D1284120

The STATE of
Tennessee

MILES

Ref.   LLRF 112560
F   The Tennessee
436   encyclopedia of
.T525   history & culture
1998

THE

TENNESSEE ENCYCLOPEDIA

OF HISTORY & CULTURE

A PROJECT OF THE TENNESSEE HISTORICAL SOCIETY

OFFICERS AND BOARDS OF DIRECTORS, 1992–1998

President
John B. Hardcastle (1992–1996)
Dan E. Pomeroy (1996–1998)

Vice President for the State-at-Large
Ophelia T. Paine (1992–1996)
Pam B. Garrett (1996–1997)
Joseph L. May (1997–1998)

Vice-President for East Tennessee
Patricia Brake Howard (1992–1998)

Vice President for Middle Tennessee
Dan E. Pomeroy (1992–1994)
Reavis L. Mitchell, Jr. (1994–1998)

Vice President for West Tennessee
Cathy Holland (1992–1994)
Lyle Reid (1994–1996)
Perre M. Magness (1996–1998)

Recording Secretary
Yollette Trigg Jones (1992–1996)
Elizabeth Queener (1996–1998)

Treasurer
W.J. Wallace IV (1992–1996)
William P. Morelli (1996–1998)

Immediate Past Presidents
William R. Mott (1992–1996)
John B. Hardcastle (1996–1998)

Past President
Don H. Doyle (1992–1996)
William R. Mott (1996–1998)

DIRECTORS

Mary Anne Harwell (1994–1998)
Douglas Henry, Jr. (1992–1998)
James A. Crutchfield (1992–1994)
Don H. Doyle (1996–1997)

Walter T. Durham (1992–1998)
Jimmie L. Franklin (1997–1998)
Edwin S. Gleaves (1992–1998)
Russell Hippe (1992–1994)

Reavis L. Mitchell, Jr. (1992–1994)
Dan E. Pomeroy (1994–1996)
William P. Purcell III (1994–1998)
H.D. Riley, Jr. (1992–1998)

TRUSTEES

Ridley Wills II (1992–1994)
J.P. Foster (1992–1995)

William P. Morelli (1993–1996)
Joseph L. May (1996–1997)

Richard H. Knight, Jr. (1996–1998)
Robert S. Brandt (1996–1998)

EXECUTIVE DIRECTOR

Ann Toplovich (1992–1998)

Tennessee Encyclopedia of History and Culture Editorial Committee

Don H. Doyle, chair
Walter T. Durham
Edwin S. Gleaves
Patricia Brake Howard
James K. Huhta
Yollette T. Jones

Perre Magness
Reavis L. Mitchell, Jr.
Harris D. Riley, Jr.
Ann Toplovich
Carroll Van West

THE
TENNESSEE ENCYCLOPEDIA
OF HISTORY & CULTURE

CARROLL VAN WEST, EDITOR-IN-CHIEF

CONNIE L. LESTER, ASSOCIATE EDITOR

MARGARET DUNCAN BINNICKER
ANNE-LESLIE OWENS
ASSISTANT EDITORS

SUSAN L. GORDON, ILLUSTRATIONS EDITOR

TENNESSEE HISTORICAL SOCIETY
RUTLEDGE HILL PRESS®
NASHVILLE, TENNESSEE

Virginia Davis Laskey Library WITHDRAWN

Ref.
F
436
.T525
1998

Copyright © 1998 by The Tennessee Historical Society.

All rights reserved. Written permission must be secured from the publisher to use or reproduce any part of this book, except for brief quotations in critical reviews and articles.

Published in Nashville, Tennessee, by Rutledge Hill Press®, 211 Seventh Avenue North, Nashville, Tennessee 37219. Distributed in Canada by H. B. Fenn & Company, Ltd., 34 Nixon Road, Bolton, Ontario L7E 1W2. Distributed in Australia by Millennium Books, 13/3 Maddox Street, Alexandria NSW 2015. Distributed in New Zealand by Tandem Press, 2 Rugby Road, Birkenhead, Auckland 10. Distributed in the United Kingdom by Verulam Press, Ltd., 152a Park Street Lane, Park Street, St. Albans, Hertfordshire AL2 2AU.

Design by Harriette H. Bateman, Nashville, Tennessee.
Typography by Compass Communications, Nashville, Tennessee.

Library of Congress Cataloging-in-Publication Data

The Tennessee encyclopedia of history & culture / Carroll Van West,
    editor-in-chief.
        p.   cm.
    Includes index.
    ISBN 1-55853-599-3
    1. Tennessee—History—Encyclopedias. 2. Tennessee—Civilization—
Encyclopedias. I. West, Carroll Van, 1955– . II. Tennessee Historical Society.
F436.T525 1998
976.8'003—dc21   98-7899
                                                          CIP

Printed in the United States of America.

1 2 3 4 5 6 7 8 9—02 01 00 99 98

112560

SUPPORTERS

PARTNERS

State of Tennessee/Tennessee Historical Commission
Middle Tennessee State University/Center for Historic Preservation
Rutledge Hill Press

SPONSORS

The Frist Foundation
Dantzler Bond Ansley Foundation

CONTRIBUTORS

Benwood Foundation
The Maclellan Foundation
Jack C. Massey Foundation
Pilot Corporation
Douglas Henry, Jr.

ADDITIONAL MAJOR SUPPORT PROVIDED BY:

The Memorial Foundation
Ingram Industries
Walter T. Durham
John B. Hardcastle
H.G. Hill Companies
Community Foundation of Greater Memphis
Shirley Caldwell Patterson
H.D. Riley, Jr.
Nashville Community Foundation

EDITORIAL STAFF

Editor-in-Chief
Carroll Van West
Middle Tennessee State University

Associate Editor
Connie L. Lester
Tennessee Historical Society

Assistant Editors
Margaret Duncan Binnicker
Middle Tennesssee State University

Anne-Leslie Owens
Tennessee Historical Society

Illustrations Editor
Susan L. Gordon
Tennessee Historical Society

Editorial Interns
Teresa Biddle-Douglass, Tara Mitchell Mielnik, Blythe Semmer
Middle Tennessee State University

Consulting Editors
Paul K. Conkin, Vanderbilt University
W. Calvin Dickinson, Tennessee Technological University
Walter T. Durham, Gallatin
James W. Ely, Jr., Vanderbilt University
James E. Fickle, University of Memphis
Cynthia G. Fleming, University of Tennessee, Knoxville
Jimmie L. Franklin, Vanderbilt University
Glenn A. Himebaugh, Middle Tennessee State University
Charles W. Johnson, University of Tennessee, Knoxville
Robert B. Jones, Middle Tennessee State University
James C. Kelly, Virginia Historical Society
Robert Tracy McKenzie, University of Washington
Anastatia Sims, Georgia Southern University
W. Bruce Wheeler, University of Tennessee, Knoxville
Larry H. Whiteaker, Tennessee Technological University
Frank B. Williams, Jr., East Tennessee State University
Donald L. Winters, Vanderbilt University
Margaret Ripley Wolfe, East Tennessee State University

AUTHORS

John E. Acuff
June Adamson
Bill Akins
Harbert Alexander
Michael Allen
Robert B. Allen
Clinton B. Allison
Donald S. Armentrout
Stephen V. Ash
Paul Ashdown
Jonathan M. Atkins
Linda T. Austin
Meredith Morris Babb
David Babelay
Jane Bagwell
Clay Bailey
Fred Arthur Bailey
Adrion Baird
Howard Baker, Jr.
Steven L. Baker
Mark T. Banker
Meredith Fiske Bare
Garry Barker
S. Jonathan Bass
Walter Lynn Bates
Lauren Batte
Colin F. Baxter
Patsy B. Beene
Marty G. Bell
Kathy Bennett
Robert Benson
Paul H. Bergeron
Michael Bertrand
Richard D. Betterly
Teresa Biddle-Douglass
Trina L. Binkley
Charles M. Binnicker
Margaret Duncan Binnicker
Michael E. Birdwell
Cindy Stephens Blades
Pam Bonee
Robert J. Booker
John C. Bowman
Lucas G. Boyd
Carolyn Brackett
Michael R. Bradley
Robert Brandt

Roy C. Brewer
Greer Edwards Broemel
G. Donald Brookhart
Jennifer E. Brooks
John B. Broster
Margaret Lynn Brown
Mark Brown
Theodore Brown, Jr.
Bettye J. Broyles
Ruth Broyles
Charles F. Bryan, Jr.
C. Andrew Buchner
Carole Stanford Bucy
Jenny Burney
Frank Burns
Margaret Butler
Sara A. Butler
Benjamin H. Caldwell, Jr.
Wendy S. Campbell
Christopher Caplinger
Kara Carden
Lorene Cargile
Thomas M. Carlson
Cathi Carmack
Marius Carriere
Robert L. Carroll
Chelius H. Carter
Martha Carver
Margaret Cate
Jefferson Chapman
Arthur Ben Chitty
James R. Chumney
John Cimprich
Herbert Clark
Jerry E. Clark
Lissa Clarke
Charles L. Cleland
Miranda R. Clements
Fred Cloud
Carl Robert Coe
Allen R. Coggins
Robert Coles
Brenda Colladay
Curtis Collier
Mona Collett
Kevin D. Collins
Fred Colvin

Paul K. Conkin
Forrest Conklin
D. Bruce Conn
John Lawrence Connelly
Thomas H. Coode
Cynthia Cook
William G. Cook
B. Franklin Cooling
Robert E. Cooper, Jr.
George Core
Susan D. Core
Mark Corey
James X. Corgan
Robert E. Corlew
Kay Oldham Cornelius
Steve Cotham
Richard A. Couto
Stephen D. Cox
Patrick Craddock
Margaret Ellen Crawford
W.C. Crooks
Fred M. Culp
Dot Curtis
Don Cusic
Wayne Cutler
Ann Dale
Linda Williams Dale
Arthur L. David
Faye Tennyson Davidson
Ed DeBoer
Miriam DeCosta-Willis
Jayne Crumpler DeFiore
Tom Des Jean
Jerry R. Desmond
Lanier DeVours
Ward DeWitt, Jr.
W. Calvin Dickinson
James Dillon
Howard Dorgan
Edward Dotson
Marvin Downing
Don H. Doyle
Jim Draeger
Diane Dunkley
Durwood Dunn
Sara Lewis Dunne
Jeffrey L. Durbin

Walter T. Durham
David H. Dye
Wilma Dykeman
Brian Eades
Megan Dobbs Eades
Linda J. Edington
Martha Avaleen Egan
John Egerton
William B. Eigelsbach
Clifton Coxe Ellis
William E. Ellis
John T. Ellisor
James W. Ely, Jr.
G. David England
Allison Ensor
Jamie Evans
Patricia Bernard Ezzell
Timothy P. Ezzell
Evelyn P. Fancher
Charles Faulkner
Heather Fearnbach
James E. Fickle
Kenneth Fields
Vilma Scruggs Fields
Kenneth Fieth
Richard C. Finch
Angela Wallace Finley
Nina Finley
E. Michael Fleenor
Cynthia Griggs Fleming
R.C. Forrester
Russell Fowler
Ed Frank
Jay D. Franklin
Jimmie Lewis Franklin
Mike Freeman
A. Jon Frere
Bettye Freudenthal
Sara A. Frey
Bob Fulcher
Dale Fuqua
Frye Gaillard
Bonnie Gamble
George A. Garrett
Joseph Y. Garrison
Kay Baker Gaston
Michael Gavin
E. Alvin Gerhardt, Jr.
Richard P. Gildrie
Trey Giuntini
John V. Glass
Patrice Hobbs Glass
Edwin S. Gleaves
John M. Glen

Kenneth W. Goings
Leo J. Goodsell
Susan M. Goodsell
Anita S. Goodstein
Ralph C. Gordon
Susan L. Gordon
Herschel Gower
Dorothy Granberry
Marjorie Graves
Helen Gray
Janice M. Greathouse
Vivian P. Greene
Rick Gregory
Irene M. Griffey
Alan Griggs
W. Todd Groce
Kevin Grogan
John D.W. Guice
Frank Gulley
Carol Guthrie
B. Anthony Guzzi
Peter J. Haas
Cherrie H. Hall
Jere Hall
Randal Hall
James B. Hallums
Jewell Hamm
Caneta Skelley Hankins
John B. Hardcastle
John E. Harkins
Herbert L. Harper
Stacy Harris
Paul Harvey
Sara Harwell
Barbara Haskew
Jeri Hasselbring
Mrs. Burwin Haun
Harold Hazelip
Thomas E. Hemmerly
Sally S. Hermsdorfer
Glenn A. Himebaugh
Mary S. Hoffschwelle
Bob Holladay
Stacy C. Hollander
Jimmy Holt
John C. Holtzapple
Nicholas Honerkamp
Michael Honey
James A. Hoobler
Robert E. Hooper
John Linn Hopkins
Helen R. Houston
Patricia Brake Howard
Roy L. Howard

Sarah M. Howell
Harvey G. Hudspeth
Timothy S. Huebner
Betty Sparks Huehls
James K. Huhta
Lynn W. Hulan
Alex J. Hurder
Abigail R. Hyde
John Rice Irwin
Ned L. Irwin
G. Brian Jackson
George E. Jackson
Annie Laurie James
David Jellema
Gary C. Jenkins
Thelma Jennings
Charles W. Johnson
Edward A. Johnson
Leland R. Johnson
Timothy D. Johnson
Beverly W. Jones
James B. Jones, Jr.
Marlene Jones
Robbie D. Jones
Robert B. Jones
Walter L. Jordan
Thomas Kanon
Jeanette Keith
James C. Kelly
Homer D. Kemp
Brent Kennedy
William L. Ketchersid
Juanita Keys
Wali R. Kharif
Jennifer Kimbro
Dorothy W. King
John J. Kivett
Milton M. Klein
Susan W. Knowles
Mildred S. Kozsuch
Mary L. Kwas
Patti Jo Lambert
Lewis L. Laska
Frank Lee
Sara R. Lee
Anne Leonard
Bill J. Leonard
Janice M. Leone
Janene Leonhirth
Connie L. Lester
Dee Gee Lester
Dwight Lewis
Selma Lewis
Marice P. Lightfoot

Kriste Lindenmeyer
Jamie Sue Linder
Beulah Duggan Linn
T. Vance Little
Kelly Lockhart
Lisa Loehmann
Michael A. Lofaro
David R. Logsdon
John Longwith
Christopher Losson
Charles Lovelady
Bobby L. Lovett
Robert D. Lukens
Edward T. Luther
Kathy Lyday-Lee
Ethan Lyell
Sharon Macpherson
Sue W. Maggart
Perre Magness
Robert C. Mainfort, Jr.
John Majors
Mark G. Malvasi
Lonnie E. Maness
Richard Marius
Helen C. Marsh
Timothy R. Marsh
John F. Marszalek
C. Brenden Martin
Marilyn Masler
Robert H. Mathis
Beth Matter
Paul A. Matthews
Bernie Matthys
Joseph L. May
Vaughn May
Ben Harris McClary
Janice M. McClelland
Joe David McClure
Joseph E. McClure
James L. McDonough
Marshall L. McGhee
John McGlone
James W. McKee, Jr.
Robert Tracy McKenzie
Alexander McLeod
Corinne McLerran
Jon Meacham
Preston Merchant
Darlene M. Merryman
Tara Mitchell Mielnick
Murray Miles
Patricia Miletich
Gregory K. Miller
Russell Miller

Reavis L. Mitchell, Jr.
Marian Moffett
James N. Monroe
Michael Montgomery
Jack Mooney
Kenneth Bancroft Moore
Wayne C. Moore
William P. Morelli
Peter Morgan
Dorothy R. Morton
Harold D. Moser
Malcolm Muir, Jr.
Estle P. Muncy
Paul V. Murphy
Benjamin C. Nance
James H. Neal
Michael Nelson
Harvey Neufeldt
Charles F. Newman
David A. Nichols
Ruth D. Nichols
Kathy Niedergeses
Sharon Norris
Emma Nunn
Lisa N. Oakley
Marsha R. Oates
Robert Oliver
Katherine M.B. Osburn
Lois I. Osborne
Conrad Ostwalt
Roy M. Overcast, Jr.
Anne-Leslie Owens
Ted Ownby
Hilda Britt Padgett
Ophelia Paine
Wesley Paine
Betty J. Parker
Franklin Parker
Rachel Parker
Robert Parkinson
Phoebe S. Pearigen
James L. Penick, Jr.
Dana B. Perry
Elisabeth Israels Perry
Bonnie Heiskell Peters
Robert C. Petersen
Elizabeth Peterson
Etta Pettijohn
James B. Phillips
Dan Pierce
Mabel Pittard
Dan E. Pomeroy
Gregory G. Poole
Marian Bailey Presswood

Charles Edwin Price
Henry R. Price
Lisa Pruitt
Richard Quin
Bob Rains
Bets Ramsey
Milly Rawlings
Patrick D. Reagan
Madeline Reed
Yolanda Reid
Glenn H. Reynolds
Tim Reynolds
D.E. Richardson
Harris D. Riley, Jr.
Holly Anne Rine
Jere W. Roberson
Carol Roberts
Jeff Roberts
Lucy Roberts
Elizabeth Robnett
Michael Rogers
Robert Rogers
Steve Rogers
Charles P. Roland
Fred S. Rolater
Jeanette Cantrell Rudy
John W. Rumble
Fred Russell
Valerius Sanford
Ronald N. Satz
Fred W. Sauceman
Daniel Schaffer
Leonard Schlup
Glenna R. Schroeder-Lein
Gerald F. Schroedl
Christopher MacGregor
  Scribner
Lucy Akard Seay
Blythe Semmer
Leslie N. Sharp
Stephen Shearon
Charles A. Sherrill
James T. Siburt
Ellen Simak
Rob Simbeck
Jan F. Simek
John A. Simpson
Anastatia Sims
Michael D. Slate
Douglas M. Slater
David Ray Smith
Gerald L. Smith
John Abernathy Smith
Jonathan K. Smith

Kevin E. Smith
L. Thomas Smith, Jr.
Samuel D. Smith
Dale E. Soden
Jean Haskell Speer
Joe Spence
Thomas T. Spencer
Claudette Stager
Richard G. Stearns
Gus A. Steele
Betty Washburn Stevens
William R. Steverson
Dykeman Stokely
Elizabeth A. Straw
Bella Katz Stringer
Amy H. Sturgis
Sandy Suddarth
David E. Sumner
Alice Swanson
Bennett Tarleton
Mayo Taylor
Robert L. Taylor, Jr.
Stephen Taylor
Moldon Tayse
Marie Tedesco
Philip Thomason
Ruth Thompson
Bill Threlkeld
H. Bruce Throckmorton
John H. Thweatt
Mary Louise Tidwell
Nancy Tinker
Donald Todd
Elizabeth Todd
Lynn Tolley
Michael Toomey
Ann Toplovich
Jack Towry
June Towry
David Tucker
William Ray Turner
William T. Turner
Jonathan G. Utley
Beth Vanlandingham
Virginia Clarke Vaughan
Louis Littleton Veazy
Sam Venable

Rebecca Vial
John R. Vile
Bill Wagoner
Gary Wake
Celia Walker
Cornelia Walker
E.R. Walker III
Opless Walker
Randolph Meade Walker
Ronald A. Walter
Rick Warwick
David W. Webb
George E. Webb
Thomas G. Webb
Marsha Wedell
Terry Weeks
Camille Wells
Paul Wells
Albert Werthan
Carroll Van West
Mark V. Wetherington
Katherine Wheeler
W. Bruce Wheeler
Larry H. Whiteaker
Kent Whitworth
Genevieve Wiggins
Russell Wigginton
Derita Coleman Williams
Edward F. Williams III
Eleanor S. Williams
Frank B. Williams, Jr.
John Hoyt Williams
Brian S. Wills
Ridley Wills II
John Wilson
Charles F. Winfrey
Thomas H. Winn
Donald L. Winters
Charles K. Wolfe
Margaret Ripley Wolfe
Marice Wolfe
Bob Womack
Eva Jean Wrather
Lynette Boney Wrenn
Thomas S. Wyman
Linda T. Wynn
Arlene F. Young

Ed Young
Kathleen R. Zebley

ILLUSTRATIONS
Ann Evans Alley
Charlotte A. Ammons
Sharon Banker
Gail Bauer
Tammy Binford
Diane Black
Charles Brown
Joanna Bruno
Joe Culver
Jed Dekalb
Michael Dickson
June Dorman
Kathy Evans
Robert A. Green
Catherine H. Grosfils
Kassie Hassler
David B. Hinton
Marylin Bell Hughes
Carol Kaplan
Patricia M. LaPointe
Ronald A. Lee
James Lloyd
Karina McDaniel
Christopher McGee
Vince McGrath
Marilyn Z. McLaughlin
James Montague
Chaddra A. Moore
Charles Laurence Nelson
Genella Olker
Julia A. Rather
Francine Sharpe
Christy Sills
David R. Sowell
Clara Swann
Sandra B. Trybalski
Tabitha Williams

MAPS
Thomas J. Nolan
Department of Geography and
Geology, Middle Tennessee
State University

CONTENTS

USING THIS BOOK

The *Tennessee Encyclopedia of History and Culture* contains 1,500 entries arranged in alphabetical order. These entries serve as an interpretive framework to cover as many people, places, themes and events in Tennessee history and culture as possible. Additional information about key people and events not listed as individual entries is found in the more than 30 thematic entries and the individual entries for each of Tennessee's 95 counties, as well as for each city of more than 50,000 people. We also attempted to avoid the duplication of information in different but related entries. Consequently, the best way to look up an individual person or place and to find all of the information related to that topic is to **USE THE INDEX,** since it lists every person, place, and event and lists the multiple pages where pertinent information is located.

At the end of each *Encyclopedia* entry are extensive cross-references that enhance the information and interpretation provided in each individual entry. The one common exception will be the more than 30 thematic entries scattered throughout the book. Since most themes would have 40 or more cross-references, these references have been placed in the index in order to save space within the volume.

Many entries also include "Suggested Readings" that will lead to additional information about the topic. Thousands of sources were used to produce the entries of the *Encyclopedia*. Limited space precluded authors from providing a complete bibliography for their topics but the suggested readings will guide readers to hundreds of available secondary sources on Tennessee history.

Editorial work on the *Encyclopedia* began September 1995 and the first section of the volume went to the publisher in October 1997. The editors therefore requested authors to fact-check their entries carefully since time and staff constraints would limit the degree of comprehensive fact-checking we could provide at the editorial offices at Middle Tennessee State University. We used recently published books, dissertations, and articles to verify as much information as possible; we had neither the time nor the budget to travel to archives and libraries to check unpublished material. We also relied on the keen eye and judgments of a distinguished group of manuscript readers, who reviewed sections of the book during the summer and fall of 1997. Then we made corrections, deletions, or additions as necessary. The manuscript readers were: Professors Frank B. Williams, Jr., and Margaret Ripley Wolfe of East Tennessee State University; Walter T. Durham of Gallatin, Tennessee; Professor Anastatia Sims of Georgia Southern University; Professors Glenn A. Himebaugh and Robert B. Jones of Middle Tennessee State University; Professors W. Calvin Dickinson and Larry H. Whiteaker of Tennessee Technological University; Professor James E. Fickle of the University of Memphis; Professors Cynthia G. Fleming, Charles W. Johnson, and W. Bruce Wheeler of the University of Tennessee, Knoxville; Professor Robert Tracy McKenzie of the University of Washington; Professors Paul K. Conkin, James W. Ely, Jr., Jimmie L. Franklin, and Donald L. Winters of Vanderbilt University; and Dr. James C. Kelly of the Virginia Historical Society. If errors remain, or if new, pertinent information comes to light, please contact the Tennessee Historical Society so corrections and/or additions can be made in future editions of the *Encyclopedia*.

FOREWORD

The Tennessee Historical Society is proud to present *The Tennessee Encyclopedia of History and Culture,* the first comprehensive reference work of its kind produced for the great state of Tennessee. The work before you is the fruit borne of more than five years of planning and production.

The encyclopedia's official genesis occurred on January 25, 1993, at the first working session of the Tennessee Bicentennial Commission. The education committee of the commission encouraged the Tennessee Historical Society (THS) to undertake an encyclopedia project as a bicentennial legacy, and we are especially grateful to chairman Martha Ingram and commission members Wilma Dykeman Stokely, John M. Jones, Virginia Clarke Vaughan, and Secretary of State Riley C. Darnell for their early moral support. Following this meeting in early 1993, the board of directors and staff of the Tennessee Historical Society began planning for production of *The Tennessee Encyclopedia of History and Culture,* conducting a feasibility study, consulting with other state encyclopedia projects, and projecting costs and time tables.

The board of directors of the THS became fully committed to the project in 1994, and the first major partner to join our effort was the State of Tennessee. A generous matching grant provided by the Tennessee General Assembly through the Tennessee Historical Commission (THC) for fiscal years 1995 through 1998 enabled the THS to proceed with financial arrangements for the encyclopedia. THC chairmen Robert E. Corlew and Ward Dewitt, Jr., and other members of the commission served among the reviewers of our plans; THC executive director Herbert L. Harper and his staff were also of great help. Another important partner to the project came on board when Rutledge Hill Press and its president Lawrence M. Stone lent their publishing and distribution expertise to the project. A third major piece fell in place when Middle Tennessee State University and its Center for Historic Preservation agreed to provide us assistance with editorial staff and office support at their campus in Murfeesboro. The THS is especially appreciative of the support of James K. Huhta and Robert B. Jones in making this possible.

THS presidents John Hardcastle and Dan E. Pomeroy provided vision and led funding efforts for *The Tennessee Encyclopedia of History and Culture* with the assistance of vice presidents Ophelia T. Paine and Patricia Brake Howard and board members Douglas Henry, Elizabeth Queener, Walter T. Durham, and Mary Anne Harwell, among others. The generous donors to the encyclopedia are listed elsewhere, but we wish to thank here the Frist Foundation and the Dantzler Bond Ansley Foundation for their sponsorships. We are grateful too for the early commitment of the Pilot Corporation, the Maclellan Foundation, and Benwood Foundation, who shared the Society's vision for this work from its earliest days. Through the help of our partners, sponsors, and contributors, the Tennessee Historical Society has been able to provide free copies of the encyclopedia to each library and public school in Tennessee.

There are many aspects of *The Tennessee Encyclopedia of History and Culture* that could not have succeeded without a dedicated staff. Carroll Van West, as Editor-in-Chief, has given boundless energy, knowledge, and direction to the project. Only others who have undertaken such work will understand what an extraordinary accomplishment he and his editorial staff achieved between September 1995 and January 1998—producing from scratch a 3,200 page manuscript with more than 1,500 entries and over 550 authors in twenty-nine months. The THS also thanks the editorial staff members Connie L. Lester, Susan L. Gordon, Margaret Duncan Binnicker, and Anne-Leslie Owens for their heroic adherence to our ambitious timetable. And at the bedrock of the project—financial management and record-keeping—Melinda P. Clary kept everything related to the encyclopedia in good order in addition to her other duties, for which we are very grateful.

During the course of this project, approximately 1,000 individuals have provided their time, knowledge, expertise, talent, and money to make *The Tennessee Encyclopedia of History and Culture* possible. They have served on planning committees, used an ocean of publications for research, reviewed entry lists, written essays, searched for images, and kept the project rolling to completion. Without exaggerating the matter, *The Tennessee Encyclopedia of History and Culture* has been written by and for the people of Tennessee and those who love her. This work encapsulates how we see ourselves at the end of the twentieth century, and we trust it will provide useful guideposts for our course into the twenty-first century.

ANN TOPLOVICH
EXECUTIVE DIRECTOR
TENNESSEE HISTORICAL SOCIETY

ACKNOWLEDGMENTS

C reating *The Tennessee Encyclopedia of History and Culture* has been an enormous task, one shouldered by many people and institutions across the state. First and foremost, thanks go to the Tennessee Historical Society for having the vision and the courage to take on the project. This volume is the Society's lasting contribution to the Tennessee Bicentennial. I especially thank the Society's Executive Director, Ann Toplovich, and its Board of Directors, headed by President John Hardcastle in the project's first years and now led by President Dan E. Pomeroy, for their support and encouragement in bringing this book to completion. Producing the *Encyclopedia's* entry list was the contribution of the Society's Encyclopedia Editorial Committee, chaired by Don H. Doyle of Vanderbilt University, which also included historian Walter T. Durham, State Librarian and Archivist Edwin S. Gleaves, Patricia B. Howard of Webb School, Knoxville, James K. Huhta of Middle Tennessee State University, Yollette T. Jones of Vanderbilt University, Perre Magness of Memphis, Reavis L. Mitchell, Jr., of Fisk University, and Harris D. Riley, Jr., of Vanderbilt Medical Center.

Providing me with time, staff, and resources have been the primary contributions of the book's other two major sponsors. The Tennessee General Assembly through its generous matching grant provided the project's financial foundation; thanks also to the Tennessee Historical Commission for its administration of the grant. I owe thanks to Middle Tennessee State University for its many considerations during the project. Dr. Robert B. Jones, Associate Vice President for Academic Affairs, located space for the project, a difficult task given the growth of MTSU in the past decade. Our first quarters were spartan but, thanks to Dr. Jones, in 1997 we acquired new office space which created the proper working environment to allow this book to be completed on time and within budget. Dr. Donald Curry, Dean of the College of Graduate Studies, kindly provided funding for a graduate research assistant through the life of the project. Dr. James K. Huhta, Director of the Center for Historic Preservation, provided time as well as Center resources for the editorial work and contributed individual entries. I also thank the Center's Caneta S. Hankins and Edward A. Johnson for their entry contributions and Nancy Smotherman for her administrative assistance. I also very much appreciate the patience of my graduate research assistants during 1995–1998—Brian Eades, Megan Dobbs Eades, Blythe Semmer, and Rebecca Smith—who often found me a most difficult man to locate, much less discuss matters for a few minutes. Through 1997 summer internships, Teresa Biddle-Douglass and Tara Mitchell Mielnik greatly helped the project by reseaching and writing about 38 topics.

Without the promptness and good work of the 560 authors of this volume, our work would have been impossible. When the *Encyclopedia* began, we estimated that if we could find 200 authors to donate their time and expertise, we would have done quite well. Yet 560 people contributed, a surprising number until you consider how many people, from all professions and avocations, share an interest in Tennessee history and culture. I am proud of how many of these historians volunteered to lend their time and talents to the book and especially thank those who contributed ten or more entries to the book. These authors are: Jonathan M. Atkins, Teresa Biddle-Douglass, Margaret Duncan Binnicker, Carole Stanford Bucy, James X. Corgan, Walter T. Durham, Ed Frank, Ned L. Irwin, Leland R. Johnson, James C. Kelly, Lewis L. Laska, Bobby L. Lovett, Perre Magness, Tara Mitchell Mielnik, Anne-Leslie Owens, Blythe Semmer, Ann Toplovich, and Linda T. Wynn. As appropriate for our roles, the most contributions came from Associate Editor Connie L. Lester (43 entries) and myself (138 entries).

I also want to thank those hundreds of Tennesseans who have attended public meetings about the *Encyclopedia* over the last 18 months. They shared their insights and perspectives about the significant people, places, and events of the state's history, allowing us to draw together a balanced and comprehensive book. Their encouragement and excitement about the book were contagious and raised our spirits every time we took the project "on the road."

Librarians and archivists at the state's major research libraries and archives played a similar role in helping us locate authors, sharpen topics, check facts, and find illustrations. We especially appreciate the assistance of the staffs at the Tennessee State Library and Archives; Archives of Appalachia, East Tennessee State University; the Center for Poplar Music at Middle Tennessee State University; the Special Collections of the University of Memphis; the Special Collections and University Archives of the University of Tennessee, Knoxville; and Special Collections of the Heard Library at Vanderbilt University.

My deepest appreciation, however, goes to the editors who have given so much over the last 30 months. Connie L. Lester, the Associate Editor, joined the project in January 1996 and immediately made an impact through her dedication, scholarship and knowledge of the state. She also prepared the book's comprehensive index. Anne-Leslie Owens, Assistant Editor, became part of the editorial team in January 1997 and her excellent organizational, people, copy-editing, and computer skills helped us to stay on track in the demanding last 18 months of the project. Margaret Duncan Binnicker, Assistant Editor, has been with the *Encyclopedia* from the beginning, first as a graduate research assistant and then in 1997 as an Assistant Editor. She helped to create the programs of the public meetings, managed the list of possible book entries with grace and persistence, and served as a manuscript proof-reader with thoroughness and promptness. These three scholars, individually and collectively, profoundly influenced the scope and quality of this volume.

The production side of the *Tennessee Encyclopedia* team at the Tennessee Historical Society in Nashville worked hard to keep the book within budget and on schedule, making it a reality. Besides contributing 18 entries, Ann Toplovich, the THS Executive Director, took care of the necessary reports and meetings with the THS board, Rutledge Hill Press, the Tennessee Historical Commission, and the Tennessee General Assembly. Susan L. Gordon of the Tennessee Historical Society did an excellent job as the *Encyclopedia*'s Illustrations Editor and prepared four entries. Melinda Clary of the THS kept the books and made sure that our finances were in order. We all enjoyed working with Ed Curtis of Rutledge Hill Press in producing the final illustrated manuscript.

Finally my deepest appreciation goes to my family who have graciously borne my absences, long office hours, and frequent distractions. My wife Mary and my children Owen William and Sara Elizabeth gave me the support and the freedom to do this book; I cherish their love and encouragement always.

CARROLL VAN WEST, EDITOR-IN-CHIEF

PREFACE

The Significance of the *Tennessee Encyclopedia*

The *Tennessee Encyclopedia of History and Culture* is an amazing collaboration of 560 authors who have created the first updated, comprehensive study of Tennessee history since 1960. In the almost four decades since 1960 thousands of books, articles, theses, and dissertations have been written about Tennessee history and culture; new research fields have been opened while others have been more fully explored; and new collections of primary sources have been discovered and stored away at an increasing number of archival collections, historic sites, museums, and research libraries across the state. As the bicentennial of 1996 approached, all of this new scholarship was ready to be mined, analyzed, and condensed into a single volume representing the present generation's summation of an entire century worth of research and historiography.

This volume, however, is not just a generation's statement, but a statement from generations. Frank B. Williams, Jr., who published his first article in the *Tennessee Historical Quarterly* in 1943, contributed a thematic entry on higher education, prepared additional individual entries, and reviewed sections of the manuscript. Another important contributor was Robert E. Corlew, who was a student of the imminent southern historian Frank B. Owsley, Jr., published his first *THQ* article in 1951, and became one of the co-authors of that last comprehensive history of Tennessee in 1960. Wilma Dykeman also made her appearance as a Tennessee historian in the 1950s with her influential book *The French Broad* (1954). She has played a central role in the project, by advocating its creation and by co-authoring her own essay on the "meaning" of Tennessee.

That essay is the first entry of the book, appropriate due to Dykeman's position as State Historian, appropriate due to her role in writing about Tennessee for half a century, and appropriate since her essay represents her generation's thinking and understanding of the state's past, and its future. In the pages that follow other voices explore in their own distinctive way the words "meaning" and "significance" in Tennessee history. Many are established scholars from the state's major universities who have made significant contributions to the literature over the last 30 years. Members of the editorial board of the *Tennessee Historical Quarterly* from 1992 to 1997—Don H. Doyle and Paul K. Conkin of Vanderbilt University; James L. McDonough of Auburn University; Margaret Ripley Wolfe of East Tennessee State University; Paul H. Bergeron, W. Bruce Wheeler, and Cynthia G. Fleming of the University of Tennessee, Knoxville; Anita S. Goodstein of The University of the South; Kay Baker Gaston of Springfield; W. Calvin Dickinson and Larry H. Whiteaker of Tennessee Technological University; Christopher Losson of St. Joseph, Missouri; Carole Stanford Bucy of Volunteer State Community College; Robert B. Jones of Middle Tennessee State University; and Thomas H. Winn of Austin Peay State University—were among the first to lend their knowledge and prestige to the book. In addition, there are up-and-coming scholars, who are exploring new topics and creating their own distinctive narratives about the past. Historians Jonathan Atkins, Fred A. Bailey, Robert Tracy McKenzie, Kriste Lindenmeyer, Connie L. Lester, Jeanette Keith, Dan Pierce, Timothy Ezzell, Jayne C. DeFiore, Mary S. Hoffschwelle, W. Todd Groce, Paul V. Murphy, Camille Wells, Wayne C. Moore, Kenneth Goings, Ted Ownby, John A. Simpson, Linda T. Wynn, Michael Toomey, Michael E. Birdwell, and Lynette Boney Wrenn, through their own important monographs or journal articles, are among those broadening our understanding of Tennessee.

The *Tennessee Encyclopedia* also is a collaboration of different disciplines, perspectives, and approaches to history. County historians, based upon a list maintained by the Tennessee Historical

Commission, were invited to prepare brief entries on their county's history. Most county historians bring a local consciousness to bear on their narratives as well as a concern with heritage, the people and events that give identity to a certain place or time. Advocational historians, who in their careers are attorneys, business people, and physicians, add research and information about people and institutions important in their respective professional fields. College professors from departments of English, Political Science, Biology, Music, Religion, Art, Architecture, Agriculture, Anthropology, Criminal Justice, and Business, and Schools of Law, Divinity, and Medicine ensure that the narrative includes more than men of war and politics because it is the entirety of our historical experience that shapes what Tennessee is today. The group of historians who practice their craft in or for public agencies, such as the Tennessee Valley Authority, the U.S. Army Corps of Engineers, the Tennessee Historical Commission, and the Tennessee Department of Transportation, have been invaluable contributors because their work led them to study in depth often forgotten historical artifacts ranging from prehistoric mounds to early twentieth century bridges. Add to that number the curators and historians who work at the state's expanding range of museums and historic sites and the geologists, folklorists, and anthropologists who work for the state government and there is a wide range of disciplines and professional backgrounds represented by the authors of this volume. Most contributors are either natives of or work in Tennessee but since the impact of the state's history and culture has often extended beyond its borders, it is no surprise that writers about Tennessee also come from the west coast, the east coast, and many points in between. Through their eyes we gain a broader perspective on the defining people and institutions of Tennessee's past.

These diverse authors write about an equally diverse range of Tennessee people and events, from the deep past of the prehistoric age to the latest developments in the health care industry. Chosen for their national, statewide, or regional significance, the individual entries also are associated with larger historical themes, particular chronological periods, and different constituencies. Through their diversity, the hundreds of entries create a balanced yet comprehensive narrative on history and culture, one that acknowledges, for example, the importance of both politicians and musicians in creating the present sense of Tennessee identity and history.

Diversity is an obvious word to describe the contributors and contents of *The Tennessee Encyclopedia of History and Culture.* But to revel in diversity for its own sake adds little to the study and interpretation of the past. A cacophony of voices without unifying themes typically makes little sense—of all that is being said, what is important? what are the associations with other peoples from other times? why should we listen? Out of the hundreds of thousands of words from the hundreds of voices in this volume, however, clarity does emerge if we step back and think about basic ideas that all of Tennessee's different classes, races, and gender share in common. Five words—duty, courage, faith, change, and continuity—may convey best the shared meaning and significance of the many people, places, and events found within these pages.

The concept of duty, certainly defined in various ways by different people, links together such diverse people as Dragging Canoe, Andrew Jackson, Frances Wright, Sam Davis, Samuel P. Carter, Julia Hooks, Ida B. Wells-Barnett, Alvin C. York, and Theotis Robinson. In surveying the rapid changes being experienced by the Cherokees during the years of the American Revolution, Dragging Canoe saw his duty as an aggressive defense of his homeland and culture. Andrew Jackson's sense of duty led him into both heroic and foolhardy adventures and more often than not—witness the Eaton Affair—he was willing to pay the price that duty sometimes demands. Frances Wright saw her duty as building a place in the wilderness of West Tennessee where blacks and whites could live and work together as free poeple in an age when the rest of society saw no alternative to slavery. A few years earlier, but in a far different place in East Tennessee, Elihu Embree and Benjamin Lundy followed a similar sense of duty as they launched the first abolitionist newspapers.

Shared concepts of duty, honor, and responsibility propelled hundreds of thousands of Tennesseans into action during the Civil War. Placing duty to his fellow soldiers and unit above all considerations, Confederate scout Sam Davis of Rutherford County proclaimed "if I had a thousand lives I would lose them all before I would betray my friends or the confidence of my informer" before meeting a horrible death in Pulaski in 1863. In that same war, Samuel P. Carter of Carter County saw his duty as a defender of the Union. He served as a Brigadier General of the U.S. Volunteers during the Civil War, and afterwards he returned to a naval career where he rose to the rank of Rear Admiral upon his retirement. A similar sense of duty to defend the country convinced Alvin C. York to lay aside, temporarily, his religous convictions and to fight in World War I.

In late nineteenth century Memphis, two African-American women acknowledged their duty in the fight for civil rights. Ida B. Wells-Barnett took to the editorial pages to denounce extralegal violence and lynching. Julia A. Hooks, in an 1894 address at the Beale Steet Baptist Church, announced that the "Duty of the Hour" was to build the strength of character and purpose which could carry African Americans through the difficult years ahead. A later generation, represented in part by Theotis Robinson at the University of Tennessee, Knoxville, renewed this sense of duty in the late 1950s and 1960s as it grasped the mantle of leadership and strode—onto college campuses first and other public institutions next—to obtain civil rights and equal opportunity for all people.

Courage walks hand-in-hand with one's sense of duty, as shown through the stories of such Civil Rights Movement pioneers as James Lawson, Diane Nash, and Viola McFerren. It required tremendous courage to confront the forces of segregation and violence with dignified non-violent protest. Outnumbered, portrayed as quacks, insurrectionists, or worse in the media, and surrounded by the power of the state, it took a courage beyond what most people possess to stand up and be counted, much less to be a leader. The Civil Rights Movement generation was not the only one to demonstrate such courage and conviction. Many Tennesseans, from John Ross among the Cherokees to Reconstruction-era black legislator Samuel McElwee to suffrage leader Anne Dallas Dudley to Highlander Folk School founder Myles Horton, have assumed similar leadership roles when the easier course would have been to stand back and join the crowd.

During the backcountry era of Tennessee history, it also took courage to explore new lands and encounter new peoples, but the potential rewards in furs and land compelled waves of Europeans to set fear aside to come into the lands of the Cherokees, Shawnees, Chickasaws, and Choctaws. Soto, Pardo, LaSalle, Marquette, Joliet, Arthur, and Demonbreun were among the first. Later in the second half of the eighteenth century, a relative handful of trailblazers, such as legendary Thomas Spencer, left home and headed west in search of those new lands and created new patterns of exchange between English colonists and Native Americans.

Courage has distinguished Tennesseans on the battlefield ever since the Overmountain Men gathered at Sycamore Shoals and crossed the Appalachians to defeat the British at King's Mountain. A generation later, so many Tennesseans rushed to fight that the state gained its nickname—the Volunteer State. Ever since a wide range of Tennesseans—Felix Zollicoffer, Cornelia Fort, and James T. Davis among many others—have sacrificed for a greater cause.

Standing up for the "cause," for principle, lies behind many famous events and places across the state. Competing principles certainly were on trial, along with John Scopes, at the Rhea County Courthouse in Dayton in 1925. The national media circus that descended upon Dayton touted the values of modern science in contrast to the rural traditions of many local residents. To outsiders, Science and Rationality won at Dayton, no matter the verdict against Scopes. Yet within five years the advocates of modern science met a much more worthy adversary, from the halls of Vanderbilt University, in the Agrarians. This disparate union of writers, historians, and economists loudly proclaimed "I'll Take My Stand" in defiance of the alliance among science, technology, and industry in the early twentieth century. As Andrew Nelson Lytle understood, the modern age "presents an awful spectacle: men, run mad by their inventions, supplanting themselves with inanimate objects. This is, to follow the matter to its conclusion, a moral and spiritual suicide, foretelling an actual physical destruction."[1]

By the next decade, however, modern science and technology had reshaped the state's very landscape through federal projects such as the Tennessee Valley Authority, Cumberland Homesteads, and the Oak Ridge facilities of the Manhattan Project. Scientists came from throughout the world to gather at Tennessee places. Their courage was of a different kind: to step into new frontiers and dream of a brave new world, a broader universe documented 50 years earlier by the photography of astronomer E.E. Barnard.

Duty and courage could accomplish little without the faith that a courageous stand makes a difference. In the conflict between the Agrarians and the prophets of modern technology, for example, both sides possessed courage and conviction for their cause because they faithfully believed that the future would vindicate them. The Agrarian writers placed their faith in history and tradition; technocrats at TVA and Oak Ridge in the next generation placed theirs in science. Faiths about differing fundamental principles of democratic society and political economy also distinguished the rhetoric and actions of both Democrats and Whigs earlier in the heated political wars of the mid-nineteenth century. Neither Democrats nor Whigs hesitated to invoke the name of God in and for their cause as both believed that they were fighting for the future. The Democrats championed the agrarian economy of their forefathers while the Whigs looked forward to prosperity under the evolving market revolution of the antebellum age. A century later, faith in righteousness and God were strongly associated with another political upheaval, the Civil Rights Movement of the 1950s and 1960s. Faith allowed the strategy of non-violence to convince, slowly, the majority of Tennesseans of the immorality of segregation.

Faith also has led generations of Tennesseans to establish and maintain several of the most influential Protestant churches of today. Few states have had as many churches established within their boundaries or maintained national and world headquarters to the present day. Tennessee is home to the Free Will Baptists, National Baptist Convention, Inc., Southern Baptist Convention, Christian Methodist Episcopalians, Cumberland Presbyterians, Church of God in Christ, and Church of God (Cleveland, TN), while playing a formulative role in the Disciples of Christ, Church of Christ, and Assembly of God denominations. The presence of these religious faiths brought educational and publishing instititutions which, in turn, elevated higher education and the music publishing and recording industry within the state. To some, Tennessee may be derisively described as the "buckle of the Bible Belt," but without its faiths, the state would be a far different, and diminished, place.

Change and continuity are the push-pull of Tennessee history. There are few static times in the state's past. Even during the deep prehistoric period, change occurred, merely at a much slower pace than we are accustomed to. Prehistoric Tennesseans changed and adapted to climate, geography, and environment through four primary eras—Paleoindian, Archaic, Woodland, and Mississippian. Then in the mid-1500s began two centuries of contact with European explorers and traders, a time of rapid change compared to past patterns, a pace that accelerated even more with the coming of permanent European settlers in the second half of the eighteenth century. Older narratives of this process of cultural interaction often told a simple, straightforward story line: the Indians vanished before in face of the juggernaut of western civilization. The story, as witnessed in this volume, is hardly so simple, being one of complexity, change, and continuity. The Trail of Tears certainly marked a concerted federal effort to remove the Native American presence from Tennessee, for instance, but today Cherokees maintain homes and traditions throughout Middle and East Tennessee while Chickasaws and Choctaws still live in parts of West Tennessee.

Indeed, the Choctaws returned to Tennessee after World War II as part of the extensive rural migration associated with an emerging modern agricultural economy. Agriculture is another theme often assumed to change little over the decades. Our farms, especially the lands cultivated by Tennessee's Century Farm families, clearly represent continuity as fields and pastures are farmed by generations within one family. But at the same time the story of Tennessee agriculture is a dynamic one, from the evolution of the market economy in the antebellum era to the death of slavery and reorganization of agricultural labor during the Reconstruction period and on to the progressive farming revolution of the twentieth century. Farm families might be on the land of their great, great grandparents, but they raise products, such as soybeans and new livestock breeds, unheard of by their ancestors.

Nor could their ancestors imagine the high technology and mass production associated with the Nissan and Saturn automobile factories, built in the 1980s in former corn and cotton fields of Middle

Tennessee. But the heralded arrival of Nissan and Saturn are frankly the latest chapters in the state's long industrial history. Large scale, multinational investments in Tennessee resources and people began to reorder lives and landscapes in the years after the Civil War when, for example, the DuPont corporation came to Cheatham County to manufacture gunpowder. During World War I DuPont built a huge modern ammunition factory and a complete company town, now known as Old Hickory, on a bend of the Cumberland River in Davidson County. In the 1890s northern financiers, led by international banker J.P. Morgan, reorganized struggling East Tennessee railroad lines and the Memphis and Charleston Railroad as integral parts of a new regional transportation monster, the Southern Railway, which soon built impressive urban terminal gateways in Knoxville and Chattanooga. In that same decade international investors looked with favor toward mining and timber resources at Cumberland Gap, the very spot where Daniel Boone and others initially launched the movement west, which, in turn, had been the process that defined American character, according to the famous 1893 "frontier thesis" of historian Frederick Jackson Turner.

As industrial development gained momentum in the resource-laden lands of the Cumberland Plateau and Appalachian Mountains, as well as within the state's four major urban centers of Memphis, Nashville, Knoxville, and Chattanooga, it also began to transform smaller cites and towns. In the early twentieth century industrialists built a modern cotton mill village, Bemis, outside of Jackson while Pittsburgh industrialists developed a modern aluminum plant and town, Alcoa, outside of Maryville, powering the facility with electricity from a series of hydroelectric dams located throughout the Appalachian region. After World War I, New York capitalists launched major industrial plants in Kingsport, and German investors built huge rayon production facilities in Elizabethton. In the 1930s the Tennessee Valley Authority was many things to many people but in general the mega-agency represented an effort to harness a river and its resources for a new industrial future. Industry and mining have a deep, significant history in Tennessee, a story of change, reaction, failure, and success. Today abandoned hulks of once large, prosperous firms litter the landscape as new firms and industries build postmodern office complexes and factories in new locations.

Race is another constant in Tennessee history. The first European settlers brought their slaves as they carried in other essential items of property. Slavery would prove to have a complex and challenging history over the next 100 years before emancipation. African-American slaves cleared many Tennessee fields and built most of the elegant manor houses that are now historic museums. But only in selected areas were there slave gangs toiling in the cotton or tobacco fields. More frequently, farmers and their families worked the fields with their few slaves; most Tennesseans did not own slaves and developed their farms themselves. But across the state free-born African Americans found life difficult and their choices limited in the antebellum period. Slaves also encountered a more brutal legal and cultural world by the mid-century. The abolition movement found an early home in East Tennessee, but the state as a whole remained firmly wedded to slavery as an essential economic and social institution. When the Civil War came, Tennessee joined the Confederacy, although most of East Tennessee, and isolated pockets in the other two grand divisions, remained Unionist. Indeed, Greeneville resident Andrew Johnson was Republican Abraham Lincoln's second Vice President and became President after Lincoln's assassination in 1865. By that time, Emancipation and Reconstruction already had initiated a new chapter in race relations, one of hope, opportunity, and promise perhaps best embodied in new educational insitutions such as Fisk University, Roger Williams University, Lane College, Lemoyne Owen College, and Knoxville College. But progress and promise were impeded during the repression and violence of Jim Crow segregation, a nadir in Tennessee race relations for almost 70 years. Yet ironically out of Jim Crow, Tennessee African Americans established institutions like the American Baptist Theological Seminary, local NAACP chapters, and Tennessee State University that would help carry the day for equality and opportunity during the Civil Rights Movement.

Politics is another way to explore the interplay of change and continuity in Tennessee history, from the personal politics of the Jackson-Sevier rivalry to the ideological battles between Whigs and Democrats to Tennessee's very different history, compared to other southern states, of the Republican party. Democratic party dominance is often assumed to be the norm from the days of Jefferson and Jackson to recent years, but that assumption is mistaken. The Democrats had difficulty even winning elections during the Age of Jackson and when Columbia resident James K. Polk won the presidency in the 1844 election, he failed to carry the vote of Tennessee. The Whig party and platform significantly influenced the state's development in the mid-nineteenth century and many members of that party, like Samuel Arnell of Maury County and Emerson Etheridge of Weakley County, were Unionists during the Civil War and became founding members of the Republican party in the Reconstruction period. Congressional districts in East Tennessee consistently elected Republican representatives throughout the twentieth century, creating the political foundation for the party's reemergence as a statewide force during the 1960s led by Howard Baker, Jr., of Scott County. The Democratic party certainly emerged from the 1870 constitutional convention as a political power without equal. But its power and goals (except the principle of white supremacy) were often diminished by factional divisions and third party threats, especially from the agrarian revolt of the late 1880s and 1890s. Then came the personal politics exercised by urban political bosses such as Hillary Howse of Nashville and Edward H. Crump of Memphis and small town bosses like those in McMinn County, who were finally turned out of power by determined former GIs in the "Battle of Athens" in 1946. The gunfire on the streets of Athens, unfortunately, was not an isolated incident; violence in politics has a long history in Tennessee. The duels of the Jackson-Sevier days were followed by the fisticuffs and armed threats of antebellum stump speakers. After the Civil War, political violence escalated as witnessed by the rise of Ku Klux Klan, the lynchings of African Americans, state and local government suppression of labor activity, the Night Riders of the Black Patch War, the shooting of Edward W. Carmack on the streets of Nashville, and the twentieth century racial battles in Knoxville and Columbia.

Within the politically defined boundaries of Tennessee, the land itself has changed more than one would think. The earthquakes of 1811–1812 left their legacy in an expanded Reelfoot Lake and an altered course of the Mississippi River. Later in the century, people began to alter the landscape permanently through mining coal at Tracy City and copper at Ducktown; by building tunnels at the Narrows of the Harpeth and at Cowan; and by logging the hardwoods of West Tennessee and the Cumberland Plateau. Teams of soldiers and engineers from the U.S. Army Corps of Engineers reworked several rivers to improve navigation, and by the early 1900s the first hydroelectric dams and reservoirs were under construction. The efforts of TVA were just the latest in a series of attempts by Tennesseans to control nature by harnessing it and replacing it with a technological system that they could control.

These man-made alterations left a fearsome toll on the landscape: a moonscape of environmental degradation at Ducktown and Dunlap; tree stumps and eroded, deeply gullied land in Overton and Henderson counties. We have spent a good part of the twentieth century attempting to reclaim Tennessee from our own worst excesses, and in the process Tennesseans worked with outsiders to build a conservation landscape of parks, natural areas, scenic rivers, and forests that rival those of any state. Fall Creek Falls, Savage Gulf, the Great Smoky Mountains, the Big South Fork, Reelfoot Lake, Cedars of Lebanon, and Roan Mountain are more than state landmarks: they are vital natural habitats of national significance.

Duty, courage, faith, change, continuity. Many people, places, and events associated with these five words are success stories, ones of hope, determination, and inspiration. But stories of failure, violence, and greed are also part of the Tennessee experience. It has often taken a rude slap to the face to awaken Tennesseans to the reality that history is not just a steady march of progress. There are abrupt stops, sometimes even a forced march backwards. The steps forward, those backwards, and even those taken sideways combine with constantly shifting perceptions about the value of the state's rich physical setting to create a cultural understanding of who we are and, perhaps, where we are going— defining what we currently like to describe as "our sense of place." Tennessee's many parks, museums, and historic sites present the physical side of that "sense of place," but to find the spiritual side of the equation we must turn to the stories, paintings, poems, lyrics, murals, and novels of generations of Tennessee writers, artists, and musicians. Our connection to the Tennessee past may be reflected in a short story by Peter Taylor, a novel by T.S. Stribling, or the poetry of Marilou Awiakta. As seen in the craftsmanship of a Woodland era bowl, the sculpture of Will Edmondson, and a painting by Gilbert Gaul, Tennessee is not the vision of one particular group of people, but a shared place of many different meanings created by many peoples over the centuries.

Certain images from Tennessee are nationally recognized—Elvis and Graceland; the Grand Ole Opry; the Scopes Trial; stock cars at Bristol; Beale Street; antebellum mansions; Bessie Smith belting the blues; Peyton Manning and UT football; moonshiners along "Tobacco Road;" Dolly and Dollywood; Civil War battlefields; and Big Hats, Nudie suits, and *Hee Haw* Daisy Maes. They create a pastiche of stereotypes, a part of Tennessee history and culture that admittedly has its significance but that also is superficial to a longer and deeper story of challenge, failure, sacrifice, greed, creativity, violence, and faith. Below these surface images lies a rich tapestry of real people, places, and events. Their little known stories are gathered here; together they best define the past and present significance of Tennessee to its residents, and to the nation as a whole.

CARROLL VAN WEST, EDITOR-IN-CHIEF

Citation:
(1) Twelve Southerners, *I'll Take My Stand: The South and the Agrarian Tradition* (New York, 1930), 202–203.

THIS LAND
CALLED TENNESSEE

O n the wall above a stairway in the west wing of our nation's Capitol there is a mural that captures a definitive moment in America's history and vision of itself. *Westward the Course of Empire Takes Its Way*, painted by Emanuel Leutze in 1861–1862, is equally appropriate in reflecting the history and meaning of Tennessee.

The mural is a quintessential representation of the nation's popular belief summarized in 1845 as "our manifest destiny to overspread the continent allocated by Providence." It departs from the Capitol's previous grandiose paintings and sculptures depicting European discovery of the "New World" and incorporates no heroic figures of founding fathers or well-draped goddesses brandishing swords of liberty and laurel wreaths of peace. Here, instead, is a searching, exultant scene of Americans fulfilling the rite of passage to claim the great West. Afoot, on horseback, in covered wagons drawn by plodding oxen, these weary and hopeful pioneers have toiled across the plains and up the rugged mountains to reach a pass opening toward California's distant Golden Gate.

"Westward Ho!"

The popular title for the mural echoed the cry not only of this small band of struggling humanity but of the irresistible multitudes to follow. It might have been voiced by one of the leaders—in coonskin cap—who has reached the top of the pass and whose outstretched arm beckons his companions on toward the horizon. Leutze identified that distinctive and optimistic figure as "a frontiere farmer (Tennesseian)."

The German-born Leutze, whose best known painting was *Washington Crossing the Delaware,* had done his homework well. That "Tennesseian" and his family represented a new breed of American, those wishing to sever the umbilical cord to Europe and turn westward. Here are the western prototypes: buckskin-clad trapper, eager young adventurer on horseback, hunter well-stocked with two rifles, a lad whose wound is perhaps reminder of an Indian encounter.

But above all his mural suggests the migrants' reach for a place to call home. Bathed in the scene's clearest shaft of light are a mother and daughter huddled beneath the protective arm of the "Tennesseian" and awestruck by the glorious vision before them. At an earlier point on the crowded trail up the mountains another mother and child lean forward in one of the many covered wagons which, upright or awry, bear the tools and furnishings for future homes. As in the earlier westward thrust across the Appalachians in which Tennesseans had tended to bring their families with them to the frontier, it is the yearning for land as home that provides meaning and energy to overcome all doubt and hardship on the long trail.

Both ominous and promising at the center foreground of the scene, but obscured under deep shadows in contrast to the sunlit faces of the pioneer leaders, a black youth leads a donkey bearing a young Irish immigrant and her infant. Is he already free or does he represent that struggle for emancipation tearing at the nation's vitals even during the mural's creation? Is she welcome in America or has she already encountered the rising tension over immigration especially in some of the growing cities? Whichever the case, these two will remain part of the country's and Tennessee's unfolding history.

Conspicuous by their absence are the Native Americans whose spirit nevertheless broods over the scene in several vague figures along the upper border.

COURTESY OF ARCHITECT OF THE CAPITOL

"Westward the Course of Empire," mural by Emanuel Leutze, 1862, in the U.S. Capitol.

Radiant in the "Tennesseian" is the confidence and questing spirit that has driven his people to look westward across the Appalachian barrier long before they sought passage through the Rockies. They were, for the most part, English, Welsh, Scotch, French Huguenot, Germans from the Palatine, and certainly Scotch-Irish, hardy souls on a quest for independence. Religious, political, and economic subjugation that had been their lot for generations was no longer tolerable.

The same questing spirit that sent Frenchmen Marquette and Joliet down the Mississippi and Englishmen Needham and Arthur into the Tennessee Valley during the same year of 1663 also motivated, over the next century, traders for lucrative furs and long hunters who sought not only game but good land. In the Revolutionary War this spirit unfolded on the national stage as Tennessee settlers re-crossed the Appalachians, joining Patriots in the East to meet and destroy a wing of Lord Cornwallis's superior British force at a place called King's Mountain just along the North Carolina-South Carolina border. Thomas Jefferson later hailed the "memorable victory" as "the joyful annunciation of that turn of the tide of success which terminated the Revolutionary War with the seal of independence."

In 1794 the Spanish Governor of Louisiana observed the westward push of these frontiersmen toward his territory and voiced alarm at "the immoderate ambition of these new people, adventurous and hostile to all subjection." They were "a vast and restless population" whose very character was as formidable to Spain as their arms. After a visit to their state, Aaron Burr said, "Tennesseans, as the breed runs in 1806, can go anywhere and do anything."

Where they went and what they did grew primarily out of need for land. If Tennessee, not unlike America, has had a meaning to be contained in one word, that word might be land. It was opening of the Old Southwest, Tennessee, that provided Americans their legendary frontier heroes: Davy Crockett, Sam Houston, and the earliest scout of the Kentucky and Tennessee "land of the western waters," Daniel Boone. Restless men who spied out land and then moved on, they broke the paths for those to follow who would accumulate and speculate: the developers.

During the late years of the eighteenth century a Methodist Bishop, Francis Asbury, saddlebag missionary on hazardous journeys to the wild country west of the Appalachians, first recognized and warned that it was not ultimately a search for religious freedom that sent settlers across the Atlantic and over the Appalachians. In a moment of discouragement he confided in his Journal: "I am of the opinion it is hard, or harder, for people of the west to gain religion as any other . . . when I reflect that not one in a hundred came here to get religion, but rather to get plenty of good land, I think it will be well if some or many do not eventually lose their souls." However, Asbury more often saw this land as replete with souls awaiting a harvest through his ministry. In fact, early in the next century the frontier revivals, or "camp meetings," of these settlers, would spark the spread of Protestant religion with a new fervor across America.

But the good Bishop also had reason to be troubled. Balanced against the courage and vigor of the legacy shaped by these seekers for home and roots was the destruction inherent in their reach for land. Eventually they would gather a rich diversity of forests, fields, mountains, and rivers in the 42,244 square-mile domain of Tennessee. In its getting, one race of people would be uprooted and sent from the place they had known "time out of mind," while another race of people would be transported from a distant African homeland, enslaved to work for others. It was the character of the land that defined both tragedies.

And what a land it was, inviting and forbidding, watered by cold, bubbling springs and majestic rivers, its mountain ranges blanketed with forests of virgin evergreens and hardwoods, its grasslands and canebrakes and wide plains fertile with loam of centuries, a land host to great herds of buffalo, elk and deer, wolf and panthers and bear, and all manner of fur bearers and smaller mammals. Along its multitude of waterways beavers and fish were plentiful. Birds of both northern and southern latitudes nested here, ranging from the lordly bald eagle to the matronly bobwhite and cheerful mockingbird and most dramatic of all, the vast migratory flights of passenger pigeons so numerous that their approach could be heard for miles and the artist John James Audubon wrote of their passing like clouds that darkened the day at noontime. Soon the settlers would learn how delectable the pigeons were and they and their swine would feed on harvests of the plump, easily slaughtered birds. Their extinction was complete by early in the twentieth century.

In the hill country woods, maple, hickory, oak, and monarchs of yellow poplar turned each autumn landscape into a Persian carpet of color before pine and hemlock and Frazier fir gentled winter's stark landscape with their green cover. In swampy bottomlands to the west, the largest of all the splendid trees was the cypress, standing in quiet, mysterious water with hollow "knees" upthrust permitting the roots to "breathe."

Most varied of all the life on this land were its plants, 1,500 with at least 300 of medicinal value, as the Native Americans already knew. From mountain thickets of rhododendron, azalea, and laurel in brilliant springtime bloom and hidden patches of coveted ginseng in the east, across the cedar groves and bluegrass grazing region of the Central Basin to the lilies and orchids and rye grasses of the West Tennessee woodlands, there were flowers, vines, bushes, grasses, providing food for people and animals, for healing and beauty.

To a person whose ancestor might have been deported from the Old World for breaking a twig in the King's forest or poaching for a rabbit on a royal preserve, such bounty for the taking must have made this land seem a Garden of Eden. An eighteenth century British visitor tried to describe the fertility of the earth along the Mississippi: "The land is so rich and the soil so deep that in many places one may run a soldier's pike up to the head without meeting a rock or stone and capable of producing everything."

This country was not empty of people. For many generations, from the headwaters of the Tennessee to the Mississippi, this had been the Land of Peaceful Hunting for Native American parties as distant as Iroquois of the Great Lakes and Choctaws from the Gulf Coast. Later, for the Cherokees in the mountains and the Chickasaws near the Mississippi, this became their settled heartland. To these people living in villages along streams and rivers, farming, hunting, following ways of their ancestors, their world was one unit of land and all life upon it was inseparable. No individual "owned" the land but all used it, knew its gifts and dangers and Old Ones' stories attending each stream and rock, every cave below, and the starry sky above. All that lived—human, plant, and animal, bird and fish—was part of a great whole from which no one was separate.

But to the European newcomer, uprooted from an Old World and many still dispossessed in this "New World," the bountiful country beyond the Appalachians was land waiting to be dismembered, to be parceled into their homes and farms and industries. These two philosophies of "ownership" of the land met in the Tennessee country. And their most prophetic encounter came not on a battlefield but on a trading ground.

The background: Following the French and Indian War which left Great Britain in control of all former French possessions, King George III attempted to keep his native and European-American subjects separate. A Proclamation of 1763 drew a boundary down the spine of the Appalachians from Maine to Georgia and prohibited any white colonist from crossing this line. It was, however, little more than a line on a map. His Majesty had limited means of enforcing his ruling and his government was confronted with more pressing colonial problems, so restless settlers pushed into river valleys in East Tennessee, sometimes unsure as to whether their homestead was in the Virginia or North Carolina colony.

And a dramatic augury of future land transfers not only in Tennessee but across the nation occurred in 1775. In London, Edmund Burke warned his government on March 22 that the Americans "have already topp'd the Appalachian mountains," and called attention to bold settlers who defied the King's Proclamation and were claiming land by "the robust title of Occupancy."

The scene: About the time that Burke was making his speech in London a great council was taking place on the Watauga River in East Tennessee. In that same season when citizens in a Massachusetts town were throwing a tea party challenging King George's authority, a less celebrated enterprise in the broad river valley at the Sycamore Shoals was defying his Proclamation Line of a dozen years earlier.

On a chilly March day a group of settlers who had already "topp'd the mountains" and followed Daniel Boone into the wilderness, building cabins, planting crops, and even forming a democratic government of their own, were gathered at the call of a North Carolina lawyer, Judge Richard Henderson. At his home in the Piedmont, Henderson had heard Boone's glowing descriptions of the backcountry and had made an exploratory journey to discover for himself its potential worth. His response was as extravagant as the fertile land spread before him. He formed the Transylvania Land Company and invited the Cherokees to a council. His proposal was to pay 10,000 English pounds or, if they chose, a cabin filled with English goods, in exchange for some 20 million acres of land.

The Transylvania Land Company was a gigantic speculation enterprise. To the Cherokees who responded to this invitation and came to ponder the offer, examining the cabin full of trade goods which they decided on instead of money, this was an experience without precedent. For many days they gathered, twelve hundred proud, curious men, women, and children. Smoke from their council fire and campfires rose like a blue haze in the crisp spring air, blending with the rich aroma of beef (provided by Henderson) roasting over glowing hardwood coals.

Moving through the assembly were Oconostota, the Great Warrior, chief of all the Cherokees, tall and powerful, along with the smaller Attakullakulla, favorite of the white people who called him the Little Carpenter because of the many treaties he had cobbled together, and the gentle Old Tassel, admired for his eloquent oratory. But perhaps most commanding of all was Attakullakulla's son, Dragging Canoe, a stern, suspicious warrior, his face deeply pocked by the scourge of smallpox that had arrived with the white man's blankets. Daniel Boone, familiar to both the settlers and the Cherokees, waited awkwardly in the background. Palaver was not one of his skills.

For three days they talked, looked at the goods "Carolina Dick" had brought in six heavy wagons lurching and lumbering through the mountains. Here were guns and ammunition, hatchets, shirts and wristbands, brooches, ribbons, rum, and several kinds of blankets, all manner of English wares to be exchanged for an empire embracing the land that would become the state of Kentucky and that part of Tennessee drained by the Cumberland River and its tributaries. It was a trade described as "the most colossal transaction in lands by individuals or a private corporation that America has ever seen."

The prophecy: As negotiations drew to a close, the Cherokees indicated their readiness to sign the treaty. Attakullakulla spoke of past treaties with the white man. Old Tassel accepted the trade that had been set forth. There were nods and sounds of agreement. Then Dragging Canoe, son of Attakullakulla, rose and faced his people. In words as fierce as his pocked countenance he denounced his father and all others who would sell, at any price, the hunting grounds of their ancestors. There were those who said that he confronted Henderson. Others remembered that he grasped Boone by the arm. But all agreed on the curse he pronounced: "You have bought a fair land, but there is a cloud hanging over it. You will find its settlement dark and bloody." And with a group of younger warriors who shared his resistance Dragging Canoe strode from the council ground. Never again did he enter into any peace negotiation with the white Americans.

The signing of the treaty went forth with all solemnity, but even before it was finally accomplished Henderson took Daniel Boone aside and sent the ready scout and a party of axe-men on their way to begin blazing a trail westward. For his part, the impatient speculator did not linger at Sycamore Shoals to hear some of the disappointment now voiced by many Cherokees receiving their share of the trade goods. One warrior, given a shirt as his portion of the treasure, spoke for many: "We have sold the land, and I would have killed more deer upon it in a day than would have bought such a shirt."

This first of Tennessee's great land speculators was not entirely successful. The governors of Virginia and North Carolina were angered by Henderson's "illegal designs." Virginia refused to recognize the Transylvania Company's title to much of the Kentucky land. However, as consolation prize for his services rendered toward settling the west, Henderson was allowed to keep some 200,000 acres. These included the Cumberland Valley settlements, to which he now turned his attention.

Henderson first made sure that the French Lick, site of an early French trading post and eventually the site of Nashville, was not in Virginia. Then he set about pursuing large plans for settlement penetrating this fruitful expanse of real estate. Two of his colleagues soon lived up to their reputation as frontier heroes. In 1779 James Robertson and 200 men drove an assortment of livestock overland to arrive, in a cold December, at the encampment along the Cumberland River. John Donelson and a flotilla of women, children, and additional men arrived the following April after a harrowing river journey. Earlier settlers had found that good land, but Henderson now led in establishing government and naming the settlement Nashborough after a North Carolina friend and casualty of the Revolution.

For his part, Dragging Canoe made sure that Henderson and his companions did not forget his prophecy at Sycamore Shoals. He and followers, now called the Chickamaugas with their retreat along the great bend of the Tennessee River, terrorized small, scattered forts and settlers bound for the area that would be Nashville. The savagery of efforts on both sides in the struggle to take and hold this land was appalling in its revelation of the human need for place, for territory.

Even before Sycamore Shoals, Dragging Canoe had said that Cherokee land was melting away "like balls of snow in the sun" before the white man's advance. During the first half of the nineteenth century, as Tennessee began to play a major role on the national scene, the final "melting away" began.

In 1818 the last of the Chickasaw land between the Tennessee and Mississippi rivers was purchased from that tribe whose staunch friendship for the English had been crucial in rivalries against French and Spanish expansion. Following that purchase the influx of settlers into West Tennessee was so great that the price of corn rose in one season from one dollar to four and five dollars. Within six years after being cleared for white settlement, sixteen counties and the town of Memphis had been established. It was called the Western District or the Jackson Purchase, commemorating the leader who had directed the acquisition.

Twenty years later, in 1838, the long Cherokee-United States struggle over land came to an end. Despite the fact that many Cherokees had adopted the dress, the commerce , even the religion of the white people surrounding them, they would not be allowed to remain in their homeland. In concert with Georgia, Tennessee removed by force of arms some 14,000 from their mountains and valleys and rivers along a route where so many died that it became known as the Trail of Tears across the Mississippi to the Oklahoma country. The Trail of Tears might be seen as a dark counterpart to the Leutze mural, the finale to a long process that began at Sycamore Shoals.

Westward Ho! The Tennessean whose life gave substance to that cry was the state's most famous, most controversial son. It is difficult to understand Tennessee without some acquaintance with its frontier hero, Andrew Jackson. Discord over land had accompanied the fiery, unflinching, charismatic leader since birth. Even his birthplace was on land disputed between the two Carolinas (and determined to be in North Carolina only when he was five years old.) From his Scotch-Irish mother he heard bitter stories of Irish laborers oppressed by the landowning aristocracy.

After moving to Tennessee his natural affinity for land intensified on a frontier where no other possession was so highly prized by those who had recently "topp'd the Appalachians" and where land speculation was often synonymous with political leadership. For Jackson, conquest of the land, to which he contributed as a lawyer, military leader, and politician, was the ultimate symbol for opportunity.

But by the time Jackson became president, the nature of opportunity had broadened. Land was no longer significant only as wealth in itself but also as a stimulus for settlement, trade, and a widening number of professions. This vision of the land was possible above all because of the new ability to communicate across it. In Leutze's mural the "Tennesseian's" son stands by his family, holding his father's gun upright and gazing confidently, in Leutze's words, "into the future," seemingly oblivious to the moving figures around him. Tucked securely in his pocket is an item of equal significance to the gun—a newspaper. Newspapers and books, achieving much greater distribution through the new steam press, were now accessible to the average person, as were the recently invented steamboat, railroad, and soon-to-be telegraph.

Mass communications fueled a change in many established vocations, most dramatically perhaps in political parties whose power was concentrated among the elite. When the new technology was matched with the dynamism of Andrew Jackson the effect was electric. Toughness on the battlefield had earned him the affectionate name "Old Hickory", an ideal persona for winning political battles. To the dismay of Virginia and New England dynasties that had held the presidency since their country's founding, here in 1829 was a wind from the west, the first president whose family name meant only what he himself could make it mean.

Jackson looked beyond the overarching institutions of American life, linked as they were to inherited wealth. He challenged the power of Eastern banks, thereby making credit more available to the West, while resisting threats of secession from the "aristocracy" of the Deep South. By promoting the West and by holding America together, Jackson set a course for the common man within the nation. After Jackson's presidency, candidates running for office searched in their backgrounds not for degrees from the University of Virginia or Harvard but for a log cabin to incorporate in their campaign oratory.

The common man, represented in the mural by the "Tennesseian's" son ("the young American" as Leutze called him), was expected to receive spiritual guidance from his mother (who now shared influence with the new plainspoken denominational faiths) and yet to discover his profession independently of his father before founding his own home. Such nuclear families were the new building blocks of the communities, the states, and the nation (in Leutze, the Tennessee family's pyramidal shape on a nearby rock is echoed by the larger pyramid of the entire mass of struggling pioneers which is crowned by two men preparing to set the American flag on a distant crag).

With the age of Jackson, the new self-made men and their families, autonomous units set apart from tradition, were free to change residence or profession, a freedom symbolized by the western landscape. But Jackson's diligent attention to both land and the common white man reached a questionable climax in 1838 with that forced removal to the west of the Cherokees, people whose land had provided them spiritual as well as material sustenance but which was increasingly coveted by the white settlers around them. Eight years later the nation's "Indian Reservation System," for Native Americans' homelands, was established.

It was natural that the next Tennessean to become President of the United States would be an "expansionist" campaigning to bring Western states into the national fold.

The symbols of the young American and the nuclear family were now joined by manifest destiny, as America's drive westward took on a religious zeal and instilled a new nationalism, a pride in

America as one nation in possession of its continental boundaries (Leutze's mural, with the flag being planted at the passage to the Pacific, attests to this achievement). Under James K. Polk's administration more land—including Texas, Oregon, California, and New Mexico—was added to the United States than under any other President. Addition of California was achieved only after a war with Mexico.

During the Mexican War many "men of the western waters" rushed to fight for new national territory. Their reach for land was so spirited that when the government called for 2,800 Tennesseans as their quota, 30,000 presented themselves for enlistment in the service of their country. Some of those who were turned away reportedly offered $250 for the opportunity to join the fight. Their readiness to take up arms won Tennesseans the name of Volunteers, which has endured not only through subsequent wars but has become the identifying slogan for much of the state's athletic, social, commercial, and political life.

Through Polk Tennessee symbolically fulfilled its unifying role of linking East and West, a process that began when trappers, hunters, and settlers crossed Great Britain's Proclamation Line and continued with Jackson's glorification of the common man—the multitude of politicians, preachers, and tradesmen who spread government, religion, and wealth across America.

But Tennessee was twice a border state. Ironically, manifest destiny was at its height during the same years when the maelstrom of sectional controversy was unleashed. "Our Federal Union, it must be preserved!" Andrew Jackson had thundered in response to the separatism preached by his enemy John C. Calhoun. States' rights and other issues entered the debate over southern states' secession, as they had done under Jackson, but at its heart now lay the question of slavery. It was disingenuous for a people so jealous of their own independence to oppose the right of other human beings to be free.

Competition over whether new territories would permit or exclude slavery now rivaled the desire to extend the nation. The annexation of Texas and Oregon had a bitter aspect, for Northerners felt that Polk's efforts to acquire Oregon did not match his attention to Texas. And there was wide-ranging debate over how much land the United States should realize from Mexico.

Like the new territories and the nation as a whole, Tennessee was self-divided. From its beginning the land that would be Tennessee was visited by black Americans. Two "Negro slaves" were with Daniel Boone on the frontier. Several of the Patriot colonels at King's Mountain were accompanied by "servants" who took up arms against the British in the heat of battle. James Robertson and John Donelson brought slaves on their journeys to the Cumberland River country. Slavery, its existence and growth, reflected Tennessee's geography. Where the land was tilted along mountainsides and valleys were narrow, there was little profit in owning slaves, but where bluegrass meadows flourished and wide river bottoms unfolded, labor intensive crops yielded rich returns.

Thus, when the Civil War began Tennessee was in many ways a paradox. When North Carolina ceded its Over-Mountain territory to the United States in 1784 it had specified "that no regulations made or to be made by Congress shall tend to emancipate slaves." Apparently there was some suspicion about their offspring's dedication to the cause of slavery, a suspicion confirmed a few years later when the Knoxville *Gazette* urged that an abolition society should be organized. A Manumission Society of Tennessee formed in 1815 in Jefferson Country was followed by several anti-slavery newspapers, and by 1827 East Tennessee contained nearly one-fifth of all anti-slavery societies in the United States.

But the rest of the state dictated the course that Tennessee would take. Only one person in East Tennessee owned more than 100 slaves while in West Tennessee there were 86 owners who could claim that many. Overall, slaves were more than one-fourth of Tennessee's total population.

Although Tennessee joined the Confederacy, its natural and human resources as a border state helped the Union as well as the South. There were an estimated 100,000 to 135,000 Confederate volunteers (their number exceeded by no other state), but Tennessee also sent 35,000 to 50,000 volunteers to the Union cause, and some 20,000 black Tennesseans served in the war. Critical to both sides were such landscape features as railroads, the Cumberland Gap (through which Union volunteers made their way north), and the rivers that helped make the valley of East Tennessee a breadbasket (a Richmond newspaper referred to East Tennessee as "the keystone of the Southern arch"). It is not surprising that battles and skirmishes ranging from Cumberland Gap on its northern border with Kentucky to Fort Pillow on the Mississippi would leave Tennessee outnumbered only by Virginia in Civil War engagements on its soil.

From Shiloh in the spring of 1862 to the winter of 1864 in the upper Tennessee Valley, crossing and recrossing Tennessee, the suffering, often hungry, usually ill-shod soldiers wounded the land as well as each other. Fields were stripped of crops, fence rails were used for firewood, woodlands were devastated. A traveler across the state after the war found the land "a womb of desolation." To another visitor it was "one wide, wild, and dreary wasteland."

Still divided in geography and politics and now economically devastated by the destruction of farms and the loss on investments in slave labor, Tennesseans moved from war to uneasy peace and a new era. With money scarce for everyone, especially the freed slaves, and credit coming from distant banks, a vicious system of farm tenancy eventually yoked most of the ex-slaves and many small white farmers as well to the land.

Even while this new kind of rural bondage was evolving, capitalists from other regions of the country, some of whom had seen the Tennessee country while serving in the Union army, were moving to join local entrepreneurs in developing commercial and industrial enterprises across the state. Only two months after Appomattox, petroleum, coal, mining, and manufacturing companies had received state charters and by 1869 one-sixth of Knoxville's business properties were owned by northern businessmen. Chattanooga was energized by an industrial growth described by one newspaper editor as "the frozen fingers of the North" being laid "in the warm palms of the South." Only the toll of a yellow fever epidemic claiming thousands of lives delayed Memphis for a decade in joining Nashville and the other urban centers in their growth.

Gradually Tennessee was beginning its long turn from rural roots in the land to an urban, industrial state, a new frontier. It was not an easy turning, and many of the industries took advantage of the abundant natural resources and the continued poverty of many of the people that invited exploitation. Cycles of prosperity and panic, as in America as a whole, culminated in the Great Depression of the 1930s.

By this time the state's major cities had appalling numbers of people needing food, clothing, and medicine, but an even more formidable problem plagued owners and tenants still dependent on the land. The cost of growing crops—including land taxes and interest on money borrowed for seed and labor—remained fixed while markets plummeted. In 36 counties of Middle and West Tennessee prices for King Cotton declined in 1932 from 35 cents a pound to six cents. Meanwhile, in the hardscrabble mountain country of East Tennessee and the Cumberlands, the old motto of "make do or do without" took on urgent new meaning. New mining and textile industries brought jobs but also brutal labor wars, with convicts sometimes used to replace striking workers.

An essential ingredient for survival on old and new frontiers, during good times and bad, was always music. Leutze understood this when he swung a fiddle and bow across the back of one of his young Westerners. And the land that Tennesseans claimed by blood and survey and deed of ownership they also made theirs by song and story. Here, too, their varied geography, their exuberance as a border people between East and West, North and South, brought forth a diversity of voices. Several would become national icons.

In the Tennessee mountains, neighbor to North Carolina and Virginia and Kentucky, singing was said to be "more common and universal than in any other area of equal geographic size in the country." Ballads brought from Scottish highlands and the British Isles by people who lived close to the land preserved and adapted stories of unrequited love, murder, all the human passions. When labor and racial conflict erupted in East Tennessee in the 1890s the Coal Creek Wars provided situations and emotions for a new kind of ballad. People told their stories in *Coal Creek Troubles* and *Coal Creek March.*

Hard work across the land found voice when black convicts in the Cumberlands created *Lone Rock Song* and black railroad workers in upper East Tennessee chanted *Nine-Pound Hammer.* A deadly plague to the cotton crop in Middle and West Tennessee was lamented in *The Boll Weevil.* These were among the many songs that grew out of daily, sometimes deadly, labor in fields and underground.

Music that found echoes around the world was called the blues. Up the Tennessee River from Alabama and up the Mississippi from the Delta, the father of the blues, W.C. Handy, brought memories on hearing laborers sing along the riverbanks. His *Memphis Blues* and *Beale Street Blues* became classics, and when he sang in *Joe Turner's Blues* that "Sometimes I feel like somethin' throwed away," he captured the mood of many fellow Americans. His remedy was to get his guitar and "play the blues all day."

Tennessee's widest influence on the music world came with the birth of a new way to carry its sound to the rest of America—the radio—and the radio's marriage to country music in the capital city of Nashville. As its name "country" professed, this music was rooted in the country, the rural heartland of Tennessee, in the same way that ballads had risen from the mountains and the blues from river bottomlands. Its stars never abandoned that appeal. Most of the male and female musicians that made up the Grand Ole Opry were born in the country, knowing its harshness as well as its beauty, its loneliness and longings as well as its richness. Even the most legendary of stars, Elvis Presley, whose career moved him from a little frame rural birthplace in Mississippi to a Memphis mansion and who could blend rhythm with blues and sing country with a beat, somehow remained a Hound Dog country boy to fans around the world.

Words sung, spoken, or written have been everlastingly important to Tennesseans. Bellowed forth at religious camp meetings, expounded at political rallies, gathered in storytellings around a winter fire or at summer family reunions, or printed in newspapers, broadsides, and books, words have shaped and interpreted the life of the land. African Americans cherished those who could interpret their ambivalence of rage and laughter, of acceptance and resistance to the rigors of their life. Their rich culture was eventually collected in anthologies and songbooks and used in fiction by African Americans and others alike. The Cherokees knew the power of words and held their orators in as high esteem as their warriors. Their Sequoyah did what no other individual in human history had accomplished when he invented a written language for his people, making them literate—with their own written constitution and newspaper—almost overnight.

When the stern Presbyterian Reverend Samuel Doak came to Tennessee before it was even a state, he brought with him the first books in the back country, walking beside his horse while the books rode safely in sturdy saddlebags. But at their Constitutional Convention in 1796, Tennesseans made no provision for public education. Unlike New England where as early as 1637 any township with as many as a hundred households was ordered to set up a grammar school to fit youth for the university, in Tennessee the system was reversed, with the college provided first, leaving it up to the individual to prepare for admission the best way he could, usually by private tutor.

Blount College, established in 1794, eventually became the land-grant University of Tennessee with campuses from Knoxville to Memphis, but it would be 1853 before Governor Andrew Johnson, illiterate himself until he married and was tutored by his wife, pointed out the inadequacy of common—also called "pauper's"schools—and overwhelmed powerful opponents to hustle through the legislature in 1854 a bill to levy and tax "from the people of the Whole state" for public schools.

Public education made great strides—and then became a casualty of war. During the Civil War and its aftermath people who could barely eke out from the land sufficient food, shelter, and clothing to keep them alive gave little thought to the three R's. By 1872 fewer than one-fifth of Tennessee's school-age people had any means of education. It would be a quarter-century and longer before every county could claim tax-supported schools. The costly injustice of a dual system requiring separate buildings, teachers, and facilities to meet the laws of segregation left black students doubly handicapped, with appropriations only a fraction of those allowed for their white counterparts.

But Tennessee did make contributions to our nation's cultural life not only in music but in literature that grew out of long attachment to the land. The variety of their voices reached special significance in the 1930s.

In Nashville a literary discussion was initiated whose echoes may be heard today. Its theme was the tension between a life lived close to the land and a life sacrificed to less satisfying industrial progress. The name its 12 contributors based at Vanderbilt University gave themselves was, appropriately, the Agrarians. They included talented poets, novelists, historians who spoke for the survival of an agrarian way of life that was being threatened by an impersonal, centralized, technology society. In a collection of personal testimonials, *I'll Take My Stand,* published in 1930, these articulate spokesmen (no women included) saw the Southern past as an ideal of self-sufficiency represented by the small farmer who cherished the land and his own individuality. Overwhelming him was a technological juggernaut which threatened to create a standardized culture attuned to commercial outside influences, mostly from the North.

This carefully crafted credo aroused debate not only in Tennessee but across the nation as people sought renewed prosperity and financial security without sacrificing old values, sought to solve racial and economic inequities while encouraging distinctive cultural vitality. Critics labeled the Agrarians "champions of a second Lost Cause" motivated by elitist nostalgia.

Presenting a personal view of those living on a subsistence level closest to the land during those Depression years was Tennessee-born James Agee. In his unique book, *Let Us Now Praise Famous Men,* he loosed his array of talents as poet, novelist, journalist, dramatist, and social commentator in an all encompassing effort to capture the daily experience of tenant farmers. Commissioned as a magazine article it grew into a book. Accompanied by Walker Evans's starkly sensitive photographs, it was and continues to be a searing indictment of generations of exploitation of both land and people, in Alabama in this case but reflecting conditions across much of rural Tennessee and the South.

Three years before beginning work on this landmark book, *Fortune* magazine had published his article about an innovative new government agency, the Tennessee Valley Authority. In two famous sentences he captured the essential geography, history, rhythm and power of the river: "The Tennessee River system begins on the worn magnificent crests of the southern Appalachians, among the earth's older mountains, and the Tennessee River shapes its valley into the form of a boomerang, bowing its seep through seven states. Near Knoxville the streams still fresh from the mountains are linked and thence the master stream spreads the valley most richly southward, swims past Chattanooga and bends down into Alabama to roar like blown smoke through the flood-gates of Wilson Dam, to slide becalmed along the crop-cleansed fields of Shiloh, to march due north across the high diminished plains of Tennessee and through Kentucky spreading marshes toward the valley's end where, finally, at the toes of Paducah, in one wide glassy golden swarm the water stoops forward and continuously dies into the Ohio."

This exceptional valley which had once beckoned pioneers westward to its fertile land teeming with all manner of life was by 1930 the most poverty-stricken river basin in the United States. Floods ravaged its fields and cities and also those of the Ohio and Mississippi, rivers swollen by the Tennessee's waters. There was little navigation on the Tennessee or its tributaries and access to electric power was limited or non-existent. Fields were in a poor state of cultivation and hills stripped of their forest cover were scarred by erosion. Where the land suffered people suffered: the annual personal income was less than half the national average. The equation of the human condition with the condition of the landscape was simple and obvious, but the solution had to be complex and challenging.

A Nebraska senator, George W. Norris, had become interested in the possible usefulness of an abandoned hydroelectric plant built at the wild Muscle Shoals rapids in northwest Alabama during World War I. Discussion with President Franklin D. Roosevelt of the potential of this asset led to a historic message sent to Congress on April 10, 1933. The President deplored "the continued idleness of a great national investment" and asked Congress to enlarge the small Muscle Shoals development to include the entire Tennessee River.

The plan, specific and bold, was for "legislation to create a Tennessee Valley Authority—a corporation clothed with the power of government but possessed of the flexibility and initiative of a private enterprise."

TVA, as it came to be known, stood for a broad utilization of resources: hydroelectric power, flood control, soil erosion, reforestation, elimination of marginal lands from agricultural use, and industrial development. As Roosevelt concluded, TVA involved "national planning for a complete watershed involving many States and the future lives and welfare of millions. It touches and gives life to all forms of human concerns." In a state where the word "plan," especially if initiated by "outsiders," was often considered a bad word, one of history's most comprehensive resource planning efforts was under way.

A giant stairway of dams and reservoirs changed the face of the land by creating "The Great Lakes of the South" and through the years held back floods whose cost would have been in the billions. River navigation increased. Electric power flowed into remote rural areas, fed metropolitan growth, and attracted a variety of industries. Improvement of the wounded land and forests was linked to a vast fertilizer development project and, at a social level, to community leadership programs. Meanwhile, visitors from around the world came to learn how they might adapt TVA's concept of multifaceted development of an entire regional entity to their own resource situations.

Its very success made TVA controversial. From its beginning private power companies viewed it as an unfair competitor. Eventually the use of stripmined coal in its steam plants and a heavy investment in nuclear power brought into question TVA's environmental commitments and lessened public support. Once seen as radical in the extreme, it was now labeled reactionary. The balance between power plants and all they represented and care of the land and all it involved was indeed a delicate one to maintain.

TVA electric power took on a worldwide significance when it helped release the only recently discovered power of the atom. Born in mystery, the Manhattan Project was located in East Tennessee due to the available electricity, the labor supply, and especially the terrain. Secrecy demanded an inland location while possible hazardous contamination meant that it should be surrounded by valleys and ridges.

At a place called the Black Oak Ridge—later Oak Ridge—the vision of Albert Einstein for harnessing the power of the atom and a simple "O.K." by President Roosevelt appropriating two billion dollars came together to create the nation's first uranium purifying plant. Known only by the code name "Y-12," it represented a new unknown frontier.

Oak Ridge's residents were brilliant scientists and engineers gathered from universities and laboratories around the world. They were generals from the armed services, administrators, and in a great horde they were laborers laying down roads and streets in winter mud and summer dust, constructing dormitories and barracks, single and multi-family homes, trailers, stores—a city. Where there were woods and fields and scattered farmhouses a few months earlier, miles of bristling fences appeared. Questions and rumors were forbidden.

On August 6, 1945, when the atomic bomb was dropped on Hiroshima, Japan, Oak Ridge learned the immediate purpose of its existence while the world entered a new age of human existence.

Continuing research at Oak Ridge National Laboratory addressed both war and peace and stirred some of the old mystery that surrounded its beginning. Conclusions reached by J.H. Rush, a physicist who worked on the atomic project, remain relevant today. Rush believed that "the specific horror of atomic war had obscured the real meaning of the Manhattan District Project. What the project signified was that mankind was moving into a new order of power over itself and the environment, that henceforth the consequences of man's acts must be weighed with utmost caution."

Self-discipline and the wise use of nature. If the first is a supreme reminder posed by Oak Ridge, the other is best exemplified by the Great Smoky Mountains National Park. They are physically separated by an hour's drive but when the last descendant of a pioneer family still living in the national park was asked by a visitor, "How far is it from the Great Smokies to Oak Ridge?" she replied, "About a hundred years."

Her figure was off by several million years but the spirit of her answer was accurate in the Tennessee way of measuring distances between places and people by time as well as space, by personal experience as well as by immediate appearance.

Perhaps just as pathbreaking as Oak Ridge in the way it links people and nature, this is the first national park (dedicated in 1940) not granted by Washington from its public lands but rather bought by the people themselves. Tennessee and North Carolina's state funds, philanthropic gifts of the wealthy, schoolchildren's nickels and dimes, all became a legacy for future generations. For years it has attracted more visitors than any of our other national parks. Here is a green kingdom of more varieties of trees than in all of Europe, where birds can migrate vertically from the valleys to high pinnacles rather than migrating to a distant habitat, where the diversity of animal and aquatic life reached from the lordly black bear to the lowly salamander, each claiming its own territory.

Cabins, farms, a mill, a schoolhouse, a church still stand in the park as witness to the hard, independent, often rewarding life of those early settlers in this land of the western waters. And along its western boundary a segment of the Cherokee still live on the special reservation won after fierce guerrilla resistance to Removal.

Outside the park the spirit of Richard Henderson flourishes. Land speculation measures the acres in fractions rather than seven digits. Noise pollutes the air. Luxury and tawdriness vie for space and dollars. But in the quiet, fresh depths of the Great Smokies we are as close to Eden as we shall ever be in Tennessee. There is no still water in the Smokies, no lakes or ponds, only the sight and sound and smell of springs born fresh from the earth and the streams they feed that gather into rushing rivers. The great source of nourishment for all other life in the park is thereby continually revealed to us.

This interdependence of all life on the land is repeated in many inviting and informative ways in the smaller but distinctive state parks established to bring people and their place into more appreciation.

Inspired by the bountiful land across the state are noteworthy sites where dedicated idealists once sought to enlarge the old sense of family by creating Edenic communities separate from the stale or corrupt practices of long-settled societies they had fled.

In 1763 German linguist Christian Priber brought books and pen and paper to found a Kingdom of Paradise among the Cherokee mountain villages most remote from the coastal cities. He prospered until the British saw his Kingdom as a threat to their own. Captured, he was imprisoned in Fort Frederica on the Carolina coast where he died. In the country that is now West Tennessee Philadelphia merchant Samuel Hazard proposed in 1772 establishment of a vast colony dedicated to freedom of worship—for Protestants only! Further east an agrarian paradise far from the noise and strife of the complex industrial society perhaps foreshadowed later creations of suburbs and movements "back to the land." But Julius Wayland's Ruskin Colony, founded in Dickson County in 1894, was also doomed to failure.

The most wide-ranging utopias, planned earlier in the century than Wayland's, emblematized their founders' fears concerning the tremendous growth of Eastern cities—intuitions that, though new technological developments could help organize America, they would not benefit those who were not fully part of the society and could foster impersonal relationships and even civil strife. These utopias represented not merely escapes from the city but attempts, on a small scale, to balance society's complexities.

English author Thomas Hughes established his colony of Rugby in the Cumberland Mountains about 1880 to attract the English gentry's younger sons. Reared as aristocrats, they were denied the preparation necessary to maintain their gentility and earn a livelihood. In Rugby they would compete to raise the best crops and to "write the best books . . . teach best, govern best" and all this "without the risks of shop-keeping and the tricks of trade" of the city. Furthermore, Hughes felt that "a good stream of Englishmen into the Southern states" might heal some of the bitterness left from the Civil War.

Unfortunately, far from reconciling conflict within the surrounding society, Rugby itself became embroiled in disputes over land titles and government by an absentee corporation, and it suffered from the unaccustomed warm climate and an epidemic of typhoid fever. More importantly, since the young aristocrats remained aloof from their Tennessee neighbors, they were perceived as being short on the "guts, grit, and gizzard" necessary to be farmers on this land. Thomas Hughes left Rugby in 1887, never to return.

Frances ("Fanny") Wright, a wealthy Scotswoman born in 1795, fell in love with America and Tennessee and promoted ideas to make them better—ideas so advanced that wherever she went she made headlines. Economic and political reforms, women's rights, abolition of slavery, universal public education, all burgeoned in her speeches and under her pen. Seeking to put her ideas into practice, she established a farm called Nashoba in 1825 on the Wolf River near Memphis. Her primary aim was to allow slaves to work the land, simultaneously paying off their purchase price and learning to become productive citizens.

As one would expect, Nashoba encountered hostility from the surrounding slave society, a hostility that deepened when Wright decided to change social relations even further by creating what would be called today open marriage and no-fault divorce. "Affection," she said, "shall form the only marriage."

But deeper problems lay within the community itself. White people had conceived and directed the plan, without regard to the views of the blacks. Wright felt that another problem was that "there is nothing more difficult than to make men work in these parts." She sardonically summed up Nashoba's dilemma in a letter to a friend, a feeling probably shared by many of the new dwellers of America's emerging big cities: "Cooperation has well nigh killed us all." In January 1830, she sailed for New Orleans with the entire black population of Nashoba and resettled them in Haiti.

And yet Wright also stated in that year that her purpose had been "to develop all the intellectual and physical powers of all human beings, without regard to sex of physical condition, class, race, nation, or color." That message, recalling the mural's inclusion of black youth and Irish immigrant, remains on our agenda today. Indeed, although Tennessee's proposed Edens were motivated in part by the old, continuing appetite for land that brought the frontier people topping the mountains, Appalachians or Rockies, across the nation, this appetite was enlightened by the equally old desire for spiritual and civic fulfillment. This desire has persisted in Tennessee and the nation even after 1893, when the historian Frederick Jackson Turner declared that America's frontier was closed.

Westward Ho!

If Leutze were creating his mural today the outstretched arm of the farmer—"Tennesseian"—urging his companions westward might be turned back toward Tennessee. There, from Oak Ridge to medical and distribution complexes in Memphis, the challenging frontier of science and technology beckons. There, from the Great Smokies to the Mississippi, the awesome diversity and fragility of life opens before us each day. New realms of scientific and social and spiritual possibilities await exploration. Tennessee's meaning is no longer as a border state between East and West or North and South but as a borderland between yesterday and tomorrow.

WILMA DYKEMAN AND DYKEMAN STOKELY,
NEWPORT

THE
TENNESSEE
ENCYCLOPEDIA
OF HISTORY & CULTURE

ACKLEN, ADELICIA (1817–1887), one of the wealthiest women of the South, was born March 15, 1817, the daughter of Oliver Bliss Hayes, a prominent Nashville lawyer, judge, Presbyterian minister, land speculator, and cousin to President Rutherford B. Hayes. At age 22, she married Isaac Franklin of Sumner County, a wealthy cotton planter and slave trader, who was 28 years older. They had four children, none of whom survived childhood. After seven years of marriage, Franklin died, leaving his widow an inheritance valued at approximately one million dollars, including seven Louisiana cotton plantations, a 2,000-acre farm in Middle Tennessee, and 750 slaves.

Three years after Franklin's death, she married Colonel Joseph A. S. Acklen, a Huntsville, Alabama, lawyer, who signed a prenuptial contract giving his wife complete control of all her businesses, property, and assets. The couple began immediate construction of Belmont, a 20,000 square-foot summer villa, now maintained as a house museum. The Acklens lived a sumptuous lifestyle, traveling between Belmont in the summer and their Louisiana plantations in the winter. The couple had six children, two of whom died young. Joseph Acklen, a superb businessman and plantation manager, tripled his wife's fortune by 1860; he died during the Civil War.

Adelicia Acklen faced financial ruin when the Confederate army threatened to burn 2,800 bales of her cotton to keep it from falling into Union possession. Acklen boldly rushed to Louisiana and secretly negotiated with both sides to save her fortune. She secured Confederate promises not to burn her cotton, while the Union army agreed to help her move the cotton to New Orleans. Acklen ran the Union blockade and sold her cotton to the Rothschilds of London for a reported $960,000 in gold. Three weeks after Robert E. Lee's surrender in 1865, Acklen and her children left for Europe to retrieve the money made from this cotton sale.

In 1867 the 50-year-old Acklen married Dr. William Archer Cheatham, a respected Nashville physician. Cheatham also signed a prenuptial agreement. The couple was married 20 years, spending most of their time at Belmont in Nashville. In 1886 Acklen sold Belmont, left Nashville and Cheatham, and moved to Washington, D.C., with three of her adult children. The exact cause of her separation from Cheatham is not known. Acklen died on May 4, 1887, while on a shopping trip to New York City. She is buried in Nashville's Mt. Olivet Cemetery in a family mausoleum with her first two husbands and nine of her ten children.
Mark Brown, Belmont Mansion
SEE: BELMONT MANSION; CHEATHAM, WILLIAM A.; FRANKLIN, ISAAC; SLAVERY

ACTORS: See TENNESSEE IN FILM; TELEVISION AND MOVIE PERFORMERS; THEATER

ACUFF, ROY C. (1903–1992), known as the "King of Country Music" due to his long association with the Grand Ole Opry, was born in Maynardville, Union County, on September 15, 1903. At age 16, he moved with his family to a Knoxville suburb. A good athlete, Acuff played baseball until felled by a sunstroke in 1929. While recuperating, he learned to play the fiddle his father owned. In 1932 he joined a medicine show selling Mocatan Tonic, and in 1934 he performed on WROL radio in Knoxville. He then moved to the "Mid-Day Merry-Go-Round" on station WNOX, but in 1935 returned to WROL, where his group acquired the name the "Crazy Tennesseans." Sometime during this period, Acuff began singing *The Great Speckled Bird*, and it soon became so popular that the American

Record Company (later Columbia) recorded Acuff and his group in Chicago in October 1936.

Since 1934 Judge George Hay had rebuffed Acuff's attempts to sing on the Grand Ole Opry. Acuff persisted in his efforts and, on February 5, 1938, made his audition appearance on the Opry singing *The Great Speckled Bird*. The Opry received a favorable mail response and he was offered a regular spot on the show two weeks later. WSM General Manager Harry Stone insisted, however, that the group change its name to the "Smoky Mountain Boys." Stone felt that "Crazy Tennesseans" might be interpreted as a slur against the state, and he wanted to avoid confusion with "Crazy Water Crystals," an advertiser for a popular laxative.

Acuff decided to cast his future with the traditional string band sound, but his band disagreed and quit early in 1939. Acuff quickly hired Pete "Brother Oswald" Kirby, Lonnie Wilson, and Jake Tindell to replace Clell Sumney, Red Jones, and Imogene "Tiny" Sarrett. Later that year he hired Rachel Veach.

Acuff supplemented his income by compiling and selling songbooks of his songs, a venture that eventually led to the establishment of Acuff-Rose Publishing in October 1942. Acuff-Rose became a cornerstone for Nashville's growing music industry and the first successful business outside the Grand Ole Opry. During the 1940s, Acuff's hits included *Pins and Needles, Beneath That Lonely Mound of Clay, The Precious Jewel, The Wreck on the Highway, Fire Ball Mail, Wait for That Light to Shine, Two Different Worlds,* and *The Wabash Cannonball*.

Acuff began hosting "The Prince Albert" segment of the Grand Ole Opry in October 1939. The exposure on the NBC radio network broadcast made him a national star. In April 1946, Acuff left the Grand Ole Opry and the "Prince Albert" show, however, out of frustration with the Opry's requirement that he return every Saturday night to perform. Acuff's popularity kept him in constant demand for personal appearances at much higher fees than what the Opry paid. After leaving Nashville, Acuff toured the West Coast and appeared in seven movies. Red Foley, a smooth-voiced singer from WLS's "The National Barn Dance" in Chicago, replaced Acuff on the Opry. Without regular network exposure, the demand for Acuff's appearances dwindled, and he returned to the Opry to re-establish himself as a major performer.

In 1948 Acuff became the Republican nominee for governor of Tennessee and won a large vote, but lost the election. That same year, he opened his Dunbar Cave resort just outside Clarksville, where he performed regularly.

After the early 1950s, Acuff was no longer a major recording artist, though he continued to tour until he was involved in a near-fatal accident in 1965. In 1962 he became the first living artist elected to the Coun-try Music Hall of Fame. Acuff gained recognition and appreciation from young fans after the Nitty Gritty Dirt Band recorded *Will the Circle Be Unbroken* in 1971.

Acuff considered the opening of the new Opry House one of the highlights of his career. On that date, March 16, 1974, he performed with President Richard Nixon on the Opry stage.

After Acuff's wife, Mildred, died in 1981, the Opryland Music Group purchased Acuff-Rose Publishing, which was actually in her name. Roy Acuff spent his final years living in a home on the grounds of Opryland and performing on the Opry each weekend. The widely respected icon of country music died on November 23, 1992.

Don Cusic, Belmont University

SEE: ACUFF-ROSE; DUNBAR CAVE STATE NATURAL AREA; GRAND OLE OPRY; MUSIC

ACUFF-ROSE, a music publishing company, was founded by Roy Acuff and Fred Rose and officially incorporated on October 13, 1942. The company's start-up capital included $25,000 from Acuff (which was never touched) and $2,500 from BMI, a performance rights organization. Roy Acuff wanted the company to supplement his income from performances. He had been selling songbooks and, by 1942 this sideline had become so extensive that Acuff approached Fred Rose with a plan to establish a music publishing company.

Fred Rose (1897–1954), a pop music songwriter, had written songs like *Deed I Do* and *Honest and Truly,* and played piano for Paul Whiteman's band. In 1938 he gave up a popular show on WSM and moved to Hollywood to write songs for Gene Autry movies. When Autry joined the Army Air Corps as a pilot in 1942, Rose returned to Nashville and quickly landed an afternoon radio show.

Acuff chose his future partner well. Rose was an ASCAP songwriter with connections in New York, Chicago, and Hollywood. A gifted editor and talent scout, Rose willingly offered his expertise to other songwriters. A practicing Christian Scientist, Rose held himself to the highest ethical standards and gained a reputation for honesty and fairness. Fred Rose was in a unique position. He knew the people at WSM and the Opry, he had learned about the huge market for country music—and the money involved—through his work with Autry and the singing cowboys in the movies, and he was a pop songwriter who came to Nashville as country music was changing from a folk-based music into a major commercial music. Rose would play a major role, introducing the pop song format with country topics to replace the folk song format. This had already been done with western music, most of which was composed by Tin Pan Alley writers who used pop song structures with western themes. Fred Rose would take that same process to Nashville and apply it to southern-based country music.

In September 1946, Acuff-Rose signed songwriter Hank Williams and soon obtained a recording contract for him with the Sterling label. Although Williams later switched to MGM, his songs became the cornerstone for the Acuff-Rose catalog. Their first major pop hit was *Tennessee Waltz* by Patti Page in 1950. In addition to the songs of Hank Williams, such as *Your Cheatin' Heart*, *Jambalaya*, *I'm So Lonesome I Could Cry*, and *Hey, Good Lookin'*, Acuff-Rose also published songs by Pee Wee King, Don Gibson, Felice and Boudeleaux Bryant, the Everly Brothers, Roy Orbison, John D. Loudermilk, Marty Robbins, Bob Luman, Leon Payne, Doug Kershaw, and Mickey Newbury. Their published songs include *Bye Bye Love*; *I Can't Stop Loving You*; *Dream, Dream, Dream*; *When Will I Be Loved*; *Oh, Lonesome Me*; *Oh, Pretty Woman*; *I Love You Because*; *Lost Highway*; *Making Believe*; and *Blue Eyes Crying in the Rain*.

Don Cusic, Belmont University

SEE: ACUFF, ROY C.; ROSE, K. FRED; WILLIAMS, HANK

ADAMS, JESSE F. (1891–1964), rural Middle Tennessee medical pioneer and entrepreneur, was born in Cannon County, Tennessee, on October 19, 1881. He married Laura Elizabeth Hudson, a Texas native, in 1907 and they had nine children. Adams graduated from Vanderbilt University Medical School in 1911 and established a practice at Short Mountain in Cannon County. In 1912 he shifted his practice to Bradyville; in 1918–19 he served one year active duty in the U.S. Army Reserve Medical Corps. In 1924 Adams moved his practice to Woodbury, the county seat, where he purchased and converted the remaining dormitory of the Baptist Female College of 1859 into his private home and office. This house is listed in the National Register of Historic Places.

His vast medical contributions to this rural region included two terms as county health officer and establishing the first county hospital, the Good Samaritan Hospital, from 1933–34 during the Great Depression. Few rural Tennessee counties at that time had such modern facilities at their disposal. Adams created the hospital as his own "public works" project and accepted no direct governmental assistance. He also was a small-town example of a "civic capitalist," playing an instrumental role in Woodbury acquiring the Armour and Company Cheese Plant in 1935. Twelve years later, he helped to convince the Colonial Shirt Corporation to establish a Woodbury factory. The Colonial factory was the county's chief industrial employer for the next 40 years. Adams served, as well, as the president of the Bradyville Bank, the Cannon County Banking Company, and the Woodbury Bank of Commerce.

In 1950 Adams donated the hospital to the county and announced his retirement. But by 1955, he was back in practice and continued so until his death on May 4, 1964. He and his wife Laura, who died in 1973, are buried in the Riverside Cemetery, Woodbury. Their son, Carl E. Adams, continued the family tradition of local medical service as a founder of the neighboring Murfreesboro Medical Clinic and as a founder of National Health Corporation, a major medical company based in Murfreesboro, managed now as National Healthcare by his sons W. Andrew Adams and Robert G. Adams.

Carroll Van West, Middle Tennessee State University

SEE: CANNON COUNTY; MEDICINE

AGEE, JAMES R. (1909–1955), was born in Knoxville, Tennessee, on November 27, 1909. His father, Hugh James Agee, was of Southern Appalachian yeoman background; his mother, Laura Tyler, came from a family of means and education. The couple also had a younger child, a daughter, Emma. When the boy was six, his father was killed in an automobile accident. Shortly before his tenth birthday, Agee was enrolled in the St. Andrew's boarding school for boys, which was run and staffed by the Episcopalian monastic Order of the Holy Cross near Sewanee, Tennessee. It was there that Agee got to know Father James Harold Flye, a priest and teacher—their many letters, back and forth, would eventually see the light of day. Agee stayed at St. Andrew's until 1924. His mother had taken a house close by, but that year she returned to Knoxville because of her father's failing health, and so her son attended high school there during the school year of 1924–1925, after which he was sent to Phillips Exeter Academy, in New Hampshire. While at Exeter he began his writing career in earnest. He published fiction, poetry, and book reviews in the school's literary magazine, *The Monthly*. Soon enough he was at Harvard (1928), where he wrote for *The Advocate*—again publishing fiction, poetry, and essays. He became president of *The Advocate* in 1931, graduated in 1932, and thereafter became a reporter, then staffwriter, for *Fortune* magazine, where, between 1932 and 1936, he wrote major pieces on a broad range of subjects: "Housing," "Sheep and Shuttleworths," "Strawberries," "Steel Rails," "Cockfighting," "U.S. Ambassadors," "The American Roadside," "Drought," "Williamsburg Restored," and not least, "T.V.A." The latter was an important subject matter to him, and one that required a return to his native state, in an effort to understand the (then) hugely ambitious (and controversial) attempt to gain control of the mighty and sometimes aberrant Tennessee River.

Meanwhile, in 1933, he married Olivia Saunders, whom he had met as a Harvard undergraduate. In 1934 his poetry, which he had been publishing since his Exeter years, was collected under the title of *Permit Me Voyage* (Hart Crane's phrase), hence published by Yale Press, and he was given the Yale Younger Poets award, a most auspicious and distinguished beginning for a 25-year-old man.

In 1936 *Fortune* commissioned Agee and his photographer friend Walker Evans to do a major study of the rural South's agricultural life—a landmark assignment that would change the very nature of his personal and writing life. In Hale County, Alabama, the two men lived with white tenant farm families, observed carefully their way of life, the work they did, and the manner in which they spent their time. Agee never would do justice to that experience as a writer for *Fortune*. Instead, he devoted himself to a prolonged literary and documentary "study" of the three families he had come to know best. The result, in the autumn of 1940, was *Let Us Now Praise Famous Men*, an idiosyncratic masterpiece that willfully defies description or categorization. It is a great, sprawling, lyrical, provocative, immensely edifying, soulful, and engaging celebration of humble but worthy farm folk, and too, a mix of social reportage, narrative rendering of a particular human landscape, moral introspection, spiritual yearning. The book's appearance was untimely—the nation was by then turning its attention away from its social and economic problems in favor of its possible international role in a European war whose stakes were by then high, indeed. The book, too, was stubbornly, at times fiercely *sui generis*, and so a real challenge to reviewers who were limited by the demands of their work and the confines of the space allotted them. Soon enough, the book was out of print, a financial failure for its publisher, Houghton Mifflin.

In 1939 Agee had embarked upon his second marriage, to Alma Mailman—their son Joel Agee (now a writer of both fiction and nonfiction) was born a year later. Agee had begun writing (unsigned) book reviews around 1941 for *Time*. In 1942 he began writing signed film reviews for *The Nation*. He quickly became a much respected authority on the movies. His generous spirit, keen eye for detail, fluent writing, wonderful sense of humor, and knowing mastery of the techniques that enabled a good "moving picture" earned him a wide, devoted audience of readers.

After the war, in 1946, he entered into a third and final marriage, to Mia Fritsch, which would produce two daughters, Julia and Andrea, and a second son, John. During those last years of the 1940s, he moved from writing about film to the writing of film scripts. He wrote the commentary for Helen Levitt's film about a troubled Harlem boy, *The Quiet One*, and wrote scripts for *The Blue Hotel* and *The Bride Comes to Yellow Sky* (both movies based on Stephen Crane stories), and he worked with John Huston on the script for *The African Queen*.

In the early 1950s, he published *The Morning Watch*—another return to Tennessee: a story of a boy's unfolding adolescence, his awakening to the world, to his body. He did two more film scripts, one for *Noa-Noa*, based on Paul Gauguin's diary, and another for *The Night of the Hunter*. Years of heavy smoking, heavy drinking, all-night bouts of exuberant conversations in Manhattan bars, restaurants, apartments—a life lived intensely, sometimes recklessly—had worn down his once tall and powerful body. He developed coronary heart disease, suffered repeated bouts of angina—and on May 16, 1955 (the same day his father was killed, thirty-nine years earlier) he died in a taxicab on his way to see his physician at Manhattan's New York Hospital. At the time he had been completing a novel, *A Death in the Family*, published posthumously in 1957, which won the Pulitzer Prize, and was eventually turned into a successful Broadway play, *All the Way Home*. The novel turned out to be James Agee's final "visit" to his native Tennessee—the reader is told, in hauntingly evocative prose, of a young boy's loss of his father. The Knoxville of this century's second decade is poignantly, suggestively evoked—and as in Dickens's *David Copperfield*, family loss, in all its melancholy and perplexity, is chronicled through a child's eyes and ears, his mind and heart and soul. A 45-year-old novelist's voice became, finally, one which (calling upon an experience of early sorrow in Tennessee) would teach people across the nation and abroad how the young come to terms with life's disappointments, tragedies, and turmoil.

Robert Coles, Harvard University

SEE: LITERATURE; TENNESSEE IN FILM; ST. ANDREW'S-SEWANEE

THE AGRARIANS. The Agrarians were a group of social critics centered around Vanderbilt University in the 1930s. They drew their name from their frankly reactionary resistance to industrial capitalism and their insistence that southern rural and small-town culture offered its best antidote. The theory of agrarianism, they argued in their anthology of essays, *I'll Take My Stand: The South and the Agrarian Tradition* (1930), "is that the culture of the soil is the best and most sensitive of vocations, and that therefore it should have the economic preference and enlist the maximum number of workers."[1]

I'll Take My Stand grew out of a circle of Vanderbilt students and professors who began meeting informally to discuss ideas in the 1910s. The membership and interests of the group changed over time; in the 1920s, a collective shift toward poetry resulted in the *Fugitive*, a literary magazine published between 1922 and 1925. The Agrarian effort, organized by Vanderbilt professors and poets John Crowe Ransom and Donald Davidson and their former student, poet

Allen Tate, represented a distinctive intellectual offshoot of the old circle. Of the twelve contributors to *I'll Take My Stand*, six were current or former members of the Vanderbilt faculty (Ransom, Davidson, psychologist Lyle Lanier, economist Herman C. Nixon, historian Frank L. Owsley, and English professor John Donald Wade) and four were former students (Tate, Henry B. Kline, Andrew Nelson Lytle, and Robert Penn Warren). The final two contributors—critic Stark Young and poet John Gould Fletcher—were literary acquaintances of Tate.

The Agrarians were bound tightly by ties of mutual affection, but only loosely by shared intellectual commitments. The contributors attempted to adopt a unified tone and platform, but differed in rhetoric, approach, and social attitudes. Some were frankly elitist, identifying with the aristocratic pretensions of the antebellum southern slaveholding elite; others were populist, upholding the hardy folk culture of the southern yeoman farmer. Although appearing on the cusp of the Great Depression, the volume represented a fundamental act of resistance to the consumer-driven mass culture that emerged in the 1920s. The book was a complex amalgam of southernism and economic radicalism.

The leading Agrarians—Ransom, Davidson, and Tate—were discouraged by the banal sloganeering of American culture, and yet they were equally disgusted with conservative cultural critics such as the New Humanists, led by classicists Irving Babbitt and Paul Elmer More. In Tate's view, the Humanists proposed nothing better than an ersatz religion of great books; in Ransom's mind they were 100 percent schoolmasters who made no effective appeal to the American public. Ransom, Davidson, and Tate envisioned an alternative southern humanism. Unlike the literary program of the Humanists, Agrarianism was an economic program. The Agrarians disdained the notion that social change occurred as elites introduced cultural material "from the top." As Davidson wrote, "A movement of reform must begin at the base of our life—that is, with its economic base. And the Humanists have practically nothing to say on the subject of economics."[2]

The Agrarians believed industrial society undercut the dignity of human labor. Modern man, they argued, was bereft of vocation and glutted with the surfeit of consumer goods churned out by the industrial economy. Industrialism eviscerated local cultures; it was antithetical to religion, arts, and the social "amenities," including manners, conversation, hospitality, sympathy, family life, and romance. The Agrarians rejected not only northern economic imperialism, but also the cultural imperialism of an incipient commercial juggernaut. They favored subsistence over commercial agriculture. "Do what we did after the war and the Reconstruction," Lytle memorably enjoined his fellow southerners. "Return to our looms, our handcrafts, our reproducing stock. Throw out the radio and take down the fiddle from the wall."[3]

Despite their robust call for economic resistance to consumer capitalism, the Agrarians' actual economic program was rather thin. In the mid-1930s, the Agrarians attempted a strategic alliance with the Distributists, a group of Anglo-American thinkers, who advocated a return to small property-holding. Their joint manifesto, *Who Owns America? A New Declaration of Independence* (1936), was a lackluster follow-up to *I'll Take My Stand*. In addition, their decision to adopt the pose of unreconstructed southerners (the original symposium included a rather moderate defense of racial segregation authored by Warren) left them open to damaging attacks from critics, who accused them of romanticizing the Old South, overlooking the South's inequalities, ignoring the impoverished reality of much southern farm life, and fruitlessly attempting to roll back progress.

Furthermore, the Agrarians were deeply divided among themselves. Ransom, Tate, and Warren saw southernism as an alternative mythology for modern Americans. In a disenchanted age, an intense emulation of an older southern culture held out the promise of a more secure sense of moral values. At the time of the writing of *I'll Take My Stand*, all three embraced religious skepticism, but yearned for the certainties of a faith they could not accept. Their concerns tended to be universal in nature. Tate wearied of the book's sectionalism early on and was horrified by the title, a lyric from the Confederate tune "Dixie," which was adopted over his strenuous objections. Davidson viewed the Agrarians' southernism not as myth, but as an alternative faith he wholeheartedly accepted. As the attention of Ransom, Tate, and the other leading Agrarians wandered to new projects, Davidson dug deeply into regionalist commitments. His ability to re-interpret the Agrarian project as a politics of cultural identity and a thorough-going resistance to the "leviathan" nation-state profoundly affected the legacy of Agrarianism. Davidson's fusion of a generalized traditionalism with a conservative politics of anti-statism and anti-cosmopolitanism shaped postwar neo-Agrarian thinkers, such as Richard M. Weaver and M.E. Bradford. Agrarianism survived into the postwar period not only as a much-studied literary episode involving some of the South's most accomplished writers, but also as a vital source for southern conservatives, who remembered *I'll Take My Stand* less as an anti-capitalist manifesto than as the taproot of their conservative politics of philosophical anti-liberalism and cultural traditionalism.

Paul V. Murphy, Truman State University

CITATIONS:

(1) Twelve Southerners, *I'll Take My Stand: The South and the Agrarian Tradition*, Introduction by Louis D. Rubin, Jr., (Baton Rouge, 1977 [1930]), xlvii.

(2) Paul V. Murphy, "The Social Memory of the South: Donald Davidson and the Tennessee Past," *Tennessee Historical Quarterly* 55(1996): 260.

(3) *I'll Take My Stand,* 244.

SUGGESTED READINGS: Paul K. Conkin, *The Southern Agrarians* (1988); Daniel J. Singal, *The War Within: From Victorian to Modernist Thought in the South, 1919–1945* (1982)

SEE: DAVIDSON, DONALD; FUGITIVES; LYTLE, ANDREW NELSON; NIXON, HERMAN C.; OWSLEY, FRANK L.; RANSOM, JOHN CROWE; STEWART, RANDALL; TATE, JOHN O. ALLEN; VANDERBILT UNIVERSITY; WARREN, ROBERT PENN

AGRICULTURAL JOURNALS. Over the last 200 years, a number of agricultural journals have been published in Tennessee. The first, *The Tennessee Farmer,* began publication in 1834 and ran through 1840, when it and the short-lived *Southern Cultivator and Journal of Science and Improvement* (1839–40) merged with a new journal, *The Agriculturalist and Journal of the State and County Societies,* which itself lasted only until 1845. These three periodicals not only initiated a long line of farm publications, but their experience also typified the history of antebellum agricultural journalism.

Most magazines existed for a few years, experienced a set of common problems, and ended up dissolving or merging with another magazine. They were usually founded and managed by well intentioned men who had an abiding interest in the advancement of agriculture, but with little journalistic or publication experience. Their editors—often the same people who initiated the projects—came from various occupations, including educators, businessmen, employees of state government, ministers, and successful farmers. Although internal disputes over content and external disputes over leadership within the agricultural community sometimes weakened the journals, their main problems involved financial insolvency. Most found it impossible to attract advertisers and subscribers sufficient to meet their expenses. None of the antebellum journals survived the Civil War; neither did the agricultural community's penchant for founding journals. The occasional new periodical appeared in the late nineteenth century and throughout the twentieth century, only to fail a short time later. For instance, there was sporadic publication of a magazine under a version of the appellation *The Tennessee Farmer;* one by the name of *The Tennessee Farmer and Homemaker* was published as late as the 1960s.

Despite their short lives and numerous problems, these magazines performed useful functions in the rural community. The most important was to inform their readers of recent developments in technology and practice. They discussed new tools and machinery and suggested guidelines to aid farmers considering possible adoption. They evaluated and compared imported livestock strains to assist those wishing to upgrade their animals through the introduction of blooded lines. They recommended changes in farming routines, such as the use of better cultivation techniques, more effective fertilizers, and improved seed varieties. Less frequently, they advised readers on commercial and financial matters—on what products offered the greatest profit potential, on marketing strategies, and on investment options. Even less frequently, they commented on political issues of concern to farmers, *e.g.,* tariffs, banking policies, and internal improvements. The journals also surveyed farming conditions across the state, reported on agricultural fairs and conventions, and carried letters and other communications on matters of interest to rural residents. Not everything dealt directly with the crops and animals. Women received hints on managing the household, children on performing their responsibilities, and the entire family on proper moral conduct.

Over time, farm journals played a declining role in rural life. Other media—the state agricultural college and experiment station, extension service, demonstration trains, agricultural groups, and suppliers of farm goods and services—assumed the journals' function as a dispenser of information.

Donald L. Winters, Vanderbilt University

SEE: CURREY, RICHARD O.; GORDON, FRANCIS H.

AGRICULTURAL SOCIETIES. County agricultural societies played an important role in rural affairs in the period before the Civil War. Local leaders formed the organizations for the purpose of exchanging information and promoting agricultural improvement. The first of these, the Cumberland Agricultural Society, appeared in Davidson County in 1819; the second, the Washington Agricultural Society, appeared in Washington County five years later. Gradually other counties followed these early examples, and by the 1840s a number of societies were in operation.

The organizational movement waned in the late 1840s, in part because many farmers came to view societies as elitist in their membership and dilettante in their activities. But the legislature's establishment of the State Agricultural Bureau in 1854 breathed new life into the movement. The bureau subsidized the formation and operation of county societies that met certain membership and financial conditions. In addition, the bureau actively encouraged their creation, arguing that the advancement of agriculture in the state depended upon cooperation and union among farmers, beginning at the local level. The agency's involvement also instilled a more egalitarian and practical orientation in the movement, which attracted the support of a wider portion of the rural community. The bureau's activities invigorated existing societies and stimulated the formation of more societies. By the end of the 1850s, organizations operated in many counties.

The early county societies were primarily discussion groups. They met, often at the farm of a member, to discuss a predetermined topic, review a piece of new equipment, or observe the results of an improved farming technique. Sometimes they sponsored guest speakers or stock shows, to which the entire community was invited. With the proliferation of societies in the 1850s came a shift in focus. Several agricultural societies had held county fairs in the 1840s; a decade later, fairs became the primary activity of all the organizations. The main purpose of the fairs was to demonstrate improved farming methods and to encourage their adoption. Expert judges evaluated samples of crops and livestock produced by local farmers and equipment displayed by manufacturers, and awarded prizes for the top entries. Most importantly, those in attendance had the opportunity to inspect the best of the county's produce and the latest in farm technology. The county societies also cooperated with the State Agricultural Bureau in organizing fairs at the three divisional levels and at the state level. A few of the larger ones, like in Davidson County, held their own conventions and exhibitions. All of the activities emphasized conveying useful knowledge to practicing farmers.

The county societies disappeared during the Civil War and were not revived. The legislature's failure to renew subsidies to the organizations doubtlessly contributed to their demise. But the major factor was that other agencies usurped their role of providing information to farmers. In the late nineteenth and early twentieth centuries, the organization of divisional farmers' institutes and conventions, the work of the state agricultural experiment station and extension service, and the greater availability of national farm publications rendered the county societies obsolete. Moreover, local governments and commercial groups took over the county fairs, and the divisional fairs were discontinued. In 1893 the State Commissioner of Agriculture suggested restoring subsidies for resurrecting the county societies. Apparently legislative support was lacking, for the recommendation went unanswered.

Donald L. Winters, Vanderbilt University

AGRICULTURAL TENANCY is a broad, often loosely defined term used to describe a variety of land and labor arrangements in which individuals farm a plot of land that they do not own but have instead rented for a definite period of time. In Tennessee, as elsewhere across the United States, the institution has historically taken a variety of forms, with the major differences among them centering on the method of payment, allocation of risk, and degree of managerial autonomy. The most common forms of tenancy his-torically included *fixed-rent tenancy,* whereby the tenant pays the landlord a fixed amount of cash or a stipulated quantity of agricultural products (the latter often known as *standing rent*). In this arrangement the tenant assumes all the burden of risk and makes most managerial decisions independently of the landlord. Another prevalent type has been *share tenancy,* a system in which the tenant pays rent in the form of a specified proportion (or share) of all agricultural output produced on the rented acreage. Under this system part of the burden of risk shifts to the landlord, who in turn frequently demands greater control of farm operations. Technically, agricultural tenancy also includes the system of *sharecropping,* a labor arrangement in which an individual family receives (rather than pays) a share of the crop produced on a plot of land in return for their labor on the same plot. Landlord and tenant again share risk in this system, but because the landlord commonly provides work stock, tools, and seed, the landlord demands a greater degree of supervision and managerial control than under share tenancy.

Tenancy varied greatly over the last two centuries in its importance to the state's economy. Although government statistics prior to 1880 are not available, systematic study of landholding patterns in sample Tennessee counties indicates that by 1860 tenants constituted between one-sixth and one-fifth of farm operators across the state and were responsible for between five and ten percent of all farm output. The prevalence of tenancy increased dramatically after the Civil War, due to the dramatic reorganization of the state's agriculture in the aftermath of emancipation. The state's tenancy rate was 34.5 percent as early as 1880 and topped 40 percent two decades later. It remained at this high level (peaking at 46.5 percent in 1930) until it began a precipitous drop after World War II, as mechanization increasingly replaced tenant labor in the state's agricultural economy.

The precise economic effect of tenancy on Tennessee agriculture is difficult to establish. Its impact at any given point in time has probably been minimal. A study of agricultural production patterns in the late nineteenth century, for example, has shown that crop and livestock yields on Tennessee farms did not vary significantly according to the tenure of the farm operator, indicating that tenant farms were about as productive as owner-operated units. In the long run, however, the growth of tenancy may have had a detrimental impact on the state's agriculture, primarily due to the chronic restlessness of the tenant population. (A 1937 study of the U.S. Department of Agriculture found that at least one-third of all tenants changed farms annually.) Because of their indefinite tenure on the land, tenants tended to focus on maximizing their short-term income and had less incentive than owner-operators to engage in soil conservation measures and land improvements that enhance long-term productivity. Landlords efforts to require long-term improvements from tenants and monitor the extent of compliance may have mitigated the adverse effects to some (unknown) degree.

The exact social significance of agricultural tenancy is also somewhat problematic. Defenders of the institution assert that it has historically functioned as a rung on the "agricultural ladder," i.e., it has generally served tenants as a stepping stone to independent land ownership. Critics, on the other hand, view the very existence of tenancy as a sign of distress in the farm sector; according to this view, the institution has more commonly functioned as the permanent, dead-end status of a rural proletariat.

The most accurate assessment surely falls between these extremes. Undeniably, tenants always lived far closer to the margins of economic subsistence than owner-operators. On average, they worked much smaller plots than owners and received incomes only one-third to one-fourth as large. Even so, the extent of upward mobility from tenancy into independent land ownership has been impressive. A study of sample counties between 1850 and 1880 indicates that, across Tennessee as a whole, at least one-half of tenants were likely to acquire farms of their own in any given decade. Similarly, a study by the Department of Commerce in 1920 (when approximately 41 percent of all Tennessee farms were operated by tenants) found that one half of all farm owners in the East South Central United States (including Tennessee) had previously been tenants. Although the evidence is not as complete as one would desire, it does appear that the extent of movement up the "agricultural ladder" was significant. For the majority of farm tenants in Tennessee's past, hard work and perseverance evidently bore fruit, eventually, in independent farm ownership.

Robert Tracy McKenzie, University of Washington

SUGGESTED READING: Robert Tracy McKenzie, *One South or Many? Plantation Belt and Upcountry in Civil War–Era Tennessee* (1994)

SEE: SHARECROPPING

AGRICULTURAL WHEEL. The Agricultural Wheel in Tennessee traced its origins to a February 1882 meeting of seven disgruntled farmers in Prairie County, Arkansas. Concerned over continuing depressed farm prices and mounting agricultural debt, the founding farmers named their organization the Agricultural Wheel to reflect their belief that agriculture represented the "wheel" that moved the world's industrial economy—without agriculture, all other economic endeavors failed. From its humble origins, the Agricultural Wheel spread across Arkansas and into surrounding states, including Tennessee. By 1887 the National Agricultural Wheel claimed 500,000 members.

The Wheel made its first appearance in Tennessee in February 1884, when J.R. Miles organized a local wheel in Weakley County. One year later, Miles became the first and only president of the Tennessee State Wheel. By the time the National Wheel merged with the National Farmers' Alliance in 1889, Tennessee had 1,600 local wheels scattered across the state.

The Agricultural Wheel championed a radical agrarian reform program that advocated currency expansion through the free coinage of silver; an end to national banks; regulation of railroads, telegraph, and telephone, or failing regulation, nationalization of these services; restriction of the sale of public lands to American citizens; the imposition of an income tax; and the popular election of United States Senators. Wheelers recognized the need for change in state and national laws and encouraged farmers to become educated in the political economy and vote their interests. The Wheel denounced partisan politics and promised to support candidates of either party who agreed to vote the farmers' interests. In Tennessee, the Wheel was most often associated with the Democratic party; in the 1889 meeting of the Tennessee General Assembly, over 40 members claimed membership in the Wheel or Alliance.

Wheel ideology also included prescriptions for individual action and local cooperative efforts. Wheel members were urged to reduce farm expenses through self-sufficiency and good management. The state newspaper of the Wheel and Alliance, the *Weekly Toiler,* encouraged farmers to read the latest agricultural journals and attend local meetings to learn the techniques of scientific farming. Nevertheless, Wheel leaders recognized that good management counted for little unless farm expenses fell and farm prices rose. The Wheel established a cooperative system in 1888, for purchasing farm equipment and selling farm products. Financed entirely through the one-dollar assessments of individual members, the State Agency met immediate resistance from Tennessee merchants.

In 1888 and 1889 the Wheel and Alliance joined in the national boycott of jute bagging, which was used for wrapping cotton bales, to protest the precipitous rise in prices imposed by the jute trust. In Clarksville, the Wheel established a tobacco warehouse to store, grade, and sell tobacco for members. Peanut farmers on the Highland Rim worked to establish a cooperative system within the state and join their efforts with those of Virginia farmers. Locally, county wheels built mills, warehouses, and cooperative stores. With a lack of strong financial backing and in the face of considerable economic resistance, most of these efforts were of short duration.

The Agricultural Wheel's effort to reform the agricultural economy officially ended in 1889, when it merged with the Farmers' Alliance to become the

Farmers' and Laborers' Union. The Tennessee Wheel became the first state organization to ratify the new institution's constitution.

Connie L. Lester, Tennessee Historical Society

SEE: COLORED AGRICULTURAL WHEEL; COLORED FARMERS' ALLIANCE AND LABORERS' UNION, TENNESSEE; FARMERS' ALLIANCE; MCDOWELL, JOHN H.

AGRICULTURE. More than any other form of human activity, agriculture has influenced the development of Tennessee and shaped the lives of its people. It was the driving force behind the state's settlement, a vital factor in its economic growth, a major contributor to its wealthholding, the principal source of household income throughout much of its history, and a key element in the formation and perpetuation of its cultural heritage. It has affected, directly and indirectly, the relationships of Tennesseans with each other and with people outside the state, and in significant ways, it has defined their place in national and international affairs. The influence of agriculture on Tennessee's past has been diverse and sometimes ambiguous. It has embraced change and sustained tradition, embodied success and occasioned failure, stimulated advancement and resisted progress. Agriculture, in short, has played a central role in the history of Tennessee.

The vast majority of immigrants, who participated in the settlement of Tennessee in the late eighteenth and early nineteenth centuries, shared a set of aspirations. They sought to create new and productive lives for themselves, their immediate families, and their heirs by exploiting the virgin territory's rich farming potential. This objective, more than any other factor, sustained the state's dynamic population growth in the early years and accounted for its rapid transition from frontier to mature settlement. Settlers first occupied the broad eastern valleys of the Tennessee and Holston river systems and the fertile central basin encircling the Cumberland River. By the time Tennessee entered the Union in 1796, these regions already supported substantial agricultural production. Settlement soon spread to the Cumberland Plateau and the Eastern Highland Rim situated between the eastern valleys and the central basin. Although sterile soil and barren terrain slowed and restricted the growth of agriculture in this area, farming eventually became the core source of livelihood for its residents. After the removal in 1818 of the last Chickasaw, claims in the state, farmers moved across the Western Highland Rim to the western valley of the Tennessee River, the western plateau, and the bottomlands along the Mississippi River, where they established extensive farming activities soon after their arrival. Within little more than a half century, settlers transformed Tennessee from an undeveloped wilderness into a collection of flourishing agricultural regions.

As settlers spread across the state, their initial tasks were to establish a farmstead and to provide for household subsistence. After securing access to land through purchasing, renting, or squatting on private or public property, they constructed an unadorned, small dwelling, cleared and broke ground for a field or two, and put in food crops. Families survived on goods transported from their previous locations, wild fruits and game, and fast maturing garden vegetables until the first crop came in. Virtually every household planted corn as its main source of nourishment. An ideal pioneer crop, corn did well on new fields, required relatively little care during the growing season, produced high nutritional yields per acre, and provided the primary ingredient for many edibles. The few frontier households with fields suitable for broadcast crops also planted wheat or other small grains in the first few years. Some settlers brought along animals, and others acquired them from neighbors or livestock traders after arriving at their destinations. In either case, they soon supplemented their grain and vegetable diets with meat and dairy products. Swine cared for themselves, surviving on forest mast during most of the year, and their meat could be readily preserved through curing and smoking. For these reasons, pork was the preferred meat among farm families. Over the first few years, members of the household prepared additional land for cultivation, increased production of farm goods, expanded and improved their original dwelling, constructed auxiliary buildings, and made numerous other improvements to the farmstead. This routine recurred over and over in the late eighteenth century and well into the next century, until eventually all of the regions of the state had been settled and brought into agricultural production.

Tennessee's early rural families valued self-sufficiency and strove to supply from their own production as much of the household consumption as possible. But they also understood that realizing their aspirations of a better life required involvement in commercial agriculture. Almost from the beginning, they looked for opportunities to sell or barter produce from the farm. At first, these exchanges involved trading small amounts of surplus goods on the local market for cash or items they could not provide for themselves. Commercial opportunities broadened as settlement moved beyond the frontier stage, and farmers responded to the demand in more remote markets. Although they continued to meet much of their household needs, they began to emphasize the production of marketable goods for sale in distant urban centers in the United States and Europe. Cotton and tobacco became Tennessee's principal cash crops. The state also sold sizable quantities of wheat and swine, and smaller amounts of corn, beef cattle, and wool. By the outbreak of the Civil War in 1861, Tennessee supported a diversified agriculture based on a wide range of subsistence and commercial products.

The antebellum period saw other developments. As farmers concentrated on commercial goods and adapted their production schemes to particular soil, climate, and terrain conditions, regions of specialization emerged. The southwestern and south-central sectors of the state became areas of cotton cultivation, and the northwestern and north-central sectors became areas of tobacco cultivation. The central basin and the eastern valleys specialized in wheat, and the central basin and western plateau specialized in swine. Commercialization persuaded some farmers to pursue enhanced profits through expanded land and slave holdings. Because this strategy proved particularly effective in cotton production, plantation agriculture occurred more commonly in southwest Tennessee than elsewhere. Still, large-scale operations appeared throughout the state and produced a variety of commercial products. Small farms remained numerically dominant, but large plantations produced the bulk of Tennessee's marketable commodities. Involvement in the market also encouraged farmers to improve their efficiency by employing new technology and better managerial techniques. They purchased animal-drawn equipment and blooded livestock, used improved varieties of seeds and fertilizers, and practiced soil conservation. They experimented with ways to extract the greatest amount of labor at the lowest cost from their slaves and hired workers. They became more sensitive to market conditions in their business decisions. Like the size of agricultural enterprise, innovative commitment ranged from the sophisticated planter, who adopted new technology and commercial techniques, to the uninformed farmer, who used primitive hand tools in a basically subsistence regimen.

By the middle of the nineteenth century, the state's agricultural economy was well established and exercised wide reaching influence. Tennessee ranked among the top ten states in the production of cotton, tobacco, corn, wheat, swine, and sheep, and sixth in total livestock value. It produced ample amounts of several small grains other than wheat, several fibers other than cotton, and a variety of fruits and vegetables. Food production exceeded the needs of Tennessee residents; the surplus fed people elsewhere in the United States and in Europe. Domestic and foreign manufacturers depended on the state's cotton, tobacco, and wool for their raw materials. A diverse group of intermediaries emerged to service the financial and commercial needs of farmers, and their business activities depended heavily on agricultural conditions. Rural Tennesseans, of course, benefited from the state's antebellum farming development, but so too did many people in different places and from different circumstances.

The Civil War devastated Tennessee's agricultural economy. Military combat and occupation wrought extensive damage and destruction to primary dwellings, outbuildings, wells, fences, crops, and livestock. Wartime neglect also took its toll in the form of over-grown fields, dilapidated buildings, and deteriorating tools and machinery. The commercial infrastructure—financial, marketing, and transportation services—that farmers depended upon to participate in the market collapsed. Emancipation freed over a quarter of a million slaves, the cost of which was borne by the state's slave holders. Crude congressional estimates placed the property loss to Tennessee farmers at almost $200 million, 2.5 times the annual value of farm production on the eve of the Civil War.

Once the war was over, Tennesseans began the arduous task of rebuilding their agricultural system, which preserved many features of the past. Farmers retained a strong commercial orientation, cotton and tobacco remained the major cash crops, and regional specialization continued. But the postwar years witnessed a significant reorganization of Tennessee agriculture. Many former plantations, their slave labor force eliminated with emancipation, were subdivided into smaller units, with a resulting rise in the number and decline in the average size of farms. An increase in land owners—largely white operators and a smaller portion of the former slaves who also became owners—accompanied these changes. Tenancy rates rose sharply, as many whites displaced by the war and many blacks freed by the war found refuge in sharecropping and other forms of farm rental on subdivided plantations. Other members of those same groups, former slaves in particular, became workers on the large-scale operations that survived after the war. Wartime destruction of livestock and postwar shifts in land distribution and tenure markedly dropped foodstuffs production and, correspondingly, the degree of self-sufficiency among farm households declined. At the same time, cotton production more than doubled and tobacco production increased by almost 15 percent between 1860 and 1900. Under the slow and irregular pace of postwar reorganization, farmers continued to specialize in a number of commodities for sale on domestic and foreign markets, but the scale and the nature of their operations had changed profoundly.

By contrast, relatively little change occurred in the early decades of the twentieth century. Improved markets immediately after the turn of the century and strong demand during World War I, to be sure, brought temporary expansion of cotton, tobacco, and wheat production. But worldwide surpluses soon after the war drove down prices to below prewar levels and caused modest declines in cotton and tobacco acreage in the 1920s. Because they lacked the necessary financial resources, few Tennessee farmers adopted the technology—tractors, trucks, hybrid seeds, and commercial fertilizers—that became available in the 1920s and was revolutionizing agriculture elsewhere in the country. They continued, instead, to use the less efficient animal-drawn machinery, hand tools, and cultivation techniques from the nineteenth century. The Great Depression of the 1930s exacerbated conditions. With the precipitous drop in already depressed prices, the federal government fashioned schemes to reduce commodity surpluses through limitations on acreage and quotas on marketing. Farmers participated by cutting back even further on cotton and tobacco cultivation in return for government subsidies. Furthermore, federal programs had the unintended effect of reducing tenancy. Many landlords chose to idle land they had previously rented out, often forcing their tenants to leave agriculture altogether. The Depression persuaded farmers to place renewed emphasis on subsistence production, resulting in a modest return to household self-sufficiency. From 1900 to 1940, Tennessee agriculture experienced short-lived and illusory prosperity followed by stagnation and economic hardship.

World War II ushered in a new period of transformation and advancement. War-induced demand ended the depression, reinvigorated commercial activities, and brought a return of agricultural prosperity. It stimulated production of the state's traditional market commodities as well as soybeans, a crop farmers had grown earlier primarily as forage and green manure. The decline in acreage devoted to cotton and tobacco, a trend begun in the 1920s and temporarily interrupted by the war, resumed in the late 1940s. Driving the postwar trend in both commodities were worldwide oversupplies, a softening of consumer demand (due, in the case of cotton, to preference for alternative fabrics and, in the case of tobacco, to health concerns), rising labor costs, and the continuation of federal programs to limit production. In the 1980s, improvements in technology and more favorable market conditions reversed the trend in cotton. Production of the fiber, which had dropped by more than 50 percent from 1949 to 1982, exceeded immediate postwar levels by almost 30 percent in the early 1990s. While remaining an essential part of the farm economy, tobacco continued to decline in relative importance. A lucrative new crop was soybeans. Shortages of industrial and edible oils during the war, and the development of a wide array of new soybean-based products after the war, fueled an enormous increase in both domestic and foreign demand. Tennessee farmers responded by increasing their output by a factor of almost 1,000 between 1949 and 1992, making soybeans the state's most valuable crop. They also devoted more of their resources to livestock, espe-

cially beef and dairy cattle and swine. Because the state was well endowed with grasslands and animals required less labor than field crops, livestock made attractive alternatives to cotton and tobacco when domestic demand for meat and dairy goods soared in the prosperous postwar years. Farmers continued to cultivate a variety of commercial grains, principally wheat and corn; with improvements in the packaging, transportation, and distribution of perishables, some moved into large-scale production of fruits and vegetables.

The postwar transformation involved more, however, than modification in production choices. Tennessee farmers participated in a nationwide agricultural revolution that generated far-reaching change throughout the country. The driving force behind the revolution was the adoption of highly sophisticated new technology. The internal combustion engine tractor was arguably the most crucial innovation. Tractors had begun to appear on Tennessee farms even before World War II; after the war their adoption accelerated markedly. In time, they completely displaced mules and horses to drive the machinery for most field tasks. Although the initial investment was greater, tractors cost less to maintain, delivered more power, and were more dependable than draft animals. Most importantly, tractors substantially reduced the need for farm hands, a critical factor in the period of rising labor costs following World War II. The internal combustion engine also became the prime mover in self-propelled machinery designed for specialized functions, such as cotton and soybean harvesting.

In addition to mechanical innovations, farmers also took full advantage of biological and chemical developments. They adopted new strains of cotton, tobacco, corn, wheat, grain, sorghum, and vegetables, which offered higher yields, superior quality, and better adaptability to weather and soil conditions. They used synthesized fertilizers, which delivered a greater range and larger amounts of nutrients to the soil. They applied herbicides, insecticides, and defoliants, which largely eliminated problems from troublesome weeds and insects and enhanced possibilities for double-cropping. Just as new machines improved the productivity of labor, so these innovations improved the productivity of land. Livestock raising as well as crop cultivation benefited from the sweeping changes taking place. Crossbreeding created new bloodlines of cattle, swine, and poultry superior in quality and productivity, and better adapted to natural conditions in Tennessee. Artificial insemination permitted breeders more effectively to select and transmit to succeeding generations desired animal traits. Farmers across the state recognized the benefits of these developments and many were quick to capitalize on them.

These innovations also generated significant changes in management. To make a profit, heavy investments in labor-saving machinery and livestock, coupled with increased operating costs from herbicides, insecticides, and fuel, necessitated a larger scale of operation. Since the end of World War II, consequently, the number of farms has declined by two thirds and the average size has doubled. Those same conditions proved to be poorly compatible with farm tenancy, and the portion of renters has dropped from a third to less than seven percent over the same period. The entry of corporate enterprise into farm management was yet another aspect of the postwar transformation. Business firms sometimes provided supplies and services to farmers in return for contracted production of marketable commodities; they sometimes purchased land and equipment, and went into production on their own. In Tennessee, agribusiness, as these corporate arrangements have been labeled, became most common in poultry and specialized fruits and vegetables.

Despite an enduring commercial orientation, farming has from the beginning of settlement in the eighteenth century to the present played a broader cultural role in Tennessee. Rural residents have viewed farming as a way of life and as a social organization for perpetuating worthwhile values. Although they never precisely defined the substance of that life or of those values, they emphasized the desirability of household independence, family cohesion, community sharing and cooperation, and working the land. They sought to pass on these cultural objectives and goals to future generations. Since World War II, adoption of scientific agriculture, expanding size of operations, and increasing commercialization have gradually undermined that cultural function. Farming as a business has largely displaced farming as a way of life.

Tennessee never regained the national agricultural importance it held on the eve of the Civil War. At that time, no other state ranked as high in so many different products. Still, Tennessee farmers have continued to supply the country with a variety of high quality farm goods, to contribute significantly to its foreign exports, and to add substantially to its annual value of agricultural output. They have sustained their own incomes—albeit sometimes at less than satisfactory levels—and enhanced those of many others in Tennessee and elsewhere. And they have managed these accomplishments even though the economic and cultural role of agriculture has steadily eroded.

Donald L. Winters, Vanderbilt University

SUGGESTED READINGS: Harriette Simpson Arnow, *Flowering of the Cumberland* (1963); Blanche Henry Clark, *The Tennessee Yeomen, 1840–1860* (1942); Gilbert C. Fite, *Cotton Fields No More: Southern Agriculture, 1865–1980* (1984); Robert Tracy McKenzie, *One South or Many?: Plantation Belt and Upcountry*

in Civil-War Era Tennessee (1994); Donald L. Winters, *Tennessee Farming, Tennessee Farmers: Antebellum Agriculture in the Upper South* (1994)

AIRPORTS. The first scheduled airline operations in Tennessee began on December 1, 1925, when a route between Atlanta and Evansville included a stop in Chattanooga. For the next ten years, however, air traffic and airports grew slowly in Tennessee. In 1932, during the Great Depression, the state had 23 airports and landing fields, but these consisted at best of a hangar or two, a tiny terminal, and often sod runways. The federal government, through the New Deal agencies of the Civil Works Administration (CWA) and the Works Progress Administration (WPA), provided the funding and labor to bring Tennessee's airports into the modern age of aviation. Across the state, the CWA began 17 projects, which the WPA later brought to completion. By 1939 new airports were already operating at Cookeville, Jackson, Jellico, Lebanon, and Milan. The WPA also funded five major airports at Memphis, Chattanooga, Nashville, Knoxville, and McKellar Field (now Tri-City Airport), which stood in a rural location between Kingsport, Johnson City, and Bristol. The WPA state administrator was World War I veteran Col. Harry S. Berry, who was keenly interested in updating and expanding Tennessee's air transportation system.

Airports have multiplied across the state since the depression. In 1996 Tennessee had 89 public airports, with funding, construction, and maintenance provided by the Tennessee Department of Transportation, which is advised, in turn, by the Tennessee Aeronautics Commission. Almost every county seat is within easy access of an airport. Yet the five major airports of the New Deal era remain the busiest and largest terminals for freight and passenger traffic, with the Memphis and Nashville airports being the most important.

Aviation took center stage in Memphis's transportation history in 1927. Encouraged by the Memphis Aero Club, which had been established in 1925, Watkins Overton made the construction of a Memphis airport a major issue in his mayoral campaign of 1927. After his election, Overton quickly appointed five municipal airport planning commissioners, who selected an airport site on the 200-acre Ward Farm, located about 7.5 miles southeast of downtown Memphis. On June 15, 1929, the Memphis Municipal Airport opened for business. Its rudimentary operation consisted of a sod field runway and three small hangars. Yet more than 200 planes and pilots flew in to celebrate its opening. That fall, the stock market crash dampened the demand for passenger services. In 1930, for example, only 15 passengers were arriving and departing Memphis on a daily basis. But air mail and air freight kept the airport open; the major carriers were American Airways and Chicago & South. The first improvements came in 1934, when three asphalt diagonal runways were constructed. In 1937–1938 the New Deal chipped in with needed improvements as the Works Progress Administration built a new terminal and generally modernized the airport facilities and infrastructure.

With the many military-related activities in Memphis during World War II, the U.S. Army assumed administration of the municipal airport. As soon as the military relinquished its control at war's end, local officials moved quickly to respond to increased demands for passenger travel, especially on the technologically advanced Douglas DC-3 airplane. In 1947 the terminal was enlarged and the city implemented a master plan to improve the runways for larger, faster planes. By 1949 at least six major carriers landed planes in Memphis.

The 1950s witnessed steady growth in the amount of freight and passenger traffic handled by the Memphis airport, with the facility reaching the benchmark of one million passengers in 1959. Four years later, on June 7, 1963, the city dedicated a new terminal, which for its $5.5 million cost provided 22 airplane gates for seven competing airlines. Architect Roy Harrover's contemporary New Formalism-style design for the facility received national recognition by the American Institute of Architects.

Memphis air travel achieved international status in 1969 when the terminal became a point of origin and entry for international passenger and freight traffic. At that time, officials created the Memphis-Shelby County Airport Authority to administer the quickly expanding facility. Within ten years, the airport's terminal capacity doubled and the authority constructed a new runway for wide-bodied jets, an International Flights terminal, and a new control tower.

A major impetus for the airport expansion came from Federal Express, which began in Memphis in 1973. As the freight service corporation boomed over the next 20 years, Memphis became one of the nation's busiest cargo airports. Federal Express has steadily reinvested in its Memphis facilities, including a $36 million Aircraft Maintenance Facility that opened in 1995. Passenger service has grown as well in the past generation. In 1985 Republic Airlines designated Memphis as a regional hub, a designation retained when Republic merged with the much larger Northwest Airlines the following year. The airport's future development was outlined in a new master plan produced in 1986. Among its improvements, it called for a new International Flights terminal (opened in 1995); a third parallel runway (completed in late 1996); and extension of an existing major runway (completed in 1997).

The first airfield in Nashville was Hampton Field, which operated until 1921, when it was replaced by Blackwood Field, in the Hermitage community, which operated from 1921 to 1928. McConnell Field was open from 1928 to 1939, but much of Nashville's air traffic shifted to the Sky Harbour Airport, an isolated rural location in neighboring Rutherford County, along the newly completed Dixie Highway. Both American and Eastern airlines landed planes at Sky Harbour. This airport served the city from 1929 until the 1937 opening of the modern Berry Field airport (named in honor of Col. Harry S. Berry), also adjacent to the Dixie Highway, in southern Davidson County.

Berry Field was one of the region's first major WPA airport projects. The 340-acre airport center had a three-story terminal, a control tower, and paved runway. During World War II, the U.S. Army enlarged the field to over 1,500 acres as it served as home base for the 4th Ferrying Command, a key clearing station for military aircraft. Once civilian control was restored in 1946, Nashville began aggressively to expand its services. By 1958 plans for a new terminal were underway and two years later, passenger jet service arrived in the city.

In 1961 officials opened a new 145,900 square-foot terminal with a modern control tower that boasted state-of-the-art electronics. In 1963 the existing runway was extended by 800 feet and construction began on a second runway. Metropolitan government officials created, in 1970, the Metropolitan Nashville Airport Authority, which continues to operate the airport today. Under the Authority's administration, Berry Field experienced a second major expansion in 1977, when the terminal was renovated and enlarged; the airport now totaled 3,300 acres with three modern runways.

From 1984–1987 the Authority constructed a new terminal, in reaction to regional growth and the news that American Airlines had designated Nashville as a traffic hub for its system. By 1986 Nashville offered 144 daily flights to 37 cities, a level of traffic which severely taxed the older terminal. But on September 14, 1987, the Nashville Metropolitan Airport Terminal opened for business, alleviating the overcrowded situation. Designed by Robert Lamb Hart in association with Gresham, Smith and Partners, the terminal has 46 gates and three concourses that radiate from an architecturally distinctive three-story atrium. In the mid-1990s, American Airlines officially closed its Nashville hub, but other companies, such as Southwest Airlines, took over many of the American gates.

The growth of the airports at Nashville and Memphis is associated with general industry patterns that reflect the impact of airline deregulation in the late 1970s. Larger metropolitan airports have prospered, often to the detriment of nearby municipal airports. That is certainly the case in Tennessee. Knoxville and Chattanooga maintain modern facilities, but face tough competition for flights from the much larger airports at Nashville and Atlanta. The McGhee Tyson Airport, operated by the Metropolitan Knoxville

Airport Authority, has fared best. In 1997 it contained more than 2,000 acres with parallel 9,000-foot runways. Six major passenger carriers and five commuter lines operated at the airport. Due to the construction of a $9.3 million Air Cargo Complex in 1991, freight traffic has expanded significantly in recent years. The Chattanooga Metropolitan Airport, at Lovell Field, completed a $20.5 million expansion and improvement of its facilities in the mid-1990s. Managed by the Chattanooga Airport Authority, two major passenger carriers and four commuter lines served the city in 1997.

Carroll Van West, Middle Tennessee State University

ALADDIN INDUSTRIES. When Aladdin Industries located its corporate headquarters in Nashville in 1949, it also introduced a progressive industrial design to Nashville's emerging corporate landscape. The company built a modern International-style headquarters, designed by the firm of Spencer Warwick Associates, on South Nashville land between existing railroad tracks and the Dixie Highway.

Aladdin Industries Incorporated dates to 1919. The company made and sold insulated receptacles and kerosene lamps. In the late 1930s, Aladdin began to develop its first vacuum bottles. By 1949, at the time of the move to Nashville, Aladdin had merged with the Mantle Lamp Company of America, which had previously sold mantle lamps under the brand name of "Aladdin." The new company kept the name of Aladdin and in the following year, 1950, it expanded into the new market of school lunch box kits.

Production at the Nashville factory was initially devoted to the manufacture of vacuum bottles and lunch box kits. The first name character for the school lunch boxes was television and movie cowboy star Hopalong Cassidy. The new product was a huge success and, over the decades, Aladdin has produced hundreds of new school lunch box designs. A second important expansion came in 1965, when Aladdin acquired the Universal Stanley Division of the J.B. Williams Company, which made the Stanley thermos bottle. Stanley bottles are still produced at the Nashville factory.

The corporation's third major product, Temp-Rite meal delivery systems, dates to 1968. These are insulated, compartmentalized trays that maintain food at a desired temperature and are in high demand from institutional clients such as hospitals. This product's success led to a creation of a separate division, Aladdin Synergetics, Inc., which by 1972, had established offices in England, France, and Germany.

Carroll Van West, Middle Tennessee State University
SEE: DIXIE HIGHWAY ASSOCIATION; INDUSTRY

ALDERSON, WILLIAM THOMAS (1926–1996), historian and editor, was born and raised in Schenec-tady, New York. After service in the Navy during World War II, he graduated from Colgate University in 1947. He then entered the graduate program in history at Vanderbilt University, where he earned his Master's degree and completed the Ph.D. in 1952. His dissertation was a study of the Freedmen's Bureau in Virginia.

Entering a tight job market, Alderson vainly sought a full-time teaching position on the college level. As an alternative, he accepted a senior archivist's position at the Tennessee State Library and Archives. His abilities as a historian and strong people skills resulted in his rapid advancement and appointment to key positions. In 1956 he was named editor of the *Tennessee Historical Quarterly,* and the following year he assumed the duties of executive secretary of the Tennessee Historical Society. In 1959 he was named assistant state librarian and archivist, and then elevated to the state's senior position two years later.

In 1964 Alderson began to rise in national prominence in the field of public history. The American Association for State and Local History (AASLH), headquartered in Madison, Wisconsin, asked him to serve as its director. Alderson agreed to accept the job under one condition: AASLH would have to move its headquarters to Nashville. The AASLH board accepted Alderson's condition and moved the organization south. During the next 14 years, Alderson elevated AASLH to the nation's most important professional organization for historical societies and museums. During his tenure, AASLH conducted scores of educational programs, issued hundreds of publications, set high standards for museums of all sizes, and saw its membership numbers increase several fold.

In 1978, Alderson left Nashville to return to academe as the director of the museum studies program at the University of Delaware. Four years later he was appointed to the directorship of the Margaret Woodbury Strong Museum in Rochester, New York, a position he held until being named president of Old Salem in Winston-Salem, North Carolina, in 1986.

Alderson officially retired from Old Salem in 1991, but he continued a decades-long commitment to professional involvement until the day he died. During his career, he served as an officer in a number of organizations including the American Association of Museums, American Records Management Association, and the Mid-Atlantic Museums Association. In 1992 he became director of the Seminar for Historical Administration in Williamsburg, the longest running continuing education program in the country for advanced museum professionals. Several months prior to conducting his fourth seminar, Alderson died in his sleep, leaving his wife of 44 years, the former Sylvia C. Farrell, and two grown children.

Charles F. Bryan, Jr., Virginia Historical Society

SEE: AMERICAN ASSOCIATION FOR STATE AND LOCAL HIS-
TORY; TENNESSEE HISTORICAL SOCIETY; TENNESSEE STATE
LIBRARY AND ARCHIVES

ALEXANDER, LAMAR (1940–), Governor, university
president, and U.S. Secretary of Education, was born
on July 3, 1940, in Blount County, Tennessee. His parents were teachers in Maryville, and Alexander
attended public schools there. Active in the Boy
Scouts as a youngster, Alexander was awarded the
rank of Eagle Scout, the highest scouting honor. In
1962 he completed his undergraduate degree, graduating Phi Beta Kappa, from Vanderbilt University.
Three years later, in 1965, Alexander received his law
degree at New York University. In addition, Alexander has received honorary doctorates from schools
across the nation, including Christian Brothers University, Cumberland University, the University of the
South, and Tusculum College in Tennessee.

Alexander's law career began as a clerk to Judge
John M. Wisdom, of the U.S. Fifth Circuit Court, in
1965; within two years, in 1967, his political career
was underway, as a legislative assistant to Republican U.S. Senator Howard Baker. After Richard M.
Nixon's election as president, Alexander was
appointed an executive aide to Bryce Harlow, the
White House congressional liaison.

Governor Lamar Alexander.

PORTRAIT BY JOHN W. KELLEY, TENNESSEE STATE MUSEUM

In 1970 Alexander's successful management of the
gubernatorial campaign of Winfield Dunn, the first
Republican governor in 50 years, propelled him to the
forefront of the Tennessee Republican party. That year,
he also was one of the founding partners of the Dearborn and Ewing law firm in Nashville. Alexander's
first attempt to win the governor's chair failed in 1974,
as Democrats statewide, including gubernatorial nominee Ray Blanton, swept to power in the wake of the
Watergate scandal. But four years later, Alexander
waged a determined campaign, highlighted by a walk
across Tennessee—a journey of 1,022 miles—during
which he wore a red-checked flannel shirt. His quest
for the governor's office was successful and the red-
checked shirt became his trademark.

At the request of the U.S. Attorney, Alexander was
sworn in as governor three days early, on January 17,
1979, in reaction to the possibility that Governor Ray
Blanton would grant clemency to prisoners who,
according to state and federal officials, had paid bribes
for the expressed purpose of gaining executive pardons. Despite this controversial beginning, Alexander
enjoyed several achievements during his two terms in
office from 1979 to 1987. It was a time of economic
growth and expansion of incomes. Thousands of new
jobs were created in the automobile industry, with the
opening of the Nissan factory in Smyrna and the
announcement of the Saturn plant at Spring Hill. He
introduced a master teachers program and a Better
Schools program to improve public education. For
higher education, Alexander introduced a system of
Centers of Excellence and Chairs of Excellence to
enhance research and public service at the public universities. Alexander also supported the creation of a
Tennessee Parkway system, which improved highway
transportation and enhanced the state's expanding
tourism industry. His Tennessee Homecoming '86 program was extremely popular, as 812 communities
across Tennessee launched special projects and publications about state and local heritage. Spurred by federal court decisions mandating change, Alexander also
addressed the state's antiquated corrections system
and began a massive prison construction program.

The first Tennessee governor to serve consecutive
four-year terms of office, Alexander also served as
chair of the National Governor's Association and
chair of the Southern Regional Education Board, and
was chosen "Conservationist of the Year" by the Tennessee Conservation League during his years as governor. The success of Alexander's two terms
solidified the Republican party's role in state politics.
As historian Dewey Grantham observed, "the election of Lamar Alexander as governor in 1978 and his
reelection four years later demonstrated that, with
able and attractive candidates, Tennessee Republicans could win the top state offices as well as presidential contests."[1]

After returning to private life in 1987, Alexander continued to pursue his goal of improving education in America. He was chair of the Leadership Institute at Belmont University in 1987–1988 and then, from 1988 to 1991, he served as president of the University of Tennessee. There he established the institution's first full-year scholarship program and developed a new five-year comprehensive plan for the university system.

In 1991 President George Bush appointed Alexander U.S. Secretary of Education. As secretary, Alexander initiated and supported administration policy to set voluntary National Education Standards, to prohibit race-based scholarships at colleges and universities, and to implement America 2000, a program to achieve national educational goals as established by President Bush and the nation's governors.

After Bush's defeat in 1992, Alexander returned to Tennessee and was a counsel at the law firm of Baker, Donelson, Bearman and Caldwell from 1993–1995. He remained active in national Republican party activities as chair of the Republican Exchange Satellite Network from 1993–1995 and as a Senior Fellow at the Hudson Institute from 1994–1995. On February 28, 1995, he launched a national campaign for the Republican presidential nomination, but withdrew in the spring of 1996 after faring poorly in the early primaries.

Alexander has written several books, including *Steps Along the Way* (1986), and he and his wife Leslee "Honey" Alexander have four children, Andrew, Leslee, Kathryn, and William. An attorney, writer, and Republican party leader, Alexander presently lives in Nashville.

Carroll Van West, Middle Tennessee State University
CITATION:
(1) Dewey Grantham, "Tennessee and Twentieth-Century American Politics," *Tennessee Historical Quarterly* 54(1995): 222.
SEE: BAKER, HOWARD H., JR.; BELMONT UNIVERSITY; BLANTON, L. RAY; BLOUNT COUNTY; DUNN, WINFIELD; HOMECOMING TENNESSEE '86; NISSAN; SATURN; TENNESSEE IN FILM; UNIVERSITY OF TENNESSEE

ALLISON, DAVID (d. 1798), backcountry lawyer, political operative, and land speculator, was an agent for the Blount brothers, especially William Blount, Tennessee's first territorial governor. Apparently from North Carolina, Allison's date of birth and exact birthplace are unknown, but he accompanied Andrew Jackson to the Cumberland settlements in 1788, both men handling minor lawsuits along the way.

In 1790 Blount appointed Allison clerk of the Superior Court of Law and later designated him as militia paymaster. Allison served Blount in a semiofficial and semiprivate capacity as business agent, frequently traveling to Philadelphia on public and personal financial business. In 1796 Allison hand-carried the famous "Blount Journal," the official record of Governor Blount's executive acts, to Secretary of State Thomas Jefferson.

By 1795 Allison had moved to Philadelphia, the nation's financial capital, where he brokered speculative land deals and merchandise trading ventures into Tennessee. In August 1795, one of these involved Andrew Jackson, who was selling land for himself, John Overton, and others. Upon Jackson's return to Nashville, he was financially embarrassed when the notes he had given to Allison were suddenly presented for payment. Jackson struggled for years to settle the matter. In 1798 it was a factor in his resignation from the United States Senate and acceptance of the salaried post of judge on the Superior Court of Law and Equity.

Overtaken by creditors, Allison was thrown into debtor's prison in Philadelphia and died there on September 28, 1798.

Lewis L. Laska, Tennessee State University
SEE: BLOUNT, WILLIAM; JACKSON, ANDREW; OVERTON, JOHN; SOUTHWEST TERRITORY

ALUMINUM CORPORATION OF AMERICA (ALCOA). Organized as the Pittsburgh Reduction Company in 1888, the company changed its name in 1907 to the Aluminum Corporation of America, and began using the acronym ALCOA in the 1910s, after applying the acronym to company-owned sites in Tennessee. In 1909 ALCOA began purchasing riparian rights along the Little Tennessee River in a search for cheap power. Building a network of dams, ALCOA chose North Maryville, Tennessee, as a plant site in 1913. It reincorporated the community as the town of Alcoa in 1914, purchased 750 acres of land and built a smelting plant. Thus, Alcoa joined other planned industrial communities in Tennessee.

In 1919 ALCOA purchased the Knoxville Power Company, which held the rights to the power potential of dams on the Little Tennessee River. After World War I, ALCOA expanded its facilities with a rolling mill, a sheet mill, and plans for a 7,500-acre city. These plans included workers' housing and schools, which were racially segregated like the facilities of most company towns in Tennessee.

City government was tied directly to company management, with Victor Hultquist, ALCOA's construction superintendent, serving as city manager until the 1950s. Alcoa recruited no other outside investment, nor were others interested in coming to a one-company town. The lack of economic diversification bound the fortunes of Alcoa's citizens to those of the company.

During the Depression, ALCOA kept production at 1920s levels, cutting workers' hours to 30 per week to maintain employment. The company also reduced rents in company housing. Nevertheless, a wave of violent strikes erupted in Alcoa in the late 1930s in response to collective bargaining legislation. Hultquist hired a police force to suppress the strikers, and Governor Gordon Browning sent in the National Guard in July 1937. The strike ended quickly, and workers returned to the factory.

World War II brought prosperity to ALCOA, and the Tennessee operations expanded accordingly. The North Plant, constructed in 1940–41, covered 65 acres and employed 12,000, making it one of the largest plants in the world. In the postwar years, the company initially prospered due to strong demand for aluminum and related products. ALCOA's national image, however, suffered in the late 1940s and 1950s as a result of the hardline stance taken toward labor unions. In addition, ALCOA no longer dominated the aluminum market, and the Tennessee Valley Authority challenged ALCOA's hydroelectric power business.

In response, the company released its paternalistic grip on the town of Alcoa. The company continued and expanded its practice of donating land for parks, schools, churches, and municipal buildings. The company also provided funds for the development of an airport in Blount County, and continued to sell property in the public's interest, including additional land to the City of Knoxville for airport expansions. In order to improve company-town relations, ALCOA also provided Alcoa residents with recreational facilities, a retirement club, and tuition support at local universities.

By the 1950s, the company dispensed with company housing, selling houses to renters and Alcoa workers. ALCOA also transferred its electric utilities to the city in 1955, and the water utility in 1960, placing ALCOA's former power monopoly under the control of the Tennessee Valley Authority. Over the last 30 years, the evolving world market for aluminum, the demands of labor, modern transportation, and the environmental movement together have reshaped the policies and products of this corporation. According to 1997 state figures, ALCOA remains Blount County's largest manufacturing employer with 2,050 workers.

Tara Mitchell Mielnik, Middle Tennessee State University
SEE: BLOUNT COUNTY; INDUSTRY; LABOR; WORLD WAR II

AMERICAN ASSOCIATION FOR STATE AND LOCAL HISTORY (AASLH) is a not-for-profit professional organization of individuals and institutions working to preserve and promote history. Its roots stem from the early Conference of State and Local Historical Societies, formed at the 1904 annual meeting of the American Historical Association in an effort to serve the needs of state and local historical societies. The AHA disbanded the Confer-

ence in 1940, and from it the Association was created. Its purpose as stated in its first constitution was "the promotion of effort and activity in the fields of state, provincial, and local history in the United States and Canada."

From its headquarters in Nashville, Tennessee, AASLH provides its more than 5,000 individual and institutional members with a variety of programs and services. Among these are the quarterly magazine, *History News*; monthly newsletter, *Dispatch*; a video library lending service; regional and national seminars and workshops; an annual meeting; and a national Awards Program.

AASLH is a co-sponsor of the Seminar for Historical Administration held each year at Colonial Williamsburg. The goal of the seminar is to develop and strengthen leadership within historical organizations and the museum community. AASLH also co-sponsors National History Day, a national program for school children to enrich their understanding of history and its impact on their lives.

Through its diverse programs and services, AASLH works to ensure the highest-quality expressions of state and local history whether provided through publications, exhibitions, or public programs.
Susan Goodsell, Plano, Illinois
SEE: ALDERSON, WILLIAM THOMAS

AMERICAN MUSEUM OF SCIENCE AND ENERGY, in Oak Ridge, was initially established in 1949 as the American Museum of Atomic Energy. Its opening, on March 19, 1949, coincided with the opening of the security gates to the once top-secret city of Oak Ridge. The museum quickly became a key institution to orient visitors and newcomers to the scientific and technological achievements associated with the Manhattan Project and atomic energy research at Oak Ridge. In 1959, with congressional approval and support, the museum developed a special program, "This Atomic World," and took it on a national tour of American school systems in addition to presentations at many community events and state fairs. Program highlights during the next decade included an exhibit and program in 1969 on recently acquired "moon rocks," which were being studied by scientists at the Oak Ridge National Laboratory.

In February 1975, again with federal support, especially the efforts of Congressman Joe L. Evins, the museum moved from its original facility on Jefferson Circle in Oak Ridge to a new two-story, four-wing museum building at 300 South Tulane. The museum has remained and prospered at this location ever since. In 1978 the museum was renamed The American Museum of Science and Energy, in an effort to better reflect the mission and energy policies of the recently established U.S. Department of Energy. Four years later, in 1982, the museum received 180,000 visitors during the six-month duration of the Knoxville World Fair.

The American Museum of Science and Energy, an educational institution funded by the U.S. Department of Energy, maintains active and broad educational programs to help place into context the past, present, and future of the varied research activities at Oak Ridge. Current permanent exhibits include: "The Oak Ridge Story," "Age of the Automobile," "Exploration Station," "Energy: The American Experience," "World of the Atom," "Earth's Energy Resources," and "Y-12 and National Defense," which connects the Manhattan Project to later national defense programs of the 1960s and 1970s.
Prepared from material supplied by Lissa Clarke, American Museum of Science and Energy
SEE: EVINS, JOSEPH L.; OAK RIDGE

AMES PLANTATION. The 18,567-acre Ames Plantation, owned and operated by Trustees of the Hobart Ames Foundation under provisions of the will of Julia C. Ames, is located in Fayette and Hardeman counties. Serving as an Agricultural Experiment Station within the University of Tennessee system, the Ames Plantation is the location of intensive research efforts focusing on agriculture and natural resource management. Each February, the Ames Plantation serves as the site of the National Championship Field Trial for all-age bird dogs. First held in 1896, this field trial has been conducted annually at the Ames Plantation since 1915.

The Ames Plantation property contains over 200 nineteenth century historic sites. The manor house, an antebellum mansion constructed in 1847 as part of Cedar Grove Plantation, is the architectural centerpiece of the property. In 1901 Hobart Ames purchased the plantation, one of the region's largest, and turned it into a private rural retreat. The manor

Students at Underwood School, Powell Valley, 1946.

TENNESSEE STATE LIBRARY AND ARCHIVES. PHOTO BY JOE CLARK

house furnishings are early twentieth century and appear much as they did when the Ames family departed in 1950.

In addition, the Ames Plantation is home to a replica mid-nineteenth century family farmstead, typical of those that dotted the antebellum landscape. The "Farmstead" consists of restored and furnished log buildings and is utilized as a cultural resource education facility. Other historic sites of interest include the earliest marked burial site in Fayette County, dated January 7, 1827, and a restored one-room schoolhouse from 1900.
Jamie Evans, Grand Junction
SEE: FAYETTE COUNTY; HARDEMAN COUNTY; HUNTING DOGS; NATIONAL FIELD TRIAL

ANDERSON COUNTY. Before Tennessee became a state, and before Anderson County received its name, Native Americans occupied lands in present-day Anderson County, according to archaeological investigations. Permanent white settlement dates to 1796, when Thomas Frost built a cabin. After statehood, settlements soon expanded, including the arrival of German immigrants in 1800. In December 1801 Anderson County was created from parts of Knox and Grainger counties. The county was named after Joseph Anderson, a prominent U.S. Senator, and former territorial judge in Knoxville. The first seat of government in Anderson County was Burrville, named after Vice President Aaron Burr. After Burr killed Alexander Hamilton in their famous duel, and became implicated in a land speculation scheme, the Tennessee General Assembly changed the name of Anderson County's county seat to Clinton, honoring Vice President George Clinton or his nephew, DeWitt Clinton.

Agriculture was the key occupation in the county's early history, but a number of small businesses supplemented subsistence farming. Land speculation, especially in coal mining areas, began in the 1830s and continued throughout the nineteenth century. Once the county was linked to regional railroad networks during the middle decades of the nineteenth century, coal mining became its leading industry.

Education also played an important role in Anderson County. Union Academy, established in Clinton in 1806, began admitting female students along with males in 1817. By the 1840s, Clinton Seminary and Clinton Grove Academy opened and affiliated with the Baptist and Methodist churches, respectively. New education laws in the post-Civil War era prompted County Education Superintendent Charles D. McGuffey to campaign for funding for schools in Anderson County. By 1892 Anderson County operated 58 public schools, five for black students.

No major Civil War battles were fought in Anderson County, but, as in many other East Tennessee counties, local loyalties were divided between Union and Confederate sympathizers. Violence settled too many arguments; "bushwacking" was common. When Confederates established a conscription center at Clinton, Union sympathizers used "Eli's Cabin" as a safe-house to escape to Kentucky and join the Union army.

In the late Victorian era, several locations along the railroad lines experienced new investments in tourism and coal mining. In the 1890s Oliver Springs, at the corner of Roane, Morgan, and Anderson counties, became a popular tourist spot. Accessible by rail, a large resort hotel attracted guests to its mineral springs from all over the United States and Europe. In July 1891 the coal mines at Briceville became the site of a violent strike, prompted by the increasing use of convict labor to replace more expensive free labor. In the resulting "Coal Creek War" miners attacked the prisoners' stockade, released the convicts, and demanded the end of the convict-leasing system in Tennessee. Months of negotiations between the miners, Governor John Buchanan, and the Tennessee General Assembly failed to resolve the issue. The convict-lease system came to an end in 1895, when the leases expired. At the same time, the General Assembly enacted prison reforms and established Brushy Mountain State Penitentiary in Morgan County.

In the 1930s and 1940s, the federal government made its presence known in Anderson County, and propelled the county and the state to national prominence. In 1933 President Franklin Delano Roosevelt signed the Tennessee Valley Authority into law and changed the Tennessee landscape, especially that of Anderson County. TVA launched its first major construction project with the building of Norris Dam, the planned community of Norris, and public parks at Norris and Big Ridge. The dam provided jobs, flood control, and electricity to Anderson County.

World War II led to new federal initiatives. Anderson County's location and resources, and the proximity of Tennessee Eastman in Kingsport, attracted federal planners searching for a site for the development of the atomic bomb. The resulting city of Oak Ridge became the fifth largest city in Tennessee within two years. "The Atomic Capital of the World" brought national and international attention to the state in 1945, when the first atomic bomb exploded over Hiroshima.

Anderson County again garnered national attention in the wake of federally mandated school desegregation in the 1950s. When Clinton High School opened its doors to black students in 1956, a riot ensued, and Governor Frank Clement called out the National Guard to restore order in Clinton. White students boycotted classes, and in 1958 the high school building was bombed. Clinton High School students attended classes in Oak Ridge while their school was rebuilt. The events in Anderson County received national television coverage when Edward R. Murrow and CBS television analyzed the desegregation trouble in Clinton.

From its establishment in 1801 to recent historical events, Anderson County has influenced the role of the state in the nation, and the role of the nation in the world.

Tara Mitchell Mielnik, Middle Tennessee State University
SEE: AMERICAN MUSEUM OF SCIENCE AND ENERGY; CAIN, ROBERT, JR.; CIVIL RIGHTS MOVEMENT; CLINTON DESEGREGATION CRISIS; CONVICT LEASE WARS; LABOR; MINING; NORRIS; NORRIS DAM; NORRIS DAM STATE PARK; NORRIS FREEWAY; OAK RIDGE; TENNESSEE VALLEY AUTHORITY; WORLD WAR II

ANDERSON, WILLIAM ROBERT (1921–), U.S. Navy Captain and Congressman, is best known as the commander of the submarine *USS Nautilus,* when it made the first underwater crossing of the North Pole in 1958. Anderson was born on June 17, 1921, in the Sycamore Landing community of Humphreys County, Tennessee, into a family distinguished by prominent farmers and political leaders. In 1942 he graduated from the U.S. Naval Academy. He received the Bronze Star and other combat awards for eleven submarine patrols in the Pacific Ocean during World War II.

After the war, Anderson became a protégé of Admiral Hyman G. Rickover, the "father" of the Navy's nuclear submarine program. In 1957, he received the command of the *USS Nautilus,* the world's first atomic-powered submarine. Few people knew Anderson's destination the following summer when his ship left Pearl Harbor on a 6000-mile voyage to Great Britain. On August 3, 1958, the *Nautilus* crossed under the geographic North Pole, climaxing the first undersea voyage in history from the Pacific to the Atlantic by way of the ice-blocked Arctic region. Passing 400 feet beneath the polar ice cap, the ship's crew conducted important scientific measurements and mapped the ocean floor in a previously unknown part of the world.

Commander Anderson and his crew received a hero's welcome and a ticker tape parade on their return to New York City. Their successful polar crossing, in the view of many Americans, helped to offset the Soviet Union's Sputnik achievement of the previous year. At a special White House ceremony, President Dwight D. Eisenhower presented Anderson with the Legion of Merit.

In 1962 Anderson retired from the Navy after twenty years of service and embarked on a campaign for Governor of Tennessee. Surprisingly, for a political novice with no financing, he ran a respectable second to Governor Frank Clement and garnered more than twice the number of votes of the Republican challenger. Anderson's congressional career began in 1964, when he was elected representative from Tennessee's Sixth District, which included his home county of Humphreys. He did well in this conservative rural district, serving four consecutive terms, despite being tagged as a liberal for his criticism of FBI Director J. Edgar Hoover and his staunch opposition to American involvement in Vietnam.

William R. Anderson retired from public life after his defeat in the 1972 election. He now lives in Florida with his second wife, Patricia Walters, and their two children. Captain Anderson was one in a long lineage of Tennesseans who won fame for their military exploits and went on to distinguished careers as elected officials.

Wayne C. Moore, Tennessee State Library and Archives
SUGGESTED READING: William R. Anderson, *Nautilus 90 North* (1959)

ANDREWS v. STATE (1871) is the single most important case regarding the right to bear arms under the Tennessee Constitution. Article I, Section 26 of the constitution provides "That the citizens of this State have a right to keep and bear arms for their common defense; but the legislature shall have power, by law, to regulate the wearing of arms with a view to prevent crime."

In *Andrews,* the defendants were charged with possession of a revolver in violation of law. They challenged the law under both the Second Amendment to the U.S. Constitution, and under the right to bear arms provision of the Tennessee Constitution. Since constitutional doctrine at the time held that the federal Bill of Rights did not apply to the states, the Tennessee Supreme Court dismissed this count. But on the Tennessee Constitutional issue, the statute was struck down in part.

The Attorney General of Tennessee argued before the Court that the right to keep and bear arms was a mere "political right" that existed for the benefit of the state and hence could be regulated at pleasure by the state. The Court did not agree. "*Bearing* arms for the common defense," it said, "may well be held to be a political right, or for the protection and maintenance of such rights, intended to be guaranteed; but the right to *keep* them, with all that is implied fairly as an incident to this right, is a private individual right, guaranteed to the citizen, not the soldier."[1] The court concluded that citizens have the right to keep military-type weapons, and to engage in the necessary practice, repair, and transportation of such weapons, without any specific connection to state activities such as the militia. Those parts of the statute that applied to military-type weapons were struck down, though the provisions relating to stilettos, derringers, and such (weapons regarded as having no usefulness except to criminals) were sustained.

Andrews remains the law today. Citizens have the right to keep and bear arms, subject to legislative regulation only for the purpose of preventing crime—there is no general legislative power to regulate arms for other purposes. *Andrews,* along with an earlier case of *Aymette v. State,* sheds light on the proper interpretation of the Second Amendment to the United States Constitution. *Aymette* says that the Tennessee provision was adopted "in the same view" as was the Second Amendment, and the only U.S. Supreme Court case of this century addressing the Second Amendment relied heavily on *Aymette.* Should the U.S. Supreme Court address Second Amendment issues again, it seems likely it will rely heavily on Tennessee case law.

Glenn H. Reynolds, University of Tennessee School of Law
CITATION:
(1) *Andrews v. State,* 50 Tenn. at 156, 3 Heisk. at 182.
SUGGESTED READING: Glenn H. Reynolds, "The Right to Keep and Bear Arms Under the Tennessee Constitution: A Case Study in Civic Republican Thought," 61 *Tennessee Law Review* 647 (1994)

APPALACHIAN EXPOSITION OF 1910 was held in Knoxville, Tennessee, from September 12 to October 12, 1910. Although large expositions were commonplace at the turn of the century, and county, regional, and state agricultural fairs predated this Knoxville convention, the Appalachian Exposition of 1910 was the first one held in the southern Appalachian region. The intention of the fair was to demonstrate progress in southern industry and commerce. Moreover, it promoted the conservation of the region's natural resources, advocating their responsible exploitation for utilitarian (to serve the public good), not aesthetic or ecological purposes. The fair's broad message applied the popular idea of a "New South" to southern Appalachia: the social and economic modernization of the South was to imitate and surpass northern prosperity. Through the promotion of conservation and the government intervention and long-term investments that it required, the exposition's founders beckoned the more conservative businessmen of Knoxville to contribute to the creation of a grand industrial city.

Director General and Secretary of the Knoxville Commercial Club, William M. Goodman, first envisioned the Appalachian Exposition in 1900. Not until 1908, however, when a massive publicity campaign rallied public support behind the event and Chilhowee Park was chosen as its site, did the club fully embrace the idea. In 1909 the Appalachian Exposition Company was established with local businessman William J. Oliver as president. Oliver and other company officers were responsible for the event's planning and management.

Exposition exhibits at the fairgrounds were housed in separate buildings. The 80,000 square-foot Main Building held a myriad of displays including hardwood products, agricultural machinery, and var-

Administration Building at the Appalachian Exposition.

ious state and county exhibits. Exhibits in the Women's Building included contests for the best household products, such as needlework or canning items, and urged the adoption of "domestic science," the application of efficient time-saving techniques to housework, cooking, and child care. The Black Department, held in a building erected by the local black community, was designated to present the progress of African Americans to visitors. By separating the Women's and African Americans' departments from the rest of the fair, traditional boundaries were reinforced. But members of each group viewed their exhibits as significant boosts to their collective self-worth. Three cabins on the fairgrounds portrayed Appalachian highlanders as churlish and peculiar, but more importantly, also as a group with the potential to participate in regional progress. The midway of the exposition hosted attractions ranging from "Muhall's Wild West Show" to "The Infant Incubator." Aeroplanes at the fair were the first to be seen in East Tennessee. Former President Theodore Roosevelt visited the fair and praised the promise of the fair, and of the region.

The success of the 1910 fair led to the 1911 Appalachian Exposition and the 1913 National Conservation Exposition. These fairs preached, with a few modifications, the same New South message. The fairs had beneficial short-term effects, such as profitability and publicity, but failed to achieve their ultimate goal, the transformation of Knoxville into a model New South city.

Robert D. Lukens, University of Tennessee, Knoxville

SEE: KNOXVILLE

APPALACHIAN REGIONAL COMMISSION. In the 1960s, much of the Appalachian region lagged behind the rest of the nation in income, educational attainment, access to health care, and efficient transportation. The Council of Appalachian Governors, an ad hoc group of nine governors of the Appalachian states of Alabama, Georgia, Kentucky, Maryland, North Carolina, Pennsylvania, Tennessee, Virginia, and West Virginia, lobbied for external assistance for the mountainous portions of their states. Meeting with John F. Kennedy, a presidential candidate in 1960, the governors convinced him of Appalachia's needs. Campaigning in West Virginia, Kennedy encountered living conditions that further convinced him of the need for government intervention to solve the region's problems.

In 1963 Kennedy created the President's Appalachian Regional Commission to assist in advancing legislation to bring federal dollars to Appalachia. Harlan Mathews, later a U.S. Senator, was Tennessee's first representative with the planning commission. Middle Tennessee congressman, Joe L. Evins, supported the legislation through his role as a member of the House Public Works Committee, which he chaired from 1966 to 1975. When the legislation, the Appalachian Redevelopment Act, was passed in 1965, creating the Appalachian Regional Commission as a federal agency, Mathews was Tennessee's first designated representative.

Today the Appalachian Regional Commission consists of the governors of the 13 states designated as Appalachian (the original nine, plus New York, South Carolina, Mississippi, and Ohio), each governor's designated state representative, and a federal co-chair, appointed by the President, who serves with one of the governors as states' co-chair. The states provide 50 percent of the funding to match the federal government's 50 percent funding. Program administration is conducted through local development districts, groups of counties designated by the state government for economic development. Programs for which the Appalachian Regional Commission initially provided funding included the Appalachian Development Highway System; construction of health facilities, vocational educational facilities, and sewage treatment plants; timber development; mining area restoration; water resource planning; and land stabilization and conservation control.

Throughout the 1960s and 1970s, the Appalachian Regional Commission demonstrated improvements in the region's economic development and quality of life. In 1981, in response to the Reagan administration's efforts to eliminate the programs, the Appalachian governors prepared a resolution calling on the President to continue the Commission; two of the states' co-chairs, Governor Lamar Alexander of Tennessee and Governor John Y. Brown, Jr., of Kentucky, helped offset many Commission budget cuts. The Commission survived, though reduced in its ability to serve the needs of the region.

Attitudes toward the Commission changed, first with the election of George Bush, and continuing during the administration of Bill Clinton. A new strategic planning process, begun in 1994, reinvigorated the Commission and culminated in the 1996 publication of *Setting a Regional Agenda*. The strategic plan called for developing a knowledgeable and skilled population, strengthening the region's physical infrastructure, building regional capacity in leadership and planning, creating a dynamic economic base, and fostering healthy people. The Appalachian Regional Commission continues to serve as a model of federal-state-local planning and partnership.

Jean Haskell Speer, East Tennessee State University
SEE: ALEXANDER, LAMAR; EVINS, JOSEPH L.

APPALACHIAN TRAIL. The Appalachian Trail is a continuous marked footpath extending 2,140 miles through 14 states from Springer Mountain, Georgia, to Katahdin, Maine. The route crosses eight national forests, eight units of the national park system, and 60 state parks and wildlife areas. The trail's 284 miles along Tennessee's eastern border are mostly within the Cherokee National Forest and the Great Smoky Mountains National Park. The trail reaches its highest point in Tennessee at 6,643 feet on Clingman's Dome in the Great Smokies.

Benton MacKaye of Massachusetts first proposed the trail in a 1921 issue of *Journal of the American Institute of Architects.* The Appalachian Trail Conference

(ATC) was formed in 1925 and coordinated planning and building the trail, which was completed in 1937. Much of the early trail ran along rural roads and across private property; over the years public lands have been acquired for rerouting. The trail received big boosts in 1968, when Congress designated it a national scenic trail, and again in 1978, when Congress authorized funds for acquisition of a corridor for the entire trail.

The ATC coordinates trail maintenance by more than two dozen volunteer organizations and publishes detailed hiker guides. Each year, several hundred "thru hikers" hike the trail from Georgia to Maine, but many thousand more use the trail for day hikes or shorter backpacks. Primitive shelters are spaced at intervals along the trail.

Robert Brandt, Nashville
Source: Materials produced by Appalachian Trail Conference, Harpers Ferry, West Virginia
SEE: CHEROKEE NATIONAL FOREST; CLINGMAN'S DOME; CONSERVATION; GREAT SMOKY MOUNTAINS NATIONAL PARK

ARCHAIC PERIOD (10,000–3,000 B.P.). The Archaic in Tennessee is the longest defined prehistoric cultural period, spanning approximately 7,000 years. The beginning of the Archaic Period roughly coincides with the Pleistocene/Holocene glacial boundary at about 10,000 years ago. The period ends with the fluorescence of both ceramic technology and more intense horticulture, hallmarks of the succeeding Woodland Period. One of the original defining features of the Archaic Period, in fact, was the absence of pottery.

In general, small groups of highly mobile hunter-gatherers characterized Archaic settlement patterns. Aggregation locales, where larger groups of people congregated at certain times of the year, were not uncommon, especially as the Archaic Period progressed. Archaic people subsisted on acorns and other plant foods, in addition to hunting game animals, primarily white-tailed deer, as well as some smaller animals. Archaic hunters did not have bow and arrow technology, but instead used spears. Unlike their Paleo-Indian precursors, they were aided in this endeavor by the atlatl, or spearthrower, which allowed them to hurl their projectiles with greater velocity. Spear points were, on average, much larger than those used in the later Woodland Period. The lifeways of Archaic people, however, were not uniform and homogenous for the entire 7,000 year period. Archaeologists have historically divided the Archaic Period into three phases—the Early, Middle, and Late Archaic periods—to delineate significant cultural changes. Some researchers also define a Terminal Archaic phase, which marks the Archaic/Woodland Period cultural transition.

The Early Archaic Period (10,000–8,000 B.P.) was one of great transition. The end of the Pleistocene brought environmental changes in both flora and fauna. Megafauna, such as the mammoth and mastodon, that dominated the Pleistocene epoch became extinct. The early Holocene was cool and moist, but warmer than the previous epoch, one factor that may explain the megafauna extinctions. In addition, oak/hickory forests replaced grasslands and savannahs all over the Southeast. These changes do not appear to have adversely affected prehistoric peoples. Rather, they adapted well to them.

In Tennessee, two major cultural variants of the Early Archaic are represented by projectile point/knife (PPKs) types—the earlier Kirk and later Bifurcate traditions. Two forms of Kirk PPKs are recognized. One is a generally large corner-notched point, while the other is a straight-stemmed and often serrated edge form. The corner-notched form chronologically precedes the latter. Kirk people subsisted largely by hunting deer and turkey, but also relied on acorn and hickory nuts. There is evidence for seasonal base camps at the Icehouse Bottom and Rose Island sites on the Little Tennessee River.

The Bifurcate Tradition differed from the Kirk primarily in the shape of their PPKs. Bifurcate points were notched both on the sides and bases. Subsistence was very similar to that of the Kirk people.

At the end of the Early Archaic Period, the region became very warm and much drier. This climatic change, termed the Altithermal, marks the beginning of the middle Archaic Period at about 7500 B.P. The number of recorded Middle Archaic sites is lower than that recorded for the Early Archaic, suggesting that perhaps this climatic change precipitated migrations to and from certain biotic provinces. Subsistence appears to have remained largely the same, although with the addition of a new pattern. Middle Archaic people intensively harvested fresh water marine resources, especially shellfish. The archaeological record shows vast accumulations known as shell middens; these can be several feet thick at Middle Archaic base camps, like the Eva and Hayes sites. In Tennessee, two regional variants are distinguished, again primarily by PPK types. Eva points are basally notched and this variant characterizes the western Tennessee River Valley, while Morrow Mountain is typical of the eastern valley. Morrow Mountain points are very similar, but commonly have rounded bases. Ground stone atlatl weights (or bannerstones) used to hone balance and velocity, made their appearance in the Middle Archaic. Increasing evidence also exists of intentional burial of the dead during this time.

The Late Archaic Period begins at the apex of the Altithermal about 5000 B.P. Conditions approximating those of the present day were reached by 4000 B.P. In evolutionary terms, many changes rapidly oc-curred during this last phase of the Archaic Period. Population size increased significantly. The number of larger aggregation sites far exceeded that in the Middle Archaic. Ceramic technology began during the late Archaic. Late Archaic pottery from Tennessee is thick and crude and often fiber-tempered. The beginnings of plant domestication and horticulture also first appear during this time. Intensive deep cave exploration and utilization occurred as well. Late Archaic people produced the earliest cave art. Projectile point forms become more variable during the Late Archaic. Early on, both the eastern and western valleys are characterized by large, asymmetrical, straight-stemmed types. In the western valley, however, this type is called Ledbetter and made of chert or flint. In the eastern valley, they are termed Appalachian-Stemmed and made largely of quartzite. Later point forms became more varied. Deep corner-notched forms are found in the western valley, small straight-stemmed types from the eastern valley, and shallow side-notched forms from the Cumberland Plateau region.

Thus, the Archaic Period, including its constituent phases and traditions, is essentially defined by its great age, lack of pottery until late in the period, and projectile point forms. Small, mobile groups of hunter-gatherers, exploiting a wide variety of terrestrial and marine resources, dominated the landscape. Larger groups of people aggregated at certain times of the year at seasonal base camps in the major river valleys in order to form alliances and find mates. Archaic hunter-gatherers explored and exploited a vast and diverse array of ecological niches across Tennessee.

Jay D. Franklin, University of Tennessee, Knoxville

SUGGESTED READINGS: J.A. Bense, *Archaeology of the Southeastern United States* (1994); Jefferson Chapman, *Tellico Archaeology: 12,000 Years of Native American History* (1987); J.T. Dowd, *The Anderson Site: Middle Archaic Adaptation in Tennessee's Central Basin* (1989); T.M.N. Lewis and M.K. Lewis, *Eva: An Archaic Site* (1961)

SEE: EVA SITE; PREHISTORIC CAVE ART

ARCHITECTURE, VERNACULAR DOMESTIC.

The majority of Tennessee residences were neither designed nor built by architects or master craftsmen. Nor were they designed with one particular architectural style in mind. They were, however, "vernacular architecture." This term is used broadly to describe housing forms that include true or folk vernacular houses, houses that imitate academic styles, and houses produced by industrialization and cultural standardization. For example, the elaborate or "high style" designs of the early Victorian era required skilled artisans to complete ornamentation in brick or stone. As a result, only the wealthy could afford to hire architects, builders, and craftsmen to complete these houses. However, the emerging middle class could rely on designs shown in the popular press, magazines, or plan books. Instead of hand-crafted elements, their houses were constructed using stamped metal or cast plaster molds. By the early twentieth century, the standardization of lumber size, the availability of catalogues of standard millwork, and the publication of house plan books made the vernacular interpretations of conventional academic styles easier.

In addition to the use of design elements that mimicked academic styles, vernacular house styles adapted to such regional variations as the local landscape, available building materials, and the skills of local craftsmen or builders. This type of domestic architecture also includes houses found in locally produced plan books, pre-cut houses from mail-order catalogues, and houses built for planned communities and company towns. Vernacular houses may also be houses constructed as speculative buildings in streetcar suburbs and suburban areas of the major cities.

The description of vernacular types generally focuses on the exterior form of the house, although the original form may have undergone change, particularly on the rear elevation. The number of stories, roof, and roof orientation are primary features used to define the forms. Exterior materials and construction methods are sometimes used to help define a vernacular form.

Two important floor plans dominate Tennessee vernacular architecture: the hall and parlor plan and the central hall plan. One of the earliest floor plans for Tennessee houses was the hall and parlor plan and its variant, the three-room plan, sometimes called the Penn plan. Generally found on most extant eighteenth century houses and early nineteenth century houses, the hall and parlor plan consists of two rooms. One room served as the more formal and public parlor, while the second room was used as the living and sleeping space for the family. In the Penn variation, one room was partitioned into two smaller rooms. This floor plan may also have a corner chimney, an indication that the house was constructed around the turn of the eighteenth century in Tennessee. Existing hall and parlor plans may be difficult to recognize because additions to the building sometimes disguised the original floor plan. As its name suggests, the central hall plan is composed of a center hall flanked by at least one room on each side. The hall, unlike today's halls, was a wide space that could function as a reception area or, more likely, living space for the family. At least one of the side rooms served as a formal, public parlor, with the other rooms reserved for family use.

Tennessee vernacular buildings are typically defined by four basic traits: materials used, construction techniques, shape of building, and design elements. Stone houses were generally constructed in East and Middle Tennessee in the period 1780 to 1820, with some construction as late as 1850. Settlers from Pennsylvania and Virginia often built or owned these homes. The houses are customarily two stories in height, with a central passage or hall and parlor plan. They feature side gable roofs, some with gable returns, and facades with multi-light, double-hung windows and three or five bays arranged symmetrically. Typically the houses have Federal or Greek Revival style embellishments, which are seen in entrances with sidelights and/or transoms. Interior doors and fireplaces may also show elements of Federal or Greek Revival designs.

Houses constructed of hewn logs, held together by corner notching and mud or wood chinking, were built in East and Middle Tennessee in the 1780s and 1790s, though some log houses were common as late as 1900. Log houses are not always recognizable when exterior logs have been sheathed in weatherboard, and interior walls have been covered with plaster or wood. The width of a building's walls can indicate that it is a log structure. Log houses are divided into four sub-types based on their exterior form: single pen, dog trot, saddlebag, and double pen. Single pens were one- or two-story rectangular or square buildings, featuring gable roofs, stone pier foundations, and stone chimneys. The dog trot house was usually one story with two single pens of the same size separated by an open hall or breezeway, which may have been enclosed at a later date. Many were built on stone pier foundations and have gable roofs and stone chimneys. Saddlebag construction consisted of two adjacent single pens with a central stone chimney, stone pier foundations, and gable roofs. The double pen was a one- or two-story residence consisting of two adjacent single pens with two exterior stone chimneys, constructed with stone pier foundations and gable roofs.

The braced frame house, also called the post and beam or heavy timber frame, was one or two stories in height, rectangular in plan with a gable roof, and featuring wall posts and beams supported with diagonal braces that were often hand hewn. Spaces between the posts and beam were filled with nogging such as brick. Frequently covered by weatherboard, these houses were built before 1860, and several examples can be found in Knoxville and Knox County.

Many styles of houses are classified by form and design features that were popularized during specific eras. An early example is the Cumberland House, the name originating in Middle Tennessee. This one- or two-story house, erected with logs or braced framing, is characterized by two single-leaf entrances on the facade, leading into two separate rooms. Rectangular in plan, the house has a side gable roof and weatherboard siding, and either a center chimney or two gable end chimneys.

One- and two-story I-Houses date from the early nineteenth century, but continued to be built until the 1900s. They are primarily frame, with gable roofs and stone or brick foundations. The three- or five-bay facades are symmetrical in design, and often there are two gable end chimneys. The interior plan of the I-House is likely to be central hall, although early I-Houses may have a hall and parlor plan. Many I-Houses contain Greek Revival, Italianate, sawn or milled wood trim, or Colonial Revival embellishments, which can be contemporary to the house or later additions.

In Middle and West Tennessee, Piano Box Houses were erected from the mid-nineteenth century into the early part of the twentieth century. The name for these one-story houses derives from their similarity to square, or box-shaped pianos. The houses feature rectangular plans with integral porches and various embellishments.

The Gable House includes at least three different forms: Center Gable, Gable Front, and Gabled Ell House. The Center Gable House was built between 1850 and 1890. As the name implies, the distinguishing feature is a center gable that extends from the wall on the facade, sometimes called a dormer wall. This gable is generally smaller or narrower than the primary roof gable. The roof is a side gable roof, but may be a cross gable roof if the facade center gable extends to the roof ridge. The facades may also have paired gables or tripled gables. Because of the gables, these houses are considered to have a Gothic Revival influence. Gable Front Houses were constructed in cities and planned communities, circa 1870 to 1930. Generally of two-story, weatherboarded frame, they occasionally feature one- or two-story porches. The Gabled Ell House, found in both urban and rural Tennessee, consists of a gable front section with a side gable section attached at right angles to produce an L-plan or T-plan. The Gabled Ell House is sometimes called an Upright and Wing House or a Gable Front and Wing House because of its shape.

Shotgun Houses were built in urban and rural areas and as worker housing or tenant housing circa 1860–1930. They have narrow rectangular plans with gable front or hip roofs. Shotgun Houses are one to four rooms deep, occasionally with a side hall or no interior hall.

Queen Anne Influence Houses, circa 1880–1920, are weatherboarded frame, but can be brick or stone veneer. The one- to two and one-half-story houses are characterized by complex rooflines and massing. They feature a variety of stylistic ornamentation and later versions have strong elements of the Colonial Revival style.

The Pyramid Roof House was built circa 1900–1930 as worker housing in both rural and urban areas. It is generally one story in height and is characterized by a steeply pitched hip or pyramidal roof. The frame house is usually weatherboarded and built on a square plan with four rooms.

Bungalow Influence Houses, circa 1895–1935, are most often weatherboard frame or brick veneer, although stone, stucco, and shingles are also used. The houses are rectangular or irregular in plan with interior floor plans that are often open and informal. Although most are one or one and one-half stories in height, there is a variation called Airplane Bungalow that has a one-room second-story addition. Roofs are hip or gable and are characterized by a low pitch and overhanging eaves. Bungalow Influence Houses may have varied stylistic elements, including Craftsman or Colonial Revival. Memphis has a large number of bungalows with different characteristics and variations of the basic form.

The Four Square House, circa 1900–1940, is two stories with a square or near square plan. The frame house can be sheathed in weatherboard or brick veneer; sometimes stone or rock-faced concrete blocks are used as a surface treatment. They have a hip or pyramidal roof and at least one central dormer on the facade. The facade porch is one story with a gable roof or half-hip roof and generally covers the facade or three-quarters of it. The interior plan has four rooms and a side stair on each floor. The Four Square House was a popular plan book or mail order house.

Between 1915 and 1940, many communities expanded into suburbs. New houses were often built as revivals of earlier styles in the new neighborhoods. The common feature of these Period Revival Influence Houses is not the form as much as the fact that all are modern vernacular adaptations of academic styles. They evoke the feeling of the earlier styles, but their use of materials and floor plans differs. These house forms include the Cape Cod Revival House, the Tudor Revival House, the English Cottage House, and the Colonial Revival House.

The Minimal Traditional House is an early to mid-twentieth century (1930–1950) house. As the name suggests, it has minimal characteristics of other styles, such as Tudor Revival and Colonial Revival. It has a rectangular plan and a roof that is generally side gable. The house is frame and can be covered with wood siding, brick, or stone veneer. Usually one or one and one-half stories, the details or embellishments appear flat and are often only around the porch or entry. The gable roof has little or no overhang. Chimneys are wide and are sometimes found on the facade. Considered the forerunner of the Ranch House, this house can be found throughout the state.

Claudette Stager, Tennessee Historical Commission

SUGGESTED READINGS: The Vernacular Architecture Forum publishes a *Perspectives in Vernacular Architecture* series that contains articles on vernacular design; Herbert Gottfried and Jan Jennings, *American Vernacular Design* (1985); Herbert Gottfried and Jan Jennings, *American Vernacular Interior Design* (1993); John A. Jakle, et. al., *Common Houses in America's Small Towns* (1989); James C. Massey and Shirley Maxwell, *House Styles in America* (1996); Virginia McAlester and Lee McAlester, *A Field Guide to American Houses* (1984)

ARMFIELD, JOHN (1797–1871), slavetrader and businessman, descended from North Carolina Quakers who were Loyalists during the American Revolution. While still a boy, Armfield ran away from home, vowing not to return until he had acquired more wealth than his father, Nathan Armfield. In the 1830s, Armfield fulfilled his vow as the partner of slavetrader Isaac Franklin.

With headquarters in Alexandria, Virginia, Franklin and Armfield conducted gangs of chained and shackled slaves down the Natchez Trace and sold them in the slave pen on the edge of the Mississippi town. The arduous journey took seven or eight weeks, but wealthy cotton planters paid Franklin and Armfield well for their traffic in African flesh. Armfield's biographer, Isabel Howell, estimated that the pair averaged sales of 1,200 slaves per year for every year from 1828 to 1835.

In 1831 Armfield courted and married Franklin's niece, Martha Franklin. A rich man when he retired in 1845, Armfield soon acquired social acceptance and began investing in Tennessee real estate. About 1850, he visited Beersheba Springs, a resort on Broad Mountain in Grundy County. Taken by the beauty of the springs and the possibility for development, Armfield purchased several hundred acres in 1854 and began renovations on the hotel. With its neo-classical facade, two-story galleries, and white columns, the hotel opened in May 1856 and inaugurated the glorious era of Beersheba and Armfield's success as host and entrepreneur. Armfield also erected a saw mill, a brick kiln, grist mill, and tannery, remnants of which survive. An Episcopal supporter of the proposed University of the South, Armfield built cottages at Beersheba for Bishops James H. Otey and Leonidas Polk in 1859. Both houses still stand, along with the hotel and twelve other structures.

Armfield died childless in 1871, his fortune diminished by the Civil War. He is buried in the little private cemetery on Armfield Avenue, across the road from his Beersheba home on the bluff.
Herschel Gower, Dallas, Texas
SEE: BEERSHEBA SPRINGS; FRANKLIN, ISAAC; GRUNDY COUNTY; OTEY, JAMES H.; POLK, LEONIDAS; SLAVERY

ARMY OF TENNESSEE. The Army of Tennessee, known by various names in the course of its existence, was the Confederacy's principal army on the western front. From the Appalachian Mountains to the Mississippi River, this force fought most of the major battles that took place in the region.

The army traced it origins to the early spring and summer of 1861, when Tennessee Governor Isham G. Harris spearheaded the effort to raise the Provisional Army of Tennessee. The army, one of the largest and best organized of the southern forces, transferred to Confederate service in July 1861. Placed under the command of General Albert Sidney Johnston, it became the core of the southern army in the Western Theater. In the opening days of the war, the army defended the northern frontier of the Confederacy, along the Tennessee-Kentucky border, before retreating following the Federal capture of Fort Henry and Fort Donelson on the Tennessee and Cumberland rivers in February 1862.

The army concentrated at Corinth, Mississippi. General P. G. T. Beauregard, second in command, styled the 44,000-man force the "Army of the Mississippi." On April 6–7, 1862, this army engaged General Ulysses S. Grant's Army of the Tennessee in the battle of Shiloh, the first large-scale battle of the war. An apparent Confederate victory on the first day turned into defeat on the second. The army limped back to Corinth, having suffered more than 10,000 casualties, including the death of Albert Sidney Johnston.

Although Beauregard succeeded to command of the army, his conflicts with President Jefferson Davis soon led to his replacement by General Braxton Bragg. For the next year and a half, Bragg led the army through some of the hardest marching and toughest fighting of the war. In November 1862, soon after the culmination of Bragg's first campaign at the Battle of Perryville and the subsequent retreat into Tennessee, the army officially became known as the Army of Tennessee, the designation it carried for the rest of the war.

In the last days of December 1862, the 38,000-man Army of Tennessee took up a position thirty miles southeast of Nashville, along the banks of the west fork of the Stones River, near the small town of Murfreesboro. The Confederate forces faced a 44,000-man Union army under the command of General William S. Rosecrans. Both armies straddled the Nashville Turnpike and the railroad leading into that city.

Early on December 31, 1862, the Army of Tennessee struck the enemy's right flank and drove the Federals back to the turnpike and railroad. But the initial success could not be sustained. After three days of fighting, Bragg withdrew and the Federals claimed victory, although both sides suffered an almost equal number of casualties.

The Army of Tennessee held the Nashville & Chattanooga Railroad near Tullahoma for the next several months. In the summer of 1863 Rosecrans adroitly maneuvered Bragg's forces from their defensive position, sending them into retreat to North Georgia, just south of Chattanooga. Reinforcements from General James Longstreet's Virginia corps bolstered the Army of Tennessee. On September 19–20, the army attacked Rosecrans along the banks of Chickamauga Creek, fighting one of the fiercest engagements of the war. Confederate casualties numbered more than 18,000, while the Union forces lost more than 16,000 men. Despite its losses, the battle became one of the Army of Tennessee's greatest tactical triumphs. The southern forces drove the Union army back to Chattanooga; only the skillful action of General George H. Thomas prevented the retreat from becoming a rout.

But Bragg failed to follow up his advantage. Criticism of the general, which had been mounting since the retreat from Kentucky and the battle of Stones River, reached new heights. Jefferson Davis visited the army and raised expectations that he would relieve Bragg of his command. Davis, however, decided to sustain the general. Then, in late November 1863, General Ulysses S. Grant, who replaced Rosecrans as Union commander, decisively defeated Bragg in the battles for Chattanooga, forcing him to withdraw to North Georgia, making the costly triumph at Chickamauga strategically worthless. Davis relieved Bragg of his command and named General Joseph E. Johnston to head the Army of Tennessee.

Johnston strengthened the army's morale and numbers, but faced an enormous task in the spring of 1864. General William T. Sherman, with superior numbers, launched his campaign to capture Atlanta. Gradually, Johnston fell back before Sherman's advance, presumably seeking an opening to strike the Union forces at an unguarded moment. Johnston found only one opportunity, and even then, General John Bell Hood, who had been expected to lead the attack, held back, fearing a Federal attack on his flank if he moved forward. The Confederates continued to retreat under pressure of Sherman's enveloping maneuvers.

A disenchanted Jefferson Davis removed Johnston from command and gave the Army of Tennessee to General John Bell Hood, who had been sending Davis criticisms of Johnston for continually retreating. Hood's engagements around Atlanta cost the army a terrible price in the numbers of dead and wounded, all to no avail. On September 2, 1864, Sherman captured Atlanta.

Hood then moved the Army of Tennessee northward, hoping to draw Sherman away from Georgia. Instead, Sherman headed for Savannah, leaving General Thomas to cope with Hood's forces in Tennessee. Crossing the Tennessee River and moving into Middle Tennessee, Hood led the Army of Tennessee into an ill-advised frontal assault at Franklin on November 30, 1864. This battle resulted in 7,000 casualties, including the deaths of six Confederate generals.

Nevertheless, Hood decided to move on to Nashville, where the army was decisively defeated on December 15–16, 1864; the remnants of the Army of Tennessee managed to reach safety on the Tennessee River. Hood lost his command, and Johnston returned to lead the weakened, hard-luck army into the Carolinas, where they fought once more at Bentonville before surrendering at Durham, North Carolina, in late April 1865. The Army of Tennessee gained a reputation as a tough, hard-marching, hard-fighting force. Usually outnumbered and led by inept commanders, the Army of Tennessee nevertheless achieved an impressive record as a fighting force.

James L. McDonough, Auburn University

SUGGESTED READINGS: Thomas L. Connelly, *Army of the Heartland: the Army of Tennessee, 1861–1862* (1967) and *Autumn of Glory: the Army of Tennessee, 1862–1865* (1971); Stanley F. Horn, *The Army of Tennessee* (1941)

SEE: BRAGG, BRAXTON; CHEATHAM, BENJAMIN F.; CHICKAMAUGA AND CHATTANOOGA, BATTLES OF; CIVIL WAR; CLEBURNE, PATRICK R.; FORT DONELSON; FORT HENRY; HARRIS, ISHAM G.; FRANKLIN, BATTLE OF; HOOD, JOHN BELL; JOHNSTON, ALBERT S.; JOHNSTON, JOSEPH E.; NASHVILLE, BATTLE OF; POLK, LEONIDAS; SHILOH, BATTLE OF; STONES RIVER, BATTLE OF; TULLAHOMA CAMPAIGN

ARNELL, SAMUEL MAYES (1833–1903), Reconstruction legislator and congressman, was born at Zion Settlement in Maury County on May 3, 1833. After attending Amherst College, Arnell returned to Tennessee, studied law, and practiced in Columbia.

Although a slaveholder, Arnell sided with the Union during the Civil War and traversed Middle Tennessee urging Tennesseans to maintain their allegiance to the United States. His relentless, vocal opposition to the Confederacy earned him many enemies, forcing him to flee to Nashville for safety. A Whig before the war, Arnell subsequently became a Radical Republican and represented Lewis, Maury, and Williamson counties in the General Assembly of 1865–66. Arnell wrote and introduced two franchise bills to prevent ex-Confederates from voting in state and national elections; they were signed into law in June 1865 and May 1866.

In the fall of 1865, after a disputed election in Tennessee's Sixth Congressional District between Arnell and Dorsey B. Thomas, Governor William G. Brownlow awarded the election certificate to Arnell. He remained in Congress until 1871, having chaired the Committee on Expenditures in the Department of State and served on the Committee on Education and Labor. The Arnell family continued to live in Washington, D.C., for a few years before returning to Columbia. From 1879 to 1885, Arnell served as the Columbia postmaster before becoming Superintendent of Public Schools. At the expiration of his term, in 1888, Arnell and his family returned to Washington, D.C., until 1894, when his declining health forced them to move to Johnson City, Tennessee. He died there on July 20, 1903.

Kathleen R. Zebley, University of Tennessee, Knoxville
SUGGESTED READING: Kathleen R. Zebley, "Unconditional Unionist: Samuel Mayes Arnell and Reconstruction in Tennessee," *Tennessee Historical Quarterly* 53(1994): 246–59
SEE: BROWNLOW, WILLIAM G.; MAURY COUNTY; RECONSTRUCTION

ARNOLD, EDDY (1918–) was the most successful commercial artist in country music for the years immediately after World War II. Arnold's success in country music sales centered on two eras: the 1945–1953 period, when he dominated country sales and even outsold most pop music artists in the live radio era; and the 1964–1970 era, when country music embraced the "Nashville Sound" and became the music of the middle class.

Richard Edward Arnold was born May 15, 1918, on a farm in Henderson, in Chester County. He first appeared on radio in Jackson, Tennessee, before moving to Memphis and St. Louis with fiddle player Speedy McNatt. In 1940 Arnold joined Pee Wee King and the Golden West Cowboys in Nashville. From the end of 1941 to the end of 1942, the Golden West Cowboys appeared on the Camel Caravan to entertain U.S. military troops throughout the country.

At the beginning of 1943, Arnold went solo and appeared on the Grand Ole Opry. He obtained a recording contract with Victor Records, and in December 1944, became the first artist to record in Nashville with a major label. His first hit was *That's How Much I Love You* in 1946. It was followed by a number of other top selling hits, including *Bouquet of Roses, I'll Hold You In My Heart,* and *Don't Rob Another Man's Castle.* Beginning in November 1947, he hosted a Mutual network radio show. In September 1948 Arnold left the Opry. That same year, he began a daily network noon show, which opened with his signature song, *Cattle Call;* he dominated country music like no other artist has before or since, having the top chart record for 50 of the 52 weeks of 1948.

Arnold's next reign as a top-selling country act occurred in the mid-1960s, with songs like *Make The World Go Away,* and *What's He Doing In My World.* During this period, he recorded with lush string sections and contributed to the middle-of-the-road sound that brought country music to American middle-class listeners.

Throughout his career, Eddy Arnold appeared on network shows, first on radio, then television. His popularity expanded the boundaries of country music, and he served as a bright, articulate spokesman for the industry.

Arnold was elected to the Country Music Hall of Fame in 1966, the same year he headlined a show at Carnegie Hall. He was the first Country Music Association "Entertainer of the Year" in 1967.

In addition to his success as a country music artist, Eddy Arnold has been a successful businessman and community leader, active in developing and promoting Brentwood, a suburb of Nashville.

Don Cusic, Belmont University
SEE: CHESTER COUNTY; COUNTRY MUSIC HALL OF FAME AND MUSEUM; GRAND OLE OPRY; MUSIC

ARNOLD ENGINEERING DEVELOPMENT CENTER (AEDC). Located on 39,000 wooded acres in Coffee and Franklin counties, AEDC is the world's most diverse complex of aerospace ground simulation test facilities and one of the most unusual U.S. Air Force installations. Approximately 3,000 civilian scientists and support personnel work with a military staff of several hundred, operating over 50 aerodynamic and propulsion wind tunnels, rocket and turbine engine test cells, space chambers, arc heaters, and ballistic ranges to simulate flight conditions, from sea level to outer space and from subsonic speeds to over Mach 20. Virtually every modern aircraft's design, engine and weapons system, missile, space vehicle, and probe have been tested in the center's three major test complexes. World War II vintage equipment from the Bavarian Motor Works in Munich forms the original core of the Engine Test Facility (ETF), which also includes the world's three largest rocket test cells. The von Karman Gas Dynamics Facility (VKF) honors famed scientist, Dr. Theodore von Karman. The Propulsion Wind Tunnel complex (PWT) is an International Historic Mechanical Engineering Landmark.

In 1951 President Harry S. Truman vowed that the U.S. would become the international leader of aeronautical development when he dedicated AEDC to the memory of the Army Air Force's visionary commander, General Henry H. "Hap" Arnold. Alarmed by the rapid advances of German aeronautical technology during World War II, Arnold enlisted Dr. Theodore von Karman to lead the Scientific Advisory Group (SAG) in assessing the situation in Europe in relation to national security. SAG's report, "Toward New Horizons," became AEDC's blueprint, including Dr. Frank Wattendorf's recommendation to provide leading civilian and military scientists with German equipment at a state-of-the-art testing and evaluation center.

Officials selected U.S. Army Camp Forrest (1940–1946) near Tullahoma as the site of the new facility. The site provided ample power and water resources, while its remoteness protected civilians from testing hazards and provided security. Surrounding communities quickly adopted space race slogans and symbols. Tullahoma became "The Wind Tunnel City," and Motlow State Community College incorporated a rocket launch on its 1969 official seal.

Arnold Research Organization (ARO) Inc. designed and operated Arnold Center until 1980. The expression "going out to ARO" continues in the local lexicon, though the company no longer exists.

As the area's largest employer, AEDC heavily influences south central Tennessee, both economically and culturally. An annual budget exceeding $360 million attracts related industries, subcontractors, and employees from across the nation and around the world. The culturally diverse work force merging into the local scene lends a cosmopolitan flavor to surrounding communities.

With the end of the Cold War, security pressures diminished. AEDC held its first open house in 1986. AEDC's mission continues to broaden, including commercial testing, the consolidation and transfer of Navy jet engine testing, and the creation of service and support alliances with neighboring institutions and municipalities.

The U.S. Air Force Materiel Command manages AEDC, with a Navy captain as vice commander. Sverdrup Technology, Inc., operates all test facilities with ACS providing Center support.

Darlene M. Merryman, Motlow State Community College
SEE: CAMP FORREST; COFFEE COUNTY

ARROWMONT SCHOOL OF ARTS AND CRAFTS,

a visual arts complex in Gatlinburg, Sevier County, grew out of the manual arts curriculum of the Pi Beta Phi Settlement School. The Pi Phi teachers taught handicraft skills to the community while seeking to revive traditional crafts among these mountain people. With an active weaving, furniture, and basketry program, the fraternity marketed the crafts to its national membership to supplement and stimulate the local economy. In 1926 the Pi Phis started the "Arrow Craft" Shop (later Arrowcraft) to market the products to a growing tourism industry. Although materials, instructions, and ideas came from outside of Appalachia, local residents interpreted the crafted items in their own way and returned the finished products to the Shop for selling. In 1940, in reaction to the opening of the Great Smoky Mountains National Park, the fraternity built a new Arrowcraft building to house the work of over 90 artisans. In the mid-1940s, the fraternity chose to enhance its offerings by establishing a summer program.

The fraternity approached the Department of Crafts and Interior Design, of the College of Home Economics at the University of Tennessee, about using the Gatlinburg premises during the summer to expand the influence of both entities in the crafts field. In 1945, this cooperative effort produced its first summer craft workshop. Under the leadership of Marian G. Heard the summer workshop blossomed. While the Arrowcraft Shop continued to market crafts from the local people, the summer workshops attracted students and instructors from around the world. The quality instruction and the platonic surroundings created an atmosphere in which artists and craft workers could concentrate on developing their skills. The university also offered college credit through the Pi Beta Phi workshops.

The availability of locally-made craft items attracted tourists, while an available market brought more crafts workers to town. In 1948 the Southern Highlands Handicraft Guild sponsored its first Craftsman's Fair at the Pi Beta Phi School, exhibiting local craft work and helping to establish Gatlinburg as a thriving craft center. At the 1964 Pi Beta Phi Convention, the fraternity decided to establish an arts and crafts school as a part of its centennial celebration.

The rapid modernization of the area around Gatlinburg changed the fraternity's mission from a three-way focus of academics, health care, and manual instruction to a single emphasis on the arts and craft work. In 1965 the fraternity closed its medical clinic. The same year, Sevier County assumed control of the school facilities, leaving only the arts and crafts curriculum. The fraternity focused its energy on building a reputable arts and crafts school. In 1969 it changed the name of the school to Arrowmont and within a year, Arrowmont had been formally established and ensconced in its new 38,000-square-foot facility. It contains galleries, workshops, and libraries, while dormitories house students, instructors, and artists-in-residence. Marian Heard retired as director in 1977. Two years later, Sandra J. Blain, a University of Tennessee professor and nationally known potter, became director.

In 1994 the Southern Highlands Handicraft Guild assumed operation of the Arrowcraft Shop to market products from all over the southern Appalachian region, leaving Arrowmont to focus on the instruction rather than marketing. Emphasizing art as a part of everyday experience and expression, the school offers seminars, conferences, community classes, and an Elderhostel program featuring internationally-known instructors. Although handwoven products have not been in high demand in recent years, Arrowmont continues to lead in the arts and crafts field through its diverse program and eclectic outlook.

Kevin D. Collins, University of Tennessee, Knoxville
SEE: ART; DECORATIVE ARTS, APPALACHIAN; PI BETA PHI SCHOOL; SETTLEMENT SCHOOLS; SEVIER COUNTY

ART. Tennessee, which until recently was rural, egalitarian, and lacking in concentrated wealth, never has been a center of art patronage or production. The first generation of pioneers lacked both time and money for art, and there is hardly any documentation of art done in Tennessee before 1800. But, once the land was cleared and the Indians vanquished, there was a demand in this family-centered society for portraits. The needs of the second generation of settlers were largely met by itinerant painters who were essentially craftsmen peddling a trade. There simply was not enough work in any one place to enable an artist to settle, and economic survival often required versatility. For example, in 1825, Robert Titus advertised in a Knoxville newspaper as both a portrait painter and watchmaker.

The first resident professional artist was probably Ralph E. W. Earl, who took up residence in Nashville when he acquired a patron. Earl came to Nashville in 1817 to paint a portrait of Andrew Jackson, married into Old Hickory's family, and lived with him at The Hermitage. He painted portraits in Nashville until 1829, when he moved to Washington to live with Jackson in the White House. The following year, Washington Bogart Cooper opened a studio in Nashville. He produced 30–35 portraits annually for half a century and more than earned his sobriquet, "the man of a thousand portraits."

With the proceeds of his early work, Washington Cooper funded European study for his brother, William, who returned to Tennessee and settled in Memphis. Like other artists of the era, William Cooper worked in Tennessee and the surrounding states. John Wood Dodge, Tennessee's premier portrait miniaturist, followed a similar pattern. From 1840 to 1861, he maintained a studio in Nashville, but frequently traveled to Kentucky towns, resorts, and such Mississippi river cities as Memphis, St. Louis, Natchez, and New Orleans.

On June 1, 1840, the *Nashville Whig* informed readers that "if a portrait is wanted, Mr. Cooper is *the* artist . . . but if a miniature is preferred for mother, wife, or 'ladylove' call upon Mr. Dodge." So prolific was the work of these two, that a century later, when collectors brought pictures to Nashville's Hooberry Bookstore for identification, the proprietor almost always told them that the oils were by Cooper, and the miniatures by Dodge. Actually, by the 1840s, the size and prosperity of Nashville and Memphis attracted many portraitists and miniature painters, although most of them stayed only briefly. An exception was George Dury, a German painter, who arrived in Nashville in 1850. He became Washington Cooper's chief rival by flaunting his prior work for European royals.

By the 1850s even Clarksville was prosperous enough to support two resident portraitists, Robert Loftin Newman and William Shackelford. Newman sought out commissions for full-length portraits because of the greater compositional challenge. No doubt, an additional incentive was the fact that the price of portraits was proportional to the size. Following an emerging trend of including landscapes in portraits, Samuel Shaver executed portraits of various sizes with estate views in the background.

William Harrison Scarborough worked in Kingston, Rogersville, and Knoxville in 1833, before moving to South Carolina two years later. Samuel Shaver may have painted earlier, but from 1845 until after the Civil War, he was the leading artist in East Tennessee.

The first Tennessee paintings with a large element of landscape were the overmantel caprices at the Carter Mansion in Elizabethton, circa 1790. The next earliest Tennessee landscapes were topographical views, essentially portraits of places, such as *A Full View of Deadrick's Hill, Jonesboro,* now at the Tennessee State Museum. This painting was commissioned in 1810 by a store owner whose shop is pictured at the center of the work. In 1832 John H. B. Latrobe completed the earliest painting of Memphis. The painting was done in watercolors, the favored medium of travelers like Latrobe. Another traveler, Charles-Alexandre Lesueur, drew pencil sketches of the Mississippi and Cumberland rivers in 1828 and 1832. Among the earliest Tennessee views, these drawings were completed for scientific, not artistic purposes, and the originals, in Le Havre, France, have never been shown in Tennessee.

The War of 1812 fueled a sense of national patriotism that combined with the first impulses of the Romantic Movement and transformed this topographical transcription into landscape art. The chosen subject was the American landscape. The favored format was the panorama.

The greatest Tennessee practitioner of panoramic landscapes was James Cameron. A Scot who settled at Chattanooga, Cameron possessed that inestimable thing that only Earl had had—a single, wealthy patron. Although Cameron did pure landscapes, he is best known for works that combine group portraiture with a panoramic view. The most famous is that of his patron, *Colonel Whiteside and Family* (Hunter Museum of Art, Chattanooga), a charming picture, but one whose parts do not quite come together into a coherent whole. The diminutive size he gave the African Americans in the picture has provided a fertile field for analysis.

Most of Cameron's landscapes show nature succumbing to settlement. Another landscape artist of the 1850s, possibly James Wagner (of whom nothing is known), painted two exquisite views of Nashville emphasizing the newly-completed capitol building (Tennessee State Museum, Nashville; First Tennessee Bank, Memphis). Generally, Tennessee artists shunned scenes of wild nature such as the New York artist Alexander Wyant's *Tennessee* (Metropolitan Museum of Art, New York). Their clients preferred to show off the state's man-made improvements and their dominion over nature, possibly to tout Tennessee as an investment opportunity to eastern capitalists.

Before the Civil War, art was taught only in schools for girls as a fashionable accomplishment, but not as training for professional artists. Men who sought to become professional artists apprenticed with a master. Newspapers were uniformly complimentary to artists and welcomed every new artist to town, but no critical art literature developed in Tennessee. Nor were there galleries for exhibitions; artists generally exhibited their work at their studios, or in shops.

A unique artistic event in antebellum Tennessee was the staging of the 1858 benefit exhibition of 350 paintings at the State Capitol to enable the Tennessee Historical Society to purchase Washington Cooper's series of portraits of Tennessee governors. A remarkable feature of the series is that it was painted on speculation with no assurance of purchase.

Although the Methodist Episcopal Church commissioned portraits of its bishops, and the Grand Masonic Lodge in Nashville paid Washington Cooper to paint portraits of its Grand Masters, antebellum public commissions were exceedingly rare. One exception was the 1859 commission granted by the Tennessee General Assembly to George Dury to execute a posthumous likeness of former U.S. Senator and Attorney General, Felix Grundy.

The Civil War virtually ended the Tennessee art market, and artists struggled throughout the war. John Wood Dodge was driven out of the state because of his wife's abolitionist views. James Cameron left at the end of the war to escape the devastation. Union soldiers, or "special artists" sent to report on the war for *Harper's Weekly* or *Leslie's Illustrated Newspaper,* produced most of the surviving datable art from the Civil War era.

The East Tennessee Art Association, a pro-Confederate organization formed in October 1862, commissioned Samuel Shaver to depict various Confederate generals, but apparently the project miscarried. Shaver was a staunch Confederate supporter, but other artists proved more flexible in their allegiances. Early in the war, George Dury exhibited a portrait of Jefferson Davis, but later accepted commissions from the Reconstruction legislature for paintings of Governor William G. "Parson" Brownlow and Union General George C. Thomas.

The Civil War marked an end to the nation's innocence. Artists no longer sought inspiration in America's uniqueness. Rather, artists were once again drawn to Europe, and Tennesseans were no exception. After the war, the itinerant faded away except in remote areas, the expected standard of art rose, and European training became a distinct advantage.

The postwar era produced an increased demand for portraits by institutions such as colleges, banks, and foundations, as well as individual capitalists and professionals. Refined homes were expected to have pictures on the walls, although in Tennessee, more often than not, these were prints rather than paintings. For the first time, Tennessee developed a market for still lifes, "negro studies," allegories like those completed by Carl Gutherz upon his return to Memphis from Paris in 1873, and landscape and genre painting in the Barbizon style.

The popularity of genre painting in France beckoned some Tennessee artists, such as Willie Betty Newman of Rutherford County, who specialized in peasant scenes from Brittany and won honorable mention at the Paris Exposition of 1900 for *En Penitence.* Tennessee genre painting, however, was largely done by outsiders, such as Elizabeth Nourse and John Stokes. His *Smoky Mountain Wedding* (Tennessee State Museum, Nashville) of 1872 combined the two picaresque elements northerners expected in a southern painting—blacks (with watermelons) and hillbillies.

Another branch of painting that blossomed was historical genre. Gilbert Gaul came to Tennessee in 1881 and, eight years later, won a bronze medal at the 1889 Paris Exposition for *Charging the Battery* (Birmingham Museum of Art), a Civil War picture. He was the first important Tennessee artist who did not paint portraits. After Lloyd Branson returned from Europe to Knoxville in 1878, portraits constituted his mainstay until his death in 1925, but the expanding market also enabled him to paint scenes from early Tennessee history, including *Rendezvous of the Overmountain Men at Sycamore Shoals, 1780* (Tennessee State Museum, Nashville). Influenced by the Barbizon painters, Branson's *Hauling Marble* (Frank H. McClung Museum, Knoxville), which won a gold medal at the Appalachian Exposition in Knoxville in 1910, was a classic Continental exhibition piece, albeit with a local theme.

Another postwar development was the emergence of the professional woman artist in Tennessee. The prevailing cult of domesticity discouraged careers for women, but art was grudgingly accepted as a suitable pursuit for women because of their presumed greater sensitivity. In 1887 Adelia Lutz returned to Knoxville from European study and commenced a career painting portraits, landscapes, and flower studies (especially hollyhocks) until her death in 1931. After Willie Betty Newman returned from her studies in France, she won a number of commissions for official portraits, including governors James Frazier and Ben Hooper. An important addition to the artistic community was Ella Sophonisba Hergesheimer, a great-great-granddaughter of the Philadelphia painter Charles Willson Peale. She came to Nashville in 1907 to paint a portrait of Methodist Bishop Holland McTyeire, but she stayed until her death in 1937, painting portraits and landscapes, although still lifes were perhaps her best work. The state's most notable Impressionist was a woman—Knoxville's Catherine Wiley. Impressionism did not become fashionable in Tennessee until the turn of the century, an example of the *retardataire,* or cultural lag of the state. She painted a few landscapes, and fewer portraits, just family and friends. Most of her subjects were individual women in quiet interiors or a few women outdoors. Among her best works are *Woman in Blue at a Desk,* perhaps also known as *The Letter* (Tennessee State Museum, Nashville), *Sunlit Afternoon* (Greenville County Museum of Art, South Carolina), and *Willow Pond* (Metropolitan Museum of Art, New York).

The end of the century also witnessed the tentative beginnings of an art establishment. Clarksville's Robert Loftin Newman and Nashville's George Dury failed in 1872 to find support for an Academy of Art in Nashville. However, in 1885, the Watkins Institute opened with a successful program of coeducational art instruction. The Nashville Art Association was founded in 1878, the Knoxville Art Circle a few years later. Both sponsored annual exhibitions.

The increasing popularity and availability of photography produced a devaluation of transcription in art. After the Civil War, the artist was expected to reveal himself in his work, interpretation gained importance, and artists stressed subject matter less than form. The cult of the artist as a genius migrated from Europe and replaced the earlier idea of the painter as craftsman. However, Tennessee artists worked in a somewhat different climate, offering little room for Bohemianism or eccentricity. Catherine Wiley's nervous breakdown, far from being compared to Van Gogh's, was hushed up for decades. Nor was art a vital part of everyday life. One artist ruefully conceded that in Nashville, "Art was a rather nice thing done by someone's maiden aunt or a courtly and slightly hungry old gentleman, and it was appreciated in a rather detached way by the gentle ladies of the women's clubs."[1]

Impressionism had not come to Tennessee until it was thoroughly respectable, even passé, in Europe, but once here it lingered into the 1930s. By then, most artists wanted to move on. Nashville's Ella Hergesheimer was quoted in the *Nashville Banner* on February 26, 1938, praising the Post-impressionists for having "done something wonderful for us. They have given us design which in a great measure was lost by the impressionists, but which the great masters of the past always had."

However, the successors of the Post-impressionists were not well received in Tennessee art circles. Mrs. Louis C. Audigier of Knoxville's Nicholson Art League reported from Rome, "I have seen the Cubists and the Futurists, and I think it reprehensible for any government to permit the exhibition of such works—as to allow a madman the freedom of the streets."[2] Nonetheless, these influences reached Tennessee a generation later as evidenced in the work of such artists as Nashville's Charles Cagle, Clarence Stagg, Avery Handly, and Philip Perkins, Memphis's Burton Callicott, and Chattanooga's George Cress. But, until the

1960s, not much Tennessee art went beyond semiabstraction because of the state's cultural conservatism.

Indeed, during the 1930s the New Deal encouraged a resurgence of realism, called Regionalism. The federal government commissioned local artists to paint murals in some 30 Tennessee post offices, including *Farm and Factory* by Horace Day at Clinton; *Manpower and the Resources of Nature* by William Zorach in Greeneville; and *Farmer Family* by Wendell Jones at Johnson City. Other public buildings also received murals, such as those by Dean Cornwell in the Davidson County Court House and the John Sevier State Office Building in Nashville, and Burton Callicott's murals for the Memphis Museum of Natural History. These works contained didactic content largely absent from earlier Tennessee art.

Another regionalist, who worked in a semipointillist style very different from that of the muralists, was Carroll Cloar, one of the best-known Tennessee artists of the twentieth century. His paintings include *The Appleknocker* (private collection) and *Historic Encounter Between E. H. Crump and W. C. Handy on Beale Street* (First Tennessee Bank, Memphis). Cloar observed that his family album was a source for his work, although as many of his paintings relate to his Arkansas boyhood as to his Memphis adulthood.

African-American artists did not come into their own until the mid-twentieth century. Before then black artists had almost no opportunities for study, exhibition, and patronage. After emancipation, African Americans themselves relied on photographs and painted photographs for their portraits and prints for other artistic needs. Blacks were the subjects of what were called Negro studies, but these were artworks by whites for a white clientele. Perhaps the first important African-American artist in Tennessee and the first to concentrate on black subject matter was Aaron Douglass. He had made his reputation as a painter of the Harlem Renaissance with geometric and stylized forms drawn from African art. He was on the faculty of Fisk University from 1936 until his death in 1969. At Fisk Douglass painted murals in the university library (now administration building), those at the north end depicting the black man in Africa, those at the south end the black man in America. Another major work of his Tennessee period is *Building More Stately Mansions* (also Fisk University, Nashville). Under his influence the Fisk University Galleries became the first in Tennessee to emphasize African and African-American art.

The art infrastructure of Tennessee expanded phenomenally in the twentieth century. The Nicholson Art League of Knoxville was founded in 1906. The Brooks Museum in Memphis was founded in 1913. The Memphis Art Association began in 1914, and the Memphis Academy of Arts commenced in 1936. The Arrowmont

School for Arts and Crafts in Gatlinburg was formed in 1945. Chattanooga's Hunter Museum of Art dates to 1951, and the University of Tennessee at Chattanooga's art gallery was founded a year later. Nashville's Fine Arts Center at Cheekwood opened in 1957 as an outgrowth of the earlier (1924) Nashville Museum. The Dulin Gallery (now Knoxville Museum of Art) was founded in 1962, the Carroll Reece Museum in Johnson City in 1965, and the University of Memphis Art Museum in 1969. Since 1971, when the Tennessee State Museum (founded in 1937) came under the administration of the Tennessee Arts Commission (founded in 1967), it has sponsored periodic purchase competitions of Tennessee art, held retrospectives of such artists as Carroll Cloar, Arthur Orr, Paul Harmon, and Carl Sublett and undertaken survey exhibitions of landscape painting and portraiture in the state. The other institutions also touted local talent and gave art a visibility it previously lacked. Art was taught in the public schools, and college art departments turned out artists in increasing numbers.

The contemporary art scene in Tennessee is incredibly varied. There are several art schools, many museums and commercial galleries, numerous exhibitions, frequent competitions, and far more artists than ever before. They work in almost every style and medium found elsewhere in the world. Nevertheless, no artist of the first rank has come from Tennessee, and perhaps the most renowned living Tennessee artist, Red Grooms, is best known for his installations based on life in Chicago and New York. A telling statistic is that Tennessee seems mired near the bottom in per capita state spending on the arts.

James C. Kelly, Virginia Historical Society

CITATIONS:

(1) Nashville *Banner,* May 18, 1930.

(2) Quoted in Frederick C. Moffatt, "Painting, Sculpture, and Photography," in Lucile Deaderick, ed., *Heart of the Valley: A History of Knoxville, Tennessee* (Knoxville, 1976), 432.

SUGGESTED READINGS: William H. Gerdts, "Virginia," in *The South and the Midwest: Art Across America: Regional Painting in America, 1710–1920* (1990); James C. Kelly, "Landscape and Genre Painting in Tennessee, 1810–1985," *Tennessee Historical Quarterly* 44 (1985): 7–152; James C. Kelly, "Portrait Painting in Tennessee," *Tennessee Historical Quarterly* 46 (1987): 193–276; Frederick C. Moffatt, "Painting, Sculpture, and Photography," in Lucile Deaderick, ed., *Heart of the Valley: A History of Knoxville, Tennessee* (1976): 424–438; Jessie Poesch, *The Art of the Old South, Painting, Sculpture, Architecture, and the Products of Craftsmen, 1560–1860* (1983)

ASBURY, FRANCIS (1745–1816), bishop of the Methodist Episcopal Church in America, was born near Birmingham, England, to Joseph and Elizabeth (Rogers) Asbury and apprenticed as a blacksmith. At an early age, Asbury joined the Methodist movement under John Wesley's leadership and became a lay preacher. In 1771, when the fledgling Methodist movement in the American colonies called for leadership, Asbury offered himself. He was elected bishop in 1784, when the Methodists in America formed themselves into the Methodist Episcopal Church.

Recognized as the preeminent leader of the denomination, Asbury became known as the father of American Methodism and the principal guide and shaper of the movement. He insisted that Methodist preachers travel constantly, winning converts and organizing new congregations. Under Asbury's leadership, Methodists established churches in every state along the eastern seaboard from New England to Georgia, and circuit-riding preachers moved westward with the pioneers into the wilderness of Tennessee and Kentucky. Like his preachers, Asbury was no armchair administrator. He was constantly on the move, making the rounds of all sections of the church to superintend the work. He adopted the motto: "Live or die, I must ride, "and traveled an average of 6,000 miles annually for 45 years.

Asbury first visited Tennessee in 1788, six years after the establishment of the Holston Conference at the headwaters of the Yakin and Holston rivers. Between his first trip in 1788 and his last in 1815, Asbury visited the state 17 times and recorded his observations in the daily journal he kept for 45 years. Critical of the frontier fondness for whiskey and concerned about the moral effects of cheap land, Asbury seldom failed to praise the generosity of Tennessee people.

Asbury died in 1816 in northern Virginia, while on his way to the meeting of the General Conference in Baltimore. He was buried in the Eutaw Church in Baltimore; in 1854 his body was moved to a prominent Methodist graveyard in Mount Olivet Cemetery in Baltimore.

Frank Gulley, Vanderbilt University

SUGGESTED READING: Elmer T. Clark, et. al., eds., *The Journals and Letters of Francis Asbury* (1958)

SEE: HOLSTON CONFERENCE

ASHWANDER ET AL. v. TENNESSEE VALLEY AUTHORITY (1936). On February 17, 1936, U.S. Supreme Court Chief Justice Charles Evans Hughes delivered the principal opinion in this 8–1 ruling on the constitutionality of the Tennessee Valley Authority. Dissenting stockholders in the Alabama Power Company challenged TVA's right to produce electric power at the World War I-era Wilson Dam in Muscle Shoals, Alabama, by filing suit against the directors of the company and the government-operated TVA.

TVA directors implemented the original vision of multiple use planning for navigation, flood control, reforestation, and regional economic development with a system of dams throughout the Tennessee River Valley; they started with electric power generation as a yardstick for inexpensive power to inhabitants of the seven-state area. TVA competition with private power companies to supply electricity, purchase transmission lines from private firms, and sell power to private companies and individuals quickly generated controversy. Dissenting Alabama Power stockholders sought to overturn a January 4, 1934, contract between the company and TVA that expanded power lines from Wilson Dam to seven surrounding counties with a population of 190,000 and 10,000 electrical customers. A district court ruled in favor of the stockholders, but the circuit court of appeals reversed the decision, setting the stage for a Supreme Court hearing on December 19–20, 1935.

The plaintiffs' lawyers presented a constitutionally based argument, favored by many conservatives at that time, contending that TVA had no legal right to exist; therefore, Alabama Power had possessed no right to enter into the original contract. Attorneys for the stockholders based their constitutional argument against the legality of TVA on the commerce clause, the Tenth Amendment reservation of rights to the states, and the Ninth Amendment restrictions on federal powers not expressly granted under the Constitution. They also argued that the federal government had no authority to create a commercial business, engage in commercial business, allow TVA to regulate navigation, or even establish the TVA commercial electric program. TVA lawyers countered that commerce and war powers included in the National Defense Act of June 3, 1916, gave the federal government authority to generate, sell, and transmit power at the Wilson Dam, and that the Ninth and Tenth Amendments did not apply in this case. The court ruled in favor of TVA, holding that Congress had authority to construct dams and sell electricity, a by-product. Justice Louis Brandeis concurred, taking the position that the constitutional issue should not have been addressed in a case involving stockholder dispute. Justice James C. McReynolds, from Tennessee, dissented.

Significantly, while the Supreme Court's narrow interpretation applied only to the Wilson Dam, leaving open future decisions about the broader authority of TVA, it set a positive constitutional precedent in favor of this key New Deal program early in the presidential election campaign of 1936. The decision was later affirmed by *Tennessee Power Company v. TVA* in 1940.
Patrick D. Reagan, Tennessee Technological University
SUGGESTED READINGS: Thomas K. McCraw, *TVA and the Power Fight, 1933–1939* (1971); Erwin C. Hargrove and Paul K. Conkin, eds., *TVA: Fifty Years of Grass-roots Bureaucracy* (1983)

SEE: LAW; TENNESSEE VALLEY AUTHORITY

ASSOCIATION FOR THE PRESERVATION OF TENNESSEE ANTIQUITIES (APTA). Thirty Nash-ville women founded the APTA in 1951, to "acquire, restore, and preserve Tennessee's historic buildings and landmarks." On November 8, 1951, approximately 100 charter members attended the first official APTA meeting at the Noel Hotel in Nashville, where they heard an address by Dr. Robert H. White and elected Mrs. Allan Van Ness as the first president.

A chartered non-profit Tennessee corporation, the APTA's mission "promotes and encourages active participation in the preservation of Tennessee's rich historic, cultural, architectural and archaeological heritage through restoration, education, advocacy, and statewide cooperation." A statewide Board of Directors governs the Association, and chapter presidents serve ex-officio on the board.

In 1982 APTA established an endowment fund to provide grants to chapters for restoration work and educational programs. An independent board of Trustees administers the fund. An APTA Board of Trust must approve new chapters when real property is involved, or for the purchase or sale of real property.

Membership in the APTA is open to anyone interested in preserving Tennessee's cultural heritage. Membership may be through a local chapter or directly with APTA headquarters in Nashville. APTA membership fees support historic preservation and entitle members to free admission at all APTA sites, a newsletter, APTA-sponsored tours, and an annual membership meeting at Belle Meade Plantation in Nashville. Membership through a local chapter brings additional benefits established by that chapter.

The Association's sites are: Belle Meade Plantation (1807), which serves as statewide APTA headquarters, administered by the Nashville Chapter; The Athenaeum Rectory (1835) in Columbia, Maury County Chapter; Buchanan Log House (1800–10), Donelson, Donelson-Hermitage Chapter; Ramsey House Plantation (1795–97), Knoxville Chapter; Glenmore Mansion (1868–69), Glenmore Chapter, Jefferson City; Crockett Tavern Museum (1796, authentic log cabin replica), Hamblen County Chapter, Morristown; Fort Blount (1796, proposed reconstruction), Fort Blount Chapter, Gainesboro; Rachel K. Burrow Museum (1905), Historic Post Office (1900) and Log Cabin, Arlington Chapter; The Pillars (1826–29) and Little Courthouse (1824), Hardeman County Chapter, Bolivar; Hannum-Wirt-Rhea House (1832), Somerville, Fayette County Chapter; and Woodruff-Fontaine House (1870) and Goyer-Lee House (1871), Memphis Chapter. Four other chapters in Bedford, Hawkins, Rutherford, and Sullivan counties promote local heritage programs in their communities, but do not currently maintain sites.

A board of directors, with the responsibility for preserving, maintaining, and interpreting the site, governs each APTA chapter. Volunteers and employed staff members mount seasonal exhibits and hold fund-raising events. Chapters provide numerous educational programs designed to reach people of all ages and cultural backgrounds to help them learn more about the way their ancestors lived.

Cherrie H. Hall, Association for the Preservation of Tennessee Antiquities

ATHENAEUM is a historic Gothic Revival building in Columbia that was once part of a women's college and finishing school which operated between 1852 and 1903. The Reverend Franklin Gillete Smith, a Vermont native who came to Columbia to head the Columbia Female Institute, an Episcopal school, established the Athenaeum. Dismissed from the Institute by Bishop James Otey over alleged improprieties with a student, Smith organized his own school on an adjacent tract. Smith believed that female intelligence was equivalent to that of men, and his Athenaeum school offered courses, such as physics, calculus, and marine biology, previously taught only to male students. The school had a 16,000-volume library and a museum with 6,000 specimens. The General Assembly chartered it as a college in 1858.

The main school complex of twelve buildings stood until about 1915 on land now occupied by the Maury County Board of Education. Only the Rectory and a small cottage, used by Reverend Smith as a study, survive. The castellated Rectory is of eclectic Gothic design, featuring elements of Moorish, Italianate, Greek Revival, and other styles. It was constructed in 1835 by Maury County builder Nathan Vaught for Samuel Polk Walker, but he never lived there. In 1973, the Smith family deeded the Rectory to the Maury County Chapter, Association for the Preservation of Tennessee Antiquities, which restored it as a house museum.

Richard Quin, National Park Service
SEE: MAURY COUNTY; VAUGHT, NATHAN

ATHENS, BATTLE OF. Officially, the Battle of Athens in McMinn County began and ended on August 1, 1946. Following a heated competition for local offices, veterans in the insurgent GI Non-Partisan League took up arms to prevent a local courthouse ring, headed by State Senator Paul Cantrell and linked to Memphis political boss Ed Crump, from stealing the election. When Sheriff Pat Mansfield's deputies absconded to the jail with key ballot boxes, suspicious veterans took action. A small group of veterans broke into the local National Guard Armory, seized weapons and ammunition, and proceeded to the jail to demand the return of the ballot boxes. The Cantrell-Mansfield deputies refused, and the veterans, now numbering several hundred, opened fire. The ensuing battle lasted several hours and ended only after the dynamiting of the front of the jail. The

surrender of the deputies did not end the riot, and the mob was still turning over police cars and burning them hours later. Within days, the local election commission swore in the veteran candidates as duly elected. The McMinn County veterans had won the day in a hail of gunfire, dynamite, and esprit d' corps.

The Battle of Athens stands as the most violent manifestation of a regional phenomenon of the post-World War II era. Seasoned veterans of the European and Pacific theaters returned in 1945 and 1946 to southern communities riddled with vice, economic stagnation, and deteriorating schools. Undemocratic, corrupt, and mossback rings and machines kept an iron grip on local policy and power. Moreover, their commitment to the status quo threatened the economic opportunities touched off by the war. Across the South, veterans launched insurgent campaigns to oust local political machines they regarded as impediments to economic "progress."

In Athens, the Cantrell-Mansfield ring colluded with bootleg and gambling interests, shook down local citizens and tourists for fees, and regularly engaged in electoral chicanery. While communities such as Knoxville, Oak Ridge, and Chattanooga boomed, Athens languished, and veterans returned to a community beset with more problems than opportunities. When Cantrell and Mansfield employed their typical methods to nullify the veterans' votes and reform efforts, the ex-soldiers resorted with the skills and determination that had brought them victory overseas.

Although recalled 50 years later with a certain amount of local pride, the Battle of Athens initially proved a source of embarrassment, and many residents abhorred the violent, extra-legal actions of the veterans. The image of gun-wielding hillbilly ex-soldiers shooting it out with the Cantrell-Mansfield "thugs" that blazed across national and regional newspaper headlines enhanced East Tennessee's reputation for violence and lawlessness. The Good Government League empowered by the veteran's victory scored few successes in its efforts to eradicate the vice, corruption, and arbitrary rule of machine government. Nevertheless, the Battle of Athens exemplified the southern veteran activism of the postwar period and defined the disruptive political impact of World War II.

Jennifer E. Brooks, Tusculum College
SEE: MCMINN COUNTY

ATKINS, CHESTER BURTON "CHET" (1924–), one of country music's greatest instrumentalists, producers, and promoters of the Nashville Sound, was born the son of a fiddler in Luttrell, Union County, Tennessee. He took up guitar at an early age, but first performed on Knoxville's WNOX as a fiddler, a sideman for Johnnie Wright and Jack Anglin, and Kitty

Wells. Atkins moved on to Cincinnati's WLW, Nashville's WSM, and Springfield, Missouri's KWTO, backing artists such as the Carter Sisters and Red Foley during the 1940s.

In 1950 Steve Sholes of RCA offered the guitarist his first contract. Atkins returned to Nashville and immediately became a prominent studio artist. His musical talents and friendship with Sholes led to his appointment as Sholes's Nashville assistant in 1952. When RCA built its own studio in 1957, Atkins managed it. Before long, Sholes turned over RCA's country operations to his protégé and by 1968, Atkins was a RCA vice-president.

Atkins supervised other producers, produced many of his own recordings, and signed such artists as Waylon Jennings, Willie Nelson, Dolly Parton, Jerry Reed, and Charley Pride. As an instrumentalist and producer, Atkins broadened the country music sound to compete with the growing popularity of rock music. By shaping the Nashville Sound, he strengthened the city's position as a recording center and helped establish its fame as Music City.

Throughout his career, Atkins legitimized the role of the country guitar soloist with dozens of albums showcasing his unique "galloping guitar" picking style. Known by many as "Mr. Guitar," the Gretsch and Gibson guitar companies even brought out guitar models built to Atkins's specifications.

As of 1997, Atkins has received 14 Grammy awards and in 1973, became a member of the Country Music Hall of Fame, at that time the youngest individual to be so honored. He retired from RCA in 1981, but continues to perform and record.

Anne-Leslie Owens, Tennessee Historical Society
SEE: MUSIC; RECORDING INDUSTRY; UNION COUNTY

ATTAKULLAKULLA (ca. 1700–1780), was a powerful eighteenth century Overhill Cherokee leader, who played a critical and decisive role in shaping diplomatic, trade, and military relationships with the British Colonial governments of South Carolina and Virginia for over 50 years. He effectively led and acted as the primary spokesman for the Overhill Cherokees in the 1750s and 1760s, although apparently he never attained the official title of Uko, or foremost chief, within Cherokee society. He was probably born in the early 1700s, most likely along the French Broad River. In 1730 he was one of seven Cherokees who accompanied Sir Alexander Cumming to England. From about 1743 to 1748, Attakullakulla resided as captive among the Ottawas of eastern Canada, where he was afforded considerable freedom and became well regarded among the French.

He returned to the Overhill country about 1750, and quickly became second in authority to Connecorte, or Old Hop, the Uko at Chota, who was probably his uncle. By this time, whites knew Attakullakulla as Little Carpenter. Popular stories attributed his name to his ability to construct amicable relationships with whites, but it more likely referred to his small stature and to his wood working skills. James Mooney suggested the derivation of Attakullakulla from the words for "wood" and for "something long leaning against another object."

In the 1750s Attakullakulla negotiated repeatedly with the Virginia and South Carolina colonies as well as the French and British traders in the Ohio Valley to improve the abundance and availability of trade goods to the Cherokees. He also argued for increased colonial military presence in the Overhill villages, which led to the construction of the Virginia Fort and Fort Loudoun near the Overhill villages in 1756. In 1759 Chief Oconastota and 28 of his followers were taken hostage at Fort Prince George as the result of misunderstandings concerning a joint military action with the British against the French. Although Attakullakulla secured Oconastota's release, some of the hostages were killed; the Cherokees retaliated with the siege of Fort Loudoun. Attakullakulla worked to prevent an escalation of violence. Placing himself at great personal risk, he managed to save John Stuart from massacre along with most of the Fort's garrison. Stuart was subsequently appointed superintendent of Indian affairs south of the Ohio. Attakullakulla remained an active leader and negotiator for the Cherokees into the 1770s. When American Revolutionary forces, under the command of William Christian, occupied the Overhill villages in 1776, Attakullakulla arranged for their withdrawal and played a leading role in the 1777 peace negotiated at Long Island on the Holston. His influence diminished as Dragging Canoe, his son, and other young leaders continued Cherokee resistance to the Americans. Sometime between 1780 and 1785, Attakullakulla died.

Gerald F. Schroedl, University of Tennessee, Knoxville
SUGGESTED READING: David Cockran, *The Cherokee Frontier: Conflict and Survival, 1740–1762* (1962); James C. Kelly, "Notable Persons in Cherokee History: Attakullakulla," *Journal of Cherokee Studies* 3 (1978): 2–34
SEE: DRAGGING CANOE; FORT LOUDOUN; OCONASTOTA; OVERHILL CHEROKEES

AUERBACH, STANLEY IRVING (1921–). A founder of the science of radiation ecology and staff leader at Oak Ridge National Laboratory (ORNL), Auerbach was born in Chicago in 1921. He studied at the University of Illinois and Northwestern University, earning his Ph.D. in zoology in 1949. He taught zoology, biology, and ecology at Northwestern and Roosevelt universities until 1955, when he moved to Oak Ridge to become a health physicist and chief of radiation ecology.

Auerbach's specialty, radiation ecology or radioecology, investigated the transport of radionuclides and their concentrations in ecosystems, especially useful considerations for siting nuclear power plants and disposing of radioactive wastes. These studies encouraged the use of radioactive tracers to track the movement of animals, decomposition of forest litter, fish migrations, and other environmental relationships. Auerbach concentrated on analysis of radioactive waste cycling in terrestrial ecosystems, and directed studies of the eastern deciduous forest biome during the 1970s. These pioneering studies led to his election as president of the American Society of Ecology (1971–72) and leadership of other professional organizations.

In 1972 Auerbach became Director of the Environmental Sciences Division at ORNL and managed its studies and expansion until he retired in 1986. In retirement, he continued his ecosystem studies as consultant for many agencies, notably on the Environmental Advisory Board for construction of the Tennessee-Tombigbee Waterway.

Leland R. Johnson, Clio Research Institute

SUGGESTED READING: J. Newell Stannard, *Radioactivity and Health, A History* (1988)

SEE: OAK RIDGE NATIONAL LABORATORY

AUSTIN PEAY STATE UNIVERSITY, located in Clarksville, Tennessee, was founded on April 26, 1927, and named for Governor Austin Peay, a Clarksville resident.

The campus had been the location of educational institutions dating back to 1806. The first on the site was an academy that operated until 1848, when the Masonic Order established a college that continued until Stewart College was created in 1855. In 1875, the Presbyterian Church opened Southwestern Presbyterian College in Clarksville, where it remained until 1925. The Presbyterian Synod then moved the college to Memphis to be nearer its student population base in West Tennessee.

The loss of Southwestern represented a severe blow for the upper Middle Tennessee area, and efforts began immediately to replace it. With support from Peay and Perry L. Harned, the state Commissioner of Education, Montgomery Countians pushed to acquire a state normal school for the vacated Southwestern facilities on College Street.

On August 4, 1927, Southwestern Presbyterian deeded the 30-acre campus to the state. After a hard political fight, the General Assembly produced a bill that proposed the establishment of "a Normal School in Clarksville for the purpose of training white teachers for the rural public schools of the state." When Austin Peay died suddenly on October 2, 1927, it seemed appropriate to place his name on the newly established Normal School.

Austin Peay Normal School officially opened September 23, 1929, in a ceremony attended by Governor Henry Horton and World War I hero Alvin C. York. The new normal school offered a two-year curriculum designed to prepare graduates to pass the state certification requirements for teachers in elementary schools, or receive a junior college diploma. Compared to contemporary standards, the curriculum required few course hours, but upheld rigorous course requirements.

Perry L. Harned, a vigorous advocate of teacher preparation and certification, selected Dr. Philander P. Claxton to serve as the school's second president after the sudden death of President John S. Ziegler. Claxton, a former U.S. Commissioner of Education under Woodrow Wilson and organizer of the University of Tennessee Summer School of the South, joined Harned in promoting the need to rehabilitate rural life through education. When Harned's tenure as education commissioner ended in 1933, Claxton continued his efforts to foster rural education. On February 25, 1939, Austin Peay Normal was elevated to the status of a three-year institution, with provisions to add a fourth year in 1941. The school received the designation of a college in February 1943.

President Claxton retired in 1946, and was succeeded by former Austin Peay history professor, administrator, and former State Commissioner of Education Halbert Harvill. In Harvill's first year of service, the Southern Association of Colleges and Secondary Schools accepted Austin Peay College for membership, thereby conferring national accreditation on its programs.

Between 1946 and 1962, Harvill led a major building program that included the expansion and modernization of the school's academic buildings, residence halls, and administration building. The college became a member of the American Association of Colleges for Teacher Education in 1951, a boost for the former normal school's teacher preparation program.

Within the campus community a number of significant changes occurred as Austin Peay College adjusted to contemporary events. Typical of the relatively peaceful integration of the state's school system, the first African American, the Reverend Wilbur Daniel, gained admission to Austin Peay in January 1956. He enrolled in the graduate school and received an M.A. degree in 1957. By 1958 black students entered the undergraduate population, and at present, compose approximately 16 percent of the enrollment. A benchmark for Austin Peay occurred in November 1966, when the State Board of Education approved the school for university status. This move, effective September 1, 1967, promoted more serious campus conversation concerning the traditional mission of an university—instruction, research, and community service. The long-simmering debate over the direction of the institution dating back to the 1920s, which pitted teacher training against emphasis on the liberal arts and sciences, was renewed with greater intensity.

In terms of faculty size, the three colleges of the university during the 1970s continually moved toward a predominantly liberal arts and sciences college, with the college of business and that of education receding to second and third place, respectively. Austin Peay provided courses at nearby Fort Campbell, Kentucky, where its role evolved from the establishment of "Eagle University" in 1972 to the present-day Fort Campbell Center, which offers both associate degrees and a bachelor's degree.

Austin Peay State University completely departed from its original mission as a "teacher college for rural white schools" when, on December 14, 1984, the State Board of Regents recommended that it be designated as a liberal arts institution. A transitional period in terms of funding requirements followed the designation as the University made adjustments to higher admissions standards to secure more academically capable students.

By September 1996, Austin Peay State University had become a regional institution with its chief mission being liberal arts and science. Enrollment had grown to 7,816 on its expanded College Street campus of 140 acres. The dreams of Perry Harned and Philander P. Claxton had borne fruit, and Austin Peay State University prepared to enter the twenty-first century "known for thoroughness in subject matter and for teaching independent thought to its students."[1]

Thomas H. Winn, Austin Peay State University

CITATION:

(1) Perry L. Harned, "Remarks at the Opening of Austin Peay Normal School," September 23, 1929.

SEE: CLARKSVILLE; CLAXTON, PHILANDER P.; EDUCATION, HIGHER; RHODES COLLEGE

AWIAKTA, MARILOU (1936–), Cherokee and Appalachian poet, storyteller, and essayist, was born in Knoxville in 1936 and reared in Oak Ridge. She graduated *magna cum laude* from the University of Tennessee in 1958.

Awiakta's unique fusion of her Cherokee and Appalachian heritage with science has brought her international recognition. In 1985 the U.S. Information Agency chose her books, *Abiding Appalachia: Where Mountain and Atom Meet* and *Rising Fawn and the Fire Mystery* for the global tour of their exhibit, "Women in the Contemporary World."

Awiakta's third book, *Selu: Seeking the Corn-Mother's Wisdom* (Fulcrum, 1993), applies Native American philosophy to contemporary issues. Quality Paperback Book Club chose it as a Fall 1994 selection. The audio tape of the book (Audio Literature), with music by Joy Harjo, was nominated for a 1996 Grammy Award. A quote from *Selu* is engraved in the River Wall of the Bicentennial Capitol Mall in Nashville. "Motheroot," a poem from *Selu*, is lined in marble along one border of the new Fine Arts Walkway at the University of California, Riverside.

Awiakta received the Distinguished Tennessee Writer Award (1989) and the Outstanding Contribution to Appalachian Literature Award in 1991. She is profiled in the 1995 *Oxford Companion to Women's Writing in the U.S.* and in *Contemporary Authors, 1996*. Three anthologies from the University of Tennessee Press contain Awiakta's works: *Homewords, Homeworks*, and *The Poetics of Appalachian Space*. She is featured in a PBS film "Telling Tales" and in Appalshop's program for National Public Radio, "Tell It On the Mountain: Women Writers of Appalachia."

Formerly chair of the Literary Panel of the Tennessee Arts Commission, Awiakta serves on the boards of the Tennessee Writers' Alliance, the Tennessee Humanities Council, and the National Wordcraft Circle of Native Writers and Storytellers.

Alice Swanson, Tennessee Arts Commission

SEE: LITERATURE; TENNESSEE ARTS COMMISSION; TENNESSEE HUMANITIES COUNCIL

B

BAGGENSTOSS, HERMAN (1904–1992), conservationist, was a native of Grundy County, the son of Swiss settlers who founded the Dutch-Maid Bakery in Tracy City in 1903. An alumnus of the University of the South, Baggenstoss served as superintendent of the Civilian Conservation Corps Grundy Camp P-62 at Tracy City in the 1930s, taking part in the establishment of Grundy State Forest, Grundy Lakes, and the Fiery Gizzard Creek hiking trail.

One of the founders of the Tennessee Federation of Sportsmen in 1934, Baggenstoss became its executive secretary in 1936 and began the bulletin "Turkey Feathers, Boar Bristles and Fish Fins." Renamed *Tennessee Wildlife* magazine in 1937, the publication became *The Tennessee Conservationist* in 1939. In 1939 Baggenstoss was also instrumental in the creation of the Conservation Commission to advise the Tennessee Department of Conservation. In 1940 he resigned from the Federation and served in the Seabees during World War II.

In 1946 Baggenstoss was a founding member of the Tennessee Conservation League. Continuing his work in forestry, Baggenstoss and his wife, Mary Elizabeth, also purchased the *Grundy County Herald,* which they published for twenty years. Baggenstoss became nationally known for his environmental advocacy and served as president of the American Forest Association, Forest Farmers Association, "Keep Tennessee Green," and Tennessee Outdoor Writers Association. Baggenstoss was appointed to the first state Board of Reclamation, overseeing the renewal of strip mine sites. He also served on the first Tennessee Forestry Commission.

Baggenstoss is credited as the driving force for the establishment of the South Cumberland State Recreation Area, which includes Grundy Forest, Fiery Gizzard, Stone Door, and Savage Gulf in Grundy County and Natural Bridge and Buggy Top Cave in Franklin County. His work received many awards, including those from the National Conservation Resource Society, Soil Conservation Society of America, and U.S. Department of Agriculture Forest Service, for his role in the establishment of the U.S. Forest Service Research lab at Sewanee. His dedication continued through the weeks prior to his death in 1992, as he opposed chip mills on the Tennessee River.

Ann Toplovich, Tennessee Historical Society

SEE: CONSERVATION; GRUNDY COUNTY; GRUNDY LAKES PARK AND GRUNDY FOREST STATE NATURAL AREA; SOUTH CUMBERLAND STATE RECREATION AREA

BAILEY, DEFORD (1899–1982), a virtuoso harmonica player who won fame on the early Grand Ole Opry, has a more significant place in history as the first African American to win fame in the field of country music as well as blues. He is recognized today as one of the South's most gifted traditional musicians, as well as one of the Opry's key figures in the 1920s and 1930s. His harmonica playing had an immense impact on the performing styles of both white and black players.

Bailey was born in the community of Bellwood in Smith County, Tennessee, on December 14, 1899. He grew up in the rural hill country there, surrounded by what he called "black hillbilly music." His grandfather was a local champion fiddler, and other members of the family played guitars, banjos, harmonicas, and other traditional instruments. His own interest in the harmonica dated from the time he was stricken with polio at age three; the disease stunted his growth, and left him too frail to do much of the farmwork. He spent his days mastering the harmonica, imitating trains and natural sounds, and developing a battery of complex trills, harmonics, lip puffs, and blended notes for his harmonica.

Moving to Nashville in 1918, Bailey worked as a domestic for wealthy white families on the city's West End, and in his spare time haunted local theaters to hear the age's great blues singers like Bessie Smith and Ma Rainey. By 1925 he was working as an elevator operator at the National Life and Accident building when Dr. Humphrey Bate, himself a harmonica player and charter member of the Grand Ole Opry, got him an audition for the show. Bailey soon became an Opry regular; by 1928 he was appearing on the show more often than any other performer. He became best known for his novelty pieces in which he did imitations on his harp—pieces like *The Fox Chase* and *Pan American Blues*. In 1927 he journeyed to New York to record eight tunes for the Brunswick Company, and the following year he participated in the very first recording session to be held in Nashville—one done by RCA Victor. In spite of his radio popularity, though, these records were not commercially successful—most of the Victor recordings were never released—and he did not try to record again for decades.

During the 1930s Bailey toured widely with Opry groups throughout the South. Often he was refused accommodations at hotels on the tours and had to seek lodging with local black families. Audiences on these tours were often surprised to see that Bailey was black—the Opry had not emphasized this on the radio shows—and publicity soon began to patronizingly refer to him as the Opry "mascot." The Opry fired him in 1941, for a variety of complex reasons, including a feud between two music licensing organizations, changing musical tastes, and the increasing professionalization of the Opry. Hurt and angry, Bailey retired from performing and opened a shoeshine stand in downtown Nashville.

In the 1960s a group of young folk music enthusiasts—including Dick Hulan, Archie Allen, and James

Talley—rediscovered Bailey; he began to appear at local coffeehouses and festivals, and in 1965 he gave a concert at Vanderbilt University. But he turned down national offers to record, to appear at the Newport Folk Festival, and even to take a role in major Hollywood films, like *W.W. and the Dixie Dancekings*, which was largely filmed in Nashville. In 1974 he began to work with a young housing authority agent named David Morton, who convinced Bailey to return to a series of special guest appearances on the Opry, and to dictate his biography for later generations. DeFord Bailey died on July 2, 1982, and is buried in Nashville's Greenwood Cemetery. His son, DeFord Bailey, Jr., has kept some of his father's harmonica music alive.

Charles K. Wolfe, Middle Tennessee State University
SEE: GRAND OLE OPRY; MUSIC

BAKER, HOWARD H., JR. (1925–), U.S. Senator, Senate Minority Leader and Majority Leader, and White House Chief of Staff, was born in Huntsville, Scott County, Tennessee, on November 15, 1925, the son of the future congressman, Howard Baker, Sr., and his wife, Dora Ladd Baker. He attended the University of the South, Tulane University, and the University of Tennessee, where he was the 1949 student body president. He also received his law degree from the University of Tennessee. World War II and his service as a lieutenant and PT boat officer in the U.S. Navy in the South Pacific interrupted his college studies. Baker married Joy Dirksen, the daughter of U.S. Senator Everett Dirksen of Illinois, in December 1951.

Baker's Scott County legal practice flourished. In 1959, while representing the Stearns Coal and Lumber Company, Baker won a $1 million judgment from the United Mine Workers for their use of violence and sabotage to disrupt Stearns's contract with a rival union. After his father's death in January 1964, Baker turned to politics. That November, as the Republican nominee, he lost to Democrat Ross Bass in a race to fill the unexpired U.S. Senate term of the deceased Estes Kefauver. Baker, however, ran a very strong campaign. Two years later, he easily defeated former governor Frank Clement in a second bid for the Senate. Baker was the first popularly elected GOP senator in Tennessee history and the first Republican to win a statewide election since 1920.

Baker proved himself a moderate conservative in Congress, urging the Nixon administration to implement a revenue sharing program with the states. In 1972 Baker won reelection by carrying all three of the state's grand divisions and defeating Democrat Ray Blanton. He even received considerable support from the black community at a time when many African Americans had abandoned all ties with the Republican Party.

Senators Sam Ervin, Jr., and Howard Baker, Jr., at the Watergate hearings, November 1973.

Baker served as Republican leader and vice-chairman of the 1973–74 Senate Watergate Committee, asking the pivotal question, "What did the President know, and when did he know it?" Baker's performance in the hearings brought national attention, and he received praise from both sides of the political spectrum as a fair and thoughtful legislative leader. In 1976 Baker considered a run for the presidency, but withdrew his bid when incumbent Gerald Ford decided to seek the nomination. Baker gave the keynote speech at the 1976 Republican national convention. In 1977 he was elected Senate Minority Leader , and in 1980, after a failed Presidential campaign bid, he became the Senate's Majority Leader in the wake of the Reagan landslide. As Majority Leader, Baker was very popular on both sides of the aisle, with many of his strongest boosters among the Democratic Senators.

In 1985 Baker retired from the Senate amid speculation that he would be a candidate for the presidency in 1988. However, during the midst of the Iran-Contra controversy in 1987, Baker accepted an offer from President Ronald Reagan to be White House Chief of Staff. The appointment of Baker instantly restored much credibility to the administration. Six months before Reagan left the White House, in 1988, Baker resigned to be with his critically ill wife Joy, who died shortly thereafter of cancer. In 1996 Baker married former Kansas Senator Nancy Kassenbaum.

Since leaving the public arena, Baker has maintained an active life. His law practice, Baker, Donelson, Bearman, and Caldwell, is among the state's largest firms, with offices in Knoxville, Nashville, Jackson, Mississippi, and Washington, D.C. Baker serves on the boards of directors of such corporations as Federal Express, United Technology, and Pennzoil. His principal hobby is photography, and he has taken particular interest in the outdoor recreational activities of his native state. In 1993, Baker authored an article for the *National Geographic* magazine on the Cumberland River's Big South Fork National Recreation Area, which had been developed under legislation sponsored by him. Most recently, Baker was active in the failed 1996 presidential campaign bid of his former political protégé, Lamar Alexander.

Michael Rogers, University of Tennessee, Knoxville

SUGGESTED READING: J. Lee Annis, Jr., *Howard Baker: Conciliator in an Age of Crisis* (1994)

SEE: ALEXANDER, LAMAR; BAKER, HOWARD, SR.; BIG SOUTH FORK NATIONAL RECREATION AREA; SCOTT COUNTY

BAKER, HOWARD H., SR. (1909–1964), Republican Congressman, was born in Somerset, Kentucky, in 1902, the son of James F. and Helen K. Baker. The Baker family had been prominent in Appalachian history for generations. Baker's grandfather, George Washington Baker, was an important Unionist during the Civil War, and his father, James Francis Baker, was a late nineteenth century attorney and newspaper publisher in Huntsville, Tennessee. James F. Baker's many business concerns extended into Kentucky. It was there that he met and married Helen Keen and saw the birth of their son, Howard. The Bakers returned to Huntsville in 1909.

In 1918 the Bakers moved to Knoxville, where Howard began classes at the University of Tennessee at the age of 16. An outstanding student, Baker served as debate team captain and was elected class president in 1922. After graduation, Baker entered the university's law school, where he served as editor of the *University of Tennessee Law Review* while completing the three-year course of study in two years. After law school, Baker married Dora Ladd and returned to Huntsville to become a partner in his father's practice. Their son, Howard Baker, Jr., was born in Huntsville in 1925.

In 1928 Baker won a two-year term in the Tennessee General Assembly as a Republican. Four years later, he became chairman of the Scott County GOP, a position he held for the next 16 years. In 1934 voters elected him Attorney General of the Nineteenth Judicial Circuit in East Tennessee. During these very active years, Baker experienced personal adversity in the death of his wife, Dora, from complications of gall bladder surgery.

In 1938 Baker won the GOP nomination for governor, but lost in the general election to Democrat Prentice Cooper. Two years later, Baker lost to Kenneth McKellar in a race for the U.S. Senate. Baker's willingness to carry the Republican standard demonstrated his party loyalty since it was almost impossible in these years for any Republican to successfully challenge any Democrat in a statewide race. In 1948 Baker chaired the Tennessee delegation to the national GOP convention.

Two years later, Baker ran a successful campaign for Congress from the heavily Republican Second Congressional District, emphasizing the themes of anti-communism and pro-atomic energy research, a popular issue among second district residents associated with the laboratories at Oak Ridge. While Baker held basic conservative principles throughout his congressional service, he also maintained strong ties with African Americans throughout Tennessee, like George W. Lee of Memphis. In 1956 Baker refused to sign the "Southern Manifesto," which called for resistance to the U.S. Supreme Court's decision in *Brown v. Board of Education* (1954).

Baker represented the second district in Congress from his election in 1950 until his unexpected death by heart attack on January 8, 1964. His second wife, Irene, succeeded him in Congress.

Michael Rogers, University of Tennessee, Knoxville

SEE: BAKER, HOWARD H., JR.; SCOTT COUNTY

BAKER v. CARR, 369 U.S. 186 (1962). This case, filed by urban voters against Tennessee's Secretary of State and Attorney General in the U.S. District Court of Middle Tennessee, was one of the Warren Court's most important decisions. After the District Court dismissed their case, the Supreme Court decided in favor of the plaintiffs following two separate rounds of oral arguments in which the U.S. Solicitor General intervened on their behalf.

The voters argued that Tennessee's system of state legislative apportionment debased their votes under the equal protection clause of the Fourteenth Amendment. Tennessee was using an electoral system that gave weight to counties as geographical units rather than equalizing population among districts. Despite a state constitutional provision mandating reapportionment every ten years, Tennessee had not reapportioned since 1901. In the interim, the state's population had grown from just over two million to more than three and one-half million.

Prior to 1962 the Supreme Court had ruled that issues of state legislative apportionment were "political questions," inappropriate for judicial resolution. The Court's plurality opinion in *Colegrove v. Green* (1946) reflected this position. It, in turn, rested on *Luther v. Borden,* an 1849 case arising under the Guarantee Clause in Article IV of the U.S. Constitution.

Given these precedents, Justice William Brennan's 6–2 majority opinion in *Baker* focused on the threshold issues of justiciability and standing rather than on formulating specific remedies. In addressing the jurisdiction issue, Brennan decided that apportionment was a federal claim arising under the Fourteenth Amendment and amenable to judicial scrutiny. Brennan further ruled that voters initiating this case had standing to claim that their votes were being arbitrarily impaired or debased. Finally, in addressing justiciability and the "political questions" doctrine, Brennan sidestepped *Luther* and *Colegrove* by distinguishing claims brought under the equal protection clause from those under the Guarantee Clause. Brennan outlined six categories of political questions. These involved foreign affairs and conflicts among the three branches of government rather than federalism issues. The Court accordingly remanded the case to the district court for further action.

Justices William O. Douglas, Tom C. Clark, and Potter Stewart filed concurring opinions. Justice Clark's noteworthy opinion argued that Tennessee's apportionment system was arbitrary and observed that, without initiative or referendum mechanisms, judicial intervention was the only effective remedy.

Justices Felix Frankfurter and John M. Harlan II authored vigorous dissents. Both objected to the Court's departure from precedent, to intervention in potential mathematical quagmires, and to the lack of standards by which to resolve apportionment issues under the Fourteenth Amendment.

Baker resulted in an avalanche of suits in other states as well as an ultimately unsuccessful movement to call a national convention to propose a repeal amendment. Meanwhile, the Court proceeded in *Gray v. Sanders* (1963) to invalidate Georgia's county-unit system of primary elections. There Justice Douglas formulated a "one person one vote" standard that the Court applied to both houses of state legislatures in *Reynolds v. Sims* (1964). These basic standards remain in force throughout the nation.

John R. Vile, Middle Tennessee State University

SUGGESTED READINGS: Richard C. Cortner, *The Apportionment Cases* (1970); Jene Graham, *One Man, One Vote: Baker v. Carr and the American Levellers* (1972)

SEE: GOVERNMENT; LAW

BARBER & MCMURRY ARCHITECTS. The Knoxville-based architectural firm Barber and McMurry designed landmark residential, civic, and commercial buildings in Knoxville and across the southeast. In 1915 Charles Irving Barber (1887–1962) joined his cousin, D. West Barber, and Ben McMurry (d. 1969) to form the firm. Their strengths complemented each other as Charles Barber was the principal designer, McMurry operated as the business manager, and West Barber took charge of the production of working drawings.

Charles Barber's interest in architecture may have originated with his father, George Franklin Barber, also an architect. The elder Barber moved to Knoxville in 1888 from Illinois and quickly established his practice. By the early 1900s George Barber's firm was the largest in Knoxville with approximately 30 draftsmen and 20 secretaries. In conjunction with his architectural practice, George Barber started the American Home Publishing Company to distribute his house designs in the form of pattern books and mail-order catalogs for house kits. He designed in a variety of styles, and Barber houses were built in every state and overseas. Many of his houses are now on the National Register of Historic Places. When George Barber died in 1915, his successful firm was absorbed by the fledgling firm, Barber & McMurry.

Aside from experience in his father's office, Charles Barber's education involved a three-month Grand Tour of Europe in the summer of 1907 to study architecture in Italy and Greece. In 1909 he enrolled at the University of Pennsylvania to gain a Certificate of Proficiency in Architecture. While at the university, he studied under Paul Cret, a French architect trained at the Ecole de Beaux Arts, and learned the tenets of the philosophy of the Beaux Arts. Ben McMurry and West Barber also enrolled in the same program and graduated shortly after Charles Barber. All three men worked in various architectural firms before they formed their successful partnership.

Charles Barber's residential designs drew on historical American and European prototypes, incorporating Beaux Arts architectural elements on a functional layout of rooms. Designed to accommodate twentieth century lifestyles and tastes, historic precedent was only a basis for Barber's original designs. Public and private areas were separated, and interior spaces flowed through French doors or picture windows to exterior terraces and landscaped gardens. Charles Lester, a local landscape architect, collaborated with Barber on many garden designs. Prominent houses in Knoxville designed by the firm include the Alex Bonnyman house (1916) on Kingston Pike, the Calvin Holmes house (1922) on Melrose Place, and the John Craig house (1926) on Westland Drive.

In addition to residential design, Barber & McMurry was known for its school and church designs. The firm designed, among others, Sequoyah Elementary School (1929) and the Maryville High School (1933). The Hoskins Library (1930) on the Knoxville campus of the University of Tennessee is an example of the stately campus Gothic style and was one of four projects the firm designed for the university in that year alone. During the 1940s and 1950s Barber & McMurry was recognized for its church designs. Knoxville's Church Street Methodist Church stands as one of its most distinguished works. Working in collaboration with the New York architect John Russell Pope, Charles Barber designed the neo-Gothic church that Franklin D. Roosevelt praised during a Knoxville visit.

Barber & McMurry was nationally recognized in both lay and professional journals. The entire June 1930 issue of *Southern Architect and Building News* was devoted to its work. In 1929 the firm won the Neel Reid Medal for a residence costing under $20,000 with their design for the Goforth house. Charles Barber extended his interest in affordable housing during the mid-1930s while he was chief architect of the Tennessee Valley Authority. During his tenure he designed low- and mid-cost housing for Norris, Pickwick, and Wheeler dam sites. In 1938 the Knoxville Small House Bureau published a brochure of small house designs, a number of which were the work of Barber & McMurry.

The last of the original three partners left the firm in 1969. In 1976 the Dulin Art Gallery held an exhibition of Barber & McMurry's work, focusing on the period 1915–1940. Barber & McMurry has persisted as a leader in design in Tennessee and now focuses on larger scale projects, such as the John J. Duncan Federal Office Building in Knoxville and numerous other civic, medical, and educational projects.

Katherine Wheeler, University of Virginia

SEE: NORRIS; TENNESSEE VALLEY AUTHORITY

BARNARD, EDWARD EMERSON (1857–1923), astronomer and astronomical photographer, was born in Nashville. To help support his fatherless family, Barnard worked in the photographic gallery of Van Stavoren, where he assisted in the use of a solar camera to make photographic enlargements. Working on the roof of the gallery, Barnard also made early astronomical observations, developing the skills that eventually made him "the foremost observational astronomer in the world."[1]

In 1877, the American Academy for the Advancement of Science met in Nashville, and the young Barnard sought the advice of noted astronomer Simon Newcomb on a possible career in astronomy. Newcomb advised him to become proficient in mathematics. Barnard traveled to Pittsburgh and purchased a five-inch telescope to begin his observations. In 1881 and 1882, he discovered two comets. In 1883 Vanderbilt University invited Barnard to take charge of its six-inch telescope and take special courses in mathematics and languages. While at Vanderbilt (1893–1887), he discovered seven of the 19 comets observed worldwide and independently discovered the Gegenschein, a faint path of light seen directly opposite the sun.

Barnard graduated from Vanderbilt in 1887 and joined the new Lick Observatory. In January 1899 he made his first photographs of the solar corona and began to take highly significant photographs of comets and the Milky Way. His first collection of photographs appeared in 1913 as Volume 11 of the *Publications of the Lick Observatory*.

In 1895 Barnard was appointed astronomer at the Yerkes Observatory, University of Chicago, where he worked with a 40-inch refractor. He observed the satellites of Saturn, Uranus, and Neptune and developed a method for measuring the color of new stars. He continued the Milky Way photography, which was financed by Catherine W. Bruce of New York. In 1923–24 the Carnegie Institution published Barnard's *Atlas of the Milky Way*.

Barnard received honorary degrees from Vanderbilt University, Queen's University, and the University of the Pacific. The French Academy of Sciences awarded him a gold medal, and the French Astronomical Society presented him with the Janssen Prize. He received the Gold Medal of the Royal Astronomical Society and the Bruce Gold Medal of the Astronomical Society of the Pacific. His life work included nearly 4,000 photographs and 840 separate addresses and articles.

Barnard married Rhoda Calvert in 1881; they had no children. His niece, Mary R. Calvert, assisted his work. Barnard died in 1923 and was buried in Nashville, after a funeral in the rotunda of the Yerkes Observatory.

Connie L. Lester, Tennessee Historical Society

CITATION:
(1) J.A. Parkhurst, "Eulogy," *Journal of the Astronomical Society of Canada* (April 1923): 98.
SEE: SCIENCE AND TECHNOLOGY; VANDERBILT UNIVERSITY

BARNS, CANTILEVER. Cantilever barns are nineteenth-century vernacular farm structures found principally in two East Tennessee counties, Sevier and Blount. Their characteristic feature is an overhang, or cantilever, which supports a large second-story loft atop one or more log cribs on the base story. In studies of mountain buildings made in the early 1960s, Henry Glassie identified these barns as characteristic of the southern highlands, indicating that they were found in North Carolina, Kentucky, and West Virginia. In the 1980s fieldwork by Marian Moffett and Lawrence Wodehouse found only six cantilever barns in Virginia and another three in North Carolina. By contrast, 316 cantilever barns were located in East Tennessee, with 183 in Sevier County, 106 in Blount County, and the remaining 27 scattered from Johnson to Bradley counties.

A cantilever barn usually has two log cribs, each measuring about 12 feet by 18 feet, separated by a 14- to 16-foot driveway. The topmost logs of each crib extend 8 to 10 feet out to the barn's sides, becoming the cantilevered primary supports for a whole series of long secondary cantilevers, which run from front to back across the entire length of the barn. A heavy timber frame, aligned over the corners of the cribs and the outer ends of the cantilevers, supports eave beams and heavy purlins, which are the major structural features of the loft. Most barns have a gable roof. Lofts were originally used for hay storage, loaded conveniently from wagons pulled into the driveway between the cribs. Cribs were livestock pens, while the sheltered area under the overhanging loft provided space for storing equipment and grooming animals. Barns still in active use now tend to be used for drying burley tobacco. Most have concealed their distinctive structures behind later enclosures and extensions, so they are not obvious from the roadside.

Documentary evidence on these barns is very scarce. Most seem to have been built from 1870 to about 1915, by second- or third-generation settlers. Cantilever barns were constructed on self-sufficient farms, where accommodations for seed corn, feed, livestock, and equipment were basic needs. The unusual design may derive from German forebay barns in Pennsylvania, built into the hillside with an overhang along the out-facing side. Pioneer blockhouses in East Tennessee and elsewhere had modest overhangs on all four sides of the upper story, and these may have inspired the shape of later barns.

Moffett and Wodehouse have hypothesized that the barn's form was an invention, pulling together ideas from several sources into an original design that enjoyed local popularity for 30 to 50 years. Cantilever barns used readily available tools, materials, and construction techniques to meet practical needs. The design also fit well with the mountain climate, a rainy environment with high humidity for much of the year, making protection from damp a continuing challenge. Rain falling on the barn's roof drips off the eaves at a distance well removed from the supporting cribs, so that the overhang protects both structure and livestock, while the space between the cribs works with the continuous vents in the upper loft walls to encourage air circulation that would dry the loft's contents.

The most accessible cantilever barns are preserved at the Cable Mill and Tipton Homeplace in Cades Cove of the Great Smoky Mountains National Park. Two others are owned by the Museum of Appalachia in Norris.

Marian Moffett, University of Tennessee, Knoxville
SUGGESTED READING: Marian Moffett and Lawrence Wodehouse, *East Tennessee Cantilever Barns* (1993).

BARRET, PAUL WEISIGER (1899–1976), banker, merchant, planter, businessman, and political and civic leader, was closely connected with the economic progress and government of Shelby County from the 1920s through the 1970s. Paul W. Barret Parkway, a controlled-access highway named for him, spans the northern and eastern sections of that county.

Barret was born in Barretville, in northeast Shelby County, the son of James Hill Barret, who was a member and chairman of the Shelby County Quarterly Court (later the Shelby County Commission), and the grandson of Anthony R. Barret, for whom the community of Barretville was named. After graduating from Memphis University School, Barret enlisted in the U.S. Army during World War I.

At the age of 21, Barret founded Barretville Bank & Trust Company, and served as its president for more than 40 years. Under his leadership it became one of the state's largest and most successful rural banking systems, with eight branches in five towns in Shelby County. His banking interests also included control of Somerville Bank & Trust Company, Rossville Savings Bank, and First State Bank of Henderson. He established The Barret Company, Inc., dealers in cotton, and expanded his father's chain of cotton gins to five. He had extensive farming interests in Shelby and Tipton counties, and for many years owned and operated J. H. Barret & Son General Store, founded in 1856.

Barret held public office continuously for 40 years and won every elective office for which he was a candidate. He served on the Shelby County Quarterly Court from 1942 until 1966. For a long period, he was the senior member and acknowledged leader of that body, championing the interests of rural and suburban areas of Shelby County and promoting education, road building, and fiscal responsibility.

Barret was active in the political organization of Edward Hull "Boss" Crump, and by 1958 was generally recognized to be its leader. Barret's name and that of the Stewartville voting precinct were synonymous, and for decades "Paul Barret's box" unfailingly turned out practically unanimous votes for the organization's candidates.

Barret and his wife of 57 years, Sarah Dickey Barret (1898–1978), are interred at Pleasant Union Cemetery, near Barretville.

Paul A. Matthews, Memphis

SEE: CRUMP, EDWARD H.; SHELBY COUNTY

BARROW, GEORGE WASHINGTON

BARROW, GEORGE WASHINGTON (1808–1866), U.S. and Confederate diplomat, editor, soldier, and statesman, was born in Nashville on May 10, 1808, to Wylie Barrow and Ann Beck, his second wife. Barrow spent a privileged and comfortable youth at the family home "Barrow Grove." He attended Davidson Academy and in 1826 became one of the first graduates of the University of Nashville. He read law and was admitted to the Tennessee Bar in 1827. In that same year, he married Anna Marian Shelby, daughter of Dr. John Shelby, one of the state's wealthiest men. In 1836 Barrow volunteered for service in the Seminole War as a member of the Second Tennessee Mounted Gunman and received promotions to Major and Adjutant.

Barrow returned to Nashville in 1837, and won election to the General Assembly. By 1840 Barrow was active in the Whig presidential victory and was rewarded with an appointment as Minister to Portugal. After three years of diplomatic service abroad, Barrow returned to Nashville and the editorship of the powerful *Nashville Republican Banner*. This position led to Barrow's election to the U.S. Congress in 1847, where he befriended the young Abraham Lincoln and joined him in opposition to the Mexican War. Returning home in 1849, Barrow was a delegate to the Nashville Convention of 1850. He also founded and served as the first president of the Nashville Gas Light Company.

After several years of seclusion following family tragedies, Barrow returned to public life just in time to become a leading advocate of secession, representing the state in negotiations with the Confederacy. In April 1861 Barrow voted for the secret declaration of Tennessee's alliance with the southern states and became a signatory of the document, which Tennessee voters ratified in June 1861. Barrow raised and equipped Company C of the 11th Tennessee Cavalry, which became known as "Barrow Guards." He served in the Confederate State Senate until February 1862, when Tennessee government collapsed with the approach of the Union army.

Following Nashville's surrender, Military Governor Andrew Johnson arrested Barrow and other prominent Confederates for treason. Barrow was first imprisoned in Nashville, before Johnson shipped him to prisons at Detroit, Fort Mackinac, and Johnson's Island. Barrow refused to take the Oath of Allegiance, but was eventually exchanged in March 1863. Barrow returned to Tennessee, ran unsuccessfully for Confederate governor of the state, and spent the balance of the war as a private with the retreating Army of Tennessee. Barrow returned to Nashville, broken in health and financially ruined. He died within the year.

John McGlone, Murfreesboro

SEE: ARMY OF TENNESSEE; NASHVILLE CONVENTION

BASEBALL, MINOR LEAGUE

BASEBALL, MINOR LEAGUE. Although Memphis fielded a professional baseball team in 1877, organized minor league baseball in Tennessee dates to 1885 and the founding of the Southern League of Professional Clubs (SL), a circuit which lasted through 1899. From 1885 to the present, 26 Tennessee towns and cities have had entries in a number of leagues, including the Southern Association (SA), Appalachian League (Appy), South Atlantic League (Sally), Kentucky-Illinois-Tennessee League (Kitty), and the "new" Southern League organized in 1964. From 1902 to the present, Tennessee has had both large cities and small towns represented in minor league circuits.

Formally organized in 1911, essentially out of the 1910 Southeastern League, the Appalachian League was a Class D circuit, with Morristown, Knoxville, Cleveland, and Johnson City as the inaugural Tennessee representatives. The designation "Class D" reflected a classification scheme based on the population of a team's city (the largest was A, the smallest D), established by the National Association of Professional Baseball Leagues in 1902. The Johnson City team—called the Soldiers in honor of the local Soldiers' Home—won the pennant in the Appy League's first year. Throughout the Appy's existence as a Class D league (to 1962), and as a short season Rookie league (1963 to present), Johnson City and Kingsport have been the mainstays of the league. Beginning in the 1930s Appy League teams ceased to be independent and became farm teams of major league teams. Today the Appalachian is a ten-team circuit with teams from Virginia, West Virginia, and Tennessee. Tennessee teams include Johnson City, Kingsport, and the smallest of the league cities, Elizabethton.

In West and Middle Tennessee, a number of smaller towns organized teams in the Kitty League, a Class D loop that existed from 1903 through 1906 and intermittently from 1910 through 1955. Jackson, Clarksville, and Union City fielded teams in this league.

Memphis, Nashville, Knoxville, and Chattanooga have extensive baseball histories.

TSLA

Unidentified Tennessee baseball team, 1907.

Memphis's first professional team, the Red Stockings, played in 1877 in the League Alliance, a circuit that lasted only one season. Between 1878 and 1885, Memphis fielded a number of semi-pro teams, including the Blues, Riverdales, and Eckfords. In 1885 the Memphis Leaguers became a charter member of the original Southern League. The team played in Olympic Park, located at the present site of the Memphis Area Transit Authority Bus Terminal. Subsequently known as the Grays, Fever Germs, and Giants, the team won the 1894 pennant (as the Giants). But in 1895 the team disbanded, the result of poor financial support.

When the Southern Association began play in 1901, Memphis again entered organized professional baseball with a team known either as the Egyptians or the Leaguers; in 1907 they became the Turtles. Eights years later, after a string of dreadful seasons, the team changed its moniker to "Chicks," probably to recall the successes of an 1890s amateur team called the Chicks—short for Chickasaws. The Egyptians played at Red Elm Park (or Bottoms), a 3,000 seat facility built in 1896. In 1915 owner Russell E. Garner renamed the park Russwood and increased the seating to 6,000 (later increased to 11,000). The Memphis entry in the Southern Association won pennants in 1903, 1904, 1921, 1924, and 1930. The 1944 Chicks were known for their one-

armed outfielder, Pete Gray, who earned MVP honors that year. On April 18, 1960, Russwood Park burned down. The Chicks played at Hodges Field and Tobey Field, but both proved unsatisfactory. Financial losses, the fire, and lack of a home playing field caused the Chicks to withdraw from the SA after the 1960 season.

In 1968 Memphis became a member of an expanded Texas League as the Blues, which played at a field located at the fairgrounds near the Liberty Bowl. This facility was rebuilt in 1967–68, and christened Blues Stadium (later Tim McCarver Stadium and Chicks Stadium). The Blues left the Texas League and entered the Dixie Association for one year, 1971, and returned to the Texas League for one last season in 1972. The following year, the Chicks entered the AAA International League as a farm team of the Montreal Expos. In 1977 Avron Fogleman purchased the team to be a farm club for the Kansas City Royals. The Chicks entered the SL. The Chicks subsequently changed parent club affiliation, first to the San Diego Padres and then to the Seattle Mariners, the current parent team in 1997. In 1998, however, the team is moving to Jackson and Memphis will be awarded a Triple A American Association expansion team.

Nashville, like Memphis and Chattanooga, was a charter member of the original SL in 1885. Prior to that the city fielded club teams in the late 1860s and

1870s. Some sources contend that the Union army of occupation brought baseball to Nashville in 1862. The Nashville SL team, the Americans, played at Sulphur Spring Bottom at Athletic Park. The Americans became the Blues in 1887 and left the SL at the end of that season. Nashville fielded the Tigers in 1893–94 and the Seraphs in 1895.

Nashville's next foray into organized minor league baseball came in 1901 with the founding of the Southern Association. From that year until the league's disbanding in 1961, Nashville boasted an SA entry called the Volunteers or Vols—although the 1901 and 1902 teams may have been called the "Fishermen," for manager Newt Fisher. Nashville teams won pennants in 1901–02, 1908; 1916, 1939–44, 1949–50, and 1953.

After a one-year sojourn in the Sally League in 1963, Nashville did not have a professional baseball team until 1978, when the Cincinnati Reds placed a SL team, the Sounds, in Herschel Greer Stadium. In 1980 the Sounds changed affiliation and became a New York Yankees farm team. In 1985 the team moved to the AAA American Association when owner Larry Schmittou bought the Evansville Tripletts and moved that team to Nashville. The SL league moved Nashville's franchise to Huntsville, Alabama. From 1985–86 the Sounds were a Detroit Tigers farm team, from 1987–92, a Cincinnati Reds team, and from 1993 to the present, a Chicago White Sox team.

One of Chattanooga's first organized and probably semi-pro teams was the 1880 Chattanooga Roanes, which represented the Roane Iron Fence Company. Five years later Chattanooga became one of the charter members of the SL. The city fielded teams in 1885–86 and 1892, before its entry was sold to Mobile, Alabama, in 1895.

Chattanooga was also a charter member of the Southern Association when it began play in 1901. After the 1902 season, however, owner Mims Hightower sold the team to interests in Montgomery, Alabama. In 1909 O.B. Andrews brought baseball back to the city with a team called the Lookouts in the Sally League. The Lookouts returned to the SA in 1910, where the team remained except for a two-year absence in1943–44, until the league folded in 1961.

Andrews and Z.C. Patten engineered the team's return to the SA, when in 1910 they purchased the Little Rock SA franchise and moved it to Chattanooga. Andrews built a field—which he named for himself—at Third and O'Neal Streets, the later site of Engel Stadium. Andrews owned the club until 1919, when Sammy Strang Nicklin purchased it. Initially successful, the team consistently finished near the bottom of the SA standings by the end of the 1920s.

In 1929 Clark Griffith bought the Lookouts to be a farm team for the Washington Senators and sent Senators scout Joe Engel to run the team. Engel built a stadium on the Andrews Field site (Engel Stadium), which was first used during the 1930 season. Engel quickly established himself as the "Baron of Ballyhoo" for his game promotions. Attendance soared and in 1932 Chattanooga won its first league championship in 22 years and then defeated Beaumont of the Texas League in the Dixie Series.

From 1933 to 1938, the Lookouts recorded five consecutive seventh place finishes. Attendance plummeted. Griffith put the team up for sale in 1937, but Engel saved the club by offering the public five-dollar shares in the team. The team rewarded its fans, and its 1,700 shareholders, by winning the 1939 SA pennant. Griffith reclaimed ownership in the early 1940s and held the team throughout the World War II years. In 1952 the Lookouts won the SA championship and attracted 252,703 fans who watched such future major-league stars as Harmon Killibrew and Jim Kaat.

In 1960 the Lookouts became a farm team of the Philadelphia Phillies. After the SA dissolved in 1961, the city did not field a team in 1962. In 1963 another Lookouts team joined the Sally League, which had been elevated from A to AA. In 1964 Chattanooga entered the new SL, which had become the AA loop. But team success did not happen and attendance declined. There was no franchise in the city after the 1965 season. SL baseball returned to Chattanooga in 1976, when the Oakland A's sponsored a team in the newly renovated Engel Stadium. The Lookouts subsequently affiliated with Cleveland (1978–82), Seattle (1983–86), and Cincinnati (1987 to present).

As early as 1878, Knoxville had "base ball" clubs, the most famous of which was the Reds team, the result of a merger of the East Tennessee University team and a local team. The original Reds and their successors played from 1878 through 1880 at the Asylum Street grounds. In 1894 Frank Moffett organized the city's first pro team, the Knoxville Reds or Indians, who played at Baldwin Park. In 1902 and 1903 Moffett organized and managed a "New Reds" (later Indians) team. Knoxville had an entry in the 1904 Class D Tennessee-Alabama League, but it is not clear if the 1905 Knoxville Indians played in the non-sanctioned Interstate League, or as a city club. The city had no organized minor league team from 1906 to 1908, but in 1909 Knoxville fielded the Appalachians, a replacement for the Charleston team in the Class C Sally League. The following year, Moffett led the Appalachians into the Class D Southeastern League, where the team won the pennant.

With the 1911 formation of the Appalachian League, Moffett led a team called the Pioneers into the new circuit. The Appy disbanded in 1914, and Knoxville did not have another professional entry until the 1921 reorganization of the league. In that year, owner/manager Moffett fielded a team, which played at Caswell Park and won the 1923 and 1924 Appy League pennants before withdrawing from the league in 1925.

From 1925 through 1930, the Knoxville Smokies played in the Sally League, now a Class B circuit. Financial difficulties forced the withdrawal of the Smokies in 1930, but the following year, the Mobile SA team transferred its franchise to Knoxville, where the team played in the new Smithson Stadium, built on the site of the razed Caswell Park. The Smokies remained in the SA until midway through the 1944 season, when the franchise returned to Mobile. From 1946–1952, the Smokies played in the Class B Tri-State League, which consisted of teams from Tennessee, North Carolina, and South Carolina. In 1953, the club switched to the Class D Mountain States League, before returning to Tri-State in 1954. In 1953, Smithson Stadium burned and was replaced on the same site by Knoxville Municipal Stadium (later Bill Meyer Stadium).

From 1956 to 1958, Knoxville's SL team affiliated with the Baltimore Orioles, then the Detroit Tigers, from 1959–1963. Knoxville entered the new AA Southern League in 1964 as a Cincinnati Reds team, an affiliation that lasted through 1966. From 1967 through 1971, there was no minor league team in Knoxville. But in 1972 the Chicago White Sox moved its AA Southern League franchise from Asheville. The Toronto Blue Jays, the current parent team, replaced the White Sox in 1979. During these years, the team name changed three times and is now the Smokies. In 1996 the Knoxville city government voted to provide money for a new stadium, but as of 1997, the team's future in Knoxville remained in doubt.

Marie Tedesco, East Tennessee State University

SUGGESTED READINGS: Robert Obojski, *Bush League. A History of Minor League Baseball* (1965); Bill O'Neal, *The Southern League. Baseball in Dixie, 1885–1994* (1994); Marie Tedesco, "Appalachia Becomes Mainstream: From Down-Home Baseball to the Rookie League in Johnson City, Tennessee," *Journal of East Tennessee History* 64 (1992).

BASEBALL, NEGRO LEAGUES. As early as 1871, Nashville had African-American baseball clubs. But it was not until 1886, when the nation's first professional league of black teams was organized. The Southern League of Colored Base Ballists (SLCBB) fielded teams from Jacksonville, Savannah, Atlanta, Charleston, New Orleans, and Memphis, which had two teams, the Eurekas and the Eclipses. The Eclipses won the only SLCBB championship. Chattanooga possibly placed a team in the league as well. Beset by financial problems, the SLCBB lasted for only one season.

Tennessee teams next played in organized professional leagues in 1920. The legendary Andrew "Rube" Foster, owner of the Chicago American Giants, founded the first Negro National League (NNL), a major league which lasted through the 1931

season. The Negro Southern League (NSL) was a minor league founded in 1920. The second NNL (1933–48), founded by Pittsburgh Crawfords' owner Gus Greenlee, and the NAL, the Negro American League (1937–60), also featured Tennessee teams. Memphis, Nashville, Chattanooga, Knoxville, and Oak Ridge participated in Negro Leagues baseball.

The Memphis Red Sox and the Nashville Elite Giants were Tennessee's best known Negro League teams. A.P. Martin, a local African-American barber, established the Red Sox in 1919, but by 1922 the team transferred to Robert Lewis, a local black funeral home owner. Lewis also managed the team and financed the construction of Lewis Park. By 1929 Lewis was in financial straits and sold the Red Sox; in 1929 the club became the property of two prominent Memphis African-American doctors, brothers W.S. and J.B. Martin (no relation to A.P.), who had been part of the 1929 group of owners. Shortly thereafter, A. T. and B.B. Martin, also brothers and doctors, bought interest in the club. In 1940 J. B. Martin ran afoul of the Crump political machine and fled Memphis for Chicago, where he became co-owner of the Chicago American Giants of the NNL, and later president of the NAL. The Red Sox and the stadium remained in the hands of the remaining Martins until 1960, when prior to the baseball season, the team disbanded and the stadium was sold. The stadium was razed in 1961.

Apparently the Red Sox team was an NSL charter member and remained there until 1923, when it either became independent for that year, or joined as an "associate" member of the NNL. In the second half of the 1924 season, the Sox entered the NNL as a fullfledged member. From 1925–30, Memphis was in the NNL, except for 1926, when they returned to the NSL for that season. In 1932 the club joined the new East-West League, which failed to survive the season.

From 1933 until the 1937 season, when the Red Sox became a founding member of the NAL, the team apparently operated as an independent, barnstorming outfit. The Red Sox remained in the NAL into the 1959 season, when the Raleigh (North Carolina) Tigers replaced it. Noteworthy Red Sox players included pitcher Verdell Mathis, Dan Bankhead, Ted "Double-Duty" Radcliffe (also a catcher and manager); infielder Marlin Carter; first baseman Bob Boyd; and catcher Larry Brown.

Tom Wilson, an African-American nightclub operator, founded the Nashville Elite Giants either in 1918 or 1921. It played as an independent team until 1926 when the club joined the NSL. In 1930 Nashville moved to the NNL. In that year, Wilson moved the Giants into Wilson Park, a 4,000 seat stadium located in Trimble Bottom, north of the fairgrounds. The following year, 1931, Wilson purchased pitcher Satchel Paige's contract from the Birmingham Black Barons, and moved the team to Cleveland, Ohio, seeking greater profit from Paige's presence on the team. After the 1931 season, the first NNL dissolved and for the 1932 season, Wilson moved the Giants back to Nashville as a member of the NSL. The team played in Sulphur Dell, where spectators were segregated by race. In 1935, seeking more profits, Wilson left Nashville for Columbus, Ohio.

Chattanooga fielded the NSL Black Lookouts in 1920 and 1926–27. Satchel Paige signed his first professional contract with the 1926–1927 Chattanooga team. Chattanooga apparently functioned as the farm team of the Homestead Grays of the NNL. Early Chattanooga baseball promoters included Bo Carter, Bud Haley, and W. C. Hixson. Beck Shepherd owned and operated the Choo Choos from 1940 through 1946, when he went broke. In 1945 Shepherd discovered Willie Mays, a fleet, hard-hitting 16 year-old outfielder. Although never under contract, since Mays' mother insisted that her son finish high school, Mays played for the Choo Choos in 1945 and briefly in 1946.

Other Negro League teams and independent black teams played in Tennessee. In 1902 the Villiains played in Nashville. Knoxville fielded the Black Giants, a NSL team from 1920–24. This team played at Brewer's Park in East Knoxville and featured a one-armed outfielder named Wing Maddox. In the 1940s, Nashville had an NSL team, first named the Black Vols, and then the Cubs. Oak Ridge had a team first called the Bombers and then the Pioneers. In 1945 Tennessee had four NSL teams: the Nashville Black Vols, the Memphis Grey Sox, the Chattanooga Choo Choos, and the Knoxville Grays or Smokies.

Non-league barnstorming enjoyed a long history in the South and Midwest. From the early twentieth century into the 1940s, black teams barnstormed Tennessee, often playing ball in the afternoon and providing musical entertainment in the evening. One well-known team, Brown's Tennessee Rats, was based in Warrensburg, Missouri.

Marie Tedesco, East Tennessee State University
SUGGESTED READINGS: Robert Peterson, *Only the Ball Was White* (1970); James A. Riley, ed., *The Biographical Encyclopedia of the Negro Baseball Leagues* (1994); Dick Clark and Larry Lester, eds., *The Negro Leagues Book* (1994); Kurt McBee, "The Memphis Red Sox Stadium: A Social Institution in Memphis' African-American Community," West Tennessee Historical Society *Papers* 49(1995); "Black Diamonds, Blues City: Stories of the Memphis Red Sox," video, produced by John R. Haddock and Steven J. Ross, University of Memphis, 1995.

BASKETBALL. See: ENTRIES FOR INDIVIDUAL SCHOOLS, COLLEGES, AND UNIVERSITIES; MEMPHIS TAMS; SUMMITT, PAT HEAD; TENNESSEE SECONDARY SCHOOL ATHLETIC ASSOCIATION, WALLACE, PERRY; WOMEN'S BASKETBALL HALL OF FAME

BASKETMAKING. Basket weaving is one of the most ancient of all arts, the spontaneous invention of people in all parts of the globe. As white explorers moved into the area that would become Tennessee, they found that Native Americans substituted baskets for many articles Europeans made of metal or wood. Indians carried water in baskets coated with tree gum and floated down rivers in basket boats caulked with pine pitch. They cooked in clay lined baskets, filling them with water and dropping in hot rocks to make the water boil. They sifted corn meal through basket sieves. They wove sturdy sandals for footwear and basket hats for protection from sun and rain.

Cherokees, Choctaws, Creeks, and Chickamaugas all used locally available river cane and white oak. Basket forms followed function of use for a variety of needs. East Tennessee Cherokee cane baskets were the most highly developed and refined in technique, construction, and design. White settlers in the mountains of East Tennessee brought the techniques and traditions of basketry forms learned in England, Scotland, and Ireland. The same traditional forms produced in East Tennessee today trace their origins to fourteenth and fifteenth century England, Scotland, and Ireland. The adaptations of these forms to local Tennessee native materials—oak, hickory, birch, pine needles, willow, corn husks, and river cane—made them unique.

The two prominent techniques used by the early Tennessee settlers were slat and ribbed baskets, which were generally constructed from swamp white oak splits. Slat baskets are made from white oak strips that have been scraped, but not prepared in any other way. They are thick and rough to the touch. In making splits or splints (interchangeable terms) the proper selection of timber is crucial. The tree should be a sapling with a diameter of four to six inches. Its trunk should be absolutely straight and unmarred by limbs, knots, or imperfections for a least a length of seven feet. A six-to-nine foot section of perfect trunk is the only piece used. Stripped of bark, the log is cut into eighths length-wise. After the heart wood is cut out, the process of stripping the splits begins by lining up a pocket knife blade with the growth rings of the timber.

Ribbed baskets are the best known style in Tennessee. They are constructed of three different elements: ribs, hoops, and splits. The traditional egg basket, or gizzard basket, is the prominent style or form produced by this technique. Different parts of the basket require splits of different lengths. The splits are woven between the ribs and gradually increase in width towards the middle of the bottom of the basket. The ribs themselves are strips of white oak usually about three times as wide as they are thick, shaved until they are rounded to an elliptical shape in cross section. The ribs are widest in the midsection and gradually taper to points at both ends. The two hoops or strips of white oak, much thicker and wider than the ribs; range from three to five times wider than thick. The hoops are carved with a pocket knife until the desired length, width and smoothness are achieved. The splits are shaved thoroughly because they must be the thinnest, most flexible parts of the basket. Shaving makes a very smooth form so the splits do not stick out and damage the contents.

Today, Cannon County still provides the best examples of the fine ribbed baskets, or typical egg basket forms, in part because of the plentiful supply of swamp white oak. Trevel Wood has taught the craft at the Campbell Folk School in North Carolina and the Arrowmont School in Gatlinburg, Tennessee.

West Tennessee cotton and work baskets provide good examples of the slat oak split basket. Cotton plantations used these baskets to harvest and transport the fiber. Made of hickory, ash, and birch, they were usually hamper-shaped with two handles and splits rough cut. The baskets were usually about four feet tall and constructed by the traditional in-and-out basket weave. Farmers used the same type basket to harvest potatoes and vegetables and gather wood.

Tobacco baskets were utilitarian flat-slat tray-like forms. They were usually four feet square with a shallow depth of four to five inches. They were woven very loosely and held together by a frame and nails. Cut tobacco was piled high on these flat baskets to move the tobacco from field to curing barn, and also to transport the cured leaves to market.

Tennessee Indian baskets were colored with vegetable dyes to emphasize the earthiness, charm, and beauty of the baskets. Vegetables dyes were made from roots, bark, leaves, hulls, flowers, fruits, stems, seeds, or the complete plant. The cane or splits were boiled in the dye. Tennessee basketmaking has continued largely unchanged into the twentieth century. The only exception has been the incorporation of nails, which occurred during the Industrial Revolution of the nineteenth century. Baskets of all forms and materials can be found at a variety of craft fairs and retail craft stores throughout Tennessee. Although many people do not use the baskets for the intended design purpose, the techniques for basketmaking remain the same as those of the past.

Roy M. Overcast, Jr., Brentwood

SEE: CANNON COUNTY; DECORATIVE ARTS, APPALACHIAN

BATE, WILLIAM BRIMAGE (1826–1905), lawyer, Confederate general, Governor, and U.S. Senator, was born at Castalian Springs in Sumner County on October 7, 1826, the son of James H. Bate and Anna Weathered Bate. His education was limited to a few years in a log schoolhouse known as the Rural Academy. Following his father's death, Bate secured a job as second clerk on the steamboat *Saladin,* which traveled between Nashville and New Orleans. At the outbreak of the Mexican War in 1846, Bate volunteered for service in a Louisiana regiment; at the expiration of his enlistment, he re-enlisted and served as lieutenant of Company I, Third Tennessee Infantry.

At the end of the war, Bate returned to the family farm in Sumner County and established a Democratic newspaper, the Gallatin *Tenth Legion.* In 1849, he was elected to the Tennessee General Assembly. After graduation from the Cumberland Law School in Lebanon in 1852, Bate opened law practice in Gallatin. He served a term as district attorney general. In 1856 he married Julia Peete, daughter of Colonel Samuel Peete of Huntsville, Alabama, a distinguished lawyer and veteran of the War of 1812. In 1859 Bate declined the Democratic nomination for Congress.

A strong believer in states rights and secession, Bate volunteered for service as a private in the Second Tennessee Infantry, C.S.A. Elected Colonel, he served with his regiment, first in Virginia and later in campaigns, which included Stones River, Chickamauga, Missionary Ridge, Franklin, and Nashville. Before the end of the war, he attained the rank of major general. Bate was wounded on three different occasions, most severely at Shiloh. While with the army at Wartrace in 1863, he declined the Tennessee gubernatorial nomination.

After the war, Bate opened law practice in Nashville and continued to be involved in Democratic party politics, becoming identified with the "Bourbon" wing of the party. In 1868 he became a member of the State Democratic Committee and the National Democratic Executive Committee. Elected governor in 1882, he was re-elected two years later. Under Bate's administration, the state debt controversy, which had divided the party since 1877, ended with a compromise agreement that funded the debt at 50 cents on the dollar with three percent bonds. In 1886 he was elected to the United States Senate to succeed Washington C. Whitthorne, and remained in that office until his death on March 9, 1905.

In the Senate, Bate supported legislation to reduce taxation, create a Weather Bureau, improve the efficiency of the Army Signal Corps, and provide support for common schools. He voted in favor of the admission of Oklahoma, Arizona, and New Mexico to statehood and secured the passage of a resolution for the erection of a Government Building at the Tennessee Centennial Exposition in 1897.

John H. Thweatt, Tennessee State Library and Archives

SEE: ARMY OF TENNESSEE; MEXICAN WAR; STATE DEBT CONTROVERSY; SUMNER COUNTY

BATTLE GROUND ACADEMY. Named for its location on the Franklin Civil War battlefield, Battle

Ground Academy opened for classes on September 3, 1889. A group of local stockholders organized and chartered the school. The board of directors selected S.V. Wall and W.D. Mooney to administer the new school; both men had taught with and received their early training under the well-known Tennessee educator, Sawney Webb.

The stockholders provided the six-acre campus and building, and allowed Wall and Mooney to operate the school as a proprietorship, which prospered under their administration. Enrollment grew to 120 students, most of whom were local youths, though a number came from great distances and lived in local boarding houses during school sessions. Most students were boys, but a few outstanding women were allowed to enroll.

BGA offered a classical college preparatory curriculum and was soon widely recognized among southern schools, becoming a charter member of the Southern Association of Colleges and Schools in 1895. BGA is one of three remaining secondary charter members of this Association.

Athletics assumed an important role in the school early in BGA's history. Few southern secondary schools fielded football teams when BGA organized its first in 1891. The team found most early opponents among local colleges.

In the spring of 1902, fire destroyed the original building. The school purchased ten acres of land two blocks south and west of Columbia Pike and constructed a new building. This structure also burned in 1910, but another facility was built on the same foundation. The school added other buildings and increased its land holdings over the years; now the 21-acre site serves as a Middle School Campus, grades 5–8.

In 1929 the school built its first dormitory and converted to an all-male student body. For the next fifty years, BGA was a boys' boarding and day school. By the early 1970s, the school began phasing out the boarding students, and in 1979 admitted girls again. Female students now comprise 40 percent of the enrollment. In 1994 the school purchased a 58-acre tract of land north of Franklin and began construction of a new high school campus, which opened in the fall of 1996.

As Battle Ground Academy continues into its second century, it still offers students a good, sound, basic preparation for college and for life as it imparts knowledge and stimulates students to a lifelong love and pursuit of knowledge.

Lucas G. Boyd, Battle Ground Academy

SUGGESTED READING: Ridley Wills II, "The Old Boys' Schools of Middle Tennessee," *Tennessee Historical Quarterly* 56(1997): 56–69

BATTLE, MARY FRANCES "FANNIE" (1842–1924), Confederate spy and social reformer, was born in the Cane Ridge community of Davidson County on her family's plantation. Educated at the Nashville Female Academy, Battle was living at home when the Civil War began. Her father and brothers enlisted in the Confederate army and saw action in the battles of Fishing Creek, Fort Donelson, and Shiloh. Two brothers died at Shiloh, and the father, Joel Battle, was taken prisoner.

When the Union army occupied Nashville in March 1862, shortly after the surrender of Fort Donelson, Battle and a sister-in-law joined a group of scouts and spies, who gathered information about Federal forces stationed in the city. Battle obtained a Federal pass and entered the city without difficulty. Many of the Confederate spies were young women, who dated Union soldiers in order to obtain information about troop movements and the strength of Federal defenses in Nashville. When Battle was caught smuggling documents, she was imprisoned in the Tennessee State Penitentiary before being transferred to the Old Capitol Prison in Washington, D.C., where she was incarcerated with other female Confederate spies. Battle returned to Nashville at the end of the war and accepted a position as a teacher at Howard School. She taught at various Nashville schools from 1870 to 1886.

In December 1881, following the flooding of the Cumberland River, Battle persuaded prominent Nashville civic leaders to organize a relief society for the impoverished flood victims, who lived in the low-lying areas near the river. The Nashville Relief Society dispensed food, clothing, and coal to more than 1,000 people left homeless by the flood. A separate Ladies Relief Society formed the next year, and Battle served as its treasurer.

After meeting the critical needs of the flood victims, Battle and other leaders of the society organized the United Charities. When United Charities faced difficulties raising money to pay a competent secretary to manage the organization, Battle left teaching to accept the post. She served as secretary-general of United Charities until her death.

As secretary, Battle became keenly aware of the many Nashville children who were neglected while their parents worked. Battle rented a room in a North Nashville neighborhood, near the cotton mills that employed women mill workers, and established a daycare program. The program grew quickly, and Battle recruited physicians and other professionals to donate services to the children. The program became the Addison Avenue Day Home, Nashville's first daycare facility. Fannie Battle died in 1924 and is buried in Nashville's Mt. Olivet Cemetery.

Carole Stanford Bucy, Volunteer State Community College

BAXTER, JERE (1852–1904), New South railroad entrepreneur, challenged the Louisville and Nashville (L&N) Railroad's control over Middle Tennessee commerce by building the Tennessee Central Railroad to connect Nashville and Knoxville. Baxter was born in 1852, the son of a prominent Nashville politician, Judge Nathaniel Baxter. After adventures in travel, law, legal publishing, and real estate, the young, energetic Baxter turned to railroading. While still in his twenties, he became president of the Memphis and Charleston Railroad Company and went on to help organize companies promoting the development of coal fields in northern Alabama and eastern Tennessee. He was involved in the founding of South Pittsburg, Tennessee, and Sheffield, Alabama.

In 1893 Baxter organized the Tennessee Central Railroad Company (TC). Baxter planned to build a rail line to span the state from Knoxville to Memphis and break the L&N monopoly over rail connections to Nashville. The Panic of 1893 stymied construction and left the TC bankrupt. Baxter turned to Louisville capitalists, who created a syndicate to buy the TC and placed him back in control. At the turn of the century, Baxter used convict labor to build a railroad line from Monterey, in Putnam County, to Harriman, and then to Knoxville. The purchase and construction of connecting branch lines enabled Baxter to provide rail connections from Knoxville to Nashville and west to Clarksville.

Baxter's attempt to break the L&N's control over Nashville commerce earned applause from many Nashvillians, who supported TC construction with city bonds. Baxter started his own Nashville newspaper to counter adverse reports in the city's two L&N-controlled newspapers. In 1900 the L&N ignored public indignation and refused to allow TC trains to use the newly opened Union Station. In 1903 Baxter won election to the State Senate, where he pushed for legislation to force the L&N to open Union Station to TC traffic. With the defeat of the bill, the TC lost its last chance to become an equal contender for Nashville's railroad business. Baxter died in February 1904 of kidney disease.

Baxter failed in his confrontation with the L&N, but his railroad exerted a lasting impact on economic development in the Eastern Highland Rim and Cumberland Plateau. The TC reached areas without river or highway connections and provided a link to the national economy. Farmers shipped produce on the TC, sawmills and coal mines sprang up along the line, and cash replaced barter as the region entered the larger market economy. Until the 1920s the TC remained the chief link to the outside world for the Upper Cumberland and the Plateau. Baxter became a hero to many people in the hill country, and one small town in Putnam County changed its name to honor him.

Jeanette Keith, Bloomsburg University of Pennsylvania
SEE: NASHVILLE UNION STATION; PUTNAM COUNTY; RAILROAD, TENNESSEE CENTRAL

BAYLOR SCHOOL. In 1893, a group of men prominent in the professional, industrial, and civic life of Chattanooga invited noted educator John Roy Baylor to the city and cleared the way for the founding of the University School. Among the founders were Dr. J.W. Bachman, Robert Pritchard, Theodore G. Montague, H.S. Chamberlain, Foster V. Brown, and Lewis M. Coleman. By 1897, Dr. Baylor's name would be forever associated with his school.

The school began with only 31 students and a determination to educate young men in preparation for entrance into universities throughout the United States. For the first 18 years, the school was located in downtown Chattanooga. In 1915 the school moved to its present location, a 30-acre campus on the banks of the Tennessee River, five miles from downtown Chattanooga. Locals referred to the site as Locust Hill.

Among the many men who figured prominently in the history of Baylor School, John Thomas Lupton, Chattanooga capitalist and philanthropist, played an essential role in translating Dr. Baylor's dream into bricks and his vision into stone and mortar. Lupton headed a group of men whose generosity made it possible to relocate the school and expand its program.

Baylor School underwent many changes during its long history. In 1917 the school established a military tradition that ended in 1971. From the three original buildings on Locust Hill, the physical plant has grown to more than 24 academic and athletic buildings and numerous playing fields. In 1985 Baylor's Board of Trustees decided to make the school coeducational. Today, it is close to achieving a 50/50 ratio of male-to-female students.

In 1996, 800 students were enrolled at Baylor, and the campus had grown to encompass 600 acres. Baylor School is a fully accredited, coeducational, independent, college-preparatory school for students in grades seven through twelve. It offers a boarding program for students in grades nine through twelve, serving not only students from the southeast, but those from across the United States and foreign countries. Baylor graduates attend top-ranked colleges and universities throughout the United States. In 1954 Baylor was invited to become one of the pilot schools in the national experiment known as the School and College Study of Admission with Advance Standing (now known as the Advanced Placement Program).

Athletics became a formal part of the Baylor experience in 1907. Since that time, Baylor has become a school nationally recognized for its outstanding athletic program and facilities. The school's athletic curriculum emphasizes both interscholastic and intramural activities. Baylor's athletes represent the school well, having won state and national titles in many sports.

In 1993 Baylor celebrated its Centennial. It is the oldest independent school in Chattanooga, and one of the oldest in Tennessee. In its second century, Baylor School continues to prosper. In the fall of 1996, the school broke ground for a multimillion dollar Fine Arts facility. A new Science & Technology Building is in the planning stages.

Milly Rawlings, Baylor School

SEE: CHAMBERLAIN, HIRAM S.; LUPTON, JOHN T.

BEALE STREET, stretching from the Mississippi River toward the east, became Memphis's most famous avenue. On the infamous section of Beale Street, between Main and Lauderdale streets, the "Blues was born." As Beale Street's reputation for a culturally rich, African-American urban life spread, visitors arrived from all over the region.

For decades, the area beyond Beale Street was the southern boundary of downtown Memphis. Racial segregation prohibited African Americans from the main business district except as workers and customers who entered side ("Colored") entrances to be waited on last. As a result, African Americans frequented Beale Street, where Jewish immigrants, other European Americans, and black businessmen offered them exclusive services and low-priced goods. Just a few blocks away, on Lauderdale Street, wealthier African-American families built fine homes and extended their community further into South Memphis.

From 1862 to 1867, the Civil War and Union army occupation produced a phenomenal growth in the African-American population. The population tripled until blacks accounted for 16,509 of Memphis's 27,703 inhabitants by 1865. Almost all these rural migrants lived in contraband camps, including Camps Dixie and Shiloh ("New Africa"), south of Beale Street near Fort Pickering and President's Island. Some of the migrants would make their fortunes in Memphis, providing goods and services to the large, postwar freedmen population.

Beale Street soon became the cultural center and the local headquarters for civil rights, politics, and religion for African Americans. Joseph Clouston, an African-American barber, invested in Beale Street real estate. From 1866 to 1874, 20 black-owned businesses and a Freedman's Bank existed in the area. African Americans controlled the barbering and local taxi (hack) and freight (dray) businesses until the streetcar system and immigrant competition put them out of business by the 1880s.

Tennessee's oldest surviving African-American church edifice was built on Beale Street in 1864, when Beale Street Baptist Church erected a frame structure. In October 1866 the congregation and the Reverend Morris Henderson (1802–1877) purchased a lot and began construction of a brick and stone building. At the time of Henderson's death, the building had not been completed, but the congregation numbered over 2,500 members. Former President of the United States, Ulysses S. Grant, visited the church on April 14, 1880, escorted by Edward Shaw, Memphis's leading African-American politician. Pastor Taylor Nightingale ran for the city Board of Education in January 1886. Ida B. Wells, later a nationally known civil rights activist, assumed coeditorship in the *Free Speech and Headlight* newspaper as a result of her friendship with Nightingale and her attendance at the Beale Street Baptist Church. After the turn of the twentieth century, Beale Street Baptist Church's George A. Long led the opposition against Mayor Edward H. Crump, the Democratic leader of the corrupt political machine that ruled Memphis for decades. Crump and the local police were infuriated when Pastor Long allowed the radical Negro union leader and civil rights activist, A. Philip Randolph, to hold a rally in the church. But Long replied that "Christ, not Crump, is my Boss."

Robert R. Church, Sr. (1839–1912), a freedman who migrated into the city during the Civil War, helped to transform Beale Street from an upper-middle class neighborhood for European Americans to a commercial street for Negroes. By the 1880s, European-American families started their flight from Beale Street. In 1899 Church, Sr., responded to the city's segregation practices by purchasing six acres of land to build Church Park and Auditorium for Negroes. The two-story auditorium seated 2,000 persons and included a parlor, meeting rooms, and a refreshment stand. Church hired William C. Handy as the park's orchestra leader. A college-educated man who put the rural blues to written music, W.C. Handy became known as the "Father of the Blues." Among the famous visitors to the park was President Theodore Roosevelt, who addressed some 10,000 persons in 1902. Church's auditorium became the meeting place for the Lincoln Republican League under the leadership of Robert R. Church, Jr. (1895–1952), whose offices were located at 392 Beale. During the 1940s, after a racially motivated city hall changed Church Park and Auditorium's name to Beale Avenue Park in retaliation against Robert Church, Jr., Matthew Thornton (1873–1963), "Mayor of Beale Street," led a successful African-American movement to restore the Church name. In 1969 the Memphis Sesquicentennial Commission erected a plaque on the Church Park grounds. The city redeveloped the park in 1987.

In his book, *Beale Street: Where the Blues Began,* George W. Lee recalled "all nite Halloween Balls, and Big Jitterbug Contests" on Beale Street. Mac Harris, "King of the Gamblers," strutted down Beale in a cutaway coat, striped trousers, a wide felt hat, twisted mustache, a beard, and a cane. Jimmy Turpin ran the Old Monarch gambling joint. During the early 1880s,

Lymus Wallace operated a saloon at 117 Beale Street. George Jackson opened the first black drugstore on Beale by 1893. Around 1903, Lucie E. Campbell (1885–1963), Tennessee's famous writer of gospel songs and music pageants, organized a group of Beale Street musicians into the Music Club. Bert Roddy (1886–1963) and Robert Lewis, Jr., opened the Iroquois Cafe across from Church Park. Roddy was the first president of the Memphis branch of the NAACP. In 1917 Beale Street's African-American businessmen included William Burrows (contractor), George R. Jackson (pharmacist), L.J. Searcy (real-estate), Paul Sneed (bookkeeper), A.F. Ward (cashier), and C.A. Terrell (physician). Church's Solvent Savings Bank and Trust Company was on Beale. During the Great Depression, owners of the secondhand clothing stores on Beale stood on the sidewalks and enticed customers inside to buy coats for $1.95 and dresses for 25 cents. Before his exile to Chicago during the 1940s, Elmer Atkinson, a political ally to Church, Jr., operated his Beale Street Cafe. By the 1960s pawn shops, clothing stores, movie theaters, nightclubs, restaurants, and back-street apartments filled Beale Street. Blues singer B.B. King and gospel singer Mahalia Jackson, among others, performed in Church's Auditorium. There also the annual Negro Cotton Carnival ("Cotton Makers' Jubilee") and parade were held.

After the riots of 1968, Beale Street and the downtown area began to decline. Businessmen and developers shifted their center of operations to East Memphis. In 1969 the city undertook urban renewal projects, including Beale Street I and Beale Street II, which erased the area's housing, demolished 474 buildings, and placed a blockwide barrier of empty lots and parking spaces between African Americans and Beale Street. This project left a thin commercial (blue light district) between 2nd and 4th Avenues, where African-American businesses were forced out through condemnation of buildings and high property resale prices. The *Memphis Press-Scimitar* (June 10, 1979) declared the "Urban renewal destroyed Beale Street." In 1979 a preservation and neighborhood revitalization movement emerged too late to save the Beale Street local African Americans knew.

Beale Street became a National Historic Landmark historic district, with businesses reopened to attract European-American tourists. Beale Street remained home to several African American institutions: Church Park, Beale Street Baptist Church, the R.Q. Venson Center for the Elderly, Mohammed Ali Movie Theater, and the main branch of Tri-State Bank, among a few others. The Beale Street Baptist Church, isolated by vacant lots at the far end of the street, and outside the Beale Street historic district, was listed individually in the National Register of Historic Places.

Although the auditorium no longer exists, Church Park was placed on the National Register in 1994 and became part of the Beale Street historic district.

Bobby L. Lovett, Tennessee State University

SUGGESTED READINGS: George W. Lee, *Beale Street, Where the Blues Began* (1934); Margaret McKee and Fred Chisenhall, *Beale Black and Blue: Life and Music on Black America's Main Street* (1981); Robert A. Sigafoos, *Cotton Row to Beale Street: A Business History of Memphis* (1979)

SEE: CHURCH, ROBERT R., JR.; CHURCH, ROBERT R., SR.; CONTRABAND CAMPS; HANDY, WILLIAM C.; HUNT-PHELAN HOUSE; MEMPHIS MUSIC SCENE; RODDY, BERT; SOLVENT SAVINGS BANK; WELLS-BARNETT, IDA B.

BEAN, JAMES BAXTER (1834–1870) was perhaps the single most important dental surgeon of the Civil War. Born in Washington County, Tennessee, June 19, 1834, James Bean's heritage included the first white settlers of the state. He was the great-grandson of William and Lydia Bean, grandson of Russell Bean, and son of Robert and Mary Hunter Bean. Since Dr. Bean practiced dentistry in other states, left no direct heirs, died on Mont Blanc and was buried in Chamonix, France, his brilliant dental accomplishments during the Civil War have largely escaped the attention of his own state.

Bean attended Washington College Academy, studied medicine, and later practiced in Micanopy, Florida, where he also collected many wildlife and ornithological specimens for the Smithsonian Institution. He received his dental degree from Baltimore College of Dental Surgery in 1860. He married Hester M. Bovell, daughter of Dr. William W. Bovell, in Jonesborough, Tennessee, October 30, 1860. After the outbreak of the Civil War, Bean moved to Atlanta where he offered his services to the Confederate medical authorities. His dental device, the "Bean splint," allowed him to treat successfully over 100 cases of gunshot wounds to the jaw and face, while preventing facial disfigurement and deformity that frequently resulted from such wounds. In January 1865, the Confederate Medical Board in Richmond, Virginia, unanimously recommended adoption of the Bean splint. Bean supervised Richmond dental surgeons in the use of his device.

After the war, Bean established a dental practice in Baltimore. He pioneered in the use of aluminum for dental plates, and in 1867, took out a patent for an aluminum denture base. Although his painstaking experiments were not successful, Bean's method of casting aluminum plates was an important step in the development of the casting process in dentistry.

Bean died in 1870, at age 36, when he and ten others were caught in a blizzard on the summit of Mont Blanc. Bean's notebook, recovered on his body, recorded his last hours as he froze to death. Mark Twain included extracts from the notebook in *A*

Tramp Abroad (1879).

Colin F. Baxter, East Tennessee State University

SUGGESTED READING: Colin F. Baxter, "Dr. James Baxter Bean, Civil War Dentist: An East Tennessean's Victorian Tragedy," *The Journal of East Tennessee History* 67(1996): 34–57

BEDFORD COUNTY was established by the Tennessee General Assembly December 7, 1807, from land taken from Rutherford County. The first court met at the home of the widow, Ann Payne, in what is now Moore County. Settlement of the area progressed slowly after an initial expedition in 1783 led by Alexander Greer, who later settled at Greer's Lick on land he marked during the expedition. Samuel Barton and the Edmiston Land Company carried out other early expeditions. Few settlers arrived until after 1806. Some brought Revolutionary War grants from North Carolina; others came with Tennessee grants, awarded from 1800 to 1810. In 1808 Andrew Erwin purchased 55,000 acres from Norton Pryor. A bitter title dispute arose between Andrew Jackson, who served as Pryor's agent, and Erwin. Litigation continued until 1824, when a compromise settlement was reached.

Shelbyville, the county seat, was established in 1810 from land donated by Clement Cannon, an early resident and the operator of the first grist mill. Shelbyville was ideally suited as a trading center, with fords on the southern and eastern ends of the town. In 1852 the commercial value of the town increased with the construction of the Nashville and Chattanooga Railroad. In the antebellum period, Shelbyville experienced its share of tragedy. A tornado swept through the town on May 31, 1830, destroying the courthouse and inflicting five casualties. Three years later an Asiatic cholera epidemic caused great panic and many deaths. Cholera outbreaks would recur in 1866 and 1873 with similar results. In 1934 the Bedford County Courthouse was destroyed a second time when a lynch mob burned it. Several days of threatened violence preceded the act of arson. One hundred national guardsmen were called to the scene to protect a young black man, E.K. Harris, accused of assault. Disguised as a guardsman, the accused man was removed from the jail and sent to Nashville for safekeeping. The mob burned the courthouse in retaliation for the removal of Harris.

In the early twentieth century, Shelbyville was a thriving industrial center. In 1923 Shelbyville had a population of 2,912 and boasted an electric light plant, water works, a textile factory, a hub and spoke factory, a foundry, saw mills, and planing mills, in addition to banks, churches, schools, and two newspapers. Shelbyville Mills was a large textile factory and company town, complete with a school and church. The Musgrave Pencil Company is one of the world's largest pencil manufacturers. On the factory grounds is the historic Turner Institute Building, a former African-American private school designed by Nashville architect Moses McKissack. Shelbyville achieved worldwide prominence in the twentieth century through the promotion of the Tennessee Walker. In 1939 Shelbyville became the home of the Walking Horse National Celebration, earning the designation as the "Walking Horse Capital of the World."

The main line of the Nashville and Chattanooga Railroad created the towns of Bell Buckle, Normandy, and Wartrace. Now one of the most visited railroad towns in Tennessee, Bell Buckle is the home of Webb School. Founded in 1886 by Sawney Webb, the school has a well-deserved reputation as one of the leading preparatory institutions in the South. The establishment of Normandy as a railroad town brought about the demise of the village of Rowesville (Roseville). Despite enthusiastic expectations for the growth of Normandy, it remained a village, attaining its largest population of 250 in 1917. Wartrace, established in 1852, benefited from the rise of the walking horse industry in the county. Wartrace's historic railroad hotel has become a virtual museum to the Tennessee Walking Horse, and the champion of the first Celebration, "Strolling Jim," is buried on the grounds.

Bedford County furnished soldiers for every war since the War of 1812. During the Civil War, Bedford County was divided in its loyalties and supplied nearly equal numbers of troops to the armies of the North and the South. The pro-union stance of Shelbyville earned that city the title of "Little Boston." One of the South's best known generals, Nathan Bedford Forrest, was born in Bedford County in 1821 and took his middle name from his birthplace.

Bedford County has been the home of two Tennessee Governors, and an Arkansas Governor, and the residence of a third Tennessee Governor. William Prentice Cooper served three consecutive terms as Governor of Tennessee from 1938–1945. His marriage to Hortense Powell Cooper produced three sons, one of whom, Jim Cooper, represented the fourth district in the U.S. Congress, 1982–1992. Jim Nance McCord was born at Unionville in Bedford County. He succeeded Cooper as Governor of Tennessee in 1945 and served until 1949. His most important accomplishment was the institution of the sales tax to fund education. Archibald Yell, second Governor of Arkansas, grew to manhood in Bedford County and practiced law in Shelbyville. A friend of Andrew Jackson and James K. Polk, he was killed at the Battle of Buena Vista, Mexican War, in 1847. Tennessee's present Governor and his wife, Don and Martha Swanson Sundquist, were residents of Shelbyville from 1962 to 1970.

Two other Bedford Countians of note are George DeForest Brush and James L. Bomar. Brush (1855–1941) was a Shelbyville native who achieved prominence as a painter. Bomar, born at Raus in

Bedford County, became a Shelbyville attorney before serving in both houses of the Tennessee General Assembly, where he was Speaker of the House and Lieutenant Governor. He is the former President of Rotary International.

Timothy R. and Helen C. Marsh, Shelbyville

SEE: COOPER, PRENTICE; FLY MANUFACTURING COMPANY; FORREST, NATHAN B.; GILLILAND HOUSE; KEY, WILLIAM; MCCORD, JIM N.; MUSGRAVE PENCIL COMPANY; SHELBYVILLE MILLS; SHOFNER, AUSTIN CONNER; SUNDQUIST, DON; TULLAHOMA CAMPAIGN; WALKING HORSE NATIONAL CELEBRATION; WEBB SCHOOL; WEBB, WILLIAM R.

BEECHLAWN, on Pulaski Pike (U.S. 31) south of Columbia, is one of southern Middle Tennessee's most imposing Greek Revival homes, distinguished by a full-temple front supported by four monumental Ionic columns. The house was built in 1853 for Major A.W. Warfield and takes its name from the grove of enormous beech trees which surrounds it. Warfield, a native of Maryland, moved to Maury County in 1852, and soon began construction of the home. During the Civil War, the home was headquarters for Union General John M. Schofield during his retreat before the advancing army of Confederate General John B. Hood, and afterwards served as Hood's own headquarters. Beechlawn's gardens were established by Mrs. Warfield when the house was built; the boxwood, brought from Virginia, have grown to enormous size.

Richard Quin, National Park Service

SEE: FRANKLIN, BATTLE OF; HOOD, JOHN B.

BEERSHEBA SPRINGS, a historic resort village in north Grundy County, began attracting visitors after Mrs. Beersheba Porter Cain of McMinnville discovered a large chalybeate spring in 1833, and suggested the water, with its high iron content, contained medicinal properties. Several freestone springs gave visitors a variety of water, and the altitude of 2,000 feet provided lowlanders a respite from the fevers and other summer ills.

Early accommodations consisted of several log cabins and a tavern built by George R. Smartt and Dr. Alfred Paine of McMinnville. They formed the Beersheba Springs Company, which the Tennessee state legislature incorporated in 1839. Although residents staged balls at the resort as early as 1837, Beersheba Springs did not achieve social prominence and attract visitors from the deep South until the 1850s, when ex-slavetrader John Armfield acquired the property. Armfield incorporated several cabins and built a two-story porticoed hotel with a fine view of the Collins River Valley. In the rear, two quadrangles of cabins opened onto two courtyards separated by a cross row. The hotel featured a large dining hall with a ball-room above it. Armfield imported chefs and musicians from New Orleans to entertain his guests and compete with the fashionable Virginia watering places. He also built 20 cottages for affluent friends, who enjoyed the last great social season in 1860.

In 1875 the hotel brochure advertised Beersheba as a quiet family retreat rather than a fashionable resort. This description identifies the community today. The family-owned Armfield cottages are passed down from one generation to the next. Families have added other cabins—several are constructed of logs hauled from other sites—and the rustic atmosphere prevails.

Beersheba's local population, which the 1990 census reported as 577, is comprised largely of families in crafts, agriculture, commerce, and community affairs. In his poem, "Mountain People," Leonard Tate compared the character of Beersheba residents and their neighbors to the lasting qualities of granite. Local residents also are active in volunteer fire and rescue squads.

In 1973 the Tennessee General Assembly authorized the preservation of 10,000 acres of wilderness in the Savage Gulf area near Beersheba, and set aside the area for recreational purposes. In 1980 the historic district of the town was placed on the National Register of Historic Places. That same year, a group of local and summer residents, led by Margaret Brown Coppinger, formed the Beersheba Springs Historical Society. The society's projects include the 1983 publication of an illustrated history for Beersheba's sesquicentennial celebration.

In 1941 the United Methodist Church acquired the hotel and uses the property for group retreats. The surrounding area offers a number of recreational attractions that include hiking, swimming, bird watching, and canoeing. Many nearby archaeological and geological sites tell the earth's history as well as that of much earlier Native American occupants.

Today Beersheba is governed by three elected commissioners, who elect a chairman. The town includes several churches, two firehalls, a local library, a museum, and a post office. An annual Arts and Crafts Fair draws thousands of visitors during the fourth weekend in August.

Herschel Gower, Dallas, Texas

SEE: ARMFIELD, JOHN; GRUNDY COUNTY; RESORTS, HISTORIC

BELL, JOHN (1796–1869), was one of antebellum Tennessee's most prominent politicians and an acknowledged leader of the state's Whig party. The son of a farmer and blacksmith, Bell was born in Davidson County and graduated from Cumberland College in 1814. After his admission to the bar in 1816, he opened a law practice in Franklin in Williamson County. A year later, his political career began with his election to the State Senate, but he declined re-election after one term. Perhaps because he recognized the limitations of a provincial town for an ambitious youth, he moved to Murfreesboro, then Tennessee's capital, before finally settling in Nashville, the state's commercial center. By the time Nashville became the capital in 1826, Bell had established himself as one of the city's most prominent attorneys.

In 1827 Bell returned to politics and won the first of seven congressional terms in a bitter contest against former Congressman Felix Grundy. He entered the House of Representatives as a supporter of Andrew Jackson, despite Jackson's endorsement of Grundy. Toward the end of Jackson's presidency, however, Bell worked with the administration's opposition. Never a member of the president's inner circle, Bell's close connections with Nashville's mercantile community—solidified by his 1835 marriage to Jane Erwin Yeatman, the widow of one of the city's wealthiest merchants—encouraged a sympathy with the developing Whig party's advocacy of federal government promotion of national economic development. At the same time, he apparently recognized that Jackson's preference for rival politicians would hinder his own aspirations. In 1835, although he still proclaimed loyalty to the administration, Bell accepted opposition support to win election over James K. Polk, who was Jackson's choice as Speaker of the House. Later that year, he openly broke with the president when he became one of the leaders of the movement to elect Tennessee Senator Hugh Lawson White, rather than Democratic party nominee Martin Van Buren, as Jackson's successor.

After White's loss in the 1836 presidential election, Bell successfully worked to move White's support into the national Whig party, and the party ultimately rewarded him for his service with an 1841 appointment as Secretary of War for the first Whig president, William Henry Harrison. Bell served only six months in the War Department before he and other cabinet members resigned after the party repudiated John Tyler, who became president following Harrison's death. Returning to his law practice in Nashville, Bell spent the next six years watching political developments and waiting for the chance to return to public office. His opportunity finally came in 1847, when he agreed to serve a term in the state House of Representatives, where he gathered sufficient support to win election to the United States Senate.

Re-elected to a second term in 1853, Bell's years in the Senate coincided with the national debate over slavery's expansion into new territories. Although a slaveowner, Bell quickly distinguished himself as an advocate of compromise. He became the only senator from a southern state to vote against passage of the Kansas-Nebraska Act in 1854. Four years later, he defied instructions from the Democratic-controlled General Assembly and voted against Kansas's admission to the union as a slave state. By the latter date, the legislature had already elected a Democrat to succeed him in the Senate, but his reputation as a defender of the Union made him an ideal presidential candidate in 1860 for the hastily formed Constitutional Union party. In a contest characterized by sectional division, Bell finished last among four candidates, but he won the second largest number of popular votes in the southern states and carried the electoral votes of Tennessee, Kentucky, and Virginia.

When the lower South seceded after Abraham Lincoln's presidential victory, Bell at first urged Tennesseans to remain in the Union, and he met with the new president to encourage him to pursue a peaceful policy toward the South. After Fort Sumter and Lincoln's call for volunteers to put down the rebellion, Bell became convinced that the Republicans intended to impose a military dictatorship upon the South. He then reluctantly endorsed Tennessee's withdrawal from the Union. As the champion of a broken Union, Bell's political career came to an abrupt end. He avoided the Union army's occupation of Tennessee by moving to Alabama and, later, Georgia. After the war he spent his remaining years near the family's iron foundry in Stewart County.

Despite the oblivion of his later years, Bell had been among the most prominent southern politicians in the antebellum era. His career presents a reminder that Tennesseans were united neither behind Andrew Jackson's Democratic party nor behind the extreme advocates of the defense of southern rights.

Jonathan M. Atkins, Berry College

<small>SUGGESTED READING</small>: Joseph H. Parks, *John Bell of Tennessee* (1950)

<small>SEE</small>: GRUNDY, FELIX; JACKSON, ANDREW; POLK, JAMES K.; WHITE, HUGH LAWSON

BELL, MADISON SMART (1957–), author, was born and raised near Nashville, and attended Ensworth School and Montgomery Bell Academy. He went to Princeton University, where he studied in the creative writing program, working with, among others, George Garrett and William Goyen. He graduated in 1979 Phi Beta Kappa and *summa cum laude*. After a year in New York City, where he lived in the heart of Brooklyn and worked as a sound technician for an Italian television crew and as a security guard at a Greenwich Village boutique, Bell attended Hollins College and received an M.A. in English and Creative Writing in 1981.

He taught at a number of institutions, including Johns Hopkins, Iowa Writers Workshop, the Poetry Center at the 92nd Street YMHA, and Goucher College where he was awarded the Chair of Distinguished Achievement in 1995. Among his other honors are the Lillian Smith Award (1989), Guggenheim and National

Endowment for the Arts fellowships, and nominations as a finalist for the National Book Award and the PEN/Faulkner Award. He was named by *Granta* magazine as one of "the best American novelists under 40" (1996). His short stories have been highly praised and widely anthologized, having been selected four times for the annual *Best American Short Stories*. He has also published essays, criticism, book reviews, and journalism in a variety of newspapers and national magazines. Bell's books have been translated into eight languages, and all but *Save Me, Joe Louis* (1993) have been published in Britain. Critically his work has earned respectful attention and high praise for its energy and artistry. Bell is married to the poet Elizabeth Spires, and they have one daughter.

Beginning with the publication of *The Washington Square Ensemble* (novel) in 1983, Bell has produced nine novels, two collections of stories, a non-fiction book, *The History of the Owen Graduate School of Management* (1988), and an anthology-textbook, *Narrative Design* (1997), as well as a dozen *Readers' Guides* for the Franklin Library dealing with authors from Aristotle to Henry James and Mark Twain. He has also written a number of screenplays.

Bell is clearly a southern writer by inheritance and in his love for language, emphasis on story telling, fondness for eccentric characters, and sense of the mysterious power of place. Although Bell has written both novels and stories set in the South, most of his work is placed elsewhere. *The Washington Square Ensemble* (1983), *Waiting for the End of the World* (1985), *Straight Cut* (1986), and *The Year of Silence* (1987) are chiefly set in a vividly realized New York City; *Doctor Sleep* (1991) takes place in London, *Ten Indians* (1996) in Baltimore, and the widely praised *All Souls Rising* (1995) in historical Haiti. He is one of the most effective contemporary writers at evoking the dingy, dangerous milieu of inner-city America.

Prolific, imaginative, brilliant, and compassionate, Bell has already created an impressive body of work by any standards and seems more than likely to become a major figure in contemporary American literature.

George Garrett, University of Virginia

SEE: LITERATURE; MONTGOMERY BELL ACADEMY

BELL, MONTGOMERY (1769–1855), early Tennessee industrialist and ironmaster, was born in West Fellowfield Township, Chester County, Pennsylvania, the youngest of ten children, to John Bell and Mary Patterson (spelled by some members of the family as "Pattison"). Too young for active service in the Revolution, he watched as five brothers marched off to war. Bell had little opportunity for formal education. He was apprenticed at the age of 16 to a tanner, but soon joined his brother, Patterson Bell, in the hatter's trade. At age 20, he moved to Lexington, Kentucky, where his recently widowed sister lived and opened a hatter's shop; he employed 20 men in the making and selling of hats. He also operated grist mills and lumber mills in Lexington and apparently met with considerable financial success.

In 1802 Bell moved to Tennessee's Cumberland region, where he bought James Robertson's interest in the Cumberland Iron Works and 640 acres of land for $16,000. He obtained the purchase money from the sale of his Lexington enterprises, supplemented by a year's work for Robertson. Why Bell entertained an interest in iron manufacture is not known. He was no doubt aware of the enormous growth of the Cumberland area and as a youth, he had been acquainted with iron smelting in Chester County. The acreage he purchased was necessary because of its iron-rich soil and the virgin timber, which could be converted into charcoal for the smelting process.

The iron works lay some 20 miles south of Clarksville, a frontier county seat on the Cumberland River. The area's growth created new counties in the following year, and Bell quickly became active in the civic affairs of the new Dickson County. He was appointed as one of five justices of the peace and became a member of a committee to choose a county seat. Later, he was named to a county board of education designed to form a school authorized by the legislature.

Bell pursued the iron business with characteristic vigor and success. In 1805 he bought the Yellow Creek Iron Works, which had just been opened by a competitor in Montgomery County. In 1808 he bought a 4,800 acre stand of timber and iron ore. By the following year, he produced more than 200 tons of pig iron annually. In 1809 his brother, Patterson Bell, anticipating war with England or France, urged Bell to cast cannon balls and offer them to the United States Army. Accordingly, in the following year, he offered to the Secretary of War "12-, 18-, and 24-pound ball" to be delivered at New Orleans for "ninety-two dollars a ton." Soon Bell had government contracts to supply not only cannon balls for the Army, but also canister for the Navy, to be delivered at the Gulf.

The labor for Bell's iron works came from two sources. He hired white immigrants from North Carolina and Virginia, and he used slave labor. At one point, he owned more than 300 slaves and hired more in busy seasons from among slaveowners in the neighborhood.

After the War of 1812, Bell suffered from the decline of government contracts and increasing competition from ironmasters like Richard Napier, who built a large and successful furnace nearby. In 1825 Bell sold Cumberland Furnace to Anthony Van Leer for $50,000. Bell built his last furnace near present-day Dickson in 1845 and named it "Worley Furnace," after one of his trusted slaves. By that time, Tennessee ranked third among the states in iron production, and most of the state's pig iron came from Middle Tennessee.

Bell was well into his seventies by the 1840s, and his iron manufacturing activities declined substantially after that. Already he had moved to Nashville, where he enjoyed horse racing and other sports. Increasingly, he considered the future welfare of his slaves. Representatives of the state chapter of the American Colonization Society convinced him that colonization in Liberia would insure their safety and happiness, and he sent several groups to Monrovia in the early 1850s. One group of 38 cost him $3,000 in transportation costs and several thousand more in tools and supplies sent with the slaves for their use upon arrival.

At the time of his death, Bell lived in an old dilapidated house near the Narrows of the Harpeth, where earlier he had constructed a tunnel to facilitate iron manufacture at a furnace he called Valley Forge. Friends and servants buried him near the banks of the Harpeth. Today, a stone marks his grave in an all but abandoned small cemetery.

Bell's will provided for $20,000 to be used for the establishment of a school for boys to be located in Nashville and $1,000 for the First Presbyterian Church in Nashville. The funds for the school were invested wisely and ultimately used to establish Montgomery Bell Academy. Other lands and funds were willed to heirs of his brothers and sisters.

Robert E. Corlew, Middle Tennessee State University

SUGGESTED READING: Robert E. Corlew, *A History of Dickson County, Tennessee* (1956)

SEE: CUMBERLAND FURNACE; DICKSON COUNTY; MONTGOMERY BELL ACADEMY; PATTERSON FORGE; SLAVERY

BELL, PERSA RAYMOND "P.R." (1913–), Oak Ridge scientist, advanced the art of scintillation spectrometry, using radioactive tracers scanned with a scintillator and collimator for medical diagnosis. Born in Fort Wayne, Indiana, in 1913, Bell attended Howard College and the University of Chicago, joining the scientists mobilized for World War II and contributing to development of improved radar systems at the Massachusetts Institute of Technology Radiation Laboratory from 1941 to 1946.

After the war, P.R. Bell joined the physics group at Oak Ridge National Laboratory (ORNL), then moved into the thermonuclear group seeking to develop fusion energy sources. He led a scientific team at Oak Ridge that improved the scintillation spectrometer, an electronic device for detecting and recording small pulses of light (scintillations) emanating from phosphorescent substances when energized by radiation. This device had practical applications for the ORNL fusion research program and also for medical science, when it was modified for use as a scanner to locate brain tumors through the uptake of radioactive

iodine, permitting diagnosis without intrusive surgery. Subsequent modifications permitted use of the scanners for diagnosis of cancer and diseases of many internal organs as the instruments became basic tools of modern medical science.

Leland R. Johnson, Clio Research Institute

SUGGESTED READING: Douglas A. Ross, "Thermonuclear's Stepchild: the Medical Instrumentation Group and How It Grew," *Oak Ridge National Laboratory Review* 2 (1968): 14–19

SEE: MEDICINE; OAK RIDGE NATIONAL LABORATORY

BELL WITCH. Along U.S. Highway 41, in Adams, Robertson County, a state highway historical marker documents the place and the story of the Bell Witch, perhaps Tennessee's most famous ghost tale. John and Lucy Williams Bell, a prosperous couple with several children, migrated from North Carolina in 1804 to Middle Tennessee, then on the western frontier. For over a decade after their arrival the Bells lived a quiet and uneventful life, developing their farm on the Red River and participating in the activities common to rural America.

Sometime around 1816, the Bells became aware of the occurrence of bizarre events, but initially said nothing to neighbors about the disturbances. Apparitions appeared and strange noises increased for a year or more, at times becoming so violent that the house reportedly shook as if it was being buffeted by a storm. Soon after the "spirit" arrived, John Bell began to experience peculiar and painful physical symptoms. Other family members were slapped, pinched, taunted, and otherwise harassed, but the spirit exhibited only kindness toward Lucy Bell. Often cantankerous, "Kate," as "she" was called, stripped the covers from beds while people slept, pestered the slaves, and prevented young Betsy Bell from marrying her sweetheart.

First trusted friends and then a variety of visitors, including Andrew Jackson, came to the Bell home to assist in solving the mystery. When the spirit began to speak, it recited prayers, imitated the voices of local people, and argued Scripture. At weekly prayer meetings, it sang along with the church congregation.

After suffering great physical torment, John Bell died on December 20, 1820. According to the spirit, Bell was a victim of a toxic liquid she had given to him. The following spring, after a four-year stay, the spirit left, but returned less spectacularly in seven years, as it had promised.

Today it is difficult to grasp the uneasy ponderings of the nineteenth century community as one views the quiet Bell family cemeteries, the old farm well now abandoned, and traces of the lane down which General Andrew Jackson rode on a visit to see for himself the unknown force troubling his friends and neighbors. A log dwelling, allegedly once a slave or tenant house on the Bell property, has been moved

to the grounds of the old public school at Adams.
William T. Turner, Hopkinsville Community College
SUGGESTED READING: Charles B. Bell, *The Bell Witch, A Mysterious Spirit* (1934)

BELLE MEADE PLANTATION was founded by John Harding in 1807. From his initial 250-acre purchase on the "Old Natchez Road," seven miles from Nashville, Harding built Belle Meade into a 1,200-acre plantation. During three decades of his management, Harding sold blacksmith services, farm products, and dressed lumber and established an important stud farm.

Harding's son, William G. Harding, a college-educated general in the state militia, managed Belle Meade from 1839 until 1883. By the 1850s he was one of Tennessee's wealthiest men and larger landowners. In 1854 William Harding greatly enlarged his home into a Greek Revival showplace. During the Civil War, Federal authorities arrested Harding, a Confederate supporter, and imprisoned him for six months. During his incarceration, his wife, Elizabeth McGavock Harding, managed Belle Meade and looked after her "family of 150 persons," mostly slaves.

Belle Meade's greatest fame came after the Civil War, when it became one of the best known thoroughbred breeding farms in the world. Iroquois and Bonnie Scotland became the stud's most famous stallions. Credit for the post-war renaissance goes both to Harding and his colorful son-in-law, ex-Confederate Brigadier General William Hicks Jackson.

Soon after Jackson's death in 1903, Belle Meade passed out of the Harding-Jackson family. In 1953 the State of Tennessee purchased the house and 24 acres and deeded the property to the Association for the Preservation of Tennessee Antiquities, which maintains the property as a historic site.
Ridley Wills II, Franklin
SEE: ASSOCIATION FOR THE PRESERVATION OF TENNESSEE ANTIQUITIES; HARDING, WILLIAM G.; THOROUGHBRED HORSE RACING/BREEDING

BELMONT MANSION. Originally named Belle Monte, Italian for "beautiful mountain," this lavish 180-acre Nashville estate was the summer home of Joseph and Adelicia Acklen. Built between 1849 and 1853, with additions made until 1860, the Belmont estate consisted of a 36-room, 20,000 square-foot villa built in an Italian architectural design, expansive circular gardens, fountains, art gallery, water tower, greenhouse and conservatory, bowling alley with billiards parlor, bear house, artificial lake, zoo, deer park, and aviary. Located two miles from downtown Nashville, a refinery at the estate provided gas for lighting Belmont.

Located today in the center of the Belmont University campus, Belmont Mansion is open for guided tours. Approximately half of the house is open to the public, and restoration is on-going. The 105-foot water tower remains on the grounds, as well as evidence of the ornamental gardens. Original gazebos and marble statuary adorn the grounds. Belmont also boasts the largest collection of nineteenth century cast iron garden ornaments in the United States. The mansion still displays an impressive collection of marble statuary, oil paintings, gasoliers, marble mantels, and gilded mirrors original to the Acklen family. Victorian furnishings and decorative items, both original and collected, show the splendor in which Adelicia and her family lived. Much of the original Venetian glass still adorns the windows, doors, and transoms of Belmont. Covered porches with cast iron balconies surrounded the house to protect windows from the sun. Atop the house, a ten-foot octagonal cupola vented the house during the summer months and provided an "astronomical observatory" for viewing the estate and downtown Nashville. Adelicia Acklen hosted some of Nashville's most elaborate parties in the house. The 58-foot long Grand Salon, added in 1859–1860 by Prussian-born architect, Adolphus Heiman, is considered one of the most elaborate domestic interiors built in antebellum Tennessee. The magnificent room features a 22-foot tall barrel-vaulted ceiling, ornate plaster cornice, Corinthian columns with cast iron capitals, and an impressive free-standing staircase. The family living quarters at Belmont consisted of ten bedrooms, two dining rooms, a library, impressive front hall, and a host of family and entertaining parlors. The kitchen and other service areas were housed in the 8,500 square-foot basement.

Despite a two-week occupation by Union General Thomas J. Wood prior to the battle of Nashville, the house and its contents went undamaged during the Civil War. Only the grounds, where 13,000 Union troops spent those first two weeks of December 1864, suffered damage.

Months before her death, Acklen sold Belmont. In 1890 it opened as a women's academy and junior college. The school merged with Ward's Seminary in 1913, and was renamed Ward-Belmont. The Tennessee Baptist Convention purchased the school in 1951, and created a four-year, co-educational college. Today the mansion is owned by Belmont University; it is operated and preserved by the Belmont Mansion Association.
Mark Brown, Belmont Mansion
SEE: ACKLEN, ADELICIA; BELMONT UNIVERSITY; HEIMAN, ADOLPHUS

BELMONT UNIVERSITY. The history of Belmont University begins with Adelicia Acklen, mistress of Belmont Mansion; the first Belmont College (1890–1913); and Ward-Belmont (1913–1951). Both were schools for women. After a century of education on the campus (as willed by Acklen), the coeducational Belmont College became a university.

As an institution of the Tennessee Baptist Convention, Belmont College grew from an initial 135 students to more than 2,800 in its 40-year history (1951–1991). Belmont benefits from strong leadership, with only three presidents having served the institution: R. Kelly White (1952–1959), Herbert C. Gabhart (1959–1982), and William E. Troutt (since 1983). Their vision and fervor have shaped the modern history of the institution, which stresses three basic values: be honest; treat every person with respect; and listen and learn from everyone.

The hallmark buildings lining Wedgewood Avenue provide a visual sense of the progress of the university. Music Row leads directly to the school's front door at Freeman Hall, flanked by two other historic buildings—Fidelity, built during the Ward-Belmont era, and Barbara Massey Hall, home of the elegant dining halls and originally called Founders Hall. Freeman Hall connects to The Jack C. Massey Business Center. The Massey Center (1990) and Freeman Hall (1890) exhibit an architectural and ideological blend of the preservation of the past and the state-of-the art construction for the future. Indeed, the campus today mixes the past, present, and future through the blending of nineteenth century gazebos and artifacts created for Acklen's country estate, as well as modern classrooms and laboratories for the twenty-first century.

Representing almost every state and more than 40 foreign countries, Belmont's 3,000 students choose from academic programs in more than 50 major areas of study. Seven undergraduate and eight graduate degrees are offered through the schools of Business, Humanities/Education, Music, Nursing, Religion, Sciences, and The Jack C. Massey Graduate School of Business.

The second largest private school in the state, Belmont University, for two consecutive years (1995 and 1996), was the state's only higher education institution honored with a Tennessee Quality Achievement Award. In 1995 Belmont received the highest Innovative Management Achievement Award from the National Association of College and University Business Officers for its comprehensive management initiative.

A leader in continuous quality improvement (CQI) among colleges and universities nationwide, Belmont has developed partnerships with the Nashville business community to support organizations that encourage lifelong learning. The Peer Learning Network brings together Nashville's young executives to study world-class leadership. The Frist Center (senior living industry), The Center for Family Business (family-owned entrepreneurships), and The Center for Quality and Professional Development provide customized learning with worldwide reach.

Belmont University's vision is to be a premier teaching university, bringing together the best of liberal arts and professional education in a consistently caring Christian environment.

Mona Collett, Belmont University

SEE: ACKLEN, ADELICIA; BELMONT MANSION; EDUCATION, HIGHER; MASSEY, JACK C.

BEMIS. Developed by the Jackson Fibre Company (a division of the Bemis Brothers Bag Company) beginning in 1900, the town of Bemis rose from the cotton fields of Madison County as a model company town created by the vision of Judson Moss Bemis (1833–1926) and his son, Albert Farwell Bemis (1870–1936). Though the elder Bemis was interested in building a model manufacturing community as early as 1865, it was his son Albert Bemis, following his graduation from the Massachusetts Institute of Technology (M.I.T.) in 1893 with a degree in civil engineering, who created a model town, with the help of his college contemporaries and the resources of M.I.T.

Judson Moss Bemis founded his St. Louis company in 1865, producing cotton bagging and jute sacks for sale. By the 1890s, the Bemis Brothers Bag Company had become one of the first American packing companies and one of the nation's earliest multi-national corporations. Postwar southern industrialization encouraged the Bemis company to develop a new manufacturing plant in Tennessee. Bemis wanted a mill in the center of a major cotton growing region, with its own gin, so that the company could buy cotton directly from the farmer and avoid the costs of brokers' fees, ginning, compressing, and shipment. With the new mill located on the Illinois Central Railroad line, the Bemis company anticipated no additional costs beyond shipment of the final product. The strategy proved enormously successful; the company followed this initial experiment with the construction of another bagging mill in 1917 at Bemiston, Alabama.

Within a year, a 300-acre site in the open fields of Madison County was transformed into the town of Bemis. Along with the mill, 60 to 75 houses for mill workers rose to the north in an area called "Old Bemis." Unlike most company towns, Bemis intended for his site to become a corporate-sponsored experiment in town planning and the development of affordable housing for American workers.

The development pattern of Old Bemis gave the town the appearance of a community that had grown over time, rather than the indifferent sameness of mill villages throughout the nation. Bemis designed several "neighborhoods" around the industrial core, with a variety of house forms set on wide, tree-lined streets. The first neighborhoods, known as Old Bemis and Bicycle Hill, were built at the same time as the industrial facilities, in 1900 and 1903 respectively. An area of segregated housing for the town's small population of African-American workers arose on Congo Street (now Butler Street) in 1903–1905. As the company grew, other housing areas were added, each with site plans and house styles noticeably different from the original neighborhoods.

The basic house forms used in the earliest Bemis neighborhoods derived from familiar southern house types, including shotguns, double shotguns, cubical cottages, L-plan cottages, and hall-and-parlor cottages. The staff of Lockwood, Greene and Company, one of the South's oldest and largest industrial engineering firms, prepared at least one of these plans. The Bemis Company Engineering Department, headed by Albert Farwell Bemis, conducted the original site planning, assisted by M.I.T. graduates employed directly by Bemis or as consultants.

The original building program included community facilities to support the town. Bemis had its own company farm, company stores, a post office, hotel, boarding house, rail depot, schools, playgrounds, churches, an auditorium, a YMCA building, a swimming pool, parks, a bath house, and a six-hole golf course. Unlike most company towns, the choice of residence remained with the employee and never became an obligation of employment. Regular jitney and train service provided adequate transportation to off-site residences.

The second major building program began in 1919 and lasted until 1921, producing the Silver Circle neighborhood and several prominent buildings. For this work, the Bemis Company hired The Housing Company of Boston, a town-planning and design firm created by Albert Farwell Bemis in 1918. In a notable change of procedure, a local architect, Reuben A. Heavner (b. 1875), in 1926 designed the final residential area, which was West Bemis (called Ragtown).

The Bemis Company's congenial relationship with its workers lasted more than a half-century; the Bemis mill closed only once for a brief strike in the 1950s. Diminishing profits resulted in the privatization of the town's housing stock in 1965; houses sold on the basis of seniority to mill employees through a company-sponsored financing plan. In 1975 the City of Jackson annexed Bemis, which further hampered the profitability of the mills, eventually forcing their sale by the Bemis Company in 1980. The mills were operated by two other companies through the 1980s, but closed in 1991. Bemis remains an identifiable town with a distinctive character, but is also nationally significant as an example of American welfare capitalism.

John Linn Hopkins and Marsha R. Oates, Memphis

SEE: ARCHITECTURE, VERNACULAR DOMESTIC; INDUSTRY; JACKSON; LABOR; MADISON COUNTY; SHOTGUN HOUSE

BENTON COUNTY was created on December 19, 1835, by the General Assembly from portions of Humphreys and Henry counties and organized in February 1836 in a small log cabin at the site of a local post office in what is now west Camden. Initially, the county name honored Thomas Hart Benton, a leading Jacksonian Democrat, but in 1852, the state legislature approved an act that retained the original name but honored "David Benton, an old and respected citizen" of the county.

The county lies partially in the western valley of the Tennessee River and partially in the plateau of West Tennessee. Its eastern boundary is the Tennessee River, whose shoreline includes a part of Kentucky Lake. The northern most section of the county is hilly, with deep, broad valleys; numerous steep bluffs overlook the river. Near the village of Eva is Pilot Knob, one of the highest elevations in West Tennessee, at some 650 feet above sea level. Otherwise the county is topographically rolling and heavily forested.

The county has a considerable prehistory, but at the time of its first settlement by blacks and whites, the Chickasaws claimed the area as a hunting range and maintained a few scattered habitations. Following the Jackson Purchase, settlers from Virginia, the Carolinas, and other eastern states arrived. Black settlers generally came as bondsmen of the whites, although several free blacks lived in the county during the antebellum period.

Benton County remains essentially a rural entity with several small towns and villages. Named for Camden, South Carolina, the site of a Revolutionary War battle, Camden was established in 1836 on the high ground above Cane Creek, a tributary of the Tennessee River. The courthouse occupies the center of the public square, though in recent years, businesses have moved to the west and northwest sections of the town. Benton County supports two radio stations and an airport. Camden has several churches, factories, and financial institutions. U.S. Highway 70 and U.S. 641 provide transportation links for Camden and Benton County. Located 20 miles south of the town, Interstate 40 can be reached via U.S. 641. Benton County's first banking institution, the Camden Bank and Trust Company, opened in 1889.

Big Sandy, named for the river on which it borders, owes its existence to local railroad development from about 1860. Its present incorporation dates from 1903. This prosperous rural town enjoyed considerable growth from the area's extensive tourism. Within a radius of 40 miles, there are 35 resorts, restaurants, and boatdocks.

Eva, a village named for Eva Steele, was originally known as Bartlett's Switch and began as a result of railroad development. Eva faces Kentucky Lake and provides a small rivercraft landing and a park. These attractions, along with the town's proximity to

Nathan B. Forrest State Historical Area and to Lakeshore, the United Methodist campground, make it attractive to tourists and local citizens.

Faxon, a village locked in the hills of northern Benton County, was established in 1881 and named for its postmaster, George B. Faxon. It is located on the Bass Bay Road, seven miles east of Big Sandy; several fishing facilities are located nearby.

Holladay, a village 15 miles south of Camden in the rolling landscape of Birdsong Valley, began as a small settlement in the 1840s, but had its firm beginning in 1887, with the establishment of a post office honoring the village's principal merchant, John M. Holladay. One of the county's most notable schools, the Holladay Independent Normal, operated there.

Politically the county has been overwhelmingly Democratic throughout its history. It was the birthplace of Thomas C. Rye, Governor of Tennessee, 1914–1918.

Principal county loyalty rested with the Confederacy during the Civil War, although a firm, but subdued Unionist element existed in the county. Troops under General Nathan Bedford Forrest destroyed the large supply depot at Johnsonville, across the river from Pilot Knob, in November 1864. The site is now the Nathan B. Forrest State Historical Area.

Tennessee took a leading role among the southern states in the passage of woman suffrage, when the state legislature enacted a limited suffrage bill on April 17, 1919. Five days later, Mary Cordelia Beasley-Hudson of Benton County cast the first female ballot in the state in the Camden municipal election.

The Tennessee Valley Authority changed the eastern landscape of the county and improved cultural life. The TVA attracted a small, but consistent, industrial development and boosted the local economy. Electrical power is distributed by the Benton County Board of Public Utilities in Camden.

Benton County has always had a strong religious commitment. The earliest congregation organized the Cypress Creek Baptist Church in November 1821. County denominations include Baptist, United Methodist, Church of Christ, Pentecostal, and Roman Catholic.

The Camden Chronicle, established in 1890, embodies the best local newspaper traditions, reporting county events and boosting economic development. The Benton County Library organized in 1942. Led for three decades by Ruth Priestley Lockhart, the library developed into one of the foremost small libraries in the state. The Benton County Genealogical Society, chartered in July 1986, has been active in the preservation of the county's heritage and its public and private records. The county is well served by a general hospital in Camden and several medical practitioners.

Jonathan K. T. Smith, Benton Co. Historian emeritus

SEE: EVA SITE; FORREST, NATHAN B.; JOHNSONVILLE, BATTLE OF; MUSSELING; RYE, THOMAS C.; TENNESSEE VALLEY AUTHORITY; SORGHUM-MAKING; TENNESSEE SHELL COMPANY

BENTON, THOMAS HART (1782–1858), the famous Missouri Senator, spent 15 of his most formative years as a resident of Williamson County, Tennessee. It was here that he was admitted to the bar and elected to his first political office. Thomas Hart Benton was born March 14, 1782, in Hillsboro, North Carolina, to Jesse and Ann Gooch Benton. His father, a lawyer, died in 1791, leaving a widow and eight small children. Before his death, the elder Benton had been involved in the ill-fated Transylvania Company and land speculation in Middle Tennessee. In 1800 Ann Benton brought her family to a 2,500-acre tract on Leipers Fork in Williamson County. The settlement was originally called Bentontown and later Hillsboro for their hometown in North Carolina.

Educated at the University of North Carolina, Thomas Hart Benton briefly taught school in Maury County. In 1804 he began to study law and was admitted to the Franklin bar in 1806; his name appears on more lawsuits than any other lawyer in that town.

Benton's political career began in 1809, when he was elected to the Tennessee General Assembly. He sponsored a number of bills, including one calling for judicial reform, which resulted in the establishment of the circuit court system in Tennessee. He also sponsored a bill guaranteeing slaves the right to a trial by jury in matters outside the jurisdiction of their master.

Benton helped persuade Andrew Jackson to raise an army to fight in the Creek Indian Wars and the War of 1812; he himself commanded a regiment of men. After the war, Jackson sent Benton to Washington to investigate travel pay for the soldiers, which he successfully obtained.

In 1813 Jackson and Benton became involved in a dispute that almost ended their friendship. Benton's brother Jesse and William B. Carroll fought a duel, and Jackson acted as Carroll's second; neither Benton nor Carroll was seriously injured. Thomas Hart Benton, who was absent when the original duel occurred, believed Jackson should have prevented the duel or refused to act as Carroll's second. In September, the Bentons met Jackson in a Nashville tavern, where a brawl broke out, and Benton shot Jackson in the left shoulder, severing an artery. The wound required a protracted recuperation, but Jackson and Benton later reconciled.

In 1815 Benton moved to Missouri, prompting gossips to speculate that Tennessee was not big enough for both Benton and Jackson. Five years later, Benton was elected to the U.S. Senate, where he served for the next 30 years. In the Senate, Benton supported the establishment of the Pony Express, the telegraph system, interior highways, a transcontinental railroad, and a sound currency, for which he received the nickname "Old Bullion." Above all else, Benton stood for the preservation of the Union and violently opposed secession.

T. Vance Little, Brentwood

SEE: CARROLL, WILLIAM B.; CREEK WAR OF 1813–1814; JACKSON, ANDREW; WILLIAMSON COUNTY

BENWOOD FOUNDATION is a charitable Chattanooga foundation created in 1944 by Coca-Cola bottling magnate George Thomas Hunter in memory of his uncle and aunt, pioneer bottler Benjamin Franklin Thomas and Anne Taylor Jones Thomas. The name Benwood was taken from the Thomas summer home on Lookout Mountain. According to legend, on viewing the beautiful site Thomas had purchased, seemingly too steep for building, Anne Thomas remarked, "Well, Ben would."

The foundation's purpose was and remains "to promote religious, charitable, scientific, literary, and educational activities for the advancement or well being of mankind." While only 10 percent of the Thomas bottling interests were estimated to come from Tennessee sources, some 90 percent of disbursements have been to Tennessee organizations. The bulk of Hunter's estate, 70 percent of the bottling company stock, went to the foundation after his death in 1950. The benefaction led to a precedent-setting lawsuit, when family members sued regarding the tax status of the donation. A 1952 court ruling stated that the foundation did not have to pay death duties, which became the responsibility of the residuary estate (from which family members benefited). Upheld on appeal, the ruling saved Benwood millions of dollars, which could be used for charitable causes and has likewise benefited other Tennessee foundations with regard to probate law.

Ned L. Irwin, East Tennessee State University

SEE: HUNTER, GEORGE T.; THOMAS, ANNE T.J.; THOMAS, BENJAMIN F.

BERRY, GEORGE LEONARD (1882–1948) was president of the Tennessee-based International Pressmen's and Assistants Union (1907–1948), prominent labor leader and advisor who served on several New Deal labor committees during the 1930s, and U.S. Senator from Tennessee (1937–1938). Born in Lee Valley, Hawkins County, on September 12, 1882, Berry was self-educated, and became independently wealthy and politically influential through hard work and perseverance. Fatherless at the age of three, he worked at a variety of jobs, both within and outside the printing industry, before his election as president of the International Printing Pressmen's and Assistants Union at the age of 25.

As IPPAU president, Berry took the struggling union with its small membership and barren treasury and made it a successful and influential labor organization. By the time of his death in 1948, the IPPAU had a membership of 86,000 and assets of nearly five million dollars. A major part of Berry's legacy as president was the construction of the Pressmen's Home, Sanitarium, and Technical Trade School for printers near Rogersville, Tennessee.

Berry's reputation and influence extended beyond the IPPAU. As a member of the American Federation of Labor, he served on several national committees, and for a brief time as executive officer of the union. In 1913, after a trip to Europe at the invitation of European labor leaders, he published a book, *Labor Conditions Abroad.* In 1918 President Woodrow Wilson named him as a liaison to his staff at the Versailles Peace Conference.

A life-long Democrat with an interest in politics, he sought both elected and appointed office. He ran unsuccessfully for the Democratic gubernatorial nomination in Tennessee in 1914, competed for the Democratic vice presidential nomination in 1924, and headed the party's labor division during the Presidential campaigns of 1924 and 1928. During the 1930s, Franklin D. Roosevelt appointed him to a number of New Deal labor committees established under the National Industrial Recovery Act, including the coal arbitration board, cotton textile board, and National Labor Board.

In 1936 Berry headed Labor's Non-Partisan League, which proved influential in securing Roosevelt's reelection. In 1937 he was appointed to the U.S. Senate by Governor Gordon Browning to complete the term of Nathan Bachman, who died in office. As Senator, Berry supported the cause of labor, but broke with Roosevelt over personal and political issues. In 1938 he campaigned as an anti-Roosevelt candidate and lost in the Democratic primary for Senator.

Following his brief tenure in the Senate, Berry continued to head the IPPAU and speak and write publicly about cooperation between labor and management. In 1946 Berry incurred serious financial and legal problems as a result of back taxes owed the Internal Revenue Service. Subsequent investigations by Congressional labor committees questioned his leadership and handling of union funds, although such inquiries stopped short of outright condemnation of his leadership. Berry died of a gastric hemorrhage on December 4, 1948, at Pressmen's Home, Tennessee.

Thomas T. Spencer, Indiana University South Bend

SEE: HAWKINS COUNTY; IPPAU AND THE PRESSMEN'S HOME; LABOR

BERRY, MARY FRANCES (1938–), a leading historian, civil rights advocate, legal scholar, and human rights advocate, was born in Nashville. After enduring an impoverished childhood, Berry received a Ph.D. and J.D. from the University of Michigan. During the 1960s and 1970s, she held several posts in academia, including Chancellor of the University of Colorado and senior fellow at Howard University's Institute for the Study of Educational Policy. In 1987 Berry accepted the Geraldine R. Segal chair as Professor of American Social Thought at the University of Pennsylvania.

Berry entered public service in 1977, when she was appointed Assistant Secretary of Education, a post she held until 1979. Berry joined the U.S. Commission for Civil Rights in 1980, serving as its vice-chairman until 1982. An outspoken critic of the Reagan administration, Berry charged that the Commission was becoming too compliant in its relations with the administration. Her prominence increased after a federal court ruled that Reagan did not have the authority to remove her from the Commission.

During the remainder of the 1980s, Berry continued to provoke public debate about civil and human rights. She helped found the Free South Africa Movement and was arrested outside the South African embassy in 1984 for protesting against apartheid.

Berry has also made distinguished contributions to historical and legal scholarship. Her book *Black Resistance/White Law* (1971) became a controversial, but groundbreaking work on the relationship between racism and the Constitution. Among Berry's other works are *The Black Experience in America* (1982, with John Blassingame) and *Military Necessity and Civil Rights Policy* (1977).

Carol Guthrie, University of Tennessee, Knoxville

BETHEL COLLEGE, in McKenzie, Carroll County, Tennessee, is one of two institutions of higher learning for the Cumberland Presbyterian Church. In 1842 the college began in nearby McLemoresville as the Bethel Seminary, established by the West Tennessee Synod, Cumberland Presbyterian Church. Reverend Reuben Burrow was the principal. Incorporated in 1847, the institution became Bethel College in 1850. As McKenzie grew as a railroad junction town in the years after the Civil War, college leaders in 1872 decided to move the school to this rapidly developing town.

In 1919 the college was presented to the General Assembly, Cumberland Presbyterian Church, which decided to upgrade the academic program, facilities, and staff of the college. Four years later, in 1923, Bethel College was re-organized and a new and larger endowment, with $100,000 alone coming from the Iowa estate of John T. Laughlin, was established. From 1924 to 1928, four new brick buildings to house a modern four-year college and seminary were constructed. At the center of the new McKenzie campus was Campbell Hall, the college's main administration building, which was designed by architect A.F. Lindsey.

Bethel College weathered the depression decade to grow and expand into a larger campus, still centered on Campbell Hall, in the second half of the twentieth century. A religious, educational, and cultural center for McKenzie and Carroll County, Bethel College celebrated its sesquicentennial year in 1992.

Carroll Van West, Middle Tennessee State University

SEE: CARROLL COUNTY; CUMBERLAND PRESBYTERIAN CHURCH

BETHLEHEM HOUSE, NASHVILLE, an example of early interracial cooperation among southern women, opened in 1913 at the corner of Tenth and Cedar Streets, as a joint effort of the Methodist Training School, Fisk University, and the Woman's Missionary Council of the Methodist Episcopal Church, South. In 1907 Sallie Hill Sawyer, a Fisk graduate and the first housemother of the Bethlehem House, asked Estelle Haskins, deaconess of the Methodist Training School and eventually the first Bethlehem House supervisor, to include Nashville's neglected African Americans in the settlement work of the city's Methodist women. The resulting Bethlehem House settlement work was governed by an interracial board of representatives from its supporting institutions and other Nashville citizens, and received its principal support from the Woman's Missionary Council. The interracial staff included volunteers, social workers, teachers, and students from Fisk University and George Peabody College for Teachers. Participants in the Bethlehem House programs enjoyed a variety of activities, including kindergarten, the Knights of King Arthur boys' club, cooking and sewing classes, Camp Fire Girls, and mothers' clubs. In 1915 Bethlehem House moved to improved facilities at Eighth and Cedar Streets; in 1923 it moved to its current location at Fourteenth Street and Charlotte Avenue.

In 1970 Bethlehem House merged with two other Methodist settlement houses to form the United Methodist Neighborhood Centers, with the renamed Bethlehem Center serving as the administrative agency. In 1992 another name change designated the three settlement houses as the Bethlehem Centers of Nashville. Today, the Bethlehem Center, financed primarily through the Board of Global Ministries of the United Methodist Church and the United Way, provides social services, job opportunities, child care, and youth and family recreation programs to the Nashville community.

Janice M. Leone, Middle Tennessee State University

BICENTENNIAL CAPITOL MALL STATE PARK, located in Nashville, honors 200 years of statehood with an innovative urban park of 19 acres. Designed by Tuck Hinton Architects, with Ross/Fowler Landscape

Architects, the park opened in 1996 and was the site of the state's grand bicentennial celebration on Statehood Day, June 1, 1996.

The park stands near the location of the old "French Lick," an early settlement area and trading post in Middle Tennessee, and creates a new vista of the State Capitol, saving that distinguished landmark from the shadows of the city's modern skyscrapers. "A major point of the park," observes architect Kem Hinton, "is to preserve a view of the State Capitol." Landscape architect Mike Fowler adds: "the Bicentennial Mall is in many ways a huge outdoor museum," where "people will take a sense of Tennessee away with them."[1] Accordingly, the park features a varied portrait of Tennessee history conveyed by a granite map of Tennessee at its entrance; fountains representing the state's 31 primary rivers; a Court of Three Stars in honor of the state's three grand divisions; a Wall of Tennessee History, which marks major events in the state's history and appears crumbling at a point representing the Civil War; and a Walk of the Counties, where time capsules from all 95 counties have been buried. An outdoor amphitheater capable of holding 2,000 people, as well as landscaped gardens, walks, and an inspiring monument honoring Tennesseans in World War II, complete this modern landmark.

Adjacent to the Mall is the new Farmers Market (1994–96), designed by Tuck Hinton Architects. The new 40,000 square-foot building replaced one that had served local florists and farmers for many years. Recalling a large shed barn and silos, executed in concrete and decorated by brightly painted cornstalks, the Farmers Market reflects the historic relationship between rural life and the urban beat of Nashville.

Carroll Van West, Middle Tennessee State University
CITATION:
(1) Both quotes are from David R. Logsdon, "Take a Stroll Along Bicentennial Mall," *Nashville Banner,* 28 May 1996, A, 1–2.
SUGGESTED READING: Kem G. Hinton, *A Long Path: The Search for a Tennessee Bicentennial Landmark* (1997)

BIG RIDGE STATE PARK contains 3,642 acres of reclaimed land, headquartered in Union County, about 12 miles east of Norris. Developed in tandem with the Tennessee Valley Authority's project at Norris Dam, park construction began October 20, 1934, with Company 4495 of the Civilian Conservation Corps providing the labor. This CCC company was originally part of a TVA work crew, designated TVA-P8-Company 1208. Under the administration of the National Park Service and the TVA Housing Division, the company built many recreational structures, including log cabins, lodge, swimming area, bathhouse, beach, trails, picnic shelters, and a blacksmith shop. It also restored a circa 1825 grist mill to docu-

ment the lifestyle of the rural people of Lone Mountain and Blue Mud, who lived there before the Norris project. The quality of craftsmanship, the use of log and stone in the buildings, and the successful land reclamation became distinguishing characteristics. A 1961 description noted that "Big Ridge has been able to capture a rustic impression in its buildings and general area which cannot be found in any other park in the system."[1] Many of these historic CCC buildings, including the restored grist mill, remain today, making Big Ridge an excellent example of the landscape created by TVA and the CCC during the New Deal era. As one of its five reclamation and recreation demonstration parks, TVA operated Big Ridge until transferring it to the park system of the State of Tennessee in 1949.

Carroll Van West, Middle Tennessee State University
CITATION:
(1) "Big Ridge State Park," *Tennessee Conservationist* 28(November 1961): 18.
SEE: CIVILIAN CONSERVATION CORPS; CONSERVATION; NORRIS DAM; TENNESSEE VALLEY AUTHORITY; UNION COUNTY

BIG SOUTH FORK NATIONAL RIVER AND RECREATION AREA of the Cumberland River drains an area of 1,382 square miles in Tennessee's Scott, Fentress, Pickett, and Morgan counties, and in Kentucky's Wayne and McCreary counties. It threads through 106,000 acres of federally protected recreation area, established by Congress in 1974, giving the river traveler a true sense of wilderness.

This is an ancient river, cutting through gorges more than 250 million years old and is one of only three rivers in the United States designated by Congress as a "national river," distinguished by its historical significance as well as its wild and scenic beauty. The Big South Fork is also one of the few rivers in the eastern United State that has not been dammed for power generation or flood control. The U.S. Corps of Engineers first proposed to dam the river in 1933, and construction was authorized several times in the 1950s and 1960s by the U.S. Senate, but the House of Representatives never agreed.

Canoers, kayakers, and rafters of every skill level—from novice to expert—can find a stretch of the Big South Fork that offers them relaxation or challenge. The river's rapids range in difficulty from Class I to Class V. The best period to be on the river falls between March and the first part of June, before the water supply becomes problematic.

The Big South Fork National River and Recreation Area features spectacular scenery. Looking down from the Cumberland cliffs into the Big South Fork gorge hundreds of feet below, visitors have the feeling of standing on top of the world, and there is nothing quite like it. No visitor to the Cumberland wilderness can miss the extraordinary stone formations sculpted by the violent collision of continents and by the patient insistence of water flowing over—and after millions of years—through solid rock. Thousands of rock shelters and scores of natural arches are in the area, but the most spectacular are the Twin Arches, one of the largest natural bridges in the world. Within the Tennessee section of the park, the larger South Arch has a clearance of 70 feet and a span of more than 135 feet. The North Arch has a clearance of 51 feet and a span of 93 feet.

The area has massive sandstone bluffs carved in semicircles, white and scarlet oaks, tulip poplars, sugar maples, umbrella and cucumber magnolias, white ash, willows, sycamores, sweet gums, river birch, and hickory trees. There are dogwood, holly, sassafras, the spreading branches of hemlocks, the smooth bark of the gray beech, and a profusion of rhododendron, mountain laurel, and azalea.

Animals are plentiful and include white-tailed deer, black bear, wild hogs, southern flying squirrels, gray squirrels, red and gray foxes, chipmunks, beaver, muskrat, mink, otter, bobcats, coyotes, long-tailed weasels, cottontail rabbits, and eastern spotted skunks. Birds—132 catalogued varieties—are seen everywhere, including the ruffed grouse, the bobwhite, the hairy and pileated woodpecker, the screech owl, the red-tailed hawk, an occasional osprey, the scarlet tanager, the crow, the whippoorwill, the cardinal, the mockingbird, the turkey, and the turkey vulture.

Human history in the Big South Fork area began about 12,000 years ago with the nomadic tribes of hunters who followed the elk, bison, deer, bear, and other large game animals to what is now Tennessee and Kentucky. The rockshelters that nature created were used as homesteads by these hunters, and about 4,000 such shelters can be found within the Big South Fork National River and Recreation Area. The National Park Service lists 8,000 archaeological sites in the area. (The Park Service also estimates that at one time there was one moonshine still for every 116 acres of the Big South Fork.)

There is evidence at these ancient sites of tremendous activity between 12,000 and 7,000 years ago. There is evidence of mussel gathering and of intentional burning of forests to clear land for primitive planting. Evidence also indicates that beginning about 7,000 years ago, and for the next 20 centuries, human life in the Big South Fork area virtually vanished.

When they returned, after two millennia, the people of the Big South Fork were hunting smaller game, collecting plants, living in primitive campsites, and moving with the seasons. Between A.D. 900 and 1000, these people left the plateau for good and founded agricultural communities along the Tennessee and Cumberland rivers. Occasional hunting forays into the mountains were all that linked people with the Big South Fork for the next thousand years.

Long hunters changed all that when they first came to the area in the late 1700s. By 1800, several permanent homesteads had been established, but the fact that life was as hard for these settlers as their prehistoric predecessors is obvious from their choice of place names, such as Difficulty, Troublesome, and No Business. Identified historic farm sites include the Clara Sue Blevins Farm and Oscar Blevins Farm near the park's Bandy Creek Visitor Center.

The nature of hardscrabble agriculture helped to make local settlers more Blue than Gray during the Civil War. Unlike planters further south, farmers in the Big South Fork region could not grow cotton and did not rely heavily on slaves. Most residents were fiercely loyal to the Union, sending more troops to serve in the Grand Army of the Republic than with the Confederacy. Indeed, when Tennessee finally seceded from the Union, Scott County seceded from Tennessee and briefly became the Independent State of Scott. The world little noted, nor long remembered, these passionate politics. On most maps of the era, this part of the country was referred to as simply "wilderness."

A portion of that "wilderness" now makes up the Big South Fork National River and Recreation Area. Planned and constructed by the U.S. Army Corps of Engineers, this multi-purpose facility is now under the management of the National Park Service. The Park Service is determined to manage this area in a manner that is responsive to the varying needs and desires of a wide constituency of users, while protecting and preserving the diversity of its natural and cultural resources.

The Big South Fork is a wilderness area from the bluff lines down, which means in the parlance of the Park Service, "no vehicles, comforts, or conveniences." On the plateau, however, the Park Service must foster peaceful coexistence among four-wheel drive vehicles, bikers, horses, hikers, hunters, fishermen, and even trappers. Mountain biking and horseback riding continue to be the major draw to the area, which makes for an interesting mix, because horses do not much care for bicycles, nor cyclists for horses. Those coming to view fall colors must remember that they share the area with those in pursuit of deer—so we are all learning to share this very special place.
Howard Baker, Jr., Knoxville
SEE: CONSERVATION; SCOTT COUNTY

BILLS, JOHN HOUSTON (1800–1871), born in Iredell County, North Carolina, was one of the founders of Bolivar, in Hardeman County, and a leader of the Tennessee Democratic Party in the nineteenth century. He came to the West Tennessee area in 1818, with members of the family of James K. Polk. In 1823 Bills married Prudence Polk McNeal, a cousin of Polk. Bills also began a cotton factoring company with her brother, Ezekial McNeal, which they called Bills and

McNeal, and acquired two plantations, one near Bolivar and the other in Mississippi.

Bills was one of the first commissioners for the new town of Bolivar in 1824, and with his brother-in-law, one of the leading industrialists and planters in West Tennessee. He purchased his home, known as "The Pillars," in 1837, from a Philadelphia newspaperman, John Lea, and traveled throughout the eastern United States to furnish it in appropriate style. The mansion is now a historic house museum administered by the local chapter of the Association for the Preservation of Tennessee Antiquities. Bills entertained several notable Tennesseans and southerners at his home, including Andrew Jackson, James K. Polk, Sam Houston, Leonidas Polk, and Jefferson Davis. After his wife died in 1840, Bills continued making trips throughout the East and Europe. In 1849 Bills married a widow from Virginia, Lucy Anne Duke.

Union troops burned the town of Bolivar in 1864, destroying the business district, including Bills's cotton plant. Bills, however, proclaimed himself neither unionist nor secessionist, and thus protected his home and much of his wealth from military reprisals. He continued traveling, entertaining, and aiding in the rebuilding of his business and of Bolivar, until his death at home in November 1871.

Tara Mitchell Mielnik, Middle Tennessee State University
SEE: ASSOCIATION FOR THE PRESERVATION OF TENNESSEE ANTIQUITIES; HARDEMAN COUNTY; HILL, NAPOLEON

BIRCH, ADOLPHO A. (1929–), a pioneering African-American jurist, became the first black man to hold several judicial posts in Nashville and the first to assume the chief justice position of the Tennessee Supreme Court. Birch was born in Washington, D.C., the first child of an Episcopal minister of the same name, who had migrated to the United States from British Honduras (now Belize) in 1894 seeking an education. When the boy was six, his mother died during the birth of a third child. Birch was raised alone by a father, who believed in stern discipline, but with the affection of his father's church members. After graduation from Washington D.C.'s famous Dunbar High School, Birch attended Lincoln University in Pennsylvania, but transferred to Howard University in D.C. where he received in 1956 both his undergraduate and law degrees at the same time.

After two years in the military, Birch moved to Nashville, where he worked in the office of an African-American attorney for office space and $12.50 per week. Later he entered into private practice with well-known African-American attorney Bob Lillard, who mentored him. In 1966 Birch began a series of firsts for African-American lawyers in Tennessee. A Democrat, he received appointment as the first black assistant attorney general in Nashville. In 1969 Gov-

ernor Buford Ellington appointed him to a general sessions judgeship, the first state judicial post held by an African American in Tennessee; he was reelected twice. In 1978 Governor Ray Blanton appointed Birch as criminal court judge. Known for his stern bearing toward litigants and lawyers, Judge Birch received the endorsement of the Nashville Bar Association for his candidacy; he was reelected to the position. In 1987 Governor Ned McWherter elevated him to the court of criminal appeals (again the first African American to hold the seat). Judge Birch was appointed to the Tennessee Supreme Court in 1993, and was later elected to a full term.

He married the former Janet Scott (deceased) and they had three children—twin daughters and a son.
Lewis Laska, Nashville
SEE: LAW; TENNESSEE SUPREME COURT

BLACK PATCH WAR. During the first decade of the twentieth century, violence erupted in the tobacco belt of western Kentucky and northern Middle Tennessee as farmers tried to ease their economic distress. Collectively, these acts of violence became known as the Black Patch War. The term black patch referred to the region of the two states noted for the growth of dark-fired tobacco. The Black Patch War constituted one of the most serious domestic threats to civil government in twentieth century America. The armed and hooded vigilantes, who participated in these violent acts, became known as the tobacco night riders.

Violence was only one method employed by the growers to raise the price of tobacco. The area had suffered a prolonged depression since the late 1890s caused by falling tobacco prices. On September 24, 1904, tobacco growers formed the Dark Tobacco District Planters' Protective Association of Kentucky and Tennessee (PPA) to cooperatively market the staple. The PPA intended to withhold tobacco from the market until purchasing companies agreed to pay higher prices. Growers, who refused to pool, and the monopoly of buyers, led by the American Tobacco Company and the Italian Regie, presented threats to the PPA plan. PPA members called the non-poolers "hillbillies" and the buyers' monopoly "The Trust."

In 1905, when the PPA efforts failed to raise tobacco prices in the Black Patch, some growers turned to vigilantism in frustration. Area residents had a long history of using group violence to redress real and perceived grievances. Indian warfare, several regulator and vigilante movements, guerrilla warfare during the Civil War and Reconstruction, and lynching characterized the Black Patch history long before the onset of the tobacco war. In October 1905, 32 members of the Robertson County Branch of the PPA met at the Stainback schoolhouse in the northern part of the county and adopted the "Resolutions of the committee of the Possum Hunters Organization." The possum hunters outlined their grievances against the Trust and the hillbillies and stated their intention to visit Trust tobacco buyers and hillbillies in groups of no less than five and no more than 2,000 and use "peaceful" methods to convince buyers and nonpoolers to adhere to the PPA. The example of the Robertson County possum hunters spread throughout the region, and most Black Patch counties adopted similar resolutions. The peaceful visits soon turned violent, however, and gave rise to the night riders.

The night riders were organized into a secret fraternal society known as the "Silent Brigade" or the "Inner Circle" and structured along military lines. Dr. Frank Amoss, a physician from Caldwell County, Kentucky, reportedly led the order. Over the next few years, the night riders engaged in attacks on both property and people. They scraped or salted tobacco plant beds, destroyed tobacco in the fields, killed livestock, burned barns and warehouses filled with tobacco, dynamited farm machinery, and assaulted hillbillies and tobacco buyers. At the height of their power, the night riders staged spectacular night raids and captured entire towns. The Kentucky towns of Princeton, Hopkinsville, and Russellville suffered this fate. Most of the night riding activity took place in western Kentucky and in Montgomery and Robertson counties, Tennessee. The violence peaked in 1907–1909, and diminished over the next few years.

The PPA denied any relationship with the night riders. Even so, the violence helped the cooperative raise tobacco prices and kept them at profitable levels from 1905 to 1914. There can be little doubt that most night riders were also PPA members, and that many of the organization's members and leaders rode with the silent brigade in spirit, if not in body.

Several factors converged to end night riding. Kentucky Governor A.E. Wilson (1907–1911) dispatched troops to trouble spots, and several victims successfully brought civil suits against individual night riders. But most importantly, the base of popular support and community consensus that protected the night riders eroded as tobacco prices rose and as a growing number of people objected to the mass violence. The PPA ceased to operate in 1914, when World War I closed most European markets for dark-fired tobacco. The remaining vestiges of night riding died with the PPA.

Rick Gregory, Pleasant View

SUGGESTED READINGS: Tracey Campbell, *The Politics of Despair: Power and Resistance in the Tobacco Wars* (1993); Suzanne Marshall, *Violence in the Black Patch of Kentucky and Tennessee* (1994); James O. Nall, *The Tobacco Night Riders of Kentucky and Tennessee, 1905–1909* (1939); Christopher Waldrep, *Night Riders: Defending Community in the Black Patch, 1890–1915* (1993)

SEE: AGRICULTURE; DARK TOBACCO DISTRICT PLANTERS' ASSOCIATION; GLENRAVEN PLANTATION; MONTGOMERY COUNTY; ROBERTSON COUNTY; TOBACCO

BLACKBURN, GIDEON (1772–1838), Presbyterian minister, college president, and missionary to the Cherokees, was born in Augusta County, Virginia, on August 27, 1772. Orphaned in his youth, Blackburn moved to what is now East Tennessee in 1787 to live with his grandfather and uncle. In that same year he became an evangelical Presbyterian and decided to train for the ministry. He received his education at Martin's Academy, studied theology with Dr. Robert Henderson of Dandridge, and in 1792 received his license to preach from Abington Presbytery, which ordained him two years later.

In his twentieth year Blackburn moved to Fort Craig, near Maryville, where he established a farm, a distillery, and the New Providence church. For the next two decades he presided over congregations in Maryville and Eusebia, and acquired a reputation as a powerful and effective public speaker. Meanwhile, he married his cousin, Grizzel Blackburn (October 1793), with whom he had seven daughters and four sons.

Blackburn served as an itinerant chaplain in the Tennessee militia during the war with the Chickamaugas and Creeks (1788–1794). He later claimed his military experience exposed him to the problems of the Cherokees and induced him to missionary work. More likely, the evangelical revival of 1800, which added 550 new members to Blackburn's congregations, convinced him to engage in more ambitious apostolic enterprises. In 1803 the Presbyterian General Assembly approved Blackburn's proposal to establish a school for Cherokee children and gave him $200 for living expenses. He obtained an additional $730 from private donors and (following a meeting with President Thomas Jefferson) the United States government. In the fall of 1803, Cherokee leaders granted him permission to begin his work.

Blackburn's school, on the Hiwassee River near present-day Charleston, opened in the spring of 1804; a second school, the Blackburn Mission, opened in 1805. Intended to instill Christian religious precepts and "civilized" standards of behavior, the curriculum emphasized lessons in dress and comportment as well as instruction in reading, math, music, and the catechism. Neither school used interpreters and thus had only limited appeal for non-English-speaking Cherokees. In 1804 and 1805, most of the one hundred or more students were bicultural Cherokee boys seeking to improve their English and gain knowledge of the three "Rs" before entering careers as traders or shopkeepers.

Blackburn confined his activities to fundraising and holding biennial public academic exercises. As part of his "civilizing" mission, however, he urged the Cherokee National Council to adopt laws respecting patrilineal inheritance, private property, solemnized marriage, and other Anglo-American cultural and legal institutions. He became a staunch ally of the powerful acculturationist chief Doublehead, to whom he offered sanctuary shortly before Cherokee nationalists assassinated him in 1807. Deeply shaken by the execution, Blackburn moved the Hiwassee school to safer ground at the abandoned Tellico blockhouse.

In the spring of 1809, the Creeks implicated Blackburn, his brother Samuel, and the Cherokee chiefs John McIntosh and The Ridge in a scheme to illegally ship whiskey through Creek territory to Mobile. The resulting scandal severely damaged Blackburn's reputation and contributed to a brief period of anti-mission sentiment among the Cherokees. In 1810, the minister closed both schools and moved his family to Middle Tennessee.

In the spring of 1811, the Blackburns settled in Franklin, where he became the principal of Harpeth Academy. He continued his work as an itinerant preacher, helping to found five new congregations (including First Church of Nashville) and the Presbytery of West Tennessee, and serving as the clerk and moderator of the Tennessee Synod. He also raised a company of volunteers for service under General Andrew Jackson during the Creek War, and became a mentor and confidante of Jackson's wife Rachel.

In 1823, perhaps in consequence of financial difficulties in Tennessee, Blackburn moved to Kentucky, where he served as the pastor of the First Church of Louisville (1823–27), the president of Centre College (1827–1830), and a minister in Versailles (1830–33). He also advocated African-American colonization and became an agent and lecturer for the Kentucky Temperance Society. In 1833, at the request of Edward Beecher, Blackburn moved to Macoupin County, Illinois, where he established two more churches and worked as a financial agent for Illinois College. He also organized a small public land company whose profits were to endow a non-sectarian theological seminary. The Panic of 1837 and protracted litigation delayed the completion and opening of the school (present-day Blackburn College) until 1859. During the winter of 1837–38, Blackburn fell and broke his hip and died the following August at his home in Carlinville.

David A. Nichols, University of Kentucky

SUGGESTED READINGS: William McLoughlin, *Cherokees and Missionaries* (1984); Walter Posey, *The Presbyterian Church in the Old Southwest* (1952); V. M. Queener, "Gideon Blackburn," East Tennessee Historical Society's *Publications* 6 (1934): 12–28

SEE: BLOUNT COUNTY; BRADLEY COUNTY; CHUQUALATAQUE; CREEK WAR OF 1813 AND 1814; MONROE COUNTY; WILLIAMSON COUNTY

BLANTON, LEONARD RAY (1930–1996), three-term Congressman and one-term Governor, was born in April 1930, in Hardin County, Tennessee, and grew up on a farm close to the small town of Adamsville in McNairy County. His "dirt-poor" upbringing in the cotton fields of West Tennessee permanently endowed Blanton with a rough-hewn populist tendency that endeared him to the working classes and many state employees.

After graduating from the University of Tennessee, Blanton taught briefly in Indiana before returning to Adamsville to help build the family road construction business. In 1964 he was elected to the State House of Representatives, where he distinguished himself by his habit of sitting in the back of the chamber, wearing his sunglasses, and observing the proceedings. In 1966 he won the first of three terms in the U.S. Congress. In 1972 he received the Democratic nomination for the U.S. Senate, and campaigned as a George Wallace-like pro-segregation populist. Republican incumbent Howard Baker handily defeated Blanton in the November general election.

In the 1974 Democratic primary, Blanton won the governor's nomination with only 23 percent of the vote in a twelve-man race. In the general election, he defeated Lamar Alexander, selling himself as a reform Democrat in the year of President Richard Nixon's resignation following the Watergate scandal.

Blanton's term as governor ranks as one of the most controversial in Tennessee's history. Despite the corruption that surrounded his administration, however, there were also numerous solid accomplishments. He created the Department of Tourism, the first in the nation. Blanton traveled extensively for the state, making numerous trips to Washington, D.C., and three overseas trips, to recruit foreign investment. Although critics questioned his large travel expenses, the explosion of interest in Tennessee by British, Japanese, and German investors paid enormous dividends. Further, Blanton joined the legislature in upgrading the state's retirement system into one of the most actuarially sound systems in the country. He also emphasized programs promoting equality for women and African Americans and tax relief for senior citizens.

Unfortunately, the image of Ray Blanton in the minds of many Tennesseans dates to the hasty evening swearing-in of Governor-Elect Lamar Alexander on January 17, 1979, three days early. Problems over pardons and paroles arose early in the Blanton administration. Marie Ragghianti, a Blanton appointee and chairwoman of the Tennessee Board of Pardons and Paroles, was abruptly fired in August 1977, when she refused to release certain prisoners who, as later events proved, bribed members of the Blanton administration. Ragghianti retained Fred Thompson, later a U.S. Senator from Tennessee, as her lawyer and won a $38,000 settlement against the state. Peter Maas brought her story to national attention in the book *Marie,* which became a 1986 movie of the same name, starring actress Sissy Spacek in the title role. On December 15, 1978, the FBI swarmed over Tennessee's capitol and seized the office of Blanton's legal advisor, T. Edward Sisk, on suspicion of a cash-for-clemency scandal. They arrested three state employees, including Sisk, and Blanton appeared before a federal grand jury on December 23, 1978, denying any wrong doing.

On January 15, 1979, Blanton pardoned 52 prisoners, claiming the need to do so under a court order to reduce the prison population. One pardon went to Roger Humphreys, the son of a Blanton patronage leader in East Tennessee, who had been convicted of murdering his wife and a male companion. Even before the pardon, Blanton allowed Humphreys to live outside the prison and serve as a state photographer. Fearing further paroles, the FBI approached U.S. Attorney Hal Hardin, Lieutenant Governor John Wilder, and State House Speaker Ned Ray McWherter, and they agreed to Alexander's early inaugural. Blanton later claimed to be the only recent Tennessee governor who left office poor and he was never convicted of receiving payments for pardons.

In June 1981 Blanton was convicted of mail fraud, conspiracy, and extortion for selling liquor licenses and served 22 months in a federal penitentiary. This scheme, which principally involved Blanton associates Jim Allen and Jack Ham, attempted to corner the highly competitive Nashville liquor store market by controlling the stores directly or forcing the owners to kick back 30 percent of the stores' profits. Blanton spent the next ten years, from 1986 until his death on November 22, 1996, trying to restore his reputation. Nine of the charges were overturned in January 1988 by federal court action.

One of Tennessee's most controversial governors, Blanton remained a politician, who played the game to reward his friends and punish his enemies. His efforts on behalf of tourism and economic development, as well as state retirement security, contributed enormously to the general prosperity of the state. Nevertheless, the scandals eventually overwhelmed his reputation.

Fred S. Rolater, Middle Tennessee State University

SEE: ALEXANDER, LAMAR; MCWHERTER, NED RAY; THOMPSON, FRED

BLEDSOE, ANTHONY (1733–1788), pioneer and surveyor, was born in Spotsylvania County, Virginia, and became a product of the rolling frontier of his day. He was a justice of the peace for Augusta County in 1769, Botetourt in 1770 and 1771, and Fincastle in 1773 and 1774. He served on the Fincastle Committee of Safety in 1775–1776. In 1777 Bledsoe was elected to the Virginia House of Delegates and re-elected in 1778.

In 1779 Bledsoe was a surveyor with the commissioners of Virginia and North Carolina to establish the line between the western lands of those states. In 1780 he became a justice of the peace for the new county of Sullivan, North Carolina, and in 1781 and 1782 was its state senator. In 1783 he was one of the commissioners selected to survey the North Carolina military land grant reservation. He became a justice of the peace for new Davidson County in 1783, and in 1785–86 he represented the county in the State Senate. When Sumner County was created in 1786, Bledsoe assumed the same duties there, becoming chairman of the county court in 1787.

He shouldered military responsibilities wherever he was. He was captain of militia in Botetourt in 1770 and volunteered for Lord Dunmore's Colonial Army in 1774 in the French and Indian War. After taking up the cause of independence, he commanded the patriots at Fort Patrick Henry on the Long Island of the Holston in 1776. He served as lieutenant colonel commandant of Sullivan County in 1781, Davidson County in 1783, and Sumner County in 1787.

A recognized leader of the Cumberland settlements, Bledsoe brought his wife, Mary Ramsey Bledsoe, and their ten children to settle near Bledsoe's Lick in 1785. He and his family paid dearly for their relocation, however. Anthony Bledsoe died at the hands of Indians in 1788, as did his brother Isaac five years later. The same fate befell Bledsoe's sons, Anthony, Jr., and Thomas, his nephew, Anthony, and his brothers-in-law, Henry and William Ramsey.

Walter T. Durham, Gallatin

SEE: BLEDSOE, ISAAC; LAND GRANTS; SOUTHWEST TERRITORY; SUMNER COUNTY

BLEDSOE COUNTY, the oldest and most northern county in the Sequatchie Valley, became Tennessee's thirty-third county by an act of the Tennessee legislature in November 1807. It was named for Anthony Bledsoe, a Revolutionary War patriot who migrated to Tennessee from Virginia in the late 1700s.

Nature divided Bledsoe County's 404 square miles into three distinct regions: Sequatchie Valley, Cumberland Plateau, and Walden Ridge. In 1795 John McClellen and Charles McClung explored the area of the Sequatchie Valley that would become Bledsoe County. They praised the rich soil as equivalent to any land in the world, but settlers generally avoided the area until after the Third Tellico Treaty of 1805. Several early settlers accepted Sequatchie land as payment for service in the Revolutionary War.

In 1816, when the decision was made to move the county seat from its first location at Madison, Charles Love of Virginia sold 30 acres of land on Sequatchie Creek to the commissioners for the establishment of Pikeville; the price was $110.25. Located on the stage route from Knoxville to Huntsville, Alabama, the town developed as a trade and supply center for farmers. The town has changed little since the early twentieth century, with houses surrounding the county courthouse, a neoclassical building listed in the National Register of Historic Places. The Lincoln School, an early twentieth century African-American school and community center, stands on the north end of town. The school, which is also listed in the National Register, was constructed in 1925–26 with support from the Julius Rosenwald Fund. There have been three colleges associated with the Methodist Church in or near Pikeville: the People's College, Bledsoe College, and Sequatchie College.

The first schools in Bledsoe County were one-room log buildings, which served both as schools and as churches. In 1826 the State of Tennessee authorized the establishment of Lafayette Academy in Pikeville. The school operated until after the Civil War. In 1990 Bledsoe County operated three elementary schools, on the Cumberland Plateau, on Walden Ridge, and at Pikeville in addition to the centrally located high school at Pikeville.

During the nineteenth century, the Methodists exerted the strongest religious influence in the county, followed closely by the Baptists. The first religious services were held in the settlers' homes. One of the earliest church buildings was the log structure erected by Thomas Swafford sometime between 1820 and 1827 and named Swafford Chapel. First replaced by a larger frame building in 1853 and then rebuilt after the Civil War, the present church was completed in 1912. In addition to the Methodists and Baptists, the Cumberland Presbyterian and the Christian Church established congregations in Bledsoe County in the nineteenth century. The 1990 census counts more than 60 churches located in the county, almost half of which are Baptist.

Bledsoe County provided several notable political figures. Isaac Stephens (1782–1862) served three terms in the Tennessee General Assembly, beginning in 1813. He was commissioned as a captain in the 31st militia regiment, a large portion of which volunteered for service in the War of 1812. James Standifer (1776–1837) began his long political career as a member of the first Bledsoe County Court. He represented Bledsoe County in the State Senate, 1815–1823. Elected to the U.S. House of Representatives in 1822, he served five terms, 1823–25 and 1829–37, and died in 1837 on his way to Washington. A farmer and surveyor, Standifer had business interests in Vicksburg, Mississippi and New Orleans. James B. Frazier, an attorney with little political experience, won the gubernatorial election in 1902 as a Democrat. In 1906 he was re-elected, but resigned after his inauguration to fill the unexpired term of U.S. Senator William B. Bate, who died in March 1907.

Bledsoe Countians had divided sentiments over the Civil War. The county voted against secession, but after Tennessee withdrew from the Union in 1861, several Confederate companies were organized in the county. Other Bledsoe men served in the Union army. James G. Spears, a Democrat and slave owner, joined the Union and advanced to the rank of brigadier general.

Today, the population of Bledsoe County stands at approximately 10,000, of which 1,800 reside in Pikeville. The 33-bed Bledsoe County Hospital, the 49-bed Bledsoe County Nursing Home, the Pikeville Clinic, and the Bledsoe County Public Health Department serve county health needs. TVA supplies electric power to the Sequatchie Valley Electric Cooperative, and the Dunlap Natural Gas System supplies Pikeville with natural gas. Bledsoe Countians enjoy the benefits of modern communications systems, including a local radio station (WUAT) and a weekly newspaper, the *Bledsonian-Banner*. Nearby Fall Creek Falls State Park offers recreational opportunities. In 1834, while touring the area in search of coal and limestone deposits, Gerard Troost, state geologist, visited the "gulf," a large chasm on the Cumberland Plateau that was later incorporated into the park. The Fall Creek Falls Lookout Tower, located near the park, is listed in the National Register.

Elizabeth Robnett, Pikeville

SEE: FALL CREEK FALLS STATE PARK; FRAZIER, JAMES B.; GEOLOGICAL ZONES; LAND GRANTS; SEQUATCHIE VALLEY; TROOST, GERARD; WALDEN RIDGE

BLEDSOE, ISAAC (1735–1793), was born in Culpepper County, Virginia, but as a young man settled with his brother Anthony on the Holston River a few miles west of Bristol. After serving with British colonial troops in Lord Dunmore's War, he hunted and explored extensively along the Cumberland River. In 1772 he discovered Bledsoe's Lick and Bledsoe's Creek in an area of North Carolina that later became Sumner County, Tennessee. He was a captain in Colonel William Christian's Cherokee expedition in 1776; the next year he commanded a company to protect the border settlements. During the autumn of 1779 Commissioners Thomas Walker and Daniel Smith chose him for the party to survey the Virginia-North Carolina state line. They selected him for his first-hand knowledge of the western country, but he went in order to select a site for the stockaded fort he had agreed to build near Bledsoe's Lick as part of the proposed Cumberland settlements. One of the court of triers of the original Cumberland Association, Bledsoe was a justice of the peace in the first Davidson County Quarterly Court in 1783, first major of the county militia, and a guard for the surveyors of the North Carolina Military Reservation. When Sumner County was created from eastern Davidson in 1786, Bledsoe served in the first Sumner

County Quarterly Court, was first major of the county militia, and became lieutenant colonel commandant in April 1788.

In 1772 Isaac Bledsoe married Katherine Montgomery, a sister of the veteran frontiersman Colonel John Montgomery. The Bledsoe family lived at Mansker's fort in 1782–83, but moved into Bledsoe's fort about 1784. They had eight children. Indians shot and killed Isaac Bledsoe while he was working in a field near his fort on April 9, 1793. Eleven months later, his son Anthony fell mortally wounded in an Indian attack near Daniel Smith's Rock Castle home.
Walter T. Durham, Gallatin

SEE: BLEDSOE, ANTHONY; FRONTIER STATIONS; MANSKER, KASPER; SMITH, DANIEL; SOUTHWEST TERRITORY; SUMNER COUNTY; WALKER, THOMAS

BLOUNT COUNTY, one of the oldest counties in Tennessee, was established in 1795 before statehood and was named in honor of Territorial Governor William Blount. Prior to white settlement, and the establishment of a county, Blount County was home to the Cherokee Indians, who established their capital at Chota and occupied a village at Chilhowee.

White settlers arrived in the mid-1780s, and established a permanent settlement at Houston's Station in 1786. The county seat of Maryville, named after Governor Blount's wife, Mary Grainger Blount, was established and laid out in the 1795 act creating Blount County. Throughout the nineteenth century, Maryville was a medium-sized prosperous county seat, noted as the home of Maryville College. Originally established in 1819 as the Southern and Western Theological Seminary, Maryville College was among the first southern schools to open its doors to Native Americans, African Americans, and women. As industry arrived in the county at the turn of the century, Maryville boomed as a rail junction. Important properties associated with the boom include the Blount County Courthouse (1906), a Classical Revival design by Bauman and Bauman of Knoxville; the Southern Railway freight depot; and the Indiana Avenue historic district.

Smaller rural settlements are scattered throughout the county. In 1796 a settlement of Quakers from North Carolina established Friendsville, west of Maryville. Cades Cove was settled in the 1820s. By the 1870s, a close community had evolved, linked by isolation and kinship. In 1927 Cades Cove residents launched an unsuccessful court battle to protect their homes from inclusion in the Great Smoky Mountains National Park. Many of the homes, barns, and mills of Cades Cove have been preserved or reconstructed as a reminder of the past heritage of Blount County.

Sam Houston, one of the most famous Blount County residents, moved there with his family from Virginia in 1807. In 1812 Houston taught school in a one-room schoolhouse near Maryville, now preserved as a state historic site.

For almost 100 years, Blount County was home to a series of resort hotels at Montvale, near several springs at the foot of Chilhowee Mountain. During the 1850s, Irish expatriate John Mitchell lived there, and the family of author Sidney Lanier owned the hotel from 1856 to 1863, inspiring his novel, *Tiger Lilies.* William G. Brownlow was also a frequent guest. After the Civil War, several less successful hotels followed at Montvale, and the last hotel burned in 1933. Other smaller resorts operated near springs throughout Blount County into the early twentieth century.

In 1844 lawmakers attempted to establish a new county from the southern portion of Blount County and part of Monroe County. The new county would be called Jones, in honor of Governor James C. Jones, and the capital would be Ashley, a settlement near the former Cherokee town of Chilhowee. Surveyors mapped the area in 1844 and 1845, but the population was evidently not sufficient to warrant the creation of the new county.

During the Civil War, many residents of Blount County supported the Union, as did much of East Tennessee. General William T. Sherman quartered in Maryville with approximately 30,000 men in December 1863. Quakers at Friendsville helped over 2,000 Tennessee men to escape, avoiding conscription in the Confederate army.

Company towns played a large role in Blount County's history. In 1901 the Little River Lumber Company was chartered, and a mill town, named Townsend in honor of the company president W.B. Townsend, grew up around the lumber operations in Tuckaleechee Cove. Although the Little River Lumber Company sold much of its land for the creation of the Great Smoky Mountains National Park, Townsend remains as a reminder of the importance of the lumber industry in Blount County. Walland, halfway between Maryville and Townsend, was home to the Schlosser Leather Company, which processed raw hides mostly imported from South America.

In 1914 the Aluminum Corporation of America (ALCOA) reincorporated the area of North Maryville into a company town called Alcoa, and built several plants for aluminum production. The company also established the town of Calderwood on the Little Tennessee River in southern Blount County to house workers. The company exercised immeasurable importance in the economic life of the county and East Tennessee, in jobs, schools, economic advancement, and municipal additions. By 1960 ALCOA's investment in Blount County brought the county from eighty-fifth of Tennessee's 95 counties in assembled wealth to the top ten. ALCOA also provided much of the money and land to build McGhee-Tyson Airport, serving Knoxville and East Tennessee.

Much of eastern Blount County lies in the Great Smoky Mountains National Park, authorized by Congress in 1926. The establishment of the park was not without controversy for local residents. With funds from schoolchildren to large benefactors, $2.5 million was raised for the purchase of park land, along with another $2.5 million given by the states of Tennessee and North Carolina, and a $5 million donation by the Rockefeller family. After land had been purchased, it was deeded to the federal government. Congress formally established the Great Smoky Mountains National Park in June 1935, and President Franklin D. Roosevelt dedicated the park on September 2, 1940.

Tara Mitchell Mielnik, Middle Tennessee State University

SEE: ALEXANDER, LAMAR; ALCOA; BLACKBURN, GIDEON; BLOUNT, WILLIAM; CADES COVE; CHOTA; CIVIL WAR; GREAT SMOKY MOUNTAINS NATIONAL PARK; HOUSTON, SAM; HOUSTON, SAM, SCHOOLHOUSE; MARYVILLE COLLEGE; OVERHILL CHEROKEES; RESORTS, HISTORIC

BLOUNT MANSION, Knoxville's only National Historic Landmark, was constructed between 1792 and 1830, with the first period of construction between 1792 and 1796 as the home and office of William Blount, the Governor of the Southwest Territory. Blount Mansion replaced Rocky Mount as the capitol of the Southwest Territory. In contrast to the surrounding log homes, Blount constructed a frame house to demonstrate his political and economic status in the community. His "mansion," the largest house in the area, was a traditional hall and parlor plan, with two rooms on the first floor, a basement, and an attic sleeping loft. The Native American name, "the House With Many Glass Eyes," testified to the number of six-over-six glass windows on the front and rear elevations of the house.

After Blount's death in 1800, the house passed through his extended family and later became the home to prominent Knoxvillians such as Matthew McClung and James White and Knoxville mayors Matthew M. Gaines and Samuel B. Boyd. These and other owners made alterations to the house, dramatically changing its original appearance, including the addition of the completed second floor, the west wing, an attached kitchen, and a front porch. By 1925 Blount Mansion faced destruction by the city of Knoxville to make room for a parking lot in the downtown area.

The Bonny Kate Chapter of the Daughters of the American Revolution purchased an option on Blount Mansion in 1925 and in 1926 chartered the Blount Mansion Association (BMA). The BMA removed the Victorian front porch and determined to interpret the house in the territorial capitol period of 1792–1800. Blount Mansion opened as a museum in 1930.

Since 1955, Blount Mansion has undergone many changes, including the dismantling of later period buildings and additions, restoration of the Governor's Office, archaeological investigations, and paint and structural analyses. In a recent architectural analysis of the house, Michael Emrick and George T. Fore concluded that the house had experienced six distinct phases of construction and/or alteration and did not acquire its current overall form and size until the fourth phase circa 1815–1830. For the study of Tennessee architecture, it is "a more complex and interesting structure because of its phased construction."[1] Blount Mansion continues to preserve Knoxville's eighteenth-century history, and the restored office, gardens, and kitchen add to its interpretation as the frontier capitol of Tennessee.

Tara Mitchell Mielnik, Middle Tennessee State University

CITATION:

(1) Michael Emrick and George T. Fore, "Blount Mansion: Architectural Analysis and the Reinterpretation of a Tennessee Landmark," *Tennessee Historical Quarterly* 55(Winter 1996): 318

SEE: BLOUNT, WILLIAM; SOUTHWEST TERRITORY; TENNESSEE GOVERNOR'S OFFICE

BLOUNT, WILLIAM (1749–1800), Territorial Governor and U.S. Senator, was born on Easter Sunday (March 26, 1749), the eldest child of Jacob and Barbara Gray Blount of Bertie County, North Carolina. As a lad, Blount received informal training in commerce at the side of his father, who operated a farm and a mill, and sold tar and turpentine. With maturity, Blount assumed a more active role in his father's businesses. Blount's business acumen gained respect, and in 1776 he was named paymaster of the Third North Carolina battalion of the Continental troops.

At the age of 31, Blount entered politics, when he won election as New Bern's representative to the North Carolina House of Commons; he assumed his post in late January 1781. Within a year, he was elected to the Continental Congress, an office he held for approximately one year before returning to the North Carolina legislature. Blount's local legislative efforts reflected his growing interest in the western lands. He successfully promoted a bill to provide land grants west of the mountains to North Carolina soldiers with two years military service. Since most soldiers sold their grants instead of moving west, Blount and others—including his friend John Sevier—seized the moment and purchased grants representing hundreds of thousands of acres.

In October 1784 Blount was re-elected to the North Carolina legislature and subsequently won an internal vote for speaker of the house. In December 1785 he was elected to the Continental Congress, where he served briefly before returning to North Carolina. Blount increased his ties with the west by working for the formation of Davidson County in the Cumberland region and the establishment of a judicial district there.

Governor William Blount.

In February 1790 North Carolina ceded its western land holdings to the United States. A few months later, the area became the newly-created Territory of the United States South of the River Ohio (the Southwest Territory). President George Washington appointed Blount Territorial Governor and Superintendent of Indian Affairs for the Southern Department.

Without a public building in which to conduct the affairs of the territory, Blount selected the spacious home of William Cobb, at the fork of the Holston and Watauga rivers, as his temporary capitol. The room at Rocky Mount Blount selected for his office had windows and a fireplace, affording him a location from which to conduct business in comfort and style.

Relations between Indians and settlers represented the most pressing problem in the new territory. Blount invited representatives of the tribes to meet with him and negotiate treaties, a time-consuming effort that initially produced favorable results for the settlers. The treaties soon failed, undercut by settlers moving beyond treaty boundaries and by hostile responses from various Indian groups. Native Americans complained that once the treaties were translated for formal viewing, promises had been altered to their disadvantage. Disappointment soon gave way to aggression. Blount found himself in the precarious position of trying to appease two groups

with opposing interests. On the one hand, the settlers of the territory demanded a military campaign to extinguish the hostilities directed against them, while federal officials urged restraint and prohibited retaliation. In the summer of 1794 settlers launched an unauthorized attack on the Chickamauga towns at Nickajack and Running Water. The attack further strained the relationship between Blount and his superiors in the federal government.

Blount's most lasting achievement was Tennessee statehood. He called a meeting of the territorial legislature in June 1795, in order to request a referendum for statehood. The request was favorably received, and the referendum submitted to the voters. When the people approved the statehood proposal, Blount sought and won a bid to represent the new state in the U.S. Senate.

As a senator, Blount became involved in a risky plan initiated by John Chisholm to attack Spanish Florida with the aid of British and Indian allies. Blount later claimed that his motives were pure, arguing for the necessity of the action to keep western land open for future expansion. When his alleged involvement became public news, his participation as an American official in a plot against another country created a considerable stir. A Senate committee called for his expulsion, and impeachment proceedings began soon thereafter. Blount returned to Tennessee and avoided the embarassment of being formally removed from office.

The episode did little to dampen support for Blount in Tennessee. In 1798 he successfully ran for a seat in the State Senate to represent the citizens of Knoxville. Two years later, on March 15, 1800, after sitting on his porch reading, Blount complained of a chill. His discomfort gradually increased and led to more serious complications. Six days later he died.
Terry Weeks, Middle Tennessee State University
SUGGESTED READING: William Masterton, *William Blount* (1954)
SEE: ALLISON, DAVID; BLOUNT MANSION; BLOUNT, WILLIE; GOVERNMENT; ROBERTSON, JAMES; ROCKY MOUNT; SOUTHWEST TERRITORY

BLOUNT, WILLIE (ca.1767–1835), Governor, was born in Bertie County, North Carolina, to Jacob Blount and his second wife, Hannah (Salter) Baker Blount. He was half-brother to Tennessee's Territorial Governor William Blount. Willie (pronounced Wiley) Blount studied law at Princeton and Columbia before returning home to read law with a North Carolina judge. When William Blount began his term as governor of the Southwest Territory in 1790, Willie accompanied him, serving as one of his brother's three private secretaries.

In 1794 Blount secured a license to practice law and in 1796 the new state legislature elected him as a judge on the Superior Court of Law and Equity, a

PORTRAIT BY WASHINGTON B. COOPER, THS COLLECTION, TENNESSEE STATE MUSEUM.

position he declined. Settling in Montgomery County about 1802 with his wife and their two daughters, he represented the county in the state legislature from 1807 to 1809.

Blount was first elected governor in 1809 and then re-elected in 1811 and 1813. Throughout his tenure as governor, Blount sought to open up new areas of Tennessee for white settlement. During the Creek War, he provided his friend Andrew Jackson with funds and volunteer soldiers, which enabled Jackson and his troops to effectively destroy the military power of the Creek Indians. During the War of 1812, Blount led the initiative to raise over $37,000 in funds and 2,000 volunteer soldiers, which earned Tennessee the nickname, "The Volunteer State."

At the end of his third term, Blount returned to Montgomery County. In 1827, he ran again for governor, but was defeated by Sam Houston. Blount served as a member of the state's Constitutional Convention of 1834. He died September 10, 1835, in Nashville and is buried at the Greenwood Cemetery in Clarksville.

Anne-Leslie Owens, Tennessee Historical Society

SUGGESTED READING: Elizabeth H. Peeler, "The Policies of Willie Blount as Governor of Tennessee, 1809–1815," *Tennessee Historical Quarterly* 1(1942): 309–327

SEE: BLOUNT, WILLIAM; CREEK WAR OF 1813 AND 1814; WAR OF 1812

BLUES MUSIC: See BEALE STREET; GARRETT, ROBERT; HANDY, WILLIAM C.; JAZZ; MEMPHIS MUSIC SCENE; MUSIC; SMITH, BESSIE; THOMAS RUFUS; WDIA; WLAC

BOND, JAMES (d. ca. 1870), one of the wealthiest slaveholding planters in Tennessee, if not in the entire South, came to the state during the late 1820s or early 1830s. Bond and two brothers moved from Bertie County, North Carolina, to the Forked Deer region of West Tennessee, and rapidly acquired large landholdings in Haywood County.

By the eve of the Civil War, Bond had amassed property holdings in Haywood County alone of more than 17,000 acres and approximately 220 slaves. In 1859 his five plantations yielded more than 1,000 bales of cotton and nearly 22,000 bushels of corn. The federal manuscript census for 1860 estimated his total wealth at just under $800,000. (By comparison, the total value of all farm land, buildings, and other improvements in the entire county of Johnson—situated in the mountainous northeastern country of the state—was just under $790,000.) In addition to investing heavily in land and slaves, Bond participated in a variety of other economic endeavors. For example, he owned or invested as a silent partner in a variety of mercantile establishments in the county seat of Brownsville. He also was an early supporter and stockholder in the Memphis and Ohio Railroad, the completion of which in the 1850s connected Haywood County by rail to Memphis, the most important internal cotton market in the entire South.

A Unionist during the secession crisis in 1861, Bond readily swore an oath of loyalty to the Union upon the occupation of Haywood County by federal troops in June 1862. Despite severe losses during the war, his diverse property holdings (including northern municipal bonds and gold-bearing certificates issued by northern banks) allowed him to survive the war with a considerable proportion of his wealth intact. Until his death during the 1870s, Bond remained the richest planter in Haywood County and among the wealthiest landholders in the state.

Robert Tracy McKenzie, University of Washington

SEE: COTTON; HAYWOOD COUNTY

BOND, SAMUEL (1804–1862), cotton planter, physician, and Tennessee legislator, was born in Knox County on December 10, 1804. Bond's family moved to northern Alabama, before locating in Shelby County, Tennessee, in 1831. After a brief period of economic struggle, the family prospered, and the community in which they lived became known as "Bonds Station."

Bond engaged in a variety of interests. He studied medicine at Cumberland University (University of Nashville) and practiced until the mid-1840s. A Whig, he served one term in the Tennessee General Assembly (1847–1849), but showed no further interest in politics. Bond played a role in the incorporation of the Memphis and Holly Springs Railroad, but apparently participated in no other railroad activities.

Cotton provided the key to Bond's prosperity. He entered his cotton in the 1851 Crystal Palace Exhibition in London and won a "Prize Medal." Bond cultivated cotton throughout the boom decade of the 1850s and mortgaged his Shelby County holdings to purchase another plantation in Carroll Parish, Louisiana.

Ruined by the Civil War, Bond was broke when he died in October 1862. He is buried in Pisgah (Ellendale) Cemetery (near Bartlett, Tennessee). His 1840s home, "The Avenue," still stands in Ellendale.

Marius Carriere, Christian Brothers University

SUGGESTED READING: Perre Magness, *Good Abode: Nineteenth Century Architecture in Memphis and Shelby County, Tennessee* (1983)

SEE: COTTON; SHELBY COUNTY

BONTEMPS, ARNAUD W. (1902–1973), Harlem Renaissance writer and Fisk University librarian, was born in Louisiana in 1902, but grew up in Los Angeles after his family moved to California when he was three. In 1923 Bontemps graduated from Pacific Union College; three years later he married Alberta Johnson; they had six children.

Bontemps's writing career flourished during the 1920s and 1930s as his teaching and writing became associated with the Harlem Renaissance. He initially taught at Harlem Academy and won awards from both the National Urban League and the NAACP for his poems. In 1931 his first novel, *God Sends Sunday,* was published. This later spawned the Broadway musical, *St. Louis Woman,* which became a star vehicle for Pearl Bailey. Bontemps left New York to accept a position at Oakwood Junior College in Huntsville, Alabama. His writing interests turned to historical novels. *Black Thunder,* an acclaimed novel about black uprisings, was published in 1936. Two years later, the Julius Rosenwald Fund gave him a fellowship to study in the Caribbean.

The late 1930s and early 1940s were pivotal years in Bontemps's career. In 1941 he edited W. C. Handy's autobiography, *Father of the Blues.* He began his graduate studies, worked with the Illinois Writers Project, and in 1943, received his MLS degree from the University of Chicago. With that degree in hand, and his reputation in literary circles secured, Bontemps became the head librarian and director of University Relations at Fisk University in 1943. He played the key role of developing the library's significant collection of African-American resources from his colleagues in both the literary and music fields. He continued to write; during the 1950s he published a series of biographies of George Washington Carver and Frederick Douglass. In 1949 Bontemps collaborated with Langston Hughes in editing *The Poetry of the Negro,* a collaboration repeated nine years later in editing *The Book of Negro Folklore.* Bontemps's *The Story of the Negro* earned the Jane Addams Award in 1956. Through his writing and editing, Bontemps became one of the key figures in the mid-twentieth century development of African-American literature and history.

Bontemps retired from Fisk in 1965, and the following year he accepted a position at the University of Illinois, Chicago Circle. His writing continued to focus on historical topics; his *Great Slave Narratives* (1966) became an important collection of primary documents for scholars and students interested in the field of African-American history. From 1969–1971 he curated the James Weldon Johnson Collection at Yale University. Bontemps returned to Nashville in 1971 as writer-in-residence at Fisk. He died in Nashville on June 4, 1973 and was buried in Greenwood Cemetery.

Carroll Van. West, Middle Tennessee State University

SUGGESTED READING: Arthur P. Davis, *From the Dark Tower: Afro-American Writers, 1900–1960* (1974); Linda T. Wynn, "Arnaud Wendell Bontemps," in *Profiles of African Americans in Tennessee* (1996), 14–15

SEE: FISK UNIVERSITY; HANDY, WILLIAM C.; JULIUS ROSENWALD FUND; LITERATURE

BOOKER T. WASHINGTON STATE PARK is located in southeastern Tennessee on Chickamauga Reservoir northeast of downtown Chattanooga. The park was established as a state recreation area in 1938, the state's second African-American recreation area, preceded by T. O. Fuller State Park near Memphis. The Tennessee Valley Authority (TVA) originally leased land for the park to the state and restricted land use for "recreational development." In 1950 the state purchased the site for a token price of one dollar and added 150 acres to the reservation. Today, the Tennessee Department of Conservation owns and operates the 353-acre park.

In 1937, when the state opened negotiations for the development of an African-American park in East Tennessee, two sites appeared suitable. State officials favored Norris Lake near Knoxville, where the Civilian Conservation Corps (CCC), Works Progress Administration (WPA), and TVA already had started development. In addition, African Americans enjoyed the use of Norris Lake, which had not been designated as a segregated park. Chickamauga Reservoir, another TVA area, just north of downtown Chattanooga, also received consideration. Hamilton County Regional Planning Commission strongly supported a park near Chattanooga and cited the city's large African-American population as justification. In 1937, 38,000 African Americans (28 percent of the population) lived in Chattanooga, and another 49,000 African Americans resided within a 50-mile radius of the city. Officials agreed that Hamilton County presented more immediate needs than Upper East Tennessee. The park, officially established in 1938, was named for the well-known African-American educator, Booker T. Washington.

Park construction began in 1937, when Company 3459 of the Civilian Conservation Corps (CCC) started clearing the land. Company 4497, a Junior African-American company, replaced the first group in 1938. Both groups worked under the supervision of the Tennessee Department of Conservation, National Park Service, and TVA. Initial building plans called for the construction of a lodge, personnel quarters, ball fields, tennis courts, picnic areas, outdoor cooking units, boating facilities, cabins, and a dam. World War II interrupted these plans, however, and most improvements were not made until after 1946. Planners abandoned many scheduled improvements because of postwar cost inflation and cost estimates. Pre-war CCC development was limited to land clearance and planning; none of the current recreational structures date to the Depression-era relief programs. At its 1950 dedication, the park included a swimming pool, bathhouses, picnic tables and shelters, camp sites, ball fields, and a fishing area. The state's Division of State Parks completed the construction using contracted labor.

No official records of park attendance at Booker T. Washington Park exist prior to 1949, but visitation estimates for that year reach as high as 16,000. In 1959–60, the park recorded its largest attendance, an estimated 85,000, rating it sixteenth out of 20 parks. The park continued to rank low in revenues, as a result of poorly developed camping facilities and overnight accommodations. Today, Booker T. Washington State Park offers group camp sites, a group lodge, swimming, picnic areas, nature trails, fishing, and boating facilities. The park is considered historically important for its connection to the CCC and the Depression era, as well as an early example of an African-American state recreational area.

Ruth Nichols, Nashville

SEE: CIVILIAN CONSERVATION CORPS; CONSERVATION; HAMILTON COUNTY

BOONE, DANIEL (1734–1820), is perhaps the best known of the early "long hunters," who ventured across the Appalachian Mountains to hunt and explore in the area of present-day Tennessee and Kentucky. Born on November 2, 1734, in Oley, Berks County, Pennsylvania, he was the sixth child of Squire and Sarah Boone. By 1752 Daniel Boone was living in the Yadkin River Valley in what is now Davie County, North Carolina. He was already recognized as an able hunter and an expert marksman. In 1755 he signed on as a wagoner with General Edward Braddock's expedition to capture Fort Duquesne and was caught up in the rout that followed. While on this expedition, Boone heard his first eyewitness accounts of rich lands and abundant game west of the mountains.

Returning to North Carolina, Boone married Rebecca Bryan in August 1756. Sometime the next year, he began exploring across the Blue Ridge Mountains into what is now upper East Tennessee. Boone recorded his presence in Washington County in 1760, when he carved an inscription on a tree, "Cilled a Bar." He continued to hunt and explore the region for the next several years, sometimes alone and sometimes in the company of other long hunters.

By 1769 Boone had formed an association with North Carolina promoter Richard Henderson, who planned to purchase large regions of the trans-Appalachian land from Indian tribes and create a fourteenth colony. Boone and six others, including his brother Squire, set out in that year to explore Kentucky in preparation for the proposed purchase. Some of his companions soon abandoned the expedition, but Boone persisted, locating and passing through the Cumberland Gap and along the Warrior's Trace into Kentucky. He explored the region until spring 1771. At about this time, Boone relocated his family to the Watauga settlements in upper East Tennessee, perhaps as a more convenient base from which to explore

and gain information about the region where Henderson planned to establish his settlement.

A delay in Henderson's purchase prompted Boone to formulate his own plans for starting a settlement in Kentucky. In September 1773 Boone led a group of settlers, including many of his in-laws, through Cumberland Gap. The expedition was abandoned, however, following an Indian attack in Powell's Valley, Tennessee, in which Boone's son, James, was killed.

The onset of Lord Dunmore's War the next year further stalled Boone's plans for settlement. Unable to continue his explorations of Tennessee and Kentucky, Boone was employed to locate surveying parties in the mountains and beyond and alert them to the war and the consequent threat of Indian attacks. He was commissioned a lieutenant in the militia and later promoted to captain.

By early 1775 Richard Henderson was completing preliminary negotiations with the Cherokees for the purchase of a huge tract of land in what is now Kentucky and Middle Tennessee. Boone played an important role in the purchase. By then he had acquired substantial knowledge of the West, and his association with the project promised to boost interest and sales. More important, Boone was expected to clear a road to the settlements and provide assistance to settlers as they migrated west.

In March 1775 the Cherokees signed a treaty at Sycamore Shoals, which formalized Henderson's Transylvania Purchase. As a condition to the purchase, the Cherokees also agreed to an access corridor known as the "Path Deed," which was to run from the treaty site through the Cumberland Gap and on to the settlements in Kentucky. Boone set out with a company of 30 axmen to start construction even before the treaty was formalized. By early April, the "Wilderness Road" was completed, terminating at the Big Lick near the confluence of Otter Creek and the Kentucky River. Boone's party started construction of a few cabins, but most of their time was spent in locating and claiming the best lands in the vicinity. When Henderson and additional settlers arrived at the site, later known as Boonesborough, the stockade, which was supposed to be completed, had not been started.

The next few years were difficult ones for Boone. His leadership at Boonesborough was critical to the successful defense of the settlement. On one occasion, however, he was forced to surrender a small company of men to Shawnees. Although they eventually escaped, Boone was forced to defend his actions in a court-martial. He was acquitted, but his leadership role was never as strong afterwards. A different problem confronted Boone with regard to his land titles, many of which had come to him as pay for his service to Henderson's land company, and thus were questionable after the Virginia legislature invalidated the

Transylvania Purchase in 1777. Most of his other land claims were either improperly filed, or successfully challenged by new claimants, leaving Boone virtually propertyless. As a result of these difficulties, Boone relocated first to western Virginia and eventually to Missouri, where he died on September 21, 1820.

Michael Toomey, Knoxville College

SUGGESTED READING: John Mack Faragher, *Daniel Boone: The Life and Legend of an American Pioneer* (1992)

SEE: CARTER COUNTY; CUMBERLAND GAP; EXPLO- RATION, EARLY; LAND GRANTS; SYCAMORE SHOALS STATE HISTORIC AREA; TRANSYLVANIA PURCHASE; WASHINGTON COUNTY; WILDERNESS ROAD

BOSTON, RALPH (1939–), former Tennessee State University track star and medalist in the 1960, 1964, and 1968 Olympic games, was born in Laurel, Missis- sippi, on May 9, 1939. Boston attended Tennessee State University, where in 1960 he won the national collegiate long jump title. Named to the United States Olympic team, Boston broke the long jump world record, long held by Jesse Owens, with a jump of 26 feet, 11 1/4 inches in a pre-Olympic competition. He then won the gold medal at that summer's Olympic games. Boston won the silver medal in the long jump at the 1964 games and followed with a bronze medal in the same competition at the 1968 Olympic games. Boston retired from competition in 1968 and entered college administration and coaching, as well as serv- ing as an expert commentator for television coverage of track and field events. He was inducted into the Hall of Fame of the USA Track and Field in 1974 and selected to the U.S. Olympic Hall of Fame in 1985. The Tennessee State University Archives maintains a col- lection covering Boston's years at the Nashville uni- versity as well as his later sterling Olympic career.

Carroll Van West, Middle Tennessee State University

SEE: TENNESSEE STATE UNIVERSITY

BOUDINOT, ELIAS (1802–1839), Cherokee publisher and signer of the removal treaty, was born around 1802 in what is now North Georgia and given the name Buck Oo-watie Galagina—Stag. In 1818 he went to mission school in Cornwall, Connecticut, where he took the name of the Philadelphia philan- thropist who had befriended him, Elias Boudinot. He also married an Anglo woman, Harriet Ruggels Gold. Boudinot completed his education at Andover Theo- logical Seminary and returned to the Cherokees as a missionary in 1826.

In 1828, with funds he raised from missionary groups, Boudinot established the first Cherokee news- paper, the *Phoenix*. A full blood and staunch national- ist, Boudinot adopted an editorial policy endorsing Cherokee sovereignty against Anglo encroachment.

By 1832, however, he realized the inevitability of removal and used the *Phoenix* to call for a public dia- logue. Tribal chief John Ross forbade publication of any pro-removal sentiments and pressured Boudinot to resign as editor. When the Cherokee National Council refused to negotiate a removal treaty, the United States government turned to a small faction of the Cherokees willing to relocate. In 1835 Boudinot, acting as a leader of this faction, signed the Treaty of New Echota authorizing removal. The Cherokee constitution labeled this action as treason, a capital offense.

In an 1837 pamphlet, Boudinot justified the actions of the treaty faction by pointing to the supe- rior power of the United States. He lamented the social and cultural changes brought about by encroaching whites and the consequent removal pres- sures, and believed that removal to the west would protect the Cherokees from further moral harm.

Recent interpretations, however, stress the eco- nomic and political motives of the treaty party. A study of these men's lives reveals that most had been somehow slighted by the elite Cherokees who con- trolled the national government. Some were thwarted in their attempts to gain permits for commercial ven- tures, some failed in elections for national govern- ment, and others owed large debts to powerful elites. Relocation to the West appeared to offer new oppor- tunities for economic and political advancement. Fur- ther, the U.S. government promised generous land grants in the West, payment of their debts, and pro- tection of their property from deep financial losses during removal. While undoubtedly sincere in his moralism, Boudinot also acted as the representative of a rising middle class of Cherokees who sought removal for personal enrichment.

On June 22, 1839, as Boudinot worked in his yard in the Indian Territory, Oklahoma, three Cherokee men approached him soliciting medicine. As he turned to accommodate their request, the men attacked him and hacked him to death. In this way, he was executed for crimes against the Cherokee nation. After Boudinot's execution, the Cherokees underwent seven more years of political turmoil before the bitter factions forged an uneasy peace in 1846.

Katherine M. B. Osburn and Jennifer Kimbro, Tennessee Technological University

SEE: CHEROKEE PHOENIX; ROSS, JOHN; TREATIES

BOWEN, GEORGE THOMAS (1803–1828) was the first prominent scientist recruited to teach in a Ten- nessee college. A Rhode Island native, in 1819 he was admitted to Yale, with sophomore standing. He graduated in 1822, then went to the University of Pennsylvania, earning a M.D. in 1824. As an under- graduate, Bowen became deeply involved in scien- tific research. The Yale faculty gave him total access to the chemistry lab. The medical school faculty was equally supportive. Most of his studies concerned the chemistry of minerals. He published in the leading journals of the era.

Bowen joined the University of Nashville faculty in May 1826. He was 23, with an earned doctorate and nine major publications. Bowen was to teach chemistry, optics, and natural history. The optics course introduced him to a new reality. On December 20, 1826, the Board of Trust of the University of Nashville approved a resolution stating that optics was best taught by a mathematician but that temporarily the Board would allow Dr. Bowen to offer the course. Bowen enraged at least one colleague, perhaps because he used the laboratory mode of instruction in science courses, which was an innovation that may have seemed barbaric to some. Actually, Bowen began a tradition of excellence in science teaching at the University of Nashville.

In Nashville, Bowen studied the chemistry of spring water and obtained a Tennessee meteorite for analysis. Before he could publish results of his studies, he died of tuberculosis on October 25, 1828. While his untimely death makes it difficult to assess his influence on the intellectual history of antebellum Tennessee, it is clear that he brought the laboratory mode of instruction to Tennessee colleges.

James X. Corgan, Austin Peay State University
SUGGESTED READING: James X. Corgan, "George Thomas Bowen (1800–1828)," Wyndham D. Miles and Robert F. Gould, eds., *American Chemists and Chemical Engineers* (1994), II, 27–28

SEE: SCIENCE AND TECHNOLOGY

BOWEN, WILLIAM (1742–1804), Cumberland pioneer, was born in 1742 in Fincastle County, Virginia, and migrated to the Cumberland Valley in 1784. He and his family first lived at Mansker's Station, and next they lived in a log house nearby the station. His two-story Federal style brick home, built in 1787 near Mansker's Creek, stands as a monument to the period. It was the first such brick house in Middle Tennessee.

Both before and during the Revolutionary War, Bowen served under William Russell, a distinguished officer with a noteworthy war record. During the French and Indian War, Bowen was a member of the colonial army of Virginia. With Russell, he fought against Cornstalk, the formidable Shawnee chief. He was part of Russell's Rangers when they aided Fort Watauga, and also fought in Lord Dunmore's War. Bowen rose to the rank of captain by the end of the Revolution.

Bowen married General Russell's daughter, Mary Henley Russell, in 1777. They became the parents of nine children; one of whom, John Bowen, was elected to the U.S. Congress. A grandson, William Bowen Campbell, served as Governor of Tennessee from 1851 to 1853.

William Bowen died in 1804. Before his death, he had witnessed the changes that accompanied the development of the Cumberland country of North Carolina into the State of Tennessee.

Bettye Freudenthal, Mansker Station, Moss Wright Park
SEE: BOWEN-CAMPBELL HOUSE; CAMPBELL, WILLIAM B.; SUMNER COUNTY

BOWEN-CAMPBELL HOUSE. Captain William Bowen brought his family to what is now Sumner County, Tennessee, in 1784. He first built a double log cabin on the bank of Mansker's Creek, before erecting the present brick home in 1787. Now within the present limits of Goodlettsville, the Bowen-Campbell House is the oldest brick house in Middle Tennessee. In 1995 archaeologists uncovered the original brick kiln, also the oldest in the region, 50 feet east of the house. The bricks on the original hall-parlor portion of the house were laid in Flemish bond. Family records indicate brick and stone masons, as well as window glass, were imported from Lexington, Kentucky. The house was restored by The Bowen-Campbell House Association, Inc., in conjunction with the Tennessee Historical Commission, in 1976. Archaeological recovery and rebuilding of the plantation's outbuildings and appurtenances is presently (1996) in progress. Archaeologists discovered the family cemetery in 1995 and restored it in 1996.

Captain Bowen was a veteran of Lord Dunmore's War, the French and Indian War, and the American Revolution. His grandson, Brigadier General William Bowen Campbell, born in the house, served in the Seminole, Mexican, and Civil wars. Campbell served one gubernatorial term, 1851–1853 and three terms as U.S. Congressman, 1837–1843. He was also president of the Bank of Middle Tennessee. Bowen's daughter, Celia, married Barton W. Stone, co-founder of The Disciples of Christ church. Bowen's son, John, served one term in the U.S. Congress, 1813–1815.

Douglas M. Slater, Goodlettsville
SEE: ARCHITECTURE,VERNACULAR DOMESTIC; BOWEN, WILLIAM; STONE, BARTON W.; SUMNER COUNTY

BOY SCOUTS OF AMERICA, TENNESSEE. The Boy Scout program came to both the United States and Tennessee in 1910 only three years after General Robert Baden-Powell founded the program in Great Britain. In 1909 William Perry "Buck" Toms read an article on the scouting movement in Britain and sent two shillings to Baden-Powell for a copy of his book, *Scouting for Boys*. In 1910 Toms formed a Boy Scout organization in Knoxville. The next year, East Tennessee's Troop 1 received a formal charter from John Alexander and the New York City YMCA, which had assumed leadership of the American program.

In Brentwood, the brothers Lawrence and John Hirsig read of the scout movement in the *Literary*

Digest and approached their uncle, Curtis B. Haley, with a request to form a troop. In September 1910 Middle Tennessee's Troop 1 received its charter.

Scout troops appeared all across Tennessee and the United States during the 1910s and 1920s. In 1916 the Boy Scouts of America received a national charter from Congress, thanks in part to the efforts of Tennessee's Senator John K. Shields.

The scout program found its greatest acceptance in towns and cities rather than the rural areas. By 1915 Chattanooga had ten troops with over 200 boys. Troops also were established in Memphis, Franklin, Bell Buckle, and Johnson City, among other towns and cities.

The Tennessee scouting program received a boost in February 1912, when Baden-Powell visited Nashville as part of an American tour. The general shared the stage with the governor at the Ryman Auditorium, which was filled with scouts and community leaders. At that meeting, Baden-Powell declared that "the central idea of the movement is to [get a boy] . . . back close to nature, so that when he comes to be fully grown he will have developed those sturdy qualities so necessary in true manhood."[1]

Though the scouting program has retained its focus on an appreciation of nature and an emphasis on the camping experience, the program has been revised several times over the years. Despite these changes, the requirements that boys advance through levels of ranks by learning various skills and earning merit badges has remained basically the same. The scout program has acquired land throughout the state, including reservations at Boxwell near Nashville and Watts Bar near Knoxville. These reservations anchor the outdoor experience and merit badge work, provide summer camp for boys, and sites for adult training.

The most momentous decade in Tennessee occurred in the 1930s, when the first African-American troops organized, the Cub Scout program for younger boys began, and a troop for blind boys was organized. In the 1940s the scouting program employed the first African-American professional leaders, and during the 1960s racial segregation of the troops ended. In the 1970s the Boy Scouts admitted girls to the Explorers, a program designed for older boys, with an emphasis on gaining professional experience.

Today, the scout program in Tennessee is administered through six regional councils, the Sequoyah (Johnson City), Great Smoky Mountains (Knoxville), Cherokee (Chattanooga), Middle Tennessee (Nashville), West Tennessee (Jackson), and Chickasaw (Memphis). Adult volunteer leadership at the troop level and sponsorship by local organizations, such as churches and businesses, are still the essential ingredients to making scouting work. Since 1910,

over five million boys in Tennessee have experienced scouting and have benefited from a program that continues to promote "patriotism, courage, self-reliance, and kindred virtues" by emphasizing "codes for character development, citizenship training, and mental and physical fitness."

Dan E. Pomeroy, Tennessee State Museum
CITATION:
(1) Wilbur F. Creighton, Jr., and Leland R. Johnson, *Boys Will Be Men: Middle Tennessee Scouting Since 1910* (1983), 22.

BOYD, HENRY ALLEN (1876–1959), founder of the *Nashville Globe,* was the son of Richard Henry Boyd, founder and manager of the National Baptist Publishing Board. As the son of one of Nashville's most prominent black businessmen and public figures, Boyd learned early the importance of both the political and economic struggle to create and protect Nashville's black "world-within-a-world." In 1906 Henry Allen Boyd and three other local businessmen founded the *Nashville Globe,* and later the Globe Publishing Company. Boyd assumed daily editorial charge of the paper, while his father's money (and frequent advertisements for National Baptist Publishing Board literature) helped to bankroll the paper. The *Globe* provided an invaluable record of Nashville's black community. By the late 1920s some 20 percent of the city's African-American families subscribed to the *Globe.* The newspaper relentlessly advertised and promoted black businesses. From the largest undertakers to the smallest barbershops, Boyd ceaselessly advanced the idea that business enterprise offered the best mechanism to advance "the race." The *Globe*'s motto was "Nashville Offers Opportunity." And, for Henry Allen Boyd, it did.

In addition to managing the Globe Publishing Company, Boyd also owned significant stock in the One-Cent Savings Bank (later the Citizens Savings Bank), a black-owned and managed enterprise that practiced fiscal conservatism to protect small depositors and directed black capital into fruitful enterprises. Boyd also remained as politically active as the Jim Crow era would permit and served as the African-American representative on various city boards.

Through the 1910s and 1920s, Boyd maintained the relatively aggressive editorial policy the paper originally assumed during a streetcar boycott of 1905–1906. Although the *Globe* operated primarily for the promotion of the black entrepreneurial spirit, the paper also publicized police abuses and provided a forum for local black protest. It demanded that more African Americans be added to the Fisk University faculty and protested the 1913 change from ward-based elections to at-large city elections, a move which diluted the black vote. A stalwart in local Republican party politics, Boyd was instrumental in obtaining land grant money for what later became

Tennessee State University. From the pages of his newspaper, he called attention to the pittance African Americans received for teacher education through the Peabody Fund and directed a campaign to build a black YMCA.

After the death of his father in 1922, Henry Boyd continued the elder Boyd's successful work in religious publishing. He produced the *National Jubilee Melody Song Book,* one of the first African-American religious hymnals, which set to notation the nineteenth century slave spirituals.

After a long and productive career, Henry Allen Boyd died in 1959, leaving behind a legacy of public service and a business tradition to the Nashville African-American community.

Paul Harvey, University of Colorado, Colorado Springs
SEE: BOYD, RICHARD H.; NASHVILLE GLOBE; NATIONAL BAPTIST PUBLISHING BOARD

BOYD, JOHN W. (ca. 1841–post 1885), was one of the first African Americans to serve in the Tennessee General Assembly. Born in Georgia to Jackson and Martha Boyd in ca. 1841, John grew up probably in both Georgia and Tennessee. His family is documented in the 1870 census as living in Tipton County. Boyd married Martha Dogette of Mason, Tipton County, and they had at least five children. An attorney in Tipton County during the Reconstruction era, Boyd was a member of the Republican party and his political career began in 1878, when he was elected as magistrate of the 9th Civil District of Tipton County. He served as a member of the Tennessee House of Representatives from 1881 to 1885. He was an effective spokesman for African-American rights in a chamber increasingly dominated by the Bourbon Democrats, who sought to enhance their party's ascendency by denying basic civil rights to black Tennesseans. Boyd died at an undetermined date and is buried in Magnolia Cemetery at Mason.

Carroll Van West, Middle Tennessee State University
SEE: RECONSTRUCTION; TIPTON COUNTY

BOYD, RICHARD HENRY (1855–1922), a founder of both the National Baptist Convention and the National Baptist Publishing Board, was born in Texas late in the antebellum era. After receiving an education at Bishop College, an institution for black Baptist men supported by white northern Baptists, in Marshall, Texas, Boyd moved to Nashville in the mid-1890s and became instrumental in the formation and early years of the National Baptist Convention. In 1896, Boyd and a group of nine other men chartered the National Baptist Publishing Board. Over the next 25 years it grew into the nation's largest African-American publishing enterprise. Boyd's company supplied black churches with religious literature, church pews, church fans, and a variety of other items for church life. The Board and its subsidiary agencies employed over 110 African-American workers, making it a substantial black enterprise. Boyd also either started or supported the National Negro Doll Company, the first business to market black dolls to black consumers; the One-Cent Savings Bank, a financial institution, which met the needs of small African-American depositors; the Globe Publishing Company, which published the *Nashville Globe,* the city's black newspaper; the *National Baptist Union-Review,* an African-American denominational newspaper; and the Home Mission Board of the National Baptist Convention, which distributed religious literature and supported missionary efforts.

As vice-president of the National Negro Business League, Boyd represented the trend in African-American thought that supported Booker T. Washington's philosophy of "industrial education" and emphasized the acquisition of property and economic independence. At the same time, as early as the 1890s, Boyd warned his fellow black Tennesseans that whites intended to turn the clock back on black civil rights. When Nashville began enforcing segregated street cars in the 1900s, Boyd and fellow ministers and businessmen supported a boycott of the public transportation, thus representing the tradition of political protest. Meanwhile, they attempted to counter segregation by forming the Union Transportation Company, a black-owned streetcar franchise. The boycott and the company eventually failed, but Boyd cemented his reputation as a "race man" through his work in fighting Jim Crow.

In the last decades of his life, Boyd became involved with an ugly controversy over the independence of his major business, the National Baptist Publishing Board. In 1915 Boyd and the forces affiliated with him split from the National Baptist Convention over this issue and formed the National Baptist Convention of America. Boyd's latter years were spent in fighting internal denominational battles. But this did not prevent him from continuing to comment on issues of the day, including the beginnings of the great African-American migration out of the South during World War I. Boyd died in 1922, but through the legacy of the National Baptist Publishing Board his influence lives on.

Paul Harvey, University of Colorado, Colorado Springs
SUGGESTED READING: Paul Harvey, "'The Holy Spirit Come to Us . . . Richard H. Boyd and Black Religious Activism in Nashville," Carroll Van West, ed., *Tennessee History: the Land, the People, and the Culture* (1998), 270–286
SEE: BOYD, HENRY A.; NASHVILLE GLOBE; NATIONAL BAPTIST PUBLISHING BOARD

BOYLE, VIRGINIA FRAZER (1863–1938) acquired the title "Poet Laureate of the Confederacy" when she was ten years old. On a visit to the Gulf Coast in 1873, she read a poem to Jefferson Davis. According to the story, he crowned her with a wreath of jessamine and proclaimed her to be "poet laureate of the Confederacy."

Boyle was born in Chattanooga on February 14, 1863, to Charles Wesley and Letitia Austin Frazer. After the Civil War, the family moved to Memphis, where her father practiced law. Boyle broke tradition by reading law in her father's office and researching cases for him.

Her literary career began when Boyle was 14 and *Harper's Weekly* accepted a poem she wrote. Her grandmother insisted she return the $25 check, saying no gentlewoman would accept money for work. They compromised by giving the money to charity.

Boyle married attorney Thomas Raymond Boyle in 1894. Her first published prose was "Hoodoo Tales," southern dialect stories. Other works included a 1905 novel, *Serena,* and a 1906 poetry collection, *Love Songs and Bugle Calls.* Each year she wrote an ode to the Confederate dead, and in 1910 the United Confederate Veterans made the title given to her by Jefferson Davis official.

World War I brought out her patriotic fervor, and her poems "Union" and "Christmas in Argonne" were translated into several languages. France honored her for her services to the Red Cross, the Women's Committee on National Defense, and the Writer's Bureau on Public Information. *Canticle, A Song of Memphis* was set to music and performed by massed choirs in 1919. She died on December 13, 1938, while working on a novel about Hernando De Soto.

Perre Magness, Memphis

SEE: LITERATURE; UNITED CONFEDERATE VETERANS ASSOCIATION

BRABSON, REESE BOWEN (1817–1863), attorney, state legislator, and U.S. Congressman, was born at Brabson's Ferry, Knox County, on September 16, 1817. He graduated from Maryville College and studied law at Dandridge, in Jefferson County. In 1844 he married Sarah Maria Keith, daughter of Judge Charles F. and Elizabeth D. (Hale) Keith, of McMinn County; their six children were John Bowen, Ada, Maria, Catherine, Mary, and Rose.

Settling in Chattanooga in 1845, Brabson practiced law in partnership with James A. Whiteside, one of the city's founding fathers. Brabson entered politics in 1848, serving the Whig party as elector on Zachary Taylor's presidential ticket. In 1851 Hamilton County elected Brabson to the Tennessee General Assembly and in 1859 to the U.S. House of Representatives.

Subsequently, responding to threats of secession, Brabson warned his southern peers in Congress against destroying their constitutional protections. A pro-Union slaveholder, Brabson remained a steadfast supporter of the federal government. When Tennessee seceded, he returned to his large, fashionable residence at Chattanooga, known as "Brabson Mansion."

Brabson refused to take up arms against either side, though each offered him a military commission. In 1862, against public opinion, he ably defended James J. Andrews, Union operative, tried for stealing a locomotive, the *General,* and attempting to destroy the rail artery between Chattanooga and Atlanta. Contrarily, Brabson gave aid to Confederate war casualties, opening his commodious house to the wounded following the Battle of Stones River.

As the war he hated continued around him, Brabson succumbed to typhoid, dying at home on August 16, 1863. He was buried at Citizens Cemetery, the location of his unmarked grave now unknown. The old mansion, still referred to as the "Brabson House," though altered extensively by subsequent owners, remains standing at 407 East Fifth Street.

Gary C. Jenkins, Chattanooga

SEE: CHATTANOOGA; CIVIL WAR

BRADFORD, ROARK (1896–1948), novelist, short story writer, and journalist, was born in Lauderdale County, where he was raised on a cotton plantation in the Nankipoo-Knob Creek area. The African Americans who worked the farm and with whom he attended church strongly influenced him. He closely observed their lives and drew on his early experiences to create his fiction.

Bradford received his education at home, in local public schools, and at the University of California, where he earned an LL.B. degree shortly before the United States entered World War I. He volunteered for military service and was posted as an artillery officer to the Panama Canal Zone; afterwards he taught military science at a Mississippi college. Following his discharge in 1920, Bradford took a series of reporting jobs in Georgia and Louisiana and eventually became Sunday editor for the New Orleans *Times-Picayune.* He left newspaper work in 1926 to devote himself to writing.

As a writer, Bradford pursued a lifelong interest in the culture and language of southern African Americans. He both admired black culture and was puzzled by it, and his prose reflects this conflict. From his studies of black speech, Bradford observed that African Americans created a beautiful and rhythmic language and he deeply appreciated black music for its expressive, creative character.

African-American religion remained at the heart of Bradford's fiction. Drawing on childhood memories and the influence of local African-American ministers, Bradford created a body of literature that pitted a good-natured God against an equally good-natured Satan. One of his first stories, "Child of God," published in *Harper's,* won an O. Henry Memorial Award in 1927. He followed that success with *Ol' Man Adam an' His Chillun* (1928), which playwright Marc Connelly adapted into a 1930 smash-hit biblical fantasy, "The Green Pastures." The play ran 73 weeks in New York and won a Pulitzer Prize.

Bradford's stories and novels sold well among contemporary readers, but today are considered racist and sentimental. Bradford's decline in popularity coincided with the Harlem Renaissance, which gave a lasting black voice to black literature. In 1946 he accepted a position in the English department at Tulane University, which was just then launching an innovative program for creative writing. Bradford died in New Orleans in 1948 from an illness he contracted during World War II while on active duty in Africa.

Susan L. Gordon, Tennessee Historical Society
SEE: LAUDERDALE COUNTY; LITERATURE

BRADLEY ACADEMY is the name given to the first school in Murfreesboro, and to subsequent school buildings located on property donated by the Murfree family in 1811. Named for a principal, students attending Bradley Academy in its early years included John Bell and James K. Polk.

A second Bradley Academy, a substantial brick building erected in the 1830s, was later used as a hospital during the Civil War. Though badly damaged, Bradley reopened as a school for African Americans in the 1880s. In 1917 construction began on a modern facility designed by the Knoxville firm of Manley and Young. This building, the first black high school in the county, also became the social and cultural center for the black community and, in the 1920s, was the site of a health clinic, supported by the Commonwealth Fund.

Bradley maintained strong academic, domestic science, and sports programs in addition to an orchestra and glee club. After Holloway High School was built in 1928, Bradley remained an elementary and junior high school until desegregation in the 1960s. At that time the building became offices and storage for Murfreesboro City Schools.

Under the auspices of the City of Murfreesboro and the Bradley Academy Historical Association (formed in 1990), and with funds from the United States Department of Housing and Urban Development, the Christy-Houston Foundation, the State of Tennessee, the MTSU Center for Historic Preservation, and private donations, the building was restored as a cultural/heritage center in 1995–97.

Caneta Skelley Hankins, Middle Tennessee State University
SEE: BELL, JOHN; CENTER FOR HISTORIC PRESERVATION;
COMMONWEALTH FUND; MURFREESBORO; POLK, JAMES K.

BRADLEY COUNTY, located in southeast Tennessee, was carved out of the Ocoee District, which had been part of the Cherokee Nation. Today, one of the top tourist sites in Tennessee is Red Clay State Historical Area, an interpretative center for the Cherokee

removal known as the Trail of Tears. The Cherokees consider the park, located on the southern end of Bradley County, sacred ground. In the 1830s Red Clay became the last capital of the Cherokees as they fought removal by appealing to the U.S. President and Congress and bringing suits in the federal courts. Further north is Rattlesnake Springs, the gathering point for the Cherokees as they left on their journey to Oklahoma. The Cleveland Public Library Historical Branch contains a collection of material on the Cherokee Indians.

The Tennessee General Assembly created Bradley County in February 1836. Its name honored Colonel Edward Bradley, a Revolutionary War veteran who served with Andrew Jackson during the War of 1812. Cleveland was designated the county seat and named for Colonel Benjamin Cleveland, a Revolutionary War hero from North Carolina, who received recognition for his exploits at the Battle of Kings Mountain. Today, Cleveland ranks eleventh in size among cities and towns in Tennessee.

Bradley County contains several other towns and communities, although the expanding size and economic domination of Cleveland has reduced the identity of some communities. The most notable is Charleston, which is located on the banks of the Hiwassee River. In 1819 Charleston, the "gateway to Indian country," provided the site for the Cherokee Agency, or Hiwassee Agency, which was the home of U.S. Agents of Cherokee Affairs. Among the men who served as Cherokee Agents were a number of notable Tennesseans, including Return Jonathan Meigs, Hugh Montgomery, and Joseph McMinn. In addition, Lewis Ross, brother of the Cherokee Chief John Ross, established a store at the agency, which remained in operation until the removal in 1838.

Today, Charleston is the home of Bowaters, a large papermill plant, and Olin Chemical, which manufactures swimming pool products. The community has a post office, an elementary school, and a high school. Although small in size, Charleston remains a vital link to Bradley County's past and provides resources and employment for the future. Other Bradley County communities include Black Fox, Blue Springs, Buck's Pocket, Chatata Valley, Eureka, Flint Springs, Georgetown, Hopewell, McDonald, Prospect, Tasso, Taylors, Valley View, and White Oak.

Bradley County boasts a thriving and diversified economy, with over 190 industries, including 11 Fortune 500 companies and another five listed in the "Top 1000." The largest manufacturing segment is in the production of stoves. Magic Chef, Hardwick, and Brown Stove dominated production until recently, when Maytag took over the local manufacturing; it is now the largest employer in Bradley County. A dynamic retail industry serves more than 150,000 shoppers. In addition, small retail and service businesses continue to grow and prosper. Finally, tourism represents a growing industry in Bradley County, as travelers visit historical and recreational sites. The county has proposed a regional museum to complement this increasing tourist activity.

Education has always played an important role in Bradley County. In 1920 the county had six high schools and 53 elementary schools. Today, both the Bradley County and Cleveland City School systems have received recognition for the outstanding work of students and teachers. Many students continue their education in one of two local colleges. Lee University, one of the fastest growing Christian schools in the United States, has established a commendable academic reputation, producing a number of medical doctors, teachers, and ministers. Cleveland State Community College is a two-year college that operates under the supervision of the Tennessee Board of Regents. It offers outstanding programs in criminal justice and nursing.

Religion has played an important role in Bradley County's history. Three denominations maintain their headquarters in the county: the Church of God, the Church of God of Prophecy, and the Church of God Jerusalem Acres. The Church of God is the third largest Pentecostal denomination in the world, behind the Church of God in Christ and the Assembly of God.

Bradley County lives up the to state's moniker "the Volunteer State," and a number of men and women served with distinction in the military conflicts of the nation. Soldiers from Bradley County fought on both sides of the Civil War, and Abraham Lincoln considered taking and holding the railroad near Cleveland a key to fighting in the western theater. The bridge at Charleston was burned several times during the course of the war. Paul Huff, a hometown hero born and raised in Bradley County, received the Congressional Medal of Honor for his actions in World War II.

Nestled in the foothills of the Appalachian Mountains, Bradley County is an ideal place to live, work, and play. With a low tax rate, a high employment rate, proximity to a major metropolitan area, the county offers opportunities for growth and expansion. A seasonal climate, access to most transportation systems, and a diversified economy of industry, commerce, and agriculture contribute to the progressive atmosphere of Bradley County.

John C. Bowman, Cleveland

SEE: CHURCH OF GOD; CHURCH OF GOD OF PROPHECY; COMMUNITY COLLEGES; HARDWICK STOVE COMPANY; LEE UNIVERSITY; MAGIC CHEF; MCMINN, JOSEPH; MEIGS, RETURN J.; RATTLESNAKE SPRINGS ; RED CLAY STATE HISTORIC PARK; TRAIL OF TEARS; TREATIES

BRADLEY, OWEN (1915–1998), musician and producer, was one of the pioneers of the Nashville recording industry and a developer of the Nashville Sound. Born in Westmoreland, Sumner County, Bradley began his musical career early by assembling musical groups to play at private parties. The Owen Bradley Orchestra, once considered the premier Nashville dance band, played from 1940 to 1964.

Beginning in 1935, Bradley worked for WSM radio, first as a spot man and later as pianist and organist. By 1948 he was serving as Musical Director, coordinating personnel, planning arrangements, and leading the orchestra. Meanwhile, Owen started working with Paul Cohen, head of the country division of Decca Records. While serving as his apprentice, Bradley learned to produce records.

In 1958 Owen left WSM to open the Nashville Division of Decca Records, serving as Vice President. When Decca and MCA merged their companies in the mid-1960s, Owen continued in this position. Before retiring from MCA in 1976, he produced such country artists as Loretta Lynn, Conway Twitty, Kitty Wells, and Patsy Cline. Like his chief rival, Chet Atkins of RCA, Bradley sought to broaden the sound of country music to appeal to larger audiences. He utilized the traditional country sound in artists like Loretta Lynn, while in other artists like Patsy Cline, he expanded the sound to incorporate non-traditional accompaniments such as piano and soft strings.

In the early 1950s Owen and his brother Harold formed Bradley's Film Studio, first occupying a building near downtown and later a rented building in Hillsboro Village. In 1954 the brothers purchased a house on 16th Avenue South, the area which would become Music Row. In an attached Quonset hut, they opened a recording studio. In it they recorded such mega-hits as Patsy Cline's *I Fall To Pieces* and Marty Robbins's *El Paso*. The Bradleys sold the studio to Columbia Records in 1962. They constructed a new studio, Bradley's Barn, in Wilson County, and continued to turn out the hits.

Bradley was inducted into the Country Music Hall of Fame in 1974 and continued working as an MCA producer until retiring in the early 1980s. As his health permitted, he completed freelance studio projects, such as k.d. lang's *Shadowland* album (1988).

Anne-Leslie Owens, Tennessee Historical Society

SEE: CLINE, PATSY; LYNN, LORETTA; MUSIC; RECORDING INDUSTRY, NASHVILLE; WELLS, KITTTY; WSM

BRAGG, BRAXTON (1817–1876), controversial commander of the Army of Tennessee from June 1862 to December 1863, was born in Warrenton, North Carolina, on March 21, 1817. He attended West Point and graduated fifth in the class of 1837. Bragg fought against the Seminoles and served with distinction in the Mexican War. He resigned his commission in 1856 to become proprietor of a sugar plantation in Louisiana. When Louisiana seceded in January 1861,

Bragg served first as commander of state forces and then as a brigadier general in the Confederate army. First assigned to Pensacola, Bragg labored to turn the troops there into disciplined soldiers. His friend Jefferson Davis rewarded Bragg by promoting him to major general in March 1861.

In February 1862 Bragg joined Albert Sidney Johnston's army in northern Mississippi. He served as a corps commander at Shiloh, spending several hours on April 6 directing a number of the piecemeal assaults against the Hornets' Nest. Later that same month, Bragg received an appointment to full general. When General P.G.T. Beauregard took an unauthorized sick leave, President Jefferson Davis replaced him as army commander with Bragg.

In his early months as commander, Bragg labored energetically to improve discipline and organization. He shifted troops from Tupelo to Chattanooga in the spring of 1862 and launched an invasion of Kentucky that summer. After a hard-fought, but inconclusive battle at Perryville, Bragg's army retreated back into Tennessee. Bragg attacked Federal forces near Murfreesboro along the Stones River on December 31, 1862, but failed to dislodge them in several days of combat and withdrew to the southeast.

After being maneuvered out of Chattanooga in September 1863, Bragg counterattacked at Chickamauga in a fierce two-day battle and drove the Union forces back into the city. He squandered the victory by quarreling with his subordinates while the Federals brought Ulysses S. Grant and heavy reinforcements to Tennessee. Thus strengthened, the Union army delivered a humiliating defeat at Lookout Mountain and Missionary Ridge that compelled Bragg to tender his resignation. Davis accepted, but softened the blow by summoning Bragg to Richmond to serve as his chief military advisor. Bragg returned to field command in late 1864 in North Carolina, and fought in the closing weeks of the war at both Kinston and Bentonville. Following the war, Bragg served as chief engineer for the state of Alabama before relocating to Galveston, Texas, where he died on September 27, 1876.

During his Civil War career, Bragg exhibited significant talent as an administrator, an appetite for hard work, and unstinting devotion to the Confederacy. These positive traits paled in comparison to his defects, which were exacerbated by chronic ill health. As an army commander, Bragg failed to inspire loyalty among many of his subordinates or the rank and file. He had difficulty adapting to unforeseen circumstances and exhibited little genius for battlefield tactics. Worst of all, Bragg fought many of his subalterns with as much zeal as he did the enemy. He occasionally distrusted men in the ranks; before Shiloh, he endorsed his wife's misgivings about the fighting qualities of Tennesseans. Bragg's relations with his commanders were particularly stormy. His tenure ultimately fractured the Army of Tennessee, which splintered into two factions aligned largely on the basis of loyalty to Bragg. Bragg's most steadfast supporters included William B. Bate and Alexander P. Stewart, while he clashed with Benjamin F. Cheatham, Nathan Bedford Forrest, and John McCowan. In fairness to Bragg, it should be noted that Leonidas Polk, William J. Hardee, Cheatham, and numerous other officers rebelled against Bragg's authority and intrigued against him. Dissident generals went so far as to petition Davis to remove Bragg from command.

Bragg contributed mightily to the enmity by his tactlessness, inflexibility, and vindictiveness. He goaded men he viewed as enemies and failed to acknowledge his own shortcomings. His persistent attempts to shift the blame for misfortunes onto the shoulders of his subordinates created deep resentment. The ongoing infighting between Bragg and his officers damaged army morale and cohesiveness; it likewise adversely affected army operations as the Confederates vainly sought to retain Middle and East Tennessee. Although Jefferson Davis sustained Bragg until after the Missionary Ridge debacle, the damage done by retaining Bragg as army commander undoubtedly contributed to Confederate defeat in the West.

Christopher Losson, St. Joseph, Missouri

SUGGESTED READING: Grady McWhiney, *Braxton Bragg and Confederate Defeat* (1969)

SEE: ARMY OF TENNESSEE; CHEATHAM, BENJAMIN F.; CHICKAMAUGA AND CHATTANOOGA, BATTLES OF; POLK, LEONIDAS; SHILOH, BATTLE OF; STEWART, ALEXANDER P.; STONES RIVER, BATTLE OF; TULLAHOMA CAMPAIGN

BRAINERD MISSION, a multi-acre mission school situated on Chickamauga Creek near present-day Chattanooga and named for eighteenth-century missionary David Brainerd, was the largest institution of its type among the Eastern Cherokees. The Boston-based American Board of Commissioners for Foreign Missions (ABCFM) received the Cherokees' approval to establish the school in October 1816, and began classes there the following March. During its two decades of operation Brainerd enrolled more than 300 male and female Cherokee students and employed 40 ministers and teachers. While the institution was a frequent source of conflict between the Cherokees and the Board, most students acquired at least basic proficiency in reading and writing, and several staff members provided Cherokee leaders with valuable political advice and assistance during the Removal crisis.

The Congregationalist and Presbyterian missionary founders, including Daniel Butrick, Ard Hoyt, and Cyrus Kingsbury, assumed that proper education for Indian children included instilling them with Christian religious precepts and Anglo-American work habits. Accordingly, they designed a curriculum which included Bible study, hymns, prayer, and vocational training (stock-raising, gardening, smithing, and carpentry for boys; domestic chores, spinning, and weaving for girls) as well as the three Rs, grammar, and geography. Lessons followed the Lancastrian plan, wherein older and more accomplished students helped instruct their younger counterparts. Rigorous discipline included corporal punishment for infractions of the school's code of behavior.

The Brainerd missionaries enjoyed some success as teachers, helping at least one hundred students achieve high levels of proficiency in English and reading, and sending several young Cherokee men to the ABCFM's Foreign Mission School in Connecticut for further instruction. Few students joined the mission's Congregational church, however, and many parents objected to the missionaries' use of corporal punishment and the agricultural chores required of male students—unsuitable work for men, according to Cherokee norms. Moreover, the missionaries' pronounced bias in favor of bicultural students alienated full blood children and their parents. Consequently, the number of fullblooded Cherokees at Brainerd fell by one-third between 1821 and 1825.

The ABCFM initially charged students $1 per week for tuition and board, but eliminated these charges in 1819 to boost enrollment. Funding for Brainerd and for the Board's seven other mission stations in Cherokee territory came from private contributions and from the U.S. government, which gave the ABCFM a large ($1,000–2,000) annual grant. Using these funds, the Brainerd missionaries provided their students with free instruction, board, and clothing, and financed the construction of an extensive mission complex, which included separate boys' and girls' quarters and schoolhouses, housing for the missionaries and other instructors, a church, two mills, and a garden. In 1824 Cherokee leaders expressed concern over Brainerd's rapid expansion and asked the National Council to prohibit further hiring by Superintendent William Chamberlain, to which the Council agreed. Tension between the Cherokee government and the Board missionaries subsided in the late 1820s, however, as the two groups joined forces to resist Removal.

In March 1830 a fire destroyed much of the central part of the mission, and classes and religious services could not resume for two years. In the mid-1830s Brainerd became a refuge for missionaries and Cherokee congregants driven from the ABCFM's smaller stations in Georgia; by 1837 the Church of Christ of Brainerd included a record 110 members. The expulsion of the Cherokees from the southeast the following year forced the ABCFM to permanently abandon the site. Brainerd's staff held their final religious services in August 1838.

David A. Nichols, University of Kentucky
SUGGESTED READINGS: William McLoughlin, *Cherokees and Missionaries* (1984); Robert Sparks Walker, *Torchlights to the Cherokees* (1931)
SEE: HAMILTON COUNTY; TRAIL OF TEARS

BRANSON, LLOYD (1854–1925), artist, was born in Union County in 1854 and spent his life in the Knoxville area. In 1871, at age 17, he exhibited at the East Tennessee Division Fair and received favorable notice. As a result, Branson moved to New York in 1873 to study at the National Academy of Design, where he won a first prize in 1875. That allowed him to travel to Europe, but in 1876 he was back in Knoxville.

The exposure to the art schools and art movements in Europe gave Branson an advantage over the other regional artists working in Knoxville in the 1870s and 1880s. In 1885 he won a medal at the Cotton States Exposition in Atlanta. In 1910 Branson won a gold medal at Knoxville's Appalachian Exposition for *Hauling Marble*. That painting is now in the McClung Museum at the University of Tennessee. His interest in regional history resulted in a number of paintings, including the historical paintings of the *Gathering of the Overmountain Men at Sycamore Shoals* and the *Sheep Shearing* incident, where John Sevier met his future wife. The Tennessee State Museum has these two paintings and a number of portraits by Branson, including those of John Haywood, J.G.M. Ramsey, John L. Cox, James B. Frazier, D.L. Lansden, Dewitt Clinton Senter, Peter Turney, Alvin C. York, Montgomery Stuart, Hester Thompson Stuart, and James Allen Smith.

In a partnership with Frank McCrary from 1885 to 1903, Branson became a leader in the East Tennessee arts community. Branson died on June 12, 1925. His wife Mollie Wilson Branson survived him until 1951.

James A. Hoobler, Tennessee State Museum
SEE: APPALACHIAN EXPOSITION OF 1910; ART; TENNESSEE HISTORICAL SOCIETY; UNION COUNTY

BREWER, CARSON (1920–), journalist and conservationist, was born in Hancock County, the son of a rural postmaster. Brewer attended Maryville College (1939–1941) before entering military service during World War II. He served in the European Theater and returned to college at the University of Tennessee (1945–1946); illness interrupted his studies and he never received a degree. Brewer joined the *Knoxville News-Sentinel* staff in 1945 and covered the federal beat, city hall, and the courthouse, among other assignments during his 40 years with the paper.

In 1948 Brewer met Alberta Trulock, who arrived in Knoxville to open the city's United Press Bureau. A respected journalist in her own right, Alberta Trulock blazed new trails for women in journalism,

becoming, among other things, the first female journalist admitted to the Vanderbilt University press
box. In 1949 Carson and Alberta married and moved
to Norris, Tennessee, where they still live in their
"honeymoon" house. They are the parents of one son,
Carson T. "Kit" Brewer, Jr.

In the 1950s, Brewer began writing a weekly
column, that soon expanded to three columns per
week. A self-described meanderer, Brewer wrote on a
variety of regional subjects, including columns on
sourwood honey, Appalachian autumns, and folklore. Brewer soon built a reputation as a conservationist, an everyman's guide to an appreciation of the
beauty and fragility of the region's natural resources.
He proved to be a tireless supporter of Knoxville's
annual Dogwood Arts Festival.

Brewer is the author of *Hiking in the Great Smokies,
A Wonderment of Mountains,* and *Valley So Wild: A Folk
History,* co-authored with his wife. Brewer has
received numerous awards for his work, including
the 1974 Golden Press Card award from the East Tennessee Chapter of the Society of Professional Journalists, Sigma Delta Chi; the 1978 best local column
award from United Press International for a column
on sourwood honey; and the 1984 winner of the Z.
Cartter Patten Award of the Tennessee Conservation
League for his contributions to conservation. In the
Knoxville News-Sentinel of February 3, 1985, TVA
Chairman Charles H. Dean, Jr., called Brewer's 1981
News-Sentinel series "TVA, a Child of Controversy,"
"one of the most valuable sources for future historians who want to understand the events of TVA's first
half century." The University of Tennessee College of
Communications awards a scholarship in Brewer's
name. Retired from the *News-Sentinel* in 1985, Brewer
continues his writing and interest in conservation.

Connie L. Lester, Tennessee Historical Society
SEE: CONSERVATION; KNOXVILLE NEWS-SENTINEL

BRILEY, BEVERLY (1914–1980), first mayor of the
Metropolitan Government of Nashville and Davidson County (1963–1975), was born in Nashville in
1914. Briley grew up in East Nashville, attended Vanderbilt University and Cumberland Law School, and
in 1932 became the youngest Tennessean ever admitted to the bar. Following his service in the Navy
during World War II, he ran successfully for election
as county judge in 1946 on the "G.I. Joe" ticket, which
was identified with reform of local government.

Briley proved to be a gifted politician and effective reformer. He became a champion of metropolitan government, and in 1963 won election against
Ben West as Metropolitan Nashville's first mayor.
Briley was re-elected in 1967 and 1971, retiring in
1975. Briley's term of service as mayor encompassed
a period of rapid growth in the city's population and
economy, fueled in part by generous federal grants.
Under Briley's leadership, Nashville experienced
desegregation and political polarization. Briley followed his mostly white suburban constituency and
moved to the political right. In 1968 he defected from
the Democratic party by endorsing Richard Nixon as
president. Briley died five years after leaving office,
at the age of 66.

Don H. Doyle, Vanderbilt University
SEE: DAVIDSON COUNTY; NASHVILLE

BRISTOL MOTOR SPEEDWAY (formerly Bristol
International Raceway) is a favorite track of
NASCAR fans across the nation. Its two annual Winston Cup events (currently the Food City 500 in April
and the Goody's 500 in August) attract the largest

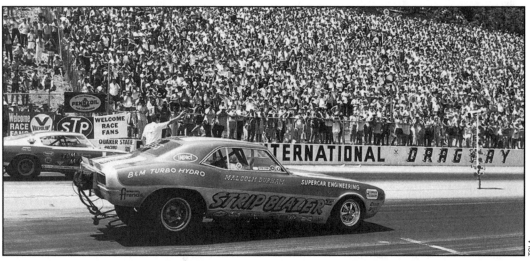

Bristol International Dragway, 1969.

crowds of any sporting events in the state of Tennessee. The "World's Fastest Half Mile" (actually .5333 mile) is legendary for its tight, competitive races and for the deafening roar reverberating off the surrounding hills as the stock cars circle the track.

Bristol entrepreneur Larry Carrier built the track in 1961 as a perfect half-mile oval with 22 degree banking in the turns. The original facility had a seating capacity of over 20,000, making it one of the larger tracks at a time when most NASCAR Grand National (now Winston Cup) venues could accommodate fewer than 10,000 fans. Carrier also built a football field in the infield of the track in hopes of attracting NFL preseason games. Johnny Allen won the first Grand National race at Bristol driving in relief of Jack Smith, who received official credit for the first victory.

In 1969 the track was reconfigured to its current .533 mile length and the banking on the turns was increased to 30 degrees, with 16 degrees banking in the straights, the steepest banking in Winston Cup racing. Seating capacity was also expanded to over 30,000. The changes on the track dramatically boosted top qualifying speeds from 88.669 mph in the spring race of 1969 to 103.432 mph in the summer race on the reconfigured track. Initially, the higher speeds caused numerous wrecks and mechanical failures, and only ten out of 32 cars completed the first race. After the race, NASCAR superstar Richard Petty complained: "If you ask me, they ruined a good race track. There's not enough room for the speeds we're running."[1] The drivers and mechanics soon adjusted to the higher speeds, however, and the attrition rate declined, although Bristol is still known as a track which combines the high speeds of the superspeedways with the rough-and-tumble bumping—"swapping paint" in NASCAR parlance—of the short tracks. The race qualifying record now stands at 125.093 mph set by Mark Martin in 1995. Tennessean Darrell Waltrip holds the record for most Winston Cup victories at the track with 12, including seven consecutive races between 1981 and 1985.

Bruton Smith's Speedway Motorsports, Inc.—owners of Charlotte Motor Speedway, Texas Motor Speedway, Sears Point Raceway, and Atlanta Motor Speedway—bought the track from Carrier in 1996. Speedway Motorsports has poured millions of dollars into the facility, making Bristol the largest and one of the most modern sporting venues in the state. Seating capacity was enlarged from 71,000 to over 130,000—including 55 skybox suites and 17 corporate suites—and mountains were bulldozed to improve accessibility to the facility. Bristol Motor Speedway now annually hosts two Winston Cup races, two Busch Grand National races, and one race each in the Craftsman Truck Series, the Slim Jim/All Pro Series, and the Goody's Dash Series.

Dan Pierce, Western Carolina University
CITATION:
(1) Greg Fielden, *Forty Years of Stock Car Racing*, Vol. 3, *Big Bucks and Boycotts, 1965–1971* (1989), 245.

BRISTOL SESSIONS. See MUSIC; RECORDING INDUSTRY; SULLIVAN COUNTY

BROCK CANDY COMPANY dates to 1906, when William Emerson Brock, a traveling sales representative with the R.J. Reynolds Tobacco Company, purchased the Trigg Candy Company of Chattanooga. Three years later, he reincorporated the company as Brock Candy Company. By the time of his death in 1950, Brock had built his family-run company into one of the largest candy companies in the United States.

Brock Candy initially produced penny candies, including southern favorites like peanut brittle and fudge, but in the 1920s it expanded production to include marshmallow and jelly candies. In the 1930s Brock Candy introduced Chocolate Covered Cherries, which quickly became a Christmas favorite. At the same time, Brock found innovative ways to deal with the problems presented by the Depression. When the bank moratorium of 1933 made it impossible for Brock workers to cash their paychecks, Brock collected his daily receipts from local retailers of his candies and paid his employees in cash.

World War II also presented challenges in the form of rationing of sugar and other supplies needed in the candy-making business. Utilizing the abundant supplies of corn syrup and peanuts, the company introduced the Brock Bar, a coated peanut roll. W.E. Brock stepped down as president in 1945, and became chairman of the board. By 1950, the company encompassed an entire block of downtown Chattanooga.

Pat Brock, a grandson of W.E. Brock, took charge of Brock Candy Company in the mid-1950s. The company continued to grow, adding a 64,000 square-foot warehouse just outside of Chattanooga in the 1960s. In the 1970s Brock acquired out-of-state candy companies, including Schuler Chocolates of Winona, Minnesota, and moved production of Brock's Old Fashioned Creme Drops, another popular candy, to this plant. In 1976 the company moved its operations from downtown Chattanooga to the 30-acre site of its distribution warehouse.

In the early 1980s Brock Candy Company became the first candy company to produce the popular "gummie" candies, including gummie bears and gummie worms. The company also introduced fruit snacks and quickly became an industrial supplier.

Brock Candy Company went public in March 1993, offering 2.3 million shares of its stock, giving asset diversification to stockholders, and providing funds for the company's planned expansion in

Europe. Brock Candy also purchased an interest in Clara Candy Company, in Ireland, in 1993, and continued its expansion in the United States. In late 1994 the E.J. Brach Corporation purchased a controlling interest in Brock Candy. Until the acquisition of Brock Candy by the E.J. Brach Corporation, Brock Candy had remained a family operation under the management of Pat Brock and his four sons and operated under the beliefs of its founder that owners, managers, and employees must have faith in the company, be optimistic, and work hard.

Tara Mitchell Mielnik, Middle Tennessee State University
SEE: BROCK, WILLIAM E., III; CHATTANOOGA

BROCK, WILLIAM E. "BILL" III (1930–), Chattanooga businessman, Republican Congressman and Senator, GOP National Party Chairman, U.S. Trade Representative, and Secretary of Labor, was born in Chattanooga on November 23, 1930, to William E. Brock, Jr., and Myra Kruesi Brock, heirs to a wealthy candy manufacturing company. Brock's family had been prominent in business and state politics for generations. His grandfather, William E. Brock, a Democrat, served in the U.S. Senate from 1929 to 1932. Bill Brock received a bachelor of science degree from Washington and Lee University before entering the United States Navy, where he served as a lieutenant from 1953 to 1956. Upon completion of his military service, Brock returned to Chattanooga and served as vice-president of the Brock Candy Company.

In 1962 Brock sought political office as a Republican and became the first GOP member to be elected from his congressional district in 42 years; he served four terms in the House of Representatives. In 1964 the Jaycees chose Brock as the "Outstanding Young Man in Tennessee." In 1970 he defeated Albert Gore, Sr., in a hotly contested race for the U.S. Senate. Brock's victory, according to many critics, was due to a sophisticated use of code words that played on white Tennesseans' racial fears and animosities. Brock, who had a conservative record and who opposed both the Civil Rights Act of 1964 and the creation of Medicare, strongly denied the allegations, noting his hopes for peaceful desegregation without the federally mandated measures advocated by Gore.

Controversy plagued Brock's service in the Senate. In 1973 Brock denied allegations that he had taken money from a secret White House slush fund. During the 1976 campaign, allegations of impropriety again surfaced, when he was accused of taking an illegal contribution of $3,000 from the Gulf Oil Company. Brock denied taking this gift, but repaid the company in hopes of settling the matter. In November 1976 Brock lost his Senate seat to Democrat James Sasser.

After his defeat, Brock remained active in national politics. He became the national GOP Party Chair-

man in the late 1970s and won praise for his leadership in revitalizing the party after Watergate, in assisting Ronald Reagan's election to the presidency, and in making possible the 1980 Republican majority in the Senate. Conservative activist and author William Bennett credited Bill Brock, more than any other GOP leader, with reorganizing the Republican Party during the post-Watergate period. During the Reagan administration, Brock served as U.S. Trade Representative before being named Secretary of Labor. In these posts, he tempered his conservative positions and became a supporter of affirmative action, parental leave, and worker re-training programs. John Seigenthaler, publisher of the Nashville *Tennessean* and a friend of Albert Gore, remarked on Brock's sensitivity and tolerance for the needs of most Americans, noting that he had developed into a good Secretary of Labor.

In 1988 Brock resigned his post in the Reagan administration to help manage the failed presidential bid of Robert Dole. After leaving politics in the late 1980s, Brock formed the Brock Group to advise foreign and domestic companies on international trade policy. In the early 1990s his firm earned almost $1 million assisting the Mexican government in the passage of the North American Free Trade Agreement. In 1990 Brock and his wife, Sandy, established residency in Annapolis, Maryland, and four years later he sought election to the U.S. Senate from that state. No candidate had ever won election to the senate from two different states since voters began directly electing senators during the Progressive Era. Brock ran against Democratic incumbent Senator Paul S. Sarbanes, one of the most liberal members of Congress. Despite the conservative landslide of 1994, Brock failed in his bid for office.

Michael Rogers, University of Tennessee, Knoxville
SEE: BROCK CANDY COMPANY; CHATTANOOGA; GORE, ALBERT A., SR.; SASSER, JAMES R.

BRODE, FREDERICK WILLIAM (1843–1931). For over half a century, F.W. Brode ranked among the leading cottonseed products brokers in the United States. His skill in developing markets for cottonseed meal helped insure the success of the infant cottonseed processing industry after the Civil War.

Born in Saxony in 1843, Brode emigrated with his family to New Orleans when he was nine or ten years old. After several moves, the family settled in Memphis in the late 1850s. A decade or so later, Brode established a brokerage business that specialized in sugar, molasses, and rice. With the growing importance of cottonseed processing, Brode decided to deal in cottonseed products as well. He promoted cottonseed meal as an ideal food for livestock, spending thousands of dollars on feeding demonstrations and writing promotional pamphlets. On his personal trips to Europe, Brode developed an extensive export trade in cottonseed meal; he also introduced it to New England cattle raisers.

A charter member of the Memphis Merchants Exchange, F.W. Brode played a leading role in developing trading rules to govern the buying and selling of cottonseed products. Since Memphis was the largest cottonseed processing center in the United States during the late nineteenth century, its trading rules were widely used. In 1897 Brode was one of the three men most responsible for organizing the Interstate Cottonseed Crushers' Association. The following year, he served as president of the Memphis Merchants Exchange. A pioneer cottonseed products broker, F.W. Brode died in 1931, at the age of 88.

Lynette Boney Wrenn, Memphis

SUGGESTED READING: Lynette Boney Wrenn, *Cinderella of the New South: A History of the Cottonseed Industry, 1855–1955* (1995)

SEE: COTTON; INTERSTATE COTTONSEED CRUSHERS' ASSOCIATION; MEMPHIS

BROOKS, CLEANTH (1906–1994). One of the foremost literary critics of the twentieth century, Cleanth Brooks achieved the breadth of his influence through his collaboration with Robert Penn Warren on the collegiate texts that revolutionized the reading of literature in mid-century America. The two, *Understanding Poetry* (1938) and *Understanding Fiction* (1946), followed the analytical practice of the "New Criticism," described by John Crowe Ransom as employing a close reading of the text in preference to biographical information, with attention to the concepts of paradox and irony, and to the effects of tone and rhythm.

Brooks and Warren exerted a significant influence on American literature both together and separately, and the parallels of their lives are striking. Cleanth Brooks was born in Murray, Kentucky, and grew up in the Kentucky and Tennessee towns where his father, a Methodist minister, served. He received his early classical education at the McTyeire School in McKenzie, Tennessee, and went on to Vanderbilt University in 1924. There he met upperclassmen Robert Penn Warren and Andrew Lytle, attended some meetings of the waning Fugitive Group, and revised his dream of the future. He studied under Donald Davidson and John Crowe Ransom, and graduated Phi Beta Kappa in 1928. After earning a M.A. degree at Tulane in 1929, he was a Rhodes Scholar at Oxford University, receiving the B.A. in 1931 and the B.Litt. in 1932.

In 1932 he joined the faculty at Louisiana State University. Brooks married Edith Amy "Tinkum" Blanchard of New Orleans in 1934. Warren also settled at LSU that year and, from 1935 through 1942, the two edited the new *Southern Review*, a leading literary quarterly. One of a number of southern humanists to migrate to northern universities, in 1947

Brooks became a member of the English Department at Yale University, from which he retired in 1975 as Gray Professor Emeritus of Rhetoric. Warren followed his colleague and friend to Yale in 1950. Together, and with additional collaborators, Brooks and Warren published eight extraordinarily influential works on literature between 1936 and 1973: *An Approach to Literature* (1936), *Understanding Poetry* (1938), *Understanding Fiction* (1943), *Modern Rhetoric* (1949), *Fundamentals of Good Writing: A Handbook of Modern Rhetoric* (1950), *An Anthology of Stories from the Southern Review* (1953), *The Scope of Fiction* (1960), and *American Literature: The Makers and the Making* (1973).

Brooks's works, *Modern Poetry and the Tradition* (1939) and *The Well Wrought Urn: Studies in the Structure of Poetry* (1947), established his reputation as an unexcelled interpreter of verse. Among his eight other literary studies, two works on Faulkner, *William Faulkner: The Yoknapatawpha Country* (1963) and *William Faulkner: Toward Yoknapatawpha and Beyond* (1978), provide benchmarks in Faulkner scholarship.

After his retirement, Brooks continued to write and lecture. He memorialized Warren, his friend of 65 years. In the early 1990s he selected for publication 22 essays that best represent the themes of his life; they were published in 1995 as *Community, Religion, & Literature*. Cleanth Brooks died May 10, 1994.

Marice Wolfe, Vanderbilt University

SUGGESTED READINGS: Thomas D. Young, ed., *The New Criticism and After* (1976) and *Tennessee Writers* (1981)

SEE: DAVIDSON, DONALD; FUGITIVES; LITERATURE; RANSOM, JOHN C.; WARREN, ROBERT P.

BROOME, HARVEY (1902–1968). A lawyer and clerk of court by profession, Knoxville native Harvey Broome spent the bulk of his time and energy in promoting an increased awareness of nature, in educating Americans on the damage that the modern industrialized world had caused to the environment, and in advocating the preservation of wilderness. He served as long-time president of the Smoky Mountains Hiking Club, worked with seven others (including such notable environmentalists as Aldo Leopold, Bob Marshall, and Benton MacKaye) in founding the Wilderness Society, and served as president of the Society from 1957 to 1968.

Broome's activities on behalf of the environment left an extensive legacy. As president of the Wilderness Society, Broome worked closely with Society executive director Howard Zahniser in the fight for the establishment of the National Wilderness Preservation System. In one of Broome's proudest moments, he stood next to President Lyndon Johnson when he signed the Wilderness Act into law on September 3, 1964. Broome also crisscrossed the country from Alaska to Florida spearheading individual wilderness preservation projects. For Broome, wilderness experiences provided an important and salutary contrast to "civilized life."

Like other environmentalists, Broome was also an accomplished writer. His work appeared in periodicals such as *Living Wilderness, National Parks Magazine,* and *Nature.* Three books containing his writings were published posthumously: *Out Under the Skies in the Great Smoky Mountains, Faces of the Wilderness,* and *Harvey Broome: Earth Man.* Benton MacKaye, founder of the Appalachian Trail, referred to Broome's journals, the basis for most of his writings, as "a marked contribution to nature findings—of fact underfoot and of thought overhead."[1]

Broome's great love in life, other than his wife and constant companion Anne, was the Great Smoky Mountains. He made his first camping trip at the age of 15 to Silers Bald in the Smokies. Over the next 50 years he hiked most of its mountains and hollows, sighted much of the Appalachian Trail through the Smokies, and worked tirelessly to keep the region free of intrusive development. In October 1966 he organized the "Save-our-Smokies" hike. Over 1,300 people participated in this "hike-in," which effectively blocked the building of a road across the Smokies from Bryson City, North Carolina, to Townsend, Tennessee.

The Smokies never ceased to awe and delight Broome. He wrote lovingly of the sensory experience that awaited those willing to get off the road and truly explore the Smokies; of the sight of "aqua-blue fading on the horizon" and "the innumerable pinkish purple blossoms of the *Rhododendron nudiflorum;*" of the sounds of the "soft mystery in the whispers of the air through the evergreens;" of the "bold piping of the veery and the thin, spirited, long sustained arias of the winter wren;" of the "all-pervasive cascadings of thunder just before the rain;" and the "fragrances of fresh balsam growth."[2]

Broome died of a heart attack at his Knoxville home, in sight of his beloved Smokies, on March 8, 1968, while building a wren's house out of a hollow log.

Dan Pierce, Western Carolina University

CITATIONS:

(1) "Harvey Broome: July 15, 1902-March 8, 1968," *Living Wilderness,* 31(Winter 1967–68): 5.

(2) Harvey Broome, *Out Under the Sky of the Great Smokies: A Personal Journal* (1975), 145–147.

SEE: APPALACHIAN TRAIL; CONSERVATION; GREAT SMOKY MOUNTAINS NATIONAL PARK

BROWN, AARON V. (1795–1859), Governor and legislator, was born in Brunswick County, Virginia, the son of Reverend Aaron and Elizabeth Melton Brown. Brown attended school at Westrayville Academy and graduated as valedictorian from the University of North Carolina in 1814. While he was in college, Brown's family moved to Giles County, Tennessee. After graduation, Brown also came to Tennessee and read law in Nashville; he was admitted to the bar in 1817. Brown began his practice in Nashville, but soon settled in Pulaski, where he formed a partnership with James K. Polk of Columbia. At an undetermined date, Brown married Sallie Burrus of Giles County, and they had four children. After Sallie's death, Brown married Mrs. Cynthia Pillow Saunders, sister of General Gideon J. Pillow, in 1845. They had one son.

An ardent Democrat, Brown had a long political career. He served in the Tennessee State Senate, 1821–1825 and 1827–29, representing Giles and Lincoln counties, and one term in the Tennessee House, 1831–1833. He served three terms in the U.S. House of Representatives, 1839–1845. Brown was a delegate to the Democratic National Convention in Baltimore that nominated Polk for the presidency. Although Polk lost the Tennessee vote in the general election, Brown won the gubernatorial election, serving from 1845–1847. While governor, Brown issued the call for 2,600 men for the Mexican War and got 30,000 volunteers. By the end of his term, many Tennesseans were weary of the war, which the Whigs made an issue in the gubernatorial campaign. Brown lost his re-election bid to Neill S. Brown, also from Giles County.

Brown was a delegate to the Nashville Convention, which met in the summer of 1850 to debate the issue of slavery in the new western territory. Credited, along with Gideon Pillow, as the author of the "Tennessee Platform," Brown worried about northern intentions, but adopted a conciliatory stance and advised southerners to put the past behind them.

In 1857 President James Buchanan appointed Brown to the post of Postmaster General, where he served until his death in March 1859. Brown was buried in Mt. Olivet Cemetery in Nashville.

Connie L. Lester, Tennessee Historical Society

SEE: GILES COUNTY; JACKSONIANS; MEXICAN WAR; NASHVILLE CONVENTION; POLK, JAMES K.

BROWN, ARTHUR (1922–1991), virologist and head of the University of Tennessee Department of Microbiology (1969–1988), was born in New York City, the son of Samuel S. and Ida Hoffman Brown. He received his B.A. in biology and chemistry from Brooklyn College in 1943 and his Ph.D. from the University of Chicago in 1950. In 1963–1964, Brown received a Senior Fellowship with Professor Werner Arber (Nobel Prize winner, 1978) at the Institute of Molecular Biology, University of Geneva, Switzerland. Brown's area of specialization included viral pathogenesis and immunity.

Brown served as an instructor in the Department of Microbiology and Immunology, College of Medicine, State University of New York, Brooklyn, New York, 1951–1955. From 1956 to 1968, he was adjunct professor for teaching and research at University of Wisconsin, Georgetown University, George Washington University, and University of Maryland. In 1957 he became Chief Virologist at the Biological Labs, Fort Dietrick, Frederick, Maryland, a post he held until he became chairman of the Department of Microbiology at the University of Tennessee in 1969.

Brown published more than 65 peer-reviewed publications. He was a Fellow and Diplomate in the American Academy of Microbiology. Honored both as a researcher and a teacher, he served as 1975 Macebearer at the University of Tennessee, Knoxville, where he also received the 1979 Chancellor's Research Scholar Award and was named 1983 Distinguished Service Professor.

Brown was married to Elaine Belaief Brown; they had four children. He was a member of Heska Amuna Synagogue.

Connie L. Lester, Tennessee Historical Society

BROWN, CLARENCE (1890–1987), film producer and director, was born May 10, 1890, in Clinton, Massachusetts. Brown took a double degree in mechanical and electrical engineering from the University of Tennessee in 1910 and began his career as an automobile dealer in Alabama. Fascinated with the movies, Brown went to the Peerless Studios at Fort Lee, New Jersey, in 1915. There he met French director Maurice Tourneur and became his apprentice for the next six years.

In 1920 Brown co-directed with Tourneur the film, *The Last of the Mohicans,* starring Wallace Beery. Over the next six years, Brown directed five movies, including *The Eagle* (1925), with Rudolph Valentino. In 1926 Brown signed with M-G-M Studios, which remained his film home for the rest of his career. Brown's work in the late 1920s and 1930s with star

Greta Garbo was especially notable, including the films *Anna Christie* (1930) and *Anna Karenina* (1935). Other popular stars who worked with Brown included Norma Shearer (*A Free Soul,* 1931), Joan Crawford (*Chained,* 1934), Spencer Tracy (*Edison the Man,* 1940), Elizabeth Taylor (*National Velvet,* 1945), and Gregory Peck (*The Yearling,* 1947). After the latter film, Brown directed only five more features before retiring in 1952; the last film he produced was *Never Let Me Go,* starring Clark Gable, in 1953. In all, Brown was nominated for the Academy Award for best director six times and his films won eight Oscars out of 38 total nominations.

Despite the long, productive career in Hollywood, Brown never forgot his years at the University of Tennessee. In 1987, at his death, Brown left a $12 million bequest to the university, contingent upon the death of his wife. Added to a previous donation of $1 million, Brown became the largest donor in the university's history. The funds support the Clarence Brown Theatre Company, fund renovations to the Clarence Brown Theatre, and provide scholarships and faculty salary supplements. Brown's papers and professional memorabilia are housed in the Special Collections of the University of Tennessee Library.

Connie L. Lester, Tennessee Historical Society

SUGGESTED READINGS: Kevin Brownlow, *The Parades Gone By* (1968); Diane MacIntyre, *The Silents Majority,* On-Line Journal of Silent Film, at mdle@primenet.com.

BROWN, DOROTHY LAVINIA (1919–) surgeon, legislator, and teacher, rose from humble beginnings in Troy, New York, to become the first female African-American surgeon in the Southeast and the first African-American woman to serve in the Tennessee General Assembly. She was born in Philadelphia on

Clarence Brown with the MGM lion.

SPECIAL COLLECTIONS, UNIVERSITY OF TENNESSEE, KNOXVILLE

January 7, 1919, to Edna Brown. When she was only five months old, her mother placed her in an orphanage in Troy, New York, where she would live for the next twelve years. During her stay at the orphanage, Brown underwent a tonsillectomy at the age of five and caught a glimpse of the world of medicine. From that day on she dreamed of being a surgeon.

Just prior to her thirteenth birthday, Brown's mother tried to reenter her life by bringing her daughter to live with her. Brown ran away from home five times, always returning to the Troy orphanage. At the age of 15, Brown ran away again, this time to enroll at the Troy High School. With assistance from her principal, Brown was taken in by foster parents, Samuel Wesley and Lola Redmon, whom she affectionately referred to as Grandma and Grandpa. Under their guidance Brown completed high school, working summers and after school as a domestic to earn money for college.

With assistance from the Methodist Women of Troy Conference, Brown attended Bennett College in Greensboro, North Carolina, a small Methodist college named for a local Troy minister. After graduation, she worked for two years at the Rochester (New York) Army Ordnance Department until she began medical school at Nashville's Meharry Medical College in 1944.

Brown spent her year-long internship at the Harlem Hospital in New York City, returning to Meharry's Hubbard Hospital in 1949 for her residency. Matthew Walker, then head of surgery, was initially reluctant to admit a woman into the strenuous five-year training program in general surgery, but finally consented. Brown's persistence, dedication, and hard work earned her the appointment of chief of surgery at Nashville's Riverside Hospital, a position she held from 1957 until the hospital's closing in 1983.

During this time, an unmarried patient approached Brown, begging her to adopt the woman's newborn daughter. Brown legally adopted the infant in 1956, becoming the first known single woman in Tennessee to adopt a child, a daughter whom she named Lola Denise Brown after her foster mother.

In 1966 redistricting offered the successful doctor and community leader yet another challenge, a seat in the Tennessee House of Representatives. She won the election, becoming the first African-American woman elected to the Tennessee General Assembly. Concerned with the issues of health, education, and welfare reform, Brown introduced a controversial bill to reform the state's archaic abortion law. At that time, Tennessee law permitted abortions only in cases where the mother's life was in danger. Brown's bill would have legalized abortions caused by rape or incest. The bill met great resistance and fell two votes short of passage. Also during her term in the 85th General Assembly, Brown was instrumental in getting a Negro History Act passed. It required all Tennessee public schools to conduct special programs during Negro History Week to recognize accomplishments made by African Americans.

After 1968 Brown, known as Dr. "D," returned to her medical practice full-time. In addition to serving as chief of surgery at Riverside Hospital, Brown also has been attending surgeon at Hubbard and General Hospitals, educational director of the Riverside-Meharry clinical rotation program, and clinical professor of surgery at Meharry Medical College. The many honors and distinctions bestowed upon Brown include: Fellow, American College of Surgeons, 1959, the third woman to be so honored; the naming of the Dorothy L. Brown Women's Residence at Meharry Medical College, Nashville, 1971; and honorary doctorate degrees from Russell Sage College in Troy, New York and Bennett College in Greensboro, North Carolina. Brown continues to live and work at her home in Nashville. Over the last few years she has scaled down her medical practice to allow her time to work on her autobiography, *Driven.*

Anne-Leslie Owens, Tennessee Historical Society
SEE: MEDICINE; MEHARRY MEDICAL COLLEGE

BROWN, JOHN CALVIN (1827–1889), Governor, was born in Giles County on January 6, 1827, to Duncan and Margaret (Smith) Brown. He was the younger brother of former governor Neill S. Brown. After graduating from Jackson College in Columbia, Brown was admitted to the bar in 1848 and launched a successful law practice in Pulaski.

In the 1850s, as Tennesseans wrangled with the question of secession, Brown emphatically supported the Union. With the outbreak of war, however, Brown joined his fellow Tennesseans in the Confederacy. Enlisting as a private in the Confederate army, he was soon elected to captain and by May 1861 he became colonel of the Third Tennessee Infantry Regiment. At Fort Donelson, he commanded the Third Brigade of General Simon Buckner's division. When the fort surrendered on February 16, 1862, Union troops captured Brown, and he remained imprisoned at Fort Warren, Massachusetts, for six months.

After his release through a prisoner exchange, Brown was commissioned as a brigadier general and assigned to duty with General Braxton Bragg in the Army of Tennessee. During the Kentucky campaign, Brown was wounded at the Battle of Perryville in 1862. The following year he saw action at Chickamauga and Missionary Ridge. For his heroic efforts in the Dalton-Atlanta campaign, Brown was promoted to the rank of major general in August 1864. Brown commanded Cheatham's Division during General John Bell Hood's Tennessee campaign. He last served at Franklin, Tennessee, on November 30, 1864, where he was severely wounded.

After the war, Brown resumed his Pulaski law practice. President of the 1870 Constitutional Convention, Brown was elected Tennessee's nineteenth governor after voters adopted the new constitution; he was re-elected in 1872. Formerly a Whig, Brown joined the Democrats and was leader of the party's Bourbon faction.

When Brown took office in 1871, he faced an overwhelming state debt of $43 million bonded and a floating debt of $3 million. The state began to incur such an enormous debt in 1833, when it issued interest-bearing bonds for the establishment of a bank and other property purchases, including the construction of the Capitol. By 1861 the state's debt had climbed to $3 million. The desire for internal improvement in the late antebellum era prompted the state to lend its credit to turnpike companies, plank-road companies, and railroads. When the Civil War destroyed these companies, their debt of nearly $14 million fell to the state. Between 1865 and 1869, bonds issued to pay the interest on the former bonds created what has been called the "Brownlow debt." In the early 1870s Brown and the state legislature reduced the state debt to $20 million, paid the large floating debt, and re-established the state's credit.

In 1873 Brown's administration also sponsored legislation that provided for a state superintendent of public instruction, county and city superintendents, a board of directors for each school district, and the organization of separate schools for black and white children. To support these schools, Brown levied a small state tax and gave cities and counties the power to raise additional taxes.

After serving as governor, Brown ran for the United States Senate, but lost to former governor and former president Andrew Johnson. Retreating from political life, Brown returned to his home and law practice in Pulaski.

Brown married twice. His first wife, Anne Pointer of Spring Hill, died in 1858. In 1864 Brown married Elizabeth "Bettie" Childress of Murfreesboro, who became the state's first lady. While in Pulaski, the Browns lived in a Greek Revival mansion, which is now on the campus of Martin Methodist College. They were the parents of four children. Their oldest daughter, Marie, married Benton McMillin, who was Tennessee's governor from 1899 to 1903 and served in the U.S. House of Representatives from 1879 to 1899.

In his later years, Brown accepted positions in industry. He moved briefly to Texas to serve as receiver and then president of the Texas Pacific Railway Company in 1888. In 1889 he became president of the Tennessee Coal and Iron Company, then the largest industrial company in the South. On August 17, 1889, Brown died at Red Boiling Springs in Macon County and was buried at Pulaski.

Anne-Leslie Owens, Tennessee Historical Society

SEE: ARMY OF TENNESSEE; EDUCATION; GILES COUNTY; GOVERNMENT; MCMILLIN, BENTON; RECONSTRUCTION

BROWN, LIZINKA CAMPBELL (1820–1872), a founder of a prominent late nineteenth century stock farm, was the daughter of former U.S. Senator George W. Campbell of Tennessee, who also served as Secretary of the Treasury in the administration of James Madison and Minister to Russia under James Monroe. Lizinka Campbell was born in St. Petersburg on February 24, 1820, and named for the Russian Czarina, who had been her mother's friend.

On April 25, 1839, Campbell married James Percy Brown, an attaché in the American Embassy in Paris. After he died in 1844, Brown returned to Nashville and the home of her father on Charlotte Avenue. When Union forces occupied Nashville in 1862, Brown fled to Virginia, and Military Governor Andrew Johnson lived in the house.

While in Virginia, Brown nursed her wounded cousin, Richard Stoddert Ewell, a general in Robert E. Lee's Army of Northern Virginia. The two, who had corresponded for years, fell in love and married on May 25, 1863. The eccentric Ewell often referred to Brown as "my wife, the widow Mrs. Brown."

After the war, Brown and Ewell moved to a farm in Spring Hill, Tennessee, on land she inherited from her father. Their Ewell Farm, later expanded by Lizinka's son, Major Campbell Brown, became one of the region's great stock-breeding plantations. The farm introduced some of the first Jersey cattle to the South and bred some of the first harness-racing horses in the country. Its horse races, cattle sales, and stock auctions were attended by the rich and powerful from throughout America. Bisected by the railroad, the farm had its own depot and huge warehouse along the tracks.

In January 1872 Ewell, Brown, and her two children were stricken with a respiratory infection. The children recovered, but Ewell's illness extended over several weeks. Brown contracted the infection while nursing him and died within a week, on January 22, 1872. When the family reluctantly informed Ewell of his wife's death, he asked to see her. He died 48 hours later. The two were buried in Nashville's Old City Cemetery. Due to its significance in agriculture and architecture, the Ewell Farm is listed in the National Register of Historic Places.

Bob Holladay, Franklin

SEE: CAMPBELL, GEORGE W.; LIVESTOCK; WILLIAMSON COUNTY

BROWN, MILTON (1804–1883), chancellor, congressman, and railroad president, migrated to Nashville from his home in Ohio in 1823 and studied law in the office of Felix Grundy. Upon admission to the bar, he practiced law in Paris, Tennessee, and in 1832

relocated to Jackson, where he became active in the temperance and internal improvement movements and earned fame as an orator.

In 1834 Brown was appointed to represent the legendary criminal, John Murrell, who was known as "The Western Land Pirate," due to his wide-ranging criminal exploits. Although convicted, Murrell escaped the death penalty, and Brown won recognition as one of the best lawyers in the state.

Governor Newton Cannon appointed Brown Chancellor of West Tennessee in 1837 following the resignation of Chancellor Pleasant Miller. In 1839 Brown resigned and ran as a Whig nominee for the U.S. House of Representatives. Winning the contest, Brown emerged in Congress as a leader of the southern Whigs and a champion of the Whig program of high tariffs, internal improvements, and the Bankruptcy Act of 1841. His ceaseless attacks on Democratic leaders in Congress and in Tennessee provided endless frustration to his opponents. In 1843 James K. Polk confronted Brown in a colorful debate in Jackson on the issues separating the parties. However, Brown is best remembered for his 1845 deadlock-breaking resolution to admit Texas to the Union.

After leaving Congress in 1847, Brown was often promoted for high office, including the Tennessee Supreme Court and the U.S. Senate, but such efforts failed to interest him. Instead, he turned his attention to transportation and remained a tireless promoter and manager of railroads during his tenure as president of the Mississippi Central and Tennessee (1854–1856) and the Mobile and Ohio (1856–1871). He is credited with doing more to cover West Tennessee in rails than any other man.

Brown was also instrumental in the founding of Union, Lambuth, and Vanderbilt universities, as well as being one of Tennessee's greatest charitable and Methodist lay leaders. Brown died one of the wealthiest men in Tennessee in 1883.

Russell Fowler, Memphis

SEE: JACKSON; MADISON COUNTY; MILLER, PLEASANT M.; MURRELL, JOHN A.; RAILROADS

BROWN, NEILL SMITH (1810–1886), Governor, was born in Giles County on April 18, 1810, to Duncan and Margaret Smith Brown. He received his early education through self study and briefly attended a neighboring academy. To finance his college education, he taught school in Giles County for several years. In 1831 he entered Manual Labor Academy, later Jackson College, outside Spring Hill in Maury County. After a brief time in Texas, he returned to Giles County and began studying law at Pulaski. Admitted to the bar in 1834, he began practicing law in Giles County the next year. In 1836 he enlisted in the 1st Tennessee Mounted Volunteers for service in the Seminole War. After this conflict,

in 1839, he married Mary Ann Trimble, and they had eight children.

Brown was one of the founders of the Whig party, providing leadership throughout the 1830s and 1840s. He served as a presidential elector on the Whig ticket of Hugh Lawson White in the 1836 election. He represented Giles County in the General Assembly from 1837 to 1839. In 1844 he again served as a presidential elector, this time on the Whig ticket of Henry Clay. In these contests he displayed a well-known talent for political rhetoric. In the 1847 gubernatorial election, Neill "Lean" Brown defeated the incumbent Democrat Aaron V. "Fat" Brown to become the second native son to hold the office. The major issue of this election was the Mexican War and President Polk's war policy, which Neill Brown and other Congressional Whigs opposed. Neill Brown won by only 1,000 votes, but the Whig party gained a majority in both houses of the legislature. During Brown's administration, the legislature passed an act to establish public schools. Brown lost his bid for re-election in 1849 to William S. Trousdale, "the War-horse of Sumner County."

In 1850 President Zachery Taylor appointed Brown as Minister to Russia, a position he held until 1853. Brown returned to the General Assembly (1855–1857), representing Davidson County and the American, or Know-Nothing, party, and serving as Speaker of the House. In 1856 he served as a presidential elector on the American party ticket of Millard Fillmore and Andrew Jackson Donelson. In anticipation of the impending war, Governor Isham G. Harris appointed him as a member of the Military and Financial Board in 1861. In 1870 he became a member of the state's Constitutional Convention and served with his brother John Calvin Brown. Afterwards, he took no further part in politics although former Whigs continued to regard him as one of their greatest leaders. Brown died on January 30, 1886, and was buried in Mt. Olivet Cemetery in Nashville.

Anne-Leslie Owens, Tennessee Historical Society

SUGGESTED READING: Joseph O. Baylen, "A Tennessee Politician in Imperial Russia, 1850–1853," *Tennessee Historical Quarterly* 14(1955): 227–252

SEE: BROWN, JOHN C.; GILES COUNTY; MEXICAN WAR; TROUSDALE, WILLIAM S.

BROWNING, GORDON WEAVER (1895–1976), three-term Governor and U.S. Congressman, was born in Carroll County in 1895. He attended local schools and opened a law practice in Huntingdon in 1915. He served in the National Guard in World War I. In 1922 he entered politics, winning a Congressional seat and serving six consecutive terms with little opposition to his reelection.

In 1934 he ran for a two-year term in the U.S. Senate against Nathan Bachman, who had been appointed to fill the vacancy created in 1933 by the appointment of Cordell Hull as U.S. Secretary of State. Browning failed to win, in part because the voters of East Tennessee did not want two senators from West Tennessee (Kenneth McKellar of Memphis was the other senator). E. H. Crump's support for Bachman was another reason for Browning's defeat.

In 1936 Browning entered the gubernatorial race. Governor Hill McAlister decided not to run for re-election and backed his ally Burgin Dossett. Initially, Crump claimed neutrality, not liking either candidate. Browning conducted an effective and energetic stump campaign. He promised to clean up corruption in state government, maintain prohibition, reform the state financial structure, and support TVA. Dossett advocated a repeal of the state's "bone dry" prohibition law and accused Browning of wanting to cripple TVA. Late in the campaign, when Browning's lead became apparent, Crump joined his cause. Consequently, Browning won the primary by more than a two-to-one margin and easily defeated his Republican opponent, P. H. Thach, in the fall.

When Browning became governor in January 1937, he found the state in severe financial difficulty. From 1924 to 1937, the state debt rose from $16 million to $129 million, and the servicing of the debt crippled efforts to accomplish other objectives. In May 1937, Browning persuaded the legislature to adopt six important measures to reorganize state debt and move forward on various social programs. The Debt Reorganization Act brought all state debts into a single plan for orderly retirement and enacted additional taxes for retirement of the debt. By 1948 the debt of Tennessee had been reduced by 40 percent. Other measures created a Department of Conservation, implemented the state's portion of the Social Security Old Age Pension programs, further increased cooperation with federal welfare programs, significantly increased state appropriations for public education, and created a civil service merit system for the state.

The death of Nathan Bachman in April 1937 opened the U.S. Senate seat for legislative appointment. Since he wanted to accomplish his state reforms, and was unwilling to openly solicit the office from the General Assembly as previous governors had done, Browning took no action on his own behalf. He reportedly offered to support Crump in a race for the Senate against McKellar in 1940, if Crump would support him for senate and Lewis Pope for governor in 1938. Browning appointed labor leader George L. Berry to fill Bachman's term until the next general election.

Any deals between Browning and Crump became moot when a major break occurred between the two men. Crump refused to run against his old friend McKellar, and Browning decided to run for reelection

as governor. The Browning-Crump split occurred for several reasons. The dominant personalities of the two men refused compromise. Crump represented the urban progressive succession to the planter aristocracy, while Browning always based his power on rural small farmers. Finally, Browning successfully personified Crump as the epitome of evil in state government, in essence a Judas of Tennessee. In 1938 Browning lost the gubernatorial election to Prentice Cooper, but the split eventually realigned Tennessee's entire political structure.

After serving in various World War II appointive positions, Browning returned to politics in 1948, and mounted a campaign against the reelection of incumbent governor Jim McCord. Browning won the Democratic primary by focusing on McCord's unpopular enactment of the state's first sales tax. Both Browning and Estes Kefauver, who successfully ran for the U.S. Senate, recognized the voter willingness to reject boss-controlled politics and used the 1948 race to destroy Crump's statewide power.

In 1949 Browning launched another period of reform. In education, he signed legislation guaranteeing a minimum salary for teachers, increased funding for school construction, raised appropriations for higher education, and established the first effective teacher retirement system. The legislature accepted without change his $48 million appropriation for farm-to-market roads. Finally, a series of election reforms provided for permanent voter registration, abolition of the poll tax for women and veterans in primary elections, open meetings for the State Elections Board, and improved absentee voter regulations.

In 1950 Browning won the Democratic primary in a close race over Clifford Allen, which gained him a second term, since the Republicans failed to run a gubernatorial candidate for the first time since the Civil War. In his third term, Browning successfully enacted a call for a limited Constitutional Convention. When voters adopted the measure in 1952, it became the first Constitutional Convention in the state since 1870.

In the 1952 election Browning faced his most formidable candidate, the charismatic, 32-year old Frank G. Clement. Clement toured the state with a ten-point "indictment" of the Browning administration on charges of corruption and favoritism. Clement easily mastered the new medium of television, a feat that proved impossible for the older Browning. Saddled with explaining the high cost of a lease-purchase agreement for state office space in the Memorial Apartments near the Capitol Building, and forced to battle voter unhappiness over his recent Democratic Convention endorsement of Estes Kefauver at the expense of the Virginia delegates, Browning's support lagged behind that of the energetic Clement. Clement won the Democratic primary by more than 50,000 votes.

Two years later, over the objections of many supporters, Browning ran against Clement again, and lost every county except Carroll. Browning then went into semi-retirement and returned to his law practice in Huntingdon, where he lived as Tennessee's elder statesman until his death in 1976. Browning's six years as governor witnessed significant legislative achievements and helped to break the power of Boss Crump. The former McKenzie post office, built by the New Deal's Works Progress Administration, now houses a museum and archives centered around the career of Gordon Browning.

Fred S. Rolater, Middle Tennessee State University

SUGGESTED READING: William R. Majors, *Change and Continuity: Tennessee Politics Since the Civil War* (1979)

SEE: CARROLL COUNTY; CLEMENT, FRANK G.; CRUMP, E. H.; GOVERNMENT; MCCORD, JAMES N.

BROWNLOW, WILLIAM GANNAWAY "PARSON"

(1805–1877), minister, journalist, and Governor, was one of those unique individuals who influenced Tennessee culture, politics, and government during the middle half of the nineteenth century. Born in Wythe County, Virginia, orphaned at age 11 and possessing limited formal education, he joined the traveling ministry of the Methodist Church in 1826. During the next decade, he rode Methodist circuits in southern Appalachia in a crusade to save souls from the devil and other denominations. His marriage, however, forced Brownlow to abandon the church's traveling ministry in search of work to support his family.

Parson Brownlow's flair for writing attracted him to journalism, and in 1838 he became editor/owner of an Elizabethton newspaper popularly known as *Brownlow's Whig*. The Parson dedicated the paper to promoting the Whig party and to championing Henry Clay for president. After a year, he moved his paper to Jonesborough, publishing it there for a decade before moving the paper a second time to Knoxville in 1849. The influential *Whig* reached some 11,000 subscribers across the country by the eve of the Civil War.

A thirst for controversy, which surfaced during his circuit-riding days, became the mainstay of Brownlow's journalistic and political careers. His clashes with adversaries were marked by their personal and caustic nature. This truculence inspired others to crown him the "Fighting Parson."

Brownlow captured public attention by stationing himself in the eye of many social and political controversies, and he boasted that he had never been neutral on any issue. He always defended Methodism from its detractors. With T.A.R. Nelson, Brownlow became an architect of the Whig party in East Tennessee; he later emerged as a principal spokesperson for the "Know-Nothing" party in Tennessee after the collapse of the Whigs. He was a major southern advocate for the Sons of Temperance and a prominent apologist for slavery. Brownlow also promoted commercial interests in East Tennessee. Most significant, the Parson stood in the front ranks of southerners who rejected secession and the Confederacy.

Although he had battled Andrew Johnson "on every stump in Tennessee" for a quarter century, the Parson temporarily joined with his political enemy in resisting secession. Together they led East Tennesseans into rejecting both 1861 votes for secession by more than two-to-one margins. The first referendum failed, but the second passed four months later due to strong majority votes in Middle and West Tennessee. The anti-secession sentiment in East Tennessee became so intense, however, that Confederate authorities controlled the region only by military occupation.

After Tennessee withdrew from the Union, Brownlow continued castigating the Confederacy in the vituperative style he had mastered. Confederate authorities took no action against him at first—perhaps in the hope he would mute his attacks. This tactic failed, and after several months, they suppressed his paper. The Parson then fled to safety in the Smoky Mountains.

Brownlow wanted to relocate in northern territory, and so reached an agreement with Confederate military leaders to surrender himself, providing they

William Gannaway Brownlow.

TENNESSEE HISTORICAL SOCIETY COLLECTION, TSLA

would not hand him over to local civil authorities who were personal and political enemies. The agreement was violated, and the Parson was thrown into the Knoxville jail, charged with treason for his anti-secession and anti-Confederate editorials. While in jail, he observed Union sympathizers imprisoned on the slightest pretext and witnessed drumhead execution of men accused of burning railroad bridges between Bristol and Chattanooga. He became seriously ill, but, three months later, Richmond authorities ordered his expulsion from the Confederacy.

Upon reaching Union territory, Brownlow launched a six-month speaking tour that took him to major cities throughout the North. The tales he related of his experiences in Confederate hands made him an instant hero and celebrity. Proceeds from his speaking tour and royalties from a book relating his experience in Confederate custody generated sufficient funds to re-establish the *Whig* when he accompanied Union troops to Knoxville in the fall of 1863. With his paper again in print, the Parson resumed lambasting secessionists and Confederates.

Tennessee Unionists chose Brownlow to succeed Andrew Johnson as Governor in March 1865, and he served two consecutive terms. Brownlow allied his administration with reconstruction policies of Congressional Republicans in opposition to those of President Andrew Johnson. By influencing the state legislature to ratify the Fourteenth Amendment in mid-1866, he swayed Congress to restore Tennessee fully to the Union. The Parson, as a result, saved Tennessee from the political reconstruction experienced by other Confederate states.

Governor Brownlow enfranchised former slaves despite his antebellum advocacy of slavery. This action provoked former Confederates to form the Ku Klux Klan for intimidating blacks and other Republican voters. The Parson undertook actions to suppress the Klan although his initiatives were somewhat ineffective.

Military operations during the war destroyed many public facilities in Tennessee, but state government was without funds for rebuilding. Brownlow led the state in backing government bonds to build railroads and other public improvements. This action indebted Tennessee for many years, but Brownlow enjoyed few other options for restoring the state's economic health. Unfortunately, some administration officials were guilty of graft and embezzlement—none of these cases, however, involved Brownlow personally.

The Tennessee General Assembly elected Brownlow to replace D.T. Patterson, Andrew Johnson's son-in-law, as U.S. Senator, beginning in 1869. He served one term before returning home to Knoxville. In semi-retirement, the Parson resumed editorial work for his former newspaper, but the ill health he had suffered over a score of years depleted his strength and he died on April 28, 1877.

Forrest Conklin, University of Northern Iowa

SUGGESTED READINGS: E. Merton Coulter, *William G. Brownlow: Fighting Parson of the Southern Highlands* (1937); James W. Patton, *Unionism and Reconstruction in Tennessee, 1860–1869* (1966)

SEE: JOHNSON, ANDREW; KNOXVILLE; KU KLUX KLAN; NELSON, THOMAS A.R.; OCCUPATION, CIVIL WAR; PUBLISHING; RECONSTRUCTION; RELIGION

BRYAN, CHARLES FAULKNER (1911–1955) was one of Tennessee's greatest composers, musicians, and collectors of folk music. Bryan was born on July 26, 1911, in McMinnville, Tennessee, the second of five children born to Clarence Justus and Allie May Bryan. At the age of 19, Bryan entered the Nashville Conservatory of Music. During his four years there, Bryan organized the Nashville Junior Concert Orchestra and conducted the Nashville Philharmonic Orchestra. He received his bachelor's degree in music in 1934 and was invited to become the head of the Music Department at Tennessee Polytechnic Institute (now Tennessee Technological University). His interest in folk music and folklore peaked during his four years in Cookeville and that inclination determined the future of Bryan's musical work.

In 1939 Bryan was awarded a graduate fellowship at George Peabody College for Teachers in Nashville. While at Peabody, he befriended Vanderbilt professor and fellow folklorist Charles Pullen Jackson, with whom Bryan co-authored a textbook for the teaching and performance of folk music in public high schools. Bryan composed a folk symphony to fulfill his master's requirements. On March 27, 1942, the Cincinnati Symphony Orchestra performed his *White Spiritual Symphony* at the University of Tennessee; the work eventually gained him a Guggenheim Fellowship.

During World War II, Bryan served in the civilian defense arm of the military, directing southeastern efforts in 1942 and 1943 and gaining national recognition for his contributions to the war effort.

In 1946 Bryan accepted a one-year Guggenheim Fellowship and entered Yale University to study with Paul Hindemith. Under Hindemith's tutelage, Bryan composed his most famous musical work, the *Bell Witch Cantata,* which premiered at Carnegie Hall on April 14, 1947, by Robert Shaw and the Julliard Orchestra. In 1947 Peabody College asked Bryan to join its faculty. There, he served as president of the Tennessee Folklore Society and co-wrote a folk-opera, *Singin' Billy,* with Donald Davidson. In the fall of 1952, Bryan accepted an invitation to become Master of Music at Indian Springs, a new boys' private school in Alabama. On July 7, 1955, while returning to Indian Springs from a visit to McMinnville, Bryan,

Virginia Davis Laskey Library

who had a long history of violent headaches, died very suddenly. Although only 43 years old at the time of his death, Bryan left a distinct mark on Tennessee and American folk culture. His peers respected him as an excellent musician, and his students revered him as an energetic teacher. In 1935 he married Edith Hillis, and they were the parents of two children, Betty Lynn and Charles, Jr.

Robert Parkinson, University of Tennessee, Knoxville

SEE: MUSIC; GEORGE PEABODY COLLEGE OF VANDERBILT UNIVERSITY; TENNESSEE FOLKLORE SOCIETY; TENNESSEE TECHNOLOGICAL UNIVERSITY; WARREN COUNTY

BRYAN COLLEGE. One of the dreams of William Jennings Bryan, which he told friends when he was in Dayton for the Scopes Trial, was for a prep school and junior college to be founded in Dayton. Bryan had long believed that a Christian school, emphasizing the Bible and other subjects, should be established in the United States. George Washburn, a friend of Bryan, suggested that such a college be erected in Dayton. Bryan enthusiastically responded by pledging $25,000 to help establish the college that would bear his name.

Following Bryan's death in July 1925, within days of the close of the arduous trial, a group called the Bryan Memorial Association solicited funds for the proposed university. Groundbreaking took place in May 1927. Pledges for the university reached $700,000, but the stock market crash in 1929 ended construction. Undaunted, the founders opened William Jennings Bryan University on September 30, 1930. Holding classes at Rhea Central High School in Dayton, the university enrolled few students, but held its first graduation in 1934. Bryan experienced serious financial problems during the 1930s and 1940s. Occasionally the faculty received no salaries except in food provided by local merchants and students. From its beginning Bryan's curriculum included courses for majors in the liberal arts, religion, and related areas, culminating with bachelor degrees. A non-denominational Christian college, Bryan's faculty and student body represent diverse Christian backgrounds, including Baptists, Presbyterians, Methodists, numerous independent Bible churches, and a few Catholics.

In the 1960s, during the administration of Dr. Theodore Mercer, Bryan received accreditation from the Southern Association and changed its name to Bryan College to more accurately reflect its course offerings. Currently, the college employs approximately thirty faculty and has an enrollment of 450 students.

William L. Ketchersid, Bryan College

SEE: EDUCATION, HIGHER; RHEA COUNTY; SCOPES TRIAL

BUCHANAN, ANDREW HAYS (1828–1914), early professor of mathematics and civil engineering and topographer-surveyor, was born in Boonsboro, Arkansas, on June 28, 1828. He attended Cumberland University in Lebanon, Tennessee, and received the A.B. degree in 1853. The following year, Buchanan accepted a professorship in civil engineering at Cumberland. He remained there until 1862, when he became a topographic engineer with the Confederate Army, attaining the rank of captain. In September 1869, Buchanan returned to Cumberland University as Professor of Mathematics and Engineering.

Buchanan contributed to Tennessee culture, both as a textbook author and teacher, and as a topographer and surveyor. From 1854 to 1911 virtually everyone who attended Cumberland University enrolled in his mathematics courses, and his influence on the discipline reached far beyond the campus. He wrote a trigonometry textbook, *Plane and Spherical Trigonometry,* that eventually entered the national textbook market and influenced instruction at many schools.

Buchanan became nationally known for his work as a topographer-surveyor. He sharpened his skills during the Civil War. From 1876 through 1896 he spent his summers doing topographic surveying for the U.S. Coast and Geodetic Survey. In 1902–1903 he helped resolve the boundary line between Virginia and Tennessee. Buchanan retired in 1911, and died three years later at Lebanon.

James X. Corgan, Austin Peay State University

SUGGESTED READING: James X. Corgan, "Notes of Tennessee's Pioneer Scientists, *Journal of the Tennessee Academy of Science,* 53 (1978): 2–7

SEE: CUMBERLAND UNIVERSITY; SCIENCE AND TECHNOLOGY

BUCHANAN, JAMES MCGILL (1919–) received the 1986 Nobel Prize in Economics for "his development of the contractual and constitutional bases for the theory of economic and political decision making." In its announcement of the prize, the Royal Swedish Academy of Sciences noted, "Buchanan's foremost achievement is that he has consistently and tenaciously emphasized the significance of fundamental rules and applied the concept of the political system as an exchange process for the achievement of mutual advantages." Often identified as the father of Public Choice Theory, Buchanan's accomplishments are even more notable because of his rural southern origins and because his contributions were made outside the mainstream of traditional economic thinking.

James Buchanan was born in Murfreesboro, the grandson of the 1890 Tennessee Governor John P. Buchanan, who headed the Farmers' Alliance. James Buchanan's early years were marked by frugality and hard work. With limited resources, his collegiate choices were restricted, and he chose Middle Tennessee State Teachers College. In *Better Than Plowing,* a series of autobiographical essays, Buchanan described his life as a day student, returning home each evening to milk cows and perform chores on the family farm.

After graduation with honors in Mathematics, English, Literature, and Social Science, Buchanan chose continued academic study over a banking position and earned a master's degree in economics at the University of Tennessee in 1941. Drafted into the military, he trained as a naval officer and spent much of World War II serving at Pacific Fleet Headquarters on the operations staff of Admiral Chester W. Nimitz. After the war, Buchanan returned to his academic studies, earning a Ph.D. in economics in 1948 from the University of Chicago. Professor Frank Knight strongly influenced Buchanan's intellectual development, especially his emergence as an academic advocate of the market order. Buchanan also discovered the writings of Knut Wicksell, a Swedish economist, which provided important insights leading to his development of Public Choice Theory.

Following a series of academic positions at Tennessee and Florida universities, Buchanan was appointed professor and chair of the Department of Economics at the University of Virginia. Despite innovative scholarship and the establishment of the Thomas Jefferson Center for Studies in Political Economy, he failed to garner the support of the University administration, which considered his research too conservative and outside mainstream economic thought then advocating growing government intervention in the economy. Buchanan moved to Virginia Polytechnic Institute and State University, where with others he founded the Center for Public Choice. In 1983 he accepted a professorship at George Mason University and relocated the Center to its current site.

Buchanan is internationally recognized for his contributions to Public Choice Theory, which has provided the theoretical basis directly and indirectly for conservative political proposals such as a constitutional amendment to balance the federal budget. In addition to the Nobel Prize, Buchanan has received many honors and has provided leadership to major professional economics associations. He is a distinguished fellow of the American Economic Association and a fellow of the American Academy of Arts and Sciences. In 1997 his alma mater, Middle Tennessee State University, established the Buchanan Scholars Program to support outstanding students who exhibit the scholarly and leadership characteristics of one of its most distinguished graduates.

Barbara Haskew, Middle Tennessee State University

SUGGESTED READINGS: James M. Buchanan, *Better Than Plowing* (1992); *The Calculus of Consent* (1962) with Gordon Tullock; *The Limits to Liberty: Between Anarchy and Leviathan* (1975); *Democracy in Deficit* (1977) with Richard E. Wagner; and *The Power to Tax* (1980) with Geoffrey Brennan

SEE: BUCHANAN, JOHN P.; MIDDLE TENNESSEE STATE UNIVERSITY

BUCHANAN, JOHN PRICE (1847–1930), Governor and president of the Tennessee Farmers' Alliance, was born in Williamson County, the son of Thomas and Rebecca Jane Shannon Buchanan. He attended common schools and joined the Confederate army late in 1864, serving as a private in Roddy's escort, attached to the 4th Alabama Cavalry. In 1867 Buchanan married Frances McGill of Rutherford County; they had eight children. The war ruined his family's land, and Buchanan moved to Rutherford County, where he established a livestock farm on Manchester Pike.

Buchanan's political life was entwined with the rise of the Farmers' Alliance in Tennessee. A perennial delegate to the Democratic state conventions, Buchanan won election to the 45th and 46th General Assemblies (1887–1891), representing Rutherford County. In 1888 he became the first president of the Tennessee Farmers' Alliance. When the Agricultural Wheel merged with the Farmers' Alliance in 1889, Buchanan became the first president of the combined organization, the Tennessee Farmers' and Laborers' Union. He won the admiration of the state's farmers when he successfully steered a bill through the 1889 General Assembly to exempt the agents of the Agricultural Wheel and Farmers' Alliance cooperative stores from the state merchant tax.

In 1890 Buchanan became the Democratic nominee for governor after a spirited party convention, in which farmers surprised their opponents by their steadfast support for the Alliance president. He won easily in the general election and opened the 1891 General Assembly with 54 Alliance members in the House and Senate. The "Farmer Legislature" produced no significant legislation that reflected the special interests of the agricultural sector. Indeed, a number of Alliance supporters began to have second thoughts as the subtreasury scheme and the demand for a third party dominated the national organization. In addition, uprisings by East Tennessee coal miners who opposed the use of convict labor in the mines marred his administration in 1891–92. Caught between the demands of New South industrialists for immediate action to end the violence and Alliance calls for an end to convict leasing, Buchanan carried out the law, but appeared weak to both sides when the unrest continued and a special legislative session of the legislature failed to end the leasing system.

In 1892 Buchanan sought the Democratic nomination for a second term, which he and his Alliance supporters claimed as their right since they had meticulously supported the party platform without insisting on implementation of the agrarian demands. The Bourbon wing of the Democratic party, supported by the New South wing, mounted an intense campaign to stop Buchanan. By May, the Bourbon candidate, Peter Turney, was ahead. In June, several important Alliance leaders, including Buchanan's friend and former campaign manager, John H. McDowell, broke with the Democratic party and joined the People's, or Populist, party, which developed from the efforts of the National Farmers' Alliance. Buchanan withdrew his name from the Democratic nomination and ran as an Independent (Jeffersonian) Democrat. The Populists supported his candidacy, but Buchanan never joined the party. Buchanan lost to Turney in the general election, and the political aspirations of Tennessee farmers ended, though the Populists fielded gubernatorial candidates in the elections of 1894 and 1896.

Buchanan held no other elective offices. He died in 1930 and was buried in Evergreen Cemetery in Murfreesboro.

Connie L. Lester, Tennessee Historical Society

SUGGESTED READINGS: Roger L. Hart, *Redeemers, Bourbons & Populists: Tennessee, 1871–1896* (1975); Connie L. Lester, "Grassroots Reform in the Age of New South Agriculture and Bourbon Democracy: The Agricultural Wheel, The Farmers' Alliance, and The People's Party in Tennessee, 1884–1892," (Ph.D. Diss., University of Tennessee, 1998)

SEE: AGRICULTURAL WHEEL; CONVICT LEASE WARS; FARMERS' AND LABORERS' UNION; MCDOWELL, JOHN H.; RUTHERFORD COUNTY

BUCKEYE COTTON OIL COMPANY. Procter & Gamble organized the Buckeye Cotton Oil Company in 1901 to provide a reliable supply of cottonseed oil for the soaps and lard substitutes the company manufactured. Such popular Procter & Gamble products as Ivory soap and Crisco shortening were originally made from cottonseed oil. By 1914 Buckeye operated eleven large cottonseed oil mills in Georgia, Alabama, North Carolina, South Carolina, Mississippi, Tennessee, and Arkansas. One of its Memphis plants, constructed in 1911, was described as "a monster cotton oil mill."[1]

In order to buy enough seed to keep their large mills operating at full capacity for as many months as possible each year, Buckeye followed the common practice of loaning money to cotton ginners to help them buy the supplies needed to begin operations each fall, and to build new gins or to improve old ones. Ginners took a portion of the seed they removed as their fee for ginning, and they usually purchased the remainder of the seed. Buckeye expected ginners, who received loans, to settle their debts by selling the seed they acquired to the company.

Independent mills had to buy seed at a price that would enable them to make a profit on the sale of crude cottonseed oil, but Buckeye could pay more for

seed and make up losses from the profits Procter & Gamble earned on its manufactured products. Mills that lacked an affiliation with a large manufacturing corporation considered the practice of buying seed at a loss unfair competition.

After World War I, Buckeye moved into cellulose production. Demand for nitrocellulose, or gun cotton, during the war stimulated interest in the infant cellulose industry. In 1920 Buckeye became the first American company to manufacture cellulose from cottonseed linters, the short fibers that remain on the seed after ginning. Memphis was chosen as the site of Buckeye's new cellulose plant and as the headquarters of cellulose operations. By 1921 Procter & Gamble renamed its subsidiary the Buckeye Cellulose Corporation.

Treated with different chemicals, cellulose served as the raw material for a variety of synthetic products such as rayon, photographic and x-ray film, paper, celluloid, cellophane, plastics, tire cord, and gun powder. The relative purity of cottonseed linters made them an excellent source of cellulose, but the supply of linters could not be expanded to meet growing demand. In the period between the World Wars, research on wood pulp provided Buckeye with an additional, cheaper, and more abundant source of cellulose.

At the end of World War II, Buckeye's fourteen cottonseed oil mills produced most of the linters used in cellulose production. By that time, more vegetable oil was being made from soybeans than from cottonseed. In the early 1950s, Buckeye operated four soybean oil mills and processed both soybeans and cottonseed in other mills.

Procter & Gamble sold Buckeye's oil mills, and in 1988, renamed the subsidiary Procter & Gamble Cellulose. Memphian Robert Cannon and a group of investors bought the Memphis facility and other assets from Procter & Gamble in 1992. Today the company bears the name Buckeye Technologies, Inc.

Lynette Boney Wrenn, Memphis

CITATION:

(1) Memphis *Commercial Appeal,* "Fifty Years Ago," 8 March 1961.

SUGGESTED READING: Lynette Boney Wrenn, *Cinderella of the New South: A History of the Cottonseed Industry, 1855–1955* (1995)

SEE: COTTON; INDUSTRY; MEMPHIS

BUCKNER, LEWIS C. (1856–1924), African-American carpenter, cabinetmaker, and house builder in Sevier County, was born and raised as a slave as a young boy before the Civil War. Buckner was the son of a white father and an African-American mother. He learned his trade as an apprentice in Sevierville after the Civil War. He started his cabinetmaking business in the 1870s; the 1880 census listed him as a cabinetmaker and he found success in building furniture and dwellings.

From 1880 to 1921 Buckner built houses throughout Sevier County and embellished them with the ornate architectural elements indicative of Victorianera ebullience. He usually built an entire dwelling and lived at the building site during construction. Buckner added decorative details, such as porches and staircases, to otherwise plain farmhouses. His handsome and creative furniture, cabinets, and mantels spread throughout the region and are now prized family heirlooms. Buckner also constructed ornate pews and a pulpit for the New Salem Baptist Church at Sevierville, a historic African-American church built by Isaac Dockery in 1886.

At least 15 examples of dwellings exhibiting Buckner's extraordinary craftsmanship still exist in Sevier County. Indicative of the chronological range of his work are the Darius and Mary Robertson House near Harrisburg (ca. 1880); the Andes-Denton House near Sevierville (ca. 1890); the Trotter-Waters House at Sevierville (1895); the Sam Dixon House near Shady Grove (1914); and the Mullendore House near Pigeon Forge (1921). Buckner built his own house near Millican Grove in 1894.

Using his own interpretation of national architectural styles acquired from patternbooks, Buckner's work is extremely creative and rarely are two pieces rendered exactly alike. Several of Buckner's flamboyant-style houses are listed in the National Register of Historic Places due to their significant and unique architecture. Buckner is buried in an unmarked grave at the Union Hill Cemetery near Millican Grove.

Robbie D. Jones, Nashville

SEE: ARCHITECTURE, VERNACULAR DOMESTIC; FURNITURE AND CABINETMAKERS; SEVIER COUNTY

BUEHLER, CALVIN ADAM (1897–1988), head of the Department of Chemistry, University of Tennessee, 1940–1962, received his bachelor's degree in 1918, his master's in 1920, and his Ph.D. in 1922 from Ohio State University. He accepted a position at the University of Tennessee in 1922. Buehler was named head of the chemistry department in 1940, and it was during his term that the university initiated its first doctoral program.

The author of one book, *Survey of Organic Synthesis* (1971), and more than 42 scholarly articles, Buehler was acclaimed for his research as well as his teaching. In 1950 the *Southern Chemist*, a monthly publication of the southern section of the American Chemical Society, named him the South's outstanding chemist for his contributions to research and the development of chemical education in the South. In 1963 Buehler was selected as one of the first five University of Tennessee professors honored as Distinguished Service Professors. Buehler retired in 1965, and five years later, the university named its newly constructed chemistry building Buehler Hall in his honor.

Buehler married Grace Stone Buehler in 1937. After her death, he married Katherine Doies McCallen. He died in Knoxville in 1988 and was buried at Highland Memorial Cemetery.

Connie L. Lester, Tennessee Historical Society

SEE: SCIENCE AND TECHNOLOGY; UNIVERSITY OF TENNESSEE

BULL, CARROLL GIDEON (1880–1931), medical researcher and immunologist, was born in Jefferson County, the fourth of 11 children born to William Gernade and Nancy Emmaline White Bull. Bull graduated from Harrison-Chilhowee Academy, before enrolling at Carson-Newman College in 1901. He graduated from Peabody College in Nashville in 1907, with a Bachelor of Science degree. In 1910 Bull completed his medical degree at Lincoln Memorial University.

Bull served as Professor of Pathology and Bacteriology at LMU, from 1910 to 1912. In 1913 he became Assistant in Pathology at New York's Rockefeller Institute for Medical Research. Four years later, he identified the gas gangrene toxin and antitoxin, becoming the first American to discover an antitoxin of any kind.

The gas gangrene infection posed an immense problem for doctors treating the wounded in World War I, and claimed many lives and limbs. In November 1917, Bull accepted a major's commission in the United States Army Medical Corps, where he promoted the production and use of his antitoxin on battlefields and in hospitals. France honored him for his efforts with its Silver Medaille de Reconnaissance Francaise.

Earlier in 1917, Bull received an appointment as Associate Professor of Immunology at Johns Hopkins School of Hygiene and Public Health in Baltimore, where he helped establish the Immunology department. Bull made outstanding contributions to medicine through his work on diphtheria, malaria, pneumonia, and the agglutination of bacteria. His work helped establish the basis for current immunological theory. In 1922 Bull was promoted to Professor of Immunology. He died on May 31, 1931.

Walter Lynn Bates, Knoxville

SEE: CARSON-NEWMAN COLLEGE; LINCOLN MEMORIAL UNIVERSITY; MEDICINE; WORLD WAR I

BURCH, LUCIUS E., JR. (1912–1996), attorney, conservationist, and civil rights advocate, was born on a large farm outside Nashville on January 25, 1912, the son of Dr. Lucius E. Burch and Sarah Cooper Burch. He descended from a long line of distinguished people, including the founders of two southern cities (John Donelson of Nashville and Thomas Polk of Charlotte, N.C.); two early presidents (James K. Polk and Andrew Jackson); and the Episcopal Bishop and Civil War General Leonidas Polk. His grandfather was Secretary of the United States Senate, and his father was Dean of Vanderbilt Medical School.

Burch spent his boyhood and youth in Nashville, interrupted only by a period in Alaska. There he supported himself by hunting and killing bald eagles, an activity he later renounced as his greatest sin. That passion for the outdoors, which took him to Alaska, later transformed into a dedication to the protection of the environment, especially wildlife and wildlife habitat.

Burch attended both college and law school at Vanderbilt. After completing law school in 1936, he moved to Memphis to join the firm of Burch, Minor and McKay, then headed by his uncle, Charles Burch. Within a few years, all three senior partners died, and Burch inherited the practice of the firm. He soon brought in Jesse Johnson and John Porter, with whom he enjoyed a long partnership. Together they led the firm for some 50 years, involving it in every area of legal practice.

Burch married Elsie Caldwell in December 1935. They had four daughters, Sarah Polk Burch Gratz, Elsie Caldwell Burch Donald, Edith Montague Burch Caywood, and Lucia Newell Burch Doggrell.

Burch combined a vigorous, extensive outdoor life with a busy, productive professional and public life. He piloted a single-engine plane around the country and into Latin America and the Caribbean in pursuit of hunting, fishing, scuba-diving, hiking, and camping opportunities, surviving a number of serious crashes.

A life-long Democrat, he opposed the Crump political machine and championed the civil rights movement. He became one of the most active trial lawyers of his time and participated in many well-known trials. He represented Dr. Martin Luther King, Jr., in a successful attempt to lift an injunction prohibiting a march in Memphis, just prior to King's assassination.

Burch was a Fellow of the American College of Trial Lawyers and the American Bar Foundation; a Founder, Charter Member, and President of the Memphis Community Relations Council; Chairman of the Tennessee Game and Fish Commission; President of the Tennessee Conservation League; Member of the Tennessee Democratic Executive Committee; Honorary Life Member of the Tennessee Academy of Sciences; and Life Member of the NAACP. Among the awards he received were the Tennessee Conservation League's Cartter Patten Award; the Certificate of Merit of the Memphis Urban League; and the "Lawyer's Lawyer" Award of the Memphis and Shelby County Bar Association. He received an honorary doctorate from Rhodes College. He was the author of numerous articles on hunting, fishing, aviation, undersea exploration, civic affairs, politics and gerontology.

Burch possessed a brilliant mind, furnished with the best of Western literature and charged with intellectual and curiosity; a strong body; boundless energy; a seemingly indomitable will; absolute integrity; and a passionate commitment to the natural world, his ideals and principles, and his friends and family.

Charles F. Newman, Memphis

SEE: CIVIL RIGHTS MOVEMENT; CONSERVATION; MEMPHIS; MEMPHIS SANITATION STRIKE; VANDERBILT UNIVERSITY

BURGESS FALLS STATE NATURAL AREA, located along the Falling Water River in Putnam and White counties, contains 155 acres. Burgess Falls is one of the most dramatic in the state and has been a location for movie and television productions. Its name comes from Tom Burgess, an early settler who received the land in a Revolutionary war grant. The Burgess family used the rushing water to establish a profitable grist mill. Over 100 years later, in 1924, the city of Cookeville built a steel and earthen dam near the falls to provide municipal power. A huge flood destroyed the facility four years later, but the city rebuilt the dam in concrete. This hydoelectric installation closed in 1944, but the dam remains at the site, creating a lake that is popular for fishing.

The transformation of the Burgess Falls area into a recreational park began in 1950, when the city of Cookeville established a co-operative management agreement with the State of Tennessee. In 1971 the state formally created the Burgess Falls State Natural Area. It is a day-use park, with several trails, a playground, and picnic facilities.

Carroll Van West, Middle Tennessee State University

SUGGESTED READING: Robert Brandt, *Touring the Middle Tennessee Backroads* (1995)

SEE: CONSERVATION; PUTNAM COUNTY; WHITE COUNTY

BURRA BURRA COPPER COMPANY. The origins of the Tennessee copper mining industry can be traced back to 1843, when a gold prospector discovered copper near Potato Creek in the southeast corner of Polk County. Copper mining began in 1847, and the Hiwassee mine became the first deep mine for copper when it opened in August 1850. By the end of 1853, 11 mines operated in Tennessee. Originally no smelting was done at the mines, and ore was hauled by wagon to Dalton, Georgia, and shipped by rail to northern cities. Successful operations demanded access to railroads, however, and construction of the Copper Road from Ducktown to Cleveland, Tennessee, through the Ocoee River gorge, began in 1851 and was completed two years later.

With the increase in mining came a need for refinement of the ore. In 1854 the first smelter was built at the Hiwassee mine; others soon followed. Nevertheless, the expense of equipping mining operations slowed development of the region, and by 1858, only five mines operated regularly in Ducktown. Consolidation of smaller companies provided the only mechanism for continuing mining operations. The Burra Burra Copper Company was the result of such a consolidation.

Organized in 1860, the Burra Burra Copper Company consolidated the Hiwassee mine, the Cocheco mine, and the inactive Toccoee Mining Company. The capital stock was fixed at $1.5 million, and the company operated under the direction of William H. Peet, president; George O. Sweet, secretary; William H. Peet, John Thomas, E. MacPherson (who later served as president), and Lyman W. Gilbert, directors. The company owned 5,000 acres of land, the greater part at Turtletown, Tennessee.

The first Board of Directors' meeting named Julius E. Raht of Ducktown, a young German engineer, as superintendent of the Polk County operations. Burra Burra prepared for mining and smelting on a grand scale. Indeed, since the directors believed the company's prospects to be so bright, they chose the name Burra Burra after a famous Australian mine of the period.

Unfortunately, the Civil War proved disastrous for the mining operation, whose entire output sold to northern refineries. Between 1861 and 1863, the mines operated under Confederate supervision. When the railroad at Cleveland, Tennessee, fell to the Union army, however, the mines closed until the war ended.

In 1866 activities at Burra Burra resumed under the direction of Julius Raht. For several years, the ore continued to average from 10 to 15 percent copper. The company hoped to realize enough profit from the rich black ore located near the surface to cover expenses until deep workings tapped the more abundant yellow ore. In June 1869, with the supply of black copper nearing exhaustion, the company made earnest, but unsuccessful attempts to reach the yellow sulphurets.

In addition to the mines, Burra Burra, like Ducktown's other two companies, operated smelting works that had been completed during the war. The smelting operation consisted of nine furnaces, a 40-horsepower steam engine, and a four-horsepower water wheel. Burra Burra employed some 160 men and boys, with an average annual payroll of $60,000. The company produced an average of one million pounds of copper annually.

The company succumbed to a series of financial problems in the 1870s. The debt load became heavier with each passing year; when mortgage bonds matured in 1866, they were renewed for another five years. The company never found the necessary financial backing to restore rail service from Ducktown to Cleveland. Burra Burra desperately needed a rise in the price of copper to survive, but an increase in domestic copper prices came too late for the company. Mortgage holders instituted foreclosure proceedings in 1875, and two years later, the companies' properties sold for $25,000.

The impact of Burra Burra Copper Company, and other copper operations, continued long after its financial collapse. By 1900, mining, harvesting of forests to fuel the smelters, and emissions from the smelters combined to denude approximately 32,000 acres, creating a virtual moonscape. Today, the process has been partially reversed through ongoing soil reclamation efforts, though the effects are still visible. The Burra Burra Copper Mine is listed on the National Register of Historic Places.
Patricia Bernard Ezzell, Tennessee Valley Authority
SEE: DUCKTOWN BASIN MUSEUM; MINING; POLK COUNTY; RAHT, JULIUS E.

BURRITT COLLEGE was founded in 1848 at Spencer, Van Buren County, as a preparatory school and junior college under the auspices of the Churches of Christ. The college was an early coeducational institution, with its faculty teaching a classical curriculum, along with strict moral and religious codes.

The first president, Isaac Newton Jones, a graduate of Irving College in neighboring Warren County, left after only one year. William Davis Carnes replaced Jones in 1849. Carnes implemented coeducation and expelled students who drank alcohol. He also petitioned the Tennessee General Assembly to pass a law prohibiting the sale of liquor within a four-mile radius of a chartered school in an unincorporated area. Shortly after this law passed, the president's home and girls' dormitory mysteriously burned. Carnes left Burritt to accept the presidency of East Tennessee University (now the University of Tennessee) and was succeeded by John Powell in 1857.

The college closed during the Civil War, and Union troops occupied the buildings. Both Carnes and Powell returned to Burritt in the years following the war and re-established a strict moral, religious, and intellectual tone for the college. In 1890 William Newton Billingsley, an 1873 Burritt graduate, became the college's eleventh president.

A fire in 1906 destroyed another campus building, and the college briefly closed. After reopening, Burritt College prospered for several years, but its enrollment declined after the opening of state normal schools in Murfreesboro and Cookeville in the early 1910s. With the establishment of a public high school in Van Buren County, Burritt College could no longer compete for students and closed in 1939.
Tara Mitchell Mielnik, Middle Tennessee State University
SEE: EDUCATION, HIGHER; VAN BUREN COUNTY

BURROW, AARON KNOX (1871–1968), whose success in the trading of cotton linters assumed strategic importance during World War I, was born in Carroll County, Tennessee, the son of the Reverend Albert Gibson Burrow and Elizabeth Polk Burrow.

From age 17, when he began work for a Memphis cotton company, Burrow focused on cottonseed products, particularly linters, the short fibers from the cottonseed, which were used primarily in bedding. The outbreak of World War I generated an enormous demand for cotton linters as a foundation for explosives. Burrow headed the linters program—purchasing, assembling the shipments, and transporting them—for E. I. DuPont de Nemours & Company, which soon became the largest manufacturer of high explosives outside Germany. When the United States entered the war, Burrow also assumed responsibility for all purchases of linters by the federal government.

Burrow's business, A. K. Burrow & Company, flourished after the war, capitalizing on the expanding market for cottonseed products in the manufacture of rayon, plastics, and chemicals. The company remained in operation until 1937, when Burrow resumed representation of DuPont. He retired in 1948. Burrow also served as a director of First National Bank of Memphis, later First Tennessee Bank N.A., from 1923 to 1955.

Burrow was active in many civic and philanthropic causes, most notably the development of Rhodes College. He helped finance its move from Clarksville to Memphis during the 1920s, when it was known as Southwestern Presbyterian University, and served on the Board of Trustees for a number of years. In the early 1950s, he donated $1 million for the construction of Burrow Library on the Memphis campus. He was also a major contributor toward construction of the refectory at Rhodes, completed in 1958 and named for his wife, Catherine Walter Burrow (1878–1962). The Burrows were involved in the planning and design of both buildings, which combined innovative interior features and the Collegiate Gothic architecture for which Rhodes is renowned.

Burrow died in 1968 and is buried at Memorial Park in Memphis.

Paul A. Matthews, Memphis

SEE: COTTON; FIRST TENNESSEE BANK; MEMPHIS; RHODES COLLEGE; WORLD WAR I

BUSSARD, RAYMOND ARTHUR (1928–), nationally recognized swim coach at the University of Tennessee, was born on August 12, 1928, in Hot Springs, Virginia. After attending Ohio University on a football scholarship, Bussard transferred to Bridgewater College in Virginia, where he received a B.A. degree in physical education and was the 1952 National AAU All-Around Champion in track and field. Bussard coached football, basketball, baseball, and track at schools in Virginia before moving to Chattanooga in 1959. There he coached at Chattanooga and Red Bank High schools and became aquatics director for the city's summer swim programs.

In 1967 Bussard joined college coaching ranks, when the University of Tennessee at Knoxville hired him to build a swimming program. At the time, UT had not had a swim program since 1959. His first team, composed entirely of freshmen, concluded the 1968 season with a surprising second-place finish in the Southeastern Conference. The next year, they won the SEC championship, and Tennessee swim teams began a decade of domination that saw seven straight Southeastern Conference titles and culminated with a national championship in 1978. During those years, Bussard coached two Olympic gold medalists, Dave Edgar in 1972 and Matt Vogel in 1976.

Bussard became known for the added color he brought to the sport of swimming. Tennessee swimmers donned coonskin caps and poured jugs of water from the UT Aquatic Center into their opponents' pools before meets. At home meets, Bussard featured the Vol Timettes, women students who served as timers and scorekeepers, an innovation that many schools copied.

Bussard was named NCAA Coach of the Year in 1972 and 1978, and was SEC Coach of the Year five times. He became the sprint coach for the U.S. swim team at the 1984 Olympics in Los Angeles. That same year, he received the Outstanding Coach of the Year award from the American Swim Coaches' Association, and the College Swimming Coaches Association honored him with the National Collegiate and Scholastic Swimming Trophy for outstanding contributions made to the sport. In 1988 Bussard was inducted into the Knoxville and Tennessee Sports Halls of Fame. In June 1988 Bussard retired from the University of Tennessee, where his record was 252–20.

Margaret Ellen Crawford, University of Tennessee, Knoxville

BUTCHER, JACOB FRANKLIN "JAKE" (1936–), was a major figure in Tennessee banking and politics in the 1970s and early 1980s, the driving force behind the Knoxville International Energy Exposition of 1982, and the subject of a banking investigation, who was convicted of bank fraud and imprisoned between 1985 and 1992.

Born in Dotson's Creek in Union County in 1936, Jake Butcher was the son of Cecil H. Butcher, Sr., a general store owner, and organizer and president of the Union County Bank of Maynardville. Jake Butcher attended the University of Tennessee and Hiwassee College and served one enlistment in the U.S. Marine Corps. He founded the Bull Run Oil Company, an Amoco distributorship, and engaged in commercial farming. On New Year's Eve 1961, he met up-and-coming movie star Sonya Wilde on a blind date, and the couple married in 1962.

Butcher's interest in banking dated from his youth and work in his father's bank. In 1968 he and his younger brother Cecil H. Butcher, Jr., began acquiring banks, borrowing large amounts of capital to finance their purchases of bank stock. By 1974, the brothers controlled eight banks in Tennessee along with other business properties. In that year, Jake Butcher used borrowed capital to purchase stock in Hamilton National Bank, Knoxville's largest banking institution with 39 percent of the city's total banking reserves. After a brief takeover fight, he won complete control and changed the bank's name to United American Bank. By 1982, the United American Bank accounted for over half of the business loans in Knoxville. In that year, Jake Butcher declared a net worth of approximately $34 million.

As the Butcher brothers continued to acquire banks and other businesses, Jake developed a keen interest in politics. After failing to win the Democratic party's gubernatorial nomination in 1974, he won the nomination in 1978, only to lose in the general election to Republican Lamar Alexander. At the same time, he was instrumental in bringing the Knoxville International Energy Exposition to Knoxville in 1982, and was considering a third run for the governorship.

Federal bank examiners had long suspected that the Butcher brothers' $3 billion empire was largely a paper empire operating under improper management. On November 1, 1982, 180 FDIC investigators descended on all the Butcher banks simultaneously, thus preventing the transfer of assets from one bank to shore up another. Ultimately they found that bank acquisitions had been made through loans from Butcher-owned banks, and uncovered a pyramid of unsecured loans, forged loan documents, and bank fraud. On February 14, 1983, United American Bank, the capstone of Jake Butcher's financial empire, failed; in August 1983, he was involuntarily declared bankrupt with listed assets of $11.9 million and liabilities of $32.5 million. In May 1985 he pled guilty to federal charges of bank fraud and was sentenced to 20 years in prison. He was released on parole in 1992, after having served almost seven years of his sentence. Butcher accepted employment at a Toyota automobile distributorship and lives in quiet obscurity—his fortune of cash, real estate, automobiles, houseboats, and property swept away in a series of public auctions.

W. Bruce Wheeler, University of Tennessee, Knoxville
SEE: KNOXVILLE; KNOXVILLE WORLD'S FAIR OF 1982; UNION COUNTY

BUTLER, JOHN WASHINGTON (1875–1952), State Representative from Macon, Trousdale, and Sumner counties (1923–1927), wrote the Tennessee Anti-Evolution Act, better known as the Tennessee Monkey Law. The son of a long-settled farming family in Macon County, as a young man Butler taught school

briefly. By 1925 he was a prosperous middle-aged farmer, thresher operator, and community leader.

A Democrat and great admirer of William Jennings Bryan, Butler ran for the state legislature in 1922, promising to represent farmers' interests and work for economy in state government. Appointed to serve on a state legislative committee that oversaw schools run directly by the state, Butler discovered that such schools used textbooks teaching Darwinism. A Primitive Baptist, Butler shared with other conservative Christians the belief that teaching Darwinism would destroy belief in the Bible and undercut the moral system upon which democracy depended. This led him to write the famous "Monkey Law."

With the passage of the bill, Butler received national attention. He attended the Scopes Trial as the guest of a press syndicate and had his picture made with his hero Bryan. While national media coverage of the Monkey Trial depicted rural Tennesseans as ignorant hicks, the coverage of Butler himself was rather respectful, noting his kindly demeanor. The *New York Times* commented editorially that Butler's beliefs were logical, if one accepted his original premise that public morals depended on a belief in the Bible. After the trial, Butler finished out his term as state representative and left politics, resuming his life as farmer and thresherman.

Jeanette Keith, Bloomburg University of Pennsylvania
SEE: EDUCATION; MACON COUNTY; SCOPES TRIAL

BYRNS, JOSEPH W. (1869–1936), former Speaker of the U.S. House of Representatives, was an important political leader in early twentieth century Tennessee, serving in the Tennessee General Assembly and then 14 terms in the U.S. Congress. Born at Cedar Hill, Tennessee, in 1869, Byrns attended Vanderbilt University, graduating with a law degree in 1890. His legal practice began in Nashville and by 1895 he was elected to the Tennessee House as a Davidson County representative. A staunch, loyal Democrat, Byrns enjoyed rapid political success and during his third term in the State House, his fellow Democrats chose him as Speaker of the House. In 1901 he won election to the State Senate, but failure came in 1902 when the voters rejected Byrns' bid to be district Attorney General for Davidson County. Byrns rebounded in 1908 and won the Democratic nomination for Fifth district seat in the U.S. Congress. From that point on, Byrns never faced serious political opposition and won every Congressional election in his district until his death in 1936.

As Byrns gained seniority in the U.S. Congress, and his party's political fortunes improved during the Great Depression years, he exercised significant influence in the nation's capital. In 1928 he was chosen as Chairman of the Democratic National Congressional Committee; two years later, once the

Democrats gained control of the House, he became the chairman of the House Appropriations Committee, one of the most powerful positions in Washington. In 1933 he advanced to the position of Majority Leader, a key political role once newly elected President Franklin D. Roosevelt announced his New Deal in March 1933. Although a conservative, Byrns embraced the New Deal out of party loyalty. He introduced the bill creating the Civilian Conservation Corps and successfully maneuvered other major New Deal initiatives through Congress.

In 1935, due to his seniority, debts owed from his leadership of the Democratic National Congressional Committee, and his loyalty to the New Deal, Byrns was elected Speaker of the House of Representatives. He was an effective speaker, which surprised some of his detractors. The Republican minority leader, however, noted that it was Byrns's "intense loyalty to the Chief Executive and his adroit and skillful leadership that piloted administrative measures through the shoals and over the rocks of legislative processes."[1] Byrns's career as Speaker, unfortunately, was cut short by his sudden death from a heart attack on June 3, 1936. "Fearless, incorruptible, unselfish, with a high sense of justice, wise in victory," observed President Roosevelt, Byrns "served his state and the nation with fidelity, honor and great usefulness."[2] No Tennessean since has served as Speaker of the U.S. House of Representatives.

Carroll Van West, Middle Tennessee State University

CITATIONS:
(1) J.M. Galloway, "Speaker Joseph W. Byrns: Party Leader in the New Deal," *Tennessee Historical Quarterly* 25(1966): 75.
(2) Ibid., 76.

SEE: CIVILIAN CONSERVATION CORPS; DAVIDSON COUNTY; TENNESSEE HOUSE OF REPRESENTATIVES

C

CADES COVE, a fertile elliptical valley surrounded on all sides by the Great Smoky Mountains, had already been long inhabited by the Cherokees, who called it Tsiyahi, or otter place, when John Oliver, his wife, and young child arrived there in the fall of 1818. By 1821 other neighbors joined the Olivers from Carter County, and the expansion of farms, homes, and gardens proceeded rapidly in a pattern identical to frontier development throughout the United States. As early as 1827, a bloomery forge was constructed in the cove; by the 1830s roads for marketing agricultural surplus connected the cove to Maryville and Knoxville. In the 1840s and 1850s new waves of immigrants from other states and many foreign countries entered the cove, enriching the community with their diverse talents. Although many migrants used the cove only as a temporary way-station in their travel west, entrepreneurs like Daniel D. Foute and the abolitionist/mineralogist/physician, Dr. Calvin Post, surveyed the surrounding mountains for prospective gold and copper mines in a fever of capitalist activity. Because of its unique location, Cades Cove remained a community of farms surrounded by large stretches of mountain wilderness, an environment which provided recreation for hunting deer and bear and fur trapping.

The Civil War brought bitter division to the community, which was largely Unionist. Outlaw guerrilla bands from North Carolina periodically raided the cove, stripping the area of food and other valuables. The postwar period brought regression—fewer new families moved into the cove; most remaining families were interrelated through an extended kinship structure. By 1900 some degree of prosperity returned, and during the next two decades, cove farmers became caught up in the progressive agricultural movement manifested throughout the rest of the country. During the 1920s farm prices slumped,

bitter divisions erupted within the community over moonshining, and many cove citizens sought new jobs in other parts of the country.

For those who remained, however, the final challenge to their life as a community came with the movement to establish a Great Smoky Mountains National Park. Initially promised they would be left unmolested in their homes, many cove residents felt betrayed by subsequent inclusion of the entire cove within the boundaries of the new park. Their leading citizen, John W. Oliver, grandson of the original settler, led a lonely and protracted court battle against eminent domain, but lost finally after appealing his case three times before the Tennessee Supreme Court. The birth of what would become the most popular national park in the East thus marked the death of this historic community.

Durwood Dunn, Tennessee Wesleyan College

SEE: BLOUNT COUNTY; GREAT SMOKY MOUNTAINS NATIONAL PARK

CAIN, ROBERT, JR., "BOBBY" (1939–) became the first African-American student to graduate from a public formally segregated white high school in Tennessee during the immediate controversial years of integration following the U.S. Supreme Court decision of *Brown v. Board of Education* (1954). Now he considers it "a great honor—-a great achievement." On August 27, 1956, when Clinton High School opened as a desegregated school, Cain did not feel heroic. The only black senior eligible to graduate, he knew segregationists meant to stop him from achieving a high school diploma. David J. Brittain, Clinton High School principal in the 1950s, recognized the danger of allowing Cain to go through the graduation ceremonies and feared for his life. To protect Cain, Brittain organized a student patrol. Cain's proud father and mother accompanied him to the ceremony, but he had to go alone to change into his cap and gown. At that point, the student patrol acted as Cain's protection from would-be attackers. Bobby Cain graduated with his class.

In 1961 Cain graduated from Tennessee State University with a bachelor's degree in social work. He later completed course work toward a master's degree. After college graduation he was employed by Oak Ridge National Laboratory before being drafted into the army. He later enlisted in the reserve system, from which he retired after 21 years with the rank of captain.

Now a supervisor with the Tennessee Department of Human Services in Nashville, Cain talks of his experiences after years of reticence. His wife, Margo, and their daughter, Yvette Yolanda, a Nashville attorney, first learned the details of his achievement from others. In his view, the strong support of family and school encouraged him to stand fast in the fight for school desegregation in Tennessee.

June Adamson, Oak Ridge

SEE: ANDERSON COUNTY; CIVIL RIGHTS MOVEMENT; CLINTON DESEGREGATION CRISIS

CALDWELL AND COMPANY. Rogers C. Caldwell founded Caldwell and Company in September 1917 to market southern municipal bonds. Few investment houses considered southern bonds a good risk because of their historic default rate. This placed Caldwell and Company in a unique position to benefit from the dramatic demand for capital to finance southern construction projects in the post-World War I era. The firm grew rapidly and, by 1930, was the largest investment banking house in the region. The firm's abrupt collapse in November 1930 produced severe financial repercussions throughout the South.

A key factor in the expansion of Caldwell and Company was the Bank of Tennessee, founded by Rogers Caldwell in 1919. Under depository agreements with bond issuers, the company deposited proceeds from bond sales with banks it selected until the funds were actually needed to pay for construction costs. Caldwell and Company channeled the funds into the Bank of Tennessee and used this capital to finance expansion of the business into other areas.

With a ready supply of capital, Caldwell and Company grew dramatically. The firm opened numerous branch offices, 14 by 1925, chiefly in the South. The firm entered other areas besides securities, buying insurance companies, banks, industrial concerns, retail businesses, oil companies, and other businesses. Caldwell and Company also expanded its bond operations into the private real estate market, underwriting construction of office buildings, apartments, and hotels.

By the late 1920s, Caldwell's company, however, was experiencing serious financial difficulties. Unknown to the public, the company had never followed normal financial and business practices. Caldwell charged off his lavish lifestyle and personal expenses to the company. The firm had incurred massive debts with its acquisition program and had inadequate cash reserves.

As the company's difficulties mounted, Caldwell became increasingly involved financially and politically with Luke Lea, owner of the *Tennessean* and a major force in state politics. Caldwell and Lea purchased controlling interests in Holston National Bank in Knoxville and the Memphis *Commercial Appeal* and the Knoxville *Journal*. As a result of Lea's influence with Governor Henry Horton, Kentucky Rock and Asphalt, a Caldwell-owned company, bypassed competitive bidding and supplied building materials for state highway projects.

In the 1928 governor's race between Horton and Hill McAlister, Lea's and Caldwell's relationship and business dealings with Horton's administration became major campaign issues. Horton won the election, and Caldwell and Company continued to receive preferential treatment from state government. The company sold large amounts of bonds to finance state highway constructions and deposited the funds with the Bank of Tennessee.

After the stock market crash of October 1929, Caldwell and Company's position became increasingly desperate. The firm remained afloat largely because it continued to receive state deposits. On November 7, state examiners audited the Bank of Tennessee and declared it insolvent. This action immediately brought down Caldwell and Company and unleashed runs on other Caldwell-controlled banks across Tennessee. On November 14, 1930, the company went into receivership.

Fred Colvin, Middle Tennessee State University

SUGGESTED READING: John B. McFerrin, *Caldwell and Company: A Southern Financial Empire* (1939)

SEE: CALDWELL, ROGERS C.; HORTON, HENRY; LEA, LUKE

CALDWELL, ROGERS CLARK (1890–1968), dominated southern financial circles in the 1920s to the point that he was often called the "J. P. Morgan of the South." In a career that spanned only twenty years, he built a financial empire that collapsed abruptly in November 1930, shaking the foundations of Tennessee's economy and government.

Rogers Caldwell was the son of James E. Caldwell, a prominent Nashville banker. He attended Montgomery Bell Academy and entered Vanderbilt University in 1908. He abandoned his college studies in 1910 to run a small insurance business his father owned.

Caldwell sold general insurance before specializing in surety bonds for county and municipal construction projects. Drawn by his success in attracting bidders, local officials soon sought his assistance. Caldwell sensed the unique opportunity for southern bonds despite their historic reputation as poor risks; southern bonds attracted fewer bidders and therefore offered greater opportunities for profit. In September 1917 he founded Caldwell and Company to market securities.

Caldwell and Company's early bond offerings competed poorly with World War I Liberty Bonds, but the firm established a market presence and exploited the dramatic postwar southern construction boom. Bond sales handled by the firm played a major role in providing capital for highways, schools, and internal improvement projects in Tennessee and other southern states.

In 1919 Caldwell launched the Bank of Tennessee, which became a key to his future financial operations. The bank functioned solely as a depository for funds raised through the company's bond sales. These funds earned no interest for the bond issuer and were dispersed only when construction projects required. The deposits provided Caldwell with considerable investment capital.

During the 1920s Caldwell expanded into other areas, buying insurance companies, banks, textile mills, oil companies, department stores, and assorted other businesses. He also expanded his bond operations into the private real estate market, underwriting the construction costs of hotels and office buildings. As Caldwell's financial empire and fortune grew, he developed a lifestyle that included racehorses, lavish entertainment, membership in exclusive private clubs, and Brentwood Hall, a magnificent Davidson County estate patterned after the Hermitage.

By 1921 Caldwell's financial empire was experiencing serious difficulties. Unknown to the public, Caldwell had never followed standard business practices, and his company was overextended, with no realistic cash reserves. His personal expenses far exceeded his annual salary, with the difference charged to the company.

At that point, Caldwell's career and fate became intertwined with that of Luke Lea, politician, banker, and owner of the *Tennessean*. They purchased controlling interest in banks and two newspapers, the Memphis *Commercial Appeal* and the Knoxville *Journal*. Lea used his political influence with Governor Henry Horton's administration to bypass competitive bidding and obtain a contract for Caldwell-owned Kentucky Rock and Asphalt to supply asphalt, under the trade name Kyrock, for state highway construction projects.

During the 1928 gubernatorial campaign the "Kyrock Scandal" became a central issue in the Horton-Hill McAlister contest, as Lea's political enemies attacked Caldwell's character and operations. Horton won the race, and his administration pursued policies advantageous to Caldwell's business, appointing Caldwell associates to key positions in the state banking department and the State Funding Board, which supervised the issuance of state bonds. Caldwell's company won a bid to sell millions in Tennessee bonds, and the state dramatically increased its deposits in his Bank of Tennessee.

The stock market crash of October 1929 sealed Caldwell's financial fate. State deposits kept him afloat until November 1930. Persistent rumors about Caldwell's financial condition forced state banking examiners to audit the Bank of Tennessee. Examiners declared it insolvent on November 7, and Caldwell and Company went into receivership several days later.

In 1931 the states of Tennessee and Kentucky indicted Caldwell on several charges. He was convicted on one count of breach of trust in Tennessee, but the state supreme court granted his appeal for a new trial. Tennessee never retried Caldwell, and he successfully avoided extradition to Kentucky.

After the collapse of his company, Caldwell retired from business, living at Brentwood Hall until 1957, when legal action by Tennessee finally resulted in the seizure of this property. He spent the last years of his life in Franklin, Tennessee, where he died on October 8, 1968.

Fred Colvin, Middle Tennessee State University

SEE: CALDWELL AND COMPANY; HORTON, HENRY; LEA, LUKE

CALHOUN, FRANCES BOYD (1867–1909), author, was born in Mecklenburg County, Virginia, in 1867, one of five children of a newspaper editor and publisher. In 1880 the family moved to Covington, Tennessee, where Frances Boyd attended Tipton Female Academy. She displayed her intelligence early by winning a scholarship awarded to the Tipton County female who graduated with the highest honors. After graduation, she taught school and wrote for her father's newspaper. In 1903 she married George Barret Calhoun, who died a year later.

As a lingering illness made continuing to teach impossible, Calhoun, from her lawn chair swing, turned to writing and regaling friends (youths and adults, alike) with her remarkable skill for story-telling.

Calhoun was best known as the bright and talented author of the 1909 best-selling children's book, *Miss Minerva and William Green Hill*, in which Calhoun portrayed friends and town youths from Covington. She submitted her manuscript to Messers. Reilly and Britton (now Henry Regnery Publishing Company) and awaited a response. When she received no answer, Calhoun penned the following rhymed letter:

> On the seventh of March, nineteen hundred and eight,
> Mr. Reilly, I sent you my book,
> And sure since that date for a letter from you
> Each day, I've continued to look.

Is it pigeon-holed now where the bookworm alone
May laugh and grow fat on each joke,
Where canker and rust will eat out the hearts
Of my dear little, quaint little folk?

Or, alas, has it vanished from all human ken,
The hard work of two long, long years?
Will the public ne'er know of its merit and worth,
Its laughter, its sighs and its tears?

Or has it already been published in full
And the 'steenth printing given it fame?
And instead of the title I gave it myself
Is it christened with some other name?

If naught has befallen it, may I still hope
You'll send my lost child back to me?
And I'll start it anew on its difficult path
Please ship it at once C. O. D.[1]

The unique letter caught the publisher's eye. He read the manuscript and excitedly passed it to others, who also were enthralled with her story of the determined Miss Minerva to civilize William Green Hill. Through wit and vivid characterizations, Calhoun depicted the chasm between blithesome youthfulness and agonizingly responsible adulthood.

Still in print today, *Miss Minerva and William Green Hill* was published in February 1909, just a few months before Calhoun's death on June 8. She never realized the book's great commercial success, nor the multitudinous reprints. The University of Tennessee Press has undertaken the most recent reprint.

Bella Katz Stringer, Nashville

CITATION:

(1) Frances Boyd Calhoun, *Miss Minerva and William Green Hill,* with introduction by Robert Drake (Knoxville, 1986), 214.

SEE: LITERATURE; TIPTON COUNTY

CALVERT, EBENEZER (1850–1924) and **PETER ROSS** (1855–1931). Brothers Ebenezer and Peter Ross Calvert were successful photographers and painters in Nashville at the turn of the century. Both were born in Yorkshire, England, near Leeds, and studied art there before arriving in Nashville in the 1870s.

The Calvert brothers worked for several Nashville galleries before setting up their own studio in the old Cole Building, now the site of First American National Bank. They taught art and did oil and watercolor paintings, pastels, crayon drawings, and miniatures on ivory. Peter Ross was an accomplished miniature painter at a time when the specialty enjoyed a revival. In 1896 they went into partnership with Sam Taylor as Calvert Brothers and Taylor. The partnership was dissolved four years later, and the firm became Calvert Brothers. Both brothers continued to paint, but photography was their livelihood, with class photographs serving as their specialty.

James C. Kelly, Virginia Historical Society

SEE: ART

CAMERON, ALEXANDER (ca. 1720–1781), British Indian agent, was a native of Scotland, who emigrated to Georgia in the 1730s and enlisted in the British army during the Seven Years' War. In 1764 the British appointed him commissary to Chota in the Cherokee territory, and he lived among the Tennessee Cherokees for the next 15 years. In early 1776 Cameron attempted to mediate between white settlers, who had moved into disputed territory at Watauga and Nolichucky, and the Cherokees, who demanded their removal. When the settlers refused to leave, the Cherokees attacked, and the settlers blamed the unrest on Cameron, accusing him of inciting the Indians.

Cameron denied that he had encouraged the Cherokee attack, but as the Revolutionary War commenced, British Indian agents sought the support of Native Americans throughout North America. John Stuart, head superintendent of Indian Affairs, died in early 1779, and in August, Cameron was appointed superintendent for the Southwest in an attempt to gain Cherokee loyalty. Cameron also tried unsuccessfully to gain the support of the Creeks and Choctaws in Florida.

During his 15 years among the Cherokees, Cameron became influential in tribal decisions and fathered three children. In 1780 an illness prevented his plans to travel through the Indian territories, and he died in Savannah in December 1781.

Tara Mitchell Mielnik, Middle Tennessee State University

SEE: CHOTA; OVERHILL CHEROKEES

CAMERON, JAMES (1817–1882), portrait and landscape painter, was born in Grennock, Scotland. He came to Philadelphia with his family about 1833. When he was 22, he moved to Indianapolis to become a portraitist, but he was back in Philadelphia by 1847. That year, he married another artist, Emma Alcock, and they took an extended wedding trip to Italy. From Rome, Cameron sent an Italian landscape to the 1848 American Art Union exhibition. In 1849 and 1851 he sent Italian subjects to be exhibited at the Pennsylvania Academy of Fine Arts.

Cameron came to Nashville in the 1850s, but was soon enticed to Chattanooga by the railroad entrepreneur, Colonel James A. Whiteside, who provided the artist with studio space, lodging, and portrait commissions. Cameron did several portraits of his patrons, but he preferred landscapes, especially Chattanooga; he often included landscapes in his portraits. With his wife's help, he bought property in downtown Chattanooga in an area now called Cameron Hill. In 1859 he briefly had a studio in the St. Cloud Hotel in Nashville.

Ranger training at Camp Forrest, 1943.

SPECIAL COLLECTIONS, UNIVERSITY OF MEMPHIS

Cameron's whereabouts during the Civil War remain uncertain, but by 1865 the devastation wrought at Chattanooga so disillusioned him that he gave up painting. After a failed attempt at business, he entered the Presbyterian ministry and moved to Oakland, California. He died there on January 5, 1882, while preparing to move to Hawaii for his health.

James C. Kelly, Virginia Historical Society

SEE: ART; WHITESIDE, HARRIET, L.S.

CAMP FORREST, at Tullahoma, was one of the largest U.S. Army training bases during World War II. The camp served as a training facility for 11 infantry divisions, two battalions of Rangers, numerous medical and supply units, and a number of Army Air Corps personnel. In addition, the camp provided logistical support for the massive Tennessee Maneuvers conducted at intervals from 1941 through early 1945. The camp also employed thousands of civilians in various support roles and housed German prisoners of war.

In 1940 the United States began limited preparations for war and established Camp Forrest as a training facility for draftees. The projected $13 million facility was expected to cover 40,000 acres; eventually Camp Forrest cost $36 million and covered 78,000 acres. The Hardaway Construction Company of Columbus, Georgia, and the Creighton Construction Company of Nashville formed a temporary partnership to build the 1,300 buildings, the 55 miles of roads, and the five miles of railroad track that made up Camp Forrest. Over 20,000 people were employed in constructing the camp.

In March 1941 the camp was officially named for Confederate General Nathan Bedford Forrest. While some old arguments arose over General Forrest, more pressing concerns caused the past to be quickly forgotten. The 33rd Infantry Division of the Illinois National Guard and the 75th Field Artillery Brigade of the Tennessee National Guard arrived later that month. After the attack on Pearl Harbor, two other infantry divisions, the 80th and the 8th, were assigned to the post.

As an induction and training center, housing proved to be a recurring problem, and many soldiers bivouacked in tents during their assignment at the post. Camp Forrest employed 12,000 civilians who ran the post exchanges, operated the 9,000 square-foot laundry, performed maintenance on military vehicles, repaired tanks and artillery pieces, and staffed the Induction Center, where some 250,000 young men received their initial physical exams for the army. Army trainees received instruction in house-to-house combat in the first village mock-up. The Second Ranger Battalion trained at the base and later won fame when they scaled the 90-foot cliffs of Point-du-Hoc on D-Day.

Approximately 800 alien civilians were interned at Camp Forrest from January until November 1942, making the camp the first civilian internment camp in the nation. Prisoners of war replaced the civilian internees in 1943, and by the end of the war, just over 24,000 members of the Wehrmacht were under guard at the facility.

After the D-Day invasion of France in June 1944, training at Camp Forrest was reduced drastically. The camp was declared "surplus" in September 1945 and given "inactive" status in February 1946. The War Assets Corporation sold off the buildings for lumber; all equipment, from machine shops to kitchen utensils, was auctioned, although the state retained the land. Today the Arnold Engineering Development Center of the United States Air Force occupies the site. Only a few overgrown concrete foundations remain of Camp Forrest.

Michael R. Bradley, Motlow State Community College
SEE: ARNOLD ENGINEERING DEVELOPMENT CENTER; SECOND ARMY MANEUVERS; WORLD WAR II

CAMP MEETINGS were outdoor religious revival meetings popularized on the southern frontier during the early nineteenth century. These meetings generally lasted several days and attracted participants who traveled significant distances and camped on site for the duration of the meeting.

The camp meeting developed out of the Great Revival of the latter part of the eighteenth and early nineteenth centuries. As a result of the rural setting, the sparse population, and the small number of churches on the southern frontier, camp meetings flourished by providing a central location for crowds that numbered from a few hundred to several thousand.

Historians disagree on the exact origins of the camp meeting, but most suggest that James McGready led the first revival recognizable as a camp meeting in July 1800 at Gasper River in Logan County, Kentucky. This and similar meetings were followed by the best known camp meeting in August 1801 at Cane Ridge in Bourbon County, Kentucky. Led by Barton Stone, this meeting boasted an attendance variously estimated at 10,000 to 30,000 people. Brothers William and John McGee attended one of McGready's early camp meetings and brought the revival spirit to Tennessee. John McGee, a Methodist minister, held the first known Tennessee camp meeting at Drake's Creek, Sumner County, in August 1800, and revivalism quickly spread throughout the fall of 1800 and into 1801.

Other scholars recognize antecedents to these revivals in the Carolinas and Georgia from the 1780s to the 1790s. Certainly these early meetings of the Great Revival provided some of the characteristics that eventually defined the camp meeting movement.

The outdoor setting, where participants camped for the duration of the meeting (usually four days), provided the most distinguishing characteristic of the camp meetings. Most services took place in a "brush arbor," a cleared area surrounded by trees with overhanging limbs that formed a shelter. Fixed structures later replaced the brush arbors. Camp meetings normally occurred in the late summer and provided a break from the hard work routines of farm life. Thus, the gatherings became as much a social event as a spiritual one and provided a meeting place for old friends and new ones, a respite from work, and an opportunity to find suitable marriage partners. An atmosphere of recreation and spiritual renewal permeated the revivals. It is not surprising that camp meetings were marked by extreme emotional and physical "exercises," with participants shouting,

"jerking," "barking," falling down, or dancing about in spiritual ecstasy. Lorenzo Dow, a famous itinerant frontier evangelist, described the jerking exercises he witnessed while preaching at Knoxville. Dow noted that these spiritual exercises affected men and women of various ages, races, and economic levels.

Critics pointed out these examples of unseemly or antisocial behavior and denounced the camp meetings as extreme, if not dangerous events that diverted attention away from true spirituality and religion toward more lustful pursuits. The controversies that accompanied these critiques divided some congregations along revivalist and non-revivalist lines, or along Calvinist and Arminian theological lines, and led to schism among many established congregations. Arminianism constituted a revision of Calvinistic determinism of election and allowed an element of free will in the appropriation of salvation through grace. Arminianism proved more compatible with revivalism and allowed a strong evangelistic strategy that appealed to the human will and the idea of conversion. Despite the theological controversies promoted by the revivals, these meetings were quite successful in bringing converts into the church, as proponents of the camp meetings quickly pointed out when confronted with opposition to the revivalist movement.

William McKendree, bishop of the Western Conference of the Methodist Church, embraced the camp meeting style and systematized the method. The camp meeting method worked in tandem with the Methodist system of circuits and led to rapid expansion of Methodism in Tennessee in the early nineteenth century. In addition, the camp meeting emphasis on repentance and grace worked well with the Methodist Arminian theology. The Methodists continued to hold camp meetings through the 1840s, long after the Baptists and Presbyterians abandoned the outdoor revivals. Eventually "protracted meetings," held in established meeting houses, almost completely replaced the camp meetings.

The camp meeting revival movement of the early nineteenth century provided one of the most colorful and controversial developments in American religious history. These meetings certainly played a significant role in the development of revivalism in Tennessee and in the success of Methodism. Remnants of the movement survived in the later Chautauqua lecture circuit and in the established religious campgrounds still operating in the South. The spontaneous, boisterous gatherings of the early nineteenth century, however, gave way to more controlled revival techniques.

Conrad Ostwalt, Appalachian State University
SUGGESTED READING: John Boles, *The Great Revival, 1787–1805* (1982)

SEE: CARTWRIGHT, PETER; MCKENDREE, WILLIAM; NATIONAL CAMPGROUND; RELIGION; STONE, BARTON

TENNESSEE HISTORICAL SOCIETY, TSLA

Barrage balloon crew at Camp Tyson during World War II.

CAMP TYSON was the nation's only World War II barrage balloon training center. Established at Paris, Henry County, the camp trained servicemen to fly, build, and repair barrage balloons, which were helium or hydrogen filled balloons, measuring 35 feet in diameter and 85 feet in length, used in aerial coastal defense. Made of a two-ply cotton fabric impregnated by synthetic rubber and lofted 9,000 to 12,000 feet into the air, the balloons were nicknamed "big bags," "air whales," and "sky elephants." The massive quantities of rubber needed to construct the balloons drove up the cost of construction to between $5,000 and $10,000 apiece and became a factor in wartime rationing of rubber products and tires.

The nearly invisible steel cables that anchored the small blimps posed the greatest danger to enemy aircraft. Arranged in concentric circles, the cables provided a shield around important buildings, factories, or strategic areas. Effective in World War I anti-aircraft protection, a renewed need for barrage balloons arose in the midst of the Nazi blitz on England and the Battle of Britain. Concerned about security of coastal cities, the U.S. War Department established the barrage balloon training center about eight miles south of Paris, in August 1941.

The 2,000-acre camp was named for Brigadier General Lawrence D. Tyson, a distinguished World War I veteran and prominent citizen of Knoxville. Construction began in the early fall of 1941, and at its peak in December, construction crews employed over 8,000 laborers working on 450 buildings, including wooden barracks, a 400-bed hospital, a 2,500-seat theater, and a modern water system. In March 1942, officers and enlisted men arrived in detachments of 5,000 or 6,000 men; by the end of the war, Camp Tyson's occupancy ranged from 20,000 to 25,000 soldiers. A 1943 expansion of the camp tripled the original 2,000 acres. A well-known Henry County antebellum home, "Bowdenville," was destroyed to accommodate the expansion.

British instructors, who held first-hand knowledge of aerial bombing, helped to instruct Americans on proper balloon training. Recruits learned how to quickly inflate and send balloons afloat and repair any punctures or damages the rubber skins received. A good crew could fully inflate and launch a balloon in less than 30 minutes.

Like several other training camps in Tennessee, Camp Tyson also served as a prisoner of war camp for German and Italian POWs. While at Camp Tyson, prisoners worked on the land and assisted in the development of area roads.

At the end of their training, balloon crews were billeted out for anti-aircraft coastal duty. They sent up balloons, assisted with anti-aircraft guns, and manned the searchlights that crossed the skies.

As the world entered the nuclear age with the dropping of the atomic bomb, barrage balloons became an anachronism. Although originally intended as a permanent military post, Camp Tyson closed after the war.
Robert Parkinson, University of Tennessee, Knoxville
SEE: TYSON, LAWRENCE; WORLD WAR II

CAMPBELL, ALEXANDER (1788–1866), editor and religious reformer, was born in County Antrim, Ireland, the son of Jane Corneigle (Corneigh), a French Huguenot, and Thomas Campbell, a minister in the Anti-Burgher Seceder Presbyterian Church. Reared in the Church of England, Thomas Campbell rejected the concept of a state church but not Anglican theology and attempted to reunite warring religious factions. In 1807, his health broken, Campbell sailed for America and settled in Pennsylvania. His family left for America in 1808 but was shipwrecked off the Hebrides. They settled in Scotland for the winter so that Alexander Campbell could attend the University of Glasgow. There he formally repudiated the strictures of John Knox. When the family reunited in 1809, Alexander learned that his father, having been excluded from the American Seceeders, was preparing to publish his response, a *Declaration and Address*, which was both a charter for Christian unity and an American religious declaration of independence.

After marriage in 1811 and the birth of his first child, Campbell began a study of Hebrew and

Greek scripture which convinced him that immersion of believers best fulfilled the New Testament design of baptism. The decision led to an invitation to join a Baptist Association. In 1823 he began publication of the iconoclastic *Christian Baptist* in which he attacked the sins of the historic church and advocated a "restoration" of the unity and purity of the New Testament church. The alliance between the Calvinist Baptists and the Campbells, who were dedicated to Renaissance learning rooted in the philosophy of John Locke and Thomas Reid, was an uneasy one. By 1830 the Baptists had read the Campbell Reformers out of fellowship, and Campbell began publication of *The Millennial Harbinger.*

The Nashville congregation remained in the forefront of reform, and Campbell lauded it as "a golden candlestick to the Lord." Two of his daughters married into Nashville's Ewing family, and between 1827 and 1858, Campbell made six preaching tours to Middle Tennessee and one to Memphis. In 1827 Andrew Jackson entertained Campbell at the Hermitage. On his 1830 visit to Nashville, Washington Cooper painted Campbell's portrait. On Christmas day that year, he engaged in a debate with the Presbyterian pastor, Obadiah Jennings, after which Campbell baptized 30 people in the Cumberland River, including John Harding of the Belle Meade plantation. Campbell also held five formal debates: three with Presbyterians, one with the British skeptic and socialist Robert Owen, and one with Roman Catholic Bishop John Purcell. In 1840 Campbell founded Bethany College in Bethany, Virginia (now West Virginia), where he served for two decades as president and professor.

While demanding independence for local congregations in the internal government, Campbell advocated cooperation through delegate assemblies, and in 1849 was elected president of the American Christian Missionary Society. He also played an active role in a number of reform efforts. He was a leader in the crusade for free public schools. He denounced the federal government's treatment of Native Americans, particularly the "Trail of Tears." In 1829 Campbell served as a delegate to the Virginia Constitutional Convention, where he was noted for his radical support of Jacksonian democracy. Campbell declared himself anti-slavery, but separated himself from abolitionism.

The Campbell movement issued in three communions: the ecumenical Christian Church (Disciples of Christ), the Church of Christ (anti-organ and anti-organization), and the independent Christian Churches.
Eva Jean Wrather, Nashville
SUGGESTED READING: Eva Jean Wrather, *Alexander Campbell: Adventurer in Freedom* (forthcoming)
SEE: CHURCHES OF CHRIST; DISCIPLES OF CHRIST; RELIGION

CAMPBELL, ARCHIE (1914–1987), a nationally known comedian and country music artist, was born in Bulls Gap, Tennessee, a small railroad town in Hawkins County. He began his performing career on several Knoxville radio stations. In the 1930s, Campbell was a creator of the "Tennessee Barn Dance" radio show and introduced his "grandpappy" character, and later joined Roy Acuff, Chet Atkins, The Carlisles, Homer and Jethro, Pee Wee King, and Eddie Hill on WNOX "Mid-Day Merry-Go-Round." After serving in the Navy during World War II, he started his own show, *Country Playhouse,* featuring such stars as Carl Smith, Carl and Pearl Butler, and Flatt and Scruggs on WROL-TV.

He and his wife, Mary, whom he called "Pudge," and their two sons moved to Nashville in 1958 when he was hired to record for RCA records and to perform a three-minute broadcast on the Grand Ole Opry every Saturday night. On *Hee Haw,* he played a barber, a doctor, and judge and was credited by fellow cast members as a major reason for the television show's longtime success. He joined the show in 1969, the same year he was named Comedian of the Year by the Country Music Association.

Most remembered for his earthy humor, trademark cigar, and "spoonerisms,' (fairy tales using mixed-up syllables), Campbell also achieved a successful musical career. His RCA Victor recordings included *The Men in My Little Girl's Life, Trouble in the Amen Corner, Twelfth Rose, Hockey Here Tonight, Pee Little Thrigs, Rindercella, Beeping Sleuty, The Drunk, The Cockfight,* considered by some the greatest record of his career, and *Make Friends,* the gospel hit that became his theme song. His album *Bedtime Stories for Adults* remained the Number One country comedy album in sales for three decades.

Campbell also devoted much time to charity work and his hobbies, painting and golf. Before commencing his career, he studied art for two years at Mars Hill College in North Carolina and sold many of his paintings later in life. The Archie Campbell Museum at Bulls Gap interprets his life and contributions to country music.
Beth Matter, Nashville
SEE: GRAND OLE OPRY; HAWKINS COUNTY; TELEVISION AND MOVIE PERFORMERS

CAMPBELL, ARTHUR (1743–1811), a political and military leader in Virginia and frontier Tennessee, was born in Augusta County, Virginia, on November 3, 1743. A band of Wyandotte Indians captured 15-year-old Campbell and took him to the area of present-day Detroit where he lived with the tribe for two years. He escaped in 1760 and joined British troops in the area, serving as a guide for the remainder of the Seven Years War.

After the war, Campbell returned to Virginia and took up farming. He married Margaret Campbell in

1772. Campbell served on the first Fincastle County Court in 1773, opened a grist mill, and led militia forays in Southwest Virginia and along the Clinch and Holston rivers in present-day Tennessee. In 1776 Fincastle County elected Campbell to the Second Continental Congress. When Washington County was carved out of Fincastle County, Campbell was appointed to the top militia post and served as county lieutenant and justice of the peace for the new county.

During the Revolutionary War, Campbell led expeditions against Native Americans, the British, and their loyalist supporters. Campbell's militia unit joined those of John Sevier and Isaac Shelby in the victory at the Battle of King's Mountain, although Campbell did not fight. Convinced that the Cherokees represented a true threat, Campbell and Sevier combined forces to raid the principal Cherokee towns of Chota, Tellico, and Hiwassee.

Campbell and Sevier believed the frontier settlements should be admitted to the new republic as separate states but could not agree on the terms. Campbell wanted the new state, "Frankland," to include portions of western North Carolina, southwestern Virginia, and part of Kentucky. Sevier favored the name "Franklin" and limited the territorial boundary to western North Carolina. In 1784 delegates to a general convention at Jonesborough favored Sevier's smaller State of Franklin and petitioned the United States for admission as an independent state. North Carolina refused to cede the western lands and blocked the petition, while Virginia brought charges of treason and misconduct against Campbell. Although the treason charges were dismissed, Campbell was removed as justice of the peace in Washington County in 1786; he was reinstated in 1789. President George Washington later commissioned Campbell as an Indian agent in the Southwest Territory.

A Federalist in the new political world of the United States and in poor health, Campbell retired from service in 1799, as the Jeffersonian Republicans gained power. After retirement, Campbell led a quiet life and began writing a history of the Revolutionary War in the Southwest, which he never completed. Campbell died at his home in Virginia in August 1811. He was buried in the Cumberland Gap, at the juncture of the three states that shaped his life.

Tara Mitchell Mielnik, Middle Tennessee State University
SEE: FRANKLIN, STATE OF; OVERMOUNTAIN MEN; SOUTHWEST TERRITORY

CAMPBELL COUNTY was created by an act of the Tennessee General Assembly on September 11, 1806, from land taken from Anderson and Claiborne counties. The twenty-sixth county was named in honor of Colonel Arthur Campbell, a Revolutionary War soldier and Indian fighter. Jacksboro is the county seat.

The primary attraction for early settlers was the wide fertile Powell's Valley. This lovely valley, coupled with wide navigable rivers and numerous tributaries, provided an ideal setting for the settlers. Although farming was the first organized activity, numerous coal and iron deposits began to attract attention in the early 1800s. The harvesting of timber also provided an early boost to the local economy. Most early settlers clustered in Powell's Valley, but a few hardy pioneers ventured into the more remote mountain areas of the county. Town locations reflect these early concessions to geography.

The 1990 federal census reported a population of 35,079 for Campbell County, with a population density of 73 people per square mile. Most Campbell Countians live in the country, and even in the four incorporated towns, where slightly more than 20 percent of the population lives, a rural character predominates. Jellico and LaFollette are the two largest towns, with Caryville and Jacksboro each reporting fewer than 2,000 inhabitants. Two of the oldest settlements in Campbell County are the unincorporated communities of Fincastle and Speedwell.

The town of Jacksboro was founded in 1807 and served as the hub of the county and its government activities. Jellico was founded in 1885 and is strategically located on the Kentucky-Tennessee border. Grace Moore, the famous international opera star in the 1940s, was educated in Jellico.

Originally known as Big Creek Gap, LaFollete's history goes back to 1893, when Harvey LaFollette, an Indiana educator and engineer, purchased the mountain land for its iron and coal reserves. In 1897 the town of LaFollette was organized, and a railroad link established to the Southern Railway. With this railway link, LaFollette expanded its iron furnace to employ as many as 1,500 workers. The furnace closed in 1926.

Railroad development in the county transformed the economy from subsistence farming to coal mining and lumber production. Except for temporary slumps, coal ruled the economy for three-quarters of a century. By the mid-1930s Campbell County men found employment in the coal mines, while women worked in the growing textile industry. New Deal agencies had a significant impact in the county as the PWA built a school in Caryville, the CCC developed Cove Lake State Park, and the WPA added a post office in LaFollette. TVA's development of Norris Lake provided the most important New Deal change.

With the completion of Interstate Highway 75, tourism boosted the county economy. The Chamberland Mountains, which separate Jellico from the rest of the county, and the 750 miles of Norris Lake shoreline attract tourists, boaters, fishermen, and retirees to the county. The interstate highway not only sparked an increase in tourism, but also provided improved access for diversified industrial development. This new growth coincided with the final decline of "King Coal" in the early 1980s. Today, more than 40 small and medium industries provide 2,294 jobs, constituting more than 25 percent of the county's work force. Tourism and the service industry employ more than half of the county's workers.

Campbell County has produced some outstanding military, political, and corporate leaders. Major General Joseph A. Cooper, a Campbell County native, commanded the U.S. Sixth Tennessee Regiment during the Civil War. Captain Winston Baird commanded an all-volunteer military brigade during the Spanish-American War and received a Presidential citation for his leadership and heroism. Two members of the U.S. House of Representatives, John J. Jennings and J. Will Taylor, were born and raised in LaFollette. Four-star General Carl W. Stiner was born on a Powell Valley farm and educated in Campbell County schools. General Stiner commanded the military forces in Operation Just Cause, the invasion of Panama. He retired to his Powell Valley farm, and his brother, retired Colonel Tom Stiner, serves as county executive. Harry Stonecipher, chief executive officer of McDonald-Douglas Corporation, was born and raised in Campbell County, as was the late Dr. Burgin Dossett, a well-known Tennessee educator.

Adrion Baird, Lanier DeVours, Marshall McGhee, Gregory Miller, and Charles Winfrey, Campbell County
SEE: CAMPBELL, ARTHUR; CIVILIAN CONSERVATION CORPS; FRATERVILLE MINE DISASTER; LABOR; MINING; MOORE, GRACE; NORRIS DAM; PUBLIC WORKS ADMINISTRATION; TENNESSEE VALLEY AUTHORITY; WORKS PROGRESS ADMINISTRATION

CAMPBELL, DAVID (1753–1832), Revolutionary war captain, State of Franklin supporter, and early Knox County settler and merchant, was born in Augusta County, Virginia, in 1753. His distinguished career began in 1774, when he served in the Virginia militia during Lord Dunmore's War; the next year, he served as clerk of court at Fincastle, Botetourt County, Virginia. During the American Revolution, he fought at the Battle of Long Island Flats in 1776 and was Captain of the Virginia militia during the Battle of King's Mountain in 1780.

In about 1782, Campbell moved his family to present-day Washington County, Tennessee; then at an unknown time, he moved to a new farm near Strawberry Plains in present-day Jefferson County. By circa 1787, Campbell resided in western Knox County and built a blockhouse, known as Campbell's Station, along the present-day Kingston Pike, where he lived for the next 36 years.

His military record led to a political career, first in North Carolina, then the new state of Tennessee. He served in the North Carolina House of Commons in 1787, was a member of the Assembly of the State of Franklin, and was in the Tennessee House of Representatives from 1801 to 1805. In Knox County, Campbell managed his farm as well as a mercantile business, in partnership with Charles McClung of Knoxville. At the end of 1822, he sold his Knox County property and moved to Wilson County, where he lived until his death in 1832. Campbell is buried in the Leeville churchyard in Wilson County.
Carroll Van West, Middle Tennessee State University
SEE: CAMPBELL, WILLIAM B.; FRONTIER STATIONS; KNOX COUNTY; OVERMOUNTAIN MEN; WILSON COUNTY

CAMPBELL, DAVID, JUDGE (1750–1812), State of Franklin official and early territorial and state judge, was born in Augusta County, Virginia, in 1750. He served in the Continental Army during the American Revolution, obtaining the rank of major. After the war, circa 1783, he moved to present-day Greene County, Tennessee, where he practiced law and served as a judge on the newly declared Supreme Court of Franklin. He is credited as being one of the authors of the Franklin constitution along with being a member of the First Franklin Convention in 1784 and the Third Franklin Convention in 1785. But of the major Franklin leaders, Campbell "was the least wedded to the separatist movement."[1] In 1787, in fact, he became a member of the North Carolina assembly, and later that year he was elected Judge of the Superior Court of North Carolina, Washington District, where he served until 1790. However, Campbell refused to abandon his Franklin friends entirely. When John Tipton and others attempted to have John Sevier arrested for treason, Campbell refused to issue the arrest warrant.

With the establishment of the Southwest Territory, Territorial Governor William Blount appointed Campbell as territorial judge in 1790; he served in that position until Tennessee's statehood in 1796.

Success and controversy marked Campbell's career as a Tennessee state judge. From 1797 to 1809, he served as a Judge of the Superior Court, but early in his term, Campbell became embroiled in a heated, bitter dispute with William Blount, John Sevier, and others over the boundary of the Treaty of Holston. The survey of the treaty, completed in 1797, placed the home of Judge Campbell and others in Cherokee territory and state officials did nothing to prevent federal troops from evicting Campbell and the other settlers. A furious Campbell lashed back at Blount and Governor Sevier. When Campbell refused to even consider a suit Blount wanted the court to adjudicate, Blount asked Governor Sevier to reply in kind. Sevier convinced leaders in the Tennessee House to bring impeachment charges against Judge Campbell.

When the removal trial came before the State Senate in December 1798, William Blount, who had been impeached as a U.S. Senator, was awaiting word from Philadelphia on whether the U.S. Senate would convict him. He had already been expelled by the U.S. Senate and upon returning to Tennessee, Blount arranged to be elected to the State Senate, where he also was chosen the Speaker of the Senate. In the Campbell removal trial, therefore, Blount was the Senate's chief prosecutor of a case in which he held a considerable personal and political interest. Campbell avoided conviction and removal, but by just one vote.

Five years later, in 1803, Campbell faced a second impeachment, this time for bribery. With the support of the Jackson faction, the Senate voted nine to three for Campbell's acquittal.

Judge David Campbell received a federal appointment as a Mississippi territorial judge in 1811, but he never served in the post. He died in Washington, Rhea County, in 1812.

Carroll Van West, Middle Tennessee State University

CITATION:

(1) Cortez A.M. Ewing, "Early Tennessee Impeachments," *Tennessee Historical Quarterly* 16(1957): 293.

SEE: BLOUNT, WILLIAM; FRANKLIN, STATE OF; GREENE COUNTY; SEVIER, JOHN; SOUTHWEST TERRITORY; TIPTON, JOHN; TREATIES

CAMPBELL, FRANCIS JOSEPH (1832–1914), a leading educator for the blind in the United States and Great Britain, was born in Franklin County, Tennessee, on October 9, 1832. A childhood accident left Campbell blind at the age of four. He attended regular schools until the age of 12, when his parents enrolled him in the newly opened Tennessee School for the Blind at Nashville, where he excelled in the study of music, especially piano.

In 1850, while a senior at the school, Campbell was appointed teacher of music and interim superintendent. The education of the blind became his calling. Campbell left Tennessee in the mid-1850s to pursue his education in Massachusetts, where he met and married Mary Bond in 1856. The Campbells briefly returned to Tennessee but, because of their abolitionist views, left the state under duress. Campbell then taught music and physical education at the Perkins Institute in Boston.

In 1868 the Campbells traveled to Europe, where Francis studied music in Germany. His chance meeting with Dr. T.A. Armitage of London led to their creation of the Royal College for the Blind in London in the early 1870s. Campbell insisted that this college be equal in social, physical, and intellectual aspects to colleges for sighted people. Under his guidance, the Royal College became a highly respected institution.

Two years after the death of his wife Mary in 1873, Campbell married Sophia Faulkner, a teacher at the Royal College. He became a naturalized citizen of Great Britain and in 1909, he was knighted by King Edward VII. Campbell retired in 1912, and Guy M. Campbell succeeded his father at the Royal College. Campbell returned to the United States after his retirement and died on June 30, 1914, leaving behind an international reputation as a musician and educator.

Tara Mitchell Mielnik, Middle Tennessee State University

SEE: FRANKLIN COUNTY

CAMPBELL, GEORGE WASHINGTON (1768–1848) served as a U.S. Senator, Secretary of the Treasury, Ambassador to Russia, and U.S. District Court Judge of Tennessee. He was born in Scotland, the son of a physician, Archibald Campbell, and Elizabeth Mackay Campbell, and migrated with his family to Mecklenburg County, North Carolina, in 1772. After the death of his father, Campbell worked on his mother's farm and taught school. He entered the junior class at Princeton, finished the work of two years in one, and graduated with high honors in 1794. Campbell adopted Washington as his middle name during this period when classmates at Princeton nicknamed him "George Washington" after the fame of the new President. He studied law, opened a practice in Knoxville, and soon ranked among the leading lawyers. Perhaps Campbell's most important case was his successful defense of Judge David Campbell in his impeachment trial before the Tennessee Senate.

With the support of Judge Andrew Jackson, George Washington Campbell was elected to the U.S. House of Representatives in 1803, where he served until 1809. During his tenure in the House, Campbell chaired two of the most politically powerful committees, the Ways and Means Committee and the Committee on Foreign Relations. As a Jeffersonian Republican, Campbell's support of the president and his administration included a duel with Barent Gardenier, a Congressman from New York, who claimed the House was under French control. Fought on Bladensburg grounds, which afterward became a noted dueling place, Gardenier was seriously wounded.

In 1809 the Tennessee General Assembly appointed Campbell and Hugh Lawson White to serve as the first Justices on the newly formed Tennessee Supreme Court of Errors and Appeals. Campbell served two years before being elected to the U.S. Senate in 1811 on a platform advocating war with Great Britain. While in the Senate, Campbell, a Warhawk, served as Chairman of the Committee on Military Affairs. In 1812 he married Harriet Stoddert, daughter of Benjamin Stoddert, Secretary of the Navy in Jefferson's cabinet.

On February 9, 1814, Campbell resigned from the Senate to accept the position of Secretary of the Treasury in James Madison's cabinet. Due to the unsettled nature of the period, Campbell's tenure in the Treasury is often viewed as a failure. In order to gain badly needed funds to finance the war, Campbell arranged to borrow money from Europe through the assistance of American businessman John Jacob Astor. Overwhelmed by the failures of the Treasury Department and his own poor health, Campbell resigned his Cabinet post in September 1814.

Campbell's wife, Harriet Campbell, made her own contribution to history during the British invasion of Washington. Upon hearing the news of the impending arrival of the British army, Harriet Campbell urged her friend, Dolley Madison, to leave the President's house. With the help of Harriet Campbell and Charles Carroll, Mrs. Madison removed the Gilbert Stuart portrait of George Washington from its frame and fled before the British burned the house and the city of Washington.

In 1815 Campbell returned to the U.S. Senate, where he served until 1818. In December 1815 he and John Williams were commissioned to negotiate the extinguishment of the Indian claims in the chartered limits of Tennessee, a process that culminated in the Jackson Purchase.

In 1817, when James Monroe took office, he offered Campbell the position of Secretary of War, but Campbell declined. A zealous supporter of the Monroe administration, Campbell chaired the Senate Finance Committee and advocated the charter of the Second Bank of the United States. In 1818 Monroe appointed Campbell Envoy Extraordinary and Minister Plenipotentiary to Russia. In accepting the position, Campbell became the first Tennessean to be appointed to a major diplomatic post. Under Secretary of State John Quincy Adams's direction, on the way to his post in Russia, Campbell adjusted Denmark's claims against U.S. privateers for disruption of commerce during the War of 1812. He served in Russia until 1820, when he was granted permission to resign after three of his children died of typhus in St. Petersburg.

Following his diplomatic service, Campbell returned to the state and accepted an appointment as Judge of the U.S. District Court of Tennessee. He also served as a member of the 1831 commission to study French war claims and was named a director for the Nashville branch of the Bank of the United States.

On December 11, 1843, Campbell sold a tract of land known as "Campbell's Hill" to the City of Nashville for $30,000, which was transferred to the State of Tennessee as the permanent site for the state's capitol. Campbell died in Nashville on February 17, 1848, and was buried in the family plot in the Nashville City Cemetery.

Louis Littleton Veazey, Hendersonville
SUGGESTED READING: Weymouth T. Jordan, *George Washington Campbell of Tennessee: Western Statesman* (1955)
SEE: CAMPBELL, JUDGE DAVID; DUELING; JACKSON, ANDREW; JACKSON PURCHASE; TENNESSEE COURTS, PRIOR TO 1870; WAR OF 1812

CAMPBELL, WILL DAVIS (1924–), a civil rights advocate and author, was the only white person present at the founding of Dr. Martin Luther King's Southern Christian Leadership Conference. Campbell was born July 18, 1924, in the rural farm country of Amite County, Mississippi. His father, Lee Campbell, was a gentle and tolerant man, who instilled the values that became the foundation for Will Campbell's support for civil rights.

At the age of 17, Campbell preached his first sermon at the nearby East Fork Baptist Church; he was later ordained as a Baptist minister. He completed his undergraduate work at Wake Forest University, served in the army during World War II, and saw action in the Pacific. In 1952 Campbell received his Bachelor of Divinity degree from Yale University. After a brief stint as pastor of Taylor Baptist Church in Louisiana and two years as Director of Religious Life at the University of Mississippi, Campbell moved to Nashville, where he became Director of the Southern Office of the Department of Racial and Cultural Relations for the National Council of Churches.

In that capacity, Campbell traveled to many of the civil rights hot spots in the 1950s and 1960s, including Little Rock, New Orleans, Nashville, and Atlanta. In Little Rock in 1957, he and two other white ministers accompanied eight black students through harassing mobs, as they sought entry to the previously all-white schools. Shortly afterward, civil rights advocate Bayard Rustin invited him to Atlanta to attend the founding meeting for the Southern Christian Leadership Conference, which soon became the cornerstone organization for the civil rights movement in the South.

Campbell continued to support the movement, but in the 1960s he broadened his ministry to other causes, including opposition to the Vietnam War. He also reached out to those he had opposed in the past, including members of the Ku Klux Klan. Throughout his work, Campbell preached a message of radical forgiveness and the call of God for reconciliation.

In 1977 he wrote his first memoir, *Brother to a Dragonfly*, in which he expanded on those themes. The book drew widespread national acclaim and received a nomination for the National Book Award. Campbell soon became known as one of the most provocative southern authors. His 15 other books include *The Glad River, Covenant, Providence,* and *Forty Acres and a Goat*. Campbell lives with his wife Brenda on a family farm outside Mt. Juliet, Tennessee.

Frye Gaillard, Queens College

SEE: CIVIL RIGHTS MOVEMENT; LITERATURE; WILSON
COUNTY

CAMPBELL, WILLIAM BOWEN (1807–1867), lawyer, soldier, state legislator, congressman, and Governor, was born on Mansker's Creek, Sumner County, on February 1, 1807, the son of David and Catherine (Bowen) Campbell. He studied law at Abingdon, Virginia, with his relative, Governor David Campbell. He returned to Tennessee in 1829, settled in Carthage, and was admitted to the bar in 1830. In 1831 Campbell was elected as district attorney, and four years later, his district sent him to the Tennessee General Assembly. That same year, he married Frances Owen, daughter of Dr. John Owen of Carthage. He resigned his seat in the legislature to serve as Captain of a mounted volunteer company in the Creek and Seminole War under Colonel William Trousdale. When he returned from the war in Florida, he was elected and served as a Whig member of the 25th, 26th, and 27th sessions of the United States Congress.

When the Mexican War broke out in 1846, Campbell was elected Colonel of the First Tennessee Volunteers, which saw action at Monterey, Vera Cruz, and Cerro Gordo, earning recognition as the "Bloody First." At the storming of Monterey, Campbell's command, "Boys, follow me!" became the slogan for the Whig party in the Tennessee gubernatorial campaign of 1851. In the summer of 1847, Campbell was elected judge of the circuit court, where he served four years.

In 1851, Campbell ran as the Whig candidate for governor and defeated Democratic incumbent William Trousdale. After serving one two-year term as governor, Campbell retired to private life in 1853 and accepted the presidency of the Bank of Middle Tennessee. In 1859 he returned to public service as circuit court judge.

During the presidential campaign of 1860, Campbell supported John Bell, the Constitutional Union candidate. Following the election of Lincoln, he canvassed the state in opposition to secession. Commissioned as Brigadier General of volunteers in the Union army by President Lincoln in 1862, Campbell resigned later that year because of poor health.

Following the readmission of Tennessee to the Union in 1866, Campbell was elected as a Democrat to the U.S. Congress, where he supported the conservative reconstruction policies of President Andrew Johnson. Campbell died at Lebanon on August 19, 1867, and was buried at Cedar Grove Cemetery.

In 1942 the War Department established a World War II army training camp on the Kentucky-Tennessee border, between Hopkinsville, Kentucky, and Clarksville, Tennessee. The Adjutant General of the United States Army named the camp in honor of William Bowen Campbell to perpetuate the memory of this outstanding soldier, lawyer, judge, and public figure, who devoted nearly four decades to the service of his state and country.

John H. Thweatt, Tennessee State Library and Archives

SEE: CIVIL WAR; FORT CAMPBELL; MEXICAN WAR; SMITH
COUNTY; TROUSDALE, WILLIAM

CANNON COUNTY was established on January 31, 1836, when the state legislature took portions of Rutherford, Smith, and Warren counties to create the new county of Cannon, named in honor of Whig Governor Newton Cannon. (Two years later, the legislature added a portion of Wilson County, creating the present county boundaries.) The county's first settlers moved to present-day western Cannon County, around the Readyville and Bradyville areas, during the late 1790s. Hugh P. Brawley operated a grist mill at Brawley Fork as early as 1808.

The first village of any size, however, was Danville, which became the initial county seat. Its name was soon changed to Woodbury, to honor Levi Woodbury, the Democratic Secretary of Treasury. In 1836 Henry Trott and William Bates laid out new lots for Woodbury, and their plan adapted the earlier linear street plan of Danville into a central courthouse square plan. The present Cannon County Courthouse, built in 1935, features a striking Colonial Revival design by Nashville architect George Waller and is listed in the National Register of Historic Places. Other local properties in the National Register are the Houston House, a vernacular Greek Revival-styled I-house associated with Democratic Congressman William C. Houston; the Adams House, the last remaining dormitory of the Baptist Female College and the later home of prominent physician Jesse F. Adams; the Wharton House, a vernacular Queen Anne dwelling from the late nineteenth century, and the Readyville Mill, a nineteenth and twentieth century grist mill complex.

Woodbury has always served as the county's seat of government and primary town. It never had a railroad connection and remained largely isolated from major transportation networks until the completion of the original Memphis-to-Bristol Highway (now U.S. Highway 70S) during the late 1920s. The new highway promoted commercial development; many of the historic stores around the town square date to the 1920s and 1930s. As travelers sped through the county on the new highway, their presence indirectly boomed the already-established market of making white oak baskets and wood furniture for sale at stands and shops along the road. Cannon County is now recognized as an important regional center for folk decorative arts. The new road also spurred local leaders, especially Dr. Jesse F. Adams, to create and invest in new businesses, like the Good Samaritan Hospital (early 1930s) and the town's first modern factory, the Armour Cheese Plant, in 1935. After World War II, in 1947, Adams and the Woodbury Lions Club combined forces to convince the Colonial Shirt Corporation to establish a Woodbury factory; a branch factory was later opened in Auburntown. Another key entrepreneur was Selmer Mason Jennings, who used the new highway and his solid business ability to gain a Ford Motor car dealership for the town during the 1920s. Jennings Ford still operates today. Woodbury also is the county's educational center, being home to the Laurens Academy and the Baptist Female College during the antebellum era, Woodbury College during the Victorian era, and the public Cannon County High School, which was established in 1920.

Villages in Cannon County include Readyville, Auburntown, Bradyville, and Gassaway. Crisp was a smaller African-American village centered around a segregated black school and church.

During the Civil War, Cannon County residents raised seven infantry companies for the Confederacy. Union soldiers also came from the county; most served in the Fifth Tennessee Cavalry, which was largely based in Liberty in adjacent DeKalb County. Small skirmishes and reconnaissance movements characterize most of the military activity within the county. Guerrilla warfare also was common. During World War II, the maneuvers of the Second Army included parts of Cannon County, and local citizens in Woodbury established a USO center for the soldiers.

Since its creation, Cannon County has been Democratic in its political loyalties and has produced two notable party leaders. In the late 1800s and early 1900s, William Cannon Houston was the county's most prominent politician. Cannon established the Woodbury newspaper, practiced law, and served in the state legislature as a young man; from 1904 to 1918, he served in the United States Congress and often entertained important southern Democratic leaders at his home on the outskirts of Woodbury. Throughout the mid-1900s, Jim Cummings was an influential member of the Tennessee General Assembly. He was first elected to the state legislature in 1929 and stayed there until 1972, except for a four-year stint from 1949–1952, when Cummings was Secretary of State under Governor Gordon Browning. Cummings was the Speaker of the House during the 85th General Assembly. Historian Robert Mason noted about "Mr. Jim" Cummings: "he evoked the essence of a more gracious, gentler time—of friendly towns and family farms and hills and valleys and country roads."[1]

Carroll Van West, Middle Tennessee State University

CITATION:
(1) Robert L. Mason, *History of Cannon County, Tennessee* (Murfreesboro, 1984), 266.

SEE: ADAMS, JESSE F.; BASKETMAKING; CANNON, NEWTON; DECORATIVE ARTS, APPALACHIAN; HIGHWAYS, HISTORIC; MACON, DAVID HARRISON; SHORT MOUNTAIN

CANNON, NEWTON (1781–1841), Tennessee's first Whig governor, was born in North Carolina. His family settled in Williamson County, Tennessee, in 1790, where Cannon received a common school education. He attempted several occupations before establishing himself as a wealthy planter. His public career began with his election to the State Senate in 1811, and over the next decade he served as a volunteer in the Creek War, an Indian commissioner, and United States Congressman. After losing to Sam Houston in the 1827 gubernatorial election, Cannon returned to the State Senate and later served as chair of the Committee of the Whole at the 1834 state constitutional convention. He sought the governor's office again in 1835, when his endorsement of Senator Hugh L. White's presidential candidacy, along with public uncertainty over incumbent William Carroll's eligibility under the new constitution, helped him win an easy victory.

Cannon's first administration produced the passage of an act providing state aid for internal improvements by authorizing the governor to subscribe for stock in railroad and turnpike companies. In 1836 he called the first special session of the state legislature in the state's 40-year history, in order to determine what to do with Tennessee's share of the federal distribution of surplus revenue funds. Despite criticism of his handling of a call for volunteers for service in the Second Seminole War, Cannon easily won re-election in 1837. During his second term, the General Assembly passed legislation expanding state support for internal improvements and creating a new state bank, designating its profits to assist in the funding of public education. Cannon soon faced public condemnation, however, over locations for branches of the state banks, which were made by his appointees to the board of directors. He also received criticism for his strict interpretation of the internal improvement laws, which he claimed prevented him from approving sites for companies in East and West Tennessee. These developments, along with his failure to become an insider among the leaders of Tennessee's emerging Whig party, weakened Cannon's bid for a third term.

In 1839 Cannon faced his strongest competitor, when Speaker of the U.S. House of Representatives James K. Polk retired from Congress to run for governor. In his campaign, Polk stressed national politics to force Tennessee voters to choose between the maturing Whig and Democratic parties. Cannon, who had long identified himself as a Whig, argued that national issues should not influence a state election, but he defended the national party's program.

The incumbent's slow and ponderous speaking style proved no match for the polished Polk, and the challenger defeated Cannon—although by a mere 2,500 votes—in an election that clearly defined the two parties in the state. Despite the narrow margin of his loss, Cannon played no further role in state politics, and he died in retirement on his plantation near Franklin in Williamson County.

Jonathan M. Atkins, Berry College

SEE: CARROLL, WILLIAM; JACKSONIANS; POLK, JAMES K.; WHITE, HUGH L.; WILLIAMSON COUNTY

CANSLER, CHARLES WARNER (1871–1953),

African-American educator, was born in Maryville, Tennessee, one of several children of Hugh Lawson and Laura Ann Scott Cansler. Cansler's mother became Knoxville's first African-American teacher in 1864, when she obtained permission from General Ambrose Burnside to open a school for free blacks during the Union occupation of Knoxville.

Young Cansler attended the Freedmen's Normal Institute in Maryville before enrolling at Maryville College. Although he never graduated, he taught school in several East Tennessee counties before accepting a position in the Knoxville city schools.

At age 19 Cansler took an examination and was hired as a substitute railway mail clerk. Although the position paid no salary, he hoped his experience would make him eligible for regular employment at the end of six months. The first African American hired by the railway line, Cansler soon felt the resentment of white mail clerks. Rather than use Cansler as a substitute, clerks "doubled" and denied him the opportunity to be paid for his work. Disgusted with the situation, he abandoned the hope of gaining full-time employment, although he continued to work as a railway clerk and bookkeeper in the Navy Yard at Portsmouth, Virginia, during summer vacations.

Cansler read law with Judge W.C. Kain and passed the Knoxville bar in 1892, when he was 21 years old. He became a Republican candidate for the Tennessee General Assembly in 1894. Following his electoral defeat, Cansler decided to give up his law practice and involvement in politics, and devote himself to education. Knoxville's African-American schools felt his influence for the next half century.

Cansler began teaching at Austin High School in 1900, and became principal in 1911. The following year, he organized the East Tennessee Association of Teachers in Colored Schools. In 1914 Cansler introduced night classes for working people who wanted to continue their education. He led efforts to obtain funding from the Andrew Carnegie Foundation to establish a library for blacks in 1917. In 1919 he influenced the General Assembly to pass an act enabling descendants of ex-slaves to inherit real estate. Cansler retired from education in 1939.

Known as a "mathematical wizard," Cansler traveled the country demonstrating his skills in calculating; he challenged the speed of adding machines in totaling long columns of figures. He wrote two booklets describing his methods. He also published *Three Generations: The Story of a Colored Family of Eastern Tennessee*, a history of the Cansler family. Cansler died on November 1, 1953.

Robert J. Booker, Beck Cultural Exchange Center, Inc., Knoxville

SEE: EDUCATION; KNOXVILLE; MARYVILLE COLLEGE

CAPITAL CITIES. Four Tennessee towns have served as the State Capital. Knoxville was the first capital city, from the drafting of the state constitution and the first meeting of the General Assembly in 1796 to 1812, when the General Assembly moved to Nashville for the next five years. In between, Kingston served as capital for one day, when the General Assembly met there in 1807 in order to fulfill a treaty obligation made with the Cherokee Indians. In 1817 the capital again returned to Knoxville, but in 1818, the General Assembly moved to Murfreesboro, the geographic center of the state. There it met at the local Presbyterian Church until 1826, when it moved to Nashville for a second time.

The 1834 State Constitution mandated that the legislature of 1843 choose a permanent state capital. After much debate, with the Whig Party generally favoring Nashville and the Democratic party generally in support of Murfreesboro's claims, the General Assembly chose Nashville as the permanent capital of Tennessee in 1843.

Carroll Van West, Middle Tennessee State University

CARAWAN, GUY (1927–) and wife Candie Anderson Carawan are noted for their long association with Highlander Research and Education Center in East Tennessee, their work in documenting southern folk music, and their participation in the civil rights movement of the 1960s. Born in July 1927, in Los Angeles, to parents native to North and South Carolina, Carawan developed a strong interest in folk music by the early 1950s. He met and toured with many folk revivalists, including Pete Seeger, Peggy Seeger, Jack Elliott, and Frank Hamilton. By 1959 Myles Horton invited him to join the staff of Highlander as music director, along with Candie, whom he married in 1961. Carawan's contributions include collecting original folk songs and integrating new forms of those songs into the social movements supported by Highlander, in part through field work in the Carolina sea islands and the mountains of east Kentucky.

Carawan is widely credited with contributing new lyrics to the Baptist hymn, *I'll Overcome Someday* to create the essential civil rights anthem, *We Shall Overcome*. Carawan himself assigns primary credit to

Zilphia Horton, wife of Myles and first music director for Highlander, but recalls disseminating the song to civil rights protesters in Nashville in 1960 and at the founding convention of the Student Non-violent Coordinating Committee (SNCC).

Carawan is responsible for nearly 30 albums, many in association with Candie, both of their own performances and of folk performers. His respected books include *Ain't You Got a Right to the Tree of Life?*, *Sing for Freedom*, and *Voices from the Mountains*.

Mayo Taylor, Middle Tennessee State University

SUGGESTED READING: Pete Seeger, *Everybody Says Freedom* (1989)

SEE: CIVIL RIGHTS MOVEMENT; HIGHLANDER FOLK SCHOOL; HIGHLANDER RESEARCH AND EDUCATION CENTER; HORTON, MYLES; HORTON, ZILPHIA JOHNSON

CARDEN, ALLEN DICKENSON (1792–1859) was a singing-school teacher and compiler of tunebooks using four-shape notation. He compiled and published *The Missouri Harmony* (St. Louis, 1820, though printed in Cincinnati). It was probably the most widely used tunebook in the southern and western United States until William Walker published *The Southern Harmony and Musical Companion* (1835). Although Carden had no further connection with *The Missouri Harmony*, nine later editions with numerous reprints were published by others through 1857.

Shortly after the publication of *The Missouri Harmony*, Carden returned to Nashville where he taught singing schools and published and printed two other tunebooks, *The Western Harmony* (1824 with S. J. Rogers, F. Moore, and J. Green) and *United States Harmony* (1829). Neither of these books achieved the success of his earlier effort. There is no record of a second edition for either book. However, all of Carden's tunebooks are significant because of his stated purpose to provide music for church services. Tunebooks of this period were typically not used in regular church services. They were intended for use in singing societies or schools. *The Western Harmony* also is uniquely significant in that it was the first music published with a Nashville imprint.

During the last 25 years of his life, Carden acquired substantial landholdings in several counties in Middle and West Tennessee, but whether he maintained his involvement in musical matters after the publication of his final tunebook is unknown.

Timothy J. Reynolds, Nashville

CARL, KATE AUGUSTA (1854–1938) is best known for her portrait of Tzu Hsi, the last Empress Dowager of China, painted for the 1904 Louisiana Purchase Exposition in St. Louis. Carl was born in New Orleans in 1854 and came to Memphis with her widowed mother shortly after the Civil War. In 1878 she took up the study of art in Paris under Charles Muller, portraiture being her specialty. After two years, she returned to Memphis, finished her studies at the State Female Academy, and opened her own studio, where she conducted art lessons. In 1884, she returned to Paris, where she attended the Académie Julian. A student of William Adolphe Bouguereau, Tony Robert-Fleury, and later Hector Le Roux, she continued to paint portraits and genre scenes, which were accepted in the Paris salons from 1886 to 1889 and 1895 to 1899. She also participated in the Tennessee Centennial Exposition in 1897. In 1903 Carl spent ten months in Beijing painting the Empress Dowager's portrait. The honor of this commission was obtained through the diplomatic contacts of her brother, China's Commissioner of Customs. One of the few foreigners allowed to live at the Imperial Palace, she published a book of her experience, *With the Empress Dowager of China*, in 1905. Although Carl lived in China until 1930, she was one of the original trustees of Memphis Brooks Museum of Art at its founding in 1916, and was a member of its board and acceptance jury for many years. After returning to the United States, she maintained a studio on Washington Square in New York, where she died in 1938.

Marilyn Masler, Memphis Brooks Museum of Art

SEE: ART; MEMPHIS BROOKS MUSEUM OF ART

CARMACK, EDWARD WARD (1858–1908), a powerful figure in turn-of-the-century Tennessee politics and a leader in the state's temperance movement, was born in Sumner County. His father, a Christian Church minister, died during Carmack's infancy, leaving the child to be raised amid hardship and poverty. Carmack overcame these obstacles and went on to attend Cumberland University, where he studied law. He then settled in Columbia, Tennessee, where he maintained a legal practice until he won a seat in the Tennessee General Assembly in 1884.

Carmack served one term in the legislature before returning to Columbia to pursue a career in journalism. He edited the *Columbia Herald* briefly, then moved to Nashville and established that city's *Democrat*. In 1888 the *Democrat* was acquired by the Nashville *American*, and Carmack was named editor-in-chief of the newly-expanded publication. Carmack quickly garnered a reputation as a combative journalist and a champion of popular causes. While at the *American*, he also developed a close relationship with the paper's owner, Duncan Brown Cooper.

In 1892 Carmack left the *American* to become editor of the *Memphis Commercial*. He remained there until 1896, when he resigned to run for the U.S. House of Representatives in a bitter and close contest that unseated the incumbent, Josiah Patterson. He served two terms in the House and, in 1901, was elected to the U.S. Senate. During his tenure in Washington, Carmack earned a reputation as a reformer, opposing the interests of railroads and other monopolies. He was also an ardent foe of American imperialism, fighting both the annexation of Hawaii and the expansionist policies of President Theodore Roosevelt.

Throughout his early political career, Carmack had been a moderate on the issue of prohibition and consistently favored the regulation, rather than the abolition, of alcohol. In the early twentieth century, however, he became a strong proponent of temperance. In his 1905 senatorial campaign, Carmack portrayed himself as an enemy of liquor interests, a position which may have cost him the race. A short time later, he publicly proclaimed his support for statewide prohibition.

Carmack's announcement instantly made him a favorite among Tennessee's temperance backers. Buoyed by this groundswell of support, Carmack declared his candidacy in the 1908 gubernatorial election. His opponent in the Democratic primary was Malcolm R. Patterson, the incumbent governor and the son of his old foe, Josiah Patterson. The prohibition issue bitterly divided Tennessee's Democratic party. Carmack attacked Patterson as a tool of the liquor interests. Patterson portrayed Carmack as an opportunist who converted to prohibition out of political expediency. The governor's position earned him the support of Tennessee's wet forces, including a majority of the state's urban residents. It also won him the endorsement of Duncan Brown Cooper, who had earlier broken with Carmack.

With strong urban support, Patterson narrowly won the Democratic primary and easily prevailed against his Republican challenger in the subsequent general election. Carmack, indignant over his loss, returned to journalism and became editor of the *Nashville Tennessean*, a prohibitionist daily. There he unleashed a barrage of attacks against Patterson, while he belittled Duncan Brown Cooper.

Outraged by such comments, Cooper sent a stern warning to Carmack to halt his attacks. Carmack, however, ignored these threats and continued to malign his former friend. The situation came to a head on November 9, 1908, when Cooper and his son Robin encountered Carmack on a downtown Nashville street. Fearing an ambush, Carmack fired on the pair, wounding the younger Cooper. Robin Cooper returned fire, killing Carmack instantly.

Carmack's violent death created an uproar across Tennessee. Prohibitionists deemed the shooting an assassination and transformed Carmack into a slain martyr. Public opinion, incited by temperance propaganda, shifted in favor of prohibition. As a result, the Tennessee state legislature voted overwhelmingly to ban the sale, manufacture, and consumption of intoxicants in January 1909. At the same time, representatives also authorized the erection of a statue of

Carmack, by sculptor Nancy McCormack, on the capitol grounds as a tribute to the fallen hero. Today, though prohibition is now a distant memory, that statue still stands, a lasting tribute to a controversial and significant figure in Tennessee history.

Timothy P. Ezzell, Knoxville

SUGGESTED READINGS: Paul E. Isaac, *Prohibition and Politics: Turbulent Decades in Tennessee, 1885–1920* (1965); William J. Majors, *Editorial Wild Oats: Edward Ward Carmack and Tennessee Politics* (1984); James Summerville, *The Carmack-Cooper Shooting* (1994)

SEE: COOPER V. STATE; MCCORMACK CUSHMAN, NANCY COX; NASHVILLE TENNESSEAN; PATTERSON, MALCOLM R.; PUBLISHING; TEMPERANCE

CARNTON PLANTATION is a historic house museum located in Franklin. Randal McGavock (1768–1843), builder of Carnton, emigrated from Virginia in 1796 and settled in Nashville. He was involved in local and state politics and eventually served as mayor of Nashville, 1824–1825. Around 1826, McGavock moved his family to the recently completed Carnton to farm and raise thoroughbred horses until his death in 1843. After his death, his son John inherited the plantation and continued to farm the land until his own death in 1893. The McGavocks grew wheat, corn, oats, hay, and potatoes, in addition to raising thoroughbred horses.

Randal McGavock named his property after his father's birthplace in County Antrim, Ireland. The Federal style plantation house became a social and political center, where McGavock entertained Andrew Jackson and James K. Polk and presided over an estate that grew to 1,420 acres. For many years, the main house was joined to the smokehouse by a two-story "wing," that was actually the first structure on the site (ca. 1815). The "wing" was damaged by a tornado in 1909 and torn away soon after, though its outline remains clearly visible on the wall of the house.

In 1847 John McGavock added a two-story Greek Revival portico and two dormers in the attic just prior to his 1848 marriage to his cousin, Carrie Winder of Ducros Plantation in Louisiana. A few years later, they added a two-story porch onto the rear of the house, which extended at one end to take advantage of southerly breezes. The interior was also updated in the 1850s, with the addition of fashionable wallpapers, carpets, and paint. The central passage now appears much as it did during the Civil War years, with restored paint colors and an original wallpaper pattern reproduced from a fragment that remains in place at the top of the stairs. The parlor was upgraded by adding a Greek Revival mantel, new wallpaper, and wall-to-wall carpeting.

Following the Battle of Franklin, November 30, 1864, the house became a Confederate field hospital.

During the night following the five-hour battle, the McGavocks and their two children Hattie (age nine) and Winder (age seven) assisted the surgeons and tended to the needs of the wounded. Several hundred eventually came to Carnton and 150 died that first night. Bloodstains are still visible in several rooms. They are heaviest in the children's bedroom, which was used as an operating room. The bodies of Confederate Generals Cleburne, Granbury, Strahl, and Adams were brought to Carnton's rear porch and placed on its lower level awaiting removal to their final burial places. Most of the over 1,750 Confederate dead were buried on the battlefield, the graves marked by wooden headboards inscribed with the soldier's name, company, and regiment. Over the months, the writing faded, and the markers began to disappear.

To preserve the graves, John McGavock designated two acres of land adjoining his family cemetery to which the remains could be removed for a more secluded and protected resting place. He, and other concerned Franklin citizens, raised the necessary money to have the bodies disinterred and reburied in order by states in the spring of 1866. The inscriptions on the grave-marker, which had remained in place on the battlefield, were carefully preserved by Carrie McGavock in the *Cemetery Record Book*. The numbers on the present markers correspond to numbers in the book. John and Carrie McGavock cared for the McGavock Confederate Cemetery for the rest of their lives.

Winder McGavock lived at Carnton with his family until his death in 1907. His widow sold the house out of the family in 1911. The McGavock Confederate Cemetery has been maintained since then by the Franklin Chapter of the United Daughters of the Confederacy.

Carnton passed through several owners from the time it left the McGavock family until September 1978, when the Carnton Association acquired the house and ten acres and opened it as a historic site. Today, Carnton is listed in the National Register of Historic Places and designated a National Historic Landmark for its role in the Battle of Franklin.

Leo J. Goodsell, Plano, Illinois
SEE: CLEBURNE, PATRICK R.; FRANKLIN, BATTLE OF

CARPENTER, J. EDWIN R. (1867–1932), nationally renowned architect of high rise apartments in New York City, was born in Mt. Pleasant, Tennessee, in 1867. His undergraduate training came at the University of Tennessee in 1885 and then the Massachusetts Institute of Technology, where he received a degree in architecture in 1887. After graduation, Carpenter worked at the Boston office of McKim, Mead, and White, a nationally significant firm, but he returned to Tennessee to establish his own practice by 1890.

From 1900 to 1901 Carpenter studied at the Ecole des Beaux Arts in Paris, France, where he was a classmate of the American architect John Russell Pope.

His first Tennessee commissions came in his native Maury County, where he designed the Columbia military arsenal, later the Columbia Military Academy, in 1890–91. In the next decade, Carpenter moved his office to New York City, but maintained an active Tennessee practice. He designed the Maury County Courthouse (1904–6) in Columbia. His major Nashville commissions included the Stahlman Building (1903), the city's first skyscraper; rebuilding Kirkland Tower at Vanderbilt University (1905–6); and the Hermitage Hotel (1908–1910). Carpenter also designed Lynmeade, a Nashville mansion for his brother James Carpenter, in 1913. The Hermitage Hotel and Lynmeade are exceptional Nashville examples of Beaux Arts Classicism.

Carpenter's national successes came in New York City. With offices on Madison Avenue, Carpenter became a popular architect of Renaissance Revival style apartment complexes and was called the father of modern apartment design in the city. He successfully fought a city regulation that limited the height of residences on Park Avenue and Fifth Avenue to 75 feet in height. Soon an apartment and office complex boom was underway in this part of New York City. His most important designs include the apartment houses at 116 E. 58th Street, 960 Park Avenue, 630 Park Avenue, E. 75th Street, and the Lincoln Building (1930), a 53-story high-rise on E. 42nd Street. His practice was not exclusively limited to New York. In 1925, for example, he joined Howard Major in the design of the apartments of the El Patio Marino resort at Palm Beach, Florida.

Carpenter received gold medals from the New York City chapter of the American Institute of Architects in 1916 and 1928. He died in New York City in 1932.
Carroll Van West, Middle Tennessee State University
SEE: HERMITAGE HOTEL; MAURY COUNTY

CARROLL COUNTY was created by an act of the Tennessee General Assembly on November 7, 1821, and named for the governor, William Carroll. The area from which the county was taken had been part of the Western District, which was controlled by the Chickasaws until ceded in the Jackson Purchase of 1818. Settlers began to move into the area in 1820, where they found abundant game, fertile land, and large forests. Grass-covered areas known as "barrens" provided pasturage for livestock and easy cultivation. Realizing that the temperate climate and natural resources offered a bright future, the settlers established firm roots in the county and founded a number of communities and towns that continue today, including McKenzie, Trezevant, Bruceton, Atwood, McLemoresville, Clarksburg, and Huntingdon.

Agriculture provided the economic base for Carroll County for most of its history. In 1920 the county contained over 4,000 farms producing corn, cotton, wheat, fruits, and livestock. Fruit and poultry raising were especially important then. In more recent years, the economy has shifted toward manufacturing and commercial enterprises and today Carroll County offers a healthy balance between agriculture, industry, and services. As of 1997, the county has five textile manufacturers, including Henry I. Siegel Company, Inc., which produces women's jeans. Other companies produce upholstered furniture, ammunition, aluminum foil, steel doors and frames, dishwashers racks, lawnmowers and garden equipment, molded rubber products, pet food, and lighting fixtures.

Good transportation systems account for much of Carroll County's industrial growth. In the early 1930s, the Memphis-to-Bristol Highway passed through the center of Huntingdon and led to rebuilding and economic realignment. The town built a new courthouse and post office and added gas stations and the Court Theater to take advantage of the changes brought by highway traffic. Today, the county is served by Interstate 40, three U.S. highways, and ten state highways. Located at the junction of the NC&St.L railroad and the Memphis branch of the L&N, McKenzie is a classic example of a West Tennessee railroad town. Today, CSX serves the county's rail needs. In addition, Carroll County has a county airport with a 5,500-foot runway.

Carroll County has a long history in education. In 1843 Bethel Seminary was established in the rural village of McLemoresville under the auspices of the Cumberland Presbyterian Church; in 1847 the state granted the school a charter. In 1872 Bethel College moved into three new buildings at McKenzie, where it remains. More than 500 students attend this fully accredited college, which is the only four-year institution sponsored by the Cumberland Presbyterian Church.

Like Bethel, another private school had its origins in Carroll County. After the Civil War, the Methodist Church sponsored McTyeire Preparatory School at McKenzie. Attended by a number of well-known men and women, this boarding school offered a Christian education to prepare students to enter Vanderbilt University. The school remained in operation until the Great Depression, when the costs of maintaining the facility forced it to close in 1931.

In 1920 more than 8,000 children attended ten high schools and 90 elementary schools. Today, Carroll County operates seven four-year high schools as independent school districts across the county. In 1965 McKenzie received one of the first State Area Vo-Tech schools, which provide post-secondary training in order to expand the pool of local skilled labor.

Carroll County enjoys the benefits of recreational and health facilities. The county has two hospitals, three nursing homes, 22 physicians, and nine dentists. In the 1930s the U.S. Department of Agriculture acquired some 42,000 acres of eroded and abused land as part of the federal reclamation project. In 1939 Tennessee leased the reforested land to create the Natchez Trace State Park. Located in Carroll, Henderson, and Benton counties, the Natchez Trace State Park offers a variety of recreational opportunities to local residents and visitors, including camping, hiking, swimming, and fishing.

Carroll County was the home of two Tennessee governors: Alvin Hawkins and Gordon Browning. Hawkins, the only Republican governor from 1871 to 1911, served one term from 1881 to 1883. Gordon Browning, a Democrat, served three terms, 1937–1939 and 1949–1953. Browning's memory lives on in the Browning Museum and Genealogical Library in McKenzie.

Joe David McClure, McKenzie

SEE: BETHEL COLLEGE; BROWNING, GORDON W.; BURROW, AARON K.; HAWKINS, ALVIN; HIGHWAYS, HISTORIC; NATCHEZ TRACE STATE PARK

CARROLL, WILLIAM (1788–1844), served as Tennessee's governor for all but two years between 1821 and 1835. He was a prominent figure in the state's early Democratic party, and his career symbolized the era's popular protest against established political interests. Carroll was born near Pittsburgh, Pennsylvania, and was the oldest son of the nine children of Thomas Carroll, a merchant who was an associate of Albert Gallatin, the Secretary of the Treasury for Presidents Thomas Jefferson and James Madison. The younger Carroll received only a limited education that emphasized practical fields like bookkeeping, surveying, mathematics, English language and grammar, and probably farming and rudimentary military training. Most of what he learned came from experience working in his father's hardware store and other mercantile ventures, and he devoted his early years toward providing the foundation for his own business career. Carroll possessed a natural intelligence, however, and in his later years compensated for his lack of formal training through his own reading. At his death, the *Nashville Republican Banner* obituary commended his private pursuit of knowledge and declared him a success in overcoming his early educational deficiencies.

Carroll came to Nashville in 1810 at the age of 22, with a letter of introduction from Gallatin to Andrew Jackson, which Carroll used to establish the local connections to enable him to open a hardware store and nail factory. The success of these businesses put him at the forefront of the town's development throughout the 1810s. In 1816 Carroll purchased the *General*

PORTRAIT BY WILLIAM B. COOPER, TENNESSEE STATE MUSEUM

Governor William Carroll.

Jackson, the first steamboat on the Cumberland River. The next year, he and other leading merchants attempted to bring a branch of the Bank of the United States to Nashville. When the legislature blocked this effort, he was named to the Board of Directors of the newly-created Bank of Nashville.

Carroll gained his military reputation during the War of 1812. He organized and served as captain of a volunteer company, and Jackson appointed him Brigade Inspector for the campaigns to Natchez in 1812 and against the Creek Indians in 1813. On the latter campaign, he participated in several battles before sustaining a severe wound during Jackson's victory at Horseshoe Bend. Notwithstanding this injury, he returned to the field when he was elected to succeed Jackson as Commander of the Tennessee militia, after Jackson was promoted to Major General in the regular army. Carroll's troops provided Jackson with crucial reinforcement that helped to turn the Battle of New Orleans into an American triumph. Because of his contributions at New Orleans, Carroll emerged from the war with a reputation second only to that of Jackson himself.

Following the war, Carroll returned to his businesses and prospered until the financial Panic of 1819 forced him into bankruptcy. The Panic ruined Carroll commercially, but it launched his political career. Hard times promoted a popular resentment against Tennessee's banks. A political faction of planters and land speculators led by John Overton controlled the

banks and suspended specie payment, to the detriment of debtors and small farmers. In 1821 Carroll, as military hero and bankrupt entrepreneur, emerged as the ideal candidate to oppose the Overton faction. Carroll supporters presented him as a poor man standing against the pretensions of the wealthy. In promotional circulars Carroll declared himself "no friend of banks" and speculated that "we would . . . have done better, if we had never seen one in the state." Still, he rejected radical proposals to abolish the banks because "their *sudden* downfall would be ruinous to the interest of the people."[1] Instead, he favored compelling the banks to resume specie payments, with continued supervision over future operations. This moderately conservative approach actually differed little from that of his opponent, Colonel Edward Ward, who proposed consolidation of Tennessee's banks into one central institution. Carroll's image as a self-made man ruined by the panic, however, contrasted sharply with Ward's standing as the candidate of the Overton faction and as a well-educated scion of inherited wealth, and he defeated Ward by a more than four-to-one margin.

When Carroll first took office, the 1796 state constitution severely limited gubernatorial authority, but Carroll's popularity and personality gave him considerable influence in the General Assembly. At his urging, the legislature passed a law compelling the banks to resume specie payments by April 1824, although it later moved the date for resumption back to September 1, 1826. Likewise, in 1825 the Assembly repealed a prohibitive tax on banks operating in Tennessee without a state charter, and with Carroll's support the Bank of the United States finally opened a Nashville branch the next year. The 1796 constitution's restriction on gubernatorial service to no more than six years in any eight-year period forced Carroll's retirement in 1827, but in 1829 he was again eligible for office and won the first of another three consecutive terms. The legislature again proved receptive to his proposals, and during the next six years the Assembly funded internal improvements, established a penitentiary and mental hospital, reorganized the judicial system, and revised the penal code. During this second phase of Carroll's leadership, the last remaining bank from the Panic of 1819 closed, and Tennessee established new banks that provided the state's financial system until the Civil War.

As a champion of "the people" against entrenched interests, Carroll foreshadowed on the state level Andrew Jackson's rise to national prominence. Still, the governor hesitated to commit himself fully to Jackson's presidential prospects, probably because he believed that the hero lacked the experience and reputation necessary for a serious run for the nation's highest office, but perhaps also because he was aware of his former commander's opposition to banks and preference for an exclusively specie currency. In any case, despite his pubic endorsement of Jackson and his work as campaign treasurer for the 1824 election, Carroll remained a regular correspondent and advisor of one of Jackson's opponents, Kentucky's Henry Clay. When Jackson won a plurality of the popular vote, but lost the presidency in the House of Representatives, Carroll abandoned Clay and avidly supported Jackson's successful candidacies in 1828 and 1832. He worked arduously to ingratiate himself with Jackson, who was aware of Carroll's earlier duplicity. By the early 1830s he had returned to Jackson's favor and, once readmitted to the leadership of Jackson's forces in Tennessee, remained a loyal supporter of the Democratic party. This loyalty even led him to endorse Jackson's preference, Martin Van Buren, as Old Hickory's successor in the 1836 presidential election, instead of following the dissident Tennessee movement for Senator Hugh Lawson White.

Carroll's political career came to an end shortly before Van Buren's election. In 1834 a convention revised the 1796 constitution, but retained the previous limitations on the governor's term of office. Nevertheless, Carroll attempted to remain in office for a fourth term by claiming that he was eligible for a first term under the new frame of government. The majority of voters disagreed with this interpretation, however, and former Congressman Newton Cannon easily defeated the incumbent. Following this loss, Jackson appointed Carroll as an Indian Commissioner to conclude negotiations for the Cherokee removal, and in 1838 President Van Buren appointed him a special agent to the Creeks. Critics charged that Carroll used these positions to enrich himself through illicit land speculation. Never proved or disproved, these charges probably stemmed from political motives to foil his future candidacy for the governorship or a congressional seat. Despite Democratic encouragement, Carroll never again stood for public office after his 1835 loss. By the early 1840s his health had declined significantly, and he died at his Nashville home in 1844.

Carroll held the office of Tennessee's governor longer than any other person, and despite the partisan rancor of the 1840s, his death was widely mourned. The *Republican Banner*, a Whig newspaper, reflected that "the country has lost a great and useful man; who has served her in war and in peace with eminent advantage, success and glory."[2] He was the first chief executive to lead the General Assembly in undertaking significant reform, while his image as the champion of the people against wealth and power brought to Tennessee the new democratic style of politics that is usually associated with the emergence of Jackson as a national leader.

Jonathan M. Atkins, Berry College
CITATIONS:
(1) *Nashville Clarion*, June 27, 1821.
(2) *Nashville Republican Banner*, March 25, 1844.
SUGGESTED READINGS: Jonathan M. Atkins, *Politics, Parties, and the Sectional Conflict in Tennessee, 1832–1861* (1997); Paul H. Bergeron, *Antebellum Politics in Tennessee* (1982)
SEE: CREEK WAR OF 1813 AND 1814; JACKSONIANS; OVERTON, JOHN; TENNESSEE LUNATIC ASYLUM; WAR OF 1812

CARSON-NEWMAN COLLEGE, a four-year liberal arts institution located in Jefferson City, Tennessee, traces its roots to the founding of the Mossy Creek Baptist Seminary. The seminary opened its doors for the first session in September 1851; Reverend William Rogers served as its first president of the institution. The curriculum included courses in Latin, Greek, literature, philosophy, morals, mathematics, history, and natural sciences. In 1855 the seminary conferred a baccalaureate degree on its first graduate, Richard Scruggs, who later became a physician. In 1856 the institution changed its name to Mossy Creek Baptist College. In 1859 the graduating class had six members, and the 1860 class numbered thirteen.

In June 1862, the college closed during the Civil War. Not only was it located in a highly contested area, but most of its students enlisted in the army. During the next three years, Federal troops occupied the campus and destroyed the buildings. When the college re-opened in 1868, its officials filed a claim for damages against the Federal government. In 1896 the institution finally received $6,000 in compensation.

By 1870 the college enrolled 100 men. In January 1880 the school changed its name to Carson College to honor J. H. Carson of Dandridge, a longtime trustee and benefactor. In 1889 the trustees of Carson College and the trustees of nearby Newman College for Women (established in 1878) agreed to merge the two institutions. To celebrate, the men of Carson College—including future Tennessee governor Ben W. Hooper—marched to the grounds of Newman College and staged a mock wedding. Townspeople, students, and faculty of both colleges looked on as the two institutions were united in "matrimony."

With more than 50 majors and special programs, Carson-Newman provides a superior educational and social experience in a Christian atmosphere for approximately 2,200 students from across the United States and various countries. Carson-Newman students excel in music, religion, business, biology, chemistry, education, nursing, psychology, history, and social sciences. In addition to the Bachelor of Arts and Bachelor of Science degrees, Carson-Newman offers graduate degrees in nursing, counseling, and education. In 1996 Carson-Newman received recognition as one of the best liberal arts colleges in the South. The college also excels in the athletic field, winning the NAIA National Baseball Championship in 1965 and five NAIA National Football Championships in 1983, 1984, 1986, 1988, and 1989.

As many as five succeeding generations of families have received their education at Carson-Newman and contributed to its rich tradition. Dr. Cordell Maddox has served as the president of Carson-Newman since 1977.

Walter Lynn Bates, Knoxville

SEE: EDUCATION, HIGHER; HOOPER, BEN WALTER.; JEFFERSON COUNTY

CARTER COUNTY, located in the northeast corner of Tennessee, was created from Washington County in 1796 and named in honor of Landon Carter, treasurer of the Washington and Hamilton districts of North Carolina and the State of Franklin's speaker of the Senate and Secretary of State. Carter's 348 square miles blend mountains, the Watauga and Doe rivers, and beautiful valleys into an inspiring Appalachian landscape. The Appalachian Trail passes through the county and most of eastern Carter County is within the Cherokee National Forest. Roan Mountain State Park, at the county's border with North Carolina, is one of the most beloved scenic spots in the state.

Carter County is extremely significant in Tennessee's settlement history. Permanent settlers arrived along the Watauga River in the late 1760s; William Bean was one of the earliest and his farm was eight miles west of the Sycamore Shoals of the Watauga River. James Robertson established a river valley farm in 1770 and stayed there until moving to the Cumberland River in 1779. Valentine Sevier, Sr., the father of John Sevier, lived near Sycamore Shoals. Also in the early 1770s, John Carter established his plantation just north of present-day Elizabethton. This notable Revolutionary patriot was the father of Landon Carter, for whom the county was named. In 1772 the settlers along the Watauga established the Watauga Association. Three years later, in 1775, land speculator Richard Henderson and Cherokee leaders met at Sycamore Shoals to negotiate the Transylvania Purchase. During the American Revolution, Fort Watauga provided refuge from attacks by Old Abram and other Cherokee warriors. In 1780 approximately 1,100 Overmountain Men gathered at Sycamore Shoals before marching to King's Mountain. The Sycamore Shoals State Historic Area preserves key historical places, including the Overmountain Men muster ground, the Shoals, the reconstructed Fort Watauga, and the John and Landon Carter Mansion.

Elizabethton, the county seat, was established in 1797 and remained a small rural village until the railroad and industrial age. William G. "Parson" Brownlow established a newspaper here in 1839. Duffield Academy, founded in 1809, was the town's leading antebellum school. During the Civil War, the town

and county were equally divided in their support of the Union and Confederate causes. The county's most famous soldier was Samuel P. Carter (1819–1891), a Naval Academy graduate, who was appointed Brigadier General, U.S. Volunteers in May 1862, and led an East Tennessee cavalry raid that same year. He later returned to the Navy as a commander and after his retirement in 1881, Carter was named a Rear Admiral on the retired list.

The Doe River Covered Bridge, built in 1882, allowed for commercial and residential expansion. Educational opportunities grew with Milligan College, established in 1882, which grew out of the earlier Buffalo Male and Female Institute (1866). Two leading late nineteenth century Tennessee politicians came from Carter County: Robert Love Taylor and his brother Alfred A. Taylor, who waged the famous "War of the Roses" in 1886. Bob Taylor was governor from 1887–1891 and 1897–1899; brother Alf served as governor from 1921–1923.

Carter County's modern history began with the arrival of the East Tennessee and Western North Carolina Railroad in the late 1880s. The county's first major industry, Line and Twine, came in 1892. Although the depression of 1893–94, followed by a disastrous flood in May 1901, dampened rapid economic growth, investors did not forget about the county's industrial potential. In the mid-1920s German capitalists located the Bemberg and Glanzstoff rayon plants between Elizabethton and Sycamore Shoals. The massive factories thrust local residents, and hundreds of other Appalachian families, into the industrial age. When hundreds of employees, mostly women, struck the companies in 1929, it was "the first concrete sign of Southern disenchantment with a textile industry financed by Northern capital and operated in an exploitative manner."[1] The strike failed, however, and rayon companies remained the town's key industries.

Another significant development in modern Carter County history was TVA's construction of Watauga Dam and Lake in the 1940s. Completed in 1948, the lake created by the earth-filled dam covers approximately 6,430 acres.

The career of Judge Ben Allen (1891–1977) is closely associated with the main themes of the county's modern history. A veteran of the 117th Infantry in World War I and a graduate of the Cumberland School of Law in Lebanon, Allen's political career began with his election as District Attorney General in 1926. In the 1930s he was a founding member of the Mountain Breeders Co-op, which aimed to enhance the county's livestock industry. In 1934 he was elected Circuit Court Judge of the First Judicial District, a position Allen held until 1942, when he resigned to become the General Manager and Vice President of the Bemberg and

North American Rayon plants. The U.S. government seized control of the German-owned factories as a wartime measure; officials selected Allen because of his reputation for honesty and fairness. Allen remained manager of the two factories until 1956, when he began an active retirement and became a founding member of the Watauga Historical Association, which eventually created the Sycamore Shoals State Historic Park. Allen's historic Renfro-Allen Farm was recognized as the county's only registered Tennessee Century Farm in 1976 and has been listed in the National Register of Historic Places.

Carroll Van West, Middle Tennessee State University

CITATION:

(1) Jim Stokely, "Elizabethton Rayon Strikes," Jim Stokely and Jeff D. Johnson, eds., *An Encyclopedia of East Tennessee* (Oak Ridge, 1981), 178.

SEE: APPALACHIAN TRAIL; CARTER MANSION; CARTER, JOHN; CARTER, LANDON; CHEROKEE NATIONAL FOREST; DONELSON, JOHN; FORT WATAUGA; LABOR; MILLIGAN COLLEGE; NORTH AMERICAN RAYON CORPORATION AND AMERICAN BEMBERG; OVERMOUNTAIN MEN; ROAN MOUNTAIN STATE PARK; STRIKE, RAYON PLANTS AT ELIZABETHTON; SYCAMORE SHOALS STATE HISTORIC AREA; TAYLOR, ALFRED A.; TAYLOR, ROBERT L.; TENNESSEE VALLEY AUTHORITY; TRANSYLVANIA PURCHASE; WAR OF THE ROSES; WATAUGA ASSOCIATION

CARTER, GEORGE LAFAYETTE (1857–1936), rail and coal magnate and founder of modern Kingsport, shaped the economic transformation of northeast Tennessee and southwest Virginia. Known as the "empire builder of Southwest Virginia," Carter built the Carolina, Clinchfield and Ohio Railway and envisioned the modern industrial city of Kingsport.

Born January 10, 1857, in Hillsville, Virginia, Carter was the son of Walter Carter and Lucy Ann Jennings. As a youth, he worked in the Hillsville General Store, but soon found employment at Wythe Lead and Zinc Company in Austinville, Virginia. He and railroad contractor George T. Mills pursued the development and sale of iron ore properties. Carter purchased small mines to provide coke for the Dora furnace at Pulaski, Virginia, where he served as general manager. He also founded the Toms Creek Coal and Coke Company. In 1898 Carter combined all his holdings into the Carter Coal and Iron Company. The following year, he organized the Virginia Iron, Coal and Coke Company, a ten million dollar corporation, headquartered in Bristol.

Carter held iron ore properties from Georgia to Virginia, as well as steel plants and iron ore rolling mills. During this time, he organized the Clinchfield Coal Company from 300,000 acres of coal lands in Dickenson, Russell, and Wise counties, Virginia. At the height of his holdings, Carter held 9,000 acres of land on the present site of Kingsport and 250,000 acres in Russell and Dickenson counties in Virginia. The South and Western Railway Company, headquartered in Bristol and later Johnson City, provided access to his properties.

Carter's most enduring legacies were the construction of the Carolina, Clinchfield and Ohio Railway and the creation of modern Kingsport. In order to build his railroad, Carter obtained the financial backing of the powerful New York capitalist Thomas Fortune Ryan, who invested a reported $30 million. The railroad project also benefited from the involvement of John B. Dennis, of Blair and Company, New York, who rescued the project and supported the development of Kingsport. In 1908 the northern syndicate rechartered the South and Western Railway Company as the Carolina, Clinchfield and Ohio Railway (CC&O). Crossing the Blue Ridge Mountains from Elkhorn City, Kentucky, to Spartanburg, South Carolina, and joining with other lines, the Clinchfield connected Charleston with Cincinnati. The construction of the railroad, a true engineering feat through the rugged terrain, promoted regional industrial development.

As early as 1905, Carter envisioned a modern industrial city at the site of Kingsport. The *Johnson City Comet* reported that Carter's Unaka Corporation, a land holding company, planned "to boom a town at Kingsport." In 1906 Carter hired a Philadelphia engineer to inspect the area and draft a street arrangement. A few years later, he sold 6,355 acres of land to Kingsport Farms, Incorporated, which was controlled by the New York firm of Blair and Company. The Kingsport Improvement Company, headed by Clinchfield land agent and Carter brother-in-law J. Fred Johnson, was soon chartered to purchase land for the proposed town from Kingsport Farms. John B. Dennis held a controlling interest in both companies, providing the financial backing for the new industrial town.

Between 1907 and 1920, Carter lived in Johnson City, where he was instrumental in the creation of a teacher's college—now East Tennessee State University—through his donation of the 120-acre site for the construction of the institution. At one point, Carter owned the *Bristol Herald,* now the Bristol *Herald-Courier.* He owned the Fort Chiswell estate near Wytheville, including several thousand acres of land, and maintained homes at Coalwood, West Virginia, and Hillsville, Virginia.

Other related business interests included the Carter Coal and Dock Company, which operated in New York, Boston, Providence, and Bridgeport. Carter maintained offices in Washington, D.C., New York, Cleveland, Chicago, and Cincinnati, and was living in Washington, D.C., at the time of his death. He is buried in Hillsville, Virginia.

Martha Avaleen Egan, Kingsport Public Library and Archives/King College

SUGGESTED READING: Margaret Ripley Wolfe, *Kingsport, Tennessee: A Planned American City* (1987)
SEE: EAST TENNESSEE STATE UNIVERSITY; JOHNSON CITY; JOHNSON, J. FRED; KINGSPORT; RAILROADS; SULLIVAN COUNTY

CARTER HOUSE. Located in historic Franklin, the Carter House was built in 1828 and completed in 1830 by Fountain Branch Carter. The Carter property included a farm of 288 acres, where Carter, a gentleman farmer, raised cotton, corn, wheat, and rye. He owned 28 slaves, who lived in the seven slave cabins on the property. In 1860, at the beginning of the Civil War, Carter's worth was $62,000.

The house is constructed of bricks, glass, and squarehead nails, which were all made on the farm. The wood in the house is mostly tulip poplar, said to deter termites. The house contains many decorative elements, including ashlar treating, graining, marbling, and wall paper. The house represents the home of a wealthy planter of the mid-1800s. The kitchen, smokehouse, slave cabin, and farm office still stand.

Before the Battle of Franklin, Union General Jacob D. Cox set up his headquarters in the parlor. When the Carter family inquired if they should leave, Cox assured them of the unlikely possibility of a battle and suggested that they remain to protect their property. The Carter family stayed. But the Battle of Franklin, one of the bloodiest of the war, came to almost the front door of the Carter House and the family sought shelter in their basement. One of the Carter sons, Captain Tod Carter, was severely wounded in the battle and was brought to the house, where he died. Two other sons, Moscow and Francis, fought with their brother in the Twentieth Tennessee. After the battle, the parlor of the Carter House became a Confederate field hospital. Although the Carter House survived the Battle of Franklin, many scars and bullet holes remain in the wood and brick of the outbuildings.

The Carter House is a National Historic Landmark owned by the State of Tennessee and operated by the Carter House Association. The site includes a visitors center with museum and a battlerama video program about the Battle of Franklin.
Meredith Fiske Bare, Nashville
SEE: FRANKLIN, BATTLE OF

CARTER, JOHN (1737–1781), early Tennessee settler and Revolutionary war officer, was born in Virginia in 1737. As an adult John lived in Amherst, Virginia, where he was a merchant. He married Elizabeth Taylor about 1758, and the couple had three sons, Landon, John, Jr., and Emmanuel.

In 1770 Carter moved to Tennessee and established a trading post with William Parker on the west side of the Holston River in an area that later became Hawkins County. In 1772, after a robbery by Indians, Carter moved his family to Watauga Old Fields [Elizabethton]. In 1775 he acquired title to a section [640 acres] of land in Elizabethton. In the 1780s, perhaps John Carter, but more likely his son Landon, built the Carter Mansion, an impressive two-story weatherboard dwelling with a Penn-plan interior, wood paneling, and overmantel paintings. Carter also extended his property. By the time of his death, he had added more than 2,000 acres to the original holding, making him one of the largest landholders west of the mountains at that time.

In 1772 John Carter headed the government established by the Watauga Compact. In 1776 he commanded the fort that defended settlers against Indian attacks associated with the Revolutionary War. Appointed Colonel by the North Carolina government in 1777, he continued his defensive activities against Indian attacks throughout the Revolutionary period. In 1778 and 1781 Carter served as Senator to the North Carolina General Assembly from Washington District. He died of smallpox in 1781.
W. Calvin Dickinson, Tennessee Technological University
SEE: CARTER, LANDON; CARTER MANSION; WATAUGA ASSOCIATION

CARTER, LANDON (1760–1800), Revolutionary war officer and State of Franklin official, was born to John and Elizabeth Carter in Virginia, on January 29, 1760. He moved to northeast Tennessee, now Hawkins County, with his parents in 1770. In 1784 he married 18-year-old Elizabeth MacLin, a neighbor in the Watauga settlement, present-day Carter County. The couple had seven children, one of whom died in infancy. The other six lived in the Carter Mansion in Elizabethton, built either by Landon or by his father in the 1780s. In addition to wealth inherited from his father, Landon was given 10,000 acres by the state of North Carolina.

Landon was educated in North Carolina and served in the Revolutionary War as a captain. In 1780 he went with John Sevier on the campaign against the Cherokees and participated at the Battle of Boyd's Creek, now Sevier County. In company with Charles Robertson, John Sevier, and Francis Marion, he fought in South Carolina between 1780 and 1782. In 1788 North Carolina appointed Carter a major of horse; in 1790 Governor Blount made him lieutenant colonel in the territorial militia; in 1792–93 he rose to the rank of colonel.

In government activities, Carter served North Carolina, the State of Franklin, the Southwest Territory, and the State of Tennessee. In 1784 and 1789 Carter represented Washington County in the North Carolina General Assembly. In the unrecognized State of Franklin, he was Speaker of the Senate, member of the Council of State, and Secretary of

State. Under the territorial government, he served as treasurer of the Washington and Hamilton districts. He represented Washington County in the Tennessee constitutional convention in 1796. He was a trustee at Martin Academy, now Washington College, and at Greeneville College, now Tusculum College.

Carter County, created in 1796, was named for Landon Carter, and the county seat, Elizabethton, was named for his wife. Landon Carter died on June 5, 1800. The Knoxville *Gazette* of June 25, 1800, called his death "an irreparable loss."

W. Calvin Dickinson, Tennessee Technological University

SEE: CARTER COUNTY; CARTER, JOHN; CARTER MANSION; FRANKLIN, STATE OF; TUSCULUM COLLEGE; SEVIER, JOHN; WATAUGA ASSOCIATION

CARTER MANSION. The John and Landon Carter Mansion on the Watauga River at Sycamore Shoals, Elizabethton, is one of the oldest and most architecturally significant houses in Tennessee. Local tradition holds that the house was built by John Carter, an early settler and political leader of the Watauga Association, who died in 1781. Documentary evidence does not refer to such a large house until the 1790s, indicating that his son, Landon Carter, may be responsible for building the house prior to his death in 1800. Based on its architectural styling, typical of the 1780s, either Carter could be responsible for the house's construction.

John Carter traveled to Tennessee from Virginia in 1770, and by 1775 he gained title to the section of land where the mansion stands. John Carter's most famous son, Landon, may have resided with his parents for he did not marry until 1784. Serving as administrator of his father's estate, Landon inherited the 640-acre home place in 1781. References to such a grand house do not appear until 1796 and 1800, when French botanist Andre Michaux and Governor John Sevier visited the Carters.

The imposing two-story frame house combines a common Pennsylvania interior floor plan with interior details typical of more academic design. It is composed of six rooms, three on each floor, plus a cellar and garret. Its first floor follows the Penn plan with a large hall on the right and two smaller rooms with corner fireplaces on the left. The builder embellished this plan by raising the first-floor ceiling to nine feet and employing carpenters and painters to create an elegant interior.

Typical of fine homes of the eighteenth century is the floor-to-ceiling paneling throughout the first floor and its distinctive chimney pieces. The great hall features a fireplace adorned with a curvilinear pediment resting on fluted pilasters. At the rear of the great hall is a small cabinet stair with square, fluted newels and turned balusters. Of the two smaller rooms, the south parlor is the most completely academic room with a

quartered and reversed circle design above the mantel and a hanging wall cabinet. These elements and the doorways of this room are embellished with finely carved keystones.

The second floor's fine styling is evident in its wainscoting and painted details. The smooth, flat, pine surfaces were painted to simulate marble, wood veneer, and wood paneling. The large second-floor bedroom contains an overmantel painting featuring a hunt scene, with hounds chasing a stag. The unknown artist created a similar country scene for the fireplace of the north parlor on the first floor.

The unadorned stone cellar with its dirt floor and large fireplace was most likely used for storage since it lacks access to the first floor. The large garret finished with wide boards may have been used as sleeping quarters for children although there is no evidence of partitioning, nor did it have a fireplace.

The house remained in the Carter family until 1882. In 1973 the State of Tennessee bought the house and several acres. After restoring the mansion to its original appearance, the state opened it to the public as part of the Sycamore Shoals State Historical Area.

Anne-Leslie Owens, Tennessee Historical Society

SEE: ARCHITECTURE, VERNACULAR DOMESTIC; ART; CARTER COUNTY; CARTER, JOHN; CARTER, LANDON; HOUSES, VERNACULAR PLAN; MURALS, DECORATIVE INTERIOR; SYCAMORE SHOALS STATE HISTORIC AREA

CARTWRIGHT, PETER (1785–1872), frontier Methodist circuit rider, was born in Amherst County, Virginia, shortly before his parents moved to Logan County, Kentucky. When he was 15 years old, Cartwright attended one of the religious meetings that were part of the camp meeting phenomenon known as the Great Western Revival. There he was converted and soon became known for his testimonies. In 1802, when his family moved farther west, Cartwright received a letter commissioning him to create a new frontier circuit. With no formal religious education, but a passion for the gospel, Cartwright began his duties, eventually riding circuit in Kentucky, Ohio, Indiana, Tennessee, and Illinois. During the course of his journeys, he engaged in a personal reading program to provide background for his sermons.

Cartwright became known for his battles, both verbal and physical, with scoffers and law breakers. His militant spirit brought him into conflict with other denominations, which he denounced as readily as sin. When the Tennessee Conference met in Nashville in 1818, Cartwright admonished Andrew Jackson to save his soul, a warning that terrified other ministers, who feared Jackson's reaction. According to Cartwright, Jackson admired his independence and fearlessness.

Cartwright abhorred slavery, but found abolitionism equally despicable. He preferred an approach that would finally free the slaves without meddling with the politics of slavery. In 1824 he moved his family to Illinois to remove his children from the influence of slavery. When slavery proponents attempted to legalize it in Illinois, he entered politics, winning terms in the Illinois House in 1828 and 1830. In the 1830 election, Cartwright defeated Abraham Lincoln. Cartwright's last political campaign occurred in 1846, when he unsuccessfully ran against Lincoln for Congress.

A champion of education, Cartwright was one of the founders of Illinois Wesleyan University and McKendree College. His habit of carrying books and pamphlets on his circuit and passing them on to frontier congregations brought religion and learning to people without much of either. In his later years, Cartwright turned to writing and published two volumes: *Autobiography* (1855) and *Fifty Years as a Presiding Elder* (1871). Cartwright retired to his farm near Pleasant Plains, Illinois, where he died in 1872.

Connie L. Lester, Tennessee Historical Society

SEE: CAMP MEETINGS; RELIGION

CASH, JOHNNY (1932–). See MEMPHIS MUSIC SCENE; MUSIC; PHILLIPS, SAMUEL C.; ROCKABILLY MUSIC; TELEVISION AND MOVIE-PERFORMERS

CATRON, JOHN (ca. 1786–1865) served as first Chief Justice of the Tennessee Supreme Court and later as Associate Justice of the U.S. Supreme Court. He was probably born in Virginia in the mid-1780s and received a meager education in the common schools of Virginia and Kentucky. In 1807 Catron married Mary Childress, a native of Nashville. Five years later, the couple moved to Tennessee, where they settled at Sparta on the Eastern Highland Rim. After serving briefly under General Andrew Jackson in the Alabama campaigns against the Creek Indians, Catron returned to Sparta, studied law, and began to practice his profession before moving to Nashville in 1818.

Despite his lack of formal education, Catron built a reputation in the law. He gave up his Nashville practice for a two-year term as attorney general for the third circuit, which covered seven Middle Tennessee counties. In 1824 the legislature elected him Judge of the Tennessee Supreme Court of Errors and Appeals, and in 1831 he became its first Chief Justice.

During his 12 years of service on the court, Catron wrote important opinions regarding conflicting land titles, homicide and self-defense, slavery and free blacks, and the status of Native Americans. Perhaps most notable at the time was Catron's opinion in *Love v. Love* (1828), which resolved a decades-long dispute by ruling that legal titles from the state were unnec-

essary for land ownership when the occupants had continuously resided on the property for seven years.

Catron's political activities tarnished his competent judicial career. An avid Jacksonian and leader in the Tennessee Democratic Party, Catron supported the presidential ambitions of Martin Van Buren, President Jackson's hand-picked successor, which angered the supporters of favorite son Hugh Lawson White. In 1835 the legislature retaliated by removing Catron from the state bench and electing Nathan Green in Catron's place. The following year, the ex-chief justice managed Van Buren's campaign in Tennessee.

Just before leaving office, President Jackson appointed Catron to the U.S. Supreme Court, and Catron took his seat as Associate Justice on May 1, 1837. He served for the next 28 years and took part in a number of cases of constitutional significance. In the famous *Dred Scott v. Sandford* (1857), Catron wrote a separate opinion in concurrence with the majority. He agreed that the slave Scott remained a slave despite his occasional residence in a free territory, and concurred that Congress possessed no power to interfere with slavery in the western territories.

Despite his pro-slavery judicial record, Catron opposed secession and in 1861 he traveled to Nashville to convince state leaders to remain in the Union. Warned that his life would not be safe in the secessionist-leaning city, Catron fled and did not return until June 1862, when the federal occupation of Nashville allowed him to convene the U.S. District Court there. John Catron died in his Nashville home on May 30, 1865.

Timothy S. Huebner, Rhodes College

SUGGESTED READINGS: Joshua W. Caldwell, *Sketches of the Bench and Bar of Tennessee* (1898); Melvin I. Urofsky, *The Supreme Court Justices: A Biographical Dictionary* (1994)

SEE: JACKSON, ANDREW; JACKSONIANS; LAW

CAULKINS STOCKWELL, TRACY (1963–), ranks among Tennessee's most successful Olympians. She began swimming at age eight and, under the aegis of the Nashville Aquatic club, qualified for the Olympic Trials five years later. At 14, Caulkins won her first national title, and *Swimming World* named her American Woman Swimmer of 1977. She broke or tied 27 world and U.S. swimming records in 1978. European sports editors voted her UPI Sportswoman of 1978, and less than a month after turning 16, Caulkins became the youngest recipient (and only Tennessean besides Wilma Rudolph) selected for the Sullivan Award, given annually to the nation's top amateur athlete. UT football star Peyton Manning of Louisiana won the 1997 Sullivan Award.

Though the U.S. boycott of the 1980 Olympic Games in Moscow stunted Caulkins's momentum, she graduated from Harpeth Hall in Nashville, entered the University of Florida, and set five world records, over 60 U.S. records, and won 48 national titles following the Sullivan Award. In the 1984 Olympic Games in Los Angeles she captained the U.S. swim team. Caulkins won gold medals in the 400 and 200 meter individual medleys and the 400 meter medley relay. Her time of 2:12.64 in the 200 meter event set an Olympic record. Though she held 63 individual national titles, more than any other swimmer in U.S. history, Caulkins did not develop the professional persona upon which some athletes have capitalized.

A member of the Halls of Fame for Tennessee Sports, Women's Sports, International Swimming, and the U.S. Olympics, she resides in Brisbane, Australia, with her husband and their twins.

Margaret D. Binnicker, Middle Tennessee State University

CEDAR GLADES. Open areas within otherwise forested regions captured the attention of both early settlers and botanists. Among these are cedar glades—open, rocky areas of variable size and shape. The designation "cedar" comes from the Eastern red-cedar trees, a conspicuous component of the mixed woods that surround glades. Found principally in the Central Basin of Middle Tennessee, cedar glades are ecosystems of considerable biological and geological significance.

The limestone that underlies cedar glades was formed during the Ordovician geological period some 500 million years ago. The weathering of this rock has resulted in thin soils that support an interesting assortment of plants, some of global importance. Several species are endemics found nowhere else.

Glade plants tend to be associated with soils of a particular range of soil depths. These zones are recognized as: (1) *exposed rock* (no soil; lichens), (2) *gravely glades* (soil 0–2 inches; several herbs, including Nashville glade-cress, Gattinger's lobelia, limestone fame flower), (3) *grassy glades* (soil 2–8 inches; annual grasses, also Nashville breadroot, Gattinger's prairie-clover, and Tennessee coneflower).

The cedar glade microenvironment is a harsh, imposing one. Summers are hot and dry, and the thin, exposed soil dries out soon after rains. Winters are cold and wet; rains are more frequent, and evaporation rates much slower. Plants and other organisms must have life cycles synchronized with these changing conditions.

Once occupying approximately five percent of the Central Basin, cedar glades have been considerably reduced in extent by man's activities. As a result, some of its plants are in peril. The conservation of glades and other special habitats is, therefore, imperative.

Thomas E. Hemmerly, Middle Tennessee State University

SUGGESTED READING: Jerry M. Baskin and Carol C. Basin, "Cedar Glade Endemics in Tennessee and a Review of Their Autecology," *Journal of Tennessee Academy of Science,* 64(1989): 63–74; Thomas E. Hemmerly, *Wildflowers of the Central South* (1990)

SEE: CEDARS OF LEBANON STATE PARK; ECOLOGICAL SYSTEMS; GEOLOGICAL ZONES

CEDARS OF LEBANON STATE PARK. During the Great Depression, the federal government worked to adapt the nation's marginal farmlands to better use. To that end, Congress first appropriated $20 million for reclamation and later approved another $50 million. The State of Tennessee applied for a share of the funds for use to reclaim areas where submarginal soil had been stripped of every profitable source of income.

Early in December 1934, county extension agent Louis Sawyer and forest service representatives surveyed a portion of southern Wilson County for inclusion in the reclamation plan. The original cedar forest in this area supported a substantial industry that used the red cedar wood for many purposes, especially in the manufacture of pencils. After the forest was logged out, area families tried to make a living from the shallow rocky soils and submarginal lands. Later that same month, State Forester James O. Hazard approved the area for a reforestation project.

The Wilson Cedar Forest Project, later renamed the Lebanon Cedar Forest Project, intended to develop a cedar forest through reforestation techniques on the glady land, place the forest development under government control, and provide employment for citizens in the economically depressed area. In September 1935 President Franklin Roosevelt approved the Lebanon Cedar Forest Project.

Two months later, the Resettlement Administration of the U.S. Department of Agriculture began development in what is now Cedars of Lebanon State Park, which was among the first state parks in Tennessee. The Works Project Administration hired workers, from among the farmers whose land made up the project, to build roads, install power lines, complete boundary surveys, and construct buildings, cabins, and shelters from the red cedar wood and abundant limestone rock. The best example of the WPA's work is the Cedar Forest Lodge, which initially served as the park office, recreation hall, and superintendent's residence. It is listed in the National Register of Historic Places. A lookout tower and nursery were also built on the site. Over 750,000 seedlings were grown and replanted to restore the once large cedar forest.

On September 10, 1937, Lebanon Cedar Forest formally opened. Dixon Merritt, editor of the *Lebanon Democrat,* who had been instrumental in gaining approval for the project, presided over the dedication and laying of the cornerstone. The Tennessee

Department of Conservation took over the management of the area in March 1939, with the U.S. Forestry Service as custodial agency. The project area was renamed Cedars of Lebanon after the dense cedar woodland that existed in the Biblical lands of Lebanon. The Cedars of Lebanon State Park and Forest operated as a reclaimed forestry area and a recreation facility, complete with swimming pool, lodge, cabins, picnic tables, shelters, and athletic fields for public enjoyment.

During the years of World War II, the park area operated mainly for the purpose of providing recreational activities to the soldiers of the Second Army, who were on maneuvers in Middle Tennessee. From 1942 through 1944, military personnel accounted for 90 percent of park attendance.

The federal government formally deeded Cedars of Lebanon State Park to the state on August 12, 1955. Since then, the Division of State Parks and the Division of Forestry have shared its management. Cedars of Lebanon has continued to expand its recreational facilities and now contains 117 modern campsites, a group lodge that will sleep 80 people, an Olympic-size swimming pool, 11 picnic shelters, nature center, recreation hall, nine modern cabins, and eight miles of hiking trails. Rangers provide security and information for visitors. A park naturalist is available to interpret the natural, cultural, and historic aspects of the park. As the twenty-first century approaches, Cedars of Lebanon continues to provide a place for visitors to enjoy the outdoors and reflect back on the dedication and work of those who built one of Tennessee's early state parks.

Sandy Suddarth, Cedars of Lebanon State Park

SEE: CONSERVATION; SECOND ARMY MANEUVERS; WILSON COUNTY; WORKS PROGRESS ADMINISTRATION

CEMETERIES, NATIONAL. The Department of Veterans Affairs maintains 114 National Cemeteries in 38 states and Puerto Rico (as well as 33 "soldiers' lots" and monument sites). Five cemeteries are in Tennessee: Chattanooga National Cemetery, Mountain Home National Cemetery, Knoxville National Cemetery, Nashville National Cemetery, and Memphis National Cemetery. The Department of Interior also maintains several cemeteries at various historic sites in Tennessee, including Fort Donelson National Battlefield, Shiloh National Military Park, Stones River National Battlefield, and the Andrew Johnson National Historic Site.

The idea for creating national cemeteries emerged in the midst of the Civil War. President Abraham Lincoln signed legislation authorizing the creation of national cemeteries on July 17, 1862, "for the soldiers who shall die in service of the country." After the war, recovery teams disinterred roughly 250,000 remains from makeshift burial sites. By 1870 these had been concentrated in 73 national cemeteries.

Eligibility for burial in national cemeteries has gradually expanded to include all veterans of the United States armed forces, except those dishonorably discharged. American war veterans of allied armed forces—like the American pilots who flew with the Royal Air Force prior to American entry into World War II and the "Flying Tigers," who flew under Chinese command—and veterans' spouses and dependent children, members of the reserve forces who died in training or on active duty, or amassed 20 years of service, are also eligible for burial in national cemeteries. The federal government provides headstones and markers.

More than 70,000 burials take place each year in Department of Veterans Affairs cemeteries. This number has been increasing steadily and will likely continue into the twenty-first century due to the large number of World War II veterans. Two Tennessee cemeteries, Chattanooga and Mountain Home, remain "open" for burials. The other three Veterans Affairs cemeteries and the Department of Interior cemeteries are no longer accepting new internments. They do make allowances, however, for spouses and children, and accept cremated remains.

All National Cemeteries, of course, have interesting local histories in addition to their famous and not so-famous internees. Fort Donelson is arguably the most diverse cemetery, as home to veterans of seven different wars. Shiloh's moss-covered walls serenely surround thousands of unidentified graves. Chattanooga National Cemetery, founded on November 26, 1863, the day after the battle of Missionary Ridge, is a good example of the history associated with these places. Union General George Thomas personally supervised many aspects of the internment. When asked if he wanted the men buried according to their states, as had been the custom, Thomas replied, "No, no; mix 'em up, mix 'em up; I'm tired of states' rights!"[1]

Chattanooga's most famous internees are likely James Andrews and seven of his men, who stole a locomotive near Kennesaw, Georgia. Confederate forces pursued and captured them near Ringgold, in what came to be known in Civil War legend as "The Great Locomotive Chase." All eight raiders were later hanged in Atlanta. All the men, except the civilian Andrews, received Congressional Medals of Honor and were among the first to be awarded this honor. Chattanooga is also the final resting place of Medal of Honor winners from World War II and the Korean War.

Jeff Roberts, Tennessee Technological University

CITATION:

(1) Shelby Foote, *The Civil War: A Narrative* (New York, 1963), II, 866.

CENTER FOR APPALACHIAN STUDIES AND SERVICES at East Tennessee State University in Johnson

City is a Tennessee Center of Excellence established in 1984 during the administration of Governor Lamar Alexander. The Center supports research and artistic endeavors focusing on the Appalachian region, improves resources for research and education about the region, and provides programs of community service. Among the Center's outstanding components are the Reece Museum, which offers art and history exhibits representative of Appalachia, educational programs, and a permanent collection of over 10,000 artworks and artifacts, and the Archives of Appalachia, the nation's premier Appalachian archive, with ten million manuscripts, 250,000 photographs, and over 5,000 sound and moving image recordings from the region. In addition, the Center administers the Appalachian-Scottish & Irish Studies Program that involves international exchange with the University of Edinburgh and the Ulster Folk and Transport Museum; *Now & Then*, the Appalachian magazine; and the only program in bluegrass music at a four-year institution in the nation, a program that produces Grammy Award-winning alumni. The Center is noted for its leadership in regional concerns and for its contribution to promoting understanding of the Appalachian region. Center staff have expertise in such diverse areas as dance heritage, regional health care, heritage tourism, sustainable economic development, Native American studies, and regional planning. The Center's *Encyclopedia of Appalachia* project, as well as work on regional bibliographies and atlases, make it a national and international resource on one of the nation's most complex and interesting regions.

Jean Haskell Speer, East Tennessee State University

SEE: EAST TENNESSEE STATE UNIVERSITY; EDUCATION, HIGHER; MUSIC

CENTER FOR HISTORIC PRESERVATION. In 1984 the Tennessee General Assembly and Governor Lamar Alexander, as part of a comprehensive statewide education reform program, proposed a special project to recognize Tennessee's national leadership in higher education through a competition to create specialized research centers involving the flagship academic programs in Tennessee's public universities and colleges. One of the first created was the Center for Historic Preservation at Middle Tennessee State University in 1984. The Center designation acknowledged the international reputation of the MTSU Historic Preservation program (founded 1973) and its affiliated Mid-South Humanities Project (1978–83, a National Endowment for the Humanities-funded project emphasizing the use of heritage resources in K-12 school rooms).

The Center is a leading catalyst for promoting tourism and other economic development through a planned use of local heritage resources. Since its founding, the Center has developed a regional strategic plan for the broader Mid-South region. In addition, honoring devotion to families and land, the Center published (with the Tennessee Department of Agriculture) a book on the almost 800 Tennessee families who have lived on and worked the family farm for at least a century. A continuing Century Farms program looks toward a second publication.

The success of the earlier 10-state Mid-South Humanities Project has been continued with continuing research on Heritage Education. In 1996 the Center undertook a national survey for the National Park Service on the status of heritage education in the United States. The report was published in fall 1997 and has led to the development of a pilot national database on heritage education materials and practices accessible through the Center's web site (http://www.mtsu.edu/~histpres/).

In the technical area, the Center has undertaken work on a national scale with research focused on historic paint analysis and a standard nomenclature and policies for architectural artifact collection.

In 1997 the Center prepared to embark on its largest project to date. In 1996 the Congress approved a program of five new national heritage areas including one proposed by the Center on the Civil War in Tennessee. The planned 15 year project, The Tennessee Civil War National Heritage Area, will work to improve the visitor experience in Tennessee through new programs to evaluate and explain the total Civil War experience in Tennessee.

James K. Huhta, Middle Tennessee State University

SEE: FARMS, TENNESSEE CENTURY; MIDDLE TENNESSEE STATE UNIVERSITY; RURAL AFRICAN-AMERICAN CHURCH PROJECT; TENNESSEE CIVIL WAR NATIONAL HERITAGE AREA

CENTER FOR POPULAR MUSIC. The Center for Popular Music was established at Middle Tennessee State University in 1985. Its mission is to foster research and scholarship in American popular music, and to promote an awareness of and appreciation for America's diverse musical culture.

The Center maintains one of the country's largest and best music research collections. It includes extensive holdings of books, sound recordings, sheet music, scores, song broadsides, periodicals, songsters, photographs, posters, playbills, trade catalogs, news clippings, and various other materials that support the study of popular music in its musical, social, cultural, historical, technological, and commercial contexts. Rather than focusing on any single genre of popular music, the Center advocates and supports an integrated approach to the study of popular musics. The collection is particularly strong in its holdings of materials that support the study of rock and its roots; the music of the southeast; and various forms of vernacular religious music.

In addition to this broad genre coverage, the Center's collection reflects considerable historical depth. It takes as a chronological starting point the introduction of European and African cultures to North America, and continues into the present. The holdings are strong in nineteenth century sheet music, broadsides, songsters, and song books, and include a sizable body of materials from the eighteenth century as well. Visiting scholars have termed the Center a "world-class archive" and "the South's premiere Music collection."

In addition to building and maintaining its research collections, the Center has produced many public programs, seminars, conferences, publications, and media productions that serve to disseminate information to the public at large. The Center also operates a fully-equipped Audio Restoration Lab that serves a variety of academic, government, and commercial clients.

Paul F. Wells, Middle Tennessee State University

SEE: MIDDLE TENNESSEE STATE UNIVERSITY; MUSIC

CENTER FOR SOUTHERN FOLKLORE, located in

Memphis, is a non-profit corporation dedicated to documenting and presenting the people and traditions of the South. Through films, video tapes, records, books, exhibits, and festivals, the Center presents the life of indigenous and ethnic cultures in the region, and preserves folk culture through its sound, photographic, and slide archives.

Founded in 1972 by a young filmmaker, Judy Peiser, and folklorist William Ferris, the Center's first film, *Gravel Springs Fife and Drum,* immediately won film festival prizes. Other films like *Ray Lum, Mule Trader; Mississippi Delta Blues; Fannie Belle Chapman, Gospel Singer; Hush Hoggies Hush: Tom Johnson's Praying Pigs;* and *All Day and All Night: Memories from Beale Street Musicians* attracted national attention. The Center received grants from the National Endowment for the Arts, the National Endowment for the Humanities, and the Rockefeller Foundation to develop a series of films, records, and books on southern culture.

The work of the Center appeals to a variety of audiences. Tourists to Beale Street read the outdoor informative signs that tell the history of the street. The Center reaches schools, museums, and libraries with multimedia presentations like *If Beale Street Could Talk; Got Something to Tell You: Sounds of the Delta Blues;* and *Colors, Shapes, and Memories: Three Folk Artists* and books like *The Heritage of Black Music in Memphis: A Teaching Resource.* Popular audiences enjoy records, like *Memphis Rocks: Rockabilly in Memphis* and *James 'Son' Thomas: Highway 61 Blues,* and exhibits like "Taylor Made Pictures," photographs chronicling life in the Memphis black community from the 1920s to the 1950s, and "Memphis Soul:

Music of the 60s and 70s," photographs and artifacts from the Stax and Hi recording era.

A series of small festivals and collaboration with the Smithsonian Institution led to the annual Mid-South Music and Heritage Festival, beginning in 1988. Occurring in mid-July, the festival features the food, music, dance, and folk art of the Mid-South, including that of recently arrived residents like the Hmong, Vietnamese, Indian, and Latino communities.

Today, the Center works with writers, journalists, theater producers, school groups, and tourists to interpret the culture of the South through its resources of archives, exhibits, films, records, books, and live performances.

Perre Magness, Memphis

SEE: BEALE STREET; MEMPHIS; MEMPHIS MUSIC SCENE

CHAMBERLAIN, HIRAM SANBORN (1835–1916), a

founder of the modern iron industry in the South, was born in Franklin, Ohio, on August 6, 1835, to Vermont natives Leander and Susanna Chamberlain. The fourth of eight children, Chamberlain attended the Eclectic Institute (later Hiram College), where he was a student and friend to future President James A. Garfield. With the outbreak of war in 1861, Chamberlain enlisted as a private in the Second Ohio Volunteer Cavalry and was stationed in Kansas and Missouri for two years. He was appointed quarter-sergeant during his first month of enlistment and was commissioned second lieutenant and regimental quartermaster. He served as divisional quartermaster under General Ambrose Burnside in Knoxville when the city was taken from the Confederates in September 1863. In May 1864, President Abraham Lincoln promoted him to Captain and assistant quartermaster and he served out the war in that position.

Chamberlain entered the iron industry in 1871, when he and five Welsh ironmasters created the Knoxville Iron Company. The Knoxville Iron Company collected pig iron from small furnaces and mills all over East Tennessee and manufactured railroad spikes, nails, and iron bars. In 1868 Chamberlain also entered into partnership with A.J. Albers in a retail drug store. Eventually the business became completely wholesale and exists today as the Albers Drug Company. These industrial and commercial ventures represented early southern revitalization and the success of northern business investment in building the New South.

In 1871 Chamberlain left his enterprises in Knoxville and moved to Chattanooga to become vice-president and general manager of the Roane Iron Company, a pig iron manufacturing plant that Chamberlain organized with fellow ex-Union officer John T. Wilder in 1867. He ascended to the presidency of Roane Iron in 1880 and served in that capacity until his death in 1916. Through Roane Iron and other endeavors and responsibilities, Chamberlain quickly became a leading citizen of Chattanooga. In 1882 he founded and directed the Citico Furnace Company, and was vice-president of the Chickamauga Trust Company and the Columbian Iron Works, along with his 30-year service as vice-president of the First National Bank of Chattanooga. Chamberlain served many years as the President of the Board of Trustees of the University of Chattanooga and as President of the School Board of Chattanooga.

Chamberlain died on March 15, 1916, at the age of 81. He married Amelia I. Morrow of Knoxville, and they had six children.

Robert Parkinson, University of Tennessee, Knoxville

SEE: CHATTANOOGA; INDUSTRY; ROANE COUNTY; UNIVERSITY OF TENNESSEE AT CHATTANOOGA; WILDER, JOHN T.

CHATTANOOGA. Tennessee's fourth largest city, Chattanooga enjoys a rich and often contentious past. The city lies on a bend in the Tennessee River, near a natural opening in the southern Appalachians. Surrounded by mountains and ridges, the river's banks formed a secure, temperate, and fertile plain well suited for human habitation. Archaeological excavations reveal that Native Americans first settled the site more than 8,000 years ago. Various tribes inhabited the land in the following centuries, culminating around AD 1300, when the area became a center of Mississippian era culture. In the mid-1500s Mississippian natives interacted with the region's first white visitors, when the expeditions of Spanish Conquistadores camped nearby. With the advent of the tribal era in the seventeenth century, the area fell under the control of the Cherokees, who dubbed the spot "Chado-na-ugsa," meaning "rock that comes to a point," a reference to nearby Lookout Mountain.

Permanent white settlers came to the site in the early 1830s and established Ross's Landing, a trading post located near the foot of present-day Broad Street on the Tennessee River. The community thrived and in 1839 its occupants incorporated the settlement as the town of Chattanooga. Starting with just 53 families, the village quickly grew into a center for river commerce. The development of the railroad furthered the town's progress. The city's first line, the Western and Atlantic, arrived in 1850 and initiated an immediate economic boom. Other lines followed and by 1860 Chattanooga was a vital link in the region's rail system.

Known as the site "where cotton meets corn," Chattanooga served as the doorway to the Deep South. Whether by river or rail, much of the cargo passing in and out of the region traveled through the city. Warehouses overflowed with goods in transit, and freight sometimes spilled into public streets. Throughout the period, citizens retained strong social and economic ties to the Deep South. Many felt the city shared that region's social, political, cultural, and commercial tendencies. Such feelings became apparent in 1861 during Tennessee's secession crisis. Though most of East Tennessee remained loyal to the Union, Chattanoogans voted overwhelmingly to join the Confederacy.

Given the city's strategic importance, Chattanooga immediately became a center of military activity. The first Confederate troops arrived in late 1861 to protect the community from East Tennessee Unionists. By 1863, the junction was a critical southern administrative center and supply depot. Soon it was also a target of federal forces. As Union armies moved through Tennessee that year, they increasingly turned their attention toward the city. Even

Market Street, Chattanooga, 1909.

CHATTANOOGA-HAMILTON COUNTY BICENTENNIAL LIBRARY, HIENER COLLECTION

Abraham Lincoln recognized the town's importance and predicted that "If we can hold Chattanooga and East Tennessee, I think the Rebellion must dwindle and die."[1]

In the fall of 1863, Union forces launched a major attack on the city, resulting in some of the bloodiest fighting of the war. Residents, terrified by the conflict and the prospect of Yankee rule, fled the city *en masse*. Most would never return. The battles at Chickamauga and Chattanooga inflicted over 47,000 casualties on both armies and resulted in a costly Union victory. Northern forces secured Chattanooga that November and thus began a lengthy and lucrative occupation.

The Union army transformed the sleepy river town into a sprawling fortified military complex. Within weeks, Chattanooga became one of the North's most important supply and transportation centers. The town also served as staging point for Sherman's March in Georgia and South Carolina, and northern troops worked around the clock erecting dozens of warehouses, stockyards, and hospitals to support his vast army. Chattanooga also became an important link in the Union's rail system, and military engineers constructed shops and manufacturing facilities to help rebuild the South's shattered transportation network.

While in Chattanooga, Union officers made note of the community's location and of the region's abundant resources. Of particular interest was the town's proximity to rich iron deposits in East Tennessee and North Alabama. Following the war, a determined handful of these officers set about to exploit these resources and transform Chattanooga into the "Chicago of the South." Men such as Henry Clay Evans, Hiram S. Chamberlain, and John T. Wilder built successful manufacturing and commercial enterprises, and their success attracted other northern entrepreneurs.

Chattanooga's northern elite not only dominated the local economy, they also maintained local political hegemony. Northern Republicans controlled the city's government for over two decades following the Civil War. Over time, however, they found themselves outnumbered by local southern voters and increasingly northern leaders had to rely on black voters to maintain their control. As a result, black Chattanoogans possessed an extraordinary amount of political power and they used it to gain schools, patronage, and a voice in municipal government. Black residents regularly won seats on the town's powerful Board of Aldermen, held important positions in city government, and even served on the local police force.

During the 1880s, Chattanooga was an industrial boom town and it quickly became the center of both national and international attention. Local boosters, led by *Chattanooga Times* publisher Adolph S. Ochs, successfully lured investors from both sides of the Atlantic, and real-estate speculators drove the price of local property to astronomical levels. The carnival-like atmosphere was short lived, however, for property values soon crashed, and the local iron and steel industry, beset by competition from nearby Birmingham, collapsed.

The Panic of 1893 only increased the city's economic woes, and throughout the 1890s Chattanooga experienced hard times. Hardest hit were the city's black residents who, in addition to widespread poverty, also suffered the loss of their political franchise. New Jim Crow laws, combined with a decline in local Republican fortunes, robbed local blacks of their votes and denied them their hard-earned voice in local government.

Recovery came to Chattanooga in 1898, when thousands of soldiers came to the city on their way to the Spanish-American War. Following the war, civic leaders ensured continued growth by developing a balanced economy based on banking, insurance, manufacturing, and tourism. Perhaps the greatest boon to the city came in 1899, when three local men, Ben F. Thomas, Joseph B. Whitehead, and John T. Lupton, secured the exclusive bottling rights to Coca-Cola. Chattanooga Coca-Cola Bottling grew to become one of the city's most successful businesses, pouring millions into the local economy, and its founders have consistently been among the city's most ardent philanthropists.

As with most of the nation, Chattanoogans endured poverty and hardship during the Great Depression. Their plight was eased, however, in 1933 with the arrival of the Tennessee Valley Authority. Chattanooga became a center for TVA's development efforts and local construction projects, such as Chickamauga Dam, employed hundreds of local residents. World War II brought an end to the Depression in Chattanooga, and the city's factories soon reached new levels of productivity. The local manufacturing boom continued after the war, with Chattanoogans producing everything from Chris-Craft boats to Buster Brown socks. The city's industrial growth brought residents a new level of prosperity, but also inflicted considerable environmental damage. By the late 1960s, Chattanooga was among the nation's most polluted communities. Civic leaders responded with strict pollution control laws and the city became a successful example of environmental regulation. By far, the greatest challenge facing Chattanooga in the post-war period has been that of desegregation. During the 1950s local blacks joined the national movement for social and political equality, staging "sit-ins" and other means of non-violent protest. In March 1962 federal courts ordered the desegregation of the city's public schools. The following years, Mayor Ralph Kelly opened all city owned facilities to blacks. Local businesses, under pressure from Kelly and other civic leaders, soon followed suit. Although local blacks universally hailed such moves, they were strongly resisted. As a result, racial tensions remained high throughout the 1960s and 1970s, and the city experienced a number of violent racial incidents.

Modern Chattanooga seems to have overcome many of its past problems. Although racial divisions still exist, the community now boasts an expanding black middle class and a growing appreciation for its African-American heritage. The city's government, once the archetype of machine politics, is now cited as a model of public administration and planning. Much of the credit for this transformation is due to the efforts of the Lyndhurst Foundation. This nonprofit body, established by members of the Lupton family, is now a guiding force in the city's development and deserves much of the credit for the community's recent renaissance. Today, as visitors tour the new Tennessee Aquarium, they stand within sight of Ross's Landing, and bear witness to the city's burgeoning promise.

Timothy P. Ezzell, Knoxville

CITATION:

(1) James L. McDonough, *Chattanooga: A Death Grip on the Confederacy* (Knoxville, 1984), 44.

SUGGESTED READINGS: Timothy P. Ezzell, "Yankees in Dixie: The Story of Chattanooga, 1870–1890," (Ph.D. dissertation, University of Tennessee, Knoxville, 1996); Gilbert E. Govan and James W. Livingood, *The Chattanooga Country, 1540–1976: From Tomahawks to TVA* (1977)

SEE: CHAMBERLAIN, HIRAM S.; CHATTANOOGA TIMES; CHICKAMAUGA AND CHATTANOOGA, BATTLES OF; CIVIL RIGHTS MOVEMENT; CIVIL WAR; EVANS, HENRY C.; HAMILTON COUNTY; LUPTON, JOHN T.; LYNDHURST FOUNDATION; OCHS, ADOLPH S.; ROSS, JOHN; TENNESSEE AQUARIUM; TENNESSEE VALLEY AUTHORITY; THOMAS, BENJAMIN F.; WHITEHEAD, JOSEPH B.; WILDER, JOHN T.

CHATTANOOGA BAKERY COMPANY, founded in 1903, is best known for the production of a single product—Moon Pies. The company began operations as an attempt at vertical integration by Chattanooga's Mountain City Flour Mill, in order to take advantage of its excess flour production. During its early years, the bakery produced a variety of cookies, crackers, fig bars, and other baked goods. About 1919, one of the company's traveling salesmen returned with client requests for a baked good that was more than a cookie, something both filling and cheap. Experimentation led to the creation of a concoction of marshmallow creme smeared on a cookie and covered with chocolate. Thus was born the Moon Pie, a large snack, which cost only a nickel. The product quickly caught on, becoming a staple snack across the South.

Today, Moon Pies are available throughout most of the United States. After the mid-1950s, the company focused solely on the Moon Pie line. By the early 1990s, the bakery produced some 300,000 Moon Pies per day. Over the years, various flavors joined the basic chocolate, widening the snack's appeal. The Mountain City Milling Company was eventually acquired by Dixie Portland Mills, and later by ADM Milling Company, but Chattanooga Bakery remains an independent, family-owned enterprise.

Ned L. Irwin, East Tennessee State University

THE CHATTANOOGA BLADE, the city's leading African-American newspaper in the late 1800s, was recognized for its rare quality as an African-American publication, edited and produced by African Americans. *The Blade* was published weekly by Randolph Miller, one of the few ex-slaves who published and edited a newspaper in the United States during that period. Miller came to Chattanooga in October 1864 and worked for several local newspapers before launching his own publishing venture.

Randolph adopted a bold and exciting writing style and addressed hard issues without pulling his punches. In 1905, for example, *The Blade* sparked protest against the application of Jim Crow laws to city street cars. On July 5, 1905, Miller and his associates launched a street car boycott and on July 16, organized hack lines with "three vehicles of sorry appearance" to help transport African Americans in dignity. Within a few weeks, black businessmen applied to start their own bus company. White officials and businessmen moved quickly to quash the effort. In an October 1905 issue of *The Blade*, Miller complained, "They have taken our school to the frog pond; they have passed the Jim Crow Law; they have knocked us out of the jury box; they have played the devil generally; and what in thunder more will they do? No one knows."[1]

Randolph Miller died in 1915, but *The Chattanooga Times* regularly reprinted excerpts from Miller's editorials after his death under the heading "Flashes from the Blade."

Vilma Scruggs Fields, Chattanooga African-American Museum

CITATION:

(1) *The Blade* statement was reprinted in the Chattanooga *Daily Times*, October 12, 1905.

SEE: MILLER, RANDOLPH; PUBLISHING

CHATTANOOGA CHOO-CHOO HOTEL, or the Southern Railway Terminal (1907–1909), is located on Market Street in downtown Chattanooga. Designed by Beaux-Arts-trained architect Donn Barber of New York City, this magnificent architectural gateway to the Deep South opened during the Christmas season of 1909. The new terminal was the centerpiece of a massive urban renewal plan, initiated by city officials, real estate developers, and the Southern Railway, to redesign the downtown built environment. On 23 acres centered around the 1400 block of Market Street, the railway began construction in 1907. The company demolished the historic Stanton House, a circa 1870 luxury hotel, and numerous dwellings and warehouses to make way for the new terminal and its associated warehouses and railroad yards. Once completed, the Southern Railway Terminal, with its imposing classical styling, symbolized the key role that railroads played in the economic development of Chattanooga.

The terminal served passenger travelers until the Louisville and Nashville's passenger train Georgian completed its final run on May 1, 1971. Two years later, in one of the earliest examples of historic preservation rehabilitation in Chattanooga, the terminal was re-opened as the Chattanooga Choo-Choo, a complex of hotel rooms, shops, and restaurants designed to attract the patronage of the millions of automobile passengers who passed through Chattanooga via the city's interstate highways. The hotel's name derived from the song, *The Chattanooga Choo-Choo,* made popular by Glenn Miller during the Big Band era of the mid-twentieth century.

Carroll Van West, Middle Tennessee State University
SUGGESTED READING: Carroll Van West, *Tennessee's Historic Landscapes: A Traveler's Guide* (1995)
SEE: CHATTANOOGA; RAILROADS

CHATTANOOGA FREE PRESS owes much of its success to its founder and long-time publisher, Roy McDonald. Originally a grocer, McDonald began the *Free Press* in 1933 as a small flyer to promote his chain of Home Stores. It proved popular and quickly became an inexpensive alternative to the dominant *Chattanooga Times.* In April 1936 McDonald added news features and comics to the Sunday weekly and began charging five cents. The following August he began daily publication of the *Free Press* and began direct competition with the morning *Times* and the afternoon *Chattanooga News.*

In 1939 McDonald purchased the *News* and launched a new afternoon daily, the *Chattanooga News-Free Press.* Marketing the paper towards local blue collar workers whose shifts ended at four P.M., McDonald filled his publication with folksy, hometown news and upbeat business features. Circulation steadily increased and the *News-Free Press* soon emerged as a serious challenger to the established and respected *Times.*

The two papers soon found themselves engaged in relentless competition. Beset by their fierce rivalry and wartime shortages, the two publications called a truce in 1942 and formed a joint publication agreement. The two papers shared advertising, circulation

and production departments, but maintained separate news and editorial staffs.

During the 1950s the circulation of the *News Free-Press* continued to grow. The paper's appeal was helped in large part by an increasingly conservative editorial policy and by its outspoken opposition to the desegregation movement. The *Times,* in contrast, emerged as a steadfast supporter of civil rights. Conservative southern readers abandoned the *Times* in droves, and by the 1960s the *News Free-Press* was becoming the city's dominant publication.

In 1966 McDonald nullified the joint publishing agreement and resumed head-to-head competition with the *Times.* The conservative and upbeat tone of the *News Free-Press* found a welcome audience among Chattanooga's anxious middle class. Circulation was also helped by McDonald's increasing use of photographs of all sorts of events.

In 1980, after more than a decade of intense competition, the *Times* and *News Free-Press* entered into another joint publishing agreement. This arrangement was similar to the earlier 1942 agreement with one notable exception: in the new accord the *Times* was pointedly referred to as a "failing newspaper."

Roy McDonald died in 1990, but his journalistic legacy continues. Although his newspaper, renamed the *Chattanooga Free Press,* is often dismissed and derided by critics, it continues to be a powerful and popular institution among city residents and one of the most formidable conservative voices in the state.

Timothy P. Ezzell, Knoxville
SEE: CHATTANOOGA; PUBLISHING

CHATTANOOGA GLASS COMPANY was founded in 1901 by Charles Rief to provide glass bottles for his brewery. Soon the company also began producing bottles for the infant Coca-Cola bottling industry, established in the city in 1899. With the advent of prohibition, the company abandoned the production of beer and whiskey bottles, and concentrated almost exclusively on producing bottles for the soft drink industry, becoming one of the chief producers of the famous "Coke" bottle. In the early days, the "Hutcheson" stopper system was used to seal Coke bottles. The rubber stopper on the inside of the glass bottle made a loud "popping" noise when pressed to open, giving the soft drink the nickname "pop." The metal crown seal was adopted later. In 1916 the introduction and adoption of the famous "hobble-skirt" Coke bottle gave uniformity to drink bottles.

Coke bottler J. Frank Harrison a relative of pioneer Chattanooga bottler John Thomas Lupton, bought the business in 1925, and expanded it to provide bottles for various cola producers. In 1960, Dorsey Corporation acquired the company. Since 1985 the company has been a part of Diamond

Container General, Inc., with corporate offices in Philadelphia, Pennsylvania.

Ned L. Irwin, East Tennessee State University
SEE: LUPTON, JOHN T.

CHATTANOOGA MEDICINE COMPANY was

founded in 1879 by Chattanooga businessman Zeboim Cartter Patten and a group of friends. The company's first two products, Black-Draught and Wine of Cardui, were so successful that they were sold well into the twentieth century. Patten procured the formula rights to Black-Draught, a senna-based laxative, from the grandson of its originator, Dr. A.Q. Simmons. The name, Black-Draught, probably derived from the dark drink given to sailors in the British navy. Wine of Cardui was a uterine sedative, whose name derived from *Carduus benedictus,* a synonym for botanical *Cnicus benedictus.* According to tradition, Wine of Cardui originated among the Cherokee Indians.

Fred F. Wiehl was the company's first president, but Patten, in the role of secretary, guided the business to success. By the 1880s Patten had acquired almost total ownership of the company. Wiehl was succeeded as company president, first by the newspaper publisher Adolph S. Ochs, followed by developer Col. A. M. Johnson, before Patten took the title of president in 1891.

Successful at finding new products to sell, Patten used imaginative promotional techniques to market his products, becoming one of the early practitioners of mass-market advertising. He made the widely-distributed Cardui Calendar and the *Ladies Birthday Almanac* popular throughout the South. The company became one of the region's largest drug manufacturers. In 1906 Patten and his son-on-law, John Thomas Lupton, sold their controlling interests in the business to Patten's nephew and assistant, John A. Patten, who created a legendary force of salesmen and expanded sales into foreign countries.

For most of its history, the company specialized in producing medicinal products to relieve pain and discomfort. In 1935 Dr. Irvine W. Grote of the University of Chattanooga developed the analgesic balm known as "Soltice" for the company. In 1939 the company expanded its products, modernized its production and research facilities, and developed a chemicals division. During World War II, the company became the largest producer of K-rations and a major supplier of ammonia. Postwar products include Pamprin, Flexall, Icy Hot, pHisoderm, and Norwich aspirin. Today the company operates under the name of Chattam, Inc. In 1995 the specialty chemicals division was sold.

Ned L. Irwin, East Tennessee State University
SUGGESTED READING: Alexander Guerry, *Men and Vision: . . . a brief history of the Chattanooga Medicine Company* (1963)
SEE: LUPTON, JOHN T.; OCHS, ADOLPH S.; PATTEN, ZEBOIM C.

THE CHATTANOOGA TIMES. On the 14th floor of *The New York Times* Building on West 43rd Street in Manhattan, the home of the nation's most influential daily newspaper, in a lavishly paneled executive board room, stands a bust of Adolph S. Ochs, the founder of the modern *Times* and patriarch of the family that rules it still. It is a gift from the people of Chattanooga, a postbellum city that seems a world away from the busy center of New York. But there is a deep, and important, family connection between the two: the bust was sent North to thank Ochs for constructing a lovely gold-domed building for *The Chattanooga Times* in that city on the banks of the Tennessee River. In 1878 Ochs had bought the struggling Chattanooga paper, 18 years before he moved to Manhattan and bought another financially strapped publication, *The New York Times.* From a financial point of view, the second investment worked out much better, but the Ochs-Sulzberger family has always kept a spot in its heart—and its publishing empire—for the small southern paper, which in fact played a significant role in the nation's most compelling twentieth century domestic drama: the civil rights movement and the emergence, by fits and starts, of the New South.

Ochs was not the first owner of the paper. *The Times* had been founded in 1869 by three Chattanoogans—T.B. Kirby, Frank DeGorgis, and Patten L. Gamble. The three founders bought the used equipment of a failed newspaper, *The Chattanooga Republican,* but their *Times* was not a raging success: it passed through several hands, including those of T.H. Payne and Z.C. Patten, before ebbing to 200 subscribers in 1878, the year Ochs came along. Though not yet 21, he was an energetic businessman and had already put together a city directory—an enterprise that enabled him to make contacts with Chattanooga's principal businessmen. With $200 (his father co-signed the note) young Ochs bought the publisher's title and a half-interest in the paper.

More than just a savvy investor (he quickly became sole owner and improved the paper's fortunes), Ochs was a key player in the journalistic revolution of the period. Until roughly the 1870s, American newspapers were essentially partisan, house organs for political parties or the whims of the publication's owner. There was no difference between the news and editorial columns: the entire paper was given over to provocative, necessarily unbalanced reporting. Ochs helped change that, deciding to keep the news columns evenhanded and confining overt political opinion to separate editorial pages. His motto was: "To give the news impartially, without fear or favor." In Chattanooga he crusaded for city improvements: closed sewers (after yellow fever outbreaks); better fire protection (after a big downtown blaze); and bond issues for streets and bridges.

By 1896, however, Ochs found himself in financial trouble not because of the *Times* but because of his sundry real-estate investments. To bail himself out, he determined to make money doing what he knew best: turning around a newspaper. He bought—at a sheriff's auction—the then-failing *New York Times* and moved to Manhattan to rebuild that paper. Though he never returned to the South permanently, he always considered himself a Chattanoogan, retaining the title of publisher of that city's newspaper until his death, during a visit to Chattanooga, in 1935.

Four other members of his family then held that title, but one—Ruth Sulzberger Holmberg—was the most significant, serving as publisher from 1964 to 1992, then as chairman of *The Chattanooga Times*. In 1992 Paul Neely became the first non-Ochs publisher of the *Times* since 1878. The paper is not part of *The New York Times Company*, a public company, but has only four shareholders, all Ochs descendants: Ruth Holmberg, her brother Arthur O. Sulzberger, Jr., the chairman of *The New York Times Company*, and their two sisters, Marian S. Heiskell and Judith P. Sulzberger.

Perhaps the Chattanooga paper's finest hours came in the 1950s and 1960s, when it was the informal center of national coverage of the civil rights movement that slowly took shape after the Supreme Court's 1954 school desegregation decision. The key figure in these years was John N. Popham, a Virginian, who was sent South by *New York Times* managing editor Turner Catledge in 1947 to be the first full-time national correspondent covering the region. Catledge, a Mississippian, sensed that important changes were in the air, and Popham became New York's man on the scene, traveling 60,000 miles a year from the Potomac to Eagle's Pass. He was jailed in Jackson, Mississippi, and shot at in Clinton, Tennessee, and he became a mentor to the stream of national reporters who journeyed south to cover milestones like the crisis at Little Rock's Central High School. Popham would interpret the local customs and ease the outsiders' way around the hot spots, keeping order on both sides in those tempestuous times. In 1958 Popham left *The New York Times* to become managing editor of its Chattanooga cousin, serving until 1978. But even though he was off the road, reporters in search of insights about the changing South found their way to Chattanooga, and to Popham.

In the ensuing years the *Times* frequently championed causes that provoked controversy in a city that, though heavily industrial and part of a border state, remains basically conservative. For example, it backed the civil rights acts of the mid-1960s, the original Clean Air Act, and supported a successful lawsuit by black plaintiffs who sued in the late 1980s to replace Chattanooga's at-large governing board to one divided into districts—a shift that gave African Americans a larger voice in municipal affairs.

The *Times* continues to enjoy a reputation as a tough, challenging, well-edited newspaper, with superior writing and reporting.

Jon Meacham, New York, New York

SEE: OCHS, ADOLPH S.; PATTEN, ZEBOIM C.; PUBLISHING

CHEATHAM, BENJAMIN FRANKLIN (1820–1886), Confederate general, was born on a plantation near Nashville on October 20, 1820. His maternal ancestors included James Robertson, the founder of Nashville. Cheatham served in the Mexican War as a captain in the First Tennessee Regiment and later as colonel of the Third Tennessee. He participated in the California gold rush, returning home in 1853. Before the Civil War he farmed, served in the Tennessee militia, and was active in Democratic politics.

When Tennessee seceded, Cheatham won an appointment in the Provisional Army of Tennessee, then was commissioned a brigadier general in July 1861. His actions at Belmont in November 1861 won him a promotion to major general in March 1862. For most of the war, Cheatham led a division composed largely of Tennessee regiments. Buoyed by devotion to their commander and united by state pride, Cheatham's men acquired an enviable combat reputation in virtually every campaign.

Controversy also dogged Cheatham's Confederate career. He clashed repeatedly with General Braxton Bragg, commander of the Army of Tennessee (June 1862-December 1863). Bragg regarded Cheatham as an incompetent political appointee, resented his close ties to Leonidas Polk, and sought unsuccessfully to have Cheatham removed from command. The relationship degenerated after Bragg accused Cheatham of drunkenness at Murfreesboro. After Chickamauga, Bragg stripped most of Cheatham's Tennessee regiments from his command and dispersed them, consigning Cheatham to a much smaller division. Richmond authorities denied Cheatham's request to be relieved from duty, and he returned as a prominent member of the anti-Bragg faction.

One of Joseph E. Johnston's first acts upon replacing Bragg as army commander was the restoration of Cheatham's Tennessee division. The reconstituted command distinguished itself during the Atlanta campaign, particularly at Kennesaw Mountain in June 1864, where they repelled a determined Union assault. After John Bell Hood replaced Johnston, Cheatham led Hood's old corps at Peachtree Creek and the Battle of Atlanta. Following William J. Hardee's departure in September 1864, Cheatham assumed command of Hardee's corps and guided it throughout Hood's invasion of Tennessee.

Debate still swirls about Cheatham's actions near Spring Hill on November 29, 1864. His corps was in the advance that day, but he failed to attack the Federals at Spring Hill or block the turnpike between

Columbia and Franklin. As a result, after nightfall much of the Union army marched unimpeded northward along the pike while Confederate units encamped nearby. The Union escape enraged Hood, who began a rancorous debate with Cheatham the next morning that extended into the postwar era. At Franklin the next day, Cheatham's corps bore the brunt of the fighting and suffered appalling casualties. Cheatham fought at Nashville two weeks later and retreated with the remnants of the army afterwards; he surrendered with Johnston in North Carolina.

After the war, Cheatham farmed in Coffee County, lost an 1872 congressional race, and served as superintendent of the state prison system. He was postmaster of Nashville at the time of his death on September 4, 1886.

Christopher Losson, St. Joseph, Missouri

SUGGESTED READING: Christopher Losson, *Tennessee's Forgotten Warriors: Frank Cheatham and his Confederate Division* (1990)

SEE: ARMY OF TENNESSEE; BRAGG, BRAXTON; FRANKLIN, BATTLE OF; JOHNSTON, JOSEPH E.; MEXICAN WAR; TENNESSEANS IN CALIFORNIA GOLD RUSH

CHEATHAM COUNTY was created by the Tennessee General Assembly on February 28, 1856, from parts of Davidson, Robertson, Montgomery, and Dickson counties. The county name honors Edward Saunders Cheatham, Speaker of the State Senate. At the first county court meeting at Sycamore in May 1856, the commissioners purchased 50 acres of land on the north side of the Cumberland River from James Lenox for the establishment of Ashland City. Proceeds from the sale of town lots financed the construction of a courthouse and jail. The courthouse, completed in 1858, was replaced by a larger, brick structure in 1869. The log jail has been replaced three times: first with a brick jail in 1886, a second jail following a fire in 1935, and a new jail in 1986.

Several archaeological sites, including ones included in the National Register of Historic Places, document activities by Native Americans who once lived in the county. Early white settlers in the county established settlements at Sycamore, Pleasant View, and Ashland City. To provide for the safety of the first settlers, a blockhouse was erected at the fork of Half Pone and Raccoon creeks.

In an effort to make education more widely available, the Tennessee General Assembly incorporated the Millwood Female Academy in 1852. Despite its name, males as well as females attended the school, which remained in operation until shortly after the Civil War. Millwood Institute, located at Sycamore Mills, became the largest private school in Cheatham County. Established in 1859, the school had closed by the end of the nineteenth century. Ashland Institute, established in 1880, Link School at Thomasville,

founded in 1902 by S. A. Link, and Pleasant View School, opened in 1884 by W.I. Harper, also provided early educational opportunities.

The first significant manufacturer in the area was Montgomery Bell. In 1818 he blasted a tunnel throught the "Narrows of the Harpeth River" to create a 16-foot fall of water. He erected two water wheels at this site to operate hammers for forging pig iron into pots, pans, kettles, and other iron products.

In 1835 Samuel N. Watson established Sycamore Mills, located on Sycamore Creek four miles north of Ashland City. In 1842 he sold half interest in the operation and 5,000 acres of land to Richard Cheatham, at which time the name was changed to Cheatham, Watson and Company. The operation included a cotton gin, grist mill, and a powder mill, but the manufacture of gunpowder was the most important product. As one of only two large powder mills in the South, Sycamore Mills became a target for both Federal and Confederate armies in the opening days of the Civil War. In 1862 it quickly came under Union control and suspended operations until the close of the war. In 1869 the Cheatham heirs sold their interest in the mills to the Sycamore Manufacturing Company, Inc. The company purchased the machinery of the destroyed Confederate Powder Works in Augusta, Georgia, and moved it to the mills in Cheatham County. In 1893, E.I. DuPont de Nemours Company purchased the mills. At the time of the closing of the mills in 1904, the daily production reached 400 kegs of powder.

Today, Cheatham County retains its reputation as a manufacturing center. With 2,700 employees, State Industries of Ashland City is the world's largest producer of water heaters.

Early agriculture and industry depended on the Cumberland River and its tributaries. In 1897, the DuPont company at Sycamore Mills purchased a steamboat, which was renamed *The Sycamore*, to haul gunpowder from Ashland City to Nashville. In 1848 the state chartered Hyde's Ferry Turnpike to extend from Nashville across the Cumberland River. The road remained in operation until 1916, when Cheatham County, following the lead of Davidson County, bought its portion of the road and freed it of tolls. By 1920 Cheatham County boasted 28 miles of railway, owned by the Nashville, Chattanooga, and St. Louis Railway and the Tennessee Central Railway. Today, Interstates 24 and 40 and U.S. Highways 70 and 41A traverse the county. At Ashland City, a new bridge over the Cumberland River has been recently finished to replace one built in 1931.

Cheatham County first acquired a local newspaper service in 1877 when H.B. Stewart established the *Cheatham County Plaindealer*. In 1896 William Thomas Clark bought *The Reporter* (established in 1883) and renamed it the *Ashland City Times*. This paper, which continues in operation, was purchased by the Community Newspapers Incorporated in 1944 and resold to Multimedia of Greenville, South Carolina, in 1973.

In recent years animal wildlife has become a source of revenue for the county. The Tennessee Wildlife Resources Agency operates a game reserve of 21,000 acres on the south side of the Cumberland River, where deer, turkey, and small game are hunted in the appropriate hunting seasons. Non-hunters can view wildlife at the Nashville Zoo, which opened on Ridge Circle Road in Pleasant View in 1991.

The 1990 federal census lists 500 families actively engaged in the farming of 58,000 acres. Tobacco and beef cattle produce the county's largest farm incomes.

More than 29,000 people live in Cheatham County. In addition to the county seat of Ashland City, there are two other incorporated towns, Kingston Springs and Pegram. Two libraries, 59 churches, 12 schools, and a hospital meet the educational, spiritual, and health needs of the county residents. Seven parks and two golf courses provide recreational opportunities. An active historical and genealogical association preserves the county's heritage.

James B. Hallums, Ashland City

SEE: BELL, MONTGOMERY; CUMBERLAND RIVER; MOUND BOTTOM; PATTERSON FORGE

CHEATHAM, WILLIAM A. (1820–1900), antebellum medical reformer, was born in Springfield in 1820, the second son of Robertson County's General Richard Cheatham (1799–1845) and Susan Saunders (1801–1864). He received his medical degree in 1843 from the University of Pennsylvania Medical School. In 1847 he married Mary Emma Ready of Murfreesboro. They had two children, Martha S. and Richard B.

Cheatham was practicing medicine in Nashville when the legislature appointed him superintendent and physician of the newly constructed Tennessee Lunatic Asylum on March 1, 1852. The hospital was constructed in response to the reform movement which swept Tennessee in the 1830s, in particular to the crusade of reformer Dorothea A. Dix, who stated in 1858 that few institutions anywhere were superior to it. The program, which incorporated the most advanced theories of moral treatment, was praised not only by Dix on her frequent visits there, but also by Dr. W.K. Bowling, editor of the *Nashville Journal of Medicine and Surgery.* Sterling Cockrill and other trustees, upon unanimously electing Cheatham to a second eight-year term in 1859, gave him much of the credit for the hospital's reputation as one of the best in the nation.

The Civil War and the Union occupation of Middle Tennessee disrupted the work of the institution and its administrator. On July 25, 1862, Andrew Johnson, Military Governor of Tennessee, informed Cheatham of his dismissal as superintendent. Subse-

quently, he and Mrs. Cheatham were arrested and ordered to be confined to federal prison in Alton, Illinois, but as they journeyed north, the order was rescinded due to Mrs. Cheatham's failing health. She died in Nashville on April 27, 1864.

Cheatham established a private practice in Nashville, which he continued almost to the year of his death, in 1900. In 1867 he remarried, choosing as a wife the wealthy Adelicia Hayes Franklin Acklen, mistress of Belmont.

Kay Baker Gaston, Springfield

SEE: ACKLEN, ADELICIA; TENNESSEE LUNATIC ASYLUM

CHEEKWOOD-NASHVILLE'S HOME OF ART AND GARDENS began as the Leslie Cheek family's opulent Colonial Revival country estate, with the grand three-story limestone manor house and magnificent gardens designed by New York landscape architect Bryant Fleming in the late 1920s. Although the house is varied in its design details and building materials, the combination of these different elements at Cheekwood is never forced; the result is a perfect statement of the stylistic eclecticism characteristic of Colonial Revival interior design. By creating numerous vistas both to and from the mansion, Fleming's landscape design complements the mansion's architecture, reflecting a successful unity between the landscape and domestic architecture.

In 1959 Walter and Huldah Cheek Sharp deeded the estate to the Tennessee Botanical Gardens and Fine Arts Center, which was a non-profit organization chartered in 1957. Center officials converted the mansion into an art museum and landscape gardening showplace. In 1971, with funds raised by the Horticultural Society of Davidson County, the museum added Botanical Hall, a contemporary-styled exhibit center and office. The Anita Stallworth Galleries were added in 1980. Today the museum features a year-round schedule of special exhibits and events and has developed a strong core collection in nineteenth and twentieth century American art, especially the work of major regional and Tennessee artists, allowing it to become one of the state's leading art institutions.

Carroll Van West, Middle Tennessee State University

SEE: ART

CHEROKEE NATIONAL FOREST, Tennessee's only national forest, consists of approximately 626,400 acres of land along the Tennessee and North Carolina border. The Great Smoky Mountains National Park divides Cherokee National Forest into two sections. The northern section of over 327,000 acres extends north from the park to the tri-state area where Tennessee, North Carolina, and Virginia meet. The southern section extends from the southern boundary of the park to the Georgia state line and includes almost 299,000 acres.

Cherokee National Forest is home to 120 bird species, including the wild turkey, golden eagle, and peregrine falcon; 47 mammal species, including the black bear, red wolf, wild boar, and coyote; and 30 reptile species, such as the rattlesnake, copperhead, and salamander. The forest also provides habitation for many threatened and endangered species of plants and animals, including the bald eagle, northern flying squirrel, and two varieties of mussels.

Cherokee National Forest is the site of earlier Cherokee tribal lands along the Little Tennessee, Hiwassee, and Tellico rivers. White settlements also claim early associations with the area, and the Overmountain Victory National Historic Trail, commemorating the American victory over the British at King's Mountain, passes through Cherokee National Forest. Clearing of the forest for agricultural and livestock production expanded with the rising East Tennessee population. By the early twentieth century, timber companies had moved into East Tennessee to harvest what was left of the virgin forests. Clear cutting, wildfires, and erosion ravaged the forests and left much of the land unfit for cultivation. Mining operations also contributed to the denuding of the land in the extreme southern section of the Cherokee National Forest.

In 1912 the federal government began purchasing land to protect the headwaters of navigable rivers, including land in southeastern Tennessee and northern Georgia. In 1920 President Woodrow Wilson officially declared these federally held lands to be the Cherokee National Forest. In 1936, during the New Deal, the boundaries were redrawn to place the forest entirely within Tennessee, and lands were added to the northern section from Unaka and Pisgah National Forests. The Civilian Conservation Corps created many of the trails currently in use in Cherokee National Forest. The construction of dams and reservoirs by the Tennessee Valley Authority flooded some Cherokee Forest land and raised ecological and environmental concerns.

Cherokee National Forest is managed under national forest regulations, which differ in important ways from those governing national parks. For example, timber regulations in national forests permit clear-cutting of up to 40 acres. Approximately 132,000 acres, or 21 percent, of Cherokee National Forest is protected under other designations, however, and includes wilderness areas, scenic areas, and primitive areas, as defined by the U.S. Forest Service.

Wilderness area designation provides the most protection by prohibiting commercial timber harvesting, motorized vehicles, and construction and development in order to leave these areas as natural as possible. Today, 66,000 acres of Cherokee National Forest fall under wilderness protection. Although Congress passed the Wilderness Act in 1964, providing for such designation, wilderness areas in Cherokee National Forest were not included until 1974, when small portions were added under the Eastern Wilderness Areas Act. Supporters of the Cherokee National Forest lobbied for more wilderness areas, but faced opposition from hunters, timber cutters, and off-road vehicle enthusiasts, as well as local citizen groups. In the mid-1980s, however, Congress passed legislation designating another 10 percent of the forest as wilderness area.

Other areas are protected under the Cherokee National Forest Management Plan of 1988 as scenic areas or primitive areas. Logging is prohibited and vehicle use limited in scenic areas, which are valued and protected for their beauty. Almost 20,000 acres of the Cherokee National Forest is classified under the scenic area designation, 19,000 acres of which are in the northern sector. Currently, over 46,000 acres are designated as primitive areas and managed to protect the resources and attributes desirable for outdoor recreation in a primitive, non-motorized environment. Both scenic and primitive areas come under review by the U.S. Forest Service every ten to 15 years, with no continued protective designation guaranteed.

The Cherokee National Forest offers many recreational opportunities, including hiking, camping, horseback riding, swimming, boating, and whitewater sports on the Nolichucky, French Broad, Hiwassee, and Ocoee rivers; the Ocoee was the site of the 1996 Olympic whitewater events. There are over 650 miles of hiking trails in the Cherokee National Forest, including 170 miles of the Appalachian Trail. Six district offices are at Parksville, Etowah, Tellico Plains, Greeneville, Erwin, and Elizabethton. Forest headquarters are in Cleveland.

Tara Mitchell Mielnik, Middle Tennessee State University
SEE: APPALACHIAN TRAIL; CIVILIAN CONSERVATION CORPS

CHEROKEES: See OVERHILL CHEROKEES

CHEROKEE PHOENIX. Among the many accomplishments of the Cherokees was the publication of the first Native American newspaper, the *Cherokee Phoenix*, from 1828 to 1834. Soon after the adoption of the Cherokee Constitution in 1828, the National Council provided for the establishment of an official federal newspaper. Published in what is now New Echota, Georgia (the first capital of the Cherokee Nation), the *Phoenix* served as a vital link between the Cherokees living in Tennessee and their sovereign government.

Beginning with the inaugural issue of February 21, 1828, it reached the broadest possible audience of traditional full blood Cherokees, who neither spoke nor read English, and the European-influenced Cherokees of mixed descent. Printed in parallel columns of English and Cherokee syllabary, the *Phoenix* served Cherokee citizens of all backgrounds.

Rather than simply reporting Cherokee national news, the *Phoenix* served as a primary medium of communication; frequently, it addressed questions of tremendous social, political, and economic importance. Perusal of issues reveals not only the distribution of official documents, such as the Cherokee Constitution in the first issue, but also information on progressive animal husbandry and agriculture. Front page articles included heated discussions of the international slave trade and the Indian Removal Act that eventually resulted in the Trail of Tears.

The success of the *Phoenix* in distributing information was ultimately its downfall. When the *Phoenix* distributed detailed information about the impending removal of the Cherokees to the West, the Georgia militia confiscated and destroyed the newspaper's presses in 1834. While the *Cherokee Phoenix* never rose from the ashes of its destruction in Georgia, the tradition of a national newspaper re-emerged in Oklahoma in 1844 as the *Cherokee Advocate*. From 1828 to the present, over 2,000 Native American newspapers and periodicals have followed in this tradition.

Kevin E. Smith, Middle Tennessee State University
SEE: SEQUOYAH; TRAIL OF TEARS

CHESTER COUNTY, the last county formed in Tennessee, was created by the Tennessee General Assembly from parts of neighboring Hardeman, Henderson, McNairy, and Madison counties. In 1875, this land was used to create a county named Wisdom County, but Wisdom County was never organized, and in 1879, the General Assembly repealed this act and created Chester County out of the same land in March. Litigation brought on behalf of opponents of the new county delayed formal organization until 1882.

Chester County was named for Colonel Robert I. Chester, a quartermaster in the War of 1812, an early postmaster in Jackson, and a federal marshal for the Western District. The county seat, Henderson, was founded along the Mobile and Ohio Railroad line in the late 1850s, and first known as Dayton. In 1860 Polk Bray opened the town's first store. The town name was later changed to Henderson Station, and then Henderson, shortly after the Civil War, to honor Colonel James Henderson, a veteran of the War of 1812. Incorporated in 1901, Henderson is home to two twentieth century county landmarks: the Classical Revival-styled Chester County Courthouse (1913), which was used in scenes in the movie *Walking Tall* about McNairy County sheriff Buford Pusser and is listed in the National Register of Historic Places; and Freed-Hardeman University. In 1907 local businessmen asked educators A.G. Freed and N.B. Hardeman, who had taught at the earlier Georgie Robertson

Christian College, to head a new school named the National Teachers' Normal and Business College. In 1919 the name changed to Freed-Hardeman College and in 1990 this Church of Christ institution acquired university status.

Chester County villages include Enville; Mifflin, established in 1833 by Colonel John Purdy; and Jacks Creek, which was established in the 1820s and was the former home of J.M. Stone, later a governor of Mississippi.

Scattered military activity took place in what is now Chester County during the Civil War. In October 1862 a Confederate force under the command of Major N.N. Cox attacked a Union occupying force in Henderson, which was guarding the railroad line. Cox and his soldiers destroyed the train station, fired the railroad bridge, and tore up track. In December 1863 General Nathan B. Forrest's cavalry fought an all-day engagement with Union forces at Jacks Creek. After the Civil War, a large family led by Colonel Fielding Hurst settled in what is now the western portion of Chester County. Known as the Hurst Nation, this family was made up of Tennessee Unionists, since Fielding Hurst had been a Union Scout.

A survey of Tennessee in 1923 described Chester County as a largely agricultural landscape, with 1,667 farms producing many types of crops with cotton being the largest cash crop. Public education had been established and the Julius Rosenwald Fund had supported the construction of modern African-American schools in Henderson in 1921–22 and later at the Gibson community in 1927–28. But hard use of the land, and little practice of any soil conservation, left the county's sandy soil in poor shape. During the New Deal era of the 1930s, a large portion of the western end of Chester County became part of the Chickasaw State Park and Forest project of the Farm Security Administration. Originally, planners wanted to include 35,000 acres in the reclamation project, but settled for a park and forest project of over 13,000 acres. The Civilian Conservation Corps performed initial work in 1934 before the project came under the control of the Resettlement Administration. The present Chickasaw State Park and Forest has 1,280 acres for recreation and 13,104 acres of protected timberland.

Famous residents of Chester County include vocalist and television performer Eddy Arnold and women rights activist Sue Shelton White.

Tara Mitchell Mielnik and Carroll Van West, Middle Tennessee State University
SEE: ARNOLD, EDDY; CHICKASAW STATE PARK; FREED-HARDEMAN UNIVERSITY; WHITE, SUE SHELTON

CHESTER INN, a historic tavern building in Jonesborough, Washington County, is one of the oldest extant buildings in Tennessee's oldest town. Dr. William P. Chester built the original Federal-style inn circa

1797–1798. The frame building measures 82 feet in length and 26 feet in width and stands flush to the sidewalk in a manner reminiscent of town lots in Maryland, Virginia, and western Pennsylvania. According to historian Paul Fink, the inn "has no distinctive style of architecture, but its timbers display distinctive marking to show that a sawmill of sorts, either a man-powered saw-pit or a primitive water-powered operation, had by this time come into use."[1] Located on what was once the major road from the Tennessee settlements to the national capital and the important urban markets of Richmond, Baltimore, and Philadelphia, the inn served thousands of visitors during its existence. Andrew Jackson was honored with a reception at the inn during his presidency. Other famous patrons include James K. Polk, Andrew Johnson, and William G. Brownlow. In about 1880, owners updated the inn with an elaborate Victorian-style projecting porch, adding Italianate-influenced brackets to the building's cornice.

The Chester Inn was listed as part of the Jonesborough Historic District in the National Register of Historic Places in 1969. Four years later, it served as a center for the first National Storytelling Festival, which is held every October by the National Association for the Preservation and Perpetuation of Storytelling.

Carroll Van West, Middle Tennessee State University

CITATION:

(1) Paul M. Fink, "The Rebirth of Jonesboro," *Tennessee Historical Quarterly* 31(1972): 228.

SEE: JONESBOROUGH; NATIONAL STORYTELLING FESTIVAL

CHICKAMAUGA AND CHATTANOOGA, BATTLES OF.

The Battle of Chickamauga (September 19–20, 1863) developed from the struggle to control the strategic railroad town of Chattanooga, the gateway to the deep South, whose seizure President Abraham Lincoln viewed as comparable to the capture of Richmond. In the summer of 1863, Major General William S. Rosecrans, commander of the Union's Army of the Cumberland, successfully forced Braxton Bragg's Army of Tennessee to retreat first from Middle Tennessee and then from Chattanooga. The Federal forces occupied Chattanooga at a cost of only a handful of casualties, shocking the South and elating the North.

Perhaps overly confident, Rosecrans believed Bragg's forces to be in pell mell retreat and decided to deal the Army of Tennessee a severe blow. He sent three corps into northern Georgia in pursuit of the fleeing army. But the Federal forces traveled on widely separated routes, too far apart to support one another. Unknown to Rosecrans, Bragg halted his retreat and bolstered his army with reinforcements from Mississippi, Knoxville, and Virginia.

By the night of September 18, 1863, the two armies faced each other along the banks of Chickamauga Creek, a name soon translated as "River of Death." A short distance south of Chattanooga, the Federals faced east, with their backs to Missionary Ridge, and in position to protect the road through McFarland's Gap. The Union army numbered approximately 58,000 men, while the Confederates mustered some 66,000 troops, one of the few times the Army of Tennessee fought with a numerical advantage.

The Confederates attacked on the morning of September 19. Bragg planned to envelop the Union left flank, cutting off their line of retreat through McFarland's Gap and pinning them against the ridge. Major General George H. Thomas's Corps, drawn up in a curved line, received the weight of the southern attack. Fighting occurred all along the line, with attacks and counter-attacks alternating through the dense woods and scattered clearings. The Confederates forced back the Federal troops for a mile or more from the point where the fighting first began, but achieved few tactical gains before nightfall ended the first day's struggle.

During the night, Lieutenant General James Longstreet arrived with the last of the Confederate reinforcements, and Bragg placed him in charge of the army's left wing. Major General Leonidas Polk commanded the right wing. When the Confederates renewed their effort against the Federal's northern flank, Longstreet attacked the enemy's right center.

Just as the battle seemed destined to end in a draw, fate intervened. Through a misunderstanding at Federal headquarters, an entire division vacated its place in the Union line and created a gap in the line at the point where Longstreet's forces attacked. Rosecrans, two of his three corps commanders, and thousands of Union troops quickly retreated and headed for Chattanooga in a virtual rout.

Thomas, known ever afterward as "the Rock of Chickamauga," averted disaster by holding the crest of Snodgrass Hill, with the help of Major General Gordon Granger's reserve forces, until nightfall covered his withdrawal to Chattanooga. The tactical triumph at Chickamauga cost the Army of Tennessee 18,000 casualties; the Union suffered 16,000 casualties. With Chattanooga still in Union hands, however, the victory at Chickamauga held little strategic meaning for the Confederacy.

Within a few days, Bragg's army moved forward and laid siege to Chattanooga. The main force entrenched on Missionary Ridge, facing Chattanooga on their west, while other troops occupied Lookout Mountain, on the southwest side of the town. A third group settled in at Brown's Ferry, across the bend of the Tennessee River, west of Chattanooga. The Confederate positions controlled the railroads to Atlanta and Knoxville, and blocked both the river and the Memphis & Charleston Railroad, cutting off Federal communications with Bridgeport, Stevenson, and

Nashville. Confederate morale at the top levels of command sank so low that President Jefferson Davis visited the army in early October. He listened to Bragg's critics, but kept the unpopular general in command.

On the Union side, President Abraham Lincoln replaced Rosecrans, who seemed incapable of recovering from the shock of the loss at Chickamauga. On October 18, Lincoln named Major General Ulysses S. Grant as commander of the forces at Chattanooga. At the same time, the Federals prepared to reinforce their position with Major General William T. Sherman's Army of the Tennessee and Major General Joseph Hooker's troops from the Army of the Potomac.

Grant reached Chattanooga on October 23 and learned the seriousness of the Federal supply situation. In a surprise attack, the Union troops drove off Confederate troops and erected a pontoon bridge across the Tennessee River. A second skirmish at Wauhatchie secured Federal communications lines. By late November, the Union forces in and around Chattanooga numbered almost 70,000. The Confederates depleted their fighting strength to about 40,000 after sending Longstreet's men to Knoxville in a futile effort to take that city.

Grant devised a simple plan of attack. He placed Hooker on the right and Thomas in the center to create diversions at Lookout Mountain and the southern center on Missionary Ridge. He assigned Sherman to the main task of assaulting the northern end of Missionary Ridge to break the Confederate right flank and sweep down the ridge.

The battle did not develop as planned. On November 23, Thomas occupied Orchard Knob, a foothill far in front of the Confederate center on Missionary Ridge. The next day, Hooker drove back the southerners between the river and Lookout Mountain. The troops he sent up the mountain disappeared in the mists, but succeeded in taking the pinnacle, from which the United States flag flew the next morning. Newspapers romanticized the episode by calling it the "Battle Above the Clouds."

On November 25, Sherman attempted to carry out his mission, while Hooker fought for a position on the Confederate left, and Thomas moved against the center. Sherman's troops made no headway against the one (reinforced) division of Major General Patrick R. Cleburne. The Federals added two more divisions to no avail. The limited space to deploy Union troops, the determined fighting by Confederates, and Cleburne's masterful choice of position undermined the Union plan.

About three o'clock in the afternoon, a concerned Grant ordered Thomas to move out and occupy the enemy's rifle pits at the base of the ridge. After advancing and seizing this objective, the troops from the Army of the Cumberland, without orders,

charged up the steep slope of the ridge in one of the most remarkable and decisive acts of the war. The avalanche of blue-clad soldiers poured over the crest of the ridge, routing the badly positioned Confederate center and forcing the entire army to fall back into North Georgia. Each side suffered about 6,000 casualties. Bragg lost command of the Army of Tennessee, while Grant now possessed the most enviable reputation of any Union general. For the first and only time in the war, the four most successful Union generals—Grant, Sherman, Thomas, and Philip H. Sheridan—served together. More importantly, however, the Union forces controlled the strategic town of Chattanooga.

James L. McDonough, Auburn University

SUGGESTED READINGS: Thomas L. Connelly, *Autumn of Glory: The Army of Tennessee, 1862–1865* (1971); James L. McDonough, *Chattanooga: A Death Grip on the Confederacy* (1984)

SEE: ARMY OF TENNESSEE; BRAGG, BRAXTON; CLEBURNE, PATRICK R.; LONGSTREET, JAMES; THOMAS, GEORGE H.; U.S. ARMY OF THE CUMBERLAND

CHICKAMAUGAS were a diverse group of Cherokees, Creeks, dissatisfied whites, and African Americans, who stymied white settlement in Tennessee for approximately 19 years. On March 19, 1775, one month before the outbreak of fighting in the American Revolution, Richard Henderson signed the Treaty of Sycamore Shoals with the Cherokees led by Attakullakulla, or Little Carpenter. The private treaty ceded Central Kentucky and northern Middle Tennessee to Henderson. Little Carpenter's son, Dragging Canoe, led the opposition warning the whites they were buying a "dark and bloody ground."[1]

In 1776, the Shawnee chief Cornstalk came south to persuade the Cherokees and other southern tribes to join the British and resist American settlement across the Appalachian mountains. Dragging Canoe and many of the younger Cherokees were quite sympathetic, and eventually the majority of the 2,500 Cherokee warriors attacked the Upper East Tennessee settlements. The Watauga settlers drove away the attackers, and soldiers from the Carolinas and Virginia destroyed most of the Cherokee villages east of the mountains. The most anti-white Cherokees, led by Dragging Canoe, Bloody Fellow, Young Tassel, and Hanging Maw, moved into several abandoned Creek towns, including Citico and Chickamauga along Chickamauga Creek, and began calling themselves Chickamaugas, meaning river of death.

The British provided the group with 2,000 pounds of supplies early in 1779, in preparation for a major raid on the East Tennessee settlements. In a preemptive strike, Evan Shelby and 900 Virginia and North Carolina troops descended the Tennessee River by boat and surprised the Chickamaugas. The whites burned the villages and seized the supplies. The raid produced few Indian casualties, however, and Dragging Canoe moved the group to the more defensible territory west of Lookout Mountain, setting up the five Lower Towns: Running Water and Nickajack in Tennessee, Lookout Mountain in Georgia, and Long Island and Crowtown in Alabama.

By this time, the Chickamaugas, who started out as dissatisfied Overhill Cherokees, included many Upper Creeks, Shawnee, French "boatmen," some blacks, and Scots traders. Daniel Ross settled among them by 1785. Cheesekau and his younger brother Tecumseh also lived with them.

The Donelson river voyagers to Fort Nashborough fought their way through the Chickamauga area during the spring of 1780. In the course of their voyage, several members of the party were killed. In the fall of 1780 the Chickamaugas struck at the Cumberland settlements and destroyed Mansker's Station in Goodlettsville. The following April, they attacked Fort Nashborough but lost the Battle of the Bluffs. In December 1780 the Chickamaugas lost 80 men to forces under John Sevier at Boyd's Creek, near the Little Tennessee River. The Chickamaugas kept the Cumberland settlements isolated in 1787, and even attacked Fort White (Knoxville) in 1788. On a river trip, Joseph Brown also was captured; he spent a year at Nickajack. In 1792 they struck Buchanan's Station, just four miles south of Fort Nashborough. Travelers between East and Middle Tennessee were forced north on the Wilderness Trail, and even there, some 100 deaths occurred. Then, on February 29, 1792, the day after a victory celebration, Dragging Canoe died suddenly, and the mantle of leadership passed to Young Tassel.

The specific end of the Chickamauga period came on September 12, 1794, when a Southwest Territory militia unit under Major James Ore, and led by former prisoner Joseph Brown, crossed Monteagle Mountain and wiped out Nickajack and Running Water. By the end of the year, the remaining Chickamaugas joined the Overhill Cherokees to make treaties with the white Tennesseans.

Indian resistance continued, as the towns of Lookout Mountain, Long Island, and Crowtown realigned themselves with the Upper Creeks. Raids into southeast Middle Tennessee continued on a regular basis. The area from Murfreesboro to Beech Grove could not be settled until 1800; Warren County opened to white settlement in 1806; and whites settled Sequatchie County between 1807 and 1810. No effective white settlements, except the trading post of Daniel Ross, reached Chattanooga until 1817. The Chickamauga movement finally ended with Andrew Jackson's victories over the Red Stick Creeks in the 1813–1814 Alabama campaign.

Fred S. Rolater, Middle Tennessee State University

CITATION:
(1) Mary French Caldwell, *Tennessee: The Dangerous Example, Watauga to 1849* (Nashville, 1974), 35.

SUGGESTED READING: Ronald N. Satz, *Tennnessee's Indian Peoples: From White Contact to Removal, 1540–1840* (1979)

SEE: ATTAKULLAKULLA; DONELSON, JOHN; DRAGGING CANOE; MANSKER'S STATION; OVERHILL CHEROKEES; SEVIER, JOHN; TRANSYLVANIA PURCHASE

CHICKASAW ORDNANCE WORKS. Sometimes called the Memphis, or Millington, Ordnance Plant, this huge explosives manufactory had its origin in 1940, when the Anglo-French Purchasing Board formed the Tennessee Powder Company to produce munitions for the Allied war effort. After the French surrendered, the British assumed control and contracted with E.I. DuPont de Nemours Company to manage the construction and operation of the facility. The 6,000-acre site north of Memphis met the plant's needs for land, labor, bulk transportation links, and access to an ample supply of cotton linters, which were chemically treated to produce "smokeless powder" (actually a high-explosive cake, or "guncotton") for small arms and artillery, as well as TNT.

The installation required its own power plant, a separate spur from the main Illinois Central Railway line, and new artesian wells that pumped enough water (22 million gallons per day) to supply the city of Memphis. U.S. Highway 51 was enlarged to a "four-lane super roadway" from Memphis to the Tipton County line to accommodate the workers' automobiles. Though some workers commuted by public bus, the complex was a foretaste of the automobile culture that burgeoned after the war.

Construction began in June 1940, and proceeded on a round-the-clock schedule with a peak workforce of over 9,000 black and white workers. In early 1941 the plant operated with 1,500 employees and shipped its first lots of explosive. It set a world safety record by operating for 2 million (later 3.6 million) work hours without a major injury. From November 1940 to May 1943 the plant maintained continuous night and day operations for 871 days (except Christmas Day 1942).

In May 1941 the U.S. government acquired the plant and later changed the name from Tennessee Powder Works to Chickasaw Ordnance Works before enlargement of the facility began. DuPont continued to manage the plant for the U.S. Army; it received the first Army-Navy "E" award given to a southeast war plant, and received "E"s for four successive six-month periods. By October 1944 the plant employed more than 8,000 women and received an Army Ordnance safety award. Its overall accident rate remained less than half that of all other such plants.

Ironically, after more than $50 million in American and foreign investment, the award-winning plant was deemed too dangerous for conversion to civilian uses after the Army deactivated it in mid-1946, and carefully dismantled it.

Ed Frank, Mississippi Valley Collection, University of Memphis Libraries

SUGGESTED READING: Robert A. Sigafoos, *Cotton Row to Beale Street: A Business History of Memphis* (1979)

SEE: SHELBY COUNTY; WORLD WAR II

CHICKASAW STATE PARK, named for the Chickasaws who once inhabited West Tennessee and North Mississippi, includes approximately 1,400 acres. It is located in West Tennessee, along the border of Hardeman and Chester counties, and was one of the state's 20 New Deal-era state parks. The Farm Security Administration (FSA) originally designated the area as a utilization project to reclaim eroded and submarginal lands. Initially, state interests concentrated on reforestation, but eventually expanded to include recreational development of a 13,104-acre park and adjacent state forest.

The FSA's Chickasaw Land-Use Project outlined three overall goals during the early 1930s: (1) to relocate local residents from eroding and submarginal lands to fertile areas and introduce them to updated agricultural methods; (2) to redevelop eroded, overused land through reforestation; and (3) to create a wildlife preserve and recreational area. The Civilian Conservation Corps (CCC) and Works Project Administration (WPA) performed the preliminary work. In 1934 President Franklin D. Roosevelt approved reclamation of the area before turning it over to the Resettlement Administration (RA). Limited state and federal funding reduced the original 35,000-acre site plan to 20,000 acres. By 1939 the main recreational area included a 54-acre lake, boating and picnic facilities, a lodge, baseball fields, trails, cabins, a group camp, and a recreational building.

The Chickasaw Land-Use project also provided funding for the restoration and development of historic and prehistoric sites near Bolivar and Henderson that included Pinson Mounds, the vacation home of President James K. Polk, and Civil War earthworks. Regulators of the land-use project wanted to expand the program to include a segregated recreational area within the park for African-American use; however, state officials failed to address this issue and it was abandoned.

Chickasaw State Park rapidly became a popular recreational site with more than 170,000 visitors recorded during 1939–1941. Attendance before and after World War II more than doubled that of other state parks. Chickasaw State Park and Forest remained under jurisdiction of the Tennessee Division of State Parks until 1949, when the site's administrative responsibility was transferred to the United States Forestry Service, with the exception of the lakes, which remained under the supervision of the state's Game and Fish Commission. In 1955 all administrative park duties returned to state control, and the park and forest lands were deeded to the state. The Tennessee Department of Environment and Conservation now manages the park.

Ruth D. Nichols, Nashville

SEE: CHESTER COUNTY; CHICKASAWS; CIVILIAN CONSERVATION CORPS; CONSERVATION; PINSON MOUNDS; WORLD WAR II

CHICKASAWS, a small but courageous tribe whose principal towns headed by local chiefs, were located in northern Mississippi and Alabama before European contact. These Muskogean-speaking Indians subsisted by a combination of hunting, gathering, gardening, fishing, and trading with neighboring tribes. An expansive people, the Chickasaws claimed an extensive hunting range that included all of West Tennessee and a portion of Middle Tennessee.

During the winter of 1540–1541, Chickasaw warriors boldly resisted Hernando de Soto's effort to force them to assist him in his search for gold. When, by the close of the seventeenth century, European traders firmly established themselves among these Indians, mixed blood children of native women became important intercultural brokers for the tribe, setting the economic and social tone and serving as the principal spokespersons for the Chickasaws for over a century.

European traders engaged in the deerskin trade were the vanguard of troops and settlers. Competition among colonial powers for political and economic supremacy led to a long and bloody contest for control of the lower Mississippi Valley during which both the English and the French attempted to enlist the Chickasaws as allies.

The Chickasaws were not so immersed in the European wars of empire, however, as to neglect their own immediate interests. In 1715 and 1747, they combined forces with the Cherokees to expel the Shawnees from Middle Tennessee. And, in 1769, when the Cherokees challenged their eastward movement into Middle Tennessee, the Chickasaws soundly defeated their former allies.

Chickasaw-European contact accelerated rapidly after 1763, and the avenue to tribal leadership rapidly shifted from clan leaders known for their wisdom and/or bravery to mixed bloods like the Colbert family, the offspring of a Scottish father and his native wives, who were able to serve as intermediaries with Europeans. Out of deference to full bloods who made up three-fourths of the tribal population, mixed bloods preserved some components of the old order. Although full bloods sought to retain more of the traditional ways, the real power in Chickasaw politics increasingly resided with mixed bloods who emulated British planters and traders. While traditionalists viewed Europeans as disruptive forces, they too had become dependent on them and the mixed bloods for a variety of goods and services.

During the American Revolution, most Chickasaws sided with England. American inroads on tribal hunting grounds, especially the construction of Fort Jefferson and Fort Nashborough and the arrival of settlers along the Cumberland River, were viewed as acts of aggression.

British withdrawal from the lower Mississippi Valley after the war left the Chickasaws in a precarious position. Tribes in the Old Northwest threatened war. Surveyors from the Cumberland settlements were in the tribal hunting territory, and Virginians were demanding a land cession. Nevertheless, the competitive struggle between Spain and the United States for control of the lower Mississippi Valley after 1783 provided opportunities for the Chickasaws to secure favorable attention and treatment from both powers. In 1786 American officials formally recognized Chickasaw land claims in Tennessee and sent trade goods and weapons for distribution at the Lower Chickasaw Bluffs on the Mississippi River (present-day Memphis area) as part of their strategy to curb Spanish influence. Six years later, in 1792, William Blount secured a treaty of peace and friendship with the Chickasaws, a treaty that proved very costly to the tribe.

The Spanish-supported Creeks retaliated by raiding Chickasaw villages and ambushing their hunters along trails leading to the Tennessee and Cumberland rivers. The Chickasaws served as a barrier between the Cumberland settlements and hostile tribes. By the end of 1795, the Creeks finally sued for peace with the Chickasaws when, thanks in large measure to the Pinckney Treaty with Spain, the United States won the contest for the control of the lower Mississippi Valley.

As economic distress in the East drew attention to western lands, the United States established a trading house near Fort Pickering on the Lower Chickasaw Bluffs in 1802. American officials encouraged Chickasaws to buy goods on credit so as to establish individual debts that might later be paid off by the sale of tribal lands. Negotiations with mixed bloods who controlled tribal affairs paved the way for land cessions. In treaties negotiated in 1805, 1816, and 1818, General Andrew Jackson and other treaty commissioners used threats, economic coercion, and bribery to acquire nearly 20 million acres of land in Tennessee from the Chickasaws and open vital lines of communication lying within the tribal domain.

Chickasaws continued to frequent the lower bluffs to trade for goods for more than ten years after the Jackson Purchase Treaty of 1818 extinguished all remaining tribal land claims in Tennessee. Their hunting grounds had been so drastically reduced that many men found it necessary to pursue small game traditionally left for children. Some hunters, in violation of the 1818 treaty, traveled as far north as present-day Weakley County in search of game to use in bartering with traders in Memphis.

Andrew Jackson's elevation to the presidency foreshadowed the removal of the Chickasaws to the West. Following passage of his administration's Indian Removal Bill in 1830, Jackson met with tribal leaders in Tennessee and secured a provisional removal agreement. The Chickasaws postponed their removal until 1837. In the meantime, they made a determined effort to regain control of the Lower Chickasaw Bluffs from Tennessee by claiming that the southern border of the state had been incorrectly surveyed. Continuing pressure from white settlers, speculators, and federal as well as state officials, however, finally forced tribal leaders to capitulate.

Chickasaw removal to the West, which began in the summer of 1837, brought great misery and suffering to the tribe, largely as a result of the poor planning of American officials and the callousness of the businessmen who provided them with food and supplies en route. By early 1838 most of the tribe had moved across the Mississippi River. Today, more than a century and a half later, a government elected by the Chickasaws helps provide for the general welfare of the tribe on their reservation in Oklahoma where, out of a total tribal enrollment of some 36,000, about 12,369 live. In 1990 only 82 people claiming Chickasaw ancestry lived in Tennessee.[1]

Ronald N. Satz, University of Wisconsin-Eau Claire

CITATION:

(1) Marlita A. Reddy, ed., *Statistical Record of Native North Americans*. 2nd ed. (Detroit, 1995), 207, 1027

SUGGESTED READINGS: David Baird, *The Chickasaw People* (1974); Arrell M. Gibson, *The Chickasaws* (1971); Charles M. Hudson, *The Southeastern Indians* (1976); Ronald N. Satz, *Tennessee's Indian Peoples* (1979); Ronald N. Satz, *American Indian Policy in the Jacksonian Era* (1975)

SEE: JACKSON PURCHASE; SOTO, EXPEDITION; TRAIL OF TEARS; TREATIES

CHOCTAWS. The Choctaws of West Tennessee are the only native-speaking American Indian community in Tennessee. In fact, they have retained their language to a greater extent than virtually any other Native American group. The importance of being Choctaw is best expressed when they say, "Chata hapia hoke" (We are Choctaw), a statement which underscores the widely held native view that the loss of language is the loss of identity. While other native languages of Tennessee have been lost, the Choctaw language and culture remain a vibrant part of the state heritage.

In 1830 the Choctaws relinquished the last of their ancestral lands by signing the Treaty of Dancing

Rabbit Creek. The majority of Choctaws, some 19,200, moved to Indian Territory, but about 8,000 remained. The smaller group became sharecroppers and tenant farmers on local cotton farms. A few held title to their own lands, but the majority were farm laborers during the growing season and lived off the land during the winter.

By 1960 some 3,200 Choctaws resided on or near the reservation near Philadelphia, Mississippi. With economic opportunities steadily declining in the Mississippi hill country, the Choctaws maintained a tenacious grip on their former territory.

In 1952 two families from Neshoba County, Mississippi, responded to the labor recruitment efforts of a farmer in Lauderdale County, Tennessee, and moved to the Golddust community. The area was appropriately named, for the Choctaws saw the rich Mississippi alluvial floodplain as the land of opportunity. The population steadily increased from the few families of the 1950s to some 200 individuals by 1960. After 1960 the bottomland sharecropper way of life gave way to more mechanized agriculture. Some Choctaws moved to more financially rewarding factory jobs in Ripley, the county seat, while others returned to the reservation. By the early 1990s, some 26 families, representing approximately 150 individuals, remained in the Golddust area.

A Choctaw community in Memphis also developed and it too numbers about 150 members. The Memphis Choctaws, like their Lauderdale County neighbors, maintained close contact with Mississippi relatives. Many Memphis Choctaws migrated to Tennessee in response to the 1953 Federal Termination Act, which advocated assimilation and rapid termination of aid and protection for Native Americans.

Today, West Tennessee Choctaws maintain a common identity based on shared language, similar customs, and collective cultural heritage. Choctaw migration occurred through kinship networks with strong links to the parent communities in Mississippi. The Choctaws have accepted some cultural values from their non-Native American neighbors, but their traditional ways of life are reinforced by travel to the Mississippi reservation to receive health services from traditional doctors and herbalists. Weddings, funerals, and festivals, such as the annual Choctaw Fair, help to retain and reaffirm traditional values.

The first generation of Lauderdale County Choctaws worried about the loss of native culture, but crafts such as cane basket and mat weaving and bead weaving, as well as the traditional dances, songs, and stick ball games are taught to younger generations. In their early days at Golddust, the Choctaws built the First Indian Baptist Church, where services are often conducted in the Choctaw language. The church has since moved to Ripley, where it serves as a focal point for the community.

The annual Choctaw festival at Chucalissa Indian Village in Memphis, begun in 1964, helps foster group solidarity. The Chucalissa Choctaw Heritage Festival informs the public about Choctaw culture and serves as a homecoming for West Tennessee Choctaws. Beginning in 1987 Lauderdale County Choctaws initiated a similar festival at Fort Pillow and later moved it to Henning, Tennessee.

In 1991 a United States Department of Education grant, Project Smoke Signal, began to correct the steady erosion of self-esteem experienced by Choctaw children attending public school. Through after-school programs, which emphasized traditional beliefs, crafts, and culture, along with a strenuous study program, the drop-out rate among Choctaw youths has decreased significantly.

The West Tennessee Choctaws continued to benefit from their association with the federally recognized tribal government in Mississippi. In 1992, through the efforts of Choctaw community leaders in Lauderdale County and the Mississippi Band of Choctaw Indians, the federal government purchased 172 acres near Henning for government housing. Seventeen families now live in this Choctaw community. The Lauderdale County community of Choctaws is also the only local Tennessee population governed by a body of elected leaders. The American Indian Affairs of Tennessee, organized in 1986, insures the continuation of traditions and the Choctaw way of life. The ability to adapt to a changing world assures the Choctaws a place in Tennessee's future.

David H. Dye, University of Memphis

SEE: CHUCALISSA VILLAGE; LAUDERDALE COUNTY

CHOTA was an Overhill Cherokee village located in the Little Tennessee River valley of eastern Tennessee in present-day Monroe County. Chota, or Itsa'sa, is also spelled Echota and Chote. The original meaning has been lost. Chota probably developed from its close neighbor Tanasi, which it superseded in size and population by the 1740s. Contemporary descriptions of the village in the 1750s and 1760s, generally confirmed by archaeological studies, indicate that it consisted of a central village plaza with an octagonal townhouse, or council house, where public ceremonies and social events took place. An open rectangular building, or pavilion, where public affairs took place in warm weather, stood adjacent to the townhouse. Approximately 60 individual domestic households surrounded the plaza and public buildings and extended along the river for nearly a mile. Each household included a circular winter house, an adjacent summer house, and their associated corncribs and outdoor work areas. Probably 300 to 500 individuals populated the village.

By the mid-eighteenth century, both Europeans and Native Americans recognized Chota for its military power, political authority, and economic influence, and regarded it as the capital of the Cherokee nation. Among the Cherokee leaders residing at Chota were Connecorte (Old Hop), Attakullakulla (Little Carpenter), Oconastota, Kanagatuckoo (Standing Turkey), Old Tassel, and Hanging Maw. British colonial traders resided at the town, and a steady flow of emissaries representing the British colonies visited it throughout its history. Henry Timberlake's 1762 journal conveys particularly vivid images of Cherokee life at Chota. In 1780 American Revolutionary War forces destroyed Chota, but it had been rebuilt by 1784. In 1788 the Cherokee capital was moved from Chota to Ustanalli in northern Georgia. By 1807 only 30 people resided at Chota, and by 1813 the population had diminished to a single household. The land occupied by Chota was finally ceded to the United States in 1819.

In 1939, and again from 1969 through 1974, the University of Tennessee conducted extensive archaeological investigations at Chota, recording the townhouses, 37 domestic structures, and hundreds of refuse-filled pits and human burials. This work has contributed substantially to the description of eighteenth century Overhill Cherokee culture and the changes it experienced as a result of European contact. Prior to the completion of the Tellico Reservoir in 1979, the central portion of the site in the vicinity of the townhouses was covered with fill by the Tennessee Valley Authority. By agreement with TVA, this area is now managed by the Eastern Band of the Cherokee. Two monuments, one dedicated to Tanasi and the other commemorating the Chota townhouse, were placed at the site in the 1980s.

Gerald F. Schroedl, University of Tennessee, Knoxville

SUGGESTED READING: Gerald F. Schroedl, ed., *Overhill Cherokee Archaeology at Chota-Tenasee* (Report of Investigations 38, Department of Anthropology, University of Tennessee, Knoxville)

SEE: ATTAKULLAKULLA; MONROE COUNTY; OCONASTOTA; OVERHILL CHEROKEES; TIMBERLAKE, HENRY

CHRISTIAN BROTHERS UNIVERSITY.

In 1864 the Brothers of the Christian Schools had applied to begin a school "of higher education" in Memphis. Yellow fever epidemics in Galveston and New Orleans, however, killed several brothers and the Brothers canceled the project. Another attempt in 1871 succeeded and from this date until the present, the Brothers have continuously contributed to Memphis education.

The Memphis clergy was determined to establish Catholic education in Memphis. The clergy envisioned not only elementary and secondary education, but college education, too. Ironically, a number of unforseen difficulties arose that resulted in the Brothers making a place for themselves in Memphis.

The closing of the Memphis Female College made that property available, but the Chicago Fire of 1871 assured the beginning of Christian Brothers College in Memphis. That fire destroyed the Brothers' Academy in Chicago and left a number of Brothers available for other duties. Several came to Memphis and Brother Maurelian came from Pass Christian, Mississippi, to be the school's first president. Dedication of the college on Adams Avenue occurred on Sunday, November 19, 1871.

The nineteenth century was mainly a period of struggle for Christian Brothers College. Recovery from the Civil War and Reconstruction was tedious, but yellow fever and financial difficulties particularly plagued the city and the Brothers' community. Three epidemics in the 1870s took their toll on Memphis and the college. Also in debt, the college barely survived the financial Panic of 1873. The final problem of this century arose over the prohibition of the teaching of Latin in the colleges of the Christian Brothers in the United States. The Memphis Brothers objected, but they adjusted and began the instruction of modern languages.

Despite the school's growth in the early twentieth century, the Memphis college would be sacrificed to another Brothers' college in St. Louis. Not surprisingly, the Saint Louis District of the Christian Brothers had concluded that there were not adequate resources to support two colleges within the District. Therefore, in June 1915, the college awarded its last college degrees for several decades; Christian Brothers College became a high school.

From the end of World War I through the 1920s and the Depression, the school grew. Its enrollment outgrew the Adams Avenue facility, and in 1940 the school moved to the suburbs on East Parkway. In addition to inaugurating a new phase of its history on East Parkway, the school opened a junior college department. World War II, however, forced the closure of the junior college.

The last 35 years have been among the most active in the college's history. Physical and academic expansion continued; in 1965 the college and high school separated, with the high school moving further east, and in 1971 the college admitted women. In the 1990s, Christian Brothers became a university, reinstituted a teacher's education program, and began three master's programs. During 1996–1997, university athletics entered Division II of the NCAA. From its beginning on Adams Avenue with four brothers and 87 students, Christian Brothers has grown to a university offering both bachelors and masters degrees, with a faculty of over 100 and a student body of more than 1,800 in day and evening programs. On November 17, 1996, the University celebrated its 125th anniversary.

Marius Carriere, Christian Brothers University

SUGGESTED READING: W.J. Battersby, F.S.C., *The Christian Brothers in Memphis: A Chronicle of One Hundred Years, 1871–1971* (1971)
SEE: EDUCATION, HIGHER; SHELBY COUNTY

CHRISTIAN METHODIST EPISCOPAL CHURCH.

Although a majority of African-American Methodists split from the white-dominated church after the Civil War and joined the African Methodist Episcopal Church or the African Methodist Episcopal Zion Church, others initially chose to remain in the Methodist Episcopal Church, South (MECS) in a segregated but parallel organization. Tensions between black and white members grew during Reconstruction, especially in regard to the white domination of church leadership and the desire of some black Methodists for ordination as bishops. By December 1870, it became apparent that the white leaders of the MECS would have to relinquish some authority to black church leaders.

On December 21, 1870, William Miles and Richard Vanderhorst, both former slaves, were ordained as Bishops of the Methodist Episcopal Church at the General Conference of the MECS held in Memphis. Led by these two bishops, the black members of the MECS announced their decision to form their own denomination, which would be known as the "Colored Methodist Episcopal Church," an acknowledgment and acceptance of the MECS religious heritage. Although the ordination of Miles and Vanderhorst signified the exodus of the African-American members, it represented a peaceful and harmonious transition. CME was one of the first religious denominations developed by southern blacks and consisted almost solely of former slaves. Unlike the northern-based AME churches, CME stressed its religious history with MECS, while acknowledging cultural and racial differences.

Other African-American churches frowned upon the new CME church and its close relationship with the white MECS. They called it the "kitchen church" or "slavery church" and accused the former slaves of still doing the bidding of their former masters. CME remained the smallest of the African-American churches, but many former slaves identified more closely with CME leaders, who were also newly emancipated, than the northern, educated leaders of other black churches. In the establishment of CME, ex-slaves consciously broke with white churches, but refused to join northern-based separate African-American churches. At the same time, the creation of CME churches represented some of the first institutional foundations of racial segregation in the South.

In 1882 CME Church, with the assistance of Bishop Isaac Lane, founded a high school in Jackson, Tennessee. Lane's daughter, Jennie Lane, served as the school's first teacher. In September 1883 Reverend (later Bishop) Charles Henry Phillips became director of the school. Under his administration, the school's name was changed to Lane Institute. In 1896 the name changed to Lane College, a reflection of the broadened curriculum of classics and natural and physical sciences. Lane College became the primary church institution for the education and training of CME ministers.

Throughout its early history, CME Church avoided political roles, but by 1925 Bishop Charles H. Phillips reported the active involvement of the church in the anti-lynching campaigns. In 1956 CME dropped the word "Colored" from its title, replacing it with "Christian." The headquarters of the Christian Methodist Episcopal Church are in Jackson.

Tara Mitchell Mielnik, Middle Tennessee State University

SUGGESTED READING: Katherine Dvorak, *An African American Exodus: The Segregation of Southern Churches* (1991)
SEE: LANE, ISAAC; LANE COLLEGE; RELIGION

CHRISTIE, AMOS URIAH

CHRISTIE, AMOS URIAH (1902–1986), nationally known medical educator and pediatrician, was the only child of Edna Davis and Frederick Absolom Christie, born August 13, 1902, in Eureka, California. His father, a lumberman, died when Christie was only four years old; his mother, a cook/dietitian at the Union Labor Hospital in Eureka, raised him.

Christie attended the University of Washington on a football scholarship and played twice in the Rose Bowl. In 1924 he entered the University of California Medical School in San Francisco and graduated June 1929. In medical school, Christie joined the Army ROTC, and on May 15, 1929, he was commissioned as a first lieutenant in the Army and became a flight surgeon. He received residency training in pediatrics at Babies Hospital, Columbia University College of Physicians and Surgeons in New York. In 1934 he married Margaret Cunningham Clarke, a Broadway actress.

In 1936 he became a research associate and specialist in pediatrics to the Children's Bureau in Washington, while also serving as director of the newborn service at the Johns Hopkins Hospital. In the fall of 1937 he studied at the Harvard School of Public Health. He returned to the University of California, where he advanced to the position of acting head of the department of pediatrics by 1940.

Shortly after the attack on Pearl Harbor, at the urging of the U.S. Surgeon General, Dr. Christie accepted the position as assistant director of medical and health services of the American Red Cross in Washington and headed up the development of a blood products program for the armed forces. Invited to become chairman of the department of pediatrics at the University of California, he decided to remain with the Red Cross medical program. His research at Johns Hopkins on the immunology and other aspects of syphilitic infections, along with certain other studies, resulted in his election to the Society for Pediatric Research, and in 1938, to the American Pediatric Society, the premier pediatric societies for clinical investigators.

On October 1, 1943, Dr. Christie began his duties as professor and chairman of the department of pediatrics at Vanderbilt University School of Medicine. He immediately became an integral part of the University, developing a department of pediatrics that became a model for teaching and patient care. Nationally and internationally-known as a pediatrician, teacher, academic leader, researcher, and humanitarian, Christie received many important medical honors, including the prestigious John Howland Award, the highest award of the American Pediatric Society; the Jacobi Award of the Pediatric Section of the American Medical Association; and the John Philips Memorial Award of the American College of Physicians. In 1965 he was named the first recipient of the Branscomb Distinguished Professor at Vanderbilt; in 1971 he received the Chancellor's Cup at Vanderbilt. Christie took pride in his success as a developer of pediatric leaders. Out of his Vanderbilt department came the largest number of heads of departments of pediatrics and professors of pediatrics of any department in the United States.

Christie also received the Frank H. Luton Award for outstanding accomplishments in the field of mental health in Tennessee. For his contributions to the Nashville community, he was presented the second annual Edward Potter, Jr., Leadership Award, conferred on those who have done the most to advance the socio-economic conditions of the Nashville community. In 1983 he was named Physician of the Year in Tennessee by the Tennessee Medical Association.

Christie was chiefly responsible for defining the natural history of histoplasmosis, the most important fungus disease in this country. His publications on that topic, other diseases, and various aspects of pediatric medicine were numerous and wide-ranging. Christie died on February 8, 1986 at the age of 84.

Harris D. Riley, Jr., Vanderbilt University Medical Center
SEE: MEDICINE; VANDERBILT UNIVERSITY MEDICAL CENTER

CHRISTOPHER, PAUL REVERE (1910–1974), labor leader, was born in Easley, South Carolina, the son of Clarence Christopher, a craft unionist. Christopher graduated from high school in 1930 and attended Clemson Agricultural College. In 1931 he returned to the textile mills, where he had worked part-time since age 14. In August 1932 Christopher married Mary Elizabeth Lybrand; they had two children.

Christopher joined the United Textile Workers of America (UTWA), becoming local president in 1933 and vice-president of the North Carolina Federation of Labor in 1934. That same year, he was designated UTWA strike coordinator for western North Carolina. After the 1934 textile strike failed, he continued organizing in the Carolinas, joining the Textile Workers Organizing Committee (TWOC) in 1937. In May 1939 he was appointed Textile Workers Union of America (TWUA) South Carolina director and elected a vice-president of the national TWUA.

Christopher resigned from TWUA, moving to Tennessee in October 1940, to become Tennessee CIO State Industrial Union Council secretary-treasurer. Appointed CIO regional director for Tennessee in 1942, he acted as special mediation representative for Region Four National War Labor Board, led the Tennessee CIO "Operation Dixie" from 1946 to 1952, headed the Tennessee Volunteer Organizing Committee, combated management dilatory tactics spawned by the Taft-Hartley Act, and worked to minimize AFL raiding of newly certified CIO locals. Appointed CIO regional director for Region Four (Tennessee, Kentucky, North Carolina, and Virginia) in 1953, he supported the merger efforts of the AFL and CIO, and was appointed AFL-CIO director for Region Eight (Kentucky and Tennessee) in 1964, a position he retained until his death in February 1974, in Knoxville.

Joseph Y. Garrison, Tennessee Historical Commission
SEE: LABOR

CHUCALISSA VILLAGE, an important Mississippian period archaeological site located within T.O. Fuller State Park in Memphis, was accidently discovered by workers from the Civilian Conservation Corps (CCC) during the park's initial development in 1939. According to the Memphis *Press-Scimitar* of February 27, 1940, the site "was literally ankle-deep in crumbling bones, bricks and ancient pottery." Once informed of the discovery, federal officials in Washington stopped the CCC work; by the spring of 1940, a Works Progress Administration (WPA) team of 20, under the supervision of George Lidberg, was excavating the site. The WPA team found a large Mississippian village, where ceremonial and burial mounds had been constructed from approximately A.D. 1000 to 1400. But Memphis WPA officials refused to approve further funding for a state archaeological park, or even an interpretive wayside for the site. Investigations at Chucalissa stopped in April 1940. During the 1950s, the Memphis Archaeological and Geological Society resumed the site's development. In 1962, 187 acres of Fuller Park associated with Chucalissa was formally transferred to the present University of Memphis, which has since operated the site for research and education purposes. The reconstructed village portrays the site as it would have appeared ca. A.D. 1400.

Archaeological research over the last 30 years indicates that Native Americans occupied the Chucalissa area over 3,000 years. Scattered tools and projectile points left by people of the late Archaic and then the Woodland periods have been uncovered. The first permanent Mississippian settlement was brief, dating probably ca. A.D. 1000. Corn agriculture, supplemented by beans, hunting, fishing, and trade, was the economic foundation of the settlement. The town was arranged around a central plaza, dominated by a large ceremonial mound for the dwelling of the settlement's headman and surrounded by a series of small mounds for the houses of other important village leaders. The size of the dwellings reflected owner status and position within the settlement. The headman's house might be as large as 50 feet on each side, with large cypress posts supporting a thatched pyramid roof. Dwellings around the plaza ranged between 18 to 22 feet per side, while others behind the main mound measured 14 to 18 feet on a side. While the settlement's leaders lived in substantial houses within or surrounding the mound complex, other villagers lived outside the complex, along a nearby ridge or on top of several nearby hills.

Carroll Van West, Middle Tennessee State University

SUGGESTED READINGS: Edwin A. Lyon, *A New Deal for Southeastern Archaeology* (1996); Carroll Van West, *Tennessee's Historic Landscapes: A Traveler's Guide* (1995)

SEE: CIVILIAN CONSERVATION CORPS; MISSISSIPPIAN CULTURE; WORKS PROGRESS ADMINISTRATION

CHUQUALATAQUE (DOUBLEHEAD) (ca. 1760s-1805), one of the lesser known of the Cherokee chiefs, was born into the Paint Clan as "Blue Hawk," probably in the early 1760s. This clan was the kin group of many noted Cherokee chiefs, including Dragging Canoe and Hanging Maw. Chuqualataque grew up in the Chickamauga town of Running Water, and his early years were undoubtedly disrupted by frequent fighting over British and later American interactions. As a result of these incessant conflicts and the atrocities committed by all sides, Chuqualataque and a small band of Cherokee warriors began raiding throughout East Tennessee and the Cumberland River area. His band was responsible for many acts of frontier violence including an attack that killed three nephews of General John Sevier.

By the late 1790s Chuqualataque became more reconciled to increasing American settlement and attended treaty negotiations at Washington, D.C., and Holston and Tellico, Tennnessee. During these treaty talks, he arranged concessions favorable to his interests, including the Fort Southwest Point ferry payments and large personal concessions in cash and goods. At the Second Tellico Treaty in 1805, Chuqualataque signed over all Cherokee claims to the Upper Cumberland lands for large personal land

concessions. Following this, while he attended the Annual Cherokee Ballgame near the Hiwassee Garrison, he was attacked by Major Ridge and others. He fought fiercely, even though wounded in the jaw and arm, but was eventually tomahawked to death.

Tom Des Jean, Big South Fork National Recreation Area

SEE: RIDGE, MAJOR; TREATIES

CHURCH OF GOD. With a worldwide membership approaching three million, this denomination grew from humble beginnings in the mountains of eastern Tennessee and western North Carolina. The doctrines of the church combine traditional Protestant tenets with others that are Pentecostal. The latter include the need to be born again, sanctification and baptism in the Holy Spirit as specific events in a Christian's life, prophetic utterance, spiritual healing, and speaking in tongues.

The first congregation was established in 1886, as the Christian Union at Barney Creek Meeting House in Monroe County, Tennessee. The first pastor was Richard G. Spurling, Sr., an ordained Missionary Baptist preacher. In 1896 this congregation moved to nearby Camp Creek in Cherokee County, North Carolina, joining with a like-minded group of worshippers there. The church experienced a Pentecostal revival marked by evangelistic preaching, fervent prayer, weeping, shouting, and speaking in tongues. The leaders preached a doctrine denouncing the worldliness of modern churches and promoting a conversion experience and holy lifestyle for each believer.

During the following decade the congregation grew, but its leaders battled against both fanaticism within the church and persecution from without. Enemies of the church destroyed a large section of the log structure at Camp Creek in a nighttime dynamite attack. Repairs were made, but a mob attacked the church on a Sunday afternoon, tore it down log by log, and burned the timbers as the church families watched. The persistent believers continued to meet in homes, and new churches were formed in Tennessee and northern Georgia.

In 1906 the leaders of the four churches then comprising the group assembled and selected the name Church of God. In 1907 Ambrose J. Tomlinson, pastor of the church in Cleveland, was appointed the denomination's General Overseer. Tomlinson, a skilled preacher and administrator, was an Indiana native who had come to the area as a Bible salesman. He presided over the growing church for 15 years, establishing a publishing house and orphanage and raising the membership from 1,000 to 21,000. In 1922 church leaders charged Tomlinson with misappropriation of funds and other wrongdoing. A series of bitter hearings ensued, and Tomlinson eventually left. Several congregations followed Tomlinson and became known as the Church of God of Prophecy, also headquartered in Cleveland. The majority of members stayed and since the church has since been listed as Church of God (Cleveland, Tennessee).

The Church of God Bible School opened in Cleveland in 1918. It moved to Sevierville in 1937, but in 1948 the church purchased buildings in Cleveland being vacated by Bob Jones College. The Bible School reopened in 1949 as Lee College, named for early church leader Flavius J. Lee. Today, Lee University is an undergraduate school with about 2,500 students in 56 degree programs. On an adjoining property is the Church of God School of Theology, a graduate school opened in 1975, with a reported 1996 enrollment of 262 students. The denomination presently claims 51,051 members in Tennessee.

Charles A. Sherrill, Tennessee State Library and Archives
SUGGESTED READINGS: Charles W. Conn, *Like A Mighty Army Moves the Church of God* (1955); Mickey Crews, *The Church of God: A Social History* (1990)
SEE: BRADLEY COUNTY; CHURCH OF GOD OF PROPHECY; LEE UNIVERSITY; RELIGION

CHURCH OF GOD IN CHRIST (COGIC), estimated
to be the second largest black religious denomination in the United States, is characterized as a Pentecostal denomination. Followers of Pentecostal faiths embrace the spiritual gifts that early Christians first received on the day of Pentecost (the fiftieth day after the Resurrection of Jesus). COGIC emphasizes all the gifts of the Spirit, particularly speaking in tongues, which is testimony to the baptism of the Holy Spirit.

Although the convening of the first Pentecostal General Assembly of the church in Memphis during November 1907 is regarded as the official founding date, the antecedents of the Church of God in Christ date much earlier. COGIC's architect was Charles Harrison Mason, who was born on September 8, 1866. In November 1878, at the age of 12, he became a professing Christian at the Mt. Olive Missionary Baptist Church near Plumerville, Arkansas. In 1893 the Mt. Gale Missionary Baptist Church in Preston, Arkansas, licensed Mason into the ministry. During his first year, Mason became intrigued with the doctrine of sanctification.

In 1895 Mason met C.P. Jones, J.E. Jeter, and W.S. Pleasant. These radical holiness preachers conducted a revival in Jackson, Mississippi, the following year. The dogmatic teachings of Mason resulted in his alienation from the Baptist Church, but this did not stall his ministry. His meetings continued to take place in an abandoned cotton gin house in Lexington, Mississippi. Despite Mason's independent stance, persecution still followed him. Five pistol shots and two double barreled shotgun blasts disrupted one meeting, wounding several worshippers.

Such attacks failed to discourage Mason and his followers. Instead, they founded the holiness sect known as the Church of God. In 1897, while walking along a street in Little Rock, Mason envisioned the name "Church of God in Christ," and the name change gave Mason's church its own distinct identity.

1907 marked a maturation point in Mason's efforts of establishing a distinctive church when he and Elders D.J. Young and J.A. Jeter attended the Azusa Street Revival in Los Angeles. There, under the teaching of W.J. Seymour, Mason became a believer in the outpouring of the Holy Spirit and in tongues as witness to this baptism. Upon his return to Memphis, where his church was now located, Mason proclaimed speaking in tongues a New Testament doctrine. C.P. Jones split with Mason over this issue and led the non-Pentecostal faction of COGIC, which eventually became known as the Church of Christ (Holiness), U.S.A. Mason's followers retained the COGIC name and convened the first Pentecostal General Assembly in Memphis in 1907. Representatives from 12 churches attended the initial meeting.

Between 1907 and 1914, the Church of God in Christ was the only incorporated Pentecostal body in the nation. Mason ordained both white and black clergy, since both needed licenses of ordination, but whites and blacks generally gravitated to separate congregations. Many of the white clergy ordained by Mason helped to form the Assembly of God Church in 1914.

When Mason died in 1961, a brief leadership crisis ensued. Mason's son-in-law, J.O. Patterson, Sr., became Presiding Bishop in 1968. Since then an orderly and timely succession of leadership has resulted in Louis H. Ford and Chandler Owens occupying the Presiding Bishopric in 1989 and 1995, respectively. The World Headquarters of the Church of God in Christ is in Memphis. There, in 1968, at Mason Temple, The Rev. Martin Luther King, Jr., gave his final major public address, the "I've Been to the Mountaintop" sermon, the night before he was assassinated at the Lorraine Motel.

Randolph Meade Walker, LeMoyne-Owen College
SUGGESTED READING: C. Eric Lincoln and Lawrence H. Mamiya, *The Black Church in the African American Experience* (1990)
SEE: RELIGION

CHURCH OF GOD OF PROPHECY, headquartered
in Cleveland, Tennessee, has more than 300,000 members worldwide. Its New Testament theology is evangelical in nature, and its worship style is Pentecostal. The early history of the denomination is entwined with that of the Church of God and the holiness movement. The church doctrines are founded on biblical inerrancy. Baptism by the Holy Spirit as evidenced by speaking in tongues, and total abstinence from tobacco and alcohol are among the teachings of the church.

A. J. Tomlinson (1845–1943) established the denomination in Cleveland, Tennessee, in 1923, following his forced resignation from the position of General Overseer of the Church of God. Tomlinson had been an early leader in the Church of God, but dissension over issues including financial control led to a division. Tomlinson and a few congregations in Tennessee and elsewhere formed a new organization, initially called the Tomlinson Church of God. The splinter group, much smaller than the parent organization, became involved in extended litigation over the use of the name "Church of God." In 1953 the Bradley County Chancery Court decreed that the suffix "of Prophecy" be added to the name for use in secular and business affairs. Internally, however, the denomination still uses the name "Church of God."

Tomlinson led the church throughout the 1930s, when the denomination achieved considerable growth, especially through missionary outreach in foreign nations. Today, 75 percent of the membership lives outside the United States.

In 1943 Tomlinson's death created a critical void in the church's leadership, and his sons, Milton and Homer, vied for appointment as General Overseer. Milton Tomlinson was selected and served in that capacity until his retirement in 1990 at the age of 84. During his tenure, the church continued to hold its General Assembly annually in Cleveland, inundating the small city with as many as 20,000 delegates from around the world to participate in the week-long church business meeting and worship services.

Homer Tomlinson moved to Queens, New York, and founded another church, The Church of God. Until his death in 1968, he remained a flamboyant preacher. He pronounced himself "king of the world" and took a throne on worldwide trips. Tomlinson ran for U.S. President four times as head of the unregistered Theocratic party.

Billy D. Murray became the first General Overseer outside the Tomlinson family in 1990. Although a splinter group separated from the denomination after his selection, efforts toward worldwide evangelism have been revitalized under Murray's leadership. Leaders also tackled some of the historical misunderstandings about the church and made efforts toward spiritual reconciliation with the Church of God. In 1997 the church reported approximately 2,000 congregations in the United States, of which 133 are in Tennessee.

Charles A. Sherrill, Tennessee State Library and Archives
SEE: BRADLEY COUNTY; CHURCH OF GOD; RELIGION

CHURCH, ROBERT R., JR. (1885–1952), a prominent Republican, civil rights leader, and businessman, was born in Memphis on October 26, 1885, the son of millionaire Robert R. Church, Sr., and his wife Anna Wright Church. Robert Church, Jr., married Sara P. Johnson of Washington, D.C., in 1911 and they had one child, Sara Roberta Church.

Church, Jr., was educated at Morgan Park Military Academy in Illinois, Oberlin College in Ohio, and the Packard School of Business in New York. He also received two years of training in banking on Wall Street. One of his first jobs was managing Church Park and Auditorium on Beale Street. He later became cashier of the Solvent Savings Bank and Trust Company, founded by his father, whom he succeeded as president after his father's death in 1912.

Active in civil rights and politics, Church, Jr., founded and financed the Lincoln League in Memphis in 1916. The Lincoln League organized voter registration drives, voting schools, and paid poll taxes for African-American voters, who were largely disfranchised from mainstream politics. Within months of its creation, the League had registered 10,000 voters. A Lincoln League ticket, which included an African-American candidate for Congress in West Tennessee, entered the 1916 election. The ticket lost, but its attempt established the Lincoln League as a viable and respected political force in Memphis, one which later expanded into a statewide and a national organization.

One year after establishing the Lincoln League, in 1917, Church organized the Memphis Branch of the NAACP, the organization's first branch in Tennessee. In 1919 Church was elected to the national board of NAACP.

Church was a Memphis delegate to eight successive Republican National Conventions from 1912 to 1940. His political organization, the Black and Tans wing of the Memphis Republican party, supplied the swing votes that carried Republicans to victory in several elections in Memphis and Shelby County. National party officials acknowledged his leadership by consulting with him about federal patronage. Republican Presidents and other high party officials also consulted with Church about political strategy, in recognition of his controlling influence on the Lincoln League. Church served on many important policy committees of the Republican party, but was not interested in prestigious positions for himself. In 1922, for example, he declined a Presidential appointment to be Chairman of the U.S. Commisssion to Study American Relations with Haiti; two years later, he rejected a similar position with a study commission about American relations with the Virgin Islands.

In 1924 the Congressional Country Club in Washington D.C., invited Church to become a Founder Life Member. This was probably the first time an African American had been invited to join a prestigious predominantly white country club. But he rejected the invitation because he was the only member of his race to be so invited. Church was active in a number of other social organizations, including the Iroquois

Club of Memphis, the Frogs of New York City, and Omega Psi Phi fraternity.

During the New Deal era, Church's political organization and influence began to diminish, due to President Franklin Roosevelt's appeal to African-American voters, and, more importantly, the increasing power of the Boss Crump political machine. Church, Jr., and Crump were not allies or partners in political activities. They had totally different political philosophies and maintained autonomous political organizations.

In 1940 the city administration under Crump's direction moved to destroy Church's political base by seizing his real estate holdings, allegedly for taxes. Church had no effective redress. He subsequently established himself in Washington, D.C., and was active in national Republican politics. He died of a heart attack on April 17, 1952.

Ronald A. Walter, Memphis

SUGGESTED READINGS: Annette E. Church and Roberta Church, *The Robert R. Churches of Memphis: A Father and Son Who Achieved in Spite of Race* (1974); Gloria B. Melton, "Blacks in Memphis, Tennessee, 1920–1955: A Historical Study," (Ph.D. diss., Washington State University, 1982)

SEE: BEALE STREET; CHURCH, ROBERT R., SR.; SOLVENT SAVINGS BANK; CRUMP, EDWARD H.; MEMPHIS; NAACP

CHURCH, ROBERT R., SR. (1839–1912), noted Memphis businessman, philanthropist, community activist, and political leader, was born in Holly Springs, Mississippi, in 1839, the son of Charles B. Church of Memphis, who owned several Mississippi River steamboats. His mother, Emmeline, lived with a family in Holly Springs and died when Church was only 12 years old. Robert Church then lived with his father until an adult. In his early years, he was a cabin boy, later becoming a steward.

During the 1860s, Church established himself as a successful Memphis businessman. At various times, he owned a saloon, hotel, restaurant, and real estate investments. During the Memphis Race Riot of 1866, a white mob attacked Church's saloon, shot him, and left him for dead. Church recovered, however, and refused to leave Memphis, despite the violence. Church stayed in the city during the terrible Yellow Fever Epidemic of 1878 and was able to invest cheaply in local real estate. When Memphis was reduced to a Taxing District, Church was the first citizen to buy a bond, for $1,000, to restore the City Charter.

In 1882 Church ran unsuccessfully on both the People's Ticket and the Independent Ticket as a candidate for the Board of Public Works. Yet, his business investments continued to prosper. Church was recognized as the South's first African-American millionaire. He was a generous contributor to many civic causes. The Memphis *Press Scimitar* stated in an 1899 article: "It may be said of Robert Church that his word is as good as his bond. No appeal to him for the aid of any charity or public enterprise for the benefit of Memphis has ever been made in vain. He is for Memphis first, last and all the time."

In 1899, for example, Memphis lacked public parks for black citizens. Church bought a tract of land on Beale Street, built an auditorium, landscaped the grounds, and called the venture Church Park and Auditorium. The modern auditorium seated 2,000 and was a cultural, recreational, and civic center for African Americans. It was the only one of its kind in the United States, owned and operated by a person of color for members of his race. W.C. Handy, who later became famous for creating the blues, was employed as orchestra leader at the park and auditorium. In 1902, President Theodore Roosevelt spoke to 10,000 people at the auditorium and on the grounds. His appearance acknowledged Church's political prominence. Two years earlier, in 1900, he had been a Memphis delegate to the Republican National Convention, which had nominated William McKinley as President and Roosevelt as Vice President.

In 1906 Church founded the Solvent Savings Bank and Trust Company, the first black-owned and -operated bank in Memphis. The bank survived the financial panic of 1907, which closed older and larger banks. To ward off a bank run, Church placed sacks of money in the bank's windows with notes asserting that he had adequate reserves to pay off depositors.

Church married twice, and two children were born to each marriage. His first marriage to Louisa ended in divorce. Their daughter, Mary Church Terrell, became one of the South's most prominent black women of the early twentieth century. Church married Anna Wright in 1885, and they became the parents of Robert, Jr., and Annette.

Ronald A. Walter, Memphis

SUGGESTED READINGS: Annette E. Church and Roberta Church, *The Robert R. Churches of Memphis: A Father and Son Who Achieved in Spite of Race* (1974); Lester Lamon, *Black Tennesseans, 1900–1930* (1977)

SEE: BEALE STREET; CHURCH, ROBERT R., JR.; MEMPHIS; MEMPHIS RACE RIOT OF 1866; SOLVENT SAVINGS BANK; TERRELL, MARY CHURCH

CHURCHES OF CHRIST are a primitivistic body of Christian believers, ideologically related to some extent to the German and Swiss Anabaptists. While they have an intellectual interest in doctrinal developments throughout the history of Christian thought, their purpose is to reproduce the beliefs and practices of the earliest Christians in their assemblies and lives. Historically, they are the more conservative heirs of the American Restoration Movement, which began between 1790 and 1810. First generation leaders included Thomas (1763–1854) and Alexander Campbell (1788–1866) in Pennsylvania, and Barton W.

Stone (1772–1844) in Kentucky. The Stone and Campbell movements formally united in Lexington, Kentucky, on January 1, 1832. The Disciples of Christ and the Independent Christian Churches also have their roots in this Restoration Movement.

The original leaders of this movement were scattered from North Carolina to New England, and unknown to each other. They shared a concern over divisions among believers in Christ, which they attributed to perpetuation of strict adherence to historic creeds. They further believed those creeds included departures from, and corruptions of, Biblical doctrines. They urged the unity of all believers, a goal attainable by a return to the Bible as the sole guide for all religious practices. Early success led to membership growth from approximately 22,000 in 1832 to 192,000 in 1860 and 1,120,000 in 1900.

By the middle of the nineteenth century, divisions began to plague the movement. Among the several controversial issues, heightened by geographical and social divisions, the use of instrumental music in worship and organized societies for mission work proved to be crucial. By 1906 the divisions were complete, and the United States census added the new listing of Churches of Christ as separate from the Disciples of Christ.

Churches of Christ were, and continue to be, heavily concentrated in the southern and southwestern regions of the United States. The 1906 census recorded 159,658 members, almost two-thirds of whom lived in the 11 former Confederate states. Over 41,000 lived in Tennessee, and Nashville became a center of the movement.

According to the most recent world-wide statistics (1990), there are 13,908 congregations outside the United States and its territories, composed of 747,568 members. Churches of Christ are found in 121 of the world's 177 nations. Serving in other countries are 660 American missionaries from Churches of Christ. In the United States, according to 1994 statistics, there are 13,013 Churches of Christ, with a total membership of 1,260,838. The largest concentrations are found in Texas (290,190 members) and Tennessee (168,190 members). Tennessee and its eight contiguous states include over 5,000 congregations and 500,000 members—40 percent of the U.S. membership.

Churches of Christ are completely autonomous, with no central governing authority. Centers of influence tend to be associated with Christian universities, periodicals, and area-wide lectureships.

Of the 19 colleges and universities associated with Churches of Christ, two are in Tennessee—Lipscomb University and Freed-Hardeman University. A self-perpetuating Board of Trustees governs each of the schools.

Approximately 75 periodicals are in publication. Two of the more widely circulated are housed in Nashville—*Gospel Advocate* and *21st Century Christian*. Individually- or family-owned commercial enterprises, these publications are not subject to any control by the churches except through influence or paid subscriptions.

Congregations and individual members of Churches of Christ support several service and outreach programs in Tennessee. These include a Federal Prison Ministry, 12 K-12 schools, 12 child and family service organizations, nine preacher training schools (non-accredited), nine campus ministries on state university campuses, and 12 camps (largely in summer) for teens.

Separatistic, Churches of Christ seldom participate in common causes with other religious groups. Of the two earliest goals of the Restoration Movement, the goal of unity of all believers has become subordinated to the goal of strict restoration—conforming to the New Testament in all congregational practices. Churches of Christ, however, accept much of mainstream historical orthodoxy as Biblical. Their view of human knowledge of God is that God reveals himself primarily in scripture, ultimately in Christ, but also in nature. The Bible is accepted as entirely trustworthy. They understand God in Trinitarian terms—as Father, Son, and Holy Spirit. They believe God created everything that exists *ex nihilo*. Evil entered the human experience through the fall of Adam and Eve; original (inherited) sin is not accepted. Jesus is understood to be both God and man; his death accomplished sacrificial atonement for all human beings who genuinely trust in him. The Christian hope is for eternal life in heaven; eternal punishment is a reality as well.

Their principal points of difference center on the doctrine of the church. Congregations use strictly *a cappella* music, members administer the Lord's Supper each Sunday, and they practice believer's baptism for the remission of sins as new converts are received into membership. Worship practices also include prayers, scripture-oriented sermons, and voluntary contributions of money. During the past decade congregations have experienced more diverse worship styles, particularly in hymnody. Worship assemblies vary from quite formal to very informal.

Historically marked by internal and external controversy, the Churches of Christ remain committed to their ideals. While some representatives have claimed these churches include the only known Christians, others insist that their commitment is to be "Christians only"—an ideal which reflects the original goals of unity (non-denominational) and restorationism (restoring primitive practices of the earliest churches).

Harold Hazelip, Lipscomb University

SEE: CAMPBELL, ALEXANDER, FREED-HARDEMAN UNIVERSITY; LIPSCOMB UNIVERSITY; RELIGION; STONE, BARTON

CISCO, JAY GUY (1844–1922), a distinguished journalist, historian, businessman, diplomat, and archaeologist, was born in New Orleans on April 25, 1844. After serving in the Confederate army during the Civil War, he traveled in Europe and worked briefly as a newspaperman. In January 1870 Cisco married Mildred George Pursley. The couple had eight children.

In 1875 Cisco settled his family in Jackson, Tennessee, and established Cisco's Bookstore. His discovery of ancient Native American relics in small mounds on Market Street and on a nearby farm awakened a passion for local archaeology. Throughout the 1880s, Cisco excavated many of Madison County's eleven mound sites and displayed relics in his small office museum.

Cisco is best known for his efforts as editor and historian. In 1883 he established and edited *The Forked Deer Blade*, a newspaper recognized for its breezy, excellent writing and vigorous editorial policies. His stand on many controversial topics, such as his support for prohibition, occasionally prompted Cisco to carry a gun for protection. Following appointment by President Grover Cleveland as U.S. Minister to Mexico in 1888, Cisco returned to Nashville, where he served as Assistant Industrial and Immigration Agent for Tennessee with the Louisville and Nashville Railroad. During this period, he established his reputation as a historian. His writings include "Madison County" for *The American Historical Magazine* (1902) and *Historic Sumner County, Tennessee* (1909). He died in Nashville in 1922.

Dee Gee Lester, Hendersonville
SEE: JACKSON; MADISON COUNTY; PUBLISHING

CITIZENS BANK (1904–), is the oldest, continuously operated African-American bank in the United States. In 1902 Richard H. Boyd, James C. Napier, and other Nashville African-American leaders formed a chapter of the National Negro Business League (NNBL) to promote black business interests. African Americans in Nashville had had no bank since the collapse of the Freedmen's Savings Bank and Trust Company (1865–1874), and European-American banks treated black customers with indifference and disdain. On November 5, 1903, nine executive committee members of the local NNBL met at attorney James C. Napier's office and agreed to establish a bank. A week later, seven others joined, and they founded the One Cent Savings Bank and Trust Company with $1,600 in capital. The One Cent Savings Bank opened on January 16, 1904, in the Napier Court Building at 411 North Cherry Street.

The principal founders and officers included such important Nashville leaders as Richard Henry Boyd (president), James C. Napier (cashier-manager), and Preston Taylor (chairman). C.N. Langston (teller), J.B.

Bosley, William Haynes, J.W. Grant, E.B. Jefferson, T.G. Ewing, and J.A. Cullom were other key officers and founders. The One Cent Bank helped finance African-American civil rights movements in 1906, when it served as the depository for the Defense Fund of the Afro American Council.

Citizens Bank survived the Great Depression, because Boyd and his successor operated the institution with efficiency and frugality. According to Boyd, bank stockholders understood "that this institution [the bank] was born out of necessity. It is not . . . a loan company, an investment and industrial insurance company, not a pawn shop, and the idea of 'getting rich quick' was never in the minds of the officers of this institution"—it was organized for the uplift of African Americans.[1] In 1920 One Cent Savings Bank's name changed to Citizens Savings Bank and Trust Company to give it a more populist appeal. In February 1922 Citizens Bank moved to the Colored YMCA building on Cedar Street. Seven years later, the *Journal of Negro History* and the Pittsburgh *Courier* paid tribute to Citizens Bank's 25 years of service. At its 1958 meeting, the National Bankers Association awarded an "Outstanding Certificate of Achievement" to Citizens Bank.

The bank's leadership remained stable after the deaths of R.H. Boyd, Napier, and Taylor. Henry A. Boyd served as president (1922–1959) and chairman (1931–1959); T.B. Boyd, Jr., chairman (1959–1979); and T.B. Boyd, III, chairman (1979–). Beginning in July 1959, Citizens Bank hired full-time presidents, including Meredith G. Ferguson, Richard Lewis, Henry Hill, Rick Davidson, and current president, Deborah Scott Ensley. Today, Citizens Bank operates a main branch on Jefferson Street, a branch on Monroe Street, and a headquarters and operations building on Heiman Street in Nashville.

Bobby L. Lovett, Tennessee State University
CITATION:
(1) Bobby L. Lovett and Linda T. Wynn, *Profiles of African Americans in Tennessee* (Nashville, 1996), 36–37.
SEE: BOYD; HENRY A.; BOYD, RICHARD H.; FREEDMEN'S SAVINGS BANK; NAPIER, JAMES C.; TAYLOR, PRESTON

CIVIL RIGHTS MOVEMENT. Like other states of the American South, Tennessee has a history of both slavery and racial segregation. In some ways, however, relationships between the races in the "Volunteer" state differed from the Deep South, resembling instead those of a border state. Although chattel slavery and the social attitude that undergirded it existed in Tennessee, slavery never achieved as much of a stranglehold upon the state as it did in most places of the American South. Indeed, some parts of Tennessee reflected a hostility toward the institution, and portions of the state objected strongly to participation in a Civil War in which slavery played a prominent role.

PHOTOGRAPH BY BILL PRESTON

John Lewis passes Krystal on Church Street in Nashville, 1960.

The bloody clash between North and South, nevertheless, did not alter most white Tennesseans' belief in the racial inferiority of African Americans, no matter where they lived. Even as a border state, however, Tennessee witnessed its share of occasional violence and brutality, even lynching and race riots; and the state could take little pride as the home of the Ku Klux Klan, founded in Pulaski, shortly after the war.

Following the Civil War, Tennessee moved quickly to reenter the Union and, consequently, race did not muddy the political waters as dramatically as it did in the other ten southern states that left the Union in 1860–61. Even though legal segregation of the races did not appear immediately after the war, established social customs and tightly fixed racial etiquette dictated private and public contact between blacks and whites. White Tennesseans expected blacks to "know their place" and to stay within prescribed political, social, and economic boundaries. The violation of custom by blacks carried the terrible risk of embarrassment, even possible bodily harm. Black Tennesseans briefly glimpsed the sight of freedom in the early years following the war, but the appearance of more conservative forces on the political horizon soon dashed their bright hopes for the future.

Near the end of the nineteenth century, white racial attitudes in Tennessee and the country hardened. Various legislatures framed laws not only to regulate race relations, but to control many aspects of the African-American community. "Jim Crow" had arrived! In 1896 the country gave legal sanction to segregation in the historic *Plessy v. Ferguson* decision that established the principle of "separate but equal." For nearly 60 years *Plessy* displayed remarkably enduring strength, producing in Tennessee and in America a decidedly separate, but unequal society. Blacks, however, did not quietly succumb to racial oppression, and for the next half century, they carried out both overt and covert attempts to defeat Jim Crow. Activists, such as newspaper publisher Ida Wells-Barnett of Memphis, and other local leaders fought for black civil rights. Black Tennesseans who were able to vote used the ballot as a weapon in their own behalf, often punishing those who ignored the interests of the black community. Unfortunately, restrictions on the franchise stifled progress within the black community and delayed democratic equality in the state.

The World War II period helped to fuel a powerful movement in Tennessee and in other parts of the United States that moved the country away from *Plessy* and the discrimination that usually accompanied it. Participation in that conflict acquainted Americans with the visible results of racial and religious bigotry, and the consequences for the country's national fiber. The performance of black soldiers, including thousands of Tennesseans, during the war, and the patriotic support of African Americans on the home front, argued well against an old system that kept racism alive and black persons second-class citizens.

Black Tennesseans contributed to the success of the war effort, and they also took part in the intellectual assault that led to the eventual demise of segregation. In Tennessee a number of public school teachers and college professors became involved with the Association for the Study of Negro Life and History that attempted to counter the effects of the shoddy scholarship that ignored black contributions to American history, or that deliberately misrepresented the race. No scholar in Tennessee played a more crucial role in helping to bring about reform in race relations than sociologist Charles S. Johnson of Fisk University. Johnson came to Fisk in 1927, established the Race Relations Institute in 1934, and became the University's president in 1937. He moved quietly but forcefully in his approach to the race problem. His research efforts and conferences, designed to bring blacks and whites together, had a meaningful impact on racial attitudes in Tennessee, and in other parts of America, where committed reformers worked for good race relations.

The new spirit generated by World War II and the efforts of scholars, such as Johnson, brought about some social changes in Tennessee before the mid-1950s. Although African Americans in the Volunteer state chipped away slowly at the edifice of Jim Crow, white attitudes changed slowly. Blacks waged a vigorous and persistent attack upon racial oppression through a number of self-help and protest organizations, including the National Association for the Advancement of Colored People (NAACP). The NAACP and a number of local groups worked to equalize teacher salaries, to abolish segregated public accommodations, and to invalidate the hated Tennessee poll tax, which restricted the black franchise in several parts of the state. Where blacks did have the ballot, they often used it wisely to exact gains from urban politicians in Nashville, Knoxville, and Chattanooga. In Memphis, blacks represented a powerful part of the political machine that controlled the city for many years. Their activity provided an argument *against* the poll tax, since opponents of the political leadership in Memphis during the era of Edward H. "Boss" Crump alleged that his political "machine" paid poll taxes for blacks and dictated their vote. Some Tennessee blacks found themselves at odds with members of their own race because of the close alliance between some Memphis blacks and Crump, who often flexed his muscle in statewide politics.

Segregation was a strong, resilient, social and political force. By the 1950s, Jim Crow remained intact, despite the new spirit that prevailed. Its death would come painfully, slowly. More than ever, black Tennesseans now questioned their mandated role in society. They sometimes walked off jobs or went on strike when treated unfairly in employment, challenged private citizens and municipalities in court for alleged wrongs, and pressured the state to abolish racially exclusive laws. The Supreme Court's decision in *Brown v. Board of Education of Topeka* (1954) further emboldened black Tennesseans, for it not only mandated desegregation of the public schools, but it also destroyed the props that gave support to racial segregation and discrimination in general. No other development in the social sphere threatened to create as much possible disruption as the case that turned *Plessy* upside down and abolished the legal principle of separate but equal.

Brown generated hostility among many white Tennesseans and other southerners, who visualized chaos within their land. To them the case meant not only desegregated schools, but also social integration throughout society; and increased social contact between the races on equal terms they believed, would lead inevitably to interracial courtship, even marriage between the races. A haunting fear gripped those who believed in the old order. To insist that young white children become pawns in a broad social experiment proved unacceptable to most white Tennesseans, who had never known anything other than a society guided by the *Plessy* decision. Federal court intervention, they said, had gone too far in the lives of the people, had exceeded constitutional limits by infringing upon the rights of the states, and in the process had threatened to sacrifice their children.

For Tennesseans, then, *Brown* represented more than a mere legal abstraction. Although the case disturbed most white citizens, they moved cautiously in their response to the decree. The city of Knoxville provided a good index to the attitudes of whites in the state at that time. A city of less than ten percent black population in 1954, some observers regarded Knoxville as the least racially sensitive of the state's largest cities. An opinion poll in 1958, however, revealed that 90 percent of white citizens strongly disapproved of desegregation. It showed further that not a single white person of the 167 polled would agree to enrolling even one white child in a black school; and nearly 72 percent would oppose sending a black child to a white school. Ninety-four percent of those polled opposed sexually and racially mixed classes. Such figures were a powerful commentary. Ironically, however, those whites who had defended *Plessy* as the law of the land now found themselves painted into a legal corner in a country that supposedly honored the rule of law.

For blacks, desegregation of the schools pointed toward progress in education, but *Brown* also brought some unexpected problems. Many black Tennesseans, including ones who had fought relentlessly to overthrow segregation and racism, had not pondered how thoroughly their lives had become culturally and economically interwoven with the African-American school. As an institution, only the family and the church were more central to black community life. Because of its social attractions and its many extracurricular activities, the black school served as a powerful agent for racial cohesiveness. Although many African Americans in Tennessee applauded the death of Jim Crow in education, they lamented the passing of special school activities that had once fostered a vital sense of community among them—athletic contests, choral renditions, dramatic productions, and other functions. Desegregation raised in an unexpected and striking manner not only educational questions, but cultural ones as well.

Despite white dissatisfaction with *Brown*, desegregation proceeded with less recalcitrance and violence than in most other states of the South. But violence was not totally foreign to the state, since public schools in Nashville and Clinton did experience damage to two of their schools from bomb blasts. In the case of Clinton, tensions remained high until Governor Frank G. Clement called out the National Guard to restore calm. Although most Tennessee localities, and the state government itself, connived at ways to slow desegregation, they faced a losing battle. Various plans to stall desegregation, or to delay implementation of court orders to achieve integration, ultimately failed when they confronted federal action, the resistance of the black community, and a state newspaper press that, by and large, encouraged obedience to the law.

Some citizens hoped that the institution of cross-town busing would offer a panacea for desegregation of the public schools, especially in urban areas of Tennessee. They were wrong. By the mid-1990s opposition to busing still remained strong, and some cities, such as Nashville, had begun to study other approaches to desegregation. Ironically, integration had made some of its most notable advances where persons had least suspected, and where hard-core racial attitudes had once prevailed—rural areas. Rural white children had ridden buses for long distances to school for many years, and the debate over busing took on a slightly different meaning in places where an entire surrounding area constituted a "neighborhood."

If desegregation of schools offered Tennessee a difficult challenge, so did direct-action protest techniques to abolish segregation in public facilities. Through the efforts of young black students, especially in Nashville at Tennessee State University, Fisk University, Meharry Medical College, and American Baptist Theological Seminary, the state would bequeath to the national civil rights campaign valuable lessons in protests, and would raise to prominence a number of young, notable black leaders. In Knoxville, African Americans and a small number of white protesters would also wage a determined campaign against public Jim Crow. As previously noted, before the mid-1950s black Tennesseans had already begun to use their institutions as vehicles to fight the forces of segregation. By the time of *Brown,* then, a social consciousness, anathema to inequality and the idea of black inferiority, existed in the state among African Americans. In the 1960s—during a period often alluded to as the "Movement" days of Civil Rights—black college students and their allies aided reform with an idealistic crusade that found segregation intolerable and public demonstrations a legitimate technique for battling societal wrongs.

The Nashville civil rights demonstrations stood out among the most noted sit-in activities in Tennessee. But in other cities of the state during the sixties and early seventies, indigenous black leadership contributed to the abolition of societal restraints that made democracy more real for many Tennesseans. Significantly, the movement in Nashville developed from a rather old political base and institutional arrangements that gave protest more of a possibility of success.

Sit-ins by African Americans, of course, predated the modern civil rights movement that followed *Brown.* In Nashville, they owed much of their success to effective leadership of the black clergy. Two persons in particular stand out in the history of protest in the city and the state—Kelly Miller Smith and James Lawson, although historians now realize that a much larger leadership base existed throughout Tennessee than was once known. Smith was the youthful pastor of First Baptist Church, Capitol Hill. A handsome, articulate, charismatic figure, he had a powerful appeal to both young and old. In early January 1958 Smith and other black activists organized the Nashville Christian Leadership Conference (NCLC), an affiliate of Martin Luther King, Jr.'s, Southern Christian Leadership Conference (SCLC), with which Smith himself already had affiliation. King, of course, was the acknowledged leader of the civil rights movement from the mid-1950s until his untimely death at Memphis April 4, 1968. The NCLC and SCLC had as their ultimate objective a frontal attack on the immorality of discrimination, and the unification of ministers and laymen in a common effort to bring about "reconciliation and love" in a racially just society.

James Lawson, another young clergyman, worked to hone the technique of non-violent resistance that finally triumphed in Nashville, other places in Tennessee, and the South. He had come South from Ohio to attend the Divinity School at Vanderbilt University. A serious student of non-violence who had spent time in India, Lawson began conducting workshops in 1958 at Smith's First Baptist Church. As he and Smith developed a strategy for social action through NCLC, they recognized that the city of Nashville could serve as an important laboratory for testing non-violent protest methods and as a model for other such activities. Lawson knew the power of grassroots movements and the vulnerability of a segregated society if participants willingly sacrificed and suffered to defeat the evil of injustice. When Vanderbilt University ordered Lawson to cease his activity or face suspension, he persevered, and the University dismissed him.

During the later part of 1959, the NCLC commenced its direct action campaign against downtown stores with two so-called "test" sit-ins. When whites-only establishments refused blacks service, youthful demonstrators left the facilities, after discussing with management the injustice of segregation and their denial of service. What these early public efforts demonstrated was the clear presence of discrimination in the city of Nashville. By January 1960 Smith, Lawson, and student protesters had decided to launch a full-scale, nonviolent attack against businesses that discriminated against blacks, if they did not voluntarily alter their policies. Before the students could act, however, other protesters in Greensboro, North Carolina, initiated sit-ins in that city, which precipitated demonstrations in other southern cities. Leaders of the Nashville movement now decided to move decisively. Led by Diane Nash, John Lewis, James Bevel, Cordell Reagon, Matthew Jones, and Bernard Lafayette, students from the city's black colleges began more intense sit-in activity that led, in May 1960, to the initial desegregation of some Nashville businesses. A number of factors accounted for their success. Undoubtedly the students' determined and courageous efforts played a pivotal role in tearing down restrictive racial barriers, but a highly effective economic boycott of downtown Nashville stores by the black community also had a measurable impact. The attitude of the city's mayor, Ben West, who openly acknowledged that the immorality of discrimination helped to create a more moderate climate following violence against the students and some other black citizens.

Other cities in Tennessee also struggled with changes on the civil rights front in the 1960s and 1970s. Indigenous leadership in Knoxville produced considerable civil rights activity in that East Tennessee city. Protests there came after black citizens failed to negotiate successfully the end to segregated public facilities. Led by students at Knoxville College and a white minister at that institution, Merrill Proudfoot, the movement set out to change laws and customs in a city that prided itself on "healthy" race relations. A broad-based movement, the Knoxville campaign drew support from a large number of African Americans who lived in the city, a sizable number of white moderates, and city officials willing to listen and act with reasonable restraint. Following the initiation of sit-ins in June 1960, white city leaders and politicians of Knoxville convinced businessmen to desegregate by mid-July.

The courageous acts of young black demonstrators and their supporters united the black community in Tennessee and challenged the consciences of those whites who casually—sometimes unthinkingly—accepted the laws and customs of contemporary society. The African Americans of Tennessee made an important contribution to the reform tradition in America by assisting the birth of a powerful social movement that changed the country, giving truth to the Declaration of Independence and the Constitution of the United States, and supporting the faith in individual growth and progress that so many other persons had sought in Tennessee. Tennesseans did much to foster the idea of non-violent protests during the era of Martin Luther King; and how ironic it was that the movement era came to an end with the assassination of King in April 1968, when James Earl Ray's bullet ripped through his body.

The four decades since *Brown* produced measurable progress in black civil rights in Tennessee and the nation. The country saw the passage of a civil rights bill, a voting rights act, and housing legislation, and the federal government instituted a number of social programs designed to redress past grievances. In 1952 the courts had forced the state to admit its first blacks to its graduate, professional, and special schools. Nine years later, the University of Tennessee admitted undergraduates to its Knoxville campus, although six blacks were already matriculating at the institution's Nashville campus, which under court order later became part of previously all-black Tennessee State University. By 1965 the state could announce that all seven of its institutions of higher learning had technically integrated and that color was not a precondition for admittance. High school graduation rates, too, were encouraging. At the time of the first major sit-in in Tennessee, less than nine percent of African Americans had finished high school, but by the mid-1990s that figure exceeded 40 percent.

Strides in the political arena also proved impressive. In 1964 Tennessee elected its first black state legislator since the late nineteenth century, A. W. Willis, Jr.; two years later the first African-American woman, Dr. Dorothy Brown, earned a seat in that body. By 1993, 12 African Americans sat in the legislature, and a total of 168 blacks served in various political positions in a state where 16 percent of its citizens were African-American. In January 1992 black votes in Memphis helped to catapult into the office the city's first black mayor, Willie W. Herenton. In the fast-growing metropolis of Nashville, an African American, Emmet Turner, earned the right to head the Metropolitan Police force in 1996.

In recent years, however, disturbing signs have appeared on the civil rights horizon. Despite recognizable progress, overcoming the past effects of discrimination and the achievement of full rights of citizenship remained a daunting task for African Americans. A number of programs designed to aid blacks, such as affirmative action, faced biting criticism in the mid-1990s. Notable discrepancies still existed between black and white incomes, and the federal courts threatened to dilute the effect of black political power with some of its decisions. In 1996 the unexplained burning of a number of black churches in Tennessee, and other southern states, reflected the continuing bigotry of some die-hard reactionaries who wanted to turn back the civil rights clock. As late as July 1996, the United States Commission on Civil Rights noted that Tennessee was sitting on "powder kegs" of tensions, which could ignite into violence.

The Civil Rights Commission did not misread the times. But it may not have accounted for the considerable number of blacks and whites who wanted to create a better Tennessee, citizens who had the determination to fight the racial conservatism that threatened to damage the state and its reputation. Opinion polls bore out the contention that most Tennesseans did not want to overturn the fundamental changes made since *Brown*, or to return to the ugly days of harsh segregation. But it was hard for many of them to make the personal or political sacrifices necessary to adjust the wrongs of the past. Yet, a desegregated, pluralist society remained a healthy ideal for most Tennesseans, especially for the younger ones born in the post-*Brown* era. In the words of one hopeful native, who had lived through the era of segregation, the state had moved "too far to turn back." That optimism, more than anything else, characterized the spirit of the African-American community at the time of the state's Bicentennial. It also registered the hope of more than a few white Tennesseans of good will, who had come to decipher the real meaning of democracy, justice, and fair play.

Jimmie Lewis Franklin, Vanderbilt University

SUGGESTED READINGS: No full-scale study exists on the Civil Rights Movement in Tennessee. The following works, however, will give the reader an appreciation for what took place in the state of Tennessee. Cynthia G. Fleming, "We Shall Overcome: Tennessee and the Civil Rights Movement," *Tennessee Historical Quarterly*, 54(1995): 232–245; Hugh D. Graham, *Crisis in Print: Desegregation and the Press in Tennessee* (1967); Lester C. Lamon, *Black Tennesseans, 1900–1930* (1977); Merrill Proudfoot, *Diary of a Sit-in* (1990); Linda T. Wynn, "The Dawning of a New Day: The Nashville Sit-Ins, February 13–May 10, 1960," *Tennessee Historical Quarterly*, 50(1991): 42–54

CIVIL WAR. In 1861, as the nation divided, so did Tennessee. In the state's three grand divisions, Confederates and Unionists fought their own political war to determine which way Tennessee would go as the Confederate States of America took form in neighboring Alabama. West Tennesseans, led by Governor Isham G. Harris, overwhelmingly wished connection with the Confederacy, while in East Tennessee most residents remained fervidly loyal to the Union. In the state's middle section, the counties in the Central Basin leaned heavily toward secession, but those on the basin's rim were more ambiguous in their support, leading to divided communities and divided families and preparing the way for a vicious neighbor-against-neighbor guerrilla conflict when the Civil War commenced.

In 1861 Governor Harris summoned the legislature into a special session to consider secession. To obtain a better view of the voters' sentiments, the legislature called for a February referendum to decide whether a secession convention should be held. At this point, the secession fever that had gripped the Deep South remained much more muted in Tennessee and the other border states. By a vote of 69,000 to 58,000, a majority of Tennesseans rejected the call for a secession convention, with West Tennessee supporting the convention, East Tennessee rejecting it overwhelmingly, and Middle Tennessee almost equally divided. Secessionists continued to agitate, and Franklin countians even threatened to secede from the state and join Alabama.

The firing on Fort Sumter in April, and President Lincoln's subsequent call for 75,000 state militiamen to put down the southern rebellion, forced many residents to re-evaluate their secession stand. Even many of those who had been staunch Unionists in February could not abide the use of force against fellow southerners. Yet others, seeing the swelling secession tide, began to contemplate taking their counties—or even all of East Tennessee—out of the state in order to remain part of the Union.

In May, seizing the new momentum, Governor Harris and the legislature declared the state's independence, made a military alliance with the Confederacy, and began raising an army to defend the state from Union invasion. To validate their actions, the legislators called another referendum for June 8. On that date, approximately 105,000 Tennesseans voted for secession, while only 47,000 voted against, but East Tennesseans voted more than two-to-one (33,000 to 14,000) to stay with the Union, indicating an enormous anti-secession and anti-Confederacy pocket east of the Cumberland Plateau. Even as the state proceeded to join the Confederacy, Scott County announced that it was declaring independence from the state, and delegates from several East Tennessee counties met in Greeneville to draw up a petition to the legislature to allow East Tennessee to form a separate state. Secessionists viewed these county and regional secessionists as traitors and soon sent the state army to "occupy" the hostile counties.

For Confederates, the summer and autumn of 1861 were times of celebration and optimism. Young men rushed to join the army units forming in their counties and towns. The soldiers elected their company officers and, after being feted and cheered by their neighbors and families, set off to Confederate training camps such as Camp Trousdale in Sumner County. For Union sympathizers, the same months brought harassment from local Confederates, arrests, and violence. Many Union men fled the state to Kentucky and other points north, where hundreds enlisted in the armies forming to invade the South. Ultimately, some 31,000 Tennesseans joined the Federal forces, constituting more soldiers than all the other Confederate states together provided to the Union side.

In September 1861 General Albert Sidney Johnston arrived to take charge of Tennessee's defenses. Governor Harris had already ordered the construction of forts to guard the Mississippi River, but Johnston saw the Tennessee and Cumberland rivers as more likely routes for Union troops. Johnston accelerated work on Fort Henry on the Tennessee and Fort Donelson on the Cumberland and built a defensive front that ran from the Cumberland Gap in the east along a rather ill-defined line through southern Kentucky to Bowling Green and on to Columbus, Kentucky, on the Mississippi River. Johnston himself took up headquarters in Bowling Green.

The first crack in the line came on January 19, 1862, at the Battle of Mill Springs (or Fishing Creek) near Somerset, Kentucky. There a Union army commanded by General George H. Thomas defeated a Confederate force under Generals George Crittenden and Felix Zollicoffer. Thomas compelled the Confederates to abandon their eastern defenses and retreat into Middle Tennessee.

To the west, a combined Union army and navy force under General Ulysses S. Grant's command assaulted Fort Henry on the Tennessee River. Poorly designed and unfinished, the fort quickly fell after a barrage of cannon shells by the Union gunboats on February 6. Grant then marched his army overland to Fort Donelson, 12 miles to the east, and laid siege to it as gunboats came up the Cumberland to attack the fort from the other side. On February 16, after a vigorous, but confused, defense of the fort, the Confederates surrendered the fort and some 13,000 soldiers. In less than two weeks, the Confederate defensive line had collapsed, the Tennessee and Cumberland rivers were under Union control, and Nashville lay at the mercy of the Union armies. On February 23, Union troops entered Nashville, making it the first Confederate state capital to fall.

Having retreated from Bowling Green to Murfreesboro, General Johnston and what was left of his army continued southward to Corinth, Mississippi. There Johnston and his second-in-command, General P.G.T. Beauregard, reorganized and called upon fellow Confederates for reinforcements and supplies. Meanwhile, Grant's army was encamped on the Tennessee River near Pittsburg Landing, waiting for another union force under General Don Carlos Buell to join it. Hoping to surprise the overly-complacent foe, Johnston and Beauregard decided to march back into Tennessee and strike before the two Union armies combined.

On April 6, 1862, Johnston's rebels smashed into Grant's soldiers near Shiloh Church, beginning the bloodiest battle yet fought on North American soil. At the end of the day, Confederates had driven the Federals almost into the Tennessee River, but among the many dead was Albert Sidney Johnston himself. During the night Grant regrouped his forces and welcomed the units arriving from Buell's army. On April 7, the Union soldiers took the offensive and reversed the battle's flow. Beauregard's defeated army retreated once more into Mississippi.

The Shiloh victory not only solidified the Union hold on Middle Tennessee, but made the Confederate control of West Tennessee extremely tenuous. Memphis, the temporary home of the state government after Nashville's fall, became even more vulnerable as the Union gunboats attacked and seized the river forts to the north. On June 6, after defeating the Confederate fleet protecting the city, Union forces took Memphis, forcing Governor Harris and state officials to flee once again.

Regrouping in the spring and summer, Confederates in Mississippi created the Army of Tennessee and placed General Braxton Bragg in command. Bragg and the East Tennessee commander, Kirby Smith, decided to launch a northern campaign by their two armies, which, if successful, would regain Tennessee and bring Kentucky into the Confederacy. Screened by cavalry raids into Middle Tennessee led by Nathan Bedford Forrest and John Hunt Morgan, Bragg moved his forces to Chattanooga. In August, General Kirby Smith left Knoxville for Kentucky by way of the Cumberland Gap, while Bragg took the Army of Tennessee through Carthage and Gainesboro to central Kentucky. In October, the Kentucky campaign ended in failure after the Battle of Perryville. Unable to elicit much support from Kentuckians, Bragg's army retreated into East Tennessee and then moved westward to Murfreesboro. Union forces, now under General William Rosecrans, consolidated at Nashville.

In December, Forrest's cavalry launched spectacular raids into West Tennessee, defeating Union cavalry units and taking garrisons at Trenton, Dyer, Union City, and several other towns. Meanwhile, the Union Army of the Cumberland, under the command of General William S. Rosecrans, left Nashville to engage the Army of Tennessee to the southeast. On December 31, Bragg's forces made a surprise attack on Rosecrans' army, initiating the Battle of Stones River. After a lull on January 1, the battle resumed the next day, ending with the repulsion of the Confederate attack. Unable to achieve a victory, Bragg abandoned Murfreesboro and retreated toward Tullahoma to enter winter quarters.

In June 1863 Rosecrans resumed his campaign against the Army of Tennessee. In a series of flanking maneuvers, his Union army forced Bragg to abandon Tullahoma and retreat toward Chattanooga. By July 7, Bragg had entered the city itself, leaving most of Middle Tennessee under Union occupation. In August General Ambrose Burnside completed a pincers movement against the Confederates and descended from Kentucky into East Tennessee with his Army of the Ohio to capture Knoxville and bring deliverance to the East Tennessee Unionists. The Confederates abandoned Knoxville, and in early September Burnside's soldiers entered the city to the welcome of cheering crowds.

On September 8, the outflanked Army of Tennessee evacuated Chattanooga and pulled back into northern Georgia. Here Bragg regrouped and began to receive reinforcements from other Confederate commands, including General James Longstreet's troops from Robert E. Lee's command in Virginia. On September 19, about 12 miles south of Chattanooga, the Battle of Chickamauga erupted as the Confederates attacked Rosecrans' forces. On the battle's second day, General James Longstreet's soldiers broke through on the Union right, causing a large portion of Rosecrans' army—including the general—to retreat in panic to Chattanooga. Only valiant resistance from the troops of George H. Thomas kept this from being a Union disaster. With the Union army once more in Chattanooga, Bragg decided that the best plan was to seal it off and starve it into submission. By early October, soldiers and civilians alike in Chattanooga suffered from food shortages.

To avoid disaster, President Lincoln named Ulysses S. Grant the overall commander in the region. General Thomas, the "Rock of Chickamauga," replaced Rosecrans as commander of the Chattanooga army. Acting swiftly, Grant sent reinforcements to the beleaguered city and forced open a new supply line. When he arrived in Chattanooga, he laid plans to assault the Confederates occupying Missionary Ridge and Lookout Mountain. Meanwhile, Bragg quarreled with his generals and weakened his position even more by sending Longstreet and about one third of the army on an expedition to retake Knoxville.

On November 23–25, Grant's forces struck Bragg's army. First, the Union army took control of Lookout Mountain in the famous "Battle Above the Clouds." On November 25, Thomas's troops attacked the middle of the Confederate line on Missionary Ridge, routed the defenders, and sent them reeling back into Georgia. Bragg's siege collapsed, and the Army of Tennessee straggled in defeat all the way to Dalton. Longstreet's attack on Knoxville fared no better. On November 29, he launched an assault against Fort Sanders, the city's northwestern bastion. In just 20 minutes, Longstreet's units suffered over 800 casualties, while the fort withstood the attack and lost only 13 men. The Confederates soon withdrew to Russellville, made winter headquarters, and the following spring returned to Virginia. All of Tennessee was technically under Union control.

In 1864 the main action in the western theater shifted to Georgia, but the war's hardships and violence in Tennessee became more widespread. Dozens of Confederate guerrilla bands, which had arisen earlier in West and Middle Tennessee to belabor Union patrols and harass Unionist civilians, continued to operate. Nathan Bedford Forrest and other Confederate cavalry commanders attacked Union garrisons, disrupted railroad operations, destroyed or confiscated supplies, and took hundreds of prisoners.

Civilian woes continued to increase. In many counties, government collapsed, and institutions such as churches and schools ceased operations. As law and order declined, outlaw bands formed and terrorized communities, stealing livestock and food, burning houses, and murdering their owners. With ordinary commerce disrupted, commodities such as flour, sugar, salt, and coffee became so difficult to obtain that people searched for substitutes. Honey and sorghum molasses replaced sugar, while ground-up okra seeds and dried sassafras made do for coffee.

In Nashville and Memphis, authorities had to cope with an influx of new residents, including numerous prostitutes, thieves, and gamblers. Andrew Johnson, former U.S. Senator, now the Military Governor of Tennessee, relied more on the Union army to keep the peace than on Nashville's pro-Confederate government. To suppress Confederate support, Johnson ultimately locked up the mayor and city council, closed four newspapers, and shut down the presses of the Methodist and Baptist churches.

A major impact of the Union occupation of the state was the de facto end of slavery. Thousands of blacks fled plantations and farms and made for the Union army camps. In August 1862 General Grant ordered the building of camps for the refugees, known as contraband camps, and by 1864 Clarksville, Pulaski, Hendersonville, and several other Tennessee cities had facilities where fugitives from slavery received shelter, army rations, clothing, medicines, and jobs. In Nashville, some 2,700 black laborers, for example, helped build Fort Negley and other facilities to protect the city. Thousands more worked on similar projects around Memphis. In 1863 those who wished to fight for the Union were allowed to enlist in the army and navy. Of the 179,000 African Americans who fought for the United States in the war, some 20,000 came from Tennessee.

In September 1864 General William T. Sherman's Union army forced the Army of Tennessee to abandon Atlanta. In desperation, its commander, John Bell Hood, devised a grandiose plan to invade Tennessee, take Nashville, and conquer Kentucky, before passing through the mountains to relieve Robert E. Lee's besieged army in Virginia. Rather than follow Hood, Sherman dispatched George H. Thomas to Nashville to await Hood with an army of 60,000 soldiers, nearly twice the size of Hood's army.

The Army of Tennessee's flanking maneuvers at Pulaski and Columbia against General John Schofield's smaller Union force compelled the Union soldiers to withdraw toward Nashville. At Spring Hill, the Confederates almost trapped their enemy before miscommunications among the Confederate commanders allowed Schofield to escape to Franklin. An irate Hood ordered an ill-advised and ill-conceived attack on Schofield's entrenched forces. In the Battle of Franklin on November 30, the Army of Tennessee suffered some 6,300 casualties including 12 generals (six killed) and 54 regimental commanders. During the night, Schofield withdrew to Nashville to join Thomas's larger force, while Hood's army—too weak to threaten Nashville and too damaged to retreat—could do no more than follow and take up defensive positions south of the city.

The last major Civil War battle in Tennessee began on December 15, 1864, when Thomas's army smashed into Hood's Confederates in the Battle of Nashville. On the following day, Thomas resumed his attack, and the out-manned Confederates finally broke and retreated. The remnants of the once-proud Army of Tennessee did not stop until they had reached Mississippi. Although sporadic cavalry raids and guerrilla attacks would continue until the spring of 1865, for all meaningful purposes, the war had ended in Tennessee.

The war left much of Middle Tennessee in ruins, with the other two sections bearing deep scars as well, but it also brought enormous changes. Many Tennessee women, for example, assumed new roles. They ran plantations and farms, managed businesses, served as nurses, and spied on the enemy. The war ended slavery, and with its demise came a new era of race relations and a future for the state's African Americans that contained much uncertainty and hardship. Economically, it would take the state years to achieve the level of prosperity that it had enjoyed before the war. Tennessee had sent over 120,000 soldiers to fight for the Confederacy and over 31,000 to aid the Union and had had more battles fought within its borders than any other state except Virginia. Civilian violence had taken a heavy toll as well. Families across the state had lost husbands, fathers, and sons. Nothing before and nothing afterwards would have such an impact on the state as did the Civil War.

Larry H. Whiteaker, Tennessee Technological University

SUGGESTED READINGS: Stephen V. Ash, *Middle Tennessee Society Transformed, 1860–1870: War and Peace in the Upper South* (1988); Thomas L. Connelly, *Civil War Tennessee: Battles and Leaders* (1979); Thomas L. Connelly, *Army of the Heartland: The Army of Tennessee, 1861–1862* (1967); James M. McPherson, *Battle Cry of Freedom: The Civil War Era* (1988); Digby G. Seymour, *Divided Loyalties: Fort Sanders and the Civil War in East Tennessee* (1982)

CIVILIAN CONSERVATION CORPS (CCC). On March 31, 1933, President Franklin D. Roosevelt signed legislation to create the Civilian Conservation Corps, the first of the New Deal agencies. The CCC employed young men and gave them an opportunity to develop new skills and prepare them for future employment as the nation recovered from the Great Depression.

Originally established as the "Emergency Conservation Work Program," the CCC was renamed in 1937. In the absence of official records, estimates of the number of young men who participated in the nine-year program reach approximately three million. Congress extended the program to include African Americans, Native Americans, and World War I veterans. Enrollees performed a variety of conservation activities, including reforestation, soil conservation, road construction, flood and fire control, and agricultural management. The CCC also completed a number of tasks associated with the development

Company 1473, Camp Evan Shelby, Bristol, 1930s.

and construction of state and national parks. The CCC provided food, clothing, and shelter, as well as education, vocational training, and health care. The Department of Labor, the War Department, and the Department of the Interior administered the CCC; state and local labor offices assisted with selection and enrollment procedures.

The CCC's Fourth Corps area, District C, included Tennessee plus western North Carolina, northern Georgia, Alabama, and Mississippi. Organized on April 25, 1933, District C fielded 40 companies, including three "Veteran White," one "Veteran Colored," two "Junior Colored," and 34 "Junior White" camps. Tennessee supported 11 district headquarters located in Memphis, Union City, Jackson, Paris, Columbia, Nashville, Tullahoma, Cookeville, Chattanooga, Knoxville, and Johnson City; and 15 branch offices located in Dyersburg, Murfreesboro, McMinnville, Shelbyville, Clarksville, Springfield, Cleveland, LaFollette, Maryville, Loudon, Rockwood, Morristown, Elizabethton, Kingsport, and Bristol. The state's first CCC company set up headquarters at Camp Cordell Hull near Limestone Cave in Unicoi County in 1933. By the following year, Tennessee sponsored 30 companies.

Enrollment was offered to single men between the ages of 17 and 28; however, reinstitution in 1937 limited enrollment to men between the ages of 17 and 23. Applicants had to prove their marital status, exhibit evidence that they had been unable to find employment for at least two months, and that their families could not provide education or training comparable to that made available to members of the corps. Enrollees signed up for a minimum of six months and few members participated for more than one or two years. The state's motto, "select, rather than collect," reflected the high honor associated with participation in the CCC. Tennessee's CCC boys earned $30 per month, $25 of which went to families or was deposited with the War Department until the corps member received his "honorable discharge."

Tennessee's total number of CCC companies reached its peak in July 1937, when the state supported 46 camps. By the time the CCC disbanded, more than 70,000 Tennesseans had served. In 1942 changing American ideas about the CCC and Congressional pressure to end the program resulted in the agency's dissolution. In Tennessee, the CCC completed work in 17 state parks and the Great Smoky Mountains National Park. The national success of the CCC is directly attributed to Roosevelt, who seldom compromised his values concerning the need for a national conservation movement.
Ruth Nichols, Nashville

SUGGESTED READING: John A. Salmond, *The Civilian Conservation Corps, 1933–1942* (1967)

SEE: APPALACHIAN TRAIL; CHEROKEE NATIONAL FOREST; GREAT SMOKY MOUNTAINS NATIONAL PARK; INDIVIDUAL STATE PARK HISTORIES

CLAIBORNE COUNTY was formed in 1801 by the Fourth General Assembly, from parts of Grainger and Hawkins counties and named for William C.C. Claiborne, Tennessee's first congressional representative. The most important historic feature of Claiborne County is the Cumberland Gap, located south of the convergence of Tennessee, Virginia, and Kentucky. Native Americans used this natural gateway to the north and west as the Warrior's Path. In 1750 Dr. Thomas Walker claimed discovery of the gap and named it Cumberland Gap in honor of William Augustus, Duke of Cumberland, the son of King George II and Queen Caroline. In 1775 Daniel Boone led 30 men through the gap and opened a road west to settlement.

The first settlement occurred in the Powell Valley along the Clinch River. Shortly afterwards settlements were began along Sycamore Creek and Fort Butler. In 1801 the town of Tazewell was laid out as the county seat of Claiborne County. The town received a post office in 1804, and James Graham served as the first postmaster. The county court met three times in the homes of John Hunt and Elisha Walling, before a small frame courthouse was erected in 1804 on land belonging to John Hunt, Sr., probably the first settler in the area and the first sheriff of Claiborne County. A jail was constructed at the same time as the courthouse, and a second jail was built in 1819. Luke Bower, one of the first Watauga settlers, was the first attorney in Claiborne County. The first merchant was William Graham, a native of Ireland. Graham had extensive real estate holdings and circa 1800, he completed a stone residence known as the Graham-Kivett house. Other historic buildings include the Parkey house, also thought to have been built by Graham, which was used as a hospital during the Civil War and survived the great fire of 1862. A frontier church at Springdale on Little Sycamore Creek was erected by Drew Harrell and the Reverend Tidence Lane sometime around 1796.

Tazewell did not have a church building until 1815, but settlers probably worshiped in open-air assemblies and in homes prior to that time. William Graham, a Presbyterian, erected the first church building, which was probably used by all denominations. In 1844 the Baptists and Methodists both erected buildings on Russell and Church streets respectively.

Children of the early Tazewell settlers received no formal education until Walter Evans opened a small school in 1822, although a few Tazewell children attended a school opened at Yoakum's Station in the Powell Valley in 1820. Michael Miles, the teacher at Yoakum Station, and Evans collaborated in the writing of text books. In 1835 a boys' academy opened in Tazewell near the town spring, but the Tazewell Female Academy was not organized until 1854. In 1856 Tazewell Academy was raised to the rank of college.

Claiborne County and the Cumberland Gap figured prominently in the Civil War strategy of both the North and the South, changing hands four times. Today, traces of the old military road that connected battlements on the pinnacle above Cumberland Gap can be discerned. Battery No. 6 still remains at the tri-state peak facing Cumberland Gap. Rifle pits dug around most batteries can be located with little difficulty. Although no major battles were fought in the county, there were several bloody skirmishes. On November 11, 1862, a fire broke out in Tazewell and destroyed some 20 buildings, including the courthouse, a large hotel, and several businesses.

On February 12, 1897, the State of Tennessee chartered Lincoln Memorial University, named for Abraham Lincoln, who had urged O.O. Howard of the Freedmen's Bureau to do something for the people of the area. Howard accepted Lincoln's charge and played an important role in the creation of the institution. The university proved a boon for tri-state area residents, who could not afford college tuition but were able to work their way through LMU by working on the college farm. Today, LMU rents the farm for pasture. The 1,000-acre campus, which presently serves 2,000 students, incorporates traditional architecture and modern technology. The Abraham Lincoln Museum, which holds one of the largest Lincoln collections, is located on the campus.

Today, Claiborne County consists of 277,963 acres. Its population grew from 13,373 in 1880 to 23,286 by 1920. The rapid growth was attributed to intensive mining developments and logging operations. By 1950 the population had increased to 24,788, but over the next decade, Claiborne County began to experience out-migration as people left the area for industrial employment in the Midwest. The population dropped to 19,067 in 1960, before beginning a slow rise that boomed in the 1980s and 1990s. The 1996 population was estimated at 28,542.

Today, Claiborne County has a mixed economy, with a growing industrial sector. Agriculturally, the county farmers produce tobacco and vegetables. The largest industrial employer in the county is England Upholstery Manufacturing Company. Other furniture manufacturers in the county include Brooks Furniture Manufacturing, Bushline, Inc., and Oakwood Furniture Manufacturing. Four textile manufacturers, two pre-built and mobile home manufacturers, and a large medical supply manufacturer (DeRoyal Industries, Inc.) keep the county's unemployment rate low. The 1996 opening of the Cumberland Gap Tunnel on U.S. Highway 25W, a model of transportation planning, promises to further enhance the economic outlook of the county in the twenty-first century.

John J. Kivett, Tazewell

SEE: BOONE, DANIEL; CUMBERLAND GAP AND CUMBERLAND GAP NATIONAL HISTORICAL PARK; LINCOLN MEMORIAL UNIVERSITY; MINING; WALKER, THOMAS

CLARK, ED (1911–), internationally recognized *Life* photographer, was born in Nashville in 1911. Clark dropped out of Hume-Fogg High School to pursue an early interest in photography and work as a photographer's assistant at the Nashville *Tennessean*. For 13 years he served as staff photographer, photographing such events as the Shelbyville Riot of 1934, which destroyed the local courthouse.

Clark's work attracted the attention of the new picture-oriented magazine, *Life*, and in 1936 he began working for the publication as a stringer. A Tennessee photo opportunity came his way in 1942, when Sergeant Alvin York, famed World War I hero, registered for the "old man's draft" in Pall Mall. Clark's photo of York so impressed *Life* editors that they invited him to New York and hired him as a staff photographer. During World War II, Clark covered the home front and later served as a correspondent in postwar Europe, covering the Nüremberg Trials.

Clark's photographic exposés captured the prosperity and change of postwar America. The best known Clark image is that of a grieving Graham W. Jackson playing *Goin' Home* on his accordion in honor of President Franklin Roosevelt's funeral procession in 1945. His 1946 image, *The Harvest That Saved the World*, portrayed the abundant fields of the Midwest. A series of 1948 photographs brought attention to the West Memphis School District in Arkansas and led to construction of a new building for African-American students.

In the 1950s and early 1960s, Clark's work took him from Washington to Hollywood and around the world. He photographed Presidents Franklin Roosevelt, Harry Truman, Dwight Eisenhower, John Kennedy, Lyndon Johnson, and Richard Nixon, and such Hollywood celebrities as Marilyn Monroe, Humphrey Bogart, and Clark Gable. In 1955 an unexpected invitation to Russia gave him the distinction of being the first Western photographer in the Soviet state in 30 years.

Retrospective shows in Birmingham, Nashville, Jackson, Mississippi, and New York showcased his 30 years of work. Clark now lives in Sarasota, Florida.

Anne-Leslie Owens, Tennessee Historical Society

SUGGESTED READING: Frank Herrera, *Ed Clark; Decades: A Photographic Retrospective, 1930–1960* (1992)

SEE: NASHVILLE TENNESSEAN

CLARK, SAM LILLARD (1898–1960), nationally known anatomist, scientist, and educator, was born in Nashville on October 5, 1898, a son of Martin and Margaret Ransom Lillard Clark. His grandfather, Dr. William Martin Clark, was a founder and owner at one time of the Nashville *Banner*.

Clark was educated in Nashville's public schools. He received the B.A. degree from Vanderbilt University in 1922, the M.S. degree in anatomy from Northwestern University, and the Ph.D. degree in anatomy from Washington University in St. Louis. In 1930 he was awarded the Doctor of Medicine degree from Vanderbilt.

Clark served as assistant professor of anatomy at Washington University and later at Northwestern University. In 1930 he was appointed to the faculty of Vanderbilt University School of Medicine; by 1937 Clark was full professor and chairman of the department of anatomy. His interpretation of anatomy permitted a breadth of interest in his department that encompassed almost the entire scope of medicine. He attracted to his laboratories not only the first-year student but advanced scholars and clinicians as well. Throughout his academic career, he was an active investigator and contributor to the literature of his specialty of anatomy and to broader fields. In promoting research he was interested in the cultivation of individual capabilities as well as in the solving of problems; he used research effectively as a means of teaching. He had a particular interest in neuroanatomy. Many of his own inquiries concerned morphological aspects of neuroanatomy, but perhaps the most significant ones were experimental and involved physiological phenomena, usually related to the central nervous system. His thoughtful and scholarly "On Becoming an Anatomist" and "Life Within the Brain" are of interest to many in academic medicine.

Clark was highly respected as a scientist. He served as president of the American Association of Anatomists and was editor of the *American Journal of Anatomy*. He revised and co-edited *Anatomy of the Nervous System*, the standard textbook used in most if not all American medical schools of his time. For many years Clark was an influential member of the medical fellowship committee of the National Research Council and later an advisor to the National Science Foundation, the American Cancer Society, the National Multiple Sclerosis Society, and the National Board of Medical Examiners. He served as a member of the overseers committee for the medical and dental schools of Harvard University.

A consummate gentleman, Clark brought distinction to Vanderbilt Medical School as a teacher, researcher, lecturer, and writer on his specialty and as an administrator. He established there a diagnostic electroencephalographic laboratory. For ten years Clark served as chairman of the admissions committee for the Medical School. From 1945 to 1950 he was associate dean of the Medical School and in June 1958 was named acting dean until the appointment of a permanent successor. He was a director of the Bill Wilkerson Hearing and Speech Center and served many years as a member of the state anatomical board.

The distinguished scientist Ernest Goodpasture had this to say about Clark: "Traditionally, it is given to the Department of Anatomy of most Medical Schools to introduce the new-coming students not only to the texture of bones and muscle, organs and tissues, but to medical education and to the profession of Medicine as a whole, that is, to medical culture. This is a difficult and unique assignment . . . . Professor Clark initiated his students into Anatomy and interpreted Medicine to them with an elegance that left an inspiring impression on several hundred of those who entered the first year class at Vanderbilt Medical School during the years of his departmental administration."[1]

Clark was married September 4, 1924, to the former Nettie Lee Petrie. She died in 1941. They had two daughters and two sons, the latter both physicians. Clark died on July 1, 1960, of lung cancer.

Harris D. Riley, Jr., Vanderbilt University Medical Center
CITATION:
(1) *Vanderbilt University, Inside the Medical Center,* 1 (No. 2, 1960): 1.

SEE: MEDICINE; VANDERBILT UNIVERSITY MEDICAL CENTER

CLARKSVILLE, the county seat of Montgomery County, is the state's fifth largest city, with a population of 89,246, and is the second oldest municipality in Middle Tennessee, established in 1784 by the North Carolina legislature as the seat of Tennessee County. Named for the Revolutionary war hero, George Rogers Clark, the town was part of a reservation set aside by North Carolina to compensate its Revolutionary War soldiers.

Clarksville grew rapidly because of the navigable Cumberland River and the rich Highland Rim soil that produced the acclaimed dark-fired tobacco. In 1788 the town was designated a tobacco inspection point to help insure the quality of tobacco shipped to market. Consequently, the river town became an important trade center for its agricultural hinterland.

Following statehood in 1796, the fortunes of Clarksville improved with the rest of Middle Tennessee. The Clarksville *Chronicle* was established in 1808, and a local resident, Willie Blount, was elected governor a year later. The Transportation and Market Revolutions of 1815–1860 brought profound change to the nation and to Clarksville. In 1820 the steamboat first appeared at Clarksville, eventually turning the Cumberland and other navigable rivers into two-lane river highways, lowering transportation time and costs while vastly expanding the tonnage shipped. This promoted the building of more and better roads, extending Clarksville's economic pull further into the countryside. Cave Johnson, a Democratic U.S. Congressman, and Gustavus A. Henry, the local Whig Party leader, characterized the town's vigorous political contests of this era.

Clarksville's economy, centered on its agricultural base in dark-fired tobacco, reached its pre-Civil War zenith in 1858. More than 18,000 hogsheads of dark-fired tobacco were shipped to international markets, returning more than $2.3 million. Clarksville's type 22 tobacco became the most famous strain in the markets of England, France, Germany, and Italy. Individual enterprise in the sale of tobacco, however, gave way to large, consolidated tobacco companies, which maintained warehouses along the river and adjacent to the city's developing railroad network.

The introduction of rail traffic in 1859–60 by the Memphis, Clarksville, and Louisville Railroad, which opened a modern bridge over the Cumberland River, tied the city to larger transportation systems. Such access had great economic significance, but it also increased Clarksville's strategic value in the Civil War. Union armies invaded the region in 1862 to grab control of the rail and river systems and to close production at pig iron furnaces in Montgomery and surrounding counties. Ironically, Clarksville residents initially had opposed secession. Former rivals Cave Johnson and Gustavus Henry both supported the Constitutional Union ticket of John Bell in the 1860 presidential election. Generally, residents seemed content to allow the Lincoln administration to govern in the spring of 1861, but events at Ft. Sumter, and Lincoln's call for volunteers to squash the rebellion, pushed residents to favor secession. Clarksville voters support the secession vote in June 1861. Henry responded by serving in the Confederate Senate. Cave Johnson withdrew from public affairs.

Recognizing Clarksville's strategic importance, Confederate commanders directed the construction of two earthern forts, Fort Defiance and Fort Clark, at the confluence of the Red and Cumberland rivers. Neither fort was fully completed or armed when a Federal flotilla, under Flag Officer Andrew Foote, approached Clarksville in February 1862. Confederate forces evacuated the forts and, after firing the Cumberland River railroad bridge, fled for Nashville. But citizens extinguished the bridge fire, saving this vital transportation link for local commerce, although later guerilla warfare along the line generally kept the line closed until 1865.

The Union occupation of Clarksville ended in September 1865, and, in the following month, both the tobacco market and the new First National Bank opened their doors for business. Normalcy did not immediately return, however. Conflicts over Reconstruction politics, rioting, and Ku Klux Klan activity

marked the years 1865–1869. Whites consistently resisted black education and impeded whenever possible the activities of the Freedmen's Bureau. Yet, newly freed African Americans established such community institutions as St. Peter's AME Church and made numerous attempts to establish public schools. A major commercial venture was established in 1868 when ex-Confederate Frank Gracey opened the mercantile business, F.B. Gracey and Brothers. Gracey and his kinsman, Julian Gracey, developed a very lucrative enterprise.

Agricultural trade remained the foundation of the local economy through the late nineteenth century. The town also was a center for the agrarian revolts of the time. The Grangers were introduced locally via the White's Chapel Agricultural Protest, headed by Joseph B. Killebrew, who was clearly the most important Clarksvillian since Cave Johnson. Killebrew abhorred secession, freed his slaves, placed them on wages, and established a black school on his large farm. Killebrew supported the New South crusade and boosted public education and scientific agriculture. State Superintendent of Public Instruction in 1872, Killebrew wrote the key work, *Introduction to the Resources of Tennessee*, in 1874. Congressman John House and U.S. Senator James E. Bailey, who replaced Andrew Johnson in 1877, were other prominent late nineteenth century residents.

Racial conflicts persisted in the 1870s, and black businesses were especially hurt by the great arson Fire of 1878 that destroyed 15 acres of the central business distict. Since the city's population at this time was roughly equal in the numbers of whites and blacks, African-American residents used their voting power to place several blacks into local government. John Page was a black city alderman while Jerry Wheeler was a black county commissioner. J.H.M. Graham, a black newspaper publisher, was elected to the Tennessee General Assembly. The most promient African American was Dr. Robert Burt, who opened a Clarksville clinic in 1904. Serving both blacks and whites, it evolved into the city's only public hospital until the late 1940s. Without fanfare, both white and black doctors utilized Burt's clinic. Mercifully, life can transcend race.

But reason could not submerge race completely. Nace Dixon, a black Republican city councilman, became active in the successful attempt to eliminate saloons in Clarksville. His activism for prohibition led the local Democratic organization to target him for defeat in 1907. Ward voting was secretly eliminated and replaced by city-wide elections, effectively eliminating black political power in the name of progressivism.

During this same decade, Clarksville was a focal point of the Black Patch War. As a major producer of dark-fired tobacco, local planters and farmers were involved intensely in the efforts to break the monopoly of the American Tobacco Company. Farmers established the Eastern Dark-fired Tobacco Growers Association to organize and agitate for their interests. Extralegal night riders supported these goals from 1902 to 1912.

In 1919 Mrs. Brenda Runyon and others established the Women's Bank of Tennessee in Clarksville. This was the first bank in the nation controlled entirely by women. Prominent residents during this era were Horace Lurton, U.S. Supreme Court Justice; Perry L. Harned, educator and promoter of public schools; and Austin Peay, Governor of Tennessee. Peay and Harned proved an effective team in creating a modern public education system, consolidating control of state administration in the governor's office, and creating an improved state highway system.

The 1920s and 1930s witnessed a flowering of literature from writers either from the Clarksville area or then living in the region. Robert Penn Warren graduated from Clarksville High School in 1921. Caroline Gordon used Clarksville for the setting of much of her writing. She and her husband Allen Tate established a literary oasis at their home on the banks of the Cumberland River. Such important writers as Katherine A. Porter, Edmund Wilson, Robert Lowell, Herbert Agar, and Stark Young visited Gordon and Tate at their Clarksville home. Evelyn Scott, born Elsie Dunn, wrote the well-received novel *Background in Tennessee*, among other works.

In 1941 the War Department established Camp Campbell as a military training installation of 42,841 acres just north of Clarksville. Camp Campbell brought Clarksville into the vortex of wartime economic prosperity and created a cosmopolitanism in the community due to the increased contacts between Clarksvillians and people from other parts of the country. When the camp became a permanent military installation, Fort Campbell, in 1950, residents knew that their future was fixed as part of the national scene. Fort Campbell remains the single most important force in the local economy and culture.

In 1954 Clarksville was one of the first communities in the nation to participate in the modern urban renewal programs of the federal government. The civil rights movement challenged public segregation throughout the city. Desegregation of education started when Austin Peay State College admitted its first black student, Wilbur Daniel, in 1956. But attitudes hardened and, when Dr. Robert McCan advocated integration, he was forced to resign from the city's largest white Baptist church in 1960. Ironically, this happened in the same year that Clarksville resident Wilma Rudolph amazed the world with her multiple gold medals at the 1960 Summer Olympics. She received a public welcome from her hometown but still was unable to dine at a local chain restaurant.

The 1960s and 1970s produced school system consolidation, annexation of new areas into the city, continued economic expansion, and the rise of Austin Peay State College to university status. The completion of Interstate Highway I-24 in 1975–76 established a new, modern transportation link to replace the earlier reliance on the river and railroad. The town's population, economy, and society have changed dramatically in the last 20 years as Clarksville seeks to assert its current marketing slogan, "Gateway to the New South."

Thomas H. Winn, Austin Peay State University

SEE: BLACK PATCH WAR; BLOUNT, WILLIE; DARK TOBACCO DISTRICT PLANTERS' PROTECTIVE ASSOCIATION; FORT CAMPBELL; FORT DONELSON; GORDON, CAROLINE; HENRY, GUSTAVUS A.; JOHNSON, CAVE; KILLEBREW, JOSEPH B.; LURTON, HORACE; MONTGOMERY COUNTY; 101ST AIRBORNE; PEAY, AUSTIN; AUSTIN PEAY STATE UNIVERSITY; PORT ROYAL STATE HISTORICAL AREA; RUDOLPH, WILMA; SCOTT, EVELYN; TATE, JOHN O. ALLEN; TOBACCO; WARREN, ROBERT PENN; WORLD WAR II

CLAXTON, PHILANDER PRIESTLEY (1862–1957), the "Crusader for Public Education in the South," was born in a log cabin in rural Bedford County in 1862. He attended several "cabin" schools and received a secondary education at a backwoods academy, where, at age 16, he taught classes for a remission of fees. He attended the University of Tennessee and graduated from its classical curriculum in two-and-one-half years, second in his class of 16. He later studied Teutonic languages at The Johns Hopkins University, but did not earn a degree.

Claxton taught and served as an administrator in several small school systems in North Carolina. From 1893 until 1902, he taught pedagogy at North Carolina Normal and Industrial College. In 1902 Charles W. Dabney, president of the University of Tennessee and a leader in the campaign to create better public schools in the South, employed Claxton to administer the Southern Education Board's (SEB) promotional efforts, including editing its journal, *Southern Education*. With support from the SEB and the interlocking Rockefeller-financed General Education Board (GEB), Dabney and Claxton created a department of education at the University of Tennessee. They also organized the Summer School of the South with GEB funds. Claxton served as head of the Department of Education and superintendent of the Summer School of the South from 1902 until 1911. During that period, more than 20,000 teachers attended the school, which became the largest summer school in the United States.

Together with R.L. Jones, S.G. Gilbreath, Seymour Mynders, J.W. Brister, and P.L. Harned, Claxton led a political struggle for state financial support for Tennessee's public schools, which culminated in the passage of the far-reaching General Education Bill of 1909. During the campaign, Claxton and the others covered the state, speaking to an estimated 100,000 people. The law significantly increased appropriations for public schools, established three normal schools, and provided for permanent state funding for the University of Tennessee budget.

In 1911 Claxton was appointed U.S. Commissioner of Education and served through both the Taft and Wilson administrations. One of the best-known peace advocates among World War I-era educators, Claxton became the target of angry attacks from members of patriotic societies, who accused him of distributing pacifist literature at government expense. He further angered his critics by resisting attempts to prohibit the teaching of the German language.

Claxton served as provost at the University of Alabama (1921–1923) and superintendent of schools in Tulsa, Oklahoma (1923–1929). He was president of Austin Peay Normal School in Clarksville from 1930 to 1946, retiring at the age of 83. While at Austin Peay, he led a second, but much less successful statewide public school campaign. Claxton made no pretense of being a scholar, but he was a prolific writer of position papers and opinion columns in journals, newspapers, and pamphlets. In 1957, shortly after his death, officials at the University of Tennessee, Knoxville dedicated the Claxton Education Building in his honor.

Clinton B. Allison, University of Tennessee, Knoxville
SEE: DABNEY, CHARLES W.; EDUCATION; EDUCATION, HIGHER; GENERAL EDUCATION BOARD; SUMMER SCHOOL OF THE SOUTH; UNIVERSITY OF TENNESSEE

CLAY COUNTY was created by an act of the Tennessee General Assembly on June 16, 1870. It was taken from the northern sections of Overton and Jackson counties. With no roads and only a few trails, the citizens of the new county believed they had a better opportunity to participate in self-government in their own county rather than as part of larger county governments. The first session of the county court met in Mary Roberts's store in the Butler's Landing community. Celina was chosen as the county seat by a narrow margin. Local craftsman D.L. Dow built the Clay County Courthouse (1872–1873), which is listed in the National Register of Historic Places.

In 1870 Clay County was a dense forest of virgin timber. Freight and manufactured goods came into the county by river or the Great Road, part of a stage road that linked Georgia and Alabama to Cookeville. Bordering on Kentucky, the area was deeply divided during the Civil War, and hard feelings between the ridge dwellers and the river people inhibited economic growth and political development. Some families moved west, but those who remained soon became engaged in harvesting the timber. By 1880 the timber industry in Clay County was big business, and in 1890 the timber harvest produced millions of feet of cut boards at more than twenty sawmills. In addition, lumbermen cut, rafted, and floated logs to Nashville during the spring high water. During the peak of timbering, the county's assessed valuation reached nearly $11,000,000, and the population topped 9,000. By 1930 the timber was gone, the land washed away, and river traffic had been replaced by the automobile. The loss of the timber industry and the Great Depression struck the Upper Cumberland hard.

The family of Cordell Hull, U.S Secretary of State under President Franklin D. Roosevelt and Nobel Prize recipient, played a large role in the county's development. Hull's first law office was located just off the square in Celina. Hull's father, Billy Hull, constructed several Celina buildings that are still in use today. Bob Riley, one of the most widely known rivermen, lives on in his tales and stories of the rafting days, and Riley's log cabin still stands on the banks of the Obey River. Calvin Hamilton of the Free Hill community was another well-known riverman, still remembered in Cumberland River stories.

In addition to serving as the county seat, Celina, located at the confluence of the Obey and Cumberland rivers, became an important stop in the logging and steamboat trade. The Kyle family operated a rafting business that employed about 100 men. Rafters found Celina, with its two hotels—the New Central Hotel and the Riverside Hotel, a hospitable place to stop on the seven-day journey to Nashville. Steamboats also made regular stops to bring mail and manufactured goods and haul away chickens, lumber, and other farm products. The steamboats continued to meet the transportation needs of Celina and Clay County until the 1920s and 1930s, when highway construction and automobiles ended the trade.

North of Celina is Free Hill, an African-American community dating perhaps as early as 1830. Robert "Bud" Garrett of Free Hill acquired considerable regional renown for making flint marbles used by blacks and whites alike in the popular local game of rolley hole marbles. During the 1940s he purchased a schoolbus with the proceeds from his marble making and shuttled community resident to jobs in Celina.

The Obey and Cumberland rivers provided transportation and a link to Nashville and beyond, but they also flooded periodically, with devastating results. In 1943 the U.S. Army Corps of Engineers finally achieved a long-sought goal and built the first dam on the Obey, creating the huge Dale Hollow Reservoir. Dale Hollow Dam tamed a wild river and drew tourists and fishermen to the vacation and recreation area, but destroyed valuable farmland. The community of Willow Grove disappeared completely under the waters of the reservoir.

In 1950 the garment industry moved into the county. For the next 40 years, the needle work factories ranked among the largest employers in the county; in 1990, however, the textile plants began moving to other countries. Timber and lumber industries still account for a large segment of the county economy in the form of pallet mills and the log home business. Seasonal tourist jobs also employ a number of people.

Despite modern transportation advances, Clay County still experiences some of the isolation common to the nineteenth century. The location of the county along the Kentucky border and the number of rivers that cross the county separate communities and people in important ways. The west end of the county maintains a high school and grade school in the Hermitage Springs community. In the middle section of the county school children attend the high school and grade school in Celina. The east end, now cut off by Dale Hollow Lake, can be reached only by entering Overton County, but residents transport their children to schools in Celina. Nevertheless each area maintains its own fire halls and a spirit of community citizenship.

Corinne McLerran, Clay County

SEE: FREE HILL; GARRETT, ROBERT; HULL, CORDELL; RILEY, BOB; ROLLEY HOLE MARBLES; STEAMBOATING; U.S. ARMY CORPS OF ENGINEERS

CLAY, ROBERT E. (1875–1961), a pioneer of rural education for African Americans in Tennessee, helped to build hundreds of rural, county, and city schools. Clay was born on June 25, 1875, in Bristol, Virginia, to Harry and Frances Clay. He married Obelia M. Goins, and the couple had one son, Hairston, who settled in Bristol, Tennessee.

Clay began his career as a disciple of Booker T. Washington. He worked diligently in Washington's National Negro Business League until Washington's death in 1915. In 1917 Clay became the Julius Rosenwald Fund's Negro agent for Tennessee. He worked as a Rosenwald agent, building schools and developing educational programs for African Americans until 1937, when the Rosenwald Fund closed its southern office. Clay later worked as a developer of African-American education for the State Department of Education.

As Rosenwald agent, Clay held public meetings to persuade European Americans and African Americans to support the construction of local school houses. He convinced reluctant European Americans to attend the Rosenwald meetings and courses, offering them free Rosenwald school plans to build their own schools. His diplomatic methods gained the confidence of local elites, and Clay erected Rosenwald schools in racially-tense counties like Haywood and Tipton, as well as in divided cities like Kingsport.

Before his retirement in 1955, Clay became a notable figure at Tennessee A & I State College, where he received his degree in 1932. Like Booker T. Washington, Clay believed in educating the whole person and, accordingly, headed Sunday School classes on the campus almost until his death. The students found him amiable and eager to give wise counsel and guidance. "Daddy Clay," as they affectionately called him, enlisted faculty members and Greek-letter organizations to direct the Sunday School lessons in the University's auditorium. In November 1949 President Walter S. Davis proclaimed the "Robert E. Clay Sunday School, " which operated under the motto, "God First, others second, and myself last."

Robert E. Clay died on June 23, 1961. He was honored with a memorial service on the Tennessee State University campus on June 27. In 1968 the new education building was named R. E. Clay Hall.

Bobby L. Lovett, Tennessee State University

SUGGESTED READING: Mary S. Hoffschwelle, *Rebuilding the Rural Southern Community: Reformers, Schools, and Homes in Tennessee, 1914–1929* (1998)

SEE: EDUCATION; JULIUS ROSENWALD FUND; TENNESSEE STATE UNIVERSITY

CLEBURNE, PATRICK RONAYNE (1828–1864), Major General in the Army of Tennessee, was born on St. Patrick's Day in County Cork, Ireland, and immigrated to the United States in 1849. Cleburne settled in Helena, Arkansas, where he rose in social position and community esteem through diligent work, uncompromising honesty, and loyalty to his friends.

In the spring of 1861, Cleburne cast his lot with the Confederacy, explaining to his brother that although he owned no slaves, he would fight with the friends who had always supported him. The citizens of Helena elected Cleburne captain of the local militia. Drawing upon his three years of experience in the British army, Cleburne quickly advanced to the rank of colonel in the Fifteenth Arkansas Infantry Regiment. Within a year, he was a brigadier general in command of a brigade of General William J. Hardee's Corps in General Albert S. Johnston's Army of Mississippi.

On April 6, 1862, Cleburne and his brigade (comprised mostly of Tennesseans) spearheaded the attack of Hardee's Corps against the Union army around Pittsburg Landing, where he faced the troops of General William T. Sherman, the first of several encounters between the two. After heavy resistance, Cleburne's untested brigade forced the Union troops into retreat, past Shiloh Church, to within 400 yards of the Tennessee River.

After the Army of Tennessee's ill-fated Kentucky campaign in the autumn of 1862, Cleburne's troops retreated to Middle Tennessee. While visiting the Confederate camp at College Grove in December

1862, President Jefferson Davis personally commissioned Cleburne Major General.

During the Battle of Stones River, less than three weeks later, Cleburne's men spearheaded Hardee's attack on the Union right, driving the Federal line back three miles, until it doubled on its own left and center. When Confederate commander Braxton Bragg failed to capitalize on this advantage, Cleburne's division acted as the rear guard for the southern retreat to Chattanooga.

During the Battle of Chattanooga, Cleburne's division anchored the Confederate line on Missionary Ridge around Tunnel Hill. On November 25, 1863, the Union attack once again pitted Cleburne's troops against those under the command of Sherman. Despite overwhelming odds (Cleburne commanded 5,500 men to Sherman's 15,000), the southern forces mortally wounded three Union generals, inflicted heavy casualties on Sherman's troops, and captured eight stand of colors. When the center of the Confederate line collapsed, Cleburne's troops, under his distinctive "Blue Flag," acted as the rear guard for the southern retreat. The Cleburne division was in the thick of the fighting throughout the North Georgia Campaign of 1864.

The final chapter in the life of the Irish general was written at the Battle of Franklin. As the Confederate army prepared for its assault on the Union earthworks at Franklin, one of Cleburne's brigade commanders predicted that few of his soldiers would return to Arkansas, to which Cleburne reportedly replied, "if we are to die, let us die like men."[1]

As Cleburne's troops made their assault up the Columbia Pike, the general had two horses shot from under him. Finally, advancing on foot and within 50 yards of the Union works, a single minie ball pierced his chest. Two days before the Battle of Franklin, as the army passed St. John's Episcopal Church, near Columbia, Tennessee, Cleburne commented that it would be worth dying to be buried in a place so beautiful. His body was laid to rest in the churchyard after the Battle of Franklin. Later it was removed to his adopted home of Helena, Arkansas.

Patrick Craddock, Franklin

CITATION:

(1) Craig Symonds, *Stonewall of the West: Patrick Cleburne and the Civil War* (Lawrence, KS, 1997), 255.

SEE: ARMY OF TENNESSEE; CHICKAMUAGA AND CHATTANOOGA, BATTLES OF; FRANKLIN, BATTLE OF; SHILOH, BATTLE OF; STONES RIVER, BATTLE OF

CLEMENT, FRANK G. (1920–1969). In the history of southern statehouses, there have been numerous incandescent governors, whose rhetorical skills and platform theatrics mesmerized voters. None was more skillfully trained or more spectacular than Frank Clement, Tennessee's governor from 1953 to 1959, and again from 1963 to 1967. Clement was the last Tennessee governor to use the evangelical style of oration on the eve of the television era of voter appeal. Seemingly destined for national greatness, Clement enthralled audiences in Tennessee and across the country with his speeches. He became an unofficial contender for the 1956 Democratic presidential nomination, while at home he initiated humanitarian changes that continue to benefit Tennessee citizens.

The product of a political family, Clement often remarked that he launched his campaign for the governor's office at age ten, when he told his Dickson classmates that someday he would run the state. At about that time, he began speech training with a favorite aunt, often practicing at night and on weekends. Historians agree with Clement's assessment that his youthful training laid the foundation for his later success.

After graduation from Cumberland Law School and a brief stint with the FBI, Clement gained notoriety as a money-saving, taxpayer-friendly young attorney with the state Railroad and Public Utilities Commission. Taken under the wing of powerful *Nashville Banner* publisher James Stahlman, many state Democrats viewed Clement as the political antidote to the statewide influence of the Memphis-based Crump machine. His initial, expedient alliance with E. H. "Boss" Crump, however, earned Clement the eternal, bitter opposition of the Democratic Nashville *Tennessean.*

Clement won his first gubernatorial election in 1952, after prevailing in a bitter primary against veteran Democrat Gordon Browning, the strong and popular governor, who called the 32-year-old Clement a "pipsqueak" and a "demogogue." Clement repeated his victory over Browning in 1954, at a time when Republicans in East Tennessee offered little effective opposition in the general election.

Clement quickly consolidated his local constituencies with visits to every county. Appearing on the courthouse square, he shook hands and made speeches, ingratiating himself with rural voters, who felt isolated from the political process. Clement's folksy style and his road-paving program gained him the rural vote.

Constitutional changes also enhanced Clement's public appeal. Early in his first term, Tennesseans approved the first changes to the state constitution since 1870. The eight new amendments included one that lengthened the governor's term from two to four years, a political windfall for Clement.

In 1954, as the state's first chief executive elected to a four-year term, Clement simultaneously sponsored social service legislation and accelerated his campaign for national recognition. Clement created the state Mental Health Department, which one publication described as the state's greatest step forward in a century. Clement also promoted the first free textbook program for all public school grades. He presided over the state's transformation from an agricultural- to an industrial-based economy and the expansion of employment opportunities that accompanied the change.

Meanwhile Clement criss-crossed the country, building his reputation among voters and party officials. Democrats increasingly viewed him as a potentially formidable candidate. His credentials included the pleasing personal portrait of a young, dynamic, untainted family man, a strong sense of patriotism, and charming good looks. A moderate on civil rights, he was the first southern governor to veto a segregation bill. From the perspective of many, his most valuable asset was his God-given talent to arouse people with his words. With so many attributes, Clement soon got a national forum.

In 1956 the Democratic party desperately needed a strong candidate to offset the popularity of the heroic, yet avuncular Dwight Eisenhower. Impressed with Clement's qualities, party officials chose the Tennessee Governor to give the keynote address at the convention in Chicago. In effect, this was the moment for which Clement had prepared all his life. Determined to succeed, Clement prepared rigorously, reviewing films and scripts of previous keynotes and pushing his staff to produce numerous revisions of his speech.

Appearing before the delegates and a national television audience, Clement delivered a rousing, old-fashioned Tennessee stump speech attacking the Republicans as the "party of privilege and pillage" that would soon pass over the Potomac River in the "greatest water crossing since the children of Israel crossed the Red Sea." President Eisenhower, Clement claimed, peered down the "green fairways of indifference," a reference to the President's love of golf. Clement referred to Vice President Richard Nixon as the "vice hatchet man." His repeated use of the phrase, "How long, America, O how long . . ." remains a hallmark of his address.[1]

While the speech impressed some people, many were repulsed by Clement's attacks, his stump speech style, and his emphatic mannerisms. The speech was a failure. In 43 minutes, Clement ended his national political hopes.

With his national political hopes in shambles, Clement resumed his work in Tennessee. He delivered an impassioned plea to end capital punishment and almost succeeded in abolishing the state's death penalty. Clement never succumbed to the politically popular attitude of hard-core segregation adopted by other southern governors, but carefully cultivated his image as a civil rights moderate, treading a fine line between the demands of blacks and whites.

In the 1960s, Clement played political leap frog with his former aide Buford Ellington, as the two men rotated their gubernatorial terms. Clement's final term, marked by health problems and a public battle with alcohol, was not as distinguished as his earlier years in office. He lost two races for the U.S. Senate.

Frank Clement thrived on politics. He was a God-fearing, hard-working, Bible-quoting man, whose flaws cost him votes, friends, credibility, and self-esteem. Yet he aroused and inspired the lowly, cajoled and convinced the powerful, and lifted the cause of the needy to new heights of public awareness.

At age 49, Frank Clement died in a November 4, 1969, automobile accident near Nashville amid speculation of a fourth campaign for governor.

Alan Griggs, United Methodist Communications

CITATION:

(1) Many sections of the keynote address are cited in Robert E. Corlew III, "Frank Goad Clement and the Keynote Address of 1956," *Tennessee Historical Quarterly* 36(1977): 95–107.

SUGGESTED READING: Lee S. Greene, *Lead Me On: Frank Goad Clement and Tennessee Politics* (1982)

SEE: BROWNING, GORDON W.; CRUMP, EDWARD H.; CUMBERLAND UNIVERSITY; DICKSON COUNTY; ELLINGTON, BUFORD; GOVERNMENT; NASHVILLE TENNESSEAN; STAHLMAN, JAMES G.

CLIFTON PLACE, the antebellum home of General Gideon J. Pillow near Columbia, is one of the more lavish examples of Greek Revival architecture in southern Middle Tennessee. The nearly intact plantation is centered around a large five-ranked house distinguished by a fine central portico, flanking wings, and an exquisite interior.

The house was built by Maury County master builder Nathan Vaught for Gideon Johnson Pillow (1806–1877), attorney, planter, and political figure. Pillow inherited a large tract of prime agricultural land from his father, a pioneer settler, and established one of the largest plantations in Maury County, as well as large farms elsewhere.

Vaught built the large brick house in 1838 and 1839. One-story side wings and a connecting gallery across the back were added in 1846, and in 1852 the roof was raised and a monumental pedimented portico supported by Ionic columns was added to the facade. The original floor plan featured four rooms on each of the two main floors, separated by a large central hall. The 1846 additions provided additional rooms to the sides and at the rear. In addition to the main floors, the house has an attic divided into two rooms and a basement with two finished rooms and a provisions cellar.

The plantation retains most of its original dependencies, including an office, kitchen, smokehouse, carriage house, barns, and other farm buildings, as well as many of the original slave quarters. Conforming to the model for many large plantations, the service buildings are located some distance away. It was named Clifton Place after the Clifton Turnpike, built in 1840 by the Pillows and their neighbors, the Polks, as a means to ship their cotton to the Tennessee River at Clifton, Tennessee.

Clifton Place was confiscated by the federal government during the war, but under the general amnesty following the war, it was returned to an impoverished General Pillow. He soon left Maury County for Memphis to practice law with Isham G. Harris, and Pillow died at Helena, Arkansas, in 1878. After the death of Mrs. Pillow, who remained behind, Clifton Place passed to son-in-law Melville Williams in 1872, and was purchased by another relative by marriage, Colonel J.W.S. Ridley, in 1877. The Ridley family retained the property until 1972, when it was acquired by Mr. and Mrs. John R. Neal, who have begun a complete restoration of the house.

Richard Quin, National Park Service

SEE: MAURY COUNTY; PILLOW, GIDEON J.; VAUGHT, NATHAN

CLINE, PATSY (1932–1963), country music star, was born Virginia Patterson Hensley on September 8, 1932, in Gore, Virginia. She was an entertainer from an early age, but nearly lost her voice and her life when complications from a serious throat infection stopped her heart. She recovered and found herself with a voice of new depth and volume. When her father left the family in 1947, 15-year-old Virginia quit school to work in a drugstore during the day and sing with local bands at night. One of the local bandleaders, Bill Peer, first called her Patsy. She began to make a name for herself in the Washington, D.C. area and in 1949 wrangled a Grand Ole Opry audition with Jim Denny, but she was not offered a regular spot. She returned to Virginia, continued to build a local audience, and slowly made inroads into the music industry.

In 1953 she returned to Nashville as Patsy Cline, after marrying her first husband, Gerald Cline, and made an appearance on Ernest Tubb's "Midnight Jamboree" radio show. Then in 1954, she earned a spot on the syndicated radio program, "Town and Country Time." Soon after, she signed a recording contract with 4-Star Music Sales. Cline hoped the contract would increase her appearance fees, but she made little or nothing from the deal. In 1955 Decca Records arranged to lease Cline's contract from 4-Star and paired the singer with producer Owen Bradley.

Cline had to be cajoled into recording the song that signaled a turning point in her career. She lambasted the song, *Walkin' After Midnight*, as a "Pop song" and resisted recording it. When she sang it on the *Arthur Godfrey Talent Scouts* show in January 1957, the "Pop song" became an overnight sensation, eventually reaching number three on the country charts and number 15 on the Pop charts. This success should have opened the door to stardom for Cline, but 4-Star owner Bill McCall failed to invest the time and money to follow up the hit.

In 1959 Cline moved to Nashville with her new husband, Charlie Dick, and their baby. When the contract with 4-Star ended in 1960, Cline signed a new contract with Decca and gained membership in the Grand Ole Opry. The Decca contract again placed Cline in the hands of Owen Bradley, who supplied her with a steady stream of material from the best songwriters in Nashville. This resulted in a string of pop-tinged hits penned by Willie Nelson, Hank Cochran, and Don Gibson. In 1961 Cline traveled to New York City with a troupe of Opry performers to play Carnegie Hall.

On March 5, 1963, Cline's rise to the top of the Country and Pop charts was cut short in a plane crash at Camden, Tennessee. The crash devastated the Nashville music community, taking the lives of Hawkshaw Hawkins, Cowboy Copas, and Randy Hughes in addition to Cline. Female singers of Country, Pop, and Jazz remember Cline both for her unforgettable voice and her assertiveness in both personal and business relations. Her continued popularity three decades after her death testifies to the power of her rich voice and emotional style.

Brenda Colladay, Middle Tennessee State University

SEE: BRADLEY, OWEN; GRAND OLE OPRY

CLINGMAN'S DOME, the highest point in Tennessee, crowns the Great Smoky Mountains at an elevation of 6,643 feet. It is created from folded, fractured, and faulted Precambrian rocks. On the Smokies's rugged shoulders one will find primarily the ancient Ocoee Supergroup exposed—four layers of moderately metamorphosed sedimentary rock overlaying the earlier one-billion-year-old Precambrian layers exposed in the Unakas to the north of the Smokies. Part of the Great Smoky Mountain National Park, Clingman's Dome is accessible by road and a one-half mile trail from the parking lot to an observation tower at the summit, rising above the fir and spruce forests.

By some accounts, the Cherokees called the mountain Kuwahi, "the mulberry place." Although the Tennessee-North Carolina line was surveyed through the mountains in 1821, the field notes contained few place names, and it was not until the 1858 explorations of naturalist S. B. Buckley that many of the peaks were specifically identified. In his report, Buckley called the peak Mount Buckley after himself, but most of his names did not survive.

In 1859 the Swiss-born geographer Arnold Guyot made the first comprehensive study of the interior of

the Great Smoky Mountains and named Clingman's Dome for his patron. His research had its roots in the dispute over the highest peak in the Appalachians, an argument begun in 1844 between Elisha Mitchell, a professor at the University of North Carolina, and U.S. Senator Thomas L. Clingman, who had been a soldier and mountain explorer. Mitchell advocated a peak called Black Dome near Asheville, North Carolina, while Clingman was convinced the peak sometimes called Smoky Dome was the highest. In June 1857, Mitchell began to run a series of altitude levels in the Black Mountains, but drowned in a stream on the dome. Clingman supported Guyot's survey, arranging for a six mile path to be cut up the favored mountain so that Guyot's horse and equipment could ascend to the top. The argument was settled when Guyot found Clingman's Dome was 6,643 feet, while Black Dome, now named Mt. Mitchell, was 6,684 feet.
Ann Toplovich, Tennessee Historical Society
SEE: GEOLOGICAL ZONES; GREAT SMOKY MOUNTAINS NATIONAL PARK

CLINTON DESEGREGATION CRISIS. In January 1956 the United States District Court in Knoxville ruled that the Anderson County high schools should be desegregated by the fall term of that year (*Joheather McSwain et al. v. County Board of Education of Anderson County, et al.*). The ruling brought to an end a protracted period of litigation and opposition to integration by the county school board. Registration for Clinton High School's fall classes was held without incident on August 20, 1956; of the 806 students enrolled, only 12 were African Americans.

Two days before classes began, John Kasper, executive secretary of the Seaboard White Citizens Council, arrived in the city and issued a call for mass meetings of pro-segregationists and the organization of picketers. Asa Carter of the Birmingham White Citizens' Council later joined Kasper; crowds gathering at the courthouse to protest desegregation soon numbered approximately 1,500. Rioting broke out over Labor Day weekend. Crowds blocked traffic; cars containing blacks were stopped and their occupants harassed and threatened. When Clinton's small police force could not control the mobs, Governor Frank G. Clement ordered state highway patrolmen and National Guardsmen to quell the rioting in Clinton.

Public support for high school principal Douglas Brittain and the peaceful integration of the school remained very high, with most citizens adhering to the view that the "law of the land" must be obeyed. Nevertheless, even after crowds dispersed, segregationists continued to engage in intimidation tactics. Crosses were burned on the lawns of some high school faculty members, as well as at the homes of civic leaders who supported integration. Other inci-

dents included rock throwing and threatening phone calls. As the intimidation escalated, shots were fired at the home of two black students attending Clinton High School, and dynamite blasts punctuated the peace of the county.

Clinton High School closed temporarily but reopened on December 10. At a general assembly of the student body, the county attorney read U.S. District Court Judge Robert L. Taylor's injunction forbidding interference with desegregation. Sixteen Clinton agitators, cited for violation of the injunction, were arrested and arraigned before the U.S. District Court. Four more bombings occurred in the first weeks of 1957, but when the high school suffered extensive damage following an early morning bombing on Sunday, October 5, 1958, public opinion galvanized against further violence.

Many observers of the Clinton desegregation crisis contend that the high school's problems resulted from the dual influence of "outsiders," who came to town to agitate the crowds, and the presence of the media, who exacerbated the situation. At one time, over 80 reporters were in town, representing a variety of publications and news agencies, including *Life, Time, U.S. News and World Report,* CBS, NBC, Associated Press, United Press, and the International News Service of the BBC. Others, however, believe that Clinton's mob protests were actually a protest against the city's civic leaders, who supported peaceful integration and who had come to represent an unwanted federal mandate for change.
Janice M. McClelland, Norris
SUGGESTED READING: June N. Adamson, "Few Black Voices Heard: The Black Community and the Desegregation Crisis in Clinton, Tennessee, 1956," *Tennessee Historical Quarterly* 53 (1994): 30–41.
SEE: ANDERSON COUNTY; CAIN, ROBERT, JR.; CIVIL RIGHTS MOVEMENT CLEMENT, FRANK G.

CLOAR, CARROLL (1913–1993), artist, was born in Earle, Arkansas, on January 18, 1913. His childhood memories of his birthplace defined his art during the latter part of his career and gained him national recognition. Flat color forms and decorative patterning are elements of his distinctive style.

Cloar came to Tennessee in 1930 and attended Southwestern University at Memphis as an English major. After a trip to Europe, he returned to Memphis and enrolled at the Memphis Academy of Art, studying with George Oberteuffer. From 1936 to 1940 he attended the Art Students League in New York, studying under Arnold Blanch, William McNutty, Harry Sternberg, and Ernest Feine. During this period, he produced a series of lithographs based upon the landscape and community of Earle, Arkansas, which gained him the McDowell Traveling Fellowship in 1940. Cloar spent this time journeying through the western United States and Mexico, before joining the Army Air Corps during World War II.

After the war, Cloar revisited Mexico on a Guggenheim Fellowship, which he received in 1946. He continued to travel extensively throughout Central and South America until 1950. In 1955, after he clearly determined the direction of his art, Cloar established a permanent residence in Memphis in order to remain closer to his southern roots. The year of his return, Cloar produced 14 works, among them his well-known, *My Father was Big as a Tree*. He held his first one-man show in Memphis in 1953 followed by a New York showing in 1956, which firmly established his career and gave him national exposure. In the ensuing years, he had more than ten exhibitions at Tennessee museums, in addition to his New York showings. Museums across the country and private collectors acquired his works.

Cloar drew images of churches, graveyards, schoolhouses, and individuals from old Kodak photographs found in his family albums. He also obtained photographs from the estate of an African-American photographer in Arkansas, and transformed them into paintings, such as *The Wedding Party* (1971) and *The Pastor* (1970). Termed "a poetic expression of a child's vision and memory," his interpretation of these people, places, and incidents represents a distillation of his personal Arkansas boyhood experiences in the early twentieth century.[1] Cloar described these images as "American faces, timeless dress and timeless customs . . . the last of old America that isn't long for this earth."[2] Cloar died in Memphis in 1993.

Marilyn Masler, Memphis Brooks Museum of Art

CITATIONS:

(1) Beverly Joyce, "The Past Within the Realm of the Present," *World in Art, Carroll Cloar and the Truths of Fiction* (Memphis, 1991), 36.

(2) Guy Northrop, "Introduction," *Hostile Butterflies and Other Paintings by Carroll Cloar* (Memphis, 1977), 24.

SEE: ART; MEMPHIS COLLEGE OF ART; RHODES COLLEGE

CLOGGING AND BUCKDANCING are popular forms of percussive dancing that originated in the southern Appalachian mountains. Though the eighteenth-century Scottish and Irish settlers brought with them the clog, a step dance characterized by a very erect upper body, the additional influences of the traditional dance of Native Americans with its toe-heel, toe-heel movement and the African-American buck dances with the arms hanging loosely at the dancers' sides made for a distinctly American style. The basic step cloggers and buckdancers use consists of a double toe shuffle, where the toe and then the heel of the free foot brushes forward, followed first by weight on that foot, then rocking onto the other foot, before stepping back onto the foot that had originally been free. The leg is generally raised a little more than six inches off the ground in clogging, while the feet stay close to the ground in traditional buckdancing.

The term "clogging," first applied in the 1930s, signified coupled dancers completing individual step dance together in group configurations. Described as freestyle (or traditional) clogging, the dancers performed spontaneous footwork, which allowed them to improvise while moving about the dance floor in time to live music provided usually by string bands. The addition in the 1940s of taps, costumes, and the concept of teams for the dancers indicated a shift underway from clogging being viewed as family or community entertainment to public performance. The Tennessee Travelers, a group featured on "National Barn Dance" radio shows in the 1940s, may have helped generate another form of clogging called precision clogging that developed in the 1950s. Precision (or modern) cloggers synchronize their steps, emphasizing identical footwork choreographed to be done in unison.

Margaret D. Binnicker, Middle Tennessee State University

SEE: GRAND OLE OPRY; MUSIC

COCA-COLA BOTTLING COMPANY. On July 21, 1899, Chattanooga attorneys Benjamin F. Thomas and Joseph B. Whitehead signed an agreement with Asa Candler, president of the Coca-Cola Company, to receive exclusive rights to bottle the soft drink throughout most of the United States. Fellow Chattanooga attorney John T. Lupton soon became the third partner to help finance the first bottling plant in Chattanooga. By September 1899 the plant had opened at 17 Market Street, and the first advertisement appeared offering the soft drink in bottles. The venture took "Coke" from the southern drugstore counter and made it a national and international drink.

The Coca-Cola Bottling Company, parent bottling company to all others, was chartered in Tennessee on November 30, 1899. At the December inaugural meeting of the company directors, Whitehead was selected as the first president, Lupton as vice-president, and Thomas, secretary-treasurer. In this latter role, Thomas oversaw the business on a day-to-day basis. Early in 1900 Whitehead moved to Atlanta to open a second bottling plant.

Within months, it became apparent to the partners that they needed a franchise system to expand as rapidly as the contract with Candler required. They decided to split the territory between them. Thomas received control of most of the eastern United States, from Chattanooga north, plus California, Oregon, and Washington. Whitehead and Lupton shared control of the rest of the country, primarily in the South and West. Each partner established "parent" bottlers, who granted franchises to local bottlers in their territory. Thomas's company, which was rechartered in

1900 as Coca-Cola Bottling Company, kept its headquarters in Chattanooga.

In 1902 Thomas sold the Chattanooga bottling plant in order to concentrate on franchise development. This, the first franchised "Coke" bottler in the world, still operates as the Chattanooga Coca-Cola Bottling Company. Hereafter, the "parent" bottling companies did not actually bottle anything but acted as middlemen, buying syrup from the Atlanta Coca-Cola Company and selling it to the franchise bottlers in their territory. By the 1950s, there were some 1,100 franchises descended from the "parent" bottlers. Beginning in the 1920s, the Coca-Cola Company began a long and expensive process of buying back all the bottling franchise rights Candler sold in 1899 for one dollar. The corporation repurchased Coca-Cola Bottling Company (Thomas) in 1974 and the Lupton interests in 1986.

Ned L. Irwin, East Tennessee State University

SUGGESTED READINGS: Ned L. Irwin, "Bottling Gold: Chattanooga's Coca-Cola Fortunes," *Tennessee Historical Quarterly* 51(1992): 223–37; *60th Anniversary of Coca-Cola Bottling Works, 1900–1907* (1960)

SEE: LUPTON, JOHN T.; THOMAS, BENJAMIN F.; WHITEHEAD, JOSEPH B.

COCKE COUNTY was created from Jefferson County in 1797 and named for William Cocke, a Revolutionary War soldier, who supported the establishment of the State of Franklin, helped write Tennessee's first state constitution, and served as one of the state's initial U.S. Senators. Cocke County, in upper East Tennessee, rests against the Great Smoky Mountains and is traversed by the French Broad and Big Pigeon rivers. The first white settler was John Gilliland, who planted a corn crop at the mouth of the Pigeon River in 1783 to establish his claim to the land. Although Cocke County settlers had few violent encounters with Native Americans, most early settlers located near one of several forts in the area: William Whitson's fort, Abraham McKay's fort, Wood's fort, or John Huff's fort.

The creation of Cocke County gave local citizens better access to courts, and made it easier to attend general musters and elections. The first county court was held in the home of Daniel Adams. After some controversy, the county seat was located on 50 acres of land on the French Broad River, donated by John Gilliland, the son of the original settler. The town was named New Port, and construction began immediately on a log courthouse. In 1828, a new brick courthouse was built.

Controversy over the location of the county seat continued into the Reconstruction period, and Cocke County, along with Obion County, was singled out in the Constitution of 1870 for permission to allow a simple majority of the voters to determine the location of county government. In 1867 the Cincinnati, Cumberland Gap, and Charleston Railroad came to Cocke County and, under pressure from railroad officials and interested capitalists, the county seat moved to a new site at the bluffs overlooking the French Broad River, but retained the name "Newport." Thereafter, the original county seat was designated Oldtown. Its only remnant is the O'Dell House, a brick structure in the Federal style, built by Abel Gilliland in 1814 and now on the National Register of Historic Places. Fire destroyed the new courthouse and most of the county records in 1876, and government returned to Oldtown, where it remained until 1884, when a new brick courthouse was constructed. The current Colonial Revival-styled courthouse, built in 1930, is listed in the National Register.

The emergence of Newport as permanent county seat was closely connected with the financial and industrial schemes of a group of British, American, and Canadian investors, headed by A. A. Arthur, who formed the Scottish Carolina Timber and Land Company, Limited. With the completion of the Western North Carolina Railroad in 1882, Cocke County had access to a modern transportation corridor linking it to both Knoxville and Asheville. Interestingly, the new courthouse in Newport was not located at the center of the downtown commercial district; that place was reserved for the railroad depot, an unmistakable sign of the power of the new capitalists compared to that of the local government.

In 1898 Anna Stokely, her two sons, James and John, and Colonel Swann established a cannery in Jefferson County that grew to become an international concern under the name Stokely-Van Camp. Initially funded by $3,900, it shipped canned tomatoes down the French Broad River to Chattanooga for sale to housewives. Using local labor and local produce, the business soon expanded into the southeastern region and offered a variety of canned fruits and vegetables. In 1933 the Stokely brothers bought the Van Camp company, considered to be the model of the canning industry. With this acquisition, Stokely-Van Camp moved into national production.

Parrottsville, the second largest town in the county, is one of the oldest communities in the state. A group of German immigrants, whose descendants continue to reside in Cocke County, settled here in the 1780s. Hamilton Yett, son of one of the original German immigrants, built the National Register-listed Ellison House in 1857.

The first church in the county, the Big Pigeon (Primitive) Baptist Church, was organized in the home of James English in 1787. Seven years later, the Baptists erected a building. In 1800 the Methodists joined the Baptists in Cocke County, when John Adam Granade preached in the courthouse. In addition to their churches, the Methodists established a campground on the north side of the French Broad River. When the denomination divided over the slavery issue in the 1840s, Cocke County maintained congregations of both. The Presbyterians appeared briefly in 1809, but did not become established in Cocke County until 1823. In addition to these denominations, others organized through the years; the Lutherans in 1845; the Christian Church in 1923; the Roman Catholics in 1913; and the Episcopal Church in 1967.

In 1814 Anderson Academy became the first school in Cocke County. However, for most children, a few months of instruction in modest one-room schools was all the education they received. In 1875 the Parrottsville Academy was established in the Robert Roadman mansion. The county later used it until 1922 and the Methodists bought it in 1924, when the Parrottsville School was built. The Southern Baptists erected Cosby Academy, a boarding school, in 1912–13 and sold it to the county Board of Education in 1936. The first Cocke County High School was constructed in 1917; the present facility was built in 1962–63, with additions in 1975–76.

At least four notable Cocke County residents deserve special mention. Upon his inauguration in 1911, Ben W. Hooper became the first Republican Governor of Tennessee (1911–1915) in 30 years. This prohibitionist received the support of the WCTU, the Anti-Saloon League, and churches across the state. Grace Moore (1901–1947), who was born near Del Rio, received international acclaim as an outstanding operatic soprano. Wilma Dykeman (1920–) and James Stokely (1913–1977) were a husband-wife team whose writings focused on the region and the character of mountain people. Their best known collaborative effort was *Neither Black Nor White*, published in 1954. Dykeman's work includes *The French Broad, The Border States, The Tall Woman, The Far Family, Return the Innocent Earth,* and *Tennessee: A Bicentennial History.*
E. R. Walker III, Newport

SEE: CHEROKEE NATIONAL FOREST; COCKE, WILLIAM; DYKEMAN, WILMA; HOOPER, BEN W.; INDUSTRY; MOORE, GRACE; STOKELY, ANNA; SWAGGERTY BLOCKHOUSE

COCKE, WILLIAM (1748–1828), was a distinguished Revolutionary war veteran, experienced legislator, Sevier faction partisan, one of Tennessee's first two U.S. Senators, and the first Tennessee jurist to be impeached and removed from office. After serving as a captain in the Fincastle, Virginia, militia during the Revolutionary war, Cocke moved from his native Virginia to a new farm on Renfroe's Creek in present-day Sullivan County, Tennessee, in 1779. Already a veteran of the North Carolina House of Commons (1775, 1777–78), Cocke passed the bars of both Sullivan and Washington counties in 1782. He then served in the

North Carolina Senate in 1782, followed by another stint in the North Carolina House of Commons, representing Hawkins County, in 1788. This term followed his move from Renfroe's Creek to a new plantation, called "Mulberry Grove," near present-day Mooresburg. Cocke owned 960 acres, operating a farm as well as a small ironworks, grist mill, and sawmill.

Cocke was a partisan in the State of Franklin controversy and is credited with helping convince John Sevier to serve as Franklin's first governor. Cocke was a member of its constitutional convention and served the new "state" on its council of state and as its brigadier general. As historian Cortez A.M. Ewing observed, "Sevier and Judge [David] Campbell may have wavered at times, but Cocke stood firm for the integrity and independence of the new state."[1] As a member of the Southwest Territory legislature, Cocke was an early supporter of education, serving as a trustee for Greeneville College, Blount College, and Washington College.

Cocke was a member of the first state constitutional convention in 1796; later that year the Tennessee General Assembly selected Cocke as one of the state's initial U.S. Senators. He served from 1797 to 1798 and from 1799 to 1805.

In 1807 Cocke moved to Grainger County. He ran for governor twice, but lost in 1807 to John Sevier and in 1809 to Willie Blount. Then in 1812, while he served on the state's first circuit court, Judge Cocke became the first Tennessee jurist to be impeached, tried, and removed from office for using his position for private gain.

Cocke's judicial disgrace, however, did not end his political career. In 1813 he vindicated himself by winning election to the Tennessee House of Representatives. The following year, Cocke left Tennessee when President James Madison appointed him as federal agent for the Chickasaws. He lived in both Alabama and Mississippi and served in the Mississippi legislature, giving him the unique distinction of having served in the legislature of the Transylvania (Kentucky) colony, the assembly of Virginia, the North Carolina legislature, the Franklin council of state, the Southwest Territory legislature, the Tennessee house, the U. S. Senate, and the Mississippi legislature. He died on August 22, 1828, in Columbus, Mississippi. Cocke County, Tennessee, was named to honor his long political career.
Carroll Van West, Middle Tennessee State University
CITATION:
(1) Cortez A. M. Ewing, "Early Tennessee Impeachments," *Tennessee Historical Quarterly* 16(1957): 301.
SEE: FRANKLIN, STATE OF; GOVERNMENT; SOUTHWEST TERRITORY

COCKRILL, ANN ROBERTSON JOHNSTON (1757–1821) was the only woman among the early

Cumberland settlers to receive a land grant in her own name. In 1784 the North Carolina legislature awarded this honor for her contribution to the "advance guard of civilization."

Born in Wake County, Virginia, Ann Robertson moved to the Watauga settlement. In July 1776, when Fort Caswell, near the present site of Elizabethton, came under Indian attack, she mobilized the women to pass caldrons of boiling water to her position overlooking the palisades. Although she sustained several injuries, Robertson continued at her post until the Indians retreated.

When her husband, a justice of the peace in the Washington District of East Tennessee, was killed in an accident, she and her three small daughters joined Colonel John Donelson and a group of pioneers, including her sister-in-law Charlotte Robertson, in the migration to the Cumberland settlement. During the journey by flatboat, she taught the children, according to tradition, by making small wooden boxes, filling them with river sand, and drawing letters and numbers in the sand.

When the flotilla reached the confluence of the Tennessee and Ohio rivers, the flatboats had to navigate against the rain-swollen current to reach the mouth of the Cumberland. Some members decided to turn south to Natchez, Mississippi. Ann Robertson took a man's place as the pilot and steered the boat near the bank so the remaining men could pole upstream.

In the fall of 1784 Robertson married John Cockrill, and they had eight children. They established a home at Cockrill Springs at the present site of Centennial Park, where today there is a monument to her memory. She is buried in the Nashville City Cemetery.
Carole Stanford Bucy, Volunteer State Community College
SEE: COCKRILL, MARK R.; DONELSON, JOHN; ROBERTSON, CHARLOTTE

COCKRILL, MARK R. (1788–1872) was known in his day as a leading authority on agriculture and livestock, earning the sobriquet, "Wool King of the World," from the awards he received for his Tennessee-bred sheep. His success in wool-culture and stock breeding gained for him a prominent place as an innovator in agricultural methods.

Cockrill was born December 2, 1788, to John and Ann Robertson Cockrill, sister of Nashville "founder," James Robertson. John Cockrill had been one of the original settlers of Nashville and established his farm and homeplace on the present-day site of Centennial Park. Mark Cockrill possessed a natural love of the soil and early in life gained a reputation as an authority on livestock husbandry. In 1815 he acquired a part of a flock of Merino sheep brought to his country by the American consul to Portugal, William Jarvis. Cockrill also introduced the "short horn" Durham cattle from England and

became a pioneer in horse breeding.

In 1822 he married Susan Collinsworth, also from one of Tennessee's leading pioneer families, and established a vast farm of 5,600 acres, called "Stock Place," six miles from Nashville on Charlotte Pike. He also owned a cotton plantation in Mississippi, and in 1854 bought an additional 1,000 acres, the famed Tulip Grove estate, from Andrew J. Donelson for over $53,000.

Cockrill's crowning achievement occurred at the 1851 Crystal Palace Exposition in London. Samples from his Merino sheep were awarded first prize for the finest wool in the world. Queen Victoria presented Cockrill with a gold medal. His sheep also earned him awards in Vienna, Paris, and Lexington, Kentucky, where he beat out Henry Clay's prized sheep—the silver cup awarded him on this occasion bore the inscription "Clay's Defeat." In 1854 the Tennessee General Assembly, in an unprecedented move, awarded Cockrill a gold medal for his achievements as Tennessee's "favorite son" of agriculture.

His worth on the eve of the Civil War was estimated at $2 million, making him one of the richest men in the state. The Civil War considerably diminished Cockrill's wealth, since the Union Army confiscated much of his property, including hundreds of blooded livestock, 20,000 bushels of corn, 200 tons of hay, 2,000 bushels of oats, and 2,000 pounds of bacon. An unrepentant secessionist, Cockrill admitted to loaning the Confederacy $25,000 in gold.

Even after his death on June 27, 1872, Cockrill's work continued to receive prizes and awards. His Merino sheep won recognition at the Centennial Exposition in Philadelphia in 1876 and in 1944 a bronze plaque was unveiled at the state capitol in Nashville to honor the election of Cockrill to the Tennessee Agricultural Hall of Fame.
Wayne C. Moore, Tennessee State Library and Archives
SEE: AGRICULTURE; COCKRILL, ANN R.; FARRIS AGRICULTURAL MUSEUM; LIVESTOCK

COE, FREDERICK H. (1914–1979), leading producer and director during the "golden age of television" of the 1950s, was born in Mississippi, but raised in Nashville and called Tennessee home. Described by media critic Richard Corliss as "one of TV's smartest, boldest pioneers," Coe was the primary creative force behind the *Philco-Goodyear Playhouse,* a highly regarded live performance anthology produced in New York City.[1] Coe's guidance in the Philco series, as well as other anthologies such as *Playhouse 90,* produced such television drama classics as *Marty* by Paddy Chayefsky, *The Trip to Bountiful* by Horton Foote, *The Death of Billy the Kid* by Gore Vidal, *Days of Wine and Roses,* and the musical *Peter Pan,* starring Mary Martin, which was the highest rated program yet on television when it

Levin Hudson Coe.

COURTESY OF CARL ROBERT COE

aired in 1955. Coe was famous for nurturing the creative side of television: its writers, directors, and actors. He supported writers like Chayefsky, Foote, Vidal, Tad Mosel, and J.P. Miller, directors Delbert Mann (also from Nashville) and Arthur Penn, and young actors such as Grace Kelly, Paul Newman, Nancy Marchand, and Rod Steiger. Coe also convinced current movie stars, such as Henry Fonda, Jose Ferrer, Humphrey Bogart, and Lauren Bacall, to do television productions.

Coe's success in television led to opportunities both on the stage and the movie screen. On Broadway, he produced *The Miracle Worker* and *All the Way Home*, which won a Pulitzer prize. In 1965 he directed the film classic, *A Thousand Clowns*. This work largely ended Coe's period of significance in American drama. He died in 1979.

Carroll Van West, Middle Tennessee State University
CITATION:
(1) Richard Corliss, "How Golden Was It?" *Time* (August 18, 1997): 72.
SUGGESTED READING: Jon Krampner, *The Man in the Shadows: Fred Coe and the Golden Age of Television* (1997)
SEE: AGEE, JAMES R.; MANN, DELBERT

COE, LEVIN HUDSON (1806–1850). Of those who carried the Tennessee Democratic banner during the middle decades of the nineteenth century, few were as colorful, magnanimous, diligent, or fearsome as General Levin Coe. As a political warrior, Coe had few peers in either party.

After graduation from the University of Pennsylvania, where he received a law degree, Coe returned to Tennessee. In 1837 he won election to the Tennessee General Assembly, representing Fayette, Hardeman, and Shelby counties. Re-elected in 1839, the House conferred upon him the honor of Speaker of the Twenty-third General Assembly.

When Polk became president in early 1845, Coe received consideration for both a cabinet position and the Tennessee Democratic gubernatorial nomination. He was appointed inspector general of the Tennessee Militias.

In July 1846 President Polk offered Coe the position as quartermaster in the Army of Occupation in Mexico, with the rank of Major, which he declined. In 1848 he was again a strong contender for the Democratic gubernatorial nomination. That same year, at the Democratic National Convention, his name was placed in nomination for Vice President of the United States.

In June 1850, while serving as Memphis attorney general, Coe was shot in the back by Joseph C. Williams during a gun battle on the streets of Memphis, an attack precipitated by allegations of fraud concerning a local bank. He died August 10, 1850, at the age of 44.

Carl Robert Coe, Marysville, Ohio
SUGGESTED READING: Carl R. Coe, "Politics and Assassination: The Story of General Levin Hudson Coe," *Tennessee Historical Quarterly* 54(1995): 30–39
SEE: FAYETTE COUNTY; JACKSONIANS; MEXICAN WAR; POLK, JAMES K.

COFFEE COUNTY, located in Middle Tennessee, was established from parts of Bedford, Warren, and Franklin counties in 1836 and named in honor of

PHOTO BY CARROLL VAN WEST

Coffee County Courthouse.

General John Coffee, who was a close political ally of Andrew Jackson. The county has several important prehistoric sites, the most significant being Old Stone Fort State Archaeological Area at the forks of the Duck River. Woodland Period people constructed a large ceremonial enclosure here. Carbon-dating within the walls has produced construction dates of A.D. 30, A.D. 230, and A.D. 430, indicating that the site was used for at least four centuries. Whites began to arrive in the county during the 1790s. Fort Nash, which protected travelers and encouraged permanent settlement, was established in 1793 on Garrison Fork near Beech Grove.

When the county was created in 1836, Manchester was named county seat on 200 acres belonging to James Evans and Andrew Haynes. The first courthouse opened in 1837 and served the county until it burned and was replaced by the present Coffee County Courthouse in 1871. This Italianate-styled courthouse is listed in the National Register of Historic Places.

The construction of the Nashville and Chattanooga Railroad during the 1850s reshaped the county's landscape and economy. Railroad officials created the town of Tullahoma as the mid-point of the railroad's line and established extensive works there, including a spur line from Tullahoma to Manchester to McMinnville, which eventually continued to coal mines and timber holdings in White County. The presence of the railroad brought both armies to Coffee County during the Civil War. Due to its importance as a rail center, both sides occupied Tullahoma at different times, destroying much of the original town. In August 1862 the Confederate cavalry of Nathan B. Forrest suffered 180 casualties in its attempt to destroy a federal post protecting the railroad at Guest Hollow. The Tullahoma campaign of 1863 touched many families and several county villages. At Beech Grove, for instance, a cemetery holds the remains of Confederate soldiers who died during the defense of Hoover's Gap.

A quickly rebuilt railroad returned prosperity in the Reconstruction era. Tullahoma grew rapidly into Coffee County's largest and most prosperous town. Important businesses included the retail firm of Dunn and Campbell, headed by Michael Ross Campbell; the Hurricane Springs resort, which was six miles south of Tullahoma; the Tullahoma Woolen Mill; and the M.R. Campbell Hub, Spoke Rim, and Handle Works. Manchester added the Hickerson and Wooten Paper Company in 1879. The county's distillery business thrived in these decades, led by Maclin H. Davis's Cascade Distillery, founded in 1882 and now known as George Dickell Distilleries, which opened in 1959.

Transportation remained crucial to Coffee County's growth in the twentieth century. Tullahoma became a railroad division headquarters in 1920. Automobile traffic became increasingly important once the Dixie Highway located through the county, largely running parallel with the railroad tracks, during the 1920s. The prospect of good transportation, for example, attracted the Lannom Manufacturing Company, which after 1922 made baseballs, softballs, and gloves. Coffee County emerged as a national leader in the sporting goods industry, led now by the Worth manufacturing corporation.

County leaders and civic officials in Tullahoma used the existing transportation network, and free railroad land, to convince government officials to locate a military base within the county. In 1926 the state established Camp Peay, a training facility for the national guard, near Tullahoma. The surrounding countryside became the site of the guard's annual maneuvers and exercises.

The Great Depression slowed growth. The Works Progress Administration built a Colonial Revival-styled post office in Manchester. In 1934 investors established in Tullahoma a clothing and shoe company called the General Shoe Corporation, which was the precursor of the major American corporation known today as Genesco.

World War II boosted the county as had no other event before. In January 1941 the General Assembly created the volunteer Tennessee State Guard, which received federal training at Camp Peay. That June, the U.S. Second Army came to Coffee County for maneuvers; headquarters were established at the high school in Manchester. The Second Armored Division, under the command of Major General George S. Patton, used the Coffee County terrain along the river to demonstrate the value, speed, and maneuverability of armored forces in a large-scale combat operation. After the attack on Pearl Harbor on December 7, 1941, government officials convinced the army to take control of Camp Peay and turn it into a federal induction center, renamed Camp Forrest. During the war, an estimated 250,000 soldiers passed through the gates of Camp Forrest, stimulating a commercial boom countywide but especially in Tullahoma. One estimate has the town's temporary population, counting service personnel, reaching 75,000 during the war years.

After Camp Forrest closed in 1946, local and state officials urged the federal government to transform the old military base into a modern technological and research center. On June 25, 1951, President Harry S. Truman formally dedicated the Arnold Engineering Development Corporation Center (AEDC), named in honor of General "Hap" Arnold, who commanded the Army Air Forces during World War II. AEDC ever since has been an important employer as well as an attraction for other high-tech personnel and firms to locate in the area. In the late twentieth century,

Motlow State Community College and the Tullahoma Fine Arts Center have emerged as key institutions shaping modern cultural life in Coffee County.

Carroll Van West, Middle Tennessee State University

SEE: ARNOLD ENGINEERING DEVELOPMENT CENTER; CAMP FORREST; DISTILLERIES, HISTORIC; HIGHWAYS, HISTORIC; RAILROAD, NASHVILLE AND CHATTANOOGA; OLD STONE FORT; SECOND ARMY MANEUVERS; TULLAHOMA CAMPAIGN; WORLD WAR II; WORTH INC.

COHEN, STANLEY (1923-), the second Vanderbilt University Medical Center professor to win the Nobel Prize, joined Vanderbilt in 1959 as a professor of biochemistry. The Nobel Prize committee recognized him for his work with Rita Levi-Montalcini in their discovery of nerve growth factor and his independent discovery and research of epidermal growth factor, a hormone-like protein that stimulates cell growth.

Levi-Montalcini, a developmental biologist, discovered nerve growth factor in the early 1950s while working with Viktor Hamburger at Washington University in St. Louis. She concluded that the tumor released a nerve-growth-promoting factor that affected certain types of cells. Cohen, then a postdoctoral fellow in biochemistry at Washington University, isolated the nerve growth protein from the salivary glands of the mouse.

After seven years of work at Washington University, Cohen independently continued and expanded his work at Vanderbilt University. His work on epidermal growth factor—which stimulates many different processes in the body including proliferation of cells in the skin, cornea, immune system, liver blood cells, thyroid, ovaries, and pituitary gland—may help scientists understand how to stop cancerous growth. His discoveries on cell growth and multiplication already aid burn victims and hold promise in the areas of senile dementia and muscular dystrophy.

A native of Brooklyn, New York, Cohen has been honored with many top medical research awards, including the 1986 National Medal of Science, the 1985 Gairdner Foundation International Award, and the 1986 Albert Lasker Basic Medical Research Award, which is considered second only to the Nobel Prize.

Kelly Lockhart, Murfreesboro

SEE: MEDICINE; VANDERBILT UNIVERSITY MEDICAL CENTER

COHN, WALDO (1910-), founder and first conductor of the Oak Ridge Symphony Orchestra, the state's oldest continuing symphony, came to Oak Ridge in 1943 with a biochemistry Ph.D. from the University of California at Berkeley via science experience at the University of Chicago. Immediately he instigated chamber music sessions in his home. When the group grew too large, rehearsals moved to the high school. As the Oak Ridge Symphonette, it gave its first concert in June 1944. By November, having combined with brass and woodwind players, the first fullfledged symphony concert was presented. Cohn continued as conductor for the next 11 years. Although classic composers were standard, the conductor also introduced works by Americans such as Edward McDowell and Henry Cowell.

Isaac Stern appeared as soloist in 1948 as a favor to Cohn and to help get the Oak Ridge Civic Music Association started. Other early soloists included Percy Grainger, Yalta Menuhin, Nadia Reisenberg, and Samuel Sanders.

Cohn today plays the cello in the Oak Ridge Symphony Orchestra.

June Adamson, Oak Ridge

SEE: MUSIC; OAK RIDGE; SYMPHONY ORCHESTRAS

COLDITZ COVE STATE NATURAL AREA, located in Fentress County east of the historic town of Allardt, is one of the state's most recently designated natural areas. The state acquired the area's approximately 70 acres from a donation of the property owners, Rudolph and Arnold Colditz, and the Nature Conservancy assisted in the transfer of the land from private to public ownership. The Cumberland Mountain Chapter of the Tennessee Trails Association developed the area's trail system.

The highlight of Colditz Cove is Northrup Falls, named for a family who once homesteaded nearby. The trail passes through a large rockshelter behind Northrup Falls; during the winter, large and beautiful ice formations cover the cliffs. The trail features an overlook, virgin hemlocks, growths of rhododendron, and picturesque sandstone cliffs.

Carroll Van West, Middle Tennessee State University

SEE: CONSERVATION; FENTRESS COUNTY

COLE, EDMUND W. "KING" (1827–1899), a leading late nineteenth century railroad entrepreneur, financier, and philanthropist, was born in Giles County, Tennessee, a descendent of a prominent Virginia family. Cole's father died when he was three months old, leaving his mother with a large family to support. Cole worked on the family farm until he was 18 and had little schooling or few advantages. In 1845 he left the farm for Nashville, where his life became a Tennessee version of the Horatio Alger story of rags to riches. Cole worked as a store clerk and attended night school. In 1851 he became a bookkeeper for the Nashville and Chattanooga Railroad; in 1868 he was the company's president.

Over the next decade, "King" Cole transformed this dilapidated railroad into a formidable contender among the rail systems of the central South, linking Nashville to St. Louis to the north and Atlanta and

Savannah to the southeast. Cole envisioned Nashville as the gateway linking the growing Midwest commerce in grain and meat to the cotton-producing South. In 1879–1880 Cole moved to implement his scheme to build a grand trunk line linking the Midwest to the Southeast and a line of transatlantic steamers. As he was putting his plan into place, the rival L&N system secretly organized a coup and took over Cole's railroad, which by then was known as the Nashville, Chattanooga, and St. Louis (NC&St.L). The merger, one of several that established L&N's regional dominance, ended competition for railroad service to Nashville, except for a brief and futile challenge by Jere Baxter and the Tennessee Central.

Cole resigned from the NC&St.L following the takeover, and for the next two years he served as president of the East Tennessee, Virginia, and Georgia Railroad, which also controlled the Memphis and Charleston Railroad. Cole resigned in 1882 and channeled his business energies into Nashville banking and real estate, becoming a major property owner and developer. He financed the construction of downtown office buildings, including the Cole Block at Union and Cherry (now Fourth Avenue). Much of his entrepreneurial energy and capital also went into the founding of several different Nashville banking institutions. During the 1880s, when the city laid its foundations as a regional financial center, Cole was among the leading financial architects. Chief among his banking enterprises was the American National Bank, which he founded in 1883.

Cole became a prominent philanthropist in the late 1880s, a southern version of the many American capitalists of the Gilded Age, who supplemented and offset their reputation for acquisitive fortune building with public spirited charities. A civic-minded man, Cole served on the State Board of Health and was active in the Tennessee Historical Society. A devout Methodist, he donated his time and fortune to the promotion of Methodist missionary and educational work. He was an important donor to the Methodists' Vanderbilt University; among other contributions, he endowed a lecture series, which continues to bear his name. In honor of his late son, Cole also donated to the State of Tennessee property for Randall Cole Industrial School, designed to educate orphaned and wayward boys. Established in 1885, it was renamed the Tennessee Industrial School in 1887. In an 1890 biographical sketch, Cole depicted his life as an American parable of success, which owed much to his strict Methodist mother and her lessons of hard work and self-denial, in particular abstinence from drink, tobacco, gambling, and dancing. These values guided Cole's philanthropy as well.

Cole married twice, first to Louise McGavock Lytle, of Williamson County, who died in 1869, and in 1872 to Anna V. Russell of Augusta, Georgia.

Among Cole's survivors was his son, Whitfoord R. Cole, who continued in his father's footsteps as a successful railroad magnate with the L&N and a leading supporter of Vanderbilt University.

Don H. Doyle, Vanderbilt University

SEE: RAILROAD, NASHVILLE AND CHATTANOOGA; RAILROADS; TENNESSEE HISTORICAL SOCIETY; VANDERBILT UNIVERSITY

COLORED AGRICULTURAL WHEEL, organized in the mid-1880s, shortly after the establishment of the Agricultural Wheel in Tennessee, supported the same demands for economic and political changes that white Wheelers advocated. Similarly, the Colored Wheel adopted secret passwords and rituals, and operated under a hierarchy of officers like that of the white organization. Members of the Colored Wheel published news of local, county, and state wheels in *The Weekly Toiler,* the official organ of the Tennessee State Wheel. They bought and sold through the Wheel's State Business Agency in Nashville and Memphis.

The Colored Wheel endured a greater degree of white supervision over their internal affairs than was true for the Colored Alliance, perhaps a reflection of the organization's economic weakness (the Colored Wheel had to borrow money from the white organization in order to obtain a charter). John H. McDowell, editor of the *Toiler,* attended a July 1888 meeting of the Tipton County Colored Wheel and reported favorably on the proceedings, praising the attentiveness of the audience and the enthusiasm for the cause of agrarian reform. That same month, the state conventions of the two organizations met simultaneously at Dunbar Cave near Clarksville. The two Wheels held one joint meeting and exchanged representatives for other sessions. They ended their conventions by reaffirming their commitment to Wheel demands.

The Colored Wheel experienced conflicts with the white Wheel and the Colored Farmers' Alliance. McDowell lambasted James Y. Bernard, the president of the Tipton County Colored Wheel and later State President of the organization, for his insistence on using only African-American organizers, apparently to prevent divulging the secret work to whites. When the Colored Alliance moved into West Tennessee, the two organizations battled briefly over members before resolving the conflict. The Colored Wheel and Colored Alliance never achieved the unification of the two organizations that their white counterparts achieved in 1889, and the Colored Wheel faded from view before 1890.

Connie L. Lester, Tennessee Historical Society

SEE: AGRICULTURAL WHEEL; COLORED FARMERS' ALLIANCE; DUNBAR CAVE STATE NATURAL AREA; MCDOWELL, JOHN H.

COLORED FARMERS' ALLIANCE AND LABORERS' UNION, TENNESSEE. This grassroots agrarian cooperative movement was founded in 1886 by 16 African-American farmers in Houston County, Texas, and spread rapidly across the South. Similar to the white Farmers' Alliance, the Colored Alliance advocated a program of uplift that promoted black education and agitated for better prices and market conditions.

C. D. Vaughan of Tipton County organized the first Colored Alliance in Tennessee in the spring of 1888. By June he had commissioned 17 organizers in the county and more than 40 statewide, even as he competed for members with the other grassroots farmer organization in the the the state, the Colored Wheel. W. A. Lewis, a black minister from Munford, served as the county business agent. Throughout the summer, as the organizating effort intensified, Vaughan advertised for 1,000 organizers, either white or black. By December the Colored Alliance and the Colored Wheel counted a combined 421 lodges across West and Middle Tennessee. Whites recognized the need to include African-American farmers in the demands for agrarian reform, and they encouraged the separate organization by granting column space in the state newspaper, *The Weekly Toiler*. In addition, the white organization extended to black farmers the right to make purchases through the state business agency, though they clearly expected the Colored Alliance to establish a separate business agency as soon as possible.

In June 1889 delegates from Shelby, Lincoln, Tipton, and Giles counties met in Memphis to create a state Colored Alliance. National General Superintendent R. M. Humphrey, a white Baptist minister, was the featured speaker. The delegates elected J. W. Brown of Giles County as Tennessee General Superintendent to replace Vaughan. They extended their appreciation to the *Toiler* for printing organizational news and pledged to support the business agency. When the state organization met again in Pulaski in August 1891, delegates reaffirmed their solidarity with white farmers.

Political and economic events of the early 1890s acted in conjunction to bring about the demise of the Colored Alliance in Tennessee. As the Farmers' Alliance became more active politically, the Democratic party used associations between African-American voters and the Republican party to discredit the movement and generate hostility within the organization. In addition to the political tensions, in 1891, the Colored Alliance in the South organized a cotton pickers boycott to protest the combination of planters and merchants to control wages and prices. Organization of the strike proceeded without the knowledge of white Alliance members. Without adequate coordination, the strike collapsed as black pickers struck in a piecemeal fashion over several days. Tennessee pickers did not strike, but planters, fearing the worst

and concerned about losing the crop, raised wages for the season. In the long run, however, the proposed strike reinforced the political distrust and contributed to the demise of the Colored Alliance.

By the end of 1891, no further references to the Colored Alliance can be found in Tennessee. What many viewed as an opportunity to overcome racial tension and create a new political and economic future for white and black farmers ended with the re-emergence of white paternalism and self-interest.

Connie L. Lester, Tennessee Historical Society
SUGGESTED READINGS: Gerald H. Gaither, *Blacks and the Populist Revolt: Ballots and Bigotry in the "New South"* (1977) and "The Negro Alliance Movement in Tennessee, 1888–1891," West Tennessee Historical Society *Papers* 27(1973): 50–62
SEE: AGRICULTURAL WHEEL; COLORED AGRICULTURAL WHEEL; FARMERS' AND LABORERS' UNION

"COLORED MEN'S" APPLICATIONS FOR PENSION. In 1921 the Tennessee General Assembly enacted a law "to provide for those colored men who served as servants and cooks in the Confederate Army." Senator Edgar Jones Graham of Hickman County proposed the bill, which entitled former slaves to ten dollars per month if they could show proof of remaining with the army until the close of the war. Widows were ineligible.

More than 280 ex-slaves presented applications to the Board of Pensions between 1921 and 1935, including the body servant of President Jefferson Davis and two men formerly owned by Nathan Bedford Forrest. The questionnaires, similar to those for white Confederate veterans, provide valuable social, military, and personal family information heretofore largely ignored. The most revealing aspect of the collection, which is stored at the Tennessee State Library and Archives, includes the supporting documents submitted with many of the questionnaires. Since each petitioner was required to prove his army service, dozens of files contain correspondence and notarized statements detailing the writer's knowledge of the applicant. Some files contain handwritten notes from former slaves. Although most of the men identified themselves as servants and cooks, a few provided more details about their work, including builder, supply wagon driver, blacksmith, forager, orderly, soldier, message runner, hospital laborer, porter, and miller at the Loudon Mill. The greatest number of applications came from West Tennessee, and several men were active in local and regional veterans' organizations. The last of the pensioners died in 1943.

Susan L. Gordon, Tennessee Historical Society
SEE: TENNESSEE CIVIL WAR VETERANS' QUESTIONNAIRES

COLUMBIA RACE RIOT, 1946, occurred in Columbia, Tennessee, on the night of February 25–26, 1946. Like other outbreaks of violence in the South in the immediate post-World War II era, this incident involved military veterans who were unwilling to accept prevailing racial norms upon returning to their hometowns. In 1946 Columbia contained about 5,000 whites and 3,000 blacks. Race relations in the county had often been tense in the prior generation; since 1925, for example, three lynchings had taken place there. But racial violence decreased during World War II and the postwar months witnessed few indications of future trouble.

On February 25, 1946, James Stephenson, a Navy veteran from the Pacific theater, accompanied his mother, Gladys Stephenson, to a local department store to pick up a radio that Mrs. Stephenson had left for repairs. She and a young white male clerk began to argue about the repair order; he became verbally aggressive and then he struck her. James Stephenson stepped between the two and struggled with the clerk, who ended up crashing through a window in the department store. Local police arrested both Stephensons for disturbing the peace. They pleaded guilty and paid a $50 fine.

The incident was seemingly over until, on that same day, the police again arrested James Stephenson, this time due to a warrant brought by the white clerk's father. The new warrant charged Stephenson with assault with the intent to commit murder, a felony. Julius Blair, a local black businessman, posted bond, however, and Stephenson was able to return home that evening.

On the night of February 25 a white mob gathered around the Maury County Courthouse. A block south, along the segregated black business section known as the Mink Slide, black citizens and military veterans gathered as well. The Columbia police chief sent four patrolmen to the Mink Slide. Someone shouted for the officers to stop; when they failed to do so, shots were fired, leaving all four wounded. Within hours, state highway patrolmen and the state safety commissioner, Lynn Bomar, arrived in town. Together with some of the town's whites, they surrounded the Mink Slide district. During the early morning of February 26, highway patrolmen first entered the district (followed later by deputized Guardsmen). The officers fired randomly into buildings, stealing cash and goods, searching homes without warrants, and taking any guns, rifles, and shotguns they could find. When the sweep was over, more than 100 blacks had been arrested and about 300 weapons from the black community had been confiscated. None of the accused was granted bail nor allowed legal counsel.

The Columbia "riot" made headlines across the state and the nation. Walter White and Thurgood Marshall of the National Association for the Advancement of Colored People immediately flew to Nashville in order to organize a legal defense. White

met with Govenor James N. McCord and announced the creation of a national defense committee. Marshall turned to Tennessee attorneys Z. Alexander Looby of Nashville and Maurice Weaver of Chattanooga for assistance.

Matters intensified on February 28 when Columbia policemen killed two black prisoners in custody. During an interrogation of James Johnson, William Gordon, and Napoleon Stewart, the police reported, two prisoners grabbed guns from white officers and began shooting. In defense, the police retaliated, killing two and wounding the third suspect. This ended the immediate violence in Columbia, but the case continued throughout the spring and summer of 1946. A federal grand jury was convened to investigate the charges of misconduct by the white policemen, but the local all-white jury absolved the officers of any wrong doing. Eventually, 25 blacks were tried in Lawrenceburg for the shootings of the white officers, but none was found guilty. Only one black male, Lloyd Kennedy, served any time in jail, for shooting at a white highway patrolman.

By November 1946 the case was over, but racial harrassment continued. As Marshall, Looby, and Weaver left Columbia for the final time, a convoy of patrolmen followed. The police stopped the three civil rights attorneys twice for alleged highway violations. The third time, they arrested Marshall for drunk driving, placed him in a patrol car, and sped away. Looby and Weaver followed, fearing for Marshall's life, but after a long journey through the countryside, the police stopped at a local magistrate's office, where the charge of drunk driving was dropped. Marshall was free to go, but this time the attorneys asked Columbia friends to mount their own convoy to escort the three men safely to Nashville. "The Columbia incident and the reaction to it," concluded historian Dorothy Beeler, "were major events of the late 1940's, which helped create a base from which black organizations gathered strength for the civil rights push of the 1950's and 1960's."[1]

Carroll Van West, Middle Tennessee State University

CITATION:

(1) Dorothy Beeler, "Race Riot in Columbia, Tennessee, February 25–27, 1946" *Tennessee Historical Quarterly* 39(1980): 60–61.

SUGGESTED READING: John Egerton, *Speak Now Against The Day: The Generation before the Civil Rights Movement in the South* (1994)

SEE: ATHENS, BATTLE OF; CIVIL RIGHTS MOVEMENT; LOOBY, Z. ALEXANDER; MAURY COUNTY

COLUMBIA/HCA HEALTHCARE CORPORATION,

one of the nation's largest healthcare companies and largest private employers, is based in Nashville. The present company represents the merger of several hospital and healthcare companies, primarily the

Hospital Corporation of American (HCA) and the Columbia Hospital Corporation. HCA was a Nashville-based healthcare corporation, established as one of the first private healthcare corporations in the country by Jack Massey, Thomas F. Frist, Sr., and Thomas F. Frist, Jr., in 1968. Frist, Sr., began the company by organizing Park View Hospital in Nashville in 1956. After the creation of Medicaid and Medicare in 1965, the number of for-profit hospitals across the country began to grow. At that same time, Frist and the other doctors at Park View decided to sell Park View Hospital to a new management company to operate the property. Frist, Sr., and Frist, Jr., then asked Nashville businessman Jack Massey for assistance, and the three established their own management company, called Hospital Corporation of America. The new corporation relied on solid leadership and sound financial decisions to quickly become one of the most important private healthcare providers in the country. By 1979 HCA owned or managed 140 hospitals; by the mid-1980s, the hospital chain included over 200 hospitals and held contracts to manage 200 more.

Over the last ten years, from 1987 to the summer of 1997, the size and structure of HCA changed to meet the opportunities and challenges of the competitive healthcare industry. In 1987 HCA sold 104 hospitals to the newly created Healthtrust corporation. In February 1994, it formally merged its 97 hospitals with the Columbia Hospital Corporation to create Columbia/HCA, an immediate national leader in the industry. Richard Scott, who established the Columbia Hospital Corporation in Texas in 1987, became the new corporation's CEO. In 1991 Scott's Columbia had a base of 12 hospitals; it then acquired Basic American Medical (eight hospitals) in 1992, Galen Health Care Corporation (71 hospitals) in 1993, and then the 97 hospitals of HCA, as well as the 96 ambulatory surgical centers of Medical Care America in 1994. Columbia's expansion was not over; in 1995 it acquired the 117 hospitals of Healthtrust. According to a 1997 tally, Columbia/HCA owned and operated over 340 hospitals, with properties in 36 states and two foreign countries.

Scott's success story, however, unraveled in the summer of 1997. Federal investigators raided hospitals in seven states in search of evidence of fraud in Columbia's billings to the federal Medicare program. By July 24, 1997, Scott had resigned as CEO, replaced by Thomas Frist, Jr. Frist immediately announced that "the new CEO of this company is very serious about addressing the government's concerns, and understands the gravity of the situation."[1] By the end of August, according to the Associated Press, ten states were investigating Columbia/HCA for possible Medicaid fraud. Yet, by the end of the summer, Frist's new management style and willingness to cooperate with

the healthcare industry, investors, and government investigators was already paying dividends for the Nashville-based corporation as it faced pressing legal and competitive challenges in 1997 and 1998.

Carroll Van West, Middle Tennessee State University
CITATION:
(1) New York *Times,* On-line edition, July 26, 1997.
SEE: MASSEY, JACK C.; MEDICINE; NASHVILLE

COLYAR, ARTHUR ST. CLAIR (1818–1907), attorney, political leader, newspaper editor, and industrialist, was born in Jonesborough, one of 13 children of Alexander and Katherine Sevier Sherrill Colyar. Colyar received his education in the Washington County common schools, and in 1828 he and his parents moved to Franklin County. He was first employed as a teacher and later read law before his admission to the bar at Winchester in 1846. Politically, Colyar supported the Whigs in a traditionally Democratic stronghold. By 1860 he owned approximately 30 slaves and was a member of the Constitutional Union party. Colyar opposed secession until Tennessee joined the Confederacy in 1861.

In October 1861, while campaigning for a seat in the First Confederate Congress, Colyar contracted pneumonia. He recuperated and practiced law in Winchester until 1863. One anecdote holds that he defended a Union man unlawfully jailed by Confederate authorities at the risk of his own life. He left Winchester soon after the abortive Confederate General Assembly met there, following the Tullahoma offensive by General W. S. Rosecrans in June 1863.

In November 1863 Colyar was elected to the Confederate Congress, serving from May 1864 until March 18, 1865. Although he supported direct taxation, the agricultural tax-in-kind, and taxes on corporate profits, he opposed economic controls, a stance he repudiated after the war. He opposed the suspension of the writ of *habeas corpus.* Colyar recognized the wisdom of opening peace talks and refused to support a motion to banish Senator Henry S. Foote for undertaking peace negotiations in early 1865.

At the end of the war, Colyar received a quick presidential pardon in September 1865. Thereafter, he lived in Nashville, where he returned to his law practice, engaged in state politics, and became involved in a variety of political and industrial matters. On three occasions, Colyar ran unsuccessfully for governor on an independent ticket. In 1870 he was an unsuccessful candidate for the gubernatorial nomination of the Conservatives and Democrats. In 1871 he allied with the Reunion and Reform Association, but abandoned that organization, and ran as an independent candidate for governor in 1872, before retiring from the election in favor of John C. Brown. In 1876 he was one of the organizers of the Greenback Party, a delegate to that party's national convention, and an unsuccessful candidate for the General Assembly. He was elected as an independent to represent Davidson County for the first and extra sessions of the 1877 legislature. In 1878 he ran unsuccessfully for the Democratic gubernatorial nomination.

His political activities always were associated with his diverse business interests in industry, mining, and commerce. Colyar's interest in coal mining and the iron furnace industry began in 1858, when he purchased the old Sewanee Mining Company. After the war, that company became Tennessee Coal and Iron Company, and later developed into Tennessee Coal, Iron, and Railway Company, one of the region's most important firms. Colyar sold ownership interest in 1881, but his interest in the company remained substantial. In 1882 he joined with Joseph B. Killebrew and others to organize the Rockdale Company and the Rock City Real Estate Company to acquire and develop mineral rights in Maury County. He also had interests in Rising Fawn Furnace, the Chattanooga Furnace, and Soddy coal mines. In 1881 he purchased controlling ownership of the Nashville *American,* which he edited and published until 1884.

A New South proponent, Colyar encouraged industrial development through the promotion of northern capital, agricultural diversification, and foreign immigration. As Vice President of Tennessee Coal, Iron, and Railway Company, he avidly supported the state program of convict leasing, which supplied convict labor to replace free miners. In 1885 the *Nashville Banner* exposed Colyar's involvement in the convict lease system. A legislative investigation and a libel suit resulted. Colyar successfully thwarted an early penal reform movement and escaped censure.

Colyar's interests were varied. He was involved in the building of the University of the South at Sewanee in the postwar years. In 1904 he published the two-volume *Life and Times of Andrew Jackson.* At an unknown date, Colyar married Agnes Erskine Estill of Winchester; they were the parents of 11 children. Two years after the 1886 death of his first wife, Colyar married Mrs. Mary McGuire of Louisville, Kentucky. Colyar died in Nashville in 1907 and is buried in Mount Olivet Cemetery.

James B. Jones, Jr., Tennessee Historical Commission
SUGGESTED READINGS: Clyde Ball, "The Public Career of Col. A. S. Colyar, 1870–1877," *Tennessee Historical Quarterly* 12(1953): 24–47, 106–128; 213–238; Sarah M. Howell, "Editorials of Arthur S. Colyar, Nashville Prophet of the New South," *Tennessee Historical Quarterly* 27(1968): 262–276
SEE: CONVICT LEASE WARS; FRANKLIN COUNTY; INDUSTRY; KILLEBREW, JOSEPH B.; MINING; UNIVERSITY OF THE SOUTH

COMMERCE AND URBAN DEVELOPMENT. Ten-
nessee's early patterns of commercial exchange deter-

mined the location and growth of its urban centers. Commercial centers typically formed at some junction of land and water that required a break in the mode of transportation, usually from animal-powered overland wagons to some waterborne method of transport. In Tennessee, the major trade centers all formed along rivers at points conducive to navigation and protection from flooding. The advent of railroads allowed more flexibility in the location of new commercial centers of activity, but railroads also tended to reinforce the initial advantages gained by the earliest urban river sites.

The primary commercial exchange of early Tennessee involved the export of agricultural goods and the importation of eastern and foreign finished products. Because of Tennessee's geographic isolation from the major commercial ports along the eastern coasts, its commercial economy prior to the railroad age was largely limited to local exchange. Much of the population depended on semi-subsistence and a locally contained economy before the Civil War. Most food, cloth, clothing, shoes, home furnishings, farm implements, leather goods, and blacksmith products were produced and consumed within Tennessee or adjacent western states for all but the wealthiest segments of society who could afford to import eastern or European products.

The main agents in the commercial economy of early Tennessee were the cotton plantations of the Nashville Basin, which became part of the expanding cotton frontier after 1800. Cotton and tobacco soon superseded the furs, skins, and other items of export that figured in the Indian trade before this time. Goods gathered in Nashville could be shipped down the Cumberland, Ohio, and Mississippi rivers to New Orleans by flatboat or keelboat. Wagon trains from Philadelphia carried eastern and foreign goods overland to Pittsburgh and then by water down the Ohio and up the Cumberland, reinforcing Nashville's early role as the main entrepot connecting Middle Tennessee to the outside world. With the advent of the steamboat in the 1820s, Nashville's role as a commercial center grew apace, and the city's population rose from a mere 345 in 1800 to 10,165 by 1850.

Knoxville emerged as the major port on the Tennessee River for the eastern part of the state; Chattanooga eventually played a similar role down river serving southeastern Tennessee. Their populations stood at only about 2,000 and 1,000 respectively in 1850, a reflection of the comparatively minor role of commercial exchange in the economy of the mountainous eastern region of the state where the rural population remained more devoted to semi-subsistence production. The steamboat made both these cities more accessible, but the mountainous terrain and lack of any significant cash crop in their surrounding hinterlands left them as minor players in the commercial and urban development of the state before 1850.

Memphis, preceded by a Chickasaw trading post established in 1794, was not laid out as an American city until 1819. It served as the major trading center for the expanding cotton frontier as it advanced into West Tennessee and northern Mississippi with the removal of the Chickasaws, which was completed by 1840. With several million acres of rich Chickasaw land thrown open to American settlement, Memphis quickly established itself as the leading inland cotton market in the South and the chief trade center for all of northern Mississippi and eastern Arkansas, as well as West Tennessee. By 1850 the population of Memphis had climbed to 8,841, standing a little behind Nashville as one of two major urban centers of the trans-Appalachian South. In the next ten years, with the expansion of its railroads and the growth of the cotton empire, Memphis shot to front rank among cities in Tennessee and the region, standing at 22,623 in 1860, while Nashville settled into its notch as the state's second ranked city with 16,988. On the eve of the Civil War, Memphis was shipping over 360,000 bales of cotton, having surpassed New Orleans long ago, and claimed close to ten percent of the total U.S. cotton market.

The upheaval that came with the Civil War brought great change to the state's commercial and urban development. There were short term disruptions to the entire economy along with booming wartime prosperity in some locales. Few southern cities benefited more from the war than Nashville which, after its fall in February 1862, became the major supply center for the western theater of war. The Louisville and Nashville Railroad remained a vital link between the North and South, and Nashville's warehouses bulged with war materiel and provision brought into the city by the railroad to supply Union forces as they advanced southward. Memphis fell to Union forces in June 1862, but much of West Tennessee and northern Mississippi remained contested by the two warring armies. Memphis thrived on the contraband trade that flowed southward to the Confederacy in the form of food and supplies, while blockade runners and speculators from the Deep South brought in confiscated and smuggled cotton. Few of Tennessee's cities suffered extensive damage during the war, several thrived under Union occupation, and the recovery of commerce was generally robust in the years that followed.

The defeat of the Confederacy, the destruction of slavery, and the impact of both on the planter class helped open the state to new currents of economic change after the war. In addition to transforming former slaves into much larger producers and consumers in the marketplace, the New South's economy pulled large numbers of white farmers out of their past semi-subsistence practices into the commercial agriculture of the future. By the end of the century, growing numbers of the white and black populations were forsaking the farm for new lives in the towns and cities. The decline of cotton prices was symptomatic of the general unpredictability and cruel indifference the marketplace showed to former yeomen and former slaves who had entered into market production since the Civil War.

The New South era is most often associated with the crusade for regional industrial development. In Tennessee the industrial spirit was particularly notable in the mountain regions of the East where textiles, mining, metallurgy, and other industries made important inroads during the late nineteenth century. Knoxville and Chattanooga both profited from industrial development. Nashville and other smaller cities in Middle Tennessee also enjoyed a degree of industrial progress, much of it linked to the iron and coal industries. But Nashville and Memphis remained primarily commercial cities with only limited industrial bases, and it was in the commercial sector of the Tennessee economy that the most dramatic transformations took place during the New South era. The expansion of the railway system and the general shift from subsistence to commercial agriculture stimulated vast changes in Tennessee's commercial development.

The advent of the steam railroad reduced Tennessee's dependency on river transportation as the major avenue of commerce, and it offset some of the former disadvantages of the state's inland isolation and mountain barriers to the east. The railroads fostered the mushroom-like growth of a number of new urban trade centers within the interior of the state. New towns emerged along the railways and by 1900, Tennessee claimed 22 urban places (defined as places with at least 2,500 population). Dozens more smaller trade centers flourished as well, all feeding the arteries of commerce as a growing portion of the rural population abandoned the traditional semi-subsistence economy in favor of producing for urban markets. In turn, country stores in rural hamlets across the state now stocked goods that were eagerly purchased by rural consumers, who quickly developed an appetite for store-bought goods. Groceries became a major item of trade in the new economy of the late nineteenth century: canned food, cured meat, and prepared coffee, flour, and corn-meal, along with tobacco products, liquor, and candy became common items of consumption for urban dwellers and rural folk alike. Ready-made clothing and shoes from the factory rapidly replaced home-made products as the subsistence economy gave way to the cheaper, more fashionable products that were now made readily available by the railroad, the factories, and the advent of farmers who were now consumers as well as producers. The commercial revolution of the late nineteenth century extended into nearly every corner of Tennessee, transforming both the traditions of production and habits of consumption in ways that were both unsettling and invigorating.

At the turn of the century Memphis was the state's leading city with 102,320 people. Following a devastating wave of Yellow Fever epidemics in the 1870s and a major financial crisis in its city government, the Bluff City staged a remarkable comeback in the 1890s during which it enjoyed an almost 60 percent rate of growth. Nashville, which had briefly surpassed its western rival and stood as the premier inland city of the New South era, slowed its growth during the depression years of the 1890s and returned to its second rank with 80,865 population in 1900. Knoxville (32,637) and Chattanooga (30,154) both grew dramatically in the new age of the railroad and industry, but each continued to occupy the same rank order it had in antebellum times. Now the four major cities stood on top of a larger and more elaborate urban hierarchy knit together by rail, river, and roadway.

The accelerated commercial and urban development of the late nineteenth century sustained rapid gains in the first four decades of the twentieth century. The number of urban places proliferated (from 22 in 1900 to 57 by 1940), while urban residents mounted to over one third of the population by the onset of World War II. Most of this urban development strengthened traditional patterns of concentration in the four major cities, but there were also the additional growth of the urban-industrial complex in Northeast Tennessee identified as the Tri-Cities: Bristol, Kingsport, and Johnson City. The rise of the truck and automobile and the beginnings of a new highway system to serve this expanding mode of transportation generally reinforced the preceding railroad system. By 1935 Tennessee claimed over 7,000 miles of new state highways, most of it constructed since 1920.

Nashville benefited especially from the expansion of the highway system, which opened up adjacent territory in its hinterland to intensified commercial development. The Good Roads Movement of the 1920s improved rural roads and brought truck and automobile traffic to the hilly and remote regions of the Cumberlands and Western Highland Rim surrounding the Nashville Basin. While Nashville continued to trade in a variety of consumer products, Memphis relied more heavily on its traditional role as a cotton market, a role that flourished with the opening of the rich Mississippi Delta lands that were now protected by levees. The Memphis cotton market recovered in spurts following the Civil War and Reconstruction, and by the end of the century it had

nearly doubled its annual volume of bales received. Once the vast railroad network of the South allowed some decentralization of inland cotton markets, Memphis's share of the total cotton market declined. Nonetheless, the city grew in commercial importance. Its central location in the lower Mississippi Valley and its extensive railway connections made Memphis the region's leading commercial city, which led some to refer to it as the "Chicago of the South." By 1900 the city's trading area extended down river to eastern Texas and Louisiana, across much of northern Mississippi and Alabama, and up to southeastern Missouri. Memphis so dominated the commercial life of northern Mississippi that it came to be known as the capital of Mississippi. As more farmers and sharecroppers in the cotton growing region turned exclusively to cotton production, Memphis served as the major supply center for this part of the Mississippi Valley. Above all, it became headquarters to hundreds of cotton factors, who bought cotton and supplied cotton plantations and country stores with provisions. A multitude of dry goods, grocery, and other wholesalers also catered to the new market of consumers the cotton economy provided in the New South era.

Memphis also grew to rely on its increasing importance as the center of southern hardwood lumber, a role it shared with Nashville. As timber supplies in the North Woods regions of the upper Middle West were exhausted, the lumber industry turned south. Massive rafts made of timber lashed together floated down the Cumberland to Nashville and down the Mississippi to Memphis, while new railways penetrated the virgin woods of the Delta and lower Mississippi Valley to bring timber to Memphis. The timber from the countryside went into the city for housing and wood products of every variety. Lumber soon rivaled cotton as a major item of trade in the Memphis economy.

Both Memphis and Nashville grew in importance as exchange points between the South and other regions within the larger national network of trade. Nashville, for example, imported wheat from Minnesota and the plains states and exported processed flour to much of the South, while Memphis gathered cotton and lumber from its hinterland and shipped it eastward to factories in the southeast and northeast. While the smaller cities continued to serve as commercial nodes of smaller trade areas within Tennessee and adjacent states, Memphis and Nashville now served a vastly expanded and more regionally integrated national economy. Nashville's commercial influence extended well into the southern counties of Kentucky and into northern Alabama, and commanded almost half the state, into the Cumberland Plateau to the east and the Tennessee River to the west. Memphis served a trading region that extended deep into Mississippi and Arkansas and dominated most of Tennessee west of the Tennessee River.

Following the Great Depression, which momentarily arrested the growth of commerce and urban development in the state, World War II brought a new energy to both forces. In the half century between 1940 and 1990, Tennessee experienced a great implosion of its rural population, this time reducing the percentage from 65 percent non-urban dwellers to 40 percent. At the same time, the number of urban places more than doubled, climbing from 57 to 138, with most of this growth occurring on the bottom tier of the urban hierarchy, producing a multitude of small retail centers throughout the state. Most of the growth took place between 1940 and 1970, with the pace of urbanization leveling off markedly in the last twenty years.

The advent of the automobile made urban centers more accessible to rural dwellers who commuted to work or to shop without moving to town. Likewise, the automobile opened up a vast new suburban frontier that expanded rapidly beyond the city limits of all the major metropolitan areas, even Nashville, whose metropolitan government in 1963 encompassed most of the surrounding county. The older central city populations displayed very slow growth and even population loss in the face of suburban development, but this disguised a vigorous growth in the larger metropolitan area population, which the census officials began to chart with more care beginning in 1940.

Though Nashville and Memphis were converging in population, Memphis's superiority as the leading commercial city of the state was firmly established in the post-World War II era. The four major cities of Tennessee dominated between 80 and 90 percent of the total wholesale trade after World War II, while the second tier of cities—Jackson, Clarksville, and the Tri-cities—took over a good portion of the remainder. More striking was the shift from agricultural and forest products toward industrial goods. Memphis's leading line of trade became motor vehicle parts and supplies, followed by groceries, with farm products now third. Other major cities showed similar patterns in the wholesale trade, with metal, electrical goods, and petroleum products taking an unprecedented role in the state's commerce. Though every Tennessee city continued to campaign hard to attract industry into the local economy, the commercial and service sectors sustained the greatest urban growth in the post-war era, as they had during most of Tennessee's history.

Don H. Doyle, Vanderbilt University

SUGGESTED READINGS: Gerald M. Capers, Jr., *The Biography of a River Town—Memphis* (1966); Don H. Doyle, *Nashville in the New South* (1985) and *Nashville Since the 1920s* (1985); Anita Shafer Goodstein, *Nashville, 1780–1860: From Frontier to City* (1988); Gilbert E. Govan and James W. Livingood, *The Chattanooga Country, 1540–1976: From Tomahawks to TVA* (1977); Michael J. McDonald and Willam Bruce Wheeler, *Knoxville, Tennessee: Continuity and Change in an Appalachian City* (1983); Robert A. Sigafoos, *Cotton Row to Beale Street: A Business History of Memphis* (1979); Margaret Ripley Wolfe, *Kingsport, Tennessee: A Planned American City* (1987)

COMMONWEALTH FUND has played an important part in the development of public health and medical education in Tennessee since the 1920s. Anna Richardson Harkness created the Commonwealth Fund in 1918 as a philanthropic outlet for the fortune amassed by her late husband, Stephen V. Harkness, one of John D. Rockefeller's original partners in Standard Oil. Their son Edward S. Harkness, the

Health lesson at the Cemetery School, Rutherford County, ca. 1925.

TENNESSEE HISTORICAL SOCIETY COLLECTION, TSLA, HARRY MUSTARD PHOTOGRAPH ALBUM

Fund's first president, and director Barry Conger Smith charted its early course into child welfare and public health issues. The Commonwealth Fund was a major contributor to the child guidance movement from 1922 to 1945. Its experience in public health issues led to the adoption of medical education as the primary philanthropic subject by the late 1940s. In recent decades, the Fund has broadened its scope to include social and public policy issues in medicine. It still offers the graduate fellowships to British students in the United States initiated by Edward Harkness in 1925.

Tennessee was one of the Commonwealth Fund's major laboratories for public health, hospital construction, and medical education programs. Between 1924 and 1928, the Fund operated one of its four experimental child health demonstration programs in Rutherford County. The Rutherford demonstration, headed by Dr. Harry S. Mustard, operated children's and maternity clinics and sponsored health education programs in public schools. Demonstration staff also functioned as Rutherford's public health department.

The Commonwealth Fund's success in Rutherford County resulted in Tennessee becoming one of its three target states in the 1920s and 1930s. The Fund's Division of Rural Hospitals built the Rutherford Hospital in Murfreesboro (1927) and contributed to the Holston Valley Community Hospital in Kingsport (1935). In the late 1920s and early 1930s, its Division of Public Health operated field units in Rutherford, Sumner, Gibson, and Sullivan counties, and provided funds for a mobile field unit to the state health department. The Commonwealth Fund, the University of Tennessee, and the Tennessee Health Department jointly sponsored a state health education program instituted in 1930. Rutherford County also received a health department building as a gift from the Commonwealth Fund in 1931 in recognition of its central role in the Fund's rural health work. Later, the Fund granted monies for the construction of public health clinics in both Trenton, Gibson County (1937), and Gallatin, Sumner County (1946).

From 1927 until 1949, the Commonwealth Fund offered fellowships to physicians on its hospital staffs for post-graduate study at Fund-sponsored medical schools such as Vanderbilt University. Medical and nursing students at those medical schools came to the Rutherford Hospital for training in rural public health practice. At Vanderbilt, the Commonwealth Fund donated undergraduate pre-medical scholarships and fellowships for nursing students and advanced medical study and research. The Fund began offering fellowships to African-American medical students at Meharry Medical College in 1949. In the late 1960s and early 1970s, the Commonwealth Fund's grants to Meharry and Vanderbilt included the construction of biomedical sciences and basic sciences buildings at Meharry and expanded medical facilities and a clinical research center at Vanderbilt.

Mary S. Hoffschwelle, Middle Tennessee State University
SUGGESTED READING: Mary S. Hoffschwelle, "Organizing Rural Communities for Change: The Commonwealth Fund Child Health Demonstration in Rutherford County, 1923–1927," Carroll Van West, ed., *Tennessee History: The Land, the People, and the Culture* (1998), 373–391
SEE: MEDICINE; MEHARRY MEDICAL COLLEGE; MUSTARD, HARRY S.; VANDERBILT UNIVERSITY MEDICAL CENTER

COMMUNITY COLLEGES. Tennessee's system of community colleges traces its origins to a 1955–1957 study, *Public Higher Education in Tennessee*, undertaken by the legislative council of the Tennessee General Assembly and directed by Truman Pierce and A. D. Albright. The study outlined fundamental changes in the state's post-war economy and population distribution, including a rapid increase in wealth brought about by industrial development and a decline in the importance of agriculture, and the associated shift in population from rural to urban areas. As a result of these changes, an increasing number of students sought post-secondary education, particularly in technical fields. While a substantial portion of the population lived within 50 miles of one of the state-supported colleges or universities, there were several exceptions, most notably in the Chattanooga, Columbia-Pulaski, and Jackson areas. The study concluded that a need existed for the creation of three new colleges in these areas, apparently in anticipation of the establishment of four-year institutions. By the time the development of the new colleges got underway, sentiment had shifted to the creation of two-year community colleges as a result of pressure from communities seeking such institutions, the concerns of existing colleges and universities, and federal funding programs enacted in the early 1960s.

In 1963 Governor Frank G. Clement and the new State Commissioner of Education J. Howard Warf determined that it was time to act. The legislature funded a $100,000 per annum appropriation to study the feasibility of establishing community colleges and initiate preliminary planning. In 1964 the committee—T. M. Divine of Kingsport, Dale F. Glover of Obion County, Mrs. B. A. McDermott of Nashville, J. Frank Taylor of Huntingdon, and Edward L. Jennings of Liberty—recommended proceeding with the construction of a two-year college in the Columbia area. The committee foresaw a multi-purpose college that would permit the transfer of course credits to four-year institutions and provide vocational-technical programs, community services, and continuing adult education.

In February 1965 the State Board of Education adopted the committee recommendations to establish three two-year colleges, one in each of the three Grand Divisions. The program began with a $4 million construction grant and a $500,000 operational grant. Community groups across the state waged campaigns to gain approval for a college in their towns. In order to provide an orderly process for determining potential sites, the state established strict requirements for all applicants. A city or county must make a one-time contribution of $250,000 for construction and provide 100 acres or more for the building site, plus utilities. The criteria established a fundamental relationship between local and state support for the colleges. In June 1965 the State Board of Education named three sites: Cleveland, Columbia, and Jackson.

The colleges created by these efforts were state-funded (aside from the initial community contribution) and charged modest fees for coursework, making higher education more readily available to a wider range of students. Educational planners envisioned the creation of teaching institutions that would be accredited under the standards of the Commission on Colleges of the Southern Association of Colleges and Schools. The schools would award associate degrees and certificates, employ regular faculty with at least a Master's degree, maintain an open admissions policy, and conduct day and evening classes year-round. The colleges were called "community colleges" rather than "junior colleges" to emphasize the partnership between state and local efforts.

Columbia State Community College enrolled 393 students in the fall of 1966 and held classes in a variety of locations, including the First Baptist Church and an old post office. The winter semester enrollment climbed to 538. On March 15, 1967, First Lady Lady Bird Johnson, accompanied by her husband, President Lyndon Johnson, dedicated the campus. Dr. Harold S. Pryor became the first president of Columbia State. The 1996 enrollment was 3,968.

Cleveland State Community College opened in the fall of 1967 with 681 students and held classes in the educational building of the North Cleveland Baptist Church until construction of the campus could be completed. Winter quarter classes began on the new campus with an enrollment of 766. Dr. D. F. Adkisson served as the first president of Cleveland State. The 1996 enrollment was 3,276.

Jackson State Community College opened in September 1967, with Dr. Francis E. Wright as president. The expected enrollment of 400 mushroomed to 640 students from 21 counties, an indication of the popularity of community colleges. Jackson State has expanded to a 1996 enrollment of 3,486.

In 1967 three additional sites were added to the list of community colleges. Dyersburg State opened in 1969 with an enrollment of 588, which grew to 2,321 in 1996. Dr. Edward B. Eller served as the first president. In 1969 Motlow State Community College opened in Tullahoma under the leadership of Dr. Sam H. Ingram. The initial enrollment of 551 has since grown to 3,160 in 1996. Walters State Community College in Hamblen County enrolled 414 students when it opened in 1970. Dr. James W. Clark served as the first president. The 1996 enrollment reached 6,028.

In 1969 the State Board of Education approved the creation of three more community colleges in Roane, Sumner, and Shelby counties, bringing the total number of two-year institutions to nine. Dr. Hall Reed Ramer, president, opened Volunteer State Community College in Gallatin in 1971 with an enrollment of 581 students from Sumner and 11 surrounding counties. The college moved onto its permanent campus on U.S. Highway 31-E in the winter of 1972. Vol State's 1996 enrollment was 6,887. Dr. Cuyler A. Dunbar became the first president of Roane State Community College, which opened at Harriman in 1971 with an enrollment of 323. Students met in temporary classrooms until the fall quarter of 1973. The 1996 enrollment reached 5,670. Shelby State Community College did not enroll students until fall 1972 and opened amid controversy over the direction of higher education. President Jess H. Parish promoted the school to area citizens as a multi-campus, comprehensive institution. The multi-campus aspect of the college complicated the issue of the community appropriation of $250,000 and land for construction of a campus. The campus finally located on 100 acres of land on the Shelby County Penal Farm in east Memphis, with a second site in the mid-city area. Desegregation suits challenged the proposal of building two simultaneous sites, causing delays in construction. The college opened in temporary quarters at the old Veterans Hospital and enrolled nearly 1,000 students in September 1972. In 1996 enrollment stood at 5,862.

Chattanooga State Technical Community College opened in 1965 as Chattanooga State Technical Institute, the first technical institute in the state, as well as the first state-supported institution of post-secondary education in Chattanooga. The institute moved to its present site on the Tennessee River in 1967. The 1974–1975 academic year marked the beginning of the college parallel program at Chattanooga State, enrolling approximately 150 students. The 1996 enrollment was 9,334.

Pellissippi State Technical Community College in Knoxville and Northeast State Technical Community College in the Tri-Cities area also trace their origins to technical institutes, and both institutions made the change to community college status in 1988. Pellissippi State operates on three campuses and recorded a combined 1996 enrollment of nearly 8,000.

Northeast State's 1996 enrollment was 3,636. State Technical Institute in Memphis is also part of the community college family. Its 1996 enrollment reached 10,195. The Nashville State Technical Institute opened in west Nashville in 1970; its 1994 enrollment was over 6,500.

The State Area Vocational Technical Schools were transferred from the State Department of Education in 1963 and became part of the State University and Community College System, governed by the Tennessee Board of Regents, when the system was created in 1972. In 1994 the names of these 26 schools were changed to the Tennessee Technology Centers. Enrollment in that year at all of the Technology Centers was 30,174.

From the visions of educators of the 1950s and 1960s, the reality of the community college system has provided Tennesseans with expanded opportunities for higher education, continuing adult education, and the acquisition of technical skills to remain competitive in the changing job market.

Connie L. Lester, Tennessee Historical Society
SEE: EDUCATION, HIGHER; WARF, JOHN HOWARD

CONFEDERATE SOLDIERS' HOME AND CEMETERY. In January 1889 the Frank Cheatham Bivouac of the Association of Confederate Soldiers forwarded a bill to the Tennessee General Assembly to establish a home for indigent and disabled Confederate veterans on the grounds of The Hermitage. The General Assembly approved the measure, but excluded the Hermitage Mansion, the tomb of Andrew and Rachel Jackson, and 25 acres surrounding the house, which it entrusted to the Ladies' Hermitage Association. The legislature also appointed a nine-member Board of Trustees to oversee construction and management of the veterans' home. Funding came from the state and Confederate veterans organizations, especially the United Daughters of the Confederacy.

The new building opened on May 12, 1892, and could house 125 inmates in its two dormitory wings that adjoined a center section used for dining and relaxation. The Tennessee Confederate Soldiers' Home provided shelter, comfort, and medical attention to nearly 700 veterans during its 41 years of service. Most men who entered the home were poor farmers before the Civil War, and their financial situation further deteriorated after it. Many were physically and mentally disabled, not only from wounds but by the harsh conditions some had experienced as prisoners of war. Most veterans living at the home fought in Tennessee units, but some were veterans of units from other states. Normally, men who died at the home were buried in the Tennessee Confederate Soldiers' Home Cemetery. The cemetery, adjacent to the Hermitage Presbyterian Church, contains the remains of 487 veterans.

The Tennessee Confederate Soldiers' Home closed on November 22, 1933, and the six veterans still living at the home moved to the Girls Infirmary at the Tennessee Industrial School. The home's last inmate died in 1941.

B. Anthony Guzzi, The Hermitage
SEE: HERMITAGE; LADIES' HERMITAGE ASSOCIATION

CONFEDERATE VETERAN magazine was founded and edited by Sumner Archibald Cunningham in 1893. The Nashville-based monthly was originally designed to inform patrons on the status of the Jefferson Davis monument fund spearheaded by Cunningham. Eventually, the magazine evolved into a clearinghouse for information related to events and rituals honoring Confederate traditions like reunions, battle enactments, and the erections of granite memorials. The magazine also reported on local and regional activities of the United Confederate Veterans and United Daughters of the Confederacy. But Cunningham's magazine played its most important role as a mouthpiece for rank-and-file reminiscences. It stood in sharp contrast to the *Southern Historical Society Papers*, edited by J. William Jones in Virginia, which stressed grand debates about strategy and command-level war aims.

At a subscription rate of only one dollar per year, Cunningham made his monthly available to a wide audience. In the early years, however, the *Confederate Veteran* suffered from publication problems, including poor paper quality, messy ink, dark photographs, and limited advertising. The editor eventually overcame these problems and, by 1904 his magazine boasted a readership of 22,000, one of the largest magazine subscription lists in the turn-of-the-century South. The majority of patrons hailed from the western portion of the former Confederacy. The physical format of the magazine expanded from a modest 24-page layout to special souvenir numbers of 64 pages.

The *Confederate Veteran* was an outstanding example of personal journalism, closely reflecting the opinions and prejudices of its proprietor. In one case, Cunningham enveloped the magazine in a fierce rivalry that unfolded between several southern cities to build the "Battle Abbey," a planned museum of Confederate war relics patterned after Westminster in Great Britain. Cunningham lobbied on the editor's page on behalf of a Nashville site. In 1901 his libelous statements against other contenders led to bitter litigation that nearly destroyed the monthly. On a more positive note, Cunningham broadcast the forgotten story of Sam Davis, "the boy hero of Tennessee." His diligent effort to educate Tennesseans on the exploits of Davis led to construction of a monument on Nashville's Capitol Hill in 1909. Cunningham considered the Davis memorial the "crowning glory" of his professional career.

After Cunningham's death in 1913, his secretary, Edith Drake Pope, assumed the editorial duties and kept the *Confederate Veteran* operational until 1932. Today, the magazine stands as an invaluable resource to professional historians and genealogists.

John A. Simpson, Kelso, Washington

SEE: CUNNINGHAM, SUMNER; POPE, EDITH D.

CONLEY, SARA WARD (1859–1944), a noted Nashville artist of the late nineteenth and early twentieth centuries, was born on December 21, 1859, to Dr. William and Eliza Ward. Following an education at Nashville's Ward Seminary (a school for young women founded by her father), she received scholarships to study art in Paris and Rome.

Ward returned to Nashville and pursued an art career, as a teacher and painter of portraits and murals. Among her works are two portraits of the William Blount family for the Blount Mansion in Knoxville and an impressive mural for the Battle Creek Sanitarium. In 1883 she married John W. Conley. She was widowed early and her only daughter died in childhood.

In 1896 Conley was named architect of the Woman's Building for the Tennessee Centennial Exposition. In contrast to the open, barn-like design of the other Exposition buildings, Conley's Woman's Building included two floors connected by a grand stairway and featured a library and model kitchen as well as separate exhibit rooms decorated by women's groups from various organizations, counties, and cities.

Conley also chaired the Centennial Arts Committee, which selected art works for display at the Exposition. Conley's pastel portrait entitled *Portrait of Elia* (also known as *June Rose*) was among the works exhibited in the Parthenon galleries.

The Tennessee Centennial Exposition was Conley's last major project. Stricken with typhoid fever later that year, she was confined to a wheelchair for the remaining 47 years of her life. Conley continued to teach art until her death on May 6, 1944. She is buried in Nashville's Mt. Olivet Cemetery.

Dee Gee Lester, Hendersonville

SEE: ART; TENNESSEE CENTENNIAL EXPOSITION

CONSERVATION. After Reconstruction, the exploitation of Tennessee's natural wealth rose to a scale unknown before the Civil War. Northern and foreign investors bought and cut timberlands, set up land companies, financed railroads, and extracted the state's coal and iron. Logging in the Southern Appalachians reached its peak between 1880 and 1909, removing the finest wood and laying waste to less desirable timber. Through its Canadian manager Alexander A. Arthur, the Scottish Carolina Timber and Land Company bought up much of the Cocke County timberland and reshaped Newport. In 1886, after a disastrous flood wiped out the log booms and mill on the French Broad River, Arthur led a new group of foreign investors (the American Association) to lands at Cumberland Gap, where they made another effort to make a frontier landmark into an industrial city.

Unlike the Unaka timber operations, small farmers harvested the Upper Cumberland forests and rafted the logs down the Cumberland River to Nashville. The logging boom, which began in the 1870s, had ended by the 1910s. During the same decades, loggers cut the West Tennessee bottom lands and shipped the timber to Memphis, which became the largest inland hardwood market in the world. The cutting of millions of board feet of timber changed the landscape, the function of watersheds and ecosystems, and led to the first major species extinctions in the region.

Perhaps the greatest environmental disaster occurred in the 40-square mile Copper Basin of Polk County. Mining of the copper deposits near Ducktown began approximately 1850, but the worst environmental damage occurred between 1890 and 1907. The open-roasting process used to remove copper from the ore required acres of timber to fuel the smelters, clearing the forests for miles around the basin. The release of sulfuric dioxide, created during the extraction process, added greater insult to the environment, as the corrosive gas mixed with rain to settle sulfuric acid on the land, killing all the remaining vegetation and the marine life of the Ocoee River. The red clay hills, barren as the Moon, eroded further with each downpour. In 1908 a process to capture the sulfuric acid through closed smelting was put into place, but visible aspects of the damage remain after 90 years, despite past (and partially successful) conservation efforts by the Civilian Conservation Corps and the Tennessee Valley Authority.

During the state's industrial boom, an intellectual revolution in regard to nature and wilderness also occurred, even as Tennesseans and other Americans exploited the earth's resources. The late eighteenth century Romantic view that depicted the wilderness as a sublime place where humans could face the majesty of God began to supplant the view of nature as something to be conquered. The Romantic view merged with the late nineteenth century fear that the American frontier, the crucible of democracy in the national mythology, had vanished. In 1888 Theodore Roosevelt and others established the Boone and Crockett Club (named for the two most famous early market hunters, Daniel Boone and David Crockett) to embody the aims of a new movement to protect and conserve wild areas and wildlife for sportsmen.

In Tennessee, the earliest conservation protections had economic roots. In 1870 the state enacted legislation to protect the rivers' fisheries from overuse by commercial fishers. The exportation of game was prohibited in 1887, as was the market hunting of bob white quail in 1889—a law from which 65 counties promptly exempted themselves. In 1895 the state put a five-year moratorium on hunting deer in Cumberland, Claiborne, Scott, Morgan, and Anderson counties to prevent their complete extinction there—Haywood County, with an 1896 deer population of 20, might have benefited from similar legislation. Finally, in 1903, the General Assembly declared that all game and fish were the property of the state and established the Game, Fish, and Forestry Department two years later. Hunting licenses were required for the first time in 1907.

In 1913 the first National Conservation Exposition, held in Knoxville, crowned the earliest efforts to conserve the state's wildlife. The National Conservation Commission, appointed by President Theodore Roosevelt in 1908, sponsored the exposition. The Knoxville event focused on the need to protect renewable natural resources such as forests, soil, water, and wildlife, but also addressed the environment's role in public health.

In June 1920 the U.S. Forest Service acquired three units in East Tennessee—the Unaka, Pisgah, and Cherokee—as part of the national effort to protect the country's woodlands. In 1936 the three were combined into Cherokee National Forest, with a combined area of 625,350 acres. Large commitments of human resources to the conservation of natural resources were left to the New Deal era of the 1930s.

Within weeks of Franklin D. Roosevelt's inauguration as president in 1933, Congress created the Civilian Conservation Corps (CCC). Thirty-five work camps for young men were established in Tennessee, and 7,000 Tennesseans enrolled by 1937. The CCC units planted millions of pine seedlings for forest reclamation, developed state parks, built fire observation towers, and began reforestation of the Copper Basin, before the organization's work ended in 1942. With the Works Progress Administration, the CCC built six Game and Fish Commission-controlled lakes between 1938 and 1940.

The New Deal legislation also created the Soil Conservation Service (SCS) to heal gullied, overworked farmland, plant trees on contoured hillsides, and add protection to watersheds. The SCS persuaded farmers to participate in small farm-game management efforts to restore fishing and hunting opportunities. The combined efforts of federal and state government to acquire cut over and badly eroded land for state parks and state forests produced a splendid conservation legacy for the latter half of the twentieth century. Tennessee state parks now number 51, with 36 satellite areas, totaling 131,000

acres. Tennessee has more state forests (13) than any southern state, totaling 146,000 acres.

In 1933 Congress created the Tennessee Valley Authority. The transformation of the free-running Tennessee River into a series of impounded lakes produced extensive environmental changes to the river and its tributaries and created new management problems. Dam construction immediately destroyed the habitats of dozens of shallow water mussels and fish, many of which became extinct or are now endangered species. The Forestry Relations Department of TVA positively affected conservation as well, with fishery biology studies, waterfowl programs, and wildlife management. The Watershed Protection unit undertook reforestation and erosion control, and the Forestry Investigations unit became the research arm of the department.

Private citizens also contributed to the conservation efforts. Z. Cartter Patten, Sr., and his friends established the McRae Club of Chattanooga, a hunting club that owned land for private use. Such clubs had existed in the state since at least 1865. In 1934 several local hunting clubs met in Murfreesboro and created the Tennessee Federation of Sportsmen (later the Tennessee Wildlife Federation). The Federation published a conservation newsletter, which the Tennessee Department of Conservation took over along with other public education work when it was created in 1937. The Federation disbanded in 1940. After World War II, erstwhile Federation leaders formed the Tennessee Conservation League (TCL) during a meeting at the Read House in Chattanooga. The TCL advocated wildlife and conservation throughout the remainder of the century and continued to be involved in hunting and fishing issues.

As early as 1927, Governor Austin Peay targeted pollution from sawmills, textile mills, and acid plants as the cause of fish kills and suggested that added appropriations to fund game wardens were useless unless the state stopped the poisoning of streams. Despite this early warning, meaningful protective legislation against pollution was not enacted until the 1950s. In 1954 the Stream Pollution Control Board tackled the need for sewerage treatment plants. Strip mining proliferated in the Tennessee coal fields in the 1950s, as giant diesel-engine shovels ripped up soil, rock, and coal, replacing the labor-intensive deep mining of the past. The first attempt to pass legislation to regulate strip mining came in 1959, but all efforts failed until 1967, when Oak Ridge-area legislators succeeded in getting the state's first land reclamation act passed.

The current environmental movement began to take form in the 1960s and 1970s. In the view of many environmentalists, man and nature were at odds—wilderness became a place of escape, where nature's resources were defended against man's use. Advocacy groups, such as the national Environmental Defense Fund (1967) emerged to lobby for environmental protection laws and bring court action against violators. Between 1965 and 1972, the U.S. Congress enacted more than a dozen major environmental laws, including the Clean Water acts of 1966 and 1972 and the Clean Air acts of 1963 and 1970. The National Environmental Policy Act of 1969 established the Environmental Protection Agency and required environmental impact statements on all projects involving federal funds and permits.

Tennessee followed the national lead and enacted companion laws, including the Tennessee Air Pollution Control Act in 1967 and the Tennessee Solid Waste Control Act in 1969. Environmental protection became so popular that Republican gubernatorial candidate Winfield Dunn ran on a strong environmental platform in 1970. Elected as the first Republican governor since 1920, Dunn's administration oversaw the passage of the Tennessee Water Quality Control Act of 1971 and the Tennessee Surface Mining Act of 1972. In 1970, the year of the first Earth Day, the Tennessee Conservation League, League of Women Voters, American Lung Association, and the Tennessee Federation of Garden Clubs united with other groups to form the Tennessee Environmental Council, an environmental advocacy group to provide research and policy suggestions.

By the end of the 1970s, print and broadcast media reported environmental news daily. Tennessee received national attention in 1977 and 1978 as opposition developed against TVA's proposed Tellico Dam and Lake on a 33-mile stretch of the Little Tennessee River, the last major free-flowing river in the state. The inundation of the "Little T" threatened to flood the richest archaeological district in Tennessee and destroy the only known home of the snail darter fish. Discovered by University of Tennessee ichthyologist David Etnier in 1973, the snail darter was added to the federal endangered species list in 1976.

Although a coalition of farmers, Cherokees, archaeologists, trout fishermen, and even the Boeing Corporation opposed the dam, TVA charged forward with the project, which would bring little in additional electrical generating capacity to the agency. In 1977 a lawsuit (*Hill v. Tennessee Valley Authority*) was brought against TVA for violating the Endangered Species Preservation Act of 1966, and the Sixth District Court of Appeals upheld the charge, forbidding construction of the dam. In 1978 the U.S. Supreme Court upheld the decision by ruling in favor of the endangered species act. Congress circumvented the court's decision, when it created the Endangered Species Committee to review projects halted by the act. In 1979 the so-called "God Squad" ruled against a future for the snail darter, and the dam's floodgates were closed in 1980. Later

that year, other small snail darter populations were found in Tennessee River tributaries.

Although the environmentalists ultimately lost the battle for the Little Tennessee, activism continued in Tennessee. Groups of citizens and government agencies addressed the channelization of West Tennessee rivers and the resulting loss of wetlands; the need for a TVA dam on the Duck River near Columbia; designation of new federal wilderness areas for the Cherokee National Forest; habitat and steam destruction by the Tennessee Department of Transportation's massive road-building program; solid waste landfills; recycling; Champion Paper Mills' 90-year pollution of the Pigeon River; and the introduction of chip mills. Environmental organizations, politicians, government agencies, and business interests struggled with the best way to accommodate the needs of Tennesseans and the preservation of natural resources.

At the end of the twentieth century, some things remain similar to the ways of the first Native Americans. Corn is planted each spring in creek-side fields. Herb gatherers take advantage of the region's more than 200 botanical species of medicinal herbs. Ginseng hunters collect "sang" for shipment to world markets, but carefully sow the plant's red berries. In the fall, bow hunters and black powder musket enthusiasts stalk the white tail deer.

Literary critic Raymond Williams wrote in *Problems in Materialism and Culture* (1980): "the idea of nature contains, though often unnoticed, an extraordinary amount of human history." As humans, we cannot avoid shaping the world around us. But Tennesseans now strive to create balance with wilderness rather than dominion.

Ann Toplovich, Tennessee Historical Society

SUGGESTED READINGS: Richard A. Bartlett, *Troubled Waters: Champion International and the Pigeon River Controversy* (1995); Alfred Cowdrey, *This Land, This South* (1996); Marge Davis, *Sportsmen United: The Story of the Tennessee Conservation League* (1997); Carroll Van West, *Tennessee's Historic Landscapes* (1995)

SEE: AGRICULTURE; BAGGENSTOSS, HERMAN; BIG SOUTH FORK NATIONAL RECREATION AREA; BURCH, LUCIUS; CIVILIAN CONSERVATION CORPS; ECOLOGICAL SYSTEMS; GEOLOGY; INDUSTRY; MINING; U.S. ARMY CORPS OF ENGINEERS; TENNESSEE CONSERVATION LEAGUE; TENNESSEE ENVIRONMENTAL COUNCIL; TENNESSEE EXECUTIVE DEPARTMENTS; TENNESSEE STATE FORESTS; TENNESSEE VALLEY AUTHORITY

CONTRABAND CAMPS (1864–1866). During the Civil War, many of Tennessee's 275,000 slaves abandoned farms and towns in anticipation of the approach of the Union army. In the summer of 1862, as the army of General Ulysses S. Grant entered the heavily slaveholding territory of West Tennessee, hordes of hungry and poorly-clad fugitive slaves surrounded the Yankees. Grant ordered Chaplain John Eaton to requisition surplus tents, blankets, rations, and tools and establish a camp for the fugitives, who supplied forced labor for the Confederate army as teamsters, construction laborers, and body servants. The African Americans were considered contraband under the Confiscation Act, thus the name contraband camps. Eaton established the first contraband camp at Grand Junction in August 1862. By March 1863 the contrabands at Grand Junction numbered 1,713. Two years later, contraband camps stretched throughout the occupied parts of the Mississippi Valley. In late 1862 northern missionaries and church leaders had arrived to establish schools, religious and medical services, and even political education for contrabands. The army put the able freedmen to work at 50 cents per day, on abandoned farms, government-supervised plantations, and military projects.

By 1866 Tennessee had contraband camps in each of the three Grand Divisions. The largest camps were in the urban areas: Memphis (4), Nashville (3), Chattanooga, Knoxville, Hendersonville, Clarksville, as well as Grand Junction, Bolivar, Pulaski, Jackson, LaGrange, and Somerville. Large settlements of contrabands also existed in Chelsea (East Memphis) and Brentwood (Williamson County).

Approximately 20,000 male contrabands were inducted into the Union army as U.S. Colored Troops (USCT). By 1866 USCT regiments comprised 40 percent of the Union army troops raised in Tennessee. Some 31,000 white Tennesseans served in the Union Army of Tennessee, while an estimated 115,000 served in the Confederate forces. The manpower provided by African-American troops and the contraband camps gave the Union a decided edge to sustain the occupation in Tennessee and win the war in the western theater.

The contraband camps became the foundation for postwar African-American neighborhoods and for the institutionalization of African-American society in Tennessee. These camps facilitated the process that produced the rapid urbanization of the former slaves, most of whom lived in rural areas. Fugitive slaves from the Arkansas delta, western Kentucky, northern Mississippi, and rural West Tennessee flowed into Memphis until freedmen outnumbered whites in 1865. Missionaries, Freedmen's Bureau agents, and ministers performed and recorded the first legal marriages for thousands of former slaves in these camps. Filled with log cabins, frame buildings, and often tents with dirt floors, the camps became so large and filled with blacks that northern missionaries and local newspapers often named them "New Africa." The large camps on Memphis's southern boundary were called Camp Shiloh and Camp Fiske (near Union

army Fort Pickering) and Camp Dixie (President's Island). Camp Shiloh had over 300 houses and 2,000 residents, as well as churches, schools, saloons, lunchrooms, and barbershops. The contrabands in Camp Dixie cultivated 300 acres of cotton and built a sawmill and a school in 1863. Many of the soldiers who manned Fort Pickering anxiously watched over the parapets for their families at Camp Shiloh. In Nashville, the camps were located south (Edgehill), west (Northwest Camp), and east (Edgefield) of the city's boundaries. Between December 1863 and December 1864, when the Union army temporarily lost some areas to invading Confederate armies, contrabands from small towns were placed on railroad cars and relocated to Memphis, Nashville, and Chattanooga. Over 1,600 contrabands transferred from Holly Springs and Corinth, Mississippi, to Memphis's Camp Chelsea.

In 1863 the Freedmen's Department of the army was established under John Eaton to manage the camps. In March 1865 Congress created the Bureau of Freedmen, Refugees, and Abandoned Lands (the Freedmen's Bureau) to assist the contrabands in making the transition to freedom. In late 1865 the Bureau initiated a program to relocate thousands of freedmen from the camps and back to the countryside, but the former slaves and their descendants continued to pour into the cities, establishing a pattern that eventually led, according to the 1990 census, to over 80 percent of African Americans in Tennessee living in urban areas.

Bobby L. Lovett, Tennessee State University

SEE: FREEDMEN'S BUREAU; UNITED STATES COLORED TROOPS

CONVICT LEASE WARS. From 1866 to 1896 Tennessee state government adopted the widely-used convict lease system to make prisons self-supporting and provide revenue to fund the state debt. Under this system, the state leased prisoners to private companies and made them responsible for feeding and housing the convicts. In July 1866 Tennessee leased its first convicts to furniture manufacturers. In 1884 the Tennessee Coal and Iron Company (TCI) leased the state penitentiary for an annual fee of $101,000. After 1889 TCI obtained the authority to sublease prisoners to other companies; TCI employed 60 percent of the prison population as miners and subleased the others. Flying in the face of *laissez-faire* capitalism, the system cheapened the wages of honest free laborers, but netted the state a profit of $771,391 between 1870 and 1890 and gave TCI "an effective club to hold over the heads of free laborers," in the words of company vice-president A. S. Colyar.[1]

The system fostered a number of abuses. African Americans made up most of the prison population. Tennessee's "Zebra Law" put men in prison stripes for crimes as petty as theft of a fence rail. Moreover, prison conditions were abominable—guards enforced discipline through beatings; food and sanitation were vile; and inmates were brutalized and subjected to unspeakable degeneration.

The first revolt against the lease system occurred in January 1871, when white miners in Tracy City struck TCI for higher wages and the end of the system. There was panic in Nashville as winter temperatures dropped. The miners mounted an assault on the guards to prevent the convicts from working, but this early example of industrial labor violence ended as a victory for the company. Minor eruptions of labor insurrection followed over the next two decades until the outbreak of the Coal Creek War in 1891.

On July 14, 1891, the miners launched a series of guerrilla attacks at Briceville, in Anderson County. In the initial confrontation, 300 miners surrounded the stockade, took charge of the 40 prisoners, marched them and their guards five miles to Coal Creek (now Lake City), sealed them in box cars, and shipped them to Knoxville. The miners requested the intervention of Governor John P. Buchanan to protect the rights of labor. Buchanan agreed to meet with the miners, but ordered three companies of state militia to restore order and return the convicts to Briceville. In his meeting with the miners, Buchanan advised them to seek justice through the courts. When the miners repeated their action on July 20, Buchanan agreed to call a special session of the legislature to consider the issue of convict leasing.

In cities across the state, many spoke against the practice of hiring prisoners to compete with convict labor. Nevertheless, that August the General Assembly took no action except to enhance the power of the governor to act against insurrectionaries and resolve to abolish convict leasing once the current contract expired.

Miners renewed and stepped up their anti-leasing activities on October 31, when they again surrounded the stockade at Briceville. This time they released the prisoners into the surrounding hills and valleys and burned the buildings and stockade. On November 2, the miners conducted a second raid at the Cumberland Mine in Oliver Springs. But, by the end of December, convicts returned to the mines under militia guard.

In August 1892 the miners in Grundy County revolted at two sites operated by the Tennessee Coal, Iron and Railroad Company. The attacks at Inman and Tracy City sparked renewed revolts in Anderson County. An attack on the stockade at Oliver Springs was met by gunfire, and several miners were wounded. In the end, the outnumbered militia surrendered, the convicts were shipped to Knoxville, and the stockade burned.

This final revolt produced several important results. Public support for the miners disappeared.

The violence associated with the last revolt and the public perception of Buchanan's inability to handle the problem contributed to his failure to win reelection in November. The 1893 General Assembly proved more willing to address the issue of convict leasing and passed legislation to construct a new state penitentiary and abolish convict leasing at the expiration of the lease contract in 1896. Prisoners continued to mine coal at the Brushy Mountain Prison, which the state marketed until 1937, when the legislature limited the sales to public institutions in compliance with similar federal action.

James B. Jones, Jr., Tennessee Historical Commission

CITATION:
(1) Walter Wilson, "Historic Coal Creek Rebellion Brought an End to Convict Miners in Tennessee," *United Mine Workers Journal* (November 1, 1938): 10.

SUGGESTED READINGS: Perry C. Cotham, *Toil, Turmoil & Triumph: A Portrait of the Tennessee Labor Movement* (1996); Pete Daniel, "The Tennessee Convict War," *Tennessee Historical Quarterly* 34(1975): 273–292

SEE: BUCHANAN, JOHN P.; COLYAR, ARTHUR S.; LABOR; MINING; TENNESSEE PRISON SYSTEM

COOK, ANNIE (d. 1878), prostitute and nurse, whose real name is unknown, was reportedly an attractive woman of German descent, who grew up in Ohio. She worked for a family in Kentucky, where she was remembered for aiding impoverished smallpox victims. After the Civil War, Cook moved to Memphis and operated Mansion House, an up-scale brothel on Gayoso Street. In 1872 her bagnio was one of 18 in the city.

When the yellow fever epidemic struck Memphis in 1873, Cook dismissed her girls, opened her elegant house to patients, and nursed them through the fever. She repeated her charitable act during the more devastating epidemic of 1878, gaining a reputation for expertise in caring for victims of the disease. Two of her "female inmates" followed her example and volunteered as nurses. Newspaper reports focused attention on Cook's sacrifices; even the "Christian Women of Louisville" commended her generosity and the example she set. On September 5, 1878, Cook contracted yellow fever and died on September 11.

The Howard Association, a local relief organization, later showed its regard by moving her grave to the Association's plot in Elmwood Cemetery. In the Memphis *Appeal* of September 17, 1878, she was lauded in Victorian fashion as a converted sinner: "Out of sin, the woman, in all the tenderness and fullness of her womanhood, merged, transfigured and purified, to become the healer."

Randal Hall, Rice University

SEE: YELLOW FEVER EPIDEMICS

COOK, JAMES B. (1828–1909), architect, was born in England and studied at King's College and Putney

College before becoming a supervising architect on the Crystal Palace for London's Great Exhibition of 1851.

Cook immigrated to New York in 1855. Two years later, he was sent to Memphis to work on the enlargement of the Gayoso Hotel and spent the rest of his life there, bringing his knowledge and skills to the city. Cook served in the Confederate Army, and designed submarines and a patented system for making jails escape-proof.

Cook's design for St. Mary's Catholic Church (1864–1874) was the first important work of a local architect. He was responsible for the 1881 renovation of Calvary Episcopal Church and the rebuilding of the Gayoso Hotel after an 1899 fire. He designed the Court Square fountain in 1876, the Memphis Pyramid at the Tennessee Centennial Exhibition in 1897, and many fine homes in the Memphis area.

Perre Magness, Memphis

SUGGESTED READINGS: Eugene J. Johnson and Robert D. Russell, Jr., *Memphis: An Architectural Guide* (1990); Perre Magness, *Good Abode, Nineteenth Century Architecture in Memphis and Shelby County* (1983)

COON CREEK, near the Leapwood community in northeast McNairy County, is known internationally to geologists and paleontologists for its exceptionally rich Cretaceous fossil beds. Located at the eastern edge of the Coastal Plain of West Tennessee, the area was covered by the sea's Mississippi Embayment in the Late Cretaceous Period (140 million to 68 million years before present) and much of the Tertiary Period (68 million to 2.5 million BP), leaving sand, clay, silt, and gravel.

The Coon Creek formation is a greenish-gray, glauconic, sandy marl. First described by Bruce Wade in the 1926 U.S. Geological Survey paper, *The Fauna of the Ripley Formation on Coon Creek, Tennessee,* Coon Creek fauna represent over 350 species of animals and one-celled foraminifera. The formation includes nearly perfectly preserved, delicate shells of invertebrate animals that lived on the sandy sea floor—pelecypods (clams), gastropods (sea snails), cephalopods (similar to the chambered nautilus), and arthropods (crabs). Vertebrate remains of marine fish and reptiles are also found, including sea turtles and lizard-like, flesh-eating monasaurs up to 40 feet long.

The Coon Creek locality is owned by the Memphis Museum System. Access by the public is allowed through special tours, environmental camps, and fossil digs conducted through the Pink Palace Museum, which employs a manager at the site.

Ann Toplovich, Tennessee Historical Society

SEE: MCNAIRY COUNTY; PINK PALACE MUSEUM

COOPER, DUNCAN BROWN (1844–1922), journalist, publisher, and leading figure in Tennessee's Democratic party in the late nineteenth and early twentieth centuries, was born in Maury County. Cooper served in the Confederate Army during the Civil War and was captured at Fort Donelson. After the war, he entered politics and served in both houses of the state legislature. He was also an accomplished journalist and publisher of the *Nashville American,* a conservative Democratic daily.

Cooper is best remembered, however, for his role in the shooting death of prohibitionist leader, Edward W. Carmack. Carmack, a former friend of Cooper, had served as editor of the *American* from 1888 until 1892. In the years after Carmack's departure, the friendship soured and by 1908 the relationship between the two men was quite hostile. That same year, Carmack ran for the Democratic gubernatorial nomination against the incumbent Malcolm Patterson. Cooper acted as an advisor to the Patterson campaign and helped him secure a narrow victory in a bitter and divisive contest.

Angered by his defeat, Carmack, now editor of the Nashville *Tennessean,* levied a barrage of libelous attacks against Cooper in the pages of his paper. Their fight soon moved to the streets of Nashville, where on November 9, 1908, Cooper and his son Robin encountered Carmack on a Nashville street. Fearing attack, Carmack fired on the pair, wounding Robin Cooper. The younger Cooper returned fire and killed Carmack.

Vilified by the temperance press, Duncan Cooper was unable to receive an impartial trial, and both he and his son were convicted of second-degree murder. Governor Patterson granted a controversial pardon to the elder Cooper and saved him from jail. A short time later, Robin Cooper was granted a new trial and released. Though a free man, Duncan Brown Cooper continued to be shunned by many Tennesseans. He died in 1922 in Nashville.

Timothy P. Ezzell, Knoxville

SUGGESTED READING: James Summerville, *The Carmack-Cooper Shooting: Tennessee Politics Turns Violent, November 9, 1908* (1994)

SEE: CARMACK, EDWARD W.; PATTERSON, MALCOLM R.; TEMPERANCE MOVEMENT

COOPER, JERE (1893–1957), a prominent member of the U.S. House of Representatives for almost 30 years, was born in Dyer County on July 20, 1893. Cooper attended local schools and graduated in 1914 from Cumberland University Law School. He was admitted to the bar in 1915, and began practicing law in Dyersburg. Cooper served in World War I with the 119th Infantry Company in France and Belgium and was promoted to captain.

After the war, Cooper returned to Dyersburg and his law practice. He was elected to the city council in 1920, elected State Commander of the American

Legion in 1921, and served as the first scoutmaster of the Dyersburg chapter of the Boy Scouts of America. Cooper, a Democrat, won election to Congress in 1928. He married Mary Rankley in December 1930; the couple had one son, Leon Jere Cooper, who died as a child.

During Cooper's congressional years, he served as the chairman of the House Ways and Means Committee and on the Joint Committee on Internal Revenue Taxation. In 1941 Cooper was selected as one of five men to aid President Franklin D. Roosevelt in drafting the resolution announcing the United States's entry into World War II. Cooper also served on an investigative committee studying the conditions at Pearl Harbor at the time of the Japanese attack. Cooper is best remembered as a champion of the Tennessee Valley Authority and improved flood control and navigation of Tennessee's rivers. Cooper served Tennessee in the U.S. House of Representatives until his death in Bethesda, Maryland, on December 12, 1957.

Tara Mitchell Mielnik, Middle Tennessee State University
SEE: BOY SCOUTS OF AMERICA, TENNESSEE; CUMBERLAND UNIVERSITY; DYER COUNTY; TENNESSEE VALLEY AUTHORITY; WORLD WAR I

COOPER v. STATE (1910). An important ruling on the concept of self-defense resulted from one of the most famous murder trials in Tennessee history. On November 9, 1908, Robin Cooper shot and killed Edward W. Carmack in downtown Nashville. Cooper was the son of Duncan Cooper, an important Nashville publisher and close friend and advisor to Governor Malcolm Patterson. Carmack was the editor of the Nashville *Tennessean*, a former U.S. Senator, and a leading champion of the prohibitionist cause.

Carmack and the elder Cooper had once been friends, but the two split over prohibition. When Cooper supported the anti-prohibition gubernatorial campaign of Malcolm Patterson, Carmack responded with a series of editorials defaming both Patterson and Cooper. Tensions mounted, and Carmack and the Coopers armed themselves in anticipation of a violent confrontation. On November 9, 1908, both Coopers spotted Carmack on a Nashville street. When Duncan Cooper crossed the street and shouted to get Carmack's attention, the startled editor pulled his gun. Robin Cooper stepped between the men and drew his gun. Carmack fired twice, hitting Robin Cooper in the shoulder and his coat sleeve. The younger Cooper shot three times, killing Carmack.

Both Coopers were tried and convicted of murder in early 1909, and immediately appealed their convictions. The Tennessee State Supreme Court heard *Cooper v. State of Tennessee* in 1910. In a divided decision that gained national attention, the justices reversed Robin Cooper's conviction "for jury instruction errors and remanded for retrial." Robin Cooper "was put in jeopardy on remand, whereupon the prosecutor requested and the judge directed a verdict of acquittal."[1] However, the Tennessee Supreme Court upheld the conviction of Duncan Cooper, although he never fired a single shot, on the grounds of "proximate cause," that he provoked the incident by approaching Carmack on November 9, 1908. Nashville's three newspapers printed every word of the judges' opinions in the days following the trial.

Within the hour of the Supreme Court's decision, Governor Patterson issued a pardon for his old friend Cooper. Prohibitionists revolted against the pardon of Carmack's killer, destroying Patterson's chances for a third term as governor and opening the way for the election of Ben W. Hooper, Tennessee's first Republican governor since Reconstruction.

Tara Mitchell Mielnik, Middle Tennessee State University
CITATION:
(1) Donald F. Paine, "The Cooper Trial and Impeachments by Bad Acts," *Tennessee Bar Journal* (Nov./Dec., 1994): 26.
SEE: CARMACK, EDWARD W.; COOPER, DUNCAN B.; LAW; PATTERSON, MALCOLM R.

COOPER, WASHINGTON BOGART (1802–1888), portrait painter, was born near Jonesborough on September 18, 1802, the third of nine children. The family moved frequently, and young Cooper lived near Carthage and Shelbyville. He briefly received some art instruction in Murfreesboro before settling in Nashville in 1830. The next year Cooper went to Philadelphia to study and returned to Tennessee in 1832. According to his account books for the years 1837–1848, Cooper averaged 35 portraits per year. At this rate, he would have produced 2,100 portraits during his working life, deservedly earning his sobriquet "the man of a thousand portraits."

In 1839 Cooper married Dublin native Ann Litton, who bore four children: James (1840–1843), James Litton (1844–1924), Kate (1846–1919), and Joseph Litton (1849–1936). Their father portrayed the last three children in a portrait which is exhibited at the Tennessee State Museum. The family still owns a portrait of Ann Litton Cooper, painted circa 1842. More introspective than his other work, the atypical portrait shows his wife in profile, seated and reading. The setting was most likely suggested by Fragonard's *A Girl Reading*, which Cooper may have seen as a print.

Cooper completed three large sets of commission portraits. The Tennessee Historical Society commissioned him to paint portraits of the Tennessee governors whose images were known. The Methodist Episcopal Church South and the Grand Lodge of Free and Accepted Masons of Tennessee also commissioned portraits of their leaders. The governors' portraits are exhibited in the Capitol and in the Tennessee State Museum. The Masonic portraits are in the Grand Lodge in Nashville, but the bishops' portraits burned during a fire at Vanderbilt University in 1905.

The Tennessee State Museum has more than 50 works by Cooper. One of the most interesting is a self-portrait, which he did in 1885, and bequeathed to the Tennessee Historical Society. He died of pneumonia on March 30, 1888.

James A. Hoobler, Tennessee State Museum

SEE: ART; TENNESSEE HISTORICAL SOCIETY; TENNESSEE STATE MUSEUM

COOPER, WILLIAM PRENTICE, JR., (1895–1969), Governor, was born in Shelbyville to William Prentice and Argentine S. Cooper. He was educated in Bedford County schools, including Hannah's School at Shelbyville, Butler's Creek Elementary School, and the Webb School at Bell Buckle. He attended Vanderbilt University from 1913 to 1915 before transferring to Princeton University, where he received a bachelor's degree in 1917. He later received honorary degrees from Lincoln Memorial University, Harrogate, in 1940; Muhlenberg College in Allentown, Pennsylvania, in 1942; and Hartwick College, Oneonta, New York, 1943.

After graduation from Princeton, he volunteered for service in World War I and was inducted into the U.S. Army as a private. He received officer training and rose from master gunman to sergeant to second lieutenant. He served with Battery E of the 307th Field Artillery until May 1918, when he was transferred to Fort Monroe, Virginia. The Armistice was signed before he could be shipped to France, and he was honorably discharged on January 23, 1919.

Cooper studied law at Harvard University and received an LL.B. degree in 1921. He was admitted to the bar the following year and returned to Shelbyville to open a law practice next door to his father, a prominent lawyer and banker. He practiced law in Shelbyville and Lewisburg between periods of public service.

In 1923 Cooper began his extensive Democratic political career in the Tennessee House of Representatives, representing Bedford County. He was later elected district attorney general of the Eighth Judicial Circuit and then city attorney of Shelbyville. From 1937 to 1939 he served in the State Senate, representing Bedford, Coffee, and Moore counties.

Cooper served as governor for three consecutive terms, from 1939 to 1945. During his administration World War II was fought and won, with Tennesseans playing many important roles both at home and abroad. Cooper took an active role in mobilizing the state for war. In anticipation of national events, he appointed a Tennessee State Defense Council in 1940, the first such council in America. He also initiated a million dollar national defense bond to purchase Sewart Air Base in Smyrna. When the war began, Tennesseans participated in every phase of the military effort. Over 300,000 Tennesseans served in the armed forces, while the state's home front activities were critical to the victory. Defense plants were built across the state, including the powder plant in Millington; an aircraft plant in Nashville; and a shell-loading plant at Milan. Industries producing clothing, arms, and food employed thousands of Tennesseans; war contracts brought millions of dollars to the state's economy.

In addition to his war efforts, Cooper amassed an important domestic record. Under his administration, the legislature passed the first civil service act for state employees. He achieved the largest debt reduction in the state's history. He increased funding for education by 66 percent, doubled old age assistance, saw that free textbooks were provided to children in the lower grades, established a statewide tuberculosis hospital system, and added lands to state parks and forests.

After his final term as governor, he was appointed Ambassador to Peru. His mother, who had served as first lady to the bachelor governor, accompanied him to Peru to act as official hostess. Cooper served as ambassador from 1946 to 1948. When he returned to Tennessee, he was selected as a delegate to the 1953 State Constitutional Convention.

On April 25, 1950, the former governor married Hortense Powell, the daughter of Ferdinand and Margaret McGavock Hayes Powell. They had three sons: William Prentice III, James H. S., and John N. Powell. He and Mrs. Cooper actively participated in state historical organizations, Lutheran Church activities, and civic affairs. Cooper died on May 18, 1969, at the Mayo Clinic in Rochester, Minnesota, a victim of cancer. He was buried in Jenkins Chapel Cemetery in Bedford County.

Anne-Leslie Owens, Tennessee Historical Society

SEE: BEDFORD COUNTY; GOVERNMENT; WORLD WAR II

CORN. Corn was the chief agricultural product almost from the beginning of human settlement in Tennessee. Referred to as "Indian corn" throughout the 1800s, the cereal was widely cultivated by the Cherokees and formed a basic element of their diet. Most southern tribes practiced some form of the summer "green corn" festival in celebration of the life-giving grain.

The fact that corn could, with reasonable success, be grown in newly-cleared ground made it the staple crop on most pioneer farms. Planted as soon as land was cleared (or even before, in hills between the stumps), corn was cultivated through May and June, "laid by" in July and August, then picked by hand in early autumn. It provided the basic sustenance for pioneer farmers. Corn whiskey was the distinctive drink of the Scots-Irish pioneer—a home distilled palliative easy to make and far cheaper than imported rum or wine. The adoption of cornmeal and pone was a benchmark of Americanization, that is, of the settler's removal from the European and coastal preference for wheat flour and bread.

Corn was admirably suited to the southern growing season; it produced a large amount of starch and glucose for fattening livestock; it was susceptible to few diseases or insect pests; and it yielded a larger food product than any other cereal. The amount of corn grown was closely tied to the production of hogs, for which it was the principal feed. Corn and hogs complemented one another perfectly and offered a type of farming well-suited to the state's many small landholders. As the basic ingredient in fattening animals for meat and in its other forms— meal, grits, hominy, whiskey—corn constituted the staple of most Tennesseans' diets.

By 1840 Tennessee was the leading corn-producing state in the Union, with 12 percent of the nation's total. Ten years later, the state grew enough corn to feed its three million hogs, the most in the nation. It made an ideal commercial crop since it could be readily transformed into marketable commodities like cured pork, whiskey, and cornmeal. Such products were easily stored and shipped by riverboat to the

Corn field along Duck River, Humphreys County, 1986.

PHOTOGRAPH BY CARROLL VAN WEST

cotton-growing areas of the Deep South. As plantations concentrated on cotton before the Civil War, the granaries of border states like Tennessee grew correspondingly. Tennessee produced twice as much "Indian corn" between 1850 and 1860 as all other grains combined, and its prolific corn-hog agriculture served as a breadbasket for the Cotton South.

Corn continued to play a prominent role in post-Civil War agriculture, although prices did not recover to their prewar level for several decades. While corn was grown universally before the war as a means of self-sufficiency, afterwards production began to follow market prices. Middle Tennessee counties such as Maury, Bedford, Wilson, Williamson, and Rutherford were the powerhouse corn producers for most of the nineteenth century. The extent of production was highest in 1900 with 3.37 million acres planted, yielding an average of 28 bushels (or about 5 "barrels," as corn was then measured) per acre. Traditionally, Tennesseans preferred single-ear, white varieties like White Dent and Tennessee Red Cob, although yellow, multi-eared varieties such as Neal's Paymaster were gaining acceptance by the twentieth century.

The value and amount of corn harvested peaked in 1920, after which Tennessee agriculture in general began a slow decline. The corn harvest lost half of its value from 1920 to 1925. The introduction of modern hybrids, tractors and mechanical pickers, chemical insecticides, and fertilizers greatly increased the yield (and cost) of corn farming, even as acreage and the number of farmers declined. Extensive dam construction in Tennessee also reduced the availability of river bottoms—land which had been devoted almost exclusively to corn.

The productivity of corn farming quadrupled following World War II, with higher yields being produced on considerably less land. Cultivation also migrated westward in the state. By 1954 nine of the top ten corn-producing counties were in West Tennessee, with Weakley, Gibson, and Obion leading the way. Also during the 1950s, cotton and tobacco finally surpassed corn in terms of cash value. Once vital to the subsistence and commercial life of rural Tennesseans, corn continues to play a significant, though much diminished, role in the state's farm economy.

Wayne C. Moore, Tennessee State Library and Archives
SEE: AGRICULTURE

CORNWELL, DEAN (1892–1960), illustrator and mural painter, was born in Louisville, Kentucky, on March 5, 1892. Cornwell began his professional career as a cartoonist for the *Louisville Herald*, but soon relocated to Chicago, where he worked in the art department of the *Chicago Tribune* and studied at the Art Institute. In 1915 he moved to New York City, where he studied under Harvey Dunn and became a successful illustrator for many national magazines.

Desiring to study mural painting, Cornwell traveled to London, where he served as an apprentice under the internationally recognized British muralist, Frank Brangwyn. After his return to America, Cornwell painted murals for several years at the Los Angeles Public Library and the Lincoln Memorial Shrine in Redlands, California. Other notable commissions include the Eastern Airlines Building in Rockefeller Plaza, the U.S. Post Office in Chapel Hill, North Carolina, the Raleigh Room at the Hotel Warwick in New York City, and the General Motors Exhibition at New York's World Fair in 1939.

In Tennessee, Cornwell is best known for murals created for the Davidson County Courthouse in 1937 and for the Sevier State Office Building in 1941. The Public Works Administration funded the construction of both buildings during the New Deal era. The murals in the main lobby of the Davidson County Courthouse feature heroic figures representing Industry, Agriculture, Commerce, and Statesmanship superimposed over maps of Nashville and Davidson County. The Sevier State Office Building murals, titled *The Discovery of Tennessee* and *The Development of Tennessee*, depict important figures in Tennessee's history. Both murals were created under the auspices of President Franklin D. Roosevelt's New Deal cultural programs. Cornwell died December 4, 1960, in New York City.

Anne-Leslie Owens, Tennessee Historical Society

SUGGESTED READING: Patricia J. Broder, *Dean Cornwell, Dean of Illustrators* (1978)

SEE: ART; MURALS, DECORATIVE INTERIOR

COTTON. Cotton was not an aboriginal crop in Tennessee, nor was it widely cultivated by the earliest settlers in mountainous East Tennessee. Gins for separating cotton seed from fiber were brought into Middle Tennessee during the 1780s, and soon appeared on estate inventories and tax rolls. Andre Michaux, the French botanist visiting Nashville in 1802, spoke enthusiastically on the wealth to be made from growing and selling cotton. Prices at the New Orleans cotton market were avidly followed by the early Cumberland settlers. On the frontier, cotton doubled as an export commodity sent downriver to market and as an important article of domestic manufacture. Families ginned, carded, and spun the fiber to make thread for a heavy homespun cloth.

Middle Tennessee's importance in terms of cotton production was eclipsed as richer lands became available. Large scale cultivation of cotton did not begin until the 1820s with the opening of the land between the Tennessee and Mississippi rivers. The upper wedge of the Mississippi Delta extended into southwestern Tennessee, and it was in this fertile section

Field laborer toting cotton in West Tennessee, 1946.

that the Cotton Kingdom took hold. Despite the importance of the crop in Shelby, Fayette, Hardeman, Haywood, and Madison counties, the state's agriculture as a whole was never devoted exclusively to cotton, as it was in other southern states.

"King Cotton" had a seasonal cycle and work regimen all its own. As the principal cash crop before the Civil War, cotton was planted year after year on the same land; it required, therefore, a deep, rich soil such as West Tennessee offered. The region grew a high grade cotton with a long and heavy staple. Raising and picking cotton demanded a great deal of hand labor, and the crop, typically, was worked by slave gang labor on large plantations. The identification of cotton with slavery was central to this distinctive brand of antebellum agriculture. In that section of Tennessee where cotton was grown, the demands of the crop and the slave/planter system that nurtured it flavored the entire character of life.

The growing of cotton and the entrepreneurial activities surrounding its movements through the world market were responsible for much of the antebellum economic growth in Tennessee. By 1850 Tennessee held fifth place among the cotton growing states, and the ensuing decade's high prices fueled a tremendous surge both in cotton production and the number of slaves. Memphis laid claim to the title of "Biggest Inland Cotton Market in the World" and became a headquarters for cotton factors, the financial intermediaries who provided planters with operating capital and marketed the crop. The Civil War had an especially destructive impact on cotton farming, and Tennessee's output 50 years later was still below what it had been in 1860.

Following emancipation, West Tennessee cotton planters needed a new labor system to replace slavery, and for the next 60 years the sharecropper system of tenancy dominated the region. Mostly African-American sharecroppers worked for one-half or one-third of the cotton crop, from which was deducted the cost (plus interest) of seed, mules, and supplies that had been advanced to them by the landlord at the start of the season. Despite chronically low prices for cotton (4 1/2 cents per pound in 1894), the dependency of the Delta on this single crop grew stronger over time. In one of the worst years ever, 1930, over a million acres were in production statewide, an all-time high.

Traditional cotton agriculture was shaken by the successive jolts of the boll weevil, the migration of blacks to the North, the collapse of farm markets after 1920, the 1927 Mississippi River flood and the severe drought three years later, the worst depression in history, and New Deal crop reduction programs. Together they transformed the old labor intensive and tenant-based system. Tractors replaced tenants, sharecropping declined, and surplus rural laborers migrated to the cities.

After the onset of mechanical pickers in Tennessee during the 1940s, West Tennessee cotton agriculture, which had higher yields than other states, became even more productive. By the 1950s, cotton ranked first among Tennessee's farm commodities in the value of production. Two derivative industries—cottonseed processing in Memphis and textile manufacturing, mainly in East Tennessee—have become important parts of the state's economy. There are only scattered remnants today of that century or so when cotton dominated the fortunes of much of the state. A way of life that typified rural West Tennessee since Reconstruction has disappeared, and few mourn its passing.

Wayne C. Moore, Tennessee State Library and Archives
SEE: AGRICULTURE; AGRICULTURAL TENANCY; BOND, SAMUEL; COTTON GINS; MEMPHIS; SLAVERY

COTTON GINS. Without the cotton gin, Tennessee never would have evolved into a major antebellum cotton market because the cotton fibers produced here were too short for hand ginning or roller ginning, which could be performed on the long-staple cotton found along the southeastern coasts. To separate short-staple cotton from the seeds, Eli Whitney developed and patented the first cotton gin in America in 1793. Three years later, H. Ogden Holmes patented the more efficient saw gin. All early gins in Tennessee were of the saw gin type. The first gin in West Tennessee, the state's major cotton producing

region in both the nineteenth and twentieth centuries, was at Jackson in 1821. Seven years later, both Jackson and Brownsville had operating gins.

In the nineteenth century, most planters operated their own gins, which were usually housed in a two-story building that included the storage bin, saw gin, and lint room. Outside stood a wooden screw press that turned the processed cotton into huge bales ready for shipping. By 1902 Tennessee had 833 cotton gins. The gin operator, who usually managed a general store and feed and seed business in addition to the gin, slowly put the plantation gins out of business. In 1938 only one plantation gin remained. But that same pattern of consolidation eventually closed most independent gin operators; by 1958 for example, only 297 gins operated in Tennessee. By this time, the rule of King Cotton in the Old South had diminished as western states became the nation's primary cotton producers.

The type of cotton processed by gins also has changed the modern ginning industry. Machine-picked cotton, compared to the earlier hand-picked cotton of the slave era and later tenant farmer period, demands automatic feeders and powerful dryers as well as expensive machinery for cleaning and extracting. Modern gins today, typically found adjacent to county seats along major highways in West and southern Middle Tennessee, are complicated industrial complexes rather than the simple machines of the past.

Carroll Van West, Middle Tennessee State University
SEE: AGRICULTURE; COTTON

COUNTRY MUSIC ASSOCIATION (CMA) is one of Tennessee's most important musical trade associations, dedicated to guiding and enhancing country music's development and demonstrating its viability to advertisers, consumers, and media throughout the world. During the late 1950s, as country music record sales faced a serious challenge from rock-n-roll, country music performers, disc jockeys, and songwriters joined music publishing, recording, management, talent booking, and broadcasting executives to promote country music and increase its radio and TV exposure. In mid-1958 the older Country Music Disc Jockeys Association disbanded, and the broader-based CMA was organized in Nashville that fall. Nashville music publisher Wesley Rose became CMA's founding board chairman. Harry Stone, formerly manager of Nashville radio and TV station WSM, served briefly as executive director, but was succeeded by Orlinda, Tennessee, native Jo Walker-Meador. Nashvillian Ed Benson took over this post in 1991, when Walker-Meador retired.

After a 1961 CMA-sponsored survey found only 81 full-time country stations, the Association focused on persuading public officials to proclaim an annual

Country Music Month and sponsored special package shows in cities across the nation. Exploiting a national trend toward radio market specialization, CMA commissioned demographic research, developed sales kits for country broadcasters, and made special sales presentations to conventions of broadcasters and advertisers in an effort to prove country music's effectiveness and potential as an advertising tool. As a result, full-time country stations passed the 600 mark by decade's end, and country made similar gains in television.

In 1961 CMA established the Country Music Hall of Fame to increase recognition for country artists and executives. Initially, the Tennessee State Museum displayed the Hall of Fame plaques within its displays at the War Memorial Building in downtown Nashville. In 1967, following an extensive fund drive, CMA created a permanent display with the opening of the Country Music Hall of Fame and Museum. CMA held its first awards show in Nashville that same year; 1968 marked the program's first national telecast.

Thanks in part to CMA, country music now claims over 2,300 full-time stations in North America, while CMA membership exceeds 7,000 individuals and companies from 30 nations. Using ever more sophisticated demographic analysis, CMA works to keep country music strong in today's competitive markets. CMA-supported seminars for songwriters, broadcasters, and talent buyers attract thousands every year, while CMA plays a key role in Country Music Week and Fan Fair (established in Nashville in 1972). Fan Fair has become the major country music industry event in Nashville every summer.

Close-up, CMA's monthly magazine, keeps readers informed about artistic and commercial developments affecting the country industry. As in the past, CMA monitors important legal issues and publicizes country music, thus ensuring the organization's longstanding reputation as an aggressive and effective association.

John W. Rumble, Country Music Foundation

SEE: COUNTRY MUSIC FOUNDATION; COUNTRY MUSIC HALL OF FAME; MUSIC; WALKER-MEADOR, JO; WSM

COUNTRY MUSIC FOUNDATION (CMF) is a tax-exempt, not-for-profit organization dedicated to collecting and preserving artifacts and disseminating information about country music's development as an art and a business. The State of Tennessee chartered CMF in 1964.

In 1967 the Country Music Hall of Fame and Museum opened, providing a home for CMF's activities and educational programs. Until 1971, CMF shared staff members with the Country Music Association (CMA), but that year CMF gained a staff of its own and established a library in the basement of the building. Today, library holdings include more than 175,000 recorded discs, 8,000 books, 450 periodicals, 60,000 photographs, and thousands of song books, films, business documents, and other materials. Open by appointment, the library serves as a resource not only for CMF staff, but for schools and colleges, the music industry, and the media.

CMF underwent considerable expansion in the mid-1970s, including the construction of new museum and library wings to house the rapidly growing collections and the launching of educational programs, first in Middle Tennessee schools, but eventually expanding to schools in Kentucky and Georgia. CMF established an oral history project to document the contributions of singers, songwriters, business executives, and others involved in country music, both past and present. The Foundation created a publications department to publish books and the CMF's *Journal of Country Music.* Since then, CMF has produced such landmark works as *Country: The Music and the Musicians* (1986, rev. ed. 1994), and is now jointly issuing new and formerly out-of-print titles with Vanderbilt University Press. Late in the 1970s, the first historic reissue recording appeared on the Country Music Foundation Records label, including *The Bristol Sessions* (1987), which features historic recording sessions made in Bristol, Tennessee, in 1927, and *Hank Williams: Rare Demos, First to Last* (1990), a collection of previously unreleased demonstration recordings by one of country music's greatest singer-songwriters. In addition, the organization also began serving as a consulting and production company for other labels reissuing historical performances, producing boxed sets featuring artists like Patsy Cline, Bill Monroe, and Merle Haggard.

Employing more than 30 full-time professionals in the fields of library science, publishing, history, education, design, museum administration, and marketing, CMF is now the world's largest research center devoted to a single form of popular music, with annual attendance at the Hall of Fame and Museum exceeding 300,000. The Foundation also operates RCA Records' Studio B as an historic site and offers a trolley tour of Nashville's Music Row and the Foundation-owned Hatch Show Print, a Nashville show-business printing firm founded in 1879. Through its museum, library, publications, and educational programs, CMF continues to advocate country music's importance in American popular culture.

John W. Rumble, Country Music Foundation

SEE: COUNTRY MUSIC ASSOCIATION; COUNTRY MUSIC HALL OF FAME; MUSIC

COUNTRY MUSIC HALL OF FAME AND MUSEUM. One of the most-visited popular arts museums in the United States, the Country Music Hall of

Fame and Museum opened on April 1, 1967, and is operated by the not-for-profit Country Music Foundation. Located in Nashville's world-famous Music Row district, the facility boasts some 20,000 square feet of exhibit space, featuring more than 3,000 items, including costumes, instruments, recordings, song manuscripts, historic cars, and film footage representing hundreds of country music personalities, past and present.

Drawing upon the vast resources of the Foundation's museum and library holdings, exhibits are designed to be both educational and entertaining, and explore today's country scene as well as the music's history as art and enterprise. The jewel of the museum is the Country Music Hall of Fame proper, whose plaques honor performers, songwriters, executives, and other outstanding individuals in country music. Many native Tennesseans, such as Roy Acuff, Chet Atkins, Eddy Arnold, Uncle Dave Macon, Owen Bradley, Tennessee Ernie Ford, and Minnie Pearl, are showcased, along with persons from other states. Other permanent exhibits include *Songs and Songwriters, Country Music and the Movies,* and *Styles of Country Music.* The Walkway of Stars, in the museum lobby, recognizes prominent contributors to the growth of country music. The museum often displays *The Sources of Country Music,* the last work of legendary painter Thomas Hart Benton, but loans this classic mural to other institutions from time to time.

Two of the museum's most recent and most popular exhibits are *Stars and Guitars,* which celebrates the centennial of the Nashville-based Gibson Guitar Corporation, and *The Treasures of Hank Williams,* a large collection of rare Williams song manuscripts, correspondence, and personal memorabilia assembled by country star Marty Stuart, supplemented by costumes, instruments, and recordings from the Foundation's own holdings and Williams's beautifully restored 1948 Packard touring car.

The museum also provides a special trolley tour of Music Row and a behind-the-scenes look at RCA's historic Studio B—a birthplace of the Nashville Sound—which the Foundation now operates as a working studio, where visitors view actual recording sessions. Museum guests may also visit the Foundation-owned Hatch Show Print, a downtown Nashville printing firm, in the Lower Broadway historic district, that has catered to the Mid-South's entertainment industry since 1879. Hatch specializes in posters made from hand-carved wooden blocks and offers some 100 prints for sale.

John W. Rumble, Country Music Foundation

SEE: ACUFF, ROY; ARNOLD, EDDY; ATKINS, CHESTER B.; BRADLEY, OWEN; COUNTRY MUSIC FOUNDATION; FORD, TENNESSEE ERNIE; MACON, DAVID H.; MINNIE PEARL; WILLIAMS, HANK

COX, ELIZABETH (1942-), poet, short story writer, essayist, and novelist, was born in 1942 in Chattanooga into a family of teachers and writers. She attended the University of Tennessee in Knoxville, the University of Chattanooga (now the University of Tennessee at Chattanooga), and the University of Mississippi, where she completed her B.A. degree in 1964; she received her M.F.A. in writing from the University of North Carolina at Greensboro in 1979. Cox has published numerous short stories and poems in a variety of periodicals and anthologies, including *Antaeus, Anthology of North Carolina Poets, Carolina Quarterly, Crucible, Fiction International, Graywolf Annual: Short Stories, Green River Review, Greensboro Review, Hyperion, St. Andrews Review,* and *Southern Poetry Review.* One of her short stories "Old Court" was adapted for broadcasting on National Public Radio (1989). She has also published two novels: *Familiar Ground* (1984) and *The Ragged Way People Fall Out of Love* (1991). Cox has won several prizes for her short stories, including a citation for excellence in *The Best American Short Stories* and a Pushcart prize, both in 1980, for her short story "Land of Goshen." In addition, she has been awarded fellowships from Yaddo (1982) and the MacDowell Colony (1983). She divides her time between Boston, Massachusetts, and Durham, North Carolina; she teaches (alternate semesters) at Bennington College and Duke University. Cox's writing, whether in the form of essay, short story, or novel, is marked by its strong emphasis on the surroundings and by the influence that place exerts on memory and finally on character.

Susan D. Core, St. Andrew's-Sewanee School

SEE: LITERATURE

COX, JOHN ISAAC (1857–1946), Governor, constitutionally inherited his position when prior Governor James Frazier (1903–1905) resigned the office to assume the U. S. Senate seat of the late William B. Bate. Before becoming governor, Cox was a consummate public official, as Bristol's city attorney, a Sullivan County judge, and a member of the state's General Assembly in both the House and Senate for 32 consecutive years.

Cox hailed from a distinguished Jamestown family, but grew up in poverty after his father, Henry W. Cox, was killed while fighting for the Confederacy. Orphaned at age eight, Cox struggled to support his mother, two sisters, and brother during the hard years of Reconstruction. His mother's perseverance during times of financial difficulty strongly shaped Cox's bootstrap ethic. Among other duties, Cox's work included carrying mail at age 16 and serving as justice of the peace at age 21, burdens that sharply constrained any attempt at formal education. Engaged mostly in private study, Cox attended Blountville's Jefferson Academy for two terms and later studied law in the office of Judge W. V. Deaderick. Cox married Lorena Butler in 1905, the educated daughter of a former Confederate army surgeon.

During his gubernatorial administration, Cox acquired a reputation for fiscal prudence and general economic conservatism. His earlier success as county judge in reducing Sullivan County's $20,000 debt as well as lowering the county's tax rate made him popular among business interests. As governor, Cox described as one of his greatest accomplishments the dispatching of state troops to protect replacement workers during a Tracy City coal strike, an action that merited predictably little support among labor groups. Other major events during his two-year stint included a renewed attack on yellow fever and the adoption of Lee Roy Reeves's state flag. Cox also lobbied to improve the pensions of Civil War veterans and widows, an effort, no doubt, cemented by his mother's hardships, and one he continued even after leaving office.

After losing a bid for a second gubernatorial term to Malcolm Patterson in 1907, Cox resumed a career in the State Senate until retirement in 1912. Cox spent most of his retirement overseeing his 600-acre farm in Bristol, periodically furnishing vocal support for various Tennessee politicians, including Memphis political boss E. H. Crump. At the national level, the former governor was an ardent supporter of Franklin Roosevelt and his TVA initiatives.

Suffering with a kidney ailment, Cox died at age 90 in Abingdon, Virginia. In one of his last interviews, he attributed his longevity to his temperate lifestyle, asserting a personal conservatism that closely mirrored his public governing style.

Vaughn May, University of Tennessee at Martin
SEE: FRAZIER, JAMES B.; LABOR; SULLIVAN COUNTY

COX MOUND GORGET, or Woodpecker, gorget style is a particularly beautiful and enduring symbol of Tennessee's prehistoric inhabitants. A gorget was a pendant, or personal adornment, worn around the neck as a badge of rank or insignia of status, and was thought to be symbolic of both earthly and supernatural powers. A variety of gorget styles, or designs, are known. Archaeologist Madeline Kneberg studied the artifact variations in gorget motifs. As a class of artistic expression, this type of artifact falls within the "Southeastern Ceremonial Complex," formerly known as the "Southern Cult."

Just over 30 Cox Mound style gorgets have been found since the late nineteenth century, primarily from prehistoric Mississippian stone box graves and villages along the lower Tennessee, Cumberland, Duck, Harpeth, and Buffalo rivers of Middle Tennessee, and the middle Tennessee River valley of northern Alabama. As a result of the frequent mortuary association of Cox Mound gorgets with certain

pottery types, namely Matthews Incised, as well as other artifacts, it has been postulated that Cox Mound gorgets date to the period A.D. 1250–1450. One rich grave from the famous burial mound at the Castalian Springs site in Sumner County, Tennessee, produced two Cox Mound gorgets.

Typically, Cox Mound gorgets were manufactured on exotic marine shell and were white in color. Other materials, such as black slate in Putnam County and human skull fragments in Hardin County, were used rarely. Engraving the intricate design on the hard shell or slate without metal tools took many hours of skilled labor and is thought to have been a winter activity.

A Cox Mound Gorget has three important iconographic elements. In the center is a cross inside a rayed circle or sun motif. The cross is symbolic of the sacred fire, or council fire. The sun represents the sky deity and/or mythical ancestors. Surrounding the cross and sun is a scroll-like design element known as the looped square. This feature may represent wind, or possibly the litter on which a chief was carried by subordinates. Typically the looped square is composed of four lines, but in some cases only three lines are used. Four crested bird heads, which most scholars interpret as woodpeckers, are found on the outer edge. The woodpecker heads always are oriented in a counter-clockwise direction, suggestive of the prehistoric Native American swastika.

The woodpecker, like the falcon, was probably a symbol of war to the prehistoric Mississippian Indians. The war symbolism of the bird probably derived from the red head of the bird, similar to a bloodied scalping victim. The Cherokees associated the red-headed woodpecker with danger and war, and the woodpecker was always invoked for aid by the ball game players. The birds's pecking is similar to an Indian warrior striking the war post at the Victory dance. For the Cherokees, the color red is associated with male attractiveness and fertility, as well as bravery and war. Groups of woodpeckers are thought to be a sign of war to the Creeks and Seminoles. While war is typically associated with males in Native American society, it is important to note that Cox Mound gorgets have been found in both male and female burials.

Other interpretations include the identification of the four woodpeckers as the four thunders at the world quarters. A recent folklorist interpretation speculated that the Cox Mound gorget style is a prehistoric expression of the Yuchi myth of the Winds. Cox Mounds gorgets are displayed by the Tennessee State Museum and Pinson Mounds State Archaeological Area.

C. Andrew Buchner, PanAmerican Consultants, Inc.
SUGGESTED READINGS: C. Andrew Buchner and Mitchell R. Childress, "A Southeastern Ceremonial Complex Gorget

from Putnam County, Tennessee." *Tennessee Anthropological Association Newsletter* 16(#6, 1991): 1–4; Madeline Kneberg, "Engraved Shell Gorgets and Their Associations." *Tennessee Archaeologist* 15(#1, 1959): 1–39

SEE: MISSISSIPPIAN CULTURE; PINSON MOUNDS; PREHISTORIC NATIVE AMERICAN ART; TENNESSEE STATE MUSEUM

CRAB ORCHARD STONE is a rare sandstone quarried from the Crab Orchard Mountain of the Cumberland Plateau. This mottled stone is predominately rose in color, but streaked in irregular patterns by different shades of brown. Its unique and beautiful color was used mostly for chimneys and foundations in the immediate region until the late nineteenth century, when Cumberland County officials built a courthouse with the stone and erected stone curbing and sidewalks in Crossville. During the mid-1920s, Crab Orchard stone gained a more statewide—even national—reputation after architect Henry Hibbs decided to use it as the primary building material for Scarritt College in Nashville. New Deal agencies used the stone extensively in their nationally significant Cumberland Homesteads project. Since that time, Crab Orchard stone has been used in a wide variety of buildings and locations across the country. The most concentrated area of Crab Orchard stone buildings, however, remains in Cumberland County, Tennessee, where the courthouse, old post office, numerous houses, several churches, schools, and even a theater are built with this distinctive material.
Carroll Van West, Middle Tennessee State University
SEE: CUMBERLAND COUNTY; CUMBERLAND HOMESTEADS

CRABB, ALFRED LELAND (1884–1979), author of historical novels, was born in Warren County, Kentucky, and educated at Bethel College, Peabody College, the University of Chicago, and Columbia University. He received his Ph.D. degree in 1925 from Peabody. In 1911 he married Bertha Gardner; they had one son, Alfred Leland Crabb, Jr. Interspersed with the years of his formal education, he was teacher and later principal at several rural schools in Kentucky and Louisiana. After receiving his doctorate, he taught at what is now Western Kentucky University, where he soon became dean. In 1927 Peabody president Bruce Payne invited Crabb back to Peabody, where he became professor of education, retiring in 1949. Crabb assumed the editorship of the *Peabody Journal of Education* in 1932, a position he retained until 1970. For this publication, and for the *Peabody Reflector*, he wrote hundreds of articles, essays, editorials, and poems.

Crabb was best known for his trilogy of historical novels, published between 1942 and 1945, and memorably titled for Nashville landmarks: *Dinner at Belmont, Supper at the Maxwell House,* and *Breakfast at the Hermitage.* The historical sites and traditional south-

ern meals of their titles reflect Crabb's preoccupation with the southern way of life in Nashville during the last half of the nineteenth century. These three novels cover 40 years of the city's history, from the eve of the Civil War to 1897, the date of the Tennessee Centennial Exposition, years of upheaval for the city, state, and nation. Almost as popular as Crabb's Nashville trilogy was the Civil War trilogy that followed: *Lodging at the Saint Cloud, A Mockingbird Sang at Chickamauga,* and *Home to Tennessee.*

Detailed descriptions of Tennessee's flora and fauna, southern food, folk music, and tall tales became the hallmarks of Crabb's writing. Two of his most colorful creations, the nameless driver, and his sidekick, College Grove (named for his place of nativity), were used to impart a wide variety of southern and rural folklore and music.

Like many historical novelists of his time, Crabb adopted an old-fashioned style. Though writing in the modern era, he shared the values of the pre-modern society he described. His works featured everything that modernism was not: continuity, certainty, and closure. Most importantly, Crabb revealed his pre-modernist sensibilities in the power he gave his characters to shape events rather than be shaped by them. His protagonists always viewed their lot as meaningful fate, never as random happenstance.

In addition to the Nashville and Civil War trilogies, he authored *Journey to Nashville: A Story of the Founding,* in which he described the adventures of the Robertson and Donelson parties on their trek through the wilderness and waters of Tennessee to establish the settlement first called Nashborough. *Home to the Hermitage,* a novel about Andrew and Rachel Jackson toward the end of her life, was dramatized and presented on the "Cavalcade of America" radio program in 1948. In *Nashville: Personality of a City* (1960) he described the various people, places, and subjects for which he had demonstrated a fondness in his fictional work.
Sara Harwell, Vanderbilt University
SEE: LITERATURE; GEORGE PEABODY COLLEGE OF VANDERBILT UNIVERSITY

CRAGFONT, the Georgian mansion located on a craggy eminence above Bledsoe's Creek seven miles east of Gallatin, was erected by James and Susan Black Winchester during the period 1798–1802. They built their two-story house of gray, rough-finished native limestone quarried near the site. When completed, it was the most elegant residence on the Tennessee frontier, the first to reflect the grandeur and style of the fine eighteenth-century homes of Maryland and Virginia.

Cragfont was T-shaped with the front section representing the top of the T and the rear wing its stem.

At first the rear wing was erected of a single story, but a second floor for a ballroom was added circa 1810 using brick walls covered with stucco.

The first floor included the parlor, entrance hall, office, library, a cross hall, dining room, kitchen, and, separated by a massive stone fire wall, a smokehouse. The owners' bedroom, a hallway, two other bedrooms, a ballroom, and card room were upstairs. From the ballroom a stairway rose to a partially finished attic. Broad porticoes flanked the rear wing at both levels.

An elaborate garden was situated on the east side of the house. Some 60 yards north was the family cemetery. Slaves lived in row quarters in an area west of the cemetery; the slave quarters have not survived.

Cragfont was always home for Susan and James Winchester's family of eight daughters and six sons. James died in 1826, but Susan lived there until her death in 1862.

In 1958 the Tennessee Historical Commission acquired Cragfont, which is listed on the National Register of Historic Places and now is open to the public.
Walter T. Durham, Gallatin
SEE: ARCHITECTURE, VERNACULAR DOMESTIC; SUMNER COUNTY; WINCHESTER, JAMES

CRAIGHEAD, THOMAS BROWN (c. 1750–1825), a 1775 "New Light" graduate of the College of New Jersey (now Princeton), became Nashville's first minister, when James Robertson and other pioneering settlers invited him to the Cumberland region to establish a Presbyterian church and school. The residents promised to purchase 640 acres of land for his use and pay him 50 pounds, about $125, annually for three years. Before coming to Nashville, Craighead held preaching engagements in South Carolina, North Carolina, and Virginia. Craighead began his Nashville career shortly after his arrival by mounting a stump and preaching to all who would listen. Like most frontier areas, the Cumberland region was characterized by profanity, drunkenness, and crime, but very little religion. Although Craighead arrived in Nashville in 1785, the Presbyterians did not formally organize a church there until 1814. Craighead not only preached, but he also established Davidson Academy, chartered by the legislature of North Carolina in 1786. Like other schools of the period, Davidson emphasized classical education, with heavy emphasis on Greek and Latin. The enrollment remained small.

Although described as calm, sober, even eloquent in his preaching, Craighead's ministry was often controversial with Presbyterians as well as other denominations. Other ministers chastised him and leaders of his own church admonished him for his "liberal beliefs." During a period of religious revivals, when emotion sometimes overcame common sense, Craig-

head challenged his listeners to think. Craighead denied the Augustinian doctrine of total depravity and gave man some responsibility for his own destiny. He believed in "freedom of the will" and denied original sin, arguing that sin was a thing of will and not of nature. He relegated "Divine Grace" to a secondary role by asserting that the human will must take the initiative in determining salvation. Few frontier Christians accepted his controversial views and in 1811 his own synod suspended his ministry. Despite this action, Craighead continued to teach and preach and in 1824 the Assembly of the Presbyterian Church restored him to the ministry.

Shortly after his vindication, Craighead died at Spring Hill, where he had lived since his arrival in Nashville, suffering from the misfortunes of poverty, ill health, and blindness. He was buried near his home and school. At the time of his death, friends and colleagues remembered him as a scholar, an independent thinker, and a man of dauntless courage.
John Lawrence Connelly, Nashville
SEE: DAVIDSON COUNTY; RELIGION

CRAVENS HOUSE. Robert Cravens, a leading industrialist in Chattanooga, purchased a thousand acres of land on the side of Lookout Mountain in 1854, where he maintained an orchard and built several cabins as a summer retreat for his family. In 1856 the Cravens became the first family to maintain a permanent home on the mountain. Originally a white, L-shaped, one-story home with six rooms, the Cravens house was a prominent feature on the mountainside.

After the Battle of Chickamauga, September 19–20, 1863, Confederate troops occupied Lookout Mountain. By securing Lookout Mountain, Missionary Ridge, and the valley between, the Confederates held the Federals in Chattanooga. Confederate forces built defenses that passed through the Cravens land, making the "white house" a target for the Federal artillery on Moccasin Bend. Although the house was struck six times, the family remained until mid-November.

On November 24, 1863, General Joseph Hooker and his Union troops attacked Lookout Mountain. The Confederates made a stubborn resistance at the Cravens' house, but retreated by mid-afternoon. Once in the possession of the Union troops, the Cravens' house became the headquarters for General W. C. Whitaker's command.

Returning home, the Cravens found only the stone basement and dairy house remaining. Cravens rebuilt his home and remained on the mountain until his death in 1886. Today, the National Park Service maintains the home as a significant part of the Lookout Mountain battlefield.
Patrice Hobbs Glass, Chattanooga
SEE: CHICKAMAUGA AND CHATTANOOGA, BATTLES OF

CREEK WAR OF 1813 AND 1814, also known as the First Creek War, actually began in the spring of 1812, when a party of Creek warriors, returning from a visit to the British in Canada, attacked a small white settlement at the mouth of the Duck River. These warriors killed several people and took a captive, Mrs. Martha Crawley, south into the Creek country. The Creek Council, at the insistence of United States Agent Benjamin Hawkins, executed the warriors and their leader, Little Warrior, for their crimes. The executions sparked a long-simmering revolt by nativist Creeks. The nativists, known as Red Sticks, sought to wrest control of the Creek Nation from the council chiefs, whom they blamed for white encroachment on Creek territory and toleration of corrupting white influences on Indian life. The Red Sticks also sought alliance with the British and membership in a confederacy of northern Native Americans under Tecumseh in order to push American settlers from the Indian heartland. During the course of their revolt, the Red Sticks attacked Fort Mims on the lower reaches of the Alabama River, killing approximately 275 of the fort's white and Creek mixed blood inhabitants. At that point, what had been a Creek civil war became a struggle between the Red Sticks and the United States and merged with the larger War of 1812 between the Americans and Great Britain.

The Fort Mims Massacre shocked the white citizens of the United States, and they determined to crush the Creek uprising. With their long history of border conflict with the Creeks and their fear of Britain's northern Indian allies, Tennesseans took the lead in the war. Without waiting for federal authorization, Governor Willie Blount asked the legislature to call out 3,500 state volunteers to march against the Creeks. The irate legislators granted the request, and the Tennessee army took to the field in two contingents. Major General Andrew Jackson, the overall commander, led the troops from West Tennessee; General John Cocke led the East Tennessee force, which included a number of Cherokee warriors. Though armies from Georgia and the Mississippi Territory also converged on the Red Sticks, the Tennesseans did most of the fighting. They destroyed several Upper Creek towns, and defeated the Red Sticks at the battles of Tallushatchee and Talladega in the fall of 1813, before delivering the death blow to the Creek uprising in March 1814 at the famed Battle of Horseshoe Bend. Following close on the heels of his victory, General Jackson assumed command of the Seventh Military District of the United States Army, extracted a 22 million-acre land cession from the Creek Council, and brought a decisive end to the War of 1812 by defeating the British at the Battle of New Orleans.

White Tennesseans, and westerners generally, reaped great rewards from their participation in the Creek war. The close of the conflict, along with the end of the War of 1812, promoted western expansion. More people moved into Tennessee, while simultaneously, some state residents departed, moving south to the lands taken from the Creeks, settling below the Tennessee River and down through Jones Valley to the town of Tuscaloosa. In 1819 representatives of these settlers took an active role in creating the state of Alabama, one of a number of western states formed in the wake of war with Britain and British Indian allies. Furthermore, several Tennesseans, including Sam Houston and David Crockett, made names for themselves in the war. Andrew Jackson's conquests promoted his rise to the presidency of the United States.

Tennessee's Native Americans suffered as a result of the war. The Creek uprising helped turn western whites against the old Jeffersonian policy of civilizing and assimilating the Indians. Instead, westerners became convinced that Native Americans could not be tamed and must be removed to insure the nation's security. Andrew Jackson, representing the growing political power of the West, took the lead in advocating removal when he became president. Unfortunately, he did not spare even the acculturated Cherokees of East Tennessee. He made them move west, even though they had demonstrated their ability to coexist with whites by helping Jackson defeat the Red Sticks.

John T. Ellisor, University of Tennessee, Knoxville
SUGGESTED READINGS: Joel W. Martin, *Sacred Revolt: The Muskogees' Struggle for a New World* (1991); Frank Lawrence Owsley, Jr., *Struggle for the Gulf Borderlands: The Creek War and the Battle of New Orleans* (1981)
SEE: BLOUNT, WILLIE; CROCKETT, DAVID; HOUSTON, SAM; JACKSON, ANDREW; WAR OF 1812

CROCKETT COUNTY. The desire for more convenient access to county government brought together the citizens of the outlying regions of Dyer, Gibson, Haywood, and Madison counties to petition the Tennessee General Assembly for the formation of a new county, first in 1832 and again, 13 years later, in 1845. Both petitions were unsuccessful. In November 1871 the legislature provided relief for the isolated farmers by enacting legislation to form Crockett County, named for the famous Tennessean David Crockett. Appropriately, the county seat was named Alamo, after the historic mission in San Antonio, Texas, where Crockett died in 1836. Two commissioners from each county from which land was taken met to establish county government. The county courthouse, which was completed in 1874, continues to serve local needs.

The 265 square miles of Crockett County lying in the Mississippi River drainage area are covered with fertile farm land that has few hilly sections. Since no town has a population of over 2,500, the entire county is classified as rural. When the Tennessee Department of Agriculture established its Century Farms program in 1976, it identified 11 historic family farms, the oldest of which was the Frog Jump Farm that Dr. Samuel Oldham, Sr., established with 1,500 acres in 1830. Cotton was Oldham's primary crop, but nineteenth century agriculture in Crockett County was diverse. Wheat, small grains, corn and livestock were other important farm products. In the twentieth century, several families turned to specialized cash crops. At the Hillcrest Farm, Columbus H. Conley managed fruit orchards, strawberry patches, and a honey bee yard while operating a sorghum mill. In Alamo, he established the Bank of Alamo, a classically-styled brick building that has been listed in the National Register of Historic Places. Soybeans are another important twentieth century agricultural crop in the county.

Cotton, however, remains "king" in Crockett County. In 1995 almost 89,000 acres were planted in cotton, followed by 10,000 acres of soybeans, 3,000 acres of corn, 2,500 acres of wheat, and 137 acres of sorghum. The county ranks second in the state in the number of acres planted in cotton, but boasts the highest yields per acre. In the mid-1990s, cotton gins operated in Gadsden, Mason Grove, Alamo, Bells, Cairo, Maury City, and Crockett Mills.

The success of agriculture in Crockett County is closely tied to the history of railroads. In 1858–59 the Memphis, Clarksville, and Louisville Railroad built through the eastern half of what later became Crockett County. The presence of the tracks led to the creation of the new towns of Gasden, Fruitvale, and Bells. After the Louisville and Nashville Railroad assumed control of the earlier line in the mid-1870s, freight and passenger trains hummed through Crockett County on a daily basis. The train traffic encouraged the creation of cotton gins at towns along the line and also provided a ready market for the many perishable fruits being produced in the county during the early twentieth century. For many years, the railroad town of Bells, rather than the county seat of Alamo, was the largest town in the county, even though its population only totaled 919 in 1940.

The African-American community in Crockett County was one of the region's more active participants in the Rosenwald school building program. Blacks, with support from the Fund and public sources, built one-room schools at Antioch, Cross Roads, and Fruitvale. Two-room schools were constructed at Hudson Grove and Maury City while three-room schools were erected in Alamo, Bells, and Porter's Grove. Overall, Crockett County blacks raised almost $12,000 for the new schools.

A statistical atlas published in 1941 documents the rural quality of Crockett County during the first half of the twentieth century. The population was over 17,300 people, with African Americans comprising almost 20% of the population. In general, almost 85% of all adult males were engaged in agriculture and 65% of farm operators were tenants. Few independent farmowners had survived the Great Depression, with only 30% of white farm operators actually owning their land. This ratio slipped to 9.5% of black families who owned their own farms. Crockett County farms were small, as well, averaging only 45 acres in size across the county.

The population of Crockett County was estimated at 13,441 in 1994. The county includes five incorporated towns: Alamo, Bells, Friendship, Gadsden, and Maury City. According to the 1990 census, Alamo at 2,426 residents is the largest town. Bells is next, with 1,643 residents. In addition, a number of unincorporated communities, including Fruitvale, Crockett Mills, Johnson Grove, Cairo, Walnut Hill, Perry's Elizabeth, Old Field, Pond Creek, Lebanon, Jetton's Mason Grove, and Coxville, offer nearby residents the convenience of small stores and agricultural services. The county is governed by a county executive and 24 commissioners.

Several public recreation facilities enhance the lives of Crockett countians. The David Crockett Lake, in the eastern part of the county, covers 87 acres and offers fishing, boating, and picnic areas. Crockett Mills is host to the West Tennessee Cotton Festival held throughout the month of August, with varied events each weekend. A variety of civic and service

Stone engraving of David Crockett, 1834.

TSLA. COPY PHOTOGRAPH BY KARINA MCDANIEL

clubs, including Chamber of Commerce, Ruritan Clubs, Lions, Rotary, Jaycees, and the Veterans of Foreign Wars, offer opportunities for fellowship and community activities. Ninety-seven churches fill the religious needs of the county.

Annie Laurie James, Humboldt

SEE: COTTON, COTTON GINS, CROCKETT, DAVID; FARMS, TENNESSEE CENTURY

CROCKETT, DAVID "DAVY" (1786–1836), frontiersman, Tennessee legislator and U.S. congressman, folk hero, and icon of popular culture, was an intriguing composite of history and myth. Both the historical figure who died at the Alamo and the legendary hero kept alive in the media of his day and ours, Crockett partly invented his own myth. History melted even more easily into myth as eager writers, editors, and producers provided an omnivorous public with an increasing number of remarkable tales about the heroic frontiersman and turned the flesh-and-blood David into the legendary Davy.

Born on August 17, 1786, in Greene County in East Tennessee, Crockett grew up with the new nation and helped it grow. He lived in Tennessee for all but the last few months of his life and promoted the gradual westward expansion of the frontier through Tennessee toward Texas. In his search for a better life for himself and his family, he participated in a process that we now call the American dream.

David was the son of John Crockett, magistrate, unsuccessful land speculator, and tavern owner, and Rebecca Hawkins Crockett. Preferring to play hooky rather than attend school, he ran away from home to escape his father's wrath. His "strategic withdrawal," as he called it, lasted about 30 months. When he returned home in 1802, he had grown so much that initially his family did not recognize him. He soon found all forgiven and reciprocated their generosity by working for a year to settle his father's debts.

David married Mary "Polly" Finley on August 14, 1806, in Jefferson County, Tennessee. They remained in East Tennessee until 1811, when the Crocketts and their two sons, John Wesley and William, settled in Lincoln County, Tennessee. In 1813 they moved again, this time to Franklin County, where Crockett twice enlisted as a volunteer in the Indian wars from 1813 to 1815; following the wars, David was elected a lieutenant in the 32nd Militia Regiment of Franklin County. Soon after his discharge, Polly gave birth to Margaret, their third child; Polly died that summer. A year later, he married Elizabeth Patton, a widow with two children. The family moved to Lawrence County in the fall of 1817.

Although he served as a justice of the peace, Lawrenceburg town commissioner, and colonel of the 57th Militia Regiment of Lawrence County, Crockett was relatively unknown before his 1821 election to the Tennessee legislature, representing Lawrence and Hickman counties. Reelected in 1823, but defeated in 1825, he won election to the U.S. House of Representatives from his new West Tennessee residence in 1827. He campaigned as an honest country boy and an extraordinary hunter and marksman—someone who was in every sense a "straight shooter." Reelected to a second term in 1829, he split with President Andrew Jackson and the Tennessee delegation headed by James K. Polk on several important issues, including land reform and the Indian removal bill. Crockett was defeated in 1831, when he openly and vehemently opposed Jackson's policies, but reelected in 1833.

Notoriety gave Crockett's image a life of its own. By 1831 Crockett had become the model for Nimrod Wildfire, the hero of James Kirke Paulding's play, *The Lion of the West,* as well as the subject of books and articles. Crockett said he was compelled to publish his 1834 autobiography, *A Narrative of the Life of David Crockett of the State of Tennessee,* which he wrote with the help of Thomas Chilton, to counteract the outlandish stories printed in *Sketches and Eccentricities of Col. Crockett, of West Tennessee* a year earlier. He clearly recognized the power of his popular image and sought to manipulate it for political gain. Anonymous eastern hack writers took up the more outrageous stories and spun out tall tale yarns for the Crockett Almanacs (1835–1856). In their hands, the fictional Davy became a backwoods screamer. With the death of the historical Crockett at the Alamo in 1836, the floodgates opened for the full-blown expansion of the legend. Crockett could not only "run faster, -jump higher, -squat lower, -dive deeper, -stay under longer, -and come out drier, than any man in the whole country," but he could save the world by unfreezing the sun and the earth from their axes and ride his pet alligator up Niagara Falls.

Touted by the Whigs as the candidate to oppose Jackson's hand picked successor, Martin Van Buren, in the 1836 election, Crockett was defeated in his 1835 Congressional bid with the help of Jackson and Governor William Carroll. The election of Adam Huntsman, a peg-legged lawyer, temporarily disenchanted Crockett with politics and his constituents, prompting him to make the now-famous remark: "Since you have chosen to elect a man with a timber toe to succeed me, you may all go to hell and I will go to Texas." His last letters spoke of his confidence that Texas would allow him to rejuvenate his political career and finally make his fortune. He intended to become land agent for the territory and saw the future of an independent Texas as intertwined with his own.

He and his men joined Colonel William B. Travis at San Antonio De Bexar in early February 1836. Mexican General Antonio Lopez de Santa Anna arrived on February 20 and laid siege to the Alamo. Travis wrote that during the first bombardment, Crockett was everywhere in the Alamo, encouraging the men to fight and fulfill their duties. The siege of 13 days ended on March 6, 1836, when Mexican troops overran the Alamo at about six o'clock in the morning. According to the eyewitness account in the diary of Lieutenant José Enrique de la Peña, Crockett and five or six other survivors were captured. Several Mexican officers asked that the prisoners be spared, but Santa Anna ordered them bayoneted and shot.

Many thought Crockett deserved a better fate, and they provided it, from thrilling fictions of his clubbing Mexicans with his empty rifle until cut down by a flurry of bullets, bayonets, or both, to his survival as a slave in a Mexican salt mine. The more heroic story provided the basis for the movie portrayals by Fess Parker in the well-known Walt Disney productions, and that of John Wayne, who produced, directed, and starred as Davy in *The Alamo*.

Clearly the present image of Crockett in American popular culture is the descendant of the tradition of Davy as the hero of romantic melodrama. From his characterization by Paulding as Nimrod Wildfire to Frank Mayo as author and star of the long-running play *Davy Crockett: Or, Be Sure You're Right Then Go Ahead*, the heritage was passed on through a series of silent and modern films that culminated in the Davys played by Fess Parker and John Wayne. Nineteenth century drama and twentieth century film always presented a heroic, kind Crockett. Courageous, dashing, and true blue, this nobleman of nature protected his country and all who were helpless with equal fervor.

The Walt Disney-Fess Parker-inspired Crockett craze of the mid-1950s was without question the high water mark of the impact of the legendary Crockett. A media-generated event, it occurred at the moment when television first began to reach a mass market, and Disney launched his enterprise with the innovative premise that children represented a renewable audience. At the height of the craze, American youth drove their parents crazy with countless renditions of *The Ballad of Davy Crockett* and demands for coonskin caps and fringed deerskin jackets and pants. Department stores set up special Crockett sections to sell clothes and Crockett paraphernalia such as records, lunch boxes, towels, wallets, athletic equipment, baby shoes, and even women's panties. Grosset and Dunlap's sales for the book *The Story of Davy Crockett* increased to 30 times the 10,000 copies per year that constituted normal sales before 1955. The total Crockett industry realized sales of approximately $300 million. And Disney was right about the recyclable nature of his market; today children meet Crockett on the Disney Channel on cable television.

Although Davy's perennial best-seller status means that economic motives support the creation of different Crocketts, that fact need not tarnish our enjoyment of them. Neither should the Gordian tangle of man and myth obscure the essential unity of Crockett. Crockett, David and Davy, was frontiersman, congressman, blazing patriot, boisterous braggart, and backwoods trickster, with all the roles dissolved by a puckish good humor and recast into a single, fun-loving presence. The Crockett of history and culture is large and mirrors the ever-changing self image of the United States. Invested in him—man and myth—are the hopes and beliefs, the virtues and values, and the shortcomings and triumphs of each generation of Americans who take him up as one of their heroes.

Michael A. Lofaro, University of Tennessee, Knoxville
SUGGESTED READINGS: David Crockett, *A Narrative of the Life of David Crockett* (1834); Michael A. Lofaro, ed., *Davy Crockett: The Man, the Legend, the Legacy, 1786–1986* (1985); James A. Shackford, *David Crockett: The Man and the Legend* (1956)
SEE: CARROLL, WILLIAM; DAVID CROCKETT STATE PARK; HUNTSMAN, ADAM; JACKSON, ANDREW; LITERATURE

CRUMP, EDWARD HULL (1874–1954), Democratic boss of Memphis and state political power during the Great Depression, was born in Holly Springs, Mississippi, in 1874, the son of a planter and former Confederate officer, who soon died of yellow fever. Crump grew up poor. He moved north to Memphis

Edward Hull Crump.

MEMPHIS/SHELBY COUNTY ROOM, MEMPHIS/SHELBY COUNTY PUBLIC LIBRARY & INFO. CENTER

as an ambitious 17-year-old bookkeeper, married the daughter of a wealthy merchant, and bought the carriage manufacturing firm where he worked.

In 1905 businessman Crump entered politics as a Chamber of Commerce candidate for efficient, progressive government, winning election as a councilman and then, in 1909, as the mayor who began the commission form of government. His political success came without making a single political speech. Devoid of oratorical ability himself, Crump displayed a genius for understanding human nature and organizing others who could make the main street speeches and negotiate on the back streets with the 600 saloon keepers and ward bosses.

Crump's talent was administration. He ran an efficient city government, getting more effort from the health, fire, and police departments. His administrative ability also built a personal political machine. On taking office, Crump conducted a brief publicity war on vice, but then permitted the underworld to run wide-open. The underworld of gambling, prostitution, and alcohol contributed protection money. Police Chief William J. Hayes later testified in court that as much as $80,000 was contributed in a single year. In addition to his use of tainted money for private purposes, Crump also purchased a sufficient number of poll taxes to control elections.

Municipal corruption never led the voters to throw Crump out of office. Moralistic progressives turned to the courts to oust the Crump machine. In 1909 Tennessee adopted a state-wide prohibition law that seemed to make Crump vulnerable to removal. When Crump refused to enforce the law in Memphis, Governor Ben Hooper pushed an ouster law in 1915, which provided the judicial method for removal of public officials from office who refused to enforce state laws. Crump resigned his office just ahead of court action.

While loss of office embarrassed Crump, he never admitted guilt. Instead, he presented himself as a victim of conspiracies by evil private power corporations that feared his plan for public power corporations. Crump's public relations campaign succeeded so completely that his fabrication was accepted as true even though no evidence supported the alibi.

In business, Crump turned to insurance and Coca-Cola franchising, becoming a millionaire. He remained out of city government for a decade before returning in 1927 as a political boss, who no longer ran for office, except for a single congressional term, but who elected his entire slate of candidates. In 1932 his candidate for governor, Henry H. Horton, won, and for the next 16 years, Crump influenced the outcome of statewide elections. With Tennessee voter turn-out low, as a result of the poll tax, Crump's heavy Shelby County vote controlled state elections.

Crump understood the vanity of individuals and devoted enormous energy and industry into making individuals feel important. Always cordial, he worked hard, over the course of many years, to oblige the demands of individuals and groups. After more than 20 years of this kind of political effort, Crump commanded absolute authority in Memphis and Shelby County. He benefited enormously from the Great Depression, which shattered people's self-confidence and made them look to paternalistic leaders for relief. The New Deal patronage—the WPA jobs—boosted his power. Those who needed work or feared they might need assistance could not afford to oppose the machine. During the thirties, political candidates even stopped running for office against Crump's local slate.

Under Crump's absolutism, the city services worked. City employees undertook election work to keep the machine in power and did the people's work too. Garbage was picked up daily, the streets cleaned, the fires put out, and the criminals arrested. People went to Crump to solve problems. He kept the taxes low and even reduced property taxes a few pennies a year. Crump government was modest and frugal in its expenditures because cheap government was good politics.

Crump's absolutism, however, required a social cost—a loss of individual freedom. Criticism and public opposition had to be abandoned. All were forced to pay homage to the boss. Newcomers learned how the system worked. A jeweler opening a business on Main Street learned that city inspectors would not approve his building unless he purchased an insurance policy from E. H. Crump and Company.

Freedom of expression did not fully exist. Reporter Turner Catledge was beaten for getting too close to election fraud. A chemist's complaining letter to the newspaper resulted in his loss of a job. Black druggist and baseball executive J. B. Martin was run out of town. The political organization especially sought to intimidate black leadership as well as CIO labor organizers.

The dictatorship eventually produced an uprising from the middle-class, blacks, and labor during Estes Kefauver's 1948 senate race. Crump's absolutism was broken with the election of Kefauver, but his control over Memphis government continued until his death on October 16, 1954. Memphis honored the Boss with an eight-foot tall statue in Overton Park, making him the only political leader the city ever remembered in bronze. Boss Crump, a Confederate warrior, and two entertainers have been the only bronzed heroes of Memphis.

David Tucker, University of Memphis

Suggested Readings: Dewey W. Grantham, "Tennessee and Twentieth-Century American Politics," Carroll Van West, ed., *Tennessee History: The Land, The People, and The Culture*

(1998), 343–372; William D. Miller, *Mr. Crump of Memphis* (1964); David Tucker, *Memphis Since Crump: Bossism, Blacks, and Civic Reformers, 1948–1968* (1980)

SEE: BROWNING, GORDON W.; COOPER, WILLIAM PRENTICE, JR.; KEFAUVER, CAREY ESTES; MCCORD, JIM N.; MCKELLAR, KENNETH D; MEMPHIS; SHELBY COUNTY

CUMBERLAND COMPACT. Richard Henderson, land speculator and representative for North Carolina on the western Virginia/North Carolina survey team, drew up the Cumberland Compact in 1780. Signed on May 1, 1780, by 250 men of the new Cumberland settlement, it served as a guide for land transactions and as a simple constitutional government for settlers. With the inclusion of additional provisions on May 13, the compact became the document by which the settlement governed itself until North Carolina created Davidson County in 1783.

The Compact called for a representative form of civil government. Each of the seven stations (or forts) of the Cumberland settlement was entitled to a specific number of elected representatives to form a 12-man "Tribunal of Notables," which dispensed justice, received and dispersed funds, settled claims, and regulated the land office.

In 1775 Henderson privately purchased a large area of land in Kentucky and the part of Tennessee drained by the Cumberland River from the Cherokee Indians. Known as the Transylvania Purchase, Henderson hoped North Carolina and Virginia would accept his purchase, and the land provisions of the Compact awaited endorsement by these states. Both North Carolina and Virginia disallowed the purchase, and the settlement came under frequent Indian attacks. The settlement succeeded, but by 1784 approximately one third of the original signers of the Compact had been killed in battles with Native Americans.

Kenneth Fieth, Metropolitan Archives for Nashville and Davidson County

SEE: DAVIDSON COUNTY; FRONTIER STATIONS; TRANSYLVANIA PURCHASE

CUMBERLAND COUNTY existed as an Indian hunting ground when Tennessee became a state in 1796. Bands of settlers making the perilous journey from Virginia, Maryland, and North and South Carolina to the Cumberland River settlements and beyond rested at the inns located along the toll roads that crossed the region. Kemmer's Stand, Mammy, Burke, Genesis, Lowery's Stand, and Grimes (Graham's) Stand were familiar names to early travelers. Movement across the region became so common that Helen Krechniak, author of *Cumberland County's First Hundred Years,* referred to the county as "The Road to Somewhere Else." Many of the roads were mere trails, partially maintained between toll gates; other roads were better maintained and offered more substantial accommo-

dations. Crab Orchard Inn, Kemmer's Stand, and Johnson's Stand (Mayland) serviced Walton Road. That road was established by the legislature to connect Southwest Point (Kingston) to Nashville. Today, Interstate 40 follows much of the original route across Cumberland County.

In 1856 the Tennessee General Assembly created Cumberland County from the eight surrounding counties of Bledsoe, Roane, Morgan, Fentress, Rhea, Putnam, Overton, and White. Covering 679 square-miles of the Cumberland Plateau, the new county rose from an elevation of 800 feet to a height of 3,000 feet, with an average elevation of 2,000 feet. Crossville (Scott's Crossroads), near the center of the county, was chosen as the county seat despite the fact that several other communities, including Crab Orchard, Grassy Cove, Mayland, and Pleasant Hill had larger populations.

The Civil War halted most economic development on the Plateau. Confederate and Union forces, as well as guerrilla bands masquerading as Confederate and Union soldiers, pillaged the county. No major battles were fought in the county, but the thinly populated area suffered as much as other Tennesseans living near the battlefields. The population was evenly divided between pro-slavery and anti-slavery sentiments; brother fought brother, sons left their families, some to the Union and some to the Confederacy.

After the war local coal and timber resources received the attention of northern developers. In agriculture, the county's reputation for fruits and vegetables, as well as grasses, grew. Artist John W. Dodge established extensive fruit groves at Pomona. The arrival of the Tennessee Central Railroad in 1900 attracted new settlers and opened the agricultural and livestock markets of Nashville and Knoxville to area farmers.

In World War I, Cumberland County recruited a company of volunteers who served in Company G, 119th Infantry, 30th Infantry Division. Sgt. Milo Lemert received the Congressional Medal of Honor. Sgt. Litton T. Thurman received the Distinguished Service Cross in the same action. Sgt. Alvin C. York came "home" to the Tennessee Central Depot in Crossville, where he was welcomed by his friends from Pall Mall in nearby Fentress County. In 1940 York came to the Hotel Taylor in Crossville to sign the contract for the making of the movie *Sergeant York.*

In the decade following World War I, Cumberland County underwent a new phase of development with the construction of highways linking Crossville to Pikeville, Sparta, Spring City, and Jamestown. As part of the New Deal recovery program, the federal government, under the Subsistence Homestead Division of the Department of Interior, established the Cumberland Homesteads. The program, which provided land and homes for impoverished, deserving families to engage in subsistence farming, made provisions for 250 families. Although economically unsuccessful, the community survived and the Homestead houses of Crab Orchard stone are among the most prized dwellings in the county. The project also left a public recreational facility, what is now Cumberland Mountain State Park.

During World War II the development of the Manhattan Project at Oak Ridge and the establishment of a prisoner of war camp near Pomona kept employment high. The POW camp was commonly referred to as the "Jap Camp," although it held only German and Italian prisoners. Mayor Fiorello LaGuardia of New York made a "secret" visit to the camp to confer with Italian generals who were among the prisoners. Soldiers from the county served in all branches of the service and in every theater of war, from Guadalcanal to Burma and Europe to Africa. Many of them continued to serve after the war ended and later retired to the Plateau.

The area experienced its most rapid growth during the postwar period. The most important factor in the advancement of agriculture, industry, and tourism was the construction of Interstate 40 through the county. The development of retirement facilities such as Fairfield Glade, Lake Tansi Resort, Renegade Mountain (now Cumberland Gardens), and Pleasant Hill brought thousands of people to visit, build homes, and retire. Manufacturing and distribution centers found Cumberland County's improved access to urban centers and smaller local markets a plus. Crossville's locally owned and developed publications, *Trade-A-Plane, Rock and Dirt, Boats and Harbors,* and *Tradequip* receive national distribution.

Cumberland County is one of the fastest growing counties in the state. Although it remains 75% forested, it is no longer a rural county. Cumberland Medical Center, the nationally known Cumberland County Playhouse, and the availability of technical and higher education provide the county's citizens with the benefits of more populated areas.

G. Donald Brookhart, Crossville

SEE: CUMBERLAND HOMESTEADS; DODGE, JOHN W.; HIGHWAYS, HISTORIC; OZONE FALLS; RAILROADS; THEATER; WALTON ROAD; WHARTON, MAY C.; YORK, ALVIN C.

CUMBERLAND FURNACE in northern Dickson County is the site of the first ironworks in the future Middle Tennessee region. The village is the oldest community south of the Cumberland River between Nashville and Clarksville. It made Dickson County a manufacturing area from its frontier beginnings.

General James Robertson, like other pioneer surveyors, soon discovered that the Western Highland Rim contained abundant iron ore deposits. In 1793 Robertson and William Sheppard purchased 640 acres from James Campbell, a private in North Carolina's Continental Line. On this tract, located on the west branch (now Furnace Creek) of Bartons Creek, Robertson erected the furnace for his ironworks. The forge was built closer to the mouth of the creek. The furnace went to blast in 1796.

Eight years later, Montgomery Bell, a native of Chester County, Pennsylvania, bought the furnace from Robertson for $16,000. Bell improved the efficiency of the furnace and made his iron plantation more self sufficient. Sometime between 1810 and 1820, Bell erected a second furnace. By 1812 he had a contract to furnish the national government with cannon shot, gunpowder, and whiskey.

During the War of 1812, Bell became the chief supplier of heavy ammunition for both the navy and General Andrew Jackson's army. The 1820 manufacturer census showed Montgomery Bell's new furnace producing 300 tons of hollow-ware, 50 tons of pig iron, and six tons of machinery, with 70 men, mostly slaves, working the furnace.

In 1825 Anthony W. VanLeer, also a native of Chester County, Pennsylvania, with Isaac H. Lanier and Wallace Dickson, purchased the furnace from Bell for $50,000. Montgomery Bell built other furnaces and forges in Dickson County and became Tennessee's first capitalist and industrialist, as well as a legendary figure in state folklore.

In 1833 VanLeer bought Lanier's and Dickson's interests for $70,000. He dismantled the first furnace, rebuilt Bell's second furnace, and later introduced steam power. In 1860 Cumberland Furnace produced 1,831 tons of pig iron with a mostly slave work force of 93 men and seven women.

After the fall of Fort Donelson in February 1862, Cumberland Furnace ceased operations for the duration of the war. Unlike other ironworks in the Cumberland River counties, it was not destroyed. On the death of Anthony VanLeer in July 1863, two grandchildren, Vanleer Kirkman and Mary Florence Kirkman, inherited the Dickson County furnace. Mary Florence and her ex-Union officer husband, Captain James P. Drouillard, reopened the furnace after the war. In 1870 Mary Florence Drouillard bought her brother's share for $20,000 and her interest in the Nashville properties.

The Drouillards operated the furnace as a family business, making it a successful enterprise even during the 1874–1879 recession years. They rebuilt the furnace and by 1880, were producing 20 tons of pig iron a day with 250 employees. In 1882 James Drouillard formed the Drouillard Iron Company, a stock company which he served as president. The new company paid the Drouillards $170,000 for the furnace and land totaling over 17,000 acres.

In October 1889 the Drouillard Iron Company sold out to the Southern Iron Company, an Alabama corporation controlled by the Warner family, for $140,000. With a six-mile spur connecting to the newly constructed Mineral Branch Railroad, Southern Iron Company built a modern coke-fuel furnace. As a result of the 1893 panic, the new owners declared bankruptcy in 1895. The Warner brothers reorganized the Buffalo Iron Company and reopened the furnace in 1896, but were out of business two years later.

Determined to stay in the iron business, the Warner family formed the Warner Iron Company in 1899. In 1917 the furnace and all property were conveyed to Joseph Warner, who increased production by updating the facility. In the mid-1920s Jeff Gray sued Warner over a patent right to manufacture ferrophosphorus iron. The seven-year trial cost Warner the railroad and depleted his finances. During the Great Depression, the furnace operated intermittently until 1938, when Warner declared bankruptcy.

In July 1940 Chancery Court transferred the property to Cumberland Iron Company, a Nashville corporation headed by Rogers Caldwell. In 1942 Caldwell obtained a loan from the Reconstruction Finance Corporation and reopened the furnace. It operated only a few months before auditors found irregularities, and the government closed the facility. In October 1943 Sol Chazen, a Chattanooga scrap dealer, purchased the property and dismantled the furnace for the wartime scrap metal drive.

In 1988 the village of Cumberland Furnace, with over 30 buildings and sites associated with the iron industry, was listed as a historic district in the National Register of Historic Places.

George E. Jackson, Dickson

SUGGESTED READING: George E. Jackson: *Cumberland Furnace: A Frontier Industrial Village* (1994)

SEE: BELL, MONTGOMERY; CALDWELL, ROGERS; DICKSON COUNTY; DROUILLARD, MARY F.; INDUSTRY; MINING; ROBERTSON, JAMES; SLAVERY

CUMBERLAND GAP AND CUMBERLAND GAP NATIONAL HISTORICAL PARK.

Few areas in the United States symbolize the American pioneer spirit more than Cumberland Gap. Crossing the Gap meant encountering America's first western frontier and symbolically severing European ties. Between 1760 and 1850, more than 300,000 people walked, rode, or were carried over the Appalachian Mountains through Cumberland Gap.

Formed by a stream and enlarged by wind and weather, the Gap is 1,500 feet above sea level, and was named by surveyor Thomas Walker for his English patron, the Duke of Cumberland, son of George II of England. Various types of sediments, including shells, shale, limestone, and gravel surround the area and attest to the great earth disturbances that formed the Gap.

Settlers followed a trail over the Gap initially used by Native Americans, who had enlarged it from an animal trace. They were entering a prized hunting ground, coveted by the Shawnees to the north and Cherokees to the south. The French and Indian War, followed by the American Revolution, briefly halted white settlement. But with the restoration of peace, the flow of hunters, settlers, and land speculators through Cumberland Gap was resumed. Perhaps the most famous traveler was Daniel Boone, who agreed to take settlers north into Kentucky after first making several hunting trips through the Gap.

By 1800 the states of Kentucky, Tennessee, and Virginia claimed the area through the Gap. After 1840 a weekly stage carried freight, mail, and passengers and gave the area a prosperous commercial appearance. During the Civil War, the Gap changed hands four times as the North and South fought for control of this strategic gateway. Initially considered part of Kentucky, and therefore under Union control, the first troops to occupy the Gap were Confederate forces under the command of Brigadier General Felix K. Zollicoffer. Union commander Brigadier General George W. Morgan took the "American Gibraltar" on June 18, 1862. Morgan did not remain at the Gap, and Confederates reoccupied the area immediately. After a year of inactivity, Union forces reappeared, and Major General Ambrose E. Burnside demanded and received unconditional surrender. The Gap was not seriously threatened again during the remainder of the war.

New South developer Alexander Arthur promoted a railroad through the mountains near the Gap and, by 1888, completed the first tunnel from Cumberland Gap to Middlesboro, Kentucky. After resolving boundary disputes, the three states that bordered the Gap sponsored an "Object Lesson Road" through the historic pass. This federally funded road encouraged business travel, and a macadamized road soon followed. Automobiles, trains, salesmen, and tourists continued to pour through the Gap.

Meeting in Cincinnati, Ohio, on May 30, 1922, several business leaders from Middlesboro, Kentucky, proposed the establishment of Lincoln National Park. Local residents were in favor of the idea, as well as representatives from the surrounding three state governments. In 1938 representatives of the National Park Service agreed to support a park, provided the lands would be donated to the United States. Cumberland Gap National Historical Park, established to celebrate the passing of the first barrier West, received Congressional approval in 1940. Kentucky, Tennessee, and Virginia bought the land and deeded it to the federal government in July 1955. Formal dedication of the 20,184-acre park occurred July 4, 1959.

Numerous trails, camping and picnic areas, a visitor center, and museum offer visitors the opportunity to explore the historic Cumberland Gap. From the Pinnacle Overlook, visitors enjoy a view of the Great Smoky Mountains, 80 miles away, and the Gap itself, 900 feet below. The completion of twin tunnels through the mountains in 1996, and the restoration of the Gap to its 1750 appearance, provide an opportunity to experience part of the journey described by Daniel Boone as he led settlers into the wilderness.

Rebecca Vial, Great Smoky Mountains National Park

SUGGESTED READING: William W. Luckett, "Cumberland Gap National Historical Park," *Tennessee Historical Quarterly* 23(1964): 303–320

SEE: BOONE, DANIEL; CLAIBORNE COUNTY; SHAWNEES; WALKER, THOMAS; ZOLLICOFFER, FELIX K.

CUMBERLAND HOMESTEADS, a rural resettlement community established during the Great Depression, is located in Cumberland County, Tennessee. This homestead community encompasses approximately 10,250 acres, less than half of the original total of 27,802 acres held by the cooperative association in 1938. The community, now incorporated into the city limits of Crossville, derives its distinct identity from the architectural style of the houses, outbuildings, and public buildings. The landscape of the Cumberland Homesteads is primarily rolling hills interspersed with hollows, deep ravines, and several small creeks. Cumberland Mountain State Park, built by the Civilian Conservation Corps (CCC), is located in the center of the project. The 1,300-acre park includes timberland and a stone dam and bridge that form Byrd Lake.

Work on Cumberland Homesteads began in 1934 with the clearing of land by Civil Works Administration (CWA) workers and prospective homesteaders. William Macy Stanton, a Pennsylvania architect, designed the site plans, including the road pattern and the houses, outbuildings and community buildings. Stanton previously worked on the house designs for Norris, Tennessee.

Plans for Cumberland Homesteads intended to create 351 farms on lots ranging in size from ten to 160 acres; the average homestead consisted of 16 acres. Areas determined unsuitable for farming remained timberland. Originally 8,903 acres were farm tracts; 1,245 acres were common land (grazing, woodland, cooperative enterprises); 11,200 acres were set aside for further development; and the cooperative association owned 5,505 acres. Unemployed miners and timber workers from nearby counties, many of whom had been out of work for several years, built the homesteads.

Properties included a residence and a range of outbuildings. Several farms still retain their original buildings. The distinctive houses are primarily one

and one-half stories in height with indigenous Crab Orchard sandstone walls and gable roofs. Stanton designed approximately 15 different house designs throughout the community, but repeated only 11 plans. Most houses were four to seven rooms, contained one or two fireplaces, with paneled walls, built-in bookcases, and batten doors with "Z" braces and hardware. The wood used in construction of the houses came from land immediately surrounding the homesteads. The majority of the interior walls and woodwork are of white or yellow pine, with some poplar and oak. Hardware, such as door hinges, was made in the community blacksmith shop. All houses had plumbing and wiring added at the time of construction. The Tennessee Valley Authority provided electricity to Cumberland Homesteads in December 1937. Homesteaders could make minor changes to the plans, but the most significant differences reversed the house plan, re-oriented the house to the road, or varied interior room designs.

Most homesteaders first lived in a gable roof, wood frame barn on their property while awaiting the completion of their houses. The chicken houses, sheds, smokehouses, and miscellaneous outbuildings were of frame construction with gable roofs or shed roofs. Siding was either flush boards, weatherboard, or board and batten. Some smokehouses had raised Crab Orchard stone foundations. A few gambrel roof barns were constructed on the larger farm homesteads. Generally outbuildings were located behind the residence in a standardized pattern that still remains on many of the farm homesteads.

A design of the Cumberland Homesteads house appeared in the 1939 publication "Small Houses" by the Farm Security Administration as an example of a well-designed small house. During the time of their construction, however, many complained that the design and cost were extravagant. Senator Harry F. Byrd of Virginia condemned the costly absurdities of electricity, refrigerators, and indoor privies for country people. Likewise Senator Kenneth D. McKellar of Tennessee complained that the Resettlement Administration constructed stone mansions and voiced his resentment that relief workers lived in houses better than he did.

In addition to the homesteads, workers built a number of community buildings, including an eight-story water tower that housed offices and meeting rooms in the cruciform base. Cumberland Homesteads Tower is prominently located at the intersection of U.S. Highway 127 and State Route 68. The Homestead elementary and high schools are located behind the tower and are constructed in a unique pod style; free-standing classrooms are connected by covered walks. Cooperative buildings include two factories, a cooperative store, a government garage, and a loom house.

On July 28, 1938, the Cumberland Homesteads Community celebrated the completion of the project. Of the original units planned, only 251 were completed. Cumberland Homesteads is the largest of the communities built by the Division of Subsistence Homesteads in the nation. The community remained intact, in spite of an uncertain economic future. The cooperative ventures eventually failed, the hosiery factory failed, and the farms proved too small with soil too poor to support the families. The men left for jobs in Detroit, Akron, and Dayton, as well as Douglas and Watts Bar dams, sending money back to pay for the farm homestead. The turnover rate in the community was relatively low and by 1941 only 44 families had moved out, with six of those evicted.

Although the community failed to fulfill some of its original purposes, it provided work and shelter for many destitute Tennesseans during the Depression. The community has remained largely intact, with houses looking much as they did when constructed, and the landscape retaining the form of the planned subsistence farms. The Cumberland Homesteads historic district is listed in the National Register of Historic Places.

Elizabeth A. Straw, Tennessee Historical Commission

SUGGESTED READINGS: Sidney Baldwin, *Poverty and Politics: The Rise and Decline of the Farm Security Administration* (1968); Paul K. Conkin, *Tomorrow A New World: The New Deal Community Program* (1959); Phoebe Cutler, *The Public Landscape of the New Deal* (1985)

SEE: CIVILIAN CONSERVATION CORPS; CUMBERLAND COUNTY; MCKELLAR, KENNETH D.; NORRIS

CUMBERLAND PRESBYTERIAN CHURCH grew out of the revivals on the Tennessee-Kentucky frontier in the early decades of the nineteenth century. The formation of the independent Cumberland Presbytery on February 4, 1810, at Dickson, Tennessee, by ministers Finis Ewing, Samuel King, and Samuel McAdow, and the subsequent establishment of the Cumberland Synod (1813) and General Assembly (1829) followed controversies over Calvinist theology and church order raised by the "New Side/Old Side" division within the Presbyterian Church in general, and more specifically, the frontier revivals.

The Cumberland Presbytery, consisting of churches in north Middle Tennessee and south-central Kentucky, was created out of the Transylvania Presbytery in 1802. It was the only presbytery in Kentucky with a majority of "New Side" (pro-revivalist theology and methodology) ministers. After the success of James McGready in Logan County, Kentucky, camp meeting revivals culminated in the Cane Ridge sacrament in 1801 and spread throughout the region. Many who led the revivals challenged the strict Calvinistic theology of the Presbyterian Church and created a demand for more ministers to care for the growing congregations. The specific issues of controversy included strict adherence to the Westminster Confession of Faith, the educational qualifications for ministers (the Cumberland Presbytery was accused of ordaining unqualified men and lowering the standards for ministry), the use of the revival as a valid methodology for evangelism, and the locus of ecclesiastical authority in the Synod or the Presbytery.

Five years after bringing charges against the Cumberland Presbytery, the Synod of Kentucky dissolved the Presbytery in 1806. The failure of repeated efforts at reconciliation led to the founding of a separate Cumberland Presbyterian Church. The church quickly spread throughout Tennessee, Kentucky, and eight other states. When the members formed the General Assembly in 1829, it included four synods and 18 presbyteries. In 1814 the church adopted a Confession of Faith, which revised the Westminster Confession and outlined a "medium theology" between Calvinism and Arminianism that rejected strict predestination, unconditional election, and limited atonement. Reflecting the methodology of the revival, Cumberland Presbyterians confessed the mystery of God's sovereign grace (retaining the doctrine of the perseverance of the saints) while also acknowledging a significant role for human choice in salvation.

The church grew five-fold in membership from 1835 to 1860 and survived the Civil War without division. In 1869 a contingent of African-American ministers, representing approximately 30,000 black members of the Cumberland Presbyterian Church, petitioned for the formation of independent "presbyteries of colored ministers." The General Assembly of what is known currently as the Cumberland Presbyterian Church in America was established in 1874 in Nashville, Tennessee. In 1883 the Cumberland Presbyterian Church revised its Confession of Faith to further eliminate elements of strict Calvinism.

An effort at reunion with the Presbyterian Church in the United States of America (Northern) in 1906, following that denomination's 1903 revision of the Westminster Confession's teaching on divine sovereignty, achieved partial success. A significant minority of the Cumberland presbyteries (51 out of 111), however, objected to the union on theological and constitutional grounds and perpetuated the Cumberland Presbyterian Church as a separate denomination.

The Cumberland Presbyterian Church reported 92,240 members in 782 churches in 1995, located primarily in the southern and border states, and in significant missionary works throughout the world. It maintains ecumenical cooperation through the World Alliance of Reformed Churches (since 1956) and also through "union churches" with the Presbyterian Church (U.S.A.). Its institutions of higher learning are

Bethel College in McKenzie, Tennessee, and Memphis Theological Seminary. Denominational headquarters are located in Memphis, and official church literature needs are served by Frontier Press. Its chief publications are *The Cumberland Presbyterian* and *The Missionary Messenger*.

L. Thomas Smith, Jr., Johnson Bible College

SEE: BETHEL COLLEGE; MCADOW, SAMUEL, RELIGION

CUMBERLAND RIVER.

From its headwaters in Lechter County, Kentucky, to its mouth at Smithland on the Ohio River, the Cumberland River travels almost 700 miles and drains a watershed of 18,000 square miles. Over 300 miles of the river flows through Tennessee, which contains 11,000 square miles of the watershed. Seven major tributary river systems to the Cumberland rise in Tennessee: the Big South Fork of the Cumberland, which enters at Burnside, Kentucky; the Obey-Wolf; the Roaring River; Caney Fork; Stones River; Harpeth River; and Red River systems. All but the last enter from the south side of the Cumberland.

A portion of the upper reaches above Lake Cumberland in Kentucky is designated a wild river for its many rapids and shoals, and an additional 100,000 acres on the Big South Fork are a national river and recreation area. This section of the river from the 63-foot tall Cumberland Falls to Burnside, Kentucky, is bounded by 300 to 500-foot high cliffs of conglomerate and sandstone. Smith's Shoals were the biggest impediments to early navigation, in some places only six inches deep at low water. Burnside was the head of low-water steam navigation, 358 river miles above Nashville. At low water, 16 shoals and bars impeded navigation on this stretch of the river. River-width from Burnside to Carthage varied from 550 to 600 feet, and the valley from one-half to one mile wide. At Carthage, the valley widens south into the Central Basin, until the river re-enters the Highland Rim fourteen miles below Nashville. Navigation on the Upper Cumberland could only occur during the wetter months of December through May, and during the "tide" some plucky captains took their steam packets as far up the twisting Caney Fork as Frank's Ferry in White County.

Navigable year round, the Lower Cumberland winds 192 miles from Nashville to Smithland. Flowing through the ridges and valleys of the highlands, the river bottom is generally a mile wide. Limestone bluffs limited the river to a width of 600 to 700 feet in its natural state. Before reaching the Ohio, the Cumberland enters the upheaved sandstone and coal of western Kentucky. At least ten major shoals obstructed the river, with the most serious the 4.3 mile length of rocky ledges and gravel bars of the Harpeth Shoals.

Human use of the river began toward the end of the last Ice Age, when hunters skirted the glacier-laden lands north of the Ohio River and entered the game-rich valleys of the Cumberland River system. Virtually every terrace along these streams bears the site of Native American occupation, from isolated Paleo-American hunting camps to great Mississippian towns. In the early 1700s, the Shawnees attempted to establish their claim to the Cumberland valley, until banished by the Cherokees and Chickasaws to the Ohio country.

Although the French learned of the river in the 1670s, naming it Riviére des Chauouanons for the Shawnees, it was Dr. Thomas Walker who gave the river its permanent name. Traveling with a small party of explorers down Yellow Creek from the gap he named for William Augustus, Duke of Cumberland, Walker came to a narrow river he also named Cumberland. For 30 years, Long Hunters visited the river, seeking game and furs, and some major tributaries bear their names—Stones River for Uriah Stone, Obey River for Obediah Spencer—while minor streams also mark their passing, including one named for Ambrose Powell's dog, Tumbler, killed by a bull elk at the stream's edge.

British army engineer, Lt. Thomas Hutchins, first charted the river in 1769 and referred to it as "Shawanoe." In 1775 the river became a boundary for Richard Henderson's ambitious Transylvania Purchase. Hutchins's maps were not published in America until after the American Revolution, and John Donelson did not know the details of the maps, when his party ascended the Cumberland during the last leg of the flatboats' rendezvous with James Robertson in 1780.

Over the next 40 years, the Cumberland region grew in population and agricultural wealth as keelboats and other craft ran produce such as tobacco and cotton from Nashville down to New Orleans. In the early 1800s sailing ships, like the 74-ton *Concordia*, were built at Cairo in Sumner County, sailed downriver to New Orleans, and sold for use in coastal and foreign commerce. In March 1819 the steamboat *General Jackson* arrived in Nashville. Nashvillians financed the construction of the steamboat and it was registered to the Port of Nashville. By 1828 boats were steaming up to the Caney Fork, and in 1833 the *Jefferson* reached Burnside, Kentucky.

In 1825 increasing steamboat trade led the Tennessee legislature to petition Congress for a survey of the Cumberland, which had become the main shipping path for Middle Tennessee produce. Between 1832 and 1838, Congress appropriated $155,000 for river improvements, viewing the potential production from eastern coal fields of eastern Kentucky as justification for navigation improvements. The U.S. Army Corps of Engineers began alterations that included clearing snags and constructing wing dams to deepen the channel. The improvement project ended, however, with the Panic of 1837 and did not resume until the 1870s.

The Cumberland River also was of strategic importance during the Civil War. Confederate Fort Donelson, constructed 50 miles from its mouth on the Ohio River, guarded the river approaches to Nashville. When the fort fell to U.S. troops in February 1862, Flag Officer Andrew Foote soon brought that section of the river under Federal control. Union boats patrolled the river to Carthage throughout the Civil War, but Confederate guerrillas often threatened the stretch between Nashville and Clarksville. The Upper Cumberland proved hard to defend also, and Confederate troops often crossed between Hartsville and the state line to carry out raids in Kentucky. In 1865 peace brought a new boom to the river.

In the early 1870s timber became a major industry on the river. Hardwood logs from the Upper Cumberland forests were rough sawn into hundreds of thousands of board feet at mills scattered from Carthage to Kentucky. Assembled into rafts up to 100 by 30 by 8 feet in dimension, the timber was floated on high tide to Nashville and other markets for finishing. Cal Hamilton, an African American from Celina, became one of the most famous pilots of these rafts. Other famous rafters from Celina included Bob Riley.

In 1871 Colonel S. T. Abert surveyed the river for the Corps of Engineers. His work generated two estimates for navigational improvements. The more expensive proposal, and the one favored by the Corps, called for the construction of 30 locks and dams for slack water navigation. The Corps justified the expense as providing access to the great coal fields of Kentucky, the timber of the Upper Cumberland, and the iron of the Western Highland Rim below Nashville. In 1887 engineers designed the first lock and dam (No. 1) to be built on the Cumberland above Nashville, and canal construction began in 1888. In 1892 Congress authorized construction of Lock and Dam A at the Harpeth Shoals. By 1900 six stone or concrete and timber dams had been built below Nashville and eight above. In 1924, 15 locks and dams raised the river to a minimum of six feet from Burnside to Smithland, but by that time, traffic from steamboats and log rafts had diminished significantly. The last steamboat, *Rowena,* left the trade in 1933. Gasoline-powered towboats took over the river scene, while railroads handled much of the freight.

New uses of the Cumberland system included flood control and hydroelectric power. In 1923 the Cumberland Hydro-Electric Power Company applied to the Corps for three dams in Kentucky. In 1926 the corps recommended three dams of its own between Carthage and Burnside; the great Cumberland floods of December 1926 and January 1927 lent urgency to the request.

By 1936, six Corps of Engineers reservoir sites were selected: Wolf Creek on the Upper Cumberland (completed 1952), Dale Hollow on the Obey (1948), Center Hill on the Caney Fork (1951), Stewarts Ferry (later Percy Priest, completed 1968) on the Stones River, Three Islands on the Harpeth, and Rossview on the Red River. The latter two were not constructed. In 1946 three more dams were authorized. Old Hickory, just above Nashville, was completed in 1956, and Cordell Hull at Carthage in 1973. A proposed dam at Celina was not built. Two later dams were designed and completed: Cheatham near Ashland City (1959) and Barkley in Western Kentucky (1966). By the 1970s, eight dams controlled the river from Burnside to its confluence with the Ohio River.

At the end of the twentieth century, the Cumberland continues to be used for the movement of coal, oil, and gravel, but recreation on Corps lakes has become a major part of the river economy. Environmental groups, such as the Cumberland Compact, Inc., have emerged to focus attention on the river and its water quality. For the 29 counties containing the Cumberland system, the river remains a vital part of their identity.

Ann Toplovich, Tennessee Historical Society

SUGGESTED READINGS: Byrd Douglas, *Steamboatin' on the Cumberland* (1961); Leland R. Johnson, *Engineers of the Twin Rivers* (1974); James McCague, *The Cumberland* (1973)

SEE: LONG HUNTER STATE PARK; DONELSON, JOHN; FORT DONELSON; RILEY, BOB; SHAWNEES; STEAMBOATING; U.S. ARMY CORPS OF ENGINEERS; WALKER, THOMAS

CUMBERLAND UNIVERSITY was established as Cumberland College at Lebanon in 1842, under the patronage of the Cumberland Presbyterian Church, and received a charter as a university in 1843. Except for the period from 1962 to 1982, when the name was officially Cumberland College of Tennessee, the institution has operated continuously as Cumberland University, the oldest institution of higher education in the central South operating under its original chartered name. Shortly after its founding, Cumberland University occupied a large new Greek Revival-style building. Robert L. Caruthers, lawyer, soldier, jurist, and congressman, took a leading role in the subscription drive that produced $10,000 for the new college; he became the first president of the board of trustees. In 1847 trustees at Cumberland University established a school of law. It opened a theological school and a school of engineering in 1853. By 1859 the law school was among the largest in the United States. Cumberland University can be justly proud of its many distinguished alumni, including three Pulitzer Prize-winning authors; the founder of Highlander Folk School, Myles Horton; president of Rotary International, James L. Bomar; president of the National Association of Manufacturers, John

Edgerton; Secretary of State and winner of the Nobel Prize for Peace, Cordell Hull; and Congressional Medal of Honor winner (Vietnam), Robert Ray.

Activities during the Civil War devastated Cumberland University. Military action in 1864 produced a fire that destroyed the main building, leaving only two Corinthian columns standing. W. E. Ward, a alumnus and founder of Ward Seminary, returned to the ruins and wrote on a column with a piece of charred wood: "E Cineribus Resurgam" ("From Ashes I shall arise"). The words and the Phoenix, the mythical bird ever born again, became the motto and emblem of the university. In 1871 the law school adopted a one-year program of instruction and a new model for legal education. An outstanding list of trial lawyers emerged from the stern discipline of the university's program.

In the twentieth century, the two World Wars took their toll. In 1942 the Second Army took over Memorial Hall as Maneuver Director Headquarters to direct the training of over 800,000 soldiers for the conquest of Europe. While the operation was underway, the tents of 10,000 soldiers covered the 50-acre campus.

In 1946 officials transferred the school to the sponsorship of the Tennessee Baptist Convention. At that time, it also merged with the Tennessee College for Women in Murfreesboro. In 1951, after the Convention acquired other property in Nashville, Cumberland returned to its former independent board. Only the law school operated until 1955, when Cumberland re-opened a two-year liberal arts college. Cumberland became a member of the Southern Association in 1962. With the addition of a School of Nursing and graduate programs in education and other areas, the school resumed the university designation in 1982. From 1963 to the end of the century, Cumberland University constructed a number of new buildings and athletic facilities. Dr. Clair Martin became president of Cumberland University in 1995.
Frank Burns, Garland, Texas

SEE: CUMBERLAND UNIVERSITY LAW SCHOOL; HORTON, MYLES; HULL, CORDELL; SECOND ARMY MANEUVERS; TENNESSEE COLLEGE FOR WOMEN; WILSON COUNTY

CUMBERLAND UNIVERSITY LAW SCHOOL. "The Lebanon Law School" opened its first term in October 1847, the first school of law in the Old Southwest. The first graduate, Payne Prim, became Chief Justice of the Oregon Supreme Court. Prim took his classes from Professor Abraham Caruthers. Nathan Green, Sr., a State Supreme Court Justice; his son, Nathan, Jr.; and Bromfield Ridley soon joined Caruthers. By 1859 Cumberland, Harvard, and Virginia were the three largest law schools in the country.

Caruthers established a new model for legal education. He assailed the old method of lectures, as well as the reading of court cases in law offices. He believed the law was a science, best taught from textbooks by Socratic questioning under the direction of an experienced jurist, with additional experience in Moot court.

In the post-Civil War era, Nathan Green, Jr., and Andrew B. Martin served as the principal teachers until their deaths in 1919 and 1920. Other faculty members included W. R. Chambers, Sam Gilreath, Frank Fancher, and Arthur Weeks. In 1871 Cumberland University took the revolutionary step of instituting a one-year law course. The Bachelor of Laws degree was awarded after two semesters of study, examination, Moot court, and debate. Students were taught one subject at a time for the entire three-hour class period. Cumberland University followed this very successful method until 1938–1939, when the school returned to a two-year course. Women were admitted in 1901. The school received full accreditation in 1947.

In the foyer of Caruthers Hall, "The Law Barn," the class pictures attest to the quality of the Cumberland education. Among the graduates are governors, senators, state and U. S. Supreme Court Justices (Horace Lurton and Howell Jackson), and a Secretary of State, Nobel Peace laureate, Cordell Hull.

In 1961 the law school was removed to Birmingham, Alabama, under the aegis of Samford University.
Frank Burns, Garland, Texas

SEE: CUMBERLAND UNIVERSITY; GREEN, NATHAN; HULL, CORDELL; JACKSON, HOWELL E.; LAW; LURTON, HORACE H.; WILSON COUNTY

CUNNINGHAM, SUMNER A. (1843–1913) was the founder and editor of the Nashville publication, the *Confederate Veteran*. The magazine was one of the New South's most influential monthlies and made Cunningham a central figure in the "Lost Cause" movement of the late nineteenth century.

Born in rural Bedford County on July 21, 1843, Cunningham grew up on a prosperous farm, among middle class supporters of the slave economy, but not strong secessionists. Following the secession of Tennessee, Cunningham joined the local home guard in October 1861; his unit was quickly assimilated into Company B, 41st Tennessee Infantry, C.S.A. After brief military training at Camp Trousdale, Private Cunningham was stationed at Fort Donelson and captured when the fort fell. Sent to Camp Morton in Indianapolis, he spent six months as a prisoner of war before being exchanged in mid-1862. Rejoining the regiment in Mississippi, Cunningham fought at Port Hudson, Yazoo River, Jackson, and Raymond. He succumbed to a series of illnesses, including pneumonia, malaria, and sciatica, that kept him away from combat for much of the remainder of the war. In 1863 he received a post-battle promotion to Sergeant-

Major and returned to the ranks in time to participate in the Tennessee campaign. He fought with determination at the battles of Franklin and Nashville, but deserted in December 1864. His account of the former battle in postwar publications became a standard treatment from the Confederate perspective. His other publication, *Reminiscences of the 41st Tennessee Infantry* (1871), is a brief but major contribution to the regimental histories of Tennessee.

After the war, Cunningham returned to Shelbyville and worked briefly in the mercantile trade. His interest in journalism surfaced when he bought and edited the *Shelbyville Commercial* (1871), *Chattanooga Times* (1876), and *Cartersville* (Georgia) *Express* (1879). In 1883 Cunningham entered the magazine field with a bold new venture—*Our Day*—a monthly published in New York City, but directed at southern audiences. Mismanagement and financial failure marked each business venture. In 1885 he joined the *Nashville American* as a staff correspondent. Columns such as "That Reminds Me!" and "Towns of the State" earned "SAC" instant popularity as a writer. In 1892 the star reporter was assigned responsibility for collecting funds to erect a monument to the recently deceased former president of the Confederacy, Jefferson Davis. He established a newsletter to keep patrons informed of the drive's progress. The *Confederate Veteran* magazine grew out of that original publication.

Cunningham died on December 13, 1913, at age 70, seated at his editor's desk, while working on his proposed monument to commemorate the life of Daniel Decatur Emmitt, the minstrel and composer of the famous battle song, "Dixie." The *Confederate Veteran* continued publication until 1932.

John A. Simpson, Kelso, Washington

SUGGESTED READING: John A. Simpson, *S.A. Cunningham and the Confederate Heritage* (1994)

SEE: ARMY OF TENNESSEE; CONFEDERATE VETERAN

CURREY, RICHARD OWEN (1816–1865), the first person with an earned doctorate to teach science at what is now the University of Tennessee, was a prolific author, an innovative educator, and a newsworthy minister. A Nashville native, Currey graduated from the University of Nashville in 1836. He taught at Nashville Female Academy and volunteered with the Tennessee Geological Survey.

Currey studied medicine at Transylvania University in 1837–1838, before working under Dr. Thomas Reid Jennings in Davidson County. Currey received his M.D. in 1840, from the University of Pennsylvania. He returned to Nashville, resumed his medical career, and rejoined the Geological Survey. In 1842 he married Rachel Jackson Eastin.

Four years later, Currey became Professor of Chemistry, Experimental Philosophy, and Natural History at East Tennessee University in Knoxville. He

introduced laboratory instruction in botany and modernized science education. Currey supplemented his salary by practicing medicine and publishing an almanac. He left the university in September 1850 to accept a better-paid professorship at the University of Nashville. Medicine remained his livelihood, however, when cholera epidemics and financial problems forced the closing of the school.

In 1851 Currey published two issues of the *Southern Agriculturist* as well as a second almanac, which advertised his new business, an apothecary shop called Chemical Hall. In 1852 Currey joined the State Medical Association, chairing a committee on the adulteration of drugs and another on medical botany. He also helped plan the *Southern Journal of the Medical and Physical Sciences.* It began publication in January 1853, with four co-editors, but became Currey's journal. Over five years, Currey offered 57 major articles on regional geology, medical practice, and other topics. He also wrote brief reports, editorials, and book reviews. He authored a laudable book on the geology of Tennessee and one on the geology of western Virginia.

By May 1853 Currey was involved in the construction of a hospital in Knoxville. At the same time, he unsuccessfully sought an appointment as State Geologist. When the appointment failed to materialize, Currey relocated to Knoxville, taking the *Southern Journal* with him. He practiced medicine with an emphasis in gynecology, and became associated with Dr. B. F. Frazier in the establishment of the School of Medicine and Surgery for Private Instruction. Currey was a leader in medical organizations and, perhaps, part owner of a hospital. Currey continued geological work throughout the southeast, perhaps occasionally as a paid consultant.

In 1857 Currey's son died, the *Southern Journal* folded, and his medical school disbanded. Shelby Medical College opened in Nashville in 1858, and began publishing the *Nashville Monthly Record of Medical and Physical Sciences,* with Currey as co-editor and professor. This time, Currey's family remained in Knoxville, and he soon left the college to return home.

In Knoxville again, Currey studied theology, received ordination, and in 1859 became pastor of Lebanon-in-the-Fork Presbyterian Church. He also operated the distinctive Daughter's Collegiate Institute. To help young ladies learn more of human anatomy, Currey decorated the school grounds with nude statues, which were not widely appreciated. In 1861 Currey entered Confederate service as a chaplain-surgeon. By 1865 he was caring for Union prisoners in North Carolina, where he died while working in a disease-infested hospital.

James X. Corgan, Austin Peay State University

SEE: AGRICULTURAL JOURNALS; GEOLOGY; MEDICINE; UNIVERSITY OF TENNESSEE

D

DABNEY, CHARLES W., JR. (1855–1945), proponent of New South scientific agriculture and respected president of the University of Tennessee from 1887 to 1899, was born in Hampden-Sydney, Virginia, to Robert Lewis and Lavinia Morrison Dabney. Dabney received his early education from his father and completed undergraduate study at Hampden-Sydney College. In 1873 he entered the University of Virginia, graduating in 1877 with a master's degree in chemistry. He accepted a teaching position at Emory and Henry College in southwestern Virginia, but left after one year, disillusioned with the demands of his teaching load and the failure of the college to support his stringent course requirements. In 1878 he enrolled at University of Gottingen in Germany, where he completed his studies in geology and chemistry under Friedrich Wohler, and received his doctorate in 1880.

Dabney returned to the University of North Carolina. That year, he courted and wed Mary Brent of Paris, Kentucky. In 1881 he accepted a position as director of the North Carolina Experiment Station and was named official state chemist, a position that made him responsible for analyzing chemical fertilizers to combat fraud. Dabney joined the Watauga Club, an organization of southern reformers instrumental in establishing North Carolina's first agricultural and mechanical college.

In 1887 Dabney's rising reputation in agriculture and education produced an invitation from the University of Tennessee Board of Trustees to accept the position of university president and director of the agricultural experiment station. Dabney came to UT, but only after acquiring assurances that he would be permitted to administer the university without interference, and that all departments would be responsible to him. The Board of Trustees reluctantly agreed.

At age 32, Dabney became the first Ph.D. to hold the presidency of the University of Tennessee. He joined the university at a pivotal moment in American higher education, as colleges and universities moved from the goal of building character through classical education to emphasis on research, science, and practical application. Dabney acted quickly to refocus the curriculum, requiring courses in agriculture and mechanics for all students, although few accepted the challenge to make scientific agriculture their life's work. During Dabney's tenure, UT added six new four-year courses in science and updated the physics curriculum. He added a home economics program, and by 1893, 48 women were enrolled. In 1890 he created a law department under the direction of former Tennessee Supreme Court Justice Thomas J. Freeman. Dabney's interest in education extended to public schools, and he played a prominent role in the development of the programs of the Southern Education Board, a Rockefeller-financed organization that promoted support for public education. In 1901 Dabney hired Philander Claxton to plan and organize the Summer School of the South, a teacher-education program held annually on the Knoxville campus.

In 1894 Dabney took a leave of absence from the university (though he continued to hold the position of president) in order to accept an appointment by President Grover Cleveland as Assistant Secretary of Agriculture. Many questioned the soundness of the arrangement, just as rural reformers had debated the efficacy and long-term consequences of yoking the agricultural experiment station to the university. Dabney returned to UT in late fall 1897. He continued to shape Tennessee's higher education and agricultural institutions, moving education from the classics to science, and agriculture toward a reliance on university-directed programs of farm management conducive to modern agribusiness.

In 1904, he accepted the presidency of the University of Cincinnati. Dabney died in 1945.

Connie L. Lester, Tennessee Historical Society

SEE: CLAXTON, PHILANDER P.; EDUCATION, HIGHER; SUMMER SCHOOL OF THE SOUTH; UNIVERSITY OF TENNESSEE

DANCE COMPANIES. For more than fifty years, dance companies have encouraged and supported the development of a high quality of dance throughout Tennessee. Through professional, civic, and educational affiliations, these ballet, jazz, tap, modern, and contemporary dance companies provide excellent opportunities for performance and education in dance to Tennessee's citizens and visitors. In the process, they play a valuable role in the state's rich artistic and cultural heritage.

Most of Tennessee's professional ballet companies originated as civic ballet associations and owe their development to dedicated volunteers, whose financial and time commitments promoted the companies to their present status. Examples include the Nashville Ballet (which became a professional company in 1986) and Ballet Memphis (1986). The City Ballet of Knoxville became a professional company in 1988, though it traces its roots from a partnership between the Knoxville Arts Council and the Cincinnati Ballet. In 1996 the City Ballet of Knoxville changed its partnership to the Tulsa Ballet. Through this innovative arrangement, partner cities share professional dancers, but each city retains a separate organizational and governing structure.

The repertoire of these professional companies includes classical, contemporary, and modern works. In addition to performance opportunities, these companies maintain affiliated schools to serve their respective communities. The school curricula are designed to meet the diverse interests of students, from a dance career, to physical exercise, or as an outlet for creative movement. Students may apprentice with professional companies and participate in dance performances. Although each company performs a dance series in their respective communities, they also tour regionally to promote cultural enrichment and make dance available to a wider range of Tennesseans.

Tennessee has a strong commitment to modern and contemporary dance, as seen in the success of the Tennessee Children's Dance Ensemble (which became a professional company in 1981), Tennessee Dance Theater (1986), and the Nashville Dance Project (1992). These companies present well-known modern works as well as new and innovative pieces, introducing audiences to original and thought-provoking works by local and guest artists. The Tennessee Children's Dance Ensemble, founded by Dr. Dorothy Floyd, is the only professional, modern dance company in the United States whose artists are children (ages 10 to 17). The group has performed around the world and worked with choreographers from the nation's leading dance companies.

Civic companies provide opportunities for talented, volunteer dancers to perform and improve their technique and offer the public a chance to learn about dance. A majority of these companies are ballet-based, but some emphasize modern, jazz, and contemporary dance. These civic association companies provide dance education for the participants and audience through formal concerts, lecture/demonstrations, and master classes. The civic companies continue to provide high quality dance experiences through the dedicated efforts of teachers, volunteers, and students. These companies have produced many students who perform professionally in major companies in the United States and Europe.

Over 15 Tennessee dance companies are affiliated with public and private high schools and colleges. These affiliations provide a broad dance experience, which allows students to study technique, develop and produce choreography, and perform a varied repertoire. In addition to performing for their individual schools, members of these companies have been chosen to tour in the United States and Europe. Terpsichord, the modern dance company of Girls Preparatory School in Chattanooga, founded in 1954 by Peggy Evans Thomas, is one of the oldest modern companies in Tennessee.

Phoebe S. Pearigen, The University of the South

DANIEL, ROLLIN A., JR. (1908–1978), a pioneer in cardiac and thoracic surgery, was born June 14, 1908, in Georgia. Shortly thereafter, his parents moved to the Nashville area, and he grew up in Middle Tennessee. Daniel graduated from Goodlettsville High School and Branham Hughes Military Academy in 1926. He received his B.A. degree from Vanderbilt University in 1930 and his M.D. from Vanderbilt University School of Medicine in 1933. Daniel served an internship in surgery at Vanderbilt University Hospital. He was an assistant resident at Barnes and Children's Hospital affiliated with Washington University in St. Louis, 1934–1935. Daniel then returned to Vanderbilt University Hospital, where he was an assistant resident for two years and then resident in surgery from 1937 to 1938. Upon completion of the residency, Daniel was appointed to the faculty of the Vanderbilt University School of Medicine, where he rose to the rank of full professor of surgery. He served as chief of the thoracic surgery service at Vanderbilt University Hospital, where he developed a superb program in cardio-thoracic surgery. He served as chief of the surgical services at St. Thomas Hospital 1962–1965 and 1970–1978. In 1968 he was president of the St. Thomas medical staff.

Daniel was certified by the American Board of Surgery and also the American Board of Thoracic Surgery, where he served as a member of the Founders Group, Chairman of the Credentials Committee, and Chairman of the Board (1965–1967). He was a member of the Society of University Surgeons and served as President of both the Nashville Academy of Medicine and the Nashville Surgical Society.

Daniel authored 56 publications. His first paper, co-authored with Drs. Alfred Blalock and Sam Upchurch, appeared in 1933 in the journal *Surgery, Gynecology and Obstetrics*. His publications cover a wide range of surgical problems, but from 1944, they reflect his concentration of interest in thoracic and cardiovascular surgery. His papers range from the descriptions of his studies on the regeneration of defects of the trachea and bronchi and the experimental production of "wet lung" to the surgical management of a wide variety of thoracic and cardiovascular disorders.

Daniel successfully achieved the difficult balance between medical educator, investigator, and practitioner. Well known as a dedicated teacher, he had few peers in surgical judgment and technical ability. Always known as a "doctor's doctor," his practice included many physicians and their families as patients. A warm and sympathetic person and loyal colleague, Daniel exemplified the best in American medicine.

Harris D. Riley, Jr., Vanderbilt University Medical Center
SEE: MEDICINE; VANDERBILT UNIVERSITY MEDICAL CENTER

DARK TOBACCO DISTRICT PLANTERS' PROTECTIVE ASSOCIATION.

On September 24, 1904, tobacco growers in western Kentucky and northern Middle Tennessee formed the Dark Tobacco District Planters' Protective Association of Kentucky and Tennessee (PPA) hoping for relief from their economic hardships. A steady decline in dark-fired tobacco prices since the turn of the century had brought deprivation and suffering to the farmers of the region. The area had endured periodic depressions caused by low tobacco prices since the Civil War, prompting many growers in the region to support the Grangers, Greenbackers, Farmers' Alliance, Populist Party, and other organizations promising relief from agrarian problems.

Although the principal goal of the PPA was to raise tobacco prices by the cooperative marketing of the crop, the organization also strove to make the federal and state governments more responsive to agrarian needs and to convince tobacco growers to embrace the gospel of diversification, science, and efficiency. The PPA operated for over a decade and was one of the nation's most successful tobacco cooperatives until the formation of the various New Deal tobacco associations. During the PPA's existence, tobacco prices rose and remained at profitable levels. Remembering the fate of the Southern Farmers' Alliance and other earlier farm organizations, the PPA refused to become embroiled in party politics.

Even though the PPA operated in over 20 counties in Tennessee and Kentucky, the organization was dominated by four growers from Robertson County, Tennessee: Joseph E. Washington, Felix G. Ewing, Charles H. Fort, and Joel B. Fort. Ewing, who emerged as the cooperative's most important leader, lived on the Glenraven plantation near Cedar Hill. He served as chairman of the cooperative's executive committee and so dominated the organization that it was often called the "Ewing Association." PPA officials contended that collusion among buyers was the primary factor suppressing tobacco prices. They identified the American Tobacco Company and the Italian Regie as the most important culprits and called this monopoly of buyers, "The Trust." The goal of the cooperative was to convince growers to sign pledges to withhold their crops from "The Trust" and sell only through the farmers' organization. When the early efforts of the PPA proved ineffective in convincing tobacco companies to buy through the cooperative, some disgruntled growers formed a second organization, "the night riders." This covert group used violence and intimidation to raise tobacco prices, initiating a period known as the Black Patch War. The joint efforts of the PPA and the night riders contributed to a general rise in prices.

The PPA declined in strength after 1908. Growing popular opposition to the violence, Trust incentives designed to lure growers away from the PPA, Ewing's increasingly dictatorial management style, and the increased prosperity that came with higher prices contributed to the deterioration of the organization. The PPA officially ended in 1914 when World War I closed most European markets for dark-fired tobacco, which was primarily an export crop.

Rick Gregory, Pleasant View
SUGGESTED READINGS: Rick Gregory, "Robertson County and the Black Patch War, 1904–1909," *Tennessee Historical Quarterly* 39(1980): 341–359; and "Desperate Farmers: The Dark Tobacco District Planters' Protective Association of Kentucky and Tennessee, 1904–1914," (Ph.D. diss., Vanderbilt University, 1989); Christopher Waldrep, "Planters and Planters' Protective Association in Kentucky and Tennessee," *Journal of Southern History* 52(1986): 565–588
SEE: AGRICULTURE; BLACK PATCH WAR; GLENRAVEN PLANTATION; WESSYNGTON PLANTATION

DAUGHTREY, MARTHA CRAIG

(1942–), attorney, law professor, and judge, was born on July 21, 1942, in Covington, Kentucky. She received a B.A. (*cum laude*) from Vanderbilt University in 1964, and graduated from Vanderbilt University School of Law in

1968. Her academic honors included election to Phi Beta Kappa and Order of the Coif.

Daughtrey was admitted to the Tennessee bar in 1968 and after a brief period in private practice in Nashville, she joined the U.S. Attorney's office as an Assistant U.S. Attorney (1968–1969). From 1969 to 1972 she was an Assistant District Attorney for Davidson County.

In 1972 Daughtrey became the first woman appointed to the faculty of Vanderbilt University School of Law, serving as an assistant professor, 1972–1975. She also taught there as lecturer (1971–1972 and 1976–1988) and adjunct professor (1988–1990).

Daughtrey served as a judge on the Tennessee Court of Criminal Appeals from 1975 through 1990, and as an Associate Justice on the Tennessee Supreme Court from 1990 through 1993. She was the first woman on both the Tennessee Court of Criminal Appeals and the Tennessee Supreme Court.

In 1993 President Bill Clinton selected Daughtrey to serve as a circuit judge on the U.S. Court of Appeals, 6th Circuit (Nashville), the first Tennessee woman to be appointed to the 6th Circuit. Although conservative groups opposed her nomination, because of the perception that she opposed the death penalty, elected officials and Tennessee Bar leaders offered overwhelming support, and her nomination received swift confirmation.

In addition to her legal duties, Daughtrey provided leadership in a number of professional and judicial activities. She served on the faculty of the Appellate Judges Seminar at New York University (1977–1989, 1994-present), and the National Judicial College (1989). She accepted leadership roles in the American Bar Association, including service as a council member of the Judicial Administration Division (1984–1985, 1987-present, chair 1989–1990), House of Delegates (1988–1991), executive committee of the Appellate Judges' Conference (1978–1986, chair 1985–1986), member of the Standing Committee on Continuing Education of the Bar (1992–1994), and a member of the commission on Women in the Profession (1994-present). She has been a member of the Board of Editors of the *ABA Journal* since 1995. During April 1991 she participated in an ABA-sponsored delegation that consulted with the drafters of the new Romanian constitution.

Daughtrey also served as a member of the Editors' Board of *The Judges Journal* (1979–1982), president of the National Association of Women Judges (1985–1986) and president of the Women Judges Fund for Justice (1983–1984, 1985–1986). She has been a director of the Nashville Bar Association (1988–1990) and the American Judicature Society (1988–1992), president of the Middle Tennessee-based Lawyers Association for Women (1986–1987), and on the Board of Visitors of Memphis State University School of Law (1978–1986).

Daughtrey's professional contributions have been recognized nationally and internationally and include *Ladies Home Journal*'s Thirty Women to Watch, the Athena Award from the National Athena Program (1991), and Woman of the Year, Women Professionals International (Nashville, 1976).

Daughtrey is married to Larry G. Daughtrey, with whom she has one adult daughter, Carran.

Dana B. Perry, Chattanooga
SEE: LAW; TENNESSEE SUPREME COURT

DAVID CROCKETT STATE PARK, located outside of Lawrenceburg, contains over 1,000 acres of land, including the original sites of a grist mill, distillery, and powder mill once owned by David Crockett, the legendary frontiersman, antebellum politician, and martyred hero of the Battle of the Alamo. For many years, the Lawrence County Historical Society had been interested in the public acquistion of the Crockett sites. Following the resurgence of interest in Crockett during the mid- to late 1950s, the lobbying of the Lawrence County Historical Society finally met with success. The park opened on May 31, 1959, as a segregated facility; two years later, a separate section and facilities were opened for African Americans. The park was integrated during the mid-1960s.

The park today enjoys a full range of recreational facilities and hosts an annual celebration, David Crockett Days, in August. The park's amphitheater is used for all sorts of programming and in the past has featured *The Gentleman from the Cane,* a musical drama about Crockett's life in southern Middle Tennessee written by Dolly Leighton.

This state park is the largest of several facilities that preserve and interpret important historic sites associated with Crockett and his family. In Greene County, the David Crockett Birthplace State Historical Area features a reproduction of the log cabin where Crockett was born near the Nolichucky River. A later Crockett dwelling, from the 1820s, was moved and restored as a historic site in Rutherford, Gibson County. The Crockett Tavern Museum, a historic site administered by the Hamblen County Chapter, Association for the Preservation of Tennessee Antiquities, is located in Morristown.

Carroll Van West, Middle Tennessee State University

DAVIDSON COUNTY, the oldest county in Middle Tennessee, dates to 1783, when the North Carolina legislature created the county and named it in honor of William L. Davidson, a Revolutionary War officer who died at Valley Forge. Its county seat, Nashville, is also the oldest permanent white settlement in Middle Tennessee, founded by James Robertson and John Donelson during the winter of 1779–1780. The initial white settlers established the Cumberland Compact in order to establish a basic rule of law and to protect their land titles. Through much of the early 1780s, the settlers also faced a hostile response from Native American tribes. As the county's many known archaelogical sites attest, the resources of Davidson County had attracted Native Americans for centuries. In fact, the first whites to encounter the area were fur traders, then long hunters, who came to a large salt lick in present-day Nashville to trade with Native Americans and to hunt the abundant game.

Nashville has always been the region's center of commerce, industry, transportation, and culture, but it did not become the capital of Tennessee until 1827 and did not gain permanent capital status until 1843. Its story is best told through its individual entry and the hundreds of other entries in this volume that cover significant people, events, and institutions associated with Nashville as the capital city of Tennessee.

But Davidson County is more than the history of Nashville. It is a large, sprawling landscape that has contained several other significant and distinctive towns and villages in its history, although that diversity has been often forgotten since the formation of the Metropolitian Government of Nashville and Davidson County in 1963. Railroads and turnpikes criss-crossed the county in the mid-nineteenth century and these new transportation routes led to the establishment of several villages, including White's Creek, Joelton, Nolensville, Madison, Antioch, Goodlettsville, and Bellevue. Historic sites in the more rural areas of the county convey a sense of what past life was like outside the glare of the big city lights. The Hermitage of Andrew and Rachel Jackson represents the large planter landscape once common in the antebellum era. The Ellington Agricultural Center in south Davidson County developed from the Brentwood Hall estate of Rogers Caldwell and contains an excellent museum of rural and agricultural history. Newsom's Mill near Bellevue is another reminder of the agrarian economy once dominant in the county. Radnor Lake State Natural Area and the Warner Parks conserve forests and rolling hills in the west side of the county. The Natchez Trace Parkway ends in Davidson County.

War has shaped Davidson County in direct and indirect ways. Federal troops occupied the city early in the Civil War. Fort Negley, a significant post in the history of African Americans and the Civil War, was one of many marks left behind by the occupation army. Throughout the county are many markers and monuments that document the activities of both armies during the Battle of Nashville in December 1864. World War I brought the massive industrial development of the DuPont ammunition factory and company town at Old Hickory, creating a bustling city where nothing had been before. World War II brought additional industrial expansion, such as the Vultee aircraft factory, now Aerostructures, along Briley Parkway. In both Old Hickory and Vultee, modern industry transformed areas of the county that were once rural and thinly populated into much larger suburban additions to the city. After World War II, that process of change continued with the construction of such facilities as the Ford Glass Plant, Genesco, and the Metro Airport.

All three Tennessee Presidents lived in Davidson County; both Andrew Jackson and James K. Polk died and were buried here. But they are just three of many distinguished Tennesseans who called Davidson County home at some time in their lives and careers. Others come from music (DeFord Bailey), architecture (Adolphus Heiman), literature (John Crowe Ransom), politics (Anne Dallas Dudley), civil rights (Avon Williams), and sports (Tracy Caulkins). Davidson County also is home to many of the state's most famous educational and cultural institutions, including Belmont, Fisk, Lipscomb, Tennessee State, Trevecca, and Vanderbilt universities; the Grand Ole Opry; the Tennessee State Museum; and the Tennessee Performing Arts Center.

Carroll Van West, Middle Tennessee State University
SEE: INDIVIDUAL NAMES, PLACES, AND INSTITUTIONS GIVEN ABOVE; NASHVILLE

DAVIDSON, DONALD (1893–1956), poet, writer, and social critic, who played a major role in shaping Southern Agrarianism, left a distinguished body of writings based on Tennessee and southern materials. Born in Campbellsville, near Pulaski, in 1893, Davidson's father, William Bluford Davidson, was a teacher and school administrator, and his mother, Elma Wells Davidson, a music and elocution teacher. Davidson was educated at Lynnville Academy, where his father was co-principal, and Branham and Hughes preparatory school before enrolling at Vanderbilt University in 1909. He earned both his bachelor's and master's degrees in English from Vanderbilt before joining the English faculty. He remained at Vanderbilt for his entire career.

Davidson became a founding member of the circle of Vanderbilt students and professors that published the distinguished *Fugitive* poetry magazine from 1922 to 1925. He and a few others, most notably John Crowe Ransom, Allen Tate, Andrew Nelson Lytle, Frank L. Owsley, and Robert Penn Warren, published the anti-capitalist and anti-modern Agrarian manifesto, *I'll Take My Stand: The South and the Agrarian Tradition*, in 1930. Davidson was a vital member of both the Fugitive and Agrarian groups. Although bound to the modernist poets Ransom, Tate, and Warren by deep bonds of affection and a common southern sensibility, Davidson's relationship with them and the rest of the group was often marked by friction. Defensive and somewhat insecure, the recalcitrant and serious Davidson did not participate fully in their revelries and sometimes seemed prone to obstinacy and inaction.

The personal frustration marked a deeper intellectual division. Although some of the poems in Davidson's *The Outland Piper* (1924) bear the mark of Ransom and Tate's modernist aesthetic, the romantic Davidson never shared in their irony or philosophical skepticism. For Ransom and Tate, the South's steadfast religious faith and strong sense of tradition made it a useful symbol of value for alienated moderns. But Davidson saw the South as no mere symbol. A deep and abiding faith that a people's own history served as the vital source of meaning and value for modern Americans became the touchstone of Davidson's career. His minor epic, *The Tall Men* (1927), horrified Tate and Ransom with its unabashed lyricism and open-hearted identification with the crude and violent pioneer "tall men." In *The Tall Men,* Davidson attempted to construct a racial myth of the South and to call his fellow southerners to remain loyal to their blood through sacraments of remembrance. Much of his later poetry, including the noted "Lee in the Mountains" (1934), embodied this theme.

Davidson shared the Agrarians' general distaste for industrial capitalism and its destructive effect on American culture. Davidson's romantic outlook, however, led him to interpret Agrarianism as a straightforward politics of identity. As twentieth century Americans became citizens of a homogenized and commercialized world, Davidson called them back to their regional identities. "American" identity is "characterless and synthetic," he argued. Americans are "Rebels, Yankees, Westerners, New Englanders or what you will, bound by ties more generous than abstract institutions can express, rather than citizens of an Americanized nowhere, without family, kin, or home," he argued in 1933.[1] *The Attack on Leviathan: Regionalism and Nationalism in the United States* (1938), a volume of essays in social and cultural criticism, represented the fullest statement of Davidson's regionalism.

Davidson harnessed his politics of identity more tightly to anti-statism after World War II. Davidson raged against a blurred "leviathan" composed of the national government and America's metropolitan culture. He rejected federal civil rights legislation on anti-statist grounds, but his defense of racial segregation in the 1950s was a logical extension of his version of Agrarianism. To Davidson, who considered African Americans racially inferior, white southerners developed segregation as a social institution to preserve their culture and identity. In the 1950s he headed the pro-segregation Tennessee Federation for Constitutional Government, the state's generally ineffective version of a White Citizen's Council.

In his evocative two-volume history of the Tennessee River published in the 1940s and his lyric poems edged with prophecy, Davidson enacted the role of southern "memory-keeper" in the postwar period. He bequeathed to neo-Agrarians both an intense southernism and an anti-pluralist and anti-cosmopolitan interpretation of Agrarianism, one much more philosophically anti-liberal than the original Agrarian symposium. He retired from Vanderbilt after a distinguished career of teaching in 1964 and published a volume of collected poems, but his racism and anti-liberalism damaged his literary standing. In the years after his death in 1968, however, Davidson's romantic Agrarianism obtained a wider audience among southern conservatives.
Paul V. Murphy, Truman State University
CITATION:
(1) Paul V. Murphy, "The Social Memory of the South: Donald Davidson and the Tennessee Past," *Tennessee Historical Quarterly* 55(1996): 263.
SEE: AGRARIANS; FUGITIVES; LITERATURE; LYTLE, ANDREW NELSON; RANSOM, JOHN C.; TATE, JOHN O. ALLEN; VANDERBILT UNIVERSITY; WARREN, ROBERT PENN

DAVIES MANOR, recognized as the oldest extant dwelling in Shelby County and perhaps West Tennessee, is at Brunswick, Shelby County. The west section of the two-story, white oak log, central hall plan house dates circa 1807 and has been attributed to an unknown Native American owner and builder. A mound probably dating to the Middle Woodland Period is directly adjacent to the dwelling.

In 1831 Joel W. Royster enlarged the house into a fashionable two-story, three-bay farmhouse. The house became known as Davies Manor sometime after its acquisition by Logan E. Davies in 1851. Logan and his brother James B. Davies eventually operated a plantation of 2,000 acres, especially noted for its production of Berkshire swine.

Davies Manor is listed in the National Register of Historic Places and was included in the 1976 and 1986 surveys of Tennessee Century Farms. In 1976 Ellen Davies-Rogers donated the house to the Davies Manor Association, which operates it as a historic house museum of antebellum life in Shelby County.
Carroll Van West, Middle Tennessee State University
SEE: ARCHITECTURE, DOMESTIC VERNACULAR; FARMS, TENNESSEE CENTURY; SHELBY COUNTY

DAVIESS, MARIA THOMPSON (1872–1924), artist and author, was born in Harrodsburg, Kentucky, in 1872 to an upper-middle class family. Before she was eight years old, her sister and her father died, and her mother moved the family to Nashville. Daviess became active in Nashville society and studied art at Peabody College. After graduation, she traveled to Europe and continued her artistic endeavors, visiting museums and meeting famous people, including Pope Leo XIII, Rodin, and Empress Eugenie. Michelangelo's magnificent art so overwhelmed Daviess that she resigned herself to photography and miniatures. She excelled at both and displayed her miniatures at a Paris salon.

In 1904 Daviess returned to America to teach art. She developed an interest in literature and eventually put aside visual art for writing. She wrote 13 novels and an autobiography during her 15-year career. Her most famous novel, *Miss Selma Lue*, typifies her style of the excessive optimism associated with the Pollyanna school.

As Daviess wrote her novels, she adapted them to the stage. *Phyllis* played in Boston and was optioned for film, though there is no evidence it was produced. Some of her work developed from her devotion to woman suffrage, a cause she helped to win in Tennessee. Daviess was a charter member of the Nashville woman suffrage organization and founded the Madison organization after moving to Sweetbriar farm in 1915. She was living at her home in Madison when she wrote her autobiography, *Seven Times Seven* (1923). At the time, Daviess was fighting severe articular rheumatism. She died as a result of the disease in 1924.

Gary Wake, Henderson

SEE: LITERATURE; WOMAN SUFFRAGE MOVEMENT

DAVIS, ANNE M. (1875–1957), a native of Louisville, Kentucky, moved to Knoxville in 1915 with her husband Willis P. Davis, the president of Knoxville Iron Company. She soon developed a life-long love for the Great Smoky Mountains. She and her husband spent much of the 1920s working for the establishment of a national park in the Smokies.

Davis is credited with inspiring the park movement in Knoxville in 1923, when she asked her husband about the feasibility of a park as the couple returned from a trip to the western parks. Willis Davis threw his considerable energies into organizing the local business community for the promotion of a Smokies park. He became a charter member and first president of the Great Smoky Mountains Conservation Association, which played a key role in making the park a reality.

Anne Davis's most important contribution came in 1924, when she declared her intention to run for the Tennessee General Assembly on the Republican ticket. Davis won the election, becoming only the third woman elected to the Tennessee House. She sponsored legislation for the purchase of 78,131 acres of mountain land owned by the Little River Lumber Company. When the bill encountered opposition, Davis organized an inspection trip for the entire legislature and effectively swayed critics, who previously characterized the area as "stump land." In an

appropriate tribute to Davis, Tennessee Governor Austin Peay gave her the pen he used to sign the bill into law.

Davis served only one term in the House and never again ran for public office. After her husband died in 1931, she moved to Gatlinburg to be closer to the mountains she loved. Davis remained active in civic life as a member and officer in the League of Women Voters and led the successful movement to establish a public library in Gatlinburg.

Dan Pierce, Western Carolina University

SEE: CONSERVATION; GREAT SMOKY MOUNTAINS NATIONAL PARK; SEVIER COUNTY; TENNESSEE GENERAL ASSEMBLY

DAVIS, LOUISE LITTLETON (ca. 1915–1995), historian and journalist, was born in Paris, Tennessee, one of five children of LaRue Lucetta Littleton, a musician, and Grover C. Davis, a career U.S. Army officer. Davis's scholarly bent took her first to Murray State College in Kentucky, where she earned a bachelor's degree, and then to Vanderbilt University for a master's degree in Latin.

As an author and Metro Nashville's official historian, Davis brought the past to life with her witty and straightforward style and meticulous attention to detail. Davis is credited with sparking the movement that preserved the Union Station from demolition and with the establishment of the Friends of the Metro Archives.

Her journalistic career began in 1943 covering the legislature for the Associated Press. At the close of that session, she joined the staff of *The Tennessean*. As a reporter in the news department, Davis covered topics ranging from agriculture to juvenile crime. Later she moved to the newspaper's magazine, where she gained a reputation for her knowledge of history, love of research, and tenacity in fighting for column space for her stories. Semi-retired in 1977, she continued working part time at *The Tennessean* until 1984. She was a long-time member of the editorial review board of the *Tennessee Historical Quarterly*.

Davis's books include *Nashville Tales, More Nashville Tales, Snowballs in the White House, Children's Museum of Nashville: the First 30 Years, Frontier Tales of Tennessee*, and *More Tales of Tennessee*. At the time of her death, she was writing a biography of Captain William Driver for the Smithsonian Institution.

Mary Louise Tidwell, Nashville

SEE: NASHVILLE; NASHVILLE TENNESSEAN

DAVIS, SAM (1842–1863), "the Boy Hero of the Confederacy," was born on his family's farm near Smyrna, Tennessee, on October 6, 1842. A frail child, Davis grew up playing on the land around his home and learned the landscape of Middle Tennessee, knowledge that later aided his activities as a Confederate scout. At 19, the quiet and refined Davis left home to attend the Military Academy in Nashville. There he made the acquaintance of Bushrod Rust Johnson, headmaster of the school and later a Confederate General. Strict military life suited the idealistic Davis.

When the war fever swept the South, young Davis joined the "Rutherford Rifles," a local militia group mustered into active service as Company I, 1st Tennessee Infantry. Davis followed his regiment to Cheat Mountain, in what is now West Virginia, and fought under the command of Robert E. Lee.

In 1862, after his initial enlistment, Davis returned home. That autumn, he joined a company of cavalry known as "Coleman's Scouts," commanded by Henry B. Shaw, one of Davis's former teachers. Numbering around 100, the Coleman Scouts operated around Nashville, Franklin, Murfreesboro, and Columbia, gathering information about federal troop movements. Although considered spies by the Union army, the Scouts usually wore their uniforms and seldom used disguises.

In the fall of 1863 Davis and five others were assigned to gather information about federal forces in Tennessee. They spent much of their time learning the movements of General Granville Dodge's division as it passed from northeast Mississippi through Middle Tennessee enroute to Chattanooga. Dodge ordered his men to wipe out the Scouts, if possible.

Moving behind enemy lines and risking capture, Davis returned home to Smyrna in early November 1863. After a brief visit with his family, Davis left to rejoin the Scouts. On November 19, 1863, while scouting near Pulaski, Davis accepted a letter written to the Provost Marshal of the Army of Tennessee and several newspapers from Captain Shaw to be delivered to army headquarters. The next day, federal soldiers captured Davis in Giles County, charged him with spying and carrying mails to persons in arms against the United States, and brought him before General Dodge. Davis pleaded not guilty to charges of spying, but entered a guilty plea to the second charge. The court-martial appointed to try Davis found him guilty on both counts and sentenced him to be hanged.

One week after his capture, the sentence was carried out. Standing before the noose, he was offered his freedom if he would reveal the name of the person who gave him the papers. His answer, "I would rather die a thousand deaths than betray a friend or be false to duty," became a touchstone of the mythology of the "Lost Cause" in the postwar South. Monuments to his bravery were erected on the grounds of the State Capitol and on the square in Pulaski. Later, in the 1920s, his family home in Smyrna became a historic house museum and a shrine to Davis, who is buried there in the family cemetery. Pulaski also has a small museum in his honor, dedicated in the 1960s, which stands near the spot of his hanging in the town's Sam Davis Avenue historic district.

Patrick Craddock, Franklin

SEE: CIVIL WAR; GILES COUNTY; RUTHERFORD COUNTY

DEADERICK, GEORGE M. (ca. 1756–1816), the wealthiest Nashvillian of his time, was a wholesale merchant, real-estate dealer, and pioneer banker. Born of German stock (the family name was originally Dietrich) in Winchester, Virginia, George and his younger brother Thomas, already enjoyed modest wealth when they migrated to Nashville in 1788. In sometime partnership with Howell Tatum (1753–1822), George established a highly successful merchandising business, selling goods to other merchants and loaning money. Deaderick dealt in Nashville town lots and in return for donating land for use as an alley (now Printer's Alley), the city named a street for him.

In 1807 Deaderick asked Andrew Jackson to assist in arranging a reconciliation with his wife Mary "Polly," who reportedly held parties and attended dances while Deaderick was out of town. Jackson's efforts failed, and Mary Deaderick apparently accused Jackson of untoward conduct, which her husband did not accredit. After much marital discord, the couple divorced in 1812.

A confidante and sometime creditor of Andrew Jackson, Deaderick founded the first bank in Tennessee, the Nashville Bank, in 1807. It was the first Tennessee bank to establish branch banks, at Murfreesboro, Shelbyville, Gallatin, and Rogersville. The bank weathered several national and state financial crises, including the Panic of 1819, but closed in 1827.

Deaderick served briefly in the War of 1812 and hosted a grand dinner for Jackson on his return from the Battle of New Orleans. When Deaderick died in 1816, he was survived by two minor sons, John George M. Deaderick and Fielding Deaderick.

Lewis Laska, Tennessee State University

SEE: JACKSON, ANDREW; NASHVILLE

DE BRAHM, JOHN WILLIAM GERARD (1717–1796), engineer and cartographer, was a native of Germany. A military engineer in the army of Charles VII, he resigned his commission in 1748, and three years later led a group of immigrants to America, settling in the German Lutheran community of Ebenezer, Georgia.

De Brahm's skills as an engineer and cartographer resulted in an appointment as Surveyor General for Georgia in 1754, and a commission from South Carolina the next year to repair the fortifications of Charles Town. De Brahm was also appointed to design and supervise the construction of Fort Loudoun, a fortification to be built in the Overhill

Cherokee country. In August 1756 De Brahm accompanied the first garrison of troops, under the command of Captain Raymond Demerré, to the proposed site on the Little Tennessee River. De Brahm, however, preferred an alternative site, which was unacceptable to the Cherokees. Demerré's decision to build the fort on the original site led to such ill feelings between the two men that they were never able to establish a good working relationship. Apparently, De Brahm perceived himself as co-commander, and on at least one occasion, he issued conflicting orders. Demerré viewed this as inciting mutiny, and the officers of the garrison, with only one exception, agreed. Soon afterwards, De Brahm abandoned the project, leaving Fort Loudoun abruptly on Christmas Eve, 1756.

De Brahm continued to work as an engineer and surveyor. In 1764 his appointment as Surveyor General of Georgia ended, and he received a dual appointment as Surveyor General for both East Florida and the Southern District. His "Report of the General Survey in the Southern District of North America," completed in 1773, includes information obtained during his stay among the Cherokees. The coming of the Revolution prompted De Brahm to return to England in 1777, where he apparently experienced financial difficulties. Returning to Charleston in 1789, he soon moved to Philadelphia, where he died in the summer of 1796.

Michael Toomey, Knoxville College
SEE: FORT LOUDOUN; OVERHILL CHEROKEES

DECATUR COUNTY. Decatur County borders the Tennessee River in West Tennessee and was established in 1845. Its name honored Commodore Stephen Decatur, naval hero from the War of 1812. Carved from land originally claimed by the Chickasaws, the area was part of the Jackson Purchase of 1818. Initially part of Perry County, which is on the east shore of the river, citizens on the western side petitioned the General Assembly for a new county in 1845. In 1849 Decatur County gained an additional three-mile strip from Hardin County, making its total area 346 square miles.

Largely rural in nature, Decatur County contains several small towns and communities. Decaturville, established in 1847, near the center of the county, serves as the county seat. The county's largest town, Parsons, like many nineteenth century communities in West Tennessee, developed around newly laid railroad tracks. In 1889 local entrepreneur Henry Myracle encouraged area settlement by donating 143 acres to the Tennessee Midland Railroad Company. Initially called Parsons Flat after Myracle's son-in-law Dock Parsons, the town gained its charter in 1913.

Perryville (1825) is the county's oldest community. The twentieth century construction of the

Gilbertsville Dam, however, flooded the old town and forced many of its residents into Parsons. In 1971 Perryville's post office officially closed, changing its status from town to village. Other communities in Decatur County include Bible Hill, Sugar Tree, Bath Springs, Scotts Hill, Tie Whop, Lick Skillet, Beacon, and Jeanette.

Agriculture continues to provide the primary economic base in Decatur County, with cotton and corn as the earliest staple crops. In the 1970s, as many farmers began dividing their time between the factory and the fields, soy beans, a less demanding crop, gained in popularity. Livestock, particularly hogs, also have been an important source of income in the county, with the principal markets in Decaturville and Scotts Hill. Since the 1960s, area lakes have supported catfish farms and musseling businesses.

Decatur County's abundant resources attracted several businesses. In 1846 Brownsport Iron Company established iron smelting furnaces on 12,000 acres near Decaturville, where it continued operations until 1878. Limestone, which is plentiful throughout the county, supported a variety of gravel industries, and phosphate is found along the Beech River. The county is also rich in timber. Native hardwoods, such as white and red oak, hickory, and tulip poplar, supply local sawmills.

Decatur County gained its first manufacturing plant in 1938, when Salant & Salant, Inc., makers of men's work shirts, opened a factory in Parsons. It expanded from five to 50 operators in the first nine months, and by 1979, employed nearly 700 workers. Industrial development accelerated in the post-World War II era. By the late 1970s, industries in Parsons included Kaddis Manufacturing Corporation, makers of machine parts; Decaturville Sportswear Company, Inc.; and Thermo Dynamics, Inc., which manufactured refrigerators. A commercial refrigerator company, Kol-pak Industries, opened in Decaturville, as did Karlyn Manufacturers, an apparel producer.

Transportation provided the key factor to Decatur County's economic development. The railroad promoted settlement and initial development of the area. Trains made their first stops in Perryville in 1889, but suspended service to the county by 1936. In the early twentieth century, road construction opened the county to industry. In 1930 the Alvin C. York Memorial Bridge opened at Perryville. The one-mile span over the Tennessee River made the county more accessible to automobile and truck traffic. The construction of a municipal airport, Scott Field, in Parsons, brought Decatur County into the age of air transportation in 1959.

Teresa Biddle-Douglass, Middle Tennessee State University
SUGGESTED READING: Lillye Younger, *Decatur County* (1979)
SEE: COTTON; LIVESTOCK; MUSSELING; SOYBEANS

DECKER, CHARLES FREDERICK, SR. (1832–1914), master potter and proprietor of Keystone Pottery, was the largest producer of utilitarian and folk-art ceramics in East Tennessee between 1873 and 1906. Decker was the binding influence behind a family business that produced items made by himself, three sons, and 25 employees. Pottery-laden wagons regularly left Keystone Pottery, in Washington County, for destinations in East Tennessee, North Carolina, Virginia, and Kentucky.

Born in Langenalb, Baden, Germany, in 1832, Decker emigrated to the United States as a teenager. He first worked for Richard C. Remmey, a Philadelphia stoneware manufacturer, before establishing Keystone Pottery in Philadelphia in 1857. Decker married three times. His first marriage produced two sons, Charles Frederick, Jr., and William, but his wife, Catherine, died before the Civil War. Decker's second wife, Sophia Hinch, bore sons Fred and Richard Henry in the 1860s. A third marriage to Susan Elizabeth Broyles Gefellers produced no children.

Decker migrated southward around 1870, working initially at a pottery near Abingdon, Virginia, before moving to Tennessee. In 1872 he acquired 100 acres of land rich in clay deposits in the Chucky Valley and reestablished Keystone Pottery. Decker and his sons produced the usual kitchenware, including crocks, jugs, and churns. They also made pitchers, flower pots, paving blocks, stoneware drainpipes, chicken fountains, chamber pots, and decorated inkwells. Distinctive tombstones and large yard ornaments of gray, salt-glazed pottery decorated with deep blue lettering and designs, as well as grotesque face vessels and sculptural pieces, established Charles F. Decker as a leading southern folk potter.

Stephen D. Cox, Tennessee State Museum

SEE: DECORATIVE ARTS, APPALACHIAN; WASHINGTON COUNTY

DECORATIVE ARTS, AFRICAN-AMERICAN. African-American decorative arts embrace many forms, from the practical utility of bed quilts, baskets, blacksmithing, and wood carving to the skill in design and construction of residential architecture or boat building. Whether the objects are practical or beautiful, the artistic creations are based on decades of learned tradition and natural instinct.

The tradition of African-American folk and craft artisans began in Tennessee with the settlement of the land and the introduction of slavery to the emerging agrarian society. Slaves brought with them not only traditional skills from Africa, but also a sense of color and pattern that made their craftsmanship unique. The strong African sense of family enabled artists to learn their skills from their parents, what African-American artist and historian Pecolia Warner called "fireplace training."

Decorative arts in the early nineteenth century began as practical objects created for daily utility, such as quilts, basketry, woven goods, iron work, and funerary art. Richard Poynor (1802–1882) was a noted Williamson County craftsman. Later works, less dependent on practicality, nevertheless maintained African color schemes and design patterns, such as the gravestones of Will Edmonson of Nashville.

Although European in tradition, bed quilts were adapted to reflect distinctly African origins by altering patterns and color selections. Quilts were used not only to cover beds but also as barriers between rooms in slave quarters to provide privacy and insulation. In the twentieth century, quilts became less utilitarian and more unique pieces of fabric art. The Nashville-born fabric designer, Viola Burley Leak, has given a strong voice to African-American history through her sewn fabric pieces, which depict scenes from black experiences.

Early African-American craftsmen produced basketry to serve the needs of plantation life in everything from cotton baskets to egg and market baskets. These forms also gave way to the improvisation inherent in African-American craft tradition. Twentieth century basketmaking was no longer driven by need, but by a new monetary value, which allowed for creative license to design unique objects such as woven purses, pocketbooks, and flower baskets.

African-American artistic talent expressed itself more often in blacksmithing than in any other trade except carpentry. Unlike fabric and cloth hand crafts, which were passed in fireplace training among females, the smithing tradition was the only craft passed down by males from generation to generation. The rural blacksmiths crafted utilitarian objects from horseshoes to hinges, but had few opportunities for creative expression. These rural craftsmen acquired many opportunities to achieve independence, however, and were often able to purchase their freedom with money earned through work for their owners and neighboring farmers and plantation owners. Smithing proved lucrative enough for some freedmen to be able to purchase their families with their earned incomes. Urban blacksmiths had more opportunities to demonstrate their artistic skills than rural blacksmiths, when they were hired to produce fences and commissioned works. Twentieth century Shelbyville artist, Vanoy Streeter, carries on the African-American tradition with metalwork with his sculpture created with yards and yards of formed wire.

African-American traditions continued to thrive in Tennessee decorative art while allowing artists to rely on improvisation to guide their creations. Twentieth century artists produce the creations using the traditional techniques of their ancestors, but allowing contemporary events to influence design and form.

Susan Goodsell, Plano, Illinois

SUGGESTED READINGS: William Ferris, ed., *Afro-American Folk Art and Crafts* (1983); Robert L. Hall, *Gathered Visions: Selected Works by African American Women Artists* (1992); Maude Southwell Wahlman, *Signs and Symbols: African Images in African-American Quilts* (1993)

SEE: DOCKERY, ISAAC; EDMONDSON, WILLIAM; GILLILAND HOUSE; MCMAHAN, FRED

DECORATIVE ARTS, APPALACHIAN.

The early decorative arts of Appalachia were the hand-pieced quilts, handwoven coverlets, split oak egg baskets, and other "necessary" crafts once common to every remote household. In the Appalachian mountains of East Tennessee, art was often the result of need. The non-industrialized Appalachian people were self-reliant, making do with materials at hand, crafting the cabin itself and all its furnishings, growing the flax and raising the sheep for the carding, spinning, and weaving of cloth for clothing, making any needed household implements, farming tools, toys, and bedding from the materials at hand.

The color that came into the Appalachian household came from the natural material and the natural dyestuffs, from walnut hulls and indigo, from inventive hands and minds adding "art" to everyday living. Intricate weaving patterns and dyes added life to the traditional coverlets, and surely many households contained "showoff" quilts made for marryings and buryings.

Just as the mail order catalog and better transportation began to give the mountaineers access to consumer products and a different, less self-sufficient way of life, a regional movement to preserve and market the traditional crafts got underway. Settlement schools and missionary workers saw the crafts as a means of generating cash income for a cash-poor people, and the "revival" of Appalachia's handicrafts began. The Pi Beta Phi School in Gatlinburg was a leader in the handweaving arena, both in teaching and production, and the Arrowcraft Shop provided the early market. In Kentucky, Berea College's "Fireside Industries," and in North Carolina, Frances Goodrich's Allanstand Cottage Crafts, the John C. Campbell Folk School, Penland School, and Clementine Douglas's Spinning Wheel Shop provided similar outlets.

In 1929 these efforts merged to create the Southern Highland Handicraft Guild, the major organization devoted to Appalachian crafts, which held its first official meeting in Knoxville in 1930. In 1935 the Tennessee Valley Authority created Southern Highlanders, Inc., a crafts marketing program to work in conjunction with the Guild to operate retail stores in Norris, Tennessee, the Rockefeller Center in New York City, and in Washington, D.C. TVA's program also included craft training, such as O. J. Mattill's woodworking classes, which gave many Gatlinburg area woodworkers a start in the craft business.

During the mid-1940s, the Rockefeller Foundation sponsored Marian Heard's survey of Appalachian crafts, which led to the first Craftsman's Fair of the Southern Highlands, held in 1948 on the grounds of the Pi Beta Phi School in Gatlinburg.

The Southern Highlanders and the Southern Highland Handicraft Guild merged in 1950, extending the Guild's territory westward to Nashville. Phenomenal growth in crafts marketing and education across the region dramatically altered the craft objects, which were once the "necessary" crafts of mountain people. During the past 50 years, many artists and craftspeople from other regions have moved into Appalachia, bringing new skills and new artistic directions. As a result, the traditional self-taught or family-taught craftsperson is now part of a distinct minority.

Preservation efforts, such as the Museum of Appalachia in Norris, the Guild's recognition of "Heritage Members," and state folklife efforts, are helping to preserve and perpetuate tradition, but the face of Appalachia's decorative arts is changing rapidly. Today's working craftspeople are more likely to be college-trained professionals, whose work is derived from traditional mountain sources. But increasingly, the crafts are not intended to function in traditional ways, and have become purely decorative. For example, quilts are now decorator showpieces seldom used on beds, and while the mountain coverlet (or "kiver") is no longer a significant part of Appalachian craft production, it is perhaps the most studied of the earlier art forms.

Organizations such as the Tennessee Association of Craft Artists (TACA) promote craft as art, though many members' work is very traditional; the Foothills Craft Guild in Oak Ridge has also been active for many years. The strong Appalachian craft organizations have maintained the effort begun during the 1930s, and today's craft professional benefits from the work done over the past half century.

The marketplace introduced changes in production. Better looms for weaving tighter, straighter seams were introduced early in this century; quilts are now assembled from all-new materials, often machine quilted and lighter weight than earlier quilts, which were intended for warmth. Powered saws, sanders, planers, and carving tools have allowed woodworkers to expand and experiment. Electric potter wheels, ram presses, jiggers, and casting molds have influenced pottery design and production. Baskets are often free-form, woven from commercial strapping, dyed bright colors, and seldom used for gathering eggs or carrying vegetables to the market. In almost every medium, technology has influenced the finished product.

Appalachian crafts have largely managed to avoid the popular "country" look pushed by magazines, though as always there are craft makers whose designs and production are market-driven. Nevertheless, contemporary Appalachian decorative arts have responded to general market influences and now differ little from those of most of the United States.

The crafts culture, however, remains as a direct descendant of the mountain heritage, and today's craftswork is, essentially, the modern equivalent of the work of a century or two centuries ago. Contemporary Appalachian craftspeople work for different reasons than those of their ancestors, but the common thread linking past and present is quality, material, and skill.

Garry Barker, Morehead, Kentucky

SUGGESTED READING: Allen H. Eaton, *Handicrafts of the Southern Highlands* (1937)

SEE: ARROWMONT SCHOOL; DECKER, CHARLES F.; MUSEUM OF APPALACHIA; PI BETA PHI SCHOOL; QUILTMAKING; TENNESSEE VALLEY AUTHORITY

DEFRANK, VINCENT (1915–), founder and musical director of the Memphis Symphony Orchestra (MSO) from 1960 to 1983, was born June 18, 1915, in Long Island, New York. He first studied violin from George Frenz from 1920 to 1933, before converting to cello, studying with Percy Such and Georges Miquella. He attended the Juilliard School of Music from 1937 to 1940, studying conducting with Albert Stoessel. During this period he was briefly a member of the Detroit Symphony Orchestra (1939–1940) before coming to Memphis as Director of the Second Army Headquarters Band. He was principal cellist of the MSO under Burnet Tuthill, where he remained until its disbanding in 1949. DeFrank was also a member of the Memphis Open Air Theater pit orchestra, Memphis Concert Orchestra, and both WMPS and WMC Radio staff ensembles. DeFrank was an adjunct member of the St. Louis Symphony from 1947 through 1950 and attended Indiana University from 1950 to 1952, studying cello with Fritz Magg. He returned to Memphis in 1952, where he formed the Memphis Sinfonietta, a precursor to the MSO.

DeFrank holds several honorary educational degrees and awards. He was the recipient of an award from the American Society of Composers, Authors, and Publishers in 1967; Southwestern at Memphis (now Rhodes College) awarded him a Doctorate of Music in 1974; and he received the Outstanding Tennessean Award in 1981. He is a lifelong member of the American Federation of Musicians Locals 71 and 802.

Roy C. Brewer, Memphis

SUGGESTED READING: Roy C. Brewer, "Professional Musicians in Memphis (1900–1950): A Tradition of Compromise," (Ph.D. diss., The University of Memphis, 1996)

SEE: SYMPHONY ORCHESTRAS

DEKALB COUNTY was established in December 1837 by the Tennessee General Assembly and named for Johann DeKalb, a German general who died while serving in the American Revolution. The county seat was located on 50 acres donated by Bernard Richardson and named Smithville by the General Assembly in honor of Samuel Granville Smith of Jackson County, a State Senator and Tennessee's Secretary of State. Smithville's population in 1990 was 3,791. A widely-attended Fiddler's Jamboree has been held annually on the square on the July 4th weekend since 1971.

Liberty is the oldest town in DeKalb County. By 1807 it had been laid off in half-acre lots by its founder, Adam Dale, DeKalb County's first settler, who arrived in 1797 from Maryland. Dale, along with John and Leonard Fite and probably Stephen Robinson, cut a road into the Liberty area from Nashville. In 1805 Dale's friends and relatives followed these groundbreakers to the area. In 1990 Liberty had 391 people.

Six miles northwest of Liberty is Alexandria, established in 1820 by Daniel Alexander, another migrant from Maryland. Alexandria prospered and soon contained a number of flourishing businesses and good schools. In 1856 Alexandria hosted the first DeKalb County Fair, which is still held there annually. The fair grandstand is the oldest in the state and is listed in the National Register of Historic Places. Alexandria's 1990 population totaled 730.

DeKalb County furnished almost as many Union troops as it did Confederate troops in the Civil War. Fighting occurred around Liberty in 1863, including the Battle of Snow's Hill on April 3, which engaged about 2,000 men on each side. After the armies left, guerrillas, or "bushwhackers," terrorized both Union and Confederate sympathizers in the county. Bitter feelings about the war lasted for decades and were especially strong at election time. Not long after the war, Dowelltown grew up one mile east of Liberty. Named by the postmaster, Frank Dowell, it became the home of several Union Army veterans. Its 1990 population numbered 308.

John H. Savage ranks among DeKalb County's outstanding antebellum political leaders. Savage, a Democrat, served in the U.S. Congress from 1849 to 1859. During the Civil War, he attained the rank of colonel in the 16th Confederate Infantry Regiment. His principal political opponent was William B. Stokes, who served as a colonel in the 5th U.S. Cavalry and became a Republican Congressman in the postwar period.

World War II brought many changes to DeKalb County. The war affected almost every family, as more than 700 area citizens entered active military service. DeKalb Countians on the home front got a taste of military action, when the county became the site of army maneuvers held in preparation for the assault on Europe.

Just after World War II, Joe L. Evins served as a Democratic Congressman from 1946 to 1976. State-level DeKalb Democrats included McAllen Foutch, who served in the General Assembly from 1943 to 1959 and as Speaker of the House from 1949 to 1959; and Frank Buck, a state representative elected continuously since 1973.

From its earliest settlement DeKalb County's economy depended on agriculture, but enormous economic change occurred after World War II. In 1948 the U.S. Army Corps of Engineers completed Center Hill Dam, flooding the Caney Fork area and forcing many farm families to move. By 1995 almost every farm family in the county depended on supplemental income from an outside source.

Some manufacturing occurred in the county in the antebellum period, including Jesse Allen's iron forge on Pine Creek and crockware pottery made by the Lefevre family and their relatives. Manufacturing on a large scale did not begin, however, until 1948, when a shirt factory was constructed in Smithville. Much of the county's present business supplies parts for the growing automobile industry in Tennessee.

Electricity became available in the towns in the late 1920s, but rural families did not receive the utility until the late 1940s. Telephone service from the DeKalb Telephone Cooperative began in 1951. The county had no medical facilities in 1945, but built hospitals and nursing homes since the 1960s, and now receives a wide range of medical services from Baptist DeKalb Hospital.

In the 1990 federal census, DeKalb County's population totaled 14,360, approximately the same as in 1880 and 1930. At the end of the Civil War, African Americans made up about ten percent of the population, but outmigration reduced the number of blacks to less than three percent in the 1990 census. In the 1980s Mexican laborers came to work in DeKalb's nurseries, but few have become permanent residents.

Thomas G. Webb, Smithville

SEE: EVINS, JOSEPH L.; SAVAGE, JOHN H.; SECOND ARMY MANEUVERS; U.S. ARMY CORPS OF ENGINEERS

DEMONBREUN, TIMOTHY (1747—1826), French-Canadian fur trader, first traveled to the sulpher springs near the Cumberland River at what would be known as the French Lick around 1769. Demonbreun made frequent trips to the early Nashville settlement to engage in fur trade with Native Americans. He managed two careers and two families. One was based in Kaskaskia, Illinois, where he fulfilled his duties as Lt. Commandant of the Illinois County and spent time with his family there. The second was based in the Nashville area, where he developed a thriving mercantile and fur trading business, with 17 employees, and spent time with his Native American wife and family there. Demonbreun joined the George Rogers Clark expedition and received an appointment as Lt. Governor in command of the Northwest Territory.

In 1786 he resigned from military service and moved to Nashville in 1790. By 1800 his mercantile business on Nashville's Public Square advertised such items as window glass, paper, cured deer hides, and buffalo tongues. Demonbreun built his final home on Third Avenue and Broadway.

Demonbreun had five children by his first wife in Illinois and three by his second common law wife in Nashville. When he died in 1826, Demonbreun divided his substantial fortune among his children. No record of the burial site of Nashville's "First Citizen" survived. In 1996 a monument in his honor was erected near Fort Nashborough, overlooking the Cumberland River, in downtown Nashville.

Kenneth Fieth, Metropolitan Archives for Nashville and Davidson County

SEE: FRENCH LICK; NASHVILLE

DEMPSTER, GEORGE ROBY (1887–1964), a leading twentieth century Knoxville businessman and political figure, was born in Knoxville on September 12, 1887, to Scotland natives John D. and Ann Dempster. After his high school graduation in 1906, Dempster and his brother Tom went to work on the Panama Canal, where he operated the first steam shovel in the Pacific cut. He returned to Knoxville in 1911 and married Mildred Frances Seymour. Two years later, he and two of his brothers founded the Dempster Construction Company, which built railroads, dams, and highways throughout the Southeast. In the years that followed the Depression, Dempster achieved his greatest fame as the inventor of the Dempster Dumpster. During World War II, the U.S. Navy widely used Dempster Dumpsters for collection and disposal of waste. As a result of his successes in heavy equipment manufacturing, Dempster rose to political prominence in Knoxville and East Tennessee.

Dempster was appointed city manager of Knoxville three times (1929, 1935, and 1945), and served as mayor from 1951 to 1955. During his administrations, the city constructed the Henley Street Bridge and Bill Meyer Stadium, built an extensive sewage disposal system, and dedicated four libraries. Dempster ran for governor as a Republican in 1940, but lost by a considerable margin to Prentice Cooper. Shortly before his death on October 19, 1964, at the age of 77, he received the U.S. Navy Public Service Award for the merits of Dempster Dumpsters.

Robert Parkinson, University of Tennessee, Knoxville

SEE: KNOXVILLE; WORLD WAR II

DENNIS, JOHN BARTLETT (1866–1947), financier and creator of modern Kingsport, was born in Gardiner, Maine, the eldest son of David and Julia Bartlett Dennis. David Dennis was a prominent businessman and president of the Merchants National Bank of Gardiner. John Dennis received his early education in the local public schools and attended Cornell University for three years. At the end of his junior year, he transferred to Columbia College and graduated with an A.B. degree in 1887. During the following years, he became involved in the investment and security business, working for several brokerage firms in Boston and New York. In 1890 he became associated with the newly organized private banking firm of Blair and Company of New York. Within three years, Dennis received a partnership in the firm and for the next 20 years engaged in banking, promotional, and reorganization activities.

The directors of Kingsport Farms, Inc., authorized Dennis, as the Blair and Company representative, to purchase approximately 6,355 acres of land in Sullivan and Hawkins counties from the Carter Coal Company. The Kingsport Improvement Company (KIC) then purchased land for a proposed town from Kingsport Farms. With controlling interest in both companies, Dennis provided financial backing for the establishment of Kingsport.

As proponents of progressivism and its emphasis on rationality, efficiency, and expertise, Dennis and KIC president J. Fred Johnson obtained advice from experts in city planning and government. When it was incorporated in 1917, Kingsport became the first Tennessee municipality with a city-manager form of government. From the beginning, the city was zoned for industrial, residential, and commercial development.

The planners implemented an interlocking concept of industrial development that recruited specific industries designed to complement one another and advance technological change and growth. Dennis persuaded Kodak founder, George Eastman, to locate a plant in Kingsport. Dennis served as chairman of the board of Kingsport Press, Incorporated, which became one of the largest book makers in the world. In 1924 Dennis recruited Borden Mills of Massachusetts to locate a subsidiary mill in Kingsport.

Dennis made Kingsport his primary residence and in 1928, purchased Rotherwood, a large nineteenth century estate, where he entertained potential investors and industrialists. Augusta, Georgia, native Lola Anderson, a Cornell graduate and Kingsport's resident landscape artist and nursery owner, married Dennis in 1929. Dennis sold Rotherwood to the U.S. Army in 1941, and the commanding officers of nearby Holston Defense Corporation lived there during the war. In 1946 Dennis exercised his option to repurchase the home, and then sold it to Tennessee Eastman executive Herbert G. Stone. Dennis died in Asheville in 1947 and is buried in Kingsport.

Martha Avaleen Egan, Kingsport Public Library and Archives/King College

SEE: HOLSTON ORDNANCE WORKS; JOHNSON, J. FRED; KINGSPORT; TENNESSEE EASTMAN COMPANY

DENNY, JAMES R. "JIM" (1911–1963), music publisher, booking agent, long-time manager of the Grand Ole Opry, and promoter of Nashville's music industry, was born in Buffalo Valley, Putnam County. As a young man, Denny found work as a mail clerk with the National Life and Accident Insurance Company, parent organization to WSM and the Grand Ole Opry. With a growing interest in country music, Denny was running the WSM Artists Service Bureau by 1946, booking Opry talent and other WSM acts. Denny eventually managed the Grand Ole Opry itself.

Denny, along with his predecessor, Jack Stapp, is responsible for updating the face of the Opry. As promoters and developers of talent, they helped to transform the Opry from a popular barn dance to a showcase of country superstars, ensuring its growth and long-term success. During their tenure, the cast grew enormously, most major stars became Opry members, and an Opry appearance became a must goal for many performers.

In 1954 Denny and Opry star Webb Pierce formed Cedarwood Publishing Company, for a time the most important publishing house in Nashville. Driftwood Music, a companion firm, was a partnership between Denny and Carl Smith, another Opry star. These business interests led to conflict of interest allegations by WSM and eventually Denny's dismissal.

With his knowledge of WSM operations, Denny achieved immediate success as a booking agent. The Jim Denny Bureau served most of the artists Denny had signed while at the Opry. *Billboard* magazine estimated that, by 1961, the bureau was handling over 3,300 personal appearances worldwide.

Denny died on August 27, 1963, in Nashville, leaving his sons to take over his company. He was elected to the Country Music Hall of Fame in 1966.

Anne-Leslie Owens, Tennessee Historical Society

SEE: GRAND OLE OPRY; NATIONAL LIFE AND ACCIDENT INSURANCE COMPANY; WSM

DEVELOPMENT DISTRICTS. Development Districts are regional planning and economic organizations owned and operated by the cities and counties of Tennessee. The nine Development Districts were established by the General Assembly under the Tennessee Development District Act of 1965. The Act was intended to provide the most effective and efficient means for cities and counties to organize to carry out general planning and economic development, as well as make the best use of federal, state, and other programs designed to stimulate economic development. The actual planning implementation was left to the local and state governments. In other states, Development Districts may be called regional councils, regional planning councils, or commissions, but approximately 95 percent of these multi-county regional planning agencies operate with similar structures to that of the Tennessee Districts. The First Tennessee Development District in East Tennessee was the first to form under this law.

Each Development District has a Board of Directors composed of County Executives, Mayors, the chief executive of any metropolitan government (such as Nashville/Davidson County), an industrial representative from each county, and one state senator and one state representative from each development district. Funding sources include dues paid by member governments, federal and state funded contracts, and an annual appropriation by the General Assembly.

The Development Districts have always served as neutral meeting places for diverse interests within each district. In the 1960s many federal programs required coordination between two or more local governments. Today, the Districts maintain a strong role in the coordination and communication among local governments and state and federal agencies. Local governments initially needed assistance in carrying out federal grant requirements in grant administration and accounting. Now, because the Districts are required to adopt uniform accounting systems and are bonded, the organizational structure required for many programs is already in place and administration can easily be performed.

Differences in programs and services provided by each district exist primarily in response to the differing priorities of each Board and the differences in resources in each area. Many functions have changed over the years as requirements for federal and state programs changed.

The economic development staff of each District carries out many tasks originally envisioned by state enabling legislation. These include providing assistance to local governments in applying for and administering state and federal grants for infrastructure improvements such as water, sewer, roads, rail, housing, and community livability using the Tennessee Industrial Infrastructure Program (TIIP) and Community Development Block Grant (CDBG). These programs are available through the Tennessee Department of Economic and Community Development. The districts prepare and maintain long-range plans, strategies and policies for regional development including transportation; water and wastewater infrastructure; water and air quality; solid waste management; and open space and recreation planning.

Seven of the districts serve the elderly as Area Agencies on Aging. These AAAs administer, monitor, and evaluate services to older people. State and federal funds support programs such as nutrition senior centers, home delivered meals, transportation, legal services, elder abuse programs, and the public guardianship for the elderly.

All Development Districts contract with the Tennessee Department of Housing Development (THDA) to provide housing technical assistance and data. The Districts also prepare applications for Parks and Recreation grants administered through the Department of Environment and Conservation. All Districts are official Sub-State Data Centers for U.S. Census information, serve as Regional Review Clearinghouses for Federal loans and grants, and provide technical assistance to member governments and other state coordinating agencies.

Five Development Districts are Certified Development Corporations (CDCs) through the Small Business Administration (SBA) to make 504 Small Business loans in partnership with private lending institutions. Seven Districts administer Revolving Loan Funds (RLFs) for small business loans through the Economic Development Administration with 50 percent matching funds from other state sources and the Rural Development Intermediary Relending Program (IRP). Districts also support economic development and orderly growth through promoting tourism, supporting 911 Enhanced Emergency Telephone Systems, providing transportation for special populations, and supplying technical assistance to local industries and businesses including short line railroads.

Greer Broemel, Nashville

SUGGESTED READINGS: *Tennessee Development District Association FY 1996 Annual Report* (1997); Frank S. So, Irving Hand, and Bruce D. McDowell, eds., *The Practice of State and Regional Planning* (1986)

DIBRELL, GEORGE GIBBS (1822–1888), Congressman and industrial entrepreneur, was born and raised in Sparta, Tennessee. He returned to White County after attending East Tennessee University (now University of Tennessee) in Knoxville. In 1842 he married Mary E. Leftwich, and they had eight children, one of whom went on to become a state senator. In 1848 Dibrell was elected county court clerk, a position he held until 1860. In October 1861 he became White County's Democratic representative to the 34th General Assembly, but left after the opening session to join the 25th Tennessee Infantry. He organized the White County "Partisan Rangers," which eventually joined Nathan Bedford Forrest's brigade. Dibrell became a brigade commander in 1863 and ultimately obtained the rank of Brigadier General.

After the war, Dibrell became a successful industrial entrepreneur. Owner of over 15,000 acres in White County, he established the Bon Air Coal & Coke Company, which became one of the county's leading industries and largest employers. He was also a key figure in the development of the Southwestern Railroad, which connected Sparta with the Nashville and Chattanooga line.

Dibrell resumed his political career in 1870 as a delegate to the state constitutional convention. Beginning in 1875, he repeatedly won election to the U.S. House of Representatives and served from 1875 to 1885 in the 44th through 48th Congresses. In 1886 he was one of three candidates for the Democratic gubernatorial nomination. A former Whig and secessionist, Dibrell was a conservative "redeemer" Democrat, who opposed railroad regulation and favored the interests of businessmen. Divisions within the party, however, weakened support for Dibrell, and the nomination went to Robert L. Taylor, who went on to win the race for governor.

Teresa Biddle-Douglass, Middle Tennessee State University
SEE: CIVIL WAR; MINING; WHITE COUNTY

DICKSON COUNTY, located 35 miles west of Nashville on the Western Highland Rim, was formed October 25, 1803, from the counties of Montgomery and Robertson and named for Congressman William Dickson, a Nashville physician. An industrial county from its inception, Dickson County was part of the frontier until 1818. The first court justices included several well known Tennesseans: Montgomery Bell, William Doak, William Russell, Sterling Brewer, Gabriel Allen, Lemuel Harvey, Jesse Craft, Richard C. Napier, and William Teas. They organized the county on March 19, 1804, at the home of Robert Nesbitt on Barton's Creek. Later sessions of the court met at the homes of Colonel John Nesbitt and John Spencer until the courthouse was completed in 1810.

Charlotte, the county seat and named for James Robertson's wife, was built on 50 acres purchased from Charles Stewart for $5,000. On May 30, 1830, a tornado devastated the town, destroying most of the businesses and homes, and the jail and courthouse, along with many county records. A new brick courthouse was completed in 1832 and is now the oldest courthouse in the state.

As a part of the Military Reserve, Dickson County was attractive to many settlers, who established farms along the rich bottom lands of the Cumberland, Piney, and Harpeth Rivers, as well as Jones, Turnbull, Bartons, and Yellow creeks. Although the soil and climate of Dickson County were not conducive to the production of cotton, early farmers raised the crop to take advantage of the high cotton prices. In 1807 Robert Jarman began operating his own cotton gin,

which he claimed was superior to all others due to the "hollow neck teeth saw" design. By 1860 wheat, rye, oats, corn, and tobacco had overtaken cotton in economic importance.

During the antebellum years, Dickson County was one of the leading iron producers in Tennessee. In 1796 James Robertson began manufacturing the first iron products west of Tennessee's Allegheny Mountains from his Cumberland Iron Works at Cumberland Furnace. In 1804 Robertson sold his furnace to Montgomery Bell, who became the state's wealthiest capitalist and industrialist. Other important iron manufacturers included Anthony and Bernard Van Leer and George F. and Richard C. Napier. Much of the iron production was accomplished with slave labor, and throughout the antebellum period iron makers held approximately one-fourth of the slaves in Dickson County. Although iron production declined in importance in the post-Civil War period, the furnace was still in production in the early 1940s.

Dickson County played a pivotal role in the development of the Cumberland Presbyterian Church. Influenced by the religious fervor associated with the Second Great Awakening, some members of the Presbyterian Church chafed under the Calvinist doctrines and church rules regarding ordination of ministers. On February 4, 1810, Samuel King, Finis Ewing, and Ephraim McLean met at the home of Samuel McAdow on Acorn Creek (now in Montgomery Bell State Park) to discuss the conflict. After a night of prayer, they organized the Cumberland Presbytery, the foundation of the Cumberland Presbyterian Church.

Although a school board was appointed in 1807, public education received little support during the nineteenth century. The first four-year high school was established in 1919. From the 1820s to the 1920s private secondary schools and colleges followed the fortunes of ministers and professors who moved into the county. Included among those early schools were Tracy Academy, Charlotte Female School, Alexander Campbell School, Edgewood Academy and Normal College, Dickson Academy, Dickson Normal School, Glenwylde Academy, and Ruskin Cave College.

On June 8, 1861, the county voted overwhelmingly to join the Confederacy. Dickson County supplied six infantry companies and an artillery battery to the southern cause. Yellow Creek and Cumberland Furnace were favorite rendezvous areas for guerrilla forces. No major skirmishes took place, but frequent attacks occurred along the railroad constructed by the Union army.

After the war the Nashville and Northwestern Railroad (on the NC&St.L main line), which traversed the southern portion of the county, became a magnet for immigrants from the north, who settled in the new railroad towns of Dickson (originally called Smeedville), Tennessee City, White Bluff, and Burns. With two railroad branch lines terminating in Dickson, the town became the county's railroad "hub," and by the early 1900s was the financial and commercial center of the county. The growth of Dickson produced bitter conflict with Charlotte, whose economic fortunes were in decline, over the best location for the county seat.

Among the new immigrants to Dickson County was Julius Augustus Wayland, who founded the Ruskin Cooperative Association in August 1894. The cooperative was first located at Tennessee City, but soon moved to the great cave (since named Ruskin) on Yellow Creek. Internal disagreements led to the dissolution of the colony in 1899.

Montgomery Bell State Park, the county's major recreation area, was established as a project of the National Park Service and the Civilian Conservation Corps during the New Deal. After World War II administration of the 3,782 acre park was transferred to the state. Montgomery Bell offers camping, hiking, boating, fishing, and golf to park visitors.

Frank Goad Clement, three-term governor of Tennessee, was born in Dickson at the Halbrook Hotel, which is listed in the National Register. Clement's administration in the 1950s and 1960s oversaw a pivotal time in the state's political life, as he dealt with the changes brought about by urbanization and desegregation. He drew national attention when he delivered the keynote address at the 1956 Democratic National Convention.

The old county court system, composed of magistrates from each of the civil districts, was phased out in the 1950s when the General Sessions Court was established. Presently, the county is administered by an elected county executive and two commissioners elected from each of the 12 representative districts.

The northern section of the county remains primarily rural. Modern highways and an industrial park has further urbanized southern Dickson County, with the town of Dickson the retail and industrial center. In addition to Dickson and Charlotte, other incorporated towns are Burns, White Bluff, Vanleer, and Slayden.

George E. Jackson, Dickson

SEE: BELL, MONTGOMERY; CLEMENT, FRANK G.; CUMBERLAND FURNACE; CUMBERLAND PRESBYTERIAN CHURCH; DROUILLARD, MARY FLORENCE; MCADOW, SAMUEL; MONTGOMERY BELL STATE PARK; ROBERTSON, CHARLOTTE; RUSKIN COOPERATIVE ASSOCIATION

DISASTERS. Natural and technological tragedies, as well as epidemics, have shaped the Tennessee experience. Many resulted in massive property damage and/or loss of life and immeasurable human suffering.

Storms have inflicted terrible damage in Tennessee throughout the last 200 years. Slow rise and flash floods have been the most common, recurrent disasters. The worst of the former occurred in 1926–27, 1936–37, and 1973. The great Tennessee, Cumberland, and Mississippi river floods of 1927 gave way to even greater floods in 1937. A number of flash floods have occurred, the worst on June 13, 1924, when 15 inches of rain fell in an eight-hour period. This flood produced a ten-foot-high wall of water, which plummeted down a narrow valley in Carter County, killing 11 people and injuring others. Eyewitnesses claimed that one could not stand out in that rain without strangling.

The state has averaged about six dangerous tornadoes per year since 1916, when the National Weather Service began keeping official records. Both individual and swarms of tornadoes have occurred, some with devastating results. Forty-five people were killed and 600 injured in a series of 13 East Tennessee tornadoes in April 1974. Six twisters killed 52 and injured 552 in six counties in March 1933. Called the East Nashville Tornado, this incident damaged or demolished 1,600 structures in that area alone. The worst ever was in March 1952, when 67 people died and 282 were injured as ten twisters touched down in ten counties. Damages exceeded $5.5 million.

Extremes in heat and cold also have affected Tennesseans. Records indicate that 16 episodes of severe drought have occurred in the past 200 years. The worst was the decade of the 1980s, the driest overall period in our state's history. A severe heat wave in 1980 took 150 lives when temperatures hovered in the hundreds for days at a time. Most victims were elderly, urban, West Tennessee residents. In other years came record frigid temperatures, snow and ice. In the twentieth century, challenging blizzard seasons happened in 1945, 1951, and 1993. The landmark winters of the nineteenth century were in 1835 and 1898. February 5, 1835, was called "Cold Friday" because many cattle and hogs froze to death that day.

The worst series of earthquakes to occur in North America took place in West Tennessee and the Central Mississippi River Valley in 1811 and 1812. Seasonal wild fires have been destructive, especially during periods of drought. Some of the worst were recorded in 1925, 1935, and the 1980s. These fires, usually caused by lightning strikes, have destroyed incalculable acres of cropland as well as wildlife, domestic livestock, homes, businesses, and other structures.

Man-made technological disasters have devastated different Tennessee communities through the twentieth century. Several dam or reservoir failures have occurred. The worst such incident was in Claiborne County, two miles south of New Tazewell, on August 3, 1916. A mill dam failed on Big Barren

Creek, sending a giant wall of water downstream and breaching several other smaller dams in the process. Twenty-four people died amidst the immense property damage caused by the roaring water.

Explosions of dangerous materials have made their mark in the pages of history. In 1906 a railroad car of dynamite exploded in a rail yard at Jellico in Campbell County, killing nine people, injuring 200, and leaving 500 homeless. In 1978 the Humphreys County town of Waverly was the site of a devastating liquid propane gas explosion that killed 16 people and injured 97. In 1983 an explosion at an illegal fire works factory, near Benton in Polk County, killed 11 workers, injured one, and demolished several buildings. Five years later, in December 1988, a liquid propane gas truck overturned and exploded in a gigantic fire ball on I-240 in Memphis. Nine people were killed on the highway, and additional lives were lost when the flaming 10,000 gallon liquid propane tank became airborne and crashed into a nearby duplex, setting several buildings on fire.

Eleven horrific mine disasters have occurred in Tennessee, all but one within the last 100 years. Eighty-four out of a crew of 89 perished in an explosion and flash fire in Cross Mountain Coal Mine No. 1, near Briceville (Anderson County) in 1911. Just nine years before that, the worst coal mine accident in Tennessee history took place at the nearby Fraterville Mine, where 184 lives were lost.

The state's worst urban fire disaster was the great East Nashville Fire of 1916. Pushed by dry, westerly, 50 mph winds, it destroyed 700 homes and businesses within a 32-square-block area of that city. A so-called "million dollar" fire occurred in Knoxville in 1897. It destroyed several warehouses and large retail stores along a section of lower Gay Street. Fire fighters came by train from as far away as Chattanooga to fight the blazes. Many individual structural fires have also occurred across the state. One was the Columbia (Maury County) jail fire that trapped and killed 42 inmates and visitors in 1977. During a fire fighters's strike in 1978, 255 fires broke out almost simultaneously around Memphis. According to officials, this was either a rash of arson fires or a most extraordinary case of coincidence. Most incidents occurred in abandoned or condemned buildings. On Christmas Eve in 1989, 16 people died, 50 were injured, and 145 were left homeless by a fire at the high-rise retirement home in Johnson City.

Tennessee's worst boat accidents date to the nineteenth century, the heyday of inland marine commerce. The worst such wreck in United States history occurred in 1865, eight miles north of Memphis, on the Mississippi River, when the *Sultana* river boat exploded and burned to the water line, claiming over an estimated 2,000 lives.

A number of railroad accidents have taken place across the state. The New Market wreck in Jefferson County killed 63 and injured another 100 on September 24, 1904. The worst passenger railroad accident occurred near Nashville in 1918, when 101 people died in the Dutchman's Grade railroad accident.

Commercial airline accidents have also occurred in Tennessee. On July 9, 1984, a United Airlines passenger plane crashed near Newport, Cocke County, killing 39. Ten died in a crash near Tri-Cities Airport in 1959, and two incidents in Memphis, in 1947 and 1944, killed 20 and 21 respectively. A 1932 crash in Smith County caused 5 deaths, and a crash near Oliver Springs a year earlier took the lives of 11.

The single worst automobile accident occurred when 12 people were killed and 50 injured in a fog-related, 99-vehicle chain reaction pileup on I-75 near the Hiwassee River bridge in 1990.

Epidemics were great killers in the 1700s and 1800s. The worst culprits were smallpox, polio, influenza, measles, cholera, and yellow fever. There have been seven great epidemics of cholera and eight of yellow fever in Tennessee history. The last great yellow fever episode occurred in 1878. Smallpox and measles epidemics were particularly devastating to Native Americans, who had no natural immunity to the diseases brought to the New World by European, African, and Asian immigrants. Almost half of the Cherokee population of Tennessee is believed to have been annihilated by intentional introduction of smallpox in blankets and other trade goods in 1738. At the end of World War I, a killer Spanish flu pandemic (a world-wide epidemic) struck Tennessee, killing over 7,700 people. Not since the Great Plague (Black Death) of the Middle Ages had such a disease killed so many so quickly.

Allen R. Coggins, Knoxville

SEE: DUTCHMAN'S GRADE RAILWAY ACCIDENT; EARTHQUAKES; FLOOD, 1936–37; REELFOOT LAKE STATE PARK; SULTANA DISASTER OF 1865; YELLOW FEVER EPIDEMICS

DISCIPLES OF CHRIST. The Christian Church (Disciples of Christ) came into being in 1832 in Lexington, Kentucky, with the union of Barton Stone's Christians and Alexander Campbell's reformers. The uniting groups shared the catholic vision of restoring unity based on the authority of Scripture to the divided church.

Both Campbell's reformers and Stone's Christians had established congregations in Tennessee before the Lexington unity event. In 1796, as a young Presbyterian minister, Barton Stone made his way from North Carolina to Kentucky by preaching his way across Tennessee. In 1801 he was host pastor to the great Cane Ridge, Kentucky, communion that launched his movement toward unity, "our polar star." He then left the Presbyterian church. In 1810 he moved to Tennessee, where he lived until 1814. Ministering as an itinerant evangelist, he established the first Christian congregation at Hopewell, Sumner County, in 1811. By the time of the 1832 union with Campbell's followers, there were approximately 25 congregations and 2,000 members in Tennessee.

Campbell's reformers came to Tennessee in the person of Philip S. Fall. This young English immigrant was a Reformed Baptist, converted by Campbell's teachings. Fall moved from Louisville, Kentucky, in 1826, and began work in Nashville as a preacher and teacher. In two ministries in Nashville, he developed his congregation (today's Vine Street Christian Church) into the largest church among Campbell's followers. The membership was almost evenly divided between blacks and whites.

At the time Tennessee celebrated its bicentennial in 1996, it was the home of 67 Disciples congregations with 23,350 members. The Disciples's largest North American congregation is located in Memphis: the 9,000-member Mississippi Boulevard Christian Church, an African-American congregation. The Disciples Divinity House at Vanderbilt University, Nashville, is one of the Disciples centers for education of ministers. The Disciples of Christ Historical Society of Nashville is the world-wide archival center of the Stone-Campbell Movement, which now encompasses three denominations.

Peter Morgan, Nashville

SEE: CAMPBELL, ALEXANDER; STONE, BARTON W.; VANDERBILT UNIVERSITY

DISFRANCHISING LAWS. In 1889 the Tennessee General Assembly passed four acts of self-described electoral reform that resulted in the disfranchisement of a significant portion of African-American voters as well as many poor white voters. The timing of the legislation resulted from a unique opportunity seized by the Democratic Party to bring an end to what one historian described as the most "consistently competitive political system in the South."[1] In the political campaign of 1888, the Democrats waged a battle unparalleled in corruption and violence to gain quorum control over both houses of the legislature. With Republicans unable to stall or defeat anti-party measures, the disfranchising acts sailed through the 1889 General Assembly, and Governor Robert L. Taylor signed them into law. Hailed by newspaper editors as the end of black voting, the laws worked as expected, and African-American voting declined precipitously in rural and small town Tennessee. Many urban blacks continued to vote until so-called progressive reforms eliminated their political power in the early twentieth century.

The disfranchising acts included the Myers Law, Lea Law, Dortch Law, and the imposition of a poll tax. The Myers Law, named for Bedford County Representative Thomas R. Myers, required voters in districts or towns that cast more than 500 votes in 1888 to register at least 20 days before every election. The Dortch Law, named for Representative Josiah H. Dortch, provided for the implementation of a secret ballot. Initially the Dortch Law, which applied to 78 civil districts in 37 counties, permitted voters to obtain assistance in marking their ballots if they voted in 1857. It disfranchised black illiterate voters, while initially protecting older white illiterates. The Lea Law, named for Benjamin J. Lea, provided for separate ballot boxes for state and federal elections. It was intended to circumvent expected congressional legislation (Lodge Election Bill) to supervise federal elections. When Congress failed to pass the Lodge Bill, the Tennessee State Legislature rescinded the Lea Act in 1893. The final act of disfranchisement came with the implementation of the poll tax. The Tennessee State Constitution of 1870 provided for a poll tax at the discretion of the General Assembly, with revenues to be used for the common school fund. At the time, critics like former President Andrew Johnson had recognized the potential harm inherent in the poll tax and vehemently protested it as a method to disfranchise the poor. Nevertheless, the provision remained in the constitution, and the 1889 legislature implemented the tax. Payment was required to vote, but no county officer came to collect the tax. Taxpayers could choose not to pay and suffered no penalty except giving up the right to vote in that year's election. Unlike some states, Tennessee's poll tax was not cumulative; payment of a single year's tax permitted one to vote in that year.

Support for the new laws came from Democrats and members of the Farmers' Alliance. Later, as Alliancemen moved into the People's party, they recognized the devastating effect the laws also had on poor whites and vowed to overturn them if elected. Yet, successive legislatures expanded the reach of the disfranchising laws until they covered the state. In 1949 political scientist V. O. Key, Jr., argued that the size of the poll tax did not inhibit voting as much as the inconvenience of paying it. County officers regulated the vote by providing opportunities to pay the tax (as they did in Knoxville), or conversely by making payment as difficult as possible. Such manipulation of the tax, and therefore the vote, created an opportunity for the rise of urban bosses and political machines. Urban politicians bought large blocks of poll tax receipts and distributed them to blacks and whites, who voted as instructed.

The poll tax vexed would-be reformers and stifled change. In the 1930s and 1940s, the Tennessee Press Association led the fight to repeal the poll tax. In 1941 the Shelby County delegation, under the influence of Edward H. Crump, successfully fought back

a legislative attempt to repeal the poll tax. Two years later, the legislators rescinded the tax, only to have their action declared unconstitutional by the Tennessee Supreme Court. Provisions for the poll tax were removed by the 1953 constitutional convention.
Connie L. Lester, Tennessee Historical Society
CITATION:
(1) J. Morgan Kousser, *The Shaping of Southern Politics: Suffrage Restriction and the Establishment of the One-Party South, 1880–1910* (New Haven, 1974), 104.
SUGGESTED READINGS: Dewey W. Grantham, "Tennessee and Twentieth-Century American Politics," *Tennessee Historical Quarterly* 53(1996): 210–12; Jennings Perry, *Democracy Begins at Home* (1944)
SEE: CRUMP, EDWARD H.; FARMERS' ALLIANCE; GOVERNMENT; TAYLOR, ROBERT L.

DISTILLERIES, HISTORIC. Tennessee's natural limestone springs, ample timber, and fertile soil for growing grain made the state an ideal location for whiskey production. Whiskey was an important part of frontier life as both an easily portable diet staple and a medicinal drug. Distilling began as an additional activity on many farms and grew to a major industry in Tennessee by the middle of the nineteenth century. Jack Daniel and George Dickel, the best-known Tennessee distilleries, have long histories. Some of the earliest distilleries in the state, however, were established in Robertson County.

Distilleries in Robertson County date back to the early 1790s when settlers Thomas Woodard and Arthur Pitt established small stills on their property. Their sons continued the process and developed whiskey production into a prosperous business. Wiley Woodard inherited his father's farm and distillery in 1836 and doubled his whiskey sales by 1841. Soon he was shipping large quantities of whiskey throughout Tennessee and other southern states. Wilson Pitt, Arthur's son, experienced similar success. As the whiskey industry soared, competition increased. Charles Nelson's distillery in Greenbriar became Woodward and Pitt's largest competitor, producing over 8,000 barrels of whiskey per year. Business began to decline in the 1880s, as tobacco surpassed whiskey in production, and anti-whiskey pressure rose from temperance groups. State and then national Prohibition stopped the production of whiskey altogether, and the industry never resurfaced in Robertson County. Several extant buildings of the Pitt Distillery are listed in the National Register of Historic Places.

Jasper "Jack" Newton Daniel, born in 1848 near Lynchburg in Moore County, began working at a local distillery at age 12 and became a full partner with its owner, Dan Call, at age 15. In 1866 Daniel bought Call's interest in the business and established a distillery on 500 acres near his birthplace. Daniel's

business prospered, and his product won national acclaim by taking a gold medal at the 1904 Louisiana Purchase Exposition in St. Louis. Although he never married, Daniel kept his business in the family by transferring it to his nephew Lem Motlow four years before his death in 1911. Motlow moved the business to St. Louis in 1910, after prohibition was enacted in Tennessee. Following the repeal of national prohibition, Motlow campaigned to reestablish the distillery in Moore County, which had chosen to remain "dry." In 1938 county citizens voted in a close race to allow the company to manufacture whiskey in Lynchburg. The Jack Daniel Distillery has remained in Lynchburg and is now one of the nation's oldest leading distilleries; it is listed in the National Register of Historic Places.

Another leading distillery is that of George A. Dickel & Co. in Tullahoma, Tennessee. In the late 1860s successful Nashville merchant George A. Dickel formed a partnership with the Schwab and Davis families of Nashville and and began to market whiskey, which they obtained from several regional sources. The most popular brand was a whisky from a distillery along Cascade Creek in Coffee County. An astute businessman, Dickel had become familiar with Nashvillians' taste in whiskey and developed a popular recipe. After his death in 1894, Dickel's wife, Augusta, and his partners managed the business. During Prohibition, the company moved to Louisville and continued to produce its product under a medicinal license. In a situation similar to that of the Jack Daniel Distillery, Dickel's original home of Coffee County remained "dry" after the repeal of Prohibition, necessitating a special referendum to approve the manufacture of whiskey locally. Approval came in 1958, and George Dickel whiskey is still manufactured at a distillery outside of Tullahoma.
Teresa Biddle-Douglass, Middle Tennessee State University
SEE: GEORGE DICKEL DISTILLERY; JACK DANIEL DISTILLERY; MOORE COUNTY; ROBERTSON COUNTY

DIXIE HIGHWAY ASSOCIATION. Constructed between 1915 and 1927, the Dixie Highway was part of the new road system built in response to the growing number of motorists in the early decades of the twentieth century. When completed, the highway extended from Ontario, Canada, south 5,706 miles to Miami, Florida. The Dixie Highway Association provided the driving force behind the development of the highway. Motor enthusiasts and/or entrepreneurs formed the Dixie Highway Association and similar groups to promote the construction of roads that would connect cities to each other. The idea for the Dixie Highway came from Carl G. Fisher, an Indiana entrepreneur and land speculator. By 1914 Fisher and Michigan businessman W. S. Gilbreath had gained enough support for this north-south highway to bring the idea to the annual meeting of the American Road Congress in Atlanta.

Governor Tom C. Rye of Tennessee and Indiana Governor Ralston called an organizational meeting of the Dixie Highway Association for April 3, 1915, in Chattanooga. Over 5,000 people attended this first meeting, including governors from Indiana, Illinois, Ohio, Kentucky, Tennessee, Georgia, and Florida.

The Chattanooga Automobile Club, newly formed in 1914, was an enthusiastic supporter of the project and remained closely allied with the Dixie Highway Association throughout its history. Five local members of the Chattanooga Automobile Club and eight other men pledged $1,000 each for the formation of the Dixie Highway Association.

The purpose of the Dixie Highway Association was to build a permanent highway from a point on the Lincoln Highway near Chicago through Chattanooga to Miami, with an eventual extension north to Ontario, Canada. Both the eastern and western divisions of the highway passed through Tennessee. The western route headed south from Springfield through Nashville, Murfreesboro, Shelbyville, Tullahoma, Winchester, Cowan, and Monteagle to Chattanooga. The eastern division went south from Cumberland Gap through Knoxville, Rockwood, and Dayton to Chattanooga.

The Dixie Highway Association headquarters were located in the Patten Hotel in Chattanooga, roughly the halfway point of the highway, and the incorporators, who were delegated to create a charter for the association, all came from Chattanooga. These prominent businessmen emerged as the biggest proponents of the highway in Tennessee. Chattanooga Judge Michael M. Allison was elected to serve as president of the Dixie Highway Association, after C. E. James, a Chattanooga builder, declined to serve. Allison remained an extremely active president throughout the life of the Dixie Highway Association until it disbanded in 1927. *The Dixie Highway* magazine was published in Chattanooga and prominently featured the city and region in articles and advertisements. Monteagle Mountain in Marion County was the last highway link to be completed, creating national concern because of its crucial location on the road.

Leslie N. Sharp, Historic Preservation Division, Georgia Department of Natural Resources

SUGGESTED READINGS: Howard L. Preston, *Dirt Roads to Dixie: Accessibility and Modernization in the South, 1885–1935* (1991); Leslie N. Sharp, "Down South to Dixie: The Development of the Dixie Highway from Nashville to Chattanooga, 1915–1940," (M.A. Thesis, MTSU, 1993)

SEE: CHATTANOOGA; HIGHWAYS, HISTORIC

DIXIE SPINNING MILLS. At the turn of the century, Chattanooga emerged as a textile manufacturing center, particularly for cotton hosiery. The 1913 introduction of the process of mercerizing, which gives yarn a fine silk finish, enhanced local industry and generated a new corporation, Dixie Mercerizing Company, controlled by local capitalist John T. Lupton. In 1922, this company's success led to the establishment of Dixie Spinning Mills to supply yarn. Situated on 1,000 acres north of the Tennessee River at a company town known as "Lupton City," outside of Chattanooga, the spinning mill began production in 1923 with 12,000 spindles; within two years, 30,000 spindles were in operation.

In order to secure and maintain a sufficient labor force, Dixie Spinning Mills built housing for its workers near the factory, a common practice among many New South textile firms. By 1929 Lupton City's first 60 houses had grown to 200. For one dollar per room per week, the employees received houses equipped with such modern conveniences as electricity and indoor plumbing. The village had concrete sidewalks, a school, post office, church, and general store. As the number of employees grew, the company eventually added recreational facilities, including a gym, movie theater, and swimming pool. A company doctor and dentist also provided services to the workers.

Dixie Mills drew its work force from the surrounding farms, and many farmers abandoned the vicissitudes of agriculture for steady factory wages of $10 to $14 a week. The work week was five and a half days long, at 12.5 hours per day for men and 10.5 hours per day for women. Financially strapped workers obtained credit from the company in the form of credit scrips, or tokens, redeemable at the company store. Workers' lives revolved around the mills, which not only paid their wages, but controlled housing, material needs, and social activities within the "model" mill village of Lupton City.

With the increasing availability of reliable transportation after World War II, workers took advantage of opportunities to live and shop elsewhere. In the 1950s Dixie closed the company store and sold all but two of its mill houses, with workers receiving first option for purchase. At the time of the sale, less than 50 percent of Dixie workers lived in Lupton City housing. Dixie Yarns still operated its Lupton City plant during the mid-1990s. Many retirees reside in the previously company-owned houses of Lupton City. Together, the mill and the village incorporate economic and social developments characteristic of the industrial transformation of Chattanooga and Hamilton County.

Teresa Biddle-Douglas, Middle Tennessee State University

SUGGESTED READING: Marirose Arendale, "Lupton City: Chattanooga's Model Mill Village," *Tennessee Historical Quarterly* 43(1984): 68–78

SEE: BEMIS; CHATTANOOGA; LUPTON, JOHN T.

DIXON GALLERY AND GARDENS, with its paintings by Impressionist and Post-Impressionist artists such as Renoir, Degas, Cezanne, and Monet, its collection of eighteenth century porcelain, and its stunning gardens, has long been one of Memphis's key attractions. With the recent acquisition of the $15 million Montgomery H. W. Ritchie Family Collection, which includes a number of Post-Impressionist works, the Dixon truly is one of Tennessee's finest museums. In addition to the museum's own holdings, special exhibitions regularly present art from outstanding public and private collections.

The history of the Dixon began with Margaret Oates Dixon (1900–1974) and Hugo Norton Dixon (1892–1974), philanthropists and community leaders, who bequeathed their home, gardens, and art collection for the enjoyment and education of future generations. Their gift enriched the cultural life of Memphis residents and visitors.

Hugo and Margaret Dixon spent nearly 35 years creating their exquisite estate in East Memphis. Their home, one of three in Memphis designed by architect John Staub, was completed in 1941. The imposing house—with its hipped roof, windows, and doors—is in the Georgian Revival style, while both the front and back porticoes are reminiscent of classical designs by the nineteenth century American architect Robert Mills.

The gardens were conceived as an integral part of the overall design of the estate and reflect the Dixons's taste, their visits to gardens throughout Europe and the United States, and their lifestyle and appreciation of nature. Carefully carved out of 17 acres of native Tennessee woodlands, the gardens were landscaped in the manner of an English park with open vistas and intimate formal gardens. Blooming dogwood trees and colorful azaleas give a fairyland quality to the gardens during the spring.

The Dixons began purchasing art in the mid-1940s and continued to collect throughout their lifetimes, amassing their collection with great care. By narrowing the focus of the collection to French and American Impressionism, Post-Impressionism, and related schools, they created a collection that was moderate in size but high in quality.

The residence first opened to the public as a museum in 1976. The following year, a wing was added to house a growing fine and decorative arts collection. A second addition in 1986 more than doubled the size of the complex, adding an auditorium, a large special exhibition gallery, a series of smaller galleries, a museum shop, and service areas. A cutting garden, greenhouses, and new horticultural complex facilities were completed in 1998.

Today, in accord with the Dixons' interests, the Dixon Gallery and Gardens continues to seek significant works by artists who exhibited in Paris at one of the eight Impressionists exhibitions between 1874 and 1886, as well as works by other artists of the period—both Impressionists and Realists—including American Impressionists and American expatriates working in France. The decorative arts collections consists of the Warda Stevens Stout Collection of eighteenth century German porcelain, one of the finest in the United States. The gallery also houses the Adler Pewter Collection, comprised of over 600 pieces.

Prepared by staff of the Dixon Gallery and Gardens
SEE: ART

DOAK, SAMUEL (1749–1830), minister and pioneer, founded the earliest schools and many of the Presbyterian churches of East Tennessee. The son of Irish immigrants, Doak was born August 1, 1749, in Augusta County, Virginia. He grew up on a frontier farm and began his education with Robert Alexander, who later founded the Academy of Liberty Hall (now Washington and Lee University). After attending an academy in Maryland, he entered the College of New Jersey (now Princeton), from which he graduated two years later in 1775

Doak married Esther Houston Montgomery of Augusta County in October 1775, and taught at Hampden-Sydney College in the spring of 1776. There he studied theology under Samuel Stanhope Smith, president, and completed his theological training in 1777 at Liberty Hall. He assumed his first pastorate in Abingdon, Virginia, and also began to "ride circuit" in eastern Tennessee. In 1778 he settled in Sullivan County, Tennessee, and was ordained a minister. In 1780 he moved to Washington County, Tennessee, where he formed Salem Church and a school, which was chartered as St. Martin's Academy in 1783, the first chartered school in the region. In 1795 it became Washington College.

Doak's best-known sermon was probably the one delivered at Sycamore Shoals in 1780 as the "Overmountain Men" assembled on their way to defeat British Colonel Patrick Ferguson and his troops at the Battle of King's Mountain. In 1784 he was a delegate to the convention that formed the short-lived State of Franklin.

Doak served as president of Washington College (1795–1818) before turning it over to his oldest son, John Whitfield Doak. Esther Doak had died in 1807 and in 1818 he moved with his second wife, Margaretta Houston McEwen, to Tusculum Academy (later Tusculum College) and taught there with his son Samuel W. Doak until his death on December 12, 1830. He is buried at Salem Church.

E. Alvin Gerhardt, Jr., Tusculum College
SEE: EDUCATION; RELIGION; FRANKLIN, STATE OF;
SYCAMORE SHOALS STATE HISTORICAL AREA; TUSCULUM
COLLEGE; WASHINGTON COUNTY

DOCKERY, ISAAC (1832–1910), African-American brickmason and builder, was born a freeman in the Jones Cove community of Sevier County. Dockery moved to Sevierville before the Civil War, where he worked as a merchant clerk in the home of Henry M. Thomas. During the war, Confederate soldiers captured Dockery and dragged him through the streets of Sevierville because he refused to reveal the hiding place of Thomas's grandson, McKendree Porter Thomas (1835–1913), a colonel in the Union army. After the war, Dockery married Charlotte Thomas (1838–1913), who had been one of Thomas's slaves.

In the late 1860s Dockery built a brick kiln near Middle Creek outside Sevierville and established a brick masonry business. Dockery inscribed his initials, "I D," and sometimes a date, on his bricks as a trademark. A master brick mason, Dockery taught his craft to his sons, his sons-in-law, and his grandsons.

Dockery made the bricks for several notable Sevierville landmarks, including the Murphy College building (1891), Sevierville Masonic Lodge (1893), and the Sevier County Courthouse (1896). He also built at least two commercial buildings on the original public square, which were destroyed in a 1900 fire. The New Salem Baptist Church, which he built in 1886 for the local black community, remains his most significant building. This handsome Gothic Revival-style church was originally constructed as a Union Church, which welcomed all religious denominations. The New Salem Baptist Church is the oldest remaining building in Sevierville and the second oldest church building in the county.

Several members of Dockery's family also became well-known brick masons in Sevier County, including Paris Witt McMahan, George and Stewart Burden, Bill Coleman, and Fred McMahan, who established the J, F & N McMahan Construction Company. Dockery died in 1910 at his son's home in Knoxville. He was buried in the Public Cemetery for African Americans near Sevierville.
Robbie D. Jones, Nashville
SEE: DECORATIVE ARTS, AFRICAN-AMERICAN; SEVIER COUNTY

DODGE, JOHN WOOD, (1807–1893), portraitist and photographer, was born in New York City, the son of a goldsmith and watchmaker and his Canadian-born wife. Dodge was apprenticed to a sign painter, where he began to copy, then paint original miniatures. When his apprenticeship ended, he rented a studio. During the winter of 1826–27, he studied at the National Academy of Design. He exhibited there from 1830 to 1838, and was elected an associate member in 1832. His exhibition piece was a portrait of his cousin, Mary Louise Dodge, whom he had married on December 13, 1831.

Dodge's account book begins in 1828. His standard price for a miniature was $11.50. By 1831 it was $25, and a few years later, with increasing fame, reached $75. In 1838 he left for the South, primarily for health reasons, but also to find an area with fewer competitors. For the next two years, he spent most of the winters in Huntsville, Alabama. In May 1840 he arrived in Nashville, where he worked until 1861. He also made frequent trips to other southern cities to paint and exhibit his work.

In 1842 and 1843 Dodge did life portraits of Andrew Jackson and Henry Clay. The pictures enjoyed an extensive sale in print form. In 1845 he bought a large orchard in Pomona, Tennessee. In order to pay for it, Dodge executed a series of large dioramas, which he exhibited with illumination at Nashville, Memphis, New Orleans, Louisville, New York, and Hartford. After 1850, Dodge spent more time at his "fruit ranch" in Pomona, and worked in Nashville during the winters. Increasingly, photography impaired his business, and tinting photographs became an important part of his operation.

A Unionist, Dodge left Tennessee in 1861, and arrived in New York destitute. He did an ink drawing of George Washington, which he intended as a correction of Gilbert Stuart's standard image; it sold reasonably well. In May 1865 he had a sitting from President Andrew Johnson, and the resulting portrait sold well in photographic form.

About 1869 Dodge moved to Chicago, where he produced mostly photographs, large oil portraits, and still lifes. In 1874–75 he was vice president of the local academy. In 1889 he returned to Pomona, where he worked in various media until shortly before his death of pneumonia on December 15, 1893, at age 86.
James C. Kelly, Virginia Historical Society
SEE: ART; CUMBERLAND COUNTY

DOLLYWOOD is a theme park which Tennessee singer-songwriter Dolly Parton founded in Pigeon Forge to enhance the economy of her native Sevier County. As the jaunty pun of the name implies, Dollywood involves endless layerings and juxtapositions of traditional mountain culture and glitzy commercial appeal, which are the twin hearts of Parton's own public persona. Dollywood is as purringly profit-oriented as any successful American theme park, the business of which is to conflate having fun with spending money, but it has an emotional core like no other. All involved in the enterprise understand what Dollywood has done for local prosperity, and even the most urbane of the park's components are suffused with the Tennessee hillbilly's point of view. Glittering Dollywood Boulevard, touted as a tribute to classic movies and film stars, also touchingly expresses what movies meant to people living in isolated Appalachia. While the hillbilly mystique is present and even celebrated in attractions as diverse as old-time soap-making and high-tech simulations of the white lightening chase in *Thunder Road*, depictions of the gullible hillbilly and his suspicious gun-toting cousin are emphatically excluded.

Theme parks in general owe their success to the desire of a vacationing public to travel to a new place and encounter something of its distinctive character without fear that geographic and cultural dislocation will force them into threatening or disorienting situations. That is the role of the themes—promotions of a place, a past, a commodity, or a fantasy which make even the most dense and colorful profusion of attractions seem cohesive and accessible. One reason Dollywood is now among the 25 most visited parks in America is because it offers safe, controlled proximity to a southern hillbilly culture which has simultaneously intrigued and alienated Americans for over a century.

Dollywood's origins devolve from late nineteenth and early twentieth century industrial exploitation of the mountain South. In 1961 the Robbins family rebuilt a narrow-gauge railway and locomotive which a logging company had abandoned after the federal government established the Great Smoky Mountains National Park. Adding passenger cars to the train and a general store, saloon, and blacksmith shop to its point of departure and arrival, the Robbinses established Rebel Railroad. The special appeal of each train ride was the "possibility" that Federal troops might spring from the underbrush, board the train, and steal a strongbox full of Confederate money. Promotions encouraged children to bring weapons and help fight off marauding Yankees.

Investment-minded managers of the Cleveland Browns bought this languishing business in 1970 and refashioned it into Goldrush Junction, an amusement park with an Old West theme which featured, in addition to the train and its existing accoutrements, a woodworking shop, sawmill, outdoor theater, and log cabins. Seven years later Herschend Enterprises bought the facility and renamed it Silver Dollar City. The park now emphasized old-time southern means of production, in support of which the new owners built and staffed a water-driven gristmill and a carriage-making shop. Other craft workshops followed. By 1980 the popularity of this handicraft theme was faltering, so the owners added amusement rides with dangerous-sounding names like Tennessee Twister, Blazing Fury, and Flooded Mine.

In the early 1980s, Dolly Parton began to consider establishing her own theme park in Pigeon Forge. By 1985 she had arranged a partnership with the Herschends and reached an agreement that she could invest several million dollars to enlarge, elaborate, and rename Silver Dollar City. Parton maintained the

facility's decades-long strategy of accretion as well as reinvention; all existing operations remained in place, although most received refurbishings and new names—the old Rebel Railroad, for example, became the Dollywood Express. Nevertheless, park planners reorganized the site into zones with contrasting designations and themes. They also added an entirely new complex of shops and amusements focused around a whitewater ride called Smoky Mountain Rampage and the Back Porch Theater, where Parton's relatives performed in regular musical shows. These improvements, in addition to a more scrubbed-up, service-oriented style of visitor reception, required Silver Dollar City's 300 employees to make room for 500 more by the date of Dollywood's 1986 grand opening.

Almost every year since, Dollywood has expanded to encompass a new zone of amusement with a distinctive name and theme shared in some way by its entire constellation of novel attractions. The park now encompasses 125 acres and welcomes well over two million visitors each year. In combination with the tourist attractions, restaurants, and motels which have sprouted beyond its gates, Dollywood also makes Pigeon Forge the most formidable source of revenues in Sevier County.

Parton's music and her spirit pervade Dollywood, but she is explicitly present in three locations: the Rags to Riches Museum contains chronologically arranged memorabilia from different phases of her life; the replica of her two-room childhood home offers visitors an impossibly tidy and charming depiction of the Partons' life on Locust Ridge; and the Heartsongs multi-media show romantically evokes the origins of her music in the natural beauty of the mountains. Parton has cheerfully acknowledged the artifice in these and many other park presentations, but her particular conviction about memory—that good ones should be treasured and bad ones forgotten—subtly justifies the relentlessly positive tone and commercial polish of a park where so many of the diversions play off the traditional lifeways of a people whose lot involved exhausting work and few material rewards. A similar resolution is implicit in the park's mission statement: "Create Memories Worth Repeating." The implication is that an energetic and consumption-oriented experience shared with family or friends can instantly generate joyous and relivable memories, minus the monotony, adversity, and loss which are the inevitable context of everyone's remembered happiness. If, however, such a thing were indeed possible, it would happen at Dollywood.

Camille Wells, University of Virginia

SEE: PARTON, DOLLY; SEVIER COUNTY

DONELSON, ANDREW JACKSON (1799–1871), son of Samuel and Mary Donelson, was a soldier, lawyer, politician, and diplomat. After Samuel's death circa 1804, and Mary's remarriage, Andrew was reared at the Hermitage, home of his aunt, Rachel Donelson Jackson, and his namesake Andrew Jackson. He graduated from West Point, second in his class, and served as General Jackson's aide-de-camp during the Seminole campaign. After this conflict, he resigned from the army and studied law at Transylvania University in Lexington, Kentucky.

In 1823 Donelson returned to Nashville to practice law, and within the year married his first cousin, Emily Tennessee Donelson. He inherited his father's property adjacent to the Hermitage, and the Donelsons had their home, Tulip Grove, constructed while they were in Washington with President Jackson during most of his two terms. Donelson served as the President's private secretary, and Emily acted as the official hostess of the White House. Emily died of tuberculosis in 1836, shortly after Tulip Grove was completed, leaving four small children. Donelson remarried five years later, and had eight more children with his second wife, Elizabeth Martin Randolph.

After Donelson's return to Nashville, he was appointed by President John Tyler to negotiate the annexation of Texas. His success in this undertaking led to his appointment as minister to Prussia from 1846 to 1849. In 1851 he became editor of the *Washington Union,* but left this position as the Democratic party moved toward sectionalism.

Andrew Jackson Donelson ran for vice-president on the Millard Fillmore ticket with the support of the Know-Nothing party in 1856. Their loss ended his political career. He sold Tulip Grove and moved his family and his law practice to Memphis in 1858, and refused to participate in the politics of the Civil War.
Heather Fearnbach, Middle Tennessee State University
SEE: HERMITAGE; JACKSON, ANDREW; JACKSON, RACHEL DONELSON

DONELSON, JOHN (ca. 1718–1785), land speculator and early settler of Middle Tennessee, led over 100 settlers on a tortuous water journey to the Cumberland Settlements during the winter of 1779–1780. Donelson was one of the earliest settlers of Pittsylvania County, Virginia, although the date of his arrival in Virginia is not known. His father and grandfather were involved in planting, commerce, and shipping. An educated man for his time, Donelson was the surveyor for Pittsylvania County from 1767 to 1779. He was a member of the House of Burgesses from 1769 to 1774. In 1771 he was appointed to survey the state line, revealing that three settlements thought to be in Virginia were actually within the boundaries of North Carolina. In 1775 he became county lieutenant, with rank of colonel, and served in campaigns against the Overhill Cherokees. As a result of Donelson's survey of the Cherokee line, he acquired a large

land claim west of that line, and attended the Cherokee treaty signing at Fort Patrick Henry, near the Long Island of the Holston, in 1777.

Richard Henderson selected Donelson and James Robertson to lead settlers into this Cumberland River region. Roberston made plans for an overland voyage while Donelson led another group along a water route. Donelson and approximately 30 families embarked from Fort Patrick Henry on December 22, 1779. Their boat, the *Adventure,* accommodated several families, household goods, and supplies necessary to sustain a settlement in a new land. At the mouth of the Clinch River, another group of emigrants joined Donelson's party. He led this flotilla of 30 or so canoes, flat boats, and dugouts on an expedition traversing the Holston, Tennessee, Ohio, and Cumberland rivers.

The fleet carried a large number of women and children. Donelson's own large family, including his wife Rachel Stockley, their children, and approximately 30 African-American slaves, were among the emigrants. One of Donelson's children was his 13-year-old daughter, Rachel, who would become the wife of Andrew Jackson. Others in the party included James Robertson's wife, Charlotte, and five of their 11 children.

Donelson kept an account of his historic journey and of the hardships they endured. On December 22, he made his first entry in his "Journal of a Voyage, intended by God's permission, in the good boat *Adventure,* from Fort Patrick Henry, on Holston river to the French Salt Springs on Cumberland River."[1] During the four-month voyage, the hardy pioneers suffered Indian attacks, a smallpox outbreak, hunger, exhaustion, extreme cold, swift currents, and treacherous shoals.

On April 24, 1780, Donelson's party reached the end of their thousand mile journey and were finally reunited with family and friends at the Big Salt Lick (now Nashville). Within a week of Donelson's arrival, Henderson prepared the Cumberland Compact, of which Donelson was the fifth signer.

Donelson, his family, and slaves made camp at a tract of land along the rich river bottom of Stones River. He named this site Clover Bottom and planted corn and the first cotton crop to be raised in the area. In July, the Stones River flooded, completely covering the bottom lands where Donelson had planted his corn and cotton. This disaster, as well as recent reports of Indian attacks in the Clover Bottom section, prompted Donelson to move his family to the relative safety of nearby Mansker's Station.

Once the flood waters receded, Donelson learned that his corn and cotton crops at Clover Bottom had matured and decided to attempt to save them. A party composed of his son, Capt. John Donelson, Jr., Abel Gower, Jr., and several others worked for several days to harvest the valuable crops. After gathering the corn, the Gower boat started down the river and was soon fired upon by a party of Chickamaugas. These attacks on the settlements, along with the serious shortage of food, prompted Donelson to remove his family and slaves to a more secure position in Kentucky.

Donelson continued his business dealings, traveling frequently between the lands of Kentucky, Virginia, and Tennessee. While returning from Virginia and Kentucky on business in 1785, Donelson learned that his family had returned to the Cumberland Settlements. On his journey to Mansker's Station he was fired upon and died along the banks of the Barren River.

Anne-Leslie Owens, Tennessee Historical Society

CITATION:
(1) J.G.M. Ramsey, *The Annals of Tennessee* (Charleston, 1853), 197.

SUGGESTED READING: A.W. Putnam, *The History of Middle Tennessee, or Life and Times of James Robertson* (1859); Tennessee Historical Commission, *Three Tennessee Pioneer Documents* (1964)

SEE: CUMBERLAND COMPACT; CUMBERLAND RIVER; DONELSON, SAMUEL; EXPLORATIONS, EARLY; MANSKER'S STATION; ROBERTSON, CHARLOTTE; ROBERTSON, JAMES

DONELSON, SAMUEL (ca. 1760–ca. 1804), Davidson County lawyer and landowner, was the eighth of 11 children born in Virginia to Colonel John Donelson II and Rachel Stockley Donelson. Samuel Donelson was among the party of emigrants that Colonel Donelson led to Middle Tennessee, arriving at the Cumberland settlement on April 24, 1780. The Donelson family became well established in Nashville, and Samuel Donelson's closest friends and business associates included his brother-in-law Andrew Jackson and John Caffey. These men assisted Donelson in eloping with Mary Polly Smith, the only daughter of General Daniel Smith, in 1797. The Donelsons had three sons, John Samuel (1798–1817), Andrew Jackson (1799–1871), and Daniel Smith (1801–1863). After Donelson's death ca. 1804, his sons went to live at the Hermitage with Andrew and Rachel Jackson. Mary Polly Donelson remarried six years later, to Colonel James Saunders, a wealthy planter.

Heather Fearnbach, Middle Tennessee State University

SEE: DONELSON, JOHN; JACKSON, ANDREW; SMITH, DANIEL

DONELSON, STOCKLY (1805–1888), early Nashville builder, was one of 13 children born to Captain John Donelson and Mary Purnell Donelson of Davidson County. He grew up on the family plantation, located on the Cumberland River ten miles northeast of Nashville, and continued to live with his parents in their log home after his 1827 marriage to Phila Ann Lawrence of Nashville. Five of Stockly and Phila Ann's children were born in the log house,

which was known as the mansion. In 1830 Stockly Donelson inherited the 716-acre farm and successfully managed the production of livestock, corn, cotton, wheat, and fruit. He was known for his building skills as well as his managerial skills, and supervised the reconstruction of the Hermitage, home of Andrew Jackson, and the construction of Tulip Grove, home of Andrew Jackson Donelson, from 1834 to 1836. In 1835 he began the construction of his family home, Cleveland Hall, which was completed in 1839. Three presidents, Andrew Jackson, Martin Van Buren, and James K. Polk were entertained by the Donelsons at Cleveland Hall. In 1976 and 1986, the property was included in the survey of Tennessee Century Farms as one of the region's oldest family farms.

Heather Fearnbach, Middle Tennessee State University

SEE: FARMS, TENNESSEE CENTURY; HERMITAGE

DORRIS, MARY CLEMENTIA CURREY (1850–1924), a founder and early leader of the Ladies' Hermitage Association, was born in Nashville on January 28, 1850, to Emily Donelson Martin and George Washington Currey. She graduated from Ward Seminary in 1867 and three years later married Duncan Robertson Dorris, city editor of the *Nashville American*.

At the request of Colonel Andrew and Amy Jackson, Dorris assumed much of the responsibility for the creation of the Ladies' Hermitage Association. In 1887 Dorris launched a letter writing campaign to the *Nashville American*, enlisted the support of legislators, and organized charter members of the Association. On February 19, 1889, the legislature chartered the Ladies' Hermitage Association and conveyed the mansion, 25 acres of land, and the tombs of President Andrew and Rachel Jackson to the association.

Dorris served as Association secretary from 1889 to 1904 and 1909 to 1924; she was regent from 1905 to 1909. During her term, President Theodore Roosevelt visited the Hermitage, and the Association acquired the Jackson portrait known as the Healy portrait. In 1915 Dorris wrote *Preservation of the Hermitage*, outlining her experiences with early preservation efforts at the site. Dorris served the Association until her death on April 18, 1924.

In addition to her work with the Association, Dorris was a founder of the Hero of New Orleans Chapter of the Daughters of 1812, and state regent of the Daughters of 1812. She founded the Cumberland Chapter, Daughters of the American Revolution, and was regent of the chapter.

Susan M. Goodsell, Plano, Illinois

SEE: HERMITAGE; LADIES' HERMITAGE ASSOCIATION

DOUGHERTY, NATHAN WASHINGTON (1886–1977), engineer, educator, and athlete, was born on

March 23, 1886, at Hales Mill, Virginia, the son of Samuel and Mary Ellen Vernon Dougherty. When he was 12 years old, young Dougherty and his family moved to Knox County, Tennessee, where his father operated a nursery and farm near Powell. Dougherty graduated from Powell High School and in 1905 entered the University of Tennessee, where he majored in Civil Engineering. A natural athlete, Dougherty played on the UT football, basketball, and varsity track teams and captained all three teams in 1909.

After graduation from UT in 1909, Dougherty worked briefly as a math teacher at Knoxville High School before accepting a position as an engineering instructor at Cornell University in Ithaca, New York, where he also enrolled for graduate study. He graduated in 1914 with both bachelor's and master's degrees in civil engineering.

In 1916, Dougherty received a position at the University of Tennessee. For the next 40 years, he taught at the university, rising to become Dean of the College of Engineering (1940–1956). Dougherty championed academic freedom in defiance of the university president and without faculty support, when he wrote to Governor Austin Peay in 1925 to protest the Butler Bill outlawing the teaching of evolution.

Dougherty made numerous contributions to civil engineering. In the 1920s, he advocated a statewide survey to coordinate planning of Tennessee highways, a program adopted by the state in 1936. He supported the Good Roads Movement and was instrumental in the development of the UT Engineering Experiment Stations. Dougherty served as vice-president of the American Society of Civil Engineers (1944–1945) and president of the American Society for Engineering Education (1954–1955). In 1958, he received the annual outstanding engineering award of the National Society of Professional Engineers for his lifetime achievements, especially as a champion of engineering ethics and professionalism.

Dougherty's reputation for ethics made itself felt regionally and nationally in athletics too. Always interested in student athletics, Dougherty became faculty chairman of the UT Athletic Council the year he arrived and retained that position for the next 39 years. Under his guidance, Robert R. Neyland came to UT as football coach, and Dougherty designed Shields-Watkins Field and the football stadium. In 1920, he became the first secretary of the Southern Athletic Conference and played a key role in its reorganization into the Southeastern Conference in 1933. He also became active in the National Collegiate Athletic Association and served on its executive committee from 1948 to 1950. As in other areas, Dougherty did not always take the popular view. He opposed the granting of athletic scholarships with its high pressure recruitment. Fearful of the professionalization of student athletics, Dougherty reminded

coaches and universities that their first objective should be education. In 1967, Dougherty was inducted into the National Football Hall of Fame. Three years later, he was inducted into the Tennessee Sports Hall of Fame and posthumously into the Knoxville Sports Hall of Fame in 1982.

Dougherty retired from the university in 1956, but continued to act as a consultant to Arnold Engineering Development Center until 1966. In 1964, UT dedicated the Dougherty Engineering Building on the Knoxville campus. Dougherty was married to the former Agnes Anna Montieth, and they had five children. He died in Knoxville in 1977.

Connie L. Lester, Tennessee Historical Society

SEE: ARNOLD ENGINEERING DEVELOPMENT CENTER; NEYLAND, ROBERT R.; UNIVERSITY OF TENNESSEE

DOUGLAS, AARON (1899–1979), African-American artist and professor at Fisk University, was born in small-town eastern Kansas and displayed an early aptitude for drawing. His mother recognized his talent and supported his pursuit of an art career. Douglas attended high school in Topeka and went to the University of Nebraska, where he pursued a liberal arts curriculum that included drawing, painting, and art history. During World War I, he spent one semester in a Student Army Training Camp where he painted a portrait of General John J. Pershing. When he returned to college, he studied drawing under Blanche O. Grant, later a prominent member of the Taos, New Mexico, art colony. As a senior, Douglas received a prize for excellence in drawing. He graduated from Nebraska in 1922, and the following year also earned a B.F.A. degree from the University of Kansas.

After a year of teaching at Lincoln High School in Topeka, Douglas, on the advice of friends, moved to New York City at the height of the Harlem Renaissance, a time of extraordinary creative ferment among African-American artists. His work came to the attention of Charles S. Johnson, a sociologist and editor of the Urban League publication, *Opportunity*. Through him, Douglas met Bavarian-born painter Winold Reiss and became the artist's prize student. Through Reiss, Douglas was exposed to the Vienna Secession Movement, the bold colors and forms of German Expressionism, and the abstractions of African art. Reiss encouraged Douglas to take up mural painting and explore his own cultural background for themes and subjects. The young artist studied at the Pennsylvania art school of famed collector Albert Barnes and at the Academie de la Grande Chaumiere and the Academie Scandinave in Paris.

Douglas's association with Fisk University dates from 1930, when he was commissioned to create a set of murals for the Cravath Memorial Library. In 1939 Douglas accepted a part-time teaching position while he completed a Master's Degree at Teacher's College, Columbia University. In 1944 he became a professor of art at Fisk and later chaired the department before retiring in 1966.

The themes in Douglas's art underscored the contributions of African Americans to every aspect of American cultural life. In 1971, when national attention was once again focused on him by a retrospective exhibition of his paintings, artist and art historian David Driskell said that "Douglas continues to tower over young and old artists in that he planted his feet on solid ground at a time when it was unpopular to dignify the image of the Black man."[1] He exerted a profound and lasting influence on the work of younger African-American artists.

After 1928 Douglas's work was widely exhibited. In addition to his murals at Fisk, he executed murals for the Harlem YMCA, the Countee Cullen Branch of the New York Public Library, the Sherman Hotel's College Inn ballroom in Chicago, and Bennett College in Greensboro, North Carolina. Most major museum collections and many private collectors own his works.

Kevin Grogan, Fisk University Galleries

CITATION:

(1) David Driskell, "Foreword" to the catalogue accompanying "Retrospective Exhibition: Paintings by Aaron Douglas," (Nashville, Carl Van Vechten Gallery of Fine Arts, Fisk University, 1971), n.p.

SEE: ART; FISK UNIVERSITY; JOHNSON, CHARLES S.

DOVER FLINT QUARRIES comprise one of the most significant prehistoric quarry sites in the southeast. Located in Stewart County, the Dover Flint Quarries were the primary source of the famous and beautiful Dover flint from which prehistoric peoples carved and made many ceremonial objects. Prehistoric peoples prized this flint because it could be mined in large sheets, which they could work and make into long, slender flint blades of different shapes. Thomas Lewis and Madeline Kneberg observed: "Incredible skill was required to break up the large boulders and secure slabs thin enough to be worked into the long swords. The flint from these quarries can be easily recognized by its peculiar grain and color [a brownish color with slight blue specks], and the finished objects always exhibit similiarities in workmanship."[1] The Dover Flint Quarries site was placed in the National Register of Historic Places in 1973.

Carroll Van West, Middle Tennessee State University

CITATION:

(1) Thomas M.N. Lewis and Madeline Kneberg, *Tribes That Slumber: Indians of the Tennessee Region* (Knoxville, 1958), 103.

SEE: PREHISTORIC NATIVE AMERCAN ART; STEWART COUNTY

DOWNTOWN PRESBYTERIAN CHURCH in Nashville is one of only two buildings in Tennessee designed by the notable Philadelphia architect, William F. Strickland. Constructed in 1849–1851, the church is listed as a National Historic Landmark as the outstanding example of the Egyptian Revival style in America.

The exterior of The Downtown Presbyterian Church remains essentially as Strickland designed it. In 1871, the columns and entablature were added to Strickland's supports on the front steps, and stained glass windows have replaced the original clear glass ones. Strickland painted the window and door surrounds, the caveto cornices, and rectangular inset panels just beneath the roof line to simulate stonework, and this work was never redone. The columns and entablature at the front facade were designed to resemble stone as well.

The interior experienced four decorative treatments. The congregation of the former First Presbyterian Church overbuilt, and having neither the people nor the funds to complete the interior, settled on a temporary gray finish. By 1880–1882 the fortunes of the congregation had improved to the point of accomplishing a decorative scheme. They hired Theo Knoch and John Schleicher, the two decorative painters Strickland had used in the construction of the State Capitol, to finish the sanctuary and vestibule in the Egyptian decor. The 1880–1882 work was extensive. A pair of rooms was added to the front of the sanctuary in the outer corners. Frescoes, simulating Karnak, were painted on the new walls. The organ was installed in the center of this new space and a choir loft added. In 1880–1888 a diamond-burgundy-patterned dado was added below the windows, along the side walls. In 1898 the paint was redone and the color scheme reversed, and an enlarged walnut pastoral platform was built. In 1913 an enlarged organ case was added for the new organ. In 1937 the interior was painted again. Finally, in the early 1950s, another touch-up was completed.

In 1917–1919 the congregation expanded the original church, with the addition of a $100,000 Education Building designed by Henry Clossen Hibbs. The top floor housed the Presbyterian Church U.S., Board of World Missions, while the other three floors provided space for Sunday School rooms, offices, and a chapel. Hibbs clad the street and alley facades in dressed limestone. Keeping with the Egyptian Revival style, sphinxes adorn the lamps on the steps of the building. Hibbs placed the chapel in the core of the building, providing the room with a round coffered dome and oculus at the top, similar to the design of the Pantheon in Rome. Since nothing of the chapel design projects above the roofline, visitors are surprised by its presence.

James A. Hoobler, Tennessee State Museum

SEE: HIBBS, HENRY C.; STRICKLAND, WILLIAM F.

DRAGGING CANOE (1740–1792), a Cherokee warrior and leader of the Chickamaugas, was born in one of the Overhill Towns on the Tennessee River, the son of the Cherokee diplomat Attakullakulla. Historians have identified Dragging Canoe as the greatest Cherokee military leader. Even at an early age, Dragging Canoe wanted to be a warrior. He once asked his father to include him in a war party against the Shawnees, but Attakullakulla refused. Determined to go, the boy hid in a canoe, where the warriors found him. His father gave the boy permission to go—if he could carry the canoe. The vessel was too heavy, but undaunted, the boy dragged the canoe. Cherokee warriors encouraged his efforts, and from that time, he was known as Dragging Canoe.

As the Head Warrior of the Overhill town of Malaquo, Dragging Canoe fought a number of significant battles against white settlers. By the 1770s the increasing encroachment by settlers on Indian land concerned Dragging Canoe, who worked to achieve their removal. In 1776, 14 northern tribes sent envoys to the Overhill towns to offer an alliance with the Cherokees. Dragging Canoe thought the opening of the Revolutionary War provided the perfect opportunity to strike the isolated white settlements. The Cherokees planned a three-pronged attack: Old Abram led a contingent against the Watauga and Nolichucky settlements; warriors under the leadership of the Raven struck Carter's Valley; and Dragging Canoe fought at the Battle of Island Flats, where he was wounded. The settlers suffered heavy losses initially, but the arrival of reinforcements proved too much for the Cherokees, and they were defeated.

Many Cherokee leaders argued against further fighting, but Dragging Canoe refused to submit. He fled the Overhill towns with like-minded Cherokees and established new towns on Chickamauga Creek in the winter of 1776 and 1777. This group, which included discontented members of various tribes, came to be known as the Chickamaugas. Dragging Canoe and his warriors fought the 1781 "Battle of the Bluffs" near Fort Nashborough and defeated American army troops when they invaded the Chickamauga towns in 1788.

As he aged, Dragging Canoe moved from the position of warrior to that of diplomat. He worked to preserve Cherokee culture and establish an alliance with the Creeks and Shawnees. In 1791 a federation of Indian forces defeated General Arthur St. Clair, Governor of the Northwest Territory. Shortly after a diplomatic mission with the Chickasaws, Dragging Canoe died on March 1, 1792, in the town of Running Water, one of the towns he helped found.

Patricia Bernard Ezzell, Tennessee Valley Authority
SEE: ATTAKULLAKULLA; CHICKAMAUGAS; OVERHILL
CHEROKEES

DRIVER, WILLIAM (1803–1886). Born March 17, 1803, in Salem, Massachusetts, William Driver is credited with nicknaming the American flag "Old Glory." At 13 Driver ran away from home to be a cabin boy on a large sailing ship. At 21 he qualified as a master mariner and was licensed to sail a ship. His mother and the "girls of Salem" sewed the flag, which he hoisted on his first ship and christened "Old Glory." On an 1831 voyage to the South Pacific, Driver's ship was the sole surviving vessel of six that departed Salem the same day. He subsequently escorted 65 descendants of the *Bounty* survivors from Tahiti back to their home on Pitcairn Island and is said to have been convinced that God saved his ship for that purpose.

In 1837 Driver left the sea. His wife had died, and he moved with his three children to Nashville, where his two brothers lived. Driver remarried and fathered nine more children. Employed as a salesman for various Nashville businesses, he served as vestryman of Christ Episcopal Church. Every holiday, he displayed "Old Glory" outside his house, with a rope extending from an upstairs room to a tree across the street.

During the Civil War, Driver remained loyal to the Union and sewed "Old Glory" into a quilt for safekeeping. When the Union Army occupied Nashville, Driver gave the flag to the troops to be flown for a short time over the State Capitol.

Driver died March 3, 1886, and is buried in the Nashville City Cemetery. At his request, his rescue of the Pitcairn people is inscribed on his gravemarker. "Old Glory" is exhibited at the Smithsonian Museum of American History in Washington, D. C.

Ophelia Paine, Metropolitan Historical Commission

DROMGOOLE, WILL ALLEN (1860–1934) was born in Murfreesboro, the last child of John Easter and Rebecca Blanche Dromgoole. When she was six, Dromgoole changed her middle name to Allen, and throughout her life was known as Will Allen or "Miss Will." In 1876 Dromgoole graduated from the Clarksville Female Academy and studied at the New England School of Expression in Boston. After her mother's death in 1884 and confronted with the responsibility of caring for her aging father, Dromgoole began her writing career. A sentimental novel, *The Sunny Side of the Cumberland,* was published under the name Will Allen in 1886; her first short story, "Columbus Tucker's Discontent," was published in and awarded a cash prize by the *Youth's Companion* in 1886. Dromgoole studied law with her father and in 1885 and 1887 won terms as an engrossing clerk in the State Senate. She was defeated in 1889 and 1891, possibly because unflattering portraits depicted in articles published in the Nashville *Daily American* (1890) and the Boston *Arena* (1891) on the Melungeons, an East Tennessee mountain community, angered the senators who

SPECIAL COLLECTIONS, UNIVERSITY OF TENNESSEE, KNOXVILLE

Will Allen Dromgoole.

represented them. Beginning in 1890, Dromgoole edited and contributed to *Will Allen's Journal: A Literary Society Weekly,* published in Nashville for several years.

After the public criticism following the second defeat in 1891, Dromgoole traveled to Texas, teaching, writing for newspapers, and founding the Waco Women's Press Club in 1894. On her return to Nashville, Dromgoole spent most of her time with her father, who died in 1897, and in 1898 published a tribute to their life together, *Rare Old Chums.* Continuing to reside in Nashville, Dromgoole returned frequently to the "Yellowhammer's Nest," a cabin located in Estill Springs, Tennessee. In this peaceful refuge bought with her first earnings in 1887, she enjoyed hunting, fishing, and writing. The cabin and all of its contents were destroyed by fire in 1972.

Having written for the Nashville *Banner* since 1900, Dromgoole was hired as a permanent staff member in 1902, and in 1903 began her immensely popular column, "Song and Story," which continued for 31 years. Shortly after the United States entered World War I in 1917, she volunteered her services to the U.S. Navy, and in May was recruited as a yeomanry warrant officer, perhaps being the first female to serve in this capacity. She was stationed in Norfolk, where her official responsibilities included working at the base library, recruiting young men into the navy, visiting ships, and delivering patriotic speeches. Her columns continued during this period,

but she wrote about Virginia instead of Nashville. Dromgoole returned to the *Banner* in late 1918 and was named literary editor in 1922, remaining in that position until her death in 1934.

Dromgoole was in great demand as a speaker to literary groups, patriotic clubs, and writing circles during her life; she was named Poet Laureate by the Poetry Society of the South in 1930. Among her many literary achievements are 13 books, dozens of stories, over 8,000 poems, over 5,000 newspaper columns, several non-fiction articles, an operetta, and two plays. In all of these she depicts the hill folk of East and Middle Tennessee or the residents, poor and wealthy, black and white, of Nashville.

Dromgoole is buried in the Evergreen Cemetery in Murfreesboro, Tennessee.

Kathy Lyday-Lee, Elon College

SEE: LITERATURE; NASHVILLE BANNER; RUTHERFORD COUNTY

DROUILLARD, MARY FLORENCE (1843–1905), was born in Nashville on August 23, 1843, the daughter of Hugh Kirkman and Eleanora C. Vanleer and granddaughter of ironmaster Anthony W. Vanleer and Rebecca Brady. Educated in local private schools, she completed her education at a finishing school in New York City, spending her summers in fashionable Newport, Rhode Island.

After her grandfather's death in 1863, she and her brother, Vanleer Kirkman, inherited property in Dickson County with assets over $500,000, including Cumberland Furnace and 85 slaves. On September 21, 1864, she married Ohio native, Union Captain James Pierre Drouillard, West Point class of 1861. The event sent shock waves through Nashville's society. None of her friends or family, including her godparents, Aunt Rebecca and Uncle Andrew Jackson Polk, attended the wedding.

After the war, the Drouillards moved to Dickson County to re-open the furnace. For Florence Drouillard, the old brick ironmaster home lacked grandeur. In 1870 the Drouillards built an Italianate-style residence, designed after a similar house in Newport. The mansion was built for entertaining, and included a three-story spiral stairway from which Mary Florence could make her grand entrances at the summer parties that brought guests from Nashville and as far away as New Orleans.

Mary Florence Drouillard bought her brother's share of the furnace in 1870, and turned her interest to improving the life of the villagers. She built St. James Episcopal church and a parish school for the white and black children.

In 1886 the Drouillards returned to Nashville, dividing their time between the city and Europe. Mary Florence was welcomed back into the city's society to become one of its most colorful social queens of the late nineteenth century. She died May 19, 1905 and is buried with her husband in the family plot in Mt. Olivet Cemetery, Nashville.

George E. Jackson, Dickson

SEE: CUMBERLAND FURNACE; DICKSON COUNTY

Du BOIS, W. E. B. (WILLIAM EDWARD BURG-HARDT) (1868–1963), a prolific writer and pro-

foundly original thinker, produced studies on American democracy and race relations that were decades ahead of the scholarship in several academic disciplines. As editor of *The Crisis,* the magazine of the National Association for the Advancement of Colored People, he advanced and advocated the culture and history of, by, and for African Americans.

Du Bois was born in Great Barrington, Massachusetts, on February 23, 1868. He came to Nashville in 1884 with a scholarship to study at Fisk University, where he finished his degree in 1888. Du Bois then studied at Harvard, the University of Berlin, and earned his Ph.D. in 1895 from Harvard, the first African American to do so. He was the student and colleague of some of the most brilliant men of his time, including William James and Max Weber. His prodigious scholarly accomplishments—22 books, 15 edited books, and almost 2,000 essays, articles, and poems—analyzed and chronicled American race relations better and more extensively than any other writer. His leadership and legacy in civil rights for African Americans was primarily and uniquely through the written word.

Du Bois's intellectual and social development at Fisk shaped a brilliant mind and indomitable spirit. Much later, he would assert emphatically that African-American colleges provided salvation for both the South and blacks, places where African Americans created an "inner culture." This certainly applied to Du Bois. At Fisk, during the morning prayers attended by two to three hundred fellow students, he realized "that this great assembly of youth and intelligence are the representatives of a race which twenty years ago was in bondage." At Fisk, he found increased pride in his race and solace that he could stand among colleagues who did not judge him by the color of his skin. Because institutions such as Fisk had their own cultural identity, Du Bois regarded them as the best space for an exchange of the views of black and white Americans.

Du Bois's scholarship pioneered in several fields. His dissertation on the suppression of the African slave trade was published as the first volume in the Harvard Historical Monograph Series. His book, *The Philadelphia Negro,* pioneered in the field of urban sociology for which the University of Chicago would become famous. While on the faculty of Atlanta University, he conducted studies and conferences that documented the condition and institutions of African

Americans, including economics, health, family, and church. This work preceded the monumental study of American race relations by Gunnar Myrdal, *The American Dilemma: The Negro Problem and Modern Democracy,* by more than 40 years. Myrdal recognized the scholarship and scholarly contributions of Du Bois much more than most other white social scientists and historians. Myrdal even included an appendix to his study that chastised American social science for its aversion to questions of racial equality and its legitimation of racial inequality. This was a mild rebuke compared to Du Bois's essay, "The Propaganda of History." In his piercing prose that penetrated the mind and heart, Du Bois analyzed the falsification of the history of the Civil War and Reconstruction to cover the shame of the southern battle to perpetuate slavery and the northern reliance on black troops to "save the Union, abolish slavery, and establish democracy." Only with the advent of the civil rights movement in the 1950s would his work, *Black Reconstruction in America, 1860–1880,* win the level of recognition and acceptance Myrdal provided it.

Du Bois wrote for general audiences, as well as scholars, to create shared spaces for blacks and whites. His series of essays, *The Souls of Black Folk,* used the image of a "Veil" as a literary device to explain the meaning of being African American in the early twentieth century. Du Bois sought to explain both sides of the veil to enable readers of both races to see the other more clearly.

In *Souls,* he chose to explain life "within the Veil" of race through his personal experiences near Watertown, Tennessee. As was customary for the students of Fisk, Du Bois taught school to about 30 children for two summers in rural Wilson County. His schoolhouse was a log crib used otherwise to store corn and his instruction provided the only schooling for area African-American children. Ten years later, during a visit to Fisk, Du Bois returned to Watertown to renew acquaintances and learn how his students had fared. His favorite student, Josie, had died, one event in the "heap of trouble" her family endured since Du Bois's departure. Josie's brother had fled from the legal enforcement of unfair labor arrangements of blacks and whites. The school remained derelict except for the now regular class sessions. While some families prospered, others lost their farms, or made a poor living from the stingy soil. Others moved to Nashville to find work. Marriage, children, and violence intertwined the lives of the community. Du Bois reflected on his time near Watertown and wrote, in a style that inspired major African-American writers of the twentieth century: "How hard a thing is life to the lowly, and how human and real! And all this life and live, and strife and failure,—is it the twilight of nightfall or the flush of some faint-dawning day? Thus sadly musing, I rode to Nashville in the Jim Crow Car."

Souls catapulted Du Bois into national prominence. An essay critical of Booker T. Washington, the most prominent African-American leader of the time, initiated a break in the public deference accorded Washington. Du Bois articulated the views of professional, intellectual, and wealthy African Americans, who experienced racial repression of the Jim Crow era as caste restrictions. Du Bois chided Washington for accommodating these repressive measures in exchange for support of incremental changes, including support for the schools and activities Washington sponsored. The emerging polemicist appeared in this essay, as Du Bois prophesied " . . . A double life with double thoughts, double duties, and double social classes must give rise to double words and double ideals, and tempt the mind to pretense or revolt, to hypocrisy or radicalism."

Du Bois used his new national stature to establish organizations to advocate revolt and radicalism and to litigate for the rights of African Americans. In 1905, he led in the formation of the Niagara Movement and in 1909, he helped found the NAACP. He served as editor of the organization's journal, *The Crisis,* from 1910 to 1934. More an agitator than an organization man, his time in the NAACP and Atlanta University was marred by controversy exacerbated by his conflicts with federal authorities. He argued that desegregation was not enough and advocated a distinctly African-American culture to resist assimilation into white institutions. By the time he left the NAACP in 1934, he was championing changes on behalf of the lower classes of African Americans, having moved beyond the mere removal of caste restrictions for the elite. He moved around—Atlanta University, back to the NAACP, international travel—looking for a platform for ideas that became more radical in the context of incremental integration and civil rights.

In 1963, when he died, Du Bois had bridged a century from Reconstruction to the Civil Rights Movement. Du Bois had undergone a journey as well. He began as a scholar; evolved to a political critic of the gap between the ideals and practice of American democracy; and finally became an expatriate. After profound harassment during the McCarthy era, he joined the Communist Party in 1961, and moved to Ghana, where he became a citizen. He died there on August 27, 1963. The next day, as Ghana conducted a state funeral for him, the greatest civil rights demonstration in American history, the March on Washington, occurred. Undoubtedly had he been there he would have praised and goaded the leaders of that demonstration by reminding them of the principal ideal of Frederick Douglass that became his own beacon of thought and action: "ultimate assimilation

through self-assertion, and on no other terms."

Richard A. Couto, University of Richmond

SEE: FISK UNIVERSITY; NAACP; WILSON COUNTY

DuBOSE, WILLIAM PORCHER (1836–1918), Episcopal theologian, was born at Winnsboro, South Carolina, the son of Theodore Marion DuBose and Jane Porcher, both of Huguenot descent. In 1851 he entered the South Carolina Military College, The Citadel, from which he graduated with first honors in 1855. The next year, DuBose entered the University of Virginia and received his M.A. degree in 1859. He then studied at the Theological Seminary of the Protestant Episcopal Church in the Diocese of South Carolina, Camden, which had opened in 1859. While a student at the seminary, the Civil War began, and DuBose was appointed Adjutant of the Holcombe Legion. During the war he was wounded twice, captured once and imprisoned, but later released in a prisoner exchange. During a furlough in 1863, DuBose married Anne Barnwell Peronneau of Charleston; the couple had four children. In December 1863 he was ordained deacon at Grace Church, Camden. He joined Kershaw's brigade at Greeneville, Tennessee, and began his ministry there. After the war, he became rector of St. John's Parish, Fairfield, composed of St. John's, Winnsboro, and St. Stephen's, Ridgeway. He was ordained priest on September 9, 1866. In January 1868 he became the rector of Trinity Church, Abbeville, South Carolina.

During the 1870 convention of the Diocese of South Carolina, DuBose received serious consideration for election to the office of bishop. He considered his failure to be elevated to this office a "fortunate escape." The following year, he was elected the first chaplain of the University of the South, Sewanee, Tennessee, a new Episcopal university which had opened on September 18, 1868. From 1871 until his death, DuBose's life and the history of the university were interwoven.

DuBose served as chaplain of university until 1883; from 1893–1894, he was acting dean of the School of Theology of the University of the South; and from 1894–1908, he was second dean of the School of Theology. DuBose helped establish the School of Theology, which opened as a distinct department in 1878. He taught almost every subject in the curriculum, although he was primarily professor of New Testament.

DuBose was arguably the major Episcopal theologian in the United States. He published *The Soteriology of the New Testament* (1892), *The Ecumenical Councils* (1896), *The Gospel in the Gospels* (1906), *The Reason of Life* (1911), and *Turning Points in My Life* (1912). DuBose is known as "Sewanee's Doctor," and he is commemorated in the Liturgical Calendar of the Episcopal Church on August 18. He has been called the most important creative theologian the Episcopal Church has produced.

In April 1873 Anne Peronneau DuBose died. In December 1878 DuBose married Maria Louise Yerger, who opened a school in Monteagle, called Fairmont College. DuBose died in 1918.

Donald S. Armentrout, University of the South
SEE: RELIGION; UNIVERSITY OF THE SOUTH

DUCK RIVER TEMPLE MOUNDS. More than eight centuries ago, a Native American town flourished atop the steep bluff overlooking the confluence of Sycamore Creek, Buffalo River, and the Duck River in Humphreys County. By A.D. 1150, this prosperous town was the political, economic, and religious center for villagers and farmers throughout the Lower Tennessee River valley. This ancient settlement, prominent throughout eastern North America as a center of prehistoric trade, declined and disappeared by A.D. 1500.

In 1894 digging at this town produced the Duck River Cache, perhaps the most spectacular single collection of prehistoric Native American art ever discovered in the eastern United States. The cache included two human statues representing the community's ancestral founding couple along with nearly four dozen ceremonial stone knives, daggers, swords, maces, and other striking examples of prehistoric stonework. As sacred symbols of leadership, these objects were similar, in many ways, to the crowns of European monarchs.

Eastern Native American chiefs valued the ceremonial weapons manufactured by Duck River artisans. Items created by these master stoneworkers have been excavated at Toqua in East Tennessee, Etowah in Georgia, Moundville in Alabama, Kincaid in Illinois, and Spiro in Oklahoma. Today, the products of those artisans are the centerpieces of major museums throughout the eastern United States. The Duck River Cache remains on display at the McClung Museum in Knoxville. In 1974 the State of Tennessee purchased the 90-acre core of this remarkable Native American town to preserve what remains of one of the most significant and impressive Native American civilizations of prehistoric Tennessee.

Kevin E. Smith, Middle Tennessee State University
SUGGESTED READINGS: H.C. Brehm, editor, *The Duck River Cache: Tennessee's Great Archaeological Find* (1984); H. C. Brehm, *The History of the Duck River Cache* (Miscellaneous Paper No. 6, Tennessee Anthropological Association, Knoxville)

SEE: HUMPHREYS COUNTY; MISSISSIPPIAN CULTURE; PREHISTORIC NATIVE AMERICAN ART

DUCKTOWN BASIN MUSEUM, located in Polk County at the southeastern corner of Tennessee, documents and interprets the copper mining history of Tennessee. Located on the grounds of the former Burra Burra Mine Company, overlooking the town of Ducktown, the museum preserves key elements of the area's industrial archaeology in addition to the environmental destruction associated with underground and surface mining and the smelting process. Copper mining in the "Copper Basin" dates to the 1840s; a reproduction of the Hiwassee smelter stack (approximately 1850) is on the west side of Tennessee Highway 68. Julius E. Raht became the leading manager of the various Copper Basin companies prior to the Civil War. While the conflict stopped mining in 1863, post-war production soared. From 1865 to 1878, over 24 million pounds of copper were taken from underground mines while 50 square miles of the Basin had been stripped of its timber in order to build underground mines and fuel local smelters.

The next era of sustained growth and expansion came in the late 1890s when the newly formed Tennessee Copper Company sank a giant underground shaft at its Burra Burra mine in 1899. Sixty years later, when the company closed Burra Burra mine in 1959, over 15.6 million tons of copper ore had been extracted. The company maintained a surface mining office at Burra Burra until 1976 and copper mining continued in the Basin until 1987. The museum interprets the remnants of the Burra Burra works, including ten buildings located on 17 acres as well as the only surviving mine headframe in Tennessee. Due to their significance in the state's mining history, the Burra Burra mine properties, and large portions of the towns of Ducktown and Copperhill, are listed in the National Register of Historic Places.

Carroll Van West, Middle Tennessee State University
SEE: BURRA BURRA COPPER COMPANY; MINING; POLK COUNTY; RAHT, JULIUS E.

DUDLEY, ANNE DALLAS (1876–1955), a national and state leader in the woman suffrage movement, was the daughter of a prominent Nashville family. She received her education at Ward Seminary and attended Price's College in Nashville. She married Guilford Dudley, one of the founders of the Life and Casualty Insurance Company in Nashville, and they maintained a country estate in west Nashville.

After joining a local suffrage association in 1911, she was elected in 1915 as the president of the Tennessee Equal Suffrage Association, Inc., and served until 1917, when she was elected third vice president of the National American Woman Suffrage Association (NAWSA). The circles in which Anne Dallas Dudley moved frowned upon the idea of women voting, yet she became a tireless worker, campaigning throughout the state, organizing suffrage leagues, and speaking across the United States. Under her leadership, suffrage became more acceptable and more women joined the movement. Abby

THS, TSLA ORIGINAL PHOTOGRAPH IN CATT PAPERS, BRYN MAWR COLLEGE.

Anne Dallas Dudley during her term as president of the Tennessee Suffrage Association.

Milton of Chattanooga and Catherine Kenny of Nashville worked closely with Dudley in organizing the suffrage movement in Tennessee.

Dudley's two children were frequently photographed as they led suffrage parades with their mother across Nashville. A photograph of Dudley reading with her two children was widely circulated with suffrage publicity materials. These photographs were a deliberate effort by the suffragists to counteract negative stereotypes of suffragists as mannish, childless radicals who were attempting to destroy the American family.

Dudley addressed Congressional committees and spoke to national audiences, urging passage of the Nineteenth Amendment. Adept at handling anti-suffrage arguments, she responded to criticism that equated male suffrage with military service by pointing out that "women bear armies."

In 1920 Dudley attended the Democratic national convention in San Francisco as the first woman delegate-at-large. On her way to the podium to make a seconding speech, the band spontaneously struck up the familiar tune, "Oh, You Beautiful Doll." In August of that same year, Dudley successfully worked to achieve the ratification of the Nineteenth Amendment by the Tennessee General Assembly and thereby add the amendment to the U.S. Constitution. She continued her political involvement through the fall of 1920 as a volunteer in Governor Albert H. Roberts's unsuc-

cessful re-election bid. Never active in the newly created League of Women Voters, she helped organize the Woman's Civic League of Nashville to assist elected officials in a needed "municipal house-cleaning." More than 35 years before the passage of metropolitan government in Nashville, this group fought for an end to overlapping city efforts and public education on health issues. In the 1930s Dudley served as president of the Maternal Welfare Organization of Tennessee. This group brought birth control pioneer Margaret Sanger to Nashville in 1938 to increase public awareness of birth control.

Dudley's likeness appears in the painting, *Pride of Tennessee*, which hangs in the Capitol. She is buried at Mt. Olivet Cemetery in Nashville.
Carole Stanford Bucy, Volunteer State Community College
SUGGESTED READING: Antoinette E. Taylor, *The Woman Suffrage Movement in Tennessee* (1943)
SEE: KENNY, CATHERINE T.; MILTON, ABBY C.; ROBERTS, ALBERT H.; WOMAN SUFFRAGE MOVEMENT

DUELING, private combat governed by formal rules, was a manifestation of the romantic spirit that once existed in the South. A relic of feudalism, the duel was popularized among rank-conscious southern gentry by European officers who participated in the American Revolution. Dueling involved a prearranged encounter between two antagonists who, armed with lethal weapons, usually a sword or pistol, met on the field of honor in the presence of seconds or other witnesses in order to resolve personal and familial disputes.

Local conditions modified various aspects of the code of honor in the states below the Mason-Dixon line, where the practice of chivalric warfare flourished, especially in the states of South Carolina, Georgia, Louisiana, Mississippi, and Tennessee. On May 30, 1806, Andrew Jackson shot and mortally wounded Charles Dickinson, a fellow Tennessean, despite the fact that he himself had been seriously wounded by his younger opponent. Twenty years later, Sam Houston, a political disciple of Jackson and future President of the Republic of Texas, severely injured his opponent, William A. White, in another famous affair of honor, having actually trained several days for the duel on the grounds of the Hermitage.

Adverse public reaction, encouraged by church disapproval of dueling, led to the adoption of antidueling laws in every southern state. Few, however, were as draconian as that of North Carolina's 1802 edict proscribing the death penalty. The Tennessee constitutions of 1835 and 1870 denied public office to anyone who participated in a duel, or aided and abetted the fighting of a duel; the legislature could also punish offenders. Neither constitution disqualified potential candidates who fought duels outside Tennessee. In *State ex rel. v. DuBose* (1890), the Tennessee Supreme Court ruled that the state had no power to punish the act of dueling when it was done legally outside the state.

General opposition to the *code duello* notwithstanding, the prevalence of dueling activity in the antebellum South, with its highly stratified society, may be adjudged by the fact that legal enactments failed to eradicate the institution, largely because of the unfortunate dichotomy existing between laws and actual social practice. Indeed, because newspaper editors, politicians, and other community leaders constituted a disproportionate share of its adherents, dueling thrived in the South long after the cult of chivalry had disappeared from other geographical sections, thereby contributing substantially to the tradition of violence that prevailed in states like Tennessee beyond the Civil War era.

James W. McKee, Jr., East Tennessee State University

SEE: HOUSTON, SAM; JACKSON, ANDREW

DUNAVANT ENTERPRISES AND HOHENBERG BROS. COMPANY of Memphis are world leaders in

cotton merchandising at the end of the twentieth century. Cotton marketing has been an important commercial activity in Memphis since the 1840s, thanks to the city's location on the Mississippi River and its proximity to the fertile cotton-growing territories of Tennessee, Mississippi, Arkansas, and Missouri. Where numerous Memphis firms once bought and sold cotton, only a handful carry on the trade today. Aggressive and innovative business strategies employed by the Dunavant and Hohenberg companies during recent decades made them two of the largest cotton dealers in the world, even though the center of American cotton growing moved to the Southwest and foreign countries increased their fiber production.

The Dunavant cotton company traces its beginnings to the 1929 partnership of T. J. White, Sr., and William Buchanan "Buck" Dunavant. T. J. White and Company had its offices on Front Street, the center of the Memphis cotton trade. William Buchanan "Billy" Dunavant, Buck's son, became a junior partner in 1952, learning the business from the ground up. Following White's 1960 retirement, the firm was renamed W. B. Dunavant and Company. A year later the death of W. B. Dunavant, Sr., brought Billy to the helm. Dunavant Enterprises, Inc., organized in 1971, embraces a wide range of business interests in addition to cotton merchandising.

In the immediate post-World War II years, the firm handled approximately 75,000 to 80,000 bales of cotton annually, with 85 to 90 percent sold to American customers. By the time Billy Dunavant assumed control in 1961, annual sales had grown to between 150,000 and 175,000 bales. Under his direc-

tion, the yearly total reached the million mark in the early 1970s and soon soared to a record three million bales. As volume increased, profit margins could be reduced, thereby increasing overall company competitiveness.

Dunavant Cotton Company buys and sells cotton all over the world. Dunavant participated in the first sale of American cotton to China. In order to solicit business from Japan, South Korea, and China, the company opened offices in Osaka, Hong Kong, and Singapore in 1978. A Geneva office established in the same year merchandised cotton grown in the Middle East and Russia and served as Dunavant's European headquarters. With the purchase of the McFadden Cotton Company of Memphis in 1985, Dunavant Enterprises acquired a profitable international operation with offices in Australia, South and Central America, and Asia.

The Hohenberg cotton company evolved from a country store. In 1879 two immigrant brothers, Morris and Adolphe Hohenberg, organized M. Hohenberg & Co., in Wetumpka, Alabama. Southern country stores in the postbellum period not only sold groceries and supplies, but financed farmers in return for mortgages or liens on their cotton crops. The Hohenberg brothers became so successful at marketing cotton that they made M. Hohenberg & Co. solely responsible for cotton trading and organized additional companies for their other business activities. Morris opened an office in Selma, while Adolphe managed the Wetumpka operation.

As the next generation of Hohenbergs came of age, they opened offices in cotton towns throughout Alabama and in other parts of the South. With the westward shift in cotton production, the Hohenbergs moved the company headquarters to Memphis in 1933. A decade later, following the dissolution of M. Hohenberg & Co., Elkan Hohenberg of Memphis and Charles M. Hohenberg of Selma became partners in Hohenberg Bros. Company, while both were serving in the armed forces.

After World War II, Hohenberg Bros. expanded into all parts of the world, wherever cotton was grown. Elkan Hohenberg's son, Julien, played an active role in making Hohenberg Bros. an international company. Rudi Scheidt, Julien's brother-in-law, also fostered the company's international connections, going wherever opportunities arose in the expectation that opportunities would follow the crop.

In 1975 Cargill, Inc., a large grain company, acquired Hohenberg Bros.; Julien Hohenberg and Rudi Scheidt continued to manage the firm. In 1985 Julien Hohenberg left the firm to found the Julien Company, which experienced spectacular growth before being forced into bankruptcy in 1990.

Although cotton no longer dominates the local economy as it once did, Memphis companies, such as

Dunavant and Hohenberg remain preeminent in the global business of cotton merchandising.

Lynette Boney Wrenn, Memphis

SUGGESTED READING: John E. Harkins, *Metropolis of the American Nile* (1982)

SEE: COTTON; MEMPHIS

DUNBAR CAVE STATE NATURAL AREA, located outside of Clarksville, contains 110 acres centered around a historic cave that has been a source of legend and recreation since the early history of Montgomery County.

Prehistoric peoples used the cave for habitation centuries before settlers came to Montgomery County. During the Mexican War, saltpeter for gunpowder was mined at the cave. Dunbar Cave and a nearby mineral springs known as Idaho Springs attracted their first recreational developers in 1858 when a number of cabins were built. After the Civil War, J.A. Tate acquired the springs and cave, constructed a two-story hotel, and marketed the spring water as a cure for all sorts of ailments. The place became a gathering point for dances, concerts, and fairs. An African-American barber and musician, Jim Shelton, was a popular performer. Camp meetings also took place on the property, at a site north of the hotel.

In 1931–32 a group of Clarksville businessmen acquired the old Idaho Springs and Dunbar Cave property and expanded the recreational facilities, especially at the renovated and expanded hotel, which now fronted an improved federal highway. The investors built a new dam that increased the lake size to approximately 20 acres. The new complex also included a bathhouse, tennis courts, cabins, and a modern concrete swimming pool. Throughout the Depression decade, Dunbar Cave was a popular resort, which hosted Big Band concerts, including such famous acts as Benny Goodman and Tommy Dorsey. After World War II, country music star Roy Acuff acquired the property and added a golf course to its attractions as well as performing on a regular basis. However, after a promising postwar beginning, Dunbar Cave's popularity began to fade. The hotel was gone by 1950; the swimming pool closed in 1967. Six years later, in 1973, the State of Tennessee acquired the property and transformed it into a State Natural Area. It now provides hiking, cave tours, and lake activities throughout the year.

Carroll Van West, Middle Tennessee State University

SEE: ACUFF, ROY; MONTGOMERY COUNTY; RESORTS, HISTORIC

DUNCAN, JOHN J., SR., (1916–1988), Congressman and Mayor of Knoxville, was born on a farm in Scott County, the sixth of ten children of F. B. and Cassie Duncan. Duncan attended the University of Tennessee, Knoxville, and in 1942, while a student there, married Lois Swisher. During World War II, he served as a criminal investigator for the U. S. Army. After the war, Duncan attended Cumberland University and the University of Tennessee, where he received his LL.B. and J.D. degrees in 1948. From 1948 to 1956, he served as state assistant attorney general.

Duncan's political career began with his work in Howard Baker, Sr.'s victorious 1954 campaign for Tennessee's Second Congressional seat. In 1959 Duncan was elected mayor of Knoxville. As a southern mayor during the civil rights era, Duncan worked with sit-in demonstrators to avoid violence and accomplish the peaceful integration of Knoxville businesses. In 1964 he won election to Congress to the seat previously held by Howard Baker, Sr. Duncan gained a reputation as a low-profile congressman, who focused on the problems of his constituents. Politically conservative, Duncan was a Vietnam War hawk who advocated get-tough policies against anti-war demonstrators. Still, he maintained a working relationship with many who did not support his conservative positions, including the NAACP and environmental groups concerned with protection for the Great Smoky Mountain National Park.

Duncan represented the Second Congressional District from 1964 until his death from prostate cancer on June 21, 1988. His son, John J. Duncan, Jr., was elected to replace his father in office.

Michael Rogers, University of Tennessee, Knoxville

SEE: BAKER, HOWARD, SR.; KNOXVILLE; SIT-INS, KNOXVILLE

DUNN, WINFIELD C. (1927–). In November 1970 Winfield Dunn defeated Democratic party nominee, John J. Hooker, and became the first Republican to be elected governor of Tennessee in a half century. Before his election to the governorship, Dunn had never held public office and was a virtual unknown, except to a handful of Republican activists. His election was a visible sign of the growing strength and popularity of the Tennessee Republican Party in the 1960s.

Winfield Dunn was born on July 1, 1927, in Meridian, Mississippi, to Aubert C. and Dorothy Crum Dunn. Despite his lack of political experience, Dunn was raised in a political environment; Aubert Dunn represented Mississippi in the U.S. House of Representatives, 1935–1937. Winfield Dunn graduated from the University of Mississippi in 1950, with a degree in business administration; he minored in political science. In the early 1950s, he married Betty Jane Prichard of Memphis, while attending dental school at the University of Tennessee, Memphis. He later practiced dentistry in Memphis.

Republican politics attracted Dunn, even as a college student. In 1952 he was a spokesman for the Eisenhower ticket. After settling in Memphis, Dunn failed in a bid for the state's General Assembly in

1962. In 1964 he worked with the Tennessee Republican Party on behalf of Senator Barry Goldwater's presidential campaign. Dunn was a delegate to the 1968 Republican National Convention, where he supported the presidential nomination of Richard M. Nixon. His victory in the 1970 governor's race assured Dunn's prominence in the new generation of southern Republicans. In 1973 Dunn was elected vice chairman of the Republican Governors Association and in 1974, was elevated to the chairmanship of that body. Dunn was not eligible for reelection in 1974, and was succeeded in the governor's office by Democrat Ray Blanton.

As Governor, Dunn developed a statewide kindergarten program, pushed highway construction legislation to an all-time high, reorganized major branches of the state government, and created the Department of Economic and Community Development. In the reorganization of state government, Dunn created the Department of General Services to cooordinate and administer state purchases and manage state properties. In 1972 the Department of Personnel was divided to enhance efficiency in the recruitment, examination, and training of state employees. A key theme of Dunn's administration was the lessening of the historic tensions and rivalries between the state's three "Grand Divisions." To this end, Dunn brought into government service both Republicans and Democrats from all parts of the state. His executive order to change billboards greeting motorists at the state line from the familiar "Welcome to the Three States of Tennessee" to "Welcome to the Great State of Tennessee" also demonstrated his desire for unity.

After leaving the governor's office, Dunn served as chairman of both the University of Tennessee Board of Trustees and the Tennessee State Board of Regents. Dunn remained active in both state and national Republican party politics, serving as chairman of George Bush's Tennessee Steering Committee in 1988. In 1986 he lost a close gubernatorial campaign to Democrat Ned Ray McWherter.

Since 1974, Dunn has also been active in many charitable organizations, including the Nashville Heart Association, the Nashville Conference of Christians and Jews, and the Nashville Chapter of the American Cancer Society. He served on the Executive Committee of the United Way. He was chosen Tennessee's Man of the Year three times by news and business organizations throughout the state. As of 1996, Dunn had returned to the medical field. He is currently chairman of Medshares, Inc. of Nashville, and he also serves on the Boards of Phycor, Incorporated, and Behavioral Healthcare Corporation.

Michael Rogers, University of Tennessee, Knoxville

SUGGESTED READING: William R. Majors, *Change and Continuity: Tennessee Politics Since the Civil War* (1986)

SEE: GOVERNMENT; MCWHERTER, NED RAY; MEMPHIS

DURICK, JOSEPH ALOYSIUS (1914–1994). Following the directives of the Second Vatican Council, Bishop Joseph A. Durick led Tennessee's Catholic Church into the modern era during the 1960s and 1970s. The Eighth Bishop of Nashville, Durick helped reform the church's liturgy, reached across denominational lines, and fostered greater lay participation. He also embraced the cause of racial justice and actively participated in the civil rights struggle.

Born in Dayton, Tennessee, on October 13, 1914, Durick was the seventh of 12 children. He grew up in Bessemer, Alabama, during the height of anti-Catholic violence in that state. The images of bigotry toward Catholics helped Durick later develop a sense of resolve in confronting racial injustice.

Durick gave up plans for a music career to enter the priesthood. He studied at St. Bernard College in Cullman, Alabama, as a seminarian for the Diocese of Mobile, and graduated in 1933. Three years later, he completed course work in philosophy at St. Mary's Seminary in Baltimore, and later received theological training at the seminary for missionary priests in Rome. Ordained on March 23, 1940, Durick became the assistant director of Catholic missions in north Alabama; by 1943 he was the director.

In 1955 Durick's success in the mission field led to his appointment as the auxiliary bishop to Archbishop Thomas Joseph Toolen of the Mobile-Birmingham Diocese. Toolen assigned his new assistant to Birmingham—placing Durick, the nation's youngest bishop, in the midst of the rising racial upheaval. During the 1963 Birmingham civil rights protests, Durick and seven other Alabama religious leaders criticized the timing and methods of the demonstrations. Martin Luther King, Jr., responded to their public statement with his famous *Letter From Birmingham Jail*, personally addressed to Durick and the other clergymen. (Although their names appeared, none of the eight men ever received a personal copy of King's letter).

In December 1963 Pope Paul VI promoted Durick to the post of Coadjutor Bishop of Nashville (the diocese covered the entire state of Tennessee until 1971), with right of succession to the aged Bishop William Adrian. The sweeping reforms initiated by Pope John XXIII in the Second Vatican Council inspired Durick to lead the Catholic Church in Tennessee into a new era. Durick consulted with the state's most influential Catholic laymen, as well as a number of journalists, including John Popham, John Seigenthaler, Joe Sweat, and Father Owen Champion, to help him organize and present his reforms. The journalists especially influenced Durick to move to the forefront as one of the state's leading voices of liberal social activism in Tennessee.

In addition to introducing reforms in church liturgy and encouraging lay participation, Durick also directed efforts at ecumenical cooperation with the state's Protestant and Jewish communities. Durick introduced Project Equality, a highly controversial ecumenical program designed to use the moral suasion of the church to achieve equal employment opportunities for black Tennesseans. During 1968 he played an active role in the strike of black sanitation workers in Memphis. Following Martin Luther King, Jr.'s assassination, Durick held a memorial service for the slain civil rights leader and participated in a tense march through downtown Memphis.

In September 1969 Bishop Adrian resigned, and Pope Paul VI named Durick Bishop of Tennessee, making him the first native-born Catholic bishop of the diocese. Durick launched into an intense effort to seek human dignity for all men regardless of race, political views, or church affiliation. He was an outspoken critic of the Vietnam War and opposed the death penalty, stands which led to constant criticism from conservatives both within and outside of the church.

During the 1970s, Durick increasingly turned his attention to prison reform. In 1975 he resigned as Bishop of Nashville to devote himself to full-time prison ministry. After six years of ministering to prisoners in various locations, a severe heart problem and subsequent surgery forced Durick into semi-retirement. He died in 1994.

S. Jonathan Bass, University of Tennessee, Knoxville

SEE: MEMPHIS SANITATION STRIKE; RELIGION

DUTCHMAN'S GRADE RAILWAY ACCIDENT. One of the worst passenger rail accidents in United States history occurred July 9, 1918, at the Dutchman's Grade, in Belle Meade, five miles west of Nashville. The southbound Memphis to Atlanta Passenger Express No. 1 collided head-on with a westbound local, Train No. 4, at a place where a curve, plus a slight grade (the Dutchman's Grade), wooded terrain, and an overhead bridge made it impossible for the engineers to see until it was too late. Deaths from the accident totaled 101 people.

The No. 1 Express normally arrived in Nashville at 7:10 A.M. while Train No. 4 usually left Nashville at 7:00 A.M. As a general rule, they met on a double track between Union Station and the railroad shops, two and a half miles west of town. By written orders, the Express (No. 1) always had the right-of-way; whenever it was late, No. 4 was to wait on the side track until it passed. On July 9, 1918, the No. 1 Express was about 30 minutes late and No. 4 was about seven minutes late. Coincidentally, about this same time, a switch engine pulling ten freight cars joined the traffic, passing No. 4 on the double tracks, inbound for Nashville. What happened next is anybody's guess. The engineer of No. 4 may have mistaken the smaller,

switch engine for the express. Whatever the reason, he immediately pulled his engine out onto the main track and began increasing his speed to 50 mph. Meanwhile the express was unknowingly racing toward him, also at 50 mph.

The resulting collision demolished both locomotives and many of the other rail cars. Some coaches literally "telescoped" (push into and through the cars ahead), bending, splintering, and squashing everything in their path, including passengers. No. 1 derailed to the west side of the track and No. 4 to the east side. Behind No. 1, the baggage car and the next three wooden passenger coaches were crushed and scattered around the scene. Thirty casualties were found under the baggage car alone. Five wooden passenger coaches behind No. 4 were ripped apart, and derailed. The last three cars were not derailed and only slightly damaged. Fires broke out at several locations within the wreck, hampering rescue efforts and causing additional casualties and injuries.

The collision was heard for miles, and there were several eyewitnesses. The number of dead and injured was variously reported, but the official Interstate Commerce Commission figure was 101 killed and another 100 or so injured. Some of the injured undoubtedly died later. Most of the victims were soldiers and black laborers (from as far away as Texas) en route to the DuPont munitions plant at Old Hickory.

Allen R. Coggins, Knoxville

SEE: DISASTERS

DYER COUNTY, located in West Tennessee, was established in 1823 and named in honor of Colonel Robert H. Dyer. John McIver and Joel H. Dyer donated 60 acres for the new county seat, named Dyersburg, at a central location within the county known as McIver's Bluff. In 1825 Joel Dyer surveyed the townsite into 86 lots; the first courthouse was built on the square in 1827. The present Classical Revival-styled courthouse, designed by Asa Biggs in 1911, centers a downtown historic district listed in the National Register of Historic Places.

Fertile soil and plentiful stands of timber made Dyer County rich farming country. Early profitable crops were timber, corn, and tobacco, replaced in the post-Civil War era by a reliance on cotton and the expanding timber industry. Situated at the head of steamboat navigation on the Forked Deer River, Dyersburg grew as a river town, especially once the *Grey Eagle* made the first successful steamboat trip in 1836. The county was spared the worst of the Civil War, as no major battles or activities occurred within its borders. Otho F. Strahl was a Dyersburg resident, who raised a local Confederate infantry company in 1861 and then steadily advanced to the rank of Brigadier General in the Army of Tennessee. On November 30, 1864, Strahl was killed at the Battle of Franklin.

Cotton wagons rolling into Dyersburg, 1920–1930.

The county's first industrial boom dates to 1879 when the steamboat *Alf Stevens* shipped timber from A. M. Stevens Lumber Company of Dyersburg to St. Louis markets. The Stevens company established a large sawmill in 1880 and opened a planing mill in 1885. The Bank of Dyersburg opened in 1880, while another timber industry, Nichols & Co. Wooden Bowl Factory, began operations in 1881. The arrival of the Newport News and Mississippi Valley Railroad in 1884 further expanded market possibilities; a branch line, the Dyersburg Northern, soon linked the county seat to Tiptonville. The new railroad links encouraged the creation of new industries and businesses. In 1884, for example, investors established the Dyersburg Oil Company, a cottonseed factory. This company remained locally important through the twentieth century.

In 1904 and 1907, Dyersburg hosted two huge revivals conducted by evangelist George C. Gates. The 1907 revival alone converted 700 people. The revivals preceeded Dyersburg's greatest boom as it emerged as a regional railroad hub. Between 1909 and 1914, Dyersburg became the junction point for three different lines, led by the Illinois Central Railroad. The Illinois Central expanded its facilities throughout the county, for instance, building in 1920 a new combination depot at the town of Newbern, which was a major cotton and livestock shipping point. Listed in the National Register, this depot survives and is one of two Amtrak passenger stops in Tennessee in 1998. Newbern is the county's second largest incorporated city. Smaller villages include Trimble, Fowkles, Finley, Bogota, and Heloise, the county's sole Mississippi River village.

By the 1920s the rich timber resources of Dyer County were gone; cotton was the county's leading resource. African Americans participated actively in the Rosenwald school building program, sponsoring and constructing four school across the county while white officials put up most of the money for a modern 16-room industrial training school for blacks. Known as Bruce High School, it remained a segregated facility until it closed in 1966. In 1929 the Dyersburg Cotton Products, Inc., built a modern plant, complete with company housing, on the outskirts of Dyersburg. The town's largest industrial concern, the plant consumed about six million pounds of cotton each year from local farmers. The great Mississippi River floods of 1927 and 1937 devastated western Dyer County, especially lands between the Obion and Mississippi rivers.

During World War II the Halls Air Base, located at the border of Lauderdale County and Dyer County, created many civilian jobs as it trained hundreds of B-17 bomber pilots. An emergency landing strip was built in Dyersburg. After the war, agriculture in Dyer County began to shift from cotton into new crops. By the mid-1980s soybeans composed the largest crop by far, followed by wheat, milo, corn, and cotton. Industry continued to expand and the county became a regional medical, educational, retail and distribution center. The establishment of Dyersburg State Community College in 1969 enhanced educational and cultural opportunities in the county. In the last two decades, two major projects modernized the county's transportation system: Interstate I-155, linking Dyersburg with Missouri via the only highway bridge (1976) over the Mississippi River between Cairo, Illinois, and Memphis, and the four-lane expansion of U.S. 412, connecting Dyersburg to I-40 at Jackson.

Carroll Van West, Middle Tennessee State University

SEE: COMMUNITY COLLEGES; COOPER, JERE; JULIUS
ROSENWALD FUND; RAILROADS; STEAMBOATING; WORLD
WAR II

DYKEMAN, WILMA (1920–), novelist, journalist, and State Historian, was born in Asheville, North Carolina, on May 20, 1920. In 1940 she married James R. Stokely. They resided in Newport, Tennessee, where they raised two sons. Stokely died in 1977. Dykeman holds her undergraduate degree, with a major in speech, from Northwestern University. She has received many honorary degrees and awards including the Sidney Hillman Award (shared with her husband James), a Guggenheim Fellowship, a Senior Fellow of the National Endowment of the Humanities, and the Tennessee Conservation Writer of the Year.

Dykeman launched her career as a Tennessee historian with the publication of *The French Broad*, released in 1955 as part of the Rivers of America Series of the Rinehart publishing company. Of Dykeman's three primary categories of writing, *The French Broad* addressed the first—early Tennessee history and the distinctive character of the state's mountain people. Her later *Tennessee: A Bicentennial History* (1976) is another classic text of the state's history. In 1981 Governor Lamar Alexander appointed Dykeman the official State Historian. A second category in Dykeman's writing is her concern for civil rights and human freedom. Works like *Neither Black Nor White* (1957) and *Seeds of Southern Change: The Life of Will Alexander* (1962), both written in collaboration with husband James R. Stokely, demonstrate a passionate commitment to civil liberties. A third category is Dykeman's reverence for and affirmation of life, human dignity, and the environment. This is perhaps reflected best in her novels such as *The Tall Woman* (1962), *The Far Family* (1966), and *Return the Innocent Earth* (1973). Scholar Thomas D. Young observed that a theme shared by all three novels is "the unique role of the mountain woman in her family and the community."[1]

Dykeman lives in Newport and continues to write and speak about the themes, people, and events that have shaped her native Appalachian region, the state, and the South. As State Historian, she is an effective spokesperson for the importance of history in the present and future and she was the first to raise her voice in support for the production of a Tennessee encyclopedia to celebrate 200 years of statehood.

Carroll Van West, Middle Tennessee State University

CITATION:

(1) Thomas D. Young, *Tennessee Writers* (Knoxville, 1981), 108.

SUGGESTED READING: Sam B. Smith, "Wilma Dykeman and James Stokely," Jim Stokely and Jeff D. Johnson, eds., *An Encyclopedia of East Tennessee* (1981), 163–165

SEE: CIVIL RIGHTS MOVEMENT; COCKE COUNTY; CONSERVATION

E

EARL, RALPH E. W. (ca. 1785–1838), portraitist, was the son of Connecticut painter Ralph Earl (1751–1801) and his second wife Anne Whiteside of Norwich, England. Born in England, he studied under his father in Northhampton, Massachusetts, before traveling to London in 1809, to study under Benjamin West and John Trumbull. After a year in London, he spent four years in Norwich with his grandfather and uncle before journeying to the Continent for a year in Paris. While there, he saw most of the Europe's greatest paintings, due to Napoleon Bonaparte's recent conquests on the Continent.

On January 1, 1817, Earl arrived in Nashville to paint the portrait of General Andrew Jackson, the hero of the Battle of New Orleans. Later that year, in Natchez, he met and married Jane Caffrey, Mrs. Rachel Jackson's niece. She died the next year, but Earl moved into the Hermitage and into Jackson's circle. From 1818 until 1827, he directed the Nashville Museum of "natural and artificial curiosities" on the Public Square. The museum included ten of Earl's portraits.

When Jackson went to Washington as president, Earl went with him. During the next eight years, Earl turned out numerous paintings of Jackson, some of distinction, but many repetitious in nature and mediocre in quality, political icons rather than art. Politicians, especially Democrats, knew it "did not hurt to order a portrait of General Jackson from Earl." He painted many of Jackson's friends and a few of his foes. He designed the invitation to Lafayette's ball in Nashville in 1825, as well as the guitar-shaped driveway and concentric flower beds at the Hermitage. He also executed decorative interior painting at neighboring Tulip Grove. Earl returned to the Hermitage with Jackson in 1837, and died there in September, 1838.

James C. Kelly, Virginia Historical Society

SEE: ART; HERMITAGE

EARTHQUAKES, 1811–1812. Between mid-December 1811 and mid-March 1812, a series of catastrophic earthquakes shook West Tennessee and the rest of the Central Mississippi Valley. Judging from reports and eyewitness accounts, the quakes would have measured among the highest ever recorded on the modern Richter scale. Some reports said that the quakes were strong enough to awaken sleepers in Washington, D.C., and allegedly some tremors were felt 1,200 miles away in Quebec City, Canada.

The first of these historic quakes occurred in the St. Francis River area of northeast Arkansas; the second struck five weeks later and several miles to the northeast. Two weeks after that the third and strongest of the three quakes hit the area, with its epicenter still further north, at the little river port town of New Madrid, Missouri. The last of these three quakes is estimated to be the strongest ever recorded on the North American continent.

Geologists associate this early quake activity with the New Madrid or Central United States seismic zone. This ill-defined series of deeply buried faults runs roughly parallel to the Mississippi River Valley. The zone extends from Cairo, Illinois, south through Missouri to Marked Tree, Arkansas. A side branch also extends into the Reelfoot Lake region of Northwest Tennessee.

Since the affected region was a sparsely settled frontier, few written accounts exist about the early quakes. According to a few personal diary entries and scanty eyewitness accounts quoted in local newspapers, the endless days and nights of earth tremors and thousands of aftershocks must have been dreadful to experience. Few settlers had ever experienced a quake.

The quakes caused much destruction along the Mississippi River as far south as present-day Memphis and as far up the Ohio River as Indiana. During the strongest of the quakes, great cracks and fissures opened and spewed out sand and water. Gaping crevices formed, some 12 feet wide and deep and more than 20 feet in length. Low waterfalls developed at points along the Mississippi, in the vicinity of New Madrid. They were short lived, however, in the soft sediments of the river valley. Shifting currents and changing flows along the Mississippi, Ohio, Arkansas, and other rivers created and destroyed islands, sandbars, and other familiar features. The quakes caused waves to rush over river banks. Return currents washed countless limbs and even whole trees into the main channels. Massive log jams formed, making navigation even more perilous.

Many boats were capsized, and cargoes and crews never seen again. Seasoned river boat pilots had to deal with whole new rivers. Cracks and fissures, downed trees, and other obstacles made roads and trails impassable. Massive landslides occurred along the Mississippi and Ohio river bluffs from Memphis to Indiana. Some ground areas rose or fell as much as 20 feet relative to surrounding landscape. An 18- to 20-acre area near Piney River in Tennessee sank so low that the tops of the trees were at the same level as the surrounding ground. Whole forests sank below their original level and filled with water to form swamps and shallow lakes. The 18,000 acre Reelfoot Lake was either formed or enlarged during the 1811–12 earthquake episode. In other areas, lakes and swamps rose to higher elevations. Soon their waters drained away or evaporated. In time they evolved into prairies and upland forests. Much of this land now supports Tennessee cotton and soybeans.

As devastating as these early quakes were, destruction in human terms was light. Population was sparse, and Indians, traders, and settlers were quite self-sufficient, capable, and resilient. Due to a lack of census records and other reliable counts, the exact number of people who perished as a result of the quakes will never be known.

Allen R. Coggins, Knoxville

SEE: DISASTERS; REELFOOT LAKE STATE PARK

EAST TENNESSEE HISTORICAL SOCIETY was initially founded in 1834 by prominent Knoxville civic leaders, including Dr. J. G. M. Ramsey, who served as perpetual recording secretary, and Judge William B. Reese, who was elected the first president. According to Ramsey, the Society procured and perpetuated "all that relates to the early history and antiquities of Tennessee."[1] To that end, the Society collected manuscripts and artifacts, which were stored at the Ramsey's home "Mecklenburg" in the forks of the French Broad and Holston rivers. When Union soldiers burned Ramsey's home during the Civil War, the Society's entire collection, including the papers of William Blount, John Sevier, Samuel Wear, and Alexander Outlaw, was lost in the flames.

The destruction of "Mecklenburg" and Ramsey's flight to Georgia brought the operation of the Society to a halt. In 1883 a group of former Confederate officers, including William G. McAdoo and William Henderson, reorganized the Society as an auxiliary of the Southern Historical Society. Although unable to attend, the bed-ridden Ramsey blessed the reorganization. The Society sponsored a number of popular historical lectures, but within about 20 years, the organization again lapsed into inactivity, as the veteran leaders died.

In 1925, primarily through the efforts of University of Tennessee faculty and Knox County librarians, the Society was resurrected again. The Society sponsored lectures and published its first official monograph, *Sectionalism and Internal Improvements in Tennessee* (1939) by Stanley Folmsbee. The annual *Publications* (today *The Journal of East Tennessee History*), first published in 1929, quickly became the most significant aspect of the Society. In addition to its informal affiliation with the University, the Society forged close ties with the McClung Historical Collection, which provided office space and secretarial support.

In the early 1980s, the board of directors hired its own professional staff and moved the Society's headquarters to the Old Custom House in downtown Knoxville. During the tenure of executive directors Dr. Charles F. Bryan, Jr. (1981–1986), and Dr. Mark V. Wetherington, Sr. (1986–1989), the Society experienced an era of unprecedented growth, as membership doubled, an affiliate chapter program strengthened its outreach to the greater East Tennessee community, and the publication of the tri-annual *Tennessee Ancestors* enhanced the genealogy mission. The Society further expanded its scope during the administration of Dr. W. Todd Groce (1990–1995) through the establishment of the Museum of East Tennessee History and the "First Families of Tennessee" project, which recognized over 11,000 descendants of Tennessee pioneers as a part of the state's bicentennial. The current director, W. Kent Whitworth, has expanded public programs and directed the installation of the museum's permanent exhibits. The East Tennessee Historical Society plays a key role in collecting and preserving Tennessee history.

W. Todd Groce, Georgia Historical Society

CITATION:

(1) J.G.M. Ramsey, *Address Delivered Before the East Tennessee Historical and Antiquarian Society at Its First Annual Meeting in Knoxville, May 5, 1834* (Knoxville, 1834), 10.

SEE: RAMSEY, J.G.M.

EAST TENNESSEE IRON MANUFACTURING COMPANY. One of Chattanooga's earliest industrial ventures, the East Tennessee Iron Manufacturing Company was a seminal force in the industrial development of the city and its surrounding area. Incorporated by the Tennessee General Assembly in 1847, the company benefited from the geological, technological, and economic conditions peculiar to the region. Chattanooga is located in the Dyestone Belt, a physiographic region containing hematite ore deposits that, in the nineteenth century, were considered to have the greatest economic potential of any in the state. The Western & Atlantic Railroad selected Chattanooga as the terminus for its line from Atlanta, which was completed in 1850, and the Nashville and Chattanooga connected the two cities four years later. As the company developed an iron industry in the fledgling city, the railroads provided the link between eager consumers and producers of raw and finished iron goods. Chattanooga's potential as a boom-town rail junction also caught the eye of entrepreneurs seeking lucrative investments. The formation of the East Tennessee Iron Manufacturing Company gathered these diverse forces into a single purpose.

Several prominent Tennesseans served on the company's board of directors, but Robert Cravens was the only principal partner with practical iron experience. Beginning in the early 1830s, Cravens successfully developed foundries, forges, and blast furnaces, becoming an accomplished ironmaster. He even built an experimental furnace in Roane County to measure the fuel efficiency of coke as compared to charcoal in the production of pig iron (raw iron derived from iron ore). Modern furnaces use coke as fuel, but in the mid-nineteenth century few furnaces in the entire country, and almost none in the South, used anything other than charcoal. Cravens's innovations were applied to Bluff Furnace, the company's most ambitious business venture in the 1850s.

With the support of additional investors and Cravens's conveyance of iron facilities, mills, real estate, and ore fields, the East Tennessee Iron Manufacturing Company became heavily involved in the iron industry. In 1853 the company opened a foundry and machine shop adjacent to the downtown railyards; rail wheels and freight cars were evidently produced at the complex. In 1854 a new industrial plant was built on the banks of the Tennessee River; Bluff Furnace incorporated the natural topography of a high bluff and river transportation into its location and design. The bluff beside the 40-foot high furnace stack afforded convenient access to the charging deck at the top of the furnace. There, massive quantities of charcoal fuel, iron ore, and a limestone flux were off-loaded from river barges and "charged" (placed in alternating layers) in the furnace interior. The furnace was then "put into blast" using preheated, compressed air to reduce the ore at a hotter, more efficient temperature. The furnace did not begin operation until 1856, when it produced 172 tons of pig iron in 13 weeks.

In 1859 the main stack was torn down, and under the direction of northern ironmasters James Henderson and Giles Edwards, a new coke-fired furnace was erected in its place. Unique in the South, and rare elsewhere, the iron-clad cupola furnace stood on the cutting edge of iron technology. In May 1860 the new furnace produced 500 tons of iron before it ran out of coke. In November it resumed operations, but soon succumbed to the problems generated by the political complications and demoralization of the workmen that accompanied the advent of war. Archaeological evidence at the site indicates that the furnace froze up in mid-blast and never operated again. It was demolished and its machinery recycled by other southern furnaces.

The Civil War brought an end to the East Tennessee Iron Manufacturing Company and its innovative iron furnace. But others, inspired by the Bluff Furnace example, continued in the tradition set by Robert Cravens. Chattanooga would grow into a town supported by heavy industry, one with roots reaching back to Bluff Furnace and the East Tennessee Iron Manufacturing Company.

Nicholas Honerkamp, University of Tennessee at Chattanooga

SUGGESTED READING: R. Bruce Council, Nicholas Honerkamp, and M. Elizabeth Will, *Industry and Technology in Antebellum Tennessee: The Archaeology of Bluff Furnace* (1992)

SEE: CHATTANOOGA; INDUSTRY; RAILROADS

EAST TENNESSEE STATE UNIVERSITY in Johnson City evolved from East Tennessee State Normal School, which enrolled the first students in October, 1911. In 1900 Tennesseans found their public schools in poor condition. State law required a minimum of 100 days per term. Publicly supported four-year high schools were few. Teachers for the lower grades qualified by completing the eighth grade and passing state examinations. Some teachers in the high schools had attended college, but few held bachelor's degrees. All had to pass examinations in the subjects they taught. State superintendents sponsored "state institutes," held in centrally located cities, and employed well-trained administrators and teachers to instruct those enrolled. Most of the teachers, however, lived in rural areas and attended "county institutes" that featured preachers, local orators, politicians, superficial reviews in elementary subjects, and easy examinations. State Superintendent Seymour A. Mynders complained that 40 percent of the schools could not operate if the requirements for spelling and composition were rigidly followed.

In 1903 leading educators decided that the time had come to make radical improvements, and they launched a "crusade." In the front rank were Professor P. P. Claxton of the University of Tennessee; Sidney G. Gilbreath, former state superintendent and superintendent of Chattanooga schools; Seymour A. Mynders, state superintendent; and R. L. Jones, superintendent of Hamilton County schools and soon to be state superintendent. Their "crusade" lasted for six years and resulted in the passage of the Education Act of 1909 to modernize the state school system; among the reforms was the provision for four normal schools to train teachers. Gilbreath, Mynders, Jones, and W. J. Hale were selected as presidents of the four normals located in Johnson City, Memphis, Murfreesboro, and Nashville.

The normals offered an "academic course" that included subjects taught in first-class high schools plus elementary psychology and methods for teaching in the lower grades. The "normal course" included advanced psychology, methods of teaching high school subjects, and the usual liberal arts courses for college freshmen and sophomores. In 1919 the state board eliminated the first two years of the "academic course" and added the junior year of college to the "normal course." Five years later the board dropped the "academic course" and added the fourth year of college.

At this time the board also changed the name of the normal school in Johnson City to East Tennessee State Teachers College. Changing economic, social, professional, and intellectual needs and interests justified eliminating "Teachers" from the title in 1941. The General Assembly, in 1949, authorized state colleges to develop graduate programs. Colleges of Arts and Sciences, Education, Business, and the Graduate School were organized. The first master's degrees—four in number—were awarded in 1951. In 1963 ETSC achieved university status. Since then the James H. Quillen College of Medicine, College of Applied Science and Technology, School of Continuing Studies, College of Nursing, and College of Public and Allied Health have been added to the roll.

The University Libraries include the Sherrod Library, the Instructional Media Center, Archives of Appalachia, the University Archives, and the ETSU/UT at Kingsport Library. Sherrod Library has over half a million volumes, 1.2 million units of microforms, and 3,700 periodical subscriptions. The University Archives have papers and correspondence, dating from 1909, that greatly contribute to understanding and appreciating the problems that faced presidents, politicians, faculty, students, parents, and taxpayers. B. Carroll Reece, who served as a member of Congress for 34 years, left his papers to the library. Other valuable primary sources are Johnson City Foundry and Machine Works Collections and Washington County (Tennessee) Court Records. The Archives of Appalachia include manuscripts, institutional records, photographic prints, negatives and slides, and audio-visual materials dealing with the area.

In 1995 East Tennessee State University enrolled 11,723 students including 2,060 in the Graduate School, 246 medical students, and 201 medical residents. Over 100 degree programs are available, including associate, bachelor's, master's, the Ed.S., the Ed.D., Ph.D., and M.D. degrees.

Frank B. Williams, Jr., East Tennessee State University
SUGGESTED READING: Frank B. Williams, Jr., *East Tennessee State University: A University's Story, 1911–1980,* (1991)
SEE: CENTER FOR APPALACHIAN STUDIES AND SERVICES; CLAXTON, PHILANDER; EDUCATION, HIGHER; JOHNSON CITY; QUILLEN COLLEGE OF MEDICINE; REECE, B. CARROLL

EATON AFFAIR. When Andrew Jackson became president of the United States in 1829, he chose John Henry Eaton, his biographer, leading political adviser, and Tennessee friend, to be Secretary of War.

Just a few months earlier, Eaton had married Margaret O'Neale Timberlake, the recent widow of navy purser John B. Timberlake. She was the daughter of the proprietor of one of Washington's leading boarding houses/taverns, the establishment where well-known politicians like Jackson and Eaton stayed. When her navy husband went away to sea, rumors spread that she was carrying on an illicit affair with Eaton. Their marriage only nine months after Timberlake took his own life fueled the gossip.

In the Washington of the 1820s and 1830s, women enforced strict societal standards on each other. Purity was an essential requirement for any proper woman, and since Margaret O'Neale Timberlake Eaton was believed to be immoral, she could not be accepted into society. No proper woman could exchange visits with her, invite her to social functions, or be seen exchanging pleasantries with her. Her Irish-American boarding house background and her forward cordiality and open conversations with men were other problems. She might be the wife of the Secretary of War, but she was still a suspect woman and had to be snubbed.

Andrew Jackson's own wife had earlier been the subject of similar attacks. She died in December 1828, and he believed it was the gossip which killed her. When Margaret Eaton came under attack, therefore, Jackson immediately rose to her defense. He saw the attacks against her as part of a conspiracy led by his long-time rival Henry Clay to thwart his administration. He had to change his mind, however, when he noted that his supporters, including his niece, Emily Donelson, were also snubbing Mrs. Eaton. Two Presbyterian ministers, including the pastor of his own church in Washington, urged him to rid himself of her moral blight. Most of his cabinet, the wife of his vice president, John C. Calhoun, and friends and political associates in Tennessee also refused to have anything to do with her. Jackson soon turned his anger on John C. Calhoun.

The Eaton Affair, therefore, began as an issue of societal etiquette, but it quickly expanded beyond that. Jackson, always a defender of women and especially agitated because of his wife's recent death, jumped to the defense of his friend whom he considered a wronged woman. There was already a rivalry between Vice President Calhoun and Secretary of State Martin Van Buren over who would be Jackson's successor, and this tension widened the issue. Jackson came to see Calhoun as the secret instigator of the affronts to Margaret Eaton. Martin Van Buren, being a widower, and developing a closeness with Jackson, refused to snub Mrs. Eaton, and in fact invited her to all his social functions. When Calhoun and Jackson battled over nullification and their roles in the 1818 Seminole War controversy, Van Buren benefited. He solidified his position with Jackson in 1831 when he volunteered to resign from the cabinet, thus giving the president an opportunity to force a mass resignation. In the controversy over this unique event in American history, Margaret Eaton was the center of the debate and name-calling. All the principals in the controversy blamed her in their printed defenses. In early 1832, Calhoun cast the tie-breaking vote preventing Van Buren from remaining as minister to Great Britain, where Jackson had sent him. Calhoun's action only helped Van Buren insure his position as Jackson's presidential heir apparent.

The Eaton Affair, therefore, was a societal issue that helped influence the politics of the first several years of the Jackson presidency. Margaret Eaton was not the sole determinant of the period's politics, but it was the debate over her virtue that provided the focus for the political disagreements that shaped the direction of the Jacksonian coalition and demonstrated society's attitude toward women during these important years.

John F. Marszalek, Mississippi State University

SUGGESTED READINGS: John Marszalek, *The Petticoat Affair: Manners, Mutiny, and Sex in Andrew Jackson's White House* (1998) and "The Eaton Affair, Society and Politics," *Tennessee Historical Quarterly* 55 (1996): 6–19

SEE: EATON, JOHN H.; EATON, MARGARET; JACKSON, ANDREW; JACKSONIANS

EATON, JOHN HENRY (1790–1856). Born into a prominent family, he was the son of John Eaton, a chaise maker, and Elizabeth, his wife. His father was county coroner, a member of the state assembly, and the owner of 5,000 acres of land in Williamson County, property he received from the estate of his uncle, Major Pinkerton Eaton, a soldier killed in the Revolution.

After briefly attending the University of North Carolina, the young John Henry Eaton settled in Tennessee around 1808 and began a law practice in Franklin. He participated in the War of 1812, and in

1813 he married Myra Lewis, the daughter of a wealthy landowner and a ward of Andrew Jackson. He served in the Tennessee legislature in 1815 and 1816, and in 1817 he completed a biography of Andrew Jackson, the hero of New Orleans. He entered the United States Senate in 1818, serving until 1829.

Eaton is most famous for his close relationship to an American president and for his marriage to a controversial woman. (His first wife died without issue.) He was one of Andrew Jackson's closest advisers in the 1824 and 1828 presidential campaigns, and when Jackson became president in 1829 he named Eaton his Secretary of War. On January 1, 1829, Eaton married the daughter of a Washington boarding house proprietor, the recent widow of a navy purser who had committed suicide, and a woman who was the target of rumors of sexual improprieties. Washington society women and cabinet wives refused to associate with Margaret "Peggy" O'Neale Timberlake Eaton, so her husband and the president unsuccessfully fought a two-year battle for her acceptance. What began as a social matter turned into a political fray resulting in the break-up of Jackson's cabinet and a permanent split between him and his vice president, John C. Calhoun.

To make up for Eaton's resignation from the cabinet, Jackson tried but failed to have him reelected to the United States Senate from Tennessee. He then appointed him governor of the Florida Territory (1834–1836) and later made him United States Minister to Spain (1836–1840). Upon his return to the United States, Eaton joined the Whig party and lost Jackson's friendship until just before the former president's death in 1845. Eaton spent most of his later life in Washington as a prominent attorney, but he and his wife regularly returned to Franklin during the summers. When he died in 1856, his substantial estate testified to a lifetime of monetary success.

John F. Marszalek, Mississippi State University

SUGGESTED READING: Ada S. Walker, "John Henry Eaton, Apostate," East Tennessee Historical Society *Publications* 24 (1952): 26–43

SEE: EATON AFFAIR; EATON, MARGARET; JACKSON, ANDREW; JACKSONIANS; WILLIAMSON COUNTY

EATON, MARGARET "PEGGY" (1799–1879). Born to William O'Neale, the owner of a Washington boarding house, and his wife, Rhoda, the young Margaret and her five brothers and sisters were well-known in political Washington. Leading congressmen and senators stayed at the O'Neale establishment (later called the Franklin House), and Margaret became especially popular because of her good looks and her personality. She attended one of the city's leading schools and received instruction in piano and the dance. When she became a teenager, young and old men began throwing themselves at her. She tried to elope with one of them, so her worried father put her in a boarding school in New York City under the watchful eye of DeWitt Clinton. She was there only a short time before convincing her father she should be allowed to return home.

After a whirlwind courtship, she married a navy purser named John B. Timberlake on July 18, 1816. She had three children by him, but his inability to survive financially in the store he had established in Washington forced him back to sea. She remained at home with the children, helping her family in the boarding house and the associated tavern.

Sometime during this period rumors began to circulate that she had long been a loose woman and was demonstrating this fact through an illicit relationship with a boarder, one John Henry Eaton, Senator from Tennessee and close friend of Andrew Jackson. When Timberlake killed himself and she and Eaton were married soon after, this nuptial was considered more than adequate proof of her shameless immorality.

Eaton had long been close to Jackson as political advisor and friend, so, when Old Hickory entered the presidency, he named Eaton his Secretary of War. Washington society and the cabinet wives were outraged that someone with Margaret Eaton's reputation was in such an important position. They refused to associate with her, basing their stand on woman's duty to protect society from immorality. The Eatons and Andrew Jackson fought a two-year battle to overcome this snubbing, and the social dispute quickly developed into a political war. In 1831, Jackson forced his entire cabinet to resign, and an irrevocable split developed between him and his vice president, John C. Calhoun.

Failing in his effort to return Eaton to the Senate, Jackson appointed him the governor of the Florida Territory (1834–1836) and later made him the United States Minister to Spain (1836–1840). Margaret Eaton was socially accepted in both places and when the couple returned to Washington in 1840, she received a similarly friendly reception. John Eaton established a successful law practice in the nation's capital and died in 1856.

The widow, raising the four children of her deceased daughter and son-in-law, unexpectedly married Antonio Buchignani on June 7, 1859, when she was 59 years old and he in his early twenties. They lived an apparently happy life until the fall of 1866 when Buchignani ran away to Italy with his wife's money and her granddaughter (his step child). He made the mistake of returning to the United States in 1868, however, and the jilted wife had him arrested. He jumped bond, leaving her destitute. She divorced him and spent the last of her years living a difficult existence in Washington, D.C., where she died in 1879.
John F. Marszalek, Mississippi State University

SUGGESTED READINGS: Margaret Eaton, *The Autobiography of Peggy Eaton* (1932); John F. Marszalek, *The Petticoat Affair: Manners, Mutiny, and Sex in Andrew Jackson's White House* (1998)

SEE: EATON AFFAIR; EATON, JOHN H.

ECOLOGICAL SYSTEMS. Tennessee is an upper South state approximately 432 miles long and 112 miles wide, constituting 42,244 square miles, with elevations ranging from peaks of over 6,000 feet to sea level, containing a wide variety of natural and human environments. A growing season that ranges from an average of 160 days in the mountainous east to 260 days in the southwestern corner provides another source of variation. The state contains significant portions of three of the major ecological regions, or biomes, of North America. Within each of those larger zones are also smaller environmental areas.

Much of the Unaka, or Great Smoky Mountains, of East Tennessee is in the Boreal, or Conifer Zone, where the climate and environment, due to the high altitude, more nearly resembles that of upstate New York than that of the upper South. Consequently, trees commonly associated with more northern climes—firs, spruce, hemlock—are native. The area's topographical complexity of peaks, ridges, valleys, and coves creates a setting for a wide variety of plant life, including some 1,300 species of flowering plant and 131 species of trees, compared to 85 trees for all of Europe. In the heart of the region is the Cherokee National Forest (625,350 acres) which includes the Great Smoky Mountains National Park (241,206 acres), one of the region's most popular parks.

At the opposite end of the state are the Mississippi River Bottom lands, which are some 50 miles wide and contain over 900 square miles. A swampy, deciduous forest is the ecological system dominating this geophysical region. Its almost subtropical appearance is typified by Reelfoot Lake, approximately 14 miles long and five miles wide, with its cypress and abundant waterfowl, including egrets and herons. Reelfoot Lake, in fact, is one of the state's few bald eagle nesting areas. This ecological zone, together with much of the rest of West Tennessee and the western portion of the Tennessee River Valley, is crucial to the Mississippi Flyway. Consequently the U.S. Fish and Wildlife Service maintains seven National Wildlife Refuges, totaling 91,073 acres, in the region.

The vast majority of the state's territory, ranging from the Valley of East Tennessee through the Gulf Coastal Plain bordering on the Mississippi Bottoms, is within the Deciduous Forest Zone. This zone is characterized by oaks, maples, beech, walnut, hickory, poplar, and other hardwoods mixed with pine and cedar. The wildlife complex—deer, raccoon, opossum, turkey—is typical for the American South. Given the zone's topological diversity and its complex drainage patterns and varying soils, there is considerable environmental variation.

West of the Unaka Mountains is the Valley of East Tennessee, varying in width from 30 to 60 miles and containing some 9,000 square miles drained by the eastern reaches of the Tennessee River and its tributaries. It is an undulating region of small farms with two major urban centers, Knoxville and Chattanooga. Forest patches are frequent. West of the Valley is the Cumberland Plateau, portions of which reach an elevation of 2,000 feet. To the south the Sequatchie Valley bifurcates the Plateau as far north as the Crab Orchard Mountains. The Plateau, totaling 4,300 square miles, is also cut by deep and sometimes wide river valleys, which create some of the most spectacular vistas in the state. The Plateau descends into the Eastern Highland Rim, averaging 1,000 feet above sea level. This region of some 2,500 square miles is reasonably fertile, except for the western edges where poor drainage and soils create broad "barrens" and where forests develop or recover more slowly than in other nearby regions.

The Great Central or Nashville Basin (5,000 square miles) with an average elevation just over 500 feet and scattered hills, termed "knobs," is often called "the Garden of Tennessee" for its relative fertility. It is a region of larger farms and cattle operations, comparatively cleared of forest. Nashville is the hub of the region. It is well-drained by portions of the Tennessee and Cumberland rivers with their tributaries including the Duck, Caney Fork, Buffalo, and Harpeth rivers. To the south and west are the Western Highland Rim (7,500 square miles with an average elevation of 1,000 feet) and the Tennessee River Valley, which are much more heavily forested than the Basin. Between the Tennessee River Valley and the Mississippi Bottoms is the Gulf Coastal Plain (9,000 square miles) of West Tennessee. Parallel to the Tennessee River in the eastern portion of the Plain is a belt of sand hills and mixed pine and hardwood forests about 35 miles wide, where farming is difficult. Much of this land is in the Tennessee National Wildlife Refuge. The bulk of the Coastal Plain is both flatter and more fertile and, consequently, more heavily farmed than other areas of the state.

Human occupation and exploitation, of course, have had a massive impact on these natural environments. Agriculture is the greatest of these influences. There were approximately 84,000 farms in Tennessee in 1990, constituting about 12,300,000 acres, or half the land area, despite the fact that around one-third of the state's territory is unfit for farming. About 20 percent of this farmland is in woodland and forest rather than field and pasture. Tennessee's forests, public and private, were sufficient to allow the cutting of 840,000 board feet of hardwood in 1993, making the state one of the nation's leaders in hardwood production. According to 1995 estimates, one-half of the state's area is wooded, with some 200 species of trees, of which one-third have commercial value. There are more acres (156,000) in state forests in Tennessee than in any other southern state. The Tennessee State Park system contains another 131,000 acres in 51 parks.

The rivers, streams, and lakes are vital parts of the state's ecological systems. The Tennessee Valley Authority operates 17 dams on the Tennessee and its tributaries, while the Army Corps of Engineers has built seven on the Cumberland. These projects for flood control and hydroelectric power have created a series of slack water lakes of ecological value as well as of recreational and economic importance. Also the state's five largest cities have, over the last 20 years, increasingly recognized the importance of urban ecology. For instance, there have been projects to preserve green areas and provide better public access to riverfronts for recreational and cultural uses.

Enforcement of state environmental laws and regulations rests mainly with the Department of Environment and Conservation, created in 1991 to consolidate programs from a variety of departments and agencies. Responsibilities include the State Park System, air and water pollution control, and solid waste management. The Wildlife Resources Agency is independent while the Forestry Division is part of the Department of Agriculture and maintains the State Forests.

Richard P. Gildrie, Austin Peay State University

SEE: AGRICULTURE; CHEROKEE NATIONAL FOREST; CONSERVATION; CUMBERLAND RIVER; GEOLOGICAL ZONES; GREAT SMOKY MOUNTAINS NATIONAL PARK; REELFOOT LAKE STATE PARK; TENNESSEE RIVER; TENNESSEE WILDLIFE RESOURCES AGENCY; U.S. ARMY CORPS OF ENGINEERS

EDGAR EVINS STATE PARK is headquartered in DeKalb County, along Center Hill Lake. Containing about 6,000 acres, the park is named in honor of State Senator and Smithville civic capitalist James Edgar Evins, who was the father of noted U.S. Congressman Joe L. Evins. The park was created in 1968 as a cooperative effort. The state constructed and maintains the park's varied modern recreational facilities, but leases the land from the U.S. Corps of Engineers, which administers the Center Hill Dam and Reservoir. Fed by the Caney Fork and Falling Water rivers, Center Hill Lake stretches some 65 miles, creating over 400 miles of shoreline and covering over 20,000 acres of land in DeKalb, Putnam, White, and Warren counties. Nearby are the Burgess Falls State Natural Area and Rock Island State Park. Near to the park, on 180 acres overlooking the Center Hill Lake, is the Joe L. Evins Appalachian Center For Crafts. Built with federal funding from the Appalachian Regional Commission and opened in 1979, the Center provides instruction and exhibits about a wide range of folk crafts. It is operated as part of the B.A. in Fine Arts degree program at Tennessee Technological University.

Carroll Van West, Middle Tennessee State University

SEE: APPALACHIAN REGIONAL COMMISSION; EVINS, JOSEPH L.; TENNESSEE TECHNOLOGICAL UNIVERSITY; U.S. ARMY CORPS OF ENGINEERS

EDMONDSON, BELLE (1840–1873), Confederate smuggler, was born in Mississippi. On the eve of the Civil War her family moved to a Shelby County farm on Holly Ford Road (now Airways Boulevard), about three miles from the Mississippi border and eight miles southeast of Memphis. The Edmondsons were staunch Confederates; two of Belle's brothers served in the army.

The Edmondson farm was located in a no-man's land, with parties of scouts from both armies patrolling constantly; Union pickets on the roads, and Confederate lines less than 30 miles south. According to her diaries and letters, Belle Edmondson became adept at smuggling information and supplies for the Confederates, carrying letters and money in her bosom, and medicine and supplies under her petticoats. Returning from one visit to Memphis, she made a skirt of gray uniform cloth, pinned hats inside her hoops, and tied a pair of boots under her skirts, counting on the fact that Union officers were reluctant to search women.

When her many trips back and forth attracted the attention of Union General Stephen A. Hurlburt, he issued a warrant for her arrest, ending her adventures. In 1864 she moved to a plantation in Clay County, Mississippi, for the rest of the war. She died in 1873, and was buried with her parents in Elmwood Cemetery.

Perre Magness, Memphis

"*Lion*" *by William Edmondson.*

TENNESSEE STATE MUSEUM

SUGGESTED READING: William and Loretta Galbraith, *A Lost Heroine of the Confederacy, The Diaries and Letters of Belle Edmondson* (1990)

SEE: OCCUPATION, CIVIL WAR; SHELBY COUNTY

EDMONDSON, WILLIAM (ca. 1870–1951). Few folk artists can claim the widespread recognition by the world of fine art that William Edmondson achieved during his lifetime. The first African-American artist to have a one-man exhibition at the Museum of Modern Art, Edmondson's artistic vision of form reduced to its elemental geometry and use of volumetric space continues to be recognized for its timeless power.

Edmondson was born in Davidson County, the son of former slaves. He worked as a farm laborer and a race horse swipe, and then at the shops of the Nashville, Chattanooga, and St. Louis Railway, until an accident forced him to retire in 1907. When he recovered, he worked at Woman's Hospital (later Baptist Hospital), where he remained until the hospital closed in 1931. Throughout the Great Depression, Edmondson worked as a stonemason's assistant, eventually developing his skills in carving.

Funerary practices had long provided a traditional outlet for southern black culture, and Edmondson first emerged as an artist within this framework. A devoted member of the United Primitive Baptist Church, Edmondson often credited his artistic energy and purpose to divine vision. His earliest efforts were gravestones, sometimes composed of several stacked geometric elements, sometimes also incorporating bird or animal forms. From this traditional context, Edmondson's carvings soon showed the influence of popular imagery in lambs, doves, and other forms. He expanded his repertory to include preachers, women, famous figures, and creatures of his imagination.

At the time Edmondson began to carve, there was a climate of growing appreciation for world folk and tribal arts. Edmondson's self-described "stingy" carving expressed a minimalist philosophy toward his medium that was consonant with the strong movement toward abstraction and simplified form gaining currency among the Modernists. He carved directly into the limestone, barely freeing the image from its confines, and creating a sensual play of texture and shape between the contours of the form and the hard edges of the stone. Photographs of the sculptures convey an impression of monumentality. In truth, few were as large as 20 to 25 inches; the majority were on an intimate scale, limited by the odd shapes and small pieces of limestone available to him.

Awareness of Edmondson's carvings reached the art world first through the efforts of his neighbor Sidney Hirsch, a member of the "Fugitive Poets" movement, who introduced the artist's work to Alfred and Elizabeth Starr. The Starrs brought photographer Louise Dahl-Wolfe to meet him. She documented his carvings and working environment, and introduced Edmondson's art to Alfred H. Barr, Jr., director of the Museum of Modern Art. In 1937 Edmondson's sculptures were featured in a one-man show at the museum. The following year, his work was included in the exhibition "Three Centuries of Art in the United States," that Barr organized for the Jeu de Paume in Paris. In 1939, and again in 1941, Edmondson was employed by the sculpture division of the Work Projects Administration. In 1973 he was the subject of *Visions in Stone: The Sculpture of William Edmondson,* written by Edmund L. Fuller and illustrated with over 100 photographs of Edmondson and his carvings by Edward Weston and Roger Haile. Edmondson's sculptures continue to be included in major art exhibitions, and his work is contained in many museum collections, including the Newark Museum in New Jersey, the Hirshhorn Museum and Sculpture Garden in Washington, D.C., the University of Rochester Art Gallery in New York, the McClung Museum at the University of Tennessee, Knoxville, and at Cheekwood and the Tennessee State Museum in Nashville.

The concrete solidity of Edmondson's carvings stand in ironic contrast to the fleeting record that remains of his life. His date of birth can only be guessed, after a fire destroyed the family Bible and the record of births. His place of burial in Mount Ararat Cemetery in Nashville is unmarked, and the cemetery records were also destroyed by fire. Edmondson's legacy survives in the several hundred astounding carvings he created between 1931 and 1951.

Stacy C. Hollander, Museum of American Folk Art, New York

SEE: CHEEKWOOD; DECORATIVE ARTS, AFRICAN-AMERICAN; WORKS PROGRESS ADMINISTRATION

EDUCATION, ELEMENTARY AND SECONDARY.

From Tennessee's earliest beginnings, many of the state's inhabitants expressed concern about the education of their children. In fact, even before Tennessee became a state, residents established private educational institutions. Despite these private efforts, however, the state's first constitution in 1796 did not even mention education. Official recognition of pubic education finally came in 1806 with the passage of the

Class picture at Nelson-Merry School, Nashville, 1910.

TSLA. NAGY COLLECTION.

Cession Act. This compact with the federal government required Tennessee to furnish 100,000 acres of land for two colleges and to reserve an additional 100,000 acres for the purpose of establishing an academy in each county. The same year, the General Assembly established academies in each of the existing 27 counties of the state.

After this initial concession to education in 1806, many years passed before the state made any serious attempts to establish a workable system of public schools. Although the General Assembly enacted measures in the name of public education in 1815, 1817, 1823, 1827, and 1830, the statutes generally had no impact because they lacked effective machinery to compel their enforcement and failed to provide for adequate funding. By 1834, against the background of national school reform, some Tennesseans became distressed by the state's school system. The state's inefficient public schools lacked adequate funding and were administered by independent county boards, whose members served without compensation.

This dismal reality prompted some to demand reform from the state constitutional convention in 1834. In response, Tennessee's new constitution of 1835 included a provision for education declaring that the general diffusion of knowledge was essential to the preservation of the state's democratic instituions. It admonished the Tennessee General Assembly "to cherish literature and science." The constitution further recommended that the General Assembly should be required to appoint a board of commissioners to oversee the state's public school fund.

One year later, the General Assembly passed a law designed to centralize the administration of state schools. It provided for a state superintendent of public instruction, elected to a two-year term by a joint vote of the General Assembly. The position paid $1,500 per annum. In February 1836 Robert H. McEwen was elected as Tennessee's first state superintendent of public instruction. During the four years of his administration, McEwen made a number of recommendations for improvement of Tennessee's school system, including gradation of schools, improvement of school house construction, per diem allowances for school commissioners, and authorization of the superintendent to publish a biannual periodical designed to promote education. McEwen's interest in reform was consistent with a similar contemporary reform impulse in the North. Consequently, the superintendent's official reports regularly included excerpts from a number of northern school reformers, including Horace Mann.

Despite official state interest in public school reform, however, most Tennesseans still remained much more committed to private rather than public education. McEwen succinctly acknowledged this reality when he declared, "Public schools sustained exclusively by public funds have seldom been known to succeed well for any length of time."[1] McEwen's less than efficient administration of the state school fund made matters even worse. A special investigative committee appointed by the General Assembly found that the school fund had been repeatedly plundered. In the wake of the damning report, Governor James K. Polk sued McEwen.

In 1847 the remnants of the state's educational reform forces convened in Knoxville to conduct an inquiry into the condition of the public schools. The convention concluded that the state's school districts refused to comply with the conditions of the school law, which required the regular election of school commissioners and the provision of physical facilities for schools. In response, Governor Neill S. Brown made a revolutionary recommendation, suggesting direct taxation as the most expedient means for increasing the common school fund. His recommendation fell on deaf ears, however, and the General Assembly refused to enact legislation to provide for direct taxation.

In 1853 public education in Tennessee finally received a sincere commitment from a state chief executive. In his message to the General Assembly, Andrew Johnson expressed deep concern for the inadequacy of the state's public education system. He readily admitted that the system failed to fulfill the dictates of the state constitution, but maintained that much of the blame for that failure could be traced to the inadequacy of the school fund. Johnson deplored the ineffectiveness of the public schools that did exist and charged that these inferior facilities tended to be an impediment to community initiatives and prevented other attempts to create privately-funded schools. The governor's distress over the inadequacy of the public school fund prompted him to pledge additional revenue from taxation to the system. Despite his commitment, the establishment of a state public education system was tabled with the approach of the Civil War.

When the war ended, Johnson, now President of the United States, faced the difficulties associated with the monumental task of reconstructing the nation. At the same time, the Tennessee General Assembly faced the equally difficult task of rehabilitating its war-torn state. As part of that rehabilitation process, Tennessee legislators attempted to resurrect the public school system. In March 1867 the legislature passed an act for the reorganization, supervision, and maintenance of common schools. The statute provided for the re-establishment of the office of State Superintendent of Education, furnished additional sources of revenue, and provided county supervision for the fledgling system.

Solving the system's administrative and financial woes proved to be exceedingly difficult for these legislators, but the existence of thousands of newly freed black Tennesseans clamoring for educational opportunities represented an equally difficult and emotional challenge to postwar education supporters. After much heated debate, the General Assembly reluctantly agreed to make provisions for the education of the state's black youth, but they clearly specified that those provisions would be segregated. Their determination to maintain two separate school systems had profound consequences in postwar Tennessee, with little taxable property after the devastation from the war and the emancipation of the slaves. In view of this bleak economic reality, the General Assembly's determination to establish two mutually exclusive school systems presented a most formidable challenge indeed. In this atmosphere, Tennessee's school fund grew slowly. One Freedmen's Bureau official's personal observations revealed that some counties paid only a portion of their assessment, a situation guaranteed to result in a slow accumulation of the school fund. In 1891 the permanent school fund amounted to only $150,000, on which the state paid six percent per annum.

As the end of the nineteenth century approached, two public education systems functioned in the state: one black, one white, and both impoverished. State administrators willingly admitted that segregation had a detrimental effect on the education of African-American and white students alike. One reasoned, "It is impossible to locate schools at present, as to place them within convenient reach of all the children of the population in the State, owing to the sparseness of the population in many sections. The consequence is, in some localities one race suffers; in others, the other."[2]

In the midst of all this talk of separation, the state's freedmen were determined to move forward. If the state would not provide them with adequate educational opportunities, they would do it themselves. Numerous reports issued by officials from the Bureau of Refugees, Freedmen, and Abandoned Lands recognized the eagerness of Tennessee freedmen to accumulate school property and defray the cost of teachers' expenses. According to statistical data released by the Bureau, black Tennesseans had acquired school property as early as the fall of 1866. In subsequent months, the freedmen's interest in actively promoting their own education continued to increase in intensity despite vigorous attempts by whites to discourage them. One Bureau official observed, "The desire of the freed people to own school property is increasing and 20 school houses are now reported as belonging to them. One school has been closed on account of the white people refusing to rent a building for it; and another because of

the alarming demonstrations against the teacher."[3] Despite the sometimes violent white opposition to their efforts, by May 1870, the last date for which the Bureau provided such data, the freedmen had managed to hold onto 30 school buildings.

After the Bureau ceased to exist in 1872, many of the black Tennessee schools it had helped to support were taken over by the state. Likewise, by the late nineteenth century the state also assumed control over a number of black schools that had been founded by northern church missionary societies in postwar Tennessee. Despite these additions, Tennessee's black public schools remained inadequate. At the same time, the state's white schools were only marginally better.

Many of these schools, especially in the rural areas, were only in session a few months out of every year. Furthermore, until very late in the century Tennessee's public schools concentrated on the primary level. The state legislature did not pass a statute providing for the establishment of secondary schools until 1885. This statute empowered "municipal corporations to levy additional taxes and to establish graded high schools." Consequently, only urban dwellers benefited. Then, in 1891, the General Assembly granted each county the option of establishing secondary school facilities. Not until 1899 did Tennessee law require the establishment of facilities for secondary education in each county. In that year, the General Assembly empowered each county court to levy special taxes for the establishment and support of a county high school. The legislature further stipulated that the county high schools would not be permitted to draw any money from the regular fund appropriated to the districts.

As the twentieth century approached, Tennessee clearly had made progress in the area of public education, but much remained to be done. The state operated with two functioning school systems, but both were inadequate and underfunded. The new century ushered in continued progress, but it also brought new problems. Some progress occurred because of help from outside the state, including the Julius Rosenwald Fund. Rosenwald, a northern philanthropist, established a fund to aid in the construction of rural public schools for black children. Although southern education was impoverished generally, rural black children suffered from the most extreme deficits. Between 1914 and 1927, the Rosenwald Fund contributed $214,700 to various rural communities in Tennessee for the building of schoolhouses for black children. The contributions were conditional on the raising of matching funds by the communities, and black Tennesseans donated $242,298 to these projects. At the same time, the state contributed $890,520 in tax dollars, and white Tennesseans gave an additional $21,977.

Tax revenues for Tennessee education rose dramatically during the 1920s, but during the next decade, the state's schools again suffered financial reverses ushered in by the Great Depression. Finances, however, were not the only challenge facing public education in this era. The National Association for the Advancement of Colored People initiated court challenges against unequal education based on race, and their first successes came in the 1930s. By the mid-1950s, the United State Supreme Court outlawed segregation in public education, and Tennessee, along with the rest of the South, faced one of the most difficult challenges since the Civil War. Communities all over the state feared the worst as they observed integration difficulties in surrounding states.

While there were examples of unrest and destruction of property—most notably the bombing of Clinton High School in Clinton, Tennessee—there were fewer violent confrontations in Tennessee than in surrounding states. Furthermore, the public pronouncements on integration by Tennessee public officials stood in sharp contrast to the inflammatory rhetoric of officials in surrounding states. The conciliatory tone of Tennessee Governor Frank G. Clement provides a graphic example. Clement urged his constituents to respect the Supreme Court decision outlawing school segregation because it was the law of the land.

In the years since the 1960s, Tennessee communities have continued to wrestle with the challenge of integrating faculties, administrations, and student bodies in the public schools. The process has been slow and the results incomplete. At the same time, communities have continued to search for ways to ensure adequate funding of their schools. This is often particularly difficult without a state income tax or state lottery. Thus, as Tennessee's public schools face the twenty-first century, they are still seeking to solve some of the same old problems. Nevertheless, despite the problems, the dual systems of public education, so painfully born in the aftermath of the Civil War, have finally become one.

Cynthia Griggs Fleming, University of Tennessee, Knoxville
CITATIONS:

(1) *The Annual Report of the State Superintendent of Public Instruction for Tennessee for the Scholastic Year Ending June 30, 1891* (1892), 31.

(2) *The Annual Report of the State Superintendent of Public Instruction for Tennessee for the Scholastic Year Ending August 31, 1874* (1875), 27.

Home economics class at the Tarbox School, Nashville, ca. 1920s.

(3) J.W. Alvord report, February 13, 1867, Records of the Education Division of the Bureau of Refugees, Freedmen, and Abandoned Lands, 1865–1871.

SUGGESTED READINGS: James D. Anderson, *The Education of Blacks in the South, 1860–1935* (1988); Charles W. Dabney, *Universal Education in the South* (2 volumes, 1936, r.p. 1969); Edgar Knight, *A Documentary History of Education in the South Before 1860* (5 volumes, 1950); Robert Margo, *Race and Schooling in the South, 1880–1950* (1990); William Vaughn, *School for All: The Blacks and Public Education in the South, 1865–1877* (1974)

EDUCATION, HIGHER. Historians studying the status of higher education in Tennessee in the closing years of the twentieth century can be more optimistic about the future than Lucius Salisbury Merriam was when his study of *Higher Education in Tennessee* was published in 1893. Merriam examined seven universities, 14 colleges, 20 women's colleges, five colleges for blacks, and the Winchester Normal, a privately owned institution. What he found was the perpetuation of problems that had plagued Tennessee higher education from its frontier origins: the establishment of private academies and colleges by Presbyterian, Baptist, and Methodist ministers, who supplemented their meager salaries by providing education for the children of the pioneers.

The colleges generally enrolled more students in their preparatory schools than in the "college departments." Even then, Merriam wrote, the standards were low. Alumni acquired master of arts degrees by maintaining a reputation for good moral character, attending to their businesses for several years, after which time, they paid five-dollar diploma fees and wrote short papers on any subject to fulfill the degree requirements. "Academic honors have become a cheap commodity in Tennessee," Merriam wrote. "The curse of higher education was the so-called 'colleges' and 'universities.'" Many who "style themselves" as such "do not possess the ghost of college equipment either material or intellectual." In perusing the list of faculty members in the catalogues of preparatory schools and church-sponsored colleges, one may wonder just how many of the A.M.s were earned. Many popular, articulate, more or less literate, and ambitious ministers received honorary Doctor of Divinity degrees.

Merriam considered Vanderbilt University, the University of Tennessee, the University of Nashville with Peabody Normal, the University of the South, and Cumberland University as the best the state could offer. Fisk University, he wrote, was "the highest grade purely collegiate institution for negroes in the world."

The University of Nashville evolved from nonsectarian and independent Davidson Academy (1785), which had become Cumberland College (1806), to qualify for federal funds made available through government land sales. The trustees employed Philip Lindsley, D.D., from the College of New Jersey, and changed the name to the University of Nashville in 1826. Hard times, a cholera epidemic, and declining enrollment resulted in the closing of the literary department in 1850. On the eve of his resignation in 1850, Philip Lindsley worked with Nashville physicians to establish a department of medicine, actually a proprietary medical school. The medical school remained open during the Civil War; after the war, the school shared its facilities with the normal school, Peabody Normal, established with support from the George Peabody Fund. In 1903 trustees of the Peabody Board voted to fund the construction of the George Peabody College for Teachers in the South; they selected a site for the new campus across the street from Vanderbilt. Like other proprietary medical schools of the late nineteenth century, the medical school of the University of Nashville could not meet standards set by the American Medical Society, and passed into history.

The University of Tennessee evolved from Blount College, chartered by the territorial legislature in 1794; rechartered in 1807, it became East Tennessee College and qualified to receive federal land grants. In 1840 it received university status. After the Civil War, trustees and administrators reorganized curricula and aims, with the goal of achieving recognition as *the* state university. The University established a school of agriculture with funds made available under the Morrill Act of 1862; developed a graduate school of arts and sciences; and expanded the undergraduate programs. In March 1879 ETU became the University of Tennessee by an act of the legislature, although the state legislature did not appropriate funds for its operation until 1903.

In the 1850s Bishops James Otey and Leonidas Polk, and other Episcopal leaders in Tennessee, Mississippi, Louisiana, Arkansas, and Texas initiated the establishment of the University of the South, with a school of liberal arts, a theological seminary, and a preparatory school. They planned to maintain academic standards comparable to the best in the North and Europe. The founders began fund-raising activities for $500,000 to develop a campus at the southern tip of the Cumberland Plateau. The Civil War, however, began before construction was completed and students enrolled. During the conflict, the endowment funds were lost, and the buildings were burned. When peace returned, Bishop Charles Todd Quintard took the lead in resurrecting the plans; he raised 2,500 pounds in England. In 1868 Quintard and the trustees chose a faculty described as "formidable," and opened the doors to students. Since then, the University of the South has raised endowments and survived wars and depressions to earn an enviable reputation in the liberal arts.

Cumberland College was established in 1826 by the general assembly of the Cumberland Presbyterian Church in Princeton, Kentucky. In 1842, with few students and inadequate funding, church leaders decided to move the school to Tennessee; they chose Lebanon after the town's citizens offered them a new $10,000 building. The name was changed to Cumberland University, and the curricula eventually included engineering, theology, arts, law, and business; a medical branch was located in Memphis. The law department included Judge Abraham Caruthers, Robert L. Caruthers, Nathan Green, and others with established reputations, and attracted students from southern and western states. In 1858 the law school, with 188 students, claimed the largest enrollment in the nation; Harvard was second with 146. By 1893 over 1,400 lawyers had earned degrees at Cumberland, including several U.S. Senators and Representatives, state governors, judges in state and federal courts, and state legislators in the southern and western states.

With the establishment of peace in 1865, John Ogden, superintendent of education for the Freedmen's Bureau in Tennessee, Erastus M. Cravath, former army chaplain and field secretary of the American Missionary Association, and Edward P. Smith, district secretary of the American Missionary Association, established a "beginners" school for freedmen in Nashville; they also planned to develop a college for Negroes with AMA and Freedmen's Aid Committee funds. Fisk School was named in honor of General Clinton B. Fisk, a friend and patron of the educational endeavor, who raised funds for buildings and programs; the school opened in January 1866. Ogden served as principal and developed programs to train students to teach fundamentals to recently freed blacks and their children. Two years after its opening, the school became Fisk University. Students enrolled in the departments of theology and commerce, in addition to the normal and model training schools. By 1871 the college of liberal arts was accepting students. Compared to prevailing standards, the faculty was well-trained, though salaries remained low. The Freedman's Bureau, the American Missionary Association, the Peabody Fund, and individual donors provided the operating funds, but the Jubilee Singers' tours at home and abroad saved Fisk from insolvency in the 1870s. Adam J. Spence headed the school after John Ogden's resignation in 1870, but hard times and overwork led to his resignation five years later. From 1875 to 1900, Erastus M. Cravath and his colleagues improved facilities, developed the faculty, and raised academic standards. While Booker T. Washington and others stressed trade school education, Cravath made some concessions, but continued to emphasize the liberal arts. In 1900 when Cravath died, Fisk had a national reputation for excellence.

Following the Civil War, Bishop Holland N. McTyeire and other prominent Southern Methodists renewed their efforts to establish a first-class university in Nashville. In 1873 the newly-selected board of trustees launched a campaign to raise a $500,000 endowment, but fell far short of the goal. While visiting his cousin, Mrs. Cornelius Vanderbilt, McTyeire found her husband, the "Commodore," interested in helping to heal the wounds of war. The plan McTyeire presented to the trustees provided $200,000 for land, buildings, books, equipment, and faculty, and a $300,000 endowment. As president of the board, McTyeire would exercise control over all phases of construction, faculty selection, and administration. The board accepted the money and the conditions, and changed the name to Vanderbilt University.

McTyeire persuaded Langdon C. Garland, his mentor, long-time friend, and professor of physics at the University of Mississippi, to join him as chancellor. Under McTyeire's leadership, Garland's duties were more like those of a dean rather than a chancellor. McTyeire and Garland envisioned a university equal to the leading eastern universities. In the fall of 1875, 307 students enrolled in the departments of Bible, academics, law, and medicine.

McTyeire soon became dissatisfied with his original faculty members; he fired several and reduced the salaries of others. By 1886 only Garland and Professor James M. Safford remained of the original faculty. McTyeire found replacements among the recent graduates of the doctoral programs of eastern and German universities; James H. Kirkand was one of them. McTyeire died in 1889, before he achieved his goal of bringing Vanderbilt up to the standards of Johns Hopkins, Yale, or Harvard, but at the time of his death, it enjoyed an outstanding reputation among southern universities and colleges. Chancellor Garland led the university until his retirement in 1893 at the age of 83. Before he left, he nominated James H. Kirkland (Ph.D., Leipzig) to succeed him. The trustees concurred. Kirkland served as chancellor for the next 44 years.

In 1903 outspoken advocates of public schools, Professor P.P. Claxton, Sidney G. Gilbreath, Seymour A. Mynders, R.L. Jones, and other prominent educators launched a six-year campaign that culminated with the passage of the Education Bill of 1909. The measure provided for longer school terms, consolidated schools, imposed higher qualifications for teachers, provided direct appropriations for the University of Tennessee, and stipulated that four normal schools (three for whites and one for blacks) be established in several locations across the state.

In the fall of 1911 Middle Tennessee State Normal School (Murfreesboro) and East Tennessee State Normal School (Johnson City) enrolled their first students. West Tennessee State Normal School

(Memphis) and Tennessee State Agriculture and Industrial School (Nashville) opened in 1912. Their curricula included four years of high school subjects, freshman and sophomore level courses in the liberal arts, courses in teaching methods, public health, and psychology. In 1915 the legislature approved Tennessee Polytechnic Institute (Cookeville) to join the normals under the direction of the state board of education. Although established as a technical school, TPI for many years emphasized teacher education more than engineering or sciences. In 1918 the normals dropped the first two years of high school and added the junior year of college work, and additional courses in education. Five years later, after the addition of senior level courses, the schools dropped "normal" from their titles and qualified as "Teachers' Colleges." In the mid-1920s, when Southwestern Presbyterian University moved to Memphis, Clarksville citizens persuaded legislators and the state board of education to buy the campus and buildings. In September 1929 Austin Peay Normal enrolled its first students.

About the same time that Clarksvillians were pressuring the legislature to acquire a campus, their neighbors in Martin (Weakley County) persuaded the lawmakers to buy the campus of Hall-Moody Institute, which became the campus of the University of Tennessee Junior College. In 1951 it became a four-year college and the University of Tennessee at Martin. In 1969 the University of Tennessee added another satellite campus when it acquired the University of Chattanooga, changing its name to University of Tennessee at Chattanooga. The school had been established by Northern Methodists as Chattanooga University in 1872. The name was changed to U.S. Grant University in 1889, before becoming the University of Chattanooga in 1904. As the University of Tennessee acquired off-campus centers, boosters claimed that the university's campus extended from Bristol to Memphis, and some Chattanoogans thought their city deserved a branch. Knowing they could not compete with UT, trustees of the University of Chattanooga entered into negotiations that resulted in President Andrew Holt's announcement that the school would become the University of Tennessee in Chattanooga on July 1, 1969.

In the 1930s many students found the lower fees of the teachers' colleges, and the acceptance of transfer credits from these institutions by professional and graduate schools, to be powerful incentives to enroll at the state schools. The six schools survived the Depression years on annual appropriations of $56,000 and student fees; the National Youth Administration provided funds to pay student helpers. In 1941 the legislature permitted Memphis State to drop "Teachers" from its title to become Memphis State College; Middle and East Tennessee followed suit in 1943. All

survived World War II with help from federal agencies that used faculties and facilities for training special military detachments. In 1949 the state board of education authorized state colleges to develop Master of Arts programs in liberal arts and education. With veterans and later "baby-boomers" arriving on campuses, state and private colleges prospered. Salaries increased, appropriations increased, and private and government foundations were generous when contrasted with preceding decades.

In 1955 the Legislative Council recommended a thorough study of the state-supported institutions of higher learning. A staff headed by Truman M. Pierce and A.D. Albright involved professors and administrators on every state campus for two years, as they accumulated statistics to point up strengths and weaknesses in the system. These were used to make 104 recommendations for improving administration, faculties, facilities, financing, and academic standards of state universities and colleges. Included was the creation of the Tennessee Higher Education Commission (familiarly known as THEC and pronounced "T-hec") to have oversight of the University of Tennessee and the six regional universities; it was created in 1967. Other recommendations included high level technical training, more financial aid for students, delegation of some authority to student governments, encouragement of faculty research, more counseling services, and limiting the number of institutions requiring expensive technical and professional training. A "common core of education" (liberally translated to include introductory courses in liberal arts, sciences, and social sciences) would be required of all students.

Control of the University of Tennessee remained with the Board of Trustees. A Board of Regents, with a chancellor and staff, was created to direct the affairs of the other state universities. Tennessee A & I was the first state college to become a university in 1951. Memphis State (now the University of Memphis) followed in 1957, then East Tennessee in 1963, Middle Tennessee and Tennessee Tech in 1965, and Austin Peay in 1967. State universities expanded their intellectual horizons when Memphis State acquired a law school in 1962, later named for President Cecil C. Humphreys, and East Tennessee State, in 1974, established a medical college named for U.S. Representative James Quillen.

In 1984, on the recommendation of THEC, the legislature created and funded Centers of Excellence for qualified state universities and the University of Tennessee; two years later, Centers of Emphasis were made available to the community colleges. Legislators also provided endowments for Chairs of Excellence. The centers focused on the expansion of research and economic development, regional and national recognition, recognition of the different missions among the institutions, and leverage of state funds. The Chairs of Excellence attract eminent scholars, budding scholars, and graduate students to the state's universities. In 1995 there were 94 Chairs of Excellence, 26 Centers of Excellence, and 15 Centers of Emphasis.

Changes in education curricula came at the same time that the system began to react to the Civil Rights Movement; it was a relatively peaceful transition compared to the disturbances on the campuses of other states. In 1951, three years before *Brown v. Topeka,* Judge Robert L. Taylor ruled that two African-American applicants be admitted to the graduate and law schools of the University of Tennessee because equal facilities were not available in the state's black university as required by legislation passed in 1941. The students enrolled in 1952. In the fall of 1955 Judge Marion S. Boyd ruled that state laws on segregation and the board's plan for gradual desegregation were no longer binding. East Tennessee State admitted its first black student in January 1956. Other state institutions fell into line. Peaceful integration of higher education became an accomplished fact.

In the 1960s and 1970s, however, there were demonstrations and sit-ins on the state's campuses as African-American students demanded courses in black history, the hiring of black faculty, and recognition of discriminatory practices. Protesters demonstrated against the draft, ROTC, and the undeclared war in Vietnam. Students for a Democratic Society were active on some campuses. Student demands included greater representation in university affairs, often including membership on all faculty committees. These were exciting decades, and some reforms were made in academe, which, in hindsight, do not seem so radical.

From 1966 to 1977, THEC, Regents, legislators, and governors bestirred themselves to finance, plan, and activate nine community colleges, three technical colleges, and two technical institutes strategically located to offer comprehensive vocational and technical training, and two-year liberal arts courses for students of all ages. The community colleges developed courses leading to associate degrees in 83 areas of learning and 48 one-and-two-year certificates.

Community colleges provide courses for adults who want to improve their occupational skills, professional expertise, or hobbies and leisure activities. Courses range from infant, toddler, and preschool care to fundamentals of money management, robotics, electric circuits, pipe fitting and plumbing practices, computer technology, micro-biology based medical instrumentation, and food and beverage management. Freshman and sophomore level courses are offered in the liberal arts—history, English, languages, political science, mathematics, economics, science, sociology, and art. Medical

technicians, electricians, automobile mechanics, civil servants, legal aides, computer experts, bartenders, beauticians, and others have broadened their knowledge and sharpened their skills in community college courses. Community colleges boast an impressive record of encouraging unmotivated students to excel, with many continuing their education at the state's universities.

In 1995, 37 private colleges and universities in Tennessee enrolled 48,597 students. The six state universities had 73,107 students; UT's four campuses totaled 41,935 students; and the 14 community colleges enrolled 71,217, for a total of 192,259. To finance the six state universities, the legislature appropriated $290,843,700; the community colleges received $157,855,200; UT Chattanooga, Knoxville, and Martin received $204,521,700. The medical units of UT in Memphis received $83,666,800 and $22,530,600 went to Quillen College of Medicine in Johnson City.

Of the 47 universities and colleges evaluated by Merriam in 1893, 16 have survived. One of the strongest to become victim to progress in the twentieth century was Peabody Normal. In 1910 it became George Peabody College for Teachers and moved from the University of Nashville campus to a model campus on 21st Avenue, across the street from Vanderbilt. It became the mecca, especially every summer, for several thousand public school teachers, superintendents, and professors of education from southern and southwestern states seeking masters and doctorates. Because students could earn masters by taking more courses in lieu of writing theses, some critics referred to Peabody and other colleges with similar policies as degree mills. Competition from the many state teachers colleges developing graduate programs at lower costs for students, the rising costs to universities to provide quality education, and the decrease in the number of foundations willing to support single specialty institutions forced Peabody trustees to accept a proposal in 1979 to merge with its neighbor as George Peabody College for Teachers of Vanderbilt.

Among the best criteria for evaluating universities and colleges on their undergraduate programs are endowments, appropriations, alumni, academic standards, and the number of scholarships available. One academic standard is membership in Phi Beta Kappa Society, founded in 1776. Of the seven state supported universities and 37 private colleges and universities in Tennessee, five have Phi Beta Kappa chapters. Vanderbilt became a member in 1901; The University of the South in 1926; Rhodes College (formerly Southwestern at Memphis and Southwestern Presbyterian University in Clarksville) in 1949; Fisk University in 1954; and the University of Tennessee in 1965. Several years earlier, UT had been turned down because, among other things, more scholarships were available for athletes than for academic achievers.

As they confront the needs of the twenty-first century, members of THEC are assessing whether the universities under their supervision have too many graduate programs in agriculture, business, education, engineering, health, human ecology (home economics), and protective services. The universities train more graduate students in education administration, for example, than the market can absorb. THEC members may conclude that some producers should be eliminated, but they can only recommend that the two boards drop programs that either overproduce or do not meet their quotas. As the twentieth century fades, THEC will employ an independent consultant to study the university system problems and make recommendations for THEC to pass to the regents and trustees. By A.D. 2005, the issue may be decided on the direction of higher education in Tennessee for the twenty-first century.

Frank B. Williams, Jr., East Tennessee State University
SUGGESTED READINGS: Paul K. Conkin, *Gone With the Ivy: A Biography of Vanderbilt University* (1985); Lucius S. Merriam, *Higher Education in Tennessee: Contributions to American Educational History,* edited by Herbert B. Adams, (1893); James Riley Montgomery, Stanley J. Folmsbee, and Lee Seifert Greene, *To Foster Knowledge: A History of the University of Tennessee, 1794–1970* (1984); Harvey G. Neufelt and W. Calvin Dickinson, *The Search for Identity: A History of Tennessee Technological University, 1915–1985* (1991); Roy S. Nicks, ed., *Community Colleges of Tennessee: The Founding and Early Years* (1979); Truman M. Pierce and A. D. Albright, *Public Higher Education in Tennessee* (1957); William Sorrells, *The Exciting Years: The Cecil C. Humphrey's Presidency of Memphis State University, 1960–1972* (1987); Frank B. Williams, Jr., *A University's Story 1911–1980, East Tennessee State University* (1991)

ELLINGTON, BUFORD (1907–1972), Governor (1959–1963 and 1967–1971), alternated power both times with unsure ally, Frank Clement. The differences between Ellington's first and second stint as chief executive, especially in terms of the South's ageless political issue of race, were a microcosm of the larger changes taking place across the state and region.

Born in Holmes County, Mississippi, Ellington studied religion briefly at Millsaps in Jackson before hard financial times forced him to abandon his studies. Bad economic luck did not deter his industrious nature: he edited a small newspaper in Durant, Mississippi, sold farm machinery in Memphis for several years, and supervised salesmen for the Tennessee Farm Bureau Insurance System during the Depression era. In Durant, he met visiting high school teacher Catherine Ann Cheek; they married in 1929. Cheek's roots were in Marshall County, Tennessee, a locale that greatly impressed the future governor. Marshall County quickly became home to Ellington;

he purchased a store in Verona and maintained his legal voting residence in the area. Ellington also farmed the hills of Marshall County. Indeed, throughout his political career he prided himself on his farming acumen and later founded an agricultural diagnostic laboratory in Nashville.

Before his election as chief executive, Ellington had long been a significant political player in Tennessee politics. As a congressional campaign manager for Joe Evins in 1946 and as state representative from Marshall County in 1948, Ellington emerged as a vital player in the Democratic party's conservative wing, a powerful faction, including such politicians as E. H. Crump and Jim McCord. Ellington also hitched his political rise to another formidable Tennessee politician: Frank Clement. Ellington served as campaign manager in Clement's run for governor in 1952, and Clement later appointed him as Commissioner of Agriculture. While assisting in the building of Clement's political machine, Ellington carefully tended to his own political future, eventually taking over the organization for his own run for governor.

Beginning in 1953, the Clement-Ellington team dominated statehouse politics for 18 years. Relations between the two politicians were originally close, but by 1960, the relationship revealed signs of severe strain. At the Democratic National Convention, Clement pledged support for John Kennedy, whereas Ellington served as convention floor manager for long-time friend, Lyndon Johnson. By 1966 the alliance had regressed to the point that Governor Clement reportedly called a special legislative session to spend surplus funds solely to avoid a tax surplus for the incoming Ellington administration. In contrast to his battles with Clement, Ellington's personal ties with Johnson remained strong. Ellington worked closely with the President on a number of matters between his two gubernatorial terms, culminating in a 1965 appointment as director of the U.S. Office of Emergency Planning.

Fiscal prudence marked both of Ellington's gubernatorial terms. During the economic boom of his first term (1959–1963), he fulfilled his campaign pledge not to raise taxes, while simultaneously sponsoring a $100 annual raise for school teachers during each year of the 1959–1961 biennium. Ellington re-organized Tennessee government, consolidating and eliminating several state departments.

Although this economic conservatism reigned supreme during his second term (1967–1971) as well, Ellington changed his tune on matters of race. During his first campaign for governor, Ellington had judged himself "an old-fashioned segregationist from Mississippi" and forcefully declared that he was not a "Johnny come-lately" in regard to segregation. During his second campaign for governor, he claimed that the time was ripe to "bury the word and practice of segregation" and followed his campaign apology with several progressive moves. He appointed Tennessee's first African-American cabinet officer, H. T. Lockard, and created the Tennessee Human Relations Commission. Close advisors to Ellington suggest that his service in President Johnson's administration, including a position involved in the implementation of the Civil Rights Act of 1964, transformed his view. By the end of his second term, Ellington had become a very visible national and regional player, including service as chairman of both the National and Southern Governors Conferences.

Ellington died in Boca Raton, Florida, on April 3, 1972, less than 14 months after leaving office. A number of national figures, including Vice President Spiro Agnew, attended his funeral. Although sometimes criticized for his lack of political imagination, Ellington's middle of the road approach stilled Tennessee during tumultuous political times and promoted a racial moderation that was in short supply in the 1960s South.

Vaughn May, University of Tennessee at Martin
SUGGESTED READING: William R. Majors, *Change and Continuity: Tennessee Politics Since the Civil War* (1986)
SEE: CLEMENT, FRANK G.; CRUMP, EDWARD H.; EVINS, JOSEPH L.; MARSHALL COUNTY; MCCORD, JIM N.

ELLIOTT, SARAH BARNWELL (1848–1928), novelist, short story writer, and advocate of women's rights, was born in Savannah, Georgia, the daughter of Stephen Elliott, a bishop of the Episcopal Church who was a leader in the founding of the University of the South at Sewanee. Her education consisted of private tutoring and some study at Johns Hopkins University in 1886. Though she lived for a time in New York (1895–1902), Elliott's principal home was Sewanee, where she died and was buried. She never married.

Of her six novels, *Jerry* (1891), the tragic story of a Tennessee mountain boy who grows up in the West, is probably best-remembered today. The first, *The Felmeres*, appeared in 1879. Sewanee and the surrounding area served as the setting for *The Durket Sperret* (1897), one of her best local-color novels. Her one collection of short pieces, *An Incident and Other Happenings* (1899), is notable for its treatment of southern racial and social problems.

In addition to her fiction, Elliott wrote essays, articles, book reviews, a few poems, a biography of Sam Houston (1900), *His Majesty's Servant* (a play produced in London in 1904), and a series of 16 letters describing her European travels, which was printed (with the signature "S.B.E.") in the Louisville *Courier-Journal* in 1887.

A leader in the fight to give women the right to vote, Elliott served as president of the Tennessee Equal Suffrage Association and as such authored a petition addressed to the law makers of the state, which

appeared in the Nashville *Banner,* August 17, 1912.
Allison Ensor, University of Tennessee, Knoxville
SEE: LITERATURE; WOMAN SUFFRAGE MOVEMENT

EMBREE, ELIHU (1782–1820), abolitionist, was the son of a Quaker minister, who removed from Pennsylvania in 1790 to the northeast corner of what would become the new state of Tennessee. Elihu and his brother Elijah were among the region's earliest and most prominent iron manufacturers in the region. Although a slaveowner and positive deist as a young man, Embree became an ardent abolitionist at the age of 30 and turned the same skill and energy he previously displayed in iron manufacturing to the antislavery cause. He became a leader in the Manumission Society of Tennessee, first organized in Greene County in 1815, under the leadership of Charles Osborn and John Rankin. After writing numerous abolitionist petitions to state and national governments, Embree began publishing the monthly *The Emancipator* in April 1820. The Jonesborough, Tennessee, periodical became the first publication in the United States devoted exclusively to the antislavery cause. Embree entered into the debate over slavery with a fierce, polemical spirit, calling slaveholders "monsters in human flesh," and denouncing the Missouri Compromise with the demand "Not another foot of slave territory!" Slavery, he argued repeatedly in the pages of his popular newspaper, "*is a shame to any people,*" and "freedom is the inalienable right *of all men.*" Although his untimely death in 1820 of bilious fever ended his strong and prophetic voice, Embree's ringing denunciation of slavery was as harsh and severe as any condemnation uttered in the 1830s by better-known abolitionists like William Lloyd Garrison.

Durwood Dunn, Tennessee Wesleyan College
SEE: INDUSTRY; MANUMISSION SOCIETY OF TENNESSEE; SLAVERY; THE EMANCIPATOR

EMBREEVILLE MINES. This small mountain community, located on the Nolichucky River in the southeastern corner of Washington County, has a long mining history. Ores in the Bumpass Cove area, about three miles southeast of Embreeville in Unicoi County, were first mined for lead, reportedly used in bullets fired at the British in 1780 in the Battle of King's Mountain.

Iron mining and smelting began as early as 1815, when Elijah Embree and others sporadically produced iron from Bumpass Cove ores in crude beehive furnaces made from slabs of native rock. In 1889 English investors formed The Embreville Land, Iron and Railway Company. (All successor companies corrected the spelling to "Embreeville".) Embreville Freehold purchased the 45,000-acre John L. Blair Estate, and in 1891 a railroad, later acquired by

Southern Railway Company, was completed from Johnson City to Embreeville. That same year the company formed the Embreeville Town Company to develop a town of 30,000 inhabitants. In 1892 the company completed a smelter with pig iron output of 150 tons per day. All efforts to develop commercial iron production proved futile, and in 1900 American interests took over the British holdings.

The Embree Iron Company acquired the property in 1903, but was equally unsuccessful in commercially producing pig iron. The company faced dissolution in 1913, when the presence of commercial zinc deposits was recognized. Embree Iron Company began producing zinc and then lead and quickly paid off its debts. Although ore reserves dwindled after World War I, the company continued to operate during the Great Depression. Manganese production began in 1935, and in 1939 the company was the nation's largest producer of metallurgical grade manganese concentrates with an output of 73,000 tons. Manganese reserves were rapidly exhausted, however, and the company was liquidated in 1946.

Thomas S. Wyman, Palo Alto, California
SEE: INDUSTRY; WASHINGTON COUNTY

EMBRY-RIDDLE FIELD. This Obion County airfield began operations as a training base for aviation cadets in 1942. The land was acquired in early March, construction proceeded immediately, and the first class arrived in July 1942. Riddle-McKay Aviation School of Florida, a private contractor for the U.S. government, built and operated the base under the name Embry-Riddle Field. John Paul Riddle, a pioneer in aviation training, airplane manufacturing, and airline operations, headed the company. During the war, schools operated by Riddle-McKay trained some 26,000 young men to fly. Civilian flight instructors at Embry-Riddle Field taught approximately 19 classes of cadets over a two-year period. Many of those cadets saw action in World War II theaters of operation around the world.

The original training planes were PT-Stearmans; by the end of 1942, these were replaced by Fairchild PT-19s, a part-plywood monoplane with an in-line Ranger air-cooled engine. By the end of 1943, the Fairchilds had been modified to use a radial engine and were designated as PT-23s.

Embry-Riddle Field originally encompassed 870 acres. In 1942 there were no paved runways, although there was a paved area in front of the two metal hangers (still present), and a wooden flight tower. Barracks for cadets, an administrative building, a dining hall, and several maintenance shops completed the base. In 1943 two more wooden hangers, a link trainer building, and additional barracks were built.

After World War II, the Embry-Riddle Field was given to Obion County, and the name was changed to Tom Stewart Field, in honor of U.S. Senator Stewart. The name was later changed again to Everett-Stewart Field to honor of both Senator Stewart and his one-time assistant, and later Congressman, Robert A. "Fats" Everett of Union City.

The field contains 825 acres. The airport includes two original hangers and a 3,500-square-foot terminal building, completed in 1987. In 1996 some 60 corporate jets, including planes owned by Goodyear Tire and Tyson Foods, regularly flew in and out of Everett-Stewart Field.

Rebel C. Forrester, Union City
SEE: AIRPORTS; OBION COUNTY; WORLD WAR II

ENGLEWOOD MILLS. While New England is the birthplace of America's textile industry, and the Carolinas are known for massive textile production, the small town of Englewood, Tennessee, serves as a reminder of the ties between industry, workers, and the resulting community. Covering more than 140 years of textile production, the history of Englewood Mills reflects ongoing changes in transportation, market, and consumer demands.

In 1857 John J. Dixon founded the Eureka Cotton Mills, laying the cornerstone of an industry which was central to Englewood's economic stability and livelihood. Yarn and warp products, made with raw cotton from the surrounding area, were sold in neighboring southern states. Elisha Brient shared in the operational responsibilities of the mill, and by 1875 the Brient family exercised sole proprietorship.

The township reflected the changes of mill ownership and improvements in transportation, for the settlement re-located twice and changed its name three times. The original site of the mill village, called Eureka Mills, was re-named Englewood by the Brients in 1894. Realizing that the railroad provided a more efficient means of shipping than wagons, the family moved the mill complex closer to the Louisville & Nashville railroad line, absorbing the pre-existing settlement of Tellico Junction. The communities joined in 1908, adopting the name of Englewood. The original town site received its final name of Old Englewood.

As the Eureka Cotton Mills thrived and expanded its product line to include men's union suits, the success of Englewood's textile mill plus its crucial railroad line attracted more business. The Englewood Manufacturing Company, which made hosiery, was established in 1913.

Englewood developed into a typical company town, supporting the needs of its workers with a company store, saw mill, blacksmith shop, grist mill, two churches, and a one-room school house. Living in company-owned rental housing, workers supplemented a subsistence life style by planting small vegetable gardens and raising livestock. By 1914 neighborhoods of mill houses expanded to accommodate the growing work force of 300.

The textile workers were typically white, subsistence farm families, searching for a better livelihood. They found that the company town provided modest housing, a sense of community, and the security of a steady income. In the mills, workers experienced an environment filled with loud machinery, heat, humidity, and lint-filled air. Often several generations of families spent their entire lives working in the mills, with every family member contributing to the household income. Men were supervisors and machine operators. Women worked in the spinning room, ensuring that cotton slivers were correctly spun into strands of thread. Young boys removed full bobbins, while girls performed tasks such as operating a spinning machine. Many families depended upon their children's incomes for survival.

The Great Depression forced the closure of Eureka Cotton Mills and the Englewood Manufacturing Company. Englewood survived the depression through federal and state government relief programs in 1933–1935 that provided temporary jobs in the Civil Works Administration and Tennessee Emergency Relief Administration.

During World War II, the Englewood mills depended upon women to fill the vacant positions of men in military service. The abandoned Eureka Cotton Mill building served as a United National Clothing Center, one of eight locations in the U.S. that processed clothing donations for shipment to war-torn countries. In August 1949 a workers' union came to the Englewood Garment Company, although massive unionization failed to materialize as post war America deemed textile employment a female occupation and not worthy of serious efforts.

In the last half of the twentieth century, the Englewood mills encountered adverse changes in the textile industry, including consumer preferences for synthetic fabrics, the importation of less expensive products, and the competition from newer factories with more extensive mechanization. Although Englewood was home to 24 textile mills over its history, only Eureka Sportswear, Inc., and Allied Hosiery mills remain in operation.

Visitors to the old Englewood mills can still see various structural remains, including the crumbling brick walls and rusty boilers of the 1907 Eureka Cotton Mills and the vacant 1913 brick building of the Englewood Manufacturing Company. Many workers' cottages survive as private residences, located in neighborhoods established during the company town's prosperity. The Englewood Textile Museum offers a past and present perspective of Englewood's mill, tracing the evolution of the industry and documenting the roles of the workers in the context of mill labor and community life.

Jenny Burney, Middle Tennessee State University
SEE: INDUSTRY; LABOR; MCMINN COUNTY; TERA; WORLD WAR II

ERNI, HENRI (1822–1885), Tennessee's first consulting chemist, was born in Switzerland in 1822. Erni studied at the University of Zurich, where he excelled in chemistry, although he may not have received a degree. In 1849 Erni emigrated to the United States, and Yale University hired him as an instructor in botany and a laboratory assistant in chemistry at its newly established Sheffield Scientific School. In 1850 Erni moved to Knoxville, where he taught chemistry, mineralogy, geology, botany, French, and German at East Tennessee University. In 1852 he accepted a position in Massachusetts, then moved to Vermont. The University of Vermont awarded him honorary A.M. and M.D. degrees in 1857.

Erni returned to East Tennessee University in 1857. Two years later, he accepted a professorship in chemistry and medical jurisprudence at Shelby Medical College, in Nashville, where he remained until the Civil War closed the school. The College permitted him to use its laboratories to establish a private consulting practice. Erni specialized in the chemical analysis of urine.

In 1863 Erni relocated to Washington, D.C., where he had a long and varied career as chemist, U.S. Ambassador to Switzerland, and author. Married to Mary MacFarlane of Knoxville, Erni gave Tennessee as his permanent address. He died in Washington, D.C., in 1885.

Erni's work in Tennessee included the publication of 22 papers in academic journals, seven of which were summaries of chemical papers that had appeared in foreign journals. His high level of scholarly productivity, as well as his teaching and consulting, advanced science in antebellum Tennessee.

James X. Corgan, Austin Peay University
SUGGESTED READING: James X. Corgan, "Offbeat Pioneers," *Journal of the Tennessee Medical Association* 70(1977): 873–876
SEE: MEDICINE; SCIENCE AND TECHNOLOGY

ESHMAN, ANDREW NELSON (1865–1951), minister, educator, author, and leader of the segment of the Cumberland Presbyterian Church that rejected the 1906 merger with the Presbyterians, USA, was born on June 1, 1865, in Mt. Pleasant, Tennessee, and raised on a farm in Marshall County. In 1890 Eshman graduated from Winchester Normal College in Winchester. That same year, he was ordained as a minister of the Cumberland Presbyterian Church and also was elected school superintendent at Huntsville, Alabama.

In 1892 Eshman became the president of Union Female College at Oxford, Mississippi, a school controlled by the Cumberland Presbyterian Church. In

1894 the school relocated to West Point, Mississippi, and its name changed to Southern Female College. In 1905 Eshman left Mississippi and built Radnor College in Nashville. Eshman served both as president and proprietor of Radnor College until it closed in 1914. For several years, the college received national attention as a result of the tours of the United States conducted by Eshman and his students.

Eshman was appointed as a promotional agent of the United States Sesquicentennial. As a result of his appointment, Winchester became a sub-office for the Sesquicentennial, along with such cities as Chicago, Pittsburgh, New York, and Washington, D.C.

Throughout his lifetime, Eshman pastored several churches, conducted some 40 educational tours, and wrote extensively. His writings include *Standard Home Civics* (1924), *Beauty Spots of America and the Life-Saving Brigade* (1935), and *Collingsworth's Lectures Condensed* (1939).

In 1914 Eshman's first wife, Annie L. Bone died. He married Annie Boardman Mack in 1919; four years later, their son Andrew N., Jr., was born. Eshman died on January 23, 1951 and is buried at McCains, Tennessee. A historical marker commemorating Radnor College is at the intersection of Nolensville Road and McClellan Avenue in Nashville.

Michael D. Slate, Nashville

SEE: CUMBERLAND PRESBYTERIAN CHURCH

ESKIND, JANE GREENEBAUM (1933–), first woman to win a statewide election in Tennessee, was raised and educated in Louisville, Kentucky. She attended Brandeis University, married Richard Eskind, completed her undergraduate degree at the University of Louisville, and settled in Nashville in 1956. Following the birth of a daughter Ellen and a son Billy, Eskind commenced an activist career as lobbyist for the Tennessee League of Women Voters from 1964–1969. She became a Democratic party activist after deciding the nonpartisan position of the League hindered its efforts. From her beginnings as a campaign worker and member of the Democratic Women's club, her participation in party matters accelerated in the 1970s. In 1972 and 1976 Eskind represented Tennessee on the Democratic National Platform Committee. In 1974 she won election to the Democratic State Executive Committee. Eskind made her first bid for public office in 1978, and, by winning the Democratic primary for the U.S. Senate seat held by Republican Howard Baker, Jr., she became the first woman to win either the Democratic or Republican nomination for statewide office. She did not defeat Baker in November.

In 1980 Eskind won a seat on the Public Service Commission, the first woman to win a statewide election in Tennessee. She later served as commission chair. In the 1986 Democratic primary for governor, Eskind placed second behind Ned McWherter, and in 1987 in a special election, she made an unsuccessful bid for Congress. In 1994 she became the first woman to chair the Tennessee Democratic Party. Within her political party, Eskind has also been president of the Democratic Women's Club, a member of the Democratic House and Senate Council, the Tennessee Democratic Finance Council, the National Finance Committee, and the National Finance Council for President Clinton. She sat on the board of the Tennessee Federation of Democratic Women and functioned as a trustee of the National Victory Fund.

Over the last two decades, Eskind has served on committees of the Anti-Defamation League, the International Women's Forum, and as a charter member of the Women Executives in State Government. She also chaired the Tennessee Commission on the Status of Women from 1978–1980. More recently, she has been named Trustee to the Vice President's Residence Foundation and to the Brandeis University Board of Trust. A Nashville resident, she has provided time and energy to many groups, at present sitting on the boards of Tennessee Tomorrow, Inc. and NashvilleREAD, and advising Nashville Cares, the Legal Aid Society, the Nashville Institute for the Arts, the League of Women Voters, the Kelly Miller Smith Institute on African American Church Studies, and New Leadership South, among others. She has raised money for numerous not-for-profit groups and received recognition and awards from various quarters.

Margaret D. Binnicker, Middle Tennessee State University

SEE: BAKER, HOWARD H., JR.; TENNESSEE PUBLIC SERVICE COMMISSION

ETHERIDGE, HENRY EMERSON (1819–1902), important West Tennessee Whig politician and Union loyalist, was born in Currituck County, North Carolina, in 1819. In 1833 the family moved to Weakley County, Tennessee. Etheridge became a lawyer with a practice in Dresden, the county seat, but his admiration for Kentucky Senator Henry Clay soon drew him into Whig politics. He served one term in the Tennessee House of Representatives and three terms in the U.S. House of Representatives. When the Civil War began, Etheridge remained loyal to the Union. As his third term was ending in March 1861, he was elected Clerk of the House of Representatives, where he served until December 1863. Although he staunchly supported the war to preserve the Union, Etheridge broke with President Abraham Lincoln over the issue of emancipation. His position placed him among the Conservative Unionists of Tennessee.

In 1867 Etheridge emerged as the gubernatorial candidate for the Conservative Unionists in Tennessee. The candidate campaigned against most of the acts of the William G. Brownlow administration and for the restoration of voting rights for the ex-Confederate majority. Although he was defeated in his gubernatorial bid, Etheridge's candidacy aided the movement that led to the overthrow of Radical Reconstruction in Tennessee in 1869. After one term in the State Senate (1869–1871), Etheridge abandoned politics. From 1891 to 1894 he was surveyor of customs in Memphis. Etheridge died at home in Dresden on October 21, 1902, and was buried in Mount Vernon Cemetery near Sharon, Tennessee.

Lonnie E. Maness, University of Tennessee at Martin

SEE: RECONSTRUCTION; WEAKLEY COUNTY

ETTELSON, HARRY W. (1883–1975), Rabbi of Temple Israel in Memphis from 1925 to 1954, was born in Lithuania and reared in Mobile, Alabama. Ettelson's scholarly, diverse, and broad background included a B.A. from the University of Cincinnati, where he was Phi Beta Kappa; graduate work at the University of Chicago; and a Ph.D. from Yale University. He attained his Bachelor of Hebrew Letters and his degree of Rabbi, as valedictorian of his class, from Hebrew Union College. Ettelson's first assignment was to Fort Wayne, Indiana, followed by ministries at Hartford, Connecticut, and Philadelphia. In each city, Ettelson identified himself with cultural and civic affairs.

In his installation sermon at Temple Israel, Ettelson articulated his ideal of brotherhood with other Jews as well as with all other human beings. He declared his intention to establish "fraternal relations and fullest neighborly contacts with ministers of all denominations and creeds."

This philosophy of brotherhood pervaded Ettelson's 50-year ministry at Temple Israel. He organized and became the first president of the Cross-Cut Club, which was dedicated to ecumenism among ministers and their congregations. He was an originator of the Union Civic Thanksgiving Service. The City Beautiful Commission honored him for civic and cultural activities. Ettelson served as president of the Association of Church and Professional Social Workers, and of the Synagogue Council of Memphis. He was a member of the Editorial committee of the Jewish Publication Society. Ettelson retired in 1954. He died in 1975 in Philadelphia.

Selma Lewis, Memphis

SUGGESTED READING: Helen G. and James A. Wax, *Our First Century, 1854–1954* (1954)

SEE: MEMPHIS; RELIGION

EVA SITE, a prehistoric Native American encampment named after the modern hamlet of Eva in Benton County, was excavated by University of Tennessee archaeologists in 1940. Located on an ancient bank of the Tennessee River, it was excavated before the area was inundated by the Kentucky Lake reservoir. It was a favored living site for thousands of years during the prehistoric Archaic Period. This period, now known to date circa 8000 B.C.E. to 1000 B.C.E., was a time when prehistoric native people in North America adjusted to the post-glacial environment by hunting, fishing, and gathering. Thomas M.N. Lewis and Madeline Kneberg Lewis, anthropologists at the University of Tennessee, published a monograph on the Eva site in 1961.

One of the most important features of the Eva site was the stratified or "layered" nature of the soil deposits or midden, which could be correlated with cultural and environmental changes in early post-glacial Tennessee. The stratigraphy indicated that several distinct prehistoric populations lived in Tennessee during the long Archaic period. The stratified midden also contained well preserved animal remains; Lewis and Lewis were the first archaeologists in Tennessee to examine these bones and shells in an attempt to determine prehistoric dietary patterns and hunting strategies. The site's human burials are among the earliest Native American populations studied by anthropologists in Tennessee.

Archaeologists distinguished five strata based on differences in soil and artifact content. Strata V-VI (earliest in time) contained artifacts of a group of people who were called the Eva culture. These hunting and gathering people preferred a reddish flint for their broad-bladed projectile points, which tipped "darts" hurled with a spear-thrower—white-tailed deer being the prime quarry. A radiocarbon date of 5,200 B.C.E. from these strata was the earliest date yet obtained for a prehistoric culture in Tennessee. Since 1961 archaeologists have obtained numerous radiocarbon dates for the Archaic period. Some dates from the Tellico Reservoir in East Tennessee are earlier than 7,000 B.C.E.

The Three Mile component, represented in Stratum II, was the next major occupation of the Eva site. Short stemmed projectile points and ground stone pestles and grinding stones are common artifacts in this culture. Unlike the earlier Eva people, the Three Mile occupants ate large quantities of river mussels. The Lewises believed this change in dietary patterns was caused by a drier climate in the Tennessee Valley, which occurred about 5,000 years ago. Such differences in subsistence patterns can also be caused by shifting seasonal occupation of sites and other social factors.

The Big Sandy culture, represented in Stratum I, was the latest major occupation on the site. A distinguishing feature of this stratum was the absence of river mussels, which was attributed to environmental change by the Lewises. Large stemmed and notched dart points characterize the weaponry of the Big Sandy hunters. Animal bone frequencies indicated that these people may have had to range further from their settlement in search of game.

The Eva site possessed 180 human burials. Study of the quantitative and pathological data on this population indicated that the Native Americans who lived at Eva were relatively healthy compared to later populations and were genetically as well as culturally related to other Archaic groups in the Mid-South.
Charles Faulkner, University of Tennessee, Knoxville
SUGGESTED READING: Thomas M. N. Lewis and Madeline Kneberg Lewis, *Eva, An Archaic Site* (1961)
SEE: ARCHAIC PERIOD; BENTON COUNTY

EVANS, HENRY CLAY (1843–1921), businessman and politician, was born in Juniata County, Pennsylvania, to Jesse and Anna Single Evans. In 1844 his family moved to Wisconsin, where he attended public schools, and he graduated from a Chicago business training school in 1861. In May 1864 Evans joined the 41st Regiment of the Wisconsin Volunteer Infantry, from which he was honorably discharged as a quartermaster sergeant in September 1864. For the next year, he handled clerical duties as an agent with the quartermaster department in Chattanooga, Tennessee. After spending some time in Texas and New York, he returned to Chattanooga in 1870 to join the Wasson Car Works. Two years later, he moved to the Roane Iron Company, where he held progressively important positions over the next decade. In 1884–1885, he worked as cashier of Chattanooga's First National Bank. Evans became president of the Chattanooga Car and Foundry Company and remained principal owner until 1917.

All the while, Evans maintained an interest in public affairs. He helped organize Chattanooga's public school system and became president of the board and school commissioner. In 1873 he was elected city alderman, and served as Mayor from 1881 to 1883. In 1888 Evans won election to the U.S. House of Representatives as a Republican; he lost his bid for reelection in the Democratic triumph of 1890. His loyal support of the 1890 Federal Elections Bill to safeguard African-American suffrage contributed to his electoral loss. In recognition of his party service, President Benjamin Harrison appointed him First Assistant Postmaster General (1891–1893), providing Evans with an opportunity to distribute federal patronage.

In 1894 Evans ran against Democrat Peter Turney in the Tennessee gubernatorial election. Evans won a plurality of 748 votes over his opponent, but lost in a recount ordered by the Democratically-controlled state legislature, which rejected some returns for alleged irregularities. Although Turney won the race, Evans gained a national reputation. In 1896 he ran second to Garret A. Hobart for the Republican vice presidential nomination. In 1897 President William McKinley selected Evans for Commissioner of Pensions. From 1902 to 1905 Evans served as U.S. Consul General in London at President Theodore Roosevelt's request.

Upon his retirement from diplomatic service, Evans returned to Chattanooga. When the city adopted the commission form of government in 1911, he was elected commissioner of health and education. Evans also served as a trustee of the University of Tennessee and University of Chattanooga.

Evans married Adelaide Durand in Westfield, New York, in 1869. They had three children. He died in Chattanooga on December 12, 1921, and was buried in Forest Hill Cemetery, St. Elmo, Chattanooga. Evans's papers are in the Chattanooga-Hamilton County Bicentennial Library, Chattanooga.
Leonard Schlup, Akron, Ohio
SEE: CHATTANOOGA; TURNEY, PETER

EVANS, SILLIMAN, SR. (1894–1955), was owner and publisher of *The Nashville Tennessean* from 1937 until his death in 1955. During his years as publisher, he held directorships at American Airlines and Maryland Casualty and also key positions in the state and national Democratic party. After his death, his son, Silliman Evans, Jr., was publisher from 1955 until his death in 1961 at the age of 36. The newspaper's named changed to *The Tennessean* in 1963.

Silliman Evans, Sr., was born April 2, 1894, in Joshua, Texas. The son of a circuit-riding Methodist preacher, he began his career as a 13-year-old printer's apprentice on the DeLeon Press in Comanche County, Texas. He attended Polytechnic College, which later became Southern Methodist University. He held newspaper jobs in Waco and Houston and, from 1918 to 1928, held various positions for the *Fort Worth Star Telegram*. During this time, he became not only its top political writer and Washington correspondent, but what an associate described as "the all-time, All-American diesel engine of Texas reporting." He married Lucille McCrea on November 20, 1923, and they had two sons: Silliman Evans, Jr., and Amon Carter Evans.

From 1928 to 1932 he worked for Texas Air Transport, which later became American Airlines, and advanced to assistant to the president before becoming involved in politics. In 1932 his friendship with John Nance Garner, speaker of the House of Representatives, led Evans to managing press relations for Garner's presidential campaign.

In 1932 Franklin D. Roosevelt appointed Evans as Fourth Assistant Postmaster General, a position he held until 1934. He resigned to accept the presidency of the Maryland Casualty Company of Baltimore. But within a few years, he was eager to get back into the newspaper business and wanted to create a southern editorial voice in support of Roosevelt's New Deal policies.

On January 7, 1937, Evans purchased the *Nashville Tennessean* at a public auction for $850,000. The nearly bankrupt newspaper, which had a circulation of 76,275, had been in federal receivership. Evans took over management on April 17, and within 45 days had the newspaper in the black again.

Shortly after Evans purchased the newspaper, he established a joint printing agreement with James G. Stahlman, publisher of the *Nashville Banner*. Under the terms of the agreement, Evans dropped his newspaper's evening edition and Stahlman dropped his Sunday edition. Within a year, he persuaded H.G. Hill to build and lease a new office and publishing facility at 1100 Broadway, which the two newspapers shared until the *Banner* closed in 1998.

In June 1955, against the advice of his physician, Evans traveled to Fort Worth, Texas, to attend the funeral of publisher Amon G. Carter, his long-time friend and associate, and the man for whom his younger son was named. While there, Evans suffered a heart attack and died on June 26, 1955.

David Sumner, Ball State University

SEE: HILL, HORACE G.; NASHVILLE TENNESSEAN; PUBLISHING

EVANS v. MCCABE (1932). The Tennessee Supreme Court decision in *Evans v. McCabe* held that the Tennessee Constitution prohibits the State from enacting and collecting a tax on income earned within the state.[1]

L. C. Evans, a Nashvillian who owned a farm in Maury County, and five other individuals and businesses in Tennessee brought suit against Charles M. McCabe, who was Commissioner of Finance and Taxation under Governor Henry H. Horton. The suit challenged Chapter 21 of the Acts of the General Assembly's Second Extraordinary Session in 1931. Known as the "Income Tax Act of 1931," Chapter 21 levied a tax graduated from one percent to five percent on the "entire income" of every individual in the state from "any source whatever."

In an opinion by Chief Justice Grafton Green, the Supreme Court struck down the Act as a violation of Article II, Section 28 of the Tennessee Constitution. At that time, Section 28 conferred three main powers of taxation on the General Assembly. (Section 28 has since been amended, but not so as to affect the holding in *Evans v. McCabe*.) First, the legislature could tax all property—real, personal, or mixed—but only based on the property's value (*ad valorem*) and at an equal rate for all property. Second, the legislature could tax "Merchants, Peddlers, and privileges" in such manner as the legislature may direct. Finally, in the so-called "income tax clause," the legislature had the authority to tax incomes "derived from stocks and bonds that are not taxed *ad valorem*."

The holding in *Evans v. McCabe* followed directly from the *Shields v. Williams* decision by the same court

in 1929 interpreting the income tax clause.[2] Before 1929, the state taxed stocks and bonds on an *ad valorem* basis at the same rate as other property, with the result that the tax consumed almost all of the income generated by the stocks and bonds. The General Assembly responded by passing the Income Tax Statutes of 1929, also known as the "Hall Income Tax" after its sponsor, Senator Frank S. Hall of Dickson. The Income Tax Statutes removed the *ad valorem* tax from stocks and bonds and replaced it with a five percent tax on their incomes.

Several taxpayers challenged the constitutionality of the Income Tax Statutes, claiming that they violated Section 28's requirement that all property be taxed on an *ad valorem* basis at the same rate. The Supreme Court in *Shields v. Williams* upheld the statute's constitutionality. It reasoned that the income tax clause is an exception to Section 28's general requirement that all property be taxed equally, and that it allows the General Assembly to tax the income generated by stocks and bonds rather than their value.

Three years later, when reviewing the Income Tax Act of 1931 in *Evans*, the Supreme Court expanded upon its holding in *Shields*. The Court reaffirmed that the income tax clause was an exception to the general provisions in Section 28 governing the taxation of property. Because of the inclusion of the specific exception in Section 28 the court concluded that the Constitution's drafters did not intend to recognize any other exceptions to the general property tax rule. Thus, the court held that Section 28 did not permit the legislature to impose a general income tax.

Robert E. Cooper, Jr., Nashville

CITATIONS:

(1) 164 Tenn. 672.

(2) 159 Tenn. 349.

SEE: LAW; TENNESSEE SUPREME COURT

EVINS, JOSEPH LANDON. (1910–1984) was the "Dean" of Tennessee's congressional delegation during the 1960s and 1970s. Born in 1910 in DeKalb County to James Edgar Evins and Myrtie Goodson Evins, Joe L. Evins attended Vanderbilt University, graduating in 1933. The following year, he took his law degree from Cumberland University Law School in Lebanon.

From 1934 to 1941 Evins served on the staff of the Federal Trade Commission in Washington, D.C., rising to the position of Assistant Secretary from 1939 to 1941. He served from 1942 to 1946 in the U.S. Army and was discharged as a major.

Upon his return home from the war, the young veteran entered politics and won election to the U.S. Congress as the Fourth Congressional District representative in 1946. Evins served in Congress for the next 30 years, at that time the longest period of continuous service in the House of Representatives of any other congressman in Tennessee history. By 1960 the conservative Evins had achieved enough seniority to be a minor power in Congress; in 1964 he managed the Johnson-Humphrey presidential campaign in Tennessee. Once Johnson began his new presidential term, Evins found that his loyal service during the campaign benefited him greatly in acquiring federal dollars, such as the "Model Cities" program, for his Middle Tennessee congressional district. "Seasoned Washington-watchers," noted his biographer in 1971, "have sized up Joe L. Evins as one of the most influential men in government today."[1]

Evins left Congress in 1977 and retired to his home in Smithville. Joe L. Evins died in Nashville on March 31, 1984, and was buried in the Town Cemetery in Smithville.

Carroll Van West, Middle Tennessee State University

CITATION:

(1) Susan B. Graves, *Evins of Tennessee: Twenty-Five Years in Congress* (New York, 1971), 9.

SEE: APPALACHIAN REGIONAL COMMISSION; DEKALB COUNTY; EDGAR EVINS STATE PARK

EXPLORATIONS, EARLY. The first explorations by Europeans in what is now Tennessee took place in 1540, when a Spanish expedition under the command of Hernando de Soto entered the region from the Southeast. Soto set out from Florida the year before with 625 men in search of gold and other treasures, hoping to duplicate the success of earlier Spanish expeditions in Central and South America. The exact route of the Soto expedition through Tennessee is unclear, but it is likely that they crossed the Appalachian Mountains somewhere to the north of the Great Smokies and followed the French Broad River to the Tennessee River down to what later was southeast Tennessee. There are some indications that later Spanish expeditions built forts in the vicinity of Dandridge and Chattanooga, a likely event as the presence of their forces was seen as a threat by many Native Americans.

Failing to find the treasures he sought, Soto apparently turned back to the Southwest, before heading north again and entering the bounds of Tennessee, south of Memphis. He crossed the Mississippi River and continued exploring to the west. As the health and morale of his party deteriorated, Soto brought them back to the Mississippi River, where he died from a fever. His troubled expedition returned to the coast.

Another Spanish expedition under Juan Pardo explored the western portion of North Carolina and some areas of Tennessee in 1566–1567. Like Soto, Pardo sought gold, but he also wanted to establish alliances with native tribes. He failed, however, in both of these objectives. While the Spanish expeditions maintained detailed accounts of their explo-

rations in Tennessee, including the earliest written description of the land and its inhabitants, the failure to locate anything of material value discouraged the Spanish from additional expeditions into the region.

More than a century later, in 1673, a French expedition under the command of Father Jacques Marquette, a Jesuit missionary, and Louis Joliet, a fur trader, descended the Mississippi River, stopping along the way at Chickasaw Bluffs near Memphis. In 1682 another French expedition, led by Robert Cavelier de la Salle, also explored the Mississippi River and built a fort near the mouth of the Hatchie River, naming it Fort Prudhomme in honor of a comrade who was briefly lost from the rest of the group. La Salle's explorations paved the way for the French to extend their trading network into the interior of the continent. By 1692 French traders had established posts along the Cumberland River near a salt springs, a site which later became know as the French Lick, and in 1780 served as the nucleus for the Nashville settlements. From this location, the French maintained an active fur trade with the Shawnees until 1714, when the Shawnees were driven out by a coalition of Cherokees and Chickasaws.

The English began their explorations in Tennessee when Abraham Wood, who operated a trading firm in Virginia, sent James Needham and Gabriel Arthur into what is now upper East Tennessee to establish trading relations with the Cherokees. Needham and Arthur arrived in Cherokee territory in 1673, the same year that the first French expedition sailed down the Mississippi. Although the Cherokees killed Needham soon after his arrival, Arthur remained with the tribe for over a year, initiating a commercial relationship that would continue through the next century. Similarly, the colony of South Carolina sent trade representatives into Tennessee and the Southeast. Among these was James Adair, who had begun extensive travels among the southeastern tribes by 1730, and whose interests extended well beyond trade. His observations regarding Cherokee traditions and customs were eventually published and provide a unique insight into this early period of relations with the tribe.

Eventually, Virginia and South Carolina developed an intense rivalry for the lucrative Cherokee fur trade. Their efforts to dominate trade relations with the tribe sent numerous traders from each colony into the area during the early 1700s, all of whom brought back information about the land and its potential. Their accounts encouraged land speculators to sponsor further exploration of the transAppalachian West.

One of the earliest explorers was Dr. Thomas Walker, who was sent by the Loyal Land Company in 1749, to locate and claim western lands for future settlement. Departing from southwestern Virginia,

Walker and six companions passed through the Cumberland Gap, crossed the Cumberland Plateau, and canoed over the Cumberland River, all of which he named in honor of the Duke of Cumberland. The group returned to Virginia by an overland route through Kentucky.

On a return visit to Kentucky in 1760, Walker explored the intervening Clinch and Powell river valleys, but by that time, there were other explorers in the vicinity. Collectively known as "Long Hunters," these individuals had ventured across the Blue Ridge and Appalachian Mountains by the 1750s. Like the traders who preceded them, the Long Hunters sought furs; but unlike the traders, they did not engage in barter with the Native Americans. Instead, they concentrated in extensive hunting and trapping expeditions. The best known Long Hunter was Daniel Boone; others included Kasper Mansker, who would become a leading citizen in the Cumberland settlements, and Thomas Sharp "Bigfoot" Spencer, whose wilderness prowess and physical strength became legendary.

While some Long Hunters worked alone or in small groups, they frequently traveled in parties of a dozen or more, both for security and to increase their profits. As their name implies, the time away from home for the Long Hunters sometimes extended over periods of months or years. It was not unusual for Long Hunters to work in partnership with land speculators, who financed the trip in exchange for information on the land. For this reason, certain Long Hunters were also surveyors, and they became the best sources of information about the trans-Appalachia.

The primary objective of the Long Hunters was the acquisition of furs for the lucrative international fur market. By 1770 prices ranged from one dollar for deerskins to as much as five dollars for otter pelts. The risks were not insignificant. Long Hunters contended with survival in the wilderness environment as well as encounters with Native Americans. At times, Native Americans confiscated the furs and equipment of the Long Hunters, whom they viewed as trespassers and thieves, men who offered nothing in exchange for the furs they removed.

From another perspective, the Long Hunters represented the first essential steps in the settlement process. They located the best access routes into the trans-Appalachian West and the most suitable land for settlement. They identified springs for water and sources of salt, traveled through valleys and mountain passes, and trapped along countless rivers and streams. Their names are well known—Boone, Mansker, Bledsoe, Stone, and Spencer—and became place names in the areas where they once hunted and explored.

A final source of information about the region came as the result of political objectives, as was the case in the construction of Fort Loudoun, which was begun on the Little Tennessee River in 1756. British military engineers explored different sites on the Little Tennessee before deciding on the final location. Even after the fall of Fort Loudoun, British officers and delegations continued to move among the Cherokees and explore the region of East Tennessee; their reports were often very detailed and informative. Most notable are the memoirs of Lt. Henry Timberlake, who visited the Cherokees in 1761–1762, and produced one of the region's earliest known maps.

The information and knowledge gained by early explorers encouraged migration into the region. In particular, the stories of rich land and plentiful game were instrumental in stimulating the rush of settlement, which began before the Revolution and continued through the 1780s. When territorial administration began in 1790, numerous settlements were in the Tennessee country. By the 1820s very little marketable land existed in the state which had not been claimed, although exploration of some of the more remote areas would continue for years to come.

Michael Toomey, Knoxville College

SUGGESTED READINGS: Samuel C. Williams, *Dawn of Tennessee Valley and Tennessee History, 1541–1776* (1937) and *Early Travels in the Tennessee Country, 1540–1800* (1928)

SEE: BOONE, DANIEL; CUMBERLAND GAP; FORT LOUDOUN; FORT PRUDHOMME AND LA SALLE; FRENCH LICK; LUNA EXPEDITION; MANSKER, KASPER; OVERHILL CHEROKEES; PARDO EXPEDITION; SHAWNEES; SOTO EXPEDITION; SPENCER, THOMAS S.; TIMBERLAKE, HENRY; WALKER, THOMAS

F

FAIRVUE PLANTATION. Fairvue was the home of Isaac Franklin and his young bride, Adelicia Hayes Franklin. Built in 1832, the house had identical facades facing east and west, situated at a 90 degree angle to the Nashville-Gallatin Turnpike, of which Franklin was an original stockholder. The four-over-four room house has a central hall and double portico in the Ionic style. A finished third floor attic extends the length of the house. Elliptical fan windows over the doors reflect some of the many Federal construction details. In 1839, the year the Franklins married, a south wing, consisting of seven rooms, was added to the original structure. On the opposite side of the house, an octagonal brick wall enclosed a garden with an ice house in the center. Fairvue was a 2000-acre working plantation devoted to cattle and thoroughbred horses. It included extensive stables and a training track. Brick slave quarters, an overseer's house, and blacksmith shop still remain.

In 1846 Isaac Franklin died. His will set up trusts for his children and provided for his wife until her remarriage, at which time Fairvue would become a private school, endowed by his vast Louisiana holdings. In 1849, after marrying Joseph Acklen, Adelicia Franklin Acklen contested the will before the Louisiana Supreme Court which declared it void and of no force. Without funding, the school never formed, and the house remained vacant during the Civil War.

In 1869 Adelicia Acklen purchased the property from John Armfield, the executor of Franklin's estate. In 1882 she sold the property to Charles Reed of New York. Reed spent $200,000 restoring Fairvue as a fine home and horse breeding establishment. By 1897 Fairvue had approximately 150 brood mares. Reed sold the property in 1908, and Fairvue had a succession of owners until 1929. Two weeks before the stock market crash, the Sumner County Land Company, a division of Southland Grasslands Hunt and Racing Foundation, purchased Fairvue and 80 other farms to build a fox hunting and steeplechase course. The project was ill timed, and the new owners declared bankruptcy in 1932. William Hatch Wemyss, a co-founder of Jarman Shoe Company, saved Fairvue when he purchased the property in 1934. In 1939 Wemyss married Ellen Stokes Moore, and she began the restoration of Fairvue. In 1956 320 acres of Fairvue Farms were flooded by Old Hickory Dam, leaving the house on a peninsula. Still a private residence, Fairvue is a National Historic Landmark and is listed on the National Register of Historic Places.

Mark Brown, Belmont Mansion

SEE: ACKLEN; ADELICIA; ARMFIELD, JOHN; FRANKLIN, ISAAC; SLAVERY; SUMNER COUNTY

FALK, RANDALL M. (1921–) has advanced Jewish-Christian relations and understanding as author, professor, and Rabbi of The Temple, Congregation Ohabai Sholom in Nashville. Born in Little Rock and educated at the University of Cincinnati and the Hebrew Union College, Falk began his rabbinic experience in 1947 in Erie, Pennsylvania, where his activities earned him the Man of the Year and the Community Brotherhood awards. After coming to Nashville in 1960, he confronted racial segregation and helped organize the first march of clergy in the country demanding integration of public accommodations. Falk's involvement in the community has continued through various activities and participation on organization boards, and he received the Human Relations Award from both the Metropolitan Nashville Human Relations Commission and the Nashville chapter of the National Conference of Christians and Jews. On the national level, Falk has contributed to the Central Conference of American Rabbis as officer, chairman of its Committee on

Justice and Peace, and vice chairman of its Commission on Social Action. At the same time, Falk's spiritual leadership helped double The Temple's membership by the time he retired in 1986. He had previously earned a doctorate from Vanderbilt's Divinity School and subsequently taught there and at the School of Theology at the University of the South. Since retiring, Falk co-authored with Walter Harrelson the books *Jews and Christians: A Troubled Family* (1991) and *Jews and Christians: In Pursuit of Social Justice* (1996). He and his wife Edna have three children and three grandchildren.

Margaret D. Binnicker, Middle Tennessee State University
SEE: CIVIL RIGHTS MOVEMENT; RELIGION

FALL CREEK FALLS STATE PARK is Tennessee's second-largest park, covering a total of 19,684 acres. The park is located between Spencer and Pikeville, along the border of Van Buren and Bledsoe counties. Located near the upper Cane Creek Gulf watershed, the site utilized severely eroded land that federal authorities purchased for less than seven dollars per acre. Despite the devastation, the park's landscape was compelling, even overwhelming in its rugged beauty in the fall, according to leading conservationists of the time. Initially, the National Park Service planned to purchase land that included both Cane Creek and Fall Creek watersheds, but finally limited its acquisition to approximately half the original proposal.

Park construction began in 1936 following the arrival of the Civilian Conservation Corps (CCC) and Works Progress Administration (WPA). The Resettlement Administration (RA) relocated families living in the area of development; the CCC restocked wildlife and began reforestation; and the WPA assisted with construction.

The State Forestry Service and Department of Agriculture administered the park throughout the 1930s and 1940s. The National Park Service oversaw development, which included parking areas, picnic and camping facilities, trails, shelters, scenic overlooks, a dam, a swimming pool, a lodge, and cabins. Although the park's remote location made access difficult, the National Park Service encouraged visitation by accentuating the area's multiple waterways, including the spectacular 250-foot Fall Creek Falls. In time, the multiple waterfalls secluded by cliffs and the backdrop of the Cumberland Mountains made Fall Creek Falls one of the state's most popular parks.

Park development moved slowly in order to maintain the area's "natural state." In 1940 the Park Service permitted the construction of vacation cabins, a lodge, horse barns, and horse trails to encourage visitation, but abandoned the project because of World War II labor and funding demands. In 1944 the Department of the Interior transferred the park to the State of Tennessee, but restricted land to recreation and conservation. The Tennessee State Planning Commission resubmitted the National Park Service's proposal of 1940 in 1950, and obtained state funding for the construction of recreational facilities. The park added swimming facilities in 1954, but eight years later, the recreational area still held only two man-made camping areas and prohibited boating, emphasizing the area's natural falls and scenery rather than its modern amenities.

Today, park attendance places Fall Creek Falls among the state's most heavily visited recreational sites. The park currently offers a nationally rated public golf course, a modern inn and restaurant complex, as well as natural vistas that include the park's namesake, Fall Creek Falls. Administrators have successfully retained the park's most valuable resources, including Cane Creek Gulf, Cane Creek Falls, Rock House Creek Falls, Piney Falls, numerous gorges, natural foliage, and an abundance of wildlife species. Today, the park remains, as the National Park Service remarked in the mid-1930s, "unquestionably one of the most outstanding beauty regions" in the eastern United States.[1]

Ruth Nichols, Nashville
CITATION:
(1) Beverly R. Coleman, "A History of State Parks in Tennessee," (Ph.D. diss., Vanderbilt University, 1974), p. 328.
SEE: BLEDSOE COUNTY; CIVILIAN CONSERVATION CORPS; CONSERVATION; VAN BUREN COUNTY; WORKS PROGRESS ADMINISTRATION

FANNING, TOLBERT (1810–1874), early leader of the Stone-Campbell Movement in Tennessee and the South, was born in rural Middle Tennessee in an area that later became Cannon County. Converted to the Disciples in Alabama in 1827, Fanning attended and graduated from the University of Nashville in 1835. Here he came under the influence of Philip Lindsley and Gerard Troost. While a student at the University, he preached throughout Middle Tennessee. Although baptized by a "Stoneite" preacher, Fanning came much nearer Alexander Campbell's rationalistic approach to religion; he established "Campbellite" churches in Franklin and Murfreesboro, among other places. Besides reading Alexander Campbell's *Christian Baptist* and *Millennial Harbinger*, Fanning traveled to New England and Canada with Campbell.

Early in his career, Fanning became interested in editing and publishing both religious and secular journals. The *Christian Review* (1844–1848) became his first publishing effort. In 1855 he issued the *Gospel Advocate,* a paper he continued until the Civil War and reissued with the aid of his former student David Lipscomb after the close of the conflict. With his preaching and writing, Fanning became one of the leading Disciples in Tennessee and the South.

Influenced by Gerard Troost, Fanning also became interested in all phases of agriculture and geology. In 1840 he was one of the founders of the State Agricultural Society and a principal editor of its journal, *The Agriculturalist,* a position he continued for six years. Fanning introduced a number of farm animals into Tennessee, including the Morgan horse. He was among the first in the state to encourage scientific agriculture. Fanning also made numerous teaching trips with his students throughout the South, where they studied the flora and fauna, along with geological formations. For one year (1847), he published the *Naturalist,* a scientific journal.

As a result of his interest in agriculture, he established Franklin College on his farm on the grounds of present-day Nashville International Airport. Patterned after Benjamin Franklin's philosophy of practical education, he developed a manual-labor school, where each student studied subjects in the classroom and put the ideas into practice on the farm. Differing from Franklin's view of education, however, each student studied the Bible as a part of the curriculum. The school continued until the Civil War. After the conflict, the school was set to reopen, but a fire destroyed the buildings that housed the school.

Robert E. Hooper, Lipscomb University

SUGGESTED READING: James R. Wilburn, *The Hazard of the Die: Tolbert Fanning and the Restoration Movement* (1969)

SEE: AGRICULTURAL JOURNALS; AGRICULTURAL SOCIETIES; CAMPBELL, ALEXANDER; LINDSLEY, PHILIP; LIPSCOMB, DAVID; RELIGION; STONE, BARTON; TROOST, GERARD

FARMERS' ALLIANCE (FARMERS' AND LABORERS' UNION) made its first appearance in Tennessee in the winter of 1887, when J. T. Alsup, a national lecturer, organized the first Alliance in Wilson County. Perhaps Alsup selected Middle Tennessee for his first attempts because West Tennessee farmers had already joined the Agricultural Wheel, a similar agrarian reform organization that originated in Arkansas. In March 1888 farmers organized the Tennessee State Alliance and elected John P. Buchanan, a Rutherford County livestock man, as the first president.

In 1889 the National Farmers' Alliance and the Agricultural Wheel joined forces to become the National Farmers' and Laborers' Union (still popularly known as the Alliance). Tennessee was the first state to ratify the new constitution, and the merger was accomplished easily. Buchanan became the first president of the Tennessee Farmers' and Laborers' Union, and Eth B. Wade served as its first secretary. At the time of the merger, the Agricultural Wheel claimed more than 1600 subordinate wheels, and the Alliance counted approximately 800 units. The combined membership topped 99,000 men, women, and boys.

The Alliance proposed to improve the lot of farmers by focusing attention on local, state, and national issues. The Alliance urged farmers to adopt scientific and business practices, diversify their crops, and become self-sufficient in order to break the debt cycle imposed by the crop lien system. To aid in this process, county and state Alliances instituted cooperative buying and marketing agencies to reduce the cost of farm equipment and seeds and obtain the highest prices for agricultural products. The Tennessee State Cooperative Agency had three offices in Nashville, Memphis, and Morristown to handle the buying and selling for county business agents in the three Grand Divisions. At the state and national levels, the Alliance pressured legislatures and Congress to adopt regulatory, anti-banking, and anti-monopoly laws favored by farmers.

The Alliance, like the Wheel, advocated non-partisan support for candidates who supported the organization's demands. In Tennessee, however, most candidates claiming Alliance support were Democrats. In the 1890 election, the Alliance president, John P. Buchanan, captured the Democratic gubernatorial nomination with the help of the state's farmers. Buchanan won the November election and became one of four Southern Alliance governors. The 1891 Tennessee General Assembly had 54 Alliance members.

The Tennessee Farmers' Alliance was unable to build on their initial success, however, and after the 1890 high point, declined rapidly. As national organizational demands became more radical, Tennessee farmers, encouraged by Alliance critics, became less certain of the organization and its goals. Many would-be reformers worried about the Subtreasury scheme, which called for government-sponsored construction of warehouses, where farmers could store non-perishable agricultural products to await higher prices. To meet immediate needs, farmers could obtain low interest loans on the stored cotton, tobacco, or grain, repaying the loan when the produce sold. The plan offered an escape from the crop lien and gave farmers access to capital rather than credit. In an attempt to broaden the plan's appeal, the national organization later added land as collateral for loans. Tennessee delegates to national meetings supported the first plan, but not the second one. Only Congressmen Rice Pierce of West Tennessee supported the subtreasury plan. Alliance critics used the expanded plan to argue that the organization benefited the wealthy. The Tennessee Alliance also suffered from internal problems ranging from financial instability to divisions based on political differences, historical conflicts, and diverse agricultural production.

After successfully capturing the election of 1890, and seemingly the Democratic party, the Alliance lost its advantage in 1892. The Bourbon and New South wings of the Democratic party laid aside their differences and combined their efforts to make Peter Turney the Democratic nominee and ultimately governor. When more radical Alliance members bolted and organized the People's Party (Populists) in late spring of 1892, the more conservative members had little choice but to follow, despite sentiment against the move. Buchanan announced his candidacy for reelection as an Independent, or Jeffersonian, Democrat, but his support came from the Populists. The defeat of the Alliance and the Populists in 1892 ended agrarian reform influence in Tennessee, although the Populists remained a feared force in several counties until the turn of the century.

Connie L. Lester, Tennessee Historical Society

SUGGESTED READING: Roger L. Hart, *Redeemers, Bourbons & Populists: Tennessee, 1870–1896* (1975); Connie L. Lester, "Grassroots Reform in the Age of New South Agriculture and Bourbon Democracy: The Agricultural Wheel, The Farmers' Alliance, and the People's Party in Tennessee, 1884–1892" (Ph.D. Diss., University of Tennessee, 1998)

SEE: AGRICULTURE; AGRICULTURAL WHEEL; BUCHANAN, JOHN P.; MCDOWELL, JOHN H.; TURNEY, PETER

FARMS AND THE AGRICULTURAL EXPERIMENT STATION.

Farms and farming in Tennessee have experienced great changes during two centuries of statehood. For example, the number of farms in Tennessee ranged from 72,735 in 1850 to 273,783 in 1935, before sliding to 87,000 in 1996. The average farm size during the same period experienced a reverse pattern, going from 261 acres in 1850 to 69.7 acres in 1935, before climbing to 149 acres in 1996. Other changes included types of crops grown, degree of specialization, sources of power to carry out agricultural processes, and government regulation of operations and financial incentives. The Agricultural Experiment Station has contributed significantly to both the nature of agricultural information and the ways in which that information reaches farmers.

Farms also experienced a dramatic change in character. The earliest settlers did more hunting and gathering than farming. As they settled on the land, they learned farming techniques from Native Americans and family members. The pioneer farmers provided first for their families and livestock, but quickly developed an interest in growing crops for the market, especially cotton and tobacco. These two crops continued to dominate the state's commercial agriculture for most of its history. In 1994 cotton and tobacco each accounted for 11.5 percent of the state's receipts from agricultural products. The only commodities producing large percentages were cattle and calves (19.1) and dairy products (12.2).

Through the years, farms increasingly specialized, as technology improved and markets became more demanding. As a result, farm families became more dependent on the larger society for the basic necessities of food and equipment for home and farm operation. Farm families now shop for food in area supermarkets and grocery stores.

The nature of power to carry out farm activities also changed dramatically. For much of the state's history, human labor, supplemented by animal power, provided the energy to complete farm work. In the antebellum period, slave labor made up a significant portion of the human labor force. In 1800 slaves accounted for about 20 percent of the population of Nashville; Knoxville was not far behind with 15 percent. With the emancipation of the slaves following the Civil War, a reorganization of relationships between the landowners and farm laborers occurred, resulting in the widespread development of sharecropping and tenancy.

Non-human sources of power produced changes in land use and promoted the development of specialized skills. The use of animal power required that part of the land be devoted to the production of hay or fodder. Tennessee farmers relied on animals to power farm equipment well into the twentieth century; the tractor became ubiquitous on farms in the 1940s and 1950s. Initially, farmers themselves contributed to the technology that produced improvements in equipment for tilling the soil and harvesting the crops. As equipment became more sophisticated, many farmers learned to do the work of electricians and welders. Eventually, farm equipment reached a level of sophistication that made farmers dependent upon specialists for service and repairs.

Before the creation of experiment farms and stations in the late 1800s, farmers relied on family, friends, and close neighbors for information, sometimes supplemented by letters from relatives and acquaintances. Largely self-sufficient, these farmers used agricultural information to make market decisions that made life somewhat easier or less risky. Neighbors often provided the most reliable information about local conditions, and frequently established agricultural societies to formally address farm problems. The earliest of these societies in Tennessee formed in Washington, Greene, and Davidson counties, from 1819 to 1830. There was sufficient interest in such societies for the General Assembly to pass an act incorporating a State Agricultural Society in 1842. Local societies promoted county fairs across the state, where farmers displayed farm products and learned the latest agricultural information.

Congressional passage of the Morrill Act in 1862 reflected a continuing interest in educating farmers about agriculture. This act provided funds to establish state colleges emphasizing agriculture and the mechanical arts. Teachers in these colleges soon discovered that there was little systematic information about many facets of agriculture.

In 1883 a second act, the Hatch Act, provided funds for the creation of Agricultural Experiment Stations to generate more systematic information. In 1882, before the passage of the Hatch Act, the Board of Trustees of the University of Tennessee created and inaugurated an experiment station in Knoxville. The College Farm became the site of agricultural experiments. In 1887 Dr. Charles W. Dabney became director of the UT Experiment Station. During this period the university set an important precedent that continues to this day: teachers in the College of Agriculture were also responsible for performing the experimental work in the Agricultural Experiment Station. The station began with a small staff and limited funds, but quickly organized into four divisions: Field and Feeding Experiments, Chemistry, Botany and Horticulture, and Entomology.

In the early 1900s, branch stations were established to improve the local applicability of the research results. Eventually, the state built 11 stations, with each concentrating on crop and/or livestock enterprises important to the area. By the late 1930s, for instance, the Tennessee Agricultural Experiment Station operated the Middle Tennessee Experiment Station in Maury County; administered an agricultural experiment station as well as a demonstration farm at the University of Tennessee Junior College (now UT at Martin); operated the West Tennessee Experiment Station at Jackson; ran a State Agricultural Experiment Station, Madison Extension, in Montgomery County; and partnered with the U.S. Department of Agriculture in administering a Burley Tobacco Experiment Station near Greeneville and a Dairy Experiment Farm near Lewisburg. During the 1930s the state provided limited funding, and much of the work depended on contracts with various New Deal agencies. When Harcourt A. Morgan, former director of the Experiment Station, became director of the Board of the Tennessee Valley Authority, he educated that agency in efficacy of utilizing Experiment Station knowledge and resources. TVA and the Experiment Station worked together to provide a soil survey of the state. One of the most innovative partnerships was between UT and the Atomic Energy Commission in administering a research laboratory in Oak Ridge.

In addition to its spatial expansion, there was an increase in the number of disciplines represented in the station's organization. The basic disciplines of Plant & Soil Science, Animal Science, and Agricultural Engineering have been supplemented with Ornamental Horticulture & Landscaping Design, Entomology & Plant Pathology, Agricultural Economics & Rural Sociology, Food Technology & Science, Forestry, Wildlife & Fisheries, and Agricultural Communications. Experiment Station services extend to a variety of citizens across the state, and programs developed by the UT stations are used in other states and around the world.

Charles L. Cleland, University of Tennessee, Knoxville
SUGGESTED READING: Thomas J. Whatley, *A History of the Tennessee Agricultural Experiment Station* (1994)
SEE: AGRICULTURAL SOCIETIES; AGRICULTURAL TENANCY; AGRICULTURE; DABNEY, CHARLES W.; FARRIS, OSCAR L.; MORGAN, HARCOURT A.; SLAVERY; TENNESSEE VALLEY AUTHORITY; UNIVERSITY OF TENNESSEE

FARMS, TENNESSEE CENTURY is a public program that honors family farmers who have kept continuously-owned family land in agricultural production for, at least, the last 100 years. Established by the Tennessee Department of Agriculture in 1975–76 as a special bicentennial project, the initial survey identified approximately 600 Tennessee farm families who joined the program and submitted the required farm history, certification by a county historian and/or extension agent, and photographs. In 1985 the Oscar Farris Agricultural Museum at the Tennessee Department of Agriculture asked the Center for Historic Preservation at Middle Tennessee State University to assist in updating the histories of eligible farms and to prepare a history book about the state's Century Farms. When its survey was completed in 1986, 783 eligible Tennessee Century Farms had been identified and were included in the subsequent book, *Tennessee Agriculture: A Century Farms Perspective,* by the Center's Carroll Van West. The MTSU Center for Historic Preservation continues to accept the applications of eligible farms. As part of its rural history and preservation program, it extended the initial book project into a traveling exhibit about Tennessee's family farm history, curated by the Center's Caneta S. Hankins, which toured the state in 1988–89; developed heritage education curricula centered on a family farm as a teaching laboratory; and established a program of historic preservation assistance, where eligible farm families may request that the Center prepare a nomination for their farm to the National Register of Historic Places. The Center has prepared a National Register multiple property nomination for historic family farms in Middle Tennessee. Due to the joint efforts of the Tennessee Agricultural Museum, the Department of Agriculture, county extension agents, county historians, and the MTSU Center for Historic Preservation, Tennessee has one of the most comprehensive history projects about family farms in the country.

Carroll Van West, Middle Tennessee State University
SEE: CENTER FOR HISTORIC PRESERVATION; FARRIS, OSCAR L., AGRICULTURAL MUSEUM

FARRAGUT, DAVID GLASGOW (1801–1870), first U.S. Admiral, was born James Glasgow Farragut in 1801 and raised in Stoney Point, near Knoxville. In 1806 his father received a navy commission and moved his family to New Orleans. In 1808, when a close family friend, Commodore David Porter, fell ill with yellow fever, the Farraguts nursed him; both Porter and Mrs. Farragut died of the fever and were buried the same day. In 1810 Porter's son David, also a naval officer, offered to take young James and his sister Nancy to live with his family in Chester, Pennsylvania.

Farragut changed his name to David, in honor of his patron, and entered the navy as a Midshipman in December 1810. His first posting was on the USS Essex under Porter. At age 11, he fought in the War of 1812, and his ship, the Essex, captured the HMS Alert, the first capture of a British ship in the war. Later, the Essex rounded Cape Horn, and captured the HMS Barclay in the Pacific; Farragut was prize master of the ship at age 12. As an adult Farragut earned the honor of escorting Lafayette to France on the USS Brandywine in August 1825. President Andrew Jackson sent Farragut to South Carolina during the nullification crisis in 1832.

Farragut married his second wife, Virginia Loyal, from a prominent Norfolk family, in 1843; his first wife Susan Marchant had died in 1840 after 16 years of marriage. In 1844 Farragut and his wife had a son, Loyal Farragut.

In March 1847 Farragut commanded the USS Saratoga to fight in the Mexican War, but he arrived in Vera Cruz after the Citadel had capitulated. He returned to Washington, D.C., and assisted in drafting ordnance regulations. In 1854–1858 Farragut set up a new navy yard in California. On the eve of the Civil War, Farragut was at home in Norfolk, awaiting new orders, when he was warned that those with Union sentiments were no longer safe in Virginia; his family moved to New York.

Farragut was called to duty in December 1861 and placed in command of a flotilla ordered to take New Orleans and open the Mississippi River to Federal traffic. In August 1862 he was promoted to Rear Admiral for his success in opening the river to Vicksburg. Farragut received a hero's welcome when he returned to New York in August 1863. By January 1864 Farragut was back in the Gulf of Mexico, preparing for an assault on Mobile Bay. During this August battle, while aboard the USS Hartford, he was reported to have responded, "Damn the torpedoes, full speed ahead," as the Hartford passed the USS Brooklyn to take the lead in the naval battle. Farragut took Mobile Bay that day.

Failing health forced Farragut to return to New York City in December 1864. As a token of their appreciation for his gallantry and service, the City of New York gave him a public reception and $50,000 to purchase a home there. He was promoted to Admiral in July 1866, the first person in the U.S. Navy to hold that rank. From May 1867 to November 1868, he took his final cruise, touring Europe as Admiral of the European Squadron to promote peaceful relations with the United States. Farragut's last mission took him to Portsmouth, New Hampshire, to take charge of the naval obsequies of George Peabody. Weak from a series of heart attacks suffered the previous winter, he died on August 14, 1870, at Portsmouth.

Leo J. Goodsell, Plano, Illinois

SUGGESTED READING: Charles L. Lewis, *David Glasgow Farragut* (1941–1943)

FARRIS, OSCAR L. (1889–1961), spent almost 40 years with the University of Tennessee Agricultural Extension Service. While serving in Maury County, he was responsible for the first "test and slaughter" attempt to control cattle brucellosis in Tennessee. This was four years before the United States Department of Agriculture instituted a similar program nationwide.

An agricultural reformer trained at the University of Missouri, Farris served his country in World War I, from May 1917 to April 1919, and in World War II, from March 1941 to April 1945. He rose from the rank of second lieutenant to lieutenant colonel and received the honor of the Distinguished Service Cross and the British Military Cross.

From 1920 to 1941, Farris was Davidson County's agricultural extension agent. During this period, he also worked toward the electrification of rural Davidson County and organized committees to improve living conditions for rural Tennesseans. Farris lobbied for a state agricultural hall of fame, and in 1937 the legislature created the Tennessee Agricultural Hall of Fame, the first such institution in the United States. Two of the early plaques were cast from the dilapidated statue of Mercury, which had previously topped the Union Station in Nashville, before a storm toppled it in the early 1950s. In appreciation for his many contributions and dedicated service to agriculture and farm families, a new farmers market administration building was dedicated to Farris in 1959.

During his long tenure in agricultural service, Farris saw the importance of preserving Tennessee's rural heritage. He collected and stored farm tools and household furnishings, which were quickly becoming obsolete in the wake of rapidly changing technology. When the state acquired Rogers Caldwell's Brentwood Hall, renamed Ellington Agricultural Center for former Commissioner of Agriculture and later Governor Buford Ellington, Farris moved his collection to an unused horse barn on the grounds. In 1957, by an act of the legislature, a state agricultural museum was officially created.

After retirement, Farris continued to add to the museum collection until his death in June 1961. In 1972 state agricultural officials dedicated the museum in Farris's honor, naming it the Oscar L. Farris Agricultural Museum.

Dot Curtis, Nashville

SEE: FARMS AND AGRICULTURAL EXPERIMENT STATION; FARRIS, OSCAR L. AGRICULTURAL MUSEUM

FARRIS, OSCAR L., AGRICULTURAL MUSEUM

(Tennessee Agricultural Museum) was chartered by the General Assembly in 1957. Located at Ellington Agricultural Center in Nashville, it is housed in a former horse barn, once part of the Brentwood Hall estate of financier Rogers Caldwell. The museum features artifacts relating to the pioneering days of Tennessee farm families, ranging from early farm tools and equipment to household goods and machines that were used by farm women and their children. The artifacts date from the beginning of Tennessee agriculture to objects representing agricultural developments during the mid-twentieth century. The museum is also home to the Tennessee Agriculture Hall of Fame, the oldest in the nation.

For many years, little funding was allotted the museum, and the facility was open only on an occasional basis. During 1980–81, the building was renovated, and the museum opened three days a week with a part-time curator. Guided tours begun in 1981 soon made way for educational programs with hands-on activities for students. Finally in 1984 a full-time curator was appointed, and the museum opened on a daily basis. Attendance doubled, tripled, and kept growing. Teachers took advantage of these opportunities to enhance their studies of Tennessee history.

Museum programs, coordinated with a group of teachers, are of a seasonal nature and include either pre- or post-worksheets for teachers, which cover several items on the curriculum guides for each grade level. The museum hosts several events each year, which include shingle riving, basket weaving, pottery throwing, cow milking, sheep shearing, or a Tennessee Walking Horse demonstration.

A museum association was organized in 1988 to establish direction, offer financial support, and provide a resource for community involvement. One of the major accomplishments of the association is the restoration of several log cabins adjacent to the main museum building. The cabins, once tenant houses of the Caldwell estate, are an important part of the museum's educational programs. In 1998 the institution's name became the Tennessee Agricultural Museum.

Dot Curtis and Cynthia Cook, Nashville

SEE: CALDWELL, ROGERS; FARRIS, OSCAR L.

FAYETTE COUNTY in southwest Tennessee was established September 29, 1824, by the Tennessee General Assembly and named in honor of the Marquis de Lafayette, French general and statesman. The county seat, Somerville, was named to honor Lieu-

tenant Robert Somerville, hero of the Battle of Tohopeka in Alabama. The first court proceedings took place at the home of Robert G. Thornton on the banks of the North Fork of the Wolf River on December 6, 1824.

Settlement began in the area as early as 1820, and by 1826 there were enough residents for the incorporation of the two oldest towns—Somerville and LaGrange. In both towns, restored antebellum homes symbolize the wealth and culture of the plantation period. The entire town of LaGrange, named for Lafayette's ancestral home, is listed in the National Register of Historic Places. Today there are nine incorporated towns: Braden, Gallaway, LaGrange, Moscow, Oakland, Piperton, Rossville, Somerville, and Williston.

Religious zeal soon prompted the organization of the county's churches. Somerville's First Presbyterian Church dates to 1829. Immanuel Parish in LaGrange, established in 1832, is the oldest Episcopal church in West Tennessee. Nineteenth century camp meetings live on at Joyner's Campground, where annual services are held each July in the open-air tabernacle built in 1893.

Historically, the economy of Fayette County has been based on agricultural production, principally cotton and corn. Large plantations and small farms supported the gins that were located in every town and many of the smaller crossroads communities. However, recent years have witnessed agricultural diversification, with soybeans becoming an important cash crop, followed by beef cattle, dairying, and egg production.

Slaves worked pre-Civil War plantations. Following the war, many former slaves remained in the county, with most employed as tenant farmers and sharecroppers. The county's African Americans constituted a majority of the population until the 1980 census. During the 1960s and 1970s, Civil Rights activists worked for voter registration and school integration. They established two "tent cities" to accommodate black residents, who sought refuge following their eviction from their tenant farms after attempting to register to vote. Today, Fayette County public schools and faculties are fully integrated in seven elementary schools, a comprehensive high school, and a vocational school. J. B. Summers and Joseph Martin each served long terms as county Superintendent of Schools. The only African American to serve in this role was Dr. Warner Dickerson, who ably guided the schools in the late 1980s. Three private academies also hold classes in the county.

The fields of Fayette County have favored the activities of sports enthusiasts and environmentalists. Wolf River, which meanders across the southern part of the county, is widely recognized by outdoor enthusiasts as a unique natural treasure. In 1995 conservationists aided the State of Tennessee in acquiring a vast forest area filled with cypress-studded swamps bordering the river, near LaGrange. As a result of their efforts, visitors now enjoy the beauty of the Wolf River Wildlife Management Area and the Ghost River State Natural Area. Herb Parsons Lake was named in honor of Herb Parsons, a world champion Winchester rifle exhibition shooter. The best known outdoors event of the county is the National Field Trials for bird dogs, which has been held annually since 1903 on the historic Ames Plantation in southeast Fayette County.

In the 1960s Troxel Manufacturing Company located a factory at Moscow. Now, most towns have developed one or more industrial parks to lure new companies. Historically, manufacturers have had excellent transportation facilities in Fayette County. Named the LaGrange-Memphis Railroad, the first railroad chartered by the State of Tennessee to be built was in Fayette County in 1835. The LaGrange-Memphis Railroad later became the Memphis and Charleston Railroad, before being incorporated into the Southern Railway system. Today, the Norfolk-Southern Railway traverses the southern portion of the county. In addition, the modern Fayette County Airport is equipped with a 3,500-foot runway with NBD approach and an automated weather observation system.

Politically, the county traditionally voted Democratic until recent years, when votes shifted to the Republican Party in statewide and national elections while retaining a Democratic majority in local county offices. During the 1940s the county was embroiled in the States Rights (Dixiecrat) movement. Charles Stainback, veteran Somerville lawyer, served as state chairman; Somerville was the host to the statewide convention in 1948. The best known Fayette politician is John Shelton Wilder, Democrat from Longtown, who was first elected to the State Senate in 1959, and has served continuously in that office since 1966. He has established a record-breaking tenure, acting as Speaker of the Senate and Lieutenant Governor for 13 consecutive terms.

Although Fayette County remains a rural, agricultural area, it is now in a period of transition as it faces the suburban sprawl from nearby Memphis.

Dorothy Morton, Moscow

SEE: AMES PLANTATION; CIVIL RIGHTS MOVEMENT; COE, LEVIN H.; MCFERRIN, JOHN AND VIOLA; PICKENS, LUCY; RAILROAD, MEMPHIS AND CHARLESTON; NATIONAL FIELD TRIAL; TENT CITY; WILDER, JOHN S.

FEDERAL BUILDING in Chattanooga exhibits the style known as "modernized" or "starved" classicism that became increasingly identified with American public architecture in the 1930s. The building, planned in 1931, built in 1932, and embellished with a courtroom mural and freestanding sculpture between 1934 and 1938, traces and illuminates a significant phase in the development of American public architecture. The building's design team was one of the many joint ventures between public and private architects prompted by the Depression and assembled during the 1930s to produce federal architecture. The R. H. Hunt Company of Chattanooga, an important regional practice, and Shreve, Lamb & Harmon of New York City, a firm with a national reputation as the designers of the Empire State Building, collaborated on the project under the direction of the Office of the Supervising Architect of the Treasury Department.

The Federal Building, rectangular in plan and centered on a rectangular site, possesses an additive composition of taut orthogonal masses with recessed fenestration. The memory of a classically designed, three-part composition of base, shaft, and capital, treated abstractly, underlies the elevations. Classical elements are detailed in a stripped, simplified, planar manner. Sculpture relieves the severity of the planar wall surface. Abstracted triglyphs and metopes at the towers over the pavilions and speedlines at the pavilion attic cap the composition. Eagles, which were associated with the National Recovery Administration, form a decorative frieze at the parapet of the central mass. Low relief eagles flank the entry stairs.

The organization of the fairly standard interior of the Federal Building is typical of the refinement achieved through the Office of the Supervising Architect's ongoing commitment to standardization. It is zoned vertically with major public spaces, the lobby and post office at the first floor, offices at the second, and courtroom and additional offices at the third. In the lobby, national emblems proclaim the building's public function. The masonry eagles of the exterior reappear in attenuated form on the interior at the aluminum frames flanking the transom grilles over the entry doors. Height distinguishes relative importance: less significant office and support spaces are stacked in two levels, flanking the one and one-half story volume of the courtroom. The size of the vertical dimension and the refinement of the interior finishes emphasize the prominence of the third-floor courtroom. The room, described as the "jewel" of the building, is the culmination of the path through the structure.

The focal point of the courtroom, Hilton Leech's *Allegory of Chattanooga*, embellishes the wall above and behind the judge's bench. The mural illustrates the style and ideals developed and promoted by the Treasury Section of Fine Arts during the New Deal. The dramatic compilation of heroic figures alludes to specific moments in the Chattanooga past, promoting local pride and tying the federal courtroom into local history. The mural creates a 1930s image of an ideal world, using stock Section art themes. The panorama celebrates the abundant landscape, improved through man's intervention in the form of agriculture, transportation, and the nearby hydroelectric dams, associated with the Tennessee Valley Authority. The conjunction of images representing hard work in the past and contemporary technology reinforces the optimistic New Deal message that a bountiful future was still attainable. A jewel within a jewel, the mural is the focal point of the space that is, both architecturally and symbolically, the building's most important room.

Sara A. Butler, University of Virginia
SEE: CHATTANOOGA; MURALS, DECORATIVE INTERIOR

FEDERAL EXPRESS, the largest express transportation company in the world, is headquartered in Memphis. Established in April 1973 at the Memphis International Airport, Federal Express expanded quickly to become the first U.S. corporation to achieve $1 billion in revenues within a decade, without relying on mergers or acquisitions. Frederick W. Smith, a native of Marks, Mississippi, who graduated from Yale University in 1966, founded the company. As its Chief Executive Officer since 1973, Smith is widely credited in the business press for building a model entrepreneurial success story. Today, he is CEO, Chairman, and President of a corporation that has approximately 137,000 employees worldwide, serving 315 airports in 212 countries and flying a total of 596 aircraft. In addition to its world headquarters in Memphis, Federal Express maintains its Asian headquarters in Hong Kong, its European headquarters in Brussels, and its Latin American headquarters in Miami. Its 1997 fiscal year revenues were $11.5 billion. The company has been so successful in its 25 years of existence that the phrase "FedEx" has become synonymous with the overnight delivery of packages and mail, representing a level of corporate identity shared by a mere handful of major American companies.

Federal Express is the single largest private employer in Tennessee, with approximately 26,000 employees in the Memphis area alone. The company's facilities at the Memphis International Airport serve as its central distribution point and have expanded from a small space within an old hanger to a vast complex of buildings on the edge of the airport property. Federal Express's Aircraft Maintenance Facility, which opened in 1995, services most of the company's huge fleet of airplanes, including approximately 160 727s and 60 DC-10s. Its many late-night flights has made Memphis one of the busiest airports in the nation. The average package volume of the entire Federal Express system, in late 1997, was approximately 2.9 million packages daily. In the United States alone, its delivery trucks log some 2.5 million miles a day.

Carroll Van West, Middle Tennessee State University
SEE: AIRPORTS; COMMERCE; MEMPHIS

FENIANS IN TENNESSEE. In 1858 John O'Mahony established the Fenian Brotherhood of America to provide money, arms, and military leadership for an anticipated rising against England by the Irish Revolutionary Brotherhood. An odd twist in this story of nineteenth century Irish nationalism was the role played by Tennesseans. Between 1866 and 1870, two former Nashville residents rose to top leadership positions in the United States and Ireland, and the Nashville Fenian circle served as a base for a British spy.

Tennessee's Fenian circles emerged during the American Civil War, a period of heavy Fenian recruitment. In 1863 Nashville, already under federal control, sent delegates to the first Fenian convention in Chicago. Over the years, Nashville maintained a seat in the Fenian senate, and Nashvillian Dennis Murphy was authorized as one of three U.S. agents selling Fenian bonds. Unknown to local Fenians a British spy, Thomas Billis Beach (known locally as Henri LeCaron), infiltrated the group after the Civil War.

At the 1865 convention, the Fenian Council named former Nashville resident Thomas J. Kelly as military representative to Ireland. By 1866 the militant Kelly replaced Irish Revolutionary Brotherhood founder James Stephens as "Acting Chief of the Irish Republic." In that same year, a militant branch of the Fenians devised an ambitious plan to capture and hold hostage Canadian territory to force the British to free Ireland. Fenians massed along the Canadian border. On June 1, forces, including Nashville's 13th regiment, led by Nashvillian John O'Neill, crossed into Canada and captured Fort Erie. The following day, O'Neill's troops won a minor skirmish at the battle of Ridgeway. Nevertheless, the bold Fenian plan failed, and, following days of indecision, President Andrew Johnson issued orders to arrest the Fenians. O'Neill's minor success catapulted him to national prominence as head of the Center of the Fenian Brotherhood. In 1870 O'Neill attempted a second attack on Canada. That failure forced O'Neill's resignation, and he led an Irish-American settlement to Nebraska.

Dee Gee Lester, Hendersonville
SEE: OCCUPATION, CIVIL WAR; SOUTHERN CITIZEN

FENTRESS COUNTY. The Tennessee General Assembly created Fentress County from parts of Overton and Morgan counties on November 28, 1823. The county was named in honor of James Fentress, the Speaker of the Tennessee House of Representatives, who assisted in passing the enabling legislation for the new county. Fentress County is located in northeast Middle Tennessee on the picturesque Cumberland Plateau. The county initially formed the state's border with Kentucky, but when Pickett County was established in 1881, that part of Fentress was included in the new county.

The history of the county is diverse, ranging from farming to mining to German immigration. Established in 1828, Jamestown, the county seat, also was named in honor of James Fentress. The settlement was once called Sand Springs because several fine springs bubbled up from the sandy soil. Today, a city park, named Mark Twain Park in honor of the Clemens family, who once carried water from the spring, surrounds the only remaining spring. Jamestown was a small agricultural trade center for most of its history. Important agricultural products included corn, small grains, livestock, tobacco, poultry, and pumpkins. In 1928 the York Institute constructed its modern campus on the outskirts of Jamestown and during the 1930s, the town's population expanded from 857 to over 1,200 residents. During these years, industry became more important in the county as six manufacturing firms located in Jamestown by the 1940s. Coal, barite, ore, and natural gas mining already had opened new economic avenues; indeed, the coal mining towns of Davidson and Wilder were the second and third largest communities in the county in 1941. The Fentress Coal and Coke Company and the Davidson Mining Company operated both communities as virtual company towns; they were the scenes of bitter and violent strikes in 1932–1933. Unemployed miners later worked for the Tennessee Valley Authority at Norris and for the Civilian Conservation Corps at LaFollette and Cumberland Homesteads.

Allardt is the other incorporated town in Fentress County. In 1881 Bruno Gernt established the town on the behalf of land speculators Cyrus and James N. Clarke of Nebraska. The settlement attracted a steady stream of German immigrants; by 1886 the town had three general stores, a hotel, a steam mill, a lumber mill, and other tradesmen. Allardt hosts a nationally-recognized Pumpkin Festival every October. Other older communities in the county include Clarkrange, Pall Mall, and Armathwaite.

Tourism is becoming a major part of the local economy as a result of the creation of the Big South Fork National Recreation Area. The Sgt. Alvin C. York State Historic Area, which includes the York home, mill, and grave site, attracts a number of visitors. Another attraction is Highland Manor, which is the state's oldest licensed winery.

Important residents in Fentress County history include Captain David Beaty, John M. Clemens, Alvin Cullum York, and Kate Stockton. Beaty was born in Fentress County in 1823. Known as "Tinker Dave," he formed a Civil War company that was known as David Beaty's Independent Scouts, an outfit that served under Major General George Thomas and General Ambrose Burnsides. Beaty's troops protected the county from Confederate incursions. Beaty was a leader in Fentress County during Reconstruction until his death in 1883. John M. Clemens and his wife, Jane Lampton Clemens, moved to Fentress County in the 1830s. John Clemens served as an attorney, Circuit Court Clerk, and county commissioner. He was postmaster at Pall Mall from April 1832 to May 1835, before he moved to Missouri, where his son, the famous writer Samuel Clemens (Mark Twain), was born later in 1835. The Clemens family owned land in the county for many years, and Samuel Clemens signed several of the land deeds. Alvin Cullum York is known worldwide for his exploits in France, where he became the most decorated enlisted man of World War I. But Fentress Countians admire him most for his dedication to his fellow citizens. Because of his experiences in the war, York realized the importance of education and dedicated his life to improving education in Fentress County. Under his leadership, the York Institute was established in Jamestown. In 1989 the institute received the prestigious National School of Excellence Award. York also was instrumental in getting better roads and other improvements for the county. Kate Bradford Stockton was a reform activist in Fentress County. She ran for governor on the Socialist ticket in 1936, becoming the first woman candidate for Governor of Tennessee. Reverend A. B. Wright was a Methodist preacher and local historian, who left a valuable record of the county's early years in his autobiography that was published in 1876. Another important local historian was Albert Ross Hogue, whose *History of Fentress County* (1916) has served as an excellent resource for many years.

Lorene Cargile, Jamestown

SEE: BIG SOUTH FORK NATIONAL RECREATION AREA; STOCKTON, KATE B.; WILDER-DAVIDSON COAL MINING COMPLEX; WINEMAKING; YORK, ALVIN C.; YORK INSTITUTE

FERRIES. Tennessee contains 19,200 miles of streams, including 1,062 miles of navigable waterways. These streams initially served as a major means of transportation that allowed early settlers access to markets and permitted travel between isolated communities. Future urban centers, such as Knoxville, Chattanooga, Nashville, and Memphis, developed alongside larger rivers. Other communities of various sizes rose and flourished beside smaller streams, only to decline and die as overland transportation became more accessible and reliable. Paradoxically, the same streams that brought settlers to Tennessee and served as frontier highways sometimes became barriers to expansion.

Prior to the later nineteenth century, state and local governments implemented few road building efforts. During the frontier era, settlers used old

Ferry across the Holston River near Blaine, Grainger County, 1950.

animal and Indian trails, fording most streams or building crude rafts to cross larger rivers. As more settlers arrived in the late 1770s and early 1800s, however, the need for more reliable river crossings became evident. Ferry boats, operated by individuals or corporations, soon appeared at major river crossings. Operators typically used the current to propel the vessel. Passengers paid a fee variously based on the number of persons crossing, the number of livestock, or the number of wheels on vehicles. Some 700 to 1,000 ferries operated in Tennessee in the nineteenth century.

In isolated areas, ferries served as social and commercial sites, and communities developed around the ferry crossing. Frequently, the community, often called a landing, derived its name from the ferry owner. For example, the Tennessee River landing and ferry operation of John and Lewis Ross became Ross's Landing, the forerunner of Chattanooga. The 1916 Market Street Bridge, on State Route 8, is adjacent to the site of this 1815 ferry operation.

Beginning around 1880 the Good Roads Movement strongly promoted the construction of bridges and the elimination of ferries. Both individual counties and the state improved road corridors and erected bridges to replace ferry operations. Changing traffic patterns and shifts in transportation corridors rendered many ferry crossings obsolete, and they faded into obscurity. In addition to its other road projects, Tennessee developed an ambitious and unique toll bridge program in the 1920s that replaced 17 ferries on major rivers. By the mid-twentieth century, a ferry crossing, once a symbol of a strategic location on a transportation route, indicated a secondary transportation corridor. Few, if any, traces of many of these ferry operations remain.

By the 1990s only a few ferries operated in Tennessee. In 1997 the Coast Guard licensed two ferry operations in the state, the Saltillo Ferry in Hardin County and the Cumberland City Ferry in Stewart County, but noted that a bridge to serve the Saltillo transportation corridor was under construction.
Martha Carver, Tennessee Department of Transportation
SEE: GOOD ROADS MOVEMENT; ROSS, JOHN; STEWART COUNTY

FIDDLE AND OLD-TIME MUSIC CONTESTS. Tennessee towns host over 30 fiddle and old-time music contests every year. Many of these current music festivals date only to the 1970s as Tennesseans rediscovered their local musical and folklore traditions, but fiddle contests have a long history in the state. Local competitions often took place on an informal basis on courthouse squares on Saturdays or during annual county agricultural fairs. By the late nineteenth and early twentieth centuries, local chapters of the Daughters of the Confederacy or the Daughters of the American Revolution sponsored more formal competitions in order to perpetuate and honor the "good old times" of the antebellum era. A Fiddlers' Carnival, like that held in Gallatin in October 1899, was an effective way to attract rural people to town. In the mid-1920s the Ford Motor Company sponsored national fiddle contests, where competitors first won at the local level, then with the sponsorship of a local Ford Dealer, moved into larger regional and national championships. During the mid-twentieth century, champion fiddlers traveled from town to town, challenging locals to prove who was best. Uncle Jimmy Thompson of the Grand Ole Opry, Arthur Smith from Dickson County, Paul Warren of Hickman County, Curly Fox of Rhea

County, and G. B. Grayson of Johnson County were among the most acclaimed fiddlers of this era.

In 1967 a group of musicians and admirers of old-time music created the Tennessee Valley Old Time Fiddlers' Association, which soon sponsored some of the first fiddle and old music contests in the region. By the early to mid-1970s, the state's best known music festivals were in operation, including the State of Tennessee Old-Time Fiddlers' Championships (1974) in Clarksville; the Fiddler's Jamboree (1972) at Smithville; and the Uncle Dave Macon Days (1978) in Murfreesboro. These festivals not only highlighted fiddlers, but included competitions in old-time music and bluegrass music, banjo, mandolin, guitar, dobro, clogging, and buckdancing. Other competitions in Tennessee that date at least to 1980 are the Holladay Fiddlers Jamboree (1956); Sewanee Bluegrass Convention (1971); Opryland's Grand Masters Fiddling Championship (1972); Minor Hill Fiddling Convention (1977); Elizabethton Fiddlers Convention (1972); Adams's Bell Witch Festival (1978); Mountain City Fiddlers Contest (1976); Crossville Fiddlers Contest (1976); and the Chattanooga Fall Color Cruise and Folk Festival (1974).

Carroll Van West, Middle Tennessee State University
SEE: CLOGGING; MACON, DAVID H.; MUSIC

FIRST TENNESSEE BANK, the state's largest bank, was founded as the First National Bank of Memphis on March 10, 1864. During the Federal occupation of Memphis in the Civil War, Franklin S. Davis and his associates recognized the city's need for banking and credit facilities and the potential of a national banking system once the war ended. The bank received its charter on March 25, 1864, and began to aid Memphis in regaining some of its former commercial activity. Even during the devastating yellow fever epidemics of 1873 and 1878, First National remained open to distribute relief funds.

In 1897 First National purchased German Bank, increasing the bank's deposits from $700,000 to $1,500,000. Under the Federal Reserve Act of 1913, Congress designated First National as one of five banks to assist in the incorporation of the Federal Reserve Bank of St. Louis. In 1926 First National merged with Central-State National Bank, with former Central-State president S. E. Ragland becoming president of First National. During the 1940s and 1950s, Memphis and First National experienced tremendous growth. Under president Norfleet Turner, the bank expanded its facilities and opened seven branch offices by 1952.

Shortly after Allen Morgan succeeded Turner as president in 1960, plans were made for a 25-story bank building to be constructed at the corner of Madison Avenue and Third Street. This imposing modern tower, completed in 1964, rests on square piers and sets back on a plaza. Its design reflects the modernist ideas of Mies Van Der Rohe, as interpreted by the local Memphis firm of Walk C. Jones, Jr. A low wing south of the tower contains the bank's spacious lobby where the First Tennessee Heritage Collection is exhibited. Paintings include Carroll Cloar's *Historic Encounter Between E. H. Crump and W. C. Handy on Beale Street* (1964) and murals by Memphis artist Ted Faiers and Betty Gilow depicting Tennessee history and geography.

First National, the Mid-South's largest bank by 1967, was expanded into a multi-bank holding company in 1971. Under the direction of Ronald Terry, elected chairman and chief executive officer in 1973, First Tennessee National Corporation acquired banks throughout the 1970s with First Tennessee Bank as their common name. In 1977 the First National Bank of Memphis officially changed its name to First Tennessee Bank.

In 1987 First Tennessee restructured its organization to give more authority to its 16 regions, allowing individual banks to better serve their customers and their communities. Today, First Tennessee Bank is the state's largest bank with assets of over $10 billion. Ralph Horn, chief executive officer, attributes part of the bank's success to the emphasis on fee-based banking such as bond underwriting, mortgage banking, and trust services. With help from its Memphis neighbor, Federal Express, First Tennessee has become one of the most efficient check-clearing banks in the country. Furthermore, Tennessee's fast-growing economy has enabled First Tennessee to provide banking services in more than 250 locations to serve most of Tennessee's metropolitan and suburban regions as well as parts of Arkansas and Mississippi.

Anne-Leslie Owens, Tennessee Historical Society
SUGGESTED READING: John E. Harkins, *Metropolis of the American Nile: An Illustrated History of Memphis and Shelby County* (1991)
SEE: CLOAR, CARROLL; COMMERCE AND URBAN DEVELOPMENT; FEDERAL EXPRESS; YELLOW FEVER EPIDEMICS

FIRST WOMAN'S BANK. Situated on the public square in Clarksville in the Arlington Hotel, the First Woman's Bank began operations on October 6, 1919. As a financial institution created, directed, and staffed entirely by women, its opening produced something of a sensation, and deposits totaling $20,000 came in the first day. The bank's establishment at this time, when women had recently experienced success in their war efforts and moved ever closer to gaining the vote, should have surprised no one.

Founder and president Brenda Vineyard Runyon led the 1916 drive for a city/county hospital in Clarksville. An accomplished leader in community efforts, she chaired the local Red Cross unit during World War I and served as sole female member of the school board. She also taught Sunday School at the First Baptist Church and with her husband, physician Frank J. Runyon, raised two sons.

Welcoming deposits from men and women, Runyon encouraged women to become savers and investors in the 1920s. The bank survived for several years, but when failing health necessitated Runyon's resignation as bank president, none of the directors would assume the vacated position. The banking venture, therefore, remains closely linked with Runyon, and its short life makes it seem more a novel experiment than a viable financial institution. The First Trust and Savings Bank of Clarksville absorbed the First Woman's Bank in 1926 and was itself later taken over by Commerce Union Bank, before that institution became part of Sovran Bank and then Nations Bank.

Margaret D. Binnicker, Middle Tennessee State University
SEE: CLARKSVILLE

FISHING. Tennessee boasts 649,000 acres of productive fishing waters—the finest anywhere. Twenty-nine major reservoirs, 19,000 miles of warm and cold water streams, and thousands of smaller lakes and ponds provide unlimited fishing opportunity and variety year-round.

Fish stories told in Tennessee are true (most of them anyway). Most anglers have heard of Tennessee's world record Smallmouth Bass catch caught at Dale Hollow Lake. This monster Smallmouth, caught by Kentucky angler D. L. Hayes while trolling a Bomber from a houseboat, tipped the scales at 11 lbs. 15 oz.

Walleye taken from Tennessee lakes have weighed 25 lbs. Some of the better Walleye fishing can be found in the headwaters of Center Hill Lake. An annual Walleye tournament at Rock Island State Park draws participants from hundreds of miles away.

Word of Tennessee high Striper Bass (Rockfish) traveled fast. Fishermen drive long distances to Tims Ford Reservoir, Percy Priest Lake, Melton Hill Reservoir, and other East Tennessee lakes to try their luck landing Stripers that weigh from 20 lbs. to more than 60 lbs. The state record for a Striper Bass is 60 lbs. 8 oz., and was taken from Melton Hill Reservoir's fertile waters.

Largemouth Bass are plentiful in most Tennessee lakes, reservoirs, rivers, and streams. Farm ponds produce many Largemouth Bass catches every spring. The state-record Largemouth Bass was caught at Kentucky Lake's Sugar Creek. It tilted the scales to a whopping 14 lbs. 8 oz.

Bass fishermen throughout the country know, but are reluctant to tell others, about a state which raises world-record fish and fishermen. Bill Dance, a Memphis native, is one of the most renowned Bass anglers in the United States. His many fishing tips have helped young and old enjoy a great sport here in Tennessee.

For catfishermen, there are four species: Channel, Blues, Flathead, and Brown Bullhead Catfish swimming in most Tennessee waters. Fall Creek Falls State Park boasts the record Channel Catfish catch, 41 lbs., while the French Broad River in East Tennessee claims the record for Blue Catfish at 68 lbs. Barkley Lake's 65 lb. Flathead Catfish is still discussed among avid catfishermen, and Chickamauga Lake yielded the record Brown Bullhead Catfish, 2 lbs. 14 oz. Pickwick Dam in West Tennessee has rightly earned the name, "Catfishing Capital of the World." Of course, Tennessee is as famous for its catfish and hushpuppies as it is for southern hospitality. The reason is clear: Catfish are probably the easiest to catch other than Sunfish and Bream (Bluegill).

Crappie are tagged Tennessee's bread-and-butter fish. This is especially true for natives of Lake and Obion counties, where Reelfoot Lake is located. Commercial fishermen are permitted to net Crappie from Reelfoot Lake three months a year. It is the only lake where commercial fishing is legal in the United States. Crappie are taken in nets, checked by the Tennessee Wildlife Resources Agency, tagged, cleaned, and sold by commercial fish markets in Lake and Obion counties. There is no limit on Crappie at Reelfoot Lake; again the only such lake where this is legal. It is not uncommon to hear fishermen claim catches of 300 or more Crappie. Yellow Jacks, another fun fish caught at Reelfoot, is a member of the White Bass species. Largemouth Bass fishing is also enjoyed at the lake in the spring, among the thousands of Cypress knees, stumps, and lily pads.

The Obey River's icy waters yielded a Rainbow Trout weighing 14 lbs. 8 oz., and a Brown Trout tipping the scales at 28 lbs. 12 oz. A Brook Trout, weighing 3 lbs. 14 oz. was lifted from the cold waters of the Hiwassee River.

Ounce for ounce and inch for inch, the scrappy Bluegill is the fightingest fish that swims in Tennessee waters. Summertime is Bluegill time, and when the Willow flies hatch, fishermen fill their coolers with one of the tastiest fish around. Bluegill can be caught in any body of water in Tennessee. It has been said, however, that Reelfoot Lake and Cumberland Plateau waters yield "platter-size" Bluegill.

Last is the mighty Muskellunge. Tennessee's state record is 42 lbs. 8 oz.. and was caught at Norris Dam. Musky fishing is not for the casual or impatient fisherman, and it is definitely not for the weak of heart! Musky fishing provides trophy-sized dynamite with a mouthful of teeth, and Dale Hollow Lake in late December or January, or Woods Hole Reservoir near Tullahoma offers good fishing.

In addition to the areas previously named, the Tennessee Wildlife Resources Agency stocks game fish in a number of agency-managed lakes. The agency also provides information about fishing regulations and licensing fees.

Jimmy Holt, Tennessee Department of Environment and Conservation

SEE: FALL CREEK FALLS STATE PARK; NORRIS DAM STATE PARK; REELFOOT LAKE STATE PARK; ROCK ISLAND STATE PARK

FISK, CLINTON BOWEN (1828–1890). When the Bureau of Refugees, Freedmen, and Abandoned Lands was established under the U.S. War Department by the Congress in 1865, President Abraham Lincoln proposed General Clinton B. Fisk as an appointee. The appointment was not made prior to Lincoln's assassination, but Andrew Johnson as seventeenth President appointed Fisk as senior officer in charge of the bureau in Kentucky and Tennessee. Fisk's commitment to securing civil rights for the emancipated African Americans during Reconstruction resulted in, among other things, Nashville's Fisk University, which he endowed with $30,000 and which bears his name.

Clinton Bowen Fisk, born December 8, 1828, in Clapp's Corner, New York, was the son of Benjamin and Lydia Fisk. His youth in Michigan was divided between voracious reading and boating with his father on Lake Michigan. In 1848 he married Geanette Crippins, the daughter of a Missouri business associate.

Fisk's military career began with the Missouri Home Guard, a private army organized to oppose the secession movement during the late 1850s. After America became embroiled in civil war, Fisk joined the U.S. Army on July 26, 1862, and was commissioned a colonel on September 5. After the war and Tennessee's full restoration to the Union in 1866, General Fisk, working through the Freedmen's Bureau (1865–1872) and the American Missionary Association, helped establish the first free schools in the South for both white and African-American children.

Reavis L. Mitchell, Jr., Fisk University

SUGGESTED READINGS: Alphonso A. Hopkins, *The Life of Clinton Bowen Fisk* (1882); Reavis L. Mitchell, Jr., *Fisk University Since 1866: Thy Loyal Children Make Their Way* (1995)

SEE: FISK UNIVERSITY; FREEDMEN'S BUREAU; RECONSTRUCTION

FISK UNIVERSITY. Fisk Free Colored School, predecessor of Fisk University, was established on January 9, 1866, in Nashville, Tennessee, to offer education—as a means of building better lives—to formerly enslaved African Americans.

African Americans, both slave and free, exhibited two related overriding concerns during the antebellum and Civil War period: a passion for religion and a desire for education. Prior to 1856, in Nashville, these needs were met as slaves and free blacks attended white churches or one of the eight priority (subscription) schools established for free blacks (though often attended by slaves). The racial fears preceding the Civil War produced an 1856 city ordinance prohibiting the education of all African Americans; the schools remained closed for more than a decade.

During the Civil War, the Union Army emancipated African-American slaves on its southward march. In February 1862 General Clinton Bowen Fisk (1828–1890) arrived with the Union forces occupying Nashville. One of the many Union soldiers and chaplains who became committed to instructing former slaves, Fisk exerted a lasting beneficial influence over the black community.

Fisk Jubilee Singers, 1873.

In 1865 Congress established the Freedmen's Bureau to provide federal assistance in education and health care for emancipated African Americans. John Ogden, superintendent of education of the Freedmen's Bureau in Tennessee, arrived at the Bureau's Nashville headquarters in 1865 to begin his duties. The Reverend Edward P. Smith, district secretary of the Middle West Department of the American Missionary Association, and the Reverend Erastus M. Cravath, who became the first secretary of the American Missionary Society, met with Odgen and agreed that Nashville was a suitable site for a normal school for African Americans. In late 1865 the organizers purchased a site on the fringe of downtown Nashville, and General Fisk used his influence to secure the former Union Army hospital barracks to house the school.

Following dedication ceremonies on January 9, 1866, hundreds of former slaves of all ages flocked to enroll in Fisk School. Enrollment jumped from 200 in February 1866 to 900 students by May of that year, a visible demonstration of the eagerness of local African Americans for knowledge. The first students received instruction in the primary subjects of alphabet, lettering, and counting. Four months after the school opened, the first educational audit revealed that over 200 Fisk students could read.

In the fall of 1867 the Tennessee General Assembly passed enabling legislation for the state's free public education. The law created a new demand for qualified teachers, especially African-American teachers. To meet this demand, Fisk School refocused its mission from primary to higher education, and on August 22, 1867, Fisk Free Colored School was incorporated as Fisk University.

By 1871 the decay of the school's buildings (former army barracks) and the rising enrollment presented an urgent need for a larger campus. With possible closure looming in the near future, the student choir embarked upon a fund-raising concert tour to save Fisk University. The nine-member ensemble gained fame as the Fisk Jubilee Singers, while introducing the world to the melodious Negro spiritual as a musical art form. After a year-long concert tour of Europe, the Jubilee Singers returned to Nashville in May 1874, having raised nearly $50,000 for construction of a new building—to be christened Jubilee Hall—on the new Fisk University campus.

An active building program in the 1880s enhanced the university's reputation, as did the well-educated graduates emerging from the school. In the 1890s the school's curriculum expanded to include liberal arts, theology, advanced training for teachers, and a secondary school. As the new century dawned, the second generation of freed blacks enrolled at Fisk University, and the school underwent further changes, including demands for the addition of African Americans to faculty and administrative staffs. After World War I, the enrollment of former servicemen and the African-American cultural renaissance of the 1920s and 1930s further infused a spirit of black pride and independence into the student body. In 1947 Charles S. Johnson became the first African-American president of Fisk University.

In 1955 the first dramatic manifestation of a modern revolution unfolded in the nonviolent protest against racial segregation in Montgomery, Alabama, and college students throughout the South began to build upon this new civil rights' foundation. Fisk students trained in nonviolent-protest workshops and joined others in the South in staging the first student sit-in protests in November 1959. The sit-in movement continued during 1960 and involved more than 100 cities across the South, as the student movement ushered in a decade of activism.

Over the next two-and-a-half decades, Fisk University eagerly moved forward through campus expansion, historic structure restoration and modernization, accelerated construction of new facilities, and amplified faculty credentials and professional development. Now, on the threshold of the twenty-first century, Fisk University remains committed to its historic mission to train its students for service to humanity. As in the past, excellence remains the university's motivation and aspiration, assuring that Fisk University is not measured against a standard of "Negro education" but against the standard of American education at its best.

Reavis L. Mitchell, Jr., Fisk University

SUGGESTED READING: Reavis L. Mitchell, Jr., *Fisk University Since 1866: Thy Loyal Children Make Their Way* (1995)

SEE: BONTEMPS, ARNAUD W.; DUBOIS, W.E.B.; EDUCATION, HIGHER; FISK, CLINTON B.; FREEDMEN'S BUREAU; JOHNSON, CHARLES S.; JUBILEE SINGERS OF FISK UNIVERSITY

FLATT, LESTER RAYMOND

FLATT, LESTER RAYMOND (1914–1979), a tenor and guitarist, is best know as half of the famous duo, Flatt and Scruggs, credited for pioneering in and popularizing bluegrass music. Born in rural Overton County, Flatt moved with his family to Sparta in White County when he was nine years old.

Flatt began his musical career in 1941 as a singer on station WBBB in North Carolina and then performed country, folk, and gospel music with Charlie Monroe and the KY Pardners. Two years later, Flatt and Earl Scruggs joined Charlie's brother, Bill Monroe, and his group, The Bluegrass Boys, considered by many to have been the first true bluegrass band. Bill Monroe, already a star on the Grand Ole Opry, found Flatt's vocals and Scruggs's lightning fast, three-finger banjo style perfect for making his sound distinctive from country music. In 1948 Flatt and Scruggs formed their own partnership, the Foggy Mountain Boys, and continued to perform for more than two decades. The genre of bluegrass music is based upon recordings by Flatt and Scruggs and Bill Monroe's recordings, with and without Flatt and Scruggs, during the late 1940s and 1950s.

Flatt and Scruggs created a new audience for bluegrass music in the 1960s with the version of *Foggy Mountain Breakdown* they recorded for the soundtrack of the film *Bonnie and Clyde* and *The Ballad of Jed Clampett*, the theme song for the *Beverly Hillbillies* television show. The Foggy Mountain Boys enjoyed performing in locations as diverse as college campuses and Carnegie Hall. The duo were members of the Grand Ole Opry and the Country Music Hall of Fame. Flatt often sang commercials for Martha White Flour, which sponsored the group's morning radio show on WSM.

In 1969 Flatt and Scruggs disbanded, and Flatt formed his own band, the Nashville Grass. One of his band's members was Marty Stuart, a current country music and Grand Ole Opry star who maintains a valuable collection of costumes and artifacts from earlier country music performers.

Beth Matter, Nashville

SEE: COUNTRY MUSIC HALL OF FAME; GRAND OLE OPRY; MARTHA WHITE FLOUR; MUSIC; WHITE COUNTY

FLOODS OF 1937. Moderate to heavy rainfall in December 1936 was no harbinger of disaster. However, as the rain, snow, and sleet continued through most of January 1937, soils became saturated, and the Mississippi, Cumberland, and Tennessee rivers and their tributaries overflowed into some of the most industrialized and populated sections of Tennessee and other states. It was to be a record flood year for these river systems, and rampaging waters would affect areas that had never known such destruction and deprivation. Socially and economically, this was the worst single disaster in American history to that date, rivaling the combined effects of the floods of 1926–27 and the "Dust Bowl" drought of 1930–31.

According to the National Weather Service, 21.24 inches (156 trillion tons) of rain fell in January alone. January 24 was dubbed "Black Sunday" as rivers overflowed in Tennessee and 11 other states, inundating 12,700 square miles and affecting 75,000 homes. Almost 900 people were seriously injured and 250 died of drowning and other flood-related causes. A surprising number died in flood-induced fires and explosions. No city, town, or rural community on these great rivers, or their tributaries, escaped unscathed.

On January 23, 1937, President Franklin D. Roosevelt issued a proclamation stating that the "disastrous floods in [the] Ohio and Mississippi River Valleys already have driven 270,000 from their homes." He predicted that the number would probably increase until the floodwaters crested, and that the "snow, sleet, and freezing weather added to the

suffering and made more hazardous the work of the rescue." Noting that the "victims of this grave disaster [would be] dependent upon the American Red Cross for food, shelter, fuel, medical care, and warm clothing," he promised that various agencies of the federal government would cooperate with these efforts to the fullest extent.

The U.S. Army Crops of Engineers (Memphis District) was heavily involved in rescue work along the Mississippi River from Cairo, Illinois, to Memphis. Due to the fear that the new levees, established upstream along the Mississippi after the 1926–27 floods, would fail, the Red Cross Regional Office at Memphis was assigned additional rescue responsibilities. In Tennessee, rescue parties were established from Tiptonville to Memphis to evacuate those already affected by the flooding and those who would be affected if, or when, the northern levees failed.

Thousands of highway patrolmen, National Guardsmen, and volunteers fought in vain to keep levees intact before the Corps of Engineers finally advised those downstream to evacuate. Many refused to leave the rooftops of their houses or the tops of trees, where they had built platforms, reasoning that the floods would soon subside, as they always had before.

Refugee centers (tent cities) were established throughout the flooded areas with the help of the Red Cross, Army, and National Guard units to make refugees comfortable and restore some semblance of order to their lives. The Memphis Fair Grounds boasted the largest refugee camp, where up to 60,000 people were fed, sheltered, and provided with medical assistance. Supply warehouses to meet the immediate needs of the refugees were established in Memphis, Nashville, and Knoxville.

A majority of the flood victims were sharecroppers and river-town residents. With so many hungry and chilled refugees suffering from exposure and in need of medical attention, additional emergency "hospitals" had to be established. Cases of pneumonia and influenza were widespread, and while the potential for other epidemics increased with spread of the floods, aggressive public health efforts kept disease and suffering in check. Approximately 8,000 were eventually hospitalized in the Memphis area alone.

In Middle and East Tennessee, the rivers sustained record floods, prompting Governor Gordon Browning to activate the National Guard. They worked in concert with the Red Cross and other relief agencies to provide temporary housing, flood, and clothing for thousands of additional refugees.

Allen R. Coggins, Knoxville

SEE: DISASTERS; MISSISSIPPI RIVER SYSTEM; U.S. ARMY CORPS OF ENGINEERS

FLY MANUFACTURING COMPANY in Shelbyville operated from 1916 to 1985. Like many small southern towns, Shelbyville's economy benefited from increased industrial development in the early decades of the twentieth century. In addition to large industries such as Musgrave Pencil Company, Empire Pencil Company, and the Shelbyville Mills, the town contained a number of small manufacturing outfits that competed for contracts in the textile market. Often founded by individual entrepreneurs, these small mills provided local residents with employment and boosted the town's economy.

One such successful entrepreneur was Joel Orval Fly, who moved to Shelbyville in 1915 after accumulating capital while managing an overall factory for J. S. Reeves and Company in Clarksville. After operating two small textile factories, Fly in 1925 commissioned John Morgan Raney to construct a two-story, 75 x 125 foot industrial building, which was completed in 1927. The following year, Fly hired 75 employees to operate his shirt manufacturing department. In addition to selling finished goods to large corporations such as Sears-Roebuck and Montgomery-Ward, Fly also sold his products to local stores. The diversity of contracts enabled Fly to employ workers from Shelbyville and neighboring communities throughout the Great Depression. In order to prevent the exodus of employees to other towns in search of work, Fly rotated work schedules to provide all employees with at least two to three days of work per week. During World War II, Fly obtained a contract to produce pants, jackets, and fatigues for the U.S. Army.

After the war, the Fly Manufacturing Company continued to thrive as an independent textile manufacturer until the death of Joel Orval Fly in 1960. In 1972, in the face of an increasingly competitive apparel market, the company was sold to Bayly Corporation, a Denver-based garment manufacturer, and transformed into a southeastern distribution center. Eight years later, a stockholding dispute within Bayly led to the sale of the plant to Woodway Corporation and the resumption of garment production in the historic building. In 1985, following a severe decline in business, Woodway Corporation ceased operations in the Fly Manufacturing Company building.

After a decade of neglect, the historic building was listed in the National Register of Historic Places as a significant part of Shelbyville's industrial heritage. The Bedford County Arts Council has restored the building as a cultural arts center.
Brian Eades, Shelby, North Carolina
SEE: BEDFORD COUNTY; INDUSTRY

FOGG, MARY MIDDLETON RUTLEDGE (1801–1872), writer and leader in Nashville civic affairs, was a member of one of Nashville's early families, the Rutledges, and the granddaughter of two of the signers of the Declaration of Independence. Fogg was an active member of Christ Episcopal Church and served as the President of the Ladies Aid Society. She was also a founding member of the Protestant School of Industry.

Fogg published seven books, covering a variety of fields, including poetry, fiction, religion, and education, in addition to her memoirs. In 1858, she published *The Elements of Natural Science,* a textbook used in Tennessee prior to the Civil War. Her poetry expressed her grief at the deaths of her three children, who died as young adults between 1851 and 1862. These poems were collected and published as *The Broken Harp.*

After the death of her third child, at the Civil War Battle of Fishing Creek in Kentucky, Fogg worked with Felicia Grundy Porter's Soldiers' Aid Society to collect and send articles to the war front. Her last book, *Biblical View of the Church Catechism,* was published shortly before her death in 1872. She is buried in the Rutledge family plot at Nashville's City Cemetery.
Carole Stanford Bucy, Volunteer State Community College
SEE: OCCUPATION, CIVIL WAR

FOLEY, GERALD (1900–1945), union organizer and president of the Tennessee Federation of Labor, was a native of Pennsylvania. Foley's family moved to Nashville when he was a boy. A plumber by trade, he joined organized labor while still in his teens, where he served in various official capacities. In 1930 he became the business representative for the Plumbers' Local Union No. 352 in Nashville, a position he held until his death. In 1937 he was elected by acclamation to the presidency of the Tennessee Federation of Labor. Known primarily for his organizing work, Foley was a forceful unionist who instilled confidence in new recruits. He was reelected annually until 1942. During World War II, Foley served as the Labor Coordinator for the Building Trades Council, where he oversaw smooth relationships between business and labor in the defense industry. When he died in 1945, Foley was serving his third term in the Tennessee House of Representatives as a Democratic member from Davidson County.
Christopher Caplinger, Vanderbilt University
SEE: LABOR

FOOTBALL, COLLEGE. Vanderbilt University was probably the first Tennessee college to organize a varsity team in 1886. Maryville College began playing intramural games in 1889 under coach, captain, and quarterback Kin Takahashi. In 1890 Vanderbilt and the University of Nashville played the state's first intercollegiate game. The University of the South (Sewanee) organized a team in 1890, and the

University of Tennessee had one in 1891. That same year, Sewanee began its long series of games with Vanderbilt and Tennessee. Maryville College began intercollegiate play in 1892 and Fisk University in 1893. Former players in the Ivy League, especially from Princeton, shaped the new programs in Tennessee. Other schools fielding teams in the 1890s included Carson-Newman College, the University of Nashville, Roger Williams University, Cumberland University, and Southwestern College.

By 1894 the popularity of the sport led to the formation of the Southern Intercollegiate Athletic Association, with seven charter members, including Sewanee and Vanderbilt. Dr. William L. Dudley of Vanderbilt was the primary organizer, and he served as the president of the SIAA. By 1895 the association claimed 19 members, which rose to 30 before the organization split in 1920.

Vanderbilt and Sewanee became the powerhouses of the SIAA, and the 1899 "Iron Men" of Sewanee remain legends of the game. That year Sewanee burned up the southern playing fields with a 12–0–0 season under Coach Billy Suter and manager Luke Lea. Their long-standing reputation rested on five games played during a six-day road trip that covered 2,500 miles. Sewanee beat Texas, Texas A&M, Tulane, LSU, and Ole Miss. Star halfback Henry G. Seibels later received recognition for the feat with induction into the National College Football Hall of Fame. The Sewanee Tigers won four SIAA championships between 1900 and 1910, with Vanderbilt their main rival. In many years, the traditional Thanksgiving Day game determined the championship. Another Sewanee Hall of Fame winner was Frank A. Juhan, a center from 1908 to 1910, who later became a bishop of the Episcopal Church. At the time of his induction into the Hall of Fame in 1966, he revealed that if he could be granted one wish, he would want to "part [his] hair in the middle" (in the style of the day) and "play Vanderbilt on Thanksgiving Day."

Vanderbilt also produced strong teams, including the squad on which Grantland Rice played. The golden age of Vanderbilt football arrived in 1904, when Daniel Earle McGugin became head coach of the Commodores. McGugin, an attorney, had played for Fielding "Hurry Up" Yost on the 1901 Michigan team that competed in the first Rose Bowl Game on New Year's Day, 1902. McGugin compiled a 30-year record at Vanderbilt of 197–55–19 (.762). His teams pioneered intersectional football for the South by playing Michigan, the Carlisle Indians, Ohio State, Navy, Harvard, Yale, and Minnesota. The Commodores won ten SIAA and Southern Conference championships between 1904 and 1923. The 1904 and 1921 teams were undefeated. Another Hall of Fame inductee, McGugin's biggest stars included Ray Mor-

rison (1908–1911), Joshua Cody (1914–1919), Lynn Bomar (1921–1924), and William Spears (1925–1927).

Ray Morrison starred as quarterback on the 1910 Vanderbilt team, one of the university's best. That season, the Commodores played Yale at New Haven, the first southern team the Elis played. The game ended in a 0–0 tie, for a Vanderbilt season of 8–0–1. Morrison is credited with inventing the "Statue of Liberty" play in his first season at Vanderbilt. When later asked about the innovation, Morrison claimed that he first used the play at McTyeire School for Boys in McKenzie, Tennessee. A Hall of Fame coach, Morrison was head coach at Southern Methodist University from 1915 to 1916 and 1922 to 1934, where he created the "Aerial Circus" that sold passing to the country. In 1923 Morrison coached the SMU team to a national championship. He returned to Vanderbilt in 1935, and in 1937 the Commodores first used the hidden ball play to beat Louisiana State. Morrison left Vandy after the 1939 season to coach at Temple and Austin College.

Three McGugin associates of the 1920s also made their mark on football: William Wallace Wade, Jess Neely, and Henry "Red" Sanders. Wallace, born near Trenton in Gibson County, was assistant coach under McGugin in the 1921 undefeated season. In 1923 he became head coach at Alabama, posting a 61–13–3 record, before leaving in 1931 to coach Duke University for the next 16 years. He compiled an overall record of 171–49–10 (.765). Jess Neely, a Smyrna native and captain of the 1922 team, swapped his Vanderbilt law degree for a high school coaching position before going on to coach at Southwestern at Memphis. Assistant to Wallace Wade at Alabama from 1928 to 1930, Neely became head coach at Clemson (1931–1939) and then Rice (1940–1966). A Nashville star athlete, "Red" Sanders played quarterback under McGugin from 1923 to 1926. He became Vanderbilt head coach in 1940, left for military duty in 1942, and returned to coach the Commodores from 1946 to 1948. Sanders went on to become head coach at UCLA, where he built a national power, losing only three games from 1952 to 1955. All three men—Sanders, Wade, and Neely—are in the Hall of Fame.

During the "football frenzy" years of the teens and twenties, other Tennessee teams also made history. The Fisk Bulldogs lost only one game between 1899 and 1904, and continued to field strong teams through the 1920s. Fisk won eight Southern Football championships between 1910 and 1929. Their 1916 team gained the National Black Football Championship. Henry Arthur Kean, later a great Tennessee State University coach, was an All-American on that team. Henderson A. Johnson built highly regarded teams in the 1920s, but Fisk's dominance declined after 1933.

Another Tennessee team established a record that will probably stand forever. On October 7, 1916, Lebanon's Cumberland University Bulldogs, under student coach and manager George E. Allen, played Georgia Tech, coached by John Heisman (for whom the Heisman Trophy is named). Cumberland lost to the Yellow Jackets 222–0. Georgia Tech went on to win the Southern Championship that year and the national championship in 1917. Cumberland University's loss stands as the greatest loss in college football history.

Grant University (later the University of Chattanooga and now the University of Tennessee at Chattanooga) played its first seven-game season in 1905, beating the University of Tennessee and losing only to Cumberland University. Chattanooga became a member of the SIAA in 1913, and acquired Frank Thomas as head coach (1925–1928). Chattanooga tied for the SIAA championship in 1926 and won the title in 1927 and 1928. Chattanooga left the SIAA in 1930 for the Dixie Conference of nine small colleges. They won the 1931 Dixie championship during the first year of Andrew "Scrappy" Moore's 1931–1967 tenure as the school's coach. Both Thomas and Moore were inducted into the National College Football Hall of Fame.

In December 1920, 14 of the larger SIAA schools formed the Southern Conference, with the University of Tennessee as a charter member. By 1928 the Southern had 23 members, including Vanderbilt and Sewanee. In 1921 Tennessee dedicated Shields-Watkins Field, named for its donors, Col. W. S. Shields and Alice Watkins Shields. The next year, Vanderbilt opened Dudley Field, named for football leader William Dudley; the 20,000-seat stadium was the largest in the South.

In 1925 Nathan W. Dougherty, engineering professor and chairman of the University of Tennessee athletic association (and a Hall of Fame guard at UT from 1906 to 1909), hired Robert Reese Neyland, Jr., as assistant coach and military instructor. Neyland became head coach of the Volunteers in 1926 and launched a new chapter in football history. During McGugin's tenure at Vanderbilt, Tennessee had won only two games and tied once in 21 games against the Commodores. Dougherty reportedly ordered Neyland to even the score with Vanderbilt. Neyland obeyed the command, and McGugin never won against Tennessee after 1926. Following McGugin's retirement after the 1930 season, Vanderbilt won no other conference championships in the Southern or the later Southeastern Conference.

Neyland brought football knowledge to Tennessee that he learned from the sport's greatest coaches. He first played college football in 1910 at Texas A&M under former Tennessee player Charles Barthell Moran. As assistant coach under Scobey "Pop" Warner at Carlisle Indian School, Moran was head coach at A&M from 1909 to 1914, with a 38–8–4 record, and at Centre College in Kentucky, from 1919 to 1923, where he built a 42–6–1 record. At Centre, he won national recognition when his 1921 team beat Harvard 6–0 during an undefeated season.

Neyland then transferred to West Point in 1912, where he was coached by Charles Daly. Daly quarterbacked the 1898 Harvard team. He later coached with former teammate Percy Haughton. Neyland absorbed the Haughton-Daly methods and maxims: the kick was the basis of play and perfection was required in the fundamentals. Neyland believed in their maxims: "the team that makes the fewest mistakes wins," "make and play for the breaks," and "protect our kickers, our QB, our lead, and our ball game." He passed those methods and maxims to players and assistants who later became head coaches, including Bobby Dodd, Bowden Wyatt, Allyn McKeen, Murray Warmath, Billy Barnes, Bob Woodruff, DeWitt Weaver, Jim Myers, Herman Hickman, Beattie Feathers, and Ralph Hatley. With military precision, Neyland made defense his main forte, emphasized a flawless, airtight kicking game, and was obsessed with pass defense. In 188 regular season games, Tennessee held the opponent to an average of 5 points per game. Neyland's name became synonymous with the single wing system, with its backfield of tailback, fullback, blocking quarterback, and wingback.

Neyland served as head coach at Tennessee from 1926 to 1934, when he was assigned to duty in Panama, before returning to Tennessee (1936–1940). He performed military service during World War II and rose to the rank of brigadier general. Neyland returned to Tennessee as head coach in 1946, where he remained until 1952. In his first nine seasons, Neyland amassed a 77–6–5 record, with undefeated teams in 1927, 1928, and 1929. He also led undefeated teams in 1938, 1939, 1940, and 1951. Four of the seven were perfect seasons, and his overall record was 173–31–12 (.829) over 21 years, making him one of the all-time winningest college coaches.

Eleven Neyland players entered the National College Hall of Fame for their play and/or coaching. Neyland's teams brought home the only Southern Conference championships won by Tennessee—in 1927 and 1932—and five Southeastern Conference championships.

Although Neyland stuck with the single wing system throughout his career, college football began to make major changes as early as the 1930s, as new formations and methods were adopted. The sophistication among larger teams was underscored in December 1932, when 13 major Southern Conference members from west and south of the Appalachians met in Knoxville to realign as the

Southeastern Conference. Sewanee, Tennessee, and Vanderbilt were charter members, although Sewanee left the conference after the 1940 season. In 1936 the Associated Press began its poll to rank college teams across the country. Neyland produced eight top ten teams between 1938 and 1952, but only the 1951 team attained the National Championship.

In the immediate postwar years, teams changed strategies, formations, and personnel. The dominance of teams in Tennessee changed too. Vanderbilt failed to reclaim the glory of the McGugin era, despite the efforts of "Red" Sanders and his assistant coach Paul "Bear" Bryant (1940–41). About 1960, Vanderbilt attempted to form a new conference, but ultimately remained in the SEC.

Memphis State (now University of Memphis) saw new successes. Fielding its first team in 1912 as the West Tennessee State Normal School, Memphis played as many high schools as colleges in the early years. In 1927 the "Teachers" won the Mississippi Valley Conference championship under coach Zach Curlin, a former McGugin player, and assistant Allyn McKeen, a former Neyland player. McKeen became head coach in 1937 and followed his instructions to install the Tennessee system. In 1938 Memphis recorded a 10–0–0 perfect season and was named the highest scoring team in the nation—281 to 35, with five shutouts. That year Memphis won the SIAA championship. In 1939 McKeen went to Mississippi, where he coached halfback Billy Jack "Spook" Murphy on the 1941 SEC championship team.

In 1947 Memphis State hired head coach Ralph Hatley, a Neyland star from the early 1930s, and the school soon built a major football program. Hatley coached until 1957, acquiring a 47–36–5 record. His assistant "Spook" Murphy succeeded Hatley as head coach in 1958 and earned a 91–44–1 record before his retirement in 1972. Murphy's 1963 team was the school's first undefeated team in 25 years, and Murphy was named national coach of the year.

The school with the greatest national success in its division, however, was Tennessee State University. Its first team hit the gridiron in 1912. TSU became a powerhouse largely through the vision of President Walter S. Davis, who saw the college as a great training ground for athletes of all sports. Davis hired Henry Arthur Kean, head coach for the Tigers from 1944 through 1954; Kean had been an All-American player on Fisk's national championship team. In 1946, 1947, and 1954, TSU was national champion in its division. In Kean's last season, the team compiled a 10–0 record. Kean's overall record as head coach (1930–1954) was 162–30–5 (.822). Howard Gentry, Kean's assistant, became head coach from 1955 to 1960. TSU won the National Black championship again in 1956, playing in the Orange Blossom Classic in Miami, the great bowl of black college football.

That same season, Gentry was named coach of the year. In 1961 TSU reigned as champion once again. John Merritt maintained TSU's dominance throughout the 1960s and 1970s.

The dominance of the UT Volunteers remained steady for most of the 1950s. Bowden Wyatt, captain of Neyland's undefeated 1938 team, became head coach at Tennessee in 1955. Wyatt had previously coached at Wyoming (1947–1952) and Arkansas (1953–1954), leading both schools to their respective conference championships. Wyatt's 1956 team, which included future coach John Majors, was undefeated, and Wyatt won recognition as national coach of the year.

The price of Tennessee's continuing power has been the determination of other in-state schools to defeat the Vols. In 1958 Chattanooga's upset victory over UT marked the school's first win against the Volunteers since 1905. The upset was surpassed in 1996, when the University of Memphis beat the fifth-ranked Volunteers.

Neyland died in 1962, and Bowden Wyatt left Tennessee that spring. In 1963 Bob Woodruff became athletic director and hired Doug Dickey, who had played for Woodruff at Florida, as head coach in 1964. Dickey's teams won SEC championships in 1967 and 1969.

It was an even more successful decade for Tennessee State University. John Merritt came from Jackson State to become head coach at TSU in 1963, a position he retained until 1983. The Hall of Famer was coach of the year in 1964 and 1965, and won back-to-back National Black College championships in 1965 and 1966. Merritt also coached teams to Small College National Championships in 1973 and 1979. TSU brought home ten national championships in its college division from 1946 to 1979.

TSU is now a member of the Ohio Valley Conference, where it regularly plays in-state rivals, Middle Tennessee State University, Austin Peay State University, and Tennessee Technological University. Of the old OVC rivalries, the one between MTSU and Tennessee Tech has the longest and most intense history. The two teams play an annual "Totem Bowl" game, the name being a reference to a trophy given to the winner by Fred Harvey, who owned a chain of Middle Tennessee department stores. MTSU, under coach James "Boots" Donnelly, emerged as a major Division I-AA power during the 1980s. Donnelly came to MTSU after two years as head coach at Austin Peay State University (1977–1978), where the Governors won the 1977 OVC football championship. A former MTSU defensive back, Donnelly has coached the Blue Raiders since 1979, guiding the team to four OVC championships and seven I-AA national play-off appearances. In the mid-1990s, the success of MTSU as a Division I-AA school led it to begin the transition to Division I-A status. Austin Peay State University surprised the OVC by announcing the end of college football scholarships after 1996.

In 1977 John Majors returned to the University of Tennessee as head coach. He began his career as student coach for Wyatt, and after a stint at Mississippi State, went to Arkansas under Frank Broyles. There Majors met Dickey, who was also on staff at Arkansas. As head coach at Iowa State (1968–1972), Majors became 1971 national coach of the year. In 1973 he became head coach at the University of Pittsburgh and coached Pitt to the 1976 national championship with Heisman Trophy winner Tony Dorsett. Majors coached at Tennessee from 1977 to 1992. He posted 115 SEC victories, ranking in the top ten all-time SEC coaches for wins. His teams won three SEC championships. Majors returned to Pitt as head coach in 1993 and retired from coaching in 1996.

After 1992, former assistant coach Phillip Fulmer became head coach at UT. His teams have a five-year record of 54–11–0 and have produced two Heisman Trophy candidates (Heath Shuler and Peyton Manning), and the Volunteers won the 1997 SEC title. As the 1997 season began, the University of Tennessee was among the top ten winningest teams in the country (666–283–52 for .691) and ranked ninth for most all-time victories.

John Majors, University of Pittsburgh and Ann Toplovich, Tennessee Historical Society

SEE: DOUGHTERY, NATHAN W.; LEA, LUKE; MAJORS, JOHN T.; MCGUGIN, DANIEL; MERRITT, JOHN; NEYLAND, ROBERT R.

FOOTE, HENRY S. (1804–1880), lawyer, U.S. Senator, and Confederate congressman, was born in Fauquier County, Virginia. Foote had practiced law in Virginia, Alabama, Mississippi, and California before settling in Nashville in 1859. By that time he had held a half dozen political offices, including terms as governor and United States Senator while in Mississippi. An active Democrat, he supported Andrew Jackson in the 1830s and James K. Polk in the 1840s. In Nashville, he numbered among his law partners such men of distinction as Arthur S. Colyar, Nashville lawyer and New South proponent.

More interested in politics than law, Foote soon announced his support of Stephen A. Douglas for president. He attended the nominating convention of 1860 at Charleston and boldly predicted that the election of Abraham Lincoln would produce secession and civil war. He declared Douglas the only candidate who could establish peace.

A strong unionist, Foote despaired when Lincoln won election, and he urged Tennessee Governor Isham G. Harris to call a Nashville convention of slaveholding states. He warned Harris that piecemeal secession would be disastrous for the South. Lin-

coln's inauguration and subsequent call for 75,000 volunteers pushed Foote into the Confederacy, and he worked with Harris to accomplish Tennessee's secession. In the early fall of 1861 he won election to the Confederate Congress from the Fifth (Nashville) District, in a race against two other candidates.

Foote did not serve the state well in the Congress. He had held President Jefferson Davis in contempt since his Mississippi days, and the mutual hard feelings were exacerbated as each sought to serve a new government. Davis largely ignored Foote; others found him to be especially obnoxious; a Richmond newspaper editor threatened to shoot him; and others urged the Confederate congressmen to censure and expel him. In 1862 Foote called for a widespread invasion of the North—with an expenditure of a million men and two billion dollars, if necessary—but by 1864 he urged Davis to seek a negotiated peace.

Finally, late in 1864, Foote fled the Confederacy. Lincoln ignored him, but Andrew Johnson—shortly after his inauguration as president—ordered him to stand trial for treason and rebellion, or leave the country within 48 hours. Foote escaped to Canada and settled in Montreal, but kept in contact with friends in Washington in an effort to have his citizenship restored. After he swore an oath of allegiance to the United States, endorsed black suffrage, and vowed not to enter politics again, he obtained permission to reenter the country. He lived for a year in St. Louis, but returned to Nashville in 1867. There he aligned with the Conservative Democrats.

During the next decade, Foote practiced law and divided his time between Nashville and Washington. He also wrote and published several books, including the well received *Bench and Bar of the South and Southwest* (1876). He supported Rutherford B. Hayes for president in 1876 and two years later was chairman of the Republican State Convention. Hayes rewarded him with an appointment as Superintendent of the United States Mint at New Orleans. He became seriously ill early in 1880 and returned to Nashville, where he died on May 19. He was buried in Mt. Olivet Cemetery.

Robert E. Corlew, Middle Tennessee State University

SEE: COLYAR, ARTHUR S.; HARRIS, ISHAM G.; JOHNSON, ANDREW

FOOTE, SHELBY (1916–), novelist and historian, was born in Greenville, Mississippi, the only son of Shelby Dade and Lillian Rosenstock Foote. Foote grew up in the Delta town, where he was influenced by William Alexander Percy, a local author and the uncle of Walker Percy, who later became a successful novelist himself.

In 1935 Foote enrolled at the University of North Carolina at Chapel Hill, but left in 1937 without taking a degree. After service in World War II, he held various jobs including construction work, radio copy writing, and reporting for the *Delta Democrat-Times*. Foote began his first novel, *Tournament*, before the war, but did not complete it until 1949. During the next five years, he published four novels including *Follow Me Down* (1950), *Love in a Dry Season* (1951), *Shiloh* (1952), and *Jordan County* (1954). These novels, with the exception of *Shiloh*, which chronicles the famous battle, are set in and around Bristol, a mythical Delta town.

In December 1953, Foote left Greenville permanently to settle in Memphis, where he had often traveled for research and where he began the monumental history of the Civil War on which his reputation rests. *The Civil War: A Narrative*, consisting of *Fort Sumter to Perryville* (1958), *Fredericksburg to Meridian* (1963), and *Red River to Appomattox* (1974), was widely praised for enticing readers into the sectional conflict with its vivid imagery and strong characterization.

After devoting 20 years to the Civil War histories, Foote returned to fiction with *September, September* (1978), in which a group of whites plots to kidnap an African-American child for ransom. Set in his adoptive city of Memphis, the drama takes place during a 30-day period in 1957, and is played against the background of white resistance to racial integration in Little Rock, Arkansas. Foote next embarked on another character study set in the Mississippi Delta during the 1940s. Tentatively titled "Two Gates to the City," this work in progress is still unfinished.

Millions of Americans "discovered" Shelby Foote in the fall of 1990, when he appeared as the principal guide in the hugely successful Civil War series that was produced for public television by the documentary filmmaker Ken Burns. Foote enlivened the show's eloquent still photographs with a storehouse of poignant anecdotes, becoming for many viewers the personification of the war itself.

Shelby Foote has been called the greatest living Civil War historian. His career began as a novelist, and his powerful works of fiction rose out of his closeness to the life and culture of his native region, the Mississippi Delta country. Later in his career he transformed modern historical prose by using his keen sense of the novel. His artistic distance from the elements of regionalism that lies at the heart both of his novels and his history writing gives his prose great narrative force and energy.

Gregory G. Poole, Tennessee State Library and Archives
SUGGESTED READING: Robert L. Phillips, Jr., *Shelby Foote: Novelist and Historian* (1992)
SEE: LITERATURE

FOOTHILLS PARKWAY. Originally envisioned as a 71-mile scenic route paralleling the Tennessee boundary of the Great Smoky Mountains National Park, the Foothills Parkway is the oldest unfinished highway project in Tennessee. The origins of the parkway stemmed from the federal government's decision not to build the Blue Ridge Parkway through any part of Tennessee. Disappointed by this decision, Frank Maloney, vice president of the Great Smoky Mountains Conservation Association, conceived the idea of the Foothills Parkway as a way to spur economic growth and link recreational areas on the Tennessee side of the national park.

After years of lobbying, Congress in 1944 passed an act that enabled the parkway project to proceed. The State of Tennessee received the authority to purchase rights of way, and the federal government promised to provide funds for construction and maintenance of the parkway. The Tennessee Highway Department (later the Tennessee Department of Transportation) purchased 8,835 acres in Cocke, Sevier, and Blount counties in the 1950s, but construction did not begin until 1960.

Due primarily to a shortage of federal funds, the construction of the Foothills Parkway proceeded very slowly. Sections of the parkway opened as early as 1965, but in 1978, nearly 35 years after the passage of the initial enabling act, less than one-third of the parkway had been completed. Although earthslides and soaring costs continued to plague the project, Representative James Quillen provided a strong legislative push for completion of the parkway. By late 1996, only 1.6 miles remained unfinished. The parkway now provides millions of tourists with breathtaking vistas of the mountains.

C. Brenden Martin, Museum of the New South
SUGGESTED READING: George Frye, "Foothills Parkway to Give Better Views to Smoky Park," *Tennessee Conservationist* (June 1966)
SEE: GREAT SMOKY MOUNTAINS NATIONAL PARK

FORD, HAROLD EUGENE (1945–), U.S. Congressman, was born May 20, 1945, in Memphis, the son of Vera Davis Ford and Newton Jackson Ford. He received his A.A. degree from John Gupton College, a B.S. degree from Tennessee State, and his M.B.A. from Howard University. Ford became vice-president of Ford & Sons Funeral Homes in 1969, and has remained involved in the family business. Ford served in the Tennessee House of Representatives from 1970 to 1975.

In 1974 Ford was elected to the U.S. House of Representatives and served until 1996, when he was succeeded by his son, Harold E. Ford, Jr. In Congress, Ford served on numerous committees, including chair of the House Ways and Means subcommittee on Public Assistance and Unemployment. During Ronald Reagan's presidency, Ford consistently opposed Reagan's attempt to dismantle social welfare programs. He strongly advocated welfare reform, job training and assistance, and forcing deadbeat parents to pay child support. Within the ninth district, Ford perhaps was best known for his constituent services on a wide range of issues affecting the district. Former aides remember that he often admonished them not to forget that his votes came from the ninth district, not Washington.

Kenneth W. Goings, University of Memphis

SEE: MEMPHIS

FORD, JESSE HILL (1928–1996). For a short time in the early 1960s, Jesse Hill Ford seemed to be establishing himself as an important new voice in southern literature. After winning an *Atlantic Monthly* prize in 1959 for his short story "The Surest Thing in Show Business," Ford published a promising first novel, *Mountains of Gilead* (1961), followed three years later by both the television and stage scripts of his drama *The Conversion of Buster Drumwright*, which appeared with an appreciative foreword by Donald Davidson, who had taught Ford and encouraged his early work. Ford seemed, as Davidson noted, "'inside' the tradition he explores, possessed by it while possessing it," an artist in control of his material, whose language did not "condescend to picturesqueness or vulgarity."[1]

Then in 1965 came *The Liberation of Lord Byron Jones.* Certainly Ford's best known work, a Book-of-the-Month Club selection and subsequently a movie for which Ford and Stirling Silliphant wrote the screenplay, the novel is a fictionalized account of an actual killing. In Ford's version, Jones, a prosperous black undertaker, insists on divorcing his wife, who is having an affair with a white policeman, and his insistence leads to his murder and mutilation. Although the novel was a popular success and received extravagant praise from Ralph McGill in the *Atlantic,* serious reviewers severely criticized the book both for its sensationalism and for its technical failures in point of view and characterization. Publication two years later of *Fishes, Birds, and Sons of Men,* a collection of his early stories containing some of his best work, regained for Ford a degree of critical acclaim, but *The Feast of Saint Barnabas* (1969), examining from various perspectives a Florida race riot, was generally regarded as a failure and probably disappointed even Ford himself, who had anticipated that, like *The Liberation of Lord Byron Jones,* it would be made into a film. After *The Feast of Saint Barnabas,* Ford published only one other substantial work of fiction, *The Raider* (1975), an ambitious historical novel set in West Tennessee before and during the Civil War. Like Ford's career, *The Raider* has moments that border on greatness, but, also like Ford's career, the early promise remains largely unfulfilled.

Born in Troy, Alabama, Ford grew up in Nashville, attended Montgomery Bell Academy, and received a B.A. from Vanderbilt University in 1951. After serving in the Navy during the Korean War, Ford enrolled in Andrew N. Lytle's writing program at the University of Florida, completing an M.A. in 1955. As a senior at Vanderbilt, Ford was the campus correspondent for the *Nashville Tennessean,* and he continued to work as a journalist while a graduate student in Gainesville. Then from 1955 to 1957 he worked as a public relations director, first for the Tennessee Medical Association, then in Chicago for the American Medical Association. In 1957, however, he gave up his position and moved with his first wife and their three children to his wife's hometown, Humboldt, Tennessee, where he devoted himself to his writing. In 1961 he spent a year at the University of Oslo as a Fulbright Scholar; later he was awarded a Guggenheim Fellowship (1966) and held visiting lectureships at various universities, including Memphis State (1969–1971) and Vanderbilt (1987).

In 1971 Ford was acquitted of all charges in the shooting death of a black soldier who had parked at night in Ford's driveway and who, Ford believed, was threatening one of his sons. The incident attracted widespread attention, however, especially because the soldier's female companion was a relative of the woman whose actions provided the basis for *The Liberation of Lord Byron Jones.* In the years that followed, legal debts and family problems drove Ford to Hollywood and largely anonymous work rewriting screenplays. Later, however, he returned to Nashville, and there on June 1, 1996, in failing health, Ford committed suicide.

Ford's best work is in his short stories. In the novels he never quite achieves an adequate controlling form, but in the more sharply focused short fiction—in such stories as "The Savage Sound," "To the Open Water," and "Wild Honey," for example—the prose is crisp, the vision clear, and the achievement real.

John V. Glass, Rockford College

CITATION:

(1) Donald Davidson, Foreword, *The Conversion of Buster Drumwright,* by Jesse Hill Ford (Nashville, 1964), xviii.

SEE: DAVIDSON, DONALD; LYTLE, ANDREW NELSON

FORD, JOHN NEWTON (1942–), State Senator, was born on May 3, 1942, in Memphis, the son of Vera Davis Ford and Newton Jackson Ford. Ford received a B.A. from Tennessee State in 1964, and an M.A. from Memphis State in 1978. Elected to the city council in 1971, Ford combined service there with work in the Tennessee Senate in 1974. In 1979 he left the city council, but remained a State Senator. In 1993 Ford again did double duty. Ford has worked consistently to provide help and support for the disadvantaged, particularly in the areas of Senior Services and Aid to Families with Dependent Children. He served as chairman of the Senate General Welfare, Health and Human Resources Committee, and as a member of the Finance, Ways and Means Committee. In addition to his work to provide social welfare assistance to the needy, Ford was instrumental in helping to secure state funds for the National Civil Rights Museum and the Pink Palace Museum, both located in Memphis.

Kenneth W. Goings, University of Memphis

SEE: FORD, HAROLD E.; NATIONAL CIVIL RIGHTS MUSEUM; PINK PALACE MUSEUM

FORD, "TENNESSEE" ERNIE (1919–1991), radio announcer, singer, and television personality, was born Ernest Jennings Ford on February 13, 1911, in Fordtown, Sullivan County, and raised in nearby Bristol. Ford began a radio career at Bristol's WOPI, where he worked as an announcer before studying voice at the Cincinnati Conservatory of Music.

During World War II, Ford served as a bombardier in the Army Air corps, then settled in California, where he worked for KFXM in San Bernadino and later KXLA in Pasadena. During this time, he adopted the name "Tennessee Ernie" and developed the "Pea Picker" character he made famous. Ford introduced songs in an exaggerated hillbilly voice and occasionally sang along with them. Cliffie Stone recognized Ford's potential and featured him on the "Hometown Jamboree," KXLA's new television show.

Ford's solo singing career took off in 1949, when he signed with Capital Records. During that year, he had several hits, including *Tennessee Border* and his first Number 1 selling song, *Mule Train.* In 1950 he made his debut performance at the Grand Ole Opry and continued his chart success with hits like the Number 1, *Shotgun Boogie.*

In 1954, Ford moved to network television as the game show host of NBC's *College of Musical Knowledge.* On this show he debuted his 1955 recording of *Sixteen Tons,* the coal-mining protest ballad, which became one of the fastest and biggest sellers in the record business at that time. This show was followed by NBC's *The Ford Show,* which aired from 1956 to 1961. Beginning in 1956, Ford recorded several highly successful gospel albums, including *Hymns* and *Great Gospel Songs,* but continued to make television appearances on numerous shows, such as the *Jack Benny Program* and *I Love Lucy.* In 1974 he went to Russia as the featured performer in the *Country Music USA* show sponsored by the U.S. State Department.

During his career, Ford recorded more than 100 country and gospel albums. As a pioneering performer, he adapted his country style for popular audiences and made a successful transition to television. Ford was inducted into the Country Music Hall of Fame of 1990. He died of liver disease on October 17, 1991. A small, white frame house in Bristol, where Ford once lived, has been turned into a historic house museum about his life in Tennessee and his contributions to American popular music.

Anne-Leslie Owens, Tennessee Historical Society

SEE: COUNTRY MUSIC HALL OF FAME; MARTHA WHITE FLOUR; MUSIC; SULLIVAN COUNTY

FORD v. FORD (1846), decided by the Tennessee Supreme Court, provides a valuable understanding of the Tennessee judiciary's peculiar relationship with the institution of slavery. The case arose after the death in 1842 of Loyd Ford of Washington County. Ford, a yeoman farmer, owned several slaves whom he regarded with particular affection. He drafted a will that freed the slaves and bequeathed them his real property. Before Ford's death, his children attempted to force him to destroy the will and even offered money for its destruction to the person holding the document for safekeeping. After Ford's death, his slaves presented the will to the Washington County courts for probate. The executors of the will, however, appeared and contested it. A jury found that the will was valid and the contestants appealed.

While the Supreme Court remanded the case for retrial on evidentiary grounds, the Court's opinion, authored by Justice Nathan Green, affirmed the legal right of the slaves to bring suit to probate the will. Ford's children argued that "the devisees in this case are slaves, and have no rights, either perfect or inchoate, until the will manumitting them shall be proved." Justice Green rejected this argument, which would obviously frustrate Ford's intent. More significantly, however, the Court also found the legal rights of Ford's slaves to be worthy of protection. Green wrote that: "A slave is not in the condition of a horse or an ox. His liberty is restrained, it is true. . . . But he is made after the image of the Creator. He has mental capacities, and an immortal principle in his nature, that constitute him equal to his owner but for the accidental position in which fortune has placed him . . . the laws under which he is held as a slave have not and cannot extinguish his high-born nature nor deprive him of his many rights which are inherent in man."[1] On retrial, a jury found in the slaves' favor a second time, and in 1850 they were finally freed and granted the property that Loyd Ford had bequeathed them.

Ford v. Ford demonstrated the tensions inherent in a system of civil law grounded on the notion of individual liberty operating in the context of a slaveholding culture. The antebellum Tennessee Supreme Court at least acknowledged the humanity of slaves, treating them as being "in the two-fold character of persons and property."[2] More than the U.S. Supreme Court and many other southern courts, the Tennessee courts, for the most part, acknowledged and protected the legal rights of slaves. The progressive nature of this approach becomes more evident when contrasted with the opinion of U.S. Chief Justice Roger Taney in the Dred Scott case, decided 11 years after *Ford v. Ford*. In that case, Taney found that, under the U.S. Constitution, even free blacks "had no rights which the white man was bound to respect."[3]

G. Brian Jackson, Nashville

CITATIONS:

(1) *Ford v. Ford*, 26 Tenn (7 Hum.) 92 (1846).

(2) *Jones v. Allen*, 1 Head 636 (1858).

(3) *Dred Scott v. Sandford*, 19 How. 393 (1857).

SUGGESTED READING: Arthur F. Howington, "Not in the Condition of a Horse or an Ox," *Tennessee Historical Quarterly* 34 (1975): 249–263

SEE: GREEN, NATHAN; LAW; SLAVERY

FORREST, NATHAN BEDFORD (1821–1877), one of the finest Confederate cavalry commanders and one of the foremost military figures produced by the state of Tennessee, was particularly famous for his determination to be "first with the most men." Forrest is generally known as the "wizard of the saddle."

He was born in Chapel Hill, Tennessee, on July 13, 1821. He assumed responsibility for his family at the age of 16, following the death of his father. Despite a mere six months of formal education, Forrest rose from semi-subsistence to planter status, acquiring substantial property and wealth, largely through the slave trade.

When Tennessee seceded from the Union, Forrest enlisted as a private in Captain Josiah White's Tennessee Mounted Rifles (7th Tennessee Cavalry), along with his youngest brother and 15-year-old son. Shortly afterward, Governor Isham G. Harris authorized him to raise a regiment of mounted troops. Forrest recruited and equipped his command, generally at his own expense. In December 1861, in his first major combat experience at Sacramento, Kentucky, Forrest demonstrated the traits of common sense tactics and close-hand fighting that characterized his military career.

In February 1862 Forrest established a reputation for boldness, when he led his men out of Fort Donelson rather than surrender. Elected colonel, he led his command at Shiloh, where he was wounded during the Confederate retreat. Subsequently, Forrest won promotion to brigadier general after a daring raid against a Union outpost at Murfreesboro in July 1862.

In mid-December 1862, Forrest led a raid into West Tennessee that destroyed Union supplies and disabled miles of track and trestlework. The Confederates eluded pursuit until forced into a pitched battle at Parker's Crossroads on December 31. With the battle almost won, a second Union force appeared, and Forrest was fortunate to save most of his force. Nevertheless, he succeeded in crippling

PORTRAIT BY NICOLA MARSHALL. TENNESSEE STATE MUSEUM

General Nathan Bedford Forrest.

the supply lines over which General U.S. Grant hoped to support his initial operations against Vicksburg, Mississippi.

On February 3, 1863, Forrest's command suffered a defeat at Dover, Tennessee, while under the command of Major General Joseph Wheeler. Then, following redeeming victories at Thompson's Station and Brentwood that spring, he stopped a Union raid led by Colonel Abel Streight through northern Alabama in April and May 1863. In his final confrontation with Streight, the Confederate cavalryman manipulated his forces magnificently, convincing the Federals to surrender their numerically superior forces by artificially inflating his own command.

Forrest participated in General Braxton Bragg's retreat from Middle Tennessee, known as the Tullahoma Campaign. In the wake of the Confederate victory at Chickamauga, he urged, but failed to convince, Bragg to pursue the defeated Federals. Resentful of Bragg's ineptitude and earlier treatment of him, the fiery cavalryman bitterly denounced his superior officer. He obtained a transfer to an independent command in Mississippi, and for the third time in his military career, created a new command of recruits and conscripts around a nucleus of battle-tested veterans.

Promoted to major general on December 4, 1863, Forrest conducted raids against Federal communications and supply lines in Tennessee. In April 1864 he captured Fort Pillow, north of Memphis. In the latter stages of that battle, Forrest lost control of his men, some of whom killed members of the black and Tennessee Unionist garrison as they attempted to surrender, and should have been spared. Of the fort's 585–605 men, 277–297 of them died, 64% of whom were U.S. Colored Troops. Charges of a "Fort Pillow Massacre" became grist for northern propaganda mills during the war and plagued Forrest for the remainder of his life.

Following Fort Pillow, Forrest routed a larger force of Union infantry and cavalry in June, at Brice's Cross Roads, in Mississippi, arguably his finest military feat. In July he helped blunt another Union force at Tupelo or Harrisburg, where he was wounded while directing the pursuit of retreating Federal troops. He recovered and led a surprise raid on Memphis that produced another Union retreat from Mississippi.

In the autumn of 1864 Forrest's cavalry destroyed railroad and protective blockhouses in northern Alabama and Middle Tennessee. He blockaded shipping on the Tennessee River, disabling and capturing several Union vessels before destroying the Union supply depot at Johnsonville. Immediately thereafter, Forrest joined General John Bell Hood in the disastrous Tennessee campaign of November and December 1864. His rearguard action during the Confederate retreat from Nashville undoubtedly saved the Army of Tennessee from extinction.

Returning to Mississippi, Forrest received a promotion to lieutenant general in February 1865 and took command of the cavalry in the Department of Alabama, Mississippi, and East Louisiana. In the closing months of the war, he failed to prevent the capture of Selma, Alabama. He surrendered his command at Gainesville, Alabama, in May 1865.

Forrest spent the years after the war struggling to regain the financial status he had enjoyed earlier. He undertook various business ventures, including the presidency of the Selma, Marion, and Memphis Railroad, but he was never able to reproduce his pre-war financial success.

Contrary to his expressed determination to remain quietly at home, Forrest soon embraced the Ku Klux Klan, assuming the role of the first Grand Wizard of the secret organization. Through it he sought to restore white conservative Democrats to power. Even so, he never completely adjusted to the new realities of the postwar South. In the 1870s, Forrest's health began to fail, and he died in Memphis on October 29, 1877.

Forrest established a reputation as one of the greatest cavalry generals of the Civil War. His ferocity as a warrior was almost legendary. His claim to have slain one more enemy soldier in personal combat than the 29 horses killed beneath him only added to the legend. Forrest understood, perhaps better than most, the basic premise of war: "War means fighting and fighting means killing."

Brian S. Wills, Clinch Valley College of the University of Virginia

SUGGESTED READINGS: Robert Selph Henry, *"First With the Most" Forrest* (1944); Brian Steel Wills, *A Battle From the Start: The Life of Nathan Bedford Forrest* (1992); John Allen Wyeth, *Life of General Nathan Bedford Forrest* (1899, reprint *That Devil Forrest,* 1959)

SEE: BRAGG, BRAXTON; CIVIL WAR; FORT DONELSON; FORT PILLOW; JOHNSONVILLE, BATTLE OF; KU KLUX KLAN; NASHVILLE, BATTLE OF

FORT ASSUMPTION. After La Salle's failed attempt in 1684, the French launched a new effort to colonize the lower Mississippi Valley in the early eighteenth century. Under the leadership of Jean Baptiste Le Moyne, Sieur de Bienville, the French subdued the Natchez Indians and built forts at Natchitoches, Natchez, and Arkansas Post to protect the Mississippi River fur trade.

In 1739 Bienville organized an army of 1,200 Frenchmen and twice as many blacks and Indians to eradicate the Chickasaws. He ordered the construction of a fort on the fourth Chickasaw Bluff, at a site near the railroad bridges in present-day Memphis. According to a contemporary account, the elaborate fortification included three bastions fronting the land and two fronting the river, with seven wide terraces sloping down to the river. It was finished on August 15, 1739, the Feast of the Assumption, and thus was named Fort Assumption.

During the winter, the army suffered from weather, disease, desertion, and drunkenness. The French received peace overtures from the Chickasaws, but they proved fruitless. On March 20, 1740, the Chickasaws agreed to release some hostages, and by March 31, Bienville's discouraged troops were withdrawn from the bluff. The French made a final unsuccessful foray against the Chickasaws in 1754. In 1762 the French king, exhausted by the struggle to maintain colonies in America, ceded his Louisiana possessions to Spain in a secret treaty.

Although the French claimed the fourth Chickasaw Bluff for 80 years, actual French occupation lasted only a few months. Today, all that remains of the French heritage is the name of a Memphis subdivision and a memory.

Perre Magness, Memphis

SUGGESTED READING: James T. Robinson, "Fort Assumption: The First Recorded History of White Man's Activity on the Present Site of Memphis," West Tennessee Historical Society Papers 5(1951): 62–78

SEE: CHICKASAWS; MEMPHIS

FORT BLOUNT located in present-day Jackson County, was established in 1794 at the point where the Avery Trace, which connected the Eastern and Mero districts, crossed the Cumberland River. Named for Territorial Governor William Blount, this post replaced an earlier blockhouse that had been constructed in 1792 at the eastern edge of the Mero District. Built by the territorial militia, Fort Blount was later garrisoned by federal troops, who remained at the post until about 1798.

Sampson Williams, a South Carolina native, played a vital role in the establishment of the post at the "Crossing of the Cumberland." In 1791 he obtained permission to keep a ferry there; one year later, Governor Blount authorized Williams to raise men to be stationed at the crossing. In 1794 Blount received authorization to establish a larger post and wrote to General James Robertson to report the dispatch of a militia commander to the post on the Cumberland River. The earliest known use of the name "Fort Blount" comes from a July 13, 1795, letter from Blount to Robertson in which Robertson was instructed to reduce the number of militia stationed at the fort.

Sampson Williams remained to be active in the area, running a ferry and a tavern at Fort Blount. By March 1796, his brother Oliver Williams served as militia captain in charge of the fort; in May Sampson succeeded him in that position. After Tennessee's admission to the union, the guard stationed at Fort Blount was discharged, and the fort was turned over to federal troops of the 3rd Infantry Regiment under Captain William Rickard. Although records are sketchy, the federal presence apparently lasted until about 1798. Sampson Williams continued to live in this area, which was referred to as "Fort Blount" for many years.

Archaeological investigations of the Fort Blount site began in 1989, and the Tennessee Division of Archaeology conducted work there for several seasons. Excavations revealed the remains of buildings as well as a number of artifacts related to the everyday operations of the fort.

Benjamin C. Nance, Tennessee Division of Archaeology

SEE: BLOUNT, WILLIAM; FERRIES; JACKSON COUNTY; ROBERTSON, JAMES

FORT CAMPBELL. Although the official address of the U.S. Army's Fort Campbell reads, "Fort Campbell, Kentucky," two-thirds of the installation by area is in Tennessee. Fort Campbell came into existence in 1941, as the United States prepared for war. In need of additional large training facilities, army planners chose an area northwest of Clarksville for a new camp. The site offered a substantial pool of local labor, good access to railroads and highways, reasonable proximity to Fort Knox, Kentucky, mild weather, and cheap land prices. Survey work began in August 1941. The government bought 102,000 acres of rich farmland, at an average price of $39.94 per acre, and dislocated approximately 700 families. The Army named the post in honor of William Bowen Campbell, a veteran of the Creek, Seminole, and Mexican wars and Tennessee's last Whig governor and designated it as Camp Campbell, Tennessee, reflecting its geographical location and proximity to Clarksville. The construction of the post office just over the line in Kentucky—possibly due to the influence of U.S. Senator Alben Barkley of Kentucky—brought a permanent change in the official address.

Work on the post buildings began immediately; the first troops arrived in July 1942. Camp Campbell quickly emerged as one of the major armor training centers in the country, where the 8th, 12th, 14th, and 20th Armored Divisions, plus the 26th Infantry Division, honed their combat skills. The installation also served as headquarters for the IV Armored Corps and XXII Corps. By V-J Day in 1945, 250,000 soldiers had trained at Camp Campbell. The post also housed about 4,000 German prisoners.

The influx of such a large number of men in uniform (there were almost 100,000 at the installation in 1944) had an enormous effect on the surrounding area. The Army poured $35 million into the project by the end of 1942, with an estimated 10,000 workers laboring on the physical plant. The size of Clarksville more than doubled in that year alone. The city instituted zoning to prevent "crazy, haphazard, and unattractive" expansion and widened Highway 41A. To provide off-duty soldiers some diversion, Clarksville built a football stadium and allowed theaters to show movies on Sundays.

With the end of the war, boom threatened to become bust. As its designation indicated, Camp Campbell had been built as a temporary training center. In the immediate aftermath of war, it served as a deployment post for troops returning home, including soldiers of the XVIII Airborne Corps and the 5th Infantry Division.

Despite a U.S. Army Corps of Engineers survey that advocated retention of the post, by early 1947 fewer than 2,000 soldiers remained, and area residents feared its closure. Unknown to most Tennesseans, in 1947 the military established the "Clarksville Base," a highly restricted area on the installation for the preparation of nuclear weapons. Operated by the Atomic Energy Commission (and later by the Defense Atomic Support Agency) until deactivated in 1969, the facility, with its hardened buildings, was guarded by a Marine detachment.

The status of Camp Campbell as an Army facility finally seemed assured with the arrival of the 3rd Infantry Division in March 1948. This unit was replaced the next year by the 11th Airborne Division.

The "Angels" stayed until 1955, solidifying the installation's association with the Army's elite forces. In April 1950 the Army upgraded the designation of the facility to "Fort Campbell." When the 11th Airborne moved to Germany in 1956, the unit was immediately replaced by the 101st Airborne—a division that has become almost synonymous with the post.

From 1950 to 1962 Fort Campbell operated an airborne training school, which graduated nearly 30,000 paratroopers. During the Vietnam War, Fort Campbell opened a basic training course that instructed more than 200,000 soldiers. When the 101st Airborne deployed to Vietnam, the post briefly housed the 6th Infantry Division. Following the return of the 101st (redesignated in 1974 as an air assault division), the Army launched a construction program to replace World War II-era "temporary" structures with modern facilities. In 1988 the post became home to two additional elite units: the 5th Special Forces and the 160th Special Operations Aviation Regiment.

Malcolm Muir, Jr., Austin Peay State University
SEE: CLARKSVILLE; 101ST AIRBORNE; WORLD WAR II

FORT DONELSON. Tennessee Confederates constructed the earthen fort in the summer of 1861 to defend the river approach to Middle Tennessee and Nashville; the fort was named for Daniel S. Donelson, Tennessee's adjutant-general. Principally a commanding water battery with adjacent armed camp for garrison, Fort Donelson was expanded to defend against land assault following the Fort Henry debacle. In early February, Confederate department commander Albert Sidney Johnston concentrated some 15,000 men to defend against Union General U.S. Grant's army of 17–21,000 men and Flag Officer Andrew Hull Foote's six-vessel gunboat flotilla.

Within a week of Fort Henry's capture on the Tennessee River by the joint army-navy command of Grant on February 6, 1862, nearby Fort Donelson on the Cumberland River came under siege by the same Union force. The engagement at Fort Donelson (February 13–16, 1862) pitted the faulty command by southern officers and the valor of common Confederate soldiers against Union numerical superiority, Grant's flexibility in crisis, and a crucial shift in fortunes from one combatant to the other. Johnston had dispatched four generals and their commands with vague instructions to defend the post, with eventual evacuation to save the force from capture. Grant marched unopposed from Fort Henry to Fort Donelson. Three days of subsequent land fighting, plus successful defeat of Foote's flotilla in a pivotal battle with the fort's water batteries on Valentine's Day, gave the Confederates the upper hand for much of the time. Then, a decisive Confederate breakout attempt on February 15 fell prey to command confu-

sion, when John B. Floyd, Gideon Pillow, Simon Bolivar Buckner, and Bushrod Rust Johnson disagreed whether to evacuate or hold onto the Cumberland position after routing Grant's right wing in an early morning attack.

The impact of Grant's decision to successfully counterattack despite destruction of a major portion of his command; the arrival of reinforcements from Fort Henry under Brigadier General Lew Wallace, which stymied the momentum of the Confederate drive; and the equal display of pluck and resolution by the Union army heightened the effect of the Confederate indecision. Adding to the general discomfort, the onset of bitter winter weather further disoriented officers and men on both sides.

What transpired was one of the truly *opera bouffe* episodes of the war and the key to understanding Fort Donelson. Meeting in council of war at a hotel in the nearby Stewart County seat of Dover, Floyd, Pillow, Buckner, and Nathan Bedford Forrest assessed their situation. Pillow remained adamant about defending his native Tennessee soil; Buckner abandoned his usual combative demeanor and dispaired of success against Grant's counterattacks; and Floyd, the nominal senior in command, dithered. When none of the generals could decide on a course of action, Forrest stormed out of the meeting, vowing to remove his cavalry command from Grant's entrapment. Eventually, Floyd and Pillow resolved to flee independently, while Buckner agreed to remain and surrender the remnants of the army. Forrest escaped with 1,500 horsemen and scattered infantry. Floyd and his personal 3,000-man brigade of Virginians, plus Pillow and his personal staff, similarly left the garrison to its fate.

The morning of February 16 dawned with both sides prepared to resume combat. When, instead, Grant and Buckner met to discuss surrender, Confederates were aghast and Federals jubilant. Grant demanded unconditional surrender, and the nonplussed Buckner complied. Although many escaped during the surrender proceedings, Grant telegraphed his superiors to report the capture of 12–15,000 prisoners, 20,000 stands of arms, 48 artillery pieces, 17 heavy guns, 2,000–4,000 horses, and a large quantity of commissary supplies.

Northern residents and Washington officials wildly celebrated the victory, but in the South, the unexpected news shocked Johnston. Nashvillians rioted and fled. Forrest and his cavalry eventually reestablished law and order in the capital. Floyd and Pillow returned to Nashville, but suffered the ignominy of their actions and were officially censured for deserting their responsibilities. As the Fort Donelson prisoners traveled north for incarceration (they were exchanged six months later), Johnston concentrated the remnants of his forces in northern Mississippi.

Within weeks of the fall of the river forts, Tennessee's capital fell to Union troops, and the state government fled into exile. The deep wedge driven into Tennessee so early in the conflict subsequently introduced Union political and military reconstruction, as well as popular resistance, guaranteeing the Volunteer State's status as a battleground for the duration of the war. With the loss of a Confederate field force of corps strength, the Union reclaimed much of Middle Tennessee as well as Kentucky. Hopes of early European recognition of the Confederacy evaporated, while Johnston's reputation as the South's greatest warrior vanished in Fort Donelson's surrender. Despite several attempts in 1862 and 1863 to recapture the Cumberland position, the Confederacy never redeemed the losses. Above all, Fort Donelson vaulted an unknown Union general into prominence. The road to Appomattox and the presidency of the United States began for Ulysses S. Grant at Fort Donelson. Fort Donelson National Military Park stands today as a monument to the starting point of these important events.

Benjamin Franklin Cooling, Chevy Chase, Maryland

SUGGESTED READINGS: Thomas L. Connelly, *Army of the Heartland: The Army of Tennessee, 1861–1862* (1967); Benjamin Franklin Cooling, *Forts Henry and Donelson: The Key to the Confederate Heartland* (1987); Benjamin Franklin Cooling, *Fort Donelson's Legacy: War and Society in Tennessee and Kentucky, 1862–1863* (1997)

SEE: CIVIL WAR; FORREST, NATHAN B.; FORT HENRY; JOHNSTON, ALBERT S.; PILLOW, GIDEON J.

FORT HENRY. Named for Confederate Senator Gustavus Henry of nearby Clarksville, this poorly positioned earthen field fortification was laid out on low ground by Tennessee state engineers and constructed in the summer of 1861 to defend the Tennessee River and the critical railroad route between Bowling Green, Kentucky, and Memphis. The fort, with its 17 mounted guns and an adjacent entrenched garrison camp, became the scene of the first major Union victory in the western theater on February 6, 1862. Fewer than 3,400 ill-equipped Confederate soldiers, under the command of Brigadier General Lloyd Tilghman, manned the fort, which was largely inundated by flood waters. Brigadier General Ulysses S. Grant commanded 15,000 man troops with the assistance of Flag Officer Andrew H. Foote's seven gunboats.

Tilghman quickly recognized the futility of his position and sent all but 70 artillerymen overland to reinforce nearby Fort Donelson. Foote's gunboats led the attack, with Grant's army moving by land to surround the garrison. The navy's heavy and accurate firepower quickly overcame the defenders, whose antiquated cannon proved ineffective. Foote and his officers simply rowed through the sallyport of the half-submerged fort to receive Tilghman's

"unconditional surrender," the first of the war. They found a wrecked fort and tallied Confederate losses at five dead, 11 wounded, and the remainder captive. Tilghman and his men remained in northern prison camps until exchanged six months later. The Union forces sustained casualties of 11 killed, 31 injured, and five missing.

The victory at Fort Henry belonged to the navy; Grant's footsoldiers, delayed by weather and muddy roads, did not join the fighting. With surprising ease, Foote breached the Confederate line and opened the Tennessee River to northern Alabama. Within days of Fort Henry's surrender, three gunboats raided 150 miles upstream to Muscle Shoals, destroying bridges and boats and uncovering ostensible pockets of Unionist sentiment among inhabitants along the way. Here was a spectacular demonstration of strategic military power. Moreover, Grant soon moved his land army to besiege and capture Fort Donelson, further opening the route of invasion into Tennessee and the upper Confederate heartland.

With the fall of Fort Henry, Union forces outflanked the major Confederate defensive bastion at Columbus, Kentucky, on the Mississippi River and opened West Tennessee to Union invasion and occupation. Fort Henry spawned the temporary myth of gunboat superiority over land defenses (partly offset soon by actions at Fort Donelson) and suggested a potent weapon in the hands of the Union, for which the Confederates had little defense. Fort Henry demonstrated that the Civil War in the West would be fought largely for control of the rivers—antebellum commercial arteries that became wartime barriers to effective Confederate unity and Union avenues for military, political, and economic reconstruction. The site of Fort Henry now lies beneath the waters of Kentucky Lake, although outworks remain at Land Between the Lakes.

Benjamin Franklin Cooling, Chevy Chase, Maryland

SUGGESTED READINGS: Benjamin Franklin Cooling, *Forts Henry and Donelson: The Key to the Confederate Heartland* (1987) and *Fort Donelson's Legacy: War and Society in Tennessee and Kentucky, 1862–1863* (1997)

SEE: CIVIL WAR; FORT DONELSON

FORT JAMES WHITE, or James White Fort, established in 1786, became the nucleus of modern-day Knoxville. General James White (1747–1821) traveled to the wilderness of East Tennessee from Iredell County, North Carolina, in 1785, settling with his wife Mary Lawson and five children on a 1,000-acre tract near the junction of the French Broad and Holston Rivers. To the west of First Creek, he built the first residence within what is today downtown Knoxville. The house was a one-and-a-half story "saddlebag" structure, built of hand-hewn square log construction with clay chinking. White also built three smaller houses of log construction and arranged them to form the four corners of a quadrangle with his principal residence located in the southwest corner. He then enclosed the sides of the quadrangle with an eight-foot-high wooden palisade and oriented the main gate to face First Creek.

In 1791 White's Fort was the site of the signing of the Treaty of Holston between Cherokee leaders and William Blount, Governor of the Territory South of the River Ohio. Blount selected White's Fort as the capital of the Southwest Territory and renamed it Knoxville. White hired Charles McClung to survey and divide a portion of his 1,000 acres into 64 one-half acre town lots. Reserving lots for himself, a church (now First Presbyterian Church, where White is buried), and for the formation of Blount College, he offered the remaining lots for sale by lottery at eight dollars each.

The White family established a second farm away from the fort, and the principal house was later incorporated as an ell into the brick residence of James Kennedy, Jr. By 1906 commercial growth made demolition of the house eminent and the J. Kennedy estate offered it to the Knoxville Historical Society. The Society did not have a site on which it could relocate the house, and refused the offer. Isaiah Ford, a local citizen, purchased White's house with the intent of preserving it. He carefully marked each log, dismantled the house, and reconstructed it on Woodlawn Pike in Knoxville.

In 1959 the City Association of Women's Clubs began its campaign for the reconstruction of the entire fort with the preservation and relocation of the principal house as its focal point. The CAWC established the James White Fort Association as a nonprofit organization to oversee the reconstruction. As the original site of the fort was already long-occupied, the JWFA selected a one-acre site nearby on Hill Avenue. However, it was not until three years later that Rep. Howard Baker and Sen. Estes Kefauver facilitated the passing of legislation that allowed the Knoxville Housing Authority to sell the proposed site to the JWFA for one dollar. The original James White house was again dismantled and relocated. With the construction of the palisades and other houses completed, the fort was opened to the public in 1973.

As it does not sit on its original site, the James White Fort does not qualify for historic status or local government funding. However, by 1990 White's Fort was the most frequently visited historic site in Knoxville, providing a physical link to the past through its significance as the first settlement in Knoxville and the home of the city's founder.
Katherine Wheeler, University of Virginia

SEE: BLOUNT, WILLIAM; KNOXVILLE; SOUTHWEST TERRITORY; WHITE, JAMES

FORT LOUDOUN, in present-day Monroe County, was named in honor of John Campbell, the Earl of Loudoun, who was commander-in-chief of the British forces in North America at the time of the fort's construction in 1756–1757. Interest in building a fort in the territory of the Overhill Cherokees, to cement, in a physical, symbolic sense, diplomatic and trade relationships between the British colonists and the Cherokees, dates to the 1740s. Nothing happened until the great rivalry between the British and French over the control of North America evolved into the Seven Years' War of 1756 to 1763. Fort Loudoun, designed by engineer John William G. De Brahm, stood on the south side of the Little Tennessee River near its confluence with the Tellico River. Captain Raymond Demere, who initially commanded the approximately 200 South Carolina militia troops and British regulars stationed at the post, and De Brahm clashed repeatedly over the fort's location, construction, and design. In a report to the governor of South Carolina, Demere sarcastically dismissed the fort by observing that the Cherokees "call it the Fort to put Horses, Cows, and Hogs in, but I differ in opinion with them for it would not be sufficient" for even that purpose.[1] While Demere and his soldiers moved into the fort in early January 1757, he did not consider the fort to be finished until late July. In August 1757 Raymond Demere left, transferring command to his brother Paul Demere.

Fort Loudoun featured a large log palisade, inside of which were a row of barracks, a powder magazine, a blacksmith shop (that also served as a meeting house or chapel), two corn houses, a guardroom, and various storehouses. Officers usually had private dwellings constructed for themselves and their families. Once complete, the fort was meant to be a self-sufficient military outpost on the farthest fringes of the Carolina frontier. But survival, or at least an adequate supply of food, was dependent on friendly relations with the neighboring Overhill Cherokees. Cherokee women, for instance, exchanged very desirable fresh foods, berries, and fish for trade goods. The Native Americans also liked to visit with the soldiers, and they considered the outpost as much their territory as that of the English colonists.

As relations between British forces, the colonists, and the Cherokees worsened during the war, tensions rose at Fort Loudoun. By 1760, mutual suspicion and distrust had replaced the earlier friendly relations. In March the Cherokees laid siege and cut off outside supplies to the fort. On June 10, rations for the soldiers and family members were reduced to a mere quart of corn for every three people; in July the last bread was consumed. As heat and hunger overwhelmed the fort's inhabitants in early August, a number of soldiers abandoned their comrades, leaving the officers little choice but to surrender. On

August 9, 1760, 180 men, with 60 women and children, left Fort Loudoun to begin a long overland march to South Carolina settlements. A day later, near Tellico Plains, approximately 700 Cherokees attacked the retreating soldiers and their families, killing three officers, 23 soldiers, and three women. The rest were captured and whisked away to Cherokee villages, where a few were murdered but most were ransomed to either Virginia or South Carolina.

Although the garrison and fort were lost in 1760, by that time Fort Loudoun had served its military mission of keeping the Cherokees from supporting the French cause in the early, decisive years of the war. The fort's site is now the Fort Loudoun State Historic Area, which features a replica of the fort.
Carroll Van West, Middle Tennessee State University

CITATION:
(1) James C. Kelly, "Fort Loudoun: British Stronghold in the Tennessee Country," East Tennessee Historical Society *Publications* 50(1978): 80.

SEE: DE BRAHM, JOHN W.; MONROE COUNTY

FORT NASHBOROUGH: See DONELSON, JOHN; FRENCH LICK; ROBERTSON, CHARLOTTE R.; ROBERTSON, JAMES

FORT NEGLEY, a Federal Civil War fortification built largely by African-American labor in 1862 and garrisoned in part by African-American soldiers during the Battle of Nashville of December 1864, is located in Nashville. It represented the first extensive use of newly freed blacks in the Federal war effort and its success influenced the later creation of contraband labor camps in other Tennessee towns. U.S. Army engineer James St. Clair Morton designed the fort as a polygonal-shaped structure, measuring approximately 600 by 300 feet, that was composed of dirt, stones, and timber. Fort Negley also contained an extensive system of underground magazines and storage spaces.

Federal troops occupied Fort Negley until, at least, 1867. After they left, it became a gathering place for the initial Nashville Den of the Ku Klux Klan, who used it in 1869 for its last public demonstration. Nathan B. Forrest led Klan members to the fort where they burned their robes and officially disbanded. The fort soon deteriorated, and many stones were later used in building Nashville's Eighth Avenue Reservoir.

From 1936 to 1937 the fort was restored by the Works Progress Administration, but the original park plans were never carried through and the fort once again was abandoned. At the end of the century, historians and historic preservationists are working to preserve the property and open it as a historic site associated with the Battle of Nashville

Fort Negley, October 1862.

REPRINTED FROM *HARPER'S*, OCTOBER 1862

and the efforts of African Americans during the Civil War. Fort Negley represented "the uneasy alliance between the Union Army and local blacks in their successful campaign to preserve the Union and destroy slavery."[1]

Carroll Van West, Middle Tennessee State University

CITATION:

(1) Bobby L. Lovett, "Nashville's Fort Negley: A Symbol of Blacks' Involvement with the Union Army," *Tennessee Historical Quarterly* 41(1982): 21.

SEE: CONTRABAND CAMPS; KU KLUX KLAN; NASHVILLE, BATTLE OF; UNITED STATES COLORED TROOPS

FORT PATRICK HENRY was located on the north side of the South Fork of the Holston River near the upper end of Long Island at present-day Kingsport. Its predecessor was a fort constructed in the winter of 1760–1761 by Colonel William Byrd, who was leading about 600 Virginians against the Cherokees after the Fort Loudoun massacre. This fort was named Fort Robinson in honor of John Robinson, one of Byrd's partners in a Virginia lead mine. Fort Robinson was described as a stockaded fort with bastions and supporting structures within the enclosure.

In September 1776 Lieutenant Colonel William Russell, commanding the Fincastle Rangers, established Fort Patrick Henry on or near the site of Fort Robinson. The stockade wall with bastions at the corners enclosed three acres on the bluff of the Holston River. This fort was used in the war against the Cherokees. A force of approximately 200 Cherokee warriors, commanded by Dragging Canoe, attacked the Holston settlements and was defeated in the Battle of Long Island Flats on July 20, 1776. In September of the same year, men from Virginia, North Carolina, South Carolina, and Georgia gathered at Fort Patrick Henry for a campaign against the Cherokees. The combined force of 2,400, under the command of General Griffith Rutherford of North Carolina, soundly defeated the Cherokees, who sued for peace. The conflict ended with the signing of the Avery Treaty in 1777 on the Long Island of the Holston. Fort Patrick Henry was garrisoned throughout the remainder of the Revolution.

Benjamin C. Nance, Tennessee Division of Archaeology

SEE: WARRIORS PATH STATE PARK

FORT PILLOW, a Civil War earthwork and battleground, occupies a Mississippi River bluff in Lauderdale County. Late in the spring of 1861, Confederate troops from Arkansas built a battery at the site to control a bend in the river. Major General Gideon Pillow subsequently ordered the construction of a 30-acre enclosure with numerous batteries below, in, and atop the bluff. It soon took on his name.

When upriver defenses crumbled in early 1862, Brigadier General John Villepigue arrived with reinforcements and a ram fleet to prepare the fort for action. On April 13, a Confederate gunboat fleet retreated to Fort Pillow. A superior federal flotilla followed and anchored near Osceola, Arkansas, exchanging artillery fire with the fort. Neither side did much damage; both forces sent most infantrymen to participate in the Corinth, Mississippi, campaign.

On May 10, Captain James Montgomery's Confederate ram fleet surprised the ships under Captain Charles Davis in the nearly bloodless Battle of Plum Bend. The rams fled after sinking two gunboats, which were soon raised and repaired. Federal Brigadier General Isaac Quimby then arrived with troops to storm the fort, but quickly abandoned the effort. Next, Colonel Charles Ellet arrived with army rams with which he tried to attack the Confederate fleet, only to be driven back by the fort's artillery. As a result of the Confederate retreat from Corinth, Villepigue evacuated the fort by June 4.

The Federal army irregularly used the site until fall 1862, when a garrison of cavalry and mounted infantry began patrolling the area in search of guerrillas, conscription agents, and contraband trade. The navy kept a warship near the fort to support these operations. The fort became a trading center as well as a refuge for runaway slaves and unionists, but the guerrilla war locked into a stalemate. In early 1864 the fort turned into a recruiting post.

The garrison included some 300 inexperienced white unionists and approximately an equal number of African Americans, when some 1,500 Confederate veterans under Major General Nathan B. Forrest assaulted the fort on April 12. The gunboat evacuated most civilians and ineffectually shelled the enemy. During morning fighting, the Federals retreated to a small inner fort near the bluff. Calling a truce, Forrest offered to accept the entire garrison as prisoners of war, a significant gesture as the Confederacy did not officially recognize blacks as legitimate soldiers. The Federals refused, and the next Confederate charge broke into the fort. As a result of the intense hostility toward armed blacks and southern unionists, discipline among the victors broke down, and many granted no quarter. Deaths totaled 64 percent of the black troops and at least 31 percent of the whites. Forrest alleged that the Federals refused to surrender until most had died; Federal survivors claimed that a massacre took place.

Sharp northern criticism included a Congressional report written by Senator Benjamin F. Wade and Representative Daniel W. Gooch. Abandoned after the incident, the site slowly reverted into a wilderness. In 1971, the state acquired it to develop a state historical area.

John Cimprich, Thomas More College

SUGGESTED READINGS: John Cimprich and Robert C. Mainfort, Jr., "Fort Pillow Revisited: New Evidence about an Old

Controversy," *Civil War History*, 28 (1982): 293–306; Kenneth B. Moore, "Fort Pillow, Forrest, and the United States Colored Troops in 1864," *Tennessee Historical Quarterly* 54(1995): 112–123; Tennessee Division of Archaeology, *Archaeological Investigations at Fort Pillow State Historic Area, 1976–1978* (1980)

SEE: CIVIL WAR; FORREST, NATHAN B.; LAUDERDALE COUNTY; PILLOW, GIDEON J.

FORT PRUDHOMME AND LA SALLE. René Robert Cavelier, Sieur de La Salle, was born in 1643, the son of a wealthy family in Rouen, France. At the age of 23, he went to Canada and established an Indian trading post near Montreal. Indian tales aroused his interest in the unexplored lands to the west, and he set out on his first journey in 1669.

During the next three years, he reached the falls of the Ohio River at Louisville, traveled around Lake Michigan, and explored the Illinois River country. The governor of Canada, the Comte de Frontenac, granted him land on the present site of Kingston, Ontario.

La Salle might have settled down and become a rich man, but in 1678 he returned to France to seek King Louis XIV's permission to explore further. He was granted permission, but only if the explorations entailed no cost to the King. La Salle established the first settlement of white men in what was to become Illinois, near the site of today's Peoria, and built a fort on the Illinois River. In February 1682 a party of 54 persons, including 23 Frenchmen, 18 Native American men, ten Native American women, and three children, set out in canoes down the Mississippi River, which La Salle called Colbert in honor of the French finance minister.

Within the boundaries of present-day Tennessee, the party stopped to hunt and almost lost one of its members, an armorer named Pierre Prudhomme. Thinking he might have been captured by the Chickasaws, La Salle had a stockade built on the second Chickasaw Bluff south of the Hatchie River. He called it Fort Prudhomme. After ten days, Prudhomme returned, safe but starving, and the party continued down river. Fort Prudhomme became the first structure built by whites in what was to become West Tennessee.

Although La Salle's expedition only passed by the site of future Memphis on the fourth Chickasaw Bluff without stopping, they left a name for the maps. Supposedly an Indian told them the name of the river, and thereafter it appeared as the Rivière du Loup, or Wolf River. The party proceeded to an Indian village they called Mitchigameas at the site of Helena, Arkansas. There, on March 14, 1682, La Salle erected a cross and claimed all the country on the west bank of the Mississippi in the name of the king of France.

The expedition reached the passes at the mouth of the Mississippi on April 6, 1682. They celebrated mass and La Salle claimed the land in the name of Louis XIV of France. Thus France claimed the Mississippi Valley, and it remained French until 1762. Fort Prudhomme, the first structure built by the French in Tennessee, preceded its English rivals in the eastern part of the state by 74 years.

Returning to Canada, La Salle sailed for France to get supplies and settlers for the colonies he planned to establish along the Mississippi. In 1684 he sailed for the Gulf of Mexico with four ships and more than 200 colonists. The ships were blown off course and landed at Matagorda Bay in Texas instead of the mouth of the Mississippi. The colonists attempted an overland march toward the Mississippi. Weakened by Indian attacks and illness, the men rebelled and killed La Salle in 1687.

Perre Magness, Memphis

SUGGESTED READING: William A. Klutts, "Fort Prudhomme: Its Location," West Tennessee Historical Society *Papers* 4(1950): 28–40; James Roper, *The Founding of Memphis, 1818–1820* (1970)

SEE: EXPLORATIONS, EARLY; MEMPHIS

FORT SAN FERNANDO DE LAS BARRANCAS (1795–1797). Continuous settlement of the Fourth Chickasaw Bluff, the site of Memphis, dates at least from Spain's founding of Fort San Fernando in May 1795. As a co-belligerent of the rebelling United States in the 1770s, Spain captured various British posts on the Gulf of Mexico and in the lower Mississippi Valley. At war's end, Spain claimed present-day Kentucky, Tennessee, Mississippi, and Alabama by right of conquest. At the Paris conference of 1783, however, the British ceded all their former trans-Appalachian holdings to the United States, creating conflicting claims to the area.

In the mid-1790s Spain moved to secure its northeastern flank in North America. Louisiana Governor-General Carondelet sent Lt. Governor Manuel Gayoso de Lemos to secure the Chickasaws's consent and then erect a fort on the bluff site. Gayoso proceeded with dispatch, building a small stockaded fort and a support complex at the confluence of the Wolf and Mississippi Rivers.

The fort, a hardship post, lasted less than two years. By 1798 Spain renounced its claims to territory above the 31st parallel, destroyed the fort, and withdrew across the Mississippi. Squatters in the shadow of the fort stayed on to welcome American occupation. Some of these pioneers survived well into the nineteenth century and became citizens of early Memphis at its founding. Some Spanish and French customs, usages, and a few place names carried over into the Anglo-American settlement.

John E. Harkins, Memphis University School

SEE: CHICKASAWS; EXPLORATIONS, EARLY; MEMPHIS

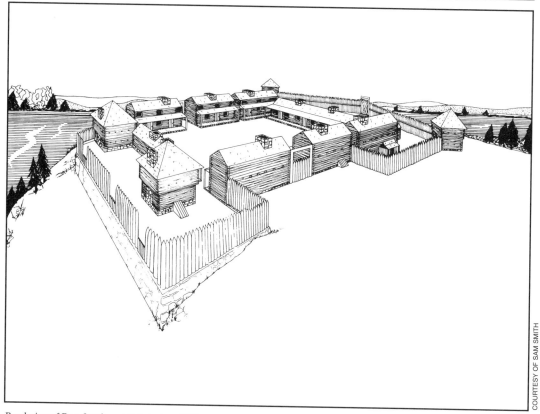

COURTESY OF SAM SMITH

Rendering of Fort Southwest Point, circa 1800.

FORT SOUTHWEST POINT was constructed in 1797 on a high knoll overlooking the mouth of the Clinch River where it enters the Tennessee River, just within the boundaries of the Cherokee territory of the "Territory South of the River Ohio," which preceded creation of the state of Tennessee. During most of the territorial period, a militia post known as the "Southwest Point Blockhouse(s)" was located a half mile above the mouth of the Clinch River, on the only east-west road connecting the Knoxville and Nashville area settlements.

The 1797 construction was the work of federal soldiers, who had been sent to Tennessee as part of an effort to control ongoing boundary disputes between Euro-American settlers and the Cherokees, who still claimed most of what is now East Tennessee. During the late 1790s, Fort Southwest Point functioned as the headquarters post for the Fourth Regiment of Infantry, commanded by Lieutenant Colonel Thomas Butler. Part of the garrison was also made up of the Third Regiment of Infantry, companies of artillery, and a troop of dragoons (cavalry).

By 1801 the number of federal soldiers in Tennessee had been considerably reduced, but Fort Southwest Point remained in use and became the headquarters for a newly appointed Cherokee Indian Agent, Colonel Return Jonathan Meigs, who also served as "Military Agent for the Federal Troops in Tennessee." Colonel Meigs's activities at Fort Southwest Point continued from 1801 to 1807, when the Agency and the United States's "Factory for Trade with the Cherokee" at Tellico Blockhouse were relocated farther into the Cherokee territory at the new Hiwassee Garrison.

Though Fort Southwest Point lost its more important functions in 1807, its buildings apparently continued to be used by the federal troops until about 1811. Its primary use during this final phase seems to have been as a supply depot for handling materials shipped overland from the east, and then by water down the Tennessee and other rivers to new posts farther along the expanding United States frontier.

Today, the city of Kingston owns the site of Fort Southwest Point. Several seasons of professional archaeological research have been conducted on this site, and from resultant discoveries some of the buildings and palisade have been reconstructed.

Samuel D. Smith, Tennessee Division of Archaeology
SUGGESTED READING: Fort Southwest Point Archaeological Site,
Kingston, Tennessee: A Multidisciplinary Interpretation (1993)
SEE: MEIGS, RETURN J.; OVERHILL CHEROKEES; ROANE
COUNTY; TELLICO BLOCKHOUSE

FORT WATAUGA, originally named Fort Caswell, was
constructed near the Sycamore Shoals of the Watauga
River near present-day Elizabethton. Settlement in
the Watauga Valley began before 1768, despite an earlier proclamation by British authorities forbidding
encroachment into Native American territory. When
a 1770 survey defined the boundary line, the Watauga
settlement was clearly inside Cherokee lands.

The Wataugans refused to leave their settlement,
and in 1772 James Robertson and John Boon negotiated a lease with the Cherokee for their lands along
the Watauga. Following this agreement, the settlers
formed the Watauga Association for the purposes of
self-government—an action taken to protect property
rights, not as a break with the British government.

After the outbreak of the American Revolution in
1775, the Wataugans feared British instigation of
Cherokee attacks on the frontier settlements. To protect against such attacks, the settlers constructed several forts and named the one at the Watauga
settlement Fort Caswell in honor of the Revolutionary Governor of North Carolina. There are no contemporary descriptions of the fort, but archaeological
testing of the site showed that it was an irregularly
shaped enclosure consisting of palisade walls probably joining blockhouses or other buildings.

In July 1776 Old Abram of Chilhowee led a group
of Cherokees in an attack on the Watauga settlement.
Repulsed in the initial attack, the Cherokees besieged
the fort for two weeks. By the time reinforcements
arrived from the Holston settlement, the Cherokees
had already abandoned the siege. In 1780 the Overmountain Men gathered at the Sycamore Shoals of
the Watauga before marching to the battle of King's
Mountain.

Benjamin C. Nance, Tennessee Division of Archaeology
SEE: CARTER COUNTY; SYCAMORE SHOALS STATE HIS-
TORIC AREA; WATAUGA ASSOCIATION

FORT WRIGHT. In April 1861 Governor Isham G.
Harris ordered Lieutenant Colonel Marcus Wright,
154th Militia Regiment at Memphis, to proceed north
and occupy a defensive position on the Mississippi
River. Wright and a battalion of men and artillery
established camp at Randolph in Tipton County.
Over the next four months, some 5,000 Tennessee,
Arkansas, and Confederate troops arrived in Randolph and fortified the Chickasaw Bluffs with
artillery batteries and earthen field defenses to guard
against the expected Union naval and land attack.
From late April through July 1861, Fort Wright

served as the forwardmost defensive position on
the Mississippi River, which represented the left
flank of the Provisional Army of Tennessee. If the
Union forces had come down that corridor, as
expected, the Battle for Memphis would have been
fought at this spot.

The significance of Fort Wright was as a place to
train soldiers, build armies, and experiment, even
make mistakes. It was one of Tennessee's first military laboratories. Here Tennesseans first attempted
to build fortifications, set up river batteries, and drill
with heavy artillery in preparation for the defense of
the Mississippi. It was here that raw recruits from the
farms, classrooms, and stores became soldiers and
learned military discipline. These soldiers went on
to the fields of Shiloh, Belmont, Murfreesboro,
Chickamauga, Franklin, and Bentonville. Fort
Wright also brought together some of the future
leaders of the Army of Tennessee and Forrest's cavalry and provided a beginning for two future lieutenant generals, Alexander P. Stewart and Nathan
Bedford Forrest.

By 1862 Confederate infantry had evacuated Fort
Wright, although southern naval and cavalry forces
would continue to occupy the site on an irregular
basis. In the fall of that year, a squad of some 10 or
15 irregular Confederate soldiers fired into the
steamer *Belle of St. Louis,* which was docked at the
landing. No damage was done, but for this rash act,
General William T. Sherman burned the entire town
of Randolph, except for an old church and one
dwelling. The remaining buildings were destroyed
by fire in 1865. Today, all that remains is the powder
magazine dug by Confederate forces at Fort Wright.
It is one of the few extant Civil War powder magazines in Tennessee.

Prepared from material supplied by Angela Wallace Finley,
Covington-Tipton County Tourism Bureau
SEE: ARMY OF TENNESSEE; TIPTON COUNTY

FORT, CORNELIA (1919–1943), aviator, was a
Nashville debutante whose love of flying led her to
become a pioneer in women's military aviation as a
member of the Women's Auxiliary Ferrying
Squadron, which later became part of the Women's
Air Force Service Pilots (WASPs) in 1943. Fort was
born to one of Nashville's wealthiest and most influential families. Her father was a founder of the
National Life & Accident Insurance Company. An
intelligent and well-liked girl, she attended Ward-
Belmont School. She was a voracious reader who was
active in the Belle Meade social scene, but ambivalent
about it as well. When her family gave her a debut
ball at age 19, Fort had to be bribed to attend.

Fort attended Sarah Lawrence College in New
York, and enjoyed the intellectual and cultural climate she found there. She attended the theater and

symphony, and wrote passionate editorials for the school's newspaper on subjects like the rise of Hitler and his abuses of power.

After her graduation in 1939, Fort reluctantly entered the world of cotillion dances and civic activities. In 1940 a chance trip to Nashville's airport with a friend changed her life; one flight opened a new interest for her. She took lessons and soloed less than a month later. The first week she had her license, she flew more than 2,000 miles in celebration. She went on to get her commercial and instructor's ratings, and became Tennessee's only female instructor.

In 1941 she took a job as an instructor in Fort Collins, Colorado, then another in Honolulu. She was giving a flying lesson on the morning of December 7, when a wave of Japanese Zeros swept past her and began the infamous bombing of Pearl Harbor. Fort landed in a hail of machine-gun fire.

After her return to the mainland, Fort traveled and sold war bonds amid heavy publicity about her Pearl Harbor experiences. She longed for service in the war effort, and found it in September 1942, when she and a handful of women were invited to become part of a new organization, the Women's Auxiliary Ferrying Squadron (WAFS), which would ferry planes from factories to military bases, freeing men for combat flight. Fort eagerly accepted and was the second woman to arrive at Delaware's New Castle Army Air Base. She was part of a pioneering group of 28 women who established an excellent record of service and safety in the face of resistance from many quarters and less-than-ideal conditions. The women often flew in open cockpits in sub-freezing temperatures without radios or other equipment now taken for granted.

In January, Fort was transferred to Long Beach, California. It was there, while on a ferrying mission to Dallas, that she was killed in a mid-air collision on March 21, 1943. Her life and love of service has been an inspiration to those around her, and her story continues to inspire new generations.

Rob Simbeck, Nashville

SUGGESTED READING: Doris Brinker Tanner, "Cornelia Fort, A WASP in World War II, Part I," *Tennessee Historical Quarterly* 40(1981): 381–394 and "Cornelia Fort, Pioneer Woman Military Aviator, Part II," *ibid.*, 41(1982): 67–80

SEE: WORLD WAR II

FORTAS, ABE (1910–1982), Associate Justice of the United States Supreme Court, was born in Memphis, the son of an English-born Orthodox Jew and cabinetmaker. While attending high school, Fortas worked nights at a shoe store and also earned money playing the violin at parties. A 1930 graduate of Southwestern College at Memphis (now Rhodes College), Fortas went on to study law at Yale Law School, serving as editor of the *Yale Law Review* before gradu-

ating at the top of his class in 1933. Fortas was influenced by his law professor, William O. Douglas, with whom he would later work at the Securities and Exchange Commission and on the Supreme Court.

Following graduation, Fortas spent four years as an assistant professor of law at Yale before entering government service at the Agricultural Adjustment Administration and the Securities and Exchange Commission, where he held a variety of positions, including Assistant Director of the Public Utilities section. He served as General Counsel for the Public Works Administration from 1939 to 1941. In 1942 he moved to the Interior Department, where he rose to the position of Undersecretary. While at Interior, he participated in the organizational meeting of the United Nations as an adviser to the U.S. delegation, a position he also filled at the first United Nations Assembly in 1946.

Resigning from government, Fortas formed the Washington, D.C., law firm of Arnold, Fortas and Porter, specializing in corporate law. In addition to his corporate practice, Fortas took cases involving civil liberties and was involved in defending individuals accused of communist activities during the McCarthy era. In 1963 he argued the case of *Gideon v. Wainwright* before the Supreme Court, which established the right of indigent defendants in criminal cases to receive free legal counsel, often viewed as one of the Supreme Court's most important decisions regarding the rights of the accused.

During his years in private practice, Congressman Lyndon B. Johnson became one of Fortas's clients. Johnson sought counsel over a dispute involving attempts to keep his name off the ballot in the Texas general election. Fortas helped resolve the conflict and became Johnson's friend and confidant. In 1965 President Johnson appointed Justice Arthur Goldberg as Ambassador to the United Nations and named Fortas to the Supreme Court, where he served until 1969.

Fortas's relatively short tenure on the Court was a mixture of scholarship and controversy. Viewed as a libertarian on individual rights, he fit within the liberal wing of the Warren Court as an ally of Douglas and a worthy successor to Goldberg. Fortas reportedly cast the deciding vote in the landmark case of *Miranda v. Arizona* (1966), enlarging the rights of criminal suspects during police investigations. Fortas authored the majority opinion in *In Re Gault* (1967), where the Court held that juveniles were entitled to the same procedural protections during juvenile criminal proceedings that applied to adult court proceedings.

When Chief Justice Earl Warren announced his retirement in 1968, Johnson nominated Fortas as his successor. With Johnson as a lame duck president, and the Republicans sensing a November victory,

Fortas's appointment soon drew fire. His friendship with Johnson, the discovery that he continued counseling the President while a Justice, and the disclosure of his acceptance of a large outside lecture fee made his Senate confirmation the subject of a filibuster, which survived a cloture attempt. Faced with a protracted confirmation fight, Johnson honored Fortas's request to withdraw his nomination.

In early 1969, *Life* magazine revealed that Fortas received, and then returned, a $20,000 fee from a family foundation of an industrialist since connected to stock manipulation. When this past association drew heated criticism from the public and Congress, Fortas resigned, becoming the first Justice forced to resign from the Court. He returned to private practice, forming the Washington, D.C., law firm of Fortas and Koven. Fortas died in 1982, two weeks after arguing a case before the Supreme Court, his first return to the Court since his resignation.

William P. Morelli, Brentwood

SUGGESTED READINGS: Laura Kalman, *Abe Fortas* (1990); Bruce Murphy, *Fortas: The Rise and Ruin of a Supreme Court Justice* (1988)

SEE: LAW; MEMPHIS

FORTRESS ROSECRANS, the largest fort built during the Civil War, is located in Murfreesboro, Tennessee. Constructed between January and June 1863 after the Battle of Stones River, the project was the responsibility of Brigadier General James St. Clair Morton, chief engineer for the Army of the Cumberland. The bastioned fort covered an area of approximately 225 acres and consisted of eight lunettes and four redoubts linked by a series of curtain walls and abatis. Numerous buildings (saw mills, quartermaster depots, warehouses, magazines, and quarters) covered the site. The fortress was placed astride the junction of the Stones River and the Nashville and Chattanooga Railroad as well as the intersection of Wilkinson Pike and the Old Nashville Pike. The fortress, never successfully assaulted by Confederate forces, provided the logistical support for the Union advance on Chattanooga and Atlanta and Sherman's march to the sea.

The west wall of the fortress and one redoubt have survived to the present. Acquired by the City of Murfreesboro in 1966—the centennial anniversary of the abandonment of the fortress—the property was transferred to the National Park Service in 1993, becoming a unit of Stones River National Battlefield. Fortress Rosecrans, Redoubt Brannan, and the national battlefield have been connected since 1997 by the 3.2 mile Stones River Greenway. The fortress is listed on the National Register of Historic Places.

Morton began work on the fortifications on January 23, 1863. The Pioneer Brigade, an elite Michigan unit experienced in building railroads and fortifications, supervised the labor of the over 40,000 men encamped in the vicinity. Initially 4,000 men worked on each of the eight-hour shifts to clear the land, position abatis, excavate moats, and create the reinforced earthen parapet walls of this massive fort. Constructed of tramped earth reinforced by wood revetments, wire, brick, and stone, the walls included lunettes, redoubts, revetments, and magazines. An enormous convalescent camp for wounded was established northwest of Fortress Rosecrans in a bend of the Stones River. Morton also published a lengthy guide for the defense of Fortress Rosecrans.

The construction pace was increased in June 1863, to allow the Army of the Cumberland to begin its advance upon Chattanooga. When Major General William S. Rosecrans departed Murfreesboro on June 24, he left behind some 2,000 troops to operate and defend the fortress under the command of Brigadier General Horatio Van Cleve. After the war, the site reverted to agricultural uses until being acquired by the City of Murfreesboro in 1966.

James K. Huhta, Middle Tennessee State University

SEE: RUTHERFORD COUNTY; STONES RIVER, BATTLE OF

FOSTER, EPHRAIM H. (1794–1854), United States Senator and early leader of the Whig party, was born in Kentucky. Foster came to Davidson County with his family in 1797 and graduated from Cumberland College in Nashville in 1813. After serving as Andrew Jackson's personal secretary on the Creek and New Orleans campaigns, Foster studied law and soon established himself as a successful Nashville attorney. His prominence as a lawyer helped him win election to three terms in the General Assembly; twice he was unanimously chosen as the Speaker of the House of Representatives.

Foster began his political career as a Jackson loyalist, but his disagreement with Jackson's fiscal policies, along with the president's opposition to Foster's 1833 candidacy for the Senate, led to his advocacy of Senator Hugh L. White's presidential candidacy in 1836 against Jackson's choice, Martin Van Buren. As the White movement developed into the Whig party, Whigs in the legislature elected Foster to the Senate in 1838. He resigned 14 months later, however, after a newly elected Democratic majority in the Assembly instructed him to support the policies of Van Buren's administration. Despite the election of a Whig majority in 1841, the "Immortal Thirteen" controversy delayed Foster's return to the Senate until 1843. His most noted action in the Senate was his introduction of a plan for the admission of Texas as a state, but he ultimately voted against Texas's admission because the admission law failed to guarantee slavery in any new state that might be created out of Texas's lands. This vote damaged his popularity, and after the expiration of his term, his loss to Aaron V. Brown in the 1845 gubernatorial election further diminished his standing. As a result, Foster had little influence in his later years with either the state or national Whig leadership.

Jonathan M. Atkins, Berry College

SEE: BROWN, AARON V.; IMMORTAL THIRTEEN; WHITE, HUGH L.

FOWLER, JOSEPH SMITH (1820–1902), United States Senator, was born in Steubenville, Ohio, to James and Sarah Atkinson Fowler. After attending Grove Academy in Steubenville, he graduated from Franklin College in New Athens, Ohio, in 1843. He spent one year teaching school in Shelby County, Kentucky, before becoming a professor of mathematics at Franklin College in Davidson County, Tennessee, a position he held from 1845 to 1849. During this time, he began to study law and after admission to the bar, practiced in Tennessee until 1861. He also served as president of Howard Female College in Gallatin, Tennessee, from 1856 to 1861.

Fowler strongly opposed slavery and secession, and in 1861 he moved his family to Springfield, Illinois. After military government was established in Tennessee in 1862, he returned to Nashville and was appointed Comptroller of the Treasury by Military Governor Andrew Johnson. He served in this position until 1865, when he was elected U.S. Senator from Tennessee as a Union Republican. During his single Senate term (1866–1871), Fowler made one of his strongest speeches in support of President Andrew Johnson during the impeachment proceedings against him. Despite much pressure to do otherwise, Fowler voted "not guilty" at Johnson's Senate trial. After choosing not to run for re-election, Fowler served as a presidential elector for the Democratic ticket of Greeley and Brown in 1872. He then resumed the practice of law in Washington, D.C., until his death on April 4, 1902. He is buried in Lexington, Kentucky.

Cathi Carmack, Tennessee State Library and Archives

SUGGESTED READING: Walter T. Durham, "How Say You, Senator Fowler?," *Tennessee Historical Quarterly* 42(1983): 39–57

SEE: JOHNSON, ANDREW; RECONSTRUCTION

FRANKLIN, BATTLE OF. Following the evacuation of Atlanta, General John Bell Hood formulated an elaborate plan to draw General William T. Sherman away from that city and place his own army in position to recapture Middle Tennessee. Hood planned to march his army north, capture the vital Union supply depot of Nashville, and take the war into Kentucky and Ohio.

Initially Hood's plan worked. Sherman withdrew from Atlanta and followed the Army of Tennessee

The Battle of Franklin, 1864.

into North Georgia. There, Sherman realized the numerical superiority of his forces and detached a portion of his army to stay ahead of Hood's advance north, while he returned with the main force to implement his March to the Sea. General John Schofield, Hood's West Point classmate, was placed in command of the 4th and 23rd Army Corps and given the task of slowing the Confederate advance to Nashville.

On the afternoon of November 29, 1864, the Army of Tennessee managed to get between Schofield's command and the federal stronghold at Nashville at the town of Spring Hill. When the Confederate forces failed to cut the road north, the Union troops marched by their enemy in the middle of the night. By the next morning, they had entered Franklin and occupied a series of earthen fortifications on the southern edge of town. During the day, Union soldiers strengthened their already formidable position, as Schofield made plans to evacuate Franklin and march to Nashville.

When Hood awoke on November 30 and found that the Union army had escaped, he blamed everyone but himself for the missed opportunity; he immediately marched the Army of Tennessee to Franklin. Arriving at Winstead Hill (two miles south of Franklin), Hood determined to make a fight despite the warnings from Generals Nathan Bedford Forrest and Benjamin Cheatham to avoid a frontal assault. The Confederate commander accepted no counsel and ordered his subordinates to prepare for the assault.

At 4:30 in the afternoon, as the sun began to set, the Army of Tennessee stepped off in a three-mile long battleline to launch the last grand charge of the war. Marching forward in near-parade formation, the leading elements of the Confederate line overwhelmed the advanced Union position one-half mile in front of the main line. Chasing the fleeing Federals, the men of Generals Patrick Cleburne and John C. Brown's divisions smashed into the Union earthworks along the Columbia Pike. Driving the Federals through the front and back yard of Fountain B. Carter's house, and into the front yard of Albert Lotz's home, the advancing Confederates met a counter charge by Colonel Emerson Opdycke's brigade. In fierce hand-to-hand fighting, the Federal soldiers forced the Confederates back to the outer ditch of the main earthworks.

The Confederates made as many as 18 separate charges, but failed to make a significant breach in the Union defenses. Some Confederate attacks occurred so late at night, the soldiers used torches to guide their lines forward. The fight lasted until 10:00 o'clock, leaving Union troops inside the works and Confederates in the outer ditches, only a few feet apart. Many soldiers sat with their backs against the works and held their muskets over their heads to fire them into the opposing ranks.

After five hours of bloodletting, the small arms fire died away. Schofield wasted no time pulling his men out of their positions and marching them toward Nashville. That night, as the temperature dropped, the wounded Union and Confederate soldiers left on the field suffered terribly. The dead and dying lay in heaps sometimes five or six deep in the outer ditch. Field hospitals in the Carter and Lotz houses, and the Carnton Mansion, treated the seemingly endless stream of wounded.

The battle exacted a disastrous toll on the Confederate forces. Hood sent approximately 23,000 soldiers against a fortified line protected by 15,000 Union soldiers and incurred 7,000 casualties, while the Federals lost approximately 2,500. Of the 100 Confederate regimental commanders, 63 were killed or wounded. The casualty toll among Confederate generals was also high—six killed, five wounded, and one captured. As the Army of Tennessee moved north toward Nashville, a colonel commanded General John C. Brown's division, and a captain led General Hiram Granbury's brigade. At the battle of Nashville, two weeks later, the Army of Tennessee was not effective, having left a sizable number of hardened veterans and officers on the field of Franklin.

Patrick Craddock, Franklin

SUGGESTED READING: Wiley Ford, *Embrace An Angry Wind* (1992)

SEE: ARMY OF TENNESSEE; BROWN, JOHN C.; CARNTON MANSION; CARTER HOUSE; CHEATHAM, BENJAMIN F.; CLEBURNE, PATRICK R.; HOOD, JOHN BELL

FRANKLIN COUNTY was established in 1807, following extinction of Cherokee claims west of the Cumberland Plateau between the Duck and Tennessee rivers. Mountain lands were added after Native American claims ended in 1819. Franklin County was named for Benjamin Franklin, whose name had already been borrowed in 1784 for East Tennessee's abortive state. The county seat was named for General James Winchester.

Whites and blacks had visited the area, notably during the 1794 Nickajack expedition, and speculators had claimed large tracts still in Indian hands. Creation of the county opened the way for settlers, mostly from East Tennessee, North Carolina, and Virginia. Among the first settlers were William Russell on Boiling Fork near Cowan and Jesse Bean in the south west. Russell's house served as the courthouse until Winchester was laid out in 1810. David Crockett made his home near Bean between 1813 and 1817. By the time of the War of 1812, Franklin County had enough settlers to answer Andrew Jackson's call for volunteers to oppose the Creek uprising in Alabama.

Franklin County was primarily a farming region. Cotton was floated down the Elk River to New Orleans early in the county history, but like much of the midstate, land was better for corn, wheat, and livestock. With the advent of improved roads and turnpikes, wagon trains moved produce to Nashville and returned with supplies, although access to Huntsville in North Alabama was also easy.

In 1854, Vernon K. Stephenson transformed the county, when he built his Nashville and Chattanooga Railroad through Decherd, tunneling the Cumberland Plateau between Cowan and Sherwood and dipping into Alabama to reach his destination and join the Western and Atlantic into Georgia and the East Tennessee and Georgia to the northeast. Within four years, the Sewanee Mining Company built a line up the mountain from Cowan, and another was completed from Decherd to Fayetteville, later extended to Huntsville and Lewisburg.

Franklin County became a Confederate seedbed. Franklin County native Isham G. Harris, a secessionist, was elected governor in 1857, 1859, and 1861. Peter Turney, a future governor, recruited a regiment which mustered into the Confederate service before Tennessee held its plebiscite on secession. Turney circulated petitions to have Franklin County secede from Tennessee if the state did not leave the Union. In the statewide vote, Franklin County reported unanimous support for secession despite pockets of resistance.

Federal troops arrived in Franklin County in 1862, although Confederates reestablished control. After the Confederate defeat at Murfreesboro in January 1863, the Southern army retreated to Tullahoma, filling Franklin County with sick and wounded until July 1863, when it abandoned Middle Tennessee for Chattanooga, exiting along local roads. Thereafter Franklin County remained under Federal control, with the Nashville and Chattanooga Railroad serving as the primary supply line for operation against Chattanooga and Atlanta.

In the postwar years, most residents of Franklin County remained farmers, but agriculture made a slow recovery. In addition to farming, the county profited from extractive industries that exploited iron, coal, timber, and stone. The Nashville, Chattanooga, and St. Louis Railroad became the preferred passenger route between midwestern cities and economic development in Florida, spawning hotels and restaurants along its route. Resorts flourished at Winchester Springs and along the Cumberland Plateau. Franklin County also became known for its educational institutions, notably Mary Sharp College in Winchester, which had pioneered in antebellum collegiate education for women, and the University of the South at Sewanee. Other colleges included Winchester Normal and Terrill in Decherd.

In the 1870s, Franklin County experienced a period of agrarian unrest, which led to the organization of granges, or the Patrons of Husbandry. The eastern side of the county experienced labor troubles when state prisoners displaced local miners. Winchester became embroiled in the temperance controversy and surrendered its charter in order to close its saloons under the Four Mile Law, which forbade alcohol sales outside incorporated towns.

Agriculture eventually recovered, especially on farms established by Swiss-German immigrants around Belvidere; their round barns gave the area a European appearance. Early in the twentieth century, farmers began planting large fields of crimson clover for seed, giving a theme to a later celebration and ball. Nevertheless, agriculture shaped the county's twentieth century character less than the World War II development of Camp Forrest as an army training facility along the county's northern border. The installation brought thousands of military families to the area. In 1952, the deserted camp became home to Arnold Engineering Development Center (AEDC) for testing advanced aerospace technology for the Air Force.

AEDC's need for water led to the damming of Elk River to create Woods Reservoir. The Tennessee Valley Authority built Tims Ford Dam, producing lakefront properties, weekend boating, and a state park. Economically, the county moved from a dependence on extractive industries to a period characterized by small textile and garment mills, to its recent introduction of automotive parts and assembly plants. Although agricultural acreage has declined, many farms remain profitable, and the expansion of nurseries east of Winchester has suggested new uses for rich agricultural lands.

John Abernathy Smith, Loretto

SEE: ARNOLD ENGINEERING DEVELOPMENT CENTER; CONVICT LEASE WARS; CAMPBELL, FRANCIS; ELLIOTT, SARAH B.; HARRIS, ISHAM G.; MARY SHARP COLLEGE; MINING; NISSAN; RAILROAD, NASHVILLE AND CHATTANOOGA; SHORE, DINAH; ST. ANDREW'S-SEWANEE; TEMPLETON, JOHN M.; TIMS FORD STATE PARK; TURNEY, PETER; UNIVERSITY OF THE SOUTH

FRANKLIN, ISAAC (1789–1846), slavetrader and planter, was born in Sumner County, the son of a Revolutionary War soldier, who had received a military land warrant in Tennessee. Franklin served in the War of 1812, and at age 18, while working for his brother on a flatboat that ran from Gallatin to New Orleans, he conceived the idea of entering the slave trade. He formed a partnership with his nephew, John Armfield, to establish a slave trading business that soon came to be regarded as the largest in the South. The company of Armfield & Franklin gained a reputation among whites, and allegedly among slaves themselves, for honesty, humane treatment, and keeping slave families together. Although lucrative, slave trading was a business that southern society considered dishonorable. Franklin retired from the business in 1835, but not before it had made him a wealthy man.

Thereafter, Franklin pursued the occupation of planter. He owned hundreds of slaves, who worked six cotton plantations in Louisiana of approximately 8,700 acres, plus a 2,000-acre plantation, Fairvue, near Gallatin, where he raised tobacco, cattle, and thoroughbred horses. In 1839, at the age of 50, the bachelor Franklin was married to Adelicia Hayes, daughter of Oliver Bliss Hayes, a Nashville Presbyterian minister, lawyer, and noted businessman.

The couple lived at Fairvue and had four children, one of whom died at birth. After seven years of marriage, Franklin died while visiting their plantation in Louisiana. According to his wishes, the body was returned to Fairvue for burial. His remains were preserved in whiskey for the riverboat trip back to Tennessee. Six weeks later, two of his children, Victoria and Adelicia, also died.

Under the terms of Franklin's will, Adelicia Franklin inherited Fairvue with the stipulation that, upon her remarriage, the property should become Franklin Institute, a private school for his children, other relatives, and worthy poor children of the area. Adelicia Franklin and her new husband, Joseph Acklen, filed suit against the will. In 1852 the Louisiana Supreme Court overturned the will on the grounds that it established a perpetuity. Adelicia Hayes Franklin Acklen and her daughter Emma inherited all the Franklin holdings in Louisiana, shortly before Emma died of diphtheria, at age 11.

Mark Brown, Belmont Mansion

SEE: ACKLEN, ADELICIA; ARMFIELD, JOHN; FAIRVUE PLANTATION; SLAVERY

FRANKLIN MASONIC LODGE is a building of many firsts. Hiram Lodge No. 7, founded in Franklin in 1809, was first affiliated with the parent Lodge No. 55 in North Carolina. The local Lodge surrendered its North Carolina charter when the Grand Lodge of Tennessee was constituted in 1813, and received its present charter in 1815. In 1817 the Masons of Franklin organized the first legal lottery in Tennessee to fund the construction of a Masonic Hall. The three-story temple, completed in 1823, was the tallest building west of the Allegheny Mountains. Hiram Lodge No. 7 has met in the Masonic Hall since its completion, making it one of the oldest continuous lodges in the same location in the United States.

In addition to the temple's long Masonic history, it has been the site of many important religious, political, and social events. In 1830 James H. Otey, later the first Episcopal Bishop of Tennessee, organized St. Paul's, the state's first Episcopal Church, at the Masonic Hall. On December 7, 1830, noted religious reformer, Alexander Campbell preached in the hall and planted the seeds for the Church of Christ, which continued to meet on the site until the congregation completed the construction of a house of worship on Fourth Avenue in 1852. United States Commissioners John H. Eaton and John Coffee accompanied President Andrew Jackson to meet in council with the Chickasaw delegation in 1830, to negotiate the sale of Indian lands, marking the first time a U.S. President had personally participated in treaty negotiations. During the Civil War, Confederate spies climbed to the roof to observe troop movements at Fort Granger, a federal post across the river on Figuers's Bluff. After the Battle of Franklin on November 30, 1864, the hall served as a hospital for wounded Union soldiers.

The Masonic Hall is also home to Franklin Chapter No. 2, Royal Arch Masons; DePaynes Commandry No. 11, Knights Templar; and Franklin Chapter No. 449, Order of Eastern Star.

Rick Warwick, Franklin

SEE: CAMPBELL, ALEXANDER; EATON, JOHN H.; FRANKLIN, BATTLE OF; JACKSON, ANDREW; OTEY, JAMES H.

FRANKLIN, STATE OF. A short-lived attempt to create a new state in the trans-Appalachian settlement of present-day East Tennessee, the State of Franklin arose from the general unsettled state of national, regional, and local politics at the end of the Revolutionary War. Under the severely limited congressional revenue powers imposed by the Articles of Confederation, the best solution for funding the new national government in the 1780s was the cession of western lands by the individual states. Congress actively encouraged this process, anticipating substantial returns. North Carolina, however, had not agreed to such a step and instead reopened its western land office in 1783. Acting on the presumption that the Cherokees had forfeited their land claims due to their alliance with the British during the Revolution, the entire trans-Appalachian West, with only a few exceptions, was made available for purchase.

The provisions of the North Carolina land act of 1783 favored those with prior knowledge of its passage. These individuals, including many of the most prominent and influential members of the North Carolina legislature, quickly claimed over four million acres of western lands in what came to be called the "Great Land Grab" of 1783. Having thus secured title to most of the area that would eventually become Tennessee, these lawmakers now gave their support to the western land cession. In 1784 North Carolina passed an act to cede its western lands to Congress, with the stipulation that all land titles would remain valid.

The cession, coupled with the apparent congressional desire to create new states, provided the final justification among the western inhabitants for an independent statehood movement. Sentiment for such a movement had been growing among the western residents largely as a result of the distance between their settlements and the seat of government, which made it difficult for eastern legislators to understand the complexities of trans-Appalachian life and for settlers to obtain relief for their complaints. Under the leadership of Arthur Campbell of southwestern Virginia and others in the Holston River settlements, a meeting was arranged at Jonesborough in August 1784, where the decision for statehood was unanimous. Delegates were elected to attend a December convention to draft the constitution for a new government.

The land grab by the North Carolina legislature created so much resentment against the land speculators who controlled the body, that voters turned out the business element in the elections of 1784. The new legislature promptly repealed the act of cession, and the western statehood movement was now technically an act of rebellion.

The convention met as planned on December 14, 1784, and reaffirmed their support for an independent state to be known as Franklin. Delegates adopted the North Carolina constitution to serve as a temporary government, but made some alterations such as the reduction or abolition of property qualifications for elective office. A second convention met in November 1785 to adopt a permanent constitution. This document, sometimes called the "Holston Constitution," provided for a unicameral legislature with specific property, religious, and moral qualifications for its members; however, the temporary North Carolina constitution continued to serve the new state. At a third convention the following March 1786, John Sevier, a popular Revolutionary War hero and Indian fighter, was elected governor; a barter system for the payment of taxes was established; and four new counties were established.

By this time, the Franklin movement enjoyed less than unanimous support. Once again land speculators dominated the North Carolina legislature, and they were eager to regain control over Franklin in order to validate their land titles. They pursued a policy of encouraging dissension in the west through conciliatory overtures to the Franklinites, while simultaneously condemning the movement. The North Carolina legislature created additional counties, courts, and a militia brigade with John Sevier as the brigadier general.

Legislative overtures made little headway until August 1786, when John Tipton emerged as the leader of the anti-Franklin faction in Washington County. Conflict between the pro- and anti-Franklin groups intensified, and became a personal feud between Sevier and Tipton as the two vied for leadership. North Carolina capitalized on the dissension and undermined support for the Franklin movement by offering pardons and a remission for two years of back taxes.

The combination of inducements and strong opposition from Tipton produced a decline in support for the Franklin movement everywhere except in the area south of the French Broad River. There, the Franklin government's aggressive policy towards the Cherokees attracted widespread support from settlers vulnerable to Indian attacks. In June 1785 a token number of Cherokee chiefs signed the Dumplin Creek Treaty, which allowed settlement well to the south of the French Broad River and into an area set aside by North Carolina as a Cherokee reservation. In November of the same year, a larger Cherokee delegation met with American representatives at Hopewell in South Carolina and established a treaty line north of Greeneville, the capital of Franklin. The two conflicting treaties soon produced open warfare between the Franklinites and the Cherokees. Franklinites interpreted the Hopewell Treaty as evidence of lack of congressional interest in their defense and opened negotiations with the Spanish authorities to explore the possibility of annexation; but the talks came to nothing. By August 1786 the Cherokees had been defeated and forced to sign the Treaty of Coyatee, which allowed settlement as far south as the Little Tennessee River.

By 1788 the feud between Tipton and Sevier escalated to the point that the two sides engaged in a minor skirmish. Later that same year, Tipton arrested Sevier on a North Carolina warrant. Sevier made bail and a new governor wisely ignored the case.

By early 1789 the Franklin movement was all but over. North Carolina continued its policy of reconciliation by allowing the locally-popular Sevier to be seated in the legislature as the representative from Greene County; as a further gesture of goodwill he was appointed brigadier general of militia for Washington County. In the settlements south of the French Broad River, support for an independent state continued and settlers organized themselves into an association known as "Lesser Franklin." When no strong leader emerged to replace Sevier, this movement also faded away.

Michael Toomey, Knoxville College

SUGGESTED READING: Samuel C. Williams, *History of the Lost State of Franklin* (1924)

SEE: GOVERNMENT; GREENE COUNTY; JONESBOROUGH; SEVIER, JOHN; TIPTON, JOHN; TIPTON-HAYNES HISTORIC SITE; WASHINGTON COUNTY

FRATERNAL AND SOLVENT SAVINGS BANK AND TRUST COMPANY

FRATERNAL AND SOLVENT SAVINGS BANK AND TRUST COMPANY was created in 1927 by the merger of two black-owned and -operated Memphis banks which had been instrumental in launching and supporting African-American businesses in the 1910s and 1920s. The bank's eventual failure, due to risky investments and poor management, devastated the local African-American community, exerting an impact similar to that produced by the 1874 collapse of the Freedmen's Savings Bank.

In 1906 Robert Reed Church, Sr., established the Solvent Savings Bank and Trust Company, which catered to entrepreneurial businessmen. By 1920 it had become the nation's fourth largest African-American bank. The Fraternal Savings Bank and Trust Company opened in 1910 and successfully followed a similar course.

With a growing Memphis population and the positive World War I economy, both banks expanded rapidly and invested heavily in a variety of business endeavors. In the 1920s, like many other banks, Fraternal and Solvent found themselves deeply in debt. In an effort to resolve their dilemma, the two banks merged in October 1927. In December, Christmas Fund withdrawals depleted the bank's cash reserves, producing a run on the bank, and the closing of the institution due to bankruptcy. Investigators traced shortages of over $500,000 dollars to bank president A. F. Ward and five other officers. Twenty-eight thousand depositors lost nearly 90 percent of their savings, and numerous African-American businesses and organizations sustained severe losses. African-American banks in Memphis did not stabilize until the 1940s.

Teresa Biddle-Douglass, Middle Tennessee State University
SUGGESTED READING: Lester C. Lamon, *Black Tennesseans 1900–1930* (1977)

SEE: CHURCH, ROBERT R., SR; FREEDMEN'S SAVINGS BANK AND TRUST COMPANY; MEMPHIS

FRATERVILLE MINE DISASTER. The worst mine disaster in Tennessee history took place on May 19, 1902, at the Fraterville mine, near Coal Creek (now Lake City), Campbell County. At about 7:30 A.M., 184 men and boys entered the mine. Minutes later a horrendous methane gas and coal dust explosion erupted, sending debris and smoke belching from the ventilation shaft and the mouth of the mine. The heat and impact of the blast instantly killed many miners. Along the main entry, the force of the explosion splintered mine cars and timbers and dismembered the bodies of miners. Some victims, found in side passages off the main entry, showed no signs of trauma. They probably lived for a short time before suffocating from the buildup of toxic gases and lack of oxygen. Others, alive but unable to escape toward the entrance, moved still deeper into the mine where they constructed barricades in a futile attempt to close out deadly gases and stifling heat. Twenty-six men were found barricaded in one side passage, some still alive as late as 2:30 in the afternoon as evi-

denced by notes found with their bodies. "It is 25 minutes after two," noted one miner. "There is a few of us alive yet. Oh God, for one more breath. Ellen remember me as long as you live. Good Bye Darling."

Rescue efforts commenced immediately, but the first party had to turn back when they encountered the first dead miner and bad air. By late afternoon, the gas had been vented to the point that rescue efforts could continue. Shift after shift of volunteers began inching their way along the partially caved-in main entry and side passages. To do this, they had to construct a venting system of bratticing, a conduit made of cloth fabric impregnated with creosote, to remove bad air. They searched one side passage after another, slowly retrieving bodies, some of which were torn apart and mutilated beyond recognition. The last body was carried from the mine four days after the ordeal begun.

At the mine entrance, a crowd of some 2,000 relatives, friends, neighbors, nearby miners, and spectators anxiously awaited word of the fate of the unaccounted-for miners. A temporary morgue was established at the Farmers Supply Company in Coal Creek. At the Leach Cemetery in Anderson County, 87 of the Fraterville miners were buried in a circle around a large monument in their honor.

The precise cause of the explosion was never determined, or never disclosed. The mine's ventilation furnace had been shut down all weekend, which could account for the accumulation of methane gas. Methane is an extremely explosive gas that can build up in poorly ventilated coal mines. When the gas exploded, probably kindled by the open flames of the miners' lamps, coal dust was blown into the air and subsequently ignited, adding even more force to the explosion.

The mine disaster devastated the small town of Fraterville, leaving both broken homes and a broken community. Only three adult male residents remained in Fraterville after the explosion. Many women lost every male member of their families, including their husbands, fathers, brothers, and sons. Unfortunately, few lessons were taken from the Fraterville tragedy; mine disasters did not end in the Southern Appalachian coal fields. From 1902 to 1927, according to the research of historian Ronald D. Eller, over 2,400 Appalachian workers died in mine explosions, with three of these disasters happening in Tennessee at Briceville (1911), Catoosa (1917), and Rockwood (1926).

Allen R. Coggins, Knoxville
SEE: CAMPBELL COUNTY; DISASTERS; LABOR

FRAZIER, JAMES BERIAH (1856–1937), Governor, was born at Pikeville in Bledsoe County, the son of Thomas Neil and Margaret M. Frazier. His great grandfather, Samuel Frazier, and grandfather, Abner

Frazier, fought at the Battle of King's Mountain during the American Revolution. His father served as circuit judge for Rutherford and Davidson counties. Frazier received his early education in the common schools of these counties and attended Franklin College near Nashville. He graduated from the University of Tennessee in 1878. During the next years, he taught school and also read law in preparation for admission to the bar in 1880. In January 1883 he married Louise Douglas Keith, daughter of Colonel Alexander Keith and Sarah Anne Foree Keith of Athens, Tennessee. Following his admission to the bar, Frazier practiced law in Chattanooga with the firm of DeWitt, Shepherd and Frazier.

Frazier was an active Democrat. His attractive personality and persuasive oratory paved the way for his political career. In 1900 he was elector at large for the Democratic presidential ticket headed by William Jennings Bryan. In 1902 he was elected governor of the state by a large majority; in 1904 he was reelected to a second term. His administration was noted for its rigid economy and the significant reduction of the state debt. Frazier supported state funding for public education, especially for the rural school systems. He sponsored legislation for coal mine safety regulation. A strong supporter of temperance legislation, he backed measures to control the sale of alcoholic beverages.

Frazier did not complete his second term as governor, but instead was elected to fill the unexpired term of William B. Bate in the U.S. Senate, where he served from 1905 to 1911. During his Senate tenure, Frazier opposed the Republican-sponsored high protective tariff, favored federal support for highway construction, and supported the adoption of a federal income tax. As the end of his term, he was not reelected by the Tennessee General Assembly.

Frazier retired to private life in Chattanooga and resumed his law practice. As an active member of the Masonic Order, Knights of Pythias, and the Methodist Episcopal Church South, his outstanding forensic skills were much in demand as a guest speaker. He died at Chattanooga on March 28, 1937.

John H. Thweatt, Tennessee State Library and Archives
SEE: BLEDSOE COUNTY; EDUCATION; TEMPERANCE MOVEMENT

FREE HILL is an African-American community established in the upper Cumberland before the Civil War. It is located northeast of Celina, Tennessee, in a remote section of Clay County, bordering Kentucky. The original inhabitants were the freed slaves of Virginia Hill, the daughter of a wealthy North Carolina planter. Hill purchased 2,000 acres of isolated and hilly land in what, at that time, was Overton County. She then freed the slaves, turned the property over to them, and left the area. Folklore suggests that among the blacks were her mulatto children (Rube, Josh, Betty, and Marie).

Free Hill refers to the surname of the original residents as well as their legal status. Thus, the community's name distinguished them from the slaves of owners with the same surname. The community conferred some degree of freedom on its residents and afforded protection for runaway slaves and black outlaws reaching the isolated region. The name also described the region's remote and hilly physical geography, which provided a haven for antebellum runaway slaves and post-Civil War freedmen.

Free Hill stands as a testament to the resolve of African Americans to retain their socio-cultural distinctiveness and promote self-help in an atmosphere of segregation and discrimination. During its heyday, Free Hill contained two grocery stores, three clubs, two eateries, two churches, a school, skilled artisans, and 300 residents. Although a small, close-knit contingent remains in the black settlement, the community has declined since the 1960s. A substantial number of residents deserted farming and moved to more prosperous areas for economic gain. In September 1993 the State of Tennessee placed a historical marker on Highway 53, identifying the entrance to this African-American community and commemorating its uniqueness. Free Hill's historic Rosenwald school was listed in the National Register of Historic Places in 1996. Folklorists also have conducted several research projects at Free Hill, documenting the community's significant place within the folk life of the Upper Cumberland.

Wali R. Kharif, Tennessee Technological University
SEE: CLAY COUNTY; JULIUS ROSENWALD FUND

FREE WILL BAPTISTS, NATIONAL ASSOCIA-TION. The National Association of Free Will Baptists, an organization of evangelical churches, has maintained its headquarters in Nashville since its formation in 1935. A derivative of Arminian or "general" Baptists, the denomination arose in the United States in the early eighteenth century when members of the prevalent "Regular" Baptists groups dissented over the issue of predestination. Rejecting the Calvinistic doctrine and believing that man has free will to accept or reject Christ, these individuals became known as "free will" Baptists. Many "free will" groups sprouted up independently of one another across the country, but significant movements developed in New England and the South around preachers Benjamin Randall and Paul Palmer. In the early twentieth century, after many followers had joined the Northern Baptist Convention, remnants of the Randall and Palmer lines eventually organized into two independent fellowships—the midwestern General Cooperative Association and the southeastern General

Conference. In 1935 these two organizations met at Cofer's Chapel in Nashville and merged to form the National Association of Free Will Baptists (NAFWB), which currently has a membership of nearly 2,500 churches and 25,000 individuals.

At its initial meeting, the National Association adopted a treatise of traditional Free Will doctrine that has remained the foundation of the organization's principal beliefs and objectives. In addition to general atonement, essential elements of the denomination's fundamentalist doctrine include the Trinity, Christ's second coming, the Lord's Supper, baptism by immersion, footwashing, sanctification, and the Bible as an inerrant authority.

Education, publications, and mission work are among the NAFWB's primary activities. Immediately after its inception, the organization made plans to establish an educational institution that reflected the denomination's concerns, and in 1942 the Free Will Baptist Bible College opened its doors in Nashville. The college offers both Associate and Bachelor degrees and emphasizes preparation for the ministry.

Closely related to its educational goals are the association's publication endeavors. NAFWB owns and operates Randall House Publications, which publishes *Contact*, the association's monthly magazine, as well as Sunday School and training literature. The NAFWB also maintains a strong missions program both nationally and abroad, and its Woman's National Auxiliary, established in 1936, actively supports this work and a variety of other benevolent causes.

Free Will Baptist organizations also exist at the regional, state, and local levels. Many of these fellowships were established long before the formation of the National Association and have a rich history of their own. The oldest Tennessee organization is the Cumberland Association, created in Middle Tennessee in 1842. The Toe River Association, a regional alliance that served churches from areas in Tennessee, North Carolina, and Virginia, originated in 1850, but in 1872 East Tennessee churches separated from the group to form the Union Association. Finally, Tennessee Free Will Baptists established a state association in 1938. Not all Free Will Baptist churches participate in the various levels of affiliation. In spite of its complex organizational structure, the denomination emphasizes the autonomy of the local church and considers each the highest authority for its congregation.

Teresa Biddle-Douglass, Middle Tennessee State University
SUGGESTED READINGS: Robert E. Picirilli, *The History of Tennessee Free Will Baptists* (1976); Melvin Worthington, *The Fifty-Year Record of the National Association of Free Will Baptists, 1935–1985* (1988)
SEE: RELIGION

FREED, JULIUS (1835–1908) was an important post-Civil War German Jewish merchant in Trenton, Gibson County. A native of Prussia, Freed in 1854 immigrated to Columbus, Georgia, where he worked as a peddler. Three years later, Freed moved to Memphis and established a dry goods business. From 1860 to April 1861 he operated a small shop in Jackson. During the Civil War, he served in the Fifteenth Tennessee Infantry of the Army of Tennessee and was wounded in the battles at Perryville, Chickamauga, and during the Atlanta campaign. Captured during Hood's attack on Nashville in December 1864, Freed became a prisoner of war until his release in May 1865.

Freed promptly moved to Trenton, where he established a partnership with another German Jewish merchant, Julius Ebert. Ebert's and Freed's store on the town square met with success and after Ebert's death in 1878, Freed continued to operate the store as a very successful business. By 1893 the store was known as J. Freed & Son (later Sons). He invested in banking and real estate, and operated a cotton gin. The economic success brought political power. Freed was a city alderman during the 1880s and was placed on a city board to manage the new town waterworks in 1897. Julius Freed submerged enough of his Jewish identity to become part of the economic and political ruling class in Trenton. Yet, he remained proud of his ethnicity, and with his family, at home, maintained Jewish cultural traditions until his death.

In 1871 Freed married Henrietta Cohn and on Eaton Street, in 1871, he built her a new Victorian-styled house, which is listed in the National Register of Historic Places. A local group of historic preservationists is guiding its restoration. The Freeds' sons were important local bankers and politicians. The family made many civic contributions, including a fountain and ball park. One of its last acts of generosity was by Dr. Frederick Freed, who gave the city a unique and valuable set of Veilleuse-Theieres (night light teapots), and this collection, housed at City Hall, has become a city symbol for Trenton.

Carroll Van West, Middle Tennessee State University
SEE: GIBSON COUNTY; JEWS, URBAN TENNESSEE

FREED-HARDEMAN UNIVERSITY, named in honor of former presidents A. G. Freed and N. B. Hardeman, represents the culmination of a succession of private schools reaching back to 1869 in Henderson, Tennessee. It is affiliated with the Churches of Christ.

In 1907 its immediate forerunner, Georgie Robertson Christian College, closed for lack of funds because of a division in the supporting church. That same year Freed and Hardeman, both of whom were associated with the preceding institution (Freed as president and Hardeman as a student and afterward a teacher), were called upon by a group of local businessmen to head a school to be named the National Teachers' Normal and Business College, with Freed as president and Hardeman as vice president. In addition to their stature as educators, both were ministers of the Henderson Church of Christ and evangelists in the Churches of Christ.

Having assumed the mortgage on the school property, the two administrators in effect owned the institution. In 1919 they turned it over to a private board of trustees, who were members of the Churches of Christ. The trustees renamed the school Freed-Hardeman College, a name it retained until 1990. It operated as a junior college from 1925 until 1975, when it began offering courses at a more advanced level.

Both Freed and Hardeman left the school in 1923; W. Claude Hall became president. Two years later Hardeman returned as associate president along with Hall C. Calhoun. The following year Calhoun left, and the board appointed Hardeman to the presidency, an office he occupied until his retirement in 1950. He was succeeded by H. A. Dixon, who, following his death in 1969, was succeeded by E. Claude Gardner. In 1990 Gardner retired as president and was succeeded by Milton R. Sewell, with Gardner becoming chancellor and later president emeritus. All of these men were ministers of the Churches of Christ.

Throughout its history the school has grown steadily both in the size of its faculty and student body and in the breadth and vitality of its programs. In 1976 Freed-Hardeman began offering the bachelor's degree in a variety of fields; in 1989 it added graduate work in the areas of education and ministry. The following year, in conformity with its expanded endeavors, its name was changed to Freed-Hardeman University. President Gardner initiated these developments. In 1994 the institution added counseling and New Testament to its graduate curriculum.

Freed-Hardeman has traditionally sought to enhance in its students what it views as the elements of man's nature: the spiritual, intellectual, social, and physical. It has drawn strength from the labors of a corps of dedicated and revered veteran faculty, including, in addition to the administrators already named, such individuals as C. P. Roland (who in addition to his teaching, served for an extended period as dean and later as vice president), the brothers L. L. and E. D. Brigance, W. Claude Hall (who returned in 1934 and remained for the rest of his career), Mary Nelle Powers (daughter of N. B. Hardeman), J. R. Ensley, and Robert Witt. Roland held the longest tenure of service and provided the clearest illustration of the institution's extraordinary quality

of continuity; he joined the faculty in 1921 and retired from the staff on July 4, 1983, his ninetieth birthday.
Charles P. Roland, University of Kentucky
SEE: CHESTER COUNTY; CHURCHES OF CHRIST; EDUCATION, HIGHER

FREEDMEN'S BUREAU. Even before the Civil War ended, President Abraham Lincoln and Congress realized that the government must offer assistance to the newly emancipated slaves. The Bureau of Refugees, Freedmen, and Abandoned Lands, commonly known as the Freedmen's Bureau, attempted this task and functioned under the direction of the War Department. After much debate about the duties and scope of the agency, Congress passed a bill authorizing the creation of the Freedmen's Bureau on March 3, 1865, and President Lincoln signed the bill the same day. Initially, the bill specified that the Bureau would expire one year after the termination of the war. President Andrew Johnson, fearful of creating a dependent class of white and blacks, vetoed a bill to renew the Bureau in 1866. Congress overrode the veto, however, and prolonged its life until the summer of 1872.

President Lincoln was assassinated before he appointed a commissioner to direct the Bureau. Notified of Lincoln's choice for the post, President Johnson agreed to follow his predecessor's wish and tapped Major General Oliver Otis Howard. To aid Howard, ten assistant commissioners directed agency work at the state and local level.

Howard designated Brigadier General Clinton B. Fisk to serve as the first assistant commissioner of the Bureau branch of Tennessee, Kentucky, and Northern Alabama. By June 1866 Kentucky no longer fell under the same jurisdiction as Tennessee. Fisk arrived in Nashville in July 1865 and organized the state into three districts, Nashville, Memphis, and Chattanooga. Two years later, Pulaski and Knoxville emerged as sub-districts.

Fisk's zealous execution of duties incensed some Tennessee legislators, particularly his efforts to introduce black testimony in courts. Operating under the guidance of federal law, Fisk created Bureau courts to guarantee the freedmen civil equality. Outraged by this bold, independent action, the Tennessee General Assembly in January 1866 deliberately passed a bill permitting black testimony, thereby placing the freedmen under the authority of state courts.

Howard considered education a key to the future advancement of the ex-slaves, and the Bureau established a number of freedmen's schools. Attendance at the schools soared as freedmen of all ages flocked to cramped buildings to learn basic reading, writing, and mathematical skills. Violent acts, such as the burning of schools, and vicious threats against teachers and students flared after the Memphis riots of

May 1–3, 1866, and tested the dedication of the freedmen and their instructors. Courageous blacks continued to enroll, and the vast number of eager pupils required more teachers. In January 1866 Fisk organized a school in Nashville, assisted by the American Missionary Association and the Western Freedmen's Aid Commission. The next year, this school became Fisk University and offered a program to train black teachers for the freedmen's schools.

In addition to managing schools, the Bureau negotiated labor contracts between the ex-slaves and white employers and even furnished legal counsel. The Bureau also organized hospitals, orphanages, and elderly homes. Whites in Tennessee, particularly in the middle and western parts of the state, vigorously opposed the goals of the Bureau. White animus stemmed from a belief that the freedmen's schools functioned as incubators of Radical Republicanism. In some areas of the state, the Ku Klux Klan frightened black residents and galvanized the whites by publicizing the bureau's efforts to achieve black suffrage and involve the freedmen in politics.

Fisk's tenure ended on September 1, 1866, and General J. R. Lewis, who had fulfilled the duties of assistant commissioner in Middle Tennessee, held the post as an interim. After three months, Major General W. P. Carlin took the helm. By the time he accepted the office, the Bureau's primary responsibility involved schools for the freedmen; but when the state assumed the management of the black schools in February 1867, the activity of the Bureau diminished until it was gradually phased out by Brevet-Major L. N. Clark in 1869. The Freedmen's Bureau in Tennessee shepherded the state's blacks on the journey from slavery to freedom by providing education, lobbying for political equality, and meeting physical needs.

Kathleen R. Zebley, University of Tennessee, Knoxville
SUGGESTED READING: Weymouth T. Jordan, "The Freedmen's Bureau in Tennessee," East Tennessee Historical Society *Publications* 11(1939): 47–61; Paul D. Phillips, "Education of Blacks in Tennessee During Reconstruction, 1865–1870," *Tennessee Historical Quarterly* 46(1987): 98–109 and "White Reaction to the Freedmen's Bureau in Tennessee," *ibid.*, 25(1966): 50–62
SEE: FISK, CLINTON B.; FISK UNIVERSITY; JOHNSON, ANDREW; KU KLUX KLAN; MEMPHIS RACE RIOT OF 1866; RECONSTRUCTION

FREEDMEN'S SAVINGS BANK AND TRUST COMPANY.

A financial institution chartered by Congress in 1865 for the newly freed black population of former slave states, the Freedmen's Savings Bank was a key component of the African-American struggle for equality and independence during Reconstruction. A total of 33 branches were established throughout the South; Tennessee branches were in Nashville (1865), Memphis (1865), Chattanooga (1868), and Columbia (1870). Although the majority of directors and upper management was white, blacks held trustee, cashier, and other positions. The banks required only a small deposit and gave up to seven percent interest on savings, which permitted many poor black Tennesseans to save and gain financial footing. The Nashville branch generated the most capital, and by 1874 the Tennessee branches combined held over $155,000 in deposits.

In 1874 mismanagement and the financial panic of 1873–74 combined to close the Freedmen's Savings Bank. The depositors, most of whom were poor, received only a small percentage of their investment. Others lost substantial sums that brought about financial ruin. Various African-American organizations and benevolent societies that had had holdings in the banks also suffered. Many who experienced considerable losses rushed to place blame on the more visible local black bank leaders rather than white officials. As a result, confidence in black-operated institutions was severely damaged. White reaction was largely unsympathetic and newspapers such as the Memphis *Avalanche* ridiculed the banks. Black-operated financial institutions did not reappear in Tennessee until 1890.

Teresa Biddle-Douglass, Middle Tennessee State University
SEE: FREEDMEN'S BUREAU; RECONSTRUCTION

FRENCH LICK. Early trading at French Lick, or the Big Salt Springs on the Cumberland River, involved all of the players in the imperial struggle of the eighteenth century. A natural magnet for wild game, French Lick drew native hunters and French and English traders. The territory between the Ohio and Tennessee Rivers was a hunting ground for many tribes. The Shawnees occupied the area in the seventeenth century, but by 1700, the Cherokees and Chickasaws were driving the Shawnees north. Traders from New Orleans and from the Illinois country came in to offer manufactured goods for pelts. James Robertson, leader of the Nashville settlement, is the source for the story that, by 1710, Jean du Charleville from New Orleans had made a deserted Shawnee fort at the French Lick into a warehouse. Charleville was thus in the vanguard of trade and imperial ambitions. French administrators hoped to hold the interior of North America with a line of forts from the St. Lawrence to New Orleans, and, in conjunction with Indian alliances, to withstand the pressure of English settlement advancing from the East. By the 1760s, however, long hunters from the British colonies had begun to penetrate the area; land speculators and settlers followed. The pioneers with Robertson reportedly found the cabin of Illinois trader Timothy Demonbreun still housing buffalo tallow, when they arrived to claim land in 1779. These new settlers also traded in hides, until settlement produced marketable crops and ultimately made French Lick into a Nashville neighborhood, found today near the site of the Bicentennial Mall.

Anita S. Goodstein, University of the South
SEE: DEMONBREUN, TIMOTHY; EXPLORATIONS, EARLY; ROBERTSON, JAMES

FRENCH, LIZZIE CROZIER (1851–1926), organizer of the Knoxville Equal Suffrage Association, president of the Tennessee Equal Suffrage Association and the Tennessee Federation of Women's Clubs, and state chair of the National Woman's Party, was one of five daughters born to John H. Crozier and Mary Williams Crozier. A civic-minded Whig attorney, John H. Crozier represented Knox County in the Tennessee House (1837–1839) and served in the U.S. House of Representatives (1845–1849).

Lizzie Crozier was educated at the Convent of the Visitation in Georgetown, then at an Episcopal female institute in Columbia. In 1872 she married William Baxter French, a grandson of presidential aspirant Hugh Lawson White. Unfortunately her husband died 18 months later. She never remarried.

Eleven years after her husband's death, and with aid from sisters Lucy Graham Crozier and Mary Hume Crozier, French opened and directed the East Tennessee Female Institute. An enthusiast of education for women, in 1885, she founded Ossoli Circle, named for feminist and transcendentalist Margaret Fuller Ossoli. By 1896 her interests had spread to the needs of working women, leading her to establish the Woman's Educational and Industrial Union.

During the second decade of the twentieth century, the movement for woman suffrage in Tennessee developed into a statewide coalition. French worked diligently on behalf of woman suffrage, rejoicing when Tennessee became the pivotal state in ratification of the Nineteenth Amendment. She ran unsuccessfully for city council in 1923.

Lizzie Crozier French became ill while attending the Baltimore Conference of the National Woman's party and died on May 14, 1926.

Jayne Crumpler DeFiore, University of Tennessee, Knoxville
SEE: OSSOLI CIRCLE; WOMAN SUFFRAGE MOVEMENT

FRENCH, LUCY VIRGINIA (1825–1881), poet and novelist, was born in Accomac County, Virginia, to a family of wealth and culture. Her parents were Mease W. Smith, an educator and lawyer, and Elizabeth Parker Smith, daughter of a wealthy merchant. She graduated with high honors from Mrs. Hannah's School, a private academy in Washington, Pennsylvania. After her mother's death and her father's remarriage, she and her sister relocated to Memphis, Tennessee, where they both became teachers. She also began writing for the Louisville *Journal* under

the pen name "L'Inconnue." In 1852 she became editor of the *Southern Ladies Book*. After her 1853 marriage to Colonel John Hopkins French of McMinnville, Tennessee, she edited a number of newspapers and magazines, including the *Southern Homestead*, the *Rural Sun*, the *Sunny South*, the *Crusader*, the *Ladies Home*, and the *Southern Literary Messenger*. She also published poetry, a five-act tragedy (*Istalilxo: The Lady of Tula*, 1856), and two novels (*My Roses*, 1872, and *Darlingtonia*, 1879). French's poetry is widely considered her best work; foremost among these pieces are "Wind Whispers," "Tecumseh's Foot," and "The Great River." On March 31, 1881, she died at "Forest Home," her McMinnville home, where she had spent her entire married life. French also kept diaries during the Civil War (now housed at the Tennessee State Library and Archives), which give detailed accounts of her family's wartime experiences, both at the plantation in McMinnville and at nearby Beersheba Springs, where they resided during 1863 and 1864.

Cathi Carmack, Tennessee State Library and Archives
SEE: LITERATURE; WARREN COUNTY

FRIST FOUNDATION, an independent philanthropic organization, was established in Nashville in 1982 as the HCA Foundation by the Hospital Corporation of America. In April 1997 the foundation changed its name to the Frist Foundation in honor of its founding directors, Thomas F. Frist, Sr., M.D., and Thomas F. Frist, Jr., M.D., who also founded HCA. In 1997 the Frist Foundation board consisted of Thomas F. Frist, Jr., chairman, Kenneth Roberts, president, Jack O. Bovender, Jr., Robert C. Crosby, Helen K. Cummings, Justice Frank F. Drowota III, and Charles J. Kane.

When first established under executive director Ida F. Cooney (1982–1991), the HCA Foundation focused on Nashville and other communities in the United States and abroad served by HCA-affiliated hospitals. The foundation became legally independent of HCA in 1985, but kept the HCA name until 1997. Following Cooney's retirement in 1991, Kenneth L. Roberts became president and chief executive officer.

The Frist Foundation emphasizes its support in four areas: arts and culture, civil and community affairs, education, and health and human services. Among the Frist Foundation's major projects are Nashville's Agenda, a citizen-based project that sets goals for the city's future, and co-founding of the Center for Nonprofit Management. The foundation has especially encouraged nonprofits' improvements in technology, strategic planning, and agency collaborations. The foundation has also provided the lead in the mid-1990s to develop an arts center of regional significance in Nashville, with the historic U.S. Post Office as the preferred site.

Today, the Frist Foundation focuses on serving the Nashville area as Middle Tennessee's largest foundation. In late 1996 the Foundation had assets of $193 million and made $4.4 million in grants in addition to reserving $6 million for a possible grant to establish a visual arts center in Nashville. From 1982 to 1997, the foundation awarded more than $35 million in grants.

Ann Toplovich, Tennessee Historical Society

SEE: COLUMBIA/HCA HEALTHCARE CORPORATION

FRIST, WILLIAM H. (1952-), nationally recognized heart surgeon and U.S. Senator, was born and raised in Nashville, a fourth-generation Tennessean. In 1974 Bill Frist took his undergraduate degree from Princeton University, where he was named a Wilson Scholar and received the Harold Dodds Award in recognition of his leadership abilities. Frist next attended Harvard Medical School, where he graduated with honors in 1978. After seven years of surgical training at Massachusetts General Hospital and the Stanford University Medical Center, Frist returned to Nashville to accept a faculty position at Vanderbilt University Medical Center. There, in 1986, he founded the university's innovative Multi-Organ Transplant Center, which quickly gained an international reputation in the field of organ transplant. As director of the Heart and Heart-Lung Transplantation program, he conducted over 200 heart and lung transplant operations. He is credited with the first pediatric heart transplant and first lung transplant in Tennessee. During his medical career, Frist has written a book, *Transplant* (1989), which explored the medical and ethical issues of organ transplantation, as well as more than 100 articles, chapters, and abstracts on medical research.

Like other members of his family, Frist is a stockholder in the Nashville-based Columbia/HCA Healthcare Corporation, which his father, Thomas Frist, Sr., helped to establish in 1968. In 1992 he received the Distinguished Service Award from the Tennessee Medical Association for his successful campaign to return the organ donation card to the back of Tennessee driver licenses. In that same year, Governor Ned Ray McWherter appointed Frist chair of the Tennessee Task Force on Medicaid.

Frist entered Tennessee politics with a decisive victory, 834,226 to 623,164 votes, over incumbent U.S. Senator James Sasser in the 1994 general election. A member of the Republican party, Frist ran on a conservative platform supporting a balanced budget, fewer government regulations, reduced federal spending, and term limits. Frist has promised to serve no more than two terms in the Senate. His upset victory produced the first practicing physician to be elected to the U.S. Senate since 1928.

Issues of health and medicine have been important concerns in Frist's first term of office. Party leaders appointed Frist to lead the Senate Republican Medicare Working Group. In the 104th Congress, 1995–1997, Frist introduced bills to establish Medical Savings Accounts and to reform the Food and Drug Administration. He sits on five key Senate committees: Budget, Commerce, Science and Transportation, Labor and Human Resources, Foreign Relations, and Small Business. On the Senate Budget Committee, Frist has supported efforts to produce a balanced federal budget and reduced federal expenditures. On the one-year anniversary of his election, Frist introduced the Citizen Congress Act, aimed at eliminating the most grievous examples of Congressional perks and privileges, including free use of military aircraft. He chairs the Senate's Subcommittee on Science, Technology and Space and its Subcommittee on Public Health and Safety. He also serves on the board of the Smithsonian Institution.

Frist lives in Nashville with his wife Karyn and three sons, Harrison, Jonathan, and Bryan.

Carroll Van West, Middle Tennessee State University

SEE: COLUMBIA/HCA HEALTHCARE CORPORATION; MEDICINE; SASSER, JAMES R.

FRONTIER STATIONS. On the Tennessee frontier before 1796, the terms "station" and "fort" were used interchangeably to mean a structure, or adjacent structures, that could temporarily house more than one family and provide protection from Native American attacks. The traditional meaning of "fort" might have been more appropriate if the frontiersmen had used the word to mean a work or works designed, constructed, and garrisoned by military personnel. Such was not the case, however.

A station or fort could be a single strong house in a central location in which persons from neighboring houses gathered for security. The terms were applied, also, to houses enclosed or connected by stockading that surrounded an interior open space. At times "fort" was used to emphasize that additional security was provided by stockading, blockhouses, and related, but improvised, defensive works. At other times, the term referred to a frontier house with no special fortification, but at which as few as two or three militiamen were on duty to help defend it from attackers. Probably the most appropriate use of the word "fort" was to dignify the modest military installations of the early period: Fort Grainger at the mouth of the Little Tennessee River, Fort Blount at the crossing of the Cumberland near Gainesboro, the blockhouse at Southwest Point near Kingston, and the post at Tellico Blockhouse.

Early stations, or forts, usually took the name of the owner-occupant of the principal or central house. Stations housed as many as 30 or 40 people, but on

Frontier stations on the Cumberland, 1783.

April 11, 1793, when settlers believed Indian attacks were imminent, 280 men, women, and children gathered in small huts at John Craig's station on Nine Mile Creek in an area that later became Blount County. Wherever large numbers crowded a station, living conditions soon became unbearable. In addition to providing shelter for people, stockaded stations sometimes enclosed open space large enough for the temporary accommodation of horses and cattle. Both Kasper Mansker's and Isaac Bledsoe's were examples of such capacity. Fortunately for the settlers, attacks were usually short-lived, and often the rush to gather for protection was the result of a false alarm.

The original Cumberland settlers planned eight stations in advance of their arrival, but probably only four had been constructed by 1780. The remaining four were completed within the next few years, although one of them, Asher's, was never permanently occupied. In the case of the Cumberland Association of 1780–83, stations served as precincts or sub-seats of government, where voters elected representatives to the ruling council of government, the court of triers. Not all stations were the result of such coordinated and advanced planning. In fact, stations usually developed quite informally as settlers acquired contiguous land and designated one loca-

tion as a place of refuge and security. In this sense, a station served as the center of the settlement community and could develop further. James White lived in White's Fort, when in 1792 he laid out 64 town lots on his adjacent land in what would become the city of Knoxville.

From 1780 to 1795, stockaded stations or forts at Nashborough, Kilgore's, Mansker's and Isaac Bledsoe's figured prominently in the defense of the Cumberland region. Similar installations at Fort Watauga and Fort Patrick Henry on the Long Island of the Holston had stood effectively against sizable assaults in the Watauga country from 1772 through 1776. Built in 1785, James Houston's fort on Little Nine Mile Creek in Blount County was a bastion for local defenses until the end of the Indian wars. But not all stations and forts were defensible strongholds. Zeigler's station, built in Sumner County circa 1790, was a huddle of three or four family cabins with no stockading. In a 1791 attack, four defenders were killed and one burned to death, four were wounded but escaped, three escaped unhurt, and 13 women and children were taken prisoner.

Once established, stations became landmarks along the frontier trails and roads. As identifiable overnight stops, they provided food and sleeping space to passing travelers.

Engraved shell gorget depicting two "Bird Men." This Late Mississippian marine shell measures 11.5 centimeters (4½ inches) in diameter and was excavated from the Hixon Site in Hamilton County. (Courtesy of Frank H. McClung Museum, University of Tennessee, Knoxville. Photograph by W. Miles Wright.)

James Robertson portrait attributed to Henry Benbridge. (Courtesy of Tennessee State Museum)

"Westward the Course of Empire Takes Its Way," mural by Emanuel Leutze, 1862, in the U.S. Capitol. (Courtesy of Architect of the Capitol)

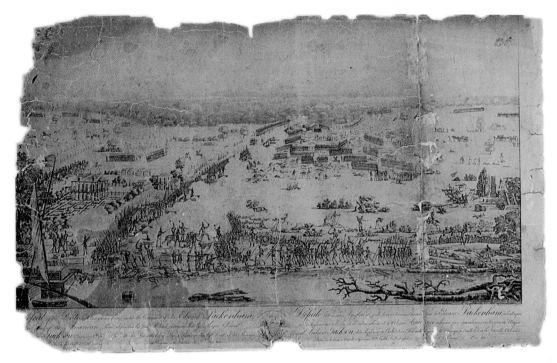

Sir Edward Packenham surrenders to General
Jackson's forces after the Battle of New Orleans,
January 1815. (Tennessee Historical Society
Collections, Tennessee State Library and Archives.
Drawing by Jean Hyacinthe Laclotte, 1815.)

Chief John Ross. (From McKenney and Hall,
History of the Indian Tribes of North America, 1836.
TSLA staff photograph by Karina McDaniel.)

[RIGHT] General Andrew Jackson, portrait by
Ralph E. W. Earl. (Courtesy of Tennessee State
Museum)

Nancy Ward gravesite in Polk County. (Courtesy of State of Tennessee Photographic Services)

Battle of Buena Vista during the Mexican War. (From Frost, *History of Mexico and the Mexican War*, 1848. TSLA staff photograph by Karina McDaniel.)

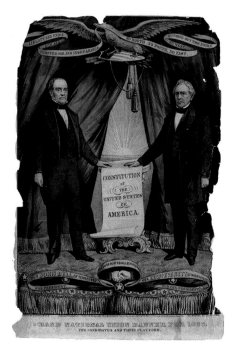

Constitutional Union Party candidates John Bell and Edward Everett, 1860. (Courtesy of Tennessee State Library and Archives. Engraving by Currrier and Ives.)

[BELOW] Slaves "sold to Tennessee" from Augusta County, Virginia. (Courtesy of Abby Aldrich Rockefeller Folk Art Collection, Rockefeller Gallery, Colonial Williamsburg Foundation)

Capture of Fort Donelson. (Courtesy of Tennessee State Library and Archives. Engraved after a painting by Chappel.)

Battle of Pittsburg Landing, also known as Shiloh, 1862. (Courtesy of Tennessee State Library and Archives. Engraving by Currier and Ives. TSLA staff photograph by Karina McDaniel.)

"Hoe in Hand," by Edwin M. Gardner, 1903. (Courtesy of Watkins Institute, College of Art and Design)

Arrest of yellow fever refugees near Memphis, 1879. (Courtesy of Tennessee State Library and Archives)

"Rafting on the Cumberland," by William Gilbert Gaul, undated. (Courtesy of Tennessee State Museum)

"Noah's Ark," by Aaron Douglas, 1944. (Courtesy of Carl Van Vechten Fine Arts Gallery, Fisk University)

Meharry Medical College graduate, circa 1915. (Courtesy of Nashville Room, Metropolitan Public Library. Copy photograph by June Dorman.)

Tennessee Centennial Exposition, 1897. The Rialto at night. (Courtesy of Tennessee State Library and Archives)

Fall Creek Falls State Resort Park, Bledsoe and Van Buren counties. (Courtesy of State of Tennessee Photographic Services)

Assembly line at the Saturn plant, Spring Hill, circa 1996. (Courtesy of State of Tennessee Photographic Services)

The Walking Horse National Celebration draws worldwide attention. (Courtesy of State of Tennessee Photographic Services)

Vice President of the United States Albert Gore, Jr. (Photograph by Tipper Gore)

Walter T. Durham, Gallatin
SEE: BLEDSOE, ISAAC; FORT BLOUNT; FORT JAMES WHITE;
FORT PATRICK HENRY; FORT SOUTHWEST POINT; FORT
WATAUGA; MANSKER, KASPER; SWAGGERTY BLOCKHOUSE;
TELLICO BLOCKHOUSE

FROZEN HEAD STATE NATURAL AREA, located in Morgan County, is one of Tennessee's largest state parks, with over 11,000 acres of beautiful, rugged land. Surrounded by the environmental scars of coal mining, Frozen Head represents the last major property of the Cumberland Mountains that is protected from surface mining. Its history began in 1893, when the state acquired over 11,000 acres for the construction of a remote prison, named Brushy Mountain State Prison, where inmates would mine coal. Coal mining, in fact, continued at Brushy Mountain until 1966. Most of the forested land was set aside later as a state forest, called the Morgan County State Forest, that was managed for hardwood timber, but few trees were ever taken. In the 1930s the Civilian Conservation Corps (CCC) located a camp at the forest, where the men constructed roads, miles of trails, and a bridge. In 1971 the Division of State Parks improved the old CCC roads and built visitor facilities. Three years later, in 1974, the Tennessee General Assembly designated the state forest a Class I Natural Area.

The park is centered around Frozen Head Mountain (elevation 3,324 ft.), which is the second highest mountain between the Great Smokies and the Black Hills of the Dakotas. The area is also noted for its rich array of wildflowers. Hiking is the primary recreational activity.
Carroll Van West, Middle Tennessee State University
SEE: CIVILIAN CONSERVATION CORPS; CONSERVATION;
MINING; MORGAN COUNTY; TENNESSEE PRISON SYSTEM

THE FUGITIVES, a group of influential early twentieth century poets and writers, date to 1914, when John Crowe Ransom and Walter Clyde Curry, both of whom taught English at Vanderbilt University, began meeting informally with a group of their undergraduates to discuss poetry and ideas. They frequently gathered at the apartment of a local eccentric named Sidney M. Hirsch, who presided over the assembly from his chaise lounge. These early, relaxed conversations gradually evolved into the regular meetings of the Fugitive poets that began a few years later.

American entry into World War I temporarily dispersed the group, several of whom enlisted in the military, but by 1920, the principals had reconvened at Vanderbilt. In addition to Ransom, Curry, and Hirsch, the original "Fugitives" included Donald Davidson, William Yandell Elliott, Stanley Johnson, and Alec B. Stevenson. After the war, a number of younger undergraduates and poets from outside the Fugitive circle also began to attend meetings. Among

their number were Merrill Moore, Allen Tate, Jesse Wills, and subsequently Alfred Starr and Robert Penn Warren. When she won the Nashville Poetry Prize in 1924, which the Fugitives sponsored, Laura Riding Gottschalk, then the wife of a professor of history at the University of Louisville, became an honorary member of the group.

By the autumn of 1921, the group was meeting fortnightly at the home of James M. Frank, a Nashville businessman and the brother-in-law of Sidney Hirsch. These meetings had no prescribed organization. Participants merely read their poems in turn, always providing copies for the audience. An intense and relentless critical discussion followed each of the presentations. No aspect of a poem escaped scrutiny. Exquisite or daring poems often excited the greatest controversy, while mediocre or conventional poems did not evoke much comment. "In its cumulative effect," Davidson recalled, "this severe discipline made us self-conscious craftsmen, abhorring looseness of expression, perfectly aware that a somewhat cold-blooded process of revision, after the first ardor of creation had subsided, would do no harm to art."[1]

At Hirsch's suggestion, the group resolved to publish a magazine of verse. Having already accumulated a substantial body of manuscripts, it remained only for them to choose the poems that would comprise the first issue. They did so by secret ballot, without designating anyone to assume editorial responsibilities. Davidson recorded the outcome of the first vote on the back of a letter from Vanderbilt Chancellor James H. Kirkland informing him that no university apartments were available.

The recommendation of a title for the magazine, and hence of a name for the group itself, came from Alec Stevenson. No one was fully certain about the meaning of *The Fugitive* or the rationale for selecting it. In his memoir about the group, Tate explained that "a Fugitive was quite simply a Poet: the Wanderer, or even the Wander Jew, the Outcast, the man who carries the secret wisdom around the world."[2]

The inaugural number of *The Fugitive* appeared in April 1922. The journal continued for more than three years, until the group, still lacking a full-time editor to perform administrative duties, suspended publication in December 1925. Unlike numerous other "little magazines" that emerged and vanished during the 1920s, *The Fugitive* did not suffer from a scarcity of funds. An annual subscription rate of one dollar and the patronage of the Associated Retailers of Nashville kept the magazine solvent throughout its brief existence.

Much of the poetry to appear in the pages of *The Fugitive* was tentative and experimental. With the exception of Ransom, who had published a slender volume entitled *Poems About God* in 1919, the rest of the Fugitives were apprentices at their craft. Yet they instinctively rejected the sentimentalism of romantic poetry and consciously embraced the formalism of traditional poetry. Preferring adaptations of traditional poetic forms to rash and careless innovation, they also questioned the fundamental tenets of modernist poetry. Although they did not categorically repudiate novelty, the Fugitives insisted that all poetic experimentation must stand up to the most demanding critiques and the most meticulous judgments.

The Fugitive poets may be unique in the annals of American literary history. With the partial exception of the New England Transcendentalists, there has never been another coterie of writers who, like the Fugitives, shared so many assumptions about nature, society, humanity, and God. Nowhere has there been a group so united in its singular devotion to poetry as were the Fugitives between approximately 1920 and 1928. Davidson portrayed this common attachment metaphorically as the "cousinship of poetry." He wrote of the Fugitives that "the pursuit of poetry as an art was the conclusion of the whole matter of living, learning, and being. It subsumed everything, but it was also as natural and reasonable an act as conversation on the front porch."[3]

The Fugitive movement effectively came to an end with the publication of the *Fugitive Anthology* in 1928. As early as 1925, some of the Fugitives had already sensed new concerns entering into their discussion, which had hitherto been focused exclusively on poetry and literary criticism. Although poetry still dominated their conversations, Ransom, Davidson, Tate, Warren, and others now began to talk and correspond about the South and to express their growing opposition to the assumptions and values that directed American political, social, economic, and cultural life. They sought to produce a manifesto in which to set forth Southern Agrarianism as a moral alternative to the "American industrial ideal," which in their conception amounted to a national myth of innocence, omnipotence, and invincibility.

I'll Take My Stand: The South and the Agrarian Tradition, which appeared in 1930, was the result of their efforts. In *I'll Take My Stand*, and in dozens of essays written during the next decade, the Fugitive-Agrarians exposed the reality of defeat and tragedy amid the growing conviction of purity and righteousness that characterized America during the 1920s. For Ransom, Davidson, Tate, Warren, and a new cadre of allies and friends, the defense of poetry had, temporarily at least, become inseparable from the defense of the South.

Mark G. Malvasi, Randolph-Macon College

CITATIONS:

(1) Donald Davidson, *Southern Writers in the Modern World* (1958), 22.

(2) Allen Tate, *Memoirs and Opinions, 1928–1974* (Chicago, 1975), 29.

(3) Davidson, *Southern Writers*, 8.

SUGGESTED READINGS: John M. Bradbury, *The Fugitives: A Critical Account* (1958); Louise Cowan, *The Fugitive Group: A Literary History* (1959); Mark G. Malvasi, *The Unregenerated South: The Agrarian Thought of John Crowe Ransom, Allen Tate, and Donald Davidson* (1997); Louis D. Rubin, Jr., *The Wary Fugitives: Four Poets and the South* (1978)

SEE: AGRARIANS; DAVIDSON, DONALD; RANSOM, JOHN C.; TATE, ALLEN; VANDERBILT UNIVERSITY; WARREN, ROBERT P.

FURNITURE AND CABINETMAKERS, NINETEENTH CENTURY. Tennessee furniture has been an overlooked and forgotten regional treasure. The simple and straight forward functional pieces produced by Tennessee craftsmen before 1850 reflect an era of outstanding craftsmanship. The furniture of this period exhibits dignity and worth of material objects from everyday life.

Early furniture-making was not limited to cabinetmakers in major settlements like Greeneville, Knoxville, Memphis, and Nashville. Many craftsmen lived in rural areas and combined their craft with farming and carpentry. Other craftsmen—turners, joiners, chairmakers, carpenters, upholsterers—produced furniture for Tennessee homes. For cabinetmakers and related craftsmen, the growing towns offered more opportunities for successful businesses.

Nineteenth century craftsmen had to be versatile in order to survive, prosper, and satisfy the needs of their community. Rural and urban cabinetmakers served as coffinmakers, which established them in the undertaking business. These craftsmen adapted their skills to the needs of their patrons.

The 1820 Manufacturers' Census from East and Middle Tennessee counties contains important information about cabinetmakers. Craftsmen listed information about the materials used, the quantity and cost of materials, and the names and pieces of finished products. Gross production ranged from less than $100 annually to as much as $6,000. The average shop operated with no more than three craftsmen, though one Nashville cabinetmaker employed five men and nine boys. The apprenticeship system, in which boys in their early teens were bound to craftsmen by the quarterly court or by parental consent, provided necessary help in the cabinetshops. The wide variety of furniture forms mentioned in the 1820 Census included chests, chairs, cupboards, tables, dining tables, clock cases, sideboards, desks, secretaries, bedsteads, presses, bookcases, and candlesticks. In one year, James Bray, a Knoxville cabinetmaker, and the four craftsmen in his shop produced 60 pieces, ranging from square tables (sold for $3 each) to secretaries and cherry presses (sold at $50 each).

Apart from the 1820 Census, the most important estate inventory is that of cabinetmaker Daniel McBean. His inventory and sale accounts provide a vivid picture of a Nashville shop in 1815. Forty-three furniture items, made in advance for sale, were on hand at the time of his death. The items, ranging from cradles to dining tables to bookcases and sideboards, were sold by the administrator of McBean's estate.

Tennessee furniture reflects the heritage of the westward migration and the individualism of the early pioneers. While isolated from the eastern mainstream influences, frontier craftsmen inherited Old World craft traditions and often showed some familiarity with academic styles. Their work was shaped, however, by their new environment and the peculiar circumstances and needs of a frontier society. The result was an individualistic combination of stylistic elements and an unconventional use of construction techniques that gave back country furniture the distinctive character so attractive to the collector and challenging to the historian of material culture. Identifying furniture made in Tennessee can be difficult. Cabinetmakers signed few pieces of furniture. Instead, artisans let style and craftsmanship identify their work. Many years later, this practice is puzzling when trying to identify regional pieces.

The patrons of Tennessee furniture makers were primarily Anglo-Americans of English, Scots, and Scots-Irish descent. They arrived from Virginia, Maryland, and Pennsylvania, the products of diverse economic and social backgrounds. As they poured over the mountains, the settlers furnished their homes as their means allowed, using design concepts brought from eastern areas.

The difficulty of the journey to Tennessee often precluded the inclusion of furniture. As a consequence, settlers purchased locally made furniture after their arrival in the new region. As wagon roads became better, and river shipping became easier, Tennessee craftsmen found themselves in competition with the skills and stylistic influences of manufacturers in Pennsylvania, Virginia, and North Carolina. Cincinnati, one of the largest furniture manufacturing cities, began shipping large assortments of furniture down river to Tennessee. Prominent citizens, like Andrew Jackson, selected wares from Philadelphia, which were shipped upriver from New Orleans.

The use of woods is useful in designating Tennessee furniture. The distinguishing characteristics of the grain and color of cherry made it the favored wood for furniture. The mellow brown color made walnut the second most frequently used wood. Other woods used for furniture included maple, mahogany, and rosewood. Two regionally abundant woods—tulip poplar and yellow pine—were used for secondary parts like drawer bottoms and sides and backboards. Tulip poplar was used in pieces made throughout the state, but yellow pine was used in the geographic regions of higher altitudes, where these trees were plentiful. Occasionally cedar and cypress were used as secondary woods.

Tennessee furniture has a simplicity in both form and decoration. Craftsmen of the region inlaid lighter woods into the native cherry and walnut for decorative appeal. An array of motifs can be found—rope and tassel, gamecocks, geometric forms, running vine, eagles, compass stars, simple line, diamond, and quarter-fans. The largest number of inlaid pieces originated in upper East Tennessee. The use of inlay declined in Middle Tennessee, and is found least frequently in West Tennessee.

The most distinguishable Tennessee forms include the sugar chest and the Jackson press. The sugar chest was developed to safeguard large quantities of sugar, a commodity of great value. Fairly simple in design, a sugar chest consisted of a large wooden storage bin set on legs. The majority of chests featured a small drawer below the bin. Since only the most affluent nineteenth century households could afford sugar in bulk, a sugar chest was a status symbol, which was displayed in public areas of the home like the dining room.

The Jackson press is also indigenous to the Tennessee region. Although the form and name were contemporary with Andrew Jackson, the exact origins of the press remain unknown. As early as 1825, the term appeared in an estate inventory in Davidson County, where Andrew Jackson lived. Most presses consisted of a shaped back splash over a rectangular top above two projecting drawers over cupboard doors set on turned feet. In the small area of Good Spring, the Levi Cochran cabinetshop produced three Jackson presses between 1833 and 1835, charging from $20 to $23 for each.

Other forms of furniture produced in Tennessee included desks, secretaries, bookcases, candlestands, work tables, tables, cellarets, sideboards, slabs, safes, cupboards, presses, dressers, tall case clocks, tall chests, bureaus, chests, clothespresses, wardrobes, bedsteads, chairs, settees, and sofas. According to the 1820 Manufacturer's Census, desks were among the most expensive articles produced, though most settlers would not have needed a desk. Necessary pieces of the nineteenth century home included candlestands and work tables. These were found in abundance in inventories of the period.

The rise of the plantation culture sparked demand for high style furniture like elaborate sideboards. In 1815, cabinetmaker Captain James G. Hicks produced a cherry sideboard for $129.99. Advertisements often pridefully listed sideboards. Another related form was the slab or slab-sideboard, which was a tall table, sometimes fitted with drawers. The safe was a piece used for storage of food, usually placed in the kitchen area. The safe consisted of a wooden case with two drawers over two doors fitted with punched tin panels. The tin varied from simplistic designs to the more elaborately punched with designs of tulips, hearts, stars, candlesticks, urns, and other geometric shapes.

Two forms of furniture necessary for storage were the cupboard—flatback or corner—and the bureau. Both of these forms survive in large numbers. The continued functional aspect of these pieces may explain why they have survived.

Three major categories of chairs appeared in Tennessee inventories—Windsor, fancy, and common chairs. Nineteenth century household accounts referred to chair sets in half dozen and one dozen lots. Most households had a half dozen Windsor or common chairs. Chairs were usually painted in a variety of colors ranging from yellow, red, green, and black to conceal a variety of woods used in their production.

The furniture produced in Tennessee during the nineteenth century imparts a sense of pride and respect for our forebearers who struggled to create homes of comfort and beauty in a new territory.

Derita Coleman Williams, Memphis

SUGGESTED READING: Derita Coleman Williams and Nathan Harsh, *The Art and Mystery of Tennessee Furniture and Its Makers Through 1850* (1988)

SEE: DECORATIVE ARTS, AFRICAN-AMERICAN; DECORATIVE ARTS, APPALACHIAN

G

GAILOR, THOMAS FRANK (1856–1935), Episcopal bishop, was born at Jackson, Mississippi, the son of Frank Marion Gailor and Charlotte Moffett. He graduated from Racine College, Wisconsin, in 1876, and then entered the General Theological Seminary, New York City. Gailor received his S.T.B. degree from General in 1879, and in that same year his M.A. from Racine. He was ordained deacon in May 1879, and began his ministry at Messiah Church, Pulaski, Tennessee. He was ordained priest in September 1880, and in 1882 became professor of ecclesiastical history and polity at the Theological Department of the University of the South, a position he held until 1893. From 1883 until 1893, Gailor was the second chaplain of the university, replacing William Porcher DuBose. Over the years Gailor and the University of the South became synonymous. From August 1890 until July 1893, he was fourth vice-chancellor of the university.

Gailor also became synonymous with the Diocese of Tennessee. On July 25, 1893, he was consecrated Assistant Bishop of Tennessee, and in February 1898 he became the third Bishop. He served as eighth Chancellor of the University from 1908 until his death.

Gailor also held leadership positions in the national Episcopal Church. In 1916 he was elected chairman of the House of Bishops, and elected president of the National Council of the Episcopal Church in 1919. He held this last position to the end of 1925.

In 1885 Gailor married Ellen Douglas Cunningham of Nashville, and they had four children.

Donald S. Armentrout, University of the South

SEE: RELIGION; UNIVERSITY OF THE SOUTH

GAINES, FRANK P. (1907–1987), Chief of the Engineering Division of Nashville District Corps of Engineers, directed the planning and design of seven multipurpose projects in the Cumberland River Basin, numerous local flood protection projects in the Cumberland-Tennessee River valleys, and the Tennessee-Tombigbee Waterway. Born in December 1907, the Westminster, South Carolina, native graduated from Clemson University in 1929 with a degree in civil engineering. He began his long career with the Corps of Engineers in 1933, arriving in the Nashville District two years later. Subsequently, he became Chief of Design.

In 1942 Gaines entered the Army Reserve. He directed the design and construction of military airfields, among them the airbase at Courtland, Alabama. After duty in the Philippines, Colonel Gaines returned to Nashville in 1946, where he directed hospital and military construction. He became Chief of Construction in 1947, directing the completion of the Wolf Creek, Dale Hollow, and Center Hill Dam projects in the Upper Cumberland area. Six years later he became Chief of Engineering.

In the remaining half of his career, Gaines oversaw comprehensive development on the Cumberland River system. During this period, the Cheatham, Old Hickory, J. Percy Priest, and Cordell Hull Dam projects were completed in Middle Tennessee, along with Barkley Dam on the Lower Cumberland. He laid the groundwork for the construction of the Tennessee-Tombigbee Waterway.

Prominent in professional and civic affairs, Gaines remained active following his 1973 retirement. He died in Atlanta in 1987.

James T. Siburt, U.S. Army Corps of Engineers

SEE: CUMBERLAND RIVER; TENNESSEE-TOMBIGBEE WATERWAY; U.S. ARMY CORPS OF ENGINEERS

GARDNER, EDWIN M. (1845–1935), illustrator, portraitist, and cartographer, was born near Pulaski, Giles County, Tennessee, but while still a young boy, he moved with his family to Mississippi, where he probably had some formal training in art. While in his teens, Gardner fought in the Civil War as a member of Forrest's cavalry. Following the war, his formal art studies began in Memphis, then moved to Europe at the Royal Academy in Brussels, with later studies in France and Italy.

Upon his return to the United States, Gardner resumed study at the National Academy of Design in New York. Afterwards, he moved to Aberdeen, Mississippi, where he taught art at a female academy. He next moved to Winchester, Franklin County, where he spent five years on the faculty at Mary Sharp College.

Gardner made his last home in Nashville, where he had his greatest artistic influence. He made the first woodcuts and pen portraits for photoengraving used in the local daily newspapers, including the first published pen portrait of Sarah Childress Polk.

Although Gardner was listed in the catalogue of the 1885 Watkins Institute art show as a teacher there, he actually taught under the auspices of the Nashville Art Association in the art room which Watkins provided. His first official association with Watkins's Night School probably came in September 1910, when he was hired to teach industrial art. (School commissioners were perhaps still uncomfortable with the term "fine" art.) Gardner's presence on the Watkins Institute faculty gave the school a teacher trained in commercial and fine arts. He encouraged his students to draw by getting more casts and using live models, and this laid the foundation for the school's Fine Art Department. *Hoe in Hand*, painted by Gardner in 1903, is reproduced in the color plate section of this book.

Madeline Reed, Watkins Institute College of Art and Design

SEE: ART; MARY SHARP COLLEGE; WATKINS INSTITUTE

GARRETT, ROBERT "BUD" (1916–1987), traditional blues musician and marble maker, was born January 28, 1916, to John Tom Garrett and Adeline Hamilton Garrett in Free Hill, a small African-American settlement in Clay County established by freed slaves prior to the Civil War. Garrett learned to play the guitar as a young man and accompanied older men in the community at local square dances. In later years, Garrett performed as a solo artist on acoustic or electric guitar, and his repertoire included a mixture of traditional and popular song styles rooted in blues, country, minstrel shows and vaudeville, big band, and western swing, as well as original compositions. In 1962 Garrett recorded two original blues compositions—*I Done Quit Drinking* and *Do Remember Me*—which were released on the Excello label.

From the late 1970s until his death, Garrett received broader attention throughout the South on music tours and at festivals, performing his music and demonstrating flint marble-making (marbles made for playing "rolley hole," a regional marble game played in the Upper Cumberland River Valley) on his machine constructed from an assemblage of spare auto parts. Appearances included the 1982 World's Fair, the Smithsonian Institute's 1985 Festival of American Folklife, and the annual Tennessee Grassroots Days in Nashville. Additional selections of his music appear on recordings of the Tennessee Folklore Society, and several interviews are housed in the Tennessee State Library and Archives. Garrett died November 24, 1987, in Free Hill, while playing marbles.

Elizabeth Peterson, Catonsville, Maryland

SEE: FREE HILL; MUSIC; ROLLEY HOLE MARBLES

GAUL, WILLIAM GILBERT (1855–1919), late nineteenth century artist, is best known for his depictions of military topics, particularly scenes of the Civil War. Born in Jersey City, New Jersey, he entered the National Academy of Design in New York City at age 17 and emerged as one of the era's leading illustrators. Gaul moved to Tennessee and established a studio on property he inherited near Fall Creek Falls in Van Buren County.

Gaul published illustrations in *Harper's* and *Century Magazine*. His Civil War paintings depicted both Union and Confederate soldiers, portraying a variety of experiences from fierce battles to quiet moments in camp. Works such as *Holding the Line at all Hazards* and *Charging the Battery* captured the war's severity and brought him awards from the American Art Association and the 1889 Paris Exposition. The height of his career came in 1893, when he received numerous awards at the World's Exposition in Chicago. Gaul also produced several landscape paintings, including *Rafting on the Cumberland River* (Tennessee State Museum).

Gaul's popularity eventually began to wane and by 1904, he had accepted a teaching position at Cumberland Female College in McMinnville. He soon opened a studio in Nashville and published the first in what was to be a series of paintings titled *With the Confederate Colors* in 1907. The project, however, met with little success, and subsequent paintings were canceled. Gaul then left Tennessee and eventually returned to his native New Jersey, where he produced paintings of World War I before his death.

Teresa Biddle-Douglass, Middle Tennessee State University

SUGGESTED READINGS: *Gilbert Gaul, American Realist*, Exhibition catalog, Tennesse State Museum and Dixon Gallery and Gardens, 1992; James F. Reeves, *Gilbert Gaul*, Exhibition catalog, Fine Arts Center at Cheekwood and Huntsville Museum of Art, 1975

SEE: ART, VAN BUREN COUNTY

GAYOSO HOTEL. A vision of grandeur for the developing river metropolis at Memphis, the Gayoso House was built by Robertson Topp, a wealthy young planter. Topp was involved in the development of South Memphis, an area of houses, commercial buildings, and a hotel designed to grace the young city with high architectural style. He commissioned James Dakin, a founder of the American Institute of Architects, to design the structure, which was constructed in 1842. Its Greek Revival portico was easily recognizable from the river. In the late 1850s Topp continued his efforts to bring architectural distinction to Memphis, when the Cincinnati firm of Isaiah Rogers, designer of the Tremont House in Boston, contributed to an addition that almost doubled the Gayoso's original 150 rooms. The addition featured wrought iron balconies overlooking the Mississippi; the supervising architect was James B. Cook, an Englishman who stayed in Memphis for the rest of his architectural career.

The Gayoso House became a Memphis landmark, an oasis of modern luxury frequented by travelers passing through the city by river, road, or rail. With its own waterworks, gasworks, bakeries, wine cellar, and sewer system, the hotel offered amenities far beyond those available to the rest of Memphis. The indoor plumbing included marble tubs and silver faucets as well as flush toilets.

The Gayoso House burned on July 4, 1899. To replace it, James B. Cook designed a new hotel. His U-shaped construction surrounded a courtyard screened from Front Street by a row of columns, which are no longer extant. Though in its recent past Goldsmith's department store used the building as a warehouse, it has now been restored for use once again for downtown apartments and residences.

Blythe Semmer, Middle Tennessee State University

SUGGESTED READING: John E. Harkins, *Metropolis of the American Nile: Memphis & Shelby County* (1982)

SEE: COOK, JAMES B.; MEMPHIS

GENERAL EDUCATION BOARD (1902–1964). One of the premier philanthropic foundations of the twentieth century, the General Education Board (GEB) invested heavily in Tennessee's educational systems. John D. Rockefeller, Sr., created the GEB in 1902 in response to son John D. Rockefeller, Jr.'s enthusiastic report of a 1901 tour of African-American schools in the South. When dissolved in 1964, the board had appropriated over $324.6 million, including $129.2 million in gifts from John D. Rockefeller, Sr.

The GEB focused initially on improving education for white and black children in the South by expanding state education departments. Beginning in 1905, the board financed a professor of secondary education at the University of Tennessee charged with promoting public high schools across the state. The board took over the Southern Education Board's programs in 1914, including support for state agents for white and black rural schools in the Tennessee Department of Public Instruction. In 1919 Tennessee hired an agent for secondary education, and in 1928 added a Division of Schoolhouse Planning, thanks to GEB funding.

The GEB's contributions also extended to agricultural demonstration work, supporting agents for Boys' Corn Clubs and Girls' Tomato Clubs in 1913 until their transfer to state and federal programs under the 1914 Smith-Lever Act. A grant from the GEB began the Seaman A. Knapp School of Country Life at George Peabody College for Teachers in 1914. Additional board support funded Peabody's Division of Surveys and Field Services, which conducted studies of state education systems and curricula.

Two philanthropies devoted to black education operated under the GEB's auspices. In 1905 Anna T. Jeanes of Philadelphia created a trust to be administered by the board to assist rural schools for blacks in southern states. The Jeanes Foundation paid the salaries of African-American industrial supervision teachers who emphasized vocational education and school improvement. Between 1909 and 1959, 105 Jeanes supervisors worked in Tennessee communities. The John F. Slater Fund, created in 1882 to support public and higher education for southern African Americans, came under the GEB umbrella when board president Wallace Buttrick became its director in 1903. Slater Fund contributions promoted the creation of 22 county training schools for black students in Tennessee. These vocational schools were often the first and only secondary schools for black students, and provided the basis for proper high schools. The Southern Education Fund absorbed the Slater Fund in 1937 and the Jeanes Foundation in 1959.

The GEB's educational programs quickly extended beyond public schools. In response to Abraham Flexner's 1910 study of medical education, the board sponsored medical schools with full-time faculty, underwriting two of Tennessee's top medical programs. Vanderbilt University received the largest infusion of GEB funds for its medical school, over $17 million between 1914 and 1960; Meharry Medical College garnered more than $8 million. Higher education increasingly concerned the board after 1920, resulting in fellowship programs and gifts to college and university endowments. GEB grants to Vanderbilt eventually exceeded $23 million, with another $5.5 million in contributions to George Peabody College for Teachers. As GEB president from 1923 to 1928, Tennessean Wickliffe Rose briefly turned its attention to research in the natural and physical sciences and focused gifts to higher education on top scientific training programs. In the 1930s and 1940s the GEB promoted regional cooperation among institutions of higher education in projects such as the Joint University Library serving Vanderbilt University, George Peabody College for Teachers, and Scarritt College. Additional board contributions strengthened endowments, library resources, and graduate education at Vanderbilt.

For decades, GEB officials and the educators they subsidized in Tennessee accepted segregated education and promoted industrial (vocational) education for African Americans. Yet the board became one of the major benefactors of higher education for African Americans in Tennessee, with gifts to Fisk University totalling over $5.2 million between 1905–52, and another half-million dollars in smaller grants to Knoxville College, Lane College, LeMoyne College, Roger Williams University, Tennessee Agricultural and Industrial College, and Walden University from 1902–1960. Some of the GEB's last grants went to the George Peabody College Center for Southern Education Studies for studies of public school systems and biracial higher education in the South in anticipation of widespread desegregation.

Mary S. Hoffschwelle, Middle Tennessee State University
SEE: EDUCATION, ELEMENTARY AND SECONDARY; EDUCATION, HIGHER; FISK UNIVERSITY; MEDICINE; GEORGE PEABODY COLLEGE OF VANDERBILT UNIVERSITY; ROSE, WICKLIFFE; VANDERBILT UNIVERSITY

GENESCO. This Nashville-based company, which grew from a small local shoe manufacturer to one of the nation's largest apparel companies, has been an important Tennessee enterprise for over 70 years. With sales exceeding one million dollars its first year in business, the company experienced strong sales and increasing success for several decades. After heavy losses and financial setbacks in the 1980s and early 1990s, Genesco is currently regaining financial ground to remain a strong competitor in the shoe industry.

Genesco began in 1924 as the Jarman Shoe Company, a small manufacturer of men's shoes. The key figure behind its prosperous development was Maxey Jarman, who saw in his father's small business an opportunity for expansion. Acquiring other companies and maximizing their potential, Jarman broadened the company's product line to include women's and children's shoes plus a wide variety of clothing. He also enhanced profits by selling through company-owned retail stores. Sales and earnings doubled approximately every six years beginning in the late 1930s until 1968, when sales reached over one billion dollars, making Genesco the nation's largest and most successful apparel conglomerate. It operated over 148 manufacturing plants and distribution centers across the United States, maintained 1,750 retail stores in North America and Europe, and its employees numbered 65,000.

In addition to his activities as president and CEO of Genesco, Jarman also pursued numerous philanthropic endeavors. A devout Baptist, he served as a trustee of the Tennessee Baptist Foundation, director of the Southern Baptist Convention Sunday School Board, and director of the Tennessee Baptist Children's Homes. Jarman was also a trustee of George Peabody College for Teachers, a member of the executive and finance committees for the Billy Graham Crusade, and co-founder of the Jarman Foundation, which funded missionary projects.

Ben H. Willingham, a Georgia native and former Vanderbilt student, joined Genesco in 1933 and quickly climbed the corporate ladder, becoming vice president in 1956 and president in 1958. When Jarman announced his retirement in 1968, Willingham became the logical choice for the next chief executive officer. He anticipated that the continuation of the management system he and Jarman perfected, which emphasized communication, flexibility, decentralized decision making, and consolidated financial control, would take sales over the two billion dollar mark by 1975. The company also opened a splashy modern-style corporate headquarters in Nashville during the 1960s. Although the company remained strong, its future proved to be less auspicious.

By the 1980s, recessions, new trends in clothing, and increased competition interrupted the company's progress. In 1985 Genesco lost $34 million and closed several factories. A year later, its stock dropped to 77 cents a share, and banks refused to extend the company credit. Newly appointed CEO William Wire II instituted drastic changes, including the sale of all Canadian operations, relocation of plants to less costly sites abroad, and downsizing of the men's suit division. When sales continued to drop, Genesco moved away from the production of dress shoes and instituted lines of rugged and athletic footwear, including two new lines in conjunction with Nautica and Levi Strauss's Dockers line. In 1993, however, sales were down to $540 million, and the company lost $51.8 million.

That year, Wire hired Douglas Grindstaff, a former marketing executive with Procter and Gamble, to enhance the company's advertising and marketing divisions. Grindstaff expanded Genesco's boot division to capitalize on the latest trend. Although this move was successful initially, the boot fad soon began to fade, taking Genesco's profits along with it. In 1994, after sales continued to decline, Grindstaff initiated a comprehensive two-year restructuring program that reduced the work force 28 percent and closed 58 retail stores and some plants, including a boot factory in Hohenwald, Tennessee. At present, the company is beginning to experience a long anticipated turnaround. During the first quarter of 1997, sales increased significantly, and earnings reached their highest point in over 20 years. Although not the multi-billion dollar corporation Willingham predicted, Genesco has survived numerous setbacks and remains a major Tennessee corporation, based in Nashville.

Teresa Biddle-Douglass, Middle Tennessee State University

SUGGESTED READING: W. Maxey Jarman and Ben H. Willingham, *The Genesco Formula for Growth* (1969)

SEE: INDUSTRY; NASHVILLE

GEOLOGIC ZONES. Tennessee is a narrow state over 500 miles long, with its long axis running east-west across the grain of the geology. Most of the geological provinces of the east-central United States are represented somewhere in Tennessee. Since geology exercises a controlling influence on topography, hydrology, mineral resources, and soil type and thickness, which in turn affect the activities of humankind, it has strongly influenced the history and development of the state.

Tennessee consists of three grand divisions, which have been recognized from the earliest days of settlement and simply called East, Middle, and West Tennessee. Each of the grand divisions is divisible into three geologic zones, all with differences in basic geology that distinguish them from each other and cause some to resemble parts of neighboring states more than adjacent parts of Tennessee.

East Tennessee includes the Unaka Mountains along the border with North Carolina, the Valley and Ridge Province (also known as the Great Valley of East Tennessee), and all or part of the Cumberland Plateau/Mountains region. In this part of the state, boundaries between regions and geologic zones run northeast-southwest rather than north-south, and geologists and geographers disagree on definitions for them. Some consider the Plateau to be in East Tennessee, others say Middle Tennessee; most compromise on an irregular, north-south line running up the middle. No matter how it is defined, parts of Middle Tennessee near Kentucky actually lie farther east than parts of East Tennessee near Chattanooga.

Middle Tennessee includes a low-lying central area called the Central (or Nashville) Basin completely surrounded by the higher ground of the Highland Rim. The valleys of the Cumberland River, flowing into the state from the north, and the Elk River, flowing southward from the Basin into Alabama, bisect the Highland Rim, dividing the area into Eastern and Western provinces.

West Tennessee begins at the northward flowing reach of the Tennessee River, where it crosses Tennessee from the Mississippi-Alabama corner to Kentucky. West Tennessee includes the Western Valley of the Tennessee, the Plateau Slope of West Tennessee, and the Tennessee portion of the Mississippi River Flood Plain at the western edge of the state.

Travelers moving from west to east across Tennessee alternately cross higher and lower topographical belts representing each of the nine geologic provinces. Parts of the Mississippi River Flood Plain, the lowest area, are less than 200 feet above sea level. East of the Chickasaw Bluffs is the Plateau Slope, some 200 to 300 feet higher, which forms a comparatively level stretch across most of West Tennessee. Near the eastern edge of the Plateau Slope, a region of eroded, sandy hills borders the 300-foot drop-off into the Western Valley, where the Tennessee River (now impounded and called Kentucky Lake) stands at a level of about 360 feet. Across the river, the elevation climbs more than 400 feet to the Western Highland Rim before descending about 300 feet into the Central Basin. Across the Basin the rise onto the Eastern Highland Rim is about 500 feet, and across the Rim, another rise of approximately 1,000 feet reaches the Cumberland Plateau. The eastern edge of the Plateau is about 750 feet higher than the lowlands of the adjacent Valley and Ridge Province. Very long, linear valleys paralleled by ridges, all running northeast to southwest, with local relief of several hundred feet or more, characterize the Valley and Ridge. The Unaka Range at the eastern end of the state has the highest elevations and the greatest local relief in the state, ranging from a high of more than 6,600 feet atop Clingman's Dome to about 1,000 feet near Pigeon Forge, more than a mile of vertical difference across half the width of Sevier County. A visual profile across the length of Tennessee forms a series of terraces stepping up and down, with the height of the terraces generally increasing to the east.

West Tennessee, except for the Western Valley, is geologically part of the Gulf Coastal Plain, with the valley of the Mississippi River cut into it and its flood plain sediments deposited on top. This part of the state is geologically young, consisting of Cretaceous, Tertiary, and Holocene age deposits. Unique in Tennessee, at a depth below the northwestern part of the region, is the New Madrid seismic zone, capable of generating devastating earthquakes.

The Western Valley, Highland Rim, and Central Basin are all part of the Interior Low Plateaus physiographic region of the east-central United States. Topography and surface geology are controlled by differential rates of erosion of rocks of Ordovician, Silurian, Devonian, and Mississippian age, modified by the tectonic uplift of broad swells and arches, such as the Nashville Dome (essentially coextensive with the Central Basin).

The Cumberland Plateau and Cumberland Mountains are part of the great Appalachian Plateau, extending from New York to Alabama. The strong relief of this coal-bearing region is due to its cap of hard, erosion-resistant sandstone layers of Pennsylvanian age.

The Valley and Ridge Province is also part of a much larger region, extending beyond the borders of Tennessee to New England and Alabama. The rocks, ranging in age from Cambrian to Pennsylvanian, have been folded and faulted repeatedly by pressure from the southeast that built the Appalachian Mountains and a number of predecessor ranges.

The Unaka Mountains are part of an extensive system of mountain ranges extending from New England to Georgia and Alabama. The system is very ancient, more than a billion years old, and has been reactivated several times. The present mountains owe their relief to uplift and erosion during and since the Permian period.

Edward T. Luther, retired geologist, Tennessee Department of Environment and Conservation

SEE: CLINGMAN'S DOME; ECOLOGICAL SYSTEMS; GEOLOGY

GEOLOGY. Records of Tennessee's diverse geology of complex mountains, rivers, valleys, rocks, minerals, soils, and earthquakes began with reports by literate travelers. The first such report was made by Father J.F. Buisson St. Cosme, who survived a Memphis-area earthquake in 1699. A legion of geological observers followed, including John D. Clifford (1778–1820), Louis Phillipe (1773–1850), and Ferdinand von Roemer (1818–1891). Of the three, von Roemer was the only specialist, a Ph.D. in paleontology, who collected Tennessee fossils and wrote descriptions of them from his home in Europe. The other two were generalists; Clifford described rock sequences, and Louis Phillipe, who later became King of France, described landscapes. Dozens of other travelers followed in their wake, publishing reports of their journeys, or leaving behind manuscripts or oral traditions.

From these various sources European geologists produced speculative maps of eastern North America, including aspects of Tennessee geology. Two early efforts were made by Jean Etienne Guettard (1715–1786) and William Maclure (1763–1840), although neither man ever visited Tennessee. Guettard's map, displayed in Paris in 1752, summarized mineral wealth. In 1809, Maclure published the first geological map of eastern North America.

By 1810 well-read Tennesseans appreciated the state's topographic complexity and the regional distribution of rocks, sediments, and resources. Popular interest in geology broadened when the 1811–1812 New Madrid earthquakes created Reelfoot Lake. By 1820 Nashville had established the Museum of Natural and Artificial Curiosities for the State of Tennessee and the related Tennessee Antiquarian Society. The museum displayed geological specimens, and the society researched, among other things, the distribution of fossils in the state.

In 1827 Gerard Troost, a Dutch geologist who had recently migrated from New Harmony, Indiana, opened a natural history museum in Nashville. He soon joined the University of Nashville faculty and began teaching the first geology course in a Tennessee college. In 1831 he became the first Tennessee State Geologist, a position that also included the duties of State Assayer. Tennessee was the fourth state to establish a geological survey. While other states quickly abandoned their efforts to provide geological information, Troost remained in his posts as state geologist and as the senior professor of science at the University of Nashville until February 1850, when he was near death. Troost came to Tennessee as an internationally esteemed scholar, and his descriptions of Tennessee geology were published in many journals, and in several languages. Initially the legislature did not provide for the publication of his work, but in 1834, it began issuing biennial geological reports.

Troost blended the duties of teaching and research by permitting students to work in the field and welcoming novice scientists from distant states as unpaid apprentices. His efforts produced a lasting legacy, as Troost's protégés performed the initial geological surveys in ten states, with many becoming professors and editors of academic journals.

As the study of geology grew more visible, it expanded into the schools. By 1836 Troost had introduced a two-term sequence of general courses—physical geology followed by earth history—to the curriculum at the University of Nashville. Although such courses are standard in today's schools, the pairing of two thematic courses in geology was new in 1836. By the late 1840s most men's colleges in Tennessee offered instruction in geology, and it was almost equally popular in female academies.

Throughout the 1830s and 1840s, orators at county fairs offered speeches on geology, and local intellectual journals published original geological articles written by professionals and amateurs. Beginning in 1819 two East Tennesseans, John H. Kain and Jacob Peck, built on their provincial interests in geology to provide contributions to the national geological literature. Middle and West Tennessee also produced non-professional local experts, such as Andrew H. Buchanan and Josiah Higgason. Backing the work of professionals like Troost, the contributions of local experts remained important from 1840 to 1860. R. R. Dashiel wrote on West Tennessee, Tolbert Fanning on Middle Tennessee, and Richard O. Currey, an East Tennessee geologist, published *A Sketch of the Geology of Tennessee* in 1857. With the arrival of the Civil War, these scientific activities ceased.

Gradually, through the efforts of professionals and amateurs, a geological literature evolved for each

Grand Division of the state. Troost maintained the broader perspective and higher academic standards. As state geologist, he crisscrossed Tennessee on horseback, studying all areas. He described soils, mapped coal beds, visited iron furnaces, and brought recognition to obscure resources. He established the sequence of rocks in all parts of the state and made chemical analyses of rocks, waters, and soils. Troost met a cross-section of the population, including mine owners, farmers, and innkeepers. He often made two long trips per year. In an era when few state officials traveled the backroads, he was almost singularly well known.

Perhaps as a result of the ongoing work of the state geologist, the legislature funded new positions for a state engineer and an assistant in 1836. Although these appointments soon lapsed, the office of state geologist remained politically and economically valuable, and Troost eventually took over the duties of planning rights of way for roads and railroads. After Troost's death in 1850, political conflicts over the appointment of a successor delayed the filling of the office for four years. In 1854, as a compromise, the Governor appointed Charles A. Proctor of Ducktown to the position of State Assayer, and the legislature made James M. Safford of Lebanon the State Geologist.

Proctor left few records of his work. The modern position, which traces its origins to Proctor's part of Troost's job, inspects mines and gathers statistical information on mineral production. Unlike Proctor, Safford left an impressive record of his solitary work, matching Troost's accomplishments in the period 1854–1860. Originally a full-time employee, Safford requested part-time status in 1856, and became a three-month appointee in 1871. Both before and after his appointment, he taught at Cumberland College in Nashville.

In 1869 Safford summarized his earlier work in a state-published masterpiece, The Geology of Tennessee. With J.B. Killebrew, another Tennessee scientist, he adapted this for use as a textbook in secondary schools. New editions appeared at least through 1900. Usually called Elementary Geology of Tennessee, the popular book enhanced the esteem of geology within Tennessee. A competing text, published by W.G. McAdoo and H.C. White in 1875, bore the same name, Elementary Geology of Tennessee. With these and other books, geology flourished in secondary schools and colleges.

In the unstable early postwar years, Safford left Cumberland and moved through several teaching jobs, before obtaining a part-time position at Vanderbilt University, where he primarily taught chemistry. He retained his position as state geologist, while working part-time for the Department of Agriculture, and apparently also for the Tennessee Board of Health. His state publications in geology, public health, water supply, and agriculture continued, and in 1876, he made a failed attempt to organize a proprietary summer field school in geology.

After the Civil War, the federal government expanded geodetic surveying, and geological reports were incorporated into the U.S. Census publications. These changes, coupled with the founding of the U.S. Geological Survey (USGS) in 1879, had a positive influence on state work. In the early 1880s USGS geologist Ira Sayles began work in East Tennessee, and others soon followed. State Geologist Safford worked closely with several federal agencies.

By the 1880s a few Tennesseans were once again affluent enough to become dedicated amateur naturalists. However, there was now a clearer separation between amateur and professional science than there had been in the antebellum years. In 1885 the Nashville-based Southern Geologist began publication to serve the interests of amateur geologists. The scientific community embraced a new professionalism, as Safford's papers grew more academic, and Vanderbilt established a short-lived D.Sc. program in geology that produced two graduates.

Safford retired as State Geologist in 1899 and left Vanderbilt in 1900. His last paper on Tennessee geology appeared in 1902. The state legislature took no action toward filling his position until two years after his death in 1907, when the General Assembly passed the Tennessee Geological Survey Act of 1909. The renewed survey, which continues today as the Tennessee Division of Geology, expanded the earlier one-person operation and provided for the orderly succession of the office of state geologist.

Despite gaps in tenure, the discontinuities from Troost to Safford and from Safford to 1909 may be more apparent than real. Once Troost began his work, the legislature always saw a need for geological services.

To generalize on legislative mandates, the survey created in 1909 was expected to: guide the state in evaluating land for purchase, sale, or other purposes; shape resource-related legislation and conserve resources; attract new capital and immigrants; aid in establishing local industries; enlarge the output of farms, mines, and factories; study geology, physics, and chemistry as they relate to resources; provide geographical data; gather information on metals and ores, fuels and fertilizers, forests, roads, water, and soils; and advise on land reclamation. Over the next decades, the Survey developed other roles in the coordination of state and federal programs, including education about the state's geology and resources; service as an archivist for geological records and specimens left by defunct companies and for items collected in compliance with resource-related laws; and home to a small, semi-independent agency, generally called the Tennessee Oil and Gas Commission.

For almost 90 years, the new survey has performed most of its tasks well. It began with notable publications, including a massive bibliography of Tennessee geology and allied disciplines, which was issued to foster research by industry, government, and academia. Survey research also promoted specific industries, such as clay and phosphate.

Initially the management of state coal and prison lands absorbed much of the agency's time and, in the case of large holdings, seemed to require on-site management. For example, one study involved a 9,000-acre block, the Herbert Domain, acquired in 1907. Gradually, however, the mission of the Survey fragmented. By 1937 forestry, parks, and geology were separate agencies. The U.S. Soil Conservation Service assumed primary responsibility for soils mapping. The study of lakes, streams, and flood prevention passed to the USGS and other federal groups. Eventually the U.S. Bureau of Mines published mineral resource data.

By the 1960s, the era of the modern Tennessee Division of Geology, groundwater studies were transferred to the USGS and to newly formed state agencies. The Oil and Gas Commission was relocated, and a Tennessee Earthquake Network evolved to record, and perhaps eventually predict, earthquakes. Robert A. Miller also led the Division to become a mainstay of the conservation movement, promoting work in environmental geology and guiding public land acquisition for aesthetic purposes. In the same period, women entered the geologic fields. Jessie K. Maniatis apparently became the first female geologist in the state when she went to work for the Tennessee Division of Geology in the late 1960s. Today, women geologists teach in colleges, develop careers in industry, and work for government agencies.

The proliferation of governmental geologists has parallels in industry and academia, though it is difficult to arrive at a precise count since geologists are spread over a number of activities, including engineering, oil, environmental consulting, water supply, and mining. The state maintains standards for the registration of geologists, who sign the state forms relative to the regulation of pollution abatement and building foundations. However, in other areas, such as academia, geologists are unregistered. Indeed, quite a few certified earth science teachers in junior and senior high schools would qualify for registration as geologists if they chose to work in industry.

In the early 1970s the state introduced earth science as a standard junior high school subject. Related courses became electives in senior high schools. Since earth science texts stress geology, most Tennessee secondary school graduates possess some knowledge of the science.

The most visible academic geologists teach in junior colleges and colleges. A survey suggests that approximately 1,300 students took freshman-level geology courses in Tennessee colleges during the fall of 1995. Eight schools offer degrees in the field. The University of Tennessee has a Ph.D. program. Information on master's degrees is less precise since some schools offer advanced degrees in geology, while others offer master's degrees in such fields as science education that can include geology.

One result of a strong presence of geology in schools is a diffuse public interest. *The Tennessee Conservationist* popularizes geology, while *The Journal of the Tennessee Academy of Sciences* offers detailed studies. Geology also plays an important role in major museums, from the Pink Palace Museum in Memphis through the American Museum of Science and Energy in Oak Ridge. Even small facilities, such as state park museums, have geological displays.

Some museums and schools are meeting grounds for adolescent and adult groups that foster a personal involvement in geology. Many Boy Scout and Girl Scout troops collect rocks and study maps while working toward geology merit badges. Memphis and Nashville have long-lived rock hound clubs. Such groups come and go in smaller towns across the state. Perhaps every college has had a cave club or a geoclub. Tennesseans subscribe to hobby magazines, such as *The Lapidary Journal,* and flock to the National Speleological Society (NSS). The Nashville Grotto of the NSS issues a newsletter, and the Tennessee Cave Survey transcends the boundaries of local grottos, publishing on all Tennessee caves.

In many ways the study of Tennessee geology is closely linked to its historical past. In the early days, Guettard made a map, Louis Phillipe described the land, Clifford recorded the rocks, and von Roemer added details. Tennesseans still need maps, analyses of landscape, rock descriptions, and added details. At least 35 government agencies, and a far greater number of businesses, regularly use topographic maps. The state is covered by 804 standard USGS maps, called 7 1/2' quadrangles. The Tennessee Division of Geology sells these maps and offers access to, or has records of, 480 maps that detail the distribution of rocks within small areas. Most modern geologic maps come with a pamphlet describing mineral resources. Map-pamphlet sets are products of the Division of Geology. Currently only four states have more complete geologic map coverage.

In 1831 a political appointment made Gerard Troost the sole member of one of the first scientific agencies in the Tennessee community. The Division of Geology now plays the same role. It serves businesses that produce coal, crushed rock, and myriad other things. The Division's newsletter reaches most mineral industries and most geologists in Tennessee.

In addition, the Division offers bibliographies, lists of mineral producers, a directory of geologists, cave bulletins, and more. Most significantly, the Division is a place where interested people can come to talk about geology. Universities, federal offices, and other state agencies also welcome geological inquiries.

James X. Corgan, Austin Peay State University

SUGGESTED READINGS: Elizabeth Cockrill, "Bibliography of Tennessee Geology, Soils, Drainage, Forestry, etc., with Subject Index," *Tennessee Geological Survey Bulletin 1-B* (1917); James X. Corgan, "Notes on Tennessee's Pioneer Scientists," *Journal of the Tennessee Academy of Science* 53 (1978): 2–7; James X. Corgan, editor, *The Geological Sciences in the Antebellum South* (1982); James X. Corgan, *History of Geology and Geological Education in the Southern and Border States. Earth Sciences History* 4 (1985); Charles W. Wilson, Jr., *State Geological Surveys and Geologists of Tennessee* (1981)

GEORGE DICKEL DISTILLERY. Only two legal distilleries remain in operation in Tennessee today, Jack Daniel Distillery and George Dickel Distillery. Located a mere 20 or so miles apart on the Highland Rim, both benefit from the rim's plentiful "good" water, with its low mineral content, a must for "good" whiskey. Reactivated in 1958, George Dickel is situated near the town of Normandy, Tennessee, in the narrow Gage Creek Hollow, fed by a year-round spring known as Cascade Spring. Here is where, in the late nineteenth century, the popular Cascade distillery operated. The original Cascade distillery consisted of a still house, cistern room, aging barns, powerhouse, and an overhead whiskey line from the still to the cistern room. The business dated to the post-Civil War period and operated until the time of prohibition, when it moved to Louisville. The historic and essential distilling features once found at Cascade have contemporary equivalents that can be seen on the distillery tour at George Dickel. Both the historic site and the modern distillery demonstrate the relationship between natural resources, such as limestone spring water and corn, and the successful distillation process.

Lynn W. Hulan, Shelbyville

SEE: DISTILLERIES, HISTORIC

GEORGE PEABODY COLLEGE OF VANDERBILT UNIVERSITY (since 1979) has a 213-year lineage through seven name changes. In 1784 Nashville set aside three land tracts for a collegiate institution, Davidson Academy (1785–1786), chartered by North Carolina 11 years before Tennessee statehood in 1796. Principal Thomas B. Craighead, followed by James Priestley, administered Davidson Academy, until it was rechartered as Cumberland College (1806–1826). Under President Philip Lindsley (whose son, John Berrien Lindsley, became chancellor after him) the name changed to University of Nashville

(1827–1875). Peabody Education Fund administrator Barnas Sears helped transform the University of Nashville's moribund Literary Department into Peabody Normal College (1875–1909).

Massachusetts-born, London-based, merchant-banker George Peabody (1795–1869) established the $2 million Peabody Education Fund following the Civil War to promote public education in the 11 former Confederate states and West Virginia. The Peabody Education Fund established model public schools before funding normal schools for teacher training. Sears wanted a state-funded normal school in Nashville to serve as a model for the South. Despite Peabody Education Fund financial inducements, the Tennessee legislature failed to pass supporting bills in 1868, 1871, and 1873. In 1874 Sears offered $6,000 annually if the University of Nashville donated land and buildings for a normal school. Relieved from spending state funds, the legislature amended the University of Nashville's charter to establish the State Normal School, officially changing the name in 1875, before changing it again in 1889 to Peabody Normal College.

State Normal College opened December 1, 1875, with 13 students and closed the year with 60 students. When the legislature rejected State Normal School funding bills in 1877 and 1879, Sears considered moving it to Georgia. This threat prompted Nashville citizens to guarantee $6,000 annually until state aid began. Stung into action, the legislature passed appropriations, which totaled $429,000 (1881–1905); Peabody Education Fund aid totaled $555,730 (1875–1909). In the 34 years under presidents Eben S. Stearns, William Harold Payne, and James Davis Porter, Peabody Normal College became a leading American normal school.

By 1910 state university departments of education were replacing normal schools in preparing teachers. This changeover coincided with the Peabody Education Fund's dissolution, which George Peabody's instructions permitted after thirty years. The trustees gave $1.5 million, which required matching funds, to transform Peabody Normal College into George Peabody College for Teachers (1911–1979).

Elsewhere in Nashville, the Methodist Episcopal Church, South, established Central University in 1872. It was renamed Vanderbilt University in 1873, after Bishop Holland McTyeire obtained a $1 million donation from Cornelius Vanderbilt. Early in the twentieth century, Vanderbilt Chancellor James H. Kirkland envisioned a strong university center and offered Peabody land adjacent to Vanderbilt. After first hesitating, Peabody officials accepted the offer.

From 1911 until 1914, the Peabody campus, modeled after Thomas Jefferson's University of Virginia design, took shape. Peabody's first President, Bruce

R. Payne (1911–1937), directed the building, raised additional funds, and assembled a first-rate faculty. Classes began in the summer of 1914.

Payne's academic cooperation with, but independence from, Vanderbilt continued under presidents S. C. Garrison, Henry H. Hill, and Felix Robb through the 1960s. Building on its reputation, Peabody College became a distinctive mini-university, including liberal arts, music, physical education, and arts departments; a library school; demonstration school; Knapp Farm for Rural Studies; and a widely used Peabody School Survey Unit. It produced more graduates with master's and doctoral degrees than undergraduates and enhanced its regional and national leadership.

Post-1970 rising energy and other costs, inflation, and a national recession adversely affected higher education, especially colleges of education. Peabody College lost 30 faculty members (1970–1972), undergraduate enrollment dropped from 1,200 to 800 (1972–1976), and graduate enrollment shrank. Despite its past reputation, the time for a single-purpose private teachers college seemed over. Peabody's best graduates—state university presidents, deans, leading professors, researchers, and textbook authors—strengthened lower cost public university colleges of education and ironically contributed to Peabody College's demise. Peabody's President John Dunworth began merger talks with Vanderbilt officials at the end of 1978. Peabody College of Vanderbilt University became Vanderbilt's ninth school on July 1, 1979.

Acting Dean Hardy C. Wilcox administered Peabody College during 1979–1980. For the next nine years, Dean Willis D. Hawley sharpened its focus, upgraded programs, added new faculty, and made it a national leader in applying computers and telecommunications to learning and teaching. Since 1992, under Dean James Pellegrino, a $14.5 million renovation of the Social-Religious Building transformed that building into the Administrative and Technology Education Center. Peabody installed state of the art computers, interactive video and audio, fiber optics, and satellite systems to sharpen and expand learning and teaching. These advances are reflected in its Center for Advanced Study of Educational Leadership, Corporate Learning Center, Learning Technology Center, and 30-year-old John F. Kennedy Center for Research on Education and Human Development. Peabody's counselor and guidance program has annually been voted among the nation's best since 1990.

Looking back, Davidson Academy, Cumberland College, and the University of Nashville spread learning and culture on what was an isolated western frontier. By providing superior teacher training, Peabody Normal College advanced public education in a war-weakened South. George Peabody College for Teachers set high teacher education standards regionally and nationally.

Faced with greater challenges than similar colleges elsewhere, Peabody and its antecedents struggled, were transformed, and arose phoenix-like to produce educational leaders. Peabody College of Vanderbilt University still proclaims George Peabody's 1852 motto: "Education, a debt due from present to future generations."

Franklin and Betty J. Parker, Pleasant Hill

SEE: EDUCATION, HIGHER; LINDSLEY, JOHN B.; LINDSLEY, PHILIP; VANDERBILT UNIVERSITY

GIBSON COUNTY was created October 21, 1823, out of lands ceded by the Chickasaws in the Jackson Purchase. It was named in honor of Colonel John H. Gibson, who served under Andrew Jackson in the Natchez campaign, the Creek Wars, and the New Orleans campaign.

In 1819 Thomas Fite built the first cabin in Gibson County, which was then part of Carroll County. Luke Biggs, David Crockett, and others followed Fite. Settlement progressed rapidly, and residents soon petitioned the General Assembly for the formation of a new county, citing the difficulty of getting to the courts of Carroll County.

Commissioners appointed by the General Assembly selected a county seat site near the center of the county, where Thomas Gibson, a brother of John Gibson, operated a trading post. Initially called Gibson-Port, the name was soon changed to Trenton. County government was organized in January 1824, when the Court of Pleas and Quarter Sessions met at the residence of Luke Biggs. Following terms of the court met in the residence of William C. Love, until April 1825, when the first term of court met in a temporary courthouse made of hewn logs.

From the beginning, agriculture played an important role in Gibson County. Fertile lands along the river bottoms of the North and Middle Forks of the Forked Deer and the Rutherford Fork of the Obion and numerous creek bottoms made farming profitable. Diversification characterized Gibson County's agricultural history. Some 60 years ago the county ranked second in the number of farm products. During the last decades of the nineteenth century and until World War I, truck crops (cabbage, tomatoes, and strawberries) were an important source of income. Difficulties in securing labor and competition from other states caused these crops to be discontinued on a large scale production. Today, agriculture still accounts for a significant portion of the county's economy, with cotton, corn, soybeans, swine, and beef the leading products.

Industrial development in the nineteenth century complemented agricultural needs. In the 1800s there were numerous grist, flour, and saw mills scattered along the waterways. Before the Civil War, at least one spinning factory operated within the county. By the 1880s Gibson County had at least one cotton mill and acquired another one at a later, unknown date. Since World War II, the county has experienced significant industrial growth. In 1941 an arsenal was located in Milan. For the first time in the county's history, employees worked around-the-clock shifts, seven days a week. In addition, the new industry employed a large number of women. Today, Gibson County's industrial sector is as diversified as its agriculture. The largest industry remains the production of ammunition, now supervised by Lockheed Martin. Other industries include automotive parts and services (Douglas & Lomason Co., A. O. Smith Automotive Products Company, Eaton Corporation), electric motors (Emerson Motor Company and Wis-Con Total Power), sporting equipment (Wilson Sporting Goods), textiles (Kellwood Company), and metal fabrication (Ceco Door Products, Ecko/Glaco Ltd., and Allsteel, Incorporated).

A number of incorporated towns hold special celebrations. Trenton, the county seat, is the home of the world's largest collection of Veilleuse-Theieres. This collection, numbering 525 porcelain pieces was donated to the city by Dr. Frederick Freed. A teapot festival is held each year. Since 1934, Humboldt has been the home of the annual West Tennessee Strawberry Festival. Both the Strawberry Festival Historical Museum and the West Tennessee Regional Center for the Arts are housed in the old City Hall. Milan is the home of the West Tennessee Agriculture Museum, where the annual No-Till Field Day is held. Dyer stages the Dyer Station Days each summer. The event takes its name from the original name of the town. Yorkville, one of the oldest settlements in the county, holds the annual International Washer Tournament each year. Rutherford observes Davy Crockett Days. The restored last Tennessee home of Crockett and the grave of his mother are found here. Kenton, on the Obion County line, is the home of the "White Squirrels," and the town holds a celebration in their honor each year. For a number of years, Bradford observed the Doodle Soup Festival. Doodle Soup, a delicacy unique to the area, is made from the drippings of cooked chicken. At one time Gibson was known as the truck farming capital of the area. Medina celebrates its location as the mid-point from the Great Lakes to the Gulf of Mexico.

David Crockett—hunter, storyteller, and politician—stands out among the notable personalities of Gibson County. Although many Tennessee counties claim Crockett as a citizen, he was living in Gibson County when he announced his candidacy for his term in the U.S. House of Representatives. Peter Taylor, the author of several novels and short stories,

is a native of Trenton. Historians Mary U. Rothrock and Samuel Cole Williams both called Gibson County home. Gentry R. McGee, an early educator, wrote *McGee's School History of Tennessee*, which was used as a textbook for over 30 years. Andrew D. Holt, a native of Milan, served as president of the University of Tennessee, 1959–1970.

Today, Gibson County has a population of over 46,000 people. The county has three hospitals and seven nursing homes. Gibson County does not have a county system of schools, but supports four special school districts and one city system.

Fred M. Culp, Trenton

SEE: CROCKETT, DAVID; FREED, JULIUS; HOLT, ANDREW D.; MILAN ARSENAL; TAYLOR, PETER H.; WILLIAMS, SAMUEL C.

GILBERT, NOEL ALEXANDER (1909–1991), violinist, was born in Scott's Hill, Tennessee, where he learned the fundamentals of the violin. In 1925 he moved to Memphis and began studies with Joseph Henkel, teacher and conductor of the Memphis Philharmonic. After joining the Memphis Federation of Musicians in 1926, Gilbert joined the pit orchestras at the Palace Theater and later the Orpheum Theater, where he absorbed the mystique and routine of the vaudeville era from older musicians.

Gilbert began advanced studies on the violin with Scipione Guidi, concertmaster of the St. Louis Symphony and former concertmaster of the New York Philharmonic. By 1939 Gilbert merited the concertmaster position of the Memphis Symphony Orchestra under the direction of Burnet Tuthill.

Beginning in the mid-1930s, Gilbert organized and conducted small orchestras for local hotels and led both the WREC and WMC radio staff orchestras. From 1947 to roughly 1980, he led an eight-week summer season at the Memphis Overton Park Shell, playing light classical and popular music.

As an educator, he taught at both the Memphis College of Music and Memphis State College (now the University of Memphis) in addition to his private students. In 1952, Gilbert was also the leader and organizer of the *Evening Serenade* on WMC-TV, a pioneering fifteen minute show that lasted only three seasons.

Gilbert was also the associate concertmaster of the Memphis Sinfonietta, which eventually became the Memphis Symphony Orchestra by 1960. From 1961 through 1985, he was an active player, contractor, and coordinator for recording sessions held at the local Sun, Stax, American Sound, Hi, and Tanner studios. He can be heard on recordings by Elvis Presley, Isaac Hayes, Al Green, Dionne Warwick, Neil Diamond, and others.

Always eager to conduct, in 1976, after his retirement from the MSO and the University of Memphis, Gilbert founded the Germantown Symphony

Orchestra, which performed four to six classical and pop concerts per season. Gilbert resigned in 1986 and immediately formed a similar group, the Memphis Civic Orchestra, which he conducted until a month before his death in 1991.

Roy C. Brewer, Memphis

SUGGESTED READING: Roy C. Brewer, "The Story of Noel Gilbert and His Contribution to the Growth of Music in Memphis, Tennessee," West Tennessee Historical Society *Papers*, 50 (1996)

SEE: MEMPHIS MUSIC SCENE; MUSIC; SYMPHONY ORCHESTRAS

GILES COUNTY was created in 1809, from land once part of North Carolina. Andrew Jackson suggested the name "Giles" to the legislature in recognition of the strong support Congressman William Branch Giles had given to Tennessee in the successful bid for statehood in 1796. Since Indian treaties had not been finalized, settlers were not permitted to move onto their land until 1806.

Both Elkton and Prospect claim the designation of first settlement in the county, followed by Lynn Creek, Campbellsville, Pulaski, Bodenham, Crosswater, Aspen Hill, and Blooming Grove. Of these, Pulaski and Lynnville exist today as incorporated towns. Other incorporated towns are Minor Hill and Ardmore.

Pulaski was designated the county seat and a courthouse erected on a square in the center of the county in 1811. The present neoclassical beauty, erected in 1909, has been placed in the National Register of Historic Places. Busts of three natives who served as governors of the state, Aaron V. Brown, Neill Smith Brown, and John C. Brown, were placed in the foyer as a Bicentennial project.

Aaron V. Brown (1795–1859) served in both houses of the Tennessee General Assembly and the U.S. House of Representatives before becoming Governor of Tennessee (1845–47). In 1847 Brown, a Democrat, was defeated in the gubernatorial race by a fellow Giles countian, Neill S. Brown, a Whig. Aaron Brown's political activities focused on national issues, particularly slavery, and he is credited with authorship of the "Tennessee Platform" in defense of national unity presented to the Nashville Convention of 1850.

The location of Giles County, on the Nashville and Decatur Railroad, made it a center of activity during the Civil War. Though no major battle was fought within its boundaries, the county fell into Federal hands after the Battle of Fort Donelson and was occupied by Union troops for several years. Grenville Dodge was in command in 1863 when Sam Davis, a young Confederate soldier and member of Coleman's Scouts, was condemned and executed for spying. A statue of Davis stands on the south side of the town square, a monument to the 21-year-old soldier whose last words were immortalized by Confederate veterans: "If I had a thousand lives, I would lose them all here before I would betray my friend or the confidence of my informer." The county contributed four generals to the Confederate cause: John C. Brown, G. W. Gordon, John Adams, and Preston Smith. More that 2,000 soldiers from Giles County filled the southern ranks.

Pulaski was the birthplace of the Ku Klux Klan. Organized shortly after the war by John C. Lester, James R. Crowe, John Kennedy, Calvin Jones, Richard R. Reed, and Frank O. McCord, the secret society spread across the state as its reputation for violence and intimidation evolved. In recent years attempts to stage Klan activities in Pulaski have met stiff resistance from the community.

Giles County was the birthplace of noted African-American architect Moses McKissack, founder of McKissack and McKissack, one of the nation's oldest African-American architectural firms in the nation. The firm's Bridgeforth School was built with support from the Rosenwald Fund in 1927. Giles County has more than 100 National Register properties, including large downtown districts in Pulaski. Elkton has the Gardner House (ca. 1896), which belonged to Matt Gardner, a black minister, merchant, and farmer.

Giles County is also the birthplace of two nationally known writers, Donald Davidson and John Crowe Ransom. Davidson and Ransom were associated with the group of poets at Vanderbilt University in the 1920s who were known as the Fugitives. These men and women have been credited with the literary flowering that emerged as the Southern Renaissance. Davidson and Ransom were also involved in another famous literary group, the Agrarians, whose 1930 anthology, *I'll Take My Stand: The South and the Agrarian Tradition* received widespread attention.

From its inception, education played an important role in the history of Giles County. Pulaski Academy, later known as Wurtenburg Academy, then Giles College, chartered by the legislature when the county was organized, was the first of many academies, colleges, and schools. Martin Methodist College, established in 1872, was a gift from Thomas Martin in honor of his daughter, Victoria, an advocate for female education. The college, which recently achieved four-year status and is administered by the Tennessee Conference of the United Methodist Church.

A county library, donated by the late C. A. Craig, a founder of the former National Life and Accident Insurance Company in memory of his wife, serves the public in a renovated building. The building also houses a county genealogy room and a museum containing artifacts brought to the county by the early settlers. A Civil War museum, "The Sam Davis Museum," organized by the United Daughters of the

Confederacy, is located on Sam Davis Avenue and is administered by the historical society.

In the post-World War II era, a number of institutions, including the U.S. Department of Agriculture, local banks, the Chamber of Commerce, and the Retail Merchants Association developed a diversified economy to carry the county into the twenty-first century.

Margaret Butler, Pulaski

SEE: BROWN, AARON V.; BROWN, NEILL S.; BROWN, JOHN C.; DAVIDSON, DONALD; DAVIS, SAM; KU KLUX KLAN; MARTIN METHODIST COLLEGE; MCKISSACK AND MCKISSACK; RANSOM, JOHN C.

GILLILAND HOUSE in Shelbyville is a unique vernacular stone building completed by locally renowned African-American stone mason James S. "Jim" Gilliland in the late nineteenth century. Born near Shelbyville on November 15, 1858, Gilliland began as a builder of stone foundations, retaining walls, and fences, but soon developed extraordinary abilities in the detailed stone work associated with window and door openings, chimneys, tombstones, and carved decorative objects. In addition to his thorough knowledge of working stone, he was an accomplished brick mason. Gilliland's stone and brick work became an integral part of many public, commercial, and residential buildings in Shelbyville. Gilliland died in 1949, after a long life dedicated to his masonry craft and to civic affairs.

Gilliland's house is an excellent example of his craftsmanship. According to tradition, beginning in 1898 Gilliland erected the 15-inch thick stone bearing walls around an existing log building, which was subsequently dismantled and the logs removed. The skillfully laid coursed ashlar limestone walls incorporate stone lintels and sills as well as a prominent water-table course, testifying to Gilliland's exceptional craftsmanship.

The single-story stone building is two rooms wide (about 32 feet) and two rooms deep (about 28 feet), surmounted by a hipped roof with a single dormer. The asymmetrical facade includes a substantial off-center doorway and two windows. One of the two original internal brick chimneys still survives. Some original exterior features have been lost, including the wooden denticulated cornice and front porch. In the 1960s, a rear concrete block addition was added to serve as a bathroom and interior surfaces were covered with modern materials.

The Gilliland House was placed on the National Register of Historic Places in 1975. The Gilliland Historical Resource Center, Inc., acquired the property in 1996 and plans to rehabilitate and operate the building as a multicultural museum and educational center. The restoration will return the building to its original appearance, with a few minor concessions to modern functionality. The restored building will focus on the contributions of James Gilliland and will also interpret the lifestyles of African-American families from 1890 to 1920. Thus, the Gilliland House will become a resource for studying family and community history in Bedford County.

Edward A. Johnson, Middle Tennessee State University

SEE: ARCHITECTURE, VERNACULAR DOMESTIC; BEDFORD COUNTY; DECORATIVE ARTS, AFRICAN-AMERICAN

GIOVANNI, YOLANDE CORNELIA "NIKKI" (1943–) expresses her version of the late twentieth-century African-American experience through poetry and essays. Though her parents left Knoxville after her birth, Giovanni returned for summers with her grandparents and graduated from Knoxville's Austin High School before entering Fisk University, her grandfather's alma mater. She came of age at the height of the civil rights and black power movements, and her political activism in combination with her creative writing brought her to the forefront of the Black Arts Movement. Giovanni has maintained that high profile for three decades through her writing and her teaching.

Giovanni's early poetry, published in *Black Feeling, Black Talk* (1968), *Black Judgment* (1969), and *Re:Creation* (1970), came out after brief stints in graduate programs at the University of Pennsylvania and Columbia University. The intense nature, reflective quality, and disciplined writing of this period led to public recognition and the inclusion of her work, often the poem "Knoxville, Tennessee" from her first volume, in textbook anthologies in American literature.

During the 1970s Giovanni released several recordings of her poetry and the first of several books of poetry for children, and new works appeared: *The Women and the Men* (1975) and *Cotton Candy on a Rainy Day* (1978). She also published essays on the black experience in *Gemini* (1970), and participated in discussions on the same topic, published as *A Dialogue: James Baldwin and Nikki Giovanni* (1972), and *A Poetic Equation: Conversations Between Nikki Giovanni and Margaret Walker* (1974), and began her teaching career. After appointments at Queens College of CUNY and at Livingston College of Rutgers University, Giovanni taught creative writing at Virginia Polytechnic Institute and State University in 1987 and remains a member of the English faculty there. She continues writing, most recently in *Conversations with Nikki Giovanni* and *Racism 101* (1994). Eighteen of her nineteen books are still in print, and she holds several honorary degrees.

Critics of Giovanni's poetry, even those sympathetic to her work, find her more often depending upon her personality in place of honing her craft. Certainly the message conveyed is as important as the medium to her. While the fierceness found in her early work has mellowed, Giovanni herself and African-American publications still consider her to be a messenger for the youth of her race. In 1994 she wrote the following in reference to her grandparents and what she learned from them, but the idea applies to Giovanni's view of her place in American society as well. "I'm glad I understand that while language is a gift, listening is a responsibility. There must always be griots . . . else how will we know who we are?"[1]

Margaret D. Binnicker, Middle Tennessee State University

CITATION:

(1) Nikki Giovanni, "Griots" from *Racism 101* (New York, 1994), 19.

SEE: KNOXVILLE; LITERATURE

GIRL SCOUTS U.S.A., TENNESSEE. Girl Scouting came to Tennessee as word of the movement spread across the United States during World War I. Individual, or lone troops, unaffiliated with any council, established independently in Tennessee cities during this era of patriotic fervor. Girls wore military-like, khaki uniforms, and troop activities included marching and drilling. A group of Memphis girls promoted the establishment of the city's first troop in 1916. The first Knoxville troop was organized in 1917, but did not affiliate with the national organization. Troops were organized in Chattanooga at the Pilgrim Congregational Church, the Bonny Oaks School, and the Standard Coosa Thatcher School. The Sunflower Troop of Morristown registered as a lone troop in 1917, and assisted at the canteen for World War I troop trains passing through the city. The Young Women's Christian Association sponsored the first Nashville troops. The YWCA organized in public schools and established a leadership training course for volunteer troop leaders. Nashville troops did not affiliate with a council, which served as a regional organization officially affiliated with the national Girl Scouts office, but paid national dues and purchased uniforms, handbooks, and other materials from the national Girl Scout office. In 1920 the Nashville YWCA discontinued its sponsorship of Girl Scouting, citing costs as the reason for their decision. They replaced scouting with Girl Reserves, a national YWCA program.

After the initial enthusiasm, scouting declined in Tennessee, in part as the result of the lack of a regional or statewide organization of troops. In Knoxville, however, the Knoxville Community Service Council obtained a charter from the national organization in 1922 for the Knoxville Girl Scout Council, Tennessee's first council. Chattanooga established a council in 1926, and began organizing troops across the city. By the fall of 1927 there were at least eight lone troops in Nashville. That year, troop leaders met and applied for a charter for Nashville's first Girl Scout Council.

Although closely identified with urban areas, Girl Scout troops began to appear in rural communities by the mid-1920s. In 1925 troops were established in Cookeville and Cumberland Furnace (Dickson County). Another troop organized in Maury County in 1928. During the 1930s Girl Scouting continued its expansion into rural areas, but troops established outside large cities functioned as lone troops, unaffiliated with any council.

During the 1920s Tennessee's few lone troops for African-American girls were not able to sustain their program and died out. In the 1940s urban councils began offering segregated Girl Scouting opportunities for African-American girls. Councils operated a two-tiered program and recruited African-American women to organize black troops. At its Nashville headquarters, the Cumberland Valley Girl Scout Council has identified and commemorated Josephine Holloway's efforts for Nashville African-American girls from the days of segregation to eventual integration. Integrated troops appeared in Tennessee in the 1950s, but did not become widespread until the 1960s.

Scouting continued to gain members during the Great Depression and World War II by offering outdoor opportunities and camping experiences for girls as well as teaching patriotism. Even the secret city of Oak Ridge organized a Girl Scout troop, which could not formally register with the national council in order to protect the security of the installation and the Manhattan Project.

In 1957 the national organization launched the Green Umbrella plan to bring unaffiliated troops outside the urban areas under the jurisdiction of regional councils. Sixteen Middle Tennessee and three Kentucky counties merged with the Nashville and Davidson County Council to become the Cumberland Valley Girl Scout Council, a name that had previously been used by the Clarksville Council. Lone troops clustered near Shelbyville established the Volunteer Council, while the Highland Rim Council formed in Cookeville. Knoxville established the Tanasi Council to include surrounding counties, and Memphis expanded into Arkansas and northern Mississippi to form the Tenn-Ark-Miss Council. With headquarters in Johnson City, the Appalachian Council served upper East Tennessee. The Reelfoot Council was chartered in 1959 to serve 16 West Tennessee counties. In the early 1960s the Volunteer Council and part of the western section of the Highland Rim Council merged with Cumberland Valley. The eastern counties of the Highland Rim Council joined the Tanasi Council in 1965. In 1975 a special pilot project called "Pixies" was instituted in Memphis to serve five and six year olds. This later became Daisy Girl Scouts.

Today, six councils with service centers in Johnson City, Knoxville, Chattanooga, Nashville, Jackson, and Memphis provide services to Girl Scouts from kindergarten through grade 12 in every county of Tennessee.

Carole Stanford Bucy, Volunteer State Community College

SUGGESTED READING: Elisabeth Israels Perry, "'The Very Best Influence': Josephine Holloway and Girl Scouting in Nashville's African-American Community," *Tennessee Historical Quarterly* 52(1993):73–85

SEE: BOY SCOUTS OF AMERICA, TENNESSEE

GIRLS PREPARATORY SCHOOL, the largest independent secondary day school for girls in the country, was founded in 1906 by three highly-respected public school teachers. Tommie Duffy, a history and science specialist, Eula Jarnagin, a language teacher, and Grace McCallie, a mathematician, petitioned the Chattanooga School Board to allow girls to take college preparatory courses. When their initial attempts were rebuffed, the women took matters into their own hands.

The three women pooled $300, bought used desks, and transformed McCallie's Oak Street house into a school for girls and a home for themselves. They hired Chloe Thompson to teach English and opened the school with 45 students; their curriculum required daily physical activity as well as classroom studies.

After ten years at the Oak Street address, they moved to a larger building on Palmetto Street. Following the death of McCallie in 1918, Duffy and Jarnagin continued to guide the school until the mid-1940s, when GPS was turned over to a Board of Trustees, who acquired the present site in north Chattanooga. In 1991 GPS was designated a National School of Excellence.

Students no longer answer "present" to a daily roll call, memorize Bible verses, or recite the kings of England. They do take a full range of college preparatory courses, and 99% of graduates continue their studies at four-year colleges and universities. The "school walks" and basketball of early days have given way to 13 varsity sports and frequent district, regional, and state championships. The yearbook, student newspaper, and May Day remain strong traditions, supplemented by 60 other extracurricular activities.

The Founders' original mission—to educate girls for "useful lives in their careers, homes, and communities by instilling a lifelong love of learning and the importance of honesty, integrity, and consideration for others"—remains the same.

Margaret Cate, Chattanooga

SEE: EDUCATION

GLENRAVEN PLANTATION, located near Adams, Robertson County, is the last large-scale, consciously designed tobacco plantation landscape in Tennessee. Its founders were Felix Ewing, a wealthy Nashville businessman and Arkansas Delta plantation owner, and his wife Jane Washington Ewing, who inherited the plantation's initial 865 acres from her prominent Robertson County family, who owned the nearby Wessyngton plantation. After their marriage in 1891, the Ewings began Glenraven's development. By the turn of the century, Glenraven contained a massive three-story Classical Revival manor house, numerous Arts and Crafts styled residences for foremen and tenants, a church, school, post office, store, power plant, dairy, mill, and store. Taken as a whole, Glenraven functioned as a self-contained economic unit, but was dependent on dark-fired tobacco sales to a broad national and international market.

Felix Ewing was a prominent leader of the planters, farmers, and businessmen allied against the American Tobacco Company in the Black Patch Tobacco War of the early 1900s. In 1904 Ewing and others created the Dark Tobacco District Planters' Protective Association of Kentucky and Tennessee; Ewing became the chairman of the executive committee, gaining the nickname of the "Moses of the Black Patch." The Ewings owned Glenraven plantation until 1931 when the Metropolitan Life Insurance Company foreclosed on the property. It is still a private farm, with livestock the primary agricultural commodity, owned and operated by the J.S. Moore family of Springfield.

Carroll Van West, Middle Tennessee State University

SEE: BLACK PATCH WAR; ROBERTSON COUNTY; TOBACCO; WESSYNGTON PLANTATION

GLENMORE. This 27-room, five-story Victorian house of hand-made brick was built in 1868–1869 in Mossy Creek (now Jefferson City). Considered one of the state's most nearly perfect examples of Second Empire style, Glenmore is now an Association for the Preservation of Tennessee Antiquities (APTA) property. Only two families owned and occupied the house, originally named the Oaks. John Roper Branner, president of the East Tennessee, Virginia, and Georgia Railroad, built the house. In the 1870s his brother Joseph established the Branner Institute for Young Ladies in the mansion. Milton Preston Jarnagin purchased the mansion in 1882. A banker, businessman, and lawyer, Jarnagin graduated from Maryville College in 1846. During the Civil War, he was appointed judge advocate and later practiced law in Memphis, where he married Agnes Watkins. The Jarnagins had five children; they renamed the house Glenmore in honor of a son, who died in infancy. Son Frank and his wife Mary lived at Glenmore for 53 years.

The architectural gem of the T-shaped house is the graceful winding staircase with the beautifully carved newel post. A small replica of the stairway is also in the "Dolltown" portion of the mansion, where the family lived in winter. The carved woodwork of solid walnut and cherry came from Baltimore. The arched frames over the doors, recessed arch windows, and fanlights are Victorian delights. Today's visitors to the mansion can enjoy Glenmore's beauty and tradition for hospitality.

Helen Gray, Glenmore Mansion

SEE: ARCHITECTURE, VERNACULAR DOMESTIC; ASSOCIATION FOR THE PRESERVATION OF TENNESSEE ANTIQUITIES; JEFFERSON COUNTY

GOLDEN CIRCLE LIFE INSURANCE COMPANY

was first established in 1950 as a fraternal organization through the efforts of Charles Allen Rawls, a Haywood County mortician, who believed that the African-American community should unite and create a cash benefit fund for struggling families living in black farm communities in West Tennessee. Poverty prevented many of the potential members from burying their deceased family members with dignity.

In 1950 Rawls assembled a small group of concerned men and women to assess the financial situation of the African-American community of Haywood and surrounding counties and discuss the possibility of developing a cash benefit fraternal organization. The group designated Rawls to make contact with the Businessmen Association of Washington, D.C., and the Department of Insurance and Banking to initiate the process of securing a charter. Rawls also sought the advice of State Senator Hugh B. Helm of Nashville and Attorney Joe Lutin, Professor of Law at Vanderbilt University. Further assistance was provided by J. H. Hudleston of the Afro-American Fraternal Organization and Dr. L. T. Miller, head of the Afro-American Hospital staff.

On July 5, 1950, the Sons and Daughters of the Golden Circle was organized in the First Baptist Church of Brownsville, Tennessee. With the help of Attorney Cluster L. Johnson, legal counsel for the Afro-American Fraternal Organization, the Sons and Daughters of the Golden Circle functioned according to the laws governing the state of Tennessee. The first members and early organizers included C. A. Rawls, G. W. Rawls, J. Z. Rawls, Reverend E. W. Selby, Reverend C. W. Allen, Alex Hill, John R. Bond, Reverend W. R. Hill, Mrs. Nola Bond, Ms. C. Y. Russell, Mrs. Mary Jane Willis, Mrs. Mabel Leigh, Louis T. Minor, and Joe Transou. Through their efforts, 33 units of the Sons and Daughters of the Golden Circle were organized in Haywood County. Reverend A. E. Campbell of Memphis initiated several other units in Shelby County, the first at Columbus Baptist Church.

Money collected was used to insure individuals and provide loans to help save farms and homes in the African-American communities. In 1951 an attempt to build a "Black Only" medical facility in Brownsville was initiated to aid blacks unable to receive adequate medical care in the white hospital in Haywood County.

In 1958 the Department of Insurance and Banking suggested that the organization convert to an Old Line Legal Reserve Stock Life Insurance Company. On May 16, 1958, the Sons and Daughters of the Golden Circle became known as the Golden Circle Life Insurance Company and operated in Brownsville, Memphis, Nashville, and Knoxville. Members who were too old to be insured in the conversion retained membership in what was then known as the Tribes of Judea.

Three hundred thousand dollars were needed to write the first policy. On May 28, 1958, Frank Chapman, president of the Brownsville Bank contacted A. B. Benedict, president of First American Bank in Nashville, and authorized issuance of series G treasury bonds for the purpose of capitalizing the company. From 1950 to 1997 the company has gone from zero assets to more than $9 million. According to *Black Enterprise* magazine (June 1996), Golden Circle ranks ninth among the top ten black-owned insurance companies in America. Cynthia Rawls Bond is president and CEO of the company.

Sharon Norris, Nutbush Heritage Productions, Inc.

SEE: COMMERCE; HAYWOOD COUNTY

GOLDSMITH'S, a well-known Memphis department store, traces its origins to the antebellum period and a German immigrant, Louis Ottenheimer, who operated a provisions store in Arkansas. Moving to Memphis, Ottenheimer opened a store on Main Street with partner Moses Schwartz. In 1867 Ottenheimer brought his nephews, Isaac and Jacob Goldsmith, to the United States and employed them in his Memphis store. As soon as the Goldsmith brothers saved $500, they opened their own store, grossing $25 on the first day of business. The Goldsmiths soon expanded to larger quarters on Beale Street. Memphis experienced several outbreaks of yellow fever during the 1870s. During the epidemic of 1878, the Goldsmiths kept the store open at least three hours a day.

By 1881 the brothers had bought their uncle's store, renaming it I. Goldsmith and Brother. The Goldsmiths prospered by adhering to a customer-friendly philosophy. Jacob Goldsmith became president of the store when his brother died. He instigated a Christmas Parade, which preceded Macy's famous event by more than a decade, and in 1960 the store opened the popular "Enchanted Forest" for children.

Goldsmith's became a true department store, among the first in the South, when it arranged merchandise by departments in 1902. It was the first Memphis store to install air-conditioning, escalators, a bargain basement, and a mechanical credit system called Charga-Plate.

When Jacob Goldsmith died in 1931, his sons Elias and Fred assumed management of Goldsmith's. In 1959 the store became an affiliate of Federated Department Stores.

Selma Lewis, Memphis

SUGGESTED READING: Paul Coppock, *Memphis Sketches* (1976)

SEE: COMMERCE; MEMPHIS

GOOD ROADS MOVEMENT. By the early twentieth century, the inadequate road system in Tennessee, and the South generally, impeded the region's economic progress. Dust in the dry season and mud in the wet, delays in waiting for ferries to cross the many rivers, and roads that led nowhere or wandered aimlessly across the countryside characterized Tennessee's road system. Beginning in the early part of the century and culminating in the 1920s, the Good Roads Movement organized to improve Tennessee's economic prospects by upgrading and expanding its road system.

The Good Roads Movement had its roots in the "Country Life Movement," an outgrowth of Populism, which sought to improve rural life and reverse the exodus of young people to the cities. These good roads proponents urged the building and improvement of farm-to-market roads, which would not only facilitate the movement of farm produce to market, but also provide rural residents with access to urban entertainment and cultural attractions, while remaining on the farm. In addition, farmers wanted to break the railroad's virtual monopoly on the shipment of farm products. By the early twentieth century, good roads associations began to appear statewide, led by the East Tennessee Good Roads Association formed in Greeneville in 1901. In 1912 the American Highway Association listed 13 affiliated good roads organizations in Tennessee.

By the mid-teens, however, the impetus and focus on good roads shifted to the cities, where young, middle-class bankers, merchants, businessmen, real-estate investors, road builders, and auto dealers touted interstate highways as a way of attracting tourists and northern investors. Several Tennesseans took leadership in this national movement of "highway progressives." Governor Tom Rye helped organize the first meeting of the Dixie Highway Association in Chattanooga in 1915, and Chattanooga attorney and circuit judge Michael Morrison Allison became the association's first president. Tennesseans also participated in later interstate highway associations, including the Robert E. Lee Highway, the Andrew Jackson Highway, and the Cincinnati-Lookout Mountain Scenic Highway. These "highway progressives" organized the Tennessee Good Roads Association in 1922 to promote increased state funding and publicize the need for good roads.

Despite the publicity and efforts of both farmer-led groups and "highway progressives," and the infusion of federal dollars from the Federal-Aid Road Act of 1916, Tennessee's roads had improved little by the 1920s. In 1923 Tennessee had only 244 miles of paved roads. Part of the problem stemmed from the differing goals and tactics employed by the two groups of good roads advocates. The farmers' emphasis on farm-to-market roads and a conservative pay-as-you-go approach to financing conflicted with the strategy of "highway progressives," who wanted interstate highways funded by long-term bonds. It required an individual with a foot in each camp, Governor Austin Peay, to energize the stalled road improvements initiative in the 1920s.

Peay first reorganized the State Highway Commission, an agency long characterized by inefficiency and waste. Critics of the three-member commission charged that state and federal highway money disappeared into a black hole of county highway departments, who received little state supervision. Indeed, some observers complained that the only paved roads in the state were those leading to the hometowns or property of commission members. Peay replaced the commission with a single State Highway Commissioner and gave him complete authority over the routing, building, and maintenance of state roads. Peay also appointed talented and energetic men to the new offices, first James G. Creveling and then C. Neil Bass.

To finance a system of state roads, Peay followed the more conservative position advocated by farmers. He pushed through a gasoline tax and used vehicle registration fees and short-term bonds. This action not only produced the revenue needed for construction and maintenance, but also relieved farmers of the burden of financing the system through the property tax. By Peay's second term, more that half of all state expenditures went to road building, with the total during his three administrations exceeding $75 million.

By the late 1920s Tennessee had satisfied the demands of both farmers and urban businessmen by completing a paved highway connecting Memphis to Bristol, building four state highways that crossed the state north to south, constructing 17 bridges over major rivers, and completing most of a statewide system of over 4,000 miles of paved roads that connected every county. These roads transformed the state. They brought millions of tourists to visit Tennessee attractions like the newly established Great Smoky Mountains National Park, Rock City, Ruby Falls, and the Grand Ole Opry. Memphis, Jackson, Nashville, Chattanooga, and Knoxville expanded as regional trade centers. And the day of the one-room school house effectively ended as rural areas became more accessible, and buses provided transportation to newly consolidated schools.

Dan Pierce, Western Carolina University

Suggested Reading: Howard L. Preston, *Dirt Roads to Dixie* (1991)

SEE: DIXIE HIGHWAY ASSOCIATION; HIGHWAYS, HISTORIC; PEAY, AUSTIN

GOODLETTSVILLE LAMB AND WOOL CLUB.

Organized by 19 farmers in May 1877, the Goodlettsville Lamb and Wool Club has the distinction of being the oldest cooperative livestock organization in the United States. This farmer-owned association was the progenitor of future cooperative marketing organizations that, by 1950, encompassed nearly one million members in similar clubs across the United States.

At the close of the Civil War, Tennessee farmers struggled to recover their once prosperous lands from the war's devastation. The Granger Movement, which sought to improve the farmer's standard of living through cooperative enterprises, met with limited success in the South. Nevertheless, the movement educated farmers about business dealings with manufacturers and middlemen in an increasingly complex agricultural market. The depression created by the Panic of 1873 was especially severe to southern farmers, who sank deeper and deeper into debt. Several crusades, including the Agricultural Wheel of the 1880s and the Farmers' Alliance of the 1880s and 1890s, developed from these conditions.

Sheep farmers in the northern Davidson County town of Goodlettsville had long submitted to the sheep buyer's practice of "guessing" the weight of spring lambs and paying the farmers accordingly. When buyers apparently were underestimating the actual weight of the lambs, 19 sheep growers, headed by William Luton, banded together to insist on proper weighing of their livestock. They called themselves the Goodlettsville Lamb Club and, the next year, changed the name to the Goodlettsville Lamb and Wool Club. In 1920 the name again changed to the Goodlettsville Wool Club.

Club bylaws protected members by keeping sales records of lambs and wool. The association guaranteed buyers that no underweight lambs would be sold and required members to sell lambs and wool only through the club. The club's success meant increased profits for sheep farmers, improvement in their farms, and a better community spirit. The success also inspired the founding of similar organizations, not only in Tennessee, but in other states. The Goodlettsville Lamb and Wool Club showed that cooperation was the best way to combat the pressures from buyers of farm products.

Wayne C. Moore, Tennessee State Library and Archives

Suggested Reading: Mason McGrew, "The Story of Goodlettsville Lamb and Wool Club" reprinted in *Makers of Millions* (1951)

SEE: AGRICULTURAL WHEEL; DAVIDSON COUNTY; FARMERS' ALLIANCE; LIVESTOCK

GOODPASTURE, ALBERT VIRGIL (1855–1942),

writer, editor, and Tennessee historian, was born on November 19, 1855, in Overton County. He attended school in Cookeville and New Middleton, and received his B.A. from East Tennessee University in 1875, having absorbed the view of the university's president, Thomas Hume, that young men should take an interest in Tennessee and southern history. Goodpasture received his law degree from Vanderbilt University in 1877, and a master's degree in history from the University of Tennessee in 1882; his thesis was a *History of Overton County*.

Goodpasture moved to the Oakland community in Montgomery County, where he became active in the Tennessee Agricultural Wheel and the Tennessee Farmers' Alliance, and served as a state representative from 1887 to 1889, state senator from 1889 to 1891, and Clerk of the Tennessee Supreme Court from 1891 to 1897. From 1897 to 1914, he and his brother William H. Goodpasture ran the Goodpasture Book Company in downtown Nashville, which often served more as a club for book lovers than a bookstore.

It was in this capacity that Goodpasture assumed editorial duties for the *American Historical Magazine*, the publication of the Tennessee Historical Society and the predecessor of the *Tennessee Historical Magazine* and the current *Tennessee Historical Quarterly*. The *American Historical Magazine* originated with Peabody Normal College American history professor William R. Garrett. Goodpasture edited the magazine for six years and served as secretary of the Tennessee Historical Society from 1903 to 1912. He became one of the original members of the Tennessee Historical Commission in 1919, and served on that body until his death.

In 1914 Goodpasture retired to his Montgomery County farm, where he continued to write about Tennessee history. His works include *History of Overton County*, *Early Times in Montgomery County*, and *Life of Jefferson Dillard Goodpasture*, co-authored with his brother. His most influential contribution was a school text *History of Tennessee*, co-authored with Garrett, and sponsored by the textbook commission under Governor Benton McMillin. In later years, Goodpasture wrote numerous articles on Tennessee history, the best of which were a series in the *Tennessee Historical Magazine* entitled "Indian Wars and Warriors of the Old Southwest." Goodpasture died in Nashville on December 3, 1942.

Fred S. Rolater, Middle Tennessee State University

SEE: AGRICULTURAL WHEEL; FARMERS' ALLIANCE; OVERTON COUNTY; TENNESSEE HISTORICAL COMMISSION; TENNESSEE HISTORICAL SOCIETY

GOODPASTURE, ERNEST WILLIAM (1886–1960)

was a distinguished figure in pathology and a pioneer in modern virological research. He contributed significantly to the advance of knowledge in many fields, particularly the pathogenesis of infectious diseases, the problems of parasitism, the laboratory cultivation of viruses, and the mechanism and course of a wide variety of viral and other infections.

Goodpasture was born on a farm near Clarksville, Montgomery County, Tennessee, October 17, 1886, the son of Albert Virgil and Jennie Wilson Dawson Goodpasture. Ernest Goodpasture received his B.A. degree from Vanderbilt University. He then entered Johns Hopkins Medical School, graduating in 1912. He was appointed a Rockefeller Fellow in pathology at Johns Hopkins under Professors William Welch and George H. Whipple. In 1915 he joined the faculty of Harvard Medical School. This period, which included two years of wartime service in the United States Navy, was followed by appointments at the University of the Philippines School of Medicine at Manila and at William H. Singer Memorial Laboratories in Pittsburgh. In 1924 he was invited to return to Vanderbilt as Professor and Chairman of the Department of Pathology in the reorganized Vanderbilt University School of Medicine.

In 1919 Goodpasture, while studying the influenza pandemic, described a progressive and usually fatal disease in which glomerulonephritis was associated with coughing of blood. Most of the patients died of kidney failure. This has been known since as Goodpasture's syndrome.

For over 30 years, the work at his Vanderbilt laboratory produced a series of noteworthy contributions, which brought national and international recognition in the field of infectious diseases, especially virus infections. He introduced the chick embryo as an experimental host in the investigation of infection and in the production of vaccines.

These studies made possible the practical application on a large scale of the development of present-day vaccines against viral diseases. The eminent virologist Sir F. MacFarlane Burnet went so far as to say that Goodpasture's discovery made possible modern abilities to control viral diseases.

Goodpasture's experiments were classic examples of simplicity in plan, detailed observations, and objectivity. Perhaps the most remarkable were those designed to test the hypothesis of the neural spread of herpes simples virus. Equally impressive were the investigations demonstrating the infectivity of inclusions in fowl pox and the determination of the relationship of these inclusions to Borrel bodies.

In subsequent years, using the chick-embryo technique, Goodpasture and his co-workers elucidated the natural history of numerous viral diseases. These included studies of vaccinia infection, which resulted in improved vaccination against smallpox and identification of the virus which causes mumps. His technique proved adaptable to studies of rickettsia, bacteria, fungi, and protozoa, as well as viruses. He and his workers also carried out novel studies of experimental skin infection and the role of humoral factors in the immune process.

For his many contributions, he was invited to give some the nation's most prestigious lectures, including the Harvey, DeLamar, Hetkoen, Loeb, Shattuck, and Alvarenga Lectures. He received honorary degrees from Yale University, Washington University, the University of Chicago, and Tulane University. He was the recipient of the Passano Foundation Award, the Howard Taylor Ricketts Award, the Kober Medal, the Sedgwick Memorial Award, the Kovalenko Medal of the National Academy of Science, and the Gold Headed Cane of the American Association of Pathologists and Bacteriologists. He was elected to the Board of Directors of the International Health Division of the Rockefeller Foundation, to the National Academy of Science, to the American Philosophical Society, and to the Board of Trust of Vanderbilt University. For many years he was a member of the American Association of Pathologists and Bacteriologists and the American Society of Experimental Pathology, in each of which he served as president. He also served on the Board of Editors of *The American Journal of Pathology* and was for a period its editor-in-chief.

During and after World War II, he served on the original Armed Forces Epidemiological Board, the Institute for Nuclear Studies at Oak Ridge, the Advisory Committee on Biology and Medicine of the Atomic Energy Commission, a scientific director of the International Health Division of the Rockefeller, and on the commission on growth of the National Research Council.

Goodpasture was a dedicated teacher, and those who were privileged to be his students were fortunate indeed. Because of his strong sense of loyalty to Vanderbilt, Goodpasture agreed in later years to take on administrative responsibility. He served as Associate Dean of the Vanderbilt School of Medicine from 1942 to 1945, and as Dean from 1945 to 1950.

In 1955, after more than 30 years at Vanderbilt, Goodpasture reached the age of retirement. He was invited to assume what was to become one this country's principal posts in his field, the scientific directorship of the Armed Forces Institute of Pathology in Washington, D.C. Goodpasture led the institute through a period of reorganization, expansion, and an enormous output of research, in which civilian pathologists throughout the country contributed heavily. He remained at the Armed Forces Institute for four years, when he resigned his position to return to Tennessee. His retirement was not to last long. He died suddenly in September 1960 of a myocardial infarction, while engaged in yard work at his home.

Harris D. Riley, Jr., Vanderbilt University Medical Center
SEE: MEDICINE; VANDERBILT UNIVERSITY MEDICAL CENTER

GOODSPEED HISTORIES. In the early 1880s Westin A. Goodspeed, a successful Nashville-based publisher, discovered that volumes combining local history, biography, and state historical records sold well in Ohio, Pennsylvania, New York, and several other northern states. In the South, except for Kentucky, Virginia, and Georgia, little compilation of resources had occurred since the Civil War; Goodspeed acted to fill that gap in Tennessee.

Goodspeed proceeded by asking more than 100 "prominent citizens," including Governor William B. Bate, State Librarian Mrs. S. K. Hatton, and the Secretary of the Tennessee Historical Society, James A. Cartwright, to submit material for a general history of the state. The 742-page summary depicted the state's geography, Native American history, white settlement, pre-statehood political development, economic development, plus judicial, political, and religious history. The compendium emphasized military history, although it also covered government and private institutions and included biographies of 17 individuals. The choice of individuals was particularly interesting and included the three Tennessee presidents, Sam Houston, William Carroll, David Crockett, John Bell, John Sevier, and James Robertson, plus the odd combination of Nathan Bedford Forrest, Felix Zollicoffer, and William G. Brownlow. The section on the Civil War covered 140 pages, though the 66 pages devoted to Native Americans represented the most ambitious attempt to develop that theme until the 1940s.

The company issued another ten volumes that covered smaller areas within the state. Each volume contained the section on state history and biography followed by sections on local history and biography, organized by county. Some counties, such as Shelby and Hamilton, made up separate volumes. Thirty-four counties were covered before the publication was discontinued. As in the state history, local citizens compiled the county histories, with little editing. They often consisted of lists of officers or prominent citizens. For those 34 counties, however, no more complete record of early government officers, business development, educational progress, or religious history exists. In the 1970s, both Woodward and Stinson of Columbia and the Elder's Bookstore

of Nashville brought out reprint editions, which are more available than the originals.

Fred S. Rolater, Middle Tennessee State University
SEE: BATE, WILLIAM B.; TENNESSEE HISTORICAL SOCIETY

GORDON, CAROLINE (1895–1981), novelist, was born into the Kentucky line of the extensive Meriwether family in 1895. Exploration of the family's past and its evolution is a major theme of her fiction. She grew up at Merry Mont in Todd County, near Clarksville, Tennessee. Her father, James Morris Gordon, came from Virginia to tutor the Meriwether children, married Nancy Meriwether, and established an academy in Clarksville, where his daughter received her early education. She earned a Bachelor of Arts degree from Bethany College in 1916. Gordon is the idealized subject of Caroline Gordon's second novel, *Alec Maury, Sportsman* (1934), and the central character in her much-anthologized story, "Old Red."

Caroline Gordon taught briefly; then, as a journalist, became one of the first reviewers to comment favorably on a new Nashville-based magazine of poetry, *The Fugitive*. During the summer of 1924, Robert Penn Warren, a Todd County neighbor, introduced Caroline Gordon to Allen Tate. Within a year they were married and living in New York City, where she gave birth to their daughter, Nancy Meriwether. With Tate, she began a period of life abroad, devoted to writing, and sustained by various fellowships granted to one or the other. In London, Gordon was secretary to the influential British writer Ford Madox Ford, who provided the couple with quarters in Paris and introduced them to the American expatriots.

In 1930 the Tates returned to the United States and settled in Clarksville in a house provided by Tate's brother Ben and called "Benfolly." Both Tates were exceptionally hospitable to friends and encouraging to younger writers. Both were prolific correspondents, generous with constructive criticism. (Gordon eventually became mentor to several writers, most notably Flannery O'Connor). Although she had to wrest time for her writing from domestic and social obligations, the eight Benfolly years were especially productive for Gordon, who published four novels and several stories before 1937. The first novel was *Penhally* (1931), followed by *Alec Maury, Sportsman* (1934), *None Shall Look Back* (1937), and *The Garden of Adonis* (1937), studies of the southern family during the Civil War and Great Depression.

Academic appointments of the 1940s took the Tates throughout the southeast and to Princeton, where they established a home near their daughter, who married psychiatrist Percy Wood in 1944. During this time Gordon published her fifth novel *Green Centuries* (1941). Her second related group of novels, *The Woman on the Porch* (1944), which deals with a troubled marriage; *The Strange Children* (1951), based on life at Benfolly; and *The Malefactors* (1956), is informed by her conversion to Roman Catholicism. Her own marriage suffered during this period. The Tates were divorced briefly in 1946, then remarried. Together they wrote *The House of Fiction* (1950), which was followed by Gordon's *How to Read a Novel* in 1957. The marriage was permanently dissolved in 1959.

Gordon maintained her home at Princeton until 1973, teaching and writing, including *The Glory of Hera* (1972). An appointment in the creative writing program drew her to the University of Dallas. When her health began to fail in 1978, she moved to San Cristobal de las Casas in Chapas, Mexico, with the Wood family. She died there on April 11, 1981.
Marice Wolfe, Vanderbilt University
SEE: CLARKSVILLE; LITERATURE; TATE, JOHN O. ALLEN

GORDON, FRANCIS HAYNES (1804–1873), pioneer in scientific agriculture, was born in Gordonsville, Smith County, Tennessee, on August 6, 1804. Though he rarely left Smith County, he exerted a lasting influence on Tennessee antebellum agriculture. In 1830 he joined a group that organized Porter's Hill Academy near Carthage; three years later he led an effort to restructure the curriculum and incorporate Porter's Hill Academy as Clinton College. Gordon served as the primary instructor, though he had no formal education beyond local schools and a few years at Campbell Academy in Lebanon. By February 1842 Clinton College had failed, and its lands were being offered for sale.

During his years at Clinton College, Gordon played a critical role in the history of scientific agriculture in Tennessee. In 1838 he guided the organization of the Smith County Agricultural Society. In 1839 he led a successful drive for a state-wide Tennessee Agricultural Society. He was the Society's secretary for several years, publishing frequently in the Society's journal, *The Agriculturist*. Early in 1842 he moved to the national level, drafting a constitution for the American Agricultural Society. Gordon was one of two Tennessee delegates who attended the first meeting of the national society in Washington, D. C., in 1842.

In 1844 and 1845 Gordon resumed his education at the University of Louisville, earning an M.D. From 1848 to 1852 he occasionally taught medicine at a little-known proprietary medical school in Memphis that was sometimes a satellite of Cumberland University in Lebanon. While Gordon pursued his career as a professor of medicine and as a physician, scientific agriculture remained his great interest. He contributed more than 50 articles to agricultural journals before he died of consumption, at Gordonsville, in 1873.

Gordon's imprint is still evident in the landscape of rural Tennessee. He is credited with introducing bluegrass to the state. He also promoted the concept of the farm yard, mowed land surrounding the farm house, as a replacement for the early practice of planting crops adjacent to homes.
James X. Corgan, Austin Peay State University
SUGGESTED READING: Robert H. White, "A Sketch of the Life and Contributions of Francis Haynes Gordon, M.D.," manuscript, TSLA
SEE: AGRICULTURAL JOURNALS; AGRICULTURAL SOCIETIES

GORE, ALBERT A., JR. (1948–), 45th Vice President of the United States, was born on March 31, 1948, to former Congressman and U.S. Senator Albert A. Gore and Pauline LaFon Gore. He attended St. Albans Episcopal School for Boys in Washington, D.C., and graduated with honors from Harvard University in 1969. Gore subsequently volunteered for service in the U.S. Army and saw duty in Vietnam.

As a young person, Gore seemed destined for and was apparently preparing for a career in public service. He was, however, greatly disillusioned by Tennessee voters' rejection of his father's attempt for a fourth Senate term in 1970. Following his discharge from the army, Gore took employment in Nashville as a newspaper reporter at *The Tennessean* and enrolled in Law and Divinity classes at Vanderbilt University.

At *The Tennessean,* Gore demonstrated characteristics that many have identified with his subsequent career in elected office. John Seigenthaler, then Editor of *The Tennessean,* recalls that Gore was equally thorough and serious in his approach to assignments whether on the police beat, covering country music, or exposing major corruption in local government. During his years as a reporter, Gore's appreciation for public service slowly revived as he covered public policy issues that frequently brought him into contact with public officials at all levels of government. Although he passed up an opportunity to run for Congress from the sixth district in 1972, by 1976, following the announcement that Congressman Joe L. Evins would not seek re-election, Gore enthusiastically jumped into a crowded field and emerged with the Democratic nomination. In November, he was elected by a comfortable margin. Following four terms in the House of Representatives, Gore challenged for, and was elected to, the United States Senate.

In the House and Senate, Gore became particularly well versed on scientific and technological issues, ranging from genetic engineering to nuclear arms control. He strongly identified with so-called "environmental" issues and, in 1992, chaired the U.S. delegation to the Earth Summit in Rio de Janeiro, Brazil. He outlined a plan for an international approach to dealing with environmental issues in his best selling book, *Earth in the Balance: Ecology and the Human Spirit.*

In 1988 Gore unsuccessfully sought the Democratic Party nomination for United States President. Two years later, Tennessee voters awarded him a second term in the U. S. Senate, shattering modern precedent by giving him winning margins in all 95 counties.

On July 9, 1992, Democratic Party presidential nominee Bill Clinton chose Gore to be his running mate. Successful in the November elections, they were inaugurated President and Vice President of the United States in January 1993, and were re-elected in 1996. Gore's influence and responsibilities as Vice President were broad and significant. During the second term, many members of his staff were assigned primary responsibility for promotion and administration of Clinton Administration programs.

As Vice President, Gore continued to emphasize public policies pertaining to enhancement of society through appropriate utilization of science and technology. He had introduced the concept of the "information superhighway" into the public debate many years earlier and, as a Senator, had been the prime force behind the High Performance Computing Act. As Vice President, Gore gave leadership to the development of the National Information Infrastructure, the Global Information Infrastructure, and other initiatives to enhance electronic communication. He continued his commitment to environmental issues, particularly in the areas of greenhouse gas emissions, national wetlands policy, and development of fuel efficient vehicles.

Consistent with the traditions of Albert Gore, Sr., and Cordell Hull, Gore staunchly supported free trade, especially the North American Free Trade Alliance (NAFTA). He also was responsible for developing procedures to reduce the size of the national bureaucracy.

Gore is married to Mary Elizabeth "Tipper" Aitcheson, whom he met while still enrolled at St. Albans. They have four children: Karenna, Kristin, Sarah, and Albert III. Both Vice President and Mrs. Gore have been highly visible in addressing issues identified with children and families. In her best selling book, *Raising PG Kids in an X-Rated Society,* Tipper Gore addressed the impact of the entertainment industry on the development of personal and social values in children. Vice President Gore has focused on the role of fathers in modern society and each year has hosted a high profile conference to address different issues pertaining to that role.

The Gores own a small farm near Carthage, Tennessee, and attend the New Salem Missionary Church there.

James H. Neal, Middle Tennessee State University

SEE: GORE, ALBERT A., SR.; NASHVILLE TENNESSEAN; SMITH COUNTY

GORE, ALBERT ARNOLD, SR. (1907–), Congressman and U.S. Senator, was born in Jackson County, Tennessee, on December 26, 1907, the son of Allen and Margie Denny Gore. Raised on a farm, Gore witnessed the loss of his family's entire financial resources during the Great Depression, when three local banks collapsed during a single week. Gore obtained his formal education in one-room schools and at Gordonsville High School. He worked his way through college at the University of Tennessee, Knoxville and at the State Teachers College in Murfreesboro (now Middle Tennessee State University) by teaching school, fiddling at barn dances, and working at various other jobs during the fall semester to pay tuition in the spring. A varsity basketball player, Gore graduated from State Teachers College, Murfreesboro in 1932 with a major in history. He served as Smith County superintendent of schools from 1932 to 1937, while attending night classes at the Nashville YMCA law school, from which he graduated in 1936.

Interested in public service from a very young age, Gore's efforts to reform the Tennessee Young Democrats brought him to the attention of Congressman Gordon Browning, who asked him to manage his unsuccessful race for governor in 1934. Successful in his second run for governor, Browning named Gore Commissioner of Labor in 1937. In that office, Gore established Tennessee's first unemployment compensation program and implemented a viable coal mine safety inspection program.

In 1938 Gore won election to represent the Fourth Tennessee District in the U.S. House of Representatives, succeeding Congressman Ridley Mitchell. Thus began 32 years of public service representing Tennessee in the House (1939–1953) and the U.S. Senate (1953–1971). Although he strongly supported Franklin D. Roosevelt's New Deal, Gore's first House speech challenged an administration housing bill. The speech contributed to the defeat of the measure and brought Gore into the national spotlight. Gore developed a close relationship with House Majority Leader Sam Rayburn, who appointed him to the Appropriations Committee and called on him for a number of extraordinary assignments. Among these was service on a secret House committee that surreptitiously secured appropriations for the wartime Oak Ridge nuclear project.

In 1952 Gore successfully challenged the Senate seat held by Kenneth D. McKellar, the powerful chairman of the Senate Ways and Means Committee and an ally of Edward H. Crump in Memphis. Gore's victory helped to undermine the statewide influence of the Crump political machine. Gore immediately forged a political alliance with Estes Kefauver, Tennessee's senior U.S. Senator and also a local opponnent of the Crump machine, and together they gave to new look to the Tennessee Democratic party.

Fiercely loyal to the Democratic party, partisanship did not, however, determine his legislative record. Gore waged high profile battles against the party establishment in Congress and against administration programs he could not support during the presidencies of Roosevelt, Harry S. Truman, and John F. Kennedy. He often supported Dwight Eisenhower's initiatives, especially in the area of foreign policy.

From the New Deal to the social programs of the Lyndon Johnson administration, Gore generally supported domestic legislation designed to benefit those he saw as inadequately served by their government. He vigorously opposed policies he believed inordinately beneficial to the privileged and powerful. Gore opposed bonuses to defense contractors, tax breaks to stimulate industrial expansion, and the 27 1/2 percent oil depletion allowance. Like his mentor, Cordell Hull, Gore believed in progressive taxation and resisted across-the-board tax cuts, while favoring increases of the individual tax exemption. He supported the Taft-Hartley Labor bill, the federal minimum wage bill, and a variety of public works projects. He is regarded as the father of Medicare, his legislation being the first federal health insurance program to be enacted into law. He authored bills for construction and financing of the Interstate Highway System, the largest public works program in history, and successfully blocked an Eisenhower proposal to use long-term debt to finance it. Gore was a leading contender for the Democratic vice presidential nomination in 1956 and 1960, and was a member of a five-person committee that coached John Kennedy on national policy issues during the 1960 presidential campaign.

Gore's record in civil rights was progressive compared to his Southern colleagues. In the mid-1950s, he was one of two senators (the other was Estes Kefauver) from states of the old Confederacy to refuse to sign the "Southern Manifesto" to oppose racial integration as ordered by the U.S. Supreme Court. His consistent support for voting rights bills was in keeping with his views on the right of franchise in a democratic society. Gore also supported early civil rights bills which set goals and policies but that took later legal mechanisms to ensure compliance. The Civil Rights Act of 1964 possessed significant enforcement and compliance measures, but Gore questioned whether the bill embraced excessive federal involvement and enforcement. He perceived the legislation as a "sledgehammer" approach to solving serious racial inequities.

Throughout his career, Gore promoted reciprocal trade and other internationalist philosophies of Cordell Hull. He opposed arms embargoes in 1939, and voted for lend-lease in 1941. After World War II, he supported authorization of UNRRA, extension of the Marshall Plan, aid to Greece and Turkey, and assistance to Korea in 1950. He was the first Senator to call for suspension of nuclear tests in 1958, and helped negotiate the arms control measures ratified during the Eisenhower administration. He was a delegate to the Interparliamentary Union and to the United Nations. Unlike most Senators, Gore initially in the 1950s questioned U.S. policy in former French Indo-China, and as the Vietnam War escalated, Gore became strongly opposed to American policy, a stance that cost him politically.

In 1970 Republican William Brock, III, defeated Gore for the U.S. Senate as part of the Nixon-Agnew "Southern Strategy" to gain Republican victories in the South. Brock's successful campaign capitalized on Gore's anti-war stance, his record on civil rights, and Gore's perceived aloofness from the values and wishes of Tennessee voters.

In 1971 Gore lectured at Vanderbilt University and was a Fellow at Harvard University. He devoted his energies to writing and to the practice of law before becoming Chairman of the Board of Island Creek Coal Company and Director and Executive Vice President of Occidental Petroleum Corporation, from September 1972 through August 1983. He continues on the Occidental Petroleum Board of Directors.

Gore is the author of two books: *Eye of the Storm* (1970) and *Let the Glory Out* (1972). He married Pauline LaFon Gore of Jackson, Tennessee, in 1937. They had two children: Nancy LaFon Gore Hunger (1938–1984) and Albert A. Gore, Jr., (1948–). They also have four grandchildren: Karenna, Kristin, Sarah, and Albert III. The Gores reside in Carthage, where they own and operate Gore Farms.

James H. Neal, Middle Tennessee State University

SEE: BROCK, WILLIAM E.; BROWNING, GORDON; KEFAUVER, CAREY ESTES; HULL, CORDELL; MCKELLAR, KENNETH D.; SMITH COUNTY

GOSPEL MUSIC: See JUBILEE SINGERS OF FISK UNIVERSITY; MUSIC; SHAPE-NOTE SINGING; VAUGHAN, JAMES D.; VERNACULAR RELIGIOUS MUSIC

GOVERNMENT. Government, in the basic sense of a structure or system for management of a group or geographic region, has a long history in the state. Archaeological studies of habitation sites of prehistoric Native Americans give intriguing hints of political and religious systems we will never know a great deal about. Bands of ice age hunters who came to the area 10,000 years ago, and those that came later, were probably led by chieftains who exercised authority over their followers. The Old Stone Fort in Coffee

County, an impressive earthen structure built by Woodland people and carbon-14 dated as early as A.D. 30, may have taken several hundred years to build. It stands as evidence of the presence of leadership and the authority of rules, or laws, that in combination led to the erection of a remarkable ceremonial edifice.

In what would become Tennessee, Native Americans such as the Cherokees, Creeks, and Chickasaws established patriarchal systems of governance centered on chiefs, sub-chiefs, and councils of advisors in principal villages. The Cherokees had a primary town, where the most powerful chief lived. They gave a place in their council to an Honored Woman, who decided the fate of captives taken in warfare. Creeks had provinces with capital towns, that functioned as ceremonial and administrative units. A chief, or miko, assisted by a group of elders, called beloved men, dealt with matters of war and peace, ceremonial obligations, and contacts with non-Creek people. Cherokees, Creeks, Chickasaws, Choctaws, and Shawnees all utilized a clan system of family identification that provided a foundation of relationships interwoven with political and religious elements of life.

The brief stay in 1540 of the Spanish adventurer Hernando de Soto in East Tennessee heralded a new era in Tennessee history. Over a century later, in 1663, the region fell within the borders of the newly chartered English colony of Carolina. English rule was nominal as the French and English struggled for control of the interior of eastern North America and its lucrative fur trade with Native Americans. The year 1763 brought the Treaty of Paris, which formalized the victory of England over France by giving the British control of Canada and most of North America east of the Mississippi River. The British immediately issued a proclamation establishing a line down the crest of the Appalachian mountains and instructing colonists to remain east of the line; the west was designated for Cherokees and other Native Americans. Tennessee lay west of the line, outside the official border of settlement. Fur trappers and settlers would not be held back from the west by a distant government's scribble on a map.

North Carolina claimed the land that would become Tennessee under the provisions of their colonial charter. In three separate instances, settlers, believing they were beyond the effective reach of North Carolina government, took the initiative to establish order on their own terms. In 1772 Watauga and Nolichucky residents assembled and formed the Watauga Association. They created offices to maintain peace and protect themselves from Cherokee attacks. The Association did not last long, and records have not survived. Eight years later, pioneers at the French Lick on the Cumberland River

drew up the Cumberland Compact for similar purposes. The Compact provided for 12 elected judges but, like its predecessor to the east, it did not endure. It was superseded in 1783, the year the United States won its independence, when North Carolina asserted its authority and established Davidson County in the region.

Settlers from the Holston and Watauga areas held meetings at Jonesborough in 1784 to organize a new state. North Carolina ceded control of its western lands to Congress in June, but repealed its action in November. Supporters of statehood petitioned Congress, claiming that the actions of North Carolina had caused Indian attacks on settlements and the state should not be permitted to reassert its claims over a "country whose prayers she has rejected and whose interests she has forsaken."[1] Their hopes rested with Congressional approval of a new, separate state named for Pennsylvania's Benjamin Franklin. John Sevier reluctantly assumed leadership of the State of Franklin movement, serving as governor under a constitution that closely resembled that of North Carolina. Franklin failed, dying slowly over a period of several years, a victim of North Carolina's opposition, internal division, and a Confederation Congress reluctant to become involved.

Statehood came, however, before the end of the century. On December 12, 1789, North Carolina lawmakers passed another statute transferring western land to the new national government under the Constitution. This time there was no change of mind by Carolina, and the United States accepted the region, naming it the Territory of the United States South of the River Ohio, known as the Southwest Territory. North Carolina stipulated that slavery be permitted in the territory, but in all other respects the provisions of the Northwest Ordinance of 1787 were to apply to the western area it relinquished. The ordinance held forth the promise of eventual statehood for the future Tennessee.

The Northwest Ordinance set forth three stages of governance based on population. The Southwest Territory moved swiftly through the steps, carried forward by a tide of new settlers moving into the territory from the east and the northeast. Following a census and referendum in 1795 that showed a majority favored statehood, Territorial Governor William Blount called for the election of delegates to a constitutional convention. Fifty-five delegates, five from each county, were chosen and assembled in Knoxville on January 17, 1796, to begin work. Blount was elected to chair the convention.

In a three-week period, the delegates fashioned a constitution that Thomas Jefferson was later to call "the least imperfect and most republican"[2] of such documents. A bicameral legislature dominated government. The franchise was extended to all free males who were at least 21 years of age, owned property, and had lived in the county for six months. The legislature filled most county and state offices. There was no distinct judicial branch of government, as the legislature was empowered to create courts and appoint judges as needed.

The state would have a governor, who served a two-year term, and no governor could be elected for more than three consecutive terms. The governor, having little real power, was charged with the execution of the laws, but had no veto over legislative actions. At the end of the text, the delegates included a Declaration of Rights, derived significantly from the North Carolina constitution of ten years earlier. The constitution of Pennsylvania was another major source for some passages, including the article on the powers of the governor and another addressing impeachment. Finally, the delegates from Tennessee County agreed to surrender their county's name so that it might become the designation of the state.

Following the directives of the convention, Governor Blount proceeded to hold an election for governor and the legislature. Tennesseans intended to have a government in place and ready to function when Congress approved the petition for statehood and the state constitution. John Sevier was elected governor, and the new general assembly convened on March 29, 1796. All steps were taken on the assumption that Congress would act favorably on the request for admission to the Union. Approval came, but not without a struggle. Federalists, who supported John Adams in the upcoming presidential election, opposed admission, fearing the new state would favor Republican Thomas Jefferson in the close fall balloting. Supporters of the state prevailed, and on June 1, 1796, President George Washington signed legislation admitting Tennessee as the sixteenth state.

In the first half of the nineteenth century, a number of states, responding to social forces pressing the case for a greater role for the average white citizen, revised their constitutions. Tennessee became part of this trend when, on May 19, 1834, 60 delegates assembled in Nashville in a constitutional convention and selected William Carter, of Carter County, as president of the proceedings. The principal interests of the delegates concerned the provisions of the 1796 constitution dealing with taxation and representation. The constitutional provision that had required equal taxation of all land, except for town lots, which could be taxed at the rate for 200 acres of land, was rewritten to call for all property to be taxed on its value. This removed the long-standing grievance of small farmers, who resented the fact that, under the old constitution, owners of fertile lands, with a great many improvements on them, paid no more per acre in taxes than the owners of the less developed farms on less fertile soil.

White citizens received greater opportunities for political expression and office-holding. The size of the legislature increased to 99 seats in the lower house, with the senate set at one-third the number of representatives, when the population of the state reached one and a half million. Voters received the right to elect trustees, sheriffs, and all other county officials, who now served for fixed terms. All property requirements for voting were eliminated. However, the new-found concern with the "common man" extended to whites only. In making suffrage changes, the delegates restricted the vote to white men, thereby disfranchising free black males, who had voted under the 1796 Constitution.

A variety of other issues were addressed. Antislavery groups petitioned for the abolition of slavery, but the delegates rejected their appeals. Instead, the convention added language requiring the approval of slaveowners for the passage of any future acts of emancipation. On the topic of the permanent location of the state capitol, the legislature was expected to make a final decision by early 1843. Lotteries were prohibited in the new constitution. The procedure for amending the constitution was changed somewhat, but remained difficult to alter. When presented to the voters in March 1835, the new constitution was ratified by a vote of 42,666 in favor to 17,691 against.

A little over a quarter of a century later, Tennesseans faced an unprecedented crisis of governmental loyalty. The election of Abraham Lincoln to the presidency in November 1860 raised the long running sectional controversy over slavery to a new level of intensity, causing several states of the Deep South to sever their connection with the United States. A majority of Tennesseans hoped to stay within the Union and on February 9, 1861, rejected a proposal to call a state convention to consider secession. However, Lincoln's call for volunteers to defend Federal authority, following the attack on Fort Sumter in April, produced a reaction in Middle and West Tennessee that identified with the new Confederate States of America. On June 8, voters ratified secession and affiliation with the Confederacy by a vote of 104,913 to 47,238. Only staunchly Unionist East Tennessee gave a majority for the Union.

In 1862 Union successes on the battlefields in Middle and West Tennessee put Confederate Governor, Isham G. Harris, to flight and led Lincoln to appoint Greeneville resident and outspoken Unionist, Andrew Johnson, military governor of the state. The tide of the Civil War ran steadily in favor of the Union as more and more of the state came under Union control. In January 1865, five hundred Unionist delegates assembled in Nashville to amend the constitution and set in motion a return to loyal civil government. The delegates prepared an amendment that abolished slavery and a "schedule" that revoked the state's secession, declared the actions of the Confederate government null and void, and confirmed the appointments made by Johnson as military governor. The delegates set in motion the process for election of a Unionist legislature and William G. Brownlow as governor. The actions of the convention were approved on February 22, 1865, by a vote of Unionists only. Readmission to the Union occurred over a year later on July 23, 1866, when President Andrew Johnson signed a congressional resolution approving the action.

Four years of control of state government by Radical Republican supporters of Governor Brownlow ended in 1869 with the restoration of voting rights to ex-Confederates. In that year, the people approved a proposal to elect delegates to a constitutional convention, which assembled on January 10, 1870, at the courthouse in Nashville. The convention was dominated by Conservatives cognizant of the unspoken presence of federal oversight, but determined to wipe out the legacy of the Radical Republican period and prevent future domination of public affairs by a minority. John C. Brown, an ex-Confederate general, was elected chair of the convention. Compared to some ex-Confederates, Brown led the convention in a moderate direction as it went about the process of altering the constitution.

In conformity with federal requirements, slavery was explicitly forbidden. Suffrage was then the key issue, and the convention's critics expected the delegates to act to disfranchise former slaves. Many ex-Confederates deeply resented the 1867 enfranchisement of the freedmen, when they had been denied the same right. Ultimately, although African-American men retained the right to vote, the inclusion of a provision for the levy of a poll tax portended disfranchisement when it became a prerequisite to voting. Although the poll tax was justified by its proponents as a school tax, its inclusion reflected the attitude of many whites against what they perceived as an uneducated black electorate, whose votes would not be cast wisely. However, many critics expressed concern that the tax could be used to reduce the number of poor white voters, as well as the number of black voters.

Reflecting the resentment felt by ex-Confederates toward the actions of former Governor Brownlow and the Radical-controlled legislature, the delegates restricted the powers of the legislature and the governor. The length of paid legislative sessions was restricted; the general assembly could not lend money or credit to any private corporation. The governor's power to use the state militia was curtailed, and the writ of habeas corpus could be suspended only by action of the general assembly. In addition, the chief executive could not appoint county officials. However, one action increased the power of the governor. The governor received veto power over any bill passed by the legislature, but a veto could be overridden by a simple majority vote of the houses of the legislature.

Opposition to Radical control of the supreme court led to an increase in the size of the court to five members, and the requirement that no more than two justices could be residents of the same grand division of the state. The attorney general's term was increased from six to eight years, and the post, which had been filled by popular election in the past, would now be an appointed one, decided by the supreme court.

The difficult process of legislative amendment of the basic law was not changed in the constitution of 1870. The 1834 document contained a procedure whereby the constitution could be changed by legislative action. This process was retained in the 1870 text. A proposed amendment must be approved by a majority of both houses of the legislature and published six months prior to the beginning of the next session. The next general assembly must approve the change by a two-thirds vote of each house. Finally, a majority of the voters in the next election for state representatives must ratify the proposed change.

The delegates approved another process for amending the constitution by means of a convention such as their own. The first constitution of 1796 contained a provision for this method, but the 1834 constitution did not. Under the provisions for amending by convention, lawmakers must pass a call for a convention, and a majority of voters must endorse it in a vote on the call. The delegates in convention may propose changes. However, the proposed changes must be submitted to the people for approval by a majority of those voting. This has been the avenue used in most successful attempts to amend the constitution since the 1870 document was ratified. On March 26, 1870, the work of the convention was approved by a vote of 98,128 to 33,972.

Delegates and voters had no way of knowing that the document they crafted and approved would remain the basic law of the state for almost a century. Three conventions, in 1796, 1834, and 1870, in less than one hundred years, might have led to predictions of more change in the next century, but this has not been the case. Remarkably, the constitution remained unchanged until 1953. In that year, ex-governor Prentice Cooper chaired a convention that proposed changing the governor's term of office from two to four years, but forbade the incumbent from serving a second term in succession. The governor received the line item veto, and wording permitting the poll tax, ruled unconstitutional by the United States Supreme Court some years earlier, was dropped.

Under the proposed provisions, the General Assembly received an increase in per diem, and the state's cities were given the option of home rule. In regard to the amending processes, the delegates favored dropping the limiting requirement that a specific amendment, which originates in the legislature, could be offered for consideration no more frequently than once in six years. Such amendments now had to receive a majority vote of those voting for governor, rather than for representatives, to be incorporated into the constitution. In regard to the constitutional convention procedure for amending, the delegates decided to place a six-year limit on the frequency of such conventions. As in the past, all recommended revisions put forward by a convention were subject to approval by the voters.

The 1953 body, the first limited constitutional convention, spawned four successors at the minimum six year intervals permitted. Delegates assembled in 1959, 1965, 1971, and 1977. In 1959 they proposed extending the terms of county trustees. The 1965 gathering changed the criteria for apportioning seats in the legislature, extended senate terms to four years, and abolished biennial meetings of the legislature in favor of annual sessions. County courts were permitted to fill legislative vacancies, and for the first time, lawmakers were paid a salary, plus per diem. Six years later, delegates met in a convention restricted to the purpose of addressing property classification for taxation. The 1977 convention had a broader agenda.

On March 7, 1978, voters approved 12 of 13 changes recommended by the convention of the preceding year. The proposals of greatest interest included those allowing the governor to serve two terms in succession, authorizing the legislature to set maximum interest rates, and requiring a balanced budget. Language establishing the post of county executive and a county legislative body of not more than 25 members was endorsed. In addition, the General Assembly received authority to permit alternate forms of county government. Federal court rulings required changing the voting age to 18, striking wording forbidding interracial marriages, and purging a provision that called for segregated schools. Not approved by the voters were proposed changes in the judicial articles of the constitution.

All three of Tennessee's constitutions have met the perceived needs of the state's citizens, but the 1870 fundamental law has had a remarkable life span. Written by a convention heavily influenced by events of the post-Civil War era, it also carries a substantial legacy of the 1796 and 1834 constitutions imbedded in its provisions. Its most significant shortcoming is the difficulty of the amending procedure; indeed scholars have termed it "the most difficult of all state constitutions to amend."[3] As a result, at times, the constitution has not reflected changes in society and the United States Constitution, including Supreme Court interpretations of the national Constitution. A number of amendments implemented by means of the convention process would probably have been made by legislative initiative, if the legislative process was not so difficult as to prove practically impossible to use to implement change. Nevertheless, the constitution reflects a people's basic efforts, imperfect as they have been in some regards, to construct a society of laws with an enduring framework of democratic, representative government.

Robert B. Jones, Middle Tennessee State University

CITATIONS:

(1) Samuel Cole Williams, *History of the Lost State of Franklin* (Johnson City, 1924), 79–80.

(2) J.G.M. Ramsey, *The Annals of Tennessee to the Eighteenth Century* . . . (Charleston, S.C., 1853), 657.

(3) Lee F. Greene, David H. Grubbs, and Victor C. Hobday, *Government in Tennessee* (4th. ed., Knoxville, 1982), 11.

SUGGESTED READINGS: Robert E. Corlew, *Tennessee: A Short History* (2nd ed., 1990); Lee F. Greene, David H. Grubbs, and Victor C. Hobday, *Government in Tennessee* (4th ed.; 1982); Anne H. Hopkins, Neva Lyons, Michael MacDonald, and H.P. Hamlin, *Issues in the Tennessee Constitution* (1976); Lewis L. Laska, "A Legal and Constitutional History of Tennessee, 1772–1972," *Memphis State University Law Review* 6(1976): 563–672; Lewis L. Laska, *The Tennessee State Constitution: A Reference Guide* (1990)

GRACELAND. Elvis Presley's Graceland ranks with Mount Vernon and Monticello as the most popular of American house museums. Though this may startle many and outrage some, there is a congruence to the heavy visitation these three sites annually receive. Since each is a place where its hero not only lived but also died and was interred, to each is imparted the aura of a shrine. While all three sites function as diversions for the curious and attractions for the historically dutiful, they also beckon pilgrims who come to honor the era-shaping magnitude of one man's achievements. Two centuries ago, George Washington and Thomas Jefferson founded an American republic on new and important ideals about human equality and rights of self-determination. Four decades ago, Elvis Presley demonstrated how unimpeded this American opportunity for self-determination might be. His life and music also cast into sharp public relief the deep and persistent fissures between social and economic classes which challenge the myth that equality of voice and dignity—if not of fortune—is an American birthright.

Graceland was built south of Memphis in 1939 according to the design of local architects Max H. Furbringer and Merrill Ehrman. Sited on a hill facing U.S. Highway 51, the house dominates the 14-acre remnant of a substantial farm which belonged to the prominent Toof family for several generations. Ruth Moore, a Toof on her mother's side, built the house with her well-to-do husband and gave it her family's name for the old farm: Graceland. Constructed with a facing of pale Mississippi limestone, the house has the two-story height, two-room depth, classical details, and domineering white portico which evoke sustained gentility in an unmistakably southern architectural drawl.

When Graceland was new, the Memphis *Commercial Appeal* wrote approvingly of its aloofness amidst a "grove of towering oaks" from the road it overlooked, but a suburban neighborhood was already replacing Graceland's rural setting, and Highway 51 itself was starting to attract commercial development. In 1945 the Moores divorced and offered their expensive house for sale to whomever would tolerate the incrementally widening highway and its multiplying roadside offenses.

Such surroundings did not faze the young man who at last purchased Graceland in 1957. Elvis Presley was born dirt-poor and raised hungry in Tupelo, Mississippi, but his capacity for original vocal fusions of country, blues, and southern gospel singing traditions made him rich and famous. His singing, combined with a knee-weakeningly erotic style of performance and velvety, haunting beauty, permanently upset the course of popular music and entirely transformed what it means to be young in America. Though only 22 when he gained title to Graceland, he already had received the homage he retains to this day: Elvis was the King of Rock and Roll.

Of course Elvis did not intend Graceland to be his alone. Like the plain, deferential southern boy he was, Elvis moved his parents to Graceland and treated them, in many respects, as heads of the household. Ensuing years saw the arrival at Graceland of an array of kin and friends, not to mention the 16-year-old "ward" whom Elvis eventually married. When Pricilla Beaulieu Presley left him in 1972, other live-in girlfriends arrived to fill the void. There also was room at Graceland for the famous "Memphis Mafia," a gang of good old boys who stayed round-the-clock available to Elvis for assistance or play.

Elvis initiated his 20-year involvement with Graceland by securing its perimeter in a way that both distanced fans and attracted their attention. The protective pink limestone wall practically invited admirers to scrawl their adulation, while the central iron gates, distinguished with guitar-strumming figures and wafting musical notes, held their own alongside other signs on the burgeoning commercial strip. At night brilliant multi-colored floodlights bathed Graceland's facade. In these ways, Elvis's house contended for attention—it was just one more visual attraction on Highway 51.

This exuberance for dramatically enhancing Graceland's form extended indoors as well. The look of the interior at any one time is difficult to grasp—changes occurred often—but generalizations are possible. For each component of the house, Elvis retained conventional room designations with their customary formal or casual qualities. Furthermore, every phase of interior treatment shares richly colored assemblages of thick carpet, costly fabrics, large-scale furniture, complicated lamps, and novelty accents. To override any suggestion of layaway purchases, installment plans, or results gradually accrued, redecorations always reflected rigorous continuities of design. From the start and even today, visitors to Graceland often miss the point of all this glisten and gush. Elvis's rise to fame and fortune was dizzyingly swift, at times overwhelming. Along the way, he snatched what he could learn about wealthy living from lavishly appointed theaters and auditoriums, luxury car and tour-bus interiors, Hollywood sets, and Las Vegas suites. Then he brought it all back to the house he proudly owned. As one analyst put it, Graceland is how a poor boy lives rich.

Although Elvis discovered soon and under piteous circumstances that chilly-eyed observers thought his house was in staggeringly bad taste, he continued to decorate Graceland as he pleased—adding a new defiant edge and a willingness to embrace the outrageous. His choices also manifest an evolving sense of Graceland as a haven—even a fortress—rather than a showplace. Heavy drapes perpetually drawn, walls covered in pleated fabric or tufted gold upholstery, ceilings lowered and softened with green shag carpet: all are manifestations of Elvis's intensifying need for enclosure and containment. Of course this muffling of Graceland is only the most obvious expression of the isolation and embattlement that accompanied his unparalleled stardom and threatened at last to engulf him. To deal with his turbulent feelings, Elvis escalated his resort to drug abuse and wanton overeating, habits he had indulged for years. Both exacerbated the disorienting effects of his longstanding nocturnal existence amidst a closed circle of accommodating friends and pliant relatives. To all of this his heavy body and aching heart at last succumbed on August 16, 1977.

Because they shared the sensibilities of those who dismissed Graceland as worthlessly gaudy, most journalists initially ignored the death of an overfed has-been; but fans of every background and description turned the death of Elvis Presley into a populist event of unique scale and significance. Motivated by the countless ways in which Elvis touched his audiences, they converged on Memphis by the tens of thousands, virtually paralyzing the city until his funeral and burial were over. Afterward their tributes and vigils made an impossibility of Elvis's conventional resting place in Forest Hills Cemetery; within weeks of his death the Presleys moved his remains to the Meditation Garden behind Graceland's gates. Thus the site became the vital abode of Elvis's spirit, just as it had been the emotional locus of his life.

Since Graceland opened to the public in 1982, Elvis's grave has figured as the destination for organized tours through the house itself and past the displays of costumes, memorabilia, and awards sheltered in auxiliary buildings. The grave also has become central to Tribute Week, the annual observation of Elvis's death. The event's climactic candlelight vigil begins in Meditation Garden at twilight on August 15 and lasts until sunrise on the fateful morning, when all participants extinguish their flames. Old-family Memphians flinch or sneer at this most intensely worshipful of all "Dead Elvis" adulations. Even Elvis Presley Enterprises keeps its distance, although permission to stay at Graceland overnight is the corporation's to grant or withhold. It hardly matters; the faithful would crowd against Graceland's embellished gates if that were as close as they could get. They sense that Elvis Presley and Graceland are inextricably bound, and that both belong, beyond all contest, to the American everybodies and nobodies who love them.

Camille Wells, University of Virginia

SUGGESTED READINGS: *Elvis Presley's Graceland: The Official Guidebook* (1996); Greil Marcus, *Dead Elvis* (1991); Karal Ann Marling, *Graceland* (1996); Gilbert B. Rodman, *Elvis After Elvis* (1996)

SEE: MEMPHIS; PRESLEY, ELVIS

GRAINGER COUNTY holds the distinction as the only Tennessee county named for a woman, Mary Grainger Blount, the wife of Territorial Governor William Blount. The state legislature formed the county in 1796 from parts of Hawkins and Knox counties, and it once included parts of Campbell, Claiborne, Hamblen, and Union counties. The county seat rotated meeting places until 1801, when a courthouse was built in Rutledge.

Nestled between the Holston and Clinch rivers, Grainger County retains much of its rural nature. Rutledge, the county seat, has a population approaching 2,500. Founded in 1798, the town was named in honor of General George Rutledge of Sullivan County. Blaine, now a suburb of Knoxville, traces its origins to the 1700s, when it was known as Blaine's Crossroads because of its proximity to the residence of Robert Blaine. George Bean, Sr., goldsmith, jeweler, and gun maker, settled Bean Station, the county's most recently chartered town (1997). Bean Station served as a crossroads along the Old Kentucky Road (Highway 25-E) and the New Orleans to Washington Road (Highway 11-W). These towns lie to the south of Clinch Mountain, which splits the county into two geographical sections. Communities north of the mountain include Thorn Hill, Washburn, and Powder Springs.

Agriculture still accounts for a significant portion of the county economy, with tobacco the major money crop, though cattle raising continues to make important gains. Grainger County tomatoes have become a national trademark.

Small businesses represented a second source of economic development. Grist mills, hatters, saddle makers, tailors, lawyers, and dry goods merchants supplied the necessities for isolated agricultural communities. Taverns, such as the nationally-renowned Bean Station Hotel along the New Orleans to Washington Road, provided accommodations and refreshments to weary travelers.

By the late 1800s a tourism industry had developed around the mineral springs flowing from Clinch Mountain. The most famous, Tate's Springs, flourished until the Great Depression. It included mineral baths and waters, an enormous hotel, cabins, and a golf course. The resort declined and closed following the Great Depression and a major fire. Today a gazebo is the most important reminder of its former grandeur. More recently, the Tennessee Valley Authority's construction of lakes of both sides of the county, Cherokee Lake to the south and Norris Lake to the north, revived the recreational industry. Fishing, camping, water sports, and development of lakefront property contribute to the county's economy.

Grainger County's industrial growth has been marginal. The Shields family operated Holston Paper Mill, one of the earliest local industries. The Knoxville and Bristol Railway, which once ran through the Richland Creek Valley, succumbed to flooding. The vegetable canneries of the 1910s closed after a tomato blight destroyed their primary produce. Locally-owned Clinchdale Lumber Company logged the county's timber in the early part of the century. Later, timbering gave way to knitting mills and zinc mining. Black marble is quarried in Thorn Hill. In 1974 the county built an industrial park to spark economic growth, with mixed results. Almost half the people of the county now travel to surrounding towns for employment. Overall, the county remains one of small businesses and agriculture.

During the Civil War, a state of near-guerrilla warfare brought economic, political, and social chaos. A major skirmish occurred near Blaine around Christmas of 1862. A year later, the Battle of Bean's Station pitted the forces of Confederate General James Longstreet against a Union army under General J. M. Shackleford in a planned surprise attack that failed through the blunders of Longstreet's staff.

Grainger County claims a number of notable citizens. James Ore, pioneer Indian fighter and Knoxville merchant, was one of the county's first settlers.

Several members of the Cocke family, including John Cocke (1796–1801, 1807–1813, 1843–1845), Sterling Cocke (1815–1819), William Cocke (1813–1815), and William Michael Cocke (1855–1857), served in the state and national legislatures. The Lea family associated with Sam Houston, founded a city in Texas, surveyed the Iowa territory, and taught at the University of Tennessee. Andrew Johnson operated a tailor's shop in Rutledge. DeWitt Clinton Senter, successor to Governor William G. Brownlow, grew up in Grainger County, as did Spencer Jarnagin, a U.S. Senator (1843–1847). John K. Shields held posts as Tennessee Supreme Court Chief Justice and U.S. Senator (1913–1925). His brother, a Knoxville banker, provided the land for the University of Tennessee football stadium. John Williams served as U.S. minister to Turkey. Dr. Herbert Acuff achieved national recognition as a surgeon. Roy H. Beeler became Attorney General of Tennessee. Theo Tate was U.S. Treasurer, and Bob Taylor Jones became Governor of Arizona.

The strength of the county lies in its people. Independent and hard-working, they retain strong family and community ties.

Kevin D. Collins, Rutledge

SEE: BROWNLOW, WILLIAM G.; COCKE, WILLIAM; JOHNSON, ANDREW; RESORTS, HISTORIC; SENTER, DEWITT C.; TENNESSEE VALLEY AUTHORITY

GRAINGER v. STATE (1830) was one of the most controversial homicide cases decided by the Tennessee Supreme Court during the nineteenth century. The case involved a conflict between two men—Grainger and Broach—who had been drinking at a tavern. The two parted on seemingly good terms, but as Grainger rode home by horseback, Broach overtook him and violently struck him on the breast. The frightened Grainger rode to a neighbor's house, where he dismounted and sought asylum. Shouting for help, Grainger moved toward the house as Broach followed. Armed with a rifle, Grainger warned Broach that he would shoot him, if he came closer. When Broach continued to advance, Grainger killed his assailant and was subsequently convicted of murder.

On appeal, Tennessee Supreme Court Judge John Catron overturned Grainger's conviction, concluding that no malice accompanied the defendant's actions. Catron characterized Grainger's behavior as cowardly and timid, but argued that he believed he was alone and in imminent danger; for these reasons, Catron deemed the homicide excusable. Yet, Catron carelessly omitted an important phrase from the holding in the case. "If the jury had believed that Grainger was in danger of great bodily harm from Broach, or thought himself so, " Catron concluded, "then the killing would have been in self-defense."[1] Had Catron included the words "upon sufficient grounds" after "thought

himself so," the opinion would never have stirred the controversy that surrounded the subsequent interpretation of the ruling.

In the case of Grainger, the grounds for his fears were clearly sufficient, which probably explained why Judge Catron omitted this language. Two later Tennessee Supreme Court rulings confirmed that Catron had not intended to expand the definition of self-defense by omitting the requirement of sufficient grounds. Nevertheless, many lawyers and legal authorities literally interpreted *Grainger* and ignored the court's subsequent interpretation of the case. Attorneys especially interpreted Catron's opinion to mean that legal excuse lay within the reach of killers who merely believed themselves in danger. Across the state, lawyers invoked the principle of self-defense to excuse murderous acts and cited *Grainger* as precedent.

Nearly three decades after the ruling, the Tennessee Supreme Court definitively declared this literal interpretation of the law a corruption of the original opinion. In *Rippy v. State* (1858), Judge Robert L. Caruthers succinctly restated the rule of self-defense in Tennessee. "To excuse a homicide, the danger of life, or great bodily injury, must either be real, or honestly believed to be so at the time, and upon sufficient grounds."[2] Writing of *Grainger,* Judge Caruthers observed, "No case has been more perverted and misapplied by advocates and juries."[3]

Timothy S. Huebner, Rhodes College

CITATIONS:

(1) *Grainger v. State*, 13 Tenn. 459, 462 (1830).

(2) *Rippy v. State*, 39 Tenn. 217, 219 (1858).

(3) *Rippy v. State*, 39 Tenn. 217, 219 (1858).

SEE: LAW; TENNESSEE SUPREME COURT

GRAND ARMY OF THE REPUBLIC, the preeminent organization for Union veterans, was founded in Springfield, Illinois, by physician Benjamin F. Stephenson in the spring of 1866. Posts were quickly organized within ten states and the District of Columbia, and the first national encampment took place in Indianapolis that November.

The GAR grew slowly at first. Many veterans quit the organization when they suspected that it was a vehicle for partisan political aims. The GAR revived and achieved its greatest growth in the 1880s, when successful agitation for a liberal pension act and other benefits for veterans spurred enrollment. At the height of its power, both political parties courted the GAR. Membership peaked in 1890, when the rolls reached 427,981. The GAR's influence inexorably waned as the years passed, and it ceased to play a major political role after 1900.

The organization also served as a means of solidifying fraternal bonds among Union veterans. Local camps offered opportunities for veterans to socialize and reminisce about their wartime experiences. Camps often undertook projects such as monument-building, either in local areas (such as in Cleveland and Greeneville in Tennessee) or on distant battlefields and cemeteries. As the ranks dwindled, GAR members became honored guests at community celebrations on national holidays. In turn, the veterans actively sought to instill patriotism in subsequent generations, especially school children. They vigilantly monitored history textbooks, condemning authors they felt misinterpreted the Civil War era.

In Tennessee, the GAR went through two distinct phases. The first occurred between 1866 and 1868, when posts were comprised almost exclusively of two groups: black veterans and federal employees who were avowed supporters of Radical Reconstruction. These short-lived early posts aroused the enmity of former Confederates; Nathan Bedford Forrest told a Cincinnati newspaper correspondent that the Ku Klux Klan developed in the state to protect against Loyal Leagues and the Grand Army of the Republic.

The moribund GAR movement in the South resuscitated in the 1880s. Grand Army members in Tennessee worked diligently to deflect the lingering hostility of many of their fellow citizens. They held joint reunions with Confederate veterans and occasionally marched alongside former foes in parades. The Nashville *Grand Army Sentinel* continually stressed that southern "disloyalty" had disappeared, endorsed a conciliatory policy towards former Confederates, and lauded the establishment of United Confederate Veteran camps.

The revitalized GAR also adopted southern attitudes concerning race. In 1885 the Department of Tennessee and Georgia reported 1,145 white members and 88 blacks. While the enrollments of blacks in GAR camps became a volatile issue within the national organization, the Tennessee posts remained predominantly white.

An educational mainstay of the GAR in Tennessee was Grant Memorial University in Athens, established in 1867 to serve the children of Union loyalists. The school eventually offered a free scholarship to a veteran's son in every post in Tennessee, Georgia, and Alabama. While the attitudes of some GAR members in the South hardened once the UCV also began to scrutinize history texts, most Tennessee GAR members were keenly aware of their minority status. They walked a delicate line, extolling Union victory while generally striving not to alienate former Confederates.
Christopher Losson, St. Joseph, Missouri

SEE: CIVIL WAR; RECONSTRUCTION; TENNESSEE WESLEYAN COLLEGE

GRAND OLE OPRY. No mass media event has been more associated with the state of Tennessee than the WSM radio program called "The Grand Ole Opry." Not only is it the longest-running radio show in U.S. history, but it has become the cornerstone for the dynamic commercial art form called country music. It and its various offspring have become one of the state's major tourist attractions, and its commercial power and attraction have been the primary reasons for Nashville's emergence as a recording and music center.

Cast of the Grand Ole Opry at the Ryman Auditorium, ca. 1960.

Essentially the Opry is a radio variety show in which a series of performers come on stage to sing one or more songs, or perform comedy routines, all of which are broadcast live before a theater audience. The performers comprise a regular repertoire company, which at various times has numbered from 20 to 100 acts, representing a cross-section of country music's sub-genres.

The program had its origins in October 1925, when the Nashville-based National Life and Accident Insurance Company decided, with much fanfare, to open radio station WSM (the initials standing for the company motto, "We Shield Millions"). Within a few weeks, the company hired George D. Hay (1895–1968) as station manager. A native of Attica, Indiana, Hay started his career as a news reporter in Memphis, but soon became the announcer for the paper's new radio station WMC. By 1924 he had been lured to WLS in Chicago, where he was announcer for one of the nation's first country radio shows, "The National Barn Dance." After his arrival in Nashville, Hay announced his intention to start a similar program in Tennessee and began inviting local string bands and performers to appear informally on the station; however, it was on November 25, 1925, when he invited 78-year-old Laguardo fiddler Uncle Jimmy Thompson to appear, that he really caught the fancy of his new listening public. Responding to a flood of letters and telegrams, Hay announced, on December 26, that WSM would present a regular Saturday night "barn dance" of old-time tunes. In May 1927 the "barn dance" was renamed "Grand Old Opry."

During the first decade of the show, many of the regulars were local string bands and singers, who worked at "day jobs" in and around Nashville. Determined to bolster the "down to earth" image of the show, Hay gave the groups colorful names, like The Fruit Jar Drinkers and The Possum Hunters. The first star of the show—the first artist who had recorded and played professionally in vaudeville—was banjoist and singer Uncle Dave Macon. He was soon joined by another professional group, a singing trio called the Vagabonds, in 1933, and by the mid-1930s singers like the The Delmore Brothers were building national reputations.

In order to support a cast of professionals, WSM started The Artists Service Bureau in 1934 to help get the show's acts paying jobs doing tours and concerts. This "professionalization" was accomplished through the efforts of Harry Stone, who had been hired in 1930 as the station's general manager, a practical, hard-headed business manager, who could take Hay's romantic ideas and commercialize them. This trend resulted in the Opry gaining a slot on the nationwide NBC network in 1939, and becoming the subject of a Hollywood film in 1940.

During the 1930s and 1940s, Opry management continued to develop a live audience for their radio show; early venues included the original WSM studio at the downtown National Life building, the Hillsboro Theater, the Dixie Tabernacle on Fatherland Street, the War Memorial Auditorium downtown, and starting in 1943, the venerable Ryman Auditorium. It was this latter structure, originally designed as a "gospel tabernacle," that became the "mother church of country music" and home of the Opry until 1974. The World War II years saw the show gain even more national attention through its popularity on the Armed Forces Radio Network and a series of military base tours called The Camel Caravan. Roy Acuff, who joined the show in 1938, had by now become a national star of the rank of Bing Crosby and Benny Goodman, with a string of hit records and a series of Hollywood musicals.

Important changes in music occurred on the Opry during the 1950s. Modern instruments, such as the steel guitar and electric guitar became common, and the older sentimental songs and banjo tunes were replaced with modern honky-tonk songs and musical styles of the west and southwest, represented by artists like Ernest Tubb and Hank Williams. During the late 1950s, the Opry, like most country music, was seriously shaken by the challenge of the new rock and roll, and the show suffered from controversy and rancor. Though it continued to attract major stars like Marty Robbins, Grandpa Jones, Hank Snow, Jim Reeves, and others, for a time it seemed to be marking time. Younger artists felt confined by the Opry's demands that they appear on a required number of shows per year, giving up lucrative touring dates.

This began changing in 1974, when National Life built a new 5,000-seat Opry House in a rural area north of town: the dedication show, held on March 16, 1974, attracted President Richard Nixon as a guest, and garnered a wealth of national media attention to the show and its history. A nearby theme park, Opryland, created by designers from Disneyland, opened; in 1987 the park added a large convention center, The Opryland Hotel. The new state-of-the-art Opry House, with its television capacity and advanced technology, helped attract new audiences and new performers to the show; the roster of Opry acts grew to 60, then to 75, and in the 1990s to 100. Though the National Life company was acquired by the Oklahoma-based Gaylord Broadcasting Company in 1983, the Opry was able to maintain its autonomy and soon developed close ties with another key Gaylord enterprise, the cable television channel called The Nashville Network. This channel telecasts a 30-minute segment of the Opry every Saturday night. By the mid-1990s the Opry could once again claim in its membership most of the major performers in country and bluegrass music.

Charles K. Wolfe, Middle Tennessee State University
SEE: ACUFF, ROY; MACON, DAVID H.; MUSIC; NATIONAL
LIFE AND ACCIDENT INSURANCE; OPRY HOUSE; RYMAN
AUDITORIUM; WILLIAMS, HANK; WSM

GRAVES, JAMES R. (1820–1893), Southern Baptist preacher, editor, and publisher, became the dominant leader of Landmarkism, a movement whose advocates asserted the sole validity and unbroken succession of Baptist churches from the New Testament era. Born into a Congregational family in Vermont, he joined a Baptist church at age 15. Although a self-educated man with little formal training, Graves diligently pursued private study and became a schoolteacher. He taught at Kingville, Ohio (1840–1842), and later in Jessamine County, Kentucky (1842–1843). Ordained into the Baptist ministry in 1842, he preached in Ohio (1843–1845) before taking a teaching position in Nashville in 1845.

In 1848, after a brief pastorate in Nashville, Graves became editor of *The Tennessee Baptist.* He made his greatest contributions in journalism and publishing. By the eve of the Civil War, *The Tennessee Baptist* had the largest circulation (13,000 in 1859) of any southern denominational paper. Not strictly a religious newspaper, *The Tennessee Baptist* provided controversial commentary on numerous contemporary political and social topics. In addition to its impact in Tennessee, it was the denomination's journal for Mississippi, Louisiana, Arkansas, and most of the lower Mississippi Valley. Graves also formed a publishing company that became one of the most influential and prolific religious presses in the South during the first few decades after the Civil War. Through his controversial writings, Graves attempted to make Landmarkism appeal both to Christian primitivism and popular American concepts of democracy.

Marty G. Bell, Belmont University
SUGGESTED READING: J. E. Tull, *Shapers of Baptist Thought* (1972)
SEE: PUBLISHING; RELIGION

GREAT SMOKY MOUNTAINS NATIONAL PARK, one of the "crown jewels" of the national park system, covers over 500,000 acres of scenic beauty—the largest wilderness area east of the Mississippi River. The area includes highland meadows, waterfalls, clear mountain streams, several of the highest mountains, and the largest stands of old-growth forest in the eastern United States, and encompasses one of the most biologically diverse ecosystems in North America. Because of its beauty and its proximity to the nation's population centers, the park consistently ranks first among national parks in the number of annual visitors. In 1994, for example, 8.7 million visitors to the Smokies generated approxi-

mately $689 million in consumer spending in East Tennessee and Western North Carolina, making the park a key economic resource.

The exceedingly difficult and complex process of establishing the Great Smoky Mountains National Park took place from 1923 to 1940. When a group of Knoxville boosters began active promotion of a park in 1923, most thought the odds insurmountable. Unlike most western parks, where land already in the federal domain simply reverted to the National Park Service for administration and development, land for the Great Smoky Mountains National Park had to be purchased by the states and turned over to the National Park Service. Boosters not only faced a daunting task in raising the estimated $10 million needed to buy the necessary land, but 6,000 landowners, especially the large timber companies that owned most of the land, resisted acquisition.

In the early 1920s boosters such as pharmacist David Chapman and steel executive W. P. Davis of Knoxville, and North Carolina author and outdoorsman Horace Kephart began educating residents on the value of a national park. Led by the Great Smoky Mountains Conservation Association in East Tennessee and Great Smoky Mountains, Inc., in Western North Carolina, and with the cooperation and support of the major Asheville and Knoxville newspapers, boosters launched a massive campaign to publicize the potential value of a national park and raise private funds to buy land. Most boosters had little interest in conservation, or modern notions of environmentalism, but they were interested in regional economic development. As Knoxville booster Cowan Rodgers argued: "When the park

Winter scene in the Great Smoky Mountains.

President Franklin D. Roosevelt dedicating the park, September 1940. Among those sitting behind the president are Anne M. Davis, Cordell Hull, Prentice Cooper, Kenneth McKellar, and Eleanor Roosevelt.

becomes a reality millions will annually come through our gates and scatter the golden shekels in our midst."[1] In 1926 residents pledged over one million dollars toward the purchase of park land. Donations came from every strata of society and included the pennies of school children, the dollar bills of hotel bell hops, and the hundreds and thousands of dollars pledged by regional elites.

Politicians on both the national and state level soon responded to the popularity of the park movement. On May 22, 1926, President Calvin Coolidge signed a bill committing the federal government to administer the land for a national park in the Great Smokies as soon as Tennessee and North Carolina donated 150,000 acres, and to begin park development when the states donated 423,000 acres. In 1927 the North Carolina and Tennessee state legislatures each committed two million dollars in bond funds to purchase land for the park. In 1928 John D. Rockefeller, Jr., donated the final five million dollars needed for land purchases in memory of his mother, Laura Spellman Rockefeller.

With the money in hand, the state-appointed commissions faced the daunting task of buying land from people who did not want to sell. The large lumber companies pulled out all stops, first to derail the project and, when that failed, to get the best possible price for their land. The Champion Fibre Company, owners of the largest land holdings in the proposed park, hired famed attorney Charles Evans Hughes to represent them—it lost his services when he was named Chief Justice of the Supreme Court—and even bribed a lawyer hired by the Tennessee Park Commission to influence jury selection in a condemnation hearing. The process of taking all five of the major timber companies to court—in the case of the Suncrest Lumber Company to the U.S. Supreme Court—delayed the purchase of land until the late 1930s. Litigation costs and loss of pledge money due to the Great Depression quickly used up the available funds for land purchases.

With land purchasing bogged down in the courts and insufficient funds to complete the project, the New Deal administration of Franklin D. Roosevelt came to the rescue. Although the original park bill declared that no federal funds would be used to purchase park lands, the Department of the Interior and its head, Harold Ickes, found ways to circumvent this proviso. In 1933 President Roosevelt issued an executive order to allocate $1,550,000 to complete land purchases in the park, justifying the expenditure as a means to "enhance the effectiveness and enlarge the opportunity" for Civilian Conservation Corps work in East Tennessee and Western North Carolina.[2] When this proved insufficient, Congress reversed its position and appropriated an additional $743,265.29 to secure the required 423,000 acres; Roosevelt dedicated the park on September 2, 1940. In 1943 the Tennessee Valley Authority transferred 45,920 acres from the Fontana Dam project in North Carolina to the Park Service.

The removal of over 4,000 residents from the site was difficult and controversial. To forestall a potentially explosive issue, the National Park Service allowed people, who lived in areas not designated for immediate development, to sell their land and lease it back from the government. Many older people considered this to be a satisfactory arrangement. The five elderly Walker sisters lived in their cabin in the Little Greenbriar area well into the 1950s and became quite a curiosity for park visitors. For most families, however, long-term leasing was not a viable alternative. As one resident put it: "They tell me I can't break a twig, nor pull a flower, after there's a park. Nor can I fish with bait, nor kill a boomer, nor bear on land owned by my pap, and grandpap and his pap before him."[3] One by one, families left their homes, businesses, schools, churches, and cemeteries behind. The Park Service preserved some structures—most notably in Cades Cove and Cataloochee—but most were either dismantled and sold for scrap lumber, or burned. The vestiges of this human habitation still abound in the park, providing a sometimes ghostly reminder of the history of the Great Smoky Mountains before the coming of the national park.

No one individual, group, or governmental agency could have overcome all of the obstacles that park supporters faced in the 17-year struggle to bring a national park to the Smokies. The successful establishment of the Great Smoky Mountains National Park serves as a testament to what can be accomplished through the combined and cooperative efforts of private citizens and local, state, and federal government.

Dan Pierce, Western Carolina University

CITATIONS:

(1) *Knoxville Journal*, 8 December 1925.

(2) Harold Ickes to Franklin Roosevelt, 28 July 1933, Laura Spelman Rockefeller Memorial Papers, Series 3, Box 13, Folder 148, Rockefeller Archives Center, Pocatico Hills, New York.

(3) Laura Thornborough, *The Great Smoky Mountains* (New York, 1962), 154.

SEE: BLOUNT COUNTY; CADES COVE; CIVILIAN CONSERVATION CORPS; DAVIS, ANNE M.; SEVIER COUNTY

GREEN, NATHAN (1792–1866), noted Tennessee Supreme Court judge, was born on May 16, 1792, in Amelia County, Virginia, the son of planter Thomas Green. The young Green left his home state and relocated to Tennessee, settling first in Winchester and later in Lebanon. In 1827 he represented Wilson County in the Tennessee Senate. That same year, the legislature established three Chancery Divisions, one for each of the state's three Grand Divisions; Green was elected Chancellor of the East Tennessee Division, thus ending his political career.

In 1831 Green was elected to the Supreme Court of Errors and Appeals. He served in that capacity for three years, until the adoption of the Tennessee Constitution of 1834. Green was then reelected to his former post and served on the reorganized Tennessee Supreme Court until his retirement in 1852. He authored an important slave manumission decision in *Ford v. Ford* in 1846. During his tenure on the bench, Green spent vacations teaching and lecturing at the new Law Department of Cumberland University. After his retirement from the court, he accepted a full professorship there.

As a member of the Cumberland University faculty, Green penned an open letter opposing secession. Confederate sympathizers demanded Green's removal to the North and criticized Cumberland University for employing him. Once Tennessee left the union, however, Green professed his loyalty to his home state and supported his son's decision to fight for the Confederacy. He even attempted a return to the political arena, becoming an unsuccessful candidate for the Confederate Congress.

Green remained on the Cumberland University faculty until his death on March 30, 1866. His contribution to Tennessee legal history continued beyond his lifetime. His son, Nathan Green, Jr., followed his father's footsteps to Cumberland University, where he served as head of the law school. Green's grandson, Grafton Green, served on the Tennessee Supreme Court, eventually as Chief Justice. On February 4, 1868, the Middle Tennessee bar adopted a resolution in memory of Nathan Green, noting that "he was the pillar of the judicial system, the keystone of its arch. And there was something grand and awe-inspiring about him . . . "

Amy H. Sturgis, Vanderbilt University

SUGGESTED READING: Arthur F. Howington, "Not in the Condition of a Horse or an Ox," *Tennessee Historical Quarterly* 34(1975): 249–263

SEE: CUMBERLAND UNIVERSITY LAW SCHOOL; FORD V. FORD; LAW; TENNESSEE SUPREME COURT

GREENE COUNTY lies in the Great Valley of Tennessee in the northeast corner of the state. Its valleys are enriched by the disintegrated limestone that lies below them. Bays Mountain, one of three sets of high ridges that run through the valley, is located on the north side of the county and is drained by Lick Creek. The Unaka Mountains to the east slope down to the Nolichucky River. The resources of Greene County, including the creeks and rivers, plentiful game, and good bottomlands, attracted generations of Native Americans. Places like the Camp Creek site, along the banks of the Nolichucky River, document Native American activities during the Woodland Period.

Settlement began about 1772 when Jacob Brown and a couple of families from North Carolina moved to a camp on the banks of the Nolichucky, the first in its valley. In 1775 Brown leased from the Cherokees a large tract, which was titled to him as part of the Washington District of North Carolina. In 1777 Henry

Earnest, a Swiss immigrant, established Elmwood Farm along the Nolichucky River. It is the oldest Tennessee Century Farm. A great influx of settlers between 1778 and 1783 made residents of the area anxious for separate government, which was achieved through the efforts of Daniel Kennedy and Waightstill Avery. Greene County, part of North Carolina, was established in 1783, and named in honor of General Nathanael Greene of Rhode Island, under whom many settlers had fought during the Revolutionary War. Greene County participated in the State of Franklin movement along with fellow upper East Tennessee counties Sullivan and Washington. The split that precipitated the end of the State of Franklin occurred during the 1785 constitutional convention held at Greeneville.

Presbyterian ministers dominated education during the early history of the county. Dr. Samuel Doak, educator and minister of Mount Bethel Church, obtained a charter for a private Presbyterian academy in 1784, which became Washington College in 1795. Doak served as its president until 1818, when he resigned to establish, with his son Samuel Witherspoon Doak, another classical school that was called Tusculum College. In 1794 Dr. Hezekiah Balch founded Greeneville College, the first college west of the Alleghenies. Tusculum and Greeneville colleges merged to form the Tusculum College that endures today. The county also is associated with the founding of Methodism in Tennessee as the site of Ebenezer Church, which was established in 1792 by the Earnest family. An early Quaker meeting took place at New Hope Meeting, near Ripley Creek, in 1795.

Greeneville is strongly associated with its most famous citizen and former alderman and mayor, Andrew Johnson, who became the controversial seventeenth President of the United States after the assassination of Abraham Lincoln in 1865. Johnson moved to Greeneville from North Carolina as a runaway apprentice and set up a tailor's shop. This building is now preserved inside a brick structure and is one of three sites in the Andrew Johnson National Historic Site. The others are the cemetery on Monument Hill where he is buried and Johnson's South Main Street home during 1851–1875, the years he served as governor, vice-president and president of the United States, and U.S. senator.

Other historic sites in Greene County are the Tusculum College historic district, which includes the only Tennessee building designed by famous American architect Louis Sullivan, and the Earnest Fort-House, an unusual late eighteenth-century fortified stone and log house, which is part of Elmwood Farm. The recently restored Dickson-Williams House in Greeneville documents antebellum life and architecture. Greene County is also the birthplace of famous frontiersman David Crockett. A replica of his family's

cabin has been constructed near Limestone as part of the David Crockett Birthplace State Historical Area.

Greene County played a pivotal role in the Civil War in East Tennessee. The county was largely Unionist in sentiment and the Greeneville Convention of 1861 was the state's largest, and most important, pro-union meeting in the weeks immediately prior to the Civil War. After the Confederate disaster at the Battle of Knoxville in 1863, General James Longstreet placed his troops in winter quarters at Greeneville. In September 1864, Confederate cavalry commander John Hunt Morgan died in Greeneville, after he and his officers was surprised by a Union force from the command of Alvan C. Gillem.

Greene County agriculture is historically known for burley tobacco production. It was the crop that led to prosperity in the late nineteenth century, when Greeneville developed into the region's most important tobacco market. The U.T. Extension Service operates a Burley Tobacco Experiment Farm outside of Greeneville. Tobacco, beef cattle, and hay remain important products from the county's rich farmland. The economic growth that accompanied burley tobacco cultivation also stimulated commerce and industry in Greeneville, and the city displays a collection of late Victorian commercial buildings that were constructed during Greeneville's years as an important stop on the Southern Railway. The Brumley Hotel, built by entrepreneur Colonel John H. Doughty in 1884, has recently been restored as the centerpiece of a downtown revitalization effort known as Morgan Square.

Greene County's economic focus has shifted, along with the other counties of upper East Tennessee, to include large industrial employers such as Five Rivers Manufacturing, which produces television sets, and Plus Mark, Incorporated, the maker of greeting cards and gift wrap. Today the population of Greene County is well over 55,000, but it retains significant reminders of its place in Tennessee's history from the earliest days of the state's settlement.

Blythe Semmer, Middle Tennessee State University

SUGGESTED READING: Richard H. Doughty, *Greeneville: One Hundred Year Portrait, 1775–1875* (1975)

SEE: CROCKETT, DAVID; DOAK, SAMUEL; FARMS, TENNESSEE CENTURY; FRANKLIN, STATE OF; MORGAN, JOHN H.; JOHNSON, ANDREW; JOHNSON, ANDREW, NATIONAL HISTORIC SITE; LONGSTREET, JAMES; TEMPLE, OLIVER P.; TOBACCO; TUSCULUM COLLEGE

GROOMS, CHARLES ROGERS "RED" (1937–) emerged in the 1960s to become one of the most important figures in the world of contemporary American art. He has captivated audiences with a creative genius that has expressed itself through a wide variety of mediums, including sculpture, film, drawing, and painting. With an irrepressible sense of humor, Grooms pokes fun at cultural icons in a good natured way.

Born in Nashville in 1937, Grooms's creativity was recognized early by his parents, who enrolled him, at age 10, at the Nashville Children's Museum. He later studied with Juanita Green Williams and Joseph Van Sickle. At Hillsboro High School, Grooms studied art and worked at Lyzon Gallery.

After high school, Grooms studied fitfully at the Art Institute of Chicago, the New School of Social Research in New York City, and Peabody College in Nashville, but he never remained in the classroom more than a few months. In 1957 he went to Provincetown, Massachusetts, where he collaborated with a number of other young artists. There he acquired the name "Red," a tribute to both his personality and his hair.

In 1958 Grooms moved to New York City, where he and some friends opened their own gallery. In 1960 the Reuben Gallery featured him in a one-man show, but just as he gained notoriety, he left for Europe, where he studied art and architecture on his own. Grooms returned to America in 1961 and soon attracted attention with his comic views of Europe and the United States, including his three dimensional *City of Chicago* (1967) and *Ruckus Manhattan* (1975).

Grooms's off-beat and good-natured humor continues to act as a counterpoint to the sometimes stuffy American cultural landscape. His works have been featured at the nation's leading museums, including the Art Institute of Chicago, the Wadsworth Athenaeum, the Smithsonian Institution, the Whitney, the Pennsylvania Academy of Fine Arts, the Guggenheim, and the Museum of Modern Art. Both the Tennessee State Museum (1985–86) and the Knoxville Museum of Art (1997) have featured him in major retrospective exhibitions.

Dan E. Pomeroy, Tennessee State Museum

SEE: ART; KNOXVILLE MUSEUM OF ART; TENNESSEE STATE MUSEUM

GRUETLI. During the 1840s, an organization, known as the "Tennessee Clonisation Gesellschaft," was formed to encourage Swiss settlements on the Cumberland Plateau. Four settlements resulted from the effort, but it was not until 1869, when Gruetli began, that a permanent Swiss colony occurred in Grundy County. Captain Eugen Plumacher, the Commissioner of Emigration to the United States, and Peter Staub, a Swiss emigrant living in Knoxville, purchased 15,000 acres of land south of Beersheba Springs in Grundy County. Advertisements extolled the climate and inexpensive arable land. Poor economic and social conditions in Europe produced many German-speaking Swiss willing to emigrate to the United States to start a new life. Nearly 100 Swiss families, including farmers, artisans, merchants, and professionals, arrived in Gruetli by the late 1870s.

The deceptive promotional broadsides failed to depict Grundy County as the isolated and heavily forested region that it was. When confronted with the reality of their new home, some newcomers left, but those who remained drew up a constitution and elected officers. Among the first officers was Anton Stoker, a farmer, who served as treasurer. Christian Marugg, the owner of a farm implement company, returned to Switzerland and recruited others to move to Grundy County. By 1880 the Swiss population in Grundy County reached 227, more than any other county in the state.

The Gruetli community reestablished or maintained many practices common to the Swiss culture. Land was set aside for a school and church, where both school lessons and church services were conducted in German until the early part of the twentieth century. A communal pasture and a community store were established in the 1870s.

Although isolated from much of the state, Gruetli's location on the stagecoach road from McMinnville to Chattanooga drew it into the commercial world of travel. Circa 1875, Christian Marugg built an inn for travelers that included finely crafted interior woodwork similar to that found in the Stoker farm house.

The principal occupation of Gruetli's settlers was agriculture, primarily grain production, dairy farming, and cheese-making. The Swiss farmers organized an agricultural association, or farmers' union. The Gruetli (or Swiss) Agricultural Society acted as a cooperative in the purchase of seeds and provided agricultural education for the members. The society met regularly, often in the home of Anton Stoker, until 1917. The intensive farming methods practiced by the Swiss proved valuable during a period of economic depression in the 1890s, when Gruetli farmers fared better than their Grundy County neighbors.

In addition to grain and dairy farming, Gruetli developed several other interests. Fruit trees and grapes were also cultivated, and several saw mills were operated by the Swiss. In the 1910s the community of "Laager" developed as a result of mining operations in nearby Palmer. Situated on a branch railroad line east of Gruetli, it was first known at Henley's Switch, and changed to Laager in 1920. In 1980, the community incorporated with Gruetli to become Gruetli-Laager.

Claudette Stager, Tennessee Historical Commission

SEE: GRUNDY COUNTY; SWISS SETTLERS, KNOXVILLE

GRUNDY, ANN PHILIPS ROGERS (1779–1847), was born December 8, 1779, in Lunenberg County, Virginia, to John and Sarah Dougherty Rodgers. She married lawyer Felix Grundy on May 11, 1797, in

Springfield, Kentucky. In 1808 she and her husband moved from Bardstown, Kentucky, where he served as Chief Justice of the Kentucky Supreme Court, to Nashville, where he became the law partner of James K. Polk.

Ann Grundy joined the First Presbyterian Church of Nashville shortly after it was organized and became active in its women's activities. In 1817 she and other women in the church organized the Female Bible and Charitable Society of Nashville. Patterned after a similar organization in Philadelphia, the Society distributed Bibles and clothing to the poor of the city. In 1820, the year that Ann Grundy gave birth to her tenth child, she joined forces with Reverend Samuel P. Ament, a Methodist minister who had recently moved to Nashville, to begin a non-denominational Union Sunday School to provide instruction for poor children whose parents could not afford to send them to school or to church. A deeply religious woman, Grundy believed that the Bible could not be properly understood by persons who were unable to read it.

The Sunday School met outside near the center of town every Sunday morning while the weather permitted. Each session consisted of Bible study and spelling class, using the Bible and *Webster's Bluebacked Speller,* interspersed with prayers and hymn singing. Since the school had to dismiss in the winter because of the weather, its sponsors requested permission to meet in one of the local churches, but none would allow the program inside its facilities. Many church leaders criticized the Sunday School as a violation of the Sabbath since the teaching of spelling and reading were secular projects inappropriate for Sunday. Nashville ministers preached sermons which described the Sunday School as "a scheme of the devil to capture the youth of the city." The minister of McKendree Methodist Church eventually adopted the program and within three years every church in Nashville sponsored a Sunday School where students were required to read the Bible and memorize Bible verses. Grundy's own church, First Presbyterian, later established around the city other Sunday School missions, which later became Presbyterian churches.

Active in other voluntary women's organizations, as well as her church-related associations, Ann Grundy was among the original Board of Managers of the House of Industry for Females. This institution, organized in 1837, provided a home for orphan girls and young women and gave them marketable domestic skills as an alternative to prostitution. In the 1890s the Young Women's Christian Association continued this work.

Ann Rodgers Grundy's daughters and later descendants followed her example by working in numerous charitable endeavors and voluntary associations in Nashville. When Ann Grundy died on Jan-

uary 27, 1847, her obituary in the *Republican Banner* listed none of her accomplishments and said only that she was "Mrs. Grundy, widow of the late Honorable Felix Grundy, a lady universally respected and beloved." Ann Grundy is buried in the Grundy family plot at Mt. Olivet Cemetery.

Carole Stanford Bucy, Volunteer State Community College
SEE: GRUNDY, FELIX; RELIGION

GRUNDY COUNTY was established in 1844 from parts of Warren, Coffee, and later, Marion counties. It was named in honor of Felix Grundy, a Virginian, who migrated to Tennessee by way of Kentucky. Grundy served in both the U.S. House and U.S. Senate and was Attorney General under President Martin Van Buren.

The first County Court was held at Beersheba Springs and then at several individual homes near the present site of Altamont, which was established as the permanent county seat in 1848. The founding of Beersheba Springs and Pelham predated the formation of Grundy County.

Long associated with the economic history of the county, coal was discovered in the area of present-day Tracy City in the 1840s, while Ben Wooten's sons were digging out a groundhog from beneath a stump. In 1848 a young Irishman, Leslie Kennedy, followed the construction of the Nashville & Chattanooga Railroad in search of moneymaking opportunities. While hiking through the Cumberland Plateau, he became interested in coal outcroppings and returned to Nashville to seek financial backing for a coal mining venture.

Nashville attorney William N. Bilbo listened to his scheme, bought the Wooten land and vast tracts belonging to the Samuel Barrell heirs, before heading to New York to find developers for the coal lands. Samuel Franklin Tracy and a group of financiers traveled to Tennessee and purchased Bilbo's holdings, which they used to form the Sewanee Mining Company with Tracy as president.

When the Sewanee site proved less productive than expected, the mining company extended their tracks ten miles farther to the Wooten site, which became the town of Tracy City. The first coal was shipped from the site on November 8, 1858.

After the Civil War, creditors in New York and Tennessee won judgments against the company and bought the property. Arthur St. Clair Colyar, a Tennessee attorney, became the president of the new company, which became the Tennessee Coal, Iron, and Railroad Company in 1882. Colyar recognized the need for coke in the iron smelting industry and experimented with its production. In 1873, at Tracy City, the company erected the famous Fiery Gizzard Coke Iron Furnace and produced 15 tons of iron before it collapsed. That original furnace demonstrated the efficacy of Tracy City coal and determined the economic future of the city.

In 1869 developers Eugen H. Plumacher, John Hitz, and Peter Staub established a Swiss settlement, Gruetli. Among the Swiss immigrants to the settlement were the Angst, Amacher, Bonholzer, Schild, Flury, and Scholer families.

Monteagle, first called Moffat Station, was founded by John Moffat, an organizer in the temperance movement. In 1870 Moffat purchased the 1,146 acres of forest land on the Cumberland Plateau that became Monteagle. In 1882 the Monteagle Sunday School Assembly incorporated to promote the "advancement of science, literary attainment, Sunday School interest and promotion of the broadest popular culture in the interest of Christianity without regard to sect or denomination." Andrew Nelson Lytle, the Vanderbilt Agrarian, did much of his writing at Monteagle, including his biography of Nathan Bedford Forrest.

The Summerfield community lies between Tracy City and Monteagle. There May Justice wrote more than 60 children's books. The community was also the site of the controversial Highlander Folk School from 1932 until 1962. This school, headed by Myles Horton, began as a training facility for labor organizers. In the 1950s, it became famous for its promotion of civil rights and the training of civil rights leaders.

In 1903 the Sewanee Coal, Coke and Land Company began mining coal in Coalmont, first called Coaldale. In 1908 the Sewanee Fuel and Iron Company bought the holdings and built coke ovens on the site. Coalmont is now the location of the new Grundy County High School.

In 1918 the railroad was extended to Palmer, where the Tennessee Consolidated Coal Company opened up new coal mines. Pelham, located in the valley part of Grundy County, is a farming town and contains several small manufacturing businesses. In addition to these small industrial plants, Grundy County's economy includes a growing nursery industry and several hundred chicken broiler houses.

In 1972 the long efforts of Herman Baggenstoss of Tracy City led to the creation of the South Cumberland Recreation Area. It included the Stone Door, Savage Gulf, Grundy Lakes, and Fiery Gizzard parks, which receive thousands of visitors each year.

Like so many Appalachian areas, Grundy County citizens have suffered through trying times, but continue to prosper.

William Ray Turner, Tracy City

SEE: BAGGENSTOSS, HERMAN; BEERSHEBA SPRINGS; COLYAR, ARTHUR S.; CONVICT LEASE WARS; GRUETLI; GRUNDY, FELIX; GRUNDY LAKES PARK AND GRUNDY FOREST STATE NATURAL AREA; HIGHLANDER FOLK SCHOOL; HORTON, MYLES; LYTLE, ANDREW NELSON; MINING; MONTEAGLE SUNDAY SCHOOL ASSEMBLY

GRUNDY, FELIX (1777–1840), Congressman, U.S. Senator, and a Democratic leader, was born in Virginia, but first rose to prominence in Kentucky politics. After his admission to that state's bar at age 20, Grundy was elected to a state constitutional convention in 1799, and served in the legislature from 1800 to 1805. In 1806 Grundy was elevated to a seat on the Supreme Court of Errors and Appeals; soon afterward, at age 29, he became the state's Chief Justice. Dissatisfied with judicial work and its meager salary, he resigned the position after only a few months. In late 1807 Grundy moved to Nashville, where he quickly established himself as one of the West's most effective criminal lawyers.

Despite the success of his law practice, politics eventually lured Grundy back into the public arena. From 1811 through 1814 Grundy served in the U.S. House of Representatives, where he ardently advocated and supported the war against Great Britain. Five years after his resignation from the House, Grundy was elected to the first of three terms in the Tennessee General Assembly as a champion of public relief for those suffering from the financial Panic of 1819. As a legislator, Grundy introduced the bills that stayed the execution of debts and created the state-owned Bank of Tennessee. After serving on a commission to settle Tennessee's boundary with Kentucky, Grundy returned to the legislature to play an influential role in modifying Governor William Carroll's plan to compel Tennessee's banks to resume specie payments. In 1827 Grundy sought to return to Congress, but John Bell defeated him. Nevertheless, in 1829, the Assembly elected him to the U.S. Senate to fill the seat vacated by John Eaton's appointment to President Andrew Jackson's cabinet.

Although he and Jackson were never on intimate terms, Grundy quickly emerged as one of the president's principal defenders in the Senate. His state-rights sympathies and his friendship with John C. Calhoun initially led him to support Calhoun's theory of nullification, but he remained loyal to the president when he learned of Jackson's condemnation of the doctrine. Grundy strongly defended Jackson's "war" against the Bank of the United States, and by 1834 he was widely recognized, with James K. Polk, as a leader of Tennessee's Democratic party. Grundy's prominence made him a particular target for the rival Whig party. A Whig majority in the legislature in 1838 attempted to force Grundy's resignation, first by electing Ephraim H. Foster as his successor before the expiration of his term, and then by instructing him to oppose President Martin Van Buren's proposal to create an Independent Treasury System. Although Grundy at first refused to resign, he left the Senate later that year, when Van Buren appointed him to the Cabinet as Attorney General.

Grundy faithfully served Van Buren in the Cabinet, primarily as a political advisor, but he anxiously returned to the Senate in December 1839, after a newly elected Democratic legislature forced Foster's resignation. Over the summer of 1840, he traversed East Tennessee speaking in favor of Van Buren's re-election. This tour severely strained his health, however, and he died in Nashville in December 1840.

Jonathan M. Atkins, Berry College

SUGGESTED READING: Joseph H. Parks, *Felix Grundy, Champion of Democracy* (1940)

SEE: BELL, JOHN; CARROLL, WILLIAM; FOSTER, EPHRAIM ; JACKSON, ANDREW; JACKSONIANS; POLK, JAMES K.

GRUNDY LAKES PARK AND GRUNDY FOREST STATE NATURAL AREA, located in Grundy County, are part of the South Cumberland State Recreation Area. Grundy Lakes's history began as an environmentally devastated mining property, part of a complex of 130 coke ovens established and operated by the Tennessee Coal, Iron, and Railroad Company by 1883. In the late 1930s, after the property had been donated by the Tennessee Consolidated Coal Company, the Civilian Conservation Corps (CCC) reclaimed the land, built the lakes, planted new trees and foliage, and constructed recreational facilities. The considerable CCC effort turned a wasteland into new recreational opportunities for a community that had been devastated by the Great Depression. Grundy Forest began as another CCC project in 1935, after local residents purchased 211 acres and donated it to the state for use as a CCC camp. CCC Company 1475 moved to the site on June 29, 1935. It built the first section of Fiery Gizzard Trail, which was extended by the state parks division in the late 1970s and early 1980s to connect to Foster Falls. Fiery Gizzard refers to the name given to an experiment blast furnace built there during the height of the coal industry in Grundy County. Foster Falls, which drops 60 feet into a pool surrounded by sandstone bluffs, is the highest volume falls in the South Cumberland area. The state has designated Foster Falls as a Small Wild Area.

Carroll Van West, Middle Tennessee State University

SEE: CIVILIAN CONSERVATION CORPS; CONSERVATION; GRUNDY COUNTY; SOUTH CUMBERLAND STATE RECREATION AREA

GUILD, JO CONN (1887–1969), a Chattanooga business leader, was an outspoken critic of the Tennessee Valley Authority. He was born in 1887 in Chattanooga, the son of a prominent engineer. He attended Baylor School, the University of Virginia, and Vanderbilt University, where he earned an engineering degree. He then spent four years working on Hales Bar dam, a project begun by his now-deceased father. In 1913 Guild joined the Chattanooga and Tennessee River Power Company, which owned power rights to the Hales Bar facility. In 1915 he became general manager of the firm.

In 1922 the Chattanooga and Tennessee River Power Company merged with the Chattanooga Railway and Light Company to form the Tennessee Electric Power Company (TEPCO). Guild served as vice-president of the firm until 1933, when he was named the company's president. Under Guild's direction, TEPCO became one of the South's leading privately-owned utilities, serving over 100,000 customers in nearly 400 communities in Middle and East Tennessee, including the cities of Nashville, Knoxville, and Chattanooga.

Guild's greatest challenge came in the 1930s, with the creation of the Tennessee Valley Authority. A champion of privately-owned power companies, Guild denounced the public utility as an unnecessary and unwarranted threat to free enterprise. He soon found a powerful ally in Wendell Willkie, then president of the Commonwealth and Southern Corporation, a giant utilities conglomerate. Together, Guild and Willkie waged a five-year legal battle against the TVA, challenging the constitutionality of the public utility in federal courts. The courts upheld the TVA act, however, and in January 1939, the United States Supreme Court dismissed their suit against the federal utility. A short time later, in August 1939, TVA purchased TEPCO for $78.4 million.

Although TEPCO no longer existed, Guild retained control of the company's streetcar franchises in Chattanooga and Nashville, which he reorganized as the Southern Coach Lines. As president of this firm, he maintained the public transportation systems of these cities for several years and oversaw their conversion to bus service. He also remained active in Chattanooga's business community and served on the boards of many local corporations. He died in 1969 at the age of 81, after a colorful and controversial life.

Timothy P. Ezzell, Knoxville

SEE: CHATTANOOGA; HALES BAR DAM; TENNESSEE VALLEY AUTHORITY; TEPCO

GUILD, JOSEPHUS CONN (1802–1883), born in Virginia, came with his parents briefly to Stewart County and then to Sumner County in 1812. Both father and mother died the following year, and he became the ward of his uncle Walter Conn of Cairo. Educated locally, Guild read law in the offices of attorneys at Gallatin and Nashville, and won admission to the Tennessee Bar in 1822. He opened a law office at Gallatin, where he practiced until 1859, when he became judge of the chancery court, seventh division. In 1862, the Union Army occupation closed the courts and ended his term. Two years later he moved to Nashville and represented clients until 1870, when he returned to the bench. He resumed private practice in 1877.

Guild volunteered for the Seminole War of 1836 and was elected Lieutenant Colonel, Second Regiment, Tennessee Mounted Volunteers. He served in the field in Florida, but escaped unscathed, although he participated in several fire fights. For most of his life, Guild owned thoroughbred horses and won his share of races at Middle Tennessee tracks. He was a lead investor in a company that sent 17 local men to the California gold rush in 1849 but, predictably, all lost their invested funds.

An effective advocate for railroads during the 1850s, Guild played a key role in organizing the Louisville and Nashville Railroad. He persuaded the voters of Sumner and Davidson counties to invest public funds to assure the line's construction and later served as the L&N's vice president for Tennessee and as its corporate counsel.

A Jacksonian Democrat, Guild won elections to the State House of Representatives in 1833 and 1835. His most memorable speech to the legislature was made in 1833, in opposition to forcible removal of the Cherokees from the state. In 1837 Guild won election to the State Senate representing Sumner and Smith counties, but did not seek reelection at the end of his term. He returned to the House for a term in 1845 and another in 1851. Guild was a member of the five-man central committee of the state Democratic organization. In 1857 he was his party's nominee for Congress in the fifth district, but lost by 290 votes. He was a Democratic presidential elector in 1844 on the ticket of James K. Polk and George Dallas, and again in 1852 on the ticket of Franklin Pierce and William R. King.

Although long committed to the preservation of the Union, Guild declared for the South in 1861. He embraced armed resistance as the only option left to force the central government into negotiating the issues that had divided the country. His outspoken support for the South caused Military Governor Andrew Johnson to arrest and incarcerate him in 1862 at Fort Mackinac, Michigan, as an example of what might happen to other public figures who did not return their loyalty to the Union. He and two fellow political prisoners were held until they made oath not to assist the Confederacy against the Union. He returned to Gallatin on September 25, 1862.

During the early 1840s, Guild and his wife Catherine Blackmore built a handsome brick house on their Rose Mont plantation, one mile south of the public square in Gallatin. Their family included four daughters and two sons, one of whom was George B. Guild, a Confederate soldier and military author, who was later mayor of Nashville.

During his latter years, Josephus Conn Guild wrote a book-length memoir, *Old Times in Tennessee*.

Published in 1878, it was reprinted in 1995 by Rose Mont Foundation, Inc.

Walter T. Durham, Gallatin

SUGGESTED READING: Joshua W. Caldwell, *Sketches of Bench and Bar of Tennessee* (1898)

SEE: JACKSONIANS; RAILROAD, LOUISVILLE AND NASHVILLE; SUMNER COUNTY; TENNESSEANS IN CALIFORNIA GOLD RUSH

GUNN'S DOMESTIC MEDICINE, popular home medical guide by Dr. John C. Gunn (1795?-1863), first published in Knoxville in 1830, was followed by a proliferation of editions in Tennessee, Kentucky, Ohio, Pennsylvania, and New York. Enlarged under the author's supervision in 1857 and translated into German, the book remained Gunn's original basic text on through the National Jubilee Edition, the 160th, in 1876, down to the last recorded edition, the 234th, issued in New York in 1920.

Designed to serve as a guide for frontier and rural families, who lived great distances from even primitive medical care, the book covered virtually any possible miscarriage of health. It contained extensive references from the works of the major medical men and journals of the time, making it also a useful textbook for largely self-taught doctors in all rural areas. The emphasis in the early editions on the use of herbs most readily available in East Tennessee indicates that initially Dr. Gunn did not expect his book to have the far-ranging influence it ultimately experienced. A sense of the volume's impact is suggested by its literary use in such diverse places and times as the Mississippi River in 1884 (Mark Twain's *Huckleberry Finn*) and California in 1952 (John Steinbeck's *East of Eden*).

Ben Harris McClary, Chattanooga

SEE: MEDICINE

GUTHERZ, CARL (1844–1907). Associated with the American Symbolist movement of the late nineteenth century, artist Carl Gutherz was born in Schoeftland, Switzerland, in 1844, and immigrated to Cincinnati, Ohio, in 1851. His family settled in Memphis about 1860, where they remained throughout the Civil War. From 1869–1872 Gutherz received his academic training at the Ecole des Beaux Arts in Paris under Isadore Pils, with further studies in Munich, Brussels, and Rome.

In 1875 Gutherz accepted a teaching position at Washington University in St. Louis, where he remained for nine years, assisting Halsey Ives in establishing the St. Louis School and Museum of Fine Arts. During this period he frequented St. Paul and Memphis, painting landscapes, taking portrait commissions, and designing costumes, invitations, and floats for the annual Memphis Mardi Gras. In Memphis, he met and wed Kate Scruggs, with whom he had two daughters and a son.

From 1884–1895, he attended the Académie Julian in Paris, studying with Gustave Boulanger and Joseph Lefebvre. Here, influenced by Symbolist theories, he produced his most successful paintings—large allegorical works such as *Light of the Incarnation* (1888). He exhibited annually in the Paris salons, and his work was shown extensively in the United States as well, including the Philadelphia Centennial Exposition, Chicago Columbian Exposition, Trans-Mississippi Exposition, Tennessee Centennial Exposition, and the Louisiana Purchase Exposition in St. Louis. In 1896, he executed a mural for the Library of Congress and remained in Washington D.C. until his death in 1907.

During these last years, he completed two additional murals at the People's Church, St. Paul, Minnesota, in 1901, and the Allen County Court House, Fort Wayne, Indiana, in 1902. He also produced a design for an arts and sciences pavilion in 1906, which was the basis for the development of Brooks Memorial Art Gallery in Memphis, now the Memphis Brooks Museum of Art.

Marilyn Masler, Memphis Brooks Museum of Art

SUGGESTED READING: Marilyn Masler, "Carl Gutherz: Memphis Beginnings," West Tennessee Historical Society *Papers* 46(1992): 59–72

SEE: ART; MEMPHIS BROOKS MUSEUM OF ART

H

HALE, MILLIE E. (1881–1930) contributed significantly to the health and welfare of Nashville's African-American population in the early twentieth century by establishing a small hospital for those turned away by white institutions. A graduate of Fisk University and the Graduate School for Nurses in New York City, Hale opened the Millie E. Hale Hospital July 1, 1916, and served as its head nurse and chief administrator. Located at 523 Seventh Avenue, North, the facility grew from an original 12 beds to 75 beds by 1923 and became a training center for local nurses.

In addition to providing much needed medical care to African Americans, the Millie E. Hale Hospital formed an auxiliary branch that conducted a variety of beneficial charitable and social programs. The auxiliary gave instruction in health education and assisted the poor and the elderly with basic needs such as food and fuel. It also managed a prenatal and infant clinic in the Hale's home.

Hale's husband, John Henry Hale, a prominent surgeon and professor at Nashville's Meharry Medical College, continued to manage the hospital after her death in 1930. In 1938 Dr. Hale, the surgeon-in-chief at the Hale Hospital, was appointed Chief of Surgery at Meharry, and the Millie E. Hale Hospital closed.

Teresa Biddle-Douglass, Middle Tennessee State University
SEE: MEDICINE; MEHARRY MEDICAL COLLEGE

HALE, WILLIAM JASPER (1874–1944) was President of Tennessee Agricultural and Industrial College from its founding date (1912) until his retirement in August 1943. Under his leadership, Tennessee A & I State College became a notable African-American institution and one of Tennessee's best known colleges. By 1944 the college produced the third highest number of graduates among historically African-American universities.

W. J. Hale was born in Marion County, Tennessee, on September 26, 1874, the oldest child of four boys and two girls. The impoverished Hale went to work at an early age, but managed to save enough money while working in Dayton, Tennessee, to enroll at biracial Maryville College. After attending for several terms, Hale accepted teaching positions in Coulterville and Retro, Tennessee, before becoming the principal of Chattanooga's East First Street Grammar School.

When the Tennessee General Assembly authorized the construction of a normal school for African Americans, Hale led an effort to raise $71,000 to have the institution located in Chattanooga. Black leaders in Nashville won the bid for Davidson County, but Hale was selected as the principal of the new Tennessee Agricultural and Industrial State Normal School for Negroes. He arrived in Nashville in January 1911 to supervise construction of the facilities and develop the school's curricula. Hale hand-picked the 13 faculty members from such notable institutions as Fisk, Atlanta, and Howard universities. Tennessee A & I opened its doors on June 19, 1912, and two days later enrolled 247 students for the summer term.

A shrewd but practical man, Hale expanded the school despite the limited resources provided by a reluctant General Assembly and State Board of Education. In 1916 he received only 40 percent of the school's funds from the state, with the rest coming from federal sources, tuition, fees, and gifts from African Americans. Hale staged annual visitations and dinners to persuade the all-white legislature to continue to vote appropriations and to allay legislative Negrophobia. Faculty members loaned their cars to drive legislators to the campus, where they saw uniformed female students and men in dress shirts. Students engaged in manual labor, performed farm tasks, and cleaned dormitories under the watchful eyes of the visitors. Faculty members served as hosts at the dinners legislators attended, standing around the room like waiters, while their guests ate. At the end of the dinner, Hale presented each legislator with a freshly dressed turkey from the school's farm.

Hale knew firsthand the deep racism held by most European-American officials in Tennessee. A soft-spoken mulatto with wavy brown hair streaked with white, a strong chin, and cold gray eyes, Hale looked like a "white" man. He often endured the insults directed against blacks by state officials before they realized that the pale-skinned Hale was African American. When visiting the state office, Hale refused to be seated. He stood, hat in hand, until called into the office of the superintendent of education, a silent protest against a past insult by the office secretary. Authoritative and sarcastic, Hale required that faculty members and students observe a curfew and refrain from political activity. He demanded that faculty members sign their paychecks (face down), before counting out their pay in cash, according to verbal contracts. He used the surplus money (as many black public college presidents did) to carry the school forward. When state officials discovered his activities and realized that Tennessee A & I had a funding surplus, they demanded Hale's resignation in August 1943.

Hale married one of his faculty members, Harriet Hodgkins of Nashville. Their three children graduated from Tennessee A & I State College. Hale served as a member of the local Citizen's Bank board. He assumed leadership roles in several civic and social organizations, including the Tennessee Commission for Interracial Cooperation (1919–1921). In 1930 he became the first Tennessean to receive the Harmon Foundation's Gold Award for outstanding achievement in education. Hale completed additional studies at Columbia University and received honorary doctoral degrees from Wilberforce University (1936) and Howard University (1939). W. J. Hale died in New York on October 5, 1944.

Bobby L. Lovett, Tennessee State University
SEE: EDUCATION, HIGHER; TENNESSEE STATE UNIVERSITY

HALES BAR DAM has the distinction of being the first main river, multipurpose dam built on the Tennessee River. In order to improve navigation on the Upper Tennessee and provide electricity to the city of Chattanooga, Jo Conn Guild, Sr., a Chattanooga engineer, promoted the construction of a privately-funded lock and dam, which would be turned over to government management in return for the hydroelectric output for a specified period. Congress passed such an act, and the Chattanooga and Tennessee River Power Company began construction on the Hales Bar Dam in October 1905.

The construction of the dam and powerhouse was the largest development of its kind in the region. The dam itself measured almost one-half mile across and 63 feet high. The project employed over 5,000 men, requiring the construction of a small village to feed and house the workers. Completion of Hales Bar, originally scheduled for 1907, was delayed by flooding and problems with the limestone foundation, and the project was not completed until 1913. The Tennessee Valley Authority acquired Hales Bar Dam in August 1939, as part of the Tennessee Electric Power Company purchase. Unable to overcome the foundation and leakage problems, TVA demolished Hales Bar in 1968, and replaced it with Nickajack Dam, 6.4 miles downstream.

Patricia Bernard Ezzell, Tennessee Valley Authority
SEE: GUILD, JO CONN; TENNESSEE RIVER; TENNESSEE VALLEY AUTHORITY; TEPCO

HALEY, ALEX MURRAY PALMER (1921–1992), internationally known author, was born in Ithaca, New York, on August 11, 1921, and died in a Tennessee hospital of the complications of diabetes in February 1992. When he was a child, his family moved to his mother's home town of Henning in West Tennessee, and when his father died young, Haley was brought up by his mother, grandmother, and various aunts

Alex Haley.

whose stories he remembered all his life. In 1939 he entered the United States Coast Guard and served 20 years. In that period he slowly became a writer.

His literary fame rests on two books, *The Autobiography of Malcolm X* (Grove Press, 1964) and *Roots* (Doubleday, 1976). Both were best-sellers.

Roots sold 1.5 million copies in hardback in the United States. Within two years after its publication it had been translated into 26 languages and had sold 8,500,000 copies. The TV miniseries of *Roots,* aired for a total of 12 hours on eight consecutive nights in January 1977, became a national event. *Roots* won the Pulitzer Prize, and the TV version won 145 awards, including nine Emmys.

Haley became an adored national figure, enthralling college audiences with the thrilling story of how he had written his masterwork. He ambled to the platform always with an air of becoming modesty. He faced his audience with a genial reserve, and he spoke in a conversational baritone reeling off stories of his childhood, of women rocking on a front porch, the sound of their rockers going "thump-thump" as they mused over the oral history of their ancestors. Especially the older women remembered tales of an African named Toby who insisted that his real name was Kin-te.

In *Roots* Haley told of visiting the British Museum on an assignment for *Reader's Digest* and seeing the Rosetta Stone that opened the way to translation of ancient Egyptian hieroglyphics. He remembered the many *k* sounds in the stories about Kin-te, and he wondered if he might use them as a key to the discovery of his own ancestors.

On a trip to Gambia Haley met a *griot,* an elder supposedly able to recall in remarkable detail the oral history of the tribe as Homer recalled the *Iliad.* From him Haley heard the story of his own ancestor, Kunta Kinte, captured by slave traders and not seen again. Haley claimed he had discovered that Kunta was shipped to America in 1767 to land at Annapolis, Maryland, and sold to a plantation owner in Virginia. He said that further painstaking research provided a remarkably complete story of his ancestors. That story became *Roots.* It appeared in 1976, the bicentennial year, and Haley dedicated it "as a birthday offering to my country within which most of *Roots* happened."

Doubleday marketed the book as "non-fiction," and Haley claimed steadfastly that the facts had come out of his research. But the book is clearly cast in the form of a novel with dialogue, thoughts, and acts that could not have come from a historical source. From the beginning *Roots* was subjected to harsh criticism by historians who found in it numerous errors. But it quickly became required reading in college courses all over America. Literary critics noted its klunky style and its clichés and stereotypes of both whites and blacks.

Behind the national enthusiasm, Haley had troubles. He was sued twice for plagiarism. One case was summarily dismissed, but the other, brought in 1978 by a white specialist in African folklore, Harold Courlander, went to trial. Haley said under oath that he had never read Courlander's novel, *The African,* published in 1967. Haley claimed that 81 parallel passages in *Roots* and Courlander's work came from notes intended to be helpful and received from audiences at his lectures. Judge Robert Ward later told *Village Voice* writer Philip Nobile that he would have ruled against Haley and that he considered charging him with perjury. But on the eve of Judge Ward's decision, Haley agreed to pay Courlander $650,000, and the case was immediately closed.

Attacks on *Roots* continued while Haley lived extravagantly. When he died in 1992, he was $1.5 million in debt, and his reputation among serious scholars was in ruins. In February 1993 Nobile's long and measured article in the *Village Voice* was a devastating final shot. Nobile used the Haley papers deposited at the University of Tennessee, Knoxville, and interviewed a multitude of people connected to the book. One by one Haley's stories collapsed under Nobile's scrutiny. His conclusion in the article: "Beyond the plagiarism and the massive perjury to cover it up, *Roots* as Haley well knew was a hoax, a literary painted bird, a Piltdown of genealogy, a pyramid of bogus research."

Saddest of all, the story of the *griot* who allegedly told Haley about Kunta Kinte appears to have been arranged by a collusion between Haley and authorities in Gambia who knew a prospective tourist attraction when they saw one. Haley told them what he needed; they produced the stereotypical old man who, through an interpreter, gave him what he required. A tape of the interview does not resemble Haley's account of the meeting in *Roots.*

Even Haley's authorship is suspect. The manuscript evidence demonstrates that Murray Fisher, Haley's editor at *Playboy,* rewrote huge parts of it, not merely revising Haley's prose but cutting it out altogether.

No one answered Nobile's attack. In a long article in *Critical Quarterly,* Helen Taylor tries to redeem Haley in part, but she does not doubt that he lied habitually. She notes that Haley remained popular with audiences to the end. But among scholars, especially black critics, he is ignored. She declares, somewhat sadly, "None of the major African-American literary critics—Henry Louis Gates, Jr., Houston A. Baker, Jr., Toni Morrison, bell hooks [sic], or Hazel V. Carby—even cites the man, book, or phenomenon." She calls *Roots* an "autobiography" that like much black autobiography tells a story of community, bondage, flight, and freedom, a tale intended to be didactic and inspirational. Haley came as close to anyone, she says, of becoming the American *griot*, the custodian of the black community's oral history in America.

It may be more accurate to see Haley, as Nobile suggests, as a writer who created a fictional life for himself and could not escape it once the public had rewarded him so handsomely. Had *Roots* been marketed as the novel it is, and had Haley not spun tall tales about his agonizing "research," the book would retain an honorable place in southern literature. It is no more inaccurate than William Styron's *The Confessions of Nat Turner*. As it is, it will always be suspect.

No doubt that during an important period in our history, *Roots* helped give white Americans sympathy for what black Americans had suffered in bondage. Unfortunately, the book will be remembered as a phenomenon of popular culture rather than as a serious and enduring study of black history.
Richard Marius, Harvard University
SEE: HOMECOMING '86; LITERATURE

HALEY, ALEX, STATE HISTORIC SITE, is located at 200 S. Church Street in Henning, Lauderdale County. This one and one-half story weatherboard bungalow was the house of Alex Haley's grandfather, Will Palmer, who operated a respected and profitable lumber business and mill in Henning. In 1918–1919 Palmer and his wife Cynthia built the ten-room house, complete with music room and library, that rated among the most modern and fashionable residences in this rural town. Two years later, in 1921, their daughter Bertha Palmer Haley brought her baby son, Alex, back home to Henning to stay with her parents as her husband, Simon Haley, pursued graduate studies at Cornell. Haley lived here from 1921 to 1929 and afterward visited the home during many summers. As he later recounted in his popular book, *Roots: The Saga of an American Family* (1976), and in many interviews, his Grandmother Palmer was an immense influence on his telling of the family history, especially her colorful and compelling stories of past, but not forgotten, family members. Haley heard those stories, and began to develop his own sense of imagination and place while living at this bungalow dwelling. His writings and lectures inspired millions to search for their family history and to learn how their families have played a role in the drama of the American past. The Alex Haley Boyhood Home was listed in the National Register of Historic Places in 1978 and was opened as the first state historic site devoted to African-American history later that decade. After his death in 1992 Haley was buried in the front yard of the boyhood home he recalled so fondly.
Carroll Van West, Middle Tennessee State University
SEE: HALEY, ALEX M.; LAUDERDALE COUNTY

HALL, WILLIAM (1775–1856), Governor, was born in Surrey County, North Carolina, in February 1775, to Major William Hall and Elizabeth Thankful Doak Hall. The family moved to Tennessee in 1785, but lost seven family members during an Indian confrontation. Hall married Mary "Polly" Brandon Alexander and settled and farmed in the Bledsoe Lick area of Sumner County, now known as Castalian Springs. The couple had seven children.

Hall was commissioned a second major in the Sumner County regiment of the Tennessee militia in 1796. He enlisted as a colonel in the Tennessee Volunteer Infantry in 1812 and became a brigadier general during the Creek Indian War.

Hall began his political life in 1797, when he won election to the Tennessee House of Representatives, where he served until 1805. He was elected to the Tennessee State Senate in 1821, serving in the 14th, 15th, and 16th General Assemblies. With Governor Sam Houston's resignation in 1829, Hall, as Speaker of the Senate, assumed the governorship. During his brief term, Hall maintained many polices initiated by William Carroll, including revision of the penal code, establishment of the penitentiary, and strengthening of the educational system.

Hall did not run for re-election in the 1829 race, but returned to his Sumner County farm, Locustland. A Jackson supporter, he was elected to Congress in 1831 and served one term. In his retirement, Hall recorded his frontier experiences for the June 1856 issue of the *Southwestern Monthly*. He hosted several pioneer reunions at Locustland where he died on October 7, 1856, and was buried in the family graveyard.
Anne-Leslie Owens, Tennessee Historical Society
SEE: CARROLL, WILLIAM; HOUSTON, SAM; SUMNER COUNTY

HAMBLEN COUNTY, third smallest county in the state, is located between the Holston and the Nolichucky Rivers in a fertile, well-watered valley, sheltered from the north winds by Clinch Mountain and from southern storms by the Smoky Mountains.

Hamblen County was formed in 1870 from parts of Jefferson, Grainger, and Hawkins counties. After much controversy, the county was named for Hezekiah Hamblen, a lawyer in Hawkins County. Morristown, which was incorporated in 1855, was named county seat, but it would be four years before a county courthouse was constructed. This building, designed by architect A. C. Bruce, is listed in the National Register of Historic Places.

Cherokees, Chickasaws, Creeks, and Shawnees roamed the East Tennessee hills and valleys in the days before settlement began in what would become Hamblen County. In 1783 Robert McFarland and Alexander Outlaw migrated from Virginia to claim land grants on the "Bend of Chucky." Gideon Morris and his brothers, Daniel and Absalom, were the next settlers; they took land grants within the present city limits of Morristown, providing the community with its name. More settlers arrived when a road connecting the stage routes from Abingdon, Virginia, and Knoxville was constructed in 1792. William Chaney, Thomas Daggett, Richard Thomas, and John Crockett were among those who lived along the road. By 1800 several communities had been established, including Russellville, Whitesburg, Springvale, and Panther Springs.

Panther Springs boasted a store, church, and academy in addition to several residences. The ever-flowing spring, with its vast volume of water, continues to be an object of interest. Panther Creek State Park, encompassing 2,000 acres, is located on this historic spot. Nearby Cherokee Lake, created by TVA's Cherokee Dam, provides additional opportunities for outdoor activities.

Russellville, another early settlement, is rich in colorful history and, at one time, was larger than Morristown. The famous Boone Trace and Buffalo Trail of the Indians, running from Kentucky through Tennessee to North Carolina, passed through Russellville. Colonel James Roddye built the first home in Russellville soon after his return from the Revolutionary War Battle of King's Mountain. By the late 1850s, the town boasted a drugstore, railroad station, theater, and an academy.

The first industry in the county was Shields' Paper Mill, located at Marshalls Ferry on the Holston River. The mill operated from 1825 to 1861 and produced a fine paper from rags, lint, and wheat straw. Two books were printed there. Other early businesses included the Morristown Manufacturing Company and J. F. Goodson Coffee Company (maker of JFG Coffee), which now operates from Knoxville. In the first half of the twentieth century, textile mills and furniture companies dominated local industry.

A number of Hamblen County residents made their mark on Tennessee history. David Crockett, the son of John Crockett, lived in Hamblen County until shortly after his marriage to Polly Finley. He later served as a member of the Tennessee State Legislature and as a Representative in the U.S. Congress. His colorful personality and heroic death at the Alamo in 1836 made him a legend. DeWitt Senter served as Governor of Tennessee, 1869–1871. Joseph Anderson, a U.S. Senator, lived at Lowland, 1797–1815. He became Comptroller of the U.S. Treasury after 11 years in the Senate. Helen Topping Miller, noted author, lived at Arrow Hill until her death in 1960. Herbert Sanford Walters served in the U.S. Senate, was Chairman of the State Democratic Executive Committee, and National Democratic Committeeman. Z. Buda, Mayor of Morristown 1972–1978, was noted for his efforts to keep taxes low and for his fight to prevent the construction of a regional prison in the city. He remains the largest donor to Walters State Community College (WSCC), having established several scholarships for needy students. Two residents of Hamblen County, Alvin Ward and Edward R. Talley, received the Congressional Medal of Honor in World War I.

Agriculture continues to be an important factor in the county's economy. The fertile farms produce beef, dairy products, and vegetables. Tobacco annually boosts the economy in excess of $5 million. A two-century farm on Leeper's Ferry Road, known as the Lewis and Lucinda Leeper Farm, originated from a 200-acre land grant of August 1780, awarded to Captain Thomas Jarnagin for services in the Revolutionary War.

Hamblen's recent economic development has been phenomenal. Two large industrial parks (East and West) house a variety of businesses.

Hamblen County's citizens enjoy a wide variety of social and cultural advantages. The county's school system is widely recognized for its excellence. In 1881 the Methodist Episcopal Church established Morristown College, a historic African-American school. In the late twentieth century, it became a branch of Knoxville College. Walters State Community College, named for Herbert S. Walters, offers continuing educational opportunities to students throughout the region. Twenty-five religious denominations maintain churches in the county. Many fraternal and civic clubs, as well as a Theater Guild, offer service and recreational activities for residents. The Hamblen County Chapter, Association for the Preservation of Tennessee Antiquities made the reproduction of the Crockett Tavern an international attraction. Rose Center (1892), the oldest school in Morristown, was restored as a civic center and is listed in the National Register of Historic Places. "Mountain Makin's," a local festival, is held there annually.

Mrs. Burwin Haun, Russellville

SEE: ASSOCIATION FOR THE PRESERVATION OF TENNESSEE ANTIQUITIES; CROCKETT, DAVID; FARMS, TENNESSEE CENTURY; HAUN, MILDRED E.; PANTHER CREEK STATE PARK; SENTER, DEWITT C.; TENNESSEE VALLEY AUTHORITY

HAMILTON COUNTY was created by the Tennessee General Assembly on October 25, 1819. Rhea, Marion, and Bledsoe counties bounded the new county, and it extended south to the state line. The creation of the new county on the southwestern frontier was brought about by a treaty with the Cherokees in 1817. By the terms of the Hiwassee Purchase, the Indians yielded large sections of Alabama and Georgia, as well as the Sequatchie Valley, and the area that became Hamilton County. Initially, Hamilton County did not extend south of the Tennessee River. This area, including the site of Cherokee Chief John Ross's landing in present-day Chattanooga, did not become a part of the county until the disputed Treaty of 1835 that led to Indian removal and the Trail of Tears. The county was named in honor of Alexander Hamilton, Secretary of the Treasury in George Washington's administration. Hamilton was the name of the district of which this section had formerly been a part.

This beautiful region, where the Tennessee River winds through the convergence of several mountain ranges, was the last stronghold of the Cherokees. When their valiant effort to retain their homeland failed, Ross's Landing became one of the main staging areas for the trek west.

At the time of the 1820 census, Hamilton County counted 821 residents, including 16 free blacks and 39 slaves. Approximately 100 Cherokees lived on six private family reserves. The settlers were clustered mainly at Sale Creek, at Poe's Crossroads (Daisy) and at the farm of Asahel Rawlings (Dallas). Hasten Poe had a popular tavern at a crossroads near the foot of Walden's Ridge, and this was used for the holding of the first courts. The courts were later moved nearby to the farm of John Mitchell before a log courthouse was built at Dallas on the Tennessee River. The county seat was shifted across the river to the new town of Harrison in 1840. Chattanooga, whose growth far outstripped that of Harrison, became the seat of government in 1870.

Principal towns, in addition to Chattanooga, are Red Bank, Soddy-Daisy, Ooltewah, Collegedale, East Ridge, Lookout Mountain, and Signal Mountain. The old towns of Dallas and Harrison were inundated by waters of Lake Chickamauga in 1939, when Hamilton County became a center for the Tennessee Valley Authority.

Chattanooga's future as a railroad center was assured when the Western and Atlantic Railroad selected it as its northern terminus. This line reached the city in 1849, and the Nashville and Chattanooga Railroad was completed in 1854. The East Tennessee, Virginia, and Georgia Railroad, the Cincinnati Southern, and other rail lines later were extended to the growing city.

A rail center and "the Gateway to the South," Chattanooga became a focal point in the Civil War, especially in the summer and fall of 1863. The Army of Tennessee under General Braxton Bragg fell back from the city and fought a bloody battle at nearby Chickamauga, Georgia, on September 19 and 20, 1863. From the surrounding mountains, the Confederate forces besieged Chattanooga until the arrival of Union forces under General Ulysses S. Grant and General William T. Sherman. The Union won victories at Wauhatchie and Lookout Mountain prior to the famous charge up Missionary Ridge on November 25, 1863.

After the Civil War, Chattanooga experienced a cholera epidemic in 1873 and a yellow fever scourge five years later. There were also devastating floods in 1867 and 1886. The city still managed to develop as a manufacturing center and underwent a real estate "Boom" in the late 1880s. Later, it became the site of the first franchised bottling of Coca-Cola and the headquarters for several major insurance companies. Combustion Engineering, DuPont, and McKee Baking were also key employers. The Krystal hamburger, the Moon Pie, and the Little Debbie snack cake originated in Hamilton County. Hamilton Place Mall, one of the state's largest shopping malls, opened in 1987.

Chattanoogans who made their mark in national politics include Senator and Postmaster General David Key, Senator and Treasury Secretary William Gibbs McAdoo, Senator Estes Kefauver, and Senator and Labor Secretary Bill Brock. Adoph Ochs went from publisher of the *Chattanooga Times* to develop the *New York Times* into a leading newspaper. Soddy's Ralph McGill became an award-winning editor of the *Atlanta Constitution*. Grace Moore was an opera and film star before meeting a tragic end in an airplane crash; she is buried in Chattanooga. Bessie Smith rose to fame as "Empress of the Blues," and Roland Hayes had an outstanding singing career.

With such attractions as Rock City, Ruby Falls, and the Incline Railway on Lookout Mountain, Chattanooga has been a favorite tourism center. An abandoned railroad station was converted to the Chattanooga Choo Choo family entertainment complex in 1973. Chickamauga and Chattanooga National Military Park has units at Chickamauga, Lookout Mountain, Signal Mountain, and Missionary Ridge. A recent focus has been development of the downtown riverfront, including erection of the Tennessee Aquarium, the Children's Discovery Museum, the IMAX Theater, and the Chattanooga Visitors Center. Other museums include the Chattanooga African-American Museum, Chattanooga Regional History Museum, Houston Museum of Decorative Arts, Hunter Museum of American Arts, Mary Walker Museum, National Knife Museum, and the Tennessee Valley Railroad. The Walnut Street Bridge was restored as a popular pedestrian walkway, and the handsomely-landscaped Tennessee Riverwalk was built along the river. Engel Stadium is the historic home of the Chattanooga Lookouts minor league baseball team. Chattanooga, which had a remarkable cleanup of its polluted air, is developing a reputation as "the environmental city," featuring electric buses, greenways, and an expanded convention center with an environmental design.

Colleges and universities in Hamilton County include the University of Tennessee at Chattanooga, Chattanooga State Technical Community College,

Southern University, Tennessee Temple University, and Covenant College.

Chattanooga's population is 152,446, and that of Hamilton County is 285,536. Hamilton County encompasses 542 square miles. Chattanooga and Hamilton County operate under separate governments, and the county includes nine municipalities.

John Wilson, Hamilton County

SEE: BROCK; WILLIAM E.; CHATTANOOGA; CHATTANOOGA BAKERY COMPANY; CHATTANOOGA CHOO-CHOO; CHATTANOOGA TIMES; CHATTANOOGA AND CHICKAMAUGA, BATTLE OF; HUNTER MUSEUM OF AMERICAN ART; MCADOO, WILLIAM G.; MCKEE BAKING COMPANY; OCHS, ADOLPH; ROSS, JOHN; UNIVERSITY OF TENNESSEE AT CHATTANOOGA; TENNESSEE AQUARIUM; TRAIL OF TEARS

HAMILTON, JOSEPH H. (1932–), the Landon C. Garland Distinguished Professor of Physics at Vanderbilt University, was born in Ferriday, Louisiana. Hamilton has led research into the discovery that nuclei of atoms have many possible coexisting shapes rather than a fixed shape. He has been a driving force behind Tennessee's emergence as a world center for graduate education and research in nuclear physics.

Hamilton pioneered and entrepreneured the first major research facilities in the United States to study nuclei far from stability. Creating unique partnerships with the State of Tennessee, the federal government, and public and private universities, he founded the University Isotope Separator at Oak Ridge (UNISOR) in 1971, a consortium of 12 universities. In 1981 he founded the Joint Institute for Heavy Ion Research (JIHIR) in Oak Ridge, which brings scientists from around the world to Tennessee to do research. He continues to direct both facilities.

In 1996 he was honored with the American Association for the Advancement of Science Award for Development of International Cooperations. The award recognized Hamilton for his leadership in developing significant individual international cooperations, having published research with more than 210 scientists in 30 countries, and the Joint Institute, which has successfully engaged in more scientific international collaborations than any other group in the United States.

Hamilton has won numerous awards for his teaching and research. He has lectured around the world and is the author of more than 600 research papers, numerous research books, and textbooks on physics. Hamilton has directed the research of nine senior theses, 25 master's theses, 54 Ph.D. theses, and more than 80 postdoctoral research associates. He received his bachelor's degree from Mississippi College, his master's and doctorate degrees from Indiana University, and honorary doctorates from Mississippi College and the University of Frankfort in Germany.

Beth Matter, Nashville

SEE: SCIENCE AND TECHNOLOGY; VANDERBILT UNIVERSITY

HAMILTON PLACE at Ashwood, Maury County, is an exquisitely crafted example of the Palladian style of architecture. It was built by (1829–1831) Lucius Junius Polk (1802–1870), one of the five sons of Colonel William Polk of North Carolina, who each relocated to Maury County to establish large cotton plantations. The 1,400-acre plantation occupied a quadrant of the 5,648-acre "Rattle and Snap" tract acquired by Colonel Polk after the Revolution. Lucius Polk became one of the wealthiest planters in Maury County. He served in the State Senate in 1831, and was adjutant-general for the state from 1851 to 1853. The house was begun in 1829, and completed two years later by crews sent out from North Carolina. Lucius named it Hamilton Place after his recently deceased brother, Alexander Hamilton Polk. The earliest and best detailed of the Polk mansions at Ashwood, the house embodies elements copied from high-style precedents. The design of the front was adapted from Palladio's Villa Pisano for the Montagnardas, and an interior arcade is taken from Brunelleschi's design for the hospital in Florence, Italy. The floor plan is loosely based on that of the White House, where Lucius Polk married Andrew Jackson's niece, Mary Ann Eastin, in a ceremony in 1832. Polk's large fortune was devastated by the Civil War, but Hamilton Place remained in the family until the 1970s.

Richard Quin, National Park Service

SEE: MAURY COUNTY; RATTLE-N-SNAP; ST. JOHN'S CHURCH

HANCOCK COUNTY is one of the earliest settlement areas in Tennessee. In a 1673 letter to John Richard of London, Abraham Wood reported the travels of James Needham and Gabriel Arthur's journey into the area: "Eight dayes jorny down this river lives a white people which have long beards and whiskers and weares clothing, and on some ye other rivers lives a hairey people." In 1784 John Sevier recorded in his journal that his party encountered white men in the same region, and they had been living there for some time. The word used to describe these people was "Melungeon," initially thought to be derived from the French word "melange," meaning mixture (as in mixed breed). Recent research by Dr. Brent Kennedy has produced evidence that the term was a sixteenth century Afro-Portuguese word meaning "white person."

The Melungeons were a Mediterranean looking people, who had olive and copper complexions, straight or slightly wavy black hair, beards, and both brown and blue eyes. They spoke broken English and possessed English surnames, but claimed to be

Portuguese. Despite their insistence on their origins, the Scots-Irish settlers declared them "persons of color" and quickly confiscated their land. Denied access to legal recourse, education, or other advantages of citizenship, the Melungeons withdrew to the most isolated, least desirable mountain locales. Today, thousands of Appalachian people trace their ancestry to the Melungeons. Names frequently associated with the Melungeons are Collins, Mullins, Goins, Gibson, Denham, Bowlin, and Sexton. A 1969 gene study on 177 Melungeons concluded that they possessed no appreciable Native American or African gene traits. Instead, and as they had always claimed, they are Caucasian people and do not differ significantly from populations in such North African nations as Libya, Algeria, and Morocco; Cyprus, southern Italy, southern Spain, and Portugal.

As Anglo-Europeans arrived in the area, the first settlers included Joseph Lamb, Jonas Lockmiller, John Ray, Enos Matthais, William McCully, and Daniel Slavins. The first settlers were joined by families with the following surnames: Greene, Purkey, Bray, Cantwell, Trent, Mitchell, Amis, Boulden, Anderson, Bryant, Campbell, McGhee, Mills, Ramsey, Winkler, Wilder, Jarvis, and Wallen. The earliest ministers were John Givens, Moses Williams, and Zachariah Seal. Initial settlement occurred in the area surrounding Greasy Rock, a large stone that protruded into a creek that ran into the Clinch River. The rock acquired its name because it was used by hunters to clean game.

At one time, Hancock County was part of Hawkins County, North Carolina, which later became Hawkins County, Tennessee. During the brief rule of the State of Franklin, Hancock was part of Spencer County. The creation of Hancock County in Tennessee was a complicated process. The 1844 act creating the county from parts of Hawkins and Claiborne counties violated some provisions of the state constitution. A second act passed in 1846, and commissioners were appointed to organize the county and fix boundary lines. When some Hawkins County residents filed a bill enjoining commissioners from further action, all county business was suspended from 1846 to 1848 until the Tennessee Supreme Court ruled in favor of Hancock County. W. H. Sneed, a Knoxville attorney, represented Hancock County in the court action, and commissioners named the new county seat (at the site of Greasy Rock) Sneedville in his honor. The county name honored John Hancock, the Revolutionary War patriot. The first court was held at the house of Alexander Campbell, and afterward at the old Union Church until 1850, when a small brick courthouse was built.

Hancock County has been the home of many men and women of character and ability. Among them were Ben Testerman, a Knoxville lawyer; W. T. Tester-

man, a member of the State Highway Commission; Judge H. Tyler Campbell; Hon. Alonzo Tyler; Judge W. T. Coleman, Judge A. T. Bowen; Col. Grant Trent; Hon. Lewis Cass Jarvis; Hon. Alfred Tylor Drinnon, a legislator and attorney; and Burkett Wallen, superintendent of Rogersville schools. The grandparents of U.S. Senator Mark Hatfield moved from Hancock County to Oregon. Governor Clyde Pearson of Virginia was born in Hancock County. Hancock native Alex Stewart, master cooper and world renowned Appalachian artisan, received the National Heritage Award at the Smithsonian Institution in Washington, D.C. At the time he received the award, Stewart was the only Tennessean who had been so honored. Bluegrass singer and musician Jimmy Martin calls Hancock home and wrote a popular song about the county. Martin became a major star during his years as part of Bill Monroe and the Bluegrass Boys and expanded his popularity in the early 1970s when he performed on the *Will the Circle Be Unbroken* album by the Nitty Gritty Dirt Band.

Sneedville is the only incorporated town in the county, with a population of approximately 1,400. WSJK-TV, Channel 2, at Sneedville was the first state-owned public television station to sign on the air in Tennessee. Other communities in the county include Mulberry Gap, Kyles Ford, Treadway, and Vardy. At one time Hancock County had at least 57 post offices, but today most mail is delivered through Sneedville.

Hancock County reported a 1990 population of 6,739 in 230 square miles. Traditionally, its economy has been based on agriculture and small businesses. In the 1950s zinc was discovered at Treadway. Mining operations continued until 1971, and at its peak, the mine employed more than 220 men. Present manufactures include a furniture factory, a laminated desk top factory, a roof truss factory, an electric motor plant, a concrete plant, and a wholesale craft manufacturer. A number of family-owned businesses operate alongside modern franchise establishments. The county has two banks, with combined assets of over $112 million.

The county's labor force numbers 3,120, and in 1991 unemployment stood at 5.1 percent. Currently, natural gas and oil wells are being developed, and gas lines are under construction. The county is also developing an industrial park on the Clinch River. State Highway 31 into Sneedville from US 11 W is being widened and straightened, and a new bridge across the Clinch River is under construction.

William G. Cook, Thorn Hill

SEE: EXPLORATIONS, EARLY; MELUNGEONS

HANDLY, AVERY (1913–1958), painter and portraitist, was born in Nashville and graduated from Wallace University School and Vanderbilt University, where he majored in English and was influenced by the "Fugitives." His first art instruction, at age 12, was from Miss Emma Cantrell at Watkins Institute in Nashville. Later he studied with Thomas Hart Benton at the Kansas Art Institute and with Grant Wood at the University of Iowa.

After serving overseas in the Navy, Handly settled in Winchester, Franklin County. He painted semiabstract, cubist, and abstract works. He did landscapes, still lifes, social comment, and modern pictures based on religious and theological themes. Late in life, he was a convert to Roman Catholicism. Throughout his work, he continued to reconcile abstraction and representationalism. He painted, perhaps, five self-portraits, portraits of family members, as well as portraits of Harry Tatum, Mrs. Harvey Templeton, Jr., Miss Avery Templeton, and Bishop Ferrani from a photograph. He believed that "all paintings have to start with a basis of magnificence. By certain deft twists and tricks, you turn magnificence into meanness—or *vice versa*."[1]

During the late 1940s and 1950s, Handly had one-man shows at the University of the South, the Hunter Museum of American Art in Chattanooga, and the Centennial Club in Nashville. His most important one-man show as held at the Ward Eggleston Gallery in New York in early 1950. He died in Winchester on October 22, 1958. A memorial exhibition was held at the Nashville Arts Festival in 1960.

James C. Kelly, Virginia Historical Society
CITATION:
(1) James C. Kelly, "Portrait Painting in Tennessee," *Tennessee Historical Quarterly* 46(1987): 270.
SEE: ART; HUNTER MUSEUM OF AMERICAN ART; WATKINS INSTITUTE

HANDY, WILLIAM CHRISTOPHER, "W. C." (1873–1958), African-American composer, bandleader, publisher, and "Father of the Blues," combined the contemporary ragtime and Latin rhythms he encountered in vaudeville, minstrel shows, and extensive travels with the black folk music of his heritage into the unique 12-bar harmonic structure that became known throughout the South as the blues. Handy's 1912 publication of *The Memphis Blues*, the first published blues composition, gained him national attention and designated Memphis as the "Home of the Blues." A truly American musical style, the blues played a key role in the development of jazz and other popular forms.

Handy was born November 16, 1873, in Florence, Alabama. The son of former slaves, he understood plantation life and the struggles of post-emancipation African Americans. The music and struggles absorbed in his childhood inspired Handy's own compositions. Both his father and paternal grandfather were ministers and had hopes that Handy would follow in their footsteps. Much to his parents' dismay, music captured his imagination at an early age. The Handys considered musicians a disreputable lot, and when young Handy proudly showed them the guitar for which he had been anxiously saving for months, they strongly disapproved and made him exchange it for a dictionary.

Handy's love for music grew in spite of their lack of encouragement. At school he learned basic music principles through vocal instruction and began to share his teacher's interest in folk singing. As a teenager, he met Memphis violinist Jim Turner, who had come to Florence to begin an orchestra. Enticed by Turner's glamorous talk of Beale Street, Handy

Musicians jamming with W. C. Handy.

MEMPHIS/SHELBY COUNTY PUBLIC LIBRARY

obtained a cornet and practiced secretly. Handy worked with Turner's group, earning a decent salary. He hoped his efforts would win his parents' approval, but by this time, nothing could deter Handy from his musical ambitions. Against his parents' wishes, Handy played, sang, and attended dances. At age 15 he joined a local minstrel show as first tenor.

Before embarking on a full-fledged musical career, Handy taught school and worked for an Alabama pipe company. He continued to sing and play with various groups, most of which were temporary informal troupes. In the early 1890s Handy's first real attempt to make music his profession landed him in St. Louis, broke and alone. A low point in his life, the hard times he experienced in that city later inspired his most famous work, *St. Louis Blues* (1914).

In August 1896 Handy's luck changed when he received an offer to join Mahara's Minstrels, a Chicago-based musical company, as a cornet player. With this group, Handy gained valuable experience and matured as a professional musician and composer. He advanced quickly to the position of bandleader and began to add his own compositions and arrangements to their repertoire. The group's extensive travels throughout the United States, Canada, Mexico, and Cuba expanded Handy's musical knowledge and skill by introducing him to a variety of new rhythms and sounds. In 1900 Handy, by now married, left the Minstrels to accept a position at the Agricultural and Mechanical College in Huntsville, Alabama. After only two years of leading the school's band and orchestra, however, Handy rejoined the Minstrels for one additional year. By this time his reputation as a bandleader was becoming well known, and in 1903 he received offers from both a white Michigan municipal band and a black orchestra associated with the Knights of Pythias in Mississippi. Handy chose the latter even though it was a less prestigious and profitable position.

Handy made frequent trips to Memphis and in 1907 he decided to make the city, with its strong African-American entertainment scene, his home. The Gayoso Street theater district, which included Beale Street, was home to such popular venues as Tick's Big Vaudeville, the Dixie, the Lyric, and the Savoy. Here, Handy published his first work, *The Memphis Blues*. Initially titled "Mr. Crump," it served as a 1909 campaign song for Memphis mayoral candidate Edward H. Crump, who had hired Handy's band to promote his platform. The crowds went wild for the tune Handy composed, and in 1912 he published the sheet music under the new title, after it was rejected by several popular music publishers. With limited sales and mounting expenses, Handy sold the rights to *The Memphis Blues* to a New York composer for $100. The new owner added lyrics and repub-

lished the song, selling over 50,000 copies by 1913. Although Handy did not benefit financially from his work, he gained a huge following, which established him and Memphis as important sources of the new musical style.

Handy, now wiser to the business side of music, formed a partnership with lyricist Harry H. Pace and began to capitalize on his recent notoriety. Located on Beale Street, the Pace and Handy Music Company published a series of blues hits including *Yellow Dog Rag, Joe Turner Blues,* and *Hesitation Blues*. Handy's success increased with each new release and paralleled the rising popularity and mainstream acceptance of the blues. His third published composition is perhaps his most successful and best known work. An immediate hit upon its release in 1914—and again in 1925, when it was recorded by Bessie Smith and Louis Armstrong—*St. Louis Blues* still remains a classic blues number.

In 1917 Pace and Handy moved their business to New York City. The partnership eventually dissolved, but Handy continued to perform and write successfully, and in later life he published his autobiography. By the time of his death in 1958, the blues music that Handy helped make a commercial success was a well-established and widely accepted American musical style. Handy's works have remained timeless classics over the years and affirm his reputation as "Father of the Blues."

Teresa Biddle-Douglass, Middle Tennessee State University
Suggested Reading: W. C. Handy, *Father of the Blues* (1941); Lynn Abbot and Doug Seroff, "'They Cert'ly Sound Good to Me': Sheet Music, Southern Vaudeville, and the Commercial Ascendancy of the Blues," *American Music* 14(1996): 402–455
See: BEALE STREET; CRUMP, EDWARD H.; MEMPHIS MUSIC SCENE; MUSIC; SMITH, BESSIE

HANKINS, CORNELIUS HALY (1863–1946) was born near Guntown, Itawamba County, Mississippi, the sixth of eight children of Reverend Edward Locke Hankins and Annie Mary McFadden Hankins. He contracted smallpox after his mother cared for Confederate soldiers. As a result, he was deaf until he was eight years old and had to be tutored at home.

In 1883 Hankins studied with Nashville professor Edwin M. Gardner and taught art at Mrs. Creek's (or Miss Clark's) Select School for Girls in Eagleville in Rutherford County. Later he studied in St. Louis with Robert Henri, leader of the Ashcan School, and with William Merritt Chase in New York.

From 1894 to 1899 Hankins worked and taught in Richmond, Virginia, where he exhibited at the first three exhibitions of the Art Club of Richmond. In 1898 he married Sophia Maude McGehee (1875–1968), an artist who specialized in china painting, miniatures, and watercolors. During this period, Hankins was commissioned to paint posthumous portraits of 12 Confederate generals from photographs. In 1901 the Tennessee General Assembly commissioned him to paint a portrait of Robert E. Lee.

About 1904 Hankins and his wife moved to Nashville, where he was first associated with George W. Chambers of the Nashville School of Art. Hankins painted still lifes and landscapes, especially Tennessee wheatfields. But his bread-and-butter came from portraits, and he painted over a thousand of them. Fifteen bust portraits were painted for the Shelby County Court House. Hankins painted a number of prominent Tennesseans, including Confederate Generals Benjamin F. Cheatham and Nathan Bedford Forrest, Admiral Albert Gleaves, Senator William B. Bate, and Governors Albert Roberts and Benton McMillin. At the time of his death, nine of his portraits were hanging in the Tennessee State Capitol, six in the Alabama State Capitol, two in the Mississippi State Capitol, and one in the Louisiana State Capitol.

James C. Kelly, Virginia Historical Society

SEE: ART; GARDNER, EDWIN M.

HARBISON, WILLIAM JAMES (1923–1993), Tennessee Supreme Court justice, was born in Columbia, Tennessee, the son of William Joshua Harbison and Eunice Elizabeth Kinzer Harbison. Harbison (B.A, *magna cum laude,* Vanderbilt University, 1947; J.D., Vanderbilt University School of Law, 1950) attended The Citadel, served in the U.S. Army (1943–1946), and was a member of Phi Beta Kappa. At Vanderbilt's School of Law, he was first in his graduating class, was elected to the Order of the Coif, served as editor-in-chief of the *Vanderbilt Law Review,* and was awarded the Founders Medal for Scholarship. Harbison began the practice of law with Trabue & Sturdivant in Nashville and soon became a partner in that firm.

In September 1966 Governor Frank G. Clement appointed Harbison as Special Justice of the Tennessee Supreme Court to serve for the ailing Justice Weldon B. White, a post which he held until Justice White's death in April 1967. Harbison was elected to the Tennessee Supreme Court in 1974, served two terms as the Court's Chief Justice (1980–1982, 1987–1989), and remained on the bench until retirement in 1990.

The election of Harbison and four other new justices to the five-member Tennessee Supreme Court in 1974 was viewed as an electoral mandate to reform and update Tennessee law and judicial procedure, and their election ushered in an unprecedented period of judicial activism. Harbison quickly emerged as the intellectual and inspirational leader of this "new Court." Soft-spoken and good-humored, the collegial Harbison brought to the task a remarkable memory and an almost encyclopedic knowledge of the law, tempered by his fundamental understanding and respect for the rule of law and the role that the judiciary should play in government and society.

The new Court wasted little time before beginning its revision of the state's often outdated, arcane rules of substantive and procedural law. The Court abolished "the last vestige of the common law disability of coverture in Tennessee" and laid the groundwork for potentially significant changes in the anachronistic, much criticized marital estate of tenancy by the entirety, at least with respect to personal property; embraced the modern doctrine that a prenuptial tort claim by a woman for personal injury is not extinguished by her marriage to the alleged tortfeasor; adopted the modern standard recommended by the *Restatement (Second) of Torts* requiring an independent contractor to exercise reasonable care for the protection of third parties, who may reasonably be endangered by the contractor's negligence even after the owner's acceptance of the work; held that actions under the federal Civil Rights Act of 1871, 42 U.S.C. section 1983, may be brought in the Tennessee state courts; created an exception to the 1884 judicially created employment-at-will doctrine for bad-faith discharges when the discharged employee has exercised a statutory privilege such as filing a workers' compensation claim against the employer; and held that an insurer has a duty to deal fairly and in good faith with its insureds.

The new Court's reform of the criminal law in Tennessee included precedent-setting decisions by which the Court expanded the legal protections accorded juvenile defendants by holding that juveniles charged with offenses constituting a felony are entitled to a jury trial, unless specifically waived, and by prohibiting the adjudication of juveniles by judges who are not licensed attorneys; enunciated for the first time the standard required for determining the scope of the Tennessee Constitution's protection against double jeopardy; abandoned the old *M'Naghten* test in cases involving the defense of mental incompetency in favor of the standard for determining criminal responsibility recommended by the American Law Institute's Model Penal Code; increased the standard of competence required for criminal defense attorneys; abandoned the so-called *Allen* deadlocked jury charge in favor of guidelines promulgated by the American Bar Association; declared the state's mandatory death penalty statute unconstitutional under the U S. Constitution's 8th and 14th amendments; broadened the scope of criminal discovery; refined the law of searches and seizures under the Tennessee Constitution; adopted the majority rule allowing multiple homicide convictions when more than one death results from a single automobile accident; and established modernized standards for trial courts to use in determining whether defendants convicted of multiple offenses should be given consecutive sentences.

Of perhaps even more enduring significance, the new Court under Harbison's guidance also made extensive use of its supervisory powers over the courts and the legal profession in Tennessee to effect long-needed reforms. The new Court, for example, established a unified bar, created the Commission on Continuing Legal Education, the Tennessee Board of Professional Responsibility, the Tennessee Lawyers' Fund for Client Protection, and the Interest On Lawyers' Trust Accounts (IOLTA) program, and adopted the current rules of criminal, appellate, and juvenile procedure. Harbison, the primary drafter of the Tennessee Rules of Civil Procedure (adopted by the Court in 1970), chaired the Court's Advisory Committee on the Rules of Civil Procedure and was instrumental in the promulgation and implementation of the Tennessee Rules of Evidence. Before Harbison's tenure on the Court, Tennessee's courts had functioned without any uniform rules of procedure.

Under Justice Harbison's leadership, the new Court became recognized as one of the most significant courts in the state's history. A hard working court, Harbison himself authored more than 400 decisions (published and unpublished, including concurring and dissenting opinions), many of which were subsequently cited and relied upon by the appellate courts of other states.

Harbison served as president of the Nashville Bar Association (1970–1971), chairman of the Tennessee Code Commission, and co-chairman of the Commission's study of the state's appellate courts (1990). He represented Tennessee on the Commission for Uniform Legislation. He took a special interest in, and served as president of, the Tennessee Bar Foundation, whose functions include funding legal services to the indigent, a high school mock trial program, law student scholarships and loans, public education projects, and programs to improve the administration of justice. Recognizing the power of knowledge as an agent for improving lives, Harbison devoted much of his time to education. He organized the first bar review course for aspiring young lawyers in Tennessee; served as a lecturer (1950–1967) and adjunct professor (1967–1993) at Vanderbilt Law School and as an instructor at the Nashville School of Law (1991–1993); served as president of the Tennessee Historical Society (1983–1985) and as a member of the Metropolitan Government of Nashville and Davidson County Board of Education (1970–1974); and taught a Sunday School class for 30 years.

Upon his retirement from the Court in 1990, he returned to the practice of law with the Nashville firm of O'Hare, Sherrard & Roe, where his son was a partner. He was married to Mary Elizabeth Coleman Harbison. The Harbisons had two children, William L. and Mary Alice.

Harbison's abilities and reputation were such that periodically he was recommended for appointment to the U.S. Supreme Court and to the U.S. Court of Appeals for the Sixth Circuit. More telling testimonies to his character, however, were to be found among the many tributes that came from friends and colleagues in the aftermath of his untimely death, wherein the terms modest, compassionate, generous, and fair are those that most frequently occur.

Theodore Brown, Jr., Atlanta, Georgia

SUGGESTED READINGS: Frank F. Drowata III, et al., "In Memoriam: William J. Harbison," *Tennessee Law Review* 51(1994): 395–402; "The Tennessee Supreme Court: Judicial Activists?" *Memphis State University Law Review* 24(1994): 179–323; John W. Wade, et al., "A Tribute to Justice William J. Harbison," *Vanderbilt Law Review* 47(1994): 943–52

SEE: LAW; TENNESSEE SUPREME COURT

HARDEMAN COUNTY is located in the upper plateaus of southwestern Tennessee, near the headwaters of the Big Hatchie River, with an area of 655 square miles. The county was formed from the Jackson Purchase and attached to Hardin County, then to Madison County, before the Tennessee General Assembly created Hardeman County in 1823. The county was named in honor of Colonel Thomas Hardeman, veteran of the War of 1812, who served as the first county court clerk. He was commissioner of Bolivar before moving to Texas in 1835.

Settlement of the county began almost immediately, with most settlers migrating from Middle Tennessee, Virginia, South Carolina, North Carolina, and Kentucky. Among the early settlers were Ezekiel Polk, the grandfather of President James K. Polk; William Polk, the son of Ezekiel Polk; Thomas McNeal, the son-in-law of Ezekiel Polk; and Rufus P. Neely, the grandson of Thomas Hardeman.

The county seat was established first on Hatchie River and named Hatchie Town. In April 1824 the commissioners chose the present site on land offered by William Ramsey and called the town Bolivar in honor of the South American patriot Simon Bolivar. The town was incorporated in 1847, and was governed by a mayor, recorder, and five aldermen.

Today, Bolivar incorporates both the old and the new. City residents enjoy recreational facilities that include a city park, city swimming pool, and the Hardeman County Golf and Country Club. The city has a weekly newspaper, *The Bolivar Bulletin-Times*, two radio stations, and cable television. City government consists of a mayor and city council. Bolivar took steps to preserve the architectural worth of the many antebellum houses still in use, and in 1973 created the Historical and Cultural District of 20 sites in the uptown area. A Victorian Village was established with the district.

The town of Grand Junction became synonymous with railroads as a result of the 1854 junction of the Memphis and Charleston and the Mississippi Central railroads. By 1858 Grand Junction had a newspaper, the *Quid Nunc*. Today, the town is the home of the National Bird Dog Museum and Field Trial Hall of Fame. Grand Junction acquired these facilities because of its proximity to the Ames Plantation, where the annual National Bird Dog Field Trial takes place each spring. The Hobart Ames Foundation operates the plantation for the benefit of the University of Tennessee. On the plantation grounds is "Cedar Grove," the plantation house built by John Walker Jones in 1847.

Other Hardeman County towns also owe their existence to the railroads. Hickory Valley is situated on the old Mississippi Central Railroad. In 1920 H. H. McMurtree and Luke Wadley built a sassafras mill near Hickory Valley. Pulliam's Crossing was established around the same time the railroad was built in 1855. In 1897 H. B. Duryea built a noted stock farm for short-horn cattle on 3,000 acres near the rail crossing.

The first flourishing settlement at Hornsby was called Bright Prospect, before it took the name Crainville. The town's reputation rested on the discovery of artesian wells in 1915. By 1923 the town boasted nine artesian wells and had become a favorite spot for political candidates to hold rallies and barbecues.

Middleton began as a small settlement called Slab Town. In 1946 the Tennessee Gas Transmission Company (now Tennessee Gas Pipeline), a major supplier of natural gas in the United States, located in Middleton. Recently, the town has emerged as a major retail and industrial center. Labor Day weekend is celebrated with the Fur, Fin, and Feather Festival. Middleton also celebrates the M-Town Variety Show in November and the Christmas Parade and Christmas Yard and Business Decorating Contests in December.

Saulsbury was incorporated in 1856, and quickly became a leading area cotton market. As a result of the importance of Saulsbury, the county polling place moved from Berlin to Saulsbury. The town also engaged in sand mining, and James H. Godsey established a leather goods manufacturing industry. Today, Saulsbury holds an annual community celebration with the lighting of the Christmas tree.

Eight cousins established the town of Silerton, which was incorporated in 1923. Jim Rowland served as the first mayor. Silerton became the center of the county's timber trade. Toone, named for James Toone, became a major shipping point for the northern part of the county, when the railroad came through in 1856. T. C. Conner established a pottery there, the only one of its kind in West Tennessee.

Whiteville, which was incorporated in 1854, first emerged in the early nineteenth century, when Dr. John White opened a trading post. John S. Norment built the first and only cloth manufacturing factory near Whiteville. In 1900 the community supported a newspaper, *The Whiteville News.* Today, Whiteville is the site of a Tennessee Technology Center. The town celebrates Children's Day, a Harvest Festival, and a December Parade. Anderson's Fruit Farm maintains markets at Whiteville and Cloverport.

Pocahontas in the southeastern part of the county was the site of a Civil War battle at Davis Bridge, part of the Corinth campaign. Today, visitors reach the National Register-listed site via a walking trail. Pocahontas is also the home of the Big Hill Pond State Natural Area, a scenic park abounding in wildlife, with fishing, nature trails, and scenic areas. Middleburg, once a thriving community, was destroyed during the Civil War. Only Lax's Ole Country Store survives as a reminder of the former community.

Several Tennesseans of note came from Hardeman County. Elizabeth Avery Meriwether, an ardent nineteenth century supporter of women's rights was born in Hardeman County. She wrote numerous articles and essays in support of her cause. Two books, *Recollections of 92 Years* and *The Master of Red Leaf, Black and White* were written by Meriwether. John Houston Bills, a Hardeman County planter, maintained private journals for the years 1843 to 1871, which are an invaluable source to the history of the county. His house, The Pillars, is a historic house museum in Bolivar. Another historic building, the Little Courthouse (circa 1824), is the county's official museum, administered by the county chapter of the Association for the Preservation of Tennessee Antiquities. John Milton Hubbard, another diarist, wrote *Notes of a Private.* Hubbard was head master of Bolivar Male Academy when he marched away to the Civil War with his students. Egbert Haywood Osborne—educator, Baptist minister, Confederate soldier, and lawyer—published a book of poems. Charles Austin Miller, 1890 Tennessee Secretary of State, compiled the *Official and Political Manual of Tennessee.* Jesse Christopher Allen and James H. White worked to establish schools for black children in the 1930s.

For much of its history, Hardeman County's economy has depended on agriculture and lumbering. Quickly identified as a favorable site for cotton production, the county early attracted planters, who built plantations and worked the cotton fields with slave labor. No longer dependent upon cotton, the county's farmers now engage in livestock production and plant a variety of crops. Hardeman is still the leading hardwood producing center in West

Tennessee. McAnulty's Woods, a conservation site within the town of Bolivar, is the only known virgin forest remaining in West Tennessee.

Since the 1940s Hardeman County's economy has shifted toward industrial production. Like other Tennessee counties, Hardeman workers are engaged in the production of automotive parts and textiles. In addition, factories in the county produce elevator appliances, pyrotechnics, electrical switches, and absorbent clay products.

Faye Tennyson Davidson, Bolivar

SEE: AMES PLANTATION; ASSOCIATION FOR THE PRESERVATION OF TENNESSEE ANTIQUITIES; BILLS, JOHN H.; CONTRABAND CAMPS; HUNTING DOGS; MERIWETHER, ELIZABETH A.; NATIONAL FIELD TRIAL; ROSE, WYCLIFFE; TIMBER INDUSTRY; WESTERN STATE MENTAL HOSPITAL

HARDIN COUNTY. The story of Hardin County begins with the prehistoric mound builders of the Woodland and Mississippian periods. Savannah, the modern county seat, is built partially within a wall and trench, and amid a line of fourteen mounds on a bluff parallel to the Tennessee River. These prehistoric peoples also built a considerable structure covering approximately four acres in the northwest corner of the county near Middleton and several mounds at Pittsburg Landing in what is now the Shiloh National Military Park. After the Mississippian era, Hardin County, along with most of the rest of West Tennessee, became an area shared by various Indian tribes as a rich hunting ground.

Geologically, Hardin County lies in the Western Valley of the Tennessee River. The river enters the county at the middle of its southern border and flows northward in a west to east direction. The western side of the river, making up one-third of the county's 600 square miles, is rich bottom land, with some hills and ridges. The land east of the river is higher, with a steadily increasing elevation moving toward the eastern boundary. East Hardin County also contains numerous rich bottom land along the lower portion of several creeks and on the inside river bends.

In 1780 John Donelson led the river party that rendezvoused with James Robertson's overland party in the establishment of Nashborough. According to Donelson's journal, his group stopped at what was probably Diamond Island, near Pittsburg Landing, in the Tennessee River, becoming the first known record of whites on Hardin County soil.

In 1783 the North Carolina legislature designated land in West Tennessee for settlement by Revolutionary War veterans. The act creating land bounties anticipated a treaty with the Chickasaws, who claimed the area, and probably anticipated Tennessee statehood. The North Carolina Act allowed claims to be surveyed, and in 1786, either Isaac Taylor or W.A.

Farrar laid off 5,000 acres for Andrew Kerr and 3,000 acres for Joseph Hardin.

After the Jackson Purchase, the Tennessee General Assembly in November 1819 created Hardin County, which extended from Wayne County to the Mississippi. Eleven days later, Shelby County was created, which removed present Shelby County and most of Fayette County from the western reaches of Hardin County. In 1823 the legislature created McNairy County, which established the current western boundary of Hardin County. Bits and pieces were added or taken away over the years, until the county's present boundaries were established in 1856.

Hardin County was named for Colonel Joseph Hardin. He was born in Richmond, Virginia, removed to North Carolina at an early date, and came to Greene County and later Knox County, following the Revolutionary War. He served as a representative of Washington and Greene counties in the State of Franklin and in the Tennessee Territorial Assembly. Hardin died sometime between 1791 and 1801 in Knox County. Among the first settlers were Hardin's sons, a daughter, and their extended families. Like the Nashborough settlers, the Hardin families arrived in two groups: one by land and one by river. The boat party arrived in July 1816, with the land party not far behind.

The first session of County Court of Pleas and Quarterly Sessions was formed January 3, 1820, at the home of Colonel James Hardin near Cerro Gordo. The July 1822 session was held at Hardinville (now called Old Town) near the confluence of Turkey and Boone's creeks. This site was determined to be the center of the county. The citizens of the county living west of the river strongly objected to the long trip, which included ferry costs, and initiated a successful effort to move the county seat. In 1829 Rudd's Ferry was selected as the county seat; the name was changed to Savannah in 1850, when the state legislature incorporated the town.

Mostly rural and agricultural, Hardin County had a mixed experience in the Civil War. Its allegiances were divided, with most of the western side of the river favoring the southern cause and much of the eastern side supporting the North. Hardin was one of the few counties outside East Tennessee to vote against secession in both plebiscites. The war moved across the county several times. On April 5–7, 1862, the Battle of Shiloh took place in an area between Shiloh Church and Pittsburg Landing. It is commemorated by a 3,000-acre national park that attracts thousands of visitors each year.

Another Civil War attraction is the Cherry Mansion. Built on the bluff overlooking the river by David Robinson in 1830, the Mansion became the headquarters of General Ulysses S. Grant during the Battle of Shiloh. The Cherry Mansion is one of several nineteenth century houses found in Savannah and Hardin County; perhaps the oldest is the James Graham house built circa 1825.

The history of the county is tied to the waterways. Early industry included mills built along the creeks throughout the county. The first mills were used to grind grain, but later mills were built to take advantage of the natural resources of timber, rock, and minerals. Commercial goods moved into the county and various products from the forest or farm moved to markets by river transportation. In 1930 the Milo Lambert Bridge at Savannah became the first span across the river in the county. Further downriver, Shannonville became Saltillo, and White's Ferry became Cerro Gordo. Hamburg and Crump's Landing fell victim to the impoundment of the river into a TVA lake. Pickwick Dam, completed by the Tennessee Valley Authority in 1938, created a recreational area, which steadily increased the size and importance of Counce. The Tennessee River Museum, located in a historic post office building in Savannah, documents the river's influence on local history and folkways.

Savannah's population reached almost 1,000 in 1880, and in 1996 numbers more than 7,000. As the county seat, it has always been the political hub of the county. In 1963 the completion of the Estes Kefauver Bridge over the Pickwick Dam made it also the county's commercial hub. Like Savannah, the county has grown considerably, with the 1990 census showing more than 22,600 people.

Although the economic importance of the clothing industry has decreased considerably in the past two decades, Kraft paper, steel, mobile homes, plastics, chemicals, and wood related products have added to the industrial base. Yet even with an increased emphasis on attracting industry and increases in jobs associated with recreational attractions, many Hardin countians still depend on the farm for at least part of their livelihood. Increased traffic on the Tennessee-Tombigbee Waterway, improvements to U.S. Highway 64, and a new connector to Interstate 40 promise to open Hardin County to new and increased industrial opportunities.

James B. Phillips, University of Tennessee, Knoxville
SEE: FERRIES; PICKWICK LANDING STATE PARK; SHILOH, BATTLE OF; TENNESSEE RIVER; TENNESSEE-TOMBIGBEE WATERWAY; TENNESSEE VALLEY AUTHORITY

HARDING, WILLIAM GILES (1808–1886), a leading Tennessee agriculturist and a nationally acclaimed stock breeder, was born in 1808 near Nashville. Harding was educated at the American Literary, Scientific, and Military Academy in Middletown, Connecticut. Two years after his first wife, Mary Selena McNairy, died in 1837, he assumed full responsibility for managing Belle Meade, his father's 1,200-acre plantation on the "Old Natchez Road."

In 1840 Harding, then a brigadier general in the state militia, married Elizabeth McGavock. They had two daughters, Selene and Mary, who would grow to maturity. Harding also had a son, John, by his first marriage.

In 1853–54 Harding transformed the Federal style house his father had built in 1820 into the Greek Revival mansion that stands today. He also raced horses, won premiums for his thoroughbreds, and established Belle Meade as a nationally recognized horse nursery.

Early in the Civil War, Harding headed the Military and Financial Board of Tennessee, which spent five million dollars arming and equipping soldiers for the defense of the South. In 1862, as the result of his activities, Harding was imprisoned by Federal authorities for six months. During his absence, his wife managed the plantation under dire circumstances and looked after "a family of 150 people," mostly slaves.

Following the war, Harding and his son-in-law, W. H. Jackson, developed Belle Meade into one of the world's greatest horse-breeding establishments. When he died in 1886, the *Chattanooga Times* called Harding "a monarch in his own domain."
Ridley Wills, II, Franklin
SEE: BELLE MEADE PLANTATION; THOROUGHBRED HORSE BREEDING AND RACING

HARDWICK STOVE COMPANY. A family business that grew from a backyard foundry to a major commercial enterprise, Hardwick Stove Company shaped Bradley County's industrial history for over 100 years. Its founder, Christopher Hardwick, began building cast iron stoves in his Cleveland, Tennessee, backyard in the 1870s. A farmer and merchant prior to the Civil War, Hardwick's support of the Confederacy left him penniless at the war's end. Industrious and resourceful, he established The Stove Foundry with two of his sons, Joseph and John. In 1880 Hardwick also launched a second venture, Cleveland Woolen Mills, which became another Bradley County industry. He was one of Cleveland's most influential businessmen, joining the ranks of the New South capitalists.

Hardwick's small backyard project expanded and prospered rapidly. By the late 1880s the foundry, then called Cleveland Stove Works, employed 15 workers, produced 12 stoves per day, and was valued at over $10,000. The company sold stoves across the South and tripled its work force by 1894. The company remained under family control, as authority passed from Hardwick to his son Joseph, and then to Joseph's son C. L., who spent a total of 63 years with the firm, serving as manager and president for nearly 50 years before his death in 1961.

Much of Hardwick's success rested on expansion, as it kept abreast of new developments, and offered a variety of styles and products. From 1942 to 1945 production of stoves halted, while the company manufactured World War II aircraft components. During this period, the factory developed a system of inspection and quality control that converted to postwar production when the company returned to the manufacture of stoves. In the 1950s Hardwick added electric ranges to its line of gas stoves. Throughout its process, Hardwick controlled every facet of stove production. Presses in the die shop cut and stamped large sheets of metal, and a pipe shop division manufactured gas lines for gas ranges. Only the heat controls were produced elsewhere.

Under the direction of Reeves Brown, president from 1962 to 1975, the Hardwick Stove Company opened a national service center and introduced continuous cleaning ovens. Harold C. Almond assumed the role of company president in 1975, and by the 1980s Hardwick employed over 1,000 people and produced over 250,000 stoves annually. In its more than 100 years of production, Hardwick Stove Company made the transition from wood stoves to gas and electric ranges and microwaves, manufacturing over 9,750,000 stoves of all types. In the 1990s, Hardwick and the other major stove manufacturers were acquired and combined into Maytag Cleveland Cooking Products, a corporation with 2,400 employees in 1997. A second associated company, Maytag Customer Service, employs 300. The Hardwick name remains, however, as part of the former woolen mills operation, now Hardwick Clothes, Inc., an employer of 665 in 1997.

Teresa Biddle-Douglass, Middle Tennessee State University
SEE: BRADLEY COUNTY; INDUSTRY

HARLINSDALE FARM. This Williamson County property is the most significant extant historic farm associated with the modern Tennessee Walking Horse industry. In 1935 Wirt Harlin established the farm, which included the historic Maney-Sidway House, on the northern outskirts of Franklin on U.S. Highway 31. Over the next 11 years, Harlinsdale Farm became a place of great reknown in the fledging Tennessee Walking Horse industry. Its landscaped entrance, the open fields next to the highway, and the prominent siting of the horse barn were not accidental, but part of an overall landscape design that has since become the standard pattern for Walking Horse farms. The careful landscaping and the huge horse barn told potential investors in the new industry that Harlinsdale Farm was a classy, progressive, and successful livestock farm. This image of graciousness was vital for the industry's success since a large part of the marketing charm of the Tennessee Walking Horse lies with its association with the image of genteel Southern culture and tradition.

The prominence of Harlinsdale Farm in the industry was insured when the Harlins acquired a colt that they named Midnight Sun. This famous horse took second in the Shelbyville national celebration in 1944 and then won first place in 1945 and 1946, becoming the first repeat National Champion. The success of Midnight Sun in the ring, and as a sire, has never been matched by any other Tennessee Walking Horse. Adored by the fans, Midnight Sun became one of the most popular horses in history and many champions today are traced to him. Harlinsdale Farm became a shrine to this famous horse and a granite stone to the immediate east of the horse barn marks Midnight Sun's final resting place. The Harlin family continues to operate the farm as a showplace for the Tennessee Walking Horse.

Carroll Van West, Middle Tennessee State University
SEE: WALKING HORSE NATIONAL CELEBRATION

HARPE, MICAJAH "BIG" (ca. 1768–1799) and **WILEY "LITTLE"** (ca. 1770–1804) were notorious outlaws on the frontier of the Old Southwest. The two committed murder and highway robbery indiscriminately around the frontier town of Knoxville and in other parts of East Tennessee and Kentucky. The legend of their atrocities survives as one of the most disturbing accounts of blood-lust in Tennessee history.

Little is known about the background or family of the Harpes, who were most likely brothers. They moved from North Carolina to East Tennessee in 1797, settling on Beaver Creek, about eight miles west of Knoxville, with at least one woman they brought with them. Little Harpe reputedly married a woman who lived near Knoxville. Though they began farming peacefully, the two soon plundered hogs, sheep, and horses from their neighbors. Their murders started in Knox County, where the community was alarmed at the fate of victims like a man named Johnson, whose body the Harpes cut open and filled with stones before throwing it in the Holston River. Stories of the Harpes's inhuman violence maintain that the men even killed their own children. They left for less populous areas, terrorizing settlers and travelers along the Tennessee and Kentucky border.

Big Harpe met his end in the summer of 1799 after he slit the throats of the wife and infant of Moses Stegall, a former Knoxville resident living in what is now Union County, Kentucky. A posse caught up with the brothers and shot Big Harpe, although Little Harpe managed to escape. According to witnesses' reports, the enraged Stegall cut off Big Harpe's head with a butcher knife, while the outlaw was still conscious. Stegall collected no reward, but he placed the head in a tree in Highland Lick, Kentucky, as a warning to other outlaws.

Little Harpe continued his career as a cohort of Samuel Mason, robbing and killing travelers along the Natchez Trace in Tennessee and Mississippi. The Trace was fertile territory for these outlaws because of the number of traders and travelers who carried gold on their journeys between Nashville and Natchez. Little Harpe's movements largely remain a mystery, but the story of his execution survives. Mason was captured in 1803, but escaped during a storm while being transported to Natchez. When two men later appeared with Mason's head to request a reward, John Bowman of Tennessee identified one as Little Harpe. Harpe and his partner escaped, but were captured hours later in Greenville, Mississippi. After their trial in January 1804, the heads of the two hanged criminals were placed on stakes on the Trace near Greenville.

The exploits of the Harpes were immortalized in Robert M. Coates's *The Outlaw Years* (1930) and O. A. Rothert's *Outlaws of Cave-in-Rock* (1924). Histories also presented sensationalized accounts of the Harpes, such as *Life As It Is* by J. W. M. Breazeale (1842). These and other writers made the brothers two of the most notorious outlaws in Tennessee history.

Blythe Semmer, Middle Tennessee State University
SUGGESTED READING: John D. W. Guice, "A Trace of Violence?" *Southern Quarterly* 29(1991): 123–43
SEE: KNOX COUNTY; NATCHEZ TRACE

HARPETH HALL SCHOOL AND WARD-BELMONT.

Harpeth Hall School opened in 1951 in Nashville on a 26-acre campus that had previously been the Estes estate. While new in name and location, the school continued in spirit and manner the education of girls and young women that had been Ward-Belmont's mission from 1913 to 1951. The earlier high school and junior college, situated on Adelicia Acklen's estate, had developed from two nineteenth-century female educational institutions: Ward Seminary and Belmont College.

From its opening, Ward-Belmont attracted to its junior college students from across the country. As the first junior college in the South to be fully accredited, it was always a popular choice of young southern women, but the number of students matriculating from outside the South often represented 40 percent of the class. Day students from Nashville and the surrounding area also enrolled in the college and in the college preparatory school that shared the campus, but the boarding department dominated the school. In its early years and at the end of its existence, the student population included 550 boarding students along with 300–400 day students.

Until the Great Depression, Ward-Belmont prospered, and enrollment reached 1,200. The college achieved national recognition, particularly in music and speech, and the customs established at the school's founding became venerated traditions. The Depression broke the school's momentum, and Ward-

Belmont fell deeply into debt. Though successive administrations reduced the amount owed, the school never recovered. In 1951 Ward-Belmont's governing board sold the campus and its buildings for the remaining debt to the Tennessee Baptist Convention, which opened Belmont College (now University) on the site.

This sudden action surprised and shocked alumnae, faculty, students, and the Nashville community. Efforts to reopen negotiations with the Tennessee Baptist Convention or to propose an alternative failed. The junior college and preparatory school known as Ward-Belmont ceased to exist. A small group of determined Nashvillians, however, took steps to open a girls college preparatory school. Some faculty from Ward-Belmont became the first teachers and first headmistress, and some of Ward-Belmont's most loved traditions carried over to Harpeth Hall.

Today, Harpeth Hall has a life and history of its own and a proud memory of its forebearer's past. Enrollment stands at more than 525 girls in grades 5–12, with 100 percent of each year's senior class entering colleges across the country. Ward-Belmont had been led by upstanding men: J. D. Blanton, John Barton, A. B. Benedict, Joseph H. Burk, and Robert Calhoun Provine, but Harpeth Hall has had only one man as Head of School, David Wood (1980–1991). Instead, Harpeth Hall has been indelibly marked and shaped by its headmistresses: Susan S. Souby (1951–1963), Idanelle McMurry (1963–1979), Polly Fessey (Interim Headmistress 1979–1980), and Leah S. Rhys (1991–1998). The recent development in the arts curriculum that includes acting, chorus, and four levels each of studio art and photography, might seem reminiscent of Ward-Belmont, but it is actually one of several energetic thrusts of the school. Harpeth Hall excels equally in the traditional core curriculum areas and in athletics, while the annual three-week winterim provides life experiences, independent study, and service opportunities for every student. The physical plant has expanded to seven buildings equipped with modern facilities and current technology. But the faculty has always been crucial to the school's success. Generations of girls and young women have benefited from the instruction they received and their association with adults who value the idea of single-sex education for adolescent girls.

Margaret D. Binnicker, Middle Tennessee State University
SEE: BELMONT UNIVERSITY; EDUCATION

HARRIMAN, WALTER C.,

(1849-d.date not identified), managing director of the East Tennessee Land Company, was born in New Hampshire, the second of the three children of Walter and Almire Harriman. During the Civil War, Colonel Walter Harriman (later General) led his Eleventh New Hampshire Regiment out of Cincinnati and across the Cumberland Plateau to join General Ambrose Burnside's army in Knoxville. The Colonel had no horse, but walked with his men through the mountainous countryside of southern Kentucky and northeastern Tennessee. During this arduous 20-day journey, Harriman and his regiment camped for several days on the Emory River near the future site of Harriman. General Harriman did not visit Tennessee after the war, but returned to New Hampshire to serve two terms as governor of the state.

Walter C. Harriman served as an orderly to his father during the Civil War, but was not with him during the Tennessee campaign. After the war, Walter C. became a journalist and the editor of a county newspaper in New Hampshire. He studied law and was admitted to the bar in 1876. He practiced law in Portsmouth, Exeter, and Boston, and served as solicitor for Rockingham County, New Hampshire, for five years. He was twice elected to Congress from New Hampshire.

In 1878 Walter C. married Mabel A. Perkins; they had two children. Shortly after his marriage, his health began to weaken, and the family moved to Tennessee in 1881. In 1889 he joined the East Tennessee Land Company venture in Roane County. Frederick Gates and other company directors wanted to create a model industrial city based on the ideals of prohibition. Harriman moved his family to the new city and became managing director of the company until 1891.

The directors of the company considered the name "Fiskville" for their town, to honor General Clinton B. Fisk, nominal president of the company. They changed their minds after a conversation with an elderly man, who fondly remembered Colonel Harriman and recalled the colonel saying that there should be a town near the site. On the basis of this memory, the directors decided to name the town "Harriman."

Walter C. Harriman built a large house in the new town and acted as one of the moving spirits of the community. He was treasurer of the S. K. Paige Lumber and Manufacturing Company and, from 1890 until 1898, served as the first president of the First National Bank of Harriman.

W. Calvin Dickinson, Tennessee Technological University
SEE: ROANE COUNTY; TEMPERANCE

HARRIS, GEORGE WASHINGTON (1814–1869),

seminal southwestern humorist, was a Democrat and a Presbyterian, in that order. He was born in Pennsylvania, but grew up in Knoxville. Although involved in many aspects of East Tennessee frontier development ranging from surveying to river and rail transportation, his major achievement was the creation of Sut Lovingood, a stereotypical "panther streak" mountaineer. Beginning in 1854 as occasional news-

paper pieces, Harris's stories of Sut's exploits were picked up by other publications, soon giving him a national reputation.

A strong supporter of the Confederacy, Harris was ruined by the war. Trying to recoup some of his losses, he collected 24 of the Sut stories, issued in book form as *Sut Lovingood: Yarns* (1867) by New York publisher Dick and Fitzgerald. Praised at the time by young Mark Twain, through the years the volume continued to have a selective reading public willing to decipher the provincial dialect and able to appreciate the often coarse imagery and rough humor. William Faulkner, Irvin S. Cobb, Stark Young, and Flannery O'Connor were among the notable fans of this volume. A detractor, Edmund Wilson, was less than appreciative, describing it in a May 7, 1955, issue of the *New Yorker* as "the most repellent book of any real literary merit in American literature."

From the original plates, the *Yarns* remained in print until 1960, by which time the exploration of American frontier culture had secured a place for Harris, Sut, and the folk humor of the old Southwest in the historical outline of American humor.

Ben Harris McClary, Chattanooga
SEE: LITERATURE

HARRIS, ISHAM GREEN (1818–1897), Governor and

U.S. Senator, was born near Tullahoma, Franklin County, on February 10, 1818, the son of Isham and Lucy Davidson Harris. Raised on his father's farm, where a small number of slaves worked the land, Harris attended public schools and Winchester Academy. In 1832 Harris moved to Paris, Tennessee, where he earned a living as a merchandise store clerk. Within a short time, he moved again to Tippah County, Mississippi, where he studied law at night and operated his store during the day. Left penniless after a local bank failure, Harris returned to Paris and resumed his earlier business partnership. In 1841 he obtained admission to the Tennessee bar and quickly acquired a reputation for honesty and legal proficiency.

Harris's long political career began with his election to the Tennessee State Senate in 1847. The next year, he won election to the U.S. House of Representatives. Re-elected in 1850, he declined a third term two years later to practice law in Memphis. In 1857 Harris was elected Governor of Tennessee. He won re-election in 1859 and 1861.

Events leading to secession and war overshadowed Harris's gubernatorial years. Harris urged secession after Abraham Lincoln's election as president in November 1860. On April 25, 1861, following the bombardment of Fort Sumter, South Carolina, and an earlier unsuccessful attempt to persuade Tennesseans to secede, Harris pushed through the General Assembly an ordinance of independence and another one allying Tennessee with the Confederacy, both of which won voter approval in a June plebiscite. In a tense atmosphere of polarization and danger, Harris prevented the separation of East Tennessee when the state seceded from the Union. He raised 100,000 troops for the Confederacy and remained as governor until forced to flee the state after the Union capture of Nashville in 1862. He volunteered as an aide-de-camp on the staffs of Albert S. Johnston, Braxton Bragg, John B. Hood, Joseph E. Johnston, and P.G.T. Beauregard. At Shiloh (1862) General Albert Johnston died in Harris's arms. Serving in the Confederate army at headquarters of the Army of the West for the last three years of the Civil War, Harris participated in all the important battles in Tennessee and those of the Army of the West except Perryville (1862).

Following Robert E. Lee's surrender at Appomattox Courthouse in April 1865, the impoverished Harris fled South to avoid capture and imprisonment. He escaped to Mexico, where he lived for 18 months before spending a year in England. In 1867 he returned to Memphis to resume his law practice and attempt a political comeback.

In 1877 the legislature elected Harris to the U.S. Senate; he won re-election in 1883, 1889, and 1895. Popular at home and respected by congressional colleagues, Harris served in the Senate during the period of party stalemate and equilibrium when national power was vested in Congress, not the presidency. For 20 years, he shaped national legislation as an advocate for low tariffs, state rights, bank reforms, limited government, currency expansion, strict constitutional construction, and protection for workers and farmers from exploitation by moneyed interests. He carefully and shrewdly distributed federal patronage to enhance his political base at home. Harris emerged as the leader of Tennessee's conservative Bourbon Democrats, who championed the rights of the individual states and the existing social order, especially white supremacy. As he built up seniority, Harris became an influential member of the upper chamber during Gilded Age America. He gained appointments to various important committees, including finance, claims, rules, the District of Columbia, and the Democratic advisory or "steering" committee. After Democrats assumed control of Congress in 1893, Harris was elected president pro tempore of the Senate, serving in that capacity until March 1895.

Harris voted with the southern Democrats on the major issues before the Senate. He supported tariff reduction to meet government obligations only, preferring the Wilson bill in 1894 to the McKinley Tariff of 1890. Harris denounced the Federal Election Bill as an abridgment of states' rights and a racial question. Throughout his career, Harris was involved in the currency question. He favored the Bland-Allison Act

of 1878 and the Sherman Silver Purchase Act of 1890, both of which permitted limited coinage of silver. In 1893 Harris led silver Democrats against President Grover Cleveland's demand for unconditional repeal of the Sherman Silver Purchase Act. In 1895 he attended a convention of over 2,000 pro-silver delegates in Memphis and later emerged as chairman of the Democratic Silver Committee. Harris joined the William Jennings Bryan campaign for the presidency in 1896. His political disappointment over Bryan's defeat aggravated his failing health, and Harris died in Washington, D.C., on July 8, 1897. He was buried in Elmwood Cemetery in Memphis.

Leonard Schlup, Akron, Ohio

SUGGESTED READING: George W. Watters, "Isham Green Harris, Civil War Governor and Senator from Tennessee, 1818–1897" (Ph. D. diss., Florida State University, 1977)

SEE: CIVIL WAR; FRANKLIN COUNTY; RECONSTRUCTION

HAUN, MILDRED EUNICE (1911–1966), author of stories of mountain life, was born in Hamblen County, on January 6, 1911, to James Enzor and Margaret Ellen Haun, but was raised in Haun Hollow in the Hoot Owl District of Cocke County in a large family of strong, independent mountain farmers whose roots could be traced back to 1779. Planning to become a granny woman/midwife and needing more education, 16-year-old Haun traveled to Franklin County, Tennessee, to live with relatives and attend high school. After graduation in 1931, she attended Vanderbilt University, became interested in literature, and enrolled in John Crowe Ransom's English course. In this class she used the songs and stories handed down through oral tradition in tales of her home and people. Haun's narrator was Mary Dorthula White, a granny woman, born, coincidentally, on January 6, 1847 (Old Christmas), a date that mountaineers believed ensured eternal life. Encouraged by Ransom, Haun continued to write stories after graduation, while teaching high school in Franklin. In 1937 she completed an M.A. in English at Vanderbilt, studying under Ransom and Donald Davidson, both of whom signed her unpublished thesis, "Cocke County Ballads and Songs."

Haun's only collection of fiction, *The Hawk's Done Gone* (1940), includes several of the stories she had written in college. This work consists of a group of stories linked by the narrator, Mary Dorthula White, and members of several families. It combines modern realism with ancient beliefs and superstitions, creating a disturbing, yet intriguing look at mountain life in the period from the Civil War to 1940. The themes of witchcraft, infanticide, incest, and miscegenation reveal a dark side of the author. But amid the talk of spirits and age-old prejudices is Haun's use of dialect, mountain beliefs, and songs. The collection is not quite a novel, but more than a series of stories. Herschel Gower edited and published posthumously ten additional stories by Haun in 1968 (*The Hawk's Done Gone and Other Stories*).

From 1942 to 1943 Haun served as book editor for the *Nashville Tennessean* and later as an editorial assistant to Allen Tate on the *Sewanee Review, 1944–1946*, occasionally returning to Cocke County to care for her aging mother while her brothers were in military service during World War II. From 1950 to 1963 Haun worked as an editor and information specialist for the Arnold Engineering Development Center in Tullahoma, Tennessee, writing speeches, news releases, correspondence courses in engineering and technical subjects for military personnel, training manuals, and featured articles of the Department of Agriculture. She was sent to Europe and the Near East in 1965 to report on agricultural projects under American foreign aid. At the end of 1965, a serious illness forced her to return to Nashville for hospitalization and treatment. Haun died on December 20, 1966, in Washington, D.C., after months of hospitalization, and is buried in Morristown, Tennessee, next to her mother in the Haun family plot.

Kathy Lyday-Lee, Elon College

SEE: ARNOLD ENGINEERING DEVELOPMENT CENTER; COCKE COUNTY; DAVIDSON, DONALD; HAMBLEN COUNTY; RANSOM, JOHN C.; TATE, JOHN O. ALLEN

HAWKINS, ALVIN (1821–1905), Reconstruction judge and governor, was seven years old when his family moved to Carroll County, Tennessee. After attending McLemoresville Academy and Bethel College, he tried his hand as a farmer, blacksmith, and teacher before determining to become a lawyer. Following admission to the bar in 1843, he opened an office at Camden, but soon returned to Huntingdon, the seat of Carroll County. In 1847 he married Julia Ott of Murfreesboro.

In 1853 Hawkins won election to the Tennessee House of Representatives as a Whig, after an unsuccessful attempt in 1845. With steadfast loyalty to the Union, he supported John Bell's presidential campaign in 1860 and the Republican party thereafter. Following the Union occupation of West Tennessee, Hawkins traveled the region on behalf of Military Governor Andrew Johnson to report on "men and matters" to aid in the formulation of plans for the reconstruction of civil governments. In 1864 President Abraham Lincoln appointed Hawkins U.S. District Attorney for West Tennessee; Hawkins was appointed to the Tennessee Supreme Court in 1865.

During Reconstruction, Hawkins served with great distinction on the State Supreme Court, which demonstrated remarkable independence from the Radical Republican regime headed by Governor William Brownlow. In 1868 he left the court for a brief time to serve as Consul-General in Havana, Cuba. He was elected to a full term on the State Supreme Court in 1869, but the approval of a new State Constitution ended Reconstruction government and his term as judge in 1870.

In 1880 Hawkins won election as the first Republican governor since Reconstruction due to division in the Democratic ranks over the state debt question. Although a strong believer in full payment of the debt, he was unable to devise a solution to settle the controversy. However, his honest, efficient government helped to erase the stigma carried by his party as a result of Brownlow's rule. He also earned a reputation as a champion of judicial and educational reform.

The reunited Democratic party defeated Hawkins in his 1882 reelection bid, but he left office amid bipartisan acclaim for his integrity. He returned to Huntingdon, where he practiced law and was active in Methodist affairs. He died at the age of 84.

Russell Fowler, Memphis

SEE: CARROLL COUNTY; STATE DEBT CONTROVERSY, 1878–83; TENNESSEE SUPREME COURT

HAWKINS COUNTY. One of the oldest Tennessee counties, Hawkins County was first established as a separate North Carolina county on January 6, 1787, when the state legislature divided Sullivan County, North Carolina. The original county was quite large, extending from the North Fork of the Holston River southwestwardly to the "Big Suck" near present-day Chattanooga. Other counties, or parts of counties, later created from Hawkins include Hancock, Grainger, Jefferson, Knox, Roane, Meigs, and Hamilton. Prior to its creation by North Carolina, the county was Spencer County, State of Franklin.

The act creating Hawkins County empowered seven commissioners to select a central place for the county seat, where a court house, prison, and stocks would be built, and to levy a tax for the support of local government. The first meeting of the commissioners took place at the home of Thomas Gibbons on Big Creek on June 4, 1787, at which time Joseph Rogers's land on Crockett's Creek was selected as the location for the county seat. During the summer of 1787 the courthouse, jail, and stocks were erected, and the little community took the name Hawkins Court House. The first elected county officials were John Hunt, sheriff, William Mashall, register, and Thomas Hutchins, clerk. William Marshall and Nathaniel Henderson were elected the first Representatives to the North Carolina House of Commons, and Thomas Amis was elected the first Senator to represent the new county in the legislative assembly.

In 1789 Thomas Amis presented a petition from the community to the North Carolina General Assembly to establish a town at the Hawkins Court House site and to name the town Rogersville. Approval of the petition, which was granted on November 7, 1789, empowered county commissioners to lay out a town in half-acre lots, with convenient streets and lots reserved for public buildings.

The Main Street of Rogersville was defined by the route of the Great Wilderness Road, which attracted a steady stream of settlers through the town on their way to Bean Station, Cumberland Gap, and Kentucky. Tennessee's first newspaper, *The Knoxville Gazette*, was published in Rogersville by George Roulston(e) and Robert Ferguson in 1791, before moving the paper to Knoxville.

The history of Bulls Gap also centers on transportation. In 1792 John Bull received a grant for 55 acres near the east-west passage over Bays Mountain. Capitalizing on his location, Bull operated a stage line through the passage that quickly became known as Bulls Gap. In 1858 the East Tennessee and Virginia Railroad used slave labor to lay the first tracks through the area. During the Civil War the strategic location of the tracks made Bulls Gap the frequent scene of fighting between Union and Confederate forces, though the railroad and Bulls Gap remained under Federal control throughout the war. In the postwar period the railroad dominated the economic life of Bulls Gap. At the turn of the century the Southern Railway System gained control over the lines passing through Bulls Gap and built a small maintenance center and railroad yard. The automobile and the construction of modern highways signaled the decline of railway influence over the town.

From the 1840s through the 1870s, the marble industry developed in Hawkins County, and the area became famous for its pink and red variegated marble. Local furniture manufacturers used much of the marble, which was cut from various quarries and hauled to Rogersville on wagons pulled by 16- or 20-mule teams. From there, the marble was floated down the Holston River on rafts, or later shipped by railroad. Marble from Hawkins County was used in the Washington Monument in Washington, D.C., as well as the balustrades and stairways of the Capitol. Huge columns of Hawkins County marble were used in the South Carolina State Capitol and in the municipal buildings of Baltimore.

For 56 years (1911–1967) the International Printing Pressmen and Assistants Union maintained the Pressman's Home on 2,700 acres of Hawkins County land. The Pressman's Home included a farm, a sanitarium, a retirement home, and a technical school where more than 3,000 union members received training before modern medicine and advancing technology rendered the operation obsolete.

Today Hawkins County has a population of 46,600. Church Hill is the largest city, followed by Rogersville, Mount Carmel, Surgoinsville, and Bulls Gap. The principal sources of farm income are beef cattle and burley tobacco. The 4,545 farms with tobacco quotas produce an average yield of 2,369 lbs. of tobacco per acre, making Hawkins County the second largest producer of burley tobacco in the state. No one industry dominates Hawkins County, but the industrial payroll for the county is approximately $145 million annually. The Hawkins County school system supports 12 elementary schools, three middle schools, three high schools, and an enrichment center. Twelve colleges and universities lie within a 75-mile radius of the county. Personal enrichment and recreational opportunities are readily available. The county supports four public libraries, and the H. B. Stamps Memorial Library offers a special collection of genealogy and local history. Local parks and golf courses provide activities from picnicking and baseball to championship PGA golf. Rogersville hosts an annual three-day festival in October called Heritage Days, and Bulls Gap celebrates Archie Campbell Homecoming Day each Labor Day.

Henry R. Price, Rogersville

SEE: BERRY, GEORGE L.; CAMPBELL, ARCHIE; IPPAU AND PRESSMAN'S HOME; PUBLISHING; RAILROADS; TOBACCO

HAYNES, GEORGE EDMUND (1875–1960), was born in Pine Bluff, Arkansas, the only child of Louis and Mattie Sloan Haynes. At a young age he moved with his parents to New York, where he spent his youth. In 1903, he received his B.A. from Fisk University. He earned his M.A. from Yale University in 1904, and in 1912 became the first African American awarded the Doctor of Philosophy degree from Columbia University.

In 1910 George Haynes married Elizabeth Ross of Montgomery, Alabama; they became the parents of one child, George Edmund Haynes, Jr. After their marriage, the couple resided in New York, where Haynes studied social science and economics. He developed an acute awareness of the impact of socio-economic readjustment upon African Americans who migrated northward from the South. Shortly after his marriage in 1910, he joined with Frances Kellor and Ruth Baldwin to establish the National Urban League for assisting those making the transition from agrarian to urban living.

Haynes accepted a faculty position at Fisk University in 1912. His intense interest in America's changing social fabric prompted his leadership in establishing Fisk's department of social sciences and an academic program to train professional social workers. By 1914 he had developed the first college-level course on the history of African Americans. His research on the African American adjustment to a predominately white society earned Haynes acclaim as a leader in the study of racial affairs.

Haynes emerged as a leader in efforts to bring Nashville's white and African-American communities together. Bethlehem House, a settlement house first proposed in 1907 by Fisk graduate Sallie Hill Sawyer and enlarged in 1913 by the addition of a kindergarten and clinic, became the "hands-on" training center for Professor Haynes's social science students. The settlement house concept, patterned after the British movement of the 1880s, had become an American movement in the early 1900s. By 1915 the Bethlehem Settlement House was the product of very advanced social theory put into action—especially in the turn-of-the-century South. Fisk University's involvement with Bethlehem House supported the reality of whites and African Americans working together to provide social services.

In 1916, when a fire devastated East Nashville, the African-American community suffered extensively. In the charred aftermath of this horrendous fire, Haynes's Fisk University students offered assistance to the fire victims as they struggled to cope with their losses.

Two years later, Haynes left Tennessee for Washington, where he was appointed special assistant to the U.S. Secretary of Labor, serving until 1921, when he became co-founder and first executive secretary of the Department of Race Relations of the Federal Council of Churches of Christ in America. For the next 26 years, he remained with the council in New York City and became a visionary leader of the city's African-American community. In the late 1940s, for example, Haynes organized the Interracial Clinic, which promoted interracial understanding and easing of racial tensions. In 1955 he was appointed to the New York University Board of Trustees, becoming the first African American appointed to a major American university's board. After his wife's death in 1953, Haynes remarried in 1955 to Olyve Jeter of Mount Vernon, New York, where the couple made their home. Haynes died in 1960 at Mount Vernon.

Reavis L. Mitchell, Jr., Fisk University

SUGGESTED READING: Reavis L. Mitchell, Jr., *Fisk University Since 1866: The Loyal Children Make Their Way* (1995)

SEE: BETHLEHEM HOUSE; FISK UNIVERSITY

HAYWOOD COUNTY, named for Judge John Haywood, was part of Madison County, when the Tennessee General Assembly created it in 1823–24. Later, part of Haywood County was taken to create Lauderdale and Crockett counties. The state legislature designated Brownsville as the county seat, and in 1823 Thomas M. Johnson sold the county 50 acres of land for the county seat for $1 and a town lot. The county court met in the home of Richard Nixon, the first settler in the area that became Haywood County, until 1825, when the first log courthouse was completed. A second courthouse was built in 1826; in 1845 it was rebuilt with brick. In 1868 the county added a west wing to accommodate the convening of the

Supreme Court for West Tennessee. The courthouse underwent complete renovation in 1989. The first jail was built in 1825; in 1872 it was replaced with a brick and iron jail. In 1974 a new jail was located four miles east of Brownsville.

Cotton agriculture provided the basis for the Haywood County economy for much of its history. Early settlers soon established a plantation system based on slave labor. In the aftermath of the Civil War, the cotton economy returned, although tenant farmers and sharecroppers now worked the fields. In 1828 James Bond settled in Haywood County and built one of the largest fortunes in the state through the cultivation of cotton.

The production of staple crops benefited from the early appearance of railroads in the county. Trains first came to Tennessee in 1846. Both the Holly Springs and Brownsville Railroad and the Mississippi and Ohio Railroad (later the L&N) served Brownsville. Passenger service through Brownsville ended in 1968. Today, Interstate 40 parallels the old Louisville & Nashville track to Memphis.

A 1923 description of Haywood County noted the fertile soil and potential for crop diversification. It listed cotton, corn, fruit, grass, and livestock as the most important agricultural products. Today, those crops remain important, together with soybeans. In 1939–40, the federal Farm Security Administration established the Haywood County Farm Project near Stanton, to provide small farms for black residents, which they could rent with an option to buy. Some 39 local families participated in the program. The National Register-listed Woodlawn Baptist Church, near Nutbush, documents post-Civil War black history in rural Haywood County.

Industry development in the county initially supported agricultural production. In 1828 Hiram Bradford began operation of the county's first cotton gin. Although declining in number (there were only 297 cotton gins operating in Tennessee in 1972), cotton gins still dot the county's landscape. In 1829 a horse-propelled grist mill began operation, and by 1874 the county had a cotton mill employing mostly women. Significant changes in industrialization came during World War II, as farmers and farm laborers left the fields, and agriculture mechanized. Today, several manufacturers employ local residents in industries ranging from the production of riding lawn mowers to the manufacture of vinyl garden hose, PVC pipe fittings, and powdered ball bearings.

The county's first newspaper, the *Phoenix*, began publication in 1833. Nine other papers appeared during the next century and a half. The *States Graphic* issued its first publication in 1900, and continues publication today.

The county's first Sunday School opened in Brownsville in 1831. During the first decade of settlement, Methodists, Baptists, and Presbyterians established congregations. The Episcopal Church arrived in 1834, and the Catholics and Cumberland Presbyterians built churches circa 1870. Temple Adas Israel (1882) stands as a reminder of the migration of Jews into rural communities in the nineteenth century.

Haywood County's first school was built by Howell Taylor in the Tabernacle neighborhood in 1827. Early schools were subscription schools, and public schools were not available until 1897. Among the county's many historic schools were Union Academy, Brownsville Male Academy, Brownsville Female Institute, Dancyville Female Institute, Brownsville Seminary, Cageville Male and Female Academy, and Wesleyan Female College. The Dunbar School for African American children became Haywood County Training School circa 1920, then Carver High School in 1950. Brownsville Baptist Female College (1850, later a high school) became the nucleus for the National Register-listed College Hill Historic District. The former college's Center Building now houses a comprehensive Lincoln Collection and the Haywood County Museum. Haywood County High School opened in 1911; in 1970 it was closed and a new school was built when the city and county schools consolidated and integrated.

Brownsville residents have enjoyed a variety of services throughout the history of the community. The Brownsville Savings Bank, organized in 1869 (reputedly the second oldest continuously operating bank in the state), became the Brownsville Bank in 1899. Since 1997 it has operated as part of the In-South Bank system. Brownsville received telegraph service in 1848; Bell Telephone opened an office in 1895. County residents began to receive rural free mail delivery in 1903. In 1872 a gas works came to Brownsville, and the city received natural gas in 1934. Rural electrification reached the county in 1936. In 1909 $7,500 from Andrew Carnegie's library program built a free public library, which was replaced in 1992 with the Elma Ross Library. In 1909 Brownsville built at the library a Public Ladies Rest Room, the first such known facility in Tennessee, to accommodate the needs of farmwives as they shopped. Ridley and Mann Wills established the Haywood County Memorial Hospital in 1930; Methodist Hospital Systems now provides medical services.

Haywood County has grown from a population of 265 families in 1826 to a population that now exceeds 19,000. A county executive and county court governs the county. Brownsville's population rose from 400 in 1832 to more than 10,000 in the 1990s. The town is governed by a mayor and five aldermen.

Emma Nunn, Brownsville

SEE: BOND, JAMES; CIVIL RIGHTS MOVEMENT; COTTON; COTTON GINS; GOLDEN CIRCLE LIFE INSURANCE; HAYWOOD, JOHN; MCELWEE, SAMUEL; RAILROADS; SMITH, HARDIN; TEMPLE ADAS ISRAEL; TURNER, TINA

HAYWOOD, JOHN (1762–1826), pioneer jurist and historian of early Tennessee history, was born in Halifax County, North Carolina in 1762, the son of prosperous tobacco producer, Egbert Haywood. Despite limited educational opportunities on the colonial frontier, Haywood taught himself law and in later life became widely read. Admitted to the bar in 1786, he quickly gained a reputation as one of the best legal minds in the state. After serving as clerk of the North Carolina State Senate and then the lower house, he became the state's solicitor general in 1790 and attorney general the next year. In 1794 he was appointed to the North Carolina Supreme Court but resigned in 1800 to defend a long-time friend, North Carolina Secretary of State James Glasgow, who, along with several other prominent citizens, had been charged with land warrant fraud. This scandal proved so unpopular that Haywood's own reputation was injured in defending Glasgow. Following the trial in which Glasgow was convicted, Haywood moved to Raleigh and returned to private law practice, in addition to beginning a career as an important legal scholar.

His North Carolina *Reports* (1806) and *A Manual of the Laws of North Carolina* (1808) were the first important compilations of the state's statutes. He produced equally important legal texts for Tennessee, including *A Revisal of all the public acts of the state of North Carolina and of the state of Tennessee* (1809), *Duty and Authority of Justices of the Peace* (1810), and *The Statute Laws of the State of Tennessee* (1831), completed after his death by Robert L. Cobbs.

Haywood owned land in Tennessee, and, at the encouragement of his friend John Overton, he moved his family to Davidson County. He built a home called Tusculum some eight miles south of Nashville and soon added two log offices, where he trained young men for the law, in what may have been the first "law school" in the Old Southwest. As in his native state, Haywood quickly established an enviable legal reputation. In 1816 he was appointed to the Tennessee Supreme Court of Errors and Appeals, a position he held until his death in 1826.

An active and energetic man, though he weighed over 350 pounds in his later life, Haywood researched and wrote on religion and history in addition to his legal work. *The Christian Advocate*, published in 1819, was his first non-legal work, a slenderly eccentric religious study. He is best known for his histories of Tennessee, including *The Natural and Aboriginal History of Tennessee* (1823), an attempt to prove that the native tribes of Tennessee were descendants of ancient Hebrews, and *The Civil and Political History of the State of Tennessee* (1823), a comprehensive history from prehistoric times to statehood in 1796. *The Civil and Political History* became an influential source for future Tennessee historians, especially J. G. M. Ramsey. Haywood's histories made him the pioneer in Tennessee historiography. In researching his histories, Haywood examined early colonial and state records and interviewed many of the pioneers or their descendants. Though later criticized for inaccuracies, the books were groundbreaking works in preserving and interpreting the state's history. An outgrowth of Haywood's research was the formation of the state's first historical society, the Tennessee Antiquarian Society, in 1820; Haywood served as president for all of its two-year existence.

Haywood and his wife, the former Martha Edwards, had ten children. Haywood died on December 22, 1826, and was buried on Christmas Eve at his home. Tennessee's Haywood County, created in 1823, is named for him.

Ned L. Irwin, East Tennessee State University

SEE: LAW; OVERTON, JOHN; RAMSEY, J. G. M.; TENNESSEE COURTS PRIOR TO 1870; TENNESSEE HISTORICAL SOCIETY

HEARD, GEORGE ALEXANDER (1917–), Chancellor of Vanderbilt University during the tumultuous years from 1963 to 1972, was committed to pluralism, freedom of expression, and self-government, which opened up the staid campus and avoided many of the painful and divisive confrontations occurring on campuses across the nation. Born in Savannah, Georgia, the son of Richard and Virginia Heard, he received a degree in political science from the University of North Carolina. Heard became involved in public policy issues by chairing the Carolina Political Union, a student forum that brought speakers from across the political spectrum to the campus. After a year of graduate school at Columbia University, Heard spent six years in government service before returning to graduate school and receiving his Ph.D. He worked as a research assistant to V. O. Key, Jr., the leading political scientist, at the Bureau of Public Administration at the University of Alabama on Key's pathbreaking work, *Southern Politics in State and Nation* (1949). Thereafter Heard married Laura Jean Keller and returned to the University of North Carolina as an associate professor of political science. In 1952 he published a revised version of his dissertation, *A Two Party South?*. In 1960 Heard completed *The Costs of Democracy*, one of the earliest studies of campaign financing. His work brought professional prominence: the presidency of the Southern Political Science Association and an appointment by President John F. Kennedy to the Chair of the Commission on Campaign Costs.

When Vanderbilt University sought a new chancellor in 1963, Heard, then dean of the graduate school at the University of North Carolina, had abundant qualifications as well as a noncombative and compromise-building leadership style that made him acceptable to Vanderbilt's various constituencies—Board of Trust, alumni, faculty, and students. Heard's leadership emphasized unity and recognition of commonalities, anticipation of problems, and consensus building.

Once on campus, Heard fostered freedom of expression through his open forum policy, self-government by enlarging the responsibilities of the University and then renamed Faculty Senate, and pluralism through the diversification of the make-up of the university from the board and faculty down to the student body. During his years as chancellor, Heard oversaw the expansion of the academic programs (eventually absorbing Peabody College for Teachers and the Blair School of Music), the raising of admission standards, the doubling of the campus area, and the launching of a building boom. Whether confronting the challenges of fundraising, demands for more rights and better treatment for women and African Americans on campus, or demonstrations for and against the Vietnam War, Heard's administrative style of encouraging input, careful study, and process decision-making often avoided painful confrontations.

In 1982 Heard retired to head the Alfred P. Sloan Foundation's study of presidential elections in America. Heard retained his professorship in political science and worked from the Vanderbilt Institute of Public Policy Studies. The Board honored Heard by renaming the library the Jean and Alexander Heard Library.

Patricia Miletich, University School

SUGGESTED READING: Paul K. Conkin, *Gone With the Ivy: A Biography of Vanderbilt University* (1985)

SEE: EDUCATION, HIGHER; VANDERBILT UNIVERSITY

HEIMAN, ADOLPHUS (1809–1862), stonecutter and architect, was born in Potsdam, Prussia. Trained as a stonecutter, Heiman came to the United States in 1834. He was in Nashville by 1841, and perhaps as early as 1837. Heiman worked in Nashville from his arrival until the eve of the Civil War in 1860. In his commissions for churches, government buildings, private homes, schools, and other community landmark buildings, Heiman incorporated the Gothic Revival, Greek Revival, and Italianate styles.

Although little is known about Heiman's work in Nashville from 1837 to 1846, he designed at least part of the First Baptist Church (1837–1841) on Fifth Avenue. Like so many of Heiman's designs, this building has been demolished (in 1940). By 1841 Heiman had his own business and was one of four Nashville architects listed in the December 20, 1845, *Orthopolitan*.

Heiman's architectural career took off in the late 1840s, after he returned from the Mexican War as a hero. He had been promoted to the rank of major

Adolphus Heiman in Mexican War uniform.

TENNESSEE HISTORICAL SOCIETY COLLECTION, TSLA

after surviving a raid on Monterey in which two-thirds of his regiment was killed.

Heiman soon became a popular choice for designing community landmark buildings. One of his first major commissions came in 1849, when he was selected to build a 250-bed state Hospital for the Insane. The building incorporated the most modern innovations, including steam heat. Completed in 1855, the Gothic Revival-style hospital was one of the most inventive public buildings in the country.

Other Nashville buildings designed by Heiman included The Cathedral of Our Lady of the Seven Dolors (today known as St. Mary's Catholic Church) in the Greek Revival style, the now demolished Italianate-styled Adelphi Theater, the Greek Revival-styled Medical Department and the Gothic Revival-styled Literary Department at the University of Nashville, Belmont Mansion in the Italianate style, as well as several homes. Heiman also designed buildings in other cities, including the Giles County Courthouse, St. John's College in Little Rock, the Arkansas Masonic School, and the First Presbyterian Church in Huntsville. He also gained a reputation as a bridge engineer in the 1850s.

Heiman's career ended abruptly with the Civil War. A colonel in the Tenth Tennessee Regiment, he was captured in 1862 and died while a prisoner of war. He was buried in Mississippi, but in 1869 he was reinterred to the Confederate Circle of Mt. Olivet Cemetery in Nashville.

Leslie N. Sharp, Historic Preservation Division, Georgia Department of Natural Resources

SUGGESTED READINGS: John G. Frank, "Adolphus Heiman: Architect and Soldier," *Tennessee Historical Quarterly* 5(1946): 35–57; James Patrick, "The Architecture of Adolphus Heiman, Parts 1 and 2," *Tennessee Historical Quarterly* 37 (1979): 167–187 and 277–295

SEE: BELMONT MANSION; ST. MARY'S CATHOLIC CHURCH; TENNESSEE LUNATIC ASYLUM

HENDERSON COUNTY was created in West Tennessee by an act of the Tennessee legislature on November 7, 1821, and named for Colonel James Henderson, who served under Andrew Jackson and commanded Tennessee troops at the Battle of New Orleans. Several of the county's early settlers served under Henderson's command during the War of 1812 and during the Natchez and Creek Indian campaigns. The original area contained the present county, a large part of Chester County, and smaller portions of Decatur and Madison counties. Major John Troxell Harmon surveyed the county seat of Lexington in 1822, and laid out the town facing northeast, making it crosswise to traditional orientation. At 720 feet, Lexington is also highest in elevation of all the West Tennessee county seats.

The Tennessee Highland Ridge (also known locally and historically as Feather Ridge and Purdy Range) divided the county into two distinct cultural and geographical sections. All water falling east of the ridge flows to the Tennessee River, while water west of the ridge flows to the Mississippi River. The Tennessee Highland Ridge enters Henderson County at the Chester County line near Laster, separates the Middlefork and Palestine communities, following a northerly pattern west of Lexington across Sand Ridge to separate Bargerton and Union Cross before entering Carroll County. Most of the plantation and slave-owning settlers of the county lived west of the ridge, where the ground was less hilly. The land east of the ridge becomes increasingly hilly toward the Tennessee River and was largely unsuitable for plantation farming.

Three rivers, the Beech, White Oak, and Forked Deer, drain the county. Nine recreational lakes dot the county, including two within Natchez Trace State Park. The trace that gives the park its name was a route used on the western side of the Tennessee River. Though not as famous as its Middle Tennessee counterpart, this trail proved just as important to the area's early settlement and economic development. Today, the park contains 48,000 acres, making it one of the largest in the state park system. Within the park is one of North America's largest pecan trees. The park contains hiking trails, camping and picnic sites, swimming, fishing, and playing fields.

In 1823 Middle Fork Primitive Baptist Church became the first organized congregation in the county. It was followed by Jacks Creek Baptist Church in 1828, Mud Creek Primitive Baptist in 1830, Mt. Gilead Cumberland Presbyterian in 1826, and a Methodist Church near the Olive Branch in 1832.

Mifflin, now in Chester County, was the earliest and largest of the settlements in Henderson County and the site of the first county commission meetings, until the surveying of Lexington. Lexington has been the home of four courthouses. One burned during the Civil War and another was destroyed by fire during the 1890s, leaving the county with few of the early records. Governor William Carroll appointed the first commissioners: James Baker, John Crook, John Essary, John Haliburton, Jere Hendricks, Dewey Middleton, John Purdy, William Ray, Abner Taylor, John Wilkes, and Samuel Wilson. Jere Hindricks was the first executive. John Purdy surveyed the first roads, and the original county seat of McNairy County, Purdy, was named in honor of him. The first sheriff was John Troxell Harmon.

The county supplied regiments for both sides during the Civil War, with the western portion of the county following the Confederacy, and the areas east of the Highland Ridge remaining with the Union. County Confederate units were attached to the 13th, 27th, 51st, 52nd, and 154th Confederate infantries, and the 18th, 21st, and 55th southern cavalries. Both Lexington and Parker's Crossroads were battlesites during General Nathan Bedford Forrest's West Tennessee Campaign of 1862. Parker's Crossroads Battlefield has been nominated for listing in the National Register of Historic Places. Interpretive signs explain the course of events during the battle. The Federals organized six companies in the 7th Tennessee Cavalry. In later years, these areas organized politically along the same lines, with former Confederate areas voting Democratic, and former Union areas supporting the Republican party. In the last few decades, much of this historic separation and adherence to old alliances has eroded, but regional voting patterns still can be discerned.

In the course of its history, Henderson County has been the site of a number of mysteries and oddities. Stories have long circulated that a large amount of gold was buried and lost by Federal troops on Owl Creek near Lexington. Various outlaw gangs, including John Murrell and the Moore Gang roamed the countryside from the 1830s through the 1870s. Henderson County was the site of a turn-of-the century resort called Hinson Springs. And one of the world's largest men, Mills Darden, is buried near the Chapel Hill community.

Today, Henderson County contains over 21,000 people; incorporated areas include Lexington, Parkers Crossroads, Scotts Hill and Sardis. Other villages include Huron, Luray, Life, Crucifer, Broadway, Juno, Blue Goose, Poplar Springs, Independence, Union Cross, Rock Hill, Chesterfield Darden, Safford, Middleburg, Shady Hill, Reagan, Cedar Grove, Hickory Flats, Union Hill, Lula, Stegall, Center Hill, Wright Town, Garner Town, Farmville, Moore's Hill, Warren's Bluff, and Stringtown. Henderson County lost the villages of Jacks Creek, Clarks Creek, Mifflin, Roby, and Center Point in 1882 with the creation of Chester County.

With easy access to Interstate 40, Henderson County has turned from agriculture to industrial development. The largest employers in the county, Magnetek and Johnson Controls Incorporated, have a combined employment of over 2,200 workers. The county has one hospital, two nursing homes, and ten schools. Over 60 percent of the county's high school graduates receive some postsecondary education, with many attending area colleges and technical schools.

W. C. Crooks, Lexington

SEE: FORREST, NATHAN BEDFORD; MURRELL, JOHN A.; NATCHEZ TRACE STATE PARK

HENRY COUNTY was created by the Tennessee General Assembly on November 7, 1821, and named in honor of Revolutionary War patriot and statesman Patrick Henry. Henry County became the gateway for the settlement of West Tennessee and beyond.

The Henry County Court House was erected in 1823 in Paris, West Tennessee's oldest incorporated municipality.

During the Civil War, military units, including the Fifth Tennessee Infantry Regiment, organized on the courthouse lawn. Henry County sent more than 2,500 volunteers to the Confederacy and earned the title "Volunteer County of the Volunteer State." In March 1862 General Ulysses S. Grant ordered four companies and a battery of artillery into Paris. The Union forces attacked an encampment of 400 Confederate soldiers, but retreated toward Paris Landing after a short engagement. In October 1864 General Nathan Bedford Forrest began his Johnsonville campaign at Paris Landing, where he captured four Union gunboats, 14 transports, 20 barges, 26 pieces of artillery, $6,700,000 worth of property, and 150 prisoners.

Beginning with Isham Green Harris, Henry County provided Tennessee with three governors. Born in Franklin County in 1818, Harris moved to Paris as a young boy. He served in both state houses before his election as governor in 1859. As Tennessee's only Confederate Governor, Harris served as Brigadier General aide-de-camp to Generals Albert S. Johnston, Braxton Bragg, and Joseph E. Johnston. In March 1864 Harris was involved in a brief skirmish with Union troops near Mansfield in Henry County, which left two Confederate soldiers wounded. After the war, he served 20 years in the U.S. Senate and was president protempore of the Senate at his death in 1897.

TSLA

Paris Fish Fry, 1956.

James Davis Porter, born in Paris in 1828, was elected to the state legislature in 1859. He helped organize the Army of Tennessee and was General Benjamin F. Cheatham's chief of staff. Porter was elected governor for two terms beginning in 1874. He later served as Assistant Secretary of State, Minister to Chile, president of the NC&St.L Railway, president of the University of Nashville, and chancellor of Peabody College. Porter died at his home in Paris in 1912.

Thomas Clarke Rye, born in Camden in 1863, moved to Paris in 1902. He was governor during World War I, serving from 1915 to 1919. Rye became Chancery Court Judge in 1919 and served 20 years. He died at his home in Paris in 1953.

Other political figures from Henry County include General J.D.C. Atkins, a Confederate Congressman and five-time member of the U.S. Congress, chair of the House Committee on Appropriations, and later Commissioner of Indian Affairs. John Wesley Crockett, the eldest son of the legendary David Crockett, took his father's old congressional seat in 1837. Justice Howell E. Jackson was U.S. Senator before he became a justice on the U.S. Supreme Court in 1893.

Henry Countians who have had an impact on education include Dudley M. Clements, who began the nation's first vocational agricultural program following the passage of the Smith-Hughes Act. E. W. Grove-Henry County High School, Tennessee's first privately endowed public high school, honored Edwin Wiley Grove, who headed the Paris Medicine Company and Grove Laboratories, which produced "Grove's Tasteless Chill Tonic." Henry County pro-duced a number of university presidents, including Dr. C.C. "Sonny" Humphreys, Memphis State University; Dr. Thomas D. Jarrett, Atlanta University; Dr. Mordecai Johnson, Howard University; and Dr. Joe Morgan, Austin Peay State University.

Entertainers from Henry County include Rattlesnake Annie, country music singer; Bobby Jones, award-winning gospel performer; Buster Jones, host of *Soul Unlimited*; Cherry Jones, Tony Award-winning actress; Merle Kilgore, country music writer and manager; Keith Lancaster, founder of the Acapella Music Group; Ula Love, Hollywood starlet and member of the Ziegfield Follies; Harry Neal, member of the duo-piano team of Nelson & Neal; Ricky Revel, country music singer; Jackie de Shannon, pop music singer; and Hank Williams, Jr., Country Music Association Entertainer of the Year.

Other prominent Henry Countians include Vernon Jarrett, newspaper columnist and social commentator; Virginia Weldon Kelly, syndicated columnist; Ethel McFadden, the first Miss Tennessee; Christine Reynolds, the state's first female cabinet member; "Miss Pearl" Routon, artist and one of those responsible for naming the iris as Tennessee's official cultivated flower; and Dr. Henrietta Veltman, who delivered over 4,000 babies during her 50 years of practice.

Vernon McGarity received the Congressional Medal of Honor for his actions in the Battle of the Bulge during World War II. Camp Tyson, built near Routon in 1941 and named for Brigadier General Lawrence D. Tyson, was the U.S. Army's only barrage balloon training center during World War II.

Henry County's first tourist attraction, Sulphur Well, was created by accident in 1821, when an artesian well of sulphur water was struck in an attempt to locate a large salt bed on a former Chickasaw reservation. Eventually a summer resort was erected at the site to accommodate the large numbers of people who came to drink the water, which was believed to have health benefits. Many sought refuge at Sulphur Well during the 1837 yellow fever epidemic.

In 1944 Sulphur Well was covered by TVA's Kentucky Lake, the largest man-made lake in the United States and the second largest in the world. After the creation of Paris Landing State Park in 1945, the lake soon became a popular recreation destination. Paris acquired the name "Capital City of Kentucky Lake," and tourism took an important role in the area's economy. The "World's Biggest Fish Fry" at Paris emerged as one of Tennessee's premier festivals and draws tens of thousands of visitors, and politicians, into Paris and Henry County during the last full week of April.
David W. Webb, Mansfield

SEE: CAMP TYSON; CHEATHAM, BENJAMIN F.; FORREST, NATHAN B.; HARRIS, ISHAM G.; JACKSON, HOWELL E.; PARIS LANDING STATE PARK; PORTER, JAMES D.; RYE, THOMAS C.; TENNESSEE VALLEY AUTHORITY

HENRY, GUSTAVUS A. (1804–1880), Whig party leader and Confederate Senator, was born in Scott County, Kentucky, on October 8, 1804, to William Henry and Elizabeth Flournoy Henry. Gustavus graduated from Transylvania University in Lexington, Kentucky, in 1835. Soon, thereafter, he was admitted to the Kentucky bar and established his practice in Hopkinsville. From 1831 to 1833 he served in the Kentucky legislature, where he was a stalwart supporter and friend of Henry Clay.

In 1833 Henry married Marion McClure of Clarksville, Tennessee, and within months he moved his practice to this Tennessee river town. By 1835–36 Henry emerged as a leader of the Whig party in Montgomery County and strongly supported Whig candidate Hugh Lawson White in the 1836 presidential election. In the 1840 contest Henry was chosen as a Whig elector for William Henry Harrison; the Clarksville attorney canvassed the state in Harrison's cause. Three years later, he ran for U.S. Congress against the popular incumbent Cave Johnson, but lost by 228 votes.

A superb orator, Henry continued supporting the Whig cause as a presidential elector in 1844. Seven years later, he returned to political office as a member of the State House of Representatives from 1851–53. His success in promoting the Whig agenda of internal improvements, new banks, and the compromise of 1850 led the party to nominate him for governor in 1853. Henry lost the election to Democrat Andrew Johnson.

The defeat in 1853 was "a turning point in his career."[1] Never again did he run for public office, although he served with distinction in the Confederate Senate for three years in a position selected by the state legislature. Despite the ups-and-downs in his political life, Henry managed a successful legal career and operated three plantations. After the Civil War, he joined the Democratic party and was chairman of the state convention in 1874. Six years later, in 1880, he died at his Clarksville home, Emerald Hill. He was buried in the Greenwood Cemetery in Clarksville. His Emerald Hill home is now the Alumni Center for Austin Peay State University.

Carroll Van West, Middle Tennessee State University
CITATION:
(1) Lewright B. Sikes, "Gustavus Adolphus Henry: Champion of Lost Causes," *Tennessee Historical Quarterly* 50(1991): 181.
SEE: CLARKSVILLE; JOHNSON, CAVE; WHITE, HUGH L.

HENRY HORTON STATE RESORT PARK, located along the Duck River in Marshall County, was constructed in the early 1960s on the former farm of Henry Horton, who was governor of Tennessee from 1927 to 1933. Horton's gravesite is located within the park boundaries. The park features the first 18-hole golf course to be built in a Tennessee state park. The course is named the Ellington Golf Course, in honor of Governor Buford Ellington, who, like Horton, was also a resident of Marshall County. In addition to the golf course, state planners provided the park with a wide range of facilities, including a restaurant, inn, conference rooms, an Olympic-sized swimming pool, "Frisbee" golf course, ball fields, and a myriad of playground equipment. The park also contains the site of the Wilhoite Village, a nineteenth century crossroads village, and the Wilhoite Mill and Dam site, which was constructed along the Duck River in 1845–46.

Carroll Van West, Middle Tennessee State University
SEE: ELLINGTON, BUFORD; HORTON, HENRY; MARSHALL COUNTY

HERGESHEIMER, ELLA SOPHONISBA (1873–1943), painter of portraits and still lifes, was born in Allentown, Pennsylvania, the daughter of Elamanda Ritter and Charles Patterson Hergesheimer. Hergesheimer was the direct descendant of Charles Willson Peale, artist and founder of Peale's Museum, part of whose collections later became the Smithsonian Institution. She attended the Philadelphia School of Design and the Pennsylvania Academy of Fine Arts, studying with Cecilia Beaux and William Merritt Chase, including one summer at Shinnecock on Long Island in 1900. She also studied in Europe for three years.

After her work was included in a 1905 traveling exhibit by the Nashville Art Association, Hergesheimer received a 1907 commission to paint the portrait of Methodist Bishop Holland N. McTyeire of Vanderbilt University. She remained in Nashville for the rest of her life, establishing her studio in the downtown area on Church Street and, later, at Eighth Avenue and Broadway.

Hergesheimer's two most notable portraits are that of former Speaker of the House Joseph W. Byrns, on view at the U.S. Capitol Building, and that of Commodore Matthew Fontaine Maury, which hangs in the U.S. Naval Academy at Annapolis, Maryland. Among her numerous Tennessee subjects are Nashvillians Mr. and Mrs. Samuel J. Keith, Mr. and Mrs. Percy Maddin, and Joseph H. Thompson. Cheekwood owns her 1931 self portrait, painted when she was 58.

Hergesheimer was also known for her still lifes, landscapes, and printmaking. Her early subdued palette was replaced in the works from the 1930s with her better known bright coloration. She exhibited extensively throughout the South, winning numerous awards, including the gold medal at the Knoxville 1910 Appalachian Exposition.

Celia Walker, Cheekwood-Nashville's Home of Art and Gardens
SEE: APPALACHIAN EXPOSITION OF 1910; ART; BYRNS, JOSEPH W.; CHEEKWOOD; MAURY, MATTHEW F.; MCTYEIRE, HOLLAND N.

THE HERMITAGE. The home of Andrew Jackson, now a public museum, is 11 miles east of Nashville. Andrew Jackson bought the Hermitage farm in 1804; it was his home for the remainder of his life. The Jacksons had lived previously on two other Davidson County farms: Poplar Grove in present-day Hadley's Bend and, due north of The Hermitage on the Cumberland River, Hunter's Hill, a well-developed property that had to be sold to meet outstanding debts.

When the Jacksons moved to The Hermitage, it comprised only 425 acres with a cluster of assorted log buildings for housing and storage. For the next 17 years the Jackson family received visitors as distinguished as President James Monroe in these simple accommodations.

In 1819 Jackson began construction of a large brick house, financially warranted at last by virtue of his second income as peacetime General of the U.S. Army. The family occupied the house upon their return from Florida in 1821. Typical of southern Federal-style houses, there were four rooms downstairs and four rooms upstairs, all opening into a broad central hall. Visitors commented little on the interior design, aside from the Dufour scenic wallpaper in the entry hall, the same pattern that hangs there now. A professional gardener from Philadelphia, William Frost, laid out an acre of pleasure garden on the east side of the house for Rachel Jackson. When she died in December 1828, the significance of The Hermitage changed entirely for Jackson. His interest in the property focused on the garden where he buried her; later he prepared a place for himself under the monument built over the grave.

By the time of Jackson's inauguration as president, The Hermitage comprised 1,000 acres. One hundred slaves, under the direction of an overseer, provided all the labor for the agricultural enterprise. Jackson never cultivated more than 400 acres; 200 in cotton and the rest in hay, oats, wheat, corn, and root vegetables. The Hermitage maintained a dairy herd, about 150 sheep, and 300 or more hogs. African-American slave artisans operated a blacksmith shop, spinning and weaving shops, a mill, and a cotton gin. About ten slaves regularly worked in the mansion, kitchen, garden, and family stable. These slaves lived in brick two-room structures with lofts, housing two families, which stretched from the rear of the mansion to the cluster of field-slave houses about a third of a mile north. By Jackson's death in 1845, the slave population numbered nearly 150.

In 1833 Jackson completed a remodeling of the house and added a dining room wing and attached a library-reception room to his bedroom. A fire late in 1834 severely damaged the house, destroyed the second story, and ruined the interior finishes. The rebuilding was left largely to the taste of Jackson's adopted son, Andrew, Jr., and his daughter-in-law, Sarah. The post-fire house emerged in the fashionable Greek Revival style, with appropriate furniture, wallpapers, and textiles purchased in Philadelphia. Jackson spent his final eight years in this remodeled house.

Andrew Jackson, Jr., was not a successful cotton farmer. Despite efforts to diversify with dairying, to operate a lead furnace in Kentucky, and to acquire more productive farm lands elsewhere, Jackson's accumulation of debt forced the sale of the farm to the State of Tennessee in 1856.

Tennessee intended to offer the property to the federal government as a western branch of the U.S. Military Academy, but the Civil War prevented this. In 1860 the Jackson family returned from a failed farming venture in southern Mississippi to take up residence once again in The Hermitage mansion as tenants at the will of the state.

In 1888 the General Assembly considered turning the property into a home for indigent Confederate veterans. To protect the property, a group of Nashville women secured a charter to operate the site as a public shrine. The Ladies' Hermitage Association continues to the present in its uninterrupted management of The Hermitage.

Elsewhere on the 500 acres, the state constructed a large brick home for Confederate veterans. The facility remained largely self-sufficient through the operation of a farm. In the cemetery near The Hermitage church, 489 Confederate Home veterans were buried. The home closed in 1933, and the state gradually added the land to the Ladies' Hermitage Association holdings.

Andrew Jackson III, his wife, and two sons were the last family occupants of the house. They left with all the furniture and memorabilia in 1893. Eventually, the Ladies' Hermitage Association bought nearly all the things the family inherited and returned them to the house and other public spaces on the grounds.
Sharon Macpherson, The Hermitage

SEE: CONFEDERATE VETERANS' HOME; DONELSON, STOCKLY; DORRIS, MARY C.; JACKSON, ANDREW; JACKSON, RACHEL; LADIES' HERMITAGE ASSOCIATION

HERMITAGE HOTEL. The last grand turn-of-the-century hotel in Nashville, the Hermitage Hotel was built between 1908 and 1910. It is the city's best extant example of a Beaux-Arts style commercial building. Its original architect was Tennessee native Edwin Carpenter, who received his architectural training at the Massachusetts Institute of Technology and the famed Ecole des Beaux Arts in Paris, France. Carpenter designed a building of abundant classical details, with coupled Ionic columns, polychrome terra cotta detailing, and an enriched entablature highlighting the east facade entrance. The main lobby and mezzanine are spectacular examples of early twentieth century interior design in Tennessee. The hotel quickly became a favorite gathering place for the rich and politically powerful. In the mid-century, a big band radio show was broadcast from its basement restaurant and dance floor.

Of the many famous gatherings and political events that have occurred at the Hermitage Hotel, the most significant came in 1920, when supporters and opponents of woman suffrage both used the hotel as a headquarters for their campaigns to sway the votes of state legislators. The suffragists won and Tennessee became the 36th and final state needed for the ratification of the woman suffrage amendment.

Changing transportation preferences and downtown stagnation contributed to a steady decline in the hotel's business and it closed its doors in the late 1970s, seemingly destined for the wrecking ball. In 1980 the Nashville firm of Gresham, Smith, and Partners restored the building into hotel suites. Another round of restoration in 1994–95, directed by architect Stan Topol, returned the Hermitage to its past architectural grandeur.

Carroll Van West, Middle Tennessee State University
SEE: CARPENTER, J. EDWIN; NASHVILLE; WOMAN SUFFRAGE MOVEMENT

HERTEL, KENNETH L. (1898–1976), internationally known researcher in cotton fibers, was born in Van Wert, Ohio. In 1920 Hertel received a bachelor's degree in engineering from Ohio State University and completed his Ph.D. in physics in 1926 at University of Chicago. He joined the faculty of the University of Tennessee in the fall of 1926 as an assistant professor of physics. Hertel served as chairman of the UT Physics Department from 1935 to 1956. From 1938 to 1968 he was Director of the UT Fiber Research Laboratory, a regional laboratory supported by the UT Agricultural Experiment Station and the U.S. Department of Agriculture. Hertel was one of seven founding members of the Fiber Society and served as president in 1949. He was vice-president of the American Society for Testing Materials in 1956–57.

In 1934 Hertel became a founder of the University of Tennessee Research Corporation, an independent non-profit organization, whose primary goal is the promotion of research at the various UT campuses; he served as president of the corporation from 1954 to 1969. The corporation covers legal and marketing expenses associated with the commercialization of patented processes developed by UT faculty members working in UT laboratories. The corporation shares the profits with the university's faculty inventors. Hertel invented several instruments for the measurement of cotton fibers, including the Fibrograph and the Arealometer, which, with improvements and modifications, remain in use today. To honor his work with UTRC, the corpora-

tion sponsors "Hertel Events," academic events designed to promote and increase public awareness of academic research.

As department head, Hertel promoted a closer association between UT and Oak Ridge. The results of his efforts and those of like-minded scientists included the establishment of the Oak Ridge Institute of Nuclear Studies (now Oak Ridge Associated Universities) and the creation of a Ph.D. program in physics.

Hertel retired from the University of Tennessee in 1968, after 42 years of service. He continued to consult on a number of projects. In 1970 the Committee on Textile Materials of the American Society for Testing and Materials awarded Hertel the Smith Award for outstanding achievement in the science of textile fiber utilization.

Hertel married the former Winifred Hayler. They were the parents of two sons, Robert and Gordon. Hertel died in Knoxville in 1976.

Connie L. Lester, Tennessee Historical Society
SEE: COTTON; OAK RIDGE; OAK RIDGE ASSOCIATED UNIVERSITIES; UNIVERSITY OF TENNESSEE

HIBBS, HENRY CLOSSEN (1882–1949), designer of academic and medical architecture, influenced the institutional landscape of Tennessee in the twentieth century. Born in Camden, New Jersey, in 1882, Hibbs received his education at the University of Pennsylvania. He worked in Philadelphia and New York before moving to Nashville in 1914 as the local head of the New York firm of Ludlow and Peabody. Hibbs supervised the construction of the new George Peabody College for Teachers, whose campus Ludlow and Peabody had designed to resemble "The Lawn" at the University of Virginia.

After completing his work on the Peabody campus, Hibbs went on to design a number of other Nashville landmarks including the Obstetrics and Pediatric Building at Meharry Medical College, the Fisk University Library, the Nashville City Market Building, the Education Building to the Downtown Presbyterian Church, and the American Trust Building. He won the American Institute of Architects gold medal for the planning and design of Scarritt College in 1929. He designed buildings for Vanderbilt University, Ward-Belmont College, and Middle Tennessee State University.

Hibbs's work was not confined to projects in Nashville or Tennessee. He also designed schools in the neo-Gothic style for Rhodes College at Memphis; Davidson College in North Carolina; Mary Baldwin College, Staunton, Virginia; Hendrix College, Conway, Arkansas; Galloway College, Searcy, Arkansas; and the University of Tulsa in Oklahoma. In West Tennessee, his buildings include the West Tennessee Insane Asylum and Kennedy General Hospital in Memphis.

James A. Hoobler, Tennessee State Museum
SEE: GEORGE PEABODY COLLEGE OF VANDERBILT UNIVERSITY; SCARRITT COLLEGE

HICKMAN COUNTY. The history of Hickman County began before Tennessee achieved statehood in 1796. In April 1791 Edwin Hickman, a native of North Carolina, led a surveying party into what is now Hickman County. Hickman's party included James Robertson, later known as the Father of Middle Tennessee; Robert Weakley, who also played a prominent role in early state history; and others. The party camped at the mouth of a small creek on the north side of Duck River opposite the present site of Centerville.

The next morning, as Hickman and Robertson built a pre-dawn fire, Indians fired on the party, killing Hickman and wounding Robertson in the hand. The party retreated to the Cumberland settlement, but returned several days later to bury Hickman's body in a shallow grave at the spot where he was killed. In December 1807, when the Tennessee General Assembly created a new county, then Representative Robert Weakley attached an amendment to the bill specifying that the new county should be named in honor of Edwin Hickman. In 1994 the Hickman County Historical Society placed a monument at Hickman's grave and built a fence around the grave site.

In 1807 the county extended all the way to the present Alabama state line, and Vernon, on the Piney River, became the first county seat. By 1820 several new counties had been created out of Hickman County, and a movement began to move the county seat to a more central location. In 1823 the new town of Centerville became the county seat. As a result of the bitterness over the change, the old log courthouse at Vernon was dismantled at night and hauled to Centerville, along with the court records. Other Hickman County communities in addition to Centerville and Vernon include Aetna, Bon Aqua, Coble, Farmers Exchange, Little Lot, Lyles, Nunnely, Only, Pinewood, Pleasantville, Shady Grove, and Wrigley.

Hickman County is now the eighth largest county in the state, containing 610 square miles. There are more springs and scenic waterfalls in Hickman County than in any other county in Middle Tennessee. A number of sulphur water springs were commercially developed as nineteenth century recreational sites, including Bon Aqua Springs, Primm Springs, and Beaverdam Springs. These health resorts included hotels, individual cottages, and recreation facilities. Bon Aqua Springs was known as the Queen of the southern spas. Neither Bon Aqua nor Primm Springs is still active, but Beaverdam Springs is operated as a church camp by the Presbyterian Church as Na-Co-Me.

The county's early industry centered around the iron furnaces. Indeed, Goodspeed's 1886 *History of Tennessee* rated Hickman County's iron ore as the best in the state. The Lee and Gould Furnace on Sugar Creek opened in 1832. Five years later, Madison Napier built a furnace near Aetna, which was destroyed by Union troops during the Civil War. Furnaces also opened on Mill Creek near Wrigley at an early date. Standard Charcoal Company opened a furnace at Goodrich in 1882; and a new furnace was built at Aetna in 1885. All iron works in the county were discontinued before 1940.

In addition to iron manufacturing, Hickman County's economy has centered on agriculture and timbering. In 1997 local industry includes manufacturers of packaging materials, metal buttons, men's pants, various wood products, structural steel, and pies.

Two native Hickman County women gained national fame: Beth Slater Whitson and Sarah Ophelia Colley. Whitson wrote several hundred songs, including *Let Me Call You Sweetheart* and *Meet Me Tonight in Dreamland.* Colley gained world acclaim as Minnie Pearl on the Grand Ole Opry and the television show *Hee Haw.* A number of men played important roles in the county's history. Jerome Spence published *Spence's History of Hickman County* in 1900. S. L. Graham built a large cotton mill at Pinewood in the 1850s. Halbert Harvill began his career in education teaching in a one-room school house. He later taught history and organized and coached the first baseball team and the girls' basketball team at Austin Peay Normal School. Harvill was Dean of the school and president of Austin Peay State University, before becoming Tennessee Commissioner of Education. He served in the Tennessee Senate from 1965 until 1981.
Edward Dotson, Centerville
SEE: INDUSTRY; MINNIE PEARL; RESORTS, HISTORIC; ROBERTSON, JAMES; WHITSON, BETH S.

HIGHLANDER FOLK SCHOOL. The history of the Highlander Folk School reflects the course of organized labor and civil rights movements in the South, as well as the struggles of southern activists between the 1930s and early 1960s. Established near Monteagle in 1932 by the Tennessee-born Myles Horton and a young Georgian named Don West, Highlander's programs were based upon the conviction that education could be used to help ordinary people build upon the knowledge they had gained from experience and work collectively toward a more democratic and humane society. This approach made the adult education center a source of inspiration and the most controversial school in modern Tennessee history.

Residential workshops at its 200-acre campus played a central role in Highlander's efforts to achieve its overall goals. Workshops lasted from two days to eight weeks and attracted 15 to 40 organizational leaders of various cultural, economic, and educational backgrounds. They focused on specific, concrete subjects in order to address particular community problems.

The process of analyzing and responding to the problems was as important as the proposed solutions. The school gave no grades, credits, examinations, or degrees; the needs of the students largely determined the curriculum of the sessions. Faculty members refrained from imposing a preconceived set of ideas. Instead, they used visiting speakers, movies, audio recordings, drama, and music to identify common issues, offer broader perspectives, and introduce promising strategies. Workshop participants evaluated their findings, assessed their new understanding of their concerns, and made plans to initiate or sustain activities when they returned to their communities.

Indeed, the Highlander faculty regarded the workshops as only part of a learning process that began before students arrived at the school and continued well after they left. Once labor education, literacy training, leadership development, or voter education classes had been firmly developed, Highlander transferred responsibility for the programs to organizations with larger resources, thereby remaining both a resource and catalyst for future action.

During its early years Highlander achieved modest success in organizing and educating mine, mill, timber, and unemployed workers in the surrounding area. It also operated several community programs for Grundy County residents. The school's reputation grew as faculty members became directly involved in the southern organizing drives mounted by the Congress of Industrial Organizations in the late 1930s. For most of the next decade, they helped unionize textile workers in Tennessee and the Carolinas, directed large-scale labor education programs in 11 southern states, and developed a residential program that promoted a broad-based, racially integrated, and politically active labor movement. But post-World War II differences over the priorities of organized labor broke up the Highlander-CIO relationship and prompted the staff to attempt a revival of the southern wing of the Farmers' Union and the formation of a regional farmer-labor coalition.

Frustrated by the continued reluctance of existing organizations to overcome racial barriers to change, Highlander's teachers began holding workshops on public school desegregation in 1953, nearly a year before the U.S. Supreme Court's momentous decision in *Brown v. Board of Education* and the subsequent emergence of the Civil Rights Movement in the South. Residential workshops gradually encompassed the challenges of community-wide integration. The sessions attracted Rosa Parks, shortly before the Montgomery bus boycott; Martin Luther King, Jr.; and hundreds of other black and white activists. Highlander-sponsored Citizenship Schools, first held in 1957 on the South Carolina Sea Islands, taught thousands of blacks in Tennessee, Georgia, and Alabama the literacy skills they needed to secure the right to vote. In the early 1960s, as sit-in protests erupted in Nashville and across the South, college students gathered at the folk school to explore the possible directions and goals for a new era of black protest; they also learned "freedom songs" adapted by Highlander musicians, including "We Shall Overcome." Through these programs Highlander became the educational center of the early civil rights movement.

The folk school's involvement in the southern labor and civil rights movements earned it both accolades and enmity. Even as Eleanor Roosevelt, Reinhold Niebuhr, educators, ministers, union leaders, philanthropists, and reform groups voiced their support, staff members endured a barrage of threats and denunciations from industrialists, politicians, self-styled patriotic groups, and journalists for unfriendly newspapers. As Highlander became more prominent in the struggle for racial justice, outraged southern white segregationists launched a sustained assault against what they described as a "Communist training school." Although faculty members defended the school's ideology and pedagogy eloquently and often persuasively in the face of such attacks, their understandable, but loose institutional practices made them vulnerable in the 1950s. Following a headline-grabbing investigation by state legislators, a police raid, and two dramatic trials, the state of Tennessee revoked Highlander's charter and confiscated its property in 1962.

This did not mean the end of Highlander. Before the final court decision on the folk school's fate, Highlander officers secured a charter for a new institution to be named the Highlander Research and Education Center. First based in Knoxville, and since 1972, near New Market, the center continues to pursue, in a new context, the folk school's original purpose, as given in its mission statement: to educate "rural and industrial leaders for a new social order" while enriching "the indigenous cultural values of the mountains."
John M. Glen, Ball State University

SEE: CARAWAN, GUY; CIVIL RIGHTS MOVEMENT; GRUNDY COUNTY; HIGHLANDER RESEARCH AND EDUCATION CENTER; HORTON, MYLES; HORTON, ZILPHIA J.; LABOR; SIT-INS, NASHVILLE

HIGHLANDER RESEARCH AND EDUCATION CENTER. Chartered in 1961, the Highlander Research and Education Center is the institutional successor of the Highlander Folk School. The adult education center operates in a considerably different context, however, working with more diverse, complex, and far-reaching issues and constituencies. Its central challenge has been to contribute as much to education and progressive change during the late twentieth century—a time without a unifying movement for social action—as the folk school had during the 1930s southern labor movement and the civil rights movement of the 1950s and early 1960s.

Highlander directed its efforts toward facilitating alliances among grassroots groups and linking local and regional problems to global developments. Through voter education projects, citizenship and political education schools, and workshops for southern black political candidates, Highlander continued to be an important part of the black freedom struggle into the 1960s. The center also confronted a segregationist backlash, as denunciations of the "Communist Training School" appeared on area billboards. In 1968 a federal court injunction blocked a proposed legislative investigation of Highlander, and Tennesseans reconciled themselves to the school's presence.

Even as the attacks subsided, Highlander's teachers moved in new directions. Inspired by the Poor People's Campaign of 1968, they promoted the formation of a multiracial coalition that broke apart in the 1970s. Meanwhile, a new generation of faculty members returned to Highlander's roots to focus again on the problems confronting Appalachia. Residential workshops examined issues, such as strip mining and occupational and environmental health hazards, that would sustain community organizations. Research projects critically analyzed regional institutions and forced the Tennessee Valley Authority to open its decision-making process to public scrutiny. A leadership-development initiative connected Highlander to leaders in the Appalachian coal fields and fostered communication among them.

This reorientation was one of several signs that Highlander was making a transition from its folk school legacy. In 1972 the center moved from its original Knoxville headquarters to its current location, a 104-acre farm near New Market. Administrative leadership passed from Myles Horton to Mike Clark. In the 1970s and 1980s, workshops brought together several thousand Appalachian residents on an extensive range of issues. Area residents became involved in research that uncovered environmental threats and inequitable land ownership patterns. A Southern Appalachian Leadership Training Program honed the organizational skills of indigenous leaders.

Realizing that the crises facing Appalachian communities were also found in other parts of the region and the world, Highlander expanded the geographic scope of its work and placed it in the global context of the 1980s and 1990s. Under the direction of Hubert Sapp, John Gaventa, and Jim Sessions, staff members pursued several related priorities: community empowerment, economic and environmental justice, leadership development, participatory research, building international grassroots linkages, and maintenance of the center as a meeting ground for diverse cultures. Highlander endures as a place that nurtures strategies for resistance, democratization, and experiential education.

John M. Glen, Ball State University

SEE: HIGHLANDER FOLK SCHOOL; JEFFERSON COUNTY

HIGHWAYS, HISTORIC. Until the late nineteenth century, the United States emphasized the construction of railroads rather than highways. Few cohesive road networks existed, and most roads were in a deplorable condition. The Good Roads Movement began about 1880, peaked with the passage of the Federal Aid Act of 1916, and ended about 1926 with the development of the U.S. routing system.

The Goods Roads Movement, led by farmers and railroad interests, initially stressed local road improvements, often termed "farm-to market" roads. About 1910 the Good Roads Movement splintered when individuals in the automobile and tourism industries began promoting the development of transcontinental or interstate roads to connect primary towns. Interstate corridors sometimes required the construction of new roads, but more often, highway associations overlaid the interstate designation onto an existing route. In order to receive the designation, however, local officials had to agree to improve the route to pre-determined standards.

Perhaps the best known of these interstate routes was the 1912 Lincoln Highway, which stretched from New York City to San Francisco. By the mid-1920s, 12 widely known interstate highways existed in the South. The two most traveled were the Bankhead Highway through the Deep South, which clipped the southwest corner of Tennessee as it crossed the Mississippi River at Memphis, and the north-south Dixie Highway, which crossed the state in both Middle and East Tennessee.

Other prominent routes in Tennessee included the Lee Highway, the Andrew Jackson Highway, and the Jefferson Davis National Highway. Less well-known interstate corridors that passed through Tennessee included the Magnolia Route, the Beeline Highway, the Florida Short Route, the Cincinnati-Lookout Mountain Air Line Highway (Dixie Air Line Highway), the Taft Memorial Highway (Alvin C. York Highway), the Mississippi Valley Highway, and the Mississippi River Scenic Highway.

The 500-mile long Memphis-to-Bristol Highway, although not originally an interstate route, tied in with other highways and functioned in much the same way. Local businessmen formed the Memphis to Bristol Highway Association in 1911 to promote its development. Soon after its creation in 1915, the Tennessee State Highway Department designated this corridor as State Route 1 and made it the number one road priority. In 1926 the state designated about two-thirds of it as U.S. 70, the major east-west corridor in the region. In the late 1920s, the entire route became part of the Broadway of America Highway from California to New York. State Route 1 remained the main east-west route through the state until the completion of Interstate 40 in the late 1960s.

The State Highway Department designated Tennessee's portion of the Dixie Highway, which stretched from Sault Sainte Marie, Michigan, to Miami, Florida, as the state's second highway priority. This route became the most influential interstate highway in Tennessee and the only one to have its national headquarters in the state. Businessmen and politicians formed the Dixie Highway Association in April 1915 at a meeting in Chattanooga, the city that would be its national headquarters throughout its existence. Although an independent association, it functioned as an outgrowth of the Chattanooga Automobile Association, and members of that group played a pivotal role throughout the association's history. Foremost among its members was Judge M. M. Allison, who served as President of the Dixie Highway Association from 1915 until the association ceased active operation in 1927. In 1924, in honor of his work, the association erected a monument in a roadside park in Marion County, the highest point on the route and roughly its mid-point.

Unlike the continuous road of most interstate routes, the Dixie Highway meandered more than 4,000 miles in two parallel routes with connectors and side roads to special attractions. The Western Division ran along Lake Michigan, through Indianapolis, Louisville, Nashville, Chattanooga, Atlanta, and Tallahassee. The Eastern Division followed Lake Huron and passed through Detroit, Cincinnati, Lexington, Knoxville, Chattanooga, Atlanta, Savannah, and Jacksonville. In 1918 the association added the Carolina Division through East Tennessee, North Carolina, South Carolina, and Georgia.

By 1926, over 600 highway associations operated in the United States with roughly 70 percent of their routes overlapping. Virtually all of these early interstate routes became state routes and played pivotal roles in local as well as regional and national traffic patterns. In 1926 the U.S. routing commission, under pressure from many of these associations, deliberately chose to splinter these routes. With a solid network of federal and state financing and maintenance, the associations gradually disbanded.

Martha Carver, Tennessee Department of Transportation

SUGGESTED READING: Howard L. Preston, *Dirt Roads to Dixie* (1991)

SEE: DIXIE HIGHWAY ASSOCIATION; GOOD ROADS MOVEMENT

HILL, HORACE GREELEY (1873–1942), groceryman, real estate entrepreneur, banker, and philanthropist, was born in Hickory Valley, White County, Tennessee, in 1873. He opened the first H. G. Hill Grocery Store at age 23 and became a pioneer in such grocery retailing innovations as self-service, cash-and-carry, and newspaper price advertising. Hill quickly built a large Middle Tennessee chain of stores and expanded into other states. At one time, he operated more than 500 grocery stores in the South, including stores in Birmingham, Alabama, and Louisiana.

Hill preferred to own the properties in which his stores operated, and he enjoyed investing and dealing in real property. By the time the H. G. Hill Realty Company incorporated in 1926, Hill held one of the major real estate portfolios in Tennessee.

In 1933 Hill agreed to use his financial resources, reputation, and management skills to rescue the Nashville Trust Company, one of the oldest banking institutions in the South. He served as its Chairman until his death in 1942.

Hill was privately known for his many acts of unrecognized generosity and kindness. His public philanthropy included providing leadership and significant financial assistance to George Peabody College for Teachers, the Young Men's Christian Association, and the Presbyterian Church. Highly respected and active in business and community affairs, Hill served as president of the Commercial Club of Nashville from 1919 to 1920.

Hill died in October 1942 and was survived by his widow, Mamie Wilson Hill.

John B. Hardcastle, Nashville

SEE: COMMERCE AND URBAN DEVELOPMENT; NASHVILLE

HILL, NAPOLEON (1830–1909), the merchant prince of Memphis, was born in 1830, the second of 11 children of Duncan and Olivia L. Bills Hill. Hill's physician father died in 1844, leaving his widow an estate valued at more than $40,000, including Longwood plantation in Marshall County, Mississippi. At age 16, Hill moved to Bolivar, Tennessee, where he clerked in a dry goods store. Three years later, he joined the California Gold Rush and reportedly accumulated several thousand dollars before returning to Tennessee. By 1857 Hill was back in Memphis after a brief stopover in Bolivar. He opened a wholesale grocery and cotton commission house on the eve of the Civil War.

In postwar Memphis, Hill became one of the leading businessmen among the cotton and merchant houses of the day. He also invested in banking and real estate, as well as New South industrial development. As Memphis rose to prominence as the world's leading cotton spot market and one of the nation's largest wholesale grocery distribution centers, Hill became wealthy, powerful, and socially prominent.

The city's cotton merchants organized the Memphis Cotton Exchange in 1873, which Hill headed in the early 1880s. Unlike other southern cities, Memphis cotton men (instead of the railroads) owned and operated the city's cotton compress and storage facilities. In 1887 Hill succeeded founder Henry Montgomery as head of the Merchants' Cotton Press and Storage Company, with its giant warehouses and daily compress output of 6,000 bales. In 1885 Hill, Sam Tate, and Robert B. Snowden formed Citizens Railway Company, a street car line serving the Fort Pickering, Cole's Mill, Scotland, Elmwood Cemetery, and Leath Orphan Asylum area. The line was soon absorbed by Memphis City Railroad Company. Hill's biggest investment was in Hill, Fontaine and Company, a cotton and wholesale grocery business. In addition to his other investments, Hill owned 1,250 shares of Pratt Coal and Coke Company, developers of the Birmingham, Alabama, steel industry. He was also a strong investor in Union and Planters Bank and served as a bank director.

Hill lived ostentatiously in a mansion he built at the present site of the Sterick Building. He died in 1909 and is buried in Elmwood Cemetery.

Connie L. Lester, Tennessee Historical Society

SUGGESTED READINGS: John Harkins, *Metropolis of the American Nile: Memphis & Shelby County* (1982); Robert A. Sigafoos, *Cotton Row to Beale Street: A Business History of Memphis* (1979)

SEE: COMMERCE AND URBAN DEVELOPMENT; MEMPHIS COTTON EXCHANGE; TENNESSEANS IN CALIFORNIA GOLD RUSH; UNION PLANTERS BANK

HINE, LEWIS (1874–1940), was an established documentary photographer when Arthur E. Morgan, first chairman of the Tennessee Valley Authority (TVA), approached him to document life in the region. Recognized as a socially concerned photographer, Hine documented the abusive conditions of child labor in mills and mines and the 1918 European relief work undertaken by the Red Cross.

Such work made Hine the natural choice to capture conditions in the Tennessee Valley. He photographed and captioned 197 images in East Tennessee. The subjects of his work included families from Loyston in the Norris Reservoir area, workers at the Kingsport Press, the Civilian Conservation Corps, and early construction work on Norris Dam. Many of these images, such as "Washday at Stooksbury Farm," have been published repeatedly to illustrate Appalachian life.

Initially Hine was quite enthusiastic about the TVA project, but as he continued his work, he felt the agency did not take full advantage of the publicity possibilities for the pictorial material. In January 1934 *Survey Graphic* published an article by Morgan about the Tennessee Valley and used several of Hine's images without his byline. The photographer believed Morgan had deliberately failed to credit his work. This episode, along with his disenchantment with the TVA bureaucracy, led to the dissolution of his contract with the agency. Nevertheless, his images captured a lifestyle TVA was determined to change.

Patricia Bernard Ezzell, Tennessee Valley Authority

SEE: TENNESSEE VALLEY AUTHORITY

PHOTOGRAPH BY LEWIS HINE, TENNESSEE VALLEY AUTHORITY COLLECTIONS

Washday at Stooksbury homestead near Andersonville, 1933. The 350-acre estate was flooded after the construction of Norris Dam.

HINTON, ELMER (1905–1979), columnist for *The Tennessean*, was born April 26, 1905, on a farm near Mitchellville. Hinton's first foray into journalism came in 1925, when he married Lucille Woods. They established the weekly *Upper Sumner Press* in Portland, publishing it until 1948. He placed his column, called "Hog Head and Hominy," on the front page.

Hinton joined *The Tennessean* in 1942, and worked as police reporter, copy reader, and state editor. He achieved a lasting niche in Tennessee journalism with his homespun column "Down to Earth," a mixture of folksy philosophy, nostalgia, and gentle humor that attracted thousands of readers for nearly 30 years. "Down to Earth" was populated with recurring fictional characters like Cousin Nud and Old Bluestreak and real life personalities gleaned from the "keg-sitters" at the United Farm Supply mill in Portland, where Hinton hung out in his spare time. Readers, too, contributed to the column in an important way.

Hinton made community involvement another priority. He served six years as mayor of Portland and 18 years as a magistrate on the Sumner County Court. In addition, he originated the Portland Strawberry Festival and the Down to Earth all-day gospel sings in Alexandria, Tennessee.

Hinton retired from full-time employment at *The Tennessean* in 1972, but continued to write his weekly column until he suffered a heart attack and died December 5, 1979. In 1982 the Elmer Hinton Memorial Library opened in Portland.
Glenn Himebaugh, Middle Tennessee State University
SEE: NASHVILLE TENNESSEAN; SUMNER COUNTY

HISTORIC PRESERVATION: See AMERICAN ASSOCIATION FOR STATE AND LOCAL HISTORY; ASSOCIATION FOR THE PRESERVATION OF TENNESSEE ANTIQUITIES; CENTER FOR HISTORIC PRESERVATION; CONSERVATION; FARMS, TENNESEE CENTURY; INDIVIDUAL HISTORIC SITES AND PARKS; LADIES' HERMITAGE ASSOCIATION; RURAL AFRICAN-AMERICAN CHURCH PROJECT; TENNESSEE CIVIL WAR NATIONAL HERITAGE AREA; TENNESSEE HISTORICAL COMMISSION.

HIWASSEE COLLEGE is a two-year coeducational liberal arts institution located near Madisonville in Monroe County, Tennessee. Originally a Methodist campground school known as Bat Creek, the college was established in 1850 as one of Tennessee's oldest educational facilities. A typical school of its era, Hiwassee was designed to provide local young males with an affordable education, and although it was church-affiliated, the college did not have rigid denominational restrictions. Hiwassee's first president, Reverend Robert Doak, a Presbyterian, also served as its senior professor. The only college-educated staff member, he was accompanied by only one mathematics instructor and a school administrator. Students entered the college around age 14 and graduated in their late teens or early twenties. David M. Key, Hiwassee's first graduate, went on to become the Postmaster General under President Rutherford B. Hayes. Future governor Albert H. Roberts was a graduate in 1889. Hiwassee's literary societies, Eromathesian and Erolethian, were an important and popular part of campus life as the primary source of recreation. Each had a designated room in the school's original building where it held weekly debates on a variety of political, philosophical, and social issues.

By 1893 Hiwassee had six buildings on 95 acres to accommodate its 100 students. In the late nineteenth century, Hiwassee came under the control of the Holston Conference of the Methodist Episcopal Church, South and has remained so to the present. Today, the campus occupies 60 of the school's 400 acres and includes 18 buildings and four residence halls.
Teresa Biddle-Douglass, Middle Tennessee State University
SUGGESTED READING: James X. Corgan, "Toward a History of Higher Education in Antebellum Tennessee," East Tennessee Historical Society *Publications* 60(1988): 39–66
SEE: HOLSTON CONFERENCE; MONROE COUNTY

HOHENWALD. One of Tennessee's few immigrant communities, Hohenwald began as a crossroads store and house owned by Warren and Augusta Smith. Augusta Smith, a German immigrant, named the community Hohenwald, which means high forest, a reflection of the surrounding countryside and its location on the Western Highland Rim.

In the 1890s, as the community developed and gained railroad access, it attracted the interest of officials of the Nashville, Chattanooga & St. Louis Railway, who recognized opportunities to establish immigrant agricultural communities and develop mineral resources. A Swiss American, J. G. Probst, advanced a scheme to establish two Swiss colonies, one in Middle Tennessee and one in Arkansas. Probst purchased 13,000 acres in Lewis County for his colony and founded the Swiss Pioneer Union to attract potential immigrant settlers. He drew attention to his scheme through advertisements in German-language newspapers. Railroads distributed pamphlets extolling Middle Tennessee farmland to midwestern passengers. The venture attracted considerable attention, and a number of Swiss immigrants sold their midwestern farms and bought stock in the Pioneer Union.

The first Swiss settlers arrived by train on November 17, 1895, expecting to find a well-developed town and established farms. When the train stopped at the boxcar depot, many would-be settlers despaired at the sight before them and remained on the train, returning to the farms they had abandoned. Those who stayed barely survived the winter in tents and makeshift barracks.

The settlers laid out a new town, which they called New Switzerland. It was platted in perfect squares, with wide streets, and immediately adjacent to Hohenwald. Conflict quickly developed between the original citizens of Hohenwald and the immigrant settlers of New Switzerland. Language, customs, and economic expectations fueled the escalating tensions and soon produced a courtroom battle which resulted in the merger of the two towns under the name of Hohenwald. In 1897 Hohenwald became the county seat of Lewis County. Its population totaled 1,200 inhabitants in 1910, over half of whom claimed Swiss heritage.

Well into the twentieth century, Hohenwald retained its Swiss distinctiveness. The Swiss settlers founded a singing group called Alpenroesli (Little Alpine Rose) and a band, Echoes of Switzerland, which played for the General Assembly. The women organized the Frauerein, an organization similar to home demonstration clubs. During World War I, anti-German sentiment forced the abandonment of the German language and cultural identification. Within a few years, most of Hohenwald's Swiss families no longer spoke German-Swiss. Only in recent years, have descendants returned to their heritage.

Connie L. Lester, Tennessee Historical Society

SEE: GRUTELI; LEWIS COUNTY; RAILROADS

HOLLAENDER, ALEXANDER (1898–1986), director of the Biology Division, Oak Ridge National Laboratory, and professor of radiation biology at the University of Tennessee, was born in Germany in 1898. He emigrated to the United States, where he studied physical chemistry at the University of Wisconsin, earning his Ph.D. in 1931. Serving as senior biophysicist at the National Institutes of Health and the Office of Scientific Research and Development until 1945, he studied the interactions of ultraviolet and ionizing radiation on biological systems. His experiments provided the first clear indication that genes are composed largely of nucleic acid.

As Director of the Oak Ridge Biology Division, 1946–1966, Hollaender recruited an unsurpassed team of radiation biologists, managing multidisciplinary studies of the effects of radiation on organisms. He edited *Radiation Biology, Chemical Mutagens,* and other professional studies and journals, and fostered biological research at universities throughout the Southeast and abroad. The encouragement he provided for biological research in Latin America, and the scientific conferences he organized at Gatlinburg were major professional contributions.

Elected to the National Academy of Sciences and the American Academy of Arts and Sciences, Hollaender received many awards and honorary degrees.

He was a founder and president of the National Council for Research Planning in Biological Sciences in Washington, D.C., where he died in 1986. His papers are preserved in the Special Collections at the University of Tennessee, Knoxville.

Leland R. Johnson, Clio Research Institute

SEE: OAK RIDGE NATIONAL LABORATORY

HOLLOWAY, JOSEPHINE GROVES (1898–1988) became the first African-American professional worker at the Cumberland Valley Girl Scout Council (CVGSC) in Nashville in 1944. She began her interest in girl scouting in 1923, when, as a recent graduate of Fisk University, she chose scouting as her means of "girls' work" at Bethlehem Center, a Nashville social settlement house.

After her marriage to Guerney Holloway, she resigned this work, but remained committed to scouting. When her oldest daughter turned six in 1933, Holloway asked Nashville's Girl Scout Council to register a troop, but the council declined, citing the high cost of maintaining separate facilities for Negroes. Holloway organized an unofficial troop, enlisted friends to start new troops, and continued to seek official status.

In 1942 the growing number of "Negro" troops forced the Council to recognize them. By 1944, when African Americans accounted for 15 percent of Nashville's Girl Scouts, the Council hired Holloway as field advisor. Her troops, soon numbering 40, thrived on a segregated basis. Integration of the Council and troops began in 1951, when the Council moved Holloway's office into its own building; in 1962 it abolished its separate "Negro" district. Integrated camps soon followed. Years later, Holloway expressed some ambivalence about the end of separate Girl Scouting programs, saying that integration lessened her girls' exposure to "examples of black strength and pride."[1] Holloway retired in 1963. The CVGSC gave her special recognition at their 1976 Bicentennial celebration, and in 1990 constructed a permanent gallery at its headquarters for the display of her memorabilia. Holloway died December 7, 1988, at the age of 90.

Elisabeth Israels Perry, Nashville

CITATION:

(1) Elisabeth Israels Perry, "'The Very Best Influence': Josephine Holloway and Girl Scouting for Nashville's African-American Community," *Tennessee Historical Quarterly* 52(1993): 82.

SEE: BETHLEHEM HOUSE; GIRL SCOUTS U.S.A., TENNESSEE

HOLSTON CONFERENCE is the organization of nearly 1,000 United Methodist churches in 33 East Tennessee counties, 17 southwest Virginia counties, a county and portions of two others in northwest

Georgia, and one church each in Alabama and West Virginia. There are nearly 1,000 pastors, chaplains, and other clergy, and nearly 175,000 lay members. The Conference took its name from the three forks of the Holston River, which rises in southwest Virginia and flows into the Tennessee River.

The first official Methodist pastor, Jeremiah Lambert, came to the Holston country in 1783. Initially one "circuit" covered nearly half the present territory. The conference organized in 1824, with Robert Richford Roberts as its first bishop. Until the 1880s Holston Conference encompassed several counties in western North Carolina and two or more West Virginia counties until 1939. Almost all the land in the Cherokee Nation once fell within the Holston Conference, including parts of South Carolina, North Carolina, and Georgia, as well as southeast Tennessee.

From 1865 to 1939, two Holston Conferences covered essentially the same territory—Holston Conference of The Methodist Episcopal Church (ME, sometimes called the "Northern" Church) and Holston Conference of the Methodist Episcopal Church, South (MES, sometimes called the "Southern" Church). The Methodist denomination split in 1844, partly over the issue of slavery. There were no "northern" churches within Holston between 1844 and 1865, but some members left the "southern" church, and many congregations were unsettled. During the Civil War, some congregations lost their buildings as a result of military occupation.

From 1830 until 1939 the Virginia District of the Methodist Protestant Church covered some of the same territory as the ME and MES Holston Conferences. In 1939 the three came together in The Methodist Church. In 1968, when The Methodist Church merged with The Evangelical United Brethren Church (EUB), what had been in some years the East Tennessee Conference of The United Brethren Church (UB), comprising much of the same geographical area, became part of Holston Conference of The United Methodist Church (UMC).

Through approximately 175 years, the bodies that today make up Holston Conference have placed a great deal of emphasis on education and social service, as well as on preaching, worship, and salvation. Today, the Conference owns two senior colleges and a junior college; at various times there were at least four other colleges and several high schools and elementary schools.

Today, the Conference also operates a hospital, a children's home (started by Methodist women) with several branches, six retirement homes, and six camps. Many local congregations operate daycare centers and a wide variety of community services; many provide meeting places for secular and ecumenical endeavors. Some are biracial, and a few are bilingual. In 1824 there were three districts with 24 circuits. Today, there are 11 districts. Twenty percent of the churches are still on circuits in which a pastor serves more than one church. Many of these pastors are bi-vocational.

An uncounted number of missionaries, both lay and clergy, have gone from the Holston Conference to other parts of the United States and around the world in the name of Christ. In addition, the churches and the Conference together support many other religious, medical, and social ministries and missions.

Roy L. Howard, Chattanooga

SUGGESTED READINGS: Robert L. Hilten, *Pillar of Fire: The Drama of Holston United Methodism in a Changing World* (1994); R. N. Price, *Holston Methodism From Its Origin to the Present Time,* 5 vols. (1912)

SEE: HIWASSEE COLLEGE; RELIGION; TENNESSEE WESLEYAN COLLEGE

HOLSTON ORDNANCE WORKS (HOW), sprawled over 6,000 acres along the Holston River in Sullivan and Hawkins counties around Kingsport, manufactured a powerful explosive for the military during World War II. Construction of the munitions plant, at an original estimated cost of almost $77 million, began in 1942 and was not completely finished until January 1944. Managed by Tennessee Eastman Company (TEC), the Holston works produced Composition B, a highly explosive amalgamation of RDX (cyclonite, or Research Development Explosive) and TNT (trinitrotoluene), which was used by the Allies in detonators and as an ingredient for bursting charges in bombs and projectiles. RDX was too sensitive to be used alone and the combination with TNT created a more stable substance.

Holston Ordnance Works was fully operational by mid-1943, and the following year became the largest maker of high explosives in the world. At its peak, HOW employed nearly 7,000 people, 40 percent of them women. In 1943 TEC and HOW were awarded the coveted Army-Navy "E" for their contributions to the war effort. Employee morale was high at the Holston works, and the facility recorded only three work-related deaths between 1942 and 1945, none of them due to explosives.

The wartime economic boom which accompanied HOW was a double-edged sword for Kingsport. Massive industrial construction and the influx of thousands of workers displaced families and created serious housing shortages, but most townspeople accepted the inconveniences in a spirit of patriotism. Although the number of employees has never matched its World War II peak, Holston still operates outside of Kingsport.

Susan L. Gordon, Tennessee Historical Society

SEE: KINGSPORT; TENNESSEE EASTMAN COMPANY; WORLD WAR II

HOLT, ANDREW DAVID (1904–1987), educator and president of the University of Tennessee, was born in Milan, Tennessee, on December 4, 1904. In 1927 Holt earned his bachelor's degree from Emory University in Atlanta, and went on to receive his master's and doctoral degrees from Teacher's College of Columbia University in New York. He also received an honorary doctor of laws degree from Union University in Jackson, Tennessee, in 1950. Holt married Martha Chase in 1938, and they raised three children.

Holt began his long and distinguished career in education in West Tennessee. He taught fifth through eighth grades in his home town of Milan and later joined the high school faculty in nearby Humboldt. As his career advanced, Holt became principal and professor of education at the Demonstration School of Memphis State College and was named high school supervisor for West Tennessee. In 1937 Holt moved to Nashville where he became the executive secretary of the Tennessee Education Association. He remained at this position for 13 years.

Holt's career as an educator progressed to a national level in 1949, when he was elected president of the National Education Association. He served on the organization's board of directors from 1950 to 1958. Holt served on numerous national education committees throughout his career, including the Council of Advisors of the U.S. Commissioner of Education, the Education Advisory Council of the National Association of Manufacturers, the National Commission to Promote the Eradication of Adult Illiteracy, and the Advisory Committee of the Great Smoky Mountains Historical Association. He chaired the U.S. delegation to the World Organization of the Teaching Profession in Berne, Switzerland, in 1949 and was a delegate to the Mid-century White House Conference on Education and Youth in 1950. He also served as the national chairman of the U.S. Treasury Department's School Savings Committee.

Holt came to the University of Tennessee in 1950 as executive assistant to president Dr. C. E. Brehm and was promoted to vice president in 1953. Six years later, Holt was named president of the university. During Holt's ten years as president, the university experienced its greatest growth: student enrollment tripled, faculty increased substantially, and academic programs expanded over 30 percent. Holt retired in 1969, soon after endorsing a controversial open speaker policy at the university. A group of students and faculty filed a federal lawsuit against the university after school officials denied civil rights activist Dick Gregory and counterculture guru Timothy Leary permission to speak on campus. The school's policy was ruled unconstitutional and replaced by an "open" policy that gave student organizations full authority in the selection of speakers. With his endorsement of the new policy, Holt added progress in free speech and student rights to his long list of contributions to Tennessee education.

Holt died in August 1987 and is buried in Woodlawn Cemetery, Knoxville.

Teresa Biddle-Douglass, Middle Tennessee State University
SEE: EDUCATION, HIGHER; GIBSON COUNTY; UNIVERSITY OF TENNESSEE

HOMECOMING '86 was a year-long celebration in almost every Tennessee community. The focus of the event, according to state officials, was to be "part hoedown, part history lesson and part homecoming celebration." Many communities put into place organizations that continued through the state's bicentennial in 1996.

The project began during the administration of Governor Lamar Alexander with the establishment of 39 pilot communities in 1983 to initiate preparations for Homecoming '86 and serve as examples to other communities. After the pilot communities created a workable development plan, state organizers worked with communities statewide. Local community organizations kept the celebration locally-based. Regional coordinators provided assistance in local organization and activities, and relayed information to the state. The state sanctioned "Official Homecoming Communities" for active participants in the celebration. More than 800 communities received this designation.

Each community focused on two major goals: researching the community's history and planning a project to preserve, promote, or enhance the qualities of the community. Homecoming Communities created four working committees: heritage, vision, project, and Homecoming '86.

Tennesseans responded enthusiastically to the Homecoming '86 concept, using the occasion as an opportunity to clean up their towns, develop new museum and parks projects, and set future goals.

The state Homecoming staff developed a promotional campaign and a Homecoming logo to publicize the celebration. A promotional film titled "3,000 Places Called Home," explained the concept of Homecoming '86. Alex Haley and Minnie Pearl served as honorary co-chairpersons for the celebration. Statewide activities included: a traveling musical production, "Comin' Home Tennessee;" school educational programs to enhance state pride; a reunion of Tennessee journalists; Tennessee Storytelling at the National Storytelling Festival in Jonesborough; and a 12-car passenger train, "Homecoming '86 Special," which traveled across the state with Governor Lamar Alexander, Alex Haley, and the "Comin' Home" musical production. Finally, the Smithsonian Folklife Festival in Washington, D.C., focused on Tennessee culture.

Carolyn Brackett, Nashville
SEE: ALEXANDER, LAMAR; HALEY, ALEX M.; MINNIE PEARL; NATIONAL STORYTELLING FESTIVAL

HOOD, JOHN BELL (1831–1879), commanding general of the Army of Tennessee, was born June 1, 1831, at Owingsville, Kentucky. The son of a physician-planter, Hood grew up in the comfortable life his family's position offered. After private schooling, Hood's congressman uncle secured him an appointment to the U.S. Military Academy at West Point. While at the Academy, Hood accumulated 374 demerits, 196 in his senior year alone, suggesting an early lack of responsibility and command.

Following his 1853 graduation, Hood served with the Fourth Infantry Regiment in California. In 1855, he was reassigned to a new cavalry regiment, the Second Cavalry, being organized at Jefferson Barracks, Missouri. The unit owed its distinction to the officers associated with it in the 1850s. Colonel Albert Sidney Johnston commanded; Lieutenant-Colonel Robert E. Lee served as second in command; and William J. Hardee and George H. Thomas were majors in the new regiment. The unit marched to Texas and served there until sectional differences led to the Civil War.

In 1861 Hood requested and received an eight-week furlough. From his home in Kentucky, Hood resigned his commission; three days later, on April 20, 1861, he was commissioned as a first lieutenant of cavalry in the Confederate army.

Hood's fighting reputation followed him into the Confederate ranks and served him well. By the early spring of 1862, he had risen to the rank of general and commanded a brigade of Texans in the Army of Northern Virginia. After seven months, he received a promotion to major general. Hood performed well as a division commander, and Robert E. Lee trusted his judgment. He exhibited a tenacity on the battlefield that enhanced his reputation as a hard fighter. Under the watchful eye of his Corps commander, Lt. General James Longstreet, Hood delivered the battlefield punch when needed. Longstreet recognized Hood's limitations, however, and always halted the general's impetuous advance before he over-extended his line. This command and control system worked well for the Army of Northern Virginia as long as Hood served under Longstreet and Lee.

Hood received two life-threatening wounds. The first came at Gettysburg, when an artillery shell left him without the use of his left arm. During Hood's convalescence in Richmond, Confederate authorities sent Longstreet's Corps to Northern Georgia to assist General Braxton Bragg's Army of Tennessee in halting the Union advance through Middle Tennessee. Hood, recovering from his wound, accompanied the division into Georgia.

On September 18, 1863, Longstreet's Corps reached the banks of Chickamauga Creek. The next day, as Hood rode forward, a minie ball pierced the upper portion of his right thigh. Doctors amputated his leg just below the hip. In less than seven weeks, Hood lost the use of one arm and underwent the amputation of his leg. The injuries entitled him to a medical discharge, but Hood remained in the army and received a promotion to corps commander in the Army of Tennessee (February 1, 1864).

Throughout the summer of 1864, General Joseph E. Johnston, commander of the Army of Tennessee, conducted a campaign to slow the advance of General William T. Sherman's march to Atlanta. Disgusted with Johnston's inability to stop Sherman's progress, President Jefferson Davis replaced Johnston with Hood.

In July 1864, when Hood assumed command of the Army of Tennessee, he had more than 50,000 soldiers. By November, battle casualties reduced the number to less than 30,000 soldiers. The worst was yet to come. Hood's campaign through Middle Tennessee in the early winter of 1864 reduced the Army of Tennessee by another 13,500 men. The army counted 7,000 casualties assaulting the Union's earthworks at Franklin. Two weeks later, on the outskirts of Nashville, the Confederate army lost another 6,500 men in a vain attempt to defeat a Union army three times its size. By Christmas, 1864, the Army of Tennessee was reduced to a mob of armed men.

In January 1865 Hood requested to be relieved of command. He died in New Orleans of yellow fever in 1879.

Patrick Craddock, Franklin

SEE: ARMY OF TENNESSEE; CHICKAMAUGA AND CHATTANOOGA, BATTLES OF; FRANKLIN, BATTLE OF; JOHNSTON, ALBERT S.; JOHNSTON, JOSEPH E.; NASHVILLE, BATTLE OF

HOOKS, BENJAMIN LAWSON (1925–), civil rights attorney, minister, judge, and executive director of the NAACP, was born in Memphis, the son of Robert B. and Bessie Hooks and the grandson of Julia Britton and Charles Hooks. Young Hooks grew up working at his father's Hooks Brothers photography studios, one of the city's oldest black businesses, on Beale Street. He graduated from Booker T. Washington High School in 1941 and attended LeMoyne College and Howard University before joining the army in 1943, rising to the rank of staff sergeant as he served in Italy. Leaving the service in 1946, Hooks attended DePaul University in Chicago, where he received his J. D. degree in 1948.

Hooks returned to Memphis and entered private practice. In 1955 he became the co-founder and later chairman of the Mutual Federal Savings and Loan Association.

The next year, he added the title Reverend to his name as he became the pastor of Greater Middle Baptist Church, a position he continues to hold, and would later also pastor (1964–1994) the Greater New

Mt. Moriah Baptist Church in Detroit. He joined other African-American ministers in the Civil Rights Movement and served on the board of the Southern Christian Leadership Conference for ten years.

In 1959 Hooks announced his candidacy for Juvenile Court judge, running on the Volunteer ticket with Russell Sugermon, Reverend Henry Buntyn, and Reverend Roy Love. Despite a vigorous campaign and a strong effort to register black voters, Hooks and his fellow candidates lost the election. Two years later, Hooks joined the public defender's office, where he served until 1964. In 1965 Governor Frank G. Clement appointed Hooks to the judgeship of the new Criminal Court Division IV, making him the first African American to hold such a post in Tennessee since Reconstruction. In 1966 Hooks won election to an eight-year term in the office. In a 1967 interview with the Memphis *Commercial Appeal*, Judge Hooks outlined his views on civil rights and the long, hot summers of the late 1960s. While expressing his empathy with the frustrations of young African Americans who were taking to the streets, he stated his firm belief in non-violent direct action as the means of achieving change. He practiced what he "preached" as a board director of the Southern Regional Leadership Conference from 1968 to 1972.

In 1972 President Richard M. Nixon appointed Hooks to the Federal Communications Commission (FCC), the first African American appointed to the agency. During his service, Hooks made good his promise to voice his criticism of media presentations of minorities in stereotypical roles. He repeatedly chastised broadcasters for their disregard of black cultural events and their failure to air African-American news. Broadcasters worried that Hooks would advance to chair the FCC following the election of Jimmy Carter in 1976. Hooks, however, resigned his position on the FCC to succeed Roy Wilkins as Executive Director of the National Association for the Advancement of Colored People (NAACP).

During his years as Executive Director (1977–1993), Hooks worked to increase the membership, financial standing, and prominence of the NAACP in a time of severe setbacks for African Americans and their quest for civil rights. Under Hooks's leadership, the NAACP launched ACT-SO, the Afro-Academic, Cultural, Technical, Scientific Olympics to foster academic excellence. He championed African-American inclusion in American corporate offices and continued to press for voter registration and participation. For his lifetime commitment to civil rights, Hooks received numerous awards, including honorary doctorates from Howard University, Wilberforce University, and Central State University, as well as the 1986 Spingarn Award, the NAACP's highest honor.

After "retiring" from the directorship of the NAACP, Hooks returned to Memphis where he served as founding chair of the National Civil Rights Museum and continues to pastor and lecture on the Civil Rights Movement. Hooks is married to the former Frances Dancy. They are the parents of one daughter, Patricia Gray. In 1976 the Memphis Round Table of the National Conference of Christians and Jews awarded its Sixteenth Annual Brotherhood Award jointly to Benjamin and Frances Hooks, honoring the couple for their "tireless dedication to the vision of a society in which goodwill in the human family prevails both in attitude and behavior."[1]

Kenneth W. Goings, University of Memphis

CITATION:

(1) Memphis *Press-Semitar* (n.d.) from the Benjamin L. Hooks file; Cossitt Library, Memphis.

Source: The Editor-in-Chief thanks Selma Lewis and Connie L. Lester for their contributions of material on the life of Judge Hooks.

SEE: CIVIL RIGHTS MOVEMENT; CLEMENT, FRANK G.; HOOKS, JULIA B.; NAACP; NATIONAL CIVIL RIGHTS MUSEUM

HOOKS, JULIA BRITTON (1852–1942), African-American clubwoman known as "The Angel of Beale Street," was born free in 1852 in Frankfort, Kentucky. Her parents, Henry Britton, a carpenter, and Laura Marshall Britton, encouraged her training in classical music. In 1869 this musical prodigy enrolled in Berea College in an interracial program that allowed her to study music and instruct white students in piano. In 1872 Julia Britton moved to Greenville, Mississippi, to teach school. She married Sam Wertles; he died in the 1873 Yellow Fever epidemic. She participated in the successful campaign of Blanche K. Bruce, one of the first blacks to serve in the U.S. Senate. In 1876 Julia Britton Wertles moved to Memphis to teach and married Charles Hooks.

Julia Hooks became a leader in African-American cultural and educational affairs. In 1883 she and Anna Church, the wife of Robert Church, Sr., launched the Liszt-Mullard Club to promote classical music and raise money for scholarships for promising black musicians. She founded the Hooks School of Music, whose students included W. C. Handy, Sidney Woodward, and Nell Hunter. Dissatisfied with the poor quality of public education for Memphis black children, she opened the Hooks Cottage School (kindergarten and elementary education) in 1892.

Hooks worked to relieve the suffering of impoverished black Memphians. In 1891 she became a charter member of two institutions: the Colored Old Folks Home (later Hooks-Edwards Rest Home) and the Orphan Home Club. These institutions provided shelter for elderly black women and orphans. In 1902

Memphis established a juvenile court for African-American offenders; Julia and Charles Hooks supervised the detention home, which was next door to their own home. In 1917 Charles Hooks was killed by an escaping juvenile, but Julia Hooks continued to provide counseling and guidance to the juvenile facility.

Hooks deplored the racial inequality and Jim Crow segregation of her day and championed personal character building as well as government protection for embattled black citizens. In March 1881 she was escorted from a Memphis theater, arrested, and fined $5 for refusing to move from the white section to the "colored balcony." She was widely quoted on the subject of character building, and her essay "The Duty of the Hour," was published in the 1895 edition of the *African-American Encyclopedia*. A member of the Memphis chapter of the NAACP, Hooks was the grandmother of the national director of the organization, Benjamin J. Hooks. She died in 1942, at age 90.

Selma Lewis, Memphis

SUGGESTED READING: "Hooks, Julia Britton," in *Black Women in America: An Historical Encyclopedia,* Darlene Clark Hine, Elsa Barkley Brown, Rosalyn Terborg-Penn, eds. (1993); Selma Lewis and Marjean G. Kremer, *The Angel of Beale Street: A Biography of Julia Ann Hooks* (1986)

SEE: CHURCH, ROBERT, R., SR.; CIVIL RIGHTS MOVEMENT; HANDY, WILLIAM C.; MEMPHIS; NAACP

HOOPER, BEN WALTER (1870–1957), Governor, was born Bennie Walter Wade in Newport, Cocke County, on October 13, 1870, the illegitimate son of Sarah Wade and Dr. Lemuel Washington Hooper. The child and his mother moved to Dandridge, Mossy Creek (now Jefferson City), New Market, and finally Knoxville, where his mother placed the boy in the care of St. John's Orphanage of the Episcopal Church. At the age of nine, he was legally adopted by his father, who changed the boy's name to Hooper and raised him in Newport.

After graduating from Carson-Newman College in 1890, Hooper studied law under Judge Horace Nelson Cate and was admitted to the bar in 1894. From 1893 to 1897 he served two terms in the state House of Representatives and was captain of Company C, Sixth U.S. Volunteer Infantry during the Spanish-American War. After the war, he married Anna Belle Jones and practiced law in Newport until he received an appointment as Assistant U.S. Attorney for the Eastern Tennessee District, a position he held from 1906 to 1910.

Prior to the 1910 gubernatorial election, prohibition and the related issue of machine politics were at the center of political strife across Tennessee. While leading Republicans supported the temperance cause, the dominant element of the Democratic Party rejected it, despite fierce objection by former U.S. Senator and fiery prohibitionist, Edward Ward Carmack. The breach among Tennessee Democrats grew wider when Governor Malcolm R. Patterson, an opponent of statewide prohibition, used his control of party machinery to block its adoption. The murder of Carmack in 1908 and Governor Patterson's pardoning of his killer further agitated relations among Tennessee Democrats.

Republicans, seizing the opportunity to take control of the governor's office, nominated Hooper, a capable East Tennessean who had embraced the moral reform efforts sweeping across the state and nation. As an ardent prohibitionist, Hooper earned the endorsement of the prohibition faction of the Democratic party. With this bipartisan support, Hooper defeated former governor Robert L. Taylor by a vote of 133,074 to 121,694 and served as Tennessee's only Republican governor between 1880 and 1920.

Hooper dealt with an ongoing conflict over prohibition and election laws; regular Democrats wanted to amend the laws passed by the 1909 legislature, while Fusionists (Independent Democrats and Republicans) fought to keep them as enacted. Despite the turmoil, this administration enacted a child labor law, a law ensuring that the pay of working women would be given only to them, a pure food and drug law, and authorization for counties to issue bonds to buy school property and establish hospitals for treating contagious diseases.

Hooper won reelection in 1912, defeating another former governor, Benton McMillin. During his second term, the legislature increased state revenue for education, initiated mandatory school attendance for children ages eight to 14, and authorized county boards of education to transport students to and from school. Other laws provided for an official examination of the state banking system, a parole system for deserving prisoners, a change in the death penalty to replace hanging with electrocution, and pensions for Civil War veterans and their widows. At Hooper's insistence, the legislature passed the "Jug Bill" to prohibit intrastate shipment of liquor or the delivery of more than one gallon from outside the state, and the "Nuisance Bill," which permitted ten citizens to petition the court to close saloons and gambling houses.

Hooper ran for a third term, but lost to Thomas C. Rye in 1914. Upon leaving the governor's office, Hooper resumed his law practice in Newport. He ran for the U.S. Senate twice, in 1916 and 1934, but was defeated both times by Kenneth D. McKellar. In 1920 President Warren G. Harding appointed Hooper to the U.S. Railroad Labor Board in Chicago where he became a national figure in labor-management arbitration by averting a railroad strike scheduled for October 30, 1921. Upon returning again to Newport,

Hooper served as a chief land purchasing agent for the Great Smoky Mountain National Park and served as vice chairman for Tennessee's Limited Constitutional Convention in 1953. Hooper authored *Elections in Tennessee* (1946). His autobiography, *The Unwanted Boy,* was published posthumously in 1963. Hooper died of pneumonia in 1957 and was buried in Newport.

Anne-Leslie Owens, Tennessee Historical Society

SEE: COCKE COUNTY; GOVERNMENT; GREAT SMOKY MOUNTAIN NATIONAL PARK; SPANISH-AMERICAN WAR; TEMPERANCE

HOPE, JOHN (1868–1936), educator and university president, noted for his ability to impart encouragement and stimulation to his students, began his distinguished academic career in Tennessee during the racially turbulent 1890s. John Hope was born in Augusta, Georgia, in 1868, into a prosperous family headed by James and Mary Frances Hope. The oldest child, he received his early education in area schools under the tutelage of teachers and community leaders such as William Jefferson White, George Williams Walker, and Lucy Laney. He went from Augusta to Worcester Academy in Worcester, Massachusetts, and from there to Brown University in Providence, Rhode Island, where he graduated Phi Beta Kappa in 1894.

Hope then joined the faculty of Roger Williams University in Nashville. At Roger Williams, he taught natural science, Latin, and Greek, and volunteered as football coach. He also spoke out for African-American rights beyond the vision then prevailing among black leaders like Booker T. Washington. At a speech in Nashville in 1896, Hope remarked: "Let us not fool ourselves nor be fooled by others. If we cannot do what other freemen do, then we are not free. Yes, my friends, I want equality. Nothing less. I want all that my God-given powers will enable me to get, then why not equality?."[1] In late 1897 he married Lugenia Burns from Chicago, Illinois. The Hopes had two children, Edward and John, Jr.

In 1898 he took a position at Atlanta Baptist College, now Morehouse College, and the remainder of his career would be based in Atlanta. He continued his teaching and coaching, and became increasingly involved in community issues. He was active in the Niagara Movement that led to the founding of the National Association for the Advancement of Colored People (NAACP), wrote newspaper articles, and gave speeches on a broad array of topics. In 1906 John Hope became the first African-American president of Morehouse College. He was awarded many prizes and honors for his accomplishments, including the Harmon Award in Education in 1929, and honorary degrees from Bates College, Brown, Bucknell, Howard, and McMaster universities. He served as president of the Association for the Study of Negro Life and History, a board member of the National Council of the YMCA, and during World War I, as special secretary of the YMCA in France. He was awarded the Spingarn Medal from the NAACP after his death in 1936.

Dorothy Granberry, Tennessee State University

CITATION:

(1) Richard Couto, "Race Relations and Tennessee Centennials," *Tennessee Historical Quarterly* 54(1996): 182.

SEE: CIVIL RIGHTS MOVEMENT; ROGER WILLIAMS UNIVERSITY

HOPE, THOMAS (ca.1757–1820), one of Tennessee's earliest and finest master carpenters and cabinetmakers, was born in England circa 1757. By 1788 Hope was in Charleston, South Carolina, where his reputation spread to the part of the western North Carolina frontier that would become Tennessee. Hope arrived in Knoxville on the eve of statehood and quickly acquired his first commission. Francis Alexander Ramsey enlisted the master carpenter to design, build, and furnish his new marble and limestone home at Swan Pond in east Knox County. Ramsey House was built between 1795 and 1797.

Hope's reputation as the skilled and versatile "house carpenter and joiner" grew following his success with Ramsey House. At least three more Knox County projects followed: Charles McClung's State's View, built about 1805; the Kain plantation's Trafalgar, built from 1806 to 1807; and Joseph Churchill Strong's Knoxville house, built in 1814. Hope's final work, Frederick Augustus Ross's Rotherwood in Sullivan County, was a work in progress at the time of his death in 1820. Architectural historian James Patrick evaluated Hope's work as some of the region's best early domestic architecture.

In addition to his design and construction of remarkable houses, Hope also built the furnishings and carved the interior and exterior details. Like many carpenters of the period, Hope discovered that his talents in carving and furniture making pleased his frontier clients and gave his services broader appeal.

The surviving examples of Hope's work in Knox County—Ramsey House and State's View—as well as the existing pieces of his furniture testify to the craftsman's skilled hand and eye, as well as his appreciation of contemporary design principles. Like many master carpenters of the period, Hope often used his copy of the *Builder's Golden Rule* pattern book, but endowed his creations with his own unique style and quality. His preference in style leaned toward Georgian, rather than the popular Federal style, but he always found a way to bring the two styles together, while incorporating the needs and preferences of his clients.

In addition to his architectural legacy, Hope contributed to the professional development of the carpentry trade in Knoxville. In 1801 Hope and four other Knoxville carpenters founded a carpenters' guild, which established standard prices for such items as framing, weatherboarding, doors, detailing, and stairs. Hope's reputation, derived from his experience in England, Charleston, and East Tennessee, gave leadership and focus to the growing community of skilled craftspeople, as well as providing a model for future carpenters and cabinetmakers.

Lisa N. Oakley, East Tennessee Historical Society

SEE: FURNITURE AND CABINETMAKERS; RAMSEY HOUSE

HORN, STANLEY F. (1889–1980), historian, businessman, and editor, was born at Neeley's Bend in Davidson County, on a farm that had been in his family since the eighteenth century. Horn's mother instilled in him an interest in history, as she read to him and his brother from Sir Walter Scott, Shakespeare, and other classics. At Nashville's Hume Fogg High School, Horn's work on the school newspaper and in the literary club stimulated his interest in writing. When he graduated in 1906, Horn was accepted for admission to Vanderbilt University, but since neither he nor his family could afford the $100 tuition, he took a job with the Cumberland Telephone Company.

In late 1908 Horn joined the *Southern Lumberman,* a young, but important trade paper. His association with this paper continued for the next 72 years, 63 of those as editor, except for a brief period in 1914 as an editorial writer with the *Philadelphia Evening Ledger.* Under Horn's direction, the *Southern Lumberman* became the voice of the lumber business in the South. Horn became a major advocate of such progressive changes as reforestation and sustained yield management.

Increasingly, Horn turned his attention to state and Civil War history. From a lifelong admiration of Robert E. Lee came Horn's first book, *Boy's Life of Robert E. Lee,* which was published in 1935 by Harper's. In 1938 he published *The Hermitage: Home of Old Hickory* and *Invisible Empire: The Story of the Ku Klux Klan* in 1939. In 1941 Horn's classic, *The Army of Tennessee: A Military History,* was published in response to a recognized dearth of collected information on the topic. It became the standard history for the Western Theater and the Army of Tennessee. Six years later, he published *Gallant Rebel: The Famous Cruise of the CSS Shenandoah,* and in 1949 *The Robert E. Lee Reader* appeared, a skillfully prepared "mosaic portrait" of General Lee. In 1956 Horn wrote *The Decisive Battle of Nashville,* which covered Hood's campaign of 1864, and the Battle of Nashville; it soon became the definitive work on the latter. As a feature of Tennessee's Civil War Centennial observance, Horn compiled and edited *Tennessee's War, 1861–1865,*

a compendium of contemporary writings and speeches from civilians, soldiers, and politicians. In all, Horn wrote and published nine books dealing with the Civil War, while at the same time, overseeing his editorial and business enterprises.

Horn was the recipient of many awards and honors, including the Building Journalism Award of the National Lumber Manufacturers Association. He was honored by the University of Tennessee at Chattanooga with an honorary doctorate of literature degree. Vanderbilt University made him an honorary member of its Alpha Chapter of Phi Beta Kappa, the only person so elected who did not attend the university. He was an honorary member of the Chicago Civil War Roundtable, which had selected him as the recipient of the special Nevins-Freeman Award before his death in 1980.

A proud Tennessean, Horn delved deeply into the state's history, knew every detail, and could speak on any aspect of it. He was a life member of the Tennessee Historical Society, serving as president from 1942 until 1953, and again from 1961 to 1965. He served as chairman of the Tennessee Civil War Commission from 1961 to 1965. When he retired from the Tennessee Historical Commission, the governor appointed him State Historian.

Horn was a renowned cultivator of irises and an accredited judge of the American Iris Association. He took an active role in the preservation of historical homes and sites and contributed to the survival of several important landmarks in Tennessee, including the old City Cemetery and the Carter House at Franklin.

Horn's personal library was one of the finest and largest historical libraries in the South. After his accidental death in 1980, his collection was located in the Heard Library at Vanderbilt University.

Harris D. Riley, Jr., Vanderbilt University Medical Center

SEE: CARTER HOUSE; TENNESSEE HISTORICAL COMMISSION; TENNESSEE HISTORICAL SOCIETY

HORSERACING TRACKS, EARLY. Long before Tennessee became famous for the Tennessee Walking Horse in the mid-1900s, the state was known throughout the country as the center for thoroughbred horses. For most of the nineteenth century, Tennessee, not Kentucky, was acknowledged as the center of horse breeding and horse racing in the United States, with Sumner County supplying the majority of southern race horses.

In 1804 the first official horse race in Tennessee was held in Gallatin. Andrew and Rachel Jackson attended the race, in which Jackson ran his horse Indian Queen against Dr. R. D. Barry's horse Polly Medley. Although Jackson's horse lost the race, he became known as the leading breeder and racer in the state. He soon purchased a famous Virginia thoroughbred, Truxton, and Greyhound, a horse which had previously beaten both Indian Queen and Truxton.

Jackson purchased an interest in one of Tennessee's most important racetracks in 1805, at Clover Bottom. By 1807 Clover Bottom, Gallatin, and Nashville each had a Jockey Club. Jackson's horses ran several races at Clover Bottom before he sold most of his horses in 1816. After becoming president, Jackson took three horses to Washington to race them there. He was the last president to race horses in the nation's capital.

By 1839 there were at least ten established race tracks in Tennessee, and over 20 organized Jockey Clubs, including clubs at Bean Station, Clarksville, McMinnville, Winchester, Murfreesboro, Franklin, Mount Pleasant, Shelbyville, Nashville, Paris, Jackson, Bolivar, and Memphis. Horse racing attracted many famous Tennesseans, including Jackson, Felix Zollicoffer, Reverend Hardy Cryer, William Carroll, Frank McGavock, Andrew Jackson Donelson, Stockly Donelson, Montgomery Bell, and Balie Peyton, who owned one of the premier horse farms in Sumner County. In 1839 William Giles Harding placed Belle Meade at the center of the horseracing region and noted the necessity of investing in blood stock in order to remain fashionable. Belle Meade remained a famous stud farm from the 1830s to the turn of the century, and Harding became president of the Nashville Jockey Club in 1856.

From 1828 to 1886, the Nashville race track, known as the Burns Island track, was located near Second Avenue North and Van Buren, along the Cumberland River. On October 16, 1843, the Peyton Stakes, sponsored by Balie Peyton, was run at this track. With a purse of $35,000, the Peyton Stakes was the richest race run anywhere in the world to that point. The winner, Peytona, was owned by Thomas Kirkman of Nashville. The Burns Island track and horse racing survived the Civil War, but since the track flooded periodically, it was replaced by West Side Park in 1887.

In 1906 the Tennessee General Assembly passed an anti-betting law, bringing an end to horseracing in Tennessee for many years. Breeding of horses continued, however, and in 1940 the Milky Way Farm near Pulaski had the Kentucky Derby winner, Hallahadion. In 1938 Nashville began construction on a $45,000 steeplechase course in conjunction with the Works Progress Administration-funded Percy Warner Park. The first Iroquois Steeplechase ran there in 1940.

Tara Mitchell Mielnik, Middle Tennessee State University
SUGGESTED READING: James D. Anderson, *Making the American Thoroughbred Especially in Tennessee, 1800–1845* (1916)
SEE: BELLE MEADE PLANTATION; HARDING, WILLIAM G.; IROQUOIS STEEPLECHASE; JACKSON, ANDREW; MILKY WAY FARM

HORTON, HENRY (1866–1934), Governor, was elected with the support of Luke Lea, head of a powerful faction of the Democratic party, and was little more than a front man for the Lea political machine. When Lea's political and financial empire crashed with the stock market in 1929, Horton faced charges of corruption that led to calls for his impeachment.

Born in Alabama in February 1866, Horton graduated from Winchester College in 1888, and attended the University of the South at Sewanee, 1891–1892. He opened a law practice in Marshall County and launched his political career when he ran for school district director. A Prohibition Democrat, Horton served one term in the State House, 1907–1909. He returned to Nashville in 1927, as State Senator, and was chosen to be Speaker of the Senate. The political fortunes of the obscure Marshall County Senator took a dramatic turn when Governor Austin Peay died unexpectedly, and Speaker Horton fulfilled his constitutional duty of finishing out Peay's term.

The inexperienced Horton turned to Luke Lea of Nashville for guidance. Lea, a former U.S. Senator, owned several powerful state newspapers and was a highly successful investor in real estate, banks, and other enterprises throughout the South. Like Horton, Lea entered state politics as a prohibitionist and supported Austin Peay's reorganization of state government and his programs to improve the state's roads and schools. Under Lea's tutelage, Horton implemented Peay's road building program and initiated the state's first eight-month school terms.

Peay's reorganization and rationalization of state government increased efficiency, but it also enlarged the political patronage system and consolidated it under the governor's control. Or, as proved the case during Horton's term of office, under the control of his chief advisor, Luke Lea. Getting and holding a job in state government depended upon the will of Luke Lea. Through the exercise of patronage, Lea emerged as the chief rival to Memphis's Ed "Boss" Crump.

By the late 1920s Lea's political and financial fortunes were closely linked with those of Nashville financier Rogers Caldwell, who built his wealth on the marketing of southern bonds. Lea invested heavily in Caldwell's projects, which included banks, newspapers, and manufacturing establishments. Among his other enterprises, Caldwell owned a company that produced road building materials, Kyrock. Horton allowed the state highway department (run by a Lea ally) to award contracts to Kyrock without competitive bidding. More seriously, Horton placed state funds in Caldwell-owned banks, where they were used to bolster the Caldwell financial empire; the Superintendent of Banks, a former Caldwell employee and Lea appointee, warned Caldwell of imminent state audits.

When Horton ran for re-election in 1928, Kyrock became a symbol of Lea's domination of the candidate. Hill McAlister, the supposed Memphis machine candidate, and Lewis L. Pope, an independent Democrat, opposed Horton, but the governor won re-election with the help of a Caldwell-financed slush fund. Riding high, Lea attacked Crump, threatening to use state patronage to undercut Crump's control of Memphis. Crump and Lea cut a deal: Lea backed out of Memphis and Boss Crump swung his formidable political machine behind Horton in 1930. Horton won his second term easily.

Lea's Caldwell connection brought down both Horton and his advisor. The Caldwell empire was already tottering when the stock market crashed in 1929. Caldwell and Company collapsed only a few days after Horton won the 1930 election, and carried with it banks throughout the South—including the banks in which the state deposited its funds. Almost seven million dollars of public funds disappeared. An investigation by the General Assembly produced charges that Horton had conspired with Lea and Caldwell to let them effectively run certain branches of the state government for their own financial gain, in exchange for Lea's political support. Boss Crump led the charge to impeach Horton. Ironically, the fact that Crump wanted him removed probably saved Horton; many rural legislators feared that a vote to impeach the governor would be seen as a vote for Crump, thus strengthening the Memphis machine. The House voted 58 to 41 against impeaching Horton, and the aging governor was allowed to serve out his term and retire to Marshall County. He died of a probable stroke in 1934.

Jeanette Keith, Bloomsburg University of Pennsylvania
SUGGESTED READING: William J. Majors, *Change and Continuity: Tennessee Politics Since the Civil War* (1986)
SEE: CALDWELL, ROGERS; CRUMP, EDWARD H.; LEA, LUKE; MARSHALL COUNTY; MCALISTER, HILL; PEAY, AUSTIN

HORTON, MYLES FALLS (1905–1990), a founder and director of both the Highlander Folk School and the Highlander Research and Education Center, was a progressive educator whose programs not only contributed significantly to the labor and civil rights movements, but also made him a controversial figure in Tennessee and the South for most of his adult life.

Born in Savannah, Tennessee, in 1905, Horton's lifelong commitment to the use of education for social change began in 1927. While conducting a Bible school in the Cumberland Plateau town of Ozone, Horton found that bringing adults together to develop their own solutions to common concerns was an effective approach to community problems. Searching for a way to act upon this discovery, he completed his undergraduate degree at Cumberland University in 1928, studied under Reinhold Niebuhr at Union Theological Seminary, attended the University of Chicago, and toured the folk schools of Denmark. When Horton returned to Tennessee, he and a Georgian named Don West established the Highlander Folk School near Monteagle in 1932.

During the 1930s and 1940s Horton and his colleagues made Highlander a vital center of labor education in the South. Horton's improvisational teaching style and faith in the working class often marked residence sessions for potential union leaders. In extension programs, he aided striking coal miners, woodcutters, millhands, government relief workers, and union members across the South; in 1937 he joined the staff of what was then called the Committee for Industrial Organization (CIO) and organized one of the first CIO locals in the southern textile industry.

In the late 1940s Horton and the Highlander staff broke with the CIO over its demand that the school compromise its ideological independence and advocacy of interracial unionism. For a time he attempted to promote a farmer-labor coalition in the South, but once again he found that racial discrimination remained a formidable barrier to such efforts. Horton and his colleagues decided to confront the problem and began holding workshops on school desegregation in 1953, nearly a year before the historic *Brown v. Board of Education* decision. Over the next two decades, much of Horton's work was devoted to creating programs that would help empower African-American leaders and groups. During the 1960s, he extended those programs to Appalachia, seeking to build a multiracial coalition pushing for fundamental change in America.

For his outspoken support of union, civil rights, and poor people's organizations Horton endured arrests, threats, violence, and denunciations from industrialists, politicians, and segregationists. Ultimately, the State of Tennessee closed the folk school in 1962. Undaunted, Horton secured a charter for the Highlander Research and Education Center, currently located near New Market.

Married twice, the father of two children, and author of *Long Haul* (1990) and *We Make the Road by Walking* (1990), Horton worked through Highlander to advance his conviction that education could help ordinary people discover their capacity to take action on the issues that concerned them. Both he and the center were nominated for the Nobel Peace Prize in 1982. Horton died in 1990.

John M. Glen, Ball State University
SUGGESTED READING: John M. Glen, *Highlander: No Ordinary School* (1996)
SEE: CIVIL RIGHTS MOVEMENT; HIGHLANDER FOLK SCHOOL; HIGHLANDER RESEARCH AND EDUCATION CENTER; HORTON, ZILPHIA J.; LABOR

HORTON, ZILPHIA J. (1910–1956), activist and artist, was born in Paris, Arkansas, as Zilphia Mae Johnson. A graduate of the College of the Ozarks, she grew up determined to use her musical and dramatic talents on behalf of the southern working class. In January 1935 she attended a labor education workshop at the Highlander Folk School, located near Monteagle, Tennessee. Two months later, she married Myles Horton, one of the founders of the school. Over the next two decades, as a Highlander staff member, Zilphia Horton directed workers' theater productions, junior union camps, and various community programs; organized union locals; and led singing at workshops, picket lines, union meetings, and fundraising concerts. Though disillusioned with the post-World War II retrenchment of organized labor, she nevertheless worked to revive the Farmers' Union in the South. In the 1950s she helped initiate Highlander's Citizenship School voter education project on the South Carolina Sea Islands and was instrumental in transforming "We Shall Overcome," originally a gospel hymn, into a civil rights anthem.

Sensitive to her roles as activist, artist, spouse, and the mother of two children, Horton sought to establish a balance in her life between independence and dependence, individualism and collective action, traditional gender expectations and creativity. Her efforts to achieve that balance was an experience shared by women at Highlander for most of its history. Horton died of uremic poisoning in 1956.

John M. Glen, Ball State University

SEE: CARAWAN, GUY; CIVIL RIGHTS MOVEMENT; HIGH-
LANDER FOLK SCHOOL; HORTON, MYLES; LABOR

HOUK, LEONIDAS CAMPBELL (1836–1891), congressman and judge, was born near Boyds Creek, Sevier County. The death of his father in 1839 left him and his mother impoverished. His formal education consisted of only a few months at a country school; thereafter, he educated himself through diligent reading. As a youth he earned a living as a cabinetmaker and Methodist preacher, while studying law at night. In 1859 he was admitted to the Tennessee bar and opened an office in Clinton. A Union loyalist at the outbreak of the Civil War and member of the Union convention in East Tennessee in 1861, Houk organized the First Tennessee Infantry, which functioned as a Union army in Kentucky. He served as a private, lieutenant, and quartermaster; in 1862 he was colonel of the Third Regiment, Tennessee Volunteer Infantry. Poor health forced him to leave military service in 1863, and he spent the next two years writing pro-Union articles for the press and following military activities. A presidential elector in 1864 for the Lincoln-Johnson ticket, he participated in the state constitutional convention in 1865 to reorganize Tennessee's postwar government. There he took a moderate stand on issues and won recognition for his ability.

From 1866 to 1870 Houk served as circuit judge of the state's 17th judicial district. In this capacity, he favored equal rights for former Confederates and refused to hear cases of treason, contending that Tennessee had ceased to exist as a state when it left the Union in 1861. Despite his moderation in some cases, he issued decidedly partisan opinions in others. After resigning his judgeship, Houk practiced law in Knoxville with Henry R. Gibson, who later founded the *Knoxville Republican,* edited the *Knoxville Daily Chronicle,* represented his district in the state legislature, and served in Congress. Gibson & Houk became one of the most prominent law firms in East Tennessee. Both men also remained politically active.

Houk was devoted to the Republican party. He loyally supported Ulysses S. Grant for president in 1868 and 1872, even favoring him as a Stalwart for a third nomination in 1880. Houk served as a presidential elector in 1872 and 1876; he was a delegate to virtually every national Republican convention in the postwar years. A member of the Southern Claims Commission in 1873, he served in the Tennessee House from 1873 to 1875. There he sponsored a state school law and chaired the ways and means committee.

In 1878 Houk won election to the U.S. House of Representatives, where he remained until his death. A nationalist Republican who followed party doctrine, Houk was a southern representative who showed more concern for the plight of poor farmers and agricultural depressions than many of his northern urban Republican colleagues.

Houk married twice. In 1858 he married Elizabeth M. Smith, by whom he had eight children. After his first wife's death in 1879, he married Mary Belle Von Rosen in Baltimore in 1880. They had one daughter. Houk died in Knoxville on May 25, 1891, and was buried in Old Gray Cemetery. Houk's papers are in McClung Historical Collection, Lawson McGhee Library, Knox County Public Library, Knoxville.

Leonard Schlup, Akron, Ohio

SUGGESTED READING: Verton M. Queener, "The East Tennessee Republicans in State and Nation, 1870–1900," *Tennessee Historical Quarterly* 2(1943): 99–128

SEE: KNOXVILLE; RECONSTRUCTION

HOUSES, EARLY VERNACULAR PLANS. For early houses in Tennessee, three house plans were common: the central passage plan, the hall-parlor plan, and the Penn-plan. The central passage plan, also called an I-house by cultural geographers, is a house with two rooms on either side of a passage, usually built to two stories. When the central passage house is two rooms deep, it is often called a Georgian plan. Although they are similar, scholars believe that the I-house and the Georgian-plan house developed for very different reasons that reflect social attitudes. Moreover, a great deal of experimentation in house forms occurred around 1800 to produce a large variety of house types. The result of this experimentation was a decided preference for a two-story, two-room house divided by a central passage.

Early examples of central passage houses in Tennessee date from the 1790s, but this house type did not become popular until the second quarter of the nineteenth century, when it finally began to replace the hall and parlor plan. Two-story central passage houses were often framed, but many brick and stone examples survive.

Scholars once believed the passage to be a response to the southern climate, where large central spaces running the depth of the house were built to catch cool summer breezes. This did not explain, however, the popularity of the I-house in other areas of the country. Scholars of eighteenth century Virginia agree that the gentry introduced the passage as a means of enforcing their own notions of social hierarchy. The passage, which usually contained a staircase, served as a circulation space. It created a buffer between the public and private spaces of the interior and allowed access to rooms without having to pass through other rooms.

Central passage houses often had a wing or 'ell' built perpendicular to the main house giving the entire plan the appearance of an L or T in shape. These wings often contained kitchens and other service rooms. Scholars continue to investigate the significance of these ells, but it appears they were built in an effort to accommodate the presence of slaves as they served the household. The ell allowed the master to observe the coming and going of slaves even as he maintained a segregation and hierarchy of both space and race. Although these theories of the central passage and ell might apply to some regions of the South, scholars have yet to systematically study this house type in Tennessee, especially in East Tennessee where fewer slaves were held.

Some scholars identified minor aesthetic developments with the appearance of the central passage in Tennessee. For example, the central passage house usually has the placement of the chimney on the outside of the gable wall in houses built of brick or stone. During the eighteenth and early nineteenth centuries, chimneys were placed inside the gable walls of brick and stone houses, creating recesses which received closets or stairs. As early as 1797, however, some builders preferred outside chimneys. In general, the central passage house is associated with newfound wealth based on a growing antebellum economy and a desire on the owner's part to present a facade to the world that announced his success and place in society.

"Hall and parlor" is the modern term architectural historians use to describe a house that was one room deep and two rooms wide. The plan derives from medieval Welch and English types and was common in seventeenth and eighteenth century Virginia. Settlers moving down the Shenandoah Valley and into the Tennessee Valley brought this house type with them and reproduced it with a few variations in frame, brick, stone, and even log construction. The hall was the larger of the two rooms and was the center of household activity. It always had a fireplace in the gable end, and it provided a circulation space for sitting and eating. Often the head of household slept in the hall. A stair, usually enclosed and often located in one of the corners next to the fireplace, gave access to a loft used for sleeping. A partition often divided the loft into two sleeping areas corresponding to the hall and chamber below. The parlor, or chamber as it was more often called in the eighteenth century South, was more private and used primarily for sleeping. The parlor often had a fireplace and door to the outside on the gable end.

In Virginia, the hall-and-parlor plan generally gave way to the central passage plan during the late eighteenth century, and scholars agree that the introduction of this central passage signaled the desire of Virginians to regulate more closely visitors' access to their domestic spaces. In Tennessee, however, the hall-parlor plan was remarkably persistent through time, and surviving examples of it date from as late as the 1820s. During the eighteenth century the facade of the hall-parlor plan was expressed as three asymmetrical bays in a window-door-window arrangement. As early as 1797 John Hays at Antioch arranged the three bays of his substantial brick house symmetrically, giving the illusion that the interior had a central passage. The symmetrical fenestration on Hays's hall and parlor house might be an attempt to present a fashionable face to the neighbors. Should those neighbors visit Hays, however, they would enter directly into his domestic living space. Hays's juxtaposition of a symmetrical facade and traditional, asymmetrical room arrangement shows how the house embodied Hays's notions of his place in Middle Tennessee society. Clearly Hays sought to portray himself as a fashionable and even discriminating man of taste. His ideas of spatial hierarchy, however, differed little from those of his neighbors, many of whom probably built log houses of the same type.

The Penn-plan is another example of house types represented in Tennessee's architectural history. The plan is named for the room arrangement that William Penn recommended to Quaker immigrants to Pennsylvania in 1670. Penn's explicit instruction for a house 30 feet long and 18 feet wide, partitioned near the middle and at the end of the house, describes a number of houses still extant in East Tennessee, though historians have not found conclusive documentary evidence linking this house type to Penn's ideal. Nevertheless, the Penn-plan is well represented among the many types that settlers brought with them in the eighteenth and early nineteenth centuries.

The Penn-plan is a variation on the hall-and-parlor plan in which the smaller of the two rooms is divided by a partition parallel to the long wall. the two smaller rooms normally share a chimney and have fireplaces set diagonally in the corner of each room. Most surviving examples of the Penn-plan are two stories accessed by stairs located next to the fireplace in the corner of the hall. The house is usually built of stone and banked into a hill so that one of the long facades is three stories. Eighteenth-century examples of the Penn-plan have kitchens located in the basement, a practice common in Pennsylvania, where the plan originated.

The earliest house of this type found thus far is the stone house Thomas Embree built south of Jonesborough ca. 1790. As late as 1830, however, Aaron Hoffman built a frame Penn-plan house near present-day Kingsport. These later examples of the Penn-plan show a preference for removing the kitchen from the house proper, building it perpendicular to the rear and connecting it to the house by an open passage. This segregation of service areas follows the trend of most southern builders, who sought to define more clearly the spatial limits of white and black members in their households and might indicate that Hoffman held slaves. Historians need to study further the development and demise of the Penn-plan to determine its ultimate significance within the social landscape of Tennessee.

Clifton Coxe Ellis, University of Virginia

SEE: ARCHITECTURE, VERNACULAR DOMESTIC; BOWEN-CAMPBELL HOUSE; CARTER MANSION; CRAGFONT; EMBREE, ELIHU; HOPE, THOMAS; NETHERLAND INN; RAMSEY HOUSE; ROGANA

HOUSES, SHOTGUN. Of all historical housing forms found in Tennessee, the shotgun house is perhaps the least understood and most burdened with confusion and misconceptions. The shotgun sometimes represented the worst evidence of the treatment of the impoverished and, therefore, was viewed as simply a small house that afforded its occupants the first step in upward economic and social mobility.

Simply defined, the shotgun is a narrow house, one room wide and at least three rooms deep, oriented with its gable end facing the street. The prototypical shotgun has only one window and a door on its front facade, and it is typically 12 feet wide. The floor plan of the shotgun is always laid out with no hallway separating the rooms, a feature which many legends maintain gave the shotgun its name: i.e., that a shotgun could be fired through the front door, and its pellets would emerge from the rear of the house without hitting an interior wall.

In spite of nearly two generations of treatment by scholars of vernacular architecture, the origin of the shotgun house is not clearly understood. In 1968 Henry Glassie suggested that the shotgun was originally an African house plan re-established in Haiti by colonial era slaves. Later work by John M. Vlach followed this hypothesis. Vlach argued that migrating Haitian freedmen brought the shotgun with them to New Orleans after the Haitian Revolution of 1791. The house type spread from New Orleans with the out-migration of the Haitians in the 1820s and 1830s.

The earliest known shotgun houses in New Orleans and the surrounding area, however, date from the 1840s. A survey of other state historic preservation offices in southern coastal states reveals no evidence of earlier extant examples, nor is there archaeological evidence of the shotgun house in the South before the 1840s.

Architectural historians and cultural geographers generally agree, however, on several points related to the shotgun houses. The shotgun is primarily an urban house type, despite the common misconception that associates it with rural settings. The earliest shotguns are found in cities, and the form migrated from the city to small towns and rural communities late in the nineteenth century. Further, there appears to be no specific connection between the shotgun house and the architecture of slavery. Finally, there are three accepted and identifiable periods of shotgun house construction.

The earliest extant shotguns in the South date from the 1840s and 1850s and can be found in New Orleans and parts of Alabama, although shotguns dating from the late 1830s are known to exist in the upper Ohio River Valley in the area between Louisville and Cincinnati. Shotguns built during this period were used by owner-occupants and by tenants, depending upon location and individual situations.

The second wave occurred in the late 1860s and 1870s, in what may be considered the "flowering" of the shotgun house. This was when the shotgun was introduced to Tennessee. In New Orleans, Memphis, and Louisville, many shotguns built by owner-occupants featured fanciful Italianate architectural detailing. The Greenlaw and Vance-Ponotoc areas of Memphis still contain some of these early frame shotguns, although they are disappearing rapidly. Documentary evidence from New Orleans shows that millwork companies there were prefabricating highly decorated shotguns; local companies probably produced the decorated shotguns of Memphis.

The third wave of construction of the shotgun houses began in the 1880s and continued until World

War II, with the majority of southern shotguns built
in this period. Like the rest of the South, most Tennessee cities and towns included at least a small
cluster of shotgun houses, built by developers as
rental units to accommodate the growing demand
for working-class housing. This wave of construction coincided with the industrial growth of the
urban South and the concurrent surge of rural-to-
urban migration that resulted from farm mechanization. These rental shotguns for the working class
featured little ornamentation. Although the neighborhoods of shotguns in Memphis and other Tennessee towns are commonly thought to have served
African-American tenants, research into areas such
as the Delmar-Lema neighborhood of Memphis
shows that they were not segregated enclaves, but
originally places where African Americans and
whites of the working class lived side by side. Racial
separation occurred in the decade following World
War I, perhaps as the production of affordable housing caught up to white demands. With more limited
opportunities for economic and political mobility,
African Americans remained behind in the only
housing available to them.

A single, definitive source for the origin of the
shotgun may never be identified. Instead, it may be
that the constraints of lot sizes and density in city and
town environments influenced the development of
the shotgun more than any cultural factor. The earliest shotguns appeared in high density residential
areas and stood on narrow lots little more than 20 feet
wide. The shotgun simply may have been the largest
free-standing house that could be built under the constraints of space and budget.

If that is the case, it is ironic, then, that present
real estate forces exert a significant influence on the
preservation of the shotgun house in Tennessee.
While a cluster of shotguns near downtown Jackson,
Tennessee, is seen as slum housing, across town in
the industrial suburb of Bemis, owners and the community highly prize their shotgun houses. The same
is true in other Tennessee towns, including Memphis, where shotgun neighborhoods are being
demolished at the same time that shotguns in other
areas sell readily for middle class housing. Perhaps,
as with all real estate, the perception of value is
shaped more by location than by historical and architectural association.

John Linn Hopkins and Marsha R. Oates, Memphis

HOUSES, VERNACULAR LOG TYPES. The log
house is perhaps the most enduring architectural icon
associated with Tennessee. Scholars continue to
debate how the knowledge of log construction was
diffused through the cultural patterns of the colonial
South, but it is generally agreed that Scandinavian
settlers first introduced log construction into the

Delaware Valley during the 1630s. German settlers
brought their own forms of log technology when they
arrived in Pennsylvania in the early eighteenth century. Anglo-Americans and the Scots-Irish adopted
log construction as they moved south and west
during the middle and late eighteenth century. These
settlers from the British Isles, however, used very different floor plans in adapting log construction to their
needs, producing the now familiar log building
types. Although these types are most commonly
found in log construction, they were also built in
frame, brick, and stone.

The single pen is the basic log house. To make a
single pen, builders join four walls by cutting or
notching the log ends in such a way that they inter-
lock when laid horizontally. There are variations on
these notches, but the most common are the v-notch,
the full-dovetail, and the half-dovetail. Henry Glassie
identified two basic shapes of single pen structures,
the square and the rectangle. The square single pen
derives from British tradition and has a gable roof
parallel to the front with an end chimney at one of
the gable ends and single door on the front. The rectangle pen is Scots-Irish in origin and also has a gable
roof parallel to the front with an end chimney in one
of the gables. The rectangle pen, however, has both a
front and back door and, usually, a window to one
side of the front door. John Morgan found the rectangle to be the most common shape in his study of log
houses in East Tennessee. These pens had dimensions
ranging between 18 by 13 feet and 36 by 18 feet. Most
commonly, they had one-and-a-half stories, but a few
were one story, and fewer still had two stories. In
some cases, the first story was divided into rooms by
a partition made of boards laid vertically or horizontally. Limestone is easily available in much of the
Upland South and builders in Morgan's study usually chose this stone for their chimneys, although
they sometimes built chimneys of brick and, in a few
surviving examples, of sticks and mud.

The saddlebag-type house, so-called because it
looks like a saddlebag draped over a house, is made
by adding another pen to the chimney gable of an
existing pen. The gap on either side of the chimney is
used as a passage or filled by closets and stairs to the
loft above. The roof line might be continuous, or it
might be of different heights reflecting the addition.

The dogtrot is made by adding another pen opposite the chimney gable of an existing pen and leaving
an open passage between the two. The two pens and
passage are covered by a continuous gable roof and
the new pen has a chimney on the gable end opposite the passage. The new pen usually has a door
opening onto the passage, but it might have only a
door opening on the front, or both. Dogtrots were
more often built in one building campaign, however,
with doors to both pens opening onto the passage.

Morgan identifies this type primarily in southeast and Middle Tennessee.

The Cumberland house, named for the Cumberland Plateau where this type is most often found, is a dogtrot without the passage. Like the old pen, the new pen has a door on the front wall and possibly a new door cut to connect the two pens. A continuous roof covers both pens and the new pen usually has a chimney opposite that of the old pen.

Single pen construction lends itself to the building of additions. Some telltale signs of an addition are an interrupted roof line, a different notch, a different species of tree used to make the logs, different dimensions, or a different shape of the new pen. It was not unusual, however, for a builder to put up a multi-pen dwelling in one building campaign. Morgan found at least one-third of the multi-pen dwellings in his study to be the result of one building campaign. The question then arises whether the different types developed because of the additive nature of pen construction or whether the types were always recognized, thus making additions conform to accepted types.

Log houses remained popular through the nineteenth century and even into the twentieth century. Although the house type endured over this period, construction techniques and cultural attitudes changed dramatically. Log houses of the late nineteenth and early twentieth centuries are, generally, inferior in their construction and finish. The logs are usually not hewn and the notches not carefully fitted. This change in attitude is a result of the way people viewed their relationship with a particular place. As the economy of Tennessee diversified and as more people took employment outside the home and away from the farm, the home lost its role as the basic economic unit. Time once devoted to the careful hewing and notching of logs for a house was now spent in wage work at factories or mines. Log construction became a temporary solution to housing needs, a prelude to the new balloon-frame house technology that wages could buy. Cultural attitudes toward log construction changed accordingly. People began to associate log construction with inferior materials and craftsmanship and sought to disguise their log houses by cladding them in weatherboards or other types of siding. The significance of log houses will be better understood as scholars study such social evolutions in their local context.

Clifton Coxe Ellis, University of Virginia

SUGGESTED READINGS: Terry G. Jordan, *American Log Buildings: An Old World Heritage* (1985); Charles E. Martin, *Hollybush: Folk Buildings and Social Change* (1984); John Morgan, *The Log House in East Tennessee* (1990); James Patrick, *Architecture in Tennessee, 1768–1897* (1981); Dell Upton and J. Michael Vlach, eds., *Common Places: Readings in American Vernacular Architecture* (1986)

SEE: ARCHITECTURE, VERNACULAR DOMESTIC; CADES COVE; LOG CONSTRUCTION; MUSEUM OF APPALACHIA

HOUSTON COUNTY was established by an act of the Tennessee legislature on January 21, 1871, and named for Sam Houston, Governor of Tennessee and hero of Texas. The people voted to establish the new county in 1871 because they were too far from their respective court houses in Dickson, Humphreys, and Stewart counties to properly conduct business. Even after Houston County formed, however, a kindred social, historical, and economic relationship remained between Houston and these parent counties.

Wells, Guise's, and Yellow creeks, of present Houston County, attracted many settlers in the late eighteenth century. After Chickasaw land cessions, many residents were ready to cross the Tennessee ridge to divide and claim lands on White Oak, Cane, and Hurricane creeks. There they had downhill access to either the Cumberland or Tennessee rivers for shipment of natural and manufactured products such as whiskey, tobacco, cotton, Indian hemp, and timber. Settlers also shipped iron products made at local forges on Well's Creek, Yellow Creek, and Hurricane Creek; an 1806 iron furnace on Well's Creek is the first mentioned in the area. A type of clay suitable for fire brick for furnaces was found on what is now Booster branch of Well's Creek (Byron Forge Creek), and the fire brick no longer had to be imported.

In the 1850s the railroad came to Houston County. The Clarksville and Louisville Railroad Company, chartered in 1852, began the section from Guthrie to Paris, and the Memphis and Ohio Railroad Company, chartered 1852, began the section from Memphis to Paris. While crews were blasting the railroad bed in the 1850s, a rock strata was found at an angle rather than the typical flat formation. State Geologist James Safford studied and reported the find, which has received extensive analysis since. Safford named the site Well's Creek Basin. This place is circular and about two miles in diameter; it was core-drilled several miles deep to determine if its origin was volcanic or meteoric. The latest geological opinion defines it as meteoric.

By 1857 the Memphis, Clarksville and Louisville Railroad had been built from Guthrie to near the Tennessee ridge, where a depot was built at a village later known as Erin Station, located about one-half mile east of the present town of Erin. Further construction stalled because of slides in the cuts of the trestle west of Tennessee Ridge, and the railroad to Paris was not completed until April 1861. Initially a ferry crossed the Tennessee River, until the bridge was completed in November 1861.

The Civil War began just as the bridge was completed. Confederate General Simon Buckner took charge of the bridge and railroad to move southern troops and supplies. When the Union army captured the area, Federal soldiers and supplies traveled in the opposite direction. In the course of the war, the bridge was damaged and rebuilt several times.

After the war, repairs to the railroad system helped launch an industrial boom. Danville became a rail and river port, moving farm products from the surrounding area and northern Alabama. Marketable products from Alabama arrived by steamboat and were reloaded at Danville. A spur line extended from Danville to Stribling and the LaGrange iron furnace. McKinnon built coke ovens to fuel the iron furnaces, and Stewart launched its lime industry, which spawned stave mills for making barrels to hold the lime. Tennessee Ridge acquired a railroad depot and a spur line to Carlisle and Bear Springs furnaces. Erin became a lime and timber manufacturing center, and Cumberland City (originally in Houston County) was a rail and river port for shipping farm products from the areas of Well's, Guise's, and Yellow creeks.

Arlington was the first seat of government in Houston County. Its location on the grade of the Tennessee ridge prevented trains from stopping there. Instead, they halted at the nearby village of Erin, near the spot where later the county seat was relocated. A favored legend has it that the Irish living there had a "wee too much to drink" and decided the area resembled their beloved Ireland, thus naming it Erin. Today, Erin celebrates its ethnic heritage with an annual Irish festival. A week of activities concludes with a parade on the third Saturday in March.

Recreation is a growth industry in Houston County. Erin features a two-mile greenbelt walking trail, a park, and the L&N Railroad Memorial Pavilion along an abandoned stretch of the former L&N Railroad. The National Guard Armory at Tennessee Ridge offers ball fields, tennis courts, and a walking trail. There are three boat launching facilities on the Tennessee River, with nearby motels.

The timber industry remains a vibrant part of the county economy with five large mills and processing plants. Trinity Hospital was the first hospital built from the ground up by Hospital Corporation of America (HCA). The county has a state-of-the-art nursing home with adjoining assisted-living apartments. Southern Gage found Houston County in the 1950s, and now many manufacturing companies call the county home. Stewart-Houston Industrial Park contains three manufacturing facilities, with four additional facilities in the planning stages. Erin's water plant, which supplies the county, was named number one water plant in Tennessee in 1996. Violent crime is a rarity, and churches of most faiths are spread throughout the county. Born into a history of industrial success, the progress of Houston County is as rich as the surrounding hills.

Charles Lovelady and Nina Finley, Erin

SEE: COLUMBIA/HCA HEALTHCARE CORPORATION; INDUSTRY; RAILROADS; SAFFORD, JAMES; TENNESSEE RIVER

HOUSTON, SAM (1793–1863), Governor and Texas hero, was born to Samuel and Elizabeth Paxton Houston in 1793, near Lexington, Virginia, and raised with five brothers and three sisters. His father, a militia colonel, died in 1806. The following year, his mother led her family west, settling near Maryville, the seat of Blount County, Tennessee. Never comfortable with his family, the all-but-unschooled, hulking teenager frequently wandered away and lived with a band of Cherokees for long periods. The leader, Oo-Loo-Te-Ka, became a surrogate father, teaching Houston the language and ways of the Cherokees.

Once, while living in Maryville, Houston opened and taught in a school, but becoming bored, he joined the army in 1813. He rose swiftly from raw recruit to become an officer. Serving in the Seventh Infantry, he participated in Andrew Jackson's Creek Indian campaign and received two severe wounds at the Battle of Horseshoe Bend in 1814. His conspicuous bravery brought him to the attention of Jackson, who posted him to his regional headquarters near Nashville after the war. There, Houston became enmeshed in politics as a member of Jackson's famous "Tennessee Junto," a powerful political machine devoted to furthering the General's career.

In 1817 Houston won appointment as sub-agent to the Eastern Cherokees, but ran afoul of Secretary of War John C. Calhoun, who became a lifelong enemy. Houston quit the army in 1819 to study law in Nashville. He opened his practice in Lebanon to be close to Jackson. That same year he was named Adjutant General of the Tennessee Militia, and was soon Attorney General for Davidson County.

With heavy support from Jackson and his machine, Houston won election to the U.S. House of Representatives, using his position to champion his mentor's bid for the presidency. After serving a second term, he successfully ran for governor in 1827.

At age 41 Governor Sam Houston stood on the brink of a national career, but his own character flaws undermined his chances. Over the years Houston acquired a legendary drinking problem; public drunkenness virtually became his trademark and caused growing concern among his admirers. While campaigning for a second gubernatorial term, Houston married Eliza Allen of Gallatin after a scandalously brief courtship. When this daughter of an "old," politically powerful Tennessee family left him after less than 80 days, Houston's future in the state became bleak.

Humiliated, he resigned the governorship and fled the state in disguise to join his Cherokee friends, by then resettled in "Indian Territory" in today's Oklahoma. There, near the border with Mexican

Texas, Houston took an Indian bride, became a trader and Cherokee citizen, drank, and fantasized about freeing Texas and becoming a millionaire. Fronting for New York financiers engaged in Texas land speculation, Houston crossed the Sabine River and settled in Texas in late 1832. He established a law practice in Nacogdoches, dabbled in politics, and plotted rebellion against Mexico.

When tensions between Mexico and the largely Anglo-Saxon settlers of Texas boiled over in 1835, the settlers made Houston one of their military leaders, with the rank of major general. After the Texans suffered defeats at the Alamo and Goliad, however, Houston retreated to restore the fighting ability of his "army" before finally turning to attack a large Mexican force at San Jacinto on April 21, 1836. Painfully wounded, the Texas general led his outnumbered forces to victory. With the U.S. Congress unwilling to admit Texas as a state, the voters overwhelmingly elected him President of the Republic of Texas.

Houston did not seek immediate re-election. He served in the Texas Congress and, in 1840, married Margaret Lea of Marion, Alabama, with whom he had eight children. Re-elected president in 1841, he spent his second term working to achieve annexation to the United States, which occurred in 1845.

In 1846, he won election to the U.S. Senate, where he served until 1858, making a name for himself as a strong Unionist, a promoter of the transcontinental railroad, and a critic of the army. He campaigned (though somewhat tepidly) for the presidency in 1852, 1856, and 1860.

Texas secessionists made it clear in the late 1850s that they could and would prevent a third senatorial term for Houston. He returned to Texas and traded on his tremendous popularity to win the governorship in 1859. Governor Houston worked to prevent Texas secession. He even counseled that if Texas left the Union, it should revert to the status of independent republic rather than join the Confederacy, which he correctly foresaw as leading to war. To his surprise and dismay, most Texans clamored for secession and the Confederacy, and Houston resigned after the Texas secession convention and plebiscite in March 1861. Texas authorities watched him closely, fearing that the charismatic and popular Houston might attempt a coup. When he died in July 1863, Texas secessionists breathed a sigh of relief.

John Hoyt Williams, Indiana State University

SUGGESTED READINGS: Llerena B. Friend, *Sam Houston: The Great Designer* (1954); John H. Williams, *Sam Houston: A Biography of the Father of Texas* (1993)

SEE: BLOUNT COUNTY, CREEK WAR OF 1813 & 1814; HALL, WILLIAM; JACKSON, ANDREW

HOUSTON, SAM, SCHOOLHOUSE. In 1792, according to tradition, a North Carolina Revolutionary War veteran named Andrew Kennedy settled with his family on a parcel of land along Little River near Maryville in Blount County. Sometime after his arrival in Tennessee, probably in 1794, Kennedy and Henry McCulloch joined with some neighbors to construct a small log schoolhouse in a clearing less than a mile from the Kennedy home. No definitive explanation can now be given for the decision to locate the schoolhouse at the somewhat unusual site more than a half mile from Little River. Presumably its proximity to the refreshing spring which flows nearby, and perhaps its central position in relation to the original builders' homes, were factors in the selection of the site. The school's first teacher was Henry McCulloch, but beyond this nothing is really known of the history of the building until the arrival of the colorful character with whose name it is now inseparably linked.

Born in 1793, and thus hardly older than the little schoolhouse, Sam Houston was one of nine children of a moderately prosperous militia officer in Virginia's Shenandoah Valley. Reverses in family fortunes around 1807 brought the recently widowed Elizabeth Houston and her youngsters to start anew in Blount County, where they settled on a farm some miles from Maryville. Young Sam, however, could not for long be kept tied to family concerns. Restless and romantic, he tried farm work, school, and storekeeping in quick succession and found none of them to his liking. His spirit of adventure led him to seek out the companionship of the nearby Cherokees, with whom he lived at intervals for several years. His purchases of trinkets and supplies from local merchants eventually put him in debt and forced him to seek employment. That he chose teaching was typical of his brazen self-confidence, for his own formal education hardly totaled six months. He did have a bright mind, however, and a taste for literature.

At the age of 18 Sam left his Indian friends and began conducting classes in the log schoolhouse of Andrew Kennedy and Henry McCulloch. Since his family's homestead was nearly 15 miles away he undoubtedly took quarters somewhere in the school neighborhood. Local tradition says that Sam boarded in his pupils' homes until his mother moved to the area to care for him while he taught. Though initially he had some difficulty recruiting students, he soon had a surfeit of them. Among his pupils were all nine children of Andrew Kennedy and, according to tradition, even some men of age 40 or 50. In order to more quickly repay his creditors, Sam set the tuition rate at eight dollars per year, well above the standard six-dollar fee. As hard currency was difficult to obtain, he allowed one-third to be paid in corn, one-third in cotton cloth, and the remainder in cash.

Sam did not envision teaching as a permanent career, however, and as soon as he had earned enough

to cover his debts he closed the school and returned to a local academy for more schooling of his own. An unsuccessful bout with geometry ended that endeavor and, in March 1813 he enlisted in the U.S. Army to begin the first chapter of a long, successful, and dramatic career in politics and war. But his experience in the little schoolhouse did not leave him unaffected, for he retained a lifelong commitment to popular education as well as some fond memories of his teaching days. Years later, when asked which of the prominent positions he had held had given him the greatest satisfaction, he replied: "When a young man in Tennessee, I kept a county school . . . I experienced a higher feeling of dignity and self-satisfaction than from any office or honor which I have since held."[1]
Marlene Jones, Maryville

CITATION:

(1) Stephen V. Ash, "The Sam Houston Schoolhouse: A Mirror of the Changing Past," *Tennessee Historical Quarterly* 37(1978): 383.

HOWSE, HILARY (1866–1938), significant Nashville politician and mayor in the early twentieth century, was born in Rutherford County. In 1884 Howse came to Nashville, found work in a furniture store, and helped five of his siblings get started in the city. By 1900 he and his brother opened their own downtown furniture store and entered politics. Howse began as a party operative for the local Democratic organization and was elected first to the County Court and then to the State Senate, where he assumed a role as leader of the powerful Davidson County delegation.

As the prohibition movement gained strength, Howse joined forces with the "wets." He ran successfully for the office of Mayor of Nashville in 1909 on the promise that he would not enforce the laws closing saloons. Howse was well known in the "Gentleman's Quarter" around Nashville's Printer's Alley as a man who frequented saloons. "I'm not a drinking man," he once told incredulous reporters, "but as long as I stay in a free country I will eat and drink as I please."[1] On another occasion, when challenged as to whether he actively protected the saloons from prosecution under the prohibition laws, he retorted: "Protect them? I do better than that. I patronize 'em."[2]

Howse won financial support from the liquor interests, but he earned popular support from the white and black working-class poor in the inner-city districts. The Howse "machine" extended personal aid to poor families in need of coal and groceries and used patronage to reward loyal party supporters. Howse welcomed black and poor white voters shut out of the political process by restrictive voting laws. He paid their poll tax and perhaps treated them to a drink on election day. The Howse machine was a political organization with a style much like the boss politics that emerged among immigrant neighborhoods of large northern industrial cities. These types of urban political machines were based on a more personal style of politics in which leaders exchanged favors for votes and used government to help the city's poor. Howse stands as an example of how this American political style was adapted to the southern urban environment, where there were fewer foreign immigrants and more African Americans.

As mayor, Howse expanded the public park system, cleaned up some of the worst slums in Black Bottom and North Nashville, sponsored free health dispensaries and milk stations in poor neighborhoods, and instigated a major addition to the city hospital. He also worked to improve the city's public schools and sponsored the construction of a new city high school, later named Hume-Fogg High School.

Howse reached out to black as well as white voters. Among the more notable political plums he offered to black voters were Hadley Park (the first major city park for blacks in America), a county hospital for black tuberculosis victims, a Carnegie Branch Library for Negroes, and Tennessee Agricultural and Industrial Normal School for Negroes (now Tennessee State University). Howse's 1911 reelection ticket included Solomon Parker Harris, the city's first black councilman since the early 1880s.

On the other side were progressive-era advocates of good government, who thought the business and professional elites should run the city. These leaders, often referred to as "goo goos" by their opponents, struck back with a series of government reforms intended to destroy the Howse machine's foundations in neighborhood politics. They introduced the commission plan of government in 1913, which they hoped would remove the "odor of politics" from city government. When Howse managed to win re-election under the new charter in 1913, the "goo goos" took another line of attack by exposing what the local press decried as a serious financial scandal in which several Howse compatriots were accused of graft and corruption. The 1915 crisis ended in Howse's resignation, after some accounting books were declared missing.

Between 1915 and 1923 Nashville's city government came under the control of the downtown business elite, but instead of good government efficiency and moral reform, a period of chronic factionalism and spotty leadership ensued. Howse married, joined a church, denounced his past ways, and prepared his comeback. Women voters, persuaded by his personal reform, proved important to his re-election in 1923. Nevertheless, Nashville remained "wide open" for illegal saloons, bootleggers, gamblers, and petty political corruption. Howse's brand of "urban liberalism" with its emphasis on health, schools, hospitals, slum cleanup, and other human welfare policies counted for more among the city's working people than did the moral concerns of his enemies.

During the next 15 years, Nashville enjoyed stable government during a period of rapid growth in the 1920s and severe economic crisis in the 1930s. The new suburban neighborhoods of Hillsboro, Belmont, and Sylvan Park joined the city in a major annexation in 1925. But other wealthy suburbs, Richland and Belle Meade in particular, resisted falling under the control of the city machine, and for his part Howse cared little for bringing more "silk stocking" districts into the city to vote against him. During the New Deal of the 1930s, Howse managed to turn federal welfare projects to local political advantage and, in the process, bring large federal grants to Nashville projects. Charges of corruption continued to hound Howse, who died in office in January 1938. Howse had served Nashville as its mayor 21 years. A new high school named in his honor was later renamed West End High School after voters and students protested.

Don H. Doyle, Vanderbilt University

CITATIONS:

(1) *Nashville American,* 13 October 1909.

(2) George Barker, "The Era of Nickel Beer, Free Lunch," and "Behind the Waterfront," in *Tennessean Magazine,* June 6 and 13, 1965.

SEE: NASHVILLE; TEMPERANCE

HUBBARD, GEORGE WHIPPLE (1841–1924), founder and first president of Meharry Medical College, was born on August 11, 1841, in North Charlestown on the Connecticut River in New Hampshire. His paternal grandfather, David Hubbard, had been among the first settlers of the older village, Charlestown, and his maternal grandfather had been one of the founders of Crydon, New Hampshire. Whipple had served as a deacon in the Congregational Church and as a Continental Army captain during the Revolutionary War.

George Hubbard was educated in North Charlestown public schools until the age of 17, when he enrolled in Pomfret Academy in Pomfret, Vermont. He later continued his education at the New Hampshire Conference Seminary at Sanbornton Bridge and the Scientific and Literary Institute in New London, New Hampshire. His first employment was as a teacher in the Calumet School in Charlestown.

In 1864 Hubbard volunteered to serve as a delegate and missionary chaplain of the U.S. Christian Commission. He served six weeks in the Army of the Potomac near Confederate lines in Virginia, then moved south to serve as military chaplain with General William T. Sherman's army, then besieging Atlanta. Arriving in Nashville, in August 1864, Hubbard discovered that the forces of General Nathan B. Forrest had destroyed the railroad between

Nashville and Chattanooga. While he waited for repairs to the railroad, Hubbard took a temporary assignment as a teacher in a school conducted in Nelson Merry's Baptist Church, the first African-American Church in Nashville. His assignment was extended for an entire year. In July 1865 Hubbard was invited to teach soldiers in the 110th United States Colored Troops, stationed in Gallatin. He joined the soldiers, and in October, went with the regiment to Huntsville, Alabama, where he remained until the unit was mustered out of the service in February 1866.

During the autumn and winter of 1866, Hubbard taught school in Clinton, Kansas, then returned to Nashville, where he taught school for the Freedmen's Aid Society of Pittsburgh, Pennsylvania. Later that year, he was elected principal of Bellevue public school in a western Davidson County farming community. He held that position for seven years. In 1875 Hubbard enrolled at the University of Tennessee and graduated the following year. He then enrolled at Vanderbilt University School of Medicine, from which he received his degree as a medical doctor in 1879.

In October 1876 Hubbard worked under the direction of Dr. John W. Braden, assisted by Dr. W. J. Sneed, a Confederate veteran, to open the Meharry Medical Department of Central Tennessee College. Initially the college enrolled fewer than a dozen students. In 1886 the dental department opened at Meharry, followed by a pharmaceutical department in 1889. With the closing of Central Tennessee College, Meharry Medical College emerged as an independent medical-training institution, of which Hubbard served as president for 45 years. Upon his retirement in February 1921, Hubbard became the first president *emeritus* of the college. Meharry's students and alumnae presented Dr. and Mrs. Hubbard (*nee* Annie Lyons) a residence on the South Nashville campus of Meharry Medical College. At that time the Hubbards had been married almost 52 years.

The January-March 1921 issue of the *Journal of the National Medical Association* published a tribute to Hubbard, noting that his "remarkable genius and devotion made successful practitioners, good citizens, and useful men of the early graduates of Meharry . . . .Dr. Hubbard has laid a substantial foundation for a great institution, an institution whose worth and influence will gather momentum with passing years."

Hubbard died August 8, 1924, and was buried beside his wife in Nashville's Greenwood Cemetery.

Reavis L. Mitchell, Jr., Fisk University

SUGGESTED READING: James Summerville, *Educating Black Doctors: A History of Meharry Medical College* (1983)

SEE: MEHARRY MEDICAL COLLEGE; UNITED STATES CHRISTIAN COMMISSION; UNITED STATES COLORED TROOPS

HUGHES, LOUIS (1832-after 1897), author and businessman, was born a slave in Virginia in 1832. Hughes remained in bondage over 30 years and spent most of that time in Tennessee. While still in slavery, Hughes secretly learned to read and write and later published a remarkable autobiography, *Thirty Years a Slave*. He not only relayed his experiences of slavery, escape, and freedom, but also pictured plantation and slave life in extraordinary detail.

At age six, Hughes was separated from his mother forever, when he was sold in a local Virginia slave market, an event that left an indelible mark on his life. In 1844 wealthy Mississippi planter Edmund McGee purchased Hughes as a Christmas gift for his wife; Hughes remained with the family for the next 20 years. Initially an errand boy, Hughes became the McGee's butler in 1850 when they built an extravagant home outside Memphis. As a house servant, Hughes did not often engage in heavy labor, but he did experience the wrathful whims of his mistress. "Some weeks it seemed I was whipped for nothing," Hughes recalled, "just to please my mistress' fancy."[1] He was severely beaten for repeated attempts to escape; his fifth attempt in June 1865 proved successful.

Hughes and his wife Matilda, the McGee's cook who escaped with him, ultimately settled in Milwaukee, where they established a successful laundry business. Hughes eventually capitalized on the medical skills McGee taught him as a slave and pursued a career in nursing. His autobiography, published in 1897, has remained a rare source for documenting numerous aspects of slave life.

Teresa Biddle-Douglass, Middle Tennessee State University
CITATION:
(1) Louis Hughes, *Thirty Years A Slave: From Bondage to Freedom* (Milwaukee, 1897), 19.
SEE: SLAVERY

HULL, CORDELL (1871–1955), Congressman, U.S. Secretary of State, and Nobel Laureate, had a remarkable career. Born to a poor family in the isolated "Mountain Section" of upper Middle Tennessee, he was educated first at home, then free schools, and, as the family income increased, at private schools. Education took him to law and law to politics. As a politician, Hull was a staunch Democrat and opponent of the protective tariff. When he made his first political speech at age 16, it was against the tariff. Twenty years later, he delivered his maiden speech in the House of Representatives on the evils of the protective tariff. Between those events, Hull served his party, won election to the Tennessee General Assembly, practiced law, and became a circuit court judge. Elected to Congress in 1906, Hull earned a footnote in history in 1913, when the Democrats lowered tariffs and turned to this moderate Progressive to write an income tax law that was progressive but not too radical.

This parochial, hard working, party man changed during World War I. He had always seen the tariff as a local issue, but the Great War changed his perspective, and he came to believe that world peace and progress depended upon nations having free access to the raw materials and markets of the world. He twice urged his government to host an international conference to establish a postwar economic order. But he was one World War ahead of his time; he would not get his conference until World War II.

Defeated in the Republican landslide of 1920, Hull learned that global issues would not win votes. He turned his attention to his party (and became Democratic National Committee Chairman) and his constituents, was re-elected in 1922, and watched his influence within the Democratic Party grow during the years of the Republican ascendancy. In 1930 he was elected to the Senate and became a supporter of Franklin Roosevelt. In 1933 president-elect Roosevelt asked him to be Secretary of State. Hull agreed, seeing an opportunity to establish his free trade principles.

During the first half of Hull's 11-year tenure as Secretary of State, he fostered free trade and promoted the Good Neighbor Policy toward Latin America. He spent the second half of his secretaryship seeking to avoid war and then helping to create a postwar system that would avoid another war. For his efforts in establishing the United Nations, he received the Nobel Peace Prize, but his greatest impact on American policy came from his work on free trade.

In 1933 Americans did not support free trade. Economic nationalists, who comprised Roosevelt's "Brain Trust," sought to restore prosperity by managing an economy isolated from the world. Their success in 1933 led to a humiliating experience for Hull at the London Economic Conference. But Hull had survived for a quarter of a century in Washington politics, and he knew how to fight. Through deft political moves, he triumphed over his opposition and escorted through Congress a reciprocal trade agreements program that moved the nation away from its high tariff tradition.

Tariff issues are pretty dull stuff. What won Hull popular acclaim was his work with Latin American nations. At the Montevideo conference in the winter of 1933–1934, Hull disarmed South American critics and won popular support for the United States by adopting an egalitarian style, flattering the other foreign ministers, and pledging that the United States would not intervene in the internal affairs of other nations. These successes and the highly principled position he took in dealing with Japan so enhanced Hull's popularity with the American people that he

Cordell Hull, U.S. Secretary of State, signing the Moscow Pact, 1943. Seated, left to right, are Fu Ping-Sheung, China's Ambassador to the USSR, Hull, Vyacheslav Molotov, USSR Commisar of Foreign Affairs, and Sir Anthony Eden, the United Kingdom's Secretary for Foreign Affairs.

NATIONAL ARCHIVES AND RECORDS ADMINISTRATION. PHOTO BY ACME

was the likely Democratic candidate for president had FDR not decided to seek a third term in 1940.

Though popular, Hull's dealing with Japan was notably unsuccessful in avoiding war. When Japan invaded China in 1937, the secretary lamented the violation of treaties and principles, but believing no vital American interests were at stake, refused to confront Japan. He waited for Japan to crumble under the weight of its war in China. But Japan did not crumble. Instead it sought to expand its control over Southeast Asia and the South Pacific. Japan's objectives were antithetical to the liberal commercial world order Hull passionately believed in. To Hull this was no petty squabble over trade. He believed that if great powers were allowed to establish exclusive control over the markets and raw materials of large sections of the world, it would destroy the political and economic progress achieved over the last five centuries. Hull urged Japan to abandon its world view. But the Japanese were no more willing to accept Hull's world order than Hull was prepared to accept theirs. When diplomacy failed, war resulted.

During the war, Hull played a marginal role in foreign policy management; Roosevelt personally handled matters of state and ignored Hull. In addition, Hull's health deteriorated. For years, he had been suffering from tuberculosis (a closely guarded secret), and as the disease advanced, the secretary spent longer and longer vacations recuperating. He was not without influence in Washington, however. He forced out Under Secretary of State Sumner

Welles, whom Hull believed had been disloyal to him; he kept foreign policy out of the 1944 presidential election; and he played an important role in creating bipartisan support in Congress for the United Nations.

Ill and exhausted by the summer of 1944, Hull remained in office only long enough to see FDR elected to his fourth term. In retirement, his medical condition teetered between serious and stable, recovering enough so he could oversee the ghostwriting of his memoirs. Though he kept well informed about international affairs, Hull played no role as an elder statesman. He lived out his years in his comfortable apartment in Washington, never returning to his native Tennessee or to the mountains from which he had sprung. He died on July 23, 1955, and was interred in the crypt of the National Cathedral.

Jonathan G. Utley, University of Illinois at Chicago

SUGGESTED READINGS: Cordell Hull, with Andrew H. T. Berding, *The Memoirs of Cordell Hull* (1948); Cooper Milner, "The Public Life of Cordell Hull: 1907–1924," (Ph. D. diss., Vanderbilt University, 1960)

SEE: HULL, CORDELL, BIRTHPLACE; PICKETT COUNTY; SMITH COUNTY

HULL, CORDELL, BIRTHPLACE AND MUSEUM.

Located near Byrdstown, Pickett County, the Cordell Hull Birthplace and Museum is a 16.2-acre site acquired by the Tennessee Historical Commission in 1990. It is the birthplace and memorial of Pickett County's most famous son, "Father of the United

Nations," Cordell Hull. The site is operated by the Friends of Cordell Hull.

Cordell Hull was born October 2, 1871, to William and Elizabeth Riley Hull. The small log cabin where he was born stands on the site, although rebuilt in 1952 and again in 1995. It is the only Pickett County site that is directly associated with Cordell Hull.

Hull and his wife, Rose Frances Witz Hull, had no children. He left most of his belongings to his niece, Katherine Hull Ethridge, with the understanding that they would go to the Friends of Cordell Hull in Byrd-stown, when adequate facilities were in place. In 1996 the Friends of Cordell Hull, along with the State of Tennessee, completed an impressive museum to house the collection. The Cordell Hull Birthplace and Museum is open daily.

Meredith Fiske Bare, Nashville

SEE: HULL, CORDELL; PICKETT COUNTY

HUMPHREYS COUNTY. Situated next to the Tennessee River on the western edge of Middle Tennessee, Humphreys County's history is intimately linked to its location and natural resources. It contains fertile agricultural land along its major waterways—the Tennessee, Duck, and Buffalo rivers—and in the creek-lined lands of its innumerable rolling hills. A strong agricultural tradition and proximity to the Tennessee River have been the county's mainstay since its 1809 creation from parts of Stewart County.

Prior to white settlement, Native Americans lived and hunted on the land that eventually became Humphreys County. Of these indigenous groups, Woodland and Mississippian groups left the most visible remains. Many mound sites are located in the western section of the county, with the most prominent being the Link and Slayden sites situated near Hurricane Mills on the Duck River. Partially excavated in 1936 by the Works Progress Administration, the Slayden site revealed a small circular village with two community houses and a nearby cemetery. The Link site contained six mounds and several cemeteries.

In 1811 the county established its first seat, Reynoldsburg, on the Tennessee River, where a stage line to Nashville crossed. Reynoldsburg thrived as an important transportation center until 1835, when the county was divided, and Waverly became the new county seat. Selected for its central location and access to the stage line, by 1838 Waverly included a courthouse, jail, businesses, and many log dwellings.

Humphreys County grew steadily and by 1860 claimed a population of 9,096 whites, 1,463 slaves, and 14 free blacks. Most residents were farmers. In addition to livestock, farms situated along the rich river bottoms and fertile valleys yielded wheat, rye, oats, tobacco, and cotton, with Indian corn the major cash crop.

Although Humphreys County lies in the once-rich iron ore area of the Western Highland Rim, only two iron operations existed. The Fairchance Furnace produced pig iron from circa 1832 to 1835, while the iron forge at Hurricane Mills operated sporadically from circa 1814 into the early 1850s.

The 1860 census shows 1,118 people in Humphreys County employed in the construction of the Nashville and Northwestern Railroad. Mostly Irish immigrants, the workers later settled the town of McEwen. The Civil War and the Union capture of Forts Henry and Donelson temporarily interrupted railroad construction. In January 1863 General William S. Rosecrans ordered the completion of the railroad from White Bluff to Johnsonville and the stationing of Union troops along the railroad line, at the Hurricane Creek stockade, and at both Fort Hills in Waverly and Johnsonville.

Humphreys County was the scene of occasional skirmishes and one Civil War battle. On November 4, 1864, General Nathan Bedford Forrest commanded the bombardment of Johnsonville, which served as a Federal supply center on the Tennessee River. After 40 minutes of cannon and gun fire, the Union troops set fire to the remaining boats and retreated to Waverly and Nashville. The battle destroyed three gunboats, eight steamboats, 18 barges, and all the warehouses.

In the decades following the war, Humphreys County grew steadily; by 1890 it had a population of 11,720 and nearly 1,400 farms. Most of the best farmland had been claimed before the war, and new growth occurred in the hilly, marginally fertile areas. Unsuitable for commercial crop farming, the land was good for timber and livestock grazing. The timber industry flourished, meeting new demands for board lumber, local stave mills, and railroad crossties. While corn continued to be an important crop, the peanut industry had the greatest impact on the county's economic development from the 1880s into the first decades of the twentieth century. At its height in 1910, the county produced one-third of the state's peanuts, with approximately 6,126 acres devoted to the legume. Peanut farming required a great deal of hand labor and supported the tenancy system as well as the small hill farmer. Large peanut warehouses in Waverly and Johnsonville stored the crop until it was shipped on Tennessee River barges. The peanut industry and the general agriculture market experienced a sharp decline around 1920, as a result of post-World War I deflation. The agricultural stagnation that followed haunted Humphreys County throughout the 1920s, reducing the county's population.

The New Deal brought progressive agricultural programs to demonstrate soil conservation, crop diversification, crop rotation, mechanization, and promotion of livestock raising and dairying. Federal involvement helped stabilize the eroding agricultural environment and promote industrial growth. As early as 1934, the Public Works Administration constructed a city water works in McEwen, which helped bring Kraft Cheese Company to the area. The Works Progress Administration built new roads, bridges, streets, a gymnasium, and other recreation and conservation projects. From 1935 to 1938 WPA spent $432,360 in Humphreys County; in 1940 WPA employed 441 people in the county.

In 1937 the Tennessee Valley Authority began surveying the western, Tennessee River side of the county to establish the zone that would be inundated by the creation of Kentucky Lake and Dam. From 1938 to 1942 TVA purchased 36,160 acres of the richest agricultural land in the county, displacing people, businesses, industries, and whole towns. TVA became the greatest vehicle for change in the history of the county, diverting the economic character from agricultural dependency to industrialization. The new potential for hydroelectric power gave the county a great advantage after 1945. By the early 1950s the recently created river town of New Johnsonville claimed TVA's first steam power plant, a large chemical plant, manganese factory, and an aluminum reduction plant. Today Humphreys County relies upon both its industrial and agricultural heritage, while also enjoying recreational attractions and wetland preserves created by TVA's legacy. A major tourist site is the Hurricane Mills estate of country music star Loretta Lynn.

Trina L. Binkley, Alabama Historical Commission

SUGGESTED READING: Wayne C. Moore, "Farm Communities and Economic Growth in the Lower Tennessee Valley, Humphreys County, Tennessee, 1785–1980" (Ph. D. diss., University of Rochester, 1990)

SEE: ANDERSON, WILLIAM R.; JOHNSONVILLE, BATTLE OF; LYNN, LORETTA; RAILROADS; TENNESSEE VALLEY AUTHORITY; TIMBER; WORKS PROGRESS ADMINISTRATION

HUMPHREYS, WEST H. (1806–1882), a jurist whose sympathy for and relationship with the Confederacy led to impeachment, was born in Montgomery County on August 5, 1806. His father, Parry W. Humphreys, was a state judge and a representative to the Thirteenth Congress, before turning to banking and moving to Missouri.

Humphreys studied law in his father's office. He then entered Transylvania University, at Lexington, Kentucky, to complete his training, but returned home when his health failed. He was licensed to practice law in 1828. Humphreys moved to Somerville in newly established Fayette County, and represented the Western District at the Constitutional Convention of 1834. His service as the chairman of the committee on legislation earned him attention as an able legal mind. In 1835 he was the first West Tennessean to seek the office of governor, but, according to historian Paul Bergeron, Humphrey's "purpose in seeking the state's highest office remains a mystery."[1]

From 1835 to 1838 Humphreys served in the lower house of the General Assembly. In 1839, he became Attorney General of Tennessee and Reporter of the State Supreme Court. He served in both capacities for 11 years and distinguished himself by editing the 11-volume *Reports of Cases in the Supreme Court of Tennessee, 1839–1851*. He was a delegate to the Nashville Convention of 1850. After returning to private practice, Humphreys was appointed a U.S. District Judge by President Franklin Pierce in 1853.

Humphreys supported secession, and after Tennessee broke with the union, he accepted an appointment for the Confederate district judgeship of Tennessee. In 1862 the U.S. Senate tried Humphreys on seven articles of impeachment, including the charges that he had publicly called for secession, given aid for the armed rebellion, conspired with Jefferson Davis, served as a judge for the Confederacy and, acting in that capacity, had ruled for the confiscation of the property of Military Governor Andrew Johnson and U.S. Supreme Court Justice John Catron. Humphreys was found guilty of high treason. On June 26, 1862, Humphreys was impeached and forbidden to hold any office under the federal government. He held his Confederate position until the end of the war.

Humphreys never returned to active practice after the war. He argued for prohibition of alcohol, and returned to his writing. His publications included *Suggestions on the Subject of Bank Charters* (1859), *Some Suggestions on the Subject of Monopolies and Special Charters* (1859), and *An Address on the Use of Alcoholic Liquors and the Consequences* (1879). He died at the age of 76 at the residence of his son-in-law, near Nashville, on October 16, 1882.

Amy H. Sturgis, Vanderbilt University

CITATION:

(1) Paul H. Bergeron, *Antebellum Politics in Tennessee* (Lexington, 1982), 46.

SUGGESTED READINGS: Richard L. Aynes, "The Impeachment and Removal of Tennessee Judge West Humphreys," *Georgia Journal of Southern Legal History* 2(1993): 71–98; Kermit L. Hall, "West H. Humphreys and the Crisis of the Union," *Tennessee Historical Quarterly* 34(1975): 48–69

SEE: FAYETTE COUNTY; LAW; NASHVILLE CONVENTION; TEMPERANCE

HUNT, REUBEN HARRISON (1862–1937) was the principal-in-charge of one of the South's most prominent regional architectural practices in the period from the 1880s through the 1930s. His career reflected in microcosm the changes in architectural practice during the late nineteenth and early twentieth centuries. While Hunt apparently was not inclined toward the development of architectural theory, he was extremely alert to new ideas and fashion, and prompt to exploit their practical values to the fullest. From an early career as a builder, Hunt educated himself through periodicals and on-the-job experience to establish a large regional practice through personal contacts resulting from extensive travel in the South and the use of publications as vehicles for peddling his firm's architectural services. The Hunt practice specialized in churches, public buildings, and the new American innovation, skyscrapers. He designed a large number of all three building types, from Virginia to Texas.

Biographical details of Reuben Harrison Hunt's life are sketchy and contradictory. He was born in Elbert County, Georgia, on February 2, 1862. The son of Reuben Smith Hunt, a Civil War planter, and Nellie McCrary Hunt, the younger Hunt was educated in the public schools. From 1876 to 1881 he worked as a carpenter and builder. Moving to Chattanooga in 1882, he found a job with Adams Brothers, though his exact duties and the extent of his formal architectural training are unknown. By 1886 he was practicing architecture as Hunt and McDaniel, described as a firm of architects, contractors, and builders. Between 1890 and 1892 the firm's name changed to Hunt and Lamm. Sometime after 1886 Hunt dropped his contractor and builder business and shifted to a strictly architectural practice, a business decision similar to that of many post-Civil War architects. In 1890 Hunt's advertisement in the *Chattanooga City Directory* announced "church and public buildings [are] a specialty." Hunt consistently gravitated toward larger scale projects, shunning domestic work. By the early 1900s he had formed the R. H. Hunt Company, which he operated until his death on May 28, 1937.

The R. H. Hunt Company was widely known in its time. A 1907 advertisement in the *Chattanooga Star* documented a portfolio of 131 finished projects, 30 years before Hunt's death at age 75. The list included 60 churches, 28 schools, 22 business houses, 11 courthouses, five hotels, and five city buildings. For the remainder of his career, church designs dominated the work of the firm. For churches of modest resources, the design was often provided free of charge.

To accommodate the firm's extensive business, branch offices were opened in Jackson, Mississippi, in 1905 and Dallas, Texas, in 1919. Often described locally as the "master builder of Chattanooga," Hunt's regional prominence justifies the description as one of the South's leading architects.

The visibility of Hunt's work was increased by the appearance of the firm's buildings in the major journals of the day, including *Architecture and Building, The Inland Architect, Pencil Points,* and *The Architec-*

tural Record. An association with Mouzon William Brabham resulted in additional exposure for Hunt's office. Brabham's *Planning Modern Church Buildings* (1928) developed out of the American pattern book genre. In the introduction, Brabham praised the designs of the R. H. Hunt Company and thanked R. H. Hunt for reading the manuscript. At least 17 designs by the Hunt office illustrated Brabham's work, which was a resource and guide for congregations contemplating a new church building. Additionally, Hunt's firm produced in-house and distributed its own pattern book of church designs. Similar to the pattern books for domestic design produced by both the Palliser Brothers, as well as George R. Barber of nearby Knoxville, Tennessee, Hunt's publications focused on a specific building type to market his firm's designs and services to a large audience. Illustrations included a plan, perspective, and a cost estimate for the potential church building congregation. The firm's pattern books demonstrate the R. H. Hunt Company's aggressive marketing to a widely scattered, regional clientele.

Hunt's firm produced work in a variety of medieval and classical revival styles. The Romanesque revival of Chattanooga's Second Presbyterian Church and the Beaux Arts classicism of the Hamilton County Courthouse are typical. The firm's competent designs reflected the eclectic architectural climate of the time. While not stylistically innovative, the firm's work was significant for two reasons. It produced a large number of buildings that incorporated contemporary forms, styles, and technology. The Hunt office also linked Chattanooga and the South to the important production of architects in larger, and primarily northern, urban centers. Through the firm, contemporary architectural thought and values were collected, filtered, and disseminated across the South.

Sara A. Butler, University of Virginia

SEE: BARBER AND MCMURRY; CHATTANOOGA; FEDERAL BUILDING

HUNT-PHELAN HOUSE. Located on Memphis's historic Beale Street and called the city's "best kept secret," this restored Greek Revival house recently opened to public tours. Completed in 1832 by George Wyatt, the house featured several architectural flourishes, including an escape tunnel. Eli and Julia Driver purchased the house from Jesse Tate in 1850. The couple made improvements, including the addition of a kitchen ell, landscaping, moving the original front portico to the side, and constructing a two-story portico of Ionic columns.

Driver's son-in-law, William Richard Hunt, owned the house through the Civil War. Confederate General Leonidas Polk used the house as his headquarters while he planned the battle at Corinth, Mississippi. Before the fall of Memphis in 1862, Confederate officials provided a boxcar for the removal of family furnishings. Union General Ulysses S. Grant headquartered in the house from June 27 to July 12, 1862, and planned the Vicksburg campaign in the library. Gun emplacements encircled the house, and Union forces used the tunnel to relay messages.

Between 1863 and 1865, the Union's Western Sanitary Commission used the mansion as a soldiers' home and housed Freedmen's Bureau teachers. In 1865 President Andrew Johnson returned the house to Hunt, who began years of repairs.

In the twentieth century, the house passed to Stephen Rice Phelan, a Standard Oil geologist. Phelan wrote a history of the house but neglected its maintenance. The house, heavily coated in gray paint and isolated from the surrounding community by barbed wire, padlocks, and weeds, slowly deteriorated.

Bill Day, a nephew of the reclusive Phelan, inherited the house, and in the 1990s embarked on an extensive restoration project. Using old photographs and maps, teams of restoration architects and artists worked to return the house to its former glory and re-introduce the Hunt-Phelan house to Memphis.

Dee Gee Lester, Hendersonville

SEE: BEALE STREET; FREEDMEN'S BUREAU; MEMPHIS; POLK, LEONIDAS; RECONSTRUCTION

HUNTER, GEORGE THOMAS (1886–1950), Chattanooga businessman and philanthropist, was the nephew of pioneer Coca-Cola bottler Benjamin Franklin Thomas. A native of Maysville, Kentucky, Hunter joined his childless uncle and aunt in Chattanooga in 1904, becoming a surrogate son and business heir. While a student at Baylor School, Hunter worked at the bottling company and learned the soft drink business from the ground up.

Hunter served as secretary of Coca-Cola Bottling Company from 1906 until Thomas's death in 1914, at which time he took control of the business. In 1929 Hunter renamed the company the Coca-Cola Bottling Company (Thomas) in honor of his uncle. Hunter took the title of chairman of the board in 1941 and hired DeSales Harrison from the Atlanta-based Coca-Cola Company to succeed him as company president.

Hunter increasingly took an interest in civic philanthropy. The culmination of his work was the 1944 creation of the Benwood Foundation, named for his uncle's summer home on Lookout Mountain. Upon the death of his aunt, Anne Taylor Jones Thomas, Hunter inherited the remainder of the Thomas estate, along with her home on Bluff View and the summer home. At his death in 1950, the bulk of Hunter's sizable estate was left to the charitable foundation. His foundation benefaction led to a precedent-setting ruling in Tennessee probate law, when Chancellor Alvin Ziegler ruled in 1952 that the death taxes would be borne by the residuary estate. The Benwood Foundation and the Hunter Museum of American Art, which opened in 1952, have become his lasting legacies in Chattanooga.

Ned L. Irwin, East Tennessee State University

SUGGESTED READING: Ned L. Irwin, "Bottling Gold: Chattanooga's Coca-Cola Fortunes," *Tennessee Historical Quarterly* 51(1992): 223–37

SEE: BENWOOD FOUNDATION; COCA-COLA BOTTLING COMPANY; HUNTER MUSEUM OF AMERICAN ART; THOMAS, ANNE T.; THOMAS, BENJAMIN F.

HUNTER MUSEUM OF AMERICAN ART. Built on a 90-foot limestone bluff overlooking the Tennessee River, and housed within a 1904 Classical Revival mansion and contemporary-styled 1975 structure, the Hunter Museum of American Art features one of the finest collections of American art in the Southeast. The majestic mansion was once the home of George Thomas Hunter, Chairman of the Board of the Chattanooga Coca-Cola franchise and the nephew of Benjamin F. Thomas, founder of the world's first Coca-Cola bottling franchise. A respected local philanthropist, Hunter established the Benwood Foundation, a private charitable and educational trust. A year after his death in 1951, funds from Benwood, along with the gift of the Hunter mansion, were donated to the Chattanooga Art Association. On July 12, 1952, the association opened Chattanooga's first permanent exhibiting institution as the George Thomas Hunter Gallery of Art.

In 1975 a new addition was added to the Hunter mansion to host changing exhibitions, public programs, and education activities, provide storage, preparation areas, and staff offices. Simultaneously, the Chattanooga Art Association and the George Thomas Hunter Gallery of Art consolidated to form the Hunter Museum of Art. At this time, the Hunter board decided to focus its collection on American art.

The Hunter collection spans the history of American art from the colonial period to the present and covers a wide variety of media, including painting, sculpture, contemporary studio, glass, and crafts. To complement the permanent collection, the Hunter presents a diverse schedule of changing exhibitions and offers a wide range of educational programs designed to bring art education and a knowledge of the Hunter collection to the public.

From fall 1996 through summer 1997, the mansion and the new building underwent extensive renovation. Restoration work in the mansion preserved the beautiful historical detail of this Classical Revival building. The new building was renovated to give it more character in keeping with the historic mansion; it has also been redesigned to provide more exhibition space. The Hunter Museum of Art strives to enrich the cultural lives of generations of Tennesseans by preserving the past and welcoming American art into the twenty-first century.

Ellen Simak, Hunter Museum of American Art

SEE: ART; BENWOOD FOUNDATION; HUNTER, GEORGE T.; THOMAS, BENJAMIN F.

HUNTING. Tennessee's early white settlers found bountiful supplies of wildlife, including deer, bear, elk, bison, and wild turkey, which the continued westward expansion rapidly depleted. The last two reports of bison were recorded near Nashville in 1795; the last known Tennessee elk was killed in 1849. The unrelenting, one-two punch of habitat destruction and unregulated hunting, accelerating particularly in the late nineteenth and early twentieth centuries, brought many other game animals to the brink of extinction.

Several restoration attempts with pen-reared animals were made in the 1930s, 1940s, and early 1950s. Most of them ultimately proved futile. In 1949 the establishment of the Tennessee Game and Fish Commission, precursor to the present Tennessee Wildlife Resources Agency, marked the beginning of wildlife management on a professional, scientific basis.

Restoration was achieved by live-trapping selected animals from the few remaining wild stocks and releasing them into unoccupied habitat. This slow process, coupled with protective regulations and reforestation efforts across the state, has seen native populations of white-tailed deer, black bear, and wild turkey—and the subsequent harvest by hunters—balloon to record numbers. In 1995, for example, hunters in Tennessee bagged 145,132 deer out of an estimated herd of 850,000, far more than likely existed in the early days of statehood.

The opposite trend occurred with rabbit and quail populations, upland species that thrive best in a farm environment. These animals were the mainstay of Tennessee hunters throughout the first half of the twentieth century and are still sought by thousands of small-game hunters today. Both species experienced an overall decline throughout the 1980s and 1990s, however, as small "patch" farmlands continued to disappear.

Deer, wild turkey, and squirrels rank among the most popular animals with Tennessee hunters. Hound enthusiasts also pursue raccoons and foxes statewide. In the Southern Appalachian and Cumberland mountains, ruffed grouse, bear, and wild boar (offspring of European imports) are highly prized by hunters willing to stretch their legs.

Hunting for wildfowl, predominantly mourning doves and ducks, also is popular across the state. In the early fall, dove shoots over harvested grain fields are a southern social tradition, often replete with country music and dinner on the grounds. Later in the year, native wood ducks, plus mallards, black ducks, teal, widgeons, scaup, and other migratory fowl provide excellent hunting in the wetlands along the Tennessee, Cumberland, Mississippi, Obion, Forked Deer, Hatchie, Wolf, and Duck river systems, as well as famed Reelfoot Lake in northwest Tennessee. Local, non-migratory populations of Canada geese have flourished in Tennessee since the mid-1980s, and now provide excellent hunting opportunities, particularly in the middle and eastern portions of the state.

In 1994–95, 266,149 Tennesseans and 11,140 nonresidents purchased hunting licenses. Most hunting takes place on privately owned land. A network of 64 wildlife management areas (encompassing 1,320,000 acres) and 31 refuges (27,250 acres) is available to the public.

Sam Venable, The Knoxville News-Sentinel

SEE: CONSERVATION; HUNTING DOGS; TENNESSEE WILDLIFE RESOURCES AGENCY

HUNTING DOGS. Europeans brought hunting dogs when they began their exploration of the North American continent. Mountain Curs and American coonhounds were the most prominent imported breeds. With the exception of the Plott, all breeds of coonhounds have a common ancestry deeply rooted in the English Foxhound. Many of the breeds were introduced to North America by prominent colonial settlers like George Washington, an avid fox hunter.

The first mention of hounds in America appears in the diaries of men serving under the explorer Hernando de Soto. Soto used the hounds for hunting Indians rather than fox, raccoon, or rabbit. In 1799 Moravian missionaries Abraham Steiner and Frederick C. De Schweinitz came to Tennessee to bring the gospel to the Overhill Cherokees. They traveled across the state to Nashville and kept a journal of their observations and adventures. At a spot near where the Caney Fork River meets the Cumberland River, they encountered "numerous companies of people that were on a bear hunt," and noted that often one hunter "had 12 to 15 powerful dogs with him." They took lodging with a settler named Mr. Shaw, who made his living selling provisions to travelers. Schweinitz noted that "His (Shaw's) possessions of special value consist in hunting dogs, of which he regards the worth of a well-trained one as being as high as that of a horse."[1]

The American Black and Tans, Blueticks, English Coonhounds, Redbones, and Treeing Walkers were all developed early in the state's history and were used for bear and raccoon hunting. Early settlers also used the dogs for protection. Today these dogs are used for either raccoon hunting (still popular statewide), bear hunting, or for show in field trials, where they are judged for speed, agility, barking, treeing, and tracking abilities.

In 1852 a Black and Tan hound, named Tennessee Lead, was stolen and taken to Madison County, Kentucky, where he became the foundation sire of all Walker, Trigg, and Goodman Foxhounds. These three strains make up the major portion of what is today called American Foxhounds by the American Kennel Club.

In the late 1800s, quail hunting preserves became popular for sporting gentlemen. Hunters used well-bred and trained bird hunting dogs to compete for titles and money. In 1902 Hobart Ames, of North Easton, Massachusetts, bought 400 acres near Grand Junction, Tennessee, where he hosted the first annual National Championship Field Trial. He built the famed Ames Plantation and eventually bought up to 25,000 acres for use as one of the country's most renowned hunting preserves. Since that first event, bird dog clubs across the country hold annual qualifying events that lead to the national contest. The kennels located on the plantation produced some of the world's most famous bird dogs. Today Grand Junction is the home of the National Bird Dog Museum, where 40 breeds of pointing, retrieving, and spaniel breeds are honored.

Etta Pettijohn, Greeneville

CITATION:

(1) Samuel Cole Williams, ed., *Early Travels in the Tennessee Country* (Johnson City, 1928), 518–519.

SEE: AMES PLANTATION; HUNTING; NATIONAL FIELD TRIALS

HUNTSMAN, ADAM R. (1786–1849), attorney and Congressman, was born in Charlotte County, Virginia, February 11, 1789, to Jacob and Mary Devine Huntsman. Huntsman attended schools in Virginia, before migrating to Knoxville around 1807. There he studied law and was admitted to the bar. Huntsman began his law practice in Overton County, where he remained until 1821, when he moved to the newly settled Madison County in West Tennessee. In addition to his law practice, he took part in land speculation and shared a merchant partnership.

Closely associated with Andrew Jackson and the rising Democratic party, Huntsman fought in the Creek Indian War, apparently losing his leg during this conflict; thereafter he wore a wooden leg. From 1815 to 1821 Huntsman represented Overton, Jackson, and Smith counties in the Tennessee General Assembly. In 1824 he was appointed one of three commissioners to improve the navigable rivers of the Western District. He returned to the legislature as State Senator for Madison, Fayette, Hardeman, Haywood, Shelby, and Tipton counties from 1827 to 1831. Huntsman served as a delegate to the Tennessee Constitutional Convention of 1834. He was the "timbertoed" Democratic candidate who defeated David Crockett in the 1834 Congressional race, which prompted Crockett to declare his intention to go to Texas. Never a Democratic front-runner, Huntsman, nevertheless, served the party well as a dependable "war horse." He influenced legislation on banking, tariffs, and internal improvements.

Huntsman married three times: first to Sarah Wesley Quarles in 1825; then to Elizabeth Todd in 1829; and finally to Nancy (last name not known), sometime in 1847 or 1848. Huntsman was the father of four children. He died on August 23, 1849, and is buried in Old Salem Cemetery in Madison County.

Connie L. Lester, Tennessee Historical Society

SUGGESTED READING: Chase C. Mooney, "The Political Career of Adam Huntsman," *Tennessee Historical Quarterly* 10(1951): 99–126

SEE: CROCKETT, DAVID; JACKSONIANS; MADISON COUNTY

HUTCHINS, STYLES L., (1852-d.date not identifed), noted African-American attorney in Chattanooga, was born November 21, 1852, in Lawrenceville, Georgia. He attended Atlanta University and after completing his studies, Hutchins taught in local schools until 1871. In that year, he became principal of Knox Institute in Athens, Georgia. But in 1873 Hutchins left his position and moved to South Carolina, where he graduated from the University of South Carolina Law School in 1876. Admitted to the South Carolina bar at the end of the Reconstruction era, Hutchins first served as a Republican state judge, but the restoration of Democratic power led to his resignation.

Hutchins returned to Georgia, fought for admission to the state bar in Atlanta, and after a six-month struggle, he became the first African-American attorney admitted to the Georgia bar. In 1881 Hutchins moved to Chattanooga and opened a law office. He also partnered with other local African Americans to establish a newspaper, *The Independent Age,* which Hutchins edited. In 1886 Hutchins was elected to a single term to the Tennessee General Assembly as a Republican. He was the second Chattanooga black to serve in the legislature; the first was William C. Hodge. Hutchins also once held a patronage position in the revenue department of the U.S. Treasury and was ordained a minister of the United Brethen in Christ in 1901.

Hutchins's most important legal case in Chattanooga involved a lynching. In 1906 Ed Johnson was accused and quickly convicted of raping a white woman. While his habeus corpus petition, prepared by Hutchins and fellow black attorney Noah W. Parden, was before the U.S. Supreme Court, a Chattanooga mob lynched Johnson, in what proved to be the last lynching in the city's history. At the urgings of Hutchins and others, federal officials cited the Hamilton County sheriff and other officials for contempt of court for not preventing the lynching. In

United States v. Shipp (1909), the U.S. Supreme Court found the Hamilton County sheriff and the others guilty. Hutchins's and Parden's success at the federal level, however, quickly destroyed their Chattanooga careers. Threats and intimidation came from many quarters and both attorneys left for Oklahoma. In honor of Hutchins's accomplishments and courage, the S. L. Hutchins Bar Association has been established in Chattanooga.

Carroll Van West, Middle Tennessee State University, Judge Curtis Collier, Chattanooga, and Vilma S. Fields, Chattanooga

SEE: CHATTANOOGA; LAW; LYNCHING

HUTCHISON SCHOOL, MEMPHIS. In 1902 Mary Grimes Hutchison established a place of learning that today is known as Hutchison School. The Old Love Place on Union Avenue was the site of Miss Hutchison's School for Girls from 1916 until 1925, when increased enrollment encouraged the board of directors to build a new school at 1925 Union Avenue. After Miss Hutchison's retirement in 1947, Dr. and Mrs. William R. Atkinson became the owners of the school. A new library and gymnasium were built, and the school became a non-profit foundation under the direction of a board of trustees. The demands by parents for excellence in education and the high standards of Hutchison School have increased enrollment from more than a dozen children to over 800 students today. Dr. Robert D. Lynn, headmaster from 1959 to 1979, oversaw the purchase of the 50-acre campus at 1740 Ridgeway Road and initiated the expansion program of four buildings. Jack B. Stanford, School Head from 1979 to 1995, presided over the opening of the Wiener Theater and the Buxton Fine Arts Center. An Early Childhood Center, housing a new program for three-year-olds, was dedicated in 1990. In 1995 Linda MacMurray Gibbs was appointed the fifth Head of School in its uninterrupted 95-year history. Hutchison is a leading college preparatory school for young women in Memphis and the Mid-South. Its rigorous academic program, its variety of extracurricular activities, its dedication to honor and integrity, and its promotion of the love of learning have given the school its state and national prominence.

Sara A. Frey, Hutchison School

SEE: GIRLS PREPARATORY SCHOOL; HARPETH HALL AND WARD-BELMONT

I

IMMORTAL THIRTEEN refers to the Democratic members of the State Senate in the 1841–1842 session of the General Assembly. These 13 Democrats maintained a one-seat majority in the Senate, but the rival Whig party's majority in the House of Representatives gave that party a two-vote advantage in a joint session of the legislature. Traditionally, the General Assembly elected U.S. Senators in a joint session, but with both Senate seats vacant, the "Thirteen" attempted to use their edge in the State Senate to force Whigs to accept a Democrat's election to at least one of the national seats. Thus, they refused to meet with the House in a joint session and claimed that the U.S. Constitution required senatorial candidates to receive approval from both chambers in their separate capacities.

Hailed as the "Immortal Thirteen" by their party, the Democratic senators' stance backfired. Whigs refused either to accept a Democrat's election or to compromise on the mode of election, while few voters found plausible the Thirteen's claim to have discovered the true interpretation of the constitution. Despite numerous efforts, Democrats could find no honorable way to retreat from their position. The controversy ultimately consumed the session and prevented the passage of any substantial legislation. No senators were elected before the session's adjournment, and Tennessee remained unrepresented in the U.S. Senate for two years. The controversy proved a major liability for Democrats in the 1843 state elections, in which Whigs won control of both chambers and subsequently elected Ephraim Foster and Spencer Jarnigan to the U.S. Senate.
Jonathan M. Atkins, Berry College
SEE: JACKSONIANS

INDUSTRY. The popular image of Tennessee is dominated by country music, Opryland, Elvis, the Smok-

ies, Jack Daniel's, and other icons of mass culture. The essence of the Volunteer State, however, is found in its history of hard working people tilling the soil, extracting raw materials from the earth, and fabricating products for shipment across the nation and around the world. Late twentieth century Tennesseans, while not totally abandoning their agricultural heritage, have moved into an age of advanced technology and global competition symbolized by electronics, chemical production, and automobile manufacturing. Tennesseans today may wear cowboy hats and listen to the Grand Ole Opry, but at work they are more likely to produce automobiles or sophisticated machinery than to till a small farm or make country crafts.

Most pioneer Tennesseans were farmers, who produced many of their own goods through household manufacture. Early settlers made yarn and cloth at their spinning wheels and looms; produced farm implements, tools, and furniture; ground wheat and corn to produce flour and meal; processed hides to craft clothing, saddles, shoes, and other leather goods; and produced lumber at small sawmills. Early industrial activity happened in the towns. Knoxville produced flour, cotton, and leather goods. Cotton factories were operating in Davidson County around the turn of the nineteenth century. Some claim that the South's first cotton mill was established near Nashville in the early 1790s. The most important early industries utilized local raw materials. Leaders in the antebellum period included iron, machinery, hardware, lumber, flour and meal mills, leather products, cotton goods, tobacco products, and liquor. Iron manufacture was most significant in the early period, although by the eve of the Civil War, grain milling and sawmilling led the state in investment and production value.

East Tennessee may have had some iron and lead production as early as the Revolutionary era. By the early 1830s several producers were turning out nails, cast iron ware, and other products for both local and regional markets. Some operations were fairly extensive, including furnaces, forges, bloomeries, nail manufacture, rolling mills, factories, and mining operations. Iron production in Middle Tennessee began in the 1790s. There were over 50 operations by the mid-1850s. Early iron operations were located on rivers or streams, since the metallic iron was produced by water-powered trip-hammers in small forges or bloomeries. Cast, wrought, and rolled iron came from water-powered bellows in blast furnaces and from crude rolling mills. By 1860 Tennessee ranked third nationally in bloomery output.

None of Tennessee's other antebellum industries were of national significance. While there were textile operations in Knoxville, Nashville, and several smaller towns by the middle of the century, Tennessee's production trailed far behind neighboring states, not to mention those of New England. Tennessee ranked at about the middle among the states in manufacturing throughout the pre-Civil War period. Even within the state, industry lagged far behind agriculture. Economic, political, and social power and prestige were primarily associated with landowning and such cash crops as tobacco and cotton. State leaders lauded the economic and moral superiority of agriculture, and many small farmers were prejudiced against work in factories.

The Civil War brought an upheaval in economic thought and priorities. After the war, many southern leaders advocated economic reconciliation with the North and industrial development as the keys to a better future. The attraction of capital and industry from the North and foreign countries became a continuing pursuit, and the South became, as some have put it, "industrially articulate." Inspired by promoters like Henry W. Grady of Atlanta, the concept of a "New South" with a balanced economy of agriculture and industry became a regional crusade. States and cities issued promotional literature and provided tax breaks and various other kinds of subsidies for industrialists who would invest in their communities.

Tennesseans joined in enthusiastically. Politicians, promoters, and newspaper editors preached the gospel of industrialization. Tennessee's larger cities were the greatest beneficiaries. Speculators and promoters rushed into the Tennessee mountains hoping to exploit their iron deposits and virgin timber. Knoxville and Chattanooga were centers of activity for the agents of northern financiers who were investing in the area. Knoxville attracted a large iron manufacturing company and factories producing paper, flour, soap, and other products. By 1870 Chattanooga had some 58 industrial operations, including iron works, furniture factories, sawmills, gristmills, and other factories. During the decade, capital investment in the city increased by nearly 450 percent! Nashville had new liquor distilleries, sawmills, paper mills, gristmills, stove factories, and a petroleum refinery. Memphis became the nation's largest cottonseed processor and attracted many other industries. Other large operations included woolen mills in Tullahoma and Jackson. Jackson also acquired a flouring mill and benefited as well from the migration of Mid-

U.S. Pipe & Foundry Company, Chattanooga, ca. mid-1900s.

western lumbermen, who established sawmills and woodworking plants.

By 1870 Tennessee's industrial production exceeded prewar levels. The value of manufactured goods had nearly doubled since the beginning of the previous decade. Throughout the late nineteenth century, however, Tennessee ranked in the lower half among the states and territories in the number of industrial establishments, and its total value of products was dwarfed by the leading manufacturing states. Tennessee industries tended to be labor intensive, depending upon low-skilled, cheap labor. The most important, by value of product, were flouring and grist mills, iron works, and lumber manufacturing.

Despite the hopes of promoters, Tennessee did not become a major force in the textile industry during this period. By the middle of the 1870s no cotton mills were in Chattanooga, Knoxville, or Memphis. By the 1890s southern textile manufacturing was booming, but while there were significant gains in Tennessee's production of cotton and wool goods, the state lagged far behind the leaders. On the positive side, by 1885, Chattanooga was an iron-making center. The city had nine furnaces, with 17 foundries and machine shops, and was regarded as the iron-making center of the South. Memphis remained the national leader in cottonseed oil manufacture. During the 1880s over 100 new factories were built in Knoxville, including new flouring mills with the latest technological improvements. By 1890 the value of products from Tennessee's flour and grist mills ranked eleventh among the 50 states and territories.

Lumber products also were important during the late nineteenth century. Significant logging and lumbering occurred in the hardwoods and cypress of the Big Hatchie Bottoms of West Tennessee and in the mountainous regions of East Tennessee. By 1909 Tennessee led the nation in the production of oak, yellow poplar, and hickory. In addition to lumber and paper, wood from the southern highlands was used for the manufacture of photographic print stock at Kingsport, and wood pulp for the production of rayon at Elizabethton. After the turn of the century the timber industry of the Cumberland Plateau gave ground rapidly to the coalmen. Logging continued in the Smokies until the last great tree was cut or until the federal government took the land for national parks and forests.

The Census of 1890 reported that, for the first time, Tennessee manufacturing led agriculture as a producer of wealth. The state moved into a new era. The number of manufacturing establishments had not changed much during the 1880s, but their total capitalization had more than doubled. The state's leading industries, however, continued to be low-wage and labor intensive. This remained the case long into the new century, and Tennessee ranked about midway among the states in industrial importance. The leading industries continued to include grain milling, lumbering, and iron production, but by World War I, lumbering and the iron industry were declining. Apparel manufacturing, chemical products, and printing and publishing began to appear among Tennessee's leading industries based on value added by manufacture. World War I stimulated industrial development, with some plants constructed to turn out war-related goods converting to civilian production in the postwar period. By the 1920s Memphis remained the world's largest center for the manufacture of cottonseed products and was the largest hardwood lumber producer in the United States. Nashville had more than 500 manufacturing enterprises, and Chattanooga was second in the country in the production of steam boilers and hosiery products. Kingsport was home to the nation's largest book-manufacturing plant, the Kingsport Press.

The Great Depression of the 1930s hit Tennessee hard, but recovery was faster than in many other states. Tennessee benefited greatly from the creation of the Tennessee Valley Authority in 1933. TVA created construction jobs, provided cheap power for developing industries, and became active in industrial promotion. The state's industrial mix did not change significantly, and it remained at about the midpoint of manufacturing output among the states. World War II helped Tennessee recover from the depression and also facilitated the transition from an agricultural to an industrial economy. In Memphis the two largest manufacturing facilities converted from automobile parts to aircraft parts production. Nashville turned out aircraft, submarine chasers, and mine sweepers. The Hercules Powder Company in Chattanooga produced TNT. In Kingsport the Tennessee Eastman Company became a significant manufacturer of explosives through the Holston Ordnance Works.

After the war Tennessee renewed its efforts to attract investment. Communities competed feverishly with one another to secure industries and jobs. During the period there were intensive efforts to unionize southern workers, including the CIO's "Operation Dixie." Tennessee's industrial appeal largely rested on a plentiful supply of cheap and tractable non-union labor and the assurance that community leaders would help prevent workers from organizing. Opposition arose in some southern circles to the influx of higher-wage or unionized firms that might alter traditional business and labor patterns. Local communities subsidized incoming industries with tax breaks and even in some cases compulsory employee contributions to help finance free facilities for their employers. Also, southern leaders traditionally held a tolerant attitude toward pollution and exploitation of natural resources. In fact, some critics argue that other industrial nations, such as Germany and Japan, removed polluting industries from their own countries and dumped them in the American South.

The composition and location of Tennessee's industrial mix changed as many plants located in rural areas and small towns rather than the major cities. By 1947 chemical production was the state's leading industry. Food and kindred products and textile manufacturing ranked second and third respectively. Industrial establishments had increased more than 50 percent since World War II began, and the total value added by manufacturing had more than tripled. Among states with 250,000 or more industrial jobs, Tennessee made the greatest gains during the decade 1955–1965.

By the time of the "Sunbelt" ballyhoo of the 1970s Tennessee was considered one of the South's major success stories. During the first half of the decade, increases in the state's gross product exceeded the growth rate of the Gross National Product by more than ten percent and moved closer to per capita equality with the nation. Apparel manufacturing recorded the greatest employment growth of any industry, but most of the state's increase occurred in high wage operations, such as transportation equipment and machinery and chemicals. By 1976 manufacturing accounted for a greater share of total employment in the Volunteer State than in the rest of the nation. With the increasing importance of manufacturing, however, the state became more vulnerable to economic fluctuations and outside factors. The Tennessee Valley region suffered more severely than other areas in the 1975 and 1980–82 recessions.

Now industrial promoters were forced to consider "quality of life issues" as they courted industry. Lawrenceburg constructed a municipal golf course in order to woo an electronics firm, and Union City, after losing a plant, undertook a civic improvement campaign to upgrade its schools, hospital, and recreational facilities. Tennessee also began to build vocational education facilities and community colleges as another inducement for industry to locate in the Volunteer State. Following the old patterns of industrial subsidies, Tennessee offered tax exemptions to industries that would utilize pollution abatement facilities. Meanwhile, state leaders continued to use opposition to organized labor as a selling point to prospective industrial investors.

A 1985 TVA report observed that the pace of economic development in the Tennessee Valley region from 1959 to 1979 was extraordinarily rapid, but that future manufacturing employment would decline in the face of foreign competition. Changes in manufacturing employment were already underway that reflected basic structural shifts in the economy. Some factories improved their productivity through new equipment and technology, which made them less labor intensive, while many of the traditionally low-paying, labor intensive operations disappeared or moved to third world countries. Other trends in the national economy, however, promised an even better future for Tennesseans. These included the tendency of many large companies to manufacture their products at lower cost in branch plants away from their corporate headquarters.

The completion of interstate highways and the improvement of air transportation services facilitated decentralization. The Tennessee Valley's excellent access to growing Sunbelt markets combined with labor surpluses, abundant water and energy sources, pleasant communities, and the pro-development attitude of the region's leaders to attract branch manufacturing plants. Then, in the 1980s, Tennessee attracted two major companies which built enormous plants and established the state as a major force in the automobile and motor vehicle supply industries.

First to arrive was the Nissan Motor Manufacturing Corporation, U.S.A., which began to produce small trucks near Smyrna in 1983. Tennessee won this plant in 1980 after intense competition with Georgia and other states. The state and local community offered a lucrative package of tax incentives, infrastructure construction, and other inducements. They were rewarded with a plant that would cost more than $300 million to build, produce roughly 10,000 small trucks per month, and employ more than 2,000 workers at roughly twice the average yearly wages prevailing in the Smyrna area. By the early 1980s a dozen Japanese companies operated in Tennessee, but the Nissan plant represented the largest foreign manufacturing investment ever made by a Japanese company. It was the largest by any new industry in Tennessee history and represented one-sixth of all Japanese industrial investments in the United States.

The Nissan operation was significant not only because of the number of jobs and income it brought to the state, but also because of its advanced technology, innovative participatory management practices, and "just in time" production parts supply system. Tennessee was immediately thrust into the forefront of U.S. motor vehicle production and achieved national recognition as a "hot" location for industrial investment. The spin-off opportunities for secondary suppliers and service providers were obvious.

General Motors soon joined Nissan in Tennessee. Less than two years after the first truck was produced in Smyrna, General Motors formed the Saturn Corporation. In a process very similar to that of its Japanese competitor, the American giant searched for a factory site, put together its preliminary staff, and in return for various inducements from the state and local governments and TVA, announced the decision to locate its production facilities near Spring Hill.

Nissan and Saturn affected the perceptions of Tennessee by outsiders and changed the state's industrial mix. The 1982 U.S. Census of Manufactures showed that the top five industries of Tennessee, on the basis of value added by manufacture, were chemicals and allied products, food and kindred products, machinery, electric and electronic equipment, and apparel. Transportation equipment ranked tenth. By 1987 apparel had fallen to tenth place and transportation equipment had risen dramatically to third. Other manufacturing areas which supplied the motor vehicle industry, such as tire producers, showed dramatic gains. By 1993 chemicals, transportation equipment, and industrial and commercial machinery were by far the state's leading exports based on dollar volume.

In the 1990s Tennessee enjoyed stronger economic growth than the nation as a whole, despite a declining employment share in manufacturing and stagnant industrial productivity growth. Manufacturing fell to second place behind the service sector as an employer. Tennessee ranked third nationally in number of manufacturing jobs created from 1991 to 1994, third in overall automotive parts production, and in the top ten in more than 75 industrial classifications. In 1995 state exports totaled more than eight billion dollars, led in order by transportation equipment, chemicals and allied products, non-electric machinery, and electronic and electrical products. Tennessee shipped products to 157 countries and the export trade was responsible for more than 100,000 jobs. Danger signs included labor shortages in Middle Tennessee, high unemployment in some other areas of the state, weaknesses in automobile sales, and the continued slippage of the textile and apparel sectors.

To ensure continued industrial growth Tennessee offers an extensive package of incentives that are consistent with the spirit of southern industrial promotion programs dating all the way back to the late nineteenth century. They include various kinds of sales tax exemptions; investment, excise, and job tax credits; and community development block grants, which may be used to assist industries. According to Governor Don Sundquist, the major economic selling points of Tennessee include "a pro-business climate; a high-quality, right-to-work labor force; [and] a superior transportation network." A state promotional booklet boasts that "'Goldbricking' is not part of the Tennessee mindset. Tennesseans take a hearty attitude toward work that matches the state's right-to-work status."[1]

State promoters make sure that their message reaches industrialists and investors across the country and around the world. In recent years state advertising supplements have been printed in such publications as *Plants Sites & Parks, Business Week, Financial World*, and *Site Selection*, and in slick and colorful brochures and booklets issued by state government agencies, various city and county chambers of commerce, industrial development agencies, and the TVA. The Volunteer State has come a long way from its pioneering agricultural roots in the mountains and valleys of East Tennessee.

James E. Fickle, University of Memphis

CITATION:

(1) "There's Gold in Tennessee," Special promotional supplement in *Plants Sites & Parks* (September/October 1996). SUGGESTED READINGS: Constantine G. Belissary, "Industry and Industrial Philosophy in Tennessee, 1850–1860," East Tennessee Historical Society's *Publications*, 23(1951): 46–52; Belissary, "The Rise of Industry and the Industrial Spirit in Tennessee, 1865–1885," *Journal of Southern History*, 19(1953): 193–215; James C. Cobb, *The Selling of The South: The Southern Crusade For Development, 1936–1980* (1982); John Egerton, *Nissan in Tennessee* (1983); Patricia Brake Howard, "Tennessee in War and Peace: The Impact of World War II on State Economic Trends," *Tennessee Historical Quarterly* 51(1992): 51–65.

INFLUENZA PANDEMIC OF 1918–1919 was the most serious outbreak of influenza (also known as grippe, grip, or flu) in Tennessee history, with 7,721 recorded deaths from the disease. What happened in Tennessee was part of an international pandemic, or a worldwide epidemic, multiplied in its effect by the dislocation and homefront demands of World War I. Two great waves of influenza occurred. The first was relatively mild, but the second literally covered the globe within a period of two months. This second wave, called "Spanish flu," appeared in the United States in August 1918. The name "Spanish flu" was a misnomer since no evidence existed that the disease either arose in Spain or was any worse there than in other parts of the world. It is possible that it was called Spanish flu because the first influenza epidemic in the Americas came from Valencia, Spain, in 1647. In addition, more information about the epidemic came from Spain, a neutral country, with no need to hide its vulnerability, unlike other European nations at war in 1918.

The disease, it is now believed, entered the United States through sailors disembarking at the port of Boston. From there, it quickly spread to populated areas along the east coast. By the fall of 1918 it reached burgeoning army training camps and other densely populated areas throughout the country, infecting military personnel and civilians alike.

Wherever the disease occurred, it would strike hard, spread for a week or two, cause much suffering and death, and then quickly subside. It is estimated to have killed 20 to 40 million people worldwide, two to four times the number killed in World War I. Not since the bubonic plague (Black Death) that killed an estimated 62 million Europeans from 1347 to 1350, had there been such a pandemic. Never had a disease spread so rapidly or invaded practically every corner of the world. Even isolated South Pacific islands were affected, and some native Alaskan settlements were completely wiped out. There were about 20 million cases of flu in the United States in 1918–19, and 548,452 were fatal.

In Tennessee, small towns were infected as severely as larger cities; the DuPont company town of Old Hickory, near Nashville, was hardest hit. On September 28, 1918, influenza struck many workers at the E. I. DuPont Munitions Plant. This plant was particularly vulnerable due to its large labor force (over 7,500 people) and their close proximity during working hours. Since flu was easily transmitted to others through airborne droplets from sneezes and coughs, it spread rapidly through the plant and out into the community. As one in four citizens contracted the flu, public gatherings, including religious services, civic events, movies, school classes, and court sessions, had to be canceled. Temporary hospitals were established wherever space could be found, and doctors and nurses were recruited from Nashville and surrounding areas to deal with the crisis. More than 1,300 Nashvillians (most from Old Hickory) died of the flu in 1918–19. In fact, so many died that the basement of the Nashville YMCA, converted to a temporary morgue, literally overflowed with bodies.

Allen R. Coggins, Knoxville
SEE: DISASTERS; OLD HICKORY

INGRAM, ERSKINE BRONSON (1931–1995), was Tennessee's only billionaire when he died of cancer at the age of 63 on June 15, 1995, in his Nashville home. His net worth was estimated at $1.3 billion. In 1994 *Forbes* national business magazine placed Ingram 56th in the annual listing of the richest Americans, and the magazine ranked Ingram Industries 14th in the 500 biggest privately held companies.

Ingram was born November 27, 1931, in St. Paul, Minnesota, to millionaire Orrin Henry and Hortense Bigelow Ingram. O.H. Ingram, whose wealth stemmed from his grandfather's Weyerhaeuser timber fortune, began investing in the oil refining business in the 1930s and 1940s. The need to haul crude oil to a refinery near St. Louis brought him into the river barge business. O.H. Ingram brought his family to Nashville in 1948.

Bronson Ingram completed his freshman year at Vanderbilt University, then transferred to Princeton University. He graduated in 1953 with a degree in English and a commission in the navy. As a young man in Minnesota, he had enjoyed summer sailing on the lakes around St. Paul, but training as a naval offi-

cer left a different impression. "I went to Panama in a destroyer," he recalled in a September 11, 1989, story in *The Tennessean*. "It was sleeping in hammocks and pitching around with what seemed like 6 million people stuffed inside the ship." Ingram resigned his commission in 1955 and, at the age of 24, went to work for his father's company, Ingram Corporation. On a trip to New York City, Ingram met Martha Robinson Rivers of Charleston, South Carolina, and they married in 1958. They later moved to New Orleans, headquarters for the Ingram business. In 1961 the couple moved to Nashville to raise their family, which eventually included a daughter, Robin, and three sons, Orrin, John, and David. Martha Ingram became a significant contributor to Nashville's cultural life, assuming leaderships roles in the development of the Tennessee Performing Arts Center in the late 1970s and the state Bicentennial Celebration of 1996.

When O. H. Ingram died in 1963, Bronson Ingram became president and his brother, Frederic B. Ingram, became chairman of Ingram Corporation, the family's $2 million oil, barge, and lumber business. In the brothers' hands, the corporation generated more than $900 million over the next 15 years. A 1975 Illinois investigation led to ultimate conviction of Frederic Ingram on a bribery charge stemming from a contract between Ingram Contractors and the Metropolitan Sanitary District of Chicago to haul sludge by barge. Bronson Ingram was acquitted of the same charge. In 1978, while Frederic unsuccessfully appealed his four year imprisonment conviction, the brothers divided the Ingram family business. Frederic kept Ingram Corporation, which included the oil refineries and pipeline system, based in New Orleans. Bronson took Ingram Book Company, Ingram Materials, Ingram Barge Company, Tennessee Book Company, and Bluewater Insurance Company. He named his business conglomerate Ingram Industries, Inc.

The new corporation steadily prospered. By 1995 Ingram's barge business, for example, had evolved into Inland Marine Transportation Group, the third-largest inland waterway carrier in the United States. Ingram Industries also branched successfully into new ventures, though not always by design. In 1964 Ingram purchased Tennessee Book Company, a school textbook depository. In 1970 the company began distributing books to retail stores and Ingram Book Company was formed. By 1995 the company controlled about 52 percent of the wholesale book distribution market to American retail bookstores.

The book business led into distribution of computer software through a new company, Ingram Software, Inc. In 1989 the company acquired Micro D Incorporated and formed a new company, Ingram Micro Incorporated, which, at Ingram's death, was the largest distributor of microcomputer hardware and software in the world. Ingram expanded on its distribution experience and background to form Ingram Entertainment, the largest wholesale distributor of pre-recorded videocassettes.

At Ingram's death, Ingram Industries employed about 11,000 people around the world. Though Ingram was a private man who avoided publicity, he was president of the Nashville Area Chamber of Commerce in 1987. As head of the Vanderbilt University Board of Trust in 1991, he led a five-year campaign to raise $350 million. He made the initial donation of more than $25 million in a drive so successful the goal was raised to $500 million in 1994. "You can't raise money unless you know where the heck it is," Ingram explained in a March 3, 1991, story in *The Tennessean.* In 1993 Ingram nominated the first African American accepted for membership in the exclusive Belle Meade Country Club of Nashville.

Ingram is buried in the family plot in Nashville's historic Mount Olivet Cemetery.

David R. Logsdon, Nashville
SEE: COMMERCE; INDUSTRY

INTERSTATE COTTON SEED CRUSHERS' ASSOCIATION

operated from 1897 to 1929. Organized in Nashville in 1897, the Interstate Cotton Seed Crushers' Association was the second cottonseed trade association, the first having been disbanded in 1887, after the American Cotton Oil Trust absorbed most of the cottonseed oil mills and refineries. A decade of mill building by independent businessmen led to the creation of a new trade association. While membership in the first organization had been limited to operators of cottonseed oil mills, the Interstate Cotton Seed Crushers' Association welcomed refiners, brokers, machinery manufacturers, oil chemists, and other interested businessmen. The association provided uniform trading rules, arbitrated trade disputes, promoted cottonseed products, and lobbied for the industry.

When the United States entered World War I in 1917, the federal government regulated essential industries in cooperation with their trade associations. Since cottonseed oil and meal were important food products, and linters, the fuzz left on cottonseed after ginning, was the raw material for nitrocellulose or gun cotton, the Interstate Cotton Seed Crushers' Association could no longer ignore the need for a full-time employee to handle the regulatory duties. When the association hired a presidential assistant in 1917, it made Memphis the permanent headquarters. During the 1920s, other staff members were added as the association undertook to promote and regulate oil mills more aggressively.

In 1929 the Interstate Cotton Seed Crushers' Association was reorganized, strengthened, and renamed the National Cottonseed Products Association. Under that name the association has now embarked on its second century of service to the cottonseed processing industry.

Lynette Boney Wrenn, Memphis
SUGGESTED READING: Lynette B. Wrenn, *Cinderella of the New South: A History of the Cottonseed Industry, 1855–1955* (1995)
SEE: COTTON; INDUSTRY; MEMPHIS

INTERSTATE HIGHWAY SYSTEM, TENNESSEE.

Until the end of the nineteenth century, the United States largely depended on rivers or railroads as the primary means of overland transportation. By the early twentieth century, the growing number of automobiles created a demand for roads suitable for year-round travel and roads that formed a network from state to state. This need resulted in the first "interstates," such as the Lincoln Highway or the Dixie Highway. These early interstate roads consisted of a route designation overlaid on a loose network of existing one- or two-lane roads. In the 1910s and 1920s, state highway departments across the United States completed these highway corridors, and this system of two-lane, open access highways served the country until after World War II.

By 1955, 70 percent of families in the United States owned cars, totaling 61 million vehicles, greatly straining existing roads. President Dwight Eisenhower strongly supported the creation of a national network of modern limited-access highways. His support resulted from his World War II experience with the rapid German troop movement made possible by the autobahn system. Eisenhower contrasted the German roads with his 1919 experience as a member of a military truck and tank convoy that crossed the country from Washington to San Francisco on the Lincoln Highway to dramatize the need for better highways and to showcase the military and its equipment. The deplorable road conditions, on what was then considered the country's best transcontinental highway, led Eisenhower to dub the trip a trek "through darkest America." Eisenhower and other road proponents also argued that an interstate system would be essential to evacuate cities in the event of a nuclear attack and even staged a well publicized mock evacuation of Washington, D.C., in which Eisenhower participated, to demonstrate the difficulties of such a procedure with the existing road system.

In 1954 Eisenhower appointed a committee to study a national interstate program. Consequently, Congress, with bipartisan support, passed the 1956 Federal Highway Act, sponsored by Senator Albert Gore, Sr., of Tennessee, and Representative Hale Boggs of Louisiana. The most significant transportation development in post-World War II America, the act established the Interstate and Defense Highway

System, a new 41,000- mile network of super high-ways to connect every major city in the United States. This was and remains the biggest peacetime construction project of any description ever undertaken by the United States. Planners originally intended to bypass large metropolitan areas, but urban politicians forced a compromise measure that resulted in interstate routes through cities. One unique design feature quickly differentiated the interstate system from other roads: a divided four-lane highway with median, limited access control, and grade separations with cross roads. Eisenhower originally proposed a system of self-financing toll highways, but agreed to a compromise measure that funded construction on a pay-as-you-go basis financed by taxes levied on trucks, tires, gasoline, and related products. However, in 1958, Congress removed the pay-as-you-go provision. Under the new legislation, the federal government paid 90 percent of the cost of the new highways, and each state paid ten percent. Planners originally predicted that the interstate system would be completed in 13 years. However, 40 years and $130 billion later, the system is only 99.9 percent complete.

Tennessee's first interstate project, built between April 1957 and November 1958, was a 1.8-mile bypass of Ardmore in Giles County, that contained a figure-eight interchange on I-65 with State Route 31. In 1987 the state completed the final segment of Tennessee's original interstate allotment, I-440 in Davidson County. Today, Tennessee's 1,062 miles of interstate routes carry 27 percent of the state's motor vehicular traffic, but comprise only 1.2 percent of the state's public road mileage. Tennessee's interstates include I-40, that runs east-west from Memphis to Newport; I-65, that runs north-south through Nashville; I-24, that runs from Clarksville to Chattanooga; I-75 that runs north from Chattanooga to Jellico; I-55 that runs through Shelby County; and I-81 from near Knoxville to Bristol. Nashville is one of only four cities in the United States to have six legs of interstates to converge within its limits.

Martha Carver, Tennessee Department of Transportation
SEE: GORE, ALBERT, SR.; HIGHWAYS, HISTORIC

IPPAU AND PRESSMEN'S HOME. The International Printing Pressmen and Assistants' Union of North America (IPPAU-NA), was organized in 1889, when disgruntled pressmen and press feeders left the International Typographical Union (ITU) and, with the combined membership of 13 locals, formed a new pressmen's union. At its peak, with a membership of more than 125,000, the IPPAU-NA became the largest printing trades union in the world.

For 65 years the union maintained its headquarters at Pressmen's Home, Hawkins County, Tennessee. The Pressmen's Home Community, located in the mountains of northeastern Tennessee, was a

2,700-acre complex with its own phone system, post office, electrical system, and farm. In addition to its headquarters, the union maintained a retirement home, a sanatorium, and a printing trades school at the site.

The East Tennessee location of the IPPAU-NA headquarters was the dream and accomplishment of George L. Berry, president of the IPPAU-NA from 1907 until his death in 1948. Berry was a dominant and controversial president, and the union's progress and growth were intertwined with Berry's life. The IPPAU-NA moved its headquarters to Pressmen's Home from Cincinnati in 1911, because Berry and the union leadership believed the location (originally a mineral health resort known as Hale Springs) was suitable for a tuberculosis sanatorium and a technical trade school for retraining pressmen in the new offset printing methods.

The school eventually became the largest trade school of its kind in the world. While pressmen were also trained on letterpress at the school, its main function was to retrain letterpressmen and educate young printers in the offset craft. The training of thousands of printers at the technical school, along with the correspondence courses the school established, enabled the union to meet the demand for offset printers following World War II.

In 1916 the tuberculosis sanatorium opened and played an important role in combating the disease, the principal cause of death among union members. Besides the physical facilities at Pressmen's Home, the union undertook an extensive campaign to educate the membership about tuberculosis and methods to prevent contamination. By 1961, the year the sanatorium closed, the union facility took credit for saving hundreds of lives through the treatments offered to its members.

In 1966 the union's board of directors decided that the changing times and conditions dictated the removal of the headquarters to a more cosmopolitan location; the following year, the headquarters moved to Washington, D.C. The technical school also closed with the relocation, although the union continued the correspondence courses from its new headquarters.

The IPPAU-NA disappeared from the union registry in 1973, when the union merged with the International Stereotypers', Electrotypers', and Platemakers' Union of North America (ISE&PU) to form the International Printing and Graphic Communications Union (IPGCU). In 1983 the IPGCU merged with the Graphic Arts International Union to become the Graphic Communications International Union (GCIU).

Jack Mooney, East Tennessee State University
SUGGESTED READING: Jack Mooney, "The Establishment and Operation of the Technical Training School of the International Printing Pressmen and Assistants' Union in Ten-

nessee, 1911–1967," *Tennessee Historical Quarterly* 48(1989): 111–122; Jack Mooney, "The Sanatorium of the International Printing Pressmen and Assistants' Union of North America, 1910–1961, at Pressmen's Home, Tennessee," *Tennessee Historical Quarterly* 48(1989): 162–173

SEE: BERRY, GEORGE L.; HAWKINS COUNTY; LABOR

IROQUOIS STEEPLECHASE, a rite of spring for horse enthusiasts held every second Saturday in May, began in 1941. The amateur horse races take place at a three-mile course of wood, water, and brush jumps at Nashville's Percy and Edwin Warner Parks, attracting an audience of some 50,000. The course was a controversial Works Progress Administration project of the late 1930s. In 1936 the WPA spent $215,000 to improve roads, entrance gates, trails, and shelters at the Warner Parks. Two years later, the agency spent another $45,000 to build a steeplechase course as well as adding $12,000 for a riding academy. William I. DuPont, Jr., joined with local horse owners and the city park commission to design the course. DuPont called it "the finest course in America and one that compares favorably with famous plants in foreign lands."[1] Agency critics, however, charged that the public funds were wasted on an elite sport that could, and should, be supported by the monied class who participated in the "sport of kings." In time, the controversy faded and the Iroquois Steeplechase evolved into an annual ritual for many Tennesseans.

CITATION:

(1) Don H. Doyle, *Nashville Since the 1920s* (Knoxville, 1985), 92.

Carroll Van West, Middle Tennessee State University

SEE: HORSERACING TRACKS, EARLY; WORKS PROGRESS ADMINISTRATION

ISLAND #10, BATTLE OF. The opening of hostilities between the Confederate States and the United States in the spring of 1861 found both belligerents woefully unprepared for the struggle ahead. Confederate strategists realized that the Mississippi River offered a broad avenue of invasion into the South which must be defended if southern independence was to be realized. Confederate control of the Mississippi River was vital to the unification of the seceding states east and west of the Mississippi Valley and could effectively cripple the agricultural economy of the midwestern states of the Union.

Early in the war, the Confederate forces under the direction of General Leonidas Polk fortified Island #10, near the Kentucky-Tennessee state line. In 1861 Island #10 was part of a chain of islands in the Mississippi River, lying below Cairo, Illinois, that led into the heart of the Confederacy. It was so named for its position as tenth in this chain from north to south.

A Confederate force of approximately 7,000 troops manned the island defenses. General W.W. Mackall was in command at the time of the Union attack in March 1862. Seven Union gun boats under the command of Flag Officer Andrew H. Foote bombarded the island for three weeks. Heavy bombardment, high water, and the successful movement of the Union gunboats past the Confederate guns forced the surrender of the island on April 7, 1862. Polk evacuated as many soldiers as possible on an assortment of river transports, while under fire from two of Foote's gunboats. Union soldiers pursued the retreating Confederates into the swamps and captured over 6,000 prisoners near Tiptonville, Tennessee.

With the collapse of Island #10's defenses, military activities moved farther south, effectively ending Confederate control of Northwest Tennessee for the duration of the war.

Bill Threlkeld, Union City

SUGGESTED READING: Lonnie White, "Federal Operations at New Madrid and Island Number Ten," West Tennessee Historical Society *Papers* 17(1963): 47–67

SEE: CIVIL WAR; LAKE COUNTY; POLK, LEONIDAS

J

J.C. BRADFORD & COMPANY, the largest brokerage firm headquartered in the southeastern United States, was founded in 1927 by James Cowdon Bradford, Sr. Bradford was born in Nashville to Alexander and Leonora Bradford on November 24, 1892. Alexander Bradford died suddenly, shortly after his son's birth, and his widow returned to her native Louisiana, where the younger Bradford spent the early years of his life. He returned to Nashville in 1907 to attend Montgomery Bell Academy, living with an uncle, Judge James C. Bradford. After completing high school, Bradford enrolled in Vanderbilt University, leaving in 1912 to enter the business world.

Bradford spent his early business career in insurance. During World War I, he was commissioned in the field artillery, serving as an instructor at Fort Sill, Oklahoma. After the war, he managed Davis, Bradford, & Company insurance agency until 1923, leaving to assume the presidency of Piggly Wiggly Stores, Inc. In 1922 Clarence Saunders, founder of the Memphis grocery chain, had borrowed heavily to finance efforts to stop a Wall Street raid on Piggly Wiggly stock. Operating under the lax enforcement of New York Stock Exchange rules, Saunders went for a corner on the market and seemingly had it, but when Piggly Wiggly stock plummeted in value, Saunders could not repay his loans to banks and pools. Pool leaders forced Saunders out and hired Bradford to salvage the company. From 1923 to 1926 Bradford led the reorganization efforts and restored Piggly Wiggly to profitability.

After resigning from Piggly Wiggly, Bradford returned to Nashville, serving briefly as a vice president with American National Bank. In May 1927 Bradford purchased a small securities firm for $10,000 and launched his own brokerage business. J.C. Bradford & Co. began business during the era of the great bull market of the late 1920s and did well until the stock market crash of 1929. The crash concerned Bradford, but he remained optimistic. In 1930 J.C. Bradford & Co. purchased a seat on the New York Stock Exchange for $400,000, the first Nashville-based firm to do so. Within months of purchasing the seat, the firm experienced a declining market that persisted throughout much of the Great Depression. Bradford's firm was the only Nashville-owned broker business to survive the depression, largely because of its small size and the reduction of expenses.

In 1934 the state commissioner of insurance and banking appointed Bradford chairman of the board of a voting trust to oversee the management of Life and Casualty Insurance Company; he served in this capacity until 1951. When life insurance companies emerged as a major investment area after World War II, Bradford's expertise allowed the firm to develop a national reputation in this area.

J.C. Bradford & Co. opened its first branch office in Knoxville in 1943. This expansion continued after the war and included nine offices in four states by the late 1950s. Nevertheless, the firm remained a small, regional concern, concentrating its efforts in industrial revenue bonds, municipal bonds, general stock sales, and life insurance stocks. In 1955 Bradford organized Life Insurance Investors, Inc., a mutual fund invested exclusively in life insurance company stocks. During the 1950s and early 1960s the firm established a national reputation in the brokerage business for its expertise and dealings in life insurance companies, negotiating company sales as well as organizing syndicates for purchasing portions of life insurance companies.

In 1959 Bradford's son, James C. Bradford, Jr., joined the firm. Educated at Groton and Princeton, the younger Bradford worked at Lehman Brothers on Wall Street before returning to Nashville. Over the next two decades, the firm moved into its modern era. While Bradford, Sr., remained the senior partner until his death in December 1981, the small company became a major regional firm. Under J.C. Bradford, Jr.'s leadership, the firm diversified its products and services. Beginning in the 1960s the firm grew dramatically, expanding in Tennessee and the South, as well as opening offices in the midwest and California. By the 1990s J.C. Bradford & Company had grown to over 80 offices in 15 states.

Fred Colvin, Middle Tennessee State University

SEE: COMMERCE; LIFE AND CASUALTY INSURANCE COMPANY; SAUNDERS, CLARENCE

JACK DANIEL DISTILLERY, the oldest registered distillery in the nation, is located in Lynchburg in Moore County. Established by Jasper "Jack" Daniel in 1866, the distillery produces sour mash whiskey. Daniel located the distillery near his birthplace, but also recognized the natural advantages that made what is now Moore County an ideal site for whiskey production, including the presence of iron-free water from the distillery's cave and the ready availability of corn, rye, and barley malt to produce the fermentable mixture called mash.

Daniel's whiskey quickly won national recognition and in 1904 received the gold medal at the Louisiana Purchase Exposition in St. Louis. In 1907 Daniel transferred the distillery to his nephew Lem Motlow, who moved the operation to St. Louis in 1910, after Tennessee enacted prohibition. In 1938, after a vigorous campaign by Motlow, Moore County, which chose to remain "dry," voted to permit the return of Jack Daniel Distillery to its historic site.

Today, the distillery attracts more than 250,000 people annually, who make the journey to Lynchburg to tour the barrelhouse, distillery, and rickyard. Although whiskey production accounts for a major segment of the Moore County economy, the county remains "dry," and visitors are restricted to the purchase of commemorative bottles of Jack Daniel's Tennessee Whiskey. Many visitors also dine at Miss Mary Bobo's Boarding House, where they are served southern, family-style dinners, presided over by Lynne Tolley. The boarding house, listed in the National Register of Historic Places, is one of the oldest buildings in Lynchburg. Its most famous proprietor was Mary Bobo, who operated a boarding house and restaurant in the Greek Revival-styled dwelling for most of the twentieth century. The historic office and early works of the Jack Daniel Distillery also are listed in the National Register.

In addition to Jack Daniel's Tennessee Whiskey, the distillery produces Gentleman Jack Rare Tennessee Whiskey, Jack Daniel's Country Cocktails, and Jack Daniel's Single Barrel Tennessee Whiskey. Adjacent to the distillery is the Lynchburg historic district, also listed in the National Register.

Lynne Tolley, Lynchburg

SEE: DISTILLERIES, HISTORIC; MOORE COUNTY

JACKSON, on land acquired by treaty from the Chickasaws on October 19, 1818, is located in the geographic center of Tennessee's western district. The Tennessee General Assembly created Madison County on November 7, 1821, shortly after settlers began moving into the area. The town of Alexandria was designated as the county seat, and in 1822 the name was changed to Jackson to honor Andrew Jackson, who negotiated the cession treaty with the Chickasaws.

Jackson's central location on the Forked Deer River made it a natural crossroads for the western district. In the early years, the rich alluvial soil of the surrounding region fostered a cotton economy and supported a plantation culture. By 1860 Madison County included 11,400 whites, 10,012 slaves, and 83 free persons of color. Even today, the rural landscape surrounding Jackson is dotted with cotton fields, and the population still reflects the early racial mix.

Transportation played an important role in the development of Jackson from a small frontier outpost into a major regional commercial and cultural center. In the antebellum period, the Forked Deer River, which was large enough to accommodate keelboats, flatboats, and even small steamboats, served as the chief transportation artery. Traffic on the Forked Deer carried crops to market in New Orleans and brought consumer goods to plantation households. In 1857 the first rail transportation arrived in Jackson and opened a new commercial era.

The Mississippi & Tennessee Central and Mobile & Ohio were the first railroads to serve Jackson. The Civil War interrupted rail development, but in the postwar years, new construction, the expansion of connections, and the consolidation of rail lines redefined the systems serving Jackson. The three largest rail companies serving Jackson were the Louisville & Nashville, the Illinois Central, and the Gulf, Mobile, & Ohio. Jackson's most legendary figure, Casey Jones, was an engineer for the Illinois Central, when he lost his life in a collision with a freight train near Vaughn, Mississippi.

Transportation development continued into the twentieth century as Jackson was linked with major state highways. The Memphis-to-Bristol Highway (later designated as U.S. 70) passed through Jackson, where it joined with U.S. 45, a major north-south highway corridor. In the late 1960s came Interstate I-40, while in the 1990s the expansion of U.S. 412 to a four-lane highway has linked Jackson with the Mississippi River bridge of Interstate I-155 west of Dyersburg.

The city suffered little physical damage during the Civil War, although events in the surrounding area significantly influenced people's lives. A few small skirmishes were fought around Jackson, and Federal troops occupied the town for approximately one year. Both sides used the main building of West Tennessee College as a military hospital. The city also served as an important recruiting station for Confederate forces. A prominent citizen of Jackson, Robert Cartmell, kept a diary during the period that provides a firsthand look at Civil War life on the homefront.

The impact of industrialization on Jackson began with its development as an important rail link between the commercial centers of the Midwest and the Gulf coast port cities. The key player in this process was the Illinois Central Railroad. In the final two decades of the nineteenth century the IC completed acquisitions that extended its service from Cairo south to New Orleans. It established an engine shop in Jackson that represented the city's first major unionized industry. By the turn of the century, the earlier cotton crossroads community of Jackson was transformed into a bustling commercial and industrial city. Other significant industries represented were Southern Engine and Boiler Works, Southern Seating and Cabinet Co., and Jackson Fibre Co, a subsidiary of Bemis Bro. Bag Co. Built in 1900 three miles south of Jackson, the textile mill soon became the largest single employer in the county. The parent company also established a planned self-sufficient community named Bemis.

Jackson's long educational tradition began with the establishment of Jackson Male Academy in 1823. Other schools, including some female academies, appeared shortly thereafter. In 1844 West Tennessee College began operations as the city's first institution of higher education. Postwar concerns for the education of freedmen led to the opening of the Colored Methodist High School in 1882. Jackson's education tradition continues today with a consolidated city-county public school system, four primary/secondary private schools, and four institutions of higher learning: Jackson State Community College, Lambuth University, Lane College, and Union University.

The Methodists, Presbyterians, Anglicans, and Baptists organized the first churches in Jackson. In 1820 the Tennessee Annual Conference appointed two Methodist ministers to serve in the newly opened west district and report on the needs of the area. Six years later, the members organized First Methodist Church in Jackson. Records of the Western Tennessee Presbytery indicate that the Presbyterians organized St. Luke's Parish in Jackson on July 23, 1832. Although Baptists formed congregations in rural Madison County during the 1820s, Jackson's First Baptist Church was not organized until 1837. Catholic families apparently settled in Jackson prior to the Civil War, but St. Mary's Parish did not record baptisms and marriages until 1867. A small Jewish community organized a congregation in 1885, and named it B'Nai Israel.

Steve Baker, Union University

SUGGESTED READINGS: Emma Inman Williams, *Historic Madison: The Story of Jackson and Madison County Tennessee* (1946); Emma Inman Williams, Marion B. Smothers, and Mitch Carter, *Jackson & Madison County: A Pictorial History* (1988)

SEE: BEMIS; COMMUNITY COLLEGES; HIGHWAYS, HISTORIC; JACKSON, ALEXANDER; JACKSON PURCHASE; JONES, JONATHAN "CASEY"; LAMBUTH UNIVERSITY; LANE, ISAAC; LANE COLLEGE; MADISON COUNTY; MATTHEWS, MARK A.; RAILROADS; SOUTHERN ENGINE AND BOILER WORKS; UNION UNIVERSITY

JACKSON, ALEXANDER (ca. 1802–1879) was an articulate advocate of scientific agriculture. Jackson completed a medical degree at the University of Pennsylvania in 1824, and came to Tennessee five years later, establishing a medical practice at Paris, in Henry County. Jackson soon demonstrated his interests in both medicine and agriculture. In 1833 he spoke to the Medical Society of Tennessee on "The Medical Topography of the Western District of Tennessee." In May 1839 he became the founding president of the Henry County Agricultural Society, which soon held the first county fair in that area of the state.

In 1840 Jackson moved to Madison County, where he once again established a medical practice and became involved in agriculture. By 1847 he retired from medicine and focused his energy in new directions; he served as a trustee of West Tennessee College, founded in 1844, and helped to bring railroads to West Tennessee. From 1849 through 1853 he was a member of the Tennessee General Assembly, before serving as mayor of Jackson, 1854–1856. Jackson's interests in agriculture found a new outlet in politics.

Jackson's entry into the legislature coincided with a new governmental emphasis on scientific agriculture. An extraordinarily active legislator, first-term representative Jackson sponsored or co-sponsored 32 bills, petitions, or resolutions. Some of the legislature's concerns in this session involved agricultural issues, including the creation of a Tennessee Agricultural Society. During his second term, the legislature initiated activities that led to the establishment of a State Agricultural Bureau in 1854.

Throughout the 1850s, Jackson provided dynamic leadership for agricultural interests in West Tennessee. In February 1854 he helped organize the Madison County Agricultural and Mechanical Society and became the group's first president. The society sponsored county fairs and served as the nucleus for the Western Division Fair, funded by the state legislature. In 1855 Jackson presided over the first Western Division Fair, presenting the principal oration. His commitment to the advancement of agriculture also took him to Washington, D.C., as a Tennessee delegate to the U.S. Agricultural Society.

After the Civil War, Jackson never again played a key role in agriculture or politics. Nevertheless, his work during the antebellum era places Alexander Jackson among the noteworthy pioneers of science and technology.

James X. Corgan, Austin Peay State University

SEE: AGRICULTURAL SOCIETIES; JACKSON; JACKSON, HOWELL E.; MADISON COUNTY

JACKSON, ANDREW (1767–1845) was the seventh President of the United States, serving from 1829 to 1837. As war hero and the "savior of his country," he was one of a handful of Americans who dominated the first half of the nineteenth century. As president, he redefined and strengthened the executive office, championing the concept of a united nation against rising threats of disunion. In all estimates, he was one of the strongest presidents, as well as one of the most controversial. He lent his name to a movement, Jacksonian Democracy, and to an era, the Age of Jackson.

Jackson was born in the frontier settlement of the Waxhaws in South Carolina, the youngest son of Andrew and Elizabeth Hutchinson Jackson, both Scots-Irish from Carrickfergus in northern Ireland. His father died a few months before he was born. Encouraged by his mother to enter the ministry, Jackson obtained a modest education and taught school for a brief time. The Revolutionary War interrupted his education, and Jackson volunteered his services to the American cause. In 1779 his brother Hugh died from war injuries. In 1781 his other sibling, Robert, died of smallpox, which he and Jackson contracted while British prisoners of war at Camden, South Carolina. Jackson recovered, but later that year, his mother succumbed to cholera, while nursing sick family members in Charleston. At 14, Jackson was an orphan, having only distant maternal relatives to supervise his continuing education, which he resumed after a brief residence in Charleston.

About 1784, Jackson arrived in Salisbury, North Carolina, where he read law for three years with two distinguished lawyers; he received his license to practice in 1787. Jackson commenced his profession in North Carolina's western district, in Washington County (now in Tennessee). By October 1788, he had received an appointment as district attorney in Mero District (now Middle Tennessee) and moved to Nashville, where he resided at the home of Rachel Stockley Donelson, the widow of John Donelson, a founder of the town.

There he met the widow's daughter Rachel, who soon became his wife and the love of his life. Unhappily married to Lewis Robards of Mercer County,

Kentucky, she had recently returned to her mother's home. When efforts at reconciliation failed in early 1790, Rachel visited friends in Natchez to escape further mistreatment. Later in the year, her estranged husband solicited a divorce decree from the Virginia assembly, but the legislature remanded the petition to the courts of the Kentucky district (then a part of Virginia). Apparently presuming that Robards would proceed with the action, Jackson went to Natchez and married Rachel in August 1791. Robards, however, delayed divorce proceedings (on charges of adultery) until 1792, and the court issued its decree on September 27, 1793. When Andrew and Rachel received news of the court decision, they remarried on January 18, 1794, before a Davidson County justice of the peace.

The Jacksons settled in Nashville, and, over the next few years, Jackson practiced law, speculated in land, bought the Poplar Grove farm in Davidson County (near the Hermitage), and commenced general merchandising in partnership with family and friends. Failed business ventures forced him to sell Poplar Grove and purchase the cheaper Hermitage property (eventually expanded to about 1,000 acres), which remained his home for the rest of his life. The Jacksons "adopted" a nephew, Andrew Jackson Donelson (known as Andrew Jackson, Jr.), reared several Indian orphans, and served as counselors for numerous children of relatives and friends. The Hermitage farm, generally managed by overseers and worked by slaves, was a model for Middle Tennessee agriculture, with orchards, gardens, livestock, staple crops, cotton gins, and stills. In the early 1820s, the Jacksons built a larger house on the site, where they hosted innumerable visitors. Fire destroyed a portion of the dwelling during Jackson's presidency, and in rebuilding, he enlarged the house and added the front and rear porticos.

Jackson's interest in politics continued even as he built his plantation. As the new Territory South of the River Ohio organized for statehood, Jackson accepted election to its first constitutional convention, and in the fall of 1796, Tennessee voters sent him to Philadelphia as their first representative. A year later, the legislature elected him United States Senator. Jackson's role in both bodies was undistinguished, and he resigned in 1798 to become a judge of the Superior Court (now the Tennessee Supreme Court). For the next six years, he rode circuit over the state, resigning in April 1804. By 1806, Jackson had abandoned his legal practice and storekeeping to devote his time to farming, with occasional interruptions for local militia musters.

Jackson's military duties markedly increased upon his election as Major General of the Tennessee militia in 1802 and continued for the next 20 years. Though this period brought national honor, personal and political controversy clouded his fame. In 1803, he quarreled with John Sevier and almost dueled with the governor. In January 1806, he caned Thomas Swann; in May, he killed Charles Dickinson in a duel; and in September, he tacitly endorsed Aaron Burr's controversial western schemes. Early in 1807, Jackson ran a sword through Samuel Jackson. And in September 1813, he brawled with brothers Jesse and Thomas Hart Benton, taking a bullet in the arm; the bullet was removed during his presidency.

Jackson's emergence as a popular national figure resulted from his distinguished service as Major General in the War of 1812. His first major assignment came when the war department in Washington ordered his Tennessee soldiers to Natchez in 1812, and there dismissed them. Jackson disobeyed orders and refused to abandon his men. Under severe hardships that earned him the name "Old Hickory," he marched the forces back to Tennessee. A year later, he added to his reputation when he led his men into battle against the Creek Indians, defeating them at Talladega in November 1813, at Emuckfau and Enotochapco in January 1814, and at Horseshoe Bend in March 1814. The Treaty of Fort Jackson, concluded in August 1814, sealed the capitulation of the tribe and transferred most of their land in Alabama and southern Georgia to the United States.

Having been commissioned Major General of the U.S. Army in May 1814, Jackson soon received orders to defend the Gulf coast against an expected British invasion. He led his troops into Florida, seized Pensacola, and in early December, marched to New Orleans. There, in the early morning of January 8, 1815, a few weeks after the signing of the Treaty of Ghent, he resoundingly defeated the British. That victory brought immediate fame. To many, Jackson was second only to George Washington in service to the republic. Some, however, found his New Orleans military record disturbing: approval of the military execution of six mutinous militiamen, imposition of martial law, suspension of the writ of habeas corpus, and defiance of the orders of a federal judge. Jackson defended his actions on military necessity and muted criticism for a time. Over the next several years, he negotiated land cessions in Georgia, Alabama, Mississippi, Tennessee, and Kentucky at treaties with the Cherokees, Choctaws, and Chickasaws, presaging his controversial presidential policy of Indian removal to accommodate advancing white settlement. In 1818, he led troops into Florida to suppress the Seminoles, again seized Pensacola, and ordered the execution of two British subjects suspected of arming the Seminoles. The action precipitated a brief international crisis and a long congressional investigation. Jackson's vindication came in 1821, when he supervised the transfer of the Floridas to the United States under the 1819 Adams-

Onís Treaty; he served as governor during the establishment of territorial government.

Jackson resigned his army appointment on June 1, 1821, and retired to Tennessee. In 1822, the state legislature nominated him for president of the United States, a move seconded by other states, and in 1823 elected him to the U.S. Senate (he resigned in 1825). Jackson consistently denied that he sought the presidency, but declared it his duty to serve if elected. In the presidential campaign of 1824, Jackson received both a popular and an electoral plurality in a contest among William H. Crawford, John Quincy Adams, Henry Clay, John C. Calhoun, and Jackson. When the House of Representatives gave the presidency to Adams, and he appointed Clay Secretary of State, Jackson labeled the transaction "a corrupt bargain" that violated the will of the voters. On that charge, Jackson's advisors launched the presidential campaign of 1828.

The ensuing presidential canvass was one of the nation's dirtiest. Pamphlets and partisan newspapers probed the public and private lives of Jackson and Adams, particularly Jackson. The parade of "juvenile indiscretions" seemed endless, but the insinuations of moral depravity as evidenced by the Jackson's marriages proved most painful. Jackson, however, was elected president that fall. On December 22, 1828, Rachael Jackson died, and her husband charged that the event had been hastened by the campaign slanders.

In January 1829, the widowed Jackson left Tennessee for his inauguration. Reform was the keynote of the bereaved Jackson's inauguration address in March 1829, and reform remained the theme of his two terms as president. He departed from practice by rejecting Adams's cabinet. As the Senate recessed in mid-March, Jackson initiated a series of removals and appointments that his opponents denounced as the spoils system. Jacksonians defended the practice as a restoration of honesty and integrity and the destruction of entrenched privilege. Cabinet squabbles erupted during Jackson's first term that ended in a reconstitution of the cabinet and the resignation of Vice President John C. Calhoun. Nevertheless, Jackson maintained his commitment to reform and executed his will through the exercise of the veto, killing the Maysville Road bill and the recharter of the Bank of the United States.

The recharter of the bank became the focus of the presidential campaign of 1832 between Jackson and Clay. The real issue, however, was Jackson. Analysis of Jackson's election victory showed a decline in his support and the rise of a strong opposition. During his second administration, Jackson continued to use the veto and took unprecedented actions: in 1833, without congressional approval, he ordered federal deposits removed from the Bank of the United States and placed in state banks, forcing the resignation of a cabinet officer who refused his directive; and in 1836, he issued the Specie Circular, requiring the payment of government debts in hard money. Jackson's 1833 proclamation against nullification defining the Union as indissoluble assaulted state's rights. In consequence, his opponents denounced him as a tyrant, "King Andrew," and united to form the Whig party. By the end of the decade, the second American party system had emerged in all the states.

Jackson returned to the Hermitage in early 1837. Many still considered him a hero and the spokesman of the common man. He spent the remainder of his years in retirement, consulting with numerous politicians on the issues of the day, entertaining frequent visitors, and managing his farm. His health, much damaged by dueling wounds and the rigors of military campaigns, continued to decline. In 1845, at age 78, Jackson died at the Hermitage and was buried in the Hermitage garden two days later.

Harold D. Moser, University of Tennessee, Knoxville

SUGGESTED READINGS: Harold D. Moser et al., *The Papers of Andrew Jackson*, 5 vols. to date (1981–); James Parton, *Life of Andrew Jackson*, 3 vols. (1860); Robert V. Remini, *Andrew Jackson*, 3 vols. (1977–1984); Daniel Feller, *The Jacksonian Promise: America, 1815–1840* (1995)

SEE: BENTON, THOMAS H.; CREEK INDIAN WARS OF 1813 & 1814; EATON AFFAIR; HERMITAGE; JACKSON, RACHEL; JACKSONIANS

JACKSON COUNTY. Located in the picturesque foothills of the Cumberland Mountains, most of the eastern part of Jackson County lies within the Highland Rim physiographic province situated at the foot of the Higher Cumberland Plateau to the east and is part of the Interior Low Plateau. The western part of Jackson County lies within the Nashville Basin. There is much rolling land between sharply incised stream valleys. Jackson County is known as the "Switzerland of the Cumberlands."

Jackson County, named in honor of Andrew Jackson, was created by the Tennessee legislature in November 1801. It is the second oldest of the 23 counties named Jackson in the United States; only the Jackson County in Georgia is older. Temporary county seats were used until about the year 1806, when Williamsburg was named as the county seat of Jackson County. Williamsburg was named for Sampson Williams, an early pioneer in the area.

In 1817 Gainesboro was selected as the permanent county seat and was incorporated in 1820. The land was donated by David Cox. Gainesborough, as it was then spelled, is one of the oldest towns in the state and was named for General Edmund Pendleton Gaines, who fought with Jackson at the Battle of New Orleans. The Gainesboro Historic District, which includes the town square and the 1927 Jackson County Courthouse, is listed in the National Register of Historic Places.

The same mountains that give Jackson County its beauty also made travel difficult in the days before paved roads and steel bridges. Both the Cumberland and Roaring rivers cross the county. River boats of bygone days came through the county weekly, carrying passengers, merchandise, agricultural produce, and lumber products. Timber and farming have been primary occupations in the county since its establishment. With the flooding of the Cumberland River in 1963 by the Cordell Hull Dam, which was built by the U.S. Army Corps of Engineers, and the opening of a deepwater port in 1981 near Gainesboro, the river once again became very important to Jackson County.

Sportsmen in Jackson County can be active year-round because there is an abundance of wildlife—from deer to quail and bass to catfish. The American bald eagle and the whooping crane can still be seen. Canada geese winter in Jackson County. The Granville Marina on the Cordell Hull Lake offers every pleasure in outdoor recreation—from boating to camping. Two U.S. Army Corps of Engineers recreation areas are at Roaring River and Salt Lick Creek.

Jackson County offers one of the most important historic sites in the upper Cumberlands: Fort Blount and the nearby old townsite of Williamsburg. Governor William Blount ordered this frontier fort to be built in 1794 to protect the increasing number of settlers moving over the trail on their way west. William Gilespie operated a tavern and ferry there. The site is located near the Cumberland River about 16 miles downstream from Gainesboro. The Fort Blount-Williamsburg site is listed in the National Register of Historic Places. Future projects of the Jackson County Historical Society include the restoration of Fort Blount and the creation of an interest in, and appreciation of, the Old Avery Trace, the first road to enter Jackson County. A bicentennial project traces its roots to a visit to Fort Blount by noted French botanist and explorer Andre Michaux on March 1, 1796.

In 1992 the state legislature passed a law designating the yellowwood as Tennessee's official bicentennial tree. Efforts by Jackson County citizens have placed yellowwood trees across the state, including one on the grounds of the State Capitol in Nashville.

Much of the material for a comprehensive history of Gainesboro and Jackson County was destroyed when the courthouse burned on the night of August 14, 1872. All county records were lost in the blaze except those of the Chancery Court. The Chancery Court records survived because Robert A. Cox, Clerk and Master, maintained his office in a private building away from the courthouse. The loss of the records of the Circuit Court Clerk, the County Court Clerk, the Register of Deeds, and the Tax Assessor generated great confusion for many years.

Agriculture is the oldest occupation or business in Jackson County. In 1940, for instance, of the 194,000 acres listed in the county, over 172,000 acres were farmland. Tobacco, livestock, and corn continue to be important farm products. The land area of Jackson comprises 327 square miles and the population of Gainesboro, as reported in the 1990 census, is 911. That same census listed Jackson County with a population of 9,297.

Moldon Tayse, Gainesboro

SEE: CUMBERLAND RIVER; FORT BLOUNT; U.S. ARMY CORPS OF ENGINEERS; TOBACCO

JACKSON, HOWELL EDMUNDS (1832–1895), U.S. Senator (1881–1886), Sixth Circuit Court (1886–1892), Sixth Circuit Court of Appeals (1892–1893), and Associate Justice of the U.S. Supreme Court (1893–1895), was best remembered for his role in the *Pollock* Income Tax Decision of 1895. He was the second of six children born to Dr. Alexander Jackson, a prominent Whig politician and planter, and his first wife, Mary Hurt. In 1840 the family moved to Jackson, Tennessee, where young Howell attended Jackson Male Academy and West Tennessee College. He finished his education at the University of Virginia and Cumberland Law School in Lebanon, where he graduated in 1856. Opening his legal practice in Jackson in 1857, his first recorded case involved the implied warranty on the health of a slave.

Relocating to Memphis in 1857, Jackson opened a partnership with future Confederate Congressman David Currin. In 1859 Jackson married Sophia Molloy; their 14-year marriage produced five children. Notwithstanding his Unionist Whig sympathies, Jackson secured appointment as Confederate Receiver of Sequestered Property for the Western District of Tennessee in October 1861. He held this position until the fall of Memphis in June 1862, after which he made unsuccessful attempts to secure a judicial commission in the Confederate Army. Jackson and his family spent the remainder of the war as refugees in LaGrange, Georgia.

Jackson returned to Memphis at war's end and in 1866 secured a formal pardon from President Andrew Johnson. With the subsequent dismissal of charges of treason, Jackson was instrumental in helping Nathan Bedford Forrest post bond in a case involving similar charges. He practiced business and corporate law in Memphis until 1874. Jackson lost his first wife during the Memphis yellow fever epidemic of 1873, and, 13 months later, he married Mary Harding of Belle Meade Plantation. This marriage produced three children.

Following his marriage, Jackson relocated to Jackson and entered a legal partnership with former Confederate General Alexander Campbell. In 1875 he was appointed to the state Court of Arbitration. Three years later, he made a strong, but unsuccessful effort to secure nomination to the Tennessee

Supreme Court. A postwar Democrat, Jackson became associated with the anti-repudiation "State Credit" faction of the party during the controversy over payment of the state's postwar debt. In 1880 Jackson won election to the state legislature. When an evenly divided legislature deadlocked on the selection of a U.S. Senator, Jackson was chosen as a compromise candidate by a bi-partisan coalition of Democrats and Republicans.

Taking office on March 4, 1881, he spent the next five years supporting such issues as restriction of Chinese immigration and the creation of the Interstate Commerce Commission. He also favored internal improvements, a lowered tariff, and civil service reforms. A member of the Committees on Pensions and Claims, Jackson occasionally clashed with Indiana Republican Benjamin Harrison on the issue of granting pensions to able-bodied veterans. During his final year as a senator, Jackson took a prominent role in the campaigns to increase presidential power over federal appointments and to secure federal aid to state education.

Democratic President Grover Cleveland appointed Jackson to the Sixth Circuit Court in April 1886. He rendered roughly 90 opinions during his seven years on the bench; his most notable decision in the 1892 case of *In re Greene* later served as the constitutional basis for the Supreme Court's 1895 decision limiting the power of the 1890 Sherman Anti-Trust Act in *E.C. Knight*.

In 1892 Jackson was elevated to the Sixth Circuit Court of Appeals, where he served with the future President William Howard Taft. Upholding the authority of federal agents to enforce civil rights law in *United States v. Patrick* (1893), Jackson positioned himself to become the last important judicial appointment of outgoing Republican President Benjamin Harrison. Formally sworn in as an Associate Justice of the U.S. Supreme Court on March 4, 1893, Jackson was stricken with tuberculosis shortly after the Court's first term. Authoring just 46 opinions and four dissents, he nevertheless left a strong record of growing opposition towards government regulation of the economy. Leaving his death bed in May 1895 to participate in the rehearing of *Pollock v. Farmer's Home Loan,* Jackson's opinion sustaining the constitutionality of the 1894 federal income tax proved futile when the Court majority invalidated the measure. Returning to his West Meade home in Nashville after the Court's decision, Justice Jackson died on August 8, 1895.

Harvey Gresham Hudspeth, Mississippi Valley State University

SUGGESTED READINGS: Melvin I. Urofsky, *The Supreme Justices: A Biographical Dictionary* (1994); Terry Calvani, "The Early Legal Career of Howell Jackson," *Vanderbilt Law Review* 30(1977): 39–72

SEE: BELLE MEADE PLANTATION; JACKSON, ALEXANDER; MADISON COUNTY; STATE DEBT CONTROVERSY

JACKSON PURCHASE included the area of West Tennessee and southwestern Kentucky between the Tennessee and Mississippi rivers. The Chickasaws historically occupied this large tract, which they ceded in the Treaty of Tecumseh, negotiated by Andrew Jackson and Isaac Shelby in 1818.

After statehood, Tennessee continued to be troubled by conflicting land claims by Native Americans and settlers. Governors John Sevier, Archibald Roane, Willie Blount, and Joseph McMinn looked to the federal government for help, and a series of treaties forged between 1798 and 1819 reduced the land occupied by Native Americans to a small Cherokee claim in the southeast corner of the state. In 1818 Andrew Jackson and former Kentucky governor Isaac Shelby were appointed to oversee negotiations for an agreement with the Chickasaws. In 1783 the tribe had established a boundary at the watershed between the Tennessee and Cumberland rivers, but in the intervening years, they had dropped claims to territory in Middle Tennessee that conflicted with Cherokee cessions. Their claim to land west of the Tennessee River was unopposed, however, and the state government had a flood of North Carolina land warrants to honor. Jackson and Shelby argued that the land warrants prevented federal action to deter settlement, and the Chickasaws agreed to sell the tract for $300,000.

In 1819 the region opened for settlement, and the General Assembly created Hardin County that same year. Speculators John Overton, James Winchester, and Jackson quickly established the town of Memphis. Within six years of its opening, the Jackson Purchase contained 16 counties.

Blythe Semmer, Middle Tennessee State University
SEE: CHICKASAWS; JACKSON, ANDREW; SHELBY, ISAAC

JACKSON, RACHEL (1767–1828), daughter of John Donelson and Rachel Stockley and wife of President Andrew Jackson, was born in Pittsylvania County, Virginia. In December 1779 her family set out for the west, arriving at Fort Nashborough (now Nashville) in April 1780. The Donelsons settled on land bordering Stones River, but a few months later moved near Harrodsburg, Kentucky, then a part of Virginia. In March 1785 Rachel Donelson married Lewis Robards, a native of Mercer County, Kentucky, and the couple moved in with Robards's widowed mother.

From the outset, the marriage was an unhappy one. According to later accounts, quarrels erupted over the flirtatious nature of the vivacious and beautiful Rachel. By 1788 the Robards had separated, and Rachel moved in with her mother, then living near Nashville.

Efforts at reconciliation failed as Robards observed on occasional visits Rachel's friendship with Andrew Jackson, a young lawyer from North Carolina now boarding with her mother. By 1790 the Robards had separated permanently, and Rachel visited friends in Natchez to escape further mistreatment by her estranged husband. In December, Robards appealed to the Virginia legislature for divorce, and that body remanded the issue to the courts of the Kentucky district. When Jackson learned of the Virginia authorization, he went to Natchez and married Rachel in August 1791, not realizing that Robards had failed to pursue the case. Robards finally took the issue to the Mercer County court in January 1792, charging adultery, and on September 27, 1793, the court granted his petition. On January 18, 1794, Andrew and Rachel remarried before Robert Hays, a Davidson County justice of the peace.

The marriage proved a happy one. The Jacksons had no children, but adopted her nephew, Andrew (1808–1865), cared for several Indian orphans, and served as guardians for numerous children of friends and family. Rachel assisted in managing their farm during Jackson's absence and took great interest in gardening and in the construction of a new house at the Hermitage. She accompanied her husband on various trips—to Washington in 1815, to New Orleans for celebrations in Jackson's honor, to Pensacola when he served as Florida governor, and to Washington during his stint as senator in the mid-1820s. But Rachel preferred the farm to city life, and she found peace and security in the scriptures and sermons she read at home and heard at the Presbyterian church on their property. As she aged, she gained weight, developed respiratory illness, and suffered from depression. The presidential campaign of 1828 contributed further to her deteriorating health, as Jackson's opponents dredged up the unusual circumstance of their marriages to demonstrate his moral flaws. The rumors probably contributed to the development of Rachel's final illness, which first manifested itself on December 17, 1828, some four weeks before the Jacksons' scheduled departure for the inauguration. Five days later, on December 22, Rachel died, apparently from a massive heart attack. Her funeral and burial followed in the Hermitage garden she had so carefully maintained over the years. Jackson ordered a tomb constructed for her remains and cherished her memory and virtue to his own death. The account of their love and devotion to each other is legendary even today, recounted in biographies, film, fiction, drama, and music.

Harold D. Moser, University of Tennessee, Knoxville
SUGGESTED READING: Harold D. Moser, et al., *The Papers of Andrew Jackson*, 5 vols. to date (1981–); Catherine W. Cruse, *An Amiable Woman: Rachel Jackson* (1994)
SEE: DONELSON, JOHN; HERMITAGE; JACKSON, ANDREW

JACKSONIANS were President Andrew Jackson and his circle of advisors who were recognized as leaders of the Democratic party both nationally and within Tennessee. Jackson's Tennessee associates included Judge John Overton; Senator John H. Eaton; Major William B. Lewis; Andrew Jackson Donelson, the president's nephew and private secretary; Nashville postmaster Robert Armstrong; Governor William Carroll; and Congressman James K. Polk. Among prominent secondary figures, more associated with Polk, but equally devoted to Jackson's presidency, were Supreme Court Justice John Catron, Congressmen Aaron V. Brown and Cave Johnson, and Senator Felix Grundy. The first group played a major role in elevating Jackson to the White House and were among his principal advisors early in his presidency. The latter figures defended Jackson's political principles as national and state politics divided into the nation's first modern political party system. With Polk's election to the presidency, they helped to establish Jacksonian ideals as federal government policy until the Civil War.

The inner circle of advisors for Jackson's first administration came together during the 1820s out of a Tennessee politics riven by factionalism. Most, including Jackson himself, were associated with a group of planters and land speculators, led by Overton, that had long dominated state politics. The Overton faction's pre-eminence, however, had recently been shaken by Carroll's election as governor in 1821 as the opponent of the Overton clique's control of the state's banks. Grundy, a former "War Hawk" congressman, meanwhile acted as a maverick in state politics by seeking to return to power as the champion of public relief for those suffering from the effects of the financial Panic of 1819. Jackson's initial nomination for the presidency by the state legislature in 1822 appears to have been orchestrated by the Overton group as a way to restore its credibility with Tennessee's voters. With Overton, Lewis, and Eaton most actively promoting his candidacy, the general's unexpected but widespread popularity brought most Tennessee politicians into open support of his election. Jackson won a plurality of popular votes in the 1824 election, but his failure to gain a majority in the electoral college left the choice of the president to the House of Representatives. The House, however, chose runner-up John Quincy Adams over Jackson. When Adams appointed House Speaker Henry Clay as Secretary of State, it provoked charges of a "corrupt bargain." Virtually all of the state's leading figures united behind Jackson's election in 1828. He became the champion of "the people" against the "bargain, intrigue, and corruption" that had "stolen" the presidency in 1824.

Jackson and his associates viewed his overwhelming triumph over Adams in 1828 as a restoration of Jeffersonian Republican principles, for he had been promoted on a platform calling for a return to a strict construction of the constitution, the retrenchment of public expenditures, and the payment of the national debt. Over the course of Jackson's two terms, his presidency became more closely identified with opposition to Clay's "American System," a series of policy proposals by which the national government would encourage economic development through chartering a Bank of the United States, providing tariff protection for American manufacturers, and funding the construction of internal improvements. Jackson's hostility to the American System lay the foundation for a new Democratic party, for he believed that such policies—despite their promise of national prosperity—would unfairly benefit a privileged, wealthy elite at the expense of farmers, laborers, and mechanics. Instead, he concluded that the government should withdraw from the economy as much as possible and provide its favors equally for the rich and poor.

Acting upon this belief, Jackson pitted his presidency against the economic nationalism that had dominated federal policy since the War of 1812. He vetoed several bills to appropriate funds for local internal improvements, and—especially after tariff revenues had helped to pay off the national debt by 1835—he encouraged free trade through a reduction in tariff rates. In 1832, in the most controversial move of his presidency, Jackson vetoed a bill to recharter the existing Bank of the United States. He then initiated a "war" to destroy the Bank by ordering the withdrawal of the federal deposits. Despite the severe recession caused by the Bank's retaliation to the removal of the deposits, Jackson's perseverance with this policy led to the lapsing of the Bank's charter—with popular approval—in 1836. Following the Bank's demise, the president more aggressively promoted a money supply that consisted exclusively of gold and silver coin, for he believed that such "hard money" possessed a standard, inflexible value, while the fluctuating value of paper money issued by state banks could defraud hard-working Americans of their labor and property. Shortly before the end of his presidency, he issued an order directing government officials to accept only specie in payment for public funds.

While Jackson's policy developed, the president and his associates also came to accept the need for a well-disciplined party organization to perpetuate his administration's principles. Following the rationale of his first Secretary of State, Martin Van Buren, Jackson believed that the absence of organization had led to the fractionalization of the Jeffersonian Republicans in the 1820s. This division among the Republican leaders ultimately thwarted the people's will by allowing unscrupulous demagogues to secure

Adams's election to the presidency. A party organization rooted in local public meetings that would elect delegates to state conventions, which in turn selected delegates to a national convention, would permit the people to speak in a unified voice on both policy and leaders. The use of party discipline and rewards, mostly through patronage appointments, would compel politicians to obey the popular will. By the end of his first term, Jackson and his allies were encouraging the formation of committees at the local, state, and national level to direct the party's electioneering activities. At the same time, his policy of "rotation in office," through which he had dismissed and replaced about one tenth of the federal office-holders, increasingly came to be used to secure party loyalty. In 1832 party leaders organized the first national Democratic convention to nominate Martin Van Buren as vice-president for Jackson's second term. In 1835 the nomination by another national convention of Van Buren as Jackson's successor in the presidency became, for Jackson, the ultimate test of party loyalty.

Although Jackson's reliance on particular advisors always shifted, the development of the Democratic party marked a move away from the Tennessee politicians who had initiated his presidential candidacy toward newer leaders who understood the realities of party politics. In particular, Polk and Grundy, assisted by Brown and Johnson, strongly endorsed the Bank's destruction and cooperated with the creation of a party structure. By 1835 Polk and Grundy were acknowledged openly as the leaders of the Jacksonian forces in Tennessee. The defining of Jackson's principles also produced a more coherent national opposition. Supporters of Adams and Clay, calling themselves first "National Republicans" and, after 1834, "Whigs," defended the American System while accusing Jackson of abusing executive power. Deriding the president as "King Andrew I," Whigs charged that Jackson's vetoes both violated the constitution and negated the will of the people as expressed through their elected representatives. Whigs decried his dismissal of federal officials and subsequent use of patronage as a "spoils system" that removed faithful public servants to make room for unqualified and subservient party hacks. The Whigs condemned the new emphasis on party loyalty as the sacrifice of freedom of opinion to follow the dictates of self-anointed party leaders.

In Tennessee, as in other southern states, Jackson's overwhelming popularity delayed the emergence of an opposition, even though politicians with connections to merchants, bankers, and other advocates of commerce doubted the wisdom of destroying the Bank of the United States. The opportunity to challenge the president came when he made clear his preference that Van Buren succeed him and his insistence that Tennesseans support the New Yorker as the Democratic nominee. John Bell and Ephraim H. Foster led the dissenters, claiming that the convention did not represent the people's will, but instead had been packed with Van Buren supporters. By demanding party loyalty, they claimed, Jackson attempted to "dictate" his will and deny Tennesseans the right to express their preference for the presidential nomination. To strengthen this appeal, Bell and Foster promoted the candidacy of popular Tennessee Senator Hugh Lawson White, whom they proclaimed more loyal than Van Buren to the original Jacksonian principles of 1828. The state legislature in 1835 unanimously nominated White, and although he finished third in the 1836 election behind Van Buren and William Henry Harrison, he won 58 percent of the vote in Tennessee, while carrying the electoral votes of his home state and of Georgia. By carrying 49 percent of the southern vote, White's candidacy destroyed southern unity behind Jackson and made possible the establishment of a permanent opposition party.

The presentation of White as a loyal Jacksonian who challenged the president only on the question of succession meant that most Tennesseans viewed the 1836 contest as a dispute within the Democratic party. For the next few years, the distinction between Jacksonian Democratic and White supporters remained unclear. The division into competing political parties within Tennessee followed the clarification of the national political division that occurred after the financial Panic of 1837, which began an economic depression that lasted until the mid-1840s. In a special session of Congress, President Van Buren introduced, as his response to the Panic, a plan to create an Independent Treasury, or "subtreasury," that would hold the government's money separately from the nation's banking system. The effect of the Independent Treasury, Van Buren explained, would be to "divorce" the government from the banks, and its creation would fulfill Jackson's desire to remove the government's influence from the national economy. White supporters, now accepting the label "Whig," condemned the subtreasury as impractical and claimed that it gave the executive too much control over the government's money. Still, party lines in Tennessee remained vague until, in 1839, Polk challenged the Whig incumbent Newton Cannon for the governorship, demanding that voters choose between "Polk, Van Buren, and the Subtreasury," and "Cannon, Clay, and a National Bank." Polk won a narrow victory over Cannon as Democrats gained control of the state legislature. More significantly, the 1839 state elections established a permanent party division within Tennessee. Over the next two decades, Democrats and Whigs competed in a series of close contests that followed the patterns established in 1839, with party loyalties now deeply entrenched in the electorate.

Tennessee's two parties each won the allegiance of roughly half of the state's voters, so party competition became particularly heated since victory seemed possible for either party in every election. Party support cut across the state's three grand divisions, although Whigs enjoyed a majority in East and West Tennessee, while Democrats held an advantage in Middle Tennessee. In general, Whigs tended to win the votes of those living in towns, county seats, and regions with relatively easy access to commercial markets. Democratic voters, meanwhile, tended to live in regions more distant from the world of commerce. This geographic divergence resulted from the Whigs' advocacy of government action to promote economic development, a policy that they encouraged on the state as well as on the national level. In the General Assembly, Whigs supported, while Democrats opposed, legislation that would expand the state's banking capital; allow the state's banks to suspend specie payments during hard times; increase the availability of paper money; grant unlimited liability to corporate stockholders; and permit corporations to operate in the state without the threat of interference by the legislature. These policies, along with the promise of relief offered by their advocacy of a new national bank, made the Whigs' appeal especially strong during the depression of the early 1840s, and throughout the decade they enjoyed a slight advantage over the Democrats. Between 1839 and 1853 each party won the governor's office four times, but Whigs carried Tennessee in all four presidential elections. Whigs also controlled the state legislature five times; Democrats won a majority only twice, while in one session both parties won 50 of the Assembly's 100 seats.

Despite Polk's victory in 1839, Democrats entered the 1840s in a weak condition. Polk twice lost re-election contests for the governorship to Whig James C. Jones. His continued support for Van Buren, who lost the presidency to William H. Harrison in 1840 but remained the expected Democratic nominee in 1844, provoked dissatisfaction with his leadership of the state party. Yet Polk's and the Democrats' prospects revived when John Tyler, who became president at Harrison's death, opened negotiations with the independent republic of Texas to annex that region to the United States. Anticipating Whig candidate Henry Clay's opposition to annexation, Democrats adopted the Texas issue as their own. When Van Buren unexpectedly announced his own opposition to annexation, Jackson—long in retirement at the Hermitage—used his remaining influence to promote Polk's candidacy instead. Astute maneuvering at the national convention by Johnson, Brown, and Gideon J. Pillow secured Polk's nomination. In the campaign Democrats stressed American expansion as their defining issue by joining Texas annexation with a call for

American possession of the Oregon territory, which the United States had occupied jointly with Britain since 1818. With the economy beginning a slow recovery without the enactment of the American System, expansion proved a popular issue. Although Polk lost in his home state by 123 votes, he upset Clay in one of the closest presidential elections in American history.

Polk's victory completed the shift in leadership of the Jacksonians from the older to a newer generation. Against Jackson's wishes, Polk fired Lewis from his position in the Treasury Department, and he helped to organize a new, quasi-official administration newspaper to replace the *Washington Globe*, which had been the Jackson administration's organ and which was still edited by one of Jackson's closest advisors, Francis Preston Blair. Nevertheless, Polk's presidency marked the triumph of the Jacksonians. By endorsing and signing into law acts that established the Independent Treasury and reduced tariff rates, and by vetoing a bill to provide federal funding for river and harbor improvements, Polk established Jacksonian principles as national policy. They remained the government's guiding principles for more than a decade after the end of Polk's term. Polk's administration also carried out the Democrats' expansionist aims. Tyler completed the Texas annexation before Polk's inauguration, but the new president negotiated a settlement of the Oregon boundary with Britain and led the nation into a war with Mexico that brought the southwestern lands between Texas and California under the authority of the United States. The question of whether slavery would exist in these territories, however, brought a new concern to the forefront of national politics and ultimately became the issue that took the country on the road to the Civil War.

The Jacksonians had a significant impact on the history of both the United States and Tennessee. Their ideological justification for Jackson's elevation to the presidency furthered the national enshrinement of "Jacksonian Democracy"—the belief that the government should execute the will of the people as represented by a majority of a mass electorate. Their role in the creation of the Democratic party helped to establish the nation's oldest political party. Their organization of the party's machinery and their competition with the Whigs promoted the acceptance of the idea of a party system as a component of American politics. The Jacksonian policy helped to legitimate what later came to be known as *laissez faire* as an acceptable relationship between government and society. Ironically, after the Civil War, the *laissez faire* doctrine was twisted so that it ultimately aided the corporations and special interests that the Jacksonians had opposed.

Jonathan M. Atkins, Berry College

SUGGESTED READINGS: Jonathan M. Atkins, *Parties, Politics, and* the Sectional Crisis in Tennessee, 1832–1861 (1997); Paul H. Bergeron, *Antebellum Politics in Tennessee* (1982); Donald B. Cole, *The Presidency of Andrew Jackson* (1993); Richard B. Latner, *The Presidency of Andrew Jackson: White House Politics, 1829–1837* (1979); Marvin Meyers, *The Jacksonian Persuasion: Politics and Belief* (1957); Charles Sellers, *James K. Polk*, Vol. 1, *Jacksonian, 1795–1843* (1957), Vol. 2, *Continentalist, 1843–1846* (1966)

SEE: BELL, JOHN; BROWN, AARON V.; CANNON, NEWTON; CARROLL, WILLIAM; CATRON, JOHN; DONELSON, ANDREW J.; EATON, JOHN H.; FOSTER, EPHRAIM H.; GRUNDY, FELIX; JACKSON, ANDREW; JOHNSON, ANDREW; JOHNSON, CAVE; JONES, JAMES C.; LEWIS, WILLIAM B.; OVERTON, JOHN; PILLOW, GIDEON J.; POLK, JAMES K.; WHITE, HUGH L.

JAMES COUNTY was the first county in the United States to be consolidated with another, a unique venture in government, and the only such instance in Tennessee history. Organized in 1871, largely from Hamilton County and a fraction of Bradley County, its 48-year history was plagued with political strife and ended in bankruptcy in 1919.

The Tennessee General Assembly passed the act creating a new county in January 1871, and Governor Dewitt Senter signed the law. The Honorable Elbert Abdiel James, a representative from Hamilton County, introduced the measure. The county was named in honor of his father, Reverend Jesse J. James. A Methodist minister and native of Sullivan County, Reverend James moved his family to Chattanooga around 1854, where they became prominently identified with the industrial and financial growth of the city.

Political motives played a role in the creation of the new 285-square mile county. The citizens of James County were predominately Republican and rural, while Chattanooga residents were largely Democratic and urban. In the 1870 census, the population of the area that encompassed James County was reported at 5,000 people of Scots-Irish, English, German, and Huguenot ancestry, with some blacks, and a few mixed-blood Indians and Melungeons.

Thirteen towns or communities lay scattered across James County, including Ooltewah, Harrison, Apison, and Thatcher's Switch (Collegedale). Ferries along the Tennessee River played a vital role in the lives of James countians and included Vann's Ferry, Field's Ferry, Teenor's Ferry, McCallie's Ferry, Daughtery's Ferry, and Blythe's Ferry. In 1920 James County turned over only 12 miles of poorly kept graveled roads to Hamilton County. Although the creators of the county expected the overflow from Chattanooga's flourishing economy to provide the tax base for building schools and roads for the rural area, the revenues never materialized. In 1919 James County made its quiet exit from politics and the American scene. Created out of political rivalry, plagued by chicanery throughout its history, insufficiently capital-

ized to provide proper services, deficient in natural resources, and unable to take advantage of nearby industrialization, the county's agrarian economy rested on the efforts of self-sufficient farmers, whose labors provided an inadequate tax base, and resulted in sub-standard banking, communication, and transportation facilities.

James N. Monroe, Ooltewah

SUGGESTED READING: Polly W. Donnelly. ed., *James County, A Lost County of Tennessee* (1983)

SEE: FERRIES; HAMILTON COUNTY

JAZZ IN TENNESSEE. Memphis is known for blues and early rock & roll traditions, and Nashville is famous for country music, but both also moved to the strains of jazz. In no part of Tennessee, however, did jazz ever enjoy commercial or popular success, or make a lasting cultural impression. Nevertheless, Tennessee can claim to have shaped national jazz personalities and contributed several native-born musical talents who influenced jazz.

At the turn of the century, Memphis musicians played classical and popular forms of music in theaters and musical shows, while local parade and military bands performed standard American fare. In addition, the Memphis nightlife also attracted smaller groups that played a rural blues music. It was these players, from the Delta and Memphis, who inspired W.C. Handy to compose the forms and lyrics that brought him fame. Unlike Handy, most musicians bypassed Memphis for work in Chicago.

Two major female jazz figures had their start in Memphis. Alberta Hunter was born on Beale Street and learned to sing there before moving first to Chicago and then New York, where she made some early blues recordings. Lil Hardin was born in Memphis, got her musical training there, and studied music at Fisk University in Nashville. She too relocated in Chicago. While playing piano with King Oliver's Creole Jazz Band, she met and married young Louis Armstrong. At her encouragement, Armstrong left Oliver to go to New York to launch his own career. Hardin's compositions offered ample harmonic structures for his innovative solo work. In the 1930s, she led a number of groups (including an all-female group) and continued to perform, record, and tour.

Erskine Tate, born in Memphis, received his musical training in Chicago and organized an orchestra that played the Vendome Theatre, the Savoy Ballroom, and the Cotton Club. During his tenure, the Vendome was an important stepping stone in the careers of many jazz musicians. Although not native to Tennessee, Jimmy Lunceford taught music in a Memphis school after taking a music degree at Fisk. In Memphis, he formed the nucleus of another important band that changed the sound of dance music in the 1930s and 1940s. Among Lunceford's ranks were Tennesseans Moses Allen (tuba and bass); George Clarke (tenor saxophonist) who performed, recorded, and toured with Stuff Smith, Cootie Williams, and Jonah Jones; Rozelle Claxton (pianist and arranger), who played in the bands of Bennie Moten and Harlan Leonard and toured with Pearl Bailey; and Jimmy Crawford (drums), who played with Ben Webster, Billy Taylor, Louis Armstrong, Benny Goodman, Billie Holiday, Fletcher Henderson, Ella Fitzgerald, Dizzy Gillespie, and on Broadway.

Memphis produced a number of other musicians of note. Buster Bailey, clarinetist, played with Handy, Erskine Tate, Joe Oliver, Fletcher Henderson's Orchestra, John Kirby, Wilbur De Paris, Henry "Red" Allen, and Louis Armstrong's All Stars. George Coleman, saxophonist, played alto with B.B. King and tenor with Walter Perkins, Max Roach, Miles Davis, and Herbie Hancock. Johnny Dunn, trumpeter, studied at Fisk and did solos in Memphis before joining Handy's band in New York. He played and recorded with Mamie Smith, led his own band, and toured Europe. Fred Robinson, trombonist, played with many prominent African-American bands in Chicago and New York. He recorded with Louis Armstrong's Hot Seven. John "Bearcat" Williams, saxophonist and clarinetist, played with Andy Kirk and Cootie Williams. Johnny Williams, bassist, began with southern territory bands, played or recorded with notables like the Mills Blue Rhythm Band, Benny Carter, Coleman Hawkins, Armstrong, Teddy Wilson, and Johnny Hodges, and toured later in life. Phineas Newborn, Jr., pianist, was a colleague and inspiration to a group of Memphis musicians, including Booker Little, Jr., George Coleman, Frank Stozier, Hank Crawford, and Harold Mabern, who is noted for his associations with Lionel Hampton and Charles Mingus.

In post-World War I, Nashville enjoyed the forms of popular music that Memphis had before the war. With the opening of radio station WSM in 1925, Nashvillians heard regular broadcasts of popular dance and novelty tunes in the performances of Francis Craig and Beasley Smith. Craig operated a long-standing "hotel" band. Beasley Smith's groups played more "hot" music and seasoned many musicians who went on to other successes, including Matty Matlock, the clarinet player who replaced Benny Goodman in the Ben Pollock Orchestra and went on to join Bob Crosby's bands. Another musician who launched his career with Smith was Ray McKinley, the drummer who eventually played with singer Smith Ballew, the Dorsey Brothers, Jimmy Dorsey, Will Bradley, the Glenn Miller Orchestra, and his own groups. For the next 20 years, Smith was musical director of WSM and finished his career composing and publishing songs.

The universities in Nashville, especially Fisk, not only provided work and study opportunities for African Americans, but provided music gigs as well. A number of black jazz and dance bands performed in Nashville, including those led by John Douglass "Chick" Chavis and Don Q. Pullen. Perhaps the best-known jazz figure to emerge from Nashville was Adolphus Anthony "Doc" Cheatham, who played trumpet. While on tour in Chicago, Lil Hardin got Cheatham work at the Dreamland Cafe, and he substituted for Louis Armstrong at the Vendome Theatre. Cheatham also recorded with blues singer Ma Rainey. He eventually played with Chick Webb and toured Europe with Sam Wooding's revue *Chocolate Kiddies.* He also played with McKinney's Cotton Picker, Wilbur De Paris, and Cab Calloway while recording with Benny Goodman. He remained musically active with tours and recordings until his death in 1997.

Chattanooga also contributed some unique and important talent to the jazz world. Bessie Smith was perhaps the most prolific and influential of the early blues women. Lovie Austin, a pianist, gained her musical training touring the vaudeville circuit in the South, led her own groups, and recorded with jazz musicians and blues singers in Chicago. Jimmy Blanton, the young bass player who enhanced the sound of Duke Ellington from 1939 until his death in 1942, re-configured bass ensemble and solo concepts and set the stage for bebop bass rhythms. Yusef Lateef, reeds player and composer, who has played with Dizzy Gillespie, Charles Mingus, and Cannonball Adderley, incorporated unusual eastern rhythms and instruments into his playing and compositions. Other Tennessee-born jazz figures include Dickie Wells (trombone), Bob Shoffner (trumpet), and Jimmy Cleveland (trombone).

David Jellema, Middle Tennessee State University

SEE: HANDY, WILLIAM C.; MEMPHIS MUSIC SCENE; MUSIC; SMITH, BESSIE; WSM

JEFFERSON COUNTY. When Goodspeed published his well-known history of Tennessee in 1887 he concluded that "No Tennessee county has a more honorable record or a more interesting history than Jefferson." The second of 26 American counties so named, its early settlers were men of intelligence, education, and patriotism, whose influence is still felt seven generations later.

Geography influenced the development of this East Tennessee valley county. From 1784 to 1788, under the government of the State of Franklin, this area was part of Caswell County. Jefferson County, as created by Territorial Governor William Blount on June 11, 1792, encompassed approximately 1,200 square miles. The Holston River formed its northern boundary, and the French Broad River bisected it. These two water highways, the result of the area's heavy rainfall, support a large variety of plants, animals, and freshwater fish. Early settlers used these rivers as their primary means of transportation to the new frontier of Tennessee. North Carolinians came down the French Broad, and Virginians arrived by way of the Holston River.

The first permanent settlement at Dandridge dates to 1783; the village became the county seat in 1793. One emigrant, Dr. William Moore, set up practice as the first physician in Dandridge. Dr. Moore's wife was Cassie Paxton Moore. This lady of culture kept a large library. Her first cousin, Sam Houston, spent weeks with the Moores, immersed in the books that would prepare him for later public service in Tennessee and Texas.

Fertile soil and favorable treaties with the Indian tribes of the area attracted hundreds of settlers to Jefferson County. By 1795 Knox and Jefferson counties each reported populations of approximately 7,500. Many of the early settlers were Revolutionary War soldiers of Scots-Irish background, who migrated to the region to claim war land grants. The rivers that brought them to the area would also provide farm-to-market roads for the corn, wheat, and cattle these industrious pioneers produced. The rivers remained the primary transportation system in the county until the first railroad was constructed in 1858.

The Civil War touched Jefferson County in a variety of ways. Divided in its loyalty, members of a given family often fought on opposing sides. On Christmas Eve, 1863, at Dandridge, Federal cavalry engaged Confederate soldiers from the command of General James Longstreet, who was moving to the Morristown-Dandridge-Greeneville area for winter headquarters. Both Union and Confederate troops foraged the area in search of food. By winter's end the land was devastated; even the fence rails had been burned. The buildings of Carson-Newman College, established in 1851, had been vandalized. Unlike many other institutions, Carson-Newman recovered and is now among the largest church-supported colleges in Tennessee. With over 2,200 students, 350 faculty and staff, and 30 buildings on 90 acres in the heart of Jefferson City, no other institution or industry contributes as much to the county's economy.

The fertile land and seasonal climate accounted for much of the agricultural recovery in the post-Civil War period. The success of the county's agricultural production encouraged the establishment of canning factories, such as Stokely and Bush Brothers in the early twentieth century. Today, Bush's baked beans controls over 50% of that product's market.

The outbreak of World War II gave final impetus to the building of Douglas Dam as part of the Tennessee Valley Authority. Construction of the dam threatened valuable farmland, and Tennessee Senator Kenneth McKellar had fought on behalf of the interests of the canning industry against TVA plans for Douglas Dam. Indeed, Jefferson County lost 40.5 square miles of the most fertile farm land to TVA. But war demands for hydroelectricity took precedence over other concerns. The Cherokee Dam blueprint was used to build Douglas Dam. More than 6,000 laborers worked around the clock and completed construction in 382 days, a world record for a project of this size. The hydroelectricity from Douglas and Cherokee Dams furnished power for two critical war industries, aluminum production and the Manhattan Project at Oak Ridge.

In 1914 valuable zinc ore deposits were discovered by Mark Newman, a geologist with American Zinc Company. In the 1930s Dr. Charles R. L. Oder, of Universal Zinc Company, and Jack Crawford and Howard Miller, two nationally recognized geologists, found additional deposits. By 1960 four major companies were mining zinc in Jefferson County. From 1950 to 1995 Jefferson County claimed the distinction of being the largest producer of zinc ore in the United States. Declining deposits have reduced the number of mining companies operating in the county to two.

Currently Jefferson County encompasses 273.83 square miles, having contributed land to the formation of Sevier County (1795), Cocke County (1797), and Hamblen County (1870). The population of Jefferson County is 36,945. There are five incorporated cities: Baneberry, Dandridge, Jefferson City, New Market, and White Pine. Jefferson City is the largest with a population of 5,600.
Estle P. Muncy, Jefferson City

SEE: BULL, CARROLL G.; CARSON-NEWMAN COLLEGE; GLENMORE MANSION; HIGHLANDER RESEARCH CENTER; MINING; TENNESSEE VALLEY AUTHORITY

JENKINS, RAY HOWARD (1897–1980), trial lawyer and chief counsel for the U.S. Senate in the Army-McCarthy hearings, was born in Cherokee County, North Carolina, in 1897. The family soon moved to the community of Rural Vale in Monroe County, Tennessee, and then to the neighboring logging town of Tellico Plains. Jenkins's early years were shaped by his distinct personal character, his family, and the rural life of the early 1900s, which included the limitations of local schools, hunting and fishing experiences, participation in sports, summer odd jobs, and the antics and escapades of boyhood. These influences contributed not only to Jenkins's nickname, "Terror of Tellico Plains," but also affected his courtroom style.

In 1916, after high school graduation, Jenkins volunteered with the Tennessee militia to fight Pancho Villa along the U.S and Mexican border. During World War I, he joined the Navy and spent his enlistment in San Diego, California. In 1920

Jenkins graduated *cum laude* from University of Tennessee Law School, having already passed the bar exam and received his license in 1919.

Jenkins began his career in the Knoxville office of Alvin Johnson. The court appointed the fledging attorney to represent indigent defendants, in addition to his work collecting debts and defending clients before the justice of the peace. By 1922 Jenkins had established his own practice and quickly developed a reputation as a courtroom dramatist and orator. U.S. District Court Judge Robert Taylor identified Jenkins's legal knowledge, his handling of witnesses, and his forceful arguments as the qualities of an extraordinary lawyer. When Jenkins defended clients in the courtroom, people came to witness the event.

In 1954 Jenkins received national attention when he was appointed chief counsel for the U.S. Senate committee investigating the Army-McCarthy hearings. Jenkins worked closely with minority counsel Robert Kennedy to ferret out the truth of the conflict between Secretary of the Army Robert Stevens and Senator Joseph McCarthy. Although Jenkins adapted his emotional courtroom style to accommodate the more conservative expectations of Washington, D.C. courtrooms, his skills became evident to the millions of television viewers who witnessed the hearings. Now a national figure, Jenkins's picture appeared on the cover of *Time* magazine. In perhaps the most interesting result of the Army-McCarthy exposure, cartoonist Al Capp adapted Jenkins's likeness and personality for the creation of "Cragnose," a character in the "Li'l Abner" comic strip.

Many Tennesseans expected Jenkins to pursue a political career following his national exposure. Jenkins returned to Knoxville, however, and resumed his practice in criminal and civil law. While his public reputation evolved from the more than 800 homicide defendants he represented, civil law accounted for more than 90 percent of his practice. In 1979 Jenkins published his autobiography, *The Terror of Tellico Plains: The Memoirs of Ray H. Jenkins.* He died in 1980.
Lisa N. Oakley, East Tennessee Historical Society
SEE: LAW; MONROE COUNTY

JEWS, URBAN TENNESSEE. The settlement of Jews in urban Tennessee reflected larger migration and settlement patterns of Jews within the United States over the last two centuries. These patterns created distinctive forms of Jewish life in the major Jewish communities of Tennessee: Memphis, Nashville, Knoxville, and the Tri-Cities.

The earliest Jewish settlers arrived in Tennessee in the 1830s and 1840s, having fled the political turmoil of the German-speaking areas with other Central Europeans. Most Jewish immigrants of this period came from small towns and villages and, in general, were not Orthodox in religious practice. Often they

were drawn to the South because of its rural character, warmer climate, and economic opportunities. Many established themselves as peddlers, shopkeepers, and artisans as they gradually spread into the small southern towns and cities. A number of Jewish merchants founded successful shops and general stores throughout the state, but especially in West Tennessee, including Schwab's (Memphis), Levy's (Halls), Kahn's (Bolivar), Felsenthal's (Brownsville), and Freed's (Trenton).

As the number of Jewish settlers increased and stabilized, thoughts turned to religious life. During the 1840s and 1850s, Jews established community organizations wherever there were enough Jews to sustain the efforts. Cemeteries or Hebrew Benevolent Societies generally developed first, with congregations following a few years later. For example, Memphis Jews established the first Jewish cemetery in 1847 and chartered a synagogue (the forerunner of the current Temple Israel) in 1854. A similar pattern emerged in Nashville, with the founding of the Hebrew Benevolent Burial Association in 1851, followed by the first synagogue in 1854.

The Civil War disrupted the slow development of Jewish life in Tennessee. During the war, Jews could be found on both sides, although most supported the loyalties of their local communities. Julius Ochs (whose son Adolph Ochs later bought and developed the *Chattanooga Times* and the *New York Times*) became a notable exception. Ochs remained a staunch Unionist, while his wife, Bertha, supported the Confederacy. As a result of their role in commerce, many southern Jews became involved in smuggling goods around the Union embargoes.

After the war, Jewish life in urban Tennessee changed considerably. Many local communities initially organized to deal with the Jewish wounded and dead. As a result, southern Jewish communities established closer ties with the larger Jewish communities of the North and Midwest. In some cases, northern Jewish soldiers, who remained in the postwar South, encouraged the creation of these expansive efforts. During this period, both Chattanooga and Knoxville established the first burial societies and congregations in those cities. The postwar economic recovery and industrialization spurred growth in the Jewish communities, especially in Memphis and Nashville. In addition, a number of national Jewish organizations established chapters in the revitalized Jewish communities of the South, including the Order of B'nai Brith, which founded chapters in Brownsville, Chattanooga, Memphis (3), and Nashville.

The next major wave of Jewish immigration began in 1881 and lasted until World War I, fueled by political upheaval in Russia and other areas of Eastern Europe. The Jews in this wave of immigration were more traditional and Orthodox in their religious life than their German predecessors. In the majority of cases, these immigrants arrived penniless and without marketable skills and remained in the port cities of Boston and New York, where they could fulfill their need for Jewish communal institutions such as synagogues and kosher butchers. As a result, large traditional, Yiddish-speaking ghettos emerged in the cities of the Northeast. This immigrant wave brought some 2.5 million Jews to America to add to the American Jewish population of 250,000.

Relatively few of the new immigrants migrated South. Those who did usually followed commercial routes down the Mississippi River and produced significant East European Jewish settlements in port cities like Memphis. By the turn of the century, Memphis included a Yiddish-speaking ghetto known as "The Pinch," which was located along Auction, Market Commerce, and Beale Streets. To deal with the social and religious needs of the new immigrants, well-established German Jews and some Eastern Europeans created new organizations and associations. By the time the Russian Revolution and World War I ended this wave of immigration, Jewish life in Tennessee consisted of a complex web of intersecting and sometimes competing organizations, clubs, synagogues, and associations. Today, Memphis continues to boast the largest single Orthodox congregation in the country.

In the years following World War I, the new immigrants gradually acculturated and assimilated as their children attended public schools, went to college, and moved out of their Jewish neighborhoods. By the 1950s, Tennessee Jews, whether of German or Eastern European background, were well assimilated into the life of the state.

During World War II, Tennessee's newest Jewish community was founded with the establishment of Oak Ridge. A number of Jewish scientists and engineers from across the country found themselves thrown together to aid the war effort. Many remained to staff the postwar laboratories and research facilities. As they established their own communal organizations during the 1940s and 1950s, these Jews created Tennessee's most diverse Jewish community.

In the last decades of the twentieth century, the Jewish population of Tennessee underwent significant demographic change. Jewish communities in the smaller towns disappeared as older members died, and younger generations of Jews left for college and careers. In addition, large numbers of Jewish professionals and businesspeople moved into the state from other areas, enlarging the urban communities and bringing new interests and needs. In 1996, the Jewish population of Tennessee numbered just under 20,000, with almost 9,000 in Memphis and close to 6,000 in Nashville.

Peter J. Haas, Vanderbilt University

SUGGESTED READINGS: Eli N. Evans, *The Provincials: A Personal History of the Jews in the South* (1973); Leonard Dinnerstein and Mary Dale Palsson, ed., *Jews in the South* (1973); Fedora Frank, *Five Families and Eight Young Men: Nashville and Her Jewry, 1850–1861* (1962) and *Beginnings on Market Street: Nashville and Her Jewry 1861–1901* (1976)
SEE: COHN, WALDO; ESKIND, JANE; ETTELSON, HARRY W.; FALK, RANDALL M; FREED, JULIUS; PLOUGH, ABE; SHORE, DINAH; TEMPLE ADAS ISRAEL; WERTHAN, JOE; ZIMMERMAN, HARRY AND MARY K.

JOHNSON, ANDREW (1808–1875). Born in a log cabin (December 29, 1808) in Raleigh, North Carolina, Andrew Johnson knew abject poverty and personal tragedy almost from the very beginning of his life. Jacob Johnson, Andrew's father, a landless and illiterate worker in Raleigh, died unexpectedly a few days after Andrew's third birthday. At ten years of age, Andrew was apprenticed to work for James J. Selby, a tailor. In that shop, Andrew learned two valuable lessons: how to perform the tailor's craft and how to read. After five years in Selby's shop, Johnson ran away from Raleigh. He returned some two years later in an unsuccessful attempt to make peace with Selby. In 1825, or early 1826, Johnson headed west to seek a better fortune.

He wandered to Mooresville, Alabama, and then to Columbia, Tennessee, and secured employment in tailor shops at both places. After a few months, however, Johnson returned to Raleigh and escorted his mother and stepfather Turner Doughtry to Tennessee. They eventually arrived in Greeneville in September 1826. Johnson found work in a tailor shop; but more important, he found Eliza McCardle. In the spring of 1827 the two teenagers (Johnson was 18 and Eliza 16) married and made Greeneville their permanent home.

Two years later, 20-year-old Andrew Johnson was chosen alderman, a post to which he was reelected several times; in 1834 he became Greeneville's mayor. Meanwhile, his tailoring business prospered, and his family increased to include two daughters and two sons. As a consequence Johnson purchased a tailor shop and a fine brick residence. Once he learned to write, Johnson became increasingly absorbed in intellectual pursuits as he prepared himself for more impressive and prestigious areas of public service.

In 1835 Johnson successfully ran for a seat in the lower house of the state legislature. At this point in his early political career he generally maintained political independence, but leaned toward the newly emerging Whig party. In fact, he backed Hugh Lawson White for president in 1836. His refusal to support internal improvements legislation, however, cost him reelection in 1837, since his constituents favored such measures. Two years later, Johnson

Andrew Johnson, portrait by William B. Cooper.

TENNESSEE HISTORICAL SOCIETY COLLECTION, TENNESSEE STATE MUSEUM

regained his legislative seat. By this time, he had made an irrevocable commitment to the Jacksonian party. Democrats named him to be one of the two state-at-large presidential electors in 1840, and Johnson campaigned throughout the state. Subsequently, he sought and won a state senate seat the next year. But after three legislative terms, Johnson looked for new challenges.

He found them in the U.S. House of Representatives, where he served for ten years, 1843–1853. Here he first introduced his famous Homestead Bill in the spring of 1846, and persisted until the House (but not the Senate) finally approved it in 1852. He sparred with President James K. Polk over patronage, supported the Compromise of 1850, and introduced constitutional amendments to provide for the direct election of the President and U.S. Senators. During his tenure as Representative, he bought a larger house in Greeneville; a year later, in 1852, his fifth child, Andrew, was born. In that year, the Whig-dominated legislature redrew the Congressional districts to make Johnson's reelection nearly impossible.

Faced with that reality, Johnson made a successful race for governor; he was reelected in 1855. The gov-

ernor's office was weak by design, and Johnson accomplished very little, other than an increase in the revenues to support public schools. His principal achievement was to gain extensive public exposure and, thereby, enhance his future career.

In the fall of 1857 the legislature's choice of Johnson as U.S. Senator surprised few. Once in the Senate, he immediately proposed his Homestead Bill, and he reintroduced it two years later. The bill finally emerged from both houses of Congress in late spring 1860, only to be vetoed by President James Buchanan—much to Johnson's dismay. That year's real excitement emanated from the presidential campaign, which involved four political parties. Johnson had flirted with the possibility of his own nomination, but the breakup of the Democratic party at the Charleston convention ruined those plans. Johnson campaigned for John C. Breckinridge, the Southern Democratic candidate, but the state went for John Bell, the Constitutional Union nominee.

In the wake of Abraham Lincoln's election and threats of secession, Johnson returned to Washington. A few days later he delivered his famous speech against secession, in which he staked out his claim as a Southern Unionist. In a February 1861 referendum, Tennessee voters refused to endorse a secession convention call, yet Johnson knew he had to return home to fight against the surging tide of secession sentiment. He finally left in April, the month the Civil War began.

Back in East Tennessee, Johnson quickly allied with his former political opponents, such as Thomas A. R. Nelson, William G. Brownlow, Horace Maynard, and others who shared his strong support of the Union. Accompanied by these new friends, he toured the region and railed against secession and the Confederacy. After the June referendum, in which Tennessee voters embraced secession, a fearful Johnson hastily left the state and made his way into Kentucky and eventually back to Washington.

At that juncture he could scarcely have imagined his next assignment: Military Governor of Tennessee. Thanks to the Federal capture of Forts Henry and Donelson, followed by the occupation of Nashville (all in February 1862), President Lincoln sent Johnson to Tennessee for the purpose of restoring civil government and bringing the state back into the Union. Johnson arrived in Nashville in late March, and for the next three years, he struggled to accomplish this goal. In the process, he was often ruthless, dictatorial, accommodating, and strongly pro-Union. He arrested and imprisoned newspaper editors, local officials, and clergymen—anyone deemed to be a threat. But Federal and Confederate military activities in Tennessee had as much bearing upon Johnson's role as governor as anything else. Indeed, both his office and his person were jeopardized from time to time by Confederate successes in the Middle Tennessee area.

The slavery question drove a wedge between the state's Unionists, and Johnson eventually took a stance in favor of abolishing slavery, while the more conservative Unionists refused to do so. This schism hampered the governor's efforts to restore civilian government. Moreover, Johnson set forth more stringent loyalty oaths than Lincoln required, further alienating substantial numbers of Unionists—particularly at the time of the 1864 presidential campaign.

Johnson, needless to say, had more than a passing interest in that election; after all, Lincoln had placed him on the ticket as the vice-presidential nominee. In the victorious campaign's aftermath, Johnson still had some unfinished business, namely, the establishment of civilian government in the state. Accordingly, he sanctioned a call for a January 1865 convention of Unionists. That unofficial Nashville gathering established dates for a referendum to abolish slavery and an election of gubernatorial and legislative officers. By late February, Johnson could delay his departure no longer, if he was to arrive in Washington for the inauguration ceremonies. But the question of the readmission of Tennessee remained unresolved.

This longtime Democrat and resident of a Confederate state arrived in town to be sworn in as vice president. Johnson's apparent intoxication that March day stirred negative reactions, but not for long. Six weeks later, on the night of April 14, an assassin's bullet ended Lincoln's life. The next morning, Johnson was sworn in as the seventeenth president.

The stunned nation expectantly awaited Johnson's leadership. He did not disappoint; indeed, the next several months constituted his "finest hour." With Congress adjourned, Johnson had a free hand, and he took advantage of the situation. In May, for example, he extended amnesty and pardon to all ex-Confederates who took an oath of allegiance (except for those who fell under 14 different exemptions). Moreover, he appointed provisional governors for seven of the former Rebel states. Throughout the summer and fall months, these states went about the business of holding elections and constitutional conventions. Meanwhile, Johnson granted thousands of individual pardons to repentant ex-Confederates. When Congress convened in December, the President bragged that the restoration of the southern states had been accomplished.

But Congress had different ideas. Its members ushered in 1866 with two significant measures: the Freedmen's Bureau bill and the Civil Rights bill. Johnson vetoed both and thus assured that the year would be one of developing tension between the executive and legislative branches. Congress also approved the Fourteenth Amendment, but the President openly discouraged southern states from ratifying it. Ironically, his home state of Tennessee accepted the amendment (all other Confederate states rejected it) and thereby successfully gained readmission to the Union in July 1866. This enabled Johnson's son-in-law, David Patterson, to claim his seat in the U.S. Senate and permitted Tennessee to escape Congressional Reconstruction.

If 1866 was a period of developing tension, the following year was one of open warfare between the President and Congress. Johnson chose to veto every major piece of legislation, including the three Reconstruction bills, the Tenure of Office act, and the District of Columbia Franchise law. Congress had no problem overriding these vetoes. Johnson fought back in the summer of 1867 by removing two of the five district commanders and by suspending Secretary of War Edwin Stanton. These actions fueled Radical intentions to get rid of the President.

Not surprisingly, in 1868, the House voted to impeach Johnson, and the Senate convened to hear the case against him. The chief charge revolved around the President's alleged violation of the terms of the Tenure of Office act (by the removal of Stanton), but the real issue was political power. Eventually, in May, the Senate acquitted Johnson of the impeachment charges, but by then he was a greatly diminished leader. Yet he continued to veto Congressional measures, including the admission of seven ex-Rebel states that had finally ratified the Fourteenth Amendment and sought to reenter the Union.

Even in his dark moments, Johnson clung to the unrealistic hope that he might be nominated for president by the Democratic party in July. But Democrats named Horatio Seymour to be their standard-bearer and Republicans rallied around General U.S. Grant. All knowledgeable persons accurately predicted Grant's victory in November. Meanwhile, Johnson simply marked time as he awaited the end of his troubled presidency in March 1869.

Cheered by friendly crowds, he returned to Tennessee. Shortly afterwards, a restless Johnson hit the campaign trail in order to line up support for election to the U.S. Senate. Despite his best efforts, however, he lost by a close legislative vote in October 1869. Undaunted by this setback, three years later he once more campaigned for public office; he did not seem to know what else to do. This time he sought the at-large U.S. Representative seat, but finished third in the contest. That defeat only whetted his appetite for new challenges, and in 1874 he launched another bid for a U.S. Senate seat. In the January 1875 legislative voting, Johnson finally emerged victorious. "Thank God for vindication," was his ardent response. He assumed the seat vacated by his longtime foe, William Brownlow, when he participated in a special session of the Senate in March. At the session's end, he returned to Greeneville, a place he had come to despise because it lacked the allure and fulfillment of the political arena. Four months later, he suffered a stroke and died on July 31. Wrapped in an American flag with his head resting on a copy of the Constitution, he was buried in Greeneville to await the judgment of history and historians.

Paul H. Bergeron, University of Tennessee, Knoxville
SUGGESTED READINGS: LeRoy P. Graf, Ralph W. Haskins, and Paul H. Bergeron, eds., *The Papers of Andrew Johnson*, 14 vols. to date (1967–); Peter Maslowski, *Treason Must be Made Odious: Military Reconstruction and Wartime Reconstruction in Nashville, Tennessee, 1862–1865* (1978); James E. Sefton, *Andrew Johnson and the Uses of Constitutional Power* (1980); Hans L. Trefousse, *Andrew Johnson: A Biography* (1989)
SEE: BROWNLOW, WILLIAM G.; FREEDMEN'S BUREAU; GREENE COUNTY; JACKSONIANS; JOHNSON, ANDREW, NATIONAL HISTORIC SITE; JOHNSON, ELIZA M.; MAYNARD, HORACE; NELSON, THOMAS A.R.; OCCUPATION, CIVIL WAR; RECONSTRUCTION

JOHNSON, ANDREW, NATIONAL HISTORIC SITE.

The Andrew Johnson National Historic Site in Greeneville honors the life and work of the nation's seventeenth president and preserves his two homes, tailor shop, and grave site. The National Park Service administers the site, which includes a visitor center and presidential museum. The tailor shop, where Johnson worked and obtained his education, remained in the hands of his heirs until 1921, when the State of Tennessee purchased it. The shop is now enclosed in the brick Memorial Building.

Across the street from the visitor center is one of the houses where the Johnson family lived from the 1830s until 1851. This house includes exhibits and information on Johnson's early years and his climb to the presidency. The Homestead, which Johnson purchased in 1851, is one and one-half blocks from the visitor center. Ten rooms, furnished with original family furniture and possessions as well as period furniture, are open to visitors by way of ranger-guided tours.

Approximately one mile from the visitor center is the national cemetery where Andrew and Eliza Johnson are buried with other family members. The marble monument over Johnson's grave has a likeness of the Constitution and the Bible; an American Eagle perches on top. His belief in democracy and his faith in the common man are commemorated by the words: "His faith in the people never wavered." At Tusculum College, just east of Greeneville, the President Andrew Johnson Museum and Library maintains exhibits and many Johnson family books and papers. Across the street from the library is a representation of Johnson's birthplace in Raleigh, North Carolina.

Mark Corey, Andrew Johnson National Historic Site

JOHNSON BIBLE COLLEGE was founded as "The School of the Evangelists" in 1893 by Ashley S. Johnson at Kimberlin Heights, Tennessee (approximately 12 miles southeast of Knoxville). Johnson, a Knox County native and successful evangelist, author, and educator, transformed his "Correspondence Bible College" (established in 1886) into an institution to provide education for poor young men who desired to preach the gospel. The name of the school was changed to Johnson Bible College in 1909 in honor of its founder. It remains a single-purpose educational institution offering a Bible major and specialty programs for students seeking church-related vocations. This non-denominational college draws most of its students and support from Christian Churches and Churches of Christ.

Ashley S. Johnson (president, 1893–1925) and his wife, Emma E. Johnson (president, 1925–1927), provided a Bible-centered curriculum to train ministers, as well as an academy for those who had not completed high school; a work program aided students who could not pay for their education. The difficult years of the Great Depression severely strained the college's resources and the efforts of Alva Ross Brown (president, 1927–1941), but the college experienced modest growth. Robert M. Bell (president, 1941–1968), long-time preacher and professor of economics at the University of Tennessee, restored the college to a solid financial base. Throughout its existence, a small number of women enrolled at the college, but it officially became co-educational in 1948. The college has undergone increased growth throughout the administration of David L. Eubanks (1969-present), illustrated by the graduation of a record 100 students in its centennial year. The second oldest continuing Bible college in the United States, it was one of the first two Bible colleges to be accredited by the Commission on Colleges of the Southern Association of Colleges and Schools.

L. Thomas Smith, Jr., Johnson Bible College
SEE: CHURCHES OF CHRIST

JOHNSON, CALDONIA "CAL" FACKLER (1844–1925), entrepreneur and philanthropist, was born to slave parents Cupid and Harriet Johnson in Knoxville on October 14, 1844. The Johnson family, slaves of Colonel Pless McClung, lived on the site of the old Farragut Hotel Building at the corner of Gay and Church streets. In his early teens, Johnson moved to McClung's Campbell Station estate, where he tended his master's horses and developed a lifelong interest in horses.

At the close of the Civil War, Johnson found work exhuming bodies from the temporary battlefield graves for reburial in proper cemeteries. As a result of the hard times and lack of economic opportunities associated with the aftermath of war, Johnson turned to alcohol and soon became a destitute drunkard, living on the streets of Knoxville.

Johnson recognized the futility of his life, vowed to stop drinking, and took a job first as a cook, then as a bartender. By 1879 he had saved $180, which he used to lease a building at the corner of Gay and Wall and open a saloon. Reinvesting his money in the business, Johnson soon operated three saloons: Popular Log, Popular Log Branch, and Popular Log Center Branch. His establishments became the most popular whiskey houses in the city, patronized by the leading men of the era. Johnson operated his saloons in strict accordance with the law: he sold neither to minors, women, nor those who appeared to be intoxicated.

Horses remained Johnson's first love, however, and he acquired an enviable stable of race horses that compared to the best in the state. He attended every major race in Tennessee and the surrounding states. In 1901 he bought the famed mare Lennette at Frankfort, Kentucky, for $6,000. He also owned George Condit, the 1893 Columbian Exposition's champion standard Bred Trotter. Johnson owned the only horseracing track in the city of Knoxville. Today, Speedway Circle, the site of the track, maintains the original shape. The track held regular races until the General Assembly outlawed the sport in 1907.

Although saloons and horses remained Johnson's principal sources of income, he also had other business interests, including vast real estate holdings. In 1906, he donated a house at the corner of Vine and Patton streets to be used as the first black YMCA building. At the presentation ceremony on May 14, 1906, Mayor S.G. Heiskell proclaimed to the large crowd of African Americans that Johnson's gift represented the largest ever given by a black person to the YMCA.

From 1883 to 1885 Johnson served on the Knoxville Board of Aldermen. In 1922 Knoxville established the Cal Johnson Park in his honor. In 1957 the Cal Johnson Recreation Center was erected in the park.

Johnson married twice, but had no children. At the time of his death on April 7, 1925, his estate was estimated at $300,000—$500,000.

Robert J. Booker, Beck Cultural Exchange Center, Inc., Knoxville

SEE: HORSERACING TRACKS, EARLY; KNOXVILLE

JOHNSON, CAVE (1793–1866) served as a Democrat in the U.S. House of Representatives (1829–37, 1839–45), Postmaster General of the United States (1845–49), and president of the Bank of Tennessee (1854–60). Johnson was born near Springfield in Robertson County, the second son of Thomas Johnson and Mary Noel Johnson. He attended Cumberland College in Nashville. There at the start of the War of 1812, he and others formed a volunteer unit,

electing Johnson as captain. Andrew Jackson declined their offer to join him, saying that the country's interest would be served better by the boys remaining in college. Johnson's college career, however, concluded the following year in 1813, when he was expelled for refusing to follow the prescribed curriculum. Johnson next studied law with Justice William Cocke for a year before serving under Jackson in his father's militia unit during the Creek War of 1813. He then returned to his legal studies and was admitted to the bar in 1814.

By this time, Johnson was in love with Elizabeth Dortch, but she rejected him in 1815; Johnson vowed never to address another lady. Dortch married another but was later widowed. Johnson then renewed his attentions. This time she accepted and they were married on February 20, 1838.

Following his appointment as Attorney General of the Tenth District in 1817, Johnson moved to Clarksville. In the Jacksonian landslide of 1828, Johnson was elected to the U.S. House of Representatives, where as an ardent Jacksonian he was notable for his economic conservatism. Johnson's attempts to control spending led Congressman John Quincy Adams to label the Tennessean "the nuisance of the House."

Cave Johnson became a close friend and advisor to James K. Polk, a fellow Democratic House member, and the two Congressmen, along with Senator Felix Grundy, became leading pro-Jackson loyalists. When Polk became the Democratic presidential candidate in 1844, Johnson assumed the role of campaign manager and was rewarded by the victorious Polk with the post of postmaster general.

Johnson's tenure oversaw the creation of the modern postal service. The introduction of the adhesive postage stamp in 1847 placed the service on a sounder financial basis by requiring the sender to finance the cost rather than the recipient. Further reforms included the urban collection of outgoing mail, a practice that became a standard feature of the postal service.

When Polk's administration ended in 1849, Johnson returned to his home in Clarksville where he practiced law until 1860 and served in several appointed posts, including circuit court judge; President of the Bank of Tennessee, 1854–59; and a Claims Commissioner of the United States, 1860. Johnson took a leading role in the resistance to the southern rights cause and secession. Like other old-line Jacksonians, he was alarmed by the new Democrats who were tinged with the old Calhoun "heresies" against majority rule and the Union.

He was a reluctant Confederate, sitting out the Civil War with resignation. When the Union gunboats arrived in Clarksville on February 20, 1862, Johnson surrendered the town to the federal forces. Johnson received a presidential pardon and in 1866 was elected to the State Senate, but was refused his seat by the Brownlow forces. His final word on the subject of the Union came shortly before his death in a letter to his son, Polk Johnson, dated March 17, 1866: "We should always bear in mind the distinction between the *Government* and the *administration* of the *government*. Our *government* is the best ever made and *its administration* for a few years past the *worst*. We should not therefore destroy or attempt it but by a change of Rulers in the legal mode." (emphasis in original; TSLA)

Thomas H. Winn, Austin Peay State University

SUGGESTED READINGS: Clement L. Grant, "The Public Career of Cave Johnson," *Tennessee Historical Quarterly* 19(1951): 195–223 and "Cave Johnson: Postmaster General," *Tennessee Historical Quarterly* 20(1961): 323–49

SEE: CLARKSVILLE; COCKE, WILLIAM; GRUNDY, FELIX; JACKSONIANS; POLK, JAMES K.

JOHNSON, CHARLES S. (1893–1956), distinguished sociologist and African-American leader, was born in 1893 in Bristol, Virginia. He was educated at Wayland Academy in Richmond, the Virginia Union University, and the University of Chicago, where he undertook graduate work with the distinguished scholar Robert E. Park. Johnson worked with Park on *The Negro in Chicago: A Study of Race Relations and a Race Riot* (1922).

In 1921 Johnson moved to New York to head the Urban League. He established its journal *Opportunity* and through its pages, Johnson became one of the leading patrons of the Harlem Renaissance. He influenced the careers of such artists and writers as Langston Hughes, Zora Neale Hurston, Aaron Douglas, and Arna Bontemps.

In 1928 Johnson arrived at Fisk University to be chair of the Social Science Department, which had been founded and funded by the Laura Spelman Rockefeller Memorial. With additional funds at his disposal from the Julius Rosenwald Fund, Johnson made Fisk a significant research center in race relations. Johnson and his colleagues produced several important reports documenting the many manifestations of African-American economic disadvantages in the South. Their series of reports on counties and individual communities in Tennessee is an important documentary source of rural and African-American life in the mid-twentieth century. His book, *The Negro in American Civilization* (1930), became a widely accepted sociological text. His later books included *Shadow of the Plantation* (1934) and *Growing Up in the Black Belt* (1941).

During World War II, Johnson openly attacked segregation for the first time. In 1943 he prepared *Patterns of Negro Segregation* for the use of Gunnar Myrdal in his monumental study, *The American Dilemma* (1944). With the help of Edwin Embree, chief executive of the Rosenwald Fund, Johnson published *The Monthly Summary,* which provided 8,000 subscribers with the status of race relations in various parts of the country, documented by several thousand items. Beginning in 1944, also with the assistance of the Rosenwald Fund, Johnson led annual Race Relations Institutes, attended by leaders from all over the country. These meetings were extremely influential in the developing Civil Rights Movement. While there was intense local opposition in the beginning, Ben West, then Nashville's vice mayor, spoke to the Institute in 1949. During the 1950s, Tennessee Governor Frank Clement addressed the Institute.

Johnson applauded the removal of racial barriers in various areas of society, but he, like many African-American leaders, was particularly interested in ending school segregation. NAACP attorney Thurgood Marshall was a frequent speaker at Race Relations Institutes of the 1950s and Johnson provided him with evidence to use in his legal briefs for *Brown v. Board of Education* (1954). The failure of white moderate Southerners to embrace the court's decree quickly bitterly disappointed Johnson.

Johnson achieved the pinnacle of his academic career in 1947, when he became president of Fisk University. By the late 1940s, his achievements in the worlds of education and civil rights finally brought him recognition from various national and international organizations. He was one of ten United States delegates to UNESCO (1946–47), a member of the Fulbright Board of Foreign Scholarships (1947–1954), and a delegate to the Assembly of the World Council of Churches (1948). He also advised three American presidents on educational and civil rights issues.

On October 27, 1956, Johnson died suddenly of a heart attack. World leaders mourned his passing and noted his important role in the Civil Rights Movement.

Sarah M. Howell, Middle Tennessee State University

SUGGESTED READINGS: Patrick Gilpin, "Charles S. Johnson: An Intellectual Biography," (Ph.D. diss., Vanderbilt University, 1973); Reavis L. Mitchell, Jr., *Fisk University Since 1866: Thy Loyal Children Make Their Way* (1995)

SEE: BONTEMPS, ARNAUD; CIVIL RIGHTS MOVEMENT; DOUGLAS, AARON; FISK UNIVERSITY; JULIUS ROSENWALD FUND

JOHNSON CITY. Located in the mountainous, northeast corner of Tennessee, Johnson City is the sixth largest city in the state, with a population of nearly 53,000 (1996), and is one of the regional Tri-Cities that includes Kingsport and Bristol. Johnson City had its roots in the building of the East Tennessee and Virginia Railroad. The railroad, chartered in 1849, began development of its line from Bristol to Knoxville in the early 1850s. In anticipation of the route, Henry Johnson built a store, depot, and post office in 1854 at the junction of the proposed railroad line and the existing stage road. Prior to the Civil War, the emerging village became known as Johnson's Tank because trains took on water for their steam engines at the site; when trains began stopping to load and unload passengers and freight, the name became Johnson's Depot. During the Civil War, the town took on the name Haynesville, in honor of Confederate senator Landon Carter Haynes, despite the fact that most East Tennesseans supported the Union Army.

After the Confederate defeat, the town name reverted to Johnson's Depot, and life in the area returned to peacetime pursuits. In 1868 a private academy named Science Hill Male and Female Institute opened; it is now Science Hill High School, a comprehensive high school rated a National School of Excellence. On December 1, 1869, the town received a state charter and the name Johnson City; Henry Johnson was its first mayor. For most of the remainder of the century, Johnson City was a boom town, where businesses and industry flourished, and the population steadily increased. The completion of the railroad line into North Carolina and the anticipation of another line from Chicago to Charleston, South Carolina, promised to make the city an iron and steel manufacturing hub. When the proposed railroad failed, and the nation's economy collapsed in the Panic of 1893, Johnson City's fortunes also declined for several years.

Shortly after the turn of the century, significant railroad traffic returned when the Carolina, Clinchfield and Ohio Railway was created, extending rail lines for nearly 300 miles. Johnson City soon emerged as a regional retail and wholesale distribution center that attracted other enterprises. The National Home for Volunteer Soldiers, now the Quillen Veterans Affairs Medical Center at Mountain Home, opened in 1903. In 1911 the East Tennessee Normal School, now East Tennessee State University was established. Construction of the Memphis-to-Bristol Highway opened the city to further industrial and tourism development. In the 1920s Johnson City became a diversified community that boasted a growing number of banks, phone service, a new public library, a major hotel, theaters, and the Appalachian School of Nursing; by 1930 it was the fifth largest city in the state.

The Depression and World War II produced profound changes. The Civilian Conservation Corps and the Works Progress Administration built new facilities in the area, including the McKellar Tri-City airport, now Tri-Cities Regional Airport. The establishment of the Tennessee Valley Authority brought dams, recreational lakes, and cheap electricity to the region. The city began an era of civic leadership development under a new charter authorizing a council-manager form of government (under which the city still operates).

From the 1950s to the present, Johnson City developed as an industrial center, retail and entertainment hub, and a burgeoning health care and educational center for the Tri-Cities and surrounding mountain area. East Tennessee State University, the largest institution of higher education serving the region, added a medical school in 1974, emphasizing primary and rural health care with medical outreach programs to surrounding communities. The medical school, the Quillen Veterans Affairs Medical Center, and the growing number of specialty hospitals in Johnson City have led to plans for a biomedical-clinical research and industry corridor (the "Med-Tech" corridor) to be developed for the twenty-first century. The growth of the university, health care, business, and industry have led to a vision of the city's future that includes a continuing education center, a new, technologically sophisticated public library, and proposed cultural district.

Jean Haskell Speer, East Tennessee State University

SEE: CARTER, GEORGE; EAST TENNESSEE STATE UNIVERSITY; QUILLEN COLLEGE OF MEDICINE; TAYLOR, ROBERT L.; TIPTON-HAYNES HISTORIC SITE; WASHINGTON COUNTY

JOHNSON COUNTY in the extreme northeastern corner of the state lies on the western slope of the Appalachian Mountains. It is bounded by Virginia on the north and North Carolina on the south and east. The county covers approximately 290 square miles. A hilly and mountainous area, the highest elevation is Snake Mountain at 5,574 feet. The most fertile and flat land can be found along the Little Doe River and Roan and Beaverdam creeks.

Before white settlers, the Cherokees, Creeks, and Yuchis used the area as a hunting and burial ground. Evidence of prehistoric mound builders has been found. The first white settlers were mostly English, but also included some Scots-Irish and Germans. The first settlement occurred at the confluence of a buffalo trail and three wilderness trails. The settlement name, Trade, attests to its importance as a meeting place where settlers, frontiersmen, and Native Americans swapped goods and stories.

Daniel Boone hunted and explored the area between 1761 and 1769. Numerous settlers followed Boone's trail through the wilderness, including John Honeycutt, who built a cabin on Roan Creek. Honeycutt entertained several well-known frontiersmen, including Boone and James Robertson, who achieved fame in the Watauga and Cumberland settlements. Before the end of the century, additional settlements had been established at Little Doe, Shady Valley, and Laurel Bloomery.

Settlers on Roan Creek included Joseph Haskins; George and Samuel Neatherly; Thomas, John, and Charles Asher; Richard and Benjamin Wilson; John and Henry Grimes; Joseph Gentry; John Jesse, John

Haskins; and John Higgins. Nathaniel Taylor erected an iron works on Roan Creek. The first Little Doe settlers were Jacob Perkins, George Brown, George Crosswhite, Ed Polly, Joseph Timpkins, and David Stout. John Vaught operated a mill and a "still house," which he left to his son Joseph Vaught. Shouns Crossroads bore Leonard Shoun's name, and David Wagner lived east of Shouns. Laurel settlers included James Keys, Charles Anderson, Peter and John Wills, Daniel Cuthbert, Peter Snyder, Abraham Dorson, Joseph Sewell, John and Garland Wilson, Robert and John Walters, William Wandley (now Widby), William Neatherly, and Anthony and William Fisher.

Johnson County shared its early history with Carter and Washington counties. Johnson County was created by the General Assembly in 1836 and named for Thomas Johnson, one of the early settlers, who came to Doe Valley from Virginia. Johnson died in 1835, but the first session of the county court was held in the home of his son, William Johnson, who served as a member of the court. Other members included Andrew Wilson, James Wright, John Ward, James B. Morley, Joseph Robinson, Jered Arrendell, Jessie Cole, M.M. Wagner, James Brown, Andrew L. Wilson, Phillip Shull, and John Dugger.

The commissioners appointed to locate the seat of justice purchased 25 and one-half acres from William P. Vaught and laid off a town, which they named Taylorsville, in honor of Colonel James P. Taylor. The first courthouse was completed in 1837, and two years later, the county built a jail. A second courthouse was erected in 1894. The third and present courthouse was built in 1958.

In 1866 Taylorsville was incorporated, and J.M. Wagner served as the first mayor. In 1885 the town changed its name to Mountain City. In 1844 W.R. Keys founded the *Taylorsville Reporter*; in 1885, the newspaper's name changed to the *Tennessee Tomahawk*, and in 1915 it was called the *Johnson County News*. Mac Wright owned and published another small paper called the *Johnson County News Bulletin*. In 1950 he purchased the *Johnson County News* and continued with the *News Bulletin* until 1956, when he sold it to new owners, who renamed the paper the *Tomahawk*.

In 1900 Johnson County acquired railroad service, and the line reached Mountain City in 1910. Built to haul timber and manganese into Virginia and North Carolina, the railroad attracted miners and timber cutters, who established camps along the line. In 1922 the Merchant and Traders Bank was founded to handle the company payrolls for the mining and timber operations. The bank, now the Farmer's State Bank, competes with two others, the Johnson County Bank and Elizabethton Federal.

The county's economy remains somewhat dependent on agriculture. Today, tobacco remains the largest cash crop, with a few land owners leasing tobacco allotments from smaller farms. Corn, apples, strawberries, and other fruits and vegetables are raised on small farms and sold locally. In the first half of the century, Johnson County was known as the "Green Bean Capital of the World."

The largest industrial employers in the county are textile mills, including Sara Lee Knit Products, Bike Athletic Company, Mountain City Glove Manufacturing Company, Incorporated, and Levi Strauss. Johnson County has experienced some industrial downsizing due to recent changes in the textile industry. In response to these changes, the county economy has shifted toward tourism and the creation of specialty shops. The Appalachian Trail, for example, crosses U.S. 412 at the Johnson-Sullivan county line; most of the county's natural resources are within the Cherokee National Forest. The TVA-created Watauga Lake (1949) provides recreational opportunities at Butler.

Johnson County and Mountain City have undertaken a number of improvements. Mountain City boasts two new parks, a swimming pool, tennis courts, and a downtown revitalization project. The Johnson County Welcome Center is one of the largest in the state, and the Mountain City Municipal Airport, which can accommodate small jets, boasts 4,500 feet of runway. The Roan Valley Golf Course hosts a number of golf tournaments.

Jewell Hamm, Shady Valley

SEE: APPALACHIAN TRAIL; BOONE, DANIEL; CHEROKEE NATIONAL FOREST; ROBERTSON, JAMES

JOHNSON, ELIZA McCARDLE (1810–1876), wife of President Andrew Johnson, was the daughter of Sarah Phillips and John McCardle, a Greeneville shoemaker, who once also operated an inn at Warrensburg. After her father's death, Eliza McCardle helped her mother make quilts to support the family. She met Andrew Johnson soon after he arrived in Greeneville in September 1826. Their wedding, performed by a justice of the peace, took place in Warrensburg on May 17, 1827, when she was 16 and he was 18.

Johnson was better educated than most women in her town. According to tradition, she taught her husband to read, but actually he was already literate. She may have taught him to write, but, in any case, she did encourage his further education.

Considered to have a modest, retiring temperament, Johnson's personality contrasted sharply with her husband's more aggressive, outgoing nature. Despite frequent, lengthy periods of separation while he held political office in Nashville or Washington, D.C., the couple were apparently devoted to each other and Andrew Johnson always expressed concern for her well-being. They had five children: Martha

(1828), Charles (1830), Mary (1832), Robert (1834), and Andrew, Jr., known as "Frank" (1852).

Remaining in East Tennessee after the state seceded from the Union, Johnson, as the wife of a notorious Unionist, was harassed and expelled from Greeneville by the Confederates. She stayed with her daughter Mary (Mrs. Daniel) Stover in Carter County until October 1862, when she was forced to leave again. General Nathan Bedford Forrest at first refused to let her through the lines to join her husband, by then Military Governor of Tennessee, in Nashville.

By this time Eliza Johnson had been ill for some years with tuberculosis. While her health periodically worsened or improved somewhat, she remained an invalid, generally withdrawn from the public eye. Johnson did not go to Washington, D.C., until June 1865, after her husband succeeded to the presidency. Even then, the couple's oldest daughter, Martha (Mrs. David T.) Patterson served as White House hostess, often assisted by her sister Mary. Johnson, usually confined to her room, rarely even attended a reception.

After the Johnsons left the White House and returned to Greeneville, her health remained poor, and she was in serious decline by the spring of 1875. Johnson was unable to attend her husband's funeral in August 1875. She died at her daughter Mary's home in Carter County six months later.

Glenna R. Schroeder-Lein, University of Tennessee, Knoxville

SUGGESTED READINGS: LeRoy P. Graf, Ralph W. Haskins, and Paul H. Bergeron, eds., *The Papers of Andrew Johnson* 14 vols. to date (1967–); Hans L. Trefousse, *Andrew Johnson: A Biography* (1989)

SEE: JOHNSON, ANDREW

JOHNSON, J. FRED (1874–1944), Appalachian entrepreneur and promoter of the model city of Kingsport, was born on June 25, 1874, in Hillsville, Virginia, the son of J. Lee Johnson and Mary Pierce Early Johnson. A nineteenth-century American value system, heavily imbued with the Protestant work ethic, shaped his private life, and New South philosophy and Progressive ideals influenced his public career. From 1916 to 1944 he devoted himself to the promotion of the planned industrial city of Kingsport, Tennessee. His life provides an example of a native Appalachian entrepreneur allied with northern investors to promote economic development in the Upper South.

Johnson's father died when the boy was a teenager, and he dropped out of school to rescue his father's general store and support his mother and two sisters. He managed to pay his father's debts with interest and continued his education by reciting his lessons to an old schoolmaster and later reading law. His marriage to Ruth Carter led directly to his business association with her brother, George L.

Carter, the principal promoter of the Carolina, Clinchfield & Ohio Railway. When Carter encountered financial difficulties, John B. Dennis of Blair and Company, New York, salvaged the project. In 1916 Dennis persuaded Johnson, who heretofore had been involved in optioning land for the railroad and in managing commissaries along the construction route, to assist him with the development of the CC&O's model city of Kingsport.

Under the auspices of the Kingsport Improvement Corporation, Dennis envisioned, financed, and directed the establishment of the new town; and Johnson provided the practicality to make the plan possible. When Johnson died on October 4, 1944, having spent almost 30 years as a one-man chamber of commerce, Kingsport stood as a monument to him. Affectionately known among residents as "the Father of Kingsport," Johnson had contributed to the successful establishment of a diversified industrial town and an urban culture in Appalachia dominated by a middle-class American value system.

Margaret Ripley Wolfe, East Tennessee State University

SUGGESTED READING: Margaret Ripley Wolfe, "J. Fred Johnson, His Town and His People: A Case Study of Class Values, the Work Ethic, and Technology in Southern Appalachia, 1916–1944," *Appalachian Journal* 7(1979–80): 70–83

SEE: CARTER, GEORGE L.; DENNIS, JOHN B.; KINGSPORT

JOHNSONVILLE, BATTLE OF. Soon after the fall of Atlanta on September 2, 1864, Confederate Lt. General John Bell Hood began a westward flanking movement originally intended to cut the supply lines of Union General William T. Sherman and draw him north to Tennessee in pursuit of Hood's army. In mid-October, a month before Hood's invasion, Major General Nathan Bedford Forrest moved north from Corinth, Mississippi, to menace Federal defenses. He reached the west bank of the Tennessee River at the Kentucky line on October 28, with some 3,500 cavalry and infantry. Capturing a gunboat and a transport as a diversion, Forrest secretly positioned his ten cannons across the river from a heavily-fortified supply depot and the western terminus of the Nashville and Northwestern Railroad at Johnsonville, named in honor of Military Governor Andrew Johnson.

On the afternoon of November 4, Forrest's gunners opened fire on three gunboats, 11 transports, and 18 barges. Union forces numbered about 2,000 men under the command of Lt. E.M. King and Colonel C.R. Thompson. Assuming Forrest was ready to cross the river with more than 13,000 troops, the Union commanders burned the vessels to prevent their capture. The fire spread to the docks and warehouses, and Federal batteries positioned above the depot could not eliminate the well-entrenched guns across the river. In the confusion, the stationmaster headed east with a train loaded with supplies and 400 men, some of whom looted the stores. The boxcars were abandoned at Waverly, and the tender and engine continued on to Nashville, 78 miles to the east.

The blazing docks and warehouses illuminated the river sufficiently to enable Forrest to evacuate his position during the night and move his forces six miles south. An artillery detachment left behind as a rear guard continued shelling the town the next morning. By the time reinforcements arrived from Nashville, Forrest's artillery had been removed. Forrest arrived in Corinth on November 10 with 150 prisoners, and reported to Hood in Florence, Alabama, on November 14.

The Confederates reported two dead and nine wounded, with the capture of 150 prisoners. Union losses were eight killed and wounded. Forrest estimated the value of the vessels and equipment he destroyed to be $6.7 million, although Union estimates were considerably lower. Forrest's movements caused panic, and one report had him near Chicago with 14,000 men. Major General Joseph Hooker took the report seriously enough to move troops from Indianapolis and St. Louis to defend the city. Ultimately, the Johnsonville raid failed to impede the well-supplied Sherman on his march to the sea, nor did it prevent the destruction of Hood's forces at Franklin and Nashville. The New Johnsonville State Historical Area contains excellent examples of Federal Civil War fortifications. The Nathan B. Forrest State Historical Area interprets the Confederate role in the battle.

Paul Ashdown, University of Tennessee, Knoxville

SEE: FORREST, NATHAN BEDFORD; HOOD, JOHN BELL

JOHNSTON, ALBERT SIDNEY (1803–1862), first commander of Confederate forces in the Western Theater, was born at Washington, Kentucky, on February 2, 1803. Johnston graduated from the United States Military Academy in 1826. While there, he developed a friendship with another cadet, Jefferson Davis.

After serving in several western outposts, Johnston resigned his commission in 1834, to join the revolutionary army of Texas as a private. By 1836 he was the senior brigade commander of the Texas forces. After the admission of Texas to the Union, Johnston rejoined the U.S. Army in 1849, as colonel of the newly formed Second Cavalry, an elite regiment that included some of the best officers in the country. In part, Johnston owed his command position to his reputation as an able officer, but more importantly, to his friendship with the Secretary of War, Jefferson Davis.

By 1861 Johnston commanded the Department of the Pacific, but when Texas seceded from the Union, he resigned his commission. Offering his services to the president of the new Confederate States, Johnston received an appointment as a full general in August 1861. The Kentuckian commanded all Confederate forces west of the Allegheny Mountains, an area encompassing approximately two-thirds of the Confederacy.

Johnston assumed the task of defending a 300-mile front, stretching from the Mississippi River across Tennessee and Kentucky to the Cumberland Gap. To defend this line against approximately 60,000 Federal soldiers, Johnston mustered only 30,000 southern men.

Despite his tenuous position, Johnston maintained the confidence of Davis and the citizens of the South. His successful prewar career and his martial bearing led many to exaggerate his military capabilities. At 59, Johnston stood over six feet tall, with gray-streaked hair and a large mustache. Usually wearing a well-fitted gray uniform, Johnston looked like a general.

In the spring of 1862 Johnston's image as the most capable officer in the Confederacy collapsed. When he moved to strengthen the garrison at Bowling Green, Kentucky, General Ulysses S. Grant took advantage of the weak defenses on the western rivers and captured Forts Henry and Donelson. As the Confederate forces retreated south, the state capital of Tennessee fell to the Union Army. Tennessee delegates to the Confederate Congress petitioned for Johnston's removal as commander in the West.

Resolving to reclaim the lost territory, Johnston gathered a strong force at Corinth, Mississippi. He planned to strike the Union forces under Grant, then encamped at Pittsburgh Landing, Tennessee, before they could be reinforced. The resulting Battle of Shiloh, April 6 and 7, 1862, was the largest engagement of the Civil War fought to date.

Taking advantage of their initial success, Johnston's forces were driving the Federal soldiers before them when word reached him that one regiment refused to advance. Johnston decided to lead personally this regiment, the 45th Tennessee Infantry, in a charge against what came to be known as the Hornet's Nest. Johnston led a bayonet charge that drove the enemy back several hundred yards. The general returned to his staff, flushed with excitement, with several bullet holes in his uniform but no visible injuries.

Johnston sent his staff to various parts of the battlefield, but he remained behind the battle line. The first of his staff to return, volunteer aide and Tennessee governor Isham G. Harris, found the general slumped in his saddle. Harris led him to a ravine and laid him under a tree, where Johnston died a short time later. During the charge with the 45th Tennessee Infantry, a ball entered Johnston's leg just above his boot and severed an artery. Command of the Confederate forces fell to General P.G.T. Beauregard. The following day, after reinforcements arrived from

Nashville, the Federal troops drove the Confederates from the field.

Patrick Craddock, Franklin

SUGGESTED READING: Charles P. Roland, *Albert Sidney Johnston: Soldier of Three Republics* (1964)

SEE: CIVIL WAR; SHILOH, BATTLE OF

JOHNSTON, JOSEPH E. (1807–1891), the most underrated Confederate commander in either theater of the Civil War and the only man to command armies in both theaters, was born at Farmville, Virginia, in 1807. A classmate of Robert E. Lee at West Point, Johnston rose to the rank of brevet brigadier general in the U.S. Army before resigning his commission in April 1861, to join the Confederate forces. Johnston was made a brigadier general in the southern army and given the command of Harper's Ferry, Virginia. From there, Johnston moved his command by rail to Manassas, where he won the first major battle of the Civil War. Promoted to full General, Johnston commanded the army in Virginia during the Seven Days battles. Though outnumbered, his army halted General George McClellan's advance on Richmond. Johnston was wounded during the Battle of Seven Pines. While he convalesced, Davis replaced him as commander of the Virginia army with a friend, Robert E. Lee.

When he returned to duty, Johnston received the command of the western military department. After General Braxton Bragg's fiascoes in Middle Tennessee, Kentucky, and North Georgia, Johnston was placed in command of the Army of Tennessee. In contrast to Bragg's strict discipline, "Uncle Joe" Johnston's relaxed and gentle character instantly won the respect and confidence of the Tennessee soldiers. During the Atlanta campaign, Johnston retained the trust of his army despite their desperate campaign against overwhelming odds. Some critics viewed Johnston as unaggressive for his decision to fight from entrenched defensive positions rather than grant his opponent, General William S. Sherman, the choice of battle ground. Johnston was relieved of his command and replaced by General John Bell Hood.

Following Hood's near destruction of the army during his late 1864 campaign in Tennessee, Johnston again assumed command. From February to April 1865, Johnston led the remnants of the Army of Tennessee to North Carolina, where he successfully blocked his old antagonist, Sherman, from combining forces with Grant against Lee. On April 26, 1865, two weeks after Lee surrendered the Army of Northern Virginia, Johnston capitulated to Sherman at Greensborough, North Carolina.

Johnston, the commander of the Army of Tennessee, never led that army in a battle on the soil of the state. Nevertheless, he remained the most respected and beloved leader of that army; to the soldiers, he was always "Uncle Joe."

Patrick Craddock, Franklin

SUGGESTED READING: Gilbert Govan and James Livingood, *A Different Valor: The Story of Joseph E. Johnston* (1956)

SEE: ARMY OF TENNESSEE; CIVIL WAR

JONES, JONATHAN LUTHER "CASEY" (1863–1900). In an era when spectacular train wrecks were common, the fate of Illinois Central engineer Jonathan Luther Jones should not have aroused popular interest. Yet "Casey Jones, The Brave Engineer" has become one of Tennessee's great folk heroes and a prominent character in American railroad lore. The legend of Casey Jones owes its creation to a black engine wiper at the Illinois Central Roundhouse in Canton, Mississippi. Wallace Saunders composed the verses about his engineer friend that embellished the events of April 30, 1900, and made Casey Jones a legend.

Jones was born on March 14, 1863. His schoolteacher father moved the family to Cayce, Kentucky, when Jones was in his teens. There he watched the locomotives at the Mobile and Ohio Railroad yards and decided to make railroading his career. In 1878, at the age of 15, Jones left his family to work on the Mobile and Ohio. The road transferred him to Jackson, Tennessee, where he met and married Janie Brady in 1886. Jones established a reputation for staying on schedule while running the freight route between Jackson and Water Valley, Mississippi. He always announced his approach with a blast of the calliope whistle, which sounded like a whippoorwill in the night.

In January 1900 Jones was transferred to a passenger run between Memphis and Canton, Mississippi, which made up one leg of a four-train run linking Chicago and New Orleans. The "Cannonball Express" had a reputation for speed, but so did Jones. He completed his day's work on the morning of April 29 and pulled train Number 1 into Memphis's Poplar Street Station. The regular engineer for the Canton run was ill, and Jones agreed to double up. He asked that his favorite engine number 382 be readied for the return trip. The train was 95 minutes behind schedule when it left the station, but Jones and fireman Sim Webb were determined to make up the time over the 188-mile run. Nearing Vaughn, Mississippi, Jones was only two minutes behind schedule and within 15 miles of his destination. A freight train with a mechanical failure was unable to move off the main line onto a siding. When Jones saw the lights of the caboose, he yelled for Webb to jump. The fireman escaped with minor injuries. No one but Jones died in the wreck when the engine slammed into the freight train's caboose. Jones stayed on the train to apply the brakes, saving the lives of his passengers.

The Illinois Central claimed to have issued warnings regarding the stalled trains, but Webb contended they saw no signals.

Wallace Saunders's version of the story spread through the vaudeville circuit, and in 1909 Lawrence Seibert and Eddie Newton altered the lyrics and copyrighted a version of *Casey Jones, The Brave Engineer*. Their version popularized the song and became the basis for over 200 later versions by everyone from the Boy Scouts to the Grateful Dead. Jones has been immortalized by a postage stamp, books, and the Casey Jones Home and Railroad Museum in Jackson, Tennessee. Although the songs often misrepresent the facts, they made the courage and heroism of the railroad man an American legend.

Blythe Semmer, Middle Tennessee State University

SUGGESTED READINGS: Norm Cohen, "'Casey Jones': At the Crossroads of Two Ballad Traditions," *Western Folklore* 32 (1973): 77–103; T. Clark Shaw, "The Legend of Casey Jones," *West Tennessee Historical Society Papers* 36 (1992): 65–71

SEE: JACKSON; RAILROADS

JONES, EDWARD CULLIATT (1822–1902), architect, was born in Charleston, South Carolina, and educated there and in Northampton, Massachusetts. He began his career as an architect in Charleston in 1848. After serving in the Confederate Army, Jones moved to Memphis in 1866, where he accepted as his first job the remodeling of the Brinkley Block of stores at Main and Monroe.

In partnership with Matthias Harvey Baldwin, Jones built the Woodruff-Fontaine House (1870), renovated the Goyer-Lee House (1871), and constructed Beale Street Baptist Church (1867–1881). Extant Memphis buildings of his design include the main building at Porter Leath Children's Center (1875), First Presbyterian Church (1884), Second Presbyterian Church, now Clayborn Temple (1891), and the first skyscraper south of St. Louis, built for the Continental Bank (1895), now the D.T. Porter Building.

James Patrick, author of *Architecture in Tennessee*, noted that Jones's career spanned two eras. His first buildings in the Greek Revival style would have been produced using tools and techniques common to the sixteenth century. By the 1890s Jones had made the transition to steel and rivets to produce skyscrapers. As Patrick notes, this situation is testimony to the versatility of architects like Jones and the rapidity of fundamental changes in construction.

Perre Magness, Memphis

SUGGESTED READINGS: Eugene J. Johnson and Robert D. Russell, Jr., *Memphis, An Architectural Guide* (1990); Perre Magness, *Good Abode, Nineteenth Century Architecture in Memphis and Shelby County* (1993); James Patrick, *Architecture in Tennessee, 1768–1897* (1981)

SEE: MEMPHIS

JONES, JAMES CHAMBERLAIN (1809–1859), one of the most popular Whig politicians in antebellum Tennessee, was born in Wilson County. Reared by an uncle after his father's death, Jones learned farming by working for his guardian. He occasionally attended common schools and briefly studied law, though he never practiced. Following his marriage in 1829, he established himself on his own farm near Lebanon. Jones's first recorded political activity occurred in 1836, when he attended several public meetings in support of Hugh Lawson White's presidential candidacy. In 1839, Jones was elected to the State House of Representatives, where he quickly gained a reputation as a devoted Whig and effective speaker. As a candidate for presidential elector for William Henry Harrison in 1840, Jones became highly regarded as a master of popular campaigning. In the next year, at age 32, Whigs nominated him to challenge incumbent James K. Polk for the governorship. Dubbed "Lean Jimmy" because of his six-foot, two-inch, 125-pound frame, Jones bested Polk in a series of debates across the state in which he used his popular campaigning style in defense of the national Whig policies of a national bank and government sponsorship of economic development. He upset Polk by a three-point margin. Two years later, Jones again defeated Polk, by championing the presidential candidacy of Henry Clay—whom, ironically, Polk would defeat a year later in his own triumphant presidential race.

Jones's two terms as governor occurred during a period of rabid partisan politics and economic depression. The "Immortal Thirteen" controversy preoccupied most of his first term, though in an 1842 special session, the General Assembly passed several relief measures, including the abolition of imprisonment for debt. In his second term, the legislature's major accomplishments included establishing Nashville as the state's permanent capital and creating state schools for the blind and for the deaf. Declining to run for a third term, Jones remained politically active after his governorship by promoting the construction of railroads and serving as a presidential elector for Zachary Taylor in 1848. In 1850 he moved to Memphis and became president of the Memphis and Charleston Railroad Company. The next year, a Whig majority in the Assembly elected him to the U.S. Senate. As a Senator, Jones spoke frequently, but otherwise achieved no significant distinction, although he did play an influential role in winning sufficient southern support at the 1852 Whig convention to secure Winfield Scott's presidential nomination. With the demise of the national Whig party, Jones refused to follow other southern Whigs into the nativist American party. Instead, he maintained his independence as an "Old Line Whig," and in 1856, he supported the Democrat James Buchanan for the presidency. After the expiration of his term, he spoke in Illinois in 1858, in favor of Senator Stephen Douglas's re-election campaign against Abraham Lincoln. Shortly before his death, Jones publicly endorsed Douglas as his candidate for the presidency in 1860.

Jones was the first Tennessee governor to have been born in the state. His ambition often put him at odds with other state party leaders, but Jones's rapid rise to prominence, his effective campaign style, and his victories over Polk made him an important figure, who helped to establish Tennessee's party as one of the strongest Whig organizations in the South.

Jonathan M. Atkins, Berry College

SUGGESTED READING: Ray G. Osborne, "Political Career of James Chamberlain Jones, 1840–1857," *Tennessee Historical Quarterly* 7(1947): 195–228 and 322–34

SEE: IMMORTAL THIRTEEN; POLK, JAMES K.; RAILROAD, MEMPHIS AND CHARLESTON; WILSON COUNTY

JONES, JOSEPH (1833–1896), Nashville's first health officer, was born in Liberty County, Georgia, the son of Charles Colcock Jones. Educated at Princeton University, he received his M.D. degree from the University of Pennsylvania in 1856. A fierce proponent of secession, Jones served as a Confederate medical officer during the Civil War, principally operating as an epidemiologist in the study of camp diseases and wounds.

Jones received an appointment as Nashville's first health officer in April 1867 and joined the faculty of the University of Nashville medical college. He characterized Nashville the dirtiest place he had ever seen, a stunning comment considering his wartime knowledge of Andersonville prison. In 1868 Jones presented a scientific paper to the Tennessee Medical Society entitled "On the Use of the Thermometer in Disease." His contract with Nashville was not renewed in 1868, and his tenure as editor of the *Nashville Journal of Medicine and Surgery* ended as the result of a faculty squabble.

While in Nashville, Jones also found time for a pathbreaking archaeological study, based on his perception that Nashville had been built on an extensive Indian burial ground. In 1870 the Smithsonian published his findings, *Aboriginal Remains of Tennessee.*

After leaving Nashville, Jones taught medicine at the University of Louisiana and became the president of the Louisiana Board of Health. He pioneered in the efficacy of the germ theory, concurrently with Louis Pasteur. Jones died in 1896, after publishing his *Medical and Surgical Memoirs.*

James B. Jones, Jr., Tennessee Historical Commission

SUGGESTED READINGS: James O. Breeden, *Joseph Jones, M.D., Scientist of the Old South* (1975); Robert W. Ikard, "The Short and Stormy Nashville Career of Joseph Jones, Tennessee's First Public Health Officer," *Tennessee Historical Quarterly,* 48(1989): 209–217

SEE: MEDICINE

JONES, MADISON PERCY (1925–), novelist, was born in Nashville and grew up on a farm located on Franklin Pike. After military service in and immediately after World War II, Jones completed a B.A. at Vanderbilt University, where he studied under Monroe Spears and Donald Davidson. He earned an M.A. at the University of Florida, where he studied fiction writing under Andrew Nelson Lytle, and then completed additional graduate work. In 1954 Jones won a *Sewanee Review* fellowship. He then taught at the University of Tennessee (1955–56). In 1956 he began his long teaching career at Auburn University, from which he retired as writer-in-residence in 1987. Jones and his wife, Shailah, continue to live in Auburn, Alabama; but the country of his imagination is Tennessee, where he began his life and his career.

From the beginning, Jones seemed to realize that the novel was his natural mode. He has written short stories, and indeed, some of his novels, including his penultimate one, *To the Winds,* are constructed of sequences or chapters that can stand alone as stories. He also wrote the novellas *An Exile* (1967) and *Nashville 1864: The Dying of the Light* (1997). But, from *The Innocent* (1957) through *Last Things* (1989) and *To the Winds* (1996), Jones showed himself the quintessential novelist. In addition to fiction, he occasionally publishes criticism in the *Sewanee Review, Southern Review,* and elsewhere.

Although comedy plays a role in his fiction, Jones's view of the world and man's place in it is tragic. There is humor in such sequences as "Zoo" in *To the Winds,* and Jones's version of frontier humor is antipastoral, recalling the comedy of William Faulkner. But Jones has an unflinching view of man's depravity and its consequences. William Hoffman correctly views Jones as a bedrock Calvinist, whose characters remain flawed and whose submission to sin requires punishment. Jones repeats this pattern throughout his novels, although the tragic vision of *Nashville 1864* is more nearly that of communal rather than individual fate. As Allen Tate recognized, Jones seems to have been most influenced by Thomas Hardy.

Jones's career has seen many vicissitudes. First published by such large trade houses as Harcourt Brace, Viking, and Doubleday, Jones's work is now distributed by smaller houses such as Longstreet Press and J. S. Sanders & Company. *An Exile* was made into a movie, though an undistinguished one. Hollywood purchased an option on what critics consider his best work, *A Cry of Absence* (1971), and actively considered *Nashville 1864.* Neither work has yet been filmed.

Jones exhibits a rich and exact sense of place and a keen ear for spoken language, including various southern idioms. He is a natural maker of strong scenes and moving sequences of consequential actions. His work, like that of others of his generation, has not achieved the popularity or respect it deserves. A special issue of *Chattahoochie Review* (Volume 18, Fall 1996) helps to repair the critical neglect that has often accompanied his fiction. Madison Jones is a novelist of enduring power, and his vision of humankind is illumined by a durable fire.

George Core, The Sewanee Review

SEE: DAVIDSON, DONALD; LITERATURE; LYTLE, ANDREW

JONES, SAMUEL (d. 1906), flamboyant Methodist evangelist, came to Nashville in 1885 as the result of a boast he made in Memphis that no church in the "city of churches" would be able to contain the crowds he would attract. When Jones made his first appearance on Eighth and Broadway, he preached to a crowd estimated at 10,000.

Jones's frequent and violent outbursts against those who sold whiskey drew the interest of Captain Tom Ryman, a Nashville riverboat magnate. Raised a Methodist, Ryman provided free shipping for church-related materials. Since his riverboats also contained gambling casinos, he was offended by Jones's condemnation of sellers of whiskey and also worried about the potential loss of business. He attended Jones's meeting with the intention of confronting the evangelist. Seizing the initiative, Jones preached, Ryman listened, and a loyal follower of Jones and Temperance was born. As a result, Ryman built the Union Gospel Tabernacle for the purpose of encouraging religion in Nashville. The building eventually became known as the Ryman Auditorium, the home of Nashville's Grand Ole Opry for many years.

Nashville was the scene of the greatest days of Jones's revival movement. Thousands converted under his preaching, and local churches carried on the message he brought. His relentless attacks on alcohol led to Nashville becoming a center for the prohibition movement. Returning to the city on numerous occasions, Jones always railed against Nashville's saloons and taverns.

Kenneth Fieth, Nashville/Davidson County Metropolitan Archives

SEE: NASHVILLE; RYMAN AUDITORIUM; TEMPERANCE

JONESBOROUGH, the oldest town in Tennessee, was chartered by the State of North Carolina in 1779 and laid out in 1780. Named for Willie Jones, a resident of Halifax, North Carolina, who supported the western settlements, the town once served as capital of the State of Franklin in 1784–1785. Jonesborough was incorporated in 1815 and is the seat of government for Washington County, which had been established by North Carolina in 1777. A year earlier, in 1776, this large region of present-day Tennessee was designated the Washington District.

Most of historic Jonesborough is within a National Register of Historic Places district, which includes important places of early settlement and political history as well as a fine range of architectural types from the vernacular log structures of the late 1700s to the Colonial Revival movement of the 1930s. Landmark buildings include the Chester Inn; the Christopher Taylor House, a two-story log dwelling; Sisters Row, an 1820s brick row house; the Presbyterian Church of 1845–1847, one of the state's most impressive Greek Revival church buildings; the Cunningham house, home of railroad investor Dr. Samuel B. Cunningham; the Holston Baptist Female Institute of 1853–1855, which later served as a Freedmen's Bureau school; and the Washington County Courthouse, designed by the Knoxville firm of Baumann and Baumann in 1913. The town's visitor center and museum provides walking tour brochures and exhibits about the town's two centuries of history. Jonesborough is also the host every October of the National Storytelling Festival, one of the nation's premier folklife events.

Carroll Van West, Middle Tennessee State University

SEE: CHESTER INN; FRANKLIN, STATE OF; NATIONAL STORYTELLING FESTIVAL; WALTON, JESSE

JUBILEE HALL AT FISK UNIVERSITY. Fisk Free School opened its doors in January 1866 in Nashville near what is today the site of Union Station. At the time, the campus's only buildings consisted of small, wooden hospital barracks originally built to serve Union soldiers who occupied Nashville during and after the Civil War.

By the early 1870s, the wooden barracks were insufficient to serve the population of African Americans who wished to be educated at Fisk School. Through the efforts of Fisk's Jubilee Singers—who introduced Negro spirituals to the world beyond the South—funds were raised to relocate the school on more than 40 acres of land in North Nashville.

Funds raised by the Jubilee Singers during an 1871–1874 international concert tour were used to construct the school's first permanent building, Jubilee Hall. This imposing six-story building, named in honor of the Jubilee Singers, was designed by architect Steven D. Hatch of New York. Construction began in 1873 and was completed in 1876. The massive Victorian Gothic structure, which first housed the entire college, features a towering steeple. Complementary elements near the entrance are magnificent doors and a beautifully carved staircase created from wood sent from Sierra Leone, West Africa, by a former student.

In Jubilee Hall's first-floor Appleton Room hangs a floor-to-ceiling portrait of the original Jubilee Singers. The portrait was created by artist Edward Havell, portrait painter for the court of

Queen Victoria, who commissioned this portrait in the 1880s and later presented it to Fisk University. The Appleton Room was totally refurbished in 1992 as a gift to the university from the William Randolph Hearst Foundation.

Jubilee Hall, dedicated in January 1876, is one of the oldest structures continuously in use for educational purposes by the African-American community. Today, the six-story building serves as a residence for first-year female students. Over the years, as many as three generations of women in the same family—grandmother, mother, and daughter—have at different times occupied the same dormitory suite, making Jubilee Hall one of the most cherished buildings on the campus. Jubilee Hall has received recognition from the State of Tennessee in the form of a historical marker denoting the structure's significance. In 1976 Jubilee Hall was designated as a National Historic Landmark by the National Park Service.

Reavis L. Mitchell, Jr., Fisk University

SUGGESTED READING: Reavis L. Mitchell, Jr., *Fisk University Since 1866: Thy Loyal Children Make Their Way* (1995)

SEE: EDUCATION, HIGHER; FISK UNIVERSITY

JUBILEE SINGERS OF FISK UNIVERSITY.

In 1871, only four years after the incorporation of Fisk Free School as Fisk University in Nashville, the school for emancipated African Americans faced impending closure. Classrooms and living quarters continued to be housed in the decaying barracks of the Union army hospital, where leaking roofs and inadequate facilities posed a serious problem for the expanding student population. Fisk University clearly needed a larger and more suitable campus. To overcome this crisis, the school's student choir embarked upon a series of fund-raising concert tours.

As early as 1867, university treasurer George White developed an appreciation for the students' a cappella singing and began organizing small choral groups. When White proposed a tour by a singing student troupe, he met opposition from the American Missionary Association, which sponsored the school. In 1871 the school's financial crisis became so severe that the local university trustees decided—in what must have been a monumental decision at that time—to allow the students to undertake a northern musical tour without the support of the association. Students selected for the nine-member ensemble were Isaac Dickerson, Maggie Porter, Minnie Tate, Jennie Jackson, Benjamin Holmes, Thomas Rutling, Eliza Walker, Green Evans, and Ella Sheppard.

Following a successful southern concert tour in the fall of 1871, the troupe traveled through several northern states and New England. During that northern tour, the singers performed Negro spirituals as an encore to their concert of "mainstream" sacred songs. As a result of the enthusiastic response to the

spirituals—or slave songs, as they were often called—a larger portion of each performance began to be devoted to spirituals, from which the singers derived their name. After a night of prayer and thanksgiving for the auspicious beginning of the singers' tour, manager George White remembered the Biblical reference (Leviticus 25: 8–17) to the Hebrew "year of jubilee," that marked the end of slavery. Realizing that the spiritual message of the singers reflected a similar jubilation or jubilee, he bestowed the name Jubilee Singers upon the Fisk students.

The success of the 1872 tour paid many of the school's debts and provided for the purchase of a new campus in Nashville. The tour was also profitable in another way: the Jubilee Singers's dignified, yet profoundly poignant performances erased white misconceptions of African-American education and culture and created new images of both. In addition, the Singers' presentation of the Negro spiritual popularized the songs within a wider audience and aided in preservation of the songs for the historical record.

In 1873 the Jubilee Singers and George White boarded a ship for England for a successful British tour. Their numerous performances created a storm of approval and culminated in a performance for Queen Victoria.

The troupe triumphantly returned to Nashville in May 1874 with news that they had raised nearly $50,000 for Fisk University's first permanent structure. The imposing Victorian Gothic six-story building, named in honor of the Jubilee Singers, was dedicated on January 1, 1876. A floor-to-ceiling portrait of the Jubilee Singers, which has become a universally recognized symbol of the spirit of Fisk University, hangs in Jubilee Hall.

The contributions of the original nine Jubilee Singers and their successors to the growth of the university and the establishment of the spiritual as an authentic musical expression are immeasurable. The young singers revealed themselves as intelligent, accomplished, well-rounded people, completely competent to assist their school and themselves. They totally confounded critics who questioned the fitness of African Americans for education, especially higher education.

Reavis L. Mitchell, Jr., Fisk University

SUGGESTED READING: Reavis L. Mitchell, Jr., *Fisk University Since 1866: Thy Loyal Children Make Their Way* (1995)

SEE: FISK UNIVERSITY; JUBILEE HALL; MUSIC

JULIUS ROSENWALD FUND (1917–1948).

Sears, Roebuck and Co. magnate Julius Rosenwald created the Rosenwald Fund in 1917 to coordinate his contributions for African-American education. Guided by Booker T. Washington, Rosenwald supported the expansion of public education for rural southern blacks within the context of segregation and vocational training. Not wishing to duplicate the efforts of other philanthropies such as the Slater Fund or General Education Board, Rosenwald agreed with Washington on a program for the construction of new school facilities for black children in the South, administered through Tuskegee Institute from 1913 to 1920. State agent for black rural schools Samuel L. Smith obtained the first Rosenwald aid for Tennessee school buildings in 1914.

In 1920 JRF officials in Chicago set up a southern office in Nashville with Samuel Smith as director of the rural school building program. Smith, who had studied rural school architecture with Fletcher B. Dresslar at George Peabody College for Teachers, designed most of the "Community School Plans" required for Rosenwald aid. Smith was instrumental in securing Rosenwald Fund support for the Interstate School Building Service at George Peabody College in 1929.

JRF aid also paid for an African-American agent in the state education department to coordinate efforts within black communities and with white county and state officials. Rosenwald building agent Robert E. Clay helped African-American Tennesseans raise the required community contributions of cash and labor to match the Rosenwald grant of $500 to $2,100, depending on school size. The Rosenwald Fund also matched local funds for the construction of teachers' homes and shops. These contributions convinced white-controlled county school boards to appropriate public funds for new black schools. By the building program's end in 1932, Tennessee communities had built 354 schools, nine teachers' homes, and ten shops. JRF aid provided $291,250; African Americans contributed $296,388, and whites $28,027; the bulk of construction funds came from tax revenues of $1,354,157. The rural school program also offered assistance for longer school terms, pupil transportation, industrial high schools, school and county libraries, and school beautification projects.

In 1928 the Rosenwald Fund revamped its programs to address broader issues in education and health for African Americans and race relations. New president Edwin R. Embree inaugurated programs for higher education that resulted in major gifts to Fisk University for its Department of Social Sciences, library, and endowment, as well as donations to Meharry Medical College and Tennessee Agricultural and Industrial State College for buildings and equipment. The JRF fellowship program supported hundreds of promising black leaders (and later, white scholars), including sociologist and Fisk president Charles S. Johnson and Arnaud Bontemps, author and Fisk librarian.

Concerned about the lack of medical facilities and treatment for southern African Americans, the JRF donated building and equipment funds to Knoxville Hospital and sponsored health education programs for teachers and public health nurses, as well as studies of syphilis and tuberculosis in Tennessee. Race relations questions dominated later JRF projects, as the Fund moved beyond special assistance programs to ensuring equal opportunities for all Americans. The JRF was a major supporter of the Commission on Interracial Cooperation and later the Southern Regional Council. Tennessee race relations projects included JRF subsidies for a department of race relations at the Nashville YMCA Graduate School and an educational program for industrial and farm workers at the Highlander Folk School.

Mary S. Hoffschwelle, Middle Tennessee State University

SUGGESTED READINGS: Edwin R. Embree and Julia Waxman, *Investment in People: The Story of the Julius Rosenwald Fund* (1949); Mary S. Hoffschwelle, *Rebuilding the Rural Southern Community: Reformers, Schools, and Homes in Tennessee, 1914–1929* (1998)

SEE: BONTEMPS, ARNAUD; CLAY, ROBERT E.; EDUCATION; FISK UNIVERSITY; GENERAL EDUCATION BOARD; GEORGE PEABODY COLLEGE OF VANDERBILT UNIVERSITY; HIGHLANDER FOLK SCHOOL; JOHNSON, CHARLES S.; MEHARRY MEDICAL COLLEGE; TENNESSEE STATE UNIVERSITY

K

KABALKA, GEORGE W. (1943–), pioneer in the use of organoborane chemistry in the area of radiopharmaceuticals containing short-lived nuclides, was born in Wyandotte, Michigan, February 1, 1943. He earned his undergraduate degree from the University of Michigan in 1965 and his Ph.D. from Purdue University in 1970. Kabalka joined the Department of Chemistry at the University of Tennessee, Knoxville in 1970. Presently he is a Distinguished Service professor of chemistry, and in 1994 he became the first endowed professor of the Robert H. Cole Chair in Neuroscience. He is director of research in radiology at the U.T. Graduate School of Medicine. Kabalka is also a consultant with the Oak Ridge National Laboratory in the Chemistry Division, the Medical and Health Sciences Division, and the Nuclear Medicine Group, Health and Safety Research Division. In 1993 he won the American Chemical Society award for the South's most distinguished chemist.

Kabalka's pioneering research on boron has resulted in the development of procedures for detecting cancer and reducing patient exposure to radiation, and his work holds promise for tumor-specific cancer treatment. A method developed by Kabalka, boron neutron capture therapy (BNCT), has shown some promising results in the treatment of brain cancers in clinical trials at Brookhaven National Laboratories in New York. In addition to the medical uses of boron, Kabalka teamed with Dr. Charles Anderson of the U.T. chemistry department and Dr. Peter Gresshoff, who holds the U.T. Chair of Excellence in plant molecular genetics, to develop a method for using magnetic resonance imaging (MRI) to produce images of microscopic soybean roots.

The use of MRI allows scientists to view soybean metabolism without having to cut and kill the plant. It offers the opportunity to learn more about nitrogen fixation and breed healthier, hardier plants.

Connie L. Lester, Tennessee Historical Society

SEE: SCIENCE AND TECHNOLOGY

KEEBLE, EDWIN A. (1905–1979), important twentieth century architect, was born in Monteagle Assembly, Tennessee, the fourth of six children of John Bell and Emmie Frazer Keeble. John Bell Keeble was a Nashville attorney and later the Dean of the Vanderbilt University Law School. Consequently, Edwin A. Keeble's early education took place in Nashville, where he attended Montgomery Bell Academy before entering Vanderbilt to study engineering at the age of 16. Keeble completed his Vanderbilt engineering degree in 1924 and that fall he entered the University of Pennsylvania for training in architecture. After two years there, Keeble spent the summer of 1926 at the Ecole des Hautes Etudes Artistiques at Fontainebleau and then used the next year to study under Georges Gromort at the Ecole des Beaux Arts in Paris.

Keeble returned to the United States and completed his architecture degree at the University of Pennsylvania in 1928. He practiced privately in Nashville until entering into an association with engineer and architect Francis B. Warfield. This firm operated for the next 15 years, producing a series of distinguished buildings for both private and public clients, including a series of Tennessee National Guard armories funded by the Works Progress Administration during the late 1930s.

Keeble was commissioned a lieutenant in the United States Navy in 1944. In 1946 he reopened a private practice in Nashville, completing numerous projects in Tennessee and across the nation until his retirement in 1970. Important Tennessee buildings associated with either Keeble, or the firm of Warfield and Keeble, are Nashville's Westminister Presbyterian Church, Woodmont Christian Church, and Vine

Street Christian Church; several buildings at the University of the South; facilities at Vanderbilt University, and the landmark Life and Casualty Tower, Nashville's and the state's best extant example of a 1950s modernist skyscraper.

In addition to his prominence as a designer, Keeble also educated promising students and young architects. He taught briefly at the University of Pennsylvania and Vanderbilt and helped to organize the Nashville Architectural Studio during the late 1920s and early 1930s. He died in Sewanee, Tennessee, in 1979.

Carroll Van West, Middle Tennessee State University
SEE: LIFE AND CASUALTY INSURANCE COMPANY; WORKS PROGRESS ADMINISTRATION

KEEBLE, SAMPSON W. (ca. 1832–ca. 1885), barber, businessman, and politician, became the first African American elected to the Tennessee General Assembly. Keeble was born circa 1832 in Rutherford County, Tennessee, to slave parents, Sampson W. and Nancy Keeble. From the age of 19 until 1863, he served as pressman for two weekly newspapers in Murfreesboro. Near the end of the Civil War, Keeble moved to Nashville, and by 1866 he had established the Rock City Barber Shop. He became an active leader as a member of the advisory board of the Freedmen's Savings and Trust Company Bank and treasurer of the board of directors of the Colored Agricultural and Mechanical Association.

During the Reconstruction era, Keeble joined other local blacks in the Davidson County Republican party. In 1872 he won the Republican nomination for a seat in the Tennessee House of Representatives. Helped by a heavy black vote for presidential candidate General U.S. Grant and some local white voters, who viewed him as a moderate black man, Keeble was barely elected to the Tennessee General Assembly in November 1872.

While in the legislature, Keeble served on the House Military Affairs Committee and the Immigration Committee. Before his term ended in 1875, Keeble introduced three unsuccessful bills: to amend Nashville's charter to allow blacks to operate businesses in the downtown area, to protect Negro laborers and their wages, and to gain state funds for the Tennessee Manual Labor University.

After service in the General Assembly, Keeble was elected a magistrate in Davidson County and served from 1877 until 1882. He sought to return to the General Assembly in 1878, but was defeated by a Greenback party candidate.

Linda T. Wynn, Tennessee Historical Commission/Fisk University
Source: Adapted from Bobby L. Lovett and Linda T. Wynn, *Profiles of African Americans in Tennessee* (1996): 70–71

SEE: FREEDMEN'S SAVINGS BANK AND TRUST COMPANY; TENNESSEE HOUSE OF REPRESENTATIVES; TENNESSEE MANUAL LABOR UNIVERSITY

KEFAUVER, CAREY ESTES (1903–1963), Congressman and U.S. Senator, was the Democratic vice-presidential nominee in 1956. Kefauver was born in Madisonville, Tennessee, and received his education at the University of Tennessee (1924) and Yale Law School (1927). He practiced law in Chattanooga (1927–1939) and married Nancy Pigott, a native of Scotland, in 1935.

Kefauver won election to the U.S. House of Representatives in 1939 as a supporter of President Franklin Roosevelt and the Tennessee Valley Authority. In the House (1939–1949), he served on the Judiciary Committee and the Select Committee on Small Business; advocated congressional reform and federal aid to education; and co-sponsored the Kefauver-Celler Antitrust Act, the Legislative Reorganization Act of 1946, and the GI Bill of Rights. A defender of civil liberties, he voted for the abolition of the poll tax and against the Taft-Hartley Act, the House Un-American Activities Committee, and the Federal Employment Loyalty Program.

Kefauver's successful revolt in 1948 against E.H. Crump, whose political organization had controlled Tennessee for decades, was a watershed in Tennessee politics. In full-page advertisements in the state's major newspapers, Crump portrayed Kefauver as a furtive raccoon-like instrument of the communists. Using the ads to his advantage, Kefauver pulled on a coonskin cap during a speech in Memphis, Crump's stronghold, and retorted, "I may be a pet coon, but I'm not Boss Crump's pet coon." Kefauver won, and the coonskin cap became his trademark.

Kefauver rose to national prominence in 1950 as chairman of the Senate Special Committee to Investigate Organized Crime in Interstate Commerce, where he established a reputation as fair and thorough. Kefauver alienated key Democrats in urban machines who had alliances, or at least friendships, with crime figures. Among the first televised congressional inquiries in American history, his crime hearings attracted an estimated 20–30 million viewers and firmly established Kefauver in the public mind as a crusading crime-buster and opponent of political corruption. A popular choice among many Democrats for President in 1952 with victories in 14 of 17 presidential primaries, he lost in the convention to Adlai Stevenson. A similar fate awaited him four years later, though delegates in the 1956 convention bypassed Senator John F. Kennedy to nominate Kefauver as Adlai Stevenson's vice-presidential running mate.

Kefauver overcame substantial odds to win reelection to the Senate in 1954. Depicted as a traitor

Kefauver with President John F. Kennedy, Governor Frank Clement, and Senator Albert Gore, Sr., 1963.

PHOTOGRAPH BY JACK CORN, TENNESSEE STATE MUSEUM COLLECTIONS

to the South because of his refusal to denounce the U.S. Supreme Court's landmark desegregation decision in *Brown v. Board of Education* (1954), Kefauver supported the Court's ruling as "the law of the land" and won with more than 68 percent of the vote, carrying all of Tennessee's congressional districts and losing only four of the state's 95 counties. In March 1956 Kefauver and Tennessee's other U.S. Senator, Albert Gore, Sr., were the only southern senators who refused to sign the Southern Manifesto, a demagogic anti-*Brown* statement of intent to block school integration. Kefauver voted for the Civil Rights Acts of 1957 and 1960. Overcoming strong segregationist opposition, he won a third Senate term in 1960 with 65 percent of the vote.

Kefauver assumed leadership roles in creating foreign and domestic policy at a pivotal time in American history. He supported American participation in the United Nations, the North Atlantic Treaty Organization (NATO), and the Atlantic Union. He chaired the American delegation to the Seventh Conference of NATO Parliamentarians in Paris in 1961. He co-sponsored the Twenty-fourth Amendment abolishing the poll tax in federal elections. An early advocate of consumer protection, he tried to establish a cabinet-level Department of Consumers, pushed for the development of fuel efficient automobiles, and

alerted the public to the dangers of such drugs as thalidomide. His exhaustive investigation of the pharmaceutical industry resulted in the Kefauver-Harris Drug Control Act of 1962.

Kefauver died after suffering a heart attack on the Senate floor. At his funeral, observed Wilma Dykeman in an August 18, 1963, story in the *Knoxville News-Sentinel*, there were thousands of "neighbors, fellow Tennesseans, commonplace people who appeared somehow more dignified, a little taller than usual"—those who had trusted Kefauver for leadership by voting for him, even when they disagreed with him. He was buried on the Kefauver family farm near Madisonville, beneath a simple stone cross bearing the epitaph:

"Courage, Justice, and Loving Kindness."

Theodore Brown, Jr., Atlanta, Georgia

SUGGESTED READINGS: Charles L. Fontenay, *Estes Kefauver: A Biography* (1980); Joseph B. Gorman, *Kefauver: A Political Biography* (1971); William H. Moore, *The Kefauver Committee and the Politics of Crime, 1950–1952* (1974)

SEE: CRUMP, EDWARD H.; GORE, ALBERT, SR.; MONROE COUNTY

KELLY v. BOARD OF EDUCATION is a lawsuit filed by several African-American families in 1955 to desegregate the Nashville public schools. The case dramatically altered education patterns, and its various remedies continue to generate debate. The longest-running case in Tennessee history (the federal court in Nashville still has jurisdiction over the suit in January 1997) was prompted by the U.S. Supreme Court decision in *Brown v. Board of Education*, which outlawed the separate system of white and black schools nationally.

In 1957 the Nashville federal court approved a grade-a-year plan whereby African-American first graders would attend formerly white schools. Several white groups resisted the plan, and there was some scattered violence. City officials, church leaders of both races, and educators strove for consensus and progress. Nevertheless, Nashville schools made minimal progress in overall desegregation even after the 1962 establishment of metropolitan government unified city and county schools. African-American lawyers, Z. Alexander Looby and Avon N. Williams, Jr., brought the plaintiffs' case before the district court several times to object to delays and ineffective plans.

In 1971 the U.S. Supreme Court approved busing to achieve racial balance in a North Carolina case. Federal authorities then introduced busing to the Nashville desegregation case, and prepared to move children of both races to "paired" schools. The busing of 15,000 students met widespread criticism, mostly from whites. Private schools quickly sprang up, and by 1978 white public school enrollment dropped by 20,000 students.

Further hearings, negotiations, plans and appeals continued until 1983, when the school board and the court approved a new comprehensive desegregation plan. This plan was based on student age and projected a goal of 18 to 48 percent black enrollment. Continued white flight to private and neighboring county schools impeded the plan, leading to modifications and refinements that included the creation of specialized "magnet" schools.

In 1995–1996 a new plan, "Commitment to the Future" proposed massive upgrading and enrichment of the Nashville schools. As the decade closed, Nashvillians still struggled to find a way to provide equal educational opportunities for all.

Lewis Laska, Tennessee State University

SUGGESTED READING: Richard A. Pride and J. David Woodard, *The Burden of Busing: The Politics of Desegregation in Nashville, Tennessee* (1985)

SEE: CIVIL RIGHTS MOVEMENT; LOOBY, Z. ALEXANDER; WILLIAMS, AVON N., JR.

KENNY, CATHERINE TALTY (1874–1950), suffragist and political activist, was born in Chattanooga in 1874. She married John M. Kenny of Atlanta in 1899 and moved to Nashville, where her husband became president of the Nashville Coca-Cola Bottling Company. Catherine Kenny became active in the Nashville Equal Suffrage League and in local Democratic party politics. In 1915 she co-chaired with Chattanoogan Abby Crawford Milton the campaign committee of the Tennessee Equal Suffrage Association, Incorporated. This campaign committee organized local suffrage societies across the state. By the time the Nineteenth Amendment for national woman suffrage passed both houses of Congress and was sent to the states for ratification, Tennessee had a suffrage club in almost every county.

Kenny was the intellectual of the Tennessee suffrage movement and was highly regarded for her organizational skills. According to Abby Crawford Milton, Kenny's organizational skills, her strength in the cause of woman suffrage, and her political common sense made the difference in the Tennessee ratification movement. In 1919 Kenny became the chairman of the ratification committee of the Tennessee Equal Suffrage League and organized a statewide effort to ratify the Nineteenth Amendment. Her strategy for ratification was based on organization by congressional districts. When Governor Albert H. Roberts agreed to call a special session of the General Assembly to vote on the amendment, Kenny's organization personally lobbied every member of the General Assembly.

After the passage of the suffrage amendment, Kenny became the second president of the Tennessee League of Women Voters. Kenny served as Democratic national committeewoman from Tennessee and held several position with the state Democratic party. She was also chairman of the Nashville City Hospital Commission for eight years, where she worked to improve working conditions for nurses and other female employees. Upon the death of her husband in 1926, Kenny left Nashville. She died in New York City in 1950 and is buried in the Catholic Cemetery in Brooklyn.

Carole Stanford Bucy, Volunteer State Community College

SEE: MILTON, ABBY CRAWFORD; ROBERTS, ALBERT H.; WOMAN SUFFRAGE MOVEMENT

KEY, WILLIAM (1833–1909), veterinarian and horse trainer, was born a slave in Winchester, Tennessee, and took the name of his owner, William Key, a Shelbyville planter and entrepreneur. As a child, he demonstrated a remarkable talent for working with horses and mules. Key read veterinary texts and experimented with animal remedies until he became a successful veterinarian and equine dentist. Known as Dr. William Key, he also practiced dentistry and other healing arts for slaves.

With the outbreak of the Civil War, Dr. Key accompanied his master's two sons to Fort Donelson. There he constructed his own dugout, log-covered shelter, Fort Bill, in which he took refuge and offered protection to his masters during Union bombardment. When Fort Donelson surrendered, Key helped his masters escape to Confederate forces commanded by Nathan Bedford Forrest. After the Battle of Stones River, the Sixth Indiana regiment captured Key as he tried to smuggle another black man through union lines. He was sentenced to hang, but the execution was postponed when it was learned that he was a good cook and poker player. Playing poker with Union officers, Key purchased his release in exchange for their gambling debts. Captured and sentenced to hang on another occasion, Key purchased a delay of execution with $1000 he had sewn between the soles of his shoe. Confederate raiders liberated him the next day.

After the war, Dr. Key and his former masters found the family estate in ruins. The elder William Key had died, leaving the family lands heavily mortgaged. Key developed and marketed Keystone Liniment for various animal and human ailments. With proceeds from gambling winnings and Keystone Liniment sales, he quickly paid off the mortgage for his former masters and subsequently underwrote their education.

Key owned a hotel and wagon shop, but the liniment business became so profitable, he promoted it across the South. He organized a traveling minstrel and medicine show, at which his animals performed skits to demonstrate the apparent effectiveness of his medications. While in Tupelo, Mississippi, Key bought a badly abused Arabian bay, Lauretta, from a defunct circus. He nursed the mare back to health and bred her to Tennessee Volunteer, a Standardbred stallion. She produced a colt so sickly that Key considered having it destroyed. Instead, he named it Jim, after the town drunk, who had a similarly wobbly gait. Key nursed the colt to good health, but otherwise ignored it until he noticed that the animal let itself out of gates, opened drawers to retrieve apples, and responded with affirmative and negative nods to questions. Key put Jim on a rigorous training routine that lasted for seven years. When finally exhibited, Jim could spell, distinguish among coins and make change, write letters and his name on a blackboard, identify playing cards, play a hand organ, and respond to political inquiries, among other amazing feats.

Key first exhibited "Beautiful Jim Key," at the 1897 Tennessee Centennial exhibition in Nashville. Albert R. Rogers, wealthy officer of the American Humane Association, witnessed the performance and was especially gratified that Key's training methods consisted entirely of positive rewards for performance. Rogers negotiated the right to exhibit the horse nationally, advanced Key a large sum of money, and promised that Jim would not be separated from Key as long as either lived. Key, Beautiful Jim, and grooms Sam and Stanley Davis of Shelbyville, traveled to the Rogers estate in New Jersey where, for several months, Key prepared Beautiful Jim for his New York City debut. In August 1897 Beautiful Jim amazed viewers and the New York City press and quickly became a celebrity.

For nine years, Key, Rogers, and Beautiful Jim toured major cities east of the Rocky Mountains. Hundreds of thousands of children received Jim Key Band of Mercy cards by pledging to be kind to animals, and local humane societies received sizable shares of admission sales. In 1906, after appearing before almost two million spectators, Key and Beautiful Jim retired to Shelbyville, where Key lived comfortably until his death in 1909.

James H. Neal, Middle Tennessee State University
SEE: BEDFORD COUNTY; FORT DONELSON; STONES RIVER, BATTLE OF; TENNESSEE CENTENNIAL EXPOSITION

KILLEBREW, JOSEPH BUCKNER (1831–1906), New South advocate and first Commissioner of Agriculture, was born May 29, 1831, in Montgomery County, the son of Bryan Whitfield and Elizabeth Smith Ligon Killebrew. In 1835 Bryan Killebrew bought a farm in adjoining Stewart County and moved his family there. The following year, Elizabeth Killebrew died and Joseph Killebrew began a series of changes in residence that variously placed him in the home of his aunts, his grandfather, and his father and stepmother.

In 1851 Killebrew entered Franklin College, the Middle Tennessee school operated by Tolbert Fanning. By the following December, he had exhausted his funds, however, and accepted a position teaching mathematics at the Clarksville school of John D. Tyler. In 1853 George S. Wimberly, a widower who had married Killebrew's aunt Judith Kesee, recognized the intellectual capabilities of Killebrew and offered to finance his college education at the institution of his choice. Killebrew chose the University of North Carolina at Chapel Hill, where he graduated in June 1857.

Killebrew returned to Clarksville, read law and entered the bar. In August 1857 his benefactor Wimberly died, having named Killebrew as the executor of his estate. In December Killebrew married Wimberly's daughter and only surviving child, Mary Catherine. The Killebrews were married for over 48 years and were the parents of seven children, six of whom survived to adulthood.

With the marriage, Killebrew assumed responsibility for the management of the Wimberly lands and 22 slaves. By 1865, with the addition of the dowager lands and a neighboring farm, the estate included 900 acres of land. By avoiding antagonizing either army and through skillful management of his lands, Killebrew emerged from the war years debt-free and with his property intact.

In 1870 Killebrew became agricultural editor of the Nashville *Union and American* and began his public advocacy of New South principles: improvement and extension of the system of public education, encouragement of immigration to the South, development of natural resources for industrialization, and improvement of agriculture. His writings attracted immediate attention. He tied agricultural development to industrialization and advocated a four-part agricultural program that included the breakup of large landholdings into smaller, independent farms; the diversification of crops to reduce southern agricultural dependence on cotton and tobacco; enrichment of the soil through subsoiling, crop rotation, and use of commercial fertilizers; and a program to attract European immigrants to farm unoccupied and idle land.

Killebrew proved to be as skilled at speechmaking as he was in writing, and he frequently traveled to courthouses to address farmers on the benefits of his programs. Despite his superior education, farmers apparently perceived him as one of their own and clamored to hear his speeches.

At Killebrew's urging, along with the demands of like-minded farmers, the Tennessee General Assembly established a Bureau of Agriculture in December 1871. Made up of two appointed citizens from each of the three Grand Divisions, the bureau published crop reports and provided information about the timber and mineral resources of the state. As Secretary of the Bureau, the task of gathering, preparing, and publishing this information fell to Killebrew. In 1875 the state legislature reorganized the Agricultural Bureau and placed it under the administration of a commissioner; Killebrew was appointed the first Commissioner of Agriculture, a position he held until 1880.

In 1872, Killebrew, with the backing of a number of prominent Middle Tennessee farmers, published the first issue of the *Rural Sun,* which served as an organ of the Bureau of Agriculture, promoting immigration, development of timber and mineral resources, and industrialization. In 1874, Killebrew published *Introduction to the Resources of Tennessee,* a volume of almost 1,200 pages outlining the agricultural, mineral, and timber resources in each county.

With the election of Republican Alvin Hawkins in 1880, Killebrew left the Agricultural Bureau. Thereafter, he devoted his time to iron, coal, and railroad interests, although he continued to write about agriculture, particularly tobacco cultivation. In the 1880s, he conducted geological surveys for iron and coal deposits, and traveled to Mexico to support his interests in the Refugion Gold and Silver Mining Company. During the Depression of 1893, Killebrew lost considerable money as the result of the collapse of the iron industry in Tennessee. In 1894, he became immigration agent for the NC&St.L Railroad.

Killebrew retired to his Montgomery County farm in 1904 and died in March 1906, only weeks after the death of his wife. As his biographer noted, Killebrew began his career as an agrarian, but ended as a Whig-industrialist.

Connie L. Lester, Tennessee Historical Society
SUGGESTED READING: Samuel B. Smith, "Joseph Buckner Killebrew and the New South Movement in Tennessee" (Ph.D. diss., Vanderbilt University, 1962).
SEE: AGRICULTURE; AGRICULTURAL WHEEL; AGRICULTURE; FARMERS' ALLIANCE; GEOLOGY; RAILROADS

KING COLLEGE. The Holston Presbytery founded King College in 1867 in Bristol, Tennessee, and named the school for James King, an eighteenth century settler in the region. Both the acreage and physical plant of the college have more than doubled in 130 years. The four-year coeducational institution is independently governed, but it maintains its covenant affiliation with the Presbyterian Church (U.S.A.) and the Evangelical Presbyterian Church.

The main portion of the campus comprises a quadrangle surrounded by red brick buildings of Georgian colonial design, planned by C.B. Kearfott and dating from 1917. Situated on this quadrangle, along with dormitories and classroom buildings, are the Memorial Chapel, site of college convocations and religious services; the Student Center, which also houses the dining hall; and the E.W. King Library, with its worldwide electronic access and the college administrative offices.

The faculty and administration express their commitment to a liberal arts curriculum for their 600 students through the offering of 19 academic majors and the development of eight pre-professional tracts, as well as through advisory groups. The college defines its mission as the combination of academic rigor with Christian nurture and provides opportunities both for study abroad and far-ranging service projects. In its efforts to provide diversity for all undergraduates, the college supports nine intercollegiate athletic teams for men and women. King College is accredited by the Southern Association of Colleges and Schools and holds membership in the Association of Presbyterian Colleges and Universities and the Coalition for Christian Colleges and Universities.

Margaret D. Binnicker, Middle Tennessee State University
SEE: EDUCATION, HIGHER; VANCE, JAMES I.

KINGSPORT was the first economically diversified, professionally planned, and privately financed city in twentieth-century America. Neither an Appalachian hamlet nor a company town, Kingsport developed as a self-proclaimed "All-American City." Affected by mergers, buy-outs, and shifting economic trends, contemporary Kingsport is a Janus-faced offspring of twentieth century professional planning and historical forces. Nonetheless, Kingsport represents one of the more successful and complex ventures in modern town planning in the United States. Located along the Holston River in Sullivan and Hawkins counties in Northeast Tennessee, the city in 1996 claimed a population of 41,213.

Produced by the marriage of New South philosophy and Progressivism and born of a passing historical moment when capitalists turned their attention to Southern Appalachia, the "model city" was a direct offshoot of the Carolina, Clinchfield & Ohio Railway. As early as 1906, George L. Carter of Hillsville, Virginia, the mastermind behind the CC&O, had recognized the potential for an industrial city at Kingsport. Beset with financial difficulties, Carter sold his holdings to John B. Dennis and Blair and Company of New York around 1914. The next year, Dennis organized the Kingsport Improvement Corporation and enlisted J. Fred Johnson, Carter's brother-in-law, as the principal promoter for the new town.

Kingsport's initial planning included the social and economic as well as the physical. Cheap land, low-cost nonunion labor, natural resources, and the desire to create traffic for the railroad represented Kingsport's underpinnings. Interlocking industries that did business with each other while developing outside markets provided the economic base. The Kingsport Improvement Corporation, controlled by Dennis and Johnson, opted to sell land and encourage home ownership.

Dennis and Johnson sought advice from a variety of experts, but never forfeited decision-making to them. For the physical plan, they hired the Cambridge, Massachusetts-based firm of John Nolen; for private housing and public building design, Clinton MacKenzie, Thomas Hastings, Grosvenor Atterbury, and Evarts Tracy; and for landscaping and gardening, Lola Anderson (later Mrs. John B. Dennis). For assistance with the development of a school system the KIC looked to Columbia University and the nearby state normal school at Johnson City; for sewerage, sanitation, and disease-prevention, F.S. Tainter of New York, the Tennessee Board of Health, and Dr. T.B. Yancey. KIC lawyers prepared a draft of the articles of incorporation, submitted the document to several southern authorities for evaluation, and consulted the Bureau of Municipal Research in New York. Incorporated in 1917, Kingsport seems to have been the first municipality in Tennessee to be established under a city manager-board of mayor and alderman government.

The success of the efforts of Dennis and Johnson depended on their ability to attract industries. A decade after incorporation, the town claimed ten manufacturing facilities, employing 3,383. During the grim years of the Great Depression, Tennessee Eastman Company became Kingsport's largest employer and made the new town an enigma—an industrial city experiencing growth. During the early 1940s, scientists from that same company developed a process for continuous flow production of RDX, an explosive capable of penetrating the hulls of the World War II German submarines. Consequently, Eastman received the contract to build and operate Holston Army Ammunition Plant (Holston Ordnance Works), which by the end of the war became the largest explosive manufacturing facility in the world. Because of Eastman's success with HAAP, General Leslie Groves of the Manhattan Project arranged for Tennessee Eastman and its parent company, Eastman Kodak, as Clinton Engineering Works, to operate the Y-12 plant at Oak Ridge. That facility produced the U-235 that was used in the atomic bomb dropped on Hiroshima, Japan.

During the post-World War II era, Kingsport has confronted challenges common to other American cities: decline of the downtown, urban sprawl and pollution, unsightly strip development, and annexation battles. Although there is much to criticize, there is also much to commend: the neighborhoods, the churches, a very good public school system, the civic clubs, a sound economic base, and cultural opportunities. Kingsport's past is an American paradigm, involving capitalistic dreams and the plans they spawned, loss of effective leadership, blurred vision, and the quest for a new consensus. Attempting to position the town for the challenges of the twenty-first century, city officials and civic leaders have pinned considerable hope on *Vision 2017*, a community "visioning" process that anticipates the hundredth anniversary of incorporation, and the economic potential of a new convention center and hotel complex.

Margaret Ripley Wolfe, East Tennessee State University

SUGGESTED READINGS: Edward L. Ayers, "Northern Business and the Shape of Southern Progress: The Case of Tennessee's 'Model City.'" *Tennessee Historical Quarterly* 39(1980): 208–222; Margaret Ripley Wolfe, *Kingsport Tennessee: A Planned American City* (1987)

SEE: CARTER, GEORGE L.; DENNIS, JOHN B.; HOLSTON ORDNANCE WORKS; JOHNSON, J. FRED; OAK RIDGE; RAILROADS; SULLIVAN COUNTY; TENNESSEE EASTMAN COMPANY

KINGSPORT PRESS (ARCATA GRAPHICS/QUEBECOR) initially was established in 1922 by Blair and Company, the New York bankers who financed the Clinchfield Railway and the Kingsport townsite, with John B. Dennis as chairman of the board of Kingsport Press, Incorporated. As an integral component in fulfilling the interlocking concept of industry upon which Kingsport's founders created the planned industrial community, Kingsport Press served as a catalyst for the development and expansion of related industries, including Mead Paper Company.

The company began in four unused concrete structures acquired from Grant Leather Company. The initial company president was Louis Adams, who secured the company's first contract with the Woolworth chain for the mass production of a miniature clothbound series of the classics. When Colonel Elbridge Woodman Palmer (1886–1953), former president of the bindery of J.F. Tapley Company, was recruited as president in 1925, he systematically restructured Kingsport Press by remodeling the plant, retraining and increasing the labor force, and creating a sales department. Walter F. Smith, a subsequent company president, observed that Palmer understood that books needed to be made, but also needed to be marketed, and to reach their intended audience for the Press to be successful. Palmer diversified the Press's fields of publications to include textbooks and encyclopedias, increased company floor space from a few hundred square feet to 12.5 acres, and added additional shifts making the Press operational 24 hours a day.

Palmer served as president for 29 years and quickly became a nationally known industrialist as well as a civic leader receiving international recognition. Serving as president of the Tennessee Society of Crippled Children and Adults for 18 years, he also was president, trustee, and treasurer of the national Society for Crippled Children and Adults. Locally, Palmer was founder of the Kingsport Building and Loan Association, an original incorporator of the Holston Valley Community Hospital, and a supporter of the Kingsport Public Library.

During World War II, Palmer was Deputy Director of the War Production Board's Printing and Publishing Division, which produced such materials as Bibles and equipment instruction manuals for U.S. troops. In 1943 he received the honorary rank of colonel for his work in the Adjutant General's Department, where he served until 1945. After the war, he received the Legion of Merit for his distinguished service.

Chemist Walter F. Smith succeeded Palmer as president in 1953, and in his first year as president Smith developed new methods of cloth manufacture and gold stamping. Under his direction, the company enjoyed continued growth, with 1961 marking a major expansion of the company's facilities. Elected chairman of the board in 1961, Edward J. Triebe was the fourth company president. He guided the Press through a period of rapid technological change as well as another expansion that included the construction and start-up of a second plant—a highly automated operation in Hawkins County, 12 miles from Kingsport. Triebe's tenure also witnessed a major transition in printing emphasis, from letterpress to offset lithography. Kingsport Press during his tenure had 2,500 employees.

One of the nation's longest strikes occurred at Kingsport Press from March 11, 1963, continuing into the spring of 1967. National union officials and federal labor mediators were unable to resolve the situation and as negotiations broke down, picket lines went up, accompanied by vandalism and violence. In 1964 over 5,000 people applied for Press jobs and by April 28, 1967, both the new and returning company employees rejected the unions.

In 1969 Kingsport Press merged with Arcata National Corporation, becoming a wholly owned subsidiary of the graphics, communication, and information services company. When Triebe was elected Chairman of the Board of Kingsport Press in 1969, G. Robert Evans left U.S. Gypsum to become the fifth company president. Two years after the merger of Kingsport Press and Arcata National, Evans was selected to direct the newly created Arcata Graphic Services Group. In 1971 Hugh F. Swaney came to Kingsport from the Mexican operations of U.S. Gypsum to serve as the Press's president.

Today, Quebecor Printing of Canada owns the former Kingsport Press and ranks as one of the largest book-making plants in the world. The company's customers include the nation's leading publishers, producing all types of hardbound and soft-cover books. Products of this graphic communications industry include elementary, high school, and college textbooks and workbooks; reference sets; book club selections; Bibles and hymnals; blank books and specialty binders; juvenile books; university press books; dictionaries; and school yearbook covers.

Martha Avaleen Egan, Kingsport Public Library and Archives/ King College

SEE: DENNIS, JOHN B.; KINGSPORT; LABOR; PUBLISHING

KINNEY, BELLE (1890–1959) was an important early twentieth century sculptor, who graced Nashville with works at the War Memorial Building, the State Capitol, and the Parthenon. Born in Nashville in 1890, one of four children of Captain D.C. and Elizabeth Morrison Kinney, she won the youth sculpting competition at the Tennessee Centennial Exposition of 1897. As a teenager, she attended the Art Institute of Chicago; later she served as an instructor in the institute's sculpture department.

Her first Nashville work came at the age of 17, when she sculpted in bronze a statue to Jere Baxter, president of the Tennessee Central Railroad. This extant work is now located at Jere Baxter School in Nashville. Her best work came during the 1920s when she received the commissions for the bronze monuments to the Women of the Confederacy (1926), which stand in the courtyard of the War Memorial Building in Nashville and at Jackson, Mississippi. Her major project at the War Memorial, however, was designed in collaboration with her husband, Austrian sculptor Leopold F. Scholz, whom she had married in 1921. Their massive, heroic bronze statue of "Victory" dominates the atrium of the building.

Kinney and Scholz also collaborated in the reconstruction of the Parthenon at Nashville's Centennial Park during the 1920s. Basing their designs on the Elgin Marbles at the British Museum in London, as well as drawings dating to 1674 by Jacques Currey, they re-created the figures at the east and west pediments of the building. Where archaeological evidence did not exist, Kinney and Scholz used their research in Greek art and their study of live models to create appropriate interpretations of the missing pieces. In 1956 Kinney supervised the repair of the plaster models used in the original reconstruction of the figures.

Throughout her career, Kinney received commissions to prepare memorial statues and busts of famous Tennesseans. This work includes her statue of Andrew Jackson at the U.S. Capitol, her bust of Admiral Albert Gleaves at Annapolis, Maryland, and her busts of Andrew Jackson and James K. Polk at the Tennessee State Capitol. The designs of Jackson and Polk were among her last. Kinney died at her studio in Boiceville, New York, on August 28, 1959.

Carroll Van West, Middle Tennessee State University

SEE: ART; PARTHENON; TENNESSEE CENTENNIAL EXPOSITION

KNIGHTS OF LABOR. Founded in 1869 by a group of Philadelphia tailors, the Noble and Holy Order of the Knights of Labor grew slowly as a secret organization under the leadership of Uriah Stephens. By 1879, the organization claimed fewer than 10,000 members, when Terence V. Powderly, a machinist and former mayor of Scranton, Pennsylvania, became grand master. Under his leadership membership swelled to more than 700,000 by 1886.

The Knights of Labor accepted both skilled and unskilled laborers into membership. Female, immigrant, and African-American workers joined the Knights of Labor, although blacks and whites met in separate unions locally. The Knights proposed an ill-defined cooperative society between employers and workers as an alternative to the competition of nineteenth century industrialization. Although the organization opposed strikes as antagonistic to the goals of cooperation, the Knights of Labor engaged in some of the most famous strikes of the day, including the southwestern railroad strike against Jay Gould in 1886.

The Knights of Labor entered the South around 1878, but as a result of the opposition tactics of employers, their activities have remained obscure. By 1883 Tennessee had 11 local assemblies located in Nashville, Memphis, Knoxville, Chattanooga, and in the coal mines of Anderson and Grundy counties. Organizing efforts in Chattanooga apparently produced the greatest results among the urban assemblies. In 1885 Powderly visited the city on his organizing swing through the South, and in 1889 the head of the women's department, Mrs. Leonora Barry, lectured on the evils of child labor and the need for shorter hours for female workers. The Chattanooga Knights demonstrated their strength in 1886, when they elected John J. Irvine, an African-American machinist, to the position of circuit court clerk. The stunned white political community readily attributed the victory to the labor union.

The Knights also found adherents in the coal fields of the Cumberland Plateau and East Tennessee. In 1884 Tracy City miners organized a local assembly and elected Tom Carrick the first master workman. Under his leadership the union swelled to 400–500 members. As the Farmers' Alliance simultaneously spread across the state, the Grundy County Knights urged greater cooperation between the two organizations, anticipating a day when farmer and laborer would end the economic hegemony of the "trusts" and "monopolies." The Grundy County union faded under the threat of blackballing by the mine owners and finally surrendered its charter; the $700 in the Tracy City union's treasury went to the support of local schools.

The Anderson County Knights remained active well into the 1890s. During the convict lease wars that convulsed the county in 1891 and 1892, Eugene Merrell, a Knights of Labor organizer, played a prominent role as spokesman and leader. In a confrontation with Governor John P. Buchanan, Merrell demanded that the state enforce all the laws and protect miners against the use of scrip, unfair weighing practices, and "yellow dog" contracts in addition to imposing order. As late as 1893 the Clinch River Assembly No. 93 still advertised weekly meetings in the hall above Hill's grocery in Clinton.

The Knights of Labor succumbed to union organization by craft, and their cooperative vision fell to more realistic goals centered on wages, hours, and safety issues. Nevertheless, the union made important contributions to southern labor in its insistence on the inclusion of all workers, regardless of skill level, race, or gender.

Connie L. Lester, Tennessee Historical Society

SUGGESTED READINGS: Perry C. Cotham, *Toil, Turmoil, & Triumph: A Portrait of the Tennessee Labor Movement* (1995); Melton Alonza McLaurin, *The Knights of Labor in the South* (1978)

SEE: BUCHANAN, JOHN P.; CONVICT LEASE WARS; LABOR

KNOX COUNTY. In 1786 James White built a fort five miles below the junction of the French Broad and Holston rivers on the southernmost edge of frontier settlement in present-day East Tennessee. William

Blount, Governor of the Territory of the United States South of the River Ohio, selected the site of James White's Fort as the territorial capital in 1791 and gave it the name Knoxville, in honor of the Revolutionary War hero, General Henry Knox (1750–1806), who served as the first U.S. Secretary of War from 1785 to 1794.

Knox County, also named for Henry Knox, was created from parts of Greene and Hawkins counties on June 11, 1792, by Governor Blount and has the distinction of being one of only eight counties created during territorial administration. Knoxville served as the county seat of Knox County from the date of the county's creation. Portions of Knox County were later removed to create Blount County (1795), Anderson County (1801), Roane County (1801), and Union County (1850). Knox County currently contains 509 square miles and lies at the geographical center of the Great Valley of East Tennessee. The Tennessee River originates near the center of the county, from the union of the Holston and French Broad rivers.

Governor Blount designated Knoxville as the capital of the Territory South of the River Ohio from 1791 to 1796. Knoxville also served as the capital of the State of Tennessee from 1796 to 1812, with the exception of one day in 1807, when the legislature met in Kingston, and briefly again in 1817–1818. Frontier leader General John Sevier, a resident of Knox County, served as Governor of Tennessee from 1796 to 1801 and 1803 to 1809, most of Knoxville's years as the state capital. Since no state capitol building was constructed until work began on the present capitol building in Nashville in 1845, the General Assembly met in taverns and public buildings. Blount Mansion (1792), the home of territorial Governor Blount, is the most historically significant dwelling surviving in Knox County from the pre-statehood era and is the only National Historic Landmark in the county.

Knoxville enjoyed an early advantage from its status as the capital city of the new and growing state and from its central location in the Great Valley of East Tennessee, and quickly became the largest commercial center of the region. The first newspaper in Tennessee, the *Knoxville Gazette*, was established in 1791 by George Roulstone. Following its early growth, Knoxville lagged behind Nashville and Memphis in the decades prior to the Civil War, in part as the result of the difficulty of transportation on the Tennessee River. When the East Tennessee and Virginia Railroad and the East Tennessee and Georgia Railroad met in Knoxville in 1855, the transportation problem was solved.

Location and the railroads made Knoxville and East Tennessee strategic targets for both the Union and Confederate armies during the Civil War. The Battle of Fort Sanders (1863) confirmed Union control of the city for the rest of the war. With Federal occupation of the city, William Gannaway ("Parson") Brownlow (1805–1877), Unionist leader, author, and newspaper editor, returned to Knoxville in triumph in 1863. He later served as Governor of Tennessee (1865–1869) and U.S. Senator from Tennessee (1869–1875).

Post-Civil War recovery was initially slow and difficult, but Knoxville retained its role as the major center of commerce in East Tennessee. By 1900 Knoxville had a population of 32,000 and appeared to have enormous potential for continued growth. In 1910 and 1911 Knoxville hosted the Appalachian Exposition and, in 1913 the National Conservation Exposition, symbols of the city's growing regional and national importance. The major industries of the early twentieth century were textiles, coal, lumber, marble, and zinc. Growth had slowed again by the 1930s. As a result of the New Deal initiatives, the Tennessee Valley Authority located its headquarters in Knoxville in 1933 and became a significant employer. A group of Knoxvillians, led by Colonel David Chapman, were instrumental in the creation of the Great Smoky Mountains National Park in 1934, which eventually generated a booming tourism industry in East Tennessee. The explosive post-World War II growth of the University of Tennessee and nearby Oak Ridge had a major impact on the city's economy. Knoxville hosted the 1982 World's Fair, which drew visitors from across the nation and the world. By 1990 Knox County reported a population of 335,749, with Knoxville's population at 165,121. The principal industries of the 1990s included apparel and textiles, metal products, and food products.

Education played an important role in Knox County's history. The University of Tennessee grew out of Blount College, which was founded in Knoxville in 1794. The University of Tennessee, Knoxville, the home campus of the statewide University of Tennessee system, serves 25,000 students in 297 degree programs in 15 colleges and schools. Knoxville College, founded in 1875 to provide a unique educational experience for African Americans, remains the oldest historically black college in East Tennessee. Pellissippi State Technical Community College, established in 1974, currently enrolls 8,000 students in programs for associate undergraduate degrees and vocational training. Knox County operates a consolidated city and county public school system with an enrollment of over 52,000 students in grades K-12. Lawson McGhee Library, the main library of the Knox County Public Library System, is the oldest continuously functioning public library in East Tennessee.

Growing communities in Knox County include the town of Farragut (incorporated), the fastest growing area of Knox County, and the unincorporated communities of Concord, Halls, Karns, and Powell.

Some historic communities in Knox County include Asbury, Ball Camp, Byington, Cedar Bluff, Corryton, Dante, Ebenezer, Gibbs, Graveston, Harbison's Cross Roads, Heiskell, Kimberlin Heights, Mascot, Millertown, Riverdale, Skaggston, Solway, Spring Place, Stock Creek, and Thorn Grove.

A number of individuals who made significant contributions to Tennessee and United States history have lived in Knoxville and Knox County. Among important writers with Knoxville connections are James Agee, Frances Hodgson Burnett, Nikki Giovanni, George Washington Harris, Joseph Wood Krutch, Cormac McCarthy, J.G.M. Ramsey, and Tennessee Williams. Military leaders from Knox County include Admiral David Glasgow Farragut and Brigadier General Lawrence D. Tyson. Country music star, Roy Acuff, and blues musician, Walter "Brownie" McGhee, both spent their formative years in Knoxville. Inventors George Dempster and Weston Fulton called Knoxville home, as did Harvey Broome, a founder of the Sierrra Club.

Steve Cotham, Knoxville

SEE: AGEE, JAMES; APPALACHIAN EXPOSITION OF 1910; BLOUNT, WILLIAM; BROOME, HARVEY; BROWNLOW, WILLIAM G.; CIVIL WAR; DAVIS, ANNE M.; DEMPSTER, GEORGE; FARRAGUT, DAVID G.; FORT, JAMES WHITE; GIOVANNI, NIKKI; GREAT SMOKY MOUNTAINS NATIONAL PARK; HARRIS, GEORGE W.; KNOXVILLE; KNOXVILLE COLLEGE; KNOXVILLE WORLD'S FAIR; MCCARTHY, CORMAC; RAMSEY HOUSE; RAMSEY, J.G.M.; RAILROADS; SEVIER, JOHN; SOUTHWEST TERRITORY; TENNESSEE VALLEY AUTHORITY; TYSON, LAWRENCE; UNIVERSITY OF TENNESSEE

KNOXVILLE. Founded as White's Fort in 1786, Knoxville served as the capital of the Territory South of the River Ohio (or Southwest Territory) and early capital of Tennessee and eventually grew to become the state's third largest city and a major commercial, industrial, and educational center.

White's Fort's principal founder, James White, was a Revolutionary War veteran who took advantage of the land grab act to purchase a large tract of land between First and Second Creeks, which emptied into the Tennessee (then Holston) River. In 1786 he built a fort overlooking the river and named it for himself. In 1791 William Blount, governor of the Southwest Territory, chose White's Fort as the capital of the territory and renamed it Knoxville, in honor of Secretary of War Henry Knox. In that same year, following Charles McClung's survey, White laid off 64 one-half acre lots and formally organized the town of Knoxville, with street names borrowed from Philadelphia and Baltimore. Two lots were set aside for a church and cemetery (First Presbyterian Church), and four were reserved for Blount College, the town's first school. In 1792 Governor Blount built his residence, an early frame house west of the moun-

tains, which also served as the territory's capitol. Soon George Roulstone began publishing the *Knoxville Gazette,* Tennessee's first newspaper. In 1793 the town and a U.S. Army fort (near the present corner of Gay and Main streets) came under attack by Creeks and Cherokees and would have been overrun if the assailants had pressed their advantage. After killing 13 settlers at Alexander Cavet's fortified house, the attackers retreated without making a determined assault on Knoxville.

From its founding until the Civil War, Knoxville served primarily as a way station for travelers to the West and an alternately quiet and rowdy river town. Population grew slowly, especially after 1818, when the state's capital moved permanently to Middle Tennessee. From a population of only 730 in 1810, Knoxville grew to 2,076 by 1850 and to around 5,000 by 1860. The rapid growth in the 1850s probably reflected the arrival of the East Tennessee and Georgia Railroad in 1855, an event that promised to make Knoxville a railroad and commercial center.

The railroad also made Knoxville an important strategic center during the Civil War. With economic ties to the South (Charleston and Savannah), the majority of Knovillians voted to secede from the Union in the June 1861 referendum, putting the city's population at odds with most East Tennessee Unionists, especially the fiery editor of *Brownlow's Whig,* William G. "Parson" Brownlow. The importance of the railroad in supplying General Robert E. Lee's Army of Northern Virginia brought Confederate General Felix Zollicoffer's occupying force to Knoxville to keep the rail lines open. When East Tennessee Unionists responded by burning railroad bridges and harassing Zollicoffer's troops, the initially lenient commander undertook a campaign of persecution and repression that filled the jail and sent numerous Union supporters fleeing to safety.

When Confederate troops fell back to northern Georgia in the fall of 1863, Union soldiers under General Ambrose Burnside rushed in to take Knoxville and cut the Confederacy's important railroad lifeline. Fearing a rebel counterattack, Burnside rapidly built a series of forts around the town. In need of supplies and to protect against a Federal invasion of southwest Virginia, General Robert E. Lee detached two divisions of the Army of Northern Virginia under General James Longstreet to recapture Knoxville and reopen his supply lines.

Longstreet took up his position northwest of the town (ironically, on the present campus of Knoxville College) and laid siege to the city. Longstreet believed he could not wait until Burnside was starved into surrender, and on November 29, 1863 launched an ill-conceived attack on Fort Sanders, an earthen fort named in honor of General William Sanders, a Union cavalry officer who had been killed by a sharpshooter

Tennessee River at Knoxville before construction of Fort Loudon Dam. The University of Tennessee can be seen on the hill at right.

TSLA

west of the town (on Kingston Pike) while the Federal troops fought a delaying action against Longstreet's advance. The Battle of Knoxville lasted under 30 minutes, as Confederate troops found it impossible to surmount the icy and slippery earthenworks and withdrew with 813 casualties. For the rest of the war, Knoxville remained firmly in Union hands. Unionists, who fled earlier, returned and retaliated against the town's Confederate sympathizers.

After the Civil War, Knoxville made great strides toward becoming a major urban center, with the railroad as a key factor in the city's progress. Knoxville became a distribution center for shipments to country stores and town merchants across East Tennessee. By 1896 the city boasted that it had become the third largest wholesaling center (in dollar volume) in the entire South, eclipsed only by Atlanta and New Orleans. Over 50 wholesaling houses bustled with activity, the largest being Cowan, McClung and Company, which was also the state's largest taxpayer in 1867. Many of these establishments located in, or around, Jackson and Depot streets, in the heart of Knoxville's present "Old City."

In the 1870s and 1880s the city also witnessed a major manufacturing boom. Between 1880 and 1887, 97 new factories turned out iron and railroad prod-

ucts, textiles, shoes, clothing, and processed food products. Capital investment in manufacturing multiplied sixfold between 1870 and 1890; and between 1900 and 1905 the city's manufactured goods increased over 100 percent. From 1895 to 1904 over 5,000 new homes were constructed. The nearby town of West Knoxville (the present Fort Sanders area, annexed in 1897) contained some of the state's loveliest mansions and became the site for James Agee's famous novel *A Death in the Family.*

Although the railroad promoted most of the postwar growth, a bold group of business leaders deserves at least part of the credit. Many of these men came to Knoxville from outside the South before, during, and after the war to take advantage of the opportunities the railroad town held. In 1869 Massachusetts native Perez Dickinson founded the town's Board of Trade, a parent of the present Chamber of Commerce. Knoxvillians welcomed other "carpetbaggers," including the founders of the Knoxville Iron Company, Albers Drug Company, Woodruff's furniture wholesalers and retailers, Dixie Cement Company, the Clinch Avenue Viaduct, and the Knoxville, Sevierville and Eastern Railroad, which was nicknamed by its passengers the "Knoxville Slow and Easy."

By 1900 Knoxville's population had jumped to 32,637, about one-third under the age of 15. Many of those who arrived in Knoxville after the Civil War were African Americans. When Burnside's troops took the town in 1863, African Americans abandoned farms and East Tennessee's comparatively few plantations and came to Knoxville in search of freedom and opportunity. By 1880 over 32 percent of the city's population was black. Plentiful jobs fostered a comparatively placid racial atmosphere. Knoxville College was established in 1875 to provide educational opportunities for African Americans.

As with other postwar American cities, rapid growth generated problems. Massive commercial, industrial, and residential burning of coal gave the city a grimy and unhealthy appearance; an adequate supply of safe drinking water was not available until the 1890s; and an 1897 fire destroyed a number of businesses on Gay Street, the city's major business avenue. As the wealthy moved out of the city to their own protected enclaves, race relations took a decided turn for the worse, and blacks and white, now residing in close proximity to one another, clashed continuously. In 1894, white political leaders of both parties quietly gerrymandered Knoxville's black voters into virtual political impotence. Earlier they had removed an African American from the city's school board. In 1919 the city experienced a disturbing, but brief, race riot.

From 1900 to the present, Knoxville has continued to grow, face urban problems, and try to solve them. Economic activity diversified and no longer relied on iron, railroad, textiles, and apparel. Air and water quality improved dramatically. The city hosted the 1982 World's Fair as a vehicle to showcase Knoxville to the world, with modest results. The city continues to tinker with its governmental structure in apparent dissatisfaction with political forms, leaders, or some combination of both. Knoxville has had five major changes in government structure in the twentieth century, although Knox County voters rejected a sixth change to metropolitan government in November 1996. Suburbanization and malls threaten downtown economic activity, but the central business district remains active as a financial, legal, entertainment, and retail center. Two 1995–1996 studies clearly decried the city's poor race relations.

From its founding in 1786 as White's Fort, the city of Knoxville has grown to be Tennessee's third largest city. From 64 lots, Knoxville in 1996 included approximately 170,000 people. Modern office buildings now overlook William Blount's house. In Knoxville, the past and present stand side by side.

W. Bruce Wheeler, University of Tennessee, Knoxville

SUGGESTED READINGS: Lucile Deaderick, ed., *Heart of the Valley: A History of Knoxville, Tennessee* (1976); Michael J. McDonald and William Bruce Wheeler, *Knoxville, Tennessee: Continuity and Change in an Appalachian City* (1983)

SEE: AGEE, JAMES; BLOUNT, WILLIAM; FORT, JAMES WHITE; KNOX COUNTY; KNOXVILLE, BATTLE OF; KNOXVILLE COLLEGE; KNOXVILLE IRON COMPANY V. HARBISON; KNOXVILLE JOURNAL; KNOXVILLE MUSEUM OF ART; KNOXVILLE NEWS-SENTINEL; KNOXVILLE RIOT OF 1919; KNOXVILLE WORLD'S FAIR; LONGSTREET, JAMES; UNIVERSITY OF TENNESSEE; ZOLLICOFFER, FELIX

KNOXVILLE, BATTLE OF. The 18-day siege of Knoxville from November 17 to December 4, 1863, was the result of two interrelated causes. First, General Braxton Bragg, commander of the Army of Tennessee, desired to divert troops from the Federal army holding the city of Chattanooga. Second, Bragg wanted to rid himself of Lieutenant General James Longstreet. In September 1863 Longstreet's First Corps of the Army of Northern Virginia had been transferred to help repel the Federal thrust against Chattanooga and into north Georgia. Bragg's and Longstreet's combined forces badly defeated the Union Army of the Cumberland at Chickamauga and hemmed it inside the fortifications around Chattanooga. Shortly after this victory, Longstreet led an abortive cabal to remove the incompetent and unpopular Bragg from command, hoping to be named in Bragg's stead. When this revolt failed, Bragg detached Longstreet and his corps and ordered them to recapture Knoxville, which had fallen in early September to a Union force under the command of Major General Ambrose Burnside.

On November 5, Longstreet headed northward up the Tennessee Valley. He soon found himself in a foot race with Burnside, who decided not to contest Longstreet's advance and quickly fell back from his forward position near Loudon. Longstreet failed in his attempt to get between the Federals and Knoxville, as Union soldiers fought a rearguard action at Campbell's Station, while Burnside withdrew into the fortifications surrounding the city.

Longstreet's troops sealed off all approaches to Knoxville, hoping to starve the garrison into submission. Longstreet and his chief engineer, Brigadier General Danville Leadbetter, determined that the old Confederate Fort Loudon (renamed Fort Sanders by the Federals in honor of Brigadier General William Sanders, who was killed in a rearguard action near the city) offered the weakest link.

The November 29 attack, led by Major General Lafayette McLaws, failed completely. Confederate soldiers lost the element of surprise after capturing the Federal picket line the night before and alerting the garrison. In the predawn darkness, the advancing column became entangled in telegraph wire strung across the line of attack. The Confederates discovered that the ditch they thought to be shallow was in actuality four to eight feet deep. The walls of the fort were slippery with ice from water poured upon them by the defenders; and even worse, the necessary scaling ladders could not be found. Additionally, the attacking column converged to a narrow front that jammed the units together in the ditch, creating a slaughter pen. The Federals laid down a murderous artillery and musket fire and hurled axes, lighted shells, and billets of wood upon the crowded southern infantry. The few Confederates who made it inside the fort were quickly killed or captured.

It was all over in about 20 minutes. The Confederates suffered 813 casualties, a quarter of whom were prisoners, who surrendered rather than run the gauntlet of fire back to their own lines. Federal losses totaled five dead and eight wounded. When Longstreet learned of Bragg's rout from Chattanooga, and Sherman's approach from the south, he lifted the siege on December 4 and withdrew into winter quarters in upper East Tennessee.

W. Todd Groce, Georgia Historical Society

SEE: BRAGG, BRAXTON; CIVIL WAR; LONGSTREET, JAMES

KNOXVILLE COLLEGE. Immediately after the Civil War, scores of northern missionaries traveled south to educate the newly freed slaves. These missionary efforts resulted in the establishment of a number of black colleges and universities. One of these schools was Knoxville College, a small liberal arts college established by the Presbyterians and located in Knoxville, Tennessee. These early schools often contained elementary and high school programs to prepare their students for college work. Hardships and setbacks punctuated the college's 121-year history. Despite these difficulties, however, the college managed to offer quality education to generations of African Americans.

The first Presbyterian missionaries centered their efforts in Tennessee on Nashville. By 1875 competition from other denominations influenced the decision of the Freedmen's Board of the United Presbyterian Church to move their operation to Knoxville. The relocated school received its first permanent building in 1876, and in 1877 it was designated as a college. During that same year, the Freedmen's Board of the United Presbyterian Church appointed Dr. John S. McCulloch, a white Presbyterian minister, as president of the new Knoxville College. McCulloch was quite surprised to learn that the new freedmen's school had been designated a college, and after his first view of the campus, he had serious doubts about the accuracy of such a designation. He lamented, "What a wilderness the college grounds appeared."[1] At the same time, the institution's first "college" students were a little uncertain about exactly what a college was, but they were fiercely proud. One recalled, "we had quite a vague conception of the scope of the word college . . . [but] when asked what school we attended we somewhat proudly replied, 'out to the college.'"[2]

Despite such tentative beginnings, Knoxville College steadily expanded its student body, its facilities, and its curriculum in the waning years of the nineteenth century. Along with its college courses in the normal, theological, classical, scientific, and industrial departments, the college established a Medical Department in 1895. A number of this department's graduates went on to become practicing physicians, but in 1900 mounting expenses forced the Freedmen's Board to discontinue the Medical Department.

The firm academic foundation built in the nineteenth century served the college well in the twentieth century. Through two world wars, the Great Depression, the Civil Rights Movement, and the new challenges posed by the post-integration era, Knoxville College has continued to pursue its mission of providing a quality liberal arts education to African-American students. As the school faces the twenty-first century, it continues to be plagued by extremely difficult financial challenges. In meeting these challenges, Knoxville College has developed increasing support from the local business community, and it continues to attract black students from all over the South and the nation.

Cynthia G. Fleming, University of Tennessee, Knoxville

CITATIONS:

(1) United Presbyterian Church, *Historical Sketch of the Freedman's Missions of the United Presbyterian Church, 1862–1904* (Knoxville, 1904), 25.

(2) *The Aurora,* February 8, 1929.

SEE: EDUCATION, HIGHER; FREEDMEN'S BUREAU; KNOXVILLE

KNOXVILLE GAZETTE: See HAWKINS COUNTY; KNOXVILLE; PUBLISHING

KNOXVILLE IRON COMPANY v. HARBISON, 183 U.S. 13 (1901). In this case the U.S. Supreme Court upheld an 1899 Tennessee statute requiring cash redemption of store orders and other noncash payments to employees. At issue was a suit brought against the Knoxville Iron Company by a licensed securities dealer who had purchased 614 coal orders (at 85 cents on the dollar) from the company's employees and unsuccessfully tried to redeem them.

The company paid its approximately 200 employees in cash on the Saturday of each month nearest the 20th for all work prior to that month, thus keeping workers at least 20 days in arrears. It allowed employees to collect coal orders, at twelve cents a bushel, in lieu of cash, on any Saturday afternoon.

Knoxville Iron Company, whose case was argued by Tennessee's Edward Sanford, a future Supreme Court Justice, challenged the script law as a violation of freedom of contract and a deprivation of due process of law guaranteed by the Fourteenth Amendment to the U.S. Constitution. The chancellor of Knox

County, Tennessee's Court of Chancery Appeals, and the Tennessee Supreme Court all rejected the company's claims before the company appealed to the U.S. Supreme Court.

Justice George Shiras authored the Court's 7 to 2 majority opinion; Justices David Brewer and Rufus Peckham dissented without recording their reasoning. Shiras quoted extensively both from the Tennessee law and the Tennessee Supreme Court opinion. Acknowledging that the law abridged contract rights, Shiras approvingly noted that it was not class-based, but applied equally to all. Shiras further concluded that the law was a legitimate exercise of state police powers equalizing the relationship between employers and employees and promoting peace and good order.

Shiras cited three precedents: *Holden v. Hardy*, an 1898 Utah case in which the Supreme Court had upheld state-mandated limits on the hours of underground miners; *St. Louis, Iron Mountain & Railway v. Paul* (1899), requiring railroads to pay employees on the dates of their discharge; and *Atchison, Topeka & Santa Fe Railroad v. Matthews* (1899), authorizing states to penalize railroads that allowed fires to escape from their locomotives.

In *Dayton Coal and Iron Company v. Barton*, a companion to *Knoxville Iron*, the Supreme Court rejected another challenge to Tennessee's script law by requiring stores to pay cash on demand for store orders issued in lieu of wages. Justice Shiras rested this second decision on the reasoning in *Knoxville Iron*.

Scholars traditionally characterized the Fuller Court as a bastion of *laissez-faire* capitalism by referring to *Lochner v. New York* (1905), where it invalidated a New York state regulation of the hours of bakers as a violation of freedom of contract. Recent scholars have argued that this characterization was overdrawn, and that the Fuller Court often upheld state exercises of police powers, especially when such laws did not have a perceived class bias. The decisions in *Knoxville Iron Company* and *Dayton Coal and Iron Company* support this newer understanding.

John R. Vile, Middle Tennessee State University

SEE: LAW; SANFORD, EDWARD T.

KNOXVILLE JOURNAL. When the *Knoxville Journal* ceased operation in 1991, a Knoxville institution died. Although the paper's exact ancestry was sometimes in dispute, the *Journal* itself liked to claim that it was the descendant of the irascible William G. "Parson" Brownlow's feisty *Whig*. The connection between the two papers lies not in their institutional histories, but in the fact that Brownlow's apprentice on the *Whig*, Captain William Rule, eventually launched the *Journal*.

In the mid-1870s the two men joined forces to publish the *Knoxville Chronicle and Whig*, a Republi-

can paper which revived the old *Whig* motto "Cry Aloud and Spare Not." Brownlow died in 1877, but Rule continued to run the paper until it was sold in 1882. Not content to stay out of the newspaper business, Rule launched the *Journal* in 1885 with partner Samuel Marfield. Rule eschewed the sensationalism which had been creeping into American journalism and announced his intention to concentrate on local news. Throughout his long association with the paper, Rule used the *Journal* to support national Republican policies, but maintained a neutral position on local political issues—even when Democrat Luke Lea purchased the paper in 1928.

Lea's fortunes declined rapidly during the Depression, and the *Journal* followed suit. The paper went into receivership in 1930 and remained there until Knoxville mill owner Roy Lotspeich purchased the paper in 1936. Guy Smith, a staunch Republican, was hired as editor in 1937, and his personality dominated and shaped the paper for the next 30 years. He seemed a worthy successor to the crusading Brownlow. He used the paper to champion state and national Republican causes, while simultaneously influencing Knoxville politics and policies. The *Journal* pressed the city government to control smoke emissions, renovate deteriorating areas in the business district, and develop new industrial parks to encourage business relocation to Knoxville. In the 1950s Smith launched a crusade for the state legislature to apportion its seats on the principle of "one man, one vote," thereby increasing representation of populous Republican East Tennessee. In the 1960s, he used the paper to fight for the controversial proposal to annex county land to enlarge the city. He also used the paper to raise funds for local causes ranging from the East Tennessee Children's Hospital to Old Diamond, an elephant belonging to the Knoxville Zoo.

Under Smith, the *Journal* also kept up a bitter feud with its afternoon rival, the Scripps-Howard *Knoxville News-Sentinel*. The two papers took opposing sides on almost every civic or political issue, with the *Journal* generally taking the more conservative stance. One of the earliest controversies surrounded the creation of a municipal-owned utility company, which the *Journal* opposed. Other battles soon followed. The war between the papers abated somewhat when, in 1957, to everyone's surprise, the owners of the papers signed a Joint Operating Agreement in which the *News-Sentinel*, the financially healthier paper, dominated the partnership. Under the agreement, the newspapers combined their production, advertising, and circulation departments, but kept separate editorial offices. The *Journal* published the morning paper, while the *News-Sentinel* retained the more lucrative afternoon market. The *Journal* ceased publication of a Sunday paper, but received a proportion of the revenue generated by the joint operation.

Smith remained as editor of the *Journal* until his death in 1968. In 1981 the Lotspeich family sold the *Journal* to the Gannett newspaper chain. Five years later, Gannett agreed to move the *Journal* to the afternoon market and allowed the *News-Sentinel* to take over the increasingly lucrative morning market. The paper was then sold to successive newspaper chains until, in 1991, its last owner, a Honolulu-based company, suspended its operation as a daily newspaper and ended the life of the paper. It had been, until 1981, one of the oldest family-owned dailies in the country.

Beth Vanlandingham, Carson-Newman College

SUGGESTED READINGS: Lucile Deaderick, ed.,. *Heart of the Valley: A History of Knoxville, Tennessee* (1976); Michael J. McDonald and William Bruce Wheeler, *Knoxville, Tennessee: Continuity and Change in an Appalachian City* (1983)

SEE: BROWNLOW, WILLIAM G.; LEA, LUKE; PUBLISHING

KNOXVILLE MUSEUM OF ART was established to bring fine arts to East Tennessee. Opened in 1961 as the Dulin Gallery of Art, the Knoxville Museum of Art was originally housed in an early twentieth century neighborhood mansion. As the museum grew, however, the limitations of the private home became evident. Inferior security and inadequate climate control prevented the Dulin from being accredited by the American Association of Museums and therefore limited the museum's ability to attract important exhibitions.

With the intent to become a regional fine arts museum, the board of trustees decided in 1984 to build a state-of-the-art facility, in the heart of Knoxville, on the 1982 World's Fair site. Plans for the new museum were met with great support from the community as $9.5 million was raised for the building fund.

In 1987 the Dulin Gallery of Art underwent a formal name change and became the Knoxville Museum of Art. The museum moved from the Dulin mansion to an interim location in the "Candy Factory" building on the World's Fair site, adjacent to the construction site of the new museum. On March 25, 1990, more than 5,000 people attended the greatly anticipated grand opening of the new Knoxville Museum of Art building. Celebrated New York architect Edward Larabee Barnes designed the modern 53,200 square-foot building that currently houses the museum. The steel and concrete building, faced in Tennessee pink marble, is often referred to as the "crown jewel" of the World's Fair Park.

The Knoxville Museum of Art contains 12,700 square feet of exhibition space in five galleries, as well as a Sculpture Terrace, an Exploratory Gallery, a computer-interactive ARTcade, and two large outdoor garden areas. Other features include the Great Hall with a panoramic view of the city, a 170-seat auditorium, and the museum gift shop.

In addition to its growing collection of American contemporary art, the museum has hosted more than 120 traveling exhibitions since 1990. Notable recent exhibitions were *The Passion of Rodin: Sculpture from the Iris and B. Gerald Cantor Collection* and *American Grandeur: Masterpieces from the Masco and Manoogian Collection.* These exhibits combined with strong interactive educational programs with area schools and popular public programs, such as the "Alive After Five" jazz series, films, lectures, workshops, and symposiums, to contribute to the increasing success and growing stature of the museum.

The Knoxville Museum of Art provides a wide variety of exhibitions, intensive educational outreach, exciting public programs, and art acquisitions that enable the museum to effectively serve the cultural needs and interests of diverse communities throughout East Tennessee.

Lucy Akard Seay, Knoxville Museum of Art

SEE: ART; KNOXVILLE

KNOXVILLE *NEWS-SENTINEL*. Now the only daily newspaper in Knoxville, the *News-Sentinel* began in December 1886 as the evening *Sentinel,* published by John Travis Hearn, a native of Shelbyville, Kentucky. The first four-page edition of the *Sentinel* was printed on a steam-operated flat-bed press in a room above a liquor store. Hearn revolutionized the local distribution of newspapers by selling the papers directly to newsboys, who pocketed all the profits. The first newsboy, Wiley Morgan, stayed with the *Sentinel* and later became general manager and part-owner of the newspaper.

In 1892 Hearn sold the paper to J.B. Pound of Chattanooga, who then sold it to another Chattanoogan, George F. Milton, in 1899. In 1912 Curtis B. Johnson, formerly a reporter for the *Knoxville Tribune,* bought the paper. During the 1920s, the *Sentinel* began publishing a Sunday edition.

In November 1921 the Scripps-McRae (later Scripps-Howard) newspaper chain launched the publication of *The News,* edited by Edward J. Meeman, with Myron G. Chambers as business manager. Meeman published a non-partisan paper that crusaded against government corruption and fiscal irresponsibility. *The News* promoted the establishment of the Great Smoky Mountains National Park and denounced the Butler Law against the teaching of evolution.

In November 1926 *The News* acquired the *Sentinel* from General Lawrence D. Tyson, a World War I hero, who had used the evening paper to further his political ambitions. The first edition of *The Knoxville News-Sentinel* appeared on November 21, 1926. Meeman continued to edit the *News-Sentinel* until 1931, when he moved to Memphis to edit another Scripps-Howard newspaper, the *Memphis Press-Scimitar.*

In 1957 the *News-Sentinel* entered into a joint operating agreement with the *Knoxville Journal*. Under the terms of the agreement, the two papers combined their advertising, circulation, and production departments into a single operation, and the *News-Sentinel* assumed printing responsibilities for both papers. This cooperative arrangement lasted until 1991, when the *Knoxville Journal* ceased publication. In 1986 the *News-Sentinel* became a morning paper.

The longest tenured editor of the *News-Sentinel* was Loye Miller, who assumed control of the paper in 1940 and edited it until his retirement in 1966. Ralph Millet, Jr., succeeded Miller and remained with the paper until 1984. Millet led the fight to open public records to public inspection. Millet was succeeded by Harry Moskos, who is the current editor of the century-plus East Tennessee newspaper.

Connie L. Lester, Tennessee Historical Society

SUGGESTED READING: Jack Mooney, *A History of Tennessee Newspapers* (1996)

SEE: KNOXVILLE JOURNAL; MEEMAN, EDWARD J.; PUBLISHING; TYSON, LAWRENCE

KNOXVILLE RIOT OF 1919. The Knoxville Riot took place on August 30–31, 1919. Although many historians question whether it was a "race riot" in the classic sense, it bore many characteristics of that phenomenon.

The arrest of Maurice Mayes, a mulatto and sometimes deputy sheriff, touched off the riot. Mayes, a well-known political figure, was rumored to be the illegitimate son of Knoxville Mayor John E. McMillan. In the early morning hours of August 30, police charged Mayes with the murder of Mrs. Bertie Lindsay, a white woman; Mayes had been identified as the assailant by the victim's cousin, Ora Smith, who was with Lindsay at the time of the assault.

That afternoon, fearing trouble, Sheriff W.T. Cate arranged for Mayes to be removed to Chattanooga. In spite of these precautions, a crowd gathered around the Knox County jail, broke down the door, and searched the building for Mayes. In the ensuing melee, no black prisoners were disturbed, but a dozen white inmates were freed, the liquor storage room was pillaged, and the jail demolished.

As rumors of violence circulated, the crowd broke into downtown hardware stores, armed themselves, and headed for the black section of town. A detachment of the National Guard, hurriedly called to the scene, proved to be little use in controlling the crowd; guardsmen joined the white mob and fired into black-occupied buildings, while blacks returned the fire. One National Guard officer was killed accidentally by his own men, and one African American was also shot and killed. On the morning of Sunday, August 31, several hundred additional guardsmen restored order.

Thirty-six whites were arrested, but an all-white jury refused to convict any of them. Mayes was convicted of murder and sentenced to death. In 1920 the Tennessee Supreme Court ordered a new trial, but it also ended in conviction. Mayes was electrocuted, despite an increasing belief that he was innocent.

Because no black prisoners were harmed in the mob's assault on the jail, many historians believe that Mayes was the only target of the crowd. The subsequent march to the African-American section of town and the ensuing firefight has convinced other historians that while the Knoxville Riot of 1919 may not have begun as a race riot, it ultimately became one. Mayor McMillan's earlier attacks on the Ku Klux Klan and the city's comparatively placid racial atmosphere demonstrate a progressive attitude among many whites that stands in sharp contrast to the mob action of August 30–31, 1919.

W. Bruce Wheeler, University of Tennessee, Knoxville

SEE: KNOXVILLE; KU KLUX KLAN; LYNCHING

KNOXVILLE WORLD'S FAIR OF 1982, the Knoxville International Energy Exposition, was held for 184 days from May until October 31, 1982, on a 67-acre area a few blocks west of the city's central business district. The idea of a world's fair in Knoxville was first conceived by W. Stewart Evans, a retired military officer and president of the Downtown Knoxville Association, a coalition of downtown business leaders. The organization's members were looking for ways to lure more shoppers to the central business district and away from the growing number of suburban shopping malls. In 1974, while on a trip to Tulsa, Evans met the man who had organized an earlier world's fair in Spokane, Washington. The Knoxville businessman immediately recognized that such an exposition in Knoxville would leave the city with a large tract of downtown acreage that could be used for downtown redevelopment after the exposition closed.

Evans's vision excited Mayor Kyle Testerman, who named local banker Jake Butcher to head an investigative committee to determine the feasibility of an international exposition in Knoxville. In 1976 the Knoxville International Energy Exposition, Incorporated (KIEE), a private, non-profit organization, was formed; the Bureau of International Expositions (BIE) in Paris was contacted to obtain official approval and listing on the bureau's calendar of approved events; local and out-of-town banks raised money to supplement an $11.6 million city bond issue; and exposition backers gradually acquired a 67-acre tract in the lower Second Creek area. The driving force behind the exposition movement was Jake Butcher, whose banking empire supplied the funds to lure foreign participants and loaned money to Butcher friends and associates seeking quick profits from the fair. Insiders called the event "Jake's Fair."

President Ronald Reagan and a host of dignitaries attended the May 1982 opening day ceremonies. The United States and 19 other nations participated in the exposition, which took as its theme "Energy Turns the World." The fair counted approximately 11 million visitors, although many local people visited the exposition several times. Despite considerable skepticism and some local opposition, the fair ended on a note of success, and KIEE almost broke even financially. Nevertheless, many who hoped for a financial windfall through short-term rentals or commercial ventures were sorely disappointed.

More disappointing was the fact that no major downtown redevelopment took place on the fair site. The United States pavilion, lacking a tenant, was demolished, as were all the other buildings constructed for the fair. Fifteen years later, the site remains a park, with some convention and restaurant facilities. In 1990 the Knoxville Museum of Art opened its new facilities on the site.

W. Bruce Wheeler, University of Tennessee, Knoxville
SEE: BUTCHER, JACOB F.; KNOXVILLE; KNOXVILLE MUSEUM OF ART

KRYSTAL COMPANY, Chattanooga-based hamburger chain, was founded in 1932 by Rodolph B. Davenport, Jr., and J. Glenn Sherrill. Loosely patterned after the successful midwestern White Castle hamburger chain, which had begun in 1921 in Wichita, Kansas, Krystal capitalized on the economic hard times of the era by offering customers nickel hamburgers and "a good cup of coffee." The first restaurant was a small, white porcelain, and stainless steel building at the corner of Seventh and Cherry Streets in Chattanooga. Its steamed, small, square hamburger, covered with chopped onions has become part of southern culinary lore. Mrs. Mary McGee Davenport selected the company name after noticing a crystal ball on a neighbor's lawn. The name she chose, "Krystal Klean," reflected the cleanliness of the restaurant; the name was later shortened to Krystal. A crystal ball became a symbol outside all Krystal restaurants.

Davenport served as company president until his death in 1943, when he was succeeded by his partner, Sherrill, who served until 1961. R.B. Davenport III, son of the founder, succeeded Sherrill as president, remaining until his resignation in 1990. The appearance of Krystal restaurants has changed over the years. Drive-throughs were added, and smaller versions, called Krystal Kwiks, with limited menus and drive-through service only, have become popular in locations unable to sustain a full-sized restaurant. The menu expanded beyond the "Krystal" burger and a cup of coffee, but the little square hamburger remains a keystone in the company's success.

In 1982 Krystal acquired the Po Folks restaurant chain, later spinning off the chain as a separate company. Krystal also became the largest franchisee of Wendy's Restaurants. In 1992 Krystal issued stock and became a publicly-traded company, ending its claim as the nation's largest privately-held restaurant chain. The company filed for bankruptcy reorganization in 1995 as a result of mounting claims of lawsuits from current and former employees involving overtime pay. In 1997 the Krystal Company announced a merger of its 250 stores with Port Royal Holdings, Inc., a corporation formed by an executive of the Coca-Cola Enterprises Inc.

Ned L. Irwin, East Tennessee State University
SEE: CHATTANOOGA

KU KLUX KLAN was organized in May or early June of 1866 in a law office at Pulaski, Tennessee, by six bored Confederate veterans (the "immortal six"). The Ku Klux Klan was, in its inception, a social club for young men seeking amusement and entertainment. It adopted some of the oaths and rituals of Kappa Alpha, a college fraternity, as well as the initiations and pranks. The name "Ku Klux" was a derivation of the Greek word *kuklos,* meaning band or circle. For the remainder of 1866 there is little evidence that the Klan was involved in vigilantism as new "dens" were formed for social purposes in many of the surrounding counties.

In February 1867 Tennessee enfranchised freedmen, and Republicans established local chapters of the Union League, a political arm of the party, to mobilize the new black voters. In some respects the KKK became the conservative ex-Confederates' answer to the Union League, a rallying point for white Democrats determined to drive freedmen, Republicans, and their allies from the polls. During the spring of 1867 the KKK's innocent beginnings began to give way to intimidation and violence as some of its members sought to keep freedmen in their traditional place.

The official reorganization of the Klan into a political and terrorist movement began in April 1867, when the state's Democratic party leadership met in Nashville. An invitation sent by the Pulaski den to others in the state called for a gathering of members, who met at the Maxwell House hotel, where Tennessee's conservative Democrats provided for greater control of an expanding KKK. A prescript established administrative protocols and emphasized the need for secrecy. Subsequently, former Confederate General Nathan Bedford Forrest was elected the first and only Grand Wizard. In 1868 a revised prescript declared the Klan the defender of the Constitution of the United States and the protector of the orphans and widows of Confederate dead. Klansmen were required to swear that they had never been members of the Union army, the Union League, or the Republican party, and they supported re-enfranchising ex-rebels and upholding the South's constitutional rights.

Prior to 1868, however, the KKK essentially assumed a defensive posture aimed at protecting the white community from the perceived threats represented by Union Leaguers and the state militia. Indeed, early in 1867, some white conservatives still hoped to win over black voters to the Democratic cause. When the freedmen flocked to the Republican banner during the elections of that year, however, conservative Democrats, incensed over their political losses, decided that a new strategy of intimidation and violence was needed.

The violent tactics of the KKK soon spread to parts of Middle and West Tennessee, where bushwhacking and general lawlessness were already common, and throughout much of the South in 1868. Klan activity was especially strong in Giles, Humphreys, Lincoln, Marshall, and Maury counties in Middle Tennessee, and Dyer, Fayette, Gibson, Hardeman, and Obion in West Tennessee. The Klan was less successful in Unionist and Republican East Tennessee, with the exception of some activity in the vicinity of Bristol, a pocket of pro-Confederate sentiment.

Irrespective of time and place, a major problem of the Klan's expansion from a leadership standpoint was a lack of control. Once the dens set aside social activity as their primary purpose and took up political terrorism and racial violence, they fed on local reaction to threats to conservative political control and white supremacy rather than to any coordinated direction on the state, or even county, level. This aspect of the KKK's character became clear when the violence did not disappear after the elections of 1868, but continued with little or no link to political activity. Klansmen attacked, whipped, and murdered black men and women whenever they found their activities offensive, no matter how innocent or trifling these were. Freed people who exhibited too much independence, established schools, or assumed positions of leadership were singled out for harsh treatment.

In an effort to curb the violent acts of the KKK, Governor William G. Brownlow called for an extra session of the legislature, which following the investigation of a Ku Klux Klan committee, reestablished the militia and gave him the power to declare martial law in any county necessary. Members of the Klan and other secret societies engaged in terrorism were subject to arrest by any citizen, a $500 fine, and imprisonment for up to five years under a so-called Ku Klux Klan Act. Brownlow, who wished to see prominent KKK leaders and ex-Confederates tried and convicted to make examples of them, employed a Cincinnati private detective, Seymour Barmore, to infiltrate the Klan and gather names. When Barmore's body turned up in the Duck River on February 20, 1869, with a rope around his neck and bullet hole in his head, Brownlow declared martial law on the same day in nine counties in Middle and West Tennessee. Five days later, Brownlow resigned as governor to fill a seat in the U.S. Senate. Subsequently, Nathan Bedford Forrest, believing that the Klan had served its purpose, called for the members to destroy their robes.

After a hiatus of almost 50 years, the revival of the Ku Klux Klan at Stone Mountain, Georgia, in 1915 stimulated a new interest in the KKK in Tennessee, the South, and the nation. In the aftermath of World War I, the Red Scare, the Scopes trial, and rising nativism, many conservatives saw the KKK as the protector of traditional American values. Working class whites in Tennessee's urban areas, feeling threatened by economic competition with blacks and immigrants, joined the Klan. By 1923 over 2,000 white men had enrolled in Knoxville, for example, and soon became involved in local and statewide elections. The political influence of the KKK in Tennessee helped elect Governor Austin Peay in 1923 and U.S. Senator Lawrence D. Tyson in 1924. Membership, however, declined sharply during the Great Depression, and the Klan disbanded as a national organization in 1944.

During the post-World War II years, various groups of individuals have organized under the Klan name and in turn have disbanded, depending upon conservative white reaction to perceived threats during the Civil Rights and school desegregation movement. Jerry Thompson, a journalist for the Nashville *Tennessean*, infiltrated the KKK and in 1980 and 1981 produced an award-winning series of newspaper articles on Klan activity. In 1997 the U.S. Klans, Knights of the Ku Klux Klan, Inc., received incorporation from the Secretary of State's office as a nonprofit organization at Camden, Tennessee.

Mark V. Wetherington, The Filson Club Historical Society
SUGGESTED READINGS: Thomas B. Alexander, "Kukluxism in Tennessee, 1865–1869," *Tennessee Historical Quarterly* 8(1949): 195–219; Allen W. Trelease, *White Terror: The Ku Klux Klan Conspiracy and Southern Reconstruction* (1979)

SEE: BROWNLOW, WILLIAM G.; FORREST, NATHAN BEDFORD; GILES COUNTY; LYNCHING; RECONSTRUCTION

L

LABOR. In its broadest context, "labor" is very diverse: slave and free labor; craft and industrial labor; farm and factory labor; and blue, pink, and white collar labor. Because there are few theses, dissertations, or secondary works on this topic, one might conclude that there was very little labor history in the Volunteer State. Such misconceptions need correction as future historians broaden and amplify this initial narrative and analysis.

Any study of Tennessee labor should focus upon issues of wage, hour, and job security, and the right to organize, for these were essential to any worker's sense of well-being. Would employers or workers ultimately control wages, hours, and job security? Would state and local government policy makers ally with the private sector to diminish workers' influence on wage and job security, or unite with the workers to ensure it? These are among the central questions in the history of Tennessee labor.

The history of wage-earning workers in Tennessee is inevitably one of change, conflict, displacement, routinization, and collectivization. As the numbers of skilled craft and industrial workers grew during the second quarter of the nineteenth century, so did their sense of identity with both work type and work place. Scattered mutual aid and burial insurance associations evolved into local chapters of organized labor unions. Both organized workers and their unorganized brethren attempted to counter the hardships created by the baser aspects of capitalism upon their wages, hours of work, and conditions in the workplace.

While labor organization is generally thought to be a product of the late nineteenth century, wage earners much earlier were both conscious of their shared identity and capable of organizing to foster their goals. For example, in March 1852, Nashville journeymen tailors struck successfully for higher wages. Similarly, in March 1853, iron workers in Nashville struck for a ten-hour day and a six-day work week. The aspirations of Tennessee's antebellum wage earners for the shorter work day are expressed in a letter published in the Nashville *Daily Gazette* of March 5, 1853. The shorter work day gave "the working man an opportunity of devoting more of his time to intellectual improvement . . . [and] . . . time for recreation after he has sweated and toiled through the labor of the day."

One of the earliest struggles in Tennessee that gave urban white skilled workers a sense of mutual identity and a reason to organize was the competition for work between free white and black slave construction hands. In the 1830s and 1840s, white Nashville "mechanics" openly challenged the practice of hiring out slave construction workers as unfair competition, but to no significant effect. Truly, free workingmen were not valued in antebellum Tennessee. Nowhere is this more clearly demonstrated than in the contempt for free labor demonstrated by the state when it opted to use slave and convict labor to build the capitol building. After the Civil War, when former slaves—now free blacks—competed for work, white urban workers retained their former antipathy. It was racism, however, not unfair competition, that nurtured this black-white dichotomy and generally prevented white workers from perceiving common interests with their black wage-earning brothers. For example, in 1892 United Mine Worker organizer W.R. Riley, an African American, reported that only when local white miners needed added strength during a strike did they call for the unity of the races.

Black and white Tennessee wage workers also had to contend with the importation of cheap foreign labor. In 1849 Nashville mechanics challenged the hiring of imported labor by local contractors. Such competition continued to pose a threat to Tennessee's resident wage-earners.

Many industrial workers in nineteenth century Tennessee were forced to compete against a government-sanctioned form of corporate welfare known as "convict leasing."

The state leased prisoners to Tennessee corporations at a lower cost than that free wage-earning workers would demand. As early as 1843 a committee of Greeneville mechanics (including the tailor and future president Andrew Johnson) protested that the town board had used convict labor instead of free white workers. Between 1870 and 1900 the convict leasing system predominated in Tennessee mines. There was unavailing resistance to the leasing system as early as 1871, but in July 1891 miners made an effective protest. Some 300 armed miners surrounded the Tennessee Coal and Iron Company prison compound and forced the 40 guards to release the convicts housed there. The miners then escorted the prisoners to Coal Creek, loaded them all aboard a train, and sent them to Knoxville. So began the Great Tennessee Miners' Rebellion of 1891–1892, which ended the convict lease system.

Information on wages is spotty at best; what little there is indicates that the average wage earner in nineteenth century Tennessee was discernibly underpaid. One report found in the Nashville *Union and Dispatch* provides a review of prevailing wages in January 1866. Carpenters earned $3.50 per day; brick masons $4.00; house painters $3.00; foundry laborers $2.00; and flour mill hands $1.50. Another rare survey of wages in Nashville for 1896 shows that typically workers toiled ten hours a day, six days a week. Carpenters earned $40 a month; brick masons earned $65 a month; house painters and decorators earned $1.75 a day; and coopers earned $8.50 a week. The highest wage went to bricklayers and steam engine engineers, who earned $65 a month. The presence of retail clerks (1,000) in the survey indicates a change in the work force in Nashville from manufacturing to retail. A total of 2,950 workers were listed in this labor survey, with trades including printers, hod-carriers, laborers, machinists, brewers, bottle washers, cigar makers, coopers, and barbers.

The strike was the chief recourse against the convict leasing system, the importation of cheap foreign labor, low wages, long hours, and other infringements against wage earners during the nineteenth and early twentieth centuries. But early in our nation's history, the strike was repugnant and perhaps even treasonable to moneyed Americans. Andrew Jackson, for example, was the first American president to use federal troops to put down a strike of workers in 1834. Trade associations like the National Typographical Union (NTU), which held its fourth annual meeting in Memphis in May 1855, were

faced with this anti-strike sentiment. NTU delegates from Chicago, New York, Philadelphia, Detroit, Boston, Louisville, New Orleans, Cincinnati, Nashville, and Memphis passed a resolution in which they, as "working men," declared their reluctance to strike, but "still we believe . . . 'strikes,' like revolutions, are sometimes necessary to a proper vindication of the rights of the working man."

Sporadic strikes continued in Tennessee for the next three decades after the end of the Civil War, but with only marginal results. These were local, single issue strikes for the most part. In August 1885 drivers for the Memphis City Railway Company—a horse-drawn, urban, mass transit service—struck for higher wages. In March 1886 workers at the Chesapeake, Ohio and Southwestern Railroad carried out one of the few successful strikes in Memphis. That May, 100 wagon makers working for the Cole Manufacturing Company in Memphis struck.

Several national unions called for work stoppages during the depression of 1893–1897. Coal miners in Jellico and Coal Creek struck for higher wages in support of the United Mine Workers in April 1894. As national unions grew in influence, local strikes became a matter of following the directions of the national union.

Strikes, labor unions, and the notion of collective bargaining threatened most Tennessee managers. Conflict over union recognition predominated during the years 1890–1930. Typical were the union recognition strikes called by Nashville theater employees in February 1899, Nashville woodworkers in August 1889, copper miners in Ducktown in September 1899, and coal miners at Coal Creek and Cripple Creek in July 1900. While such strikes demonstrated that organized labor could no longer be discounted, they were not particularly successful at assuring wage earner control of wages, hours, and working conditions.

As Tennessee became more industrialized, local governments touted low wages as a tool to attract businesses to their areas. In their support for management, government officials became increasingly antagonistic to organized labor, whose strikes contended against their anti-union views. In Memphis, from 1910 through the end of the Second World War, Edward H. Crump's political machine was especially notorious for co-opting local union leaders and sometimes even endorsing violent anti-unionism by Memphis city government employees. In East Tennessee, the famous rayon mill strikes at Elizabethton in 1929 illustrated how city and state officials worked closely with local management to impede union activity.

The end of World War I brought with it rising expectations among Tennessee labor, but also a growing fear within the general public about labor-related violence. In April 1919 Tennessee Governor Albert Roberts signed into law a bill that created a state police force. This law authorized him to dispatch state police to any outbreak of violence in Tennessee. To organized labor, this law was a tool for breaking up strikes in the name of thwarting "Communist" insurrection. When 250 members of the Amalgamated Association of Street and Electrical Railway Employees struck in Knoxville in October 1919, residents decried the strike in local press as an example of "reds" attempting to take over the nation. Only the "return to normalcy" quelled the "Red Scare" both in Tennessee and in the remainder of the nation. Yet strikes did not completely disappear as the three-month work stoppage by female workers at the Bemberg and Glanzstoff rayon mills in Elizabethton in 1929 demonstrates.

The "normalcy" of the 1920s gave way to the despair of the Great Depression. Jobs disappeared and wages fell. Nationally and locally called strikes for higher wages, secure employment, and union recognition occurred throughout the era. Employers hired "goons" to attack union members. Replacement workers crossed union picket lines because they needed to work at any wage to provide for their families. Nationally, and in Tennessee, the American Federation of Labor's member unions became increasingly identified with skilled craft workers, while the newly created Congress of Industrial Organizations' member unions became increasingly identified with industrial workers. National strikes in textiles, like that in Harriman in 1934, and in mining and metal founding in 1937 had their Tennessee counterparts. Only the near full employment brought on by the massive defense contracts of the Second World War quieted the anxieties of wage and job that had arisen with the Great Depression.

After the Second World War, labor unions pressed employers to hire only union workers in workplaces whose employees had overwhelmingly voted for a "closed shop." Employers, however, favored an "open shop" that allowed employment of non-union members, thus diminishing organized worker influence. The Tennessee General Assembly solved the issue by establishing an "open shop" state. Government policies of protection for the commercial and industrial sectors appear endemic to the Volunteer State.

In more recent times, the issues that bind labor together have remained much the same as in the past. Tennessee wage earners still do not welcome competition with imported low-wage workers, nor do they want to work excessive hours at low pay. Numerous Tennessee workers want the help of a trade union, while management insists the labor movement is not in the interest of the working class. Agricultural, craft, and industrial workers still do many of the jobs their pioneer ancestors did, and their descendants will surely continue to do so, most likely within a predominantly non-unionized environment.

Joseph Y. Garrison and James B. Jones, Jr., Tennessee Historical Commission
SUGGESTED READINGS: Constantine G. Belissary, "Behavior Patterns and Aspirations of the Urban Working Classes of Tennessee in the Immediate Post Civil War Era," *Tennessee Historical Quarterly* 14(1955): 24–43; Roger Biles, "Ed Crump Versus the Unions: The Labor Movement in Memphis During the 1930s," *Labor History* (Fall 1984): 533–552; Lennie Austin Cribbs, "The Memphis Chinese Labor Convention, 1869," West Tennessee Historical Society *Papers* (1983): 74–81; Michael K. Honey, *Southern Labor and Civil Rights: Organizing Memphis Workers* (1993); and James B. Jones, Jr., "Class Consciousness and Worker Solidarity in Urban Tennessee: The Chattanooga Carmen's Strikes of 1899–1917," *Tennessee Historical Quarterly* 52(1993): 98–112; and "Strikes and Labor Organization in Tennessee During the Depression of 1893–1897," *Tennessee Historical Quarterly* 52(1993): 256–264

LADIES' HERMITAGE ASSOCIATION was organized in 1889 to honor President Andrew Jackson by preserving his home, The Hermitage. Mrs. Andrew Jackson III and Mary C. Dorris suggested a women's association similar to The Mt. Vernon Ladies' Association. Dorris had become fearful that the State of Tennessee would dispose of the property by giving it to the Confederate Soldiers' Home Association as a home for indigent Confederate veterans. In January 1889 Dorris appointed a committee of women to write a charter for the organization.

While they waited for the passage of the bill assigning responsibility for The Hermitage to the women's group, the organizers determined to obtain a state charter. On February 19, 1889, Mrs. Rachel J. Lawrence, Mary W. May, Mrs. Mary Hadley Claire, Mrs. E.L. Nicholson, Louise Grundy Lindsley, Mrs. Henry Heiss, and Mary C. Dorris applied for the state charter, stating that the Ladies' Hermitage Association would acquire the residence, tomb, and land of The Hermitage in order to "beautify, preserve, and adorn the same throughout all coming years, in a manner most befitting the memory of that great man [Jackson]."[1]

In the final days of the 1889 legislative session, both houses passed a bill giving the The Hermitage estate to the Confederate Soldiers' Home, but amended the bill to exempt the house, tomb, and 25 acres of land surrounding the house. The Senate then passed a bill deeding the house to the Ladies' Hermitage Association. In the House, John H. Savage, a former Confederate officer from McMinnville, strongly opposed deeding the property to the women's organization. On the day before adjournment, Savage, who was known as the "old man of the mountain," made an impassioned speech against the bill. At the urging of John Berrien Lindsley, the Ladies' Hermitage Association lobbied on behalf of their cause, and Savage changed his mind.

As soon as Governor Robert L. Taylor signed the bill, the Ladies' Hermitage Association began renovating the house and grounds. In the early years, the organization devoted most of its efforts to fund-raising—sponsoring plays, concerts, and shows, and holding barbeques and luncheons to raise needed funds. In 1897 the Association began to purchase possessions and furniture that had belonged to Jackson. After a visit by President Theodore Roosevelt in 1907, Congress made a financial contribution to the Association so that a water system could be installed. Later Congressional appropriations allowed the Association to acquire portraits of Jackson as well as to make needed repairs. The state conveyed additonal land to the Association in 1923 and 1935. The National Park Service designated The Hermitage a National Historic Landmark in 1961. Four years later, the Association acquired the old Hermitage Church and in 1971 it began its support for the collection and publication of the *Papers of Andrew Jackson*. The Ladies' Hermitage Association continues to manage the home and property, which receives more than 250,000 visitors annually.

Carole Stanford Bucy, Volunteer State Community College
CITATION:
(1) *The Hermitage: A History and Guide* (Nashville, 1967), 16.
SEE: CONFEDERATE SOLDIERS' HOME; DORRIS, MARY C.;
HERMITAGE; LINDSLEY, JOHN B.; LINDSLEY, LOUISE G.;
LINDSLEY, SALLIE M.; SAVAGE, JOHN H.

LAKE COUNTY is located in the northwest corner of Tennessee and is bounded by Kentucky on the north, Obion County on the east, the Mississippi River on the west, and Dyer County on the south. One of the smallest counties in the state, Lake County covers 210 square miles. Its flat terrain contains some of the richest soil in the state. The county was named for Reelfoot Lake, formed by a series of earthquakes from December 1811 to mid-March 1812. Despite popular legends that attribute the name of the lake to "Chief Reelfoot and his Indian Bride," the lake was named for Bill Jones, whose clubfoot gained him the nickname "Reelfoot Jones." Jones died in March 1839, when he slipped from a footlog, fell into Spring Creek, and drowned. Thereafter the creek was known as "Reelfoot Creek," and since it fed the lake, the shallow body of water acquired the name Reelfoot also.

The Tennessee General Assembly organized Lake County in June 1870, and Tiptonville was designated as the county seat. The first session of court was held on September 5, 1870. Settlers established homesteads along the river and the lake as early as 1827. Until the organization of Lake County, area residents were part of Obion County and traveled to Troy to conduct county business. In recognition of the difficulty associated with crossing the "scatters of the Lake" (a swampy area extending south from the lake to the Obion River), a special Circuit Court was established in 1858 for the portion of Obion County lying west of Reelfoot Lake. The first term of this court was held in June 1858 in the Masonic Hall in Cronanville, the largest village. The men living in this area were exempted from militia duty in Troy. The scatters of the lake were brought under control by digging a dredge ditch from the lake to the Obion River along the boundary line between Lake and Obion counties. Bridges crossing the ditch replaced the earlier ferry boats.

Lake County's economy is based on agriculture, with cotton and soybeans the chief crops. Farmland has remained in the same families for generations, and Lake County has several Tennessee Century Farms, including the Ed Sumara Farm, the Wynn Farm, and the Carter Farm. In the nineteenth century and early twentieth century, cotton gins operated alongside the tracks of the Illinois Central Railroad, ginning as much as 40 bales per day. In 1997 only one gin operates in the county, turning out a bale of cotton every five minutes. Continental Grain Company ships corn, wheat, and soybeans by river and has replaced several earlier soybean companies. Lake County Seed Company, which operated a cottonseed oil mill in Tiptonville from 1906 to 1971, now stands abandoned.

In 1861 the last major Confederate fort on the Mississippi River fell in the Battle of Island No. 10, which lies in the great river bend near Tiptonville. The Confederate loss at Island No. 10 opened the Mississippi River to Union forces and assured the occupation of Memphis in June 1862.

Lake County and Reelfoot Lake returned to national prominence in 1907, when lake residents waged a violent battle against the West Tennessee Land Company for control of the lake. In a series of slick legal moves, the land company acquired title to the lake and developed plans for draining the lake for cotton production. Local commercial fishermen and lake residents fought back, and the conflict escalated into a series of nightrider attacks, in which armed and masked men terrorized the company and its supporters. The attacks resulted in the kidnapping and death of company attorney Quinton Rankin of Trenton and the arrest of 300 men accused of being nightriders. The cases against the men were eventually dropped, and the state acquired the lake for public use in 1914.

Lake County contains 22 villages, including the communities of Ridgely, Tiptonville, and Wynnburg. Located on a spur of the Illinois Central Railroad, Ridgely was once the site of several cotton gins, whose abandoned operations are still visible. In the great Mississippi River flood of 1927, Ridgely became the site of one of the 154 emergency relief camps established by the American Red Cross. Today the community operates two schools for students in the south end of the county; one is kindergarten through sixth grade; the other is a junior high school.

Wynnburg was created by Samuel F. Wynn, when he divided his farm in 1907 to accommodate the construction of a branch line of the Illinois Central from Dyersburg to Tiptonville. Wynn donated land for a depot, schools, and churches, and the town acquired its name from the family.

Tiptonville, the county seat, dates from 1857 but was not incorporated until 1900. Located on a small rise known as the Tiptonville Dome, the town also served as an emergency relief camp during the flood of 1927 and again during the flood of 1937. Tiptonville serves the educational needs of the northern end of the county with kindergarten through sixth grade and the county high school. The Lake County High School football team won the state championship in 1980 and 1985, and has been runner-up in 1977, 1979, and 1994.

Today Lake County has several factories, including Georgia Gulf, which produces PVC, a vinyl compound. The Illinois Central Railroad still plays an important role in the county's economy. Formerly, the county was served by trains making two round trips daily for passengers and freight. Today, it makes one trip daily for freight.

General Clifton Bledsoe Cates, a four-star General and nineteenth Commandant of the U.S. Marine Corps, was born at Cates Landing in 1898. He was raised in the county, attended elementary school here, and called the county "home." Cates died in 1970. Tiptonville also was the early home of Carl Perkins, whose combination hillbilly music and rhythm and blues influenced early rock 'n' roll.

Abigail Hyde, Ridgely

SEE: COTTON GINS; DISASTERS; EARTHQUAKES; FARMS, TENNESSEE CENTURY; FLOODS, 1936–37; ISLAND NO. 10, BATTLE OF; NIGHT RIDERS OF REELFOOT LAKE; PERKINS, CARL; RAILROADS; REELFOOT LAKE STATE PARK

LAMBUTH UNIVERSITY. On December 2, 1843, the Memphis Conference of the Methodist Episcopal Church received a charter from the Tennessee General Assembly authorizing the establishment of a young women's prepatory school and college, to be named the Memphis Conference Female Institute (MCFI), in Jackson, Tennessee, on five acres of land that had been the site of a Presbyterian college. The new college soon won renown for its quality education as a result of the work of its presidents, Dr. Lorenzo Lea, Dr. Amos W. Jones, and Dr. A.B. Jones, who succeeded his father. During the Civil War, the college buildings served as a hospital for Union troops, while the school continued to operate in the home of Dr. Amos Jones.

The degree of Mistress of English Literature was conferred on the early graduates who completed the English course; those who completed additional work in Latin or one of the modern languages received the A.M. A bachelor of arts degree was added in 1912, as was a Conservatory of Music and a School of Expression, Art, and Domestic Art.

In the early twentieth century financial difficulties led to the decision to make the institution coeducational. The MCFI charter was amended on January 3, 1923, to provide for coeducation and to change the name to Lambuth College in honor of the Reverend Walter R. Lambuth, M.D. To expand its facilities, the college moved from the corner of Chester and Institute streets to its present location on Lambuth Boulevard. In the fall of 1924 Lambuth College admitted its first class of male students.

Lambuth College had five presidents from 1924 to 1991, when the college achieved university status. Dr. Richard E. Womack became the first president in 1924 and served until 1952. Although his tenure spanned the difficult years of the Great Depression and World War II, several new buildings were erected on the campus. Dr. Luther L. Gobbel assumed the duties of the presidency in October 1952 and served until the fall of 1962. In July 1962 the board of trustees elected Dr. James S. Wilder, Jr., as Lambuth's third president. In 1964 Wilder initiated a master plan, known as the "Great Challenge," that resulted in a period of extraordinary academic and fiscal growth. During this period, Lambuth added four new buildings, including the science building which contains the mid-South's finest planetarium. Dr. Harry W. Gilmer became the fourth president of Lambuth College in June 1980, and served until October 1986. Under Gilmer's leadership, the college launched a $15 million sesquicentennial campaign for scholarships, endowment, and campus renovation.

In July 1987 Dr. Thomas F. Boyd became the last president of Lambuth College; on July 1, 1991, the school became Lambuth University. Boyd enhanced the academic and athletic programs. When Boyd resigned in April 1996, Dr. Joseph R. Thornton was appointed acting president. After a six-month search, W. Ellis Arnold III, an Arkansas educator, was named president.

Through many generations and with able leaders, Lambuth University, still a United Methodist institution, has continued to educate students with a commitment to the belief that a liberal education must be dedicated to the cultivation of the mind and spirit.

Robert H. Mathis, Lambuth University

SEE: EDUCATION, HIGHER; JACKSON

LAND BETWEEN THE LAKES is a federal recreation area located along the Tennessee-Kentucky border in northwest Middle Tennessee. Established by Congress in 1964, Land Between the Lakes (LBL) is a 170,000-acre peninsula between the Tennessee Valley Authority-created Kentucky Lake (1944) and the U.S. Corps of Engineers-created Barkley Lake (1965). The Tennessee Valley Authority (TVA) received administrative responsibility for the park. Creation of the recreational area required the acquistion of 103,000 acres and the relocation of approximately 2,700 people from 900 families in the Kentucky communities of Fenton, Golden Pond, Hematite, and Energy and the Tennessee communities of Model, Blue Spring, Hays, and Mint Spring.

Most local residents bitterly resented and opposed their relocation and the consequent destruction of their rural communities. In return, residents were to receive an enhanced local economy, based on tourism and recreation. This new economic potential, however, has never been fully developed. Budget cuts at TVA have diminished outdoor and public programs at the park significantly in the late 1980s and 1990s. Some commentators, in fact, have called for the closure of the park or, at least, its transfer to a consortium of state and local governments.

The Tennessee portion of LBL contains several important historic sites. A portion of the outer works of Fort Henry is preserved within the park. The Homeplace-1850 is a living history museum that documents and interprets the agrarian lifestyle of Stewart County farm families in the decade prior to the Civil War. The ruins of the Great Western Iron Furnace, a key contributor to the late antebellum iron industry in Tennessee, lie directly on "The Trace Road" that runs the length of the park.

On the Kentucky side, LBL maintains the Woodlands Nature Center, where adults and school children learn about wildlife, geology, geography, botany, and the environment. The Golden Pond Visitor Center features a planetarium. Approximately 7,000 students annually spend a portion of their school year at LBL's two resident camps, Brandon Spring (Tennessee side) and the Youth Station (Kentucky side). Thousands more visit LBL on day trips about history and the environment.

The recreation area also contains an extensive system of hiking trails, campgrounds, biking trails, and one of the nation's largest publicly-owned herds of buffalo, an animal once found in abundance in Tennessee. Bald eagles and osprey also were re-introduced at LBL in the 1980s. In 1991 the United Nations Educational, Scientific, and Cultural Organization designated Land Between the Lakes a world biosphere reserve, as an internationally significant representative of the world's major ecosystems.

C.arroll Van West, Middle Tennessee State University

LAND GRANTS. After the Revolutionary War, North Carolina had little or no money in its treasury. Faced with accumulating debts to soldiers and military suppliers, the state began to grant or transfer its western land to individuals to pay for war service and supplies in lieu of cash. The process of receiving land was not easy. After the claimant selected or "located" a desired tract, he paid the necessary fees and registered his entry in the appropriate entry taker's office, where he obtained a warrant authorizing the survey. The plat (an official scaled drawing by the surveyor) and survey (legal description of boundary lines), together with the warrant (ownership authorization) were forwarded to the Secretary of State, who issued the grant. Registration of the grant in the county where the land lay completed the process. Litigation, brought about by overlapping boundary lines, later clogged the courts.

Entry taker offices opened in the newly erected counties of Washington in 1777 and Sullivan in 1779; these offices closed in 1781. Two years later, John Armstrong's office opened in Hillsborough, North Carolina, for redemption of war provision certificates and specie issued during the war, and for sale of the western land. Ignoring Indian rights, the entire western area—now Tennessee—was opened for sale, except the military bounty land reservation in northern Middle Tennessee and the extreme southeastern corner of the state, where the Cherokees lived. North Carolina legislative acts of 1780, 1782, and 1783 established the military reservation, which covered much of the area originally designated as Davidson County.

Discouraged by North Carolina's failure to provide military assistance against the Indians and worried by the Spanish closing of the Mississippi River, settlers in the area that would become northeastern Tennessee illegally formed the State of Franklin, which existed from 1784 to 1788. Acting within the context of the new "state," settlers moved south of the French Broad and Holston Rivers. Although unable to obtain title to their land for many years, the claims or preemption rights of these settlers were protected by Tennessee's first constitution.

In 1784 North Carolina accepted fees for the transfer of title to individuals for much of the Tennessee area. Following the example of other states that credited their western lands to the newly formed Confederation of States, North Carolina also offered to cede its unappropriated western land (Tennessee) in 1784. Although withdrawn before it was accepted, this offer permanently closed the John Armstrong office in Hillsborough, North Carolina. A second cession made in 1789 paralyzed Tennessee land grants. Unlike North Carolina, the United States did not permit the occupation of territory not obtained through treaties. This left most of the state free of settlement, and until 1805, a wilderness existed between the settlements of northern East Tennessee and the Cumberland River area in northern Middle Tennessee. North Carolina had sold most of the Chickasaw area west of the Tennessee River in 5,000-acre grants, but the United States closed this area to white settlement until the Chickasaw treaty of 1818 was signed.

North Carolina had accepted money for patchwork grants throughout Tennessee and was legally obligated to honor these sales as well as the military bounty land promises. Therefore, North Carolina's cession deed to the United States included the following restrictions: 1) all entries and surveyor's warrants, which had been made and for which grants had not been issued, would be honored and completed into grants; 2) North Carolina reserved the right to continue issuing military warrants until all the veterans were paid, even if it meant issuing warrants outside the reservation; 3) land promises made to members of Evans Battalion, who had come to the aid of Cumberland settlers during Indian attacks in the 1780s, would be honored; and 4) special promises made to commissioners, surveyors, hunters, and their guard for laying off the military reservation, and preemption rights to those settlers who occupied the land prior to its official opening, would be honored.

When the United States accepted the cession deed containing the restrictive clauses, it found that the title conveyed only an undetermined amount of residue land, and it was impossible to determine if any land would remain after all North Carolina promises were honored and Indian claims respected. In 1790 Tennessee became the Territory South of the River Ohio, but the only territory land granted by the United States was 640 acres for Pulaski, the county seat of Giles County. Under these existing and conferred conditions, Tennessee achieved statehood in 1796.

The Compact of 1806 between the United States, North Carolina, and Tennessee authorized Tennessee to complete North Carolina's obligations by making land grants. A congressional reservation line separated the land obtained by Indian treaty from land otherwise obtained. The two areas were designated as land East and land West of the Congressional Reservation line. The land was divided into surveyor's districts, with the survey using the rectangular system in townships and ranges similar to that of other federally owned land. Boards of Commissioners were provided for East and West (Middle) Tennessee to determine the validity of North Carolina warrants. Only those grants initiated by North Carolina and grants for occupancy were issued at this time. Later, the bits and pieces lying between the patchwork grants were sold. Certain portions of the land—section 16 in each federally surveyed township, as well as most of the Ocoee and Hiwassee districts—were reserved for the benefit of schools.

As the Chickasaws released their land west of the Congressional Reservation Line and the Cherokees released their reservations (in the land south of the French Broad and Holston rivers, and the Hiwassee and Ocoee districts), the granting of these lands followed earlier practices. Only the Ocoee and Hiwassee districts were free of North Carolina warrants.

Irene M. Griffey, Clarksville

SUGGESTED READINGS: Thomas Abernathy, *From Frontier to Plantation in Tennessee* (1932); Walter T. Durham, *Before Tennessee: The Southwest Territory, 1790–1796* (1990); John Haywood, *The Civil and Political History of the State of Tennessee from its Earliest Settlements up to the Year 1796* (1823); Henry D. Whitney, *The Land Laws of Tennessee* (1893)

SEE: BLOUNT, WILLIAM; CHICKASAWS; CUMBERLAND COMPACT; FRANKLIN, STATE OF; JACKSON PURCHASE; SOUTHWEST TERRITORY

LANDMARKISM, a Baptist movement arising in the South, west of the Appalachians, during the nineteenth century, asserted the sole validity and unbroken succession of Baptist churches from the New Testament era. This exclusivistic ecclesiology promoted the idea that the term church always refers to a local and visible institution. This emphasis on an unbroken succession of local and visible Baptist churches as the only true churches of Christ controverted the practices of ecumenism. Landmarkers believed that Baptists, who participated in "pulpit exchanges" with other denominations, accepted immersion performed outside the auspices of a Baptist church, or celebrated communion beyond the confines of local church membership, removed an ancient landmark that was essential to Baptist identity. These ideas deeply influenced Baptist life in the South. The more radical Landmarkers withdrew from participation in the Southern Baptist Convention, either forming their own organizations or maintaining a strict localism that forbade any denominational participation beyond the local church. Other Landmarkers remained within the Southern Baptist Convention, forming one of the major traditions in Southern Baptist life, especially in the late nineteenth and early twentieth centuries.

The dominant figure of the movement was James R. Graves of Tennessee, who was perhaps the most influential Baptist clergyman in the nineteenth century South. James M. Pendleton of Kentucky and Amos C. Dayton of Mississippi joined with Graves in the promotion of Landmarkism. The three were known by their followers as "The Great Triumvirate." Pendleton coined the term Landmark in an essay he wrote in 1854, which Graves published under the title *An Old Landmark Re-set.*

Marty G. Bell, Belmont University

SUGGESTED READING: H. Wamble, "Landmarkism: Doctrinaire Ecclesiology Among Baptists," *Church History* 33(1964): 429–47

SEE: GRAVES, JAMES R.; RELIGION; SOUTHERN BAPTIST CONVENTION

LANE COLLEGE. In 1882 Lane College, then the "C.M.E. High School," was founded by the Colored Methodist Episcopal Church (now Christian Methodist Episcopal Church, CME) in America. Initially Bishop William Henry Miles, the first Bishop of the CME Church, presided over the Tennessee Annual Conference at which Reverend J.K. Daniels presented a resolution to establish a school to educate African-American students and to develop CME clergy. The Conference appointed a committee made up of Reverends C.H. Lee, J.H. Ridley, Sandy Rivers, and J.K. Daniels to solicit funds to purchase the land. On January 1, 1880, the church purchased four acres of land in East Jackson, Tennessee.

The school opened in November 1882 as the "C.M.E. High School," and Jennie E. Lane, daughter of the founder, Bishop Isaac Lane, served as the first teacher and principal. In January 1883 J.H. Harper of Jackson took over the work and finished the unexpired term of Jennie Lane. The following September, Reverend Charles H. Phillips succeeded Harper. During the Phillips administration, the school was chartered, and the name was changed to Lane Institute.

In 1887 T.J. Austin presided over Lane Institute's first graduating class. That same year, Reverend T.F. Saunders, a former white slaveowner, and a member of the Memphis Conference of the Methodist Episcopal Church, South, was appointed the first president of Lane Institute. In 1896 the college department was organized, and the Board of Trustees voted to change the name to Lane College.

In 1903 Reverend James Albert Bray was elected president, a position he held until 1907. During his administration, the present Administration Building was erected. Dr. James Franklin Lane, the son of the founder, succeeded Bray and served as president for 37 years. During his administration, the college improved its educational facilities, expanded its curriculum, and enlarged its physical plant.

In 1936 the Southern Association of Colleges and Schools (SACS) approved Lane College and gave it a "B" rating. The rating was upgraded to "A" in 1949, and Lane College was admitted into full membership in SACS in 1961.

When Lane died in 1944, Reverend P. Randolph Shy briefly served as acting president, until the election of Dr. D.S. Yarbrough to the presidency in 1945. Yarbrough served until 1948, when J.H. White succeeded to the position. Upon the resignation of White in 1950, Dr. Richard H. Sewell, the Dean of Instruction, was elected acting president. He served until Reverend Chester Arthur Kirkendoll was elected in July 1950. Kirkendoll served for the next 20 years, during which time the college received accreditation by SACS and six modern buildings were added to the campus.

Dr. Herman Stone, Jr., who served as the dean of the college for ten years, was elected president in 1970. During his presidency, the college's accreditation was reaffirmed twice, and the J.F. Lane Health and Physical Education building was added to the campus. Stone retired in 1986 and was succeeded by Dr. Alex A. Chambers. During his administration, the college received a grant to refurbish several historic buildings, which had been listed in the National Register of Historic Places. Following the death of Chambers in 1992, the Board of Trustees named Dr. Arthur L. David, Dean of the College, as the interim president.

In August 1992 Dr. Wesley Cornelious McClure was elected the ninth president of Lane College. McClure completed the construction of a multimillion dollar communications center and library and supervised the general upgrading and improvement of the campus appearance. More than a century after its founding, Lane College continues to serve as a source of inspiration and a symbol of Christian education.
Arthur L. David, Lane College

SEE: CHRISTIAN METHODIST EPISCOPAL CHURCH; JACKSON; LANE, ISAAC

LANE, ISAAC (1834–1936), fourth bishop of the Colored (Christian) Methodist Episcopal Church, was born March 4, 1834, in Madison County in West Tennessee. Lane grew to manhood as a slave on the plantation of Cullen Lane. At age 19, Isaac Lane married Frances Ann Boyce, an 18-year-old slave woman from neighboring Haywood County. The couple became the parents of 12 children, who became ministers, educators, and physicians.

In 1870, during the chaos of Emancipation and Reconstruction, freedmen established the CME Church, and Isaac Lane quickly rose to prominence among the clergy of the fledgling congregations. In 1872 Lane was elected a bishop of the church and assigned to the Tennessee area.

In 1882 Lane founded a CME. school in Jackson, Tennessee, to provide education for freedmen. Bishop Lane's daughter, Jennie Lane, became the first teacher and principal of the new school. When the school applied for college status, Lane chose a white Methodist minister, Thomas F. Saunders, to serve as the first president. His choice reflected the racial reality of the period and allowed the new college to establish a stronger position in the Jackson community. In 1907 Bishop Lane's son, James Franklin Lane, completed his Ph.D. degree and became the president of Lane College. His distinguished service to the college continued for the next 37 years. During his tenure, Lane College lived up to the belief of Bishop Lane that education must keep pace with the changing times and needs of the people.

During World War II, in recognition of the contributions of Bishop Lane to the field of education, the United States named a Merchant Marine Victory ship in his honor. The *USS Lane*, based in San Diego, is the only WWII Victory ship still in service. It remains a fitting tribute to this great man of color, this ex-slave, who touched the lives of so many men and women who matriculated at Lane College.

Bishop Lane died in 1936, at the age of 102, a centenarian who dedicated his life to the education of both the soul and the mind of African-American youth, as they rose, phoenix-like, from the fiery ashes of slavery.

Arthur L. David, Lane College

SEE: CHRISTIAN METHODIST EPISCOPAL CHURCH; LANE COLLEGE; JACKSON

LAUDERDALE COUNTY was established by the Tennessee General Assembly in November 1835 from portions of Tipton, Dyer, and Haywood counties. The county was named for Lt. Colonel James Lauderdale, who was killed in the Battle of New Orleans. The county covers 477 square miles and is bounded by the Forked Deer River, the Mississippi River (although some areas, such as Forked Deer Island are now on the west side of the river), and the Hatchie River. The eastern part of the county lies on the Gulf Coastal Plain while the western portion is in the Mississippi Bottom.

Native Americans used the rich resources of Lauderdale's river bottoms and hardwood forests for thousands of years before European explorers arrived. Woodland and Mississippian period sites, many with mounds, dot the landscape. By the late seventeenth century, the Chickasaws claimed West Tennessee. Robert Cavelier de La Salle and his party observed their villages, and the Europeans constructed Fort Prudhomme near the mouth of the Hatchie. Despite the Chickasaw claims, North Carolina sent Henry Rutherford to the area in 1785 to survey for land warrants. Rutherford and his party established "Key Corner" as a landmark for marking off claims by carving his initials and a large key into a huge sycamore on the first high ground east of the Mississippi and south of the Forked Deer. Following the Jackson Purchase in 1818, Rutherford, his brothers, Benjamin Porter, and a man named Crenshaw settled near Key Corner. Native Americans returned to Lauderdale County during the 1950s, when two Choctaw families migrated to the county to work in the cotton fields.

Today two Choctaw communities are in Ripley and Henning.

The earliest settlements of whites and African-American slaves were located at Key Corner and Porter's Gap. Griffith Rutherford built the first grist mill in the county at Key Corner in 1826, and Joseph Jordan and William Champers added a cotton gin the following year. Fulton, on the Mississippi River, was settled in 1819, and Judge James Trimble laid out Lauderdale's first town there in 1827. Fulton prospered as a steamboat landing, but today much of the town has been consumed by the Mississippi River. Durhamville was established in 1829, and that same year, a church—Turner's Chapel—was built there. Edith Kenley opened the first school in her home at Double Bridges. General William Conner promoted Ashport, a speculative town on the Mississippi. Other early towns included Golddust, Nankipoo, and Hales Point. Nankipoo became the home of Roark Bradford, a popular writer of the 1920s, 1930s, and 1940s. Bell Irvin Wiley also was raised near Nankipoo and later achieved fame as the author of more than 20 history books on the Civil War, including *The Road to Appomattox*, *The Life of Billy Yank*, and *The Life of Johnny Reb*; the latter two remain authoritative studies of the common soldiers of the war.

Ripley was established as the county seat in February 1836 on 62 acres purchased from Thomas Brown and named for General E.W. Ripley, a veteran of the War of 1812. J.N. Smith opened the first mercantile store in a log cabin, and the town quickly became a center for trade between Dyersburg and Covington. In 1936 the Public Works Administration built Lauderdale County's fourth courthouse. Designed by the Nashville firm of Marr and Holman, the building displays the PWA Modern style so popular in the New Deal era. Works Progress Administration funds were used to construct the post office in 1941, which was designed by Louis A. Simon in a Colonial Revival style. A mural, *Autumn*, produced through the federal artists' program still decorates the post office interior. Painted by Marguerite Zorach, the mural reflects hunting and nutting in the West Tennessee country.

During the antebellum period, cotton dominated the county's agriculture. Steamboats carried cotton bales from landings on the Forked Deer, Mississippi, and Hatchie rivers. In 1850 there were 304 slaveholders in Lauderdale County, 96 of whom owned ten or more slaves—the two largest planters were Hiram Partee, who had 86 slaves, and Thomas Fitzpatrick with 84.

The Civil War devastated the county's farms and plantations. After Fort Pillow's fall to Union forces in June 1862, occupation of the county seesawed between Confederate and Union troops, both of whom bivouacked in Ripley at different times. Skirmishes occurred at Double Bridges and Woodville in October 1862, Knob Creek in January 1863, and Durhamville in September 1863. The most controversial engagement took place at Fort Pillow on April 12, 1864, when a Confederate force under General Nathan Bedford Forrest overran the Union outpost and killed almost half the garrison of 600, mostly African-American, troops.

The county recovered from the war slowly, returning to cotton as the primary crop, with some tobacco raised for the market at Memphis. Railroads reached the county in the 1870s. Henning became the first railroad town; it was established on the line that at various times was named the Newport News and Mississippi Valley line, then Paducah and Memphis (1872), Memphis and Louisville (1874), Memphis Paducah and Northern (1878), Chesapeake, Ohio and Southwestern (1881), and finally Illinois Central (1887). In 1873 Carrie White became the first African-American teacher in Henning. In 1918–1919 Will Palmer, an African-American businessman, built his home in Henning. The town's most famous son, Alex Haley, spent his boyhood there with his Palmer grandparents. He later wrote the international best-seller *Roots* from the stories he heard from his grandmother and aunts. The railroad reached Ripley in 1874 and eventually reached the towns of Gates (1882), Halls (1883), and Curve (1884), which was touted as the strawberry capital of the world.

By the late 1890s Ripley acquired an electric system. Telephone lines strung by the Cumberland Telephone and Telegraph Company reached Halls in 1900. The Bank of Halls organized in 1899, followed by the Farmers and Merchants Bank of Henning (1901), Ripley Savings Bank and Trust (1903), and Gates Banking and Trust Company (1904). Building on a school tradition that included Ripley Academy, Lauderdale Institute, and Ripley Female Institute in the 1800s, public high schools were built between 1900 and 1910 at Curve, Ripley, and Halls. Timber became an important industry in the county. Anderson-Tulley, a Memphis veneer company, purchased 17,000 acres of Lauderdale timberland, which now serves as the Anderson-Tully Wildlife Management Area.

During World War II the U.S. Army constructed an air base at Halls. Some 7,700 troops trained on the 2,450-acre site, many of them as B-17 bomber pilots. The base closed after the war, and the land was sold at auction in 1955. A portion of the land was developed as an industrial park, and Lauderdale County acquired its first plant when Tupperware opened one of three national plants in 1969, employing 750. Although Tupperware closed its manufacturing facility in 1991, Lauderdale has attracted a number of industrial employers. In 1997 the largest private employers were Marvin Windows with 640 employ-ees and Magnatek with 575. Other industrial plants included Siegel-Robert Inc., Komatsu Dresser Co., Anderson Hickey Company, and Master Casual Wear. The two largest public sector employers were the Lauderdale County School System (566 employees) and the State of Tennessee's Cold Creek Correctional Facility, formerly Fort Pillow Prison Farm (271). In 1996 the population of Lauderdale County was 23, 972.

Ann Toplovich, Tennessee Historical Society
SUGGESTED READING: Clarice H. Hellums and Kara H. McCauley, *Visions of Lauderdale County, Past and Present* (1996)
SEE: BRADFORD, ROARK; CHICKASAWS; CHOCTAWS; COTTON; FORREST, NATHAN B.; FORT PILLOW; FORT PRUDHOMME; HALEY, ALEX M.; HALEY, ALEX, BOYHOOD HOME; JACKSON PURCHASE; LAUDERDALE, WILLIAM; PUBLIC WORKS ADMINISTRATION; RUTHERFORD, GRIFFITH; TENNESSEE PRISON SYSTEM; WORKS PROGRESS ADMINISTRATION

LAUDERDALE, WILLIAM (ca. 1780–1837), a planter-soldier, for whom Fort Lauderdale, Florida, is named, was born in Virginia between 1780 and 1785, the son of a prominent Sumner County family. Lauderdale first served as a lieutenant under Andrew Jackson in the Tennessee Volunteers, who were dispatched to New Orleans in 1812. Although the troops were discharged before they saw combat, the experience made Lauderdale a member of Jackson's inner circle. Lauderdale left his Goose Creek plantation in Hartsville again to fight in the Creek War. He became Jackson's chief quartermaster in the campaign that culminated in the battle of New Orleans in 1815. Lauderdale's brother James, for whom Lauderdale County is named, was the highest-ranking Tennessee officer killed in that conflict.

Lauderdale took up arms again as a militia captain during the Seminole Indian campaigns of 1836. Jackson recommended Lauderdale's return to Florida in the war against the Seminoles. In the fall of 1837, Lauderdale formed a battalion of mounted spies. This company helped push American claims far south in Florida, establishing a post on the New River named Fort Lauderdale. The volunteers were ordered to Baton Rouge to be mustered out, and Lauderdale died there of a pulmonary disorder May 11, 1837. Lauderdale's various military exploits, though fought in Jackson's shadow, marked him as a Tennessee volunteer in the age of American expansion.

Blythe Semmer, Middle Tennessee State University
SUGGESTED READING: Kirk Cooper, *William Lauderdale: General Andrew Jackson's Warrior* (1982)

LAW IN TENNESSEE. The origins of law in Tennessee can be traced to a variety of sources, notably English common law and colonial North Carolina statutes. The 1796 Constitution provided that all laws then in force should continue until replaced by the legislature. This, in effect, adopted the substantive law of North Carolina, which included common law so far as compatible with circumstances in colonial America, as the basis for Tennessee jurisprudence. The organization of Tennessee as a state, therefore, did not entail any sharp break with existing legal principles. Indeed, the Supreme Court of Tennessee eventually held that English common law as it stood in 1775 was part of the law of the state.

In contrast to certain other states, little evidence exists of hostility to English law in early Tennessee. Governor John Sevier, however, declared in 1803 that "the common law of England, or any other European nation, are not suitable for republican states to adopt," and urged the legislature to supplant English laws.[1] Yet an unconvinced state senate committee did not recommend any action in response. Lawyers and judges regularly cited English authorities and employed English judicial procedures during the first decades of statehood.

The Constitution of 1796 did not provide for a fully independent judicial branch of government. Rather, the Superior Court and lower courts were created by and subordinate to the legislature. Many observers decried the defective nature of the judicial system, and the legislature revamped the court structure several times in the early period of Tennessee history. Most of the cases heard by the courts involved private law disputes between individuals. All lawsuits were brought in the style of one of the common-law forms of action, such as trespass on the case, covenant, and ejectment. The bulk of the litigation concerned collection of debts, enforcement of contracts, conflicts over ownership or possession of land, and torts. The early judges clarified much of the land law and adjusted the laws inherited from North Carolina to new circumstances.

Although preoccupied with private law matters, the Tennessee judiciary did not neglect constitutional issues. The highest court moved gingerly to assert the right of judicial review over legislation. As early as 1818, the Supreme Court of Errors and Appeals declared that "the Constitution is the paramount law of the land; that it is not competent to the Legislature to act in derogation of this principle; and if they attempt it their acts are void."[2] The Court also insisted that the judiciary could determine whether legislative acts violated the Constitution. Judges first wielded judicial review to protect the integrity of judicial procedures. In *Bank of the State v. Cooper* (1831), for instance, the Court invalidated legislation creating a special tribunal to resolve suits against officers of the state bank on several grounds. Among other concerns was the right to a jury trial. Since the special tribunal would hear cases without a jury, the act unconstitutionally deprived the defendants of the

right to a trial by jury. In *Fisher's Negroes v. Dabbs* (1834), the Court struck down an act, which directed that a proceeding to manumit certain slaves be stricken from the chancery court docket. The Court reasoned that the legislature had no power to close the courts and thus, in effect, determine the outcome of cases pending judicial resolution.

In language derived from the Magna Carta, the Declaration of Rights of the 1796 Constitution provided that no person shall be "in any manner destroyed or deprived of his life, liberty, or property, but by the judgment of his peers or the law of the land." Tennessee judges early treated the law of the land clause as a vehicle to protect individual liberty from legislative infringement. In a separate opinion in *Vanzant v. Waddel* (1829), Judge John Catron commented: "The clause 'Law of the Land' means a general and public law, equally binding upon every member of the community."[3] He maintained that the liberty and property of every individual must be governed by general laws binding on the whole community. In Catron's view, partial laws directed at individuals in violation of this principle of equal treatment were void. Judge Nathan Green amplified this theme in *Bank of State,* emphasizing that the law of the land clause was intended to prevent the legislature from affecting the rights of any citizen unless the rights of all others similarly situated were equally affected. Reflecting the tenets of Jacksonianism, this judicial approach sought to protect the rights of individuals by requiring that laws be generally applicable and not single out politically vulnerable groups. This stress on equality under the law helped to shape the doctrine of substantive due process and anticipated the aversion of state and federal courts to class legislation following the Civil War.

Criminal law received little attention in the decades immediately following statehood. Corporal punishments, such as whipping and branding, remained common. In 1829 the legislature enacted a measure to erect a penitentiary and reformed the penal code to substitute imprisonment for corporal punishment. In another development, the Supreme Court of Errors and Appeals in *Grainger v. State* (1830) adopted a generous understanding of self-defense as a justification for killing an assailant.

Tennessee judges repeatedly asserted that the judiciary was a separate and coordinate branch of government. The Constitution of 1834, which expressly provided for a Supreme Court, firmly established this principle. The Supreme Court now had a constitutional foundation and could no longer be controlled by the legislature.

The 1834 Constitutional Convention also added a section urging the legislature to encourage internal improvements. Legislators and judges shared the widespread enthusiasm for improved transportation, and devoted particular attention to fledgling railroads. Starting in 1831 the legislature granted numerous charters with broad privileges to railroads. During the antebellum era, moreover, various acts provided for the state to purchase railroad stock or endorse bonds, and authorized counties to subscribe for railroad stock. The Supreme Court upheld this use of public funds in *Louisville & Nashville Railroad Co. v. County Court of Davidson* (1854), on grounds that better trade and commerce served a public purpose. Likewise, the Court sustained the delegation of eminent domain to private railroad companies. But in *Woodfolk v. Nashville & Chattanooga Railroad Co.* (1852), the judges insisted that the owner must receive the fair value of the land taken by the railroad, and could not be compensated by the incidental benefits of a project. The Court supported rail construction, but it carefully safeguarded the rights of individual owners.

The antebellum era witnessed numerous moves to improve the state legal system. Edward Scott published a valuable compilation of statutes in 1821. Thereafter, the legislature directed several revisions of the state's statutes. Finally, the legislators enacted a code of public statutes in 1858, revising the law in many respects and streamlining civil procedure. The legal literature was also strengthened. In 1809 the legislature required that the judges of the Supreme Court submit written opinions, laying the basis for the publication of case reports. John Overton, a prominent jurist, collected and published the first volume of court decisions in 1813.

Tennessee's decision to secede from the Union in 1861 ushered in years of conflict, which disrupted orderly legal process. In the face of Union military victories, the legislature adjourned in March 1862, and the court system ceased to operate. After a period of military rule, Governor William G. Brownlow organized a Reconstruction government in 1865 and appointed judges to the Supreme Court. Although long dismissed as a carpetbagger court of slight consequence, the Reconstruction Court, in actuality, was composed of jurists who served ably during probably the most trying phase of Tennessee judicial history. The Reconstruction Court confronted a huge backlog of cases and most of its decisions dealt with ordinary civil litigation. But its handling of matters arising from the Civil War and Reconstruction has fixed the court's image. As would be expected of unionist judges, the Supreme Court in *Smith v. Ishenhour* (1866) upheld a measure invalidating the ordinance of secession. More controversial was the Reconstruction Court's handling of laws designed to disfranchise ex-Confederates. In *Ridley v. Sherbrook* (1867), the judges sustained the franchise law of the Brownlow government. In part, they were motivated to avoid antagonizing the Radicals in Congress, and

thus spare Tennessee from military governance. In *State v. Staten* (1869), the Court demonstrated its independence by striking down Brownlow's practice of disfranchising voters who he thought had fraudulently registered.

Reconstruction came to an end with the Constitution of 1870. This document, as amended, remains the basic framework for Tennessee law and government. Following the Civil War and Reconstruction, the Tennessee legal system addressed the new issues that emerged from the economic and social transformation of the state and union. Increased concern about personal violence, for instance, sparked legislative efforts to curb the practice of carrying concealed weapons in public. In *Andrews v. State* (1871), the Supreme Court affirmed the constitutional right to bear and use arms, but held that the legislature could regulate the time and manner of carrying arms to protect the community. The emancipation of slaves created new possibilities for interracial marriage. To forestall this result, the Constitution of 1870 and implementing legislation prohibited interracial marriage. Stressing the state police power to regulate marriage, the Court in *Lonas v. State* (1871) found the prohibition to be valid and not in violation of the Fourteenth Amendment. The constitutional barrier to interracial marriage was removed in 1977.

Cases involving corporate enterprise and private property rights occupied a place of importance on the Supreme Court's docket in the late nineteenth century. The Tennessee Constitution provides that monopolies shall not be allowed in the state. This declaration was first written in 1796, long before the growth of modern public utilities. The constitution does not define monopoly, and in *City of Memphis v. Memphis Water Co.* (1871) the Court ruled that the prohibition is inapplicable when a particular trade or business is not of common right. The judges then upheld the exclusive privilege of the Memphis Water Company. Occasionally the Supreme Court has invalidated business arrangements as a monopoly. In *Noe v. Mayor and Aldermen of Town of Morristown* (1913), for instance, the Court ruled an exclusive municipal franchise for slaughtering animals was an unconstitutional monopoly. But during the twentieth century, the Court has drained the monopoly provisions of much meaning by recognizing a broad legislative power to confer exclusive licenses under the police power to promote public safety and welfare.

When the state takes private property for public use, both the state and federal constitutions require that the owner be compensated. The Supreme Court adopted a broad definition of taking in *Barron v. City of Memphis* (1904), holding that a physical invasion which destroyed the usefulness of land constituted a compensable taking. The Court ruled that there need not be an actual appropriation of the property to secure constitutional protection. Yet the abatement of a common law nuisance is not an unconstitutional taking of property. Thus, in *Theilan v. Porter* (1885), the judges pointed out that a city could destroy a house deemed a health hazard under the police power to guard the public.

During the twentieth century, the states lost a good deal of their autonomy to fashion law. The Supreme Court of the United States gradually federalized many areas of law, such as criminal procedure and race relations, by applying constitutional norms under the Fourteenth Amendment to the states. Congress preempted many fields with extensive regulatory legislation, effectively displacing state authority. Business transactions increasingly involved persons in more than one state. Accordingly, there was a push for uniformity among the states in various areas of private law. To meet the demand, the Tennessee legislature enacted numerous modern codes, such as the Uniform Commercial Code and the Uniform Residential Landlord and Tenant Act.

Despite these developments, Tennessee legislators and judges retained considerable latitude in making law to meet societal needs. Economic issues predominated in the early years of the twentieth century. Adjusting to the hazards of the industrial workplace, Tennessee abrogated common law rules limiting recovery by injured workers against employers and adopted worker's compensation in 1919. The Supreme Court initially looked with skepticism upon price-fixing schemes. In *State v. Greeson* (1939), for instance, the Court determined that a statute setting the prices charged by barbers represented an unconstitutional deprivation of the freedom of contract. Subsequently, however, the judges sustained the Tennessee fair trade law, which permitted manufacturers to stipulate the retail price of their goods. Labor relations were largely governed by federal law after 1935, but the legislature passed a right-to-work act in 1947, outlawing contracts which restricted employment to union members. The Tennessee Supreme Court affirmed the validity of this measure in *Miscari v. International Brotherhood of Teamsters* (1948).

More important, in a series of decisions starting with *Evans v. McCabe* (1932), the Supreme Court ruled that the Constitution of 1870 only authorized the legislature to tax income derived from stocks and bonds, and that other sources of income were not taxable. In recent years, the Attorney General has taken the position that a general state income tax could be found constitutional. But the matter remains unresolved.

By the late twentieth century, the Tennessee courts were demonstrating a degree of judicial activism in reshaping both private and public law. The Supreme Court changed tort law in *McIntyre v. Balentine* (1992) by adopting a scheme of comparative fault rather than contributory negligence in negligence actions.

Of greater potential significance, appellate judges in Tennessee have shown a new interest in state constitutional law. They have begun to invoke the Tennessee constitution to expand personal rights beyond the federal minimum standard. In *Tennessee Small School Systems v. McWherter* (1995), for instance, the Supreme Court determined that the equal protection provisions of the Tennessee Constitution imposed on the legislature a duty to maintain a public education system that afforded substantially equal opportunities to all students. Instead of imposing a remedy, however, the Court deferred to the legislature to fashion a plan to equalize funding available to school districts. Similarly, the Court of Appeals in *Campbell v. Sundquist* (1996) relied on a right of privacy implied from several provisions of the state constitution to invalidate statutes prohibiting sodomy. In these cases the Tennessee courts have exceeded federal constitutional requirements. The outcome represents a departure from the historic Tennessee practice of treating the state constitution as conferring essentially the same rights as the federal constitution.

Tennessee law is the product of evolution rather than upheaval. Innovation has usually been incremental, and the state has rarely been at the forefront of legal change. Yet from 1796, both legislators and judges have sought to adjust traditional legal principles to meet the challenge of economic growth and societal change.

James W. Ely, Jr., Vanderbilt University

CITATIONS:

(1) Robert H. White, *Messages of the Governors of Tennessee,* Volume I (Nashville, 1952), 137–138.

(2) *Huntsman's Lessee v. Randolph,* 5 Haywood (Tenn.) 263, 271 (1818).

(3) *Vanzant v. Waddel,* 10 Tenn. 259, 270 (1829).

SUGGESTED READINGS: Joshua W. Caldwell, *Sketches of the Bench and Bar of Tennessee* (1898); Joshua W. Caldwell, *Studies in the Constitutional History of Tennessee,* 2nd ed. (1907); James W. Ely, Jr., and Theodore Brown, Jr., eds., *Legal Papers of Andrew Jackson* (1987); Lewis L. Laska, "A Legal and Constitutional History of Tennessee, 1772–1972," *Memphis State University Law Review* 6(1976): 563–672

LAWRENCE COUNTY was created October 21, 1817, by an act of the Tennessee General Assembly from territory acquired by treaty with the Chickasaw Indians. A section of Hickman County and a small portion of Giles County were included in its boundaries. Local government was established in 1818.

Both the county and the county seat were named in honor of Captain James Lawrence, U.S. Naval hero of the War of 1812. Lawrenceburg, the county seat, was sited near the center of the county, but an important consideration in determining its location was the presence of Jackson's Military Road on the eastern border of the town. As a major thoroughfare from

Natchez, Mississippi, to Nashville, Tennessee, the Military Road played a significant role in the economic development of the county; in April 1821 the road was relocated through the center of town.

David Crockett served as one of the first commissioners and justices of the peace in Lawrence County. In the four or five years he lived in the area, he operated a water-powered grist mill, a powder mill, and a distillery. Today David Crockett State Park is situated on the site of the frontiersman's land. The park attracts tourists from across the United States, especially during the annual David Crockett Days.

In addition to the county seat, a number of smaller towns and communities dot the landscape, including Summertown, Henryville, Ethridge, Leoma, Loretto, St. Joseph, West Point, and Iron City. The past vitality of these towns was associated with their proximity to Jackson's Military Road or the mining of iron ore.

A number of citizens of the county achieved regional and national prominence. George Henry Nixon, Confederate officer and politician, was the person most responsible for bringing the railroad to Lawrence County. James Jackson Pennington, a well-known local inventor, patented a working model of an "Aerial Bird," a flying machine similar to a zeppelin, in 1877. Thomas H. Paine, lawyer, politician, and educator, was appointed State Superintendent of Public Instruction in the 1880s by Governor William B. Bate. In 1899 he was appointed Tennessee Commissioner of Agriculture.

Lawrence County has long been known for its gospel singers. One person in particular, James D. Vaughan, transformed Lawrenceburg into the undisputed capital of gospel music in America. The James D. Vaughan Music School attracted students from across the South. The James D. Vaughan Publishing Company printed gospel music books and operated branch offices in South Carolina, Mississippi, and Texas.

Throughout the nineteenth century and well into the twentieth century successive migrations brought settlers to Lawrence County from other southern states and foreign nations. Initially Lawrence County was settled largely by people migrating from the Carolinas. Wealthier farmers brought slaves, although Lawrence County never had a large percentage of slave-owning farmers. Farmers among the early immigrants planted cotton while entrepreneurs built sawmills, grist mills, and cotton mills or mined the iron ore. Mining expanded with the arrival of the railroad in 1883.

In the early 1870s a large number of German Catholics arrived in Lawrence County in search of better land, bringing many skilled tradesmen with them to such communities as Loretto and St. Joseph. A third migration between 1908 and 1915 brought families from Cullman, Winston, and Morgan counties in Alabama to southern Middle Tennessee. Most of these twentieth century settlers were cotton growers or timbermen. Cotton continued to play a major economic role in Lawrence County until the late 1960s.

Certainly one of the more interesting migrations into Lawrence County was that of the Amish in 1944. Bringing with them their strong religious and cultural beliefs, these immigrants established their community in the area around Ethridge. Their rejection of war and worldly pleasure and their reluctance to incorporate the conveniences of industrial society have made them a source of interest to local residents and visitors to the area. Their skills as farmers and craftsmen receive widespread admiration.

In the mid-twentieth century, the relocation of the Murray Ohio Manufacturing Company, one of the world's largest producers of bicycles and lawnmowers, to Lawrence County refocused the county's economy toward industrial production. Dozens of other, smaller factories, manufacturing a wide variety of items, including automobile windshields, windshield wipers, kitchen counter tops, fishing lures, clothing, printed packaging, church pews, and caskets, followed Murray Ohio into the county.

The population of Lawrence County in a 1994 census was 35,303. Thirteen public schools and four private schools serve 7,120 students. Columbia State Community College maintains a branch in Lawrenceburg. County government operates under the County Executive and a board of 18 commissioners. The city government of Lawrenceburg is made up of a mayor and four commissioners. The Lawrenceburg Town Square is a National Register-listed historic district while the Natchez Trace Parkway passes through the western portion of the county.

Kathy Niedergeses, Lawrence County Archives

SEE: CROCKETT, DAVID; DAVID CROCKETT STATE PARK; NATCHEZ TRACE PARKWAY; VAUGHAN, JAMES D.

LAWRENCE, WILLIAM (1930–), a Nashville native, rose to the Navy's top ranks and received national honor after six years as a prisoner of war in North Vietnam, during which time he wrote "Oh Tennessee, My Tennessee," the official state poem. Lawrence excelled at academics and sports at Nashville's West High School and entered the U.S. Naval Academy in 1947. He was class president and brigade commander his senior year and graduated eighth in a class of 725, with a degree in electrical engineering. He attended flight school and won his aviator's wings in 1952.

After serving in a fighter squadron in the Korean War, Lawrence was sent to Patuxent Naval Air Test Center. He was part of an elite group that included John Glenn, Alan Shepard, Pete Conrad, and Wally

Schirra, all of whom became astronauts, an honor Lawrence missed only because of a mild aortic valve leakage.

Lawrence was the first Naval aviator to fly Mach 2 in a Navy aircraft, and he took part in the flyover at the funeral of President John F. Kennedy. As fighting in Vietnam intensified, he was assigned to the aircraft carrier *USS Ranger,* and then to the *USS Constellation,* as an F-4 Phantom squadron commander. By mid-1967 he had flown 75 combat missions. Then, on June 28, flying an F-4 Phantom, he was shot down during a bombing raid over Nam Dinh, North Vietnam.

Lawrence was held six years in the Hoa Lo prison, nicknamed the "Hanoi Hilton." He was tortured and spent 14 months in solitary confinement. As a result of the torture and poor sanitation, he developed health problems. Still, his forbearance and leadership served as inspiration to many other American prisoners. In 1971, during a two-month confinement in a tiny, sweltering shed (called "Calcutta" by the prisoners), immobilized by pain and heat, he wrote a poem about Tennessee to maintain his sanity. That poem, "Oh Tennessee, My Tennessee," was named official state poem in 1973.

Upon his release early in 1973, Lawrence returned to a hero's welcome. He had been promoted to captain during his imprisonment. Over the course of his naval career, he would receive three Silver Stars, four Distinguished Service Medals, the Legion of Merit, the Distinguished Flying Cross, and two Purple Hearts. Vice Admiral Jim Stockdale, senior Navy POW, praised Lawrence for his loyalty, bravery, toughness, and compassion. He was an inspiration to all prisoners.

Lawrence threw himself into Navy life. He was named Rear Admiral in 1974 and made Commander of the Navy's Light Attack Wing in the Pacific. After a stint at the Pentagon, he was named Superintendent of the U.S. Naval Academy. In 1983 he was appointed Deputy Chief of Naval Operations and Chief of Naval Personnel, a position that placed him only under the Chief of Naval Operations. He held that post until his retirement in 1986.

Following his retirement, Lawrence occupied the Chair of Naval Leadership at the Naval Academy, wrote on many issues for newspapers, including the *Nashville Banner* and *The Tennessean,* and co-authored a major report on the military and the news media for the Freedom Forum First Amendment Center at Vanderbilt University.

Lawrence lives near Annapolis, Maryland, with his wife, the former Diane Wilcox Rauch.

Rob Simbeck, Nashville

SEE: TENNESSEE STATE SYMBOLS

LAWSON, JAMES E., JR. (1928–) is best known in Tennessee history as the Vanderbilt Divinity School student who was expelled in 1960 over his leadership in the Nashville lunch counter sit-ins. Lawson also helped organize the Student Nonviolent Coordinating Committee (SNCC) in Raleigh, North Carolina, in April 1960, and became one of the organization's key leaders. He later served as a Methodist pastor in Memphis from 1962 to 1974, where he led the sanitation workers' strike that provided the occasion for Martin Luther King, Jr.'s assassination in 1968.

Already an ordained Methodist minister, the 30-year-old Lawson came to Nashville in 1958 to continue his ministry as southern regional director for the Fellowship of Reconciliation and to complete his divinity degree at Vanderbilt. The Fellowship of Reconciliation is an international Christian organization emphasizing pacifism and nonviolence. While in Nashville, he became projects director for the Nashville Christian Leadership Conference, the local affiliate of King's Southern Christian Leadership Conference.

In this role, he began teaching workshops in nonviolence to students from Nashville's four predominantly black institutions of higher education. This led to the organization of the Nashville Student Movement, which initiated the sit-ins that began on February 13, 1960. The sit-ins ended on May 10 with the successful integration of the city's downtown lunch counters.

The Vanderbilt controversy began on March 2 following a *Nashville Banner* report in which Lawson was quoted as saying he would encourage students to "violate the law." Although Lawson denied the remarks, Vanderbilt Chancellor Harvie Branscomb gave him the choice of being expelled or giving up his leadership role in the sit-ins. Lawson accepted expulsion, which was supported by the University's Board of Trust. An ensuing controversy at Vanderbilt lasted for several months. An eventual compromise between the administration and Lawson's faculty supporters gave him the option of completing the remaining courses for his degree elsewhere and transferring them to receive a Vanderbilt degree. Lawson refused the offer, however, and eventually completed his bachelor of sacred theology degree at Boston University's School of Theology. However, he did return to Vanderbilt in 1970–1971 to work on a doctor of ministry degree.

Lawson, who was born September 22, 1928, in Uniontown, Pennsylvania, graduated from Baldwin-Wallace College in Ohio in 1952. When he received a draft notice during the Korean conflict, Lawson, who had become a pacifist after registering for the draft, refused to report for duty. As a result, he was tried and convicted for draft evasion. After serving a 13-month sentence, he was paroled in order to work as a missionary teacher at Hisloe College in Nagpur, India, from 1953 to 1956.

After graduation from Boston University's School of Theology, Lawson served as pastor of Centenary United Methodist Church in Memphis from 1962 to 1974. Here he received a number of civic and community awards, including "Man of the Year" from the Catholic Interracial Council in 1969. After leaving Memphis, he became pastor of Holman United Methodist Church in Los Angeles, where he remained at the time of this writing in 1996. He is married to the former Dorothy Wood, and they have three sons.

David Sumner, Ball State University

SUGGESTED READING: David Sumner, "The Publisher and the Preacher: Racial Conflict at Vanderbilt University," *Tennessee Historical Quarterly* 56(Spring 1997): 34–43

SEE: CIVIL RIGHTS MOVEMENT; SIT-INS, NASHVILLE; MEMPHIS SANITATION STRIKE; STAHLMAN, JAMES G.; VANDERBILT UNIVERSITY

LEA, ALBERT MILLER (1805–1891), Chief Engineer of the State of Tennessee, was born in Knoxville in 1805. Lea learned his engineering skills in the Army. He entered West Point and graduated fifth in a class of 33 in 1831. In 1836 Lea assumed the newly created post of Chief Engineer. His first, and only, report shows that Lea and his staff ran long lines of precise interconnected altitude determination. Such data were essential in planning transportation routes. When the state published Lea's report, it also published a dissenting opinion written by the Assistant Engineer, C.W. Nance. Nance questioned Lea's judgment and skills. Perhaps as a result of the disharmony, the office of State Engineer was not continued.

After his stint as State Engineer, Lea worked for the federal government, determining the boundary between Iowa and Missouri. Next, he became an engineer for the Baltimore and Ohio Railroad, a general in the Iowa militia, and chief clerk for the U.S. War Department. Lea returned to East Tennessee University (now University of Tennessee), where he earned a master's degree in 1844 and joined the faculty as Professor of Mathematics and Natural Philosophy. In 1850 he declined reappointment, but taught for part of 1851 before leaving the university. From 1849 to 1854 Lea served Knoxville as city engineer, perhaps the first city engineer in Tennessee. From 1851 to 1853 he also managed an East Tennessee glass manufacturing business. About 1855 Lea moved to Texas. He served as an engineering officer in the Confederate Army. In 1874 he bought a farm at Corsicana, Texas, where he died in 1891.

Lea's service as city and state engineer demonstrates the public recognition of the need for government-sponsored engineering services. Today, Lea is known chiefly for work done in the 1830s in the Upper Mississippi Valley. He was probably the first to use the name Iowa to designate a portion of the American midwest. The city of Albert Lea, Minnesota, is named in his honor. He is esteemed in Texas and many other states, and in Tennessee he should rank as a major figure in the development of science and technology.

James X. Corgan, Austin Peay State University

SUGGESTED READINGS: James X. Corgan, "Notes on Tennessee's Pioneer Scientists," *Journal of the Tennessee Academy of Science* 53(1978): 2–7; Stanley J. Folmsbee, "East Tennessee University: Pre-war Years, 1840–1861," East Tennessee Historical Society *Publications* 22(1950): 60–93

SEE: SCIENCE AND TECHNOLOGY; UNIVERSITY OF TENNESSEE

LEA, LUKE (1879–1945), a key figure in the reform and prohibition movements, was prominent in Tennessee history during the early twentieth century. A descendant of the pioneer Overton and Cocke families, Lea was the son of Ella Cocke and Overton Lea. He was born and reared at Lealand, the family's 1,000-acre farm on the outskirts of Nashville.

Lea was tutored at home until he entered the University of the South at Sewanee in the spring of 1896. While at Sewanee, he managed the fabled 1899 football team. He received his bachelor's degree in 1899 and his master's in 1900. In 1903 he earned a law degree from Columbia University, where he edited the *Columbia Law Review.*

After graduation, Lea returned to Nashville to practice law. He burst upon the political horizon when he seized the gavel at the chaotic 1906 Democratic state convention and brought the delegates to order. An ardent prohibitionist, he battled to free the state from what he considered the corrupt domination of the liquor interests and railroads. With his crusading spirit, supreme self-confidence, and incredible energy, he made bitter political enemies and staunch friends. Like many men drawn to reform and politics, Lea established a newspaper, *The Nashville Tennessean,* in 1907.

In 1911 a Fusionist coalition of dry Democrats and Republicans elected Lea to the U.S. Senate. There he worked for passage of far-reaching progressive measures. On the state level, he continued to support election law reform and enforcement of temperance legislation. Following the attainment of those goals, he attempted to reunify the splintered Democratic party, but was defeated in the first popular primary held 15 months before the expiration of his term.

When the United States entered World War I, Lea put aside his own aversion to the war and raised and commanded a volunteer regiment. The 114th Field Artillery distinguished itself in France in the battles of St. Mihiel, the Meuse Argonne, and the Woevre Plains.

After the armistice, Lea gained worldwide attention by leading a small group of American soldiers into Holland, where the former German Kaiser had been granted asylum. Lea hoped to persuade the Kaiser to go to Paris and risk being tried for war crimes rather than place the German people under the burden of heavy war reparations, an outcome that Lea correctly foresaw as sowing the seeds for a future world conflict. A washed-out bridge over a branch of the Rhine obstructed Lea's plans, and the Versailles meeting proceeded without the Kaiser.

Lea returned home and played an influential role in the founding of the American Legion. He also resumed active management of his newspaper and leadership of the rural progressive faction of the state Democratic party. His political activities once again placed him in opposition to the Nashville and Memphis machines, especially Edward H. Crump of Memphis, except during brief periods of "armed" truce.

An increasingly strong voice of support for Governor Austin Peay, Lea influenced Tennessee public policy in the 1920s. He strongly supported highway construction, public education, tax revision, and modernization of state government. He advocated the veteran's bonus, taxes on luxuries such as tobacco, unionization of labor, woman suffrage, and the establishment of the Great Smoky Mountains National Park.

During the 1920s, often in alliance with financier Rogers Caldwell, Lea established a publishing empire. He acquired two other city newspapers, the Memphis *Commercial Appeal* and the *Knoxville Journal*. He invested in Nashville real estate, especially in the prestigious residential suburb of Belle Meade. In 1927 he donated the original 868 acres of Percy Warner Park to the city of Nashville, with the request that the park be named for his father-in-law. At the zenith of his financial and political influence, Lea declined an appointment to the U.S. Senate in 1929.

With the onset of the Great Depression, and the spectacular failure of Caldwell and Company in 1930, Lea's political and publishing empires began to crumble. He lost control of the Memphis and Knoxville newspapers. In 1933 the *Nashville Tennessean* was placed in receivership. Creditors foreclosed on many of his large real estate holdings. The General Assembly launched an investigation into the loss of state funds deposited in banks associated with Lea and threatened his ally, Governor Henry Horton, with impeachment. Investigators scrutinized Lea's transactions, but brought no charges.

In Asheville, North Carolina, however, indictments were returned against Lea as a result of the failure of the Central Bank and Trust Company. Certain of his innocence, Lea waived his legal rights and voluntarily traveled to North Carolina to answer the charges. When the trial began, the original indictments were quashed and new ones returned, on which he was forced to stand trial immediately. The

trial took place in a highly charged atmosphere, and Lea was convicted of banking law violations. He appealed the verdict and waged a lengthy, but unsuccessful battle to remain free. While incarcerated in the North Carolina state prison, an independent audit by A.M. Pullen & Co. proved his innocence. He was paroled in 1936, after 23 months in prison, and received a full pardon the following year. He spent the rest of his life involved in public relations work in Washington, D.C.

Lea married Mary Louise Warner in 1906, and they had two sons, Luke Lea, Jr., and Percy Warner Lea. Lea's first wife died in 1919, while he was aboard ship on the return voyage from France after World War I. In 1920 he married Percie Warner, the youngest sister of his first wife. They had three children, Mary Louise, Laura, and Overton.

Mary Louise Tidwell, Nashville

SEE: CALDWELL, ROGERS; CRUMP, EDWARD H.; HORTON, HENRY; KNOXVILLE JOURNAL; MEMPHIS COMMERCIAL APPEAL; NASHVILLE TENNESSEAN; PEAY, AUSTIN; PUBLISHING; TEMPERANCE; WORLD WAR I

LEAGUE OF WOMEN VOTERS OF TENNESSEE was formed prior to the ratification of the Suffrage Amendment when 35 of the required 36 states had ratified the amendment. Tennessee suffragists attended the last national suffrage convention in February 1920 and returned home to Tennessee to organize Tennessee's League as the successor to the state suffrage association. Suffragists saw the League as a broad-based educational and political organization made up of women who were active in both political parties. The state founders envisioned the League as a coalition of women's groups, that would come to the League for education about government issues and work with the League on specific legislative agendas.

The Tennessee suffragists convened the first meeting of the Tennessee League of Women Voters on May 18, 1920, at the State Capitol in Nashville. Throughout the two-day meeting, representatives from each political party encouraged the League to become active in party politics once women gained the vote. Anne Dallas Dudley called for Tennessee to become the thirty-sixth state to ratify the Nineteenth Amendment. When the meeting adjourned, League members began to pressure Governor A.H. Roberts to call a special session of the Tennessee General Assembly to ratify the amendment; the amendment was ratified on August 18, 1920.

After the passage of the amendment, the newly elected officers of the League found it difficult to maintain the momentum that accompanied the suffrage association. The League had more success in gaining support for their legislative program than in electing members to public office. Throughout the

1920s, the League held citizenship schools and pushed for specific legislation to benefit women and children. Although the League earned statewide respect, it could not maintain sufficient membership to pay its national dues. In 1933 the national League withdrew the Tennessee League's affiliation.

The Tennessee League reorganized just three years later, when a number of women with League experience in other states moved to Tennessee as a result of the establishment of the Tennessee Valley Authority. East Tennessee women created a new League in 1936, but the organization gained little support in Middle and West Tennessee. At the first convention of the reorganized League in 1936, the members adopted as their major program item the abolition of the poll tax as a voting prerequisite. The League pressed for a state constitutional convention, which was not held until 1953.

Realizing that they were not represented fairly in the Tennessee General Assembly, League members in Johnson City and Knoxville launched a movement in 1955 that eventually resulted in the favorable *Baker v. Carr* (1962) decision by the U.S. Supreme Court. The Tennessee League of Women Voters remains active on a number of legislative issues statewide.
Carole Stanford Bucy, Volunteer State Community College
SEE: BAKER V.CARR; DUDLEY, ANNE D.; ROBERTS, A.H.; WOMAN SUFFRAGE MOVEMENT

LEE, BRENDA (1944–) was born Brenda Mae Tarpley in Atlanta's Emory University Hospital charity ward on December 11, 1944. By age three, she showed a remarkable ability to memorize and sing songs she had heard only once or twice. At age five, she won first prize in a Conyers, Georgia, singing contest.

In 1953 the death of her father left Brenda, by now a local radio and television star, the principal breadwinner for her mother and three siblings. The Tarpleys moved to Augusta, where Brenda was discovered by Red Foley, the host of ABC-TV's *Ozark Jubilee*. In March 1956, Foley booked the young star for the first of several appearances on the Jubilee. He also brought her to Decca Records in Nashville.

During the next two decades, Brenda Lee had dozens of pop hits on Decca, including *I'm Sorry*, *Rockin' Around the Christmas Tree*, and *Sweet Nothin's*. At four feet, nine inches, Lee became known in the U.S. as "Little Miss Dynamite." Abroad, the idol's small stature gave rise to rumors that she was really a 35-year-old midget.

By the 1970s Lee was recording country music for MCA Records, where the Oak Ridge Boys joined her on one of her recordings. Her recordings for Elektra, Monument, and Epic also made the charts. She recorded duets with Willie Nelson and George Jones. Brenda Lee has sold an estimated 100 million records.

Lee married Charles "Ronnie" Shacklett in 1963.

They live in Nashville. In 1997 she was elected to the Country Music Hall of Fame.
Stacy Harris, Nashville
SEE: COUNTRY MUSIC HALL OF FAME

LEE, GEORGE W.: See BEALE STREET; LINCOLN LEAGUE

LEE UNIVERSITY. On January 1, 1918, 12 students from four states met with Nora Chambers in an upstairs room of the Church of God Publishing House in Cleveland, Tennessee. This first class meeting of the Church of God's Bible Training School (BTS) led to the founding of Lee University. Initially Chambers served as the only faculty member, and the dozen students made up the entire student body. The first two graduates earned their diplomas in April 1919. A correspondence program was initiated in September 1919, which increased the school's overall enrollment to 788 students. During the following decades, BTS enlarged its faculty and curriculum and moved to a campus in Sevierville in 1938.

In 1947 BTS moved back to Cleveland, occupied a recently purchased larger campus, and was named Lee College in honor of Flavius J. Lee, an early leader in the denomination and second president of the school. The college expanded its emphasis to include both biblical studies and traditional liberal arts in a four-year curriculum. In 1959 Lee's Bible College was accredited by the Accrediting Association of Bible Colleges, and in 1960 a junior college was accredited by the Southern Association of Colleges and Schools (SACS). In 1969 SACS granted Lee full accreditation as a four-year liberal arts college. From the 1970s into the early 1990s, Lee experienced tremendous growth, increasing its enrollment to more than 2,600 students, making it one of the largest and fastest growing private colleges in Tennessee. In the 1990s the college added its first graduate program, a Master of Church Music, to its 28 undergraduate majors. In 1996 students from 46 states and 27 foreign countries attended classes on the 60-acre campus in downtown Cleveland.

In 1996 the Lee College Board of Directors resolved to change the school dramatically by launching a plan for the institution that called for reorganization and designation as Lee University. On August 1, 1997, Lee University was formally in place; it included four academic units: a College of Liberal Arts and Sciences, a School of Music, a School of Ministry, and a College of Education. The board left unaffected the mission, institutional goals, policies, and operation procedures of the institution. Thus, Lee University's strong ties to its parent denomination and its commitment to providing a high-quality, affordable education in a Christian context continues to guide the institution's priorities. Lee University has remained coeducational since its founding and, in keeping with its Pentecostal heritage, operates the Pentecostal Research Center, which boasts the most extensive collections available on Pentecostalism. Determined to maintain its more broadly based Christian identity, Lee University identifies itself as "A Campus Where Christ is King."

David Bruce Conn, Berry College

SEE: BRADLEY COUNTY; CHURCH OF GOD; EDUCATION, HIGHER; RELIGION

LEMOYNE OWEN COLLEGE in Memphis opened its doors in 1871 as LeMoyne Normal and Commercial School, but it traces its ancestry to the schools for ex-slaves organized by members of the American Missionary Association (AMA) during and after the Civil War. In 1870 Dr. Francis Julius LeMoyne, a Pennsylvania doctor and abolitionist, whose house had been a stop along the Underground Railway, donated $20,000 to the AMA for a Freedmen's School in Memphis. He instructed that "The institution should be so conducted as to give a good practical and scientific education."

The school opened with fanfare on October 1, 1871, at 284 Orleans, with J.H. Barnum, who had formerly worked with the Freedmen's Bureau, as principal. The demand for black teachers was so great that many students left to take jobs before completing the full four-year course. There were three divisions: the normal school for teachers, a commercial department, and a music department. The first two diplomas were granted in 1876.

The school survived the yellow fever epidemics of the 1870s, when three members of the small faculty died. In 1901 a high school was added to prepare students for the normal school course. In 1914 the school moved to its present location at 804 Walker Avenue, and Steele Hall, which is listed in the National Register of Historic Places, was built. LeMoyne became a junior college in 1924, but the high school division continued until 1934, when the State of Tennessee chartered the school as LeMoyne College, a four- year institution granting the bachelor's degree.

Dr. Hollis Price became the first black president of the college in 1943. He was a founding member of the United Negro College Fund, and the first black moderator of the United Church of Christ, into which the American Missionary Association had been absorbed.

In 1954 the Tennessee Baptist Missionary and Educational Convention opened a junior college on Vance Avenue named for the Reverend Samuel Augustus Owen. Owen was pastor of the Metropolitan Baptist Church adjacent to the LeMoyne campus, and a leader in his denomination and community. Owen Junior College merged with LeMoyne in 1968. The college maintains its ties with the Tennessee Baptist Convention and the United Church of Christ.

The college awarded its first Master of Science degrees in education in the spring of 1994. Today, there are over 1,200 students. Throughout its history, LeMoyne Owen College has educated teachers, doctors, judges, and leaders in the black community. Distinguished alumni include the mayor of Memphis, Dr. W.W. Herenton; author and Duke University professor Dr. C. Eric Lincoln; former president of Morehouse College, Dr. Hugh Gloster; author and Spelman College professor, Dr. Gloria Wade-Gayles; and Benjamin Hooks, former president of the National Association for the Advancement of Colored People.

Perre Magness, Memphis

SEE: EDUCATION, HIGHER; FREEDMEN'S BUREAU; HOOKS, BENJAMIN L.

LENOIR CAR WORKS, located on 93 acres along the Tennessee River in downtown Lenoir City, was once the largest and most important business in Loudon County. The earliest operation was the Bass Foundry and Machine Company, which produced iron railcar wheels; in 1907 the company produced 300 wheels per day. The Lenoir Car Works, a small plant for building and repairing freight cars, was founded in 1904 and purchased by Southern Railway the following year. Soon after, the Bass Foundry became part of the industry. By 1907 the Car Works produced ten to 12 cars per day and employed approximately 500 men.

During World War I, the work force swelled to 2,700 men. The average number of employees varied between 800 and 900 men, and most area families depended on the plant for economic survival. The only major strike occurred in the early 1920s and resulted in the death of one striker and the involvement of the Ku Klux Klan. The local Klan sent threatening notes to non-union "scabs" and burned crosses in their yards.

The complex contained a machine and blacksmith shop, a wood shop, an erecting shop, and a boiler and engine house, topped by an imposing smokestack. The engine house powered the complex and supplied electricity to parts of Lenoir City. In the mid-1920s wooden freight cars were declared unsafe, and orders decreased, although the steel foundry, the iron foundry, and the old brass foundry continued to produce 400–500 wheels per day. During World War II the machine shop was converted to a second steel foundry and produced various castings for ocean-going freighters and other craft.

After World War II diesel engines made the old steam engines obsolete, and the grey iron foundry closed in 1957. Steel and wrought iron wheels replaced iron wheels and led to the closing of the steel foundry in 1963. In 1980 Sarten Metal Reclaiming Company purchased thousands of patterns and molds from the original pattern shop and moved many of them to the Tennessee Valley Railroad Museum in Chattanooga. The last area to close was a newer, more modernized brass foundry, where journal bearings and insulated glued rail joints were produced.

Joe Spence, Lenoir City

SEE: INDUSTRY; KU KLUX KLAN; LOUDON COUNTY; RAIL-ROADS

LENOIR COTTON MILL is one of a series of five mills built by the family of General William Lenoir along Town Creek in what is now Lenoir City. In 1810 Major William Ballard Lenoir, son of Revolutionary War General William B. Lenoir, arrived with his family to occupy a 5,000-acre military grant given to his father. He developed the land, known as Lenoir's Station, into an important commercial and manufacturing community. The first industrial structure on the site was a burr and roller flour mill with a 150-barrel capacity. By 1834 the site included a cotton mill built with slave labor. At one time, the large brick structure was equipped with 1,000 spindles, producing cotton yarn and batting. Cotton fiber to supply the spindles was imported from states in the lower South. Lenoir built his home, which still stands, close to the mills.

When the Civil War arrived in East Tennessee, the mills came to the attention of General Ambrose Burnside. A force of approximately 1,500 men under the command of Colonel W.P. Saunders arrived at Lenoir's Station on June 19, 1863, and burned the general store, the railroad depot, and a quantity of military stores. As they prepared to burn the cotton mill, Dr. Benjamin Ballard Lenoir, the son of the mill's founder and an active Mason, moved among the troops giving a secret Masonic sign. The mill was spared and continued in operation into the late nineteenth century. In the 1890s the Holston Manufacturing Company used the building to house a hosiery mill. The mill was then converted to a flour mill and continued operation until the 1950s. The building eventually became the property of Lenoir City and remained unused for many years.

The building was included in the Historic American Buildings Survey as an early and unique example of industrial architecture, and placed on the National Register of Historic Places in 1976. The building reflected the naive and unpretentious indigenous architecture of the time, which grew out of two contradictory forces, progress and romanticism. Some of the internal structure, particularly the unique placement of brick abutments within the walls to serve as landings for the internal beams, is considered to have been far ahead of its time.

In 1980 the American Studies Class at Lenoir City High School, with support from interested citizens,

formed the Lenoir Cotton Mill Association (LCMA) to preserve and restore the historic building. The organization raised over $100,000 and completed a number of restoration projects before arsonists burned the structure in 1991. In 1996, after the Lenoir City Council rejected a revised plan to rebuild the mill, the LCMA approved a plan to protect the site and preserve the ruins of the building.

Joe Spence, Lenoir City

SEE: INDUSTRY; LOUDON COUNTY; OCCUPATION, CIVIL WAR

LeQUIRE, ALAN (1955–), creator of the monumental *Athena Parthenos* for The Parthenon in Nashville, is one of Tennessee's most accomplished sculptors. He is best known for his public commissions, such as the life-size bronze sculptures at Blair School of Music and near Kirkland Hall at Vanderbilt University. A handsome, heroic bronze of Timothe DeMontbrun, French fur trapper and an early Nashville inhabitant, was completed in 1996 and now stands on the west bank of the Cumberland River. Tennessee's Vietnam Veteran's Memorial, a well-composed grouping of three figures in action is located on War Memorial Plaza in downtown Nashville. In progress are two monuments to the Woman Suffrage Movement. For downtown Knoxville, he is creating a sculptural group featuring life-size portraits of Elizabeth Meriwether (Memphis), Anne Dudley (Nashville), and Lizzie Crozier French (Knoxville) to be installed in a downtown park. In Nashville, a large bronze relief for the State Capitol will commemorate the passage of the Nineteenth Amendment in 1920.

LeQuire is also an accomplished portrait artist whose commissioned pieces are most often portraits of individuals. At times, he also must become a historian. His research on Athena (for which there is no existing model), DeMontbrun, the conflict in Vietnam, and the Woman Suffrage Movement in Tennessee contributed to the interpretation of these historical subjects. LeQuire has stated that by representing the human figure, his pieces must consider humanity and its relationship to the past. The ideas behind the work emerge from what LeQuire perceives as the collective cultural history. The forms themselves reconnect us to the noble figurative tradition in art, which continues unbroken to the present. LeQuire sees the central mystery of sculpture as bringing life to the inanimate and having the viewer recognize in the piece the power of another human soul.

LeQuire was raised in Nashville. His father is retired from the Vanderbilt University School of Medicine, where he served on the faculty as a physician and researcher. His mother is a painter, art teacher, and writer. LeQuire's interest in three-dimensional form early on took precedence over other inclinations. While an undergraduate at Vanderbilt University, he studied independently under professor of sculpture Puryear Mims and Middle Tennessee State University sculptor Jim Gibson. He spent his senior year in France, studied art history, and earned a degree in English. After a year in Rome learning bronze casting as an assistant to New York artist Milton Hebald, LeQuire entered the University of North Carolina at Greensboro, where he earned a Master of Fine Arts degree. He won the commission for *Athena Parthenos* in 1982, was a Tennessee Arts Commission Fellow in 1986, and received a Tennessee Governor's Citation in 1987. In 1990 he was awarded an American Institute of Architects Design Award for *Athena Parthenos*.

Susan W. Knowles, Nashville

SEE: DEMONBREUN, TIMOTHY; PARTHENON

LEWIS COUNTY was established in 1843 from parts of Perry, Hickman, Maury, Lawrence, and Wayne counties and named in honor of Meriwether Lewis, the famed explorer of the Lewis and Clark expedition, who died within the county's boundaries. The first courts were held in the home of John Blackburn on Swan Creek. The first county seat was located there in 1846, and named Gordon, in honor of Powhattan Gordon of nearby Columbia. Two years later the county seat moved to Newburg, a 50-acre tract donated by Hugh B. Venable and Robert O. Smith, which stood on the dividing ridge between Big and Little Swan creeks. Demands for a more central location for the county seat, coupled with the economic decline of Newburg, led officials to move the seat of government to Hohenwald in 1897; the town received its charter in 1923.

Located on the western Highland Rim, Lewis County's thin and flinty soil has not been conducive to agriculture. Corn, wheat, oats, grasses, and especially peanuts constituted the principal crops. The wealth of the county consisted of iron ore deposits, primarily in the southern part of the county. In 1834 Napier & Catron erected Napier Furnace, which produced approximately ten tons of pig iron per day and employed 25 laborers. By 1880 it had ceased operations. The Rockdale Cotton Factory opened in 1825. Producing cotton yarn and employing mostly female workers, the factory operated until late in the Civil War. Other antebellum manufacturing included sawmills, grist mills, and barrel making.

During the Civil War the county furnished three companies for the Confederate army: Company H, 3rd Tennessee Infantry, Company C, 48th Tennessee Infantry, and Company H, 9th Tennessee Cavalry. In all, approximately 400 men served. No battles were fought in the county, but farmers suffered extensive property losses from foragers.

In the late nineteenth century, three groups of German and Swiss immigrants inscribed the area with a unique cultural heritage. German immigrants arrived in 1878 and established the community of Schubert. They were followed in 1885 by Swiss settlers from Milwaukee, whose colony attracted a third settlement a decade later by the Swiss Pioneer Group from Omaha, Nebraska. The Swiss settlers established New Switzerland and Hohenwald (High Forest). The cultural life of Lewis County quickly assumed the flavor of the new immigrants, with music filling the air from the Swiss Singing Society and a band called "Echoes of Switzerland," waltzes at Hohenwald's Society Park, and an annual production of the Wilhelm Tell play. Both the Swiss Reformed and German Reformed Churches conducted services in German. The German and Swiss cultural heritage survived until the anti-German propaganda of two world wars and the forces of Americanization eroded the preservation of folk knowledge and history.

In 1903 the Kurshedt Manufacturing Company of New York established a lace factory in Hohenwald. Employing Swiss labor, the factory produced Hamburg lace for baby clothes. During World War I, the factory was converted to the manufacture of embroidered military uniform emblems, and the plant closed shortly after the war's end.

Lewis County has catapulted into national prominence on at least two occasions. In 1809 Meriwether Lewis died while lodging overnight at Grinder's Inn on the Natchez Trace. The death of Lewis, who was enroute to Washington, D.C., to explain irregularities in his administration of Upper Louisiana, prompted an investigation by his patron and friend, Thomas Jefferson. The death was never satisfactorily explained, and debates continue as to whether the death was a suicide or a murder. Lewis was buried nearby. In 1925 the federal government designated the grave site as a National Monument. Today the Meriwether Lewis National Monument features picnic areas and nature trails, in addition to Lewis's grave and a replica of Grinder's Inn.

On August 10, 1884, a local mob attacked a group of Mormon missionaries and their followers, an episode that was subsequently labeled "The Tennessee Massacre" in Mormon church history. A small Mormon community had lived quietly on Cane Creek until that fateful Sunday morning when a party of masked men descended on the home of James Condor. The intention of the mob has been disputed, but gunfire quickly erupted, resulting in the deaths of four Mormon men and one member of the mob and the wounding of Mrs. Condor. The small Mormon community soon fled the county, some moving to Utah and others settling in nearby counties.

Several small villages have existed in Lewis County. Kimmons once was a large peanut shipping center and railway stop. Allen's Creek, Napier, and Gordonsburg were iron ore and phosphate mining towns. The oldest village was Palestine, which was a voting precinct in Hickman County in 1820. The villages of North Riverside and Hinsontown have survived the reverses of changing economies and population shifts.

Today the citizens of Lewis County enjoy a diverse economic base, an A+ school system, a state vocational school, and opportunities for civic, religious, and recreational activities. Industrial employment is divided among textile, rubber hose, and bootmaking factories. The Natchez Trace Parkway and the Meriwether Lewis National Monument draw tourists to the area and provide recreation for local residents. Local trucking companies, railroads, and an airport provide transportation and shipping.

Marjorie Graves, Hohenwald

SEE: HOHENWALD; MERIWETHER LEWIS NATIONAL MONUMENT; NATCHEZ TRACE

LEWIS, JOHN ROBERT (1940–), civil rights leader and congressman, was born on February 21, 1940, in Troy, Alabama, to Eddie and Willie Mae Carter Lewis. One of ten children reared approximately 50 miles from Montgomery, on a small farm without electricity or plumbing, Lewis attended the public schools of Troy. In 1957, he became the first member of his family to complete high school.

After completing his secondary education, John Lewis entered American Baptist Theological Seminary (now American Baptist College) in Nashville. A year later, he became involved in the workshops on nonviolence directed by the Reverend James Lawson, under the sponsorship of the Nashville Christian Leadership Conference (NCLC). Inspired by the Reverend Martin L. King, Jr., and the Montgomery Bus Boycott (1955), Lewis actively participated in the movement to secure African-American civil rights.

In November and December 1959, John Lewis joined other students in the first unsuccessful attempts by the NCLC to desegregate Nashville lunch counters. On February 13, 1960, he participated in Nashville's first full-scale sit-in. Seven days later, after whites verbally tormented the students at the Walgreen's lunch counter, Lewis formulated the rules of conduct that became the code of behavior for protest movements throughout the South. His participation in workshops at the Highlander Research and Education Center further strengthened his belief in nonviolent direct action.

Like other Nashville students, John Lewis demonstrated against the city's segregated movie theaters. As he did during the sit-ins, Lewis refused to post bail when arrested. In April 1960, he became a found-ing member of the Student Nonviolent Coordinating Committee (SNCC) in Raleigh, North Carolina. A year later, he graduated from American Baptist Theological Seminary and joined the freedom rides. In 1963 he was a principal speaker at the August 28 March on Washington. Delivering one of the most stinging declamations of the day, Lewis predicted, "By the force of our demands, our determination, and our numbers, we shall splinter the segregated South into a thousand pieces and put them back together in the image of God and democracy."[1]

After his graduation from Fisk University in 1963, Lewis served as chairman of SNCC. He resigned in 1966 in protest to the organization's increasing militancy and was replaced by Stokley Carmichael (now Kwame Ture). A leader of the Selma-to-Montgomery Voting Rights marches, Lewis sustained a fractured skull when Alabama law enforcement officials charged the crowd of peaceful protesters during the first march in 1965. From the beginning of his civil rights career in Nashville, Lewis was beaten unconscious four times and arrested at least 40 times during the 1960s.

From 1970 to 1977 Lewis served as director of the Voter Education Project (VEP) of the Southern Regional Council. In 1975 he received the Martin Luther King, Jr., Peace Prize, the highest award given by the Martin Luther King, Jr., Center for Social Change. Eight years later, Lewis was awarded the Martin Luther King, Jr., Award for his contributions to voter education and registration.

In 1982 Lewis won election to the Atlanta City Council and served as councilman-at-large until 1986. In that year he ran as a Democrat and was elected to the U.S. House of Representatives from Georgia's Fifth Congressional District. To date, Lewis has been continuously reelected to his congressional seat.

Linda T. Wynn, Tennessee Historical Commission/Fisk University

CITATION:

(1) Juan Williams, *Eyes on the Prize: American Civil Rights Years, 1954–1965* (New York, 1987), 201.

SUGGESTED READINGS: Clayborne Carson, *In Struggle: SNCC and the Black Awakening of the 1960s* (1981); Linda T. Wynn, "The Dawning of a New Day: The Nashville Sit-Ins, February 13-May 10, 1960," *Tennessee Historical Quarterly* 50(1991): 42–54

SEE: CIVIL RIGHTS MOVEMENT; HIGHLANDER RESEARCH AND EDUCATION CENTER; LAWSON, JAMES; SIT-INS, NASHVILLE

LEWIS, WILIAM B. (1784–1866), an associate and advisor of Andrew Jackson, was born in Virginia, but moved to Nashville in 1809. Little else is known of his earliest years except that he received a good education and developed a strong friendship with Jackson, who appointed him as quartermaster for the

1813 Creek Indian War campaign. In the 1820s Lewis became one of the earliest advocates of Jackson's presidential candidacy and played a crucial role in securing the General's election to the Senate in 1823 and in the 1828 election by answering charges about the candidate's marriage. Once President, Jackson appointed Lewis as Second Auditor of the Treasury and invited him to reside in the White House.

During Jackson's first term, Lewis stood as an important member of the president's "Kitchen Cabinet" and helped promote Martin Van Buren's claims as Jackson's heir apparent. His disagreement with Jackson over the spoils system and the Bank of the United States, however, weakened his influence. Lewis never openly opposed the president, and their friendship remained intact, but he was only a minor figure in Jackson's second administration. He retained his office after Jackson's retirement, but subsequent presidents, including Van Buren, largely ignored him until President James K. Polk, over Jackson's objections, fired him shortly after Polk's inauguration. Lewis then retired to his Davidson County plantation, from whence he provided information to James Parton for use in his biography of Jackson. During the Civil War, Lewis supported the Union, but after his election to the state House of Representatives in 1865, he became part of the Conservative opposition to Governor William G. Brownlow's harsh treatment of former Confederates. He died in 1866.

Jonathan M. Atkins, Berry College

SUGGESTED READING: Louis R. Harlan, "The Public Career of William Berkeley Lewis," *Tennessee Historical Quarterly* 7(1948): 3–37 and 118–51

SEE: BROWNLOW, WILLIAM G.; JACKSON, ANDREW; JACKSONIANS; POLK, JAMES K.

LIBRARIES IN TENNESSEE. Although Tennessee libraries developed slowly from early statehood until the twentieth century, early Tennesseans placed a high value on their collections of books. Given the demands of frontier life and the relatively high cost of books, it is not surprising that early private collections were small. When John Sevier died in 1815, his library contained 35 volumes. In Middle Tennessee, Lardner Clark willed his 47 volumes to the Davidson Academy in 1795. As the state developed, private collections grew accordingly, and dues-paying members established social or subscription libraries well before the Civil War. By 1860 29 independent subscription libraries had been created throughout the state, but only two lasted more than ten years. Colleges and universities also founded libraries early in the state's history. In 1860 most college libraries in Tennessee held no more than 3,000 to 6,000 volumes. By far the largest were the University of Nashville, with 14,000 volumes, and East Tennessee University in Knoxville, with 8,000 volumes. The collections of

the college literary societies often rivaled those of the college libraries.

The Tennessee State Library and Archives was founded in 1854 as the Tennessee State Library; Return Jonathan Meigs served as the first State Librarian. The library had acquired 15,000 books by the time of the Civil War. In 1871 the *Catalogue of the General and Law Library of the State of Tennessee* listed 18,383 volumes. The State Library merged with the State Archives in 1919, with historian John Trotwood Moore serving as the first State Librarian and Archivist. The State Library and Archives occupied space in the State Capitol until the mid-twentieth century, when it moved into the newly constructed State Library and Archives Building. Current collections total well over a million books, periodicals, documents, microforms, photographs, tapes, and nonprint material, and 27 million official documents and 4.8 million manuscripts.

Public and school libraries were virtually nonexistent in Tennessee before the twentieth century. Legislation enacted around the turn of the century provided for the establishment of city libraries, but few cities took advantage of the law. In 1933 only 16 of Tennessee's 95 counties supported public libraries; there were only 25 public libraries in the entire state. Several of these public institutions, like the libraries in Brownsville and Harriman, were built with support from the Carnegie Library building program of industrialist Andrew Carnegie. Two-thirds of the state's population was without public library service. School libraries were equally scarce, as few possessed funds to establish libraries. The existing libraries rarely exceeded a few hundred outdated volumes.

Public library service made dramatic improvement with the coming of the Regional Library System, which began in 1939 at the Watts Bar Dam site in a cooperative project between the Tennessee Valley Authority, the Knoxville Public Library, and the Division of Public Libraries of the State of Tennessee. The project resulted in the establishment of the Fort Loudoun Regional Library. The Regional Library System now consists of the four metropolitan libraries (Chattanooga, Knoxville, Memphis, and Nashville) and the twelve multi-county regions. The multi-county regional libraries promote public library development by acquiring, processing, and distributing materials found in Tennessee's local public libraries, while also operating bookmobile service within their regions. They also provide in-service education for local librarians and library trustees. The multi-county regions and the sites of the regional library centers are the Blue Grass Regional Library, Columbia; Caney Fork, Sparta; Clinch-Powell, Clinton; Forked Deer, Halls; Fort Loudoun, Athens; Highland Rim, Murfreesboro; Nolichucky, Morristown; Reelfoot, Martin; Shiloh, Jackson; Upper

Cumberland, Cookeville; Warioto, Clarksville; and Watauga, Johnson City.

Currently, the state of Tennessee is rich in libraries and the resources and services they offer. School libraries, the most numerous, are found in virtually all public and private schools. Despite recent local and state funding cuts for school libraries, their roles expanded as media and computer centers. In 1996, a special statewide initiative connected all school and public libraries to the Internet.

Colleges and universities account for 40 academic libraries, and two-year colleges and technical schools add another 18. A dozen libraries, mostly associated with universities, hold more than 50 percent of the bookstock in Tennessee libraries. Vanderbilt University holds the largest collection with over two million volumes, followed by the University of Tennessee and the University of Memphis.

Tennessee's special libraries vary in size and purpose. Fifty-eight special libraries serve industry, associations, clubs, foundations, institutes, and societies. Other special libraries include four armed forces libraries, 14 government libraries, 16 law libraries, 36 medical libraries, and 28 libraries of religion. Budgets and holdings of special libraries vary according to size and function, and range from small business and institutional libraries to large scientific libraries, such as those of the Lockheed Martin Energy Systems in Oak Ridge and the Eastman Chemical Company in Kingsport. Most special libraries in Tennessee are found in the metropolitan areas.

In 1996, 125 public libraries and library systems in Tennessee met the Tennessee minimum standards for non-metropolitan public libraries. Library systems in Chattanooga, Knoxville, Memphis, and Nashville include 60 libraries and branches. In recent years, local appropriations for library services in Tennessee exceeded $40 million per annum, or $8 per capita, which ranks nationally in the lowest quartile. State government subsidizes local library service through the Regional Library System. Federal funds administered through the State Library and Archives are used for coordination of statewide activities such as networking and other special projects. Public libraries in Tennessee, including the regional libraries, jointly hold over 10 million items, the largest being the Memphis-Shelby County Public Library and Information Center with over 1.7 million items.

While the holdings of libraries are traditionally given in terms of books, periodicals, and certain non-print materials, many public libraries now turn to computerized systems, not only for processing their materials, but also for storing and locating information. The impact of the Internet and the World Wide Web on library and information services, already substantial, has yet to reach its full potential. Even so, it appears that electronic resources will not replace existing formats so much as supplement them with value-added services.

Edwin S. Gleaves, Tennessee State Library and Archives
SEE: MOORE, JOHN T. AND MARY D.

LIFE AND CASUALTY INSURANCE COMPANY

(L&C) was established by Andrew M. Burton, Guilford Dudley, Sr., Helena Haralson, Dr. J.C. Franklin, and Pat M. Estes in Nashville in 1903. It initially offered industrial (health and accident) insurance to working-class blacks and later concentrated on ordinary life insurance to middle-class whites. Together with the rival National Life and Accident Insurance Company, L&C made Nashville one of the South's leading insurance centers during the twentieth century. In 1963 for instance, financier Sam Fleming described Nashville as "more like Hartford Connecticut than any other city I know. It is hard to meet very many people here before you run into someone connected with an insurance company."[1]

Andrew M. Burton, company president, established and managed the Life and Casualty Insurance Company as a family enterprise even as it expanded its market share throughout the South and later the nation. In 1909 L&C salesmen entered Mississippi, followed by Louisiana in 1911 then Arkansas and South Carolina in 1913. During World War I, in 1918, Life and Casualty established offices in Florida and North Carolina, followed by offices in Kentucky in 1922 and Missouri in 1923.

Due to increased competition from black-founded insurance companies, and the growing popularity of life insurance during the 1920s, L&C began to move away from its earlier reliance on industrial insurance for blacks. In 1927 company officials announced the goal of creating a "Lily White Company," which specialized in ordinary life insurance for white middle-class customers. As part of its new marketing strategy, L&C acquired a radio station, WDAD, in 1926. Through the airwaves, L&C advocated a gospel of thrift, with one 1926 effort aimed at convincing 50,000 children to establish a dollar-a-week savings account. Within two years, the station's name had changed to WLAC and its 5,000-watt signal reached much of the Mid-South. The company's strategic shift in market emphasis worked. In 1938 the company set the goal of reaching $1 billion of insurance in force. It achieved that goal by 1953, three years after Burton's retirement to his Nashville home.

Paul Mountcastle was company president from 1950 to 1952, when he was promoted to chairman of the board. His successor as president was Guilford Dudley, Jr., son of one of the company's founders. Mountcastle and Dudley aggressively expanded L&C's horizons. The company had been among the state's pioneers in radio with its powerful WLAC station. In 1954, to complement the radio station, L&C acquired a television station, WLAC-TV, affiliated with the CBS network. Three years later, Mountcastle and Dudley presided over the grand opening of the splashy L&C Tower, a modernist Nashville skyscraper designed by architect Edwin Keeble that became an instant corporate and city landmark. The 31-story, $7 million structure was the tallest commercial building then in the southeast. As architect Keeble explained in the *Nashville Tennessean* of April 28, 1957, the tower "speaks as pleasantly as possible, with dignity and repose, of its purpose in the service of one of Nashville's greatest institutions." By 1961 L&C had over $2 billion of insurance in force.

The Mountcastle/Dudley years, however, also witnessed sales of company stock to wealthy investors from outside of Tennessee. Texas oilman Clent W. Murchison, later the owner of the Dallas Cowboys, bought $40 million in stock, roughly 24 percent of the company, in 1959. Dudley remained as company president until 1969, when Murchison's American General Group acquired control of the Life and Casualty Company. American General reorganized L&C's Nashville operations as a central headquarters for several of its associated companies in the region. Allan Steele, former general counsel, was named L&C president in 1970, ending the Dudley era as well as L&C's independent influence on the economies of Nashville and Tennessee.
Carroll Van West, Middle Tennessee State University
CITATION:
(1) Don H. Doyle, *Nashville Since the 1920s* (Knoxville, 1985), 129. The Editor-in-Chief also acknowledges Professor Doyle's prior research on this company in his two-volume history of Nashville.
SEE: DUDLEY, ANNE DALLAS; KEEBLE, EDWIN A.; NASHVILLE; NATIONAL LIFE AND ACCIDENT INSURANCE COMPANY; WLAC

LILLARD, ROBERT EMMITT (1907–1991), Nashville councilman, judge, and civil rights activist, was born March 23, 1907, in Nashville, to John W. and Virginia Allen Lillard. He received his education at Immaculate Mother's Academy and in local public schools, before attending Beggins Commercial College. Lillard's longtime ambition was to become a lawyer. In 1932, while working as a city garage attendant, Lillard entered Nashville's Kent College of Law, attending law classes five nights a week. He graduated in 1935 and passed the bar examination the following year.

Lillard worked for Nashville's Fire Engine Company No. 11 and became actively involved in local black politics. In 1932 he organized the 15th Ward Colored Voters and Civic Club. He persuaded local politicians to pay the $2 poll tax for over 100 black men and women in the 15th ward.

In 1951, after receiving a disability pension from the fire department, Lillard entered the predominantly black third district, second ward city councilman race against a white incumbent, Charles Castleman. Castleman had the support of Democratic Mayor Thomas Cummings, and white politicians reportedly offered Lillard money and jobs to withdraw from the election. Lillard responded that he would not be bought out or frightened out; white politicians would have to beat him out. Lillard won the May runoff election and joined Z. Alexander Looby as the first African Americans elected to Nashville's city council since 1911.

Lillard served the city council for 20 years, never missing a regular meeting. He served as chairman of several council committees, including the Public Election Committee. He helped persuade the city to transform Cameron Junior High School into the second high school within the city limits for local blacks and successfully gained an ordinance to desegregate the Parthenon in Centennial Park. Lillard believed that a metropolitan form of government would dilute black voting strength and opposed the plan to consolidate the city and county governments. Before retiring from the Metro City Council in 1971, Lillard became the first African American to serve as Vice Mayor Pro Tem (1967). He made unsuccessful campaigns for vice mayor and councilman-at-large.

Meanwhile, Lillard's political activism and law practice continued to thrive. He gained admission to the federal district court (1955), the U.S. Court of Appeals, the Sixth Circuit Court (1957), and the U.S. Supreme Court (1962). Lillard founded the Tennessee Federation of Democratic Leagues and campaigned for the election of President John F. Kennedy in 1960. He refused the offer to become Nashville's Assistant U.S. Attorney; however, in 1964 and 1967 Lillard was appointed to the Tennessee Board of Pardons and Paroles by two Democratic governors. In March 1978 Governor Ray Blanton appointed Lillard as judge of the First Circuit Court, Tenth Judicial District. On August 31, 1978, Lillard retired from the bench. Lillard died on November 6, 1991, and is buried in Greenwood Cemetery in Nashville.
Linda T. Wynn, Tennessee Historical Commission/Fisk University
Adapted from Bobby L. Lovett and Linda T. Wynn, *Profiles of African Americans in Tennessee* (1996)
SEE: LOOBY, Z. ALEXANDER

LINCOLN COUNTY is located in southern Middle Tennessee, with most of the county in the Central Basin and the remainder on the Highland Rim. The Elk River runs through the county from the northeast to the southwest, dividing the county into two nearly equal parts. The Cherokees and Chickasaws ceded the land that comprises Lincoln County in

1806. Settlers arrived almost immediately, although surveyors and prospective settlers came as early as 1784 to establish boundaries for Revolutionary War land warrants. Some of the first settlers included Drury Abbott; Ezekiel Norris; Joseph Alexander, and Andrew Greer; William and Thomas Edmonson; Robert Farquharson; and James Bright. The county, which contains 570 square miles, was established by an act of the General Assembly in 1809 and named for Revolutionary War hero General Benjamin Lincoln.

Commissioners John Whitaker, Sr., Wright Williams, Eli Garrett, Littleton Duty, and Jesse Woodruff were appointed to purchase 100 acres near the center of the county to establish a county seat. Ezekiel Norris sold the land near the Elk River that became the town of Fayetteville, and the commissioners laid off town lots which were sold in 1810. The first court was held in the home of Brice Garner, the first county clerk. In 1811 the first courthouse was constructed of logs. The present Colonial Revival-styled courthouse was built in 1970 and is the fourth one in the county's history.

The "Town Spring," located on one of the lots, provided most of the town's water until additional springs were discovered five miles south of Fayetteville at Rainy Falls. In 1899 the Fayetteville Gravity Flow Water System, completed at a cost of $37,000, brought fresh water to the town. This unique gravitational flow system excited the interest of engineers from as far away as New York and brought visitors to see the system in operation. Water flowed into a large reservoir located on a hill above Fayetteville at a rate of 225,000 gallons daily. The system provided water for families and mills until the 1920s when Fayetteville's needs surpassed the capacity of the springs.

Lincoln County provided 21 companies of volunteers to the Confederate cause. Although no major battles were fought in Lincoln County, the area suffered severely from troop movements and the bands of armed men who raided, abused, robbed, and murdered defenseless people. Fortunately for the history of Lincoln County, the courthouse was not burned, and the county records were safely hidden by concerned citizens.

A number of small communities and villages dot the countryside. Most of the communities developed around local post offices, schools, churches, or stores. Today, the schools have been consolidated into the county system, many stores have been closed, and most post offices were moved to Fayetteville, but many communities still maintain their sense of pride and history. A few of the larger communities are Blanche, Taft, Coldwater, Dellrose, Elora, Flintville, Kelso, and Mulberry.

From 1875 to 1920 the Lincoln County economy depended on railroads. Petersburg, the county's second largest town, was once a thriving railroad village. Located on the Marshall County line, Petersburg's access to the NC&St.L Railroad made it an important center for trade. It also was home to Morgan School, a well-respected prep school from the late nineteenth to mid-twentieth century.

During the twentieth century, Lincoln County has supported a number of industries. Construction of the Elk Cotton Mills began in 1900, and the plant remained in operation until 1997. The Borden Milk Plant moved to Lincoln County in 1927 and is credited with the area's economic survival during the Great Depression. The plant closed in 1962, and the National Register-listed facility now houses the Lincoln County Museum. Fayetteville had an electric system long before the Tennessee Valley Authority, and even some rural areas had electricity in the 1920s. Nevertheless, the arrival of TVA in 1935 brought enormous change to the lives of most Lincoln County residents. County industries presently include Delmet, Frito Lay, Summa, B & M Wire, Franke, Amana, Beowolf, and Lampi.

From its origins, agriculture has played a vital role in the county's economy. Its rich and varied soils are suitable for a variety of crops, including corn, cotton, hay, tobacco, and Irish and sweet potatoes. In the 1930s and 1940s many local farmers entered the dairy business and supplied milk to Borden and Kraft Milk plants. Lincoln County now ranks among the top beef producers of the state.

Among Lincoln County's most notable citizens is Retired Admiral Frank Kelso, who served as Commander and Chief of Naval Operations during the Persian Gulf War. He, along with less notable Lincoln Countians, including many descendants of early settlers, have made significant contributions to the state.
Jack and June Towry, Fayetteville
SEE: AGRICULTURE; OCCUPATION, CIVIL WAR; TENNESSEE VALLEY AUTHORITY

LINCOLN LEAGUE was founded by Robert R. Church, Jr., on February 12, 1916, in Memphis and named for Republican President Abraham Lincoln. Church, whose father had been one of the first black millionaires in the South, wanted white Republicans representing the national office to recognize and appreciate the support African-American voters made to the party. Since the 1870s black Memphians had been actively involved in city and state politics, but their participation did not produce solid political patronage. Recognizing the potential influence of black voters, Church organized several black business and professional men to form the League. T.H. Hayes, J.B. Martin, Levoy McCoy, J.B. Martin, Bert M. Roddy, and J.T. Settle were among the first to back the organization. From the beginning, the League had an impact on Republican politics in West Tennessee.

Mass meetings were held in the black-owned Church Park Auditorium, on Beale Street, where members rallied against racism and violence. The League organized clubs in black wards, collected money to pay the poll taxes of poor blacks, established night schools to educate African Americans about voting, and nominated candidates for state and national political offices. In August 1916 close to 1,600 African Americans from Hardeman, Tipton, and Fayette counties joined with the Memphis-Shelby County contingent to nominate candidates for the November elections. The League quickly earned the national Republican Party's attention. Church became a key politician for the party in the South and helped organize a Lincoln League of America. The Lincoln League made an important contribution to the modern civil rights movement by promoting African-American racial solidarity.

Gerald L. Smith, University of Kentucky

SUGGESTED READINGS: Lester C. Lamon, *Black Tennesseans 1900–1930* (1977); David M. Tucker, *Lieutenant Lee of Beale Street* (1971)

SEE: BEALE STREET; CHURCH, ROBERT R., JR.; CHURCH, ROBERT R., SR; RODDY, BERT M.

LINCOLN MEMORIAL UNIVERSITY. In 1897 the Reverend Arthur A. Myers, his wife Ellen, and General O.O. Howard founded a mountain school that expanded to become an accredited four-year institution, Lincoln Memorial University. Supported by the American Missionary Association, the Reverend and Mrs. Myers arrived in Cumberland Gap, Tennessee, in 1888. They began construction of a Congregational Church and school just as New South economic development collapsed in the area surrounding the Gap. Soon after they moved their Harrow School into one of the bankrupt hotels in Cumberland Gap. In 1895, hearing that the "Christian General" and former head of the Freedmen's Bureau, O.O. Howard, would speak in Chattanooga, Myers arranged for Howard to speak at Harrow School's commencement. Following the ceremony, Myers took the general to the site of another postwar bankruptcy and impressed the visitor with his dream of a larger school on a 600-acre former plantation. As Howard recalled his last conversation with Abraham Lincoln and the President's desire to reward East Tennessee mountaineers for their support of the Union, he vowed to make the school a living memorial to the slain president. School brochures reflected Howard's desire "to pay our country's debt to these Highlanders of America by educating the children of the G.A.R. on slave soil." The school offered a broad range of studies, from classical Greek and Latin to medicine and farm management.

Donations of Civil War and Lincoln memorabilia by General Howard and his friends form the core of artifacts and books housed today in the Abraham Lincoln Museum. The museum sponsors exhibits and symposiums, and hosts visiting scholars and researchers from around the world. The modern, private, independent, non-sectarian campus, in a rural setting, welcomes students from many states and foreign countries who receive a liberal arts education. New classroom buildings, a large athletic arena, the library and resource center, an auditorium, and dormitories now occupy the campus. Among its 10,000 alumni are 3,000 Japanese students. The university is also the home of the J. Frank White Academy, a selective, private, college preparatory school for grades 7 through 12. The television station and computer science department connect Lincoln Memorial University to a world undreamed by Reverend Myers and General Howard in 1897. A spirit of cooperation infuses today's students with the same enthusiasm and dedication as the students of the nineteenth century experienced when they first joined the blue and gray at Lincoln Memorial University.

Rebecca Vial, Great Smoky Mountains National Park

SEE: CLAIBORNE COUNTY; EDUCATION, HIGHER; GRAND ARMY OF THE REPUBLIC

LIND, SAMUEL COLVILLE (1879–1965). Called the father of radiation chemistry in America, Samuel Lind was born in McMinnville, Tennessee, in 1879, the son of a Swedish immigrant and Union Army veteran, who practiced law in McMinnville. He studied classics at Washington and Lee University until his senior year, when a chemistry professor awakened Lind's interest in the subject. After graduate studies at the Massachusetts Institute of Technology, Lind earned his Ph.D. in 1905 at the University of Leipzig in Germany.

Lind taught chemistry at the University of Michigan until 1910, when he took sabbatical to study radioactivity with Madame Marie Curie in Paris and with Victor Hess, the discoverer of cosmic rays, in Vienna. After returning to America, Lind worked with the Bureau of Mines at Denver, Colorado, separating radium, then a precious metal, from carnotite, and in 1923 he became chief chemist for the Bureau of Mines. From 1926 to 1947 he taught at the University of Minnesota, becoming dean of its institute of technology.

Upon retiring from academic life, he joined Union Carbide in Oak Ridge as consultant for research in experimental radiation chemistry of gases, performing most of his work at Oak Ridge National Laboratory and serving as acting director of its Chemistry Division from 1951 to 1954. He edited the *Journal of Physical Chemistry,* published classic studies of radiation chemistry, and earned many honors. During the 1950s, he was the sole member of the National Academy of Sciences living in Tennessee. Although physically contaminated by radium, it had no apparent effects on his health. An avid fisherman, he lost his life in 1965 at age 86, while fishing in the fast waters of the Clinch River at Oak Ridge.

Leland R. Johnson, Clio Research Institute

SUGGESTED READINGS: Ellison H. Taylor, "Samuel Colville Lind," *Journal of Physical Chemistry* 63(1959): 773–776; "The Memoirs of Samuel Colville Lind," *Journal of the Tennessee Academy of Science* 47(January 1972): 1–40

SEE: OAK RIDGE NATIONAL LABORATORY; SCIENCE AND TECHNOLOGY; WARREN COUNTY

LINDSLEY, JOHN BERRIEN (1822–1897), educator, physician, Presbyterian minister, author, and civic leader, was born in Princeton, New Jersey, and came to Tennessee with his family at the age of two, when his father, Philip Lindsley, accepted the presidency of the University of Nashville. He was educated at the University of Nashville and at the medical school of the University of Pennsylvania, where he received his M.D. degree in 1843. In 1846 Lindsley was ordained as an evangelist in the First Presbyterian Church and appointed to a pastorate at the Smyrna Church in Rutherford County. The next year he began preaching as a domestic missionary, ministering to the poor and the slaves.

In 1850 Lindsley helped to make one of his father's fondest hopes a reality, by participating in the establishment of the Medical Department of the University of Nashville, which he served as its first dean and professor of chemistry and pharmacy. In 1851 he was elected to the American Medical Association and to the Board of Trustees for the common schools of South Nashville, serving as chair of its first meeting.

All but the Medical Department of the University of Nashville suspended operations in 1850, due to the city's cholera epidemic and the resignation of President Philip Lindsley. In 1855 John Berrien Lindsley was elected chancellor of the university and given the charge to revitalize its Literary Department (liberal arts program). While the father was a man of impressive scholarship and discipline, the son was a man of prodigious energy and versatility. He completed negotiations for the merger of the Western Military Institute and the University of Nashville. He undertook an ambitious program for the renovation of the curriculum and buildings of the university. Throughout the Civil War, Lindsley served as post surgeon of Nashville hospitals and alone protected the library and laboratory of the University of Nashville from the occupying army. In 1857 he married Sarah McGavock, daughter of Jacob McGavock and granddaughter of Felix Grundy.

In 1866 Lindsley was appointed Superintendent of Nashville Public Schools. The following year, he arranged for the establishment of Montgomery Bell Academy, and petitioned the Peabody Education Fund to appropriate funds for a normal school (teachers' college) at the university. In 1870, discouraged by the university's inability to recover from the decline caused by the Civil War, Lindsley resigned as chancellor and helped in organizing the Tennessee College of Pharmacy.

During the last two decades of his life, Lindsley's efforts on behalf of public education, public health, and prison reform claimed most of his attention. He served at various times as president of the Tennessee State Teachers' Association, Health Officer of the City of Nashville, a director in the National Prison Association, treasurer of the American Public Health Association, and Executive Secretary of the Tennessee State Board of Health, and he guided the city through the 1878 outbreak of yellow fever. He wrote widely circulated pamphlets: *On Prison Discipline and Penal Legislation, Practitioners of Medicine as Men of Science, Public Health Movement, On the Cremation of Garbage,* and *Popular Progress in State Medicine.* In 1886 he edited and published the monumental *Military Annals of Tennessee. Confederate.* Lindsley was a founder of the Tennessee Historical Society and the American Association for the Advancement of Science, a charter member of the American Chemical Society, a fellow of the American Academy of Medicine, and a fellow of the Historical Society of London and of the American Historical Society. He died in 1897.

Sara Harwell, Vanderbilt University

SUGGESTED READING: John E. Windrow, *John Berrien Lindsley: Educator, Physician, Social Philosopher* (1938)

SEE: GEORGE PEABODY COLLEGE OF VANDERBILT UNIVERSITY; LINDSLEY, PHILIP; MEDICINE; MONTGOMERY BELL ACADEMY; TENNESSEE HISTORICAL SOCIETY

LINDSLEY, LOUISE GRUNDY (1858–1944), Regent of the Ladies' Hermitage Association and woman suffragist, was born in Nashville on March 12, 1858, the daughter of John Berrien and Sallie McGavock Lindsley. She grew up in Nashville and graduated from the State Normal College in 1879. In 1889 she was recruited by her mother to sign the charter for the Ladies' Hermitage Association, when a legal opinion issued on the charter stated that the signatures of unmarried women were needed. During her mother's tenure as Regent of the Ladies' Hermitage Association, Louise Lindsley designed the organization's badge, a wreath of green hickory leaves with "LHA" in white enamel.

After her mother's death in 1903, Lindsley took a more visible role in Nashville civic affairs and became Regent of the Ladies' Hermitage Association in 1912. During her term as Regent, the association purchased the remainder of the acreage of Andrew Jackson's property from the state and continued renovations on the house itself. She provided national visibility and awareness of The Hermitage by speaking to visiting conventions in Nashville.

While performing these duties, Lindsley addressed the Southern Commercial Congress at the Ryman Auditorium. The president of the Congress, a national organization in the New South tradition of commercial promotion, recruited Lindsley for the Women's Auxiliary of the Congress to organize the Tennessee Women's Division. She called together women from across the state, who were active in other voluntary associations, to work together to promote the goals of the Congress and to educate rural women. One of the highlights of her work with the Congress was a trip in 1914 to Panama where she walked in the Canal prior to its opening. By 1915 she was national president of the Women's Auxiliary to the Southern Commercial Congress. The auxiliary focused on vocational education for women and sought to empower rural women to improve local communities in such areas as schools, roads, and public health.

When the United Stated entered World War I in 1917, Lindsley presided over the initial meeting of the Tennessee Division of the Woman's Committee of the Council of National Defense and was appointed by the National Bureau of Speakers as speaker for the South. Her work in support of the war effort led to her appointment as organizing chair of the Nashville Housewives' League, a local branch of a national organization supporting the war effort by making housekeeping more efficient and scientific.

An active member of the Tennessee Equal Suffrage Association, Lindsley was 62 years old when the Nineteenth Amendment to the U.S. Constitution was passed giving all American women the right to vote. Throughout her life, she continued her involvement in various local women's groups and served in a variety of leadership positions in the Thomas Jefferson Memorial Association, the United States Good Road Association, the Daughters of the American Revolution, the Daughters of 1812, and the Centennial Club. Lindsley died in July 1944 in Nashville. She is buried in the McGavock-Lindsley family plot of Mt. Olivet Cemetery.

Carole Stanford Bucy, Volunteer State Community College
SUGGESTED READING: Carole Stanford Bucy, "Quiet Revolutionaries: The Grundy Women and the Beginnings of Women's Volunteer Associations in Tennessee," *Tennessee Historical Quarterly* 54(1995): 40–53

SEE: LADIES' HERMITAGE ASSOCIATION; LINDSLEY, JOHN B.; LINDSLEY, SARAH M.; WOMAN SUFFRAGE MOVEMENT; WORLD WAR I

LINDSLEY, PHILIP (1786–1855), educator, Presbyterian minister, and classical scholar, was born in Basking Ridge, New Jersey. He was educated at private

academies and at the College of New Jersey (now Princeton University) and joined the faculty as Latin and Greek tutor in 1808. In 1813 Lindsley was made Professor of Languages, Librarian, Inspector (Dean), and Secretary of the Board of Trustees. The same year he married Margaret Elizabeth Lawrence, daughter of Nathaniel Lawrence, the Attorney General of the State of New York.

By the time he was elected vice-president of the College of New Jersey in 1817, Lindsley was recognized as one of the foremost classical scholars in the United States. In 1822 he was made acting president of Princeton. The next year he was offered the permanent presidency not only of Princeton, but also of several colleges and universities, including the struggling Cumberland College in Nashville, but he declined them all. In 1824, he changed his mind and accepted the position in Nashville. The next year, at Lindsley's instigation, the college's name was changed to University of Nashville.

The institution's new name was an indication of Lindsley's aspirations. He wished to create a center of learning and civilization in the midst of a region, the old Southwest, that was barely out of its frontier phase. It was Lindsley who first suggested that Nashville be the "Athens of the Southwest," a sobriquet changed to "Athens of the South" 70 years later at the celebration of the Tennessee centennial. In his effort to develop the university into a nationally-prominent institution of learning, Lindsley brought some of the most eminent scholars of the day to teach classics, languages, mathematics, and geology, among other subjects. Early in his administration, he unveiled an ambitious plan for the implementation of many new academic programs, so that the university might truly live up to its name by encompassing the "universe of learning," with appropriate colleges for each division of knowledge.

In many areas of endeavor and thought, Lindsley was ahead of his time. His attitude toward education reflected his forward-looking philosophy. He was among the first academics to urge the formal training of teachers in special colleges, then called normal schools. He was also an early advocate for education of all citizens. In a pamphlet he wrote during the 1830s, entitled *A Lecture on Popular Education*, he urged that school children receive a well-rounded education in Greek, Latin, arithmetic, algebra, geometry, geography, and English. As much as any one man, Lindsley can be credited with bringing an appreciation for learning to the old Southwest, helping to raise the standards of education in the region. He planted the seeds; his influence was enduring.

In 1850, after Nashville's cholera epidemic decimated the ranks of students, the university suspended operation, and Lindsley resigned as president. Four years after his first wife had died in

1845, he married Mary Ann Myers, widow of Elias Myers, the founder of New Albany Theological Seminary. Lindsley moved with his wife to New Albany and became professor of Ecclesiastical Polity and Biblical Archaeology at the seminary. His son, John Berrien Lindsley, became chancellor of the University of Nashville when it was revived in 1855. Philip Lindsley died that year while visiting Nashville as Commissioner to the General Assembly of the Presbyterian Church.

Sara Harwell, Vanderbilt University

SUGGESTED READING: John F. Woolverton, "Philip Lindsley and the Cause of Education in the Old Southwest," *Tennessee Historical Quarterly* 19(1960): 3–22

SEE: EDUCATION, HIGHER; LINDSLEY, JOHN B.

LINDSLEY, SARAH "SALLIE" McGAVOCK (1830–1903), Regent of the Ladies' Hermitage Association, was born in Nashville, Tennessee, on July 19, 1830, the daughter of Jacob and Louisa Grundy McGavock. She married John Berrien Lindsley, the founder of the medical school of the University of Nashville, in 1857. Although Sallie Lindsley's brother, Randal McGavock, former Mayor of Nashville, enlisted in the Confederate army and was killed at the Battle of Raymond, Mississippi, in 1863, her husband was opposed to secession and kept the medical school open throughout the war. The Union army ultimately occupied the grounds of the Lindsley home, but it was not destroyed in the Battle of Nashville in 1864.

Lindsley worked in various voluntary organizations in Nashville and was a charter member of the United Daughters of the Confederacy when it was organized in Nashville in 1894. Mary C. Dorris appointed her to a committee of women to write a charter for a new women's organization similar to the Mount Vernon Ladies' Association that would preserve The Hermitage, the historic home of President Andrew Jackson. The Hermitage was being used as the Confederate Soldiers' Home and Lindsley was serving as president of the Ladies Auxiliary of the home. After the charter was drafted, Lindsley worked to convince the General Assembly to deed The Hermitage and 25 acres surrounding it to the Ladies' Hermitage Association and personally lobbied individual members who expressed opposition to the plan. Lindsley died July 5, 1903, during her term as regent of the Ladies' Hermitage Association. She is buried in the McGavock-Lindsley family plot at Mt. Olivet Cemetery.

Carole Stanford Bucy, Volunteer State Community College

SUGGESTED READING: Carole Stanford Bucy, "Quiet Revolutionaries: The Grundy Women and the Beginnings of Women's Volunteer Associations in Tennessee," *Tennessee Historical Quarterly* 54(1995): 40–53

SEE: CONFEDERATE SOLDIERS' HOME; DORRIS, MARY C.; HERMITAGE; LADIES' HERMITAGE ASSOCIATION; LINDSLEY, JOHN BERRIEN; LINDSLEY, LOUISE GRUNDY

LIPSCOMB, DAVID (1831–1917), second generation Stone-Campbell Movement leader, was born in Franklin County, Tennessee. Educated at Franklin College in Nashville, he matriculated between 1846 and 1849. Tolbert Fanning baptized Lipscomb while he was a student at the college, and he spent the remainder of his life within the Disciples of Christ and a seceding fellowship, the Churches of Christ. He married Margaret Zellner of Maury County in 1862. They had one son, Zellner, who died at age nine months.

Lipscomb's early training did not suggest that he would spend his life preaching and editing a religious magazine. The disruption of the Nashville Christian Church by Jesse Ferguson, who advocated a form of universalism, during Lipscomb's student years at Franklin College convinced him to do what he could to advance the Christian religion. The Civil War also had an impact on his life. When the conflict divided families and churches, Lipscomb embraced a pacifist view on war and a separatist position toward Christian participation in government. After the war, he edited the *Gospel Advocate*, a journal that became the leading voice of southern Disciples of Christ (after 1906, Churches of Christ). He remained in the position for 47 years. Because of his opposition to missionary societies, the use of instrumental music in worship, and higher criticism, Lipscomb reluctantly led the Churches of Christ out of the larger Disciples of Christ. The religious census of 1906 recognized Churches of Christ as a separate religious fellowship.

Prior to the Civil War, Lipscomb became interested in education. He encouraged education through the pages of the *Gospel Advocate* and helped establish the Fanning Orphan School in 1884. His most important educational endeavor, however, was the 1891 establishment, with James A. Harding, of the Nashville Bible School, later David Lipscomb College (now Lipscomb University). Lipscomb never became president of either school, but served as chairman of the board of trustees of both institutions.

Besides editing the *Gospel Advocate*, Lipscomb wrote *Civil Government, Biography and Sermons of Jesse Sewell*, and several commentaries on New Testament books. Articles, along with questions and answers, have been compiled into other volumes.

During the national bicentennial of 1976, the *Nashville Banner* polled members of the Tennessee Historical Society to ascertain the ten most outstanding Tennesseans in American history. David Lipscomb finished in fourteenth position, higher than any other religious and educational leader in Tennessee's history.

Robert E. Hooper, Lipscomb University

SUGGESTED READING: Robert E. Hooper, *Crying in the Wilderness: A Biography of David Lipscomb* (1979)

SEE: CHURCHES OF CHRIST; FANNING, TOLBERT; LIPSCOMB UNIVERSITY; RELIGION

LIPSCOMB UNIVERSITY was established as the Nashville Bible School on October 5, 1891, by David Lipscomb and James A. Harding. Lipscomb and Harding believed there was a need for a school which would prepare students completely through high quality studies in general subjects as part of a Bible-centered curriculum. Lipscomb, who was editor of the *Gospel Advocate,* stated the school's purpose: "to teach the Bible as the revealed will of God to man and as the only and sufficient rule of faith and practice, and to train those who attend in a pure Bible Christianity . . . Such other branches of learning may be added as will aid in the understanding and teaching of the Scriptures and as will promote usefulness and good citizenship among men."[1]

Nine boys enrolled for the first session. In 1997, Lipscomb University includes the Campus School, which enrolls 1,551 in grades K-12, and 2,552 students in bachelor's and master's degree programs. More than 100 major programs of study are offered in 17 academic departments leading to bachelor degrees, with master's degrees available in Bible and education. In keeping with the original purpose of the school, students attend Bible class and chapel daily.

The school moved to its first "owned" campus in 1893, when property was purchased near the city reservoir on South Spruce Street, about halfway between sites known then as Fort Negley and Fort Morton. By 1903 the school had outgrown these facilities. Lipscomb gave his farm to the school, where Lipscomb University stands today, between Nashville's Lealand Lane and Belmont Boulevard.

For the school's first ten years, Harding taught classes and served as superintendent. Twelve men have served as superintendent, or president, in 16 administrations, including Harding and current president Stephen F. Flatt.

Lipscomb was chairman of the Board of Trustees and taught classes until age 82. Four years later, in 1917, Lipscomb died. The school was renamed David Lipscomb College the following year in his honor.

The Lipscomb Expansion Program (LEP) began in 1944 to raise money and add facilities. A.C. Pullias was named director of the LEP, and Willard Collins was associate director. Pullias and Collins became president and vice president, respectively, in 1946. Pullias set the school on course to graduate its first senior college class in 1948. Six years later, the Southern Association of Colleges and Schools accredited the school for the first time. Collins succeeded Pullias in 1977.

The Collins years marked a return to the vigor experienced in the LEP's early years. A gymnasium and athletics complex were added for the high school; a new women's residence hall and the first major classroom building since the 1960s were built for the college. Enrollments reached record highs. Bible study remained as the core of the curriculum, and Lipscomb's first graduate work in Bible studies was offered in 1983.

Harold Hazelip became president in 1986. Improvements in the graduate program resulted in Level III accreditation of Lipscomb by the Southern Association. In February 1988 the board of directors voted to advance Lipscomb to university status. Two major buildings and a campus-wide fiber-optic network were constructed. Connections to the network are available in every dormitory room, faculty office, and classroom. Resources associated with the network make Lipscomb one of the most technologically advanced institutions, from middle school through university, in the South. *U.S. News and World Report* and *Peterson's Competitive Colleges* recently have honored Lipscomb for its quality and affordability.

Lipscomb University is committed to offering its students a twenty-first century education as it retains its commitment to presenting that education within its unique philosophy of the highest quality academic subjects combined with daily Bible study. This combination has prepared young people well for successful living for more than a century.

G. David England, Lipscomb University

CITATION:

(1) *1996–97 Lipscomb University Undergraduate Studies Catalog,* p. 7.

SEE: CHURCHES OF CHRIST; EDUCATION, HIGHER; LIPSCOMB, DAVID

LITERARY CLUBS. Before the Civil War, voluntary associations of women existed in Knoxville, Memphis, and Nashville as well as some rural areas. Most groups organized through local religious institutions to provide charitable services to the needy. With the establishment of these early groups, women also began meeting informally to share information and discuss books. The Ingleside Club of Memphis held its first meeting on March 4, 1837. This early example of a women's literary club purchased books and distributed them among the members.

One of the effects of post-Civil War urban growth was an increase of educated women with leisure time. These women gathered in their homes to exchange books and discuss academic topics. Although these early literary clubs were often short-lived and lacked continuity, they established an organizational pattern that became widespread in Tennessee in the 1890s. Literary clubs generally limited membership and confined activities to the study of literature and other academic subjects. Meetings followed a set agenda centered on a formal presentation by a club member and group discussion. Some literary clubs expanded their focus to current events and local community problems, eventually evolving into the broader realm of women's clubs.

The Thackery Book Club organized in Memphis in 1876. Like the earlier Ingleside Club, this organization limited its membership, purchased books, and rotated them among the members. The Women's Club of Memphis traces its origins to 1892, when members of the Nineteenth Century Club established an organization for cultural and literary discussion.

When the Ossoli Circle was founded in Knoxville in 1885, its members studied authors and presented papers at club meetings. Although it had its origins as a literary club, Ossoli Circle is regarded as Tennessee's first women's club and became active in the advocacy of a number of women's issues, including woman suffrage.

Between 1885 and 1898, Nashville women established three literary clubs, with membership limited by marital status and religious views. In 1885 the Query Club was founded for unmarried women who wanted to continue their education. Seven years later, a similar club, the Review Club, emerged for married women. In 1898 Nashville's Jewish women established the Magazine Circle.

Six women who exchanged books established Kosmos, Chattanooga's first women's literary club. When the Tennessee Federation of Women's Clubs was established in 1896, many of these literary clubs joined. Literary clubs continued throughout the twentieth century, and bookstores report a recent upsurge in literary societies and clubs.

Carole Stanford Bucy, Volunteer State Community College
SEE: NINETEENTH CENTURY CLUB; OSSOLI CIRCLE; TENNESSEE FEDERATION OF WOMEN'S CLUBS

LITERATURE. Where does Tennessee literature begin? With the poems and stories composed and handed down orally by the Native Americans long before the white explorers and settlers came? With the accounts of the Spanish expeditions of Hernando de Soto and Juan Pardo? If one limits consideration to material written in English, then the literature of Tennessee perhaps begins with the accounts written by early travelers, especially those chronicling their journeys between Nashville and Knoxville as they passed through the "wilderness," the land controlled by the Native Americans as late as 1838. Among them were the Methodist Bishop Francis Asbury; Andre Michaux, the French botanist; Louis Philippe, Duke of Orleans and future King of France; and the Moravian missionaries Abraham Steiner and Frederick Schweinitz—all of whom left a record of their journeys made between 1795 and 1802.

The first fictional journey from Nashville to Knoxville is accomplished in the first novel set in Tennessee, Anne Newport Royall's *The Tennessean; A Novel, Founded on Facts* (New Haven, 1827). The melodramatic plot places the action in such cities as Boston, New York, Philadelphia, New Orleans, and even Mexico City, but there are scenes in Tennessee, usually in Nashville or the nearby Rutherford County. At one point the narrator, Charles Burlington, and others make a three-day journey on horseback through the wilderness from Nashville to Knoxville, where the narrator catches the stage for Philadelphia.

The Tennessean was written by an outsider and published in New England. It remained for Charles W. Todd, a man about whom little is known, to write the first novel by a Tennessean, the first to be published in Tennessee: *Woodville; or, The Anchoret Reclaimed. A Descriptive Tale* (Knoxville, 1832). Much of the setting is in the mountains of an unnamed Southern state, presumably Tennessee, and some of the action takes place at "the —— Springs," presumably based on Montvale Springs, a popular resort south of Maryville.

The novels by Royall and Todd could not hope to rival in popularity or longevity a book published in 1834, the *Narrative of the Life of David Crockett*. Of all the books to which Crockett's name was attached, this appears to have been the only one to which he contributed in any way. Almost equally famous were the *Crockett Almanacs*, which appeared for years after Crockett's death at the Alamo in 1836.

Excerpts from the Crockett almanacs frequently appear in national anthologies of humor and of American literature, and the same may be said for the work of George Washington Harris, a Southern frontier humorist who lived in Knoxville for a number of years before the Civil War. Harris created a rustic central character from the copper mining section of southeastern Tennessee, Sut Lovingood, who appears in story after story, recounting his latest adventures to his city friend George. The first Sut story, "Sut Lovingood's Daddy 'Acting Horse,'" appeared in New York's *Spirit of the Times* in 1854, and numerous others appeared over the years, frequently in Tennessee newspapers. They were later collected in *Sut Lovingood. Yarns Spun by a "Nat'ral Born Durn'd Fool"* (New York, 1867), a classic of nineteenth century Southern humor. Despite the difficulty of Sut's dialect (the spelling of almost every word is changed to reflect its pronunciation), the seeming delight in cruelty and pain, and the male-oriented humor, the Sut Lovingood stories are more likely to appear in a college anthology of American literature than anything else written in Tennessee before the twentieth century.

The years following the Civil War saw the rise of the local color movement in American fiction. In New England, in the West, and in the deeper South, writers such as Sarah Orne Jewett, Bret Harte, and George Washington Cable devoted themselves to depicting the scenery, customs, the ways of speaking, thinking, and acting of those who lived there. Tennessee was not to be left behind. Although most attention was paid to Mary Noailles Murfree, who wrote under the masculine pseudonym Charles Egbert Craddock, there were at least three other women who wrote about the Tennessee mountains in short stories and novels published in the North.

Murfree's best book was her first, a collection of stories previously published in the *Atlantic Monthly* called *In the Tennessee Mountains* (Boston, 1884), which she followed up with her best mountain novel, *The Prophet of the Great Smoky Mountains* (Boston, 1885). Unquestionably Murfree put the Tennessee mountains (she depicted both the Cumberlands and the Great Smokies) on the literary map. Much admired in her own time, Murfree was later rejected as an outside interpreter and creator of stereotypes of people she did not really understand. It was, of course, hard for a Philadelphia-educated Episcopalian from Murfreesboro to identify completely with the mountaineers, and her summers at Beersheba Springs and Montvale Springs were less than ideal circumstances for learning about the people she described for her readers. Nevertheless, Murfree does present some rather admirable women characters, such as Cynthia Ware of "Drifting Down Lost Creek," the first story in the collection.

Less well-known than Murfree's was the work of Will Allen Dromgoole and Sarah Barnwell Elliott, who also wrote of the Tennessee mountains and mountaineers. A fourth woman, Sherwood Bonner, though not a Tennessean, wrote of the Cumberland Mountains in a series of stories for *Harper's Weekly.* These were collected in *Dialect Tales* (1883).

Mention should also be made of an Englishwoman of the same time period, Frances Hodgson Burnett, best-known for her novels *Little Lord Fauntleroy* (1896) and *The Secret Garden* (1911). Burnett lived first in New Market and later in Knoxville (1869–1873) and wrote several stories and novels making use of Tennessee settings.

If the nineteenth century women local colorists were "outsiders", the first "insider" to write seems to have been Emma Bell Miles of Walden's Ridge and Chattanooga whose book *The Spirit of the Mountains* appeared in 1905. A non-fiction work, it describes in some detail such cultural elements as education, religion, superstition, and music as they were to be found in the mountains she knew.

Of course, not all of Tennessee literature concerned itself with the mountains or came out of East Tennessee. By the early 1920s a group of writers associated with Nashville's Vanderbilt University began to take center stage in the state's literature. Under the leadership of such men as John Crowe Ransom, a group of professors and students gathered to discuss literature and philosophy and to read their works to each other. Beginning in 1922, they published a "little magazine" called *The Fugitive,* and the name came to be applied to the group, which included Ransom, Donald Davidson, Allen Tate, Robert Penn Warren, and Walter Clyde Curry. The one female Fugitive was Laura Riding; another closely connected with the group, though an important novelist in her own right, was Caroline Gordon, who married Allen Tate in 1924.

The last issue of *The Fugitive* appeared in December 1925. At Vanderbilt the old Fugitive group was replaced by the Agrarians, though some—Ransom, Davidson, Tate, Warren—were members of both groups. The Agrarians concerned themselves with political and economic issues and especially with their application to the South. In 1930 the group published its manifesto, *I'll Take My Stand,* the title a line from the song "Dixie." For the most part the essays set forth conservative positions, with Warren's "The Briar Patch," dealing with the racial question, a notable exception. To many the collection of essays seemed a futile attempt to turn back the clock, to reject "progress," embracing as it did an agricultural way of life and attacking industrialism. Others praised what seemed an incisive critique of many elements of life in the 1920s.

Although the work of Ransom and Tate regularly appears in the major national anthologies—especially Ransom's "Bells for John Whiteside's Daughter" (1924) and Tate's "Ode to the Confederate Dead" (1930), the most widely known member of the Fugitive and Agrarian groups is surely Warren. Looking back from 1986, Douglas Paschall declared that Warren was "indisputably Tennessee's most significant man of letters." His Pulitzer Prize winning novel *All the King's Men* (1946), based on the career of Louisiana governor Huey Long, is perhaps the most distinguished in a group of novels, which includes several set in Tennessee, among them *The Cave* (1959), *Flood* (1964), and *Meet Me in the Green Glen* (1971). One of Warren's most frequently anthologized stories, "Blackberry Winter," is set in Middle Tennessee during an exceptionally cold June.

Warren was also a poet, winning the Pulitzer Prize for *Promises* (1957), and in collaboration with Cleanth Brooks, another Vanderbilt alumnus well-known for his books of literary criticism, he edited the highly influential textbooks *Understanding Poetry* (1938) and *Understanding Fiction* (1943). Brooks and Warren, along with Ransom, Tate, and others, practiced what was called "new criticism" (after the title of Ransom's 1941 book, *The New Criticism*), in which the critic focuses on the work of art itself, subjecting it to close analysis.

In time most of the prominent Fugitives and Agrarians left Vanderbilt. Tate ended his teaching career at Minnesota; Warren ended his at Yale. Ransom left Vanderbilt for Kenyon College in 1937 and taught there until his retirement. Only Davidson finished his teaching at Vanderbilt.

Naturally not all Tennessee writing during the time was done by those connected with Nashville. East Tennessee's Anne Armstrong published in 1915 a novel set in Knoxville (though the city is called "Kingsville"), entitled *The Seas of God,* a phrase from Whitman's "Passage to India." In 1930 she published a better-known novel, *This Day and Time,* set in Sullivan County before the completion of the South Holston Dam. Evelyn Scott of Clarksville, a rebel against middle-class morality, who in 1913 at the age of 20 ran off with a married man and lived with him in a common-law marriage in Brazil for six years, wrote a series of novels. The best-known is *The Wave* (1929), set during the Civil War. Her Brazilian experience is detailed in the autobiographical *Escapade* (1923).

Though little remembered now, T.S. Stribling of Clifton published a number of novels in the 1920s and 1930s. *The Store* (1932), second in his trilogy on Southern life which extends from the Civil War to the 1920s, received the first Pulitzer Prize awarded to a Tennessean. Another almost-forgotten novelist of the time was Harry Harrison Kroll; the most noted of his 20 novels was *Cabin in the Cotton* (1931), which was made into a film starring Bette Davis.

Over the years the Vanderbilt group exerted a strong influence on certain young Tennessee writers. Mildred Haun of Cocke County, for example, studied at Vanderbilt in the 1930s, where she was encouraged by Ransom and Davidson. In 1937, under the latter's direction, she completed a thesis on the ballads and songs of her native county, and three years later she published *The Hawk's Done Gone* (1940), a book of interconnected stories of the East Tennessee mountains told by an elderly "granny-woman."

A very different writer, who studied with Ransom and Davidson at Vanderbilt, was Randall Jarrell, who received his bachelor's degree in 1935 and then began graduate work, later following Ransom to Kenyon College. Though he published one novel, *Pictures from an Institution* (1954), Jarrell is best known for his poetry, especially one short poem taken from his World War II experiences, "The Death of the Ball Turret Gunner."

Still another strongly influenced by the Vanderbilt group was Peter Taylor. In the 1930s Taylor had Allen Tate as his freshman English teacher at Southwestern in Memphis (later Rhodes College). So impressed was Tate with the young Taylor that he urged him to transfer to Vanderbilt in order to study under Ransom. When Ransom left, Taylor followed him to Kenyon, just as Jarrell did. Though he taught for many years in North Carolina and at the University of Virginia, Taylor did not forget his connection with Tennessee, as evidenced by his Pulitzer Prize winning novel *A Summons to Memphis* (1986) and *In the Tennessee Country* (1994).

Another Pulitzer Prize winner among Tennessee writers is James Agee, who grew up in Knoxville and used the circumstances of his father's death in a May 1916 automobile accident as the basis for the novel *A Death in the Family* (1957). Not only did the novel win the Pulitzer; the drama based on the novel and retitled *All the Way Home* (1960), also won a Pulitzer. The novel's separately published prologue, "Knoxville: Summer of 1915," has become still better known through a setting for soprano and orchestra by composer Samuel Barber.

Cormac McCarthy, who also grew up in Knoxville, wrote a notable series of novels set in East Tennessee, beginning with *The Orchard Keeper* (1965) and including *Suttree* (1979), which portrays the darker underside of Knoxville some 40 to 45 years ago. Again and again critics have compared McCarthy with Faulkner, and some readers found his prose too filled with violence, horror, and the macabre, but McCarthy has earned a wide following.

Many who were unaware of Memphis's Shelby Foote as a writer came to know him as one of the narrators in the PBS television series on the Civil War, a subject he had explored in detail in his three-volume trilogy *The Civil War: A Narrative* (1958–1974) and still earlier in the novel *Shiloh* (1952).

Surely no Tennessee writer has achieved greater fame than Alex Haley. *Roots* (1976), tracing his family's origins back to the African Kunta Kinte, achieved phenomenal success and inspired a popular eight-part ABC television miniseries in 1977, as well as a sequel, "Roots: The Next Generation," which was broadcast two years later.

Other notable African-American authors associated with Tennessee include the poet Nikki Giovanni, a Knoxville native whose *Black Feeling, Black Talk* (1968) established her as one of the new wave of black poets, and Ishmael Reed, a poet and novelist originally from Chattanooga, whose clearest link with the state is the collection *Chattanooga: Poems* (1973). Richard Wright, author of *Native Son* (1940), one of the most distinguished early African-American novels, lived for a time in Memphis, as recorded in his autobiographical *Black Boy* (1945).

Among earlier black writers are Arnaud Bontemps, the noted poet, novelist, and short story writer, who participated in the Harlem Renaissance and was associated with Nashville's Fisk University for some 25 years. Another writer having a long association with Fisk was the poet James Weldon Johnson, well-known for *God's Trombones* (1927), *The Autobiography of an Ex-Coloured Man* (1912) and *Lift Every Voice,* which became a kind of national anthem for African Americans. Still earlier was George Marion McClellan, a Fisk graduate of 1885 who published three collections of poetry and a collection of short stories, *Old Greenbottom Inn* (1906).

Many other names could be added to the preceding, according to the taste of those proposing or objecting to the inclusion of a particular writer. New writers are appearing constantly, and older writers are adding to their works. The inclusion of more than 100 writers in a bicentennial anthology, *Home Works* (1996), amply testifies to the fact that Tennessee literature is alive, thriving, and constantly growing.
Allison Ensor, University of Tennessee, Knoxville
SUGGESTED READINGS: Paul K. Conkin, *The Southern Agrarians* (1988); Douglas Paschall and Alice Swanson, eds., *Homewords: A Book of Tennessee Writers* (1986); Phyllis Tickle and Alice Swanson, eds., *Home Works: A Book of Tennessee Writers* (1996); Ray Willbanks, ed., *Literature of Tennessee* (1985); Thomas Daniel Young, *Tennessee Writers* (1981)

LIVESTOCK. From earliest settlement, Tennesseans herded livestock—horses and mules, cattle, sheep, and swine—in addition to farming. Indeed, livestock became as important to Tennessee's antebellum economy as cotton or tobacco. Many early observers pointed to the grassy range-land and the natural mast, and noted the suitability of the region for livestock. The large herds of deer and buffalo underscored the thriving conditions for livestock.

White settlers brought livestock of bloodlines that mingled breeds introduced by British, French, and Spanish colonists. In a preview of American cowboy culture, the Tennessee settlers allowed their cattle and hogs to range freely, rounded them up, and often branded them for long drives to market. In the Carolinas, mounted slaves sometimes tended cattle and became adept horsemen. The use of such cowboys spread across the South and into Texas as families moved west.

Faced with poor shipping opportunities, East Tennessee livestockmen drove cattle, hogs, and even turkeys up the Great Wagon Road to Virginia and over the Charles Town (Charleston) Road to South Carolina. David Crockett's father hired the youth as a drover to Jacob Siler on a cattle drive from Jefferson County, Tennessee, to Rockbridge County, Virginia. The road from Newport to Asheville, North Carolina, witnessed huge annual caravans of drovers and their hogs moving to market. Native Americans also took up livestock raising, and an 1828 census of the Cherokees shows they owned 22,400 cattle and 7,600 horses. The state's large herds of cattle and hogs led to the development of tanneries, and leather became a significant Tennessee export. Many early towns list a tannery among the first industries.

Settlers from North Carolina, Virginia, and Pennsylvania brought Shorthorn, Ayrshire, and Devon stock. East Tennessee highland "native" cattle bore a striking resemblance to the forest-bred herds of the Scottish Black Kerry and Ayrshire, and were likely brought from Scotland into North Carolina. These cattle were extremely hardy, smaller than Shorthorns,

Stock farm near Cookeville, 1940.

angular, surefooted, and seldom of a solid color unless black. Hard to fatten, they gave a very rich milk. The cattle of the East Tennessee valley and Middle Tennessee were larger and easier to fatten, more valuable for beef, with traces of Shorthorn and Devon bloodlines. West Tennessee cattle were similar to those of Middle Tennessee, but until the late nineteenth century, western counties raised cattle in smaller numbers than the rest of the state.

Cattle received little breeding attention until the 1830s, when competition promoted by agricultural fairs encouraged improved stock through introductions of blooded cattle from England and elsewhere, with attention given to Patton, Teeswater, and English breeds. A revival of breeding interest occurred about 1855, as interest in fairs spread across the state.

As Tennessee lost its frontier aspect, horse breeding gained interest. Andrew Jackson led efforts to bring the best horses of East Tennessee to the midstate, and breeders imported stallions and mares from the eastern states and Europe. Sumner, Davidson, Giles, and Maury counties became well-known for their fine stock. By the mid-1800s the state had gained a reputation for fine stock, and Tennessee horses were exported to other regions. Tennessee is the only state to lend its name to one of the world's most popular horse breeds, the Tennessee Walking Horse. Harlinsdale Farm in Williamson County produced Midnight Sun, one of the breed's most famous horses. By 1860 Tennessee also had become the leading state for mule production, serving the increasing demand for mules in the cotton-producing states.

Many livestock men viewed Middle and West Tennessee as ideal in climate and pasture for sheep production. Some early settlers brought sheep and used the wool for home consumption. In the 1820s Merino sheep were introduced, and later Cotswold, Southdown, Leicester, and Oxfordshire sheep were brought to the state. Clifton Place in Maury County was known for its sheep production. Many farmers permitted their sheep to range half-wild, which decreased the amount and value of the wool. In sharp contrast to this practice, Mark R. Cockrill experimented with breeding a superlative animal. His efforts paid off when the Davidson County farmer won the gold medal for the finest wool in the world at the 1851 Crystal Palace Exposition in London.

By the mid-1800s Tennessee ranked as the top southern state for swine production, becoming the leading state in the nation in 1850. Hogs thrived in the state's mild climate, which supported rich, mast-producing forests of chestnut, oak, and hickory, in addition to corn production. Free-roaming pigs sometimes became feral, establishing the wild "razorbacks" of the South. Swine breeders took pride in their stock, importing lines from Europe and elsewhere. The Berkshire breed gained the most advocates, like at the Davies Manor plantation in Shelby County, but other popular breeds included Essex, Poland China, Neapolitan, and Sussex swine. On the eve of the Civil War, Tennessee's hog population numbered about 1.5 million.

The Civil War devastated the livestock industry, as occupying armies confiscated or killed meat-producing herds, horses, and draft animals. In 1874 Agricultural Commissioner Joseph B. Killebrew wrote that Tennessee provided a larger number of cavalry horses to both armies than any other state. The war so reduced cattle herds that ten years later, Tennessee cattle numbered only 700,000 head, a 30 percent reduction from 1860 figures. So few cattle remained after the war that livestockmen had to replace their herds with cattle imported from Kentucky and other states. Several farms that specialized in livestock sales were established, like that of Lazinka Brown Ewell and Richard Ewell in Williamson County. Breeders recommended shorthorns for all of Tennessee except the East Tennessee highlands, where Devons were suggested. Jerseys and Ayrshires were preferred for dairy production or for the city family that kept a cow. For many plain folk, herding ended, and livestock production continued only for household and farm use. Farmers unable to afford blooded cattle "made do" with free-ranging scrub cattle. During the late nineteenth century crop farmers and blooded livestock producers entered into a protracted dispute with poorer farmers over attempts to legislate requirements for fencing. The dispute centered on who should be required to fence—crop farmers or cattle producers—as well as the definition of legal fencing. County extension agents and business progressives like the members of the Kiwanis Club banded together in the early twentieth century to rid the state of scrub cattle and replace the poor stock with blooded cattle. In Hamblen County in the mid-1920s, in fact, agents and businessmen staged "trials," where scrub cattle were "condemned" to death and sent to the nearest packinghouse for their "execution."

Dairying rose in popularity after 1865, and Holstein lines were added to Jerseys. In 1872 the Tennessee Jersey Cattle Club was formed, and it is now the oldest farmers' organization in the state. A U.S. Dairy Experiment Station, specializing in Jersey cattle, was established near Lewisburg in 1929. Private landowners, like Frank Mars of the Milky Way Farm of Giles County, also bred Jersey cattle for optimal milk production. From 1936 to 1940 Marshall County was the leading Jersey cattle county in the nation. Major national corporations located milk product plants at places like Fayetteville (Borden) and Murfreesboro (Carnation). By 1950 Tennessee ranked fifth in the nation for cheese production. Similarly beef cattle production rose during the postwar period.

In the 1990s livestock farms dot the state, and Tennessee still remains the chief mule center of the nation. In 1995 annual cash receipts for the state's farmers totaled $2 billion, of which livestock production accounts for more than half. Farmers in East and Middle Tennessee now derive more income from beef cattle and dairy herds than from crops. Nearly one million cattle, hogs, and sheep are exported for sale annually, continuing Tennessee's long heritage in livestock production.

Ann Toplovich, Tennessee Historical Society

SEE: AGRICULTURE; BROWN, LAZINKA C.; CLIFTON PLACE; COCKRILL, MARK R.; DAVIES MANOR; HARLINSDALE FARM; MILKY WAY FARM; MULES; U.S. DAIRY EXPERIMENT STATION

LOG CONSTRUCTION. The log cabin is a familiar symbol of Tennessee's pioneer period. Although its use as shelter is well known, its quaint image has tended to obscure its importance as a bridge between civilization and the wilderness. The western settlement movement of the first half of the nineteenth century owes its greatest debt to the humble log cabin and the adaptive techniques of log construction.

Log construction came to Tennessee in the eighteenth century with the first Europeans to enter the area. The earliest uses of this technology occurred at opposite ends of the state. Deep within the Great Smoky Mountains, traders from South Carolina built log cabins in the Overhill towns of the Cherokees as secure storehouses for deerskins and the British goods used as barter with the Native Americans. In the west, on the Chickasaw Bluffs overlooking the Mississippi River, French military engineers erected log palisades and blockhouses for protection from Indians.

The most important and enduring use of log construction occurred in the dwellings, barns, and related outbuildings of the thousands of independent farmsteads that were established throughout the state. Building with logs proved to be an efficient use of the trees that needed to be cleared for agricultural production in the fertile areas of the Upland South, and the thick wood walls afforded ample protection from all types of predators. Houses are the most studied example, but logs were used for the construction of smokehouses, tobacco barns, stock barns, corn cribs, blacksmith shops, and for other related agricultural products and practices. Of the outbuilding types, only cantilever barns, found exclusively in East Tennessee, have been studied in detail.

No matter the function of the building, the most important and distinctive feature of log construction is the corner notch. Coupled with the combined weight of the logs above, this device locks the lower logs firmly in place and ensures structural stability. Seven different notch types have been identified on log buildings in Tennessee: the saddle, V, half dovetail, full dovetail, square, half, and diamond notches. Of these, the half dovetail is by far the most common, due to its relative ease of construction (compared to the full dovetail) and its superior stability when compared to the saddle and V notches.

The basic unit of domestic log construction consists of four walls notched at the corners. This is known as a pen (or crib, when referring to farm buildings). The typical log cabin found throughout Tennessee was a small (approximately 20' x 18') single pen house that had a rock pier foundation, side gables, off-centered doors on the front and rear eave walls, and a chimney on one of the gable ends. It could be either square or rectangular, reflecting cultural traditions, and one, one-and-a-half, or two stories tall.

More complex houses could be formed either by attaching additional units to the original one or from the subdivision of a larger pen into two or three units. A log pen joined to one side of another formed a double pen, or Cumberland house; a pen built a short distance from the first with a roof over both pens and the passage became known as a dogtrot house; and two pens separated by the shared chimney was referred to as a saddlebag house.

Notched log construction is a building technique, not a type or style. The vernacular houses built during the period when log construction flourished were also built of frame, brick, or stone. Although all of the important elements of log construction in the Upper South have their roots in the Old World (Scandinavia and German-speaking states), the form that the Tennessee log house finally assumed had evolved along the back country roads emanating from the cultural hearths of southern Pennsylvania and the Carolina Piedmont. Hewn log construction reached its zenith in Tennessee in the mid-nineteenth century, but it continues to be practiced in isolated areas at the present time.

Michael Gavin, Summertown

SEE: ARCHITECTURE, VERNACULAR DOMESTIC; BARNS, CANTILEVER; HOUSES, VERNACULAR LOG TYPES

LONG HUNTER STATE PARK is located along 30 miles of shoreline of Percy Priest Lake in Davidson and Rutherford counties. In 1968 the U.S. Army Corps of Engineers acquired the property for park development as part of its Percy Priest Dam and Reservoir project. Four years later, it leased 2,400 acres to the state for the creation of Long Hunter State Park. Conservation is an important park mission, but Long Hunter contains large picnic, camping, and recreational areas, including trails, a boat dock, and a fishing pier. Archaic-period Native Americans once hunted and gathered food within the park boundaries; an archaeological site yielded significant information about their activities before it was covered by the reservoir. The name Long Hunter is associated with prominent early white hunters, such as Colonel James Smith, Uriah Stone (Stones River is named for him), James Knox, John Baker, and Kasper Mansker, who once hunted game in this area during the 1760s and early 1770s.

Carroll Van West, Middle Tennessee State University

SEE: EXPLORATIONS, EARLY; MANSKER, KASPER; U.S. ARMY CORPS OF ENGINEERS

LONG ISLAND, described as the most historic, yet little known, site in East Tennessee, played a significant role in the state's early history. Situated on the outskirts of present-day Kingsport, the island was located on the route of the "Great Indian Warrior Path," a historic route traveled by the Cherokees, early traders and settlers, and later by wagon and stagecoach passengers. Located midway on the trail, Long Island emerged as a neutral area for settling tribal disputes.

Whites coveted the ground that Native Americans held sacred. William Cocke claimed to have bought the island when he purchased "corn rights," and, without a legal claim, he sold it to Samuel Woods in 1776. The Cherokee claim to Long Island was strengthened by the Long Island of the Holston Treaty (1777). In 1792 Samuel Woods's daughters inherited Long Island, but they made no attempts to occupy the land until 1810, after the Cherokees had ceded the island in the Dearborn Treaty (1806). Richard and Margaret Woods Netherland accepted ownership of the site in the early nineteenth century and laid plans for their 814-acre plantation. The island supported agriculture until the mid-1920s, including the financially successful Leeper Dairy Farm.

In 1925 the Leeper family subdivided the area south of Horse Creek Road (the main thoroughfare) and named the area Long Island Gardens. The community, situated across the river from the Tennessee Eastman Company, was solidly working class. Grocery stores, barber shops, dry cleaners, restaurants, churches, and an elementary school were located within convenient walking distance. The school and the "Big Field," a large open field, became the community center. Long Island grew at an astounding rate, reaching its peak between 1955 and 1963, with 517 residences and approximately 1,800 people. Although many upstanding citizens lived on Long Island, the neighborhood acquired a local reputation for violence and bootlegging.

After the mid-1960s Long Island experienced a gradual decline due to several factors. In 1967 the Holston River Bridge, which connected the Island's main street to the Tennessee Eastman Company site and to Kingsport, collapsed and was not rebuilt. At the same time, the community's young adults emigrated to other areas, followed by some older residents who moved to newer homes. Many of the latter migrants kept their island homes as rental property. Finally, the island acquired a more industrial appearance, and today a coal gasification plant stands on the site of Big Field and the old elementary school. Over the course of its history, Long Island demonstrates, in microcosm, the successive development of many areas of Tennessee, from Native American use to disputed territory to agriculture to urban and industrial development.

Patricia Bernard Ezzell, Tennessee Valley Authority

SEE: COCKE, WILLIAM; KINGSPORT; NETHERLAND INN; TENNESSEE EASTMAN COMPANY

LONG, STEPHEN H. (1784–1864). Engineers who modify the fluvial landscape of Tennessee should feel strong ties to Stephen Harriman Long, who served as an Army engineer at a time when the role of government in engineering projects had not yet been defined. In the course of his career, he designed roads, advised on the construction of railroads, created new types of bridges, revolutionized ship design, and modified rivers. Many of his projects altered the landscape of Tennessee.

In 1827 Long came to Tennessee to satisfy popular demand for improved navigation. That year the Tennessee General Assembly sanctioned five lotteries to fund engineering projects for river improvements in Middle Tennessee. Long's initial work involved improvements to the Cumberland and Tennessee rivers, but his river work in the state continued into the 1840s.

In addition to his modifications of Tennessee rivers, Long mapped the topography of proposed railroad routes and built "Long's Road," connecting Knoxville and Bristol. He published an abundance of topographic data and geological observations, the bulk of it in U.S. Congressional documents. Despite his publications and extensive landscape alteration, no assessment of Stephen H. Long's work in Tennessee has been undertaken.

James X. Corgan, Austin Peay State University

SUGGESTED READING: Richard G. Wood, *Stephen Harriman Long, 1789–1864; Army engineer, explorer, inventor* (1966)

SEE: GEOLOGY

LONGSTREET, JAMES (1821–1904). One of the most controversial Confederate generals, Longstreet was born in Edgefield District, South Carolina, January 8, 1821, and reared in Georgia. After graduating near the bottom of his West Point class in 1842, "Old Pete" fought in Mexico, where he won two brevets for gallantry. He resigned his commission in the paymaster's department to join the Confederacy. Longstreet competently commanded a brigade at First Manassas and a division at Seven Pines and in the Seven Days campaign. His tactical abilities at Second Manassas and Sharpsburg won the admiration of General Robert E. Lee and led to his appointment in October 1862 as Lieutenant General and Commander of the First Corps, Army of Northern Virginia. In this new capacity he fought brilliantly at Fredricksburg, but with less distinction at Gettysburg, where his performance is still debated.

Chafing to gain independent command, Longstreet engineered the transfer of his corps to the Army of Tennessee in September 1863, perhaps with hopes of wresting command of that army away from the incompetent and unpopular Braxton Bragg. His troops played a key role at Chickamauga on September 19, but his participation in an abortive attempt to oust Bragg from command shortly thereafter led Bragg to detach Longstreet's troops from the army. Bragg sent Longstreet on a forlorn campaign to retake Knoxville, which had fallen to Major General Ambrose Burnside's Union forces in early September. After losing a foot race with Burnside to Knoxville, Longstreet laid siege to the city and attempted to starve the garrison into submission. Longstreet ordered an assault on Fort Sanders, which he thought was a Federal weak link, on November 29, but was repulsed with heavy casualties. When he received news of Bragg's rout at Chattanooga and the approach of a Union relief column from the south, Longstreet lifted the 18-day siege and retreated into winter quarters in upper East Tennessee. While his army rested around Morristown and Greeneville, Longstreet launched a savage attack against his senior officers, blaming division commanders Lafayette McLaws and Evander Law for his failures. Both generals were sacked and their commands given to Longstreet supporters.

By April 1864 Longstreet was back in Virginia, where he participated in the final campaigns of Lee's army. Following the war, Longstreet entered into a protracted and bitter feud with former Virginia officers over his role in the Confederate defeat at Gettysburg. His undistinguished attempt at independent command in East Tennessee and his attacks on his own officers did little to enhance his reputation. Lee's "Old War Horse" died January 2, 1904, at his home in Gainesville, Georgia.

W. Todd Groce, Georgia Historical Society

SEE: CIVIL WAR; GREENE COUNTY; HAMBLEN COUNTY; KNOXVILLE, BATTLE OF

LOOBY, ZEPHANIAH ALEXANDER (1899–1972),

attorney and civil rights activist, was born in Antigua, British West Indies, on April 8, 1899, the son of John Alexander and Grace Elizabeth Joseph Looby. After the death of his father, young Looby departed for the United States, arriving in 1914.

Looby received a bachelor's degree from Howard University, a Bachelor of Law degree from Columbia University, and a Doctor of Juristic Science from New York University. In 1926 he came to Fisk University as assistant professor of economics and remained until 1928. At various times he later served as a lecturer at Fisk University and Meharry Medical College. In 1929 Looby was admitted to the Tennessee bar and practiced law in Memphis for three years. He returned to Nashville and helped to found the Kent College of Law, Nashville's first law school for African Americans since the Central Tennessee College's department of law (1877–1911).

In the Civil Rights Movement of the World War II era, Looby rose to a position of local leadership. From 1943 to 1945 he presided over the James C. Napier Bar Association. He lost a 1940 run-off election to a white opponent in a race for city council. In 1946 the National Association for the Advancement of Colored People hired Looby, Maurice Weaver, and Thurgood Marshall to represent the African Africans charged with murder following the recent race riot in Columbia, Tennessee. Looby's legal defense helped acquit 23 of the defendants. He crisscrossed the state in the company of other black lawyers, arguing against Jim Crow and discrimination. Looby is credited with desegregating the Nashville airport dining room and the city's public golf courses.

Soon after the momentous U.S. Supreme Court decision of *Brown v. Board of Education of Topeka* (1954), Looby filed a suit against the local public schools on behalf of A.Z. Kelly, a barber whose son Robert was denied access to a nearby white school. During the sit-in demonstrations and civil rights marches of the 1960s, Looby and other black attorneys provided money and legal services for local college students who were arrested and jailed. On April 19, 1960, his Meharry Boulevard home was destroyed by dynamite.

Looby viewed politics as a way to change an oppressive system. In 1951 he and fellow attorney Robert E. Lillard became the first blacks to be elected to the city council since 1911. In 1962 he lost a bid for a seat on the Tennessee Supreme Court. A year later, Looby became a member of the Metropolitan Charter Commission. In 1971 he retired after serving on the old city council and the new Metropolitan Council for a combined total of 20 years.

Looby died on March 24, 1972. Ten years later, the Nashville Bar Association, whose white members had denied Looby's membership application in the 1950s, posthumously granted a certificate of membership in his name. His contributions to Nashville are recognized in the Z. Alexander Looby Library and Community Center erected by the city on Metro Center Boulevard.

Linda T. Wynn, Tennessee Historical Commission/Fisk University

Adapted from Bobby L. Lovett and Linda T. Wynn, *Profiles of African Americans in Tennessee (1996)*

SEE: CIVIL RIGHTS MOVEMENT; COLUMBIA RACE RIOT, 1946; KELLY V. BOARD OF EDUCATION; LILLARD, ROBERT E.; NAACP

LOOKOUT MOUNTAIN, part of the Cumberland Plateau, extends 83 miles through Tennessee, Georgia, and Alabama, and is famous for its northern end at Chattanooga. Point Lookout, the extremity overlooking the river valley at Moccasin Bend, has attracted tourists since antebellum days. The 1863 Civil War battle fought on its slope brought additional fame to Lookout Mountain.

In 1818 Elias Cornelius, a cleric visiting Brainerd Mission, the Cherokee school, left the first written account of a tour atop Lookout. In 1838, following the Cherokee Removal and the founding of Chattanooga, the State of Tennessee granted James A. Whiteside a large tract encompassing the point. During the 1850s Whiteside built the Lookout Mountain Turnpike from an ancient Indian path leading up the mountain and developed the northern summit. The University of the South's organizational meeting was held at this site in 1857. Whiteside built a resort hotel in the Early Classical Revival style to accommodate visitors. Summer visitors from as far away as Virginia and Louisiana came to enjoy the mountain climate and see the sights. Natural attractions included Rock City, Lula Falls, Natural Bridge, Umbrella Rock, and Point Lookout, which afforded what many regarded as one of the most magnificent views in America.

During the Civil War, the Confederate army held Lookout Mountain until 1863. In November, following the Union's defeat at Chickamauga, General Joseph Hooker's army stormed up the mountainside. Fought in heavy fog, the engagement received the romantic name the "Battle Above the Clouds." Subsequently, the Union army established a military hospital complex on the summit.

During the 1880s and 1890s, tourism flourished on Lookout Mountain. A modern turnpike, two incline railways, and a broad gauge railroad provided transportation to the summit. In 1896 the U.S. War Department purchased Robert Cravens's mountainside property, the scene of the Battle Above the Clouds, and integrated the reservation into the Chickamauga and Chattanooga National Military Park. In 1898 the government purchased the point property from the Whiteside estate and added it to the park system as Point Park.

Tourism and residential development increased during the twentieth century. Ruby Falls and Rock City opened to visitors. To stem the tide of overdevelopment, Adolph S. Ochs, publisher of the *Chattanooga Times*, led a preservation movement. It eventually brought over 2,000 acres under the supervision of the National Park Service. Ochs Highway and Ochs Museum and Observatory were named in honor of the civic-minded publisher. Today, the Lookout Mountain Protection Association and the Lula Lake Land Trust continue similar preservation efforts. Over a million people visit Lookout Mountain's scenic, military, and commercial attractions annually.

Gary C. Jenkins, Chattanooga

SUGGESTED READINGS: Gary C. Jenkins, *Taking the Old Mountain Road: The Lookout Mountain Turnpike and Its Possessor, Harriet L. Whiteside* (1994); John Wilson, *Lookout: The Story of an Amazing Mountain* (1977)

SEE: CHICKAMAUGA AND CHATTANOOGA, BATTLES OF; CRAVENS HOUSE; OCHS, ADOLPH S.; WHITESIDE, HARRIET

LOTTERIES appeared in Tennessee before statehood in 1796, were prohibited by constitutional amendment in 1835 and 1870, and continue to generate public debate today. By definition, a lottery is any contest that involves three factors: the payment of money, for a chance, to win a prize.

The first recorded lottery within the present boundaries of Tennessee occurred in 1787, while the region was still a part of North Carolina. Its proceeds were designated for building a road from the south end of Clinch Mountain to Bean's Lick. Widely advertised, lotteries became common in the early nineteenth century. Private lotteries were held without government control for the benefit of individuals, usually to dispose of property or to encourage business. In 1809 the legislature outlawed these types of lotteries, saying they encouraged idleness and dissipation. However, the continuing existence of "underground" lotteries calls to question the effectiveness of the legislation.

Quasi-public lotteries to allow an individual to devise his own lottery scheme in order to pay debts through the sale of his property required legislative approval. In Tennessee, at least 11 such lotteries were approved between 1819 and 1829.

After 1809 the legislature approved lotteries for the benefit of projects of public interest. In order to insure honest administration of public lotteries, the legislature imposed regulations, appointed respectable trustees, and required the lottery managers to take an oath of honesty. Private organizations, such as Masonic lodges, petitioned for authorization to conduct lotteries. Lotteries for educational purposes and for public improvements, primarily in transportation, received the highest approval rates. Public lotteries helped to finance several schools and higher education, benefiting Nashville College and Cumberland College (later the University of Nashville and after that Peabody College). The City of Nashville built wagon trails, a waterworks, a hospital, and a town clock through public lotteries.

Despite their positive contributions, lotteries experienced a variety of problems. Due to their initial popularity, the market was soon saturated with them. Notable Tennessee lotteries, such as an 1810 lottery to benefit what is today the University of Tennessee, experienced difficulties selling a sufficient number of tickets to fund the drawing. Other lotteries encountered the same problem, and many drawings had to be postponed. Although there were no accusations of the fraud and corruption common to the lotteries in other states, private publications began to point to social ills, such as drunkenness, laziness, and even suicide, as direct effects of lotteries. By the late 1820s public sentiment had turned against lotteries.

In 1829 the Tennessee Supreme Court dealt a serious blow to the lottery. In *State v. Smith*, the court held that participation in a private lottery was gambling and subject to a criminal penalty of disqualification from holding public office. But Judge John Catron drew no distinction between public and private lotteries when he denounced the lottery as "odious gambling" and the cause of ruin, beggary, and drunkenness.

Though limited to private lotteries, *Smith* sounded the death knell for all lotteries. That same year, the Tennessee legislature codified *Smith* by outlawing "unauthorized" lotteries, followed by an act in 1832 that made the sale of any lottery ticket illegal. In 1834 the Committee on Private and Local Legislation submitted a report to the Tennessee Constitutional Convention in which lotteries were defined as legalized gambling. The committee advocated the prohibition of legislative authority to license them. The Convention incorporated this recommendation as Article XI, Section 5 of the Tennessee Constitution of 1834, which states that "The legislature shall have no power to authorize lotteries for any purpose; but shall pass laws to prohibit the sale of lottery tickets in the State." The same provision was incorporated in the Constitution of 1870 and remains the fundamental law today.

Despite legal provisions, the lottery persists as a controversial issue. In 1989, in *Secretary of State v. St. Augustine Church/St. Augustine School*, the Tennessee Supreme Court, in effect, outlawed "charitable" bingo by holding it to be a lottery under the state's constitution and striking down statutes enacted to protect such gaming. Yet the court also held that the constitution did not prohibit gambling, leaving confusion as to what constitutes a "lottery." As surrounding states enact lotteries to fund public education and siphon money that might otherwise be wagered in Tennessee, the lure of instant wealth and the need for public funds has prompted many to question the existing law and urge the establishment of a state-run lottery.

Lewis L. Laska, Tennessee State University

SUGGESTED READINGS: Lewis L. Laska and Severine Brocki, "The Life and Dealth of the Lottery in Tennessee, 1787–1836," *Tennessee Historical Quarterly* 45(1986): 95–118; Mike Roberts, "The Constitutionality of Gaming in Tennessee," *Tennessee Law Review* 61(1994): 675

SEE: GOVERNMENT; LAW

LOUDON COUNTY was established on June 2, 1870, from portions of Roane, Monroe, and Blount counties. On September 5, the county court was organized, and the Loudon (formerly Blair's Ferry) town square was donated as the site for the courthouse. The county court selected the building plan submitted by A.C. Bruce, and brothers J. Wesley and Ira Napoleon Clark built it for $14,200. By September 1872 the courthouse was ready for occupancy and has served since as the seat of government.

With 229 square miles, Loudon County lies on both sides of the Tennessee River and extends north to the Clinch River. The territory south of the river contains the fertile valleys of Sweetwater, Pond, Fork, and Town creeks. To the north are the broad bottoms of the Tennessee River. The Little Tennessee River also passes through the county. The first occupants were Native Americans. The part of the county lying south of the rivers formerly belonged to the Hiwassee District and was not settled by white men until 1819–1820, but settlements were made on the north banks of the Tennessee and the Little Tennessee before 1800.

In 1790 white families settled on the north bank of the Tennessee River, near the present location of the Loudon bridge. The William Tunnell family was the first to settle on the south side of the river. As other settlers, including the Carmichaels and Blairs, came, a ferry was established, and the settlement was called Blair's Ferry. In 1850 a formal plan for the town was established, and the name was changed to Loudon in 1858. The East Tennessee and Georgia Railroad was built to Blair's Ferry in 1852, and by 1855 a railroad bridge spanned the river northward, and the flourishing river traded declined.

Lenoir City traces its origins from the extensive land holdings of General William B. Lenoir, a prominent and wealthy North Carolinian, who served at the Battle of King's Mountain. For his service, Lenoir received 5,000 acres of land, which he deeded to his eldest son, Major William B. Lenoir, who moved his family to the area in 1810. By 1821 Major Lenoir had developed a prosperous and well-managed plantation widely known for cattle and hog production, and several small industries, including a cotton mill and a flour mill. When Major Lenoir died in 1852, four of his sons formed William Lenoir and Sons and controlled about 2,700 acres of the estate. Eventually, the land was sold to the Lenoir City Company, which developed the town. Lenoir City was incorporated in 1907.

Workers at Taubel Scott Company knitting machines, Lenoir City, ca. 1920.

In October 1813 an act of the state legislature established the town of Morgantown, located at the mouth of Baker's Creek, on land owned by Hugh and Charles Kelso. Originally called Portville, the town's name was changed to honor Gideon Morgan, Sr., a Revolutionary War soldier. The town did not survive the economic decline it suffered in the late 1800s, when the L&N Railroad was built through the area and ended the thriving river trade. The waters of Tellico Lake inundated the townsite.

In the fall of 1821 William Knox and Jacob Pearson established the town of Philadelphia, six miles southwest of Blair's Ferry. The town's largest and most successful industry was the Philadelphia Hosiery Mill, which was established by Edward Waller in 1921. For more than 40 years, the corporation expanded and grew, but in the early 1960s, the mill was sold and reopened as Bar Knit Hosiery, which closed in the early 1970s.

During the 1800s, the town of Greenback was established as the result of railroad construction. It occupied land once owned by Robert Thompson and J.B. Hall. Greenback is primarily an agricultural community, but one with strong civic pride.

Loudon County did not escape the destruction and devastation of the Civil War. No major battles were fought in Loudon County, but there were massive troop movements through the area. As the only East Tennessee railroad bridge across the Tennessee River, the bridge at Loudon provided a strategic link between Knoxville and Chattanooga. The bridge remained under constant surveillance during the war and was partially burned twice by retreating Confederate forces.

Following the Battle of Chickamauga on September 19–20, 1863, General James Longstreet moved north to capture Knoxville, and Union General Ambrose Burnside sent 10,000 men to the Loudon area. During October and November, cavalry skirmishes took place around Philadelphia and Loudon, as the armies moved north. After the Battle of Knoxville, Confederate troops burned the Loudon railroad bridge and sank three locomotives and 48 cars to deny General William T. Sherman access to the bridge. Loudon County and East Tennessee remained under Union control for the rest of the war.

Industrialization developed slowly after the Civil War. The Lenoir family rebuilt the depot and general store burned by Union troops and built a new burr and roller flour mill to replace the one that burned in 1860. The Lenoir City Company, founded in 1890, attracted new industries, including the Bass Foundry and Machine Shop, which eventually built railroad cars for the Southern Railroad Company under the name Lenoir Car Works. The Holston Manufacturing Company also operated a hosiery mill. The Tennessee Valley Authority completed Fort Loudon Dam in 1943 and added Tellico Dam in the 1970s. The creation of Tellico Lake and Tellico Village, a residential community, contributed significantly to the local economy.

Loudon's progress was slower and tied to agriculture. In 1906 Charles H. Bacon established Loudon's first significant industry, a hosiery mill. Shortly thereafter, the Lutz Mantel Company and Don P. Smith Chair Factory also were established; only the chair factory remains. In recent years, several new industries have located in Loudon: Viskase Corporation,

Maremont, the Staley Corporation, Honda Distribution Center, and Kimberly Clark.

Joe Spence, Lenoir City

SEE: FERRIES; LENOIR CAR WORKS; LENOIR COTTON MILL; TENNESSEE VALLEY AUTHORITY

LUNA EXPEDITION. In 1560, 20 years after the Hernando de Soto entrada traversed the Upper Tennessee Valley in its search for gold, burden bearers, and food, a second Spanish expedition crossed into Tennessee near present-day Chattanooga. The Tristán de Luna expedition sought to validate Spain's claim to *La Florida*, the present southeastern United States, by creating a flourishing colony. A veteran of the Coronado expedition in the west, Tristán de Luna y Arellano was appointed to establish a town at Ochuse in Pensacola Bay and open roads to the Mississippian Coosa chiefdom in northern Georgia, and from there to Santa Elena in South Carolina.

Luna's fleet anchored in Pensacola Bay on August 14, 1559. Five days later, a hurricane destroyed most of the ships, tools, supplies, and food. The stranded colonists eked out a living in the bay area, but by February, they were forced to move north to the Mississippian town of Nanipacana on the Lower Alabama River. The people of Nanipacana, however, fled their towns, destroying their stored food supplies as they left.

On April 15, Luna, again desperate for food, sent Mateo del Sauz north to Coosa with a translator, two friars, 40 cavalry, and 100 infantry. The translator was a woman taken from Coosa by the Soto expedition 20 years earlier. Soto had reported an abundance of food in Coosa, and Luna hoped Sauz also would find food there. Two and a half months later, Sauz and his weary party straggled into the main Coosa town, near present Carters, Georgia.

Some of the principal men of Coosa complained to Sauz that their former vassals, the Napochies, who lived near the Tennessee River, refused to send them tribute. The Coosa suggested the hungry Spanish might receive more food if the Napochies became Coosa vassals again. Sauz reluctantly consented to a combined Spanish-Coosa attack against the Napochies. About August 21, 25 Spanish cavalry and 25 infantry, in addition to 300 Coosa warriors advanced north and west toward the Napochie province.

The Coosa-Spanish force stormed the first Napochie town they encountered, but found it abandoned. The Napochies from here as well as a second Tennessee River town, had already crossed to the other side of the river earlier in the day. The Spaniards and the outraged Coosas pursued the Napochies, who escaped to a nearby island, possibly Chattanooga Island.

Trapped and outnumbered, the Napochies sued for peace, consenting to become Coosa vassals and renewing their deliveries of game, fruits, and nuts three times a year. Sauz's expedition and the Coosa warriors left the Tennessee Valley Napochie towns at the end of August 1560 and returned to Coosa.

David H. Dye, University of Memphis

SEE: EXPLORATIONS, EARLY; HAMILTON COUNTY; PARDO, JUAN; SOTO, HERNANDO DE

LUNDY, BENJAMIN (1789–1839), pioneering abolitionist, was born in New Jersey on January 4, 1789, to Quaker parents, Joseph and Eliza Lundy. In 1808 Lundy moved to Wheeling, Virginia, to pursue a career in saddle-making. There Lundy experienced his first contact with slavery and developed a lifelong commitment to end the practice.

In order to escape the daily sight of slavery and its conflict with his Quaker religion, Lundy moved to Ohio in 1815. That year he and his newlywed wife, Esther Lewis, settled in St. Clairsville, Ohio, where Lundy opened a successful saddle-making business. In 1816 Lundy founded his first anti-slavery society, the Union Humane Society, and soon began writing abolitionist articles which first appeared in Charles Osborn's reform newspaper, *Philanthropist,* in 1817.

After Osborn sold his newspaper, Lundy began publishing his own anti-slavery newspaper, *The Genius of Universal Emancipation,* in January 1821. Following the death of Tennessee abolitionist Elihu Embree, who had published *The Emancipator,* state abolitionists recruited Lundy to continue the work. Lundy purchased Embree's printing equipment and moved to Greeneville in 1822, where he continued publication of *The Genius of Universal Emancipation.*

Lundy believed that abolitionism would be most effective if it emanated from a slave state. He circulated the *Genius* in more than 21 states and kept the abolitionist movement alive in the Upper South, especially in Tennessee, Kentucky, and North Carolina. The paper was not a financial success, however, and in 1822 he began publishing a second newspaper, *The American Economist and Weekly Political Recorder,* which reported farm prices, published poetry, and relayed local and national economic and political news.

While in Greeneville, Lundy joined the Humane Protecting Society and became president of the Greeneville branch of the Tennessee Manumission Society. As president, he attended the 1823 national meeting of the American Convention for Promoting the Abolition of Slavery, held in Philadelphia. This contact with well-financed eastern abolitionists induced Lundy to move his family and newspaper to Baltimore in 1824.

From the columns of his newspaper, Lundy had always advocated gradual emancipation and colonization as the most effective methods to end slavery. In 1825 he published a plan for the "Gradual Abolition of Slavery in the United States without Danger or Loss to the South," a plan written by Francis Wright for her work at Nashoba in Tennessee. Dissatisfied with the initial lack of interest in his proposal, Lundy traveled to Haiti in the summer of 1825 to look for possible colonization sites. While he was there, his wife died giving birth to twins. On his return, Lundy placed the infants and his three older children with various family members and continued his abolition work.

In 1829 Lundy recruited William Lloyd Garrison as associate editor of the *Genius*. After a falling out with Garrison, Lundy suspended the publication of the *Genius* and devoted himself to the search for suitable colonization sites for freed blacks; his search took him to Haiti, Canada, and the Texas republic. In 1838 Lundy rejoined his children in Illinois and reestablished the *Genius of Universal Emancipation*. He published 12 issues prior to his death on August 22, 1839. His is buried in McNabb, Illinois.

Tara Mitchell Mielnik, Middle Tennessee State University

SEE: EMBREE, ELIHU; GREENE COUNTY; MANUMISSION SOCIETY OF TENNESSEE

LUPTON, JOHN THOMAS (1862–1933), Chattanooga capitalist and philanthropist, was born near Winchester, Virginia. Lupton received a law degree from the University of Virginia and settled in Chattanooga in 1887, following a visit to the home of a fellow student, Lewis Coleman. His first law partner was William Gibbs McAdoo, later Secretary of the Treasury and son-in-law of Woodrow Wilson. Lupton served as legal counsel for the Chattanooga Medicine Company, eventually becoming vice president and treasurer of the company (1891–1906). His marriage to Elizabeth Olive Patten, the daughter of the company's president, Z. Cartter Patten, was a major social event of Chattanooga's 1889 season. The couple had one son, Thomas Cartter Lupton.

In 1899 Lupton joined Benjamin Franklin Thomas and Joseph Brown Whitehead in a partnership to bottle Coca-Cola, in an agreement that gave the three exclusive bottling rights for most of the United States. Lupton served as vice president of the newly chartered Coca-Cola Bottling Company and became the most successful of the three bottling pioneers. In 1900 the partners split the bottling territory, with Lupton and Whitehead receiving most of the western United States and the South. They established "parent" bottling companies to grant local franchise bottling rights. Following Whitehead's death in 1906, Lupton took a more active role in management, serving as president or director of many of the bottling companies.

In addition to the soft drink business, Lupton maintained various other business interests. In 1906 he joined his father-in-law in organizing and promoting the Volunteer State Life Insurance Company. He served as president of the Stone Fort Land Company, developers of important real estate holdings in downtown Chattanooga. In 1910 he purchased and oversaw the revival of the Thacher Medicine Company. Around 1920, he completed construction of the Dixie Mercerizing Company and served as president of the mill, which became a leader in the southern textile industry. Today, the company operates as Dixie Yarns. Adjacent to the plant site, he developed a modern planned company town, known as Lupton City, now a part of Chattanooga.

In later life, Lupton concentrated on philanthropy as much as business. He became a major financial supporter of several southern colleges and universities, including Oglethorpe College, the University of the South, the University of Chattanooga, George Peabody College, Agnes Scott College, and his alma maters, Roanoke College and the University of Virginia. He served as trustee for many of these schools. He was the leader in the acquisition of land and the construction of new buildings for Baylor School, a Chattanooga preparatory school and frequent recipient of his generosity.

In 1909 Lupton built "Lyndhurst," at the time one of the largest estates in the South, in the Chattanooga residential community of Riverview. He died at his summer home near Sapphire, North Carolina, following complications from an appendectomy. He was buried in Chattanooga's Forest Hills Cemetery.

Ned L. Irwin, East Tennessee State University

SUGGESTED READING: Ned L. Irwin, "Bottling Gold: Chattanooga's Coca-Cola Fortunes," *Tennessee Historical Quarterly* 51(Winter 1992): 223–37

SEE: BAYLOR SCHOOL; CHATTANOOGA; CHATTANOOGA MEDICINE COMPANY; COCA COLA BOTTLING COMPANY; DIXIE SPINNING MILLS; LYNDHURST FOUNDATION; MCADOO, WILLIAM GIBBS; PATTEN, ZEBOIM C.; THOMAS, BENJAMIN F.; WHITEHEAD, JOSEPH B.

LURTON, HORACE HARMON (1844–1914), the third of six Tennesseans appointed to the U.S. Supreme Court, was born in Newport, Kentucky, on February 26, 1844. In the 1850s the family moved to Clarksville, Tennessee. Lurton attended Chicago's Douglas University (now defunct), but left in 1861 to return to Tennessee, and joined the Confederate army.

In February 1862, Lurton received a medical discharge because of a lung infection, but soon reenlisted and was captured by Union troops at Fort Donelson. He escaped and joined General John Hunt Morgan's cavalry. Morgan's band of raiders engaged in sabotaging Union railroads, bridges, and communication lines. In July 1863 Union solders captured Lurton for the second time, and he spent the rest of the war in a Lake Erie prisoner-of-war camp. During his detention, he developed tuberculosis and took a loyalty oath to the Union to secure his release.

In 1865 Lurton enrolled in Cumberland University law school and received his law degree in 1867. That same year, he married Mary Frances Owen; the couple became parents to three sons and two daughters.

After graduation, Lurton opened his law practice in Clarksville and became an active Democrat. From 1875 to 1878, he served as chancery judge before returning to private practice. In 1886 he was elected to the Tennessee Supreme Court, becoming chief justice in 1893. Only four months later, President Grover Cleveland nominated him to the U.S. Sixth Circuit Court of Appeals in Cincinnati, a post he held for the next 16 years. In addition, Lurton taught constitutional law at Vanderbilt University from 1898 to 1905 and served as dean of the law school from 1905 to 1909.

On December 13, 1909, President William Howard Taft, a friend and former colleague from the Sixth Circuit Court, crossed party lines to appoint Lurton to the U.S. Supreme Court. Lurton wrote 87 opinions during his more than four years on the court, voting most frequently with Oliver Wendell Holmes, Jr., yet he did not author any major decisions. Lurton also became deeply involved in the effort to reform the equity rules in federal courts.

On July 12, 1914, Lurton suffered a fatal heart attack while vacationing in Atlantic City, New Jersey. He is buried in Greenwood Cemetery in Clarksville.

Ed Young, Nashville

SUGGESTED READING: Melvin I. Urofsky, *The Supreme Court Justices: A Biographical Dictionary* (1994)

SEE: CLARKSVILLE; MORGAN, JOHN HUNT; TENNESSEE SUPREME COURT

LYNCH, MATTHEW SIMPSON (1912–1981), labor organizer, lobbyist, and administrator, was the grandson of an organizer of New England shoe workers. Lynch began working in a Chattanooga hosiery mill and joined his first union as a teenager. In 1934 he graduated from the Chattanooga College of Law and began organizing for CIO-affiliated groups in Tennessee and Georgia. Following a stint in the Navy during World War II, Lynch became the executive director of the Tennessee Industrial Union Council, where the bulk of his energy was spent lobbying for union issues. When the Tennessee AFL and CIO merged in 1956, Lynch became its first secretary-treasurer, a post which allowed him to forge strong relationships with Tennessee politicians. From 1963 until he retired in 1979, Lynch served as the president of the Tennessee State Labor Council and the chief labor spokesman in the state. Throughout his career as a labor lobbyist, Lynch worked 80-hour weeks championing labor issues such as higher minimum wage laws, repeal of the state's poll tax, simplified voter registration, and the repeal of the open shop law. Not always successful, Lynch was nonetheless a shrewd politician and one of Tennessee's most effective labor leaders.

Christopher Caplinger, Vanderbilt University

SUGGESTED READING: Perry C. Cotham, *Toil, Turmoil, and Triumph: A Portrait of the Tennessee Labor Movement* (1995)

SEE: LABOR

LYNCHING was one of many expressions of violence directed mostly towards African Americans following Reconstruction and lasting well into the twentieth century. According to one set of statistics, lynch mobs in the old Confederate states, including Tennessee, killed 2,805 people, roughly one victim every week, between 1882 and 1930. Tennessee had 214 confirmed lynch victims during this period; 37 victims were white, 177 were African American. An additional 34 remain as unreconciled listings. Tennessee ranked sixth in the nation in the number of lynchings, behind Mississippi, Georgia, Texas, Louisiana, and Alabama.

Most Tennessee lynchings occurred in West and Middle Tennessee. Various causes were cited for lynchings, including rape, murder, theft, trouble with a white man, arson, attempted rape, criminal assault, mother of arsonists, barn-burning, preaching Mormonism, keeping a white woman, bad character, testifying, fighting a white man, conflict over fishing rights, and manslaughter.

The National Association for the Advancement of Colored People created a lynching profile, which included four components: 1) evidence that person was killed; 2) the victim met death illegally; 3) a group of three or more persons participated in the killing; and 4) the group acted under the pretext of service to justice or tradition. Sociologists and authors E.M. Beck and Stewart A. Tolnay compiled a new inventory of southern lynchings through careful research of the files of the NAACP, Tuskegee Institute, and *The Chicago Tribune*, which they compared to contemporary newspaper coverage to confirm actual lynchings.

Lynchings occurred in 70 Tennessee counties. Shelby County ranked first in the state with 18, and Obion County was second with 17. The largest documented group lynching took place in August 1894 in Shelby County, where six men, accused of arson, were lynched. Davidson County recorded three lynchings, Hamilton County four, and Knox County one, during the same period. Local newspapers frequently described a spectacle or celebratory atmosphere that accompanied lynchings. Announcements and promotions of lynchings prior to their occurrence were printed in newspapers or spread by word of mouth, via railroad conductors. The *Memphis Press* declared the burning of prisoner Henry Lowery "an outstanding lynch success."[1] Tennessee's "greatest lynching carnival" was held in Memphis in May 1917, when Ell Person, the allegedly confessed ax-murderer of a 16-year-old white girl, was burned to death in the presence of 15,000 men, women, and little children. The mother of the murdered child cheered the mob as they poured oil on the man and set him afire. The *Memphis Press* said that "the mob fought and screamed and crowded to get a glimpse of him and the mob closed in and struggled about the fire."[2]

African-American victims, both men and women, were regularly tortured with methods that included eye-gouging, cutting off of the ears and nose, and cutting off fingers and toes joint by joint for souvenirs. Lynch mobs used corkscrews to tear flesh and wire pliers to extract teeth. African-American men were usually unsexed as part of the lynching; African-American women were raped. According to the evidence, white male lynching victims were not tortured before death, nor were white females raped.

Social, cultural, economic, and political forces supported lynching in the South. Although the Civil Rights Act of 1875 legislated open access to public transportation and public facilities, the U.S. Supreme Court nullified the law in an 1883 decision. The continuation of the plantation system, economic exploitation through the crop-lien system, and dependency on the paternalism of landlords made it difficult for African-American workers to escape poverty and degradation. Southern political leaders crusaded on the theme of racial superiority.

Lynchings created a form of social control that effectively limited full access to the story of lynching: victims' families, friends, and community members lived in fear and adopted a code of silence. Coroner's juries attributed the cause of death for lynching victims to have occurred "at the hands of parties unknown," or suggested suicide in the case of hanging. The identity of lynchers was rarely hidden, and local police often helped with traffic control and assisted in the protection of participants. Lynchers were chiefly young men, ranging in age from late teens to 25 years of age. They came from an unattached group of people who exercised the least responsibility and were farthest removed from institutions and agencies determining accepted standards of conduct. Ninety-nine percent of mob members escaped arrest and punishment.

Anti-lynching efforts included those of African-American journalists T. Thomas Fortune and Memphis resident Ida B. Wells; Jessie Daniel Ames, Director of Women's Work in the Commission on Interracial Cooperation; and the Association of Southern Women for the Prevention of Lynching. In 1897 Tennessee became one of three states to enact an anti-lynching law, making lynching a felony. Two

anti-lynching bills failed Congress: the Dyer Bill of 1920, which made lynching a federal crime and imposed a minimum five-year jail sentence for any state or federal employee who did not attempt to prevent a lynching, and the Wagner Bill of 1938. According to statistics kept by Fisk University, Elbert Williams of Haywood County became the last recorded lynching victim in Tennessee, in June 1940, when he attempted to register to vote and establish a NAACP chapter in Brownsville.

Kathy Bennett, Nashville

CITATIONS:

(1) Frank Shay, *Judge Lynch* (1938), 92

(2) Ibid, 131.

SUGGESTED READINGS: Judith Jackson Fossett and Jeffrey A. Tucker, eds., *Race Consciousness: African-American Studies for a New Century* (1997); Donald Lee Grant, *The Anti-Lynching Movement, 1883–1932* (1975); Stewart E. Tolnay and E.M. Beck, *A Festival of Violence: An Analysis of Southern Lynchings, 1882–1930* (1995)

SEE: CIVIL RIGHTS MOVEMENT; HUTCHINS, STYLES L.; NAACP; WELLS-BARNETT, IDA B.

LYNDHURST FOUNDATION, a Chattanooga charitable foundation, was organized in 1978 by Coca-Cola bottling heir, John T. (Jack) Lupton II, and family, following the death of his parents, Thomas Cartter Lupton and Margaret Rawlings Lupton. Named for the former Lupton family estate in the Riverview community, the foundation was originally organized by Cartter Lupton in 1938 as the Memorial Welfare Foundation, the first private foundation established in Tennessee.

Lyndhurst's philosophy centered on the "search for new ideas related to learning in the fields of health, education, and the arts." The foundation provided funds and encouragement for a number of Chattanooga projects, including the Tennessee Aquarium and the Lupton Library at the University of Tennessee at Chattanooga campus. Much of the economic and cultural growth of the city, especially downtown renewal, would not have been possible without the contributions of the foundation. In 1991 Jack Lupton retired as board chairman, and his four children were appointed to the board. The foundation's scope has expanded over the years to cover not only Chattanooga, but the southeastern United States. New headquarters opened in the renovated Thomas McConnell house in downtown Chattanooga in 1995.

Ned L. Irwin, East Tennessee State University

SEE: LUPTON, JOHN THOMAS; TENNESSEE AQUARIUM

LYNK, MILES VANDERHORST (1871–1956), physician, journalist, and educator, was born in Brownsville, Tennessee, on June 3, 1871, the son of former slaves. His father was killed when Lynk was only six years old, and he was running the farm by the time he was 11. His mother insisted that he attend school five months a year, and Lynk supplemented his education by reading at home in what he later called "Pine Knot College." He began teaching in Fayette County when he was 17, saving his money for further education. Lynk graduated from Meharry Medical College in 1891.

Lynk became the first black physician in Jackson, Tennessee, and founded the first medical journal published by an African American, *The Medical and Surgical Observer*, published monthly from 1892 to 1894. He also published a literary magazine from 1898 to 1900. Lynk was a co-founder of the National Medical Association for African-American Physicians in 1895.

In 1900 Lynk founded the University of West Tennessee, with departments of medicine, law, dentistry, pharmacy, and nursing. In 1907 the school moved to Memphis. Dr. Fanny Kneeland, one of the first women to practice medicine in Memphis, was a member of the faculty. The Jane Terrell Baptist Hospital provided clinical training. When the school closed in 1924, it had issued 216 medical degrees.

Lynk was also a founder of the Bluff City Medical Society and an active member of Collins Chapel CME Church. He wrote several books and numerous articles.

In 1893 Lynk married Beebe Stephen, a Lane College graduate, who taught chemistry and medical Latin. They were married for 55 years. After her death in 1948, he married Ola Herin Moore. Lynk died on December 29, 1956.

Perre Magness, Memphis

SEE: HAYWOOD COUNTY; JACKSON; MEDICINE; MEHARRY MEDICAL COLLEGE

LYNN, LORETTA (1935–), influential country music performer and songwriter, and member of the Country Music Hall of Fame, was born Loretta Webb in Johnson County, Kentucky, in 1935. She married Oliver V. "Mooney" Lynn in 1948, and soon thereafter the Lynns moved to Washington State. By the late 1950s Lynn began her musical career, performing at local clubs. In 1960 Buck Owens booked her on his popular radio show produced at Tacoma, Washington. Zero Records, based at nearby Vancouver, British Columbia, recorded and released her first single, *I'm A Honky Tonk Girl*.

The song became a hit, and by 1961 Lynn landed her first appearances at the Ernest Tubb's influential "Midnight Jamboree" on WSM Radio and the Grand Ole Opry in Nashville, appearing on the Opry for 17 consecutive weeks before joining the cast. Kitty Wells, Patsy Cline, Ernest Tubb, and producer Owen Bradley influenced Lynn's development. Since 1960–1961 Lynn has been a Tennessee resident, living first in Nashville before acquiring 1,200 acres at Hurricane Mills in Humphreys County in 1966. There she and Mooney Lynn established their home and later the Loretta Lynn Dude Ranch, which is a popular tourist destination.

Lynn has significantly influenced country music, especially the role of women as performers and songwriters. Named to the Country Music Hall of Fame in 1988, the zenith of her career was during the 1970s. In 1972 Lynn was the first woman to be named "Entertainer of the Year" by the Country Music Association. Her autobiography, *Coal Miner's Daughter* (1976), became a bestseller and later an award-winning movie. Lynn formed a popular duet with Conway Twitty, who also was a huge fan favorite in the 1970s. During the decade, she won many "Female Vocalist of the Year" awards from various institutions and was named the "Artist of the Decade" by the Academy of Country Music in 1979.

Although Lynn's number of recordings and performances have decreased from her height of popularity in the 1970s, she continues to perform and record. Her classic songs about women of strength and emotion, like *You Ain't Woman Enough*, endure and continue to influence such recent women writers as Nanci Griffith and Mary Chapin Carpenter.

Carroll Van West, Middle Tennessee State University and Ethan R. Lyell, Hurricane Mills

SEE: BRADLEY, OWEN; COUNTRY MUSIC ASSOCIATION; COUNTRY MUSIC HALL OF FAME; GRAND OLE OPRY; HUMPHREYS COUNTY; MUSIC; TUBB, ERNEST

LYTLE, ANDREW NELSON (1902–1995), writer, editor, critic, and teacher, was born the day after Christmas, 1902—like a "wet fire-cracker," his grandmother remarked. He would spend nearly the rest of the century pondering the remote world into which he had been born: the rural farmland and agrarian life of Middle Tennessee, the heart of the yeoman South. Writer, editor, teacher, farmer, critic, and famously hospitable host, Lytle was the most enduring member of the Agrarians, the collection of essayists at Vanderbilt University who published the 1930 manifesto *I'll Take My Stand*. It was a formidable assembly of talent: Robert Penn Warren, Allen Tate, John Crowe Ransom, and Donald Davidson. And it was, for the era, a powerful message: deeply suspicious of central authority and industrialization; Lytle and his comrades made a case for preserving the economy, habits, and values of the farm and small town. Coming after World War I and in the midst of the Great Depression, the book resonated in a region long soaked in sentimentality.

Eventually, most of the Vanderbilt figures moved North. But Lytle stayed in the South. Living mainly in his ancestral log house in Monteagle, Lytle taught at The University of the South and edited *The Sewanee Review*, the oldest continuously published literary quarterly in the country, that he helped turn into a showcase for the old Confederacy's best writers at the pinnacle of the southern renaissance, including Warren, Tate, Caroline Gordon, Flannery O'Connor, Peter Taylor, Katherine Anne Porter, and Cleanth Brooks.

Lytle was the center of this enduring circle, a man of enormous charm, lyrical story-telling gifts, and a fixed world view that lasted until his death in December 1995 at Monteagle. Celebrated more in the South, particularly in upcountry states like his native Tennessee, than in the rest of the country, he was chiefly an artist, a literary man whose history, novels, and stories rank, in quality, with the better-known work of William Faulkner. Lytle kept his eye on the permanent things; he always thought in epic, mythic terms—then brought overarching themes down to earth. "Now that I have come to live in a sense of eternity," he wrote in his family chronicle *A Wake for the Living* (1975), "I can tell my girls who they are." He spent his life telling his three daughters, and the rest of us, exactly where we all came from.

Born in Murfreesboro, in Rutherford County, Lytle was the son of Robert Logan Lytle, a farmer and lumberman, and Lillie Belle Nelson. (In 1938, Andrew married Edna Barker, and they had three daughters.) A founding family of the Middle Tennessee town—a Revolutionary War ancestor had donated the land for the city—the Lytles raised their son there and in northern Alabama. Andrew attended Sewanee Military Academy, on the grounds of The University of the South, then graduated from Vanderbilt with a Bachelor of Arts in 1925. That year he was accepted at Exeter College, Oxford, but was summoned home on the death of his grandfather. After discharging his familial duties, he moved north, to New Haven, Connecticut, as a student at the Yale School of Drama from 1927 to 1929. Always theatrical, he supported himself as an actor in several plays in New York City.

Lytle's serious literary career began in the late 1920s, as he worked on a biography of Nathan Bedford Forrest. His book turned into *Bedford Forrest and His Critter Company* (1931), in which he used the wild Confederate general to muse on the nature of the hero in decidedly unheroic times. It is a marvelous narrative, one that helped inspire another southern writer, Shelby Foote, as he wrote his epic history of the Civil War decades later.

Lytle soon turned his attention to serious fiction, writing a powerful and enduring short story, "Jericho, Jericho, Jericho," which contains perhaps the finest dramatic narrative of the moment of death in the English language. Then came *The Long Night* (1936), a novel of revenge set during the Civil War. It was followed by *At the Moon's Inn* (1941); *A Name for Evil* (1947); and his masterpiece, *The Velvet Horn* (1957). He also authored three collections of essays and one collection of stories, as well as a ruminative book on Sigrid Undset, published near the end of his life.

For many years, Lytle also kept up a punishing teaching schedule. He lectured on American history for a year at the old Southwestern at Memphis (now Rhodes College); taught at the Iowa Writers Workshop (one of his students there was Flannery O'Connor); and founded the writing program at the University of Florida, where he was resident from 1948 to 1961. He also taught at Kenyon College and the University of Kentucky. In 1961 he returned to Sewanee to edit *The Sewanee Review* and teach English and creative writing at The University of the South. He retired from his official university duties in 1973. Among his honors are two Guggenheim fellowships, a Kenyon Review fellowship, a National Institute of Arts and Letters fellowship, and a special achievement award from the Fellowship of Southern Writers in Chattanooga, of which he was a founding member.

Lytle then opened the long final chapter of his life and career, becoming the South's most gracious man of letters. On his vine-covered porch in summer and before his stone fireplace in winter, Lytle presided over a salon featuring bourbon in sterling silver cups and his own ruminations, ranging from theological musings to backwoods tall tales, from the proper use of olive oil to the decline and fall of the Episcopal Church. By turns formal and earthy, he fascinated generations of undergraduates and transfixed aspiring writers and journalists who, in search of the authentic South, gathered around him, dining and listening—always listening to his incomparable, subtly sophisticated voice. Still a fierce defender of Agrarianism—at several points in his life he had in fact attempted to write and farm at the same time—he would nevertheless dress in Brooks Brothers shirts and, for a time in the 1980s, drove a black Mercedes around the Mountain.

At heart, however, Lytle belonged to another age. "I'm in a precarious position," he would say to guests at the log cabin, and he did not just mean his health. Reflecting on his Forrest biography, he once said: "The world over which Forrest's men rode and fought was closer to Henry II's than it is to ours. They are centuries apart, yet those centuries knew the orderly return of the seasons, saw the supernatural in the natural, moved about by foot, by horse and at sea by the wind. We have put our faith in the machine." It was quintessential Lytle: erudite, authoritative, unapologetic. In the end, he was more artist than polemicist, though, and as he lay dying all of his work was in print. "If three generations are reading my book," he said, "then it's holding up—that means, it's not just a provincial thing." His art is indeed universal, and will endure.

Jon Meacham, New York, New York

SEE: AGRARIANS; BROOKS, CLEANTH; DAVIDSON, DONALD; FORREST, NATHAN BEDFORD; GORDON, CAROLINE; RANSOM, JOHN CROWE; RUTHERFORD COUNTY; THE SEWANEE REVIEW; TATE, JOHN O. ALLEN; TAYLOR, PETER; WARREN, ROBERT PENN; UNIVERSITY OF THE SOUTH

M

MACLELLAN BUILDING in Chattanooga was built as the home office for Provident Life and Accident Insurance Company. Founded in 1887 in Chattanooga, the Mutual Medical Aid and Accident Insurance Company specialized in providing accident coverage to the "uninsurables"—miners, railroad workers, and lumber mill hands. Incorporated in December 1887 as Provident Life and Accident Insurance Company, the business was an outgrowth of the southern industrial boom of the 1880s.

In 1894 the company founders sold Provident to Thomas Maclellan and John McMaster. Within six years, Maclellan was the sole owner. In an environment of failed insurance companies, he built a highly successful business around the theme of stability. During the twentieth century, the specialized company grew into a strong national company and a large multi-line insurance carrier with its home office in Chattanooga.

Provident leased space in a series of buildings during its first 20 years of operation before moving into the James Building Annex in 1911. By 1919 Provident was ready for a home of its own and selected R.H. Hunt, the designer of the James Building Annex, as its architect. The final design became the Hunt firm's skyscraper masterpiece, a tribute to and symbol of the company molded by the ideals of the owner and architect. However, the symbol was costly: the final price tag of $640,000 represented over one-third of Provident's assets. At the building's opening, the *Chattanooga News* called it a "monument to courage."

The three-part facade of the Maclellan Building knits the existing James Building Annex into the final composition. A two-story base with attic provided the platform for the thin, brick shaft with limestone trim, which springs from the center portion of the base. The use of materials and elaborate ornamentation differen-

tiated the building's vertical divisions and contributed to the impression of the Maclellan Building's height.

The Maclellan Building uses symbolism and iconography to reinforce and enrich its message. The Hunt firm's proposal cleverly duplicated the James Building Annex on the opposite side of the site. The two stood as pavilions flanking the 13-story shaft infill. Physically and symbolically the old home effectively became part of the new. The building's decorative program contributed to the overall theme of corporate success and stability. The elaborate portal used a colossal Ionic order with decorative sculpture, the eagle holding the earth in his claws, to express the company's strength and economic ambitions. The interior elevators, finished as Pullman cars, were a gesture acknowledging the importance of the city's railroad connections both to Chattanooga and to Provident. Finally, the building itself became a company logo used on letterheads and policies, as a symbol of Maclellan's and Provident's success and stability.

The Maclellan Building was also an important civic symbol. The elegant shaft surmounted by the green tile, mansard roof was the only fully three-dimensional tower in Hunt's Chattanooga work, dramatic and complete when viewed from any angle. The skyscraper continued to house and symbolize the Provident corporation until growth necessitated new corporate headquarters in 1960. The Maclellan Building is leased as office space and remains a significant component of the Chattanooga skyline.

Sara A. Butler, University of Virginia
SEE: CHATTANOOGA; HUNT, REUBEN H.

MACON COUNTY, located on the Eastern Highland Rim Plateau of the Upper Cumberland and bordering Kentucky, was formed by the Tennessee General Assembly in 1842 from parts of Smith and Sumner counties. It was named in honor of Nathaniel Macon, a North Carolina Revolutionary War soldier, U.S. Senator, and Speaker of the House of Representatives. Lafayette, the largest community in the county and the county seat, was named for the French general and hero of the American Revolution, Marie Joseph Gilbert de Motier, Marquis de Lafayette. Lafayette has had four courthouses: an 1844 two-story brick courthouse that burned in 1860, a two-story brick courthouse begun in 1861 and finished in 1866 that burned in 1901, and a 1901 two-story brick and stone structure with a domed clock tower that burned in 1932. The present two-story brick courthouse was completed in 1933 and renovated in 1972.

Macon County encompasses 307 square miles, and the 1990 federal census reported a population of 16,146. It is one of the few Tennessee counties that has never contained a rail line. A municipal airport is located west of Lafayette.

Macon County's economy has depended largely on agriculture. For most of the twentieth century, burley tobacco was the most common cash crop. In 1995 the county's 35,777 acres under production included 25,000 acres in hay, 3,800 acres in soybeans, 3,750 acres in burley tobacco, 2,800 acres in corn, 350 acres in wheat, 61 acres in fruits and vegetables, and 16 acres in dark tobacco. The American Greeting Card Company is the county's largest industrial employer, with 288 employees in 1997.

Red Boiling Springs is the county's second largest community. In the 1840s Samuel Hare recognized the commercial potential and medicinal value of the area's unusual boiling springs. He fenced the springs, built cabins, and developed the area as a "watering place." A thriving community in the 1850s, the Civil War and land disputes halted development and resulted in the demolition of most of the original buildings. In the 1880s New York businessman James F.O. Shaughnesy purchased 200 acres, including the boiling springs, and began to develop the area as a summer resort, which became famous for its mineral springs. At its peak, in the 1920s and 1930s, the resort boasted nine hotels and more than a dozen boarding houses. In addition to the mineral springs treatments, the resort featured horseback riding, tennis, a dammed lake that served as a swimming pool, bowling alleys, and a dance hall. Three of the historic hotels remain and are listed in the National Register of Historic Places. Spring houses still feature five kinds of mineral water: white, red, black, double and twist, and free-stone. Each has a distinctly different mineral composition related to rock formations in the Highland Rim area, and each is considered a cure for different ailments. Red Boiling Springs hosts an annual Folk Medicine Festival on the last weekend in July.

Other notable landmarks include what is reputedly the world's largest sundial near Pleasant Valley, a large concrete structure that Elmer White built

about 1920. The Morrison House, a one-story brick residence built in about 1829, is probably the only pre-Civil War brick building in the county and the oldest building located on its original site. Macon County also boasts one of an increasingly rare artifact of the automobile culture, the Macon Drive-in Theater, on State Route 10 north of Lafayette. Built in 1950, the drive-in is open nine months a year, seven nights a week. Three early twentieth century frame schoolhouses are listed in the National Register. One of these, the Galen Elementary School, northeast of Lafayette, houses the county's Heritage Museum.

One of the county's most famous residents is Nera White, who set various amateur and professional basketball records, beginning in the 1950s. She received numerous national and international awards, and in 1992 became the first female basketball player inducted into the National Basketball Hall of Fame.

Martha Carver, Tennessee Department of Transportation
SEE: RESORTS, HISTORIC; TOBACCO

MACON, DAVID HARRISON "UNCLE DAVE"

(1870–1952), Grand Ole Opry star, born in Warren County in 1870, learned the craft of entertainment from vaudeville actors and actresses that boarded at his parents' rooming house in Nashville. After traveling the vaudeville circuit for a time, Macon acquired a log cabin in Rutherford County from which he founded and operated the Macon Midway Mule and Wagon Transportation Company. As a muleskinner, Macon absorbed the folklore and music of white and black workers in farming communities, on the railroads and rivers, and in the mines. These songs and stories, which became a part of his repertoire, document and preserve an important segment of the changing South.

In 1926 Macon joined WSM's Grand Ole Opry as its first vocalist. His combination of banjo music and homespun humor immediately won many fans from people who identified with his songs and anecdotes about working class people and hard times. Until his death in 1952, "Uncle Dave" Macon regularly performed on the radio show. The National Register-listed log house in which Macon lived for over 50 years still stands on the Old Woodbury Highway, and he is buried in Coleman Cemetery just down the road and across Cripple Creek—the subject of one of his most performed songs.

The celebrated comedian and musician is remembered each July at "Uncle Dave Macon" Days in Murfreesboro, as hundreds gather for the festival featuring "old time music." Macon's contributions are a significant part of the legacy of country music.

Caneta Skelley Hankins, Middle Tennessee State University
SUGGESTED READING: Bill C. Malone, *Country Music USA* (1985)
SEE: FIDDLER AND OLD-TIME MUSIC CONTESTS; GRAND OLE OPRY; MUSIC; RUTHERFORD COUNTY

MADISON COUNTY. Before statehood, West Tennessee was occupied by prehistoric Native Americans, who camped and hunted there as early as 9,000 B.C., as well as much later historic tribes such as the Choctaws and Chickasaws. Woodland Culture peoples developed the large mound village site now protected by the Pinson Mounds State Archaeological Park, the site of three separate mound groups. First discovered in 1820 by a surveyor, Joel Pinson, the mounds remained of local interest until the 1880s, when a Smithsonian Institution archaeologist, William E. Myer, surveyed and mapped the site. Pinson Mounds is the largest Middle Woodland period mound group in the United States and includes one mound, measuring 72 feet, the second tallest mound in the country.

Twenty years after Tennessee statehood, the Chickasaws signed the 1818 treaty that secured the area for settlement. The first farm families came to Madison County in 1819 and settled east of Jackson in Cotton Gin Grove. In the following year, additional pioneers settled further west on the banks of the Forked Deer River in a community they named Alexandria. In 1822 Alexandria changed its name to Jackson in honor of Andrew Jackson. Jackson's sister-in-law Jane Hayes lived in the city, and the general played an important role in the early history of Madison County.

Jackson became the county seat in September 1822, after the Tennessee General Assembly created Madison County in November 1821. In 1835 Congressman David Crockett made an angry speech on the courthouse steps, following his defeat for reelection, in which he told the people of Jackson: "The rest of you can go to hell, for I am going to Texas." A year later he and another Jackson resident, Micajah Autry, were dead at the Alamo. In the antebellum period, Jackson became a transportation center for agricultural products on the Forked Deer River.

During the Civil War, Madison County contributed two Confederate generals, Alexander W. Campbell and William H. "Red" Jackson. The county became the scene of several small battles and skirmishes, the most important of which was the Battle of Britton Lane. A small park in the Denmark area commemorates the engagement in which Confederate cavalry under General Frank C. Armstrong clashed with Federal infantry, leaving more than 170 Confederate dead. Because of its importance in the regional railwork network, Federal troops occupied Jackson for most of the Civil War. In 1864 Federal raiders demanded a ransom or they threatened to burn Jackson. Although the city met the demands, most of downtown Jackson was burned.

The town of Denmark once rivaled Jackson for prominence and size. A number of man-made and natural disasters, including fires, tornadoes, and the relocation of the railroad contributed to its demise. Today only a few houses remain along with a historic antebellum Presbyterian church.

The town of Bemis arose from the cotton fields of Madison County when the Bemis Brothers Bag Company decided to construct a cotton bagging plant and a town along the Illinois Central Railroad. Begun in 1900, the model town developed in several stages and incorporated the designs of graduates from the Massachusetts Institute of Technology as well as local architects such as Reuben A. Heavnor. Jackson annexed Bemis in 1980.

The first railroad appeared in Madison County in 1858 as a result of the promotional efforts of Judge Milton Brown. In addition to serving the transportation needs of commercial agriculture, the railroads developed a labor base for later industrial development. Jackson resident I.B. Tigrett was the president of Gulf, Mobile & Ohio Railroad, which boasted 3,000 miles of track. The legendary Illinois Central Railroad engineer Casey Jones made his home in Jackson. His house is preserved at Casey Jones Village.

Today Madison County offers a wide variety of economic, cultural, and educational benefits. It is the home of Lambuth University, Union University, Lane College, and Jackson State Community College. For many years, Jackson has hosted the Miss Tennessee pageant. Several musical artists claim Madison County as their home, including Sonny Boy Williamson, a legendary blues and harmonica artist; Big Maybell, a gospel and blues recording artist; and Carl Perkins, Mr. "Blue Suede Shoes." Once largely agricultural, the county's economy now rests on a diversified industrial and commercial base. In 1997 the three largest industrial plants were Procter & Gamble, Porter Cable Corporation, and Murray Incorporated, and each of the three employed more than 1,000 workers. Transportation continues to be important to county development, and Madison County is served by Interstate 40, three railroads (Norfolk-Southern, CSX Transportation, and West Tennessee Railroad), and McKeller-Sipes Regional Airport.

At the hub of West Tennessee's agricultural and industrial production, Madison County and the more than 84,000 people who live and work there benefit from a rich history and a bright future.

Harbert Alexander, Jackson

SEE: BEMIS; BROWN, MILTON; CROCKETT, DAVID; HUNTSMAN, ADAM R.; JACKSON; JONES, JONATHAN "CASEY"; LAMBUTH UNIVERSITY; LANE COLLEGE; LANE, ISAAC; MATTHEWS, MARK A.; PERKINS, CARL; PINSON MOUNDS; UNION UNIVERSITY

MAGEVNEY, EUGENE (1798–1873), Memphis entrepreneur and Catholic leader, was born in 1798 in County Fermanagh, Ireland. He studied for the priesthood but changed his mind and became a school teacher. In 1828 he emigrated to the United States and settled in Memphis in 1833. Magevney supported himself by teaching in a small private school, where he accepted land as payment from cash-strapped families.

Within a few years, Magevney's land acquisitions had become large enough to permit him to leave teaching and concentrate on real estate development, where he made his fortune. Soon recognized as a community leader, he served as an alderman and, in 1848, led the fight to establish public schools. Always ready to defend his fellow Irishmen, Magevney wrote editorials in the local newspaper protesting the prejudice to which they were subjected.

A devout Catholic, Magevney helped to establish the city's first Catholic church and parochial school. In 1839 the first mass was celebrated in Magevney's house on Adams Avenue, where the first marriage (his own) and the first baptism (his daughter Mary) were also celebrated. Magevney was also one of those responsible for the founding of St. Peter's Catholic Church, which was located next to his house. In 1941 the Magevney heirs donated the house to the City of Memphis. It is now part of the Memphis Museum System and open to the public.

Anne Leonard, Memphis

SUGGESTED READING: Charles W. Crawford and Robert M. McBride, "The Magevney House, Memphis," *Tennessee Historical Quarterly* 28(1969): 345–55

SEE: MEMPHIS; RELIGION

MAGIC CHEF, now a branch of the Maytag Corporation, a major manufacturer of appliances, is based in Cleveland, Tennessee. It began in 1916 as a family-owned and operated company known as Dixie Foundry. Company founder, S.B. Rymer, Sr., was a native of Polk County, but his family later immigrated to what was then Oklahoma Territory. In 1916 Rymer and his family returned to Tennessee, settling at Cleveland, where he established several retail businesses and the Dixie Foundry Company. Dixie Foundry initially produced cast-iron holloware, used for corn stick molds, fireplace grates and frames, sugar pots, and teapots. In 1921 the company began to make coal and wood ranges for the kitchen; thereafter, ranges of different sorts have been the company's main items. In 1924 production expanded to coal and wood heaters. Gas ranges came off the company's lines in 1928, and in 1952 Dixie Foundry produced its first electric ranges.

In 1958 Dixie Foundry acquired Magic Chef, which had been a St. Louis-based manufacturer of gas ranges and an industry leader since the 1930s. Two years later, company officials decided to capitalize on the consumer name recognition of "Magic Chef." They changed the company's name from Dixie Foundry to Magic Chef. Within a year, the company had reasserted its leadership in the national market for gas and electric ranges, and by 1969 the corporation had achieved 11 percent of the market share in the United States.

In 1964 the Rymer family gave up its total control of the company's stock in order to raise new capital through a public offering of stock. By 1970 Magic Chef was listed in the New York Stock Exchange and had significantly diversified its factories and products. In 1957 the company had acquired Dixie-Narco, a manufacturer of soft drink vending machines, and invested in refrigerator production. During the 1960s, it had expanded into air-conditioning manufacturing, especially after its acquisition and consolidation of the Gaffers and Sattler company of Los Angeles in 1969–1970. During the next two decades, Magic Chef aggressively moved into the production of microwave ovens in response to consumer demand. By the late 1970s, Magic Chef employed 1,800 workers at its modern factories in Cleveland, making it one of the region's key private employers. In the 1990s the company was merged with other local firms into Maytag Cleveland Cooking Products, a division with 2,400 employees in 1997.

Carroll Van West, Middle Tennessee State University

MAJORS, JOHN TERRILL (1935–), University of Tennessee football player and coach, was born May 21, 1935, in Lynchburg, Tennessee, the son of Shirley and Elizabeth Majors. Shirley Majors coached football, first as a high school coach and then at the University of the South. All five of his sons played college football; three at the University of Tennessee, one at Florida State, and one at the University of the South. John Majors graduated from Huntland High School in 1953, where he played for his father and scored an astonishing 565 points. Majors enrolled at the University of Tennessee and became an All-American tailback under Coach Bowden Wyatt. The 1956 Volunteer team won the Southeastern Conference Championship. That year, Majors was named the SEC's Most Valuable Player and made every All-American team. He was runner-up to Notre Dame's Paul Hornung for the Heisman Trophy.

After graduation in 1957, Majors joined the UT coaching staff as a student coach. In 1960 he became assistant coach at Mississippi State University, before joining the coaching staff of Frank Broyles at the University of Arkansas in 1964. There he met fellow staff member Doug Dickey. In 1968 Majors became head coach at Iowa State, where he led the Cyclones to two postseason bowl games and was named Big Eight Coach of the Year in 1971. In 1973 Majors accepted the head coaching position at the University of Pittsburgh. When he arrived at Pitt, the Panthers had won only one game the previous season. That fall, Majors produced a 6-5-1 record, followed by a 7-4 record in 1974 and an 8-4 record in 1975. The 1976 team, with Heisman Trophy winner Tony Dorsett, won the national championship.

In 1977 Majors returned to the University of Tennessee as head coach. He first led the Vols to the Astro Bluebonnet Bowl against Purdue in 1979, and thereafter, Majors and the Vols seldom missed a postseason bowl. At Tennessee Majors posted 115 SEC victories, placing him among the top ten all-time SEC coaches for wins, and UT won three SEC championships. In 1993 Majors returned to Pitt and retired from football in 1996.

In 1973 the Football Writers Association and the Walter Camp Foundation honored Majors as National Coach of the Year, the same year his father, Shirley Majors, won honors as Small College Coach of the Year. In 1976 both the Football Writers Association and the American Football Coaches Association named him National Coach of the Year. Majors is a charter inductee into the Tennessee Sports Hall of Fame. He was selected to the All-SEC team picked by sports writers and broadcasters for the years 1950 through 1974.

Majors is married to Chattanooga native Mary Lynn Barnwell Majors. They are the parents of two children, a son John Ireland and a daughter Mary Elizabeth.

Connie L. Lester, Tennessee Historical Society
SEE: FOOTBALL, COLLEGE; UNIVERSITY OF TENNESSEE

MALLORY-NEELY HOUSE, located at 652 Adams Avenue, in the Victorian Village historic district of Memphis, is a splendid example of the Italian villa architectural style. Constructed in 1852 for banker Isaac Kirtland and his family, the house later became the home of the Babb, Neely, Mallory, and Grant families. From 1864 to 1883 it was the residence of cotton factor Benjamin Babb. In 1883 another cotton factor, James Columbus Neely, purchased the house and lived there with his wife, Frances, and their five children. The Neely's youngest daughter, Daisy, who married cotton factor Barton Lee Mallory in 1900, returned to the mansion with her husband, where they raised their three children, William Neely and twins, Barton Lee and Frances. Daisy's sister, Pearl Neely Grant, also resided there with her family for a time.

The Neelys renovated the house extensively during the 1880s and 1890s. The two-and-one-half story house was expanded into three full floors, and the central tower was enlarged, creating a 25-room, 16,000-square-foot mansion. The family redecorated it in high Victorian style, featuring ceiling stenciling, ornamental plasterwork, faux grained woodwork, heavily carved etagere mantelpieces, and parquet flooring. The uniqueness of the Mallory-Neely House is its remarkable state of preservation, with much of

the late nineteenth century decor intact, providing valuable insights into Victorian social customs. Most of the eclectic, turn-of-the-century furnishings are original. Stained glass windows from the Neely family's visit to the Columbian Exposition in Chicago in 1893, exquisite pieces brought from the Chinese exhibit at the Louisiana Purchase Exposition in St. Louis in 1903–1904, as well as paintings, sculpture, and decorative objects from world travels still enhance the entrance hall, parlor, dining room, and library of the house.

Barton Mallory died in 1938, but his widow, Daisy Neely Mallory, remained in the residence until her death in 1969 at the age of 98. Daisy Mallory wanted the house to be preserved as a museum, and in 1972 her family deeded the mansion and its furnishings to the Daughters, Sons, and Children of the American Revolution. Since 1987, the house has been operated by the Memphis Park Commission and Memphis Museums, Inc., as a facility of the Memphis Museum System. The Mallory-Neely House is listed in the National Register of Historic Places.

Wendy S. Campbell, Murfreesboro
SEE: MEMPHIS

MAMANTOV, GLEB (1931–1995), internationally recognized chemist in molten salt chemistry, was born in 1931 in Kapsava, Latvia, the son of physicians Alexander V. and Elena Pribikov Mamantov. When, in 1944, the Soviets overran the Baltic States, the anti-Communist Mamantov family fled westward and lived in a displaced persons camp in Kleinkotz, Germany, from 1945 to 1949. He was 18 years old when the family immigrated to the United States; Mamantov became a U.S. citizen in 1955.

At Louisiana State University, Mamantov earned a B.S. in 1953, a Master's degree in 1954, and a Ph.D. in 1957. In 1958 he entered the U.S. Air Force and served in rocket propulsion at Edwards Air Force Base in California. In 1961 Mamantov became an assistant professor of chemistry at the University of Tennessee; he served as department head from 1979 until his death in 1995. Mamantov edited nine books, including five volumes of *Advances in Molten Salt Chemistry and Characterization of Solutes in Non-Aqueous Solvents*. He authored or co-authored 32 book and proceedings chapters and more than 100 publications in scientific journals. He held three patents.

His international recognition includes the Meggers Award of the Society of Applied Spectroscopy (1983). He made a trip to Latvia in 1993, where he was honored for his achievements in chemistry and made a lifetime member of the Latvian Academy of Sciences. In 1994 he received the Max Bredig Award for outstanding scientific contributions to molten salt chemistry. Mamantov was a Fellow in the American Institute of Chemists and in the American Association for the Advancement of Science. He served as a consultant to the Oak Ridge National Laboratories from 1962 until his death in 1995.

Mamantov was married to Dr. Charmaine Bienvenu Mamantov, also a chemistry professor in the UT Evening School. The Mamantovs were the parents of three children. Mamantov died in 1995 at age 63.

Connie L. Lester, Tennessee Historical Society

SEE: OAK RIDGE NATIONAL LABORATORY; SCIENCE AND TECHNOLOGY; UNIVERSITY OF TENNESSEE

MANN, DELBERT (1920–). An award-winning director of many television and cinema productions, Mann was born in Kansas in 1920, but grew up in Nashville. In a career that has included 109 live television shows and more than 50 films, Mann has captivated audiences by his treatment of contemporary dramas, classics from England and the continent, comedies, and historical pieces.

The foundation for this spectacular career was laid in Nashville, where he learned drama from Inez Alder at Hume-Fogg High School and from Fritz Kleibacker and Fred Coe at the Nashville Community Playhouse. After graduation from Vanderbilt, where he had been a student leader, Mann served with distinction as a bomber pilot in World War II. He then studied at Yale Drama School and directed the Town Theatre in Columbia, South Carolina.

Fred Coe brought Mann into the world of live television drama in 1949, where Mann won acclaim for *Marty* in 1953. The Hollywood version of this play won several Academy Awards. In the 1960s Mann became a director of box-office successes like *Lover, Come Back* and *That Touch of Mink*. In 1967 he was made president of the Directors' Guild of America.

Awards received by Mann include a Golden Globe Award for *All Quiet on the Western Front* (1979) and Christopher Awards for *Jane Eyre* (1971), *The Man Without a Country* (1973), *The Ted Kennedy, Jr. Story* (1986), and *Against Her Will: An Incident in Baltimore* (1992). He received Emmy nominations for *Our Town* (1955), *Breaking Up* (1978), and *All Quiet on the Western Front* (1979), as well as five Directors' Guild nominations. Mann's papers are at the Jean and Alexander Heard Library of Vanderbilt University, where he has long served as a member of the Board of Trust.

Sarah M. Howell, Middle Tennessee State University

SEE: COE, FREDERICK

MANSKER, KASPER (ca. 1750–ca. 1820), long hunter and early Middle Tennessee settler, was born on an immigrant ship bound for the American colonies. Little is known about his German ancestry or his early life. Mansker married Elizabeth White of Berkeley County, Virginia, at an unknown date and place.

The couple moved to the head of the Holston River, where Mansker began his hunting career at least by June 1769. A journey taken in 1772 introduced Mansker to the rich resources of Middle Tennessee, especially what is now Sumner County and Davidson County. Near a salt lick and a large creek, known as Mansker Creek, in the present-day city of Goodlettsville, Mansker established his own fortified station, Mansker Station, in 1780. Also that year Mansker signed the Cumberland Compact. Due to repeated Indian raids in the area, settlers left Mansker Station during the winter of 1780–1781 and soon thereafter, Indians burned the abandoned fort. In 1782–1783 Mansker built a new fort about one mile north of the first one. This second Mansker Station became an important early settlement area in Middle Tennessee, where Mansker lived for the remainder of his life. Throughout the years, boarders at the station included such notables as Isaac Bledsoe, Andrew Jackson, and John Overton. Visitors included the French botanist André Michaux.

In 1783 Mansker was a surveyor of the military reservation land that North Carolina planned to grant its Revolutionary War veterans. Four years later, he was elected major of the Sumner County militia and served on the first Sumner County grand jury. When the Southwest Territory was established in 1790, Territorial Governor William Blount appointed Mansker lieutenant colonel of the Sumner County militia. Mansker later participated as a volunteer in the 1794 campaign on the Chickamauga villages. During the War of 1812 he served in the Second Regiment of the Tennessee Volunteer Mounted Gunmen and fought at the Battle of New Orleans in 1815. Five years later, he died at his Sumner County residence and was buried there. In 1956 Mansker's remains were removed to a public park in Goodlettsville. His many contributions to the region's history are now interpreted at Mansker Station, a reconstructed frontier station, in Moss Wright Park in Goodlettsville.

Carroll Van West, Middle Tennessee State University and Betty Freudenthal, Mansker Station historic site

SUGGESTED READING: Walter T. Durham, "Kasper Mansker: Cumberland Frontiersman," *Tennessee Historical Quarterly* 30(1971): 154–177

SEE: BLEDSOE, ISAAC; CUMBERLAND COMPACT; FRONTIER STATIONS

MANUMISSION SOCIETY OF TENNESSEE. In December 1814 Charles Osborn and other Quakers met to form the first anti-slavery society in Tennessee. By February 1815 these men had drawn up a constitution and established the "Tennessee Society for Promoting the Manumission of Slaves." Branches of this society appeared in other East Tennessee counties, and in November 1815 its first convention met in

Greene County, where the delegates adopted the constitution of the Manumission Society of Tennessee.

The constitution of the Manumission Society advocated gradual abolition rather than immediate emancipation and forbade members to vote for public officials who did not support manumission. Slaveholders were permitted to join the society, but they were encouraged to free their slaves and educate them. Charles Osborn wanted the society to take a stronger abolitionist stand, and when he failed to achieve that he moved to Ohio, where he continued his efforts on behalf of emancipation. In November 1816, at the second annual convention, which also met in Greene County, Elihu Embree, another Quaker, took a prominent role in the Manumission Society. At this convention, delegates confirmed the society's objective to achieve the gradual abolition of slavery.

After Embree's death in December 1820, Tennessee abolitionists recruited Benjamin Lundy to continue publication of an abolitionist journal in Tennessee. Although Lundy's *Genius of Universal Emancipation* was not officially linked with the Manumission Society, he became an active member and president of the Greeneville branch. Lundy also published the minutes of the annual convention of the Manumission Society of Tennessee in the *Genius.*

By 1823 the Manumission Society of Tennessee supported colonization as a method to solve the problem of slavery. The society claimed 20 branches with a membership of over 600. In 1825 the society "excommunicated" all slaveholding members who refused to educate their slaves. By the end of the 1820s, amid rumors regarding the group's activities, the society forbade members to assist runaway slaves or provide means of escape for slaves. Although the Manumission Society promoted gradual emancipation, it never attempted to free slaves through activities that were illegal under Tennessee law.

As more radical and powerful abolitionist societies appeared in the North, southern anti-slavery societies faced increasing opposition. In 1830 James Jones, president of the Manumission Society of Tennessee, died, and after his death the society foundered and dissolved in the early 1830s.

Tara Mitchell Mielnik, Middle Tennessee State University
SEE: EMBREE, ELIHU; GREENE COUNTY; LUNDY, BENJAMIN; SLAVERY

MARATHON MOTOR WORKS provides a spectacular though short-lived example of new industry during one period of Nashville boosterism. Augustus H. Robinson, Maxwell House Hotel owner, masterminded the removal from Jackson of the automotive division of Southern Engine and Boiler Works to Nashville in 1910. From then until 1914, the company produced motor cars at 1200 Clinton Avenue in what had been a vacant cotton mill. Marathon Motor Works became the South's premier attempt to compete nationally in the pre-World War I automotive industry. Marathons were the only automobiles completely manufactured in Tennessee before the 1980s.

Initially the Marathon was named the Southern. William Collier, a Southern Engine and Boiler Works engineer, designed an automobile in 1906, and by 1910 approximately 600 cars were made in Jackson and sold as Southerns. The two models, a rumble-seat roadster and a five-seat touring car, sold for $1,500. The discovery of another auto also called Southern led Collier to name his models Marathon.

After the move to Nashville, the line expanded to five models in 1911 and to 12 models on four chassis in 1913. The work force also grew from 75 to 400 employees. The factory building was enlarged, and an administration building was constructed in 1912. The production rate rose to 200 cars monthly, with predictions of building 5,000 cars annually.

Tennessee Highway Department officials used Marathons when determining the Memphis-to-Bristol Highway route in 1911. Nationally-run advertisements showed different Marathon models before Nashville's Parthenon and Belmont Mansion. Marathon first sold cars overseas in 1912. They added cheaper models along with the top-of-the-line Champion. For this car, Collier lengthened the wheelbase and enlarged the four-cylinder engine to 45 horse power. He also continued his practice of using aluminum for some parts and acquiring patents for innovations later used throughout the industry.

Collier disagreed with the company president in 1913 and was demoted. Marathon had three presidents in four years, and its board of directors, composed of Nashville business leaders, did not watch the company closely. Collier filed charges of mismanagement; suppliers of parts claimed lack of payment. In 1914 Marathon stopped building cars, though the factory produced parts until 1918. After that time, Marathon faded from public memory. The buildings survive, having served several businesses before renovation and adaptive reuse in the 1990s. The factory at 1200 Clinton Avenue is listed on the National Register of Historic Places.

Margaret D. Binnicker, Middle Tennessee State University
SEE: INDUSTRY; SOUTHERN ENGINE AND BOILER WORKS

MARBLE SPRINGS is a state historic site that documents the Knox County farmstead of General John Sevier, who was the first governor of the State of Tennessee. As a soldier in the Revolutionary War, Sevier received 640 acres from North Carolina in 1785; his property was located at the foot of Bays Mountain, where deposits of marble had been found as well as large springs. Thus, Sevier named his farm "Marble Springs." He established his farm residence before 1792, and he and his family periodically lived in this Knox County three-room log residence, as well as in a fine Knoxville dwelling, until his death in 1815. Three years later, the property was sold to James Dardis.

Restoration efforts at Marble Springs date to 1941, when the state purchased the remaining original log residence and 40 acres. The John Sevier Memorial Commission directed the property's restoration, with the assistance of the Tennessee Historical Commission. Since 1964 the John Sevier Memorial Commission, the Sevier Family Association, and the Sevier Community Club have promoted and maintained the site. In 1971 the property was listed in the National Register of Historic Places. Eight years later, in 1979, the Tennessee Historical Commission appointed the Governor John Sevier Memorial Association to manage and guide future restoration at Marble Springs.

Carroll Van West, Middle Tennessee State University
SEE: KNOX COUNTY; LOG CONSTRUCTION; SEVIER, JOHN

MARBLES COMPETITIONS. The game of marbles is an ancient and universal pastime, with Roman, French, and British roots. In Tennessee, Indian burials of the Mississippian culture yielded clay and stone spheres speculatively interpreted as game pieces. Archaeologists also discovered marbles at Tennessee's early outposts and settlements, including Fort Loudoun, Blount Mansion, and Southwest Point. Excavation of slave quarters at The Hermitage yielded stone, clay, and painted china marbles.

Players maintained varied games through informal marble-playing, often with localized rules and vocabulary. A popular game from pioneer times, primarily played by adult men throughout Tennessee and Kentucky, became known as Euchre, Old Bowler, Big Tennessee, Tennessee Square, Dollar Man, and Big Marbles. It usually requires five or nine large target marbles (1 1/4" diameter), all placed on the edge of a square, except for a center marble. In recent years, Macon County emerged as the most noted locale for this game, with "marble yards" scattered beside country stores and homes.

Until the late 1960s, children brought marbles to Tennessee's school yards. Though many parents and principals outlawed "playing for keeps" as a form of gambling, the fantastic reward of bulging pockets tempted children to break the rules. In one version of "keeps," an entrepreneur loaded a tin can or glass bottle with a few marbles, and challenged all comers to drop their marbles into the container from belt or head height. The owner of the container kept all marbles that missed, while paying out the container's contents for an accurate drop.

Another very common game, called Ring or Circle Marbles, required contestants to place a number of their target marbles inside a ring, marked in the dirt with a stick. Each player owned a favorite marble for shooting, known as a "taw" or "shooter," and attempted to knock the marbles out, while keeping the shooter within the ring. Target marbles were usually glass or clay, although in desperate circumstances children even played with acorns.

In 1922 the traditional ring game became formalized through the National Marbles Tournament, a contest for children. In the 1930s and 1940s city recreation programs, schools, and newspapers in Tennessee sponsored preliminary competitions for this national tournament. Eddie Cox (1934), J. Will Disney (1939), and O.L. Dabney (1940), all from Coal Creek/Lake City, won the All-Southern regional championships, and traveled to Wildwood, New Jersey, for the final rounds with other regional champs. In 1992 Tennessee resumed its participation in the National Marbles Tournament, and two Clay County girls, Amanda Burns (1993) and Molly Reecer (1996), have claimed national championships in the past five years.

Rolley Hole, known as Three Holes, Poison, Granny Hole, or Rolley Holey, has also been widely played in Tennessee, but became especially identified with Clay County and Standing Stone State Park. Since 1983, Standing Stone has hosted the National Rolley Hole Marbles Championship. Partners Wayne Rhoton and Ralph Roberts of Clay County have won more than half the competitions, which include from 16 to 32 teams.

Standing Stone State Park also hosted an International Marbles Festival with competitions and demonstrations of marbles games from Tennessee and around the world.

Bob Fulcher, Clinton
SEE: CLAY COUNTY; MACON COUNTY; ROLLEY HOLE MARBLES; STANDING STONE STATE PARK

MARION COUNTY, located in the southern part of the Cumberland Plateau and the Sequatchie Valley, encompasses 500 square miles. Established in 1817 out of Cherokee lands, the county was named for General Francis Marion, a Revolutionary War leader in South Carolina. When Tennessee became a state , the Sequatchie Valley was a part of Roane County. The upper end of the valley was established as Bledsoe County in 1807. This county included all of the valley, but treaties with the Cherokees kept white settlers out of the lower end. The first white settlers are thought to have been Amos Griffith and William and James Standifer in 1805, while the area was still part of Roane County.

Native Americans have played an important part in the history of present-day Marion County. They built their towns on the rivers and were living here when the white men came. These newcomers kept the Indian names Tennessee and Sequatchie for this area. Recent research indicates that in 1560, Spanish soldiers from Tristan de Luna's expedition entered the Tennessee River valley in the vicinity of Marion County, visiting the main town of the chiefdom of Napochies. More than a century later, the next Europeans to make contact with the Native Americans found a number of tribes in what later became Tennessee. The Cherokee dominated this area later in the 1700s and early 1800s.

In 1789 Chiefs Catetoy and Vann, accompanied by 40 warriors in canoes, intercepted the boat of Colonel James Brown who, with his family and party, was enroute to Middle Tennessee to take up land awarded him for Revolutionary War services. The Indians killed the men and captured the women and children, including Joseph Brown, a youth who later escaped and guided the Cumberland settlers' expedition to Nickajack in 1794 to destroy the native towns of Nickajack, Running Water, and Long Island. After the Cumberland expedition, the Indians made a treaty allowing whites in the lower part of the valley.

The first court in 1817 was held in the house of John Shropshire in what is now Whitwell. Then court was held for one year in the old Cheek house, a two-story double log house located south of Whitwell in a place called Cheekville, later named Liberty, where court had been held while this county was still in North Carolina. In 1819 the county seat was moved to Jasper, named in honor of Sergeant Jasper of Revolutionary War fame. The commissioners to select and establish the county seat were: William Stone, David Oats, Burgess Matthews, Alexander Kelly, William King, William Stevens, and Davis Miller. Betsy Pack, a Cherokee Indian woman, sold these commissioners 40 acres, and the courthouse built in 1820 was near the center of the tract where the present one now stands. John Kelly was the first clerk of the court and Alan Griffith the first registrar.

During the Civil War, sentiment in the county was so divided that frequently members of the same family could be found in both the Confederate and Federal armies. The presence of the railroad and major turnpikes meant that troops from both sides often passed through the county.

Industry and mining marked the county's post-war history. In 1877 James Bowron and associates from England brought sufficient capital into the valley to develop the iron and coal industries. Coal mines opened in Whitwell; coke ovens operated in Victoria; iron ore came from Inman; and smelters dominated South Pittsburg. In the early 1890s J.C. Beene installed a small steam plant at South Pittsburg to serve the city. It became an industrial town for several important iron-making firms and manufacturing companies. The still-operating Lodge Cast Iron is one of the state's oldest manufacturing firms. Industrialist Richard Hardy established Richard City as a com-

pany town for the Dixie Portland Cement Company in the early 1900s. Today the county is famous for its manufacture of fireworks.

The development of hydroelectric power came with the completion of Hales Bar Dam in 1912. In 1933 Congress created the Tennessee Valley Authority for the purpose of flood control, navigation, and the sale of cheap hydroelectric power in the Tennessee Valley. The lake created by its Nickajack Dam covered the earlier Hales Bar Dam. The dams that TVA built on the Tennessee River and its tributaries changed the look of the area without damaging its beauty, while covering sites used by first settlers but improving navigation on the river.

In this lovely Sequatchie Valley today lie the graves of countless military heroes and politicians: Brigadier General William Stone, War of 1812; General Adrian Northcut, Mexican War; U.S. Senator Hopkins Turney; Governor and U.S. Senator James B. Frazier; U.S. Senators Foster V. Brown, James Whiteside, and Tom Stewart; Congressmen Joe Brown, Sam D. McReynolds; and Judges Leslie R. Darr, Alan Kelly, Sam Polk Raulston, Paul Swafford, and John T. Raulston.

Patsy B. Beene, South Pittsburg

SEE: CHICKAMAUGAS; HALES BAR DAM; LUNA EXPEDITION; MINING; TENNESSEE VALLEY AUTHORITY

MARIUS, RICHARD (1933–), historian and novelist, was born in Martel, Tennessee, the son of a Greek father and a Methodist mother from Bradley County. Looking back on his childhood, Marius later identified three elements that contributed to his writing career: a love of the English language, the experiences of a vividly remembered childhood, and his profession as a historian. Among those childhood memories, he recalled his mother reading to him from the Bible and the classics of English and American literature, and growing up in rural East Tennessee during the Great Depression and World War II.

After attending public schools in Lenoir City, Marius graduated *summa cum laude* in journalism from the University of Tennessee in 1954. He earned his B.D. from Southern Baptist Theological Seminary (1958), but not finding the ministry to his liking, he took his M.A. (1959) and Ph.D. (1962) from Yale. He taught history at Gettysburg College and the University of Tennessee before becoming director of Expository Writing at Harvard University, where he now teaches English.

While at the University of Tennessee, Marius wrote his first novel, *The Coming of Rain* (1971), a period novel, heavy with memory, set in fictional Bourbonville in East Tennessee 20 years after the Civil War. In characterization, plot structure, imagery, and pure craftsmanship, *The Coming of Rain* ranks among the finest novels written by a Tennessean about Tennessee. The author recently dramatized the work for stage production. Marius followed with *Bound for the Promised Land* (1976), an episodic novel of a Tennessee man in search of his father in the American West; *After the War* (1992), set once again in Bourbonville after World War I, with Paul Alexander, a Greek immigrant like Marius's father, as the protagonist; and *An Affair of Honor* (1998), also set in Tennessee.

Other writings include *Luther* (1974), *Thomas More: A Biography* (1985), *The McGraw-Hill College Handbook* (with Harvey Weiner, 1985), *A Writer's Companion* (1994), and *The Columbia Book of Civil War Poetry* (co-edited with Keith Frome, 1994). A major reconsideration of Martin Luther is in progress.

Edwin S. Gleaves, Tennessee State Library and Archives
SEE: LITERATURE

MARKS, ALBERT SMITH

MARKS, ALBERT SMITH (1836–1891), lawyer, soldier, and governor, was born at Owensboro, Kentucky, on October 16, 1836, the son of Elisha S. Marks. He grew up on his father's farm in Daviess County. After the death of his father, Marks received little formal education, but spent as much time as possible reading fiction, history, biography, and the Greek and Roman classics. When he was 19, Marks moved to Winchester, Tennessee, to accept a position in the law office of a relative, Arthur S. Colyar. There he read law and was admitted to the bar in 1858. He practiced in the firm of Colyar, Marks and Frizzell until the outbreak of the Civil War.

Marks supported the Southern Democratic ticket of Breckinridge and Lane in the presidential election of 1860. Strongly opposed to secession, he ran as a Union candidate for district delegate to the state convention, but was defeated by Peter Turney. When Tennessee voted to withdraw from the Union, he enlisted in the Confederate Army, was elected captain, and later promoted to colonel of the Seventeenth Tennessee Infantry. At the Battle of Stones River on December 31, 1862, Marks was wounded while leading a charge against a Federal battery. As a result, surgeons amputated his right leg, and he endured a long hospital convalescence. When he recovered, Marks was attached to the staff of General Nathan Bedford Forrest as judge advocate and served in that capacity until the end of the war.

Colonel Marks married Novella Davis, daughter of John R. Davis of Wilson County, in April 1863, at the Marshall County home of her uncle, J.M. Knight. After the war, Marks resumed his law practice, first with Colyar until 1866, and then with James B. Fitzpatrick and T.D. Gregory until 1870, when he was elected Chancellor of the Fourth Chancery Division.

Marks was selected as the Democratic candidate for Governor in 1878, and elected that fall. The most pressing problem of his administration involved the matter of the state debt, over which the state was badly divided. At the Democratic convention in 1880, Marks declined a nomination for a second term. Following his term in office, he resumed his law practice at Winchester and continued to be active in state and national politics. In 1888 he was a delegate to the Democratic National Convention. He died at Nashville on November 4, 1891.

John H. Thweatt, Tennessee State Library and Archives
SUGGESTED READING: Margaret I. Phillips, *The Governors of Tennessee* (1978)

SEE: COLYAR, ARTHUR S.; FORREST, NATHAN BEDFORD; STATE DEBT CONTROVERSY; STONES RIVER, BATTLE OF; TURNEY, PETER

MARR AND HOLMAN ARCHITECTURAL FIRM

MARR AND HOLMAN ARCHITECTURAL FIRM, founded by Thomas Marr in 1897, grew rapidly in the 1910s and 1920s as it specialized in the design of theaters, schools, hotels, and other commercial buildings. Marr began his career as a draftsman for Nashville architect George Thompson, and two years later, he enrolled in an architectural program at Massachusetts Institute of Technology. Marr opened his Nashville architectural practice as a residential architect, but house commissions accounted for little of the firm's overall work.

Joseph Holman started his career as an office boy in Marr's firm and rose rapidly to partnership. Holman built the firm into a major power, aggressively pursuing both public and private contracts. He courted long-term clients such as Tony Sudekum's Crescent Amusement Company, for which the firm designed numerous theaters. In the 1920s the firm developed a close relationship with Nashville's powerful financial empire, Caldwell and Company. Caldwell financed numerous Marr and Holman commissions including the Andrew Jackson Hotel, Harry Nichol Building, and Cotton State Life Building. Holman offered access to project financing to other firms in Georgia, Florida, North and South Carolina, in exchange for making his firm a partner in their projects. This relationship helped account for the firm's tremendous growth during the 1920s, placing it in a very advantageous position over its competitors, until the demise of the Caldwell empire in 1932.

The development of the Marr and Holman firm presents a microcosm of the evolution of architectural firms in the United States. Marr began as a draftsman and became one of Tennessee's first technically trained architects. His fortuitous association with Holman reflected a movement within larger firms toward divisions of responsibilities according to individual strengths, as Marr assumed responsibility for project design and office supervision, while Holman's personal connections and business acumen enhanced the firm's growth.

James Draeger, State Historical Society of Wisconsin
SEE: CALDWELL AND COMPANY

MARSHALL COUNTY was established by the Tennessee General Assembly in 1836 from parts of Giles, Bedford, Lincoln, and Maury counties. Its name honors former U.S. Supreme Court Chief Justice John Marshall of Virginia. The members of the first county court, with William McClure, chairman and David McGahey, secretary, met at the home of Abner Houston, who donated land for a county seat. James Osborne, William Williams, Joel Yowell, Aaron Boyd, and James C. Record then served as a committee to build a courthouse and jail, layout the new town's streets, and sell lots. The county seat was named Lewisburg in honor of Meriwether Lewis, of the Lewis and Clark Expedition, who died in adjacent Lewis County. Lewisburg today is an attractive rural town of 9,879. The town square is dominated by the Marshall County Courthouse (1929), a Colonial Revival-styled building designed by the Nashville architectural firm of Hart Freeland Roberts and later modernized by the same firm in the mid-1970s. Other Lewisburg landmarks include the National Register-listed Adams House, a Queen Anne-styled dwelling built by local civic capitalist and town mayor Joe C. Adams circa 1900; the Art Deco-styled Dixie Theater; a Colonial Revival-styled post office constructed by the Works Progress Administration in 1935; and the Ladies Rest Room, the first known independent building (1924) constructed in Tennessee for the sole purpose of providing a place for country women to relax, rest, and eat when they visited the town square in the early twentieth century. The National Register-listed Ladies Rest Room remains in service for visitors in 1998.

Chapel Hill, the county's second largest town with 833 residents, is at the north end of Marshall County. Confederate General Nathan Bedford Forrest was born at a nearby farm; the Forrest homeplace is currently under restoration by the Sons of Confederate Veterans. Cornersville is another important country town, at the south end of Marshall County. Several outstanding antebellum homes are nearby and the Cornersville United Methodist Church (1852), a Greek Revival-styled brick building, is listed in the National Register. Other villages in Marshall County include Belfast, Farmington, Verona, and Berlin, famous as a location for political stump speeches during the antebellum era.

Little research has been undertaken about the county's black history. During the 1920s the Rosenwald Fund's school building program constructed new black schools at Farmington, Chapel Hill, and Lewisburg. This positive development, however, occurred within a context of four verified lynchings in the county from 1900–1931, one of the highest numbers in a Tennessee county in these years.

Agriculture has dominated the county's economic history, with specialized stock breeding representing a distinctive contribution to the modern history of Tennessee agriculture. In the late 1920s the U.S. Department of Agriculture, at the urging of several local government leaders and businessmen, including future Governor James N. McCord, established the U.S. Dairy Experiment Station on the highway between Lewisburg and Cornersville. The experiment station, now part of the University of Tennessee Extension Service, was extremely significant in assisting the county's rise to national prominence in production of Jersey cattle. By the late 1930s, for example, Marshall County was the nation's largest Jersey producer and several dairy products companies established local factories. The *WPA Guide for Tennessee* noted: "one of the condenseries here has an annual capacity of 25 million gallons, and a co-operative creamery produces approximately 2 million pounds of cheese and 2 million pounds of butter each year."[1] The success of the Dairy Experiment Station further encouraged McCord and other local residents to establish the first official register for Tennessee Walking Horses in Lewisburg in the mid-1930s. That registry is still maintained at the Lewisburg headquarters of the Tennessee Walking Horse Breeders and Exhibitors Association.

Henry Horton State Park, named in honor of a former Tennessee governor from Marshall County, was constructed in the 1960s along the Duck River near Chapel Hill. It contains the first golf course specifically constructed for a Tennessee state park.

Besides former Governors Horton and McCord and General Nathan Bedford Forrest, other Marshall Countians of note include Governor Buford Ellington, who moved in 1941 to Verona where he operated a farm, ran a general store, and began his political career. Isaac Rainey (1763–1826), a Revolutionary War veteran from North Carolina, moved to the area in 1823 and died at his Duck River farm near Chapel Hill in 1826. Another Revolutionary War veteran was John Medearis, who lived near Belfast. John William Burgess (1844–1931) was a native of Cornersville who later, in 1890, became a dean at Columbia University, where he gained fame for his expertise in international law.

Carroll Van West, Middle Tennessee State University
CITATION:

(1) Federal Writers Project, *WPA Guide to Tennessee* (New York, 1939), 385.

SEE: ELLINGTON, BUFORD; FORREST, NATHAN B.; HORTON, HENRY; HORTON, HENRY HORTON STATE PARK; JULIUS ROSENWALD FUND; LIVESTOCK; MCCORD, JIM NANCE; WALKING HORSE NATIONAL CELEBRATION; U.S. DAIRY EXPERIMENT STATION

MARTHA WHITE FOODS pioneered the development of self-rising flour, self-rising corn meal, and later the packaged-mix southern hotbread. In 1963

the company introduced the first in the line of family-serving size packages, BixMix, to offer the young homemaker the chance to make the same kind of biscuits her mother made, but more easily. A full line of pouch mix products followed.

Unlike many brand symbols, Martha White was a real person. In 1899 her father, Richard Lindsey, named his Royal Flour Mill's finest flour brand for her. Cohen E. Williams and his sons, Cohen T. and Joe D., acquired the Royal Flour Mill and the Martha White name in 1941; the name has symbolized quality baking products ever since. Martha White Flour Company benefited from strong individual leadership, with Williams as chairman while his son, Cohen T. Williams, served as president. In 1967 Cohen T. became chairman with James R. King and then Robert V. Dale as president. In 1975 Martha White merged with Beatrice Companies Inc. and remained a wholly-owned subsidiary of Beatrice until 1987. Though the company changed hands several times from that point until 1994, Dale remained president until the Pillsbury Company purchased it in 1994.

In the early years Martha White concentrated on country music, another important product of Nashville, to carry its advertising message. Starting in 1947, the company-sponsored 5:45 A.M. radio program called "Martha White Biscuit and Cornbread Time" helped many Grand Ole Opry performers get their start in Nashville. Martha White sponsored its first show on Nashville's famed Grand Ole Opry in 1948 and remains today part of that Saturday night tradition. In 1953 the company hired Lester Flatt, Earl Scruggs, and the Foggy Mountain Boys to tour the South as spokesmen for Martha White. The group went on to become the nation's number one Bluegrass music group, and over the years its name became synonymous with Martha White. During an appearance at Carnegie Hall, Flatt and Scruggs played the famous Martha White jingle after requests were shouted from the audience. After Flatt and Scruggs disbanded, Tennessee Ernie Ford became spokesman for Martha White in 1972. His down-home personality combined with his tremendous popularity helped Martha White bridge the gap between rural and urban consumers, and Ford's association with the company continued through the 1980s. In 1995 Martha White sponsored Alison Krauss and Union Station's 1996 and 1997 tours, carrying on Martha White's long tradition of support for country and bluegrass music.

Linda Williams Dale, Nashville

SEE: FLATT, LESTER; FORD, TENNESSEE ERNIE; GRAND OLE OPRY; WSM

MARTIN, JOSEPH (1740–1808), Revolutionary War hero and Indian agent on the Virginia-Tennessee frontier, was born in Albemarle County, Virginia, in 1740.

As early as 1763, he attempted to settle in Powell's Valley at a place known as Martin's Station. He was a resident there by 1769 and he lived in the western frontier from 1777 to 1800, but, according to the *Biographical Directory of the Tennessee General Assembly,* he never brought his Virginia family to his frontier home. His reluctance is perhaps explained by the fact that Martin took a Cherokee wife, Elizabeth "Betsy" Ward, daughter of the famous Cherokee Beloved Woman, Nancy Ward, and South Carolina trader Bryant Ward. Martin and Betsy Ward had children, but there is no known record of how many.

A member of the North Carolina Constitutional Convention of 1777, Martin served in the North Carolina House of Commons in 1782, then in the North Carolina Senate in 1783, 1786, 1787, and 1789, representing Sullivan County. But his true significance in the early settlement era is as a military leader. He was a Lieutenant in Lord Dunmore's War in 1774 and Captain of Virginia militia in 1775. He commanded troops at the Treaty of Long Island in 1777 and served with distinction in various conflicts between the colonists and Cherokees along the western frontier from 1777 to 1780.

Due to his own family connections with the Cherokees, Martin was often involved in treaty negotiations. In 1777 Governor Patrick Henry appointed him as an Indian agent; six years later, he was one of three Virginia commissioners empowered to negotiate with the southern tribes. Considering his responsibilities as Indian agent, his marriage to Betsy Ward was a politically astute decision. In 1787, the North Carolina assembly chose Martin as brigadier general of the Washington District.

General Martin was an important surveyor, having surveyed the boundary between Virginia and Tennessee in 1795 and 1800–1802. Married twice to white women, and the father of 18 children, Martin died at his "Belmont" farm, in Henry County, Virginia, in 1808.

Carroll Van West, Middle Tennessee State University

SEE: SULLIVAN COUNTY; TREATIES; WARD, NANCY

MARTIN METHODIST COLLEGE, located in Pulaski, evolved from the 1870 bequest of Thomas Martin, a prominent business leader known well beyond Giles County. In his will he fulfilled a promise made to his daughter, Victoria, to establish a school for young women. In its early years, Martin Female College operated as a four-year boarding college with an elementary division for the town's children. After becoming the property of the Tennessee Conference of the Methodist Episcopal Church, South in 1905, the institution was renamed Martin College. In 1938 the school became coeducational and, by 1966 it was among the first private colleges in Tennessee to be racially integrated.

The current campus is comprised largely of buildings built since the 1950s. Administrative offices are planned for the rehabilitated l853 Batte-Brown-Blackburn House (Colonial Hall). Listed on the National Register of Historic Places, Colonial Hall was the home of Thomas Martin in addition to John C. Brown, Governor of Tennessee from 1871–1875. An endowed professorship is named for Senator Ross Bass who was a U.S. Senator, postmaster, Giles County native, and Martin College alumnus.

Martin Methodist College, affiliated with the Tennessee Conference of the United Methodist Church, became an accredited four-year college in 1995. In addition to the Pulaski Campus, Martin operates an Evening College Program at the Belmont United Methodist Church in Nashville. Degrees offered include Church Vocations, Elementary Education, Human Resources, Childhood Learning, and English.

Caneta Skelley Hankins, Middle Tennessee State University
SEE: BROWN, JOHN C.; EDUCATION, HIGHER; GILES COUNTY

MARY SHARP COLLEGE, formerly the Tennessee and Alabama Female Institute, was chartered in Winchester in 1850. Opening in 1851 the school was named for an early benefactor. Under the direction of Dr. Z.C. Graves and the Baptist Church, Mary Sharp College, which opened ten years before Vassar College, was the first women's college in the United States to offer degrees equivalent to those offered at men's colleges.

Graves patterned the classical curriculum at Mary Sharp College after those offered at Amherst College, Brown University, and the University of Virginia. He emphasized religious and moral training, and required every student to attend chapel. Students at Mary Sharp, unlike those at other female colleges and academies, studied algebra, geometry, and trigonometry; Latin and Greek; English literature, grammar, and composition; ancient, English, and American history; philosophy and rhetoric; geography and geology; and botany, chemistry, astronomy, and physiology. Graves believed that not only were women physically and mentally capable of obtaining a liberal arts education, but that such courses contributed to their personal improvement and that of their families. Three women received the first A.B. degrees in 1855.

Mary Sharp's influence was far-reaching. Many of Franklin County's early teachers were graduates of Mary Sharp College. In addition, Dana Slaughter Miller, a missionary and teacher at Shanghai Baptist College, and Florence Skeffington, first woman faculty member and second dean of women at the University of Tennessee, graduated from Mary Sharp.

Although most students were from Tennessee, girls came from as far away as Vermont, California, and China. Over 4,000 girls attended Mary Sharp between 1856 and 1896, and 350 girls graduated during the college's 40-year history. Mary Sharp College closed in 1896, a casualty of the financial depression of the early 1890s. Mary Sharp Elementary School in Winchester stands on the site of the former college.

Tara Mitchell Mielnik, Middle Tennessee State University
SEE: EDUCATION, HIGHER; FRANKLIN COUNTY

MARYVILLE COLLEGE, a distinguished higher education institution in Blount County, was among the first colleges in the country to open its doors to African Americans and Native Americans, as well as white males, and admitted women students as early as 1869. The college dates to 1819 and the efforts of Dr. Isaac Anderson (1780–1857) to build the Southern and Western Theological Seminary to train men for leadership in the Presbyterian Church. Anderson's goal later broadened to reach out to local whites, blacks, and Cherokees, who could benefit from higher education. The seminary was known as a center for southern abolitionist thought. But divisions within the Presbyterian Church and the lack of financial support led Anderson to broaden the school's audience from being just a seminary to a literary college. In 1842 Maryville College was chartered. As part of its education program, Maryville College established a preparatory school, which remained in operation until 1925. In the late nineteenth century, the college was notable for its policy to have blacks and whites attend together; its doors remained opened to African Americans until Jim Crow legislation in the early twentieth century forbade blacks to attend the college. Once the U.S. Supreme Court announced its decision outlawing public segregation in *Brown v. Board of Education* (1954), Maryville College immediately ended segregation policies and welcomed back African Americans. It was the first college in Tennessee to do so.

The first campus was located in downtown Maryville, but Civil War activity destroyed or damaged these buildings. The college was closed from 1861 to 1866. In 1869 Maryville College moved to a new 60-acre location on the outskirts of town, where an impressive array of buildings, many financed by leading reform institutions or philanthropists, were constructed over the next 50 years. For example, the Freedmen's Bureau, industrialist William Thaw of Pittsburgh, and John C. Baldwin of New York provided funds for the construction of Anderson Hall, named in honor of the school's founder, in 1869. Benjamin Fahnestock designed this impressive Second Empire-style building. Daniel B. Fayerweather of New York funded the construction of Fayerweather Science Hall, designed by Baumann Brothers of Knoxville, in 1898. Philanthropist Mrs. Nelle

McCormick of Chicago, the YMCA, and the students themselves provided the money and labor for Bartlett Hall, designed by George F. Barber of Knoxville in 1901. In the 1910s capitalist Andrew Carnegie provided funds for the five-story Carnegie Hall, which was designed by R.F. Graf and Sons of Knoxville and completed in 1917. Thaw Hall (1923) was built with donations from Mrs. Mary C. Thaw of Pittsburgh. Much of the campus's expansion came during the presidency of Samuel T. Wilson, who also had graduated from the college. All of these buildings, along with other historic structures, comprise the Maryville College Historic District, listed in the National Register of Historic Places. The beautiful campus, and rich institutional history, of Maryville College are sources of pride for the college's thousands of graduates.

Carroll Van West, Middle Tennessee State University

SUGGESTED READING: Harold M. Parker, Jr., "A School of the Prophets at Maryville," *Tennessee Historical Quarterly* 34(1975): 72–90

SEE: BLOUNT COUNTY; EDUCATION, HIGHER

MASSEY, JACK C. (1905–1990), international businessman, was the first person to take three companies to the New York Stock Exchange. He was head of the Winners Corporation when it secured a place on the Exchange in 1984, having previously served as chairman when Kentucky Fried Chicken Corp. and Hospital Corporation of America (HCA) were listed in 1969 and 1970, respectively.

A native of Sandersville, Georgia, Massey began his career as a pharmacist and retail druggist in Nashville. From a chain of six drugstores, he founded Massey Surgical Supply Inc., in 1930. He managed the profitable company until 1961, when he sold it to a division of the Brunswick Corporation. He retired briefly at the age of 56, but quickly returned to business and civic endeavors. His most important involvement came in the late 1960s with the founding and development of HCA, which became Columbia/HCA Healthcare Corporation in 1997.

A Nashville resident for more than 50 years, Massey left a living philanthropic legacy to the city. His generous contributions are visible as the Jack C. Massey Business Center on the Belmont University Campus. He contributed to Nashville's cultural life as the first chairman of the Tennessee Performing Arts Center. In addition, Massey made substantial contributions to Montgomery Bell Academy, Vanderbilt University Law School, and Cheekwood.

Massey died in 1990 at his winter home in Palm Beach, Florida. Known throughout his business career for backing people, not propositions, Massey believed that wealth could not be measured fully by making money, but through accomplishments.

Mona Collett, Belmont University

SEE: BELMONT UNIVERSITY; COLUMBIA/HCA

MATTHEWS, MARK ALLISON (1867–1940), developed a national reputation as a pastor in the Pacific Northwest, but he laid the foundation for his work and established his pattern of ministry in Jackson, Tennessee, between 1896 and 1902. Compared to other southern clergy, Matthews fashioned an unusual combination of religious conservatism and social conscience. His national fame developed during his ministry at Seattle's First Presbyterian Church from 1902 to 1940. He built his congregation into the denomination's largest with nearly 10,000 members, and played an assertive role in Seattle politics, while displaying a personal flamboyance in the pulpit that was matched by few of his contemporaries.

Born in Calhoun, Georgia, on September 24, 1867, Matthews grew up in the war-ravaged South. He sought his religious calling in the Cumberland Presbyterian Church. Later ordained in the Presbyterian Church in the United States (Southern), Matthews never went to seminary. He served churches in Calhoun and Dalton, Georgia, before moving to Jackson in 1896. At the First Presbyterian Church, he was a popular preacher and an activist in civic life. He founded a night school for working people, persuaded Andrew Carnegie to donate funds for the town library, organized a Presbyterian hospital, and started an unemployment bureau for Jackson's poor. Organizing local chapters of the YMCA and the Humane Society, Matthews introduced elements of the Social Gospel during his six years in Tennessee, making his ministry unusual among southern churches of that time.

Dale E. Soden, Whitworth College

SEE: JACKSON

MAURY COUNTY was established by an Act of the Tennessee General Assembly on November 16, 1807. Taken from parts of Williamson and Dickson counties, the new county was named for Abram Maury, a State Senator from Williamson County.

Columbia, the county seat, was laid out and lots sold in 1808. At that time, the town consisted of four square blocks. In 1996 Columbia's city limits stretched 15.5 miles from Spring Hill to Mt. Pleasant, towns that were settled at the same time as Columbia. Columbia was incorporated in 1817, Mt. Pleasant in 1824, and Spring Hill in 1901.

From the beginning the rich soil of Maury County attracted settlers, who planted cotton and tobacco and raised livestock. The Polk family plantations at Ashwood became regionally famous for their rich array of agricultural products. After the Civil War, farmers shifted from cotton to grain and livestock raising, although tobacco is still the county's largest cash crop. In the twentieth century, progressive agricultural practices were demonstrated and made popular through programs at the Middle Tennessee

Agricultural Experiment Station near Spring Hill. Today Maury County leads the state in the production of beef cattle and remains a major producer of corn, wheat, grain, sorghum, and cotton.

The county's long history of agricultural success can be attributed, in part, to the richness of the Maury County soil with its underlying layer of phosphate rock, once the bottom of an ancient seabed. In 1888 William Shirley's discovery of high grade brown phosphate rock at Mount Pleasant launched a mining industry that flourished for more than 100 years. With the arrival of processing plants in the 1930s, Maury County moved from an agricultural to an industrial economy. Thousands of Maury Countians worked in the phosphate industry for such companies as Hooker, Monsanto, Occidental, and Stauffer, until environmental concerns and dwindling resources forced its decline in the mid-1980s.

Phosphate made Mt. Pleasant a "boom town," but the arrival of the Saturn Corporation in the 1980s produced phenomenal growth at Spring Hill. With over 9,500 employees, this automotive manufacturing company is the largest employer in the county, followed by Maury Regional Hospital and the Maury County School System.

Maury County is serviced by a good rail system, an excellent trucking industry, the Maury County Airport, four radio stations, a daily newspaper, and a weekly newspaper. Columbia State Community College was the first community college in the state.

In recent years, Maury County has emerged as an important tourist center. Except for the resort counties, Maury County annually welcomes a larger number of tourists than any other rural county in Tennessee. Visitors pour into Columbia for the annual Mule Day celebration in April. Throughout the year, tourists visit the large number of historical sites scattered throughout the county, including the James K. Polk Home, the Athenaeum, and Elm Springs in Columbia. Visitors to Spring Hill tour Rippavilla and Oaklawn, both of which figured in the Civil War fighting of November 1864. Civil War reenactments take place at Elm Springs and in the Spring Hill area.

Just inside the Mt. Pleasant city limits stands St. John's Episcopal Church, one of the few remaining plantation churches in the country. Nearby is Rattle-N-Snap, built for George Polk in 1845; the National Historic Landmark is considered one of the great houses in North America. Across the highway is the first of the Polk family plantations, Hamilton Place. In downtown Mt. Pleasant, tourists visit the Mt. Pleasant/Maury Historical Phosphate Museum and the Mt. Pleasant Public Library, which features the "Bigby Grey Flag," made in 1862 for local Confederate volunteers. The Maury County Chapter of APTA and the Maury County Convention and Visitors Bureau sponsor an annual tour of the many fine homes and sites in the county.

A number of Maury Countians contributed to Tennessee and national history, including James K. Polk, Governor of Tennessee, Speaker of the U.S. House of Representatives, and eleventh President of the United States. A.O.P. Nicholson served Tennessee as state representative, state senator, U.S. Senator, and Chief Justice of the Supreme Court of Tennessee. William J. Harbison served as state Chief Justice for 20 years in the late twentieth century. Edward W. Carmack, Henry Cooper, and W.C. Whitthorne served in the U.S. Senate. Dr. Marion Dorsett discovered a method for producing a serum to prevent hog cholera. Lindsey Nelson was a famous radio and television announcer of football games for the University of Tennessee, the University of Notre Dame, and the CBS network.

Maury Countians also made their mark in the military. Fran McKee, a Maury County native, became the first female line Admiral in the U.S. Navy. Captain Meade Frierson received the Distinguished Service Cross for action in World War I. Colonel Wibb Earl Cooper, who fought in World Wars I and II, received the Distinguished Service Cross with Oak Leaf Cluster for exceptional heroism in combat during World War II. John Harlan Willis was awarded posthumously the Congressional Medal of Honor for gallantry in action in World War II. Sons and daughters of Maury County have fought and died in every conflict from the War of 1812 to the Gulf War, contributing to the history of the state and nation.

Marise P. Lightfoot, Mt. Pleasant

SEE: ARNELL, SAMUEL M.; ATHENAEUM; CARMACK, EDWARD W.; CLIFTON PLACE; COLUMBIA RACE RIOT, 1946; HAMILTON PLACE; HARBISON, WILLIAM J.; MINING; MULES; NICHOLSON, A.O.P.; OTEY, JAMES; PILLOW, GIDEON J.; POLK, JAMES K.; POLK, JAMES K., ANCESTRAL HOME; POLK, LEONIDAS; RATTLE-N-SNAP; ST. JOHN'S EPISCOPAL CHURCH; SATURN; VAUGHT, NATHAN; ZION PRESBYTERIAN CHURCH; ZOLLICOFFER, FELIX

MAURY, MATTHEW FONTAINE (1806–1878), oceanographer and author, was born on January 14, 1806, in Fredericksburg, Virginia. His family moved to Williamson County, Tennessee, when he was five. Maury attended Harpeth Academy in Franklin and studied under Gideon Blackburn and James Otey, first Episcopal Bishop of Tennessee. He joined the navy as a midshipman at age 19 with his first posting on the *USS Brandywine,* the ship chosen to escort Lafayette home to France. While on board the *Brandywine,* Maury met the future Admiral David Farragut.

In 1834 Maury married Ann Hull Herndon, and they lived in Fredericksburg, Virginia, for seven years. During this time, Maury published a number of books and articles, notably *A New Theoretical and*

Practical Treatise on Navigation (1836). The *Treatise*, better known as *Maury's Navigation*, became the standard text for the Naval Academy at Annapolis.

In 1842 Maury was named superintendent of the Navy Depot of Charts and Instruments, later known as the Naval Observatory. He published papers on the gulf stream and ocean currents in 1844 and the books *A Scheme for Building Southern Commerce; Wind and Current Charts*; and *Sailing Directions*. He called a general maritime conference in Brussels that standardized the logs kept by captains. In 1856 he published *The Physical Geography of the Sea*.

When Virginia seceded, Maury resigned from the U.S. Navy and entered the Confederate Navy in June 1861 with the rank of Commander. He was sent to Europe to continue earlier experiments on torpedoes. Eventually, Maury invented a method of arranging and testing torpedo mines using an electrical detonation system. He was ready to put his system into operation when Robert E. Lee surrendered.

Maury returned to the United States and became a professor of physics at Virginia Military Institute, where he continued to write books on the sea and geography. Maury died on February 1, 1873, in Lexington, Virginia, and is buried in Richmond, Virginia.

Honored all over the world as the founder of a new science, Maury was the first man to describe the Gulf Stream and to mark sea routes across the Atlantic Ocean. He instituted the system of deep-sea sounding and suggested the laying of transoceanic telegraph cables, which later became a reality. His work earned him the nickname "Pathfinder of the Seas."

Leo J. Goodsell, Plano, Illinois
SEE: OTEY, JAMES H.; WILLIAMSON COUNTY

MAXWELL HOUSE HOTEL, formerly at the northeast corner of Fourth Avenue, North, and Church Street in downtown Nashville, was for years the center of Nashville's social and political life. Colonel John Overton, Jr., built the hotel named for his wife, Harriet Maxwell Overton. Construction of the Maxwell House, designed by Isaiah Rogers, began in 1859 using slave labor. During the Civil War, the partially finished brick building served as both barracks and prison hospital for the occupying Union Army.

After the war, Overton resumed construction of what became Nashville's largest hotel, which local citizens initially called "Overton's Folly." Opening in the fall of 1869, the five-story, 240-room hotel cost $500,000. The Maxwell House advertised steam heat, gas-lighting, and a bath on every floor. Rooms were $4 a day, meals included. The building fronted on Fourth Avenue and the infamous Men's Quarter; an entrance for women opened onto Church Street. Eight Corinthian columns flanked the main entrance; the elegant main lobby featured mahogany cabinetry, brass fixtures, gilded mirrors, and chandeliers. There were ladies' and men's parlors, billiard rooms, bar rooms, shaving "saloons," and a grand staircase to the large ball or dining room.

The heyday of the Maxwell House Hotel was the 1890s to the early twentieth century. The hotel became famous for its Christmas dinner, featuring such delicacies as Calf's Head, Leg of Cumberland Black Bear, and Tennessee Opossum. Seven presidents stayed at the Maxwell House Hotel, including Theodore Roosevelt, whose comment that the coffee was "good to the last drop" launched the advertising slogan used for years to promote the nation's first blended coffee. Other visitors included Thomas Edison, "Buffalo Bill" Cody, General Tom Thumb, Cornelius Vanderbilt, and George Westinghouse. The Maxwell House burned on Christmas night 1961.

Ophelia Paine, Metropolitan Historical Commission
SEE: NASHVILLE

MAYFIELD DAIRY FARMS INC., an important late twentieth century dairy and milk products corporation based in Athens, began as an antebellum family farm in McMinn County that continues as a family-run business into the late twentieth century. In 1833 Thomas Brummitt Mayfield and Sarah Rudd Mayfield established a farm on 510 acres east of Athens on the Madisonville Road. After the Civil War, their son, Thomas B. Mayfield, Jr., expanded the farm to 600 acres and introduced specialized breeds of livestock, especially Jersey cattle. He established the farm's dairy business, which sold products to the growing towns of southeast Tennessee. In 1914 the farm passed to Thomas B. Mayfield, a fourth-generation grandson, who upgraded the dairy into a formidable regional business. In 1976 Mayfield Farm was designated an official Tennessee Century Farm. In the mid-1980s, Goldie D. Mayfield and her children operated a 1,400 acre farm, while the company expanded sales across the state. Dean Foods of Franklin Park, Illinois, acquired Mayfield in 1990s but kept everyday affairs in the capable hands of the Mayfield family.

Carroll Van West, Middle Tennessee State University
SEE: FARMS, TENNESSEE CENTURY; MCMINN COUNTY

MAYNARD, HORACE (1814–1882), Congressman, diplomat, and Postmaster General, was born on August 30, 1814, in Westboro, Massachusetts. After graduating from Amherst College in 1838, Maynard moved to Knoxville, where he worked as a tutor in the preparatory department of East Tennessee College (later the University of Tennessee). The college appointed Maynard principal of the preparatory department in 1840; the next year he became teacher of mathematics and ancient languages at the college.

While teaching, Maynard studied law and, in 1844, was admitted to the bar. One of his most famous cases involved the defense of Union County against a suit filed by disgruntled citizens of Knox County, who protested the establishment of Union County from a portion of Knox County. In gratitude for his successful defense of their county, Union County residents named the county seat Maynardville.

Maynard was initially elected to the U.S. House of Representatives in 1857, on the American Party, or Know-Nothing ticket. His constituents reelected him twice: in 1859, as a member of the Opposition Party, and in 1861, as a candidate on the Unionist ticket. Along with other East Tennessee politicians, Maynard canvassed the region in the aftermath of Abraham Lincoln's election to the presidency, in an effort to persuade Tennesseans to vote against secession. Even after secession, Maynard continued to serve in the U.S. Congress.

In 1863 Andrew Johnson, Military Governor of Tennessee, appointed Maynard Attorney General of the state. Two years later, Maynard returned to Congress to represent Tennessee's second district until 1875, when President Ulysses S. Grant appointed him Minister to Turkey. In the summer of 1880 President Rutherford B. Hayes recalled Maynard and appointed him to the cabinet position of Postmaster General, a post he held until March 5, 1881. Maynard returned to Knoxville and died on May 3, 1882.

Kathleen R. Zebley, University of Tennessee, Knoxville
SEE: RECONSTRUCTION; UNION COUNTY

McADOO, WILLIAM GIBBS (1863–1941), was a leading figure in American politics in the early twentieth century. He was born in Marietta, Georgia, in 1863, but later moved with his family to Knoxville, where his father taught at the University of Tennessee. McAdoo attended that institution for three years, then went to Chattanooga where he practiced law, participated in Democratic politics, and invested in local development. While there he also developed a life-long interest in public transportation. In 1889 he undertook an ambitious plan to electrify Knoxville's streetcar system. The scheme failed, however, and left McAdoo virtually penniless.

Broke and embarrassed, McAdoo moved to New York City and soon established himself as a successful corporate attorney. He remained interested in transportation and in 1901, led a bold venture to construct a series of railroad tunnels under the Hudson River. The successful completion of the Hudson Tubes brought McAdoo considerable notoriety, and he soon became a trusted advisor to New Jersey governor Woodrow Wilson. McAdoo enthusiastically backed Wilson's bid for the bid for the presidency in 1914, and served as vice chairman of his national election committee. In return, the victorious Wilson named McAdoo his Secretary of the Treasury.

As Treasury Secretary, McAdoo oversaw the formation of the Federal Reserve system and pushed

innovative programs designed to help farmers and revitalize the nation's merchant marine. He also helped finance America's participation in World War I and served as director general of railways during the conflict. In 1919 McAdoo left Wilson's administration, but remained active in national politics. He was a leading candidate for the Democratic party's presidential nomination in 1920 and 1924. In 1933 he was elected United States Senator from California, and served until 1938. He died in 1941, after a life devoted to public service.

Timothy P. Ezzell, Knoxville
SEE: CHATTANOOGA

McADOW, SAMUEL (1760–1844), one of the founders of the Cumberland Presbyterian Church, was born on April 10, 1760, in Guilford County, North Carolina, the son of Scots and Irish immigrants. Raised a Presbyterian, McAdow attended the church and school led by Dr. David Caldwell. He studied at Mecklenburg College for three years before returning to Caldwell's tutelage to prepare for the ministry. McAdow was licensed to preach in 1794 and ordained prior to 1799.

That same year, McAdow left North Carolina to begin work in Kentucky. He spent the summer in Tennessee, where over 100 families appealed to him to remain as their pastor. From 1800 to 1806 McAdow served in the Cumberland Presbytery in Kentucky, though he occasionally journeyed to Tennessee to preach. McAdow participated in the revivals of the period and became involved in the conflicts that gripped the frontier Presbyterian Church over the proper response to the emotionalism associated with the western revivals. In 1806 the Presbyterian Church dissolved the Cumberland Presbytery and prohibited pastors who had participated in the Great Revival from preaching or administering sacraments.

During this period, McAdow left Kentucky and settled in Dickson County, Tennessee, in an area that is now part of the Montgomery Bell State Park. At his home on February 4, 1810, McAdow met with other revival pastors, including Finis Ewing and Samuel King, and organized the Cumberland Presbytery, independent of the Presbyterian Church, which quickly became known as a new denomination, the Cumberland Presbyterian Church.

McAdow and his family moved to Illinois in 1828, where he continued his work in the Cumberland Presbyterian Church. He founded the Mount Gilead Church in 1828, and several members of his family are buried in the church cemetery, including two sons, a daughter, and his wife Hannah. Samuel McAdow was married three times. In 1788 he married Henrietta Wheatley in North Carolina. They had five children, three of whom died in infancy. His first wife died in 1799, and the next year McAdow married Catherine Clark of Logan County, Kentucky. She died in 1804. McAdow married for the third time in July 1806 to Hannah Cope, who died in 1839. McAdow died on March 30, 1844. A replica of McAdow's log dog-trot dwelling has been constructed in Montgomery Bell State Park to commemorate the foundation of the denomination.

Tara Mitchell Mielnik, Middle Tennessee State University

SEE: CUMBERLAND PRESBYTERIAN CHURCH; DICKSON COUNTY; MONTGOMERY BELL STATE PARK; RELIGION

McALISTER, HILL (1875–1960), Governor and attorney, began his political career as the city attorney for Nashville. He served several terms in the State Senate, and the General Assembly elected him to four terms as State Treasurer. He lost close races for the Democratic gubernatorial nomination in 1926 against Austin Peay and in 1928 against Henry Horton. When McAlister won election to the governorship in 1932, his possibilities for action were severely limited. At the time of his inauguration in 1933 the State of Tennessee and the nation were in serious financial straits. The state government faced an operating deficit of $6 million and banks had failed all over the state, including the Bank of Tennessee which had held $3,418,000 in state funds. With the New Deal administration of Franklin Roosevelt, McAlister also found himself in a situation where federal programs became more important to most Tennesseans than their state government.

His association with Memphis political boss E.H. Crump also limited McAlister's options. Beginning in 1926, McAlister's political career was both cursed and blessed by the support of the controversial Crump. In 1926 Austin Peay effectively played on Crump's endorsement of McAlister and the Memphis boss's manipulation and use of the African-American vote to defeat McAlister in the ostensibly all-white Democratic Party primary. Crump's support paid off, though, in 1932 when McAlister won a tightly contested Democractic primary by 10,000 votes primarily due to the 25,000 vote majority that Crump delivered in Shelby County. Crump's support came with a price, however, and throughout his four years as governor McAlister felt tremendous pressure to toe the Crump line.

Despite these handicaps, McAlister was determined to help Tennessee out of the Depression. For McAlister and for Crump, this meant strict economy in government. In his inaugural address, McAlister announced: "we do not face a mere desire to reduce governmental costs, but an absolute necessity to do so."[1] By scaling back expenditures, the governor balanced the budget in his first two years. Along with other governors, he declared March 6, 1933, a six-day bank holiday that, along with new federal measures, helped restore confidence in Tennessee's banks.

Much of McAlister's career as governor was spent in coordinating efforts to bring federal money and programs to the state. An avid supporter of the New Deal, he won reelection by a large margin in 1934 on a platform of continued support for Roosevelt.

McAlister's political career came to a virtual end in 1935 when he broke ranks with Crump and introduced a sales tax measure designed to reduce state indebtedness and aid the ailing public school system. Crump vehemently opposed the revenue bill, marshalled his forces to insure its defeat, withdrew his support from McAlister, and later referred to him as an incompetent governor. Crippled politically, McAlister did not run for reelection in 1936. He retired to his Nashville home but returned to public life a few years later as a bankruptcy referee. He died in 1960.

Dan Pierce, Western Carolina University

CITATION:

(1) John Dean Minton, *The New Deal in Tennessee, 1932–1938* (New York, 1979), 55.

SEE: CRUMP, EDWARD H.; PEAY, AUSTIN

McCALLIE SCHOOL opened September 21, 1905, with eight teachers and 48 students on the family farm located on the western slope of Missionary Ridge donated by Presbyterian minister T.H. McCallie to his sons, James Park and Spencer J. McCallie, for this enterprise. Today, educational experts consider McCallie School to be one of the finest secondary schools in the South. With a campus of more than 100 acres, an endowment in excess of $40 million, and an enrollment of 750, it has produced some of Tennessee's and the nation's top leaders, including cable television mogul Ted Turner, former Senate Majority Leader Howard Baker, Jr., and former Senator and Ambassador William Brock.

McCallie, an all-boys school, has day and boarding students in grades seven through 12. It stresses strong academic achievement in the core curriculum and consistently leads the state in the numbers of National Merit Scholarship Semifinalists and Finalists as well as Advanced Placement Scholars. Committed also to the physical and moral development of its students, McCallie participates in 14 varsity sports. It was the first in the state to begin organized competition in non-traditional sports such as lacrosse, rowing, and water polo.

Since 1985, McCallie has had a formal coordinate program with Girls Preparatory School in Chattanooga. Students at the two schools exchange classes and participate in a variety of organized social events.

William R. Steverson, The McCallie School

SEE: BAKER, HOWARD H., JR.; BROCK, WILLIAM E., III; GIRLS PREPARATORY SCHOOL

McCARTHY, CORMAC (1933–), author of seven novels and two dramas, spent his childhood in

Knoxville where he graduated from Catholic High School in 1951 and attended the University of Tennessee. Although he never received a degree, he left the university with two novels in progress. *The Orchard Keeper* (1965), his first published novel, received the William Faulkner Foundation Award for that year. Following the publication of his fourth novel, *Suttree* (1979), McCarthy moved to El Paso, Texas, where he researched and wrote *Blood Meridian* (1985) and the first two volumes of the Border Trilogy: *All the Pretty Horses* (1992) and *The Crossing* (1994). McCarthy has avoided the literary limelight, refusing to do interviews, book signings, readings, or lectures. In an age fascinated by artistic personalities, McCarthy's privacy has cost him some readers, but it has served also as a reminder of the primacy of the writer's work.

McCarthy's first four novels are set in East Tennessee. No writer, not even Faulkner or Flannery O'Connor to whom he is often compared, has written better dialogue or realized more vividly the character of the plain folk of his region. Without sentimentality or condescension, McCarthy's evocative prose brings mountain people to life, rendering their cautious reserve, their dignity, and resignation flawlessly. *The Orchard Keeper* is a novel about murder and friendship in a remote rural community. *Outer Dark* (1968) is a horrifying tale of incest and apocalyptic violence. *Child of God* (1973) tells the story of Lester Ballard, a homicidal necrophiliac, who stashes corpses in caves. *Suttree*, set mostly in Knoxville, is a darkly humorous chronicle of the adventures of Cornelius Suttree, an intelligent dropout living among the failures and rejects of modern society. With *Blood Meridian*, McCarthy turned to the southwest, to the border country. This story of a band of scalphunters led by John Glanton has been compared to *The Iliad* in terms of bloodiness. His latest novels are both about young men coming of age through harrowing experiences in Mexico. *All the Pretty Horses*, which won the National Book Award for Fiction, is less pessimistic and violent than the earlier novels, but *The Crossing* ends bleakly.

McCarthy is unquestionably a major American novelist whose work is just beginning to get the critical attention it deserves. All of his work takes a dim view of human nature and of the projects of modernity. Abstract optimism and easy confidence in human perfectibility cannot endure in the face of the grim particulars of human wickedness and perversity which fill his tales, acts beyond psychological explanation or cure. McCarthy's fiction is a direct assault on the bloodless naiveté of modern secular imagination, and he writes as if trying to shock his readers out of their willful innocence by the details of gory violence. His suspicion of schemes and social programs is deep, and the violence and brutality to which man reverts in a state of nature is convincing and unforgettable because the language is both exact and beautiful.

Robert Benson, University of the South
SEE: LITERATURE

McCORD, JIM NANCE (1879–1968), Governor, progressive agricultural reformer, publisher, and public official, was born in Unionville, Bedford County, in 1879. His parents, Thomas N. and Iva Stelle McCord, were farmers and the young McCord learned the value of hard work on the family farm. Striking out on his own at the age of 17, McCord was a traveling salesman for ten years. He learned about the needs and aspirations of rural Tennesseans as he honed a personable style grounded in his great skill and ease as a public speaker. In 1901 he married Vera Kercheval of Lewisburg, the Marshall County seat; they remained married until her death in 1953 and had no children.

In 1910 McCord began his newspaper career, during which he edited and published the Lewisburg *Marshall Gazette* and was chosen president of the Tennessee Press Association. Through the newspaper, McCord became a spokesman for agricultural reform. For instance, in 1923–1924, McCord strongly supported efforts by local officials to build and equip a Ladies Rest Room in downtown Lewisburg, so country women would have a proper place to rest and eat during trips to town. Listed in the National Register of Historic Places, this building still operates as one of the few Ladies Rest Rooms in the country that is located in its original building. By this time, McCord was in the midst of his long stint as mayor of Lewisburg, a total of 13 terms and over 25 years of public service. He also was a member of the Marshall County Court for over 27 years. During the Great Depression, his newspaper supported Franklin D. Roosevelt and New Deal programs brought a new electrical system to Lewisburg as well as building a modern post office.

McCord was extremely interested in the progressive effort to improve Tennessee livestock, especially Jersey cattle. McCord headed most local efforts at improving cattle breeds and served as president of the American Jersey Breeders' Association, for whom he also conducted cattle auctions. He also helped to convince federal agricultural officials to locate a U.S. Dairy Experiment Farm, which specialized in Jersey cattle, on a 500-acre tract south of Lewisburg. This facility is now part of the University of Tennessee's Extension Service program. By the 1930s Lewisburg was a milk producing center, with several large dairies in operation. In 1935 McCord played an important role in creating the official registry for Tennessee walking horses, records which are still maintained in a Lewisburg headquarters. He was the first secretary-treasurer of the Tennessee Walking Horse Breeders Association of America.

McCord entered the larger arena of Tennessee politics in 1942, when he was elected the Fourth District's U.S. Congressman. He spent only two years in Washington before returning to Tennessee to run for governor. McCord served two consecutive terms, from 1945 to 1949, and "earned a place as one of the strongest friends of education in the history of the state."[1] In his first term, McCord convinced the legislature to raise all basic appropriations for public education and to make a special $4 million appropriation to give every full-time teacher and principal a monthly raise of $25. The General Assembly also set aside $500,000 in higher education funding to benefit returning war veterans eager to take advantage of the GI Bill. McCord also gracefully presided over the Sesquicentennial of Tennessee in 1946. Addressing the Tennessee Historical Society at the Hermitage Hotel in Nashville, McCord proclaimed that "there are important lessons for us and our children to learn from the annals of the past. In these perilous days of controversy and contention, world-wide in scope, let us seek to indoctrinate our youth with the golden leaven of reason, justice and humanity."[2]

For his second term, McCord envisioned further educational reforms, but more money would be needed and McCord wanted to pass a two percent general sales tax to better fund Tennessee's schools. But E.H. "Boss" Crump of Memphis, the undisputed kingmaker of Tennessee Democrats and McCord's patron within the party, had always opposed a sales tax. McCord personally lobbied Crump to support the tax increase. Crump grudgingly lent his support and the General Assembly passed the sales tax as well as a state retirement law for teachers and other state employees. The legislature used the new sales tax money to significantly expand the infrastructure of public education. The revenues built new schools; bought new buses; and established the state's first comprehensive minimum school program for grades one to 12.

Despite the benefits of increased educational funding, the public never fully approved of the sales tax. McCord quickly found himself in political hot water, which only got hotter once he signed anti-labor legislation calling for open shop, or "right to work," rules in Tennessee. His support of the legislation greatly angered labor organizations. Faced by a formidable challenger in former Governor Gordon Browning, McCord failed to secure a third term as governor when he lost the Democratic primary to Browning in 1948.

After his defeat, McCord returned to Lewisburg and resumed his duties at the newspaper. He was a member of the 1953 State Constitutional Convention and served as Commissioner of Conservation under Governor Frank G. Clement. McCord died in 1967 and is buried in Lone Oak Cemetery in Lewisburg.

Carroll Van West, Middle Tennessee State University
CITATIONS:
(1) Robert L. Corlew, et al., *Tennessee: A Short History* (Knoxville, 1969), 543.
(2) Jim N. McCord, "Tennessee's Sesquicentennial," *Tennessee Historical Quarterly* 5(1946): 110.
SEE: BROWNING, GORDON W.; CLEMENT, FRANK G.; CRUMP, EDWARD H.; MARSHALL COUNTY; TENNESSEE HISTORICAL SOCIETY; U.S. DAIRY EXPERIMENT FARM

McCORMACK CUSHMAN, NANCY COX (1885–1967), internationally recognized sculptor, was born August 15, 1885, in Nashville to Nannie Morgan Cox and Herschel McCullough Cox. After the deaths of her parents, she attended an Arkansas boarding school but soon returned to Nashville, entered Ward Seminary in 1900, and received art training under the direction of Willie Betty Newman. In 1903 she married Mark McCormack in Nashville, but by 1911 their marriage had ended in divorce.

McCormack began her sculptural training in 1909 at the St. Louis School of Fine Arts of Washington University and later at the Chicago Art Institute. Her professional career spanned the years 1911–1960. During this time she sculpted the likenesses of some of the most important personalities of her time. Her American and European subjects included Benito Mussolini, Primo de Rivera, Henry P. Fletcher, Jane Addams, Clarence Darrow, Mahatma Gandhi, and Ezra Pound.

Between study and work in New York and abroad, McCormack completed two Nashville commissions of Doctor Matthew C. McGannon and Edward Ward Carmack. She made a death mask and portrait bust of McGannon, founder of the Women's Hospital, Nashville, in 1920. Between 1922 and 1924 McCormack created the heroic Carmack monument honoring the slain politician and newspaper editor. Erected in 1925, it stands over the Charlotte Avenue entrance to the State Capitol Tunnel.

In 1939 McCormack married Charles Thomas Cushman of New York City but continued to sculpt and tour, living briefly in Sicily, Rome, and Florence. She died in 1967 in Ithaca, New York.

Anne-Leslie Owens, Tennessee Historical Society
SEE: ART; CARMACK, EDWARD W.; NEWMAN, WILLIE BETTY

McDONALD, JOHN (ca. 1747-ca. 1824), first white settler in Hamilton County, immigrated from Scotland to Charleston, South Carolina, in 1766. Almost immediately, McDonald secured a position as a trader among the Cherokees and moved to Fort Loudoun, Tennessee. In 1770 McDonald was appointed Assistant Superintendent of Indian Affairs for the British. He moved south with his wife, Anna Shorey, a mixed-blood Cherokee, and established a home and store near the point where the Chickamauga Creek flows into the Tennessee River. As whites pushed further into their lands, the Cherokees moved south and developed towns around McDonald's store, which became the British commissary and outpost. In 1779 a joint Virginia and North Carolina militia expedition pushed south, destroyed the Chickamauga towns, and confiscated all the goods from McDonald's commissary. McDonald moved his family to the "Five Lower Towns" located further south along the Tennessee River.

After the American Revolution, the United States government was eager to establish peace among the southern Indians. Government officials worked through McDonald to win favor with the Cherokees. The Treaty of Hopewell, signed November 25, 1785, drew a boundary to restrict white settlement within the Cherokee lands and gave the government the exclusive right to trade among the Cherokees.

From his home near present-day Rossville, Georgia,. McDonald maintained influence with the Cherokees until his death in ca. 1824. His family's influence in Cherokee matters continued through his grandson, John Ross, who became the Cherokee principal chief in 1828.

Patrice Hobbs Glass, Chattanooga

SEE: CHATTANOOGA; CHICKAMAUGAS; HAMILTON COUNTY; ROSS, JOHN; TREATIES

McDOWELL, JOHN H. (1844–ca. 1911), newspaper editor and leader in the Agricultural Wheel and Farmers' Alliance, was born December 12, 1844, near Trenton in Gibson County, the son of John Davis and Nancy H. Irwin McDowell. Young McDowell attended St. Andrews College until the Civil War interrupted his education. He joined Company H of the Twelfth Tennessee Infantry but was discharged as underaged. Undeterred, McDowell joined a cavalry regiment and served under generals Earl Van Dorn and Nathan Bedford Forrest.

After the war, McDowell returned to farming, first in Arkansas and then Obion County. In addition to farming, he edited the *Union City Anchor* and became involved in Democratic party politics. In 1882 McDowell won his first term in the Tennessee General Assembly. He served two terms in the Tennessee House of Representatives (1883–1885 and 1905–1907) and one term in the Senate (1887–1889). McDowell shepherded a constitutional amendment to impose prohibition through two legislatures and brought it to a statewide vote, where it was defeated in 1887. He also championed an anti-Sunday baseball law to prevent semi-professional baseball games (and gambling) on Sundays.

In addition to his prohibition and anti-gambling reform efforts, McDowell became a leader in the growing agrarian movements of the 1880s. A member of the earlier Patrons of Husbandry (Grange), he joined both the Agricultural Wheel and the Farmers' Alliance, becoming a national vice president in both organizations. In 1888 McDowell became owner and editor of *The Weekly Toiler*, the state organ of the Wheel, which was published in Nashville. From the pages of the *Toiler*, McDowell marshaled support for the farmers' organizations, the cooperative efforts of the Wheel and Alliance, the jute boycott, and the election of agrarian-friendly legislators. In the fall of 1890 McDowell left the *Toiler* to manage the gubernatorial campaign of John P. Buchanan, the president of the Tennessee Farmers' Alliance and Laborers' Union. Governor Buchanan rewarded McDowell with the prize state patronage position of Coal Oil Inspector. McDowell succeeded Buchanan as state president in the Alliance.

McDowell resisted reform efforts that called for the formation of a third party, both in the temperance and agrarian movements. By 1892 many Democratic leaders openly worried that the Alliance would soon dominate the party. As a result, Buchanan's campaign for a second term became an acrimonious battle for control of the party, and McDowell became the lightning rod for the fears of traditional party leaders. When Democrats invoked party discipline that precluded support for Alliance demands, many Alliance members withdrew to establish the People's Party (Populists), and McDowell reluctantly joined them. Politically unsuccessful, the Populists nevertheless remained a thorn in state politics for the remainder of the century.

In 1896–1897 McDowell headed the agriculture department of the Tennessee Centennial Exposition. Into the new century, he continued to make temperance speeches, often sharing the platform with men who earlier opposed his agrarian efforts.

McDowell married Emma Sandeford of Gibson County, and they were the parents of seven children. McDowell died sometime after 1911.

Connie L. Lester, Tennessee Historical Society

SEE: AGRICULTURAL WHEEL; BUCHANAN, JOHN P.; FARMERS' ALLIANCE; TEMPERANCE MOVEMENT; OBION COUNTY

McELWEE, SAMUEL A. (1857–1914), was born in slavery in Madison County, struggled to achieve a college education and law degree, and served his race for three terms in the Tennessee General Assembly (1882–1888), where he was recognized as a "magnetic speaker, forcible debater, and indefatigable worker," making him one of the state's most influential African-American men of the 1880s.[1] Following emancipation, McElwee's father, Robert McElwee, the son of a white man, moved his family to Haywood County, where Samuel attended freedmen's schools for a few months each year. In addition to his schooling, McElwee was strongly influenced by the words of Frederick Douglass, which he read in the latter's newspaper, the *National Era*.

In 1875 McElwee attended Oberlin College in Ohio, where he met his school expenses by doing menial work. After a year, he returned to the South and for the next three years, he taught school and peddled books, Bibles, and patent medicine. The desire for more education remained uppermost in his mind, and he continued to study Latin, German, and algebra with a white Vanderbilt student, who tutored him twice a week. In 1878 McElwee enrolled at Fisk University, after the tutor made university officials aware of his industrious student. He graduated in 1883, opened a store in Haywood County, and began reading law on his own. In 1884 he was a delegate to the Republican National Convention, where a black newspaper favorably noted his self-confidence and drive. Following the death of his wife in 1885, McElwee placed his two small children with his wife's parents and entered Central Tennessee College in Nashville, receiving a law degree in 1886.

At the same time he was pursuing his education, McElwee also served two terms in the Tennessee General Assembly. During his first legislative session, McElwee introduced legislation to increase the appropriation for the education of black teachers. His appeal for support from white legislators rested on the foundation of African- American contributions to the history of the state and their opportunities in the future progress of the "New South." Although McElwee failed to achieve his goal of adequate educational funding, his legislative skill and speaking ability soon earned respect from his assembly colleagues.

In 1885 McElwee received the Republican nomination for Speaker of the House, an honorary gesture in view of the Democratic domination of the House. As his name was placed in nomination, McElwee was endorsed as the equal of any House member. The nominee received 32 votes; the next year he was elected temporary chairman of the Republican gubernatorial convention. Soon McElwee's reputation extended beyond the borders of Tennessee. Booker T. Washington invited him to be a commencement speaker at the 1887 graduation of Tuskegee Institute due to McElwee's accomplishments and his skill as a public speaker.

In 1887, during his third term, McElwee lectured the House on race relations in a powerful speech delivered in the wake of the horrific lynching of a black woman in West Tennessee. He had proposed a bill that would make sheriffs responsible for prisoners who "escaped," a deterrent to the common excuse for allowing mobs to "capture" escapees and lynch them. As the legislators listened, McElwee thundered his protest and demanded reform. "I stand here today and enter my most solemn protest against mob vio-

lence in Tennessee, " he thundered, "Great God, when will this Nation treat the Negro as an American citizen? . . . As a humble representative of the Negro race, and as a member of this body, I stand here today and wave the flag of truce between the races and demand a reformation in Southern society."[2] Despite his emotional plea, the bill was tabled by a vote of 41 to 36.

McElwee served during the era when the restrictive racial legislation known as "Jim Crow" law was passed. As a result, McElwee and his black colleagues are sometimes accused of "selling out." However, with other black legislators, he fought against overwhelming odds to introduce bills to protect laborers, improve education, and provide for the civil rights of African Americans.

Voting fraud and intimidation cost McElwee reelection in 1887, and he left Haywood County under threat of his life. Settling in Nashville, he married Georgia Shelton. In 1888 his last foray into political life came when he attended the Republican National Convention and made an unsuccessful attempt to obtain an appointment as Minister to Haiti. He largely withdrew from public life after 1890, although he continued to give well-received speeches at black colleges and events, and he edited a newspaper. In 1901 McElwee moved his wife and daughters to a white neighborhood in Chicago, where he developed a lucrative law practice, specializing in suits against street car companies. He died in October 1914.

Lewis L. Laska, Tennessee State University

CITATIONS:

(1) Nashville *American*, June 9, 1888.

(2) Parts of the speech were reprinted in (Nashville) *The Tennessean*, February 13, 1971; also see Joseph H. Cartwright, "Black Legislators in Tennessee in the 1880s: A Case Study in Black Political Leadership," *Tennessee Historical Quarterly* 32(1973): 282–283.

SUGGESTED READING: Richard A. Couto, *Lifting the Veil: A Political History of Struggles for Emancipation* (1993)

SEE: DISFRANCHISING LAWS; FISK UNIVERSITY; GOVERNMENT; HAYWOOD COUNTY; LYNCHING; RECONSTRUCTION; TENNESSEE HOUSE OF REPRESENTATIVES

McEWEN, HETTY MONTGOMERY KENNEDY (1796–1881), Civil War Unionist, was born in Nashville. Her husband, Robert McEwen, a veteran of the Battle of King's Mountain, served as superintendent of Nashville's schools. As the Civil War approached, the McEwens remained strong Unionists and opposed Tennessee's secession. Hetty McEwen defied local Confederate sentiment and continued to fly a homemade American flag from the top of her house on Spruce Street. Once a Confederate government was in place in Nashville, she was advised to remove the flag. McEwen refused, asking her husband to load a shotgun so she could defend the flag and reminding him that her four uncles fell at King's Mountain. Later, when Confederate Governor Isham G. Harris ordered all firearms brought to the state capitol and sent soldiers to the McEwen residence to confiscate their weapons, Hetty McEwen refused to surrender her guns to anyone but the governor himself.

The Union occupation of Nashville in March 1862 meant that the McEwens could fly the United States flag without fear of punishment for the remainder of the war. After the war, McEwen became active in the Nashville Protestant School of Industry, a home for girls with no family. McEwen died in 1881 and is buried with her husband in Mt. Olivet Cemetery.
Carole Stanford Bucy, Volunteer State Community College
SEE: HARRIS, ISHAM G.; OCCUPATION, CIVIL WAR

McFERREN, JOHN AND VIOLA. Two years after the passage of the 1957 Civil Rights Act, civil rights activists John and Viola Harris McFerren (now divorced) led voter-registration drives in Fayette County, Tennessee. Unyielding proponents of the right of African Americans to exercise the franchise, the McFerrens were among those who organized Fayette County's Freedom Village, a makeshift community of army tents. Better known as "Tent City," the village assembled when white farm owners evicted hundreds of African-American tenant farmers who registered to vote.

The modern Civil Rights Movement thrust the mantle of leadership upon many unlikely leaders. In Fayette County, African-American World War II veterans assumed leadership roles. Having tasted democracy in their experiences outside the South, they found the county's discriminatory racial practices and disfranchising tactics intolerable. John McFerren—Fayette County native, World War II veteran, farmer, grocer and gas station proprietor—came to the forefront (along with Harpman James and others) to lead African Americans in the fight for civil and voting rights. McFerren explained that after the war, he "came back here and made a home," and he believed the battle for African-American rights was "just as important as World War II."[1] Although Viola McFerren initially attempted to dissuade her husband from active participation, she soon joined him. The McFerren home became the center of the Civil Rights Movement in Fayette County, and Viola McFerren furthered the civil rights cause as she provided for the needs of workers and fulfilled her domestic obligations.

In 1959 John McFerren became a founder of the Original Fayette County Civic and Welfare League (OFCC&WL). In June and July, League members persuaded a number of African Americans to register to vote. In the August Democratic primary, however,

registered African Americans were barred illegally from casting their ballots. On November 16, 1959, League members filed a federal lawsuit against the Fayette County Democratic Executive Committee. In April 1960 the court ruled in favor of the plaintiffs.

As leaders in the Fayette County voter-registration drive, the McFerrens endured economic and physical hardships. John McFerren reasoned that economic independence held the key to the acquisition of African-American civil rights. When the White Citizens Council banned African Americans from the marketplace, McFerren traveled 50 miles every other week to stock his store. Until the Tennessee Council of Human Relations threatened to prosecute, the local Coca-Cola Bottling Company refused him sales. Tennessee agents for the major oil companies denied him gasoline for his station. The McFerrens traveled to Memphis for the birth of their third child after local white physicians stopped offering medical services to blacks.

The steadfastness of the McFerrens and their neighbors was rewarded on July 26, 1962, when a federal consent decree permanently enjoined the defendants from interfering with the voting rights of any eligible voter. Motivated by their victory in the battle for voting rights, the McFerrens became successful plaintiffs in the county's school desegregation cases. When African Americans continued to encounter racism, they initiated a refusal-to-purchase offensive against local white merchants. Ever vigilant for the cause of racial justice, the McFerrens became stalwart soldiers in the Fayette County campaign for human rights in the modern civil rights era.
Linda T. Wynn, Tennessee Historical Commission/Fisk University
CITATION:
(1) "Cold War in Fayette County," *Ebony Magazine* (September 1960), 28.
SUGGESTED READINGS: Robert Hamburger, *Our Portion of Hell, Fayette County, Tennessee: An Oral History of the Struggle for Civil Rights* (1973); Linda T. Wynn, "Toward a Perfect Democracy: The Struggle of African Americans in Fayette County, Tennessee, to Fulfill the Unfulfilled Right of the Franchise," *Tennessee Historical Quarterly* 55(1996): 202–223
SEE: CIVIL RIGHTS MOVEMENT; FAYETTE COUNTY; TENT CITY

McGILLIVRAY, LACHLAN (1719–1799), a trader and diplomat among the Upper Creek Indians in Georgia and Alabama, played an important role in British-Indian relations on the southern colonial frontier. Born in Inverness, Scotland, McGillivray emigrated to Georgia in 1735 and established relations with the Creeks through his family's trading company. He soon mastered the Creek language and, by 1741, was interpreting for British diplomatic agents. He successfully gained Creek alliances for the British against both the Spanish in Florida and the French in Tennessee, Georgia, and Alabama. McGillivray received a license to trade among the Creeks in 1744, which led to a successful career as a trader among the Creek villages throughout the region, and as an Augusta and Savannah merchant and land speculator. He married a Creek woman, Sehoy Marchand; their son Alexander McGillivray (b. 1750) was the famous Creek chieftain.

After the Choctaw Revolt (1746–1749), McGillivray served as ambassador of the South Carolina Commons House to the Choctaws, weakening French ties to the Choctaws and strengthening British ties with Choctaws and Chickasaws, as well as the Creeks. He was instrumental in the formation of the Creek and Chickasaw alliance against the Cherokees, preventing the Creeks from joining the Cherokee uprising against Fort Loudoun in Tennessee in 1759–1760. McGillivray assisted in the negotiations for the Treaty of Augusta (1763), which extended the northern border of Georgia, the Chickasaw land cessions in 1763 and 1773, and the boundary line of 1763 against the Cherokees. Lachlan McGillivray later returned to Scotland and died at Dunmaglass in 1799.

L. Thomas Smith, Jr., Johnson Bible College

SEE: CHICKASAWS; CHOCTAWS; FORT LOUDOUN; OVER-HILL CHEROKEES; TREATIES

McGUGIN, DANIEL EARLE (1879–1936), the most successful coach in Vanderbilt University football history, was born on July 29, 1879, in Tingley, Iowa, the son of Benjamin Franklin and Melissa A. Crutchfield McGugin. McGugin graduated from Drake University in Des Moines in 1901, where he played varsity football for two years. He graduated from the law school at the University of Michigan in 1904 and was admitted to the Michigan bar.

While at Michigan, McGugin played guard for two years under coach Fielding Harris "Hurry Up" Yost, one of early football's greatest innovators. The 1901 team was one of Michigan's most successful, and McGugin played with his team at the first Rose Bowl in 1902. Although he had just entered law practice, McGugin accepted the position of head coach at Vanderbilt University for the 1904 season. That year, his team remained undefeated, a feat his team repeated in 1921. For five years, McGugin coached Vanderbilt football in the fall and returned to his Michigan law office for the rest of the year. In 1909 he moved to Nashville and established a corporate law office.

From 1904 to 1923 McGugin's Vanderbilt teams won ten conference championships in the Southern Intercollegiate Athletic Association and the Southern Conference. His career record was 197–55–19 for regular season play. Maintaining his private law practice, he taught and coached at Vanderbilt until his retirement in 1934, when he became the school's ath-

letic director. In 1920 McGugin was elected for one term in the Tennessee Senate on the Democratic ticket. He also served as a trustee for Fisk University and was president of the American Football Coaches Association in 1933. In 1951 McGugin was inducted into the National College Football Hall of Fame for his exceptional career as a coach.

McGugin married Virginia Louise Fite in 1905, and Fielding Yost served as best man. The colleagues had even closer ties after Yost later married Fite's sister. McGugin died on January 19, 1936, and is buried in Nashville's Mount Olivet Cemetery.

Ann Toplovich, Tennessee Historical Society

SEE: FOOTBALL, COLLEGE; VANDERBILT UNIVERSITY

McINTYRE v. BALENTINE (1992). Until recently, Tennessee followed the doctrines of "contributory negligence." Under contributory negligence, a person harmed by a defendant's negligent act may be unable to recover anything in damages if that person contributed, even in a small way, to the harm. Thus, for example, a person exceeding the speed limit by two miles per hour might be unable to recover damages from a drunk driver who was exceeding the speed limit by 50 miles per hour and driving on the wrong side of the road.

The Tennessee Supreme Court had refused on previous occasions to consider abandoning contributory negligence. Although the doctrine, like most rules of tort law, was judge-made to begin with, the Court wished to give the General Assembly a chance to abolish contributory negligence by statute.

In *McIntyre* (1992) the Tennessee Supreme Court abolished the doctrine of contributory negligence and replaced it with a system of comparative negligence. Under the new rule, so long as the plaintiff's fault is less than the defendant's, the plaintiff can adopt a pro-rata share of the damages. If the jury finds that the plaintiff is 25 percent at fault, for example, and the defendant 75 percent at fault, then the plaintiff can recover three-fourths of what he or she would receive if the fault were entirely that of the defendant.

Comparative negligence now is the rule in most states. It is seen as less harsh than contributory negligence, which could deny a seriously injured person any recovery at all even where the victim's negligence is minor in relation to that of the defendant.

Glenn H. Reynolds, University of Tennessee, School of Law

SEE: LAW

McKEE FOODS CORPORATION. As the creator and producer of Little Debbie Snack Cakes, O.D. and Ruth McKee ended their bakery career with a terrific success that their two sons have turned into a business worth $770 million in annual sales. Before the introduction of the individually wrapped snack cakes in 1960, the McKees experienced four distinct periods in their business. As a young couple in the depressed 1930s, they bought a small bakery in Chattanooga and operated it with Ruth McKee's father. When the bakery prospered, the McKees sold their interest and moved to Charlotte, North Carolina, where they opened another bakery. In the early 1950s, the couple sold the enterprise, intending to retire. The McKees returned to Chattanooga and again helped Mrs. McKee's family with the old bakery. They purchased the bakery for themselves, naming it the McKee Baking Company. The business relocated to Collegedale in 1957, where the company headquarters has remained for 40 years.

The idea of boxing 12 separately packaged snack cakes and marketing the cartons as family packs at the low price of 49 cents proved innovative. The addition of the name "Little Debbie" and the image drawn from a picture of the McKee's granddaughter provided an identity both wholesome and easy to remember.

Today the cost of the family pack runs from two to four times its 1960 price, depending upon the variety purchased. The line has expanded to 66 varieties of snack cakes and leads all competition in unit sales. The two plants in Collegedale, one in Virginia, and one in Arkansas employ a total of 5,000 people and operate around the clock six days a week. Ellsworth McKee became company president in 1971 and passed the title to his brother Jack in 1996. McKee Baking Company changed its name to McKee Foods Corporation in 1991, and introduced a line of Sunbelt snacks and granola cereal bars that runs slightly more in cost than the Little Debbie snack cakes. The company recently diversified into merchandising with a line of Funware (tee shirts, caps, and mugs) and a Little Debbie-style Barbie doll.

The association with the Seventh-day Adventists of Southern Adventist University in Collegedale and the McKee's commitment to involvement in the community have led the company's management to support education of its employees for job advancement. The McKee Education Center for Children and Adults provides resource information for parents, child-rearing tips, and activities for the family. The legacy of O.D. and Ruth McKee continues through the philosophy the corporation espouses.

Margaret D. Binnicker, Middle Tennessee State University
SEE: INDUSTRY; SOUTHERN ADVENTIST UNIVERSITY

McKELLAR, KENNETH DOUGLAS (1869–1957), U.S.

Senator, was born in Dallas County, Alabama, on January 29, 1869. Young McKellar was schooled by an older sister and his parents before his father died when the boy was 11. Working at different jobs, borrowing money, and with help from an older brother, he earned three degrees from the University of Alabama. Soon, along with most of his siblings—he

was the fifth of nine children—he moved to Memphis where he began to practice law.

At once interested in politics and civic affairs, McKellar was part of a group of young Democrats who organized the Jackson Club, and it was during these years that he formed his long political and personal association with Memphis political leader, Edward H. Crump. With their allies, the Crump-McKellar tandem would form one of the most powerful political teams in the history of Tennessee.

In 1911 McKellar was elected to fill the unexpired term of Representative George W. Gordon of Tennessee's Tenth Congressional District. He was reelected in 1912 and 1914. With Democrat majorities in the House of Representatives and with Southern Democrats in both houses of Congress enjoying their greatest influence in national affairs since before the Civil War, McKellar began his Congressional career at an opportune time. Even as a short-timer in Congress, McKellar in 1916 persuaded President Woodrow Wilson to support federal highway legislation which distributed $75 million of federal funds to the states. McKellar had already found his formula for political success—using federal money to promote economic development in the states, especially Tennessee. In time, control over the jobs that came with the money became a major preoccupation of the patronage-minded Memphian.

As a member of the House, McKellar supported the Constitutional amendment which provided for the popular election of U.S. Senators, and he became one of its first beneficiaries. In the 1916 Senate race in Tennessee, he not only defeated both incumbent Senator Luke Lea and former Governor Malcolm Patterson in the Democratic primary, he then defeated former Republican Governor Ben Hooper in the general election. It was the beginning of a long and often stormy Senatorial career for McKellar—the only Tennessean ever elected to six terms in the U.S. Senate.

In his first years in the Senate, McKellar supported President Wilson's progressive reform program as well as the President's unsuccessful attempt to convince the Senate to ratify the Treaty of Versailles after World War I. During the Republican-dominated 1920s, McKellar continued to support progressive legislation that usually failed in Congress while insisting that despite the nation's general prosperity, Tennessee and the South needed federal economic aid. However, McKellar, who first won reelection in 1922 and then defeated House Democratic leader Finis Garrett in a spirited primary in 1928, primarily used these years to build his seniority in a system which has always favored longevity in office.

These years proved profitable for McKellar when the Democrats won in 1932 and President Franklin D. Roosevelt launched the New Deal the following year. With his seniority as Chairman of the Senate Committee on Post Office and Post Roads and as a ranking member of the Senate Appropriations Committee, McKellar controlled countless jobs through federal programs which operated during the New Deal and World War II. Loyal to the New Deal program, McKellar supported federal aid for farmers, New Deal relief programs, and, of course, he helped lead the fight in Congress for the Tennessee Valley Authority (TVA) Act in 1933.

McKellar's considerable success in Washington was matched by that back home in Tennessee. From the mid-1930s to the late 1940s, the Crump-McKellar political machine rolled from one political victory to another. McKellar was reelected in 1934 and 1940 with little opposition and few in the state questioned his considerable political strengths.

At the same time, as the years passed, McKellar increasingly took conservative stands on major policy issues and became personally irascible. He began to differ with FDR over patronage matters, TVA operations, and several of the President's top-level appointments. The split became such that only weeks before he died in 1945, President Roosevelt asked Crump to withdraw his support from McKellar in 1946, a request that Crump refused to honor.

After the war, McKellar's position in the Senate remained secure. He headed the powerful Senate Appropriations Committee and for several years was the Senate President pro tempore. But at the same time, he spent less and less time in Tennessee and, always prone to confrontational politics, his feuds with political foes distracted him from more useful political pursuits. In the early years of McCarthyism, McKellar often opposed presidential nominees on the basis of their political and social associations. Against his friend Crump's advice, and weakened by the machine's political losses in 1948, McKellar was defeated four years later in the Democratic primary by Congressman Albert Gore, Sr.

A lifelong bachelor, the aging McKellar then retired to his suite at the Gayoso Hotel in Memphis where he died on October 25, 1957. He is buried in Elmwood Cemetery there and his papers are housed in the Memphis-Shelby County Library.

Thomas H. Coode, Volunteer State Community College

SUGGESTED READING: Robert D. Pope, "Senatorial Baron: The Long Political Career of Kenneth D. McKellar," (Ph.D. diss., Yale University, 1976)

SEE: CRUMP, EDWARD H.; GORE, ALBERT, SR.; TENNESSEE VALLEY AUTHORITY; WORKS PROGRESS ADMINISTRATION

McKENDREE, WILLIAM (1757–1835), the first American-born bishop of the Methodist Church, was closely associated with the establishment of the Methodist Church in Tennessee. Born in Virginia in 1757, McKendree visited Nashville as early as 1797. Three years later, he became the church's Western District field marshal, with the responsibility of organizing new churches and circuits and recruiting new preachers. McKendree proved to be "the superintendent who most significantly influenced the development of Methodism in Tennessee."[1] Elected Bishop in 1808, McKendree moved to Nashville permanently and lived there until his death. In 1812, with Bishop Francis Asbury, McKendree organized the Tennessee Conference, the general governing organization for Methodism in Tennessee.

His last sermon came at Nashville's McKendree Methodist Church upon its dedication on November 23, 1834. McKendree died in 1835 and was buried in Nashville; later his remains were reinterred at Vanderbilt University.

Carroll Van West, Middle Tennessee State University

CITATION:

(1) Herman A. Norton, *Religion in Tennessee, 1777–1945* (Knoxville, 1981), 28.

SEE: RELIGION; NASHVILLE

McKISSACK AND McKISSACK ARCHITECTS. The McKissack and McKissack architectural tradition dates back to the first Moses McKissack (1790–1865) of the West African Ashanti tribe, who was sold into slavery to William McKissack of North Carolina and became a master builder. In 1822 he married Mirian (1804–1865), a Cherokee, and they had 14 children. The ninth child, Gabriel Moses McKissack (1840–1922), continued in the building trade he learned from his father. Like his father, Gabriel Moses II taught the building skills to his son, Moses McKissack III (1879–1952).

Moses McKissack III was born in Pulaski, Tennessee, and received his formal education in the segregated Pulaski public schools. He initially worked with his father, but in 1890 a Pulaski architect employed him to draw, design, and assist in his construction business. Moses III's adroitness in the trade earned him a reputation as an excellent craftsman. From 1895 to 1905 he built houses in Decatur, Alabama, as well as in Mount Pleasant and Columbia, Tennessee.

In 1905 Moses III moved to Nashville and opened his construction business. That same year, he built a residence for the dean of architecture and engineering at Vanderbilt University. This led to commissions to design and build other residences in Nashville's West End area. McKissack's first major commission was in 1908 for the construction of the Carnegie Library at Fisk University. In 1909 he advertised as an architect in the *Nashville City Directory*. By 1920 McKissack was designing buildings for clients throughout Nashville and the state.

McKissack's brother, Calvin Lunsford McKissack (1890–1968), assisted on most projects. In 1921, when the state professional registration law became effective, the McKissacks were among Tennessee's first registered architects. A year later, Calvin joined his brother as a business partner, and McKissack and McKissack became Tennessee's first professional African-American architectural firm. The firm's architectural projects were located across the South, with most being African-American educational and religious facilities and churches.

McKissack and McKissack received several federal Works Progress Administration contracts in the late 1930s. In 1942 they were awarded a $5.7 million contract for construction of the 99th Pursuit Squadron Air Base (an African-American combat air unit) in Tuskegee, Alabama. This World War II contract was the largest ever granted by the federal government to an African-American company. The McKissacks also designed several federal housing projects. During President Franklin Roosevelt's administration, Moses McKissack III received an appointment to the White House Conference on Housing Problems.

Following the death of his brother, Calvin McKissack became president and general manager of the firm until his death in 1968. Leadership of the company then passed to Moses III's son, William DeBerry McKissack (1925–1988), who served until a debilitating stroke compelled him to resign. The leadership of the nation's oldest African-American architectural firm transferred to his wife, Leatrice Buchanan McKissack. With the assistance of her daughters, she opened three satellite offices in Memphis, Washington, D.C., and New York City. The McKissack women perpetuate the architectural legacy and family tradition of McKissack and McKissack.

Linda T. Wynn, Tennessee Historical Commission/Fisk University

SUGGESTED READINGS: Linda T. Wynn, "Leatrice B. McKissack," in *Notable Black American Women, Book II*, edited by Jessie Carney Smith (1996), 450–454; Linda T. Wynn, "McKissack and McKissack Architects, 1905," in *Profiles of African American in Tennessee*, edited by Bobby L. Lovett and Linda T. Wynn (1996), 87–89

SEE: FISK UNIVERSITY; GILES COUNTY

McLEMORE, JOHN CHRISTMAS

McLEMORE, JOHN CHRISTMAS (1790–1864), West Tennessee land speculator, was born January 1, 1790, in Orange County, North Carolina. In 1809 he moved to Nashville, where he became a surveyor's clerk. Five years later, he succeeded his uncle William Christmas as Surveyor General of the Tennessee Military Tract. His name appeared in most county land books as a grant or land locator or as an official. Because of his character, generosity, and business acumen, contemporaries considered McLemore a potential gubernatorial or senatorial candidate, but he never ran for either office. Both Nashville and Memphis named an early street in his honor, an indication of his community status.

In addition to his popularity and impressive good looks, McLemore's rise to prominence benefited from his marriage to Elizabeth Donelson, daughter of John Donelson, a longtime friend of Andrew Jackson. Before 1820, Jackson and McLemore cooperated in land development in northern Alabama with fellow brother-in-law and Jackson favorite, General John Coffee.

McLemore invested heavily in West Tennessee's development. Evidently he lent his name to McLemoresville and Christmasville in Carroll County. More importantly, the Jackson-McLemore tie resulted in the latter's early interest in Memphis and made him the fourth founding father of the city, along with Jackson, John Overton, and James Winchester. In competition with Overton and Winchester, McLemore speculated in risky ventures, namely Fort Pickering and the LaGrange and Memphis Railroad. Nearly bankrupt, he tried to recoup his losses in California's gold boom of 1850. Within a decade, McLemore returned to Memphis, where he died May 20, 1864.

Marvin Downing, University of Tennessee at Martin

SEE: DONELSON, JOHN; JACKSON, ANDREW; MEMPHIS; TENNESSEANS IN CALIFORNIA GOLD RUSH

McMAHAN, FRED

McMAHAN, FRED (1895–1980) was an African-American brick mason and builder from Sevierville. McMahan learned the trade from his grandfather, Isaac Dockery. He attended Knoxville College where he met his future wife, Mary Bond (1896–1983), in the late 1910s. McMahan earned a master's degree in architectural engineering from the University of Illinois, Urbana-Champaign. Around 1920, he returned to Sevierville, and, along with his brothers James and Newt McMahan, he established the J, F & N McMahan Construction Company.

One of the company's first projects was the construction of the Pleasant View School on a section of McMahan's farm just outside Sevierville. Completed in 1922 with financial assistance from the Julius Rosenwald Fund, this elementary school is the county's only Rosenwald school and one of the few extant brick Rosenwald schools in Tennessee. McMahan's wife was the county's first female teacher to earn a master's degree (in education from the University of Cincinnati in 1938) and was the sole teacher at Pleasant View until 1960. The school remained in use until 1965, when the county integrated its elementary schools.

This firm constructed several buildings in and around Sevierville including the Pigeon Forge Methodist Church (1921); the Murphy Collegiate Institute's Administration Building (1923) and Female Dormitory (1925); the First Baptist Church of Sevierville (1926); the Watson Motor Company (1928); the Townsend Motor Company & John Sevier Service Station (1930); the Rawlings Funeral Home (1937); and the Sevierville Post Office, which was built with Work Progress Administration (WPA) funds in 1940.

The most important building that Fred McMahan built, however, may be the Dwight and Kate Wade House, which was completed at Sevierville in 1940. This house was based on plans provided by Verna Cook-Salomonsky of New York City, one of the country's leading female architects. The Wade House is a replica of an Art Moderne-style house featured at the "Town of Tomorrow" exhibit at the 1939–1940 New York's World Fair. The Wades visited the world's fair on their honeymoon and brought the Town of Tomorrow's brochure home with them, where they picked out Salomonsky's "Garden Home" design and sent off for the architectural plans. The Wade House may be the first documented replica of a Town of Tomorrow house in America; it is certainly the first in Tennessee.

Other buildings constructed by Fred McMahan's company include the Cash Hardware Store at Sevierville (1941); the Beech Springs School at Kodak (1952); and buildings at the Junior Community College for African Americans at Morristown and at Knoxville College. Fred McMahan's own house still stands outside Sevierville.

Robbie D. Jones, Nashville

SEE: DOCKERY, ISAAC; JULIUS ROSENWALD FUND; KNOXVILLE COLLEGE; SEVIER COUNTY; WORKS PROGRESS ADMINISTRATION

McMILLIN, BENTON (1845–1933), Congressman, Governor, and diplomat, was born on September 11, 1845, in Monroe County, Kentucky, the son of John and Elizabeth Black McMillin. After completing preparatory studies at Philomath Academy in Tennessee, he attended the Kentucky Agricultural and Mechanical College (later University of Kentucky) at Lexington. At the outbreak of the Civil War, McMillin's father, a wealthy planter, withheld his permission for his youthful son to join his two older brothers in the Confederate Army. When Union troops captured the young McMillin, he refused to swear allegiance to the federal government and was imprisoned briefly. After the war, McMillin read law under Judge E.L. Gardenshire in Carthage, Tennessee. Admitted to the Tennessee bar in 1871, he established his practice in Celina, before moving to Carthage.

McMillin's long political career began in 1874, when he was elected to the Tennessee House of Representatives as a Democrat. In 1875 Governor James D. Porter commissioned McMillin to negotiate with Kentucky officials on a territorial purchase. Two years later, the governor appointed him as special court judge of the fifth judicial circuit. McMillin served as a presidential elector in every election from 1876 to 1932, except the 1916 contest and attended every Democratic National Convention except that of 1920, earning the sobriquet of "Democratic War Horse."

In 1878 McMillin won election to the U.S. House of Representatives, serving continuously from 1879 to 1899. Known for his impromptu oratorical powers and his skill as a parliamentarian, he served on the Rules Committee, where he frequently challenged House Speaker Thomas B. Reed, a Maine Republican. McMillin served 14 years on the important Ways and Means Committee. He opposed government extravagance, condemned Republican tariff policies, favored antitrust laws, denounced the Federal Election Bill, castigated imperialism, warned against federal court encroachments, and supported currency expansion, including the free coinage of silver.

Beginning in 1879, McMillin advocated an income tax as an equitable means of raising revenue. When Democrats introduced a tariff reform bill in 1894, McMillin attached an income tax provision for a two percent tax on incomes above $4,000. President Grover Cleveland allowed the Wilson-Gorman Tariff, with McMillin's income tax amendment, to become law without his signature. After the U.S. Supreme Court invalidated the income tax in *Pollock v. Farmers' Loan and Trust Company* (1895), a disappointed McMillin lobbied for a constitutional amendment to allow such a tax. This finally occurred with the adoption of the Sixteenth Amendment in 1913.

Unsuccessful in a contest for the U.S. Senate in 1897, McMillin quit Congress to run for governor. He served as the state's chief executive from 1899 to 1903. During his administration, McMillin reduced the state debt by creating a sinking fund and presiding over a strict management of the treasury. He also signed legislation establishing uniform textbooks for public schools, providing for factory inspection, and changing the minimum age for factory employment from 12 to 14 years. After his second term, McMillin engaged in the insurance business in Nashville. He never again held elective office, though he sought a Senate seat in 1910 and 1930, and ran for governor in 1912 and 1922.

In 1913 President Woodrow Wilson appointed McMillin as Minister to Peru, where he served until September 1919. After six years in Peru, McMillin was transferred to Guatemala, where he served until 1922.

McMillin married Birdie Brown, daughter of Tennessee Governor John C. Brown, in 1869. She died a few years after their marriage, leaving him with a son. In 1887 he married Lucille Foster, by whom he had a daughter. McMillin died in Nashville on January 8, 1933, and was buried in Mt. Olivet Cemetery.

Leonard Schlup, Akron, Ohio

SEE: SMITH COUNTY

McMINN COUNTY, located in southeast Tennessee, was established by the Tennessee legislature in 1819. Named for Governor Joseph McMinn, the county was created from lands ceded by the Cherokees in the Hiwassee Purchase.

Calhoun, the first town and county seat, was established in 1820 across the Hiwassee River from the Cherokee Indian Agency. The need for a more centrally located seat of government led to the county seat's removal, in 1823, to Athens, 15 miles northward. Athens was chartered in 1822. By 1830 McMinn County had a population of over 14,000, including 1,250 slaves.

The Hiwassee Railroad began construction of one of Tennessee's first railroads in McMinn County in 1837. Plans called for a line from Dalton, Georgia, through McMinn County to Knoxville, a distance of 98 miles. Financial problems, and a general economic depression statewide, halted construction in 1839 after the completion of 66 miles of graded roadbed and a bridge at Calhoun. Work was resumed in 1849 by the East Tennessee and Georgia Railroad with Athens as the railroad's headquarters until 1855 when the central office was moved to Knoxville.

With the arrival of the railroad came the new towns of Riceville, Sanford, and Mouse Creek (now Niota) which developed along the line. During the Civil War, the railroad gained added significance, serving as a vital link for transporting troops and supplies between the lower and upper South.

Like most East Tennesseans, McMinn Countians experienced divided loyalties during the Civil War. Although Tennessee joined the Confederacy in 1861, the county furnished troops to both Confederate and Union armies. While no major battles were fought within the county, thousands of troops passed through the area which suffered severe economic hardships.

Following the war, lack of capital hampered growth and development, but by the late nineteenth century, recovery, spurred by the railroad, was well under way. Two new towns, Jellico Junction (later Englewood) and Etowah, were established along railway lines. Etowah came into existence in 1905 as a railroad town, the Atlanta Division headquarters of the Louisville & Nashville. By the 1920s employment reached over 2,000, and some 20 trains passed through Etowah daily.

In 1920 McMinn County's young representative to the Tennessee legislature, Harry T. Burn of Niota, cast the deciding vote approving the Nineteenth Amendment which granted women the right to vote. The Senate had passed the measure, but a tie vote occurred twice in the House. Having previously voted with the opposition, Burn switched his vote, breaking the tie, and making Tennessee the required thirty-sixth state to approve ratification.

In 1921 McMinn County became the site of the construction of the first concrete highway in Tennessee, a 14-mile stretch of the Lee Highway (U.S. 11)

from Athens to Calhoun. A small section of this road is still in use today.

McMinn County suffered severe economic hardship during the Great Depression. Etowah was most affected since its economic base was tied to a single industry. When repair shops were closed and the division headquarters of L&N moved to Knoxville, employment fell to fewer than 100. While World War II brought a temporary revival, the boom days of the railroad town were over.

Perhaps the most notable event in McMinn's history occurred on August 1, 1946, when returning GIs overthrew a corrupt political machine with ties to Ed "Boss" Crump. A large number of armed deputies took ballot boxes to the county jail to be "counted" behind barricaded doors, refusing requests for GI observers to witness the counting. After several hours of a raging gunfire battle, those inside the jail were dynamited into surrendering. This "Battle of Athens," in which, miraculously, no one was killed, resulted in governmental reform. The County Court system of government was replaced by a County Council-Manager system, the first in Tennessee.

Following World War II, McMinn County experienced rapid growth and economic development as existing industries and businesses expanded and several corporations, including Bowaters, the world's largest newsprint producer, established major plants in the area. Educational opportunities also increased with expansions at Tennessee Wesleyan College and Lee University and the opening of Cleveland State Community College. Also, dairy farming increased during the first three decades following the war. Mayfield Dairy Farms, one of the largest dairy processors in the southeast, helped to stimulate the growth in dairying.

McMinn County's primary historical attractions are the exhibits at the L&N Depot, Etowah; the Englewood Textile Museum; and the McMinn County Living Heritage Museum, Athens. The latter institution interprets the county's history from the days of the Cherokees to the economic transformations of the 1940s with 30 exhibits. Antebellum landmark buildings include the Old College of Tennessee Wesleyan College and the Cleague Building, both in Athens.

Bill Akins and Genevieve Wiggins, Tennessee Wesleyan College

SEE: ATHENS, BATTLE OF; ENGLEWOOD MILLS; MAYFIELD DAIRY; MCMINN, JOSEPH; TENNESSEE WESLEYAN COLLEGE; SENTER, DEWITT; WOMAN SUFFRAGE MOVEMENT

McMINN, JOSEPH (1758–1824), farmer, state legislator, Indian agent and Governor, was born at Westchester, Pennsylvania, on June 22, 1758. McMinn served in the Continental army during the American Revolution. After the war, he moved to the future Tennessee, and bought a farm in Hawkins County in 1786.

In 1790 Territorial Governor William Blount appointed McMinn to county office, and in 1794 he represented Hawkins County in the Territorial General Assembly. As a member of the State Constitutional Convention in 1796, McMinn was chosen to deliver a copy of the state constitution to U.S. Secretary of State Timothy Pickering in Philadelphia. He was elected to the first Tennessee State Senate and later served three times as Speaker of the Senate. He was Governor of Tennessee for three terms between 1815 and 1821. During his tenure, the Jackson Purchase was completed, the State Capitol was moved from Knoxville to Murfreesboro, and the Bank of Tennessee was incorporated.

After retiring from the gubernatorial office in 1821, McMinn bought a farm near Calhoun. Two years later, he was appointed as Agent of the United States to the Cherokees. He died on November 17, 1824, at the Cherokee Agency on the Hiwassee River and was buried near Calhoun. Both McMinn County and McMinnville in Warren County are named in his honor.

John H. Thweatt, Tennessee State Library and Archives
SUGGESTED READING: Charles W. Crawford (ed.), *Governors of Tennessee* (1979)

SEE: HAWKINS COUNTY; JACKSON PURCHASE; MCMINN COUNTY; TREATIES; WARREN COUNTY

McNAIRY COUNTY was created on October 8, 1823, from a part of Hardin County and named in honor of John McNairy, whom President George Washington had appointed as one of the three judges of the Southwest Territory. The first courts were held in the home of Abel V. Maury until a log courthouse could be constructed. The first county seat was named Purdy in honor of John Purdy, the government surveyor who laid out the town lots. Benjamin Wright, a veteran of the Creek Indian Wars, soon emerged as the driving force behind the economic development of the town. Located on the stage road that ran from Nashville to Mississippi, Purdy developed a reputation as a beautiful town. In 1831 the county built a new courthouse, where both David Crockett and James K. Polk made political speeches.

In 1855 the citizens of Purdy refused to raise the $100,000 in subscriptions for the Mobile and Ohio Railroad to route its line through the town. The decision resulted in the gradual decline of Purdy and in 1870 an effort began to move the county seat to a location near the rail line. In 1890, when P. H. Thrasher, an Alabama investor, built a courthouse and donated it to the county at Selmer, voters agreed to move the county seat to the railroad town, where it remains. In addition to Purdy and Selmer, McNairy County has eight other incorporated towns: Adamsville, Bethel Springs, Michie, Milledgeville, Finger, Ramer, Eastview, Stantonville, and Guys.

During the 1861 secession crisis, McNairy County divided along political lines, with some 1,000 voting for secession and 800 against. McNairy Countians living north of an invisible line running east to west remained pro-Union (and later supported the Republican party), while those living south of the line supported secession, the Confederacy, and the Democratic party. Military Governor Andrew Johnson chose McNairy County slaveholder Fielding Hurst to head up the Sixth Cavalry of the Army of the Tennessee (Union). McNairy County became the scene of looting and burning throughout the war years.

In the postwar years, McNairy Countians returned to agriculture, producing cotton, corn, and hogs. By 1920 the county population totaled 18,350 people, most of whom tilled the 3,263 farms. Selmer had a population of 546, three banks, a newspaper, and various commercial establishments. The county had six high schools and 109 elementary schools.

Cheap power from the Tennessee Valley Authority promoted McNairy County's economic growth in the mid-twentieth century. In 1945 Brown Shoe Company and Myrna Mills, a textile manufacturer, became the first industries to locate in the county. These industries encouraged other textile manufacturers to build plants in McNairy County and utilize the female work force. In the 1970s E.B. Blasingame founded Aqua Glass, Inc., which quickly emerged as the county's largest employer, with approximately 1,000 employees. Today, Aqua Glass and the textile manufacturers have been joined by the General Electric Corporation, Spectrum Corporation (recycled oil products), Kolpack Mfg. Company (refrigeration), Ripley Industries, Incorporated (engine filtration), Shiloh Frozen Foods, Reitter & Schefenacker (automotive), and Jones Exhaust Systems.

McNairy County's Adamsville was the home of Tennessee Governor Ray Blanton (1975–1979). McNairy County sheriff Buford Pusser's career in combating lawlessness and illegal whiskey was chronicled in three best-selling books by W.R. Morris, three block-buster movies, and a short-lived TV series. A museum in his hometown of Adamsville recognizes his law enforcement career. Other famous residents of McNairy County include Marcus J. Wright and his brother John V. Wright, both of whom served as Confederate generals. Marcus Wright served as military governor of Columbus, Kentucky, early in the Civil War. After the war, the U.S. government hired him to compile the Official Records of the Rebellion, an effort that required 33 years and resulted in creating the most important single primary document about the war. Dew Wilson, a former Confederate army officer, served under President Grover Cleveland as Commissioner of Indian Affairs in the Oklahoma

Territory. T. Wash Scott was Counsel General to Mexico in the 1850s.

Today, McNairy County's 560 square miles of rolling hills and flatlands are dotted with homes, pastures, fields, and well-groomed towns. The Indian trail that became Davy Crockett Highway (U.S. Highway 64) is undergoing transformation to become a four-lane scenic highway that will traverse the Volunteer State.

Bill Wagoner, Adamsville

SEE: BLANTON, LEONARD RAY; COON CREEK; MCNAIRY, JOHN; PUSSER, BUFORD; TENNESSEE IN FILM

McNAIRY, JOHN (1762–1837), Andrew Jackson's early friend and mentor, was one of Tennessee's first federal judges. Variously reported to have been born in Pennsylvania or North Carolina, McNairy was the son of Francis and Mary Boyd McNairy. The young McNairy read law under Spruce Macay (as did Jackson) and was admitted to practice law in Rowan County, North Carolina, in 1784.

In December 1787 the 25-year-old McNairy was elected by the North Carolina General Assembly as the judge for the new district Superior Court of Davidson County in the state's westernmost territory. He emigrated to Nashville in the autumn of 1788. En route to his new home, McNairy was admitted to the bar in the Washington County court in Jonesborough. He presided at his initial term of court in early November 1788, and one of his first acts was to appoint his young friend, Andrew Jackson, as prosecuting attorney for the district.

In June 1790 President George Washington appointed McNairy, a protégé of territorial Governor William Blount's, as one of three judges for the federal Territory South of the River Ohio. In 1796 Judge McNairy was one of five delegates from Davidson County to the state constitutional convention that met in Knoxville, where he served on the convention's drafting committee. When Tennessee acquired statehood later that year, McNairy was elected as one of three judges to serve on the Superior Court of Tennessee, the state's court of last resort and forerunner of the Tennessee Supreme Court.

In February 1797 President Washington appointed McNairy as Judge of the United States District Court for the District of Tennessee, a position he held through various congressionally-mandated jurisdictional changes. Beginning in 1807, and continuing for the remainder of his tenure on the bench, Judge McNairy also sat as a member of the Circuit Court of the United States for the Seventh Circuit in cases arising in Tennessee. He shared his Circuit Court duties with U.S. Supreme Court Associate Justices Thomas Todd (1807–1826), Robert Trimble (1826–1828), and John McLean (1830–1833). McNairy retired from the bench in 1834, after a judicial career of more than 46

years. He was known for decisions that upheld the spirit of the law rather than the letter of the law.

McNairy's substantial landholdings (nearly 11,000 acres in Davidson and Sumner counties in 1794) included the 477-acre farm Bellview, where he and his wife, Mary Bell Robertson, lived. In addition to his judicial duties, McNairy served as a trustee of the Davidson Academy, the consolidated Davidson Academy-Federal Seminary, and Cumberland College. He was chairman of the host committee for President James Monroe's visit to Nashville in 1819 and served on a similar committee for the Marquis de Lafayette's 1825 visit to the city. McNairy briefly served as president of the Bank of Tennessee that was created in the aftermath of Panic of 1819. Although he occasionally—and strenuously—quarreled with Jackson, McNairy endorsed his initial, unsuccessful presidential bid in 1824 and served on a committee of Nashvillians who supported Jackson's second, successful race for the presidency in 1828.

McNairy died scarcely three years into his retirement. He is buried in Nashville's City Cemetery.

Theodore Brown, Jr., Atlanta, Georgia

SUGGESTED READINGS: James W. Ely, Jr., and Theodore Brown, Jr., eds., *Legal Papers of Andrew Jackson* (1987); Stephen S. Lawrence, "The Life and Times of John McNairy," (M.A. thesis, Middle Tennessee State University, 1971)

SEE: BLOUNT, WILLIAM; DAVIDSON COUNTY; JACKSON, ANDREW; LAW; MCNAIRY COUNTY; SOUTHWEST TERRITORY

McREYNOLDS, JAMES CLARK (1862–1946), the fourth Tennessean to be appointed to the U.S. Supreme Court, was born in Elkton, Kentucky, on February 3, 1862. His father was a surgeon and plantation owner, and the family belonged to a fundamentalist sect of the Disciples of Christ church. The isolation of the mountain community where young James grew up, the political and religious conservatism of his father, and the strict moral code to which he was subjected profoundly influenced him.

He entered Vanderbilt University in Nashville at age 17 where he excelled in science, edited the school paper, and graduated first in his class. He began postgraduate work in science, but soon left to attend law school at the University of Virginia. McReynolds was such a diligent and enthusiastic student of the law that he graduated in only 14 months.

Following graduation in 1884 he spent two years in Washington as a staff assistant to Senator Howell E. Jackson of Tennessee (who was to be appointed to the Supreme Court in 1893). McReynolds established a law practice in Nashville in 1886. Ten years later he was an unsuccessful candidate for Congress. It was said that his arrogance and aloofness contributed to his political defeat.

In 1900 McReynolds became a professor of law at Vanderbilt University where one of his colleagues was Horace Lurton (who was appointed to the Supreme Court in 1909). He was appointed Assistant Attorney General by President Theodore Roosevelt in 1903, and soon gained a reputation as a zealous and effective "trust buster." In 1907 he left government to practice law for a time in New York City, but returned to Tennessee after a few years and resumed his involvement in politics. He supported Woodrow Wilson in the election of 1912 and was appointed Attorney General in the new President's cabinet.

McReynolds was eminently qualified to be Attorney General, but his violent temper and abrasive personality soon began to create problems for the President. When his fellow Tennessean, Justice Lurton, died in 1914, Wilson seized the opportunity to solve two problems at once by appointing McReynolds to the U.S. Supreme Court.

James C. McReynolds served 26 years on the nation's highest court where he became well known for his inflexibility, his narrow constructionist views, and his utter failure to get along with his colleagues. He was especially intolerant of Justices Cardozo and Brandeis, and became a bitter enemy of President Franklin Roosevelt and the New Deal. McReynolds strongly opposed the growing economic regulatory power of the federal government. He authored several significant decisions in the field of civil liberties. In *Pierce v. Society of Sisters* (1925), for instance, McReynolds invoked the doctrine of substantive due process to invalidate a state law requiring that all children attend public school. He resigned from the Court in 1941 after becoming the sole surviving member of the conservative bloc. He died of bronchial pneumonia in a Washington hospital on August 24, 1946, and was buried in Elkton, Kentucky.

It is unfortunate that his acerbic personality and lack of social graces marred McReynolds's career. After his death many were surprised to learn that he had supported almost three dozen young refugee children during World War II, and that he had been a substantial contributor to other children's charities.

Ed Young, Nashville

SUGGESTED READINGS: James E. Bond, *I Dissent: The Legacy of Chief Justice James Clark McReynolds* (1992); Melvin I. Urofsky, *The Supreme Court Justices: A Biographical Dictionary* (1994)

SEE: JACKSON, HOWELL E.; LAW; LURTON, HORACE H.; VANDERBILT UNIVERSITY

McTYEIRE, HOLLAND N. (1824–1889), Methodist Bishop, is best remembered for his indispensable role in the founding of Vanderbilt University. As a key player in wresting a charter for a central university from the Methodist Episcopal Church, South, McTyeire acquired the money to make the charter a reality and shaped the early university in its location, buildings and grounds, the first faculty, and educa-

tional policies. When McTyeire died on February 15, 1889, his beloved university was well established.

Born in Barnwell County, South Carolina, in 1824 to John and Elizabeth McTyeire, he was educated at Methodist schools and earned a B.A. from Randolph-Macon College in Virginia in 1844. There followed ministerial appointments in Virginia and Alabama and marriage to Amelia Townsend of Mobile in 1847. It quickly became apparent that McTyeire's gifts were not those of an emotional, charismatic itinerant preacher, but instead those of a careful and logical writer and editor, administrator, and church leader. In 1858 McTyeire came to Nashville to assume the editorship of the *Christian Advocate*. After serving rural folk and refugees in Alabama during the Civil War, McTyeire emerged as a major force in the reorganization of Southern Methodism after the war. He was elected bishop and in 1867 returned to Nashville, where he assisted in the organization of the Colored Methodist Episcopal Church.

As a bishop of a church literally torn apart by sectional strife and war, and living in a devastated section of the nation, McTyeire identified better ministerial training as a critical need. McTyeire's vision was of a theological seminary, a separate institution from the biblical departments already in existence in Methodist colleges in the South. McTyeire's plans were controversial—some felt theological training was too intellectual, elitist, and removed from the people, while others opted for a central university stressing the liberal arts (much more in the vein of a Yale or Harvard). McTyeire joined with the proponents of a central university in 1872 when the church's conferences met in Memphis. The charter authorizing a Central University of the Methodist Episcopal Church, South, laid out a plan for an institute of higher learning that was broad-based with theological, literary, scientific, and professional schools.

The charter would have been stillborn without the efforts of McTyeire. While in New York City for a surgical procedure, McTyeire used a kinship connection with Cornelius Vanderbilt's second wife to solicit an initial gift of $500,000 that gave birth to Vanderbilt University. The Vanderbilt gift brought McTyeire great power and prestige; Vanderbilt insisted that McTyeire become the president of the university's Board of Trust, receive a salary and a free home, and hold veto power over board decisions. From the planning, the opening on October 3, 1873, and through its first 15 years, Vanderbilt University felt McTyeire's decisive hand and guidance in every important policy decision. During the years of McTyeire's reign, controversies and problems threatened to swamp the fledgling institution: contentious battles with the faculty, periods of declining and sluggish enrollment, poorly prepared students that undercut rigorous standards, and lack of financial support from the denomination. McTyeire rode out the controversies, expanded the physical plant, solicited still more money from the Vanderbilt family to bring the endowment up to $900,000, and established new Ph.D. programs. At the time of his death in 1889, Vanderbilt University was poised on the brink of its "golden age." No subsequent leader, whether president of the board or chancellor, would wield the power of a McTyeire.

Patricia Miletich, University School, Nashville

SUGGESTED READINGS: Paul K. Conkin, *Gone With the Ivy: A Biography of Vanderbilt University* (1985); John J. Tigert, *Bishop Holland McTyeire, Ecclesiastical and Educational Architect* (1955)

SEE: EDUCATION, HIGHER; VANDERBILT UNIVERSITY

McWHERTER, NED RAY (1930–), Governor and Speaker of the Tennessee House, was born in Palmersville, Weakley County, to Harmon Ray and Lucille Golden Smith McWherter in 1930. Educated in the public schools of Dresden, the seat of Weakley County, McWherter joined the Tennessee National Guard in 1948 and served until 1969, when he retired with the rank of captain. As a young man, McWherter owned and operated several local business while also managing a family farm. In 1953 he married Mrs. Bette Jean Beck Coffee (later divorced) and they raised two children, Michael Ray and Linda.

As he developed his businesses, McWherter became active in local civic groups and Democratic politics. In 1968 he sought and won the Democratic

nomination to represent Lake, Obion, and Weakley counties in the Tennessee House of Representatives. McWherter served in the Tennessee House from 1969 to 1987 and almost immediately he gained respect for his integrity and political shrewdness. In 1973, at the age of 42, he was elected Speaker of the House, a position he ably filled until his inauguration as Governor in 1987. His seven terms is the longest of any Speaker in Tennessee history.

As Speaker, McWherter largely worked with Republican governors, except during the term of fellow Democrat and West Tennessean Ray Blanton from 1975–1979. He appointed the first African-American committee chairs in the South and assisted women legislators in gaining leadership roles in the House. His legislative successes included passage of the state "Sunshine Law," which opened all governmental meetings and records to the public, and new campaign financial disclosure laws. In the 1980s he worked closely with Governor Lamar Alexander to reform and enhance the state's public education system and the state prison system. He consistently supported state highway improvement and expansion programs.

In 1986 he sought and won the Democratic nomination for governor and then defeated former Governor Winfield Dunn in the general election. He was reelected to a second term, facing only token opposition, in 1990. From 1987 to 1995 Governor McWherter built a popular record on balanced budgets, new roads, elimination of unnecessary bureau-

Governor Ned McWherter.

STATE OF TENNESSEE PHOTOGRAPHIC SERVICES

cracy, and increased appropriations for K-12 public education. His Twenty-first Century Schools program, part of the Educational Improvement Act of 1992, upgraded facilities, lowered teacher-student ratios, and addressed the inequities of public education funding between rural and urban counties. It represented the initial state response to the chancery court decision of *Tennessee Small School Systems v. McWherter* (1991), which found the Tennessee system of funding local schools to be in violation of the equal protection clause of the Tennessee Constitution. McWherter's innovative reform of the state Medicaid system, the TennCare program, has been monitored carefully by officials from other states who are interested in new programs that provide health care for needy citizens at a reasonable public cost.

In 1995 McWherter retired from political office, but remains active in Democratic politics both in Tennessee and at the national level, occasionally providing advice to President Bill Clinton, whom McWherter has known since Clinton was Governor of Arkansas.

Carroll Van West, Middle Tennessee State University

SEE: ALEXANDER, LAMAR; BLANTON, RAY; TENNCARE; TENNESSEE HOUSE OF REPRESENTATIVES; TENNESSEE SMALL SCHOOL SYSTEMS V. MCWHERTER; WEAKLEY COUNTY

MEDICINE. A rich source of herbal and root remedies derived from indigenous American plants greeted newcomers to the Tennessee backcountry in the eighteenth century. James Adair, an early white Indian trader of the trans-Allegheny region that is now Tennessee, described remedies skillfully applied by the Cherokees to heal the sick, injured, or infirmed. Indians, Adair observed, always carried with them snakeroot, or wild horehound, plantain, and other herbs to curb the life-threatening effects of snake bites. Unfortunately for the Cherokees, the bounteous medicinal offerings of the Great Smoky Mountains shrank before the decimation stemming from the smallpox white settlers brought with them to America.

While traders in the west encountered Native American healers, colonists in the east tenaciously clung to remedies originating in plants imported from their native lands or those transplanted to the New World. Only gradually did indigenous remedies meld with the knowledge colonists brought with them on their trans-Atlantic crossings. The extent of the influence of Native American healing practices upon white practices is inconcise and likely involved a process of adding to known remedies rather than supplanting them.

If the impact of traditional Indian medicinal remedies is difficult to assess, then remedies brought to America by African Americans present an even greater challenge. Self-care and medicine as practiced by African-American doctors during the colonial era is little understood. Certainly, the African tradition of relying on conjurers traveled to America. Whites had little trust in blacks' medical remedies, thus whites' and blacks' treatments often competed. Only rarely did whites adopt blacks' remedies as legitimate healing practices.

Sullivan County records the first white physician in Tennessee. Dr. Patrick Vance immigrated to America in 1754, removing to Tennessee following the American Revolution. Dr. Elkannah R. Dulaney joined Vance in 1799 or 1800. Dulaney typified the active interest many physicians took in their communities. Remuneration was meager and physicians like Dulaney, who served six terms in the state legislature, became involved in civic affairs. By the time Dulaney's son, William R. Dulaney, was born in 1800, it was customary for aspiring physicians to apprentice themselves to a physician in their community, then to attend a medical training program, usually a four-month course of lectures spread over two years, with the second course a repeat of the first. William Dulaney completed his studies in 1839 at Transylvania University in Lexington, Kentucky, a school that supplied many of Tennessee's early physicians.

Reverend Samuel Carrick, noted for his pastoral and educational accomplishments, dispensed medicines before Dr. James Cozby, Knoxville's first physician, settled in the area. In 1794 two other physicians, Dr. Thomas McCombs and Dr. Robert Johnson, joined Cozby. Dr. Joseph Churchill Strong opened his practice in 1804 and served as preceptor to a number of ambitious physicians. Dr. J.G.M. Ramsey studied with Strong for two years, then matriculated at the University of Pennsylvania, one of America's oldest medical schools.

As white settlers migrated westward to the Cumberland settlement at what is now Nashville, physicians followed. The first physician of record was Dr. James White. An exceptionally well-trained graduate of the University of Edinburgh, White was succeeded by Dr. John Sappington and his brother, Dr. Mark B. Sappington, who arrived in Nashville in 1785. In 1806 University of Pennsylvania-trained Dr. Felix Robertson opened a medical practice in Nashville. The first white male child born at the settlement, Robertson was a son of Nashville founder, James Robertson, and Charlotte Reeves Robertson. Felix Robertson grew to become a leading figure in Nashville's civic and medical circles. Besides being mayor of the city, he served as president of the Medical Society of Tennessee (1834–1840) and is credited with organizing the first local medical society in 1821. Of special significance, Robertson initiated the use of quinine for malaria victims.

West Tennessee drew settlers once the Indian threat was removed. Memphis's first physicians arrived in the 1830s. Two engaged in practice were Dr. Mark B. Sappington (a grandson of Nashville's Dr. Sappington) and Dr. Wyatt Christian. In 1842 Sappington offered to vaccinate all of the city's residents against smallpox. Christian represented Shelby County at a meeting called in 1830 to organize the Medical Society of Tennessee.

Many untrained healers practiced alongside physicians. Lay practitioners and the common people dispensing care to family members, especially in the South, were more likely to turn to *Gunn's Domestic Medicine* than to physicians for help. Published in 1830, Gunn's book recommended drugs imported from Europe, such as mercury and opium, which were readily available at local mercantile stores, rather than those gathered from medicinal plants native to Tennessee. Patent medicines, promising cures in a single bottle for every ailment imaginable, rested comfortably beside mercury and opium on mercantile shelves. In the absence of physicians, settlers carried dog-eared texts containing remedies and traded recipes for concocting them, since treatment was administered at home.

By the 1830s botanical healing movements had gained substantial favor among the common folk. An emerging abhorrence to heroic treatment, consisting of blood letting, purging, and blistering, which had arisen in the 1790s from the pen of Philadelphia physician Benjamin Rush, encouraged that interest. Samuel Thomson, an itinerant herbalist, provided the justification for using herbs in healing, proclaiming every man his own physician. Thomson had at least 29 agents in Tennessee spreading his message.

As medical sects began to establish a grip on the American public, traditionally trained physicians attempted to organize to defend their legitimacy as purveyors of healing. On May 3, 1830, 47 physicians gathered in Nashville to form the Medical Society of Tennessee. Charter members of the new organization were drawn from the ranks of the reputedly best doctors in the state. East Tennessee provided 45 of the 151 named physicians, with 79 from Middle Tennessee and 27 from West Tennessee. On the appointed day, the attendees wrote by-laws and on the second day elected Nashvillian Dr. James Roane as the first president.

Despite physicians' efforts to professionalize medicine, an informal 1850 census conducted in East Tennessee indicated that of 201 practicing doctors only 35 had graduated from a medical school. The others possessed professional training ranging from one course of medical lectures to no formal training whatsoever. Clearly, many of the physicians were self-proclaimed. Without licensing procedures, which did not become law in Tennessee until 1889,

anyone could declare himself, or herself, a physician. Although the Medical Society of Tennessee had the power to confer licenses, rarely did anyone apply. Initially, the state society languished before physicians' lethargy, geographical considerations, and the Civil War.

A promising development occurred in 1851, when the Medical Department of the University of Nashville opened. Physicians desiring a credible education no longer had to travel to Philadelphia or Kentucky to receive it. Enrollment swelled over the next decade until, in 1859, the school was the third largest in the United States. Three outstanding physicians on the medical faculty, Paul F. Eve, William T. Briggs, and William K. Bowling, guaranteed a propitious beginning for the new school. The Tennessee legislature relinquished operation of St. John's Hospital, formerly an insane asylum, to the faculty of the new medical department. Successful from the beginning, the school grew to enroll 456 students in the 1859–1860 session.

In Memphis, keen competition materialized between followers of Samuel Thomson and traditional physicians, and both founded their own medical schools in 1846. Regular physicians supported the Memphis Medical College, while Thomsonians favored the Botanico-Medical College.

Medical conditions on and off the battlefield during the Civil War were dismal. Dr. Samuel S. Stout, placed in charge of the Gordon Hospital founded by a ladies' benevolent society in Nashville, declared the facility unsuitable and considered the women to be an interference. Stout reorganized the facility and wrested control from the ladies. Later when Stout was reassigned to Chattanooga and placed in charge of the Army of Tennessee's hospitals, he found more of the same. Cleanliness varied considerably among hospitals. Nurses, who were untrained and in short supply, were drawn from the white and black population without regard to gender. Eventually female matrons were appointed to oversee laundry, bedding, food, and medicine in hospitals. Well-known Federal forces nurse, Mary Ann Bickerdyke, served as matron of Adams Hospital and Gayoso Hospital in Memphis. Confederate forces established 1,200 hospital beds in that city, which Federal forces increased to 5,000 when they took control in 1862. Nuns from the Sisters of Charity and Dominican nuns from St. Agnes provided nursing care.

Deplorable behind-the-line conditions for physicians attached to field troops included battlefields strewn with dead men and dead horses, and smallpox, typhoid, and dysentery that raged among the soldiers. Without clear knowledge of where diseases originated or how they were spread, physicians labored against formidable odds.

The Civil War, and postwar readjustments, influenced the future course of professional medicine in Tennessee. The Memphis Medical College reopened briefly following the Civil War, but folded in 1872. The Botanico-Medical College in Memphis suffered a similar fate. The Nashville medical school remained open, but never recovered sufficiently after the war. The newly established Vanderbilt University forged an agreement with the University of Nashville's medical department in April 1874 that shared the faculty between the schools. The winner in this arrangement was Vanderbilt, which eventually outshone the University of Nashville. Two years later, Dr. Duncan Eve, a son of Dr. Paul F. Eve, and Dr. W.F. Glenn founded the Nashville Medical College. Its faculty came from Vanderbilt and the University of Nashville. In 1879 the Nashville Medical College became the Medical Department of the University of Tennessee.

Several medical schools to train African-American physicians opened in the late nineteenth century. In 1876 Meharry Medical College was created as the Medical Department of the Central Tennessee College. The school prospered under the adept guidance of Dr. George W. Hubbard. Coeducational from the outset, Meharry enrolled more women than any other medical school in the state. As white schools increased their enrollment of women, however, Meharry's enrollment slipped, probably because of increasing expense. Still, Meharry graduate Dr. Mable Clottele Smith Fugitt served on the faculty of the University of West Tennessee College of Medicine and Surgery, a black medical training facility founded in Jackson that moved to Memphis in 1906 and closed in 1923.

Of considerable concern to the state's general population throughout the nineteenth century was the successive waves of cholera and yellow fever that afflicted towns and cities statewide. Memphis, pronounced by one contemporary writer as the filthiest town in America, often lived up to that inevitable reputation. Drinking water and sewage mixed with unimpeded freedom. Cholera, smallpox, and yellow fever made their way upstream by steamship, passing along the length of the Mississippi River. Even before the devastating epidemic of yellow fever in 1878, Memphis's mortality rates in 1872 soared above other urban areas in the South and the nation. Finally city officials sprang into action and created a Board of Health. In less than ten years, the city's death rate was cut by more than half.

The Tennessee State Medical Association (formerly the Medical Society of Tennessee) offered a bill to form a state Board of Health that passed in 1877, but as little more than a paper expression. No funds or authority accompanied the law. Rectified by an amendment the following year, the law granted power to quarantine and prescribe regulations with an appropriation of $3,000 annually. With additional pressure from the medical society, the General Assembly passed a measure to gather and record vital statistics in 1881. Improved sanitation helped curb the effects of epidemics, yet tuberculosis and influenza, scourges of the twentieth century, took a significant toll.

From the 1870s through the 1920s, leading medical educators pressed for physician training reform. Initial unsuccessful reform efforts failed to stem the proliferation of low grade proprietary medical schools. When Abraham Flexner published his report in 1910 on the condition of medical education in the United States and Canada, nine medical schools separated by race were in Tennessee. Knoxville had one white and one black medical school; Memphis had two white and one black medical schools, as did Nashville; and Chattanooga had one white medical school. Flexner recommended that the Vanderbilt University Medical Department and Meharry Medical College seize the responsibility of training physicians for the whole state. In 1911 the University of Tennessee, which had appropriated the Nashville Medical College and the Medical Department of the University of Nashville, moved its operation to Memphis and assumed the defunct facilities of the College of Physicians and Surgeons, and later those of the Memphis Hospital Medical College. At the same time, the school began to enroll women students. Lincoln Memorial University's medical training facility in Knoxville transferred its students west when that institution closed in 1914.

Hospitals, viewed at the beginning of the twentieth century as little more than a place to die, gradually moved to the forefront of medicine. Following military hospitals established during the Civil War came city- and county-supported hospitals such as the Memphis City Hospital, the Knoxville General Hospital, Chattanooga's Baroness Erlanger Hospital, and Nashville's City Hospital. Over the years, major medical centers either absorbed or replaced those hospitals. The Commonwealth Fund of New York built the nation's first modern hospital for a rural community, the Rutherford Hospital, in Murfreesboro in 1926–1927. Over the years, major medical centers either absorbed or replaced the early major hospitals. The Hospital Corporation of America, later known as Columbia/HCA Healthcare Corporation, was founded in Nashville in 1968 and grew over the next three decades into the largest privately-owned healthcare company in the country.

In recent years, the most critical problem in medicine involved providing medical care for Tennessee's citizens at a reasonable cost. Former Governor Ned Ray McWherter's TennCare initiative, begun in 1993 to serve Medicaid and uninsured citizens, sought to solve that problem. The state dispensed medical care

reimbursement through regional managed care organizations run by insurance companies. Some form of
state-managed-care program likely will endure as
Tennesseans prepare for the future.

Jayne Crumpler DeFiore, University of Tennessee, Knoxville
SUGGESTED READINGS: John C. Gunn, *Gunn's Domestic Medi-
cine* (rpt., 1986); Philip Hamer, *The Centennial History of the
Tennessee State Medical Association 1830–1930* (1936); Timothy
C. Jacobson, *Making Medical Doctors: Science and Medicine at
Vanderbilt Since Flexner* (1987); James W. Livingood, *Chat-
tanooga and Hamilton County Medical Society* (1983); Samuel J.
Platt and Mary L. Ogden, *Medical Men and Institutions of
Knox County Tennessee 1789–1957* (1969); Glenna R.
Schroeder-Lein, *Confederate Hospitals on the Move: Samuel H.
Stout and the Army of Tennessee* (1994); Marcus J. Stewart,
William T. Black, Jr., and Mildred Hicks, eds., *History of Med-
icine in Memphis* (1971); James Summerville, *Educating Black
Doctors: A History of Meharry Medical College* (1983)

MEEMAN, EDWARD JOHN (1889–1966), journalist
and newspaper editor, was born in Evansville, Indiana, to German-born, Catholic, working class parents; his father was a cigar-maker and a local union
official. Meeman received his education in Evansville
public schools, graduating from high school in 1907.
Following a brief service in the U.S. Navy during
World War I, Meeman took his first newspaper job as
a four-dollar-a-week reporter for the *Evansville Press.*
He later served as editor there, reported for the *Terre
Haute* (Indiana) *Times,* and wrote for the Newspaper
Enterprise Association, a Cleveland-based feature
story and editorial syndicate.

In 1921 the Scripps-Howard Company selected
Meeman to organize and edit the *Knoxville News,*
later the *News-Sentinel,* an afternoon daily. After a
decade of Meeman's management, the newspaper
dominated its rivals in advertising revenue and circulation. Meeman used his editorial position to
advocate federal spending for the improvement and
development of the Tennessee River. He also supported the conservation and recreational development of what later became the Great Smoky
Mountains National Park.

In 1931 Scripps-Howard sent Meeman to
manage another languishing property, the *Memphis
Press-Scimitar.* Meeman again supported local economic development. Anticipating the extension of
benefits to West Tennessee, Meeman was an early
advocate of the Tennessee Valley Authority. He also
promoted public health and played a prominent
role in raising support for the modernization of
local medical facilities.

Meeman soon found himself at odds with the
political machine of Edward Hull "Boss" Crump in
Memphis and Shelby County. Meeman supported
reforms such as a council-manager form of municipal
government, permanent voter registration, the use of

voting machines, and the hiring of African Americans
as policemen. The racially liberal editor opposed the
machine's practice of buying African-American votes
through the poll tax. In 1948 Meeman led an anti-
Crump band of reformist lawyers, union leaders, and
businessmen in support of Estes Kefauver's Democratic primary victory over the machine candidate,
and subsequent election to the U.S. Senate.

Meeman considered England and Germany his
"spiritual homelands." In the early 1930s he went to
Germany to study forestry and conservation techniques; he returned as a convinced opponent of
Nazism. In the 1940s he advocated U.S. membership
in the Atlantic Union, a federation of western democ-
racies against the threat of the Soviet Union. His anti-
communism did not prevent Meeman from arguing,
as early as 1964, for an end to U.S. military involvement in Vietnam.

Nominated for a Pulitzer Prize in 1946, Meeman
retired from the editorship of the *Press-Scimitar* in
1962. Until his death on November 15, 1966, he
served as conservation editor of the Scripps-
Howard syndicate. As a young man, Meeman was
briefly a Socialist; in middle life, he became affiliated with Christian Science; and throughout his life,
he opposed what he considered to be shoddy, ugly,
and mendacious.

When he died, the former four-dollar-a-week cub
reporter left a multi-million dollar estate, of which
the largest portions went to institutions of higher
learning in his adopted hometown of Memphis. The
Meeman-Shelby Forest State Park, north of the city,
recognizes his importance in the history of American
environmentalism. The Edward J. Meeman Biological
Station, now a part of the University of Memphis,
adjacent to the forest, facilitates research in natural
history, ecology, and environmental biology.

*Ed Frank, Mississippi Valley Collection, University of
Memphis Libraries*
SUGGESTED READINGS: Edwin Howard, ed., *Edward J.
Meeman. The Editorial We: A Posthumous Autobiography* (1976);
Clark Porteous, "The Two Eds of Memphis—Meeman and
Crump," West Tennessee Historical Society *Papers,* 45(1991)
SEE: CRUMP, EDWARD H.; KNOXVILLE NEWS-SENTINEL;
MEEMAN-SHELBY FOREST STATE PARK; MEMPHIS PRESS-
SCIMITAR; PUBLISHING; UNIVERSITY OF MEMPHIS

MEEMAN-SHELBY FOREST STATE PARK, with
13,467 acres, is the most visited state park in Tennessee. Initially known as Shelby Forest State Park, it
began as a New Deal recreation demonstration area
of the National Park Service during the 1930s.
Edward J. Meeman, avid conservationist and editor
of the Memphis *Press-Scimitar,* had interviewed
Adolph Hitler and was impressed with forest reclamation projects in Germany, finding similarities
between the land there and eroded southern land. In

a series of newspaper editorials, and private conversations with public officials, Meeman insisted that forests in his region could be made to prosper once again. He worked with State Forester James O. Hazard to identify a potential park area in Shelby County and in 1933 the National Park Service gave Shelby County money and CCC labor for the park's initial development.

The National Park Service and the Resettlement Administration supervised the CCC crews, and later Works Progress Administration workers, at the park. The Tennessee Game and Fish Commission supervised wildlife control projects. Land clearing came in 1935 and early objectives focused on establishing a wildlife reserve, replanting the forests, reclaiming eroded land, and building recreational facilities. The CCC planted trees, built trails and a group camp area, and dammed a lake. The WPA built cabins and various recreational structures; the largest was the Administration Building, which housed an auditorium, recreation hall, and cafeteria. By 1941 the park had picnic areas, playgrounds, the group camp, the Administration Building, cabins, trails, and a swimming area; officials announced that more facilities, including a lake, swimming pool, and horse barn, would soon be under construction. World War II intervened, however, and the new facilities were not built. In 1944 the National Park Service transferred the park to the state. Five years later, under state supervision, park development began again.

Over half of Meeman-Shelby Forest is a wildlife management area, supervised by the Tennessee Wildlife Resources Agency under an agreement with the Tennessee Department of Environment and Conservation. Within the park, many species of birds, including the rare Mississippi Kite, may be seen; wild mammals include white-tailed deer, foxes, and raccoons. Reclamation efforts also have been very successful. As early as 1962, state conservation officials were bragging of the park's success in regenerating valuable stands of southern hardwoods. Mack Prichard, State Naturalist, observes that the park is "one of the prime examples of hardwood forest regeneration. Some of the trees there gain up to an inch in diameter a year. It's one of the fastest-growing forests we have."[1]

Carroll Van West, Middle Tennessee State University

CITATION:

(1) James and Dorothy Richardson, "Meeman-Shelby: One of Our Most-Loved State Parks," *Tennessee Conservationist* (May/June 1994): 4.

SEE: CIVILIAN CONSERVATION CORPS; CONSERVATION; MEEMAN, EDWARD J.; TENNESSEE WILDLIFE RESOURCES AGENCY; WORKS PROGRESS ADMINISTRATION

MEHARRY MEDICAL COLLEGE in Nashville originated in 1876 as the medical division of Central Ten-

nessee College, an institution established by the Freedman's Aid Society of the Methodist Episcopal Church. The founding motivation was to train aspiring care givers to serve newly freed African Americans and all who were deprived of and needed medical attention. The founder and first president of Meharry Medical College was New Hampshire native George Whipple Hubbard (1841–1921), a former Union soldier who received his medical degree from the University of Nashville. While still in school, Hubbard began the work of building Meharry with himself as sole instructor, religious advisor, and superintendent.

Meharry's dental and pharmaceutical departments were organized in 1886 and 1889, respectively. There was only one member in the first graduating class in 1890; he held the degree of Master of Arts. In 1910 the School of Nursing of Mercy Hospital was transferred to Meharry. The Hubbard Hospital was built in 1912. On October 13, 1915, Meharry Medical College was granted a charter separate from Central Tennessee College, which had changed its name to Walden University in 1900.

On February 1, 1921, John J. Mullowney, a 1908 graduate of the University of Pennsylvania and a former faculty member of Girard College in Philadelphia, became the second president of Meharry. Under his leadership, admission requirements were rigorously administered; the number of faculty members increased; research and hospital facilities were expanded, increasing the bed capacity to 100; outpatient clinics were reorganized according to specialty; and a hospital superintendent was employed. In 1923 Meharry received an "A" rating.

With contributions from the General Education Board and the Rockefeller, Rosenwald, Eastman, and Carnegie foundations, together with assistance from the City of Nashville and Meharry alumnae, the college moved from South Nashville to its present location in North Nashville, one street west of Fisk University in the late 1920s. Thus began a long, mutually beneficial relationship between the schools. Initially, some buildings served both institutions. The later Neo-Gothic and College-Gothic architecture of the two schools' buildings would reflect the symbiotic relationship between Fisk and Meharry. By the 1930s many aspiring physicians would obtain their undergraduate and pre-medical education at Fisk and later graduate with their medical degrees from Meharry.

In 1938 the distinguished scholar Edward L. Turner assumed the post of president. Turner modified the curriculum of the medical school, insisting on a more scientific approach and stressing the importance of proper clinical procedures. During this time, Meharry began to experience financial difficulties, which plagued the institution throughout the

1940s. Turner resigned in 1944. Dr. M.D. Clawson served as president of Meharry from 1945 to 1950.

An interim administrative committee directed affairs until 1952, when Dr. Harold D. West, the first black president of the school, began his term. Under West the school launched a $20 million fund drive, purchased land adjacent to the campus, and added a wing to the hospital. The school redefined its purpose, terminating the School of Nursing and the Division of Dental Technology in the early 1960s. Significant improvements also were made to the curriculum and facilities in the schools of medicine and dentistry.

From 1966 to 1968 an interim committee managed Meharry until the former dean of the medical school, Lloyd Elam, was appointed president. Meharry then established a graduate school offering the Ph.D. degree in the basic sciences and a School of Allied Health Professions in conjunction with Tennessee State University and Fisk University. New buildings for the schools of medicine and dentistry and a new hospital were constructed in the 1970s. Elam provided Meharry with 13 years of progressive leadership. He continued his service to the school as a distinguished member of the teaching faculty.

In March 1981 Richard Lester, chairman of the Department of Radiology of the University of Texas Science Center and a member of Meharry's board of trustees, assumed the duties of interim president for one year. In July 1982 David Satcher became the third black man to hold the position of president. Satcher rose to national prominence and was appointed director of the United States Center for Disease Control in Atlanta in 1993. In 1997 President Bill Clinton nominated Satcher to the position of Surgeon General of the United States, he was confirmed in 1998.

The reins of Meharry were passed to Dr. John E. Maupin, Jr., the first alumnus and graduate of Meharry's School of Dentistry to become the institution's top administrator. Maupin became the ninth president on July 1, 1994. He was charged with overseeing construction and renovation of facilities, merging the respective clinical staffs, and accomplishing the monumental job of solidifying the national community around the continued viability of Meharry Medical College. Maupin also would orchestrate the inauguration of the merged facilities on January 1, 1998.

Meharry Medical College includes the School of Medicine, the School of Dentistry, the School of Graduate Studies and Research, the School of Allied Health Professions, the Metropolitan General Hospital of Nashville-Davidson County, two health centers, and the Harold D. West Basic Sciences Center.

Reavis L. Mitchell, Jr., Fisk University

SUGGESTED READINGS: Charles V. Roman, *Meharry Medical College, A History* (1934); James Summerville, *Educating Black Doctors: A History of Meharry Medical College* (1983)

SEE: FISK UNIVERSITY; GENERAL EDUCATION BOARD; HUBBARD, GEORGE WHIPPLE; JULIUS ROSENWALD FUND; MEDICINE

MEIGS COUNTY was created in 1836 from Rhea County and named for Return Jonathan Meigs (1740–1823), a colonel in the American Revolutionary War and later an Indian agent from 1801 until his death in 1823. The county encompasses 195 square miles and is bounded on the west by the Tennessee River. The lower Hiwassee River crosses through the southern portion of the county, where it enters the Tennessee. The county contains fertile bottom land and ample timber, as well as a vein of iron ore.

The Tennessee River valley was first inhabited by generations of Native Americans, and Meigs County contains many prehistoric and Cherokee sites. Hiwassee Island, at the mouth of the Hiwassee River, is the site of a large Mississippian period town dating from the eleventh century A.D., and includes several temple mounds surrounding a plaza. The Cherokees later occupied the island. In 1809–1810 Sam Houston lived with Oolootek (John Jolly), leader of 300 Cherokees living on Hiwassee Island, also called Jolly's Island. Today the area is Hiwassee Island Wildlife Refuge, noted for its use by migrating sand hill cranes.

In the Hiwassee Treaty of 1817 and the Calhoun Agreement of 1819, the Cherokees ceded the land on the east bank of the Tennessee River north of the Hiwassee to Tennessee. The first settlements in the Meigs County area were in the Ten Mile Valley in the north, while later families settled near the site of Decatur. The territory south of the Hiwassee remained in the Ocoee District of the Cherokee nation and was not opened to white settlement until 1836. Most of the Cherokee residents were removed as part of the Trail of Tears in 1838, crossing the Tennessee in Meigs County at Blythe's Ferry. A few claimed reservation of their land and remained, notably John Miller, Richard Taylor, Colonel Gideon Morgan, and John Jolly. The Meigs County government, Tennessee Valley Authority, and Tennessee Wildlife Resources Agency have planned a monument near the Hiwassee inscribed with names of the Cherokees removed in 1838, as well as a walking trail along part of a removal route. The memorial is projected for completion in October 1998.

The only incorporated town in the county, Decatur, was laid out as the county seat in 1836 on 50 acres donated by James Lillard and Leonard Brooks. Named for Stephen Decatur, a War of 1812 naval hero, the original courthouse was built in 1837. Decatur Academy, a secondary school, opened in the 1840s, and a school for African-American children was established in 1869. When the academy closed in 1890, the Holston Conference of the Methodist

Church set up a high school that operated until 1910, when Meigs County High School was built. The Meigs County High School's girls basketball team were state AA champions in 1994 and 1995. County schools consolidated in 1997 into two elementary, one middle, and one high school. Other communities in the county include Ten Mile, Big Spring, Peakland, Union Grove, Sewee, Goodfield, and East View.

Meigs County is covered by a series of ridges and valleys running southwest to northeast, with the valleys filled with family farms. In antebellum times, commerce was linked to river boats at landings such as Cottonport, Pinhook, and Breedenton. Several ferries were also established: the Blythe, Washington, and Free ferries on the Tennessee, and the Russell and Kincannon ferries on the Hiwassee. (In the 1990s, two bridges replaced the Blythe and Washington ferries, the last ferries in the eastern Tennessee river valley.) Although a railroad was expected in the 1840s and 1850s, one would never cross the county. There were 598 farms in 1850, chiefly raising hogs (20,000 head), wheat, oats, corn, and potatoes.

In 1850 Meigs County's population consisted of 4,480 whites and 395 slaves with 4 free African Americans. By 1860 there were 4,021 whites, and the number of slaves had increased to 638, with 7 free blacks. When Tennessee voted on secession in June 1861, Meigs voted 481 for secession and 267 for the Union. The district south of the Hiwassee had the fewest slave holders and sent most of its men to the Union. In 1864 Owen Soloman, acting under the order of Military Governor Andrew Johnson, organized a new county court loyal to the Union.

Following the war, farmers in the county resumed their lives, adding apples and peaches, beef cattle and milk cows to the production of grains. In the 1880s Meigs farmers turned increasingly to tobacco as a cash crop—4,159 pounds were raised in 1880, growing to 136,791 pounds by 1940. Timber became increasingly important to the county's economy and was sent by river to Chattanooga until 1900 when the pine and poplar trees were virtually logged out. Although Meigs County contained 814 freedmen in 1870, the African-American population found little opportunity; their numbers fell after the Civil War to less than 2 percent by 1990. As late as 1940, Meigs County had only one industrial plant, the Decatur Hosiery Mills, established in the late 1930s.

The Tennessee Valley Authority brought changes to the county with the construction of Chickamauga Lake in 1940 and Watts Bar in 1942. Although Meigs's most productive acres were flooded by the lakes, 225 miles of shoreline were created within the county on the Tennessee and Hiwassee rivers. The lakes brought tourist use for fishing, hunting, boating, and photography. TVA's construction of Sequoyah and Watts Bar plants south and north of the county in the

1970s added residential growth. Several industries were established by the 1970s, when nine companies employed 432 workers.

In the late 1990s, tobacco and vegetables top the Meigs County market crops, although beef cattle and dairy herds are still raised. The county contains neither railroads nor a U.S. highway, but seven motor freight companies serve the county. Shaw Industries is the largest of 16 employers, followed by Delta Apparel. The largest public sector employer is the Meigs County School System. In 1992 Decatur's population was 1,429, while the 1997 Meigs County population stood at 13,714.

Ann Toplovich, Tennessee Historical Society

SUGGESTED READING: Stewart Lillard, *Meigs County, Tennessee* (rpt. 1982)

SEE: FERRIES; HOLSTON CONFERENCE; HOUSTON, SAM; MEIGS, RETURN J.; OVERHILL CHEROKEES; TENNESSEE RIVER SYSTEM; TENNESSEE VALLEY AUTHORITY; TRAIL OF TEARS; TREATIES

MEIGS, RETURN JONATHAN (1740–1823) arrived in Tennessee in May 1801 to fill the combined position of Agent to the Cherokee Nation and Military Agent for the United States War Department. Colonel Meigs, who was from Connecticut and later Ohio, had already completed a long and successful military career. The U.S. Congress awarded him a presentation sword for heroic behavior during the Revolutionary War.

Colonel Meigs located his first Tennessee base of operations at Fort Southwest Point, near present-day Kingston. His office and the Cherokee Agency remained at that location from 1801 until 1807. He supervised relocation of the agency and the U.S. "factory" for trade with the Cherokees at Tellico Blockhouse to a new post named Hiwassee Garrison, near the mouth of the Hiwassee River. Meigs functioned in his dual roles as Cherokee and Military Agent at Hiwassee Garrison until 1813, when the Federal soldiers stationed there were withdrawn. He remained as Cherokee Agent, but in 1815 he moved the agency a few miles up the Hiwassee River. He relocated a third time in 1817, and continued as agent at the new location until his death on January 28, 1823. Within the context of the U.S. government policy for the southern Indians, Meigs devoted his 22-year career as Cherokee Agent to promoting the well-being of the Cherokees, defending their rights during treaty negotiations, and encouraging their efforts to establish their own republican form of government.

In 1823 the remains of Colonel Return Jonathan Meigs were brought to the "Garrison Cemetery," near the Rhea County site of the former Hiwassee Garrison, and placed next to those of his wife, Grace, and son, Timothy. The adjoining county of Meigs was named in his honor.

Samuel D. Smith, Tennessee Division of Archaeology
SUGGESTED READING: Henry T. Malone, "Return Jonathan
Meigs—Indian Agent Extraordinary," East Tennessee Histor-
ical Society *Publications*, 28(1956): 3–22
SEE: FORT SOUTHWEST POINT; MEIGS COUNTY; TELLICO
BLOCKHOUSE

MELUNGEONS are a mysterious, dark-complexioned
European-featured people first encountered by English and Scots-Irish settlers when they migrated into
the Appalachian Mountains in the eighteenth century. Melungeons generally claimed Portuguese
and/or Turkish ancestry, but the state declared them
"free persons of color" and confiscated their considerable land holdings in the early 1800s. Today, most
Melungeon descendants reside in the Southern
Appalachians, particularly in East Tennessee and
Southwest Virginia.

For the past four years, a 30-member international research team, headquartered at Clinch Valley
College of the University of Virginia in Wise, Virginia, has been collecting evidence to aid in the identification of the Melungeons. While findings remain
under study, evidence suggests a significant Middle
Eastern/Mediterranean heritage. The Melungeons
may be descendants of sixteenth century Iberian settlers (Portuguese and Spanish), who were abandoned or otherwise cut off when the English overran
the Santa Elena (Beaufort, South Carolina) Colony in
1587, and several hundred Ottoman (Turkish and
other Muslim) Levants (sailors) set off on Roanoke
Island and the North Carolina coast in 1586 by Sir
Francis Drake. Drake had freed the Turks from their
Spanish captors, who utilized the Turks as slave
labor at Cartagena in the Caribbean. Current Turkish
research indicates the possibility of an even earlier
group of Ottoman sailors brought to America by the
Portuguese in 1558. Early Virginia census data also
indicates the importation of Turkish laborers in the
late 1600s. One theory indicates that both of the
above groups (Ottomans and Iberians) intermarried
with Native Americans (primarily Cherokees,
Creeks, Powhatan, Pamunkey, Catawba, and Chick-
ahominy) and that eventually the resultant populations came together in the mountains of western
North Carolina and upper South Carolina. There
they merged prior to a final push into Tennessee in
the late 1700s. "Melun can"—a Turkish term, pronounced identically to "Melungeon" (i.e. Meh-lun-
jun)—means "cursed soul" or "one who has been
abandoned by God." It has its roots in the Arabic
"Melun Jinn."

Genetic studies (gene frequency) of the Melungeon population indicate no significant differences
between them (177 individual samples from Lee
County, Virginia, and Hancock County, Tennessee,
taken in 1969 and re-analyzed in 1990) and popula-

tions in the Galician Mountain region of Spain and
Portugal, North Africa (Morocco, Libya), the Levant
(Greece, Turkey, Syria), and the Middle East (Northern Iraq and Northern Iran). Diseases consistently
identified in the Melungeon population include
established Mediterranean and Middle Eastern illnesses. [The Encyclopedia editors note that other
scholars, however, assert that it is plausible that the
Melungeons have tri-racial origins.]

Cultural and linguistic evidence offers support
for the Ottoman and Iberian origins. Southeastern
Native American dress styles include turbans
(Cherokees), and the fez (Creeks/Seminoles), as
well as the layered "Levant" style dress of both
tribes, a style similar to the uniforms worn by sixteenth century Turkish Levants. Also interesting is
the Cherokee and Creek habit of wearing the turban
or fez with a single feather, the typical Ottoman
head dress. Drawings of Cherokee Chief Sequoya,
himself perhaps part Melungeon, show a clothing
style similar to the sixteenth century Levants.

Southeastern Native American blanket and pottery designs, as well as a number of Appalachian
quilting patterns, are similar to sixteenth century
Turkish and Arabesque carpet and kilim designs
(tulip, geometrics, etc., almost always repeated in
identical squares). While quilting is an equally
entrenched Anglo and northern European tradition,
styles and designs can serve as intriguing evidence
of other cultural influences.

Many words, such as Alabama, Kentucky, Ten-
nessee, Seminole, and Cherokee may indicate Turk-
ish or Ottoman origins. Many of the words are old
Ottoman, as opposed to modern Turkish, adding
even more credence to the similarities.
*Brent Kennedy, Clinch Valley College of the University of
Virginia*
SEE: HANCOCK COUNTY

MEMPHIS. The Fourth Chickasaw Bluff, which rises
high above the Mississippi River even at flood stage,
forms a logical place for settlement. Native Americans dwelt there, but had departed prior to Hernando
de Soto's expedition through the area in the 1540s.
Ongoing settlement began by 1795, when Spain built
Fort San Fernando on the bluffs. Soldiers, traders,
and squatters occupied the area until the formal
founding of Memphis.

Prior to Spanish occupation, John Rice and John
Ramsey claimed 5,000-acre tracts, based on North
Carolina's British-based titles. John Overton pur-
chased Rice's tract from his heirs, and Andrew Jack-
son and James Winchester bought into the venture.
In 1819 they founded "Memphis," named for ancient
Egypt's capital.

For a variety of reasons, Memphis grew slowly. A
national economic depression, a river sandbar, loss of

the county seat designation to neighboring Raleigh, yellow fever, a severely restricted hinterland, depredations by raucous flatboatmen, and competition from other ports all retarded growth. By the early 1840s, however, the city's fortunes improved. Northern Mississippi opened to settlement, doubling the settled hinterland. The city became a post and stagecoach terminus, and by 1842, six miles of railroad had been laid eastward. Upstream, Randolph lost its river access with the development of a mile-wide sandbar, and Memphis quelled its flatboatmen's antics. Citizens organized a fire department, built a wharf, established a board of health, and undertook many other reforms. Moreover, they initiated such amenities as a bank, a thespian society, newspapers, and a truly grand hotel, the Gayoso House.

The 1850s brought even more explosive growth and considerable ethnic diversity to "the Bluff City." Three western rail routes converged on Memphis as the result of military planning. By 1861, the Memphis and Charleston and the Memphis and Ohio connected the city to the Southeast and Midwest. Slower development of a line to Little Rock may have cost the town its chance to become the first eastern terminus of a transcontinental railroad; the city served as an eastern terminus of the Butterfield overland mail coaches.

Despite its uneven record, Memphis grew at a faster rate than any other American city in the mid-1850s. From a population of fewer than 1,800 in 1840, the city swelled to 22,000 inhabitants in 1858. In addition to Anglo-American migrants, Irish and German immigrants contributed to the population rise.

The Irish arrived first, refugees from English oppression and successive famines following the potato blight. Displaced and largely illiterate farmers with few marketable skills, the Irish provided the labor for cutting roads, erecting buildings, and constructing railroads, levees, and canals. Irish crews also manned the area's trains and boats, and handled their cargoes. They entered politics enthusiastically and filled municipal jobs, especially fire and police ranks.

Germans came for reasons similar to those of the Irish, though after the revolutions of 1848, political motives dominated. Generally more urban and propertied than the Irish, Germans found a niche in the city's retail, commercial, and small industries sectors. They guarded their ethnic traditions more protectively than the Irish and furnished many of the city's artists, musicians, and teachers.

African Americans, both slave and free, also contributed to the boom decades. Unlike European immigrants, African Americans received few rewards for their work, and racial prejudice intensified as their scope of opportunities shrank. An 1840s repeal of Tennessee's ban on the domestic

Memphis skyline, 1960s

slave trade made Memphis a slave trading center during the 1850s.

Most urban blacks were domestic servants, but many others worked as draymen, roustabouts, barbers, and in the mechanical trades and crafts. The mobility demanded in these jobs threatened whites, and the city imposed a curfew and pass system with harsh penalties for violators.

In the generation following the boom era, Memphis suffered a succession of disasters. Prior to the election of 1860, Memphians remained loyal to the Union. Once Lincoln called for volunteers to subdue the rebellion, however, they abruptly and wholeheartedly switched to secession and the Confederacy. Styling their city the "Charleston of the West," they squelched all dissent and prepared for war. Men volunteered for military service and converted local facilities and services to meet wartime needs.

Initial confidence in a quick victory soon gave way to a more sobering evaluation as Tennessee's defenses fell early in 1862. The Confederate retreat at Shiloh left Memphis vulnerable to attack from the north and east. Confederate troops in Memphis destroyed local stores and abandoned the unfortified city. Many civilians followed the army south. With only a makeshift naval fleet left to protect the city, Memphis fell quickly on June 6, 1862. Eight converted steamboats faced 24 new Union warships, as 10,000 citizens watched the 90-minute battle from the bluff. Upon sinking or disabling seven Confederate vessels, Union forces demanded surrender and occupied the city.

Military occupation lasted more than three years and affected local attitudes more than the war itself. Memphians chafed against occupation rule and operated the city as a center of smuggling and profiteering. Approximately 15,000 African-American refugees poured into the city, and many aided the Union war effort as auxiliaries or soldiers. In August 1864 Nathan Bedford Forrest's dramatic raid on Memphis raised Confederate morale, but had no effect on the war's outcome.

As war gave way to Reconstruction, a white backlash to radical rule often made bad situations worse. In 1866 the city experienced three days of racial rioting set off by tensions between Irish immigrants and African-American soldiers. Forty-four blacks died in the violence, and 12 schools and four churches burned. Approximately three-quarters of the city's African Americans departed in the riot's aftermath.

Yellow fever posed a worse problem than Reconstruction. The city suffered through epidemics in 1867, 1873, 1878, and 1879. Thousands of people died despite the heroic efforts of physicians, clergy, volunteers, and black militia units. To escape the repeated epidemics, many Memphians abandoned the city, some permanently. Declining property values and a generation of poor fiscal management ended in bankruptcy and the loss of the city's charter in 1879.

Under the rule of the "Taxing District of Shelby County," the bluff community revived and became a modern city. Frugal government repaid municipal debts; the state restored home rule in 1893; and economic growth returned. Railroading (Memphis had 11 trunk lines and a bridge across the Mississippi by the early 1900s), hardwood lumber, cotton, and hardwood and cotton byproducts contributed to the city's economic well-being. Technology revolutionized urban life: electricity, trolleys, skyscrapers, artesian wells, sewerage and sanitation facilities, and the automobile restructured Memphis lifestyles. Rural in-migration and extensive annexation sent the city's population past 100,000 by 1900.

As Memphis rose from disease and debt, the city undertook progressive reforms. Edward Hull Crump, a rural transplant and Horatio Alger success story, gained control over local politics. In 1915 his failure to comply with state prohibition laws led to his removal from office by the courts, but he continued to exercise strong influence over municipal politics. After 1927, and for the next 21 years, his rule was unchallengeable in Shelby County and across much of Tennessee.

Memphis acquired a mixed reputation in the early decades of the century. On the one hand, it became recognized as the nation's murder capital. On a more positive note, the city lobbied for the Tennessee ratification of woman suffrage, promoted blues music, and initiated the self-service supermarket, the Piggly-Wiggly stores of Clarence Saunders. When the boom times of the 1920s gave way to the Great Depression, Memphis promoted its economic future through the organization of the Cotton Carnival. During the 1930s, Crump's political power brought many New Deal dollars for public buildings, public housing, and improvements in urban structure. World War II brought enormous military and industrial expansion, including the Memphis Defense Depot and even a German POW camp.

After the death of E.H. Crump in 1954, Memphians entered a new political era, that included the emerging demands of African Americans for full political participation. Memphis promoted a policy of gradual interracial cooperation until the mid-1960s, when racial integration intensified emotions, and polarization replaced accommodation.

In 1967–1968 Memphis replaced its city charter and instituted a mayor-city council form of government. Almost immediately the city faced the challenge of a "budget busting" sanitation workers strike. When Reverend Martin Luther King, Jr., arrived to support the strike, an assassin's bullet struck him down, and the city erupted in riot. Television provided the nation with a much-needed lesson on racial oppression, but it polarized Memphis. Race baiters, both black and white, used divisiveness to personal advantage. The election of a black mayor, William Herenton, in 1991 and a black majority in the city council in 1995 restored a measure of restraint.

Post-World War II Memphis gave the world important innovations in lodging and shipping as the birthplace of Holiday Inns and Federal Express. Elvis Presley put Memphis on the map in rock music, and St. Jude Hospital made important strides in the battle against catastrophic childhood diseases. The city lost several large corporations in recent decades, but strengthened the local economy and maintained a high employment rate by encouraging the growth of numerous small businesses.

Such symbols gave the city hope in an atmosphere of racial mistrust, declining population, and political cynicism. As Memphis rejects race-baiting opportunists and embraces equality for all, it anticipates a reversal of its postwar decline and a return to its reputation as a "city of good abode."

John E. Harkins, Memphis University School

SEE: BEALE STREET; CHICKASAW ORDNANCE WORKS; COTTON; CRUMP, EDWARD H.; DISASTERS; FEDERAL EXPRESS; FORT SAN FERNANDO; GAYOSO HOTEL; HANDY, WILLIAM C.; MEMPHIS RACE RIOT OF 1866; MEMPHIS SANI-

MEMPHIS BROOKS MUSEUM OF ART, founded as Brooks Memorial Art Gallery in 1916, was the first art museum in Memphis. Initial efforts to build a municipal art museum in Memphis were based upon a design for an arts and sciences pavilion submitted by artist Carl Gutherz (1844–1907) in 1906. This plan never came to fruition, but a decade later a Renaissance Revival building of Georgian marble, designed by James Gamble Rogers, was erected in Overton Park. Bessie Vance Brooks donated the building to the city in memory of her husband, Samuel Hamilton Brooks, to "forever uphold a standard of truth and beauty in the community."[1] Reminiscent of a portion of the Villa Guilia in Rome, this building is listed on the National Register of Historic Places and is situated within the city's park and parkway system.

Florence McIntyre was the gallery's first director, and the board and acceptance jury consisted of noted artists William Merritt Chase, Kate Carl, Cecilia Beaux, and Irving Ramsey Wiles. The museum had a small core collection of paintings and hosted American and European art exhibitions in various media. It was instrumental in introducing the Mid-South to a wide range of artists and stylistic developments. Gifts and purchases have brought the collection to over 7,000 objects, consisting of painting, sculpture, drawings, prints, photographs, and decorative arts. Of particular note are the Samuel H. Kress Collection of Renaissance and Baroque paintings, the Hugo N. Dixon Collection of Impressionist paintings, the Levy Collection of American prints, the Goodman Book Collection, and the Goodheart Collection of Carl Gutherz paintings, drawings, and archival material. The permanent collection is supplemented by long-term loans, which together present a broad survey of art that includes African and pre-Columbian artifacts as well as an extensive chronological survey of western art traditions.

To accommodate a growing collection and an active exhibition schedule, three additional structures have been added to the original building. The first, built in 1955, was designed by Everett Woods; the second, which consisted of two floors of new galleries, was designed by Francis Mah in 1973; the final 1989 addition, which included a new main entrance, was designed by Skidmore, Owings, and Merrill. Today the museum consists of 75,000 square feet of gallery, storage, and office space, and houses a print study room, a library, an auditorium, a gift store, and a restaurant. In 1983 its name was changed to Memphis Brooks Museum of Art to better reflect the function and purpose of the institution. It is accredited by the American Association of Museums and is supported by the city of Memphis and the Memphis Brooks Museum of Art Foundation, Inc. The Foundation was created in 1955, and its board continues as the main governing body.

Marilyn Masler, Memphis Brooks Museum of Art

CITATION:
(1) *In Celebration of Brooks Memorial Art Gallery's Ten Year Anniversary* (1926) n.p.
SUGGESTED READING: Douglas K.S. Hyland, "History of the Collection of the Memphis Brooks Museum of Art," Sally Palmer Thomason, ed., *Painting and Sculpture Collection, Memphis Brooks Museum of Art* (1984), 11–18
SEE: ART; CARL, KATE; GUTHERZ, CARL; MEMPHIS PARK AND PARKWAY SYSTEM

MEMPHIS COLLEGE OF ART is the only independent college in the South dually accredited by the Southern Association of Colleges and Schools (SACS) and the National Association of Schools of Art and Design. It opened on October 5, 1936, as the Memphis Academy of Arts, with classes in drawing, painting, sculpting, and crafts. In an unusual arrangement, both city money and private funds supported the school.

In the 1920s the Memphis Art Association, under the leadership of Florence McIntyre, the first director of the Brooks Memorial Art Gallery, had organized free classes in art. Classes moved from the Nineteenth Century Club in 1929 to Adams Avenue when Miss Rosa Lee of the Lee Steamship Line family donated her house (still standing in Victorian Village) to the city. The school became the Lee Academy.

A dispute split the faculty in 1936. McIntyre disapproved of "modern" art and believed in a thoroughly academic training. French-trained George and Henriette Amiard Oberteuffer withdrew from the Lee Academy. The city decided to back their school, the Memphis Academy of Arts, and offered a building. Robert McKnight became director, and Burton Callicott and Dorothy Sturm joined the faculty.

After returning to the Lee property in 1942, the school moved, under the leadership of Ted Rust, to its new location in Overton Park in February 1958. Architects William Mann and Roy Hanover won the design competition for the new building, producing one of the state's best examples of 1950s modernism.

The name was changed to the Memphis College of Art in 1985, and graduate studies were added in 1987. Having supported the school since its opening, the city gradually withdrew its financial support in the 1990s, though the college continues to grow and thrive. The college offers careers in the fine arts, advertising, graphic design, textile design, and, increasingly, interactive and digital design and applications.

Perre Magness, Memphis
Source: Adapted from material supplied by Ruth Crawford Haizlip's *Manuscript History of the Memphis College of Art* (1997)
SEE: ART; MEMPHIS BROOKS MUSEUM OF ART; NINE-TEENTH CENTURY CLUB

MEMPHIS *COMMERCIAL APPEAL*. Although the title *Commercial Appeal* dates from 1894, the roots of this newspaper reach back to the early decades of Memphis's history. One ancestor, the *Weekly* (later *Daily*) *Appeal,* began in 1841 under Henry Van Pelt. A strongly sectional and Democratic paper, by 1861 the *Appeal* was a leading voice for secessionist sentiment, equipping and manning an artillery battery that was taken into Confederate service. When Federal forces occupied Memphis in June 1862, the last train south bore the staff and press of the *Appeal,* which stayed one step ahead of the Union armies for the next three years, publishing in various cities in Mississippi, Georgia, and Alabama. The paper returned to Memphis in 1865, where it continued to be a strong Democratic voice. During the war and immediately thereafter, John R. McClanahan and Benjamin F. Dill managed the paper.

A second predecessor was the *Daily Avalanche,* whose first issue appeared early in 1858. Even more secessionist than the *Appeal,* the *Avalanche* merged with the more moderate *Bulletin* in late 1861. Union authorities found the politics of the *Avalanche* so odious that they suppressed the name and only allowed the paper to appear for the rest of the war as the Unionist *Bulletin.* Less than a year after the Confederate surrender, the *Avalanche* was back in business.

The city's fortunes revived in the early 1870s, but yellow fever epidemics that decimated the population and sent survivors fleeing also affected the newspapers. At one time, a staff of one editor and one pressman issued the *Appeal.* In 1890 the *Appeal* acquired the rival *Avalanche* and until 1894, the paper appeared as the *Appeal-Avalanche.*

The *Daily Commercial* first appeared in 1889 as a result of a split in the local Democratic Party. Though a newcomer, this paper boasted some of the most respected journalists of the city and the owners came from elite families. In 1894 the *Commercial* bought the *Appeal-Avalanche,* and on July 1, 1894, the first issue of the *Commercial Appeal* appeared with Edward Ward Carmack (1858–1908) as editor.

Two years later, Charles P.J. Mooney assumed the editorship, beginning the modern history of the *Commercial Appeal.* Mooney's two stints as editor initiated many firsts and enhanced the *Commercial Appeal's* regional and national reputation. By sharing a correspondent with a New York paper, the *Commercial Appeal* scooped the world with coverage of Admiral Dewey's victory at Manila Bay in the Spanish-American War. In 1923 the paper became among the first in the nation to acquire its own radio station and it was the first southern paper to publish a Sunday comic section.

The *Commercial Appeal* was generally liberal on the domestic issues, opposing prohibition and favoring woman suffrage. The paper received its greatest honor, a Pulitzer Prize for public service, for its campaign against the Ku Klux Klan in the 1920s. That award also recognized the outstanding talents of cartoonist J.P. Alley; ironically, Alley's popular syndicated "Hambone's Meditations" (in which a poor black man waxed philosophical about life) was itself judged racially insensitive and discontinued in 1968.

In 1936 the Scripps-Howard Syndicate bought the *Commercial Appeal,* but allowed the paper an unusual amount of freedom in policy and layout. Like all Scripps-Howard properties, the paper supported Republican candidates for President in every election (except 1964) from 1940 to 1968. Wisconsin-born editor Frank Ahlgren (1903–1995), who served from 1936 to 1968, was a key figure in securing the chain's endorsement of Dwight Eisenhower in 1952.

The morning and Sunday *Commercial Appeal* always had a larger circulation than its sister property, the *Memphis Press-Scimitar,* and remains among the top papers in circulation in the South. The *Commercial Appeal* lent its considerable influence to the establishment and enlargement of the Tennessee Valley Authority and to the creation of the modern Port of Memphis. In recent years its "Thousand Points of Light" series on volunteerism attracted the notice of then-President George Bush, while the paper's second Pulitzer Prize was awarded to editorial cartoonist Michael P. Ramirez in 1994.

Ed Frank, Mississippi Valley Collection, University of Memphis Libraries
SUGGESTED READING: Thomas H. Baker, *The Memphis Commercial Appeal: The History of a Southern Newspaper* (1971)
SEE: CARMACK, EDWARD W.; LEA, LUKE; PUBLISHING

MEMPHIS COTTON EXCHANGE. Following the organization of cotton exchanges in New York (1870) and New Orleans (1871), Memphis cotton buyers pushed for an exchange in Memphis. Initial attempts to organize the institution failed, because most of the cotton factors feared that the proposed exchange would develop a "ring" for futures trading, as the New York and New Orleans exchanges had done. Many factors, who sold cotton on commission for planters, believed that speculation in futures depressed prices.

When the Memphis Cotton Exchange formally opened at the end of 1873, it established a "spot" market with no provision for trading in futures contracts. Cotton sent to Memphis was bought and sold

Memphis Cotton Exchange, 1953.

TSLA

on the spot. Apart from two short-lived ventures into futures trading, Memphis remained a spot market.

Members formulated rules to govern the buying and selling of cotton. The regulations standardized trade practices based on past customs. The Exchange established a reliable system for grading cotton. Violations of the rules were punishable by the revocation of membership. In order to insure compliance with the rules, members could not trade with non-members.

The Exchange arranged to receive price quotations from all important cotton markets. It also kept members informed about crop conditions and other matters of interest. Cotton merchants who declined to join the Exchange soon found they could not compete without access to the information.

Arbitration became another key function of the Memphis Exchange. With verbal contracts, sales based on samples, and the many staple lengths and grades of cotton being traded, numerous disputes occurred. By keeping disagreements out of the courts the Memphis Cotton Exchange saved cotton merchants from expensive litigation. Relying on sales contracts based on honor rather than documents speeded up business transactions.

The Memphis Cotton Exchange promoted cotton bought and sold in its market and worked to increase the volume of cotton passing through its warehouses. In the past, Memphis cotton had often been marketed under the name of the port from which it was shipped. The Exchange sent samples of the different grades of cotton traded in Memphis to Liverpool, New York, and New Orleans and requested separate

quotes and prices for Memphis grades. To advertise their product, the Exchange periodically gave a prize for the best bale of cotton received in the Bluff City and sent the prize-winning bale to fairs in the United States and Europe.

With diversification of the Memphis economy, collection of cotton statistics by federal agencies, and a declining number of cotton-buying firms, the Memphis Cotton Exchange no longer sustains the commanding presence it once did.

Lynette Boney Wrenn, Memphis

SEE: COTTON; DUNAVANT ENTERPRISES & HOHENBERG BROS. COMPANY; HILL, NAPOLEON

MEMPHIS *FREE SPEECH* was founded in 1888 by the Reverend Taylor Nightingale. The paper was published on the grounds of Nightingale's church, the First (Beale Street) Baptist Church. The name of the paper changed to *Free Speech and Headlight* when J.L. Fleming, a newspaperman from Crittendon County, Arkansas, joined Nightingale. Fleming had edited *The Marion Headlight* until a white mob "liberated" the county from black rule and ran him out of town. Ida B. Wells, a local teacher and community activist, was invited to join the staff, and she bought a third share of the newspaper.

Free Speech and Headlight quickly became the most radical and talked about newspaper in Memphis. In the late 1880s, as the *de jure* segregation and black male disfranchisement movements hardened racial lines in Memphis, the editors often railed against the loss of black rights. These attacks against white rule did not go unnoticed by city authorities.

Wrongly blaming the moderate Nightingale for the attacks, city authorities used an internal church squabble to have him arrested in 1891. Nightingale understood the message and fled the city, leaving Wells and Fleming to express their more radical views on racial issues.

Free Speech received national attention in 1892 for its coverage of the so-called "Curve Riot." Not a riot at all, the Curve Riot was an attack on the People's Grocery Store by a group of undercover police serving a warrant on the black-owned business. Will Barret, the store's white competitor, had convinced a local court that the People's Grocery had became a nuisance. The court ordered the owners arrested. Fearing an attack, supporters of the People's Grocery armed themselves to defend the store. In the ensuing melee three deputies were wounded. Crying "race riot," other armed whites joined the police and eventually captured and arrested over 30 African Americans, including three of the store's owners: Tom Moss, Calvin McDowell, and Will Stewart. A mob seized the three from the jail and lynched them. Wells wrote passionately of the atrocity and advised her readers to abandon Memphis and move to the western territories. Many followed her advice.

Using the columns of *Free Speech*, Wells launched her anti-lynching campaign. In one of her most famous columns, Wells attacked the supposed reason for the lynching of black men, the rape of white women. Suggesting that white women only claimed rape after their illicit affairs with black men had been discovered, she cautioned the lynchers that their activities threatened to sully the reputations of the South's fairer sex. Fortunately, Wells was out of town when the attack occurred, and she did not return to the South for another 30 years.

No copy of the *Free Speech* survives. Like the other 25 black-owned newspapers of the era, no library or archive preserved copies. Our only knowledge of the once thriving and outspoken African-American newspaper comes from reprinted articles extant in other newspapers.

Kenneth Goings, University of Memphis
SEE: BEALE STREET; CIVIL RIGHTS MOVEMENT; LYNCHING; PUBLISHING; WELLS-BARNETT, IDA B.

MEMPHIS *LABOR REVIEW.* Founded in 1917 and edited by owner and publisher Jake Cohen (1877–1945), this weekly newspaper served as the official organ of the Memphis Trades and Labor Council, an American Federation of Labor affiliate. Prior to his journalistic efforts, the Russian-born Cohen, a reputed friend and traveling companion of Jack London, worked as a machinist and labor leader. A delegation of Memphis unionists solicited Cohen away from the presidency of the Chattanooga Trades and Labor Council to edit the paper. From 1924 to 1932 Cohen simultaneously served as president of the Memphis Trades and Labor Council and president of the Tennessee Federation of Labor.

In 1945, following the death of Jake Cohen, pro- and anti-Crump factions in the Memphis Trades and Labor Council fought for control of the paper; Cohen's will named three members of the council as trustees for the paper. From 1945 to 1948 longtime southern journalist Tom Simmons edited the *Labor Review*. An anti-Crump typographer, attorney, and sometime judge, Robert A. Tillman succeeded him. Pro-Crump plumber, Lev Loring, replaced Tillman. During Loring's management, the paper lost its official Trades and Labor Council support and Tennessee Federation of Labor recognition; in 1950 these designations transferred to the *West Tennessee Labor Review*. In 1957 that paper merged with the *Labor Journal* (a CIO organ founded in 1950) under the title *Memphis Union News*, renamed *AFL-CIO News* in 1970.

The Mississippi Valley Collection in Memphis holds copies of the *Memphis Labor Review* and successor titles, 1944–1977.

Ed Frank, Mississippi Valley Collection, University of Memphis Libraries
SEE: LABOR

MEMPHIS MUSIC SCENE is exciting, diverse, and extremely significant in the history of American culture. Today Memphis's best known landmarks are two places—Beale Street and Graceland—intimately associated with the city's place in American music history, especially that of the blues, rockabilly, and rock-n-roll. But key institutions in Tennessee's classical music history are based in Memphis and several nationally recognized artists in jazz, gospel, and rhythm-n-blues have strong associations with the Memphis Music Scene.

Blues, rock-n-roll, soul, and jazz music may still be heard nightly at the different clubs and music venues on Beale Street. The street was the center of African-American commerce and culture for blacks from the city, eastern Arkansas, West Tennessee, and northern Mississippi, a virtual northern gateway to the rich culture of the Mississippi Delta. "A meeting place for urban and rural styles," emphasized folklorist George McDaniel, "Beale served as a school where young talent was nurtured and it produced musicians who shaped the course of American music."[1] W.C. Handy, B.B. King, Jimmy Lunceford, Bobby "Blue" Bland, Furry Lewis, Booker T.W. White, Piano Red Williams, Lillie May Glover, Sleepy John Estes, McKinley Morganfield (Muddy Waters), Sam Chatmon, and Big Joe Williams were among the most important artists shaping the distinctive Memphis Blues sound of the mid-twentieth century. The city joined Chicago and New York as the creative centers of blues music. Radio announcer and Memphis history teacher Nat D. Williams observed in the Memphis *World* of November 30, 1945: "Come what may, there will always be a Beale Street, because Beale Street is a spirit . . . a symbol . . . a way of life . . . Beale Street is a hope."

This Memphis sound, and musical tradition, later shaped the early rockabilly style associated with Elvis Presley, Jerry Lee Lewis, Roy Orbison, Carl Perkins, and Johnny Cash. All five artists made their early significant recordings, under the guidance of producer Sam Phillips, at Sun Records studio which was located a few blocks away from the heart of the African-American nightclub district. Presley, Lewis, Perkins, and Cash also show how rural southern traditions mixed with the urban beat of Memphis. Presley, although living then in Memphis, was originally from northern Mississippi. Perkins came from rural West Tennessee while Lewis hailed from Louisiana and Cash from Arkansas. Presley always remained identified as a rock-n-roll star, although he took great pride in his Grammy Award-winning gospel music recordings. Lewis, Perkins, and Cash later became identified as country music performers, especially the latter two as they recorded and performed together regularly in the late 1960s and 1970s. The *Johnny Cash Show,* recorded at Nashville's Ryman Auditorium in the early 1970s, was a popular network television program, contributing significantly to the rise in popularity of country music across the nation. Interestingly, during this period, Orbison and Cash were neighbors in Hendersonville, a community northeast of Nashville. As the 1990s end, Cash is the only one of the five Sun artists to record regularly, with his recent stark releases gaining critical praise. Cordell Jackson, the "Guitar Granny," continues to record and perform the classic rockabilly sound that once defined early rock-n-roll in Memphis.

The reputation of Beale Street attracted musicians to come to Memphis. Another attraction was the city's diverse radio stations. During the late 1940s and 1950s, "radio was the key to the magic taking place in Memphis. It instilled pride; it energized emotions."[2] Just south and across the Mississippi was KFFA in Helena, Arkansas, where Sonny Boy Williamson II hosted a Saturday night blues showcase called "King Biscuit Time." In Memphis, WNBR Radio broadcast a weekly "Amateur Night" show from the Palace Theater on Beale Street, where widely different musicians performed blues, pop songs, jazz, and rhythm-n-blues numbers. Memphis's WDIA Radio in 1948 hired Nat D. Williams, a teacher, announcer, and Beale Street advocate/performer, as the region's first black disk jockey on a white radio station. WDIA introduced an all-black music format, replacing its earlier classical music format. Williams's broadcasts of rhythm-n-blues music became popular and later influenced Elvis Presley and many other white performers. WDIA played an influential role in the career of B.B. King and also introduced to the listening white audience the sounds of black gospel music. WDIA is the oldest black-oriented radio station in the nation, shaping not only the region's musical traditions but also its sense of black history, culture, and civil rights. WHBQ Radio during the early 1950s hosted the influential "Red Hot and Blue" show by disk jockey Dewey Phillips. Phillips was the first to play Elvis Presley on local radio and the station championed the rockabilly sound coming from Sun Records.

Rhythm-n-Blues or soul music in Memphis is closely associated with the rise of Stax Records and its Memphis recording studios. Estelle Stewart Axton and her brother Jim Stewart established Satellite Productions in an abandoned grocery store at Brunswick in rural Shelby County. In 1960 they moved to an old movie theater at 924 East McLemore Avenue in Memphis where they joined forces with producer Lincoln "Chips" Moman. Among the initial artists recording with Satellite Productions were Rufus and Carla Thomas, Booker T. Jones, and Steve Cropper. In late 1961 Satellite became Stax Records and Booker T. and the MG s became the label's first star act. Otis Redding soon joined the company's roster and Stax Records became a major force in American popular music, achieving its best work from 1965 to 1970.

Hi Records, led by producer Willie Mitchell, was a competing label for the best in Memphis's Soul music. Early Hi artists included Don Bryant, Ann Peebles, and especially Tina Turner, who worked with Mitchell on various album productions from 1967 to 1977. Mitchell's primary artist, however, was Al Green, who had a string of soul music hits in the early 1970s. Isaac Hayes, from nearby Covington, was another important contributor to the Memphis soul music tradition.

At the same time of this explosion of popular music, classical music institutions developed in Memphis, and sometimes artists from these institutions participated in the more popular side of the Memphis Music Scene. Beginning in the mid-1930s Noel Gilbert organized small orchestras to play at local hotels as well as conducting both the WREC and WMC radio staff orchestras. In the early 1950s he brought classical music to the new medium of television, with a nightly program titled *Evening Serenade* on WMC-TV. From 1947 through the 1970s Gilbert also conducted a summer series of classical music at the band shell in Overton Park. He even found time in the early 1960s to serve as a studio musician and coordinator at recording sessions for Sun, Hi, and Stax records. His work accompanied recordings from artists as diverse as Elvis Presley, Dionne Warwick, Al Green, and Isaac Hayes. In 1952 Vincent DeFrank formed the Memphis Sinfonietta, a precursor to the

Memphis Symphony Orchestra he founded in 1960. Today the city maintains several active classical music institutions and Opera Memphis is the state's largest opera company.

Gospel music too was important in the rise of the Memphis Music Scene. Reverend Herbert W. Brewster, of the city's East Trigg Baptist Church, began writing gospel songs in the 1930s, including the favorites *Move on up a Little Higher*, recorded by Mahalia Jackson, and *Surely, God is Able*, recorded by the Ward Singers. The Spirit of Memphis was a popular gospel group during the 1940s. Gospel, jazz, blues, soul, and rockabilly have combined to create the distinctive Memphis music tradition, a legacy still savored by music lovers across the nation.

Carroll Van West, Middle Tennessee State University

CITATIONS:

(1) George McDaniel, "Beale Street," Charles R. Wilson and William Ferris, eds., *Encyclopedia of Southern Culture* (Chapel Hill, 1989), 1044.

(2) James Dickerson, *Goin' Back to Memphis: A Century of Blues, Rock 'n' Roll and Glorious Soul* (New York, 1996), 84.

SEE: BEALE STREET; CENTER FOR SOUTHERN FOLKLORE; DEFRANK, VINCENT; GILBERT, NOEL; GRACELAND; HANDY, WILLIAM C.; JAZZ; MUSIC; OPERA; PERKINS, CARL; PHILLIPS, SAM; PRESLEY, ELVIS; ROCK MUSIC, SOUTHERN; ROCKABILLY; STAX RECORDS; THOMAS, RUFUS; TURNER, TINA; VERNACULAR RELIGIOUS MUSIC; WDIA

MEMPHIS PARK AND PARKWAY SYSTEM. Associated with the Progressive era and City Beautiful Movements of the late nineteenth and early twentieth centuries, the development of the Memphis Park and Parkway System laid the foundation for municipal park systems across Tennessee. The Memphis system also represented one of the earliest efforts in the South to introduce basic concepts of modern comprehensive urban planning and design by George E. Kessler (1862–1923), who is widely regarded as one of the fathers of urban planning in America.

The Memphis Park and Parkway System resulted from the vision of new civic capitalists, who emerged in the wake of the yellow fever epidemics of the 1870s. In 1895 these well-educated, well-traveled, and prosperous capitalists established the Greater Memphis Movement (GMM), a loose organization devoted to the promotion of a progressive civic agenda that included annexation of suburban areas to the east, establishment of a public water and gas utility, extension of George Waring's revolutionary sewer system, and the construction of a system of parks and connecting boulevards to unite the new city with the old.

Work began in 1897, following the election of Mayor John J. Williams and supportive aldermen. Initially the GMM program faced frustrating legal and legislative battles to establish the city's right to form an independent park commission, issue bonds, and exercise eminent domain in the condemnation of property for the park. While the Williams administration awaited resolution of these delays, the GMM entered into a three-year relationship with John C. Olmstead, the son of Frederick Law Olmstead, Sr., the famous landscape architect. Olmstead provided advice on the drafting of legislation and designed an alignment for a proposed parkway to connect two park sites, one on Riverside (Cow Island) Road and the other on an old farm tract known as Lea's Woods.

In 1899 the city annexed seven square miles, quadrupling its size, and in 1900 the Tennessee Supreme Court resolved the legal issues surrounding the establishment of the Memphis Park Commission, which met for the first time on November 6, 1900, and elected Judge J.B. McFarland as chairman. In less than three weeks, the mayor and city aldermen authorized the acquisition of property for the establishment of the parks. The speed with which the city and its staff moved suggests that the preliminary work had been completed and only awaited the court's decision. The purchase of Lea's Woods and the Wilderberger Farm on Cow Island Road were finalized on October 26, 1901.

In November 1901 the city accepted the bid of George E. Kessler of Kansas City to design the parks and parkway systems. Over the next 13 years, Kessler and his protégé and partner, Henry C. Wright, Sr., executed an impressive program of park development, largely based on the model presented by Kessler in Kansas City in 1891. Their designs for the site plans and structures of Lea's Woods (renamed Overton Park) and the Wilderberger Farm site (named Riverside Park) progressed with impressive speed despite the firm's simultaneous commission to design the Louisiana Purchase World's Fair grounds in St. Louis in 1903–1904.

The complex and ambitious Memphis project included the redesign and development of three of the city's four original 1819 squares; the design of three new small urban parks, including Forrest, Confederate, and Gaston parks; the design and development of Overton and Riverside parks; and the design for a new system of parkways to connect these parks and spur development in the newly annexed areas. By the end of 1906 more than 1,750 acres of parkland had been purchased, designed, developed, and opened.

Political pressure forced Kessler to address Overton Park first with a picturesque landscape design, largely derived from the design traditions of New York City's Central Park. The design was completed in early 1902, and initial development of the drives, open areas, lakes, and pavilions was completed by August. The work on Riverside Park progressed at a slower pace during 1902 and 1903, due in part to its location away from the city's residential development. At its opening in 1903, for instance, access was limited by a four-mile carriage ride from the city, or a twenty-minute trip by river steamer. Greater public access by streetcar connections was not completed until 1913.

The key to the vision of Kessler and the Commissioners lay in the creation of parkways to connect the major parks. Kessler eventually abandoned the idea of a meandering parkway in the English Romantic landscape tradition in favor of a rectilinear alignment that ran over a series of existing roads. Kessler envisioned a portion of the parkway to resemble New York's Riverside Drive, a pleasure drive designed to allow city dwellers the opportunity to race their horses and carriages. Called the Speedway, this colorful feature of the parkway survived only until 1910, when the Commission responded to public pressure and voted to enforce a speed limit along the parkways.

Development of the parkways encountered another obstacle when a lawsuit challenged the commission's authority to use eminent domain to build what many saw as merely roadways. After two years, the Tennessee Supreme Court resolved the issue in favor of the Commission in *Memphis v. Hastings.* The Commission broke ground for the parkways in November 1904 and officially completed the routes in April 1906.

The park and parkway system stimulated residential development. In 1906 the Park Commission received the power to review and comment on all development plans submitted for approval by the Mayor and Board, in order to insure that future development would enhance the appearance of the city's parks and parkways. In practice, the review process provided the Commission with *ad hoc* powers to act as a city planning commission. The relationship between the Memphis Park Commission and George Kessler ended in 1914.

The Memphis Park Commission has continued to grow over the years, currently acting as steward for 6,000 acres of parkland, the city's museum system, seven golf courses, 25 community centers, eight senior citizen centers, 13 "After School" programs, and the Mid-South Fairgrounds, among other facilities. It stands as an object of pride to Memphians and a tribute to the vision of its founders and designers.

John Linn Hopkins and Marsha R. Oates, Memphis
SEE: MEMPHIS; MEMPHIS BROOKS MUSEUM OF ART

MEMPHIS *PRESS-SCIMITAR.* The history of the *Memphis Press-Scimitar* is shorter, though no less convoluted, than that of its main rival, the *Commercial Appeal.* In 1880 George P.M. Turner (1839–1900), owner-editor of papers in Mississippi and Arkansas, leader of Texas troops under Nathan Bedford Forrest, and district attorney-general, began a Sunday morn-

ing paper called *The Scimitar,* but by late 1883 it was issued daily except Sunday. In 1894 a mass lynching in Shelby County prompted Turner's successor, A.B. Pickett, to an editorial crusade against the practice, setting a progressive tone that marked most of the paper's history. In 1904 *The Scimitar* merged with the *News* (founded in 1902) and continued as the *News-Scimitar* for the next two decades.

The *Memphis Press,* an evening daily, appeared in 1906 as a property of the Scripps-McRae League (later the Scripps-Howard syndicate). In its 20 years, the *Press*'s editors included R. Young, Harper Leech, Ralph Millett, Edward T. Leech, Tom E. Sharp, and G.V. Sanders. In the summer of 1919 Edward Leech served a ten-day jail sentence for contempt of court as a result of an editorial critical of E.H. "Boss" Crump's political machine.

In 1926 the *Press* and the *News-Scimitar* merged to form the *Memphis Press-Scimitar.* Tom Sharp and G.V. Sanders were the first editors, but the paper's greatest days began in 1931 with the arrival of Edward J. Meeman, who served as editor until 1962. Although the *Press-Scimitar* and the *Commercial Appeal* were both Scripps-Howard properties after 1936, the former was generally more liberal. Both newspapers voiced their differences with Boss Crump, but Meeman's *Press-Scimitar* pursued a running battle against the machine's dominance of state and local politics that drew the Boss's ire. The 1948 Democratic primary, in which Meeman and the paper supported anti-Crump candidates Gordon Browning (for governor) and Estes Kefauver (for senator), is generally judged the greatest blow ever landed against Crump's machine. In that year, the *Press-Scimitar* also won the prestigious public service award from Sigma Delta Chi, the national professional journalistic fraternity, and columnist Eldon Roark's syndicated "Strolling" column was awarded the National Headliners' Club's praise as the best daily feature-human interest column in the country.

Under the arts-loving Meeman, the *Memphis Press-Scimitar* became an instigator of the Memphis Shakespeare Festival (1951–1966) and, in partnership with Theater Memphis, of the Memphis Acting Competition. The Goodfellows annual Christmas party and the Cynthia Milk Fund, both targeted at poor children, originated with the predecessor papers, but continued under the *Press-Scimitar.* In the 1930s the *Press-Scimitar* and the Memphis Cotton Carnival Association created the annual Maid of Cotton pageant to highlight the continuing importance of that crop to the regional economy. Editor Meeman became a recognized leader in the conservation movement and used his position to support environmental and ecological protection.

By the early 1980s Scripps-Howard could no longer afford to maintain two dailies in a single market, even though the two had long shared management and advertising staffs, buildings, and presses. The last issue of the *Press-Scimitar* appeared on October 31, 1983. Many of its staff moved to the *Commercial Appeal* and the *Memphis Business Journal,* while its morgue file (a significant research resource of clippings, photos, and ephemera) is now housed in the Mississippi Valley Collection of the University of Memphis Library.

Ed Frank, Mississippi Valley Collection, University of Memphis Libraries

SEE: CRUMP, EDWARD H.; MEEMAN, EDWARD J.; MEMPHIS COMMERCIAL APPEAL; PUBLISHING

MEMPHIS PROS/TAMS/SOUNDS, the only major league professional basketball team ever based in Tennessee, was a member of the American Basketball Association (ABA) from 1970 to 1975. Playing primarily at the Mid-South Coliseum in Memphis, this team was one of the weakest links in the ABA, a diverse range of professional basketball teams that challenged the National Basketball Association for professional basketball dominance during the 1970s.

The ABA first came to Memphis in 1970 when the failed New Orleans franchise, the New Orleans Buccaneers, moved to the Bluff City and became the Memphis Pros (1970–1972). In its first season, the Pros played moderately well, winning 41 games, placing third in the division, and making the playoffs. Babe McCarthy was the coach and leading players included Steve Jones, Gerald Govan, Jimmy Jones, and Wendell Ladner. But the first year proved to be the franchise's best in Memphis; later teams never won more than 27 games in an 84-game season. In the 1971–1972 season, the team almost failed, but local fans bought stock in a public campaign to "Save Our Pros." Enough money was raised to keep the team in business through the season.

In 1972 Charles O. Finney, the flashy and controversial owner of the Oakland Athletics major league baseball team, acquired the Memphis Pros. He changed the team's name to the Memphis "Tams," which referred to the team's alleged fan base in Tennessee, Arkansas, and Mississippi. He replaced Babe McCarthy with Bob Bass as coach and brought in new players such as George Thompson and Johnny Neumann (an Ole Miss star). The Tams, however, were no better than the Pros and attendance remained low. Finley lost interest in his Memphis franchise and by the 1973–1974 season, with Bill van Breda Koff as coach, the team struggled so financially that it stopped printing game programs and meeting the payroll. Finally the ABA had to step in and manage the team until the end of the season.

The last year of major league professional basketball in Memphis was 1974–1975 when former ABA commissioner Mike Storen ran the franchise as the Memphis Sounds and named Jack Mullaney as the coach. With such players as Mel Daniels, Chuck Williams, and Larry Finch, who had been a collegiate star at Memphis State University and would later coach at his alma mater, the Sounds actually made the playoffs and won the only playoff game ever won by a Memphis team. However, fans stayed away from the Mid-South Coliseum, and in the summer of 1975 the Memphis Sounds were sold to a group of Baltimore businessmen, who announced plans to play the next season as the Baltimore Claws. The Baltimore venture never worked and the former Memphis Pros/Tams/Sounds faded into ABA history.

Since the ABA, several minor league basketball teams have attempted to establish permanent homes in Tennessee, but as of the 1997–1998 season, professional major league basketball has yet to return to the Volunteer State.

Carroll Van West, Middle Tennessee State University

MEMPHIS RACE RIOT OF 1866. On May 1–2, 1866, Memphis suffered its worst race riot in history. Some 46 African Americans and two whites died during the riot. A Joint Congressional Committee reported 75 persons injured, 100 persons robbed, five women raped, 91 homes burned, four churches and eight schools burned and destroyed, and $17,000 in federal property destroyed. Hundreds of blacks were jailed, and almost all other freedmen fled town until the disturbance ended. For two days, white mobs, including policemen, firemen, and some businessmen, attacked the freedmen's camps and neighborhoods.

The riot started after an alarm went out that African-American soldiers from Fort Pickering, on the south boundary of downtown Memphis, had killed several policemen who tried to arrest a black soldier. In response to the reports, Union General George Stoneman disarmed the soldiers and locked them in their barracks, leaving nearby freedmen's settlements vulnerable to the white mobs that soon attacked women, children, and defenseless men, as well as the northern missionaries who served as ministers and teachers for the freedmen.

The Memphis riots reflected the anger and frustration felt by many white citizens and particularly former Confederates, who suffered the agony of a bitter defeat at the hands of a black and white Union army. Irish immigrants, who had sided with the Confederacy, especially hated the freedmen who dominated the skilled and unskilled jobs that had previously served as a mechanism for upward mobility in the Irish community. Some downtown businessmen participated in the mob because they resented the hordes of penniless freedmen on the streets. Other rioters wanted revenge for the Union occupation. The use of African-American soldiers as patrolmen with power to order whites to "move on" was especially galling to many. Finally, the riots reflected the attitudes of most white citizens toward the former slaves who were then free and soon demanding equal rights.

One outcome of the Memphis riot (and a similar riot in New Orleans) was the Congressional move toward Radical Reconstruction. The Radical Republicans passed a Civil Rights Bill and the Fourteenth Amendment, guaranteeing citizenship, equal protection of the laws, and due process to former slaves. Tennessee was forced to ratify the Fourteenth Amendment before being allowed to return to the Union (July 1866). Paradoxically, the former slaves became citizens, voters, and officeholders in part due to the Reconstruction acts passed in response to the race riots in Memphis and elsewhere.

Bobby L. Lovett, Tennessee State University

SEE: RECONSTRUCTION

MEMPHIS SANITATION STRIKE began on February 12, 1968, and few then suspected the walkout by black sanitation workers would escalate into one of the climactic struggles of the civil rights and labor movements of the 1960s. By the time the struggle ended with a contract 64 days later, the city's intransigent anti-unionism had been defeated. Some 1,300 members of the American Federation of State, County, and Municipal Employees (AFSCME) Local 1733 had revived a dormant labor movement in Memphis and initiated a wave of public employee union organizing in other parts of the South. Yet the victory came at a great cost, as an assassin's bullet cut down the strike's most influential supporter, Dr. Martin Luther King, Jr., on April 4. Ever since that date, the city and the nation have struggled to draw meaning out of the strike and King's death.

The workers were the main leaders for this uprising of the urban poor. Guided by T.O. Jones, a sanitation worker fired for his union activities, the sanitation men had been asking the city for recognition of their union and for a resolution of their many grievances since 1963. These workers lived below the poverty level while working fulltime jobs, and 40 percent of them qualified for welfare to supplement their meager salaries. They received virtually no health care benefits, pensions, or vacations, worked in filthy conditions, and lacked such simple amenities as a place to eat and shower. They carried leaky garbage tubs which spilled maggots and refuse on them, while white supervisors called grown men "boy" and sent them home without pay for the slightest infraction. The sanitation workers walked out spontaneously, without support from the AFSCME international, after supervisors sent blacks home without pay during a rain storm while keeping whites on at full pay. A recent incident in which a malfunctioning garbage compactor had crushed two

black men to death had also fueled the men's rage at work conditions they could no longer tolerate.

The strike came to symbolize the strivings of the working poor and the general demand by the African-American community for equality. Arbitrary behavior by white supervisors, refusal by the city government to recognize the union or meet with workers to discuss their grievances, and the hostile reaction to the strike by the city's white residents, all made the strike a racial as well as an economic issue. In a city of 540,000 people, some 40 percent of them black, the election of Mayor Henry Loeb, a Republican fiscal conservative, signaled a refusal on the part of the city's white residents to take issues of racial equity seriously. Nearly 60 percent of black community residents lived below the poverty line, and they suffered disproportionately high mortality rates and deficits in basic education in a highly segregated school system. Mechanization of cotton production in the countryside and a decline of factory employment for blacks in the city both undergirded the plight of the working poor.

The strike polarized the city racially after police attacked a march by sanitation workers and ministers to city hall only a few days into the strike. Beatings and macings of prominent black leaders galvanized strike support among the city's black ministers and civil rights community, while most whites rallied to the mayor's effort to suppress the strike. All these conditions led to the strike's slogan "I Am A Man," which represented the basic demand of members of the black community, male and female alike, to be treated as citizens with equal rights.

Dr. King came to support the strike as part of his Poor People's Campaign, an effort to take the grievances of the poor directly to Washington, D.C. Mass meetings, a boycott of Memphis businesses and commercial newspapers (which African Americans felt consistently distorted the facts and issues in the strike), and daily picketing formed the back drop for King's March 18 speech to a crowd of 15,000. Made at the request of civil rights stalwart Reverend James Lawson, King's speech put national media attention on the strike, revived flagging spirits in Memphis, and led to major strike support by national and local trade unions. When King returned to Memphis for a mass march on March 29, however, tensions in Memphis had risen to a fever pitch. Window breaking by march bystanders led to confrontations with the police, who shot Larry Payne to death, leading to riots and occupation of the city by 4,000 National Guard members. The courts enjoined King from leading further marches, threatening to cancel out the credibility of his campaign for a national march on Washington. Returning to Memphis determined to lead a mass nonviolent march, King called for support of the worldwide "human rights revolution" at a mass rally on April 3 at Mason Temple. In an emotional climax to the speech, King practically predicted his own death and prophesied that "I may not get there with you, but I want you to know tonight that we as a people will get to the promised land."

King's assassination on April 4 led to massive riots all over the United States and to turmoil in the streets of Memphis. On April 7, some 8,000 Memphians, most of them white, expressed their concern in a memorial, followed by a completely silent mass march of 20,000 to 40,000 people from all over the country through the streets of Memphis on April 8. National labor leaders, President Lyndon Johnson, and Tennessee Governor Buford Ellington all pressured the city into recognizing Local 1733 and allowing check off of union dues from workers' pay checks.

In the settlement's aftermath, AFSCME became the largest union local in the city. Police and fire fighters joined public employee unions. African-American workers took on a higher profile in the labor movement and as voters. Civil rights leaders became increasingly active in city school board and other issues, while pressure from the African-American community opened up jobs to blacks in previously forbidden zones of white collar employment. Ultimately, demographic change and black activism led to the election of African-American Willie Herenton as mayor in the 1990s, while both individuals and local and state governments attempted to resolve the city's history of racial polarization by creating the National Civil Rights Museum at the Lorraine Motel, scene of Dr. King's martyrdom. The demand that America come to grips with the economic demands of minorities and poor people, represented by the Memphis sanitation strike and the Poor People's Campaign of 1968, has nonetheless remained an unresolved legacy of the labor and civil rights movements of the past.

Michael Honey, University of Washington, Tacoma

SUGGESTED READINGS: Joan T. Beifus, *At the River I Stand: Memphis, the 1968 Strike, and Martin Luther King* (1985); Michael Honey, *Southern Labor and Black Civil Rights: Organizing Memphis Workers* (1993), and *Black Workers Remember, An Oral History: Segregation, Industrial Unionism, and the Freedom Struggle* (1999)

SEE: CIVIL RIGHTS MOVEMENT; LABOR; LAWSON, JAMES E., JR.; NATIONAL CIVIL RIGHTS MUSUEUM

MEMPHIS UNIVERSITY SCHOOL (1893–1936 and 1955–)

dates to September 1893, when E.S. Werts and J.W.S. Rhea founded the school with seven students and high hopes. The school opened in a city recovering from successive bouts of yellow fever and entering a deep economic depression. Against all odds, the school succeeded.

By 1899 Memphis University School's distinctive building fronted Forrest Park and included eight grades and approximately 150 students. MUS graduates attended the nation's most competitive colleges and furnished generations of leadership for Memphis and the surrounding area. Notable alumni included writers Richard Halliburton and Nash Buckingham, and political leaders Lewis Donelson and George Grider. During the Great Depression, the school languished, then closed.

Memphis University School re-emerged during the post-World War II prosperity. Alumni of the earlier school and Second Presbyterian Church leaders worked together to create a new Memphis University School. It opened at 6191 Park Road in 1955; Ross M. Lynn and Eugene Thorn served as the first and second headmasters. MUS grew to almost 600 students and, like its namesake, boasts an honor system and strong academic and athletic traditions. Its graduates continue the tradition of attendance at the nation's most respected colleges and maintain leadership roles in business, professional, and civic endeavors. For more than a century, the two Memphis University Schools have maintained reputations as the city's premier college-preparatory school.

John E. Harkins, Memphis University School

SUGGESTED READING: John E. Harkins, *MUS Century Book* (1993)

MEMPHIS WORLD.

Launched in 1931 by the Southern Newspaper Syndicate as a tri-weekly under the editorial direction of Lewis O. Swingler (1906–1962), the *World* later claimed to be "The South's Oldest and Leading Colored Semi-Weekly Newspaper."

The *World* emphasized racial pride, black economic development, equal pay for black teachers, and the historic accomplishments of African Americans, but much of its coverage focused on crime and scandal. The *World* aimed criticism at Jim Crow laws as well as the Gandhian non-violent tactics of leaders like A. Philip Randolph. The newspaper generally adhered to a "law and order" line in the face of the rising black militancy of the 1940s and after.

During the 1940s, the *World*'s circulation peaked at more than 16,000. By comparison, the two leading white dailies in Memphis boasted a combined circulation of over 220,000 in 1942. During the war, the *World* emphasized the contrast between advances of African Americans in the armed forces with a lack of progress on the local homefront.

The *World* maintained a traditional "party-of-Lincoln" Republicanism in most matters, but also supported civil rights and fair employment legislation. Though never too openly critical of the Crump machine, the *World* applauded the anti-Crump insurgent campaign of Estes Kefauver in 1948. That same year, the *World* urged and trumpeted a major breach in the color barrier, when the city hired its first black uniformed policemen of the twentieth century.

In addition to the talents of editor Swingler, the *World* regularly carried a column by Memphis educator and entertainer Nat D. Williams, a prominent figure in the rise of black-oriented radio. In 1951 Swingler departed to establish the rival *Tri-State Defender*, and the *World* slowly declined in influence and circulation. In 1963 circulation dropped to a mere 6,000. Decreasing frequency paralleled the decline in circulation; issued twice-a-week in 1960, the *World* ended as a weekly. The Republican-oriented *World* failed to keep readers among increasingly Democratic local blacks and ceased publication in 1973.

Ed Frank, Mississippi Valley Collection, University of Memphis Libraries

SUGGESTED READING: Henry Lewis Suggs, ed., *The Black Press in the South, 1865–1979* (1983)

SEE: PUBLISHING

MENNONITES IN TENNESSEE share several commonalities despite their many differences. As Anabaptists, they trace their roots to the radical wing of the Protestant Reformation. Nearly all are part of the "Swiss Brethren" wing of Mennonites. With a few exceptions, the approximately 20 Mennonite churches and/or settlements are relatively small, usually numbering less than 100.

One part of Tennessee's Mennonites functions primarily as a church and not as an ethnic culture group. Included are the four churches which are part of the Mennonite Church—two in Knoxville, one each in Nashville (Brentwood) and Mountain City—and the three Brethren in Christ churches in Rolling Acres (McMinnville area), Dowelltown, and De Rossett (near Sparta). With one or two exceptions (such as the Concord Mennonite church in Knoxville which dates to the late nineteenth century), these churches were established as home mission efforts by Mennonite Conferences outside of Tennessee after World War II. Consequently, native Tennesseans comprise much of their membership.

The second major group of Tennessee Mennonites are comprised of church groups and/or communities that can be classified as cultural (and ethnic) as well as religious groups. Many of the members are first or second generation migrants from Indiana, Pennsylvania, Ohio, Maryland, and even Ontario, Canada. All of these groups define Christian discipleship, at least partly, in terms of resisting aspects of modern culture, such as formal high school education beyond the eighth grade, urbanization, mass communications (including television and in some cases telephones), the appropriate use or non-use of technology in farming and transportation, and occupations which remove the individual from working with the soil and/or one's hands. Included here are the Old Order Amish settlements in Lawrence, Carroll, and Hickman counties established in 1944, 1975, and 1982,

respectively, and groups classified as Beechy Amish, Mennonite Fellowship, or Christian Community near Bolivar, Paris, Winchester, Crossville, Cookeville, Sparta, and Clarkrange, as well as the Cumberland Mountain community near Monterey. At least three other Amish communities, one dating back to the nineteenth century, did not survive. Reasons these groups came to Tennessee include the search for affordable land, concern over school consolidation, and compulsory school attendance laws that were instituted after World War II in the Middle Atlantic and Midwestern states.

Harvey Neufeldt, Tennessee Technological University

SEE: LAWRENCE COUNTY; RELIGION

MERIWETHER, ELIZABETH AVERY (1824–1916), Tennessee suffragist, temperance activist, publisher, and author, was born in Bolivar on January 19, 1824. Her father Nathan Avery was a physician and farmer, while her mother Rebecca Rivers Avery was the daughter of a Virginia planter.

Financial problems led the family to move to Memphis around 1835. Nathan's death in 1846, and Rebecca's in 1847, caused economic crisis for the siblings. Brother Tom sought outside employment to support his four sisters, and Elizabeth operated a school for some 25 students in the family's dining room.

In 1852 she married Minor Meriwether, a railroad civil engineer. Carrying out the wishes of Minor's late father the couple sold part of Minor's inherited land to free his slaves and repatriate them to Liberia. She characterized the act as abolitionist, although she later accepted the gift of a household slave from her brother. Both Meriwethers spoke of their marriage as strong and happy. Elizabeth bore three sons: Avery, in 1857; Rivers, in 1859; and Lee (the namesake of General Robert E. Lee), in 1862.

With the onset of the Civil War Minor Meriwether joined the officer corps of the Confederate army. He served with General Nathan Bedford Forrest; Elizabeth was vocal in advocacy of the Confederate cause, and defiant during Union occupation. General William T. Sherman ordered her to leave Memphis in December 1862, weeks before the birth of her third son. She recounted the experience in her 1863 short story, "The Refugee."

After the war Minor Meriwether purchased a modest Memphis home for his family on the current site of the Peabody Hotel. He worked with Nathan Bedford Forrest to establish the Ku Klux Klan in Memphis; an early Klan organizational meeting took place in Elizabeth's kitchen.

Elizabeth Meriwether nettled occupation forces to reinstate the title to her girlhood home, successfully arguing that her 1851 "abolitionist" stand invalidated its seizure. Thus recognized as a property owner and tax payer, she obtained a voter registration in 1872.

She published a small-circulation newspaper, *The Tablet*, during part of 1872. It featured her unorthodox views on woman suffrage, divorce law, and pay equity for women teachers. In 1876 she made one of the first public suffragist addresses in Memphis. Elizabeth and her sister-in-law Lide Meriwether championed a number of reform causes. Both were active in the Woman's Christian Temperance Union and belonged to the National Woman Suffrage Association. Elizabeth served as a national officer of NAWSA in 1886. She presented unsuccessful suffrage petitions at both the Democratic and Republican national conventions in 1880.

Elizabeth Meriwether's published writing includes two novels, *The Master of Red Leaf* (1872) and *Black and White* (1883), and a play, *The Ku Klux Klan, or The Carpetbagger in New Orleans* (1877). Non-fiction works include *Facts and Falsehoods About the War on the South* (1904), published under the pseudonym George Edmonds, and *the Sowing of the Swords, or The Soul of the 'Sixties* (1910). An informal memoir, *Recollections of 92 Years,* was serialized in many Tennessee papers in 1916 and was published by her son Lee in 1958. Meriwether's writing idealized the Confederate cause and the traditional race ideology of the "Old South."

Elizabeth Meriwether died in St. Louis on November 4, 1916; several months earlier, each of the major political parties had adopted campaign planks urging passage of a woman suffrage amendment.

Sally S. Hermsdorfer, Memphis

SUGGESTED READINGS: Elizabeth Avery Meriwether, *Recollections of 92 Years, 1824–1916* (1958); Marsha Wedell, *Elite Women and the Reform Impulse in Memphis, 1875–1915* (1992)

SEE: FORREST, NATHAN B.; KU KLUX KLAN; MERIWETHER, LIDE; WOMAN SUFFRAGE MOVEMENT

MERIWETHER LEWIS NATIONAL MONUMENT,

in Lewis County, is located along the Natchez Trace Parkway. In 1925 the federal government designated the monument to mark the grave of Meriwether Lewis (1774–1809), a Virginian who was one of the co-leaders of the Lewis and Clark Expedition (1804–1806) and Governor of Louisiana Territory (1806–1809). In 1924 Tennessee state archaeologist P.E. Cox had written the National Park Service about the site of Lewis's grave and the old Grinder's Inn, where Lewis allegedly either committed suicide or was murdered on October 11, 1809. The National Park Service, however, did not want to set a precedent of acquiring the grave sites of famous Americans. Even after a favorable response to the proposal of a national monument from President Calvin Coolidge, the Park Service passed the proposal to the War Department, which formally accepted deed to

the property on February 6, 1925, and created the Meriwether Lewis National Monument. Later that year, President Coolidge presided at the dedication of the monument, which features a broken column, symbolizing Lewis's early and tragic death.

The War Department, however, made few significant park improvements at the grave site. When the Natchez Trace Parkway was established in 1938, the Lewis property was included in the new park's boundaries. Development of the property as a historic site along the Trace began. Today the monument site includes a visitor center, a reproduction of Grinder's Inn, walking trails, and picnic areas.

Carroll Van West, Middle Tennessee State University

SEE: LEWIS COUNTY; NATCHEZ TRACE PARKWAY

MERIWETHER, LIDE SMITH (1830–1913) was a leader of the first generation of southern feminists and social activists. She was president of the Tennessee Woman's Christian Temperance Union, serving from 1884 until 1897, and then as henorary president for life. Having organized the first Equal Rights Association in Memphis in 1889, she served as president of the Tennessee Equal Rights Association from 1897 until 1900, when she also was made honorary president for life of that group.

Lide Smith was born in Virginia and educated at the Emma Willard Seminary in Pennsylvania. Prior to her marriage, she taught school. In 1856 she married Niles Meriwether, with whom she had three daughters. In 1872 Lide Meriwether began her activism on behalf of women with the publication of *Soundings,* dedicated to bringing respectable women to the rescue of prostitutes, who were pictured as victims rather than moral untouchables. During the 1880s she traveled the state, founding WCTU local organizations, including unions of African-American women. She lobbied for prohibition, for raising the legal age of consent, for a police matron in Memphis, and notably for woman suffrage. In her suffrage petition of 1895, she argued against the classification of women with minors, aliens, paupers, criminals, and idiots and advocated legal reform that would give women title to their own clothing and earnings, guardianship of their children, and the right to vote.

Anita S. Goodstein, University of the South

SUGGESTED READING: Marsha Wedell, *Elite Women and the Reform Impulse in Memphis, 1875–1915* (1992)

SEE: FRENCH, LUCY V.; MERIWETHER, ELIZABETH A.; WOMAN SUFFRAGE MOVEMENT

MERO DISTRICT. In 1788 North Carolina established a Superior Court district to serve the Cumberland frontier. The district was named in honor of the Spanish Governor of Louisiana, Esteban Rodrigues Miro, who had served with Spanish troops assisting the Americans during the Revolutionary War. Tensions between the Spanish colonial government and the new nation were high at the time of the establishment of the Mero District. The naming of the new district is credited to James Robertson, who was scheming to establish a good relationship with Miro in order to gain the Spanish Governor's assistance in halting attacks from Creeks and Chickamaugas on the Cumberland settlements, and to open the Mississippi River to Cumberland travelers. Robertson and his allies persuaded the North Carolina legislature to name the new district Mero, inadvertently misspelling the name.

The first judge of the Mero District Superior Court was John McNairy, and one of his first actions was the appointment of Andrew Jackson as district attorney. The court served Davidson and Sumner counties, and the counties created out of them, until 1809, when the Superior Courts were abolished. The name Mero faded from use, and was virtually unknown in 1977, when Peter Taylor published his literary collection, *In the Miro District and Other Stories*. The title story is set in the twentieth century, but one character refers to the city of Nashville as the Miro District, "because he said only an antique Spanish name could do justice to the grandeur which Nashvillians claimed for themselves."[1]

Charles A. Sherrill, Tennessee State Library and Archives
CITATION:
(1) James C. Robison, *Peter Taylor: A Study of the Short Fiction* (Boston, 1988), 86.

SEE: JACKSON, ANDREW; MCNAIRY, JOHN; ROBERTSON, JAMES; TAYLOR, PETER H.

MERRITT, JOHN AYERS (1926–1983), one of Tennessee's most successful football coaches, was born on January 26, 1926, in Falmouth, Kentucky, the son of a stonemason, Bradley Merritt and his wife, Grace. After completing grade school, he moved to Louisville to live with an aunt in order to be eligible to attend Central High School, where he played football. Merritt joined the U.S. Navy after graduation. When he returned from military service, Merritt earned a football scholarship to Kentucky State College. In 1947 he married Maxine Owens, and they had a daughter Bonita (Bonnie) Merritt Traughber. After receiving his college degree, Merritt entered graduate school in 1950. He coached football at Versailles High School and Jackson State University before coming to Tennessee State University.

TSU's President Walter S. Davis hired Merritt in 1963. Over the next 20 years he continued the university's strong football tradition, winning four undefeated seasons, six national championships, and four black college football titles, while enhancing TSU's rich football history and winning tradition. Edward "Too-Tall" Jones, Waymond Byrant, and Joe Gilliam were among the many outstanding players Merritt

sent to professional football. Some 23 Merritt-coached pro players distinguished themselves, including six who played in the Super Bowl. In addition, 29 assistants, three head coaches, and five athletic directors played for Coach Merritt.

John Merritt compiled 30 straight winning seasons. In 1967 his team achieved a national defensive record for allowing opponents a measly average of 2.15 feet per carry. He was Coach of the Year in 1973. Merritt and the team received the Associated Press and the United Press International small college championships in 1975. By 1979 he had a record of 130-25-5. Merritt modestly downplayed his role in the team's success and attributed the team's winning record to "the Good Lord."

The more games Merritt won and the more players he sent to the National Football League, the more attention Tennessee and Tennessee State University gained nationally. He used a pro-type T with multiple sets, a wide open style, and an excellent set of coaches (Joe Gilliam, Sr., and Alvin Coleman), who accompanied Merritt to TSU from Jackson, Mississippi, in 1963. In 1980 President Jimmy Carter called to congratulate Merritt for his 200th victory. Nashville named John A. Merritt Boulevard (old Centennial Boulevard between 28th and 44th avenues) in his honor in 1982. By then, Merritt was in failing health. From 1963 until 1983, when he resigned, Merritt compiled a record of 172-33-7 at TSU and 232-65-11 overall. Coach Merritt died on December 15, 1983.

Not only was he considered a great coach, college professor, and family man, but "Big John" Merritt was a "people person." Men and women of all ages, races, and colors loved and respected him. He commanded the support and loyalty of local politicians and leaders for the TSU football program. He took care to see that "my boys" got their lessons and graduated. Merritt believed "A black kid doesn't understand how to win just for the sake of winning. He has to have a reason to win. . . . The same damn thing holds true here at Tennessee State University."[1] John Ayers Merritt knew how to win and how to teach generations of college students to win.

Bobby L. Lovett, Tennessee State University
CITATION:
(1) Dwight Lewis and Susan Thomas, *A Will to Win* (Nashville, 1983), 33.

SEE: FOOTBALL, COLLEGE; TENNESSEE STATE UNIVERSITY

METROPOLITAN HUMAN RELATIONS COMMISSION. The Metropolitan Government of Nashville/Davidson County created the Metropolitan Human Relations Commission in 1965 during a period of heightened racial tensions in the community and the nation. Composed of 15 persons representative of the various social, economic, religious, cultural, ethnic, and racial groups that comprised the area population, it was the first official human rights agency in Tennessee. The agency assumed broad responsibilities to promote and encourage fair treatment and equal opportunity for all persons; to promote mutual understanding and respect among the members of all racial, religious, and ethnic groups; and to endeavor to eliminate discrimination against and antagonism between religious, racial, and ethnic groups and their members.

The commission attempted to carry out these functions during its first year, 1965–1966, through the efforts of its volunteer commissioners, but the group soon concluded that it needed a staff. Consequently, it chose as its first staff members an African-American Executive Director, Warren N. Moore (1967–1970), and a Caucasian Associate Director, Fred Cloud. This black/white teamwork was continued as a matter of policy for the next two decades.

The enactment of a Fair Employment law for Nashville/Davidson County became the first priority of the newly staffed commission. After seven months of community organization and persuasion, Metro Council passed the Fair Employment Act, and it was signed into law in July 1968—the first such law in Tennessee. A considerable number of "firsts" in human rights followed this initial success: Human Relations Training for all Metro Police officers (1968); Mass Media and Race Relations Seminar (1969), which led to the hiring of several African-American reporters by Nashville newspapers; Affirmative Action plan for Metro government (1974); initiation of the Clinical Legal Education Project at Vanderbilt University Law School (1974); formation of the Mayor's Committee on Refugee and Immigration Affairs (1980); planning for International Festivals for Nashville (1983–1987); assistance in the founding of Nashville Habitat for Humanity (1985); coordination of Holocaust Remembrance (1986–1987); and planning for Martin Luther King, Jr., Birthday Celebration (1986–1990). In 1978 the commission hosted the annual conference of the National Association of Human Rights Workers when it met in Nashville.

In 1970 Fred Cloud assumed the post of Executive Director and remained in that position until 1990. In 1995 after a five-year hiatus in the life of the commission caused by a cut-off of operating funds, the budget was reinstated under Mayor Philip Bredesen. Anthea Boarman became the new Executive Director. Throughout its existence, the staff of the Metropolitan Human Rights Commission has assumed leadership roles in both state and national human rights organizations.

Fred Cloud, Nashville

SEE: CIVIL RIGHTS MOVEMENT

MEXICAN WAR. In 1846 the United States went to war with Mexico as a result of a boundary dispute fueled by an American expansionist desire to control the entire North American continent. With an army of fewer than 9,000, a number wholly inadequate to wage war in a foreign country, officials in Washington issued a call for volunteers. When Secretary of War William Marcy requested 2,800 recruits from Tennessee to fill two regiments of infantry and one of cavalry, 30,000 Tennesseans offered their services, thus preserving the reputation of "The Volunteer State."

Numerous Tennesseans played prominent roles in the conflict, starting with President James K. Polk of Columbia. Sometimes described as the first true commander-in-chief in U.S. history, Polk was actively involved and maintained oversight in the conduct of the two-year struggle. He also unsuccessfully tried to provide sufficient opportunities for Democratic party faithfuls to achieve fame and glory in Mexico so as to assure a party victory in the 1848 election. Such favoritism caused clashes with Whig generals like Winfield Scott and Zachary Taylor, who won the presidency after the war. The list of important Tennesseans who served in Mexico also includes three future governors: William Trousdale (Democrat, 1849–1851); William Campbell (Whig, 1851–1853); and William Bate (Democrat, 1882–1886). Bate, who later served as a United States Senator until his death in 1905, also held the rank of general in the Civil War. Gideon Pillow, Benjamin F. Cheatham, and George Maney also used the battlefields of Mexico as a training ground for their later role as Confederate generals.

In the summer of 1846, state officials used a lottery system to determine who, among the overwhelming number of volunteers, would serve, and who had to return home. Approximately 1,000 men from Middle Tennessee counties formed the First Tennessee Infantry Regiment commanded by Colonel William Campbell. Volunteers from the western part of the state comprised the Second Tennessee Infantry Regiment commanded by Colonel William T. Haskell, while a contingent of dragoons hailed from East Tennessee.

After joining General Zachary Taylor's army in June 1846, the First Tennessee became a part of John Quitman's brigade while the Second Tennessee was assigned to Pillow's brigade. Illness plagued the army during its stay in northern Mexico that summer, and the First Tennessee was particularly hard hit. While encamped at Camargo, Captain Frank Cheatham, company commander of the Nashville Blues, wrote home to his brother complaining that only about half the regiment was fit for duty. Despite its reduced numbers, the regiment fought admirably at the Battle of Monterey in September. At the crucial point of the engagement, it surged forward and assaulted Fort Teneria, a Mexican bastion guarding the city. Afterward one member of the unit described the density of the enemy fire as thick as a handful of thrown peas. First over the walls and into the fort, the regiment won the nickname "The Bloody First."

Both Tennessee regiments were later transferred to General Winfield Scott's army and saw action in the Mexico City Campaign in 1847. In this often overlooked but brilliant campaign, Scott landed an army of 10,000 at Veracruz in March and after a series of marches and battles, he succeeded in capturing the Mexican capital in September. Remnants of both regiments fought a small engagement at Medeline Bridge near Veracruz on March 25, but their most notable involvement came the following month.

Near the village of Cerro Gordo, a Mexican army under Santa Anna held a fortified position overlooking a mountain pass that the Americans had to travel on their march inland. Rather than assault the enemy stronghold, Scott opted to swing the bulk of his army around and assail the Mexicans in flank and rear. To distract the enemy, however, Scott ordered Pillow, who commanded four regiments of volunteers, including the First and Second Tennessee, to advance and demonstrate in the enemy's front. Despite Pillow's mismanagement of his portion of the battle plan, the flank attack succeeded, and the Mexican army fled further inland resulting in Santa Anna's characterization of Cerro Gordo as the most significant American victory of the war.

When their 12-month enlistments expired in the summer of 1847, most volunteers, including the First and Second Tennessee, opted to return home. They were discharged and allowed to leave the army prior to the fall of Mexico City, but some of them returned later in the campaign having joined new regiments raised to replace the old. Pillow returned as a division commander in time to play a controversial role in the battles that occurred on the outskirts of the enemy capital. Later he exaggerated the significance of his part in the Battle of Contreras, and as a result was court martialed for violating army regulations. (He wrote about his exploits in a letter that was published in American newspapers which was a breach of the army's code of conduct.) The court exonerated him—many believe because of his friendship with President Polk. The Third and Fourth Tennessee Regiments were raised that summer and fall, but both arrived too late to participate in the fighting around the enemy capital. They were used rather to garrison towns and guard supply lines while officials negotiated the Treaty of Guadalupe Hildago that ended the conflict.

Timothy D. Johnson, Lipscomb University

SEE: BATE, WILLIAM B.; CAMPBELL, WILLIAM; CHEATHAM, BENJAMIN F.; PILLOW, GIDEON J.; POLK, JAMES K.; TROUSDALE, WILLIAM

MIDDLE TENNESSEE STATE UNIVERSITY, located in Murfreesboro, was created by the General Education Bill of 1909 and dedicated on September 11, 1911, as Middle Tennessee State Normal School. Many local residents joined President Robert L. Jones, the faculty, staff, and state officials in the dedication day's celebration. Murfreesboro leaders and businessmen, especially Andrew L. Todd who was a member of the State Board of Education, had lobbied to locate the new state teachers college for Middle Tennessee in Murfreesboro. They donated land and pledged $180,000 to see the campus and its buildings completed. Acquiring the new higher education institution proved to be worth the sacrifice. Together with the recently established Tennessee College for Women, the normal school, later a college and then a university, would have an enormous influence on the twentieth century development of Murfreesboro and the surrounding counties.

The original campus had 100 acres, five buildings, and 125 students. Nashville architect C.K. Colley designed the school's buildings in a dignified Classical Revival style and today the President's House, Kirksey Old Main, Rutledge Hall, and the Alumni Center still form the historic core of the campus. The first men's dorm, Jones Hall, was constructed in a compatible Classical Revival style in 1922.

In 1925 the normal school became Middle Tennessee State Teachers College, a four-year institution with the power to grant a Bachelor of Science degree. Due to increased state funding for higher education during the administration of Austin Peay, the college gained a new library, science building (Wiser-Patten Hall), a teacher's training school (Pittard Campus School), and additional dormitories. It received accreditation from the Southern Association of Colleges and Schools in 1928.

Despite the new buildings, the Great Depression brought uncertainty to the college. Murfreesboro resident Mabel Pittard recalled: "they talked about closing down the school. There was an undercurrent of not knowing what was going to happen."[1] New Deal agencies helped the students, and college, stay afloat during the cash-strapped times. The National Youth Administration provided scholarships and funds so students could work and stay in school. The Works Progress Administration undertook other projects and improved the campus's landscaping. The school introduced the Bachelor of Arts degree in 1936.

In 1943 officials changed the college's name to Middle Tennessee State College. Student enrollment, however, remained depressed until the end of World War II when returning veterans took advantage of the GI Bill and entered the institution in record numbers.

Under the presidency of Quintin M. Smith, the institution developed a new identity and mission in education, liberal arts, and the sciences. It established a Graduate School in 1951. Fifteen new major buildings were constructed from 1951 to 1964 to provide additional classrooms, dorms, recreation, and a modern library. When state officials and President Quill Cope, a former State Commissioner of Education, dedicated the new Cope Administration Building in 1965, the college had firmly entered its modern era, and it officially received the designation of university.

As Middle Tennessee State University, the institution experienced a period of rapid expansion in student numbers, faculty size, and facilities during the presidency of M.G. Scarlett in the late 1960s and early 1970s. Peck Hall, a liberal arts classroom building; Keathley University Center; Davis Science Building; Murphy Athletic Center; a library expansion; and the McWherter Learning Resources Center were constructed between 1967 and 1975. The university also added the degrees of Doctor of Art in 1970 and Specialist in Education in 1974.

Growth of MTSU's facilities slowed over the next ten years, due in part to federal court decisions regarding the integration of student bodies and faculties at MTSU and Tennessee State University in Nashville. Yet, during the 1980s administration of President Sam Ingram, student enrollment continued to expand, exceeding 11,000 in 1980, and the university developed nationally recognized programs in aerospace, mass communications, historic preservation, and recording industry management. In 1984 Governor Lamar Alexander's program to improve Tennessee higher education led to the creation of the Center for Historic Preservation; a year later came the Center for Popular Music. By the end of the decade, the Bragg Mass Communications Building was under construction, signaling a new era of university expansion.

The 1990s have witnessed dramatic growth in students, programs, and facilities at MTSU. Along with its two centers of excellence, the university has eight chairs of excellence. The Business and Economic Research Center has assisted economic planning and development statewide while the Albert Gore Research Center has evolved into an important archive for twentieth century American political history. New buildings include the Cason-Kennedy Nursing Center, the Miller Equine Center and Arena, a football stadium seating over 30,000, the Business Aerospace Building, a new library, and a modern campus recreation center. This transformation of the university's facilities and related programs have come under the leadership of President James Walker, the first African-American president of a formerly all-white state university in Tennessee. In 1997 MTSU set new university records with over 18,000 students and 700 faculty members.

Carroll Van West, Middle Tennessee State University
CITATION:
(1) Carolyn Brackett, ed., "MTSU Diamond Anniversary," Special Insert to Murfreesboro *Daily News Journal*, 7 September 1986, 68.
SEE: BUCHANAN, JAMES; CENTER FOR HISTORIC PRESERVATION; CENTER FOR POPULAR MUSIC; EDUCATION, HIGHER; GORE, ALBERT, A., SR.; MURFREESBORO

MILAN ARSENAL. This important munitions facility was created in October 1945 by the combination of the Wolf Creek Ordnance Plant and the Milan Ordnance Depot. The combined physical plant of the two installations includes 88 miles of railroad track and 231 miles of roadway in a sprawling 36-square-mile tract that lies in both Gibson and Carroll counties.

Construction contracts were awarded December 31, 1940, and the builders turned the properties over to the government exactly one year later. Construction began on the Wolf Creek facility in January 1941 and on the Ordnance Depot two months later. Building on the 28,000-acre grounds required the demolition of over 1,500 existing farm structures and their replacement with approximately 30 separate assembly and storage areas. Construction costs topped $34,000,000. Operated by the Procter and Gamble Defense Corporation, the facility functioned as a shell-assembly plant where components were turned into finished products.

Although Congress investigated possible corruption in the construction of the facilities, the plant received the Army-Navy "E" for excellence award during World War II. During the Korean Conflict, a few research and development functions were added, but the primary business of the plant remained the assembly of large caliber ammunition for mortars and artillery.

Peak employment reached more than 10,000 during World War II, falling to 1,500 in 1947, rising to more than 8,000 during the Korean War, dipping to fewer than 500 in 1959, before returning to 7,000 in 1968. The small farming community of Milan boasted a population of 3,000 in 1940, but by 1971 that figure had risen to 7,000—growth largely attributable to the Arsenal. The downside of such military oriented economic progress includes the environmental concerns associated with decades of toxic-waste dumping.
Ed Frank, Mississippi Valley Collection, University of Memphis Libraries
SEE: CARROLL COUNTY; GIBSON COUNTY; WORLD WAR II

MILES, EMMA BELL (1879–1919), artist, naturalist, and author of *The Spirit of the Mountains* (1905) as well as poems, stories, and essays, was born in Evansville, Indiana, on October 19, 1879, to schoolteachers Benjamin Franklin and Martha Ann Mirick Bell. She spent her early years in the Ohio River town of Rabbit Hash, Kentucky. In 1890 the family moved to Walden's Ridge on Tennessee's Cumberland Plateau, where Emma lived among the mountain people and roamed the woods, drawing, reading, writing, and studying nature.

In the fall of 1899 Emma Bell entered the St. Louis School of Art, where she spent two winters. There she first encountered the writings of Henry David Thoreau, which strongly influenced her life and thought. Desperately homesick, she returned to Walden's Ridge resolved to remain in the mountains despite her father's hopes for her to study further in New York and Paris.

On October 30, 1901, just three weeks after her mother's death, Emma Bell eloped with Frank Miles, a mountain native with whom she had fallen in love three years earlier. The first of their five children were twins, Jean and Judith, born in September 1902. Less than a year later, B.F. Bell turned them out of the frame house on Anderson Pike which Emma's mother had left to her in a penciled will.

After the March 1904 publication of her poem "The Difference" in *Harper's Monthly*, Miles's work appeared regularly in national magazines. In November 1905 James Pott & Company of New York published *The Spirit of the Mountains*, a classic study of southern Appalachia. Her first published story, "The Common Lot," appeared in *Harper's* in December 1908.

At first Miles's writing and painting seemed barely interrupted by the births of Joe Winchester (February 1905), Katharine (January 1907), and Mark (March 1909). Her health began to deteriorate, however, and the family spent the winter of 1909–1910 in Miami, Florida. They returned to upper East Tennessee the following spring, and Miles accepted a position as artist-in-residence at Lincoln Memorial University. There a local physician diagnosed her illness as tuberculosis.

After returning to the mountains near Chattanooga, Miles supported her family through the sale of paintings, poems, and stories. The death of her youngest child was the great sorrow of her life. In the spring of 1914, she began writing the "Fountain Square Conversations," a series of columns for the *Chattanooga News* in which she expressed her views on the environment and human nature.

In February 1917 Miles entered Pine Breeze, the county tuberculosis sanitarium, later returning to Walden's Ridge, where she began a series of bird paintings. That fall she returned to Pine Breeze, where she remained, living in a tent provided by the Chattanooga Writer's Club, until a few months before her death on March 19, 1919. Bedridden most of the time, Miles managed to complete the bird book she had always dreamed of writing and illus-

trating. *Our Southern Birds* came off the press just two weeks before she died at the age of 39.
Kay Baker Gaston, Springfield
SUGGESTED READING: Kay Baker Gaston, *Emma Bell Miles* (1985)
SEE: LINCOLN MEMORIAL UNIVERSITY; LITERATURE; WALDEN RIDGE

MILKY WAY FARM. The builder of Milk Way Farm, Franklin C. Mars, was the founder of Mars Candies Incorporated, maker of the famous Milky Way candy bar for which the estate was named. Mars and his wife, Ethel V. Mars, came to Tennessee from Chicago in 1930 to establish a southern office of Mars Candies in Nashville. Soon afterwards the Mars purchased 2,800 acres eight miles north of Pulaski along U.S. Highway 31, where they began to develop plans for their home and a breeding farm for thoroughbred race horses and Hereford cattle. Mars hired architect James F. Drake to design the buildings and contracted local businessmen and farmers for supplies and labor to build Milky Way Farm. At the height of the construction work between 1931 and 1933, around 800 men were employed by Mars. During the Great Depression, Milky Way Farm was the largest employer in Giles County.

The Mars's Tudor Revival house, standing among a grove of well-established magnolia trees, was designed for entertaining. A living room with exposed beams and 40 foot ceiling, a dining room which boasted the largest private dining table in the state, and 21 bedrooms and 15 bathrooms accommodated the constant flow of guests. A swimming pool and landscaped grounds added to the grandeur of the estate. The grounds keeper's house, several barns, including one which incorporated octagonal design, stables, well-houses, and other outbuildings are extant. Native limestone was used as a primary or secondary building material in most of the farm's buildings.

Franklin Mars died in 1934 and was buried in a mausoleum on the estate. Ethel Mars continued with the plans she and her husband had made. The farm produced prize-winning cattle, and Milky Way Farm's racing colors made their first appearance in 1934. In 1936 the stable was the leading turf winner in the United States. Over the next few years, horses bred and trained at the farm were among the leaders in many races. Milky Way's Galladion won the Kentucky Derby in 1940. Ethel Mars's ill health caused her to dispose of the thoroughbred stock gradually. When she died in 1945, Milky Way Farm was sold. Franklin and Ethel Mars are now buried in Chicago, though the remains of the elaborate mausoleum still stand.

Milky Way Farm is listed on the National Register of Historic Places. The estate is currently privately owned and operated as a bed and breakfast, which also hosts special events and corporate functions.

Caneta Skelley Hankins, Middle Tennessee State University

SEE: GILES COUNTY; LIVESTOCK; THOROUGHBRED HORSE BREEDING AND RACING

MILLER, PLEASANT MOORMAN (1773–1849) was one of the most influential figures in Tennessee politics and law during the first half of the nineteenth century. Born the son of a tavern owner in Lynchburg, Virginia, Miller studied law under Judge Archibald Stewart of Staunton before moving to Rogersville, Tennessee, in 1796. Following a move to Knoxville in 1800, Miller married Mary Louisa Blount, daughter of William Blount, was elected chairman of Knoxville's governing commission, and emerged as a leader of the Blount-Jackson political faction. Aided by immense oratorical skills and wit, he became known as one of the best criminal trial lawyers in Tennessee.

In 1808 Miller was elected from central East Tennessee to the U.S. House of Representatives, where he became a spokesman for the Southwest, an early and ardent expansionist, and an ally of President James Madison. He achieved national prominence in 1810 with the publication of the "Miller letter." In this letter, Miller reported Madison's meeting with the Tennessee delegation in which he discussed the necessity of acquiring West Florida and control of the Mobile River. This report of Madison's views fanned the flames of expansion and helped to prepare the country for war. In 1811 he was elected to the Tennessee House of Representatives and secured the creation of the Bank of the State of Tennessee. He resigned in 1812 to serve in the first Seminole War and enlisted again in 1814 in the Creek Indian War.

Returning to the Tennessee House from 1817 to 1823, he assumed leadership of the East Tennessee delegation, defeated Felix Grundy's efforts to enact inflationary measures, emerged as a champion of squatter rights, secured passage of legislation stabilizing Tennessee banks and currency during the Depression of 1819, and sponsored major judicial reform. In 1822 he introduced the resolution nominating Andrew Jackson for the Presidency.

Miller moved to Jackson, Tennessee, in 1824 in order to manage his extensive land holdings and law practice. In 1829 he broke from the Jackson camp, abandoned a campaign as Jackson's candidate against Congressman David Crockett, and became a tireless organizer of the Whig party. Elected by the legislature as the first chancellor of West Tennessee in 1836, he served with great distinction until resigning in 1837 in order to campaign for Whig candidates. In 1847 he moved to Trenton in Gibson County, where he died in 1849.

Russell Fowler, Memphis

SUGGESTED READING: Joshua W. Caldwell, *Sketches of the Bench and Bar of Tennessee* (1898)

SEE: BLOUNT, WILLIAM; HAWKINS COUNTY; JACKSON; LAW

MILLER, RANDOLPH (ca.1830–1916), former slave and newspaper editor, was emancipated with hundreds of other African Americans on June 9, 1864, in Newton County, Georgia, as General William T. Sherman's army swept through the region. Miller came to Chattanooga in October of the same year and soon took a job as the pressman for the *Chattanooga Gazette*. Miller spent a few years in Richmond, Virginia, but returned to Chattanooga and became the pressman for the *Chattanooga Times*, which was edited and published by Adolph S. Ochs. In 1898 Miller started his own newspaper, *The Weekly Blade*, probably with the quiet support of Ochs.

Miller was well-known in both the white and black communities for his flamboyant personal and editorial style; he advanced his strong values from the columns of his newspaper. His relentless condemnation of racial segregation and civil rights restrictions was highlighted by his response to a 1905 Tennessee law segregating public transportation. Predating Dr. Martin Luther King, Jr., by 50 years, Miller and other black leaders in Chattanooga launched a briefly successful boycott of the streetcars. Miller subsequently editorialized that year: "They have taken our part of the library; they have moved our school to the frog pond; they have passed the Jim Crow law; they have knocked us out of the jury box; they have played the devil generally; and what in thunder will they do no one knows."[1]

Plagued by ill health and overwork, Miller stopped publication of the *Blade* after 12 years. He died at the reported age of 86 in 1916, and is buried in the Forest Hills Cemetery in Chattanooga.

Jerry R. Desmond, Chattanooga Regional History Museum

CITATION:

(1) Lester C. Lamon, *Black Tennesseans, 1900–1930* (Knoxville, 1977), 31.

SEE: CHATTANOOGA; CHATTANOOGA BLADE; CHATTANOOGA TIMES; OCHS, ADOLPH S.

MILLIGAN COLLEGE is located in Carter County in East Tennessee. Its origins go back to a Buffalo Male and Female Institute (1866) chartered by a small Christian (Disciples of Christ) congregation. In 1882 Josephus Hopwood upgraded it to a college named after a revered professor at Kentucky University. Hopwood, the dominating personality in the early history of the college, served as president until 1903, and coined its enduring motto, "Christian Education—the Hope of the World."

A new era began in 1917. The new president, Henry J. Derthick, a beloved "shepherd unto the hills," completed the four main buildings that survived World War II, and created a competitive liberal arts college to serve youth from the nearby mountains. In World War II the college converted all its facilities to a Navy V-12 program. A temporary postwar boom led all too quickly to near disaster. A scandal in the president's office, major faculty resignations, an overly costly sports program, and a sharp drop in enrollment (to under 300) led to near bankruptcy and a loss of regional accreditation.

The modern era began in the dark days of 1950. Dean E. Walker came from Butler University as the new president. He aligned Milligan with a conservative and independent faction (Christian Churches and Churches of Christ) within the Disciples movement. This helped win increased financial support from sympathetic individuals and congregations. The less regional and growing student body (866 in 1995–96) increasingly represented this fellowship. Milligan, with growing financial stability and a much expanded campus, regained regional accreditation in 1960.

Paul K. Conkin, Vanderbilt University
SEE: CARTER COUNTY; EDUCATION, HIGHER

MILLINGTON, MEMPHIS NAVAL AIR STATION.

Aviation at this facility, the largest inland naval base in the world, dates back to World War I, when the U.S. Army created Park Field as a training ground for air and ground crews. The Navy's presence began in 1942 when the Park Field site and adjacent areas became first a Naval Reserve Air Base, then a Naval Air Station and finally, in 1949, Naval Air State Memphis. The primary task of the base has remained the same—to train air and ground crews in the operation and maintenance of the Navy's sea- and land-based aircraft. From 1945 to 1955, however, no flight training took place at Millington.

Although Memphis firms supplied the architects and engineers involved in the initial construction, by mid-1942 Memphis-area builders were engaged in other construction projects, and firms from Chattanooga and Birmingham, Alabama, built the 8,000-foot runway, a project that eventually employed 4,000 workers.

As a primary flight training center in World War II, 600 to 800 aviation cadets trained at a time. The ground crew training facility was designed for 10,000 students. The entire complex, which included unpaved satellite fields in a 15-mile radius, covered an area of more than 3,500 acres.

In early 1943 the ground crew facility was named the Naval Air Technical Training Center (NATT); the headquarters of that command was transferred there in 1946, and all the operations of the NATT command were consolidated in 1947. The Korean War turned the temporary installation into a permanent one when $64 million was allocated for a six -year build-

ing program. By the late 1950s almost 13,000 uniformed and civilian employees were on the payroll, and the base became one of the largest employers in Shelby County, with an annual payroll of $39 million. By 1971 a reported 23,000 students rotated through the base annually. As recently as 1993, the 5,000 full-time uniformed and civilian employees and the 5,000 students assigned to the base contributed to the estimated $250 million annual value of the base to the local economy.

The Memphis Naval Air Station and associated installations, such as the Naval Hospital, are important factors in the local economy and provide a steady influx of non-southern-born Navy and Marine retirees (many with foreign-born wives) to the area's population.

Ed Frank, Mississippi Valley Collection, University of Memphis Libraries
SEE: SHELBY COUNTY; WORLD WAR II

MILTON, ABBY CRAWFORD (1881–1991), woman suffrage leader, became involved in the suffrage movement after marrying newspaper publisher George Fort Milton, moving from Georgia to Chattanooga, and giving birth to three daughters. Milton received a law degree from the Chattanooga College of Law, and although she never practiced law, she believed that legal training improved her mind and gained her credibility with the courthouse crowd. She was the last president of the Tennessee Equal Suffrage Association and the first president of the League of Women Voters of Tennessee. Like many dedicated suffragists, Milton traveled across the state giving speeches and organizing suffrage leagues in small communities.

During the height of the 1920 battle for the ratification of the Nineteenth Amendment to grant woman suffrage, Milton spent the entire month of August in Nashville lobbying members of the General Assembly to secure pro-suffrage votes. Carrie Chapman Catt, the national president, praised Milton's efforts and depicted the Nashville battle as one of the fiercest waged on behalf of woman suffrage. Fist fights broke out in the lobby of the Hermitage Hotel, where legislators, suffragists, and anti-suffragists lived during the Special Session of the Tennessee General Assembly. Anti-suffragists controlled the hotel mezzanine and plied legislators with liquor. Every morning, the lobby of the hotel filled with red roses, the anti-suffrage symbol.

After the legislature ratified the amendment and secured suffrage for all American women, Milton returned to Chattanooga, where she continued to push for legislative reforms to benefit women. She also worked to secure the creation of the Great Smoky Mountains National Park. She attended Democratic national conventions as a delegate-at-large, and, in

1924, she gave the seconding nomination speech for William Gibbs McAdoo in his unsuccessful run for the party's presidential nomination. In the late 1930s Milton ran unsuccessfully for the Tennessee State Senate, taking a stand in support of the Tennessee Valley Authority during a controversial period when the agency was involved in the takeover of local power companies.

Milton died in 1991 at the age of 110.

Carole Stanford Bucy, Volunteer State Community College
SUGGESTED READING: Carole Stanford Bucy, "The Thrill of History Making: Suffrage Memories of Abby Crawford Milton," *Tennessee Historical Quarterly* 50(1996): 224–239
SEE: HERMITAGE HOTEL; MCADOO, WILLIAM G.; MILTON, GEORGE F.; WOMAN SUFFRAGE MOVEMENT

MILTON, GEORGE FORT (1869–1924), Chattanooga newspaper publisher and Democratic political activist, was born in Macon, Georgia, and educated in Chattanooga, Tennessee. After attending the University of the South at Sewanee, Milton entered the banking business in Chattanooga. He left banking to become the editor and manager of the *Taxpayer*, a monthly publication devoted to tax reform and political issues. In 1895 he moved to Knoxville to edit the *Knoxville Sentinel*. Three years later, he accepted an appointment as first lieutenant in the Sixth United State Volunteer Infantry and remained with his regiment until the conclusion of the Spanish-American War.

In 1899 Milton returned to Knoxville and bought a two-thirds interest in the *Sentinel*; in 1901 he acquired the paper's remaining stock. While at the *Sentinel*, Milton led the fight to pass Knoxville's prohibition law in 1907. The next year, he supported former U.S. Senator Edward Ward Carmack in his race against Governor Malcolm Patterson for the Democratic gubernatorial nomination. In 1909 he bought a two-thirds interest in the *Chattanooga News*. After managing both papers for three years, Milton sold the *Sentinel* and returned to Chattanooga. In 1910 he supported the fusion movement, a coalition of Republicans and prohibition Democrats, which resulted in the election of Republican Ben W. Hooper as governor.

Milton continued to be interested in tax reform and served on a state tax commission in 1915 and 1917. He also supported Henry Ford's efforts to bring about peace in Europe prior to the United States entry into World War I in 1917. He visited Europe in 1915 and 1916 with the Ford Peace Party which worked to end the war.

Milton, whose second wife, Abby Crawford Milton, was president of the Tennessee Equal Suffrage League, served on the Men's Ratification Committee in support of the ratification of the Nineteenth Amendment. He also worked for improvements in the Tennessee River to make it navigable. Milton died in 1924 in Murfreesboro while campaigning for Democratic presidential candidate, William G. McAdoo. He is buried in Chattanooga.

Carole Stanford Bucy, Volunteer State Community College
SEE: CARMACK, EDWARD W.; CHATTANOOGA; HOOPER, BEN W.; KNOXVILLE NEWS-SENTINEL; MCADOO, WILLIAM G.; SPANISH-AMERICAN WAR; TEMPERANCE MOVEMENT; WOMAN SUFFRAGE MOVEMENT

MINING. Tennessee has a long, rich, and varied mining history. Although the industry today accounts for only about three-tenths of a percent of the state's gross products and two-tenths of a percent of nonagricultural jobs, Tennessee remains among the national leaders in some mining categories. Nonetheless, minerals and mining in the late twentieth century are scarcely mentioned in state promotional literature, a stark contrast with 100 years ago when abundant mineral resources were highly publicized among the state's attractions for investors and immigrants. In fact, as early as the 1840s, an eminent geologist observed that because of the mineral resources and water-power potential of East Tennessee "Nature had stamped it as country for manufacturing."[1] Three decades earlier a noted planter and amateur scientist from Natchez noted iron deposits near the Natchez Trace in what is now Lewis County and predicted a bright industrial future for the area.

East Tennessee Iron Company scrip.

TSLA. PHOTOGRAPH BY KARINA MCDANIEL

Tennessee has more than 70 minerals and chemicals in scattered deposits across the state, a larger number than any other southern state and among the top in the nation. Limestone and dolomite, bituminous coal, lead, zinc, ball clay, sand and gravel, phosphate, fuller's earth, petroleum, common clay and shale, barite and fluorite, marble, sandstone, copper, iron, gold, manganese, mica, tripoli, celestite, bauxite, granite, slate, and bentonite are among the products that have been mined or quarried. According to state geologists, there are a number of other potentially mineable minerals as well.

Historically, Tennessee's most important mining products have been iron, bituminous coal, copper, lead, zinc, and phosphate. Iron ore was the most significant during early settlement years. Interest in the iron ore of the Western Highland Rim dates back to the 1790s and even earlier in the eastern mountains. Early miners attacked the outcrops of ore on or close to the surface. They stripped the ore by hand or used horses or mules to pull scrapers, sometimes gouging the land to a depth of 30 feet. Where the overburden was unweathered, they sometimes blasted and hauled it away. From these pits miners extracted hematite (red ore), brown ore (mountain or valley ore), or limonite.

The commercially valuable iron ores were located in the valleys and mountains of East Tennessee and in Middle Tennessee and were processed in manufactories that supplied mostly local and regional markets. By 1860 the state ranked third nationally in iron bloomery production, with Western Highland Rim properties in Stewart, Houston, Hickman, Montgomery, and Lewis counties being particularly important. Early national census reports did not separate iron ore mining from iron production, but most early manufactures were associated with mines. By 1840 the census reported iron production from 82 furnaces, bloomeries, forges, and rolling mills in East Tennessee; 47 in Middle Tennessee; and four in West Tennessee. In 1870, however, the census reported only six producers of iron ore in the state producing just over 34,600 tons of ore worth nearly $132,000. Tennessee had fallen to ninth among 21 states in iron ore production, from its position of fourth in 1850. By 1910 the state reported 46 producing iron mines. Pit mining along surface outcrops had almost disappeared and was largely replaced by underground mining in the Euchee, Rockwood-Cardiff, and Chamberlain areas of central East Tennessee and the La Follette area of northeast Tennessee. At this point no deep shaft iron mining existed anywhere in the South.

In the early twentieth century iron mining became less and less important in Tennessee as the number of producing mines and ore production both dropped by roughly half from 1909 to 1919. By the latter year the Volunteer State contributed only half of a percent of national iron ore production. State geological studies of the period pointed to the abundant iron ore deposits and anticipated a prosperous future for the industry. A decade later, however, Tennessee had nearly disappeared from the ranks of iron-producing states, largely due to the relatively low quality and inaccessibility of its deposits. Since that time there have been only a few small and sporadic iron ore mining operations.

Iron's close companion in early industry was coal. Tennesseans began to mine coal in small quantities during the 1840s. Blacksmiths who used the coal in their shops undertook much of this activity. Unlike iron, however, coal production in the state has remained significant ever since. Tennessee coal is of the bituminous, or soft, variety and is found in extensive deposits along a northeast-southwest belt a little east of the center of the state.

Coal mining became a significant Tennessee industry only after the end of the Civil War. As late as 1840, the U.S. census reported only two coal producers in the state. By the eve of the war the number had risen to six, with nearly 400 employees, but only $423,662 in value of production. These figures changed only slightly during the next decade. Tennessee was tenth of 19 states in bituminous production, with output concentrated in Anderson, Campbell, Grundy, Hamilton, Marion, and Roane counties. By the 1850s large scale coal mining had begun, and in the 1860s J.D.B. De Bow, the famous promoter of southern industrialization, predicated that the extensive coal and iron resources of the Cumberlands would facilitate the rise of industry.

In the 1870s northern investors and businessmen bought up huge acreages in the mineral areas of Appalachia, and by the early twentieth century controlled most of the best coal districts. During the 1880s there was a five-fold increase in coal production, and employment rose to more than 4,000 workers laboring above ground and 3,400 below ground. The value of coal produced was nearly $2,340,000. By this time Tennessee was thirteenth of 29 coal-producing states and territories in value of production. Five large mines operated in the Jellico coal field, which stretched from Kentucky into the Tennessee counties of Campbell, Anderson, and Scott. Other important mining areas were in Claiborne, Morgan, Hamilton, and Marion counties. Fentress, White, Grundy, Roane, Overton, Bledsoe, Sequatchie, Rhea, Putnam, and Overton counties were also coal producers. The needs of industry stimulated production, as did the fact that railroad construction in the late nineteenth and early twentieth century made the state's coal deposits more accessible to both miners and markets. Consolidation and the opening of new and larger mines also contributed to the growing output.

By 1909 bituminous coal was the state's leading mining industry. A decade later coal mining constituted more than half of the mining enterprises in the state, employed 66 percent of mining wage earners, and contributed over 60 percent of the value of mining production. The bituminous coal industry continued to rank first among the mineral industries in Tennessee as late as 1939, although by that time it accounted for only about 46 percent of the total value of mineral products.

At the turn of the century about 85 coal operators were in the state. During the next four decades, the number of mines fluctuated, from a high of 145 in 1919 to a low of 78 in 1929, and back up to 123 in 1939. Production settled at around five million tons, while the value of production fluctuated wildly because of changing prices. As late as 1909 far more coal was produced by hand pick than by machine. Because of new technology, the number of workers in the industry steadily declined, settling in at around 7,500 by 1940. For the next 20 years production remained at about the same level, roughly six million tons mined each year, although a surge in production occurred during World War II. Production shot up again in the 1970s, reaching a peak of 11.2 million tons in 1972. During the same period, employment dropped due to increasing mechanization and the closing of marginal mines. In the mid-1970s Tennessee ranked eleventh nationally in coal production.

As late as 1940 underground mines produced practically all (99.9 percent) coal in Tennessee. The state's coal fields were not considered suitable for strip or auger mining because most were located under mountain peaks and contained relatively thin seams of the mineral. With the development of sophisticated machinery, however, strip and auger mining became increasingly important. By 1975 about 60 percent of the state's coal was strip-mined. By the early 1990s the number of coal mining establishments in Tennessee had fallen by more than two-thirds, the number of workers by three-fourths, and the value of shipments by nearly two-thirds. The major markets for Tennessee coal in recent decades have been utilities in Tennessee and neighboring states. A relatively small amount of high grade metallurgical coal has been exported, mostly to Japan.

Lead and zinc production also has origins in Tennessee's early history. Lead is found in East and Middle Tennessee, commonly in limestones and dolomites, and usually in association with zinc. The primary modern uses of lead are for storage batteries, gasoline additives, paint pigments, ammunition, and various alloys. The earliest deposits mined were at and near Bumpass Cove (Embreeville) in Washington and Unicoi counties. They were worked as early as the Revolutionary Era, while deposits in the Powell River district in Claiborne and Union coun-

ties were mined in the nineteenth century to make bullets. As late as the 1930s and 1940s the Kings Bend and Branch Hollow mines produced large quantities of zinc-lead concentrates, as did the New Prospect mine which operated almost continuously from 1883 to 1901. Other mining operations have been located in the White Pine district of Jefferson County. Some lead was mined before the Civil War in Davidson County, and by the Holt mine in Williamson County during World War I. In recent years no mines were worked exclusively for lead, but a small amount of the mineral was recovered as a by-product of copper mining in Polk County.

The first zinc mining in Tennessee occurred at Mossy Creek (Jefferson City) in 1854. Subsequently mining also occurred in Claiborne and Union counties. Other mining areas were in the Bumpass Cove region of Washington and Unicoi counties and in Bradley and Cannon counties. The early mines were mostly open-pit operations recovering ores near the surface. Once they were depleted, the industry was dominated by large underground operations such as those in Knox, Jefferson, Hawkins, Hancock, and Grainger counties. Some mines are more than 1,000 feet deep and are highly mechanized, with some ore hauled nearly two miles by electric trains before reaching the shaft to be hoisted to the surface.

While zinc production was relatively insignificant through the 1940s, by the 1960s Tennessee led the nation and was not surpassed until the 1990s by Alaska. Most of the modern production has come from a small number of large operators in the Mascot-Jefferson City district. Tennessee zinc ore is shipped to other states for smelting, and the concentrates are used to manufacture die-castings and paint pigments. The metal also is used in galvanizing and brass manufacture and for minting pennies and metal sheets for battery cases. Zinc metal is also used for the production of pharmaceuticals.

Tennessee was the only major southern producer of copper, which is considered second only to iron as an important industrial metal. Copper mining in the Volunteer State began in the middle of the nineteenth century in the Ducktown-Copperhill district, commonly known as the Copper Basin, of Polk County. The mineral was first discovered in the area in the 1840s. The Hiwassee Mine opened in 1850 and became the first deep underground mine. By 1864 there were 14 mines. The 1870 U.S. Census ranked Tennessee third nationally in value of copper production. The first smelter was established at the Eureka Mine in 1885, and it was soon followed by several others. By 1909 copper was the second leading mineral industry in Tennessee. Copper mining continued in the area until the Tennessee Chemical Company closed its mines in 1987, after 137 years of production (with only a 13-year gap).

In addition to the copper and other metals recovered from the Copper Basin's ores, in the early twentieth century sulfuric acid was recovered from the smelter effluents. Before this, sulfur dioxide was released directly into the atmosphere, reacting with water vapor to form sulfuric acid, which fell as acid rain, denuding the area of the remaining trees that had not been harvested to provide fuel for the early ore roasting process. Eventually the area shifted from a primary emphasis upon copper production, with sulfuric acid as a by-product, to the reverse situation. The acid was used in storage batteries, as a bleaching agent, and in the fertilizer, chemical, petroleum refining, paint pigment, and rayon manufacturing industries. The once denuded area of the Copper Basin is now recovering, and in 1988 the State of Tennessee purchased the Burra Burra copper mine, which operated for over 65 years from the turn of the century. It is now preserved as a historic complex and is on the National Register of Historic Places.

Tennessee was once a national leader in phosphate mining, and as late as 1990 ranked fifth in national production, even though the state produced only three percent of the nation's marketable phosphate. Three principal types of phosphate (brown, blue, and white) have been mined in the state, although most of the modern production has been of the brown variety. Production has come primarily from the four Middle Tennessee counties of Williamson, Hickman, Maury, and Giles, but there has been some mining in Davidson and Sumner counties. Brown phosphorous is exclusively mined by surface operators using drag lines and scrapers. Blue phosphorous is found in scattered deposits in Perry and Decatur counties of Middle Tennessee and Johnson County in East Tennessee. TVA mined it briefly in the 1930s, but it has been generally of little economic importance.

Through the 1930s, phosphate rock was primarily used to produce fertilizers, especially superphosphates, and in the manufacture of sodium phosphate. In recent years most of the phosphate mined in Tennessee was smelted in electric furnaces for the production of elemental phosphorus, which can be used to make many organic and inorganic chemicals with a wide variety of industrial uses. Among these are water softening and cleansing products, soaps and detergents, insecticides, incendiary military products, oil refining, food processing, and many other uses.

The 1900 U.S. Census reported 40 phosphate mines in Tennessee with nearly 1,600 employees. A decade later the Volunteer State was second among the states in phosphate production. Over the next several decades about half that number of operations existed, although there were variations from time to time. Production and revenues increased significantly, and Tennessee remained the second leading phosphate mining state. As late as the 1960s phosphate rock mining contributed about ten percent of the total value of Tennessee mineral production. Beginning in the 1970s, the number of operations dropped significantly, and by the 1980s only two were left. In 1991 both operators announced closings, ending phosphate mining and refining in Tennessee.

Marble quarrying in Tennessee has a long and interesting history. The first quarrying activities date back to the late 1840s, when stone was produced for use in construction of the Washington Monument. Early the next decade, production began in the Knoxville area, with some of the stone used in construction of the state capitol building. The reputation of Tennessee marble spread, and it became famous for its high quality and the variety of its coloration. It was widely used across the United States and in other countries, especially in the interiors of public buildings. Among the famous structures that feature extensive use of Tennessee marble are the J.P. Morgan Library in New York City, and the capitol building, National Gallery of Art, and Lincoln Memorial in Washington, D.C. By the 1920s there were 11 active marble companies and 28 quarries. After a prolonged slump during the Great Depression and World War II the industry momentarily recovered. By the late 1950s Tennessee led the United States in rough-dimension marble output, accounting for 42 percent of the nation's total value of production. As late as 1963 Tennessee ranked second in national production. After that time production and the number of operations dropped drastically. A significant recovery occurred in the late 1980s spurred by the use of Tennessee marble in some major construction projects, including the renovation of New York City's Grand Central Station. New markets have opened up with the production of "marble tiles," combining crushed marble with a binding polymer and coloring agent, but the industry still faces tough competition from producers in Italy and Spain.

A little-known, but significant Tennessee mining industry is the production of ball clay, an area in which the state ranks as the national leader. In recent years the counties of Henry, Weakley, and Carroll have provided about 70 percent of total national production. Ball clay is a fine-grained material with extreme plasticity and high bonding strength. The name comes from England, where it was mined by cutting and rolling it into ball-like chunks. Ball clay is primarily used in the manufacture of dinnerware, sanitary ware pottery, wall and floor tiles, electrical porcelain, and refractories. Ball clay minerals are also used in rubber, fiberglass, ceiling tile, wall board, and agricultural chemicals.

Pioneer Tennesseans used ball clay to make crocks, jugs, and other domestic items. It was not until World War I interrupted clay imports from

Europe, however, that the high quality of Tennessee clay was widely recognized. By the late 1980s ball clay ranked fifth in total annual revenue among minerals mined in Tennessee, and it was shipped to major markets in Mexico, Canada, the Philippines, and other parts of the world. The clay is obtained by open-pit mining, with the overburden removed by bulldozers and draglines. The clay is removed by backhoes or front-end loaders. Both the mining and processing are done by a small number of companies.

Another commercially important Tennessee clay is fuller's earth, which is also known as bloating or bleaching clay and soapstone. Its most important use is in pet waste absorbents, but it is also found in oil and grease absorbents, pesticide extenders, mineral and vegetable oil decolorizers, drilling mud, lightweight ceramic ware, and bricks used in refractories. Fuller's earth is found in Henry, Carroll, Madison, Henderson, Chester, and Hardeman counties. Mining and processing began in Henry County in the 1930s, and by the 1980s Tennessee fuller's earth ranked fifth in value nationally, and eighth among all mineral commodities produced in the state. Fuller's earth is surface mined and then trucked to plants for processing.

Common clay and shale have been mined for many years in Tennessee. They provide raw material for bricks, cement, clay pipe, and structural clay products. In the late 1980s common clay and shale from the state's open-pit mines ranked tenth among Tennessee's mineral industries. Tennessee also produced small quantities of bentonite, a fine-grained, sticky clay, that is used in oil refining, drilling mud, and as a component of foundry sand and a desiccant. While some bentonite is found in all three major regions of the state, the only significant commercial production has been in West Tennessee.

Other minerals still mined or quarried as late as the 1980s include sand and gravel, barite and fluorite, lightweight aggregate, and dimension sandstone. Minerals formerly produced commercially, but not mined or quarried in the late 1980s, are dimension limestone, gold, silver, manganese, mica, tripoli, celestite, bauxite, granite, and slate.

While Tennessee has never been a major producer of oil and gas, petroleum has been an important, if small, contributor to the state's economy. Oil production in Tennessee actually predates the famous Drake well in Pennsylvania. Pioneers drilling for brines to make salt discovered and drew petroleum from relatively shallow wells. The first commercial oil well in the state was drilled in Overton County in 1866. In the late 1980s crude oil and natural gas production combined ranked ninth in total value among the state's mineral commodities. The major producers of crude oil were in Morgan, Scott, Claiborne, and Fentress counties, while Morgan, Scott, and Fentress

counties contributed most of the natural gas. Most of Tennessee's natural gas is used for fuel, while the crude oil products include gasoline and diesel fuel (which make up about 80 percent of the total), jet and aviation fuel, kerosene, residual fuels, lubricants, and liquefied petroleum gases. Petroleum is used in the textile, plastics, and petrochemical industries.

Tennessee's rank among mining states has fallen rather steadily since the late nineteenth century, although mining and quarrying have remained significant industries. At the turn of the century, Tennessee had 241 mines and quarries, turning out products valued at $9,533,782. This ranked eighteenth among the states. A decade later there were 365 mines, wells, and quarries, and the value of production had risen to $12,692,547, which represented one percent of the national total. The leading industry was coal mining, followed in order by copper and phosphate. By 1919 coal continued to be the leading mineral product of the Volunteer State, but phosphate rock had risen to second in both the state and the nation, followed by lead-bearing zinc ores, marble, iron, and copper. The state ranked twenty-third nationally in value of production, and its total of $23,292,114 represented seven-tenths of one percent of the national figure. A decade later the number of mines and quarries in Tennessee had fallen to 189, but their total value of production had risen slightly, and it was twenty-second among the states. By 1940 Tennessee had fallen to twenty-seventh among the states in value of production. Coal production was still the state's leading mining industry and phosphate rock mining was second. The state led the nation in the value of products from its rough dimension marble industry, and was second nationally in the value of phosphate rock production. The state value of production from 240 mines and quarries was $21,951,517.

Since the 1950s Tennessee has continued to rank near the middle of the states in mineral production. In 1958 the state's 677 mines, quarries, and wells contributed just over $61 million in value added in mining, which represented one-half of one percent of the national total, and ranked the state twenty-sixth nationally. By 1963 Tennessee's value added in mining had risen to over $90 million, produced by 528 mining operations. The number of operations dropped to 352 by 1967, but the value added in mining increased to $116.2 million. The value added in mining had risen to $152.1 million by 1972, while the number of mining operations remained about the same. The number of mining operations increased to 481 by 1977, while the value added in mining jumped dramatically to $378.1 million. Inflation in the economy affected these figures.

In 1982 the state had 515 mineral establishments and the value added in mining totaled $497.7 million. By 1987 these figures had dropped to 341 and $458.4 million, respectively, and mining employment had decreased by 28 percent. By 1992 Tennessee had 291 establishments, which contributed $348.3 million in value added by mining, ranking the state thirty-first in the nation. It still led the nation in the production of ball clay, gem stones (mostly freshwater cultured pearls), and zinc while remaining among the leaders in barite, crushed stone, fuller's earth, and phosphate production. Tennessee's mineral industries are obviously less important in the state's economic mix today than in the past, though they continue to play a significant role in the state's economy.

James E. Fickle, University of Memphis

CITATION:

(1) Constantine G. Belissary, "The Rise of Industry and the Industrial Spirit in Tennessee, 1865–1885," *Journal of Southern History* 19(1953): 195.

SUGGESTED READINGS: Ronald D. Eller, *Miners, Millhands, and Mountaineers: Industrialization of the Appalachian South, 1880–1930* (1982); Robert J. Floyd, *Tennessee Rock and Mineral Resources* (Bulletin 66, State of Tennessee, Department of Conservation, Division of Geology, 1965, reprinted 1990); *Tennessee Minerals Annual* (Bulletin 83, State of Tennessee, Department of Environment and Conservation, Division of Geology, 1992)

MINNIE PEARL. Though arguably the most recognizable person in the history of country music, Sarah Ophelia Colley Cannon's name was never a household word. It was her alter-ego, Minnie Pearl, with her frilly dresses, hat with dangling price tag, and shrill greeting, "Howdee! I'm just so proud to be here!" who received the attention.

Sarah Colley was born to a prosperous family in Centerville, Tennessee, on October 25, 1912. Though the family suffered financial losses in the Great Depression, they sent Sarah to Ward-Belmont, a prestigious finishing school in Nashville, where she majored in expression. After graduation she taught dance, dramatics, and piano to local children in Centerville, but longed for a serious acting career. In 1934 she began to work for William P. Sewell, founder of a theater company that sent teams of field workers throughout the South to organize local dramatic productions. Colley soon became director of Sewell's school, training other field producers. While producing a play in Sand Mountain, Alabama, Colley met the woman who changed her life.

Stuck without lodging arrangements, Colley accepted an invitation from a kind mountain woman to share her family's small cabin. The woman, who Colley later credited as the inspiration for Minnie Pearl, impressed the would-be actress with her

Minnie Pearl sits between Dean Martin and David Jansen.

THE MINNIE PEARL MUSEUM, OPRYLAND USA

humorous view of life. Her droll stories and impeccable timing affected Colley deeply. Soon after she left the woman's home, Colley began repeating the stories and eventually performed them in character.

While performing at a Lions Club event, WSM radio program director Harry Stone spotted her and offered her a Grand Ole Opry audition. Soon "Minnie Pearl" was traveling with Roy Acuff's tent show. When Colley turned out to be less than the seasoned performer Acuff assumed she was, he dismissed her. More determined than ever to develop a strong comic character, Colley transformed Minnie into a man-crazy country girl with a whole cast of characters who provided material for gossip from her fictional home town of Grinder's Switch. She became a Grand Ole Opry favorite and remained so for over 50 years.

Off stage, Colley married Army Air Corps pilot Captain Henry Cannon in 1947 and he devoted himself to her career. At his request, she temporarily stopped traveling with the Opry road shows and dedicated her extra time to charities such as Vanderbilt Children's Hospital, the National Heart Association, and the American Cancer Society. Through her involvement, Cannon also managed to smooth a rift that existed between Nashville society and the country music industry. The social elite were not thrilled to see the "Athens of the South" transformed into "Hillbilly Heaven." Cannon managed to move between the two communities, offending neither. In addition to many humanitarian awards, Cannon was inducted into the Country Music Hall of Fame in 1975 and received a National Medal of the Arts in 1991.

In 1985 Cannon was diagnosed with breast cancer, and after undergoing a double mastectomy, devoted her time to education and counseling. In 1991 Centennial Medical Center dedicated its cancer unit to her name. Cannon continued to perform as Minnie Pearl on the Grand Ole Opry, and the television programs *Hee Haw* and *Nashville Now,* until she suffered a stroke in June 1991. She died March 3, 1996. A tireless entertainer and philanthropist, "Minnie Pearl" remains one of America's most beloved entertainers.

Brenda Colladay, Middle Tennessee State University
SEE: ACUFF; ROY; GRAND OLE OPRY; HICKMAN COUNTY

MISSISSIPPI RIVER MUSEUM is dedicated to the preservation and promotion of the natural and cultural history of the Lower Mississippi River Valley, a region that stretches from Cairo, Illinois, to the Gulf of Mexico. Situated on a 52-acre park in downtown Memphis, the facility was constructed in the late 1970s and opened to the public in July 1982 as part of the Mud Island river theme park. Today, the City of Memphis owns the museum and operates it under the Memphis Park Commission. The museum is comprised of 18 galleries that showcase 10,000 years of history in the lower Mississippi River

Valley and that contain a permanent collection of over 5,000 artifacts.

The first gallery presents a history of the origin of the Mississippi River, the first inhabitants to settle in the valley, the exploration and settlements by Europeans, and the basic modes of transportation employed by these cultures. Reproductions of Paleo and Archaic projectile points and tools, as well as pottery from Mississippi Woodland cultures provide examples of life in the Lower Mississippi Valley some 10,000 years ago. Interpretive panels emphasize the migratory origins of Native Americans, the distinctly colder climate, and prehistoric plant and animal life.

Four galleries trace the evolution of transportation on the river from the earliest canoes through the golden age of steamboats and finally to modern diesel towboats. The search for more efficient transportation and the economic impact of river transportation played a vital role in the development of trade routes and the growth of river cities. These galleries include numerous dioramas of river characters, detailed boat models, and a full-scale reproduction of the front one-third section of an 1870s steam packet boat.

The strategic importance of the Mississippi River during the Civil War and the military campaigns initiated by both Union and Confederate forces are emphasized in five galleries of the museum. The major battles that occurred on the Mississippi, as well as those on the Tennessee and Cumberland rivers, are highlighted. The war on the river comes alive with a simulated battle between a Confederate river battery and a scale reproduction of the front one-third section of a Union ironclad gunboat. Personal artifacts and government-issued equipment from both sides are displayed.

Five galleries trace the origins of the Blues as a distinct musical form originating in the Mississippi Delta region and emphasize the importance of its effect on other types of music including Jazz, Ragtime, urban Blues, and Rock-n-Roll. Charley Patten, W.C. Handy, Scott Joplin, Papa Dee, and Elvis Presley are represented with video programs that provide biographical histories.

The final gallery combines the mechanical and engineering aspects of river machinery with the environmental flora and fauna. It also contains a changing exhibit gallery that promotes various aspects of the people and culture of the Mississippi River.

Trey Giuntini, Mississippi River Museum
SEE: MISSISSIPPI RIVER SYSTEM; MEMPHIS MUSIC SCENE; STEAMBOATS

MISSISSIPPI RIVER SYSTEM. The 3,658 miles of the Mississippi River makes it one of the longest rivers in the world. Its drainage basin covers two-fifths of the continental United States, extending from western

Pennsylvania to Idaho and from Canada to the Gulf of Mexico. The Mississippi basin covers more than 1,245,000 square miles, and only the Amazon and Congo basins surpass its size.

The Mississippi Alluvial Flood Plain (otherwise called the Valley or Bottom) begins at Cape Girardeau, Missouri, and extends 1,000 miles down the river. The valley covers 35,460 square miles and extends the length of Tennessee's western edge, ranging in width from ten to 14 miles at an elevation of 250 to 300 feet above sea level. Spring rains and melting snows bring annual floods, carrying away 400 million tons of soil annually. Geologists speculate that the bay of the Gulf of Mexico once reached north to Cairo, Illinois, and the ancient mouth of the Mississippi. Centuries of siltation have filled the ancient bay to an area beyond New Orleans.

The river meanders over the valley in great bends and curves, creating islands, oxbow lakes (or bayous), swamps, natural levees, and fossil river beds. The river moves often. Reelfoot Lake was created from its waters during the December 1811 and January 1812 New Madrid earthquakes. Portions of Tennessee once on the east bank when the state was created, such as Centennial Island in Tipton County, now lie on the west bank. The river builds large necks of land, around which it loops until it breaks through in a cut off, creating a new channel.

The rich soils of the Mississippi Valley are also found along the river's main Tennessee tributaries— the Forked Deer River system including the Obion River and the South Forked Deer, the Hatchie River, and the Wolf River. The sluggish currents of the West Tennessee streams flow northwest between earthen banks before turning southwest some 15 miles from the Mississippi. Loess deposits, 50-foot deep drifts of soil deposited by wind as Ice-Age glaciers retreated in the Great Plains, top the bluffs above the valley and mark its edge.

Standing at Hales Point in Lauderdale County, or any one of a number of Tennessee landings, it is easy to understand the awe which gave rise to the Native American name for the river, "Father of Waters." The river became a major migration and trade route for Native Americans. Along the banks of the broad, surging river, the Mississippian culture arose with its large cities and temple mounds. Chucalissa, now in Memphis, is a reconstructed town from that period.

Once Europeans learned of the river, it became the target of diplomatic and territorial battles between the French, Spanish, and English, who viewed the river system as the key to an inland North American empire. As early as 1513 the Mississippi River appeared on Spanish maps, but the first European to see the river was probably Hernando de Soto, who reached the river with his party of Spanish explorers in May 1541 at a spot reportedly near Memphis.

By the time the French arrived only a remnant of the Mississippian nations survived, and the Chickasaws claimed the Tennessee region along the river. In birch-bark canoes Pere Jacques Marquette and Louis Joliet passed by the future state in 1673. Robert Cavelier de La Salle and his men landed near the mouth of the Hatchie in 1682, where they constructed Fort Prudhomme. Following these early explorations, the French settled the middle Mississippi Valley in the early 1700s, trading down river to the French port of New Orleans.

In 1763 the Spanish gained control of New Orleans and attempted to assert their rights in the Tennessee region, which was also claimed by England and later the United States. In 1785, in an effort to establish land warrant claims, North Carolina sent Henry Rutherford to survey the "Western District." Beginning at Key Corner, he laid out land grants on Coal Creek Bluff. In 1795 the Spanish became concerned about American activities in the territory along the Mississippi and sent Don Miguel Gayoso de Lemos to erect Fort San Fernando de las Barrancas near the Chickasaw Bluffs at the mouth of the Wolf River. The struggle for control of the east bank ended with the Treaty of San Lorenzo (1795), and the Spanish dismantled Fort San Fernando in 1797. The United States took control of the Mississippi Valley in 1803 with the Louisiana Purchase.

A brisk traffic in flatboats and keelboats carried Middle Tennessee pork, corn, whiskey, and hides down the Mississippi to New Orleans, where goods and boats were sold; crews returned home by way of the Natchez Trace. The first steamboat on the Mississippi, the *New Orleans*, passed by Tennessee in December 1811, and the crew witnessed the destructive force of the New Madrid earthquake.

In 1818 the Chickasaws relinquished their claims to the Western District, and settlement began in the Mississippi Valley. Towns quickly sprang up on the Tennessee bank of the river, and the steamboat trade flourished. By 1834 some 230 steamboats plied the Mississippi. Memphis emerged as an inland port city and a destination for immigrants arriving in the United States through New Orleans. Towns along the Mississippi tributaries benefited as well. The Forked Deer was navigable for steamboats to Dyersburg, although a few managed to reach Jackson. The Hatchie was navigable for several miles, and some boats went as far as Bolivar, though this area could not as easily engage in shipping despite its rich agricultural land.

Little was done to improve navigation on Tennessee's Mississippi tributaries except for the clearing of snags and driftwood and the removal of overhanging trees. Rotting, sunken keelboats became one of the greatest barriers to navigation on the Forked Deer. In 1838 the Tennessee General

Assembly appropriated $93,000 for improvement of the Obion, Forked Deer, and Hatchie rivers, but most improvements depended on local efforts. The Civil War disrupted the river trade and the development of Tennessee towns. Union strategy targeted control of the Mississippi River. Confederate fortifications at Island #10 fell on April 8, 1862. Federal forces took Fort Pillow on June 5, 1862, and Memphis surrendered the next day.

Beginning in 1879, with the creation of the Mississippi River Commission of the U.S. Army Corps of Engineers, the federal government assumed a more active role in making improvements, controlling floods, and maintaining navigation on the Mississippi. The Corps created cut-offs, built levees, laid revetments, and opened spillways. The grass-covered earthen levees built by the Corps along the river and its tributaries averaged 21 feet in height. Revetments, now mats constructed of connected concrete slabs, were laid on banks to prevent erosion. Twentieth century methods of flood control also include restoration of wetlands and bottom-land forests. New Deal agencies also funded and/or worked on flood control, river navigation, and recreation.

Modes of river transportation changed as well. By 1930 diesel-powered tugboats and barges had replaced the last of the steamboats. Since World War II, intensive agricultural practices and the draining of wetlands to create new cropland greatly increased erosion in the Valley. The loess soils, stable at vertical cuts, erode quickly from the flatter slopes that are plowed. Choked streams caused by the erosional run-off and siltation became a major problem in West Tennessee. In 1948 Congress authorized the West Tennessee Tributaries Project to help residents struggling with the problems associated with the rivers. Through the program, the Corps of Engineers channelized more than 20 percent of the 350 miles of streams in the Obion-Forked Deer basin. Channelization was used to minimize flooding and drain wetlands for cropland. Although providing relief to farmers in the immediate area, it often increased flooding downstream. A series of environmental law suits, most notably the landmark *Akers v. Resor,* have held up channelization as of 1996. In the 1990s the Hatchie River, designated a Tennessee Scenic River, is the only major tributary below Cairo, Illinois, to escape channelization. One of the world's natural wonders, the Mississippi River system looms large in the history and culture of Tennessee, and residents living along its banks continue to search for ways to live in harmony with its strength.

Ann Toplovich, Tennessee Historical Society

SUGGESTED READING: Norah Deakin Davis, *The Father of Waters: A Mississippi River Chronicle* (1982)

SEE: CHICKASAWS; CHUCALISSA VILLAGE; COTTON; EARTHQUAKES; FLOODS OF 1937; FORT PRUDHOMME; FORT SAN FERNANDO; FORT PILLOW; ISLAND #10; MEMPHIS; MISSISSIPPIAN CULTURE; REELFOOT LAKE STATE PARK; SOTO EXPEDITION; STEAMBOATING; U.S. ARMY CORPS OF ENGINEERS

MISSISSIPPIAN CULTURE refers to the late prehistoric cultures of the southeastern United States dating from ca. A.D. 900 to 1600. In general, Mississippian culture is divided chronologically into emergent, early, and late periods. Based on differences in culture traits, particularly ceramics and mortuary patterns, distinct Mississippian cultures are identified in West, Middle, and East Tennessee. In general, changes in Mississippian cultures chronicle the development of intensive agriculture based on the cultivation of corn and reflect associated development of complex religious, social, and political organization. These developments are expressed in the size and density of settlements; the construction of elaborate earthen mounds upon which were erected public buildings; and the occurrence of numerous burials often accompanied by elaborate grave goods.

Mississippian cultures manufactured an abundance of ceramic vessels for utilitarian and ceremonial uses. In contrast to preceding cultures, a distinguishing characteristic of virtually all Mississippian ceramics is that the clay was tempered with crushed river mussel and snail shells. Mississippian vessels included a wide variety of globular jars, bowls, shallow pans, and bottles. These were sometimes decorated with fabric or cord impressions or with incised lines, or more frequently the surface was left undecorated. Flat strap handles or circular loop handles were added to vessels. Some of the most elaborate vessels are bottles manufactured in the shape of animals such as dogs or owls, or bowls with animal and human effigies. Bottles and bowls were painted red with iron oxide overall or in broad curved patterns.

Mississippian period people also excelled in the manufacture of stone, shell, and copper objects. Besides finely made small triangular arrow points and numerous utilitarian tools for cutting, scraping, and chopping, Dover chert from West Tennessee was made into large and elaborate knives, swords, and discs used for ritual purposes. Large shells from the Gulf and Atlantic coasts also were cut into ceremonial drinking vessels or gorgets depicting supernaturally endowed creatures including woodpeckers, rattlesnakes, and spiders. Other shells were made into elaborate ear pins and hair decorations or into a wide variety of beads which were worn on the arms, legs, and neck. Cold hammered copper was fashioned into thin embossed decorations in the shapes of abstract arrows and supernatural beings which were used as parts of headdresses and ritual clothing. Beads, ear spools, and other body adornments also were constructed from copper.

An important defining criteria for Mississippian culture was the development and dependence on intensive maize agriculture. Mississippians also continued to grow plants such as chenopod, sunflowers, and squash which had been domesticated much earlier. By A.D. 1000 beans had been incorporated into the diet, and between 1200 and 1400 farming of the large fertile river bottoms that surrounded Mississippian settlements on the Tennessee, Cumberland, and Mississippi rivers and their larger tributaries was well established. Wild plants, but especially hickory nuts, acorns, walnuts, and chestnuts, were utilized. Deer, turkey, raccoon, and bear were the most important animal resources, but also used in large numbers were various aquatic turtles, fish, and birds such as passenger pigeons and migratory waterfowl.

Mississippian social and political patterns largely are inferred from the size, organization, and complexity of settlements, but more importantly from patterns in mortuary behavior. Emergent and early Mississippian cultures exhibit progressively greater cultural elaboration in this regard, which culminates in the well-known highly complex and sophisticated late Mississippian cultures. Mississippian settlement consisted of large towns, intermediate size towns, small hamlets, and individual farmsteads, as well as hunting camps, and camps for the exploitation of different plants and animals. This pattern is especially evident during the late Mississippian period after about A.D. 1400. Large towns were often enclosed by a palisade and occupied two to ten acres. The largest such sites surely served as regional civic-ceremonial centers. Within the village were square or rectangular wattle and daub houses and their associated work and storage areas for 200 to 600 people. These buildings were situated around a central plaza. At one end of the plaza was an earthen mound referred to as a substructure or temple mound. Buildings erected on the summit of these mounds were used by priests and chiefs to conduct ceremonies and rituals. In some instances the buildings also served as their residences while in other instances additional buildings were placed there for that purpose. Often located on the plaza opposite the primary mound were one or more additional mounds which usually served mortuary functions.

Mississippian people engaged in elaborate ritual that surely reflected their beliefs in the supernatural and helped them define, maintain, and replicate complex patterns of political and social organization. These patterns are especially evident from the study of mortuary ritual in late Mississippian times. Burials reflect an individual's status at death, and most individuals of all ages and both sexes are buried in village areas. These people have few or no grave associates except for utilitarian objects such as cooking vessels. Mortuary mounds and small cemetery areas, often near mounds, contain burials interred with greater ritual and more numerous and different kinds of artifacts, suggesting that they enjoyed a more privileged social position which they had likely inherited. Individuals with the highest status were almost always adult males, buried in temple mounds or cemeteries, and frequently accompanied by the best crafted stone, ceramic, shell, and copper objects. These types and styles of objects were clearly restricted to the most powerful individuals in Mississippian society—the political, military, and religious leaders of the society.

Much of the elaborate ritual and belief system evident at Mississippian sites in Tennessee was shared by cultures across the southeastern United States. This collective cultural experience is identified as the Southeastern Ceremonial Complex. Unifying aspects to this complex were warfare, fertility, and ancestor worship. Ancestor worship was critical to the ruling political and religious leaders because this was the source of their power and authority. Fertility is evident by the fact that much of the iconography found on Mississippian artifacts appears to represent or symbolize reproduction in both natural and supernatural contexts. The representations of symbolic weapons, war costumes, and the use of raptors, especially falcons, also are prevalent motifs in Southeastern Ceremonial Complex artifacts, indicating an intense and pervasive interest in war.

In East Tennessee, Mississippian cultures are well known from the upper Tennessee River valley and its major tributaries, especially the Little Tennessee and Clinch rivers. Martin Farm culture represents emergent Mississippian occupations, while Hiwassee Island and Dallas cultures respectively represent early and late Mississippian cultures in the region. Martin Farm settlements consisted of a small settlement usually smaller than two hectares. Small platform mounds upon which were built community buildings and a village plaza were the focal points for individual rectangular houses surrounding these features. Houses had wattle and daub walls on a frame of upright posts; the roofs were gabled or arched and covered with sheets of bark stripped from trees. Evidence for palisades enclosing the settlements has not been identified. Early Mississippian settlements were similar in their spatial organization, but there is evidence that individual villages were larger and more numerous than in the preceding period. Dallas culture maintains the same fundamental organizational pattern, but unlike the preceding period there are abundant human interments.

In Middle Tennessee, Mississippian cultures are best defined in the Duck and Cumberland river valleys. Regional cultures respectively representing early and late Mississippian manifestations include the Jonathan Creek and Tinsley Hill cultures in the Lower Tennessee-Cumberland River valley. Middle Cumberland culture is used to describe Mississippian occupations in the Nashville Basin, where Harpeth River, Dowd, and Thurston cultures generally represent chronological development in the region. As in most areas, some sites like Mound Bottom on the Harpeth River exhibit long and complex developmental histories. Here and elsewhere in the Middle Cumberland area large cemeteries are found with individuals interred in boxes constructed from limestone slabs, and hence referred to as stone box graves. These burials often contain associated artifacts, especially ceramic vessels. In West Tennessee along the Mississippi River and in the vicinity of Reelfoot Lake emergent, early, and late Mississippian cultures have received a variety of designations. Among the best documented is the Walls culture which includes bluff top villages such as Chucalissa near Memphis. There is evidence that after ca. A.D. 1450 much of West Tennessee and parts of the Cumberland-Tennessee valley were either abandoned by Mississippian societies or their settlements were so fundamentally reorganized that occupation is difficult to detect. What might have led to such occurrence is not known. In East Tennessee, no comparable pattern is evident.

When Europeans entered the southeastern United States in the sixteenth century, they encountered Mississippian cultures. Hernando de Soto surely visited Mississippian villages in East and West Tennessee. Largely because of warfare and European introduced diseases, Mississippian cultures with their large village populations and complex social, political, and religious organization no longer existed by the beginning of the seventeenth century. A century later, the remnants of Mississippian culture regenerated as the historic Native Americans of Tennessee—especially the Chickasaws in the West and the Cherokees in the East.

Gerald F. Schroedl, University of Tennessee, Knoxville
SUGGESTED READINGS: David Dye and C.A. Cox, eds., *Towns and Temples Along the Mississippi* (1990); Robert Ferguson, *The Middle Cumberland Culture* (1972); T.M.N. Lewis and Madeline Kneberg, *Hiwassee Island* (1946); and Charles H. McNutt, ed., *Prehistory of the Central Mississippi Valley* (1996)
SEE: CHUCALISSA VILLAGE; CHOTA; DUCK RIVER TEMPLE MOUNDS; MOUND BOTTOM; MYER, WILLIAM E.; SOTO EXPEDITION; TOQUA

MITCHELL, HARRY LELAND (1906–1989), one of the founders of the Southern Tenant Farmers Union and president of the National Farm Labor Union, was born near Halls, in Lauderdale County, the son of James Y. Mitchell, a tenant farmer and Baptist preacher. Mitchell graduated from Halls High School in 1924, and shortly thereafter became a sharecrop-

per near Ripley, Lauderdale County. He married Lyndell Cannack, a teacher, on December 26, 1926 and operated a dry-cleaning business in Tyronza, Arkansas, from 1927 to 1934. Mitchell married a second time in 1951, to Dorothy Dowe.

With 17 others, Mitchell founded the Southern Tenant Farmers Union (STFU) in 1934, serving as its executive secretary from 1934 to 1939, and from 1941 to 1944. Mitchell organized tenant farmers during 1934 and led strikes in Arkansas and Tennessee in early 1935. These brought national attention to the STFU, and by 1937 some 30,000 tenant farmers and sharecroppers had joined. Mitchell lost faith in orthodox union tactics after the failure of several strikes. He emphasized the role of the STFU as a special interest group. Mitchell affiliated with the politically-sensitized Congress of Industrial Organizations and merged, reluctantly, with the Communist-led United Cannery, Agricultural, Packing and Allied Workers of America (UCAPAWA) in 1937. After numerous quarrels with UCAPAWA president Donald J. Henderson over STFU autonomy, Mitchell left the UCAPAWA in 1939. He was elected president of the STFU in 1944, and led the union into the American Federation of Labor (AFL) under the National Farm Labor Union (NFLU). He served as president of the NFLU, from 1945 to 1955, and its successor, the National Agricultural Workers Union (NAWU), AFL-CIO, from 1955 to 1960.

Although the STFU failed to accomplish its goals in the 1930s, Mitchell and others showed considerable personal courage as they stood up to local planters. Through their efforts, the STFU gained national attention for the problems of sharecroppers and tenants and won occasional economic victories.
Joseph Y. Garrison, Tennessee Historical Commission
SEE: LABOR; LAUDERDALE COUNTY

MONROE COUNTY, named in honor of President James Monroe, is located along the North Carolina border in the southeastern corner of Tennessee. Its beautiful landscape includes the Appalachian Mountains, approximately 145,380 acres of Cherokee National Forest, the Bald River Falls on the Tellico River, and the Little Tennessee River. The modern Cherohala Skyway, a scenic byway, connects Tellico Plains to Robbinsville, North Carolina.

In 1819 the Tennessee General Assembly established the county from lands formerly belonging to the Overhill Cherokees. Despite the destruction of several Cherokee village sites by Tellico Lake in the late 1970s, Monroe County still possesses extremely significant historical sites associated with the Cherokees and the Native American heritage of Tennessee. Toqua was a large Mississippian village along the Little Tennessee River. Great Talequah was a principal Overhill Cherokee town initially visited by South

Carolina fur traders in the late seventeenth century. Tanasi was the principal Cherokee political center of the early eighteenth century while by the mid-1750s Chota emerged as the principal town, remaining so until the treaty era began in the late eighteenth century. Fort Loudoun, the first permanent English settlement in present-day Tennessee, was established along the Little Tennessee River in 1756–1757. In 1760 Sequoyah, the originator of the Cherokee syllabary, was born at the nearby village of Tuskegee. Today, the Sequoyah Birthplace Museum documents his contributions to Cherokee culture and history as well as the Cherokee legacy in Tennessee. Another important site concerning early relations with the United States and the Cherokees is Tellico Blockhouse, a former federal agency established in 1794 near the site of Fort Loudoun. The first major gold mining sites in the state also are in Monroe County, where placer mining took place along Coker Creek in 1831–1834.

Madisonville is the county seat and the National Register-listed Monroe County Courthouse (1897), designed by Baumann Brothers and Company of Knoxville in Classical Revival style, dominates the historic town square. The construction of the new courthouse coincided with plans of the Louisville and Nashville Railroad to build a new line linking Atlanta and Knoxville which would pass directly through Madisonville, giving the county its second major railroad line. The Cannon-Stickley House, a two-story brick central hall dwelling with an impressive double Greek Revival-style portico, documents the town's antebellum past. Madisonville is also home to the historic Hiwassee College, which was established in 1849, and is the birthplace of U.S. Senator C. Estes Kefauver (1903–1963), the Democratic nominee for Vice President in 1956, and John C. Vaughn (1824–1875), who served in the Mexican War and later as a brigadier general for the Confederacy. Vaughn commanded the cavalry brigade which escorted President Jefferson Davis during his flight from Richmond in 1865.

Sweetwater, located along the original route of the East Tennessee and Georgia Railroad (later the Southern Railway) and the historic Lee Highway (U.S. 11), is the county's largest town and industrial center. It is home to the former Tennessee Military Institute (TMI), established by Dr. J. Lynn Bachman in 1874 as the Sweetwater Military College. The school operated as TMI from 1902 to 1975 when it became TMI Academy. Now the campus is home to Tennessee Meiji Gakuin, a high school for Japanese students. During the Civil War, Sweetwater was a strategic railroad town, serving as a key supply depot for the Confederacy in mid- to late 1863. East of Sweetwater, on Tennessee 68, is the Lost Sea, a huge underground lake that has been an important tourist destination throughout the twentieth century.

Tellico Plains, located on the western boundary of the Cherokee National Forest, was a late nineteenth and early twentieth century logging and industrial town, controlled largely by Charles Andrew Scott (1866–1930), whose Classical Revival mansion of 1912 has been listed in the National Register. The first industrial works in the county, however, date to iron works of the early 1800s operated by Cherokee residents. James Bradley and Michael Carroll acquired the property in 1824 but Elisha Johnson bought the Tellico Iron Works in 1846, operating them until they were destroyed by Union troops in 1864. Ray Jenkins (1897–1960), a famous defense attorney, was born at Tellico Plains.

The construction of Tellico Dam by the Tennessee Valley Authority during the 1970s reshaped the county's landscape while creating new economic opportunities, especially in recreation. While TVA's plans for Timberlake City (1967–1975) never fully materialized, construction of Tellico Dam continued throughout the decade, although final completion was delayed for years due to controversies surrounding the project's impact on the snail darter, an endangered species; the environment; and historic Cherokee sites. In September 1979 President Jimmy Carter regretfully signed a federal law allowing the dam to be closed and Tellico Lake to be completed.

Carroll Van West, Middle Tennessee State University

SEE: CHEROKEE NATIONAL FOREST; CHOTA; DE BRAHAM, JOHN W.G.; FORT LOUDOUN; HIWASSEE COLLEGE; JENKINS, RAY; KEFAUVER, C. ESTES; OCONASTOTA; OVERHILL CHEROKEES; SEQUOYAH; TELLICO BLOCKHOUSE; TENNESSEE VALLEY AUTHORITY; TIMBERLAKE, HENRY; TOQUA

MONTEAGLE SUNDAY SCHOOL ASSEMBLY. In 1882, a group of Tennessee Sunday School workers organized an assembly patterned after Chautauqua, New York, which had been founded in 1873 to train Sunday School teachers during the summer. That fall, a site selection committee accepted an offer from Monteagle, Tennessee, and the Tennessee Coal and Railroad Company to establish an assembly on the Cumberland Plateau. The railroad and John Moffatt, the town's founder, each gave the assembly $5,000 grants. The railroad also donated approximately 1,100 acres of land.

The assembly's charter was drawn on October 16, 1882. During the first season in 1883, more than 1,000 people attended events. Families either camped in tents erected on the 96-acre grounds or stayed at a hotel in town. Children's activities were held in a tent.

The next year, assembly members began constructing their own cottages on leased lots. Most were one or one and one-half stories high with gable roofs and board and batten, shingle, or weather board siding. Today, Monteagle Sunday School Assembly has 161 cottages, most built before 1930.

The first public building erected was an amphitheater, built in 1883. A rough, circular building which seated 2,500, it was replaced in 1901. Today's auditorium, which seats 1,500 people, was built in 1927 after the second auditorium burned. The oldest building still standing is a gymnasium built in 1884. During its early years, the gymnasium housed annual physical education summer schools.

In 1884 the Nashville House was built to provide free lodging for Nashville public school teachers. The Memphis, Alabama, and Mississippi homes opened later in the decade.

Before 1900, a month-long Normal School, free to public and private school teachers, was popular. In 1901 Peabody College held a summer school at Monteagle. Soon, however, Peabody, the University of Tennessee, and the University of the South began offering their own summer classes, curtailing attendance at the assembly's academic schools.

Early in the twentieth century, guest orchestras presented concerts on the mall twice daily. Excursion trains brought music lovers from Chattanooga, Huntsville, and Nashville to attend the heavily publicized events.

The Monteagle Sunday School Assembly's purpose, as stated in its charter, was for "the advancement of Science, Literary Attainment, Sunday School interests, and the promotion of the broadest popular culture in the interest of Christianity, without respect to sect or denomination." Initially, most members were Baptist or Methodist. Later, more Episcopalians and Presbyterians, and smaller numbers from other Protestant denominations, became members. Traditionally, different ministers come to assembly each week of the season to conduct twilight prayers and preach on Sunday mornings.

The assembly has become increasingly secular since World War II. Almost forgotten are the days when card playing, mixed-sex swimming, alcohol, and dancing were prohibited. The swimming pool and tennis courts are heavily used, and porch parties are popular. The assembly's six-week-long program includes children's activities, twilight prayers, and lectures. Attendees often represent the sixth or seventh generation of families that have been "on the mountain." Despite changes that have occurred over the more than 100 years of its existence, Monteagle Sunday School Assembly remains a mecca for young families, whose children find a freedom there often denied them elsewhere.

Ridley Wills II, Franklin

SEE: GRUNDY COUNTY; SUMMER SCHOOL OF THE SOUTH

MONTGOMERY BELL ACADEMY. Of the more than one dozen boys' schools established in Middle Ten-

nessee at the turn of the century, only Montgomery Bell Academy (MBA) remains in operation as such at the end of the twentieth century. Founded in 1867 as the preparatory department of the University of Nashville, MBA carries the name of Montgomery Bell (1769–1855), an early Tennessee iron master, who left $20,000 in his will for the school's establishment. Through the University of Nashville and its predecessor schools—Cumberland College and Davidson Academy—MBA's roots go back to 1785, when the North Carolina General Assembly authorized the establishment of Davidson Academy.

Today, MBA is one of the leading Independent schools in the United States. Its long tradition of producing gentlemen as well as scholars and athletes, and meeting high expectations, has given the school exceptionally strong constituent support and alumni loyalty. In recent years, broad-based programs in art, drama, and music achieved the same standards of excellence that have characterized more traditional programs such as English, debate, and foreign languages.

MBA also has a long and distinguished athletic history. In 1955 the school fielded 32 teams in 11 sports. From 1950 to 1955, MBA's varsity record in those 11 sports was 655 wins against 210 losses. One of the reasons MBA's athletic programs remain strong is because of the high percentage of students who participate in team sports.

Ridley Wills II, Franklin

SEE: BELL, MONTGOMERY; EDUCATION, ELEMENTARY AND SECONDARY

MONTGOMERY BELL STATE PARK is located along U.S. Highway 70 in Dickson County, approximately 30 miles west of Nashville. This 3,782-acre recreational area bears the name of the wealthy industrialist who established the second iron furnace west of the Allegheny Mountains. The park holds several historical resources, including the remains of Laurel Furnace, one of the state's early manufacturing sites. The ore pits and furnace originally belonged to Colonel Richard Napier, who received the acreage as part of a Revolutionary War land grant. The park is also the site of the early nineteenth century house of Samuel McAdow. In 1810 the McAdow dwelling became the "birthplace" of the Cumberland Presbyterian Church, when dissident Presbyterian ministers met there and held the first Synod of the new church.

Montgomery Bell State Park originated as a project of the National Park Service. After the Park Service announced its intention of creating five parks in the Midstate, Dickson County business leaders successfully sought a park for their area. They persuaded federal representatives that the proposed site met Resettlement Administration criteria of submarginal land, and simultaneously offered a beautiful natural landscape.

Three New Deal agencies assisted the Park Service in the construction of the park: the Public Works Administration (PWA), Works Progress Administration (WPA), and Civilian Conservation Corps (CCC). The National Park Service officially designated the site as a recreational demonstration area, and construction began in 1935. Three CCC companies worked at Montgomery Bell State Park, including Company 4495, a Junior African-American group that arrived from Knoxville in December 1935. Company 4495 built Lake Acorn and Lake Woodhaven. By 1938 the park held a beach, bathhouse, boating facilities, picnic and camp area, a mess hall, administration building, and group cabins, probably constructed by Company 4495. The work of the PWA is less clearly documented, but probably included a group of Girl Scout cabins that remain in the park today.

Company 3464 arrived in 1941 from Cumberland Mountain State Park, followed shortly by Company 4497 from Wartburg, Tennessee. These two groups relieved Company 4495 of its duties and completed the park's construction during the early 1940s. The lakes are the only CCC facilities constructed at the park. The last CCC-built building, a tool shed north of the visitor's center, was razed in 1990.

Montgomery Bell State Park remained under National Park Service jurisdiction until 1943, when the original 5,000-acre tract, including the park and its surrounding forest, was deeded to the Tennessee Department of Conservation. One of the state's most heavily visited recreational sites, Montgomery Bell State Park preserves and promotes the area's rich history and sublime landscape. The park serves as the annual reunion site for Tennessee's former Civilian Conservation Corps "boys," who gather each spring to reminisce and enjoy the beauty of their work.

Ruth D. Nichols, Nashville

SEE: BELL, MONTGOMERY; CIVILIAN CONSERVATION CORPS; CUMBERLAND PRESBYTERIAN CHURCH; DICKSON COUNTY; MCADOW, SAMUEL; PUBLIC WORKS ADMINISTRATION; WORKS PROGRESS ADMINISTRATION

MONTGOMERY COUNTY. Long before the dawn of written history, humans inhabited the lands along the Cumberland and Red Rivers. In successive order Paleoindian, Archaic, Woodland, and Mississippian Indians have left evidence of their occupancy in this area. Knowledge of the Tennessee and Cumberland rivers led to the historic journey of John Donelson with his flotilla of flatboats and an excerpt from Donelson's journal notes that on April 12, 1780, Moses Renfroe and company took leave of the main party, ascended the Red River and made a short-lived settlement upstream.

By the early 1780s three principal stations were in the Cumberland-Red River area: Prince's Station, established in 1782, near Sulphur Fork and Red River; Neville's Station founded ca. 1784 between Prince's Station and Clarksville; and Clarksville, the only station to become a city, established near the confluence of the Cumberland and Red Rivers. In January 1784 John Montgomery and Martin Armstrong surveyed the present site of Clarksville and proceeded to sell lots. The town, established by North Carolina in 1785, was named for General George Rogers Clark, Indian fighter and Revolutionary War leader.

In 1796 when Tennessee became the sixteenth state, Tennessee County, of which Clarksville was a part, was divided into Montgomery and Robertson counties, with Clarksville the county seat of Montgomery County. The name Montgomery honored John Montgomery, who was a founder of Clarksville as well as a Revolutionary War leader. By 1797 Clarksville contained 30 houses, a courthouse and a jail. Cultivation of tobacco in Montgomery County antedates the county's name. Three years after its establishment, Clarksville was declared a tobacco inspection site.

The early years of the nineteenth century were progressive ones, chiefly devoted to the building of roads, railroads, and bridges, and the establishment of churches and educational institutions. The Civil War forced the residents of Montgomery County to declare their loyalty to the Union or the Confederacy. On June 8, 1861, citizens of Montgomery County cast 2,631 votes for secession and only 33 votes against. Realizing that both the Tennessee and Cumberland Rivers provided easy access to the heart of the state, the Confederates established Fort Henry on the Tennessee River and Fort Donelson at Dover on the Cumberland River in preparation for the impending Union advance. Near Clarksville breastworks atop the hill overlooking the confluence of the Cumberland and Red Rivers bore the gallant name of Fort Defiance. After the fall of Forts Henry and Donelson in February 1862, Confederate troops at Clarksville withdrew. When Federal gunboats arrived at Fort Defiance, they found it deserted and flying a white flag. Federal troops occupied Montgomery County, except for one brief skirmish, until 1865.

After the Civil War, traffic on the Cumberland River continued to be of great importance to the community, and Clarksville became well known for its production of dark fired tobacco, its primary money crop. From 1900 to 1940 Clarksville's trade and business progressed, with the growth of the town closely connected to agricultural production.

The importance of education to the people of the county was made apparent with the establishment of the Rural Academy in 1806. A long line of educational institutions followed at the same location, including

Southwestern Presbyterian University in 1875. In 1925 the school was moved to Memphis, where it remains in operation as Rhodes College. Today's Montgomery County students can continue their education at the same site, now the home of Austin Peay State University, established in 1929 as Austin Peay Normal School, which initially was a two-year school designed to train teachers for classrooms in the state's rural public schools.

During World War II, the U.S. Army established Camp Campbell from land in Christian and Trigg Counties in Kentucky, and Montgomery and Stewart counties in Tennessee. In Montgomery County, over 42,000 acres (almost two-thirds of the Tennessee total) were purchased, and in June 1942 relocation of the families was completed. The post was named Camp Campbell in honor of General William Bowen Campbell, a Federal officer, who served in the Mexican War of 1846 as well as the Civil War. On April 15, 1950, the post became Fort Campbell when it became a permanent installation.

Montgomery County furnished two governors to the state, Willie Blount (1809–1815) and Austin Peay (1924–1927); a United States Supreme Court Justice, Horace H. Lurton; and a U.S. Postmaster General, Cave Johnson. Clarksville claims the oldest bank in the state, the Northern Bank established in 1854, now First American; the state's oldest newspaper, the *Leaf-Chronicle*, established in 1808; and the first and only bank established and operated entirely by women, the First Woman's Bank of Tennessee, which opened in 1919.

Several Montgomery Countians have influenced the fields of music, literature, and the dramatic and creative arts. Well known musicians include Clarence Cameron White, Roland Hayes, and Ferdinand Lust. Important twentieth century writers associated with the county are Caroline Gordon, Evelyn Scott, Allen Tate, and Robert Penn Warren. Local dramatic talent includes Dorothy Jordan, Frank Sutton, Charles Boillin Watts, and Helen Wood. The visual art of painting is represented by internationally known artist Robert Loftin Newman, who died in 1912.

Other notable Montgomery Countians have excelled in the arena of sports, including major league baseball player Horace Lisenbee, golfer Mason Rudolph, track Olympian Wilma Rudolph, and basketball coach Pat Head Summitt.

Individuals excelling in the fields of medicine and business include Dr. Robert Burt, well known African-American surgeon who founded Clarksville's first hospital; Clarence Saunders, founder of the modern supermarket; and A.H. Patch, inventor of the famed corn sheller.

Since World War II, advances in communication and technology have produced industrial growth in Montgomery County, attracting new residents and creating a population growth that has made Clarksville the fifth largest municipality in the state and one of the fastest growing cities in the South. No longer dependent upon an agricultural base, Montgomery County has become an important transport, industrial, retail, and professional center.

Eleanor Williams, Montgomery County Historian

SEE: AUSTIN PEAY STATE UNIVERSITY; CLARKSVILLE; DUNBAR CAVE STATE NATURAL AREA; FIRST WOMAN'S BANK OF TENNESSEE; FORT CAMPBELL; GORDON, CAROLINE; HENRY, GUSTAVUS; JOHNSON, CAVE; LURTON, HORACE H.; NEWMAN, ROBERT L.; PEAY, AUSTIN; RHODES COLLEGE; RUDOLPH, WILMA; SAUNDERS, CLARENCE; SCOTT, EVELYN; TATE, JOHN O. ALLEN; WARREN, ROBERT PENN

MONUMENTS, CIVIL WAR. Memorials that honor either Union or Confederate participants exist throughout the state, symbolic of the divided allegiances of Tennesseans during the war. Despite some exceptions, most monuments are found in one of three localities: on battlefields, in cemeteries, and on courthouse lawns or public squares. While building monuments continued well into the twentieth century, a majority were dedicated in a 30-year span between 1885 and 1915.

For both sides, erecting monuments became a way to honor the sacrifices of Civil War soldiers. The inscriptions on Union and Confederate monuments sometimes conveyed comparable sentiments. A Union monument erected in Cleveland by a Grand Army of the Republic post in 1914 was dedicated "To Perpetuate The Memory of The Boys In Blue In the War of 1861–1865 Who Lived in Bradley County." Similarly, a monument erected in Dresden in 1915 bore an inscription "In Honor Of The Confederate Soldiers Of Weakley County, Tennessee 1861–1865."

The earliest war-related monument in Tennessee appeared in 1863, while the conflict still raged. That year, survivors of Colonel William B. Hazen's brigade constructed a wall and monument to honor their comrades who fell on December 31, 1862, while defending the Round Forest, a crucial salient in the Union line during the Battle of Stones River.

The economic and political turmoil in the immediate postwar years prevented most communities from recognizing their veterans with a monument. Early memorialization efforts revolved around the decoration of Confederate graves with flowers, a task undertaken by women's memorial committees in the late 1860s.

The few monuments erected to honor Tennessee Confederates in the immediate postwar years often employed funereal symbolism. The earliest monuments to the Confederate dead were erected in Union City and Bolivar. In Union City, a relatively unadorned white marker was dedicated October 21, 1869, at a cemetery containing the graves of 29 unknown Confederate dead. At Bolivar, an obelisk erected on the courthouse square was dedicated "To The Confederate Dead of Hardeman County, Tennessee." The marble shaft was surmounted by a draped flag, reminiscent of a shroud, and an urn, another popular funerary symbol.

Citizens in three of Tennessee's largest cities placed Confederate monuments in cemeteries prior to 1895. Memphians dedicated a monument in Elmwood Cemetery in 1878, Nashville did the same at Mount Olivet Cemetery in 1889, and in 1892 Knoxville erected a monument in the Confederate Cemetery. Placing monuments in the midst of Confederate dead conveyed the loss felt by many Tennesseans for the deceased and their cause.

Monument building intensified in 1890, when the federal government passed legislation creating Chickamauga and Chattanooga National Military Park, the first such venture in the country. In Tennessee, later efforts resulted in government establishment of military parks at Shiloh (1894), Stones River (1927), and Fort Donelson (1928).

At Chickamauga-Chattanooga and Shiloh, efforts to accurately mark troop positions and honor soldiers in both armies resulted in the erection of a staggering array of battlefield monuments. These included imposing state memorials, unit monuments, statues, busts, and reliefs. Among the most impressive of these artworks is the elaborate United Daughters of the Confederacy (UDC) memorial dedicated at Shiloh in 1917. Funds for these memorials came from various sources: veterans' organizations, women's associations such as the UDC, and funds appropriated by state legislatures and the federal government.

The intense interest generated by battlefield adornment coincided with increased reverence for the Confederacy. A Lost Cause ideology prevalent by the late nineteenth century venerated the Confederate experience. Women often played key roles in this process and channeled enormous energy into selecting suitable memorials. Monuments increasingly appeared in highly visible public venues such as courthouse squares. Simple markers and funerary symbols gave way to more expressive memorials. Commercial firms vied for contracts to erect monuments, advertised their successes in the *Confederate Veteran* magazine, and urged memorial committees to place statues of Confederate soldiers above a marble or granite pedestal. Towns such as Lebanon, Murfreesboro, and Union City that had earlier erected monuments in cemeteries added a second one in the heart of the community. Most monument inscriptions paid tribute to Confederate veterans from a particular locale. One town honored the 300 "Unconquered" Confederate soldiers "Who Went Out From Mulberry" in Lincoln County. Sentiments carved on monuments rarely deviated from eulogizing the Confederate era, but a notable exception appeared on a monument erected in Union City in 1909: "To The Confederate Soldier of Obion County/ Who Was Killed In Battle/ Who Was Starved In Federal Prison/ And Who Has Preserved Anglo-Saxon Civilization In The South."

The monuments represented a considerable emotional and financial investment by the individuals and groups that labored to erect them. It often took years to secure enough money for a monument. At Franklin, for example, a monument association existed as early as 1883, but progress lagged until 1897, when a United Daughters of the Confederacy chapter began soliciting funds in earnest. Their efforts paid off on November 30, 1899, the twenty-fifth anniversary of the Battle of Franklin, when a Confederate monument was dedicated on the public square.

The elaborate ceremonies attendant to the Franklin dedication were repeated throughout Tennessee at the height of the monument-building boom. A huge crowd attended the dedication of a Confederate monument at Mount Pleasant on September 27, 1907. Railroad cars conveyed a band from Fayetteville, which played "Dixie" as distinguished visitors filed off the train. Grayclad veterans fell into line and marched in a parade to the public square for the dedication ceremonies. The day-long festivities included an invocation, welcoming speeches, a poem written for the occasion, a feast at the Cumberland Presbyterian Church, and speeches in the afternoon by Senator Edward W. Carmack and Judge S.F. Wilson. The latter's eloquence reportedly moved the old Confederates in the audience to tears. At the end of the ceremony, 13 girls tugged on ribbons and unveiled the monument.

Accounts in the *Confederate Veteran* speak glowingly of similar ceremonies in Dyersburg, Lewisburg, Paris, Shelbyville, and a host of other communities. In each case, speakers lauded both the Confederate veterans and the women who toiled so diligently to build the monuments.

Monument building diminished as the wartime generation passed away. More recently, monuments have aroused occasional controversy. Groups cognizant of Nathan Bedford Forrest's status as an antebellum slave trader and Imperial Wizard of the original Ku Klux Klan agitated unsuccessfully to remove his remains and the equestrian statue over his grave from the site in Memphis. In 1996 a Williamson County man demanded the relocation of the Franklin monument. Nevertheless, Civil War monuments remain in place as silent reminders of a tragic era in the state's history.

Christopher Losson, St. Joseph, Missouri

SEE: CONFEDERATE VETERAN; GRAND ARMY OF THE
REPUBLIC; NASHVILLE NO. 1, UDC

MOON, VIRGINIA BETHEL (1844–1925), Confederate spy and philanthropist, was a student at an Ohio girls' school when the Civil War began. School officials finally acquiesced to her demands and allowed her to leave school and join her mother in Memphis. Initially Moon had supported the abolitionist cause, but as the war commenced she became more sympathetic to the Confederacy.

In the early days of the war, her sister, Lottie Moon, disguised as an Irish washerwoman, carried dispatches and papers from Memphis to Cincinnati. Ginny Moon also began to carry Confederate documents behind the Union lines and traveled to Canada on a mission for the Confederate army. She then disguised herself as an Englishwoman and entered the city of Washington where, according to legend, she rode in a carriage with Abraham Lincoln.

Moon frequently funneled important information about Union troop movements to General Nathan Bedford Forrest; she was said to have swallowed an important message to Forrest to prevent it from falling into Union hands. She crossed Union lines with supplies and medicines for Confederate troops, and once disguised herself as a Union mourner accompanying a loved one's coffin, which was filled with medicine. She was imprisoned in New Orleans shortly before the end of the war.

After the war, Moon returned to Memphis and engaged in local philanthropic projects. When her African-American cook died, Moon took in the woman's child and raised him as her own son, one of the many orphans she raised. Moon became a familiar sight on Memphis streets, and many thought she carried a revolver hidden in her ever-present umbrella. An early supporter of women's rights, Moon claimed to have voted in a Memphis election before woman suffrage. Moon died in 1925 in New York City.

Carole Stanford Bucy, Volunteer State Community College
SEE: FORREST, NATHAN B.

MOONSHINE. Simply stated "moonshine" is untaxed liquor, furtively produced quite often by the light of the moon, or at least out of the immediate reach and oversight of law enforcement. Nicknamed corn likker, white lightening, white mule, mountain dew, and numerous other local appellations, the typical moonshine is clear in color and potent, usually approaching 100 proof, or 50 percent alcohol by volume.

The process of making moonshine includes fermentation, distillation, and condensation. The basic ingredients are sugar, water, yeast, cornmeal, and malt. First the mash of fermented grain is carefully heated. At the conclusion of the process, the alcohol is condensed, using the "worm," a coil of copper pipe in a barrel of cool water. Although appearing to be a simple process, unadulterated whiskey can only be produced by well-trained practitioners under such generally primitive conditions.

Scots-Irish settlers brought with them to America the knowledge and skills of whiskey-making. Prior to the American Revolution, production was limited, with rum being the preferred ardent spirit.

The imposition of an excise tax on whiskey by the Washington administration in 1791 touched off a 1794 rebellion of farmers in western Pennsylvania who found it advantageous to convert their large corn crops into something more easily transportable. Although the revolt failed, it proved that some Americans will, whether they be nineteenth century moonshine makers or twentieth century marijuana growers, provide a product for an illicit market if the price is right and chances of prosecution are minimal.

The legal history of this cottage industry followed several trends. Between 1817, when the excise tax was lifted, and 1862, when it was reinstituted, local distillers flourished along with larger established companies. In 1878 the federal government offered a blanket pardon to moonshiners, which many accepted while still plying their trade. The *Tennessee v. Davis* Supreme Court decision of 1879 established federal supremacy in moonshine prosecution cases.

With corn the primary crop, particularly among semisubsistence farmers in the Appalachian back country, it was only natural for the production of distilled liquor to become the occupation or avocation of many farmers. Coupled with poor or corrupt local law enforcement and inhospitality to federal "revenuers," a tradition was formed that would last to the present.

Prohibition touched off a flurry of activity with syndicates connected to such mobsters as Al Capone. The end of the "Noble Experiment," the cost of sugar, changing American tastes, and the vagaries of law enforcement have dictated the ebb and flow of the market for moonshine.

Several areas in Tennessee, particularly Cades Cove, and Blount, Carter, Fentress, Hancock, Henry, Polk, and Scott counties have dominated the history of moonshining in the state. Women as well as men took part in the trade. For example, Mollie Miller led the moonshiners of Polk County and has been credited for the killing of several revenuers and informants. Another woman, who reportedly weighed 600 pounds, ran a bloody family business, comforted by the fact that lawmen could think of no way to physically transport her to the seat of justice.

The folklore and legends about moonshiners and revenuers have become a lasting part of southern history. The blockade runner, or "tripper," became legendary with the advent of fast, modern automobiles. Their flight from justice stood them in good stead as contenders on the early stock car circuit. Revenuers who served as the nemesis of their moonshining quarry became famous as well.

The cause of many well-known and countless lesser known crimes of passion, as well as times of pleasure, the moonshine trade is perhaps best described by the following verses from an old mountain folksong: "You just lay there by the juniper/ When the moon is bright/ And watch them jugs a-fillin'/ By the pale moonlight."[1]

William E. Ellis, Eastern Kentucky University

CITATION:

(1) Joseph Earl Dabney, *Mountain Spirits* (Lakemont, GA, 1974), 115.

MOORE COUNTY, with a total area of only 129 square miles, is the second smallest county in the state. Set in the heart of agrarian Middle Tennessee, Moore County contains a diverse landscape, with nearly one half of the county lying along the Highland Rim and most of the remaining area part of the Central Basin. The Elk and Mulberry rivers create fertile, heavily timbered ridges and farmland that contribute to the agricultural production as well as the lucrative whiskey industry that remains an integral part of the county's heritage.

The first settlements in modern-day Moore County were initially part of Lincoln, Bedford, Franklin, and Coffee counties. After the Civil War, residents of the remote parts of these contiguous counties petitioned the state legislature for the creation of a new county. To support their demand for a new county, the rural petitioners pointed to the distances to the county seats and described the treacherous road system that made travel difficult, and very often impossible. They argued that the distances and hazardous road conditions made legal protection offered by the courts and grand juries inaccessible to rural residents.

The Tennessee General Assembly established Moore County in 1871 in honor of General William Moore, who was one of Lincoln County's first settlers and a long-time member of the General Assembly. The new county originally surveyed at 300 square miles, but the Constitution of 1870 stipulated that no established county should contain less than 275 square miles, and that no new county line could be closer than 11 miles from the courthouse of an old county. Since the Moore County boundaries reduced Lincoln County to 255 square miles, the new act violated the constitution. Lincoln County sued to reclaim its land, and Moore County was reduced to a mere 129 square miles.

Eleven districts comprised of Lynchburg, Ridgeville, Marble Hill, Reed's Store, Tucker Creek, Wagoner's, Prosser's Store, Charity, County Line, Hurricane Church, and William B. Smith's Mill were included in the new boundaries. A county-wide election in 1872 designated Lynchburg as the county seat. Many of the townships have all but disappeared, with a few farmsites or a small store as the only indication of population. Lynchburg remains the largest and most populated district, estimated at around 350 residents, while the total population for the entire county is just over 4,700. In the 1870s Lynchburg was a regional center for the mule trade in Middle Tennessee because it was located in the center of an economic triangle that linked Tullahoma (Coffee County), Shelbyville (Bedford County), and Fayetteville (Lincoln County). Farmers traveling to and from these railroad hubs used the turnpike through Lynchburg, which later became Tennessee Highway 55. Produce, consumer goods, and livestock were traded in the county seat and contributed to Lynchburg's prominence within the county. Most of the town's character is still intact, largely because manufacturing and industry never developed fully, and with the construction of interstate highways, the region was isolated from the major industrial centers.

Moore County's fertile soils and close proximity to the Mulberry and Elk rivers were excellent for growing corn, wheat, and oats. Many farmers raised cattle, hogs, and sheep to supplement their income. Dairies are still one of the county's major agricultural producers.

Moore County has a long history in the whiskey industry. The first distillery was erected in 1825, along the West Mulberry. By 1876 at least 15 distilleries were registered in Moore County, and the product formerly known as Lincoln County whiskey became a Lynchburg specialty. One of the largest and most famous distilleries was founded by Jack Daniel, who made Tennessee Sour Mash whiskey a major commodity. Today, Jack Daniel Distillery is the central tourist attraction in Lynchburg and a primary source of tourism revenue for the county.

Although the county is sparsely populated and predominantly agricultural, Moore County is one of the most intact examples of Middle Tennessee's agrarian landscape. Visitors to Lynchburg and the surrounding area can experience the strong feeling of community and see the historic buildings that contribute to the lasting heritage of Moore County.

Megan Dobbs Eades, Shelby, North Carolina

SEE: GOVERNMENT; JACK DANIEL DISTILLERY; MOORE, WILLIAM

MOORE, GRACE (1901–1947), popular soprano in opera, musical comedy, and film, was born December 6, 1901, in Slabtown, Cocke County, and christened Mary Willie Grace. She spent her youth in Jellico, where she sang in her church choir. After studying briefly at Ward-Belmont College, she continued her musical training in Washington and New York. Early experience with a touring company was followed by her Broadway debut in 1920 in the musical, *Hitchy Koo,* by Jerome Kern. In 1923 she starred in Irving Berlin's *The Music Box Review.* Inspired by Mary Garden, and after training in France, she made her Metropolitan Opera debut as Mimi in *La Boheme* in 1928. This was also her first role at the Opera Comique in Paris and in London's Covent Garden. Long maintaining her association with the Metropolitan Opera, she sang in a variety of Italian and French operas as well as the title roles in *Tosca, Manon,* and *Louise,* which was considered her greatest success. Lured to Hollywood, she made her cinema debut in 1930 in *A Lady's Morals,* based on the life of Jenny Lind, and she achieved international fame with *One Night of Love* (1934). Other movies followed including a film version of *Louise.* She was happily married to the Spanish screen actor, Valentin Parera. Through her films she did much to popularize opera with a wide audience. In opera and concerts she delighted audiences in the United States, Europe, and Latin America. On January 26, 1947, after singing for American troops, she was killed at the height of her career in an airplane crash leaving Copenhagen. She published an autobiography, *You're Only Young Once,* in 1944. The motion picture, *So This Is Love,* was based on her career. She bequeathed her scores, books, letters, and souvenirs to Ward-Belmont. The University of Tennessee has since acquired her papers.

Charles M. Binnicker, University of the South

SEE: CAMPBELL COUNTY; COCKE COUNTY; OPERA

MOORE, JOHN TROTWOOD (1858–1929) AND MARY DANIEL (1875–1957).

When appointed as State Librarian and Archivist in March 1919 by Governor Albert H. Roberts, John Trotwood Moore was best known as a man of letters. A native of Marion, Alabama, he moved to Maury County, Tennessee, in 1885 where he became interested in writing. Over time, the theme of his work shifted from thoroughbred horses and hunting dogs to historical figures and events. His fascination with Andrew Jackson inspired a related interest in collecting original Jackson manuscripts, which eventually led to the publication of *Hearts of Hickory* (1926). After moving to Nashville in 1906, he collaborated with Senator Robert L. Taylor in publishing the *Taylor-Trotwood Magazine* that was continued until 1911. Although *The Bishop of Cottontown* (1906) is regarded as his best literary effort, his four volumes *Tennessee: The Volunteer State* (1923) was a useful reference for historical research.

Moore's success while State Librarian and Archivist in collecting historical documents was enhanced by the development of a Civil War ques-

tionnaire sent out to some 5,000 former soldiers and returned by 1,650 veterans. Through the Tennessee History Committee, records of Tennessee veterans of the World War were also collected. The crowning achievement of his efforts was the addition of the collection of the Tennessee Historical Society to the holdings of the Library and Archives.

Following the death of his first spouse, Florence W. Allen, John Trotwood Moore married Mary Brown Daniel, a native of Harrisonville, Missouri, in 1900. Mary Daniel Moore was proficient in the daily operations of the Library and Archives and shared her husband's understanding and interest in the collection and preservation of historical materials. The Moores worked well together as a team. From the time of Moore's death in May 1929, Mary Moore continued in this work until her retirement as State Librarian and Archivist in 1949.

In the collection of historical materials, Mary Moore worked closely with historical, archival, and patriotic societies and participated in the Historical Records Survey programs of the Works Progress Administration during 1935–1942. In addition, Moore contributed substantially to the understanding of Tennessee history through the publication of a number of articles in the *Tennessee Historical Quarterly* between 1944 and 1956.

Although delayed until 1947, final funding approval for the construction of an appropriate building for the State Library and Archives remains the hallmark of the Moore era in Tennessee. On June 17, 1953, the new State Library and Archives Building was dedicated as a memorial to Tennesseans who had served in World War II.

The Moore years were a period of significant archival achievement. The archives program was recognized as a vital component of state government; records were made accessible to the public; the state assumed responsibility for preserving the rich holdings of the Tennessee Historical Society; and finally, steps were taken to construct a permanent archival facility for housing the permanent value records of the State of Tennessee.

John H. Thweatt, Tennessee State Library and Archives

SUGGESTED READING: John H. Thweatt, "The Archival Tradition in Tennessee—The Moore Years," *Tennessee Historical Quarterly* 50(1991): 152–156

SEE: TENNESSEE CIVIL WAR VETERANS' QUESTIONNAIRE; TENNESSEE STATE LIBRARY AND ARCHIVES

MOORE, WILLIAM (1786–1871)

was born in a fortified blockhouse on the Green River in Kentucky to early emigrants William Moore, Sr., and Olivia Free. William Moore came to Lincoln County, Tennessee, around 1806. He first married Nancy Holman, by whom he had one daughter. His second wife, Elizabeth Lawson Moore, daughter of Lawson Moore, bore him ten daughters and three sons. On September 3, 1811, after raising a company of volunteers at Fayetteville, Moore was commissioned as captain, 39th Regiment of the Tennessee Militia; he later rose to the rank of major. His company, which included Davy Crockett, fought under Andrew Jackson in the Creek Indian Wars and the War of 1812. A staunch supporter of both Jackson and James K. Polk, Moore served in the Tennessee House of Representatives from Lincoln County 1825–1829, and from Lincoln and Giles counties in the Tennessee Senate 1833–1837. On January 1, 1840, Governor Polk appointed Moore as Adjutant General of the State of Tennessee. In 1850 William Moore and three other men formed the Town Company which developed Tullahoma. In other civic endeavors, he served as Justice of the Peace; president of the Fayetteville, Lynchburg, and Mulberry Turnpike Company; president of the Lincoln County Democratic Committee; and delegate to the 1851 Democratic National Convention. He died in Tullahoma on March 9, 1871. In December of that year, the Tennessee Legislature created a new county and honored Moore by posthumously naming it for him.

Kay Oldham Cornelius, Huntsville, Alabama

SEE: COFFEE COUNTY; CREEK INDIAN WAR OF 1813 & 1814; LINCOLN COUNTY; MOORE COUNTY

MORGAN COUNTY was organized as Tennessee's thirty-ninth county by legislative act in 1817, primarily from territory removed from Roane County. The new county ran diagonally across the Cumberland Plateau from the eastern escarpment to the Kentucky line to the north. The county and the county seat, Montgomery, were named in honor of Revolutionary War hero, General Daniel Morgan, and Major Lemuel P. Montgomery, a Knoxville resident who was killed in the Battle of Horseshoe Bend during the Creek Indian Wars of 1814.

The first permanent settlers, Samuel and Martin Hall, arrived soon after the Third Tellico Treaty opened the area to settlement in 1805. Many of the early settlers, like Samuel Hall, were Revolutionary War veterans, who claimed land grants from North Carolina for military service. Early settlers made their homes in isolated mountain valleys where the soil was relatively fertile and game abundant. The soil and the topography of the county reduced the land suitable for agriculture to less than half of the 345,000 acres within the county's boundaries. Although two rivers, the Obed and the Emory, flow through the county, neither was suitable for transportation of goods. As a result, settlers engaged in subsistence farming, and settlement and development were extremely slow. The lack of significant agricultural production limited slavery in Morgan County. The 1820 census registered 46 slaves; by 1860

the number of slaves had grown to 120, distributed among 25 owners.

The abundance of coal, hidden beneath the surface, provided the potential for the county's economic advancement. First extracted in 1819, coal quickly achieved prominence in the local economy. By 1860 two mines were in operation in the county, employing nine men, and producing $15,000 in coal annually.

In 1844 George F. Gerding, a New York businessman, organized the East Tennessee Colonization Company in partnership with Theodore de Cock of Antwerp and purchased 170,000 acres of land in Morgan, Cumberland, White, Fentress, and Scott counties in an effort to attract German and Swiss settlers to the area. The first 50 settlers arrived from Mainz in 1845, followed by two more contingents in 1846. By 1855 the German and Swiss migration to Morgan County had ended. Most immigrants settled on small farms of less than 100 acres and combined farming with the use of their skills as craftsmen. The Wartburg Piano Company, which prospered briefly, was joined by furniture makers and cabinet makers. Tobacco production in the county was utilized by a local cigar maker. The Germans planted vineyards and orchards for the production of wine and brandy. A surprising number of professional people arrived in Wartburg, including an architect, a university-trained musician, eight physicians, and a German nobleman. Most remained only briefly before moving to cities or towns where they could better utilize their skills. Conflicts over the price of land and the lack of development combined with religious disputes between the Reformed Church and the Lutheran Church and the effects of the Civil War to produce the decline of the community. By 1870 only 57 German- and 41 Swiss-born residents remained in the county.

Like other East Tennessee counties, Morgan County voted against secession, although residents divided in their support of the Confederate and Union armies. No significant clashes occurred between the two armies in the county, but foraging and looting were almost daily occurrences. County government broke down under the pressures of war, leaving the isolated farm families vulnerable to the attacks of guerrilla forces operating on the plateau. Many Union sympathizers left the county during the early years of the war, when the area came under Confederate control, and a number of them did not return.

The opening of the Cincinnati Southern Railroad in 1880 brought significant changes in the lives of the people of Morgan County. The railroad ran south to north through the county, with shorter lines extending out to the logging areas. As a result of the railroad, the extractive industries flourished, and a number of towns profited from their position along the rail line, including Sunbright, Lancing, and Oakdale. The railroad also made Morgan County accessible for the development of health resorts and spas. Deer Lodge and Franklin became the summer destination of families from as far away as Wisconsin and Louisiana.

In 1880 Thomas Hughes, the British social philosopher and reformer, bought 75,000 acres in Morgan County to create a utopian community drawn from the younger sons of the English aristocracy. Like other such endeavors, the dream proved stronger than the reality. Without the skills to create an economically viable settlement in the harsh environment, the experiment failed. By the turn of the century, the Rugby settlers, like the Germans of Wartburg, had scattered and taken up new lives.

In April 1893 the Tennessee General Assembly authorized funding for the construction of a new prison at Brushy Mountain in Morgan County. Prison reform, and particularly the question of the leasing of convicts, had occupied political debate for several years. The establishment of Brushy Mountain ended convict leasing, but not their work in the coal mines. The state purchased 9,000 acres from East Tennessee Land Company for the construction of the prison. Coal deposits on the land were mined by prisoners under the supervision of the state for state use.

In the twentieth century Morgan County benefited from a number of federally funded programs, including the establishment of a CCC camp during the New Deal. Frozen Head State Park, Catoosa Wildlife Management Area, Obed National Scenic River, and Big South Fork National Recreation Area have opened new opportunities in tourism and development for county residents. As part of the East Tennessee Development District, Morgan County used state and federal developmental funds and loans to construct water, gas, and sewer systems and develop an industrial park. Although most Morgan County residents continue to commute to jobs outside the county, a number of industrial firms have opened plants, including Red Kap in Wartburg, Blue Hole Canoe Company in Sunbright, and Advance Transformer, while traditional extractive industries continue as an important influence in the economy.
Donald Todd, Wartburg

SEE: BIG SOUTH FORK NATIONAL RIVER AND RECREATION AREA; DEVELOPMENT DISTRICTS; FROZEN HEAD STATE NATURAL AREA; LAND GRANTS; MINING; RAILROADS; RUGBY; TENNESSEE PRISON SYSTEM

MORGAN, JOHN HARCOURT ALEXANDER
(1867–1950), thirteenth president of the University of Tennessee (1919–1934) and second chairman of the board of directors of the Tennessee Valley Authority (1938–1941), was born in Kerrwood, Adelaide Township, Middlesex County, Ontario,

Canada, the child of a farming family. After receiving a bachelor of science degree from the University of Toronto's Agricultural College at Guelph in 1889, he took a position as professor of entomology at Louisiana State University. Here he conducted important research on cattle tick and boll weevil control and was credited with saving the cattle industry from the harmful effects of the tick.

In 1905 Morgan moved to the University of Tennessee in Knoxville as professor of entomology and zoology and director of the university's agricultural experiment station. In 1913 he was also named dean of the College of Agriculture. During his tenure, he persuaded suspicious Tennessee farmers that academic agriculturalists could assist them in practical ways. A series of farmers' institutes offered exhibits, demonstrations, and lectures to report the results of the experiment station's research. Morgan's informal dress, manner, and language and the revivalist intensity of his message for the improvement of agricultural practices endeared him to the state's rural population. His "lessons" not only stressed the profitability of their work, but also the need for farmers to be conscious of its environmental impact. His concept of the "oneness of the universe" became known as Morgan's "common mooring" philosophy, which stressed the integral relationship between humans and their natural environment. In application of this view, Morgan encouraged farmers to prevent soil erosion, practice crop rotation, and improve livestock breeding.

Appointed president of the University of Tennessee in 1919, Morgan enhanced the university's influence among Tennessee's farmers, adopting the motto "The State is the University's Campus." At the same time, he oversaw a considerable expansion of the university, which quadrupled the student population and added 11 buildings, as well as a new athletic field. Morgan's persuasive powers and his growing reputation in the agricultural community gave him considerable influence with Tennessee governors and led to increased appropriations for the university.

In 1933 Franklin D. Roosevelt appointed Morgan to the board of the new Tennessee Valley Administration. He became the agency's agricultural specialist and its propagandist to the state's farmers. Allied with another board member, David Lilienthal, Morgan pursued a policy of "grass roots democracy," working with state and local agencies to educate farmers in scientific agriculture and assure them that TVA promoted their interests and not those of the federal government. For three years, Morgan served as board chairman; he remained as a director until his retirement in 1948 at the age of 80.

Morgan was widely honored. In 1927 he was elected president of the Association of Land Grant

Colleges and Universities. In 1937 he received the Farm Bureau Federation's award for distinguished service to agriculture; and in 1940 the *Progressive Farmer* named him its "Man of the Year." Clemson University and the University of Western Ontario awarded him honorary doctorates. Roosevelt praised him as one of the nation's most useful public servants. Shy, modest, and self-effacing, Morgan never sought the limelight. His success derived from the simplicity and earnestness of his message: "The land, the land itself. Therein lies our wealth and that of the world."[1]

Milton M. Klein, University of Tennessee, Knoxville

CITATION:
(1) *Knoxville News Sentinel,* August 25, 1950.

SUGGESTED READING: Mouzon Peters, "The Story of Dr. Harcourt A. Morgan" in *Makers of Millions* (1951)

SEE: FARMS AND AGRICULTURAL EXPERIMENT STATIONS; UNIVERSITY OF TENNESSEE; TENNESSEE VALLEY AUTHORITY

MORGAN, JOHN HUNT (1825–1864), Confederate cavalry commander, was born in Huntsville, Alabama, on June 1, 1825. Educated at Transylvania University, he fought in the Mexican War as a first lieutenant in the Kentucky Mounted Volunteers and saw action at the Battle of Buena Vista. Morgan married Rebecca Bruce in 1848. Working as a hemp manufacturer in Lexington, Morgan became a Mason and an active community leader, serving on the school board, city council, and as captain of the fire department. From 1852 to 1854, he served as captain of an artillery company in the state militia. In 1857 he formed the Lexington Rifles and attached the unit to the state guard militia in 1860. Morgan initially supported Kentucky neutrality, but in September 1861, on his own authority, he led the Lexington Rifles in a series of guerrilla raids before officially joining the Confederacy as a captain of cavalry in October 1861.

In April 1862 Morgan was promoted to colonel and continued his raiding activities, earning the sobriquet "Francis Marion of the War." He led a squadron at the Battle of Shiloh. On a raid from Knoxville to Cynthiana, Kentucky, from July 4–28, 1862, he recruited 300 volunteers for the Confederate cause. On August 12, 1862, Morgan successfully disrupted General Don Carlos Buell's campaign against Chattanooga by burning the twin Louisville and Nashville Railroad tunnels near Gallatin, which were vital links in the Union supply line. Embarassed by this loss, Buell sent his entire cavalry force against Morgan and suffered a rout, including the capture of General Richard Johnson. Morgan's success emboldened Confederate plans for a Kentucky invasion, and Morgan's cavalry joined General Braxton Bragg in the Perryville campaign. On December 7, 1862, Morgan captured a garrison of 1,834 Union troops at Hartsville, Tennessee.

In Murfreesboro, on December 14, 1862, Morgan, widowed since 1861, married 17-year-old Martha "Mattie" Ready in what was the highlight of the city's winter social season. Most of the Confederate high command attended the ceremony which was performed by Lt. General (and Bishop) Leonidas Polk. This marriage produced a daughter, Johnnie, who was born after Morgan's death. Two weeks after the wedding, Morgan's troops participated in raids during the Battle of Stones River, diverting Union troops from assisting General William S. Rosecrans's army.

During his raids, Morgan often avoided direct combat through tactical plans which involved ruse and deception, including intercepting telegraph messages and sending out false ones to Union commands. During 1862 his command grew from 325 to a division of 3,900 and he was promoted to brigidier general on December 11, 1862.

In early 1863, as Union cavalry in the western theater gained proficiency and strength, Morgan began suffering losses in his confrontations. In an attempt to recoup some lost prestige and morale, he embarked on his legendary "Great Raid." Morgan led his troops on an unauthorized raid through Kentucky, Indiana, and Ohio. During the raid, which lasted from July 1–26, 1863, Morgan spread panic in each successive town he approached, encountering hastily convened militia who offered relatively weak resistance. Passing through southern Indiana, he crossed into Ohio at Harrison, and moved within seven miles of Cincinnati. Captured with most of his command at West Point, Ohio, Morgan escaped from the Ohio State Penitentiary on November 27, 1863, and returned to Kentucky. His "Great Raid" was the northernmost incursion of western Confederate troops and served to bolster Southern morale after Lee's defeat at Gettysburg. It also served to secure Morgan's legendary status among Civil War generals.

Despite the Confederate high command's anger at his unauthorized, impetuous raid, he was restored to command. Reports of looting by Morgan's men during an unsuccessful raid near Cynthiana, Kentucky, in June 1864 led to his suspension from command and the scheduling of a court of inquiry for September 10. Morgan was surprised by Federal soldiers in Greeneville, Tennessee, on September 4, and died attempting to escape. Originally buried in Richmond, Virginia, his body was moved to Lexington, Kentucky, in 1868.

William P. Morelli, Brentwood

SUGGESTED READING: James A. Ramage, *Rebel Raider: The Life of General John Hunt Morgan* (1986)

SEE: CIVIL WAR; GREENE COUNTY; SHILOH, BATTLE OF; STONES RIVER, BATTLE OF; TROUSDALE COUNTY

MORGAN, KARL Z. (1908–   ), called the "father of health physics," was born in North Carolina and studied physics at the University of North Carolina and Duke, earning his Ph.D. in 1934. He chaired the Physics Department at Lenoir Rhyne College and studied cosmic radiation physics until 1943, when he joined the Metallurgical Laboratory of the University of Chicago. Transferring to Oak Ridge National Laboratory, he became Director of the Health Physics Division in 1944, leading studies on the detection of ionizing radiation and protection of people and the environment from its insidious hazards.

As Director of Health Physics at Oak Ridge for 27 years, Morgan led teams that designed ionization chambers, film meters, and advanced Geiger counters for personnel monitoring and radiation surveys of buildings and environment. He became a founder and first president of the National Health Physics Society and the International Radiation Protection Association. He also edited *Health Physics Journal* and co-authored the first textbook on health physics.

Morgan became an international authority on studies of the safe limits for radionuclides in the human body. After retiring at Oak Ridge in 1972, he became professor at the Georgia Institute of Technology and continued his work in the reduction of low-level radiation from radon, medical diagnostic procedures, and nuclear power.

Leland R. Johnson, Clio Research Institute

SUGGESTED READINGS: Karl Z. Morgan and James E. Turner, eds., *Principles of Radiation Protection: A Textbook of Health Physics* (1967); Leland Johnson and Daniel Schaffer, *Oak Ridge National Laboratory: The First Fifty Years* (1994)

SEE: OAK RIDGE NATIONAL LABORATORY

MOUND BOTTOM. Almost 1,000 years ago, a thriving city of several thousand Native Americans existed in a bend of the Harpeth River, not far downstream from Kingston Springs in Cheatham County. Around A.D. 950, Mound Bottom emerged as a sacred ceremonial center for hundreds of farming families scattered throughout the Harpeth River valley. Over the succeeding 300 years, the site grew into a fortified city, serving as the social political, economic, and religious center for one of North America's most complex native civilizations.

Mound Bottom is located in a well-protected horseshoe bend, and along with the adjacent Pack mounds, comprises a 500-acre archaeological site, including at least 29 flat-topped earthen pyramids and burial mounds. An estimated five miles of earthen embankments and wooden palisades once surrounded these mounds and hundreds of houses, storehouses, craft production centers, and other buildings. Faced with increasing competition from similar towns in the Central Basin, Mound Bottom declined as an important center in Middle Tennessee

around A.D. 1300. Because this Tennessee civilization disappeared centuries before written records, archaeologists will never know the original name of Mound Bottom, nor that of the people who lived there. Instead, archaeologists refer to these eastern North American societies as Mississippian.

In Middle Tennessee, Mississippian cultures lasted from A.D. 900 to 1450. Their most significant achievements included the construction and use of large flat-topped earthen pyramids as platforms for temples and elite residences and the creation of one of the most spectacular artistic traditions of the western hemisphere. They conducted intensive agriculture based on corn, beans, squash, and many other domesticated plants. In addition, their trading networks spanned eastern North America, extending from the Great Lakes in the north to the Gulf of Mexico in the south, and from the eastern Great Plains in the west to the eastern Appalachian Mountains of the Carolinas.

Archaeological investigations over the past two centuries have demonstrated the trade connections between the ruling families of Mound Bottom and chiefs of similar civilizations: copper necklaces, earspools, and headdresses were imported from the Lake Superior and Appalachian regions; fragile pottery vessels were imported from southern Illinois and the Tennessee River Valley; and conch shell cups and jewelry from the Gulf Coast. Around A.D. 1200, probably few leaders in eastern North America were unaware of the city at "Mound Bottom."

In recognition of its importance as an archaeological site, the State of Tennessee purchased Mound Bottom in 1972. The staff of Montgomery Bell State Park and the Tennessee Division of Archaeology currently manage the area as an archaeological preserve. The site is closed to the public, and it is hoped that a future archaeological park with an interpretive center will be created to promote appreciation for the achievements of Tennessee's late prehistoric native people.

Kevin E. Smith, Middle Tennessee State University

SEE: CHEATHAM COUNTY; MISSISSIPPIAN CULTURE

MOUSETAIL LANDING STATE PARK, located along the banks of the Tennessee River in Perry County, is one of the state's most recent parks, dedicated in 1986. The park's 1,249 acres offer hiking, fishing, boating, camping, and outdoor recreational facilities. The park is centered around the original site of "Mousetail Landing," a once prominent river village during the late 1800s. Tanned goods were the major commodities shipped from Mousetail Landing; allegedly the name came from the many rodents attracted by the cowhides awaiting shipment to markets at Paducah, Louisville, Evansville, and St. Louis. The park contains several archaeological ruins from the historic era, including the original Mousetail Landing pier, a blacksmith shop, and the Parrish Cemetery.

Carroll Van West, Middle Tennessee State University

SEE: PERRY COUNTY; TENNESSEE RIVER SYSTEM

MOVIES: See TENNESSEE IN FILM

MULES. Until the widespread adoption of motor-powered machinery in the mid-twentieth century, mules powered most farm activities in Tennessee. Middle Tennessee was a major mule market. At annual "Mule Days" held at towns such as Columbia and Lynchburg, farmers and breeders from throughout the South purchased the best stock available. On the first Monday in April, Columbia still hosts an annual Mule Day celebration, which is the largest in Tennessee. According to the research of agricultural historian Pete Daniel, mules were of extraordinary value, especially to families with small farms. Their mules often were treated as unofficial members of the family.

A hybrid animal, mules are a mix of jackass studs and mare horses. Mules can be either males or females, but in the great majority of cases they are sterile and cannot reproduce. Mules were more expensive than either workhorses or oxen, but farmers who cultivated cotton and/or tobacco preferred to own them. They considered mules to be more sure-footed, smarter, and stronger than horses and oxen. According to those who owned mules, the animal rarely succumbed to disease and performed well in the hot summer. Admitting that mules had a complex—some would say stubborn—personality, a

handful of farmers countered that the animals had thicker skins than other work animals and could be beaten until they performed satisfactorily.

Mules typically responded to simple commands. Farmers yelled "gee" for a right turn, "haw" for a left turn, "whoa" to stop and "come up" to start. Farmers and mules worked together to produce the family subsistence. Perhaps that explains why rural families were so attached to their mules, giving them names and treating them as pets.

Carroll Van West, Middle Tennessee State University

SEE: LIVESTOCK; MAURY COUNTY

MURALS, DECORATIVE INTERIOR AND INTERIOR PAINTING. Historic examples of decoratively painted interiors exist across the state of Tennessee. While some of the paintings have been lost, many works from the late eighteenth century to the New Deal era have survived, indicating the wide variety of techniques, styles, and motivations for adorning both private and public interiors with architectural paintings.

Using painters' manuals and their own imagination, both itinerant and local artists employed the common and inexpensive techniques of graining and marbling to imitate rare and costly woods and marbles. Others painted landscapes to serve as a focal point of the room, often in the form of an overmantel painting or firescreen. In this century, academically trained artists created mural paintings for numerous public buildings through President Franklin D. Roosevelt's New Deal art programs of the 1930s and 1940s.

Some of the earliest examples of painted interiors indicate the transference of New England decorative traditions to Tennessee. The John and Landon Carter Mansion in Elizabethton is one of Tennessee's oldest residences, dating to ca. 1780. The mansion retains many of its original architectural features, including two rare overmantel paintings depicting pastoral scenes. The "Stencil House" located near Clifton in Wayne County is the earliest known completely painted interior to retain its original decoration. This log dogtrot house contains stenciling in both the parlor and entrance hall. The anonymous artist painted such common nineteenth century motifs as flowers, leaves, vines, weeping, willow trees, pineapples, and swags and tassels.

Many Tennessee houses contain fine examples of Victorian-era decorative painting. Together they serve to illustrate the varied and changing interior fashions of the late nineteenth century. Notable examples from across the

At 18 hands this was the largest mule in the parade at Columbia's Mule Day, 1939.

TSLA

state include the Acquilla Lane House in Hamblen County, "The Beeches" in Robertson County, the Meady White House in Hardin County, and the Julius Freed House in Gibson County. In East Tennessee, the Acquilla Lane House in Whiteburg once contained at least two decoratively painted rooms: the parlor and a second floor bedroom. These rooms are the work of W. Bakar, who signed and dated the bedroom in 1861. The parlor design is composed of colored blocks in a stretcher bond pattern. The bedroom, dismantled and transferred to the Tennessee State Museum in Nashville in 1981, features tulips, birds, heart-shaped leaves, urns, vines, pomegranates, baskets, and a woman and man holding fish. Set on a bright-blue background, these Pennsylvania Dutch-style motifs may indicate that Bakar was of German descent although no written documentation exists to support this assertion. "The Beeches" at Springfield in Middle Tennessee contains elegant tromp l'oeil paintings on the ceilings of both the entrance hall and dining room, said to be the work of an itinerant French artist. In West Tennessee, the Meady White House in Saltillo and the Julius Freed House in Trenton feature geometric designs and floral motifs similar to those recommended by painters' manuals and household critics of the late 1870s. The Meady White House contains graining, marbling, and stenciled ceiling paintings attributed to John Joseph Christie, an Irish artist. At the Julius Freed House, an anonymous artist painted landscape scenes, flowers, and geometric designs on a marbled background in the parlor and a second floor bedroom.

Four of the most ornate historically painted interiors are located in the adjoining southern Middle Tennessee counties of Coffee, Moore, and Bedford. The James G. Carroll House (not extant) in Tullahoma, the Green-Evans House and the Hinkle-Price House in Lynchburg, and the Maple Dean Farmhouse (not extant) in Flat Creek are all attributed to Fred Swanton, who, according to family tradition and a death notice in the Shelbyville *Gazette,* was a circus painter from Buffalo, New York, who painted in this area during the late 1880s. At the Carroll House and the Hinkle-Price House, Swanton created large overmantel paintings which included his signature motifs: a broken tree limb and an Indian maiden. All of the three remaining houses contain smaller landscapes featuring such pastoral subjects as a lake, waterfall, wheat field, bridge, and rural cottage amidst mountains and trees. At the Green-Evans House, Swanton painted six small landscapes on grained wainscoting. The Maple Dean Farmhouse contained his most complete interior scheme. Its bedroom ceiling and cornice contain seven small oval-shaped landscapes framed by painted scroll borders and set in a stenciled floral border. At the fireplace,

Swanton painted two landscapes: one at the center of the mantel and one as a firescreen. The Carroll House, the Hinkle-Price House, and the Maple Dean Farmhouse all had artistically painted ceilings dominated by painted medallions.

During the late 1930s and early 1940s, a more professional and systematic contribution was made to Tennessee art through the New Deal cultural programs. The Public Works of Art Project (PWAP), the federal government's fine arts project of the Works Progress Administration, authorized the creation of murals for Tennessee post offices, courthouses, and other public buildings. Reflecting the current artistic style of Regionalism, these paintings illustrate city or regional history and identity, and some even promoted New Deal projects such as TVA. *Picking Cotton* by Carl B. Nyquist in Bolivar, *Electrification* by David Stone Martin in Lenoir City, and *Wild Boar Hunt* by Thelma Martin in Sweetwater are among the nearly 30 murals created for Tennessee post offices. Other public buildings received federally funded art, such as the mural in the Davidson County Courthouse and the Sevier State Office Building, both painted by Dean Cornwell. Memphis resident Burton Callicott created a mural depicting Hernando De Soto's arrival in West Tennessee for the lobby of the Memphis Pink Palace Museum, then the Memphis Museum of Natural History. In Memphis's Ellis Auditorium, Maysie Dimond painted a seven-foot high, 152-foot long mural to serve as a pictorial history of Memphis from Spanish exploration to the twentieth century. Using the ancient buon fresco technique of applying paint to wet plaster, she ensured that the colors would remain vibrant over time. During a 1950s renovation, the mural was covered by pink marble slabs, which have since been removed.

These federally funded art programs came to an end as the United States entered World War II. Occasionally administrators sacrificed murals during building expansion and renovation. Fortunately, some have been recovered, like Dimond's murals at the Ellis Auditorium and Wendell Jones's post office mural, *Farmer Family,* now hanging at the D.P. Culp Center at East Tennessee State University. While little is known about the artists who created these New Deal paintings or those of earlier centuries, many Tennessee murals have been preserved as a testament to the rich and diverse artistic heritage of the state.

Anne-Leslie Owens, Tennessee Historical Society

SEE: ART; CORNWELL, DEAN; PINK PALACE MUSEUM; TENNESSEE STATE MUSEUM; WORKS PROGRESS ADMINISTRATION

MURDEROUS MARY, as the press called her, was a five-ton circus elephant, that was lynched from a 100-ton railroad crane car in Erwin on September 13,

1916. She had killed her trainer the day before in Kingsport. Because of East Tennessean's outrage over the incident, the owner of the circus, John Sparks, decided Mary would be killed in full public view.

An estimated 2,000 people assembled in the Clinchfield yard to witness the spectacle. A circus roustabout chained one of Mary's legs to a steel rail. Another roustabout slipped the crane car's 3/4-inch steel chain around the elephant's neck.

The chain tightened, and Mary was lifted into the air. Unfortunately, no one remembered to unchain Mary's leg, and the crane strained against itself with the elephant dangling in the middle. With a loud crack, the chain snapped, and Mary fell heavily to the ground. Onlookers scattered in an effort to escape, but Mary remained where she fell; the fall had broken her hip.

A roustabout climbed the elephant's back and attached a heavier chain. Once again, the noose was drawn, and Mary was lifted off the ground. Five minutes later, she was dead by strangulation.

Charles Edwin Price, Gate City, Virginia

SEE: UNICOI COUNTY

MURFREE, MARY NOAILLES "Charles Egbert Craddock" (1850–1922). In the latter part of the nineteenth century, Mary Noailles Murfree depicted the scenery and people of the Tennessee mountains for a national audience. At a time when local color fiction was much in vogue throughout the country, she came to prominence as the most noted writer using the southern mountains as the setting for her fiction.

Murfree was born in Murfreesboro, the name of the city having been changed to honor an ancestor of hers. When she was seven, the family moved to Nashville, where she attended the Nashville Female Academy and lived for the next 16 years. In 1867, shortly after the end of the Civil War, she attended the Chegary Institute, in Philadelphia, a "finishing school" for young women.

The Murfrees owned a cabin at Beersheba Springs, a summer resort in the Cumberland Mountains south of McMinnville, and for about 15 years Murfree went there every summer with her family. Much of what she knew of mountain scenery, speech, and manners apparently came from those summers at Beersheba, though she also visited Montvale Springs, south of Maryville, and ventured into the Smoky Mountains as far as Gregory's Bald.

Though their Murfreesboro home, Grantland, was destroyed during the Civil War, a new house was built, and in 1872 the family moved there, remaining until 1881, when they moved to St. Louis. By that time Murfree had published a number of stories, beginning with "Flirts and Their Ways" and "My Daughter's Admirers" in 1874–1875, stories which appeared under the pseudonym "R. Emmet

Mary Noailles Murfree, "Charles Egbert Craddock."

Cembry." In 1878 the prestigious *Atlantic Monthly* published her story "The Dancin' Party at Harrison's Cove," set at a summer resort modeled on Beersheba Springs. This time she used a different masculine pseudonym, "Charles Egbert Craddock," and it was by that name that she became widely known.

Murfree's first book was *In the Tennessee Mountains* (Boston, 1884), a collection of eight stories set in either the Cumberlands or the Great Smokies. All had previously appeared in the *Atlantic Monthly*. In the following year Murfree published her first mountain novel, *The Prophet of the Great Smoky Mountains.* Between the two there appeared *Where the Battle Was Fought* (Boston, 1884), set at Murfreesboro.

For years readers had been curious about the identity of the mysterious "Craddock." The Boston editors and publishers with whom she corresponded knew the author only as "M.N. Murfree," the signature on her letters to them. They assumed that the writer was male. The secret was at last revealed in 1885, when Murfree, her sister, and her father journeyed to Boston to meet with an astonished Thomas Bailey Aldrich, editor of the *Atlantic Monthly.*

In the years which followed Murfree published many more books, 25 in all, most of them about the mountains, but some focusing on Tennessee history and on the Cherokee Indians. Some of her later fiction was set in Mississippi. By 1891 she had returned to Tennessee, where she lived the rest of her life, dying at Murfreesboro in 1922. Her last novel was printed in the Nashville *Banner* after her death.

Murfree's fiction has been consistently criticized for its stereotyping of the mountaineer and for its overblown, highly romanticized descriptions of the landscape. Almost every reader notices the wide gap between the tone and vocabulary of the narrator and the mountain dialect of her characters. Like many other local color writers, she felt it necessary to provide as narrator a cultured, sophisticated intermediary, someone like the reader she hoped to reach.

Allison Ensor, University of Tennessee, Knoxville

SEE: BEERSHEBA SPRINGS; LITERATURE; MURFREESBORO

MURFREESBORO is a city of over 56,000 citizens (1997) located in Rutherford County, 32 miles southeast of Nashville. It is the geographical center of Tennessee.

Following over 20 years of earlier settlements in the 1780s and 1790s, land owner and Revolutionary veteran Colonel William Lytle gave land to establish the Public Square, a community cemetery, and its adjacent First Presbyterian Church. Initially named Cannonsburgh, after a political dignitary in the area—Newton Cannon—for 30 some days, Lytle then specified, for reasons unknown, that the new community be renamed Murfreesborough in honor of a Revolutionary War friend, Colonel Hardy Murfree. Murfreesboro was chartered in 1811 by the Tennessee legislature. The city would function under the 1811 charter until it was replaced by a more up-to-date charter in 1931. Murfreesboro, in 1811, was also designated as the county seat of Rutherford County (chartered 1803) replacing Jefferson (designated in 1803) due to the concentrated population in the Murfreesboro area. The first courthouse was completed in 1813 and served as the capitol of Tennessee from 1818 to 1826. In the 1840s Murfreesboro could have become the permanent capital but local public officials did not help state Democrats attempting to achieve the relocation by objecting to pay the $100 necessary to move the official records of Tennessee from Nashville to Murfreesboro.

The new city, adjacent to the west fork of the Stones River, was initially connected to markets by riverboat, wagon, and stage for purposes of trade and transportation, until the arrival of the railroad in 1851.

A half century after its founding, Murfreesboro became a household word during the Civil War. By the summer of 1862, the Union army occupied the city only to be driven out shortly afterward by Confederate forces under Colonel Nathan Bedford Forrest from neighboring Marshall County. In December 1862 two major armies collided. The Union forces of General William S. Rosecrans and the Confederates under General Braxton Bragg fought for three days in early winter (December 31, 1862-January 2, 1863) with casualties exceeding 24,000. A national cemetery was established as a burial ground for the Union dead. Confederate casualties were later exhumed and the mostly unidentified bodies were re-buried at the Confederate Memorial Circle in the city's new Evergreen Cemetery. Following the battle, Union forces constructed the massive Fortress Rosecrans as a base and supply depot for the planned drive against Chattanooga and Atlanta.

After the end of the war in 1865, Murfreesboro became an early market center with a bustling retail trade on its Public Square while continuing its earlier role in agriculture. One noteworthy planter and businessman, a local physician from Tidewater North Carolina, Dr. James Maney, built a landmark property beginning in the 1810s. The home today is preserved by the Oaklands Association and functions as a Civil War-era museum. The symbol of the community became the Rutherford County Courthouse constructed in 1857–59 with strong resemblance to the recently completed Tennessee State Capitol by Philadelphia architect William Strickland. The distinctive first cupola was replaced near the turn of the century with a cupola of Victorian design. In 1997 the interior restoration of the National Register-listed courthouse was completed.

Education has always been a prominent interest of Murfreesboro citizens. As early as 1806 a first academy was founded. Later (1840s) the successor building apparently bore the name of an early headmaster named Bradley. One of the most distinguished early graduates of Bradley Academy was future president James Knox Polk who also married a Murfreesboro woman he met while a student, Sarah Childress. Bradley later merged with local Union University and after the Civil War the building became a center of black education and a black community center. In 1997 the Bradley Academy was restored by the city as a heritage center. Other prominent natives of Murfreesboro include novelist Mary Noailles Murfree (writing as Charles Egbert Craddock), legendary sportswriter Grantland Rice, astronaut Rhea Seddon, and Jean Faircloth MacArthur, wife of the late General Douglas MacArthur. Today the Murfreesboro City Schools serve over 5,500 students on nine campuses. The city schools have been early leaders in education reform. One K-8 school is the first in Tennessee to combine a year-round normal calendar and the Paidea teaching method. Another school is one of only two in the state offering a dual calendar, one traditional and the other year-round. Earlier, the city schools system had received national attention for the development of its Extended School Program (ESP).

Modern higher education came to Murfreesboro in 1906 with the founding of the Tennessee College for Women. Following enabling legislation passed by the Tennessee General Assembly to create regional colleges in each of the three grand divisions of Tennessee in 1909, Middle Tennessee State Normal School at Murfreesboro was founded in 1911. In 1997 Middle Tennessee State University (MTSU) became the second largest university in Tennessee.

The presence of the colleges, and an activist Red Cross program led by Simeon Christy, encouraged the Commonwealth Fund of New York to launch an innovative rural health program in Murfreesboro during the 1920s. Eventually the project produced both the Rutherford Health Center, an early national training center in public health, and the Rutherford Hospital. The sale of the Rutherford Hospital in the 1980s has since produced a modern medical center, the Middle Tennessee Medical Center, and a key foundation, the Christy-Houston Foundation, which supports the city's quality of life through annual donations to institutions ranging from the Oaklands Association to MTSU. In the late 1930s the Public Works Administration built a modern V.A. hospital (now the Alvin C. York VA Medical Center).

After World War II, Murfreesboro leaders witnessed a decline in agriculture in the area and began to seek a more diversified economic base. The State Farm Insurance Company regional office in Murfreesboro was the first step in that direction.

Municipal government services are the ultimate responsibility of the City Council, six members elected at large and an elected mayor as chair. Policies are implemented by an appointed city manager.

One recent city project was to link its major historic sites by riverside greenways. Over five miles along Stones River and Lytle Creek had been completed by 1997. Plans were also being reviewed for a children's discovery education center at a former city waterworks site and to develop a municipal museum in a recently vacated school building.

In 1976 Murfreesboro was recognized as one of the national leaders by the American Revolution Bicentennial Administration for its "Cannonsburgh: A Living History Museum of Early Southern Life" project which today is administered by the city.

The city also took the leadership to bring together the needs of both the local Linebaugh Library and the city government for new facilities. The resulting Civic Plaza project provided space for these needs as well as underground parking for almost 900 cars and a garden area with substantial outdoor assembly space.

Murfreesboro has recently been named the "Most Livable Town in Tennessee" and its government was recognized as one of the one percent "best performing" in the United States.

James K. Huhta, Middle Tennessee State University
SEE: BRADLEY ACADEMY; COMMONWEALTH FUND; FORREST, NATHAN B.; FORTRESS ROSECRANS; MIDDLE TENNESSEE STATE UNIVERSITY; MURFREE, MARY N.; OAKLANDS; POLK, SARAH C.; RICE, GRANTLAND; TENNESSEE COLLEGE FOR WOMEN; STONES RIVER, BATTLE OF

MURRELL, JOHN ANDREWS (1806–1844), a thief and counterfeiter, spent much of his short life in prison and was a notorious outlaw in antebellum Middle Tennessee. In 1844 he died in Pikeville at the age of 38, shortly after he completed nine years hard labor for slave stealing.

Murrell acquired a reputation as a criminal mastermind soon after his imprisonment. In 1835 a small pamphlet appeared which purported to be Murrell's life story as he himself revealed it to Virgil A. Stewart (the chief witness against Murrell). Murrell's "confessions" not only described the murderous career of a monster with a grudge against the human race, they also purported to reveal the existence of a vast conspiracy, the aim of which was to bring about a region-wide slave insurrection. The pamphlet would have been consigned to richly deserved oblivion had not certain white residents of Madison County, Mississippi, believed Stewart's outrageous story. Slaves were questioned near Livingston, the county seat, and under torture revealed the existence of a conspiracy. The fear spread rapidly through the other counties of western Mississippi. White men, mostly outsiders and strangers believed to be members of the imprisoned Murrell's band, were rounded up. The hangings and whippings began, though with a semblance of legality, as committees of safety sprang up and handed down sentences. Over 50 white men and an unknown number of blacks (mostly freemen) were either hanged or savagely whipped and banished. The entire episode was inspired by the depraved Stewart's imaginary tale.

James L. Penick, Jr., Charleston, South Carolina
SEE: BLEDSOE COUNTY

MUSEUM OF APPALACHIA, located near the town of Norris in Anderson County, contains the state's largest collection of historic buildings, artifacts, and folk art associated with the diverse cultures of Appalachia. Established by John Rice Irwin, the museum is a unique monument to the mountain lifestyle and to the persistent drive of Irwin himself to amass a significant collection of Appalachian history and culture.

The 65-acre museum contains a collection of more than 35 authentic log cabins and buildings recreating an early to mid-nineteenth century Appalachian community complete with houses (including Mark Twain's family's Tennessee home), privies, corn cribs, smokehouses, barns, blacksmith shops, a school, and a church. It is one of the best places in Tennessee to view the unique cantilever barn type. Its Arnwine House, a single-pen log dwelling, is listed in the National Register of Historic Places. The various buildings are completely furnished, with every interior detail carefully addressed. "It's easy enough to bring in an old log cabin, set it up and get everything right from a structural standpoint," Irwin observed in materials submitted to the *Encyclopedia* editors. "It's much more difficult to get every item just the way it should be. It is such things as the handmade corner cupboard and the little items on the shelves that really represent the culture of the people in this area."

Irwin began his collection in 1962 when he was shocked to hear what buyers at an auction of a old farmstead near Norris planned to do with the items—changing a cedar churn, for example, into a lamp. What started as a one-man effort to preserve Appalachian history has evolved into a huge collection of over 250,000 items displayed in the restored buildings and an exhibit barn. Irwin also collected stories about the various artifacts, like a meal barrel that belonged to John Sallings, who some claim was the last veteran of the Civil War. "These old relics really don't mean very much unless you know the histories that go with them," Irwin insists.

The Museum of Appalachia also features the Appalachian Hall of Fame, which is housed in a three-story brick building. It contains exhibits, handmade and unusual musical instruments, and a large Indian collection. The museum's Tennessee Fall Homecoming, held the second full weekend every October, is one of the most popular autumn events in the region, attracting hundreds of Appalachian musicians and craftspeople as well as thousands of visitors. "Christmas in Old Appalachia" is another popular annual event. In a generation, the Museum of Appalachia has become one of Tennessee's most popular cultural institutions and its important collections have been featured in national travel magazines, the *Smithsonian* magazine, and in national and international newspapers.

Carroll Van West, Middle Tennessee State University
Source: The Editor-in-Chief acknowledges the assistance of
and material by John Rice Irwin in preparing this entry.
SEE: ANDERSON COUNTY; BARNS, CANTILEVER; DECORATIVE ARTS, APPALACHIAN

MUSGRAVE PENCIL COMPANY.

Commonplace but enduring, the wood cased pencil industry ventured onto the Tennessee industrial landscape in the first quarter of the twentieth century. The industry took advantage of the state's ubiquitous and prolific red cedar and a recycling scheme that exchanged cedar rail fences for modern wire equivalents. James Raford Musgrave sent out crews to trade and install new wire and pole fences for the old cedar rails. On some exceptionally large tracts, Musgrave's representatives purchased rails. Already dry, weathered, and pristine for the purpose, the cedar rails were perfect for cutting into pencil slats at the Shelbyville mill. The milled slats went from Shelbyville to German manufacturers, like Faber.

When World War I interfered with the exchange of goods, Musgrave turned to the close-knit American pencil manufacturers to market his slats. In 1919 the Pencil Makers Association organized to represent and unify the industry. This action promoted an exchange of raw material and technology within the domestic market. Musgrave brought a German machinist to Shelbyville and used his expertise to continue the transformation of his mill to encompass the entire operation of pencil manufacturing. As the Tennessee sources of red cedar logs and rail fences disappeared, the California Incense Cedar—a fast growing, plentiful, wood with similar characteristics—replaced it. By the time of the Great Depression, the Shelbyville company not only made its own pencils, but J.R. Musgrave nurtured the establishment of other local pencil manufacturers as well as the specialty advertising imprinting industry. During World War II, many women went to work in the pencil factory.

Situated in a designated industrial neighborhood, near the original Bedford County Fairgrounds, Musgrave Pencil Company became the workplace of generations of millhands. In recognition of its exceptional contributions to the pencil industry and the economic growth of the community and state, Governor Buford Ellington named Shelbyville "The Pencil City" in the 1950s.

Today, production focuses on a quality woodcased writing instrument for schools, offices, and specialty advertising. Recent additions to the line include the Musgrave Designer pencil, with glitz and sparkle for holidays, and messages and colors for the "techno" generation. Harvest Packaging was created for packaging multiple production items. A Tennessee product, the Musgrave pencil is a result of commitment at all levels from materials to management.

Lynn W. Hulan, Shelbyville
SEE: BEDFORD COUNTY

MUSIC.

Folk music expresses the the oldest and most basic forms of Tennessee music that were carried into the region by its earliest settlers, usually passed on from generation to generation by oral tradition. Though instrumental music—especially that of the fiddle and banjo—formed part of this tradition, vocal music was at the heart of it, and on the Tennessee frontier singing was an important and widespread recreation. One body of music was designed for public performance, in church gatherings, at dances, corn shuckings, and other community events. A second body was a domestic tradition, performed in the home for family gatherings or evening chores. Early collections of folk songs indicate that as many women sang as men, though more men tended to be fiddlers and banjo players. Most genuine traditional singers sang unaccompanied, developing highly ornamented styles, unorthodox phrasing and meter, and even "gapped" scales which relied on five or six notes rather than the standard seven.

Many of the vocal songs, especially in the domestic scene, were ballads, or narrative songs. The oldest of these had pedigrees that went back to seventeenth century England, Ireland, and Scotland, and many had been brought over by the Scots-Irish and English immigrants. Tennessee was not unique in giving a new home to these old ballads (sometimes dubbed Child ballads in honor of the Harvard professor who catalogued them); they were found all over the South and even into the New England states. But the state was unusually rich in them, was full of isolated areas that helped preserve them, and attracted the attention of numerous pioneering folk song collectors. As early as 1912, E.C. Perrow was publishing Tennessee songs in *The Journal of American Folklore,* and by 1917 the British scholar Cecil Sharp was trouping through East Tennessee gathering texts and music for his classic *English Folk-Songs from the Southern Appalachians* (1932).

Various collections made in the state reveal that songs like *Barbara Allen* and *The House Carpenter* seem to have been the most popular here. Both are sad, tragic stories that many of the old singers referred to as "love songs," and that go on for as many as 20 or 25 stanzas. Soon Americans were crafting their own ballads, modeled on the older imports. A local favorite was the murder ballad *The Knoxville Girl,* in which the narrator kills his fiancee and throws her body into the "river that flows through Knoxville town." Though many listeners have assumed the song referred to a real murder in Knoxville, it was in fact a reworking of the British *Wexford Girl,* with the place names changed. Other native ballads, though, were based on actual local events. *The Hills of Roane County* was a well-known account of a nineteenth century murder that took place in Spencer while *The Braswell Boys* described a killing and hanging in Putnam County. Broadside ballads—songs about specific tragedies or newsworthy events often sold on printed cards or sheets of paper—continued another old British tradition. *The Newmarket Wreck* described a train crash early in the century; *Shut Up in the Mines at Coal Creek* dealt with a mine cave-in north of Knoxville; *The John T. Scopes Trial* chronicled the "monkey trial" at Dayton. From the 1930s well into the 1970s, local singers were still using the broadside

form to protest the building of the Norris Dam, working conditions at a Tullahoma laundry, and highway engineering at Knoxville's "malfunction junction" or "Bloody Highway 31W."

Throughout the nineteenth century, other musical streams fed into this river of traditional song. Minstrel shows, which became popular in the 1840s, spread songs throughout the rural South, some of which (such as *Walk, Tom Wilson*) remained in repertoires until the present day. The original Davy Crockett song, a piece called *Pompey Smash,* was a minstrel show favorite that Tennesseans liked to sing for generations before the Walt Disney theme that began "Born on a mountain top in Tennessee." The Civil War spread many composed songs around the area, such as *Lorena* and *I'm a Good Old Rebel.* Sentimental parlor songs, such as *The Blind Child, Girl in Sunny Tennessee,* and *The Orphan Girl,* at one time had well-known composers and sold thousands of sheet music copies, but over the years entered folk tradition across the state, especially in Middle Tennessee. Starting in the 1920s, a similar transformation occurred with phonograph records, when songs by Jimmie Rodgers, Uncle Dave Macon, and the Carter Family were learned and put into tradition.

Following in the footsteps of Cecil Sharp came a number of dedicated folk song collectors. One of the first native Tennesseans to do this was a Fisk chemistry professor named Thomas Talley. In addition to being the nation's first African-American folksong collector, Talley was also one of the first to explore the black song traditions in Middle Tennessee; his *Negro Folk Rhymes,* originally published by a national press in 1922, revealed a wealth of non-ballad material, and showed the extent to which black and white musics overlapped. Lucien and Flora MacDowell, working from their base in the Smithville area, gathered songs and play-party games from the area, though they had to publish their best work through an obscure press in Michigan. Edwin Kirkland, an English professor at the University of Tennessee, made some of the first field recordings in the state in the late 1930s, while his student Ruby Duncan made an important ballad collection from the Chattanooga area. Other early field recordings in the 1930s were made by John Lomax (prison songs from Nashville) and Sidney Robertson Cowell (songs from the Cumberland Plateau and the Homestead project). George Peabody College professors Charles Pendleton and Susan Riley encouraged graduate students to make regional collections of songs for M.A. theses, resulting in fine material from Cannon, Macon, Maury, Overton, Carter, and Putnam counties. George P. Jackson, another Nashville scholar, explored the complex heritage of religious music starting with his classic *White Spirituals in the Southern Uplands* (1933).

Later decades saw further work by Mary Barnicle and her husband Tilman Cadle, who traveled around the Tennessee-Kentucky mountains with a portable disc cutting machine in the 1940s and 1950s. In the l960s East Tennessee State University professors Thomas Burton and Ambrose Manning continued to gather and record songs from the Appalachian area—especially the singing traditions on Beech Mountain—and made pioneering efforts to integrate the music into their college courses. In the 1950s another important academic, George Boswell, who had grown up and attended Peabody in Nashville, embarked on a major collection of folk songs not from the mountains, but from the Middle Tennessee and Nashville area. He found to his delight that these areas were as rich in song as the more colorful ones to the east, and eventually he amassed the words and music to over 1,200 songs, some of which were published in 1996 as *Folk Songs of Middle Tennessee* (ed. Charles Wolfe). In the 1980s Bob Fulcher of the Tennessee Department of Conservation initiated the State Parks Folklife Project, which involved extensive documentation of a wide variety of traditional cultural forms. Fulcher's most important discovery was Dee Hicks, from Fentress County, who had one of the richest and rarest repertoires of any modern ballad singer and who sang at the fiftieth anniversary of the Library of Congress' Archive of American Folk Song.

Instrumental music in the nineteenth century was built around the fiddle and the banjo. The former was imported from British and continental sources, replete with a battery of tunes. In pre-war times, figures like Andrew Jackson danced to the fiddling of slaves, and for much of the nineteenth century as many blacks played the fiddle as did whites. Though it was sometimes called "The Devil's Box" because of its association with parties and dancing, by the 1880s the fiddle became the central icon in the "War of the Roses" between Tennessee's "fiddling governors," Alf and Bob Taylor. The banjo, or "banjar" as it was sometimes called, was an import from Africa, played often by slaves and popularized by minstrel shows. An easy instrument to make on the frontier—a cured skin head and gut strings were common in the early days—the banjo began winning middle-class acceptance in the l880s, when it was a common instrument on the vaudeville stage. Other instruments used in vernacular music in the state included the autoharp (a favorite in East Tennessee, especially as a device to accompany singing), the harmonica (especially popular in Middle Tennessee, where it sometimes substituted for the fiddle in a string band), and the dulcimer. The latter included the familiar mountain dulcimer (in the upper east end of the state), the hammered dulcimer (a totally different instrument, often characterized by a set of as many as 52 taunt strings, and popular in Middle Tennessee), and the "Ten-

nessee music box," a square shaped instrument played like a mountain dulcimer but found primarily in the southern part of the state.

Starting in the late 1800s, various "fiddler's carnivals" or fiddlers' contests sprang up around the state, some attracting dozens of area musicians. Bigger festivals since have emerged to celebrate not only the fiddle, but other instruments, old-time buck dancing, square dancing, singing, and crafts. Among the long-running ones are ones at Smithville, Murfreesboro, Memphis, and Norris. Smaller community festivals are emerging yearly, as much to attract tourists as to maintain tradition, and by the 1990s the concept of "cultural tourism" was winning favor in the halls of state government.

During the late nineteenth century, ragtime became one of the first native American musical forms to become internationally popular. Though many fans today associate it as a musical style featuring a honky-tonk piano and the Gay 90s repertoire, serious ragtime was an important style of music composition and performance. And while Scott Joplin, the best known composer of the age, did not start publishing his rags until 1899, earlier composers helped pave the way. Tennessee played a minor but vital role in the early development of the genre.

Most Tennessee ragtime composers came from the mid-state and created compositions so distinctive and numerous (some 18 rags were published there around the turn of the century) that some historians speak of a "Nashville style" in early ragtime. Perhaps the most prolific and well-known was Columbia native Charles Hunter (1876–1906), who worked for the French Piano Company in Nashville and had many of his early works published by Frank G. Fite in Nashville. Hunter became a master of the kind of "folk rag" that pre-dated the later classic rags of Joplin; his *Possum and Taters, A Ragtime Feast* (1900) was derived from rural string bands he had heard as a boy, and *Just Ask Me* (1902) became a staple in folk ragtime repertoires. His *Tickled to Death* (1899) also became a standard of sorts, and was even recorded on early Victrola records by Prince's Band. A graduate of the Tennessee School for the Blind, Hunter later moved to St. Louis, where he worked in the red light district before his early death.

Tennessee's other great ragtime composer was Thomas E. Broady, of whom far too little is known. Though a native of Illinois, he moved to Middle Tennessee (possibly in Clarksville) and began publishing pieces through the H.A. French Company as early as 1898. Critics consider his *Mandy's Broadway Stroll* to be one of the best ragtime marches while *A Tennessee Jubilee* (1899) and *Whittling Remus* (1900) are both important links between older cakewalks and the new rag styles. Both Hunter and Broady are still performed by modern ragtime players and have been recorded on LP and CD. A third composer was Lew Roberts, who wrote and self-published numerous more derivative rags such as *The Glad Rag* in the first decade of the century.

During the l920s and l930s a number of rags were routinely featured by performers on WSM's "Grand Ole Opry," who converted the piano rags to string band style. Prominent among these were the McGee Brothers, Sam and Kirk, and the band of Dr. Humphrey Bate. In the early 1950s a young Gallatin native named Johnny Maddox began recording piano ragtime for a local label called Dot records, and soon became one of the most popular instrumentalists in the country. In 1951 a Nashville native named Adeline Hazelwood, working under the stage name Del Wood, recorded a ragtime piano version of the old pop tune *Down Yonder* for another Tennessee independent label, Tennessee. It became a national bestseller, won Wood a spot on the Grand Ole Opry, and began a long series of ragtime LPs for the prestigious RCA label.

Though the term "blues" has been traced back to the 1740s, it has historically been associated with an emotional state rather than a specific music. Only in the early twentieth century did the term become attached to a musical style, and Tennessee musicians played crucial roles in popularizing and defining it. Two of the earliest figures were composer and bandleader W.C. Handy (1873–1958) and singer Bessie Smith (1894–1937). In addition to being founders of the genre, both shared a number of characteristics: both based their music on deep-rooted African-American folk traditions, both utilized the mass media in popularizing their music, and both took their music far beyond Tennessee to achieve national popularity.

Handy, the son of ex-slaves, was actually born in Florence, Alabama, a few miles south of the Tennessee state line; there he absorbed a rural black musical culture that ranged from church music to fiddle tunes, and from minstrel shows to brass bands. As a young man, he lived in Mississippi and Kentucky before settling in Memphis about l908. In Memphis he began translating some of the black folk music to written form; his first publication was *Memphis Blues* (l912), derived from a campaign song he had written for Edward H. "Boss" Crump. In 1914 he issued *St. Louis Blues*, which was to define the blues for millions of fans and become one of the most widely performed songs in American history. During this time, Handy also led a popular dance orchestra, playing on riverboats and for fancy Memphis balls. Handy had won fame in earlier days as a cornet player, and while his orchestra (which began recording in 1917) was not very jazz-like, it was a good representation of the popular dance music of the day. In

1918 Handy moved to New York City, where his career as a performer and music entrepreneur continued. He often visited Memphis in later days, where he was honored by having a park on Beale Street named after him.

Bessie Smith, still referred to by many as "the world's greatest blues singer," grew up in Chattanooga in extreme poverty, making her first stage appearance there at the Ivory Theater at age nine. Learning from a local singer named Cora Fisher, Bessie soon found herself traveling the South in tent and minstrel shows; by l923 she started recording for Columbia Records in New York. She specialized in singing the "classic blues" or "city" blues, usually on vaudeville stages, accompanied by a piano, a jazz band, or a jazz soloist like young Louis Armstrong. Her recordings of *Gulf Coast Blues, St. Louis Blues, After You're Gone,* and *Nobody Knows You When You're Down and Out* sold thousands of copies, both to white and black audiences. By l929 her national fame was such that Hollywood featured her in a short film called "St. Louis Blues." Her turbulent life, complicated by bouts of alcoholism, was cut short when she died in an automobile accident as she was on the verge of a comeback in l937.

The golden age of blues in Tennessee was the decade of 1925-1935 when dozens of skilled musicians, mostly from West Tennessee and the Delta, recorded for major record companies at "field sessions" staged in Memphis. The Victor Talking Machine Company along with other major labels recorded annually in the city from l927 until l930. Especially popular was a group called The Memphis Jug Band, an informal street-corner assembly that featured homemade instruments such as the kazoo and jug (blown into to create a false bass), as well as harmonicas, guitars, banjos, and even fiddle. Led by a young black Memphis native named Will Shade, the band enjoyed huge hit recordings with titles like *Sun Brimmer's Blues* and *K.C. Moan*. The band recorded extensively through the 1920s, and enjoyed considerable sales during the Depression. A rival jug band group was Cannon's Jug Stompers, led by the talented songster and banjoist Gus Cannon, who was then living in Ripley, Tennessee, where he worked with his harmonica player Noah Lewis. Their signature songs included *Going to Germany, Minglewood Blues,* and *Feather Bed*. Such bands were transitional in nature, mixtures of the "pure" archaic blues with vaudeville tunes, ragtime, and even early pop music. Their infectious music attracted thousands of new fans in the 1960s when young folk music fans like Bob Dylan heard it reprinted on LPs.

During the 1920s and 1930s Memphis became the nation's leading recording center for the most basic and influential form of blues, the "Delta blues." Though the form, which featured complex figures played on an acoustic guitar as well as intricate vocals, was centered in northern Mississippi, most of its practitioners were drawn to Memphis to record or seek fame. One of the best was Furry Lewis, who recorded in the 1920s and continued to be active through the 1960s. A genuine Memphis native was Frank Stokes, a versatile guitarist who recorded widely and often performed as one-half of a duo called The Beale Street Shieks. Of the same generation was Mississippi Fred McDowell (1904-1972), who actually enjoyed his greatest popularity touring at folk and blues festivals in the 1960s. One of the new women stars from this era was Memphis Minnie (Lizzie Douglas), who started out playing on street corners in Memphis; she was a superb guitarist and singer, as well as a composer. Her first signature song was *Bumble Bee Blues*; in the 1930s she and her husband, another bluesman named "Kansas Joe," moved to Chicago, where she became one of the most-recorded singers of her time. In 1941 she wrote and recorded her most popular song, *Me and My Chauffeur,* and in 1958 returned to Memphis, where she continued to record before her death in 1973.

Areas around Memphis also produced many fine bluesmen. From Brownsville came the intense Sleepy John Estes, who featured songs about local events that were intensely autobiographical; Yank Rachel, an oft-times companion of Estes who featured the mandolin, an instrument seldom associated with blues; and Hammie Nixon, who often backed Rachel at country dances and shows. All of them knew Sonny Boy Williamson (born in Jackson in 1914), a composer and harp player who was the center of a nascent blues scene in Jackson. Though Sonny Boy (not to be confused with a later artist of the same name associated with blues radio) eventually took his music north, his records, like the memorable *Good Morning, Little School Girl,* circulated throughout the South and were widely imitated.

After World War II, new generations of West Tennesseans continued to develop and popularize the rich blues traditions. Many of these newer singers utilized modern instrumentation such as the electric guitar, drums, amplified harmonica, and saxophone. Key figures of this new era include Big Maybelle (born Maybelle Louise Smith in Jackson, 1924), who started her career singing in Memphis in the 1930s before going to New York to work with various jazzmen. In the late 1940s she became one of the pioneer rhythm and blues singers. Pianist Memphis Slim (aka Peter Chatman, born in Memphis in 1915) for years played with the legend Big Bill Broonzy before going out on his own and winning great fame overseas, especially in France. Bobby Blue Bland (born Robert Calvin Bland in Rosemark in 1930) developed a soulful, intimate blues style in the 1950s and 1960s with hits like *That's the Way Love Is* and

Turn on Your Love Light. Other second generation artists to win major fame include singer Koko Taylor, guitarist and singer Johnny Shines, pianist and singer Cecil Gant (who worked out of Nashville and often did studio work for country singers), Sparky Rucker, Little Laura Dukes, widely recorded singer and guitarist Brownie McGhee (from Knoxville), and pianist-singer Leroy Carr. Tina Turner, who became one of the country's most popular singers in the 1980s, hailed from the tiny West Tennessee town of Nutbush.

By far, though, the best known of all the modern blues giants from West Tennessee has been Riley "B.B." King. Coming from a poor sharecropping family in Indianola, Mississippi, where he was born in 1925, he started out singing gospel music until after his service in the army, and later move to Memphis in 1947. He soon got a disc jockey job on WDIA, billing himself as "The Blues Boy from Beale Street," a sobriquet which eventually was shortened to "Blues Boy" and then "B.B." Starting in the 1950s, he began recording for a variety of independent labels, eventually crafting such classics as *Lucille* and *The Thrill is Gone.* During the Rock-n-Roll era of the 1960s, he used his newly won prestige to become an articulate spokesman for the blues, for younger blues musicians, and for the historical study of the blues. In the 1990s he was serving as a spokesman for Tennessee tourism and involved with a Beale Street nightclub.

Though the term "country music" did not come into general use until the late 1940s, the commercialization of Anglo-American folk music had been underway since the early 1920s. During that decade, the traditional singing, fiddling, and banjo playing that had been endemic throughout the South gained access to the new mass media such as radio, the phonograph record, and the mass-produced songbooks. The result was a new commercial art form, as well as a new class of professional and semi-professional entertainers, one that was in many ways centered in Tennessee. Called variously "old time music," "old Southern tunes," "hill country tunes," "native American melodies," and "hillbilly music," this new hybrid music was as much folk as it was commercial.

Tennesseans played no part in the first recorded fiddle record (in 1922) or the first recorded country vocal record (in 1923), but by 1924 several Tennessee performers made trips to New York to commit their music to wax. Most were "discovered" and promoted by a Knoxville record dealer named Gus Nennsteil, who worked with the state-wide Sterchi Brothers furniture stores and had good contact with an early label called Vocalion. These pioneers included Charley Oaks, a street singer from Knoxville; Uncle Am Stuart, a fiddler from Morristown; and George Reneau, "The Blind Minstrel of the

Smoky Mountains," from Cocke County; and the most important, Uncle Dave Macon from Kittrell in Rutherford County.

David Harrison Macon (1870–1952) hailed from Smartt Station in Warren County, where his father had been a distiller and former Civil War captain. As he grew up, he learned to play different styles on the banjo, and to sing old folk songs, parlor songs, vaudeville tunes, and many comic songs drawn from African-American sources. For much of his life Macon farmed and ran a freight line between Murfreesboro and Woodbury, but when trucks put his mule teams out of business in the early 1920s, he began to play professionally, first on the Loew's vaudeville circuit, and then on the new Nashville radio show that would become the Grand Ole Opry. A superb comedian, clear-voiced singer, and dexterous banjoist, he became the first Tennessean to win national fame through music. Among his signature songs were *Keep My Skillet Good and Greasy, Cripple Creek, Rockabout My Saro Jane,* and the gospel song *How Beautiful Heaven Must Be.* During the 1930s and 1940s, Macon traveled widely with Opry show groups, became a star on the radio, and even appeared in the Hollywood film *Grand Ole Opry* (1940). He recorded for almost every major record company, amassing a total of over 170 sides. Many of his records stayed in print into the 1990s, and an annual music festival named in his honor was started in Murfreesboro in 1978. Historians view him as country music's most important link between the rural folk music of the nineteenth century and the more modern country music of the twentieth.

By 1926 the record companies were bringing their studios to the artists rather than paying for them to make long trips to New York or Chicago. The most important of these "field sessions" was the one the Victor Talking Machine Company staged at Bristol in July and August 1927. This has been referred to as the "big bang" of country music—the event that in one dramatic two-week period at once established the music's aesthetic and commercial validity. Two of early country music's greatest acts, blue yodeller Jimmie Rodgers and the singing Carter Family, were discovered here, and dozens of others had their music preserved and disseminated, including everything from a gospel quartet from Alcoa to Bristol's Tenneva Ramblers string band to a Kentucky holiness preacher and his congregation. The Bristol sessions were such a dramatic success that they set off a trend for other field recording in the state. Victor returned to Bristol again in 1928, as well as setting up shop in Nashville for that city's first recording; Columbia did sessions in Johnson City and Memphis in 1928 and 1929, while Vocalion tried its luck in Knoxville in 1929 and 1930. All of these yielded a rich trove of Tennessee music as it sounded at the dawn of the commercial

era, and a number of artists used them to establish regional reputations. From Chattanooga came the prolific vocal duet of The Allen Brothers and the eclectic fiddle music of former coal miner Jess Young. The Knoxville area could boast of the influential duet harmony singing of McFarland and Gardner, with their songs like *When the Roses Bloom Again,* the popular tenor High Cross *(Wabash Cannonball),* and the charismatic family string band The Tennessee Ramblers. Upper East Tennessee was home of the remarkable singer and fiddler G.B. Grayson *(Lee Highway Blues)* as well as the fiddler Charles Bowman. Another family band, The Weems Family, from Perry County, made what many critics deem the finest two string band sides ever recorded, *Davy Davy* and *Greenback Dollar* (1928). Around Memphis, the duet of Reese Fleming and Respers Townsend adapted the blues to their harmony singing and falsetto yodeling, and recorded dozens of sides for major record companies. Around Nashville, most of the popular acts shared their recording fame with broadcasting stints on the Grand Ole Opry.

Though Memphis was becoming the home of the blues, the older African-American instrumental traditions of fiddle, banjo, and mandolin continued to be strong in other parts of the state. The Sequatchie Valley was home of the early duo of "The Two Poor Boys," Evans and McClain, who recorded rags, hoedowns, pop songs, and blues for numerous record companies. The square dance of John Lusk was for generations popular with both white and black dancers and was finally recorded by a team from the Library of Congress in 1946. Nashville could boast a number of black string bands which did "busking" on street corners; the best of these was the duo of Nathan Frazier (banjo) and Frank Patterson (fiddle), whose remarkable archaic work survives also only through the efforts of the Library of Congress. The Nashville Washboard Band often played in front of the state capitol in the 1940s and 1950s, and the eclectic band of James Campbell was popular with dancers in Nashville for generations. Howard Armstrong and his band did similar work in Knoxville and in the 1970s were discovered by young folklore enthusiasts and won new fame as Martin, Bogan, and Armstrong. Young Brownie McGhee grew up playing both country blues in Knoxville, while guitarist-singer Leslie Riddle, from Kingsport, taught both songs and playing techniques to Virginia's famed Carter Family. The 1980s brought attention to McDonald Craig, from Linden, who featured the classic repertoire of white bluesman Jimmie Rodgers.

The Depression curtailed the field sessions (as well as sales) for most record companies, and starting in the 1930s radio became the dominant medium for country music. Among the first Tennessee stations were WOAN in Lawrenceburg (one of the state's first stations, started in 1922 by gospel music publisher James D. Vaughan), WMC in Memphis, WDOD in Chattanooga, WNOX in Knoxville, WOPI in Bristol, and WSM in Nashville; all had taken to the air in the 1920s, and in those days of pre-network feeds, all drew upon local talent for a bevy of live programs. Several of these won serious fame and influence: for example, WNOX's "Mid-Day Merry-Go-Round" in the 1930s and WJHL (Johnson City) with its "Barrel of Fun" show in the 1930s. In the 1940s Bristol's WOPI began its "Farm and Fun Time," which became a launching pad for bluegrass greats like Flatt and Scruggs and the Stanley Brothers. But most successful of all was WSM in Nashville, which took to the air in October 1925 and three months later started what would become the Grand Ole Opry.

Increasingly throughout the 1930s the stars of these radio shows were country vocal soloists. Though centers like Nashville and Knoxville were attracting more and more artists from out of state, an impressive number of native Tennesseans played key roles in the development of modern country music. Probably the most famous of these was Roy C. Acuff (1903–1992), from the Maynardville area, who grew up actually listening to old mountain ballads, as well as working in one of the last rural medicine shows. After winning fame over Knoxville radio with a strange gospel song called *The Great Speckled Bird,* Acuff joined the Grand Ole Opry in 1938, and within months had become the show's biggest star. Singing in a high, lonesome mountain tenor, Acuff specialized in sentimental and gospel songs; he was featured on the NBC network portion of the show and made a string of Hollywood musicals in the 1940s. Through the 1970s and 1980s he became a fixture on the show as "The King of Country Music," a gray-haired and gracious ambassador to visitors like President Richard Nixon. A female counterpart to Roy (and an occasional duet partner) was Kitty Wells, born Muriel Deason in Nashville in 1919. She began her career on Nashville radio (WSIX) in 1936, soon married another local singer named Johnny Wright, and began a musical career that took her from Knoxville to Shreveport, Louisiana. She developed an emotional, plaintive singing style with an ornamentive "tear" that was perfect for the new kind of "cheating songs" that were beginning to emerge in the 1950s. Her 1952 recording *It Wasn't God Who Made Honky-Tonk Angels* is considered to be the first modern country song from a woman's point of view, and its success opened country doors for women to enter this male-dominated profession.

Another contemporary of Acuff's was Eddy Arnold, "The Tennessee Ploughboy," who was born in Chester County in 1918. He won his initial fame singing with Pee Wee King on the Opry in 1940, but soon went out on his own and developed a smooth, baritone style that had more in common with Bing Crosby than Acuff; by the 1960s he was singing in tuxedo and with a large orchestra to supper club audiences, regaling them with *Bouquet of Roses* and *Anytime*. In doing so he set the stage for a whole new style of "cosmopolitan" country that would encompass later singers like Jim Reeves and Ray Price. In East Tennessee a local singer and disc jockey (who often sang along with records on the air) named Tennessee Ernie Ford (1919–1991) moved country another few notches toward pop when he moved to the west coast, started a popular TV show, and recorded one of the biggest-selling records in history, *Sixteen Tons*.

A key figure in the development of Nashville into a recording center also came from East Tennessee: guitarist Chet Atkins, who hailed from Luttrell, north of Knoxville. As a musician, Atkins learned to play "Travis style" guitar, where the instrument is finger-picked instead of strummed. Starting his career at WNOX in Knoxville, he settled in Nashville in 1950, where he quickly learned he could make a living in the record studios that were just then starting to proliferate there. His versatility and skill soon led to his becoming a producer of sessions for RCA, and a key architect of the "Nashville sound," a style of studio back-up that dominated the music for the next two generations. Another key player in the creation of the studio system was sound genius Owen Bradley, born in Westmoreland in 1915. Growing up, he was interested in big bands and pop music and served as a musical director at WSM. In 1952 he opened a film studio in downtown Nashville, but soon was busy recording artists like Kitty Wells for Decca; three years later he created a new studio that became known as the Quonset Hut. It was one of the first studios on the strip now known as Music Row, and for years its legendary acoustic qualities made it the best studio in town.

By the 1960s Nashville had become the recording center for country music, as well as music publishers and the radio empire of the Grand Ole Opry. Dozens of talented musicians from around the country settled in Nashville to work there, but there remained an impressive cadre of native Tennesseans. These included Dolly Parton of Sevierville, who parlayed her singing style, songwriting genius, and buoyant personality into a music empire that included the huge theme park, Dollywood. Others included Carl Smith (from Maynardville), Dottie West (from McMinnville), Ronnie McDowell (from Fountain Head), Melba Montgomery (from Iron City), smooth singer George Morgan (from Waverly) and his daughter Lorrie (from Nashville). From Centerville came the Opry's most beloved comedienne, Sarah Ophelia Colley (Minnie Pearl).

The 1980s and 1990s saw country music go through a number of changes, both stylistic and commercial. Bluegrass music, which Bill Monroe (though a Kentuckian) had been defining from the Opry stage since 1939, reached new heights of popularity. Key players in the sound of Monroe's music included Lester Flatt and Jimmy Martin (from Sneedville). Earl Scruggs, a North Carolina native, moved to Tennessee in 1946 and used the state as his base as he popularized his unique "Scruggs style" banjo playing, eventually winning a National Heritage Fellowship in Washington for his contribution to American traditional culture. Second (and third) generations of younger bluegrass musicians, like the award-winning Nashville Bluegrass Band, moved the style into the 1990s. The so-called "new traditionalism" of the 1980s took Nashville music back to its roots, while the "Americana" movement of the 1990s led the music into a more eclectic direction. The development of the Opryland theme park in 1974, as well as the cable system Nashville Network (TNN) in 1983, gave Nashville an even bigger boost toward becoming a national "third coast" music center.

With the exception of a few scattered venues in Memphis and Nashville, Tennessee never developed a permanent and well-defined jazz venue like the larger cities of New York, Chicago, or San Francisco. Many of the jazz musicians who came from the state had to go north to nourish and develop their art, a pattern found in many rural southern states in the 1920s and 1930s. Though a good case could be made for the state's two great blues artists, Bessie Smith and W.C. Handy, being included in jazz histories, and for many of the great Memphis country blues artists being thought of as early jazz, there was a separate cadre of purely jazz players—a cadre that influenced almost every chapter in jazz history.

At the very dawn of jazz, when Louis Armstrong was forging his new style in Chicago, he was encouraged by Lil Hardin Armstrong, his piano player (and after 1924, his wife), who was from Memphis. Though overshadowed by her dynamic husband, Lil was a forceful pianist who later played with greats like Sidney Bechet and Henry "Red" Allen. Another key traditional musician was William "Buster" Bailey, a clarinet player from Memphis who moved to New York to perform with greats like Fletcher Henderson and King Oliver. One of the few early jazzmen to receive professional training, Bailey in later years made numerous guest appearances with symphonies across the country. A third Memphis native, Johnny Dunn, was a pioneer trumpet player in New York, and considered the hottest player there until Armstrong arrived. Pianist Lovie Austin (from Chattanooga) was a key figure in the early Chicago scene, and trumpeter Bob Shoffner (from Bessie, Tennessee) played second trumpet behind the great King Oliver himself.

In the 1930s, jazz moved into its second stage, swing, and the big bands emerged as the forum for the new style. For many, the essence of this new swing was Kansas City bandleader Count Basie, and one of the cornerstones of the Basie band was the Centerville, Tennessee, native Dickie Wells. His trombone style was one of the most influential of the time, with its unexpected octave jumps and rhythmic changes, and in later years scholars singled out his solos as reflecting the very core of swing style. In addition to Basie's band, one of the other top four swing bands was that of Jimmy Lunceford, and it too came out of Tennessee. Lunceford was a high school teacher in Memphis, though his band was first formed at Fisk in Nashville. By 1934 it began to enjoy the reputation as one of the best-disciplined big bands, with difficult arrangements by people like Sy Oliver. The group remained an important force through the 1940s, and a training ground for modern greats like Jimmy Crawford and arranger Gerald Wilson. The state also boasted some of the best "territory bands," groups which decided not to go north but to carve out a niche in the mid-South. Memphis had the exciting band of Charlie Williamson, whose leader became an RCA Victor talent scout for local blues singers; of Slim Lamar and his Southerners; and of Blue Steel, one of the strangest bandleaders of the time (he reportedly had fits of violence and had a metal plate in his head). Nashville could boast of the orchestras of the fine black pianist Brenton "Doc" Banks as well as the white bandleader Francis Craig. Related to the Craigs who owned WSM, Francis Craig began his career in 1925, became a fixture at the Hermitage Hotel, and trained a vocalist named James Melton, who would later become one of the most popular tenors of the 1940s. In 1948 Craig's band had a huge nationwide hit—probably the first million seller to be recorded in Nashville—with his lilting song *Near You*. Another Nashville band, led by Beasley Smith, became a training ground for jazz greats Phil Harris, Ray McKinley (later associated with Glenn Miller) and clarinet player Matty Matlock (long associated with Bob Crosby's band). In Knoxville, the big band of Maynard Baird was a fixture at WNOX and at the concerts at Market Hall.

Later in the 1940s, as jazz continued to evolve, contributors included the boogie woogie piano of Kingsport native Cripple Clarence Lofton; the Charlie Parker-influenced alto sax of Memphis native Sonny Criss; Oakdale native King Pleasure, who developed jazz bop singing, in the manner of today's Manhattan Transfer; pianist Phineas Newborn, Jr. (Whitesville), who spent his apprenticeship with Lionel Hampton and the Tennessee State Collegians and later worked with the legendary Charles Mingus; modern trombonist Jimmy Cleveland (Wartrace); tenor saxophonist Yusef Lateef, who experimented in fusing eastern music with jazz; and saxophonist-flutist Charles Lloyd. Isaac Hayes, whose scoring for the cult film *Shaft* made him known across America, helped put Memphis on the map as a center of soul music. Also winning national acclaim in the l960s was Aretha Franklin (born in Memphis), the "queen of soul," who started singing in the church of her father, the well-known C.L. Franklin. Nashville in the 1950s was the home of popular electric organist Lenny Dee, and in the 1980s saw the emergence of pianist Begee Adair.

In terms of mainstream pop singing, the state's best-known artist was probably Winchester native Dinah Shore. Born Francis Rose Shore in 1917, she won her initial fame singing over Nashville station WSM in the late l930s. During this time, WSM was feeding a great deal of programming to the national networks, and soon Shore had moved to New York where she sang with Latin bandleader Xavier Cugat, and appeared on NBC's jazz program with the Chamber Music Society of Lower Basin Street. She soon began to record as a soloist, enjoying 75 hit records from l940 to l954 on labels like Bluebird, RCA Victor, and Columbia. These included classic pop singles like *Blues in the Night* (1942), *I'll Walk Alone* (1944), *The Gypsy* (1946), *Buttons and Bows* (1948), and *Dear Hearts and Gentle People* (1949). During the 1950s, she devoted her talents to television, first with "The Dinah Shore Show" from 1951–57, then with the "Dinah Shore Chevy Show" from 1953–63 (with its famous theme, *See the USA in your Chevrolet*), and later with a morning talk show, "Dinah's Place" from 1970–1980. She was married to actor George Montgomery from 1943–1962, and died from cancer in 1994.

Though Tennessee is most readily associated with types of vernacular music, it did produce a number of performers and composers working in the more formal European tradition. As with jazz, the lack of suitable performance venues in the state in earlier times caused many performers in this mode to seek their careers in larger northern cities. One such performer was Emma Azalia Smith Hackley (born in Murfreesboro in 1867), who was one of the first great African-American soprano soloists. She eventually settled in Chicago, where in her later years she became very active in encouraging the careers of other black artists who excelled in formal music, and fought to gain recognition for her own African-American folk song heritage. In 1910, shortly before her death, she even traveled to Japan to expose this heritage to oriental audiences.

An even better known singer in his time was Roland Hayes (1887–1977), a tenor who was born in Georgia but brought up in Chattanooga. Like Emma Hackley, he was exposed as a youngster to the rich world of black folk music, and by 1910 was singing and even recording with the Fisk Jubilee Singers from Nashville. He moved to Boston to continue his studies of vocal music, having his first solo recital there in 1917. Soon he toured Europe to great acclaim, and performed at Carnegie Hall in l923. He was an outstanding interpreter of spirituals, but was equally at home with Schubert, Brahms, and Debussy. One historian concluded that he became the leading black male singer of his time, especially as a concert tenor during the 1920s to the 1940s.

A third African-American to stride the borders between art music and vernacular music was John Wesley Work III (1901–1967), a Tullahoma native who came from a family of important black composers, collectors, and scholars. His father, John Work (b. 1873), was the Harvard-educated leader in the Fisk Jubilee singers, and his uncle Frederick Jerome Work (b. 1880) published string quartets and sonatas, as well as collections of spirituals. After studying at Fisk, Work traveled to Columbia and Yale to further his work in composition, eventually returning to Fisk in 1933 to serve in various roles. His large output ranged from orchestral pieces to piano sonatas and arrangements of spirituals; in l946 his cantata *The Singers* won wide acclaim. He also was an important pioneer in studying black folk music, expanding vastly on the interest in spirituals shown by his father and uncle and working with folksong collector Alan Lomax to gather and record blues and black string band music.

Anglo-American composers from Tennessee also sought to bring the folk song tradition into more formal musical settings. Perhaps the best of these was Charles Faulkner Bryan (1911–1955). Bryan was a native of McMinnville who grew up in the hills of Warren County listening to local folk music, Sacred Harp singing, and pioneer broadcasts of the Grand Ole Opry. An early supporter and president of the Tennessee Folklore Society, he was especially interested in the history of the dulcimer, and traveled widely to build an impressive collection of the instruments; he made early 78 rpm records for an educational company in Chicago singing and playing the mountain dulcimer. After studying at Peabody College and serving as a state director for the WPA Federal Music Project, he journeyed to Yale, where he studied composition and theory with the distinguished composer Paul Hindesmith. This yielded a Guggenheim fellowship and the time to finish his first major work, *The Bell Witch* cantata, which had its premiere in Carnegie Hall under the direction of Robert Shaw. His lush, romantic *White Spiritual Symphony* emerged in the early 1950s, and in l952 he attracted national attention with his opera *Singing Billy,* co-authored by Vanderbilt writer Donald Davidson, and built on the life and music of the nineteenth century songbook publisher William Walker. He also produced a number of folksong collections for elementary and high schools.

Later composers from or active in the state include H. Gilbert Trythall (b. 1930) and his younger brother Richard (b. 1939); both natives of Knoxville, the brothers were active as composers and teachers during their careers. Gilbert especially has been a pioneer in electronic music. David Van Vactor (b. 1906), a composer and flautist, had established an impressive career before he moved to Knoxville to establish the school of fine arts at the University of Tennessee. His works include five symphonies, including the well-received *Walden* in 1971. In the 1990s a new generation of composers emerged, sharing their serious work with careers in the Nashville recording industry; these include double bass virtuoso Edgar Meyer, as well as violinist Mark O'Connor, who premiered his *Fiddle Concerto* with the Nashville Symphony in 1995.

Throughout much of the nineteenth century, gospel and religious music was pretty much a congregational affair, and the leaders were by and large composers and publishers such as M.L. Swan, whose mid-nineteenth century songbooks were printed in Knoxville and Nashville. By the latter years of the century, though, several gospel performers began to make a name for themselves. One was the songleader and composer Homer Rodeheaver (1880–1955), who came to age in the rough mountain logging communities of upper East Tennessee, and was for 20 years a songleader for the popular evangelist Billy Sunday. During this time, he helped popularize the new type of religious song that was more lively and more personal than earlier ones, and which gave the actual name "gospel song" to the genre. Another was the group known as the Fisk Jubilee Singers, organized in 1871 as a desperate ploy to raise money for their university. During the next three decades the group traveled widely both in the United States and abroad, issuing its own songbooks, exposing millions to the rich, if somewhat orchestrated, sounds of the African-American spiritual. As early as 1909, long before any other vernacular folk music had been recorded, a quartet drawn from the Singers recorded for the Victor Talking Machine Company. The original quartet was organized by John Work II, and included James Myers, Alfred King, and Noah Rider. These recordings were the first of a large number the Singers made for a variety of pre-World War I labels. Through the years, the Jubilee Singers continued to perform in a wide number of venues, and to even have a regular radio show over WSM. They survive as a singing group in the 1990s.

White gospel music, or as it is known today "southern gospel," started in Tennessee and in neighboring states through the efforts of music publisher James D. Vaughan (1864–1941). Born near Giles County, Vaughan studied music with the Reubusch-Kieffer company in the Shenandoah Valley, and learned a special, seven-shape note system that had won favor in the South at that time. After a tornado destroyed his home in Texas, where he had moved to teach music, he returned to Tennessee and, about 1901, began to publish his own collections of locally written, new gospel songs. The first of these was *Gospel Chimes,* and soon Vaughan was producing a new book every year and within ten years was selling over 800,000 copies a year. These books were "convention books," as opposed to regular church hymnals, and were used for special singings in the church—Wednesday night singings, competitions, and singing school exercises. Sometime about 1912 Vaughan hit upon the idea of having some of the workers at his Lawrenceburg publishing office go on the road as a quartet to demonstrate the new song books for prospective congregations. To that end, he provided the singers expenses and a car, and the first "Vaughan Quartets" hit the road. This was a spectacular success with church members, who soon began to enjoy the quartet music more than the songbooks themselves; the tail began wagging the dog. By 1924 Vaughan had no fewer than 16 different quartets traveling around the country, singing for free and selling hundreds of the little songbooks out of the trunk of the car.

Starting in 1922, Vaughan began to use mass media to promote his music. He opened WOAN, one of the first radio stations in the state, and began his own record company, the Vaughan Records, the very first southern-based record company. "Now you can have a Vaughan Quartet in your home without having to feed them," announced one of the advertisements. As the quartets developed, some began to break away from the support of the publishing company and go out on their own. By the 1930s some such groups, such as The Speer Family and the John Daniel Quartet, were winning slots on local radio stations like WSM. The publishing company also ran annual singing schools in Lawrenceburg in which thousands of Tennesseans learned the rudiments of harmony, meter, and composition. After Vaughan's death and the increasing development of music in the public school curriculum, these singing schools began to decline; the Vaughan company itself, though, continued to publish through the 1990s and a variety of ownership changes.

During the highwater mark of the southern gospel movement, in the 1930s and 1940s, Tennessee also had several other noteworthy publishers/promoters to emerge. One was the Tennessee Music and

Printing Company, located at Cleveland in the late 1920s, which boasted the talents of men like Otis McCoy and Connor B. Hall. In Chattanooga, one found the eastern branch office of the powerful, Texas-based Stamps-Baxter company, and in Nashville the venerable John T. Bentson Company. In Dayton was the extremely popular company of R.E. Winsett, whose books included the venerable *Soul Winning Songs* and remained popular until the 1960s. By the 1920s the McDonald Brothers, then headquartered in West Tennessee, became the first professional group to make a living full time with gospel music, as they popularized up-tempo pieces like *Rockin' on the Waves*. Soon the "gospel quartet" style—which could refer to any configuration of small group singing—was becoming popular with local amateur and family groups as well as increasing numbers of radio and touring groups. This tradition reached a peak of sorts in 1947, when a transplanted Georgian named Wally Fowler (b. 1917) moved to Oak Ridge to organize a slick, country sounding group called The Oak Ridge Quartet. This led to Fowler starting to book gospel groups in marathon concerts that he called "All-Night Sings;" the first of these dated from 1948, and continued to be a venue for two decades.

By the 1990s several "gospel quartets" around the state maintained both the black and white gospel traditions. In Memphis, The Spirit of Memphis Quartet served as a training ground for dozens of good singers and a means for maintaining the gospel style. In Nashville, the venerable Fairfield Four, dating from the 1920s and nationally popular on radio in the 1940s and 1950s, survived numerous personnel changes to keep alive their rich harmonies and songs. In the east, the Anglo-American tradition was preserved by Kingsport native Doyle Lawson and his group Quicksilver. Though often associated with bluegrass music, the Lawson band relies best on tight vocal harmonies and even *a capella* arrangements of some of the old Vaughan and Stamps favorites. In the meantime, Nashville emerged as the locus for a powerful modern gospel scene, sparked by Bebe Winans, Take 6, Bobby Jones, Amy Grant, and Gary Chapman.
Charles K. Wolfe, Middle Tennessee State University

MUSSELING. Typically, musseling has been a part-time, seasonal occupation to supplement the income of timber workers, farmers, or fisherman living near Tennessee's great rivers, though it always held the allure of a treasure hunt. Indians of the Woodland period gathered mussels, principally for food, and left enormous shell middens, or waste heaps.

Beginning in the 1850s, the search for freshwater pearls generated bursts of activity in American river towns. In 1914 W.E. Myers reported that a "magnificent pearl . . . probably worth . . . not less than $10,000," was found on the Caney Fork about 1876

and created the first pearl stir in Tennessee.[1] Searchers attempted pearling on all of Tennessee's principal waterways, including the Tennessee, Cumberland, Calfkiller, Duck, Elk, Stones, and Obey rivers. By the mid-1890s, operations on the Clinch River dominated the pearling industry.

John F. Boepple, a German immigrant, who first established the "pearl button" industry in America in 1891, introduced many Tennessee musselers to the commercial value of their discarded shells as button material. Between 1900 and 1920, button factories operated in Knoxville, Clarksville, Memphis, and Nashville. Weber and Sons Button Company operated at Savannah, Tennessee until the 1980s, even though plastic buttons had essentially replaced shell products by the late 1950s.

In 1947 Japanese pearlers imported a barge-load of Tennessee River mussels for use in the cultured pearl industry. By the 1960s, the Japanese market brought a revival of musseling activity, which has continued, with some 1,200 commercial licenses issued annually.

Historically, shellers took mussels by "toe-digging," (collecting them by hand in shallow water); "brailing" (dragging strands of knobbed, unbaited hooks across a mussel bed); or shoveling them up with forks, rakes, or dredges. Modern musselers prefer to dive, with the aid of an air compressor and long hose, feeling around the dark river bottom for shells.
Bob Fulcher, Clinton

CITATION:
(1) W.E. Myers, "Pearl Fisheries of Tennessee," in Transactions of *Tennessee Academy of Science* (1914): 19–25

SEE: TENNESSEE RIVER SYSTEM

MUSTARD, HARRY STOLL (1889–1966), public health physician, author, professor. Dr. Mustard's work in Tennessee made him a national figure in the emerging field of public health in the early twentieth century. Mustard was educated in his native state at the Medical College of South Carolina and the College of Charleston. He began his public health career with the U.S. Public Health Service in 1916, and was health officer for Preston County, West Virginia, in 1923.

The Commonwealth Fund selected Mustard as director of its Child Health Demonstration in Rutherford County, Tennessee, from 1924 to 1928. He also served as the county's public health officer. Mustard's success in developing a rural public health program here led to his appointment as assistant to the state commissioner of health in 1929 and as assistant commissioner in 1930. He published the results of the Rutherford County demonstration in *Cross-Sections of Rural Health Progress* for the Commonwealth Fund in 1930.

In 1932 Mustard joined the faculty of the Johns Hopkins University Medical School and then the New York University College of Medicine in 1937. From 1940 to 1950, he directed the Columbia University School of Public Health, and held the DeLamar Professorship of Public Health Practice. Mustard wrote several texts, including *An Introduction to Public Health* (published in five editions from 1935 to 1969), *Rural Health Practice* (1936), and *Government in Public Health* (1945).

Mustard may have described himself when he wrote in his 1935 text that "the physician entering this field . . . must be socially minded and socially adjusted. . . . He must be conscious of his own work as but one cog in society's machine for human betterment."[1]

Mary S. Hoffschwelle, Middle Tennessee State University

CITATION:

(1) Harry S. Mustard, *Introduction to Public Health*, 1st ed., (1935), 48.

SEE: COMMONWEALTH FUND; MEDICINE

MYER, WILLIAM EDWARD (1862–1923), was a leading figure in the early twentieth century transformation of Tennessee archaeology from a casual hobby to a professional science and in the development of both overland and river transportation systems. Myer was born in Kentucky in October 1862, but at about age six, he and his family moved to Carthage, where he spent most of the remainder of his life. In 1878 he entered Vanderbilt University and began his lifelong interests in business, transportation engineering, and archaeology.

Throughout his early life, he worked tirelessly in the development of the transportation infrastructure of Middle Tennessee. His leadership as president of the Cumberland River Improvement Society and Tennessee Good Roads Association eventually resulted in bridges over the Cumberland and Caney Fork Rivers. As organizer of the Cumberland Navigation Company, Myer operated a fleet of steamers on the upper Cumberland and took an active part in the development of river navigation.

Myer retired from his commercial pursuits in 1915 to focus research on the archaeology of the Cumberland River valley. His efforts were briefly interrupted in 1917, when he was called into the service of Tennessee during World War I as U.S. Fuel Administrator. Returning to his archaeological interests at the end of the war, Myer moved to Washington, D.C., in 1919, and became a Special Archaeologist with the Smithsonian Institution's Bureau of American Ethnology. Between 1919 and 1923, Myer mapped, surveyed, and conducted excavations at some of the most significant prehistoric archaeological sites in Tennessee, including Mound Bottom in Cheatham County, Gordontown in Davidson County, Pinson Mounds in Madison County, Castalian Springs in Sumner County, and Fewkes in Williamson County.

Unfortunately, in the midst of his work, Myer died of a heart attack on December 2, 1923. Although his most significant book, *Stone Age Man in the Middle South*, has not yet seen publication, a number of posthumous publications by the Smithsonian Institution remain classics of southeastern archaeology. Unlike most of his predecessors and contemporaries, Myer left substantive records of his research in both published and unpublished forms.

As a testimony to the national respect earned by Myer as Tennessee's first professional archaeologist and as a scholar in many fields, the Engineering Association of Nashville, the Tennessee Academy of Science, the Froelac Literary Club, the Tennessee Historical Society, the American Anthropological Association, the Smithsonian Institution, and the Tennessee Ornithological Society passed resolutions praising both his scholarship and his personal qualities. The transformation of William E. Myer from an educated antiquarian into a nationally recognized archaeologist marks the beginnings of the science of archaeology in Tennessee.

Kevin E. Smith, Middle Tennessee State University

SUGGESTED READINGS: John H. DeWitt, "[Obituary of] William Edward Myer," *Tennessee Historical Magazine* 8(1924): 225–230; Warren K. Moorehead, "Mr. W.E. Myer's Archaeological Collection," *Science* 60(1924): 159–160

SEE: CUMBERLAND RIVER SYSTEM; MOUND BOTTOM; PINSON MOUNDS

N

NAIFEH, JAMES O. (1939–), Speaker of the Tennessee House of Representatives, was born and raised in Covington, Tennessee. He attended local public schools and graduated from Byars Hall High School. Attending the University of Tennessee, Knoxville, he took a B.S. degree there in 1961. Naifeh next served in the U.S. Army Infantry, with the rank of 1st lieutenant, from 1962–1964.

Speaker of the House of Representatives James O. "Jimmy" Naifeh.

OFFICE OF THE SPEAKER

After his military service was completed, Naifeh returned to Covington and entered the grocery business and other retail concerns. Taking an active role in local and regional economic development, he has served as president of the Covington/Tipton County Chamber of Commerce and the Covington Rotary Club as well as serving on the boards of First State Bank of Covington, the Tennessee Wholesale Grocers, ALSAC-St. Jude Children's Research Hospital, and other institutions.

Naifeh's state political career began in 1974 when he successfully campaigned for the District 81 seat in the Tennessee House of Representatives. Since 1975, he has continuously served that district, compiling a 22-year record of achievement and leadership. He was past chair of the House Ethics and House Rules committees; the Democratic majority floor leader during the 90th through 93rd General Assemblies; and the Democratic majority leader from the 94th through 96th General Assemblies. He has served as Speaker from the 97th General Assembly to the present.

Many different agencies and institutions have commended Naifeh for his legislative record. In 1990 he received the NCSL Leadership Award and the Caribe Award from the Tennessee State Employees Association. In 1993 he was awarded the Harry Burn Award. Several statewide organizations have honored Naifeh as Tennessee Legislator of the Year, and the Tennessee Women's Political Caucus named him the first recipient of its "Good Guys" Award.

Carroll Van West, Middle Tennessee State University

SEE: TENNESSEE HOUSE OF REPRESENTATIVES; TIPTON COUNTY

NAPIER, JAMES C. (1845–1940) was born to free parents on June 9, 1845, in Nashville, Tennessee. His father, William Carroll, was a free hack driver and a sometime overseer. James attended the free blacks' school on Line and High Street (now Sixth Avenue) with some 60 other black children until white vigilantes forced the school to close in 1856. He later attended school in Ohio once a December 1856 race riot ended black education in Nashville until the Union occupation in February 1862.

Upon returning to the Union-held city of Nashville, Napier became involved in Republican party politics. John Mercer Langston, an Ohio free black who became a powerful Republican politician and congressman, was a friend of Napier's father. On December 30, 1864, Langston visited Nashville to speak to 10,000 black Union troops who had taken part in the recent and victorious Battle of Nashville, and to address the second Emancipation Day Celebration. He later invited Napier to attend the newly opened law school at Howard University in Washington, D.C., where he was a founding dean. After receiving his law degree in 1872, Napier returned to practice in Nashville. In 1873 he married Dean Langston's youngest daughter, Nettie. This wedding was the biggest social event in nineteenth century black Washington.

Between 1872 and 1913 Napier became Nashville's most powerful and influential African-American citizen. Between 1878 and 1886 he served on the Nashville City Council and was the first black to preside over the council. He was instrumental in the hiring of black teachers for the "colored" public schools during the 1870s, the hiring of black "detectives," and the organization of the black fire-engine company during the 1880s. His greatest political accomplishment was his service as President William H. Taft's Register of the United States Treasury from 1911 to 1913.

Napier also was a successful businessman and a personal friend of Booker T. Washington. Margaret Washington was a personal friend of Nettie Langston Napier and often spent two or more weeks each summer at the Napier's Nolensville Road summer home. Washington visited the city several times a year until his death in 1915. Napier was elected president of the National Negro Business League, which Washington had founded. The league held several of its annual meetings in Nashville, and Napier organized a local chapter of the league in 1905. He was a founder and cashier (manager) of the One Cent (now Citizens) Savings Bank organized in 1904, and he gave the new bank temporary quarters rent-free in his Napier Court office building at 411 North Cherry Street (now Fourth Avenue). He helped organize the 1905 Negro streetcar strike and the black Union Transportation Company's streetcar lines. He presided over the powerful Nashville Negro Board of Trade and was on the boards of Fisk and Howard universities. Upon his death on April 21, 1940, Napier

was interred in Greenwood Cemetery near members of his family and members of the Langston family.
Herbert Clark, Nashville
Adapted from Bobby L. Lovett and Linda T. Wynn, *Profiles of African Americans in Tennessee (1996): 94–95*
SEE: CITIZENS BANK; FISK UNIVERSITY

NASH, DIANE J. (1938–). In the vanguard of the national civil rights and anti-war movements from 1959–1967, Diane Judith Nash was born on May 15, 1938, in Chicago, Illinois. Reared a Roman Catholic, Nash received her primary and secondary education in the parochial and public schools of Chicago. She began her college career in Washington, D.C., at Howard University and later transferred to Fisk University in Nashville.

At the time of Diane Nash's arrival, racial segregation permeated Nashville. Nash's encounters with the inequities, immorality, and privation of southern segregation led her to seek rectification actively. Early in 1959 she attended workshops on nonviolence directed by the Reverend James Lawson, under the auspices of the Nashville Christian Leadership Conference. A strong supporter of the direct nonviolent-protest philosophy, Nash was elected chair of the Student Central Committee. In late 1959 she was among those who "tested" the exclusionary racial policy of Nashville's downtown lunch counters.

The first phase of Nashville's movement began on February 13, 1960, and ended three months later on May 10, when Nashville became the first southern city to desegregate its lunch counters. It was in response to Nash's April 19 query about the immorality of segregation that Mayor Ben West expressed his view that lunch counters should be desegregated and set in motion the events that cracked Nashville's wall of racial segregation.

In April 1960 Nash was one of the founding students of the Student Nonviolent Coordinating Committee (SNCC). The following February, Nash participated in the Rock Hill, South Carolina, protests for desegregation. After she and other students were arrested, they chose incarceration and refused to pay bail. In May, she coordinated the Freedom Rides from Birmingham, Alabama, to Jackson, Mississippi, which were led by Nashville's "nonviolent standing army." Three months later, at a Highlander Folk School seminar, Nash became the director of the direct-action wing of SNCC. Between 1961 and 1965 she worked for the Southern Christian Leadership Conference (SCLC) as a field staff person, organizer, strategist, and workshop instructor. After her marriage to James Bevel (now divorced), the couple moved to Jackson, Mississippi, where she was jailed in 1962 for teaching African-American children the techniques of direct nonviolent protest. Her ideas were instrumental in initiating the 1963 March on Washington. She and James Bevel conceptualized and planned the initial strategy for the Selma Right-to-Vote movement that helped produce the Voting Rights Act of 1965. Dr. Martin Luther King, Jr., presented SCLC's Rosa Parks Award to Nash and Bevel in 1965.

Nash's civil rights endeavors led her to the Vietnam peace movement. She continued working for political and social transformation through the 1970s and lectured nationally on the rights of women during the 1980s. An omnipresent voice in the movement for social change, Nash continues to lecture across the country and currently is working in real estate as a resident of Chicago.

Linda T. Wynn, Tennessee Historical Commission/Fisk University

SUGGESTED READINGS: Reavis L. Mitchell, Jr., and Jessie Carney Smith, "Diane Nash," in *Notable Black American Women* (1992): 796–800; Linda T. Wynn, "The Dawning of a New Day: The Nashville Sit-Ins, February 13-May 10, 1960," *Tennessee Historical Quarterly* 50(1991): 42–54

SEE: CIVIL RIGHTS MOVEMENT; HIGHLANDER FOLK SCHOOL; LAWSON, JAMES E., JR.; SIT-INS, NASHVILLE

NASHOBA, a short-lived utopian community on the present-day site of Germantown in West Tennessee, was founded in 1826 by Frances Wright, who dreamed of demonstrating a practical and effective alternative to the South's slave-based agricultural economy. Hardly a trace of the community could be seen by 1830, but Nashoba survives in historical accounts of American utopias.

Wright and her sister, Camilla, were the daughters of a Scottish merchant and his aristocratic English wife, both of whom died when the girls were young. Reared by relatives in England and educated in London, they were, by the age of 20, fluent in several languages and possessed of a remarkable self-assurance. With a substantial inheritance from their late father, the Wright sisters came to America as young women in 1818 and traveled freely about the country. A book she subsequently wrote—*Views on Society and Manners in America*—brought Frances Wright an impressive following, including Thomas Jefferson, Henry Clay, and the Marquis de Lafayette. It also led to a close and continuing relationship between the tall, vivacious, 26-year-old Fanny, as she liked to be called, and the 64-year-old Lafayette, then a widower living outside Paris.

When Lafayette came to the United States in 1824 on a triumphant return to the scenes of his heroism in the American Revolution, Wright followed. Visiting with Jefferson and others in the highest social and political circles, she sensed the plight of otherwise-decent men caught up in the system of slavery, from which they could see no avenue of escape not tainted by financial ruin. Wright suggested one: a setting in which progressive whites and free blacks would live and work together in a sort of training school for independence.

In the summer of 1825 Wright put before Lafayette her proposal to buy a small number of slaves and set up a colony where they could be prepared to be self-supporting. She hoped such an example, if successful, might lead others to follow suit. Lafayette gave her an introduction to Andrew Jackson, who invited her to Tennessee to seek a site for the colony. Through Jackson and his Nashville friend John Overton, Wright located a 2,000-acre tract of land near Memphis, then an unincorporated village of a few hundred residents. She decided to buy the site on the Wolf River east of Memphis and name it Nashoba—the Chickasaw word for wolf.

With a small group of idealistic young whites that included her sister, Wright formally launched her experiment in the spring of 1826. With the help of about 15 former slaves whose freedom she had purchased, she and the others set about clearing land and building cabins. But the task was arduous and fraught with difficulties. Sickness and conflict within

Nashoba, from a German engraving, circa 1830.

SPECIAL COLLECTIONS, UNIVERSITY OF MEMPHIS

the little community and controversy sparked among outside critics dogged the settlers at every step.

Wright went to Europe in 1827 to raise funds for the venture, but by the time she returned, she found her idealistic dream of a new community of equals was gone; all that remained was a loose association of individuals. The white residents soon left. Only the blacks remained, their rights unrealized, their status unclear, their future in doubt. Wright herself soon moved to New Harmony, Indiana, with a fellow Scot, Robert Dale Owen. She and Owen went to New York, where she became active in a variety of social causes.

But Nashoba and its abandoned residents tugged at her conscience. In December 1829 she returned there to find 31 black residents barely holding body and soul together. She offered to take them to Haiti, where they could live as free people in a black-ruled nation, and the small group favorably received her offer. Early in 1830 the entire population of Nashoba and Wright sailed from New Orleans for Haiti. The young country's president, Jean Pierre Boyer, who had been alerted to their arrival by the ever-helpful General Lafayette, greeted the group at Port-au-Prince. Thus ended the short and stormy life of Nashoba.

John Egerton, Nashville

SUGGESTED READING: John Egerton, *Visions of Utopia: Nashoba, Rugby, Ruskin* (1977)

SEE: SHELBY COUNTY; SLAVERY; WRIGHT, FRANCES

College Street (now Third Avenue) decorated for the Tennessee Centennial Exposition.

NASHVILLE (METROPOLITAN NASHVILLE/ DAVIDSON COUNTY). With an estimated (1996) population of 529,765, Nashville is the capital of Tennessee and a national business, transportation, and tourism center for the United States. The Metropolitan Nashville-Davidson County government was organized in 1963, and the downtown stands on the banks of the Cumberland River where the city began.

Middle Tennessee's abundant natural resources and many animals attracted Paleoindians as early as 11,000 years ago. American Indians of the Mississippian culture lived here ca. A.D. 1000 to 1400. They built towns with great earthen mounds, some of which survive today. Cherokees, Chickasaws, and Shawnees followed. Middle Tennessee became known as the "bloody ground" because of the battles fought over its rich hunting grounds. In the late 1600s and early 1700s, French fur traders came to "The Bluffs" (now downtown Nashville). Around 1710 Charles Charleville operated a trading post near a salt lick just north of town, later known as the French Lick. French-Canadian Timothy Demonbreun began hunting here in the 1760s and was here when the first settlers arrived from the East.

In 1778 James Robertson of the Watauga settlement in what was then North Carolina scouted the Nashville area with eight men. The following year he returned with a group of close to 250, mostly men and boys, to establish a permanent settlement. They arrived on Christmas Day 1779. Robertson's partner, Colonel John Donelson, brought the families and provisions over 1,000 miles by boat down the Holston and Tennessee rivers and up the Ohio and Cumberland rivers to the Cumberland Bluffs, arriving April 24, 1780. Within a week, the Cumberland Compact, the first civil government in Middle Tennessee, was signed by 256 men. They named the settlement Nashborough for General Francis Nash of North Carolina. In 1784 Nashborough was changed to Nashville, probably as a result of anti-British sentiments following the Revolutionary War.

By the early 1800s Nashville was growing rapidly. In 1796 Tennessee had become the sixteenth state. Andrew Jackson's resounding defeat of the British at the Battle of New Orleans in 1815 brought new prominence to Tennessee and Nashville, his home. In 1828 Jackson was elected seventh president of the United States, the first "western" president. In 1843 Nashville became the permanent capital of Tennessee. Philadelphia architect William Strickland was hired to design the Greek Revival capitol, completed in 1859 and now a National Historic Landmark.

Its location on the Cumberland River was critical to the growth of Nashville during the first half of the nineteenth century. The arrival of the first steamboat in 1819 opened the way for trade with cities like New Orleans and Pittsburgh, and Nashville became the main distribution point for goods throughout the mid-South. Steamboats brought rice, sugar, coffee, and household goods to Nashville and returned with cotton, tobacco, corn, and lumber. In addition to properous merchants, banking, printing, and publishing industries began to grow. There were also large farms and plantations. Andrew Jackson's Hermitage, Belle Meade Plantation, Belmont Mansion, and Historic Travellers Rest are among the nineteenth century historic houses open to the public today.

The first recorded church in Nashville was a small stone structure built on the Public Square. It was commonly known as the "Methodist Church." Baptists and Presbyterians were also among the earliest congregations, followed by Episcopalians, Catholics, Jews, and others. By the beginning of the Civil War there were also African-American congregations, including two Methodist Episcopal churches and one Christian church. Clergymen and church leaders established many educational institutions.

By 1860 Nashville was a thriving city with close to 14,000 inhabitants. Because of its location on the river and the newly built railroad links connecting Louisville, Nashville, Chattanooga, and Atlanta, Nashville was an extremely important center for the distribution of supplies. In February 1862 the Union Army occupied the city and held it until the end of the Civil War. The Battle of Nashville, fought in 1864, was the last aggressive action of the Confederate Army of Tennessee. The first shots were fired from Fort Negley, a Union fort built largely by African-American labor.

After the war, Nashville experienced renewed vigor in business and industry and substantial population growth. Already a printing center, the city continued to develop as an important distribution and wholesale center. The most remarkable growth, however, was in education. In 1866 Fisk University was founded as one of the first private schools dedicated to the education of African Americans. Vanderbilt University was founded in 1873, and Peabody College, now part of Vanderbilt University, began as an institution for teacher education in 1875. In 1876 Meharry Medical College was established for the education of black doctors.

In 1880 Nashville celebrated the one hundredth anniversary of its founding. The culminating event was the unveiling of Clark Mills's equestrian statue of Andrew Jackson on Capitol Hill, presented to the state by the Tennessee Historical Society. Two other castings of this statue stand in New Orleans and Washington, D.C.

With the advent of streetcars—first mule-drawn, then electric—Nashville began to grow beyond the downtown area by the mid-nineteenth century. Germantown, Edgefield in East Nashville, and the Cameron-Trimble community were established at this time. In 1897 the Tennessee Centennial Exposition was held where Centennial Park stands today. A wood and stucco replica of the Parthenon was such a popular building that the city, already called the Athens of the South because of its educational insitutions, built a permanent reconstruction in concrete in the 1920s, now the only full-scale facsimile of the Parthenon in existence.

In the early twentieth century, Nashvillians wrestled with the same public issues and problems as most of the United States during this period: prohibition, the departure of its citizens to fight in World War I, woman suffrage, and the Great Depression. The final battle for woman suffrage was waged in Nashville in August 1920, when the Tennessee General Assembly became the 36th state legislature to ratify the 19th Amendment to the U.S. Constitution, giving American women the right to vote.

As population increased, Nashvillians continued to move west and southwest to streetcar suburbs now known as Woodland-in-Waverly, Waverly-Belmont, Belmont-Hillsboro, and Richland-West End. The Great Depression and suburban expansion led to the decline of former residential areas downtown. In 1949 Nashville launched the first postwar urban renewal program in the country, the Capitol Hill Redevelopment Project.

In the 1950s and 1960s, long unresolved problems of racial segregation and inequality came to a head in the national Civil Rights Movement. In Nashville, Kelly Miller Smith, pastor of the First Baptist Church, Capitol Hill, and other local religious leaders trained student volunteers in the principles of non-violence and organized a well-disciplined sit-in movement that became a model for similar demonstrations throughout the South. Nashville became the first major Southern city to experience widespread desegregation of public facilities. In 1963 Nashville and Davidson County merged, becoming the first consolidated city/county government in the United States.

In the twentieth century, Nashville's business economy became increasingly diversified and service oriented. Following World War I, insurance, banking, and securities dominated the economic scene with downtown's Union Street becoming known as the "Wall Street of the South." In the final quarter of the century, health care services emerged as Nashville's largest industry, beginning in 1968 with the founding of Hospital Corporation of America. Music and entertainment, printing and publishing, education, and tourism followed close behind. In the 1990s Nashville boasts 18 higher education institutions, a tourism industry that draws eight million visitors a year, and a thriving publishing and printing industry. In addition, the Middle Tennessee region is now the largest automobile production center in the southern United States.

Anglo-American folk music came to the Bluffs with the settlers, and music publishing is said to have begun in 1824 with *The Western Harmony*, a book of hymns and instruction for singing. In the 1870s and 1880s, it was Fisk University's Jubilee Singers who first brought international fame to Nashville as a music center when they toured the United States and western Europe. Nashville's reputation as a country music center can be traced to the 1920s when WSM radio launched the "WSM Barn Dance" (later the Grand Ole Opry), a radio show used as a marketing tool by the National Life and Accident Insurance Company. The "Nashville Sound" emerged in the 1950s and is given credit for the successful comeback of country music after the advent of rock music in the late 1950s. The present music publishing industry began in 1942 with Acuff-Rose Publishing Company—the first non-Opry music venture in Nashville. Fed in the early days by Opry performers, the publishing industry has continued to grow. The city's strong organized churches have also supported the growth of the gospel music industry. In the 1990s increased diversification and international recording activity has resulted in dramatically increasing employment and investment.

Ophelia Paine, Metropolitan Historical Commission, and John Connelly, Nashville

SEE: ACUFF-ROSE; BELLE MEADE PLANTATION; BELMONT MANSION; BRILEY, BEVERLY; CIVIL RIGHTS MOVEMENT; CUMBERLAND COMPACT; DEMONBREUN, TIMOTHY; DONELSON, JOHN; DUDLEY, ANNE DALLAS; FISK UNIVERSITY; FORT NEGLEY; GEORGE PEABODY COLLEGE FOR TEACHERS; GRAND OLE OPRY; HERMITAGE; JACKSON, ANDREW; JUBILEE SINGERS; MEHARRY MEDICAL COLLEGE; MUSIC; NASHVILLE, BATTLE OF; NATIONAL LIFE AND ACCIDENT INSURANCE COMPANY; PARTHENON; ROBERTSON, JAMES; SMITH, KELLY M.; STRICKLAND, WILLIAM;; TENNESSEE CENTENNIAL EXPOSITION; TENNESSEE HISTORICAL SOCIETY.; TRAVELLERS REST; VANDERBILT UNIVERSITY; WOMAN SUFFRAGE MOVEMENT; WSM

NASHVILLE BANNER. The *Nashville Banner* published its first edition on April 10, 1876. William E. Eastman, one of the founding partners, served as its first president; Thomas Achison, another partner, was its first editor. Other partners included two local newsmen, John J. Carter and Cicero Bledsoe, and two printers, Homer Carothers and Pleasant J. Wright.

The *Banner* struggled for survival during its early years. When the newspaper lost a libel suit, Major Edward Bushrod Stahlman, a local railroad executive, loaned the paper $110,000 in exchange for stock collateral. In 1893 he purchased full ownership. Three fires caused extensive damage; fire destroyed the editorial offices in October 1894.

Banner editors provided important continuity. Gideon H. Baskette was editor from 1893–1911. He was succeeded by Richard H. Yancy, who was editor until 1922. Other editors included Walter Cain (1922–1929) and George H. Armistead, Sr. (1929–1942). During those years, the *Banner* grew in circulation and became one of the state's largest newspapers. The *Banner* maintained an independent position, supporting Woodrow Wilson in 1912 and 1916, John W. Davis in 1924, Alfred E. Smith in 1928, Franklin D. Roosevelt in 1932, and Wendell Wilkie in 1940. The paper endorsed no candidates in the other presidential races of the period.

The opposing editorial policies of Nashville's morning and afternoon newspapers also developed during the early part of the century. In 1907 Stahlman's political enemy, Senator Luke Lea, launched the *Nashville Tennessean*. Lea and his political associates conspired unsuccessfully to have the German-born Major Stahlman declared an "alien enemy" after World War I began.

In 1930 James G. Stahlman, Major Stahlman's grandson, became president and publisher of the *Banner,* following his grandfather's death. Stahlman's son and James Stahlman's father had died in a boating accident in 1904. James Stahlman and his uncle, Frank C. Stahlman, purchased half interest in the *Banner* in 1937. James Stahlman bought his uncle's share and assumed full ownership in 1955.

Shortly after Silliman Evans, Sr., purchased the *Nashville Tennessean,* he established a joint printing agreement with James Stahlman. In 1938, the two newspapers built a new publishing facility at 1100 Broadway, which they shared for 60 years.

Under James Stahlman, Tennessee historian Hugh Davis Graham described the *Banner* as "the voice of Nashville's business community." Furthermore, Graham says that "while Stahlman accurately and honestly reflected the conservative convictions of Nashville's businessmen, he stubbornly and successfully over the years refused to be owned by them."[1] During the Stahlman years, the *Banner* consistently endorsed conservative and Republican views.

On January 14, 1972, Stahlman announced the sale of the *Banner* to the Gannett Corporation. Six months later, he retired after 60 years of service to the *Nashville Banner,* 42 of them as publisher. He died in 1976. On July 5, 1979, the Gannett Corporation announced the purchase of the *Tennessean* from the Evans family and sale of the *Banner* for $25 million to Music City Media, Inc., owned by three local businessmen: Brownlee Currey, Irby C. Simpkins, and John J. Hooker, Jr. In December 1980 Simpkins and Currey purchased Hooker's interest.

In 1989, through its production partnership with Gannett and the *Tennessean,* the *Banner* became part of a new printing plant with modern color presses. The first paper was printed on the new press in September 1990. The *Banner* ceased publication on February 20, 1998 after 122 years of continuous operation. The Gannett Company, owners of *The Tennessean,* bought out Simpkins and co-owner Brownlee Currey, Jr., from their 61-year-old joint operating agreement.

David Sumner, Ball State University

CITATION:

(1) Hugh Davis Graham, *Crisis in Print: Desegregation and the Press in Tennessee* (Nashville, 1967): 41.

SEE: LEA, LUKE; NASHVILLE TENNESSEAN; PUBLISHING; STAHLMAN, JAMES G.

NASHVILLE, BATTLE OF, fought December 15–16, 1864, continued the destruction of the Confederate Army of Tennessee that began when it suffered devastating casualties at Franklin. After that engagement, army commander John Bell Hood faced limited options. A withdrawal would further dishearten the army, and Hood rejected his former notion to bypass Nashville and head northward. The high toll at Franklin prevented him from seriously contemplating an assault at Nashville, another earlier scheme. Hood opted instead to bring his army to the city's outskirts and await an attack from the Federals, hoping to counterattack if the enemy left an opening.

The Confederates moved north from Franklin in early December and established a five-mile defense line. There were serious flaws in the position, since it did not come close to covering all the major roads leading from the city. The army was situated so that Frank Cheatham's corps occupied the right near the Nolensville Pike, Stephen D. Lee's corps the center astride the Franklin Pike, and A.P. Stewart's corps the left, crossing the Granny White Pike and bent back near the Hillsboro Pike. In spite of their efforts to entrench and strengthen their defenses, the Confederates were vulnerable on both flanks.

Hood's adversary, General George Thomas, enjoyed several compelling advantages. His Federals occupied extraordinarily strong works, since Nashville by late 1864 was one of the most heavily fortified cities in America. Although it had taken time for Thomas to amass his force, by mid-December he had over 54,000 effectives on hand at Nashville, well over twice Hood's numbers. Thomas's force represented a conglomeration of disparate elements, including the Fourth Army Corps from the Army of the Cumberland and John Schofield's Twenty-third Army Corps, both sent back by William T. Sherman before he began the March to the Sea. There were also 12,000 rugged troops led by Andrew J. Smith, recently arrived from Missouri. Thomas intended to use these battle-hardened units to smite Hood. He concocted a plan to keep Cheatham on the Confederate right occupied, then concentrate the bulk of his army against A.P. Stewart, wheeling around the Southern left flank with overwhelming numbers.

Bitterly cold and inclement weather pushed into Middle Tennessee the second week of December, forcing Thomas to delay his attack. This sensible decision did not set well with Union officials in far-off Washington or with Ulysses S. Grant in Virginia, who worried about Hood's lingering presence in Middle Tennessee. Grant seriously contemplated replacing Thomas, but a thaw set in on December 13 and allowed Thomas to convene his officers and issue final orders for offensive operations.

Union troops under James Steedman moved out against Cheatham early on the morning of December 15. Bitter fighting erupted when Cheatham's veterans discerned that black soldiers made up a portion of the Federal assaulting party. Although Steedman suffered heavy casualties, he effectively neutralized Cheatham while the main Yankee blow fell on A.P. Stewart. Although Stewart's men resisted valiantly, they were outnumbered ten to one and the massive pivot devised by Thomas threatened to crush the Confederates. Hood sent reinforcements, first from Lee and then from Cheatham, but relentless pressure forced Stewart back towards the Granny White Pike.

After dark, Hood ordered a withdrawal nearly two miles to the south and aligned his men in a more compact position. Cheatham replaced Stewart on the Confederate left. Thomas for his part had no intention of abandoning his plans and decided to continue with his successful tactics the next day. He did modify his strategy to attempt an envelopment of both Confederate flanks. On December 16, Thomas impatiently awaited as his units, somewhat scattered and out of position, sorted themselves out. He grew increasingly frustrated at Schofield's reluctance to attack, but Union artillery pounded the makeshift Southern defenses before the infantry assaulted. When they finally did so, Cheatham's defenses crumbled. A pivotal salient occupied by the Twentieth Tennessee held out against a fierce Union artillery barrage from three directions, but Colonel William Shy and his men atop the hill were practically obliterated when Union infantry overran the summit. The remainder of Cheatham's left collapsed, and the panic extended to Stewart's troops in the center.

Only a skillful defense by Stephen D. Lee prevented Thomas from achieving his goal of encircling the Confederates and annihilating them. Lee pulled his corps back to the Overton Hills and managed to stave off the Federals. Lee continued his rear guard actions the next day, while the rest of the army passed through Franklin. Nathan Bedford Forrest's cavalry and infantry fragments from eight brigades led by General Edward C. Walthall covered the withdrawal.

Union cavalry persistently hounded the retreat until the Confederate survivors managed to cross the Tennessee River. Thomas called off the pursuit on December 29.

Hood lost some 6,000 men at Nashville, many of them captured when they failed to make good their escape from the battlefield. Union casualties were just over 3,000. Tennessee historian Stanley Horn entitled a 1956 book about the campaign *The Decisive Battle of Nashville,* and Horn's work is aptly titled when one considers that Thomas narrowly missed destroying Hood's entire force. Yet Federal success at Nashville was aided tremendously by the earlier action at Franklin, which demoralized many Southerners and decimated Hood's best combat units. Psychologically devastated by the losses at Franklin, and unwilling to be sacrificed at Nashville, many of Hood's most courageous veterans broke and fled there.

The result of Hood's Tennessee campaign, which began with such heady optimism in the fall, was the near-total disintegration of his army. The remnants of the army finally halted at Tupelo, Mississippi, but large numbers of men deserted along the way and others did so shortly after reaching Mississippi. Hood asked to be relieved on January 13, and Richmond authorities accepted the request. Two fatal decisions by Hood, the first to launch a frontal assault at Franklin, and the second to await Thomas at Nashville, doomed his army in the campaign. And George Thomas belied his reputation as a slow, stolid commander by delivering a well-conceived knockout blow at Nashville.

Christopher Losson, St. Joseph, Missouri

SUGGESTED READING: Stanley F. Horn, *The Decisive Battle of Nashville* (1956)

SEE: ARMY OF TENNESSEE; CHEATHAM, BENJAMIN F.; FRANKLIN, BATTLE OF; HOOD, JOHN B.; STEWART, A.P.; THOMAS, GEORGE H.

NASHVILLE BRIDGE COMPANY, the most productive and important bridge firm in Tennessee, was founded by Arthur J. Dyer, an 1891 graduate of the Vanderbilt Engineering School. Dyer worked for a variety of bridge companies over the next decade before he borrowed $750 and entered a partnership with H.T. Sinnot in a bridge company known as the H.T. Sinnot Company. The firm reorganized in 1902, when Dyer purchased Sinnot's interest and renamed the firm the Nashville Bridge and Construction Company. In late

1903 or 1904 the firm underwent a second reorganization and became known as the Nashville Bridge Company. The firm built its headquarters in downtown Nashville on the banks of the Cumberland River, where a large complex containing a six-story office building remains. It maintained a Latin-American branch office in Colombia.

The commissions of Nashville Bridge Company came from throughout the southeastern United States as well as many Central and South American countries. The firm was recognized for its work in movable bridges and built several along the Gulf Coast. The company claimed to have built over half of all the bascule bridges in Florida.

As a result of federal legislation passed in 1916, the bridge building industry changed and standardized bridge plans became common. While independent bridge companies continued to design and build bridges for cities and counties, generally, their work on state projects was limited to providing steel or construction activities.

In 1915 the Nashville Bridge Company built a small floating derrick hull for the Army Corps of Engineers, which marked the beginning of its shift from bridge construction to the marine field. The company expanded by building a new plant in 1922–1923 at Bessemer, Alabama. In the late 1920s Dyer's son, Harry, took over operations of the firm's Marine Department. His crews built barges on a production line basis and launched them from pivoted arms, a technique never used before. This new method proved very successful, and the company's barge business expanded substantially. The Great

Launching a minesweeper during World War II.

NASHVILLE BRIDGE COMPANY

Depression resulted in bankruptcy and closure of innumerable bridge companies across the country. The Nashville Bridge Company's anomalous survival was due, in large part, to its diversified interests in marine production. In the early 1940s the U.S. Navy hired the firm to manufacture dozens of vessels, and the company expanded its Nashville complex.

Over the years, the Nashville Bridge Company decreased its bridge building and expanded its Marine Department. By the 1980s it had become the world's largest builder of inland barges. In 1969 the Dyer family sold the company, and there have been several subsequent owners. In 1972 the firm sold its bridge and structural building operations. Although Trinity Marine of Dallas is the current owner, it is still known locally as the Nashville Bridge Company. The company relocated to Ashland City when the city chose its downtown location as the site for Nashville's professional football stadium, and demolition of the complex began in 1997.

Martha Carver, Tennessee Department of Transportation
SEE: INDUSTRY; NASHVILLE

NASHVILLE CONVENTION. On June 3, 1850, delegates from nine southern states met at McKendree Methodist Church in Nashville to discuss common grievances in the great sectional crisis that developed with the territorial acquisitions following the Mexican War. The South demanded equality in the territories in an alarming atmosphere of increased northern resistance to proslavery measures. Senator John C. Calhoun of South Carolina played a major role in the convention call to promote southern unity, but he did not originate the idea of such an assemblage.

Because of South Carolina's radical stance on slavery, it seemed desirable that the movement for a cooperative endeavor should come from another state. A bipartisan convention at Jackson, Mississippi, in October 1849 issued the call for the Nashville Convention. The proposal defined the purpose of the convention "to devise and adopt some mode of resistance to northern aggression."

The call for a southern convention initially produced a favorable response, especially among the Lower South states. Democrats took the lead, while the Whigs remained less inclined to approve the convention. No standard method of selecting candidates prevailed; when the Tennessee General Assembly failed to appoint delegates, the counties selected delegates in county meetings. The southern movement for unity reached a peak around February 1850; thereafter the introduction of compromise resolutions in the Senate and the prospect of a satisfactory adjustment somewhat lessened support for a southern convention in most states, except South Carolina.

One hundred seventy-six delegates attended the first session of the nine-day convention. The Ten-

nessee delegation of 101 was the largest group from any state. The delegates adopted 28 resolutions asserting the South's constitutional rights in the territories and the rights and interests of Texas in the boundary dispute. The convention recommended, as an extreme concession, an alternative division of the territories by an extension of the 36°30' line to the Pacific—an ironic position antithetical to the platform of non-interference. In addition, it adopted a more radical "Address to the People" of the southern states, written by the South Carolina fire-eater, Robert Barnwell Rhett. However, the moderates gained control of the convention and adopted a wait-and-see attitude. The convention also resolved that it would reassemble in Nashville on the sixth Monday after congressional adjournment.

After President Millard Fillmore signed the five bills that constituted the Compromise of 1850, interest in the second session of the convention declined considerably. Nevertheless, more than 50 delegates from seven southern states met at Nashville in November. Although they rejected united secession, delegates approved measures affirming the right of secession, denouncing the Compromise, and recommending a southern congress. Secession had been averted, and the Union was saved.

Though the Nashville Convention recorded little concrete accomplishment, it was by no means insignificant. It failed to unite the South, but it brought national attention to the South's grievances and undoubtedly influenced the passage of the Compromise of 1850. The convention revealed the loyalty of the South in 1850 to the concept of national unity and the willingness of southerners to compromise in order to save the Union.

Thelma Jennings, Middle Tennessee State University
SUGGESTED READING: Thelma Jennings, *The Nashville Convention: Southern Movement for Unity, 1848–1850* (1980)
SEE: CIVIL WAR

NASHVILLE GLOBE, founded in 1906, promoted self-reliance and racial solidarity as the best means for Nashville's African-American community to succeed and prosper within the confines of the Jim Crow South. After an editorial run that lasted more than five decades, the bi-weekly black newspaper ceased publication in 1960. The paper survived due to its strong editorials, its extensive reporting of local news and social happenings, and its state and national bulletins. Contemporaries estimated that the *Globe's* readership neared 20,000, about one-fifth Nashville's total population, during its first decade. From 1910 to 1930 it had the largest circulation of any black newspaper in Tennessee. The financial backing of one of Nashville's wealthiest black families also contributed to the stability of the *Globe*. Richard H. Boyd, secretary of the National Baptist Publishing

Board, originally financed the newspaper, and his son, Henry A. Boyd, controlled the editorial content. The Boyds had extensive contacts within Nashville's black middle class, which made it easier to gain advertisers and readers.

The newspaper embraced the self-help message of Booker T. Washington, but at the same time it demanded constant improvements within a segregated society. The Boyds founded the newspaper during a streetcar boycott that followed the decision by Nashville authorities to extend Jim Crow laws to the city's transportation system. The new journal reported the efforts of several black businessmen to start their own streetcar company to serve the black boycotters. The streetcar business, in which the Boyds held a stake, failed after less than a year, but the newspaper persisted. While not fully rejecting accommodation, the Boyds recognized that the expansion of Jim Crow required more diligent protection of the African-American community's interests in other areas of life.

Nothing better illustrated the *Globe's* strategy of accommodative resistance than its efforts to promote black businesses. The newspaper urged Nashville's African Americans to patronize black-owned banks and stores. Such institutions would treat patrons fairly and provide opportunities for economic development, which the *Globe* touted as the surest means to racial advancement. Economic growth could create community cohesion, contribute to racial pride, and provide valuable skills.

The *Globe* promoted race pride and advancement in other ways. The newspaper pressed for equal educational opportunities in Nashville's public schools. In 1909 Henry Boyd used the newspaper to promote the successful campaign for a state normal college for blacks (now Tennessee State University). Editorials stressed the importance of political participation by reminding readers to pay their poll taxes. Generally committed to the Republican Party, the *Globe*, at times, urged independent voting if it gave Nashville's African Americans greater leverage. On some matters, such as its relentless urban boosterism and patriotic appeals during the World Wars, the *Globe* linked the success of the African-American community with the city at large.

In their message of uplift, the *Globe's* editors attempted to infuse their readers with middle-class notions of self-help and individual responsibility. Nonetheless, the newspaper also championed communitarian ideas because the editors realized only racial solidarity could overcome the inequalities of segregation. The newspaper constantly challenged the status quo if segregation meant unequal services or opportunities. The conservative message of economic advancement and social separation, however, clashed with the direct action, integrationist dimensions of post-World War II civil rights protest. As a result, the *Globe's* influence declined. The *Globe* stopped publishing in 1960, shortly after Henry A. Boyd's death.

Christopher MacGregor Scribner, Vanderbilt University
SEE: BOYD, HENRY A.; BOYD, RICHARD H.; PUBLISHING

NASHVILLE NO. 1, UNITED DAUGHTERS OF THE CONFEDERACY. The United Daughters of the Confederacy (UDC) was founded in Nashville on September 10, 1894, and Nashville No. 1 became the first chapter to apply for membership, thus earning the coveted designation of the "mother chapter." The local unit was an outgrowth of the powerful Ladies' Hermitage Association, which was dedicated to the preservation of Andrew Jackson's property. In 1894 Caroline Meriwether Goodlett announced a meeting in Nashville of all interested southern white women's societies that were similarly dedicated to "social, literary, historical, monumental, and benevolent activities with a Confederate agenda."[1] Those who proved lineal descent from a Confederate soldier or civil servant were welcome in the UDC.

Goodlett was elected to head both the UDC and Nashville No. 1; she also created the chapter's logo, "The Women Who Never Surrendered." Other officers of the "mother chapter" included Mrs. S.F. Wilson, vice president; Mrs. Kate Litton Hickman, secretary; and Mrs. John C. Aust, treasurer. Like the officers, many charter members belonged to Nashville's most elite families. Within five years, the membership roll topped 200, and Nashville No. 1 became the largest chapter in the state. The chapter later founded a children's auxiliary to provide instruction about the Confederate heritage.

Nashville No. 1 institutionalized the goals of the UDC at the local level through a wide range of programs. It maintained the Confederate Soldiers' Home at The Hermitage, planned the elaborate memorial day ceremony at Nashville's Mt. Olivet Cemetery, conducted programs on key Confederate holidays (Lee Day on January 19, Jefferson Davis's birthday on June 3, UDC Founder's Day on September 10, and Sam Davis Day on October 6), participated in local and regional fund raising campaigns to build monuments to Confederate heroes, partnered with public school administrators to screen history textbooks, and visited classrooms to distribute Confederate memorabilia.

At the height of the association's influence, No. 1 was joined by five "affiliated" UDC chapters in Nashville. During the early twentieth century, No. 1 was arguably the most politically powerful and socially important women's club in Nashville. The "mother chapter" celebrated its one-hundredth anniversary in 1994 and still maintains an active membership.

John A. Simpson, Kelso, Washington

CITATION:

(1) *United Daughters of the Confederacy, Tennessee Division, Records, Manuscript Division, Tennessee State Library and Archives.*

SUGGESTED READING: Mary Poppenheim, *The History of the United Daughters of the Confederacy* (1956)

SEE: CONFEDERATE SOLDIERS' HOME; DAVIS, SAM; LADIES' HERMITAGE ASSOCIATION

NASHVILLE PREDATORS is the first professional hockey team in Tennessee to be a member of the National Hockey League (NHL). Beginning the 1998–1999 season as a member of the NHL's Central Divsion, the Predators will play all home games at the new Nashville Arena, a facility shared with the Nashville Kats of the Arena Football League. Leipold Hockey Holdings, the majority investor, and Gaylord Entertainment Company, the minority investor, jointly own the Predators.

Craig Leipold is Chairman of the Nashville Predators. Team President is Jack Diller, a former executive with the New York Rangers. The Executive Vice President, Business Operations is Tom Ward, formerly of the Charlotte Hornets of the National Basketball Association. The General Manager and Executive Vice President, Hockey Operations is David Poile, who has previous experience with the Calgary Flames and the Washington Capitals. A highly respected hockey executive, Poile relied heavily on his former associates at the Capitals to build Nashville's initial coaching and scouting staffs. The head coach is Barry Trotz, a former Washington Capitals scout and coach of the Capitals's top minor league affiliate in Portland, Maine. The assistant coach is Paul Gardner, a former NHL first round draft selection, who scored 201 goals and 201 assists in his ten-year NHL career that included a stint with the Capitals. Craig Channell, chief amateur scout, held a similar scouting position with the Washington Capitals before coming to Nashville.

Professional ice hockey has been played in Nashville since the early 1960s when the Nashville Dixie Flyers were members of the East Coast Hockey League (ECHL), a minor league association. Over the past 30 years, other Nashville team names include the South Stars, the Knights, the Nighthawks, and the Ice Flyers. Memphis and Knoxville also have hosted minor league teams in the Central Hockey League and the ECHL.

Carroll Van West, Middle Tennessee State University

SEE: TENNESSEE OILERS

NASHVILLE *TENNESSEAN*. This Nashville newspaper traces its origins to the *Nashville Whig*, which Joseph and Moses Norvell began in 1812 when the city had a population of 1,200. The *Whig* survived

more than a dozen mergers and consolidations to eventually become the *Nashville American*. Colonel Luke Lea launched the first issue of *The Tennessean* on Sunday, May 12, 1907. Three years later, the two newspapers merged as *The Nashville Tennessean*.

The newspaper was always identified with the Democratic Party and in 1911 the state legislature elected Luke Lea to the U.S. Senate, making him, at 32, the youngest member of that body. Lea only served one term; in 1917 Kenneth D. McKellar defeated him to become the state's first popularly elected senator.

The Nashville Tennessean was published in both morning and afternoon editions until March 1933. The Depression increased Lea's financial difficulties to the point that the paper was placed in the hands of a federal receiver, Littleton Pardue, a lawyer from Ashland City. Silliman Evans, Sr., purchased the newspaper at a public auction on January 7, 1937, for $850,000. He took over its management on April 17 and, within 45 days, had the newspaper operating in the black again.

Shortly after Evans, Sr., purchased *The Nashville Tennessean*, he established a joint printing agreement with James Stahlman, publisher of the *Nashville Banner*. Under the terms of the agreement, Evans dropped the *Tennessean's* evening edition and Stahlman dropped his Sunday edition. The agreement continued until 1998, when the *Banner* ceased publication.

In 1948 Evans recalled the highly regarded Coleman Harwell from the *New York World Telegram* as editor. A Nashville native, Harwell initially joined *The Nashville Tennessean* in 1927 as a reporter and advanced to managing editor by 1931 when he left. Historian Hugh Davis Graham characterized Evans and Harwell as congenial journalists, whose New Deal support gave a liberal voice to the *Tennessean.*

During the 1950s and 1960s, several reporters who worked for the *Tennessean* went on to outstanding careers elsewhere. They included David Halberstam, Tom Wicker, Fred Graham, and Wallace Westfeldt. Albert Gore, Jr., also worked for the newspaper during the early 1970s.

The senior Evans published the newspaper until his death in 1955 at the age of 61. His son, Silliman Evans, Jr., took over as publisher and managed the newspaper until his death in 1961 at the age of 36. During his tenure, Evans, Jr., replaced Harwell with Edward Ball, formerly head of Nashville's Associated Press Bureau. Following the death of Evans, Jr., ownership of the newspaper passed to his mother, Lucille McCrea Evans, and his brother, Amon Carter Evans. In 1963 the newspaper's name was changed to *The Tennessean*, and a year later, Amon Carter Evans became publisher. Evans soon hired John Seigenthaler as managing editor. Seigenthaler had worked for the newspaper from 1948–1961, before serving as administrative assistant to Attorney General Robert Kennedy, 1961–1962.

In 1979 Evans and his mother sold *The Tennessean* to the Gannett Corporation, which continues as its owner to this day. Gannett retained John Seigenthaler as editor and publisher until his retirement in 1992. Seigenthaler also served as *USA Today's* founding editorial director.

David Sumner, Ball State University

SEE: EVANS, SILLIMAN, SR.; GORE, ALBERT A., JR.; LEA, LUKE; NASHVILLE BANNER; PUBLISHING

NASHVILLE TRADES AND LABOR COUNCIL,

organized in 1890, was most responsible for the passage of the Tennessee child labor law and the local barber's Sunday closing law. Composed of three delegates from the different unions in Nashville, the Council has been able to exert great influence throughout the state for labor's benefit. As late as 1889–1890 only three or four labor unions, including the Typographical Union and Molders' Union, existed in Nashville. Unionization increased, however, once the Nashville *Evening Herald* fired all its union printers and hired non-union workers to replace them. This stimulated the typesetters union to call a meeting of all unions in Nashville to meet at the old Olympic Theater and form a primary labor organization. By August 24, 1890, the Central Labor Union, later to be called the Trades and Labor Council, was formed and took out a charter with the American Federation Labor. The Council likewise issued a newspaper, the *Journal of Labor*.

The aims of the Nashville Trades and Labor Council illustrate the growing class consciousness among workers in Tennessee cities in the late nineteenth century. Among their objectives were: higher wages, shorter work days and "absolute Sunday rest," and the elimination of hiring children under 15 by instituting compulsory school attendance. Additionally, the Council was instrumental in having several municipalities pass ordinances to protect labor. The Council claimed its guidance had helped employers by cutting down on strikes and lockouts. Instead, the Council's conservative approach allowed reason to prevail.

James B. Jones, Jr., Tennessee Historical Commission

SUGGESTED READING: Perry C. Cotham, *Toil, Turmoil, & Triumph: A Portrait of the Tennessee Labor Movement* (1996)

SEE: LABOR

NASHVILLE UNION STATION. This National Historic Landmark symbolizes the power of railroad companies, specifically the Louisville and Nashville Railroad, over the transportation and economy of turn-of-the-century Tennessee. Built between 1898 and 1900, and designed by L&N company engineer Richard Montfort, the building is a significant Tennessee example of Richardsonian Romanesque style. The magnificent passenger train shed, which measures 250 by 500 feet with a clear span of 200 feet, was an engineering marvel for its time. In 1900 it was the longest single-span, gable roof structure in the country.

For seven decades, Union Station served Nashville passengers as a massive stone gateway to the metropolitan corridor represented by the national rail system. In 1975 the station was condemned and closed; Amtrak continued to use the shed for passenger traffic until 1979. Metropolitan Nashville officials acquired the rapidly deteriorating structure in 1985; by the following year, Union Station had been restored as a hotel and restaurant. It has served that function ever since and once again is a prominent Nashville architectural and historical landmark.

Carroll Van West, Middle Tennessee State University

SEE: RAILROAD, LOUISVILLE AND NASHVILLE

NATCHEZ TRACE. From the port of Natchez on the Mississippi River, the Natchez Trace followed over 500 miles of intertwining Indian paths through the Choctaw and Chickasaw nations across the Tennessee River to Nashville. For reasons of national security, Winthrop Sargent, first Governor of Mississippi Territory, in 1799 recommended the opening of a post road from Natchez to Knoxville to improve communications with the nation's capital. The administration and Congress concurred, but permission had to be obtained to cross Indian land. Though the Cherokees refused to allow a road from Knoxville to Nashville, in 1801 the Choctaws and Chickasaws agreed. Consequently Nashville became the northern terminus. Because the Chickasaws wisely reserved rights to operate houses of accommodation and ferries in their nation, some mixed-bloods such as George Colbert profited considerably from their businesses on the Trace.

Soon the Trace became heavily traveled by gold-laden boatmen returning to Tennessee, Kentucky, and points beyond after selling their cargoes and flatboats at New Orleans and Natchez. They were not alone. A vast assemblage of characters also marched the same route: robbers, rugged pioneers, fashionable ladies, shysters, politicians, soldiers, scientists, and men of destiny such as Aaron Burr, Andrew Jackson, and Meriwether Lewis.

Under the command of General James Wilkinson, Edmund Pendleton Gaines marked the path through the Indian nations in 1802, and over the next several years Army troops widened the trace through the Natchez District, for some 40 miles beyond, and over the final 150 miles leading into Nashville. Because such "land pirates" as Samuel Mason and Joseph Thompson Hare infested the road in its early years, the myth of violence still shrouds the Trace. Micajah and Wiley Harpe are often associated with the Trace, but most of their mayhem took place in Kentucky and Tennessee. Though the number of robberies and murders on the Trace subsided by 1805, most persons venturing up and down it traveled in convoys. It was not unusual for outlaws to disguise themselves as Indians. Indians committed few serious crimes on the Trace, and they provided considerable assistance. Occasionally, however, they hid the horses of sleeping travelers and demanded ransom to find them.

From Natchez the Trace ran northward through the Natchez District to Bayou Pierre, east of Vicksburg. From there, it veered northeastward 160 miles through the Choctaw Nation to Line Creek and another 205 miles through Chickasaw territory to the Duck River ridge. The final segment ran through a sparsely settled portion of Tennessee into Nashville. Despite the improvements at each end, much of the Trace remained a horse path through the wilderness. The postmaster general contracted with business men to deliver the mail from Nashville to Natchez; in turn, they hired riders who made the trip in ten to 15 days. John Lee Swaney is the only rider who escaped anonymity. With the founding of Columbia, Tennessee, in 1807, officials routed mail deliveries via the new town, and commercial traffic soon followed.

The trace is best known as a commercial route by which the colorful boatmen, often young and unpolished, made their way back to their homes—generally after celebrations in New Orleans and/or Natchez. Mike Fink, a riverman mythologized by Mark Twain and others, remains the quintessential riverman—half alligator, half horse. Though at first there were only a few houses of accommodation scattered among the Chickasaws, soon they dotted the trace from end to end.

Tennessee militia used the Trace on at least three occasions. In 1803 the Secretary of War ordered troops to Natchez as a precaution during the transfer of Louisiana. In 1813 John Coffee led the cavalry to rendezvous with Andrew Jackson and the militia infantrymen who arrived in Natchez on boats during the War of 1812. When Jackson received orders to dismiss his militiamen instead, he defiantly walked up the Trace with his men in a display of toughness that led to his sobriquet "Old Hickory." Following the Battle of New Orleans in 1815, Tennesseans, including the triumphant Jackson, returned up the Trace. Jackson, who first ventured to Natchez while it was under Spanish rule, by then was quite familiar with the road.

On October 11, 1809, 35-year-old Meriwether Lewis met his untimely and mysterious death at Grinder's Stand, 73 miles south of Nashville. The demise of Lewis was reported to Thomas Jefferson as a suicide, and this interpretation was not challenged until 1848 when Tennessee moved the site of his grave and constructed a monument over it that is now part of the Natchez Trace Parkway. In 1996 a group of forensic scientists convinced a Lewis County Coroner's Jury to request that Lewis's body be exhumed in order to determine his cause of death. As of 1997, no final decision has been made about this possible forensic examination.

By the late 1820s, the Trace was no longer a heavily traveled route from Natchez to Nashville. Though local traffic used segments for decades, the Trace fell victim to numerous forces such as the steamboat, construction of competing roads, and changing settlement patterns. By then, however, the Trace had served its crucial role in cementing the southwestern frontier to the young republic despite French, Spanish, and British threats. Meanwhile the frontiersmen who traveled this wilderness artery contributed to a force later known as Manifest Destiny. In this sense, the Natchez Trace was a pathway to empire.

John D. W. Guice, University of Southern Mississippi

SUGGESTED READINGS: Vardis Fisher, *Suicide or Murder? The Strange Death of Governor Meriwether Lewis* (reprint ed., 1993); John D.W. Guice, "A Fatal Rendezvous: The Mysterious Death of Meriwether Lewis," *The Journal of Mississippi History* 57(1995): 121–38

SEE: HARPE, MICAJAH AND WILEY; LEWIS COUNTY; MERIWETHER LEWIS NATIONAL MONUMENT

NATCHEZ TRACE PARKWAY, a unit of the National Park Service since May 18, 1938, commemorates the historical significance of the Old Natchez Trace which served as a frontier road linking Nashville through the wilderness to Natchez, Mississippi. The Parkway does not follow the exact route of the Old Natchez Trace, which actually consisted of several different trails, but follows the general route of the old road over 445 miles through Tennessee, Alabama, and Mississippi.

Interest in recognizing the Natchez Trace started in the early twentieth century when Mrs. Egbert Jones of Holly Springs, Mississippi, suggested to the Mississippi Society of the Daughters of the American Revolution that they erect granite markers along the Old Trace in each county through which it ran. The first marker went up in Natchez in 1909. Soon DAR groups in Alabama and Tennessee as well as other historic organizations became involved in the marker project, which lasted until 1933.

After the passage of the Federal Highway Aid Act of 1916, the Natchez Chamber of Commerce suggested reconstructing and paving the Old Natchez Trace. Enthusiasm for this project died as the United States became more involved in World War I.

Interest in paving the Old Trace increased again after the last marker was placed in 1933, when U.S. Representative Thomas J. Busby of Mississippi became involved. Believing the project to be in accord with the public works programs being established by President Franklin Roosevelt, Busby introduced two bills that, first, called for a survey of the Parkway and, second, appropriated $25 million for its construction. The President approved the survey, with funding coming from the National Park Service's Roads and Trails fund. Initial funds for the subsequent construction of the road came from the 1934 Emergency Appropriation Act.

Federal public works agencies such as the Public Works Administration, Works Projects Administration, and Civilian Conservation Corps participated in the initial construction of the Parkway. After the New Deal, construction slowed drastically and the National Park Service completed the last segment, which terminates at Highway 100 at the community of Pasquo in Davidson County, in 1996.

Just over 100 miles of the Natchez Trace Parkway are located in Tennessee running along the Western Highland Rim through Davidson, Williamson, Hickman, Maury, Lewis, and Wayne counties. Although there are prehistoric Native American sites along the original Natchez Trace in Tennessee, there are no such sites along the Natchez Trace Parkway within the state's boundaries. Historic sites along the Parkway commemorate the late eighteenth and early nineteenth period of the Old Trace, including two sections of the original trace, located at mile markers 375.8 and 401.4, that travelers may drive over. There are also several sections of the Old Trace open for hiking. Other Tennessee sites include the Gordon House (1818), a former toll house which is located near the Duck River crossing; the Meriwether Lewis National Monument, which was annexed to the Parkway in 1961; and various mining sites associated with the nineteenth century iron industry in Tennessee. Located near the Buffalo River crossing is the town of Napier where open pit iron mining took place from the 1830s to the 1920s. A tobacco barn site interprets the twentieth century practice of burley tobacco production.

The Natchez Trace Parkway offers a unique look at Tennessee history ranging from the back-country years of the early nineteenth century through the mining period of the nineteenth century to the agriculture and New Deal history of the twentieth century.

Holly Anne Rine, University of New Hampshire

Suggested Reading: Carroll Van West, *Tennessee's Historic Landscapes: A Traveler's Guide* (1995)

SEE: MERIWETHER LEWIS NATIONAL MONUMENT; NATCHEZ TRACE

NATCHEZ TRACE STATE PARK, covering 12,096 acres, is located approximately five miles east of Wildersville, Tennessee. In combination with the Natchez Trace State Forest, which includes nearly 36,000 acres in Henderson, Carroll, and Benton counties, the two sites comprise West Tennessee's largest state-owned recreational area. Initially the site included some of the state's most eroded lands, with gullies measuring up to 75 feet deep and 300 feet wide. Now the Natchez Trace State Park Visitor's Center exhibits historic photographs of these huge gullies, and a small portion of the devastated land has been preserved.

Three New Deal agencies, the Works Progress Administration (WPA), Civilian Conservation Corps (CCC), and Resettlement Administration, assumed responsibility for the park's initial planning and development. Like other early state parks, the Resettlement Administration relocated property owners from unproductive and overused farm land; the CCC and WPA began land replenishment and park construction. The CCC concentrated its efforts on reforestation work and instigated land stabilization programs that included the introduction of the Japanese vine, kudzu, to halt erosion.

In 1939 the U.S. Department of Agriculture leased land to the state for the development of Natchez Trace State Park, and the CCC and WPA began park construction. These two agencies built a lake, public lodge, bathhouse, beach, 20 brick cabins, outdoor fireplaces, picnic areas, a group camp site, hiking trails, and a recreational building. Additional building plans included an athletic field, amphitheater, assembly hall, dining hall, kitchen, ten cabins, two washhouses, and two lakes. These plans failed to materialize as state interest in the park, which was used as a resort and a fish and game refuge, declined. Six years later, the site had still not become a popular tourist attraction. The park's remote location, minimal attractions, as well as poor planning, construction, and development all contributed to lack of visitors. State officials viewed development of the site as too expensive and abandoned all work except construction of camping facilities. In 1949 a renovation program closed the park for remodeling of cabins and ranger's houses, reconstruction of the swimming area, and renovation of the administrative area.

The Division of State Parks emphasized the historical features of Natchez Trace State Park. The park's name reflects the assumption that the old "Natchez Trace" passed through the area; later research identified the original route several miles east of the park. Park officials also attempted to raise visitation by associating the area with nearby Indian burial grounds and featuring within the park a large pecan tree that measured 17 feet in circumference and approximately 106 feet in height in 1960.

Park officials now believe that the CCC and WPA completed all 1930s era buildings and structures for the park, but few of these remain intact. A firetower and water tower constructed in 1937, probably by the CCC, are still visible. The park's unique Depression-era project is Fairfield Gullies, a well-preserved area that demonstrates the former severely eroded lands of West Tennessee and the introduction of kudzu as a conservation method.

Ruth D. Nichols, Nashville

SEE: CIVILIAN CONSERVATION CORPS; CONSERVATION; WORKS PROGRESS ADMINISTRATION

NATIONAL ASSOCIATION FOR THE ADVANCE-MENT OF COLORED PEOPLE (NAACP) began in 1909 in protest of violent forms of racism, including lynching; of racial segregation; and of disfranchisement of African-American voters. Events and people from Tennessee played a major role in its formation and subsequent history.

The NAACP sought to improve the legal status of African Americans and their social, political, and economic opportunities, especially in combatting the pernicious effects of the U.S. Supreme Court's ruling in *Plessy v. Ferguson* (1896) that "separate but equal" provisions for black and white Americans were constitutional. Ida B. Wells-Barnett, a founding member of the NAACP, became well-acquainted with the meaning of separate but equal in her years in Tennessee as a teacher and journalist. In 1884 she protested her removal from a train in Shelby County, where she taught. She insisted that her first-class ticket entitled her to ride in a car "reserved" for white women and their companions. She refused to move to another, obviously less desirable car where all passengers could use tobacco and liquor regardless of race. In overturning lower court verdicts that had supported Wells, the Tennessee Supreme Court suggested that she should have just found "a comfortable seat for a short ride." This was not her nature and with her personal example of courage and duty, she infused the NAACP with a determination to protest both subtle and profound forms of racial subordination, especially the institution's early initiative to pass anti-lynching laws. Nothing expressed the racial subordination of African Americans as completely as the number and lack of punishment for lynchings of African Americans, like those protested by Wells and others in Shelby County during the 1890s.

A second NAACP founder with a significant Tennessee association was W.E.B. Du Bois, who attended Fisk University and taught briefly at a African-American public school in Wilson County. Du Bois's initial 1905 effort at a national organization of protest and advocacy, the Niagra Movement, sputtered to an end after a few years. Shortly thereafter, Du Bois and Wells, who now lived in Chicago, joined forces in a national effort for increased racial equality. Wells helped in a petition drive to use the 100th anniversary of Lincoln's birth to protest and improve the conditions of African Americans. The National Negro Conference grew from that effort and eventually grew into a committee of 50 that founded the NAACP. The basic goals of the NAACP were to end violence towards African Americans and to secure equal protection of the laws. Its strategy focused on the judicial system since NAACP leaders believed that the courts provided the best hope to challenge segregation and racial inequality.

The first NAACP chapter in Tennessee was established in Memphis in 1917. From there, similar efforts spread to other cities; by the following year chapters existed in Nashville and Chattanooga while chapters were established in Knoxville in 1919 and Jackson in 1920. The organization then slowly moved into rural counties. A local chapter of the NAACP in Brownsville, for example, began an effort to register to vote in 1940. As in many other cases in Tennessee and the South, the members of the Brownsville chapter came from the local business and professional class of African Americans, primarily; the "talented tenth," as Du Bois called them. The efforts to increase political participation in Haywood County met violent reaction. In 1940 Elbert Williams, one of their members, was lynched, the last verified lynching in the state's history. Seven other leaders of the branch were literally expelled from the county by white mobs that included law enforcement officers. Thurgood Marshall, who would later become a U.S. Supreme Court Justice, gained some of his initial experience in civil rights in these events. He investigated the Brownsville case for the NAACP. No charges were brought in the case and the local branch was suppressed. In a historic irony, Mildred Bond, the daughter of one of the expelled local NAACP leaders, would join the national staff of the NAACP and return to Haywood County for the formal organization of a new NAACP chapter in 1961. Tennessee also provided Marshall, the head of the NAACP Legal Defense Fund, his closest brush with violence. In 1946 he traveled to Columbia to assist the defense of African Americans accused of participating in a race riot that summer. One hundred African Americans had been arrested and two killed, while in police custody, but an all-white federal grand jury found that no civil rights had been violated. Eventually, charges against the defendants were dismissed, some convictions were vacated, and only one defendant served jail time. At the conclusion of the trial, Marshall was driving from Columbia to Nashville with Z. Alexander Looby, a prominent African-American attorney from Nashville, when he was stopped by local police, who separated the two attorneys. Looby refused to drive away. Instead, he followed the police car that had taken Marshall, averting violence against Marshall. After hiding in Columbia for the night, Marshall and Looby escaped to Nashville the next day.

The courageous leadership of NAACP officials and members provided a foundation for the civil rights movement in Tennessee. The first voter registration drives in Haywood and Fayette counties drew upon NAACP support. The sit-in demonstrations in Nashville found support from Z. Alexander Looby and other NAACP leaders in Nashville. At the same time, Ella Baker, field secretary of the NAACP, urged the young protestors of the emerging Civil Rights Movement to develop their own organization. Students from Nashville and other areas took her advice and formed the Student Nonviolent Coordinating Committee. At the same time, the NAACP led or joined coalitions that demonstrated for and achieved legislation that enfranchised African Americans, such as the Voting Rights Act of 1965.

From 1977 to 1993, Benjamin J. Hooks of Memphis was the NAACP's Executive Director. During these years, the Legal Defense Fund invoked the provisions of the Voting Right Act on 1965 to lower the informal remaining barriers to African-American political participation, such as at-large elections for city councils, that diluted the votes of racial minorities. Between 1969 and 1990, these efforts helped to increase the number of African-American elected officials from 1,200 to 7,000. Hooks's period of leadership, however, found that increased civil rights and legal protections had not been matched with sufficient improvement in the socio-economic position of African Americans. The changed political climate of the 1980s and 1990s also included less support for civil rights programs. Despite this, the NAACP supported major civil rights legislation successfully in the 1980s.

After Hooks's retirement in 1993, internal conflict over new directions rocked the organization for almost two years. In 1995 Myrlie Evers-Williams became chair of the NAACP board of directors and a year later, Kwiesi Mfume was elected president. The NAACP's determination to create a better future expresses the spirit of Ida B. Wells-Barnett, W.E.B. Du Bois, and the thousands of prominent and unnoticed Tennesseans who have supported it.

Richard Couto, University of Richmond

SUGGESTED READING: Lester C. Lamon, *Black Tennesseans, 1900–1930* (1977)

SEE: CHURCH, ROBERT, JR.; CIVIL RIGHTS MOVEMENT; COLUMBIA RIOT OF 1946; DU BOIS, W.E.B.; HOOKS, BENJAMIN J.; LOOBY, Z. ALEXANDER; LYNCHING; WELLS-BARNETT, IDA B.

NATIONAL BAPTIST CONVENTION, founded in 1895, has since spawned four different denominations that have roots in the original convention. It formed originally as a combination of three separate organizations—the American National Baptist Convention, the Baptist Foreign Mission Convention, and the National Baptist Educational Convention. Each group took on separate work in evangelism, missions, and education. By combining the three, the National Baptist Convention became a large and multi-faceted denominational body, delegating specific types of religious work to various boards and agencies subsumed under it.

Tennessee and Tennesseans played a major role in the early history of the convention. Richard H. Boyd, later manager of the National Baptist Publishing Board in Nashville, was present at the founding meeting of the National Baptist Convention in Atlanta, as was Sutton Griggs, for many years a black Baptist pastor and author in Nashville and Memphis. Many of the early leaders of the organization either attended, graduated from, or taught at Roger Williams University in Nashville and Howe Institute in Memphis (both now defunct). Major Tennessee congregations, such as the East First Baptist Church in Nashville and the Beale Street Baptist Church in Memphis, have played key roles in the organization's history.

Tennesseans also were instrumental in the battle which led to the splitting of the original convention in 1915. Convention leaders deemed Boyd's National Baptist Publishing Board to be an agency subsumed within the larger denomination, while Boyd himself believed that his publishing enterprise was an independent entity affiliated with, but not specifically controlled by, the convention. When, in 1915, convention leaders tried to secure control of the board, Boyd and his forces, including most Tennessee black Baptists, bolted from the meeting hall and formed the unincorporated National Baptist Convention, U.S.A. A battle for the future of the National Baptist Convention raged through court battles, and unsuccessful mediation attempts over the next several years resulted in two groups, the incorporated National Baptist Convention, U.S.A. and the unincorporated group of the same name. Both were based in Nashville. After Boyd and his main combatant, Elias Camp Morris (a former student at Roger Williams), died in the early 1920s, the conventions settled into a dual existence, each claiming to speak for black Baptists of America.

Today the incorporated group is the larger, with five million members. With the recent opening in Nashville of the National Baptist Convention U.S.A., Inc.'s World Headquarters, Tennessee will continue to play a key role in the future of this religious denomination. Its American Baptist Theological Seminary is in Nashville and produced the notable student leader, John R. Lewis, during the Civil Rights Movement.

Paul Harvey, University of Colorado, Colorado Springs

SEE: BOYD, RICHARD H.; NATIONAL BAPTIST PUBLISHING BOARD; RELIGION

NATIONAL BAPTIST PUBLISHING BOARD.

Chartered in 1896 by Richard H. Boyd and a group of black businessmen, and fully operational by 1898, the National Baptist Publishing Board grew in the twentieth century to be the largest black publishing enterprise in the United States. Located on Second Avenue North in downtown Nashville, the Board employed over 100 African Americans by 1910, and became a successful symbol of "race enterprise." Beginning with the printing of Sunday School lessons authored by whites, by 1910 the Board employed black writers to pen homilies that found their way into thousands of black churches across the nation. The Board was also instrumental in the publication of song sheets and hymn books, which became standard in black churches across the nation. Thomas Dorsey, the so-called "father of gospel music," made his name publishing songs through the auspices of the National Baptist Publishing Board before later moving on to more commercial presses. In addition, subsidiary enterprises of the Board made dolls, church pews, and accoutrements for worship.

In 1915 disputes over the relationship of the Board to the larger National Baptist Convention split black churches across the nation and split the National Baptist Convention into two different institutions. The National Baptist Publishing Board remained in Nashville. Boyd presided over its operations until his death in 1922, when his son, Henry Allen Boyd, succeeded him. Henry A. Boyd significantly expanded the company's business during his 37 years of leadership. Dr. T.B. Boyd, Jr., became chief administrator in 1959, serving for the next 20 years during which time he acquired and developed the board's modern printing plant on Centennial Boulevard. After his death in 1979, his son Dr. T.B. Boyd III became the fourth generation of Boyds to guide this important religious publishing entity.

Paul Harvey, University of Colorado, Colorado Springs
SUGGESTED READING: Bobby L. Lovett and Linda T. Wynn, eds. *Profiles of African Americans in Tennessee* (1996)
SEE: BOYD, RICHARD H.; NATIONAL BAPTIST CONVENTION; RELIGION

NATIONAL CAMPGROUND,

located in rural Loudon County, has held religious camp meetings since the late Reconstruction era. In 1873 individuals from congregations representing the Presbyterian, Cumberland Presbyterian, Baptist, Methodist Episcopal Church, South, Friends (Quakers), and the Methodist Episcopal Church faiths gathered at this spot five miles west of Greenback to establish a "union campground" where annual revivals could be held. The group incorporated under the laws of Tennessee, creating a board consisting of two trustees from each denomination. The corporation policed the proceedings and passed binding ordinances prohibiting alcohol, protecting trees and shrubbery on the grounds, and governing the use of the site for other religious and educational meetings.

The first meetings took place in 1873 under a large tent, set in about five acres of land surrounded by woods and supplied with two springs of fresh water. A year later, the trustees approved and supervised the construction of a large open-shed tabernacle, with benches constructed directly in the ground. At the time of the campground's listing in the National Register of Historic Places in 1972, the only change to the tabernacle was the addition of electrical lighting. Historians also believed that National Campground was the only rural camp-meeting tabernacle in the state where annual revivals still took place.

Reverend W.B. "Billy" Brown, a Presbyterian minister, held the first meeting at the new tabernacle in 1874. The meetings took place both day and night for an intense two-week period in the summer; thousands came by horse and wagon to attend. This summer rite continued into modern times, with the various churches rotating their ministers as speakers, although as more and more participants acquired automobiles, people stopped camping on the grounds and merely drove to the nightly meetings.

Carroll Van West, Middle Tennessee State University
SEE: CAMP MEETINGS; LOUDON COUNTY; RELIGION

NATIONAL CIVIL RIGHTS MUSEUM,

located at 450 Mulberry in Memphis, is the state's pre-eminent museum dedicated to the history of the Civil Rights Movement in the United States, from the nineteenth century to the present. The interactive exhibits especially focus on the momentous events of the 1950s and 1960s when Dr. Martin Luther King, Jr., played such a crucial role in the struggle for civil rights. The spotlight on King is appropriate because the museum incorporates a portion of the original Lorraine Motel; on its balcony Dr. King was assassinated in April 1968. The museum also preserves the room where Dr. King was staying before his murder. He was in Memphis lending support, and bringing national publicity, to the strike of Memphis sanitation workers, most of whom were African Americans. In the days of Jim Crow, the Lorraine Hotel and Motel was a popular segregated resting place for African Americans visiting in Memphis. The Lorraine's guests included Cab Calloway, Count Basie, Nat King Cole, and Aretha Franklin. It remained a motel until its conversion into the National Civil Rights Museum in the late 1980s; the museum opened to the public in 1991.

Carroll Van West, Middle Tennessee State University
SEE: CIVIL RIGHTS MOVEMENT; MEMPHIS SANITATION STRIKE

NATIONAL FIELD TRIAL. For more than 100 years, owners have brought together the top pointing dogs in the country to compete in a premier stake known as the National Field Trial Championship. Most championship competitions have been held at Ames Plantation, located near Grand Junction, about 40 miles east of Memphis.

Massachusetts manufacturing mogul Hobart Ames acquired property near Grand Junction after the turn of the century, and for more than 30 renewals the stake was held on the Hobart Ames Preserve. Upon his death in 1945 the trial was continued there under the auspices of his widow, Julia Colony Ames. Upon her death in 1950 the Hobart Ames Foundation was established, its purpose to benefit the University of Tennessee as well as provide a permanent home for the National Field Trial at Ames Plantation.

During its 101-year-history, the National Championship has been cancelled only four times, either because of weather or, in the opinion of championship officials, there was not sufficient quail on the plantation courses for the dogs to have a fair chance of winning the title. The English Setter breed dominated the winners's circle in the early days of the stake, but pointers came on in the 1920s and have been the predominant winners since. Multiple winners of the stake have been few in number, and those dogs that have won the Grand Junction classic on more than one occasion have a special place in bird dog history. The first multiple winner was Sioux, which won in 1901 and 1902. Mary Montrose, Becky Broom, Feagin's Mohawk Pal, and Ariel enjoy the distinction of "three time winners," all by 1945. Since then, Paladin (1951, 1952) and Whippoorwill's Rebel (1987, 1989) have won twice, as had Mary Blue in 1929 and 1931.

The stake draws between 32 and 40 dogs annually, and the running time will consume the better part of two weeks as dogs compete in three-hour marathon heats over the morning and afternoon course at Ames Plantation. The National Field Trial championship is one of the oldest sporting events in America.

Bernie Matthys, American Field Publishing

SEE: AMES PLANTATION

Pointer, "Jake," competing at the 1946 National Field Trials.

NATIONAL LIFE AND ACCIDENT INSURANCE COMPANY, destined to become one of the top insurance companies in the nation, barely survived its first winter. C.A. Craig bought it for $17,250 on the Davidson County courthouse steps on December 27, 1901. Previously administered by C. Runcie Clements, the company, then called National Sick and Accident Company, was sold to settle an estate.

By January 1, 1902, the company had only $23,000 in assets and about half of that was in real estate. The company's cash had dwindled to $3,200. On January 7, 1902, Craig was elected president of the company at a meeting of shareholders. W.R. Wills became secretary and treasurer and C.R. Clements became assistant treasurer. All three men owned shares and the name was changed to National Life and Accident Insurance Company.

During early days of its operation the only policies sold by the company were health and accident premiums usually for industrial workers, a large percentage of whom were African Americans. Five cents per week bought the policyholders $1.25 per week in case of illness, $2.00 per week in case of disability, and $12.50 in accidental death benefits.

Craig, Wills, and Clements were men of vision and extended their services and staff. In 1920 National Life opened its first life insurance department, with Edwin W. Craig as manager and Eldon B. Stevenson, Jr., as assistant manager. Other key executives would include Jesse E. Wills, G.D. Brooks, William C. Weaver, and Walter S. Bearden. By 1924 the company had moved into a handsome stone building on the northwest corner of Seventh and Union. It expanded its market by offering a wide range of insurance policies including whole life, endowment, and term policies.

Edwin Wilson Craig as president of the National Life and Accident Insurance Company is frequently credited with the idea for a radio broadcasting station. WSM was launched in 1925, and it won international fame through its program of country music, the Grand Ole Opry. WSM helped to spread Nashville's name through its broadcasts, and out of the Grand Ole Opry grew Nashville's popular Opryland.

In 1968 N.L.T. Corporation was created as a holding company with National Life the principal subsidiary. From its Texas headquarters, American General Corporation, which already had acquired Nashville-based Life and Casualty Insurance Company, gained control of N.L.T. in 1982. Two giant Nashville-born insurance companies were melted now into a conglomerate holding company. It was the end of an era in Nashville's economic history.

John Connelly, Nashville

SUGGESTED READING: John Egerton, *The Faces of Two Centuries 1780–1980* (1979)

SEE: COMMERCE; GRAND OLE OPRY; NASHVILLE; WSM

NATIONAL ORNAMENTAL METAL MUSEUM,

dedicated to the collection, exhibition, and preservation of fine metalwork, opened in 1979. The site was formerly a part of the U.S. Marine Hospital, constructed by the Works Progress Administration in the mid-1930s. The gallery building was the nurses' dormitory, and the adjacent duplex was housing for doctors and their families. The west duplex now provides housing for the museum director while the east duplex is a guest house for artists and consultants for the museum and other area non-profit agencies. The white building, located at the northeast section of the property, was built in 1870 and later was a center for yellow fever research. During the 1930s construction, this building was moved to its existing site.

The Schering-Plough Smithy, completed and dedicated in 1986, is a site for metalworking demonstrations for visitors, classes for area residents, and workshops for metalsmithing students and professionals. Staff metalsmiths also undertake a variety of special projects and commissions, including the barbecue trophies for Memphis in May, the restoration of the Graceland Gates, and the lion sculptures from the Memphis Zoo. The smithy contains a state-of-the-art laboratory for metals conservation and restoration. The lab, also funded by Schering-Plough, provides conservation services for private collectors and other museums. It also offers training opportunities for metalsmiths interested in careers in the field of conservation.

The Riverbluff Pavilion, overlooking the Mississippi, is constructed of castings salvaged from a building which stood on historic Beale Street in the 1800s. Richard Quinnell of England designed the Anniversary Gates. The scroll and rosette components were contributed by over 180 metalsmiths from 18 nations.

The museum's library has grown to include over 2,000 volumes, 10,000 slides, and manufacturers' catalogues, periodicals on metalworking, videotapes and drawings. The museum's collections now number some 3,000 objects.

Lisa Loehmann, National Ornamental Metal Museum

SEE: ART; MEMPHIS; WORKS PROGRESS ADMINISTRATION

NATIONAL STORYTELLING FESTIVAL, held every October in Jonesborough, is the most prestigious storytelling festival in the nation. Sponsored by the National Storytelling Association, which is headquartered in Jonesborough, the national festival began in 1973. "We all live in a network of stories. There isn't a stronger connection between people than storytelling," emphasizes Jimmy Neil Smith, the Association's executive director.[1]

The first festival in 1973 attracted about 60 people, but numbers rapidly increased. In 1975 organizers created the institutional predecessor to the current Association. By 1980, 1,000 people were attending the event and by the mid-1980s, 5,000 listeners were convening every October in the Jonesborough historic district. One of the festival's most popular places is the Swappin' Ground, where visitors can take their turns, no more than ten minutes, telling grand tales.

Celebrating its 25th anniversary in 1997, the National Storytelling Association has developed into one of Tennessee's key folklife institutions. It is developing a $10 million National Storytelling Center, featuring a story archives, in Jonesborough and has launched a site on the World Wide Web, reaching storytellers who have yet to make the fall trek to the festival.

Carroll Van West, Middle Tennessee State University

CITATION:

(1) Bruce Watson, "The storyteller is the soybean . . . the audience is the sun," *Smithsonian* 27(March 1997): 61.

SEE: CHESTER INN; JONESBOROUGH

NEAL, JAMES F. (1929–), Nashville attorney and federal prosecutor, achieved prominence as successful trial counsel in some of the nation's highest profile criminal cases from the 1960s through the 1990s. He is best known as lead trial counsel in the prosecution of high-ranking officials of the Nixon administration that arose out of the Watergate cover-up, the scandal that prompted President Nixon's resignation.

After graduating from high school in Sumner County, Neal attended the University of Wyoming on a football scholarship and graduated in 1952. Following service in the U.S. Marine Corps where he reached the rank of captain, Neal attended Vanderbilt University School of Law and finished first in the class of 1957. He earned an advanced law degree at Georgetown University in 1960.

While serving in 1961–1964 as a special assistant to the Attorney General of the United States, Neal helped prosecute Teamsters Union President Jimmy Hoffa for attempting to bribe jurors in a previous case. Following service as U.S. Attorney for the Middle District of Tennessee in 1964–1966, he entered private law practice in Nashville and was a founding partner of the firm of Neal & Harwell.

In 1973 former U.S. Attorney General John Mitchell and other ranking members of the Nixon administration were charged with obstructing justice following the 1972 burglary of Democratic Party offices at the Watergate Hotel by Republican political operatives. Neal was named lead trial counsel and successfully prosecuted the cases.

Among the more noted defendants Neal has successfully represented are Dr. George Nichopoulos (Elvis Presley's physician), Louisiana Governor Edwin Edwards, Ford Motor Company in the Pinto criminal trial, and Exxon Corporation in charges resulting from the Alaskan oil spill.

Robert Brandt, Nashville
SEE: LAW

NEAL, PATRICIA (1926–), Academy Award-winning actress, was raised in Knoxville where she studied theater and performed in various venues. In 1942, following her junior year of high school, Neal landed a summer-stock position at Robert Porterfield's Barter Theatre in Abingdon, Virginia.

After high school graduation Neal entered Northwestern University but left to move to New York, where working as an understudy she caught playwright Lillian Hellman's attention. Neal appeared in Hellman's *The Little Foxes,* and by 1947 she signed a contract with Warner Brothers. Her first important film role was in King Vidor's screen adaptation of Ayn Rand's *The Fountainhead* (1949).

The Fountainhead secured Neal's reputation and led to an affair with co-star Gary Cooper. After making *The Hasty Heart* (1949) with Ronald Reagan, she appeared with Cooper again in *Bright Leaf* (1950). Their affair became more brazen, and she endured an illegal abortion at Cooper's request. The ongoing affair took its toll emotionally on Neal, driving her to psychotherapy. Her contract was not renewed, and she moved to Twentieth Century-Fox and completed *The Day the Earth Stood Still* (1951). Neal returned in 1952 for a revival of Hellman's *The Children's Hour* in New York. While there, she met and married novelist Roald Dahl in 1953. Their first child, Olivia, was born in 1955.

Neal went to work in television, and later she played Maggie the Cat in Tennessee Williams' *Cat on a Hot Tin Roof* in an Off-Broadway production. Direc-

tor Elia Kazan created her Hollywood comeback in a dark comedy, *A Face in the Crowd* (1957), also starring new comic sensation, Andy Griffith. After appearing in the Broadway production of *The Miracle Worker* (1959) and the birth of her son, Theo, she was named Tennessee's Woman of the Year in 1962, but her daughter's death from measles at the age of seven devastated the entire family.

In the midst of her grief, Neal was offered the role that earned her the Academy Award for Best Actress: Alma in Martin Ritt's production of *Hud* (1963). More work followed, including *In Harm's Way,* but three years to the day after her daughter's death, on November 17, 1965, Neal, pregnant with her fourth child, suffered an aneurysm. Paralyzed and unable to speak, her recovery was slow and painful. Dahl devoted himself to her recuperation with sternness. Though bouts of severe depression along with her difficult pregnancy impeded her progress, by 1968 Neal was fully recovered. Her first film after her illness, *The Subject Was Roses* (1968), was a personal and professional triumph. In 1970 *Good Housekeeping* reported that she was one of the ten most admired women in America. She dedicated time and money to the Patricia Neal Rehabilitation Center, a not-for-profit research facility dedicated to stroke research and therapy. Working steadily throughout the 1970s, Neal became associated with roles of strong, wise, world-weary women. Dahl, her husband of 30 years, sued her for divorce on November 17, 1983. Neal went into retirement in 1987, devoting her full energies to the Patricia Neal Rehabilitation Center.

Michael E. Birdwell, Tennessee Technological University
SEE: TENNESSEE IN FILM; TELEVISION AND MOVIE PERFORMERS

NELSON, THOMAS A. R. (1812–1873), Whig Congressman and Unionist, attempted to steer a moderate course during the sectional crisis of the 1850s. Born in Roane County, Tennessee, March 19, 1812, and a lawyer by training, he became a founder of the state's Whig party and supported the presidential candidacy of Hugh Lawson White in 1836. As a party leader, he served as presidential elector in 1844 and 1848 and twice ran for the U.S. Senate. In 1859 he was elected to Congress, where he took a strong Unionist stance and attacked secession as radical and unconstitutional. He supported John Bell and the Constitutional Union party in the 1860 election and continued to counsel caution after Abraham Lincoln's election and the secession of the deep South states.

When the Civil War erupted in 1861, Nelson was stunned by President Abraham Lincoln's call for troops, but campaigned vigorously against secession in his own state. He was elected president of both the Knoxville and Greeneville Unionist conventions to oppose secession and agitate for a separate East

Tennessee state. After Tennessee joined the Confederacy, Nelson's constituents elected him to the U.S. Congress in August 1861. On the way to Washington, he was arrested in Kentucky and taken to Richmond. He was paroled and eventually permitted to return home and resume his law practice.

When Lincoln issued the Emancipation Proclamation in 1863, Nelson concluded that the Republican party was becoming dangerously radical. At the request of Confederate authorities, he issued a statement to the people of East Tennessee denouncing Lincoln's acts, which he considered despotic and unconstitutional. Nelson, however, became increasingly troubled by the Confederate policies of conscription and confiscation of private property and reversed his course once Federal forces occupied East Tennessee. Even so, he rejected Republicanism and supported the 1864 presidential candidacy of Democrat George B. McClellan and a compromise peace.

True to his conservatism, Nelson decried the postwar campaign of terror and retribution launched against former Confederates by Radicals such as William G. "Parson" Brownlow. He defended ex-Confederates accused of treason and other crimes and assisted them in recovering confiscated property. As Justice on the State Supreme Court, he handed down a decision in the case of *Smith v. Brazelton* (1870), which held that the Confederacy was a de facto government, a position vehemently denounced by Radicals. He also opposed congressional Radicalism by serving as counsel for President Andrew Johnson during his impeachment trial. Refusing to follow Brownlow and his supporters into the Republican party, Nelson worked with other Tennessee conservatives to create a third party based on old Whig principles, but he died in 1873 without realizing his goal.

W. Todd Groce, Georgia Historical Society

SUGGESTED READING: Thomas B. Alexander, *Thomas A.R. Nelson of East Tennessee* (1956)

SEE: BROWNLOW, WILLIAM G.; RECONSTRUCTION; TENNESSEE SUPREME COURT

NETHERLAND INN, located on the Holston River in Kingsport, was a commercial port that served the developing economy of the frontier. It was a place where traders gathered, travelers rested, and local residents gathered to hear news from a distance. Originally part of the plantation of Colonel Gilbert Christian, in 1802 the lot on which the inn stands was sold to William King, for whom Kingsport is named. King owned a number of boatyards on the Holston and Tennessee rivers, where he built flatboats and shipped salt and other merchandise. He died in 1808, and in 1814 George Hale leased the boatyard adjoining the inn from King's estate, added a large wharf, and remodeled some buildings.

The Netherland Inn building was constructed between 1810 and 1820, but the exact date of construction and the identity of the builder are not certain. Possibly King or Hale built it. However, it may be that Richard Netherland, for whom the building was named, constructed the inn after he purchased the property in 1818.

The structure, a three-story, five-bay building with stone and brick exterior chimneys on the gable ends, was set into the side of a steep slope, which angled down toward the Holston River. The first level was constructed of handcut limestone brought from a quarry northwest of the inn site. The second and third levels were made of large hand-hewn timbers, with brick nogging filling the spaces between the wall timbers. The exterior of the upper level was covered with whitewashed beaded poplar siding; walls were plastered throughout.

Floor plans for the three levels were similar; each had a large central hallway with rooms on both sides. The bar and taproom were on the first level. The second level housed the best sitting room and the dining hall. The third level contained the master bedroom and three sleeping rooms. The kitchen was attached behind the inn.

Both the river and the Great Stage Road brought guests to the Netherland Inn. During the flatboat season, farmers and merchants carrying goods down the river would use the facility. Wagoners hauling goods on the Stage Road frequented the establishment as well. Stagecoach drivers made the inn a regular stop, with approximately 14 scheduled visits a week.

The inn remained in the Netherland family until 1904. Between 1906 and 1965, H.C. Cloud operated it as a boarding house. In 1967 the Netherland Inn Association purchased the building and restored it; in 1969 it was placed on the National Register of Historic Places.

W. Calvin Dickinson, Tennessee Technological University

SUGGESTED READING: Marie Day and W. Calvin Dickinson, "The Netherland Inn," East Tennessee Historical Society *Publications* 60(1988): 67–77

SEE: KINGSPORT; LONG ISLAND; SULLIVAN COUNTY

NEWMAN, ROBERT LOFTIN (1827–1912), portraitist and figurative painter, was born in Richmond, Virginia, the second child and only son of Robert L. Newman and Sarah J. Matthews. Newman's father died when he was young, and the family moved to nearby Louisa Court House. His mother married Joseph Winston, and in 1839 they moved to Clarksville, Tennessee, where his stepfather died in 1844.

Newman soon tried his hand at portrait painting, but his clients repeatedly rejected his work. In 1846 he wrote to the famous artist, Asher B. Durand, requesting acceptance as a student. In his letter, he stated that he had abandoned portraiture and decided to "cast in another stream." Durand refused to accept him, but in 1849 the American Art Union in New York purchased his *Music at the Shop-Board*. The following year, he spent five months studying with Thomas Couture in Paris. Four years later, he was back in France, where William Morris Hunt introduced him to the Barbizon School.

In 1858 Newman opened a studio in his Clarksville home and accepted commissions for full-length portraits. During this period, he executed pendant portraits of William Wallace Warfield and son and of Adelia Boisseau Warfield and daughter. These are Newman's only known oil portraits.

Newman served in the Confederate Army twice during the Civil War. In 1861 he was elected a lieutenant of artillery but resigned after a dispute with his commanding officer. In 1864 he was conscripted and assigned to Company G of the 15th Virginia Regiment.

Newman probably lived in New York immediately after the war, but in 1872 he had a studio on Union Street in Nashville, next door to the studio of George Dury. The two artists attempted to establish an Academy of Fine Arts, but they apparently failed. The 1873 Nashville City Directory listed Newman as a portrait painter, but he also offered classes at his studio and in one of the public schools. Newman's mother died that year, and the artist moved to New York, returning to Tennessee only once.

In New York, Newman abandoned portraiture and focused on small figurative paintings of allegorical, religious, mythological, and obscure objects, such as madonnas, sapphos, nymphs, and fortune tellers. He adopted a highly individualistic style that was identified with no school. Though little appreciated in his own day, it was this work that provided him with his present fame.

In 1886 his *Little Red Riding Hood* was exhibited at the National Academy of Design. In 1894 he had a one-man show at Knoedler's in New York and partially repeated at the Museum of Fine Arts in Boston. In 1900 his *Christ Stilling the Tempest* was shown at the Paris International Exposition. On March 31, 1912, Newman died of gas asphyxiation in his New York apartment.

The Brooklyn Museum acquired the first collection of Newman's work in 1914. Major exhibitions of his work were held in New York in 1924, 1935, 1939, and 1961; in Richmond in 1942; and in Washington, D.C., and Nashville in 1975.

James C. Kelly, Virginia Historical Society
SEE: ART; MONTGOMERY COUNTY

NEWMAN, WILLIE BETTY (1863–1935), portraitist, was born on the Benjamin Rucker plantation, near Murfreesboro, the daughter of Colonel William Francis Betty and Sophie Rucker Betty. She attended Soule College in Murfreesboro and Greenwood Seminary in Lebanon, before studying art at the Cincinnati Art School under T.S. Noble. In 1881 she married I. Warren Newman, but they separated soon afterward, and she never spoke of him again.

For 12 years, she studied art in Paris, mostly at the Julian Academy, under masters that included William Adolphe Bouguereau, Jean Paul Laurens, Robert Fleury, and Benjamin Constance. She specialized in genre scenes of French peasant life. A pervasive spiritual quality existed in her work, exemplified by *Passing of the Holy Bread*, now at the Centennial Club, and *En Penitence*, now at Cheekwood, Nashville's Home of Art and Gardens. She exhibited at the Paris Salon from 1893 to 1898, and again in 1900. She received honorable mention and a certificate from the French government for her portrait of Miss Fanny Alice Gowdy, daughter of the American Consul in Paris.

When Newman returned to Nashville, she maintained a portrait studio in the Vauxhall Apartments. Newman portrayed such prominent Nashvillians as John Trotwood Moore, Joel Creek, Governor James Frazier, Mrs. James C. Bradford, James E. Caldwell, and Oscar F. Noel. She was commissioned to paint a portrait of John Sherman, Vice President under William Howard Taft, but her work was rejected as too large, and she forfeited the $4,500 fee. Congress commissioned her to do posthumous portraits of James K. Polk and John C. Bell. The Centennial Club commissioned a portrait of Mrs. Elizabeth Rhodes Eakins. The Nashville Museum of Art awarded Newman the Parthenon medal, its highest honor. She died in Nashville on February 6, 1935.

James C. Kelly, Virginia Historical Society
SEE: ART

NEYLAND, ROBERT REESE, III (1892–1962), football coach, was born February 17, 1892, in Greeneville, Texas, the son of attorney Robert R. Neyland, Jr., and Pauline Lewis Neyland. After high school graduation, he entered Burleson Junior College in Greeneville; a year later he transferred to Texas A & M, where he studied engineering and played baseball and football. In 1912 Neyland won a competitive appointment to West Point, where he continued his engineering studies and his athletic development. He played end on the 1914 and 1915 Army football teams, won 20 straight games in baseball (defeating Navy four times), and won the heavyweight boxing title three years in a row.

After graduation from West Point in 1916, Neyland was sent to the Mexican border, where he was engaged in levee work and bridge and road construction. During World War I, Neyland served in France. Before the war ended, he was assigned to

Fort Bliss, Texas. In 1920 he took additional course work in engineering at Massachusetts Institute of Technology before returning to West Point in 1921 as an assistant adjutant and assistant coach in football, baseball, and basketball. He also served as aide-de-camp to the Academy Superintendent, General Douglas MacArthur.

In 1926 Neyland was assigned to the University of Tennessee as R.O.T.C. commandant and also served as assistant to the district engineer in Chattanooga. In 1931 Neyland became district superintendent and supervised the dredging of the Tennessee and Cumberland rivers. He also oversaw the preliminary surveys for Norris Dam, which was built later by the Tennessee Valley Authority.

In 1926 Neyland became head football coach at the University of Tennessee. In the period from 1926 to 1934, Neyland's teams won 75 games, lost 7, and tied 5. They lost only one game out of the 68 played on their home field. A firm disciplinarian, Neyland stressed speed and conditioning. He required that players rehearse plays until they could execute them perfectly. To Neyland, the most important game of the season was the one against Vanderbilt. In 1927 Tennessee played Vanderbilt to a 7-7 tie in Knoxville. Thereafter, the Volunteers lost only three times to Vanderbilt in 19 games.

Coach Robert Reese "Bob" Neyland, ca. 1930.

SPECIAL COLLECTIONS, UNIVERSITY OF TENNESSEE, KNOXVILLE

The army sent Neyland to the Panama Canal Zone in 1935. When the Volunteers lost all their major games that season, the fans demanded his return. Neyland had found that he also missed football coaching more than he expected, and in 1936 he retired from the army and returned to Tennessee as head football coach. During his second round of coaching, Neyland coached George Cafego, Babe Wood, Sam Bartholomew, Jim Rike, Bowden Wyatt, and Len Coffmen. UT won 11 games in 1938; 10 in 1939; and 10 in 1940. Neyland's defense limited the opposition to 42 points in 50 games.

When the U.S. entered World War II, Neyland was called back into the service and assigned to Norfolk as district engineer. He was reassigned to Dallas, before being sent to China and then Calcutta, India, where he served as port commander. He rose to the rank of brigadier general. Neyland was awarded the Legion of Merit with two clusters and the Distinguished Service Medal from the United States, the Chinese Cloud and Banner, and the British Knight Commander.

In 1946 Neyland returned to coaching at the University of Tennessee. His 1946 team won the Southeastern Conference Championship, and the 1950 team made a post-season trip to the Cotton Bowl, ending the season with a 10-1-0 record. The next year, the Volunteers became the national collegiate champions.

By 1952 Neyland was in poor health. He retired from coaching in 1954, but continued as athletic director. The first coach in the South to use press box spotters and the telephone to assist him in making coaching decisions, Neyland never exploited his reputation as a winning coach. He refused to lecture, write books, or appear on television, believing that the only thing that mattered was his winning record. He produced nine undefeated teams, 40 All-Conference stars, 21 All-Americans, five Southeastern Conference Championships, and one national championship. He was elected to the Football Hall of Fame in 1953, named the Football Writers' Man-of-the-Year in 1954, and received the A.A. Stagg Award by the American Football Coaches Association in 1957.

Neyland died on March 28, 1962, at the Ochsner Foundation Hospital in New Orleans where he had gone for tests. He was married to Ada Fitch of Grand Rapids, Michigan. Their two sons were Robert Reese, IV, and Lewis Fitch Neyland.

Connie L. Lester, Tennessee Historical Society
SEE: FOOTBALL, COLLEGE; U.S. ARMY CORPS OF ENGINEERS; UNIVERSITY OF TENNESSEE

NICHOLS, KENNETH DAVID (1907–) had the responsibility for the design, construction, and operation of the three huge Oak Ridge plants needed for the production of U-235 and a semiworks to produce the first gram of plutonium, the fissionable materials required at Los Alamos to produce the first atomic bombs during World War II. As the district engineer for the Manhattan Engineer District (MED), Nichols was also responsible for the layout and construction of Oak Ridge housing, hospital, schools, utilities, roads, shopping centers—the whole town. Although authority for running the city was delegated to other officers, Nichols was the final arbiter. From 1943 to 1946 Oak Ridge served as his headquarters and his home, despite constant travel to oversee other MED sites, including plutonium production at Richland, Washington.

Nichols was born November 13, 1907, in West Park, Ohio. In 1929 he graduated first in his class from the Military Academy at West Point and was assigned to Fort Humphreys (now Fort Belvoir) as a second lieutenant in the Army Corps of Engineers. Nichols returned to school in 1931 and earned an undergraduate degree and a Masters of Civil Engineering degree from Cornell. An Army assignment to the Technische Hochschule and the Prussian Experimental Station in Berlin, Germany, contributed to his Ph.D. dissertation, "The Observed Effect of Geometric Distortion in Hydraulic Models." The work contained examples from all over Europe and the United States and won the American Society of Civil Engineers Collenwood Award. He taught engineering as well as military history at West Point from 1937 to 1941, during which time another trip to Europe gave him first-hand knowledge that war with Germany was inevitable.

As Nichols reveals in his book, *The Road to Trinity: A Personal Account of How America's Nuclear Policies Were Made*, his work in Oak Ridge forced him to learn to deal with Tennessee politics in order to establish a town as normal as possible, given its origins as a secret installation. The credit for the good basic construction of much of Oak Ridge's early housing goes to Colonel J.C. Marshall and later to Nichols. Tennessee's newest city was completed in spite of arguments for bulldozing down the valley and using cheaper construction. Marshall and Nichols's choice won out—to build more permanent houses on roads that followed the wooded contour of the naturally hilly landscape that helped hide the secret city. Nichols also convinced state officials that a new road was needed between Oak Ridge and Knoxville.

Nichols's success with scientists as well as politicians was due to his training and abilities. In addition to his formal education, he spent two years on assignment to the Engineer Topographical Survey in Nicaragua drilling foundations for locks and seeking a route for a new intercontinental canal. He also worked with the U.S. Waterways Experiment Station in Vicksburg, Mississippi, on engineering river structures to improve navigation and flood control of the Mississippi River and its valley.

After the war, Nichols advanced to the rank of major general and played a major role in missile development and defense planning. He became general manager of the U.S. Atomic Energy Commission (AEC), a post he resigned in 1955. He then spent several years as consulting engineer in the fields of missile research and development as well as commercial atomic power.

June Adamson, Oak Ridge

SEE: OAK RIDGE; WORLD WAR II

NICHOLSON, ALFRED OSBORNE POPE (1808–1876), prominent antebellum Democratic politician, was born in the Carter Creek's area near Spring Hill, Tennessee, in 1808. He received private tutoring before attending Woodward Academy in Columbia. In 1823 he entered the University of North Carolina, graduating four years later. After college, Nicholson studied medicine and then law, receiving his license to practice law in 1830. He married Mary Gordon O'Reilly in 1829, and they had eight children.

A Democratic stalwart, Nicholson represented Maury County in the Tennessee House of Representatives from 1833–1837; he later served in the State Senate from 1843–1845. Like many Democrats, he supported Hugh Lawson White in the 1836 presidential contest, but he returned to the Democratic fold by serving as a presidential elector on the Martin Van Buren ticket in 1840. After the death of U.S. Senator Felix Grundy in 1840, Governor James K. Polk rewarded Nicholson for his hard campaigning by selecting him to complete Grundy's term in office, from December 1840 to February 1842, when the General Assembly would either re-elect Nicholson or select a successor. But the election of any Tennessee Senators became hopelessly mired in partisan politics during 1842. Democrats, led by the "Immortal Thirteen," delayed the selection process until the Whig Party swept the 1843 elections and secured control of the General Assembly.

Nicholson also served his party as a newspaper editor. He was one of the compilers of the *Statutes of Tennessee* in 1836. He edited Columbia's *Western Mercury* from 1830–1834 and the Nashville *Union* from 1845–1846, after which he was selected as a director and later president of the Bank of Tennessee, 1846–1847. During the late 1840s, he became one of the acknowledged leaders, along with Andrew Johnson, of the anti-Polk faction within the Democratic party. After 1848, according to historian Paul Bergeron, "the anti-Polk group moved steadily toward a position of domination in the party, though it ran into some difficulties from time to time."[1]

For instance, in the 1850s, Nicholson served as Chancellor of the Middle Tennessee Division (1850), a delegate to the Nashville Convention (1850), a presidential elector on the Franklin Pierce ticket (1852), and again as U.S. Senator from 1859–1861. He also resumed his editorial career, serving as editor of the Washington *Daily Union* from 1853 to 1856 and was the public printer for the U.S. House of Representatives from 1853–1855 and for the U.S. Senate from 1855–1857.

After the Civil War, Nicholson was a member of the 1870 State Constitutional Convention and then became the new Chief Justice of the State Supreme Court, serving in that position until his death on March 23, 1876. He is buried in Rose Hill Cemetery in Columbia.

Carroll Van West, Middle Tennessee State University
CITATION:
(1) Paul H. Bergeron, *Antebellum Politics in Tennessee* (Lexington, 1982), 95.
SEE: IMMORTAL THIRTEEN; MAURY COUNTY; POLK, JAMES K.; JOHNSON, ANDREW; PUBLISHING; TENNESSEE SUPREME COURT

NIELSEN, ALVIN ANDREAS HERBORG (1910–1994), physicist in molecular spectroscopy, was born May 30, 1910, in Menominee, Michigan. Nielsen graduated from the local high school in 1927, and entered the University of Michigan, from which he earned his B.A. in 1931, M.A. in 1932, and Ph.D. in 1934.

Nielsen accepted a position as instructor in the department of physics at the University of Tennessee in 1935. He became a full professor in 1946 and succeeded Kenneth Hertel as department head in 1956. Nielsen achieved national and international recognition for his work in molecular spectroscopy. He authored 85 publications. During World War II, Nielsen joined a war research team at Ohio State University where he worked on infrared detectors. When he returned to Knoxville after the war, Nielsen became one of the first consultants employed by the Gaseous Diffusion Plant at Oak Ridge, where he led a research team that specialized in studies of halogen-substituted fomaldehydes, which have been found to be important in the pollution of the atmosphere. Nielsen's early work continues to provide information for current pollution studies.

In 1951 Nielsen became the University of Tennessee's first Fulbright Scholar, when he spent a year at the Institut d'Astrophysique de Cointe in Liege, Belgium. He proved adept at building national and international connections for UT. As department head (1956–1969), he played a major role in developing the Oak Ridge connection that provided dual appointments for UT faculty and opened federal research facilities to university scientists. With Hilton

Smith of the chemistry department, he acquired a ten-year faculty endowment grant from the Ford Foundation. In 1969 the National Science Foundation named the physics department a Center of Excellence and awarded it a $750,000 matching grant.

Nielsen was named Dean of the College of Liberal Arts from 1963 to 1977. Nine new departments or programs were added, and six new buildings were constructed. In 1972–73 he served as chairman of the American Council of Academic Deans. When Nielsen retired as Dean, the Mayor of Knoxville, Randy Tyree, declared May 23–29, 1977, as "Alvin H. Nielsen Appreciation Week." In 1980 the UT physics building was named in his honor.

Nielsen was a Fellow of the American Physical Society, of the American Association for the Advancement of Science, and of the Optical Society of America. He married Jane Ann Evans of Columbus, Ohio, in 1942. They were the parents of one daughter, Margaret A. Nielsen Wayne. Alvin Nielsen died in Knoxville on November 3, 1994.

Connie L. Lester, Tennessee Historical Society
SEE: SCIENCE AND TECHNOLOGY; UNIVERSITY OF TENNESSEE

NIGHT RIDERS OF REELFOOT LAKE. Probably no event in the region's history, with the exception of the Civil War, polarized the population of Obion and Lake counties as did the Night Rider episodes of 1908. Nearly a century later, public opinion varies greatly in regard to the character and motivation of the men and women involved in the Reelfoot violence. For seven months in 1908, masked horsemen rode roughshod over a portion of Obion County and imposed their brand of justice with whip, arson, and shotgun. But if the riders are judged guilty of excesses, their adversary, the West Tennessee Land Company, with its example of callous greed, must share in that guilt. Unfortunately, when the State of Tennessee intervened in the matter, it too showed scarcely more restraint than the other participants in the events.

Simply stated, the Night Rider episode was a dispute over title to Reelfoot Lake and the surrounding land. Created by the cataclysmic forces of the 1811–1812 earthquake, the lake and its wildlife supplemented the diets and incomes of subsistence farmers in the area. Although claims on the land existed prior to the earthquake, the local population regarded the lake as public domain. When the West Tennessee Land Company quietly purchased old claims and made plans to drain at least part of the lake and convert it to cotton production, the region's residents reacted violently.

On the night of October 19, 1908, after several weeks of increasingly violent activities, events moved swiftly to a tragic stage. Masked riders kidnapped Tennessee Land Company officers R.Z. Taylor and

Quinton Rankin from Ward's Hotel in Walnut Log. Rankin was murdered, but Taylor escaped into the swamp and was presumed dead. He survived by hiding under a cypress log and was found more than 24 hours later, wandering and disoriented.

Governor Malcolm Patterson personally took charge of matters and arrived in the lake region with the Tennessee National Guard. By the end of October, nearly 100 suspects were incarcerated in a make-shift camp set up by the Guard. The suspects received very harsh treatment while in the custody of the state, and two died while awaiting trial. Eventually, six were found guilty in the murder of Quinton Rankin and sentenced to death. The Tennessee Supreme Court overturned their convictions in 1909.

Public opinion favored the plight of the Reelfoot Lake people. As a consequence, the state acquired title to the lake in 1914, ending the threat of private ownership.

Bill Threlkeld, Union City

SUGGESTED READING: Paul J. Vanderwood, *Night Riders of Reelfoot Lake* (1969)

SEE: OBION COUNTY; REELFOOT LAKE STATE PARK

NINETEENTH CENTURY CLUB. At the urging of Elise Massey Selden, a group of elite white women assembled at the Gayoso Hotel in May 1890, and founded what was soon to become the largest and most influential women's club in Memphis. The stated objectives were "to promote the female intellect by encouraging a spirit of research in literary fields and provide an intellectual center for the women of Memphis."[1] Initially men feared that club activities would interfere with their wives's duties in the home and lead to involvement in public affairs, which ran counter to southern notions of female propriety. But the women were determined, and while they gave continuous assurances that they did not intend to usurp functions considered unsuitable for women and would not abandon their home responsibilities, they did expect to influence the moral, philanthropic, and educational future of their city. Gradually, the Nineteenth Century Club adopted the idea propounded by earlier women's clubs in the North and Northeast, that the community was but a broader household which needed the "gentler spirit" and "uplifting influence" of women; by the end of the decade the focus of the Nineteenth Century Club had shifted in the direction of civic reform. As one Nineteenth Century Club member expressed their emerging definition of municipal housekeeping: "The advancement of women in the eternal scheme of things, means the advancement of the race."[2] The club adopted the motto "Influence is Responsibility."

The club was a success from the start, with a steadily rising membership that reached a peak of approximately 1,400 members in 1926. Club members entered into public life in areas they believed to be a rightful extension of "home duties," and created for themselves a solid position as a responsible force in civic reform. They focused primarily on the needs of women and children, and they addressed problems in areas such as sanitation, health, education, employment, and labor conditions. Some notable successes included securing a police matron at the city jail and a female sanitary inspector at the Board of Health, and the formation of the Shelby County Anti-Tuberculosis Society and a new city hospital. They played an important role in bringing higher education to Memphis in the form of the West Tennessee State Normal School, now the University of Memphis. Club members also initiated a municipal "clean government" campaign, calling attention to violations of the liquor laws, widespread gambling and prostitution, and demanding the ouster of corrupt officeholders.

In 1893 the Nineteenth Century Club was instrumental in the formation of a city-wide network of club women, the Woman's Council, which helped focus and unite white women for more effective action; in 1896 a state organization, the Tennessee Federation of Women's Clubs, was founded to provide similar coordination among white women's clubs across the state. Members pledged "to strive for better homes, schools, lives, surroundings, scholarship, civic health and righteousness, the conservation of forests and places of natural beauty, and protection for unfortunate children and women laborers."[3]

At the time of its founding, the Nineteenth Century Club filled a vacuum in the lives of many women by providing an acceptable avenue by which they could develop long denied intellectual and civic opportunities. Through club work came the beginning of a public identity for these women and a heightened sense of female self-worth, with a support network entirely separate from family. But as educational opportunities for women improved and social work was professionalized, the Nineteenth Century Club gradually disappeared from the cutting edge of reform, and social functions became the central focus. The club remains in existence to this day; since 1926 it has occupied an imposing brick and stone structure on Union Avenue.

Marsha Wedell, Memphis

CITATIONS:

(1) *First Annual Announcement* Nineteenth Century Club, Memphis, 1890–91, 23.

(2) "Souvenir," 20th Annual Congress, Association for the Advancement of Women, Memphis, 1892, 16.

(3) Philip M. Hamer, *Tennessee, A History, 1673–1932* (New York, 1933), vol. 2, 715.

SUGGESTED READING: Marsha Wedell, *Elite Women and the Reform Impulse in Memphis, 1875–1915 (1992)*

SEE: GAYOSO HOTEL; MEMPHIS; TENNESSEE FEDERATION OF WOMEN'S CLUBS

NISSAN MOTOR MANUFACTURING CORPORATION, U.S.A.,

headquartered in Smyrna, Tennessee, initially represented the single largest foreign investment by a Japanese corporation anywhere in the world. Led by Marvin Runyon, president and chief executive officer, the company broke ground for its Smyrna facility in February 1981. Middle Tennessee's location, available transportation networks, and affordable labor were key attractions to the Japanese. Tennessee's "right-to-work" laws were another factor influencing Nissan's selection. Despite repeated efforts by the United Auto Workers, Nissan's Smyrna plant remains non-union. In June 1983 the first Nissan truck rolled off the modern assembly line. At that time, 1,736 employees worked at the factory, which had an annual manufacturing capacity of 120,000 trucks. Resting on a 778-acre site, part of which was once a local stock-car "Circle 8" racing track, the factory contained 5.1 million square feet and the overall company investment totaled $760 million.

In May 1984 Runyon announced that the Smyrna factory would start producing the Sentra passenger car, which would be the first Nissan passenger car produced in the United States. The following March, the first Sentra car was completed; the factory's production capacity reached 250,000 vehicles a year. When the company added a night shift in June 1985, Nissan employed some 3,000 workers.

The next major shift in the company's fortunes came under the direction of new president and chief executive officer, Jerry L. Benefield, who assumed his position in December 1987. The following April,

Benefield announced a $31 million improvement project to assemble engines and axles and to build bumper fascias. A year later, he announced that the factory would begin producing a new vehicle in 1992, requiring a $490 million expansion that would create another 2,000 jobs. In July 1989 the Smyrna facility produced its one millionth vehicle.

During the 1990s Nissan rapidly added new products to its industrial output. The first Altima passenger car rolled off the assembly line in June 1992. Two months later the factory began the engine assembly for the Nissan Quest/Mercury Villager minivan. Nissan's two millionth vehicle was produced in March 1993. While expanding into new products, company officials also updated old models. In November 1994 the company launched an all-new Sentra model while reintroducing the once popular 200SX sports coupe. Plans for a Nissan Powertrain Assembly plant in Decherd, Tennessee, were announced in 1995 and the factory went into production two years later, with a $50 million expansion planned for 1998. The latest Nissan product, the Frontier light truck, first rolled off the assembly line in September 1997.

By the time of the release of the Frontier truck, Nissan had developed into a major force in the Tennessee economy. In 1996 the company produced a total of 414,031 vehicles, including 141,000 Altimas, 105,000 Sentras, and 30,000 200SX coupes. It had approximately 6,200 employees at the Smyrna plant and its total Tennessee investment was $1.7 billion.

Carroll VanWest, Middle Tennessee State University

SEE: INDUSTRY; RUTHERFORD COUNTY

Quality control at the Nissan plant, 1996.

STATE OF TENNESSEE PHOTOGRAPHIC SERVICES

NIXON, HERMAN CLARENCE (1886–1967), historian, political scientist, and member of the Southern Agrarians, was born in Merrellton, Alabama, in 1886. He was educated at the Alabama State Normal School, the Alabama Polytechnic Institute (now Auburn University), and the University of Chicago. Nixon served in the military in World War I. While working on his dissertation on the Populist movement in Iowa, Nixon taught at several schools in Alabama, then at Iowa State College (now University), and from 1925 to 1928 he taught history at Vanderbilt University. From 1928 to 1938 Nixon taught political science at Tulane University, serving as chair of the Department of History and Political Science, 1931–1938. For the next two years he was Visiting Professor of History at the University of Missouri. In 1940 Nixon returned to Vanderbilt as Lecturer in Political Science; he was promoted to full professor in 1953, two years before his retirement. Nixon also served as Editorial Director of the Vanderbilt University Press. He was elected Second Vice President of the American Political Science Association in 1940 and President of the Southern Political Science Association in 1944. Nixon was married in 1927 to Anne Trice, and they had three children.

During the late 1920s, Nixon was recruited by the organizers of the Southern symposium *I'll Take My Stand: The South and the Agrarian Tradition* (1930) to write the chapter on the southern economy. In *I'll Take My Stand*, the Agrarians did not recommend a specific program of action but urged the people of the South not to surrender the region's "moral, social, and economic autonomy" to the increasingly prevalent industrial system. In "Whither Southern Economy," Nixon expressed concern that the region's reliance on agriculture as the basis for its society was being threatened by industrialism and admonished the region to move cautiously in embracing wholesale the industrial order, with its attendant evil of unbridled consumerism.

Nixon agreed with his colleagues about the evils of unregulated industrialization of the region's economy, but he parted philosophical company with them when it came to determining the most effective remedy for the region's economic ills. Nixon would soon be urging more cooperative, and therefore less individualistic, solutions for the poverty-stricken rural South than the other Agrarians could accept.

Remembered as the Agrarian who moved farthest from the ranks philosophically, Nixon's political views were always more liberal than those of most of the group, including African Americans in his advocacy of practical measures to lift the rural South out of poverty and supporting President Franklin D. Roosevelt's Subsistence Homesteads program and the Tennessee Valley Authority. In 1935 he lobbied Congress for the Bankhead-Jones Farm Tenancy bill, and, as chairman of the Southern Policy Committee, he coordinated hearings on the cotton tenancy programs of the New Deal's Agricultural Adjustment Administration. As a member of the Social Science Research Council's Southern Regional Committee, he conducted research projects and helped plan conferences on southern rural poverty. He was one of the organizers and first field agent of the Southern Conference for Human Welfare. Nixon never failed to support progressive, liberal initiatives whose goal it was to relieve poverty and promote social justice, often at tremendous personal cost.

Sara Harwell, Vanderbilt University

SEE: AGRARIANS; VANDERBILT UNIVERSITY

NORRIS was constructed in 1933 by the Tennessee Valley Authority to provide housing for the construction workers building Norris Dam, the agency's first hydroelectric project. The responsibility of planning the city fell to TVA's Division of Land Planning and Housing, which employed Tracy Auger and Earle Draper, two of the nation's most distinguished planners. However, Arthur E. Morgan, Chairman of the TVA Board, had his own plans for Norris. He insisted that the architecture resemble the vernacular architecture of the region, and he went so far as to make TVA architects inspect and measure existing houses in the region. One result was the traditional "dogtrot" house being one of 12 basic housing types found in Norris. Different external materials such as native stones, bricks, and shingles varied the houses. Each home was wired for electric heat, and they all had chimneys, fireplaces, and porches with screens.

Another important point in the planning and development of Norris was that the homes were to fit into the environment. The natural materials helped the houses blend in, but so did the placement of the structures. Most were placed along the natural contours of the land and a primary consideration was to take advantage of good sites without felling trees. In fact, one structure, the hillside house, was constructed specifically for use on steep slopes.

Besides its ties to TVA, Norris is significant in the field of planning because it was the first self-contained town in the United States to utilize the greenbelt principles advocated by Ebenezer Howard. The planners of Norris created a greenbelt, or a belt of rural land, around the town as a way to preserve the character of Norris.

There were other aspects of Norris besides planning that were quite experimental. For example, the TVA established demonstration dairy and poultry farms and a ceramics lab to test local clays. The Norris Creamery, the first private business under lease, was actually the first all-electric milk-producing plant in the world, and Norris was the first town in Tennessee to have a complete system of dial telephones. The Norris School was quite progressive in teaching through activities instead of traditional rote learning.

The operation of the town required continuing financial support, and Congress periodically suggested that TVA divest itself of the town. However, with the outbreak of World War II, Norris housing was needed for workers at the nearby Oak Ridge project. With the end of the war, Congress finally demanded that Norris either be self-sustaining or be disposed of. On June 15, 1948, the town was sold at public auction for $2.1 million to Henry D. Epstein, who headed a group of Philadelphia investors. They sold off all the existing houses, and then in 1953, sold their remaining real estate holding to the Norris Corporation, a local corporation formed by Norris residents.

Today little has changed in Norris. The greenbelt protects the town from encroachment; the city business district still consists of the post office, a drug store, and a grocery; and TVA's Resource Management Offices remain a vital part of the community. In today's atmosphere of generic suburbs and strip malls, Norris illustrates the purpose, the necessity, and the success of planned communities in the United States.

Patricia Bernard Ezzell, Tennessee Valley Authority

SUGGESTED READING: Walter L. Creese, *TVA's Public Planning: The Vision, The Reality (1990)*

SEE: ANDERSON COUNTY; NORRIS DAM; TENNESSEE VALLEY AUTHORITY

including acquisition of reservoir lands, was about $36 million.

The dam's engineering predates TVA, but its appearance owes everything to a young Hungarian-born architect, Roland Wank (1898–1970), TVA's first chief architect. The Bureau of Reclamation had drawn plans in 1927 for a dam at Cove Creek on the Clinch River that would increase the efficiency of the government-owned Wilson Dam at Muscle Shoals, Alabama, further downstream on the Tennessee River. When TVA was created, it inherited both Wilson Dam and the site drawings for Cove Creek Dam (as Norris was then called), along with instructions from Congress to begin construction as soon as possible to relieve the appalling unemployment in the region.

Wank felt that the unimaginative and heavy appearance of the Bureau's design lacked the simplicity that should characterize TVA work, and he proposed a sculptural recasting of the dam's elements, pulling the powerhouse and spillway face into a coherent composition. Applied ornament on the Bureau's scheme was replaced by sensitive massing, carefully proportioned window openings, and the subtle texture of concrete imparted by the formwork boards. Wank tried to make the dam look as functional as the engineers had designed it to be, even though the engineers were not pleased with his result. The distinguished industrial architect Albert Kahn was asked to choose between the original design and Wank's proposal, and his vote for Wank's scheme was subsequently upheld by the TVA Board,

NORRIS DAM. Norris was the first Tennessee Valley Authority hydroelectric project, begun in October 1933 and finished in March 1936, on the Clinch River in Anderson County. It is a straight concrete gravity-type dam, 1,860 feet long, 265 feet high, and 208 feet thick at the base, equipped with two 50,000 kilowatt generators located in a powerhouse on the right side of the dam face. The dam was named for Senator George Norris of Nebraska, a progressive Republican who for 11 years had kept alive a vision of public power in the Tennessee Valley and whose stubbornness finally bore fruit during the first 100 days of the Roosevelt administration, when TVA was created by an act of Congress. Total cost of construction,

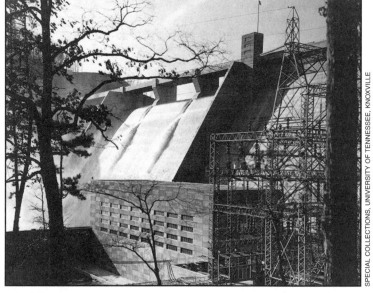

Norris Dam.

SPECIAL COLLECTIONS, UNIVERSITY OF TENNESSEE, KNOXVILLE

thus starting TVA on a course of modern design that would characterize all the Authority's projects through the end of the 1950s.

Wank was concerned with more than external appearance, however. At his insistence, the landscaping and approach route to the dam were carefully studied, with overlooks provided at appropriate locations so that the visitor would receive the impression of a great work designed in harmony with its site. Furthermore, visitors were invited into the powerhouse itself, where a reception room was furnished with illustrative displays and staffed by information officers to explain the dam's operation. In the turbine room, vibrating from spinning electric generators, an impression of modernity and technological progress was presented, the first glimpse of a better world opening to people in a relatively backward region of the country. The inscription, "Built for the People of the United States", is set prominently inside this and all other TVA projects.

Marian Moffett, University of Tennessee, Knoxville

SUGGESTED READINGS: Walter L. Creese, *TVA's Public Planning: The Vision, The Reality* (1990); Michael J. McDonald and John Muldowny, *TVA and the Dispossessed: The Resettlement of Population in the Norris Dam Area* (1982)

SEE: NORRIS; TENNESSEE VALLEY AUTHORITY

NORRIS DAM STATE PARK was created in the mid-1930s as a demonstration recreational project of the Tennessee Valley Authority (TVA), the National Park Service, and the Civilian Conservation Corps (CCC). Today the 4,000-acre park contains two distinct areas. The east side has rustic accomodations and hiking trails constructed by the CCC in the 1930s while the west side has modern chalets and a swimming pool developed by the state in 1976.

CCC Company 4493 first established camp at the park site in 1934. Thirty-six families lived on the land prior to park development. The CCC recruits built cabins, a lodge, trails, playgrounds, a boat harbor, and an amphitheater, along with other structures. Together with the National Park Service, the CCC also moved and restored a ca. 1798 grist mill as a historic site within the park. The mill is adjacent to the modern Lenoir Museum.

In November 1952 the State of Tennessee leased the park from TVA, which then formally sold the state the park for $28,969 in 1953. Norris was one of the first five state parks. The last major TVA land transfer came in 1986 when the agency gave the state an additional 95 acres and harbor limits for the marina at no cost.

Carroll Van West, Middle Tennessee State University

SEE: NORRIS DAM; TENNESSEE VALLEY AUTHORITY

NORRIS FREEWAY. The Tennessee Valley Authority (TVA) built the Norris Freeway in 1934 as a compo-
nent of its first hydroelectric project, Norris Dam. The Norris Project inaugurated President Roosevelt's most ambitious New Deal program. In addition to the dam, the generously funded agency included plans for a state park and a planned community. As construction began, TVA soon found it necessary to build either a highway or a railroad to transport materials from the railroad in Coal Creek (later renamed Lake City) to the project site and to provide better access between its administrative offices in Knoxville and Norris. TVA chose to build a roadway to meet both needs, and after considering a variety of roadway options, selected a freeway design.

A freeway is a highway with limited vehicular access from side roads and from abutting properties. It provides a high level roadway with easy grades and smooth curves to facilitate high-speed traffic. An outgrowth of the City Beautiful Movement of the Progressive Era, a few parkways or freeways had been built in other areas, but the Norris Freeway was the first limited access highway in Tennessee and "the world's first utilitarian, limited-access road."[1] The Norris Freeway, which cost $1.5 million to build, extended 34 kilometers (21 miles) between Coal Creek in Anderson County and Halls Crossroads north of Knoxville. The freeway contained two ten-foot traffic lanes with two to four-foot shoulders within a 250-foot right-of-way. TVA limited billboards and commercial uses along the freeway for aesthetic reasons and required 75-foot construction setbacks.

In the mid-1930s, TVA's architectural department, headed by Roland Wank, drew international attention for its planning and designs. European interpretations of Art Deco and Moderne styles had greatly influenced Wank, and he deliberately designed TVA's public structures in a manner that did not replicate regional or even traditional architectural styles, but rather emphasized TVA's view of itself as an experimental, modern, and forward-looking agency. Structures from tiny culverts to massive bridges, power plants, and enormous dams exhibit Art Moderne influences. Structures along the Norris Freeway, which include the Norris Dam and visitors' center, a cattle underpass, small and intermediate simple slab bridges, one haunched girder span, and one concrete arch bridge, embody a cohesive Art Moderne design. All are concrete and sleek in appearance exhibiting smooth surfaces, streamlined rails, curvilinear wing-walls, and sweeping lines. The exception to TVA's use of the Art Moderne style was its use of a rustic design in its parks and for the town of Norris.

Much of the Norris Freeway is relatively intact, but development pressures increasingly threaten it. The State Historic Preservation Office has determined that 30.4 kilometers (18.9 miles) of the original 34-kilometer (21-mile) Norris Freeway is eligible for the National Register of Historic Places.

Martha Carver, Tennessee Department of Transportation
CITATION:
(1) Phoebe Cutler, *The Public Landscape of the New Deal* (New Haven, 1985), 140.
SEE: NORRIS DAM; TENNESSEE VALLEY AUTHORITY

NORTH AMERICAN RAYON CORPORATION AND AMERICAN BEMBERG CORPORATION.

In October 1926 American Bemberg began the manufacture of "artificial silk," or rayon, at its new plant in Elizabethton, Tennessee. The parent company, J.P. Bemberg, was affiliated with Vereinigte Glanzstoff Fabriken (VGF), one of the international giants in the production of rayon. Two years later, in August 1928, VGF opened another rayon plant in the small East Tennessee town. This one, then called American Glanzstoff but known now as North American Rayon Corporation, made rayon by the viscose process, whereas Bemberg utilized the cuprammonium process. By the end of 1928 employment at the two plants exceeded 3,000 workers.

Visions of economic growth encouraged government officials in Elizabethton to make concessions to VGF concerning property taxes and charges for the huge volumes of water needed to make rayon. They also promised the German industrialists that they would have an abundant supply of docile and cheap—that is, non-union—labor. The work force soon proved anything but docile. In 1927 and 1928 there were a number of small strikes at Bemberg, which in 1927 resulted in the formation of Local 1630 of the United Textile Workers Union of America (UTW). On March 12, 1929, unorganized women workers of the American Glanzstoff plant led a walkout. Bemberg workers struck in sympathy with their Glanzstoff compatriots. A second more violent and divisive strike began on April 15 and lasted until May 25, 1929. Labor problems dominated the history of the companies through 1930.

Throughout the Great Depression the plants remained operational and, overall, continued to profit. The number of workers employed bottomed out at 2,491 in 1932, and peaked at 4,500 in 1939. During these years the international rayon market experienced highs and lows, as did the United States market. But, during the 1930s imports of rayon declined dramatically, allowing domestic producers to increase their market shares. American Bemberg, and American Glanzstoff—as of May 9, 1934, known as North American Rayon Corporation (NARC)—benefited from these market forces.

During World War II, the plants' production of rayon yarn increased and the plants altered production to meet wartime demands. Bemberg, for instance, made parachute cloth. Employment and payrolls increased. But, as a foreign corporation profits went overseas to AKU, Algemeene Kuntzijde Unie

N.V., the company created in 1929 by the union of the German VGF and the Dutch N.V. Nederlandsche Fabriek. In early 1942 the Office of Alien Property (OAP) assumed management of the factories, and initiated an investigation into AKU's ownership of the Elizabethton plants and of American Enka. But, seeking to placate the Dutch, OAP did not actually seize the assets of the plants, which in part were enemy-owned. In 1947 AKU and OAP came to an agreement which provided that the Dutch corporation waive all claims to shares of outstanding stock that it or its affiliates owned in Bemberg or NARC, together with working capital, assets, and all of AKU's interest in patents, trademarks, and other industrial property of the two companies. Bemberg and North American remained under government control until their December 1948 purchase by Beaunit Mills, a New York corporation which recently had entered into production of rayon.

Beginning in 1949, the plants entered into a long period of struggle, precipitated by failure of low-wage industries in the South to experience significant growth, and by changes in the synthetic fibers market. To ensure continued profitability, Beaunit switched part of the Bemberg plant to polyester and part of the North American facility to nylon. Moreover, Beaunit in 1961 entered into a joint venture with El Paso Natural Gas to manufacture "nylon 66" at a new plant at Etowah. The plant became operational in 1966, but incurred significant losses for Beaunit. Increased domestic polyester production, which severely depressed prices by the late 1960s, increased foreign competition in nylon, and a 1967 strike by leading tire companies compounded Beaunit's woes. In 1967, therefore, the company's shareholders approved a merger which resulted in the company becoming a wholly-owned subsidiary of El Paso Natural Gas. By 1967 employment at the Elizabethton plants had declined to 3,550—down substantially from the 6,000 of 1949. The UTW local, Watauga Rayon Workers Local 2207, continued to represent the hourly workers; their major concern was mismanagement by El Paso.

By the early 1970s Bemberg was in serious financial trouble. The cuprammonium process it used produced toxic wastes which the company dumped into the Watauga River. Bemberg found it could not comply with Environmental Protection Agency orders to clean up its wastes and still turn a profit. As a consequence, in December 1970 El Paso announced that Beaunit was going to suspend all operations at the Bemberg factory. But the following March Beaunit sold the Bemberg plant, together with 140 acres of land around the plant, for $350,000 to Abner Industries. Abner acquired an Elizabethton address and officially changed the company name to Bemberg Industries, Inc. The new president, A.A. Rosen, hired as executive vice-president Buford Goldstein, a Johnson City native who had held a similar position with Beaunit. Rosen and Goldstein became the major investors in Bemberg. The new Bemberg continued to experience financial difficulties, and again was sold in 1973 to a group of investors called RG Associates, which also changed its name to Bemberg Industries. Still, the company failed to turn a profit and had to face escalating debts. On February 16, 1974, Bemberg filed a petition for bankruptcy.

With Bemberg's demise, only North American Rayon remained operational. But in November 1976, El Paso announced that in 1977 Beaunit would be sold to a holding company named "BEM." BEM purchased Beaunit's assets, and in turn sold them to Beaunit II, an unaffiliated corporation set up for the purpose of securing those assets. The Beaunit II investment group which purchased the assets was known as TA Associates. TA continued to operate the plant under the name North American Rayon Corporation. In 1978 TA sold the company to Elizabethton businessman James Walker, who earlier had purchased the abandoned Bemberg building.

North American Rayon survived, and by the early 1980s was manufacturing rayon for apparel, home furnishings, and industrial products. But, to comply with environmental regulations, the company was faced with the prospect of building a water treatment facility. With an unstable market for rayon, NARC officials expressed doubt that profits would be large enough to finance the treatment plant. By the fall of 1985 owner Walker began negotiations with management and union officials to have the employees become company stockholders. Local 2207 voted down the proposed plan, but was instructed by the UTW international office to accept the restructuring designed to turn the workers into "employee-owners." The plan went into effect in December 1985 and, from that point through 1988, wages increased and employee-owners received dividends. In August 1988 North American Rayon acquired MKS Polyester, which it renamed North American Polyester. The company also contracted with the National Aeronautics and Space Administration (NASA) to make carbonized rayon for the lining of the nozzles of the solid rocket motors that boost the space shuttle into orbit.

But the 1990s have again ushered in hard times. Competition from imports has hurt the company. Labor relations, seldom harmonious in the past, have continued to be poor as employees feel badly informed about plant operations. In 1996 NAR Polyester closed, leaving 70 workers unemployed. Employment at the rayon plant was only at 700 in late 1996. Due to the end of the manufacture of rayon filament in late 1997, there were only 250 workers in early 1998.

Marie Tedesco, East Tennessee State University
SUGGESTED READINGS: John Fred Holly, "Elizabethton, Tennessee: A Case Study of Southern Industrialization," Ph.D. diss., Clark University, 1949; Marie Tedesco, "The Rayon Plants in Elizabethton, Tennessee: A Case Study of Appalachian Economic Development, 1925–1988," *Locus. An Historical Journal of Regional Perspectives on National Topics,* 1(1989)
SEE: CARTER COUNTY; INDUSTRY; LABOR; STRIKES, RAYON PLANTS AT ELIZABETHTON;

NURSERY INDUSTRY. In 1905 horticulturalists officially established the Tennessee Nursery Association for the advancement of the state's horticulture industry and the professionalization of standards. From its very beginning, the founders recognized the potential impact of the nursery industry on the state's economy. Through the ensuing years industry leaders, such as N.W. Hale, Richard Jones, Hoskins Shawdow, Henry Boyd, E.W. Chattin, Lee McClain, D.P. Henegar, Ed Porter, A.D. Cartwright, and Don Shawdow, have developed professional unity among the members to further intellectual, social, and business interests, and establish long-range goals.

Almost one hundred years later, the Tennessee Nursery Association has grown from a founding group of 24 to 550 active members, representing a variety of horticultural interests. Wholesale growers comprise 75 percent of the current membership. Retail and garden centers make up an important segment of the industry. Landscapers represent another segment of the membership, with a small one percent of the membership consisting of mail order and grounds maintenance personnel.

The nursery business, which was born in Middle Tennessee, now spreads statewide and boasts a national reputation for quality production. There are over 36,000 certified acres of ornamental plants in Tennessee, with approximately 300 cultivable species of woody ornamentals. The Volunteer State is the largest producer in the South of narrowleaf evergreens, ornamental trees, and deciduous plants. Tennessee nurserymen have become the leading producers and developers of new varieties of the flowering dogwood. Nursery and greenhouse production, with more than 1,000 growers and approximately $160 million in gross annual sales, represents one of the top agricultural enterprises in the state.

In the early 1900s the association provided a clearing house of information for professionals and worked to present a unified effort to resolving major problems. Meetings have now evolved into large trade shows that include educational seminars, attractive displays of products, and up-to-date marketing techniques. The nursery business also engages in professional and cooperative efforts with the Tennessee Department of Agriculture and kindred organizations. As caretakers of our environment, nurserymen have cultivated native plants and saved many species from extinction.

Although today's nurseries range from numerous small family-run operations to large corporations, they share the same bond of commitment and personal attention to quality products and customer service that the founders of the Tennessee Nurserymen's Association expressed in 1905.

Anne Dale, Tennessee Agricultural Museum
SEE: AGRICULTURE

O

OAK RIDGE. Over the years, "the Government" had come to East Tennessee in many forms, varying from the Civil War Confederacy to the Tennessee Valley Authority of the 1930s. The most dramatic and least public incursion followed quickly on the heels of the Great Depression, during the Second World War. Government officials, most of them wearing the uniform of the U.S. Army and the insignia of the Corps of Engineers, arrived quietly in the summer of 1942 to observe, study, consult maps, and leave. They were followed, more ominously, by men with surveyor's stakes.

The nation had been at war with Japan, Germany, and Italy since the preceding December. Even prior to the nation's military involvement, President Franklin D. Roosevelt had been informed of an unexpected and serious potential danger by concerned scientists. In 1939 Leo Szilard and Eugene P. Wigner persuaded Albert Einstein to sign a letter warning FDR of the possibility that Adolph Hitler's Nazi Germany could construct a revolutionary weapon through atomic fission capable of creating vast amounts of explosive power. Heeding the warning, Roosevelt began a tentative exploration of the possibilities of constructing an atomic bomb. But only after Pearl Harbor and the American entry into the war was the project pursued with urgency.

That urgency brought newly promoted Brigadier General Leslie R. Groves to East Tennessee in September 1942. He had been appointed to head the recently created Manhattan Engineer District, or, more commonly, the Manhattan Project. His task was to supervise the location, planning, and construction of whatever facilities were necessary to construct an atomic bomb before the Germans could do it.

This remote area of East Tennessee seemed to meet many of the requirements for the main work site. Approximately 1,000 families, roughly 4,000 people, lived in the area of primary interest to the government planners. Mostly farmers, the residents were clustered around small crossroads centers with names like Wheat, Elza, Scarboro, and Robertsville. Moving them would not present a large problem for the Army.

Some of the planned processes would require vast amounts of electricity, which TVA could provide. There was an abundance of clean water, a good rail line, adequate roads, and the land could be acquired cheaply. Topographically, the reservation was a long valley divided into smaller segments by ridges. This meant that the individual processing plants could be separated geographically, so that if, in an unforeseen disaster, one blew up, the others would not explode like firecrackers on a string. The town itself was sited on the eastern end of the reservation, away from the plants.

Land acquisition began quickly. In the fall of 1942 residents were informed, sometimes simply by notices nailed to their front fence posts, that they would have to leave; the government was taking their land. A year later, the eviction process was complete. Although most of the former residents accepted the government offers for their land, a few brought legal action challenging the valuations. Roane County lost approximately one-eighth of its land area to the project, but was not as directly affected by the government's activities as Anderson County. The focus of the project was east, toward Clinton and Knoxville, rather than south and west, toward Kingston and Harriman. Oak Ridge, the town created by the project, was only eight miles from Clinton, the seat of Anderson County, which gave up one-seventh of its land to the project. State Highway 61, which had run directly through the reservation site, was closed and re-routed to the north, through Motlow. The reservation site was approximately 17 miles long, averaging seven miles in width, and encompassing some 59,000 acres.

Providing security for a project of such scope and purpose involved intense planning. The Clinch River surrounded the reservation on three sides, providing a natural defense. On the exposed northern side, the Army erected a fence, which was patrolled by armed guards. Knoxville, a city of 110,000 people who provided the labor base for the construction and support work force, was 30 miles away, isolating the work site from the outside world. As a further measure of security, the site was provided with an ambiguous title, the Clinton Engineering Works (CEW). All personnel entering the site were required to have a pass and a purpose. On the site itself, Army security personnel tried to separate scientists and engineers associated with the various segments of the project to prevent them from discussing their work with one another. Of course these efforts extended to outside contacts as well. A passion for secrecy dominated the early years of the community and extended into the tension-filled era of the Cold War, marking Oak Ridge with a concern for security unique among Tennessee cities in the five decades following World War II.

The town was an adjunct to the plants. Built as well as possible in order to keep the gathering scientific and engineering personnel reasonably content, the town was planned by the prominent firm of Skidmore, Owings, and Merrill, who designed plans to house 8,000 people. The town was laid out along the south side of Black Oak Ridge, with Outer Drive at the top and Tennessee Avenue and Oak Ridge Turnpike running parallel, east to west, along the bottom of the ridge. Avenues, named for the states and arranged alphabetically north to south, connected the east-west thoroughfares. Courts, roads, and lanes branching off the avenues received names beginning with the same first letter. For example, all the streets off Delaware Avenue began with the letter "D." The simplified arrangement proved to be a great boon in a community where everyone was a newcomer.

The nearly insatiable demands of the project for additional workers placed planners and contractors in the position of constantly attempting to catch up, and constantly failing in their efforts. The well-planned family homes, "cemestoes" (bonded cement and asbestos), were supplemented by apartments and by dormitories for single workers. But they were also quickly overwhelmed, and more temporary housing of limited livability, including trailers, barracks, hutments, plywood Flat Tops, and "Victory Cottages," sprang up along the ridge and spread into the valley.

Recruitment of scientific talent took a variety of forms, including personal contacts among the members of the nation's leading academic and scientific institutions. Foreign scholars, forced out of Italy, Germany, and Eastern Europe by the Fascists and Nazis, added to the pool. Scientifically trained personnel drafted into the ranks of the army were assigned to the Special Engineer Detachment (SED), often before recruits had had much more than the basics of basic training, developing them into a creative, but often quite unmilitary, unit. The Corps of Engineers, of course, made up the major part of the military presence. Later in the war, two companies of WACs expanded the number of uniformed personnel.

At the heart of the scientific and engineering effort were the facilities designed as X-10, Y-12, and K-25. Stone and Webster Corporation was the primary contractor for these facilities. Oak Ridge would serve as a headquarters for the national military project, house a graphite reactor, and provide facilities for separating the fissionable isotope Uranium 235 from the much more plentiful U-238.

Construction for X-10 and the graphite reactor began in February 1943. It would serve as a pilot plant for creating a new, fissionable element, plutonium, and separating it chemically. Larger quantities of plutonium would be produced at the Hanford site in eastern Washington. During the war, X-10 was built and operated by a combination of contractors which included Du Pont, the Metallurgical Laboratory of the University of Chicago, and Monsanto Chemical Corporation. After the war it was designated as Oak Ridge National Laboratory (ORNL), and served as a laboratory for nuclear research, leading the nation in research in nuclear power and nuclear medicine. After 1948 supervision was transferred to Union Carbide's Nuclear Division. "The Lab" continues to conduct basic research in physics and other sciences and produces radioactive isotopes with many uses in science and industry.

Since it was not certain in 1942 which method of separating U-235 would yield the quickest and richest result, the original plan was to pursue as many methods as seemed feasible. Y-12, operated by Tennessee Eastman Corporation, used an electro-magnetic separation process. After the war, Y-12 was operated by Union Carbide and was primarily responsible for shaping nuclear components for weapons. The K-25 plant, operated from the beginning by Union Carbide Corporation, used a very different gaseous diffusion process where highly corrosive uranium hexafluoride gas was passed repeatedly through membranes, allowing the slightly lighter U-235 isotopes to be gradually concentrated. Construction on Y-12 was begun in the spring of 1943, K-25 in the fall. A third process, S-50, using thermal diffusion was begun too late to have any impact on events and was not carried to completion.

The scientists and engineers gathered together at Oak Ridge, nearly all of them very young, found themselves working terribly long hours on some of the most exciting work many of them would ever do. Repeatedly, they demonstrated that what conventional wisdom said could not be done could, in fact, be accomplished in less time than anyone thought possible. During and after the war, Oak Ridgers provided much of the theoretical and practical grounding for the developing nuclear industry.

Beginning with the arrival of construction workers in spring 1943, Oak Ridge grew to an astounding 66,000 residents by the summer of 1944, before peaking at a population of 75,000 by the summer of 1945. The reservation demanded a work force of 80,000. In 1944 the two-year old town was the fifth largest city in Tennessee with the sixth largest bus operation in the nation. Many of those who worked but did not live in Oak Ridge were bused in, some from distances of more than 50 miles. Some who lived off the reservation commuted by car, but wartime shortages of tires and gasoline limited automobile use. The right to live in Oak Ridge depended on employment there, while housing itself was designated by worker position and family size.

The original design of the town included an area in the eastern section designated as the "Negro Village," with dormitories and some well-built homes. However, the operating companies did not hire African Americans in positions that qualified them for that type of housing, and the Negro Village was quickly absorbed into the larger white community. African-American employees lived in hutments further west that were segregated both by race and by gender. The Oak Ridge community, as was the case in government projects throughout the nation, complied with local custom in racial matters, and Tennessee was, by law and custom, a segregated state in the 1940s. However, the practice of segregation met some local resistance, and in 1955 Oak Ridge became one of the first cities in the South to mandate desegregation of its public schools.

Tensions between those who came to Oak Ridge and those who gave up the land for the facilities, or who lived in close conjunction with the reservation became apparent during the war and continued to some extent after 1945. Those who had lived prior to 1942 in what was to become Oak Ridge had identified closely with the land where their families had lived and farmed, often for generations. Some who had been forced off their land harbored resentment for many years. The newcomers had no roots in Tennessee and viewed themselves as temporary residents. The majority of the new residents were young and filled with the camaraderie fostered by work on a project they felt certain would win the war. In addition to the young and enthusiastic outsiders, who had little in common with traditional area residents, the project absorbed large numbers of local workers attracted by high wages, excitement, and patriotism.

The competition for scarce labor did little to foster good relations with outside employers, especially as it extended beyond the demand for construction and laboratory personnel. In order to educate the children of Oak Ridge employees, the city demanded the best teachers available and paid significantly more than surrounding school districts to get them. The high standard of education produced in Oak Ridge became a source of pride for the city's residents, but the loss of teaching staff and the higher wages bred resentment in school districts outside the fence. Many viewed Oak Ridge as a highly secret, probably wasteful, and certainly enormous federal project. In an era of war-generated shortages, fears, and discontent, it was easy to blame the project and the people living and working there for broader problems.

Despite the tensions, the work proceeded swiftly and on schedule. The small amounts of concentrated fissionable U-235 were hand-carried to the newly created facility at Los Alamos, New Mexico, where, under the leadership of Dr. J. Robert Oppenheimer, they were shaped into the nuclear weapon nicknamed "Little Boy." Plutonium from Hanford formed the heart of the second bomb, "Fat Man." The first bomb was dropped over Hiroshima at slightly after 9:00 A.M. local time on August 6, 1945. Three mornings later, the second bomb exploded over Nagasaki. On August 14, the Japanese Emperor surrendered his nation. World War II ended with the signing of the surrender document in Tokyo Bay on September 2, 1945. In the summer of 1942 General Groves had predicted the United States would have the bomb in three years. Oak Ridgers greeted the news of the Hiroshima explosion with a mixture of enthusiasm for the expected end of the war, concern for the future, and unease growing out of the three-year period of absolute secrecy. But the overall mood was one of self-congratulation and relief.

From the earliest days of the project, the assumption had been that the Manhattan Project was a temporary, wartime endeavor that would be closed with the return of peace. At war's end, some employees promptly packed up and returned to their former lives, or made plans for new opportunities. Others lingered, interested in the announcement by Colonel Kenneth D. Nichols, the ranking Army officer on the reservation, that the project would continue for at least the immediate future. With the completion of construction, building laborers left, and the number of operating personnel also declined, though not as precipitously. By 1947, when the Atomic Energy Commission took over immediate control of the project, the town's population had fallen to under 40,000; the 1950 Census showed 30,205 residents, fewer than half its former number, though Oak Ridge was still the fifth largest city in the state. The population of Oak Ridge remained at or near that level for the following 50 years. Control of the facilities shifted from AEC to the Department of Energy in 1977, and Martin Marietta Corporation took over direction of operations from Union Carbide in 1984.

In the years following the war, the town became more "civilian-looking" as occupants painted their homes a variety of colors, Southern Bell took over the operation of the telephone company, and the guard/police force changed uniforms from khaki to blue. In 1949 the gates came down; by the 1950s houses were made available for sale, first to those who occupied them, and then to others. The heritage of cultural activities begun by the earliest Oak Ridgers continued to enrich the life of the community through a myriad of civic organizations, the playhouse, the symphony, the ballet company, the community band, and a variety of concert series.

With the increasing tensions of the Cold War and the inability of the nation to place nuclear weapons under international control, or to eliminate them altogether, Oak Ridge and other facilities of the former Manhattan Project continued to be of vital importance to the nation's defense. But research in nuclear power, radio-isotopes, and other aspects of nuclear medicine became a more significant part of the research and development work in Oak Ridge. Cooperation with industry to solve a wide variety of problems was also, by the 1980s, an increasingly large part of the community's efforts. Facing a somewhat uneasy future in the mid-1990s with the end of the Cold War and the uncertainties surrounding the use of nuclear power, the large professional/scientific community and the highly skilled work force share the belief that, even with smaller defense budgets, Oak Ridge will continue to function as a leader in high technology enterprises.

Charles W. Johnson, University of Tennessee, Knoxville
SUGGESTED READINGS: Richard G. Hewlett and Oscar E. Anderson, Jr., *The New World, 1939–1946: A History of the Atomic Energy Commission* (1962); Charles W. Johnson and Charles O. Jackson, *City Behind a Fence: Oak Ridge, Tennessee, 1942–1946* (1981); James Overholt, *These Are Our Voices: The Story of Oak Ridge, 1942–1970* (1987); George O. Robinson, *The Oak Ridge Story: A Saga of a People Who Share in History* (1950); and Michael Stoff, *The Manhattan Project: A Documentary Introduction to the Atomic Age* (1991)

OAK RIDGE ASSOCIATED UNIVERSITIES. In October 1946, the Oak Ridge Institute of Nuclear Studies (ORINS) received a charter of incorporation from the State of Tennessee, and with 14 southern universities as its charter members, the consortium of ORINS began to work toward the vision of Dr. William G. Pollard, the organization's founder. Pollard wanted to allow access for faculty and students from the University of Tennessee and other southern universities to the science and technology that had

developed in Oak Ridge during World War II as part of the Manhattan Project.

The Graduate Training Program was the first in a legacy of student research participation programs that still offer graduate students the opportunity to carry out thesis or dissertation research at the federal government's laboratories. Similarly, ORINS initiated a Research Participation Program, which brought university faculty members to the federal facilities as well. For those researchers employed by the Oak Ridge National Laboratory and living in Oak Ridge, ORINS teamed with the University of Tennessee in 1947 to offer the Oak Ridge Resident Graduate Program, which provided masters and doctoral courses in chemistry, math, and physics. ORINS provided the Oak Ridge facilities, equipment, and supplies while UT provided the faculty. Fifty years later, the organization manages more than 100 programs similar to each of these.

In 1948 the Atomic Energy Commission asked the organization to establish a clinical research program to study the use of radioactive materials in treating and diagnosing diseases. ORINS set up a cancer research hospital and accepted its first patient in 1950. Until the hospital closed in the mid-1970s, numerous patients came to the ORINS hospital, hoping to find a cure in the new treatments offered by the newly discovered powers of radiation.

In 1966 ORINS became Oak Ridge Associated Universities (ORAU) and has grown to 88 member universities with representation from New Mexico to New Hampshire and is a contractor to the U.S. Department of Energy for the management of the Oak Ridge Institute for Science and Education. The organization expanded to encompass new areas, such as research and training in workforce health, safety, and security; worldwide emergency preparedness, response and training; hazardous site characterization; and environmental cleanup verification while it has created collaborative research partnerships. ORAU continues to provide that important link between academia and federal research facilities.

Pam Bonee, Oak Ridge Institute for Science and Education
SEE: OAK RIDGE; POLLARD, WILLIAM G.

OAK RIDGE NATIONAL LABORATORY. Established during World War II by the Manhattan District, Oak Ridge National Laboratory (ORNL) occupied the X-10 site on the 56,000-acre reservation between Clinch River and Black Oak Ridge purchased by the U.S. Army Corps of Engineers in 1942. Initially called Clinton Laboratories after the nearest town, it began as a top-secret installation to produce plutonium for the first nuclear weapons.

While the K-25, Y-12, and other plants at Oak Ridge experimented with different processes to separate uranium-235 from natural uranium-238, to produce fissionable enriched uranium for nuclear bombs, the X-10 site (ORNL) experimented with the production of fissionable plutonium-239 from uranium-238. Working from the theories and processes developed by Albert Einstein, Enrico Fermi, and Glenn Seaborg, and the designs of Eugene Wigner, Alvin Weinberg, and colleagues of the University of Chicago, the world's first powerful nuclear reactor was built at the X-10 site in 1943, to transform uranium into plutonium, along with the "hot cells" needed to chemically separate the precious plutonium from uranium.

In 1944 plutonium produced at X-10 (ORNL) went to laboratories at the University of Chicago, University of California, and Los Alamos, New Mexico, for experimentation. The designs and processes developed at X-10 served as the pilot plant for the larger reactors and chemical separation plants built by the Manhattan District that year at Hanford, Washington. Plutonium became the nuclear explosive used in the "Fat Man" bomb dropped at Nagasaki, while the enriched uranium produced at other Oak Ridge installations went into the "Little Boy" bomb, which was used at Hiroshima. Using graphite to moderate neutrons, the X-10 Graphite Reactor at ORNL served the pioneering nuclear science field until 1963, when the reactor was shut down. The Graphite Reactor opened to the public during the 1980s as an educational exhibit and the world's oldest surviving nuclear reactor.

In 1948 the X-10 site was officially designated the Oak Ridge National Laboratory and managed successively by the University of Chicago, Monsanto Chemical, Union Carbide, and Lockheed Martin corporations for the Atomic Energy Commission (1947–1974), and later the Energy Research and Development Administration (1975–1977) and Department of Energy (1977-present). During its early decades, ORNL focused on developing new types of atomic reactors and training nuclear scientists and engineers. Among the 14 nuclear reactors designed at ORNL, most notable were its experimental materials testing, aqueous homogeneous, transportable package, and molten salt reactors. A participant in experimental gas-cooled and thermal breeder reactor development, ORNL contributed to the design of aero and naval propulsion, commercial, and liquid metal breeder reactors.

As national emphasis on nuclear and atomic energy waned, ORNL directors Alvin Weinberg, Floyd Culler, Herman Postma, Alex Zucker, Alvin Trivelpiece, and their associates expanded the Laboratory's scientific research programs to include fusion, fossil, and renewable energy sources along with high-energy physics, environmental, biological, robotics, advanced materials, and allied sciences of national significance. These involved many cooperative programs with universities and schools in Tennessee as well as throughout the nation. During the 1990s, ORNL became deeply involved in Department of Energy efforts to clean up and remediate the legacy of toxic and radioactive wastes generated in earlier years, both at its own facilities and throughout the nation and world. National policy mandated that ORNL speedily transfer its technologies to American industry and thereby enhance national economic competitiveness in the global marketplace.

The impact of ORNL extends from the local and economic impact of providing opportunities for highly skilled and technical employment to the global and intellectual impact of developing scientists and engineers who have contributed to the advancement of knowledge and education. Among the outstanding scientists and engineers associated with ORNL are Waldo Cohn, Alexander Hollaender, and William and Lianne Russell in radiation biology; Stanley Auerbach in radioecology; Ellison Taylor and Sheldon Datz in radiation chemistry; P.R. Bell and Karl Morgan in radiation dosimetry; and Ernest Wollan, Michael Wilkinson, and Clifford Shull in neutron physics.

Leland R. Johnson, Clio Research Institute

Suggested Readings: Alvin Weinberg, *The First Nuclear Era: The Life and Times of a Technological Fixer* (1994); Leland Johnson and Daniel Schaffer, *Oak Ridge National Laboratory: The First Fifty Years* (1994)

See: Auerbach, Stanley I.; Cohn, Waldo; Hollaender, Alexander; Russell William and Lianne; Shull, Clifford; Weinberg, Alvin; X-10

OAKLANDS, located in Murfreesboro, was a 1,500-acre plantation established by the Maney family. Initially a 274-acre land grant to Ezekial White for his Revolutionary War service, the property was purchased by his commanding officer, Colonel Hardy Murfree of Hertford County, North Carolina. After Colonel Murfree's death in 1809, his daughter Sally Hardy Murfree Maney, the wife of Dr. James Maney, inherited the property.

Around 1818 a two-room brick home was built on the property. The Maneys improved the home in the mid-1820s with a two-story Federal style addition; in the 1830s a rear wing was added. After Sally's death in 1857, Dr. Maney retired and Oaklands passed to his oldest son, Major Lewis Maney. Major Maney and his wife Adeline Cannon, daughter of Governor Newton Cannon, made one final addition, the Italianate facade, making it one of the most elegant homes in Middle Tennessee.

During the Civil War, both northern and southern armies camped on the plantation. In June 1862 Union troops under the command of Colonel William Duffield of the Ninth Michigan Regiment occupied the site as their headquarters. On July 13, 1862, Confederate General Nathan Bedford Forrest routed the Union forces from the area and accepted the surrender of Murfreesboro from the injured Duffield in a room at Oaklands. In December of that year, Confederate President Jefferson Davis and his aide, Colonel George W.C. Lee, son of General Robert E. Lee, stayed with the Maneys while visiting troops in the area.

After the Civil War, the family sold the property piece by piece. In 1884, two years after the death of her husband, Adeline Maney sold the home and 200 acres. The home passed through three other families before it became vacant in 1954. Oaklands Association, created in 1959, restored the home for use as a house museum. Listed on the National Register of Historic Places, the plantation home is open to the public.

Ed DeBoer, Oaklands Association

SEE: FORREST, NATHAN B.; MURFREESBORO; RUTHERFORD COUNTY

OBION COUNTY was created on October 24, 1823, organized on January 19, 1824, and included what is now Lake County until 1870. The county took its name from the Obion River; the word Obion is thought to be an Indian word meaning many forks. Situated in the rolling hills of northwest Tennessee, Obion County has earned the nickname "Land of Green Pastures."

Many early settlers were Scots-Irish from the Carolinas and Virginia. The first known white settler was Elisha Parker, who arrived in the area in 1819. In 1820 Colonel W.M. Wilson settled three miles southwest of the future town of Troy; organization of Obion County took place in his cabin. David Crockett was among those present on March 16, 1825, when the county seat of Troy was laid out. Crockett's association with the history of Obion County is well known; he served the area in the U.S. House of Representatives, and his claim of a record kill of 103 bears was made in Obion County.

The history of Union City, the present county seat, was tied to the railroads. Laid out in 1854 by General George Gibbs on land he received in 1829, the town derived its name from the intersection of the Nashville and Northwestern Railroad with the Mobile and Ohio Railroad.

Historically Obion County has been a region of small farms; in 1860 most farms ranged in size from 20 to 50 acres. Tobacco, corn, and wheat were the principal crops. The population of Obion County increased rapidly in the antebellum years; in 1830 the population numbered just over 2,000, increasing to 12,800 by 1860.

Obion County experienced its share of action during the Civil War. In the early months of 1861,

Camp Brown, which housed up to 10,000 Confederate soldiers, was established one mile north of Union City in preparation for General Leonidas Polk's invasion of Kentucky and occupation of Columbus in September 1861. The last important engagement in Obion County pitted the U.S. Seventh Tennessee Cavalry under the command of Colonel Isaac Hawkins against Nathan Bedford Forrest's Seventh Cavalry under the command of Colonel Duckworth. Unable to take the federal stronghold at Union City by storm, the Confederates devised a "Quaker cannon" from a black painted log and wagon wheels and successfully demanded unconditional surrender in Forrest's name.

Rebuilding and recovery occupied the years following the war. Business and manufacturing had revived by the early 1880s, and the rail lines soon made Union City a commercial center, shipping the products of the county's furniture factories and sawmills to eastern markets.

Along with the commercial vitality of Union City came demands to move the county seat from Troy. Following a lengthy public debate and court battle, Union City won a hotly contested referendum, and the county records were moved to the new courthouse in July 1890.

In the early 1900s trouble loomed at Reelfoot Lake. Fishermen felt they had a natural right to fish the lake. However, lands beneath the lake's shallow waters had been claimed under the 1783 grants, which were made prior to the earthquakes of 1811–12 that created the lake. In the meantime, settlers profited from the lake's bounty of fish and migrant waterfowl unmindful of previous claims. In the 1870s John Burdick established a dock and wholesale fish business at the lake.

In the 1890s James Harris of Tiptonville became interested in exploiting the timber and agricultural possibilities of the lake. Buying up most of the old land grants, Harris announced in 1899 that he would drain the lake. Opposed by Burdick and the fishermen, Harris's son won the initial legal battle when the lake was declared not navigable and thus subject to private ownership.

In 1907 Harris joined forces with the West Tennessee Land Company, which had acquired the remaining grants. Under pressure from the land company, Burdick chose to lease his property and obtained sole rights to purchase all lake fish, a move that embittered some of the fishermen.

Emotions among some lake residents shifted toward a more violent solution to the dispute as they lost faith in legal remedies. Soon men wearing masks and gowns, and calling themselves Night Riders, made vigilante raids around the lake, terrorizing those who opposed them and burning Burdick's dock.

On the night of October 19, 1908, Robert Z. Taylor and Quentin Rankin, attorneys for the land company, were taken from Ward's Hotel at Walnut Log by the Night Riders. When they refused demands to reopen the lake to fishing, Rankin was killed and Taylor escaped into the water of the lake, surviving to tell the story.

Captured by the state militia, eight men were tried in Union City, and six of them were sentenced to hang; the Tennessee Supreme Court overturned the verdict on several technicalities. The lake was later ruled navigable and incapable of private ownership. Today it is a part of Tennessee's park system, and its fish, game, and the winter presence of American eagles attract many visitors.

Economic development in the twentieth century rested on manufacturing. In 1923 Brown Shoe Company joined the Canvas Duck Decoy Company and Child's Specialty House (children's clothing) as the major industries located in Union City. In 1934 Salant & Salant established shirt manufacturing in that city. In 1968 Goodyear Tire, employing 3,000 workers, came to Union City. The newest industry to locate in Obion County is Tyson Foods, which established a processing plant in 1996. In addition to rail service, Obion County is served by Everett-Stewart Airport, which originally was a World War II aviation training field.

Agriculture remains a key economic contributor. In 1986 the state designated 27 Tennessee Century Farms in Obion County and these properties produced cotton, soybeans, livestock, honey, corn, and wheat.

Obion County's rich history has been carefully preserved. The first monument ever erected in memory of unknown Confederate dead was dedicated in Union City on October 21, 1869. Nearby is the Obion County Museum. On Highway 51 is Turner Kirkland's Dixie Gun Works, the world's largest supplier of antique guns and parts. The Obion County Courthouse, built by the Public Works Administration in 1939–40, and the Parks covered bridge near Trimble are listed on the National Register of Historic Places. In 1997 Main Street Union City sponsored a multiple property National Register nomination which will list over 100 additional properties in Union City, including the Capitol Theater, Mt. Zion CME Church, Central School, and the Union City Armory.

The 1990 census lists the county's population at 31,597, with Union City accounting for 10,436 of that number. Despite its industrial growth, Obion County has retained its agricultural base and ranks first in the state in the production of corn, wheat, and orchard products, second in soybeans, and third in hogs and pigs.

Rebel C. Forrester, Union City

SEE: CROCKETT, DAVID; EMBRY-RIDDLE FIELD; FORREST, NATHAN B.; MCDOWELL, JOHN H.; MONUMENTS, CIVIL WAR; NIGHT RIDERS OF REELFOOT LAKE; PUBLIC WORKS ADMINISTRATION; RAILROADS

OCCUPATION, CIVIL WAR. Tennessee's strategic location made it a prime target of the Union armies during the Civil War. It was, in fact, the only Confederate state that came entirely under Union control before the war ended.

The invasion of Tennessee began early in 1862 when Federal land and naval forces under Ulysses S. Grant moved against Fort Henry on the Tennessee River and Fort Donelson on the Cumberland River, both of which fell in February. Grant's forces proceeded to penetrate deep into the state along the Tennessee; meanwhile, another Federal army under Don Carlos Buell captured Nashville (February 25) and Confederate forces abandoned Middle Tennessee. The governor, legislators, and other state officials fled from Nashville to Memphis, which was itself captured on June 6, 1862, by Union forces advancing down the Mississippi River. The Confederate state government thereupon ceased to exist.

West Tennessee remained in Federal hands for the rest of the war. Confederate forces reoccupied the southern part of Middle Tennessee in the fall of 1862, but were again expelled from the region in July 1863 by Buell's successor, William S. Rosecrans. After that, except for the Confederate Army of Tennessee briefly occupying the southern counties in November-December 1864, Middle Tennessee remained under Union control.

East Tennessee eluded the Federals' grasp considerably longer than the other two regions. Not until late August 1863 did a Union army enter the region, advancing southward from Kentucky. That army, under the command of Ambrose Burnside, captured Knoxville on September 1. Rosecrans moved eastward and seized Chattanooga that same month. Grant then succeeded Rosecrans, and in late November 1863 he drove the Confederate Army of Tennessee into Georgia. At the same time, Burnside repulsed a Confederate force sent to recapture Knoxville. That force then withdrew into upper East Tennessee; when it moved on to Virginia in the spring of 1864, Tennessee was wholly in Federal hands.

As Union commanders seized Tennessee piece by piece, they imposed martial law and posted garrison forces in the important towns, including Clarksville, Murfreesboro, Columbia, Jackson, Knoxville, Chattanooga, Memphis, and Nashville. These last three, especially Nashville, became major Union military centers, occupied by thousands of Federal troops and support personnel, and crowded with supply depots and hospitals.

Throughout most of 1862, Federal authorities pursued a lenient occupation policy in the hope of winning over secessionist citizens, who comprised the great majority of citizens in Middle and West Tennessee. But finding that the secessionists remained hostile and defiant, the authorities adopted an increasingly harsh policy. This included the seizure and destruction of private property, the imprisonment or banishment of those who refused to take an oath of allegiance to the Union, and the forcible emancipation of slaves. (Though Tennessee was exempted from President Abraham Lincoln's Emancipation Proclamation of January 1, 1863, military authorities generally ignored that exemption when dealing with secessionist slaveowners.)

Military rule over the civilian populace was complicated by a conflict of authority between the Union army commanders and Military Governor Andrew Johnson, who was appointed by President Lincoln and sent to Nashville in March 1862 with orders to reconstruct the state government. Arguments with the generals exasperated Johnson, but even more frustrating to him was the continuing defiance of Middle and West Tennessee secessionists, who would have nothing to do with reconstruction. Nor did the capture of East Tennessee, with its predominantly Unionist population, bring the speedy revival of state government that Johnson sought, for his increasingly radical stance on such issues as emancipation provoked opposition from conservative unionists. Not until April 1865 was civil government restored in Tennessee, under a new state constitution written by radical unionists and endorsed by Johnson.

For most Tennesseans, Union occupation was a devastating experience. Many secessionist citizens, appalled by the prospect, fled at the approach of the Yankees and lived as refugees in the deep South for the duration of the war. Those who stayed faced the agonizing decision of whether, and to what extent, to resist the enemy. The great majority did resist to some degree; the boldest went beyond defiant words and noncooperation to engage in active resistance, including smuggling, spying, and even guerrilla warfare. But in doing so they risked retaliation.

Those who lived in the garrisoned towns found themselves directly under the enemy's thumb and subject to constant scrutiny. But there were compensating advantages. Army authorities, anxious to preserve order around their military posts, provided police and fire protection, health services, and courts of law. They doled out free provisions to the needy and permitted the operation of schools, churches, and markets. People in the garrisoned towns, therefore, could live a relatively normal life despite the war that raged all around them.

In the countryside, by contrast, there was famine, anarchy, and violence. Federal foraging squads stripped the farms of crops and livestock. Local government collapsed, law enforcement evaporated, and in that vacuum of authority appeared bandit gangs that preyed ruthlessly on inhabitants. Traveling about became so dangerous that most rural people simply stayed at home. Schoolhouses and church buildings stood empty.

Amid the chaos and ruin, however, there were signs of joy, not only among the Unionists, who welcomed the Federal troops as saviors, but also among the slaves, who seized the opportunity of invasion to liberate themselves. Even in the early months of occupation, when the Union army's official policy was to avoid interfering with slavery, many slaves ran off to the army camps. As Federal policy turned emancipationist, the trickle of runaways became a flood. Many of those blacks who left their masters made their way to "contraband camps" established by the Union army. There they received food, clothing, shelter, medical care, schooling, and jobs; thousands of the younger black men enlisted in the Union army. Even those blacks who chose not to desert their owners declined in many instances to act any longer as slaves; they refused to obey orders and demanded wages for their labor. Slaveowners, having always persuaded themselves that their slaves were docile and contented, were dumbfounded when the truth was revealed.

The collapse of slavery, the widespread suffering and destruction, and the incontrovertible fact of Union military rule undermined Confederate morale in the Volunteer State. Well before their comrades in most other parts of the South, secessionists in Tennessee resigned themselves to defeat and emancipation, and ended their resistance to Federal authority.

Stephen V. Ash, University of Tennessee, Knoxville
SEE: CIVIL WAR; CONTRABAND CAMPS; JOHNSON, ANDREW

OCHS, ADOLPH SIMON (1858–1935), along with Joseph Pulitzer and William Randolph Hearst, helped lay the foundation of modern American journalism. He was born March 12, 1858, in Cincinnati, Ohio, the son of Bavarian immigrants. His father, an abolitionist, and his mother, a secessionist, differed greatly on the issues of the day, and from his earliest years Ochs learned the importance of tolerance and conciliation. Driven from the North by his mother's southern sympathies during the Civil War, the Ochs family settled in Knoxville. There, at age 11, Adolph Ochs began his newspaper career delivering the *Knoxville Chronicle* to help support his impoverished family. Three years later, when he was promoted to office boy, Ochs decided to make newspapers his life's work.

At the *Chronicle* Ochs mastered the skills of newspaper composition and was soon much sought after as a printer and typesetter. In 1877, after working briefly in Louisville, Ochs took a position with the *Chattanooga Dispatch*. The paper soon failed, but Ochs remained in Chattanooga and a year later, at the age of 20, he bought another failing local publication, the *Chattanooga Times*. Starting with just $12.50 in working capital, Ochs transformed the ragged daily into one of the South's leading newspapers. A technical perfectionist and a political moderate, Ochs produced a paper which was attractive, accurate, and fair. Though an ardent Democrat, Ochs resisted the extremism of Tennessee's Bourbon leaders, and instead urged cooperation with the North and moderation towards blacks. Locally, he pressed for reform, and the *Times* became an outspoken advocate of honest, efficient government. Ochs contributed to the community in other ways as well. He helped establish the town's first public library, assisted in the effort to establish the Chickamauga-Chattanooga Military Park, and led a movement to preserve much of Lookout Mountain. Ochs was also an important figure in Chattanooga's Jewish community and contributed heavily to the town's Reform congregation.

Soon after acquiring the *Times*, Adolph Ochs emerged as Chattanooga's greatest booster, and he tirelessly pursued the city's economic development. Och's efforts helped create a local economic boom in the 1880s, and Chattanooga's rapid growth brought the young publisher considerable wealth and prestige. Emboldened by his sudden success, Ochs invested heavily in area real estate and organized vast syndicates to develop nearby lands. His plans were soon dashed, however, when land values crashed in 1887, leaving the publisher with huge financial losses.

The Panic of 1893 dealt Ochs another severe economic blow, and by 1896 his modest empire was on the verge of collapse. Desperate for income to pay his mounting debts, he drew on his remaining credit and set out to buy another failing newspaper. Equipped with "$70,000 and a letter from Grover Cleveland," Ochs acquired the nearly bankrupt *New York Times* on July 1, 1896. Applying lessons learned in Chattanooga, Ochs turned the metropolitan daily into one of the nation's great publishing dynasties, and the Ochs-Sulzberger family continues to play a leading role in American journalism.

Adolph Ochs left Chattanooga shortly after his purchase of the *New York Times*, yet he continued to have an active interest in the community and its development. He died there April 8, 1935, during a final visit to the city he loved and helped to create.
Timothy P. Ezzell, Knoxville

SEE: CHATTANOOGA; CHATTANOOGA TIMES; JEWS, URBAN TENNESSEE; PUBLISHING

OCONASTOTA (ca. 1710–1783) was a prominent eighteenth century Overhill Cherokee civil and military leader, who resided at Chota on the Little Tennessee River in present-day Monroe County. He was born around 1710. By the 1740s he had acquired the title Great Warrior of Chota. His reputation grew as he led successful war parties against the French and their Indian allies. During the 1750s the British explicitly recognized Oconastota as the military and political leader of the Cherokees. He became the Headman, or Uko, at Chota and the effective chief of the Cherokee nation in 1768.

In 1759 the British took Oconastota and 30 of his followers hostage at Fort Prince George following misunderstandings concerning service against the French. Oconastota was released, but when he murdered a British officer outside the fort, the British killed the 28 Cherokees still held captive. To avenge the deaths, the Cherokees, led by Oconastota, captured Fort Loudoun in 1760 and massacred most of its garrison as they were being marched toward Charleston. Despite British retaliation, including the destruction of the Lower Cherokee Towns, Oconastota's reputation rose among the Cherokees.

In subsequent years, Oconastota commanded campaigns against the Creeks, Choctaws, and Iroquois. He also conducted frequent negotiations with the British, as white settlers encroached on Cherokee land and forced the tribe to cede more and more territory. When Revolutionary War forces attacked the Overhill towns in 1776, Oconastota helped to negotiate their withdrawal and the peace treaty of 1777. Oconastota resigned his position as chief about 1780. He died in 1783 and Joseph Martin described his burial at Chota; archaeologists excavated his grave in 1969. Oconastota was returned to the Cherokee people and reinterred at Chota in 1987.
Gerald F. Schroedl, University of Tennessee, Knoxville

SUGGESTED READING: James C. Kelly, "Oconastota," *Journal of Cherokee Studies* 3 (1978): 221–238

SEE: CHOTA; FORT LOUDOON; OVERHILL CHEROKEES

OLD HICKORY, a planned industrial complex and town in Davidson County, dates to January 29, 1918, when the DuPont corporation and the federal government agreed to build a massive factory and town along Hadley's Bend of the Cumberland River. As planned, the factory had nine separate units, each with the ability to produce 100,000 pounds of gunpowder daily, and included hundreds of buildings within the site. At the time of its construction, it was the largest industrial facility in terms of employees and sheer scope in the state's history.

To house the thousands of workers needed at the factory, DuPont designed a permanent village, initially called Jacksonville to honor Andrew Jackson, which had over 300 dwellings by November 1918. These were reserved for company foremen, supervisors, and officials. Many homes were utilitarian, but substantial ones reflected architectural elements from popular revival styles. A "temporary" village contained over 500 residences where common laborers lived, with African Americans segregated into one area while another 41 large buildings housed a Mexican community of some 3,000 people.

The DuPont village was designed to be self-sufficient, providing a hospital, churches, gymnasiums, city hall, police station, first aid stations, fire hall, theaters, bank, commissary, mess halls, and a restaurant. A hotel could house up to 400 visitors. The YMCA built separate facilities for African Americans and whites while the YWCA built a quarters for white women. Historian Stanley Horn observed: "'They had 56,000 men (and women) on the payroll and they were recruited from everywhere. The plant was so big and had so many people on its payroll that Nashville was just turned around.'"[1]

Two months after the November 1918 armistice, DuPont officials and the federal government closed the gunpowder factory; by the end of 1919, only 500 lived in a place that had claimed as many from 35,000 to 56,000 workers a year earlier. In 1920 the Nashville Industrial Corporation bought the complex for about $3.5 million; three years later, it sold the complex to DuPont officials, who converted it into a rayon factory, constructing a cellophane installation by the end of the decade.

DuPont acquired a large part of the factory village and changed the community name to Old Hickory, again in honor of Andrew Jackson. By 1925 the DuPont Rayon Plant was in production; for the next 20 years the corporation operated Old Hickory as a company town. Many extant public and commercial buildings in the town date to this post-World War I era, including the Colonial Revival-style post office (1934), designed by federal architect Louis A. Simon, and the Colonial Revival-style library, built in 1937. Not until 1946 did DuPont begin to sell its homes to employees, ending the tradition of company control over the townscape.

Carroll Van West, Middle Tennessee State University
CITATION:
(1) Frank Burns, *Davidson County* (Memphis, 1989), 70.
SUGGESTED READING: Carroll Van West, *Nashville Architecture: A Guide to the City* (1999)
SEE: DAVIDSON COUNTY; INDUSTRY; WORLD WAR I

OLD HICKORY DIVISION.

With America's declaration of war on April 6, 1917, a general mobilization of U.S. Armed Forces was ordered. War Department General Order #95 on July 18, 1917, created a National Guard division, designated the 30th Division, to be filled by Tennessee, North and South Carolina National Guard troops.

Camp Sevier (named for John Sevier), in South Carolina was established as headquarters and con-

centration point for the 30th Divisional Camp. Once clearing of the woods and construction of camp buildings was completed, military training began. Artillery regiments, lacking armaments, trained with wooden cannon. The infantry trained in tactics of trench warfare and offensive tactics of open warfare. "Old Hickory" was selected as the Division's official name, the affectionate nickname for Andrew Jackson. Unit insignia featured an "H" within a horizontal oval "O"; the three Xs within are Roman numerals for "30."

In April 1918 the 30th Division left for Camp Mills, New York; it sailed to England, then France. Infantry regiments were sent to train with the British Second Army in Belgium, receiving instruction in trench warfare, patrol, and gas attacks. Remaining with the British Army, they participated in the September 29 drive to break the Hindenburg Line. The 30th Division's infantry advanced continuously until October 19 when they were then pulled back for rest.

Division artillery regiments and support units in France trained on the French 75mm cannon. Combining with other U.S. Divisions, they created the "All-American Army," and participated in the September 12 first "all-American drive" on the St. Mihiel salient; leading up to the Meuse-Argonne offensive and Armistice on November 11, 1918. Thus, the Old Hickory Division served under both the British and American flags in World War I.

Lt. McMurray of the Thirtieth (Old Hickory) Division, circa 1918.

TSLA. PHOTOGRAPH BY CALVERT

During World War II, the 30th Division, again known as the Old Hickory Division, compiled a distinguished fighting record in the European Theater.
Chelius H. Carter, Memphis
SEE: WORLD WAR I

OLD STONE FORT is a prehistoric enclosure consisting of embankments or "walls" constructed of undressed stacked or piled stone covered with earth. They circumscribe a 50-acre plateau at the forks of the Duck River in Coffee County. These embankments, originally ranging from four to six feet in height, would have a total length of 4,600 feet if they were continuous; however, they were only constructed where the stream bluffs are not steep. The enclosure also includes a complex entranceway consisting of a ditch, pedestal mounds on either side of the entrance, and interior parallel walls that run perpendicular to the entrance to form a cul-de-sac. The entranceway configuration convinced many early historians and antiquarians that this was a fortification built by early explorers such as the Welsh, Norse, or Hernando de Soto. These romantic myths were shattered in 1966, when archaeologists from the University of Tennessee proved that this enclosure was built 2,000 years ago by prehistoric Native American groups.

Charcoal recovered from the ditch and embankment provided radiocarbon dates for a sequence of construction phases that span an almost 500-year period, from 80 A.D. when the entrance ditch was dug to 550 A.D. when the cul-de-sac walls were completed. These radiocarbon dates closely correlate with the construction dates of similar hilltop enclosure sites such as Fort Ancient in Warren County, Ohio. The Ohio enclosures are now known to have been constructed by the Hopewell people, a mound-building group of Native Americans, who were in contact with cultures in the Southeast during the Middle Woodland period of North American prehistory, about 2,000 years ago.

Two of these groups that had contact with the Ohio Hopewell people were the McFarland and Owl Hollow cultures of the upper Duck River Valley. Small village sites of these early farming and pottery-making people were excavated by University of Tennessee archaeologists in the nearby Normandy Reservoir before inundation in 1976. Based on numerous radiocarbon dates from these villages, the McFarland people inhabited the upper Duck Valley between 200 B.C. and 200 A.D., with the Owl Hollow people succeeding them between 200 A.D. and 600 A.D. The McFarland culture apparently began constructing the Old Stone Fort in the first century of the Christian Era, the enclosure being completed almost 500 years later by the Owl Hollow culture.

There is now little doubt among anthropologists and archaeologists that the Old Stone Fort was sacred space; however, the actual ceremonial function of this enclosure is still unclear. While a small burial mound may exist outside the walls, there is no direct evidence that the enclosure was used in funerary ritual as were some of the related Hopewell sites in Ohio. The most recent hypothesis is that the Old Stone Fort was some kind of celestial observatory since the parallel entrance walls seem to point toward the position of the sun at summer solstice.

The Old Stone Fort is now a state archaeological park with an interpretive museum, near Manchester.
Charles Faulkner, University of Tennessee, Knoxville
SEE: COFFEE COUNTY; WOODLAND CULTURE

"OLD TIME" BAPTISTS. By the middle of the eighteenth century, Baptists had begun to settle the mountain valleys of what is now East Tennessee, and by 1786 their small churches were numerous enough to establish what became the second Baptist association west of the Alleghenies, the Holston Valley Association. However, these early Tennessee Baptists brought with them a doctrinal division that had flourished before and after the Great Awakening. "Regular Baptists" held an allegiance to the Philadelphia Association (established in 1707) and to that organization's creed, the Philadelphia Confession (adopted in 1742 as a heavily Calvinistic, limited atonement document). "Separate Baptists" had become non-creedal, Arminian, general atonement Baptists. Although most of the larger Baptist churches of Tennessee now are affiliated with the Southern Baptist Convention, there still are Regular and Separate congregations within the state, preserving many of their eighteenth and nineteenth century traditions.

"Old Time Baptists" or "Old Baptists" are informal titles employed by some in the Central Appalachians to indicate not only the Regulars and the Separates, but also a host of equally small denominations with titles such as Old Missionary Baptists, Old Regular Baptists, Regular Old School Baptists, Regular Primitive Baptists, and United Baptists. All of the latter are derivatives from either the Regulars, the Separates, or both, and share many of the same tenets such as the observance of such traditional practices as lined *a cappella* singing, rhythmically chanted impromptu preaching, congregational shouting, and warmly tactile worship behavior; strict adherence to "natural water" (also called "living water") baptisms and communion services that are followed by footwashings; the practice of such governance rules as Paulinian gender mandates, Paulinian directives for elders and deacons, and articles of decorum that date from the earliest history of colonial Baptists; and restrictions on divorce and "double marriage" (remarriage after divorce, while the original spouse still lives). A common liturgical format that, for example, makes the typical Regular Primitive service appear remarkably similar to those of Regular, Old Regular, and United Baptists includes—among other common liturgical elements—at least three sermons, and as many as seven or eight, depending on the nature of the service.

In terms of doctrine, these "Old Baptists" are a mixed lot. With the exception of the Separates, each of these subdenominations believe in some version of "election." However, Primitives usually interpret election as meaning that before the beginning of time God chose who would become the beneficiaries of Christ's atonement, while Regular, Old Regulars, and Uniteds generally see election as a process by which God individually "calls" the sinner to regeneration and redemption. Separates have adopted a general atonement doctrine that grants to the individual the "free will" to choose or reject redemption. One unique Regular Primitive group found in Appalachia, the Primitive Baptist Universalists, believes Christ's atonement is for all, with the result that at the "Resurrection" all of humankind will be reunited with God and Christ in heaven.

Howard Dorgan, Appalachian State University
SEE: RELIGION; SOUTHERN BAPTIST CONVENTION

OMLIE, PHOEBE FAIRGRAVE (1902–1975) was known as the "godmother" of early Tennessee aviation. Omlie started her career as a barnstormer, wingwalker, and stunt pilot. She and her husband Vernon settled in Memphis in 1922 and opened Mid-South Airways, the first flying service in the Southeast. In the late 1920s and early 1930s she attained prominence representing the Mono Aircraft Company in national air races.

Omlie was the first woman appointed to a federal aviation post. From 1933 until 1936 she served as special assistant for air intelligence with the National Advisory Committee for Aeronautics (the predecessor to NASA). From 1941 until 1952 she worked with the Civil Aeronautics Administration (the forerunner of the FAA). Omlie introduced the federal airmarking program through the Works Progress Administration, and, prior to and during World War II, she started schools for primary flight instruction and aircraft mechanic training.

In the late 1930s Omlie introduced aviation into the Memphis public school curriculum, a program that the federal government adopted for its Civilian Pilot Training Program. She and W. Percy McDonald, head of the Tennessee Bureau of Aeronautics, authored legislation that provided the state with funds to improve airports and provide pilot training. In 1942 they started the Tennessee Women's Research Flight Instructor School to ease the pilot shortage in World War II. The program graduated one class of ten and received national recognition but was not adopted and funded by the federal government.

After retiring from aviation in 1952, Omlie ranched, ran a restaurant, and traveled as a public speaker.
Janene Leonhirth, Louisville, Kentucky
SEE: AIRPORTS; WORLD WAR II

ONE HUNDRED AND FIRST AIRBORNE DIVISION. The 101st Airborne Division (Air Assault) has been since the 1960s the single major military force stationed—if only partially—in Tennessee. The unit boasts an illustrious combat record and is one of the U.S. Army's most potent quick reaction forces.

Formed from the 82nd Airborne Division on August 15, 1942, the 101st Airborne trained at Fort Bragg, North Carolina, before deploying to Great Britain in the fall of 1943. Like the other four airborne divisions in the U.S. Army in World War II, the 101st was small in numbers (about 8,400 men—half the size of a standard infantry division), but high in quality. The first combat test for the unit came during the invasion of Normandy when it parachuted behind Utah Beach on June 6, 1944. After fighting in France for a month, the 101st then took part in Operation Market Garden in September 1944. Suffering severe losses in both these engagements, the 101st was recuperating when Hitler launched his last offensive, culminating in the Battle of the Bulge. The 101st rushed forward to Bastogne, a critical road junction in Belgium. Although completely surrounded and substantially outnumbered, the paratroopers conducted so determined a resistance that the 101st received the Distinguished Unit Citation, the first such award ever made to an entire division. From February 1945 to V-E Day, the 101st fought in the Ruhr and southern Germany, ending the war at Hitler's Berchtesgaden retreat.

Inactivated in France on November 30, 1945, the 101st Airborne survived in the Army for over a decade solely as a unit designator for training centers in Kentucky and later South Carolina. Then on September 21, 1956, the division's colors moved to Fort Campbell as the unit returned to active duty. The Army frequently used the division to test new equipment and operational concepts, such as the pentomic organization designed so that a ground force might fight and survive on a nuclear battlefield. The 101st also was employed to suppress major civil disturbances at Little Rock in 1957; Oxford, Mississippi, in 1962; and Detroit in 1967.

In 1965 part of the division (the First Brigade) deployed to Vietnam; the remainder of the unit arrived two years later. Frequently in combat, the 101st changed character as it maneuvered principally by helicopter. Seventeen division soldiers won the Medal of Honor. In 1969 the Army began the official conversion of the 101st from an airborne (parachute) to an airmobile (helicopter) formation. The division was therefore redesignated as the 101st

Airborne Division (Airmobile), then as the 101st Air Cavalry Division, and finally on October 4, 1974, as the 101st Airborne Division (Air Assault). Although no longer a classic airborne formation, the unit retains a small Pathfinder element—and the title for reasons of heritage.

As the Vietnam War wound down, the 101st returned to the United States; all its men were home by February 1972. Over the next decades, 101st soldiers frequently trained in NATO exercises and with Rapid Deployment forces in Egypt. Sadly in December 1985, 248 soldiers returning from Sinai duty were killed in an airplane crash at Gander, Newfoundland.

The 101st next deployed abroad as a division in 1990. Participating in the early phases of Operation Desert Shield, in February 1991 soldiers of the 101st fired some of the first shots of the war against Iraq when their helicopters blasted holes through the enemy radar net. As part of the XVIII Airborne Corps, the division took part in the celebrated left hook which flanked the enemy out of Kuwait. On the first day of the ground campaign, the 101st in the single greatest air assault operation in history sent over 300 helicopters 50 miles into enemy territory. The 101st captured so many Iraqis that its supply of food and water had to be replenished by air drops.

Since returning to Fort Campbell, the 101st has been held in readiness for contingency operations, although some of its troops have been deployed abroad on peacekeeping missions in places as diverse as the Middle East, Somalia, Panama, or Haiti. With a strength of over 18,000 soldiers and 400 helicopters, the 101st Airborne (Air Assault) Division remains one of the most powerful military units in the world. As might be expected, such a large formation has a major impact on north-central Tennessee. Much of the growth of Clarksville, for instance, is directly attributable to the division's presence.

Malcolm Muir, Jr., Austin Peay State University

SEE: FORT CAMPBELL; WORLD WAR II

OPERA has long been performed on stages throughout Tennessee. Famous stars and opera companies of the nineteenth and early twentieth centuries often presented performances in the state's larger cities. In 1851 Jenny Lind appeared in both Nashville and Memphis. Adelina Patti gave her first Nashville concert in 1859. By the late nineteenth century, opera lovers in Memphis flocked to performances at the Memphis Grand Opera House, constructed in 1890. The Metropolitan Opera of New York City staged Bizet's *Carmen* in Memphis and Nashville in 1901. Roland Hayes of Chattanooga was a popular concert tenor from the late 1910s through the 1930s.

Tennessee, in fact, has a direct connection to the Met's tradition of traveling companies through the career of Francis Robinson (1910–1980), who was born in Kentucky but grew up in Mt. Pleasant, Tennessee. A graduate of Vanderbilt University, Robinson in the 1930s worked for the *Nashville Banner* and then WSM Radio before accepting a position at the Metropolitan Opera, where he became the manager of its national and international tours. Later advancing to Impresario of the company, Robinson received a honorary doctorate from Princeton University and the Italian Order of Merit. He also served on the Board of Trustees for Vanderbilt University. At the end of his career, Robinson donated his papers and Met Opera memorabilia to Vanderbilt's Heard Library, where the collection is a major reference source for opera scholars.

Current Tennessee-based opera companies date to the second half of the twentieth century. The Chattanooga Opera was the first, established in 1942. It merged in 1985 with the Chattanooga Symphony, creating the Chattanooga Symphony and Opera Association, the only such combined organization in the country. Opera Memphis, founded in 1955, is the state's largest company and has included such stars as Beverly Sills, Sherrill Milnes, and Memphis-born Kallen Esperian in its productions. In 1976 the Knoxville Civic Opera Company was incorporated. Its first performance in 1978 of Verdi's *La Traviata* featured Knoxville native Mary Costa. In 1983 the company moved to the Tennessee Theater on Gay Street and changed its name to the Knoxville Opera Company. In 1981 the Nashville Opera was created; it performs at the Jackson Theater of the Tennessee Performing Arts Center. Its educational tour, Opera-Net, performed in over 30 local schools in 1996, introducing a new generation to the drama, comedy, and music of opera.

Several Tennessee natives have achieved fame in the international world of opera. Grace Moore, from Jellico, made her Metropolitan Opera debut in 1928 and followed that success with performances at most of the major opera houses in the world during her distinguished career. More recently, Elizabeth Carter of Nashville has performed with the Met, Covent Garden in London, and the Vienna Staatsoper in Salzburg as well as other international opera companies. Kallen Esperian of Memphis also has enjoyed a successful international career; she won the Pavarotti Opera Company of Philadelphia International Voice Competition in 1986. The most impressive rising star from Tennessee is Nashville native Dawn Upshaw, who is now recognized as one of the major performing and recording sopranos in all of opera. Awarded prizes from the Naumburg Foundation and Young Concert Artists, Upshaw was invited to join the Metropolitan Opera Studio a year before she made her critically successful debut at the Met in 1985. Since that time, Upshaw has sung with the major international opera companies and as a soloist in concert with many leading symphony orchestras. Upshaw's performances draw from such diverse repertoire as Mozart, Messiaen, and Stravinsky. Her recordings likewise range from American popular music to lieder recitals to operatic standards. She is noted as a champion of modern music, which she performs in recital and records. By 1997 Upshaw already had won two Grammy Awards for her solo recordings.

Carroll Van West, Middle Tennessee State University

SEE: MOORE, GRACE; MUSIC; RYMAN AUDITORIUM

OPRY HOUSE AND OPRYLAND HOTEL, a Nashville entertainment and convention complex, began when the National Life and Accident Insurance Company, the parent company of the nationally famous country music radio show, the Grand Ole Opry, decided to move the Opry from the crowded conditions of the Ryman Auditorium in downtown Nashville to a new suburban location between Briley Parkway and the Cumberland River. President Richard M. Nixon dedicated the new Opry House at its opening on March 16, 1974. The Los Angeles architectural firm of Welton Beckett and Associates, with George Hammons as principal architect, received the commission to design a modern home for the Grand Ole Opry. Hammons designed a technologically modern 48,000-square foot auditorium, yet his design reflected a rural sensibility due to its shingled-like sloping roof and the red brick that wraps around the building. Inside, the Opry House contains lofty, inspirational spaces, in keeping with its role as the secular "mother church" of country music.

The Opryland theme park opened in 1972. Like other theme amusement parks of the era, its architecture reflected different historical eras and regions, from the Old West to Railroad Towns to Country Fairs to the drive-in aesthetic of the 1950s. At the end of its 1997 season, owner Gaylord Enterprises closed Opryland and announced that a new mega-shopping mall, Opry Mills, would replace the amusement park.

The Opryland Hotel complex (1977, 1983, 1987, 1996) is a fantasyland of a different sort and scale, designed in four stages by the Nashville architectural firm of Earl Swensson Associates. The exterior central block of this neo-Georgian Revival design recalls the Governor's Palace at Colonial Williamsburg. But the interior—named the Magnolia Lobby—has more in common with grand southern plantation architecture. The Opryland Hotel has evolved into one of the largest convention hotels in the country; as of 1997, it was considered the largest in the United States outside of Las Vegas, Nevada. The first major addition was the Conservatory (1983), which contains two acres of gardens underneath a huge glass and steel skylight. Four years later came the Cascades wing, with its huge fountains and man-made waterfalls, again under a giant skylight. Most recently came the Delta wing (1996), which reflects the architectural styles of the French Quarter of New Orleans and Louisiana's Mississippi River plantations.

Carroll Van West, Middle Tennessee State University

SUGGESTED READING: Carroll Van West, *Nashville Architecture: A Guide to the City* (1999)

SEE: GRAND OLE OPRY; NASHVILLE; NATIONAL LIFE AND ACCIDENT INSURANCE COMPANY

OSSOLI CIRCLE. The first women's club in Knoxville and in Tennessee, and the first club in the South to join the General Federation of Women's Clubs, Ossoli Circle was organized on November 20, 1885, when Lizzie Crozier French called 12 other women together to form a literary society intended to advance their intellectual and moral development through organization. At the suggestion of the first president, Mary Boyce Temple, they named it after New England intellectual and women's rights advocate Margaret Fuller Ossoli (1810–1850). From 1885 to 1890 the Tennessee Female Institute, where French was principal, served as the first home of the Ossoli Circle.

Mary B. Temple, educated in the library of her father, Judge Oliver P. Temple, and at Vassar, where she graduated in the class of 1877, led Ossoli Circle for its first five years. In 1886 she read before its members the manuscript of her *Sketch of Margaret Fuller Ossoli*, published in that year by the Ossoli Society. In this book, she suggested that the public "conversations" which Margaret Fuller held for the women of Boston 46 years earlier were "something akin to the aims of our own circle. They were entirely novel in their day."

By 1893 membership in Ossoli Circle had grown to 75. In 1896 Ossoli Circle issued a call for delegates from the state's 16 women's clubs to meet in Knoxville and organize the Tennessee Federation of Women's Clubs. Ossoli accomplishments in the early twentieth century included the establishment of traveling libraries, an important activity until 1913; aid to mountain schools, begun in 1901; improvement of the laws of Tennessee that affected women, an activity led by the determined and energetic Lizzie Crozier French; the establishment of a state vocational school for girls, an idea that originated in Ossoli Circle; and the Ossoli Story Telling League for Children, organized in 1907.

In 1933 Ossoli Circle moved into its own clubhouse, located at 2511 Kingston Pike, near Tyson Park, where it remains today a social, cultural, and intellectual center for Knoxville women.

Kay Baker Gaston, Springfield

SEE: FRENCH, LIZZIE CROZIER

OTEY, JAMES HERVEY (1800–1863), Christian educator and first Episcopal Bishop of Tennessee, established the Anglican church in the state and organized its first parish churches. Born in Bedford County, Virginia, on January 27, 1800, he attended the University of North Carolina. Upon his graduation in 1820 he was appointed tutor in Greek and Latin at the school. Following his marriage to Eliza D. Panhill of Petersburg, Virginia, in 1821, he moved to Maury County and took charge of a boy's school in nearby Franklin.

On returning to North Carolina to head the academy at Warrenton, he was baptized and confirmed in the Episcopal Church and chose a career with the church. He became a deacon in 1825 and priest in 1827. He then returned to Franklin and organized the state's first Episcopal Church in the Masonic Lodge there. He established several other churches and on July 1, 1829, organized the Episcopal Diocese of Tennessee at Nashville. He was elected the first bishop in June 1833 and was consecrated at Christ Church, Philadelphia, the following January. Following his election, Otey also took charge of the Diocese of Mississippi and was missionary bishop for Arkansas and the Indian Territory. He traveled for months at a time across the extensive region, establishing new churches and preaching the Gospel.

Otey was fervently interested in Christian education and helped organize schools at Ashwood, Columbia, and Jackson. His dreams for a "Literary and Theological Seminary" for the region were realized by the establishment of the University of the South at Sewanee in 1857.

Otey lived at "Mercer Hall" in Columbia from 1835 to 1852, when he relocated to Memphis. He died there on April 23, 1863. After the Civil War, he was buried at St. John's Church at Ashwood in Maury County.

Richard Quin, National Park Service

SEE: FRANKLIN MASONIC LODGE; MAURY COUNTY; RELIGION; ST. JOHN'S CHURCH; UNIVERSITY OF THE SOUTH

OVERHILL CHEROKEES refer to the settlements of the eighteenth century Cherokee people found in eastern Tennessee. The name Overhill is generally derived from the geographic location of the Cherokees and the need to travel over the mountains from South Carolina to reach them. Early historic sources also often refer to these as the upper settlements in contrast to the lower and middle settlements found east of the Appalachians.

The Overhill towns were found primarily in the lower Little Tennessee and Hiwassee River valleys and their tributaries, although some less well known towns were located in upper East Tennessee. Scholars disagree concerning the establishment of the Overhill towns. Some believe that Overhill Cherokee settlements date as early as the sixteenth century while other researchers argue that the Cherokees came into the area in the late seventeenth century. The most frequently identified towns on the Little

Tennessee are Chilhowee, Tallassee, Citico, Chota, Tanasi, Toqua, Tomotley, Tuskeegee, and Mialoquo, and on the Tellico River, Great Tellico and Chatuga. Chestue and Hiwassee Old Town were located on the Hiwassee River. Other divisions of the Cherokees included the Lower towns in northern Georgia and northwestern South Carolina, and the Middle, Valley and Out towns in western North Carolina.

Towns within each group had close linguistic, political, economic, and religious ties, and shared similar architecture and material culture, but were largely politically autonomous. Individual residents were members of one of seven Cherokee clans. Clan membership and kinship relations were established through an individual's mother. Cherokees could be virtually certain that a fellow clan member resided in any Cherokee town they visited regardless of the region. Clan membership provided a rich network of social and economic alliances that could be called upon at all times. The Cherokees also recognized social and linguistic differences among the regional town clusters which were clearly identified by English traders and settlers.

Overhill people, for example, spoke a distinctive dialect, which they shared with the Valley towns. One settlement in each region was considered a mother town. By the mid-eighteenth century Chota was considered the mother town, although early in the century its neighbor Tanasi had filled this role, and still earlier Great Tellico may have been the mother town.

Village populations numbered about 100 to 400 people. Each village had an octagonal council house or town house measuring up to 60 feet in diameter and a rectangular summer council house measuring about 15 by 40 feet. Both buildings were located at one end of a village plaza which covered an acre or more. The council houses and plaza were the site for all public meetings, including religious festivals, social gatherings, political debates, and military planning. Lieutenant Henry Timberlake in 1760 and Duke Louis Phillipe in 1797 provide particularly vivid descriptions of these buildings. The townhouse and plaza were surrounded by associated households which were scattered along a river for as far as a mile. Each household included a circular winter house and a rectangular summer house, built to the same plan as the council houses only smaller. In and around these structures, Cherokee families stored and prepared plant and animal foods, processed hides, and manufactured pottery and other household and personal items. Scattered among the houses were small family gardens. At greater distances were agricultural fields where native crops of corn, beans, and squash were raised, and where plants introduced by Europeans such as potatoes, cabbage, melons, and field peas were grown, as well as where apple and peach trees were cultivated.

The Overhill towns were the homes of a number of prominent Cherokee leaders well known in American history. These include, for example, Oconastota, the Great Warrior, and Attakullakulla or Little Carpenter, the great diplomat, both of whom resided at Chota. Ostenaco, the warrior and political leader who hosted Henry Timberlake during his well known diplomatic mission following the Cherokee war of 1760, was from Tomotley. Dragging Canoe, from Chota, was famous for his resistance to American Revolutionary War forces. He established the town of Mialoqua and led the establishment of the Chickamauga towns in the vicinity of Chattanooga. Sequoyah, the inventor of the Cherokee syllabary, came from Tuskegee, which was located near Fort Loudoun.

British traders and colonial officials were well aware of the Overhill settlements by the 1690s, while sustained contact by traders began in the early 1700s. The first official diplomatic mission was attempted in 1715, but failed to reach the primary settlements on the Little Tennessee River. In 1725 this goal was achieved when Colonel George Chicken met with Cherokee headmen at the Tanasi townhouse. Thereafter, there was a steady stream of diplomatic, economic, and military missions to the Overhills as the British came to depend on the Overhills to provide deer hides and as they recognized the importance of the Cherokees as a military buffer against the French and their Indian allies to the west. Among early missions to the Overhills was the visit of Alexander Cummings in 1730, and the expeditions led by Raymond Demere and William Gerard De Brahm in connection with the construction of Fort Loudoun near Tomotley and Tuskegee in 1756.

During the Cherokee War of the 1760s many refugees moved to the Overhills when the British destroyed the Lower and Middle towns in North and South Carolina. During the American Revolution and the hostilities that continued into the 1790s, colonial and later territorial militia repeatedly destroyed Overhill towns. People escaping these deprivations and continuing their resistance to American encroachment moved south to form the Chickamauga towns in the vicinity of present-day Chattanooga. The population of the Overhill towns was greatly reduced so that some towns were completely abandoned. At other towns council houses were maintained to serve the political, social, and religious needs of households in the vicinity, and some towns retained small resident populations. In the Treaty of 1819 the Cherokee ceded land from the Little Tennessee River south to the Hiwassee River and in so doing transferred the sites of the Overhill settlements to the United States. The treaty of 1819 also provided for Cherokees to retain residence in this area on 640- or 160-acre reservations. Some individuals reestab-

lished households at former village locations, while other families resided along smaller streams and uplands throughout the region. This effort to sustain a cultural identity and physical connection with the Overhill settlements lasted until 1838 when the Cherokee were removed to Oklahoma by the United States government.

In the 1960s and 1970s, extensive archaeological studies of the Overhill villages on the Little Tennessee River in Monroe and Loudon counties were undertaken because of their inclusion in the Tellico Dam Reservoir. In the late 1970s the village sites were inundated. A small area of the Chota townhouse and plaza were covered with fill, and two monuments, one at the site and another overlooking the site, honoring the Cherokee people were erected. The Sequoyah Birthplace Museum, located near Vonore, is dedicated to the public presentation of Cherokee history, especially the Overhill towns.

Gerald F. Schroedl, University of Tennessee, Knoxville

SUGGESTED READINGS: John P. Brown, *Old Frontiers, The Story of the Cherokee Indians from Earliest Times to the Removal to the West, 1838* (1938); David Cockran, *The Cherokee Frontier: Conflict and Survival, 1740–1762* (1962); Verner Crane, *The Southern Frontier, 1670–1732* (1929); Charles M. Hudson, *The Southeastern Indians* (1976); James Mooney, *Myths of the Cherokee* (1900); Samuel Cole Williams, *Dawn of Tennessee Valley and Tennessee History* (1937)

SEE: ATTAKULLAKULLA; CHICKAMAUGAS; CHOTA; DRAGGING CANOE; FORT LOUDOUN; OCONASTOTA; SEQUOYAH; TIMBERLAKE, HENRY; TOQUA; TRAIL OF TEARS

OVERMOUNTAIN MEN refers to those pioneers who settled on the western side of the Appalachian Mountains during the second half of the eighteenth century. The first group to venture into the region were adventurers, traders, and long hunters—temporary residents who came in search of game or trade and did not create permanent settlements. Some came for a few days, while others stayed for weeks or months. The stories they told about the unspoiled beauty of the land aroused the curiosity of Easterners.

The first wave of visitors to the West troubled British government officials. As the French and Indian War drew to a close, King George III issued a proclamation in 1763 to restrict movement across the Appalachian Mountains. The proclamation prohibited government land grants, as well as private land purchases, and reserved the land between the crest of the mountains and the Mississippi River for the Indians.

The proclamation failed to limit interest in the land. Those willing to take on the immediate risks associated with life in the wilderness felt little or no threat from a king who lived so far away. They gathered such belongings as could be carried on horseback, said good-bye to friends who stayed behind, and set out confidently toward their new home. Their reasons for making the journey varied. Some sought a life free from oppressive laws and taxes imposed by fiat. Members of the Regulator Movement in North Carolina, for example, wanted to escape from what they perceived as the tyranny of Royal Governor William Tryon. In their minds, the prospect of freedom outweighed the challenges of the wilderness. Others recognized the enticing opportunities for land acquisition. A few lawbreakers viewed the West as an opportunity to escape from the consequences of their crimes. And the entire scenario was made to order for frontier adventurers.

William Bean of Pittsylvania County, Virginia, became one of the earliest permanent settlers in the Tennessee country. Bean and his wife, Lidia, came into the area in 1769, and settled along Boone's Creek, a tributary of the Watauga River. In early 1771 James Robertson led a small group of North Carolinians into the area. Other communities developed in Carter's Valley, Nolichucky, and Holston.

Since they lived outside the boundaries of the British colonial government, the Watauga settlers met in May 1772 to form their own government. Their deliberations produced the Watauga Association, which was based on the Virginia code of laws and primarily operated to protect the property of the settlers through a court of five magistrates, a sheriff, and a militia. The Watauga Association represented the first white government in Tennessee, though it instituted neither a breakaway government nor a renunciation of British sovereignty.

Terry Weeks, Middle Tennessee State University

SEE: ROBERTSON, JAMES; SULLIVAN COUNTY; WASHINGTON COUNTY; WATAUGA ASSOCIATION

OVERTON COUNTY, named in honor of Nashville judge John Overton, was carved out of Jackson County on September 12, 1806. With over 1,000 square miles, the newly created county encompassed all of what is now Fentress County, as well as portions of Clay, Putnam, Cumberland and Scott counties. It is situated on the escarpment of the Highland Rim to the west and the Cumberland Plateau to the east, and now totals 433 square miles.

Prior to the establishment of the county the area had been used as a hunting preserve by Native Americans, and white encroachment into the area violated existing treaties with the Indians. In the Alpine community the Cherokee inhabitants were referred to as "Nettle Carrier" Indians and were friendly with white explorers. In 1763 a party of Long Hunters explored the area and camped for a time at the current location of Waterloo on Spring Creek, and later along the Roaring River. A number of the Long Hunters chose to remain, to the chagrin of the Cherokees. In 1769 one of those frontiersmen,

Robert Crockett, was ambushed in the Oak Hill area and killed; he is purported to be the first Long Hunter to die in Middle Tennessee.

In 1797 the idealistic and peripatetic Dr. Moses Fisk moved into the county. A recent graduate of Harvard who was licensed to practice law, Fisk wanted to tame the wilderness and pursue the American dream. He established a settlement at Hilham, which is one of the oldest communities in the county. Fisk, thinking Hilham was the geographical center of the entire globe, started four roads radiating out of Hilham in the four major directions of the compass, convinced that all roads would lead to his new Rome in the wilderness. In an era of male dominance, Fisk established a Female Academy at Hilham in 1806, one of the first such schools in the entire South.

After the American Revolution many veterans received land grants from the federal government and moved into the region. In 1799 Colonel Stephen Copland and his son "Big Jo" left Kingston and established a settlement near Monroe. Copland worked out a hospitable arrangement with the Cherokee chief Nettle Carrier and was allowed to establish a homesite. His success encouraged further settlement.

The first county seat was located at Monroe in the northern part of the county at the crossroads of the Kentucky Stock road and the road to Danville, Kentucky. Benjamin Totten served as its first county clerk. Both John Sevier and Andrew Jackson acquired landholdings in Overton County in such places as Monroe, Windle, Oakley, Independence, Taylor and Ozone. In 1802 French botanist Andre Michaux explored the Roaring River and trekked through the county as he moved west across the state.

John Sevier's son, Samuel Sevier, acted as the first doctor in the Upper Cumberland, and his daughter Joannah lived most of her life in Overton County; she is buried in Monroe. Sevier's widow, "Bonnie Kate," moved to Overton County in 1815 and settled in the Dale community. Dale, or Lily Dale, no longer exists. The community was one of those flooded to create Dale Hollow Lake, yet its name endures in the choice of the lake's name.

The county seat moved from Monroe to Livingston in 1835 as traffic through Monroe began to decline. Overton County representative Alvin Cullom engineered the change of location. New roads into Livingston and a burgeoning merchant district made it the logical choice for the county's government.

Though much of the land in the county is inadequate for commercial agriculture, Overton County did have a number of slaveowners. In 1860 slaveholders numbering 248 owned 1,087 slaves.

Though largely outside the fighting in the Civil War, Overton County was not untouched by the conflagration. Prior to the debacle at Mill Springs which led to his untimely death, Felix Zollicoffer's

Confederate troops encamped and trained near Monroe. In 1865 Captain John Francis and a band of Confederate guerrillas burned down the courthouse.

After the Civil War entrepreneurs and industry moved into the county. Two extractive industries, logging and coal mining, flourished side by side. Loggers, like "Uncle Billy" Hull, father of Cordell Hull, made fortunes at the turn of the century. Logs were cut and either snaked by mules to "peckerwood" mills to be roughly sawed and shipped to market or floated down to the Cumberland River for delivery in Carthage or Nashville. Coal camps were established in the rugged hills to the south and east of Livingston. Run by the Fentress Coal and Coke company and the Gernt family, towns like Twinton, Davidson, Wilder, Crawford, and Hanging Limb experienced a brief economic boom that lasted from the 1890s until the mid-1930s. The Wilder-Davidson strike over unionization led not only to the murder of organizer Barney Graham, but also precipitated the demise of the soft coal industry in the Upper Cumberland.

Concomitant with the logging and coal booms was the extension of railroads into the region. The railroad assisted the extractive industries and increased mobility in the region. Rickman, the second largest community in Overton County, was established in 1900 as a railhead. Rickman provided the only stop between Livingston and Algood, and became a burgeoning economic center as a result. That economic boom reached its peak in the 1940s, and has been on the wane ever since. The Rickman community had its own high school until 1984, when schools were consolidated and all students of high school age attended Livingston Academy. Rickman became a bedroom community for citizens who worked either in Cookeville or Livingston.

The Alpine community of Overton county was home to Governor Albert H. Roberts. A progressive governor and former educator, Roberts was instrumental in Tennessee's ratification of the Nineteenth Amendment. Ironically those very women who Roberts empowered with the right to vote chose to vote him out of office when he ran for re-election in 1920. Roberts performed the marriage ceremony of World War I hero Alvin C. York and his bride Gracie Williams in Pall Mall June 7, 1919.

The first American soldier to lose his life in Vietnam hailed from Livingston. James T. Davis was killed at Bien Hoa in an ambush on July 8, 1959, and his is the first name on the Vietnam Memorial in Washington, D.C.

The county boasts two significant recreational facilities: Standing Stone State Park and boat docks and camp grounds on Dale Hollow Lake. Tourism accounts for a considerable portion of the county's annual income.

In 1997 the population of Overton County was approximately 18,400, with only 0.3 percent of the residents being non-white. The largest employer was the furniture manufacturer Berkline Corporation.

Michael E. Birdwell, Tennessee Technological University

SEE: OVERTON, JOHN; ROBERTS, A.H.; SEVIER, BONNIE KATE; STANDING STONE STATE PARK; TIMBER; WILDER-DAVIDSON COAL MINING COMPLEX; ZOLLICOFFER, FELIX

OVERTON, JOHN (1766–1833), trusted friend of and advisor to Andrew Jackson, was an early Tennessee lawyer, jurist, banker, and political leader. Born in Louisa County, Virginia, Overton moved to Mercer County in present-day Kentucky in 1787 to begin his law career. He boarded with the family of Lewis Robards and his wife, Rachel Donelson Robards, whose subsequent divorce and marriage to Andrew Jackson, Overton defended.

Overton moved to Nashville in March 1789 and began practicing law in the Davidson County court; he was admitted to the bar in April 1790. He lodged with young Jackson, who was in the early stages of his own legal career, and the two frequently worked together to represent certain clients. The personal and professional relationship between the two men expanded into a business partnership in May 1794, when Overton became Jackson's partner in land speculation.

Overton represented Sumner County as a delegate to the 1789 North Carolina convention to ratify the U.S. Constitution. In 1795 he received an appointment from President George Washington as supervisor of revenue for the District of Tennessee, Territory South of the River Ohio. The following June, Washington appointed Overton to the post of district inspector of the revenue.

Between 1803 and 1806, Overton, as agent for the State of Tennessee, negotiated a settlement with North Carolina regarding the latter's right to dispose of land located within the new state. Under the terms of Overton's compromise, Tennessee ceded most of the western third of its territory to the United States, land warrants that had been issued by North Carolina were to be recognized throughout Tennessee, and Tennessee obtained clear title to the remaining land within its bounds.

In August 1804 Overton was elected to succeed Jackson as a member of the Superior Court of Tennessee, the forerunner of the Tennessee Supreme Court. He served on that Court until January 1810 and was one of the judges of its successor, the Supreme Court of Errors and Appeals, from November 1811 until his resignation from the bench in 1816.

In collaboration with Judge Thomas Emerson, Overton published the initial two volumes of the *Tennessee Reports* (1813–1817), the first official compilation of published decisions by Tennessee's highest courts. Judge Overton owned a substantial law library (in 1808, his collection contained some 160 volumes) and apparently served as an agent for eastern publishers of law treatises. Cumberland College awarded him an honorary Doctor of Laws degree in 1825.

After his resignation, Overton married Mary McConnell White May in 1820. He returned to the practice of law and to tutoring prospective new lawyers at his home, Travellers Rest, before turning his attention to his substantial business interests and to promoting Jackson's political career. Reputed to be one of the wealthiest men in Tennessee, Overton had long engaged in the slave trade and by 1819 had become leader of the powerful Blount-Overton political/banking organization. As head of the Nashville branch of Knoxville's Bank of the State of Tennessee, Overton and his fellow bankers opposed the resumption of specie payments and the adoption of small-debtor measures that followed the national depression triggered by the panic of 1819. Their opposition contributed to the landslide election of William Carroll, the anti-bank candidate for governor in 1821, and to the eventual closing of the Blount-Overton banks. As a founder of Memphis (1819) on land he owned with Jackson and General James Winchester, Overton devoted a substantial portion of his later years to promoting the new town's growth and development.

Whenever Jackson's interests were at stake, Overton was on hand to ensure that they were represented and protected, if not promoted. As a young lawyer, he handled legal and business matters for Jackson. In late 1821 or early 1822 Overton helped organize the Nashville Junto, a loose committee of Jackson's closest personal friends, to plan and promote the General's election to the presidency. In 1822 Overton joined with Felix Grundy and mobilized the Blount-Overton faction in the Tennessee General Assembly to nominate Jackson for president. Overton used his personal knowledge of the facts surrounding Jackson's controversial marriage to draft an effective brief defending Jackson against bitter personal attacks during the 1828 presidential campaign. Overton remained an intimate political advisor to Jackson throughout his first term as president. Although his resistance to Jackson's choice of Martin Van Buren as a running mate in 1832 concerned some of Jackson's other lieutenants, Overton was selected as chairman of the Baltimore convention to renominate the president. Ill health prevented his acceptance of the position.

Though independent and occasionally rebellious when it came to his relations with Jackson, Overton was viewed as a family member, and the two men remained close to the end. According to tradition, Overton's last words were of Jackson.

Theodore Brown, Jr., Atlanta, Georgia
SUGGESTED READINGS: Frances Clifton, "The Life and Activities of John Overton," M.A. thesis, Vanderbilt University, 1948; Henry L. Swint, "Travellers' Rest: Home of Judge John Overton," *Tennessee Historical Quarterly* 26(1967): 119–136
SEE: JACKSON, ANDREW; JACKSONIANS; LAW; MEMPHIS; SOUTHWEST TERRITORY; TRAVELLERS REST

OWSLEY, FRANK LAWRENCE (1890–1956) was a noted Vanderbilt University historian and apologist for the Old South. "The purpose of my life," he wrote to a colleague in 1932, "is to undermine . . . the entire Northern myth from 1820 to 1876." Only historians would read his books, he reasoned, "but it is the historians who teach history classes and write textbooks and they will gradually and without their knowledge be forced into our position."

The son of Lawrence Monroe Owsley and Annie Scott McGehee, he was born on his maternal grandparents' plantation near Montgomery, Alabama, and raised on a large farm where his father rented land to mostly black sharecroppers. In his youth, Owsley listened intently to aging Confederate veterans, absorbing from them a distaste for the Yankee colossus which overwhelmed the South in 1865.

Having earned a masters degree from Alabama Polytechnic Institute (now Auburn University) in 1916, he entered the University of Chicago to study under the southern historian William Edward Dodd. Although he appreciated Dodd as a teacher and shared with him an intense enthusiasm for southern history, Owsley resented his mentor's attacks upon the South's antebellum aristocracy. Awarded the doctorate in 1924, Owsley quickly emerged as a formidable scholar who eventually published three books, two textbooks, and 34 articles along with many book reviews and review essays.

Owsley began his teaching career at Birmingham-Southern College where he met and married Harriet Fason Chappell. He then joined the faculty at Vanderbilt University in 1920, remaining there until 1949 when he left to help establish the newly created Ph.D. program in history at the University of Alabama. Stimulating as a teacher and popular as a graduate professor, he directed almost 40 dissertations and powerfully influenced a generation of budding southern intellectuals.

A southern chauvinist, Owsley's career as a writer fell into three fairly defined periods. Throughout the first phase—bounded by his *State Rights and the Confederacy* in 1925 and *King Cotton Diplomacy* in 1931—he warned that southern defeat in 1865 and the South's continued subjugation in his own time resulted from internal divisions. He argued that throughout the Civil War white Southerners responded with enthusiasm to the crisis, won most of the military engagements, but in the end suffered defeat when their sacrifices were undermined by wrong-thinking domestic policies.

The second phase of Owsley's career began in 1930 and climaxed in 1940. Throughout this decade he campaigned against forces which he believed threatened southern culture: neo-abolitionist historians and northern industrialists, Communists, southern liberals, and blacks. He, along with 11 other southerner intellectuals, collaborated to produce *I'll Take My Stand* (1930), dedicating it to the support of "a Southern way of life against . . . the American or prevailing way." Owsley's essay, "The Irrepressible Conflict," condemned northern abolitionists and industrialists as hypocrites and Pharisees who campaigned to impose their corrupt culture upon an agrarian South. In one of his more controversial articles—"Scottsboro, the Third Crusade," published in the *American Review* of June 1933—Owsley castigated the defenders of nine alleged Negro rapists in Alabama as neo-abolitionists interfering with southern justice. These latter-day reformers, he proclaimed, fostered racial tension, promoted anarchy, and created fertile ground for the twentieth century cancer of communism. In 1940 he delivered his presidential address before the Southern Historical Association— "The Fundamental Cause of the Civil War: Egocentric Sectionalism." Once again he scourged the North, branding its politicians and publicists as aggressors forcing the South out of the Union in 1861.

Owsley commenced the third phase of his intellectual endeavors in 1936 by focusing on a project to present his idealized image of the Old South; it culminated in his classic work *Plain Folk of the Old South* (1949). He, his wife, and a coterie of graduate students gleaned archives to prove that the Old South was more a democracy supported by small farmers than an oligarchy dominated by a powerful aristocracy. He pioneered the use of the United States census as a valuable historical resource and documented from it that across the South small farmers resided in close association with the large planters. He overlooked, however, the censuses' economic data which showed the aristocrats' overwhelming economic domination; and he relied upon elite sources—county and local histories and the autobiographies of lawyers, physicians, and preachers— to portray the social fellowship of yeoman and planter. "The Southern folk . . . were a closely knit people," he thus concluded. "They were not class conscious in a Marxian sense, for with rare exception they did not regard the planters and men of wealth as their oppressors." Owsley suffered a fatal heart attack while researching in England; he died October 21, 1956. Across a distinguished career, his work retained a singular theme. Ending a lecture series presented to the University of Georgia's faculty and students in 1938, he relished their applause because in his words, "it was the *rebel yell* that I heard."
Fred Arthur Bailey, Abilene Christian University
SEE: AGRARIANS; VANDERBILT UNIVERSITY

OZONE FALLS STATE NATURAL AREA preserves a breathtaking 110-foot waterfall on the Cumberland Plateau near the village of Ozone in Cumberland County. The gorge of the falls features beautiful stands of hemlock, yellow birch, basswood, and magnolia trees. Recognized for many years as a scenic landmark along U.S. Highway 70, a portion of the original Memphis-to-Bristol Highway, a 14-acre state natural area was designated in the early 1970s and expanded significantly by 28 acres in 1996. Plans for new hiking trails, recreational facilities, and an additional route to the rear of the falls now are under development.
Carroll Van. West, Middle Tennessee State University
SEE: CUMBERLAND COUNTY; HIGHWAYS, HISTORIC

P

PAGE, BETTIE (1923–) has been immortalized in bronze sculpture, song lyrics, paintings, comic books, and enough tattoo ink to flood a swimming pool. As the many tributes testify, the Nashville native reigns as an American pop-culture icon. The 1950s pin-up queen was born the second of five children to Roy and Edna Page in Nashville, April 22, 1923. Bettie's early years were spent drifting throughout the South with her family as her father searched for employment. In 1933 Edna left Roy and moved back to Nashville, where she supported her children as a hairdresser.

Assessing her future possibilities, Bettie decided that education was her only means of escape from the poverty and instability she had known since birth. She excelled as a student at Hume-Fogg High School and graduated in 1940 as salutatorian, earning a scholarship to George Peabody College for Teachers. After graduating with a teaching degree, Page decided that profession was not for her. She began to travel, making a living with secretarial work in San Francisco, Miami Beach, Haiti, and New York.

At Coney Island in 1950, Page met amateur photographer Jerry Tibbs who took her first pin-up photographs and convinced her to cut her famous bangs. She began modeling for camera clubs part time, soon becoming a favorite of "gentlemen's magazines." The most infamous of Page's photographs were taken by Paula and Irving Klaw. Clad in leather, six-inch heels, metal cones, ball gags, or other fetish regalia, Bettie teased and spanked her way through hundreds of photo sessions and a few short films. After the Klaws were investigated in 1957 by a U.S. Senate subcommittee led by Tennessee's Estes Kefauver, Page left modeling. In 1959 the ex-pin-up devoted the rest of her life to the Christian faith. Bettie Page now lives quietly in California, declining offers to be photographed, adding to the mystique that attracts a new generation of admirers.

Brenda Colladay, Middle Tennessee State University
SUGGESTED READING: Bunny Yeager, *Betty Page Confidential* (1994)

PALEOINDIANS, TENNESSEE. We do not know exactly when the first people entered the "New World" from Asia. However, we do have confidence that they had reached what is now Tennessee at the end of the last Ice Age (the Pleistocene) some 13,000 years ago. These people, ancestors of all modern Native Americans, came in small family groups, of probably 25 to 50 individuals per group, and practiced a hunting and gathering way of life. This adaptation goes back many thousands of years in the Old World. It is believed, from archaeological evidence, that they primarily hunted the large game of the Pleistocene, especially extinct forms such as mammoth, mastodon, and the giant bison. Horse, camel, paleollama, and deer were probably exploited along with smaller animals and edible plants.

Individual Paleoindian groups consisted of two or three related families participating in a seasonal round of hunting and gathering based upon the movement of large animals within large expanses of territory. To date, there is scant record of the physical appearance of these people since skeletal remains are lacking. However, we do believe that general life span was relatively short, with most individuals not living beyond the age of around 40 years.

Evidence proving that Paleoindians occupied Tennessee is quite abundant. Recent archaeological investigations conducted by the Tennessee Division of Archaeology have recorded over 100 camps or archaeological sites associated with this time period. The earliest Paleoindian groups, called Clovis after the original find near the town of the same name in New Mexico, are well represented. Some of the largest Clovis camp sites in the United States have been recorded in the Western Valley of Tennessee. In fact, this area may be the most densely settled region during the Paleoindian period in the United States. An abundance of high quality chert (flint), used for making spearpoints and other tools, and the high density of large animals (megafauna) are thought to be the main reasons for this great number of Paleoindian sites in our state.

Recently, a kill/butchering site containing the remains of a mastodon was discovered in Middle Tennessee; it provided a date of over 13,000 years for an association of cut mastodon bones and stone tools from the site. This is one of the oldest dates for Paleoindians in the New World and is the first documented mastodon kill site in the Mid-South. Mammoth and giant bison kills have been recorded in the Southwest and Florida has produced evidence for several mastodon kill and butchering sites.

Paleoindian peoples thrived in the Tennessee area for at least 3,000 years until the end of the Pleistocene and the extinction of large megafauna at about 10,500 years ago. These groups quickly adapted to the ever-changing environment and became experts at the hunting of smaller game, especially deer, and expanded their use of new plant resources. This new adaptation has been called the Archaic period by archaeologists.

John B. Broster, Tennessee Department of Environment and Conservation
SEE: ARCHAIC PERIOD

PANTHER CREEK STATE PARK lies six miles west of Morristown in Hamblen County in East Tennessee. This 1,435-acre park features the recreational opportunities of Cherokee Lake, the reservoir created when the Tennessee Valley Authority built Cherokee Dam and dammed the Holston River in the 1940s. Water skiing, swimming, fishing, hiking, and picnicking are favorite activities at the park, which includes 50 campsites as well as numerous trails. Birdwatching also is popular since a 1,460-foot high ridge overview gives visitors a panoramic view of the lake and the valley. It is a popular place to observe migrating hawks and waterfowl.

The park is named for Panther Creek Springs, a landmark of the early settlement era along the Holston River Valley. The springs attracted generations of Native Americans long before the arrival of the first settlers, who allegedly named it Panther Creek Springs because one settler killed a panther there. The 1939 *WPA Guide to Tennessee* further noted that near the spring was "a rock with a depression in which early settlers ground corn into meal with the aid of a heavy pestle attached to a beam propelled by the current of the stream." This "'pounding mill' was slow, but it could be carried on without attention."(1)

At Tate's Store near the springs, commissioners met to establish Hamblen County in 1870. Today the springs still exist, but the rural village of Panther Creek is gone, with the park serving as a memorial to the early history of the Holston River Valley.

Carroll Van West, Middle Tennessee State University
CITATION:
(1) Federal Writers' Project, *WPA Guide to Tennessee* (New York, 1939), 302.
SEE: HAMBLEN COUNTY; TENNESSEE VALLEY AUTHORITY

PARDO EXPEDITION. On December 1, 1566, the third Spanish expedition into Tennessee commenced when Juan Pardo left Santa Elena on the South Carolina coast with 125 soldiers. Sent into the interior to further Spain's colonial ambitions and to relieve the food shortage in Santa Elena, Pardo traveled northward. At the eastern foot of the Blue Ridge Mountains he built a small stockade, Fort San Juan, at Joara near modern Marion, North Carolina. Pardo garrisoned the fort with 30 men under the command of Sergeant Hernando Moyano de Morales and then explored to the east of Joara before returning to Santa Elena in early March.

While stationed at Fort San Juan, Moyano aided a local chief by taking 15 soldiers and a force of warriors to attack a rival Chisca town, burning the houses and killing many of the inhabitants. Later Moyano received a threat from a "mountain chief," presumably a Chisca in the vicinity of the Upper Nolichucky River in eastern Tennessee. Moyano responded by attacking a strongly defended settlement with 20 men and perhaps native allies. Two of Hernando de Soto's men had contacted the Chiscas in this area some 27 years earlier.

Moyano then explored the Upper Tennessee Valley for four days for precious metals and gems before arriving at the palisaded main town of Chiaha on Zimmerman's Island in the French Broad River near present-day Dandridge, Tennessee. This town had been visited previously by the Hernando de Soto and Tristán de Luna expeditions. While at Chiaha Moyano's men were well fed and well treated. Moyano explored the area around Chiaha and built a small fort on the island.

Pardo departed Santa Elena for the interior again on September 1, 1567, with approximately 120 soldiers, harquebusiers, and crossbowmen. Arriving at Fort San Juan, he learned that the Chiahans had confined Moyano and his men to their fort. On his way to relieve Moyano at Chiaha, Pardo stopped at the fortified town of Tanasqui on the French Broad River on October 6. The land around Tanasqui reminded the Spaniards of Andalucia. Proceeding down the French Broad River the next day, they reached Olamico, the fortified principal town of Chiaha. There Pardo found Moyano and his men safe, but restricted to their fort. The Spaniards were impressed with the rich, broad alluvial land at Chiaha and referred to it as a *tierra de Angeles*—a land of angels.

After resting at Olamico for five days, Pardo struck out for Coosa, passing through several towns. On October 14 the Spaniards saw the highest mountains yet seen during their explorations—the Great Smoky Mountains. At the town of Satapo, near the junction of Citico Creek and the Little Tennessee River, Pardo was warned of a plot forged by the chief of Coosa and his Upper Tennessee Valley allies. The Coosas planned to ambush the Spaniards as they traveled from Chiaha to Coosa. To avoid an attack Pardo returned to Olamico and strengthened the island fort. Pardo and company continued on to Santa Elena, arriving there on March 2, 1568.

David H. Dye, University of Memphis

SUGGESTED READING: Charles Hudson, *The Juan Pardo Expeditions: Exploration of the Carolinas and Tennessee, 1566–1568* (1990)

SEE: EXPLORATIONS, EARLY; LUNA EXPEDITION; SOTO EXPEDITION

PARIS LANDING STATE RESORT PARK, located along the western shore of Kentucky Lake (the dammed Tennessee River) in Henry County, contains 841 acres and is a major recreational spot for northwest Tennessee. Located across Kentucky Lake from the Land Between the Lakes recreational area, Paris Landing was once a steamboat landing in the age of river transportation along the Tennessee. Today it is a modern park, featuring a large and modern marina, a facility designed for both sportsmen and recreational boaters. The park also has a restaurant, modern resort inn, with 100 rooms, and ten cabins. The park's 18-hole, 6,800-yard golf course is well regarded. Other recreational features include two swimming pools, campsites, hiking trails, tennis courts, game areas, and picnic grounds.

Carroll Van West, Middle Tennessee State University

SEE: HENRY COUNTY; LAND BETWEEN THE LAKES

THE PARTHENON in Nashville is the world's only exact-size replica of the original temple in Athens, Greece. For the Tennessee Centennial Exposition, Nashville drew upon its nickname "Athens of the South" and built the art building as a copy of the most famous example of Greek classical architecture. The Parthenon crystallized for Nashvillians their image of themselves and their city, and although all the buildings of the Centennial were built to be temporary, they were loathe to tear it down at the conclusion of the exposition. The exterior coating, sculpture, and decorative work, made of plaster, soon deteriorated. After repeated patching kept destruction at bay for several years, the city, with the involvement of local architect Russell Hart and archi-

tectural historian William Bell Dinsmoor, decided in 1920 to rebuild the Parthenon in lasting materials.

The roof, expanded walls, and load-bearing columns were made of reinforced concrete, the novel new building material of the twentieth century; the brick walls and non-load-bearing columns of the 1897 building were retained and incorporated into the new construction. For the permanent surface treatment Hart selected a cast concrete aggregate, taken from a formula by John Earley of Washington, D.C., for all exterior surfaces as well as the roof tiles, decorative work, and sculpture. The firm of Foster and Creighton served as general contractors. Sculptor George Julian Zolnay, creator of the pedimental sculptures on the 1897 Parthenon, returned to make the metopes of the Doric frieze, and Nashville sculptor Belle Kinney and her husband Leopold Scholz created the permanent pediment figures. To assist them in creating figures as close to the original as possible, the Park Board purchased from the British Museum a set of casts of the original marble fragments. Work on the exterior of the building was completed by 1925.

The interior of the Parthenon built for the Centennial was a series of galleries for exhibiting the enormous collection of paintings and sculptures borrowed from Europe and throughout the United States for the exposition. The permanent structure's interior, however, was to be a complete replica and as accurate as scholarship would allow. Due to various financial crises, work continued haltingly until completed in 1931. When the doors were opened to the public, two major elements were still missing: the great statue of Athena in the naos and the Ionic frieze on the exterior. Donations for the Athena accumulated over the years and in 1982 the Park Board commissioned Nashville sculptor Alan LeQuire to recreate the 42-foot statue for the interior, a task that took almost eight years. Its unveiling on May 20, 1990, generated excitement and renewal of interest in the Nashville Parthenon as an icon of the city.

Wesley Paine, The Parthenon

SUGGESTED READING: Christine M. Kreyling, et al., *Classical Nashville: Athens of the South* (1996)

SEE: KINNEY, BELLE; LEQUIRE, ALAN; TENNESSEE CENTENNIAL EXPOSITION

PARTON, DOLLY (1946–) emerged from a childhood of grim mountain poverty with formidable singing and songwriting talents which she forged first into Nashville country music fame and then into international stardom. While some of her writing strains unnecessarily for approval, most Parton songs—and all of her best ones—are rich, authentic distillations of life and culture in the upland South. Astonishingly prolific, Parton had published over 500 compositions by 1994, supplying career-enhancing material for many performers besides herself. Of course, Parton is much more than a songsmith; she is a skilled stylist whose gently vibrating, flute-like soprano shimmers and enchants.

Beyond these gifts, Parton has always cultivated a striking public presence. From the start she molded her fine-boned face, flawless complexion, and voluptuous hourglass figure into a larger-than-life display involving skin-tight costumes, gravity-defying high heels, blonde wigs of epic abundance, and lavishly applied cosmetics. Not even Hollywood could much amend her hillbilly melding of Daisy May and Mae West into what one journalist has called the "quintessential truck-stop fantasy." Parton shrewdly welcomes the publicity her appearance invites, but she preempts parody or criticism with self-deprecating humor, a disarming smile, and a just-us-girls giggle. She also carries off her frank celebration of physical attributes with feisty, forthright talk which withers any notion that she is vulnerable or available for exploitation.

Dolly Rebecca Parton was born in Sevier County on January 19, 1946, the fourth of 12 children. Through determined labor, her sharecropping parents eventually wrested the wherewithal to buy their own small farm. By all accounts, the Partons kept their children clothed, washed, and fed, but there was little comfort, no abundance. To escape this harshness, Dolly Parton relied on daydreams—especially the fantasy that she would become a famous singer. She composed her first song when she was about five years old.

Parton's maternal uncles and aunts, the musically talented Owens family, helped her realize her dream. Through their efforts, she was by age ten a regular radio and television performer in Knoxville, and she cut her first single when she was 12. Oblivious to stringent rules concerning membership and performance schedules, an Owens uncle hustled her on stage for her first Grand Ole Opry appearance when she was just 13. As a result, Parton was exceptionally well seasoned as a writer and performer of songs by 1964, when she graduated from high school and moved to Nashville.

During the mid-1960s country music was still a man's world. Despite her easily won affiliations with Mercury and Monument Records, two years passed before Parton's work received much notice. Her chance arrived when Bill Phillips recorded her tune *Put It Off Until Tomorrow*. Parton herself sang an uncredited backup of which disc jockeys made a popular mystery: who possessed this enthralling voice? Encouraged, Monument Records promoted her 1966 recording of Curly Putnam's *Dumb Blonde*. It became a top-ten hit and drew the attention of Porter Wagoner, an Opry mainstay and host of his own nationally syndicated television show. Wagoner hired

Parton as the new "girl singer" in his act. This, along with Wagoner's help arranging an RCA contract, were critical breaks in her career. Between 1968 and 1975 Parton enjoyed weekly appearances on the Porter Wagoner Show and a prolific studio career. She recorded 22 popular solo albums, plus 13 exceptionally successful albums with Wagoner. Many still regard Wagoner and Parton as among the best man-woman singing partners in country music history. Solo and duet albums alike were dominated by Parton's own poetic and gutsy explorations of traditional southern themes, including such classics as *Jolene, Coat of Many Colors,* and *Daddy Was An Old-Time Preacher Man.*

During her years with Wagoner, Parton won a dazzling array of music awards as well as membership in the Grand Ole Opry. Still she felt real stardom—and control of her own affairs—eluded her so long as she was confined to a partnership. With difficulty she broke free of Wagoner, and then spent two years experimenting with new back-up musicians, managers, and touring schedules. Though the Country Music Association named her Female Vocalist of the Year in 1975 and 1976, Parton was nearing exhaustion, certain that the price of promoting her reputation on the road was too high, and convinced that her record sales, while substantial by Nashville standards, would never provide real financial freedom. She thus hatched the idea of aiming her talents at the West Coast.

In the teeth of Nashville's disapproval, Parton signed with a Los Angeles promoter who severed her remaining ties to Porter Wagoner, arranged for her to host a weekly television show, and encouraged her to record an album friendly to pop-music fans. The television show mercifully lasted but one season and included only two redeeming episodes. One with guests Linda Ronstadt and Emmylou Harris forecast the significant *Trio* album. The other with Kenny Rogers launched a series of popular duo appearances and the hit single *Islands in the Stream.*

Parton's attempt to cross over to pop airplay was, by contrast, a genuine triumph. The 1977 album *Here You Come Again* went gold and generated three hits, including the title song. Parton frankly acknowledged that this record was far "slicker" than she had initially planned, but it brought her a larger, more diverse audience. There ensued guest appearances on national and cable television, invitations to perform in Las Vegas, and five starring movie roles. Collectively these venues gave Parton the resources and fame of her childhood dreams.

In the early 1980s, Parton began to talk of founding her own theme park at Pigeon Forge in Sevier County. By 1985 she had arranged a partnership that allowed her to enlarge, elaborate, and rename an old park called Silver Dollar City into Dollywood, which is now among the 25 most visited parks in the country. The park offers safe, controlled proximity to a southern hillbilly culture which has simultaneously intrigued and alienated Americans for over a century. Americans have long imagined and depicted the mountain South as a physically daunting landscape populated by a primitive, shiftless, and clannish sort of people. Yet when railroads first made Appalachia accessible, industrial entrepreneurs rushed to take advantage of its resources: timber, coal, copper, and an ostensibly jobless workforce. It is both ironic and fitting that Dollywood devolves from this exploitation.

Today Dolly Parton is a unique superstar, the only female performer of her particular background and talents to move with ease in the most glamorous of show-biz circles. She uses her "Professional Personality" role to promote such other-than-musical commodities as cosmetics and lingerie, but she remains a musician of undiminished power. Since *Trio* appeared in 1987 she has returned to Tennessee for most of her recording. Her latest releases include *Honky Tonk Angels,* a celebration of her Nashville heritage with fellow Opry veterans Loretta Lynn and Tammy Wynette. *Heartsongs: Live from Home* confirms her enduring ties to East Tennessee's rugged landscape. The title of her new autobiography, *My Life and Other Unfinished Business,* suggests what she has also asserted crisply in a recent interview: in her fiftieth year, Dolly Parton has no intention of "going out to pasture." No one imagined she did.

Camille Wells, University of Virginia

SEE: DOLLYWOOD; GRAND OLE OPRY; MUSIC; SEVIER COUNTY

THE PATRONS OF HUSBANDRY or Grange was the first general farm organization in the United States. Established by the Minnesota agricultural reformer Oliver H. Kelly in December 1867, it briefly flourished in Tennessee during the 1870s, providing Tennessee's small farmers with opportunities for economic, political, and social expression.

The Grange movement addressed the needs of Tennessee's small farmers in the turbulent decade immediately following the Civil War. While the state's aristocratic class felt some economic discomfort, its common folk suffered more. Mostly subsistence farmers prior to the war, they had cherished their social and economic independence, but in 1865 many returned to find their farms in tatters. Desperate to rebuild their shattered lives, Tennessee's small farmers suffered the indignity of dependence upon the wealthy planters' mercantile establishments for credit and for the opportunity to purchase seed, farm stock, and agricultural implements at inflated prices. Their plight was further exasperated by profit-hungry railroads whose high freight rates threatened the small farmers with ruin.

Tennessee's first local grange was established at Stockton in 1870, and as late as 1872 there were only four chapters. On July 2, 1873, representatives from 40 local granges convened to form a state organization, electing William Maxwell of Dyer County as Worthy Master of the State Grange. Thereafter it grew at a phenomenal rate. By October the number of granges had increased to 86 and continued to multiply: November 1873—215 granges; January 1874—350; May 1874—823. The movement peaked during the spring of 1875 with 1,050 granges and 37,500 adherents. Tennessee ranked third behind Kentucky and Texas in total membership. Two of Tennessee's more important agricultural papers—*The Rural Sun* (Nashville) and *The Southern Farmer* (Memphis)—promoted the Patrons of Husbandry, and the movement spawned its own journals: *The Southern Husbandman* (Nashville), *The Southern Granger* (Memphis), *The Patrons of Husbandry* (Memphis), *The American Farmers' Advocate* (Jackson), *The Grange Journal* (Humbolt), and *The Grange Outlook* (Knoxville).

Desperate to break the common farmers' dependence upon local merchants, Tennessee's state leaders negotiated with independent agents who offered grange members implements, seed, and machinery at discounts from 10 to 37 percent. This soon led to the establishment of grange-sponsored cooperative stores throughout the state, and in 1876 to the formation of the Southwestern Co-operative Association underwritten by the state granges of Tennessee, Arkansas, Mississippi, and Louisiana.

As a political movement, the Tennessee grange urged the General Assembly to broaden educational opportunities. Tennessee's aristocratic class had long retarded public education, preferring a private system in which only the wealthy secured sufficient knowledge to control the state's weal. The Patrons of Husbandry demanded educational reform, the expansion and improvement of the public schools system, and the implementation of a curriculum that would embrace their needs as farmers. Although Mississippi and Texas grangers strongly influenced the establishment of their states' agricultural and mechanical colleges, Tennessee grangers were less successful because the chief architect of the University of Tennessee'e agricultural college—Knoxville attorney Oliver Perry Temple—was a fervent opponent of their movement.

Tennessee's Patrons of Husbandry also campaigned for railroad reform. Seeking a fair deal from the companies, the Tennessee grange had modest success negotiating with local railroads for reduced rates, but failed in its effort to secure from the Tennessee General Assembly legislation regulating the industry.

In Tennessee, as elsewhere, the Patrons of Husbandry promoted a better social environment for the farmer and his family. Rural life was lonely and monotonous, and social opportunities provided by local granges offered an escape from the routine, humdrum existence. Picnics, barbecues, and other activities gave hours of pleasure to a people locked in the eternal cycle of planting, cultivating, and harvesting.

Tennessee's grange movement experienced only a brief period of success. Scandals associated with its commission agents and its cooperative stores, and the lack of political sophistication possessed by the state's small farmers, undermined its popularity. Early in 1876 it underwent a sudden decline and by 1877 it ceased to be an effective organization. Although a failure, it was nonetheless important. It constructed a pattern for such future agricultural associations as the Southern Farmers' Alliance and the Populist Party movement. It trained young farm leaders who in the 1880s and the 1890s would challenge Tennessee's and the South's aristocratic establishment.

Fred Arthur Bailey, Abilene Christian University

SEE: AGRICULTURAL WHEEL; AGRICULTURE; FARMERS' ALLIANCE; TEMPLE, OLIVER P.

PATTEN, ZEBOIM CARTTER (1840–1925), prominent Chattanooga industrialist and capitalist, was born in Wilna, New York, and educated at Lawville Academy. During the Civil War, he served with the 115th Illinois Infantry and the 149th New York Infantry regiments. Patten first saw Chattanooga while convalescing from wounds suffered in the Battle of Chickamauga. After the war, he and another veteran, T.H. Payne, returned to the city and opened Patten and Payne, a book and stationery store. A few years afterward, Patten sold his interests in the store and purchased *The Chattanooga Times*.

In 1879, with the profits from his previous businesses, Patten and a group of friends founded the Chattanooga Medicine Company to manufacture patent medicines. The first two products, Black-Draught and Wine of Cardui, proved so successful they became the backbone of the company's prosperity for many years. In addition to his skill in selecting products, Patten possessed remarkable marketing imagination. He is remembered for the creation and distribution of the popular Cardui calendar and the *Ladies Birthday Almanac*.

In 1903 Patten became president of the Stone Fort Land Company, which owned and developed commercial property in downtown Chattanooga, including the city's first high-rise building, the Hotel Patten. In 1906 Patten and his son-in-law, John Thomas Lupton, founded the Volunteer State Life Insurance Company, an important regional financial institution.

He was a founding director of the American Trust and Banking Company (later American National, now SunTrust); a founder and chairman of First Trust and Savings Bank; an organizer of Title Guaranty and Trust Company; and developer of the Acme Furniture Company.

Patten and his first wife, Mary Rawlings, who died young, had one daughter, Elizabeth Olive Patten Lupton. In 1901 he married Sarah Key, daughter of David M. Key, judge, former U.S. Senator, and Postmaster General. The couple had one son, Z. Cartter Patten, Jr., who became a noted environmentalist, local historian, and long-time state legislator. The elder Patten died at his estate, Ashland, and is buried in Forest Hills Cemetery, Chattanooga.

Ned L. Irwin, East Tennessee State University

SUGGESTED READING: John Wilson, *The Patten Chronicle—A Chattanooga Family* (1986)

SEE: CHATTANOOGA; CHATTANOOGA MEDICINE COMPANY; CHATTANOOGA TIMES; LUPTON, JOHN T.

PATTERSON FORGE (NARROWS OF THE HARPETH STATE HISTORICAL AREA) was constructed at the neck of an unusual bend of the Harpeth River where, after approximately four miles, the stream channel returns to within 200 yards of itself. Around 1818 Montgomery Bell purchased the site, which at the time was in Davidson County. Soon after, African-American slaves under Bell's direction began excavating a tunnel through a 100-yard wide rock ridge that separated the river beds. Designed to convey water for power, the tunnel was completed by 1820. Following a failed effort to sell the site to the United States government for construction of an armory, Bell erected a forge for the production of wrought iron, using pig iron from regional blast furnaces.

Montgomery Bell owned and operated Patterson Forge from 1832 to 1854. After this, James L. Bell ran the operation until about 1862, when it was closed during the Civil War. The forge was not reopened after the Civil War, because the iron industry in Tennessee, in general, remained depressed. In the 1880s a grist mill was established on the site to take advantage of the water power provided by the tunnel.

Today the Cheatham County site of Patterson Forge is part of the Narrows of the Harpeth State Historic Area maintained by the Tennessee Department of Environment and Conservation. The site and the nearby grave of Montgomery Bell are silent reminders of one of Tennessee's important early industries.

Samuel D. Smith, Tennessee Division of Archaeology

SUGGESTED READING: Robert E. Dalton, "Montgomery Bell and the Narrows of the Harpeth," *Tennessee Historical Quarterly* 35(1976): 3–28

SEE: BELL, MONTGOMERY; CHEATHAM COUNTY; INDUSTRY

PATTERSON, MALCOLM R.

PATTERSON, MALCOLM R. (1861–1935), one of the most controversial governors in Tennessee's history, was born in Memphis June 7, 1861, the son of Colonel Josiah Patterson, a prominent local attorney. Patterson attended Christian Brothers College and Vanderbilt University, then read law at his father's firm. In 1884 he was named attorney general of the criminal court at Memphis, a position which he held for six years. In 1900 Patterson entered the political arena and won a seat in the U.S. House of Representatives. In 1907 he was elected Governor of Tennessee, unseating the incumbent John Isaac Cox.

As governor, Patterson proved to be a competent, albeit uninspiring administrator. He oversaw creation of the State Highway Commission and led a movement for improvements in public education. Perhaps his finest moment occurred in 1909, when he quelled an uprising by the Night Riders of Reelfoot Lake, a West Tennessee vigilante group. Patterson's swift and decisive action earned him praise across the state and helped him win a second term in office.

Patterson's popularity, however, was short lived and he soon found himself mired in controversy. Many of the governor's problems arose from his seemingly inconsistent stand towards prohibition. Though Patterson pledged to support temperance during his 1907 race, he reversed his position in 1909 by vetoing a popular bill prohibiting liquor sales within four miles of a school. Though the legislature subsequently overrode the veto, it angered temperance supporters, who labeled Patterson a turncoat.

Patterson was also criticized for his liberal policy regarding pardons. In his four years in office, he pardoned over 1,400 criminals. Critics, including many law enforcement officials, accused the governor of releasing felons for partisan purposes. Though he vigorously denied such charges, Patterson was branded a machine politician and an obstacle to reform.

Patterson's association with Duncan Brown Cooper ultimately doomed his political career. Cooper, editor of the *Nashville American* and a close advisor to the governor, was engaged in a running feud with rival editor and prohibitionist leader Edward Ward Carmack. In November, 1908, Cooper and his son, Robin, encountered an armed Carmack on a Nashville street. A gunfight ensued and Robin Cooper killed Carmack. Although Patterson had worked to prevent such bloodshed, some prohibitionists accused the governor of complicity in the shooting.

Such rumors intensified in 1910 when Patterson pardoned both Duncan and Robin Cooper for their role in the shooting. Prohibitionists, already angry at Patterson for his 1909 veto, openly charged the governor with conspiring to assassinate their martyred leader. Wild tales of intrigue dogged Patterson and the controversy bitterly divided the state's Democratic party. Finding himself a pariah among many voters, Patterson declined to run for a third term and retired from politics in 1911. He returned to his home in Memphis and resumed his legal practice. He died there in 1935, his achievements clouded by his contentious past.

Timothy P. Ezzell, Knoxville

SUGGESTED READING: Paul E. Isaac, *Prohibition and Politics: Turbulent Decades in Tennessee, 1885–1920* (1965)

SEE: CARMACK, EDWARD W.; COOPER V. STATE; NIGHT RIDERS OF REELFOOT LAKE; TEMPERANCE MOVEMENT

PATTON, MARY MCKEEHAN

PATTON, MARY MCKEEHAN (1751–1836), pioneer gunpowder manufacturer, was born in England in 1751 and immigrated with her family to Pennsylvania in the late 1760s. McKeehan served an apprenticeship, possibly under her father, David McKeehan, and learned the art of gunpowder making. In 1772 she married John Patton, an Irish immigrant, who served as a private in the Pennsylvania militia early in the American Revolution.

The Pattons manufactured gunpowder in the Cumberland County region of Pennsylvania. Following the birth of two children, the couple sold their Carlisle powder mill for cash and migrated to the Overmountain region of North Carolina, now East Tennessee. With the help of family friend Andrew Taylor, they established a mill on what became known as Powder Branch, adjacent to the Taylor homeplace.

Mary McKeehan Patton earned her place in history by providing over 500 pounds of gunpowder to the 850 Overmountain Men led by Isaac Shelby and William Campbell for the Revolutionary War battle of King's Mountain. Essential to the victory over Major Patrick Ferguson's British troops was Patton's gunpowder. After the war, Patton continued to make and deliver gunpowder.

On December 15, 1836, Mary Patton died and was buried in Patton-Simmons Cemetery near Sycamore Shoals, Tennessee. The family tradition of gunpowder manufacturing continued until after the Civil War, when the powder mill was sold.

Susan M. Goodsell, Plano, Illinois

SUGGESTED READING: Robert A. Howard and E. Alvin Gerhardt, Jr., *Mary Patton: Powder Maker of the Revolution* (1980)

SEE: CARTER COUNTY; OVERMOUNTAIN MEN

PEABODY EDUCATION FUND IN TENNESSEE

PEABODY EDUCATION FUND IN TENNESSEE (1867–1914). Shocked by reports and letters about the South's Civil War devastation, George Peabody (1795–1869) founded the $2 million Peabody Education Fund (PEF, 1867–1914) to aid public education in 11 former Confederate states and West Virginia. Born in Massachusetts but a merchant in the South, he became an international banker in London (1837–69) and a philanthropist.

The war-devastated South lacked the means or will to establish public schools. First PEF general agent Barnas Sears, distinguished New England educator, used limited resources as a lever to help achieve tax-supported public schools. PEF-aided schools had to meet ten months a year and have at least one teacher per 50 pupils. PEF grants required that local citizens more than match PEF funds and that laws for tax-supported public schools be enacted.

Sears urged a state normal school (for teacher training) in Nashville as a model for the South. But state normal school legislation continually failed in the Tennessee legislature over the next six years. Rather than lose Nashville as a normal school site, Sears said that if University of Nashville trustees gave land and buildings for a normal school, the PEF would contribute $6,000 annually. The Tennessee legislature amended the University of Nashville's charter. The new State Normal School, financed by PEF's annual grant of $6,000, opened December 1, 1875, and was renamed Peabody Normal College (1889–1909).

Disappointed when the legislature refused to subsidize Peabody Normal College in 1877 and 1879, Sears considered moving Peabody Normal College to Georgia. This threat prompted Nashville citizens in April 1880 to guarantee $6,000 annually. From 1881 to 1905 the General Assembly's appropriations for Peabody Normal College totaled $429,000. In contrast, the Peabody Education Fund trustees gave $555,730 from 1875 to 1909.

In its first 30 years (1868 through 1897) the PEF gave the 11 former Confederate states and West Virginia a total of $2,478,000 to advance public schools, teacher institutes, and normal schools. Tennessee received about nine percent of this total, second highest after Virginia. Additionally the PEF enriched Tennessee with Peabody Normal College (and successor institutions). Besides its regular tuition-paying students, Peabody Normal College enrolled 3,645 higher qualified teacher candidates through PEF-financed Peabody Scholarships (1877–1904), which brought the college and Tennessee an additional $398,690.88. Educators trained at Peabody Normal College became educational leaders throughout the South and gave Peabody in Tennessee a national reputation.

Allowed to disband after 30 years, the PEF gave $1.5 million to transform Peabody Normal College into George Peabody College for Teachers. Former Governor James D. Porter (1828–1912), who had been Peabody Normal College's third president (1901–09), helped raise PEF-required matching funds from Nashville, Davidson County, and other Tennessee sources. The new George Peabody College for Teach-

ers was built opposite Vanderbilt University. In 1979 it became Peabody College of Vanderbilt University.

Amid post–Civil War chaos, the PEF financially encouraged state efforts in advancing public schools. By creating in Nashville a model professional teachers college, it helped produce educational leaders who became college and university presidents, deans, scholars, educational writers, and master teachers for Tennessee, the South, and the nation.

Franklin and Betty J. Parker, Pleasant Hill

SEE: EDUCATION, HIGHER; GEORGE PEABODY COLLEGE OF VANDERBILT UNIVERSITY

PEABODY HOTEL. In 1935 David Cohn wrote that "the Mississippi Delta begins in the lobby of the Peabody Hotel and ends on Catfish Row in Vicksburg." Since its opening on September 2, 1925, the Peabody Hotel has been the place to be seen for wealthy and fashionable society in Memphis and the Mississippi River Delta area of West Tennessee, eastern Arkansas, and northern Mississippi. Chicago architect Walter Ahlschlager was the hotel's designer. Terra cotta cornices and balustrades decorate the exterior, and the interior recalls a Spanish hunting lodge. The centerpiece of the two-story lobby is a large fountain carved from a single block of travertine marble, the home of the famous Peabody ducks. They have paddled there since 1932, when hotel manager Frank Schutt returned from a hunting trip and put some live ducks in the fountain. The twice-daily duck march has become a Memphis tradition, as visitors flock to see the Peabody's most famous residents waddle from elevator to fountain across a red carpet. The fantastic quality of the Peabody extends from the lobby to the top floor, which features an Art Deco skyway, a circular dancefloor, and a roof garden.

After a period of declining fortunes in the wake of World War II, this National Register-listed hotel underwent a major rehabilitation in 1980, injecting new life into downtown Memphis and reestablishing the Peabody as a Southern institution and one of America's grand city hotels.

Blythe Semmer, Middle Tennessee State University

SEE: MEMPHIS

PEARSON, JOSEPHINE ANDERSON (1868–1944), leader of the anti-suffrage movement in Tennessee during the 1920 fight for ratification of the Nineteenth Amendment, was born in Gallatin. Pearson grew up in McMinnville where she graduated from Irving College in 1890. She received her masters degree in 1896 from Cumberland College and held several teaching and administrative positions across the state. In 1895 she was appointed as a commissioner to the Woman's Board of the Tennessee Centennial Exposition. Pearson in the early twentieth century participated in the organization of the Dixie Highway

Council of the Cumberland Divide. As president of its women's auxiliary, Pearson lobbied for federal funds to be used for the building of this highway.

Pearson received her greatest recognition as president of and speaker for the Tennessee State Association Opposed to Woman Suffrage and the Southern Woman's League for the Rejection of the Susan B. Anthony Amendment. When Governor Albert Roberts called a special session of the Tennessee General Assembly to ratify the amendment in 1920 , Pearson came to Nashville and worked actively during July and August to defeat the amendment. Pearson established her headquarters at the Hermitage Hotel and lobbied legislators to vote against ratification. When the amendment was ratified, Pearson accepted the deanship of the Southern Seminary of Virginia where she also taught history and philosophy. Pearson lectured throughout the South and wrote numerous articles and books until her death in 1944. She is buried in the Monteagle Cemetery.

Carole Stanford Bucy, Volunteer State Community College
SEE: DIXIE HIGHWAY ASSOCIATION; HERMITAGE HOTEL; WOMAN SUFFRAGE MOVEMENT

PEAY, AUSTIN (1876–1927), a successful and progressive governor during the 1920s, was perhaps best known as the governor who signed the infamous Butler (anti-evolution) Bill into law. Through administrative reorganization and advocation of reform-minded legislation, Peay influenced the state during the four and one-half years as governor more so than any other governor of his era. By the time of his death, Peay had completely reorganized state government, improved the tax system, reformed education, expanded and improved the road system, established Tennessee's first state park, and assured the establishment of the Great Smoky Mountains National Park. Although his policies benefited most Tennesseans, Peay focused his efforts on reviving stagnant agriculture and improving the quality of rural life.

When Peay took office in 1923, he inherited the leadership of a state over three million dollars in debt, and ranked near the bottom in per capita expenditures for government services. Tennessee's educational system ranked last in teacher salaries and forty-third in per-pupil expenditure; adult illiteracy was high. The state had only 244 miles of paved state highways, and bridges spanned few of its major rivers. State appropriations often ended up in the pockets of county courthouse gangs and were funded by a property tax which unfairly weighed on Tennessee's depressed farming community.

Peay began his administration with improvements for the notoriously inefficient state government. Prior to Peay, Tennessee's governors exercised little power, other than the veto, and maintained little

Governor Austin Peay.

TSLA. PORTRAIT BY WILLIE BETTY NEWMAN

control over the bureaucracy they ostensibly supervised. In 1923 Peay pushed through the Administrative Reorganization Act, which gave the governor hiring and firing power over the executive branch bureaucrats, greater control over the state budget, and reorganized administrative agencies to make them more professional and efficient. He sought an end to the wasteful expenditure of state money and developed a reputation as a budget watchdog.

Peay also tackled Tennessee's antiquated and inequitable revenue system. Most of the state's revenue came from a property tax that produced inadequate funds for state expenditures. The governor pressed for legislation providing for new sales taxes on gasoline (for road building) and on tobacco products (for education). With new revenues from these taxes, automobile license fees, and short-term bonds, Peay cut the property tax and expanded government services. At the same time, due to new efficiency measures, the state's three million dollars deficit turned into a $1.2 million surplus.

Peay's next challenge was to improve Tennessee's roads and its educational system. Under Peay, more than half of the state's total expenditures went to road projects. By the time of his death in 1927, Tennessee's system of paved roads had expanded from 244 miles to over 4,000 miles, with a paved highway connecting Memphis and Bristol, four paved routes that crossed the state north to south, and 17 new bridges over major rivers. In education, Peay sponsored legislation that established a state salary schedule, standardized licensing requirements for teachers, and created an equalization fund that guaranteed an eight-month school year in most public elementary schools. He also greatly increased funding for the University of Tennessee, which he justified as an aid to the Tennessee farmer. His efforts produced a new agricultural junior college at Martin (now the University of Tennessee at Martin) and a teachers' college at Clarksville (now Austin Peay State University), and pushed through a one million dollar appropriation for rural school construction.

Peay took the lead in promoting public health and conservation. He professionalized the State Department of Health and more than doubled the department's budget for public immunization and for sanitation and disease control. Under the governor's leadership, the legislature created the first state park at Reelfoot Lake and passed a two million dollar bond bill for the purchase of land for the Great Smoky Mountains National Park.

Peay accomplished his reforms with a legislature that often fought him at every turn and only met for a 75-day biennial session. In his last term, he struggled with the Crump machine of Memphis (which viewed him as a potential political threat to U.S. Senator Kenneth McKellar). Crump's supporters allied with business interests that opposed much of Peay's program and with country politicians who lost power with the centralization of state government. The Democratic party was split into pro-administration and anti-administration factions. Despite these problems, his considerable political skills and his reputation for fairness and integrity made Governor Austin Peay an effective chief executive.

Dan Pierce, Western Carolina University

SUGGESTED READINGS: David D. Lee, *Tennessee in Turmoil: Politics in the Volunteer State, 1920–1932* (1979); Joseph T. Macpherson, "Democratic Progressivism in Tennessee: The Administrations of Governor Austin Peay, 1923–1927," *East Tennessee Historical Society Publications* 40(1968): 50–61

SEE: AUSTIN PEAY STATE UNIVERSITY; CRUMP, EDWARD H.; GREAT SMOKY MOUNTAINS NATIONAL PARK; HIGHWAYS, HISTORIC; REELFOOT LAKE STATE PARK; UNIVERSITY OF TENNESSEE AT MARTIN

PERKINS, CARL LEE (1932–1998), the son of Tiptonville, Tennessee, sharecroppers, was Sun Record's first certified million-selling artist. Perkins began his musical career by forming The Perkins Brothers— Jackson, Tennessee's hottest honky-tonk group. The trio featured Carl as lead singer and songwriter, older brother Jay on rhythm guitar, and younger brother Clayton on guitar.

Through Clayton, Carl Perkins befriended Johnny Cash. Cash, who later hired Perkins to become part of his road show and eponymously-titled ABC-TV series, inspired Perkins's signature song, *Blue Suede Shoes*. Perkins and Elvis Presley were well acquainted long before Presley made *Blue Suede Shoes* a hit song.

Perkins lost the momentum of his early success when, en route to New York for his network television debut on *The Perry Como Show,* he was seriously injured in an automobile accident at Dover, Delaware. None of Perkins' subsequent hits, including *Honey Don't, Boppin' the Blues,* and *Matchbox,* proved as popular as *Blue Suede Shoes*. Nevertheless, Perkins's fans include a number of internationally known music stars, who attribute their own musical style to his influence. The late Ricky Nelson, the Beatles, and the Stray Cats have been among his admiring peers.

Carl Perkins and his wife, Valda, are the parents of three sons and a daughter, resided in Jackson, Tennessee, when not recording and touring. In 1991 the city honored the singer with the establishment of the Exchange Club Carl Perkins Center for the Prevention of Child Abuse. Perkins died January 19, 1998 and is buried in Ridgecrest Cemetery in Jackson.

Stacy Harris, Nashville

SEE: JACKSON; LAKE COUNTY; MEMPHIS MUSIC SCENE; PHILLIPS, SAM; ROCKABILLY

PERRY COUNTY was created by an act of the Tennessee General Assembly on November 14, 1819. It was named for Commodore Oliver Hazard Perry, a naval officer and hero of the War of 1812. The first quarterly sessions and circuit courts were held at the home of James Yates, on Toms Creek. In 1821, the year following the county organization, the county seat was established at Perryville, on the west bank of the Tennessee River, where it remained until 1846. At that time the county was divided, and the portion west of the Tennessee River became Decatur County. The new Perry County seat was located briefly at Harrisburg before moving to a permanent location in Linden in 1848. The Perry County Courthouse, a Colonial Revival design by Nashville architect C.K. Colley completed in 1928, is listed in the National Register of Historic Places.

Some of the early communities developed as commercial centers. Farmers Valley, on the Buffalo River, included a post office, two stores, and a warehouse. Theodore, a hamlet on Hurricane Creek, presented a more industrial outlook with a wool-carding mill, a grist mill, and a sawmill. Beardstown, established in 1830 by George Beard, had a post office, two stores, a church, and a school. Britts Landing, established in 1839 on the east bank of the Tennessee River, developed as a thriving commercial center. The town's importance in the shipping of cotton, and later peanuts, continued until the 1880s. The scenic community of Flatwoods, established ca. 1844 by families from Halifax, N.C., was originally known as Whitaker's Bluff, in honor of one of the founders. In 1871 the community was renamed Flatwoods. A center of commercial activity, the town contained several stores, a bank, a photography shop, a blacksmith shop, two doctors, and a school. Little remains of this once active community. Lobelville was established in 1854 by a French immigrant, Henry DeLobel. Today Lobelville is comparable in size and population to Linden.

The topography of the county, with numerous ridges and lush valleys drained by tributaries of the Tennessee River, presents a unique beauty. Buffalo Ridge rises to a height of 300 feet above the adjacent valleys. It traverses the entire length of the county, north and south. Eight subordinate ridges radiate westward for a distance of nine miles, ending just short of the Tennessee River. Between these various ridges, streams of pure, sparkling water flow in parallel lines and empty into the Tennessee River. Parallel spurs, and the troughs they form, convey the waters from the eastern slope of the ridge into the Buffalo River. The beauty of the Buffalo River attracts nature lovers and water enthusiasts, who enjoy canoe and float trips on this unspoiled "Wild River."

In 1861, when Tennessee seceded from the Union, Perry County rallied to the Confederate cause, furnishing 600 men to the southern armies. Support for the Confederacy was by no means universal, and after an initial attempt to remain neutral, Unionists supplied approximately 200 men for the Federal armies. Considering its population, Perry County probably sent as high of a percentage of its men to this war as any other county in the state.

In 1820 Ferney Stanley taught the first school in Perry County, located on Toms Creek. Edwin H. Eldridge taught the first school in Linden, which opened in 1848. Both of these schools were probably subscription schools, financed by the parents of children who attended. Such tuition schools were the only educational opportunities until 1827 when the State of Tennessee adopted a levy to fund "free" schools throughout the state. For many years, Perry County did not contribute any local support to the free school system, leaving the schools with insufficient resources based entirely on the revenues from the state levy. The earliest schools for African-American children followed a similar pattern and were also subscription schools. Established soon after Reconstruction, they were supported entirely by the black community, which recognized education as the avenue to independence and advancement. In the beginning, these schools were taught in the community churches: Craig's Chapel on North Lick Creek, Robert's Chapel in Linden, Oak Grove in Flatwoods,

and Howard's Chapel in the Pope community on the Tennessee River. Financial resources and the demands of agriculture determined the length of the school year, though they were seldom in session for more than three months.

The population of Perry County has remained relatively constant through the years. The census of 1860 reported 5,356 inhabitants while the 1990 census lists 6,612. The timber industry provides employment for many residents. With its abundance of wild game and excellent fishing, Perry County is rapidly becoming a recreational center, especially at Mousetail Landing State Park.

Gus A. Steele, Linden

SEE: MOUSETAIL LANDING STATE PARK; TENNESEE RIVER SYSTEM

PHILLIPS, SAMUEL CORNELIUS (1923–), most popularly known as the man who first recorded Elvis Presley, is more critically renowned for combining essential elements of Southern vernacular music, black and white, to produce the sound which heralded the age of rock-n-roll. As an entrepreneur Sam Phillips helped define the role of postwar independent labels in developing and promoting new talent.

Born in January 1923 near Florence, Alabama, to tenant farmers, Phillips developed an early interest in the music of black field workers and churches in Alabama. He first visited Memphis in 1939, where he was drawn to the musical vitality of Beale Street. He began his career in radio, taking audio engineering courses at the Auburn Polytechnical Institute and working for WLAY in Muscle Shoals, WMSL in Decatur, and WLAC in Nashville before moving to Memphis in late 1944 as an announcer and technical staff for WREC. His duties there included live broadcasts of big bands and recording of acetate radio transcriptions. Phillips's success is credited to both innovation as an audio engineer and an intuitive appreciation of the converging forces of delta blues, hillbilly country music, and gospel traditions.

Phillips opened his Memphis Recording Studio in January 1950, while still employed at WREC, with one portable mixing board, a Presto tape recorder and an acetate lathe. Early proceeds came from custom recordings of speeches, but Phillips's goal was to record and release local musicians. His earliest recordings included the white country band of Slim Rhodes and black blues singer Lost John Hunter. Phillips was influenced by local, unrelated, WDIA deejay Dewey Phillips whose "Red, Hot & Blue" program disseminated black blues-based music to the mid-South, particularly its white youth, and with whom he attempted the short-lived "Phillips" label. Sam Phillips's early recordings were released through established labels, chiefly Modern/RPM in Los Angeles and later Chess in

Chicago. Memphis area artists promoted by this method included Howlin' Wolf, Riley "B.B." King, Little Milton, Rufus Thomas, Bobby Bland, Little Junior Parker, and Roscoe Gordon. Phillips's first major impact on American popular music was his 1951 recording of *Rocket 88* by vocalist Jackie Brentson with pianist Ike Turner, a Chess release which topped the Billboard R&B charts, and which some proclaim the first rock-n-roll record. Phillips's own Sun Records label debuted in 1952 with Jackie Boy and Little Walter singing *Blues In My Condition.*

Sun Records made a quick reputation as an independent label but the black musicians it fostered gradually scattered, drawn by the lure of Chicago, Detroit, and other cities outside the South. Sun had begun to intersperse its blues recordings with hillbilly artists such as Harmonica Frank when, in 1954, Phillips recorded Elvis Presley, followed soon by Carl Perkins, Jerry Lee Lewis, Johnny Cash, Roy Orbison, Charlie Rich, and others. Sun release no. 209 was an unrehearsed Presley backed by Scotty Moore and Bill Black singing *That's All Right,* with Bill Monroe's *Blue Moon of Kentucky* on the flip side. Phillips appreciated the mixed musical roots that underlay the styles of Presley and others, and melded them to produce the sound dubbed rockabilly. By 1956 Elvis Presley's single of *Don't Be Cruel/Hound Dog* topped the Billboard charts for both country and R&B to be the best selling record of the year. By then Elvis's contract had been sold to RCA, but Phillips continued to produce Orbison, Cash, the volatile Jerry Lee Lewis, and a host of lesser talents, retaining the classic Sun sound into the late 1950s.

Sun Records did not carry its vitality into the new decade. Phillips and his colleagues ventured into new styles and recording approaches, moved to a new studio, and branched out to Nashville, but none of their efforts produced the impact of the early blues and rockabilly recordings. In 1969 Phillips sold controlling interest in Sun Records to Nashville record executive Shelby Singleton and turned his attentions to other endeavors.

Mayo Taylor, Middle Tennessee State University

SUGGESTED READINGS: Colin Escott with Martin Hawkins, *Good Rockin' Tonight: Sun Records and the Birth of Rock 'n' roll* (1991); Robert Palmer, *"Get Rhythm" Country: the music and the musicians,* 2 ed. (1994); Elizabeth Kaye, "Rockabilly reunion" *Rolling Stone* 461(Nov. 21, 1985)

SEE: BEALE STREET; MEMPHIS MUSIC SCENE; MUSIC; PERKINS, CARL L.; PRESLEY, ELVIS; ROCKABILLY; THOMAS, RUFUS; WDIA

PHILLIS WHEATLEY CLUB was organized in 1895 by a group of black women, wives of prominent black leaders in Nashville's church, business, and professional arenas. The club established its headquarters at the AME Publishing House on the public square in Nashville. The club supported missions in Africa as well as charitable outreach work to the needy in Nashville.

Active primarily from 1895 to 1925, the Phillis Wheatley Club was affiliated with the National Federation of Colored Women's Clubs, and in 1897 Nashville's Phillis Wheatley Club hosted the first meeting of the National Association of Colored Women. Along with other progressive organizations in the black community, the Phillis Wheatley Club worked to raise money and to encourage the school system to provide better equipment for Nashville's African-American high school. The Phillis Wheatley Club, along with Nashville's black newspaper, the *Globe,* also campaigned for better treatment of African-American inmates in state and local prisons.

Like many other progressive organizations sponsored by women, the Phillis Wheatley Club worked among "the sick, the poor, the unfortunate, and the aged," as one of their publications reads. In 1907 the club designated departments, creating the group's basic organization. Members served in either the Temperance, Social Purity, Educational, Charitable, Mother's, Literary, or Industrial department. Under the leadership of Mrs. Lewis Winter, the Charitable Department distributed food baskets and donated clothing and shoes to Nashville's poor. The club sponsored a daycare for children who were left unattended by working parents. Club members also volunteered at Mercy Hospital, maintaining the Phillis Wheatley Room. In 1921 the club decided to purchase and maintain a home for aged women; it completed this priority project in 1925.

Tara Mitchell Mielnik, Middle Tennessee State University

SEE: BETHLEHEM HOUSE, NASHVILLE; NASHVILLE GLOBE

PHOSPHATE MINING AND INDUSTRY began in 1886 in Middle Tennessee when William Shirley, a stone cutter, discovered phosphate on Gholston Hill near Columbia. This deposit proved to be too limited to be mined economically. In 1891 Shirley found a stratified blue rock deposit around Knob Creek, north of Columbia. A small group organized the Tennessee Phosphate Company, and the following year two tons of phosphate were shipped to National Fertilizer Company in Nashville. The company also mined blue rock phosphate at Swan Creek and Gordonsburg, both in Lewis County, and the Swan Bluff area in Hickman County.

In 1896 Judge S.O. Weatherly discovered brown rock near Mt. Pleasant. This site contained brown phosphate rock of high grade and proved to be one of the most important mineral discoveries in Tennessee. As news of this find spread, mining and industry moved into the area. Mt. Pleasant became a boom town with the population increasing from 466

Physiographic Regions of Tennessee

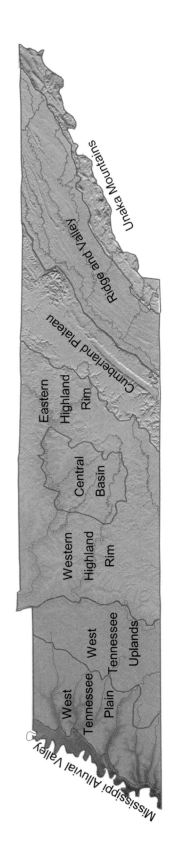

Unaka Mountains

Ridge and Valley

Cumberland Plateau

Eastern Highland Rim

Central Basin

Western Highland Rim

West Tennessee Uplands

West Tennessee Plain

Mississippi Alluvial Valley

Tennessee Interstate Highway System

County Seats and Counties of Tennessee

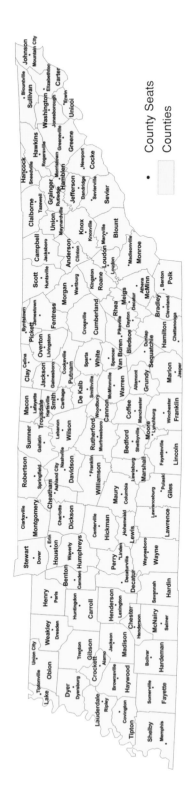

County Seats
Counties

Forests in Tennessee
Forest Coverage by County

Forest Ownership by Owner Class

Percent Forest

9.1%–32%
32%–43.74%
43.74%–57.83%
57.83%–68.9%
68.9%–87.7%

Federal
State
Forest Industry
Corporate
Farmer
Individual

Source: U.S. Forest Service, 1989

THE POPULATION OF TENNESSEE

1920 Population Per Square Mile

1990 Population Per Square Mile

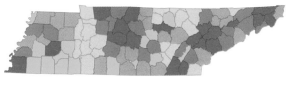

People per Square Mile

- 16–35
- 35–45
- 45–65
- 65–120
- 120–1050

Percent Change in Population, 1920–1990

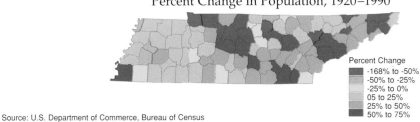

Percent Change

- -168% to -50%
- -50% to -25%
- -25% to 0%
- 05 to 25%
- 25% to 50%
- 50% to 75%

Source: U.S. Department of Commerce, Bureau of Census

NUMBER OF SLAVES BY COUNTY IN 1860
AND BLACKS AS A PERCENTAGE OF TOTAL POPULATION IN 1995

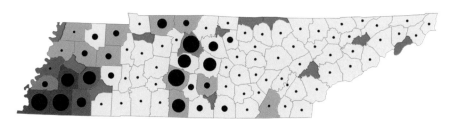

Counties Created after 1860

Number of Slaves by County

- · 1–3,000
- 3,000–7,000
- 7,000–10,000
- 10,000–13,000
- 13,000–17,000

Blacks as a percent of total population, 1995

- 0–10%
- 10–20%
- 20%–30%
- 30%–40%
- 40%–50%

Source: U.S. Department of Commerce, Bureau of Census

Percent of Land in Farms in Tennessee

Percent of Land Area in Farms, 1920

Farms as Percent of Land Area

0%–25%

25%–50%

50%–70%

70%–85%

85%–100%

1920 Average Farm Size = 77.2 Acres
1992 Average Farm Size = 146 Acres

Percent of Land Area in Farms, 1992

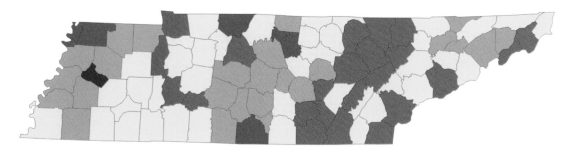

Source: U.S. Department of Commerce, Bureau of Census, 1920
Tennessee Agricultural Statistics Service, 1996

Corn Production in Tennessee

Corn Production for 1919
70,639,252 Bushels

Corn Production for 1995
63,720,000 Bushels

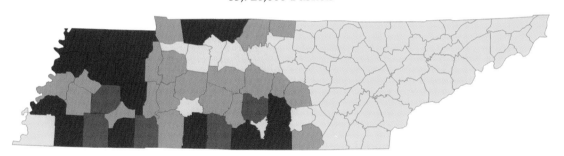

Corn Production

- Less than 250,000 Bushels
- 250,000 to 500,000 Bushels
- 500,000 to 750,000 Bushels
- 750,000 to 1,000,000 Bushels
- Over 1,000,000 Bushels

1919 Yield/Acre: 21.4 Bushels
1995 Yield/Acre: 118 Bushels

Bushels = 2,150.42 cubic inches

Source: U.S. Department of Commerce, Bureau of Census, 1920
Tennessee Agricultural Statistics Service, 1996

COTTON PRODUCTION IN TENNESSEE

Cotton Production for 1919
306,974 Bales

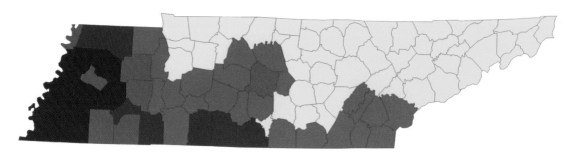

Cotton Production for 1995
724,000 Bales

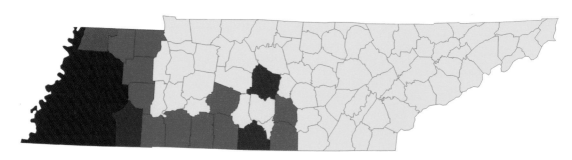

Number of Bales

None

1 to 3,999 Bales

4,000 to 7,999 Bales

8,000 to 15,999 Bales

Over 16,000 Bales

1920 Yield/Acre: 0.38 Bales

1995 Yield/Acre: 1.97 Bales

Bale = 480 pounds net weight

Source: U.S. Department of Commerce, Bureau of Census, 1920
Tennessee Agricultural Statistics Service, 1996

TOBACCO PRODUCTION IN TENNESSEE

1920 Tobacco Production

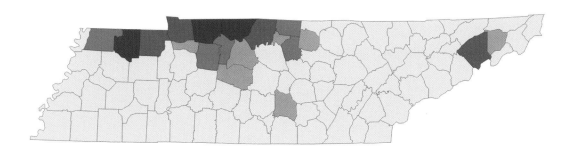

1995 Tobacco Production

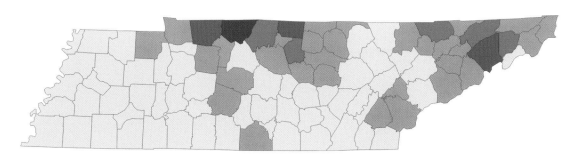

Tobacco Production in Pounds

	0 to 500,000
	500,000 to 2,500,000
	2,500,000 to 5,000,000
	5,000,000 to 10,000,000
	Over 10,000,000

1920 Yield/Acre = 811 pounds
1995 Yield/Acre = 1,797 pounds

1920 Total Production = 112,367,587 pounds
1995 Total Production = 92,907,000 pounds

Source: U.S. Department of Commerce, Bureau of Census, 1920
Tennessee Agricultural Statistics Service, 1996

Major Civil War Engagements in Tennessee

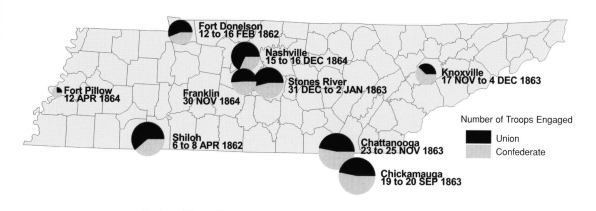

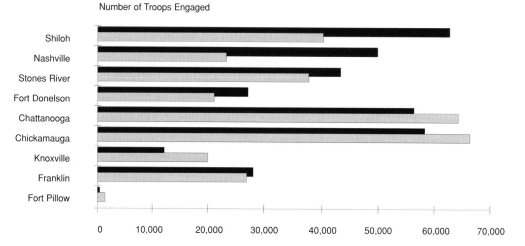

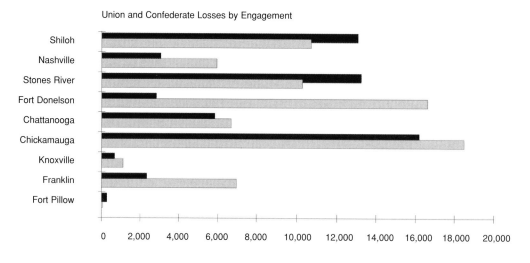

Source: Battles and Leaders of the Civil War
Boatner, The Civil War Dictionary

in 1890 to 2,000 in 1900. Fifteen companies were in operation in the early 1900s. Small companies were bought or forced out by larger companies.

Companies operating fertilizer plants in the area were Charleston Mining Company, owned by Virginia-Carolina Chemical Company; Federal Chemical Company; International Minerals and Chemical Corporation, operating in Maury and Giles counties; Hoover and Mason Phosphate Company; Ruhm Phosphate Company; and Armour Fertilizer Works. Rockdale Furnace, located south of Mt. Pleasant, manufactured ferrophosphate steel by a process of mixing phosphate and iron. This material was used for armor plating for artillery guns and battleships in World War I. The production of brown rock became the main source of supply of Tennessee phosphate. At first, all mining operations were done by hand using picks and ten-tined stone forks; ore was hauled by mule-drawn wagons. Labor was plentiful at 65 cents a day; the teams were at $1.50 per day.

According to a fiftieth anniversary company history developed by the Columbia branch of Monsanto, the initial mines typically yielded "plate rock," which was 14.5 percent phosphorus and by 1923 most of this had been mined. Companies then had to devise washing methods that could concentrate lower grade rock and make it usable. After building washing installations, companies found that they could use rock, or "muck," with as little as eight percent phosphorus, allowing them to "re-mine" some areas as many as three or four times.

In the 1930s TVA began research on the production of phosphate fertilizers by electric furnace process. TVA's electric furnaces were at Muscle Shoals, Alabama. A mining and washing division was built in Columbia. In 1936 Monsanto Chemical began construction of a plant near Columbia for the manufacture of elemental phosphorus. Victor Chemical Works located in Mt. Pleasant the following year. This company later sold to Stauffer Chemical Company. Shea Chemical built an electric furnace operation in Columbia in 1951. This plant became Hooker Chemical Company, then Occidental Chemical Corporation. A 1971 study of the phosphate industry in Maury County reported that the three phosphorus producing plants had an annual payroll of 15 million dollars. An additional 60 to 70 million dollars were put into the local economy that year in the purchasing of raw materials and in the operating and maintaining of material and supplies.

Increased operational costs, a decline in the market for phosphate materials (primarily in the manufacture of detergents), and the depletion of phosphate reserves were factors that ended the phosphate industry in this area. Mobil Chemical Company, which had purchased the Virginia-Carolina plant in Mt. Pleasant, shut down its phosphorus furnace in 1971. Monsanto Chemical Company began its shut down in 1986. Rhone-Poulenc, owner of the former Stauffer Company, and Occidental Chemical Corporation ceased operations in 1991.

For 100 years the phosphate industry played a vital role in the economic growth and material prosperity of the Maury County area. Its history is interpreted at the Mt. Pleasant/Maury Phosphate Museum in Mt. Pleasant.

Juanita Keys, Mt. Pleasant/Maury Phosphate Museum
SUGGESTED READINGS: *Monsanto, The 50ᵗʰ Anniversary of the Columbia Plant* (1986); Columbia *Daily Herald,* July 2, 1976
SEE: MAURY COUNTY; MINING

PI BETA PHI SETTLEMENT SCHOOL. The settlement house movement epitomized the drive of women toward professional careers during the Progressive Era. The Pi Beta Phi Women's Fraternity initiated a settlement in 1910 with emphasis on education, manual arts instruction, and health care. It chose Gatlinburg as the site and in 1912 hired a teacher, who taught the first session with 13 children in a single-room cabin. During the next few years, the newcomers overcame initial local resistance by providing a better trained staff and tapping greater monetary resources. From these initial programs, the fraternity established a 12-year academic, agricultural, and industrial curriculum. The fraternity built several new buildings and remodeled others to meet this growth.

They focused the manual arts program on the revival of traditional crafts in order to stimulate the local economy. In 1915 the first manual arts instructor taught carpentry and home economics to students. She soon began reviving the crafts of spinning, weaving, and basketry among adults. The response led to the opening of the Arrowcraft Shop and sponsorship of the Southern Highland Handicraft Guild in the 1920s.

The teachers also provided health care until after the 1919 influenza epidemic, during which the head resident nursed the community through the crisis. That year the fraternity hired a community nurse; they dedicated a new hospital in 1922. Their collective response to the crisis as well as continued economic support seemed to break any lingering barriers of local resistance to the school.

Most teachers only stayed one or two years. At least 31 women served on the school staff in the first ten years, while only two men taught. The rapid turnover seems to indicate a dissonance between their expectations and the hard reality of settlement life.

Today, the three-fold vision of the community continues in new forms. In 1965 Sevier County assumed control of the school, and the clinic closed the same year. The manual arts curriculum evolved into the internationally acclaimed Arrowmont School of Arts and Crafts.

Kevin D. Collins, University of Tennessee, Knoxville
SEE: ARROWMONT SCHOOL; DECORATIVE ARTS, APPALACHIAN; SETTLEMENT SCHOOLS; SEVIER COUNTY

PICKENS, LUCY PETTWAY HOLCOMBE (1832–1899), known as the "Queen of the Confederacy," was born in LaGrange in Fayette County, the daughter of Beverly Lafayette Holcombe and Eugenia Dorothea Hunt. At some time between 1848 and 1850, the family left their home, Westover of Woodstock, and moved to Marshall, Texas.

At age 13, Lucy and her sister were sent to a Quaker school in Bethlehem, Pennsylvania. She became interested in Cuban affairs, and at age 17, published a book, *The Free Flag of Cuba*. After her fiancé was killed while fighting for the Cubans, she involved herself in social activities. A charming beauty, she captivated many admirers.

In 1856, while on an annual summer visit to White Sulphur Springs, Virginia, Lucy Holcombe met Colonel Francis Wilkinson Pickens, a lawyer and secessionist, twice widowed and twice her age. She reportedly promised to marry him if he would accept a diplomatic post and take her abroad. In 1858 he accepted an appointment as Ambassador to Russia, and they were married at her home, Wyelucing, in Texas.

With her knowledge of French and Russian and her elaborate wardrobe, Pickens was soon a court favorite in St. Petersburg. Czar Alexander II and Czarina Maria showered the couple with gifts. The Czarina moved Lucy Pickens into the imperial palace and called in the royal physicians for the birth of her daughter Eugenia Frances Dorothea in 1859. The royal couple became the baby's godparents, and the Czarina christened her with the additional names of Olga Neva and the term of endearment "Douschka" (Little Darling) by which she was always known.

As the South moved toward secession, Colonel Pickens decided to return home and lend his support to the southern cause. Shortly after his return, he was elected Governor of South Carolina. Lucy Pickens joined the Confederate effort, selling jewels given to her by the Russian royal family in order to outfit the "Lucy Holcombe Legion." She became known as "Lady Lucy," and her likeness appeared on three issues of Confederate currency—the one-dollar bills of 1862 and 1863 and the one-hundred-dollar bill of 1864—making her one of the few women whose likeness has appeared on a national currency, a tribute usually reserved for heads of state. That is one of the reasons she has been called the "uncrowned queen of the Confederacy."

Francis Pickens died in 1869 at his home, Edgewood, in Edgefield, South Carolina. Lucy Pickens continued to live there, while managing three plantations with the help of her brother John, until her death in 1899.

Dorothy R. Morton, Moscow
SEE: FAYETTE COUNTY

PICKERING, SAMUEL F., JR., (1941–) was born in Nashville, attended Montgomery Bell Academy and The University of the South (Sewanee), and took advanced degrees at Cambridge and Princeton on his way to becoming a scholar of children's literature. In addition to scholarly books and articles, his writing life has been built on the familiar essay, where his wit, crusty affability, and sense of wonder often tinged with mischief shine through what he calls "forthright, workaday sentences." His topics range from wildflowers in Nova Scotia to small town gossip in Tennessee to the fusty pretensions of university life. As exercises in "gilding the mundane," Pickering's essays discover subtle ironies, juxtapose delight and melancholy, and wander afield but always return home.

Pickering's allegiance is always to the essays themselves, which are often based in fact but are not slaves to it. In "Composing a Life" from his first collection *A Continuing Education* (1985), he writes, "The trouble is that I'm not sure if the things I remember actually happened." His blend of the madcap and mundane, as he says in another piece, can "thrust him against the actual." Pickering sees truth as composite, to be picked apart by language. His books include *May Days* (1987), *Still Life* (1990), and *Walkabout Year: Twelve Months in Australia* (1995). His life, he says, is like his writing: "slow, relaxed, punctuated by fits of pique and occasionally lust, but all in all meandering and gently contemplative."

Preston Merchant, New York
SEE: LITERATURE; MONTGOMERY BELL ACADEMY; UNIVERSITY OF THE SOUTH

PICKETT COUNTY, located along Tennessee's northern border with Kentucky, lies in the picturesque Cumberland Plateau region of upper Middle Tennessee. In 1878 Lem Wright and Howell L. Pickett, legislators from Wilson County, led the move to organize Pickett County. The county was established in 1879 from sections of Overton and Fentress counties.

The county seat is Byrdstown, where the Pickett County Courthouse, designed in Crab Orchard stone by the Nashville firm of Marr and Holman, is listed in the National Register of Historic Places. Originally the county seat was to be named Wrightsville after Lem Wright, but at the last minute support went to Colonel Richard Byrd of Kingston and the county seat was named Byrdstown. During the Civil War,

Byrd had struggled to keep Tennessee in the Union and when Tennessee seceded, he joined the Union Army. Byrdstown was incorporated in 1917.

The county encompasses 163 square miles with the Obey and Wolf rivers flowing through the western half of the county. Though hilly, the landscape has supported farming with corn, wheat, oats, grass, and livestock as the primary products. In 1943 Pickett County lost most of its best farm land, as well as a fourth of its population, when the U.S. Army Corps of Engineers dammed the Obey River, creating the Dale Hollow Reservoir. The county continues to be rather sparsely populated with its 1996 population estimated at only 4,800 residents.

In addition to farming, many Pickett County residents were employed in the logging-rafting industry from the 1870s to 1930s. Pickett County farmers harvested trees from remote sections of the county, hauled them to the riverbank with mules or oxen, then floated them downstream to larger river towns. Rafting companies, such as the Kyle family's rafting business in Celina in Clay County, employed dozens of men from Pickett County who rafted the logs along the Cumberland River to Nashville where the lumber was finally processed. In addition to rafting, steamboating on the Cumberland River allowed towns as far east as Byrdstown to transport goods to and from larger markets to the west. In the early twentieth century, timber companies also acquired large tracts of land to clear-cut forests and ship the trees to sawmills in Tennessee and Kentucky.

With the end of the rafting and steamboat eras, Pickett County lost a valuable transportation link to the rest of Middle Tennessee, especially since no railroads traverse the county. The emergence of the trucking industry after World War I and state highway construction provided more efficient routes to transport goods to and from the Upper Cumberland region. These conditions, along with the large female work force, the absence of labor unions, and low-cost electricity provided by Dale Hollow Dam, led to the construction of several clothing factories such as OshKosh B'Gosh Children's Apparel and Dale Hollow Apparel. Some of the county's other major employers are Huthinson Automatic Hoses, Pickett County Schools, and Blue Grass Cooperage Co., Inc.

Pickett County's scenic beauty may be enjoyed at two outdoor recreational areas, Dale Hollow Lake and Pickett State Park. Periodic floods devastated the Upper Cumberland region until 1943, when the U.S. Army Corps of Engineers constructed the Dale Hollow Dam. Dale Hollow Lake spreads over much of the western end of the county and provides area residents with both electricity and recreation. Pickett State Park and Forest in eastern Pickett County adjoins the Big South Fork National Recreation Area. The Civilian Conservation Corps largely completed the reclamation of the forest and the park's development during the 1930s and today the park is considered one of most extant CCC-designed landscapes in the state.

Pickett County's most famous son is Cordell Hull, U.S. Congressman and Senator and Secretary of State under Franklin Delano Roosevelt. Born in a small log cabin in Pickett County, Hull initiated the founding of the United Nations and received the Nobel Peace Prize in 1945. The Cordell Hull Birthplace and Museum is located near Byrdstown. The Pickett County area also was home to Tennessee Lead, a black and tan hound of the 1850s that was acquired by George W. Maupin of Madison County, Kentucky, and this breeder turned Tennessee Lead into the foundation sire of all Walker, Trigg, and Goodman fox hounds.

Anne-Leslie Owens, Tennessee Historical Society
SEE: HULL, CORDELL, BIRTHPLACE AND MUSEUM; HULL, CORDELL; HUNTING DOGS; PICKETT STATE RUSTIC PARK; TIMBER INDUSTRY; U.S. ARMY CORPS OF ENGINEERS

PICKETT STATE RUSTIC PARK. The Michigan-based Stearnes Coal and Lumber Company acquired forested land in Pickett and Fentress counties in 1910 and used the land until 1933, when the company deeded the property to the State of Tennessee. On December 13, 1933, Tennessee Governor Hill McAllister declared the land a state forest. The Tennessee State Forester in the Department of Agriculture administered the land until 1937, when it was transferred to the Division of Forestry in the Department of Conservation. The land eventually became Pickett State Rustic Park, administered by the Division of State Parks.

In 1921 a national conference for the establishment of state parks identified Tennessee as one of 28 states with no state parks. Tennessee established a State Park and Forestry Commission in 1925, but it was not until the federal government began promoting land use planning during the Depression, that the movement to acquire land and construct state parks gained substantial support in Tennessee. Federal funding and New Deal work programs provided the means to complete the projects.

Civilian Conservation Corps (CCC) Company 1471 organized at Fort Oglethorpe, Georgia, in 1933, before moving first to Putnam County and then settling in Pickett County in 1934. There, they constructed a dam and a 12-acre lake, 22 miles of roads, telephone lines, trails, a lodge, picnic areas, cabins, and other facilities for the new Pickett Forest State Park (the area was also known as Pickett Forest Recreation Area). The CCC also built fire towers and ranger stations in the forested areas of Pickett. The National Park Service designed park buildings and structures to utilize native materials and fit in with the local landscape, providing for functionally and aesthetically related components that remained easily accessible to park visitors.

A 1937 U.S. Department of Interior master plan for Pickett Forest State Park shows picnic areas, auto and trailer camps, groups of cabins, trails, comfort stations, and shelters, many of which still exist. Historic resources (ca. 1934–1942) are constructed of rock faced coursed stone with wood trim. They are gable roofed and one story in height. Many buildings have large, impressive stone fireplaces.

Situated near the Tennessee-Kentucky state border, the park and forest contain close to 12,000 acres of reforested land. Pine growth occurs on the plateau, and hemlock and birches predominate in the ravines of the park. Rock formation, natural bridges, and caves can be found throughout the area.

Development of the park facilities continued into the late 1930s, then ceased until the 1950s, when additional cabins and the superintendent's residence were erected. In 1949 approximately 1,000 acres of the land were transferred to the Division of State Parks in the Department of Conservation. Today, the Tennessee Department of Environment and Conservation administers Pickett State Rustic Park.

Claudette Stager, Tennessee Historical Commission
SEE: CIVILIAN CONSERVATION CORPS; CONSERVATION;
PICKETT COUNTY

PICKWICK LANDING STATE RESORT PARK,
located along Pickwick Lake (the dammed Tennessee River) in southern Hardin County, began as a demonstration park constructed and administered by the Tennessee Valley Authority. Construction at Pickwick Dam, the third completed TVA dam, began in March 1935. Lake formation began in February 1938 and the dam's generators produced their first power on June 29, 1938. For the demonstration park, TVA designers followed a rustic scheme similar to that of the earlier Norris Dam State Park. They also built swimming facilities, a boat dock, playgrounds, campgrounds, and picnic areas.

At one time, the former demonstration park was operated as a private resort, but then the facilities were acquired by the State of Tennessee to establish the modern Pickwick Landing State Resort Park. The park presently features a modern inn and restaurant, ten cabins, a 48-site campground, a marina, an 18-hole golf course, three public swimming beaches, and various picnic and recreational sites. The Bruton Branch Primitive Area, located across the lake from the main park, has 347 acres, offering a boat launch, primitive campsites, a swimming beach, and a modern bathhouse.

Carroll Van West, Middle Tennessee State University
SEE: HARDIN COUNTY; TENNESSEE VALLEY AUTHORITY

PIERCE, JUNO FRANKIE (ca. 1862–1954), founder of the Tennessee Vocational School for Girls, was born during or shortly after the Civil War to Nellie Seay, the house slave of a Smith County legislator. Frankie Pierce received her education at the McKee School, a private school in Nashville for African Americans, founded by the Presbyterian Church as a mission. She also attended Roger Williams University in Nashville and taught school for a brief period of time. She then married Clement J. Pierce and lived with him in Paris, Texas, until his death.

Upon her return to Nashville, Pierce worked to found an educational institution for delinquent African-American girls. Since the African-American girls were not permitted in white juvenile institutions or schools, they were placed in local jails if they became delinquent. She was president of the Negro Women's Reconstruction League, the founder of the Nashville Federation of Colored Women's Clubs, and on the first Committee of Management of the Blue Triangle League of the YWCA.

At the invitation of suffrage leader Catherine Kenny, Pierce addressed the May 1920 state suffrage convention held in the House Chamber of the Tennessee capitol. "What will the Negro women do with the vote?" she asked her audience. "We will stand by the white women. . . . We are asking only one thing— a square deal. . . . We want recognition in all forms of this government. We want a state vocational school and a child welfare department of the state, and more room in state schools."

After the passage of the suffrage amendment, Pierce and Kenny were active in local Democratic party politics. The vocational school for African-American girls became a part of the legislative agenda of the suffragists and the newly organized League of Women Voters of Tennessee. After an extensive lobbying effort by the women the following year in 1921, the General Assembly passed the bill creating the school. The school opened its doors two years later and Pierce became its first superintendent. She held that position until 1939. Pierce had excellent political instincts and held an annual breakfast at the school for state legislators and other community leaders so that they could observe the operation of the school.

Pierce continued to live in Nashville after she retired. She served as the chairman of the Building Campaign for the Negro division to raise funds for the building of the Blue Triangle Branch of the YWCA in 1952. Frankie Pierce died in 1954 and is buried in the Greenwood Cemetery in Nashville.

Carole Stanford Bucy, Volunteer State Community College
SEE: KENNY, CATHERINE T.; ROGER WILLIAMS UNIVERSITY;
WOMAN SUFFRAGE MOVEMENT

PILLOW, GIDEON JOHNSON

PILLOW, GIDEON JOHNSON (1806–1878) was born in Williamson County and raised in Maury and Giles counties. He received a classical education at local academies and graduated from the University of Nashville in 1827. He then read law and became an attorney in 1830; the next year he married Mary Elizabeth Martin of Maury County (d. 1869); in 1872 he married Mary Dickson Trigg, young widow of a Louisiana planter.

His first major accomplishment in the law was to co-edit the highly regarded *Digest and Revision of the Statute Laws of Tennessee,* and in private practice he rapidly gained a reputation as one of the state's finest lawyers (with an income to match). In 1833 Governor William Carroll named the young Pillow as adjutant general of the state militia, ranking as a brigadier general. In this period he also became a close friend and advisor of James Knox Polk, though never actually his law partner as is often reported.

Clifton Place, his estate near Columbia, begun in 1838 and remodeled in 1852, was not only one of the grandest residences in the state, showcasing the latest fashions and taste, but also a progressive, modern farming operation utilizing the most advanced methods in horticulture and husbandry. Pillow was a respected authority on farm economics, and urged the diversification of Southern agriculture and the increased mechanization of the Southern economy. He also acquired extensive holdings of land and slaves in Mississippi and Arkansas in the 1840s.

In 1844 Pillow played a critical role in the nomination and election of his friend Polk to the presidency. In 1846 Pillow was commissioned a brigadier general of U.S. volunteers (major general in 1847) and commanded Tennessee troops in the war with Mexico. He served under Zachary Taylor and Winfield Scott, and managed to alienate both with a tendency to alter or ignore orders and to claim credit for other people's exploits. At Cerro Gordo he was personally brave but his leadership was inept; at the later battles near Mexico City his performance as a commander was far more competent, and at the storming of Chapultepec he was badly wounded in the left ankle. He expected to be involved in the negotiations with the Mexicans, but neither Scott nor the plenipotentiary Nicholas Trist accepted his pretensions.

In the 1850s Pillow maintained a Jacksonian stance in favor of continued Union with safeguards for slavery; in 1852 and 1856, despite playing a major role in his party's politics (and floating his interest in the vice presidency), he received no official post or recognition. In Tennessee, he had found a new friend and ally to replace Polk in the person of the rising Isham Green Harris. In 1857 Pillow missed becoming a Senator when he was out-manuevered by Andrew Johnson's faction, and in 1860 he was a vocal proponent of Stephen Douglas. Upon Lincoln's election he urged a convention of slave states, though as a good Jacksonian he still decried outright secession.

In May 1861 Governor Harris named Pillow as the senior Major General of the Provisional Army of Tennessee, and he threw his great energy and administrative ability into the task of raising, training, and motivating that force. In July 1861 he was commissioned as a brigadier general, which he always considered a slight, in the Confederate Service.

In February 1862 he was partly responsible for the disastrous surrender of Fort Donelson, where he displayed physical courage and some tactical competence along with a degree of strategic fecklessness: it was his decision to withdraw to the starting positions on February 15 that began the train of errors that led to the surrender. Even worse for his reputation was his decision to flee the fort, leaving the onerous task of capitulation to his old enemy Simon Buckner. For the rest of his life, Pillow would carry the taint of a failure made worse by the abandonment of his men.

Unable to procure a permanent command, he led a brigade of Tennesseans on the last day of the Battle of Stones River, where he displayed aggressiveness but not brilliance. For the rest of that year and into 1864 he was head of the Volunteer and Conscript Bureau for a vast portion of the Deep South, a role that was well suited to his talents and energy. His modern biographers hold that his efforts essentially filled the ranks of Joe Johnston's army after Bragg's removal, but again he was prone to overstepping his authority and to alienating both superiors and subordinates.

In 1864 he once again took a field command, but his one major initiative, against Sherman's line of communications at Lafayette, Georgia, in June was almost a reprise of Cerro Gordo decades before and the action proved a fiasco. He spent the remainder of the war on recruiting duty.

One of the wealthiest men in the state in 1860, Gideon Pillow had spent much of his fortune in the war effort and seen some of his properties confiscated or otherwise encumbered by the Federal authorities. After the war, he went into a law partnership with Isham Harris in Memphis, and was not above flattering approaches to his old enemies such as Grant and Sherman, but he never received office or reward for his troubles. His family life, too, became embittered, and he was involved in lawsuits against some of his numerous daughters and their husbands. He was a victim of the last great visitation of yellow fever to Memphis in 1878, and is buried in Elmwood Cemetery.

Ed Frank, Mississippi Valley Collection, University of Memphis Libraries

SUGGESTED READING: Nathaniel C. Hughes, Jr. and Roy P. Stonesifer, Jr., *The Life and Wars of Gideon J. Pillow* (1993)

SEE: ARMY OF TENNESSEE; CLIFTON PLACE; FORT DONEL-
SON; HARRIS, ISHAM G.; JACKSONIANS; MAURY COUNTY;
MEXICAN WAR; POLK, JAMES K.; STONES RIVER, BATTLE OF

PINK PALACE MUSEUM, THE MEMPHIS is both a house and a museum. In 1922 Clarence Saunders, the father of self-service grocery shopping and founder of Piggly Wiggly, began building a mansion. Memphians called his 36,500 square foot house, faced with pink Georgia marble, his" Pink Palace" and the name stuck. In 1923 he lost a battle on the New York Stock Exchange, was forced to declare bankruptcy, and never finished his house. The land was sold to developers. The unfinished mansion was donated to the City of Memphis which turned it into a museum. It opened in March l930 as the Memphis Museum of Natural History and Industrial Arts. The public, though, called it "The Pink Palace," and in 1967 the museum formally became the Memphis Pink Palace Museum.

Its early exhibits featured a collection of North American game animals, stuffed fish, and the remarkable Boshart collection of 800 taxidermied birds. For several decades the museum's collections could best be described as eclectic as the staff accepted almost any artifact someone offered. Today's museum exhibits focus on the cultural and natural history of the Memphis region, interpreting the history of Memphis, medicine in the Mid-South, and the geology and wildlife populations of the area. There is a replica of the first Piggly Wiggly grocery store, a turn-of-the-century country store, and the hand carved, automated Clyde Parke Circus.

The mansion has been renovated. It contains exhibits on the history of Memphis in the twentieth century and the evolution of the museum. One wing houses the Entrepreneur Hall of Honor, which salutes Memphians who have had an impact on business worldwide. After several expansions, the museum now contains over 170,000 square feet, making it one of the largest in the Southeast. In addition to the permanent collection, there are regularly scheduled traveling exhibits. The Sharpe Planetarium and the Union Planters IMAX Theater expand the museum's role and audience.

In addition to the Pink Palace, the Memphis Museum System has two nineteenth century historic properties, the Magevney and Mallory-Neely Houses, and the Lichterman Nature Center in Memphis. The Coon Creek Science Center in McNairy County is another part of the system. It is a major invertebrate fossil collecting site and education facility.

Anne Leonard, Memphis Museum System

SEE: COON CREEK; MAGEVNEY, EUGENE; MALLORY-NEELY
HOUSE; SAUNDERS, CLARENCE

PINSON MOUNDS, the largest Middle Woodland period (ca. 200 B.C.–A.D. 400) archaeological site in the Southeast, is located about ten miles south of Jackson, on the South Fork of the Forked Deer River. Within an area of approximately 400 acres, the site includes at least 12 mounds, a geometric earthen enclosure, and associated ritual activity areas. While the site's large size and immense volume of earth fill are very impressive, the presence of five large rectangular platform mounds (ranging in height from 7 to 72 feet) of Middle Woodland age underscores the unique nature of the Pinson Mounds site.

Archaeological excavations conducted on Ozier Mound (Mound 5) in 1981 provided the first unequivocal evidence in eastern North America for the construction of rectangular platform mounds during the Middle Woodland period. Prior to this, mounds of this type were thought to be confined to the later Mississippian Period (post-A.D. 1000).

Approximately 33 feet tall, with a ramp on one side, Ozier Mound was constructed in at least six stages. Each successive summit was covered with a thin layer of pale yellow sand. Copper, mica, and microblades of non-local chert were found in association with the uppermost mound summit. These materials have been recovered from ritual activity areas elsewhere within the site, thus providing clues about the use of Ozier Mound for rituals.

Few earthworks at Pinson Mounds were constructed specifically for burial of the dead. In fact, only three burial mounds have been identified at the site. The largest of these, the Twin Mounds (Mound 6), consists of a pair of large, intersecting conical mounds, each about 23 feet tall and 80 feet in diameter. Partial excavation of the northern Twin Mound provided a rare view of a large, undisturbed Middle Woodland burial mound.

At the base of the earthwork, four log and/or fabric covered tombs, containing the remains of 16 adults were excavated. Several of the individuals wore fiber headdresses decorated with copper ornaments, as well as necklaces of freshwater pearls. A pair of engraved rattles cut from human skull and decorated with a bird motif in the Hopewellian style were found at the knees of an elderly man. Each rattle contained a number of small quartzite river pebbles to produce sound. Also recovered from the burials were a small mica mirror, a schist pendant, and a finely crafted boatstone of green speckled schist.

Radiocarbon dated to ca. A.D. 100, the northern Twin Mound exhibited unusually complex stratigraphy reflecting the following construction sequence. First, a layer of puddled clay (moistened to thick liquid consistency) was placed over the tombs and associated ritual features. Then, over the area in which the tombs were located, a circular, flat-topped primary mound, covered with alternating bands of multi-colored earth and sand, was constructed. Numerous sharpened wooden poles were driven into the surface of the primary mound at intervals of approximately 1.7 feet. Separated from this mound by a narrow walkway was a low, sand-covered platform that supported a number of large, outslanting posts. Finally, the primary mound, the walkway, and the circular platform were covered with several distinctive layers of fill dirt, bringing the northern Twin Mound to a height of approximately 23 feet.

Like most large Middle Woodland ceremonial sites, Pinson Mounds was not built by a single small village or group of villages. Based on a variety of distinctive pottery types found at the site, it appears that individuals from as far away as southern Georgia and Louisiana participated in rituals at Pinson Mounds. For example, numerous sherds of non-local pottery were found at the Duck's Nest Sector, a ritual activity area dating to approximately A.D. 300. These include limestone-tempered wares (characteristic of the Tennessee River valley), Swift Creek Complicated Stamped (a southern Georgia type), McLeod Simple Stamped (commonly found in the Mobile Bay area), and several other types of no known local counterparts.

Other interesting features at Pinson Mounds include the second-tallest mound in the United States (Sauls Mound at 72 feet) and a circular earthen enclosure similar to earthworks found in the Ohio Valley.

Pinson Mounds has been designated a National Historic Landmark and is managed by the State of Tennessee as an archaeological park.

Robert C. Mainfort, Jr. and Mary L. Kwas, Arkansas Archeological Survey

SUGGESTED READINGS: Robert C. Mainfort, Jr., "Middle Woodland Ceremonialism at Pinson Mounds, Tennessee," *American Antiquity* 53(#1, 1988): 158–173; Robert C. Mainfort, Jr., and Richard Walling, "1989 Excavations at Pinson Mounds: Ozier Mound," *Midcontinental Journal of Archaeology* 17 (#1, 1992): 112–136

SEE: MADISON COUNTY; WOODLAND PERIOD

PITTMAN CENTER was founded by Dr. John S. Burnett, a Methodist minister and educator, who had long dreamed of establishing an educational and medical facility in one of the most isolated sections of East Tennessee. In 1921 funding for this project came from northern philanthropists through the Methodist Episcopal Church, primarily through the efforts of Dr. Eli Pittman, Superintendent of the Elmira District of the Central New York Conference. Although the center was only 42 miles southeast of Knoxville in Sevier County on the Pigeon River in the Great Smoky Mountains, the location was still extremely isolated in the 1920s, accessible only by steep and rugged mountain passes.

From its opening on August 15, 1921, Pittman Community Center filled the educational and medical needs for the surrounding communities. The building itself was a model of modern construction, electrically lighted, steam heated, with modern plumbing facilities. Numerous teachers, primarily from the North, taught the usual subjects and offered courses in home economics for women and agriculture for men. A model farm and cannery at the center provided hands-on education for the students.

By the 1960s the basic mission of the Pittman Center had been fulfilled as measured by the achievements of hundreds of center graduates. Many Pittman alumni became teachers after completing their education in colleges throughout the state and nation.

Durwood Dunn, Tennessee Wesleyan College

SEE: SETTLEMENT SCHOOLS; SEVIER COUNTY

PLOUGH, ABE (1892–1984). Within a year of his birth in 1892 in Tupelo, Mississippi, Abe Plough moved with his family to Memphis where his father, Moses, operated a clothing and furnishings store. Abe Plough attended Market Street School where a teacher taught him to calculate figures without pencil or paper. He said this "mental arithmetic" served him well in his business career since he never needed a pencil to calculate his acquisition of 30 companies for the Schering-Plough Corporation at a cost of over one billion dollars.

Plough received his only other formal education at St. Paul Street Grammar School, from which he was graduated. After school and on weekends he worked at the George V. Francis drug store without pay because he wanted to learn the drug business, determined that it would be his future. Moses Plough lent his son $125 to start his own business, Plough Chemical Company, in 1908. At age 16 Abe Plough was owner, manager, and only employee of the new business, located in one small room above his father's store. Using dishpans for mixing the chemicals, his first formula was for Plough's Antiseptic Healing Oil, a "sure cure for any ill of man or beast." On days when he was not bottling his healing oil, Plough set out in his father's horse-drawn buggy to sell his product to drug stores and country merchants.

Success came almost immediately for the new enterprise. Within two years it doubled in size, entered the patent drug business, and branched out into cosmetics. Adding aspirin to his line of products in 1920, Plough bought the St. Joseph Company, a step he called his "first on the road to the big time."

Despite the world-wide depression in 1929, Plough raised his employees' salaries and added 100 others to his drug store and factory labor forces.

Plough, Incorporated moved in 1951 to 3022 Jackson Avenue, a $2,000,000 plant encompassing 250,000 square feet on six acres of land. The business reported net sales of $254.5 million by 1954, a figure that doubled by 1962. It merged in 1971 with Schering Corporation, primarily a manufacturer of prescription pharmaceuticals. Plough was chairman of both Plough, Incorporated, and Schering-Plough.

Abe Plough retired from business in 1976 to devote his talents and energies to his other chief interest, philanthropy. His generosity to the community is legendary. His many gifts were often made as "challenge grants," his stated goal "to help the greatest number of people in order to do the most good." His legacy lives on not only in the business he created, which bears his name, but also in his deeds of generosity and leadership. The Plough Foundation continues to be devoted to the welfare of the community, and is administered in his name by his heirs.

Selma Lewis, Memphis

SUGGESTED READINGS: Memphis *Commercial Appeal*, June 15, 1951, September 15, 1984, and September 15, 1987

SEE: COMMERCE; MEMPHIS

POCKET WILDERNESS AREAS are part of a conservation program involving a corporate-state partnership. Beginning in 1970 the Hiwassee Land Company of the Bowater Southern Paper Corporation developed in Tennessee four pocket wilderness areas, defined as "a pocket of land set aside for preservation in its natural state, with no logging or development other than hiking trails permitted within its boundaries."[1] The areas contain national and state recreational trails and are designated state natural areas. The first pocket wilderness was the Virgin Falls State Natural Area, which contains 317 acres along the Caney Fork River in White County. Its most spectacular attraction is the 110-foot Virgin Falls. Laurel-Snow State Natural Area, located near Dayton in Rhea County, contains 710 acres. It includes two stunning waterfalls, Laurel Falls and Snow Falls. The Stinging Fork State Natural Area has 104 acres near Spring City; it features the 30-foot high Stinging Fork Falls. The Honey Creek State Natural Area in Scott County is within the Big South Fork National Recreational Area. Honey Creek's 109 acres lie along the creek's gorges at the junction with the Big South Fork of the Cumberland River and the area has a rugged five-mile trail. Many groups have commended the pocket wilderness program, including the Tennessee General Assembly, the U.S. Department of the Interior, the Tennessee Conservation League, and the Tennessee Trails Association.

Carroll Van West, Middle Tennessee State University

CITATION:
(1) Yvonne Callahan, "An Untouched Wilderness," *Tennessee Conservationist* 45(May/June 1979): 4.

SEE: CONSERVATION

POLK COUNTY, established by the Tennessee General Assembly in 1839 and named to honor newly elected Governor James K. Polk, is located in the extreme southeastern corner of the state, bounded by North Carolina and Georgia. Most of the county's 435 square miles lie within the Chilhowee and Unaka mountain ranges and contain some of the most scenic beauty in the country, including Parksville, the Ocoee, Conasauga, and Hiwassee Rivers, and 150,865 acres of Cherokee National Forest. The rapids of the Ocoee River are internationally known to white water enthusiasts as the scene of the Twenty-fifth Olympic kayaking events.

Polk County's known Indian heritage extends back at least 2,000 years to the early Woodland Indians. In 1540 the Spanish explorer, Hernando de Soto, camped near Columbus, a thriving trading post on the banks of the Hiwassee River. The Treaty of 1819 opened the territory north of the Hiwassee to white settlement, and the 1835 Treaty of Removal forced the Cherokees to give up their final land claims in Tennessee.

Acting on the petition of some 100 citizens, the Tennessee State Legislature created Polk County from parts of Bradley and McMinn counties on November 28, 1839. David Ragen, as acting sheriff, was authorized to hold the first election after the commissioners divided the county into seven civil districts. In the February 4, 1840, election, McKamy's stock stand, located on the Old Federal Road, was chosen for the permanent county seat and named Benton in honor of Thomas Hart Benton, U.S. Senator from Missouri. The new town was surveyed and laid out by James McKamy and John F. Hannah into 223 lots, which were sold at auction for a total of $11,386, much of which was never collected.

Copper was first discovered at Ducktown in 1843, and within four years mule teams were carrying casks of ore south to a forge at Dalton, Georgia. Sustained development of the Copper Basin began in the late 1850s after transportation improvements and company consolidation. Julius E. Raht combined many individual mining claims into the Union Consolidated Mining Company and became superintendent of both the Polk County Copper Company and the Burra Burra Copper Company. From 1865 to 1878, 24 million pounds of copper was taken from the underground mines, and 50 square miles of the Copper Basin area was stripped of its timber to fuel smelters and build mines. After 1891 production by the open-roasting process of removing copper from the ore, an environmentally disastrous method, killed vegetation for miles and left the landscape open to erosion. By the early twentieth century, a barren moonscape of red hills surrounded Ducktown and Copperhill.

During the Civil War, Polk County provided five companies for the Confederacy and two for the Union Army, as well as 90 percent of the copper for the southern cause. No battles were fought within the county; however, a November 29, 1864, raid by the notorious bushwhacker and guerrilla, John P. Gatewood, resulted in at least 16 deaths.

Polk County's remote Sylco Mountains became the site of Vineland, a unique experiment in social living by Rosine Parmentier. In the 1840s, with the aid of a New York associate, Parmentier purchased 50,000 acres of land and encouraged French, German, Italian, and Austrian colonization of the area. Their grandiose plans for a profitable winemaking industry apparently failed to materialize, and most of the colonists migrated elsewhere. Those who remained were quickly integrated into the local community, but the family names of Becklers, Miolin, Nocarina, Genollic, Sholtz, Pace, and Chable are indicators of this vanished settlement.

In 1858 W.P. Collins edited the county's first newspaper, the *Ducktown Eagle.*

The Polk County News, with editor-owners Ingrid and Randolph Buehler, now in its 113th year of publication, continues to serve the county. A recently reorganized Historical & Genealogical Society publishes a quarterly and oversees the preservation of the county's historic sites and heritage.

According to the 1990 federal census, Polk County had a population of 13,643, served by four elementary and two high schools. There are approximately 50 churches of Protestant denominations in the county. The largest denomination is Baptist, followed by Methodist, Presbyterian, Church of God, and Episcopal.

The Tennessee Valley Authority operates three hydroelectric plants on the Ocoee River and one on the Hiwassee River; TVA owns more than 3,000 acres of land in Polk County. The U.S. Forest Service controls in excess of 150,000 acres and operates several recreational sites which provide picnicking, camping, and swimming facilities for local citizens and thousands of visitors each year.

Agriculture continues to be a major factor in the economy of Polk County. The leading agricultural products include poultry, dairy products, cattle, hogs, soybeans, forestry products, and corn. Several small industries, employing approximately 400 people, produce clothing, furniture, lumber, and automobile mats.

Marian Bailey Presswood, Benton

SEE: BENTON, THOMAS H.; BURRA BURRA COPPER COMPANY; CHEROKEE NATIONAL FOREST; DUCKTOWN BASIN MUSEUM; MINING; POLK, JAMES K.; RAHT, JULIUS E.; TENNESSEE VALLEY AUTHORITY

POLK, JAMES KNOX (1795–1849), a native of North Carolina, served one term as United States President, 1845–49; won election seven times to Congress and presided over the U.S. House as its Speaker for the last four of his 14-year tenure (1825–39); served one term as governor of Tennessee, 1839–41; and represented Maury County in the Tennessee General Assembly, 1823–25. A life-long devotee of Thomas Jefferson's political creed and a loyal son of Andrew Jackson's democracy movement, Polk holds a unique place in American history as the first "dark horse" candidate for president and the first former Speaker of the House of Representatives to serve as president.

The son of Samuel and Jane Knox Polk and the eldest of their ten children, young James moved in 1806 with his family from their farm in Mecklenburg County, North Carolina, to Maury County, Tennessee, where he attended common schools from 1808 until 1810. Two years of recurring illness ended in 1812 when Ephraim McDowell of Danville, Kentucky, performed a lithotomy procedure and restored Polk to health. Less than a year after his surgery, he began preparation for college and studied Latin under the tutelage first of a local Presbyterian minister, Robert Henderson, and then Samuel P. Black, master of

James Knox Polk as president-elect, 1844.

LIBRARY OF CONGRESS

Bradley Academy in Murfreesboro. Entering the University of North Carolina as a sophomore in the fall of 1815, Polk gave himself fully to his studies and won first honors in his class at each of the college's semi-annual examinations.

Upon completion of his degree in 1818 Polk commenced legal studies in the law office of Felix Grundy, a renowned Nashville trial lawyer and member of the General Assembly. Impressed with his young law clerk, Grundy sponsored Polk's election in 1819 to the post of chief clerk of the Tennessee Senate, which then held its bi-annual sessions in Murfreesboro. Licensed to practice law the following year, Polk returned to Maury County and started a legal practice with Aaron V. Brown. Election to the Tennessee House in 1823 again took the young lawyer-politician to Murfreesboro in the fall. On New Year's Day next he and Sarah Childress, daughter of Joel and Elizabeth Whitsitt Childress, married and so formed a union of two influential families in Rutherford and Maury counties.

At the young age of 30 Polk defeated the one-term incumbent, James T. Sandford, for a seat in Congress and began a distinguished career in the House marked by four years of opposition to the administration of John Q. Adams and ten years of loyal support to Andrew Jackson and Martin Van Buren. In his first floor speech (March 13, 1826) Polk argued for a constitutional amendment that would have provided for popular election of the president and thereby avoid recurrence of the alleged corrupt bargain between Adams and Henry Clay. Polk gained notice through his opposition to Adams's appointment of ministers to attend the Panama Congress on grounds that the United States should not abandon its tradition of neutrality or participate in a diplomatic agenda where the objectives were enveloped in uncertainty and darkness. In his second and third terms in Congress he sat on the House Committee of Foreign Affairs before moving in 1832 to the House Committee of Ways and Means.

Polk's work as chairman of a House Select Committee on surplus revenue in 1830–1831 established his credentials in the area of government finance, and in his report (January 28, 1831) he expressed in the strongest of terms his opposition to what he termed political "log-rolling." First, he could find no constitutional sanction for internal improvements undertaken either directly by the general government or indirectly through the distribution of surplus revenues to the states. The framers of the Constitution did not grant the general government those consolidating powers precisely because buying voter support, apart from undermining republican notions of civic virtue, would engender prejudices, excite sectional feelings, and destroy the harmony of the Union. Instead of looking to the general welfare,

congressmen would engage in disreputable competitions for funding local works that in their appeal to special interests could only result in the corruption of public morals.

Polk led the House minority in its fight against rechartering the Second Bank of the United States in 1832, and he fully supported Jackson's veto of the Bank bill. At the start of the second session Polk moved to the Committee on Ways and Means and led minority members in exposing the Bank's attempt to block the administration's paying off the government's remaining three-percent stocks, most of which were held by European creditors. In his report Polk argued that the Bank could not be trusted to manage the people's money and hinted at the possibility of removing the government's deposits. His opposition to the Bank's re-charter and his exposure of its manipulations placed him near the top of the Bank's enemies list, but the Bank's branch in Nashville could not bring him down in the August election, which Polk won easily.

Jackson's supporters commanded a majority in the next Congress and, of course, placed Polk at the head of the Ways and Means Committee. Polk backed Jackson's removal of federal deposits to state banks, and later as Speaker he would champion creation of a treasury system entirely independent of the banking corporations. The issue remained that of sustaining the broadest diffusion of political and economic power in the agrarian republic, for the Bank war had demonstrated fully the danger of allowing limited liability corporations to set up as rival powers to the elected government.

In Tennessee the Bank party worked to undermine Jackson's control of the state by bringing forward Hugh Lawson White as the state's favorite-son presidential candidate and so making his candidacy a litmus test in the 1835 congressional and state elections. Polk saw the purposes of the nomination and campaigned against the "caucus of eleven" Tennessee congressmen and their use of White's popularity. Again Polk won vindication at the polls and the continued backing of the President, who gave the dissidents at home the back of his hand by making Polk Speaker of the House in place of John Bell, leader of the White movement in Tennessee. In the presidential canvass of 1836 Polk campaigned across the state for the national party's nominee, Martin Van Buren, but state pride ruled in favor of White. In the 1837 congressional elections only three of the Jackson loyalists held their seats against the tide of economic panic and Bank money. Polk returned to Congress for a second term as Speaker fully aware that the Tennessee Democracy could not survive another such defeat two years hence; and before returning to Washington in the fall of 1838, Polk announced his decision to run for governor in the next election.

Polk's race to recapture the state for the Democracy proved his loyalty both to Jackson and to Democrats across the Union. With the help of John C. Calhoun's friends in East Tennessee, Polk won the governorship. Depression pressures for cheap money and public works hounded the state legislature, and the new governor accepted the Assembly's "logrolling" as necessary for the survival of his party both at home and in the Union. The price of consistency would be the loss of the issue at the national level. He had hoped that hard times would pass before the 1840 presidential election and that his loyal efforts in Tennessee would win him the party's vice-presidential nomination. But the Democratic National Convention chose not to give Van Buren a running mate. Probably no one on the ticket could have spared Van Buren his defeat to the Whig party candidates, William Henry Harrison and John Tyler.

In 1841, during his own reelection campaign, Polk stood by his support of Van Buren, as he had done in four prior elections; but he lost his first election. In 1843 Polk again ran for the governorship and against the best advice of his political friends held firmly to his support of Van Buren. In doing so he demonstrated most clearly the heavy price of supporting the former president, which did not go unnoticed at The Hermitage.

Polk won the 1844 Democratic presidential nomination because Andrew Jackson had arranged for the convention to choose a loyal Democrat from the West who could bridge the widening sectional divide and who would support the annexation of Texas. By voting to impose the traditional two-thirds majority rule, delegates to the Baltimore convention assured a choice other than Van Buren. After seven ballots and careful backstage work party leaders brought Polk's name into view, and on the ninth ballot delegates ratified their best chance for electoral victory.

Although the Democrat and Whig parties engaged in spirit-building rallies and sloganeering not unlike that of 1840, the expansion issue brought the election a more serious side, for the threat of war with Britain over Oregon and with Mexico over Texas framed the political discourse of the campaign. Henry Clay hurt his candidacy by publishing extended and somewhat varied commentaries on the Texas question, and Polk helped his dark-horse bid by limiting his public utterances to a single statement on the tariff issue. The Liberty party promised to abolish slavery and chose former Democrat James G. Birney to lead their quasi-religious crusade. Democrat hopes for large-scale Whig defections to Birney did not materialize; indeed, Whig alliances with American nativists in Pennsylvania and New York cost Democrats more votes in those crucial states than were gained from Whigs choosing the abolitionist option. The presidential election of 1844 proved that the American electorate had divided almost evenly between expansion and consolidation, between free trade and protection, between immigrant toleration and native xenophobia, and in the larger context between agrarian rule and market revolution. In the midst of one the Union's most contentious elections, white male voters gave little thought to expanding the boundaries of freedom for African, native, or female Americans.

Elected by less than a majority of the voters and the narrowest of popular pluralities, Polk nevertheless took the presidential oath with a determination to direct personally the administration of the general government and to accomplish four major goals—the annexation of Texas already having been approved by the outgoing Congress. He would settle the Oregon boundary dispute with Great Britain, reduce tariffs, establish an independent Treasury, and purchase California. In the course of meeting his objectives he would lead the nation into war with Mexico in the defense of Texas annexation.

From the Mexican point of view the United States had no right to annex lands west of the Sabine River, and as promised Mexico broke diplomatic relations with the United States shortly after Polk's inauguration. Polk sought to restore amicable ties, but Mexican leaders would not accept the loss of their eastern province. For his part Polk could not fail to defend Texas sovereignty or agree to circumscribe its territorial claims, and he did not wish to pursue a long-term defensive border war defending Texas's right of self-determination. Convinced that Mexico intended to move its army into Texas, Polk sent Zachary Taylor and his troops to the Rio Grande; and on April 24, 1846, a Mexican force of 1,600 crossed the river and captured an American patrol of 60 dragoons.

Within a week of learning that the Mexican and American armies had clashed, the British cabinet decided to settle the Oregon boundary dispute and sent instructions to its minister in Washington to agree to a partition at the forty-ninth parallel. Some of Polk's advisors, Secretary of State James Buchanan included, had feared that the British would fight over their control of the Oregon Country and that the United States might find itself engaged on two fronts, a land war in Mexico and a maritime struggle with the British navy. Although militarily the United States stood unprepared for either, the President calculated correctly that Britain would not go to war over its commercial interests in Oregon, Texas, or Mexico. Polk's diplomatic successes in settling the Oregon question and his military strategy for winning the war in Mexico did not bring political consensus at home. Whigs blamed him for giving up half of Oregon and charged him with fighting an immoral war in Mexico.

Polk made every effort to resolve the Texas issue through diplomacy and offered to purchase Mexico's northern provinces, not because he believed in manifest destiny but because he knew that the agrarian republic could not close its borders and so prevent emigration. Polk's expansion policies postponed the demise of the agrarian republic but did not resolve the problems of a Union bereft of compatible economic, religious, and racial interests. In four tumultuous years he accomplished his basic goals, and true to his word he declined all interest in a second term. Although blessed with a strong constitution, "Young Hickory" fell victim to cholera and died at his home in Nashville on June 15, 1849.

Wayne Cutler, University of Tennessee, Knoxville
SEE: JACKSONIANS; MEXICAN WAR; POLK, SARAH C.

POLK, JAMES K., ANCESTRAL HOME in Columbia is the only surviving residence of the eleventh U.S. President, excluding the White House. James K. Polk was attending the University of North Carolina in 1816 when his father Samuel built the two-story, Federal-style house on Market Street (now Seventh Street). The fine brick structure reflected Samuel Polk's success as a farmer, surveyor, and land speculator. After graduating from college in 1818, James returned to Tennessee and stayed with his parents until he married Sarah Childress in 1824. While living in his father's house, he practiced law and successfully campaigned for the State Legislature. When his father died in 1827, James executed the will, which ensured that the house would remain his mother's residence. Throughout his life, he was a frequent guest at the Columbia home. Shortly after leaving the Presidency, he paid a final visit to his mother in April, 1849; he died of cholera in Nashville two months later. His mother, Jane Knox Polk, lived in the family home until her death in 1852.

After Sarah Childress Polk died in Nashville in 1891, her great-niece, Sarah Jetton Fall, began to collect and publicly display President and Mrs. Polk's personal belongings. In 1924 Mrs. Fall's daughter, Saidee Fall Grant, started the James K. Polk Association to continue these preservation efforts. Although the Association originally exhibited its historical collection in Nashville, group members saw the Polk house in Columbia as the ideal site for their museum. With help from the City of Columbia and Maury County, the Association raised half of the necessary funds to purchase the property; the State of Tennessee then matched the amount. Owned by the State and operated by the Association, the James K. Polk Ancestral Home became a Presidential historic site in 1929. Between then and 1979, a series of restoration projects revealed the structure's early nineteenth century appearance. A Victorian front porch and an enclosed side porch were removed; a metal roof was replaced by an authentic wooden shingle one; a detached brick kitchen was reconstructed. In 1961 the National Park Service designated the Polk Home a National Historic Landmark.

Today, visitors to the Home see original furnishing from James K. Polk's years in Columbia, Nashville, and Washington, D.C. The site's collections of over 1,300 artifacts and documents include books from Polk's library, memorabilia from his political campaigns, the official notification of his election to the Presidency, Inaugural mementos, White House china and decorative items, oil portraits of President and Mrs. Polk, and a daguerreotype of Polk's Cabinet, the earliest known photograph of the White House interior. The Home remains the headquarters of the Polk Memorial Association. In accordance with its stated purpose, the organization continues to "perpetuate the memory of the eleventh President of the United States."

John C. Holtzapple, James K. Polk Ancestral Home
SEE: MAURY COUNTY; POLK, JAMES K.; POLK, SARAH C.

POLK, LEONIDAS (1806–1864), Episcopal bishop and Confederate general, was born in Raleigh, North Carolina, April 10, 1806. He briefly attended the University of North Carolina before entering the U.S. Military Academy. He graduated eighth in his class in 1827. He became an Episcopalian during his senior year and resigned his commission six months after graduation to enter the ministry. He was ordained a deacon in 1830.

Polk married Frances (Fanny) Ann Devereux in May 1830 and immediately was posted as assistant to Bishop Richard Channing Moore of Monumental Church of Richmond, the church in which he and Fanny were married. In 1832 he moved his family to Tennessee, where he received a portion of the Polk lands near Mount Pleasant and built a home called "Ashwood."

He became Missionary Bishop of the Southwest in 1838 and Bishop of Louisiana in 1841. At the Louisiana Convention in 1842 he proposed that religious education should be extended to blacks. He was active in the establishment of the University of the South where he laid its cornerstone at Sewanee, Tennessee, in 1860. When the Civil War began and Louisiana seceded from the Union, Polk as Bishop, and not with the prior consent of the Louisiana Convention, pulled his convention out of the Episcopal Church of the United States.

Confederate President Jefferson Davis, friend and former West Point classmate, encouraged Polk to accept a commission in the Confederate Army, and Polk eventually exchanged his clerical vestments for a uniform. He was commissioned Major General in the Provisional Army of the Confederacy on June 25, 1861. In the early months of the conflict, he commanded the vast territory of Department No. 2 (headquartered in Memphis), which included the Mississippi River defenses from the Red River to Paducah, Kentucky. To fortify the river further he occupied Columbus, Kentucky, on September 4, 1861, violating Kentucky's neutrality. This act probably hurt the Confederate cause in the area more than it benefited it. He also organized the Army of the Mississippi, later a part of the Army of Tennessee. He was superseded in command of Department No. 2 by General Albert Sidney Johnston.

Polk commanded the Confederate right at Shiloh, leading four charges personally. At Perryville, he was second-in-command to Braxton Bragg, who criticized him for not attacking the Union forces when ordered. Bragg blamed Polk for the failure of the Perryville campaign. Polk commanded the right flank at the battle of Stones River, and his corps took the pivotal Round Forest twice before Bragg's army withdrew. At Chickamauga, Bragg relieved Polk of command, had him transferred to Mississippi, and ordered a court-martial for disobeying orders. After careful investigation, Jefferson Davis dismissed the charges. Polk took command of the Department of Alabama, Mississippi, and East Louisiana in December 1863 with its headquarters in Meridian, Mississippi.

General Joseph E. Johnston, who replaced Bragg following the Battle of Chickamauga, ordered Polk's forces to assist him in the Atlanta campaign. While examining the Federal position in company with Generals Johnston and Hardee, Polk was instantly killed by a shot to the chest at Pine Mountain near Marietta, Georgia, on June 14, 1864. At that time he commanded a corps of the Army of Tennessee. He was buried in Augusta, Georgia, until 1945, when his remains and those of his wife were re-interred in Christ Church Cathedral in New Orleans.

Leo J. Goodsell, Plano, Illinois

SEE: ARMY OF TENNESSEE; BRAGG, BRAXTON; CHICKA-MAUGA AND CHATTANOOGA, BATTLES OF; RELIGION; SHILOH, BATTLE OF; ST. JOHN'S EPISCOPAL CHURCH; STONES RIVER, BATTLE OF; UNIVERSITY OF THE SOUTH

POLK, SARAH CHILDRESS (1803–1891), wife of the eleventh president of the United States, privately strengthened the role of first lady, acting as her husband's closest political ally, while publicly dignifying her position in a manner her contemporaries held in highest esteem. The third of four surviving children, she was born to Joel and Elizabeth Whitsitt Childress near Murfreesboro in Rutherford County on September 4, 1803.

Sarah grew up in surroundings fitting for the daughter of a successful merchant, tavern keeper, and land speculator. The family dwelled in an ample frame house two miles outside of Murfreesboro, Tennessee's capital from September 1819 to October 1825.

The state's leading politicians, including Andrew Jackson and Felix Grundy, frequented the Childress home when the legislature was in session; thus Sarah became acquainted with politics and political issues at a tender age.

Acting on their desire to educate and train their daughters for the expected role of upper class white women, Joel and Elizabeth Childress sent both girls to the Daniel Elam School locally and then engaged a tutor, Samuel P. Black, the principal of the Bradley Academy to teach the girls at the school after the boys had departed for the day. Their primary education, then, exceeded that of most girls and equaled that of most boys in their community. When Sarah reached 12 or 13, she and her sister attended the Abercrombie School in Nashville for two years to acquire the accouterments deemed proper for their station. They finished their education at the Moravian Female Academy in Salem (now Winston-Salem), North Carolina.

Murfreesboro was teeming with political activity when the Childress daughters returned home. James K. Polk was elected clerk of the Senate in 1819, which gave him the opportunity to renew his acquaintance with Sarah. Polk also ran successfully for a state legislative seat. The couple's courtship blossomed into betrothal and they married on January 1, 1824, afterward settling in Columbia.

James K. Polk continued to advance politically, serving in the U.S. House of Representatives from 1825–1839, when he launched his campaign for governor in order to wrest political power from the Whig party. During his extensive absences from home, Sarah Polk acted in conjunction with Polk's closest political advisors to assure his election. She sent documents pertinent to his congressional record and kept him apprised of newspaper articles dealing with the election. Successful in 1839, Polk lost the governorship to Whig James C. Jones in 1841 and again in 1843. Sarah became despondent over her husband's losses and worried about his health throughout and following his strenuous campaigns.

In 1844 James K. Polk was the Democratic choice for president. Discreet inquiries of the Tennessee delegation as to the suitability of Sarah Polk as first lady sealed the nomination. In a close race, Polk lost his home state by 267 votes but not the presidency.

Childless, Sarah Polk devoted her life to her husband's political career. During the 14 years he served in the House of Representatives, she accompanied him to Washington on all but two occasions, his first journey and during the upheaval known as the Peggy Eaton Affair that occurred during Andrew Jackson's presidency. Becoming acquainted with the Washington social scene and hosting parties to cement political bonds served her well when she became first lady. She had already attained a reputation for graciousness and the Polks made it their policy never to speak ill publicly of even their bitterest of political enemies. Consequently, Sarah Polk moved easily among Whig and Democratic men and women.

Throughout Polk's four years as president, newspaper reporters praised Sarah Polk's deportment as first lady. She fulfilled all of the tenets of mid-nineteenth century white, upper class womanhood. Twice weekly the White House doors were thrown open to visitors and Sarah Polk greeted her guests with dignity and charm. On those occasions she became the eyes and ears of her husband, who often declined to attend owing to pressing political matters. To save her husband's energy, she read the daily newspapers, marking passages of interest. Sarah Polk's behind-the-scenes role in her husband's political career remained secret to avoid subjecting her to public ridicule. She steadfastly held to her religious upbringing, barring dancing from the White House, and barring, unsuccessfully, visitors on the Sabbath. Although both Polks suffered from illness during their four years in Washington, they rarely missed church services.

Upon completion of his term as president in 1849, the Polks undertook a long journey from Washington to Nashville, where well wishers greeted them enthusiastically en route. When they arrived at New Orleans, word of a cholera outbreak reached them. They concluded their journey from Kentucky by land in the face of shipboard cases of the dreaded disease. A debilitated James K. Polk spoke before a gathering in his honor at Nashville on April 1, 1849. Although his health improved initially, he died on June 15. As a measure of his abiding trust in his wife, Polk praised her in his will for standing by him through all vicissitudes of his public and private life.

Sarah Childress Polk outlived her husband by 43 years, only occasionally leaving her home other than to attend church services. On August 12, 1891, she became ill and died two days later. She was originally entombed beside her husband on the grounds of their home. In 1893 the remains of President James K. Polk and First Lady Sarah Childress Polk were removed to the capitol grounds in Nashville.

Jayne Crumpler DeFiore, University of Tennessee, Knoxville
SEE: BRADLEY ACADEMY; EATON AFFAIR; MURFREESBORO; POLK, JAMES K.

POLLARD, WILLIAM G. (1911–1989), nuclear physicist, Episcopal priest, and founder of Oak Ridge Associated Universities (ORAU), was a native of New York state. Pollard moved to Tennessee with his family at age 12. He received his B.A. from the University of Tennessee in 1932, the same year he married his wife Marcella, and began a graduate fellowship at Rice University. He earned a Ph.D. in physics from Rice in 1935. He also received honorary doctorates in science, divinity, law, and humane letters from 12 colleges and universities.

Pollard began his career in 1936, serving on the physics department faculty at UT.

In 1944 he undertook two years at Columbia University as a research scientist on the Manhattan Project. He conducted research on the gaseous diffusion method of extracting uranium 235—the explosive in atomic bombs—from common uranium.

After the end of World War II, Pollard and his family returned to Tennessee, and a fellow physics professor at UT suggested to Pollard that university researchers in the Oak Ridge region have access to the federal government's Oak Ridge National Laboratory. This idea sparked Pollard's interest, and he headed a committee to investigate the possibility. He built the necessary support of both the federal government and 14 southern schools to create the Oak Ridge Institute of Nuclear Studies (ORINS) in October 1946. He served as the organization's executive director until his retirement in 1974.

Pollard regularly attended the Episcopal church with his wife and four sons without considering himself particularly religious. He experienced , though, a feeling "close to terror" immediately after the atomic bomb was dropped on Nagasaki, countering his initial exuberance following the bomb-drop on Hiroshima. After Pollard returned to Oak Ridge, he became more involved in the development of St. Stephen's Episcopal Church and participation in its services. As the leader of ORINS, he considered the new organization his primary responsibility, but he found himself more interested in theology.

Pollard was ordained in 1954 and served as priest associate at St. Stephen's until his death in 1989. Throughout his studies, Pollard had to resolve in his mind a complicated marriage of science and religion. As he struggled with the issue, he came to believe, to put it simply, that science was a way of investigating the wonders of God's creations. Because his combination of careers was so unusual, he also received attention from both academia and the media. Lectures he delivered on the relationship of science and theology led to publication of several books, including *Chance and Providence* and *Physicist and Christian*.

Pollard retired from his post as Executive Director of ORAU in 1974, but he worked for several more years as a distinguished scientist in the organization's Institute for Energy Analysis. Following a long struggle with cancer, Pollard died in 1989.

Pam Bonee, Oak Ridge Institute for Science and Education
SEE: OAK RIDGE ASSOCIATED UNIVERSITIES; OAK RIDGE NATIONAL LABORATORY

POPE, EDITH DRAKE (1869–1947) was a Williamson County native who worked as the business secretary

(1893–1913) and editor (1914–1932) of the *Confederate Veteran* for the magazine's entire 40-year history. As editor, she faced mounting financial problems caused by increased death rates, among Confederate veterans, reduction in the subscription list, and meager advertising. Pope secured modest monetary grants from the United Daughters of the Confederacy (UDC), which enabled the magazine to stay in business, but only in the format of an associational newsletter. Content changed, as secondary accounts replaced the earlier tradition of printing firsthand wartime reminiscences. Pope's personal journalism created unnecessary crises, such as when she stubbornly defended untenable positions in terms of historical veracity on Whittier's poem about Barbara Frietchie. Pope also actively engaged in several commemorative projects, including the Matthew Fontaine Maury monument in Richmond, Virginia, the Sam Davis Memorial Association, in Smyrna, Tennessee, and the monument to Confederate women in Nashville.

As editor of the *Confederate Veteran*, Pope associated with some of the highest ranking people in the UDC, including Mildred Lewis Rutherford, Kate Litton Hickman, Janet Henderson Randolph, Katie Walker Behan, and Mary Poppenheim. She joined Nashville No. 1, UDC in 1914 and became chapter president (1927–1930) and recording secretary (1930–1935). In retirement, she administered the Confederate Room in Nashville's War Memorial Building from 1931 to 1938 and served as Radio Chairperson for the Tennessee Division, UDC (1941–1943). She won more than a dozen essay contests sponsored by the UDC. Pope also belonged to the Tennessee Women's Press and Author's Club, Confederate Memorial Literary Society, Association for the Preservation of Virginia Antiquities, and the Woman's Historical Association (Nashville).

Pope died on January 27, 1947, on the ancestral farm in Burwood.

John A. Simpson, Kelso, Washington

SEE: CONFEDERATE VETERAN; DAVIS, SAM; NASHVILLE NO. 1, UDC

PORT ROYAL STATE HISTORIC AREA

PORT ROYAL STATE HISTORIC AREA is a 34-acre site in Montgomery County that preserves one of Middle Tennessee's earliest settlement areas as well as a reconstructed covered wooden bridge, which initially dated to 1903–1904, that crosses the Red River at this point. The first permanent settlers arrived in 1784 and nearby was held the first meeting of the Tennessee County Court, North Carolina, in 1788. The Red River Baptist Church, one of the earliest in the region, was organized at Port Royal in 1791. The town was organized in 1797 and during the nineteenth century it grew to a population of over 1,200. During the 1840s, local investors planned to open a silk mill but it never began production. In the second half of the century, R.L. Reding operated a broom factory and received a gold medal for his product at the 1904 World's Fair in St. Louis. A renovated Masonic Lodge (1859) is the park's headquarters and it has exhibits about Port Royal's significant role in late eighteenth and nineteenth century river transportation.

Carroll Van West, Middle Tennessee State University

SEE: MONTGOMERY COUNTY; SILK

PORTER, JAMES DAVIS (1828–1912), Governor and President of Peabody Normal School, was born in Paris, Tennessee, on December 7, 1828. An 1846 graduate of the University of Nashville, and admitted to the bar in 1851, Porter was elected to the state legislature in 1859. After Tennessee seceded, he helped organize troops for the Provisional Army of Tennessee. With the transfer of these forces to the Confederacy, Porter was appointed to the staff of Benjamin F. Cheatham, a post he held throughout the war.

After the war, Porter resumed his law practice and reentered public life in 1870 as a delegate to the state constitutional convention. Shortly afterwards, he won election as a circuit judge. Porter resigned from the bench in 1874 to seek the Democratic gubernatorial nomination. He handily defeated Republican opponent Horace Maynard in the election and won a second term in 1876. Porter served as president of the Nashville, Chattanooga, and St. Louis Railroad from 1880–1884. He was Assistant Secretary of State under President Grover Cleveland in 1885 and, during the second Cleveland administration, he was appointed Minister to Chile in 1892. He later served as president of the Tennessee Historical Society.

During Porter's first gubernatorial term, he secured use of the University of Nashville campus for a normal school funded through the largesse of financier and philanthropist George Peabody. In 1901 he was appointed chancellor of his alma mater, and the next year as president of the Peabody Normal College. Early in his tenure, he began efforts to turn over assets of the University of Nashville to trustees of the Peabody Fund, a transfer which occurred in 1907. Porter's herculean efforts in securing funds from local and state sources proved indispensable when the Peabody Education Fund liquidated its assets and granted a million dollar bequest for the creation of George Peabody College for Teachers. Porter felt embittered and betrayed when fellow Peabody Fund trustees decided to abandon the University of Nashville site and locate the teachers' college near Vanderbilt University. He resigned in 1909 and retired the next year to Paris, where he died May 18, 1912.

Christopher Losson, St. Joseph, Missouri

POTTERY. Manufacturing of pottery existed throughout Tennessee during much of its history, but records are non-existent until the 1820 manufacturing census, which listed eight potteries, all in East Tennessee. Isaac Hart and John Mathorn (later Mottern) produced earthenware in Carter County. Earthenware was also made in Greene County at potteries owened by Frederick Shaffer, John Click, Thomas Ripley, and Henry Kinser. A Jefferson County pottery, the owner of which is unknown, produced earthenware. The only listed stoneware manufacturer was Samuel Smith in Knoxville. One additional pottery, according to current research, was located in Davidson County.

Potteries established throughout the nineteenth and early twentieth centuries were primarily family operations situated where abundant clay deposits existed. These potteries produced primarily handcrafted, utilitarian wares using non-industrial techniques and featuring stylistic similarities passed from master to apprentice over several generations. Only a very few of these family operations produced a limited number of pieces that can be considered art pottery.

Industrialization at the end of the nineteenth century changed Tennessee's pottery operations. Industrial wares were produced by larger firms employing non-family workers, using mechanized techniques and imported clays, and were transported to non-local markets. Most industrial potteries were situated in major towns and cities, near available rail lines. They produced primarily fire brick, sewer pipe, stove pipe, flu linings, window caps, chimney tops, crocks, churns, flower pots, and stoneware whiskey jugs.

Techniques for firing greenware and the types of pottery produced varied from region to region during the nineteenth century. In East Tennessee, pottery was fired in above-ground, circular updraft kilns, with 42 percent being earthenware and 58 percent stoneware. In Middle Tennessee, semi-subterranean, circular updraft kilns were used and produced only 11 percent earthenware and 89 percent stoneware. West Tennessee operations used mostly above-ground, circular downdraft kilns and fired 100 percent stoneware.

As the 1820 census indicates, East Tennessee works initially dominated the state's production of pottery. Kiln sites were located on a north-south line following the East Tennessee Shale Belt in the valleys and ridges of the Appalachian chain. Most of the known potteries were situated in Greene, Washington, Jefferson, Knox, and Blount counties. Dominant among family operations in this part of Tennessee was the Keystone Pottery operated by Charles F. Decker, Sr., and his sons. Other noteworthy potteries were those operated by William Grindstaff of Blount and Knox counties and William Hinshaw, William Grim, and John Click in Greene County. Moses P. Harmon of Greene County, Chattanooga Fire Clay Works in Hamilton County, Weaver & Brothers Pottery in Knox County, and Southern Potteries, which produced the famous Blue Ridge ware, in Unicoi County were successful industrial potteries.

In Middle Tennessee, family-operated potteries were concentrated in White, Putnam, and DeKalb counties on lands rich in clay deposits situated on the Eastern Highland Rim. Pottery manufacturing in this three-county area seems to have been tied to the arrival of Andrew LaFever in White County about 1824. LaFever's six sons and the three generations of the family which succeeded them had connections with most of the major potteries in the area and seem to have influenced their products. Also noteworthy among family operations were those of the Dunn, Hedgecough, Roberts, Elrod, and Spears families. The Nashville Pottery Company in Davidson County and the Cookeville Pottery in Putnam County were the leading industrial firms in Middle Tennessee. Nashville Art Pottery, created as part of the Nashville School of Art in 1884 and operated until 1889, was probably the first of its kind in Tennessee.

In West Tennessee, family potteries were primarily along the north-south West Tennessee Bedded-Clay Belt. Leading family potteries in this portion of the state were those operated by the Connor, Crave, and Reevely families of Hardeman, Henderson, and Madison counties, respectively. Grand Junction Pottery of Hardeman County, Currier-Weaver Pottery and W.D. Russell Pottery in Henry County, Pinson Pottery Company and Jackson Pottery Company in Madison County, and the Bluff City Terra Cotta Works of Shelby County were leading industrial firms.

Stephen D. Cox, Tennessee State Museum

POW CAMPS IN WORLD WAR II. During the Second World War, Tennessee was home to 11 prisoner-of-war camps. Four were large installations. Camp Crossville was built on the site of an abandoned 1930s Civilian Conservation Corps work camp. Camp Forrest and Camp Campbell were existing army installations with extra space wherein prisoners were quartered. The Memphis Armed Service Forces Depot also housed prisoners, initially serving as a branch of a camp in Como, Mississippi.

Though nicknamed the "Jap Camp" by local residents, the Crossville camp actually contained only

Italian and German prisoners. The first prisoners sent there included roughly 1,500 Germans, most of whom were veterans of General Erwin Rommel's Afrika Korps. Camp Forrest housed nearly twice as many Germans. Camp Campbell was a special-purpose camp which served as a safe-haven for dedicated "anti-Nazis." Ironically, discipline at this camp was often a problem as these German democrats quarreled incessantly among themselves. The Memphis installation housed German and Italian prisoners.

Given benevolent treatment, which was commonplace in American camps, the prisoners generally were cooperative. Italian captives in particular proved congenial. Prisoners were at times for small wages required or requested to perform labor, mostly of an agricultural variety. Commonly, they completed their tasks adequately and without incident. Those who refused to work or performed poorly were punished with reduced rations, sometimes cut to bread and water. When the cotton compresses and warehouses in Memphis suffered from a labor shortage in the fall of 1944, prisoners from the Memphis camp worked there and some were sent to Arkansas to pick cotton.

Security at the camps was rather lax. Prisoners were allowed, for example, to go for walks outside the compounds. Most always returned. Of 356,560 prisoners in the United States, only 1,583 "escaped," and of those only 22 were never recaptured.

While escape attempts were rare, they were often interesting. The first two escapees recorded jumped from a train bound for Camp Forrest in November 1942. They were apprehended a few days later. An Afrika Korps veteran walked out of Camp Forrest to nearby Tullahoma, caught the 9:25 train to Nashville, and actually went pub-crawling with an unsuspecting GI on leave before being apprehended the next day during a routine check. One escapee from Camp Crossville, who spoke English fluently, remained at large for several months before returning. Not every escape attempt had a happy ending, if the following story is believed. Three German submariners who escaped from Crossville came upon a mountain cabin. Out came "granny," who told them to "git." When they did not leave, she shot one of them dead. When a local deputy arrived and told her of the circumstances, the woman sobbed, claiming she would never have fired had she known they were Germans. "I thought they wuz Yankees," she said.

Conditions were comfortable for "prison." By the Geneva Convention, the enemy never did without. Entertainments were commonplace. For example, at Camp Campbell the inmates purchased musical instruments from canteen profits and formed two complete orchestras. Germans prisoners at Memphis also formed an orchestra. Camp authorities allowed the inmates to publish newspapers at both Crossville and Camp Campbell. Barring disciplinary problems, the prisoners were even allowed to buy beer and wine!

Educational programs were established at nearly every camp. English instruction was the most common course of study. Standard coursework in chemistry, mathematics, and the like was also offered, along with such local specialties as piano lessons at Crossville and a course on "The Symbolism of the American Funnies" at Camp Campbell.

There is little doubt that the prisoners appreciated the kind treatment which they received. They expressed this in letters and during postwar visits. Several even emigrated to the areas in which they had been imprisoned. In 1984 a group of German prisoners visited Memphis and the site of their old camp.

Jeff Roberts, Tennessee Technological University
SUGGESTED READING: Hazel Wages, "The Memphis Armed Service Forces Depot Prisoner of War Camp: 1944–1946," *Tennessee Historical Quarterly* 52(1993): 19–32
SEE: WORLD WAR II

PREHISTORIC CAVE ART. In 1979 a caver exploring a narrow subterranean passageway in southeastern Tennessee noticed scratches and lines in mudbanks that lined the cave walls. He reported the marks to Charles Faulkner of the University of Tennessee, who identified them as prehistoric drawings. These were the first ancient artworks ever found in the "dark zone," beyond the reach of light, in a North American cave. The Mud Glyph Cave images included animals, winged humans, warriors, and other emblems of the "Southeast Ceremonial Complex" (SECC), a religious iconography associated with the late prehistoric Mississippian moundbuilders. Several radiocarbon dates on cane charcoal, deposited from torches used by ancient cave visitors, clustered around A.D. 1300 and also are coincident with the Mississippian period.

Nearly 20 other deep art caves have been found since. Two caves are in Virginia, two in Kentucky, one in Alabama, and the remainder in Middle and East Tennessee. This distribution corresponds to the limestone tablelands of the Appalachian uplands, suggesting that cave art was produced everywhere caves were available for decoration. In one case, the art is located a mile from the mouth of the cave, indicating that prehistoric artists were physically and technically able to penetrate the vast underground karst systems of the Appalachian Plateau.

Three different production techniques have been identified. *Mud glyphs* are images traced into wet mud on cave walls and banks. Seven mud glyph sites are now known, including one of the earliest (Adair Cave) and the very latest site (1st Unnamed Cave). Mississippian period mud glyph caves are very elaborate, sometimes including organized compositions of hundreds of images. *Petroglyphs* are images scratched into the rock of cave walls and ceilings. Tennessee's earliest cave art (3rd Unnamed Cave at 4,000 years old) is of this type, but petroglyphs were also produced during the late Mississippian period. Some petroglyphs are associated with human burials, but most are either isolated art independent of other evidence for cave use or are associated with mining of raw materials from caves. *Pictographs* are images painted onto surfaces with mineral pigments like charcoal and clay. These date either to the Woodland or Mississippian periods and are the rarest form of prehistoric cave art; only a few examples are presently known. Thus, a great variability existed in the nature and context within which artwork was produced.

Tennessee cave art has great time depth, and it appears that the subject matter of the artwork changes over time. Radiocarbon dates from Adair Cave in Kentucky and 3rd Unnamed Cave in Tennessee suggest that artwork may have its origins more than 4,300 years ago during the Archaic period. Images in these early sites are simple (serpents, suns, chevrons) and not obviously similar to later SECC iconography. Artwork from Crumps Cave in Kentucky shows that art was also produced during the Woodland period (2000 B.C.–A.D. 1000), and the images there (humans and crude animals) are also distinctive. A number of sites associated with the Mississippian show the SECC iconography first identified at Mud Glyph Cave.

The meaning of Tennessee's prehistoric cave art is difficult to determine. In late time periods, similarities between the cave images and SECC iconography suggest that the art was primarily religious, perhaps produced by priests or shamans in the context of specific rituals. For historical tribes in Tennessee, caves were passageways to the underworld, and the underworld was also an important yet dangerous place for Mississippian peoples. Cave art depicting serpents and winged humans may reflect a belief in the power of these dark, deep places and their role in the structure of the cosmos. In earlier periods, meaning is problematic. Image themes are rather different from those during the Mississippian and sometimes associated with other activities (e.g., mining). Thus, Archaic and Woodland cave art may have served different purposes for its makers: sanctifying space, protecting people engaged in dangerous activities, marking places where resources could be found. So far removed in time, we may never know the meaning of this earliest prehistoric cave art.

Today, conservation is the most pressing problem for Tennessee's prehistoric cave art. Unauthorized digging in caves destroys the context of the images by removing datable artifacts and can damage the artwork itself. Modern graffiti are often unknowingly placed over the ancient icons, obscuring or obliterating them forever. Even simple traffic through a cave can damage art as people touch and rub against the fragile images in passing. Awareness of the presence of these treasures is the first step in protecting this important aspect of Tennessee's cultural heritage.

Jan F. Simek, University of Tennessee, Knoxville

SUGGESTED READINGS: Charles H. Faulkner, ed., *The Prehistoric Native American Art of Mud Glyph Cave* (1986); Jan F. Simek, "The Sacred Darkness: Prehistoric Cave Art in Tennessee" *Tennessee Conservationist* (March/April 1987)

SEE: ART; MISSISSIPPIAN CULTURE; PREHISTORIC NATIVE AMERICAN ART; WOODLAND PERIOD

PREHISTORIC NATIVE AMERICAN ART. Art in its broadest definition is patterned application of human skill that evokes a feeling of aesthetic sensibility. As such, art is a universal of human culture and can be traced archaeologically to at least 40,000 years ago. Art functions on two levels. First it can be decorative or purely ornamental in function, as are many of the so-called "decorative arts." Second, art can be symbolic or actually embody aspects of the value and belief systems of the cultures in which it occurs. In general, symbolic art is created using formalized styles of some time depth and is designed to elicit in the viewer clearly defined expectations and behaviors. For example, a Cherokee wooden mask manufactured in the image of a wolf would be more than a mask to a member of the tribe; it was a clan symbol, which also elicited a set of socio-religious feelings and responses. This symbolic aspect of artistic expression is not restricted to tribal societies. Today, Christian motifs, coats of arms, commemorative scenes, and political logos, for example, are added to elicit social, political, and religious feelings.

To fully appreciate and understand art, it must be studied in the context of the culture and even the individual that produced and used it. It is hard to overcome our own ethnocentrism in interpreting non-western or tribal art; it is even more difficult when that art is associated with prehistoric cultures hundreds or even thousands of years old.

Our knowledge of the art of the prehistoric Indians of Tennessee is based upon archaeological research, analogies drawn from historical documents and nineteenth century ethnographies of the Creeks and Cherokees, and the artifacts themselves. Our record of past art mediums is incomplete; Tennessee's temperate environment generally precluded the preservation of wood, fiber, feathers, and skins, and in some areas, bone and shell as well. Time also took its toll on the cultural assemblages of groups living five to ten thousand years ago.

Little has been preserved from the Paleoindian (10,000+ to 8000 B.C.) and much of the Archaic

(8000–1000 B.C.) periods that one could define as art. However, the execution of many of the chipped stone projectile points over the millennia exceeded the utilitarian and evoked aesthetic sensibilities. Likewise, the manufacture of spearthrower weights (atlatl weights, bannerstones) often ultilizing non-local stone became an art form in the Archaic period. By the Late Archaic, artistic decoration was executed in elaborate geometric carving on bone pins. The emergence of regional trade networks by 5000 B.C. and the appearance of marine shell ornaments and copper with some burials in Tennessee suggests the development of social distinctions—status—enhanced by valued objects, an ideal environment for symbolic aspects of art.

By the Woodland period (1000 B.C.–A.D. 900), the artistic embellishment of objects had increased greatly and included stone pendants and pipes delicately carved in the forms of animals and insects, and clay pots whose surfaces were impressed before firing with elaborate geometric designs. North of Tennessee, the Adena and Hopewell cultures, complex societies with earthworks and ritualism, developed formalized art styles that spread throughout the Southeast. Recent excavations at the Pinson Mounds site near Jackson found two rattles made from portions of two human skulls and engraved with typical Hopewellian abstract motifs. The occurrence of much of the art in burials of apparent high status individuals at Pinson and elsewhere suggests an association of art with social differentiation and political power.

In the Woodland period, stylistically consistent images emerged that were probably associated with specific mythic creatures and contributed to an iconographic system that reached its peak of complexity and formalization in the succeeding Mississippian period (A.D. 900–1600). The fundamental view of the cosmos for the Indians of the Southeast was a three-tiered universe. This world was a circular island that existed between the Upperworld and the Underworld; life was a constant struggle to maintain balance between order and harmony of the Upper World and disorder and disharmony of the Underworld. Mythic beings who had analogs in different animals personified these worlds; art became a way in which the Indians could symbolically depict and manipulate this construct.

The Mississippian period in the Southeast was the pinnacle of prehistoric social and political complexity; it was also the peak of artistic expression. Utilizing the mediums of marine shell, pottery, bone, copper, stone, wood, and fabric, the Mississippian Indians of Tennessee created a spectacular array of artistic objects. Additionally, there is evidence that images were applied to dwelling walls with colored clays, and recent research is indicating that art was being applied to mud and stone surfaces in the deep recesses of caves—a phenomenon that may extend back to the Late Archaic. Mississippian art is a fascinating assemblage of symbols and a virtual bestiary of creatures that have been modeled, carved, incised, engraved, or painted.

Fundamental to all this art is a formalized iconography that is based on the construct of the cosmos, veneration of ancestors, warfare, fertility, and the perpetuation of an elite class. The recognition of the frequent use of a number of motifs in Mississippian art gave rise in 1940 to the putative existence of a Southeastern Ceremonial Complex (Southern Cult, Buzzard Cult, Death Cult). Most scholars today reject the idea of a unified cult and instead see this distinctive iconography as symbols in a complex system that was social, political, and economic as well as religious. Scholars also have rejected the notion that the inspiration for Mississippian art derives from Mesoamerica; the similarities are more likely because of fundamental ideologies of great time depth shared in common by North American Indians.

Mississippian art continued into the 1600s, but disappeared with the cataclysmic impact of European intrusion and the diseases that brought decimation and social change. In the 1700s, the rapid acculturation of the Cherokees and Chickasaws all but eclipsed any traditional art with the exception of basketry.

Jefferson Chapman, Frank M. McClung Museum, University of Tennessee, Knoxville

SUGGESTED READINGS: David S. Brose, et al., *Ancient Art of the American Woodland Indians* (1985); Jefferson Chapman, *Tellico Archaeology: 12,000 Years of Native American History* (1995); Stephen D. Cox, et al., *Art and Artisans of Prehistoric Middle Tennessee* (1985)

SEE: ARCHAIC PERIOD; MISSISSIPPIAN CULTURE; PINSON MOUNDS; PREHISTORIC CAVE ART; WOODLAND PERIOD

PREHISTORIC USE OF CAVES. More than 7,000 deep caves have been recorded throughout Tennessee. Concentrated in the limestone uplands of Middle and East Tennessee, these karsts extend from the Mammoth Cave area of central Kentucky, through Tennessee, into northern Alabama, and they represent one of the most extensive cave systems in the world. Ancient Native Americans took note of these caves, incorporated them into their world view, and used them in a variety of ways.

There is no evidence that prehistoric peoples ever lived in the "dark zones" of deep caves, beyond external light. Occupations did occur in open rockshelters and in cave vestibules, but the deeper recesses were clearly considered unsuitable for habitation. Deep caves were used for more specialized purposes. Dr. Patty Jo Watson, a leading cave archaeologist, defines four types of sites based on variation in ancient underground activities. These are: footprint caves, mortuary caves, mines and quarries, and ceremonial caves. All four types are found in Tennessee.

Footprint caves preserve the imprints of human feet in mud or soft sediments and are often associated with very limited archaeological debris, suggesting ephemeral, exploratory visits to the dark zone. Charcoal from ancient torches sometimes found with footprints allows them to be dated; in several cases, footprints may be older than 4,000 years, indicating that Archaic hunter-gatherers (8000 B.C.-1000 B.C.) were willing and able to penetrate Tennessee's karst systems. Hundreds of prints might be present in a given cave, evidence for the presence of groups of people of varying ages and/or sexes. Caves where *only* footprints and torch charcoal are found bear witness to ancient cave exploration as a specific activity, but footprints also occur in mining and ceremonial caves. Ancient footprints are extremely fragile, and many have been obliterated by later, including modern, cave traffic.

Mortuary caves are holes in the ground into which human bodies, intact or cremated, were introduced for inhumation. There may be hundreds of these sites in Tennessee, but very few have been studied out of respect for their dead. Some have been examined when looters have illegally exhumed or molested the human remains. At least two sites associate petroglyphs, or cave art, with burials. In Alabama, Kentucky, and Virginia, where burial caves have been researched in detail, this practice seems to be related to the Woodland period (1000 B.C.–A.D. 1000), as initial agricultural communities were developing. The chronology of mortuary caves in Tennessee is unknown.

Mines and quarries are well known from Kentucky and Indiana, where caves were mined for minerals during the Woodland period, especially for crystalline salts (epsomite, gypsum, aragonite and mirabilite). These minerals might have been ingested for ceremonial or medicinal purposes and were probably traded among Woodland agricultural villages. No direct evidence for mineral mining has been found in Tennessee, although residues of these materials have been recovered from prehistoric containers, making it likely that such mining did occur. Chert quarries in caves are common in Tennessee, and these have been dated from the Archaic, through the Woodland, into the Mississippian (A.D. 1000–1600) periods. In one case, a Late Archaic chert mine was located more than a kilometer from the cave's mouth. It is also likely that clay was removed from some caves for use in ceramic production or as pigment.

Historical Native American groups in the Southeast saw caves as pathways to the underworld, which was an enigmatic and even dangerous world. Prehistoric ceremonial activity is evident in a number of caves in the form of cave art. This is the only dark zone cave art tradition known from prehistoric North America. Images of religious import are incised into rock (petroglyphs), painted (pictographs), and engraved into wet clay (mud glyphs). The great majority of cave art was produced in the Mississippian period, but some sites may be Woodland and even Archaic in age.

Cave use by prehistoric peoples involved a variety of activities and changed over time. In the Archaic, caves were explored, mined, and decorated with art. The same range of activities occurred during the Woodland period, with the probable use of pit caves for burial; mining of mineral salts was emphasized. Mississippian peoples decorated caves and may have performed limited mining. Tennessee's vast karst systems were an important part of the prehistoric landscape.

Jan F. Simek, University of Tennessee, Knoxville
SUGGESTED READING: Kenneth C. Carstens and Patty Jo Watson, eds., *Of Caves and Shell Mounds* (1996); Charles H. Faulkner, ed., *The Prehistoric Native American Art of Mud Glyph Cave* (1986); Patty Jo Watson, ed. *The Archaeology of the Mammoth Cave Area* (1974)
SEE: ARCHAIC PERIOD; MISISSIPPIAN CULTURE; PREHISTORIC CAVE ART; PREHISTORIC NATIVE AMERICAN ART; WOODLAND PERIOD

PRESIDENTIAL ELECTIONS, TENNESSEE PATTERNS. In the ten presidential elections from 1796–1832, Tennessee went for the winner eight times. In 1796 (Tennessee's first election for president), the state's three electoral votes were cast for Thomas Jefferson, but John Adams was elected. Tennesseans supported Jefferson again in 1800 when he won, and again in 1804 when he was reelected.

James Madison and James Monroe received the state's electoral votes for two terms each. In 1824 Andrew Jackson carried Tennessee and won the popular vote but failed to win a majority of electoral votes. In the House of Representatives, John Quincy Adams (a National Republican) was elected president. Andrew Jackson got his revenge in 1828 and was reelected in 1832, both times carrying Tennessee.

Jackson exerted little political influence on his state once his presidential career was over. From 1796–1832 Tennessee voted solidly for candidates who would be modern Democrats. Beginning in 1836, they started voting for Whigs (the predecessor of today's Republican Party). Jackson could not carry Tennessee for his handpicked successor, Martin Van Buren. The state's electoral votes in 1836 went to a native son, Senator Hugh Lawson White, a Whig.

In the nine national elections from 1836–1868, Tennessee voted in only eight of them since it did not participate in 1864 due to its membership in the Confederacy. Tennesseans voted for winners four times and losers four times. Whig candidates carried the state in 1840 (William Henry Harrison), 1844 (Henry Clay), 1848 (Zachary Taylor), and 1852 (Winfield Scott). The 1844 Tennessee election was notable since Clay defeated James K. Polk—a Tennessean who won the presidency even though losing his own state.

Only in 1856, the last election before the Civil War, did Tennessee return to the Democratic column, voting for James Buchanan of Pennsylvania. In 1860 the state rejected the major candidates—Abraham Lincoln (Republican), Stephen A. Douglas (Democrat) and John C. Breckinridge (Southern Democrat)—and supported instead another native son, John Bell (Constitutional Union), a former Whig who had been a speaker of the U.S. House of Representatives and a U.S. Senator.

Tennessee, in July 1866, became the first Confederate state to reenter the Union. With Reconstruction still at full tide, the state cast its electoral votes for Ulysses S. Grant in 1868. Tennessee would not support another Republican candidate for over a half century. In the 12 presidential elections from 1872–1916, Tennessee supported the Democrat every time, backing the winner only four times (Grover Cleveland twice and Woodrow Wilson twice). The state's electoral votes went to losers Horace Greeley (1872), Samuel J. Tilden (1876), Winfield Scott Hancock (1880), William Jennings Bryan (1896, 1900, and 1908), and Alton B. Parker (1904).

Following World War I, no clear voting pattern emerged. Warren G. Harding (Republican) carried the state in 1920, but in 1924 Tennessee rejected Calvin Coolidge and cast its votes for the Democratic candidate, John W. Davis. In 1928, however, the state returned to the Republican column and backed Herbert Hoover over Al Smith.

Tennessee swung toward the Democrats again four years later, and Franklin D. Roosevelt won the state in 1932, 1936, 1940, and 1944. In 1948 the state cast 11 electoral votes for Harry Truman, and one vote for Strom Thurmond's States' Rights party.

1952 began a 40-year domination by Republicans in Tennessee presidential elections. Of the 12 elections in this period, Tennessee voted Republican eight times. Even more significant, the state backed the winner in 11 of the 12 elections. Only in 1960, when Richard Nixon was favored over John F. Kennedy, did Tennesseans back a losing candidate. The only three Democrats who won the state during this time were Lyndon Johnson (1964), Jimmy Carter (1976), and Bill Clinton (1992 and 1996). Even in 1956 when Senator Estes Kefauver was the running mate of Adlai Stevenson, Tennessee stayed in the Republican column. Tennessee's tilt toward Bill Clinton in 1996 marked the first time since 1944 that the state voted for a Democrat in consecutive elections.

In ten Presidential elections there has been a Tennessean on the ballot for either President or Vice Pres-

ident, and six of those times resulted in victory. Tennessee, thus, has played a disproportionately important role in Presidential politics, and that tradition seems likely to hold in 2000.

Ed Young, Nashville

PRESLEY, ELVIS A. (1935–1977). Elvis. The first name alone invokes images and sounds which spark instant recognition. While he may not have invented Rock-n-Roll, few can deny that Elvis Presley helped transform a musical fad into a national and international phenomenon. In the process, he became one of the most successful entertainers of the twentieth century and one of its most controversial cultural figures.

Presley was born into anonymity in Tupelo, Mississippi, on January 8, 1935. After years of struggle against dwindling economic opportunities and eroding status, Presley and his working class family migrated to Memphis. In the West Tennessee metropolis, young Presley aspired to overcome his feelings of invisibility. Inspired by movie-stars and entertainers, he developed a penchant for flashy clothes, slicked-back hair, and long sideburns. In his quest for identity, he also turned to radio and absorbed an eclectic assortment of musical styles: rhythm and blues, country, pop, and both black and white gospel. Presley eventually synthesized these various styles into what became known as rockabilly.

In 1954 Presley made his first recordings for Sam Phillips's Sun Records Company. He also joined the Louisiana Hayride in Shreveport and toured extensively throughout the South and Southwest. By the end of 1955, when he signed with RCA, Presley had become one of the hottest commodities in country music. Yet his new manager, the flamboyant Colonel Tom Parker, sought a larger and more diversified audience for his client. In 1956 Parker booked Presley onto several network television programs, the most famous being his appearance on the Ed Sullivan Show. Beamed into the living rooms of millions of viewers, Presley's popularity skyrocketed. Following unprecedented record sales, Hollywood beckoned, and the singer became a movie idol in *Love Me Tender*. As his fame rose, furor over a black-derived and overtly sexual performance style mounted across the nation. The criticisms only heightened Presleymania. By 1958 he was the undisputed "King of Rock-n-Roll."

Between 1956 and 1965, Presley dominated popular music. Even a stint in the Army failed to stifle his popularity. After 1960 he devoted his energy almost exclusively to motion pictures. While the results did not bring him critical acclaim, he became one of the highest paid actors of the decade. Yet by the mid-1960s, Presley's creativity and influence appeared irreversibly diminished. A highly-successful television special in 1968, in which he returned to his blues roots, revived his career, and Presley returned to touring for the first time since the 1950s. To the astonishment of many, Presley recaptured the vitality which characterized his early career. After 1973, however, personal difficulties, including a failed marriage, health problems, and ballooning weight took a toll on the singer. On August 6, 1977, Presley died of heart failure and complications from drug use. A southern version of the Horatio Alger hero, who challenged contemporary boundaries regarding music, sex, taste, race, and public behavior, Presley remains a significant key to understanding the region and era from which he emerged.

Michael Bertrand, Middle Tennessee State University

SUGGESTED READINGS: Greil Marcus, *Mystery Train: Images of America in Rock 'n' Roll Music* (rev. ed., 1981); Peter Guralnick, *Last Train to Memphis: The Rise of Elvis Presley* (1994)

SEE: GRACELAND; MEMPHIS MUSIC SCENE; MUSIC; PHILLIPS, SAMUEL C.; ROCKABILLY MUSIC

PRESTON, FRANCES WILLIAMS (1934–), a Nashville native who went to work for Broadcast Music Inc. (BMI) when she was 21, serves now as that enterprise's worldwide president and CEO. While still a teenager she had joined WSM as a receptionist, and within five years she landed an informal arrangement with BMI. By 1958 she had the title of Southern Area Manager for BMI and office space in the Life and Casualty Tower.

Founded by a group of leading radio executives in 1940, BMI is a music performing rights organization that collects and distributes license fees on behalf of more than 120,000 songwriters and more than 60,000 music publishers with a repertoire of over three million works in all areas of music. Preston's endeavors on behalf of country music songwriters and publishers brought their work protection for the first time, and with it came an emerging awareness and acknowledgment of legitimacy on the part of the larger music world of the 1950s and 1960s. Preston's induction into the Country Music Hall of Fame in 1992 indicates the country music industry's view of her important role in its success over the previous 35 years.

While Preston is known to musicians, songwriters, and publishers as their champion, she has also provided a role model for women who would enter the business end of the music industry. In the 20 years following her elevation to vice president at BMI (a promotion that in 1965 made her Tennessee's first female corporate executive), she served in the capacity of president of the boards of the Country Music Association, the Country Music Foundation, and the Gospel Music Association. In 1985 Preston became senior vice president and then president of BMI the next year. She had already been labeled by *Esquire* in 1982 as "the most influential and powerful person in the country music business." In 1987 *Fortune* included her in that year's "50 most fascinating business people." In 1990 *Ladies Home Journal* ranked her among America's 50 most powerful women.

Now in her second decade as BMI's CEO and headquartered in New York, Preston's energy remains unflagging, both in business and in service projects. She has been instrumental in the establishment and ongoing funding of the Frances Williams Preston Laboratories, a division of the T.J. Martell Foundation, that provides monies for research in AIDS, cancer, and leukemia. In 1996 she became the first recipient of the Distinguished Service Award of New York's Elaine Kaufman Cultural Center.

Margaret D. Binnicker, Middle Tennessee State University

SUGGESTED READING: Mary A. Bufwack and Robert K. Oermann, *Finding Her Voice: The Saga of Women in Country Music* (1993)

SEE: COUNTRY MUSIC ASSOCIATION; COUNTRY MUSIC HALL OF FAME

PRIEST, JAMES PERCY (1900–1956). Born in Maury County on April 1, 1900, Priest went to county public schools before attending classes at the teacher's college in Murfreesboro (now Middle Tennessee State University), George Peabody College for Teachers, and the University of Tennessee in Knoxville. He then taught school and coached for several years in Maury County before joining the staff of *The Nashville Tennessean* in 1926.

At the *Tennessean,* Priest served as news editor, city editor, and ultimately the paper's managing editor. While writing public-interest articles as the daily's roving reporter in 1938–1940, he became well known among Middle Tennesseans. Affable and easily approached, Priest was familiar with the interests and concerns of area residents. His opportunity to serve them came in 1940 when he was elected to the United States Congress from Tennessee's Fifth District. He would serve eight terms in the House before his death.

Conscientious and devoted to his work, Priest enjoyed his life in Congress. Besides attending to the needs of his individual constituents, he, like most of his colleagues from Tennessee, generally supported federal aid for farmers, Tennessee Valley Authority appropriations, federal aid for vocational education programs, and federal appropriations for the indigent; he was also instrumental in securing funds for Nashville's new federal building. As Democratic Whip for a time and later as chairman of the House Interstate and Foreign Commerce Committee, Priest promoted federal public health measures and joined others in securing legislation which provided national distribution of the Salk polio vaccine.

A lifelong member of the National Press Club, Priest was very popular with the news media and well-liked and respected by his Congressional colleagues. Considered progressive, even liberal, on spending and civil rights issues, he was not always as one among Southern congressmen. In 1956, for example, Priest refused to join the more than 100 members of Congress who signed the so-called Southern Manifesto which denounced the Supreme Court's *Brown* desegregation decision and promised to fight racial integration. Later that summer, Priest won nomination for a ninth term but died on October 12, before the general election in the fall. He is buried in Nashville at Woodlawn Memorial Park.

Thomas H. Coode, Volunteer State Community College

SEE: NASHVILLE TENNESSEAN

PROFFITT'S department store was started by D.W. Proffitt in Maryville, Tennessee, in 1919. Son Harwell Proffitt opened another Proffitt's in Athens in 1965, and the first Knoxville location opened in West Town Mall in 1972. The Proffitt family expanded the business to four stores in East Tennessee before selling it in 1984 to a group of investors led by mall developer R. Brad Martin of Memphis. Fred Proffitt, the third generation of the family to run the business, retired from his position as president and chief executive officer in 1989. Martin then took over the operations of the company and formulated plans for future expansion. Proffitt's began by buying other small regional retailers and opening more of its own stores. In 1994, however, the chain's growth became more aggressive with the acquisition of McRae's, a chain of 28 stores based in Mississippi. Proffitt's then became a holding company with two divisions. Today the company has expanded to six divisions: Proffitt's with 19 stores in the upper South, McRae's with 31 stores in the deep South, Younkers with 50 stores in the Midwest, Parisian with 40 stores in the South and Midwest, Herberger's with 37 stores in the Midwest and Great Plains, and Carson Pirie Scott, the most recent addition, with 52 stores in the Midwest. Proffitt's merger with Carson Pirie Scott in October 1997 made it the fourth largest traditional department store company in the U.S., with 230 stores in 24 states. By late 1997 Proffitt's announced plans to move its headquarters to Birmingham.

Blythe Semmer, Middle Tennessee State University

SEE: BLOUNT COUNTY; COMMERCE

PROVIDENT LIFE AND ACCIDENT INSURANCE CO. See MACLELLAN BUILDING

PRUNTY, WYATT (1947–) is the author of four collections of poetry, *The Times Between* (1982), *What Women Know, What Men Believe* (1986), *Balance as Belief* (1989), and *The Run of the House* (1993), and a study of contemporary poetry, *"Fallen from the Symboled World": Precedents for the New Formalism* (1990).

Born in 1947 in Humboldt, Tennessee, he attended the University of the South (Sewanee) and took advanced degrees at Johns Hopkins and Louisiana State University, eventually returning to Sewanee in 1989 as Professor of English and Director of the Sewanee Writers' Conference.

Elegant and meditative, Prunty's poems find their subjects close to home. Player pianos, shortwave radios, and children waving from waterslides focus thought through language and act as signposts like the bent sapling in "The Elbow Tree," saying, "This way, and you will not be lost." His poems insist on order, seeking to create it where it does not yet exist, as in "A Family Portrait for Our Daughter," where the speaker muses at the delivery, "Genetically, I'd mix you like Matisse / in a garden's green concert of senses."

There is a darker side as well. A number of poems examine grief, especially at moments when order can be crippling. In "What doesn't Go Away," the speaker at his father's deathbed can say only "concentrate on your breathing" instead of "I love you" and realizes his words are "an off-speed pitch / I'll never retrieve." Similarly, "Induced Light" explores "one pain's power over another," as a soldier at an interrogation gives answers "Wrong or desperately true . . . in a place / That no opposing figure will confirm."

Preston Merchant, New York, New York

SEE: GIBSON COUNTY; LITERATURE; UNIVERSITY OF THE SOUTH

PUBLIC WORKS ADMINISTRATION (PWA). Organized with funds from the National Industrial Recovery Act of June 1933, the PWA was one of the New Deal's several attempts to revive the nation's depression-ridden economy. Designed to provide unemployed workers with wages as well as to stimulate the building industry, the PWA's main focus was on large-scale construction projects. From 1933 to 1939, the PWA spent six billion dollars in constructing 70 percent of all educational buildings built in the country; 65 percent of all the courthouses, city halls, and other nonresidential public buildings constructed; 65 percent of all the sewage treatment plants; 35 percent of the hospitals and public-health facilities; and ten percent of the roads, streets, and bridges. The PWA also completed numerous public housing and public utilities projects.

In the South, where the Great Depression had only worsened an already lame economy, where urban infrastructures were inadequate and public and private construction had virtually stopped, the PWA eventually made a noticeable difference. From 1933–1938, the South received over $500 million from the PWA. Besides the many miles of roads it surfaced and hundreds of buildings it constructed, the PWA in the South built Florida's Key West Highway, Atlanta's Techwood housing complex, the man-made port at Brownsville, Texas, the Virginia State Library in Richmond, Charity Hospital in New Orleans, and a water supply system in rural Alabama.

In Tennessee, the PWA employed thousands of jobless workers. It built, surfaced, and resurfaced over 200 miles of roads over the state, built numerous bridges and rail crossings, paved city streets, repaired power plants, constructed waterworks, and helped erect numerous public buildings, including new county courthouses in Davidson, Franklin, Lauderdale, Lewis, Madison, Obion, and Sumner counties.

In its large construction projects, the PWA especially was active in Tennessee's cities. For instance, PWA boosted Nashville's dollar-poor public education system by building several new elementary and junior high schools, West End High School, and the Pearl High School for African-American students. PWA workers also built schools in Chattanooga, Knoxville, Jackson, and Memphis.

At the same time, the PWA began over 50 housing projects in 29 states, including Tennessee. In Memphis the PWA constructed the Lauderdale Courts for white tenants and the Dixie Homes for blacks. In Nashville PWA workers built the Andrew Jackson Courts for African-American residents and Cheatham Place for whites.

In Tennessee, the presence of the PWA may have been more prominent than in other states because of its association with the Tennessee Valley Authority (TVA) in providing electric power for its citizens. Municipalities such as Knoxville and Chattanooga obtained PWA financing for the construction of public power distribution centers and local power stations; smaller towns like Lewisburg also benefited from new power distribution centers. PWA loans also helped bring TVA electricity to thousands of Tennesseans over the state.

PWA grants to cities for large-scale construction projects permanently changed urban landscapes in Tennessee. In Memphis, the PWA built a juvenile court building, the John Gaston Hospital, and dormitories at the University of Tennessee Medical School. In Chattanooga, besides its rather substantial school construction program, the PWA added a building to Silverdale Hospital, constructed the combined Public-University of Chattanooga Library building, and financed an addition to the Hamilton County Court House. In Knoxville, PWA funds added buildings to the sprawling campus of the University of Tennessee. The PWA especially was generous to Nashville. There it helped construct the Tennessee Supreme Court Building, the State Office Building, a new post office on Broadway, and the Davidson County Public Building and Court House on the city's Public Square.

By the late 1930s, growing opposition to the New Deal and the approach of World War II resulted in a shift of public spending from civilian to military construction. Ongoing PWA projects received final funding and the agency was terminated, but in Tennessee, almost 600 projects costing federal and local governments $90 million had not only provided wages for thousands of depression-weary Tennesseans but had enhanced significantly the physical portrait of the Volunteer State.

Thomas H. Coode, Volunteer State Community College

SUGGESTED READINGS: Roger Biles, *Memphis in the Great Depression* (1986); John D. Minton, *The New Deal in Tennessee, 1932–1938* (1979)

SEE: TENNESSEE VALLEY AUTHORITY; WORKS PROGRESS ADMINISTRATION

PUBLISHING. In 1875 Mark Twain published "Journalism in Tennessee," a delightful sketch about his experiences as associate editor of a newspaper called the *Morning Glory and Johnson County War-Whoop.* He had come South, he said, to improve his health, but soon found dodging bullets, bricks, and the foul language of competitors and readers to be more than he had bargained for. "Tennesseean [sic] journalism is too stirring for me," Twain concluded in announcing his intention to leave the state as quickly as possible.

Twain's fictional piece is an entertaining read, but the true story of publishing in Tennessee offers a better one. It is a story of diversity, one filled with memorable characters, many of whom rose to courageous heights in facing the hardships and challenges of their time. It is a story of commitment, one of important contributions to our society. It is a story that continues in our own day.

In 1791 George Roulstone and Robert Ferguson arrived in Rogersville in upper East Tennessee. The event is commemorated with a plaque behind the Hawkins County Courthouse. Bringing a printing press, type, and paper in a wagon, the experienced newspapermen came across the Appalachian Mountains from North Carolina to what was then the Southwest Territory at the invitation of Governor William Blount. Although they set up operation in a log cabin in Rogersville, the paper they founded and first issued on November 5, 1791, was called the *Knoxville Gazette,* since the move to Knoxville was already anticipated. In October 1792, as soon as the new town was laid out, the presses were moved by flatboat down the Holston River. It may well have been that the *Gazette* became the first newspaper in the United States named for a town not yet in existence at the time of the newspaper's founding.

Clearly, the *Gazette* served as spokesman for the Blount administration, and the governor richly rewarded Roulstone with political appointments. (Ferguson withdrew in 1793.) Roulstone became the first printer for the Territory, and later for the State of Tennessee. He is remembered both for his contributions in wording the Tennessee state constitutional provision guaranteeing a free press and as the state's first book publisher.

When Roulstone died in 1804 at the age of 36, his widow, Elizabeth, took over the *Gazette,* thereby laying claim to being the state's first woman newspaper editor and publisher. When she later married William Moore, they moved to Carthage, in Smith County, and published that town's first newspaper, the *Carthage Gazette.*

Pressmen's Home, another monument to the importance of publishing in Tennessee, and the only community anywhere totally devoted to the printing craft, is located about a dozen miles from Rogersville. In ruins today and nearly forgotten after its abandonment in 1967, Pressmen's Home was headquarters for the 125,000-member International Printing Pressmen and Assistants' Union of North America for 56 years. George L. Berry of Rogersville headed the union from 1907 until his death in 1948. The location of the Pressmen's Home in the remote mountains of East Tennessee was due entirely to Berry's efforts. In its present decay, it is hard to envision Pressmen's Home in its glory years: 2,700 acres, a lavishly equipped four-story technical school (largest of its kind in the world) in which 3,148 pressmen were trained in letterpress and newer offset printing, a sanatorium that for over 41 years served more than 900 craftsmen suffering from tuberculosis, a luxury hotel that was open to the public, a chapel, living accommodations, union offices, recreational facilities, and its own post office.

Upper East Tennessee can make other historic publishing claims. Beginning as early as 1819, three of the nation's leading abolitionist journals, including the first, were published there; two in Jonesborough and the third in Greeneville. Elihu Embree, a Quaker and leading figure in the Tennessee Manumission Society, published the two anti-slavery journals in Jonesborough, beginning with a weekly called *The Manumission Intelligencer,* which first appeared in March 1819. Embree replaced the newspaper after one year with a monthly, *The Emancipator,* which he published until his death in December 1820. Shortly thereafter, in 1821, the Reverend Benjamin Lundy was encouraged by the Tennessee Manumission Society to bring his journal, *The Genius of Universal Emancipation,* from Ohio to Greeneville, where he published it until moving to Baltimore in 1824.

Across the country today, journals published by and for Native Americans are commonplace, but perhaps few persons realize that the first of these newspapers had strong ties to East Tennessee. In reference to the *Cherokee Phoenix,* one scholar pointed out that "Cherokee journalism . . . was the first jour-

nalism in the Chattanooga area."[1] The *Phoenix* appeared as a weekly in February 1828, not long after the abolition journals.

Although the *Phoenix* was published at New Echota, the Cherokee capital in North Georgia, it owed its existence to the work of Sequoyah, a Tennessean. Born in 1776 at the village of Tuskegee, near Fort Loudoun on the Little Tennessee River, Sequoyah invented the 86-character Cherokee syllabary and taught his people to read. Working with Sequoyah, Dr. Samuel A. Worcester of Brainerd Mission near Ross's Landing (Chattanooga) developed the idea for a newspaper in the Cherokee language. Worcester then traveled to Boston to acquire a press and fonts of type in the Cherokee characters. Early issues were printed partly in English and partly in Cherokee, lending support to the argument that it was the nation's first bilingual newspaper.

In February 1829 the paper was renamed the *Cherokee Phoenix and Indians' Advocate;* regular publication continued into 1832, when Georgia authorities, upset with the journal's increasing militancy, seized it. Issues appeared irregularly for a few months thereafter; however, a plan to move the press to Red Clay in Tennessee did not materialize, ending the country's first Native American newspaper.

Not long after that, in 1838, Ferdinand Parham established Chattanooga's first newspaper, the *Hamilton County Gazette.* Parham, who had earlier published a sheet in Maryville, retitled the paper the *Chattanooga Gazette* when the city was named.

In 1816 Frederick Heiskell and Hugh Brown founded the *Knoxville Register,* which remained in circulation for 47 years and became East Tennessee's dominant newspaper prior to the Civil War. The paper, and Heiskell, attained statewide importance and political power. Brown left the paper in 1829 and Heiskell in 1837, but it continued to exert an influence until shut down by occupying Federal troops during the Civil War.

East Tennessee could claim no monopoly in the early newspaper business. Middle Tennessee's first journal, the short-lived *Rights of Man, Or, The Nashville Intelligencer,* appeared in February 1799, followed a year later by Benjamin J. Bradford's Nashville-published *Tennessee Gazette.* (The Bradford family name appears frequently in newspaper history in Tennessee and Kentucky.)

After Nashville, the next midstate community with a newspaper was Carthage, with William Moore's *Gazette* in August 1808. At least 20 papers sprang to life in nine other midstate towns before 1820 as population burgeoned.

In West Tennessee, meanwhile, publishing saw an early beginning as well. Historians usually credit *The Pioneer,* established in Jackson in 1822, as being the first journal in the region. The more successful *Jack-*

son Whig was established in 1848; it merged with the *Jackson Sun* in 1877.

Publishing in Memphis began in January 1827 with the Bluff City's first journal, *The Memphis Advocate,* which lasted until 1835. Several other papers saw life in Memphis before Henry Van Pelt arrived in 1841 and established the *Weekly Appeal,* the forerunner of today's long-standing *Memphis Commercial Appeal.*

As might be anticipated, the Civil War resulted in several publishing developments of note in Tennessee. One of the more interesting episodes involved the *Appeal,* by then a daily under the leadership of Benjamin Franklin Dill and John McClanahan. Determined to avoid closure by occupying Federal troops, Dill loaded a press and type on a flatcar and fled to Mississippi, later moving to Georgia and Alabama. The paper continued to publish all the while, earning the sobriquet "Moving Appeal" in the process. Finally, Federal troops captured the paper near Columbus, Georgia, having chased it through ten towns and four states. For more than a year, the *Appeal* was issued in Atlanta, where it was joined by two other Tennessee newspapers, the *Knoxville Register* and the *Chattanooga Daily Rebel.* Later the *Appeal* resumed publication in Memphis.

The *Vidette* (Sentinel), still published in the Middle Tennessee town of Hartsville, traces its lineage to Confederate General John Hunt Morgan, who issued a paper by that name for his troops stationed there in August 1862. Civil War journalism in East Tennessee gained national recognition in the form of the *Knoxville Whig,* published by William Brownlow. The leading "Union Screamer" (pro-Union southern newspaper), the *Whig* gained a wide following in the North because of its stance. After a speaking tour of northern cities, Brownlow renamed his paper *Brownlow's Whig and Rebel Ventilator,* a clear indication of where he stood. He went on to become the controversial governor of Tennessee during Reconstruction, before serving as a U.S. Senator.

An important milestone in Tennessee publishing, the advent of newspapers owned by and published for African-American citizens, occurred as the Civil War ended. In April 1865 William Scott, an African American from East Tennessee, began publication in Nashville of the *Colored Tennessean,* which is generally acknowledged to be the first black newspaper in the state. Two years later, Scott moved the paper to Maryville, where it underwent several name changes and became the "county newspaper," serving black and white readers alike. In 1872 the *Memphis Weekly Planet* became West Tennessee's first black newspaper. Later important African-American papers in Tennessee included the *Nashville Globe* (1906–1960), the *East Tennessee News* in Knoxville (1906–1948), the *Chattanooga Defender* (1917–1937), and two journals

in Memphis, the conservative *Memphis World* (1931–1972) and John Sengstacke's fiery *Tri-State Defender,* which appeared in 1951 and played a significant role in the Civil Rights Movement. In 1906 W.E.B. Du Bois briefly tried his hand at journalism in Tennessee, publishing the *Memphis Moon,* which, he said, was "a precursor of *The Crisis,*" the influential publication of the National Association for the Advancement of Colored People (NAACP) he would later edit.[2]

No discussion of African-American publishing in Tennessee would be complete without recognizing Ida B. Wells-Barnett, whose journalistic career began in 1889 with the *Memphis Free Speech.* After three years of reporting the poor race relations of the city for the *Free Speech,* Wells moved to New York and later Chicago, and gained national and international acclaim as a crusader against lynching. Her keen interest in the subject was triggered by an 1892 incident in Memphis in which a mob lynched three black grocers. Wells's coverage of the incident led to a two-month boycott of white businesses by the city's African-American population. After Edward Ward Carmack, editor of the *Memphis Commercial,* demanded retaliation against "the black wench," the offices of the *Free Speech* were demolished. Nonetheless, Wells had used the paper to launch a career that earned her a reputation as perhaps " the most influential black female journalist in this nation's history."[3]

Carmack is also well-known in the annals of Tennessee publishing, editing several leading papers in Memphis and Nashville, and serving in both the U.S. House and Senate, before becoming editor of the *Nashville Tennessean* in August 1908. An outspoken Prohibitionist, Carmack was shot to death on the streets of Nashville in November 1908 by Robin Cooper, son of Duncan Cooper, an associate of Carmack's bitter rival, Governor Malcolm Patterson. The incident calls to mind Mark Twain's fictional account of Tennessee's journalistic violence, but with a real life tragic result.

The Tennessean (renamed in 1972) has employed many famous staff members over the years, including Grantland Rice, often called the greatest sportswriter of all time; David Halberstam, Bill Kovach, Jim Squires, Tom Wicker, Wallace Westfelt, Fred Graham, John Seigenthaler, and Albert Gore, Jr., who went on to become a U.S. Senator and Vice President of the United States. *The Tennessean's* long-standing rival, the *Nashville Banner,* was for years associated with the Stahlman family, after Edward B. Stahlman acquired it in 1881. Tennessee native Ralph McGill worked at the *Banner* briefly before leaving in 1929 to join the *Atlanta Constitution* where, over 40 years, he would play a leading role in the Civil Rights Movement.

Edward J. Meeman founded the *Knoxville News* in 1921. For ten years, he edited it and its successor, the *News-Sentinel,* championing the establishment of the Tennessee Valley Authority and the Great Smoky Mountains National Park. In 1931 he moved to Memphis, where he edited the *Press-Scimitar* and waged an ongoing editorial crusade against political boss Edward H. Crump.

Another Tennessean with a distinguished publishing record was Adolph S. Ochs, who bought the nearly bankrupt *Chattanooga Times* in 1878. The 20-year-old Ochs turned the newspaper into a success. In 1896 he went to New York City, where he bought the venerable, but financially strapped *New York Times* at auction for $75,000. Ochs ignored the sensationalism of contemporary publishers like William Randolph Hearst at the *New York Journal* and Joseph Pulitzer at the *New York World.* Applying the same conservative formula he had used in Chattanooga, Ochs revived the *New York Times* and established the high standards the paper still maintains.

Today, in Tennessee, as across the nation, the era of personal journalism has largely been supplanted by corporate journalism, with absentee owners. Gannett, the largest of all the chains, owns numerous newspapers across the state. In Chattanooga, newspaper rivalries continue under a government-approved Joint Operating Agreement which allows competing publications to maintain separate editorial voices while combining advertising, circulation, and printing operations in cost-saving ventures.

Book publishing plays a significant role in Tennessee today, as it has from earliest times. As with newspapers, George Roulstone is credited with having published the first book, a 320-page tome titled *Laws of the State of Tennessee,* which he set up, printed, bound, and issued in September 1803. In the preface, Roulstone addressed the challenge of the undertaking, noting, "The present undertaking has been very laborious. . . ." Over the years, Nashville would become the center of book publishing in Tennessee. In 1809 Thomas G. Bradford published the first important book there, *A Revisal of All the Public Acts of the State of North Carolina and of the State of Tennessee.*

Nashville's reputation as a center for publishing religious materials began in the 1830s and received a major boost in 1854 when the Methodist Episcopal Church, South established the forerunner of the United Methodist Publishing House, which now produces some 120 new books and tapes annually, in addition to hundreds of church school curriculum items. Shortly afterward, by 1855, J.R. Graves established the Southwestern Publishing House. *The Tennessee Baptist* was its most popular publication, but the company had no relation to the later Sunday School Board of the Southern Baptist Convention

(SBC), which traces its origins to 1891. Today, the SBC's Sunday School Board claims to be the world's largest publisher of religious materials. It produces 180 monthly and quarterly products and 400 to 500 undated products annually.

The two operations are not Nashville's only religious publishers. The National Baptist Publishing Board, established in 1896 by Richard Boyd, claims to be the country's oldest African-American-owned publishing business and produces 15 million books and periodicals annually. Thomas Nelson Publishers, the world's largest Bible publisher, has called Nashville home since 1972, publishing seven translations of the Bible in addition to other religious books and music.

An important regional publishing house, Rutledge Hill Press, began operations in Nashville in 1982. Vanderbilt University and the University of Tennessee operate academic publishing centers. Elsewhere in Tennessee, the Kingsport Press has perhaps the largest book publishing operation. Founded in 1922 by John B. Dennis and the J.J. Little & Ives Company of New York, the firm initially produced inexpensive ten-cent classics (7,777,000 in the first year of operation) and trained Kingsport area farmers as printers. In 1969, it merged with Arcata National Corporation; by the mid-1980s more than 3,200 employees were producing 300,000 books a day for customers that included Time-Life and the National Geographic Society.

Publishing in Tennessee is, indeed, a far cry from Mark Twain's early description. One wonders what he would think if he were to return for a visit on the eve of the twenty-first century.

Glenn A. Himebaugh, Middle Tennessee State University

CITATIONS:

(1) Edwin B. Brinkley, "History of the Chattanooga Times, 1869–1949" (M.A. thesis., University of Missouri, 1950), 34.

(2) Karen F. Brown, "The Black Press of Tennessee: 1865–1980" (Ph.D. diss., University of Tennessee, 1982), 112.

(3) Ibid., 69.

SUGGESTED READINGS: Douglas C. McMurtrie, *Early Printing in Tennessee, With a Bibliography of the Issues of the Tennessee Press 1793–1830* (1933); Jack Mooney, ed., *A History of Tennessee Newspapers* (1996); Joseph H. Sears, *Tennessee Printers 1791–1945: A Review of Printing History from Roulstone's First Press to Printers of the Present* (undated); John Tebbell, *A History of Book Publishing in the United States, Volume I, The Creation of an Industry 1630–1865* (1972)

PURITY DAIRY, one of the most successful family-owned Nashville businesses into the 1990s, was established in 1926, as Ezell's Dairy by Miles Ezell, Sr., with 80 rented cows, a rented farm, and rented equipment. With quality products, hard work, and tenacity, the Ezells transformed their family dairy into a modern dairy company. In 1926 approximately

250 dairies were in Davidson County, each with its own plant, milk route, and clientele. In the 1940s, the public health requirement for pasteurization reduced the number of Nashville area dairies to 17; among the survivors was Ezell's Purity Dairy.

The Depression, the competitiveness of the dairy business, and the changing agricultural landscape along its Murfreesboro Pike location made Purity Dairy develop new business methods. Ezell encouraged quality control and high standards among all regional dairies. In the 1950s and 1960s the Ezells bought out their strongest competitors and strengthened Purity's position in the dairy industry. The company used creative and multi-faceted advertising. During the 1960s and 1970s Purity produced memorable advertising characters such as the punching cow and kangaroo, "Sgt. Glory," and Ernest P. Worrell's "Know what I mean Vern?" to interest customers in the quality of Purity products. The dairy regularly sold a wide variety of products, including cottage cheese, sweet acidophilus milk, and frozen yogurt. These strong business and advertising philosophies produced and still maintain Purity's number one status in the milk business. In 1998 Dean Foods of Illinois acquired Purity Dairy. The Ezell family maintains corporate control of doing business activities.

Carol Roberts, Tennessee State Library and Archives
SEE: AGRICULTURE; MAYFIELD DAIRY FARMS, INC.

PUSSER, BUFORD (1937–1974). Immortalized by three screen portrayals of his career, *Walking Tall* (1973), *Walking Tall II* (1976), and *Walking Tall III: The Final Chapter* (1977), McNairy County Sheriff Buford Pusser earned a reputation as a hard-nosed, no nonsense law officer who settled disputes with a large homemade bat. By age 32 he had been shot eight times, stabbed seven, and run over by felons in a car. On August 12, 1967, Pusser witnessed the violent death of his wife in an ambush that was meant for him. Permanently disfigured, Pusser underwent numerous reconstructive surgeries to mend his battered face and crushed jaw.

Born December 12, 1937, in Adamsville, Tennessee, Pusser moved to Oklahoma during his junior year in high school. From there he joined the Marines but was discharged due to chronic asthma. Disheartened, he returned to Adamsville in 1958 and traveled the semi-professional wrestling circuit in the Southeast until his marriage to Pauline Mullins in 1959.

The couple moved to Chicago where he found employment at the Union Paper Bag Company as a die cutter and their child, Dwana Aitoya Pusser, was born. Shortly thereafter, the Pussers returned to McNairy County. In September 1962 Pusser ran for constable and upset the incumbent by over 100 votes. Taking his job seriously, he made a crusade out of crushing the local illegal whiskey trade.

The McNairy County sheriff, James Dickey, was in cahoots with the Moonshine Ring which operated along the state lines of Tennessee and Mississippi. Incensed by the collusion of local authorities in supporting criminal activity, Pusser decided to run against Dickey for sheriff, choosing to run as a Republican in a staunchly Democratic county. His election was assured when Dickey died in an automobile accident.

In November 1964 he suffered his first assault by the members of the Moonshine Ring. Ambushed by assailants who stabbed him seven times and left him to die, Pusser survived and made war on the ring with a vengeance. In his first year as sheriff he raided 42 stills and arrested 75 moonshiners. In subsequent years he expanded his attempts to clean up the crime-ridden state line area by prosecuting prostitution rings and illegal gambling houses.

In 1969 the Tennessee General Assembly recognized Pusser for his accomplishments and made him an honorary Sergeant of Arms. His career as sheriff ended in 1970, but his fame was just beginning. He signed a contract with Bing Crosby productions in 1972 to film his life story. *Walking Tall* became a box-office smash, but Pusser died in a car wreck in 1974. His death and the success of the first story spawned two sequels, neither of which was as successful as the first.

Michael E. Birdwell, Tennessee Technological University
SEE: MCNAIRY COUNTY; TENNESSEE IN FILM

PUTNAM COUNTY was first created in 1842 from Jackson, Overton, Fentress, and White counties, but an 1844 injunction charged that it violated state constitutional requirements. In 1854 the General Assembly reestablished the county, although it was harried by boundary disputes for decades. The new county seat, Cookeville, was named after Richard F. Cooke, whose efforts were critical to the county's second attempt at creation. Putnam County's name honors Revolutionary War General Israel Putnam.

Putnam County is located in the Upper Cumberland region. It spreads across three major geographic divisions of Tennessee: the Cumberland Plateau, the Highland Rim, and the Central Basin. Most of the county falls in the Highland Rim. A principal early nineteenth century east-west migration route, the Walton Road, passes through the length of Putnam County. Many families stopped at this point about midway between Knoxville and Nashville on their journey along the Walton Road. There they established small subsistence farms, growing corn and other crops in the generally poor soil. By 1860 the population had risen to 8,591, including 718 blacks and 33 Native Americans. Settlement halted during the Civil War, when Putnam County civilians were harassed by both Confederate and Unionist guerrilla attacks that destroyed farmland and homes.

Between 1865 and 1910 the county population tripled. Part of the growth was due to the railroads that reached Putnam in the 1890s. The Nashville and Knoxville reached Cookeville from the west in 1890, and the Tennessee Central connected the Southern Railroad at Harriman to the new town of Monterey in Putnam County, founded when the tracks reached it in 1893. Other new villages were created in the wake of the railroad, including Buffalo Valley, Silver Point, Boma, Baxter, Algood, and Brotherton. Eventually the Tennessee Central ran all the way to Knoxville, and in 1902 its proprietor, Jere Baxter, bought the Nashville and Knoxville. The National Register-listed Tennessee Central depot in Cookeville contains an excellent local museum on the railroad days in Putnam County. Three years later Baxter moved the TC engine service facilities and crew change stop from Cookeville to Monterey, which became an important railroad-promoted resort area around the turn of the century. Industrialist John Wilder maintained a home and office there in the early 1900s.

Railroads brought prosperity to Putnam County farmers who finally gained access to urban markets. Railroads also served industry like the Cumberland Mountain Coal Company, the executives of which had organized Monterey, lumbering in the county's rich forests, and manufacturing. Education also grew during Putnam County's railroad years. The University of Dixie, known as Dixie College, was chartered by the General Assembly in 1909 and opened in 1912. Organized through the efforts of the Church of Christ, this school merged with the new Tennessee Polytechnic Institute (TPI), which was created in 1915. TPI included three divisions: a two-year college, a four-year technical high school, and Putnam County's Central High School.

As the twentieth century progressed, Putnam County's agriculture suffered the setbacks being felt around the country in the 1920s. More farmers turned to poultry, egg, and dairy production as corn, tobacco, and hogs declined with decreasing profits.

However, county leaders were optimistic about the prosperity that industrialization and commerce might bring. By 1928 Cookeville was calling itself the "Hub City—The Hub of the Upper Cumberland."

Roads helped deliver some of the growth that Putnam Countians awaited. Although the Memphis-to-Bristol Highway bypassed Cookeville to pass through Sparta to the south, U.S. Highway 70 North was completed through Putnam County in 1930, the first modern highway in the Upper Cumberland. The county's transportation network also benefited from New Deal programs. The Cookeville airport was built in 1934 with matching Civil Works Administration and city funds.

With only modest industrialization, the county economy suffered in the postwar period because of persistent unemployment and low wages, causing many workers to leave Putnam during World War II through the 1950s. The next decade, though, saw expansion and increasing prosperity thanks to the construction of Interstate 40, rapid industrialization, the growth of Tennessee Technological University, and federal aid. Tennessee Polytechnic Institute changed its name to Tennessee Technological University in 1965 during the massive growth of the state higher education system. Today it is the county's largest non-manufacturing employer and boasts an enrollment over 8,000. Tennessee Tech administrates the Joe L. Evins Appalachian Center for Crafts, located near Center Hill Lake, which supports the modern practice of traditional crafts. The completion of I-40 through the county in the mid-1960s attracted manufacturing jobs as well. Today Putnam County has a population of about 57,000 and is a fast-growing center for the Upper Cumberland region.

Blythe Semmer, Middle Tennessee State University

SUGGESTED READING: Mary Jean DeLozier, *Putnam County, Tennessee, 1850–1970* (1979)

SEE: BAXTER, JERE; BURGESS FALLS STATE NATURAL AREA; MINING; POW CAMPS IN WORLD WAR II; RAILROAD, TENNESSEE CENTRAL; SMITH, RUTLEDGE; TENNESSEE TECHNOLOGICAL UNIVERSITY; WALTON ROAD; WILDER, JOHN T.; WILSON SPORTING GOODS

QUILLEN COLLEGE OF MEDICINE. In 1963 East Tennessee State University President Burgin E. Dossett, Dean John P. Lamb, Charles E. Allen, M.D, various civic leaders, and legislators called attention to the need for a regional health center in Upper East Tennessee. When Dossett retired in 1968, he and his associates were ready to implement their plans. The hard work was left to his successor, Delos P. Culp, who enthusiastically and skillfully worked with local committees and legislators. Four years later, the group asked the General Assembly to appoint a joint committee to negotiate with the Veterans Administration to establish a medical school in cooperation with the Mountain Home Hospital adjacent to the university campus.

Formidable opponents, led by Governor Winfield Dunn and friends of the University of Tennessee, marshaled their forces. The climax came in February and March 1974, when Dunn and seven members of the governing Board of Regents voted eight to seven to kill a proposal for a free-standing medical school. When Culp informed the governor that supporters of the medical school would continue their work, Dunn considered removing the president from office; he changed his mind after being warned against alienating Republicans in Northeast Tennessee. In the legislature, Representatives Palma Robinson and Robert Good and Senator Marshall Nave worked to gain support for the school. With the help of Speakers Ned R. McWherter and John S. Wilder, the bill to establish the medical school passed. Dunn vetoed the bill, and both houses overrode the veto.

The next step involved qualifying for federal funds under the Teague-Cranston Act. U.S. Representative James Quillen helped to secure grants, which assured the Liaison Committee on Medical Education that ETSU would meet the standards for accreditation. The Letter of Assurance arrived on June 20, 1977, Culp's last day in office. Full accreditation came when the first class graduated in 1982.

In the fall of 1978, 24 students, chosen from 255 applicants, enrolled in ETSU College of Medicine and met their 62 professors. Four years later 23 received their degrees; the twenty-fourth had dropped out because of illness, but graduated in 1984. In 1996, 60 first-year students were selected from over 2,000 applicants; total enrollment is limited to 240 students. The full-time medical faculty consists of 185 professors. In almost two decades, 750 M.D.s and 50 Ph.D.s have been awarded, and 560 medical doctors have completed residency programs. Four endowed chairs include Cecille Cox Quillen Chair in Gerontology, Carol Hardy Long Chair of Surgical Research, Paul Dishner Chair of Medicine, and Lee Ann Brown Group Chair in General Pediatrics. In 1989 regents acknowledged and honored Congressman Quillen for his political and financial support by renaming the institution The Quillen College of Medicine.

In 1988 the colleges of medicine, nursing, and public and allied health were brought together in the Division of Health Sciences. Two years later they received a six million dollar grant from the W.K. Kellogg Foundation to develop centers for primary care in local communities where such services had never been available. The programs also made it possible for students majoring in public health, nursing, and medicine to work as teams in caring for patients.

The Division of the Health Sciences brought industries and businesses related to health care to Upper East Tennessee. In 1994 they provided 13,000 full-time jobs in Washington County alone and put $771 million into circulation.

Researchers anticipate that people living in the early decades of the twenty-first century will be better served by family practitioners than by specialists. The Quillen College of Medicine ranks eighth among 126 medical schools whose graduates enter family practice; the faculty wants to become one of the five leaders in this field. Another goal is the development of model allied health programs. A third goal focuses on working in conjunction with ETSU, the Veterans Administration, regional hospitals, and related industries to become a major force in the economic development of the region.

Frank B. Williams, Jr., East Tennessee State University
SEE: EAST TENNESSEE STATE UNIVERSITY; JOHNSON CITY; MEDICINE; QUILLEN, JAMES H.

QUILLEN, JAMES H. (1916–). When Republican Congressman James H. Quillen decided not to seek reelection to the U.S. House of Representatives from Tennessee's First Congressional District in 1996, he ended more than 30 years of uninterrupted Congressional service, a record in Tennessee political history. Quillen first began his service to the Volunteer State as a member of the Tennessee General Assembly in 1954. He attended his first Republican National Convention in 1956 and was either a delegate or parliamentarian to all subsequent GOP conventions until his retirement. Quillen served in the Tennessee House of Representatives for eight years after 1954, and he eventually held the position of minority leader. In 1962 he won his first election to the U.S. Congress.

Quillen was born in Southwest Virginia, on January 11, 1916, one of ten children of John and Hannah Quillen. The family moved to Kingsport in East Tennessee when the future congressman was a child. After high school graduation, Quillen entered the newspaper business in both Kingsport and Johnson City; in 1939 he established the *Johnson City Times*. During World War II, Quillen served as an ensign on the aircraft carrier *USS Antietam*; he was discharged with the rank of lieutenant. After the war, he entered real estate, construction, and insurance businesses. In 1952 he married Cecile Cox.

Congressman Quillen took conservative stands on most issues; he supported policies of budget restraint and lower tax rates. In 1968 he sponsored and saw passage of the first federal legislation to outlaw the desecration of the U.S. flag. Quillen served on the House Rules Committee after 1965, becoming chairman of that very important committee, and was Chairman Emeritus of it at the time of his retirement. In 1995, with the new Republican majority in Congress, he was named to the Republican Policy Committee. He also served as chairman of the Tennessee Valley Authority Caucus.

Quillen was instrumental in the long battle to establish a medical school in Northeast Tennessee, and his successful work resulted in the creation of the James H. Quillen College of Medicine at East Tennessee State University in Johnson City. He was also a supporter of higher education in his district, and East Tennessee State University in 1994 established the Quillen Chair of Excellence in Education to honor him.

Michael Rogers, University of Tennessee, Knoxville
SEE: EAST TENNESSEE STATE UNIVERSITY; JOHNSON CITY; QUILLEN COLLEGE OF MEDICINE

QUILTMAKING has been a form of needlework enjoyed by generations of Tennessee women, and men, from the first settlers' arrival to the present day. The earliest quilts, made when fabric was scarce and expensive, graced the homes of affluent families. Blankets, bed rugs, and feather beds, rather than quilts, were readily obtainable to use for bedcovers. Initially European traditions and fashion influenced styles and techniques, but gradually quiltmaking in America became an arena for invention and refinement. As cloth production increased, so did the interest in making quilts.

A survey of Tennessee quilts conducted in the 1980s failed to locate any quilts made in the state prior to 1800, but the earliest quilts brought into the state were wholecloth, medallion chintzwork, and simple geometric patterns. Numerous Tennessee-made quilts from the first half of the nineteenth century, however, were preserved, many because they had special significance. Among these were pre-Civil War brides' quilts made from fine material, lavished with exceptional needlework, and reserved for special occasions.

In the nineteenth century the block arrangement of patchwork began to replace eighteenth century styles, beginning with a format of four large squares. The squares were cut to the width of the material for minimum waste and, if the bed was especially high, nine squares were required. Plumes, Cockscomb and Currant, and Rose of Sharon were among the most popular patterns and are found in many variations. All sewing was done by hand until after mid-century. Domestic or imported cotton and linen fabrics were favored, or occasionally wool, with cotton or wool for filler. Handwoven material for backing is found on a number of early Tennessee quilts. As the century progressed, quilt blocks grew smaller in size and there were greater choices of designs for patterns.

Many hardships accompanied the Civil War. Quilts and blankets were donated to the war effort or were confiscated by marauding soldiers from both sides. The blockade caused extreme shortages of manufactured goods, and prices soared. It was almost impossible to get sewing supplies, cloth, and cards for preparing quilt batts. Weaving in the home was resumed in order to make clothes and household goods. Utility quilts made from this period are in marked contrast to the elaborate brides' quilts made before the war.

After the Civil War pieced designs increased in popularity as patterns in publications multiplied. With improved transportation and commerce, local peddlers were replaced by shops and country stores. Increased mill production in the South provided affordable cloth for every quiltmaker. If cotton was not grown at home, it was easy to obtain. Quiltmaking was practiced in nearly every household in Tennessee in the nineteenth century.

Several conclusions can be drawn from the survey of quilts made in Tennessee prior to 1930. In Rhea County the technique of adding extra stuffing to the quilting design, popular in the mid-nineteenth century, continued there until 1900 to set many Rhea County quilts apart. Fewer Tennessee quilts have borders in comparison to those of other regions, and the quilting is not particularly refined or precise. Of those patterns appearing with frequency, Rocky Mountain Road was much favored.

Interest in quiltmaking fluctuated nationally in the twentieth century, but many Tennessee quilters never diminished their activity. Local groups and individuals continue to make quilts for family and friends, for worthy causes, and for sale. State and local fairs, contests, guilds, quilt shows, agricultural extension groups, museum exhibitions, and media coverage contribute to the nurturing of quiltmaking in the state.

Anne Orr, of Nashville, was a popular needlework columnist and entrepreneur who made an impact on quilt styles nationally in the 1920s and 1930s. When a new revival took place 50 years later, annual meetings and exhibitions of the Southern Quilt Symposium in Chattanooga during the 1970s and 1980s gave emphasis to quilts as art.

Subtle differences in color, pattern, and style in some of the older quilts allow them to be recognized as Tennessee-made, but those differences are disappearing in the global quilt revival which began in the 1960s and which has resulted in a proliferation of quilting literature and instruction.

Bets Ramsey, Chattanooga

SUGGESTED READING: Bets Ramsey and Merikay Waldvogel, *The Quilts of Tennessee: Images of Domestic Life Prior to 1930* (1986)

SEE: DECORATIVE ARTS, AFRICAN-AMERICAN; DECORATIVE ARTS, APPALACHIAN

QUINTARD, CHARLES TODD (1824–1898), Episcopal bishop, was born at Stamford, Connecticut, the son of Isaac Quintard and Clarissa Hoyt. In 1847 he received his M.D. degree from University Medical College, New York University, and worked for a year at Bellevue Hospital. About a year later, he moved to Athens, Georgia, and practiced medicine there. In 1851 Quintard became professor of physiology and pathological anatomy at the Memphis Medical College and one of the editors of the *Memphis Medical Reporter.* While in Memphis, Quintard studied for the ministry of the Protestant Episcopal Church under Bishop James Otey, and was ordained deacon on January 1, 1855, and priest on January 6, 1856. He was rector of the Church of the Advent, Nashville, until he was consecrated the second Bishop of Tennessee on October 11, 1865. He served in that position until his death in 1898.

During the Civil War, Quintard was a chaplain for the Confederate Army. He also worked as a surgeon. As bishop he was instrumental in the revival of the Protestant Episcopal Church in Tennessee, and extended its ministry to blacks. He was deeply interested in education and supported the founding of a number of preparatory schools. His greatest contribution to education was in rebuilding the University of the South after the devastation of the Civil War. He served as the first Vice Chancellor of the University, February 14, 1867-July 12, 1872. Quintard made several trips to England to raise money for the University.

In 1848 Quintard married Katherine Isabella Hand of Roswell, Georgia, and they had three children.

Donasld S. Armentrout, University of the South

SEE: OTEY, JAMES H.; MEDICINE; RELIGION; UNIVERSITY OF THE SOUTH

R

RADNOR LAKE STATE NATURAL AREA, uniquely located in sprawling Metropolitan Nashville-Davidson County, is an 1,100-acre park designed to include only foot trails for passive recreation and educational purposes. In the midst of Nashville's fast-paced development, this site remains an island of serenity and beauty.

The first land owners in the park area arrived in the late 1770s. James Mulharrin and John Buchanan received Revolutionary War land grants, where they surveyed the land and built frontier stations. Mulharrin soon sold his grant to Revolutionary War veteran Alexander Campbell (this tract is now under water in the approximate middle of Radnor Lake). By the mid-1830s, settlers brought the rugged hills under cultivation and began timbering operations.

On the eve of the Civil War, Burwell Lazenby owned the majority of the current park land. Lazenby methodically gathered, conserved, and preserved documents pertaining to the original land acquisition and unwittingly provided a valuable source for modern investigation of the cultural history of the area. During Lazenby's ownership, the Louisville & Nashville Railroad became interested in the land and around 1910, the Lazenby family sold its property to the railroad.

The long, high valley bisected by Otter Creek provided the natural elevation the railroad needed to create a reservoir to provide water to the nearby Radnor Yards. A drop of 185 feet from the lake to the yards 4.9 miles away created a natural gravity water flow piping system. In 1919 one million gallons of water per day began flowing from Radnor Lake reservoir to maintain the railroad's over-the-road operations. The lake provided water for steam engines, equipment maintenance, and stockyards.

Water fowl quickly adapted to the beautiful lake, and the Tennessee Ornithological Society found the area an instant viewing platform for native and migratory birds. A young L&N employee became an avid bird watcher. His records of weather, dating, and wildlife sighting provided the data for the Tennessee Ornithological Society's 1926 petition to the railroad to make Radnor Lake a natural wildlife preserve. The railroad officials concurred and made the designation.

By 1957 the use of diesel fuel led to the demise of steam-driven trains, and the railroad terminated its use of Radnor Lake. In 1962 the Louisville & Nashville sold 773 acres of the Radnor Lake properties to a private individual. During the 1970s, planned development threatened the fragile wildlife environment and diverse ecosystems around Radnor Lake. Individuals, businesses, and state and federal agencies worked together to save Radnor Lake. In August 1973 the State of Tennessee purchased 747 acres of the Radnor Lake property. Since then, as smaller properties have become available, they have been added to the park.

Radnor Lake features seven miles of walking trails around and above the 85-acre lake. The Lake Trail winds beneath deciduous forests and through fields filled with a diversity of native plants and wildflowers. A high elevation Ridge Trail commands a spectacular view of downtown Nashville. Time spent here can be likened to a visit in an outdoor museum where both aquatic and terrestrial flora and fauna are experienced in their natural environments.

The park provides environmental education programs. Park rangers and interpretive specialists conduct ecology walks and guide field trips. The Visitor's Center presents an audio-visual program and provides space for an interpretive display of artifacts depicting the cultural history of Radnor Lake.

Dorothy W. King, Nashville

SEE: RAILROAD, LOUISVILLE AND NASHVILLE, TENNESSEE ORNITHOLOGICAL SOCIETY

RAGLAND, MARTHA RAGSDALE (1906–1996), reformer in political, health, and women's issues, was born near Russellville, Kentucky. She wanted to attend law school and later run for Congress, but the Great Depression put law school beyond her reach. She graduated from Vanderbilt University in 1927 and 1928, respectively, with undergraduate and master's degrees in economics. Her thesis on immigration restrictions attracted the attention of Yale University professor Elseworth Huntington, who hired her to research his book on immigration. In 1932 she married Thomas Ragland, but refused to wear a wedding ring. "It seemed to me a symbol of bondage, or slavery," she explained.[1] The marriage lasted until her death and produced two children, Tommy and Sandra.

When her husband's family business took the new couple to Knoxville, Ragland became active in Planned Parenthood and the Birth Control League. At that time, contraceptives were illegal in Tennessee. In 1938 Ragland persuaded the famous birth control advocate Margaret Sanger to accompany her on a speaking tour of Tennessee to generate support for adding birth control education to the state's public health clinics.

Ragland joined Dorothy Stafford in revitalizing Tennessee's League of Women Voters. An early League project stemmed from the discovery that milk was not properly and uniformly tested in Chattanooga dairies. Motivated by concern for children like their own toddlers, the two women pooled their money to purchase an ad in the *Chattanooga Times* to draw attention to the issue. As a result of the ensuing public pressure, Chattanooga officials corrected the milk testing process. Another League project in the health field focused on a drive for detection and prevention of tuberculosis.

In 1945, while president of the League, Ragland wrote the booklet, "Tennessee Needs a New Constitution" and led a drive to update the state constitution. The two goals, reform of the merit system and abolition of the poll tax, were not realized until a constitutional convention convened in 1953.

In 1948, at Estes Kefauver's request, Ragland organized women supporters for his first campaign for the U.S. Senate. In 1952 she worked in Albert Gore, Sr.'s U.S. Senate campaign. These two elections demonstrated the rising political clout of women voters in post-World War II Tennessee.

In 1952 Ragland served as a Tennessee delegate to the Democratic National Convention. At that time, delegations were predominantly male, though women made up roughly half the voters. In 1968, for example, more than 50 percent of Tennessee's voters were female, but only six of the state's 66 delegates to the national convention were women. In 1970 Ragland and Carlene Waller set up the Volunteer Women's Roundtable, from which stemmed the inde-

pendent National Democratic Women's Caucus. The Women's Caucus focused first on changes to the convention rules regarding delegates to reflect the male and female voting ratios. Ragland and Waller helped organize the National Women's Caucus to monitor the convention and take legal action against disproportionate delegations.

In 1971 Ragland fanned the coals for political reform at home. In a speech before the Volunteer Women's Roundtable, she criticized Tennessee Democratic party officials. She charged party officials with ignoring members who attempted to make motions, and accused officials of preparing resolutions in back room sessions then hammering them through legislative meetings with no discussion. She chastised the party for its disorganized and outmoded structure and called for public disclosure of party financial records. She complained that women did much of the fundraising, but had no voice in how the money would be spent.

Ragland's career included service as a member of the White House Commission on Women and Children, a founder of the Council on Aging, chairperson of the Tennessee Advisory Commission to the U.S. Commission on Civil Rights, and a member of the Federal Advisory Council on Employment Security.

Ragland died on January 18, 1996, in Nashville at the age of 89. She was survived by her husband and daughter; her son died earlier. Ragland's papers are in Schlesinger Library at Radcliffe College in Massachusetts.

David R. Logsdon, Nashville

CITATION:

(1) *Nashville Tennessean,* July 30, 1995.

SEE: KEFAUVER, C. ESTES; LEAGUE OF WOMEN VOTERS

RAHT, JULIUS ECKHARDT (1826–1875), pioneer in the mining and smelting of copper in East Tennessee, was born in Dillenburg, Duchy of Nassau, Germany, on June 26, 1826. He attended Bonn University and the University of Berlin before emigrating to the United States with his brother Charles in 1850. Raht arrived in Ducktown, Tennessee, in 1854. He made a brief return to Germany that year when he married Mathilde Dombois. Back in Ducktown by August 1854, Raht was employed as a mine captain and opened a store. By 1858 he managed the Ocoee Turnpike and Plank Road Company. That same year, Raht became superintendent of the Union Consolidated Mines. In 1859 he was superintendent of the Polk County Copper Company and, the next year, managed the Burra Burra Copper Company. By age 34, Raht managed all of the mines and smelting works at Ducktown.

During the Civil War, Raht hired a substitute to serve in his stead and moved his family to Cincinnati. Returning to Cleveland, Tennessee, he helped organize the Cleveland National Bank in 1866, becoming the first vice-president, and, in 1875, president. Locally Raht became well-known for his many acts of charity. He helped build and repair roads, schools, and churches, and contributed generously to charitable causes.

Julius and Mathilde Raht were the parents of 12 children, with six sons and two daughters surviving to maturity. Raht died on August 15, 1875, at age 53, from heart failure. In his book, *Ducktown Back in Raht's Time*, R.E. Barclay concluded, "No man ever worked harder to make Ducktown a district of moral and industrial strength . . . and, in turn, no man ever reaped greater rewards for his efforts than did Julius Eckhardt Raht."[1]

Marion Bailey Presswood, Benton

CITATION:

(1) R.E. Barclay, *Ducktown Back in Raht's Time* (New York, 1946; r.p. 1974), 249.

SEE: BURRA BURRA COPPER COMPANY; MINING; POLK COUNTY

RAILROAD, LOUISVILLE AND NASHVILLE

(L&N) The Louisville and Nashville Railroad achieved national recognition as one of the most profitable and influential railroads in the southern market from the second half of the nineteenth to well into the twentieth century. The foundation for the company's success began with the Kentucky and Tennessee state legislatures granting charters in 1850 for a railroad line to be built between Louisville and Nashville. Recognizing that a rail line was needed did not prevent conflict, as both Kentucky and Tennessee sought controlling interests in transportation for the prized upper-south commercial industry. The agreement to construct a line connecting the two cities resulted out of the desire to restrict competitors such as Cincinnati, Atlanta, and New Orleans from flooding the market. Still, due to construction problems and financial concerns, the first train did not travel from Louisville to Nashville until November 1, 1859.

Shortly after these territorial squabbles and building complications ended, the L&N faced an even larger dilemma with the onset of the Civil War. Its two major terminals were at Louisville and Nashville; this physical proximity meant that the L&N was literally caught in the middle of the war. In the early days of the war, L&N president James Guthrie spoke out in defense of the South, and the L&N shipped vital supplies for the Confederate army. But, after the ban on trade with the Confederacy, the company reduced its southern shipments and shifted support to the Union. The L&N's assistance to the Union turned out to be profitable as the company emerged from the war in comparatively stable physical and economic condition.

L&N's postwar stability enabled the company to push forward in expansion and development. In Ten-

Train departs Union Station, Nashville, 1940.

nessee, the L&N incurred the debts of the Memphis & Ohio and Clarksville railroads in exchange for management control. This led to an eventual consolidation between the L&N, Clarksville, and Memphis & Ohio railroads by 1872. Then in 1880 the company moved quickly to take control of the Nashville, Chattanooga and St. Louis Railway, when Edmund Cole's ambitions for the Nashville competitor proved too threatening. By the 1880s, L&N maintained a stronghold on the Kentucky and Tennessee markets, and expanded into numerous other southeastern territories. With an increase in rail mileage from 921 miles in 1873 to 1,840 in 1880, L&N established itself as a major player in southern transportation.

Despite continued expansion in the early 1880s, questions arose regarding the L&N's financial status. By 1880 localized control of the L&N decreased, and most financial decisions came down from financiers in New York. This change to "big city" control, questionable expansion decisions, and perceived financial incompetence by company president C.C. Baldwin, led to a downward spiral in the company's reputation. This damaged public image, along with the overall decline in security prices, reduced L&N stock value per share from $99 in late 1881 to $31 in late 1882.

By 1884 the L&N sought a savior to regain financial stability and public confidence. Longtime railroader Milton Hannibal Smith accepted the challenge. Regarded as a "representative of the people," Smith's presidential appointment was well-received in Louisville, Nashville, and the entire southeastern region. Through his managerial insight and dogged determination, Smith helped reestablish the L&N as a transportation leader. Smith's presidency lasted from 1884 to 1886 and from 1891 until his death on February 22, 1921. In his tenure, L&N track mileage expanded over 60 percent, mostly through developing eastern and western Kentucky as well as central and eastern Tennessee, rather than through major acquisitions. In Tennessee, the L&N constructed a 94-mile line from Brentwood to Athens, Alabama, via Lewisburg, and built a new line from Knoxville to Atlanta. Other Tennessee expansions included the acquisition of the Gallatin & Scottsville Railway and the Middle & East Tennessee Railway in 1906. Smith's stubborn style proved less effective in facilitating the management-labor relations. In the 1890s Smith's unwillingness to compromise with unions landed the L&N the reputation of a company unfriendly to labor.

As was the case with many United States railroads, World War I federal control policies and the subsequent Transportation Act (1920) left the L&N financially restricted. The L&N responded to the federal control by cutting back train service and reducing its labor force by approximately 10,000 workers. For remaining workers, the impact of company cutbacks most noticeably affected African Americans, who were often paid reduced wages for performing the same jobs as whites. Because African Americans continued to value railroad jobs, most accepted the conditions, albeit unwillingly. The company, however, fought through the tough times of the 1920s and 30s, suffering only one year with a deficit net income from 1920 through the Depression era.

Leading the L&N from the Depression to the 1950s were two former presidents of the NC&St.L, W.R. Cole and J.B. Hill. Because both were native Tennesseans and familiar with railroading in the state, Cole and Hill maintained an overall understanding of the importance of Tennessee to L&N success.

During the 1940s the L&N enjoyed the fruits of World War II-generated business and industrial expansion that developed along company rail lines. In Tennessee, the Milan ordnance plant, the ALCOA plant, and the Tennessee Valley Authority helped increase L&N net operating earnings more than twofold to $50 million. These tremendous increases, combined with the need to replace employees now serving as soldiers, created a broader job base for women and minorities. However, the railroad brotherhoods's continual rise in power reserved desirable skilled labor for white males only. The L&N was very much a part of these discriminatory practices, as indicated by the 1946 Supreme Court case of black employee *Steele v. the Louisville and Nashville Railroad*.

The case, won by Steele, established the principle that a majority union could not make a contract with a railroad company which unfairly discriminated against nonmember minority workers.

The L&N continued as a major southeastern railroad company through the 1950s, giving it over 100 years of activity and influence in the railroading industry. In 1957 it formally merged with the NC&St.L; in the early 1970s it became part of the Seaboard Coast Line. In 1986 it merged into an even larger corporation, CSX Railroad, which continues to maintain the line and rail facilities today.

Russell Wigginton, Rhodes College

SUGGESTED READINGS: Thomas D. Clark, *The Beginning of the L&N* (1933); R.S. Cotterill, "Southern Railroads, 1850–1860," *Mississippi Valley Historical Review* 10(1923–24); Leonard Curry, *Rail Routes South* (1969); Maury Klein, *History of the Louisville and Nashville Railroad* (1972)

SEE: COMMERCE; HENRY COUNTY; MCMINN COUNTY; NASHVILLE UNION STATION; RADNOR LAKE SNA; RAILROADS; RAILROAD, NASHVILLE AND CHATTANOOGA

RAILROAD, MEMPHIS AND CHARLESTON (M&C) was the last link in a chain of early railroads connecting the Atlantic Coast to the Mississippi River. Its route from Memphis to Chattanooga across Tennessee, Mississippi, and Alabama is still an important rail line as part of the Norfolk Southern system.

Railroad fever gripped Memphis following the Southern and Southwestern Railroad Convention held there in 1845. Out of it grew the idea for a railroad running east from Memphis toward the Atlantic Coast. Tennessee Governor James C. "Lean Jimmy" Jones led the campaign for funds. The company was chartered in 1846 and construction was completed a few years later. The new railroad incorporated two existing lines, one in North Alabama and one in West Tennessee.

The first railroad west of the Appalachians was a two-mile line for horse-drawn cars built in 1832 at Tuscumbia, Alabama, as a bypass for the Muscle Shoals on the Tennessee River. The line was soon expanded to a 43-mile steam line. The LaGrange & Memphis Railroad was launched in West Tennessee about the same time, but it was never successful.

The Memphis & Charleston provided the only rail connection between the eastern and western parts of the South. From Chattanooga, lines extended to Virginia and Georgia. Goods and passengers that had previously gone by roundabout water and overland routes could now go directly by rail. Travel time from Memphis to New York was reduced to 79 hours. The railroad was a major factor in the growth of Memphis over other Mississippi River towns in the mid- to late nineteenth century.

The Memphis & Charleston was strategically important to the Confederacy. The railroad was the scene of heavy fighting early in the Civil War—the April 1862 Battle of Shiloh was fought near it—and it was inevitable that the line would be a target for destruction. The war completely demolished much of the railroad.

Postwar recovery saw rapid consolidation of the South's fragmented rail network. Under the leadership of Richard T. Wilson, a partner in a New York banking and cotton brokerage firm who had served as the Confederacy's commissary general, the Memphis & Charleston became part of a system that included the railroads in East Tennessee. The consolidation movement continued and in 1894 the old M&C became part of the Southern Railway System, which was organized by international banker J.P. Morgan. The route remained part of the Southern until 1982 when the Southern merged with the Norfolk & Western to create the Norfolk Southern, one the nation's major rail systems.

Robert Brandt, Nashville

SEE: CHATTANOOGA CHOO-CHOO; JONES, JAMES C.; MEMPHIS; RAILROADS

RAILROAD, MEMPHIS-PACIFIC. As soon as the first proposal to build a transcontinental railroad reached Congress in 1845, Memphis area leaders launched a campaign to become the Mississippi terminus. Neither as old nor as powerful as New Orleans or St. Louis, Memphis backers hoped that their central location would make them the compromise route. The State of Arkansas supported the plan, as did powerful political figures like John C. Calhoun, John Bell, Sam Houston, and Thomas Jefferson Rusk from Texas. But sectional bickering over slavery and states' rights quickly undermined their plans. By 1854 supporters of the Memphis terminus had no hope of seeing their expectations fulfilled, despite the fact that the most practical all-weather route lay west of the city.

The proposed Memphis-Pacific Railroad also faced serious topographical as well as its political problems. Swampy, shifting soil covered the approaches to Memphis from east and west. Hundreds of miles of the proposed route lay in desolate land. The railroad's political problems proved more crippling. Opposition to federal aid for internal improvements, intrasectional rivalries, and competition from New Orleans, Vicksburg, St. Louis, and Chicago, as well as promotions for a railroad or canal across Central America, further compromised the Tennessee plans. The sectional battle over slavery largely destroyed the consideration of the Memphis terminus.

At least until 1854, Memphis leaders valiantly tried to overcome these drawbacks through the staging of commercial conventions (1845, 1849, and 1853). They invited national leaders to attend in the vain hope of producing a compromise.

The Memphis-Pacific Railroad project attracted the attention of countless southerners and mesmerized Tennesseans. This failed dream exemplifies the economic consequences of the eroding national and intersectional unity on American progress.

Jere W. Roberson, University of Central Oklahoma

SEE: MEMPHIS; RAILROADS

RAILROAD, NASHVILLE AND CHATTANOOGA (NC) created new towns, new wealth, and a new corporate landscape as it brought the industrial age to Middle Tennessee. The railroad was the first complete line to operate in Tennessee in 1854 and was one of the few railroads in Tennessee that did not fall into receivership after the Civil War.

Nashville merchants, bankers, and large landowners in Middle Tennessee were the first to articulate the vision of a railroad that would allow the conversion of the natural resources of Middle Tennessee into valuable marketable commodities. They seized the opportunity to develop a railroad when the Western and Atlantic Railroad chose Ross's Landing (Chattanooga) as the terminus for its planned line to the Tennessee River in 1838. A railroad from Nashville to Chattanooga would provide a link to the Western and Atlantic road which traveled through Georgia to Augusta on to Charleston, South Carolina. Vernon K. Stevenson, the founding president of the NC, and other Nashville merchants and landholders successfully promoted the railroad as a means of increasing prosperity among the citizens of Middle Tennessee by providing a cheaper access to lucrative long distance markets. New Orleans no longer had to serve Middle Tennessee as the primary exchange center; now ports on the Atlantic could fulfill these services, especially Charleston. Middle Tennesseans could market grains and livestock to the cotton belt to the south via the new railroad.

Stock subscriptions went on sale in 1845 with cities such as Nashville, Murfreesboro, Shelbyville, Winchester, and Charleston, South Carolina, supplying substantial investments. The construction of the railroad began in 1849, which created considerable opportunities for landholders along the route to reap the benefits of land speculation. The siting of railroad depots produced new towns and engendered a rapid rise in land prices. Railroad officials estimated land prices rose from $5.00 per acre to $15.00. Larger new towns along the line were Smyrna, Bell Buckle, Wartrace, Tullahoma, Decherd, Cowan, and Chattanooga. These new towns offered a new spatial town alignment with corporate space, meaning the railroad depot, becoming the central organizing focal point. The traditional town square pattern gave way to businesses located parallel to the railroad tracks, or perpendicular from the railroad depot. Homebuilders chose to build parallel to the railroad right of way to give visitors and passengers an impression of wealth and prestige. The goal was to project an image of the town as experienced through the windows of a train, or from the depot, that would be communicated to others as promotion for town development.

The real work of altering the landscape to accommodate the requirements of the railroad was provided largely by African-American slaves contracted out to the railroad, and Irish laborers. The Irish were important in the construction of the Cowan Tunnel, especially in the blasting, because owners of contracted slaves would expect recompense if they were harmed, while the Irish were considered expendable. Many of the Irish railroad workers settled in Cowan permanently and their descendants still live in the area. Once in full operation on February 11, 1854, the railroad immediately altered the conception of time and space as it reduced the old stage journey of 22 hours between Nashville and Chattanooga to nine hours by rail. The railroad flourished until the Civil War divided operation and management

After the fall of Nashville in February 1862 to Union forces, the Nashville and Chattanooga Railroad came under the control of the U.S. Army, while Vernon K. Stevenson and Edmund Cole operated the portion of the railroad located in Confederate-held territory. The Nashville and Chattanooga Railroad was a vital link in supplying the Union Army, with a critical connection to the L&N railroad and Union Army supplies stockpiled in Louisville. Confederate cavalry conducted several skirmishes in efforts to destroy this important rail connection. The Union Army attempted to protect the line by constructing several blockhouses and stockades along the railroad, fortifications like Fortress Rosecrans in Murfreesboro. It spent a considerable amount of time in repairing torn-up rails. The railroad had a critical role in supplying Union forces in the battles of Chickamauga, Lookout Mountain, Chattanooga, and ultimately General William T. Sherman's Atlanta Campaign.

The end of the Civil War and Reconstruction brought a great deal of hardship to southern railroads, yet the Nashville and Chattanooga proved a very resilient corporation. The old guard of management regained control when Edmund Cole was elected president in 1868, which in turn provided needed stability for the future. The turmoil of the 1870s included destructive floods, cholera outbreaks, economic depressions, fierce rate wars among railroads, increased competition from consolidated railroad lines, and governmental attempts at regulation. The Nashville and Chattanooga developed a policy of expansion as a way to combat the designs of the major railroads such as the Baltimore and Ohio, Pennsylvania, Illinois Central and L&N, of controlling southeastern markets. Additional spur lines were

developed to reach the rich coal deposits along the Cumberland Plateau. In 1873 the name of the Nashville and Chattanooga was changed to the Nashville, Chattanooga & St. Louis (NC&St.L) to reflect the railroad's goal of becoming a major trunk line. The NC&St.L purchased the Owensboro, Kentucky, to Nashville line in 1879 and acquired entry into St. Louis from the St. Louis and Southeastern Railway via Evansville, Indiana, to East St. Louis. This expansion began to alarm the corporate hierarchy of the L&N who wished for sole control of this southeastern corridor. When Edmund Cole began negotiating for the Western and Atlantic and Central Georgia railroads, the L&N made their move to extinguish the expansion dreams of the NC&St.L. In a secretive maneuver involving the major stockholder of the NC&St.L and former president, Vernon K. Stevenson, the L&N bought controlling interest in the NC&St.L. without Edmund Cole's knowledge on January 18, 1880. The action shocked Nashvillians as they realized that the city of Nashville could no longer claim importance as the headquarters of a major corporation, but was now denigrated to a large city along the line. Citizens of Middle Tennessee voiced feelings of betrayal that helped persuade the L&N to leave the NC&St.L operating as an independent division with its own president and officers, which continued until the companies formally merged in 1957. However, the major decisions of the NC&St.L were now based on the needs of the L&N corporation as it strove to control the southeastern railroad markets.

Bonnie L. Gamble, Manchester

SUGGESTED READINGS: Jesse C. Burt, Jr., "The History of the Nashville, Chattanooga and St. Louis Railroad 1873–1916," (Ph.D. diss., Vanderbilt University, 1950) and "The Nashville and Chattanooga Railroad 1854–1872: The Era of Transition." East Tennessee Historical Society *Publications* 23(1951): 58–76; Bonnie L. Gamble, "The Nashville, Chattanooga and St. Louis Railroad 1845–1880: Preservation of a Railroad Landscape,"(M.A. thesis, Middle Tennessee State University, 1993)

SEE: COLE, EDMUND W.; RAILROAD, LOUISVILLE AND NASHVILLE; RAILROADS; STEVENSON, VERNON K.

RAILROAD, TENNESSEE CENTRAL was an important late nineteenth and early twentieth competitor to the dominant Louisville and Nashville and Southern Railway systems in Tennessee. Nashville capitalist, and former Memphis and Charleston Railroad president, Jere Baxter organized the line in 1893 to link, first, Nashville to Knoxville, crossing the Cumberland Plateau and tapping rich resources of coal and timber. Despite initial financial setbacks during the Depression of 1893–1894, Baxter's work crews completed this first section by 1898.

Baxter then turned his attention to a western extension which would connect Nashville to Memphis. Executives at both the Southern and the L&N did everything within their corporate and political power to impede Baxter's progress. For example, the L&N denied the Tennessee Central terminal access to the new Union Station under construction in Nashville. The Southern also built a new, exclusive terminal in Knoxville. Legal manuevers cost Baxter additional time and money as he sought public support and funding for the western branch. Then in 1904, Baxter died at the age of 54; his dream of an independent railroad was over.

In 1905 the Tennessee Central leased its eastern section to the Southern Railway and its incomplete western branch to the Illinois Central, which was primarily interested in having a connection to Clarksville. L&N officials undermined these arrangements by building a huge concrete and brick warehouse, named Cummins Station, near the Nashville Union Station in order to draw business away from the Tennessee Central line and associated warehouses in Nashville. Within three years, in 1908, both the Southern and Illinois Central ended their arrangement with the Tennessee Central.

The Tennessee Central still was a formiable presence in the communities of the Cumberland Plateau, reshaping urban development in Cookeville and Crossville while creating new towns such as Baxter in Putnam County. But with the loss of freight and passenger business from Nashville and Memphis, the line could not sustain itself based largely on products and passengers from the Plateau. In 1912 it was in receivership. Ten years later, the company was reorganized and remained a freight carrier until it ceased operation in 1968.

Carroll Van West, Middle Tennessee State University

SUGGESTED READING: Don H. Doyle, *Nashville in the New South, 1880–1930* (1985)

SEE: BAXTER, JERE; NASHVILLE UNION STATION; PUTNAM COUNTY; RAILROADS

RAILROADS. Tennesseans considered railroads as early as 1827 when a rail connection between the Hiwassee and Coosa rivers was proposed. The General Assembly granted six charters in 1831 for railroad construction, but these early efforts failed when financial support did not materialize. Early railroad fever struck hardest in East Tennessee. Beginning in 1828 Dr. J.G.M. Ramsey of Knoxville advocated a rail connection between South Carolina and Tennessee. In 1831–1832 the Rogersville *Rail-Road Advocate* (possibly the first railroad newspaper in the United States) favored an Atlantic connection through Virginia.

West Tennesseans also envisioned connections to the Atlantic coast. The Memphis Railroad Company (chartered in 1831, renamed Atlantic and Mississippi in 1833), hoped to connect Memphis with

Charleston. Another scheme attempted to link Memphis with Baltimore.

Tennessee's legislature enacted an 1836 law requiring the state to subscribe to one-third of railroad and turnpike company stock (the subscription was raised to one-half in 1838). When the state-stock system stumbled after the Panic of 1837, the ironic outcome was completion of Middle Tennessee turnpikes rather than railroads. The state aid laws were repealed in 1840 under Governor James K. Polk.

Although in force only a few years, the state internal improvement laws spurred some railroad developers to action. The Hiwassee Railroad did not qualify for the state subscription, but began construction in 1837 near Athens. Despite achieving Tennessee's first actual railroad construction, the Hiwassee failed in 1842. The LaGrange and Memphis Railroad was the only railroad to qualify for state subscription and in 1842 it became the first railroad to actually operate a train in Tennessee. A few months later the county sheriff took possession due to unpaid court judgments.

Tennessee's railroad interest revived in the late 1840s, encouraged by successful neighboring states. Georgia's Western and Atlantic was already headed toward the Tennessee River and it reached Chattanooga by 1850, a development that renewed the hopes of Knoxville and Memphis and created the first serious railroad interest in Nashville.

In 1848 the General Assembly endorsed bonds of the Nashville and Chattanooga (N&C), but the East Tennessee and Georgia (ET&G) won a precedent-setting direct loan two years later. The General Internal Improvement Law of 1852 provided state loans to railroads at $8,000 per mile ($10,000 per mile by 1854). Every Tennessee antebellum railroad (except the N&C) received grants under this system.

The N&C was the first railroad completed in Tennessee. Incorporated in 1845, it reached Chattanooga by 1854. It was the only state-aided railroad to avoid financial loss to the state. Associated branch lines were completed in the 1850s: the McMinnville and Manchester, the Winchester and Alabama; and the coal mine branch to the Sewanee Mining Company at Tracy City. Another associated line, the Nashville and Northwestern (N&NW), was intended to connect Nashville to the Mississippi River at Hickman, Kentucky. Construction began at Hickman and ran eastward only to McKenzie by the Civil War; the eastern end extended only a few miles from Nashville when captured by the Union army, who continued it to Johnsonville on the Tennessee River (the remaining gap was completed after the war).

The Memphis and Charleston (M&C), incorporated in 1846, ran across Mississippi and Alabama, to reach Stevenson, Alabama, by 1857, where it connected with the N&C, thus linking Memphis to the Atlantic via the N&C and the Western and Atlantic.

The ET&G, chartered in 1848, revived the Hiwassee Railroad. Running from Dalton via Athens and Loudon to Knoxville by 1855, it was the second railroad completed in Tennessee. A more direct route between Cleveland and Chattanooga was completed in 1858. The East Tennessee and Virginia (ET&V), chartered in 1849, was completed from Knoxville to Bristol in 1858, ending East Tennessee's rail isolation.

Nashville gained rail access to the North through Kentucky. Louisville city subscriptions and Tennessee state aid financed the Louisville and Nashville (L&N), incorporated in Kentucky in 1850. Competitive subscriptions among local governments determined its Tennessee route. Completed in 1859, it hosted an excursion intended to preserve the Union. Several other Middle Tennessee railroads provided Nashville connections. The Nashville and Decatur (N&D) ran from Nashville through Columbia to Tennessee's southern border, where it connected with the M&C and an Alabama railroad to Decatur (it also extended from Columbia to Mt. Pleasant). The Edgefield and Kentucky (E&K), completed in 1860, ran from the Nashville suburb of Edgefield to Guthrie on the Kentucky boundary.

Memphis also established railroad access to Louisville: the Memphis and Ohio (M&O) ran from Memphis to Paris; the Memphis, Clarksville, and Louisville ran from Paris to Guthrie; and the L&N constructed a branch from Bowling Green to Guthrie.

West Tennesseans gained rail access to Mobile, New Orleans, and Columbus, Kentucky, due to the rivalry between New Orleans and Mobile to establish rail connections to the Ohio River mouth. The Mobile and Ohio reached from Columbus to Jackson, Tennessee in 1858, and to Mobile in 1861. The Mississippi Central and Tennessee connected with the Mobile and Ohio in 1860, giving New Orleans access to the Ohio a year before its rival Mobile. The Mississippi and Tennessee completed a line from Memphis to Grenada, Mississippi, in 1861, giving Memphis access to New Orleans via the Mississippi Central.

Tennesseans took preliminary steps to begin a transcontinental route through Memphis, Little Rock, and El Paso, but the Civil War dashed any hopes that the South would participate in a railroad to the Pacific.

Tennessee railroad equipment of the 1850s was primitive. Railroad track (mostly unballasted) consisted of light T-section wrought-iron rail on untreated crossties. Tennessee track adopted the usual Southern broad gauge of five feet. The typical steam locomotive was the *American* type, characterized in the Whyte system as the 4-4-0 (four leading wheels, four drive wheels, no trailing wheels). Colorfully painted and picturesquely named, they were wood fueled, requiring a distinctive balloon smoke stack. Rolling stock utilized wooden construction, link-and-pin couplers, cast iron wheels, and hand brakes. Freight cars were limited to boxcars, flatcars, and gondolas. Passenger cars were crude open air coaches, with wood stoves, kerosene lamps, and hand-pumped water. Antebellum railroad depots in larger cities were substantial brick buildings, but elsewhere they were simple wooden structures, often lacking protective canopies for passengers or freight loading ramps.

By 1860 Tennessee had completed 1,197 miles of track, which represented about 13 percent of the South's total of 9,167 miles. Southern railroads represented only about 30 percent of the total national rail mileage, and comparatively they were small organizations with inferior equipment running on lighter rail. However, Tennessee's strategic location as a border state between North and South destined its railroads to play a significant role in the Civil War.

In the spring of 1862, with the fall of Forts Donelson and Henry to Federal gunboats, Confederate General Albert S. Johnston realized that Nashville was indefensible and retreated toward Murfreesboro. Plans to evacuate supplies from Nashville faltered when panicked citizens and bridge washouts overwhelmed southbound railroads. Johnston, aware that he could not defend both Middle Tennessee and the Mississippi, decided to protect the river and Memphis. The most strategic point was the railroad junction at Corinth, Mississippi, where the Mobile and Ohio joined the M&C. Using railroads extensively, Johnston concentrated troops from all over the Confederacy at Corinth. Meanwhile, Federal General Grant gathered his forces at nearby Pittsburg Landing on the Tennessee River. The two forces met in a major battle near Shiloh Church in April 1862. Johnston was killed and the Confederates retreated, leaving Union forces in control of the only Confederate rail line between Virginia and the Mississippi River. The outcome disabled Confederate rail transport west of Chattanooga and north of Vicksburg, and permitted Union rail access southward to Alabama and Mississippi and eastward to Stevenson, Alabama, near the important rail junction of Chattanooga.

Grant was assigned to guard the railroads providing communication with the Mississippi and Buell was assigned to take Chattanooga. But Confederate General Braxton Bragg delayed federal movement toward Chattanooga with a series of harassing raids by Nathan B. Forrest and John H. Morgan against the federally occupied M&C and N&C railroads, allowing time to move Confederate troops by rail from Tupelo to Chattanooga. Grant created a defensive railroad triangle encompassing Memphis, Humboldt, and Corinth.

The state's railroad system became of even more strategic value in 1863. After the Battle of Stones River, massive quantities of supplies arrived at Murfreesboro via the N&C, and Federal forces erected enormous Fortress Rosecrans to protect this critical supply depot.

The Confederates decided to concentrate additional forces at the center where Bragg and Rosecrans were evenly matched. In a remarkable transportation feat, Confederate troops traveled by rail from Virginia (1,000 miles by a difficult indirect route, necessary because Federals had taken Knoxville), while others marched from Mississippi. In September 1863 Rosecrans advanced to Chattanooga, and Bragg withdrew to Georgia. Rosecrans recklessly pursued Bragg, until the Confederates delivered a severe blow at Chickamauga, forcing the damaged Federal army to retreat back to Chattanooga. Bragg advanced on Chattanooga, occupying Lookout Mountain and Missionary Ridge, from which vantage point his forces could control the city's transportation. With Federal forces reduced to near starvation, Secretary of War Edwin Stanton devised an ambitious plan for the massive railroad transport of Federal troops from Virginia to relieve the siege of Chattanooga. Generals George H. Thomas (who replaced Rosecrans) and U. S. Grant used these forces to conquer Chattanooga, effectively delivering all of Tennessee to Federal control. This amazing transportation feat proved that, under the control of strong centralized authority, railroads could project substantial military force across great distances within a short time.

In 1864 Confederate General John B. Hood conducted raids against the Federal rail lines to Chattanooga. Hood invaded Tennessee, hoping that the Federals would follow him to supposedly advantageous terrain. Sherman sent Generals Thomas and John Schofield to Tennessee, where they defeated the Confederates at the battles of Franklin and Nashville in late 1864. The Confederates retreated from Tennessee for the last time, leaving the state's railroads completely in Federal hands. Although the Confederate railroads served their military forces well, when Federal forces secured control of the Southern railroad network, they solidified access to the superior manufacturing capabilities of the North, which ultimately led to Union victory.

The Civil War left Tennessee's railroads damaged and most of its railroad companies in financial straits. Governor William G. Brownlow attempted to reconstruct the whole railroad system, and by 1869 the General Assembly appropriated $14 million dollars for railroad companies. However, widespread corruption among legislators and railroad officials led to fraudulent use of the funds. Tennessee defaulted on bonds maturing in 1867–1868, causing a severe drop in the state's securities and excessive speculation in its bonds. Investigative committees had little effect, and suggestions of repudiating bonds were silenced by threats of military reconstruction by Washington Radicals. Brownlow was succeeded by DeWitt C. Senter, who eventually abandoned Radicalism and worked with the Conservative legislature to reverse Radical measures. In 1879 the General Assembly and Governor Albert S. Marks uncovered the flagrant corruption of railroad and government officials.

Especially during the 1880s, Tennessee railroads expanded substantially. The railroad network nearly tripled its antebellum size to a substantial 3,131 miles by 1900. Simultaneously, railroad track and equipment evolved into more sophisticated forms for more effective passenger and freight transportation. However, the biggest change in the state's railroads was the gradual shift of finance and control from local parties to Northern interests. By the 1890s, the bulk of Tennessee's railroads were consolidated into just three major systems dominated by Northern control: the Southern, the L&N, and the Illinois Central (IC). Amazingly, these three large systems would continue to maintain their corporate identities for nearly a century!

The Southern Railway Security Company, controlled by the Pennsylvania Railroad, pioneered use of a holding company to consolidate Southern railroads: it controlled the East Tennessee, Virginia and Georgia (ETV&G—formed by the 1869 merger of the ET&G and ET&V) by 1871, and leased the M&C in 1872. The Pennsylvania abandoned its southern initiative after the Panic of 1873. The rapidly growing ETV&G absorbed the M&C by 1884, and was in turn acquired by the Richmond and Danville in 1887. These companies entered receivership in 1892, and J.P. Morgan reorganized them by 1894 to form the long-lived Southern Railway. The Southern acquired the Cincinnati Southern (Cincinnati to Chattanooga) in 1895.

The L&N remained prosperous while expanding rapidly in the late nineteenth century. This dominant Middle Tennessee line absorbed the Memphis, Clarksville, and Louisville by 1871; the M&O and the N&D by 1872; the E&K in 1879; and the Nashville, Chattanooga and St. Louis (previously formed when the N&C acquired the N&NW in 1872) in 1880. Although the railroad remained in local and southern hands into the 1880s, the Atlantic Coast Line actually controlled the L&N by 1900.

The IC absorbed several West Tennessee lines after the war, beginning with the New Orleans, St. Louis and Chicago in 1877 (a consolidation of the New Orleans, Jackson, and Great Northern and the Mississippi Central with its 1873 extension from Jackson, Tennessee, to Cairo, Illinois). The IC acquired the Mississippi and Tennessee by 1889, and the Chesapeake, Ohio and Southwestern (C.P. Huntington's

Louisville to Memphis line) in 1893, giving control of most West Tennessee railroads to Edward H. Harriman. (Tennessean Casey Jones achieved his folksong fame on the IC during a fatal run south from Memphis on April 30, 1900.)

Tennessee's railroad technology developed rapidly during the late nineteenth century. A massive 1886 effort converted the antebellum Southern broad gauge track (five feet between rails) to the national standard gauge (four feet, eight and one half inches), eliminating many costly transfers at junction points. Track was ballasted and made more robust, and steel rail was introduced in the 1870s. Railroads began to use creosote on wooden bridges and trestles (crossties remained untreated), and metal components appeared on large bridges. Locomotives grew larger and used more efficient coal fuel. Specialized freight locomotives appeared, such as the Mogul (2-6-0) in the 1870s, and the Consolidation (2-8-0) in the 1880s. By the 1890s Ten Wheeler (4-6-0) passenger engines appeared. Wooden construction still dominated rolling stock, but refinements included air brakes (1870s), steel-tired wheels (about 1880), and automatic couplers (required by the Federal Safety Appliance Act of 1893). By the 1880s passenger cars acquired gas lighting, enclosed vestibules, and steam heating. By the 1890s passenger cars had wide vestibules, air-pressured water supplies, and electric lights powered by axle generators and batteries. The Railway Post Office car appeared in 1869, and sleeping cars (invented in the North in 1864, but slowly adopted in the South) became more common. Freight cars increased in capacity, some utilizing steel underframes as early as the 1870s. Ice-bunker reefers (for refrigerated fresh produce) appeared in the 1870s.

Depots acquired formal stylistic traits, although accompanied by a divergence between urban and rural stations. Elaborate urban depots reflected Victorian Gothic, Richardsonian Romanesque, Neo-Classical, and Beaux Arts Classical styles. Many rural depots displayed Carpenter Gothic features, while others exhibited Stick, Eastlake, and Queen Anne characteristics. Some railroads adopted standardized designs and color schemes for their buildings.

Tennessee's late nineteenth century railroad growth reflected a larger economic revitalization, based on extractive industries controlled by Northern interests. Numerous small railroads developed specifically for timber/lumber, iron mining/smelting, coal, and phosphate transportation. The mountainous topography of East Tennessee led to the creation of unusual lines which were uniquely configured to accommodate sharp curves and steep grades. These railroads adopted narrow gauge (three feet) track and geared locomotives to access valuable but remote resources.

The early 1900s involved moderate growth for Tennessee railroads, culminating in the all-time maximum state rail mileage of 4,078 miles in 1920. The Southern, L&N, and IC continued incremental growth; L&N notably gained a foothold in East Tennessee by 1905, with completion of its Atlanta to Cincinnati line which passed through Knoxville.

Creosote treatment (previously confined to bridges and trestles) finally was extended to crossties around 1912. More powerful locomotives evolved, including the Mikado (2-8-2) for freight and the Pacific (4-6-2) for passenger use. Passenger cars obtained steel underframes, and by 1913–1914 all-steel coaches and diners appeared. Freight cars grew in size and developed steel-framed superstructures. Sophisticated signaling and control systems evolved, contributing to both efficiency and safety. Tennessee's most impressive depots, designed to serve multiple railroads, appeared during the early twentieth century: especially notable are Nashville Union Station (1900) and Memphis Union Station (1913).

The major effect of World War I was the imposition of Federal control on Tennessee's railroads. A centralized system which consolidated operational activities and facilities during the war replaced rivalry between competitors. Financial difficulties beset the railroads when federal control was lifted in 1920—even the relatively prosperous L&N experienced a deficit, its first since 1875.

After 1920 Tennessee railroads began a long decline. The primary cause was the development of an extensive highway network with its growing fleet of cars, buses, and trucks. Airlines contributed to the decline in rail passenger operations. New pipeline systems and improved water transport affected rail freight operations. Excessive government regulation, along with preferential funding of newer transportation modes, also contributed to overall railroad decline. Tennessee's total railroad mileage continued to diminish—to 3,573 miles by 1940—as did the railroads' share of transportation traffic.

During the 1920s and 1930s (and despite the damaging effects of the Great Depression), the railroads attempted to fight back by developing more efficient freight equipment, additional passenger comforts (especially air conditioning), and faster speeds (as suggested by the adoption of streamline design). These measures only marginally slowed the railroads' loss of freight and passenger traffic.

The increased rail traffic which came with World War II improved railroad profitability. Operating on considerably less total track mileage than in World War I, technological improvements allowed railroads to carry larger volumes of traffic during World War II. In contrast to the excessive government intrusion of the earlier war, during the second conflict the railroads remained under private control.

Diesel locomotives first appeared on Tennessee railroads during the early 1940s. Diesels were more efficient and required less maintenance than steam engines, allowing railroads to replace elaborate steam locomotive servicing facilities with simpler diesel facilities. Most Tennessee railroads were completely dependent upon diesel power by the mid-1950s.

The postwar years brought further decline in Tennessee railroads. Railroad traffic share continued to diminish, substantially in freight transportation, and to virtual extinction in passenger operations. By 1995 continued abandonment reduced Tennessee's total rail mileage to only 2,634 miles—smaller than the state's 1890 rail network.

In the late twentieth century corporate consolidation again has become a major theme in the state's railroad history. The Southern Railway became part of Norfolk Southern as a result of the 1982 consolidation of the Southern with the Norfolk and Western. The L&N became one of the Family Lines created by the Seaboard Coast Line (SCL) in 1972. Most of the Family Lines were formally merged in 1983 to form the Seaboard System Railroad, which was renamed CSX Transportation in 1986. CSX inherited the traditional Middle Tennessee dominance exercised by the L&N for nearly a century, and broadened its influence in East Tennessee through another merged Family Line, the Clinchfield Railway. Widely known for its remarkable engineering through challenging mountainous terrain, the Clinchfield crossed Tennessee (a major shop facility is located at Erwin) on its passage from South Carolina to Kentucky. The Illinois Central merged with the Gulf, Mobile and Ohio in 1972 to form the Illinois Central Gulf Railroad, owned by IC Industries, Inc. It serves primarily the western division of Tennessee, with strong connections to the Gulf coast and to northern cities.

The Tennessee Central Railroad, created by controversial promoter Jere Baxter in the 1890s, fought L&N's Middle Tennessee monopoly for many years, managing to survive until bankruptcy in 1968, after which its remaining assets were divided up in 1969 between the Southern and L&N.

Tennessee railroads continue to evolve technologically to cope with changing economic conditions. The once vast fleet of boxcars has been mostly replaced by "piggybacking" of trailer-on-flat-car (TOFC) and container-on-flat-car (COFC). TOFC/COFC is a key component of the intermodal freight concept which seeks to minimize en route-handling between various modes of transportation. Another method for lowering costs involves unit trains: long strings of high-capacity rolling stock which convey massive quantities of bulk commodities. Unit trains carry coal, Tennessee's top bulk commodity.

The Staggers Act of 1980 reduced the federal regulation of railroads, allowing rail companies to respond more effectively to market conditions in state, national, and even international settings. Tennessee's bulk freight rail traffic reflects a relatively healthy economic situation, with the state ranking ninth in total tons carried by rail. Although passenger rail traffic has virtually disappeared in Tennessee, with Amtrak operating stations in only Newbern and Memphis, severe highway congestion around major urban centers has led to interest in the establishment of commuter rail links to surrounding suburban areas.

Edward A. Johnson, Middle Tennessee State University

Suggested Readings: Stanley J. Folmsbee, et al., *Tennessee: A Short History* (1972); Kincaid A. Herr, *Louisville and Nashville Railroad, 1850–1963* (1964); John F. Stover, *The Railroads of the South, 1865–1900: A Study in Finance and Control* (1955); Elmer G. Sulzer, *Ghost Railroads of Tennessee* (1975); George Edgar Turner, *Victory Rode the Rails: The Strategic Place of the Railroads in the Civil War* (1953)

RAILWAY, CAROLINA, CLINCHFIELD AND OHIO

(CC&O), best known as the Clinchfield Railroad, provided the "Quick Service, Short Route between the Central West and Southeast," crossing the Appalachian Mountains and opening communities along its 277-mile route to distant markets and the twentieth century. The track stretched from Elkhorn City, Kentucky, where the CC&O connected with the Chesapeake and Ohio, through Virginia, Tennessee, and North Carolina, to Spartanburg, South Carolina, and its connection to the Southern. The railway operated in five states, crossed four mountain ranges and five major watersheds, included 54 tunnels (totaling almost ten miles) and 17,000 feet of bridges, and cost an estimated $40 million to construct.

The idea of a railroad along such a route emerged as early as 1836, but the first serious attempt came in 1886 at the hands of northern investor John Wilder, whose plans for the Charleston, Cincinnati and Chicago Railway collapsed in the Panic of 1893. The pieces thus far built were bought by Charles E. Hellier, renamed the Ohio River and Charleston Railroad Company, and sold off over the next ten years. George L. Carter bought the tracks from Johnson City to Boonford, North Carolina, in 1902 and named his route the South and Western Railway.

Though a native of the region, Carter turned to New York financiers for funds to meet the cost imposed by M.J. Caples, his general manager and chief engineer. Caples's insistence upon a railroad built to the highest standards meant the CC&O (as the line was rechartered in 1908) met its primary purpose of hauling coal from Kentucky and Virginia mines, through mountains and across rivers, to a distribution point beyond the Piedmont with great success. Except for the northernmost 35 miles of the route, grades were held below 1.2 percent and curves had a maximum of eight degrees. Caples also required 85 lb. rail, passing tracks on average every seven miles, and water tanks ten miles apart. Enlarging tunnels and strengthening bridges has not been necessary throughout this century because of the superior specifications Caples incorporated at the outset.

By 1909 the CC&O line ran from Spartanburg to Dante, Virginia (the section north to Elkhorn City opened six years later). Carter established the railway offices and yards in Erwin, in Unicoi County, halfway along the route. Kingsport and Johnson City also benefited from the railroad's presence and along with Erwin welcomed new industries over the next two decades. In 1924 company officials changed the line's name to Clinchfield when they leased the CC&O to the L&N and Atlantic Coast Lines. The passenger service that began in 1909 ceased in 1954. Freight trains ran on the Clinchfield Railroad until 1982, when Seaboard System Railroad (now CSX Corporation) bought all outstanding shares and continued the freight service but dropped the Clinchfield name.

Margaret D. Binnicker, Middle Tennessee State University
SUGGESTED READING: James A. Goforth, *Building the Clinchfield: A Construction History of America's Most Unusual Railroad* (1983)

SEE: CARTER, GEORGE L.; JOHNSON CITY; KINGSPORT; RAILROADS; SOUTHERN POTTERIES, INC.; UNICOI COUNTY

RAMSEY HOUSE, the home of Colonel Francis Alexander Ramsey (1764–1820), was built between 1795 and 1797 by master carpenter and cabinetmaker, Thomas Hope. Colonel Ramsey migrated to the North Carolina frontier from Gettysburg, Pennsylvania, in 1783. Settling first in the Watauga area, within a decade Ramsey purchased land along the forks of the French Broad and Holston Rivers in Knox County.

Ramsey House was constructed just inland from the forks of the rivers at a site known as "Swan Pond." The pond, which was formed by a beaver dam, was a landmark for early hunters and travelers; even after the pond was drained, the name continued to be linked to the Ramsey House property.

In some respects, the house Hope created is a traditional late Georgian style "I-house," with a simple three bay, central hall design. Ramsey House, however, is exceptional for its walls of pink marble, the detailed stringcourse of blue limestone which circles the house, the marble keystones and quoins, and the intricately carved consoles at the roof corners. This was Englishman Thomas Hope's first commission upon arriving on the Tennessee frontier from Charleston, South Carolina—a commission which would convince prominent East Tennesseans to seek his skills, making Hope one of Tennessee's most important early craftsmen.

"The most costly and most admired building in Tennessee," according to the 1800 federal census, served one of the most revered early East Tennessee families admirably for three generations. After the Civil War, however, the house was sold and began to deteriorate. In 1952 the Association for the Preservation of Tennessee Antiquities' Knoxville Chapter purchased the house and one acre of land in order to preserve this architectural and historic landmark. Today, the Ramsey House property has increased to more than 90 acres; the house is fully restored and open to the public.

Lisa N. Oakley, East Tennessee Historical Society
SEE: ASSOCIATION FOR THE PRESERVATION OF TENNESSEE ANTIQUITIES; KNOX COUNTY; RAMSEY, JAMES G.M.

RAMSEY, JAMES GETTYS MCGREADY (1797–1884) made an indelible mark on the political, economic, and social development of antebellum East Tennessee. He was a physician, public official, religious leader, banker, railroad advocate, scholar, and staunch secessionist, one of the most accomplished East Tennesseans of his era.

Ramsey's father, Colonel Francis Alexander Ramsey, migrated to the North Carolina frontier from Gettysburg, Pennsylvania, in 1783. He married Peggy Alexander of Mecklenburg County shortly thereafter. Colonel Ramsey played an instrumental role in the establishment of Tennessee in 1796, having previously held official positions in the failed State of Franklin and the Territory South of the River Ohio.

J.G.M. Ramsey's schooling began at Ebenezer Academy in Knox County and continued at Washington College. Ramsey read medicine under Dr. Joseph Strong, of Knoxville, and completed his education at the University of Pennsylvania Medical School. In 1821 Ramsey married Margaret Barton Crozier. The union produced 11 children, all of whom were raised at Mecklenburg, the Ramsey home built at the confluence of the French Broad and Holston Rivers.

After his father's death, Ramsey became the president of the Knoxville branch of the Bank of Tennessee. Economic development and railroad promotion occupied his attention thereafter. Ramsey had supported earlier efforts to build a canal system to bypass navigational hazards on the Tennessee River and provide reliable transportation for Knoxville merchants and industrialists. By the 1830s his interest turned to railroad development, and he worked diligently to establish a railroad connection between Knoxville and Charleston. Early public enthusiasm for construction of the railroad gave way to delays caused by adverse economic conditions; the East Tennessee and Georgia Railroad was established in 1848, and the first train entered Knoxville in 1855.

Ramsey's most enduring contribution came as author and historian of the state's early settlement history. In 1834 Ramsey supported the organization of the East Tennessee Historical and Antiquarian Society, which continues today as the East Tennessee Historical Society. As recording secretary, Ramsey assumed responsibility for cataloging and providing a home for the documents and relics owned by the Society. Mecklenburg took on the role of library and museum for East Tennessee's past, with Ramsey as its historian. In 1853 Ramsey published his time-honored history, *The Annals of Tennessee to the End of the Eighteenth Century.*

In 1861 Ramsey was a staunch states-rights Democrat, who publicly supported secession and served as a treasury agent and field surgeon for the Confederacy. The war proved to be disastrous to the Ramsey family: a son was killed and Mecklenburg was burned during the Union occupation of Knoxville. The fire destroyed a library of 4,000 volumes and the museum collection. Ramsey and his family spent the rest of the war in exile, moving from Atlanta to Savannah, and on to Augusta, before settling in Charlotte, North Carolina, in a home they called Exile's Retreat.

After the war, Ramsey received amnesty from President Andrew Johnson. He lived in North Carolina, where he practiced medicine and wrote his autobiography; this volume was published in 1954 as *Dr. J.G.M. Ramsey: Autobiography and Letters.*

Ramsey returned to Knoxville in the early 1870s and to his life of public service. The Tennessee and East Tennessee Medical Societies, East Tennessee University (now the University of Tennessee), Tusculum College, and Washington College all benefited from his involvement. President of the Tennessee Historical Society, 1874–1884, he also continued his work with the East Tennessee Historical and Antiquarian Society until his death in 1884.

Lisa N. Oakley, East Tennessee Historical Society

SUGGESTED READING: David L. Eubanks, "Dr. J.G.M. Ramsey of East Tennessee: A Career of Public Service," (Ph: D diss., University of Tennessee, 1965)

SEE: EAST TENNESSEE HISTORICAL SOCIETY; RAILROADS; TENNESSEE HISTORICAL SOCIETY

RANSOM, JOHN CROWE (1888–1974), Tennessee's pre-eminent poet and arguably the South's most influential literary critic and teacher, was born in Pulaski and educated at Vanderbilt where he later taught English and became the leading member of the Fugitives, whose magazine contained many of Ransom's finest poems. Ransom's students included Allen Tate, Robert Penn Warren, and such distinguished Tennessee authors as Donald Davidson, Andrew Lytle, Cleanth Brooks, Peter Taylor, and Randall Jarrell. Emphasizing close consideration of language in literature, Ransom's analytical method of reading poetry would precipitate a

movement in literary theory called the New Criticism culminating in *Understanding Poetry* (1937), an anthology prepared by Cleanth Brooks and Robert Penn Warren which revolutionized the teaching of college English in this country.

Ransom's skills as poet and critic were balanced by an interest in philosophy and theology reflecting the influence of his father, a Methodist minister who preached in several Middle Tennessee towns before moving to Nashville where Ransom entered Vanderbilt at the age of 15 and graduated first in his class in 1909. After studying at Oxford on a Rhodes Scholarship, Ransom accepted a position at Vanderbilt in 1914 where he taught until 1937 when he joined the English department at Kenyon College in Gambier, Ohio. There he founded and edited for 20 years the *Kenyon Review,* an enormously influential quarterly which promoted the New Criticism, published works by many Southern authors including Andrew Lytle and Flannery O'Connor, and attracted writers as diverse as Bertrand Russell, W.H. Auden, and Bertold Brecht. Ransom died and was buried at Gambier in 1974.

Ransom's early poetry collected in *Poems About God* (1919) reflects experiences and places from his Tennessee childhood and introduces many of the themes to be developed in later poems and essays: the division between past and present, nature and man, and the search for wholeness and place in an increasingly fractured and uprooted world. These concerns were shared by T.S. Eliot; however, Ransom, like Frost, preferred to use provincial settings and more traditional verse forms. Most of Ransom's best poems were written during the publication of the *Fugitive* (1922–1925) and were collected in three volumes, *Chills and Fever* (1924), *Grace After Meat* (1924), and *Two Gentlemen in Bonds* (1927).

In the late 1920s, Ransom turned from poetry to social criticism. Attacking industrial capitalism and a pervading belief in the perfectibility of man, he contributed "Introduction: A Statement of Principles" and the initial essay "Reconstructed but Unregenerate" to the agrarian symposium *I'll Take My Stand* (1930). His first book of prose, *God Without Thunder: An Unorthodox Defense of Orthodoxy* (1930), defends religious ritual, not doctrine, and anticipates many of the views expressed in *The World's Body* (1938) where Ransom argues that science studies nature in order to control it while poetry, even more than religion, can best represent the mysterious complexity of nature (the world's body). In *The New Criticism* (1941), which gave the movement its name, Ransom calls for a critic who can demonstrate the ways in which poetry presents the concrete body of the world through language and structure.

Ransom's literary theories mirror his poetic practice: "metaphysical" lyrics that achieve a precarious balance between intellect and emotion, irony and love. The style is restrained, the subject matter often violent and shockingly varied: dead chickens, "transmogrifying" bees, and disembodied heads. In "Piazza Piece" the grim reaper is a dirty old man in a dustcoat lurking in the vines beneath a lady's verandah. In "Amphibious Crocodile" a dislocated Southerner longs for green slime and suffers lewd nostalgic tremors. In mock ballads with mother goose rhythms, the young are deprived of their innocence and sometimes their lives while a child-like old man violently retains his innocence but loses everything else. "Captain Carpenter," like other defeated Southern men, is told he shall "bear no more arms," but fights on to lose ears, eyes, even "the red red vitals of his heart." Whether confronting the frailty of innocence or the greater vexation of mortality, the more Ransom's reserved narrators try to remain unemotional and uninvolved, the more they reveal how much they really care.

Many of his finest lyrics are iconoclastic pastoral elegies like "Bells for John Whiteside's Daughter," "Janet Waking," and "Winter Remembered," in which Latinate diction, reflecting Ransom's education in classical languages, and allusions to the rituals of an older, more formal Southern culture are countered by colloquial diction, a skeptical modern awareness of the "forgetful kingdom of death," and the poignant "cry of Absence, Absence, in the heart."

Described by Allen Tate as one of the "best elegaic poets in the language" and by Randall Jarrell as a poet whom "generations of the future will be reading page by page with Wyatt, Campion, Marvell, and Mother Goose," John Crowe Ransom received the Bollingen Award in Poetry in 1951 and the National Book Award for poetry in 1963.

Thomas M. Carlson, University of the South

SEE: AGRARIANS; FUGITIVES; GILES COUNTY; LITERATURE; VANDERBILT UNIVERSITY

RATTLE AND SNAP, at Ashwood in Maury County, is considered one of the most emphatic examples of Greek Revival plantation architecture in Tennessee. George Polk's elaborate Corinthian mansion is the largest and most pretentious of the great Maury County plantations, and its monumental front facade of ten massive columns was a conspicuous display of the wealth and taste of one of the region's largest cotton planters.

George Washington Polk, one of the five sons of Colonel William Polk of North Carolina to establish large farms in Maury County, arrived on his father's 5,648-acre tract at Ashwood in 1840. By 1843 he was making arrangements for large-scale improvements on his quadrant of the parcel, and soon began construction of his magnificent home. Polk slaves cut the timber, hewed the limestone, and dug the clay

and burned the thousands of bricks needed for the house. Woodworking plants from the upper Ohio and iron foundries from Cincinnati and New Orleans provided finished materials. The house was completed in 1845. George Polk called it Rattle and Snap, after a game of chance in which his father supposedly won the Ashwood tract from the governor of North Carolina.

Rattle and Snap reflects the pinnacle of Greek Revival architecture in Tennessee. The L-shaped house is distinguished by its monumental facade with ten great Corinthian columns supporting a heavy pedimented portico and cornice. The stately edifice rests on a dressed stone foundation and is topped by a shallow hipped roof. The east porch has a delicate iron balcony with a lacy grillwork frieze, probably shipped from New Orleans by Polk's factor; the west or garden front has a portico supported by "Temple of the Winds" columns. The elaborate interior features a large entrance foyer and a double parlor separated by more "Tower of the Winds" columns. Exquisite plaster cornices and ceiling medallions are featured in the principal rooms. The name of the architect or designer is unknown.

His fortune devastated by the Civil War and the freeing of his slaves, George Polk sold the property to J.J. Granberry in 1867. The Granberrys, who occupied the place for the next half century, renamed the house Oakwood Hall. In 1919 the farm was sold to two other Maury County planters, and for many years, farm tenants occupied the house. In 1953 Mr. and Mrs. Oliver M. Babcock, Jr., purchased and restored it. After several subsequent changes of ownership, Amon Carter Evans, former publisher of *The Tennessean*, acquired Rattle and Snap. Over the next three years, Evans carefully restored the mansion to its original grandeur. The house, a National Historic Landmark, is open to the public.

Richard Quin, National Park Service

SEE: MAURY COUNTY

RATTLESNAKE SPRINGS is located five miles northeast of Cleveland in Bradley County. In 1838 Rattlesnake Springs served as the site of the last council of the eastern band of the Cherokees, where approximately 13,000 Native Americans assembled to begin the long journey to the Oklahoma Territory, a forced migration known as the Trail of Tears. At this last council meeting, tribal officials agreed to continue their old constitution and tribal laws in their new Oklahoma homeland. Unfortunately, many did not survive the journey west, as hunger and disease claimed thousands of lives before they reached Oklahoma.

Federal troops, along with Tennessee and Georgia militia, supervised the assembly and removal of the Cherokees. Troops established two military camps near Rattlesnake Springs—Camp Foster and Camp Worth—to oversee and guard the Cherokees prior to removal. Soldiers herded the Cherokees into stockades like cattle, where they remained penned under intolerable conditions until removal. Sanitation was deplorable, while food, medicine, and clothing remained in short supply. Reportedly, over 200 Cherokees died at the springs before the removal began.

From August through December of 1838, soldiers divided the Cherokees into 13 detachments of about 1,000 people each for the journey west. On the Trail of Tears, most people walked, with only the sick, aged, children, and nursing mothers allowed to ride in wagons.

Steve Rogers, Tennessee Historical Commission
SEE: BRADLEY COUNTY; RED CLAY STATE HISTORIC PARK; TRAIL OF TEARS

READ HOUSE HOTEL, located in downtown Chattanooga at the corner of Broad Street and Martin Luther King Boulevard, was constructed in 1926 at a cost of over two million dollars. The hotel was designed by Holabird and Roche, an architectural firm from Chicago, and built by George A. Fuller & Company of Washington, D.C.

The Read House is a ten-story red brick building designed with Georgian detailing. It features a one-story limestone base with storefront windows. Terra cotta detailing decorates the exterior of the building in the form of quoining, window surrounds and pediments, beltcourses, and cornices. The interior features 237 guest rooms as well as meeting and banquet space. Two of the most notable rooms include "The Silver Ballroom" and the "Green Room." The Silver Ballroom is decorated with Waterford crystal chandeliers and silver leaf ornamental cornice and medallions. The ground floor is dominated by a two-story lobby with black walnut paneling, terrazzo and marble floors, carved and gilded woodwork, and a richly detailed plaster ceiling with two bronze chandeliers.

Dr. John T. Read built and opened the original Read House in 1872. In 1879 he sold the lease and furniture to his son, Samuel R. Read. Much of this building was demolished in 1926 and the current structure built. Read operated the hotel until 1943 then sold it to Albert Noe, Jr. Upon Noe's death in 1947, his son, Albert Noe III, began operating the hotel. In 1960 Noe converted a portion of the hotel to a motor inn. The motor inn opened in 1962 and featured 106 rooms and a 135-car parking garage. Provident Life and Accident Insurance Company purchased the Read House in the mid-1960s and contracted with the National Hotel Company to manage it in 1968. After suffering recent financial trouble and several changes in ownership, the Read House is currently owned and operated by the Radisson Hotel chain. Listed in the National Register of Historic Places, the Read House is a significant example of grand hotels built for railroad passengers in the early twentieth century.

Miranda R. Clements, Chattanooga
SUGGESTED READINGS: Linda L. Burton, *Chattanooga Great Places* (1996); John Wilson, *Chattanooga's Story* (1980)
SEE: CHATTANOOGA

"*The Parting of the Way.*" *Andrew Johnson attempts to kill the Freedmen's Bureau, 1867.*

RECONSTRUCTION. In the immediate aftermath of Confederate defeat, Northerners and Southerners alike widely recognized two clear-cut consequences of the Federal victory in the Civil War. First, the union had been preserved and the right of secession as a legitimate expression of state sovereignty had been forcibly repudiated. Second, slavery, which had flourished for nearly two and one-half centuries, was dead to rise no more. For both black and white Tennesseans, however, in the spring of 1865 the implications of these results were far from clear. Numerous questions remained unanswered. When and under what terms would the state be reintegrated into the political life of the reunited nation? What would be the legal and political implications for Tennesseans who had sided with the Confederacy and who were now branded as "traitors"? How, practically, would the devastation of the war and the disruption of emancipation affect the state's economy and its traditional patterns of race relations?

Such questions would be answered, gradually and imperfectly, during the period of "Reconstruction" that followed. Historians traditionally define Reconstruction as the period extending from the conclusion of the Civil War in 1865 to the final withdrawal of federal troops from southern soil in early 1877. Although this chronological definition makes sense for the region as a whole (at least with regard to politics), it is arbitrary and often inappropriate when applied specifically to individual states. Such is certainly the case with regard to Tennessee. Many of the most crucial political questions raised by Confederate defeat were answered in the state long before 1877. For example, by the end of the 1860s the state had already regained full representation in the national Congress and repudiated fleeting Republican rule in the state legislature. Other crucial political issues, however, most notably the influence of the former slaves in state politics, would not be resolved until the early 1890s. Similarly, most of the major economic issues of the postwar era were not effectively resolved until near the end of the century. In particular, although it was undeniable that emancipation had initiated a major reorganization of agriculture across much of the state, even as late as 1877 it was not yet certain what sort of new land and labor arrangements would come to predominate. In sum, to its very close the Reconstruction period was characterized by considerable uncertainty for Tennesseans of both races.

Of the numerous crucial questions facing Tennesseans after the war, that concerning the state's reintegration into the union was resolved the most rapidly. Immediately after the surrender of Confederate armies, radical Republicans in Congress, such as Thaddeus Stevens and Charles Sumner, lobbied for a punitive policy that would treat the ex-Confederate states as conquered enemies. President Andrew Johnson, on the other hand, prescribed a far more lenient policy in which the formerly disloyal states would be readmitted to Congress as soon as they had ratified the Thirteenth Amendment abolishing slavery, repudiated state debts accrued during the rebellion, and rescinded their original ordinances of secession. Like the other ex-Confederate states, Tennessee rapidly met these criteria and requested readmission to Congress in December 1865. At that point, however, the Republican majority in Congress refused to seat any Congressional delegation from the former Confederacy and eventually added one further prerequisite for readmission: ratification of the Fourteenth Amendment, which defined the former slaves as U.S. citizens and penalized any state that excluded them from the franchise. Unique among the ex-Confederate states, Tennessee rapidly ratified this amendment (in July 1866) and was thus readmitted to the Union before Congress imposed a more stringent reconstruction plan in March 1867. In a technical sense, "Reconstruction" in Tennessee had formally ended, only slightly more than one year after Lee's surrender at Appomattox.

Tennessee politics had not returned to normal, however, for the state continued to be dominated by a Republican minority that commanded the allegiance of, at most, one-third of the total population. Non-existent in the state prior to 1865, the party had emerged as a political vehicle for unionists and, consequently, always was strongest in staunchly unionist East Tennessee. Aided by a war-time edict of Military Governor Andrew Johnson that disfranchised Confederate sympathizers, Tennessee Republicans swept into power in March 1865, controlling the General Assembly as well as the governorship, which was claimed by the mercurial parson and newspaper publisher, William G. Brownlow. For four years the Brownlow government worked assiduously to maintain Republican supremacy. In 1865 the legislature formally disfranchised ex-Confederates. Two years later it took the drastic step of awarding the franchise to the former slaves to expand the ranks of potential Republican voters, and the following year it authorized the governor to declare martial law in individual counties in order to counter the growing influence of the Ku Klux Klan.

Despite such aggressive tactics, Republican rule in Tennessee was short-lived. Nearing the end of his second term as governor, Brownlow stepped down from office in February 1869 to accept a U.S. Senate seat and was replaced for the duration of his term by Senate Speaker Dewitt C. Senter, a conservative East Tennessee unionist. Determined to win election in his own right and facing opposition from within his own party, Senter reached out for support from the state's Democrats by effectively setting aside the franchise law and allowing thousands of Confederate sympathizers to vote. Senter won the election, but conservative Democrats reclaimed control of the General Assembly and "redeemed" the state from Republican rule. Although divisions within the Democratic party would occasionally allow Republicans to challenge for state offices, after the election of 1869 Republican influence was largely limited to East Tennessee. Although without significant political power, Tennessee blacks statewide would continue to vote Republican in large numbers until the early 1890s, when they were effectively disfranchised by a combination of registration laws and poll taxes.

In the economic sphere, Tennesseans had to address both the immediate impact of the war's physical destruction and the long-term consequences of slavery's demise. Across the state, Confederate and Union veterans returned to their homes to find dilapidated buildings and fences, deteriorated soils, broken down work animals, and depleted food supplies. A Congressional investigating committee conservatively estimated the state's nonslave property losses at approximately $89 million, or just under one-third of the total value of nonslave property in Tennessee when the war began. A recent statistical study suggests that the Congressional figures actually substantially understated the war's devastating effects. In eight counties selected from across the state for intensive scrutiny, the median value of real estate per white farm household fell during the 1860s by from one-half to three-fifths. In addition, slaveholding families (representing roughly one-quarter of all free households in the state) suffered financial losses due to the emancipation of more than 275,000 slaves, valued by Congress at just under $100 million but easily worth three times that amount on the eve of the war. In a sense, emancipation did not constitute a true loss to the state, but rather a redistribution of wealth from slaveholders to former slaves, who now for the first time legally owned their own persons.

Significantly, such severe and widespread financial injury did not lead to a notable reordering of wealth or status within the state's agricultural population. There was no revolution in land titles in the countryside, and the bottom rung on the agricultural ladder did not replace the top. Because it disproportionately affected the state's major plantation regions, emancipation did reduce drastically the pronounced disparities in levels of wealth that had distinguished the state's three grand divisions before the Civil War. At the local level, however, the war's effect on wealthholding patterns appears to have been minimal. *Gone With the Wind* images aside, Tennessee's wealthiest planters and farmers exhibited impressive resilience in the face of unprecedented physical destruction and economic upheaval. Granted, they typically suffered severe financial losses during and immediately after the war, but more often than not they landed on their feet. Noticeably weakened, they nevertheless retained their positions of economic dominance within their own communities.

Overall, given the sheer magnitude of economic and social upheaval generated by the war, the extent of continuity in wealthholding patterns is little short of remarkable. Although the concentration of personal property (which had formerly included slaves) declined noticeably between 1860 and 1870, the distribution of real estate was almost literally unaffected, and inequality in the overall distribution of total (real and personal) wealth—a prominent antebellum characteristic—proved to be an amazingly durable phenomenon despite the cataclysm of civil war. As before the war, the top five percent of agricultural households commanded from one-third to one-half of their counties' total wealth, while the bottom one-half generally controlled from three to six percent. The relative frequency with which landless farmers acquired their own farms continued to be impressive, however. As had been true of the antebellum era, during Reconstruction a highly uneven distribution of wealth coexisted in Tennessee with a social order sufficiently fluid to sustain the egalitarian ideal that hard work and perseverance would lead to economic independence.

Although evidence of continuity is impressive, it is undoubtedly clearer from hindsight than it was to contemporaries. With rare exceptions, Tennesseans who actually lived through the period were far more impressed—indeed, at times overwhelmed—by the changes that seemed likely to transform their lives. No factor contributed more to this pervasive perception of revolutionary change than emancipation. Slavery had been an indispensable pillar of the state's economy and a bulwark of traditional patterns of white supremacy and black deference. Depending upon the color of their skin, consequently, white and black Tennesseans viewed the end of slavery with either anger and anxiety or with joy and expectation. Both races recognized its undeniable significance. Neither knew what to expect in its aftermath. Poised on the threshold of the unknown, Tennesseans fashioned a number of competing visions of the postwar world, none of which was perfectly realized.

The former slaves, for their part, sought first and foremost to own their own farms and to secure as much economic independence as possible from their former masters. In the short run, their vision could only be realized by the intervention of the federal government to break up and redistribute their former masters' plantations. Any realistic hope of such a policy vanished abruptly with President Johnson's offer of pardon and full restoration of nonslave property to all who would swear an oath of future loyalty to the United States.

In contrast to the freedmen, white Tennesseans were divided in their vision for the postwar economy. Given the severe labor shortage that existed for several years after the war, many whites sought to lessen dependence on black labor. For example, urban advocates of "New South" ideals trumpeted the benefits of industrialization and championed a diversified economy in which the demand for agricultural labor would be substantially reduced.

Adopting a different approach, numerous large landowners sought to decrease the need for black labor per se by enticing northern and foreign workers to replace the freedmen in the fields. The majority of landowners, in contrast, continued to rely on black labor but hoped to immobilize the former slaves and to construct labor arrangements that resembled slavery as much as possible.

None of these strategies was successful in the short run. Industrial output did increase significantly for nearly a decade after the war, but the onset of a serious depression in the mid-1870s interrupted this expansion. Not until the 1880s did industrialization in Tennessee proceed in earnest. Similarly, although the Tennessee legislature in 1867 created a Board of Immigration to advertise opportunities for industrious immigrants, the much-desired influx of laborers never materialized. Finally, efforts to perpetuate slavery in everything but name were also frustrated, as they ran directly counter to the free labor commitment of Congressional Republicans, who were willing to use both the Freedmen's Bureau and the military to ensure a free market in labor during the early years of Reconstruction.

As a result, white landowners in need of labor negotiated with black laborers in need of land. The outcome was a gradual but thoroughgoing reorganization of agriculture that affected the entire state but was strongest in Middle and West Tennessee. Initially, white landowners attempted to rely solely on farm hands; i.e., wage laborers who worked under the close scrutiny of the employer or his agent. In order to attract sufficient labor, however, landowners increasingly found it necessary to subdivide their farms and plantations and rent small plots to laborers for either a fixed rent or a share of the crop. The result was a sharp increase in the number of farm units across the state (which doubled between 1860 and 1880), a severe decline in the average size of farms (which fell by half during the same period), and a substantial upsurge in the number of tenants (who constituted roughly one-third of all farm operators by 1880).

Ironically, poor whites were among the prime beneficiaries of these changes. Emancipation created a window of opportunity for white farm laborers, who had traditionally been forced to compete against slaves for agricultural employment. Close analysis of selected counties reveals that huge numbers of landless whites shifted from wage labor to some form of tenancy during the first 15 years after the Civil War. The ex-slaves also became tenants by the thousands, although it is not true, as historians once thought, that sharecropping almost immediately became "the South's new peculiar institution." In Tennessee, as late as 1880, between one-half and three-fifths of rural freedmen continued to work as wage laborers, the lowest position on the agricultural ladder. At the same time, however, nearly ten percent of the ex-slaves had managed to acquire their own farms, an impressive accomplishment considering their near total lack of financial resources and independent managerial experience only 15 years earlier.

Without question, Tennessee's labor system no longer bore much resemblance to its antebellum predecessor. A new system was in the process of crystallizing, yet that process was still far from complete.
Robert Tracy McKenzie, University of Washington
SUGGESTED READINGS: Thomas B. Alexander, *Political Reconstruction in Tennessee* (1950); Steven V. Ash, *Middle Tennessee Society Transformed, 1860–1870* (1988); William Gillespie McBride, "Blacks and the Race Issue in Tennessee Politics, 1865–1876" (Ph.D. diss., Vanderbilt University, 1989); Robert Tracy McKenzie, *One South or Many? Plantation Belt and Upcountry in Civil War-Era Tennessee* (1994); Gordon B. McKinney, *Southern Mountain Republicans, 1865–1900* (1978)

RECORDING INDUSTRY, NASHVILLE. The Nashville recording industry actually began after World War II, although there were several earlier events and factors that played a significant role in its success. During the 1920s and 1930s recording executives traveled across the country, making field recordings of local talent. The birth of contemporary country music is considered to have occurred in August 1927, when Victor executive Ralph Peer recorded the Carter Family and Jimmie Rodgers in Bristol, Tennessee. Peer and other recording executives visited several southern cities, but made only one stop in Nashville; in September 1928 Peer recorded a number of Grand Ole Opry acts. Nothing came of the effort, and neither Peer nor any other field recording executives returned.

During World War II, local entrepreneurs, including WSM executive Jim Denny, established small recording companies that catered to the influx of soldiers and enabled service men to record greetings and messages for their families at home. The major "recording" studios belonged to radio stations and recorded transcriptions for broadcast and advertisements. The first recording session for a major label occurred in WSM's Studio B, when Eddy Arnold recorded four songs for Victor on December 4, 1944; he recorded again the following July. WSM employee Jim Bullet, who founded Bullet Records, also recorded some sessions at WSM's Studio B.

The real beginning of Nashville recording studios came in 1946, when three WSM engineers, Aaron Shelton, George Reynolds, and Carl Jenkins, launched Castle Recording Studios. Castle initially used the WSM studios, before setting up a studio at the Tulane Hotel in 1947. The studio recorded radio commercials for local businesses as well as recording major label artists. Decca's Paul Cohen became the first A&R man to record regularly in Nashville; he recorded Ernest Tubb and Red Foley in August 1947. The same year, the Nashville studios had its first "million seller" when the Francis Craig Orchestra recorded *Near You* at the Ryman Auditorium. The song became the theme song of Milton Berle's "Texaco Theater" show. In addition to Castle Studios, the Brown Brothers Transcription Service and Thomas Productions also did recording sessions.

The post-World War II recording industry in Nashville was aided by a number of factors. After 1946, the Grand Ole Opry dominated country music as the result of its network exposure on NBC and the decline of its major competitor, "The National Barn Dance" on Chicago's WLS. Major record labels, including Mercury, Capitol, RCA Victor, Columbia, and Decca, opened offices in Nashville to tap the talent pool attracted by the Opry and those musicians generally employed by WSM for its musical shows. Later, in 1956, the death of Dallas studio owner Jim Beck sent a number of Texas country music acts to Nashville. The Nashville local of the American Federation of Musicians, under George Cooper, gave area musicians an opportunity to play, because it did not require members to demonstrate the ability to read and write music, a requirement in many other locals. Owen Bradley and Chet Atkins emerged as corporate leaders for Decca and RCA and based the country divisions of these labels in Nashville. Perhaps most importantly, the Nashville songwriting community, spurred by the strong publishing outlets, created a body of top quality songs.

In 1954 Owen and Harold Bradley moved their recording studio to 16th Avenue South to become the first business on what would be known as "Music Row." Bradley's studio was in a Quonset Hut, built to film songs for TV. The initial venture proved unsuccessful (although later this same format would be used for music videos), but the recording facility succeeded and soon attracted business from Decca and Columbia. RCA Victor used the Brown Brothers' Studio, built in the early 1950s for an advertising agency, before constructing their own studio in 1954 on McGavock Street, in space rented from Methodist Television, Radio, and Film Commission. Chet Atkins managed the McGavock Street facility.

In 1957 RCA built the first permanent record company office on Music Row; this later became known as Studio B. In 1961 they expanded the original building and three years later built an adjoining building, which housed executive offices as well as Studio A.

In 1958 Owen Bradley took over as Decca's head of country music. In 1962 Columbia purchased Bradley's Studio and made it the label's headquarters; Bradley then built Bradley's Barn in Mount

Juliet. By this point, there were a number of studios in Nashville, and the "Nashville Sound" had developed around a small group of musicians who played on the majority of Nashville recording sessions. As the major labels established permanent offices in Nashville, the demand for recording studios grew, and independent studios soon outnumbered label-owned studios.

Don Cusic, Belmont University

SEE: ARNOLD, EDDY; ATKINS, CHESTER B.; BRADLEY, OWEN; DENNY, JAMES R.; TUBB, ERNEST; WSM

RED CLAY STATE HISTORIC PARK, located 12 miles south of Cleveland, was the site of the last seat of Cherokee government before their forced removal by Federal troops along the Trail of Tears. From 1832 to 1837 it was the site of 11 general councils, some attended by 5,000 Cherokees.

Those years were troubled times for the Cherokees as they worked to insure their future. It was at the council meetings at Red Clay that the Cherokees learned that they would have to leave on *nunahi-duna-dlo-hilu-i*, the Trail Where They Cried, on their way to Indian Territory, now the state of Oklahoma. A young Cherokee, Jane Bushyhead, wrote a friend from "Red Clay Cherokee Nation March 10, 1838" with her fears that "we Cherokees are to be driven to the west by the cruel hand of oppression. . . . It is thus all our rights are invaded."[1]

At one time the Cherokees claimed all of Tennessee and Georgia, and parts of North Carolina, South Carolina, Virginia, West Virginia, Kentucky, Mississippi, and Alabama as their homeland. As the first settlers started crossing the Blue Ridge Mountains and entering Cherokee territory, they had little respect for the Cherokee's kinship with the land and saw that land as free for the taking.

By the early 1800s the Cherokees lived very much like their white neighbors. By 1826 the Cherokee Nation had its capital at New Echota, Georgia, with a surveyed city including a courthouse, printing office, houses, and streets. However, in 1832 the State of Georgia stripped the Cherokees of their political sovereignty and made it illegal for the Cherokees to meet together for any reason other than to treaty away their land. Georgia also divided the Cherokee's land by lottery. As a result, the Cherokee Nation moved its capital to Red Clay in Tennessee.

A U.S. Department of War removal treaty was presented at two Council meetings at Red Clay in 1832. After the Council unanimously rejected the treaty, they adopted a resolution to send a delegation to Washington to attend to the business of the Cherokee nation. For five years at meetings at Red Clay, the Council heard reports from various delegations and agreement or disagreement with the actions of these delegations. The Cherokees divided into factions.

Not only did the Cherokees send delegations to the President and to Congress, they took their case to the U.S. Supreme Court. In 1833 they hoped for relief from the President or Congress because the Supreme Court had decided in favor of the Cherokee Nation remaining in their ancestral land (*Worcester v. Georgia*).

In 1834 the Treaty Party, led by John Ridge, Major Ridge, and Elias Boudinot, began formal efforts for acceptance of a Cherokee treaty with the United States. Principal Chief John Ross led the Cherokee fight to keep their eastern lands and not to emigrate. By 1835 two rival delegations were in Washington to negotiate a treaty, and the factions held separate Council meetings. Seemingly a compromise was made in October 1835, but while Chief Ross was in Washington, the Ridge faction signed the Treaty of New Echota.

During the last Council meetings at Red Clay, after protests to this New Echota treaty and all views were heard, the Council appointed another delegation. A regular Council session was scheduled for 1838, but due to the collection and removal activities that meeting never happened. As many as 17,000 Cherokees were rounded up and kept in holding stations until the government was ready to move them to Indian territory. The Cherokees endured great hardships in these camps and they suffered during the trek westward. It is estimated that over 4,000 died in the camps and on the trail.

It was almost 150 years before the Cherokee met again in council at Red Clay. The Cherokee Council Reunion in April 1984 was commemorated by a return of the eternal flame to Red Clay. This symbol of the council fire remains burning to honor those Cherokee of the 1830s, those who died during the forced removal, and those Cherokee living today and tomorrow.

Today these Cherokee council grounds form the core of a Tennessee state park, which includes a museum and outdoor replicas of an 1830s Cherokee Council House, sleeping huts, and a farmstead. Red Clay State Historic Park is listed in the National Register of Historic Places, is a certified site and interpretive center on the Trail of Tears National Historic Trail, and is honored by today's Cherokees as sacred ground.

Lois I. Osborne, Red Clay State Historic Park

CITATION:

(1) Quotation is cited in *Journal of Cherokee Studies* 3(1978): 137.

SEE: BRADLEY COUNTY; RATTLESNAKE SPRINGS; RIDGE, MAJOR; ROSS, JOHN; TRAIL OF TEARS

REECE, BRAZILLA CARROLL (1889–1961), Congressman, was born in Butler, Tennessee, to John Isaac and Sarah Maples Reece. He was one of 13 children in the Reece family. Named for an ancestor, War of 1812 General Brazilla Carroll McBride, Reece never used his first name. Growing up in rural Tennessee, Reece attended Watauga Academy and Carson-Newman College, where he played basketball and football and was the valedictorian of the 1914 graduating class. After working as a high school principal for one year, he attended New York University and earned a master's degree in economics and finance in 1916.

In 1917 Reece joined the American army headed for the war in France. He served in the American Expeditionary Forces and was decorated with the Distinguished Service Cross, Distinguished Service Medal, Purple Heart, and French Croix de Guerre with Palm. He returned to Tennessee and won election to the U.S. House of Representatives from the First Congressional District in 1920. He held that position, almost without interruption, until his death in 1961; he failed to win reelection for one term (1930–1932) and spent two years as Republican Party National Chairman from 1946 to 1948.

Reece soon gained a reputation as one of the most conservative members of Congress. An opponent of Franklin Roosevelt's New Deal social policies, he also advocated isolationism in the years preceding World War II. During and after the war, Reece voted conservative economic principles in his opposition to federal wage and price controls. He supported the abolition of the poll tax and the implementation of federal anti-lynching legislation.

As 1946 Republican party chairman, Reece represented the "old guard" conservative faction, which included Ohio Senator Robert Taft. Reece and Taft met opposition from such Republican liberals as Harold Stassen of Minnesota. Independently wealthy, Reece served without salary during his tenure as GOP chair. He presided over a Republican sweep of the House and Senate in the midterm congressional elections of 1946.

In his private life, Reece became a successful businessman, serving as president of three banks in his district. He briefly published the *Bristol Herald-Courier*. In addition, Reece practiced law, having received his law degree from Cumberland University. He married the former Louise Goff, whose father and grandfather had represented West Virginia in the U.S. Senate. After their marriage in 1923, the couple had one child, a daughter named Louise. Reece died of cancer on March 20, 1961, at Bethesda Naval Hospital in Maryland and is buried at the Monte Vista Burial Park in Johnson City. His wife completed his congressional term. The Carroll Reece Museum at East Tennessee State University is named in his honor.

Michael Rogers, University of Tennessee, Knoxville

SEE: CARSON-NEWMAN COLLEGE; WORLD WAR I

REED, ISHMAEL SCOTT (1938–), a contemporary

African-American satirist, poet, playwright, and essayist, was born in Chattanooga, February 22, 1938, and lives in Oakland, California. Having left Chattanooga as a child and grown up in Buffalo, New York, he attended public schools and the University of Buffalo. In Buffalo, Reed did newspaper work for a black weekly and co-hosted a sometimes politically radical radio show. An interview with Malcolm X led to Reed's dismissal from WVFO in the early 1960s, and his move to New York City in 1962 put him in touch with other young African-American writers who offered encouragement and impressed upon Reed the need to break away from white writing models—Nathanael West, Ezra Pound, William Blake, and William Butler Yeats, for example—and focus on African-American literature. As a result, his first novel, *Free-Lance Pallbearers* (1967) combined his admiration for the work of Ralph Ellison and his gift for parody and satire; it is a parody of Ellison's *Invisible Man* which satirizes America's Vietnam-era political scene. In addition to creative writing, Reed also edited a weekly newspaper in Newark, New Jersey, and helped organize, in 1965, the American Festival of Negro Art.

Aside from the publication of his first novel, 1967 also was a landmark year for Reed, his first wife, and their daughter when they moved to northern California and Reed took a teaching job at University of California, Berkeley. His second novel, *Yellow Back Radio Broke-Down*, a Western parody, followed in 1969. Following Yeats's lead in establishing a personal mythology, Reed demonstrates in this novel his long-time interest in traditional Afro-Caribbean religion, namely Voodoo, or Vodoun. This traditional religion, imported by slaves, provides a rich source of cultural and narrative tradition which Reed has drawn on throughout his career as a writer. Reed calls his own version of vodoun mythology "Neo-HooDooism," a concept fully developed in his novel *Mumbo Jumbo* (1972), in which the *loas* or Vodoun deities or spirits act through PaPa LaBas, a trickster in search of a sacred text. Like Ishmael Reed's first novel, *Mumbo Jumbo* owes much to Ellison's only novel; in addition, many figures of the Harlem Renaissance are satirized.

The slave narrative, another traditional African-American literary form, is the inspiration for Reed's *Flight to Canada* (1976), another satiric novel in which the "Uncle Tom" character, here called Uncle Robin, ends up inheriting his master's plantation and refuses to sell his story to Harriet Beecher Stowe, preserving his right to his own story.

Other novels include *The Last Days of Louisiana Red* (1974), *The Terrible Twos* (1982), *Reckless Eyeballing* (1986), *The Terrible Threes* (1989), and, in 1993, *Japanese by Spring*. Reed's *oeuvre* includes several poetry collections, one of which, *Chattanooga* (1973), clearly

indicates his ties to his native state; other poetry collections are *Catechism of D Neoamerican Hoodoo Church, A Secretary to the Spirits,* and *Conjure*. His works range into drama: *Mother Hubbard, The Ace Boons, and Savage Wilds*; television productions: *Personal Problems, A Word in Edgewise*; anthologies: *Calafia* and *19 Necromancers from Now*; and essay collections: *Shrovetide in New Orleans, God Made Alaska for the Indians, Writin' is Fightin',* and *Airing Dirty Laundry*.

Reed is an innovator in style—often called a postmodern experimental writer—who delights in playing with all literary forms. He is also a community leader and a supporter and mentor to younger multiethnic American writers, having co-founded the Before Columbus Foundation and co-edited *The Before Columbus Foundation Fiction Anthology* which features award-winning fiction written by various multiethnic American writers. Reed continues to teach at the University of California, Berkeley, and has held teaching positions in many major American universities.

Sara Lewis Dunne, Middle Tennessee State University

SEE: CHATTANOOGA; LITERATURE

REELFOOT LAKE STATE RESORT PARK is a 300-acre park located on a 18,000-acre lake in northwest Tennessee. The New Madrid earthquakes of 1811–1812 probably enlarged a series of oxbow lakes that had existed here long before. Permanent settlement was slow to come to the lake area, due to the frequency of flooding and "unhealthy" reputation the lake had gained. An account from 1848, for instance, mentioned only a single family living along the lake. But the region was reknowned for its hunting. Allegedly David Crockett killed 105 bears in the lake area between 1825 and 1826. In time, however, the people living around the lake fell into two groups. Those on the west side, between the lake and the Mississippi River, typically practiced plantation agriculture while those on the east side were fishermen and subsistence farmers.

After the Civil War, the timber industry harvested much of the lumber in the region. One lumberman, James C. Harris of Tiptonville, announced in 1899 that he "owned" the lake and that he planned to drain it for further development. Harris's pronouncement eventually led to the violence of the infamous Night Riders of Reelfoot Lake affair in 1908. Legal battles over ownership continued until 1913 when the Tennessee Supreme Court declared the lake navigable and within the public domain.

The move toward creating a state park occurred in the 1920s due to lobbying from several citizens and local officials as well as the state government's desire to end the legal fight over the ownership of the lake. Donald V. Sabin and his wife Nonie Rhoads Sabin, who grew up in Union City, moved to Union City and opened a photography studio in 1919. They specialized in people and topics from the Obion and Lake counties area but especially focused their attention on the natural beauty of Reelfoot Lake. In 1923 the Sabins offered a series of 300 photographs of Reelfoot Lake to the State of Tennessee. State officials declined to purchase the collection, but realized that the Sabins's offer was an important example of local interest in the preservation of Reelfoot Lake. Two years later, the state purchased property surrounding the lake and established the Reelfoot Lake Park and Fish and Game Preserve.

In the 1960s to 1980s the state instituted a series of improvements, including a visitor's center/museum, lodge and restaurant, and an airplane landing strip, that led to the park's designation as a State Resort Park. Today the park is popular with fishermen and nature lovers, who especially enjoy looking for the park's small resident population of American bald eagles. The Tennessee Wildlife Resources

"The Sentinel" at Reelfoot Lake. Photograph by Verne Sabin.

Agency successfully introduced nesting eagles to the park in 1981.

Carroll Van West, Middle Tennessee State University

SUGGESTED READINGS: Mary Locker and Catherine Elick, "The Turbulent Past of Reelfoot Lake," *Tennessee Conservationist* (May/June 1987): 17–20; Obion County-Union City Museum, *Sabin: A Time Returned: 1919–1924* (Union City, 1986)

SEE: CONSERVATION; EARTHQUAKES; LAKE COUNTY; NIGHT RIDERS OF REELFOOT LAKE; OBION COUNTY

REEVES, LEE ROY (1876–1960), designer of the Tennessee State Flag, was born in Johnson City, Tennessee, in June 1876, the son of Elbert Clay and Alice D. Robeson Reeves. After graduating from the local high school and normal school, Reeves taught in the Johnson City public schools from 1896–1898. He then was admitted to the bar in 1899 and practiced in Johnson City with his father until 1905.

Reeves became interested in creating a state flag during his years as an officer in the Tennessee National Guard. In June 1903 he organized a company for the National Guard's Third Regiment, based in Johnson City, and was commissioned a captain. Two years later, Reeves approached several legislators with his flag design and asked them to sponsor legislation to have the flag designated as the official Tennessee State Flag. The General Assembly approved the bill on April 17, 1905. As described in the *Tennessee Blue Book*, Reeves's design is straightforward but effective: "The three stars are of pure white, representing the three grand divisions of the state. They are bound together by the endless circle of the blue field, the symbol being bound together in one—an indissouble trinity. The large field is crimson. The final blue bar relieves the sameness of the crimson field and prevents the flag from showing too much crimson when hanging limp. The white edgings contrast the other colors."[1]

After the approval of the state flag, which was flown first in Johnson City, Reeves went on to have a distinguished legal and military career. He resigned his captaincy in 1906, after service in Virginia and Tracy City, and subsequently was appointed Major and Judge Advocate for the Tennessee National Guard. During the Mexican border crisis of the 1910s, Reeves served as acting brigade adjutant and assistant division adjutant. With the entrance of the United States into World War I, Reeves left the National Guard to volunteer for the U.S. Army in January 1918. He was commissioned major and after general demobilization he remained in the Army, serving in the office of the Judge Advocate General. In 1920 he was commissioned a major in that Army department, and he advanced to the rank of colonel before his retirement in 1940. Reeves died in 1960 and is buried in Johnson City's Oak Hill Cemetery.

TSLA, SABIN PHOTO COLLECTION

Carroll Van West, Middle Tennessee State University

CITATION:

(1) John L. Kiener, "Lee Roy Reeves: Designer of the Tennessee State Flag," Lecture given to Washington County Historical Association, October 19, 1996, p. 1. The Editor-in-Chief thanks State Senator D.E. Crowe II for providing him with a copy of this lecture.

SEE: TENNESSEE STATE SYMBOLS

RELIGION is a word that almost defies any consensual definition. Most people reflect some of their own religious beliefs, or at least those of their own culture, in defining religion. Thus, those from the Semitic traditions (Judaism, Christianity, Islam) tend to make belief in a god or gods essential to being religious. Those from the great Eastern religions (Buddhism and Hinduism) often make the quest for enlightenment essential, not theism, since early Buddhism was non-theistic. Those familiar with African religions may key their definition to ecstatic types of experience. Fortunately, one does not have to choose among these options when writing about religion in Tennessee, for at least since European penetration into the area that became Tennessee, the Judaic-Christian tradition has been completely dominant. An essay on religion in Tennessee has to be an essay largely about Christian churches and a very few Jewish congregations and the more recent arrivals of the followers of Islam, Hindu, and Buddhism (today clustered in the larger cities).

Before the Europeans came, various Indian tribes had their own, very complex religions. Europeans were so ethnocentric, and so unselfconsciously Semitic in the cosmology, that they consistently failed to understand the nuances of Indian beliefs and practices, or illegitimately tried to understand these through Christian presuppositions. Contemporary scholars, most from a Native American background, are correcting this bias, but with such a degree of complexity as to defy any brief summary. Suffice it to say that almost all popular images of Indian religion are simplistic if not completely mistaken. In many cases, present-day Native American spokespersons, often for political reasons, have utilized such simplistic perspectives, or perhaps even believe them. Among the most prevalent is the easy, but simplistic, view that all Indian religions supported a type of piety or respect for nature.

Europeans migrated across the Appalachians and into what would be Tennessee after 1769. They came largely from the piedmont of North Carolina or southern Virginia, or down from the Great Valley of Virginia. This meant that most migrants were of British background, and in so far as they had a church affiliation (most did not) were Presbyterian, Baptist, or lapsed Anglicans. This meant that largely British versions of Protestantism, rooted in the Reformed or Calvinist rather than Lutheran tradition, dominated. This evangelical Protestantism provided the most basic cultural bridge between whites and blacks and

River baptism in Morgan County, late nineteenth century.

TSLA, RUGBY PAPERS

between the varied geographic regions of the state. Tennessee's evangelical orientation was a southern, rather than state, characteristic.

The largely English populations of tidewater Virginia and North Carolina moved west into the piedmont in the early eighteenth century. Nominally Anglican, many converted to the more evangelical Baptists, particularly in North Carolina. These Baptists, Calvinist in doctrines, were largely the product of revivals that periodically broke out from 1740 to the Revolution. The Baptist missionaries, who established congregations in North Carolina and formed the Sandy Creek Association, were originally from New England. Scots-Irish Presbyterians (Scottish Presbyterians from Ulster), who often moved south from Pennsylvania, joined the Baptists on the frontier and dominated the early settlement of the Great Valley. Thus, the early congregations in what would become Tennessee were doctrinally Calvinists.

Baptists and Presbyterians both claim the first congregations in Tennessee. In the pre-Revolution period, some Presbyterian ministers did missionary work in the Watauga settlements, and in all likelihood some lay Baptist ministers preached to congregations. In 1778 Samuel Doak, a graduate of the Presbyterian College of New Jersey at Princeton, moved to the Watauga settlements, and by 1782 he had helped establish a settled church in Sullivan County. Possibly three years earlier, Baptists from the Sandy Creek association had established congregations in both Hawkins and Washington counties. Doak has received the most attention because of his credentials and educational role. In 1784 he founded a congregation and academy (Washington College) in Limestone in Washington County and later began an academy in Greene County (it merged with Greeneville College, established by Presbyterian rival, Hezediah Balch, to become the present Tusculum College). As a result of Presbyterian commitments to education, all early Tennessee colleges had a Presbyterian heritage, including Maryville College, Blount College (later the University of Tennessee), and Davidson Academy (George Peabody College for Teachers).

The Presbyterians, at first, outgrew the Baptists and remained more numerous than Baptists in a few upper East Tennessee counties into the twentieth century. But Baptists and Presbyterians soon lost their religious monopoly. German-speaking migrants, particularly from the Great Valley, entered Tennessee early, establishing a thin sprinkling of Lutheran, Church of the Brethren (Dunkard), and United Brethren congregations. They endured, but rarely expanded, in part because they resisted the revival institutions that came to dominate the major evangelical denominations. After 1800 a few Friends (Quakers) established small, ephemeral Meetings in

Washington and Greene counties, where they began the first abolitionist publications in American history. More importantly, many English migrants proved receptive to a growing offspring of colonial Anglicanism, the Methodists. Just before the Revolution, revivals among Virginia evangelical Anglicans created a population very receptive to Methodism, which penetrated the western counties of North Carolina even before the formation of an independent Methodist Episcopal Church in 1784. Methodist circuit preachers, based in southwest Virginia, preached in what would become Tennessee during the Revolutionary period and formed the first congregation in Sullivan County in 1786. Within the next generation, Methodist growth would be explosive. By the mid-nineteenth century, the Arminian (resistible grace and non-perseverance in grace) Methodists outnumbered either of their Calvinist Baptist and Presbyterian rivals.

These three denominations, plus the New England Congregationalists, who were never strong in Tennessee, made up the evangelical mainstream in American Christianity. They dominated the religious life in all parts of the United States, but were most monopolistic in Kentucky and Tennessee. In the nineteenth century, immigrants increased the religious heterogeneity in the North (Irish and German Roman Catholics, German and Scandinavian Lutherans, and central European Jews), but not in most of the South, which attracted only a few migrating Irish workers, who established the first Roman Catholic congregations in Tennessee. The label "evangelical," one embraced by almost all Protestants, had a rather clear meaning for early nineteenth century Presbyterians, Baptists, and Methodists, and helped maintain commonalities that bridged wide, and at times rancorous, doctrinal differences. By 1800 the label identified Christians who placed ever greater emphasis upon a crisis-like conversion or rebirth, on a warm, free, and affectionate or spiritual style of worship and devotion, on a commitment to proselytizing or soul winning through various revival techniques, and on a rigorous or non-worldly and near ascetic standard of personal holiness and moral purity.

After a difficult last decade of the eighteenth century, such evangelical denominations entered a period of rapid growth at the turn of the century. A key to the beginning of this religious boom occurred in the Cumberland area of Middle Tennessee and southern Kentucky. Six ministers (five Presbyterian and one Methodist) moved to Sumner County, Tennessee, and Logan County, Kentucky, between 1796 and 1800.

There they ministered to new congregations that arrived from the piedmont of North Carolina. James McGready, a particularly effective preacher, and his colleagues revived the old Scottish tradition of four-

and five-day intercongregational communion services. Held at individual churches during the summer and attended by all nearby congregations, these services had long been the occasion for conviction or conversion, and had been responsible for several waves of revival in North Carolina and southern Virginia after 1787.

In 1800 a building religious fervor peaked in at least eight planned communions in the two counties and in Nashville. Many in attendance at the outdoor preaching fell in a near coma. This falling and other dramatic physical exercises created great excitement and had two important consequences. McGready published a long and enormously influential letter about the revival, and a meeting at Gasper River, in Logan County, stimulated the first extensive camping on the church grounds. Well publicized by the host minister at Gasper River, John Rankin, and recounted with great effects to congregations in East Tennessee and North Carolina, this precedent led to widespread development of camp grounds and annual camp meetings everywhere, but particularly in Kentucky and Tennessee. This revival in the west climaxed at Cane Ridge in central Kentucky in 1801, and only gradually abated after 1805. But its precedents— camping, falling and other physical exercises, intense conviction, new hymns of invitation, lay exhorting— remained accepted patterns in evangelical revivals, whether held at outdoor retreats or camps (soon a Methodist preference) or in extended and special proselytizing services in churches.

The fervor of the revivals, the disturbing physical exercises, created doubts and divisions among the Presbyterians, who had hosted all the most explosive early revivals. The conversions, and new ministerial candidates, that sprang from the Cumberland revivals led Kentucky Synod to create a new presbytery in the Cumberland. This Cumberland Presbytery compromised the normal classical education required for licensing and ordaining new ministers and allowed candidates to finesse the Westminster doctrine of double predestination (God elects both to salvation and to damnation). When the Cumberland's senior Presbyterian minister, Thomas Craighead of Nashville, indicted the presbytery for its educational compromises, the synod investigated, found serious doctrinal problems, and insisted upon a doctrinal examination of all young men. Supported by their seniors—McGready and the other architects of the 1800 revival—the young men refused, and the synod expelled them. The battle raged over five years, but eventually the Presbyterian General Assembly upheld the synodical expulsion.

Some of the young men, led by socially prominent Finis Ewing, refused to capitulate. In 1810 Ewing and a colleague, Samuel King, met at the cabin of an ill Samuel McAdow (one of the original migrants from North Carolina) in Dickson County to form an independent Cumberland Presbytery. This grew into a denomination, only the first of several to originate in Tennessee. By 1860 the Cumberland Presbyterians, with doctrines midway between Presbyterian Calvinism and Wesleyan Arminianism, had surpassed the membership of the parent Presbyterian Church (now the Old School Presbyterians) in Tennessee. In 1906 a majority of Cumberland Presbyterians voted to merge with the northern Presbyterian church. Several individual Cumberland presbyteries rejected this merger and, alone in Tennessee, won a court battle to keep the existing property. This left the small, surviving Cumberland Presbyterian denomination with a unique Tennessee focus. Its only remaining college (Bethel) is located at McKenzie, and its seminary, boards, and publishing are centered in Memphis.

The Cumberland schism, a lack of qualified ministers, a more ordered and sedate religious style, and the rigorous demands of orthodox Calvinism retarded Presbyterian expansion. Thus, the two confessions that gained most from the explosive revivals were the Methodists and Baptists, who remained in first and second place in Tennessee church membership throughout the nineteenth century, only to reverse the order in the twentieth. In 1916 the Southern Baptist Convention (SBC) reported slightly over 200,000 members. The two wings of the Methodist Episcopal Church, North and South, reported 223,000. Already the SBC was the largest single denomination in the state and joined with African-American Baptists to make up approximately 40 percent of all Tennessee Christians. Black and white Methodists made up only 34 percent, with the Presbyterians (Cumberland, northern, and southern) far behind at just over eight percent. By then the Restoration churches (Disciples and Churches of Christ) exceeded Presbyterians (at almost 11 percent). These four groups of churches accounted for over 90 percent of all Christians in the state (Roman Catholics had less than 3 percent).

The two largest Protestant confessions in America (Methodists and Baptists) have both retained a special tie to Tennessee. After both the main Baptist and Methodist denominations split over the issue of slavery, the southern branches created their own denominational agencies. The Methodists led the way, and through the generosity of a former Methodist circuit preacher who had gained considerable wealth, the Methodist Episcopal Church South located its publishing house in Nashville. Soon its bishops met there, and other boards and agencies located in Nashville, making it the capital of southern Methodism. With the 1968 merger of northern and southern Methodists, the merged church distributed its boards and commissions, but, as a gesture to the former southern wing, established several of its most important agencies in Nashville, including those involved in discipleship, communications, and higher education. Perhaps most important of all, both economically and in terms of widespread religious influence, it kept its publishing house in Nashville. As the SBC created a quasi-denominational structure after its break from the Baptist General Convention in 1845, it eventually chose Nashville as home. Its central headquarters (its Executive Committee), and almost all its major commissions and boards, are in Nashville, including its huge publishing house.

By the end of the nineteenth century, one could identify deep tensions within these older, evangelical denominations. To an extent, a majority of southern Methodists and Presbyterians and a minority of Baptists relaxed some of the earlier moral rigor, became more inclusive in membership requirements, transformed the rebirth experience in something closer to confirmation, changed the former revivals and camps into milder forms of education, and variously reinterpreted central doctrines or relaxed an inflexible biblicalism. In the sense of the early nineteenth century, these mainline evangelicals were no longer very evangelical. Such shifts, and the resulting intramural controversies, led to major doctrinal counterattacks, often loosely labeled as fundamentalist, and tied to a few key doctrines (Biblical inerrancy, the initiatory role of Jesus in launching a millennium, and the key doctrines tied to rebirth). At the same time others, who resisted the modernizing trends, down played doctrines and tried to retain, or recover, the emotional warmth or spirituality of the old time Evangelicalism and its resulting moral purity or holiness. From this wing of reaction came the late nineteenth century holiness movement and, in the early twentieth century, a rapidly growing Pentecostal movement, that added to the older Evangelicalism a new emphasis upon charismatic gifts (prophecy and healing), with speaking in tongues elevated to a key position as a necessary witness to spiritual baptism. In all these changes, Tennessee once again occupied a central position, one much more important in the history of Christianity than its anti-evolution legislation or the famous Scopes trial at Dayton in 1925.

The Nashville-based SBC was not unaffected by liberal and more inclusive trends in the mainline denominations. But it was much more resistant than the reunited Methodist and Presbyterian denominations, and never moved close to any union with the northern American Baptist churches. Since the early 1980s, the Convention (technically a fellowship and not a denomination) has moved, at the central level and in elected leadership, to a clear and emphatic defense of both the doctrines and the devotional style of nineteenth century Evangelicalism, and is today the largest voice for this tradition. As the largest Protestant denomination in the United States, it both reflects and fosters a religious style that is quite pervasive in Tennessee.

Even as the Baptists held firm, or moved back toward an older Evangelicalism, the largest Methodist and Presbyterian denominations more fully embraced a broad, latitudinarian approach. Since much of East Tennessee remained unionist, northern Methodists and Presbyterians remained dominant in some heavily unionist counties, and eventually both denominations ended the Civil War divisions. Today, these denominations tolerate a wide spectrum of beliefs, but have a national profile that is decidedly liberal in its inclusiveness in tests of membership, flexibility in Biblical interpretation, openness to Biblical scholarship or to the implications of scientific knowledge, and a commitment to social outreach as well as to individual salvation. Thus, in Nashville, a few blocks apart, one can observe the polarities in the formerly mainstream evangelical denominations, with a growing and ever more monolithic and exclusive SBC challenging the shrinking and tolerant United Methodists.

Other conservative or evangelical denominations have their home in Tennessee. From the eighteenth century on, a small Free Will Baptist movement, with salvation doctrines close to Methodism, challenged majority Calvinist Baptists. Many of these Free Will Baptists remain independent or associate in loose local fellowships. Membership statistics do not exist, but impressionistic evidence suggests that independent Free Will Baptists have been growing very rapidly in the last two decades, particularly in the mountains of East Tennessee. Some, but far from all, southern Free Will Baptists joined in a conference in 1921, and united with a smaller northern counterpart in 1935, to form the present National Association of Free Will Baptists. Its headquarters, Bible College, and several boards are located in Nashville.

To further establish the priority of Nashville in world Baptism, one must chart its centrality in the black, National Baptist movement. Black Baptists first organized independent boards or commissions under the guidance of American Baptists (northern), but then formed a loose National Baptist Convention in 1886. Its subsequent organizational history is complex and contested. In 1895 several black Baptist agencies combined to create the first large union of black Baptists, also named the National Baptist Convention. In 1915 the original National Convention split over publishing (the occasion was a publishing enterprise in Nashville), and now the National Baptist family includes four related but separate denominations. The largest wing of this movement, the National Baptist Convention of the U.S.A., Inc., has its national headquarters, a new and impressive world center, a seminary, and a publishing house in Nashville. This largest black Baptist denomination (over five million), when added to the 15 million Southern Baptists, means that well over 20 million American Baptists have their headquarters and publishing houses in Tennessee.

Black Methodists eventually formed three major denominations. The smallest of these, the Colored Methodist Episcopal Church (today the Christian Methodist Episcopal Church), reflected a friendly separation of blacks from the Methodist Episcopal, South. This 1866 separation, effected at a General Conference in Memphis, led to another Tennessee denomination. Its main boards, including one on publications, are now in Memphis, further documenting the centrality of Tennessee in black Christianity. The CME's school, Lane College, is in Jackson.

In the upper South, the first effective competition with the three main evangelical denominations came from the Restoration churches (variously denominated Christians, Disciples of Christ, and Churches of Christ). One branch of this movement, led by Barton Stone, originated out of the Kentucky revivals of 1801. By 1831 Stone's western churches, usually called Christian, effected a partial and unofficial merger with a movement founded by Thomas and Alexander Campbell, and by then called Disciples of Christ. Both the Stonites and Campbellites won early converts in Tennessee, and by 1850 Nashville was one of the leading centers of this movement. The Restoration churches were not evangelical, in the sense that they did not emphasize an explosive conversion or rebirth, but instead a reasoned, step-by-step response to the Gospels, climaxing in a remitting baptism. They also repudiated the extreme emotionalism associated with most revivals. Much more than most Baptists, they eschewed any denominational organization, although a major Baptist reform movement, Landmarkism, which originated in Nashville, came close.

The Restoration churches eventually splintered into three major fellowships. Even by the Civil War, tensions had developed between rural, most often southern, rigidly anti-mission or anti-organization and rigidly restorationist Disciples, and many of their northern, less rigidly congregational and separatist, ecumenically oriented brethren. One leader of the conservative, restorationist, or purist congregations was Tolbert Fanning of Nashville, who edited the most influential periodical (*Gospel Advocate*) in this very conservative faction of the movement, one that rejected any form of intercongregational organization or any instrumental music. After the war, David Lipscomb, the new editor of the *Gospel Advocate*, became the leading spokesman for the conservative wing of the movement, one with most of its strength in the defensive, post-Civil War South. These cleavages led, by 1900, to two distinct fellowships (no denomination existed), and the choice by these conservative

congregations to distinguish themselves in the religious census of 1906 from the main body of Disciples of Christ.

As a result of the influence of Fanning and Lipscomb, the conservative faction outgrew the more liberal in the Nashville area and in the state as a whole. Today, these Churches of Christ make up a loose, deeply splintered national fellowship with no headquarters. Yet, in a loose way one could argue that Nashville is at the center of the fellowship, since the Middle Tennessee Churches of Christ have a larger share of the membership than any comparable area of the United States, and David Lipscomb is one of the most influential of their universities. Nashville remains a home to the *Gospel Advocate* and other influential periodicals and is the address of a small, private publishing house and bookstore that is unofficially linked to these congregations. The more ecumenical Disciples also later split into two fellowships, with the conservative wing—Christian Churches and Churches of Christ—well established in East Tennessee, and Milligan College (its only liberal arts college) and Emmanuel (its strongest seminary) in Carter County. The largest body of historical sources on the Restoration movement are in the Disciples of Christ Historical Society library in Nashville.

In the twentieth century, the most threatening competitor of the big four religious traditions in Tennessee has been holiness and Pentecostal movements, although both Seventh-day Adventists and Mormons established scattered congregations in the state. A modern, organized Pentecostal movement began with ecstatic experience, and tongue speaking, in Topeka, Kansas, in 1901. It developed within a loose holiness movement, one with roots in Methodism. Independent holiness congregations joined in several local denominations by 1900, and stressed the Wesleyan doctrine of holiness or perfection, the attainment, in a second conversion-like experience, of a type of sanctification. This second step had gradually lost centrality in the two largest (North and South) Methodist denominations. Such holiness doctrines spread throughout the country and gained local adherents in several Tennessee cities. Following mergers in 1907 and 1908, one holiness mission in Nashville became one of the outposts of what became the Pentecostal Church of the Nazarene (after 1919 simply the Church of the Nazarene), the largest non-charismatic holiness denomination today. This led to a growing Nazarene membership in Nashville and a very influential college, Trevecca Nazarene University.

Even before 1908 important holiness ministers in Tennessee capitulated to a burgeoning Pentecostal revival. This began at an Azusa Street mission in Los Angeles in 1906, led by an African-American lay preacher, Charles Joseph Seymour. For Seymour, the

holiness second step, or sanctification, was intermediary, followed by a baptism of the Holy Spirit, testified to by tongue speaking and fulfilled through
several spiritual gifts, with healing the most visible.

The largest Pentecostal denomination today, and
one of the ten largest denominations in the United
States, the Church of God in Christ, has its headquarters in Memphis. Its founding and first half-century of
growth involved perhaps the most influential religious leader in Tennessee history—Charles Harrison
Mason—a leader all but ignored by historians, perhaps because he was black and represented a low-
status Pentecostal variety of Christianity. In the late
nineteenth century, two black holiness ministers—
Charles Price Jones and Mason—organized a small
holiness denomination in Mississippi. They soon
moved the headquarters of the Church of God in
Christ to Memphis. Mason was first persuaded of the
validity of the new Spirit baptism by a white missionary from Azusa, who visited Memphis. He then joined
two ministerial colleagues for a 1907 visit to the Azusa
Street Mission and capitulated completely to the doctrines taught in this bi-racial revival. He returned to
Memphis to persuade his denomination to convert to
Pentecostalism, but only partly succeeded. Jones was
open to tongue speaking, but never accepted its necessity as testimony of spirit baptism, and thus forced
Mason's followers out of the original church.

Mason's faction, which retained the denominational name and its episcopal form of organization
(borrowed from Methodism), was vitally important
in the first decade of an emergent Pentecostal movement. His church already had a state charter, which
enabled it to license ministers. At the time, creden-
tialed ministers alone gained valuable benefits, such
as free rail passes. Since none of the early Pentecostal
movements had a corporate charter, or could legally
license or ordain ministers, many white as well as
black Pentecostal evangelists came to Memphis to
gain a license. Later, almost all these opportunistic
ministers separated into white Pentecostal sects (most
in Mason's movement eventually joined the Assemblies of God), leaving Mason's denomination as the
strongest black Pentecostal church in the world, a
church that now claims over five million members in
the United States, with phenomenal recent growth.
Mason remained the presiding bishop of the Church
of God in Christ until his death in 1961. He seemed
to live forever, eventually becoming the often dictatorial patriarch of Pentecostalism. Mason kept his
headquarters in Memphis, at what is now the Mason
Temple. Here the church maintained its boards, publishing house, and periodicals. Numbers are unreli-
able, but the Church of God in Christ is the most
rapidly growing denomination and now the second
largest black church in Tennessee (behind only the
National Baptist Convention, U.S.A., Inc.).

The Pentecostal movement appealed to both black
and white southerners and was especially strong
among small farmers and textile workers. In 1908 the
leading Pentecostal leader in the South, Gaston B.
Cashwell, who had converted to Pentecostalism with
Mason at Azusa, visited and preached in Cleveland,
Tennessee, at the home church of a dynamic, at times
authoritarian, holiness minister, Ambrose J. Tomlinson. In 1903 Tomlinson had become a minister in a
sect that began as the Christian Union in the mountains of Tennessee and North Carolina in 1886. The
Christian Union changed its name to Holiness
Church in 1902. As early as 1896, some members of
this very emotional denomination spoke in tongues,
but as yet no one interpreted this as evidence of spiritual baptism. Cashwell converted Tomlinson to
Spirit baptism and to the necessity of evidential
tongues, and in turn Tomlinson was able to win most
of the small, but growing denomination to a three-
step form of Pentecostalism. Although now predominantly white, this denomination, which took the
name Church of God, with doctrines close to those of
Mason's Church of God in Christ and with a similar
episcopal organization, accepted black members and,
for a brief time, had integrated congregations.

The charismatic but authoritarian style of Tomlinson, plus some financial indiscretions, led to later
schisms. In 1923 a majority of Church of God congregations overthrew the leadership of Tomlinson and
after a period of litigation, began listing itself as the
Church of God. Today it is the second largest predominantly white Pentecostal denomination in
American (second to the Assemblies of God), with a
membership of over 500,000 in the United States and
an even larger foreign membership. It has its world
headquarters, boards, publications, university (Lee),
and seminary in Cleveland, Tennessee. The minority
in this split remained loyal to Tomlinson until his
death in 1943, and usually used the title of Tomlinson
Church of God. At Tomlinson's death, it split once
again, with one splinter taking the name of Church
of God of Prophecy. This small denomination has its
headquarters in Cleveland, plus a small publishing
house and Tomlinson College (which operated until
the mid-1990s), and is today probably the most successful in bi-racial cooperation of any American
denomination and has led the way in the ordination
of women.

Even this brief survey demonstrates the role of
Tennessee in American Protestantism. At least ten
denominations have a special tie to the state, and by
most calculations publishers in Tennessee lead the
nation in church literature of all types. In a comparative perspective, Tennessee remains among the three
or four states with both the highest percentage of
church members, and the highest percentage of
Protestant membership. It thus deserves the label,

both celebratory and at time pejorative, as the buckle of the Bible Belt. What so clearly distinguishes it from northern states is the low percentage of Roman Catholics (less than five percent), and the continued weakness of the more formal and confessional Protestant denominations; the Episcopal Church has just over two percent, the two major Lutheran confessions less than one percent. The Baptist dominance increases with each decade (over 50 percent), but the United Methodist Church and the Churches of Christ are still comparatively stronger in Tennessee than states to the south and southwest. As in much of the South, the older evangelical themes have remained more dominant than in much of the North, which again helps explain the continued growth of the SBC and the newer Pentecostal denominations.

Paul K. Conkin, Vanderbilt University

RESORTS, HISTORIC. Early tourist resorts in Tennessee were almost invariably close to mineral springs in mountainous East Tennessee. Reflecting a widespread belief in the efficacy of the ancient practice of hydrotherapy, or the "water cure," visitors endured arduous journeys to highland spas to drink and bathe in "health restoring" springs. While some invalids visited mineral springs in East Tennessee as early as the 1790s, resort development formally began after 1830.

Tennessee's earliest spa, Montvale Springs, was located on the western slopes of the Great Smoky Mountains in Blount County. Although one legend holds that Sam Houston discovered the springs in the early 1800s, Native Americans were likely the first visitors to partake of the mysterious subterranean waters. In 1832 Daniel Foute built a rustic log hotel at Montvale Springs to cater to southern health seekers. Advertised in 1841 as a "fountain of youth and health," visitors also came for hunting, social life, and scenery. In 1853 Asa Watson, a wealthy Mississippi Delta planter, bought the property and built the famed Seven Gables Hotel, a 200-foot-long, three-story frame structure with 125 rooms. Touted as the "Saratoga of the South," the hotel attracted a clientele of southern planters and urban elites, who sought to escape the malarial lowlands during summer. Among the famous visitors were William G. Brownlow and Sidney Lanier.

While Montvale Springs evolved into a luxurious spa, other historic Tennessee resorts originated as exclusive cottage colonies. The most famous antebellum cottage resort was Beersheba Springs in present-day Grundy County. According to legend, Mrs. Beersheba Cain discovered the spring in 1833, while on a horseback journey with her husband. After the state authorized the construction of a first class road to the mountain in 1836, Beersheba Springs became much more accessible. Wealthy families from Tennessee and Louisiana erected cottages and made annual pilgrimages to the springs. In 1854 Colonel John Armfield, a planter and slavetrader, purchased the springs, where his slaves constructed a lavish hotel and summer home. In the late 1850s the luxurious accommodations at Beersheba Springs attracted such wealthy patrons as Leonidas K. Polk and William Murfree, whose daughter, Mary Noailles Murfree, later wrote influential local color stories about mountain life that reflected her interactions with local residents at the resort.

The Civil War completely disrupted life at Tennessee's spas. During the war, some families sought refuge in their mountain retreats, but they were often harassed by pro-Union mountaineers. After Union forces swept through Beersheba Springs in July 1863, local mountain residents plundered the cottages and hotel. At Montvale Springs, Unionist sentiment in Blount county forced the Laniers, the pro-Confederate owners of the resort, to close the hotel in 1863 and flee to Georgia, never to return.

At the end of the war, Tennessee resorts faced very bleak circumstances. Most former patrons of the state's spas were either dead or financially ruined. With few patrons and a general lack of capital or credit in the South, highland resorts, like Montvale Springs and Beersheba Springs, fell into the hands of northern owners. Northern investors also financed the development of new resorts in late nineteenth century Tennessee, including Allegheny Springs, Henderson Springs, and Cloudland Hotel, a large three-story hotel built in 1885 atop Roan Mountain by midwestern industrialist John T. Wilder.

Nicholson Springs, a spa on the banks of the Barren Fork River near McMinnville, represented a notable exception to the trend of northern capital investment in Tennessee resort development. In 1881 Dr. J.W. Ransom of Murfreesboro bought the property from the Crisp family and built Crisp Springs Hotel as a summer sanitarium that attracted a middle class clientele. Ransom served as owner and physician in residence until he sold the hotel to Mrs. Electa Nicholson of Nashville, who changed the name of the resort to Nicholson Springs. Nicholson and her heirs owned the hotel until it closed just before World War I.

With the rise of modern automobile tourism in the twentieth century, Tennessee's historic resorts struggled to adapt and generally fell into decline. Montvale Springs and Nicholson Springs were abandoned and destroyed by fire in the 1930s, but Beersheba Springs survives as a quaint retreat. Red Boiling Springs in Macon County thrives, with three operating historic hotels within a National Register-listed historic district. Forgotten by modern society, these resorts provided the foundation for Tennessee's tourist industry.

C. Brenden Martin, Museum of the New South

SUGGESTED READINGS: Margaret Brown Coppinger, *Beersheba Springs, 1833–1983: A History and a Celebration* (1983); Marie Summers, "Nicholson Springs Resort Hotel: A Nineteenth Century Spa," *Tennessee Historical Quarterly* 45(1986): 244–255; Charles B. Thorne, "The Watering Spas of Middle Tennessee," *Tennessee Historical Quarterly* 29(1970–71): 321–359; Jennifer Bauer Wilson, *Roan Mountain: Passage of Time* (1991)

SEE: BEERSHEBA SPRINGS; BLOUNT COUNTY; MACON COUNTY; MURFREE, MARY N.; WARREN COUNTY

RHEA COUNTY was formed by the General Assembly on December 3, 1807, from a portion of Roane County. The new county was situated in a valley between the Tennessee River and the Cumberland Plateau. Though enlarged in 1817, parts of the county were lost in the formation of Hamilton County in 1817 and Meigs County in 1836.

Settlers began moving into this valley bottomland once Cherokees gave up claim to it in 1805. Thomas Moore, Joseph Brooks, and John Henry were the original commissioners appointed to select a suitable place for holding court. They decided upon the home of William Henry at Big Spring (north of present-day Dayton); the house served as the county courthouse until October 1812.

In 1809 and in 1811 the General Assembly appointed a commission to establish the town of Washington as a county seat. After investigating several sites, Washington (now known as Old Washington) was established in 1812 near the head of Spring Creek on land donated by Judge David Campbell and Richard Green Waterhouse. Lots in the new town were surveyed and sold on May 21 and 22, 1812. Contracts to construct the public buildings were awarded to James C. Mitchell (courthouse), John Moore (jail), and Adam W. Caldwell (stocks and pillory). By 1825 a new jail became a necessity, but it was not completed until 1836. A new brick courthouse, designed by craftsman Thomas Crutchfield, was completed in December 1832.

Washington, the center of political life in Rhea County, was also a thriving marketplace. The town contained ten stores, three taverns or hotels, a branch of the State Bank, a newspaper (*The Valley Freeman*), several blacksmiths and cabinet maker's shops, a turner (lathe operator), several saddlery and harness shops, a tannery, and three large cotton gins.

During these decades the population of the county began to increase, doubling with each ten-year period—2,504 in 1810, 4,215 in 1820, and 8,186 in 1830. In 1836 the county's population declined due to the formation of Meigs County and the founding of Chattanooga a few years later. By 1840 the population had dropped to 3,985, and by 1860 the county had gained only about 1,000 additional residents.

At the beginning of the Civil War, Rhea County had a population of 4,377 whites and 615 slaves. Although 435 men were between the ages of 18 and 45 (military age), over 700 men served in the Confederate Army and about 100 left the state to join the Union Army. Although no large-scale battles took place in Rhea County, the area was constantly under pressure and minor skirmishes were common. Throughout the war troops from both armies crossed the county and the courthouse in Washington was used as a headquarters by various officers in 1863.

During the mid-1880s the Cincinnati Southern Railway was constructed along the west side of the Tennessee Valley, completely bypassing the county seat of Washington. This lack of a railroad connection led to the decline of Washington until today it is only a small country village.

As Washington dwindled in size the town of Dayton, known until 1877–1878 as Smith's Cross Roads, rapidly emerged as a major manufacturing center. In 1883–1884 English capitalists, recognizing the wealth of coal, iron, and limestone in Rhea County, organized the Dayton Iron and Coal Company and a town soon began to grow. On March 14, 1885, the residents voted to incorporate the town by a vote of 120 to 13. The first mayor was Thomas N.L. Cunnyngham, and the first recorder was William B. Benson. By 1887 two furnaces were in operation, each turning out approximately 100 tons of pig iron daily. This company offered employment for a large number of citizens and, along with the railroad, encouraged the growth of Dayton through the turn of the century. In 1889 Rhea Countians voted to move the county seat from Washington to Dayton. The new jail was completed in 1890 and the new brick courthouse, designed by W. Chamberlin & Co. of Knoxville, in 1892.

Sulphur Springs (name changed to Rhea Springs in 1878), situated on the bank of Piney River, was settled early in the county's existence. This resort area possessed "healing" waters and a large hotel. The railroad bypassed the town, dwindling its size. The construction of Watts Bar Dam was the final blow as Rhea Springs was inundated in 1941.

After the demise of Rhea Springs, Spring City, on the Cincinnati Southern Railroad line, emerged as the important town in the northern portion of the county. Unlike most railroad towns, Spring City continued to grow after the 1930s, due mostly to the impact of Watts Bar Dam and, later, the nuclear steam plant.

Other railroad towns were Evensville, Graysville, Roddy (Prestonville), and Pinnine (Miller's Station, Sheffield). Settlements away from the railroad included Grandview, Paine Springs, Morgan Springs, Ogdon, Morgantown, Salem, and Carp.

In 1925 Rhea County became internationally famous when the Scopes Trial was held in Dayton.

William Jennings Bryan served as prosecutor while Clarence S. Darrow argued for the defense. Dayton teacher John Thomas Scopes was charged with teaching evolution in violation of the Butler Act. The population of Dayton swelled from about 1,800 inhabitants to about 5,000 at the height of the trial. After eight days, Scopes was found guilty and fined $100. The 1892 courthouse where the trial took place is still in use and is a National Historic Landmark. Only five days after the end of the trial, Bryan died. William Jennings Bryan College, founded in his honor, was first opened in 1930 and still operates today as Bryan College.

As of 1996 there were an estimated 27,400 residents of Rhea County. TVA's Watts Bar facility continues to be a major employer as are La-Z Boy Recliners, Robison Manufacturing, and Kayser-Roth Corporation.

Bettye J. Broyles, Chattanooga

SEE: BRYAN COLLEGE; DURICK, JOSEPH A.; POCKET WILDERNESS AREAS; RAILROADS; SCOPES TRIAL; TENNESSEE VALLEY AUTHORITY

RHEA, JOHN (1753–1831), pioneer, statesman, and early advocate of higher education, was born in northwest Ireland in 1753. He was the son of Joseph Rhea, a Scottish Presbyterian minister transplanted to Ireland, and Elizabeth McIllwaine, also Scots-Irish. As a child, he immigrated with his parents to Pennsylvania and later into western North Carolina, near what is now Blountville, Tennessee.

A soldier in the Revolutionary War, Rhea completed a degree in classical studies and law from Princeton University in 1780. Representing Sullivan County in the North Carolina House of Commons, he voted for the ratification of the U.S. Constitution in 1789. As Tennessee evolved from a territory into a state, Rhea sat on the constitutional committee of 1796. Representing Sullivan County during the first three sessions of the Tennessee General Assembly, he chaired the committee that drafted the guiding rules for the legislature. In 1802 Rhea entered the national political scene, and, with the exception of 1815–1816, was a member of the House of Representatives until 1823.

In his political stances, Rhea was hostile to Great Britain and antagonistic to the renewal of the national bank charter. He believed the removal of native tribes was sound policy; championed states' rights; upheld the legal rights of slaveholding states though he recognized slavery as a great moral evil; and promoted agrarian interests above commerce and industry. As a lifelong proponent of higher education, he served as trustee or incorporator of three of the earliest institutions west of the Alleghenies: Washington College, Greeneville College (now Tusculum College), and Blount College, the parent institution of the University of Tennessee.

John Rhea died in 1831 and is buried in Blountville. Rhea County and Rheatown (Greene County) carry his name.

Caneta Skelley Hankins, Middle Tennessee State University

SUGGESTED READING: Marguerite B. Hamer, "John Rhea of Tennessee," East Tennessee Historical Society *Publications* 4(1932): 35–44

SEE: SULLIVAN COUNTY; TUSCULUM COLLEGE

RHEA, MATTHEW (1795–1870), cartographer, geologist, and educator, was born near Blountville, Tennessee, in 1795. He attended Washington College and earned his living by surveying, teaching, and farming. In 1820 he moved to Maury County, where surveying and cartography became his major interests. Rhea made three significant contributions to the intellectual life of Tennessee. In 1832 he published his major work, a map of Tennessee that incorporated extensive personal observations. It clarified the geography of Tennessee and stimulated economic development. Published comments on Rhea's map assume he worked alone, but unpublished sources indicate he had help from a University of Nashville professor, Gerard Troost. On March 5, 1831, Troost wrote Rhea an apology for an error he made in calculating the elevation of Nashville for Rhea's map. How much computational work Troost did is not clear, but he had some influence on the map.

Rhea's second contribution was to geology. Although he never published an independent report on the subject, Rhea accumulated original geologic data which he contributed to at least one publication by Alexander Buchanan. Finally, Rhea was one of the first people to describe an archaeological site that involved the type of aboriginal interment that is now called a stone box burial.

In 1833 Rhea changed careers and relocated to Somerville in Fayette County. While continuing to farm, he became the only teacher, and the president, of a female academy. The school existed on paper in 1831 as the Somerville Female Academy, but first accepted pupils in 1833. A companion male school opened in 1831. By 1850 a legislative charter made the female school a college and authorized the awarding of degrees. Another reorganization in 1854 created the Somerville Model School for Young Ladies, with degree-granting privileges. Both this school and its companion, the Model School for Young Gentlemen, were boarding facilities.

By 1857 the female school had a faculty of 15. The student body of 264 included several graduate students. Young women came from California, Texas, and seven other states. Rhea no longer served as president, but was affiliated with the school through 1860. Success of the Somerville schools, both male and female, was partly rooted in Rhea's years of service. In 1870 he died at his home, near Somerville. Rhea was a creative school administrator, an innovative cartographer, and a contributor to state-level knowledge of both archaeology and geology.

James X. Corgan, Austin Peay State University

SUGGESTED READINGS: James X. Corgan, "Toward a History of Higher Education in Antebellum West Tennessee," West Tennessee Historical Society *Publications* 39(1986): 51–81; Robert M. McBride and Owen Meredith, eds., *Eastin Morris' Tennessee Gazetteer 1834 and Matthew Rhea's Map of the State of Tennessee 1832* (1971)

SEE: FAYETTE COUNTY; GEOLOGY; TROOST, GERARD

RHODES COLLEGE in Memphis has been aptly characterized as "the garden in the city," a reference to the college's lush, richly-wooded, and landscaped campus in the heart of the state's largest city. *Princeton Review's* 1995 college guide cited Rhodes as "the most beautiful campus in America." In recent years, the national media has offered numerous encomiums to Rhodes's growing reputation for academic excellence. Two figures loom especially large in the history of the college: Charles E. Diehl, president from 1917 to 1949, and James H. Daughdrill, Jr., president since 1973.

Diehl, a Johns Hopkins and Princeton-trained Presbyterian minister, became president of the college when it was still Southwestern Presbyterian University in Clarksville. The Grand Masonic Lodge of Tennessee founded the college in 1848, and it subsequently existed under a variety of names, including Masonic College and Stewart College. In 1855 the college affiliated with the Presbyterian Church, an affiliation that continues to this day. Originally all male, the school became coeducational in 1916. Despite a distinguished faculty that included theologian Joseph R. Wilson, the father of Woodrow Wilson, the college fell on hard times in Clarksville.

Diehl brought the college to its new 100-acre campus in Memphis in 1925, renaming it Southwestern at Memphis, a name tied to the college's location in the southwest region of the Southern Presbyterian Church. During his tenure as president, Diehl instituted the three practices that distinguish the college in national educational circles.

His first innovation was the consistent use of the "Collegiate Gothic" style of architecture that characterizes all the college's buildings. In 1989 University of Louisville architect William Morgan chronicled the college's successful use of the style in his book, *Collegiate Gothic: The Architecture of Rhodes College.* The second innovation was an honor system that places responsibility for the integrity of students' academic and personal conduct in the students themselves. The honor system has received considerable attention in the *Washington Post,* National Public Radio, and other

Palmer Hall at Rhodes College.

TENNESSEE HISTORICAL SOCIETY COLLECTION, TSLA

national publications for the faithfulness with which it is upheld by Rhodes students. Diehl's third innovation was a twelve-credit course called "The Search for Values in the Light of Western History and Religion," which leads students through the history, philosophy, religion, politics, and literature of the West in a discussion-intensive, primary text-centered format. The Search course spawned progeny at numerous other southern institutions, including Davidson College, the University of the South, Millsaps College, Eckerd College, and Louisiana State University. Michael Nelson and his colleagues described the success of the program in *Celebrating the Humanities: A Half-Century of the Search Course at Rhodes College* (1996).

James Daughdrill, the other leading figure in the history of Rhodes College, left a career in business and the Presbyterian ministry to become president of Rhodes in 1973, at a time when the college was struggling financially. Despite a sometime uneasy relationship with the college's faculty, all three of Diehl's innovations have flourished and grown during Daughdrill's tenure. Rhodes students single out the honor system as the best aspect of the college, the Search course is being taught and studied with greater enthusiasm than at any time in its history, and even the newest, most technologically sophisticated buildings continue to be constructed in the Collegiate Gothic style.

At the same time, Rhodes progresses toward the achievement of its recently announced goal of becoming "one of the finest colleges of liberal arts and sciences in the world." From 1973 to 1998, the size and quality of the Rhodes student body grew significantly, from 980 students with an average SAT score of 1105 to 1,450 students with an average score of 1290. With the exception of a small masters program in accounting, every Rhodes student is an undergraduate. The college reported a growth in the endowment from $6 million to over $200 million and the maintenance of a balanced budget throughout Daughdrill's tenure.

Daughdrill also initiated the change in the college's name from Southwestern at Memphis to Rhodes College. Confusion caused by the existence of many other colleges with "southwestern" in their names and the location of the college in an area no longer considered the southwest provided the impetus for the name change. The name Rhodes honors Peyton Nalle Rhodes, a longtime professor at the college and Diehl's immediate successor as president.

Michael Nelson, Rhodes College

SEE: CLARKSVILLE; EDUCATION, HIGHER; MEMPHIS

RHODES, THEODORE "TED" (1913–1969), recognized as the first African-American professional golfer, grew up in Nashville. Immediately after becoming the first person of color to win the prestigious Masters Tournament in 1997, Tiger Woods told a national television audience: "I am the first minority to win here, but I wasn't the first to play. That was Lee Elder, and my hat's off to him and Charlie Sifford and Ted Rhodes, who made this possible for me." Rhodes was more than a pioneer in the game, he also was a teacher and an inspiration to many. "Whatever has happened to me in bigtime golf, and whatever success I attain eventually, I owe to Ted Rhodes," remarked Lee Elder a day after Rhodes's death on July 4, 1969. "He took me under his wing when I was 16-years-old and completely re-built my golf game and my life. His encouragement and assistance enabled me to develop a game strong enough to compete on the PGA [Professional Golf Association] tour."

Ted Rhodes rose from humble beginnings. As a teenager, he worked as a caddy at Nashville's Belle Meade Country Club, a club where African-Americans like Rhodes were not allowed to play golf, or even belong as a member.

But Rhodes, nicknamed "Rags" because of his neat and flashy dress style, picked up the game caddying. He would slip in and play whenever he got a chance to on the golf course. He also practiced the game as a teenager with other caddies at the old Sunset Park, a baseball field in Nolensville in Williamson County.

After serving in the U.S. Navy during World War II, Rhodes was discharged in Chicago. There, he became friends with entertainer Billy Eckstine and boxing champions Sugar Ray Robinson and Joe Louis. Louis would eventually sponsor Rhodes in various tournaments, such as the Canadian Open and the Los Angeles Open. Rhodes, meanwhile, taught Louis the game of golf and served as his valet. He also traveled with Charlie Sifford, who followed Rhodes as one of the first African-American members of the PGA.

In his adulthood, Rhodes weighed about 200 pounds and had broad shoulders. He was a good dancer and that helped with rhythm and good balance for his golf game. John Bibb, retired sports editor of *The Tennessean,* recalls: "he was a helluva player. The great golfer Ben Hogan knew him. In those days, if he had been given a fair shot at everything he would have been a contender at the various golfing championships around the United States." Bibb observes: "all of the good playing he did was done out of town because he couldn't play the municipal courses in Nashville because he was black."

After traveling around the nation most of his adult life, Rhodes moved back to Nashville in the late 1960s. He died while living at the El Dorado Motel in Nashville on July 4, 1969. On March 8, 1970, 32 people attended a Nashville meeting to form the Ted Rhodes National Memorial Foundation. The foundation, a charitable non-profit organization, was organized to promote the game of golf and to encourage and assist qualified young men and women who exemplify a talent for the game of golf. "Ted Rhodes was a gentleman, full of clean humor, and a flawless striker of the ball," said William Hailey, former director of the Ted Rhodes Golf Tournament, which was established after Rhodes's death. "He mastered clubs from the 1 iron to sandwedge, the driver through 4 wood. A pupil of the late Ray and Lloyd Mangrum, he was truly great."

Today, in Nashville near the intersection of Ed Temple Boulevard and Clarksville Highway, there is an 18-hole municipal golf course named in honor of Ted Rhodes. In his later years of life, Rhodes played on a nine-hole course at the site.

Dwight Lewis, The (Nashville) Tennessean

RICE, HENRY GRANTLAND (1880–1954), the most widely-read and respected American sports writer of the first half of the twentieth century, was born in Murfreesboro and named for his maternal grandfather, Henry Grantland. He was later called "Grant" and "Granny" by personal friends. A historical marker at the southeast corner of Spring and College Streets, one block from the Public Square, notes that this son of Rutherford County became internationally famous "for his influence on sportsmanship and fair play."

Rice moved to Nashville with his family and soon acquired a life-long love of the outdoors and sports. He entered Vanderbilt University in the fall of 1897, after prepping at Wallace School. A good athlete, the slender (6'2", 135 pounds) Rice played end on the college football squad and shortstop on the baseball team. Baseball was his best sport, and in recognition of his outstanding abilities, he was named varsity captain during his senior year. A scholar as well as an athlete, Rice's favorite courses were English literature, Latin, and Greek. His grades earned him membership in Phi Beta Kappa.

Rice briefly aspired to a professional baseball career, which both his father, Bolling Rice, and grandfather opposed. In the mid-summer of 1901, Rice accepted a position at the *Nashville Daily News,* writing sports and covering the State Capitol and the Davidson County Court House.

In 1902 Rice moved to the *Atlanta Journal* as sports editor. There he became an associate of Don Marquis, Frank Stanton, and Joel Chandler Harris. He also met his future wife, Kate Hollis of Americus, Georgia. They married in 1906, and were the parents of one daughter, Florence.

Rice left Atlanta in 1907 to join the *Nashville Tennessean,* a fledgling newspaper impressively launched by Luke Lea. Owner-publisher Lea paid Rice the then princely salary of $70 a week to write and edit sports, and contribute a column to the editorial page, called "Tennessee 'Uns," a daily potpourri that usually contained a verse or two.

While covering Nashville's Southern Association baseball team, Rice is credited with changing the name of the team's playing field from Sulphur Springs Bottom to Sulphur Dell. Some years later, he explained: "It was hard to find any word to rhyme with 'bottom.'"

Rice typically worked 12- to 14-hour days producing copy for the *Tennessean* sport pages; when he filled in as theater critic, the work days were even longer. Undoubtedly this schedule, which left little time for his family, was a factor in Rice's decision, late in 1910, to take a substantial pay cut and accept a job with the New York *Evening Mail.* Perhaps another factor in the move was the *Evening Mail's* reputation for building circulation by accentuating the paper's columnists. Veteran columnists Franklin P. Adams and Rube Goldberg hailed the addition of Rice to the staff.

Rice's columns on the Giant's manager John McGraw, pitching ace Christy Mathewson, and teenage golf sensation Bobby Jones quickly created a loyal New York following. In January 1914 the *New York Tribune* used a full-page ad to announce the addition of the talented Grantland Rice to the sports staff.

When the United States entered World War I, the 38-year-old Rice enlisted as an army private. He spent 14 months in military service, mostly in France and Germany. When he was mustered out in the spring of 1919, Rice returned to New York to resume his journalistic career.

Besides his daily column, which was syndicated to 80–100 newspapers, Rice edited *American Golfer* magazine and contributed to *Collier's* and *Look.* He helped pick college football's All-America teams and narrated the weekly *Sportlight* films. Rice's talent earned him the friendship and respect of well-known members of his craft, including Ring Lardner, Heywood Broun, Damon Runyon, W.O. McGeehan, and Rex Beach; he authored several books of poems.

Sports and poetry seemed to blend perfectly for Rice, observing that "Rhythm, the main factor in both, is the main factor in life itself." His most enduring and oft-quoted stanza was: "For when the one Great Scorer comes to write against your name, He marks —not that you won or lost—but how you played the game." Grantland Rice died in 1954.
Fred Russell, Nashville

SEE: BASEBALL, MINOR LEAGUE; LEA, LUKE; MURFREESBORO; NASHVILLE TENNESSEAN; PUBLISHING

RICHARDSON, JAMES DANIEL (1843–1914), prominent turn-of-the-century Democratic leader, U.S. Congressman, and nationally recognized historian and editor, was born in Rutherford County, Tennessee, on March 10, 1843. His grandparents, James and Mary Watkins Richardson, moved to Jefferson, Tennessee, in 1814, and his father, John Watkins Richardson, was a Murfreesboro physician who served in both the Tennessee Senate and House as well as being the president of the Tennessee State Medical Society. James Daniel Richardson's mother, Augusta Mary Starnes, was from a politically prominent family of Georgia.

Richardson attended schools in Murfreesboro and Franklin Academy before enlisting as a private in the 45th Tennessee Infantry (C.S.A.) during the Civil War. While serving as Adjutant-General, Richardson rose to the rank of major and was wounded in the Battle of Resaca during the Atlanta Campaign of 1864. This wound crippled his hand for life.

In 1865 Richardson married Alabama R. Pippen, daughter of a prominent Eutaw, Alabama, planter and they had five children. After the war Richardson studied law with Judge Thomas Frazier, being admitted to the bar in 1866. He and General Joseph Palmer of Murfreesboro practiced together for 12 years. At Palmer's death, he opened a partnership with his brother, John E. Richardson.

During these years, Richardson became a leader of the state Democratic party, serving as Speaker of House in 1871, and in the State Senate for two years. In 1884 Richardson entered national politics when he was elected as the Fifth District Congressman from Tennessee to the Forty-ninth Congress. Richardson was elected to the next five succeeding congresses (1855–1905), becoming the Democratic minority whip for an interim in the Fifty-third Congress in 1894. After being a delegate in 1876, 1896, and 1900, Richardson was named the Chairman of the National Democratic Convention in Kansas City. He was Chairman of the National Democratic Congressional Committee in 1900. While serving in Congress, Richardson introduced a bill for appropriation of $125,000 to purchase land for a military park and national cemetery at the site of Stones River Battlefield.

In 1894 Congress passed a resolution requesting Richardson, a scholarly gentleman, to begin the compilation and editing of *The Messages and Papers of the Presidents* and, later, *The Messages and Papers of the Confederacy*, both valuable reference sources. Other published works by Richardson are "Tennessee Templars" and "The Ancient and Accepted Scottish Rite."

In October 1867, while still in Alabama, Richardson was inducted into the Scottish Rite Masons. In the 1870s he served as Grand Master of the Masons of Tennessee. Richardson accepted the position of Sovereign Grand Commander of Scottish Rite Masonry in 1901 and remained in that position until 1914. Richardson purchased land for building a new temple in Washington, D.C., and approved plans for its proposed facade and its interior. Unfortunately, he died before its completion, but the temple remains as a memorial to Richardson's vision of the future.

When Richardson died on July 25, 1914, a Knight Templar Kodosh funeral ceremony was held at midnight at the Central Christian Church in Murfreesboro. The next afternoon, a traditional service, attended by over 1,000 people, was held at the Central Christian Church. Richardson was interred in Murfreesboro's Evergreen Cemetery in the family plot.

Lucy Roberts, Murfreesboro

SEE: MURFREESBORO

RIDGE, MAJOR (ca. 1770–1839), whose Cherokee name meant "walking-the-mountain-tops," is best known as one of the men who signed the Treaty of New Echota in 1835, authorizing the removal of the Cherokee Indians. Once in Oklahoma, his political enemies assassinated him as a traitor who betrayed his people to the U.S. government.

Ridge, however, is not easily stereotyped. On one hand, he was a full-blooded Cherokee, careful of his people's sovereignty. In 1805 he executed chief Doublehead for accepting bribes to cede Cherokee territory. Nonetheless, Ridge was also highly acculturated. He was a wealthy slave holder who lived in a frame house, married an Anglo woman, and educated his children in missionary schools. He served the Chero-

kee nation as a member of the Lighthorse Guard (the Cherokee police force), treaty commissioner, ambassador to the Creek Indians, and member, speaker, and co-chief of the National Council.

Ridge advocated cooperation with the U.S. government. He urged the Cherokees not to join Tecumseh's resistance movement against the United States and he fought with Andrew Jackson against the Creeks and Seminoles. Eventually, Ridge came to view resistance to removal as futile and relocation as in the Cherokees' best interests. Not surprisingly, the removal treaty also protected Ridge's interests, shielding his land from confiscation during the removal process and providing him a generous land grant in the West. Whether he acted from self-interest or nationalism Ridge was a major figure in Cherokee politics and his death deprived the Cherokee of an experienced leader.

Katherine M.B. Osburn and Jennifer Kimbro, Tennessee Technological University

SEE: CHUQUALATAQUE; CREEK WAR OF 1813 & 1814; TRAIL OF TEARS; TREATIES

RILEY, BOB (b. 1855) one of the earliest and most successful raft pilots in the Upper Cumberland logging industry of the late 1800s, became a popular tall-tale figure in Tennessee folklore. Born in 1855 in the Clay County community of Fox Springs, Riley was one of the first raft pilots to take large drifts of logs from Celina to Nashville. Riley became well known for his knowledge of the river and for his cunning and courage.

Once arriving in Nashville, rafters gathered in large groups to swap stories and jokes, and characters such as Riley quickly grew to fictional proportions. In folklore, Riley became "Uncle Bob" Riley, a character who combined traits of Huck Finn and Brer Rabbit. He came to be a sympathetic trickster figure who used the anonymity of the traveler to get what he wanted and the freedom of the river to escape the consequences of his actions.

In one story, Riley stole a calf and put it on his raft. By the time the owner arrived to retrieve it, Riley had put the calf in boots and a raincoat and told the owner the calf was actually his brother who had just died of smallpox. Out of either respect for the dead or fear of the disease, the owner left the raft without looking at his calf. Uncle Bob plays the lovable rogue who used his wits to get away with petty theft.

In other stories, he was a prankster who created havoc simply for the fun of it. For example, one story portrayed him on a raft that approached a river baptism. As a Tennessee storyteller, Herman Burris, told the story in 1983, Uncle Bob suddenly appeared in the middle of the crowd "strip, stark, stark naked, not a rag on, a'bawling like a bull." According to such stories, people along the Cumberland River watched and worried that Uncle Bob Riley might be floating on a raft to do something disruptive. As with many historical figures who become folk heroes, such stories often combined real events from Riley's life with stories associated with other folk characters.

Ted Ownby, University of Mississippi

SUGGESTED READINGS: William Lynwood Montell, *Don't Go Up Kettle Creek: Verbal Legacy of the Upper Cumberland* (1983); Elizabeth Peterson and Tom Rankin, *Free Hill: A Sound Portrait of a Rural Afro-American Community, Traditional Song, Narrative, and Sacred Speech from Tennessee* (audio recording and typescript, 1985)

SEE: CLAY COUNTY; CUMBERLAND RIVER

ROAN MOUNTAIN STATE RESORT PARK, located near the Tennessee-North Carolina border in Carter County, is a 2,006-acre park that preserves Roan Mountain, a 6,285-foot peak reknowned for its annual blooming of wildflowers, especially its lush 600-acre carpet of crimson catawba rhododendrons. "Along its highest ridges, open meadows called grass balds stretch for as far as the eye can see," observes naturalist Jennifer Wilson. "The views from the highlands stretch for miles into the Tennessee and North Carolina mountains, creating indescribable scenes and moods."[1] The Cherokee National Forest surrounds the park while the Appalachian Trail crosses adjacent to the park. With cabins, a restaurant, a group lodge, a swimming pool, trails, picnic areas, and campsites, the park also features three cross-country skiing trails for winter recreation. The Daniel Miller homestead from the late nineteenth century is preserved within the park's boundaries.

Carroll Van West, Middle Tennessee State University

CITATION:

(1) Jennifer Wilson, "Longer than Springtime: Roan Mountain Wildflowers," *Tennessee Conservationist* (May/June 1990): 9.

SEE: APPALACHIAN TRAIL; CARTER COUNTY; CHEROKEE NATIONAL FOREST

ROANE, ARCHIBALD (1760–1819), second Governor of Tennessee, was born in 1760 in Lancaster County, Pennsylvania. He became a lawyer and served with distinction in the Continental Army during the Revolution. Roane arrived in Tennessee in 1788, in the aftermath of the Franklin movement and prior to the creation of the Southwest Territory. He settled first in Jonesborough and established a law practice there before moving to Jefferson County.

Roane's professional skills soon attracted the attention of Territorial Governor William Blount, who appointed him Attorney General for the Washington District and confirmed his position as one of Blount's protégés. Roane enhanced his reputation when he became the tutor of Hugh Lawson White,

son of the founder of Knoxville and a future presidential candidate. In 1796 Roane was selected as a delegate from Jefferson County to the Tennessee constitutional convention.

Roane became one of the first three judges of the Superior Courts of Law and Equity. In 1801, when John Sevier retired after his constitutional three terms in office, Roane was the nearly unanimous choice to replace him as governor—his opponent received fewer than a dozen votes statewide.

During Roane's administration, Tennessee expanded to three congressional districts, but his term of office is generally remembered more for factional confrontation and controversy than for growth. The first controversy centered around the vacant position of major general of the state militia. An election among the field officers to fill the position resulted in a tie, and Roane, as governor, was required by law to break the deadlock. The two candidates, John Sevier and Andrew Jackson, were well-placed, ambitious, and unwilling to concede the highest military position in the state. Roane eventually gave the appointment to Jackson, a decision that surprised few, given the close friendship between the two men. Sevier believed his past military record made him the more qualified candidate. His feud with Jackson escalated sharply. More important for Roane, his support for Jackson prompted Sevier to seek reelection as governor in 1803.

In an attempt to assist Roane in his campaign against the popular Sevier, Jackson provided information which implicated the former governor in a series of land fraud schemes dating back to 1795. The evidence was embarrassing for Sevier, but inconclusive to voters; Sevier won the election easily.

Following his defeat, Roane returned to his law practice until 1811, when he was elected as Circuit Judge. In 1815 he was elected as Judge of the Superior Court of Errors and Appeals. He held that position until his death on January 18, 1819. Roane is buried at Campbell's Station in Knox County. Roane County is named in his honor.

Michael Toomey, Knoxville College

SEE: BLOUNT, WILLIAM; JACKSON, ANDREW; SEVIER, JOHN; TENNESSEE COURTS, PRIOR TO 1870; WHITE, HUGH L.

ROANE COUNTY is situated at the juncture of the Tennessee, Clinch, and Emory rivers, a location of vital importance to both white settlers and Native Americans in the early years of Tennessee state history. Settlers gained control of the area through three treaties with the Cherokee Indians: the Treaty of 1794, the Third Tellico Treaty of 1805, and the Hiwassee Purchase made through the Calhoun Treaty of 1819. In 1792 John Sevier established Fort Southwest Point at the convergence of the Tennessee and Clinch rivers to protect white settlers traveling west. Initially the fort was placed near a spring rather than at a higher

Coal miners at Rockwood, early 1900s.

point, since the defenders apparently valued access to water more than strategic advantage. In 1797, when the mission of the fort changed to one of offering protection to the Indians against the encroaching settlers, the fort was expanded and moved to a hill overlooking the two rivers. The boyhood dreams of Roane County Historian J.C. Parker were fulfilled posthumously in 1996 with the completion of the restoration of Fort Southwest Point and its dedication and opening to the public.

After several petitions to the state legislature, Roane County was established in 1801, and named in honor of the second governor of Tennessee, Archibald Roane. The town of Kingston, in the shadow of Fort Southwest Point, was chosen as the county seat. In 1807 Kingston became "Capital for a Day." The Tellico Treaty of 1805 stated that Kingston would become the state capital in return for thousands of acres of Indian land. It did, for a few hours on September 21, 1807. The terms of the treaty were thus fulfilled, the capital was returned to Knoxville, and the Indian land was forfeited. A monument commemorating this infamous event stands in the center of Kingston.

It was not until the Civil War, when Union Colonel John Wilder led troops through the area, that the commercial potential of local mineral deposits was recognized. Wilder, with other northern industrialists, organized the Roane Iron Company, and in 1868 established the town of Rockwood. It was a "Company Town of the New South," shipping pig iron first by steamboat and later by rail.

The town of Harriman brought diversified industry to Roane County late in the nineteenth century. Northern industrialists of the East Tennessee Land Company, impressed by the climate, location, transportation systems, and work ethic of southerners in the area, established the town of Harriman in 1890. The industrialists were strict prohibitionists, with strong religious backgrounds and high ideals, who believed that sober workers and a variety of industries would insure a successful town and reliable profits. In February 1890 the

Virginia G. and Euskey Library

company held a "Great Land Sale" on its property. Thousands of buyers from all across the United States offered astonishing prices for lots. Within ten hours, 573 lots had been sold for more that $600,000. Utopian dreams shaped this social experiment in town building. Every contract or deed contained a provision forbidding the use, making, storage, or selling of intoxicating beverages. As a result, Harriman soon gained the reputation as a "Utopia of Temperance."

Oliver Springs, a small town at the convergence of the Roane, Anderson, and Morgan County lines, enjoyed national prominence as a mineral springs resort that attracted people from across the eastern United States in the late nineteenth century. Richard Oliver, the first postmaster of the town and the man for whom the town was named, commercialized the springs. Oliver built a four-story hotel containing almost 200 rooms, topped by a 60-foot tower. The resort featured bridle paths to the top of Walden's Ridge, a billiard room, electric elevators, wine cellars, and a dance pavilion. The resort burned in 1905 and was not rebuilt.

Roane County has its share of famous residents. Return Jonathan Meigs served as Indian Agent at Fort Southwest Point. Sam Houston lived in Kingston briefly, where he clerked in a store before volunteering for military service in the War of 1812. A little known Civil War heroine was 16-year-old Mary Love, who carried a Union message to Knoxville through Confederate lines. Sam Rayburn, long-time Speaker of the U.S. House of Representatives, was born in Roane County in 1882 and lived there until 1887, when his family moved to Texas. Roane County also has its infamous residents. Cherokee chiefs Tullentusky (variously spelled) and Doublehead attacked local settlements for several years. The Harpe brothers swept through Roane County in the early 1800s, killing and pillaging.

Today, Roane County offers the tranquil beauty of Watts Bar Lake, the community atmosphere of small town living, and the convenience of proximity to the metropolitan areas of Knoxville and Chattanooga.
Jere Hall and Rachel Parker, Kingston

SEE: CAPITAL CITIES; CHAMBERLAIN, HIRAM S.;
CHUQUALATAQUE; FORT SOUTHWEST POINT; HARPE,
MICAJAH AND WILEY; HARRIMAN, WALTER C.; HOUSTON,
SAM; MEIGS, RETURN J.; NELSON, THOMAS A.R.; STRIKE,
HARRIMAN, OF 1933–34; TEMPERANCE; TENNESSEE VALLEY
AUTHORITY; WILDER, JOHN T.

ROBERTS, ALBERT H. (1868–1946), Governor, was instrumental in obtaining state ratification of the Nineteenth Amendment for woman suffrage. His highly unpopular tax reform, his use of state troops against labor, and his support for women's rights combined to make him one of the most unpopular

Democratic governors in the state's history. He lost a reelection bid in 1920 to Alfred Taylor, Republican brother of famed Democratic governor Robert Taylor.

Born July 4, 1868, in Overton County, Roberts graduated from Hiwassee College in 1889. He married Nora Dean Bowden, the daughter of his Latin teacher, and joined his in-laws in the operation of Alpine Institute, a Presbyterian private school in Overton County. Roberts studied law, was admitted to the bar in 1894, and opened a practice in Livingston. Roberts built a successful law practice, but remained interested in education; he served as superintendent of public instruction for Overton County for five years. In 1909 Roberts and Livingston civic leaders made a successful bid to the Disciples of Christ Christian Women's Board of Missions to establish a mission school, Livingston Academy, in Overton County.

From 1910 until 1918 Roberts served as Chancellor for the Fourth Judicial Division. As a circuit judge, he traveled through 15 Middle Tennessee counties twice annually, and became a well-known figure in the district. Roberts served on Benton McMillin's 1912 gubernatorial campaign committee and made a bid for the Democratic nomination for governor in 1914, losing to Tom C. Rye in the primary. Roberts made a second bid in 1918, overcame formidable primary opposition from Clarksville's Austin Peay, and swept past the Republican candidate in the general election. Roberts's progressive commitment to tax reform and better roads and schools faced an electorate already irritated by World War I restrictions and the Democratic handling of the war. Roberts compounded his problems by alienating almost every constituency in the Democratic party.

His problems began with tax reform. Roberts designed a plan to lower property taxes through standardized assessments and a sliding scale tax rate based on two-year projected revenue needs. Theoretically, as the amount of taxed property increased, the tax rate decreased. When owners of "intangible" property failed to present their assets for taxation, the state fell back on land taxes; the tax rate on farms increased approximately 260 percent in one year.

Roberts alienated both the right and left wing Democrats. Tennesseans joined postwar workers nationwide to strike for union recognition and better pay. Roberts reacted with legislation to create a state police force, appeals for citizens to organize "Law and Order Leagues," and the dispatch of troops to quell strikes in Nashville and Knoxville. He lost the support of the right wing of his party over woman suffrage. Following Congressional passage of the Nineteenth Amendment, state legislatures took up ratification in the summer of 1920. Bowing to pressure from President Woodrow Wilson, Roberts called the General Assembly into special session to take up ratification. When the General Assembly ratified the Nineteenth Amendment and gave women the right to vote, Roberts received national applause, but conservative Tennesseans were outraged.

In 1920 the Republicans nominated Alf Taylor, who campaigned with a fiddle and a quartet, promising farmers tax relief. Prominent Democrats pulled back their support of Roberts; labor organized against him; and he faced constant attacks for his support of woman suffrage. Taylor won the election with 229,000 to Roberts's 186,000 votes.

After his defeat Roberts and his son ran a successful law practice in Nashville. The former governor remained in politics. In 1930 he served on a committee that investigated Governor Henry Horton's involvement with Luke Lea and Rogers Caldwell. He died June 26, 1946, at his home in Donelson.

Jeanette Keith, Bloomsburg University of Pennsylvania
SUGGESTED READING: Gary W. Reichard, "The Defeat of Governor Roberts," *Tennessee Historical Quarterly* 30(1971): 94–109
SEE: CALDWELL, ROGERS; HORTON, HENRY; MCMILLIN, BENTON; OVERTON COUNTY; TAYLOR, ALFRED A.; WOMAN SUFFRAGE MOVEMENT

ROBERTSON, CHARLOTTE REEVES (1751–1843), was among the earliest settlers to live in Middle Tennessee. She followed her husband, James Robertson, in a journey from the Watauga settlement of East Tennessee to the wilderness of Middle Tennessee, helping to establish settlements in each of these areas. She survived Indian attacks as well as long separations from her husband, who was frequently called away on governmental business. Indians killed two of her sons and she nursed another son back to good health after he had been scalped by the Indians and left for dead at the Battle of the Bluffs.

Charlotte and James Robertson had moved to Watauga from North Carolina shortly after their marriage. At Watauga Charlotte Robertson and the other women who lived there worked shoulder to shoulder with men, planting crops, tending livestock, and defending themselves from the Indians. At Watauga, Charlotte Robertson's husband was a leader. Because of his knowledge of the Cherokee language, he devoted much of his life to negotiating with the Indians to try to provide a permanent peace. The Robertsons and other families moved further west to acquire land. When James Robertson, a surveyor, identified the spot of the Salt Lick on the Cumberland River, 40 families at Watauga decided to leave for Middle Tennessee.

While James Robertson led a group of men by land through the Cumberland Gap to the site later known as Fort Nashborough, Charlotte Robertson traveled with John Donelson and a group of women and children by flatboats via backcountry rivers.

Almost immediately, there were conflicts with Chickamaugas who resented the settlers moving into the region. Charlotte Robertson is remembered as the heroine of the Battle of the Bluffs, April 1781. When she realized that the Indians were about to attack, she left the safety of the fort to warn the men. Returning to the fort, she realized that the men would not be able to get inside the walls because the Indians had positioned themselves between the men and the fort. At this point, she unleashed the hounds. They chased the Indians and created so much confusion that the men were able to return to the safety of the fort. Consequently, Charlotte Robertson is credited with saving Fort Nashborough.

The city of Charlotte, Tennessee, and Charlotte Pike in Nashville are named for Charlotte Robertson, who lived in Middle Tennessee until her death in 1843 at the age of 92. She is buried in Nashville's City Cemetery.

Carole Stanford Bucy, Volunteer State Community College
SEE: DONELSON, JOHN; ROBERTSON, JAMES; NASHVILLE

ROBERTSON COUNTY. The first white settlement in Robertson County was established by Thomas Kilgore who came here in 1778 claiming land and building a station in 1779 near present-day Cross Plains. Prior to statehood this area was one of the counties in Mero District and called Tennessee County, located north of Nashville on the Kentucky border.

One of the first acts of the new state was to appropriate Tennessee County's name for its own use and to divide that county into Robertson and Montgomery counties. Robertson County took its name from General James Robertson, often called the "Father of Middle Tennessee." Robertson County, established by the General Assembly on April 9, 1796, covered 477 square miles and contained 304,640 acres.

The enabling act, which created the new county, appointed commissioners and instructed them to establish the county government system, "to lay off, and appoint a place, the most centrical and convenient in the county of Robertson, for the purpose of erecting a courthouse prison and stocks," which became the county seat of Springfield. By 1798 Thomas Johnson had surveyed and laid out Springfield and the lots sold for eight dollars each.

Residents began forming churches and schools almost as soon as they arrived in the area. Red River Baptist Church in Adams was constituted on July 25, 1791, and in 1798 Mt. Zion Methodist Church was organized. Both are active churches today. Tradition has it that Robert Black started the first school in the area on Sulphur Fork in 1789, and Thomas Mosby also taught a school in the area before 1796.

Over the first half of the nineteenth century, Robertson County grew from a sparsely settled frontier community of 4,228 to a society of over 16,000 people. Most of the early white settlers in the area were of English or Scots-Irish origin, although there were also contingents of people whose backgrounds lay in the German states and other western European countries. A few of the settlers brought slaves with them and a small contingent of free blacks lived in the county in the 1790s. The earliest reference to African Americans in the area was in 1789. However, the majority of the region's inhabitants used no slave labor.

Tobacco had been raised for personal use and for sale almost as soon as people settled in Middle Tennessee. By 1820 tobacco, a crop dependent largely on slave labor, became the most important commercial crop in the county and remained so to the present as Robertson County became known as the "Home of the World's Finest Dark Fired Tobacco" by the 1920s. Another major economic force in the county was the manufacture of fine whiskey which reached its peak in the 1880s and died with prohibition in 1909. The Springfield Woolen Mills was founded in 1903 as the first major "factory" in the county.

Robertson County was occupied territory and no major battles were fought within its borders during the Civil War. However, both armies moved men and materials through and Confederate cavalryman John Hunt Morgan and his raiders destroyed parts of the Edgefield & Kentucky Railroad which ran through the county.

By 1910 the county's population was 25,466, including 6,492 black citizens. The lives of most residents still revolved around the rhythms of farm work. The lack of economic opportunity for many young citizens, black and white, and the burdens of segregation fueled an exodus of people from the county to the large industrial cities of the North from the 1940s until the early 1970s. From the 1950s through today several manufacturing companies have strengthened the industrial sector of the county's economy, and the area has experienced unparalleled growth. Such companies include the Frigidaire Range Products, Unarco Material Handling, Datrek Professional Bags, and CEI Auto Electronic Parts. Part of the growth came as Interstates 65 and 24 connected Robertson County to Nashville. Even with the rise of industry, agriculture and tobacco continue to be important elements in the economic, social, cultural, and political life of the county's 45,000 residents.

The Robertson County Courthouse and Springfield Public Square are listed on the National Register of Historic Places, along with 13 other locations within the county.

Yolanda Reid, White House

SEE: AGRICULTURE; BELL WITCH; BLACK PATCH WAR; BYRNS, JOSEPH W.; DARK TOBACCO DISTRICT PLANTERS' PROTECTIVE ASSOCIATION; GLENRAVEN PLANTATION; MORGAN, JOHN H.; ROBERTSON, JAMES; ST. MICHAEL'S CATHOLIC CHURCH; TOBACCO; WASHINGTON, JOSEPH E.; WESSYNGTON PLANTATION

ROBERTSON, JAMES (1742–1814), early leader of both the Watauga and Cumberland settlements, has been called the "Father of Middle Tennessee." Born in 1742 in Brunswick County, Virginia, he was the son of John and Mary Gower Robertson. Physically, Robertson stood close to six feet tall, with dark hair, blue eyes, and a fair complexion. All descriptions of his personality point to an individual who was soft spoken and even-tempered, a person who maintained an inner composure regardless of external circumstances. Charlotte Reeves, who married Robertson in 1768, admired these traits. The daughter of a minister, Charlotte Robertson also persevered under the harsh frontier conditions and established a reputation for resourcefulness and strength. She and Robertson had 13 children, two of whom died in infancy.

In late 1769, as Robertson grew increasingly frustrated with the provincial rule of North Carolina's Governor Tryon, he became intrigued by the stories of the land west of the Appalachian Mountains and began to consider relocating his family there. Late that year, he crossed the mountains and found a suitable site in the upper Holston Valley, near the Watauga River. To establish his claim, he planted corn and built a corncrib and a cabin. On the return trip, Robertson became lost and wandered aimlessly for approximately two weeks before hunters directed him across the mountains.

Encouraged by his favorable description of the land, several of Robertson's North Carolina neighbors decided to accompany him to the new frontier. In May 1772, when the Watauga settlers met to establish a government, they selected Robertson as one of the five magistrates to lead the Watauga Association. In addition, he was elected commander of the Watauga Fort.

In 1777 Richard Henderson of the Transylvania Land Company purchased a large tract of land from the Cherokees, including most of what constitutes present-day Middle Tennessee. In the spring of 1779, Robertson and a small party of Wataugans, acting on behalf of Henderson's claim, traveled to a site along the Cumberland River, known as French Lick. There they selected a suitable location for a new settlement. Late that same year, Robertson returned with a group of men to prepare temporary shelter for friends and relatives, who planned to join them in a few months. The men arrived on Christmas Day and drove their cattle across the frozen Cumberland River. Crude cabins were erected for immediate winter housing, and a fort was built atop a bluff along the river. The fort was named Fort Nashborough, in honor of Francis Nash, a friend of Robertson's, who fought along-side him at the Battle of Alamance in 1771.

A faction of Cherokees, known as the Chickamau-gas, opposed the Transylvania Purchase and warned the new settlers that trouble would follow their claim to the land. Attacks on the Cumberland settlement lasted several years and reached a peak between 1789 and 1794. Robertson's brothers, John and Mark, were killed, as were his sons, Peyton and James, Jr. Another son, Jonathan, was scalped. Robertson narrowly escaped death on two occasions. Once he was shot in the foot while hoeing corn. Another time he was ambushed along a trail and received gunshot wounds in both wrists.

In 1790 Congress created the Territory South of the River Ohio, and Robertson became Lieutenant Colonel Commandant of the Mero District. The fol-lowing year, President George Washington appointed him brigadier general of the U.S. Army of the same region. Under Robertson's guidance, the settlers worked together and persevered. Eventually attacks on the community decreased, and the population rose with the arrival of new settlers. As the Cumber-land settlement entered a period of prosperity, the Robertsons built a comfortable brick home.

Occasionally, Robertson acted on behalf of the federal government to assist in the treaty negotiations with various Indian tribes. In 1804 he was commis-sioned U.S. Indian Agent to the Chickasaw and Choctaw Nations. His final mission took him to the Chickasaw Agency at Chickasaw Bluff. In his seven-ties, Robertson made the trip during heavy rains that forced him to swim several swollen creeks along the way. As a result, he became ill and died on Septem-ber 1, 1814. His remains were later returned to Nashville, where he received a formal burial in the City Cemetery.

Terry Weeks, Middle Tennessee State University

SUGGESTED READING: Anita S. Goodstein, *Nashville, 1780–1860: From Frontier to City* (1989); Thomas E. Matthews, *General James Robertson* (1934); A.W. Putnam, *History of Middle Tennessee; or, Life and Times of Gen. James Robertson* (1859)

SEE: CHICKAMAUGAS; CUMBERLAND COMPACT; DAVID-SON COUNTY; FRENCH LICK; NASHVILLE; ROBERTSON, CHARLOTTE; SOUTHWEST TERRITORY; TRANSYLVANIA PURCHASE; TREATIES; WATAUGA ASSOCIATION

ROBINSON, THEOTIS, JR. (1942–), now a Special Projects Coordinator for the University of Tennessee, Knoxville, gained statewide attention in 1960 when the University of Tennessee refused to admit him due to his race. The previous spring, Robinson, who grad-uated in June from Austin High School, had partici-pated in sit-in demonstrations to desegregate Knoxville's downtown eating establishments. Those sit-ins proved successful: well before the end of the summer desegregation became a fact of life in down-

town Knoxville. While Robinson and his fellow activists were thrilled at their success, they still real-ized that much remained to be done.

That realization prompted Robinson to apply to the University of Tennessee that fall. Initially the school refused to admit him, but after a series of meetings with various school officials, the Board of Trustees allowed him to register. Thus, in January 1961 Theotis Robinson, Jr., became the first black undergraduate to attend the University of Tennessee. From this "first" Robinson went on to become the first African American to serve on the Knoxville City Council in over 50 years. He was elected to that post in 1969 and he served through the end of 1977. Since that time Robinson has continued to serve the Knoxville community in various capacities including a post as Vice President for Economic Development for the 1982 World's Fair. Currently, in addition to his university position, Theotis Robinson, Jr., writes a weekly column in the *Knoxville News Sentinel*.

Cynthia Griggs Fleming, University of Tennessee, Knoxville

SEE: EDUCATION, HIGHER; *KNOXVILLE NEWS SENTINEL*; KNOXVILLE WORLD'S FAIR; SIT-INS, KNOXVILLE; UNIVER-SITY OF TENNESSEE

ROCK CASTLE, a late eighteenth century plantation house, was once the home of General Daniel Smith, his wife Sarah Michie Smith, and their two children. General Smith (1748–1818), a well-read and classi-cally educated Virginian, attended the College of William and Mary. A military man, who was a Revo-lutionary War captain, Smith also was a licensed sur-veyor, who produced the first map showing the "Tennessee Territory" in relation to Virginia and Kentucky. Being familiar with the Middle Tennessee area, he brought his family there in 1784, and built Rock Castle on a 3,000-plus-acre land grant from North Carolina.

Building Rock Castle along the shores of the Cum-berland River (now Old Hickory Lake), Smith's laborers used limestone quarried on site. They cut lumber for construction and finish carpentry from timber on the property. When the Smiths' modest log house was burned a few years later, the family occu-pied the two rooms of the rock house that were then partially completed. The several stages of construc-tion were finished by 1796. Built largely by nephews Peter and Smith Hansborough, under the supervision of Sarah Smith during her husband's frequent absences on military assignment, Rock Castle shows a degree of architectural mastery rarely found on the Tennessee frontier. Although it strives for Georgian symmetry and balance, its two-story portico, which was added during the Greek Revival period, is not quite centered on the front facade. The interior has the common central-hall plan of the time, and the car-penters added unique fireplaces that feature central-

mantel, over-mantel, and floor-to-ceiling side cabinets placed within an integrated and painted black
walnut-paneled wall. The house is a splendid early
example of frontier transitional Federal architecture
in Tennessee.

The State of Tennessee purchased Rock Castle and
18 surrounding acres, including the family cemetery,
in 1969. Sarah Berry, a direct descendant of General
Smith, spearheaded the formation and charter of
Friends of Rock Castle in 1971. Ten years later, Historic Rock Castle opened on May 1, 1981. The Friends
of Rock Castle exist to restore, preserve, furnish,
maintain, and interpret the house and grounds as an
educational model of early Tennessee. The property
is listed in the National Register of Historic Places.
Arlene F. Young, Friends of Rock Castle
SUGGESTED READINGS: Walter T. Durham, *Daniel Smith, Frontier Statesman* (1976); Carroll Van West, *Tennessee's Historic
Landscapes* (1995)
SEE: SMITH, DANIEL; SUMNER COUNTY

ROCK ISLAND STATE PARK, located in Warren
County, was established as a state park in 1969 but its
historical significance dates to the region's early settlement. A small village called Rock Island, located
upstream from the park's boundaries, was the
county's first permanent settlement and a temporary
county seat. Logging was the area's first important
industry. The arrival of the railroad in 1881 led residents to relocate their village from its proximity to
the confluence of the Rocky and Caney Fork rivers to
a new place along the railroad tracks. Eventually the
improved transportation convinced local capitalists
to use the Great Falls of the Caney Fork River, near
the confluence of the Caney Fork and Collins rivers,
for industrial development. In 1892 Clay Faulkner,
H.L. Walling, and Jesse Walling established the Great
Falls Cotton Mill and built a small company town
known as Falls City. A flood in 1902 severely damaged the company's facilities and the owners closed
the factory, selling their property to the Great Falls
Power Company.

However, the Great Falls Hydroelectric Plant, a
800-foot structure that dams the Collins River, did
not go into operation until January 1, 1917. In 1922
the Tennessee Electric Power Company (TEPCO)
acquired the dam and its powerhouse. The conversion of the river into a lake created new recreational
opportunities at the confluence of the Caney Fork
and Collins rivers, especially once the Memphis-to-
Bristol Highway (present-day U.S. Highway 70S)
was completed adjacent to the dam and lake in the
1920s. The Webb Hotel was constructed ca. 1920. A
group of Rustic-styled summer homes were built for
urban families who still come annually to the park
area. TEPCO probably built the whimsical "Witch's
Castle" as it developed a park and trails on the

Warren County side of the lake in the 1920s. The
Tennessee Valley Authority acquired the dam and
powerhouse in 1939; the property is listed in the
National Register.

Rock Island State Park contains campsites, picnic
grounds, trails, boat launches, and an interpretive
center. Park personnel also manage Bone Cave State
Natural Area, which contains important archaelogi-
cal sites detailing prehistoric life and the mining of
saltpeter during the War of 1812 and the Civil War.
Carroll Van West, Middle Tennessee State University
SUGGESTED READING: Evelyn K. Tretter, "Rock Island State
Park," *Tennessee Conservationist* (March/April 1987): 9–11
SEE: BRYAN, CHARLES F.; TEPCO; WARREN COUNTY

ROCK MUSIC, SOUTHERN. The first record Elvis
Presley released in 1954 shows the inspired ways Ten-
nesseans merged musical traditions into something
new and exciting called rock music. The "A" side was
That's All Right, a blues song by Arthur "Big Boy"
Crudup, and the "B" side was Bill Monroe's blue-
grass standard, *Blue Moon of Kentucky.* From its very
beginnings, those two traditions—blues and country,
Memphis and Nashville—have shaped Southern
Rock music.

Rockabilly was the first rock-n-roll tradition that
Tennesseans contributed to the rock music revolution, a tradition traced to the work of Sam Phillips in
Memphis during the 1950s. In 1951 he recorded
Rocket 88, by Ike Turner and His Kings of Rhythm, a
song Phillips later called the first rock-n-roll song. It
had a rough, raucous sound, in part because the band
had broken an amplifier and Phillips repaired it with
a piece of paper that made a guitar sound like an electrified, out-of-tune saxophone. In 1952 Phillips
opened a new studio he called Sun Records, where
the recordings tended to be lean and raw, with one
track, a powerful string bass, and few backup musicians or singers. Phillips began to look for a white
musician to play the songs black musicians were
turning into hits. He supposedly claimed, "If I could
find a white man who had the Negro sound and the
Negro feel, I could make a billion dollars."

Elvis Presley turned out to be that man. Presley's
That's All Right surprised Phillips with its popularity, and his second record, *Good Rockin, Tonight,* was
even more successful. Presley's rhythm-n-blues side
is well known, but the country aspects of his early
career were equally important. The term "rockabilly" blended the new term rock music with the
popular Tennessee stereotype of the hillbilly. Elvis's
compatriots at Sun included other rockabilly pioneers such as Johnny Cash from Arkansas, Jerry Lee
Lewis from Louisiana, and Carl Perkins from Tennessee. Phillips sold Presley's contract to RCA
Records, where Elvis had success making hits out of
an extraordinary variety of music. Yet most music

writers believe Presley never had as much fun or sounded as fresh and exciting as he did in his early recordings with Sun Records.

The second Southern Rock pioneer from Tennessee was Carl Perkins, who grew up listening to country music on the radio and the blues in the cotton fields. He attributed his ability to play the guitar to a black man, John Westbrook, who, Phillips said, made the instrument "slur." In 1955 Perkins wrote *Blue Suede Shoes*, his great hit song since performed by countless rock musicians, after Johnny Cash suggested that he build a song around the common demand for respect, "stay off of my blue suede shoes." Typical of early rock musicians, he composed the song quickly and claimed to have written it late one night on an empty potato sack.

Showing both their own experiences and the strong influence of the blues, the first generation of Tennessee rock musicians showed no nostalgia for farm roots. Carl Perkins called rockabilly "blues with a country beat," but the music had virtually no tributes to farm life, plows, mules, or the security of male-female relations on the farm. Love was something musicians either sought or enjoyed and rarely something they remembered. Early rock songs were not remarkable for the sophistication of their lyrics. For example, Presley did not write his own songs, perhaps meaning that the movement lacked lyrical coherence from the start. If one can generalize, the songs performed by the early performers for Sun Records tended to demand respect for the young, to stress the essential importance of young people's search for happiness, and the frequency of physical mobility. Showing the lyrical debt to the blues, the first rock-n-roll song, *Rocket 88* by Ike Turner and His Kings of Rhythm, was about a fast car.

If the development of rock music in Memphis shows the powerful effects of the blues, rock musicians in Nashville show the clear influence of playing in the home of country music. Many musicians since the 1960s have gone to Nashville to record songs with banjoes, steel guitars, and twangy backup vocalists, and some went simply to play in a city full of recording studios and opportunities to play. Only in the 1970s did a distinctive rock music style emerge around Nashville.

Charlie Daniels became the leader of southern rock music in Nashville. Born in Wilmington, North Carolina, in 1937, and now a resident of Mt. Juliet, Tennessee, Daniels first played guitar and fiddle in bluegrass bands before moving to Nashville in 1968 to become a studio musician where he played on Bob Dylan's *Nashville Skyline* album. He formed the Charlie Daniels Band in 1970 and enjoyed about a decade of stardom playing a form of rock music generally closer to country music than the blues. Among the features that distinguished Daniels from the Memphis rockabil-

lies in the 1950s was his rabid southern self-consciousness. He performed numerous songs that mentioned southern cities and states, especially Tennessee, performed in front of a huge Tennessee state flag, and relentlessly reminded audiences of southern images and stock characters. His favorite phrase in concert was "Ain't it good to be alive and be in Tennessee."

One of the clearest statements about southern identity was Daniels's Volunteer Jam, an annual concert that started in 1975. At the Jamboree in Middle Tennessee State University in Murfreesboro in 1975, he invited fellow Southern Rock musicians from the Marshall Tucker Band and the Allman Brothers Band to play along with the Charlie Daniels Band. The show included not only its trademark country conclusion, *The Tennessee Waltz*, but also a version of *Mountain Dew*, featuring "Hee Haw" banjo player Ronnie Stoneman. The jamborees became huge events and were relocated to Nashville where Daniels invited special guests to perform. The guest list in the late 1970s and early 1980s included stars ranging from James Brown and Billy Joel, to Rufus Thomas and Carl Perkins, to Crystal Gayle and Roy Acuff.

Bringing together such diverse performers to close every concert with *The Tennessee Waltz* showed Daniels's notion that music could bring people together. His trademark 1974 song *The South's Gonna Do It* combined regional defensiveness, even urging listeners to "be proud you're a rebel," with a surprisingly wide range of identities for what it meant to be a Southerner. This anthem to a new musical movement listed the musicians of Southern Rock and urged defiance against anyone who might criticize Southerners or their music. But the song itself drew on the swing sound of Bob Wills and the Texas Playboys from the 1930s and 1940s and included a guitar solo based in African-American blues, a piano solo reminiscent of New Orleans jazz, and Daniels's country fiddle solo. Thus being a "rebel" meant a willingness to combine various southern traditions into something new and defiant.

The lyrics of Daniels's songs brought together an agrarian image of Tennessee life with fascination and respect for life on the move. In one song, he urged all potential critics of him and other Southerners to "leave this long-haired country boy alone" when all he wanted from life was leisure, good friends, and marijuana. Countless songs upheld the virtues of a stable rural life. On the other hand, he, like most Southern Rock musicians in the 1970s, portrayed life on the run as the only way for men to keep their freedom. Songs repeatedly compared musicians on the road to cowboys on the trail. In his politics, Daniels' songs moved from occasionally liberal political commentary in the early 1970s to a combative conservatism by the end of the decade. A song in 1980 told Russians "they can all go straight to hell" if they did not believe Americans would return "on the paths of righteousness." Finally, Daniels has been unique in writing songs like *Trudy* and *The Devil Went Down to Georgia* that told stories—a tendency far more common in country music than rock music or the blues.

In *The South's Gonna Do It,* Daniels sang that "All the good people down in Tennessee" listened to "Barefoot Jerry and the CDB." Barefoot Jerry exemplified an often overlooked side of the Southern Rock movement—a side that blended the typical regional defensiveness with agrarian imagery and a strong populist sensibility. The four musicians from Nashville named the band after a fiddle-playing storekeeper in the Smoky Mountains and released their first album in 1975. Their music stressed vocal harmony, a country guitar sound, and a kind of countrified innocence. In *I'm Proud to be a Redneck,* they urged people not to be ashamed of old identities but also called for a non-violent image for southern men. "We'll make peace and lots of love," they sang in an odd pairing of lines, "The South's gonna rise again." Another song offered a leftist view of American history and religion. *In God We Trust* began with Indians in "God's Eden" whose natural harmony fell when "white man came with all his greed and evil," bring slavery, environmental destruction, and religious rationales for conquest. In general, however, Barefoot Jerry songs stressed an easy-going rural good time.

Today Tennessee is home to many *memories* about Southern Rock music. Contemporary country musicians draw openly on the tradition of Southern Rock music, with performers like Marty Stuart, Travis Tritt, Hank Williams, Jr., and Garth Brooks mixing their country sound with energetic rock rhythm, high-powered amplifiers, and regional defensiveness. For a music that always tries to be new and rebellious, rock music lives in Memphis in part as history, with Sun Studio, Beale Street, and above all Presley's Graceland as places for music lovers to remember and relive a particular form of rebellion. A recent compilation of alternative rock songs is called *It Came From Memphis,* a title that suggests both the sense that rock music had roots in the city and also the notion that Memphis music can still be daring and innovative.

Ted Ownby, University of Mississippi

SUGGESTED READINGS: Colin Escott with Martin Hawkins, *Good Rockin' Tonight: Sun Records and the Birth of Rock'N'Roll* (1991); Peter Guralnick, *Last Train to Memphis: The Rise of Elvis Presley* (1994) and *Lost Highway: Journeys and Arrivals of American Musicians* (1989); Bill C. Malone, *Country Music, U.S.A.* (rev. ed., 1985); Carl Perkins, *Go, Cat, Go! The Life and Times of Carl Perkins, The King of Rockabilly* (1996)

SEE: MEMPHIS MUSIC SCENE; MUSIC; PERKINS, CARL L.; PHILLIPS, SAMUEL C.; PRESLEY, ELVIS; ROCKABILLY MUSIC; THOMAS, RUFUS; TURNER, TINA; WDIA

ROCKABILLY MUSIC. The years between 1945 and 1960 represented the South's greatest period of upheaval in the twentieth century. In music, this period of transformation focused on what popular music observers identify as the rock-n-roll revolution, with the term rockabilly representing the first outburst of this new music, one that combined a range of southern musical traditions.

While the early rock-n-roll sound of the postwar era was not unique to the South, its connection to the region was considerable and unmistakable. The large majority of first generation artists who performed in the genre hailed from below the Mason-Dixon Line. They spoke in a southern dialect and displayed characteristics which were associated with the South. Arguably the two most important recording centers for rock-n-roll music in the 1950s were New Orleans and Memphis, each of which developed a characteristic sound and style. In New Orleans, the recording studio of Cosimo Matassa produced such luminaries as Fats Domino, Little Richard, and Lloyd Price, all of whom had rhythm-n-blues hits that crossed into the pop market as rock-n-roll.

In Memphis, Sam Phillips began successfully recording blues and rhythm-n-blues artists such as Howlin' Wolf, Rufus Thomas, B.B. King, and Little Junior Parker in 1950. He also produced *Rocket 88,* a song many popular music historians consider to be the first rock-n-roll record. Phillips, however, was well aware of the racial intolerance and segregated circumstances inherent within popular music. He realized that a black rhythm-n-blues act stood little chance of gaining the broad exposure needed to achieve large-scale commercial success. Soon after establishing the independent Sun Record Company in 1952, therefore, Phillips started his search for a white man who could perform with the same feeling as black blues vocalists.

Phillips, of course, found Elvis Presley. In 1954 Presley, along with guitarist Scotty Moore, bass player Bill Black, and Phillips, combined various musical forms, including rhythm-n-blues, black and white gospel, pop, and country music in a successful synthesis that only later would be labeled as rockabilly. While his subsequent career proved that Presley was an eclectic vocalist whose style could not be easily classified, his success as a country singer who performed rhythm-n-blues nevertheless opened the door for other such singers to actively seek commercial prosperity. Phillips would release five Presley recordings; after 18 months the young singer left Sun, signed an exclusive contract with RCA Victor, appeared on national television, and began making motion pictures. He was destined to become the "King of Rock-n-Roll."

Yet Phillips would not have to look hard for other potential rockabilly stars seeking to replace Presley.

Young musicians from throughout the South, performing in a style similar to that of Elvis, traveled to Memphis to gain the attention of Phillips. They included such performers as Carl Perkins, Jerry Lee Lewis, Johnny Cash, Warren Smith, Roy Orbison, Charlie Rich, and Conway Twitty. Phillips and Sun, however, did not enjoy a monopoly on rockabilly. By the middle to late 1950s, other record labels had signed such southerners as Buddy Holly, the Everly Brothers, Bob Luman, the Rock 'n' Roll Trio (Memphis-natives Johnny Burnette, Dorsey Burnette, and Paul Burlison), and Gene Vincent. For a time, it appeared that rockabilly was set to alter forever the influence of Nashville and country music. Virtually all of the talented young white working class singers seemed intent on becoming the next Elvis, not the next Hank Williams.

Ironically, despite the Nashville music establishment's fear of rockabilly, the music itself and the performers who sang it were steeped deeply in country. Rockabilly was basically country music played with an intensity and beat borrowed from black gospel and rhythm-n-blues. The fact that many of the southern white performers associated with rockabilly returned to country music once their popularity as pop stars began to fade indicated that they had never completely abandoned their roots. Their explorations into rockabilly had simply expanded the boundaries of country music.

The rockabilly performers were not, of course, the first southern whites to have been influenced by the blues of their black neighbors. Jimmie Rodgers, the "Father of Country Music," had apparently absorbed much of his style from African Americans. And neither was he the last hillbilly singer who came under the influence of black bluesmen. Others of note would include Bill Monroe, Jimmie Davis, the Delmore Brothers, Moon Mullican, and Hank Williams. Yet while such musicians borrowed heavily from the blues, their music, style, and appearance remained conventional within country music.

What distinguished the rockabilly artists from their predecessors was their willingness to identify completely with the rhythm-n-blues singers they emulated. Through their performing styles, dress, speech, and behavior, they were attempting to relate on some level to their black counterparts. In this manner they forced their way out of the complex, yet rigid southern folk and country music tradition they were born into. Significantly, early rock-n-roll performers and audiences engaged in a degree of public interchange and acceptance of black music and culture that separated them from the region's past. Today, such country music performers as Marty Stuart and BR-549 incorporate rockabilly music into their concerts while Cordell Jackson, the "Guitar Granny," still records and performs rockabilly across the country.

Michael Bertrand, Middle Tennessee State University
SUGGESTED READINGS: Greil Marcus, *Mystery Train: Images of America in Rock `n' Roll Music* (rev. ed., 1981); B. Lee Cooper and Wayne S. Haney, *Rockabilly: A Bibliographic Resource Guide* (1990); Peter Guralnick, *Lost Highway: Journeys and Arrivals of American Musicians* (1989, 2nd ed.); Colin Escott with Martin Hawkins, *Good Rockin' Tonight: Sun Records and the Birth of Rock `n' Roll* (1991)
SEE: MEMPHIS MUSIC SCENE; PERKINS, CARL; PHILLIPS, SAMUEL C.; PRESLEY, ELVIS

ROCKY MOUNT, the home of William Cobb, served as the first capitol of the Southwest Territory. William Blount, the Governor of the Territory of the United States South of the River Ohio, presided over the newly formed territory from 1790–1792. On October 20, 1790, Blount wrote: "At William Cobb's Washington County . . . On the 11th instant, I arrived in this country, and was received with every mark of attention and gladness that I could have wished. I am very well accommodated with a Room with Glass Windows, Fireplace, etc., etc., at this place." Other notable pioneers, such as Daniel Boone, John Sevier, Daniel Smith, William Campbell, and Richard Henderson, enjoyed Cobb's hospitality. Andrew Jackson lodged at Rocky Mount for six weeks while waiting for his license to practice law in nearby Jonesborough.

Migrating from North Carolina in 1769, William Cobb was one of the first settlers and most distinguished citizens of the territory. In 1777 the North Carolina legislature appointed Cobb as one of the first county magistrates. He also served on the commission charged with laying out the town of Jonesborough.

The house at Rocky Mount, erected ca. 1770, befits the distinguished family that built it. The multiple-room, two-story log house was large by frontier standards, but not overly ornate. The glass windows that impressed Blount were indeed status symbols, but the pine mantels and paneled stairway suggested hospitality rather than high style.

Almost two centuries after it was built, Rocky Mount was bought from Cobb family descendants by the State of Tennessee in 1959. Three years later, on April 1, 1962, the Rocky Mount Historical Association opened the site to the public. Today, Rocky Mount Museum continues to receive guests with "every mark of attention and gladness." As a living-history museum that interprets life in 1791, visitors may be greeted by "Mrs. Cobb" and given a tour of the house and grounds by various "friends" and "family members." Guests are ushered into the kitchen where "servants" are hard at work preparing meals over an open hearth. Activities outside the Cobb home are equally in keeping with the period. Herbs and vegetables are grown in the yard and garden, while wool and flax are processed in the weaving cabin. A blacksmith shop, complete with forge, is located by the barn, and visitors can see wood shaped on the spring pole lathe in the wood shop. In the kitchen shed, dyeing cloth and washing clothes may be a part of the day's work.

Also on the property is the Massengill Museum of Overmountain History, which features period rooms with pottery, homemade tools, clothes, and a wagon that area pioneers used two centuries ago. Sheep shearing and herding are featured events during the annual Woolly Day. Special events are held throughout the year.

Kara Carden, Rocky Mount Museum

SEE: BLOUNT, WILLIAM; BOONE, DANIEL; JACKSON, ANDREW; JONESBOROUGH; LOG CONSTRUCTION; SEVIER, JOHN; SMITH, DANIEL; SOUTHWEST TERRITORY; WASHINGTON COUNTY

RODDY, BERT MAYNARD (1886–1963) was a well known, innovative businessperson who founded the first African-American-owned grocery chain in Memphis. He was born in Augusta, Arkansas, on August 19, 1886, to Jerry and Harriette McKenny Roddy.

When he was a young boy, he and his family moved to Memphis where he attended and later graduated from LeMoyne Normal Institute. Roddy had a great interest in promoting racial progress and participating in business and civic activities that benefited African Americans. He was one of the early stockholders of the Solvent Savings Bank and Trust Company that was established in 1906, and he became cashier of the bank in 1914. During this period, he and a friend, Robert S. Lewis, Sr., opened the Iroquois Café, a popular spot, on Beale Street. Another friend who assisted in managing this enterprise was Mordecai W. Johnson, who later became president of Howard University in Washington, D.C.

In 1916 he joined a political organization, the Lincoln League, and became a candidate for the State Senate on the Lincoln League Ticket. The ticket lost, but the Lincoln League became a respected political organization in Memphis, Tennessee, and the nation. Roddy was the first president of the Memphis branch of the NAACP established in 1917.

Roddy's business prowess drew him to establish Citizen's Cooperative Stores in 1920. There were 14 of these stores at the peak of the business's success, along with several dozen employees and a fleet of delivery trucks. The stores met their demise due to the recession of the 1920s and increased market competition.

An active church member, Roddy was a member of Second Congregational Church for many years and was superintendent of the church's Sunday School and a trustee.

Roddy organized the syndicate that launched the Supreme Life and Casualty Company of Ohio, founded by Truman K. Gibson, Sr. Later the company moved to Chicago and became known as the Supreme Liberty Life Insurance Company.

Moving to Chicago with his family, Roddy became the Assistant Agency Officer of the Supreme in 1931 and retained this position until he retired in 1957.

Ronald A. Walter, Memphis

SEE: LINCOLN LEAGUE; NAACP; SOLVENT SAVINGS BANK

ROGAN, HUGH, Sumner County pioneer, left his native County Donegal, Ireland, and sailed to the American colonies in 1775. Following the pattern of many Irish emigrants, he entered at the Port of Philadelphia, migrated into North Carolina, then moved west across the mountains into the Cumberland Valley. By the late 1770s he was a guard with the survey party led by commissioners Daniel Smith and Thomas Walker, who marked the boundaries of North Carolina and Virginia. He returned to the Cumberland Valley with John Donelson's party of settlers, who traveled by river to join with James Robertson's overland group at Fort Nashborough in 1780. One of 255 men who signed the Cumberland Compact, Rogan spent nearly two decades helping to establish and defend the stations or forts along the Cumberland River. His adventures as an Indian fighter, as recorded by his contemporaries, are legendary.

Rogan established a farm of nearly 1,000 acres in eastern Sumner County, near Bledsoe's Creek, where neighbors included Isaac Bledsoe, William Hall, and James Winchester. He brought his wife Nancy and son Bernard to this farm more than 20 years after leaving them in Ireland. Here he built a two-room stone house, patterned after an Irish folk cottage, in which a second son, Francis, was born in 1798. Additionally, Rogan and his family are credited with establishing the Roman Catholic Church in Sumner County. The nearby community of Rogana was named in honor of Hugh Rogan, who transferred many aspects of Irish culture to frontier Tennessee.

Caneta Skelley Hankins, Middle Tennessee State University

SEE: BLEDSOE, ISAAC; CUMBERLAND COMPACT; DONELSON, JOHN; HALL, WILLIAM; ROBERTSON, JAMES; ROGANA; SUMNER COUNTY; WALKER, THOMAS; WINCHESTER, JAMES

ROGANA, the historic name of the stone cottage built ca. 1800 by Irish immigrant and Tennessee pioneer Hugh Rogan, is located near Bledsoe's Creek in eastern Sumner County. The building is a rare surviving example of American architecture which is clearly based on an Irish folk house. Dressed limestone, a building material plentiful in both Rogan's native County Donegal and his adopted Sumner County, was used to construct the two-room house. While well adapted for the frontier, the house was also designed to adhere to Irish folk traditions. These included a linear floor plan, thought to be essential to long life and family harmony, and the placement of corresponding doors and windows for the safe passage of spirits. A central stone chimney provided a fireplace for each room and a source of heat for the full loft—a concession to "new world" architecture. The low gabled roof, also traditionally Irish, may first have been thatched with straw.

Rogana was the original house on the farm owned by Rogan, his family, and their descendants for several generations. Here Hugh, his wife Nancy, sons Bernard and Francis, and area Catholics met for services for nearly 50 years until the Catholic Church was formally established in Sumner County in 1837. Francis Rogan built a substantial brick residence in 1825, which was joined to the stone cottage. Near the house is the Rogan family cemetery, and about one mile away is the site of the early crossroads community also named Rogana.

Caneta Skelley Hankins, Middle Tennessee State University
SUGGESTED READING: Caneta S. Hankins, "Hugh Rogan of Counties Donegal and Sumner: Irish Acculturation in Frontier Tennessee," Carroll Van West, ed., *Tennessee History: The Land, the People, and the Culture* (1998), 56–79
SEE: ROGAN, HUGH; ARCHITECTURE, DOMESTIC VERNACULAR

ROGER WILLIAMS UNIVERSITY, one of four freedmen's colleges in Nashville, began as elementary classes for African-American Baptist preachers in 1864. Classes were held in the home of Daniel W. Phillips, a white minister and freedmen's missionary from Massachusetts. By 1865 the classes had moved to the basement of the First Colored Baptist Mission. In 1866 the "Baptist College" was officially named the Nashville Normal and Theological Institute under the auspices of New York's American Baptist Home Mission Society (ABHMS). A year later, the school moved from old Union army barracks on Cedar and Spruce streets to a two-story frame building at Park and Polk streets. In 1869 Phillips and the Nashville Normal Institute's board members tried to purchase the adjacent former Union army Fort Gillem, but Fisk University's officials gained the property and built Jubilee Hall on the new campus site seven years later.

Soon after granting its first bachelor's degree, the Nashville Normal and Theological Institute purchased Robert Gordon's farm on Hillsboro Road and started a new campus in 1874–1875. Vanderbilt University became the school's neighbor on the west side of Hillsboro Road. In 1883 Nashville Normal incorporated as Roger Williams University. African Americans held faculty positions and served on the board of trustees. In 1886 Roger Williams expanded the curriculum to include a master's degree program.

After mysterious fires destroyed its buildings in January and May of 1905, the ABHMS closed Roger Williams University and transferred students to Atlanta Baptist College (Morehouse College). George Peabody College for Teachers and area real estate developers purchased the property by 1911.

Meanwhile, nearly three years after the mysterious fires, determined African-American Baptist leaders raised money to match a gift from the ABHMS. In 1908 they reopened Roger Williams University on Whites Creek Pike, on the east bank of the Cumberland River, near the streetcar line, and closer to African-American neighborhoods. A graduate of Roger Williams University, John W. Johnson, became the institution's first African-American president. By 1922, the school had 159 students and 12 faculty members. Continuing financial problems led to the closing of the Nashville campus. On December 29, 1929, the students and teachers merged with Howe Institute (LeMoyne Owen College) in Memphis. By 1996 the American Baptist College and the World Baptist Center had occupied the last Roger Williams site.

Bobby L. Lovett, Tennessee State University
SEE: HOPE, JOHN; LEMOYNE OWEN COLLEGE

ROLLEY HOLE MARBLES. The area along the Kentucky-Tennessee border including Clay County, Tennessee, and Monroe County, Kentucky, maintains a remarkable marble-playing tradition focused on a game known locally as "rolley hole," "three holes," or simply "marbles."

In this region, rolley hole is played primarily by adult men, on cleared "marble yards" often constructed from sifted loam soil, 40 to 50 feet in length and 25 to 30 feet wide. Historically, such yards have been constructed and maintained by private individuals beside their homes, country stores, and woodlots, or cooperatively maintained by interested players at public spaces like school yards and parks. A marble yard was kept on the Clay County courthouse square early in the twentieth century, and the Monroe County Fairgrounds is currently the site of an active "indoor" yard.

The development of tournament play by the Monroe County Fair in the 1950s probably led to formalizing some of the game's rules, such as the number of players on a team, the number and arrangement of holes on the course, and the question of "knuckling down" while shooting. Many variations of minor rules continue to be debated among experienced players.

Players now exclusively use locally-made flint marbles, although prior to the use of electric or gasoline-powered grinding equipment, limestone marbles were also common, as they were more quickly made with water power.

The contemporary game pits two teammates against two opponents. Each player has one marble, and must work through a course of 12 holes, made by going up and down a line of three holes that are dug into the yard with the aid of pocket knife and a quarter dollar coin. A team wins when both partners have completed that course. Along the way, players prevent the progress of their opponents by shooting at their marbles, and knocking them "out of edge," or out of bounds. Essentially the same as croquet (a Victorian game which was probably inspired by the marble game), rolley hole players earn extra shots by hitting opponents' marbles and "making" holes.

The origin of the game and the reason for its sustained popularity in one small region are moot points. While there were numerous British and French games dating to the seventeenth century that involved rolling marbles into holes, no clear antecedent has been documented. To confuse the issue, it has recently been found that the Cherokees of Delaware County, Oklahoma, play a game with uncanny similarities, that many claim to be a pre-Removal tradition.

Their game, called "Indian Marbles," is played on a "marble field," up to 200 feet in length, often with five holes. They now use billiard balls as marbles, although they were pecked and ground from stone until the 1950s. Stone spheres of similar size have occasionally been found in Mississippian Period burial sites from Tennessee and Kentucky, interpreted by archaeologists as game pieces or marbles. Oral tradition places the rolley game in pre-Civil War times, at least.

The site of the National Rolley Hole Marbles Championship is Standing Stone State Park, located between Livingston and Celina, and held each September. The event includes scoreboards, announcers, and interpreters to assist visitors in understanding the game's intricacies and history.

Bob Fulcher, Clinton

SEE: CLAY COUNTY; MARBLE COMPETITIONS; STANDING STONE STATE PARK

ROSE, KNOWLES FRED (1898–1954), a prime mover in Nashville's rise as a music center, was born in Evansville, Indiana. Rose initially made his mark in Chicago as a pop songwriter, radio performer, and recording artist during the 1920s, when he penned such hits as *Red Hot Mama* for stars like Sophie Tucker. In 1933 he moved to Nashville radio station WSM and put down permanent roots in the city after marrying Nashvillian Lorene Dean in 1934.

Rose traveled to Chicago and New York during the mid-1930s still pursuing pop songwriting success. His conversion to Christian Science, around 1935, revitalized his personal and professional life amid the trying Depression years. Gradually Rose began to write songs with Grand Ole Opry acts like the Vagabonds. Between 1938 and 1942 he lived in Hollywood and wrote hits like *Be Honest With Me* for "singing cowboy" film stars, primarily Gene Autry.

In 1942 Rose launched Acuff-Rose Publications, Nashville's first country publishing house, with Grand Ole Opry kingpin Roy Acuff. Over the last 12 years of his life, Rose composed country classics like *Blue Eyes Crying in the Rain,* edited songs written by his protégé Hank Williams (among many others), recruited rising songwriters like Felice and Boudleaux Bryant, produced recording sessions by Williams and other artists for MGM Records, scouted talent for other labels, and vigorously promoted Nashville and country music in general. Thus, Rose's election to the Country Music Hall of Fame in 1961 was well-deserved.

John W. Rumble, Country Music Foundation

SEE: ACUFF, ROY; ACUFF-ROSE; GRAND OLE OPRY, WILLIAMS, HANK; WSM

ROSE, WICKLIFFE (1862–1931), born in Saulsbury, Tennessee, in 1862, became a leading administrator for the Rockefeller philanthropies. Rose earned degrees from the University of Nashville, the University of Mississippi, and Harvard. He began his career at Peabody College and the University of Nashville as professor of philosophy from 1892–1902, and returned as dean 1904–1907.

Rose joined the South's educational crusade in 1902 as a member of the Southern Education Board's Bureau of Investigation and Information at the University of Tennessee. As general agent of the Peabody Fund 1907–1915, member of the Southern Education Board 1910–1915 and its executive secretary 1909–1913, trustee of the John F. Slater Fund 1909–23, and member of the General Education Board 1911–1928, Rose helped to coordinate support for improved public education and teacher training for whites and African Americans in the southern states. Simultaneously, as executive secretary of the Rockefeller Sanitary Commission for the Eradication of Hookworm Disease 1910–1915, Rose directed the largest public health crusade in the American South. Rose's service earned him membership in the Rockefeller Foundation in 1913 and appointment as general director of the International Health Board 1913–1923. Under his leadership, the IHB funded research and public health campaigns around the world, most successfully against yellow fever.

From 1923 until his retirement in 1928, Rose served as president of the General Education Board. Rose also convinced John D. Rockefeller, Jr., to create the International Education Board, which Rose headed 1923–1928. A "rare combination of the scholar, investigator, philosopher, and administrator," this Tennessean shaped philanthropic policies and programs at the regional, national, and international levels.[1]

Mary S. Hoffschwelle, Middle Tennessee State University

CITATION:

(1) General Education Board, *Review and Final Report, 1902–1964* (New York, 1964), 16.

SEE: GENERAL EDUCATION BOARD; HARDEMAN COUNTY;
PEABODY EDUCATION FUND

ROSS, JOHN (1790–1866), son of Daniel and Mollie McDonald Ross, was born in the fall of 1790 in present-day Cherokee County, Alabama. At the age of seven, the Ross family settled in southern Tennessee near the northern end of Lookout Mountain. As an adult, Ross moved a few miles to the south and settled at the home of his maternal grandfather, John McDonald, in Rossville, Georgia. The log cabin where he resided is preserved today as the Chief John Ross house.

Ross was well-educated, having attended schools in Kingston and Maryville, Tennessee. In 1812 Ross received a government commission, and traveled among the Cherokees who had accepted government relocation along the Arkansas River. Upon his return, Ross joined with U.S. agent Return J. Meigs in persuading the Cherokees to align with the United States government in the conflict with the Creeks.

In 1813 Ross joined Agent Meigs's son, Timothy, in forming "Meigs and Ross." This enterprise thrived by negotiating contracts with the United States government to supply goods to the Cherokees during the Creek War. After Timothy Meigs's death, Ross's brother Lewis joined the business. Firmly established along the southern bank of the Tennessee River, the Ross's warehouse became an important supply source for Indians and settlers. The settlement that grew around the river landing and warehouse became known as Ross's Landing. In 1838 the area was incorporated under a new name, Chattanooga.

Though only one-eighth Cherokee, Ross's ability to speak the Cherokee language fluently, along with his early work with the U.S. government, propelled him into a leadership role among the Cherokees. Elected a delegate to the Cherokee National Council in 1817, Ross was present at the council meeting in which government officials demanded Cherokee cession of land north of the Hiwassee River. Despite protests from Ross and several Cherokee chiefs, the land was ceded. Ross's formal protest to the treaty stated that all the Cherokees wanted was to remain on their fathers' land and to become a civilized people.

Using the United States Constitution as a model, Ross developed the Cherokee constitution in 1827. The following year Ross was elected Principal Chief of the Cherokees. As gold was discovered in its northern mountains, Georgia annexed all Cherokee lands within the state. Ross moved his family to the tribal council grounds at Red Clay, Tennessee, and made many trips to Washington, D.C., attempting to have Georgia's action annulled. While Ross was appealing to Congress, a "Treaty Party" within the Cherokee nation signed an agreement that all Cherokees would move to land west of the Mississippi river for four and a half million dollars. In 1835 the national council repudiated the treaty and Chief Ross traveled to Washington with a petition of protest.

In early 1838 removal of the Cherokees began; the treatment was so bad throughout the first months that Chief Ross secured permission for the National Council to oversee the removal of the Cherokees. That fall, 17,000 Cherokees led by Ross began their journey west. Four thousand perished along the way on the infamous Trail of Tears.

Re-elected as Principal Chief, Ross traveled regularly to Washington on behalf of the Cherokee nation. In 1866 while on a trip east, Ross died in Philadelphia. His body was taken back to Oklahoma and buried at Park Hill cemetery near Tahlequah.
Patrice Hobbs Glass, Signal Mountain
SEE: CHATTANOOGA; HAMILTON COUNTY; MEIGS, RETURN J.; RED CLAY STATE HISTORIC PARK; TRAIL OF TEARS

ROSS, JOHN WALTON (1843–1920), Naval medical officer associated with the fight against yellow fever, was born January 11, 1843, near Clarksville, the son of educator John Ross and Mary Parker Ross. In 1861 young Ross enlisted in the Confederate cavalry and served throughout the war. In 1870 he graduated from Tulane University with a degree in medicine and entered the U.S. Navy as an assistant surgeon.

Ross became associated with the fight against yellow fever in 1878, when he worked with the Howard Association to combat the disease in Holly Springs, Mississippi. That same year, he volunteered to work in the Memphis outbreak of yellow fever and contracted the disease himself. He remained in the city two years and was rewarded for his service with a promotion.

During the early 1880s, Ross returned to sea duty and served in the Pacific. By 1886, he was back in the South, stationed at the Navy Yard and Navy Hospital at Pensacola, Florida. When a yellow fever epidemic broke out in East Florida, Ross again volunteered for duty and was placed in charge of the hospital facilities at Fernandina. He served in Florida and Cuba during the Spanish-American War and became Chief of the Department of Charities Hospitals in Havana (1899–1900). In 1901 he was placed in charge of the Yellow Fever Hospital at Las Animas, Havana, where he carried out experiments that disproved the popular theory that contact with clothing or personal items of yellow fever patients was the method of transmission of the disease.

As a result of his experience with yellow fever and his experiments regarding the transmission of the disease, Ross was named Medical Director of the Navy in 1903 and assigned duty with Colonel

William Crawford Gorgas under the Isthmian Canal Commission at the Canal Zone. By the end of 1904 he was forced to leave by an attack of estuo autumnal fever, from which he never fully recovered.

Ross retired from the Navy and moved to California in 1905. In 1900 he married Clara Clayton, daughter of Alexander Mosby Clayton, Judge of the Supreme Court of Mississippi. Ross died on February 8, 1920, at Pasadena, California. His correspondence and medical journals are available in the Tennessee State Library and Archives.

Connie L. Lester, Tennessee Historical Society
SEE: MEDICINE; MONTGOMERY COUNTY; YELLOW FEVER EPIDEMICS

ROWAN, CARL THOMAS (1925–), journalist, government worker, media personality, and author, has broken racial barriers throughout his career. He was born on August 10, 1925, to Thomas David and Johnnie Bradford Rowan and grew up in McMinnville, Tennessee. Challenged to pursue excellence by his high school teachers and Tennessee State University professors, Rowan took the national examination for admission to the Navy officer training program. He became one of the first 15 African Americans to be admitted and, in 1944, one of the first African Americans to earn a commission in the Navy.

Following his military career in 1946, he entered Oberlin College where he majored in mathematics and received a B.A. in 1947. In l948 he received an M.A. in journalism from the University of Minnesota. While in school he wrote for several newspapers and upon graduation became a copy editor for the *Minneapolis Tribune.* Eventually he was promoted to reporter, one of the few African-American reporters in the United States. In 1950 he proposed to his editors a series of articles on the conditions in the post-World War II South. Several publications grew from this series, including *Go South to Sorrow* (1957). This reporting underscored his determination to tell the truth regardless of the parties involved, to be more than the African-American reporter who reported black events, and not to be a token African-American reporter.

In 1954 he spent nearly a year in India, Pakistan, and Southeast Asia as a lecturer for the United Nations' international education exchange program. He reported his observations to the *Tribune* and other papers in the United States and Asia and ultimately wrote *The Pitiful and the Proud.* Additionally for the *Minneapolis Tribune,* he wrote articles on Native Americans; the Bandung Conference; the Civil Rights Movement; the Suez Canal crisis; and the Hungarian uprising against the Soviet Union. For his domestic reporting and foreign correspondence, he became the only journalist in American history to be awarded the Sigma Delta Chi medallion for three consecutive years.

In 1961 Rowan left the *Tribune* to serve as deputy assistant secretary for public affairs with the U.S. Department of State in Washington, D.C. He moved to Helsinki in 1963 where he served as Ambassador to Finland until 1964, when he became director of the United States Information Agency. He became not only the highest ranking African American in the federal government but also the first to attend National Security Council meetings. In 1965 he returned to journalism and was hired by the Field Newspaper Syndicate becoming the first African American with a nationally syndicated column. He also had his own radio program "The Rowan Report" and made regular appearances on the television programs "Agronsky & Co." and "Meet the Press".

Additionally, Rowan wrote and produced two documentaries on Thurgood Marshall and has written *Just Between Us Blacks* (1974), *Race War in Rhodesia* (1978), *Breaking Barriers: A Memoir* (1991), *Dream Makers Dream Breakers: The World of Justice Thurgood Marshall* (1993), and *The Coming Race War: A Wake-up Call* (1996).

In his syndicated column, lectures, and community involvement, Rowan continues to adhere to the principles which have informed his life work.

Helen R. Houston, Tennessee State University
SEE: PUBLISHING; WARREN COUNTY

ROWING, sometimes called crew, was America's first professional sport. Even today, the single largest sporting event in America is a rowing race. It is no wonder, with Tennessee's network of rivers and lakes, that crew is a popular pastime. Tennessee rowers of all ages, from teens to seniors, participate in recreational and competitive events in the state and nation.

According to popular legend, rowing came to Tennessee in 1875, with a small club of Chattanooga men. Though the club disbanded three years later, the men competed in Saratoga, New York, races made famous by the beautiful paintings of Thomas Eakins. In 1971 rowing returned to Chattanooga with the Lookout Rowing Club. The first full chartered rowing club was the Pellissippi Rowing Club in Oak Ridge. The Knoxville Rowing Association (KRC) soon followed in 1974. The early founders of Tennessee rowing include James Ramsey, Carl Parlota, Rod Townsend, Sr., and Greg Maynard, all of the KRC. Soon after the formation of the club, the first official regatta, or river race, was held in Knoxville.

The Head of the Tennessee Regatta is the second oldest river race in America and draws over 1,500 athletes from the southeast. In 1978 the Southern Intercollegiate Rowing Association (SIRA) permanently moved their collegiate regatta to Melton Hill Lake in Oak Ridge. High school and collegiate clubs sprang up in the 1980s, including the University of Tennessee at Chattanooga club in 1989. In 1995 the

University of Tennessee at Knoxville women's club became a varsity sport, marking the first SEC rowing team with NCAA status. Chattanooga brought the Women's National Team training center to the city in 1994, and Oak Ridge hosted the trials of the Pan American Games in 1995. The Women's National Team continues to train in Tennessee as they prepare for the Olympic Games in 2000.

Meredith Morris Babb, University Press of Florida

RUBY FALLS, a commercial cavern, is one of Chattanooga's major tourist attractions. Its entrance is situated in a medieval-styled stone edifice, Cavern Castle, located on the side of Lookout Mountain along Scenic Highway, from whence visitors are taken by elevator 260 feet down to the cave. Guided tours cover a distance of about 700 yards along an electrically lit passageway to the 87-foot falls. Along the way are numerous stone formations with such whimsical names as Leaning Tower, Beehives, and Hall of Dreams. Colored lights and music add drama to this natural spectacle. Upon leaving the cave visitors are treated to a panoramic view of the Tennessee River valley from atop the castle's tower.

Ruby Falls's commercial history dates to 1928 when the Lookout Mountain Cave Company was in the process of drilling an elevator shaft to the regionally significant Lookout Mountain Cave. Passage into this large cavern, explored by Indians and early settlers, and repeatedly used during the Civil War, had been recently cut off by an intersecting railroad tunnel. The cave company formed to reopen the cavern on a commercial basis. Midway into drilling the 400-foot elevator shaft, a passage opened into the falls cave. Leo Lambert and other corporate officials explored it and discovered the falls. Lambert subsequently named the falls after his wife, Ruby.

By 1930 both caves were open to the public. Ruby Falls proved far more popular, however, and tours of the lower cave eventually ceased. After years of financial struggle during the Great Depression, the Lookout Mountain Cave Company declared bankruptcy. New ownership launched an aggressive advertising campaign, based on roadside signs, and made Ruby Falls into a highly successful attraction. Each year, hundreds of thousands of visitors see Ruby Falls.

Gary C. Jenkins, Chattanooga

SUGGESTED READINGS: Thomas C. Barr, Jr., *Caves of Tennessee* (rpt. 1990); Ed Brinkley, *The History of Ruby Falls* (rpt. 1980); John Wilson, *Lookout: The Story of an Amazing Mountain* (1977)
SEE: CHATTANOOGA; DIXIE HIGHWAY ASSOCIATION

RUDOLPH, WILMA (1940–1994) **AND THE TSU TIGERBELLES.** The Tigerbelles Women's Track club at Tennessee State University became the state's most internationally accomplished athletic team in the mid-twentieth century. The sprinters won some 23 Olympic medals, more than any other sports team in Tennessee history. Mae Faggs and Barbara Jones became the first Olympic-winning Tigerbelles in 1952. The Tigerbelles won another medal in 1956. Soon, the Gold Medal winners included Edith McGuire, Madeline Manning, Barbara Jones, Martha Hudson, Lucinda Williams, Chandra Cheeseborough (2), Wilma Rudolph (3), and Wyomia Tyus (3). Tyus was the first athlete to win Gold Medals in the sprints in two consecutive Olympiads (1964 and 1968). The first star of the Tigerbelles was Wilma Goldean Rudolph (1940–1994).

Wilma G. Rudolph, the twentieth of 22 children, was born June 23, 1940, in Clarksville. Her father, E.D. Rudolph, already had 14 children when he married Wilma's mother, Blanche. Wilma Rudolph suffered a number of childhood diseases before contracting polio; she wore leg braces from age six until she was ten years old. In early 1955, when serving as a referee for a Clarksville basketball game, Tennessee A & I State College women's track coach, Edward S. Temple, saw Rudolph and invited the 14-year-old, skinny-legged basketball player to attend his summer camp. In 1956 Rudolph and five other Tigerbelles qualified for the Olympic team, returning to Nashville with several medals and plaques. In 1959 Rudolph accompanied the team to the Pan American Games, where they also won several medals. At the 1960 Olympic Games in Rome, Italy, Rudolph won three gold medals, prompting Coach Temple to assert, "I was so happy I was bursting all the buttons off my shirt."

In 1961, the year her father died, Rudolph won the James E. Sullivan Award and visited President John F. Kennedy. The next year, she retired from track and field, and completed goodwill tours abroad before returning to Clarksville to marry Robert Eldridge. Although America's first female star athlete, Rudolph's life was "no crystal stair." Rudolph described her life as "besieged with money problems." The expectations of others left her feeling "exploited both as a woman and as a black person."

In 1992, after ten years in Indianapolis, Wilma Rudolph returned to Tennessee to become a vice president for Nashville's Baptist Hospital. Two years later, shortly after her mother's death, Rudolph was diagnosed with brain and throat cancer. Thereafter she seldom appeared in public, except for quiet walks around the Tigerbelle's track with retired Coach Temple. Wilma Rudolph died on November 12, 1994, and thousands of mourners filled TSU's Kean Hall on November 17 for the memorial service in her honor. Others attended the funeral at Clarksville's First Baptist Church. Across Tennessee, the state flag flew at half-mast.

In her short life, Wilma G. Rudolph became more than an athlete: she was the epitome of the triumphant human being. Her many honors and memorials testify to the respect afforded her by Tennessee's citizens. In 1980 Tennessee State University named its indoor track for Wilma Rudolph. In 1994 she was inducted into the National Woman's Hall of Fame and received two honorary degrees. A section of U.S. Highway 79 in Clarksville was renamed the Wilma Rudolph Boulevard (1994). Throughout the summer and fall of 1995, several events honored Rudolph's memory: Clarksvillians held the Wilma Rudolph Breakfast in July; TSU dedicated a new six-story dormitory, the Wilma G. Rudolph Residence Center in August; TSU's Annual Edward S. Temple Seminars on Society and Sports named its annual luncheon the Wilma Rudolph Memorial Luncheon in October; and the Wilma Rudolph Memorial Commission placed a black marble marker at her grave in Clarksville's Foster Memorial Garden Cemetery in November. In April 1996 a life-sized bronze statue of Wilma Rudolph was completed for mounting in Clarksville.
Bobby L. Lovett, Tennessee State University
SEE: BOSTON, RALPH; TEMPLE, EDWARDS S.; TENNESSEE STATE UNIVERSITY

RUDY'S FARM, once home to the Rudy Sausage Company, was a family operation dating back to 1881. Daniel Rudy made and sold his own sausage in Nashville on a farm near the railroad on Lebanon Road. His son, Jacob Ludwig, continued the sausage operation and taught his own sons, Frank and Dan Rudy. In the cold winter months, they killed the hogs, ground them into sausage, and hauled the sausage to various merchants in wooden tubs, measuring out the desired amounts with a wooden paddle. Due to the family's dedication, this small operation managed to stay profitable, despite local competition and hard economic times in the early 1930s. When Jacob Rudy died in 1936, his sons Frank and Dan assumed the duties and expenses of the farm and slowly began its modernization and expansion into a large sausage and pork products company.

During World War II the Rudys intensified their farming effort by farming 1,200 acres, at times with the assistance of German prisoners of war. In 1945 Dan and Frank Rudy incorporated the business. Frank directed the actual hog kills while Dan was in charge of the sausage production. As the business grew they hired a sales manager, bookkeeper and secretary, and acquired a refrigerated truck. The Rudys built a 2,700 square-foot sausage plant and, by late 1950, were making about 5,000 pounds of sausage a month. In 1962 a modern plant was built to meet the U.S. government inspection standards and eventually Rudy's employed about 175 people making hundreds of thousands of pounds of sausage.

Milton Schloss of Kahn's Meats in Cincinnati, Ohio, was instrumental in the sale of Rudy's Farm to Kahn's. Kahn's was a subsidiary of Consolidated Foods, now the Sara Lee Corporation. Early in 1990, the old Rudy Sausage Company plant was physically moved to Newbern in Dyer County, where the Sara Lee Corporation keeps accounts.
Jeanette Cantrell Rudy, Nashville
SEE: DYER COUNTY; LIVESTOCK; INDUSTRY

RUGBY, a Victorian-era village at the northern tip of Morgan County, was founded by a company of British and American capitalists who cleverly traded on the popularity of Thomas Hughes, a noted English author and social reformer of the time, to draw attention to their real estate venture, later to be described as "the last attempt at English colonization in America."

Hughes, a lawyer and one-time member of Parliament, had gained a high level of name recognition and visibility on both sides of the Atlantic for his 1857 novel, *Tom Brown's School Days,* based loosely upon his own experiences at Rugby, a famous English school for boys. On a visit to the United States in 1870, he was struck by the relative ease with which young graduates of American schools moved into the broad world of work. In contrast, English schools catered almost exclusively to the sons of the upper class, who subsequently could engage in only a few elite callings, all other work being considered beneath them.

The idea for a new American colony integrated across various social barriers began to take shape in the idealistic English writer's mind, and in 1879 he became the central public figure in an Anglo-American company made up of a few wealthy Englishmen and a group of Boston capitalists who owned a large tract of land in East Tennessee. The Bostonians had acquired the property—75,000 acres, with options on another 300,000—as a relocation site for unemployed New Englanders idled by an industrial depression, but improved economic conditions had lessened interest in the venture.

With Hughes in the forefront, the developers, incorporated as the Board of Aid to Land Ownership, proceeded to make the most of a novel concept: aristocratic young Brits and energetic young Yanks working in harmony to build a model community—and, what's more, on Southern soil. Given the recent Civil War and the long history of conflict between Great Britain and its former colony, the prospects for a symbolic reconciliation and reunion in the new Tennessee village attracted broad public interest.

By the time Rugby was officially christened on October 5, 1880, the rising village had become home to a handful of young English colonists and an interesting mix of others, perhaps 100 people in all. The

Tabard Inn, named for the celebrated hostelry in Chaucer's *Canterbury Tales,* welcomed guests and temporary residents, and Christ Church, a backwoods outpost of the Church of England, brought an exotic new air of pomp and antiquity to the religious ambiance of the Cumberland Plateau. Homes and boarding houses and public buildings—most notably, a fine new library soon to be full of Victorian first editions—also were coming along. Almost from the start, Rugby had a look and feel of permanence.

The population grew to about 300 residents by the summer of 1881. Privileged young Englishmen were the most visible in press reports of the colony, but they never were a majority; in fact, Americans outnumbered all Europeans from the start. Men and women from the North and South, and from the Tennessee mountains in between, were joined by men and women from France and Germany as well as England. Thomas Hughes frequently expressed his desire "to have [a positive] influence with the poor whites and blacks," and his reconciling, inclusive spirit pervaded the utopian community.

But in Rugby, as in all Edens, snakes lurked in the shadows. In the late summer of 1881, a typhoid fever epidemic claimed the lives of seven settlers. Many residents of Rugby pulled up stakes and left in panic; by the end of the year, only about 60 people remained. With gradual recovery over the next few years, the population rebounded to about 450, and there were 65 homes and other buildings in use—but then the Tabard Inn was destroyed by fire, and all of the various plans for industry and agriculture to sustain the colony financially proved to be ineffective. Land sales never reached expectations, and legal problems cropped up, and the school that was to have been the pride of the English Rugby never reached its potential.

Inevitably, the high-born Englishmen were blamed for virtually every shortcoming, they and Thomas Hughes, but in truth it was the profit-driven English and American investors whose poor judgment was most costly. They tried to micromanage the community from London and Boston, and in so doing tied the hands of the resident leaders and managers who struggled in vain to keep the community afloat. Hughes visited Rugby almost every year through 1887, but never lived there (though his mother and brother did). In 1892, when he was past 70 and his would-be utopia was past saving, he expressed in a letter to one of the residents his abiding faith "that good seed was sown when Rugby was founded and that someday the reapers will come along with joy, bearing heavy sheaves with them."

Nothing so grand ever transpired. But in 1966 a small group of interested Tennesseans established the Rugby Restoration Association to save the historic church and library and other remaining buildings, and under the leadership of 17-year-old Brian Stagg of the nearby Deer Lodge community, the organization began a process that is now bearing significant fruit. Historic Rugby is a residential community once again, and an important tourist attraction as well. The long-ago dreams of Thomas Hughes and the more recent visions of the late Brian Stagg have not been in vain.

John Egerton, Nashville

SUGGESTED READING: John Egerton, *Visions of Utopia: Nashoba, Rugby, Ruskin and the "New Communities" in Tennessee's Past* (1977)

SEE: BIG SOUTH FORK NATIONAL RIVER AND RECREATIONAL AREA; MORGAN COUNTY

RUGEL, FERDINAND (1806–1879) was a professional field botanist who primarily collected in the Southern Appalachians, Florida, and Cuba. His collections were sold in Europe, mainly through Robert James Shuttleworth, a British-born botanist who lived in Switzerland and France. Rugel was born near Altdorf, Wurttemburg, on January 26, 1806. He became an M.D. by serving an apprenticeship with a pharmaceutical house in Berne, Switzerland, where he became interested in botany. By 1838 he was in the field collecting for extended periods and by 1839 was a professional collector. In that year he spent at least four months in the field, traveling widely.

In 1840 Rugel came to the United States to collect biological specimens in the Southern Appalachians, though he supported himself as a pharmacist. Rugel traveled to Portsmouth, Virginia, and Knoxville, Tennessee, finally venturing into Dandridge, Tennessee in 1842. In Dandridge, he met and married Laura Bell.

Until 1849, Rugel was primarily a plant collector, although he seems to have practiced medicine at Dandridge in the mid-1840s. After 1849 he moved to Knoxville, where he worked for a wholesale drug firm. Sometime after the Civil War he moved to Jefferson County, near Talbot. Before 1849 and after 1865, Rugel occasionally left Tennessee on extended collecting trips, going as far as Cuba. In his later years he began to emphasize the southwest, especially Texas. As late as 1878, Rugel still did significant field work. He died on December 31, 1879, in Jefferson County.

James X. Corgan, Austin Peay State University

SUGGESTED READING: James X. Corgan, "Notes on Tennessee's Pioneer Scientists," *Journal of the Tennessee Academy of Science* 53(1978): 2–7

SEE: JEFFERSON COUNTY

RUNYON, MARVIN T. (1924–), president of Nissan, U.S.A., Chairman of the Board of Tennessee Valley Authority, and Postmaster General, was born in Ft.

Worth, Texas, on September 16, 1924. He did not become a Tennessean until 1980 but has since maintained a home in the state. He has become one of the most important Tennesseans in the twentieth century.

Runyon began his career at the Ford Motor Company as a factory line worker in 1943. After serving as an Air Force B-29 flight engineer in World War II, Runyon took advantage of the GI Bill to get a B.S. in Engineering Management from Texas A&M in 1948. He returned to Ford, becoming Vice-President of Body and Assembly Operations in 1977. By 1980 he had become extremely frustrated at union rules and top management by accountants and not operations personnel.

In that year Marvin Runyon became President and Chief Executive Officer of Nissan Motor Manufacturing Corporation, U.S.A., when that Japanese-owned automobile company agreed to locate somewhere in the southern United States, a dream of relocation which Runyon had held for some time. Three individuals may have transformed modern Tennessee manufacturing more than any others by their choice of Smyrna as the location of that Nissan plant: Runyon, Smyrna Mayor Sam Ridley, and Governor Lamar Alexander. The choice was influenced by Tennessee's anti-union reputation and a location which was directly on the main line of the CSX Railroad from Nashville to Atlanta and also near I-24. Tennessee agreed to build an interstate connector and to train the employees extensively.

Runyon led the company to build the largest single building in use as an automobile assembly plant anywhere in the world. The company spent $63 million training its employees and adopted the latest robotic techniques and Japanese "just in time" assembly techniques which used over 2,000 parts supplied by outside companies. Originally many of these parts came from Japan but eventually almost all were produced within 100 miles of Smyrna. Runyon would become famous in Tennessee for adopting the Japanese idea that companies should be extensively involved in community support, such as for symphonies and recreational parks.

In 1988, after his first wife's death, Runyon accepted an appointment by President Ronald Reagan as the Chairman of the Board of the Tennessee Valley Authority. He found an agency that was dated in its operations and practically crippled by a failed attempt to develop nuclear power. Memphis and some other cities were threatening to buy their power elsewhere. Within a year, he had reduced the workforce by nearly one-third and economized operations so well that TVA held its wholesale costs of electricity until 1997, moving it from a high cost to a very lost cost power producer. Runyon's solution to the nuclear power problem was to shut down the proposed Hartsville plant and to end any further plans for opening new plants. Not all of this was popular with the TVA workforce but it was very popular with the general Tennessee population.

In 1992 Runyon was appointed Postmaster General of the United States by President George Bush. Runyon applied his business background to streamlining postal service operations. By 1994 he became the first Postmaster General since Benjamin Franklin to run a surplus that kept mail rates constant. He retired in 1998 and returned to Tennessee.

Fred S. Rolater, Middle Tennessee StateUniversity
SEE: NISSAN; TENNESSEE VALLEY AUTHORITY

RURAL AFRICAN-AMERICAN CHURCH PROJECT
seeks to identify and document historic African-American churches located in rural areas throughout Tennessee. Administered by the Center for Historic Preservation at Middle Tennessee State University, the program began in 1997 as a long-term effort to identify, analyze, and interpret significant African-American rural churches. Initial projects include a statewide survey of extant historic churches, a research report delineating the historical and architectural patterns associated with the churches, and nomination of individual churches to the National Register of Historic Places.

For Tennessee's African Americans, there are no more important places associated with community, history, and identity than their churches. Especially in the countryside, rural churches, often with adjacent historic cemeteries, schools, and fraternal lodges, are valuable places to study and document the African-American experience. Rural churches often became the predominant space within the built environment to express community and culture. In the 1920s rural African-American churches often sponsored the construction of Rosenwald schools, with the schools frequently constructed on adjoining property. In small towns African-American congregations also sponsored Rosenwald projects. Later, as Rosenwald schools were closed or abandoned, local churches would incorporate the buildings into their own physical plants, as at the Oak Grove CME Church in Shelby County. As the twentieth century progressed, the attention of local congregations turned towards the Civil Rights Movement, and church buildings became the sites for planning anti-segregation demonstrations and for hosting voter registration drives. Many rural historic churches are monuments to, and significant places directly involved with, the local fight for civil rights. Their importance in this regard is demonstrated by the fact that churches were sometimes bombed, burned, or defaced by those attempting to stop integration. This statewide research effort, the first of its kind in the nation, seeks to establish a long-term documentary project which would serve all Tennesseans for years to come.

Nancy C. Tinker, Charleston, S.C.
SEE: CENTER FOR HISTORIC PRESERVATION; CHRISTIAN
METHODIST EPISCOPAL CHURCH; JULIUS ROSENWALD
FUND

RUSKIN COOPERATIVE ASSOCIATION (RCA)
existed in Dickson County, Tennessee, from 1894 until
1899. Established at Tennessee City, the colony soon
moved five miles away, to a site by a large cave on
Yellow Creek which still bears the name Ruskin.
Named for English social critic John Ruskin and
inspired also by Americans Edward Bellamy and
Laurence Gronlund, this secular cooperative colony
grew from the efforts of Julius Wayland and profits
and publicity from his socialist weekly, *The Coming
Nation.* Wayland relocated the paper from Versailles,
Indiana, and it became a vital part of the RCA.
Colonists came primarily from the middle and far
West. While membership, obtained by purchasing a
$500 no-yield share and demonstrating a commit-
ment to cooperative living, never exceeded a few
hundred, the eyes of the world were upon the experimental colony.

The experiment did not lead to anything larger.
The charismatic and entrepreneurial Wayland left
after leading Ruskin for only a year, exacerbating factionalism within RCA. While some Ruskinites sought
to apply radical ideas and help bring about a
"coming nation" based on cooperation over competition and common over individual ownership, others
sought and found at Ruskin a haven for threatened
American values such as economic and political independence. Tensions between these forward and backward looking visions, which Wayland may have been
able to reconcile, ultimately destroyed the RCA.

Yet in its short existence, notable practices and
phenomena in addition to the cooperative commonwealth abounded. These included: the use of scrip
money, several entrepreneurial ventures, and the
implementation of innovative educational practices.
By fashioning a system based upon the labor theory
of value to counteract the "wage slavery" of the
industrial age, the RCA sought to reward laborer as
producer. Colonists worked for scrip money—currency based upon work hours—which could be
exchanged either for labor or for goods priced upon
the same principle. Labor included newspaper work,
farming, and preparing meals for the cooperative
dining hall. Members also operated and produced
goods for several mail order ventures undertaken to
keep RCA afloat, including the production and sale
of suspenders, natural chewing gum, and cereal
coffee. As the latter two products imply, the colony
was within the same cultural milieu as sanitaria of
the day, including those of John Harvey Kellogg and
C.W. Post. Colonists grew their own food, many practiced vegetarianism, and alcohol was forbidden on
colony grounds.

RCA also offered self-improvement through free
medical care and free education for members. From
its beginnings and, by March 1896, under the leadership of Isaac Broome, the colony sought to implement

The printery at Ruskin, 1894.

SPECIAL COLLECTIONS, UNIVERSITY OF TENNESSEE, KNOXVILLE

innovative educational ideas. In the spirit of John Ruskin, Julius Wayland and his successors saw better education as fundamental to the transformation of society, an essential if "ignorance is to be dethroned." And the coming nation would need a class of "philosopher kings" to lead it. Most colony leaders stressed childhood education, including the new concept of kindergarten, as well as higher and continuing education for adults. They fostered the latter with an extensive library and frequent lectures and performing arts events at Ruskin. Broome's crowning achievement was to have been the Ruskin College of the New Economy, which would reflect John Ruskin's own emphasis on experiential learning and the importance of fostering an aesthetic appreciation for life's endeavors.

However, the growing majority at Ruskin had little appreciation for the ideologues's efforts on their behalf. The College never developed beyond a grand vision and a groundbreaking ceremony featuring Henry Demarest Lloyd. Many Ruskinites, an embittered Broome later reflected, preferred to "smoke, gossip, and spit tobacco" rather than develop their minds. The seemingly harmless split between those who sought escape from a changing world and the more doctrinaire who sought to revolutionize society through the microcosm of the RCA ultimately destroyed the colony.

By July 1899 factionalism brought disintegration. The cooperative was placed in receivership, ending two years of lawsuits between the two factions over issues relating to ownership and control of the RCA. By this point, many from both sides had given up the cause, and efforts by several dozen of the less doctrinaire faction to continue the cooperative and the newspaper on swampy land in Duke, Georgia, were short-lived.

Clay Bailey, Montgomery Bell Academy

SUGGESTED READING: Clay Bailey, "Looking Backward at the Ruskin Cooperative Association," *Tennessee Historical Quarterly* 53(1994): 100–113

SEE: DICKSON COUNTY

RUSSELL, LIANE BRAUCH (1923–) and **WILLIAM LAWSON** (1910–) were leaders of mammalian genetics studies at Oak Ridge National Laboratory. Liane Brauch was born in Austria in 1923. She immigrated to the United States, enrolled in Hunter College, and earned her Ph.D. in zoology at the University of Chicago. William Lawson Russell was born in England in 1910, graduated from Oxford University in 1932, and immigrated to the United States, earning his Ph.D. in zoology at the University of Chicago in 1937. The Russells married and both worked at Jackson Memorial Laboratory in Maine before transferring to Oak Ridge in 1947 to conduct genetics research focusing on radiation-induced mutations.

The Russells developed efficient methods to determine the rates at which mouse genes were mutated by different radiation types and levels. They set up a laboratory, called the "Mouse House," to study mutations through generations. Their discovery that the mouse mutations' rate was several times higher than the rate for fruit flies resulted in reductions in the permissible levels for occupational radiation exposure. Liane Russell's discovery of the vulnerability of mice embryos to radiation led nationally to ending diagnostic pelvic x-rays for childbearing women, except during part of the menstrual cycle.

The Russells expanded their research to include the genetic effects on mice of chemicals from drugs, fuels, and wastes. In 1975 Liane Russell developed a fur-spot test for identifying chemicals likely to be mutagenic in reproductive cells. She subsequently expanded her research into modern molecular genetics, seeking human genes that might be responsible for malfunctions such as diseased kidneys. The Russells also formed the Tennessee Citizens for Wilderness Planning, seeking stringent control of strip-mining and preservation of wilderness areas. Their efforts fostered creation of the Big South Fork National Recreation Area in northern Tennessee and southern Kentucky. The Russells received many awards for their achievements and were recognized as one of the most fruitful scientific collaborations in American history.

Leland R. Johnson, Clio Research Institute

Suggested Readings Leland Johnson and Daniel Schaffer, *Oak Ridge National Laboratory: The First Fifty Years* (1994); W.L. Russell and Liane Brauch Russell, "Radiation-Induced Genetic Damage in Mice," in *Progress in Nuclear Energy: Biological Sciences* (1959)

SEE: BIG SOUTH FORK NATIONAL RIVER AND RECREATIONAL AREA; OAK RIDGE NATIONAL LABORATORY

RUTHERFORD COUNTY was created in 1803, from sections of Davidson, Wilson, Williamson, and Sumner counties. Named in honor of Griffith Rutherford, an Irish immigrant who served on the council of the Southwest Territory, the county's 619 square miles encompass the geographic center of the state.

Until 1794 the land that is Rutherford County was the seasonal hunting and fishing ground of the Cherokees, Chickasaws, Shawnees, Creeks, and Choctaws. Early maps depict the Nickajack Trail and the Creek War Trace converging near present-day Murfreesboro at the springs camp of Black Fox, a noted Cherokee chief. After a series of treaties negotiated between settlers and native tribes failed, militia under Nashville founder James Robertson wiped out Black Fox's camp. The Cherokees last used the camp springs site of the legendary leader as they were forcibly marched along the "Trail of Tears" to reservations in Oklahoma.

Stones River, a major tributary of the Cumberland River named for explorer Uriah Stone around 1767, provided a transportation route and water source for settlers and power for mills built throughout the county. Jefferson, a river town now covered by the waters of Percy Priest Lake, was the first county seat. Centrally located Murfreesboro gained county seat status in 1811. From 1818 to 1826, Murfreesboro was the capital of Tennessee. Smyrna, LaVergne, and Eagleville are incorporated towns within the county.

A moderate climate supporting a long growing season, proximity to Nashville, access to market by water, road, and, by the 1850s, the Nashville and Chattanooga Railroad combined to promote an agrarian base of considerable diversity and wealth. A few holdings exceeded 1,000 acres. Oaklands, established by the Murfree and Maney families in the 1820s, had 1,500 acres and, as illustrated by the 1850s Italianate house museum, was a very prosperous estate. The county now has 200,000 acres of farm land and 22 certified Century Farms (those that have been in the same family for at least 100 years). Livestock and grains continue to be the county's chief agricultural products.

Rutherford County's location between Nashville and Chattanooga made it a highly contested area during the Civil War. The Battle of Stones River was one of the bloodiest confrontations of the western theater. To supply the Union advance to the south, General William Rosecrans ordered the construction of the largest earthworks fortification built during the war—Fortress Rosecrans. Of the county's many Civil War stories, none is better known than that of Smyrna's Sam Davis, who was only 21 when captured, tried, and hanged as a Confederate spy. He is buried in the family cemetery on the grounds of his home, now a state historic site. Another noted Confederate scout from Rutherford County was Dewitt Jobe, who also was executed for spying in 1864.

Education has traditionally been a priority in Rutherford County. Nineteenth century schools included Bradley Academy, established around 1811 and attended by James K. Polk and John Bell, and Union University, Soule College, and Jefferson Academy. The Tennessee College for Women, completed in 1907, was a landmark of education as well as Classical Revival architecture. It was followed in 1911 by the Middle Tennessee Normal School, now Middle Tennessee State University (MTSU).

Denied formal education for generations, Rutherford County's African-American population took advantage of schools which opened across the county in the wake of Reconstruction and succeeding decades. Bradley Academy, reopened in the 1880s as a school for African Americans, became the county's first accredited high school for blacks.

A county hospital opened in the 1920s, as did a county health department funded by the Commonwealth Fund of New York. The Alvin C. York Veterans Administration Hospital is named in honor of Tennessee's World War I hero and its construction by the Public Works Administration represented a lasting New Deal legacy to the county. Sewart Air Force Base, near Smyrna, was a product of the country's preparations for World War II and remained in operation until the 1960s. Major employers in the county's history include the Carnation Milk Plant, Tennessee Red Cedar Wooden Ware Company, Sunshine Hosiery Mills, General Electric, National Healthcare Corporation, Bridgestone/Firestone, Inc., Ingram Distribution, and Samsonite Furniture Company. Nissan Motor Manufacturing Corporation, USA, is the largest employer in the county.

Rutherford Countians of note include Sarah Childress (Mrs. James K. Polk); Governor John Price Buchanan and grandson James Buchanan, a 1986 Nobel Prize winner; poet Will Allen Dromgoole; congressman/historian James D. Richardson; novelist Mary Noailles Murfree; writer Andrew Nelson Lytle; sportswriter Grantland Rice; country music's "Uncle Dave" Macon; Jean Marie Faircloth (Mrs. Douglas MacArthur), and NASA astronaut, Rhea Seddon.

Caneta Skelley Hankins, Middle Tennessee State University

SEE: BRADLEY ACADEMY; BUCHANAN, JAMES; BUCHANAN, JOHN P.; COMMONWEALTH FUND; DAVIS, SAM; DROMGOOLE, WILL ALLEN; FARMS, TENNESSEE CENTURY; LYTLE, ANDREW NELSON; MACON, DAVID H.; MIDDLE TENNESSEE STATE UNIVERSITY; MURFREE, MARY N.; MURFREESBORO; OAKLANDS; POLK, SARAH C.; RICE, GRANTLAND; RUTHERFORD, GRIFFITH; STONES RIVER, BATTLE OF; TENNESSEE COLLEGE FOR WOMEN

RUTHERFORD, GRIFFITH (1720–1805), was born in Ireland in 1720. Soon after his birth his parents took voyage to America. Unfortunately, both of his parents died at sea, and Griffith arrived in America a homeless orphan. It is thought that he lived with a cousin in Virginia until about the age of 19 when he went to North Carolina.

In North Carolina he distinguished himself as an Indian fighter, a member of the North Carolina legislature and later the Senate, and as a brigadier general in the Revolutionary War. He was captured by Loyalists and sent to prison in St. Augustine, Florida. He remained there for about a year in a dungeon and almost died of poor sanitation and lack of food.

Following the Revolutionary War, Griffith was one of the commissioners who surveyed military land grants in Tennessee. Intrigued with the region's potential, he sold his property in North Carolina and moved to Sumner County, Tennessee, where he lived until his death in 1805.

Among the honors bestowed upon this famous general was the presentation of a silver snuff box given to him by George Washington in recognition of his military service. Two counties have been named in honor of Rutherford, one in North Carolina and the other in Tennessee. A monument to the general, dedicated in 1946, is located at Murfreesboro, the county seat of Rutherford.

Mabel Pittard, Murfreesboro

SUGGESTED READING: C.C. Sims, *A History of Rutherford County* (1947)

SEE: LAND GRANTS; RUTHERFORD COUNTY

RYE, THOMAS CLARKE (1863–1953), Governor, was born in a log cabin in 1863 to Wayne and Elizabeth Atchison Rye of Benton County. Growing up on his father's farm, he attended county public schools. After studying law in Charlotte, North Carolina, he returned to Tennessee in 1884 to practice law in Camden, the county seat of Benton County, and in 1888 he married Betty Arnold.

Rye moved to Paris, Tennessee, in 1902, where he became district attorney general of Henry County from 1910 to 1914 and earned a reputation for strong law enforcement and a firm stand against bootleggers. As a prohibitionist unattached to party factionalism, Rye became an acceptable Democratic candidate for the 1914 gubernatorial race. In an effort to unite the party, the Democrats wrote a platform favoring prohibition. Rye received the support of Luke Lea, founder of the *Tennessean,* and former governor Malcolm R. Patterson, a recent convert to the prohibition cause. Republicans and Independents nominated Ben W. Hooper for a third term, but Rye won the election with a vote of 137,656 to 116,667.

During Rye's administration, the state's industrial growth flourished as a result of the prosperity that accompanied World War I. The Alcoa aluminum plant established near Maryville and the DuPont munitions factory established at Hadley's Bend of the Cumberland River near Nashville employed thousands of Tennesseans. Rye's administration is best known for the "Ouster Law," enacted in January 1915. This law provided for the removal of any public official for incompetence or unwillingness to enforce the law. The measure targeted Memphis mayor Edward H. Crump, whose failure to enforce prohibition laws kept saloons open in that city. The state attorney general's office filed suit in October 1915, initiating the action that removed Crump from office.

Other legislation under Rye's two-term administration included the creation of the state highway department, the founding of a governor-appointed board to control state penal and charitable institutions, the registration of automobiles and trucks, a special highway tax to match federal funds, a general budget system, the organization of a state board of education, and the levying of a tax to support state high schools. A 1917 act significantly altered partisan politics by requiring primary elections rather than conventions to nominate party candidates.

At the end of his second term, Rye returned to his Paris law practice. He died on September 12, 1953, and is buried in Paris.

Anne-Leslie Owens, Tennessee Historical Society

SEE: ALCOA; BENTON COUNTY; CRUMP, EDWARD H.; HENRY COUNTY; OLD HICKORY; TEMPERANCE

RYMAN AUDITORIUM was built as the Union Gospel Tabernacle between 1888 and 1892 and gained international renown from 1943 to 1974, when it was home to the Grand Ole Opry, the premier live country music radio broadcast of Nashville station WSM. It is recognized as the "mother church" of modern country music. With the powerful WSM signal, the Grand Ole Opry reached millions of households in the United States and Canada. It made the music careers of many country music stars, and membership in the Opry remains a coveted honor.

Funding for the construction of the estimated $100,000 original tabernacle came largely from the tireless efforts of Reverend Sam Jones and the generosity of steamboat captain and businessman Tom Ryman. Local Nashville architect Hugh Thompson designed the building in a dignified Victorian Gothic style, distinguished by its steeply gabled roof, its gable-front entrance, and tall Gothic lancet windows. In 1897 the seating capacity was expanded when the Confederate Veterans Association donated funds to construct a balcony, which has since been known as the Confederate Gallery. Other citizen groups raised money in 1901 and 1904 so that the stage could be enlarged for Grand Opera productions from the Metropolitan Opera of New York City and the French Grand Opera Company of New Orleans. After Ryman's death in 1904, Jones proposed that the building's name be changed to honor Ryman and from that point on, the building was known as Ryman Auditorium.

Throughout the years, the Ryman has hosted lectures, classical concerts, popular music performances, conventions, and dramatic plays. Speakers included the populist leader William Jennings Bryan and African-American leader Booker T. Washington, while performers ranged from Enrico Caruso to Bob Hope to Sarah Bernhardt. After the construction of the War Memorial Building in the mid-1920s, many classical music performances and plays moved to that new venue. But the Ryman regained its position as the city's focal point for live performances when the Grand Ole Opry moved its weekly broadcasts to the building in 1943. It was the center of a lively music and honky-tonk scene that centered along adjacent Broadway, spawning such local institutions as Tootsie's Orchid Lounge and Ernest Tubb's Record Shop.

In 1974 the owners of the Grand Ole Opry left the Ryman for new quarters at the Opryland complex. Once threatened with demolition, the building was saved, but it slowly deteriorated as it was used only for tours and for occasional concerts, television tapings, videos, and movies. In 1988–1990 the owners stabilized the building and in 1993 Gaylord Entertainment commissioned Nashville architectural firm Hart Freeland Roberts to restore the Ryman to its former glory as a grand public assembly hall. With 1,500 seats available, performances are scheduled throughout the year.

Carroll Van West, Middle Tennessee State University

SEE: GRAND OLE OPRY; JONES, SAMUEL; NASHVILLE; OPERA; TUBB, ERNEST; WSM

S

SAFFORD, JAMES MERRILL (1822–1907) was a geologist, chemist, and professor in Tennessee from 1848–1900. Originally, his highest qualification was training in the famous chemistry lab at Yale, but his fame is from geology. Safford was a professor at Cumberland University from 1848 to 1873. From 1873 to 1900 he was half-time Professor of Chemistry in the proprietary Medical School of the University of Nashville and Vanderbilt University. From 1875 to 1900 he was also half-time Professor in the Academic Department of Vanderbilt University where he taught geology and botany.

Safford's 54 books, reports, and maps were about, or included, geology. His 1869 book *Geology of Tennessee* is still frequently cited. Much of his work applied geology to practical uses and was supported and published by Tennessee state agencies. He was State Geologist from 1854 until retirement. For 30 years he served on the Board of Health, and he was a chemist for the Tennessee Bureau of Agriculture for several years in the 1870s and 1880s. Geological applications included topography and health, water supply, and soils as well as mineral resources. Safford and J.B. Killebrew published a voluminous report on the resources of Tennessee and later a textbook on geology of Tennessee that was used in high schools for over 25 years.

Safford was a lifelong Presbyterian. At Vanderbilt, while in the field, he led students in prayers to start each day. Students remarked on his kindly nature and tendency to punctuate lectures with bits of classical poetry.

Richard G. Stearns, Vanderbilt University
SEE: EDUCATION, HIGHER; GEOLOGY

SANDERS, NEWELL (1850-ca. 1938), was born in 1850 in Indiana and moved as an adult to Chattanooga, at the encouragement of General John T. Wilder. Recognizing the need in the South for reliable farm machinery, Wilder encouraged Sanders to produce plows. His Chattanooga Plow Company was incorporated in 1883.

Sanders soon became one of the business leaders of the rapidly growing city. The Tennessee River Improvement Association, which advocated a general program to develop the Tennessee River and its tributaries, named him president in 1898. He also served as president of the Chattanooga Steamboat Company, as director of the Nashville, Chattanooga, and St. Louis Railway, and was responsible for the surface railroad that was built on Lookout Mountain.

A politically active Republican, Sanders served on the School Board and on the Board of Alderman, where he became the protégé of fellow Chattanooga Republican, Henry Clay Evans. Sanders managed Evans's controversial 1894 gubernatorial campaign and remained active in Tennessee politics into the twentieth century. In 1912, following the death of U.S. Senator Robert L. Taylor, Governor Ben Hooper appointed Sanders to finish out the term. As a Senator one of his greatest achievements was the enactment of the Interstate Bill which prohibited the shipment of liquor from wet into dry states. He was a proponent for woman suffrage and his family's influence made Lookout Mountain the first locality in Tennessee to give women the vote. Sanders ran for the Senate in 1922 but lost to Kenneth McKellar. He continued to be active in Chattanooga's affairs until his death at age 88.

Patricia Bernard Ezzell, Tennessee Valley Authority
SEE: CHATTANOOGA; EVANS, HENRY C.; TEMPERANCE

SANFORD, EDWARD TERRY (1865–1930), influential Tennessee lawyer, civic leader, orator, and U.S. Supreme Court Justice, was born in Knoxville on July 23, 1865, the eldest of six children, whose wealthy parents stressed education and achievement. He received two bachelor's degrees from the University of Tennessee by the age of 18 and later added an A.B. and an M.A. from Harvard University. At the age of 24, he received an LL.B. from Harvard Law School, where he served as editor of the *Harvard Law Review.*

In 1890 Sanford began a Knoxville law practice, earning a reputation as an accomplished and meticulous practitioner of chancery and appellate cases. A year later, he married Lutie Mallory Woodruff of Knoxville; they became the parents of two children.

Recognized for his charm and scholarship, he became a trustee of the University of Tennessee in 1897 and the following year was made a part-time law professor. He wrote the first history of the university (initially presented as an address during the Tennessee Centennial). He was also a founding member and president of the board of George Peabody College for Teachers, in addition to holding important offices in numerous state and national organizations. He was one of Tennessee's most popular platform speakers.

In 1907 he was appointed U.S. Assistant Attorney General. Following 17 months in Washington, he was appointed U.S. District Judge of Eastern and Middle Tennessee by President Theodore Roosevelt. Though uncomfortable with some of the duties of a trial judge, Sanford had an impeccable record and gained a reputation as a lenient, thorough, and impartial judge.

In 1923, backed by his judicial record and longtime friend Chief Justice William Howard Taft, Sanford was appointed Justice of the Supreme Court by President Warren G. Harding. His 130 opinions were generally conservative, favoring strict adherence to antitrust laws. He was known for his "technical" cases, which involved the interpretation of difficult procedural or statutory matters. The most important of these was the *Pocket Veto Case* (1929), which clarified the rules by which a president could use this power, a question that had remained open for 140 years. He wrote only seven dissents, most notably in *Adkins v. Children's Hospital* (1923) in which the Court invalidated the District of Columbia minimum wage law for women.

He is best known for his majority opinion in *Gitlow v. New York* (1925), involving a socialist who had published a manifesto which advocated the violent overthrow of the government. More important than the outcome of the decision, which upheld the defendant's conviction, was Justice Sanford's statement that "we assume that freedom of speech and of the press are among the fundamental liberties protected by the Fourteenth Amendment."[1] This introduced a cornerstone of modern constitutional jurisprudence known as the incorporation doctrine, under which the guarantees of the Bill of Rights have been extended to actions of the states. Heretofore, only the just compensation of the takings clause had been applied to the states. In time, most of the other Bill of Rights have been made applicable as well, leading to important protections for persons accused of crime.

Because of his brief service on the Court, Justice Sanford received a rating of "average" in a survey of Supreme Court Justices. Even his sudden death on March 8, 1930, was overshadowed by the passing of Justice William Howard Taft on the same day.

Lewis L. Laska, Tennessee State University

CITATION:

(1) Lewis L. Laska, "Mr. Justice Sanford and the Fourteenth Amendment," *Tennessee Historical Quarterly* 33(1974): 210.

SEE: LAW; UNIVERSITY OF TENNESSEE

SASSER, JAMES RALPH (1936–), attorney, U.S. Senator, and Ambassador to the People's Republic of China, was born in Memphis in 1936, the son of Joseph Ralph and Mary Nell Gray Sasser. He attended the public schools of Nashville and was enrolled at the University of Tennessee, Knoxville, 1954–1955. He completed undergraduate studies at Vanderbilt University, Nashville, and received the B.A. degree in 1958. In 1961 he graduated with the J.D. degree from Vanderbilt Law School. Admitted to the Tennessee bar the same year, he practiced law in the Nashville firm of Goodpasture, Carpenter, Woods and Sasser, 1961–1977.

Active in the Democratic Party since his work in Estes Kefauver's 1960 senate campaign, Sasser served as chairman of the state party from 1973 to 1976. In 1976 Sasser successfully campaigned for the U.S. Senate, defeating a veteran Democratic party candidate in the primary and the incumbent Republican senator in the general election. Twice reelected, he served 18 consecutive years in the Senate. Chairman of the Senate Budget Committee, 1989–1995, he played a decisive role in the passage of the 1993 Deficit Reduction Package. He also chaired the military construction subcommittee of the Committee on Appropriations; the subcommittee on International Finance and Monetary Policy of the Senate Banking Committee; the subcommittee on General Services, Federalism, and the District of Columbia of the Senate Governmental Affairs Committee; and the subcommittee on Legislative Branch of the Committee on Appropriations.

In 1996 Sasser became U.S. Ambassador to the People's Republic of China. During 1995 he had been a Fellow in the Kennedy School of Government, Harvard University. He received honorary degrees from Tusculum College in Greeneville and Lane College in Jackson. Sasser served as a regent of the Smithsonian Institution, 1987–1995, and as a trustee of the Sgt. Alvin C. York Historical Association, 1993–1995.

In 1962 Sasser married the former Mary Gorman of Louisville, Kentucky. They are the parents of two children, Elizabeth B. Sasser and James Gray Sasser.

Walter T. Durham, Gallatin

SEE: BROCK, WILLIAM E., III; FRIST, WILLIAM

SATURN. On July 31, 1985, Governor Lamar Alexander announced that a new General Motors company—Saturn—would build a giant industrial complex in Spring Hill, a small town located 30 miles south of Nashville on U.S. Highway 31 in northern Maury County. Spring Hill had only recently passed the 1,000 population mark. The site of camp revivals in the early 1800s, the community was recognized primarily for its scenic agricultural landscape and its varied nineteenth century domestic architecture. The community's grandest plantation was Rippa Villa, where the Nathaniel Cheairs family hosted Confederate officers on the morning of November 30, 1864, prior to their departure for the Battle of Franklin.

Following the 1985 announcements that Spring Hill had been chosen over 37 other sites, the community almost immediately began its metamorphosis. Land prices escalated overnight, and farms and homes sold at spectacular prices. Spring Hill, along with Columbia and Franklin, prepared for Saturn's arrival with plans for new and improved infrastructure, apartments, homes, and support and satellite businesses. By July 1986 excavation of 2,400 acres had begun for the 4.3 million square-foot factory.

General Motors created the Saturn Corporation to reform the American automobile industry, which was languishing from continual increases in Japanese import sales. The name was derived from the Saturn space project that propelled the United States ahead of the Soviet Union in the race to the moon.

GM and the United Auto Workers joined forces in an unprecedented cooperative effort to redesign the automobile manufacturing process, including its technology, labor, sales, and service techniques. Two groups within GM began a long-range study of companies considered leaders and innovators in quality, service, and cost. They also enlisted ideas and comments from people in all aspects of the automobile industry as well as a cross-section of company employees. The result was the unique team approach, which is the Saturn hallmark.

The first Saturn rolled off the line on July 30, 1990. Later that year *Popular Science* named Saturn one of "The Year's 100 Greatest Achievements in Science and Technology." By 1991 Saturn ranked first in sales per outlet, marking the first time in 15 years that a domestic brand held that honor. Accolades accumulated, and sales surpassed expectations, producing a profit for the company by 1994. By 1995 the Spring Hill plant had produced one million cars. The company's successful product and approach had altered

American automotive history. In 1996 Saturn employed 9, 591 employees.

The changes required to accommodate Saturn have been a challenge for state and local government, private enterprise, and individual residents in Spring Hill and surrounding communities. Not all of the ensuing growth and development have been welcome, nor have they been planned as well as long-time residents and newcomers alike might wish. The relocation of many individuals and families from GM's other facilities has changed the demographics of local society as much as construction has altered the landscape. From its inception, however, the Saturn Corporation has made unprecedented efforts to orient and ease the transition for its relocated employees and its neighbors. Classes, town meetings, tours of the facility, landscape design to buffer intrusion, additional environmental controls, and contributions to many local charities and concerns have helped to ease some of the concerns and criticisms. Saturn also donated Rippa Villa to Maury County, along with funds to assist in its renovation as a visitor's center. The architecture of the past and future face each other across U.S. Highway 31, and while some vestiges of Spring Hill's pre-1985 history remain, its future is inextricably bound to the fortunes of Saturn.

Caneta Skelley Hankins, Middle Tennessee State University

SEE: ALEXANDER, LAMAR; INDUSTRY; MAURY COUNTY

SAUNDERS, CLARENCE (1881–1953) changed the way people buy their groceries. In his innovative Piggly Wiggly self-service stores no clerks fetched groceries for customers. Instead shoppers selected from items placed on shelves within easy reach. While Saunders did not open the first self-service store, he is credited with selling this idea to a public still accustomed to being waited upon in stores.

Saunders was born in 1881 to an impoverished Virginia family, who moved to Palmyra, Montgomery County, Tennessee. Young Saunders found his calling in a Clarksville wholesale grocery house. While still in his twenties, Saunders left Clarksville for a sales position in a Memphis grocery company. A bold and observant salesman, Saunders paid close attention to the business methods of his retail clients. Displeased by the lack of efficiency, he developed the idea of self-service.

On September 11, 1916, Saunders opened his Piggly Wiggly store for business. Shoppers liked the store where prices were cheaper than competing markets. Within a year he sold Piggly Wiggly franchises across the nation. By 1923 the Piggly Wiggly chain included 1,268 stores, selling $100 million in groceries, the third largest retail grocery business in the nation. Piggly Wiggly stock was traded on the New York Exchange.

Then Saunders managed to lose it all. An attempt to corner the Piggly Wiggly stock failed, costing Saunders millions of dollars. He resigned from Piggly Wiggly and filed for bankruptcy. Immediately, he opened a competing grocery, called the Clarence Saunders Sole Owner of My Name Stores, or the Sole Owner Stores. A successful endeavor until the Great Depression, Saunders once again lost his business in the 1930s.

For the rest of his life, Saunders experimented with an automated grocery store, which he named Keedoozle. It operated on the principles of the vending machine. The customer slipped a key into a coin slot next to a window display. The key activated circuits that released merchandise from the storage room chutes. The merchandise tumbled to conveyor belts and was carried to the shoppers at the cashier's desk. Saunders visualized a system that would dispense groceries quickly, with fewer errors, and simultaneously track inventory. Unfortunately, Keedoozle never operated profitably.

On October 15, 1953, Clarence Saunders died. Having built and lost two fortunes, he will be remembered as the man who brought the retail store into the twentieth century.

Mike Freeman, Memphis

SUGGESTED READING: Mike Freeman, "Clarence Saunders: The Piggly Wiggly Man," *Tennessee Historical Quarterly* 51(1992): 161–169

SEE: PINK PALACE MUSEUM; MEMPHIS

SAVAGE GULF STATE NATURAL AREA is the largest and most significant portion of the South Cumberland State Recreation Area. Located on the Cumberland Plateau in Grundy County, Savage Gulf contains approximately 11,500 acres and its wide ecological diversity has earned it National Natural Landmark status. One-third of the almost 2,300 native plant species identified in Tennessee grow in this natural area. One section of the park contains 500 acres of old growth hardwoods, a rarity in the eastern United States.

The park's name refers, first, to the Savage family who once owned part of the land and, second, to one of the primary gorges that branches out from the headwaters of the Collins River. Savage Gulf has a visitor center, where a path leads to the Great Stone Door, a 150-foot-long natural crevice that leads to an awe-inspiring view of "a vast panorama of rolling mountains and deep gorges, a true wilderness reaching all the way to the horizon."[1] The area also has 50 miles of trails, including the famed Big Creek Trail.

Carroll Van West, Middle Tennessee State University

CITATION:

(1) Terry Livingstone, "Big Creek Trail," *Tennessee Conservationist* (June/August 1991): 15.

SEE: BAGGENSTOSS, HERMAN; GRUNDY COUNTY; SOUTH CUMBERLAND STATE RECREATION AREA

SAVAGE, JOHN HOUSTON (1815–1904), Congressman, state legislator, and veteran of three wars, was born at McMinnville on October 9, 1815, the son of George and Elizabeth Kenner Savage. Savage attended common schools and the Carroll Academy at McMinnville before studying law; he was admitted to the bar in 1839. His law practice began at Smithville but moved to McMinnville after the Civil War.

Savage's political career began in 1841, when he became attorney general for the Fourth Judicial Circuit, a post he kept until 1847. He served as a presidential elector on the Democratic ticket of James K. Polk in 1844. Savage served in the U.S. House of Representatives from 1849–1853 and 1855–1859. He lost a bid for a seat in the Confederate Congress in 1863.

Savage served in three wars. In 1836 he fought in the Seminole War as a private in Captain William Lauderdale's company of mounted volunteers. More than a decade later, he served in the Mexican War, where he held the rank of major. Again in the Civil War, Savage volunteered and was commissioned as a colonel in the Tennessee Sixteenth Infantry, C.S.A. In 1862 he was wounded at Perryville and again at Stones River. In February 1863 Savage resigned his commission in anger over his failure to advance in the ranks. He believed Isham G. Harris received preferential treatment in advancements, and the two men remained bitter personal and political enemies thereafter.

After the war, Savage served three terms in the State House, 1877–1879 and 1887–1891, representing Warren County. He also served a single term in the State Senate, 1879–1881. The Tennessee General Assembly created a weak Railroad Commission in 1883, and Savage headed the three-man regulatory agency. Crippled by weak enabling legislation and stymied by a federal injunction blocking the activities of the agency, the commission made no progress against rebates, differential rates, and other abuses. The 1885 General Assembly rescinded the enabling legislation that created the commission. Many Tennesseans blamed its demise on Savage's uncompromising and "fanatical" enthusiasm for reigning in the transportation giants. Irascible, argumentative, and stubborn, Savage was a Buchanan delegate in the 1890 Democratic gubernatorial convention, but remained ardently opposed to the Populists, who emerged from the agrarian reform movement in 1892. Savage initially opposed the poll tax but supported it in 1889 as a mechanism for ending electoral corruption.

Savage never married. In 1903 he published his memoirs, *The Life of John H. Savage*. Savage died at McMinnville on April 6, 1904, and is buried at Riverside Cemetery. His papers are available at the Tennessee State Library and Archives.

Connie L. Lester, Tennessee Historical Society

SUGGESTED READING: Roger Hart, *Redeemers, Bourbons & Populists: Tennessee, 1870–1896* (1975)

SEE: BUCHANAN, JOHN P.; HARRIS, ISHAM G.; LAUDERDALE, WILLIAM; WARREN COUNTY

SCARBROUGH, W. CARL (1935–), international president of the United Furniture Workers, was born in Henderson, Tennessee, the son of Joseph Scarbrough, a farmer. Scarbrough graduated from Chester County High School in 1952, and married his wife, Faye, that same year. They had two children. Scarbrough began work in the furniture industry in Memphis and joined Local 282 of the United Furniture Workers of America (UFW). He was elected president of the local in 1962, and during the next eight years he expanded its membership from three to nearly 2,000. He was elected UFW international vice-president in 1964, and, as a result of this position, was appointed southern regional director of the union at age 29. Scarbrough was elected UFW secretary-treasurer in 1970, and, after serving in that capacity for four years, was elected to the international presidency in 1974 by the UFW executive board after the death of the incumbent, Fred Fulford.

Joseph Y. Garrison, Tennessee Historical Commission

SEE: CHESTER COUNTY; LABOR

SCARRITT COLLEGE FOR CHRISTIAN WORKERS was moved from its original home in Kansas City, Missouri, to Nashville in 1923. Established as an institution to train women missionaries by the United Methodist Church, the school was dedicated in 1892 as the Scarritt Bible and Training School. When Scarritt College moved to Nashville to be affiliated with the George Peabody College for Teachers, its Methodist leaders broadened its mission to include both male and female church workers and changed the school's name to the Scarritt College for Christian Workers. The college was located along Nineteenth Avenue South, adjacent to the Peabody campus, and, like Peabody, the Scarritt campus was distinguished for its architectural beauty. Henry C. Hibbs of Nashville was the primary architect. His Collegiate Gothic design, which used native Tennessee Crab Orchard stone and Indiana limestone in the buildings, is the best example of that architectural style in the capital city and is rivaled in Tennessee only by the campus of Rhodes College in Memphis. Scarritt's Wrightman Hall, with its 115-foot Gothic tower, was the tallest building in Nashville at the time of its completion and became the campus's landmark. In 1929 the American Institute of Architects awarded a prestigious Gold Medal to Hibbs for his Scarritt design.

The college prospered in its new setting and by the late 1930s its faculty offered a bachelor's degree and graduate education in the fields of community and family service, social work, and religious educa-

tion. After World War II graduate majors in christian education and church music became available. In the 1950s the Methodists expanded world missionary programs and enrollment at Scarritt increased; over 40 percent of their missionaries trained at Scarritt. In the 1960s, however, Scarritt faced difficult times. In 1973 J. Richard Palmer was brought in from Berea College in Kentucky to lead fund-raising and to reverse the college's dwindling enrollment. Programs in continuing education and women's studies were strengthened and expanded. Yet Palmer resigned in 1977, frustrated by internal politics and his lack of success in raising even enough money to cover the college's annual operating expenses. Within another ten years, Scarritt's time as a leading missionary college was over, although the school's program in religious music continued to be recognized as one of the best in the country. In the late 1980s, Scarritt's name and purpose changed to the Scarritt-Bennett Center of the United Methodist Women's Division of the Board of Global Missions. As president of the Women's Missionary Council of the Methodist Episcopal Church, South, Belle H. Bennett initially urged the creation of a training school for missionaries in 1887.

Carroll Van West, Middle Tennessee State University

SEE: EDUCATION, HIGHER; HIBBS, HENRY C.; RELIGION

SCIENCE AND TECHNOLOGY. The history of science and technology in Tennessee dates to the early settlement era when explorers recognized the geological and botanical diversity of the state. Soon after the initial tasks associated with homesteading were completed, a survey of the mapping and geological resources of the state began. Gerard P. Troost, who arrived in Tennessee from New Harmony, Indiana, in 1827, played the most important role in this work. In 1831 he became the first Tennessee State Geologist, adding the duties of completing a geological survey to his teaching responsibilities at the University of Nashville. Tennessee became the fourth state to undertake a geological survey, but whereas other states abandoned the effort, Troost continued this work until his death in 1850. His reports were published in several languages, and his students mapped ten other states. In addition, Troost's many protégés taught geology in numerous colleges and universities and edited scientific journals. Interest in geology and mineralogy continued in the post-Civil War era under the influence of James M. Safford and Joseph B. Killebrew.

Several other Tennesseans later achieved prominence in exploration and mapping. In the mid-nineteenth century, Matthew Fontaine Maury, who grew up in Tennessee, mapped the seas, charted the Gulf Stream, and laid the foundations for the National Weather Bureau. His oceanographic work earned him the sobriquet, "Pathfinder of the Seas." At the end of the century, Edward Emerson Barnard combined his interests and knowledge in astronomy and photography to make the first photographs of the Milky Way. He discovered one of the moons of Jupiter and a ninth magnitude star in the constellation of Ophiuchus, which is named in his honor. In the twentieth century P.V.H. Weems wrote the award winning textbook *Air Navigation* (1931); taught air navigation to Charles Lindbergh; patented the Mark II Plotter and other apparatus and methods for navigator's timekeeping; and established the Institute of Navigation. Toward the end of his life, he taught a pilot class in space navigation at the U.S. Naval Academy. William R. Anderson, another naval officer, commanded the nuclear submarine *Nautilus* in its pathbreaking voyage under the polar icecap, and Rhea Seddon became one of the first American women to travel into space and conduct experiments.

Troost maintained a collection of fossils, minerals, artifacts, and botanical specimens at his Museum of Natural History in Nashville. His research and the collection excited the curiosity of educated Tennesseans, who emulated his collections and developed impressive skills as non-professional collectors and observers. In both the antebellum period and the post-Civil War era, faculty members at Tennessee academies, colleges, and universities prided themselves on their collections of artifacts and fossils. Interest in natural science acquired such public support that both men and women studied geology in many colleges and academies.

Interest in fossils developed along with a fascination for the artifacts from earlier human activity in the state's prehistoric past. Tennesseans quickly recognized the archaeological wealth that lay below the surface, and early historical societies determined to collect, document, and preserve these artifacts. In 1877 the American Association for the Advancement of Science (AAAS) held its 26th Annual Meeting in Nashville, the first such meeting in the South since the Civil War. During the course of the meeting, much attention was given to geology and Indian culture, and some participants opened nearby Indian gravesites at Fort Zollicoffer, or joined post-meeting excursions to explore the botanical and geological characteristics of southeast Tennessee.

Like other southern states Tennessee's industrial development lagged behind its agricultural production throughout the nineteenth century. Nevertheless, the state led the South in antebellum iron manufacturing, an area where local ironmasters proved technologically innovative. Soon after Montgomery Bell purchased the Cumberland Furnace from James Robertson, he gained a reputation as a profit-minded iron manufacturer. In 1818 Bell purchased land at the Narrows of the Harpeth River—an area in Cheatham County where the Harpeth River loops back in a four-to-five-mile reverse that drops some 17 feet. There his slaves constructed one of the nation's earliest man-made tunnels through the Narrows. Bell offered the area as a site for a federal armory and after the government passed on the offer, he established Patterson Forge on the site.

In post-Reconstruction Tennessee, enthusiasm for technological progress among proponents of a "New South" outran the financial means to implement a program of statewide industrialization. Local boosters championed railroad construction, promoted the establishment of textile mills and iron manufacturing, and encouraged the expansion of telephone and electrical services. At the 1877 AAAS meeting, Nashvillians experienced their first telephone call, when copper line was strung from the home of Sarah (Mrs. James K.) Polk to the nearby home of Adam G. Adams. Though the two houses were within shouting distance, neighbors talked and played piano pieces over the wire, to their great amusement. At that same meeting, urban leaders looked to science to provide cost-effective measures to supply the cities with clean water and improve public health while educators promoted mechanical and agricultural studies in elementary and secondary schools to create a more scientifically-oriented class of farmers and workers.

Similar demands reappeared at the state's Centennial Celebration in 1897. Promoted by railroad interests, the exposition carried out a theme of technological advancement, deliberately contrasting the innovative and mechanical methods of "modern" farmers and workers with the outdated techniques of more traditional (and presumably less enlightened) farmers and laborers. Like other forms of boosterism, the Centennial Exposition promised a future made easier and more productive through technology.

By the turn of the century, many Tennesseans could take advantage of several technological innovations. Wives of prosperous farmers enjoyed the use of sewing machines and the "Busy Bee" washer. Farmers consulted the columns of urban newspapers for weather information, crop prices, and agricultural advice—all made more readily available through advances in communications, information gathering, and lowered costs in printing. Residents of the county seats built generating plants to provide electricity, installed telephones, and piped water to homes.

Many of the conveniences associated with town living were made accessible to mill workers as industrial leaders looked to the state for supplies of raw materials and low-wage workers. Employing the latest technology, refined to make use of undereducated workers in what would otherwise be complex operations, companies ranging from Bemis Brothers Bag Company in West Tennessee to rayon mills in

Elizabethton and Tennessee Eastman in Kingsport employed thousands of workers, housing them in company towns that, while not lavish, offered many modern conveniences. In Memphis, technological changes produced new uses for the area's staple product, cotton. Cottonseed and cotton linters, earlier discarded, became valuable products as the cottonseed oil business emerged with the new industrial focus on chemical production. Likewise, World War I put new emphasis on cotton linters in the production of smokeless powder, while the development of rayon fiber added to the value of the cotton by-product.

At the same time that Tennessee mill workers entered new industrial areas and began living in company towns, farmers experienced the not always welcomed intrusion of railroads and mining and timber companies. Farm families who had always maintained a self-sufficient lifestyle now found themselves drawn into a cash-based market economy. Many farmers felt the "threats" to family life more challenging than the economic changes. The market economy offered non-agrarian opportunities to young men and women, challenged traditional folk knowledge and, many believed, undermined religious training. The lightning rod that attracted the unfocused rural concerns was Darwin's Theory of Evolution.

Concern about the social and religious implications of Darwin's scientific theory of natural selection had percolated under the surface since the 1870s. Although newspapers printed jokes about evolution, and progressive-minded reformers proclaimed no conflict between science and faith, the problem occasionally surfaced in academic circles. Yale paleontologist Othniel Charles Marsh, the featured speaker of the 1877 meeting of AAAS, shocked conservative Nashvillians when he declared that evolution was scientific truth. The following spring Vanderbilt University trustees abolished the position of Professor Alexander Winchell for his defense of the theory of evolution. The degree to which Tennesseans of all intellectual talents remained skeptical of evolution or remained silent in the face of public opinion can be seen in the 1925 enactment of the anti-evolution or Butler Bill. A prosperous farmer, community leader, and Primitive Baptist from Macon County, John Butler proposed a law to prohibit the teaching of "any theory that denies the story of Divine Creation of man as taught in the Bible, and to teach instead that man has descended from a lower form of animals."[1] Neither the fledgling Tennessee Academy of Sciences nor the University of Tennessee officially protested.

Spurred by dreams of economic revival, entrepreneurs in Dayton inveighed upon John Thomas Scopes, a young high school biology instructor, to allow himself to be charged with breaking the new law and test its constitutionality. The ensuing trial brought notoriety to the town and state but hardly enhanced the reputation of either. The "Monkey Law" remained on the statute books until 1967; Scopes's conviction was overturned on a technicality; and Dayton acquired the present Bryan College. Arguably the most important outcome of the trial and the scathing publicity surrounding it was the articulation of the defense of southern tradition prepared by the Vanderbilt writers and historians known as the Agrarians. The 1930 publication of their position, entitled *I'll Take My Stand*, offered a statement of principles that attacked the "Cult of Science" and industrialization as "extravagant" and the enslaver of human energy. These intellectual agrarians argued that industrialization, the product of technology, devalued labor, rendered employment insecure, created consumer-driven societies, undermined religion and the arts, and destroyed the amenities of life.

Unfortunately for the proponents of a more traditional lifestyle, the state had arrived at the moment of monumental economic and social transformation, as first the Tennessee Valley Authority (TVA) and then Oak Ridge and related wartime industries brought a massive shift in population from the countryside into the towns and cities, and the ready availability of cheap electricity altered the way Tennesseans lived, worked, and played. In 1933 the Tennessee River Valley became the living laboratory for one of the largest technological and social experiments in history.

Having identified the South as the nation's number one economic problem, President Franklin D. Roosevelt made the transformation of the Tennessee Valley the centerpiece of his New Deal legislation. Charged with providing flood control, fertilizers, and electricity to the area, TVA uprooted farmers, provided jobs, created parklands, reforested depleted woodlands, broke the power of private utility companies, attracted outside investment, and built model communities. Suddenly, technology and science in the form of a federal agency provided answers to poverty, poor education, and limited opportunities. Though not all Tennesseans welcomed the changes, many rallied to the support of the new agency—though not always for the same reasons—because they anticipated a more technologically oriented future.

In the wake of this federally-inspired and federally-financed change, Tennessee became the backdrop for the transformation of scientific research, when Anderson County became a site of the ultrasecret Manhattan Project. Providing isolation, an abundance of cheap electricity, and a patriotic workforce, Oak Ridge became, in the words of Wilma Dykeman, the twentieth century frontier. In the development of Oak Ridge, both as a wartime research installation and in its continuing role as a national laboratory, Tennesseans participated in the transformation of science. Until the wartime institutionalization of science on behalf of national interests, American scientific research had been conducted largely by individual scientists. Working in academic, industrial, or private laboratories, they usually addressed technological problems; the development of scientific theory remained the specialty of Europeans. Often poorly funded, scientific research depended in large measure on the generosity of individual benefactors.

World War II, in general, and the Manhattan Project, in particular, transformed scientific research into "Big Science." Utilizing the theoretical knowledge of an international academic community, the technological expertise of the American industrial community, and the funding of the federal government, Oak Ridge portended the future of science. The project drew scientists from a global community, but its scope (and mandatory secrecy) compartmentalized the research, so that each team of scientists and technicians worked on a single facet of the project, without having the knowledge and/or the responsibility for the whole. The demands for technical support and specialized equipment also surpassed the financial abilities of business or educational institutions. Tennessee and Tennesseans moved to center stage as the pioneers in the nuclear age and the advent of modern scientific research.

The development of "Big Science" profoundly affected the state's higher educational system. Professors of chemistry, physics, mathematics, engineering, and biology quickly recognized Oak Ridge as an academic and research bonanza. The proximity of the University of Tennessee made it a natural beneficiary, but other public and private institutions also developed working relationships with the government's laboratories. At UT, department heads in physics and chemistry quickly moved to provide Oak Ridge scientists with joint appointments at the university and to acquire consulting appointments at Oak Ridge for themselves and their faculty. In the immediate postwar years, UT developed its first Ph.D. programs; not surprisingly, they were in chemistry, physics, and mathematics.

Graduate students and university faculty were not the only beneficiaries of the technological and scientific changes instituted by TVA and Oak Ridge and later by the Arnold Engineering Development Center at Tullahoma. The presence of three high-profile facilities attracted other industries and technological support services. By the mid-1950s state educators recognized the need for an expansion of higher education facilities to accommodate the rising numbers of potential college students (as baby boomers came of age) and to provide technical education to prepare Tennesseans for the modern job market. By the time the state implemented the recommendations advanced in the 1950s, emphasis had shifted from the establishment of a single four-year institution to the construction of several two-year community colleges and additional technology centers, which now are within easy driving distance for most Tennesseans.

Although nostalgia for a simpler life beckons Tennesseans, most of the state's citizens, like most Americans, are wedded to the scientific and technological world in their work as well as their lifestyles. A glance at local economies shows Tennesseans producing automobiles and auto parts, staffing hospitals and ancillary laboratories, and manufacturing synthetic fibers, paints, and plastics. Nobel Prize-winning scientists now conduct their research in Tennessee laboratories. Tennesseans are engaged in space exploration, genetic mapping, the development of designer drugs, transplant surgery, computer programming, environmental and ecological research, and the development of new energy sources. Tennessee courts have made new case law as they determined the fate of frozen human embryos. Local school boards grapple with the competing demands of parents who want the latest scientific knowledge for their children and those who want to insert creationism into the science curriculum. Having rescued the land from the ecological disasters of the early twentieth century, Tennesseans face renewed environmental problems, some of which have been generated within the state and others that arrive on the air currents and streams that enter from other areas. As in previous generations, Tennesseans remain more comfortable with science that provides answers than with science that theorizes. In 1996 the Tennessee General Assembly debated evolution again, this time without acting on their words. In this area, as in its new-found identification with modern science, Tennessee continues to act as a microcosm for the development of national issues.

Connie L. Lester, Tennessee Historical Society

CITATION:
(1) George E. Webb, *The Evolution Controversy in America* (Lexington, 1994), 84.

SUGGESTED READINGS: Joe P. Dunn and Howard L. Preston, eds., *The Future South: A Historical Perspective for the Twenty-first Century* (1991); Leland Johnson and Daniel Schaffer, *Oak Ridge National Laboratory: The First Fifty Years* (1994); Thomas K. McCraw, *TVA and the Power Fight, 1933–1939* (1971); James Summerville, "Science in the New South: The Meeting of the AAAS at Nashville, 1877," *Tennessee Historical Quarterly* 45(1986): 316–328; Alvin Weinberg, *The First Nuclear Era: The Life and Times of a Technological Fixer* (1994); Margaret Ripley Wolfe, *Kingsport, Tennessee: A Planned American Community* (1987)

THE SCOPES TRIAL. In mid-July 1925, much of the nation's attention was focused on the small town of Dayton, Tennessee, where John T. Scopes was on trial for teaching about evolution. Four months earlier, the Tennessee General Assembly had overwhelmingly passed a bill, introduced by Representative John W. Butler of Macon County, which made it illegal to teach "any theory that denies the story of Divine Creation of man as taught in the Bible, and to teach instead that man has descended from a lower order of animals." Governor Austin Peay quickly signed the measure, but stressed that he interpreted the Butler Act as a protest against irreligious tendencies in modern America and doubted that it would be an active statute.

The American Civil Liberties Union viewed the Butler Act as unconstitutional and offered to represent a Tennessee educator in a test case of the statute. Learning of this offer, civic leaders in Dayton decided to pursue such a case in an effort to draw publicity to their community. They approached Scopes, a football coach and science teacher at the local high school, and asked him if biology could be taught without mentioning evolution. Scopes replied that he did not think that was possible, especially as the state-approved biology text discussed evolution. Scopes also told the Dayton boosters that he had conducted a biology review session the previous April and had used the textbook. Presumably, although he could not remember this for certain, he had also discussed evolution. By the end of May, Scopes had been indicted for violating the Butler Act by a special grand jury called by local judge John T. Raulston.

When the Scopes Trial opened on July 10, 1925, the ACLU defense team included noted attorney John Randolph Neal of Knoxville, and as outside volunteers, Clarence Darrow, Dudley Field Malone, and Arthur Garfield Hays. Assuming that Scopes would be convicted, the ACLU planned to appeal the verdict to higher courts to determine the constitutionality of the Butler Act. The prosecution included Tennessee Attorney General Thomas Stewart and a local lawyer S.K. Hicks, but the most famous member of the team was William Jennings Bryan, who had been invited as a special prosecutor. Although a circus atmosphere surrounded the Dayton proceedings from the beginning, the Scopes Trial included issues of significance. Was the Butler Act, as the defense maintained, an attempt to establish the religion of Protestant Fundamentalism and thus a violation of the First Amendment? Was the act a vague statute that did not clearly define what it meant to "teach" evolution? Or was the prosecution correct in its argument that the Butler Act was a legitimate effort by the legislature to control the public school curriculum?

Such issues, however, were largely ignored during the trial, as Judge Raulston ruled out expert testimony concerning the scientific status of evolution and its harmony with the Bible, and the prosecution focused on Scopes's violation of the act. The dramatic climax of the Scopes Trial took place on July 20, when Darrow called Bryan to the stand as an expert witness on the Bible. Despite its irrelevance to the case at hand, Bryan welcomed the opportunity (as he viewed it) to defend traditional religion against the forces of atheism. During the 90-minute examination, Darrow showed that Bryan's knowledge of the Bible was imperfect and that the Great Commoner did not believe that every passage in the Bible could be taken literally. Although Bryan's faith had never been based on a rigid Biblical literalism, his testimony disappointed many of the most extreme fundamentalists.

The exchange between Darrow and Bryan convinced both prosecution and defense that the substantive aspects of the trial had been exhausted. When court reconvened on July 21, therefore, Darrow made a few brief comments to the jury, urging them to convict Scopes and outlining the defense plan for appeal. The jury returned a guilty verdict in less than ten minutes. Judge Raulston levied the minimum fine of $100 against Scopes, explaining that the local custom in other cases was for the jury to consider fines only if they wished to impose more than the minimum.

Although Bryan's death in Dayton five days later removed an important symbolic force from the anti-evolution crusade, the campaign actually gained strength from the Scopes Trial. Not only did the trial provide publicity for the movement, but Scopes's conviction showed that an anti-evolution statute could be upheld in court. Over the next few years, anti-evolution bills were introduced in legislatures throughout the United States and were passed in Mississippi and Arkansas. Even in states without anti-evolution statutes, the place of evolution in the biology curriculum remained ambiguous. Local school boards and individual teachers backed away from teaching the concept, while publishers deleted the topic from their biology texts.

As Scopes began graduate study in geology at the University of Chicago, the ACLU appealed his conviction to the Tennessee Supreme Court. A divided court issued its decision in January 1927, announcing that nothing in the Butler Act violated either the state or the federal constitution. Because the statute did not *require* the teaching of anything, it could not be seen as an attempt to establish religion. Yet Scopes's conviction could not be upheld. The Tennessee Constitution clearly stated that any fine over $50 was to be levied by the jury. By imposing a higher fine, Judge Raulston had violated the constitution. The Court not only reversed Scopes's conviction, but strongly recommended that the state not retry the case.

The Butler Act remained on the statute books for the next 40 years, until the legislature repealed the measure in 1967. Even after repeal, however, the ghost of the Scopes Trial continued to haunt the state. As was the case elsewhere, various attempts to eliminate or compromise the teaching of evolution emerged in Tennessee. Such attempts attracted local, national, and international media attention to the state, always identified as the site of the Scopes Trial decades earlier. In their campaign to gain publicity , the Dayton boosters of 1925 succeeded better than they could possibly have anticipated.

George E. Webb, Tennessee Technological University
SUGGESTED READINGS: Ray Ginger, *Six Days or Forever? Tennessee v. John Thomas Scopes* (1958); George E. Webb, *The Evolution Controversy in America* (1994)
SEE: BRYAN COLLEGE; BUTLER, JOHN W.; RHEA COUNTY

SCOTT COUNTY's location on the Cumberland Plateau abutting the Tennessee-Kentucky state line makes for beautiful landscape, poor soil for farming, and a small population. The region is blanketed with forests and parks, both in neighboring counties and Scott County's westernmost section where is found the Big South Fork National River and Recreation Area. This park extends into Morgan and Fentress counties to the south and west and into McCreary County in Kentucky to the north. Attracting tourists, hikers, rafters, kayakers, and canoers, Big South Fork protects geological features of great age and prehistoric and historic resources as well as providing employment to local residents.

Scott County was created in 1849 by the Tennessee General Assembly out of parts of Anderson, Campbell, Fentress, and Morgan counties and named for General Winfield Scott, whose military exploits in the Mexican War were fresh in the public's mind. The county seat is Huntsville, named in honor of an early hunter. The first election was held in March 1850 and the first court in July of that year. The courthouse was erected in 1851, but later courthouses replaced it, first in 1874 and then in this century. Listed in the National Register of Historic Places, the old Scott County Jail is the oldest extant building in Hunstville and its distincitve fortress design is the work of architect J.G. Barnwell of Chattanooga. Huntsville was incorporated in 1965.

The largest municipality in the county, Oneida, was incorporated in 1913. Oneida served as a way station on the Cincinnati Southern Railroad, built in the 1870s to connect Chattanooga and Cincinnati. Another line, between Oneida and Jamestown and called the Oneida and Western, prospered during the 1920s due to logging and mining work, but it and the county suffered greatly in the Depression. The line was dismantled in 1953. Other towns in the county include: Smoky Junction, Norma, Fairview, Winfield, Isham, Helenwood, Robbins, and Elgin. Robbins is home to Barton Chapel, which memorializes the social and humanitarian contributions of the Reverend William E. Barton, who established his ministry here in 1885.

Paleoindians during the last ice age visited the rock overhangs and shelters that wind and water erosion created from the area's sandstone and shale. Later Native American peoples also used these resources. Settlers in the early nineteenth century carved out small, self-sufficient farms from the wilderness. Perhaps because of the poor farming conditions, blacks as slaves and freemen did not factor at more than two percent of the county's antebellum population. In the mid-nineteenth century industry was limited to independent grist mills and whiskey production.

During the Civil War, Scott Countians were strongly Unionist in sentiment. U.S. Senator Andrew Johnson denounced secession at a courthouse speech in Huntsville on June 4, 1861, and the county voted against secession by the greatest percentage margin of any Tennessee county. In fact, local residents so opposed the Confederacy that later in 1861 the county court approved a protest resolution that announced the county's secession from the State of Tennessee and the creation of a "Free and Independent State of Scott." Guerrilla warfare occurred in the county during the Civil War, but no major battles occurred within the county's boundaries.

After the war, the construction of the Cincinnati Southern in the early 1880s opened the county to timber, mining, and New South industrial development. Extraction of natural resources served as the foundation for local urban and economic development until the Great Depression. Oneida served as a shipping point for timber, coal, farm products, and livestock, while Huntsville's chief activity was lumbering, and brick-making was the primary industry in Robbins. The construction of U.S. Highway 27 in the late 1920s opened new transportation alternatives for county residents.

In the 1990s the Scott County Hospital with 99 beds, the county government, and its school system employ the largest numbers of non-manufacturing workers. The county's biggest employers include American Bag Corporation (automobile air bags); Hartco/Tibbals Flooring Company (wood flooring); Tennier Industries (military coats); Denim Processing, Inc.; and Wabash National Corporation (trailer platforms). The county's population in 1990 was 18,358.

Perhaps the most recognized name from Scott County is that of Howard Baker, Jr., who, like his father, represented his region and state in the United States Congress for many years. Howard Baker, Sr., was in the House of Representatives for seven terms, and his wife Irene succeeded him. Baker, Jr., was a

Republican Senator for Tennessee for more than 20 years and Chief of Staff for President Ronald Reagan. Other political personalities from Scott County include Millard Caldwell, a congressman who later was governor of Florida, and John Duncan, who served in Congress from 1964 until his death in 1988.

Margaret D. Binnicker, Middle Tennessee State University

SEE: BAKER, HOWARD H., JR.; BAKER, HOWARD H., SR.; BIG SOUTH FORK NATIONAL RIVER AND RECREATION AREA; CHUQUALATAQUE; DUNCAN, JOHN, SR.; RAILROADS; STEARNS COAL AND LUMBER

SCOTT, EVELYN (1893–1963), novelist and essayist, was born Elsie Dunn in Clarksville, Tennessee, on January 17, 1893, the only child of Seely and Maude Thomas Dunn. After living in Clarksville as a young child, she moved to New Orleans and enrolled in the Sophie Newcombe Preparatory School and later briefly at Sophie Newcombe College and Tulane University. Elsie Dunn rebelled early against the limitations of her class and times, writing at 15 a controversial letter to the New Orleans *Times Picayune* advocating the legalization of prostitution as a way to control venereal disease. In 1913 she ran away to Brazil with a married man, Frederick Creighton Wellman, the dean of the School of Tropical Medicine at Tulane. To conceal their identities, they called themselves Cyril and Evelyn Scott.

During the five years she spent in Brazil, where she gave birth to a son named Creighton in 1914, Evelyn Scott emerged as a writer. At first she produced poems and critical essays published in *Poetry,* the *Dial,* and other periodicals. But publication of *The Narrow House* (1921), the first of a trilogy of novels including *Narcissus* (1922) and *The Golden Door* (1923), brought her critical recognition from H.L. Mencken and launched a career that made her a significant American writer in the decades between the two world wars. This first trilogy was followed by a second—*Migrations* (1927), *The Wave* (1929), and *A Calendar of Sin* (1931). *The Wave,* Scott's best novel, deals with the Civil War in an experimental narrative style attempting both epic sweep and accurate psychological analysis. Due to the success of this work, Scott's publisher asked her to write an essay about relative newcomer William Faulkner's *The Sound and the Fury.*

While the Scotts returned to the United States in 1919, they did not settle permanently but spent time in Bermuda, France, North Africa, and England. Evelyn Scott left Cyril for Owen Merton, father of the future Trappist monk Thomas Merton, and ended her common law marriage to Scott by divorce in 1928. She married British novelist John Metcalfe in 1930 and lived in Canada and England until the end of World War II. Scott continued to write, producing in *Eva Gay* (1932) a fictionalized version of her relation-

ships with Merton and Scott. Her later work did not have the commercial and critical success of her earlier novels. Scott's critical analysis of Soviet communism in *Breathe Upon These Slain* (1934) and *Bread and a Sword* (1937) did not appeal to readers or to a literary establishment flirting with Marxism. Her last novel, *The Shadow of the Hawk* (1941), returned to her earlier focus on family relationships.

Scott's reputation derives from the two trilogies, in particular the individual books *The Narrow House* and *The Wave,* and from her memoir *Background in Tennessee* (1937), a study of her early years. While Scott continued to write after returning to the United States in 1952, she did not find publishers. In ill health, Scott and John Metcalfe lived in a residential hotel in New York City, where she died August 3, 1963. Evelyn Scott is buried in Rose Hill Cemetery in Linden, New Jersey.

Robert C. Petersen, Middle Tennessee State University

SEE: LITERATURE; MONTGOMERY COUNTY

SECOND ARMY (TENNESSEE) MANEUVERS. In the autumn of 1942, the War Department decided to resume field maneuvers in Middle Tennessee. Large scale war games had been conducted in an area around Camp Forrest, near Tullahoma, the previous summer, and General George S. Patton had perfected the armored tactics that were to bring him fame and his divisions victory in Europe. Between the wars Erwin Rommel, as a young military attache, had visited Nashville and Middle Tennessee to study and follow the cavalry campaigns of Confederate General Nathan Bedford Forrest to help him develop a pattern for the use of tank units as cavalry. The Army, perceiving in the Cumberland River and the hilly country to the south and north a similarity to the Rhine and Western Europe, decided to send divisions into the state for their last preparation before actual combat. Between September 1942 and March 1944 nearly one million soldiers passed through the Tennessee Maneuvers area.

Lebanon was chosen as headquarters and Nashville as the principal railhead. Over the hills and valleys of 21 counties Blue and Red armies engaged in weekly strategic "problems," with troops moved in and out according to a calendar of "phases" that lasted about four weeks apiece. In the military's scenario Nashville was Cherbourg, without the bombing. The first and second problems usually took place east of Davidson County, but the third in each phase would poise attacking "Blue" troops against "Red" troops in defense around Donelson in Davidson County and Couchville in Wilson County. This force would advance to the east toward hilly terrain. In one instance at least a problem involved the defense of Berry Field in Nashville against Blue airborne troops.

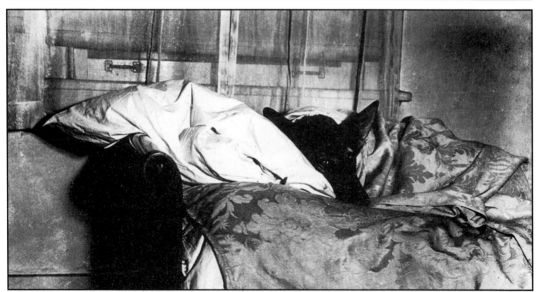

TSLA.

Morris Frank's Seeing-Eye dog "Buddy," 1937.

Maneuvers paused at noon on Thursday or Friday, when a light plane would fly over the mock battle lines, sounding a siren. Then thousands of soldiers would seek recreation in Nashville and the county seat towns. Facilities were limited, despite the best efforts of the U.S.O. and the American Red Cross; movie theaters and cafes were packed; drug store soda fountains were forced to shut down twice a day for clean-up. Each Army PX was strained to the limit. Churches opened their doors and set up lounges; schools opened their gyms for weekend dances. The Grand Ole Opry had never drawn such crowds than during these months when Middle Tennessee hosted the army's preparations for the eventual invasion of Normany in 1944.

Frank Burns, Garland, Texas

SEE: CAMP FORREST; CEDARS OF LEBANON STATE PARK; WILSON COUNTY; WORLD WAR II

SEEING EYE, INC., a New Jersey-based corporation that enhances the independence and dignity of blind people through the training and use of "Seeing Eye" dogs, has its roots in Nashville. In 1927 Nashville native Morris Frank, totally blind since the age of 16, learned about a German program which used shepherd dogs as eyes for the blind. Frank contacted Dorothy Harrison Eustis, an American author who lived in the Swiss Alps where she trained dogs to be guides for the Red Cross, police, and army. She had no experience training dogs to assist the blind, but she suggested that if Frank came to Switzerland, she would assist him in locating a dog and a qualified trainer.

Frank went to Switzerland and returned to Nashville with "Buddy Fortunate Fields," a female German shepherd and the pioneering first of all Seeing Eye dogs. Frank and "Buddy" were a common sight in downtown Nashville for years. Frank successfully challenged the "no dogs allowed" codes on streetcars, elevators, and in restaurants. The concept of service dogs sharing space with humans in public places first gained social acceptance on the streets of Nashville.

Frank's success encouraged him to establish an organization to train guide dogs for the blind. Naming the nonprofit corporation "The Seeing Eye," a reference to a story about guide dogs in the *Saturday Evening Post,* Frank served as managing director, operating from his Richland Avenue home in Nashville. During its first year, however, the corporation moved to New Jersey where it has remained ever since. As the oldest guide dog school in the nation, Seeing Eye has matched more than 11,000 trained guide dogs with blind men and women.

Susan L. Gordon, Tennessee Historical Society

SENTER, DEWITT CLINTON (1832–1898), farmer, state legislator, and Governor, was born in McMinn County, Tennessee, on March 26, 1832, the son of William T. Senter, a Methodist minister, and Nancy White Senter. He attended the public schools in Grainger County and the Strawberry Plains College. Beginning in 1852, he read law at home. He married Harriet T. Senter in 1859.

From 1855 to 1861 Senter represented Grainger County in the Tennessee General Assembly. Although a member of the Whig party before the Civil War, he later served as an elector for the Republican ticket in

1864 and 1868. In addition to his interest in farming and public service, Senter served as president of the Cincinnati, Cumberland Gap, and Charleston Railroad in 1865–1866.

In the 1866–1867 legislative session, Senter was elected Speaker of the Senate. Following the election of Governor William G. Brownlow to the U.S. Senate in October 1867, Senter served out the Brownlow term as Governor. In 1869 Senter defeated William B. Stokes in a hotly contested campaign for the governorship. As Governor, he allied himself with former Confederates and conservatives to reverse many key Reconstruction programs. In 1870 he supported the call for the State Constitutional Convention, which drafted a new constitution that restored formerly disfranchised Confederates—and the Democratic party—to power.

Senter retired to a large farm near Morristown, where he died on June 14, 1898.

John H. Thweatt, Tennessee State Library and Archives
SEE: BROWNLOW, WILLIAM G.; GOVERNMENT; HAMBLEN COUNTY; RECONSTRUCTION

SEQUATCHIE COUNTY was created from a section of Hamilton County by an act of the Tennessee General Assembly on December 9, 1857, with Dunlap as the county seat. Europeans first settled in the area in 1806. The land in the Sequatchie Valley was highly attractive for agricultural purposes.

Throughout most of the nineteenth century, inhabitants of the county practiced subsistence agriculture with a few prosperous farms located within the valley. The small farmers produced corn and raised livestock such as cattle, sheep, hogs, and poultry for themselves and the local market. Few opportunities existed to expand to a larger agricultural market until a road, Anderson Pike, was built in 1852 connecting the Sequatchie Valley to the newly constructed Western and Atlantic Railroad in Georgia. Anderson Pike was used mainly by farmers to transport their livestock out of the valley and to larger markets throughout the South. During the Civil War, in October 1863, Confederate Major General Joseph Wheeler led a cavalry raid against a Union supply train on Anderson Pike that was attempting to relieve besieged Federal troops at Chattanooga. Wheeler burned an estimated 800 to 1,000 wagons and captured livestock.

The construction of railroads in the post-Reconstruction era expanded Sequatchie County's agricultural and industrial opportunities. The Nashville, Chattanooga and St. Louis Railway constructed a line through the Sequatchie Valley in the 1880s. This line reached Sequatchie County in 1888 thus enabling coal companies to conduct large-scale mining activities by the turn of the century. The Chattanooga Iron and Coal Corporation owned and operated 16,000 acres

of coal land near Dunlap and employed 350 men. They also operated two sawmills which supplied the railroads with ties and the coal mines with shoring. In addition to mining, the company constructed and operated 268 beehive coke ovens near Dunlap, many of which can still be viewed at the Dunlap Coke Ovens historic site. Coke ovens carbonize bituminous coal by removing the majority of volatile materials in the coal by heating it in a closed oven thus preventing its burning. The coke then was used in blast furnaces to melt iron. As the southern steel industry continued to expand, the demand for coke continued to increase.

The Chattanooga Iron and Coal Corporation sold their mining and coke operations to the Southern States Iron and Coal Company in 1919. The Southern States Company closed the operations in 1922 due to the overproduction of coal. The closing of the mines also brought about the closing of many associated industries. Railroad traffic declined in the county and many people left the area in pursuit of work. Those who remained returned to subsistence farming as a living. The Great Depression seemed to start early for the residents of Sequatchie County.

The county saw some relief from President Franklin Roosevelt's New Deal programs, specifically the Tennessee Valley Authority and the National Youth Administration (NYA). The former helped bring low-cost electric power to the county and surrounding areas. The latter organization was established in the county to give young men skills to find employment while temporarily keeping them out of the depressed labor market. During its existence in Sequatchie County, NYA members, supervised by local men, learned construction skills by building the Dunlap Community Building and four schools around Dunlap and Cagle.

While Dunlap is the main town in Sequatchie County, several smaller communities are in the surrounding area. Daus, originally known as Delphi and located south of Dunlap, began as a small farming community until the railroad came in the 1880s. Daus soon experienced rapid growth and decline due to the boom and bust of coal mining. The development of the coal industry in the early twentieth century also affected Fredonia and Cartwright. Other small farming communities include Cagle, Mount Airy, and Lone Oak.

Sequatchie County has been home to several noteworthy people. William Stone of Delphi (now Daus) and James Standifer from Mount Airy both served in the U.S. Congress in the 1820s and 1830s. Arthur Thomas Stewart was born in Dunlap and served as attorney general of the 18th judicial circuit of Tennessee where he served on the prosecuting team at the Scopes Trial in Dayton. Stewart also served as a U.S. Senator during the 1930s and 1940s.

Raymond H. Cooley, also of Dunlap, served as staff sergeant in the Pacific during World War II where he earned the distinguished Congressional Medal of Honor for his courage and heroism during the 1945 invasion of the Philippines.

Holly Anne Rine, University of New Hampshire

SEE: MINING; RAILROADS; TENNESSEE VALLEY AUTHORITY; WHEELER, JOSEPH

SEQUOYAH (ca. 1770–1843) was born in the Cherokee town of Tuskegee (or Taskigi) on the Little Tennessee River in what is now Monroe County. The son of Nathaniel Gist (or Guess), a Virginia fur trader, and Wurtah (also known as Wureth or Wut-teh), daughter of a prominent Cherokee family, Sequoyah rose to international prominence as the first known individual to create a totally new system of writing.

While sometimes known by his English name of George Gist, Sequoyah was raised in the ways and customs of the Cherokees to the extent that he was largely unable to speak, read, or write English. By profession, he was a talented silversmith, but he also pursued the honored Cherokee occupations of farmer, hunter, fur trader, and soldier.

Cherokee oral tradition suggests that Sequoyah first became fascinated with the ability of Euroamericans to communicate by making marks on paper

FROM GEORGE E. FOSTER, *SE-QUO-YAH, THE AMERICAN CADMUS* (1885). DRAWING BY MISS C. S. ROBBINS, COPY PHOTOGRAPH BY JUNE DORMAN

Sequoyah teaching Ahyokey the Cherokee syllabary

while recuperating from a hunting accident in 1809. During this period of contemplation and study, he became convinced that these "talking leaves," as they were called by many Native Americans, were the key to the power of Euroamericans and must become a critical component in the future progress and success of the Cherokees.

Sequoyah became further convinced of the necessity of literacy for his people during service as a soldier on the side of the United States in the War of 1812 and the Creek War of 1813–1814. He and other Cherokee soldiers were unable to write letters home, read military orders, or make diaries and journals of events. After those experiences, he began in earnest to create a Cherokee written language.

His conviction that a written language would greatly benefit his people in a rapidly changing world was not readily accepted by all Cherokees. Despite ridicule by friends and family members, and accusations of insanity and practicing witchcraft, Sequoyah devoted the next decade of his life to creating "talking leaves" in his native tongue.

By 1821 Sequoyah had isolated 86 (later reduced to 85) syllables used in the spoken Cherokee language, and assigned written symbols to each. Unlike the English writing system, where different letters can represent the same sound (for example, "c" and "k" can both represent the same sound as in "can" and "kill"), each letter in Sequoyah's syllabary represented a distinct sound. This brilliant innovation meant that any Cherokee who simply memorized the sounds of the symbols could automatically read or write anything in the Cherokee language.

In 1821 a demonstration of the system by Sequoyah and his daughter Ayoka to Cherokee leaders was so dramatically convincing that the syllabary was officially adopted by the Cherokee Nation. Within five years, thousands of Cherokees were literate—far surpassing the literacy rates of their Euroamerican neighbors. Sequoyah had single-handedly invented the first written language of native North America.

While this brilliant linguistic achievement was rapidly recognized throughout the western world, Samuel Austin Worcester (1798–1859), a missionary to the Cherokee from the Congregational Church, was instrumental in making the new Cherokee syllabary suitable for printing. Serving from 1825–1826 in the Brainerd Mission in Tennessee, Worcester was convinced that the use of native languages was a significant way to propagate the gospel. At his urging, a hand printing press and Cherokee syllabary characters in type were prepared in 1827 by the Missionary Board and shipped from Boston to Cherokee leaders in New Echota, Georgia. On February 21, 1828, the inaugural issue of the first Native American newspaper, the Cherokee *Phoenix*, was printed in parallel columns in Cherokee and English. Using Sequoyah's syllabary, the Cherokee Nation and missionaries published newspapers, almanacs, government documents, religious tracts, hymn books, and the Christian Bible in this new written language. By 1843, the year of Sequoyah's death, more than four million pages of books, articles, and newspapers had been published in Cherokee.

While perhaps no other legacy can match the millions of printed pages preserving Cherokee history, culture, tradition and sense of nation, many other honors have been bestowed upon Sequoyah for his remarkable achievement. As early as the late 1840s, Native Americans and other concerned individuals made concerted efforts to create a new State to be called Sequoyah between Arkansas and Oklahoma City. While in 1906 the U.S. Congress finally rejected that accolade (partly as a result of lobbying efforts by oil and gas interests who feared complications dealing with Native American governments), his name has been remembered in many other fashions. His name is attached to the giant redwood trees of California, a county seat in Oklahoma, a presidential yacht, and a nuclear power plant near Chattanooga. Perhaps most significant to the memory of his achievements, however, are the statue standing in our nation's capitol and the Sequoyah Birthplace Museum constructed by the Cherokee on the shores of Tellico Lake at Vonore, Tennessee.

Kevin E. Smith, Middle Tennessee State University

SUGGESTED READING: Grant Foreman, *Sequoyah* (1938)

SEE: BRAINERD MISSION; CHEROKEE PHOENIX; MONROE COUNTY; OVERHILL CHEROKEES

SETTLEMENT SCHOOLS. At the end of the nineteenth century no universally accepted standards or requirements for any level of education existed in the South. Defeated in the Civil War and their economies devastated, the southern states had little monies to expend on education, and newly freed African Americans also now had to be figured into educational projections. The chief instrument of education in the South prior to 1860 had been private academies; now public funds must provide. The rural nature of the region with its agricultural economy made it poorer than the industrialized northeast and more dispersed in population than the midwest. Southern states strove first to develop elementary education in cities and towns, but their attention to mountainous sections lagged behind until the turn of the century.

Into these more removed areas, instead, came outsiders with the purpose of educating the young through settlement or mission schools. Different groups established this fieldwork for diverse reasons, but their programs shared certain characteristics. They included a curriculum of craft or trade training which made each school somewhat self-sufficient while also developing skills among the students. As part of the "myth of Appalachia," residents of the region were considered to be pure Anglo-Saxon stock. The discipline of self-help in the form of manual labor or crafts production would effectively remove the children, and through them the whole population, from squalor. The people of the hollows would be shaped into the images held up for them by the earnest outsiders.

This middle-class idealism was a translation of the settlement-school philosophy as developed and exemplified in Jane Addams's Hull House in Chicago. Progressive reformers believed that learning might build the community as a whole through programs involving different generations. In Appalachian settings such intergenerational endeavors acquired the name "fireside industries." The irony in these programs resulted from introduction of particular material or methods of craft production from outside the region for the "mountaineers" to incorporate in making and selling their "authentic" objects in distant markets. Attempting to impose their own standards upon another group made the outsiders' approach a paternalistic one. Rearranging local customs to fit better a preconceived notion was both manipulative and destructive. Some modern critics have called these efforts subversive colonization, instigated in order to get at and use up the region's resources.

Most settlement schools were located in Appalachia, and the majority were coeducational. In Tennessee, legislation mandating that a public high school be built and maintained in each county of the state passed into law in 1908. Spearheaded by Philander P. Claxton, this initiative included a bill that required 25 percent of the state's gross income to go to a General Education Fund to support the program. All school-age children living in a rural, mountainous county, however, might not be close enough to the one high school to attend it. By the 1930s settlement and mission schools and colleges existed in 19 East Tennessee counties extending from the northeast corner southward: Johnson, Carter, Washington, Greene, Cocke, Sevier, Blount, Monroe, McMinn, and Polk counties, with Hancock, Claiborne, Grainger, and Jefferson counties adjoining the diagonal line-up. Roane County and four counties on the Cumberland Plateau, namely Overton, Putnam, Cumberland, and Franklin, completed the set in the region. In comparison, five settlement and mission schools were reported in Middle Tennessee.

Of the 34 East Tennessee institutions, three were independent of any one church group and five schools' affiliations were not known. Denominations represented among the remaining schools were: Methodist Episcopal, Presbyterian USA, Southern Baptist, Disciples of Christ, Friends,

Methodist Episcopal South, and Episcopalian. Eight institutions were devoted to higher education (Lincoln Memorial University and Tusculum, Hiwassee, Maryville, Milligan, Carson-Newman, Tennessee Wesleyan, and Washington Colleges). The remaining 26 schools were labeled as follows: five secondary, 11 both secondary and elementary, one junior high, one both junior high and elementary, two elementary, and six unknown. The great majority, then, attempted to fill the gap in secondary education in remote areas or to prepare students to become teachers themselves. Many settlement schools closed once expanded public education reached their locales, but a few continue and operate today, though they have evolved from their Progressive-era or earlier beginnings.

Margaret D. Binnicker, Middle Tennessee State University

SUGGESTED READING: David Whisnant, *All That Is Native and Fine* (1983)

SEE: ARROWMONT SCHOOL; CARSON-NEWMAN COLLEGE; CLAXTON, PHILANDER P.; HIWASSEE COLLEGE; LINCOLN MEMORIAL UNIVERSITY; MARYVILLE COLLEGE; MILLIGAN COLLEGE; PI BETA PHI SCHOOL; PITTMAN CENTER; ST. ANDREW'S-SEWANEE SCHOOL; TENNESSEE WESLEYAN COLLEGE; TUSCULUM COLLEGE

SEVIER, CATHERINE SHERRILL (1754–1836), known as "Bonnie Kate," was the wife of John Sevier (1745–1815), Revolutionary War hero, Indian fighter, Governor of the State of Franklin, and first Governor of Tennessee. Legend has it that their courtship began after she was surprised by an Indian attack while milking a cow outside the walls of Fort Watauga in northeast Tennessee. The defenders of the fort quickly closed the gates, locking her out. She ran to the palisades and, helped by Sevier, climbed to safety. She and Sevier married in 1780, when she was 26, after the death of his first wife, Sarah Hawkins. At their home in Washington County, Bonnie Kate made soldiers' uniforms, cast lead balls for ammunition, and prepared food for her husband's victorious campaign against the British at the Battle of King's Mountain in South Carolina. On the eve of the battle, she thwarted a Tory attempt to murder her husband. Bonnie Kate held the title "First Lady" three times, first from 1785 to 1788, when her husband was Governor of the State of Franklin, and during his terms as the first and third Governor of Tennessee, 1796 to 1801, and 1803 to 1809. She was originally buried in Russellville, Alabama, but was reinterred in 1922, next to her husband on the lawn of the old Knox County Courthouse in Knoxville. The inscription on her tombstone describes her as the "brightest star among pioneer women of this state."

Fred W. Sauceman, East Tennessee State University

SEE: SEVIER, JOHN

SEVIER COUNTY has the distinction of having three birthdays: in 1785 under the State of Franklin, in 1794 under the Southwest Territory, and in 1796 under the State of Tennessee. Sevierville, the county seat, and the county were named in honor of John Sevier. The land area of 592.3 square miles has varied topography, which includes fertile lowlands along the French Broad and Little Pigeon rivers, the hilly portion drained by the Forks of Little Pigeon River, and Clingman's Dome, the highest mountain peak in Tennessee, and the majestic peaks of the Great Smoky Mountains.

The two branches of the Great Indian War Path which crossed the county became the chief migratory route for the early settlers in the 1780s. The signing of the Dumplin Treaty at Major Hugh Henry's Station in 1785 opened the area south of the French Broad for settlement.

The first court of Sevier County, State of Franklin, was held at Samuel Newell's Station on Boyds Creek in March, 1785. The first court of Sevier County, Southwest Territory, was held at the home of Isaac Thomas on November 8, 1794. Magistrates present were Samuel Newell, Joseph Willson, Joshua Gist, Peter Bryant, Joseph Vance, and Andrew Evans. Absent were Mordecai Lewis and Robert Pollock. On January 11, 1796, Spencer Clack, John Clack, Samuel Wear, Peter Bryant, and Thomas Buckingham were sent to help prepare a state constitution at the convention in Knoxville. John Clack was elected to the Senate and Spencer Clack and Samuel Wear to the House of Representatives.

Surveyors who prepared the plats for the State of Tennessee to issue land grants from 1807 to 1894 included Robert Wear, Thomas Price, Mark Moore, Guilford Cannon, Daniel Kerr, John Mullendore, G.W. Layman, Wellington McMahan, John A. Trotter, G.W.J. Hill, and Jesse Atchley.

Sevierville, originally the "Forks of Little Pigeon" community settled by the Isaac Thomas, Spencer Clack, and James McMahon families in the 1780s, became the county seat in 1795. The present courthouse with its majestic tower was built in 1896. Incorporated in 1901 with A.M. Paine as mayor, Sevierville had 7,178 residents in 1990.

Pigeon Forge, originally the "Fanshiers" community, was settled by the Wear, Fancher, and Lovelady families in the 1780s. The Pigeon Forge post office opened in 1841 with William K. Love as postmaster. Incorporated in 1961 with Xan Davenport as mayor, the city had a population of 3,027 in 1990.

Gatlinburg, originally the "White Oak Flats" community settled by the Richard Reagan and Martha Ogle families ca. 1806, was the name given to the post office in Radford Gatlin's store in 1856. Incorporated in 1945 with Dick Whaley as mayor, the city had a population of 3,417 in 1990.

Pittman Center, named for Reverend Eli Pittman of Elmira, New York, was established by Reverend E.O. Burnett as a Methodist settlement school and health center in 1921 and closed with the retirement of Dr. Robert F. Thomas in 1964. The Pittman Center community, incorporated in 1974 with Conley Huskey as mayor, had a population of 478 in 1990.

Manufacturing in the county before the Civil War included cottage industries, the Sevierville Pottery, mills, the bloomary forge at Pigeon Forge established by Isaac Love in 1817, and Sweden furnace. From the 1870s to 1920s flatboat transportation from Sevierville to the steamboats on the French Broad River increased trade. The construction of the Knoxville, Sevierville, and Eastern Railroad (K.S. & E.) and the extension to McCookville in 1920 enhanced manufacturing. The railroad ceased operation in 1961.

The logging industry flourished from 1900 to 1930 in the Great Smoky Mountains. The establishment of the Great Smoky Mountains National Park in 1930 and the construction of Highway 441 through the center of the valley in the 1950s opened the area for the development of tourism.

In 1996 with a population of 51,043 the labor force is predominantly employed in trade and finance due to the large number of retail establishments associated with the tourism industry. Manufacturing is the second largest industry.

Nancy Academy (1811–1897) and Murphy College (1892–1936) were historic educational institutions. In 1996 Sevier County has three high schools, four middle schools, one intermediate school, nine elementary schools, and a vocational center. A branch of Walters State Community College is in Sevierville. The Sevier County Library, founded by Fred P. Rawlings, opened in 1920 in the Masonic Temple.

Sevierville's African Americans have contributed to Tennessee history. Many brick buildings in Sevierville today attest to the skill of brick making, masonry, and carpentry of Isaac Dockery, Samuel Coleman, the P. Witt McMahan family, and S.H. Burden and son. The furniture of Lewis Buckner is a prized possession. Mary Bond McMahan and James Chandler were educators.

Preston B. Love published the first newspaper, *The Enterprise*, in 1882. Subsequent newspapers include *The Republican, Sevier County Republican, Star, Vindicator, Volunteer, Sevier County Republican and Sevier County Record, Gatlinburg Press, News-Record,* and *Mountain Press.* The Bank of Sevierville opened in 1888.

Ray L. Reagan, the elected county judge from 1956 until his death in 1978, led the campaign to attract new industry to broaden the county's agricultural and tourist-oriented economy. He was instrumental in the remodeling of the courthouse, the development of Sevier County Industrial Park, the Sevier County Medical Center, and the Pigeon Forge-Gatlinburg Airport. Dollywood is the largest amusement park in Tennessee.

In 1996 Sevier County is the second fastest growing county in Tennessee.

Beulah Duggan Linn, Sevier County Historian

SEE: ARROWMONT SCHOOL; BUCKNER, LEWIS; DECORATIVE ARTS, APPALACHIAN; DOCKERY, ISAAC; DOLLYWOOD; GREAT SMOKY MOUNTAINS NATIONAL PARK; HOUK, LEONIDAS C.; MCMAHAN, FRED; PARTON, DOLLY; PI BETA PHI SCHOOL; PITTMAN CENTER

Governor John Sevier, portrait by Charles Willson Peale.

TENNESSEE HISTORICAL SOCIETY COLLECTION, TENNESSEE STATE MUSEUM

SEVIER, JOHN (1745–1815), pioneer, soldier, statesman and a founder of the Republic, was Tennessee's first governor and one of its most illustrious citizens. Married and on his own at age 16, he was in the vanguard of frontier life and accomplishment from his late teenage years until his death. First and only Governor of the aborted "State of Franklin," six terms Governor of Tennessee, and Congressman for four terms from the eastern district, he was also a soldier of no mean accomplishment, having risen to the rank of general in the North Carolina militia.

Born near the present town of New Market, Virginia, Sevier was the oldest of seven children of Valentine and Joanna Goad Sevier. His forebears—the Xaviers—were of Huguenot religious persuasion who had fled France for England, anglicized their name, and became prosperous farmers. By 1740 Valentine had arrived in Virginia and settled in the Shenandoah Valley on Smith's Creek.

Not much is known of Sevier's early life. Educational opportunities were limited, but as a child he apparently learned to read and write; later his state papers and correspondence with Andrew Jackson and others exhibited a concise and direct style. Married in 1761 to Sarah Hawkins (1746–1780), a daughter of Joseph and Sarah Marlin Hawkins, the couple settled in the valley of his birth. There Sevier farmed, dealt in furs, speculated in land, ran a tavern, and fought Indians—along with raising an ever-increasing family.

By 1773 he lived on the Holston River, but three years later he had moved to a farm on the Watauga River near the present town of Elizabethton. In the same year, North Carolina authorities created the Washington District, which included the Watauga settlements, and Sevier was sent to the Provincial Congress of North Carolina as representative.

The Revolutionary War began in 1775, and in the following year Sevier was named a lieutenant colonel of the North Carolina militia and assigned first to protecting the frontier settlements. He fought elsewhere but was confined primarily to the South. The encounter for which he became best known was the Battle of King's Mountain (1780), in which he and his fellow frontiersmen fought Tories and British soldiers at a location just north of Spartanburg, South Carolina.

The British, having met with only moderate success in the middle and northern colonies, had turned in late 1780 to the soft underbelly of the rebellious provinces where they prevailed without difficulty in Georgia. Then they moved northward without serious opposition. Major Patrick Ferguson, assigned to the command of the British left flank, viewed the western settlements with disdain. Overconfident, he ordered frontiersmen to lay down their arms and give allegiance to the Crown; otherwise, he wrote, he would march over the mountains, "hang . . . western leaders and lay the country waste with fire and sword." Sevier and others, accepting the challenge, gathered at Sycamore Shoals late in September 1780, determined to engage Ferguson before he could reach Watauga. They soon found him on a narrow ridge in northwest South Carolina where he, with perhaps 1,000 men, had ensconced himself claiming that even "the Almighty" could not drive him off. But the backwoodsmen ascended the heights and assaulted him from both south and west, taking care to remain well camouflaged behind trees, logs, and rocks. Although forced to fall back several times, the westerners rallied each time, and, after about an hour of fighting, claimed victory. They had lost fewer than 100 men

while the British had lost three times that number, including Ferguson. The victory turned the British from the West, and pushed Sevier forward as the foremost figure among the transmontane people. One of Sevier's biographers thought it "impossible to state just how great an influence this exerted upon his future political career."

Several months before King's Mountain, Sevier's wife of nearly 20 years died and was buried in an unmarked grave just outside Nolichucky Fort in Washington County. She and Sevier had raised ten children. Sevier later married Catherine ("Bonny Kate") Sherrill (1754–1838) whom he had rescued four years earlier during a surprise attack by the Cherokees. They reared eight children.

Soon after the Revolution, Sevier became involved in a movement designed to secure separate statehood for the people living in Washington, Sullivan, and Greene counties. The Continental Congress in 1780 had urged that lands claimed by North Carolina and Virginia should become states soon after hostilities might end. Thomas Jefferson had presented a plan whereby 18 new states might be carved from the western territories. But North Carolina authorities objected vehemently when western leaders assembled in Jonesborough in August 1784 to make plans for statehood. When they chose Sevier as Governor and drafted a constitution, claiming an "inalienable right" to form an independent state, Governor Alexander Martin threatened to "render the revolting territory not worth possessing" if North Carolina did not retain sovereignty over it. Attempts at conciliation divided the Franklin people into factions and border warfare developed. Several men were killed or wounded, and two of Sevier's sons were captured, threatened, and held briefly.

Sevier's term as Governor of Franklin expired in the spring of 1788, and for all practical purposes the state came to an end. Sevier was arrested and charged with treason but never tried. Within less than a year he had taken an oath of allegiance to North Carolina and was elected to the State Senate. A few months later he was restored to his rank of brigadier general in the North Carolina militia.

North Carolina permanently ceded its western lands to the central government in 1789, and in the following year President George Washington signed into law a measure for the governance of the region. Sevier probably was the choice of most of the western people for the post of Territorial Governor, but Washington appointed William Blount instead. Soon Sevier became a member of the Territorial Legislative Council—a group of five men provided for under the Congressional Ordinance of 1787 designed for the governance of territories. He was among those who urged Governor Blount to call the legislature into session to make plans for statehood as required under the ordinance. Blount complied, and early in 1796 leaders drafted a constitution and applied to Congress for admission. After several weeks of debate—at times acrimonious, as Federalists and Anti-Federalists haggled over terms and reasons for admission—Congress recommended statehood, and President Washington signed into law a bill creating Tennessee as the sixteenth state.

The new constitution had provided for a two-year term for governors with the right to serve "not . . . more than six years in any term of eight." The other qualifications to hold the office of governor were simple. One must be at least 25 years of age, possess a free-hold of at least 500 acres, and be a citizen for four years. Sevier met these requirements and became the only serious candidate.

For months before the admissions bill had been enacted, Tennesseans conducted affairs as though the state had been legally admitted to the Union. Elections were held in late February and legislators convened in late March. On March 29 they examined the returns of the gubernatorial race and determined that Sevier won. On March 30, Sevier took the oath of office at Knoxville. In a brief inaugural address, he thanked voters for the confidence reposed in him and he pledged to discharge "with fidelity" the tasks of chief executive. A 16-gun salute ended the brief ceremonies. When Sevier became Governor, the total population of the new state was only about 85,000, but by the end of his gubernatorial service it had increased to nearly 250,000.

Although the office of Governor was not considered a full time task, still Sevier had the usual problems which the foibles of human nature were sure to create. Indian problems were vexatious as any and Sevier met them with characteristic vigor. The Tellico and Dearborn treaties, negotiated in 1805 and 1806 respectively, did much to clear Indian claims in both east and west, but the attitude and actions of the federal government in its strict policy of enforcement angered Tennesseans.

Many disputes over military rank tried Sevier's patience. Free men between 18 and 50 were subject to military duty, and they elected their own officers. But allegations of fraud permeated the contests in many of the counties and at all levels, and the Governor—who issued the commissions—had to decide who had been legally and duly elected. Although Sevier apparently handled these matters as judiciously as he could, he was frequently criticized in many counties for allegedly selecting political friends and favorites. His disputes with Andrew Jackson over these and other matters led to considerable bitterness between the two. Indeed Jackson's charges that Sevier was guilty of forgery and bribery in his procurement of lands brought challenges to duels and bitter words.

Internal improvements such as wagon roads interested Sevier from his early days as Governor. He also frequently mentioned a need for "the encouragement of education"—and a measure chartering schools in most of the counties was enacted in 1806. Improving conditions in the state militia and the development of a better means of settling disputes over land titles were other matters of concern.

In March, 1809—a few months before his final term ended—Sevier ran before the legislature for the U.S. Senate but was defeated by Judge Joseph Anderson. Later in that year, voters in Knox County sent him to the State Senate. Then, in 1811, he was elected to Congress. His advanced years and his unfamiliarity with federal procedures resulted in his being an ineffective legislator on the national level.

Sevier died on September 24, 1815, while on a mission to the Alabama territory where he had gone with U.S. troops to determine the proper location of the Creek boundary. He was buried on the eastern bank of the Tallapoosa River near Fort Decatur.

Sevier was a product of the frontier and a hero to Tennesseans who understood and appreciated his varied career. When in 1887 his body was reinterred on the courthouse lawn in Knoxville, a monument was erected whose inscription well describes his life of public service: "John Sevier, pioneer, soldier, statesman, and one of the founders of the Republic; Governor of the State of Franklin; six times Governor of Tennessee; four times elected to Congress; a typical pioneer, who conquered the wilderness and fashioned the State; a protector and hero of King's Mountain; fought thirty-five battles, won thirty-five victories; his Indian war cry, "Here they are! Come on boys!"

Robert E. Corlew, Middle Tennessee State University

SUGGESTED READING: Carl S. Driver, *John Sevier: Pioneer of the Old Southwest* (1932)

SEE: BLOUNT, WILLIAM; FRANKLIN, STATE OF; GOVERNMENT; JACKSON, ANDREW; KNOXVILLE; MARBLE SPRINGS; OVERMOUNTAIN MEN; SEVIER, CATHERINE S.; SOUTHWEST TERRITORY; SYCAMORE SHOALS STATE HISTORIC AREA; TREATIES

THE SEWANEE REVIEW (SR), founded by William Peterfield Trent in 1892 at the University of the South in Sewanee, Tennessee, is the nation's oldest quarterly that has been continuously published. The *SR* changed from a general journal devoted to the humanities to a literary and critical quarterly, achieving its metamorphosis during the editorships of Andrew Lytle (1942–1944) and Allen Tate (1944–1946). Poetry began to be published in the 1920s; fiction in 1943; reminiscences and other familiar essays in 1987. Literary criticism has been the magazine's staple since the mid-1940s. The *SR's* editors have included W.S. Knickerbocker (1926–1942), John E. Palmer

(1946–1952), Monroe K. Spears (1952–1961), Andrew Lytle (1961–1973), and George Core (since 1973).

The critical program chiefly entails English literature since 1500 in addition to various classical writers. Although the critical emphasis is given principally to the literature of the twentieth century, such subjects as the English Renaissance (especially Shakespeare) receive regular attention. Over the recent past there have been special issues on many subjects and modes, including Irish letters, commonwealth (or postcolonial) literature, and biography and autobiography.

The *Sewanee Review*'s regular contributors include writers from Great Britain, Canada, and India in addition to the United States. Representative writers of the last half century are Flannery O'Connor, Robert Penn Warren, Wallace Fowlie, L.C. Knights, Robert B. Heilman, B.L. Reid, Elizabeth Spencer, Samuel Hynes, Walker Percy, James M. Cox, George Woodcock, Jayanta Mahapatra, Helen Norris, Malcolm Cowley, George Garrett, Neal Bowers, F.D. Reeve, William Hoffman, Merrill Joan Gerber, Neal Bowers, Walter Sullivan, and Catharine Savage Brosman. Many of these authors have written in more than one mode for the *SR*—Warren and Garrett in nearly every genre.

George Core, The Sewanee Review

SEE: LITERATURE; LYTLE, ANDREW NELSON; UNIVERSITY OF THE SOUTH; TATE, JOHN O. ALLEN

SHAPE-NOTE SINGING is a predominantly rural, Protestant, Anglo-American music tradition that involves singing from hymnals or "tunebooks" having shaped notes (a.k.a. "character notes," "buckwheat notes," or "patent notes") as opposed to the standard "round notes." Shape-Note Singing is rooted in the Singing School Movement that began in New England during the eighteenth century, but swept west and south with settlers during the early nineteenth century. That reform movement—an attempt to raise the level of congregational singing in the colonial churches by teaching them to read music notation—spurred an increase in both the number of published tunebooks and the number of newly composed tunes and anthems. The Singing School Movement thus fostered the earliest body of indigenous American musical compositions following the arrival of Europeans. These tunebooks, in fact, are most important historically as repositories of indigenous American hymn tunes, anthems, fuguing tunes, and folk hymns of the eighteenth and nineteenth centuries. In a further effort to help students learn to read "by note," a system of four shaped notes—Fa (◣), Sol (◯), La (▢), and Mi (◇)—was invented in the early nineteenth century to be used with the four-syllable "fasola" solmization system. In the mid-nineteenth century, a system of seven shaped notes—Do (X),

Ra (D), Mi (◇), Fa (◣), Sol (◯), La (▢), and Ti (△)—was introduced to be used with the seven solmization syllables still used in music instruction. These systems, as well as the rudiments of music, are usually explained in an essay preceding the three- and four-part compositions.

The Sacred Harp, a four-shape-note hymnal first published in Georgia in 1844, is the most popular of the shape-note books, especially in Middle Tennessee, northwestern Georgia, and northern Alabama. In East Tennessee, the favorite is *The New Harp of Columbia,* a seven-shape-note hymnal published in Nashville in 1867. *The Southern Harmony,* another four-shape-note book published in 1835—and for many years used only in Benton, Kentucky—is also used by some Tennessee singers.

In keeping with the tradition's foundations in the Singing School Movement, shape-note singing typically occurs in annual, one-to-three-day "singings." These singings are not just musical, but social, pedagogical, and religious events. Each day consists of morning and afternoon sessions (or "classes") with the hosts providing "Dinner on the Grounds." The singers sit in a square formation facing the center. Each side of the square represents one of the four vocal parts. Alto and bass are sung by women and men, respectively, but the treble and tenor (or "lead") parts are sung by both sexes in octaves, resulting in a rich, six-part texture. Hymns or "tunes" are led from the center by a singer who stands facing the tenors, in whose part lies the melody. Each tune is sung first using the solmization syllables, after which one or more verses of the hymn proper are sung. The singing style is characteristically loud (sometimes piercing), often quite fast, and marked by a vigorous beat and much enjoyment among the participants.

Stephen Shearon, Middle Tennessee State University

SEE: CARDEN, ALLEN D.; MUSIC; RELIGION

SHARECROPPING, technically defined, is a land and labor arrangement whereby an individual or family receives a stipulated proportion of the crops produced on a particular plot of land in return for their labor on that same plot. The legal status of sharecroppers varied over time and from state to state. Historically, many southern states classified sharecroppers as agricultural laborers, making them legally indistinguishable from wage hands who worked on a daily, monthly, or annual basis on farms operated by others. In the 1870s, however, the Tennessee Supreme Court defined sharecroppers as "tenants in common of the crops," and ruled that the sharecropper's portion of the harvest represented personal property, not wages. Legally, sharecropping in Tennessee became a variety of agricultural tenancy rather than a form of wage labor. Practically speaking, however, sharecroppers resembled both farm laborers and tenants in fundamental ways. Like the farm laborer, the sharecropper was allocated work stock, tools, and seed by the landlord, received wages rather than paid rent, and commonly labored under close supervision from the landlord, who typically controlled most managerial decisions. Like tenants, the sharecroppers farmed a specific plot of land and worked alongside their families, rather than singly or in a labor gang.

The lack of systematic statistics limits what can be known with certainty about the prevalence of sharecropping in Tennessee before the late nineteenth century. The institution undoubtedly existed in the state long before the Civil War, but it is not likely that it was very widespread. After the Civil War, it mushroomed in importance, so that as early as 1880, sharecroppers comprised nearly one-fourth of all farm operators and fully two-thirds of all tenants. To a significant degree, this expansion resulted from emancipation. The newly freed slaves rejected the initial attempts of white landowners to employ them exclusively as wage hands. From the end of the war through the 1890s there was a gradual, but inexorable shift among blacks from wage labor to sharecropping (and to a lesser degree, to other forms of tenancy). Sharecropping in postbellum tenancy, however, was far from an exclusively African-American institution. Historically, whites constituted two-thirds or more of all sharecroppers in the state, and the initial expansion of sharecropping after emancipation—at least through the end of the 1870s—stemmed in large part from a shift among whites from wage labor to sharecropping as the end of slavery opened up new opportunities for landless whites in the former plantation districts of central and southwestern Tennessee.

Sharecropping continued to be a significant institution in Tennessee agriculture for more than 60 years after the Civil War, peaking in importance in the early 1930s, when sharecroppers operated approximately one-third of all farm units in the state. It declined steadily and rapidly after 1940, due to a combination of factors. The most important were the increasing mechanization of Tennessee farms, which rendered the labor of sharecroppers more expendable, and the growing demand for industrial labor outside the South, which enticed thousands of white and black Tennesseans to migrate to northern and western cities.

Robert Tracy McKenzie, University of Washington
SEE: AGRICULTURAL TENANCY; AGRICULTURE; RECONSTRUCTION

SHARP, AARON J. "JACK" (1904–), internationally acclaimed botanist and author of over 200 publications, was born in Plain City, Ohio, on July 29, 1904, the son of Prentice Daniel H. Sharp and Maude Herriott Sharp. His mother died when Sharp was only 16 months old, and he was sent to live with his Quaker

grandmother, whom he credits with providing him his first awareness of natural science. In 1922 he entered Ohio Wesleyan University and graduated in 1927 with a B.S. in Botany. His M.S. in Botany came at the University of Oklahoma in 1929 and his Ph.D. from Ohio State University in 1938.

Sharp came to the University of Tennessee in 1929, becoming a full professor in 1946 and serving as department head from 1951 to 1961. From 1958 to 1973 he was Associate Curator of the UT Herbarium. Sharp gained an international reputation for his work in the field of bryology, the study of mosses and liverworts. He has collected plants and mosses in every county in Tennessee, every state in the United States, and a number of foreign countries including Mexico, Japan, Taiwan, Russia, Tanzania, and Finland. An undaunted champion of environmental responsibility, Sharp served as the first botanist for the Great Smoky Mountains National Park.

Sharp co-authored *Great Smoky Mountain Wildflowers,* served on the editorial committee of *American Journal of Botany* (1948–1953), and was associate editor for *The Bryologist* (1938–1954), *Castanea* (1947–1949), and *Journal of the Hattori Botanical Laboratory,* Japan (1961–). He holds memberships in 43 professional and learned societies, including memberships in organizations of local and state interest such as the Smoky Mountains Natural History Association and the Tennessee Academy of Sciences.

In 1991 the Tennessee Environmental Education Association presented Sharp the organization's highest honor, the Distinguished Service Award. In 1992, he was elected a Fellow in the Linnean Society of London.

Connie L. Lester, Tennessee Historical Society
SEE: GREAT SMOKY MOUNTAINS NATIONAL PARK; UNIVERSITY OF TENNESSEE

SHAVER, SAMUEL M. (1816–1878), portraitist, was born in Sullivan County, Tennessee, the son of David Shaver and Catherine Barringer Shaver. He may have been influenced by William Harrison Scarborough (1812–1871), a native-born Tennessee artist, four years Shaver's senior, who did portraits of Shaver's relatives. Shaver's earliest known painting dates to 1845, but he was probably painting before that time. For the next quarter century, he was East Tennessee's standard portraitist.

In 1845 Shaver married Mary Hannah Elizabeth Powel, daughter of the late Congressman Samuel Powel. The couple lived with the congressman's widow in Rogersville and were the parents of two daughters. In 1851 Shaver was professor of drawing and painting at the Odd Fellows Female Institute in Rogersville. In 1852 he advertised in Greeneville and Knoxville papers; for several years thereafter his whereabouts are unknown. The death of his first wife in January 1856 recalled him to Rogersville, where he remained until the Civil War.

At the outset of the war, pro-Confederate Shaver moved to Knoxville, where he became one of the founders of the East Tennessee Art Association. The Association commissioned him to do portraits of 15 Confederate leaders and generals, presumably from photographs. None of the portraits has been located, and perhaps they were never painted. From 1863 to 1868 Shaver lived and worked near Russellville, Tennessee. About 1868 he joined his mother-in-law and family in Jerseyville, Illinois, near St. Louis, where he continued painting. He died on June 21, 1878.

James C. Kelly, Virginia Historical Society
SEE: ART; HAWKINS COUNTY

SHAVIN HOUSE, the only dwelling designed by Frank Lloyd Wright in Tennessee, is located in Chattanooga. In 1949 newlyweds Gerte and Seamour Shavin contacted Frank Lloyd Wright to design a home for them on Missionary Ridge in Chattanooga. Wright (1870–1959), one of the most prominent architects of the twentieth century, developed a house plan based on his vision of a democratic America that appreciated and respected nature. The result was an "Usonian" house that simplified the building process by eliminating excessive labor, materials, and spaces. His Usonian houses utilized native materials and featured open, flowing plans that were often based on a grid. The use of open spaces and large windows allowed for natural heating and cooling, as well as expansive views of the property surrounding the house.

Constructed in 1952, Wright never visited the site of Shavin's house. Marvin Bachman, an apprentice of Wright, supervised the construction. Both the exterior and interior of the house use red cypress and Tennessee Crab Orchard stone. A focal point of the house is the large stone fireplace in the living room. As in many of Wright's houses, the Shavins's Usonian house contains built-ins and furniture designed by Wright, resulting in a unified design scheme. The use of native materials, and its expansive setting overlooking Chattanooga, makes the Shavin house a model Usonian house.

Claudette Stager, Tennessee Historical Commission
SEE: CHATTANOOGA; CRAB ORCHARD STONE

SHAWNEES are one of several tribes who speak the Central Algonquian dialect. They were the most southerly located of all the Algonquian tribes. In most Algonquian languages they are called *Shawunogi*, which literally translates as "Southerners." Legends indicate that they were originally situated in Eastern Canada and migrated south prior to the arrival of Europeans. Many archaeologists associate the Shawnees with the late prehistoric Fort Ancient cul-

ture which was located in the Ohio Valley. The mixed hunting and horticultural subsistence system and the presence of stone-box graves of the Fort Ancient culture was similar to the historic Shawnee cultural practices. The fact that the earliest historic contacts with the Shawnees occurred in the Ohio Valley also lends support to such an identity.

Historically the Shawnees were a highly nomadic people and during the colonial period various groups of them could be found in nearly every region east of the Mississippi River. The earliest historical references locate them along the upper Ohio River. This location in Pennsylvania placed them into close contact with the Iroquois, who became long standing enemies of the Shawnees. It is believed that the Iroquois drove the main body of Shawnees from the east scattering them as far west as the Mississippi River, and south to Alabama where they were closely allied with the Creeks.

The Shawnees were organized into five divisions: Chillicothe, Hathawekela, Kispogogi, Mequachake, and Piqua. Each village tended to be affiliated with one or another of these divisions and the village name itself often reflected the division. It is speculated that these divisions may have been the principal villages at a time when all the Shawnees lived together as a single group. A patrilineal clan structure with totemic names likely existed early in Shawnee history. However, descriptions of these totemic name groups in historic accounts seem to indicate that children were assigned to one of these groups by a name giver and that it could be changed later if it did not seem to match his or her personality.

In historic times the village was the most important social unit for the Shawnees. Probably because they were so highly nomadic throughout the colonial period it was difficult to maintain the clan structure. The members of a village were a highly autonomous group and made their own political and economic decisions. Thus, members of villages would often ally themselves with other tribes or with European colonists during conflicts independently from other Shawnee groups.

The Shawnees were known to be fierce fighters. Their conservatism in attempting to retain their own culture and preserve the land they occupied often placed them into conflict with Europeans and other Indian tribes. In spite of their conservatism they became dependent upon trade goods provided by the Europeans. In order to obtain furs to trade for these goods they often were forced into conflict with other tribes who laid claim to the same hunting grounds they were using.

As early as the 1670s the Shawnees were hunting and trading along the Cumberland River in what is today Tennessee. They had several villages along the Cumberland which was identified as "*la riviere des*

Chaouesnons" or the "River of the Shawnees" on early French maps. Their primary village was near the present site of Nashville. This location placed them into direct conflict with the Cherokees on the east and the Chickasaws to the west. Both continually harassed the Shawnees who were located there. In 1714 the Cherokees and Chickasaws united to drive the Shawnees out of the region.

The Shawnees continued to hunt in this area, however, and in 1745 the same two tribes united once again to do battle with the Shawnees. One band of Shawnees led by Peter Chartier, a half-breed son of a French trader, settled with the Creeks in Alabama. They moved to the Cumberland in 1756 but were also expelled. In the later part of the eighteenth century the Shawnee warrior, Cheeseekau, joined with the Chickamaugans, a band of Creek, Cherokee, and white Tories, to raid white settlements in the Cumberland Valley. Tecumseh, who was attempting to recruit other tribes to join his northern confederacy, joined Cheeseekau in the fight against the Cumberland Valley settlers. In 1792 Cheeseekau was killed in a raid and Tecumseh buried him, vowing to return. Tecumseh's efforts to recruit tribes to his cause did not fare well in Tennessee. His death at the Battle of the Thames in Canada virtually ended the Indian resistance in the east.

Jerry E. Clark, Creigton University

SUGGESTED READINGS: Jerry E. Clark, *The Shawnee* (1993): James H. Howard, *Shawnee!: The Ceremonialism of a Native Tribe and its Cultural Background* (1981)

SEE: CHICKASAWS; EXPLORATIONS, EARLY; FRENCH LICK; OVERHILL CHEROKEES

SHELBY COUNTY was established by the Tennessee General Assembly on November 24, 1819, just a little over a year after the "Jackson Purchase" and Chickasaw treaty freed West Tennessee from Indian claims. The county is named after one of the successful treaty commissioners, Isaac Shelby, a Revolutionary War veteran and former Governor of Kentucky. Although sparsely populated at the time, Shelby County began its existence as Tennessee's largest (784 square miles) in area and is now also the largest county in population (over 860,000 people).

From the beginning, Shelby County enjoyed a geographical advantage as a travel and trade center. The Chickasaws had already established trails from the fourth Chickasaw Bluff (future Memphis) to future northwest Alabama and northeast Mississippi (now U.S. Highways 72 and 78 respectively) in order to gain access to early Mississippi River trade. Originally these trails followed ridge lines between river basins in order to facilitate all-weather travel. Later they would become the basic routes for early railroads, which would make Shelby County and its principal city, Memphis, the economic center of the region.

The first meeting of the Shelby County Quarterly Court was held on May 1, 1820, and authorized $125 for the construction of a log courthouse and jail along with a property tax of $6.25 per 100 acres of land. It also authorized the conduct of a county survey which officially reported three years later that the county contained only 625 acres, because of a state boundary error by James Winchester which had sliced a strip four miles wide and approximately thirty miles long off the bottom of Shelby County and recorded it as being in Mississippi. The error was not discovered until 1835, but is commemorated today by Winchester Road which follows his state boundary survey line. Shelby County property in this strip is still neatly delineated by the Mississippi survey system of section and quarter sections while the northern 80% of the county uses the older Tennessee survey system of "metes and bounds."

In 1826 Memphis was incorporated as a town, but almost two years earlier, the county seat was relocated to the village of Raleigh at Sanderlin's Bluff on the Wolf River, squarely in the center of the county. There it remained until after the Civil War, when in 1868 the clamor of lawyers and litigants brought it back to Memphis. Other early settlements include Big Creek (south of present Millington), which apparently was home to several families even before the Chickasaw treaty, and the log cabin which would expand into Davies Manor at Brunswick dates from 1807. Obviously, these early settlers had made their own arrangements with the Indians. Near Big Creek, further south towards Memphis, was the Egypt settlement, part of the exotic Egyptian-naming era which swept southern Illinois and West Tennessee around 1818 to 1820.

Other areas of Shelby County were also receiving attention. In 1825 an idealistic young Scotswoman, Frances Wright, acquired 2,000 acres of wilderness property about four miles upstream of Raleigh on the Wolf River. There in early 1826 she and her younger sister, Camilla, began a noble experiment. They established a plantation named Nashoba upon which black slaves could work and earn sufficient credit to purchase their freedom. The surplus funds would be used to buy more slaves and repeat the cycle. However, there were no profits and in 1829 Wright ended the project, but kept the property, eventually leaving it to a niece who only parted with the last remaining acreage in 1900. Today it comprises the southeast quadrant of the Shelby County Penal farm (Shelby Farms) and the western subdivision of Germantown located north of the Norfolk-Southern Railroad (earlier the Memphis & Charleston Railroad). Germantown now has a population of nearly 32,000.

During the nineteenth century, lasting towns were also established at Bartlett (currently Shelby County's second most populated with more than 35,700 people); Collierville (24,700); Millington (18,100); and Arlington (1,400). Several twentieth century incorporations have been attempted, but only one, Lakeland (1,275) has survived. Census estimates place Memphis at 600,000 in 1997.

The county government continued to be based upon the accepted statewide quarterly court pattern until the Civil War. During the years 1862–64 it neither met nor functioned. During Reconstruction it ran afoul of Governor William G. Brownlow, who used the coercive "Metropolitan Police Act" to abolish it and replace it with a five member commission appointed by him. When the State Constitution was rewritten in 1870, a section of it was aimed directly at preventing a repeat of this practice by providing that county officials must either be elected by the people or the Quarterly Court.

However, by 1910 the Shelby County Quarterly Court with its unwieldy 50 members had grown too democratic and large. Legendary political boss E.H. Crump superimposed control through a 1911 legislative act creating a three-member executive commission which could override the Court on all items except the constitutionally protected power to set property taxes. Only after Crump's death in 1954 did this arrangement become unworkable.

Not until 1975 were governance problems solved when the people voted to ratify the "Shelby County Restructure Act," creating a single executive with the title of mayor and a single 11 member legislative body (now called the "County Commission"). The third mayor, Jim Rout, now holds office and the system works well.

Edward F. Williams III, Memphis

SEE: CHICKASAWS; CRUMP, EDWARD H.; DAVIES MANOR; JACKSON PURCHASE; MEMPHIS; NASHOBA; SHELBY, ISAAC; WINCHESTER, JAMES; WRIGHT, FRANCES

SHELBY, ISAAC (1750–1826), early Tennessee settler, Revolutionary War veteran, and Governor of Kentucky, was born in Hagerstown, Maryland, in 1750 to Evan and Letitia Cox Shelby, who moved their family to Sapling Grove, the present site of Bristol, in 1771. Their son Isaac Shelby served as a lieutenant, captain, and colonel in the Revolutionary War and fought with distinction at the Battle of King's Mountain in 1780. In an address before the battle, Colonel Shelby encourged his men to fight in frontier fashion: "Let each one of you be his own officer, taking every care you can of yourselves, and availing yourselves of every advantage that chance may throw in your way. If in the woods, shelter yourselves and give them Indian play! advance from tree to tree, pressing the enemy and killing and disabling all you can."[1]

Political fame followed his military exploits. An early justice of the peace in Sullivan County, Shelby represented the county in the North Carolina House of Commons in 1782. The following year, in 1783, he married Susanna Hart at Boonesborough, Kentucky, and they had 11 children.

After the creation of the Southwest Territory and the State of Kentucky during the early 1790s, Isaac Shelby enjoyed an even more prominent Kentucky career. He was chosen Governor in 1792 and again in 1812. Between his terms as state executive, he served as sheriff of Lincoln County, Kentucky, from 1796 to 1798. His last significant contribution to the region came in 1818 when he, Andrew Jackson, and others negotiated the "Jackson Purchase," which removed control of the western districts of Kentucky and Tennessee from the Chickasaw Indians. To honor this service, the Tennessee General Assembly named Shelby County (Memphis) for Isaac Shelby. He died in Lincoln County, Kentucky, in 1826.

Carroll Van West, Middle Tennessee State University

CITATION:

(1) Samuel C. Williams, *Tennessee During the Revolutionary War* (Knoxville, 1974 [1944]), 151.

SEE: JACKSON PURCHASE; SHELBY COUNTY; SULLIVAN COUNTY

SHELBYVILLE MILLS. In 1852 Gillen, Webb, and Company established Sylvan Mills on the Duck River, outside of Shelbyville, Tennessee, as a woven cotton fabric mill. It produced fabric from raw cotton throughout the late nineteenth and early twentieth centuries. During the early 1920s, the mill changed ownership and became known as Shelbyville Mills. It produced cotton fabric to make tops for the Model T and other automobiles, and cotton cord to make rubber tires stronger and more durable.

The quality of the materials produced at Shelbyville Mills caught the attention of the United States Rubber Company. In December 1933 Shelbyville Mills became a branch of United States Rubber Company's Textile Division. The purchase and expansion of the Shelbyville Mills brought new jobs to Bedford County, which had been hard-hit by the Great Depression. For many new employees, the mill provided the first paychecks in years. Shelbyville Mills also built a company town, complete with a fully stocked store, a neighborhood school that included one of the first gymnasiums in the county, and homes for many employees.

Shelbyville Mills became an integral part of the defense manufacturing efforts of World War II, producing materials for military tires. In the postwar economic boom, the mills made additions to the facility and produced new types of cord. In 1955 Shelbyville Mills began producing synthetic cords. A totally new technique, the "hot stretch" process for producing synthetic cords, was added in 1963.

Market and process changes in the 1970s and 1980s resulted in the decline of the Shelbyville Mills.

The U.S. Rubber Company consolidated all phases of work and changed its name to Uniroyal. In the process Shelbyville Mills lost its unique identity. Finally, in 1982, Shelbyville's Uniroyal plant closed when it became clear that economic and technological changes made the plant unprofitable.

Carol Roberts, Tennessee State Library and Archives
SEE: BEDFORD COUNTY; INDUSTRY; WORLD WAR II

SHILOH, BATTLE OF (April 6–7, 1862). In February 1862 a Union army-navy offensive succeeded in capturing Fort Henry and Fort Donelson, located respectively on the Tennessee and Cumberland rivers, near the Tennessee-Kentucky border. The fall of the two forts initiated a series of Union triumphs that left the Confederacy struggling for life. The Confederate defensive line across southern Kentucky immediately collapsed, and the southern forces retreated from northern Tennessee to Alabama and Mississippi. Major General Don Carlos Buell's Federal forces occupied Nashville, a major arsenal, transportation center, and supply depot, which suddenly found itself the first Confederate state capital to fall to the enemy.

The capture of Fort Henry opened the Tennessee River to Federal penetration to the Alabama and Mississippi state lines. Forces under Major General Ulysses S. Grant advanced south to Pittsburg Landing, located on the west bank of the Tennessee River, about 20 miles north of Corinth, Mississippi. That put Union forces dangerously close to the Confederacy's most important east-west railroad, the Memphis & Charleston line, which made a junction at Corinth with the north-south Mobile & Ohio. If the Union army, designated the Army of the Tennessee, captured Corinth, not only would the Federals control the railroad, but Memphis would likely fall and open several hundred miles of the Mississippi River to Union forces. By late March, Major General Henry W. Halleck ordered Buell and his Army of the Ohio to join Grant for an offensive against Corinth.

Meanwhile, the Confederates concentrated their forces at Corinth in order to stop the Union advance before Buell could reinforce Grant. Their effort culminated in the Battle of Shiloh, named for the Shiloh Methodist Church, near the Union encampment. The Confederate commander, General Albert Sidney Johnston, marshaled about 44,000 troops for his Army of Mississippi; General P.G.T. Beauregard was second-in-command. Johnston's army moved out of Corinth on April 3, hoping to mount a surprise attack on Grant's 42,000 men before Buell's 25,000 troops arrived from Nashville. The intended one-day march became a three-day trek, as rain, complicated marching orders, rugged terrain, and inexperienced soldiers slowed the timetable. Beauregard wanted to call off the offensive, believing that the noise of the troop movement had alerted the enemy, who was now firmly entrenched. But Johnston refused to turn back and ordered the attack for Sunday, April 6.

The first fighting occurred as southern skirmishers, preceding their battle lines, engaged Union patrols at about five o'clock in the morning. The northern soldiers fought a delaying action but fell back as the main body of Confederates moved forward. Despite the action in the woods, many Union soldiers remained unaware of the danger and went about their usual Sunday morning camp routines. Suddenly, yelling Confederates poured out of the woods to the south, and in some sectors, right into the Union camps. For the next two days, 100,000 Union and Confederate soldiers fought along the banks of the Tennessee River.

At first, a Confederate victory seemed likely, as the Federal encampments lacked tactical formation, and green troops manned the advanced positions. Neither Grant, at his headquarters nine miles away, nor Brigadier General William T. Sherman, the camp commander, expected an attack. The southerners benefited from the elements of surprise and momentum, as well as a numerical advantage. Union mishaps compounded the southern advantage; the Federal division of Major General Lew Wallace never got into the April 6 fight, and some 5,000 Union soldiers fled in panic.

Nevertheless, the southern attack did not develop as originally planned by Johnston. An inefficient attack formation and confusion over whether to drive the enemy back to Pittsburg Landing or away from it slowed the Confederate momentum. The southern army lost command control as regiments, brigades, divisions, and corps became hopelessly intermingled. In mid-afternoon, Johnston sustained a leg wound and bled to death shortly thereafter. Perhaps most important, a natural defensive position, "the Hornets' Nest" as it was dubbed by the southerners, became a rallying point for Federal troops, as they fell back toward the Landing. Troops from several divisions joined the men from Brigadier General Benjamin F. Prentiss's division in defending the position against an aggressive southern attack. The action at the Hornets' Nest cost the Confederates too much time and too many men and focused their attention away from an opportunity to break through the weaker Union left nearer the river. The delay awarded Grant, who hurried from Savannah at the sound of the battle, a desperately needed chance to establish a last line of defense at Pittsburg Landing.

Beauregard, in command after Johnston's death, chose not to make an attack on the Federal position at the Landing. Buell arrived with reinforcements during the night, and Lew Wallace came up from Crump's Landing to take a position on the right side of the Union line. In all, the Federals mustered an additional 25,000 men on April 7. They drove the southerners back across the battlefield and forced them to retreat to Corinth.

The two-day carnage approached 24,000 casualties; each side counted more than 1,700 dead and 8,000 wounded in addition to the missing. With casualties totaling nearly five times those of First Bull Run, Shiloh became the bloodiest battle of the war up to that time. Both sides recognized the struggle as one of the most important in the war. The Union army turned back a major southern counter-offensive. With the arrival of reinforcements, a powerful Union army held its position on the flank of the line of the Mississippi, within a few miles of the strategic Memphis & Charleston Railroad. The battle opened the way to split the Confederacy along the Mississippi and doom the western Confederacy.

James L. McDonough, Auburn University

SUGGESTED READINGS: Larry Daniel, *Shiloh* (1996); James L. McDonough, *Shiloh—in Hell before Night* (1977)

SEE: ARMY OF TENNESSEE; CIVIL WAR; CLEBURNE, PATRICK R.; JOHNSTON, ALBERT SIDNEY; RAILROAD, MEMPHIS & CHARLESTON

SHOFNER, AUSTIN CONNER (1916–), Brigadier General Retired, a native of Bedford County, was a Marine Corps officer and soldier of World War II. Shofner's heroic exploits in the Philippines were unique for many reasons: his escape from a Japanese POW camp, his work in guerrilla resistance, and his diary. He was able to write in his diary and keep it hidden while in the POW camps, as well as protect it while hiking through the Philippine jungles. His journal is a valuable historical record of the war in the Philippines and is in the Manuscript Collections of the Tennessee State Library and Archives.

Shofner's military career began in 1941, as a lieutenant and company commander in the Fourth Marine Regiment stationed in Shanghai, China. In November 1941, the regiment was transferred to the Philippine Islands to assist the Philippine Army in its defense against the expected Japanese invasion. Shofner fought in the battles around Bataan and Corregidor, and received the Silver Star with Oak Leaf Cluster and a promotion to captain in February 1942.

In May 1942 Corregidor surrendered to the Japanese. Shofner and his group were placed in several different POW camps, where they endured many hardships. They were forced to watch as fellow soldiers were beaten and killed, or died from starvation and disease. They suffered from various battle wounds and illnesses such as malaria and dysentery without medical attention. A group of ten Marines, including Shofner, and two Filipino soldiers took advantage of work details outside the camp walls to escape the Davao POW camp.

The escapees fled through the jungles to the northwest in April 1942, with the hope of reporting POW camp conditions to General Douglas MacArthur. With the help of Filipino guerrillas, they reached Philippine army strongholds in the jungle. There the Marines organized and guided the 110th Division, a group of U.S. military personnel and Filipino guerrillas that maintained a resistance movement around Mindanao. Submarines supplied the 110th from MacArthur's Pacific Headquarters in Australia. During this time Shofner was promoted again, to major. His duties included deputy chief of staff and assistant for operations for the division.

In November 1943 Shofner and two other Marine officers boarded the supply submarine and sailed for Australia. There Shofner received the Distinguished Service Cross from General MacArthur. Major Shofner and his fellow Marines then joined the First Marine Division and participated in various Pacific Theater battles to liberate the Philippines. Shofner retired in 1959, with the rank of brigadier general.

Carol Roberts, Tennessee State Library and Archives

SEE: BEDFORD COUNTY; WORLD WAR II

SHORE, DINAH (1916–1994). Leap-year baby Fannie Rose Shore was the second daughter born to Russian Jewish immigrants Anna and Sol Shore on February 19, 1916 in Winchester, Tennessee. In 1923 the family moved to Nashville where they prospered. Poliomyelitis left Fannie Rose with a damaged leg, but perseverance, exercise, and determination kept the injury from becoming a permanent handicap. She became an excellent swimmer and tennis player.

Fannie Rose began to sing in childhood, continued in high school, and in college at Vanderbilt University she became professional, singing with the popular Francis Craig orchestra. Her talent prompted a trip to New York between her junior and senior years at college. Despite a positive reception, her father insisted she obtain her B.A. degree before moving to New York, where she changed her name to Dinah, and sought fame and fortune. Both came almost immediately, as she was hired by radio star Eddie Cantor to sing on his weekly show.

Dinah Shore's success quickly escalated. After entertaining the troops in World War II, she became a celebrity as television began its domination of the entertainment industry. On the *Dinah Shore Show* she explored important contemporary issues with guests. Many of them involved an interest and skill in cooking, from which three cook books resulted. Her voice, smile, and trademark kiss to the audience made hers a household name. She became the highest paid female entertainer of her time and continued to perform in benefit concerts until her final illness and death in 1994.

Selma Lewis, Memphis

SEE: FRANKLIN COUNTY; TELEVISION AND MOVIE PERFORMERS

SHORT MOUNTAIN is a noted feature of the Eastern Highland Rim landscape of Middle Tennessee. Located in northeastern Cannon County, the mountain looms above adjacent portions of DeKalb and Warren counties as well. Capped by Pennsylvanian sedimentary racks that have prevented its erosion, Short Mountain is a monadnock, an erosional remnant from an older landscape when the Cumberland Plateau extended further to the west. The highest point of the Eastern Highland Rim at 2,074 feet in elevation, Short Mountain now rises alone above the Central Basin, 20 miles to the west of the Cumberland Plateau's current edge. The mountain consists of several truncated and flattened conical projections and is primarily drained by Mountain Creek. Other scattered knobs within the Central Basin have a similar origin.

Several hundred acres on Short Mountain are designated as a state natural area and are overseen by the Tennessee Department of Environment and Conservation.

Ann Toplovich, Tennessee Historical Society
SEE: CANNON COUNTY; GEOLOGIC ZONES

SHULL, CLIFFORD GLENWOOD (1915–). A Nobel laureate who pioneered neutron diffraction research at Oak Ridge, Clifford Shull was born at Pittsburgh, Pennsylvania, in 1915. He attended Carnegie Institute of Technology and New York University, where he earned his Ph.D. degree in nuclear physics in 1941. During World War II, he worked for the Texas Company in New York, performing research on the physical properties of catalysts with gas absorption and x-ray diffraction techniques.

Shull joined the Oak Ridge National Laboratory (ORNL) as a senior physicist in 1946, when the field of neutron diffraction was novel. He and Ernest O. Wollan bombarded various materials with neutron beams from the Oak Ridge Graphite Reactor and carefully studied the scattering of neutrons from the materials. In this research, they systematically examined the fundamental principles of neutron diffraction and established this technique as an outstanding method for measuring various nuclear properties and for determining the atomic and magnetic structures of materials. In 1994 Shull received the Nobel Prize in Physics for his pioneering research at Oak Ridge.

Shull became professor of physics in 1955 at the Masschusetts Institute of Technology, where he and his students continued to use neutron scattering techniques for research in solid state and neutron physics. He retired in 1986 and became emeritus professor.

Leland R. Johnson, Clio Research Institute

Cliff Shull, right, and Ernest Wollan performing an experiment using the graphite reactor, circa 1950.

OAK RIDGE NATIONAL LABORATORY

SUGGESTED READING: Leland Johnson and Daniel Schaffer, *Oak Ridge National Laboratory: The First Fifty Years* (1994)

SEE: OAK RIDGE NATIONAL LABORATORY; SCIENCE AND TECHNOLOGY; X-10

SILK. For a short time in the antebellum period, many Tennessee farmers pursued what they thought was a promising commercial opportunity in the production of silk. Fueling their optimism were discoveries in the 1830s that silkworms thrived on the native mulberry tree, and that the Chinese *morus morticaulis* plant, which in Asia and Europe provided the main food for silkworms, also grew well under soil and climate conditions in the state. Because it required relatively modest investment and could utilize the labor of women and children without interrupting the work routines of the men in the household, production of the fiber ideally suited small-scale, marginal operations. It was, moreover, an attractive alternative in poor farming areas to the state's main cash crops of cotton and tobacco, since mulberry and *morus morticaulis* plants adapted well to soils of low quality.

These circumstances gave rise to a flurry of interest and activity in the 1830s and 1840s. A nursery devoted specifically to the cultivation of morus morticaulis seedlings to sell to aspiring producers went into operation in 1838. The establishment of several small silk manufacturing companies supplemented an already strong demand from outside the state. In 1840 supporters formed the Tennessee Silk Society to promote production of cocoons and use of the fabric. Two years later, the Tennessee Silk Manufacturing Company and Agricultural School opened in Port Royal to train workers in the manufacture of cloth. Farmers also received financial and promotional encouragement from the government to adopt silk culture. The state legislature offered bounties on cocoons and reeled silk, and Governor James C. Jones arrived at his inauguration in 1843 wearing a silk suit manufactured by the institute in Port Royal. Small wonder, then, that agricultural leaders and journals across Tennessee vigorously urged farmers to consider silk production as part of their commercial schemes.

The response was enthusiastic. Many farmers, particularly in East and Middle Tennessee, put in mulberry and morus morticaulis plants and purchased silkworms. By 1840, production of cocoons exceeded 1,000 pounds, which placed the state fifteenth in the country. Ten year later the state ranked first with an output of nearly 2,000 pounds. Although relatively small operators raising fewer than 100,000 worms accounted for most of the production, some large operators with as many as a million worms participated in the new fad. For awhile, it appeared that rural Tennessee had discovered a lucrative commodity that could benefit farmers of all sizes.

Optimism soon gave way to disappointment, however. In the 1850s, an unknown disease moved across the state infecting the silkworms and destroying an enterprise that had held such promise a short time earlier. The epidemic destroyed the worms of many farmers and convinced others to withdraw from production before they too were driven out. By the end of the 1850s, the devastation was nearly complete. Production plummeted to 71 pounds of cocoons and involved only a handful of operators. Tennessee farmers never again ventured into silk culture.

Donald L. Winters, Vanderbilt University

SEE: AGRICULTURE; PORT ROYAL STATE HISTORICAL AREA

SILVERSMITHS. For many years it was assumed that there were few silversmiths in Tennessee beause of its rural character and remoteness. However, by reading early newspapers and available censuses, the author compiled a checklist of 535 silversmiths and allied craftsmen who worked in Tennessee before 1860. The checklist was published in 1971 in a special issue of *Antiques* about Tennessee.

George Bean is the earliest known silversmith in East Tennessee. He was working there by 1792. One of the earliest in Nashville was Joseph T. Elliston (ca. 1798–1856), who arrived at age 18 after an apprenticeship in Lexington, Kentucky, and earned his first 50 cents in Nashville repairing a watch.

Young men aged 12 to 14 could apprentice to a master craftsman and, after a term of years (usually seven), become a journeyman. Like Elliston, most of these craftsmen combined smithing with watch, clock, and jewelry repair, often reworking the silver from old-fashioned jewelry or from Spanish milled dollars. Indeed, the most successful among them gravitated to the jewelry trade. Elliston became Nashville's fourth mayor from 1814 to 1816.

Silver was a luxury in early Tennessee and had to be ingeniously promoted. One popular way was the lottery sometimes featured in tradesmen's advertisements. Before about 1865, most silver was coin silver, 900 parts silver per thousand. The higher standard of sterling—925 parts of silver per thousand—became standard only after 1865.

Tennessee silversmiths had no distinctive style. Many had come from Kentucky, Virginia, or the Carolinas. All worked in styles prevalent throughout the eastern United States—classical forms early in the nineteenth century, and more elaborate rococo forms, often executed in repousse (hammered from the back), by the mid-1880s. Generally, simplicity of form and decoration was the keynote of Tennessee silver. Many of the more elaborate pieces were only retailed here. Also, it is dangerous to date Tennessee silver by style, because styles remained long in vogue and were slow to be changed.

The advent of the steamboat, which reached Nashville by 1816, caused a sharp reduction in transportation costs from cities such as Pittsburgh and New Orleans. Formerly, a round-trip from Nashville to New Orleans by keelboat might take a year. The streamboat covered it in 17 days. Silversmiths could import machine-pressed silver. By mid-century, features such as patterned banding and elaborate handles were available through suppliers. At first, this seemed a boon to silversmiths, eliminating some of their most tedious work. Ultimately it eliminated these craftsmen entirely by converting silver into an industry.

By the 1840s Tennessee had ceased to be a frontier and had become an agricultural commonwealth. It ranked sixth among the states in population in 1850 and fifth by 1860. Almost every town had at least one silversmith. Among the larger establishments were the brothers George R. and William H. Calhoun in Nashville, active from the 1830s to 1860, and in Memphis F.H. Clark & Company, active 1840 to 1860. Clark sold jewelry, repaired clocks and watches, and produced the usual flatware: cream pitchers, cups with handles, beakers, and ladles. The firm sold plated wares and britannia, but also made surveyor's transits and derringer pistols.

Some silver undoubtedly was destroyed during the Civil War, and some may still be buried, but probably most was bartered away during the hard times of the war and its aftermath. The revolution in silver production meant that those Tennesseans who remained in the business after 1865 were really jewelers who retailed the new machine-made patterned silver manufactured in the northeastern cities. Nonetheless, there are a few silversmiths in Tennessee even today. They really are not connected with the earlier trade. Rather they emerged in the post-World War II era as craftspeople who took up working in silver, or they were teachers in design schools.

The most comprehensive exhibition of Tennessee silver is at the Tennesee State Museum in Nashville.
Benjamin H. Caldwell, Jr., Nashville

SUGGESTED READING: Benjamin Hubbard Caldwell, Jr., *Tennessee Silversmiths* (1989)

SEE: ART; TENNESSEE STATE MUSEUM

SINGLETON, BENJAMIN "PAP"

SINGLETON, BENJAMIN "PAP" (1806–1883?) called himself the "father of the Black Exodus." Singleton and other grassroots black leaders developed the idea that former slaves should migrate to Kansas and other western homesteading sites, rather than remain in the South to suffer racial and economic oppression. Between 1869 and 1881 the Black Exodus idea swept southern black communities, none more than those in Middle Tennessee.

In September 1869 Nashville freedmen held their first meeting to discuss western migration. Randal

Brown, a former slave who suffered a recent defeat in his reelection bid for Nashville's city council, urged freedmen to resist becoming "hewers of wood and drawers of water," and take their place in society. He feared that with the "thousands . . . crowding to the West," the land would soon fill up. "Then, where in the name of God," he asked, "are you going to?" The initial meetings, however, convinced only a few hundred freedmen families to leave the region's former contraband camps to settle on homestead land in Arkansas.

A grassroots leader, Benjamin "Pap" Singleton was more successful in launching a local movement beyond Arkansas—to Kansas. Born a slave in Davidson County, Singleton escaped to New Orleans to avoid being sold by his master. When he was returned to Nashville, Singleton escaped again and made his way via the Underground Railroad to Canada, before moving to Detroit and then back to Nashville at the end of the Civil War. Singleton made a living as a cabinet-maker, mostly finishing coffins for the many freedmen who died in crowded, filthy conditions, particularly in the former Edgefield (East Nashville) contraband camp area near Singleton's residence.

"Old Pap" and a local preacher, Columbus Johnson, organized a homestead association to promote settlement of freedmen in the western states, where 160 acres of land could be gained if the applicant paid a $10 filing fee, lived on the property for ten years, and made improvements. Johnson preached and recruited in nearby Sumner County, where thousands of freedmen lived in former contraband camps in Hendersonville and Gallatin. While he peddled his services, Singleton encouraged the unemployed and landless freedmen to gain farms of their own. In 1872 his homestead association sent a committee to study settlement in Kansas. The next year, Singleton secured steamboat and railroad transportation for thousands, who left Edgefield to settle in Cherokee County, Wyandotte, and Topeka, Kansas.

In 1875 Singleton, William A. Sizemore, and Benjamin Petway called for a state convention to discuss migration to the West. The Nashville *Bulletin*, a Republican party paper, blamed the Black Exodus on "inadequate labor prices and delays in paying the same." The African-American delegates formed the Colored Emigration Society with Nashville's Nelson Walker as president. The convention concluded that "To the white people of Tennessee, and them alone, are due the ills borne by the colored people of this state."[2]

Named for the Exodus in the Bible, the Black Exodus really took off in 1876, when thousands of destitute African Americans headed West, many of whom never reached Kansas because of lack of money and supplies. Singleton's Edgefield Real

Estate Association at No. 5 Front Street held several rallies. Singleton even inspired a group of freedmen in adjacent Kentucky to settle in Kansas. In June 1879 he founded a colony at Dunlap, Morris County, Kansas. One of Singleton's settlements, Nicodemus, survived to become a modern town. Sometime after testifying to a congressional investigating committee about the phenomenal Black Exodus in 1881, Singleton died and was buried in an unknown grave in the west.

Overall, some 25,000 freedmen migrated from the South to Kansas. By 1880, according to the United States Census, 5,418 African Americans from Tennessee lived in Kansas. The out-migration of freedmen from Nashville alone numbered approximately 2,407 persons. Few Americans, including the descendants of Tennessee freedmen yet living in Kansas and other western states, are aware that a Tennessean, Benjamin "Pap" Singleton, led the Black Exodus to the West.

Bobby L. Lovett, Tennessee State University

CITATIONS:

(1) Nashville *Bulletin*, April 29, 1875.

(2) Ibid.

SEE: CONTRABAND CAMPS; RECONSTRUCTION

SIT-INS, KNOXVILLE. On February 1, 1960, four black freshmen from North Carolina Agricultural and Technical College in Greensboro, North Carolina, entered the Woolworth store in downtown Greensboro, seated themselves at the store's lunch counter, and requested service. As they expected, they were refused, but they continued to "sit-in" until the store closed. Word of their bold and dramatic action spread rapidly, and soon black college students in towns and cities all over the South began conducting lunch counter sit-ins.

One of those cities was Knoxville. On February 15, 1960, a group of Knoxville College students met and decided to begin sit-ins at downtown lunch counters two days later. When the college's president, Dr. James Colston, learned of the students' plans, however, he quickly persuaded them to postpone their protests until he could negotiate with city leaders. Colston's confidence in the negotiation process clearly indicates two of Knoxville's unique qualities that set the stage for the short and peaceful sit-ins that followed. Knoxville had a long history of open communication between local black and white leaders and there was a less restrictive form of segregation practiced in the city. In such an atmosphere many local residents were convinced that the violent protracted sit-ins affecting other cities could not happen in their community.

One of those who fervently believed that was Knoxville's Mayor, John Duncan, Sr. Duncan recalled, "I saw the problems going on in Chattanooga,

Nashville, and Memphis, bloodshed almost . . . I made up my mind that I didn't want that in Knoxville."[1] Duncan, along with other city leaders, engaged in seemingly endless negotiations in spring 1960. At one point during this process Mayor Duncan took the bold and unprecedented step of taking a delegation to New York to negotiate with chain store executives. The delegation, which consisted of the mayor, two Knoxville Chamber of Commerce officials, and two Knoxville College student leaders, wanted chain store executives to order their Knoxville branches to desegregate their eating facilities. But the executives refused to meet with the delegation.

In the meantime, Knoxville College students were becoming increasingly impatient with the slow pace of negotiations. Then in May the downtown merchants finally announced that they would not desegregate after all. Many in the black community felt betrayed. They were sure that negotiations would head off demonstrations, but with failure many knew they had no choice. Consequently, on June 9, 1960, the Knoxville sit-ins began—spearheaded by a local group, the Associated Council for Full Citizenship. Regardless of the stand taken by the downtown merchants, Mayor Duncan continued his support of lunch counter integration and directed police officers to protect the rights of sit-in protesters. In such an atmosphere Knoxville's sit-ins were peaceful and successful in record time. By July 12, after barely a month of lunch counter protests, downtown merchants capitulated and desegregation of downtown eating facilities became a fact of life for all Knoxvillians.

Cynthia Griggs Fleming, University of Tennessee, Knoxville

CITATION:

(1) Author interview with John J. Duncan, Knoxville, February 15, 1984.

SUGGESTED READING: Cynthia Griggs Fleming, "White Lunch Counters and Black Consciousness: The Story of the Knoxville Sit-ins," *Tennessee Historical Quarterly* 49(1990): 40–52

SEE: CIVIL RIGHTS MOVEMENT; DUNCAN, JOHN J., SR.; KNOXVILLE COLLEGE

SIT-INS, NASHVILLE. In 1958, following the formation of the Nashville Christian Leadership Conference (NCLC) by the Reverend Kelly Miller Smith, Sr., and others, African-American leaders and students launched an attack on Jim Crow segregation. The NCLC utilized the concept of Christian nonviolence to stage the Nashville sit-in movement to combat *dejure* and *defacto* racial segregation. The Reverend James Lawson, a devoted adherent of the Gandhi philosophy of direct nonviolent protest, trained local residents in the techniques of the belief. Early in 1959 the NCLC began a movement to desegregate Nashville's downtown lunch counters and illustrate the hypocrisy of the Jim Crow economic system. During

Citizens arrested at Cain-Sloan department store in Nashville, April 1960.

BANNER PHOTOGRAPY BY VIC COOLEY

November and December, NCLC leaders and college students made purchases in downtown stores and staged "test sit-ins" in unsuccessful attempts to desegregate the lunch counters.

On February 1, 1960, four North Carolina Agricultural and Technical College students captured America's attention when they launched the Greensboro, North Carolina, sit-in. Twelve days later, Nashville's African-American students launched their first full-scale sit-ins. They convened at the Arcade on Fifth Avenue, North, at approximately 12:40 P.M. and entered Kress's, Woolworth's and McClellan's. They made small purchases, and then occupied lunch counter seats. By 2:30 P.M., all three retail stores closed their lunch counters, and the students departed without incident. In response to white harassment at Walgreen's, students formulated ten rules of conduct for demonstrators. These became the code of behavior for later protest movements in the South. Throughout the spring, Nashville students conducted numerous sit-ins. They suffered verbal and physical abuse, arrests, fines, and incarceration, but held steadfastly to the concept of Christian nonviolence.

African-American pressure to desegregate and white resistance to integration increased throughout the early spring. Shortly before Easter, the majority of Nashville African Americans used their "dollar vote" and simply stopped making purchases in the downtown stores, creating an estimated 20 percent loss in business revenues. As racial tension escalated, segregationists lashed out at civil rights activists. On April 19, an early morning bombing damaged the home of attorney Z. Alexander Looby, defense counsel for the

students, a city councilman, and a leading figure in desegregation movements throughout Tennessee. The Loobys escaped with only minor injuries. In response, thousands of black and some white Americans marched to Nashville's City Hall. Mayor Ben West met the protesters and conceded to Diane Nash of Fisk University that he felt segregation was wrong and that lunch counters should be desegregated. On May 10, 1960, Nashville became the first major city to begin desegregating its public facilities. While the Greensboro sit-in was spontaneous, the Nashville movement had been planned over several months and drew students from the city's four predominately black colleges as well as community residents. According to Dr. Martin Luther King, Jr., the Nashville movement was one of the best organized and most disciplined movements in the South. In November sit-ins resumed, as racist practices were still customary in most eating establishments, and institutionalized racism remained intact.

The Nashville sit-in movement served as more than a model for future demonstrations against segregated accommodations, unfair employment practices, and other examples of institutionalized segregation. Its example of non-violent protest emboldened and mobilized others across the country. Many of the student participants became leaders in the struggle for civil rights.

Linda T. Wynn, Tennessee Historical Commission/ Fisk University

SUGGESTED READINGS: Taylor Branch, *Parting of the Waters: America in the King Years, 1954–1963* (1988); Linda T. Wynn, "The Dawning of a New Day: The Nashville Sit-ins, February 13-May 10, 1960," *Tennessee Historical Quarterly* 50(1993): 42–54

SEE: CIVIL RIGHTS MOVEMENT; LAWSON, JAMES E. JR.; LEWIS, JOHN R.; LOOBY, Z. ALEXANDER; NASH, DIANE

SLAVERY. In the 1760s Anglo-American frontiersmen, determined to settle the land, planted slavery firmly within the borders of what would become Tennessee. Over time, East Tennessee, hilly and dominated by small farms, retained the fewest number of slaves. Middle Tennessee, where tobacco, cattle, and grain became the favored crops, held the largest number of slaves throughout the antebellum period. West Tennessee, the area between the Tennessee and Mississippi rivers, ultimately the richest cotton producing section of the state, saw the greatest concentration of slaves. By 1860 Tennessee's 275,719 slaves represented just under 25 percent of the total population and were engaged in urban, industrial, and agricultural slavery.

When North Carolina ceded its western lands to the United States in 1790, the terms of cession prevented the new federal congress from excluding slavery in the Southwest Territory, as had been done under the Articles of Confederation's government in the Northwest Territory. Six years later, when Tennessee achieved statehood, the 1796 constitution remained mute on the status of slavery. The state operated under the laws first promulgated by North Carolina, whereby slaves were regarded primarily as chattel (the property of their owners), but sometimes as persons with legal obligations and a very few legal rights. Slaves, for example, had the right to a jury trial in those exceptional cases of crimes that were outside the master's jurisdiction. They also had the right to contest their ownership in the courts if they could present evidence and procure a white sponsor. At the same time, as in all of the slave states, the marriage of slaves and their right to their children had no legal sanction.

As Tennesseans moved westward from the 1770s throughout the 1820s, successive frontiers saw a temporary loosening of restraints on slaves and a multiplication of roles for slaves to play. Slaves traveled alone through the wilderness on their masters' errands, carried guns for protection against Indians and to hunt game, and shared tight quarters with their masters in the stockades. White men of property made unusually public alliances with women of color. Sometimes they freed and provided for their mulatto children. Agencies to enforce racial codes were weak and erratic. Ironically, however, in these years, roughly from 1770 to 1830, when legal obstacles least constrained emancipation, both the demand for slave labor and uncertain frontier finances made slave families especially vulnerable to slave sales. From the beginning slaves were among

white Tennesseans' most valuable assets; in time, both Nashville and, most notably, Memphis established permanent slave markets. From 1826 until 1853, legislation outlawing interstate trade in slaves was ignored.

East Tennessee manifested an early antislavery sentiment. Some 25 manumission societies organized before 1830 and attracted major figures in the emerging national campaign against slavery. Men like Elihu Embree and Benjamin Lundy attempted to find ways to achieve emancipation without violent upheaval. In 1829 the Tennessee Colonization Society organized to send emancipated slaves to Liberia, transporting 870 ex-slaves to Africa in the period that ended in 1866. Although this modest record had minimal impact on the institution of slavery in Tennessee, it represented the only antislavery activity tolerated in the state after the 1830s. Manumission societies disappeared and public discussion of emancipation was prohibited. The increasing militance of the abolition movement in the North, periodic white panic following rumors of slave insurrection, and above all, the increasing institutionalization of slavery as it became part of the settled agriculture of the state dictated a harsher legal code governing not only slaves, but also free blacks and white abolitionists. In 1831, for example, the law required that emancipation of a slave had to be accompanied by removal from the state, while severe penalties were enacted against the distribution of "rebellion inciting" materials. The 1835 state constitution explicitly deprived free blacks of the right to vote. Laws against the assembling of blacks, which were often observed only in the breach, were harshly enforced during slave rebellion scares.

Although most slaves, both male and female, were agricultural workers, slavery was not a uniform experience. On the farm, a slave's life was influenced, first, by the kind of operation the master ran: a subsistence farm, a corn and tobacco cash crop farm, a livestock farm, a cotton plantation, or, most likely in all sections of Tennessee, some combination of these. Secondly, the number of slaves a master housed helped determine the contours of any given slave community. Relatively few great plantations existed in Tennessee. Census records show that only one person owned more than 300 slaves in 1860 and only 47 owned more than 100. More than three-fourths of all masters held fewer than ten slaves; together they controlled under 40 percent of the slave population. Thus, by 1860, more than half of the slaves probably lived in quarters that housed more than ten, but many fewer than 100 slaves. Work assignments were dictated by the seasonal needs of the master's farm, by the domestic needs of the master's household, and often by the needs of the plots assigned to slave families to provide a portion of their subsistence. Some slaves, especially those with special talents like carpenters, weavers, or musicians, were hired out to other planters or town residents.

For the most part, rural slaves had to create their own societies. They focused first on putting together families which, given the trauma of slave sales and dispersals, meant putting together surrogate families to take in newly purchased single adults or children separated from parents. The so-called "matriarchal" families of slavery were one result, but the nuclear or extended family remained the vital institutional base of slave society. Generally slaves were housed in family units rather than in barracks, which undoubtedly reinforced the sense of family that prevailed in the slave quarters despite the ways in which slavery violated the norms of family life as understood by black people or by white people of the nineteenth century.

Religion also served as a strong survival mechanism, as slaves adopted and adapted Christianity. Frontier Methodist and Baptist churches were open to slaves in ways that were almost anomalous given the institutional constraints of slavery. Methodist circuit riders preached to whites and blacks and eagerly claimed black converts. Black church members were called upon to exhort their fellow parishioners, black and white, in Baptist churches. Within the quarters, slave preachers, who emerged from the slave community itself, interpreted Christianity; in the quarters powerful gospel music was created. This musical response to a people's travail left a historical record for modern historians, but more importantly, it provided immediate solace, hope, and solidarity. Despite the denial of literacy, some slaves learned how to read with or without the cooperation of individual masters. Thus, slaves fashioned a world of their own within the white masters' farms and plantations. Slaveowners were often conscious of this slave community outside their purview, in some sense independent of them, even subversive, but usually they chose to ignore what they could not control.

Urban slavery produced another set of experiences. In most towns and in the larger cities, slaves were ubiquitous, scattered throughout the community, visible at any public event, providing the basic manual labor of the city and much of its skilled labor as well. The black population of the village of Nashville in 1800 amounted to 45 percent of the total. As the town grew, that figure declined to just over a third of the total in the 1820s and 1830s, and then continued to decline to 25 percent in 1850, and to 23 percent in 1860. European immigrants entering the labor force accounted for much of this change, which was even more dramatic in Memphis, where the cotton boom attracted many new immigrants to fill the demand for labor and the city's black population declined from 28 percent to 17 percent in the decade before the Civil War. Urban conditions may have

meant greater opportunities for literacy and education of all sorts, for religious choices, and even a quasi-legal independence for some slaves. On the other hand, cities may have been harder on the slave family's integrity.

Most city slaveholders, living in restricted quarters, bought or rented individual slaves according to the services required, although they sometimes agreed to take on slave children with their mothers, so that in many households, the slave family centered around the mother, grandmother, or "auntie." The hiring of slaves became so common it was institutionalized: each New Year's Day, the market square drew slaves and employers to bargain for slave labor for the coming year. Self-hire, by which masters allowed slaves to bargain with employers for their own labor, simply sending back a fixed sum to the owner, was illegal but so convenient and profitable that it was difficult to stop. These quasi-free people mingled with the legally free black population, which though fewer than a thousand persons in Nashville in 1860, succeeded in creating autonomous Methodist, Baptist, and Christian (Disciples of Christ) congregations, open to slaves as well as free persons, and pastored by well known black ministers. Nelson Merry led the Baptist congregation from the 1840s until his death in 1884, when his church numbered more than 2,000 members. Schools were more clandestine operations and yet were stubbornly and courageously opened by free blacks like Daniel Wadkins, William Napier, and Sally Porter, and then reopened after white panic that forced them to close had eased.

City life was not only churches or schools, or even the excitement of the streets; it was mainly work, and slaves performed in every area, from the municipality's street hands to the hotels' kitchens. They were domestics of all sorts, coachmen, housepainters, laundresses, and midwives. They were also industrial workers. Small textile plants advertised for hands early in the nineteenth century; mines and grist mills used slave labor, often hired hands. From 1807 until 1857 iron master Montgomery Bell operated a series of furnaces, employing hundreds of slaves. The steam-driven Worley Furnace, built in 1844 in Dickson County, was named for Bell's slave and the trusted manager of his works, James Worley, and was operated with slave labor. By 1833 some of Nashville's earliest merchant bankers, Thomas Yeatman and his partners, Joseph and Robert Woods, had developed iron mines, blast furnaces, and a rolling mill in Stewart County that were operated by at least 200 slaves. By the 1850s, this operation, the Cumberland River Iron Works, employed almost 2,000 slaves and nearly as many white workers. The concentration of slave labor in the iron manufacturing industry focused suspicion on the Iron Works in 1835, when the specter of slave rebellion seemed imminent. Again in 1856, the suspicion of rebellion resulted in the torture of 65 slaves from the Iron Works to produce confessions to insurrection; nine of the "confessed" rebels were hanged at the Iron Works and another 19 at Dover.

Resistance to slavery by slaves was rarely a matter of conspiracy. Most resistance involved individual actions of sabotage, slow-downs in output, negligence with livestock and tools, and other kinds of behavior that might force concessions in work loads or rewards from overseers or masters. The most feared forms of slave rebellion were poison and arson. The runaway slave, regardless of the success of his endeavor, was the most conspicuous and the most common form of resistance throughout the history of slavery. In Tennessee slavery officially ended in April of 1865, when the Unionist-controlled legislature ratified the Thirteenth Amendment.

Anita S. Goodstein, University of the South

SEE: AGRICULTURE; ARMFIELD, JOHN; CONTRABAND CAMPS; EMBREE, ELIHU; FRANKLIN, ISAAC; HUGHES, LOUIS; LUNDY, BENJAMIN; MANUMISSION SOCIETY OF TENNESSEE; PATTERSON FORGE; SMITH, HARDIN; TENNESSEE COLONIZATION SOCIETY

SMITH, BESSIE (1894–1937), blues singer, was born in Chattanooga and lived in a section of the city called Blue Goose Hollow at the foot of Cameron Hill. Her father, William Smith, a part-time Baptist minister, died when Smith was very young and her mother died when she was nine. That same year, Smith began her career on Ninth Street in Chattanooga, singing and dancing for change to the accompaniment of her brother's guitar.

In 1912 she joined the touring Rabbit Foot Minstrels, where Gertrude "Ma" Rainey, the mother of all female blues singers, began to tutor her greatest pupil. Smith soon began touring on her own. In 1923 she signed a contract with Columbia Records and recorded *Down Hearted Blues,* which sold 800,000 copies at 75 cents each. It was Columbia's first big hit and inspired the company to start its "Race Series," aimed at the African-American market.

Billed as "The Empress of the Blues," Smith soon earned an annual income of $20,000 from her Columbia sales, and performed for $1,500 to $2,500 per week on the African-American circuit in the northeast and South. She sang with the best musicians of the day, including Louis Armstrong, who played trumpet on nine of her records. Smith wrote many of the songs she recorded, using the themes of poverty, love, and the temptation of alcohol. Her 156 known recordings include such classics as *Pig Foot and Bottle of Beer, Beale Street Blues, Beale Street Mama, Baby Doll, Standin' in the Rain Blues, Midnight Steppers,* and *Nobody Knows You When You're Down and Out.*

An imposing figure at 5'9" and 200 pounds, Smith's performance attire of satin gowns, headdresses, long strands of pearls, and feather boas became a well-known trademark. In the days before electronic microphones, her booming voice could be heard outside the largest theaters. Her only performance in Chattanooga after achieving stardom produced a memorable story. After her performance at the Liberty Theatre, Smith attended a party given by a friend, where she knocked down a drunken admirer who pestered her. The would-be admirer stabbed Smith, who chased him for several blocks before collapsing. She was taken to the hospital but returned to the stage the next night.

Smith's career declined in the 1930s due to a combination of the Great Depression, alcoholism, and the lack of radio exposure as a result of her suggestive song lyrics. In 1937 Smith was killed in a highway accident outside Clarksdale, Mississippi, while making a comeback tour of the South. Contemporary accounts that she died after being turned away from a "Whites Only" hospital have proven unfounded, although she had to wait for a "Blacks Only" ambulance.

Smith was buried in Sharon Hill, Pennsylvania, near Philadelphia. In 1970 Janis Joplin, who credited her own success to her imitation of Smith's style, contributed funds to the erection of a gravestone at the burial site. Inscribed on the headstone are the following words: "The greatest blues singer in the world will never stop singing."

Jerry R. Desmond, Chattanooga Regional History Museum

SUGGESTED READING: Chris Albertson, *Bessie* (1972)

SEE: CHATTANOOGA; MUSIC

SMITH COUNTY was created by the Tennessee General Assembly on October 26, 1799, and was named in honor of General Daniel Smith. Carved out of Sumner, the county covered a large territory of 314 square miles. Immigrants of Scots-Irish, English, and German descent established thriving towns and productive farms along the courses of the two rivers and abundant streams that flow through the fertile bottom lands. The majority of the settlers came from North Carolina, many of whom held land warrants for Revolutionary War service. Once the pioneers cleared land, planted a crop and built a shelter, churches and schools soon followed. The Presbyterians, Methodists, and Baptists all had active congregations. Clinton College at New Middleton, Geneva Academy at Carthage, Shady Grove Academy at Gordonsville were among the early schools.

In 1804 a heated election was held for selection of a permanent county seat. The contest raged between proponents (the polecats) of Bledsoesborough, a site on the Cumberland near Dixon Springs, and supporters (the moccasin gang) of William Walton whose land grant was situated at the confluence of the Cumberland and Caney Fork rivers. Walton, a Revolutionary veteran, operated a ferry and tavern at the site. An abundance of refreshments, including a full supply of whiskey furnished by Colonel Walton, may have influenced the victory claimed by the moccasins who determined Carthage, destined to become one of the most important towns in Middle Tennessee during the steamboat era, as the county seat. Throughout the winter of 1805 the town was laid out and public buildings constructed. By 1879 a new courthouse building, "the handsomest in the State," was erected and continues to grace the town square, having been placed on the National Register of Historic Places in 1979.

Crucial to the pioneer's survival were the streams that turned the mills and provided a highway to market for his products. John Lancaster operated a mill on Smith Fork and the town of Lancaster was laid out nearby. New Middleton was established on Mulherin Creek, and, further west on Round Lick Creek, the community of Jenning's Fork (Grant) was not only a mill seat but also was traversed by the Trousdale Ferry Pike, a main stage thoroughfare terminating into the Walton Road at Chestnut Mound, a scenic stage coach town on the eastern ridge of the county. Travelers along the Pike crossed the Caney Fork River at Stonewall on the ferry established by John Trousdale who settled in the area about 1804. Pleasant Shade on Peyton's Creek and Difficult and Defeated on Defeated Creek grew into trade centers for residents of the northern section of the county. Dixon Springs was settled prior to 1787 by Tilman Dixon, Revolutionary War soldier, where his historic home, Dixona, site of the first county court meeting, still stands. Maggart, Sullivan's Bend, Jonesboro, West Point have all been inundated by the Cordell Hull Reservoir. Rome, located on the Cumberland at the mouth of Round Lick Creek, rivaled Carthage as a port and trade center until it began to decline, along with the steamboats, in the early twentieth century. The historic Rome Ferry plied the river at this point.

During the 1880s railroads brought new life to communities along the rails. Brush Creek, Sykes, Hickman, Lancaster all bustled with hotels, dry goods stores, banks, livery stables. Gordonsville, founded in 1801 by John Gordon and the largest town south of the Cumberland, flourished as a busy rail center and was incorporated in 1909. One of the county's two high schools is located at Gordonsville. South Carthage, just across the river from Carthage, emerged as the rail center for northern Smith County, resulting in the building of a bridge spanning the Cumberland to replace the obsolete ferries. Opened to the public on February 1, 1908, the new structure was operated as a toll bridge and was built at a cost of $64,000.

Smith County industries, until recently, have been those associated with farm products such as distilleries, grist and flour mills, tanneries, saltpeter, tobacco, and timber. Construction of the Cordell Hull Dam on the Cumberland River in the 1960s, development of an industrial park where several large plants have located, and the mining of the county's rich deposit of zinc have been determining factors in the growth of the economy. Leading manufactures in the county include William L. Bonnell Aluminum Extrusion, Savage Zinc, Inc., and Dana Corp. Spicer Universal Joint.

Among the better-known statesmen from Smith County are William Bowen Campbell and Benton McMillin who served as Governors of Tennessee 1851–1853 and 1899–1903, respectively. Cordell Hull, Secretary of State under Franklin D. Roosevelt and recipient of the Nobel Peace Prize in 1945, practiced law and called Carthage home for many years. The unique Cordell Hull Bridge, the second to span the Cumberland, and the Dam honor his name today. Albert Gore, Sr., represented Tennessee in Congress from 1939–1971. Albert Gore, Jr., served as Representative and U.S. Senator prior to being elected Vice President of the United States in 1992 and 1996.

Sue W. Maggart, Carthage

SEE: BAILEY, DEFORD; CAMPBELL, WILLIAM B.; CUMBERLAND RIVER; GORDON, FRANCIS H.; GORE, ALBERT A., JR.; GORE, ALBERT A., SR.; HULL, CORDELL; LAND GRANTS; MCMILLIN, BENTON; MINING; MYER, WILLIAM; SMITH, DANIEL, WALTON ROAD

SMITH, DANIEL (1748–1818), pioneer, surveyor, treaty negotiator, Secretary of the Southwest Territory, and U.S. Senator, was a native of Stafford County, Virginia, who became infatuated with the trans-Appalachian West while a surveyor on the Virginia frontier. During the early years of the American Revolution, he commanded militia forces that defended the western settlements against British-inspired Indian attacks. He held public office for the first time as justice of the peace for Virginia's newly created county of Washington in December 1776, and later was sheriff for a single term. He became lieutenant colonel commandant of the county militia in 1780.

Smith came to the Tennessee country in the winter of 1779–1780 with Dr. Thomas Walker as Virginia's commissioners to survey the line separating the western lands of Virginia and North Carolina. Pausing at the future site of Nashville, he so liked the area that, in 1784, he brought his family and settled them on a tract of 3,140 acres at the confluence of Drake's Creek and the Cumberland River.

Appointed justice of the peace and county surveyor for the new county of Davidson, North Carolina, in 1783, he assisted in surveying the state military land grant reservation in the Cumberland valley. He was one of five trustees for the establishment of the City of Nashville and was a charter trustee of Davidson Academy. When the new county of Sumner was partitioned from Davidson in 1786, Smith became a justice of the peace, presided over the first session of the Sumner County court, and more than once was its chairman. He accepted appointment as commanding General of the Mero District Militia on November 29, 1788.

President George Washington appointed Smith Secretary of the Territory of the United States South of the River Ohio in 1790, with authority to act for the Governor in his absence. He served in that capacity until the territory became the State of Tennessee in 1796. Smith was a delegate from Sumner County to the convention that organized the state, and he chaired the committee that drafted its constitution and bill of rights.

The first pamphlet describing the Tennessee country, usually attributed to Smith, was published in 1793, and the next year the first map of the future state, based on his surveys, appeared in *Guthrie's Geography,* published by Mathew Carey at Philadelphia.

Treating with the Cherokees for additional land, Smith and his fellow commissioner Return J. Meigs concluded separate treaties at Tellico for relatively small cessions in 1804 and 1805. They negotiated a treaty at Washington in 1806 by which the Cherokees ceded their extensive holdings between the Tennessee and Duck rivers.

In 1798–1799 Smith served a few months of the unexpired term of Andrew Jackson in the U.S. Senate. Later the legislature elected him to a full term in the Senate beginning in 1805. He resigned because of ill health in 1809.

Smith returned to his plantation in Sumner County on which he and his wife, Sarah Michie Smith, had completed their two-story stone house, later known as Rock Castle; the house became a state-owned historic site in 1969. Smith, a man known for his unimpeachable integrity in public life and for his leadership in the establishment of the institutions of representative government on the frontier, died at his home in 1818.

Walter T. Durham, Gallatin

SUGGESTED READING: Walter T. Durham, *Daniel Smith: Frontier Statesman* (1976)

SEE: GOVERNMENT; LAND GRANTS; MEIGS, RETURN J.; ROCK CASTLE; SMITH COUNTY; SOUTHWEST TERRITORY; SUMNER COUNTY; TREATIES; WALKER, THOMAS

SMITH, EDMUND KIRBY (1824–1893), a native of St. Augustine, Florida, was one of the most despised Civil War commanders in East Tennessee. Smith graduated from West Point in 1845, saw action in the Mexican War, served on the frontier, and taught mathematics at West Point before the Civil War. He resigned his commission in 1861 and was commissioned brigadier general in the Provisional Army of the Confederate States. He led a brigade at the First Battle of Manassas, where he was badly wounded. After he recovered, Smith was promoted to major general and appointed commander of the Department of East Tennessee in March 1862, succeeding Brigadier General Felix Zollicoffer, who was killed at Mill Springs the previous January.

Smith's tenure as commander was a disaster. Declaring East Tennessee to be "an enemy's country," he completely reversed Zollicoffer's policy of reconciliation and leniency. Acting as virtual military dictator, Smith enforced martial law, suspended habeas corpus, jailed and deported suspected Unionists, and vigorously enforced the April 1862 conscription act, sending hundreds of Unionists into headlong flight to Kentucky. These heavy-handed measures only succeeded in further provoking Unionists and spreading discontent by turning previously neutral East Tennesseans into enemies. Moreover, Smith cast doubt upon the dependability and loyalty of East Tennessee troops raised for Confederate service, suggesting that these men be transferred to the deep South, where they could be molded into good soldiers, away from the pernicious influences of local Unionist leaders. By failing to draw any distinction between the loyal and disloyal, Smith turned Jefferson Davis and the army's high command against the citizens and soldiers of his department, adding to an already uneasy feeling about the region.

Smith commanded the department through the summer of 1862, repelling minor Union incursions and breaking up East Tennessee Confederate units he suspected of disloyalty. In the fall of that year, he participated in Braxton Bragg's campaign into Kentucky, winning a spectacular victory over Federal forces at Richmond. Supremely unhappy with his duties in East Tennessee, Smith engineered a transfer to the Trans-Mississippi Department, where he ruled in almost total isolation after the fall of Vicksburg. Smith's command was the last major Confederate force to surrender, laying down its arms in late May 1865. After the war, he devoted himself to education, teaching for many years at the University of the South. The last surviving full Confederate general died at Sewanee, Tennessee, March 28, 1893.

W. Todd Groce, Georgia Historical Society

SEE: CIVIL WAR; UNIVERSITY OF THE SOUTH

SMITH, HARDIN (1829–1929), was a slave and Baptist preacher, who lived and taught the principle that freedom was acquired through education. He founded churches and schools for freed slaves, and his legacy includes a rich musical heritage for African Americans of Nutbush in Haywood County.

Smith was born in Hanover County, Virginia, in March 1829, one of seven children fathered by Abner Smith, a white slaveowner. His mother, Littie, was a slave. Around 1840 Abner Smith sold Littie and her children through the slave pen in St. Louis; all were sold together, shipped, and resold in Memphis. Hardin Smith and his sister Elizabeth were sold to General William H. Loving, a lawyer, minister, and substantial landowner in Haywood County.

In his new home, Smith remembered the words of Virginia slaves, who assured one another: "We're goin' to be free, and our children's goin' to school." Ruth Loving, the wife of his new master, and her children secretly taught Smith to read, and he, in turn, secretly taught other slaves.

In 1846, at age 16, Smith received permission to minister to a select group of slaves during night services at the white Woodlawn Baptist Church in Nutbush. At the same time, he secretly preached and taught a slave congregation near the Hatchie River in Brownsville.

In 1866, Smith became one of the first African-American ministers to receive training from missionaries of the Baptist Home Mission Board of New York City. Smith, the Freedmen's Bureau, and white residents of the small community of Nutbush founded Woodlawn Colored Baptist Church. Smith became its first minister and remained for the next 56 years.

Smith and members of his congregation founded churches in surrounding communities, including Elam Baptist Church in Nutbush/Durhamville, and Spring Hill Baptist Church; they assisted in the establishment of First Baptist Church in Brownsville. In 1867 Smith and five others founded the first school for freed slaves, the Freedmen's School of Brownsville, now Carver High School.

Reverend Smith was one of the organizers of Memphis's Howe Institute of Technology (LeMoyne Owen College), the original National Negro Baptist Convention, and Roger Williams University in Nashville. Before 1900 Woodlawn Colored Baptist Church sent more students to Roger Williams College than did any other community in Tennessee. Out of this student group came some of the leading ministers, teachers, and physicians in the state, including Reverend W.F. Lovelace; J.R. Evans, Dean of Roger Williams; and J.W. Evans, M.D., who practiced in Brownsville for 40 years.

While still in slavery, Smith brought together black musicians and singers, and provided an opportunity for them to perform the spirituals sung in the cottonfields of Nutbush; he continued his musical interests in freedom. A number of musicians and singers emerged from the slave and free congregations of churches founded by Smith, including Sleepy John Estes, the Bootsie Whitelow String Band, gospel recording artist Reverend Clay

Evans, singer/actor Meshach Taylor, and performer Tina Turner.

Hardin Smith fathered 22 children and died at the age of 100.

Sharon Norris, Nutbush Heritage Productions Inc.

SEE: HAYWOOD COUNTY; LEMOYNE OWEN COLLEGE; MEMPHIS MUSIC SCENE; RELIGION; ROGER WILLIAMS UNIVERSITY; SLAVERY; TURNER, TINA

SMITH, HILTON A. (1908–1982), professor of chemistry and Dean of the University of Tennessee Graduate School, was born September 4, 1908, in Plymouth, New York, and reared in North Adams, Massachusetts. After earning a Ph.D. in physical chemistry from Harvard in 1934, he taught at Lehigh University (1935–1941) before coming to the University of Tennessee. There he helped develop the associations between scientists at Oak Ridge and the university that laid the foundation for the Ph.D. program in chemistry that UT began offering at the end of the war. In 1961 he was named Dean of the Graduate School, becoming Vice President for Graduate Studies and Research in 1966 and Vice Chancellor for Graduate Studies and Research when the university became part of a statewide system in 1968. In this capacity, Smith continued to advance the university's doctoral program. He was instrumental in starting the UT-Kingsport Graduate Center, the UT-Chattanooga Engineering Graduate Center, the UT Space Institute in Tullahoma, the Memphis Branch of the UT School of Social Work, and the UT-Oak Ridge Graduate School of Biomedical Sciences.

The author of more than 130 articles, Smith achieved national recognition for his research in the study of hydrogen isotopes. He isolated the isotope tritium, a form of hydrogen, which is used as a low-cost radioactive isotope. In 1969 he was elected a fellow in the American Institute of Chemists. Smith died in December 1982 and is buried in Knoxville's Highland Cemetery.

Connie L. Lester, Tennessee Historical Society

SEE: UNIVERSITY OF TENNESSEE

SMITH, KELLY MILLER, SR., (1920–1984) was the influential pastor of Nashville's First Baptist Church, Capitol Hill, from 1951 until his death in 1984. He was also Assistant Dean of the Vanderbilt Divinity School from 1969–1984. As president of the Nashville NAACP from 1956–1959, founder and president of the Nashville Christian Leadership Conference (NCLC) from 1958–1963, and a founding board member of the Nashville Urban League, he was one of the city's most influential black leaders.

Smith was president of the Nashville NAACP when the U.S. Supreme Court made its 1954 ruling against school segregation. To spur implementation in Nashville, Smith joined 12 other black parents in filing suit in U.S. DistrIct Court against the Nashville Board of Education. For his leadership, *Time* magazine called Smith "the one person who deserves major credit for the Nashville racial transition." *Ebony* magazine also named him "One of America's Ten Most Outstanding Preachers" in 1954.

With the NCLC, he helped organize and support Nashville students in the sit-ins leading to the integration of the city's downtown lunch counters in 1960. The NCLC was the local affiliate of Martin Luther King, Jr.,'s Southern Christian Leadership Conference (SCLC), on which Smith served from 1955–1969 on the executive board.

Kelly Miller Smith was born October 28, 1920, in Mound Bayou, Mississippi. He attended Tennessee State University from 1938–1940 and graduated from Morehouse College in Atlanta in 1942. In 1945 he received a bachelor of divinity degree from the Howard University School of Religion. He was also a Merrill Fellow at Harvard University in 1967.

Prior to coming to Nashville in 1951, he was pastor of Mt. Heroden Baptist Church in Vicksburg, Mississippi, from 1946–1951. From 1946–1948 he was also head of the Department of Religion at Natchez College in Natchez, Mississippi.

He delivered the 1983 Lyman Beecher Lecture Series at Yale University, published shortly before his death by Mercer University Press in the book *Social Crisis Preaching*. He was also author of *Microphone Messages* (1947) and *A Doorway to Bible Appreciation* (1948) and a contributor to *The Struggle for Meaning* (1977); *The Pulpit Speaks on Race* (1964); *To Be a Person of Integrity* (1975); and *Best Black Sermons* (1972). Smith was survived by his wife; his son, Kelly Miller Smith, Jr.; and four daughters.

David E. Sumner, Ball State University

SEE: CIVIL RIGHTS MOVEMENT; NAACP; RELIGION; SITINS, NASHVILLE; TENNESSEE STATE UNIVERSITY; VANDERBILT UNIVERSITY

SMITH, MAXINE ATKINS (1929–), Executive Secretary of the Memphis NAACP for over 40 years, was born in Memphis, Tennessee, on October 31, 1929. She graduated from Booker T. Washington High School in Memphis at the age of 15, received her A.B. degree in biology from Spellman College (Atlanta) in 1949 and master's degree in French in 1950 from Middlebury College in Vermont. Ironically, this civil rights leader attended Middlebury College because the University of Tennessee would not admit her or any other African-American student. The state did, however, cover her expenses at Middlebury College as an alternative.

What propelled Smith into the eye of the civil rights storm was her rejection from Memphis State University (now the University of Memphis), when she and Miriam Sugarmon Willis applied to do graduate work there in 1957. Memphis State's decision met with thunderous resistance from both Smith and Willis and they vowed to fight. Smith became active in the Memphis NAACP serving as volunteer Executive Secretary. She coordinated sit-ins, protests, and voter registration drives.

One who pushed integration, she organized the "If You're Black, Take It Back" campaigns boycotting downtown stores that would not integrate their work force. In 1961 she helped escort 13 black first graders who desegregated four white public schools. By 1962 she was the Executive Secretary of the Memphis NAACP. There was much work to be done. Many restaurants, theaters, and stores in Memphis were either closed to blacks or allowed them limited access. Employment opportunities essentially did not exist in white-owned and -operated companies. Department stores like Gerber's did not allow blacks to try on the clothes they were buying. Moreover, severe restrictions were placed on blacks' use of certain public facilities, including the zoo, lunch counters, drinking fountains, restrooms, parks, and playgrounds.

Because the Memphis City Schools remained largely segregated and were slow to change, Smith was at the forefront of Black Mondays, school boycotts initiated in 1969 to force the issue of total integration of all aspects of the Memphis City Schools. Many students, teachers, and principals stayed out of school. This effort resulted in the restructuring of the school board into district representation that led to the election of African Americans to the board.

In 1971 Smith took advantage of this restructuring and ran for and won a seat on the School Board. She was board president 1991–1992 and served the School Board until 1995. While on the Board, she saw to it that an African American, Dr. W.W. Herenton, was named superintendent of the Memphis City Schools in 1978.

Prominent in social circles in the black community, Smith is a member of the Memphis Chapter of Links, Inc., and the Memphis Smart Set and was a member of the Memphis Chapter of Jack and Jill of America, Inc., all organizations of well-to-do African Americans. She is a member of the Metropolitan Baptist Church.

Ronald A. Walter, Memphis

SEE: CIVIL RIGHTS MOVEMENT; NAACP; UNIVERSITY OF MEMPHIS

SMITH, RUTLEDGE (1870–1962), enjoyed careers in journalism, banking, and railroads. He was called "Major" by most people and was best known for his role in preparing the state for mobilization in both World War I and World War II. Born in Putnam County, Smith attended Washington Academy in Cookeville, but soon left school to work on the railroad.

At the age of 15, Smith worked as a rodman on the survey crew of the Knoxville and Nashville Railroad. From those humble beginnings, he rose through the ranks of what became the Tennessee Central Railroad to become Chief Industrial Agent in 1910, followed by promotions to executive general agent in 1913, and superintendent and executive general agent in 1914. Smith's interests in railroads overshadowed most other ventures, and in 1910 he was named president of the Tennessee, Kentucky, and Alabama Railroad Company.

Smith simultaneously enjoyed a successful career in journalism. In 1888 he acquired one-half interest in the *Cookeville Press* and acted as the paper's general manager and publisher. Primarily an organ of the local Democratic party, the *Press* was published every Thursday and boasted a readership of 2,000 subscribers. In 1893 he bought the rival *Cookeville Courier,* combining the two papers to create an expanded operation. In 1917 his involvement in other enterprises prompted Smith to sell the newspaper.

He was always involved in politics. In 1894 Smith became secretary to Congressman Benton McMillin. His move to Washington, D.C., provided the opportunity to improve his education, and Smith attended Georgetown University in the evenings. He later claimed to be a founding member of the Washington Press Club. In 1908–1909 Smith returned to Washington to act as the secretary to Senator James B. Frazier.

Smith's interests in banking date to 1906, when he took a position as cashier at the People's Bank of Cookeville. He assumed the presidency the following year. From 1907–1910 he served on the executive committee of the Tennessee Bankers Association.

Following the American declaration of war in April 1917, Smith attended a conference in Washington to formulate policy for mobilization. His advocacy of preparedness earned him the presidency of Tennessee's Council for National Defense. In addition, Defense Secretary Newton Baker appointed Smith field representative for the southeast region of the Council for National Defense, which oversaw defense activities south of the Ohio River and east of the Mississippi. Honorably discharged as a lieutenant colonel in 1919, Smith returned to civilian life with the Tennessee Central.

During the woman suffrage debate of 1919–1920, Smith and his wife, Graeme McGregor Smith, engaged in a public, though not acrimonious, difference of views. Smith was opposed to suffrage. Graeme McGregor Smith, however, became the first registered female voter in Davidson County.

During the late 1930s, Smith once again sounded the clarion for preparedness. Governor Prentice Cooper agreed and in 1940 established the Tennessee Preparedness Committee, the first such committee in the nation. He appointed Smith and Alvin C. York as advisors to the committee. Smith served as chairman of the Putnam County Home Guard during World War II.

During the 1930s and 1940s, Smith continued his interests in the Tennessee Central Railroad, serving as assistant president from 1931 until his retirement to Miami, Florida, in 1947.

Michael E. Birdwell, Tennessee Technological University
SEE: COOPER, WILLIAM PRENTICE, JR.; FRAZIER, JAMES B.; MCMILLIN, BENTON; PUTNAM COUNTY; RAILROAD, TENNESSEE CENTRAL; WOMAN SUFFRAGE MOVEMENT; WORLD WAR I; WORLD WAR II

SMITH, STANTON EVERETT (1905–), local, state, and national officer in the American Federation of Teachers, the Tennessee Federation of Labor, and the Tennessee State Labor Council, was born in Wyoming, Ohio, in 1905, the son of Charles Henry Smith, an accountant. Smith received his early education at the McCallie School in Chattanooga and graduated from high school in 1924. He earned a bachelor of arts degree from Denison University in Denison, Ohio, in 1930, and took additional courses at the University of Wisconsin and the University of Chattanooga. He married Nancy Virginia Lea, a teacher, in March 1932; they had four children.

In 1932, while teaching high school mathematics in Chattanooga, Smith joined the American Federation of Teachers (AFT); he served as the president of AFT Local 246 from 1932 to 1939. In 1937 he was elected national vice-president of the AFT and served until 1946. He also served as secretary-treasurer of the Chattanooga Central Labor Union from 1941 to 1956. He worked as education director for the southeastern region of the International Ladies Garment Workers' Union from 1942 to 1945.

Smith was elected president of the Tennessee Federation of Labor, American Federation of Labor (AFL) in 1949, serving until 1956. After the merger of the AFL and the Congress of Industrial Organization (CIO), he was elected president of the Tennessee State Labor Council, AFL-CIO, in 1956 and served until 1960. Then in 1960 he became the coordinator of state and local central bodies for the AFL-CIO and helped establish the Southern Labor School operated by 13 southern AFL-CIO state councils; he served as secretary-treasurer and president at various times.

Joseph Y. Garrison, Tennessee Historical Commission
SEE: LABOR; MCCALLIE SCHOOL

SMITH, WILLIAM MACON, (1830–1921), was the preeminent Radical Republican leader in Memphis during Reconstruction. As a judge, Smith confronted some of the most controversial legal issues of the period and led the Shelby County Republican party through decades of Democratic dominance.

Smith was born in Mecklenburg County, Virginia, and reared in Brownsville, Tennessee. He graduated from LaGrange College in Alabama in 1848 and from Cumberland Law School in 1851. After establishing a successful law practice in Brownsville, Smith was elected to the Tennessee House as a Whig in 1853; he was the youngest member of the General Assembly. He became a vehement critic of the anti-Catholic, anti-immigration, "Know-Nothing" movement.

In June 1860 Smith was elected chancellor of the vast Sixth Chancery Division, which included the West Tennessee counties of Henry, Weakley, Obion, Gibson, Dyer, Haywood, Lauderdale, Tipton, and Fayette. With the coming of the Civil War, he aligned himself with the Union and was forced to flee to occupied Memphis in 1862, where he organized Haywood County refugees to pressure Union authorities to bring their county under federal control.

At the urging of Alvin Hawkins, Smith reluctantly accepted appointment by Military Governor Andrew Johnson to the post of chancellor of the Common Law and Chancery Court of Memphis in 1864. After boldly establishing the Unionist judiciary's independence from the Union army, he upheld the constitutionality of legislation disfranchising ex-Confederates in 1865. In 1869 he enjoined Governor DeWitt Senter from removing Brownlow-appointed voter registrars who excluded ex-Confederates from the polls. His action was reversed by the Tennessee Supreme Court, resulting in the registration of ex-Confederates en masse and the demise of the state's Radical regime. Despite these controversial rulings, Smith earned a reputation as an honest jurist, in sharp contrast to many corrupt Unionist officials in Memphis.

Upon retirement from the bench in 1869, Smith declined appointment to the Supreme Court and devoted himself to a thriving Memphis law practice, Methodist Church affairs, and the Republican party. In 1880, due to division in the Democratic ranks over the state debt question, he was elected to the Tennessee State Senate, where he served as speaker and became Governor Alvin Hawkins's chief advisor. In 1882 he failed in efforts to win election to both the U.S. House and the U.S. Senate. In 1890 he was defeated as the Republican nominee for the Tennessee State Supreme Court, but regularly served as a special judge of the court.

He practiced law until 1906 and was considered the elder statesman of the Shelby County Republican party until he died in 1921, at the age of 91, the oldest member of the Memphis bar.

Russell Fowler, Memphis

SEE: HAWKINS, ALVIN; LAW; MEMPHIS; RECONSTRUCTION

SOLVENT SAVINGS BANK AND TRUST of Memphis was founded in 1906 by Robert R. Church, Sr., who had become the wealthiest African American in

Tennessee through real estate and other interests. The bank was located on Beale Street across from Church Park and Auditorium. Originally stock could be purchased for ten dollars a share, and the minimum deposit was one dollar. By 1921 the bank boasted that it was the largest bank in the world owned and operated by blacks, with resources over one million dollars.

Church and his son Robert R. Church, Jr., served as successive presidents; other early officers included Bert Roddy as cashier, and undertaker T.H. Hayes, J.W. Sanford, and attorney J.T. Settle. Directors included the Rev. T.O. Fuller of Howe Institute, Bishop N.C. Cleaves of the CME Church, Dr. R.G. Martin, owner of the Memphis Red Sox, and other leaders of the black community. When the neighboring Beale Street Baptist Church faced foreclosure in 1908, the Solvent paid the notes and saved the church.

After the failure of several borrowers in the early 1920s, the bank merged with the Fraternal Savings Bank and Trust in 1927, but its position was perilous. Robert R. Church, Jr., who had resigned from active connection with the bank in 1912, deposited $50,000 to stem the panic. State bank examiners found a shortage of at least $500,000 in 1928, and the bank president Alfred F. Ward was jailed. Black reaction ranged from shock to scorn. The failure of the Solvent Savings Bank predated by a year the crash of 1929 which shocked the entire financial system of the United States.

Perre Magness, Memphis

SEE: BEALE STREET; CHURCH, ROBERT, R., JR.; CHURCH, ROBERT, R., SR.; RODDY, BERT

SORGHUM-MAKING. The common term for sorghum syrup in Tennessee is "molasses" or "sorghum molasses." Educated agriculturists unsuccessfully campaigned against the use of these vernacular synonyms. Molasses is a by-product of sugar making and might derive from sugar cane or beets. Sorghum syrup is the pure, condensed juice of sweet sorghum cane, a sub-tropical grass first imported to America in 1853 as a possible source for commercial sugar supplies. The 1857 importation of 16 African varieties to Georgia and South Carolina made this grass a southern crop. By 1859 syrup production reached almost seven million gallons per year. The production of sorghum syrup became an enterprise of small farmers and retained the traditional language, farming practices, and syrup-making procedures of this producer class.

Currently, some 80 Tennessee producers keep 400 acres in sorghum cane, down from 3,000 acres in the 1950s. Until the early 1970s, West Tennessee ranked as the major sorghum growing region of the state, with Benton County providing up to 40 percent of

Sorghum-making near White Bluff, 1939.

TSLA

total production. A state survey from 1988 to 1990 found 85 percent of the producers in Middle and East Tennessee and 73 percent of the farmers growing five acres or less. Eighty percent of these small farmers still grew their crop from seed saved from the previous year's planting, thereby maintaining traditional varieties of cane; 87 percent cut their cane by hand; and 80 percent stripped the cane leaves by hand. Twelve percent of all producers still used horse-powered mills for squeezing juice from the cane, and 38 percent sold their product in traditional four-pound tins. A "stir-off" or gathering to press juice and cook it down to syrup has been a harvest season tradition in many families and communities since the late nineteenth century.

Not unexpectedly, the process of producing sorghum syrup also follows traditional methods. Farmers normally cut the tropical sorghum cane before frost. They strip the leaves from the standing cane and "top" it (remove the seed heads) after harvest. Sorghum cane mills are often built from refitted nineteenth century sugar cane processing machinery. The ground cane stalks may be used for fodder. Juice is always cooked on the same day of extraction. Evaporator pans, heated by hardwood coals, propane, or steam, are typically shallow, stainless steel troughs, baffled to allow juice to thicken as it passes from one section to another. As the strained, raw juice cooks down, chlorophyll and starchy material coagulates and floats to the top, and must be skimmed from the surface to avoid a bitter-tasting product. "Skimmings" may be fed to livestock, though some producers hide them in a "skimming hole," a trap into which an unwary visitor might step and amuse the crowd.

Traditionally, a sorghum-maker evaluates the readiness of syrup by observing the bubbles of the boiling juice and its thickness as it drips from a ladle. After a batch has been poured off, it is judged for its color, sweetness, texture, clarity, and flavor by the maker and the bystanders. Scorched syrup is fed to hogs and cattle.

Tennessee has been a consistent leader in the production and sale of sorghum syrup, often ranking first or second nationally.

Bob Fulcher, Clinton

SUGGESTED READING: A. Hugh Bryan, in "Sorghum Sirup Manufacture," USDA, Farmer's Bulletin 477, 1912

SEE: AGRICULTURE; BENTON COUNTY

SOTO EXPEDITION. An expedition led by Hernando de Soto conducted the earliest exploration of Tennessee by non-Native Americans in May, June, and July of 1540. The expedition of some 700 Spaniards and their slaves landed at Tampa Bay the previous May and struck north in search of food and gold. After wintering at the main town of Apalachee in present Tallahassee, Florida, Soto continued northeastward the following spring, advancing from one Mississippian town to the next. The expedition turned west in mid-May 1540, crossing the Blue Ridge Mountains at the Swannanoa Gap on May 25.

Following a trail through the mountains, they came upon the fortified town of Chiaha on Zimmerman's Island in the French Broad River near modern Dandridge, Tennessee. The well-provisioned town contained no gold. The Spaniards' horses, weak from traversing the mountain trails, were put out to pasture. During the respite at Chiaha, Soto sent two men north to the Chisca towns on the upper Nolichucky River. The Chiscas were rumored to mine copper, and perhaps gold.

The hospitable Chiahans provided the Spaniards with food and played and swam with them in the French Broad River. The good time came to an abrupt end, however, when Soto, preparing to leave, asked for 30 women. The Chiahans had attempted to pacify the Spaniard's demands, but Soto's request for women brought an end to peaceful relations. Rather than fight the Spaniards, the Chiahans left their town early on the morning of June 21, in hopes the Spaniards would leave. Soto responded by leading 30 horsemen and 30 footmen against the Chiahans, who took refuge on a nearby island. Unable to reach the sanctuary by horse, Soto accepted a negotiated truce that gave the Spaniards porters, but no women.

The expedition left Chiaha on June 28, following the French Broad River and passing through several neighboring towns. On July 1, the chief of Coste met the Spaniards and escorted them to one of his towns. At the Coste capital on Bussell Island in the mouth of the Little Tennessee River, Soto took the chief hostage to obtain guides and porters and prevent bloodshed after his men pillaged the corncribs and houses. Sick men left behind at Chiaha and those who had gone to the Chisca country came down the Tennessee River in canoes and rejoined the expedition.

On July 9, Soto left Coste. At the adjacent province of Tali, near present Sweetwater, the expedition again resupplied with corn, beans, and other food. Crossing the Hiwassee River on July 14, they reached the town of Tasqui, near modern Conasauga, Tennessee. The next day, the Spaniards crossed into northwestern Georgia and continued southward to the capital of the province of Coosa.

David H. Dye, University of Memphis

SUGGESTED READING: Lawrence A. Clayton, et al., eds., *The de Soto Chronicles: The Expedition of Hernando de Soto to North America in 1539–1543* (1993)

SEE: JEFFERSON COUNTY; MISSISSIPPIAN CULTURE; MONROE COUNTY

SOUTH CUMBERLAND STATE RECREATION AREA (SCRA) is a unique park within the Tennessee park system as it combines separate natural areas, trails, state forests, and small wild areas within one management unit. Its headquarters and visitor center are on U.S. Highway 41 between Monteagle and Tracy City but the different units include land in Franklin, Grundy, Marion, and Sequatchie counties and total over 12,000 acres of beautiful, ecologically rich land. SCRA's most visited units include: Sewanee Natural Bridge; Carter Natural Area; Hawkins Cove; Grundy Forest and the Fiery Gizzard Trail; Foster Falls; and Savage Gulf State Natural Area. The units feature hiking trails and picnic facilities.

Carroll Van West, Middle Tennessee State University

SEE: GRUNDY LAKES PARK AND GRUNDY STATE FOREST; SAVAGE GULF STATE NATURAL AREA

SOUTHERN ADVENTIST UNIVERSITY. After its founding as Graysville Academy in 1892, this educational institution evolved and expanded, changed its name twice, and moved in 1916 to what became the town of Collegedale in Hamilton County. On its new 1,000-acre campus the school, then known as Southern Junior College, continued to grow, and by 1944 its academic offerings included a four-year program, and "Missionary" replaced "Junior" in its name. Four decades later its name shifted to Southern College of Seventh-day Adventists. In 1996, when the institution initiated two Master of Science degrees in Education and in Community Counseling, it became Southern Adventist University. The institution's twenty-third president, Gordon Bietz, was installed in 1997.

The present study body numbers more than 1,600 and comes from 47 foreign countries as well as from across the United States. The majority of students are from the southeast and most take classes in Collegedale, but B.S. nursing classes are also available in three locations in Florida. Besides the new graduate program, the 21 departments at Southern Adventist University offer a range of majors for baccalaureate degrees, associate degrees, and four different one-year technology certificates. The university is accredited by the Southern Association of Colleges and Schools. Its radio station WSMC-FM broadcasts from the campus throughout the Chattanooga area, and McKee Foods Corporation has its headquarters here. The Seventh-day Adventist Church, central to the institution's identity, provides it the mission to instill students with a sense of service to others.

Margaret D. Binnicker, Middle Tennessee State University

SEE: EDUCATION, HIGHER; MCKEE FOODS CORPORATION; RELIGION

SOUTHERN BAPTIST CONVENTION. Southern Baptists in Tennessee represent a tradition born in Amsterdam and London in the early seventeenth century, transported to the American colonies in the 1630s and spreading south and west with frontier immigration. These Christians affirm the authority of Scripture, the liberty of conscience, autonomous churches composed of converts who have received immersion baptism, associational cooperation of churches, the priesthood of all believers, and religious liberty. While there are numerous types of Baptists in Tennessee, the largest single group is represented in those churches related to the Southern Baptist Convention, numbering more than a million adherents statewide.

Baptists were among the earliest settlers to Tennessee, with churches founded perhaps as early as 1758, though records are unclear. The rolls of the Sinking Creek Baptist Church contain the names of some such early colonists as Julius C. Dugger, Michael Hyder, and Baptist McNabb. Many were influenced by the Separate Baptist congregation founded by Shubal Stearns (1706–1771) and Daniel Marshall (1706–1784) at Sandy Creek in North Carolina in 1755. Certain of these Separate Baptists were forced to leave Carolina in the 1770s after Governor William Tryon blamed them (falsely) for the ill-fated Regulator rebellion. They were instrumental in the building of the Buffalo Ridge Baptist Church in 1779, often claimed as Tennessee's first Baptist church. William Murphrey established the Cherokee Church in 1783 and became the church's first pastor.

The first Baptist association in Tennessee—the Holston Association—was founded at the Cherokee Church in 1786 by several churches previously identifying themselves with the Sandy Creek Association in North Carolina. The association linked churches for fellowship, discipline, and doctrinal inquiry.

In the eastern portion of the state numerous Baptist groups developed, some in response to the antimission controversy initiated by preachers like Daniel Parker (1781–1844). Parker traveled through Tennessee, challenging those who sought to organize mission boards and send out missionaries. He insisted that God was the sole author of salvation and human means of conversion were unbiblical. The Primitive Baptists of Tennessee and other portions of Appalachia reflect Parker's legacy. They eschew Sunday Schools, revivals, and any human attempt to bring about conversion. They practice various Baptist "ordinances," including immersion baptism, the Lord's Supper, and the washing of feet. Other Baptist subdenominations in the region include the old Regular Baptists, United Baptists, and Free Will Baptists.

Nashville was the scene of another important Baptist movement known as Old Landmarkism, an attempt to trace Baptist origins to the New Testament church. Led by Tennesseans such as J.R. Graves (1781–1844) of Nashville, Landmarkists claimed that Baptist churches alone retained the marks of the true church. All other churches were merely "societies." Landmarkists rejected alien immersion—the baptism of persons in non-Baptist churches and promoted "close (or closed) communion," a practice which restricted the Supper only to members of the local congregation in which it was served. Landmarkism was a significant influence on Baptist life well into the twentieth century.

Tennessee was also a center of the Restorationist movement fostered by Alexander Campbell (1788–1866) and Barton W. Stone (1772–1844), an effort to "restore" the New Testament church which had been corrupted by all the denominations. They claimed only to maintain those practices evident among New Testament churches. They rejected denominational names and labels, calling themselves "Christians only" or Disciples of Christ. Many Baptist churches in Tennessee became Christian churches, or "Campbellites" as their critics designated them.

An initial effort in 1833 to organize a state Baptist convention failed by 1842 due to opposition from those who rejected such general alliances as unscriptural and a threat to congregational autonomy. From 1842 to 1874 there were actually three sectional organizations linking Baptists through associations in East, Middle, and West Tennessee for missionary and benevolent endeavors. A state convention uniting all those regions was finally founded in April 10, 1874. The convention funded missionary work, colleges, hospitals, evangelism, and other ministries for Baptist churches. The first corresponding secretary-treasurer (director) was William Allen Montgomery, elected in 1877. A state Baptist periodical, *The Baptist and Reflector,* was begun in 1889 through a union of two earlier papers, *The Baptist* and *The Reflector.*

The state convention also owns and operates three schools of higher education: Belmont University in Nashville, Union University in Jackson, and Carson-Newman College in Jefferson City. The Southern Baptist Convention also maintains a significant presence in Nashville where its Sunday School Board and Executive Committee offices are located. A joint effort between the African-American National Baptist Convention, Inc., and the Southern Baptist Convention led to the founding of American Baptist Theological Seminary in Nashville in 1924. The seminary provides theological education for African-American ministers.

Bill J. Leonard, Wake Forest University

SUGGESTED READINGS: Nancy T. Ammerman, *Baptist Battles: Social Change and Religious Conflict in the Southern Baptist Convention* (1990); Bill J. Leonard, *God's Last and Only Hope: the Fragmentation of the Southern Baptist Convention* (1990)

SEE: BELMONT UNIVERSITY; CARSON-NEWMAN COLLEGE; FREE WILL BAPTISTS; LANDMARKISM; NATIONAL BAPTIST CONVENTION; PUBLISHING; RELIGION; SOUTHERN BAPTIST HOME MISSION BOARD; UNION UNIVERSITY

SOUTHERN BAPTIST HOME MISSION BOARD.

When a group of ministers met in Augusta, Georgia, in 1845 to establish the Southern Baptist Convention, they simultaneously created two separate boards to oversee the domestic and foreign missionary work of the Convention. The Board of Domestic Missions, headquartered in Marion, Alabama, had as its three main purposes sending missionaries to frontier settlements, strengthening churches in the South, and evangelizing slaves. Reflecting an additional emphasis, the Convention changed the agency's name in 1855 to the Domestic and Indian Mission Board.

Financial struggle and administrative turmoil characterized the Board's history from 1845 to 1874. The year 1874, however, marked a new era. The Convention renamed the agency the Home Mission Board (HMB) and, in 1882, moved its headquarters to Atlanta. That same year, they appointed a new corresponding secretary (director), Isaac Taylor Tichenor (1825–1902), who succeeded in reversing the agency's fortunes during his 17-year career. During that period, the Board appointed a total of 2,692 missionaries, organized 2,290 churches, started 2,117 Sunday Schools, built 640 church buildings, and added 67,169 members to Southern Baptist churches. The state of Tennessee shared in all of those efforts, but Tichenor also inaugurated a particular program that would prove to be the Board's most significant investment in the state.

In 1885, addressing the annual meeting of the Southern Baptist Convention, Tichenor called for financial support for missionaries to the southern Appalachian mountains. A limited program supporting ministers and evangelists followed, concentrated primarily in East Tennessee and western North Carolina. By 1898 Tichenor had mustered sufficient support to begin a network of schools in the mountains, mostly in Tennessee, Kentucky, and North Carolina.

For the most part, the HMB established elementary and secondary schools (Harrison-Chilhowee Institute established in 1881 in Sevier County was an example), along with a few colleges that received support for their roles in training ministers and teachers for the mountain region. The schools received most of their support from local churches and associations and from tuition. The HMB administered the schools and provided part of the funds to purchase property and construct and equip buildings. They also supported some of the teachers. In addition, the Board had on its staff a full-time supervisor for the mountain schools program whose responsibilities included recruiting teachers and seeking opportunities to establish schools with local cooperation. Financial pressures from school creditors, together with a disastrous embezzlement scandal at the HMB in 1928, prompted officials drastically to reduce funding for the mountain schools program. In 1931 the HMB transferred all responsibility for the schools to locally organized boards of trustees.

The mountain schools program reflected a model of cooperation between the HMB, state-level missions boards, and local Baptist associations that has continued to govern HMB programs, many of which have been carried out in Tennessee. In 1935 the Board inaugurated a new program of evangelism and church-planting in the mountain region. That same year, defeating an effort by the Tennessee Valley Authority to prohibit missionary work among laborers building the Norris Dam, the HMB and the Tennessee Baptist Convention Board of Missions established a church in Norris, Tennessee. During World War II, the national and state boards cooperated to establish churches and other ministries for communities that grew up around industrial defense plants and military camps. Beginning in 1945, the state board and Home Mission Board also cooperated with the National Baptist Convention to provide an African-American missionary to work with the black student population in Nashville. Since the end of World War II, the Home Mission Board and the Tennessee Baptist Convention Board of Missions have cooperated in language missions, financial support for rural churches, church building loan programs, evangelism, military and prison chaplain programs, and urban social ministries.

Lisa Pruitt, Vanderbilt University

SUGGESTED READINGS: *A Heritage of Caring People: Home Mission Board, SBC* (1995); Arthur B. Rutledge, *Mission to America: A Century and a Quarter of Southern Baptist Home Missions* (1969)

SEE: SETTLEMENT SCHOOLS; SOUTHERN BAPTIST CONVENTION

SOUTHERN CITIZEN. The short-lived *Southern Citizen* was a pro-slavery newspaper in the heart of anti-slavery East Tennessee; its editor, an Irish nationalist hero of 1848, worked in the midst of anti-immigrant Know Nothings.

In October 1857 Knoxville mayor William Swan co-founded the newspaper with John Mitchel, a talented journalist and dynamic speaker whose militancy and controversial opinions repeatedly challenged authorities in Ireland, England, and the United States. As a "Young Irelander" and editor of the *United Irishmen*, Mitchel's violent anti-British writings resulted in his 1848 arrest and exile first to Bermuda, and later to Tasmania. Following his escape and arrival in New York, Mitchel edited *The Citizen*. His initial embrace by Irish-Americans cooled, however, when Mitchel (a Protestant) angered Archbishop Hughes with open attacks on papal authority. In 1855 Mitchel abandoned New York and moved his family to Tuckaleechee Cove in Blount County.

Bored with pastoral life, Mitchel moved to nearby Knoxville and, with Swan's backing, began publishing *The Southern Citizen*. The newspaper's editorial policies and selection of articles, no doubt, confused East Tennesseans as the paper vigorously embraced the notion of the enslavement of blacks in the South, while simultaneously railing against British imperialism, racism, and enslavement of people in Ireland and India.

Mitchel stirred bitter opposition from Knoxville editors William G. "Parson" Brownlow (*Brownlow's Knoxville Whig*) and John Fleming (*Knoxville Register*), and Brownlow gleefully reported the end of the *Southern Citizen* when Mitchel moved to Washington, D.C., in 1858. He died in Ireland in 1875.

DeeGee Lester, Hendersonville

SEE: BROWNLOW, WILLIAM G.; KNOXVILLE; PUBLISHING

SOUTHERN COLLEGE OF OPTOMETRY in Memphis has educated over 6,000 optometrists in its 65 years of existence. It is one of only 17 schools of optometry in the United States and has contracts with several states to educate health care professionals.

Dr. J.J. Horton owned a proprietary school in Kansas City. In 1932 he decided to move it to Memphis, opening the Southern College of Optometry (SCO) at 865 Washington with six students and two faculty members. From the beginning, the school was accredited by the Council on Optometric Education.

In 1935 Horton sold the school to Dr. Wilbur Cramer. In the mid-1940s, responding to changes in the profession, the school became a non-profit institution. The college entered a period of growth after the end of World War II because of the GI Bill. By 1950 the college occupied six buildings on Washington Avenue plus a clinic on Union.

The 1960s saw increased governmental spending in health care, as well as increased governmental regulation. The 1970s and 1980s saw more changes in the practice of optometry. States passed laws allowing optometrists to use diagnostic, then therapeutic pharmaceutical agents. The college moved to its architecturally significant 11-story building at 1245 Madison in 1970.

Students from 42 states and several foreign countries take a four year post-baccalaureate course combining classroom learning and practical experience. The school has 53 faculty members. Students have access to the latest methods and equipment, including VISIONET, a computer database, developed by the college's staff, which has all eye care and vision science literature published since 1976.

The clinic at SCO, staffed by 43 licensed clinicians assisted by 60 to 100 students on rotation, sees over 50,000 patient visits a year. In addition, the college provides services to city schools and nursing homes.

Perre Magness, Memphis

SEE: MEDICINE; MEMPHIS

SOUTHERN ENGINE AND BOILER WORKS. In 1884 two mechanics in Jackson, Tennessee, established the Southern Engine and Boiler Works to build a line of small engines and boilers. In 1895 the mechanics sold their shop to local stockholders, who constructed a new complex on North Royal Street. By 1900 the new plant employed 400 workers making high pressure boilers, steam engines, and saw mills. This steam engine industry was the largest of its kind in the South at the turn of the century. The success of the company led to the replacement of the original building with a larger plant. Built between 1902 and 1904, it consisted of five connecting brick buildings, including an office, a machine shop, a foundry, a forge and engine room, and a boiler shop.

In 1906 chief engineer William Collier created a gasoline-powered engine and automobile. Over the next four years, the company manufactured around 300 cars. The automobile was originally called the "Southerner," but was renamed the "Marathon" in 1909. The following year, a group of Nashville investors, headed by A.H. Robertson, purchased the Marathon division of the company. Relocated to Nashville, the automobile division built around 5,000 Marathons between 1910 and 1914. The Jackson plant continued to produce parts for the Marathon until management problems led to the automobile's demise in 1918. The Southern Engine and Boiler Works produced steam engines until 1926, when the company ceased operations.

The Southern Engine and Boiler Works was a major industry at the turn of the century. In addition to its prominence in Jackson's industrial development, the company spearheaded the development of the Marathon automobile, which holds the distinction of being the only mass-produced car completely manufactured in the South until recent years. Less than a dozen original Marathons are known to exist, making them among the rarest cars in the world. The remaining buildings of the Jackson complex were listed in the National Register of Historic Places in 1993.

Philip Thomason, Nashville

SEE: INDUSTRY; JACKSON; MARATHON MOTOR WORKS

SOUTHERN POTTERIES INC., under the leadership of E.J. Owens, located in Erwin, Unicoi County, Tennessee, in 1916–1917 and began operations using skilled labor brought from Ohio and local unskilled workers. Its product was known as Clinchfield ware, and the company's letterhead insisted "Clinchfield on China is like Sterling on Silver." An early switch in leadership in 1922, when Charles W. Foreman of Canton, Ohio, purchased the plant, did not change its emphasis. The pottery's period of great growth, however, emerged by 1938 with the shift from the use of decals in decoration to a new process of decorating the china with hand painting under the glaze. Southern Potteries' primary product became the mass-produced, hand-decorated dinnerware known as Blue Ridge. Its increasing popularity made Southern Potteries the largest producer of hand-painted pottery in the nation during the 1940s. Post-World War II developments of plastic dinnerware and Japanese export ceramics led to such market loss for the Tennessee pottery that it ceased operating in 1957, never to reopen. The American public's recent revival of interest in Southern Potteries' distinctive Blue Ridge patterns has led to a marked increase in the value of individual pieces among collectors, and Erwin is trying to capitalize upon this development.

The selection of Erwin in 1916 for the pottery site made sense for several reasons. Upper East Tennessee had become more accessible due to construction of the Carolina, Clinchfield & Ohio Railway (Clinchfield), completed in 1915. Businessmen of the region believed in the New South philosophy and saw its implementation as their means to prosperity. An end to the boom period in Ohio's china industry after 1910 made a move away from that region to Tennessee more appealing as well. The natural resources needed for the production of the Clinchfield dinnerware existed in the immediate area and adjacent states, and potential laborers abounded. The railroad could carry the china to markets across the country and bring department-store buyers to the pottery's doorstep. With Kingsport just up the rail line drawing several industries to its locale, Erwin investors imagined that any number of companies might soon be locating in its narrow valley beside the Nolichucky River. That rush of new businesses failed to materialize, and for 40 years Southern Potteries functioned as Erwin's second largest employer, well behind the Clinchfield. The pottery's labor force reached perhaps 1,200 in the 1940s.

The significance of Southern Potteries has yet to be definitively measured, but several features deserve mention. The product itself, mass-produced pottery, was created at a remarkable pace. In 1926, in a single day, 2,400 dozen plates could be produced, making Southern Potteries the largest plant of its kind in the South. The company maintained this level of production even after all pieces were hand-painted. At its peak, around the end of World War II, female decorators turned out 324,000 pieces of Blue Ridge ware each week. This dinnerware represented a peculiar combination of assembly-line precision and individual decoration.

The pottery operated 24 hours a day, seven days a week, with coal-fired kilns and billowing smokestacks. Converting the kilns to gas fuel by 1940 eliminated the smoky exhaust. Southern Potteries employees were members of Local #103 of the National Brotherhood of Operative Potters, though the pottery was not a closed shop. Perhaps because Erwin's largest employer, the Clinchfield Railroad, was also unionized, the town's population did not go through the same disruptions over labor issues that plagued many other Appalachian communities in the 1930s. Earlier, in the spirit of welfare capitalism, the railroad had begun construction of a model community planned by the New York architect Grosvenor Atterbury for its employees. Forty-five residences were completed in 1917. The railroad sold two-thirds of those houses in 1920 to Southern Potteries, which first rented them and then sold them to employees in the late 1930s. This planned neighborhood may have had some influence on employee satisfaction. Certainly the prospect for local women of employment as decorators and finishers had a positive economic impact in the town and surrounding counties. The liquidation of Southern Potteries in the late 1950s meant some women sought work at other small industries in Erwin, and other employees, both men and women, and their families moved away to work in other potteries.

Margaret D. Binnicker, Middle Tennessee State University

SEE: DECORATIVE ARTS, APPALACHIAN; RAILWAY, CAROLINA, CLINCHFIELD & OHIO; UNICOI COUNTY

SOUTHWEST TERRITORY, or The Territory of the United States South of the River Ohio, was created by an act of Congress on May 26, 1790. The State of North Carolina had ceded the lands and waterways encompassed by the act to the national government on December 22, 1789. The cession represented the total area of the territory, although its name suggested the possible inclusion of other lands south of the Ohio not yet in federal hands. Congress specified that the territory would be governed under the provisions of the Ordinance of 1787, the statute that established the vast Northwest Territory. The lawmakers made one important exception, however. They permitted slavery in the new territory, although they had prohibited slavery in the Northwest Territory.

Establishing a federal territory was a political mechanism by which the people, of a specific area of the country outside the bounds of the states, could be placed under federal authority until such time as its population increased to levels adequate to support the organization of state government. A newborn territory, at its first level, was virtually a fiefdom for the governor. The settlers achieved a voice in government at the second level when the population reached 5,000, a number that permitted them to elect the lower house of a general assembly and nominate the members of the upper house for appointment by the President. The third and final progression was the step to statehood, authorized when the population had exceeded 60,000.

The creation of the new territory was the result of the dynamics of four separate but related interests. First, land speculators and expansionists coveted stable government for the region because it was part of the nation's next logical growth area. Secondly, the State of North Carolina could sharply reduce the demand on its drained treasury and find relief from the responsibility of protecting western settlers by ceding the overmountain domain and waiving to Congress the potential revenues from future sales of its public lands. Next, the western settlers wanted territorial status and lobbied vigorously for it, believing that the national government would offer better protection against the Indians. Finally, the federal government was anxious to establish control over western lands England had yielded in the Treaty of 1783, but from which the king had not yet totally evacuated his troops.

The Southwest Territory contained 43,000 square miles of surface area, less than one-sixth of the area of the Northwest Territory. In 1791, however, the populations were of inverse ratio: 35,691 reported in the Southwest and 3,200 estimated in the Northwest. The western district of Virginia, lying immediately south of the Ohio River, constituted the most heavily populated transmontane area. Yet, it was a part of neither territory. After a series of conventions that began in 1784 and ended in 1790, the inhabitants negotiated an agreement with Virginia and Congress to provide statehood for the region. Congress admitted Kentucky as an equal member state of the Union on February 4, 1792.

Nowhere was the role of the speculator more directly involved with the development of the overmountain west than in the Southwest Territory. In 1790, when President George Washington appointed North Carolina businessman William Blount as Territorial Governor, Blount and his brothers claimed title to approximately one million acres of the land inside its boundaries. Earlier, in the latter 1770s, William Henderson, another North Carolinian, had made colossal purchases of western lands from the Indians only to have them invalidated later by the states of North Carolina and Virginia. He succeeded, nonetheless, in promoting settlements in separate areas that later became parts of Central Kentucky and Middle Tennessee.

The cession of the western half of the state was a difficult decision for the leaders of North Carolina. Although the General Assembly had passed an act to cede the lands beyond the mountains in 1784, the same body repealed its action before Congress could accept it. Five years later, with a treasury that was virtually empty, the state faced an assessment for its share of the national debt incurred during the American Revolution. Its portion was determined by a formula that related the assessment to the land area of the state; consequently, by reducing the size of the state, the tax share would be cut proportionally. That option guaranteed the votes to pass the cession act. Other support came from many North Carolinians

living east of the mountains who were eager to be relieved of the burden of protecting western settlers from the Indians. The frontier folk in North Carolina's western lands had lobbied passionately for cession because they believed that by accepting the area as a federal territory, the national government would be honor-bound to defend them.

President Washington gave Governor William Blount a second responsibility as Superintendent of Indian Affairs in the Southern Department, an office that placed him in contact with the neighboring Choctaw, Chickasaw, Cherokee, and Creek nations. Relations with the latter two were so difficult that Blount had to devote more time to Indian matters than to the office of governor. The combined duties of both offices did not prevent him from taking an active role in land purchases and sales, however.

The first capital of the territory was the home of William Cobb, since called Rocky Mount, in Washington County near the Watauga River. Governor Blount and Daniel Smith, a Mero District leader appointed by the President to be Secretary of the territory and acting Governor in Blount's absence, set up the territorial office there in 1790. They relocated the capital to Blount's residence in the newly laid out town of Knoxville in 1792. The three other principal officers of the government were judges John McNairy, David Campbell, and Joseph Anderson. Generals John Sevier and James Robertson commanded the militia of Washington and Mero Districts respectively. Before the area was certified as populous enough to elect its own house of representatives, the judges and the Governor constituted the General Assembly with authority to enact statutes.

Early in 1791 the governor enumerated the population and reported more than enough free white adult males to qualify the territory for its next step toward statehood, the election of a lower house. Blount did not call for elections until December 1793, nearly three years later, when the populace would wait no longer. He clearly preferred to rule without dealing with an elected house, but joined the popular cry for elections when he could put it off no longer.

President Washington assigned Blount the task of clarifying provisions of the 1785 Treaty of Hopewell and, if possible, purchasing some of the Cherokee land south of the French Broad since occupied by settlers. When the governor sought to treat with them, they responded hesitantly, but their chiefs came to the treaty grounds after Blount sent James Robertson, formerly a respected agent among them, to urge their attendance.

The Indians' interests would have been better served if they had remained at home. Blount enticed them to give up the right-of-way for a road to connect Southwest Point with the Cumberland settlements and browbeat them into signing over most of the land he sought for an annual payment by the federal government of $1,000. There was no longer a need for clarification of the Treaty of Hopewell.

The following year of 1792 was marked by both Cherokee and Creek raids into the territory. The national government, already involved in Indian wars in the Northwest Territory, would not participate in a war against the southern Indians; neither would it permit the frontiersmen to make preemptive strikes, nor pursue attacking Indians across the line into their own territory. The settlers could take defensive measures only.

That kind of response from the War Department and Congress infuriated the territorial settlers. Separate groups of unauthorized volunteers from the Holston and Cumberland leveled Cherokee and Creek villages and killed a number of warriors. On one of the few occasions when strikes against the Indians were authorized, acting governor Daniel Smith, in Blount's absence, sent General John Sevier with a regiment of militia into Cherokee territory in pursuit of a large body of Indians that had approached Knoxville but turned back after massacring the family of Alexander Cavett a few miles from town. Smith's action, though upheld by Blount, was not approved by the War Department. Pay for the militia, a federal obligation, was withheld until long after Tennessee became a state.

Other large groups of warriors also invaded the territory. On September 30, 1792, a group of more than 500, principally Creek and Cherokee Indians, marched on Nashville, and unsuccessfully laid siege to Buchanan's station. A force of an estimated 260 Creeks and Cherokees attacked Greenfield station in Sumner County on April 28, 1794, but a few alert defenders drove them off.

After elections for the territorial house were held in December 1793, the representatives chosen met at Knoxville on February 24, 1794, to nominate ten councilors from whom President Washington appointed John Sevier, James Winchester, Stockley Donelson, Parmenas Taylor, and Griffith Rutherford to make up the legislative council, or upper house, of the General Assembly.

The full General Assembly of the Southwest Territory convened its first session at Knoxville on August 26, 1794, and elected a nonvoting representative to Congress. The territory had reached its second level of progression toward statehood, and there was only one remaining.

In a special session that began on June 29, 1795, the General Assembly voted to make an enumeration of the population and authorized Blount to recommend that each county elect five delegates to be convened by him for the purpose of determining the permanent form of government for the area and adopting a constitution.

When Governor Blount tied the pay of the sheriffs taking the census to the totals reported, even skeptics joined those who believed the population would exceed 60,000. It was a very straightforward arrangement; the larger the total reported from each county, the larger the sheriff's pay for counting them.

On November 28, 1795, the collected census reports from all 11 counties indicated that there were 77,262 inhabitants in the Southwest Territory, a total comfortably exceeding the minimum required for statehood. The governor called for the election of delegates to meet in convention on January 11, 1796, to begin work on a constitution and form a state government.

Once the qualifying enumeration had been made, the final progression under the Ordinance of 1787 had been reached. But it was not clear what was yet to be done to bring the state into existence and into the Union.

Blount and his political allies decided on a bold initiative. They would establish the new state, adopt a constitution for it, elect its officials, and petition the national government to accept it on an equal basis with the other states.

Fifty-five representatives from the 11 counties of the territory met in convention at Knoxville on January 11, 1776. They elected Blount to be the presiding officer and Daniel Smith to be chairman of the committee to draft a constitution and bill of rights.

Consideration of a bill of rights was apparently of the highest priority. Smith's draft was debated and adopted before the full constitution was brought to the floor. Containing 32 separate provisions, the bill was entitled "A Declaration of Rights." The delegates incorporated it into the constitution later as its last section, Article XI.

The Declaration of Rights closely paralleled the Bill of Rights of the Constitution of the United States, but in its final form it was marked by two distinctly western concerns. Section 29 proclaimed: "That an equal participation of the free navigation of the Mississippi, is one of the inherent rights of the citizens of this state: it cannot, therefore, be conceded to any prince, potentate, power, person or person whatever." Mirroring the westerners' passion for land, Section 31 declared: "That the people residing south of French Broad and Holston between the Rivers Tennessee and the Big Pigeon, are entitled to the right of pre-emption and occupancy in that tract."

Providing for executive, legislative, and judicial departments, the constitution drew heavily upon the work of the constitution makers of North Carolina and, to a lesser extent, Pennsylvania. It broke with the North Carolina tradition by sanctioning no single church or religion. It prohibited seating ministers of the gospel and priests in either house of the bicameral legislature but simultaneously barred from any office in the civil department of the state anyone who denied "the being of God, or a future state of rewards and punishment." The constitution departed from the ways of some of the older states by providing universal manhood suffrage. All white males and all free black males 21 years of age or older were permitted to vote.

On February 6, 1796, the convention approved the constitution and the name of the new state—Tennessee—by a unanimous vote. Before adjourning the delegates instructed Governor Blount to send a copy of the constitution by express to the Secretary of State at Philadelphia, so that it could be brought before Congress before the end of its session. Governor Blount issued writs of election to the sheriffs of the several counties in order that the first election for members of the General Assembly and Governor of the new state could be held.

The adjournment of the convention left the constitution firmly in place. There was no requirement for further approval or review, except by the Congress of the United States, and that only for the purpose of determining that it and the government to be formed under its provisions were truly republican.

At the March elections, the voters chose John Sevier to be the new state's first Governor and elected members of the House and Senate of the first General Assembly. Although he was probably the most popular man in the state, John Sevier's election reflected decisions by territorial leaders to promote him for Governor, Blount and William Cocke for the U.S. Senate, Andrew Jackson for Congress, and James Winchester for Speaker of the State Senate and *de facto* Lieutenant Governor. The most powerful offices went to those living in East Tennessee, where the population was larger, but the western, or Mero District, people were mollified by the inclusion of Jackson and Winchester.

When the General Assembly certified Sevier's election, Governor Blount announced to Secretary of State Timothy Pickering that the government of the State of Tennessee was organized and established and that the government of the Territory of the United States South of the River Ohio "has terminated." President Washington placed the question of statehood for Tennessee before Congress on April 8 when he submitted (without recommendation) the constitution of the state, the enumeration of the inhabitants, and other pertinent documents to both houses.

The House of Representatives took up the issue and after considerable debate, voted 43 to 30 on May 6 to admit Tennessee to the Union. In the Senate it was a different matter. There the Federalists, who rightly expected the new state would vote against their candidate in the upcoming presidential election, delayed admission until the last day of the session, June 1, 1796. Yielding in conference committee

to House pressure to admit, the Senate was able to force the new state to elect their United States senators anew, to reduce their electoral college votes from four to three, and to accept a single congressman instead of the two contemplated, until the next federal census.

Although temporarily crippled politically by the Senate's provisions, Tennessee had become the sixteenth state of the Union and the first state to be developed from a federal territory. The Southwest Territory existed no more, but its leaders had charted a way for other territories evolving under the provisions of the Ordinance of 1787 to become equal states of the Union. They had tested and established a method by which those in succeeding westward migrations would be able to achieve full citizenship and enjoy the blessing of representative government.
Walter T. Durham, Gallatin

SUGGESTED READINGS: Clarence E. Carter, comp. and ed., *The Territorial Papers of the United States, Territory of the United States South of the River Ohio, 1790–1796.* Vol. IV. (1936); Walter T. Durham, *Before Tennessee: The Southwest Territory, 1790–1796* (1990); Walter T. Durham, "The Southwest and Northwest Territories, A Comparison, 1787–1796." *Tennessee Historical Quarterly* 49(1990): 188–196; William H. Masterson, *William Blount* (1954)

THE SOUTHWESTERN COMPANY, recognized as the oldest still operating door-to-door sales company in the United States, publishes Bibles and educational reference books which college students sell over summer vacation. The Reverend James R. Graves, a prominent Baptist minister, published religious tracts as far back as the 1840s. By 1855 Graves had founded the Southwestern Publishing House. *The Tennessee Baptist* was the company's most popular publication and helped advertise other tracts.

Prior to the Civil War, Bibles had been printed in the North and shipped south. The stock of Bibles in the South, however, was depleted during the war. "The North has no monopoly on the Word of God," Graves declared. In August 1861 the Southwestern Publishing House began to publish Bibles from stereotype plates smuggled from the North. The Bibles were pocket-sized and bound in hard covers.

This first venture, however, did not last long. Nashville fell to Union forces on February 24, 1862, and Graves, feeling vulnerable because of his stormy articles against the North, fled to Memphis. The company resumed publication of religious materials in 1867. At this time during Reconstruction, a number of colleges and training institutions were starting in the South, but jobs to earn money for school were hard to find. In 1868 Graves began to train young men as book agents to sell the company's publications from door-to-door. Some young men sold the greater part of the year, while college students sold only during the summer months. Graves retired in 1871 and sold his interest in the company. The firm remained in Memphis until 1879 when it returned to Nashville. However, its marketing strategy has never changed and its annual summer training program attracts thousands of eager student-sellers to Nashville.

Michael Fleenor, Tennessee Historical Commission

SEE: GRAVES, JAMES R.; PUBLISHING

SOYBEANS have become one of the most important cash crops in post-World War II Tennessee, ranking the top cash crop in the state by the mid-1990s. The first record of soybeans in the United States dates to 1804 but the plant was not produced in large amounts until after 1890. During the 1920s the U.S. Department of Agriculture through its extension agent program publicized the use of soybeans and their commercial production. Another boom in the plant's production came in the 1940s but the widespread growth of soybeans can be attributed to developments of the 1960s. Soybeans became known as a double-crop plant species that could be grown in tandem with small grains, primarily wheat, to produce two crops per year from the same field. In addition, soybeans proved adaptable to the no-till production movement in agriculture. New uses for soybeans as food products spurred demand for the crop and soybean meal began to be used in the manufacture of many chemical products, from paints to fire-extinguisher fluid. Finally, soybeans brought good prices—as high as $13 per bushel. Thus, farmers began to convert former pastures and hay crops to soybean fields. The boom of soybean production, however, had its downside as soil erosion increased in the 1960s and the 1970s.

West Tennessee farmers quickly adapted to the soybean revolution and over the last generation soybeans replaced cotton on many farms in the region. Of the 70 million acres planted in soybeans across the country, one million of those acres are in Tennessee, mostly in West Tennessee. According to figures from the Tennessee Department of Agriculture, Gibson, Dyer, Weakley, and Obion counties were the state's leading producers in 1995, with these four counties accounting for more than 12.3 million bushels of soybeans.

Yields in soybean production have made outstanding increases in the last few years, due to the development of new varieties and bio-technology. Yields in the 1960s typically were 20–30 bushels per acre; now that same amount of land sometimes yields 60 bushels. Soybean, "the wonder food plant" of the twentieth century has made its mark in the United States, with a promised continued bright future.

Dale Fuqua, West Tennessee Agricultural Museum

SEE: AGRICULTURE

SPANISH-AMERICAN WAR. Tennesseans participated in virtually every aspect of the Spanish-American War of 1898. Commander Washburn Maynard (a Knoxville native) of the gunboat *Nashville* is credited with firing the first shot of the war on April 22. The same vessel was assigned the leading role in cutting the Atlantic telegraph cables between Cuba and Spain.

Four Tennessee volunteer infantry regiments were mustered into federal service for the Spanish-American War. Only the First, originally commanded by Colonel William Crawford Smith, saw combat. Neither the Second, under the command of Colonel Kellar Anderson, nor the Third, led by Colonel J. Perry Fyffe, were sent overseas; both regiments were mustered out of service in early 1899. The Fourth, commanded by Colonel George Leroy Brown, served on occupation duty in Cuba for five months after the war. The four Tennessee volunteer regiments comprised 187 officers and 4,148 enlisted men.

The Federal government also authorized a number of "Immune" regiments. It was mistakenly assumed that black soldiers would be immune to tropical diseases; however, officers were white. The Sixth U.S. Volunteer "Immune" Regiment was commanded by Colonel Lawrence D. Tyson, later World War I general and U.S. Senator from Tennessee. Captain Ben W. Hooper of Company C later served two terms as governor. The regiment spent four months on occupation duty in Puerto Rico.

Individual Tennesseans did take part in the main land campaign in Cuba. With the First United States Volunteer Cavalry, the famous Rough Riders, were 17 men who claimed Tennessee as their native state. Others served with regular United States Army regiments that fought against the Spanish. Jonesborough native Alfred M. Ray served with the black Tenth United States Cavalry, the famous Buffalo Soldiers. At the battle of San Juan Hill on July 1 many of the Tenth Cavalry's white officers were either killed or wounded in the assault on Spanish positions. Sergeant Ray and other black non-commissioned officers continued the attack. Amid a hail of Spanish bullets, Ray planted the first American flag on San Juan Hill. For his gallantry in action, he received a battlefield promotion and later served in the Philippines.

The Fourth Tennessee Regiment was mustered into federal service at Camp Poland, Knoxville, on July 13, 1898, or more accurately dumped in the woods and told to be a regiment. When someone proposed that it should be called "Taylor's Tennessee Tigers," after Governor Robert Love Taylor, others suggested that a better name might be "Brown's Bloody Butchers," after its regimental commander, or perhaps "Hannah's Heroic Hornets," after Harvey H. Hannah, its second in command. Twenty-six-year-old lawyer Cordell Hull, later famous as

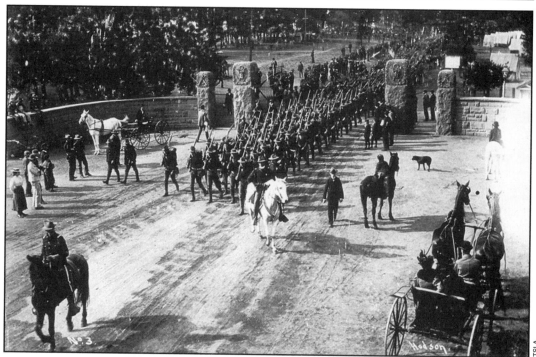

First Tennessee Infantry leaving Presidio for Manila, 1898.

Franklin D. Roosevelt's Secretary of State, raised Company H of the Fourth Regiment from men in his own Upper Cumberland section of the state. As in the Civil War, an individual or individuals recruited a company of men from their own locality. The Fourth Tennessee arrived in Cuba after the war in December 1898 and stayed until May 1, 1899. Homesickness, malaria, boredom, and their hot woolen uniforms were among their discomforts. Poker playing was a popular pastime.

The First Tennessee Regiment was mustered into federal service at Nashville's Cherokee Park on May 26. Patriotism and a desire for adventure figured prominently as motives among the Middle and East Tennesseans who volunteered for service. Selected by the War Department for service in the Philippines, the regiment went first to San Francisco where the men trained at Camp Merritt for four months. The excitement of military life turned to boredom as the war drew to a close with little prospect of the Tennesseans seeing combat. They were saved from garrison duty in California when, late in 1898, they were sent as reinforcements to hold the Philippine Islands that the United States had newly acquired from Spain. Fighting between American forces and those of Philippine leader Emilio Aguinaldo broke out in Manila in February 1899. The First Tennessee participated in the fighting. Colonel Smith, the oldest member of the

First Tennessee, became its first combat casualty when he died from heat exhaustion. Lieutenant Colonel Gracey Childers assumed command and served with distinction during the remainder of the First's time in the Philippines. The regiment took an important part in the capture of Iloilo, the Philippines' second largest city. With the outbreak of guerrilla warfare in the Philippines, Tennessee troops, like other American soldiers, became frustrated with the hit and run tactics of the Filipino insurgents. The First Tennessee suffered its only man killed in action during one such skirmish.

When the War Department authorized the formation of regular United States regiments to replace the state volunteer units then on duty in the Philippines, over 300 Tennesseans, almost a third of the First Tennessee, re-enlisted with the new 37th U.S. Volunteer Infantry Regiment. The 37th served continuously in the field until January 1901. The First Tennessee, missing the "Tennessee Battalion" of the newly organized 37th, prepared to return to the United States. Before doing so, however, they volunteered to help suppress a renewed outbreak of fighting on Cebu Island. Once again the Tennesseans emerged unscathed and sailed for the United States in October. The First Tennessee was mustered out of federal service in San Francisco on November 22, one of the most honored of the Spanish-American War state volunteer regiments and the last to leave United States service.

Colin F. Baxter, East Tennessee State University

SUGGESTED READINGS: Gregory Dean Chapman, "Taking up the White Man's Burden: Tennesseans in the Philippine Insurrection, 1899," *Tennessee Historical Quarterly* 47(1988): 27–40; Cordell Hull, *The Memoirs of Cordell Hull* (1948)

SEE: HOOPER, BEN W.; HULL, CORDELL; TYSON, LAWRENCE

SPANISH CONSPIRACY. The Spanish Conspiracy of the mid-1780s arose in the aftermath of the American Revolution, when the leaders of the Cumberland settlements, which were then still part of North Carolina, courted a possible relationship with the Spanish government in New Orleans. Following the Revolution, Spain attempted to arrest the increasing flow of Americans to the West by assisting the Creeks, under the leadership of the mixed-blood Alexander McGillivray, with their attacks on the Cumberland settlements. In addition, the Spanish controlled the Mississippi River and New Orleans. Although the Cumberland settlers were not yet producing goods that required a market outlet like New Orleans, they recognized the potential for commercial enterprises and looked to the Mississippi River as the future outlet for their trade. Spain, however, forbade American access to the river, and the North Carolina government in the east did not support the westerners in their demands for navigation rights.

Cut off from any legal outlet for trade and harassed by the Creeks, the western settlements became vulnerable to the possibility of breaking ties with the east to formulate a separate alliance with Spain or form a separate state under Spanish authority. Either option offered them access to a market for western goods and promised relief from Creek attacks. Such an alliance would provide the Spanish government in New Orleans with a buffer between Spanish-held territory and the newly formed United States.

James Robertson contacted the Spanish governor in New Orleans, Esteban Miro, concerning a plan for the western settlements to separate and join Spain. Dr. James White, serving as Indian agent, also contacted Miro, assuring him that the western settlers were prepared to set up an independent state with Spain.

Spain proposed that the westerners break relations with the United States and take an oath of allegiance to His Catholic Majesty, King of Spain. In return, the frontiersmen would be allowed access to the Mississippi and the right to manage their local affairs. Economic relations were soon established between Spain and the settlements. All trade traveling down the Mississippi to New Orleans was subject to a 15 percent duty and anyone who conducted business in Spanish territory had to sign the oath of allegiance. Those who chose to reside in Spanish Louisiana were promised large land grants, the right to practice the Protestant religion, and the same commercial rights as all Spanish subjects. Many westerners, including Andrew Jackson, took advantage of the opportunity and signed an oath in order to trade down the Mississippi.

The Spanish Conspiracy in Tennessee came to an end when North Carolina ratified the Constitution in 1789. The cession of western territory to Congress satisfied the leaders of the Tennessee settlements, who now enjoyed the protection of the United States government. In 1795, amid mounting European hostilities, Spain agreed to surrender the Louisiana territory east of the Mississippi above the thirty-first parallel to the United States, restrain the southern Indian tribes under Spanish influence, and grant the United States free navigation of the Mississippi River with the right of deposit at New Orleans.

Holly Anne Rine, University of New Hampshire

SEE: JACKSON, ANDREW; MISSISSIPPI RIVER SYSTEM; NATCHEZ TRACE; ROBERTSON, JAMES

SPARTA ROCK HOUSE, three miles east of Sparta along U.S. Highway 70, was built initially as a toll house and stage stop along a busy antebellum turnpike between Sparta and Crossville and is considered a significant and rare artifact of the turnpike era in Tennessee. Barlow Fiske built the symmetrical three-bay one-story stone structure between 1835 and 1839; as late as 1852 Fiske operated a store at the place. Another important nineteenth century owner was Samuel Denton. Famous patrons included James K. Polk, Andrew Jackson, and Sam Houston. The Sparta Rock House was listed in the National Register of Historic Places in 1973. It is a public historic site, administered locally by the Rock House Chapter of the Daughters of the American Revolution.

Carroll Van West, Middle Tennessee State University

SEE: WHITE COUNTY

SPEECH. How Tennesseans talk expresses their regional identity and often draws comment by people from elsewhere. Whether they call it a "Tennessee twang" or an "East Tennessee brogue," Tennesseans and others often consider it distinctive. It is quite difficult, however, to identify the features and usages that make it so, because the varieties of English spoken in Tennessee vary socially and geographically in complex ways. Nor are these varieties confined to the Volunteer State. Broadly speaking, East Tennessee speech is closer to western North Carolina and north Georgia (and thus classified as "Upper South" or "South Midland") than to West Tennessee, a region with cultural and linguistic affinities to Mississippi and the Lower South and historically an extension of the cotton belt showing more influence from African Americans than other parts of the state. As in many other respects, Tennessee does not form a speech region per se, but its sections (especially East and West) represent parts of larger territories that may be identified in terms of terrain, settlement history, material culture, and other factors. The *Dictionary of American Regional English* labels only a small handful of terms as confined to Tennessee, but these are far from widely known or used (e.g. *fee grabber* for law enforcement officer; *hallway* for passage between two buildings), and these are not useful in characterizing the state's speech.

For well over a century how Tennesseans use English has drawn popular and scholarly interest. Tennessee politicians from the days of David Crockett (shown especially in his autobiography) until Howard Baker have had a deserved reputation for their apt and colorful use of words and for a style of talking that is folksy, but more down home than fancy. Beginning in the 1870s the novels of local colorist Mary Noailles Murfree exposed countless readers to a literary version of Tennessee mountain speech and set a mold for writers of local and regional fiction down to the present. Since 1889, scholars have commented on speech patterns of the state's citizens in well over two hundred notes and articles. Even so, the object of scholarly interest more often than not has been words and unusual and archaic expressions (often labeled "Elizabethan" or "Shakespearean"), especially from the East Tennessee mountains. The cumulative picture is skewed and far from complete, suggesting little about the diversity of Tennessee speech—its social and regional differentiation within the state—or its ongoing changes.

Based on traditional vocabulary, scholars have differed on the number of subregions of Tennessee speech, but they agree these are not nearly so salient as popular notions about the three grand divisions. Over the past three decades two projects, the *Dictionary of American Regional English* (DARE) and the *Linguistic Atlas of the Gulf States* (LAGS), systematically interviewed speakers from across the state as parts of larger surveys. The *DARE* evidence suggests that the basic regional distinction is two-way with the Cumberland Plateau being a subdivision of East Tennessee and the Nashville Basin part of West Tennessee. The evidence from *LAGS* partially supports this view (grouping the Cumberlands with the east), but sees the Nashville Basin as a transition area and finds that West Tennessee has some vocabulary not shared with the rest of the state (e.g. *bayou* for backwater; *middlebuster* for lister plow). LAGS finds many traditional terms to be more widespread in the east (*airish* for chilly; *fireboard* for mantelpiece; *poke* for paper bag; *family pie* for deep-dish pie; *snake feeder* for dragonfly), but none of these are unrecorded in West Tennessee. The material collected by *DARE* and *LAGS* also highlights the main historical sources of traditional vocabulary; of the five terms just cited, the first two are Scots-Irish, the third is English and Scots-Irish, and the last two are new terms unknown in the British Isles.

Principal features of pronunciation throughout the state (but usually more prevalent in the east) include: 1) pronunciation of vowels in words *pen* and *hem* as *pin* and *him*; 2) shift of accent to the beginning of words with more than one syllable (thus *Tennessee* becomes *TIN-isee*); 3) clipping or reduction of the vowel in *ride*, *right*, etc. to sound similar to *rad*, *rat*, etc.; and 4) the southern drawl, the stretching of vowel sounds so that words of one syllable sometimes become two (*bed* becomes *bay-ud*). Though by no means exclusive to Tennessee, these features are widely associated with the Volunteer State. The first three features have become shibboleths of Tennessee speech.

With urban growth, traditional regional vocabulary and pronunciation often become socially differentiated by class, education level, and ethnic background, as well as regional in another sense: urban vs. rural. Though much of it is disappearing along with traditional culture, the language of the state is in no danger of homogenization with the rest of the country.

Michael Montgomery, University of South Carolina

SUGGESTED READING: Craig Carver, *American Regional Dialects: A Word Geography* (1987)

SEE: CROCKETT, DAVID; MURFREE, MARY NOAILLES

SPENCER, THOMAS SHARP (d. 1794), is usually regarded as the first white settler in Middle Tennessee, because on a long hunt to the area from 1776 to the spring of 1779, he staked out land, planted it, and built cabins on it. During the last winter, he lived alone in the hollow of a giant sycamore tree at Bledsoe's Lick. He returned to Middle Tennessee in the winter of 1779–1780 to become one of "the immortal 70" original Cumberland settlers. Spencer fought in several Indian skirmishes and, on one occasion, a ball shattered his right arm. In 1783 he guarded the party that surveyed the North Carolina Military Reservation.

His physical strength was legendary. According to one story, Spencer threw a militiaman over a high rail fence to break up a fight at a local muster. When the embarrassed trooper recovered, he begged Spencer to set his horse over the fence also. Others characterized him as having the "strength of a lion," as being stronger than "two common men," and as being "the stoutest man I ever saw." Spencer said he was afraid to strike another man in anger for fear of killing him.

On April 1, 1794, Spencer died from a gunshot fired from ambush. At the time, he was returning from Virginia across the Cumberland Mountains and had reached a hill in Van Buren County, which has since been given his name.

Walter T. Durham, Gallatin

SUGGESTED READING: Walter T. Durham, "Thomas Sharp Spencer, Man or Legend," *Tennessee Historical Quarterly* 21 (1972): 240–255

SEE: EXPLORATIONS, EARLY; SUMNER COUNTY

ST. ANDREW'S-SEWANEE SCHOOL resulted from the merger in 1981 of two older institutions, and it builds upon the heritage of three Episcopal schools founded on Monteagle Mountain in Franklin County. The junior department of the University of the South, opened in 1867, went by several different names and enrolled students of various ages but existed longest as the Sewanee Military Academy. St. Mary's School for Girls functioned from 1896–1968 under the auspices of the Sisters of St. Mary's before the Order ceased its teaching activities. St. Andrew's School, started by Episcopal monks from the Order of the Holy Cross in 1905, began as an elementary school but eventually concentrated on secondary education. Though quite different in mission in their earlier decades, changes that occurred on the three campuses in the late 1960s led to growing similarities. With St. Mary's closure, both SMA and St. Andrew's became coeducational. In 1970 the Order of the Holy Cross and its monks withdrew from St. Andrew's and turned the school over to a board of trustees. That same year the military aspect of SMA was dropped and its name changed to Sewanee Academy. The evolution of distinctly diverse schools into two campuses attracting the same types of students led to merger on the St. Andrew's campus immediately adjacent to the domain of the University of the South.

St. Andrew's-Sewanee maintains its Episcopal tradition in a location of natural beauty on the Cumberland Plateau. The school supplements its college-preparatory curriculum for day and boarding students with a range of activities in the arts, athletics, and outing programs. With deep roots in the nineteenth century and realignment and rejuvenation in the late twentieth century, the school seems well prepared for twenty-first century challenges.

Margaret D. Binnicker, Middle Tennessee State University

SUGGESTED READING: Ridley Wills II, "The Old Boys' Schools of Middle Tennessee," *Tennessee Historical Quarterly* 56(1997): 56–69

SEE: AGEE, JAMES R.; SETTLEMENT SCHOOLS; UNIVERSITY OF THE SOUTH

ST. JOHN'S EPISCOPAL CHURCH, constructed between 1839 and 1842, exemplifies rural simplification of the prevailing Gothic Revival architectural style used in Episcopal churches of the antebellum South. Five sons of the North Carolina planter William Polk, who settled on shares of his Tennessee landholdings, contributed financially and materially to the church's construction. One of the brothers, Leonidas Polk, an Episcopal clergyman, conceived the idea of building a plantation chapel, drew the church's plans, and supervised construction on a corner of his land, where four of the Polk plantations intersected. Polk slaves built the church from materials found on the plantations.

Polk's design reflected the practical qualities of rural ecclesiastical architecture, while incorporating aesthetic elements of the Gothic Revival style. Narrow slit vents in the limestone foundation allow the undercroft to breathe. Buttresses on each side wall provide structural support for the steeply pitched roof, while narrower buttresses brace the 50-foot, three-story central tower on the front facade. The tower's low parapet and corbelled corner crennels resemble a medieval castle's battlements. Pointed arches over doorways and windows complete the style's image of looking up toward Heaven. The austere interior's simple white plaster walls and exposed roof beams and trusses lack the cruciform floorplan so typical of Episcopal churches. Instead, the pews in the nave are arranged with two side aisles and no central aisle. St. John's remains one of the best surviving examples of unaltered ecclesiastical architecture in Middle Tennessee with a historic cemetery adjacent.

Richard D. Betterly, Savannah, Georgia

SEE: HAMILTON PLACE; MAURY COUNTY; OTEY, JAMES H.; POLK, LEONIDAS; RATTLE AND SNAP

ST. JUDE CHILDREN'S RESEARCH HOSPITAL, the world's only institution devoted solely to the study and treatment of catastrophic childhood illnesses, was built on one man's promise: "Help me find my place in life and I will build you a shrine where the poor and the helpless and the hopeless may come for comfort and aid." Then a struggling radio actor with $7 in his pocket, Danny Thomas offered this prayer on his knees in a Detroit church before a statue of St. Jude Thaddeus, the patron saint of hopeless causes.

Thomas dreamed of becoming a successful entertainer, but it was the Depression era and his career seemed to be going nowhere. He asked God for guidance. A few days later Thomas received his "big break" when he was hired as the headline comedian at the 5100 Club, a popular Chicago nightclub. Thomas later became the star of the classic sitcom, *Make Room for Daddy,* and the producer of many hit shows, including *The Dick Van Dyke Show* and *The Andy Griffith Show.*

The famous performer never forgot his promise to St. Jude Thaddeus. He wanted his shrine to be a hospital where catastrophically ill children could find treatment, regardless of their race, religion, or their ability to pay for treatment. He dreamed of a place where the top scientists in the world would work together to find cures for the potentially fatal diseases of childhood.

Thomas began raising money for St. Jude Hospital in the early 1950s. By 1955 Memphis business leaders began area fund-raising efforts. Thomas, often accompanied by his wife, Rose Marie, crisscrossed the United States by car raising funds at meetings and benefits. The pace was so hectic that the couple once visited 28 cities in 32 days.

The son of Lebanese immigrants, Thomas turned for help to his fellow Americans of Arabic-speaking heritage. He believed Arabic-speaking citizens should, as a group, thank the United States for the freedom given their parents. In 1957, 100 representatives of the Arab-American community met in Chicago to form ALSAC—The American Lebanese Syrian Associated Charities. ALSAC, headquartered in Memphis, has assumed full responsibility for the hospital's fund-raising efforts.

St. Jude Children's Research Hospital opened in 1962. It has become an international resource for the study and treatment of pediatric illnesses, including cancer, AIDS, sickle cell disease, and inherited immune disorders. Since 1962 the hospital has treated 15,300 children from 48 states and 58 foreign countries.

The hospital rewrote the textbooks on childhood cancer. Before the institution opened, less than 4 percent of children with the most common form of pediatric cancer, acute lymphocytic leukemia, survived. Largely because of treatments developed at St. Jude Hospital, by the 1990s more than 70 percent of children were surviving this form of leukemia.

Thomas died in 1991 and is interred in a family tomb on the grounds of St. Jude Hospital. But his dream continued after his death. A landmark event in the hospital's history came in 1996, when Peter Doherty, Ph.D., chairman of the immunology department, was awarded the Nobel Prize for Medicine for key discoveries he made about the immune system.

During the 1990s the hospital began to devote increasing efforts to develop bone marrow transplantation and gene therapy as treatments for dozens of diseases from leukemia to sickle cell disease.

Elizabeth Todd, St. Jude Children's Research Hospital
SEE: MEDICINE; MEMPHIS; NAIFEH, JAMES O.

ST. MARY'S CATHOLIC CHURCH. This Nashville landmark is one of the first Catholic Church buildings constructed in Tennessee and served as the Catholic Cathedral for almost 70 years. The oldest extant church building in downtown Nashville, St. Mary's dates to 1844–1847. Its architect was Adolphus Heiman, a German immigrant who designed several major Nashville buildings, such as the State Asylum, during the late antebellum era. Heiman chose a Greek Revival temple style for the building,

featuring a gable front entrance of two fluted Ionic columns supporting a classical pediment.

Richard Pius Miles (1791–1860), the first Catholic bishop in Nashville, is primarily responsible for the construction of St. Mary's. Consecrated bishop over a large six-state diocese at Bardstown, Kentucky, in 1838, Miles arrived in Nashville in 1844. He led the city's growing Catholic population until his death in 1860, when he was buried beneath the cathedral.

In 1926 the Nashville firm of Asmus & Clark renovated both the exterior and interior of St. Mary's, finishing the west facade in local limestone and altering the original octagonal belfry. In 1972 the congregation moved the cast iron casket of Bishop Miles to a small chapel in the church's northwest corner. St. Mary's celebrated its 150th anniversary in 1997.

Carroll Van West, Middle Tennessee State University
SEE: HEIMAN, ADOLPHUS; RELIGION

ST. MARY'S EPISCOPAL SCHOOL is the oldest private school in Memphis. It has operated continuously since its founding in 1847, and during most of its existence the school has been exclusively for girls.

During the Civil War, Headmistress Mary Foote Pope moved the school, along with many of its students, to Mississippi, to await the end of hostilities. The Sisters of St. Mary's, an order of Episcopal nuns, directed the school from 1873 to 1910. Four of them and two priests, known collectively as the "Martyrs of Memphis," died while caring for yellow fever victims during an 1878 epidemic. As Thomas F. Gailor, Bishop of the Episcopal Diocese of Tennessee, observed in 1901, the school never succumbed to "the mere social veneering which some people call 'the education of girls.'"[1]

The school was located first at Calvary Episcopal Church, and then successively at St. Mary's Cathedral, in a building at 1257 Poplar Avenue, and at Grace-St. Luke's Episcopal Church. It moved to its present location at Church of the Holy Communion in 1953.

St. Mary's currently has an enrollment of approximately 800 girls in pre-kindergarten through the twelfth grade. It is noted for the highest academic and moral standards and a tradition of service to the community.

Paul A. Matthews, Memphis
CITATION:
(1) Ellen Davies-Rodgers, *The Great Book: A History of Calvary Episcopal Church* (Memphis, 1973), 624, quoting *Journal, Episcopal Diocese of Tennessee*, 1901, p. 38.
SEE: GAILOR, THOMAS F.; YELLOW FEVER EPIDEMICS

ST. MICHAEL'S CATHOLIC CHURCH, incorporating the state's oldest Catholic church building, began as a small log meeting house near Cedar Hill in Robertson County. Four families (Byrne, Redmond,

Traughber and Watson), who settled near Turnersville between 1838 and 1840, built the 22-by-32-foot church on an acre of land bought for $5 from Joseph Washington's estate, Wessyngton. The church was completed in 1842, and on May 8 of that year it was dedicated, on the Feast of the Apparition of St. Michael. Later the logs were covered with weatherboarding. In 1846 Saint Michael's Male and Female Academy was established near the church. It was one of the earliest Catholic boarding schools in Tennessee; it closed in 1855.

An addition built across the rear of the church in 1934 gave the building a T-shape. Materials for the addition came from an old Episcopal church and school on the nearby Glenraven Plantation, between Cedar Hill and Adams. Some of the materials were used to make additional pews. The addition was formally opened and dedicated on May 12, 1935. The concrete block bell tower was added to the front in 1942, giving the church a covered entrance. The tower bell came from the cannibalized Glenraven church.

In 1973 St. Michael's Catholic Church was added to the National Register of Historic Places. The church cemetery, which includes the graves of original parishoners, was expanded in 1978 by a gift of three acres.

David Logsdon, Nashville

SEE: GLENRAVEN PLANTATION; RELIGION; ROBERTSON COUNTY; WESSYNGTON PLANTATION

ST. PAUL'S EPISCOPAL CHURCH, the Mother

Church of the Diocese of Tennessee, is the state's oldest Episcopal church and serves its oldest Episcopal congregation. It was organized on August 25, 1827, in Franklin. Built with handmade bricks 18–24 inches thick, the 40-by-83-foot church was completed in 1834.

During the Civil War, Union soldiers quartered in St. Paul's built fires on the floor and cut holes in the roof to let smoke out; they made firewood out of the pews, pulpit, and the mahogany pipe organ. St. Paul's was used as a hospital after the November 30, 1864, Battle of Franklin. Later, Union troops stabled mules in the church.

After the war, a carpenter briefly made the church on Main Street his workshop, but it was empty and neglected in June 1869, when the Reverend Edward Bradley arrived as rector. Bradley led the congregation of 17 women and four men in reclaiming and repairing St. Paul's. They eliminated the slave gallery and replaced the flat roof with a peaked roof that was 20 feet lower. Leftover bricks went into the Parish Commons Hall. The altar and sanctuary were moved to the north side, and several windows were reduced. St. Paul's was reconsecrated on January 25, 1871. In 1902 federal officials paid the congregation for damages caused by Union soldiers.

Improvements made before 1917 included installation of Louis Comfort Tiffany-designed stained glass memorial windows and paneling of the sanctuary. In 1970 offices, a library, a bigger parish hall, classrooms for the church school, and a kitchen were added. St. Paul's was added to the National Register of Historic places in 1972.

David Logsdon, Nashville

SUGGESTED READING: Sara Sprott Morrow, "St. Paul's Church, Franklin," *Tennessee Historical Quarterly* 34(1975): 3–18

SEE: FRANKLIN, BATTLE OF; RELIGION; WILLIAMSON COUNTY

STADIUMS, HISTORIC. From the Stone Castle (Bris-

tol Municipal Stadium) and its Medieval Gothic architecture to the symmetry and sleek lines of the Liberty Bowl in Memphis; from personalities like General Robert R. Neyland of the University of Tennessee to E.H. Crump, the powerful mayor of Memphis, an overview of the nine historically significant stadiums in Tennessee provides an interesting glimpse of the state's past.

Even before the Civil War, Tennesseans played baseball and other games at the Sulphur Spring Bottom in Nashville. When minor league baseball came to Nashville in 1885, the team played its games at the Sulphur Spring Bottom site in an enclosed wooden ballpark known as the Athletic Park. The owners of the Nashville club eventually built a new set of stands at the same location. By 1910 Grantland Rice, later a nationally acclaimed sports writer, penned the name "Sulphur Dell" for the Nashville ballpark. In 1927 the new owners of the Nashville baseball club constructed a new ballpark of steel and cement on the historic site. Described in the *Nashville Banner* as the "finest minor league grand stand in the country," a crowd of 7,535 attended the stadium's first game on April 12, 1927. As Nashville's population shifted away from downtown, attendance at Sulphur Dell dwindled. The 1963 season was the last for professional baseball at Sulphur Dell. At the time of its demolition in the mid-1960s, Sulphur Dell was considered the oldest baseball field in America.

Fortunately, most of Tennessee's historic stadiums fared better than Sulphur Dell. Chattanooga's Engel Stadium, which opened in the spring of 1930, benefited from several sensitive renovations in recent years and continues to serve as the home of the Southern League's Chattanooga Lookouts. Named for Lookouts president and operating officer Joe Engel, the handsome brick stadium seats 11,000 people and maintains its now famous "LOOKOUTS" sign on the center field terrace. During the Great Depression, attendance declined at ballparks around the country. As a result, in 1935 Engel Stadium became one of the first ballparks to be lighted and therefore make baseball accessible to day workers. A year later, Engel staged his most famous promotion when a record 24,839 people attended "Joe Engel's House Giveaway."

Howard Johnson Field in Johnson City, more commonly known as Cardinal Park, serves as the home of a rookie league affiliate of the St. Louis Cardinals and the East Tennessee State University baseball team. Constructed in 1923, the stadium seats approximately 2,000 and beginning in 1994, underwent a major remodeling. Howard Johnson, for whom the park is named, founded the Johnson City Parks and Recreation Board and worked for the city for 48 years.

Through the early twentieth century, baseball dominated the interest of sports fans in Tennessee and around the country. When it opened in 1921 with a college baseball game, no one could have imagined that the modest 3,200-seat stadium known as Shields-Watkins Field would become the University of Tennessee's Neyland Stadium, currently one of the largest football stadiums in the nation. Actually, Vanderbilt University's Dudley Field was the first stadium in the South erected exclusively for college football. Dedicated in 1922, the horseshoe-shaped stadium with its concrete tiers seated 20,000 spectators. The stadium was named for Dr. William Dudley, Dean of the Vanderbilt Medical School, who organized the old Southern Intercollegiate Athletic Association in 1893 and later helped organize the NCAA in 1906. In 1980 much of the original Dudley Field was demolished, and a new Vanderbilt Stadium was constructed on the same site. Today, the 41,000-seat Vanderbilt Stadium serves as the "Home of the Commodores," as well as the home of the TSSAA football championship games.

Situated on the banks of the Tennessee River in Knoxville, Neyland Stadium celebrated its 75th anniversary in 1996 with the dedication of its eleventh expansion. The double-decked bowl now seats 102,854. General Robert R. Neyland laid the foundation for this growth by leading University of Tennessee football to national prominence after being named head coach in 1926. The stadium's growth, from a capacity of 6,800 in 1926 to 52,000 at Neyland's death in 1962, reflects his impact on Tennessee football. Later innovations of note included installing a Tartan Turf playing surface in 1968, making it one of the first two artificial turfs in the nation.

In the 1960s the City of Memphis built the Liberty Bowl Memorial Stadium at a cost of $3.7 million. Inaugurated in 1965, the 62,380-seat stadium serves as the home for the University of Memphis football program and annually hosts the Liberty Bowl postseason game. The National Football League's Tennessee Oilers called the Liberty Bowl home in 1997 while awaiting their new stadium in Nashville. In 1977 East Tennessee State University opened Memorial Center, one of only seven college-owned domed stadiums in the United States capable of accommodating football. Commonly known as the Mini-Dome, the multi-purpose stadium covers approximately 4.5 acres and seats 13,000 people.

Two stadiums constructed by the Works Progress Administration (WPA) during the New Deal, Crump Stadium in Memphis and the Stone Castle in Bristol, are currently still in use. They are best remembered from the post-World War II era, when high school football received top billing around the state. Located directly behind Central High School in Memphis, the modest first phase of Crump Stadium opened in 1926; the WPA built the 1939 concrete structure that seated 28,000 people. Crump Stadium played host to numerous major college teams, including two Delta Bowl games. Nevertheless, the largest recorded attendance came in 1946, when 32,000 fans crowded into Crump Stadium to watch Central High School and Humes High School play. In 1944 Memphis businessman and politician, E.H. Crump, began a tradition that lasted more than 25 years. The E.H. Crump Blind Benefit Game, played annually on the first weekend of December, featured two area high school football teams.

Situated on the campus of Tennessee High School in Bristol, the Stone Castle Stadium opened on October 8, 1936. Officially known as Bristol Municipal Stadium, the Stone Castle served as the home football field for Bristol Tennessee High and Bristol Virginia High, as well as for Slater High and Douglas High, the respective African-American high schools in Bristol, Tennessee, and Bristol, Virginia. King College also played its home games there. Constructed of coarse rubble limestone from another WPA project at nearby Beaver Creek, the stadium seats approximately 6,000 and features most of the original Medieval Gothic details. Its unique corner towers, arched entries, and crenelated walls clearly make the Stone Castle the most architecturally significant stadium in Tennessee. Like all the stadiums in this study, the Stone Castle accommodates a variety of community activities in addition to its primary function as an athletic facility.

Kent Whitworth, East Tennessee Historical Society

SEE: BASEBALL, MINOR LEAGUE; CRUMP, EDWARD H.; FOOTBALL, COLLEGE; NEYLAND, ROBERT R.; RICE, GRANTLAND; SULLIVAN COUNTY; SULPHER DELL; TENNESSEE OILERS; UNIVERSITY OF TENNESSEE; VANDERBILT UNIVERSITY; WORKS PROGRESS ADMINISTRATION

STAHLMAN, JAMES G. (1893–1976) was publisher of the *Nashville Banner* from 1930 until 1972, when he sold the newspaper to the Gannett Corporation. He inherited part of the newspaper from his grandfather, Major Edward Bushrod Stahlman, when he died in 1930; James Stahlman's father, Edward Claiborne

Stahlman, had died in a boating accident on the Cumberland River near Williams Ferry in 1904. James Stahlman became the sole owner in 1955, when he purchased the remaining stock from his uncle.

Stahlman began working for the *Banner* on June 1, 1912, following his graduation from high school. He continued to work for the *Banner* as a campus correspondent for the next four years, until his graduation from Vanderbilt University in 1916. He did graduate work at the University of Chicago for a year and then served in World War I as an infantry private.

Stahlman returned to Nashville in 1918 to become city editor of the *Banner*. In 1925 his grandfather named him vice president and executive director. On August 12, 1930, Major Stahlman died, and 37-year-old James Stahlman became president and publisher of the *Banner*.

In 1932 Stahlman was elected president of the Southern Newspaper Publishers Association (SNPA). He worked with SNPA and the American Newspaper Publishers Association in the joint fight to defeat President Franklin D. Roosevelt's efforts to force newspapers to accept federal license under the National Recovery Act. This battle culminated in victory for the newspapers and brought Stahlman into national prominence in the newspaper field. He was director, vice president, and at 44, president of the ANPA, one of its youngest ever.

In state journalism, Stahlman carried on legendary editorial battles with his Nasville competitor, *The Tennessean*. Compared to the pro-New Deal and pro-Democratic positions of *The Tennessean*, Stahlman's paper generally was more conservative and pro-Republican.

Stahlman married Mildred Porter Thornton in 1917 and they had two daughters, Mildred and Ann. They were later divorced. In 1939 he married Effye Chumley, who was killed in a 1952 automobile accident. They had no children. In 1953 he married Gladys Breckenridge, to whom he was married at the time of his death in 1976.

Stahlman was a member of the Board of Trust at Vanderbilt University from 1927 until his death in 1976. He gave five million dollars in 1972 and 1973 to establish five chairs in the Vanderbilt School of Medicine, named in honor of his mother, father, wife, and two daughters. These and other contributions Stahlman made at the time represented the largest donations ever made by a living alumnus.

On January 14, 1972, Stahlman announced the sale of the *Banner* to the Gannett Corporation. Six months later, on June 1, 1972, he retired. That ended Stahlman's 60 years of service to the *Nashville Banner*, 42 of them as publisher. He died on May 1, 1976, following a stroke, which he suffered while attending a Vanderbilt board meeting.

David E. Sumner, Ball State University

SEE: NASHVILLE BANNER; PUBLISHING; VANDERBILT UNIVERSITY

STANDARD CANDY COMPANY began as Anchor Candy Company, founded in 1901 in Nashville by Howell H. Campbell, Sr. The son of Millard and Anna Hooper Campbell, Howell Campbell was born in 1883 in Nashville. After attending the public schools, he worked as a shipping clerk for Hooper Grocery Company for two years. He was 19 when he opened his candy company at Clark Street and First Avenue North. Campbell started with two copper kettles and about a dozen employees. In 1903 he reorganized Anchor and incorporated the business as Standard Candy Company. In 1914 a fire forced the company to move to a three-story brick building on Second Avenue North, where Standard remained for the next 65 years.

The company produced a variety of sweets, including suckers, marshmallows, Nujoy hard and bag candies, and Belle Camp fine chocolates. But it was the Goo Goo Candy Cluster that became the company's star product. Campbell and his plant superintendent, Porter Moore, developed the mound of caramel, marshmallow, and roasted peanuts, hand-dipped in milk chocolate, in 1912. Best sources about the new candy's name agree only on one thing: it was suggested to Campbell by a woman who rode the same street car to work with him each morning.

Initially, Goo Goos were sold unwrapped at candy counters. Later, they were wrapped in tinfoil by hand. Advertised as the "Nourishing Lunch for a Nickel," Goo Goo became Standard's most profitable product in the company's limited market area.

After World War II, Howell Campbell, Jr., son of Standard's founder, became president and owner of Huggins Candy Company, known for its King Leo stick candy in peppermint, lemon, and clove flavors. Later, Campbell, Jr., merged Huggins with Standard, which continued production of King Leo. Standard was now Nashville's biggest candy company. Under Campbell, Jr.'s direction, the company expanded Goo Goo's name recognition by becoming a sponsor of the Grand Ole Opry, a popular national radio show broadcast from Nashville.

In 1974 Campbell, Jr., sold Standard to Nashville businessmen Jim Fischer and James Miller. Five years later, the company moved to a bigger and more modern facility on Massman Drive. The same year, a drought increased peanut prices fivefold. The next year, high interest rates hit the company. At the time, Standard's sales were in a decline that started in 1974, and its mainstay, the 35-cent Goo Goo, was difficult to find outside of Nashville. A peanut-less version of Goo Goo had flopped in the early 1970s.

In 1981 Jimmy Spradley, Jr., persuaded his father to come out of retirement and join him in buying Miller's interest in 1982 and help run the business.

Spradley, Jr., 26, was made president of the firm and charged with expanding Standard's market and sales. He made personal calls on old customers and persuaded large retail chain stores to stock Standard's candies and feature Goo Goos as a trend-setting specialty item. This aggressive marketing made Goo Goo a nationally known candy. In 1982 Standard introduced the Goo Goo Supreme, made with pecans instead of peanuts. The 50-cent Supreme was Standard's first major new product; in less than six months, it made up 20 percent of Goo Goo sales.

In 1985 Standard purchased the Stuckey's Candy Company factory in Eastman, Georgia, from Pet, Inc. of St. Louis. At its height, Stuckey's had 320 outlets throughout the Southeast, but it had only 100 when sold to Standard. The acquisition added a popular pecan roll to Standard's candy line and gave the company another production facility. Ten years later, the Spradley family and Standard employees acquired the company through an employee stock ownership plan. In addition to its Goo Goo, pecan roll, and King Leo stick candy, Standard makes sweets for other labels and exports its candies to Canada, Mexico, Europe, and Asia.
David Logsdon, Nashville
SEE: GRAND OLE OPRY

STANDING STONE. A huge animal-shaped monolith standing beside the Avery Trace in Putnam County mystified the eighteenth century travelers who first encountered it. *McClain's History of Putnam County* (1925) describes the figure as a "sphinx-like sculpture which may have belonged to a cultured people long antedating the wild and roaming Indian." McClain recorded one early pioneer's description of the figure as "a big gray dog in a sitting position, head and ears up, looking straight out west." Native Americans venerated the monolith to such a degree that it became a religious icon. Settlers referred to the statue as the "Standing Stone," a name that was applied to the nearby town until 1901, when it was incorporated as the town of Monterey.

By the early 1890s only four feet remained of the monument that once stood over twelve feet in height. Railroad workers, blasting a road bed across Monterey mountain, reduced the remainder to a scattering of various sized stones. In 1895 a patriotic fraternity, the "Improved Order of Red Men," incorporated one of the stones into a monument in Monterey. The passing of generations all but erased the memory of the Standing Stone from the minds of the local people, but the efforts of one young girl, Nannie Ellen Buckner, preserved its significance in Tennessee history. In 1939 the State of Tennessee named Standing Stone State Park after the monolith. An annual celebration is held each October in Monterey to commemorate the Standing Stone mystery.

Opless "Op" Walker, Cookeville
SEE: STANDING STONE STATE RUSTIC PARK

STANDING STONE STATE RUSTIC PARK. Located in Overton County on the Cumberland Plateau, Standing Stone State Rustic Park was acquired from the U.S. Department of Agriculture through the Land-Use Area program of the 1930s. The program allowed sub-marginal property to be obtained from the federal government for the establishment of parks. The U.S. Department of Agriculture acquired the property through its soil and conservation resettlement programs. Lands could then be developed for erosion control, reforestation, or recreation. The Federal Resettlement Administration, Civilian Conservation Corps, and the Works Projects (later Progress) Administration (WPA) worked with states to find alternate uses for the land. Standing Stone became one of four Land-Use Areas that developed into Tennessee state parks; Chickasaw, Cedars of Lebanon, and Natchez Trace state parks were the others.

At Standing Stone, the Resettlement Administration and the U.S. Forestry Service relocated farmers, reforested the land, and implemented erosion control measures to prepare the area for further development. Federal agencies promoted the development of state parks within a day's drive from population centers. Standing Stone's location in a triangular area surrounded by highways with easy access to the county seats of Clay, Overton, and Jackson counties fit the criterion. The park's name ostensibly came from a "standing stone" that had been significant in Native American culture and that was thought to be on park land. The stone was later found in adjacent Putnam County.

Development of the park by the WPA centered on a 60-acre, man-made lake. In 1938 state plans called for a $53,213 expenditure to construct recreational facilities, including cabins, an amphitheater, a boathouse, a recreation hall, picnic shelters, a pump house, the park entrance sign, a group camp, and trails and roads. On March 23, 1939, Standing Stone was transferred to the Division of State Parks in the Department of Conservation, but the State of Tennessee did not receive full title to the property until 1955.

The park and forest consist of about 10,000 acres of land. Historic structures built between 1938 and 1942 include one-story buildings of hewn logs or board siding, resting on stone foundations; numerous low stone guard rails along the roads; cabins and group camps; picnic shelters; an amphitheater; and a recreational hall. The most impressive feature of the park is the 69-acre lake, with its stone dam. The 300-foot dam is constructed of rock-faced, coursed-stone and concrete. The lake was intended to be used for boating and fishing, but swimming was also permitted until the construction of a pool.

Work in the park ceased during World War II, but renovations resumed in 1946 with the draining and restocking of the lake. The following year, a group camp and ranger residences were erected. The Tennessee Department of Environment and Conservation now administers Standing Stone State Rustic Park.

Claudette Stager, Tennessee Historical Commission
SEE: CONSERVATION; OVERTON COUNTY; STANDING STONE; WORKS PROGRESS ADMINISTRATION

STANTON, JOHN C. (1824–1901) was a controversial railroad contractor who brought economic prosperity and ruin to Chattanooga in the post-Civil War era. A New Hampshire native, persuasive and energetic, he rose by his wits from the laboring ranks to a position of building contractor. In 1868, backed by New York financiers, he and his brother, D.N. Stanton, came south to exploit the railroad building program created by Alabama's Reconstruction legislature. With millions in state funds, Stanton organized the Alabama & Chattanooga Railroad, destined to run the width of Alabama, reaching from Chattanooga to Meridian, Mississippi.

In 1869 Stanton moved his headquarters from Montgomery to Chattanooga. The city, which had stood destitute since the war, welcomed Stanton as its savior. Employment and business boomed during the railroad's construction, and in 1870 Stanton erected "Stanton Town," a new center of commerce. The downtown addition, located south on Market Street, boasted depots, stores, and a luxury hotel, the Stanton House. This instantaneous prosperity was based upon credit, however, and in 1871, when the interest on Alabama's bonds became due, Stanton defaulted. The boom went bust.

The bankruptcy "tore Chattanooga from tower to turret." Thousands of businessmen and unpaid laborers faced ruin and hunger. Over the following years Stanton launched new business schemes while promising to pay his many creditors. In 1879 he ran for mayor under the "Greenback" banner. Representing himself as a friend of the laboring poor, he gained little support except from African Americans. Many citizens considered him a "carpetbagger." Others defended Stanton, reminded that he brought the working man a temporary relief, and convinced that he failed through no fault of his own.

After losing the election and still battling a multitude of lawsuits, Stanton left Chattanooga in 1880 and retired in New York City on his proceeds from the South. He died in 1901, aged 76, at his home, the historic Sturtevant house.

Gary C. Jenkins, Chattanooga
SUGGESTED READINGS: John W. Dubose, *Alabama's Tragic Decade: Ten Years of Alabama, 1865–1874* (1940); James A.

Ward, *Southern Railroad Man: Conductor N.J. Bell's Recollections of the Civil War Era* (1994)
SEE: CHATTANOOGA; RAILROADS

STATE DEBT CONTROVERSY raged for six years (1877–1883) as a predominant political issue. Having first been incurred in support of antebellum railroad construction, the debt dramatically increased during the Civil War as unpaid interest was allowed to accumulate. Railroad repair and expansion during Reconstruction added to the previous debt. Consequently, by 1870 the debt amounted to $43,052,625. With the state still laboring under financial difficulties created by the war, Reconstruction, and the Panic of 1873, a growing sentiment developed to repudiate the debt, either partially or wholly.

In January 1877 Democratic Governor James D. Porter asked the state legislature to create a committee to work out a permanent "honorable" settlement between the bondholders and the state. The General Assembly then requested that the state's creditors submit a plan of debt adjustment. The creditors' solution included a reduction of state expenses, the maintenance of the current rate of taxation, utilization of any surplus to refund the state's bonds with their accrued interest, and concurrent issuance of new bonds bearing three percent interest for five years. The creditors further recommended that the debt be refunded at a rate of 60 cents on the dollar in new six percent bonds.

Although the plan would have reduced the debt by 40 percent, the legislature rejected this proposal, suggesting instead that the state suspend all further payments of interest on the state's bonds, excepting only those held by the state's educational institutions. The legislature further acted to reduce the tax rate from 40 cents on each 100 dollars of property to ten cents, to be used "for current expenses only." Overriding Governor Porter's veto, the legislature effectively prevented any further interest payments on the bonds.

Governor Porter called the legislature into special session in December 1877, but his proposed compromise, which would have coupled debt adjustment with a tax levy designed to meet the interest on the proposed new bonds, failed. A second proposed compromise, calling for debt reduction by 50 percent and a refunding of this sum into six percent bonds, was rejected as well, and the debt controversy became a major issue in the gubernatorial campaign of 1878.

Badly divided on the question of the state debt, the Democrats adopted a platform that evaded pledging the party to any particular settlement. Instead, gubernatorial nominee, Albert Marks, denounced the anti-repudiationist Republican Party for running up the debt during Reconstruction and won the election by a popular landslide.

Taking office in 1879, Marks pushed through legislation that provided for the refunding of most of the debt at 50 cents on the dollar at four percent interest. As he had pledged during the campaign, however, the settlement was to become effective only if two-thirds of the bondholders approved it, followed by a majority of the state's voters in a special election. While the state's creditors gave their approval, voters rejected the proposed settlement by a margin of 76,333 to 49,772 in the August 1, 1879, referendum.

The 1880 gubernatorial election again focused on the debt controversy. Incumbent governor Marks declined the Democratic nomination, which divided the party into pro-repudiation (Low-Tax) and anti-repudiation (State Credit) factions. As a result of these divisions, Republican Alvin Hawkins won the election. On April 6, 1881, the legislature enacted the "100-3 Act," which funded the debt at 100 cents on the dollar, including unpaid interest, by issuing new three percent "compromise bonds." It excluded educational and local charitable institutional bonds and bonds held by Sarah Childress Polk, widow of James K. Polk, from this reduced interest rate while increasing the property tax from ten cents to 40 cents to pay the interest on the new bonds.

The compromise did not hold. In February 1882 the state supreme court declared the "100-3 Funding Act" unconstitutional and void, largely for its provision making the unpaid bond coupons receivable in payment of state taxes. Hawkins immediately called the legislature back into special session. On May 20, 1882, the General Assembly passed the "60-6" Act , which funded the principal and all past due interest on the state bonds at 60 cents on the dollar.

The issue of the "60-6 Settlement" dominated the gubernatorial campaign of 1882. The Low Tax Democrats' nominee, General William B. Bate, rejected "60-6" in favor of a pledge to pay in full only the "state debt proper," with the remainder refunded at 50 cents on the dollar. Bate received the support of most State Credit Democrats, who found him preferable to the Republican Hawkins. Taking office in 1883, Governor Bate and his fellow Low Tax Democrats soon enacted the "Compromise of 1883." The compromise called for the funding of the "state debt proper" ($2,118,000), with accumulated interest, at par into five and a quarter percent bonds; funding of the remainder of the debt ($18,903,000), with accumulated interest, at 50 cents on the dollar into three percent bonds; and the consequential decrease of the state's debt by approximately $14,000,000 to roughly $15,784,608.

The question of the payment of Tennessee's debt was finally settled and removed, at least on the surface, from political discussion. The deep animosities that it had aroused, however, were to linger on and thus have their influence on the state's politics for several years to come.

Harvey Gresham Hudspeth, Mississippi Valley State University
SUGGESTED READING: Robert B. Jones, *Tennessee at the Crossroads: the State Debt Controversy, 1870–1883* (1977)
SEE: BATE, WILLIAM B.; HAWKINS, ALVIN; MARKS, ALBERT; PORTER, JAMES D.

STAUB, PETER (1827–1904), a prominent figure in late nineteenth century Knoxville business, culture, and politics, was born in Switzerland on February 22, 1827. Orphaned at eight years old, Staub immigrated to the United States when he was 27. He finally settled in Knoxville in 1856, where he became a leading figure in the city's postwar development. The first of Staub's many Knoxville business enterprises was a tailor shop. In October 1872 the city's first opera house, Staub's Theater, opened on the corner of Gay Street and Cumberland Avenue. Under his management, the theater became the centerpiece of Knoxville's cultural development, bringing prominent actors and theatrical companies to East Tennessee.

Staub also played a crucial role in Knoxville city government from 1874 until his death in 1904. He was twice elected mayor, in 1874 and 1881. Under Staub's leadership, Knoxville founded a city fire department and established the city's public school district. President Rutherford B. Hayes appointed Staub to represent the United States and Tennessee as a commissioner to the Paris exposition. In 1885 President Grover Cleveland named him U.S. Consul to Switzerland.

On May 8, 1904, a runaway horse accident claimed Staub's life. He married Rosina Blum in 1847, and they had nine children, including Fritz, who followed his father in the management of Staub's Theater.

Robert Parkinson, University of Tennessee, Knoxville
SEE: KNOXVILLE; SWISS SETTLERS, KNOXVILLE; THEATER

STAX RECORDS, Memphis's great soul music recording company, was founded in 1960 by siblings Jim Stewart and Estelle Axton. Aspiring to break into the music business, Stewart, a bond salesman, convinced his schoolteacher sister to mortgage her home for $2,500. Their company, originally called Satellite Productions, began with an Ampex recorder in a rented store in Brunswick, just outside of Memphis.

In 1960 Axton and Stewart moved their operation to Memphis, renting a former movie house, the Capitol, on East McLemore Street for $100 a month. In the space they combined a record shop, run by Axton, and a recording studio. The sloping theater floor with carpeted walls and heavy bass U-8 movie theater speakers would create the distinctive sound of Stax recordings.

Soon Wayne "Chips" Moman, a producer and musician, joined the two and began producing the sessions. In 1961 a local high school band, the Mar-Keys, recorded *Last Night,* which went to No. 2 on the pop charts. The success of the recording brought the threat of a lawsuit from a similarly named record company so Axton and Stewart donated the first two letters of their names to create Stax.

Booker T and the MGs, a racially mixed band, recorded Stax's first mega hit, *Green Onions,* and became the studio band. Stax would produce such notable artists as Otis Redding, Isaac Hayes, Rufus Thomas, Carla Thomas, Wilson Pickett, William Bell, Johnnie Taylor, and Sam and Dave. The theme for the movie *Shaft* became the fastest selling album in Stax's history and won an academy award for Isaac Hayes.

Not only did Stax have an interracial sound through its house band, Stax was a racially integrated company with Al Bell, an African American, as national sales director. The riots of the late 1960s, though, led Stewart temporarily to shut down Stax, a white-owned business in the midst of an African-American neighborhood.

At the same time, Stewart learned that Warner Brothers had bought Atlantic Records and now owned all masters recorded at Stax. Stewart and Bell made a deal with Paramount and, in 1970, repurchased the company in an effort to save the label. In 1972 Bell bought out Stewart, though he remained as chief executive.

Though most of the original Stax talent had left during this chaos, the Staple Sisters, Johnnie Taylor, the Soul Children, and others continued to record hits. The once flourishing company came to an end in 1975–1976 when Stax landed in bankruptcy court and Al Bell was indicted for fraud.

Anne-Leslie Owens, Tennessee Historical Society
SUGGESTED READINGS: Rob Bowman, *Soulsville, USA: The Story of Stax Records* (1997); Peter Guralick, *Sweet Soul Music: Rhythm and Blues and the Southern Dream of Freedom* (1986)
SEE: MEMPHIS MUSIC SCENE; MUSIC; THOMAS, RUFUS

STEAMBOATING. In 1811 the voyage of the steamboat *New Orleans* ended the silent world of pre-steam Tennessee riverboatmen. When Nicholas J. Roosevelt successfully sailed his wood-fired steam craft down the Mississippi past the Chickasaw Bluffs, the "Steamboat Age" officially began in Tennessee. Actually the voyage of the *New Orleans* past Tennessee's western shore proved noisier than Roosevelt expected; the New Madrid earthquake thunderously created or expanded Reelfoot Lake during the passage of the *New Orleans.* By 1819 the steamer *General Jackson* had sailed the Cumberland to Nashville; in 1822 the steamer *Rocket* sailed the Tennessee River to Florence, Alabama. Although the Muscle Shoals of the Tennessee River delayed speedy navigation of that waterway, the once-silent Mississippi, Cumberland, and Tennessee rivers echoed with the sounds of the Industrial Revolution.

The workaday Tennessee steamboat was a small, 300-ton, low-draft (drawing only two-three feet) sternwheeled craft, with few fancy trappings, with an average life span of five years. Peak shipping time occurred during high water, when steamers carrying flour, pork, whiskey, tobacco, cotton, livestock, and passengers dotted the Mississippi, Tennessee, and Cumberland rivers. Steamers on these waterways carried crews of 12, including a captain, pilot, engineer, mate, and deck hands. The men varied in age according to their rank and occupation. The common hands included farm boys, city urchins, and an increasing number of Irish and German immigrants. Free blacks and slaves also worked aboard steamers.

From 1811 until approximately 1830, steamboat commerce increased dramatically and profits soared. Although the steamer *Atlas* somehow negotiated the Muscle Shoals and arrived in Chattanooga and Knoxville in 1828, most steamer traffic on the Tennessee River was confined to open stretches upstream and downstream from the Shoals. The *Knoxville,* christened in 1831, ran intermittently between its namesake city and Decatur, Alabama, before the Civil War. On the Upper and Lower Cumberland and the Lower Mississippi business boomed, making the Memphis quay a lively picture of steamers, bustling dockworkers, and cotton bales.

Beginning in 1827, subsidized river improvements, undertaken by the U.S. Army Corps of Engineers, accompanied the increase in steamer commerce. Captain Henry Miller Shreve developed a steam-powered snag-pulling apparatus, mounted to his steamer *Heliopolis,* that achieved fame on the Lower Mississippi as "Uncle Sam's Tooth-Puller." Between 1832 and 1837 Congress allotted $135,000 for snag-pulling on the Cumberland; the state legislature funded navigation improvements on the Tennessee. In 1836 state and federal governments financed the construction of a canal around the Muscle Shoals, but it proved useless to navigation; year-round navigability of the Tennessee remained a dream for another century, until the Tennessee Valley Authority (TVA) and the Corps of Engineers finally conquered the Shoals.

After a major setback during the Panic of 1837, the Tennessee steamboat trade stabilized but never regained its earlier profits and glamour. Ironically, as steamers supplanted the flatboats and keelboats, railroads poised to cripple all these modes of river commerce. The rise of railroads and the Civil War closed most western river commercial traffic and marked a watershed for the "Steamboat Age" in Tennessee. Postbellum statistics show a gradual shift in almost every market, except coal, from river to rail transport.

Nevertheless, the steamboats did not immediately, or entirely, disappear. Steamers continued to serve the urban centers as well as hundreds of smaller ports and landings. On the Upper Cumberland River, poor roads and the late arrival of the railroads perpetuated a vibrant market for steamers well into the opening decades of the twentieth century. Towns like Carthage, Gainesboro, and Celina boasted a limited, but stable steamboat commerce from the 1850s through the 1920s; in 1925 there were 121 steamboat landings between Carthage and Burnside, Kentucky. Steamers delivered farm equipment and consumer goods to the Upper Cumberland towns and returned to Nashville carrying cargoes of lumber, livestock, farm produce, and passengers.

Elsewhere, steamboat commerce continued, but lost its vibrancy and competitive edge. Tennessee steamboatmen pondered their fate and looked to an increase in subsidized river improvements and the development of more powerful and efficient boats to compete with railroads (and later truckers). The locks and dams of the Army Corps and TVA and the internal combustion engine redefined river transportation. By the post-World War II era, screw-propellered, diesel-powered, flat-nosed towboats dotted the Tennessee, Cumberland, and Mississippi river systems that once hosted the Steamboat Age.

An epilog to Tennessee steamboating came in the 1970s with the return of the pleasure sternwheeler to the Mississippi, Cumberland, and Tennessee rivers. The luxurious *Delta Queen, American Queen,* and *Mississippi Queen* fire their boilers with diesel oil, not wood or coal, as in the Steamboat Age. And an old steamboatman would certainly feel out of place on boats that boast swimming pools, saunas, movie theaters, and gymnasiums. Yet the sight of these huge pleasure craft, such as the *General Jackson* in Nashville, conveys a powerful image akin to that of Tennessee steamboating during its antebellum height.

Michael Allen, University of Washington, Tacoma
SEE: CLAY COUNTY; CUMBERLAND RIVER; JACKSON COUNTY; MISSISSIPPI RIVER SYSTEM; SMITH COUNTY; TENNESSEE RIVER SYSTEM; U.S. ARMY CORPS OF ENGINEERS

STEARNS COAL AND LUMBER COMPANY. With the end of the Civil War and restoration of communications and travel, investors identified and then developed many of the resources of the South. A land agent for the Stearns Salt and Lumber Company of Ludington, Michigan, traveling through virgin timber stands of eastern Kentucky and Tennessee in the late nineteenth century was impressed with the navigable, northward flowing Big South Fork of the Cumberland River and the north and south running Cincinnati Southern Railway. By 1899 agents for the company of Justus S. Stearns, a Michigan timber industrialist, had negotiated large purchases of land like the "Big Survey" which included 30,000 acres of land in Scott, Pickett, and Fentress counties, Tennessee, and Wayne County, Kentucky. The Stearns

Coal and Lumber Company was formed and papers of incorporation drawn up in 1902. At the same time the lumber industry was being established in the region and coal mining operations began. The first Stearns Company coal mine opened in 1902 and the coal shipments rolled out of the area in 1903. The Stearns Company employed area residents and established a bond of mutual respect that made the company relatively immune from the labor strife that characterized much of the mining industry during the 1920s and 1930s. The Stearns Coal and Lumber Company was the oldest continuous mining operation in Kentucky when the company sold out in 1975.
Tom Des Jean, Big South Fork National Recreation Area
SEE: BIG SOUTH FORK NATIONAL RIVER AND RECREATION AREA; MINING; SCOTT COUNTY; TIMBER INDUSTRY

STEELE, ALMIRA S. (1842–1925), teacher and missionary, founded in Chattanooga the South's first African-American orphanage. Born of Puritan forebears in Chelsea, Massachusetts, (neighboring Boston) on July 23, 1842, the daughter of Benjamin H. and Almira Sylvester Dewing, she was reared in financial affluence and Christian training. At an early age she embraced the Abolitionist movement. After completing her education and entering teaching, she was appointed principal of an elementary school. In 1870 she married Walter Steele, businessman. His death three years later left Almira a widow with an infant daughter, Mira D. Steele. In 1880 she resigned her position, sold her home and husband's store, and embarked upon what she believed was her life's calling—a ministry to black children in the South.

Under the auspices of the American Missionary Association, she opened a school for the poor in Hampton County, South Carolina. The Ku Klux Klan thwarting all her efforts, Steele transferred to Chattanooga in 1881 to conduct a similar work. Shortly, she observed a larger need than education: no orphanage existed for black children, nor could she persuade public or private sectors to establish one.

In April 1884 she founded the Steele Home for Needy Children. With three infants in care, it opened within Fort Wood's black section, on Strait and Magnolia, one block from Baroness Erlanger Hospital. The institution quickly fell into controversy; with its wards, black, and its proprietor and her young daughter, white, it effectuated a concept that did not sit well in an era of growing racial segregation. Arsonists soon destroyed the home's frame buildings. Steele, seven aides, and 54 children narrowly escaped with their lives.

Undaunted, she erected on the site a substantial three-story, brick Queen Anne building that had 44 rooms. Over the years Steele put into the mission her lifetime's accumulated wealth, including savings, legacies, and real estate investments. Donations from friends, strictly unsolicited, aided the Steele Home. Daughter Mira Steele also worked and sacrificed for it.

As a Congregationalist turned Seventh-day Adventist, the proprietor served her wards a vegetarian diet and held church services Saturday and Sunday. The home functioned as a school, offering what Steele described as "Christian education combined with industrial training." Adolescent students were sent to various trade schools or colleges. Her goal was that each child should have the skills to become a self-supporting adult. She actively managed the Steele Home for 41 years, which closed with her death at the age of 83. Between 1884 and 1925 she sheltered and educated more than 1,600 children.

Gary C. Jenkins, Chattanooga

SUGGESTED READING: Gary C. Jenkins, "Almira S. Steele and the Steele Home for Needy Children," *Tennessee Historical Quarterly* 48(1989): 29–36

SEE: CHATTANOOGA

STEVENSON, VERNON K. (1812–1884), the foremost promoter of railroads in antebellum Tennessee and the founder and first president of the Nashville & Chattanooga Railroad, arrived in Nashville in 1831. He opened a dry goods store. Hoping to ensure his financial success, Stevenson married into prominent Tennessee families. In 1834 he married Elizabeth Childress who was from an old Nashville family; in 1850 he wed Elizabeth Brown, daughter of Judge M.W. Brown; and, finally, he married in 1854 Maria L. Bass, daughter of John M. Bass and granddaughter of Felix Grundy. The Bass-Grundy connection helped Stevenson in promoting the Nashville and Chattanooga railroad as John M. Bass was the president of Union Bank in Nashville and was a past mayor of Nashville. The vast land holdings inherited from Felix Grundy provided ample opportunity for financial gain from the speculation of lands located near the proposed line.

In 1838 Vernon K. Stevenson became the most active and vocal proponent of a railroad between Nashville and Chattanooga, which would link up with the Western and Atlantic line that connected Chattanooga with Charleston. He envisioned Middle Tennessee as part of a long distance commercial market economy which would produce marketable commodities to cities in the North and South. Stevenson personally solicited stock subscriptions from citizens in Murfreesboro, Nashville, Augusta, and Charleston. He also addressed the Tennessee General Assembly on behalf of the project and argued vehemently that the railroad would benefit all citizens regardless of occupation.

The State of Tennessee granted incorporation and charter for the Nashville and Chattanooga Railroad in 1845. Vernon K. Stevenson was elected president

of the railroad in 1848 and served in that role until 1862. He and his family owned large portions of land along the railroad that were later sold at substantial profit to town developers in Tullahoma, Decherd, and Stevenson, Alabama. Stevenson also became the major stockholder in several branch railroads.

The most controversial period of his life came during the Civil War. Stevenson was a major in the Quartermaster Department of the Confederate Army in Nashville. General Nathan Bedford Forrest criticized Stevenson's actions with the Quartermaster Department in regard to the fall of Nashville to Union forces on February 23, 1862, because vast supplies of shoes, clothing, and meat were not transported south and instead fell into the hands of Union troops. Stevenson left Nashville eight days before Union troops entered the city in his own private railroad car with his family, personal belongings, furniture, carriage, and carriage horses, without finishing the transportation of army supplies south. This action did not endear Stevenson to Nashvillians left in the occupied city, nor did they admire the fact that Stevenson made a fortune selling cotton to England by running the Union naval blockade and supplying the Confederate army. At the end of the war, he moved his family and business to New York City.

In 1880 Stevenson again won the ire and dislike of many Nashvillians when the L&N railroad bought out the expanded Nashville & Chattanooga company, known as the Nashville, Chattanooga & St. Louis, through Stevenson's secret sale of a majority of stock. Stevenson's sale ended the existence of an independent railroad headquartered in Nashville.

Stevenson died in New York City on October 18, 1884, leaving an estate valued at five million dollars. He lived the proverbial American dream of starting near the bottom, as a small merchant, and rising to the top of society as a railroad president and a successful millionaire.

Bonnie Gamble, Manchester

SUGGESTED READINGS: Jesse C. Burt, Jr., "The Nashville and Chattanooga Railroad 1854–1872: The Era of Transition," East Tennessee Historical Society *Publications* 23(1951): 58–76; Bonnie L. Gamble "The Nashville, Chattanooga and St. Louis Railroad 1845–1880: Preservation of a Railroad Landscape," (M.A. thesis, Middle Tennessee State University, 1993)

SEE: RAILROAD, LOUISVILLE & NASHVILLE; RAILROAD, NASHVILLE & CHATTANOOGA

STEWART, ALEXANDER P. (1821–1908), educator and Confederate general, was born in Rogersville, Tennessee, on October 2, 1821. Known among his men as "Old Straight," Stewart graduated from the U.S. Military Academy at West Point in 1842. Three years later, he resigned his commission to become an educator. From that time until the beginning of the

Civil War, he taught mathematics and natural and experimental philosophy at Cumberland University at Lebanon and at the University of Nashville.

Initially, Stewart opposed secession, but when Tennessee seceded he offered his services to the state and the South. His first months in Confederate service were devoted to organizing camps to instruct new recruits. After commanding the heavy artillery and water batteries at Belmont, Missouri, he was appointed a brigadier general on November 8, 1861. He was assigned a brigade command under General Leonidas Polk, the fighting bishop. In 1863 he was promoted to major general, and in June 1864 to lieutenant general; he succeeded to the command of the corps following Polk's death. Stewart led his corps until the end of the war. He surrendered and was paroled with General Joseph E. Johnston's army at Greensboro, North Carolina, in May 1865.

Stewart fought in all the major battles of the Army of Tennessee—Shiloh, Perryville, Stones River, Chickamauga, Chattanooga, the Atlanta Campaign, Franklin, Nashville, and the Carolina Campaign. Stewart's brigade performed quite well on December 31, 1862, at Stones River, aiding in pushing General James S. Negley's division out of the cedar glade and capturing 12 artillery pieces. At Chickamauga, Stewart's division was part of General James Longstreet's command that broke through the Union army, commanded by General William S. Rosecrans, and put it to rout. Stewart's corps performed valiantly at Atlanta, but to no avail. In the disastrous battle of Nashville, Stewart's corps was on the extreme left of the Confederate line. Stewart's men stood up under overwhelming odds but finally retreated with the rest of General John Bell Hood's command.

After the war, Stewart resumed his professorship at Cumberland University. He engaged in business in St. Louis from 1870 to 1874, before becoming chancellor of the University of Mississippi from 1874 to 1888. After resigning his chancellorship, Stewart was appointed a commissioner of the Chickamauga and Chattanooga National Military Park. He served in this capacity until his death in Biloxi, Mississippi, on August 30, 1908. Stewart was buried in St. Louis, Missouri.

Lonnie E. Maness, University of Tennessee at Martin

SUGGESTED READING: Marshall Wingfield, *General A.P. Stewart, His Life and Letters* (1954)

SEE: ARMY OF TENNESSEE; CHICKAMAUGA AND CHATTANOOGA, BATTLES OF; CIVIL WAR; CUMBERLAND UNIVERSITY; FRANKLIN, BATTLE OF; HAWKINS COUNTY; POLK, LEONIDAS; NASHVILLE, BATTLE OF; SHILOH, BATTLE OF; STONES RIVER, BATTLE OF

STEWART COUNTY was created in 1803 from Montgomery County and named for an early pioneer and speculator, Duncan Stewart. Originally inhabited by

Bear Spring Furnace east of Dover, Stewart County.

TSLA. HABS PHOTOGRAPH BY JACK E. BOUCHER, 1971

nomadic hunters and mound builders, the area received white settlers in the 1780s, as Revolutionary War veterans arrived to claim land grants. The fertile bottom lands attracted immediate interest, but the area's substantial iron deposits also drew attention. Several factors, including the location of deposits between the easily navigable Tennessee and Cumberland rivers, the availability of slave labor to operate the furnaces, and timber for fuel, produced a thriving iron industry that lasted for over a century.

The county's boundary lines have changed repeatedly, and today the county encompasses 458 square miles and a population of approximately 10,000. State and federal agencies control over 44 percent of the land in the county. Modern highways have replaced the Tennessee and Cumberland rivers as the primary transportation arteries. A Cumberland City ferry is the last remnant of a service rendered obsolete by the construction of bridges throughout the county. However, many place names indicate the county's geography and cultural history: Tobaccoport, Bumpus Mills, Big Rock, Bear Springs, Model, Bellwood, Leatherwood, Indian Mound, and Cumberland City.

In 1805 a state-appointed commission purchased a 30-acre plot on the Cumberland River from Robert Nelson and established the county seat of Dover. By

1850, the frontier town had blossomed into a large river trade center and the second largest steamboat port on the Cumberland. During the Civil War, Union troops, which had occupied the town since the fall of Fort Donelson in 1862, set fire to Dover to prevent the town from falling into the hands of General Nathan Bedford Forrest; only four buildings survived the conflagration. Today, a mayor and four aldermen govern the 2,000 citizens of Dover. The city oversees the operation of modern utility systems, and citizens enjoy the benefits of up-to-date medical facilities. Dover has a weekly newspaper, *The Stewart-Houston Times,* and a radio station, WTWL-101.5. An automotive assembly plant and a garment factory provide employment.

Cumberland City, the second largest city, was established in 1814. Prior to 1860, it was known as Bowling Green, but changed the name to Cumberland to eliminate confusion with Bowling Green, Kentucky, which was also on the L&N Railroad. The word "City" was added by citizens who anticipated a great future for their town. The town is perhaps best known for the Cumberland City Academy, which was founded in 1893 by W.T. Thomas. Before statehood, Methodist circuit riding preachers conducted camp ground meetings at the site of the McKendree Church, the oldest church in the county. Today, Cumberland City looks much as it did at the turn of the twentieth century, except for the presence of one of the largest coal burning steam plants in the world, built by TVA in 1968. Adjacent to the steam plant is Stewart-Houston Industrial Park, which houses several modern manufacturing operations.

Many other county communities were once bustling towns. Bumpus Mills derives its name from Andrew Bumpus who built a sawmill, gristmill, flour mill, and planing mill on Saline Creek in 1846. The mills thrived and were best known for the production of Bob White Flour. Big Rock was a hub of activity for tobacco farmers at the turn of the century. A tobacco prizing warehouse established in 1915 by C.W. Joiner and William Martin attracted tobaccomen from the area. Although Big Rock remains an important county community, the development of Fort Campbell in the 1940s greatly diminished the town's size and population. Indian Mound was named for the prehistoric burial mounds located in the community. Early settlers recognized the mounds and recorded their presence in early court records and deeds. The community developed with the establishment of two iron furnaces. When the furnaces closed, the population of the community declined.

As the era of the iron industry passed, the economy depended more heavily on the earlier established farming and timber industry. Cotton was among the first crops grown in the early 1800s, but it declined in production due to low yields caused by poor soil conservation practices. Both dark-fired and burley tobacco were introduced into the area in the early 1800s, but dark-fired tobacco dominated and continues as the county's primary cash crop. In fact, the region is known as the "Dark-Fired Capital of the World." In addition to tobacco, Stewart County farmers produce corn, wheat, and soybeans.

Timber has always been one of the county's greatest natural resources. As early as the 1830s trees were harvested for the production of charcoal to fuel the iron furnaces and steam boats. As the railroad expanded local farmers provided crossties to meet increasing demand. Even today, hundreds of acres of timber are managed by Westvaco and a number of sawmills continue in operation.

Stewart County contains a number of sites of recreational, educational, and historical interest. Kentucky Lake and Lake Barkley offer opportunities for fishing and boating. Cross Creek Wildlife Refuge and the Land Between the Lakes provide nature lovers sightings of eagles, wild geese, turkey, and deer. The 1850 Homeplace, a living history farm, furnishes entertainment and education for all ages. For the Civil War buffs, Fort Donelson National Battlefield and Cemetery and Surrender House, the site of Buckner's surrender to Grant, are popular attractions.

Jane Bagwell, Dover

SEE: CUMBERLAND RIVER; DOVER FLINT QUARRIES; FERRIES; FORT CAMPBELL; FORT DONELSON; FORT HENRY; INDUSTRY; LAND BETWEEN THE LAKES; TENNESSEE RIVER SYSTEM; TIMBER INDUSTRY; TOBACCO; WELLS CREEK BASIN

STEWART, RANDALL (1896–1964) was born in Fayetteville, Tennessee. In 1898 his family moved to Nashville, where he grew up and was educated through his undergraduate years at Vanderbilt, from which he was graduated in 1917 as the founder's medalist. He did his graduate work at Harvard (M.A., 1921) and Yale (Ph.D., 1930).

Stewart's famous edition of Nathaniel Hawthorne's *American Notebooks,* in which he restored passages omitted and bowdlerized by Mrs. Hawthorne, was published by Yale University Press in 1932. It was followed by Stewart's edition of Hawthorne's *English Notebooks* (1941) and his life of Hawthorne (1948). His *American Literature and Christian Doctrine* appeared in 1958. From 1929 to 1963 he published dozens of articles and reviews on American letters from the Puritans through William Faulkner.

Stewart edited many textbooks for Scott, Foresman, chiefly with Walter Blair, Theodore Hornberger, and Dorothy Bethurum; and his textbooks included *The Literature of the South,* edited with R.C. Beatty, Floyd C. Watkins, and T.D. Young, a pioneering and durable anthology. Stewart's editing was part and parcel of his great contribution to the making of American literature as an essential part of the academic curriculum in this country and abroad.

With Louis D. Rubin, Jr., Stewart was responsible for the Fugitive reunion at Vanderbilt in 1956. That important occasion was a defining event in modern southern literary studies as well as a watershed in Vanderbilt's history and its awkward relation with the Fugitives and Agrarians, some of whom, such as John Crowe Ransom and Robert Penn Warren, are among its most distinguished graduates.

In addition to his two appointments as professor at Vanderbilt (1934–1937 and 1955–1964), Randall Stewart was long associated with Yale and Brown. Under his chairmanship, in the late 1950s and early 1960s, the Vanderbilt English department experienced the last of its salad days.

George Core, The Sewanee Review

SEE: FUGITIVES; LITERATURE; VANDERBILT UNIVERSITY

STOCKTON, KATE BRADFORD (1880–1969), a socialist and the first woman to run for governor in Tennessee, was born in Stockton, California, in 1880. She was a direct descendant of William Bradford, second governor of Plymouth Plantation. Her grandfather, Arthur Bradford of Pennsylvania, was appointed consul to Amoy, China, by Abraham Lincoln. After an unsuccessful attempt at ranching in California, the Bradford family moved in 1884 to Fentress County, Tennessee, where Kate's father took a job with the railroad. Kate attended a local subscription school founded by the Stockton family and went to Overton Academy in Livingston, where she earned a teaching certificate. She continued to teach after her marriage to Joe Kelly Stockton in 1904 and the birth of four daughters. Despite the press of her domestic duties, Kate was an early advocate of birth control and an outspoken feminist.

Joe Kelly Stockton was active in local politics, and by 1920 both he and Kate had embraced socialism. Labor activist Myles Horton boarded with the Stocktons when he worked for the YMCA in the early twenties. After a trip to Scandinavia, Horton decided to open a cooperative school in America, for which the Stocktons offered Horton several hundred acres of land. Horton filed the charter for Highlander School in Fentress County, but after one summer the school was moved to Grundy County. Horton first encouraged Kate Stockton to run for governor.

The Socialist party in Tennessee consisted of only a few hundred members. Kate Stockton became the party's candidate for governor in 1936 largely because no one else was willing to run. The only political experience Stockton had was as state committee chair. The 56-year-old candidate frequently drew on her teaching experience to explain the economic problems of the United States to women unfamiliar with economic theories and convince them to vote for Socialist candidates. The press focused on her small stature, neat appearance, and correct speech rather than her message for radical change. It was no easy task to run a statewide political campaign in Tennessee during the 1930s. The lack of paved roads in Fentress County forced Stockton to ride a horse to Cumberland County (ten miles) and catch the train to other parts of the state to meet her speaking engagements. Since the Socialist party could not provide financing for the campaign, Stockton began with a personal contribution of five dollars and asked other supporters throughout Tennessee to send one dollar a month to support the campaign. This fund raising provided two mimeographs and highway signs. A red sound truck, furnished by the national office, was used extensively to transport Stockton to her speaking engagements in major cities throughout the state. After a well attended rally in Memphis, she was warned about her denunciation of Democrat Gordon Browning. The Shelby County sheriff indicated he could not protect her from ripe tomatoes or other missles that might be thrown at her if she continued her socialist message. Undeterred, Stockton spoke whenever and wherever she could attract an audience. Stockton knew her chances of winning the governorship of Tennessee were improbable, if not impossible. She received only 3,786 of 410,814 votes.

Kate Stockton returned to her home after the election but remained active in politics. She was in Birmingham, Alabama, in 1938 with Eleanor Roosevelt, Mary McLeod Bethune, Myles Horton, and others for the organization of the Southern Conference for Human Welfare. The group met again in 1940 and 1942. By this time the F.B.I. was closely scrutinizing Stockton and others. Horton was under constant pressure from national and local authorities for his political activism, but Stockton was able to return to relative obscurity in Fentress County. In 1939 she wrote a short book explaining the advantages of cooperative living, and at the time of her death in 1969 she was working on a similar book for senior citizens. Stockton was buried near her husband in the Stockton cemetery in Fentress County.

Rebecca Vial, Great Smoky Mountains National Park

SEE: FENTRESS COUNTY; HORTON, MYLES

STOKELY, ANNA ROREX (1852–1916), who established one of the nation's major canning companies, was the daughter of James Addison and Rebecca Badgett Rorex, born in 1852 on a farm along the French Broad River in Cocke County, Tennessee. In 1872 she married John Burnett Stokely and moved to his farm downstream from her homeplace. When her husband died at age 44, Anna Stokely was left with five sons, three daughters, and good land. Markets, however, were limited because of road conditions and lack of rail transportation, and Stokely faced financial problems. A woman of strong character and religious faith, she was determined that her sons follow their father's example of hard work, joining hired hands in the fields as soon as they were physically able, and that they receive a college education.

When the second son, James, returned home from college, he suggested that the farm try canning the vegetables it grew in order to sell foodstuffs in southern markets and better support the family. On January 1, 1898, the Stokely Brothers & Company formed with Anna R. Stokely and a neighbor, A.R. Swann, investing $1,300 each, and Stokely's sons James R. and John M. Stokely putting up $650 each.

In the first season, 4,000 cases of tomatoes were packed in a crude factory and shipped from the river landing on the family farm to Knoxville and Chattanooga. With this initial success, the family bought out Swann's interest, brought in another of Stokely's sons, William B., and reorganized the company into a partnership of four equal parts. Anna Stokely helped in the store, welcomed a growing stream of salesmen and national leaders in the food industry, and provided advice and encouragement to her sons running the canning operation.

An important factor in the family's success was the distinct talent each brother brought to the company. James served as chief financial officer and president, William managed the farms and crops, and John made an excellent salesman. The other two brothers, MIT-educated George and Harvard Law School graduate Jehu, provided ideas in mechanical innovation and legal matters. With Anna Stokely at its center, Stokely Brothers grew, survived national financial panics, expanded to other sites, and yet remained a family enterprise.

On October 24, 1916, though, Anna and her son George died at a railroad crossing when their car stalled before an approaching train. John died three years later at age 43, and James died of a heart attack in 1922 at age 47. Though the three original family founders of the company were gone, the grandsons of Anna Stokely not only kept the business going but expanded it. Stokely Brothers became Stokely-Van Camp in 1933 and developed a national market. More than three decades later the company first produced Gatorade, capping its earlier successes. Anna Stokely's family business evolved and advanced through the twentieth century before being bought in recent years. Anna Stokely's finest product, though, was the sense of family bonding and commitment to community responsibility she instilled in her children.
Wilma Dykeman, Newport
SEE: COCKE COUNTY; INDUSTRY

STONE, BARTON WARREN (1772–1844), a minister and key figure in Tennessee and Kentucky frontier revivalism of the early 1800s, established a "Christian" movement that later became part of the Disci-

ples of Christ. Born in Port Tobacco, Maryland, Stone grew up in southern Virginia and enrolled in David Caldwell's Log College at Guilford, North Carolina, in 1790. After a conversion experience, he studied theology and became a Presbyterian minister. In 1796 he accepted the call to the Concord and Cane Ridge churches in Bourbon County, Kentucky.

Stone and fellow Presbyterian James McGready shared a growing concern about the need for religious renewal on the frontier. In 1800 Stone attended a revival meeting at Gasper River that lasted for several days as people came and camped at John Rankin's church in Logan County, Kentucky. Stone came away impressed by the large number of conversions. Soon after, Stone began planning his own sacramental service in Bourbon County. On August 6, 1801, thousands of people from Kentucky, Tennessee, and Ohio appeared at Cane Ridge, and for nearly a week, participated in the largest Presbyterian communion service in American history. In the intensity of the service, people cried, jerked, and above all fell to the ground.

By 1803 the Presbyterian Church accused two of Stone's closest colleagues with Arminianism. In 1804 Stone and six other ministers resigned from the Kentucky synod, and within a year adopted the name "Christians" and took the Bible as their only guide. Rejecting a church hierarchy, they contended that salvation was open to all believers and that each congregation should govern its own church.

Stone spent the years from 1804 to 1832 preaching and writing in Kentucky and Tennessee. At Lexington on January 1, 1832, Stone and representatives of his own congregation and representatives of Alexander Campbell's Disciples agreed to a form of unity that became the Disciples of Christ.
Larry Whiteaker, Tennessee Technological University
SEE: CAMP MEETINGS; CAMPBELL, ALEXANDER; CHURCHES OF CHRIST; DISCIPLES OF CHRIST; RELIGION

STONES RIVER, BATTLE OF (December 31, 1862–January 2, 1863). By the last days of December 1862, the war was more than halfway through its second year, and certainly its course had turned against the Confederacy. The fall of Fort Henry and Fort Donelson, the loss of New Orleans, the occupation of Nashville, the capture of Island #10, the capture of Memphis, the Federal triumph at the Battle of Shiloh, the Union takeover of the Memphis & Charleston Railroad, the strategic defeat at Antietam, and the failure of the Kentucky campaign provided indisputable evidence that the war had gone badly for the South. Despite the many losses, missed opportunities, and disappointments, the Confederates still exhibited a fighting spirit. Determined yet to overcome, they stood on the eve of another great battle as the end of December drew nigh.

The Union's Army of the Cumberland, some 44,000 strong, commanded by Major General William S. Rosecrans, was drawn up about 30 miles southeast of Nashville. Positioned along the banks of the west fork of Stones River, near the small town of Murfreesboro, it faced Braxton Bragg's 38,000-man Army of Tennessee. Each commander planned to strike his enemy's right flank early on the morning of December 31. Both armies rested astride the Nashville Turnpike and the railroad from Nashville.

On the night before the bloodletting began, just as soldiers of both armies prepared for what promised to be a restless night, one of the most unusual events of the war took place. In the stillness of the cold winter night, the military bands of both armies began to play their favorite pieces. For a time, the music-making assumed the characteristics of a North-South contest, as *The Bonnie Blue Flag* competed with *Hail Columbia.* After a while, one of the bands started playing *Home Sweet Home* and, one after another, various bands, Union and Confederate, joined in, until all the bands in both armies were playing *Home Sweet Home.* It was a strange prelude to one of the bloodiest battles of the war.

Early on the morning of December 31, a cold, wet, and miserable dawn, the Confederate Corps of Lieutenant General William J. Hardee struck first. Streaming out of the clumps of black cedars, in the dim morning light, they stunned Major General Alexander M. McCook's troops, who were still at breakfast. The full force of the assault on the Federal right wing fell on the brigades of Brigadier General Edward N. Kirk and Brigadier General August Willich. At the moment of the Confederate charge, Kirk's men were up and under arms, but some of the artillery horses had been unhitched and taken to water. The resulting confusion was compounded when Kirk suffered a mortal wound. Willich's men were cooking and eating breakfast, their arms stacked. Willich himself, returning from a visit with another general, rode right into the Confederates and was captured. Ironically, Rosecrans enhanced the effectiveness of the Confederate attack by deceiving the Confederate commander into thinking the Federal right flank was stronger than it was. The Union commander ordered campfires built hundreds of yards beyond McCook's right. The deception fooled Bragg, who ordered his attacking columns to move more widely to the Yankee flank. When they struck, the Confederates attacked at a better angle, and only Brigadier General Philip H. Sheridan of McCook's Corps made a fighting retreat with his division.

Hardee's Corps, supported by Lieutenant General Leonidas Polk's Corps spearheaded the southern effort and forced the Federals to retreat some two and one-half miles to the Nashville Turnpike and railroad. Once he realized the magnitude of the Confederate assault, Rosecrans called off his planned offensive and worked to build a defensive line along the turnpike to protect his line of supply and reinforcement from Nashville. By noon, the Federal corps of Major General George H. Thomas held the key sector, where the Union line bent back to the west, just south of the turnpike and railroad.

Bragg ordered Major General John C. Breckinridge's division, the largest in the army, to abandon its position east of Stones River and reinforce the effort west of the river. If Bragg could break the Federal resistance and cut them off from their Nashville base, it seemed likely he would achieve a great victory.

The fiercest fighting of the afternoon came at the angle of the Union line, in a dense, four-acre thicket of cedars, known locally as the Round Forest, and afterward dubbed "Hell's Half-Acre" by soldiers who struggled there. Thomas's men held the critical ground that covered both the turnpike and the railroad, and the Confederates lost another opportunity for triumph.

Both armies spent New Year's Day reorganizing and preparing to renew the battle. The Federals sent troops across Stones River and occupied a ridge from which enfilading fire could threaten the southern position. On January 2, Bragg ordered Breckinridge to recross the river and drive the Union forces from the high ground. Breckinridge protested the impossibility of the mission but obeyed the order. Late in the afternoon, Breckinridge attacked and drove the Federals from the hill. As the Confederates pursued the enemy toward the river, however, they were met by massed Union artillery fire from a commanding position on the opposite side of the stream. The southerners suffered heavy casualties and fell back, while the Union troops recrossed the river and once more occupied the high ground. General Rosecrans held his position the next day, and that night Bragg decided to retreat, withdrawing along the Nashville & Chattanooga Railroad for some 30 miles to Tullahoma.

Total casualties for both sides reached an estimated 24,645. No other Tennessee battle casualties quite equaled that figure, although a few hundred more men died at Shiloh than at Stones River. The Confederate retreat left the Union forces in possession of the battlefield, and General Rosecrans claimed Stones River as a Federal triumph, a claim quickly accepted in Washington, D.C.

James L. McDonough, Auburn University

SUGGESTED READINGS: Peter Cozzens, *No Better Place to Die: The Battle of Stones River* (1990); James L. McDonough, *Stones River—Bloody Winter in Tennessee* (1980)

SEE: ARMY OF TENNESSEE; BRAGG, BRAXTON; THOMAS, GEORGE H.; U.S. ARMY OF THE CUMBERLAND

STOUT, SAMUEL HOLLINGSWORTH (1822–1903),

was the son of Nashville carriage-maker and city

councilman Samuel Van Dyke Stout and Catherine Tannehill Stout. Educated at Moses Stevens's Classical and Mathematical Seminary and the University of Nashville, Stout taught school and apprenticed in medicine to his brother Josiah Stout and the latter's partner R.C.K. Martin, before graduating from the University of Pennsylvania's medical school in 1848. After a brief residence in Nashville, where he was active in the fledgling Tennessee Historical Society, Stout moved with his wife, Martha Moore Abernathy Stout (m. 1848) to Giles County, near Pulaski, where he owned land and slaves, and practiced medicine. The couple's seven children were born there.

When the Civil War began, he became surgeon of the Third Tennessee Infantry (May—November 1861), until he was placed in charge of the Gordon Hospital in Nashville (November 1861—February 1862). After the fall of Nashville, Stout was sent to Chattanooga, where he was soon in charge of all of the Army of Tennessee hospitals behind the lines. In this capacity, he supervised doctors and other personnel, selected hospital sites, and coordinated the needs of the medical department with military and civilian suppliers. During the summer of 1864, he supervised more than 60 hospitals, which were constantly relocating in Georgia, Alabama, and Mississippi.

After the war, Stout lost his farm to bankruptcy and moved to Atlanta, where he practiced medicine and helped establish the public school system. In 1882 he moved to Cisco, Texas, and eventually to Dallas, where he continued his medical and educational activities, though he never again achieved financial stability. At his death, he left a collection of 1,500 pounds of Army of Tennessee hospital records. The collection is scattered among several southern libraries, including the Tennessee State Library and Archives in Nashville. The largest collection is housed at the Eugene C. Barker Texas History Center, University of Texas, Austin.

Glenna R. Schroeder-Lein, University of Tennessee, Knoxville
SUGGESTED READING: Glenna R. Schroeder-Lein, *Confederate Hospitals on the Move: Samuel H. Stout and the Army of Tennessee* (1994)

SEE: ARMY OF TENNESSEE; MEDICINE

STREET CAR ERA. Beginning in the late 1870s Tennessee's four major metropolitan areas entered the so-called street car era. At first these interurban railways were powered by mules, and ran a very short distance, usually in the downtown area. Soon, because they offered cheap transportation beyond the city limits, "street-car suburbs" developed for middle- and working-class Tennesseans. Work places, factories, and offices in the city were now more separate from home places, which were now in wholesome and clean environments out of the city.

The street car companies were private enterprises with little control from municipal governments. That the horse drawn trolley was immediately accepted as the mass transit solution of choice is seen in the trolleymen's strike in Memphis in August 1885. This successful 20-day strike for higher wages set the pace for other such strikes in Tennessee's cities, involving militant unionism versus corporate and legal power. The strike also indicated just how dependent urbanites were upon horse drawn public transportation. Street car workers first formed local unions but soon formed chapters of the Amalgamated Association of Street Railway Employees of America (AASREA).

The first application of electricity as a street car power source in Montgomery, Alabama, and Richmond, Virginia, in 1886 ushered in the era of the electric streetcar. Nashville began its conversion to electric power in 1888, followed by Chattanooga in 1899 and Memphis and Knoxville in the 1890s. Competition was stiff and chaotic, sometimes resulting in actual combat between companies. For example two competing companies in Knoxville rioted and armed police were sent to quell the disturbance in March 1897.

Because these new trolleys required electric power, appropriate production facilities had to be developed and were followed by the growth of public utility monopolies. In Chattanooga, for example, the Electric Light Company, Chattanooga Electric Railway Company, and Chattanooga Rapid Transit Company had evolved inevitably into a local monopoly, the Chattanooga Railway and Light Company. This, in turn, would ultimately become the statewide monopoly known as TEPCO, the Tennessee Power and Light Company. In Nashville the Nashville Railway and Light Company became the local public transportation monopoly by 1902; TEPCO later subsumed it.

Until the more substantial development of hydroelectric plants in East Tennessee, small, local steam powered generators provided electricity for street car systems. Small hydroelectric plants had been in operation in the Volunteer State in isolated settings since 1901. In 1912 the Chattanooga Railway and Light Company initiated the state's first major hydroelectric plant, Ocoee No. 1, on the river by the same name. Street car and electrical generating plants were soon purchased by larger corporations, both in- and out-of-state conglomerates. For example, by 1917 the E.W. Clark Company, a regional municipal mass transit holding company, owned properties in Chattanooga, Nashville, East St. Louis, Philadelphia, and other cities.

A series of strikes in Chattanooga, Nashville, Memphis, and Knoxville in the first two decades of the twentieth century and the development of internal-combustion-engine-powered urban mass transit systems replaced the street car with the bus. The street car's existence from ca. 1870 to the 1920s added suburbs, electrical power, industry, and strong labor unions to the state's urban centers.

James B. Jones, Jr., Tennessee Historical Commission
SUGGESTED READINGS: James B. Jones, Jr., "Class Consciousness and Worker Solidarity in Urban Tennessee: the Example of the Chattanooga Carmen's Strikes of 1899–1917," *Tennessee Historical Quarterly* 52(1993): 98–112; David H. Steinberg, *And To Think It Only Cost a Nickel! The Development of Public Transportation on the Chattanooga Area* (1975)
SEE: LABOR

STRIBLING, THOMAS SIGISMUND (1881–1968),

novelist and short-story writer, became the first Tennessean to win the Pulitzer Prize for literature. Stribling was born in Clifton, Tennessee, on March 4, 1881, the son of Christopher and Amelia Waits Stribling. After abandoning teaching and the practice of law, he began to write formulaic adventure tales for leading popular magazines.

Stribling's major work as a serious writer came between 1921 and 1938. He achieved success with his first novel, *Birthright* (1921), a book dealing with the problems of a Harvard-educated African American, who returns to his hometown in Tennessee hoping to uplift his race. In the early 1930s he produced *The Forge* (1931), *The Store* (1932), and *Unfinished Cathedral* (1934), a massive 1,479-page trilogy still recognized as his most significant literary production. Set in Florence, Alabama, and its surroundings, the trilogy portrayed the history of the Vaiden family from the beginning of the Civil War through the boom period of the twenties. In these works, Stribling critically examined the factors contributing to the decline of planter-aristocrats after the Civil War and the emergence of a new breed of opportunistic, middle-class mercantilists. *The Store* enjoyed the greatest success, winning the Pulitzer Prize in 1933. His other novels dealing with the South include *Teeftallow* (1926), *Bright Metal* (1928), and *Backwater* (1930).

Stribling did not write anything of major significance after *These Bars of Flesh,* which was published in 1938. He brought his career to a close in the late 1940s and early 1950s by writing detective stories for commercial pulp magazines. After years of residence in Florida and New York City, Stribling returned to Clifton in 1959. He spent the last years of his life there, dying of cancer on July 10, 1968. His autobiography, *Laughing Stock* (1969), was published posthumously.

Combining keen insight and open receptivity to the life around him with a penchant for intricately designed plots, Stribling produced a group of novels that provided good reading and recorded social conditions during various eras. As a pioneer in the southern renaissance, Stribling helped forge a new view of the South and cleared the way for southern authors in the ensuing decades. In short, Stribling helped to create modern southern literature; in doing so, he has earned a place in the American literary chronicle.

Gregory G. Poole, Tennessee State Library and Archives
SELECTED READING: Edward J. Piacentino, *T. S. Stribling: Pioneer Realist in Modern Southern Literature* (1988)
SEE: LITERATURE; WAYNE COUNTY

STRICKLAND, WILLIAM F. (1788–1854), master

architect and designer of the Tennessee State Capitol, was born in 1788 in Navesink, New Jersey. When he was two years old, his parents, John and Elizabeth Strickland, moved the family to Philadelphia. In 1803 William Strickland was apprenticed to the British-American architect, Benjamin Henry Latrobe, under whose tutelage he learned the principles of architecture and engineering. After completing his training, Strickland supported himself through painting, engraving, and aquatinting, as well as creating designs for plasterers and carpenters.

In 1808 Strickland prepared drawings for a new Masonic building in Philadelphia. He was awarded the contract and completed the Gothic style building in 1811. Primarily identified with the Classical style, he designed a number of familiar institutional buildings, including the Second Bank of the United States (1818–1824), the tower of Independence Hall (1828), and the Merchants Exchange (1832–1837) in Philadelphia, and the U.S. Mints in Charlotte, North Carolina (1835), and New Orleans (1835–1836). In 1837 he designed a new sarcophagus to hold the remains of George Washington.

In addition to his architectural projects, Strickland also completed several engineering ventures. His Delaware Breakwater continues in operation 150 years later. As America entered the transportation revolution of the nineteenth century, Strickland's expertise was sought by a number of entrepreneurs, and his work includes numerous reports on railroad and canal projects.

In 1843 Governor James C. Jones charged the Tennessee General Assembly with the responsibility of naming a permanent capital city. Nashville won the designation after the city purchased Campbell's Hill and gave it to the state as the site for the capitol building. The legislature named William Strickland as the architect for the proposed capitol, and he arrived in Tennessee in April 1845. Construction proceeded at a slow pace. The corner stone was laid on July 4, 1845. More than eight years later, the Tennessee General Assembly met for the first time in the yet unfinished building. The final stone was set in place on March 19, 1859. The cost of construction and furnishing of the building reached a total of $879,981.48. Sadly, Strickland died five years before the completion of the capitol.

Nashville's only other surviving Strickland designed building is the Downtown Presbyterian Church. The Egyptian Revival style, which he also used in his design of Philadelphia's Mikveh-Israel Synagogue, represents a real departure from his usual Classicism. The twin towers of the Nashville church are reminiscent of the stepped octagonal twin tower of St. Stephen's Church in Philadelphia. Strickland again toyed with the use of the Egyptian Revival style in an unaccepted proposal for the gateway of Philadelphia's Laurel Hill Cemetery.

During his Nashville years, Strickland received three commissions to design grave monuments. The first, a monument to Sarah Ann Gray Walker, wife of Jonathan W. Walker, was erected in City Cemetery around 1846. An eternal torch, in stone, surmounts the monument, and a lachrymal vase sits, symbolically, in an archway at the center of it. In 1850 Strickland designed the monument for James Knox Polk, which was erected next to the former president's Nashville home, Polk Place. In that same year, he designed the John Kane monument, the most interesting of the three. Kane, a stone-cutter, was employed in the construction of the State Capitol. Erected in City Cemetery by his fellow stone-cutters, the top of the monument is covered with the tools of their trade.

Strickland also designed several area buildings, which have not survived. From a drawing in his portfolio, it is possible to attribute the Second Presbyterian Church of Nashville (1846) to Strickland. His drawing, labeled "Second Presbyterian Church," matched the interior of the building, which was leveled in 1979 for twelve parking spaces for the new Davidson County Criminal Justice Center. In 1848 Strickland designed the Wilson County Courthouse, which burned in 1881.

William Strickland died in Nashville on April 7, 1854. The Tennessee General Assembly honored the architect's wish to be interred in a niche carved into the north portico of the State Capitol he designed.

James A. Hoobler, Tennessee State Museum

Suggested Reading: Agnes E. Gilcrease, *William Strickland, architect and engineer, 1788–1854* (1950)

See: DOWNTOWN PRESBYTERIAN CHURCH; TENNESSEE STATE CAPITOL

STRIKE, HARRIMAN, OF 1933–1934. On July 1, 1933, textile workers at the Harriman Hosiery Mills (HHM) plant in Harriman, Tennessee, seized the opportunity created by Section 7(a) of the National Industrial Recovery Act to organize a local union of the Hosiery Workers, part of the United Textile Workers of America (UTW). Over the next year, hundreds of workers, most of them women, in this East Tennessee community became embroiled in a bitter strike against the town's largest employer, which produced nationally marketed women's silk stockings. The strike tore the town apart, divided managers and workers, and revealed the fragile state of labor reform in the early 1930s.

Seeking to better their lives, hopeful workers confronted the Tarwater family, the owners and operators of both the mills and the company town. Key issues in the strike involved the firing of 23 union activists in July 1933; recognition of UTW Local 1757; use of collective bargaining as a new business-labor relations tool; management resistance to union recognition and substantive bargaining over wages, hours, and working conditions; and confused labor policies of the early New Deal under the National Industrial Recovery Act of June 16, 1933.

Between late July and early October 1933, union officials Floyd Johnston, Roy Gossage, and Edna Gossage tried to discuss recognition, a contract, and the rehiring of the fired workers with HHM secretary M.W. Walker and company attorney T. Asbury Wright. The company's refusal to consider union recognition, bargaining, or a contract resulted in an overwhelming union rank and file strike vote on October 3, 1933. Union organizer Fred Held, Harriman Mayor J.G. D'Armond, and local union leaders sought accommodation with managers, but company intransigence led to hearings before both the regional labor board in Atlanta in November and the National Labor Board in Washington, D.C., in January 1934.

Over the next several months, company officials fired union activists, threatened to cancel employee insurance, insisted on reapplication of all employees, hired new operatives from outside Harriman, obtained an anti-strike injunction, and used Roane County sheriff's deputies as company guards. The half-hearted intervention by federal officials produced no favorable results for labor. By March 1934 the strike had been lost, and the community was divided into factions supporting strikers or owners. A management lockout on June 25 led to a last-minute resolution of the strike on company terms. The July 1934 agreement was arranged by federal negotiators who consulted neither union officials nor striking workers.

The course of the Harriman strike suggested that the early New Deal's attempt to provide for real improvement in the lives of ordinary working people through union organization, recognition, and collective bargaining proved to be a missed chance for textile workers in the South. It also was a missed chance for enlightened management practices in a competitive industry and for compassionate government labor policy reforms in the early years of the Great Depression.

Patrick D. Reagan, Tennessee Technological University

Suggested Reading: W. Calvin Dickinson and Patrick D. Reagan, "Business, Labor, and the Blue Eagle: The Harriman Hosiery Mills Strike, 1933–1934," *Tennessee Historical Quarterly* 55(1996): 240–255; James A. Hodges, *New Deal Labor Policy and the Southern Cotton Textile Industry, 1933–1941* (1986)

See: LABOR; ROANE COUNTY

STRIKES, RAYON PLANTS AT ELIZABETHTON, 1929.

On March 12, 1929, Margaret Bowen, a worker at American Glanzstoff, led a walkout of 523 women operatives. After other shifts joined the walkout the next day, the plant closed on March 14. Four days later Bemberg workers struck in sympathy with the Glanzstoff operatives. The workers' protests centered on low wages, unfair promotion policies, and petty regulations that applied only to females. Workers also objected to the pressure exerted to force them to rent houses at high rates from Watauga Development Corporation. At the time of the strike, Glanzstoff employed 1,099 men and 854 women, while Bemberg employed 886 men and 384 women. At Glanzstoff, although all employees had a 56-hour week, wages for women were considerably lower than those for men.

When the strike began, there was no active union local at the plants. Local 1630 of the United Textile Workers Union of America (UTW) had been chartered in November 1927, when Bemberg workers struck for increased wages. Workers reactivated Local 1630 at a March 13 meeting. Dr. Arthur Mothwurf, president of the rayon plants, refused to recognize the union and refused to consider wage increases. At Mothwurf's request, the Carter County Chancery Court injoined strikers from picketing, damaging plant property, interfering with plant workers, or assembling at the plant gates. Another injunction prohibited strike activities on roads near the plants.

Workers refused to end their strike. Charles Wood, a Department of Labor Conciliation Service mediator, and Paul Aymon of the Tennessee Federation of Labor arranged a meeting between Mothwurf and labor representatives. They reached an agreement, which provided for wage increases, assurances for strikers against discrimination, lifting of the injunctions, and recognition of an in-plant grievance committee. There was no union recognition. Initially Mothwurf refused to sign the agreement, but three days later he pledged his support, and the plants reopened on March 26. Yet management refused to hire back strikers and UTW members. William Green, president of the American Federation of Labor (AFL), sent Edward F. McGrady, the AFL's Washington, D.C., legislative representative, to investigate. McGrady reported that over 300 union members had not been rehired. Early in April, a group of prominent Elizabethton businessmen kidnapped McGrady and Alfred Hoffman, a hosiery union official. They were driven across state lines in separate cars, released, and warned not to return. When they returned, 4,000 workers rallied in outrage at the kidnappings.

On April 13 and 14, management dismissed union members of two Bemberg grievance committees. These dismissals led directly to the second strike, which began on April 15. This time the UTW partici-

pated from the start. On April 20, Governor Henry Horton appointed George L. Berry, president of the International Printing Pressmen's Union, to act as the governor's mediator. But Mothwurf refused to meet with Berry, who then resigned on May 8.

During the second strike, Dr. S.C. Rhea, an employee in the Bemberg Chemical Department, organized the "Loyal Workers of Bemberg," which soon included Glanzstoff as well. Rhea claimed to have the signatures of 700 loyal workers. Mothwurf reopened the plants on May 6. The number of returning union members is not known. The union counted only a few, but management claimed more than 1,100 employees at work on May 11. Management admitted, however, that 500 were "new hires" or strikebreakers.

With the reopening of the plant, Mothwurf persuaded Governor Horton to dispatch 800 National Guardsmen to Elizabethton, an action that turned the strike into a violent, bitter affair. Increasingly violent encounters between strikers and soldiers occurred along the roads leading to the plants. Troops used tear gas against strikers, and in one three-day stretch, from May 14 through May 16, they arrested over 300 strikers. Two houses were dynamited; two barns, one containing plant machinery, were burned. On May 16, a water main leading into Elizabethton was dynamited. The violence resulted in a deluge of requests from labor and other sources to Governor Horton, demanding the removal of the troops from the city; Horton refused.

A second mediator, Anna Weinstock, and Mothwurf on May 23 reached an agreement which stipulated that the plants would reinstate former employees; would not discriminate against union members; and would recognize worker grievance committees. Local 1630 was not accorded recognition. The plants brought in E.T. Willson, an anti-union personnel manager from New Jersey, to carry out investigations of striking workers who had not been rehired. On May 25, 2,500 workers grudgingly approved the agreement.

The strikes cost the plants an estimated $500,000 in losses. In July 1929 Mothwurf left for a two-month vacation in Germany and did not return. The issue of discrimination against union workers continued to plague the plants. By his own account, E.T. Willson blacklisted between 200 and 300 workers. Strikes over this issue occurred in June and October 1929 and March 1930; workers called off a threatened strike in September 1929. Most blacklisted workers were never rehired.

The companies never recognized Local 1630. Instead, they created the Bemberg-Glanzstoff Council, which controlled labor concerns until 1938. The local briefly affiliated with the CIO's Textile Workers Organizing Committee, when it took over UTW locals.

After the UTW was reconstituted in 1939, a NLRB election recertified the local as a UTW local in 1940.

The legacy of the 1929 strikes is multi-faceted. As a consequence of Local 1630's defeat and the treatment of the workers, bitterness and mistrust marked labor-management relations to the present. The violence of the strikes, however, generated union opposition among many workers; as the union weakened, workers dismissed it as useless. Company officials promoted their union and sponsored plant activities in the 1930s in an effort to establish a reputation as "good" employers. To an extent, they succeeded and solidified their place as the city's most important employers. A number of sources credit the Elizabethton strikes as the initiators of a wave of strikes that swept across the Piedmont textile industry in 1929 and 1930, although their exact role remains a much debated subject among southern labor historians.
Marie Tedesco, East Tennessee State University
SUGGESTED READINGS: Jacquelyn Dowd Hall, "Disorderly Women: Gender and Labor Militancy in the Appalachian South," *Journal of American History* 73(1986): 354–382; James A. Hodges, "Challenge to the New South: The Great Textile Strike in Elizabethton, Tennessee, 1929," *Tennessee Historical Quarterly* 23(1964): 343–357
SEE: BERRY, GEORGE L.; HORTON, HENRY; LABOR; NORTH AMERICAN RAYON CORPORATION

STRITCH, SAMUEL ALPHONSUS (1887–1958), Roman Catholic prelate, was born in Nashville, Tennessee, on August 17, 1887, the son of Irish immigrants. Having chosen to enter the priesthood, Stritch was ordained in Rome on May 21, 1910, at the age of 19. Returning to the United States, Father Stritch was assigned as a curate at St. Patrick's Church, Memphis, and within a year he rose to the pastorate of that church. In 1921 Pope Benedict XV appointed the 34-year-old priest a domestic prelate with the title of Right Reverend Monsignor, and later in the same year he was installed as Bishop of Toledo, the youngest American to achieve that rank in the Catholic Church.

From 1930 until 1939 Stritch served as Archbishop of Milwaukee, where he greatly expanded the role played by the Catholic Church in aiding those left destitute by the Great Depression. At the death of Cardinal George Mundelein of Chicago, Stritch was appointed to the post in March 1940. By the completion of his tenure in 1946, his ecclesiastic jurisdiction had grown to include 350 parochial schools and 400 churches with over 1.7 million parishioners. In March 1958 the Cardinal was appointed Pro-Prefect of the Sacred Congregation of the Propagation of the Faith, and was the first American Cardinal to be given the direction of a Congregation in the Roman Curia, but he died in Rome, on May 26, 1958, before assuming his duties. He was interred in Mount Carmel Cemetery, Chicago, Illinois.

Gregrory G. Poole, Tennessee State Library and Archives
SEE: RELIGION

SULLIVAN COUNTY, established in 1780, was one of the earliest settled areas in Tennessee. In 1761 troops on their way to aid besieged Fort Loudoun passed through this area of northeast Tennessee, built the Island Road, and constructed Fort Robinson on the Long Island of the Holston. Settlement of the area began shortly after the fort was constructed. The first permanent settlers came from Lancaster, Pennsylvania, in 1765. This area was known as the North of the Holston Settlement and was considered part of Virginia until a boundary survey proved it to be part of North Carolina in 1779. The county of Sullivan, named for General John Sullivan, a New Hampshire Revolutionary War leader, was officially organized in February 1780.

The Holston River crosses the county from northeast to southwest. At the southwest corner, the Holston and Watauga Rivers come together in the Forks area. The north fork of the Holston forms the county boundary with Hawkins County, which was created out of Sullivan in 1786. The Long Island's strategic location at the head of navigation on the Holston figured prominently in campaigns against the Cherokees and during the American Revolution, when Fort Patrick Henry stood on the old site of Fort Robinson. It was a docking place for boats bound for towns downriver laden with commodities like iron and salt. White settlers defeated the Cherokee in their attempts to resist settlement in the famous Battle of Island Flats in 1776. The Treaty of the Long Island of the Holston in 1777 temporarily resolved conflicts between settlers and the Cherokee, who ceded lands to both Virginia and North Carolina. At a location nearby, Colonel John Donelson assembled his family and other settlers for a voyage down the Holston to establish a settlement on the Cumberland River in December 1779. The river routes through the county, as well as the early roads cut in the area, made it a gateway for western settlement as immigrants moved down the Valley of Virginia from Delaware, Maryland, Pennsylvania, Virginia, and across the Carolinas.

Sullivan County is a place of many "firsts" in the settlement history of Tennessee. In 1773, at Taylor's Meeting House near Blountville, settlers established a Presbyterian church, probably the first of any denomination to be established within the borders of the future state. Island Road, dating to 1761, is the oldest wagon road in Tennessee. Acuff Chapel, established in 1786, was the first Methodist Episcopal Church founded in the state. The Boat Yard, across from the Netherland Inn at Long Island, was the first major river port, established in 1768. The first nail factory in Tennessee was at King's Ironworks, established south of Bristol in 1784. Rocky

Mount was the first seat of government for the Southwest Territory in 1790.

Sullivan County developed as a rich agricultural area with an economy augmented with industries such as iron works, powder mills, tanneries, gristmills, and sawmills in the early nineteenth century. Blountville, centered on a turnpike that went north to Richmond, Washington, D.C., and Philadelphia, was the county seat and a prosperous trade and commercial town. The Deery Inn served travelers from 1785 to the 1930s. Although much of East Tennessee remained loyal to the Union during the Civil War, Democratic Sullivan County voted in favor of secession.

Sullivan County is home to Kingsport and Bristol, two of the three "Tri-Cities" of Upper East Tennessee. Kingsport remained a country village until 1909, when the construction of the Carolina, Clinchfield and Ohio Railway passed through the Holston Valley. This important link to Cincinnati and the Atlantic opened the door for Sullivan County's development as an industrial center. An improvement association planned an industrial city for the land near the village of Kingsport with the aid of John Nolan, an engineer and city planner. Kingsport, which featured a circular road and park at its center from which city streets radiated, was chartered in 1917. The Tennessee Eastman Corporation, which employs 11,400 in the production of synthetic fibers, is the largest employer in Kingsport and the county today. It began operations as a methanol distillery in the 1920s and expanded operations to include the manufacture of cellulose acetate by the 1930s. The Quebecor Printing Company (former Kingsport Press) continues Sullivan County's involvement in the binding industry and is the city's second largest employer with a work force of 1,400.

Bristol's history for its first 100 years or so was that of a rural village. Evan Shelby (1719–1794) came to Sapling Grove (now Bristol) in 1771 and established a fort that became a settlement center. During the Revolutionary War, Shelby commanded expeditions against the Chickamauga towns and early planning for the King's Mountain campaign took place in his quarters at the fort. Modern Bristol dates to the late nineteenth and early twentieth centuries when an industrial town developed at the junction of the Southern Railway and Norfolk and Western Railroad. The presence of two major lines attracted rapid commercial and industrial development. In the mid-1920s Victor Talking Machine Company talent scout Ralph Peer set up a recording studio on the Tennessee side of State Street and made a series of recordings with regional artists. These "Bristol Sessions" featured the Stoneman Family, the Carter family, and Jimmie Rodgers. They marked the beginning of the modern country music industry, a fact proclaimed by a colorful mural on the side of a State Street building

in downtown Bristol. Tennessee Ernie Ford was another country music star from Bristol.

Blythe Semmer, Middle Tennessee State University

SEE: BRISTOL INTERNATIONAL SPEEDWAY; COX, JOHN I.; DENNIS, JOHN B.; FORD, TENNESSEE ERNIE; FORT PATRICK HENRY; JOHNSON, J. FRED; KING COLLEGE; KINGSPORT; KINGSPORT PRESS; LONG ISLAND; MARTIN, JOSEPH; MUSIC; NETHERLAND INN; RAILROADS; RHEA, JOHN; ROCKY MOUNT; SHAVER, SAMUEL; SHELBY, ISAAC; STADIUMS, HISTORIC; TENNESSEE EASTMAN COMPANY; TREATIES; WARRIORS PATH STATE PARK

SULPHUR DELL was the professional baseball park in Nashville, located between Fourth and Fifth Avenues, North, and Jackson and Summer streets. Union troops introduced baseball to the city in 1862, when they played in a low-lying area north of the statehouse known as Sulphur Springs Bottom. In past times, a salt lick and sulphur spring attracted animals to the thick canebreak in the Bottom and made the location a popular place for hunting. In 1885 Athletic Park was built on the site, and the Chicago White Stockings used the facility to "take the waters" and hold spring training. The next year, Nashville fielded a minor league club.

When the Southern League reorganized in 1901, Nashville was among the eight-team association and maintained its affiliation until 1961. As a member, the Nashville Vols played in the old, wood-planked stadium, renamed Sulphur Dell by the famous young sports editor of the *Nashville Tennessean*, Grantland Rice. The new electric trolley line made access to the stadium convenient for fans.

The field possessed rather peculiar dimensions and several natural obstacles. Located less than one-fourth mile from the Cumberland River, the playing surface lay below street level. As a result the field frequently flooded. A 16-foot high wall enclosed the outfield, and an open press box sat atop the grandstand in the northwest corner. The dimensions of the 6,000 seat park were intimate, with seating only 26 feet and 42 feet away from third base and first base respectively. The trademark of the stadium, however, was its short right field wall—which stood only 262 feet away from home plate, and at 236 feet, the field uniquely slanted at a 45 degree angle upward to the wall. Most right fielders positioned themselves on a 10-foot-wide shelf constructed half way up the incline. A rope was strung along the base (at 235 feet), and overflow crowds sat on the grassy outfield. Casey Stengel once reportedly bragged that he hit a bunt for a home run down the right field line at Sulphur Dell. The short porch was popular with left handed hitters, but pitchers often referred to the park derisively as "Sulphur Hell." Visiting teams nicknamed the field "The Dump" because of the stench caused by burning garbage at the city landfill located beyond the right field wall.

One of the most exciting games ever played at Sulphur Dell occurred on the last day of the 1908 season. The Vols were pitted against their arch rivals, the New Orleans Pelicans, in a winner-take-all league championship game. Reportedly over 10,000 fans crammed into the tiny stadium and witnessed a tremendous pitcher's duel between the Vol's righthanded Vedder Sitton, and the Pelican's masterful lefthander, Ted Breitenstein. Nashville won the game in dramatic fashion by scoring the game's only run with two outs in the bottom of the seventh inning. Sportswriter Rice called it "the greatest game ever played in Dixie."

Sulphur Dell was reconfigured in the winter of 1926, when the diamond was relocated in the southwest corner of the field. The faint outline of the original base paths remained forever visible in shallow center field. The stadium held the distinction of being the oldest professional baseball park in the country when it was razed in 1963. Today the original site is a parking lot for state vehicles.

John A. Simpson, Kelso, Washington

SEE: BASEBALL, MINOR LEAGUE; STADIUMS, HISTORIC

SULTANA DISASTER OF 1865. At 2:00 A.M. on April 27, 1865, the magnificent, side wheeler river boat *Sultana* was struggling against the surging current of the Mississippi River, eight miles north of Memphis. The weather was rainy and chilly, and the boat was grossly overloaded. Suddenly one of the boilers exploded, triggering the worst inland marine disaster in U.S. history.

The initial impact ripped the vessel in half, igniting flames, releasing scalding steam, and instantly killing, or mortally wounding, hundreds of sleeping passengers as well as a number of stock animals. Within seconds, bodies and body parts, along with metal fragments from the boilers, splintered wood, and other debris rained down on the boat and into the water. As the flames spread, those who survived the initial explosion began jumping overboard in the false belief that they were near the shore. Unfortunately, the river was at flood and the *Sultana* near mid-channel, a distance of more than four miles to either bank. With no life boats and little in the way of safety equipment, panicky passengers resorted to ripping wooden planks and other buoyant objects from the boat before jumping into the dark and fast-moving water. Meanwhile, the flames cast an eerie glow into the night and onto the mass of live and dead humanity thrashing or bobbing about the sinking boat. Chaos and panic ensued as those in the water either tried to help one another or competed for handholds on every available piece of floating debris.

The first rescue craft, the *Bostonia No. 2*, was 90 minutes away when her crew spotted the glow of the *Sultana* pyre in the night sky. As they approached the scene, the crew of the *Bostonia* threw bales of hay and anything else that would float to the struggling survivors. With the approach of dawn, other craft arrived and survivors were transported to shelters and hospitals in Memphis. The dead were retrieved from the water and many were later buried in mass graves in Memphis.

The *Sultana* was licensed to carry 356 passengers and crew, but on this occasion the boat may have been carrying as many as 2,485. Exact figures were never established and are still controversial. Most of those on board were Union prisoners of war from Andersonville, Georgia, and Cahaba, Alabama, homeward bound after the end of the Civil War. Among them were a number of East Tennesseans from Blount, Claiborne, Hancock, Knox, Sevier, and Union counties. Estimates of the number of dead range from a low of 1,450 to as high as 1,900. In terms of maritime disasters, the estimated death toll exceeded that of the ocean liner, *Titanic*, which sank in the North Atlantic in 1912.

Stories about the disaster quickly faded from contemporary newspapers leading some to suspect a cover-up by the War Department. However, it is more likely that the end of the war, economic problems, and the recent assassination of Abraham Lincoln account for the public's brief interest in the disaster.

A monument erected by the survivors to the memory of the East Tennessee victims of the *Sultana* disaster stands in the Mount Olive Cemetery in Knoxville. Inscribed on the monument is a modest tribute to the brave Tennesseans who suffered the toils of war and almost made it home.

Allen R. Coggins, Knoxville

SEE: DISASTERS

SUMMER SCHOOL OF THE SOUTH. From its inception in 1902 to its demise in 1918, the Summer School of the South was a major instrument of regional educational improvement, instructing some 32,000 teachers in the art of education. The Summer School was born from the desire of its founder, University of Tennessee President Charles W. Dabney, to change the then lamentable state of Southern learning. To Dabney regional educators were little better than "makeshift teachers," whose pupils received "only 3 years of schooling." For the region to advance, Southern education had to improve.

With the 1902 arrival in Knoxville of Philander P. Claxton, agent of the Southern Education Board, Dabney found the man to change this situation. Using money raised locally and nationally, Dabney hired Claxton to create a summer school for teachers—the Summer School of the South—an independent institution that would be located on the University of Tennessee campus. The dual goals of the Summer School were to improve Southern education by improving Southern educators and to turn the region's teachers into agitators for more educational resources. In sum, the school was to be a cross between a summer college and a propaganda rally.

Immediately, Claxton set to work. In two months he toured some ten southern states, where he addressed state educational assemblies, enlisted the support of local school superintendents, and talked to scores of individual teachers. To buttress these personal appeals, Claxton flooded the mails with over 100,000 posters and brochures announcing the school's first session.

Results surpassed even optimistic projections. When the school opened, over 1,900 teachers were in attendance and a distinguished faculty had been assembled to instruct them. Of the 51 faculty members, eight were present or former university presidents. Further gracing the faculty were the prominent Southern writer Walter Hines Page and the U.S. Commissioner of Education William T. Harris. Later sessions would also attract noted instructors such as John Dewey, Richard T. Ely, and U.B. Phillips.

The Summer School faculty offered teachers a wide variety of subjects to study. "Courses may be had in anything from that post graduate work of the nursery, 'Patty cake, patty cake, baker's man," T.S. Stribling wrote in his 1903 prize essay on the Summer School, "to Pre-Shakespearian Drama, from Belles Lettres to a course on Agriculture."[1] Supplementing formal instruction were cultural activities. For example, Charles Coburn and his *al fresco* players regularly appeared to perform classical plays. Among other such artists, who performed on campus, were the violinist Maude Powell and the conductor Leopold Stokowski and the Cincinnati Symphony Orchestra.

While under Claxton, the Summer School was quite a success. After Claxton's departure in 1911 to be U.S. Commissioner of Education, the school came under direct University of Tennessee control and swiftly declined. In just seven years attendance dropped more than 60 percent. University bureaucracy, competition from newer summer schools, and dislocations from World War I impeded further progress. After the 1918 session the university closed the school, ending an important epoch in Southern education.

William B. Eigelsbach, University of Tennessee, Knoxville, and Jamie Sue Linder, Knoxville

CITATION:

(1) T.S. Stribling, "The Summer School of the South," *The Florence Herald*, July 17, 1903

SEE: CLAXTON, PHILANDER P.; DABNEY, CHARLES W.; EDUCATION, HIGHER; UNIVERSITY OF TENNESSEE

SUMMITT, PAT HEAD (1952–), women's basketball coach at the University of Tennessee, Knoxville, has produced an enviable record of success both on and off the court. Born in Henrietta, Tennessee, on June 14, 1952, she attended and graduated from Cheatham County High School in Ashland City and then received her B.S. in physical education from the University of Tennessee at Martin in 1975. The following year, she received her master's in physical education from the University of Tennessee, Knoxville.

Summitt enjoyed a successful basketball career as a player at UT-Martin and in international competitions. She was on the 1975 U.S. World Championship team and at the 1976 Olympics in Montreal she and the U.S. team won the silver medal. But as a coach, Summitt has no equals in Tennessee sports history. By 1998 her teams at the University of Tennessee, Knoxville, have won six NCAA championships and her combined record was an impressive 664 wins versus 143 losses in 24 years of coaching. Her international coaching record is 63-4 and in 1984 she coached the U.S. team to the gold medal at the Olympic Games in Los Angeles. In all of college basketball history, only legendary UCLA coach John Wooden has won more NCAA championships (10). Her 660+ wins places Summitt into another elite category of excellence. Only Texas's Jody Conradt with 697 wins ranks ahead of Summitt among women college basketball coaches. Summitt has won the Naismith College Coach of the Year Award three times.

Summitt is extremely active in community affairs and as a spokesperson for the university as well as women's athletics. She takes pride in the graduation rates and careers of her players. A member of the Women's Sports Foundation Hall of Fame, she is on the Board of Directors of the Women's Basketball Hall of Fame, now being developed in Knoxville. She is married to R.B. Summitt and they have a son, Ross Tyler Summitt.

Carroll Van West, Middle Tennessee State University

SEE: UNIVERSITY OF TENNESSEE; UNIVERSITY OF TENNESSEE AT MARTIN; WOMEN'S BASKETBALL HALL OF FAME

SUMNER COUNTY. Archaeological evidence in Sumner County indicates occupation by Paleoindian, Archaic, Woodland, and Missisippian cultures in the deep past. Two prehistoric mounds are seen easily at Castalian Springs, where Native Americans for centuries came to hunt game which gathered at the springs and its salt lick. The first white long hunters included Henry, Charles, and Richard Skaggs and Joseph Drake in 1765. Among other early explorers and long hunters were James Smith and an 18-year-old male mulatto slave in 1766, and Kasper Mansker, Isaac Bledsoe, and others in 1771–1772. The first permanent settler was the fearless Thomas Sharp Spencer who earned that distinction by living several months in the hollow of a sycamore tree at Bledsoe's

Lick in 1776, then planting crops and building cabins from 1776 to 1779. By 1783 settlers erected three forts—Mansker's, Bledsoe's, and Asher's—for protection against Indian attack.

In 1786 the North Carolina General Assembly created Sumner County and named it for Revolutionary War General Jethro Sumner. The rolling hills and well-watered lands attracted pioneer leaders of the stature of Daniel Smith and Anthony Bledsoe and those of more meager means such as Hugh Rogan. However, Native Americans did not passively accept this frontier advance; periodic warfare resulted in the deaths of both Indians and settlers, including Robert Peyton, the last known Sumner settler killed by Indians. The opening of wagon roads, the influx of new settlers, and a preemptive strike at the Indian raider's base village of Nickajack ended the Indian wars by 1795.

Cairo emerged as an early trade center and important port along the Cumberland River. However, in 1801, the General Assembly authorized the purchase of 41.5 acres from Captain James Trousdale and thereon established Gallatin as the county seat.

With the exception of a two-year agricultural depression (1821–1823) and cholera epidemics in 1849 and 1852, the first half of the nineteenth century was a period of growth, development, and recognition for Sumner County. Two residents, William Hall and William Trousdale, and Sumner-born William B. Campbell served as governors of Tennessee. Advantages provided by improved roads, a stagecoach line, river trade, and ferry services led to establishment of approximately 30 communities and, according to the 1820 census, a total of 54 manufacturers, mostly distilleries and mills.

Following a tradition of building for permanence established by Daniel Smith's construction of Rock Castle and William Bowen's 1780s brick house near Mansker's Station, the county experienced an architectural boom during the 1800s. Among the more than 100 showplace homes were James Winchester's Cragfont (1802), John Bowen's Trousdale Place (1822), Josephus Conn Guild's Rose Mont (1840s), Isaac Franklin's Fairvue (1832), and Daniel Smith Donelson's Hazel Path (1857). National reputations and fortunes amassed by owners of the several estates came from plantation-based agriculture and the raising of thoroughbred racehorses.

Sumner Countians, historically united in war, furnished 821 men to Andrew Jackson in the War of 1812, three companies to the Seminole War of 1836, and three to the Mexican War. Such devoted support of the Union divided voters on the question of secession early in 1861. But following the fall of Fort Sumter, the county voted 6,465 to 69 to declare Tennessee independent in the referendum of June 8.

Over 3,000 Sumner Countians were soldiers in the Civil War and many of the first were trained at Camp Trousdale near Portland. In 1862 Confederate General John Hunt Morgan defeated Union forces at the Battle of Gallatin but soon afterward withdrew, and the county was in Federal control for the rest of the war. The Union army hired local blacks, called contrabands, as contract labor, and in Gallatin black residents enlisted in the Union army's Thirteenth and Fourteenth U.S. Colored Troops.

Following the war, freed blacks established several communities including Village Green and Free Hill, and organized the nation's first agricultural fair created by and for black citizens. The fair remained an annual event for nearly 100 years. By the twentieth century, Gallatin's black leadership had established strong churches and schools. Black businesses such as restaurants, dry cleaners, taxi services, and barbershops emerged, along with a black baseball team, the Travelers.

The early twentieth century brought added emphasis to agricultural production. Portland's strawberry industry expanded and the location of a Kraft Cheese plant in Gallatin in 1928 provided a ready outlet for increased dairy production throughout the county. Out-of-state money underwrote the formation of the Southland Grasslands Hunt & Racing Foundation, attempting to establish new steeplechase traditions in the Tennessee "bluegrass" country.

The Tennessee Valley Authority and the U.S. Army Corps of Engineers provided a defining moment in county history during the early 1950s. With the Corps' construction of Old Hickory Dam on the Cumberland River, TVA built a steam electric generating plant at Gallatin. The net result was new jobs, new recreational opportunities, and a housing boom along the hundreds of miles of lake shoreline.

Benefiting greatly from proximity to the lake and to Metropolitan Nashville, and from the advent of a growing local tourism industry, Hendersonville became the largest city in the county (32,000 in 1990) and a tourist center for country music fans. Conway Twitty and Johnny Cash once operated country music museums there. The Trinity Broadcast Network, a Christian cable television network, now uses the facilities at the former "Twitty City." Country music star Reba McIntyre owns a horse farm along the Cumberland River just south of Gallatin.

Educational opportunities within the county have expanded with the opening of Volunteer State Community College at Gallatin in 1969. Employment opportunities were further increased with the addition of 31 new industries and the expansion of over 120 others, principally at Gallatin and Portland.

DeeGee Lester, Hendersonville

SEE: BLEDSOE, ANTHONY; BLEDSOE, ISAAC; CAMPBELL, WILLIAM; COMMUNITY COLLEGES; CRAGFONT; GUILD, JOSEPHUS CONN; HALL, WILLIAM; MANSKER, KASPER; FAIRVUE; FRANKLIN, ISAAC; ROCK CASTLE; ROGAN,

HUGH; ROGANA; SMITH, DANIEL; SPENCER, THOMAS S.;
TROUSDALE, WILLIAM; U.S. CORPS OF ENGINEERS; TEN-
NESSEE VALLEY AUTHORITY

SUNDQUIST, DON (1936–), Governor of Tennessee
since 1995, was born March 15, 1936, and was the first
member of his family to finish high school and attend
college. He graduated from Augustana College and
then served two years in the U.S. Navy. In 1962 he
began his business career by joining Josten's, a
scholastic products company. Sundquist and his wife
Martha Swanson Sundquist, a graduate of Augustana
College he married in 1959, moved to Shelbyville,
Tennessee, where Sundquist rose quickly to become
plant manager of the Josten's factory.

In 1972 Sundquist left Middle Tennessee to establish his own company, Graphic Sales of America, a
printing and advertising firm, in Memphis. There he
became active in the growing Republican party of
Shelby County. He was the chairman of the county
Republican party from 1976–1979 and managed
Howard Baker, Jr.'s presidential candidacy in 1979.
Sundquist won a seat in the U.S. Congress in 1982,
serving a large, mostly West Tennessee district with
distinction until 1994, when he left Congress after 12
years to launch his gubernatorial candidacy. In Congress Sundquist established solid conservative credentials in his service as a member of the powerful
Ways and Means Committee. Along with other committee work, he served as chairman of the House
Republican Task Force on Trade and as a member of
the House Republican Task Force on Ethics Reform.

In 1994 Sundquist defeated Nashville mayor Phil
Breseden by 807,104 to 664,252 votes to become Tennessee's 47th Governor. Sundquist campaigned on a
platform of welfare reform, law enforcement, and
increased governmental efficiency. He pushed for the
elimination of the Public Service Commission, and
his "Families First" welfare reform package has
received national recognition for its attempt to save
taxpayer money and to provide better care for needy
and troubled children. He also pushed through the
General Assembly a 20-bill law enforcement package
that focused on tougher sentences, capital case
reform, domestic violence, and victims' rights. As
Sunquist remarks on the State of Tennessee Web Page
(May 26, 1997), "we want to get government out of
people's business and the people into the business of
government." His program has met with legislative
success and popular approval; as the 1998 primaries
near, it appears that Sundquist will face little opposition for a second term of office.

Don and Martha Sundquist have three children.
Tania (Mrs. David) Williamson; Andrea (Mrs. Art)
Jeannet, and Donald Sundquist, Jr., of Nashville.
C.V. West, Middle Tennessee State University
SEE: MEMPHIS; TENNESSEE GOVERNOR'S OFFICE

Governor Don Sundquist.

OFFICE OF THE GOVERNOR

SUTHERLAND, EARL W., JR. (1915–1974), a professor of physiology at Vanderbilt University Medical
Center from 1963 to 1973, was the first scientist from
a southern university to win a Nobel Prize in physiology and medicine. Many observers considered the
conferring of the prize on Sutherland in 1971 a sign
of the rise of the South as a pacesetter in medical
research, education, and clinical service.

In 1956 Sutherland and Dr. T.W. Rall discovered
cyclic AMP. Sutherland's further research demonstrated the ubiquitous nature and prime importance
of this chemical and its associated compounds,
notably adenyl cyclase, in all living things. As the
result of Sutherland's work and those who followed
his lead, it became known that hormones are not the
sole regulatory substances in the chemistry of living
organisms, as had previously been believed. In many
cases, necessary cellular reactions are triggered by
cyclic AMP, the almost universal "second messenger," responding to the hormonal signal. Sutherland's
work on hormones opened up new paths of research
into diabetes, cancer, and cholera.

Sutherland was born in Burlingame, Kansas, and
earned his medical degree in 1942 from the Washington University Medical School in St. Louis. After serving as a doctor in World War II, he returned to his
alma mater as a researcher in Nobel laureate Carl Ferdinand Cori's laboratory. In 1953 he became director

of the department of medicine at Case Western Reserve University in Cleveland, Ohio, where he discovered cyclic AMP. By 1963 Sutherland wanted to limit his duties to research and moved to Vanderbilt.

In addition to his Nobel Prize, Sutherland was named a career investigator of the American Heart Association, which awarded him its Achievement Award in 1971. In 1970 he won the Albert Lasker Award for basic medical research. In 1973 he received the National Medal of Science. He was elected to the National Academy of Sciences.

Sutherland died one year after he and his wife, Dr. Claudia Sutherland, accepted positions with the University of Miami Medical School, he as distinguished professor of biochemistry and she as assistant dean.
Kelly C. Lockhart, Murfreesboro
SEE: MEDICINE; VANDERBILT UNIVERSITY MEDICAL CENTER

SWAGGERTY BLOCKHOUSE, in Cocke County, was built ca. 1787 by James Swaggerty on land acquired from the state of North Carolina in 1786 by Abraham Swaggerty. It is the only remaining log blockhouse on its original site in Tennessee. Swaggerty built the three-story cantilevered structure in a style commonly erected on the eastern frontier to provide protection and security for pioneer settlers. Blockhouses were sometimes part of larger defensive structures such as forts or stockades. Swaggerty Blockhouse, however, appeared to be a free standing structure used by the family as a place of sanctuary in times of danger.

Resting on a one-story limestone foundation, the log structure enclosed an ever flowing spring that provided a constant source of water. The second story is of half dovetail-notched log construction 12 feet square. The third story extends (cantilevers) out four feet on all sides for a total length of 20 feet. The logs of the third story were replaced at some point with frame construction. A wooden hewn ladder, still preserved with the structure, provided access to the upper floors.

Ownership of the property passed from the Swaggerty family to Jacob Stephens in the mid-1850s. In 1921 T.J. Gillespie bought the property and his son, Gay Gillespie, has continued to preserve and protect the blockhouse.
Steve Rogers, Tennessee Historical Commission
SEE: COCKE COUNTY; LOG CONSTRUCTION

SWISS SETTLERS, KNOXVILLE. In 1848 Knox County's "Swiss Colony" began when The Reverend Adrien Chavannes and his family settled on a 275-acre farm four miles north of Knoxville. During the next 65 years, over 75 families settled in the Knoxville area, engaging in various agricultural and business pursuits. These immigrants included both French-Swiss, who came from the Canton of Vaud

in the Lake of Geneva area, and German-Swiss who came from several cantons: Appenzell, Bern, Glarus, Schwyz, and St. Gallen. These immigrants were farmers, cheese makers, gardeners, teachers, ministers, and government officials. In Switzerland, most of them lived in large multifamily stone houses, many with attached farm buildings. The small log and mainly single-family frame houses and detached farm buildings of East Tennessee contrasted greatly with those to which the immigrants were accustomed.

The first Swiss immigrants took ten weeks to reach East Tennessee, traveling by a "char a bancs" (bench wagon), "diligence" (stagecoach), and train to Le Havre, France. They sailed to New York (41 days), where they took a steamer to Charleston, then a train to Dalton, Georgia, a wagon to Chattanooga, and then by steamboat up the Tennessee River to Kingston, where another wagon took them to an early Swiss and German settlement in Wartburg, Tennessee.

The German-American "East Tennessee Colonization Company," founded in 1844 to promote land sales in Wartburg, attracted many German and German-Swiss immigrants. Arriving in 1848, the French-Swiss were "disagreeably surprised" by Wartburg's poor market and infertile soil, and they soon relocated to Knox County, where the Chavannes, Gouffon, and Sterchi families settled. During the next several years Knox County's Swiss population increased with the arrival of the Buffat, Esperandieu, Truan, Bolli, Porta, Rochat, Berney, Getaz, Andre, LeCoultre, Seilaz, Tauxe, Falconnier, Felix, Guignard, and Babelay families. By 1850 the Swiss comprised the largest European ethnic group in Knox County. There were 35–40 French-Swiss families, and an equal number of German-speaking Swiss, which included the Aebli, Benziger, Koella, Leopold, Metler, Schaad, Scheitlin, Staub, Steiner, Tobler, Wohlwend, and Zurcher families.

Within a matter of years, the Swiss and their descendants became an important part of East Tennessee's social, political, and economic life. The Knox County Courthouse (1885) and the Knoxville Market House (1897) were built by David Getaz of Stephenson and Getaz, Architects and Builders. Swiss politicians included Peter Staub, founder of Staub's Opera House and twice mayor of Knoxville (1874 and 1881), and Alfred Buffat, founder of Buffat Mill and Knox County trustee (1904–1906). In the early twentieth century, Edward Terry Sanford, son of Swiss immigrant Emma Chavannes Sanford, was appointed a United States Supreme Court justice (1923–1930).

Important Knoxville businesses started by the Swiss include Buffat Mill, Sterchi Bros. Furniture Stores, Chavannes Lumber Company, Gouffon Transfer Company, Schaad Lumber Company, A.J. Metler

Hauling and Rigging, Babelay Greenhouses, and Rochat Realty Company.

Most of the French-Swiss immigrants were members of the Open Brethren, a fundamentalist Christian group which had withdrawn from the National Protestant Church of Switzerland in 1824. The Open Brethren had a simple, scripture-based, laity-oriented practice of faith. Their worship service was characterized by spontaneous Bible-reading, prayer, and hymn-singing without musical instruments as they sat in a circle facing one another. The Open Brethren existed in Knoxville for 56 years, but their descendants became members of other Protestant denominations, a step which further assimilated them into East Tennessee culture. In 1870 some of the Open Brethren became Plymouth Brethren, a group which today numbers about 125 members, almost all of Swiss descent.

David Babelay, Knoxville

SEE: GRUETLI; SANFORD, EDWARD T.; STAUB, PETER

SYCAMORE SHOALS STATE HISTORIC AREA, in

Carter County, preserves and interprets the Sycamore Shoals of the Watauga River, a National Historic Landmark that was one of the most significant early settlement areas on the western frontier. Here in 1772 residents established the Watauga Association, recognized as the first majority-rule system of American democratic government. In 1775 land speculator Richard Henderson negotiated with the Cherokee Indians for the purchase of a huge land tract of 20 million acres—known as the Transylvania Purchase—at Sycamore Shoals. Reportedly 1,200 Native Americans attended the negotiations; Dragging Canoe strongly denounced the deal as unfair and unwise. The following year, 1776, Cherokees attacked the upper East Tennessee settlements. At Sycamore Shoals, settlers constructed Fort Watauga for defense. One Cherokee group, led by Old Abram, laid siege to the fort for two weeks that summer but, unable to force a surrender, the Cherokees retreated.

Important trails connected the Shoals to settlements in western North Carolina and Virginia as well as to all of the primary Tennessee settlements such as Fort Patrick Henry, Fort Robinson, and Sapling Grove. Therefore, in 1780, when the leaders of the Overmountain Men looked for a place to assemble before marching to the Battle of King's Mountain, they chose Sycamore Shoals. Their muster on September 25, 1780, involved about 100 men; 11 days later the Overmountain Men decisively defeated British General Patrick Ferguson at King's Mountain.

Sycamore Shoals State Historic Area contains a visitor center, trails, picnic facilities, and a reconstruction of Fort Watauga. Special events include the Overmountain Victory Trail Celebration held every September. Park rangers also manage the Carter

Mansion in Elizabethton. Listed on the National Register of Historic Places, the Carter Mansion is one of the important impressive pieces of vernacular architecture, both in its construction techniques and its interior decorative painting and craftsmanship, remaining from the early settlement era.

Carroll Van West, Middle Tennessee State University

SEE: ARCHITECTURE, VERNACULAR DOMESTIC; CARTER COUNTY; CARTER MANSION; DRAGGING CANOE; OVERMOUNTAIN MEN; TRANSYLVANIA PURCHASE; WATAUGA ASSOCIATION

SYMPHONY ORCHESTRAS. Tennessee has two professional orchestras designated as "regional" (Nashville and Memphis) and three which fall in the "metropolitan" status (Chattanooga, Jackson, and Knoxville). Other cities with part-time orchestras are Oak Ridge and Germantown, and an annual summer music festival occurs at the University of the South. Various universities also support orchestras.

There were attempts at sustaining symphonic organizations in Nashville during the late 1920s, but the current Nashville Symphony Orchestra (NSO) owes much to Walter Sharp (1911–1970). He desired to raise the cultural awareness of his fellow Nashvillians. Sharp acquired financial support for the new NSO through his connections with the Nashville elite. Under his supervision, a 27-member board of directors was elected and a five-member executive committee and an official charter were drawn up in June 1946 for the Nashville Civic Music Association.

From 1946–1951 William Strickland was conductor of the new orchestra, which debuted at 8:30 P.M., December 10, 1946, at the War Memorial Auditorium. From the onset, he insisted the new group be organized, maintained, and operated as a professional organization. Strickland demanded high standards of musicianship for its members, set strict codes for performance dress, and insisted rehearsals be held in privacy. Musicians came from local radio orchestras and vaudeville, and instructors from the Nashville Conservatory, George Peabody College, Ward-Belmont Conservatory, and Fisk University were enlisted as principles. Other Nashville conductors have been Guy Taylor (1951–1959), Willis Page (1959–1967), Thor Johnson (1967–1975), Michael Charry (1976–1982), and Kenneth Schermerhorn (from 1983). In 1980 the orchestra began performances at Andrew Jackson Hall in the Tennessee Center for the Performing Arts. Including pop concerts, the NSO has a 37-week season employing 70 core musicians.

Though there were several earlier attempts under various titles, the most successful organization and forerunner to the present Memphis Symphony Orchestra (MSO) was developed by Burnet C. Tuthill, music department head at Southwestern College who became the president of the Memphis College of

Music (1939). The orchestra benefited from the fund-raising efforts of the newly formed Memphis Symphony Society. The orchestra was open to all levels of skill, the bulk of which were amateur, and augmented by professionals performing four to five concerts per season. Their first concert was held in the Goodwyn Institute Auditorium in March 1939, featuring soloists engaged through Tuthill's connections with the Cincinnati Conservatory. World War II caused interruptions, and there were no plans made for the 1947–48 season.

Meanwhile, Noel Gilbert initiated the Memphis Concert Orchestra, a part-time pops group in 1949. With funding from the Memphis Federation of Musicians, the orchestra performed five to six concerts at the Overton Park Shell during the summer season until the mid-1970s. The remnants of this group can be found in the current Memphis Civic Orchestra and the Germantown Symphony Orchestra.

Vincent DeFrank, who had been first cellist under Tuthill, began a chamber group in 1952 with the fund-raising efforts of the new Memphis Orchestral Society and the Memphis Arts Council. He maintained the group over the next eight years as it grew into the Memphis Symphony Orchestra by 1960. In 1981 DeFrank announced his retirement. Alan Balter became the musical director in 1984. The MSO performs 100 concerts over a 38-week season, supporting 35 core musicians.

The current Knoxville Symphony Orchestra (KSO), the oldest continuing orchestra in the Southeast, was founded by Bertha Walburn Clark, who conducted the group from 1935 to 1946. She was followed by Lamar Stringfield (1946–1947), David Van Vactor "father of the modern KSO" (1947–1972), Arpad Joo (1973–1978), Zoltan Rozsnyai (1978–1985),

and Kirk Trevor (1985 to present). A 16-piece core orchestra was established in the late 1970s as well as an expanded season of 129 annual performances. The subscription orchestra maintains a 30-week season performing in the Civic Auditorium with additional classical, pops, and educational series. The KSO operates on an annual budget of $2.5 million with an endowment fund of $2.3 million.

There was symphonic activity in Chattanooga as early as 1909, and by 1932 Arthur Plettner formed the Chattanooga Symphony Orchestra (CSO). Melvin Margolin was the ensemble's first conductor in 1933. From 1956 to 1965 Julius Hegyi served as conductor and was succeeded by Charles Gabor temporarily, until Richard Cormier replaced him. Cormier remained as musical director through the 1983 season. In 1985 the CSO merged with the Chattanooga Opera Association and Vakhtang Jordania was engaged as conductor and artistic director. Robert Bernhardt has been musical director of the association since 1992, performing 19 performances per season including three operas and four pops concerts.

The Jackson Symphony was founded in 1961 and conducted by James Petty until his retirement in 1985. After a season of guest conductors, Jordan Tang became musical director and conductor in 1986. The orchestra's size and budget currently ranks fifth in Tennessee. With only 32 percent of its members residing in Jackson, supporting musicians are hired from neighboring orchestras and colleges. The JSO currently schedules approximately 12 performances each season.

Roy C. Brewer, Memphis

SEE: COHN, WALDO; DEFRANK, VINCENT; GILBERT, NOEL; MUSIC; OPERA

T

T.O. FULLER STATE PARK is located southwest of downtown Memphis, off Tennessee Highway 61. Established in 1933, it is the nation's second oldest state park created for use by African Americans. The park currently contains 1,138 acres and includes Chucalissa Indian Village, a reconstructed Native American village and museum that interprets regional archaeology. Shelby County purchased the land from the Dover Barrett estate and called the original park the "Shelby City Negro State Park." In 1949 the county deeded the land to the state for one dollar.

In April 1939 Civilian Conservation Corps (CCC) Company 1464 arrived and began park development. The group, which had just finished a project at Chickamauga National Military Park near Chattanooga, had been reduced in size to 44 men, but rapidly expanded to as many as 175 members, with the hiring of local workers. The designation of the facility for African Americans influenced the site location, which took precedence over aesthetic appeal of the landscape. Allegedly, the park encompassed one of the state's most significant historical places—the legendary site where the Spanish explorer Hernando de Soto first viewed the Mississippi River. In addition, the CCC uncovered a Native American village and burial mound dating to the Mississippian period while conducting routine excavation for a swimming area.

Following discovery of the Native American site, construction ceased while archaeologists, under the supervision of the University of Tennessee, investigated the site. Once archaeologists stabilized the area, the CCC participated in the excavation of what became known as the "Fuller Mounds" project. This work continued until the advent of World War II. Major excavation activities resumed in 1952. The state redesignated the Fuller Mounds area as an unsegregated park and renamed it Chucalissa Archaeological State Park. In 1962 the state transferred approximately 187 acres, including the excavated site, to the Tennessee State Board of Education for research purposes. The University of Memphis administers the archaeological property today.

By 1943 T.O. Fuller Park contained very few recreational facilities. Early development of the park instead centered around excavation of the Chucalissa site. Limited state and federal funding prevented the hiring of additional labor, and diminishing CCC participation crippled further development. During the 1950s, the park acquired cabins, a lodge, bathhouse, swimming pool, athletic fields, a concession building, hiking trails, and picnic areas. In 1956 the City of Memphis funded construction of a segregated golf course for African Americans. Today this park retains a rich and fascinating history as one of Tennessee's most intriguing state parks, offering a wealth of information on Native American and African-American history.

Ruth D. Nichols, Nashville

SEE: CIVILIAN CONSERVATION CORPS; CHUCALISSA VILLAGE

TANNEHILL, WILKINS (1787–1858) was born near Pittsburgh, Pennsylvania. He moved to Nashville in 1808 and was involved in politics, intellectual pursuits, Masonic activities, journalism, and publishing for most of his life.

Tannehill's political interests led him to serve as an alderman in 1813 and as mayor of Nashville in 1825–1826. He was a trustee of Cumberland College, later the University of Nashville, in 1814–1821 and 1825–1832. As one of the most literate Nashvillians, Tannehill joined the Nashville Library Company around 1810 and served as the society secretary for the Tennessee Antiquarian Society. He launched his career as an author with the appearance of a volume for Masonic use in 1824. By 1827 he had published a more general work on the history of literature. This, and other activities, led to an honorary A.M. from the University of Nashville in 1828.

An especially well-known Mason, he held high positions more often than anyone else. In the later 1840s and early 1850s, he blended his interest in Masonry with his interest in education. Partially as a result of his influence, money from area Masons supported the Montgomery Masonic College in Clarksville, Jackson College in Columbia, and small colleges at Huntingdon and Macon in West Tennessee and at Bradley in East Tennessee.

Near the end of his career, Tannehill founded a newspaper and a monthly journal. The *Daily Orthopolitan,* begun on October 1, 1845, supported intellectual causes and scientific interests. *The Port Folio; or Journal of Freemasonry and General Literature,* began in July 1847 and supported various intellectual causes. Tannehill's last great venture before his death in 1858 was the Merchants Library and Reading Room, a subscription library formed in downtown Nashville in 1849.

James X. Corgan, Austin Peay State University
SUGGESTED READING: Alfred L. Crabb, "Wilkins Tannehill: Business and Cultural Leader," *Tennessee Historical Quarterly* 7(1947): 314–331

TATE, JOHN ORLEY ALLEN (1899–1979), teacher, poet, and critic, was associated with Tennessee most of his life and lived in the state for long periods, especially during his college years at Vanderbilt University (1918–1923) and during his last years in Nashville and Sewanee (1967–1979). Tate grew up thinking that he had been born in Virginia but, in fact, like others of the Fugitives and Agrarians, was born in Kentucky—in his case in Winchester in bluegrass country.

For all of his mature life Tate was a professional man of letters. First and foremost, he was a writer, not a teacher, although he taught often, especially at the University of Minnesota (1951–1966). Tate was known chiefly for his criticism and poetry, which was also the case of his two masters, T.S. Eliot and John Crowe Ransom. He also wrote biography (lives of Stonewall Jackson and Jefferson Davis); a novel, *The Fathers* (1940); translations; tributes to such friends as Eliot, Ransom, Andrew Lytle, and Cleanth Brooks; and memoirs. With Caroline Gordon he wrote and edited a superb textbook, *The Craft of Fiction* (1951). He edited *A Southern Vanguard* (1947) in memory of John Peale Bishop and a special issue of the *Sewanee Review* devoted to T.S. Eliot (1966) and did many other comparable projects during his long career, especially the second Agrarian symposium, *Who Owns America?*, edited with Herbert Agar (1936).

Much of Tate's most important editorial work was done at the *Sewanee Review* in the middle 1940s—first when he was an unpaid advisor to Andrew Lytle (1942–1944) and then as editor (1944–1946). Lytle and Tate decisively changed the *SR* from a journal devoted to the humanities to a literary and critical quarterly. Tate created the blueprint for the critical quarterly in "The Function of the Critical Quarterly" (*Southern Review,* 1936). Not only did he remake the *Sewanee Review,* but he advised John Crowe Ransom about the *Kenyon Review* and helped with the founding of the *Hudson Review* in 1948.

Tate was endlessly helpful to countless writers and editors. He and Caroline Gordon befriended such writers as Robert Lowell, Flannery O'Connor, and Walker Percy and such editors as J. E. Palmer and Frederick Morgan. Tate had a great gift for friendship and knew practically every important British, American, and European writer during the course of his mature life—from Eliot to Yevtushenko. His literary friends and acquaintances included, in addition to the Fugitives and Agrarians (especially Ransom, Donald Davidson, Robert Penn Warren, and Lytle), Ford Madox Ford, Malcolm Cowley, Hart Crane, William Meredith, Louis D. Rubin, Jr., Joseph Warren Beach, Howard Nemerov, Edmund Wilson, Katherine Anne Porter, Ernest Hemingway, Jacques Maritain, and Elizabeth Hardwick.

Tate charmed many women and was married four times—twice to the novelist Caroline Gordon and then to the poet Isabella Gardner and finally to a former student who had been a nun, Helen Heinz. He had a daughter, Nancy, by Caroline Gordon and sons, John and Ben, by Helen Heinz.

Tate's poems are traditional in form—rhymed and metered. The severe formality of his verse may have resulted in his not writing considerably more poetry. His collections began with *Mr. Pope* (1928) and ran through *The Mediterranean* (1936) and *The Winter Sea* (1944) to his *Collected Poems* (1977).

The criticism of Tate may well outlast his poetry, a matter that would frustrate and disappoint him. He was a great critic, and most of his criticism can be found in *Essays of Four Decades* (1968) and *Memoirs and Opinions* (1975). During his lifetime Tate was blessed in the critics who wrote about him—Cleanth Brooks, Louis Rubin, Walter Sullivan, Radcliffe Squires, Howard Nemerov, M.E. Bradford, Arthur Mizener, Frank Kermode, and Denis Donoghue. He has not been nearly so fortunate so far as a critical biography is concerned. A model citizen in the realm that he called the Republic of Letters, Tate was both feared and revered in his lifetime. Since then he has been reviled often, when not ignored.

George Core, The Sewanee Review
SEE: AGRARIANS; BROOKS, CLEANTH; DAVIDSON, DONALD; FUGITIVES; GORDON, CAROLINE; LITERATURE; LYTLE, ANDREW NELSON; RANSOM, JOHN C.; *THE SEWANEE REVIEW*; UNIVERSITY OF THE SOUTH; WARREN, ROBERT PENN

TAYLOR, ALFRED ALEXANDER (1848–1931), Governor and U.S. Congressman, was born in Happy Valley, Carter County, August 6, 1848, the second son of Emma Haynes and Nathaniel Green Taylor. His father was a farmer, Methodist minister, twice First District U.S. Representative, and Commissioner of Indian Affairs under Andrew Johnson. Alf Taylor entered politics as a Republican, while his younger brother, Robert L. Taylor, became a Democrat. Together the two became cornfield debaters, fiddlers, and adept story-tellers; Alf also gained a reputation as an avid fox hunter.

After attending academies in New Jersey and Carter County, Alf Taylor read law and was admitted to the bar. In 1874 he won a legislative seat on the Republican ticket. In 1881 he married Jennie Anderson of nearby Buffalo Valley and they became the parents of ten children.

In 1886 the Republicans tried to head off Democratic plans to nominate Bob Taylor for governor by nominating Alf Taylor. The Democrats nominated Bob Taylor anyway, and the resulting campaign became famous in Tennessee history as the "War of the Roses." Alf Taylor lost, but he won the First Congressional District seat in 1888, 1890, and 1892. He supported the McKinley Tariff and the Lodge Federal Elections Bill, a measure to protect African-American voting rights under federal supervision.

After leaving Congress, Alf started a new career, once more teaming with his brother Bob. The brothers launched a joint lecture tour, titling their lectures "Yankee Doodle" and "Dixie." More lecturing and farming followed, with unsuccessful periodic forays into politics. In 1920, when Taylor was 72 years old, a division within the Democratic party provided him with the opportunity to make another race for governor. To counter criticism of his age, he introduced a story about "Old Limber," an aging foxhound who beat the pack. Three sons and a friend formed the Old Limber Quartet that opened speaking engagements. Democrats had little political ammunition beyond Taylor's support for the Lodge Bill 30 years earlier. Taylor won 55.2 percent of the vote in the first gubernatorial election in which women voted.

Tennessee struggled with an outmoded tax system, and since 1910 the state had sunk steadily into debt. Taylor proposed a new tax commission, capable of compelling county assessors to set fair rates and taxing farm land according to its earning power. Taylor made recommendations for addressing the state's "Big Four" problems—taxation, rural schools, highways, and economy in government— but legislative opposition blocked his program. In addition, some critics of the Taylor administration question his failure to prevent the execution of Maurice F. Mayes, an African American accused of murdering a white woman in Knoxville.

In 1922 Taylor faced Austin Peay in his bid for a second term. The candidates' programs were not materially different, but Peay won. Taylor returned to his East Tennessee home, where he died in 1931.

Robert L. Taylor, Jr., Middle Tennessee State University

SUGGESTED READINGS: Robert L. Taylor, Jr., "Apprenticeship in the First District: Bob and Alf Taylor's Early Congressional Races," *Tennessee Historical Quarterly* 28(1969): 24–41 and "Tennessee's War of the Roses as Symbol and Myth," *Tennessee Historical Quarterly* 41(1982): 337–359

SEE: CARTER COUNTY; PEAY, AUSTIN; TAYLOR, ROBERT L.; WAR OF THE ROSES

TAYLOR, ANTOINETTE ELIZABETH (1917–1993), historian, was the first scholar to study woman suffrage in the South. Born on June 10, 1917, in Columbus, Georgia, she received a B.A. from the University of Georgia in 1938 and an M.A. from the University of North Carolina in 1940. She taught for one year at Judson College in Alabama, where she came across the six-volume *History of Woman Suffrage*. That discovery led to her life's work; she set out to tell the story of southern women's fight for the ballot.

Taylor earned her Ph.D. from Vanderbilt University in 1943 and published an article about woman suffrage in the Volunteer State in the *Tennessee Historical Quarterly* that same year. She subsequently published *The Woman Suffrage Movement in Tennessee*, a book based on her dissertation, in 1957. It was the first book-length study of southern women's struggle to win the right to vote.

After receiving her Ph.D., Taylor accepted a position at Texas State College for Women (now Texas Woman's University) and continued her research, chronicling the woman suffrage movement in each of the southern states and publishing more than a dozen articles. Taylor retired in 1981 but remained active, encouraging younger historians who built on her work. The Southern Association for Women Historians named an award, for the best article in southern women's history, in her honor.

She died at her home in Columbus on October 10, 1993. Her last essay, which recounted Tennessee's pivotal role in the ratification of the Nineteenth Amendment, appeared in *Votes for Women! The Woman Suffrage Movement in Tennessee, the South, and the Nation* (1995). The book is dedicated to her memory.

Anastatia Sims, Georgia Southern University

SEE: WOMAN SUFFRAGE MOVEMENT

TAYLOR, ELLISON HALL (1913–), Oak Ridge chemist and administrator since 1945, was born in Kalamazoo, Michigan, in 1913 and studied physical chemistry at Cornell and Princeton, earning his Ph.D. in 1937. After teaching chemistry at Utah and Cornell, in 1942 he joined the Manhattan Project at Columbia University, where he conducted research on concentrating heavy water and development of the gaseous diffusion process for enriching uranium, used at the K-25 plant in Oak Ridge. He joined the Chemical Division of Oak Ridge National Laboratory in 1945 and directed the Division from 1954 to 1974.

In addition to molding the Laboratory's physical chemistry programs, Taylor participated in its research. He and colleagues analyzed the effects of ionizing radiation on solid catalysts, stimulating new research ventures, and devised a novel approach to measuring the absorptive forces of gases on solids. Another memorable achievement was his invention, with Sheldon Datz, of a crossed molecular-beam scattering technique for studying chemical-reaction mechanisms. By sending two focused beams of gases at high speeds on a collision course, they were able to analyze the new molecules thus created, allowing scientists to better understand the dynamic interchange of atoms during chemical reactions.

Taylor retired from the Laboratory in 1974. He remained in Oak Ridge and continued his research as consultant to the Laboratory and to Atom Sciences, Inc.
Leland R. Johnson, Clio Research Institute
SUGGESTED READING: Leland Johnson and Daniel Schaffer, *Oak Ridge National Laboratory: The First Fifty Years* (1994)
SEE: OAK RIDGE NATIONAL LABORATORY

TAYLOR, PETER HILLSMAN (1917–1994), one of the most esteemed American writers of short stories in the twentieth century, was born January 8, 1917, in Trenton, Tennessee, to a notable political family. His maternal grandfather Robert Love "Bob" Taylor, a Democrat, served three terms as governor and as U.S. Senator (1907–1912), and his maternal great uncle was Alf Taylor, a Republican, who also served as governor and U.S. Congressman. The brothers opposed one another in the 1886 gubernatorial election, which became known as the War of the Roses.

When he was seven years old, Taylor's father, Hillsman Taylor, a prominent attorney, moved the family from Trenton to Nashville, then later to St. Louis, and finally to Memphis. Taylor's childhood encompassed an era of migration from the country and its traditional life to the developing cities of Tennessee. This movement, particularly among people of property, is often the background and sometimes the subject of his stories. He is particularly interested in the transformation of the families of prosperous landowners into the fully developed urban culture of industrial and financial corporations. Taylor does not view the transformation of the Old South into the New South as the replacement of one class by another but as the transformation of the ruling class itself: the same men who ran the plantations led the new industrializing South. This transformation, however, does include deracination, particularly felt by women and the young sons of these families.

Taylor was educated at Southwestern at Memphis (where the poet Allen Tate was his freshman English teacher), Vanderbilt (where he became friends with many writers of the Agrarian movement and the southern literary renascence), and Kenyon College (where he studied with John Crowe Ransom). He also did graduate study at Louisiana State University, which had become a center of literary creativity because of the teaching of Robert Penn Warren and Cleanth Brooks. During World War II he served in the U.S. Army in England. In 1943 he married the poet Eleanor Ross of North Carolina.

Taylor returned from the war to teach at The Woman's College of the University of North Carolina (later the University of North Carolina at Greensboro), where he returned to teach at various times in his career. His first book, *A Long Fourth and Other Stories,* was published in 1948 with an introduction by Robert Penn Warren. His second, *The Widows of Thornton,* was published in 1954. His earliest stories were published in the *Kenyon, Sewanee, Southern,* and *Virginia Quarterly* reviews. He reached his largest audience when he began to publish regularly in *The New Yorker.* By the early 1960s he had achieved a national reputation as a distinguished craftsman in the short story form, but he never sought a large audience as a popular novelist. The collection which solidified his reputation were *Happy Families Are All Alike* (1959) and *Miss Lenora When Last Seen* (1963). The title story of the latter book especially treats the movement of Tennessee families from the country to the city and cultural changes which attend that shift. Early reviewers of Taylor's stories compared them to Chekhov's because of their irony, humor, and intelligence—all of which keep nostalgia or sentimentality at bay. Taylor himself on several occasions remarked that as a young man he read not only Chekhov but also and particularly Turgenev. *The Collected Stories* (1969) was followed by *In the Miro District* (1977), whose title alludes to an early name for part of Middle Tennessee. In 1979 the National Academy and Institute of Arts and Letters awarded him its gold medal for literature. In 1986 he won the PEN Faulkner Award for *The Old Forest and Other Stories* (1985); the title story had been adapted into a short motion picture of the same name, directed by Steven John Ross (Pyramid Films, 1984). His last collection of stories was *The Oracle at Stoneleigh Court* (1993), which deals with Tennessee families living in Washington, D.C., as members of his own family had done.

Taylor also wrote novels, which he tended to think of as extended short stories. They include *A Woman of Means* (1950), *A Summons to Memphis* (1986), and *In the Tennessee Country* (1994). He thought of the short story as a particularly dramatic form. Again like Chekhov, writing stories led him to try to write plays. In 1961 he was an associate of the Royal Court Theatre in London. His published plays are *Tennessee Day in St. Louis* (1956), *A Stand in the Mountains* (1971), and *Presences: Seven Dramatic Pieces* (1973).

Taylor's career as a teacher of creative writing led him beyond Greensboro to Kenyon, Ohio State University, and finally the University of Virginia at Charlottesville, which he made his home in the last years of his life. He was a visiting teacher at Indiana, Chicago, Oxford, Georgia, and Memphis State. In the later 1960s, he taught briefly at Harvard but turned down a permanent position there because he feared the public would view him primarily as a teacher rather than a writer. Nevertheless he headed the creative writing program at Virginia until his retirement. In 1984 he received a $25,000 senior fellowship from the National Endowment for the Arts in recognition of his extraordinary contribution to American literature. Throughout much of his career he maintained summer homes in Tennessee either at Sewanee or Monteagle Assembly, called Owl Mountain Springs in some of his stories. Taylor died November 2, 1994, in Charlottesville and was buried in Sewanee.

D.E. Richardson, University of the South

SUGGESTED READING: C. Ralph Stephens and Lynda P. Salamon, eds., *The Craft of Peter Taylor* (1995)

SEE: AGRARIANS; BROOKS, CLEANTH; LITERATURE; MONTEAGLE ASSEMBLY; RANSOM, JOHN CROWE; TATE, JOHN O. ALLEN; TAYLOR, ROBERT L.; WARREN, ROBERT PENN

TAYLOR, PRESTON (1849–1931), African-American businessman and religious leader, was born in Shreveport, Louisiana, on November 7, 1849, of slave parents. Taylor served as a drummer boy in the Union army during the siege of Richmond, Virginia. After the Civil War, he traveled throughout the North, settling in Mount Sterling, Kentucky, where he served as a minister. Taylor also secured a contract to build several sections of the Big Sandy Railway from Mount Sterling to Richmond, Virginia. After this business venture and extensive work in the Christian (Disciples of Christ) church, he moved to Nashville in 1884. He soon emerged as one of the city's most influential African-American business and religious leaders.

In 1887 he purchased 37 acres of land at Elm Hill Pike and Spence Lane on which he established Greenwood, Nashville's second oldest black cemetery. In 1888 he founded Taylor Funeral Company at 449 North Cherry Street (now Fourth Avenue). In 1905 Taylor purchased land at the corner of Spence Lane and Lebanon Road where he established the Greenwood Recreational Park for Negroes. The park contained elaborate fountains, gardens, a baseball park, rides, band stands, and special attractions. The annual State Colored Fair, which attracted as many as 14,000 attendees in a single day, was held on the site. Taylor's horse-drawn "pleasure wagons" met

streetcars at the Green-Fairfield Street turnaround and took customers to the Lebanon Road park entrance. Twice mysterious fires threatened to destroy the park. Otherwise, there was no challenge to Greenwood Park until Hadley Park, the first city-owned park for blacks, opened in 1912.

Taylor also served as minister of the Gay Street Christian Church, founded in 1855 as the African-American congregation of the white Vine Street First Christian Church. Following an 1891 controversy, Taylor and a part of the congregation left the Gay Street Colored Christian Church and established a church in a doctor's office building on Spruce Street (now Eighth Street). In 1903 the congregation completed a church building on Lea Avenue near Lafayette Street. After Taylor's death, the two congregations united into today's Gay-Lea Christian Church, located on Osage Street.

Among his other activities, Taylor organized the 1917 National Colored Christian Missionary Convention. He also was involved in the establishment of the Tennessee State Agricultural and Industrial State Normal School. He helped to organize several other Nashville black businesses, including the One Cent (Citizens) Savings and Trust Company Bank. As a businessman, undertaker, and influential minister, Taylor was one of Nashville's most powerful black leaders.

Taylor married Georgia Gordon, one of the original Fisk Jubilee Singers. Their son, Preston, died as an infant in 1891, and Georgia Taylor died in 1913. Taylor then married Ida D. Mallory. When Taylor died in 1931, week-long ceremonies were held before his interment in Greenwood Cemetery. In 1951 a public housing project was named in his honor.

Joseph E. McClure, Nashville

Source: Adapted from Bobby L. Lovett and Linda T. Wynn, eds., *Profiles of African Americans in Tennessee* (1996)

SEE: CITIZENS BANK; NASHVILLE; TENNESSEE STATE UNIVERSITY

TAYLOR, ROBERT L. (1850–1912), three-term Governor and one-term U.S. Senator, was born into a political family in Carter County, in Tennessee, July 31, 1850. At the time, his uncle Landon Carter Haynes, a Democrat, was serving as Speaker of the Tennessee House of Representatives, and his father, Nathaniel Greene Taylor, a Whig, farmer, and Methodist minister, had lost a congressional race to Andrew Johnson the year before. Haynes later became a Confederate Senator, and Nathaniel Taylor served two terms in Congress before receiving an appointment as Commissioner of Indian Affairs under President Andrew Johnson.

Influenced by these models and encouraged by his mother, Emma Haynes Taylor, Bob Taylor grew up in the Watauga River Valley, the third son in a

Compliments of The Nashville Tennessean

HANDS OFF THIS TOGA!

ROSIN.

Senator "Bob" Taylor

NASHVILLE ROOM, METROPOLITAN PUBLIC LIBRARY. COPY PHOTOGRAPH BY JUNE DORMAN

Robert Love Taylor as caricatured by C. H. Wellington of The Tennessean.

family of four daughters and six sons. The second son, Alfred A. Taylor, became identified indelibly with Bob as a political rival for elected office. Alfred Taylor eventually became a Republican, while Bob Taylor joined the Democratic Party of his mother and Uncle Landon. "Democracy," as he called it, eventually became his civil religion. In their youth the two boys conducted cornfield debates, learned to fiddle, and exchanged humorous stories, all of which would figure in their later political life.

Bob Taylor attended several schools, ending at East Tennessee Wesleyan University (in Athens), where his father taught for a time. Dramatics attracted Taylor, and he exhibited a remarkable talent for storytelling. Following college, he farmed, manufactured bar iron, and read law in Jonesborough. During this time, he courted Sallie Baird of Asheville, North Carolina, but delayed marriage to launch his political career.

In 1878, after Alf Taylor lost the Republican nomination for the First Congressional District, Democrats encouraged Bob Taylor to run in the general election.

Although the First District was Republican, Taylor triumphed, evidently attracting Alf's disgruntled following and setting a pattern of sibling political rivalry as well as establishing his image as a vote getter. In 1881 Taylor lost the election for the U.S. Senate in the General Assembly, but the experience inaugurated a lifelong quest for a senate seat. In this period, he helped found the Johnson City *Comet,* served as a presidential elector in 1884, and was appointed pension agent in Knoxville in 1886. That same year, he ran for governor against his brother Alf, the Republican nominee, in a race that became known as the War of the Roses. Joint campaigning, humor, and general goodwill marked the contest, which Bob Taylor won.

Taylor disliked executive office. Criticism cut him, and his association with the New South (business-oriented) wing of his party brought opposition from the Bourbons, who spoke for agrarian interests and states' rights. Taylor's style generally straddled the issues, but his support for federal aid to education and his appointments of New South men infuriated the Bourbons. In 1888 the Bourbons attempted to block his renomination and stymied his bid for a second term for 38 ballots. Taylor also garnered criticism for excessive pardoning, but though he released more prison inmates than his predecessor, he pardoned fewer than his two successors. He demanded a reformatory and, when the legislature failed to provide one, pardoned youthful offenders. The most important legislation of his second term brought no credit to Taylor or his party. In 1889 the legislature, controlled by the Democrats, passed a series of election laws, including the poll tax and registration laws, that discouraged voting and virtually disfranchised the poor, especially African-American Republican voters. Taylor supported this legislation.

In 1891 Taylor left office in ill health. During his convalescence on Alf Taylor's Nolichucky River farm, he acquired a new vocation. Alf Taylor suggested lecturing, a career his brother launched later that year. Success followed and, with it, financial well-being for his family. But financial success was not enough. In 1893 Taylor unsuccessfully challenged William B. Bate, a Bourbon Democrat, for his U.S. Senate seat. Following a joint lecture tour with Alf Taylor, Bob accepted another Democratic nomination in 1896 for the governorship, the office he disliked. Taylor's motives for acceptance were mixed: he may have entered to win favor for his next Senate race but more likely his commitment to his civil religion—his party—impelled him.

Taylor won, but the legislature did not repay him with a senate seat when Senator Isham G. Harris died in office. During his third term, he presided over the state's centennial celebration. Ill and under a financial strain, Taylor considered resigning and went into retirement after a single term, "fly[ing] away to the haven of [his] native mountains . . . safe from the talons of some old political vulture, safe from the slimy kiss and the keen dagger of ingratitude."[1]

Taylor returned to lecturing. His wife died; he remarried, divorced, and married again. In 1905 Taylor founded *Bob Taylor's Magazine*, a periodical aimed at southern readers and carrying, among many other things, reprints of several of his lectures and other personal writing. His interest in industrialization and education remained, especially in what he called "high technological training." Also, in 1905, Senator Bate, his former opponent, died. Taylor lost the legislative contest to succeed him, but the following year the Democrats held a primary for nomination to Edward Ward Carmack's Senate seat. Taylor defeated Carmack and merged his publication (which became *The Taylor-Trotwood Magazine*), before leaving for Washington. After three contented years in the Senate, Taylor recognized that his party faced defeat in the 1910 governor's race. As in 1896, when a divided party looked to Taylor, the factionalized Democratic party offered him the nomination. He reacted as he did in 1896 and accepted the nomination he did not want, risking the Senate seat that had always been his goal. Taylor lost the race to Ben Hooper, the Republican candidate. Less than two years later, in 1912, while still in the Senate, Taylor died, following a gallstone attack.

Robert L. Taylor, Jr., Middle Tennessee State University
CITATION:
(1) Robert H. White, ed., *Messages of the Governors of Tennessee, 1883–1899*, VII (Nashville, 1967), 702.
SUGGESTED READINGS: Dan M. Robison, *Bob Taylor and the Agrarian Revolt in Tennessee* (1935); Robert L. Taylor, Jr., "Demogoguery, Personality, and the Gospel of Democracy: Family Influence on Centennial Governor Taylor," *Tennessee Historical Quarterly* 55(1996): 160–175
SEE: BATE, WILLIAM B.; CARTER COUNTY; DISFRANCHISING LAWS; JOHNSON CITY; TAYLOR, ALFRED A.; TENNESSEE WESLEYAN COLLEGE; WAR OF THE ROSES

TELEVISION AND MOVIE PERFORMERS from Tennessee have enjoyed distinguished careers, as already shown in this volume's individual entries of Clarence Brown, Archie Campbell, Fred Coe, Tennessee Ernie Ford, Delbert Mann, Patricia Neal, Dolly Parton, Elvis Presley, Dinah Shore, and Oprah Winfrey. The state's music industry helped to create many of these opportunities. During the 1940s and 1950s stars from the Grand Ole Opry, such as Roy Acuff, appeared in a series of Hollywood B-movies with a country music theme and/or setting. In the 1950s and 1960s weekly television programs, featuring Grand Ole Opry stars like Ernest Tubb and Porter Wagoner, were syndicated nationally and many shows were produced in Nashville. During the late 1960s and early 1970s network television programs with a country music theme, such as the influential and long-running *Hee Haw* and the *Johnny Cash Show*, were produced in Nashville. *Hee Haw* featured Archie Campbell, Grandpa Jones, and Minnie Pearl, all Hall of Fame members. After his television show, Cash appeared in and produced movies. The *Barbara Mandrell Show* in the early 1980s provided television airtime for a host of country music performers. Today the most important Tennessee-based television network is The Nashville Network, which has featured such Nashville music industry stalwarts as radio and television host Ralph Emery, gospel music performer Gary Chapman, and talk show hosts Lorianne Crook and Charlie Chase. Writing the Oscar-winning theme music for the movie *Shaft* opened acting opportunities for rhythm-n-blues artist Isaac Hayes, who has appeared in such cult classics as *Escape from New York.*

The acting careers of many other Tennesseans, however, have had little reliance on music industry associations. Memphis in particular is either the birthplace or home of several important actors. Kathy Bates took Oscar and Golden Globe awards for *Misery.* After a distinguished stage career, Morgan Freeman won a Golden Globe for *Driving Miss Daisy.* Both Bates and Freeman have received major Hollywood roles in the 1990s. In 1971 Cybill Shepherd of Memphis first achieved stardom in the acclaimed *The Last Picture Show* and has since appeared in several major Hollywood films including *Taxi Driver.* Shepherd is best known for her television work, and her hits in *Moonlighting* during the 1980s and *Cybill* in the 1990s rank her as the state's most successful television actress. Other Memphis actors of note include George Hamilton, who has starred in movies and television since the 1960s, and Shannen Doherty, best known for her role in *Beverly Hills 90210,* a popular television show of the 1990s. Game show host Wink Martindale, a native of Jackson, graduated from the University of Memphis and hosted local radio programs before achieving stardom in daytime television.

Polly Bergen and John Cullum of Knoxville both have enjoyed distinguished careers on stage and screen. Bergen has starred on Broadway, in Hollywood movies, and on television in her career of 50-plus years. In 1957 she took an Emmy for her performance in *The Life of Helen Morgan.* Cullom won a Tony Award for *On the Twentieth Century* and starred in the program *Northern Exposure* in the 1990s. Since the 1980s Knoxville's David Keith has had a successful film and TV career. Another Knoxville native in Hollywood is director Quentin Tarantino, who is highly regarded for his recent work in *Reservoir Dogs, Pulp Fiction,* and *Jackie Brown.* One of the stars of the latter two movies is Samuel L. Jackson of Chattanooga.

Nashville native Cynthia Rhodes performed at Opryland before receiving roles in several 1980s movies, including *Flashdance*. In addition to her role in television's *Designing Women,* Annie Potts of Nashville has had major Hollywood roles, including the comedy-hit *Ghostbusters*. Claude Jarman, Jr., won an Oscar in 1946 for *The Yearling.* U.S. Senator, Nashville attorney, and Lawrenceburg native Fred Thompson also is a well-respected actor with films such as *Marie* and *Hunt for Red October* to his credit. A Hollywood actor turned Tennessee politician was Tex Ritter (1905–1973), a Texas native who gained fame as a singing cowboy in many movies of the 1930s. In his later years Ritter developed a country music following and joined the Grand Ole Opry in 1965. A resident of Nashville in this period, he unsuccessfully ran as a Republican for the offices of Governor and U.S. Senator. His son, John Ritter, enjoyed a huge television success in the late 1970s as a member of the cast of *Three's Company* and has since appeared in many Hollywood films and television programs.

Smaller towns also have produced notable actors. Michael Jeter of Lawrenceburg won a 1990 Tony Award for *Grand Hotel*. Dixie Carter of McLemoresville starred in the *Designing Women* television program. Sondra Locke of Shelbyville received an Oscar nomination for *The Heart is a Lonely Hunter,* appeared in several hit movies during the 1980s, and recently directed the movie *Ratboy.* Cherry Jones, a native of Paris, established the American Repertory Theatre in 1980 and won a Tony Award for *The Heiress.* Clarksville native Frank Sutton's best known role was the sergeant in *Gomer Pyle USMC.* Savannah native Elizabeth Patterson received an Oscar nomination for *Hail, the Conquering Hero,* a Preston Sturgis satire, in 1941. Ally Walker, star of NBC's *Profiler* and the movie *Kazaam,* was born in Tullahoma.

Carroll Van West, Middle Tennessee State University
SUGGESTED READING: Stephanie Vozza, "Home Grown Heroes," *Tennessee Bicentennial Arts and Entertainment Festival Program* (1996), 68–73

SEE: CAMPBELL, ARCHIE; COE, FREDERICK; FORD, TENNESSEE ERNIE; MANN, DELBERT; MINNIE PEARL; NEAL, PATRICIA; PARTON, DOLLY; PRESLEY, ELVIS; SHORE, DINAH; TENNESSEE IN FILM; WINFREY, OPRAH

TELLICO BLOCKHOUSE, in Monroe County, was a federal outpost on the southwest frontier, constructed in 1794–1795 at the confluence of the Tellico and Little Tennessee rivers, adjacent to the site of the earlier Fort Loudoun. For protection from aggressive settlers, the dwindling number of Overhill Cherokees in the Little Tennessee River country sought to re-establish an alliance with the newly created federal government. Federal officials in Philadelphia were also interested in a Cherokee alliance and envisioned that

a series of frontier posts would help to control and "civilize" the Native Americans. In 1794 Territorial Governor William Blount agreed to a request from Hanging Maw to build a new federal post, which would eventually serve as a military fort and trading post. At Tellico Blockhouse, federal and territorial officials implemented the Factory Act of 1795, which was a Washington administration plan to assimilate the Indians by maintaining federal "factories," or trading posts, where Indians would receive fair exchange for their furs as well as learn farming and mechanical skills.

Implementation of the Factory Act in 1795–1796 required close and at least open relations between the soldiers, traders, and the Cherokees. John McKee was the first Indian Agent at Tellico; a later agent, Silas Dinsmoor, provided cotton cards, spinning wheels, looms, and cottonseed in the hope of teaching the Cherokees how to spin and produce their own cloth. In returning for the trade goods and training, the Cherokees provided food, furs, and other valuable items. The Duke of Orleans (later King Louis Philippe of France) visited the post in 1799 and observed that the Cherokees "continually supply Tellico with game, eggs, fruits in season, etc. so that the Tellico market is always well stocked, and is certainly one of the best forts in the region. The availability of women makes it very pleasant for the soldiers. Just now there is an abundance of strawberries, which the women and girls bring in and sell at ninepence the gallon."[1]

In 1805 federal officials and the Overhill Cherokees negotiated a new land cession and treaty at Tellico Blockhouse. This agreement moved the federal agency south to the mouth of the Hiwassee River. In 1807 the federal government abandoned Tellico and moved its remaining operations to the Hiwassee River post, which was the new center of the Overhill Cherokee settlements.

Today the site of Tellico Blockhouse is part of the Fort Loudoun State Historical Area. The archaeological remains of the post are intact and partially exposed to indicate the size of the fort and the range of activities that took place there.

Carroll Van West, Middle Tennessee State University
CITATION:
(1) Carroll Van West, *Tennessee's Historic Landscapes: A Traveler's Guide* (Knoxville, 1995), 198.

SEE: MONROE COUNTY; OVERHILL CHEROKEES; SOUTHWEST TERRITORY; TREATIES

TEMPERANCE. In the early twentieth century, temperance was the key issue in Tennessee politics. The roots of the temperance movement date to Jacksonian America, when temperance reform appeared in conjunction with capitalistic economic efforts. For the next eight decades temperance leaders directed their efforts toward the weaning of agricultural and industrial laborers from consumption of alcohol in order to improve their working habits. The upper class was encouraged to exhibit restraint in alcohol consumption in order to set an example for the working class. Before and after the Civil War and into the twentieth century, southern leaders wanted to deny liquor to blacks and poor whites out of fear that alcohol would inflame passions and increase crime. The *Knoxville Sentinel* admitted on February 6, 1907: "If the southern states adopt prohibition it will be largely because of the necessity of keeping whiskey from the colored man."

Throughout the era, Protestant churches enthusiastically embraced prohibition as did the holiness movements that emerged from the early nineteenth century revivals. The revivals preached an asceticism that induced converts to abstain from the evils and pleasures of this world in order to achieve holiness and prepare themselves for the eternal world. In the context of Protestant revivalism, alcohol was both an unnecessary pleasure and one of the world's evils.

In 1826 Marcus Morton founded the American Temperance Society in Massachusetts to advocate total abstinence from the use of distilled spirits. Three years later, the first Tennessee temperance societies met in Kingsport and Nashville. The Nashville and Davidson County Temperance Society, auxiliary to the American Temperance Society (ATS), enrolled prominent citizens and held quarterly meetings. As with the ATS, the Nashville group agreed to abstain from the use of distilled spirits. Both societies discouraged the use of alcohol by their employees, and the Kingsport group pledged themselves not to vote for candidates who used liquor in their campaigns.

Support for temperance increased throughout the 1830s and 1840s. Two newspapers, the Nashville *Western Philanthropist* and the Maryville *Temperance Banner,* were devoted to highlighting the evils of alcohol in the 1830s. In 1848 the General Assembly chartered the Sons and Sisters of Temperance, and these groups received strong statewide support. One town in DeKalb County, Temperance Hall, was named for the building in which the men of the organization met in 1849.

In 1853 Nashville hosted a temperance convention, which urged Tennessee to follow Maine's example of statewide prohibition. In 1854 the State Senate passed a bill to put the question of prohibition to the voters, but the measure was defeated in the House. The next year, the liquor question became part of the gubernatorial campaign, foreshadowing its major importance in politics at the turn of the century. Democratic nominee Andrew Johnson rejected restrictions on alcohol as a threat to individual liberty, while his opponent Meredith P. Gentry favored local option. Prohibitionists rejected both positions as too liberal.

Early statutory efforts focused on the regulation of a legitimate trade without attempting to prevent the making or consumption of alcohol. In 1831 the Tennessee General Assembly began to exert some regulation of the liquor trade by authorizing licenses for operating saloons. Under the requirements of the law, applicants gave bond to the county court clerk and secured a license for a $15 tax. The number of saloons increased fivefold under the law. In 1838, under pressure from constituents, including a petition signed by 374 Nashville women, the General Assembly repealed the earlier measure and passed a "Quart Law," which restricted the sale of alcohol to containers of one quart or more. This law applied only to liquor; wine, beer, and cider could be sold without restriction, as had been the case under the old law. Eight years later in 1846, this poorly enforced law was replaced by another, which again licensed saloons to sell liquor by the drink. Saloon keepers could not sell to minors, if their parents forbade it in writing, or to slaves without permission from their owners.

During Reconstruction, Radical Republican Governor William G. Brownlow, a vituperative Methodist minister, editor, and longtime supporter of temperance, predicted that alcohol would "bring down upon us, as a State, Sodom's guilt and Sodom's doom."[1] Attempts to include local option measures in the Constitution of 1870 failed twice. In 1873 a local option bill passed both houses of the General Assembly, only to be vetoed by Governor John Brown.

Anti-liquor groups in Tennessee had more success forbidding the sale of liquor near the premises of schools, hospitals, and churches. The first such law, passed in 1824, restricted liquor sales near churches. In 1877 the legislature enacted a law forbidding the sale of alcohol within four miles of chartered rural schools. In 1887, while attention was focused on a prohibition amendment to the state constitution, the legislature amended the Four-Mile Law to prohibit the sale of intoxicating liquors within four miles of any country school, virtually banning the liquor business in rural Tennessee.

The seemingly more important event centered on the public referendum on a constitutional amendment to ban the manufacture and sale of intoxicants within the state of Tennessee. First introduced in the 1885 General Assembly, the resolution passed two different legislatures, as required by law. In February 1887 the Tennessee Temperance Alliance held a convention in Nashville to organize county committees statewide to generate public support for the amendment when presented to the voters for the final referendum. Methodist, Baptist, and Presbyterian churches participated in the campaign. In Morgan County, for example, Reverend A.B. Wright, a circuit rider in the Upper Cumberland region, served as chairman. For two weeks, he made speeches in favor of the prohibition amendment to groups assembled in schoolhouses and churches. When he arrived at an engagement scheduled at the Baptist Church in Sunbright, he discovered the preacher and his father had "locked us out," and he was forced to speak at a nearby building. Throughout his crusade, Wright found that most voters favored liquor, a perception that was confirmed by the September vote. David Lipscomb, leader of the Christian Church and editor of the *Gospel Advocate*, urged his members to boycott the polls because he did not believe Christians should become involved in politics. When the vote was counted, 145,00 voted against the prohibition amendment, and 118,000 voted for it. "A dark day for Tennessee," lamented Wright.[2]

In addition to state efforts to obtain prohibition, efforts continued with the formation of a National Prohibition Party. In 1872 James Black headed the Prohibition Party ticket, but drew only 5,000 votes nationally. The party organized in Nashville in 1883, but never offered a serious threat to the campaigns of the established parties. In 1888 General Clinton B. Fisk, the Prohibition presidential candidate, received fewer than 6,000 votes in Tennessee, while J.C. Johnson, the gubernatorial candidate, polled approximately 7,000 votes. The election of 1890 brought the Prohibition Party its greatest success. Gubernatorial candidate, D.C. Kelley, a Methodist minister in Gallatin and a former Democrat, received 11,000 votes. The party newspaper, the Nashville *Issue*, was encouraged by this showing "for another tilt with the enemy of God and man" as stated in its issue of November 6, 1890. Both Democrat and Republican parties ignored the alcohol issue in this election and the next; between 1892 and 1896 the Prohibition Party disintegrated.

One unusual aspect of the temperance movement in Tennessee involved the founding of Harriman in 1890, the only city founded on the principles of industry and prohibition. Frederick Gates of New York, a wealthy real estate developer, wanted to create an industrial city where alcohol was forbidden in order to prove the advantages of such an arrangement. He moved his family to Chattanooga in 1885 and created the East Tennessee Land Company in 1889. General Clinton B. Fisk was named president of the land company. The company purchased several thousand acres of land in Roane County, considered an ideal site for an industrial city, with both river and railroad transportation readily available. In February 1890, after an extensive advertising campaign, the great sale of town lots took place. In three days, 300 lots were sold to a crowd of approximately 3,000 people from 18 states. The deeds stipulated that the use of the site to manufacture, store, or sell liquor would render the deed null and void, and the property would revert to the land company.

Harriman never achieved the economic success envisioned by its founders. Shortly after its auspicious beginning, Harriman and the land company suffered financial losses in the panic of 1893. A tornado in 1896 caused considerable damage. The coal reserves were not extensive, and the flood of 1929 destroyed much of the town. However, no deed ever reverted to the land company because of the use of liquor. In 1893 American Temperance University opened in Harriman; 1907–1908 was the last year the school operated under this name. By its second year of operation, 345 students from 20 states enrolled, and 200 to 300 students studied at the temperance school each year.

Rugby, a utopian community founded in Morgan County in 1880 by English novelist Thomas Hughes, also included restrictions against alcohol in its bylaws. Wine was the only alcoholic beverage allowed in the colony, and the Rugby Total Abstinence Society was created to enforce the rule.

By the latter part of the nineteenth century, the Protestant churches of Tennessee had become leaders in the temperance movement, using spurious arguments from the Bible to support the charge of alcohol as a moral evil. The 1892 Tennessee Baptist Convention voiced the sentiments of several Protestant denominations: "The saloon is the enemy of all good, the friend of all evil."[3] In 1896 Nashville religious groups, including the Baptists, Methodists, and Presbyterians, called a conference to plan a renewed fight against alcohol. They organized the Local Option League as the best practical means of eliminating liquor. However, they soon encountered stiff opposition. Both political parties declined to endorse the local option position, and the General Assembly refused to enact a local option law. Some urban newspapers, including the *Chattanooga Times*, the Memphis *Commercial-Appeal,* and the Nashville *American*, opposed prohibition.

From the earliest days of the temperance movement, the saloon had been the symbol of the evil of liquor and the watering hole of the working class. Thus, in the eyes of upper class reformers, the saloon was the den of iniquity that fostered and promoted drinking among that class. If the saloon could be eliminated, then the drinking habit of the laboring class might dry up. Acting on this idea, the Anti-Saloon League was created in 1895. Seeking the cooperation of Protestant churches and industrial leaders, the League eventually adopted the idea of a constitutional amendment to establish prohibition.

Tennessee prohibition leaders quickly embraced the Anti-Saloon League. Tennessee Methodists attended the 1896 convention of the League. In 1899 the Tennessee Local Option League adopted the name of the Anti-Saloon League. E.E. Folk, editor of the *Baptist and Reflector*, was its first president. By

1901 approximately 60 league chapters with 5,000 members were in Tennessee; in 1902 the *Anti-Saloon Journal* was published. That same year the Knoxville *Journal and Tribune* declared that the Anti-Saloon League had become a power in Tennessee politics.

The Tennessee League chose the Four-Mile Law as its vehicle to bring about prohibition. The Peeler Act of 1899 extended the Four-Mile Law to towns "hereinafter incorporated" with populations less than 2,000. The Adams Bill of 1903 extended the restrictions of four miles to all towns of 5,000 population or less, which incorporated or re-incorporated after passage of the bill. Many towns immediately moved to recharter in order to eliminate liquor, and in most towns where the issue was put to a vote, the results created prohibition. Sparta, in White County, voted dry, but tiny Walling voted to remain wet, 16–1. Lynchburg also voted wet, thanks to the influence of distiller Jack Daniel. By the middle of 1903, all towns of less than 5,000 population except six had voted dry. The nine larger cities remained wet, for a total of 15 wet municipalities in 11 counties.

The Pendleton Act of 1907 extended the Four-Mile Law to the larger cities, and by the end of the year only Memphis, Chattanooga, Nashville, and LaFollette were wet. When Knoxville decided the question, a carnival atmosphere pervaded. Church bells rang each hour of the day, a parade was staged in the morning, and University of Tennessee students appeared riding a water wagon in support of prohibition. In LaFollette, citizens voted to abolish the city charter to gain prohibition, and the General Assembly passed a bill to that effect. However, LaFollette representative W.H. Potter opposed prohibition, and the governor vetoed the bill.

The Women's Christian Temperance Union (WCTU) formed its first Tennessee branch in Memphis in 1876. In 1882 the statewide organization was created with 39 "unions" and 511 members. In 1887 the national convention met in Nashville; the group was welcomed by Governor Robert L. Taylor. By 1908 there were 183 unions and 4,037 members in Tennessee. *Open Door,* the monthly publication of the state WCTU, had been published in Knoxville since 1899. This group always favored statewide prohibition, and, with this goal in sight in 1907, the WCTU state convention urged passage of the measure. Meeting in Nashville after the conclusion of the state convention, the national WCTU called for national prohibition. In 1908 prohibition was the major topic of the gubernatorial campaign. Both parties were split by the issue. Malcolm Patterson and Edward Carmack contended for the Democratic nomination. Patterson had the support of party leaders and of the liquor interests. Carmack, who had never been a prohibitionist, and who as editor of the Nashville *Democrat* and the *American* criticized the Prohibition Party, was looking for

an issue to oppose Patterson. With a campaign that favored statewide prohibition, Carmack became the candidate of the Anti-Saloon League and the WTCU. Patterson defeated Carmack in the Democratic primary with 52 percent of the vote, although Carmack thought that the election was dishonest.

The Republicans divided between Newell Sanders, a Chattanooga businessman and chairman of the state Republican Committee, and John C. Houk, former Second District congressman. The Republican convention in Nashville was so contentious that fistfights occurred and property was destroyed. Weeks later, the Sanders group nominated George N. Tillman for governor. He lost to Patterson by 20,000 votes, but the election gave the prohibitionists a majority in the state legislature.

In 1908 Carmack became editor of the *Nashville Tennessean,* a newspaper started in 1907 by Luke Lea as a prohibitionist journal. Carmack used his new position and his newspaper as a platform to express his bitterness about the election. He attacked Patterson and Duncan Cooper, Patterson's advisor. Cooper and Carmack had been on opposite sides in several political races. In 1908 the two, along with Cooper's son, Robin, met armed on a Nashville street. Robin Cooper and Carmack fired shots; Carmack was fatally wounded. The Coopers were convicted of murder, but Governor Patterson issued a pardon.

The murder of Carmack created a martyr for the prohibitionist crusade, although the rivalry between Carmack and Cooper had little to do with liquor. Silena M. Holman, president of Tennessee's WCTU, proclaimed that "the bullet that ended Carmack's life will write prohibition on the statute books of Tennessee."[4] Church leaders and prohibition crusaders used the emotion stirred by Carmack's murder and the governor's pardon of the Coopers to pressure the General Assembly for statewide prohibition. In January 1909 Senator O.K. Holladay of Putnam County offered a bill to forbid the sale of liquor within four miles of any school in the state; an identical bill was introduced in the House. Governor Patterson denounced the measure: "For a State . . . to attempt to control what the people shall eat and drink and wear . . . is tyranny, and not liberty."[5] The bill passed over Governor Patterson's veto and went into effect in 1909. A second law prohibited the manufacture of intoxicating beverages.

"Tennessee had been redeemed," wrote Luke Lea's *Nashville Tennessean* on January 13, 1909, but it was soon obvious that this was not the case. Officials in the four largest cities made little effort to stop the liquor trade. Memphis bars operated openly; Nashville bars closed only on Sunday. In 1912 both cities again licensed liquor dealers. One alcohol trade newspaper claimed that more liquor was sold in Tennessee than before prohibition.

The Democratic party was a victim of the prohibition crusade. Split between the Independents who favored prohibition and the Regulars who opposed it, the party became so weak that Republican Ben W. Hooper was elected governor for two consecutive terms, 1911–1915, becoming the first Republican governor since Alvin Hawkins in 1881. Hooper wanted to administer the prohibition laws, but the governor actually did not have the means to enforce them. He called two special sessions of the legislature to enact laws to implement prohibition, and the second session passed statutes which would close some saloons and prevent transportation of liquor between counties. The Tennessee Supreme Court invalidated the second law, and the law aimed at the closing of saloons did not eliminate the sale of liquor. Slack enforcement of the laws, bootleg dealers, and locker clubs kept the state wet. In 1915 the State Senate impeached the Shelby County attorney general and a Shelby County judge for malfeasance. The following year, the courts removed Mayor Edward H. Crump from office for his refusal to enforce prohibition in Memphis; Nashville Mayor Hilary E. Howse was removed for the same reason.

In 1917 the "bone-dry bill" of Governor Thomas C. Rye completed the prohibitionist campaign in Tennessee. This legislation made illegal the receipt or possession of liquor and prohibited the transportation of liquor into or out of the state. Ratification of the Eighteenth Amendment to the U.S. Constitution by Tennessee was a perfunctory matter in 1919. Tennessee's senators and representatives in the Congress had supported the prohibition amendment. By an overwhelming vote—only four negative votes in both houses—the General Assembly approved national prohibition. Only the *Chattanooga Times* spoke against the Eighteenth Amendment. Commenting on the destruction of American freedom, the newspaper sarcastically wondered in its issue of January 16, 1920, if the nation might next pass a law "prohibiting nature from allowing fruit juices and ciders to ferment while in storage."

National prohibition did not work in Tennessee in the 1920s any better than state prohibition had since 1909. By the time of repeal in 1933, Tennessee was discouraged with prohibition. In 1939 the state enacted local option, allowing counties and cities to permit package sales of wine and liquor by referendum.

W. Calvin Dickinson, Tennessee Technological University

CITATIONS:

(1) Robert H. White, ed., *Messages of the Governors of Tennessee, 1859–1867* (Nashville, 1959), 579.

(2) J.C. Wright, ed., *Autobiography of Rev. A.B. Wright* (Cincinnati, 1896), 261.

(3) Tennessee Baptist Convention, *Minutes,* 1897, p. 25.

(4) Paul E. Isaac, *Prohibition and Politics: Turbulent Decades in Tennessee, 1885–1920* (Knoxville, 1965), 160.

(5) Stephen Ash, ed., *Messages of the Governors of Tennessee, 1907–1921* (Nashville, 1990), 67.

SUGGESTED READINGS: Eric R. Lacy, "Tennessee Teetotalism: Social Forces and the Politics of Progressivism," *Tennessee Historical Quarterly* 24 (1965): 219–241; Grace Leab, "Tennessee Temperance Activities, 1870–1899," East Tennessee Historical Society's *Publications* 21(1949): 52–68; Leslie F. Roblyer, "The Fight for Local Prohibition in Knoxville, Tennessee, 1907," East Tennessee Historical Society's *Publications* 26(1954): 27–37; Thomas H. Winn, "Liquor, Race, and Politics: Clarksville During the Progressive Period," *Tennessee Historical Quarterly* 49(1990): 207–217; Margaret Ripley Wolfe, "Bootleggers, Drummers, and National Defense: Sideshow to Reform in Tennessee, 1915–1920," East Tennessee Historical Society's *Publications* 49(1977): 77–92

TEMPLE ADAS ISRAEL, a historic Jewish synagogue listed in the National Register of Historic Places, is located at the corner of Washington and College streets in Brownsville. Built in 1881–1882, and veneered in brick ca. 1920, the Gothic Revival-styled temple represents the impact of Jewish immigrants on West Tennessee towns and commerce in the years immediately following the Civil War. In the 1860s Joe Sternberg emigrated from Germany to the United States, eventually settling in Brownsville. He brought a century-old Torah, and by 1867 Jacob and Karoline Felsenthal provided a room in their Brownsville home for the keeping of the Torah. Together with Sternberg and other Jewish residents in Haywood and neighboring counties, they organized the Adas Israel congregation. Until the dedication of Temple Adas Israel in 1882, the congregation met in local homes, including those of the Anker and Rothschild families. This Reformed Jewish congregation never had a rabbi and, from its founding to the 1970s, it had only four lay readers. The Jewish community in rural and small town West Tennessee decreased dramatically in the twentieth century, but members kept Temple Adas Israel open. At the time of its listing in the National Register in 1979, Temple Adas Israel was the oldest such building in West Tennessee and possibly the oldest yet remaining in the state.

Carroll Van West, Middle Tennessee State University

SEE: HAYWOOD COUNTY; JEWS, URBAN TENNESSEE

TEMPLE, EDWARD S. (1927–), TSU Tigerbelles track coach, became Tennessee's most honored and accomplished track and field coach. His famous Tigerbelles Women's Track Club of Tennessee State University (TSU) won 23 Gold, Silver, and Bronze Olympic medals, 34 national team titles, and 30 medals in the Pan American Games.

Temple's Tigerbelles won their first medal in the 1952 Olympic Games, when 15-year-old Barbara Jones became the youngest woman to win an

Olympic gold medal in track and field. The team won several medals in the 1956 Olympics in Melbourne. Tigerbelle Wilma G. Rudolph became the first female athlete to win three gold medals during the 1960 Olympic Games in Rome. Wyomia Tyus, another Tigerbelle, became the first athlete to win back-to-back gold medals in the sprints in 1964 and 1968.

Temple became the most internationally recognized track and field coach in the history of Tennessee sports. In 1958 Temple trained the U.S. Women's Track Team in the first-ever American-Soviet Union track meet. In 1975 he coached the women's team for the first China-U.S.A. track meet. He served as head Women's Track Coach for two U.S. Olympics teams. Temple became a member of the National Track and Field Hall of Fame, the Tennessee Sports Hall of Fame, the Pennsylvania Sports Hall of Fame, the TSU Sports Hall of Fame, and received the Helms Award. He served on every major local, state, and national sports committee, including the U.S. Olympic Committee. TSU named its outdoor track in Temple's honor.

Edward Stanley Temple was born September 20, 1927, in Harrisburg, Pennsylvania, to Christopher and Ruth N. Temple. An all-state athlete, he attended Tennessee State University, where he completed bachelor's and master's degrees. In 1993 Coach Temple retired after 43 years at Tennessee State University. To commemorate Temple's achievements and international stature, TSU inaugurated the annual Edward S. Temple Seminars on Sports and Society in October 1993.

Bobby L. Lovett, Tennessee State University
SEE: RUDOLPH, WILMA; TENNESSEE STATE UNIVERSITY

TEMPLE, OLIVER PERRY (1820–1907), author, East Tennessee economic promoter, and trustee of the University of Tennessee, was born on January 27, 1820, near Greeneville, Tennessee. An 1844 graduate of Washington College in Washington County, Temple studied law and gained admittance to the bar in 1846. During the Civil War, Temple dedicated his time to aiding the Unionists of East Tennessee and helping organize the East Tennessee Relief Association. In 1866 Governor William G. Brownlow appointed Temple chancellor of the eighth district, a position he held until 1878.

In his later years, Temple promoted the interests of farmers by organizing the East Tennessee Farmer's Convention. During his 54 years as a trustee for East Tennessee University, later the University of Tennessee, Temple promoted agricultural and mechanical education to supplement the institution's liberal arts program. He was instrumental in obtaining federal funding for higher education and worked tirelessly to transform the university into the state's land grant institution.

Temple became a spokesman for the promotion of regional growth. He recognized East Tennessee's economic potential, encouraging the construction of a transportation system and the development of the area's coal and iron resources.

Temple also worked to preserve East Tennessee's distinctive heritage in his books, *The Convenanter, the Cavalier, and the Puritan; East Tennessee and the Civil War;* and *Notable Men of Tennessee,* which was published posthumously. Temple died in Knoxville on November 2, 1907.

Kathleen R. Zebley, University of Tennessee, Knoxville
SEE: UNIVERSITY OF TENNESSEE

TEMPLETON, JOHN MARKS (1912–), financial executive, investor, and philanthropist, was born in Winchester, Tennessee, on November 29, 1912, the son of Harvey and Vella Handly Templeton. He graduated from Yale University in 1934 and from Oxford University in 1936, where he studied law as a Rhodes Scholar. After working briefly as an investment counselor at Fenner & Beane in New York, Templeton served from 1937 to 1940 as vice president of the National Geophysical Company in Dallas, Texas. Selling his investment in this company in 1940, he founded his own initially New York-based investment company, Templeton Dobbrow and Vance, Inc. (becoming the Templeton family of mutual funds), and began his distinguished career as a financial manager and investor. Templeton pioneered the idea of investing globally in stocks of non-American companies, developing in the process the most successful international stock mutual fund (managing billions of dollars in investments), the Templeton Growth Fund, beginning in 1954. Other funds were added over the years. In the course of his career, Templeton came to be recognized as one of the century's greatest financial figures and investors, a major influence on financial markets and the securities industry worldwide. In 1992 the Templeton firm became a subsidiary of Franklin Resources, one of the world's largest investment management companies, and Templeton retired from active participation.

Templeton's significant interest in religion, influenced by his religious upbringing, led him to establish the Templeton Prize for Progress in Religion in 1972. Regarded as the "Noble Prize for religion," the prize seeks to promote creative approaches and progress in the field of religion. For his religious and philanthropic works, Templeton was knighted by Queen Elizabeth II in 1987.

Ned L. Irwin, East Tennessee State University
SEE: FRANKLIN COUNTY

TENNCARE, initiated by Governor Ned Ray McWherter on January 1, 1994, replaced the jointly federal-state funded Medicaid program in Tennessee. TennCare's mission was twofold: to cut costs and expand health care coverage. Twelve statewide managed care organizations (MCOs) were established to negotiate with physicians and hospitals to fund medical expenses at a level aimed to reduce cost. The previously uninsured working poor and those uninsurable because of preexisting illnesses, estimated at 500,000 to 700,000, were also brought under TennCare's umbrella on a sliding scale payment basis.

Problems erupted almost as soon as the plan took effect. Chief culprits were insufficient reimbursement and underfunding. Reimbursement for care was distributed annually to the MCOs for each enrollee. Treatment of the poor and chronically ill exceeded reimbursement, and patients for whom hospitals received no reimbursement continued to appear at emergency rooms. Collection of premium payments lagged behind estimates, and only $18 million out of $45 million owed was recovered.

Adding to its woes, TennCare was thrust upon an unprepared medical community, and many physicians refused to see TennCare patients. Over time physicians adapted to the new system, raising participation to 97 percent statewide. Physician complaints now fasten on the lack of standardization of rules and regulations among MCOs, which necessitates compliance with several lists of approved hospitals, specialists, pharmacies, and drugs.

Hopes to cover 1.3 million people statewide were dashed when enrollment was closed at 1.2 million, leaving 6.3 percent of Tennessee's population still uninsured. TennCare, however, significantly curbed the growth of health care costs in the state.

Jayne Crumpler DeFiore, University of Tennessee, Knoxville
SEE: MCWHERTER, NED RAY; MEDICINE

TENNESSEANS IN THE CALIFORNIA GOLD RUSH. The discovery of gold in California in 1848 inspired at least four or five thousand young Tennesseans to cross the country. Many of them, rejected for service in the Mexican War because of the overabundance of volunteers, saw this as a chance to enjoy the adventure denied them in 1846. Others, who had gone to war, viewed the gold rush as an opportunity to see and exploit the lands acquired as a result of their conquest.

Most of the early forty-niners made the crossing in companies organized to pool their resources and share the risks of travel. Coming from communities all across the state, most were young men who expected to collect their riches in one or two years and return home. The few women who undertook the journey usually went with their families and planned to settle and remain in the West.

Tennesseans usually followed one of two routes to California. Overland travelers began the crossing at one of the Arkansas or Missouri outfitting towns. The faster route involved traveling by ship across the Gulf to the Isthmus of Panama, traversing the Isthmus, and sailing to San Francisco. The overland crossings remained remarkably free of notice from the Native Americans, whose lands they crossed, but the western deserts and the Sierra Nevada regularly brought suffering and death. The Isthmus passage was easier, but seasickness, shipboard inactivity, and inadequate diets also took a toll.

Tennessee miners discovered that extracting gold was backbreaking work, typically yielding meager results. Most of their success came from working deposits of loose gravel in stream beds called placers. Several Tennessee companies tried "quartz mining," the recovery of bits of gold from quartz rock, but the process was so inefficient that most abandoned quartz operations by the mid-1850s. Later, the development of efficient stamping mills and improved methods of separating the gold from pulverized rock reignited interest in quartz mining. The new developments were capital intensive, however, and few forty-niners were able to take advantage of them.

Like others, Tennesseans fared poorly in the mines, and most returned home with little or no money. The gold rush was a vastly different experience for many who remained in California and amassed fortunes from ventures in agriculture, real estate, banking, and commerce.

Tennesseans made important contributions to the development of California statehood and government. Peter Hardeman Burnett, who had come to the nearby Oregon territory in 1846, hastened to the gold country and chaired several public meetings that led to the convention that organized the state of California and called for election of its officials. He received vital support from William McKendree Gwin, who had left Washington, D.C., with the personal goal of seeing California become a state and himself one of its two U.S. Senators. Gwin was the undisputed leader of the convention, and when the state was organized, he was elected to his first of four terms in the U.S. Senate, becoming California's most powerful political leader. Burnett won election as the first governor. He appointed William Van Voorhies secretary of state, and the General Assembly elected Richard Roman state treasurer. In addition to these former Tennesseans, two of the original 16-member state senate, David F. Douglass and W.R. Bassham, came from the Volunteer State. Voters chose Jack Hays and Ben McCullough, former Texas Rangers, but both native Tennesseans, to be the first sheriff of San Francisco and Sacramento counties, respectively. Other Tennesseans filled offices at all levels of California government.

Walter T. Durham, Gallatin
SUGGESTED READING: Walter T. Durham, *Volunteer Forty-Niners, Tennesseans and the California Gold Rush* (1997)

**TENNESSEE 200 STATE BICENTENNIAL CELE-
BRATION.** The year 1996 marked Tennessee's bicentennial. In honor of the occasion, the General
Assembly created Tennessee 200, Inc., and charged it
with developing bicentennial programs. Local and
traveling programs were developed to bring the celebration to all areas of the state.

Tennessee Treasures, a traveling historical
exhibit, inaugurated the bicentennial activities in
1993–1994 by visiting all 95 counties. The Bicentennial Capitol Mall State Park, a 19-acre urban park
located north of the State Capitol, was constructed
as the permanent monument to the bicentennial. The
mall was dedicated on Statehood Day, June 1, 1996.
Spirit of Tennessee Bicentennial Train, a traveling
exhibit focusing on Tennessee's developments in
commerce and industry, made some 35 stops across
the state in 1996. The Bicentennial Arts and Entertainment Festival presented a month-long program
highlighting the state's symphony orchestras,
operas, theater and ballet companies. Beginning on
Volunteer 200 Day on June 1, 1995, which was a state
day of volunteer service, citizens developed local
projects and participated in programs planned by
the state organization, including a Civil War Heritage Trail, an archives training prram, and a World
War II Veterans Survey. Grants from Tennessee 200
provided funds for local projects.

Carolyn Brackett, Nashville

SEE: BICENTENNIAL CAPITOL MALL STATE PARK; TEN-
NESSEE CENTENNIAL EXPOSITION

TENNESSEE ACADEMY OF SCIENCE, founded in
1912, has provided direction for Tennesseans on a
number of science issues. The Academy organizes
symposia, manages on-going programs in many
fields, and communicates with the national scientific
culture. The Tennessee Academy of Science is affiliated with two national societies and seven Tennessee societies.

The first two gatherings of the Academy in 1912
drew 29 participants, primarily college professors
and government scientists. Those first members
planned twice-yearly meetings and chose an Executive Committee to oversee the organization. Organizing on the eve of World War I, the Academy
grew slowly, and for a brief period one member
funded the publication of *The Science Record*. Three
issues of the *Record* had appeared before the Executive Committee assumed the journal's modest debt
in March 1913. Thereafter the Academy published
Transactions of the Tennessee Academy of Science in
1914 and 1917.

The Academy grew slowly, averaging 16 new
members per year. In 1923 the Academy began publishing a quarterly *Journal of the Tennessee Academy of
Science*, which continues to the present. The Academy

experienced renewed vigor after 1925 as a result of
the Scopes Trial and the publicity surrounding the
state's anti-evolution law. Strong support for Scopes
and a favorable reception of the new journal brought
in 125 new members annually for the period 1925
through 1928.

On the eve of the Great Depression, the Academy
launched several new programs, several of which
survived the economic decline. One new program
created an Academy library with a professional
librarian. A more successful innovation developed a
research center, the Reelfoot Lake Biological Laboratory, which remained in operation from 1935 to 1977.
For many years reports from the lab were offered as a
separate series of Academy publications before being
republished in the *Journal*.

Initially the Academy met twice annually, in the
spring and fall, and presented talks on diverse subjects. In 1930 the Academy held its first symposium,
a program on Tennessee caves. During the 1930s the
Academy also held separate meetings for a Botany
Section, a Geology Section, and a Physics Section. In
addition, some sections held special field meetings.
Flexible arrangements were made for luncheons, banquets, and other special events.

Although World War II provided a stressful
period for the Academy, a vigorous Junior Academy
emerged early in the decade, and new sections in
Chemistry, Mathematics, Zoology, and Psychology
appeared. Soon sectional programs prospered; still
the overall program declined, perhaps a reflection of
the gas and food rationing that inhibited travel and
the number of scientists who entered military service.
During the 1940s the spring meeting permanently
ended. From 1912 to 1944 the Academy published
proceedings of the meetings and provided materials
for the organizational archives. There were no published or archival records for 1945, but records
resumed in 1946, although archival materials became
less detailed.

The Academy began admitting African Americans
in the 1940s, and the nature of scientific research
changed to reflect the atomic age. Women had been a
part of the Academy since its founding in 1912, but
the increase in the number of women in the work
force during World War II brought an expansion in
female membership. The Academy joined a national
trend toward the funding of science education projects by private companies, academic societies, and
federal agencies. The Tennessee Academy awarded
certificates to secondary science teachers and supported high school students' research projects. The
Academy still recognizes secondary teachers, funds
secondary school research, and awards prizes to
accomplished students.

In 1952 the Psychology Section, which had
formed in 1947, left the Academy and became the

Tennessee Psychological Association, one of the Academy's seven affiliated societies. An Engineering Section started in 1955; Medical Sciences began in 1960; and in 1962 the Science and Mathematics Teachers Section was created. The Academy participated in the national interest in science education that continued through the 1970s and supervised statewide federally funded training programs for secondary school teachers. Teacher certification emerged as an Academy concern, as did a resurgence of anti-evolution legislation.

As part of the educational thrust of the Academy, it strengthened the Junior Academy and in the 1950s it formed a Collegiate Division to serve the research needs of college students. The *Journal* added two short-lived sections to serve high school readers and the Collegiate Division. In addition, the Academy established a Visiting Scientist Program to send senior scientists to area high schools. In some years the programs reached as many as 3,500 secondary students. The Collegiate Division always met with the fall annual meeting, but soon also sponsored spring meetings in each of the three Grand Divisions. In recent years approximately 125 college students participate annually. The Visiting Scientist Program, the Collegiate Division, and the Junior Academy issued handbooks, directories, and other publications to spotlight the organization's accomplishments and programs.

Academy membership, with 971 members, reached an all-time high in 1963. It also reached new audiences such as medical professionals and teachers. Much of the growth reflected federal and state funding. After federal funding ended, the State of Tennessee began subsidizing science education programs in 1968. With state funding, the meetings were well attended, and the *Journal* flourished. At the 1975 annual meeting, a symposium on a focused topic—genetic engineering—replaced the diffuse general program; similar symposiums became the norm in future meetings. In 1981 state funding stopped; most programs survived, but they were less active. Money problems may have intensified a long-term decline in enrollment. The membership bottomed at 483 in 1983, when state funding resumed. Today membership stands at 703, signaling a renewed vigor, despite another loss of state money in the 1990s.

The Academy continues to grow and change. A History of Science Section began in the 1980s, followed by an Ethics in Science and Technology Section in the 1990s. Biological programs recently diversified to develop sections in Microbiology and Cell and Molecular Biology. Several other sections have undergone name changes to reflect new research interests.
James X. Corgan, Austin Peay State University
SEE: SCIENCE AND TECHNOLOGY; SCOPES TRIAL

TENNESSEE ANTI-NARCOTIC LAW OF 1914. Tennessee's first anti-narcotic law was largely the work of Dr. Lucius Polk Brown, Tennessee's Food and Drug Commissioner. It went into effect on January 1, 1914, and reflected the moral reform atmosphere of the Progressive era. The law went further than the Harrison Act, the existing national law, in that it limited dispensing or distribution of drugs to veterinary surgeons, dentists, registered physicians, and pharmacists who received a legitimate prescription. The law specifically applied to opiates and included a provision that allowed addicts to obtain a permit entitling them to maintain their habits by registering with the state. Supporters of the law believed that cutting off the supply would bring considerable suffering to poor addicts and drive drug traffic outside of the law. Tennessee's permit system did not include cocaine because of the belief that it was habitual and not as dangerous as other drugs such as morphine.

According to Brown's statistics, 2,370 addicts registered during the first year of the law's operation. Addicts included all races and both genders, but two-thirds of the registrants were women. Brown found women prone to laudanum addiction, but men used more drugs than women, with the exception of laudanum. Fifty-nine percent of registered male addicts were between the ages of 22 and 55, which Brown ascribed to the commonly held view that men from the age 25 to 35 were most prone to take up "dissipations." Polk found that over half of the active cases of addiction in Tennessee were due to poor administration of drugs by doctors, not the result of recreational usage. African Americans used fewer opiates and more cocaine than white men. In East Tennessee the ratio of addicts to non-addicts was one addict in every 1,359, while in West Tennessee the ratio was one in only 928. Brown presented no figures for Middle Tennessee. Brown estimated that in 1914 approximately 5,000 addicts were in Tennessee, out of a national population of 269,000.

The annual cost of the drugs used in Tennessee was placed at $145,000, "a sheer waste of money" according to Brown. The use of recently introduced heroin was mainly restricted to boys and men as a result of debauchery. Brown believed that "in every place where a number of boys and young men are employed together there will be a certain amount of heroin addiction." He argued that the sale of heroin should be restricted drastically. Brown believed the "drug addict is . . . more to be pitied than censured, and every effort should be made to help him attain a fulfillment of the desire . . . . The drug addict is a sick man both physically and mentally, and should be . . . treated as a sick man and not as one always willfully delinquent."[1]
James B. Jones, Jr., Tennessee Historical Commission

CITATIONS:

All quotes taken from Lucius P. Brown, "Enforcement of the Tennessee Anti-Narcotic Law," *American Journal of Public Health* 5(1915): 323–337.

SUGGESTED READINGS: James B. Jones, Jr., "Selected Aspects of Drug Abuse in Nineteenth- and Twentieth-Century Tennessee History, circa 1830–1920," West Tennessee Historical Society *Papers* 48(1994): 2–23; Margaret Ripley Wolfe, *Lucius Polk Brown and Progressive Food and Drug Control: Tennessee and New York City, 1908–1920* (1978)

TENNESSEE AQUARIUM in Chattanooga opened May 1, 1992, as the first major freshwater life center in the world dedicated to the understanding, conservation, and enjoyment of rivers. The exhibits guide visitors on a journey from the Tennessee River's source in the Appalachian Mountains, through its midstream, to the Mississippi Delta, and on to the great rivers of the world in Africa, South America, Siberia, and Asia.

The journey takes visitors through living environments that accurately re-create the habitats of over 7,000 fish, birds, amphibians, reptiles, mammals, and insects that rely on the river for survival. Visitors leave the Tennessee Aquarium with a new appreciation of the world around them and the animals that inhabit their own backyard.

Just as the Tennessee Aquarium allows visitors to see below the surface, the Tennessee Aquarium IMAX 3D Theater takes viewers from miles above the earth to the depths of the sea. The 3D Theater, one of only 14 in the world, opened in May 1996, and is a natural extension of the educational environment guests experience in the Aquarium.

The IMAX Center also features the Tennessee Aquarium Environmental Learning Lab, using advanced computer, video, distance learning, and multimedia technologies to teach about the environment. This unique educational center blends high-tech programs with hands-on learning for children and adults to learn about the global environment. It is the first learning center in the country to integrate science programs of a major aquarium and IMAX 3D Theater.

Patti Jo Lambert, Tennessee Aquarium
SEE: CHATTANOOGA; TENNESSEE RIVER SYSTEM

TENNESSEE ARTS COMMISSION. In 1965 the Tennessee House of Representatives created a Commission on the Performing Arts to document and study artistic facilities in the state. Two years later, the study recommended the establishment of the Tennessee Arts Commission. Since its creation, the commission has assumed responsibility for arts development in Tennessee and, from time to time, such facilities as the Appalachian Center for Crafts. Today, in addition to its other activities, the commission supervises and administers the Tennessee State Museum. Bennett Tarleton has served as the commission's executive director since 1984. The Tennessee General Assembly, the National Endowment for the Arts, and private contributors provide the funding for the Arts Program division of the commission. The commission invests public money in Tennessee's not-for-profit arts industry; provides services to citizens, artists, and arts organizations; and undertakes leadership projects to enhance Tennessee's cultural life.

The commission is composed of 15 members, broadly representative of all fields of the performing, visual, and literary arts. The governor appoints the commission members from among the state's citizens who have demonstrated a vital interest in the performing, visual, and literary arts. At least one, but no more that two members must be selected from each U.S. congressional district. In 1998 Jim Hill of Chattanooga was serving as commission chairperson.
Bennett Tarleton, Tennessee Arts Commission
SEE: ART; TENNESSEE STATE MUSEUM

TENNESSEE BAR ASSOCIATION, founded in 1881, has been an influential voice in shaping Tennessee law and standards of legal education, lawyer discipline, and continuing education. Today over 7,000 of the state's 12,000 lawyers belong to this voluntary association that can boast of a president (Edward Terry Sanford) who later served on the U.S. Supreme Court and others who held important judicial and governmental posts.

An elite group of 69 lawyers formed the association on December 14, 1881, to serve as a catalyst for reforming the legal profession which had been in decline and disarray for 20 years. Licensing standards had become so loose that virtually any man could become a lawyer with minimal effort and knowledge. Formation of the Tennessee Bar Association (TBA) was part of a national movement to uplift professional standards, marked by founding of the American Bar Association (ABA) in 1879.

Annual meetings since 1881 have featured notable speakers, such as U.S. Supreme Court justices, and presentations by members on current legal topics. From the beginning, TBA has pressed for reform of Tennessee law; a speaker at its first meeting in 1882 called for woman suffrage. The TBA allowed women members before the ABA did; in 1998 it elected its first woman president, Pamela L. Reeves.

The signal achievement in the early years was implementation of the written bar examination (1904); later came the requirement of a high school diploma (1925) and two years of law study prior to taking the bar examination (1934). The association pushed for higher judicial salaries starting in 1900, a radical overhaul of the state constitution as early as 1897 (this finally occurred in 1953), and recodification of statutes in 1917 (fully achieved in 1955). The association endorsed measures such as juvenile court law (1917), compensation for job-related injuries (1919), and general sessions courts replacing justices of the peace (1937). TBA has worked to harmonize Tennessee law with other states, e.g. Model Corporation Act in 1969.

The association formally adopted the American Bar Association's 1908 code of ethics in 1912. Technically, the code and its successors only applied to association members until the State Supreme Court mandated the ABA's code of professional responsibility in 1970. TBA assisted local bar associations in actions against unethical lawyers and was instrumental in the establishment of an agency to hear complaints and discipline lawyers in 1976.

The association offered the first formal continuing legal education program in 1941 and was instrumental in the establishment of mandatory CLE in 1987. In addition to the CLE sessions offered at each annual convention, TBA sponsors 80 educational programs a year on diverse topics.

The *Tennessee Bar Journal*, published six times a year, is a descendant of TBA proceedings published since 1882, making it one of the state's oldest continuous publications. Daily operations are handled by a staff of 12, including an executive director, headquartered in Nashville. The association's Web site provides membership information and fosters member-to-member communication.

Lewis L. Laska, Tennessee State University

SEE: GOVERNMENT; LAW; SANFORD, EDWARD T.

TENNESSEE CENTENNIAL EXPOSITION, held in Nashville in 1897 to celebrate Tennessee's one hundredth anniversary of statehood, was one of the largest and grandest of a series of industrial expositions that became hallmarks of the New South era. Modeled in particular after the Chicago Columbian Exposition in 1893, it featured exhibitions on the industry, agriculture, commerce, and transportation of the state as well as displays on the educational and cultural achievements. Torn by jealousy among the three Grand Divisions and stymied by the deadening effects of the 1893 depression, the state's centennial celebration could not begin until one year after the one-hundredth anniversary of statehood. A group of Nashville businessmen took the lead in planning the exposition. The L&N Railroad provided major backing for the event which became, in part, a public relations effort to appease widespread public discontent with the railroad monopolies. Two chief officers of the Nashville, Chattanooga, and St. Louis Railroad, John W. Thomas and Eugene C. Lewis, served as president and Director General, respectively, of the exposition.

The exposition grounds were an important experiment in city planning and park design. They were built upon the model of the Chicago Columbian Exposition, which inspired the City Beautiful Movement. Laid out on the grounds of a former race track about three miles west of the city center on West End Avenue, the exposition featured neoclassical buildings, a manmade lake, curvilinear roads, and elaborate landscaping. Centennial City was also granted full powers as a separate city, and it became a model of progressive era "good government," with its strict regulations of liquor and vice.

The Centennial Exposition was, above all, a celebration of technological progress brought by the machine age. Major exhibits were devoted to Commerce, Agriculture, Machinery, and Transportation. The typical exhibits included a relic of some outmoded method or contraption and the modern technology that had replaced it. Thus, an old cotton bale press powered by a plodding mule was set in "striking contrast" to the steam-powered model of the present day, and an old hand loom or spinning wheel put beside new electric powered textile machinery. There were in addition automatic brick makers, telephones, gasoline engines, electric dynamos, electric lights strung on every building, all offered as evidence of the promise of technological progress in the New South.

The exposition also gave much attention to the social progress of the "new woman," the "new Negro," and the modern child. Tennessee women played a particularly prominent role in the exposition, which served to galvanize women reformers of the Progressive era. The Woman's Building featured displays of domestic arts and home economics and sponsored visiting lectures by Jane Addams and other leaders of the emerging feminist movement. The Negro Building was filled with displays of African-American products and educational achievements. Advocates of racial progress and cooperation were invited to address the exposition, and several Negro Days were set aside to honor the free, educated, aspiring "new Negro." The celebration of black progress at the Exposition, along with the strict segregation of the races, reflected the paradoxical racial politics of the New South. A Children's Building put on display children's art work and hosted lectures on school reform. Throughout the exposition there was an ever-present emphasis on improvement through science, technology, and education.

Along with the celebrations of technological and social progress were major exhibits devoted to art and history. To house the Fine Arts Building an exact scale model of the Parthenon of ancient Greece was erected at the center of the exposition grounds. It soon became the most admired building on the grounds. Symbol of Nashville's traditional claim as the "Athens of the South," this plaster and wood version of the Parthenon remained standing until the

1920s when it was rebuilt in concrete. The history of the state was also honored by the Tennessee Historical Society, which displayed artifacts and manuscripts from the state's early history. The Ladies' Hermitage Association, the Colonial Dames, and the Daughters of the American Revolution joined in displaying artifacts depicting the state's history. The Confederate Memorial Association, a women's organization devoted to raising monuments to the Lost Cause, organized a special display on the "late war," while the Grand Army of the Republic offered artifacts depicting the northern side of the war. One of the chief functions of this and other southern expositions was to put on display the New South spirit of reconciliation with the North. Among the more dramatic examples of this was the Confederate Veteran's Day, which drew 16,000 former rebels to Nashville to honor the Lost Cause and celebrate the South's new place within the Union.

In addition to the exhibits displaying Tennessee's economic, social, and cultural progress, the Centennial Exposition included a midway with exciting rides and exotic shows for the entertainment of the families attending. The Tennessee Centennial Exposition opened May 1, 1897, and closed six months later. It drew approximately 1.8 million visitors, the largest of any southern exposition. Afterwards the Exposition grounds were converted to Centennial Park, which became a centerpiece of Nashville's new city park system and a major magnet to the westward growth of suburban Nashville. A number of civic organizations that sprang from the Exposition continued to meet and influence politics and reform in Nashville and the state. Women reformers joined the Centennial Club to work on municipal reform and city beautification. Others who had cooperated in the successful planning of the exposition brought a new confidence in the Progressive era's faith in improvement through technology, education, and the expertise of business leaders.

Don H. Doyle, Vanderbilt University

SUGGESTED READINGS: Don H. Doyle, *Nashville in the New South* (1985); Herman Justi, ed., *Official History of the Tennessee Centennial Exposition* (1898)

SEE: CONLEY, SARA WARD; GRAND ARMY OF THE REPUBLIC; HOPE, JOHN; LADIES' HERMITAGE ASSOCIATION; PARTHENON; TENNESSEE HISTORICAL SOCIETY

TENNESSEE CIVIL WAR NATIONAL HERITAGE AREA.

In November 1996 President William J. Clinton signed legislation authorizing creation of a new national heritage areas program. The concept of a national heritage area focuses on significant themes in American history which can be better understood in a more comprehensive setting. Nine applications from 41 states were approved, with one being for the National Heritage Area on the Civil War in Tennessee. In October 1997 Congress authorized funding for the heritage areas. The Tennessee heritage area is the largest of all the national heritage areas with more square miles included than the others combined.

Tennessee's successful application was prepared by the Center for Historic preservation at Middle Tennessee State University and was introduced in Congress by Representative Bart J. Gordon in 1995 to coincide with a proclamation by Tennessee Governor Don Sundquist urging citizens and communities to preserve Tennessee's endangered Civil War resources.

Possible plans over a ten-year implementation period include an emphasis on the non-battle aspects of the Civil War era: training, logistics, religion, agriculture, transportation, economy, governance, the home front, industry, medical care, and the impact of geography. Several sub-theme areas will examine the war experience in different parts of the state. All Tennessee counties and communities will be able to take advantage of the project. The National Heritage Area on the Civil War in Tennessee will emphasize interpretation, visitor support, and community partnerships. No funds may be used for land acquisition or capital projects. The Center for Historic Preservation (www.histpres@frank.mtsu.edu) has been designated by Congress to coordinate and manage development of the heritage area.

James K. Huhta, Middle Tennessee State University

SEE: CENTER FOR HISTORIC PRESERVATION

TENNESSEE CIVIL WAR VETERANS' QUESTIONNAIRES

form an extensive collection of documents housed in the Tennessee State Library and Archives in Nashville and useful for the study of the state's nineteenth century social conditions. Its 1,650 respondents dictated their memories of life before, during, and after the Civil War, thereby providing a rich source valuable to genealogists, Civil War students, and southern scholars alike.

Largely collected between 1915 and 1923, the questionnaires solicited information from Tennessee's Confederate and Union veterans, just over 1,200 of whom were native to the state prior to 1861; the remainder had resided in states across the South. Each questionnaire constituted a short, uniform autobiography. It requested from an aged soldier information on his antebellum lifestyle: how much land did his family own; did his family have slaves and how many; what kind of house did his family occupy and how many rooms did it have; what kinds of activities were engaged in by his father and his mother; what type of work did he do as a boy; and how much education did he receive? This was followed by a series of questions devoted to the veterans' opinions concerning social class relations: did white men respect manual labor; did slave owners and non-slaveowners have friendly or antagonistic relations; was slave ownership a factor in politics; and were there opportunities for a poor man to advance economically? The men were then encouraged to relate their Civil War experiences. They were specifically asked to name their regiments; tell when and where they enlisted; and recount their first battle. This was followed by an invitation to discuss briefly their military engagements, their camp life, and, if relevant, their experiences in hospitals and prisons. The questionnaire concluded with a request that each veteran recount his life since the Civil War stating his occupation, where he lived, his church relationship, and whether he held a civic office.

Gustavus W. Dyer and John Trotwood Moore, archivists at the Tennessee State Library, collected the questionnaires between 1915 and 1923. Dyer, an eccentric Vanderbilt sociology professor, developed the questionnaire, but collected few of them before his political position was terminated. Appointed librarian in 1919, Moore revived the project and secured the vast majority of the responses. Defenders of the antebellum aristocracy, both men hoped that the questionnaires would provide the raw material for a "true history of the Old South" demonstrating the essential class harmony among the planters, the plain folk, and the poor. Ironically, when Tennessee's normally inarticulate people were given voice, they suggested significant differences in life styles, cultural expectations, and social attitudes across the nineteenth century's class structure.

In 1985 the Southern Historical Press (Easley, South Carolina) published a transcription of the questionnaires in six volumes. Although faithful to each questionnaire, its compilers abridged collateral material filed with them—newspaper articles and personal letters. This project was unique to Tennessee; no other state made a similar survey of its Civil War veterans.

Fred Arthur Bailey, Abilene Christian University

SUGGESTED READING: Fred A. Bailey, *Class and Tennessee's Confederate Generation* (1987)

SEE: MOORE, JOHN T. AND MARY D.; TENNESSEE STATE LIBRARY AND ARCHIVES

TENNESSEE COLLEGE FOR WOMEN.

In 1905 the Southern Baptist Convention authorized the establishment of a college for women to be located in Murfreesboro and to be known as Tennessee College for Women. The institution was founded on the principle of offering the very best educational advantages under a positive Christian influence. The Murfreesboro site selected for the college was on property formerly owned by Union University, another Baptist institution ruined by the Civil War.

Tennessee College for Women opened in the fall of 1907 with George J. Burnette as its first president. The first year, 199 students enrolled, and of that number 131 were boarding students. In 1909 the trustees dropped the elementary division and added the junior and senior years of liberal arts that led to a bachelor of arts degree. Music, drama, health, and physical education became integral parts of the college curriculum, with students taking part in soccer and hockey as well as field day activities such as the high jump and the 60- and 100-yard dash.

One of the most hallowed traditions of the college began about 1910, when the first "May Day" celebration took place. These festivities became an enduring part of the institution's activities, which were set among the massive oaks that dotted the campus. Each May 1, heralds led the parade which preceded the May Queen who arrived in a coach. Large numbers of townspeople came to watch the young ladies from the college as they danced around the flag pole.

World War I disrupted college activities, and from 1917 to 1923 attendance dropped due to the war and competition from the adjacent Middle Tennessee State Normal School (now MTSU). President Burnette offered his resignation and was replaced by Dr. Edward L. Atwood. Dr. James A. Kirtley, one of the best-loved administrators, served as dean.

The college encountered financial difficulties during the Great Depression and enrollment dropped to 78 students. In 1942 Dr. John Clark, former dean of Mercer University, became president. Under Clark's leadership, the school's fiscal health improved dramatically. During the depression the debt reached $24,000, but by 1945 the school was debt-free and had $135,000 in excess funds.

In 1945 the executive board of the Southern Baptist Convention closed the 40-year-old institution. The board voted to merge Tennessee College with Cumberland University, which was located in nearby Lebanon and operated under the auspices of the Presbyterian Church. Alumni and townspeople took legal steps to prevent the merger and keep the college in Murfreesboro. Their efforts, however, proved futile, and in January 1946 the merger went into effect. Unfortunately, the merger with Cumberland did not succeed and Cumberland later lost its law department to Sanford University, an Alabama Baptist institution. The remaining departments from Tennessee College at Cumberland merged with Belmont College in Nashville. The heritage and high ideals of Tennessee College were perpetuated at the new institution.

Mabel Pittard, Murfreesboro

SUGGESTED READING: Homer and Mabel Pittard, *Pillar and Ground* (1993)

SEE: CUMBERLAND UNIVERSITY; MURFREESBORO; SOUTHERN BAPTIST CONVENTION

TENNESSEE COLONIZATION SOCIETY,

a branch of the American Colonization Society, was organized as a debating society in Nashville in December 1829.

Josiah F. Polk, an agent of the American Colonization Society, recruited members throughout Tennessee, and Philip Lindsley, head of the University of Nashville, was named president.

Although the society suffered from a lack of money, Lindsley worked throughout the state to convince slaveholders to free their slaves and send them to Africa. In 1833, as a result of lobbying by colonization leaders, the Tennessee General Assembly voted to pay the society ten dollars for every freed slave transferred to Liberia from Tennessee, up to $500 per year. That same year, however, the Tennessee Colonization Society disbanded as a result of the lack of interest.

The enduring record of the Tennessee Colonization Society is mixed. Although the society was largely abandoned in 1833, and only 55 freed slaves emigrated from Tennessee to Liberia prior to 1841, Lindsley continued his work for colonization. Years later, Lindsley influenced large slaveholders like Logan Douglas and Montgomery Bell to free many of their slaves and send them to Liberia. Approximately 700 blacks left Tennessee for Africa between 1830 and 1860 as a direct result of the influence of the Tennessee Colonization Society.

Tara Mitchell Mielnik, Middle Tennessee State University
SEE: LINDSLEY, PHILIP; SLAVERY

TENNESSEE COMMISSION ON THE STATUS OF WOMEN.
On April 5, 1972, the same day that the State Senate ratified the Equal Rights Amendment, the Tennessee General Assembly created the Tennessee Commission on the Status of Women (TCSW). It was to study and highlight women's issues and to make recommendations that would ensure women's participation as "equal partners" within the state. The official commission was the successor to a series of earlier "governor's commissions," that had existed since 1963 when Governor Frank G. Clement established the first Governor's Commission on the Status of Women in Tennessee. The governor's commission did not endorse an equal rights amendment, but it did call for a series of legislative reforms, including an end to wage discrimination and inequitable property distribution laws. From 1965 to 1972 the state's governors formed several Continuing Commissions on the Status of Women. As second-wave feminism swept the nation, however, the continuing commission received some criticism from Tennessee women for its failure to recognize women's new status. In response, the legislature created the TCSW, and Governor Winfield Dunn appointed its first 11 members in January 1974. Although the caption of the 1972 law proclaimed the establishment of a "permanent commission," support for the TCSW rose and fell with the state's support of the ERA, and in 1981 it failed to get renewal under the state's sunset review.

From 1974 until 1981 the TCSW worked primarily as a clearinghouse for dissemination of information of interest to, and about, the state's women. The commission issued a number of brochures and pamphlets designed to inform women of their rights and responsibilities under the law, for example the 1978 pamphlet, "Marriage, Divorce, and Property Rights in Tennessee." It also participated in or sponsored workshops across the state on issues like job opportunities for women and family violence. In addition, commissioners and staff accepted inquiries from the public and answered women's individual complaints and questions. Another commission function was that of advocate. It lobbied for the repeal of gender-biased statutes, such as the spousal exemption for rape and women's special exemption from jury service. The TCSW also supported the ERA and commissioners issued a protest in March 1974 when the Tennessee legislature rescinded its earlier ERA ratification. This later action placed the commission under the scrutiny of the state's anti-ERA forces, who argued that state taxpayer funds should not be used to support an agency promoting the amendment. These groups stated that TCSW did not represent the interests of homemakers and other non-professional women. Although TCSW commissioners insisted that they supported the concerns of all the state's women, it could not rally enough votes in the state legislature to win legislative re-enactment and the agency officially ended on June 30, 1981.

Ruth Anne Thompson, Georgia Southern University
SUGGESTED READINGS: Governor's Commission on the Status of Women in Tennessee, *Women in Tennessee* (1965); Rina Rosenberg, "Representing Women at the State and Local Levels: Commissions on the Status of Women," in *Women, Power, and Policy,* Ellen Boneparth, ed. (1982)
SEE: CLEMENT, FRANK G.; DUNN, WINFIELD; ESKIND, JANE G.; GOVERNMENT

TENNESSEE CONSERVATION LEAGUE.
To conserve game animals for hunting, local sportsmen organized clubs in Tennessee as early as 1865, beginning with the McRae Club of Chattanooga. The first statewide organization, the Tennessee Federation of Sportsmen, was formed in 1934 to marshal local clubs into advocacy for conservation programs; the organization became the Tennessee Wildlife Federation in 1937. With the establishment of the Tennessee Department of Conservation that same year, the state assumed much of the work of the Federation, and by 1940 the organization ended. Most conservation activity slowed during World War II, although the Tennessee Outdoors Writers Association was established in 1942.

In 1945 the Tennessee Wildlife Federation attempted to reorganize, and in January 1946 the sportsmen received a charter for the Tennessee Conservation League (TCL). Louis V. Williams, an outdoor writer for the *Chattanooga Times*, was elected its first president. The purpose of the TCL included not only wildlife conservation but natural resource conservation, especially in the areas of soil, water, and forests. Other leaders in the new league were Nathaniel T. Winston, Sr., Z. Cartter Patten III, Nash Buckingham, and Walter Amann. Herman Baggenstoss, a stalwart of the earlier federations, soon joined forces with the league.

In 1949 the TCL produced model game and fish laws, which the state adopted; these state activities led to the creation of an independent Game and Fish Commission. In the 1950s the TCL became active in forest reclamation and in conservation education. In the 1960s the TCL attacked pesticide use, which killed small game, and planned the development of an umbrella environmental organization to provide information and advocacy on emerging environmental issues such as air and water pollution and energy conservation. The resulting Tennessee Environmental Council was chartered in December 1970.

In 1971, conservation leader Lucius Burch, Jr., chaired a special committee to reorganize the TCL; the following year the League hired its first executive director, Anthony J. (Tony) Campbell (1972–1992). In the mid-1970s, the TCL worked for reorganization of the Tennessee Game and Fish Commission into the Tennessee Wildlife Resources Agency. TCL also developed a strong lobbying presence, leading efforts to require deposits on drink containers, ensure sound management of natural resources, and promote conservation education. It continued its advocacy for hunting, fishing, and conservation through the 1990s. It issued an annual report, the Tennessee Environmental Quality Index, from 1990 through 1993, examining the progress of the state's environmental programs in preserving resources. Other projects included cosponsoring a biodiversity project focused on neotropical migrant birds and evaluating the Tennessee Department of Transportation's adherence to environmental regulations. In 1996 the Tennessee Environmental Boards Bill provided for a TCL appointee to the state Water Quality Control Board. Following its fiftieth anniversary, the TCL continued its work toward a future for Tennessee's environment by opening the Lucius E. Burch Center for Conservation Planning in 1997.

Ann Toplovich, Tennessee Historical Society

SUGGESTED READING: Marge Davis, *Sportsmen United: The Story of the Tennessee Conservation League* (1997)

SEE: BAGGENSTOSS, HERMAN; BURCH, LUCIUS; CONSERVATION; FISHING; HUNTING; TENNESSEE ENVIRONMENTAL COUNCIL; TENNESSEE WILDLIFE RESOURCES AGENCY

TENNESSEE CONSTITUTIONAL OFFICERS. The Tennessee State Constitution provides for three constitutional officers: the Secretary of State, the Comptroller of the Treasury, and the Treasurer. All three are elected by a joint session of the General Assembly, with the Secretary of State serving a four-year term, and the other two officers serving two-year terms.

Riley C. Darnell, a Democrat from Clarksville, was Secretary of State in 1998. According to the Tennessee Constitution, the Secretary of State is required to keep a register of the official acts and proceedings of the Governor and provide the General Assembly with all papers, minutes, and vouchers relative to the office of the Governor. In addition, the *Tennessee Code Annotated* requires that the Secretary of State serve on the following boards and agencies: State Funding Board, Board of Equalization, Board of Claims, State Building Commission, Library and Archive Management Board, Tennessee Local Development Authority, Tennessee State School Bond Authority, Publications Committee, Public Records Commission, Tennessee Housing Development Agency, Board of Trustees of the Tennessee Consolidated Retirement System, State Capitol Commission, Tennessee Competitive Export Corporation, Tennessee Higher Education Commission, and the State Trust Board of Directors.

The Secretary of State keeps all acts and resolutions passed by the state legislature and signed by the governor, making them available to the public in pamphlets or bound volumes. The office also keeps other records required by statute, including receipt and recording of corporate charters, annual reports, receipt of all trademarks, the execution of notary commissions, and the receipt of all state administrative rules and regulations.

The office of the Secretary of State is located on the first floor of the Capitol. Seven of the operating offices are located in the James K. Polk State Office Building: Division of Fiscal and Administration Services, Division of Personnel and Development, Division of Administrative Procedures, Division of Charitable Solicitations, Division of Elections, Division of Publications, and Division of Services. The Division of Library and Archives is located in the State Library and Archives on Seventh Avenue.

William R. Snodgrass, the Comptroller of the Treasury, has been elected to this office by every General Assembly since 1955. His duties, which are defined by statute, relate to the audit of state and local government entities and participation in the general financial and administrative management of state government. The Comptroller serves on the following boards and agencies: State Building Commission, State Capitol Commission, Board of Claims, Board of Equalization, State Funding Board, Tennessee State School Bond Authority, Tennessee Local Development Authority, Tennessee Housing Development Authority, Board of Standards, Tennessee Consolidated Retirement System, Health Facilities Commission, Tennessee Student Assistance Corporation, Publications Committee, Public Records Commission, State Insurance Committee, State Library and Archives Management Board, Tennessee Advisory Commission on Intergovernmental Relations, Information Systems Council, Tennessee Competitive Export Corporation, State Trust of Tennessee Board of Directors, Child Care Facilities Corporation, Governor's Council on Health and Physical Fitness, Sports Festivals Incorporated, Utility Management Review Board, Tennessee Commodity Producers Indemnity Corporation, Workers Compensation Insurance Fund Board, Wastewater Financing Board, Council on Pensions and Insurance, Higher Education Commission, Task Force on Not-for-Profit Accountability, and the 1996 Bicentennial Commission. In addition to the administration division of the Comptroller's office, there are nine other divisions, including the Office of Management Services, Division of State Audit, Division of County Audit, Division of Bond Finance, Division of Local Finance, Office of Local Government, Division of Property Assessments, and Offices of Research and Education Accountability.

Steve Adams has served as the State Treasurer since 1987. This constitutional office is charged with duties and responsibilities relating to the financial operations of state government. In recent years, the State Treasurer has also assumed responsibility for accounting for the receipt and disbursement of public funds, investing available cash balances, administering the Tennessee Consolidated Retirement System, investing the pension fund, operating the state's Unclaimed Property Program, administering the State Employees' Deferred Compensation Program, operating the State Employees' Flexible Benefits Plan, and directing the staff of the Division of Claims Administration and the Risk Management Division. The State Treasurer is a member of the following commissions and agencies: Funding Board, Board of Claims, Board of Equalization, School Bond Authority, Tennessee Student Assistance Corporation, State Library and Archives Management Board, State Employee and Teacher Group Insurance Committees, Tennessee Competitive Export Corporation, Tennessee Housing Development Agency, Local Development Authority, Defense Counsel Commission, Counsel on Pensions and Insurance, Tennessee Higher Education Commission, Public Records Commission, State Building Commission, Board of Trustees of the Tennessee Consolidated Retirement System, Investment Advisory Council, State Capitol Commission, State Trust Board of Directors, Sick Leave Bank Board, Chairs of Excellence and Baccalaureate Education System Trust Boards, Tennessee Child Care Loan Guarantee Board, Tuition Guaranty

Fund Board, Commission to Purchase Federal Property, Worker's Compensation Fund Board, Collateral Pool Board, Tennessee Sports Hall of Fame Board, and Tennessee Bicentennial Commission. The State Treasurer's office is located in the Capitol building, and the operating divisions have offices in the Andrew Jackson State Office Building. Operating divisions include Staff Services, Division of Retirement, Investment Division, Division of Claims Administration, Division of Risk Management, Accounting Division, Division of Information Systems, Division of Management Services, and Division of Financial Control.

Connie L. Lester, Tennessee Historical Society
Source: Adapted from materials in the *Tennessee Blue Book, 1995–1996: Bicentennial Edition*
SEE: GOVERNMENT

TENNESSEE COURTS PRIOR TO 1870. For Tennessee's first hundred years, Justices of the Peace were the foundation of the state's legal system. These men, often without legal training, served the citizens in their counties by resolving minor disputes, performing marriages, and serving on the quarterly court. They saved both time and expense by resolving issues without formal court proceedings. The regular courts changed and evolved through the years, but the Justice of the Peace remained the first source of help for citizens with legal problems.

The Watauga Association formed the first court in what is now Tennessee in 1772. The five members of this court served as both legislators and judges, under the leadership of John Carter. In 1776 North Carolina accepted responsibility for the Tennessee frontier and authorized John Carter to continue holding court at Jonesborough for the "Washington District." After the organization of Washington County in 1778, this court became the County Court of Common Pleas and Quarter Sessions. Appeals were technically (though not practically) grantable to the Superior Court of Law and Equity of Salisbury District, 200 miles to the east.

As the new counties of Sullivan (1779) and Greene (1783) were formed, each had its own Court of Common Pleas. In order to try appeals from the Common Pleas courts of the new counties locally, North Carolina established the Washington District Superior Court of Law and Equity at Jonesborough in 1784. The same process followed the development farther west with the formation of the Davidson County Court of Common Pleas and Quarter Sessions in 1783. The Mero District Superior Court of Law and Equity was established at Nashville in 1788 to hear appeals from western counties. This two-court system survived through the territorial period.

The 1796 Constitution of Tennessee gave Justices of the Peace sole jurisdiction over cases involving less than $50 in property or fines. It also continued the Court of Common Pleas and Quarter Sessions as an "inferior" court, and the Superior Court of Law and Equity as the "superior" court and appellate court.

The Court of Common Pleas and Quarter Sessions was comprised of a county's justices sitting in quorum. Until 1809, this group heard cases both of law and equity and handled the business of the county. They heard law cases in which the punishment did not include loss of life or limb and equity cases of modest money or property value. A clerk kept minutes of the court's proceedings and handled the court's business between sessions.

The Superior Courts of Law and Equity maintained sole jurisdiction over cases punishable by loss of life or limb and cases of greater dollar value. They also served as courts of appeal from the Court of Common Pleas. Many leading pioneers served as Superior Court judges, including Andrew Jackson, John Overton, John McNairy, Archibald Roane, and Willie Blount. The three traveling Superior Court judges heard cases in Jonesborough (Washington District), Knoxville (Hamilton District), Carthage (Winchester District), Clarksville (Robertson District), and Nashville (Mero District).

By 1809 the two-court system was overworked. To divide the case load, the legislature formed a Circuit Court, to be held in each county. The Superior Court was renamed the Supreme Court of Errors & Appeals. The division of cases among the courts varied from 1809 to 1833 as the legislature and the judges worked out the new system. In general, the Common Pleas court heard only minor cases of both law and equity, the Circuit Court heard criminal cases and appeals from the Common Pleas court, and the Supreme Court heard larger equity cases and appeals from the other two courts.

By 1829 the existing court system was strained to the limits. Adam Huntsman reported to the State Senate that year that confusion over jurisdiction, multiple appeals, and a lack of legal knowledge among justices of the peace made Tennessee's judicial system expensive and inefficient. Legal reform became a major issue driving the need for a new Constitution.

The 1834 Constitution of Tennessee reorganized the judiciary by adding a system of Chancery Courts. This provided a clear division of cases of law (Circuit Court) and cases of equity (Chancery Court). The name of the Court of Common Pleas and Quarter Sessions was shortened simply to County Court and its powers limited to trying non-indictable offenses (such as swearing, bastardy, and gambling), and tending to estate matters, roads, and other county business. The Supreme Court reduced its circuit to three districts, meeting in Knoxville, Nashville, and Jackson.

The Chancery Court was originally a district court, but gradually established one in each county.

The Chancellor (judge of Chancery) weighed the evidence in equity cases and decided on a fair division among the parties. The court heard disputes over land boundaries, the partitioning of estates, disagreements between business partners, and other matters of equity or "fairness."

In contrast, the Circuit Court heard matters of law. A jury decided each case by determining whether a specific law had been violated. The cases heard by the Circuit Court included those brought by the State for crimes against the people (criminal cases), and those between individuals (civil cases). Criminal cases included murder, unlawful retailing of liquor, lewdness, public fighting, and theft. Most civil cases resulted from unpaid debts. Beginning in 1842, the largest counties found it necessary to ease the work of the Circuit Court by forming separate Criminal Courts, but most counties did not divide the Circuit Court until after 1880.

The appellate function of the Supreme Court causes its records to reflect the operations of all the lower courts. The case files of this court, preserved in the state archives, provide an intimate look at the lives of Tennesseans through the documents filed by the parties as they dealt with issues ranging from burglary to bribery and beyond.

Charles A. Sherrill, Tennessee State Library and Archives

SUGGESTED READINGS: Theodore Brown, Jr., "The Tennessee County Courts under the North Carolina and Territorial Governments," *Vanderbilt Law Review* 32(1979): 349; Joshua Caldwell, *Studies in the Constitutional History of Tennessee* (1907)

SEE: BLOUNT, WILLIE; CARTER, JOHN; GOVERNMENT; LAW; MCNAIRY, JOHN; OVERTON, JOHN; ROANE, ARCHIBALD

TENNESSEE EASTMAN COMPANY/EASTMAN CHEMICAL COMPANY. In the 1880s, George Eastman (1854–1932) founded Kodak, a camera and photographic film manufacturer based in Rochester, New York. His Eastman Kodak Company was a multinational corporation that soon dominated the film market and led the way in the mass production of inexpensive and simple cameras. The production of film, however, remained the key to Kodak's huge profits. When World War I disrupted the German supply of photographic paper, optical glass, gelatin, and an assortment of chemicals including methanol, acetic acid, and acetone, Kodak faced a serious problem. Attracted by the forests of the Appalachian South as a source of raw materials for the manufacture of methanol and acetone and actively recruited by the planned industrial community of Kingsport and officials of the Clinchfield Railroad, George Eastman visited East Tennessee in July 1920. He purchased 35 acres and the factory buildings of the American Wood Reduction Company from the U.S. government as the base for the Tennessee Eastman Corporation. The original purchase expanded to

TSLA

Tennessee Eastman Company, Kingsport, in the 1950s.

include an additional 300 acres and represented an investment of more than $1 million.

Tennessee Eastman initially manufactured methanol, methyl acetone, and various by-products through the dry distillation of wood, but Eastman soon realized the Kingsport site would be ideal for the production of photographic chemicals, enabling him to maintain an independent supply of chemicals to his photographic processes. An ongoing federal antitrust suit against Kodak for its acquisition of other camera companies also contributed to the development of Tennessee Eastman. In 1921 Eastman ended six years of litigation by agreeing to end its attempt to create a monopoly in the camera field; instead it refocused its investments into the development of plants, like that at Kingsport, to produce the basic materials for film manufacture.

Officially incorporated July 17, 1920, Tennessee Eastman Corporation (TEC) began with $3.5 million in capital. Perley S. Wilcox (1874–1953) was elected a director and appointed as general manager; he rose to the position of vice president in 1921. As head of the Tennessee Eastman Corporation, he eventually held the honorary position of chairman of the board of the Eastman Kodak Company, but never served as president or chief executive officer. James C. White became general plant superintendent.

In the early years, wood was used to make methanol, a chemical needed for photographic film. By-products included charcoal, acetic acid, hardwood pitch, and wood preserving oil. In the mid-1920s, two developments of significance shaped the company's direction. The demand for safety film for home movies and the need for X-ray film coincided with the successful research of Eastman chemists and resulted in the production of acetic anhydride from pyroligneous acid, one of the primary ingredients used in manufacturing cellulose acetate, the base for safety film. Cellulose acetate production was transferred from Kodak Park to TEC in 1929. That same year, TEC began production of acetic anhydride. In 1930 efforts began to develop the production of cellulose acetate yarn, and by 1931 acetate yarn was produced on a large scale. In the early 1930s, TEC employed A. M. Tenney Associates to market cellulose acetate textiles. In conjunction with the acetate yarn production, TEC initiated production of Tenite cellulosic plastics, acetate dyestuffs, as well as Tenite II, a cellulose acetate butyrate molding composition. Utilized by the automobile and communications industry, these products had far-ranging ramifications for design and methods of production. By 1940 annual sales reached nearly $29 million. In 1930 Kodak also transferred the manufacture of hyroquinone from Passaic Junction, New Jersey, to Kingsport.

A hallmark in TEC and Kingsport history is the story of the company's contribution to the World War II effort. When the war halted natural rubber supplies from Asia, the Allies developed a commercial method for making synthetic rubber based on a process that depended on hydroquinone. As a result, TEC developed a close relationship with the War Production Board. In 1941 the National Defense Research Committee (NDRC) contacted TEC general manager James C. White and requested the initiation of a pilot plant for the manufacture of the powerful explosive RDX. H.G. "Herb" Stone (1897–1976) led the effort to develop RDX and served as works manager of the Holston Ordnance Works. Soon TEC was manufacturing RDX and Composition B in the large quantities needed to win the war in the European theatre. In early June 1942 TEC received official authorization from the U.S Army Ordnance and NDRC to design and operate Holston Ordnance Works (HOW). Subsequently, HOW became the world's largest manufacturer of high explosives. Now known as Holston Defense and the Holston Army Ammunition Plant, the company continues to be one of the world's largest manufacturers of explosives. In 1943 TEC and HOW received the prestigious Army-Navy "E" Award for "outstanding achievement in the production of materials of war."

General Leslie Groves, commanding officer of the Manhattan Project, recognized the TEC achievement in the production of RDX and utilized the resources of the company in the operation of the Y-12 plant (known as Clinton Engineering Works) at Oak Ridge, Tennessee. Dr. Fred Conklin served as works manager at the Y-12 plant, and Eastman scientists and engineers were transferred from Kingsport to Oak Ridge. Eastman managed the plant from January 1943 to May 1947, when the company requested permission to be relieved of the responsibility for Y-12.

In the 1950s acetate yarn became TEC's major product, with annual sales of $130 million. In the early 1950s Eastman expanded production and formed the Texas Eastman Company (Longview). The Tennessee Products Division moved from Rochester to Kingsport. Under the leadership of Wilcox and White, and with Dr. James McNally as head of research, TEC's Tenite plastics remained competitive in the emerging global market. Eastman also began large scale production of Chromspun, a dyed-in-solution acetate textile fiber and cellulose acetate filter tow for cigarettes. Verel, a modified acrylic fiber, was introduced as a part of TEC's textile fiber line in 1956. Two significant 1959 product developments included Eastman 910 Adhesive and Kodak polyester fiber.

During the next two decades and into the 1980s, Dr. L.K. Eilers, Harry D. McNeely, and Toy F. Reid continued previous efforts and spearheaded new developments. TEC began manufacturing scores of products now familiar to everyone including polyester fibers for apparel and home furnishings and plastics for automobiles. By 1960 filter tow was TEC's most lucrative product; that year company sales reached $250 million. Texas Eastman introduced Tenite polypropylene, and TEC began production of UVEX cellulose acetate butyrate sheets used for large weather-resistant outdoor signs. The formation of Eastman Chemicals Division of Eastman Kodak Company (1968) included TEC, Texas Eastman, Carolina Eastman Company, Eastman Chemical Products, Inc., and related marketing organizations, Holston Defense Corporation, Ectona Fibres Limited, Bays Mountain Construction Company, and Caddo Construction Company.

During the 1970s annual sales reached approximately $590 million, primarily as a result of polyester fibers and filter tow, and the company expanded to Batesville, Arkansas. One of the greatest product success stories was the introduction of Kodapak polyester plastic for use in the manufacture of beverage bottles. PET plastic (polyethylene terephthalate), developed in the late 1970s, enjoyed a worldwide success.

After the oil embargoes of the 1970s, Eastman recognized the advantage of independence from oil supplies and created a coal gasification facility. The plant produces acetic anhydride from coal instead of petroleum, for which it earned the 28th biennial Kirkpatrick Chemical Engineering Achievement Award. TEC became the first U.S. commercial manufacturer to produce a new generation of industrial chemicals that used second-generation coal-gasification technology to prepare feedstocks.

The 1990s have brought recognition and important changes to TEC. In December 1993 President Bill Clinton presented Eastman with the prestigious Malcolm Baldrige National Quality Award. On January 1, 1994, Eastman Kodak and Eastman Chemical Company became separate concerns. Eastman Chemical Company became an independent, publicly-owned company traded on the New York Stock Exchange. Earnest W. Deavenport, Jr., serves as chairman and CEO of Eastman Chemical Company. Now the tenth largest chemical company in the U.S. and the 34th largest in the world, ECC anticipates increasing growth, with 50 percent of sales outside the U.S. by the year 2000.

Martha Avaleen Egan, Kingsport Public Library and Archives/ King College

SEE: HOLSTON ORDNANCE WORKS; INDUSTRY; KINGSPORT; OAK RIDGE; WORLD WAR II

TENNESSEE ENVIRONMENTAL COUNCIL. The Tennessee Environmental Council (TEC) was chartered in December 1970 as an umbrella organization for groups concerned with environmental issues and as an information clearinghouse and think tank for environmental policy. Its founding leaders included Lucius Burch, Jr., Lester Dudney, and Cecil Branstetter. Among the first member organizations were the Tennessee Conservation League, League of Women Voters, Tennessee Federation of Garden Clubs, Nashville Junior League, and the Tennessee Chapter of the American Lung Association. In some years, more than 70 groups have been members of TEC.

Under its first director, Ruth Neff, (1970–1984), TEC established a reputation for objective environmental analysis and a sound understanding of the lawmaking and regulatory process. Members of the TEC staff and board served on the state's air pollution and water quality control boards and took leading roles in efforts to ban billboards, create a container deposit law, promote solar energy, encourage rural land use planning, and oppose nuclear waste storage in Tennessee. TEC also led lawsuits against air pollution from TVA coal-fired power plants and against industries that would not comply with toxic waste disposal and other pollution laws.

In the late 1980s and early 1990s, TEC aligned itself with emerging activist environmental groups. TEC's criticisms of state officials, policies, and regulations, especially regarding toxic and solid waste reduction and recycling resulted in fewer appointments from among TEC members to state regulatory oversight boards and study committees. In the late 1990s, TEC has concentrated on protecting air and water quality for public health. Focused on objective advocacy based on solid technical research, TEC continues as one of the most influential private organizations shaping Tennessee's environmental policies.

Ann Toplovich, Tennessee Historical Society

SEE: BURCH, LUCIUS; CONSERVATION; TENNESSEE CONSERVATION LEAGUE

TENNESSEE FARM BUREAU FEDERATION. Throughout the twentieth century, the Tennessee Farm Bureau Federation has made a significant contribution to the economy and way of life of rural Tennessee. The Tennessee Farm Bureau grew out of the County Councils of Agriculture, first established in Blount County in 1919. A meeting in 1921 on the necessity of farm organization led to a statewide union of the County Councils. Two years later, this temporary association changed its name to the Tennessee Farm Bureau Federation and joined the American Farm Bureau Federation.

One of the Farm Bureau's goals is to assist in organizing farmers' cooperatives. In 1923 the Farm Bureau helped to organize the Tennessee Cotton Marketing Cooperative. In 1932 the Bureau co-sponsored the Tennessee Livestock Producers' Marketing Association. The Bureau also helped to establish the Tennessee Burley Tobacco Growers' Association in 1941. These new associations aggressively sought new markets and better prices for their members.

The Farm Bureau also established education programs about federal agricultural initiatives and farming methods. It cooperates with groups such as Future Farmers and the 4-H Club to teach young farmers new methods. The Bureau publishes *Tennessee Farm Bureau News, Farm Bureau Digest,* and many educational pamphlets and sponsors daily radio and television programs on agriculture.

Lobbying quickly emerged as another key activity of the organization. Since World War II, the Farm Bureau has advocated better rural health programs, roads, and schools for farm communities. It became a powerful promoter of rural electrification. In the mid-1950s, under the leadership of President T.J. Hitch, the Bureau lobbied extensively against a proposal to allow private companies to build power plants in areas already served by the Tennessee Valley Authority.

Today, the Tennessee Farm Bureau reaches many Tennesseans through the Tennessee Farmers Mutual Insurance Company. In 1928 the organization first offered automobile insurance to its members. These programs have become a major source of income for the Bureau and provide an avenue for public visibility for the organization through the company's 550 agents and claims representatives.

In 1923 the Tennessee Farm Bureau had 3,600 members. The number tripled in the next six years, but fell dramatically during the Great Depression. In the late 1930s and early 1940s, however, the Bureau became a permanent establishment in many Tennessee counties, and by 1942 over 12,000 Tennesseans were members. Today, the Tennessee Farm Bureau counts 987,000 members, the largest state bureau in the nation. More than any other early twentieth century farm organization, the Tennessee Farm Bureau responded successfully to the changes in southern agriculture, such as population shifts, increasing agricultural diversification, new technology, and the decrease in farm tenancy to remain a vital part of the state's rural life.

Jeffrey L. Durbin, Historic Preservation Division, Georgia Department of Natural Resources

SUGGESTED READING: Carroll Van West, *Tennessee Agriculture: A Century Farms Perspective* (1986)

SEE: AGRICULTURE

TENNESSEE FEDERATION OF GARDEN CLUBS, INC. In 1926 delegates and representatives from 17 of the state's 34 garden clubs met at the Read House in Chattanooga and organized the Tennessee Federation of Garden Clubs (TFGC). Mrs. E.Y. Chapin of the Garden Club of Signal Mountain was TFGC's first president.

The fledgling federation survived the difficult years of the Great Depression to promote family gardens and beautification. Mrs. Sim Perry Long of the Garden Club of Riverview in Chattanooga promoted the planting of sustenance gardens through the donation of tools, seeds, and planting information. TFGC supported the conservation efforts of the 1930s by promoting the preservation of slow-growing evergreens and wildflowers. The clubs advocated roadside beautification through the clearing of signs and debris and promoted the planting of trees in conjunction with the George Washington Tree Planting Program. During the 1930s, TFGC also established the first Junior Garden Club. To acknowledge the work of local clubs, TFGC President Mrs. John Burch of Nashville created an awards system. The Wildwood Garden Club of Memphis won an award for planting 18,245 trees. The Fountain City Garden Club won the Award of Honor for its work in landscaping miles of roadside between Knoxville and Fountain City. In 1936 TFGC launched its first fight against billboards.

During World War II, the federation joined the governor in a program of garden therapy which supplied small plants, seedlings, and cuttings to inmates in the state's penal institutions and patients in state hospitals. TFGC also encouraged Junior Gardeners to become soldiers for gardening with promotions for vegetable gardens.

In the postwar years, TFGC has expanded into new areas. It established its first horticulture scholarship and provided 28 scholarships to the Teachers' Conservation Education Workshop. The clubs erected Blue Star Markers along Tennessee highways as memorials to the state's soldiers killed in battle. The federation expanded into world gardening programs. During the 1970s Mrs. James B. Carey promoted the erection of fences and the planting of roses to hide junkyards. Ivan Racheff presented TFGC with properties in Knoxville that included six and one-half acres of park and several buildings; Racheff Park and Gardens became the permanent home of the federation. Under the direction of TFGC President Betty Weesner, the federation promoted flower show schools, conservation workshops, and garden consultant courses.

In 1979 Anne Wilbanks of Knoxville added environmental workshops to the federation's list of activities. In 1983 President Jerry Tubb from Memphis organized the first Wildflower Workshop, the first Arboreta Conference, and the first Environments Education workshop designed for college credit. In 1987 TFGC President Martha Phillips held the federation's first Legislation Advocacy Seminar.

As TFGC entered the last decade of the twentieth century, the organization continued to improve old programs and add new ones. The first Riverboat Water and Energy Workshop was held in Clarksville. During Jo Monroe's tenure as president, the first environmental studies course was approved for con-

tinuing education for teachers. The World Gardening Program of the NCSGC launched in 1947 as "Seeds of Peace" continued to help impoverished families in Uganda, East Africa, Thailand, and Ecuador. Charlotte Branstetter of Nashville received a NCSGC Garden Therapy Award for developing a Horticulture Program for youth offenders.

In 1996 TFGC included four districts and 254 clubs with 6,954 members. That year TFGC oversaw one environmental education school, 42 flower shows, six flower show schools, and two symposia. The President's Project was the TFGC Butterfly Garden, at the University of Tennessee Challenge Center, which promotes interest in butterflies and their benefit to the natural world. In June 1996 TFGC held its Bicentennial Flower Show at the State Capitol.

The Tennessee Federation of Garden Clubs promotes gardening through audio-visual presentations and programs for radio and television. In addition, the federation supports butterfly gardening, historic preservation projects, and environmental awareness. As an example of the ways in which garden clubs have advanced with the times, the Environmental Concerns Garden Club of Clarksville established the nation's first garden club web page.

Prepared from material supplied by Linda J. Edington, Clarksville

SEE: CONSERVATION

TENNESSEE FEDERATION OF WOMEN'S CLUBS

was organized in 1896 to bring together women's clubs from across the state into one organization that would provide communication among its members. A decade after the founding of the first women's clubs in Tennessee, 20 women's clubs sent representatives to a statewide organizational meeting called by Lizzie Crozier French, a well-known teacher and activist, and the Ossoli Circle in Knoxville. The women elected Mrs. W.D. Beard as president and agreed to meet the next year in Memphis at the Nineteenth Century Club. During the Memphis meeting, the delegates adopted the club motto, "Unity of Purpose." Education was a primary purpose of the federation, and French was named chair of the educational committee.

Federation leaders soon realized that many issues before the state legislature affected the lives of women across the state. The federation created a legislative committee to monitor General Assembly meetings and inform members of pending legislation. The committee studied bills and adopted a legislative program to facilitate the passage of compulsory education laws, a bill to allow women to serve on local school boards, equal pay for female teachers, a vocational school for delinquent girls, pure food and drug laws, and bills to improve labor conditions for women and children. Although the annual convention endorsed the ratification of the Nineteenth Amendment giving women the right to vote, many local clubs were divided on the subject of woman suffrage. The federation supported traveling libraries, which brought library services to rural areas, a mountain work division to provide educational opportunities in the Appalachians, and the Hancock County Health Project. Today, the federation has more than 90 member organizations in Tennessee.

Carole Stanford Bucy, Volunteer State Community College
SEE: FRENCH, LIZZIE CROZIER; NINETEENTH CENTURY CLUB; OSSOLI CIRCLE

TENNESSEE FOLKLORE SOCIETY is a statewide organization of academics and interested citizens who are concerned with the preservation, celebration, and study of the traditional expressive culture of the state. Such culture ranges from the classic forms of folklore that include proverbs, tales, and music to more recently appreciated forms such as folk architecture, foodways, beliefs, and recreation styles. The Tennessee Folklore Society recognizes these forms in a number of ways: publishing a journal, *The Tennessee Folklore Society Bulletin* (TFSB); serving as a conduit for state and federal grants devoted to folklore projects; serving as a clearinghouse for information about folk culture and events; holding annual meetings; and producing a series of television documentaries, audio recordings, and videotapes.

The Society formed in 1934, when famed ballad collector John Lomax pointed out to his Tennessee friend J.A. Rickard that parts of the state were "the richest in folklore of any portion of the United States." Impressed, Rickard called a meeting at what was Tennessee Polytechnic Institute (now Tennessee Technological University), which attracted some 50 people, mostly educators. The group created a constitution and elected Charles S. Pendleton of George Peabody College as the society's first president. The following spring, the organization began publishing its journal, which continues today as one of the nation's oldest continuously published regional journals. As the society grew, its pioneering efforts attracted the attention of a number of notable figures who became members: Eleanor Roosevelt, Estes Kefauver, Mary Frances (Mrs. Cordell) Hull, J. Percy Priest, Carroll Reece, and Albert Gore, Sr. It also attracted the work and support of most of the country's folklore scholars, such as Richard Dorson, Stith Thompson, Dorothy Horne, and Henry Glassie. The pages of the journal were filled with riddles, proverbs, stories, and songs and became the first to call attention to such modern folk trends as "elephant jokes" and oral lore from the Vietnam war.

Originally the *Tennessee Folklore Society Bulletin* was headquartered at Tennessee Tech, where it flourished under the guidance of T.J. Farr. In 1952 it moved to Peabody College, where it was edited by William J. Griffith until 1966. Then it moved to Middle Tennessee State University, first under the editorship of Ralph Hyde, and starting in 1980 under the direction of Charles Wolfe. Later Guy Anderson of MTSU joined the staff as co-editor. Today, the society remains headquartered at MTSU.

In the 1970s the society played a role in establishing the position of Director of Folk Arts with the Tennessee Arts Commission and in supporting and encouraging the development of festivals in the state. It sought and received a non-profit charter which allowed it to receive grants from state and federal agencies. By the mid-1970s the organization began a series of documentary field recordings which ranged from "historical ballads" to the aural documentation of the rural black community of Free Hill. In 1980 the society sponsored television documentaries, including *The Uncle Dave Macon Show*, which won a regional Emmy for best documentary and was shown nationally over the PBS network. In the 1990s the society co-sponsored The Tennessee Banjo Institute, a novel teaching experiment that attracted national attention. As the organization enters its sixth decade, it remains active in its mission to curate and preserve the state's folklore.

Charles K. Wolfe, Middle Tennessee State University
SEE: MACON, DAVID H.; MIDDLE TENNESSEE STATE UNIVERSITY; TENNESSEE ARTS COMMISSION; TENNESSEE TECHNOLOGICAL UNIVERSITY

TENNESSEE GOVERNOR'S OFFICE. The executive power of the state is vested in the office of the governor, and that elected official is responsible for the enforcement of the laws, collection of taxes, and well-being of the state and its citizens. The recognized state leader of their political party, governors must be 30 years of age, a citizen of the United States, and have been a resident of Tennessee for seven years before their election. The governor is the commander-in-chief of the army and navy of the state as well as the state militia unless they are called into the service of the United States. The governor has the authority to recommend legislation to the General Assembly and to veto bills passed by the legislature which the governor judges to be not in the best interests of the state. The governor has the power to appoint judges and chancellors to fill vacancies and can grant executive clemency following all convictions, except in the case of impeachment.

Governors speak for all the people of the state in national matters, and as such represent labor, industry, commerce, agriculture, and urban and rural areas. They are elected to a four-year term and can succeed themselves one time. Receiving $85,000 annually in compensation, they receive the use of the Governor's Mansion, plus expenses for its operation. In the event of a vacancy in the office, the lieutenant governor (Speaker of the Senate) succeeds to the office, followed by the Speaker of the House, the secretary of state, and the comptroller.

The governor appoints the commissioners who head the various departments of the executive branch of government. These commissioners plus six senior members of the governor's staff make up the governor's cabinet. The cabinet advises the governor and assists him in the administration of the state's business.

Three of the executive departments began in the nineteenth century: the Department of Agriculture (1854); the Department of Commerce and Insurance (1873); and the Department of Military (1887). The greatest period of agency creation came during the progressive era from 1905 to 1925 when nine departments had their beginnings: Environment and Conservation (1905); Financial Institutions (1913); Transportation (1915); Correction (1923); Education (1923); Health (1923); Labor (1923); Revenue (1923); and Human Services (1925). Several of these departments also had nineteenth century roots in different offices and divisions.

Two departments—Personnel and Safety—were created in 1939. At the end of World War II came the Department of Economic and Community Planning (1945 and 1953); the Department of Employment Security (1945); and the Department of Veterans Affairs (1945). Executive departments established in the last 50 years are the Department of Mental Health and Mental Retardation (1953); Department of Finance and Administration (1959); Department of General Services (1972); Tourist Development (1972, 1976); and Department of Youth Development (1989). The regularly updated *Tennessee Blue Book* has extensive information about the personnel and programs of these various departments and that information also is available on the Tennessee State Government web page (www.state.tn.us).

Connie L. Lester, Tennessee Historical Society

SEE: GOVERNMENT; KILLEBREW, JOSEPH E.; PEAY, AUSTIN; TENNESSEE PRISON SYSTEM

TENNESSEE HISTORICAL COMMISSION was established as the Tennessee Historical Committee by a Joint Resolution of the General Assembly on January 23, 1919. The resolution defined the duties of the Committee to collect, compile, index, and arrange all data and information relating to the participation of Tennessee in World War I. The documents and data were assigned to the State Librarian and Archivist for safekeeping.

On March 29, 1921, the State Senate defined the Committee's duties in more detail and designated the director of the State Library and Archives chairman of the Tennessee Historical Committee. Historian and author John Trotwood Moore served as chairman until his death on May 10, 1921, after which the Committee remained inactive for almost two decades. On April 18, 1940, Governor Prentice Cooper issued an executive order to call a meeting of the Tennessee Historical Committee. Only six members attended, and Governor Cooper acted as chairman. The minutes of the meeting used the new title, "Tennessee Historical Commission," for the committee. Vacancies on the Commission were soon filled, and Judge Samuel Cole Williams was elected chairman.

Subsequent legislative actions in 1951, 1959, and 1971 further defined the Commission's membership and expanded its area of responsibility to include evaluation, acquisition, and preservation of historic sites; selection and erection of historical markers; publication of books and other documents on Tennessee history; compilation of a Tennessee Register of Historic Places; and the general administration of funds made available from public sources for historic purposes.

In 1971 the Tennessee General Assembly expanded the role of the Commission to comply with the provisions of the 1966 National Historic Preservation Act. In compliance with the federal program, the Commission's work includes a county-by-county survey of all properties 50 years or older, nomination of the most significant ones to the National Register of Historic Places, review of all projects within the state utilizing federal funds to determine potential threats to cultural resources, public assistance in the administration of tax incentive programs, and work with the Certified Local Government program.

The Commission provides grants to local non-profit organizations to assist in the operation of state-owned historic sites. It grants funds for the publication of historical materials, including the journals of the Tennessee Historical Society, the East Tennessee Historical Society, and the West Tennessee Historical Society. The Commission provides assistance to the University of Tennessee, Knoxville, for the publication of the papers of Presidents Andrew Jackson, James K. Polk, and Andrew Johnson. Other programs administered by the Commission provide awards to students, literacy advocates, preservationists, writers, and others for their achievements.

In 1994 the General Assembly created the Tennessee Wars Commission. Creation of the new agency came in recognition of the rich history and exceptional resources available in Tennessee as the site of more Civil War battles than any other state except Virginia. As a result of the legislative act, the role of the Tennessee Historical Commission was once again expanded to "coordinate, plan, preserve, and promote structures, buildings, sites, and battlefields of Tennessee associated with the American Revolution and the War Between the States."

The executive director and his staff have the responsibility of implementing the programs of the Commission under the authority of the 24 members of the Commission appointed to five-year terms by the governor.

Herbert L. Harper, Tennessee Historical Commission

SEE: MOORE, JOHN T. AND MARY D.; TENNESSEE STATE LIBRARY AND ARCHIVES; WILLIAMS, SAMUEL C.

TENNESSEE HISTORICAL SOCIETY. Early histories of the Tennessee Historical Society (THS) place its origins in the Tennessee Antiquarian Society, organized in Nashville in 1820. The purpose of the society, chaired by John Haywood, was the collection and preservation of important events in the history of Tennessee and research into prehistoric antiquities. Many of the members of this group reorganized as the Tennessee Society for the Diffusion of Knowledge in 1835. In an 1857 editorial, the Nashville *Daily Union and American* traced the 1849 creation of the Tennessee Historical Society from this organization. In her 1943 history of the Tennessee Historical Society, Mary Daniel Moore states that the missions, constitutions, and by-laws of the three organizations were similar, and that several persons are found as members of all three. These similarities and the possession by the THS of the earlier societies' minutes and collections support the claim of an 1820 founding.

The Tennessee Historical Society was reorganized from these earlier societies on May 1, 1849, with Professor Nathaniel Cross chosen as chairman. The members organized for the purpose of collecting and preserving facts related to the natural, aboriginal, and civil history of the state. The University of Nashville became the temporary depository of the THS holdings; one item immediately sought was the collection of papers of Governor William Carroll. Other early acquisitions brought 56 books, manuscripts dating to 1732, newspapers, and artifacts such as the spectacles of General Nathaniel Greene. One result of the activity was the incorporation of the Tennessee Historical Society by an act of the General Assembly on February 1, 1850. THS hired librarian William Wales as its first staff member in May 1850.

Beginning in March 1857, meetings of the THS took place in the State Library in the new State Capitol building. The holdings of the THS, which now included oil portraits, were exhibited in the library and in the federal courtroom of the Capitol. On May 1, 1858, General B.F. Cheatham rode through Nashville at the head of a parade in honor of the society. The parade, which ended with a picnic in a nearby grove, included military cadets, militia guards, veterans from three wars, teachers and students from local academies, ex-governors, judges, and pioneer settlers.

The THS continued to build its archival and museum collections, and in 1860 Jeremiah G. Harris donated one of its most popular holdings, an Egyptian mummy. The Civil War disrupted THS meetings. Some of the collections from the Capitol, especially coins and minerals, were removed just before federal occupation and stored at Polk Place under the protection of Sarah Childress Polk. Many of the manuscripts and books left in the Capitol's library were lost. The THS did not return to the Capitol building until 1874. J.G.M. Ramsey of Knoxville served as THS president from 1874 to 1884.

In the 1870s and 1880s, the THS asked historians to collect local and county biographical and historical information. Much of this material was published as county histories or used in Goodspeed's *History of Tennessee* in 1887. The THS guided activities for celebrating Nashville's centenary in 1880, and as part of its efforts purchased and erected the heroic statue of Andrew Jackson by sculptor Clark Mills on the grounds of the Capitol. In 1886 the THS moved its archival and museum collections from the State Library to larger quarters at Watkins Institute. That same year, members were allowed to invite female guests to each alternate program of the society. Women were permitted to join as corresponding members in the 1880s, and Mary Noailles Murfree's name was added to the rolls. In 1890 the society authorized full membership for women, with Sarah Polk elected to honorary membership in 1891. The Tennessee Historical Society participated in the state's centennial celebrations through a special campaign to collect papers from the settlement of the state forward through 1896 and by seeking to establish a historical exhibit at the Centennial Exposition of 1897. The celebration's History Building was constructed to accommodate the society's portraits of famous persons, historic arms, and manuscripts.

Although the THS had prepared other publications, beginning with a history of Davidson County in 1879, the society entered into an agreement with *American Historical Magazine* in 1896 to publish its transactions, a partnership that continued until 1904. In 1915 the THS began publication of its own quarterly journal, the *Tennessee Historical Magazine*. First edited by St. George L. Sioussat, the magazine continued until 1937.

The first quarter of the twentieth century brought several changes to the THS. In 1915 the Ladies Historical Society consolidated with the THS. Following World War I, the society became active in promoting the construction of a soldiers' memorial building. After the War Memorial Building was completed in 1927, the THS petitioned the General Assembly for space to display its collections, which had outgrown its rooms at Watkins Institute. In April the General Assembly adopted a resolution accepting in trust the collections of the society and committing to the society's use rooms in the memorial building plus aid in publishing the THS magazine. In the late 1990s the THS and the state still operated under this 1927 agreement.

In 1937 came the death of THS president John H. DeWitt, who had held that office since 1913. In 1941 Stanley F. Horn was elected as president, and in 1942 the THS resumed its quarterly journal as the *Tennessee Historical Quarterly*. (Under editor Carroll Van West, the quarterly entered its fifty-seventh volume in 1998.) In 1953 the Tennessee State Library and Archives moved to a new building constructed as a memorial to World War II veterans. All the THS manuscripts, printed materials, and books not on display in the museum were moved to the archives and made available for public use. In 1980 the society's museum collections were moved to the new Tennessee State Museum in the Polk Building, although a few items remained on display in the military branch of the museum at the War Memorial Building. The society's portraits of the governors hang in the State Capitol.

From the 1920s through the 1970s, the THS concentrated its efforts on publishing Tennessee history, hosting public lectures, and adding to its collections. These activities were conducted by volunteers and by the society's editor, a position provided by the State of Tennessee until the early 1980s. In 1980 the THS hired its first full-time executive director, James A. Hoobler. During the 1980s, the society expanded programs to sites across the state, planned and produced special museum exhibits highlighting the society's collections, and published new histories. In 1988–1989 James S. Summerville served as executive director, and the THS launched new public history projects, most notably "Votes for Women," a commemoration of the 70th anniversary of Tennessee's role in the passage of the Nineteenth Amendment to the U.S. Constitution. In 1990 the THS board employed Ann Toplovich as executive director and continued its commitment to new research, public programs, and publications related to Tennessee history. In the 1990s, special projects have included "Home Front Tennessee: The World War II Experience" and "'Eden of the West': The Development of Upper South Culture in Tennessee and Kentucky, 1750–1850." The THS also served as advisor to the Tennessee Bicentennial celebration in 1996. The society's major project to commemorate Tennessee's 200th anniversary was its production of the state's first comprehensive encyclopedia.

In 1970 Harriet C. Owsley noted that almost all major histories of Tennessee had been written by members of the Tennessee Historical Society, from John Haywood, A.W. Putnam, and J.G.M. Ramsey through Robert E. Corlew, Robert H. White, and Stanley J. Folmsbee. The publication by the THS of *The*

Tennessee Encyclopedia of History and Culture in 1998 was a crowning achievement in this tradition.
Ann Toplovich, Tennessee Historical Society
SUGGESTED READING: Harriet Chappell Owsley, "The Tennessee Historical Society: Its Origin, Progress, and Present Condition," *Tennessee Historical Quarterly* 29(1970): 227–242
SEE: CHEATHAM, BENJAMIN F.; HAYWOOD, JOHN; HORN, STANLEY F.; POLK, SARAH CHILDRESS; RAMSEY, J.G.M.; TENNESSEE STATE LIBRARY AND ARCHIVES; TENNESSEE STATE MUSEUM; WILLIAMS, SAMUEL C.

TENNESSEE HOUSE OF REPRESENTATIVES. The lower house of Tennessee's bicameral legislature is called the House of Representatives. Made up of representatives from the 99 districts of the state, the representatives of the 100th General Assembly (1997–1998) includes 61 Democrats (50 men and 11 women) and 38 Republicans (35 men and three women). Representatives are elected for two-year terms, and all representatives stand for election simultaneously. To qualify for election to the Tennessee House, the candidate must be 21 years old, a U.S. citizen, a Tennessee resident for three years, and a resident of the county from which the candidate is seeking election for one year preceding the election.

During the organizational session of the House, representatives elect a Speaker and Speaker *pro tempore*, who acts in the absence of the Speaker. The Speaker has the right to name any member of the House to perform the duties of the chair for no more than one legislative day. The Speaker of the House presides over the House and is second in line for succession to the office of the Governor in the event of a vacancy in that office. The Speaker appoints the members of all committees, giving consideration to the abilities, preferences, party representation, and seniority of the members. The Speaker also names the chair, vice chair and secretary of each committee, using the same criteria used in selecting committee members. The Speaker and the Speaker *pro tempore* are voting members of all standing committees, but the Speaker *pro tempore* exercises the right to vote in committee meetings if the Speaker defers to him. The Speaker serves as co-chair of the Joint Legislative Services Committee and must approve, in concurrence with the Speaker of the Senate, the directors of the Legislative Services Office, Legal Services Office, and the Legislative Administrative Office. The Speaker signs all acts, proceedings, or orders of the House and has the responsibility for all facilities, professional and clerical staffs, custodians, and security personnel of the House. James O. "Jimmy" Naifeh was the speaker of the 100th General Assembly, and Lois M. DeBerry was the Speaker *pro tempore*.

Other House leaders include the minority and majority party leaders, who are the chief floor spokesmen for their parties. In the 99th General

Assembly, Jere Hargrove was the majority leader, and Steve McDaniel was the minority leader. Elected by their respective party members in the House, these leaders serve on committees, sponsor legislation, analyze bills, develop political strategy regarding the timing of legislation, and represent their party in House discussions and debates. Party caucus chairs preside at meetings of the Democratic or Republican members of the House. The Democratic caucus chairman was Randy Rinks, and the Republican chairman was Randy Stamps.

Much of the work of the House is performed in standing committees. After bills receive a first and second reading before the entire House, they are referred to one of the standing committees. The committees originate and revise bills, study legislation, hold public hearings, and by majority vote recommend passage to the entire House. The House has 12 standing committees: Agriculture; Calendar and Rules; Commerce; Conservation and Environment; Education; Finance; Ways and Means; Health and Human Resources; Government Operations; Judiciary; Consumer and Employees Affairs; State and Local Government; and Transportation. Once the appropriate standing committee recommends passage, the bill is read before the House for the third time, and after any discussion or debate, is put to a vote of the House. In addition to the standing committees, the House has three select committees: Calendar and Rules, Ethics, and Select Committee on Rules.

Connie L. Lester, Tennessee Historical Society
Source: Adapted from materials found in the Tennessee Blue Book, 1995–1996, Bicentennial Edition
SEE: GOVERNMENT; NAIFEH, JAMES O.

TENNESSEE HUMANITIES COUNCIL. Chartered in 1974, the Tennessee Humanities Council exists to bring the study of the humanities into public awareness, thus fulfilling the mission of the National Endowment for the Humanities (NEH) at the state level. In the beginning, many associated with the council expected it to unite Tennesseans of different regions, races, and economic backgrounds through examination of their common needs and goals. The council's first funding proposal, constructed as a result of "coffee meetings" with citizens across the state, bore the title, "Them and Us: What Divides Tennesseans? What Can Unite Them?"

The first director of the Tennessee Humanities Council was Jane Crater. Noted for her public relations skills, she was quite successful in making the humanities council's mission intelligible to the public. Later directors have had to strike a careful balance between the desires of the academic world and those of the public at large. Critics of the council have expressed some of the same sentiments voiced

against the NEH: that it provides one-way communication from "those who know" (the academic community) to "those who do not know" (the general public). According to current Executive Director Robert Cheatham, state humanities councils have had to fight that image since their founding.

The Tennessee Humanities Council provides support grants to projects that involve both the academic community and the general public. Cheatham's leadership produced the Southern Festival of Books, an annual event held in downtown Nashville featuring book sales, autograph parties, and author readings in fiction, poetry, history, and other disciplines. Under Cheatham's oversight, the Council also sponsored the Tennessee Community Heritage Project, in which college faculty collaborated with local citizens to write the histories of numerous Tennessee communities. These examples are just two of the successful statewide projects supported by the Council over the last 25 years.

Stephen W. Taylor, Middle Tennessee State University
SEE: TENNESSEE ARTS COMMISSION

TENNESSEE IN FILM. The Tennessee depicted in Hollywood films is akin to the romanticized mythographic West of cowboys and Indians. Though there may be a grain of truth imbedded somewhere in the stereotypical image, it is far from representative of the state or its inhabitants. Ironically, many films in the silent era (1896–1927) depicted the state and Tennesseans in a more favorable light. Tennessee became associated with hillbilly culture in the minds of viewers only after the media coverage of the 1925 Scopes Trial depicted the state's residents as backward rubes. Newsreel footage of the Dayton citizens who crammed into the town to observe the happenings, coupled with the scathing observations of H.L. Mencken, left lasting impressions of Tennessee as the locus of the illiterate and unreconstructed. This stereotype was, perhaps unwittingly, reinforced by the growing popularity of country music heard in national broadcasts from Nashville on WSM and Knoxville on WNOX. These random events converged to cement the image of Tennessee as the home of the hillbilly.

Country music has played a key role in many films set in the state, from Ferlin Huskey's *Country Music Holiday* (1958) to Robert Altman's frenetic and disjointed masterpiece *Nashville* (1970), and to the recent *Thing Called Love* (1995). Lives of country music stars have served as grist for the cinematic mill, providing the requisite heartache, violence, alcohol and drug abuse, illicit sex, and dejection that viewers associate with the musical genre. Among the films that exploit such fare are *Your Cheatin' Heart* (1964) with George Hamilton reliving the sanitized life of Hank Williams; *Coal Miner's Daughter*

(1980) with Sissy Spacek, Tommy Lee Jones, and Levon Helm depicting the rags-to-riches story of Loretta Lynn; and Jessica Lange's role as Patsy Cline in *Sweet Dreams* (1985). Country music is also used to establish a sense of place, mood, and character and to provide a voice for male characters who otherwise are depicted as incapable of expressing their thoughts or emotions.

Prior to the 1960s, most films about Tennessee were not filmed in the state. Tennessee lacked the resources necessary for filmmakers, and California had to double for Tennessee. John Huston's classic film *Red Badge of Courage* (1951), based on Stephen Crane's novel about the Battle of Shiloh, was shot on location in California. Nor was the earlier dramatic story of *Sergeant York* (1941) shot in Tennessee. One early exception is Alan Holubar's film *The Human Mill* (1923), which was shot on location in Franklin. Based on John Trotwood Moore's romantic novel *The Bishop of Cottonwood*, the filmmaker set out to recreate the Battle of Franklin. Using Civil War veterans and extras from all over Middle Tennessee, the film marked the first Hollywood venture into the state. Unfortunately, Holubar died during the filming, and the movie was never edited for distribution; the whereabouts of the footage remains unknown. One wishes that the footage had been lost for *I Walk the Line* (1968). Filmed on location in Smith, Overton, Fentress, Jackson, and Putnam counties, directed by John Franenheimer, and starring Gregory Peck, Tuesday Weld, and Ralph Meeker, the film depicts the state in the most sordid and stereotypical terms.

Several historic figures from Tennessee's past have been depicted on film; most prominent among them are David Crockett, Andrew Jackson, and Sam Houston. Out of the dozens of Crockett films, the two most popular are Fess Parker's simplistic, sanitized Disney Crockett created from the *Crockett Almanacs* and John Wayne's larger-than-life, ultra-American Crockett from the *The Alamo* (1960). Hollywood also has interpreted key events in the state's history. Stanley Kramer's *Inherit the Wind* (1960) was about the Scopes Trial; that same year Elia Kazan looked at the impact of the Tennessee Valley Authority in *Wild River*, which starred Montgomery Clift and Lee Remick.

In the 1980s several changes made Tennessee the location for a number of Hollywood films, both about the state and as the screen-double for other states and nations. In 1983 Governor Lamar Alexander founded the 50-member Tennessee Film, Tape, and Music Commission to aggressively pursue filmmakers and encourage them to produce feature films. Filmmakers recognized the cost benefits associated with hiring local laborers and technicians in a right-to-work state and avoid paying union scale. Additionally, the various recording facilities in Nashville and Memphis facilitated post-production and editing work.

Alexander's team met with immediate success, and four films were shot in Tennessee. Mark Rydell's domestic tragedy *The River,* starring Sissy Spacek, Mel Gibson, and Scott Glenn, featured the Rogersville area as the Midwest farmbelt. Sylvester Stallone and Dolly Parton teamed up for the off-key musical romance *Rhinestone.* Jane Fonda and Levon Helm shot the tearjerking story of triumph, *The Dollmaker.* Perhaps the most interesting film shot in Tennessee that year was the science fiction film *Star Man,* starring Jeff Bridges and Karen Allen. In that film, Tennessee doubled for Minnesota, the Mid-West, and even Arizona—the desert sequences were shot around Copper Hill.

The success of the first year of filming in Tennessee encouraged further production. In 1984 the Disney corporation used Nashville locations and the State Capitol for the dramatic story of the first seeing-eye dog, *Love Leads the Way,* directed by Tennessean Delbert Mann, and starring Timothy Bottoms, Ernest Borgnine, and Ralph Bellamy. Jean Jacques Annaud filmed a portion of his virtually silent feature *The Bear,* which chronicled the life of an abandoned cub, in Tennessee locations near Memphis. The Willie Nelson feature *Songwriter* was shot in Nashville and the surrounding area. In 1985 Franklin doubled for a small town in western Pennsylvania in Michael Apted's chilling film about a family of criminals, *At Close Range,* starring Christopher Walken and Sean Penn.

Sissy Spacek portrayed Marie Ragghianti, the woman who blew the whistle on the Ray Blanton administration in the 1986 feature *Marie.* This film marked the screen debuts for two of Tennessee's biggest stars: the Tennessee State Penitentiary and Fred Thompson (now a U.S. Senator). Once slated for demolition, the prison has become a popular movie set; the HBO film *Attica* (1996) was recently shot there. Thompson has acted in several major films, including *No Way Out, In the Line of Fire,* and *The Hunt for Red October.*

During the administration of Governor Ned Ray McWherter, film production declined. A brief resurgence of state filmmaking occurred in the mid-1990s. *The Firm,* the first of John Grisham's popular thrillers, was filmed in Memphis and starred Tom Cruise. Portions of two feature films set in the exotic jungles of Columbia and India were filmed in Middle Tennessee. Location scouts chose Rock Island State Park as a site to double for the jungles of Colombia in Sylvester Stallone's action-adventure yarn *The Professional.* Another Upper Cumberland location doubled for the jungles of India. Disney shot its live-action version of *The Jungle Book* at Fall Creek Falls State Park and Lost Creek Cave.

Michael E. Birdwell, Tennessee Technological University

SEE: ALEXANDER, LAMAR; MANN, DELBERT; MOORE, JOHN T. AND MARY D.; SEEING EYE, INC.; TENNESSEE STATE PRISON; THOMPSON, FRED

TENNESSEE LUNATIC ASYLUM. The movement for an asylum in Tennessee arose in the context of the nationwide reforming furor associated with the Second Great Awakening. The asylum movement in America built its ideological arguments upon the theories of a group of European physicians, including Phillipe Pinel of France, Daniel Hawke Tuke of England, and Vincenzo Chiarugi of Italy. These thinkers advocated a system known as "Moral Treatment." The heart of this system consisted of the theory that insanity often arose in the context of a disordered environment. Treatment involved removing the patients from harmful surroundings and immersing them in a carefully controlled milieu in which they could develop the habits and modes of thought conducive to health.

The Tennessee General Assembly established the asylum in 1832, and it opened its doors to patients in 1840. The physicians and staff of the institution quickly attempted to apply the principles of moral treatment, combined with somatic therapies, such as venesection and purging, commonly used during the era. In 1845 a book titled *A Secret Worth Knowing*, purportedly written by an asylum patient named Green Grimes, appeared praising the asylum's success. The book was followed the next year by a sequel, *Lily of the West*.

Despite Grimes's praise, however, the institution quickly faced a set of interlocking, intractable problems. The legislature had been quite generous with its appropriations, at least as measured by the total size of the state budget. For most years during the antebellum era, asylum appropriations far exceeded those for the state penitentiary, the other public institution founded during this era of reform, and in fact the asylum budget often surpassed that of the entire executive payroll. But the money was never enough. Despite the fact that the staff of the asylum emphasized the crucial role of prompt treatment (within a year of the onset of symptoms) in curing mental disease, families and local governments unburdened themselves of relatives or citizens with long-standing problems. The asylum also found itself overwhelmed with pauper cases, which required state financial assistance. The latter problem was compounded by an early underestimation of the costs of caring for paupers in the asylum. Actual costs per patient for pauper care amounted to more than twice the original estimate. Finally, the assumptions of antebellum medical science may well have worked against the asylum. The institution treated persons with a wide variety of illnesses, including alcoholism, depressive disorders, mania, seizure disorders, and frank psychosis. While some of these conditions might have responded to an environment structured according to the ideas of moral treatment, others probably would not. Indeed, many of these conditions only found effective treatment with the development of modern drug therapies, and many others still cannot be treated effectively.

The asylum lurched along, chronically over budget (sometimes by as much as 200 percent) and understaffed. Its original quarters, at the corner of the present 12th Avenue South and Division Street in Nashville, proved woefully inadequate. A visit by Dorothea Dix, the itinerant champion of asylum and penitentiary reform, combined with the pleas of asylum staff, prompted the legislature to approve the construction of another facility. This building, located on Murfreesboro Pike to the southeast of Nashville, remained the home of the asylum from 1851 to 1995. During that period it underwent several changes of name, becoming first the Tennessee Hospital for the Insane, then, upon incorporation with the developing system of state mental hospitals, Central Hospital for the Insane, and finally Middle Tennessee Mental Health Institute. Its institutional history, however, stretches back unbroken to the first lunatic asylum founded by the legislature in 1837.

By 1865 even the superintendent of the asylum flatly admitted that the asylum could not hope, under existing conditions, to strive for the goals of moral treatment. Instead, the institution had become a custodial facility, harboring the chronically and irredeemably ill. Yet, the institution's continued existence, albeit with a long checkered history, into the present day attests to the power and nobility of the original vision.

Robert Oliver, University of Wisconsin, Madison

Suggested Reading: Robert Oliver, "A Crumbling Fortress: The Tennessee Lunatic Asylum, 1837–1865," *Tennessee Historical Quarterly* 54(1995): 124–139

See: CARROLL, WILLIAM; MEDICINE

TENNESSEE MANUAL LABOR UNIVERSITY, the only freedmen's college in Tennessee founded by African Americans, was established in 1867 in Nashville. Despite opposition from local whites and without northern missionary help, leaders in the Gay Street Colored Christian (Disciples of Christ) Church established Tennessee Manual Labor University. Located in several frame buildings in Ebenezer, a freedmen's settlement on Murfreesboro Road, the school's property included 136 acres of land under cultivation in corn, cotton, and sorghum. In January 1868 classes began for 100 students.

The school's prinicipal founders, Peter and Samuel Lowery, were ministers in the Christian Church. Having studied under Tolbert Fanning, proprietor of Franklin College, they promoted his philosophy of practical education combined with Bible studies. The directors of Tennessee Manual Labor University, many of whom were officials in Nashville's Colored Agricultural and Mechanical

Association, encouraged a similar curriculum consisting of agricultural science, mechanical arts, and manual labor courses. Basic liberal arts and Christian education rounded out the course of studies.

When local white churches refused their support, the school's leaders commissioned Samuel Lowery and Daniel Wadkins, local African Americans, to tour the North and raise funds. Wadkins, "the father of Negro education" in Nashville, had operated classes for local free blacks from 1839 until 1856; he reopened his classes during Union occupation. Wadkins solicited a letter of support from Frederick Douglass, who said that former slaves had no alternatives to education. Despite the thousands of dollars raised for the Tennessee Manual Labor University, the school continued to experience financial problems. In 1872 Sampson W. Keeble tried unsuccessfully to gain support for legislation to provide public funds to support the school. The school closed in 1874, and the facilities quickly fell into disrepair before eventually disappearing.

Bobby L. Lovett, Tennessee State University

SEE: FANNING, TOLBERT; FREEDMEN'S BUREAU; KEEBLE, SAMPSON W.; RECONSTRUCTION

TENNESSEE MEDICAL ASSOCIATION. The Tennessee Medical Association (TMA) is a 6,800-member professional organization for medical doctors and doctors of osteopathy dedicated to protecting the health care interests of patients and enhancing the effectiveness of physicians throughout the state. Its headquarters are located in Nashville. Founded in 1830 as the Medical Society of Tennessee, the organization developed as the result of the recognition by the Tennessee General Assembly that "health is universally acknowledged to be essentially necessary to the happiness and prosperity of society." The association gained strength in the twentieth century as the practice of medicine in Tennessee became guided by national professional standards and training. The mission of today's TMA is to provide leadership to support the unity and interaction of the state's physicians. TMA carries out this mission in four areas: promoting medical knowledge, science, and high standards of medical education; sustaining medical ethics and standards of competence in the healing arts; advocating laws and regulations that protect and enhance the physician-patient relationship and improve access and delivery of quality medical care; and promoting an understanding between the public and the medical profession.

Membership in the TMA is offered locally through 51 various chartered component or county medical societies, many of which have roots in the nineteenth century. Membership is open to all medical doctors and doctors of osteopathy who agree to stand by the founding principles of the medical society. The TMA is an effective lobbyist and manages the Independent Medicine's Political Action Committee—Tennessee, or IMPACT. The society promotes collegial development in a variety of ways: peer-to-peer networking opportunities through special membership divisions address the needs and interests of young physicians, medical students, and hospital staff physicians; annual meetings shape the practice of medicine in the state and provide opportunities to debate and develop policies; local and regional seminars and workshops offer opportunities for continuing education and collegial development; monthly magazines, newsletters, special communications pieces, a home page on the world wide web, and electronic online forums promote the exchange of ideas.

Russell Miller, Tennessee Medical Association

SEE: MEDICINE; UNIVERSITY OF TENNESSEE, MEMPHIS: THE HEALTH SCIENCE CENTER; VANDERBILT UNIVERSITY MEDICAL CENTER

TENNESSEE MILLS (KNITTING MILLS) began operations in Columbia, Tennessee, in June 1931 as Massachusetts Knitting Mills. In that year, a group of Bostonians, led by Jacob S. Gordon, bought the floundering Cadet Hosiery Mills and renamed it the Massachusetts Knitting Mills (MKM). Under the leadership of Saul Kaplan, MKM made its first shipment of full-fashioned hosiery to New Orleans in July 1931. The company maintained a large labor force of 585 employees. Potential employees worked for a trial period of two weeks at no pay before signing contracts. Mill hands often worked 10 to 12 hours a day at a rate of ten cents per hour until legislation set minimum wages and hours.

In 1941 management promoted Frank Cover to general manager of the newly renamed factory, the Tennessee Knitting Mills (TKM). The war with Japan soon limited the male labor force and restricted any available silk to parachute production. In response, TKM began hiring and training female workers and experimenting with cotton and nylon. After the war, hundreds of returning veterans resumed their TKM jobs once the mill made the transition to postwar production.

During the 1950s in an effort to improve labor relations, management created two men's baseball teams, the TKM Knitters (affiliated with the Alabama-Tennessee League) and the TKM Nighthawks (composed entirely of night shift workers). The mill also sponsored a female interdepartmental softball association and a 16-member TKM Choir.

Despite such efforts, TKM did not escape labor problems. In 1954 the American Federation of Hosiery Workers lost a National Labor Relations Board election at TKM by the close vote of 125 pro-union to 147 anti-union votes. Labor problems, economic depression in the hosiery industry, and the decline in demand for full-fashioned hosiery resulted in a drop in TKM employment to 300 workers. Union organizers continued their efforts, and in 1956 mill workers voted in the Hosiery Workers of America Union (HWAU). Cover refused to accept the union and, following a year of failed negotiations, announced that TKM would cease most operations.

During the summer of 1957, many unemployed mill hands began crossing the picket line set up by the striking knitters. After several minor scuffles, the strike erupted in violence on September 25, 1957, when shots were fired into TKM's water tank and strikers overturned a car attempting to cross the picket line. Police quickly arrested strikers and broke up demonstrations. Cover eventually rehired those knitters who wanted to return, but at a rate of one or two at a time to prevent reorganization of the union.

Economic conditions declined after the 1957 strike. In response to changes in fashion, the mill began manufacturing leotards, sweaters, and seamless nylon panty hose, marketing these items to J.C. Penney's, Sears-Roebuck, and other major chain stores. By the early 1980s, TKM could no longer compete effectively in the apparel industry, and the mill ceased operations on October 30, 1981.

Brian Eades, Shelby, North Carolina

SUGGESTED READING: Brian Russell Eades, "Early Twentieth Century Factories in Middle Tennessee: A Historical Analysis of Tennessee Knitting Mills and the Fly Manufacturing Company," M.A. Thesis, Middle Tennessee State University, 1997

SEE: INDUSTRY; LABOR; MAURY COUNTY

TENNESSEE OILERS is the first National Football League (NFL) team to be based in Tennessee. Previously established in Houston, Texas, the Oilers secured a move to Nashville in 1996 after reaching an agreement with the city that included, among other things, the construction of a new 65,000-seat stadium. The contract, however, became a point of controversy in the city, reflecting contemporary nationwide debate over the relationship between professional sports and municipalities. Divided over the issue, Nashville put the question to public vote and ultimately approved the arrangement with the team.

Oilers executives first approached Nashville officials in July 1995 when the team was in the midst of conflict in Houston. Grasping the opportunity, Nashville Mayor Phil Bredesen and Tennessee Governor Don Sundquist quickly signed an exclusive negotiating agreement with the Oilers. In mid-November, Nashville and the Oilers entered a $292 million contract to bring the team to Tennessee.

The basic terms of the agreement required Nashville to construct a 65,000-seat open air stadium, which the Oilers were obligated to lease for home games for 30 years. Negotiators chose the east bank of the Cumberland River, an industrial area facing the downtown district, as the site for the new stadium. Building the facility required moving 49 businesses, rerouting railroad tracks and sewer and water lines, refurbishing bridges, and developing greenways along the riverbank. The project is being funded in various ways. The sale of personal seat licenses (PSLs), a type of "lifetime season ticket," is expected to bring $71 million, and the state will contribute approximately $80 million. Nashville will pay its portion through revenues gained via sales tax, hotel tax, and the Oilers lease payments. The two major sources of Nashville's capital, however, are municipal bonds and an "in lieu of tax" charge levied on the local water department.

A number of Nashville citizens opposed the deal as a poor economic decision for the city. They questioned the use of public funds for private enterprise and argued that the city's money was needed to back more important civic projects such as schools. Many feared higher water rates and property taxes. Others thought the team would not draw enough support and eventually millionaire-owner Bud Adams would pull the team out of Nashville, leaving the city in dire economic straits. Those favoring the deal claimed that the stadium and team would generate substantial economic growth, create numerous jobs, and bring much needed development to the east bank. In addition to enticing conventions, tourism, and corporate relocation to the city, the Oilers would promote intangible benefits such as civic pride and an improved metropolitan image.

Project opponents formed the Concerned Citizens for Metro Nashville, and in less than three weeks collected 45,000 signatures to force a referendum vote on the issue. The "Yes" team inundated the city with yard signs, bumper stickers, and television, radio, and newspaper ads and overshadowed the grassroots, and underfunded, "No" organization. On May 7, 1996, 42 percent of registered voters (125,897) voted 58.8 percent to 41.2 percent in favor of the agreement with the Oilers.

As the Oilers became a reality, the city immediately began construction at the stadium site in anticipation of the team's arrival. Still, a few glitches developed that caused a new wave of skepticism. In April 1997 the Oilers received a 64 percent rent reduction because they chose to locate their practice field off the stadium site. Even though this was a legitimate option stated in the contract, it annoyed many taxpayers and council members. After coming close to establishing their practice facility outside the Metropolitan Davidson County area, the Oilers settled on an 18-acre site in the Nashville suburb of Bellevue. In August 1997, however, the team announced that the site would serve them only temporarily. In addition, owner Bud Adams remained reluctant to change the team's name to something more oriented toward Tennessee.

Despite these problems, the Oilers continue to enjoy strong support throughout Nashville and many expect the team to improve the city's image and economy. The team played its 1997 season at Memphis's Liberty Bowl before small crowds, but managed a winning record in home games and achieved an overall record of 8-8. The Oilers will play their 1998 games at the Vanderbilt Stadium.

Teresa Biddle-Douglass, Middle Tennessee State University

SEE: NASHVILLE PREDATORS

TENNESSEE ORNITHOLOGICAL SOCIETY (TOS),

founded in Nashville in October 1915, is an independent, non-profit, educational, scientific organization dedicated to the study and conservation of birds. The original objectives of the TOS still hold today: (1) to promote the science of ornithology in Tennessee, (2) to publish the results of its investigations, (3) to stand for the passage and enforcement of wise and judicious laws for bird protection, and (4) to promote bird study and protection by any other means that may be deemed advisable. The Society's official journal, *The Migrant,* first published in 1930, provides an important repository of sight records and articles to facilitate the tracking of changes in Tennessee bird populations and the *Tennessee Warbler* is the statewide TOS newsletter. In 1933 the TOS received widespread attention through its campaign to select a state bird (the Mockingbird), which took place through an open election. Current activities include state meetings and field trips, as well as major cooperative projects such as the Christmas Bird Counts, the Tennessee Breeding Bird Atlas Project, Teaming with Wildlife, and Partners in Flight. Over a dozen local chapters from Bristol to Memphis publish their own newsletters and carry out activities appropriate to their area of the state. By the mid-1990s electronic mail and the World Wide Web facilitated communication among the TOS chapter and members.

Edwin S. Gleaves, Tennessee State Library and Archives

SEE: TENNESSEE STATE SYMBOLS; TENNESSEE WILDLIFE RESOURCES AGENCY

TENNESSEE PRESIDENTS TRUST. Founded in 1989

as a service organization of the University of Tennessee, Knoxville, the Tennessee Presidents Trust supports financially the work of a unique documentary editing center dedicated to the publication of the papers of Tennessee's three American presidents, Andrew Jackson, James K. Polk, and Andrew Johnson. The Trust also assists in building statewide awareness and support for the university's historical research program, as well as fostering a greater appreciation of the Tennessee presidents' legacy of civic responsibility. Both the Trust and the documentary editing center are located on the second floor of Hoskins Library.

All three editorial projects undertake the same tasks of collecting, transcribing, researching, annotating, and publishing the papers of their respective president. Under the direction of Harold Moser, Wayne Cutler, and Paul Bergeron, the three projects have published a total of 27 volumes: Jackson five, Polk nine, and Johnson 13. Each of the projects has received prestigious research grants from the National Endowment for the Humanities and the National Publications and Records Commission. The Tennessee Historical Commission also makes modest continuing grants in support of the center.

In addition to support for the editorial projects, the Trust publishes a numbered issue in its Occasional Pamphlet Series and provides instructional aids for teaching American and Tennessee history in the state's primary and secondary schools. In 1992 the Trust prepared and distributed an illustrated *Tennessee Presidents Portfolio,* which provides classroom teachers with materials suitable for grades four to six. Through generous grant support from First Tennessee Bank, the Trust produced and distributed gratis a 26-minute video, entitled *Voices for Union,* to some 1,500 secondary schools in the state. The video distribution, the bank's bicentennial gift to the people of Tennessee, included a printed guide with text, graphic descriptors, glossary of terms, and map exercises for further study. In addition to its educational projects, the Trust hosts commemorative programs for its members and recognizes distinguished civic leaders in Tennessee through its newsletter, *The Legacy.*

Within eight years of its founding the Trust had reached a membership of over 900. In 1993 the Trust began a new tradition of celebrating "Tennessee Presidents Month" in February of each year to coincide with the national Presidents Day. In addition to individual memberships, the Trust offers corporate membership to civic clubs wishing to affiliate and undertake local educational and commemorative work. To date, 11 Civitan Clubs have brought their 300 members into affiliation to assist in preserving the Tennessee Presidents' legacy.

Wayne Cutler, University of Tennessee, Knoxville

SEE: JACKSON, ANDREW; JOHNSON, ANDREW; POLK, JAMES K.; UNIVERSITY OF TENNESSEE

TENNESSEE PRISON SYSTEM. Section 32 of the

Tennessee Constitution states that "the erection of safe and comfortable prisons, the inspection of prisons, and the humane treatment of prisoners, shall be provided for." In 1796 the legislature passed three separate acts to establish courthouses, jails, and stocks in three separarate counties of the state. Similar acts were subsequently passed providing for the establishment of small prisons in the county seats. In 1813 the legislature authorized the taking of voluntary contributions for the purpose of building a penitentiary, but the effort failed after only about $2,000 was subscribed.

In 1819 Governor Joseph McMinn suggested that a loan be made from the State Bank to fund the construction of a prison, but it was not until 1829 that the legislature passed a law to build one in Nashville. Work began in April 1830, and on January 1, 1831, Governor William Carroll opened the prison for the reception of convicts. The prison contained 200 cells, a warden's dwelling, a storehouse, hospital, and other structures. Carroll also was responsible for criminal code reform, abolishing whipping, branding, the pillory, and the use of stocks, as well as many crimes for which execution had been the punishment.

Tennessee's first prison was used until 1858, when new construction was completed. In 1898 it was replaced by the "modern" Tennessee State Prison, located in the Cockrill Bend area of Davidson County. This new prison resulted from the efforts of Governor Peter Turney, who also secured funding for Brushy Mountain State Penitentiary in Morgan County. The Turney administration brought an end to the convict lease system, a badly abused system of leasing inmate labor to private industry, which had been in force since 1866.

In 1930 a new building for adult female offenders was built on the grounds of the Tennessee State Penitentiary. Although the female facility was located separately, it was administratively dependent on the Tennessee State Prison.

By 1937 both state prisons were badly overcrowded, and in December, the Western Tennessee Penal Farm (later Fort Pillow State Penal Farm, now the Cold Creek Correctional Facility) was opened in Lauderdale County. This institution included about 5,000 acres of agricultural land, where inmates raised diversified crops and livestock. Also in 1937 the General Assembly approved a bond issue for $1,500,000 to establish Tennessee State Industries, which provided employment for approximately 600 prisoners. It also established the Board of Pardon and Paroles.

A number of changes took place in the 1950s. In 1955 an inmate classification system was created at the Tennessee State Penitentiary, and the Department of Institutions and Public Welfare was renamed the Tennessee Department of Correction (TDOC). Two years later, the General Assembly established the Division of Juvenile Probation, and a statewide system of juvenile probation became operational in 1958.

Operational and administrative reforms occupied prison personnel during the 1960s. In 1961 the Division of Adult Probation and Parole was established, and in 1963 the Board of Paroles appointed its first black member. In 1965 juvenile institutions were desegregated, juveniles were classified by age, and a prison school was established and accredited. Corporal punishment for adult offenders was abolished in 1966, and the Tennessee Prison for Women became operational. The Tennessee State Penitentiary initiated treatment services for the first time in 1968 and opened a halfway house for male offenders in Nashville the following year.

In the 1970s the Tennessee prison system felt the impact of continuing state reform and reorganization, as well as the effect of federal court decisions. The General Assembly authorized adult work release in 1970. Several significant events happened in 1972. A reorganization of the Board of Pardons and Paroles gave the Governor the power to appoint board members and the chair. Brushy Mountain State Prison closed following a series of labor problems. In June the U.S. Supreme Court, in *Furman v. Georgia*, declared capital punishment, as it was then applied, unconstitutional. The death sentences of Tennessee prisoners were commuted to life imprisonment. In Tennessee, the gallows preceded the electric chair, and no penitentiary records exist to indicate how many were executed in this manner. However, 78 were executed by electrocution, beginning with Julius Morgan in 1916, and ending with William Tines in 1960. In 1976 the U.S. Supreme Court, in *Gregg v. Georgia*, ruled that Georgia's revised death penalty statute met constitutional requirements; and many states, including Tennessee, rewrote their laws to conform to the Georgia model. As of 1997, however, no one has been executed under the Tennessee death penalty law.

Other significant events of the 1970s included an inmate revolt over living conditions, called the "pork chop" riot, at the Tennessee State Penitentiary in 1975, the re-opening of Brushy Mountain State Penitentiary in 1976, and the opening of the Lois M. DeBerry Institute for Special Needs Offenders in 1977. In 1978 corporal punishment for juvenile offenders was abolished. That same year, the Board of Paroles was expanded to five members; in 1979 it was separated from TDOC and became an autonomous unit.

The 1980s were a troubled decade for Tennessee's prison system. In 1982 the federal district court declared parts of the system unconstitutional in *Grubbs v. Bradley,* and appointed a Special Master to oversee improvements in the system. In the summer of 1985, overcrowding provoked violence and riots occurred throughout the prison system, causing millions of dollars in damage. The General Assembly responded by holding its First Extraordinary Session on Corrections and passing the Comprehensive Corrections Improvement Act of 1985. This act established the Oversight Committee on Corrections, the

Tennessee Sentencing Commission, and the Community Corrections Program.

All juvenile functions and responsibilities were removed from TDOC in 1989, and the Department of Youth Development was created to assume these duties. Later that year, both the Riverbend Maximum Security Institution in Nashville and the Wayne County Boot Camp became operational.

In 1992 the Corrections Corporation of America, headquartered in Nashville, began operation of the South Central Correctional Center in Clifton. This was the first private prison to operate in Tennessee. In that same year, the Tennessee State Penitentiary in Nashville was closed, and TDOC was permanently enjoined by the federal court from housing inmates there. The following year, the Special Master released TDOC from supervision.

The Tennessee Department of Correction became the first adult correctional system in America to have all of its institutions accredited by the American Correctional Association.

Frank Lee and Robert Rogers, Middle Tennessee State University

SUGGESTED READINGS: Larry D. Gossett, *The Keepers and the Kept: The First Hundred Years of the Tennessee Prison System, 1830–1930* (1992); Tennessee State Penitentiary, *History of the Tennessee Penal Institutions: 1813–1940* (1940)

SEE: ALEXANDER, LAMAR; BLANTON, LEONARD RAY; CONVICT LEASE WARS; MCMINN, JOSEPH; MORGAN COUNTY; TENNESSEE STATE PRISON; TURNEY, PETER

TENNESSEE PUBLIC SERVICE COMMISSION.

Regulation of railroads, common carriers, and public utilities in Tennessee has followed development in the technological and economic structures of those industries, changes in general professional and public attitudes toward monopolies, competition and governmental regulation, particularly as reflected at the federal level, and the vicissitudes of party and personal politics.

In 1897, following the creation of the Interstate Commerce Commission and the perceived need to regulate railroads, the legislature established the Railroad Commission, consisting of three members, one from each Grand Division, to be elected statewide for six-year staggered terms, having the power to fix freight and passenger rates, to investigate rates and practices of railroads, and to approve tariffs. Unjust discrimination, excessive rates, and undue preferences were prohibited in provisions codifying the common law.

Electric power, street railways, and telephones developed rapidly in the late nineteenth and early twentieth century. They were regulated by city franchises, state charter provisions, and the common law. In 1919, primarily at the urging of street railway officials, the legislature changed the name of

the Railroad Commission to Railroad and Public Utilities Commission. It gave that agency general regulatory power over public utilities, including the power to approve franchises, review local government regulations, fix rates and regulate practices, and the power to assess the property of such utilities for taxation.

In 1923, primarily at the urging of the electric companies, new utilities and extensions into new territories were required to obtain authority from the Commission. Public utilities were viewed as natural monopolies and competition was considered wasteful and destructive. The administration was a prototypical administrative agency.

In 1933 the Commission was given jurisdiction over motor carriers, entry was restricted, and rates and practices were regulated. In the late 1930s, with the creation of the Tennessee Valley Authority, almost all of Tennessee was served by municipality- or cooperatively-owned electric power entities which were excluded from commission jurisdiction. In 1943 street railways were removed from commission jurisdiction. In 1955 the name was changed to the Public Service Commission.

By the 1980s the prevailing policies at the federal level shifted to favor competition. Railroads and then motor carriers were substantially deregulated. Competition was introduced in long distance telephone service. New forms of price regulation were adopted. The pressure for competition began to reach the electric power and gas industries. In 1995 the legislature adopted a new telecommunications policy to bring competition to that industry.

In 1995, as a result of scandals in election practices, charges of favoritism, and efforts of Governor Don Sundquist, a Republican (no Republican had ever been elected to the Commission), the Commission was terminated effective June 30, 1996. It was replaced by the Tennessee Regulatory Authority, whose three members were appointed by the Governor, the Lieutenant Governor, and the Speaker of the House, and whose jurisdiction was limited to telecommunications, gas, and water and sewer utilities. The history of the Public Service Commission reflects the political and economic history of Tennessee for the 99 years of its existence, the continuing experiment in Federalism, and the development of administrative law.

Valerius Sanford, Nashville

SEE: GOVERNMENT; LAW; SUNDQUIST, DON

TENNESSEE RIVER SYSTEM

covers 41,000 square miles, draining portions of 60 Tennessee counties and seven states. The Tennessee River is the largest tributary to the Ohio River and is its equal in water volume. From its mouth at Paducah, Kentucky, to the Virginia headwaters of its own longest tributary, the

TSLA

Coal barge "Donna Lee" on the Tennessee River at Savannah, 1946.

Tennessee travels 1,100 miles, falling 2,000 feet in elevation along the way.

The Holston River is the largest tributary to the Tennessee and includes the Watauga within its drainage. The French Broad meets the Holston at Knoxville after gathering the waters of the Pigeon and Nolichucky rivers. The Little Tennessee River joins the Tennessee at Lenoir City, and the Clinch enters at Kingston; the Clinch and Powell confluence is now found at Norris Lake. Below Decatur, the Hiwassee brings its waters and those of the Ocoee River to the Tennessee and above South Pittsburg is the mouth of the Sequatchie River. The Flint and Elk rivers enter in the great bend of the Tennessee which flows through Alabama and the northeast corner of Mississippi. As the Tennessee River flows north through its western Tennessee valley, the Duck River (fed by the Buffalo River) joins south of New Johnsonville, and the Big Sandy joins near Paris Landing. Continuing its way across western Kentucky, the Tennessee joins the Ohio approximately 12 miles west of the Cumberland River confluence and 30 miles east of the union of the Ohio and Mississippi rivers.

The name of the Tennessee and the river's origins have changed several times since Europeans first attempted to map its course. In the late 1600s, French maps showed the river as the "Caquinampo" or "Kasqui," while early 1700 maps used "Cussate," "Hogohegee," "Callamaco," and "Acanseapi." A British map of 1755 shows the Tennessee as the "River of the Cherokees," the Little Tennessee as the "Tenassee or Satico," and the Clinch as the "Pelisipi." By the late 1700s, the main river was known as the Tennessee, and it was considered to begin at the mouth of the Little Tennessee. Through much of the 1800s, the confluence of the Clinch with the river was considered the start of the Tennessee. In 1889 the Tennessee General Assembly declared the upper limit of the Tennessee to be at Kingsport, but in 1890 a federal statute recognized the junction of the French Broad and Holston rivers as the start of the Tennessee, a designation that still stands.

Although the Tennessee was one of the largest rivers east of the Mississippi, the presence of powerful Indian nations along its banks coupled with a number of significant navigational hazards prevented the river from becoming a major migration route for European settlers moving west. The terrors of the river as it cuts a 30-mile long gorge through Walden's Ridge at Chattanooga are well dramatized in John Donelson's account of the 1780 voyage down the river. Muscle Shoals in northern Alabama formed a series of obstructions nearly 40 miles in length, with rock reefs, gravel bars, rapids, log snags, and a shallow channel that caused boats to ground. The Chickasaws controlled the region of the shoals, and the Chickamaugas controlled the gorge. Until the early 1800s, these barriers left only the upper and lower Tennessee valleys open for settlement.

Commercial keelboats carrying goods and people traveled up river as far as Tuscumbia by the 1820s. In 1821 the first steamboat, the *Osage,* traveled from the Ohio River as far as Florence, Alabama. Using the spring's high water, the *Atlas* reached Knoxville in 1828 and claimed a $640 prize as the first steamboat to reach that city. The steam lines divided service between Paducah-Florence and Chattanooga-Decatur, with limited service from Decatur to Knoxville, and regular through steam line service from Knoxville to the Ohio did not occur until 1890.

During the Civil War, the Tennessee River generally was seen as something to be crossed, not used as a military route, although the Union army did transport some troops by water, chiefly in the western valley. The Confederate Fort Henry, built to guard the Tennessee River, fell in February 1862, and by April U.S. forces occupied the lower valley. Battles took place near the river—Shiloh, Chattanooga, Chickamauga, and Knoxville—but the objective remained the capture of railroads more than waterways.

Many river towns were damaged or destroyed during the war, and in March 1867 a flood from the upper valley to Paducah washed away houses, bridges, and submerged some towns. The postwar arrival of outside capital helped revive the iron and timber industries of the eastern Tennessee valley. John T. Wilder's Rockwood iron works used the river to transfer material to Chattanooga, and the Scottish Carolina Timber and Land Company established operations on the Pigeon and French Broad rivers.

In 1875 work began on a canal and dam system around Muscles Shoals and incorporated an 1837 canal built by the U.S. Army Corps of Engineers at Tuscumbia. Opening in 1890, it was the longest steamboat canal in the world, but railroads largely had supplanted river commerce on the Tennessee. Steamboating declined sharply after 1916, and the canal ceased operation in 1918. Commercial steamers were gone by the 1930s when the age of dams arrived.

In 1900 the U.S. Army Corps of Engineers proposed a dam on the Tennessee River at Scotts Point below Chattanooga, which would provide hydroelectric power and conquer the gorge's hazards. The site was moved to Hales Bar, and the Chattanooga and Tennessee River Power Company began construction in 1905. The fearsome gorge was tamed in 1913 when the first boat locked through the dam. In 1916 a federal report recommended three dams to deal with Muscle Shoals, and the Corps of Engineers began construction of Wilson Dam near Florence in 1918. Wilson was completed in 1925, and the Corps began construction of Wheeler Dam several miles upriver in 1933, the same year the Tennessee Valley Authority (TVA) was established.

TVA took over the Wheeler project and other dams on the Tennessee system and initiated a massive building program. In its first ten years, TVA completed nine dams, with Norris Dam the first to come on line in 1936. By 1944, a nine-foot deep channel was available from Paducah to Knoxville, and that year the first modern towboat and barges arrived in Knoxville. Diesel-powered tows now dominated the river, transporting sand, gravel, coal, grain, forest products, and petroleum products. TVA continued its mission of flood control and power generation and in 1980 more than 30 dams existed on the Tennessee system.

Perhaps the last great change to the Tennessee River was the Tennessee-Tombigbee Waterway, authorized by Congress in 1946. The "Tenn-Tom" was designed by the Corps of Engineers to connect the Tennessee River near Pickwick Landing by canal and Yellow Creek to the Tombigbee River in Mississippi. This route allowed barge traffic to reach Mobile Bay and the Gulf of Mexico. The 232-mile waterway was begun in 1972 and completed in the 1980s.

In the mid- and late-twentieth century, the Tennessee River system became as much the focus of recreation and environmental preservation as the focus of commerce and industry. Tourism dominated lake use and TVA power generation shifted primarily to steam and nuclear-powered plants. Environmental activists, sportsmen, and archaeologists opposed new dam construction, losing against the Tellico Dam on the Little Tennessee River, and prevailing against the Columbia Dam on the Duck River. The battle over paper plant pollution on the Pigeon River was as active in 1998 as it was in 1908, and a new battle had formed over chip mills and their use of the Tennessee. As the century ended, the purposes of the TVA as a public agency were under examination as officials considered the best ways to manage the Tennessee River system.

Ann Toplovich, Tennessee Historical Society

SUGGESTED READING: Donald Davidson, *The Tennessee*, 2 vols. (1946 and 1948)

SEE: CONSERVATION; DONELSON, JOHN; FORT HENRY; HALES BAR DAM; OVERHILL CHEROKEES; PICKWICK LANDING STATE PARK; STEAMBOATING; TENNESSEE VALLEY AUTHORITY; TENNESSEE-TOMBIGBEE WATERWAY; TIMBER INDUSTRY; TRANSPORTATION, RIVER; U.S. ARMY CORPS OF ENGINEERS; WILDER, JOHN T.

TENNESSEE ROOM, NSDAR HEADQUARTERS.

The Tennessee Daughters of the American Revolution are represented in Washington, D.C., by the Tennessee Room of the Daughters of the American Revolution (DAR) Museum. It is located in Memorial Continental Hall, a National Historic Landmark constructed between 1904 and 1910 to house the offices and auditorium of the fledgling heritage society. State and local organizations raised money for the new building, with architectural elements named for each supporting group. The Tennessee Room was originally the office of the society's chief financial officer.

By 1920 the DAR had outgrown its original building. A new office building and a new auditorium, Constitution Hall, replaced the original offices which were returned to the sponsoring societies to be furnished as period rooms. Since 1937, the state period rooms have been part of the DAR Museum.

Today the Tennessee room represents a parlor of the Jacksonian era and includes several objects that were in the White House during Andrew Jackson's administration. Two armchairs by Georgetown cabinetmaker William King and another by French cabinetmaker Pierre Antoine Bellangé were purchased for the White House by James Monroe. The King chairs, of undecorated mahogany, contrast sharply with the elaborately carved and gilded French example. Monroe apparently never used the American chairs for they were not upholstered until Jackson's administration. Jackson himself may have considered the Bellangé chairs to be more "presidential," as he posed for portraitist Ralph E.W. Earl seated in one. This portrait now hangs in the Tennessee Room.

Diane L. Dunkley, DAR Museum

SEE: EARL, RALPH E.W., JACKSON, ANDREW

TENNESSEE SCENIC RIVERS PROGRAM. In 1998 the Tennessee Scenic Rivers Act celebrates its thirtieth anniversary. The Tennessee program, a pioneering effort, was the second state river conservation program in the nation (Wisconsin was the first, but Tennessee's program was the more comprehensive). The Scenic Rivers Act, based on an early draft of the National Wild and Scenic Rivers Act, reflected long-standing conservation ideas from the conservation and progressive movements of the late 1880s through the early 1900s. The Tennessee Scenic Rivers Act owes its existence to the efforts of Liane and William Russell of Oak Ridge, Bob Miller of Nashville, former state representative Bill Pope, and governors Buford Ellington and Winfield Dunn. The Tennessee Citizens for Wilderness Planning (TCWP) and the Tennessee Scenic Rivers Association (TSRA) also provided key support in the passage of the act. Enacted during a period of awakening awareness of environmental needs, the Scenic Rivers Program received much financial support through the federal Land and Water Conservation fund.

Through the years, the program has met local opposition, in part due to poor communication with local riparian landowners. A more fundamental conflict centers on the fact that the program's support base is drawn from urban and suburban populations, while the areas of preservation interest are rural. As the state and federal programs developed, river protection planners "learned the hard way" the importance of building local constituencies and establishing effective communication with riparian landowners. Officials also have learned of the need to set project boundaries through a carefully planned process of public education and comment.

One recent trend in river protection has been the growth of local river protection projects, particularly land trusts or conservancies and greenway projects. The Wolf River Conservancy in Shelby and Fayette counties, and the Tennessee River Gorge Natural Areas Trust and the North Chickamauga Creek Greenway in Hamilton County are outstanding examples of these efforts.

The most successful federal river preservation efforts in Tennessee grew out of the failure to place the Obed River in the state system. The Russells and TCWP played instrumental roles in designating the Obed as a National Wild and Scenic River and the Big South Fork of the Cumberland River as a National River Recreation Area.

At least three other areas deserve special notice. The Hatchie River, the largest river in the program at 185 miles, is the last major unchannelized tributary of the lower Mississippi River Basin. Surrounded by the Cherokee National Forest, the Hiwassee River in southeastern Polk County is the most heavily used recreational river in the program.

The success of the 1996 Whitewater Olympic Venue on the Ocoee River in Polk County raised the visibility of whitewater recreation for local economic development and "eco-tourism."

The Department of Environment and Conservation's Natural Heritage Section recently completed a Statewide Rivers inventory. This inventory looked at most free-flowing (non-dam) rivers and streams in Tennessee and rated them based on a number of values (recreational boating, natural and scenic quality, recreational fishing, and water quality). This inventory, available to the public in a "Summary Report," will facilitate public education and public discussion of water resource policy issues.

The State Rivers program now faces two conflicting realities. One is the likelihood of shrinking federal and state dollars that are necessary for the type of river protection efforts undertaken during the 1970s. Another "reality" is the effect of increasing growth and development pressures that accompany urbanization and suburbanization. The increase of development pressure on environmentally sensitive and historically open space and countryside necessitates enhanced support for land preservation and effective land planning.

Bob B. Allen, Nashville

SEE: BIG SOUTH FORK NATIONAL RIVER AND RECREATION AREA; CONSERVATION; CUMBERLAND RIVER; MISSISSIPPI RIVER SYSTEM; RUSSELL, LIANE AND WILLIAM; TENNESSEE RIVER SYSTEM

TENNESSEE SECONDARY SCHOOL ATHLETIC ASSOCIATION (TSSAA). In 1925 a group of high school administrators attending a meeting of the Tennessee State Teachers' Association in Nashville organized the Tennessee Secondary School Athletic Association. Commonly known as TSSAA, the founders established the Association "to stimulate and regulate the athletic relations of the secondary schools in Tennessee." The group elected G.C. Carney of Nashville Central High School as its first president and named A.J. Smith, superintendent of the Clarksville schools, the first secretary-treasurer. F.S. Elliott of Memphis Whitehaven, TSSAA secretary-treasurer from 1930 to 1942, and Pat W. Kerr, the Association's president from 1930 to 1936, also provided valuable leadership during these formative years.

The TSSAA jointly sponsored the 1927 Boys' State Basketball Tournament with the tournament's founding organization, *The Nashville Tennessean.* The TSSAA assumed full responsibility for the Boys' State Basketball Tournament in 1928. The late Blinkey Horn, sports editor of the *Tennessean,* initiated the Boys' State Basketball Tournament in 1921.

The first Girls' State Basketball Tournament took place the following year, making Tennessee one of the few states to offer interscholastic athletics for girls. The initial girls' tournament was unfortunately short lived due to financial constraints and the variety of rules used in women's basketball. Girls' basketball teams, however, continued to thrive at most high schools throughout the mid-twentieth century, and in 1958 the TSSAA sponsored its first Girls' State Basketball Tournament, which followed a six-on-six, half court format supposedly better suited to the physical endurance of girls. Girls's high school basketball switched to a five-on-five, full court format in 1980.

From its beginning the TSSAA consisted of a nine-member Board of Control, in addition to the two part-time officers. Made up of elected school officials from different athletic districts across the state, the Board of Control enforces TSSAA regulations, conducts state meetings, authorizes expenses, and registers officials. In 1935 the TSSAA created a Legislative Council to make necessary amendments to the organization's constitution and bylaws. William Osteen, principal of Millington Central High School, first served on the TSSAA's Legislative Council and then on the Board of Control from 1942 to 1971, the last 13 years as Board president.

In 1946 the Board of Control hired the TSSAA's first fulltime executive officer and opened a state office in Trenton. A.F. Bridges, formerly a teacher, coach, and administrator in several Tennessee communities and last in the Covington city schools, became the TSSAA's first executive secretary and served in that capacity until 1972. Bridges was nicknamed "Mr. TSSAA" for his dedicated leadership. In 1964 when the Board of Control took a major step toward integration by accepting black schools as affiliate members. By March 1966 the first integrated Boys' State Basketball Tournament took place at Vanderbilt's Memorial Gymnasium with Nashville's Pearl High School, led by Perry Wallace, winning the title.

Suprisingly, it was not until early in 1969 that the TSSAA approved a playoff plan for state competition in football. The plan called for schools to be split up into three classes (A, AA, AAA) based on enrollment. The plan also divided each class into four regions with regional winners advancing to the state playoffs. The first playoff games and State Football Championship games took place in November 1969. Morristown East won the Class AAA title, while Loudon claimed the Class AA crown, and South Pittsburg captured the Class A championship. The classification of football sparked a dramatic growth in the TSSAA program. In 1969, 12 teams advanced to the state playoffs with a total attendance of 23,146. In 1995, 160 teams advanced to the playoffs in five classes with overall attendance ballooning to 290,000 people. By 1973 the TSSAA introduced a classification system for basketball as well.

Gill Gideon of Jackson became the second executive secretary of the TSSAA in 1972 and held that post until his retirement in 1986. Gideon served as president of the National Federation of State High School Associations for 1981–1982. Ronnie Carter joined the TSSAA staff in 1978 from Nashville's Overton High School as the assistant executive secretary. Carter succeeded Gill Gideon as the TSSAA's executive director and continues to serve in this capacity. Perhaps the most significant change in recent years occurred in May 1996, when the TSSAA split schools into two divisions after public schools complained that private schools were offering scholarships to students based on athletic ability.

The TSSAA that began with 45 schools in 1925 grew to an organization now based in Hermitage with 375 schools in its membership and an annual operating budget in excess of $1.2 million. Nevertheless, the TSSAA remains a voluntary, nonprofit, self-supporting organization which now sponsors football, baseball, and wrestling for boys only and softball and volleyball for girls only as well as basketball, track, tennis, cross country, soccer, and golf for girls and boys.

Kent Whitworth, East Tennessee Historical Society
SEE: EDUCATION; WALLACE, PERRY

TENNESSEE SHELL COMPANY. Robert Latendresse began Tennessee Shell Company in Camden in 1954 to ship Tennessee mollusk shells to Japan. There the shells were cut, ground into round beads, and inserted by Japanese pearl farmers into mollusks in Japan's waters to be the nucleus of culturing pearls. The success of this arrangement led to shipments to China, Thailand, Indonesia, and other Pacific islands as well as to Japan, so that today all cultured pearl necklaces begin with beads from United States shells, and 60 percent of those beads come from Tennessee.

Once firmly established as a leading provider of Tennessee native shells to the East and as an importer/dealer of Japanese and Chinese pearls, Latendresse and his wife Chessy commenced extensive research and experimentation with growing their own fresh water cultured pearls in Tennessee. Two decades later, they had their first substantial harvest in 1985. By 1990 Latendresse sold Tennessee Shell Company and concentrated on a related business he began in 1961, American Pearl Company. It provides the only commercially available pearl culturing in the United States. Still family-owned and presided over by daughter Gina, this enterprise maintains pearl farms in Tennessee from which it markets loose pearls to U.S. and overseas designers as well as offering several lines of pearl jewelry and custom pieces.

Margaret D. Binnicker, Middle Tennessee State University

SUGGESTED READING: Fred Ware, "The Pearl," *National Geographic* 168(August 1985): 193–223
SEE: BENTON COUNTY; MUSSELLING

TENNESSEE SMALL SCHOOL SYSTEMS v. McWHERTER, 851 S. W. 2d 139 (1993).

The Tennessee Supreme Court decided that the system of financing public education in Tennessee violated the provisions of the Tennessee Constitution guaranteeing equal protection of the law to all citizens. The court held that the Tennessee General Assembly must maintain and support a system of free public schools that affords equal educational opportunities to students in small counties as well as large, and rural counties as well as urban.

After the U.S. Supreme Court decided in *San Antonio Independent School District v. Rodriguez* (1971) that inequality in educational opportunity based on the unequal wealth of school districts did not violate the Equal Protection Clause of the U.S. Constitution, parents and school officials from poorer school districts across the country turned to state courts and state constitutions for relief.

Tennessee Small School Systems, an unincorporated association of 77 rural school districts, filed suit against the State of Tennessee and Governor Ned McWherter on July 7, 1988, in the Davidson County Chancery Court to overturn the Tennessee system of financing local school systems. Memphis attorney Lewis R. Donelson represented the small schools, and Charles W. Burson, the Tennessee Attorney General and Reporter, represented the State of Tennessee.

After a six week trial, Davidson County Chancellor C. Allen High ruled on August 6, 1991, that the public education funding system violated the equal protection clause of the Tennessee Constitution. He found that students in rural school did not have equal access to science laboratories, computers, current and new textbooks, adequate buildings, foreign language courses, state-mandated art and music classes, and other curricular opportunities. When the state appealed, the Tennessee Court of Appeals reversed the trial court and set the stage for arguments before the Tennessee Supreme Court.

While the Small Schools case was pending before the Tennessee Supreme Court, the General Assembly passed the Educational Improvement Act of 1992 that contained a new formula, called the Basic Education Program (BEP), to replace the old statutory funding scheme. The General Assembly, however, did not vote to fund the BEP until after the Supreme Court's decision in the Small Schools case.

Chief Justice Lyle Reid, writing for a unanimous Supreme Court, agreed with the Chancellor's findings that the old system was inadequate and unequal. The court found that there was no legitimate state interest to justify a system that resulted in inadequate and unequal educational opportunities for children in small school systems and held that the existing statutory funding scheme violated the equal protection provisions of the Tennessee Constitution.

Alex J. Hurder, Vanderbilt University
SEE: EDUCATION; LAW; MCWHERTER, NED RAY

TENNESSEE STATE CAPITOL.

The cornerstone of the Capitol was laid on July 4, 1845. William Strickland designed the building and supervised construction until his death in April 1854. Two architects assisted in its completion. Strickland's son, Francis, served as architect for the next three years. The last stone was laid in the tower cupola on July 21, 1855. Francis Strickland designed the cast iron roof decorations, which were cast in Nashville by T.M. Brennan. In 1857 the building commission dismissed Strickland. One year later, it hired Harvey M. Akeroyd to design the last room in the building, the State Library. Officially, construction was completed in 1859, but grounds work continued until the outbreak of the Civil War. As a result of the war, the final two gasoliers for the stair and the east lobby of the legislative floor were never ordered.

The interior included space on the ground floor for the Governor's office, the State Archives, offices of the Secretary of State, the Treasurer, and the Register of Land, as well as the Tennessee Supreme Court, a Federal District Court, and the Repository of the Official Weights and Measures. The main floor contained the assembly halls for the House of Representatives and the Senate, legislative committee rooms, and the State Library, which is considered the finest room in the Capitol. The library features cast iron stacks, surrounding galleries, and a cast iron spiral staircase connecting the various stack levels. Wood & Perot Company provided the decorative iron work in the library, as well as the iron work for the staircases in the main building and the cupola tower. Portraits of various "worthies" decorate the ceiling of the library chamber. Beginning in the northeast corner, and proceeding south, the portraits include Dr. Gerard Troost, first state geologist; historian William Hickling Prescott; James Kent, "father of American jurisprudence;" and Dr. James Priestley, noted geologist and president of Cumberland College. In the southwest corner, and proceeding north, the portraits include the Reverend Charles Coffin, president of the University of Tennessee; Dr. Philip Lindsley, president of the University of Nashville; Matthew Fontaine Maury, "pathfinder of the seas;" and poet Henry Wadsworth Longfellow. Until the mid-1880s, the State Library also housed the Tennessee Historical Society and most of its collections.

James A. Hoobler, Tennessee State Museum
SUGGESTED READINGS: Mary Ellen Gadski, "The Tennessee State Capitol: An Architectural History," *Tennessee Historical*

Quarterly 47(1988): 67–120; James A. Hoobler, "Afterword: The 1984–88 Capitol Restoration," *Tennessee Historical Quarterly* 47(1988): 121–123

SEE: LINDSLEY, PHILIP; MAURY, MATTHEW F.; STRICK-LAND, WILLIAM; TENNESSEE HISTORICAL SOCIETY; TENNESSEE STATE LIBRARY AND ARCHIVES; TROOST, GERARD

TENNESSEE STATE FORESTS. Although recommended as early as the 1870s, the first impetus for a state forest system came in 1900 when President William McKinley asked for a report on the natural resources of the Southern Appalachians, including Tennessee. In response to the report's recommendations, the Tennessee General Assembly approved establishment of three federal reserves in Tennessee: the Unaka, Pisgah, and Cherokee, later to be combined into the Cherokee National Forest.

In 1905 the General Assembly created a Department of Game, Fish, and Forestry; the state's first general forestry law was passed in 1907. In 1914 the position of state forester was established in the Tennessee Geological Survey agency. The Division of Forestry, created in 1915, remained under the survey until 1921 when the state created the Bureau of Forestry and a State Forestry Commission within the Tennessee Department of Agriculture. It also made the teaching of forestry mandatory in public schools. In 1923 the establishment of the state's first forestry school at the University of the South aided the training of foresters. The University of Tennessee began offering courses and created a four-year degree pro-

gram in 1936. The first state forest was established in 1927 in Madison County on 38 acres donated by the county from tax-delinquent lands.

The denuded hillsides and the erosion that became the legacies of the timber boom of the 1870s through the 1920s received no attention until the Civilian Conservation Corps began reforestation and soil conservation projects in the 1930s. In 1933 CCC crews established Morgan (now Lone Mountain in Morgan County with 3,597 acres), Bledsoe (on 6,656 acres in Cumberland, White, Van Buren, and Bledsoe counties), and Pickett (15,887 acres in Pickett County) state forests. In 1935 to 1940 the Corps created Grundy (now part of the South Cumberland State Recreation Area); Stewart (4,000 acres in Stewart County); Lewis (1,257 acres in Lewis County); Franklin-Marion (6,941 acres in its namesake counties); and Scott (3,182 acres in Scott and Fentress counties) state forests. After planting more than 63 million trees and 554,457 pounds of hardwood seeds in these forests and other areas, the CCC began a reforestation project in the Copper Basin in 1941, which was interrupted by World War II. In the 1930s the Tennessee Valley Authority also established a forestry division that undertook reforestation on additional lands.

Other state forests with origins during the New Deal era include Chuck Swan (24,300 acres in Union and Campbell counties), Chickasaw (13,104 acres in Hardeman and Chester counties), Cedars of Lebanon (6,943 acres in Wilson County), Natchez

Fighting fire near Dover, 1941.

Trace (37,090 acres in Henderson, Carroll, and Benton counties), and Standing Stone (8,445 acres in Overton and Clay counties). In 1937 the Division of Forestry moved to the newly created Tennessee Department of Conservation.

In 1945 the state designated 23,759 acres purchased in Marion, Hamilton, and Sequatchie counties as Prentice Cooper State Forest. The Tennessee Division of Forestry also maintains tree nurseries in Madison and Polk counties.

In 1951 a new organization, Keep Tennessee Green (later the Tennessee Forestry Association), was formed to work for better forest fire prevention. In 1952 more than a million acres burned in forest fires in Tennessee, a disaster calling attention to prevention needs. By the late 1950s, fire protection was available in 72 counties. In 1961, after almost three decades of herculean efforts to reforest the state, Tennessee contained 13.7 million acres of forest lands, surpassing the acreage of the early 1870s.

In 1997 half of Tennessee, 13.6 million acres, was forested. More than 86 percent of this land was privately owned, the great majority by individuals, while corporations owned 17 percent of this segment (approximately 2 million acres). The remainder was owned by federal, state, or local governments, with about 1.8 million acres controlled by the federal government and a mere 156,000 by the state.

There are 178 tree species native to Tennessee, 89 percent of which are hardwoods, including white and red oaks, Virginia and shortleaf pines, hickories, yellow (tulip) poplar, red and sugar maples, blackgum, red cedar, and sourwood. Oak and hickory forests make up 72 percent of the total forested area. The wood products industry employs an estimated 60,000 workers with total wages of over one billion dollars annually.

In 1991 the Tennessee Division of Forestry transferred from the Department of Conservation to the Department of Agriculture. It continued to assume responsibility for the management of state forests, fire suppression, and various other timber production and conservation programs. The Tennessee Forestry Commission, comprised of seven gubernatorial appointees and representatives of the departments of Agriculture and Environment and Conservation and the Tennessee Wildlife Resources Agency, provides the division with guidance on program and policy development.

Studies conducted in the 1990s indicated that the ecological health of the state's forests was declining. Most forest acreage came from idle fields reverting to woodlands. The rich bottomland hardwood forests of West Tennessee had been depleted, and only 9 percent of the original forested wetlands remained in 1994. The spruce and fir forests of Tennessee's mountains were being destroyed by imported insect pests that attacked

trees weakened by the effects of air pollution—the 21,000 acres of spruce-fir forests in 1980 had been reduced to 7,000 acres by 1989. A major recent controversy is the construction of modern chip mills, such as the Champion International mill in Perry County, which environmentalists view as an invitation for wholesale clear-cutting of even the poorest forests. In 1997 the Dogwood Alliance, a coalition of 35 southern environmental organizations, asked the federal government to halt the opening of new chip mills and study their environmental and economic impact. In other recent developments, the Nature Conservancy, Southern Appalachian Highlands Conservancy, and Tennessee River Gorge Trust worked to acquire threatened but environmentally-rich forests for their management and preservation. State agencies also acquired new forests through the Wetlands Acquisition Fund, State Natural Areas, and other programs.
Ann Toplovich, Tennessee Historical Society
SEE: BAGGENSTOSS, HERMAN; CIVILIAN CONSERVATION CORPS; CONSERVATION; CUMBERLAND RIVER; TIMBER INDUSTRY

TENNESSEE STATE LIBRARY AND ARCHIVES (TSLA) collects and preserves books and records of historical, documentary, and reference value, and encourages and promotes library development throughout the state. It is the state agency responsible for preserving materials which document Tennessee's people and history.

TSLA operates within the Division of Public Libraries and Archives, which also includes the Tennessee Regional Library System. The chief policymaking body of the Division is the State Library and Archives Management Board, which consists of the Secretary of State, who serves as chairman and chief administrative officer; the State Treasurer; the Comptroller of the Treasury; the Commissioner of Education; and the Commissioner of Finance and Administration. The State Librarian and Archivist serves as Executive Secretary to the Management Board. The Secretary of State, acting through the State Librarian and Archivist and the Division of Public Libraries and Archives, is empowered by law to execute the rules, regulations, policies, and programs adopted by the Management Board.

The Tennessee State Library was founded in 1854 through the efforts of its first State Librarian, Return Jonathan Meigs, former corresponding secretary and librarian of the Tennessee Historical Society, which was founded five years earlier. Until his departure from the state just before the Civil War, Meigs and his son acquired and processed rare books that were collectors' items even in their day; many of those books survive today. Meigs also developed his own classification system, which was replaced in 1871, when Dr. George S. Blackie compiled the *Catalogue of the Gen-*

eral and Law Library of the State of Tennessee and developed his own classification scheme in the process. The *Catalogue* listed 18,383 volumes; the collection doubled over the next 30 years. In 1901 a newly formed Library Commission appointed Mary Skeffington as State Librarian; she held that position until 1919, longer than any previous librarian.

In the first decade of the twentieth century, the Tennessee State Archives, which had existed more as a concept than an institution, received legislative attention and funding. In 1919 it became part of the Tennessee State Library and Archives, with John Trotwood Moore serving as the first State Librarian and Archivist. Moore expanded the role of TSLA through his relationship with the Tennessee Historical Society and his projects to collect official records, including military records dating to the War of 1812. When he died in 1929, the office of State Librarian and Archivist passed to his wife, Mary Daniel Moore. She guided TSLA through the Great Depression and its last years in the State Capitol. Moore retired in 1949, only three years before the dedication of the current State Library and Archives Building.

From 1952 until 1971 TSLA operated under the direction of historians Daniel Robison, William Alderson, Sam B. Smith, and Wilmon Droze, who enhanced its role as a repository of historical information. Later interest in family history, or genealogy, brought a new kind of researcher to TSLA, an interest that shows no sign of waning.

With the passage of the federal Library Services and Construction Act in the 1950s, TSLA assumed a new role in the development, promotion, and construction of public libraries in Tennessee, and in the further development of the regional library system. Kathryn C. Culbertson became the first professional librarian to head the TSLA. She remained in office until 1982, when TSLA passed from the Department of Education to the Office of the Secretary of State. Through the efforts of the Secretaries of State, financial support for TSLA increased markedly, and the Division of Public Libraries and Archives achieved greater public visibility.

The World Wide Web and other on-line information systems transformed the way TSLA functions as an organization and as a provider of information services. By the mid-1990s TSLA had established a statewide catalog of all public libraries and, through federal and state funds, facilitated on-line access to the Internet.

Currently, TSLA holdings total over one million items (exclusive of original records), approximately half of which are books and periodicals. The other half consists of maps, photographs, tapes, microforms, and other non-print materials. Archival and manuscript collections, dating from pre-statehood days to the present, consist of 27 million official records and 4.8 million manuscripts, occupying some 31,000 cubic feet of space. The staff includes over 90 archivists, librarians, assistants, and specialists in microfilming, photography, and computer networking.

The holdings on Tennessee, regional, and national history—areas of primary interest to historians and genealogists—are central to its collections. TSLA features a photographic archive of nineteenth and early twentieth century pictures; special collections of sheet music, political pamphlets, and broadsides; official records of the state and the counties of Tennessee; letters, diaries, and family papers of Tennesseans; newspapers from Tennessee towns and cities; research materials on Native Americans; and a general reference collection. TSLA is a depository of all state publications and a partial depository of federal documents dating from 1784. In 1995 the State Planning Office Library was incorporated into the Public Services Section of TSLA.

In addition to the reference and information services provided by the Public Services Section, TSLA provides a range of services to special clients and populations. Since 1955 TSLA staff have recorded all sessions of the Tennessee General Assembly; these tapes are available to the legislature, other government agencies, and the general public through the Legislative History Service. The Restoration and Reproduction Section provides microfilming, document restoration and preservation, and photographic and photoduplication services for state government and the public. This section stores 54,000 rolls of camera-negative microfilm containing newspapers, archival records, manuscript collections, and local records.

The Tennessee Library for the Blind and Physically Handicapped (LBPH) cooperates with the Library of Congress in bringing free reading materials and other library services to visually and physically handicapped Tennesseans. The Technical Services Section staff acquires, processes, and catalogs materials in the collections to assure their usability. Records specialists also work with local governments on records management and preservation.

The Planning and Development Section of TSLA administers the state's contractual agreements with the Regional Library System and promotes public library development throughout Tennessee by means of continuing education, summer reading programs, direct grants to public libraries, and network coordination and development.

Edwin S. Gleaves, Tennessee State Library and Archives
SUGGESTED READINGS: Edwin S. Gleaves, "From the Vulgate Bible to the World Wide Web: Preserving the Past for Tomorrow in Tennessee," *Tennessee Historical Quarterly* 55(1996): 292–309; Mrs. John Trotwood [Mary Daniel] Moore, "The Tennessee State Library in the Capitol," *Tennessee Historical Quarterly* 12(1953): 3–22

SEE: LIBRARIES IN TENNESSEE; MEIGS, RETURN J.; MOORE, JOHN T. AND MARY D.; TENNESSEE'S ARCHIVES

TENNESSEE STATE MUSEUM, a Tennessee government agency, is devoted to collecting, preserving, and interpreting objects related to the history and culture of Tennessee. These items generally are conserved and displayed at the museum's main facility, which is at the James K. Polk Center in Nashville.

The General Assembly adopted a resolution accepting in trust the collections of the Tennessee Historical Society in 1927. This collection contained over 10,000 artifacts, including David Crockett's powder horn; Andrew Jackson's top hat; and swords and rifles from the Battle of King's Mountain. The Tennessee State Museum was founded in 1937 for the purpose of bringing together various state-owned collections. It was then housed at the War Memorial Building.

Individuals and groups, such as the United Daughters of the Confederacy, the Department of Conservation, the Game and Fish Commission, and veterans of the Spanish-American War and World Wars I—II, loaned or donated items as well, greatly expanding the museum's collection. In 1981 the State Museum opened its main facility in the James K. Polk Center. The War Memorial Building houses 7,000 square feet of military exhibits.

The current collection includes over 85,000 artifacts, many relating to famous Tennessee personalities such as James K. Polk, Elvis Presley, and Alex Haley. Within its excellent collection are Tennessee-made paintings, silver, ceramics, textiles, furniture, and firearms. Through its permanent interpretive exhibits, the museum traces the state's history from the Paleoindian era through the early twentieth century. Six distinct eras of Tennessee's history are represented in the exhibits: First Tennesseans, Frontier, Age of Jackson, Antebellum, Civil War and Reconstruction, and The New South.

Twentieth century military exhibits are maintained in the State Museum's Military Branch. It includes exhibits on America's involvement in foreign wars from the Spanish-American War to World War II. Among the objects on display are the Medal of Honor awarded to Alvin C. York and a full-scale replica of the atomic bomb dropped on Hiroshima. The State Museum also provides curatorial oversight and tours of the State Capitol, management of the National Civil Rights Museum in Memphis, and provides objects to other sites and museums across the state.

The Tennessee State Museum Foundation, a public, non-profit organization, supports the State Museum. The museum's temporary exhibits have included "Red Grooms, A Retrospective," "Magna Carta: Liberty Under the Law," and "A People at War: Americans in World War II."

Anne-Leslie Owens, Tennessee Historical Society
SEE: TENNESSEE ARTS COMMISSION; TENNESSEE HISTORICAL SOCIETY; TENNESSEE STATE CAPITOL

TENNESSEE STATE PRISON. Interest in the construction of a penitentiary dates back to 1815, when a State Senate committee recommended construction of the structure using funds obtained through public subscription. This effort failed, and political infighting in the General Assembly over the penitentiary site lasted from 1819 to 1827. Finally, in 1829, the General Assembly appropriated $25,000 for construction of a facility on Church Street in Nashville. Work began in April 1830; on January 1, 1831, the first prisoners arrived. The penitentiary contained 200 prison cells, a storehouse, hospital, and living quarters for the warden.

In 1853, in response to serious overcrowding, the legislature approved the construction of 32 additional cells. Overcrowding was particularly acute for the female inmates housed on the upper floor of the main office building (women prisoners were supervised by male guards for another 40 years). In 1858, after further construction, the capacity increased to 352 beds. Accounts differ as to whether this new construction resulted in the creation of a separate structure or simply added a wing to the existing facility. In any case, expanding housing without concomitantly increasing funding for medical care, refuse control, and sanitation only served to exacerbate already squalid living conditions. During this period, rehabilitation played a subordinate role to both retribution and the profit motive, as the state sanctioned the exploitive convict leasing system.

The convict leasing system ended in disgrace in 1893 and the state legislature enacted legislation to discontinue the practice. The same legislature voted to erect a new state penitentiary in Nashville to include a minimum of 1,000 cells and a sufficient number of workshops to provide employment for all inmates. For the first time, the legislature also provided for a separate building to house female prisoners and staffed it with matrons.

Site selection evoked claims of "irregularities," but eventually 1,200 acres at the Cockrill Bend of the Cumberland River near Nashville was chosen. The proposed prison design called for the construction of a fortress-like structure patterned after the penitentiary at Auburn, New York (made famous for the lockstep, striped prisoner uniforms, nighttime solitary confinement, and daytime congregate work under strictly enforced silence). The new Tennessee prison contained 800 small cells, each designed to house a single inmate. In addition, an administration building and other smaller buildings for offices, warehouses, and factories were built within the 20-foot high, three-foot thick rock walls. The plan also provided for a working farm outside the walls and mandated a separate system for younger offenders to isolate them from older, hardened criminals.

Construction costs for this second Tennessee State Penitentiary exceeded $500,000, not including the price of the land. The prison's 800 cells opened to receive prisoners on February 12, 1898, and that day, admitted 1,403 prisoners, creating immediate overcrowding. To a greater or lesser extent, overcrowding persisted throughout the next century. The original Tennessee State Penitentiary on Church Street was demolished later that year, and salvageable materials were used in the construction of outbuildings at the new facility, creating a physical link from 1830 to the present.

Every convict was expected to defray a portion of the cost of incarceration by performing physical labor. Within two years, inmates worked up to 16 hours per day for meager rations and unheated, unventilated sleeping quarters. The state also contracted with private companies to operate factories inside the prison walls using convict labor.

The Tennessee State Penitentiary had its share of problems. In 1902, 17 prisoners blew out the end of one wing of the prison, killing one inmate and allowing the escape of two others who were never recaptured. Later, a group of inmates seized control of the segregated white wing and held it for 18 hours, before surrendering. In 1907 several convicts commandeered a switch engine and drove it through a prison gate. In 1938 inmates staged a mass escape. Several serious fires have ignited at the penitentiary, including one that destroyed the main dining room. Riots occurred in 1975 and 1985.

In 1989 the Department of Correction opened a new penitentiary, the Riverbend Maximum Security Institution at Nashville. The old Tennessee State Penitentiary closed in June 1992. As part of the settlement in a class action suit, *Grubbs v. Bradley* (1983), the federal court issued a permanent injunction prohibiting the Tennessee Department of Correction from ever again housing inmates at the Tennessee State Prison.

Frank Lee and Robert Rogers, Middle Tennessee State University

SUGGESTED READING: Larry D. Gossett, *The Keepers and the Kept: The First Hundred Years of the Tennessee Prison Sysytem, 1830–1930* (1992); Tennessee State Penitentiary, *History of the Tennessee Penal Institutions: 1813–1940* (1940)

SEE: CARROLL, WILLIAM; TENNESSEE IN FILM; TENNESSEE PRISON SYSTEM

TENNESSEE STATE SENATE. Tennessee is divided into 33 state senatorial districts, from which the members of the upper house of the Tennessee General Assembly are elected. Senators serve four-year terms, with those from even-numbered districts being elected in the same general election, and those from odd-numbered districts being elected two years later. Senators may be elected for consecutive terms, and Tennessee does not impose term limits on either the House or the Senate. The Tennessee Constitution requires senators to be at least 30 years old, a U.S. citizen, a state resident for three years, and a resident of the district from which the senator is elected for one year immediately preceding the election.

At the organizational session of the General Assembly, the Senate elects a Speaker, who is also the state's Lieutenant Governor. At the same session, the Senate also elects the Speaker *pro tem*, Deputy Speaker, and the majority and minority leaders, who are the primary spokesmen for their parties. The chairs of the Democratic and Republican party caucuses preside over party meetings to consider and formulate party policy. The Speaker of the Senate of the 100th General Assembly is John S. Wilder, a Democrat from Fayette County. Senator Wilder is serving his fourteenth consecutive term as speaker and lieutenant governor. The Speaker *pro tem* is Robert Rochelle, a Democrat from Lebanon, who has served in the 93rd through the 100th General Assemblies.

Most of the work of the Senate is accomplished through the activities of the nine legislative committees, which study proposed legislation, hold public hearings, and recommend passage to the entire Senate. The Speaker of the Senate exerts considerable control over the legislative process through committee appointments. The nine standing committees of the Senate include Commerce; Labor and Agriculture; Education; Environment; Conservation and Tourism; Finance; Ways and Means; General Welfare, Health, and Human Resources; Government Operations; Judiciary; State and Local Government; and Transportation. In addition, there are three select committees: Calendar, Ethics, and Rules.

The Senate, like the House, has the primary function of lawmaking. The Senate has the additional power to try impeachment proceedings initiated by the House. Any officer of the state may be impeached, but two-thirds of the Senate must concur before the officer is removed from office.

The 100th General Assembly is composed of 16 Democrats (15 men and one woman) and 17 Republicans (15 men and two women).

Connie L. Lester, Tennessee Historical Society

Source: *Prepared from material found in the* Tennessee Blue Book, 1995–1996, Bicentennial Edition

SEE: GOVERNMENT; WILDER, JOHN S.

Great Seal of the State of Tennessee

STATE OF TENNESSEE PHOTOGRAPHIC SERVICES

TENNESSEE STATE SYMBOLS. Tennessee is particularly rich in official state symbols. As of 1998, the list includes the flag, capitol and seal, two birds, two flowers, two fish, two rocks, two trees, eight songs, a poem, four insects, a reptile, an amphibian, a gem, a wild animal, and a folk dance—31 in all. We know of no state with more.

Tennessee gained its symbols slowly. It had no permanent capitol for more than 50 years after achieving statehood and no flag for more than a century. Its first state flower was chosen in 1919, and more than half its symbols have been added since 1965.

Those symbols, made official by the General Assembly, serve several functions. They symbolize the state's ideals, strength, and unity. They also speak of its natural beauty and its cultural and commercial heritage. In one very real sense, many are simply the means by which we celebrate those aspects of life in Tennessee that we hold dear.

Only one symbol could be considered vital to the day-to-day operation of government, and that is our first—the state seal, required by the state's 1796 Constitution. It was not until 1802, though, that a seal was produced; in the meantime, governors John Sevier and Archibald Roane used their personal seals on state documents. Today, the seal bears the words "Agriculture" and "Commerce" and the phrase "The Great Seal of the State of Tennessee" as well as the year of the state's admission to the Union, "1796," and the Roman numeral "XVI," as Tennessee was the sixteenth state.

Construction of the state capitol was begun in 1845, shortly after Nashville was chosen as its site. It was designed by architect William Strickland, who also oversaw its construction. Cost overruns, labor troubles, squabbles between Strickland and the building commission, and even graffiti problems plagued the construction. Nevertheless, the result is acknowledged as an architectural masterpiece. Built to house all three branches of state government, it is a striking showpiece of nineteenth century Greek Revival architecture.

Of the eight state songs, the first was *Tennessee,* written by A.J. Holt to the tune of *Beulah Land* and first used at the state's Centennial celebration. The five legislated state songs are *My Homeland, Tennessee* (1925), *When It's Iris Time in Tennessee* (1935), *My Tennessee* (1955), *Tennessee Waltz* (1965), and *Rocky Top* (1982). Two Bicentennial songs were adopted in honor of the nation's bicentennial: *The Tennessee Salute* (1975) and *Fly, Eagle, Fly* (1976).

Tennessee's flag was designed by Captain Lee Roy Reeves, a Johnson City lawyer, who organized Company F of the Tennessee National Guard's Third Regiment. It was made official in 1905. Its three stars represent the grand divisions of the state. They are bound together by the endless circle of the blue field. The white and blue stripes on the free end of the flag are there to enhance the design.

In 1919 the legislature asked schoolchildren to select a state flower. They chose the passionflower, or maypop, a lovely purple-and-white flower which grows as a weed in farm fields and forest edges. Then, in 1933 the legislature also named the iris state flower. A long-running battle over the choice raged for years, with garden clubs and newspapers taking sides. The matter was not resolved officially until 1973, when the legislature named the passionflower state wildflower and the iris state cultivated flower.

The mockingbird is a highly visible and widespread resident of Tennessee. Renowned for its marvelous singing voice and its ability to imitate the songs of other birds, it is also a fearless protector of its nest and territory. It was named state bird in a statewide vote held in 1933. The bobwhite quail, whose territorial two-note call is a common springtime sound, was named state game bird in 1987.

The tulip poplar, a tree which proved highly useful to Tennessee's pioneers, was named state tree in 1947. In 1991 the legislature designated the yellowwood, used often as an ornamental tree, as state Bicentennial tree.

In 1969 the legislature named agate, a semi-precious gemstone found in several areas, as state rock. A decade later, at the urging of sixth-graders in Martin, it added limestone, an important building material which underlies much of the state.

The raccoon, a familiar nocturnal visitor to many campsites and rural homes and an animal associated with frontier legend Davy Crockett, was named state wild animal in 1971.

"Oh Tennessee, My Tennessee" was written in 1971 by then-Commander William Lawrence while he was a prisoner of war after being shot down over North Vietnam. It was adopted as state poem in 1973.

Tennessee has three state insects—four if you count the butterfly. The ladybug, a natural "pesticide" with a voracious appetite for crop pests, was chosen in 1975. The firefly, or lightning bug, a beetle whose natural taillight makes it a summer delight, was named the same year. The honeybee, whose worth as a pollinator makes it an economic powerhouse in Tennessee, was named agricultural insect in 1990.

The freshwater pearl is found in mussels, which were once ubiquitous in Tennessee waterways. The pearl is now harvested commercially at mussel "farms" and was named state gem in 1979.

The square dance, a popular pastime for many Tennesseans, was adopted as official state folk dance in 1980.

Ricky Chadwick and Jason Mobley, seventh-graders at Erin Elementary School in 1987, suggested that a state fish be adopted. In 1988 Tennessee adopted two—the channel catfish as commercial fish and the largemouth bass as game fish.

The state butterfly, the zebra swallowtail, was chosen by a biology class at Gallatin High School and made official by the legislature in 1994.

In 1995 the legislature named the box turtle, a relatively common inhabitant of rural and suburban areas, as state reptile. That same year, the Tennessee cave salamander, a rare resident of a handful of caves in Tennessee and Alabama, was named state amphibian.
Rob Simbeck, Nashville

SUGGESTED READING: Rob Simbeck, *Tennessee State Symbols: The Fascinating Stories Behind Our Flag and Capitol, the Mockingbird, Iris and Other Official Emblems* (1995)

SEE: LAWRENCE, WILLIAM; REEVES, LEE ROY; STRICKLAND, WILLIAM; TENNESSEE STATE CAPITOL

TENNESSEE STATE UNIVERSITY (TSU), opened in 1912, has become one of Tennessee's most recognized public higher education institutions, both nationally and internationally. Its athletes, including Ralph Boston, Wyomia Tyus, and Wilma G. Rudolph, have won 29 medals in the Olympic Games. The university's most famous graduate, Oprah Winfrey, became America's highest paid entertainer and television personality during the 1990s. By 1996 seven TSU buildings had been placed on the National Register of Historic Places as a historic district—the first of Tennessee's public colleges and universities so designated.

As the twentieth century began, Tennessee remained the only state with legal segregation that did not have a public college for its African-American citizens. In 1907, after learning that the General

Assembly planned to authorize publicly supported normal schools, Nashville's African-American leaders demanded the inclusion of a school for blacks. In 1909 the legislature authorized a normal school in each Grand Division and another school for the state's 472,987 African Americans. Benjamin Carr, Preston Taylor, and other African-American leaders in Nashville formed the Colored Agricultural and Industrial Normal Association and launched a campaign to locate the school in Davidson County. Taylor, Carr, Henry Allen Boyd, James C. Napier, T. Clay Moore, W.S. Ellington, and others appeared before several legislative sessions, the Davidson County government, and the governor. They solicited over $80,000, including funds gathered from a door-to-door campaign in African-American neighborhoods. On January 13, 1911, the State Board of Education decided to locate Tennessee Agricultural and Industrial State Normal School for Negroes in Davidson County.

William J. Hale, Chattanooga school principal and a friend of the State Superintendent of Education, was selected as principal of the institution. He supervised the school's construction on rocky Zollicoffer Hill, overlooking the Cumberland River. The campus eventually expanded to 165 acres. The school's early buildings consisted of the President's Home (Goodwill Manor), an industrial building, a three-story main building, two dormitories, two barns, and farm houses.

On June 19, 1912, Tennessee A & I State Normal School for Negroes opened its doors for summer school, enrolling 245 students who were taught by 13 teachers. State Normal soon served as the summer school training site for most of Tennessee's African-American educators. By fall 1912 enrollment had risen to 300; the school was formally dedicated on January 16, 1913.

Tennessee A & I Normal offered remedial elementary and secondary courses, and a high school diploma that required 16 Carnegie credits. After completion of the normal curriculum, the students received teacher certification. Students paid $101 per year for books, room, board, and fees. Chapel attendance was required, and each student worked two hours per day. By 1922 the curriculum included college courses, and Tennessee A & I graduated its first college class of eight students in June 1924. The institution's name was changed to Tennessee A & I State Normal College in 1925, and two years later the word Normal was dropped. The school's motto,"Enter to Learn; Go Forth to Serve," and the words on the school's seal, "Think; Work; Serve," gave little offense in the age of segregation when whites expected African Americans to hold subordinate and service positions.

Public school education for blacks seldom reached the sixth grade in most Tennessee counties. As a result, Tennessee A & I grappled with crowded conditions; enrollment quickly rose from 401 in 1916 to nearly 2,000 within a few years. Much of the funding for improvements in public education for African Americans came from northern philanthropists. By 1917 the Anna T. Jeannes Fund and the Rosenwald Fund maintained agents at Tennessee A & I. Improvements in secondary and high school education for black children in most counties enabled Tennessee A & I State College to abolish its normal and high school divisions by the 1930s.

In 1927 a new building phase began. African Americans raised some $65,000; the General Education Board contributed $100,000; and the state legislature appropriated $400,000. The campus design included a quadrangle on the north side of Centennial Boulevard, surrounded by three new buildings (Hale Hall, Memorial Library, and Harned Science Hall), and several original structures. Hale employed A.W. Williston, a Tuskegee landscaper, to beautify the rock-filled campus. In 1932 another building phase produced the Women's Building, the Administration and Health Building, and the Industrial Arts Building. In 1935 more improvements added a football stadium, a track field, a limestone fence along Centennial Boulevard, and recreational facilities. From 1943 to 1949 a six million dollar program completed the Engineering Building, a new heating plant, expansion of the Women's Building, and expansion of Memorial Library. During this period, A & I added a graduate school and awarded the first master's degree in 1944. By this time, A & I enrollment numbered 1,513 students, and the school claimed the third highest total number of graduates among historically African-American universities.

On September 23, 1951, the school received recognition as Tennessee A & I State University and obtained the first Air Force ROTC unit for African Americans. In 1958 the university gained land grant status. During the presidency of Walter S. Davis, the University's enrollment grew to over 6,000 students, and construction added several more buildings: Graduate Building, Clay Hall, Lawson Hall, a Home Economics Building, and new dormitories. Three older buildings were torn down, leaving only Goodwill Manor, the presidential home, from the original 1912–1915 campus.

The school's name changed to Tennessee State University in 1968, the same year that a federal court suit was filed to dismantle the recent erection of the University of Tennessee's Nashville (UTN) branch. The plaintiffs argued that downtown UTN furthered segregation in higher education and competed with TSU. On July 1, 1979, UTN's modern downtown campus merged with Tennessee State University.

Meanwhile state neglect and years of use had left TSU's main campus in a deplorable and shameful condition. A limited building phase between 1975 and 1985 added the Gentry Physical Education Complex, School of Business Building, a new library, the Torrence Engineering Building, and the CARP Research Building, plus renovations to the old Memorial Library, and Harned and McCord Halls. Beginning in 1989 TSU student leaders pressured the governor for changes. As a result, the General Assembly appropriated $122,000,000 over several years to implement a Master Plan developed under President Otis L. Floyd that included the rebuilding of the campus infrastructure, the renovation of all buildings, and the construction of new facilities. Federal funds helped to transform two old barns into an agricultural complex, to build an agricultural center at McMinnville, and to support minor renovations on the main campus.

By 1996 Tennessee State University, an urban, land-grant institution, was Tennessee's most cosmopolitan public university, enrolling over 8,600 students of all races. Over the years, TSU's student body represented 86 of the state's 95 counties, 51 nations, and 40 states. By 1996 the university employed faculty members of all ethnic groups, while claiming the distinction as America's sixth largest historically African-American university. From its founding in 1912, TSU prospered under the leadership of its acting and permanent presidents, including W.J. Hale (1912–1943); Walter S. Davis (1943–1968); Andrew P. Torrence (1968–1974); Frederick S. Humphries (1975–1985); Roy Peterson (acting, 1985–1986); Otis L. Floyd (1986–1990); George W. Cox (acting, 1990–1991); and James A Hefner (1991–).

Bobby L. Lovett, Tennessee State University

Suggested Reading: Lester C. Lamon "The Tennessee Agricultural and Industrial Normal School: Public Education for Black Tennesseans," *Tennessee Historical Quarterly* 32(1973): 42–58; R. Grann Lloyd, *Tennessee Agricultural and Industrial State Univerity* (1962)

See: BOSTON, RALPH; BOYD, HENRY A.; EDUCATION, HIGHER; GENERAL EDUCATION BOARD; HALE, WILLIAM J.; JULIUS ROSENWALD FUND; MERRITT, JOHN A.; NAPIER, JAMES C; RUDOPLH, WILMA; TAYLOR, PRESTON; TEMPLE, EDWARD S.; WINFREY, OPRAH.

TENNESSEE SUPREME COURT. Tennessee's first constitution did not create a state Supreme Court. The Constitution of 1796 provided only for "such superior and inferior courts" as the legislature should create, with the judges to be elected by the General Assembly to serve "during their good behavior." In 1809 the legislature finally created the Supreme Court of Errors and Appeals composed of two judges; on appeal cases, a circuit judge, who had not participated in the trial in a lower court, joined the two justices. Moreover, the jurisdiction of this Supreme Court was not exclusively appellate. Until 1834 the

Court exercised originial jurisdiction over the trial of equity cases, many of which involved titles to land—a very important field of the law in the early days of the state. The earlier lack of constitutional standing subjected the tenure of the judges to legislative whim, but the Court ruled on the constitutionality of many state statutes.

Tennessee's second constitution, adopted in 1834, made provision for a Supreme Court, composed of three judges. The constitution granted the Court appellate jurisdiction only and fixed the tenure of judges at 12 years. The constitution required one judge from each Grand Division of the state and stipulated that judges had to be at least 35 years old.

In 1870 Tennessee adopted its third and last constitution. It provided for a five-judge Supreme Court and required that not more than two judges could reside in any one of the three Grand Divisions. The Court is required to hold sessions in Knoxville, Nashville, and Jackson. Judges are popularly elected for terms of eight years. Judges must be residents of the state for five years and at least 35 years of age. The state legislature fixes the compensation for judges, and it cannot be increased or decreased during their term of office. According to a 1994 act, when an incumbent Supreme Court judge seeks election or re-election for a full eight-year term, the judge shall be retained in office, if, at the next regular August election, he or she receives a favorable majority vote. In August 1996 Supreme Court Justice Penny White, who had been appointed by Governor Ned R. McWherter to fill an unexpired term, was turned out of office by the voters.

Other constitutional provisions require the judges of the Supreme Court to designate one of their number as Chief Justice. In recent years, the office of Chief Justice has been rotated among the judges; in earlier Courts, one justice held the office throughout his tenure. Concurrence of three of the judges shall, in every case, be necessary to reach a decision. In the pre-Civil War history of the Court, dissenting opinions were more frequent than has been true of recent rulings. Unanimity or dissent probably reflects the state political situation and the particular makeup of the court.

According to a unique constitutional provision, the judges of the Supreme Court appoint the Attorney General and Reporter of the State for a term of eight years. The people of 43 states elect the Attorney General; in five, the governor appoints the chief lawyer of the people; and in Maine, the legislature elects the top lawyer by secret ballot. Challengers to Tennessee's controversial method of selection argue that there is a built-in conflict of interest when the State's chief lawyer is chosen by the very body before whom he or she must argue cases. So far, these challenges have been unsuccessful.

Two Tennessee Supreme Court justices, John Catron and Horace Lurton, received subsequent appointments to the Supreme Court of the United States. Of the many judges who served on the Tennessee Supreme Court, Grafton Green (1910–1947) had the longest tenure. He served as Chief Justice from 1923 until his death in 1947, and is widely recognized for his judicial skill and knowledge of the law.

Ward DeWitt, Jr., Nashville

SUGGESTED READING: Samuel C. Williams, *Phases of the History of the Tennessee Supreme Court* (1944)

SEE: BIRCH, A.A.; CATRON, JOHN; DAUGHTREY, MARTHA C.; GOVERNMENT; GREEN, NATHAN; HARBISON, WILLIAM; LAW; LURTON, HORACE; TENNESSEE COURTS PRIOR TO 1870

TENNESSEE TECHNOLOGICAL UNIVERSITY. In 1915, following an intense lobbying effort on the part of Putnam County's state representatives, the General Assembly chartered Tennessee Polytechnic Institute, located on the grounds of Dixie College in Cookeville. Established in 1909 by the Church of Christ, Dixie College suffered from a lack of financial support and never achieved college status, serving instead as an academy of secondary education.

State Democratic politics made the creation of TPI a political football. The split in the Democratic Party over the question of prohibition weakened the party and made party leaders anxious to guarantee an election victory. Governor Thomas C. Rye was given assurances that the location of a school in Cookeville would win support for him from Putnam and the surrounding counties, with the possible exception of White County. In another political move, the legislators created a technical school rather than a teachers' college in order to still opposition from the three normal schools already in operation. Although high school administrators objected strenuously, TPI's funding came from the high school fund rather than the normal school fund.

Soon after assuming control of the Dixie College campus, the legislature funded the construction of two dormitories for men and women. The old Dixie College building housed the campus classrooms, library, and administrative offices. In 1929 the General Assembly passed a million dollar bond issue to transform Tech into a college of technology equal to others in the southern states. Overcoming a threat of closure during the Great Depression, Tech received accreditation as a college-level institution from the Southern Association of Colleges and Schools in 1939. Although the name of the school and the emphasis on technology overshadowed other aspects of the curriculum, the charter of TPI charged it with the additional mission of training teachers for the Cumberland region. Women who attended Tech in the early years enrolled in the education courses.

Tech's first presidents were Thomas Alva Early (1916–1920), Quinton Smith (1920–1938), and James M. Smith (1938–1940). Everett Derryberry, who held a master's degree in English that he earned as a Rhodes Scholar at Oxford University, was president from 1940 to 1974. Derryberry expanded the campus, raised the enrollment, and improved the curriculum. His achievements can be credited to his dynamic personality and political influence, as well as his recruitment of able administrators and faculty. In addition, Derryberry's tenure spanned a period of favorable economic, social, and political conditions in the state and nation.

The campus changed dramatically during the Derryberry years. Before 1940 the campus contained seven buildings. In 1949 the new library building opened. Between 1945 and 1965 a number of dormitories were constructed to accommodate the massive influx of students entering college after World War II. Between 1965 and 1971 the campus gained 15 new buildings, all constructed in the Georgian and Classical Revival styles to maintain architectural unity.

In Derryberry's last decade several important milestones were established. In 1964 Tech began racial integration without incident, the last of the state universities to comply with the Supreme Court ruling of 1954. In 1965 its name changed to Tennessee Technological University.

Derryberry's retirement in 1974 opened a new chapter in Tech's history. Professor of education Arliss Roaden, vice provost of Ohio State University, became president. Roaden aspired to achieve national recognition for Tech by maintaining excellence in engineering while creating a multi-purpose university. He emphasized quality in the student body and the faculty, and gave increased attention and funding to the College of Business Administration. Roaden also launched a successful fund-raising campaign. During his tenure, a new fine arts building opened, and plans were made for a new library. Student enrollment passed 8,000 in 1980, and entering freshmen had the highest ACT scores of any Board of Regents school.

In the early 1980s Roaden persuaded Governor Lamar Alexander to propose research Centers of Excellence at the state's universities. Tech was awarded four of the initial centers: Center for Manufacturing Research, Center for Water Resources, Center of Electrical Power, and Center for Educational Evaluation. The latter is no longer in operation.

In 1985 Roaden resigned to become executive director of the Tennessee Higher Education Commission. During Roaden's administration, the issues of research and publication had divided the faculty, with some taking the position that the president had "violated" their conditions of employment as teachers. To restore calm, Dr. Wallace Prescott, Derryberry's chief academic officer, was called out of retirement to act as interim president after Roaden's resignation. Prescott led the school until 1988, when Dr. Angelo Volpe accepted the position as president.

Volpe's appearance symbolized a change in the character of Tech. He was the first Ph.D. (chemistry, University of Maryland) to be named as permanent president of Tech. He was also the first non-southerner and non-Protestant to be president. In many ways, Volpe reflected the spirit of Roaden's philosophy. Tech had escaped, to some extent, its regional image; it was reaching out to broader horizons. The changing faculty and student body also reflected these new characteristics.

W. Calvin Dickinson, Tennessee Technological University
SUGGESTED READINGS: Harvey G. Neufelt and W. Calvin Dickinson, "'Dark and Mysterious Channels': The Creation of Tennessee Polytechnic Institute," *Tennessee Historical Quarterly* 48(1989): 144–150; Harry G. Neufelt and W. Calvin Dickinson, *The Search for Identity: A History of Tennessee Technological University, 1915–1985* (1991)
SEE: ALEXANDER, LAMAR; DECORATIVE ARTS, APPALACHIAN; EDUCATION, HIGHER; PUTNAM COUNTY; RYE, THOMAS C.

TENNESSEE VALLEY AUTHORITY (TVA) is an independent public corporation founded by Congress in 1933 to control flooding, improve navigation, assist farmers, provide cheap electric power, and make "surveys of and general plans for [the Tennessee River] basin and adjoining territory . . . for the general purpose of fostering an orderly and proper physical, economic, and social development" of the Tennessee Valley. In an address to Congress on April 10, 1933, President Franklin Roosevelt asked Congress to create such an agency. Congress moved swiftly, and Roosevelt signed the TVA Act on May 18, 1933, making it a part of the New Deal's First Hundred Days.

Prior to the creation of TVA, large parts of the Tennessee Valley were in dire economic conditions. Soil erosion had ruined or damaged seven million acres of farmland. Per capita income in 1933 was only 44 percent of the national average. In Union County, Tennessee (near where TVA built Norris Dam, its first project, begun in 1933 and finished in 1936), there were no electrical utilities in 1926, crude birth rates were more than double the national average, out-migration was heavy, and only 1 percent of farm owners had indoor plumbing, 4 percent had telephones, and 8 percent had radios. In some areas of the Tennessee Valley, by 1933, the situation was desperate.

Throughout the 1920s, Nebraska Senator George Norris had tried to interest the federal government in initiating a multipurpose development project centered at Muscle Shoals, Alabama, where the government owned a large nitrate plant that was used for

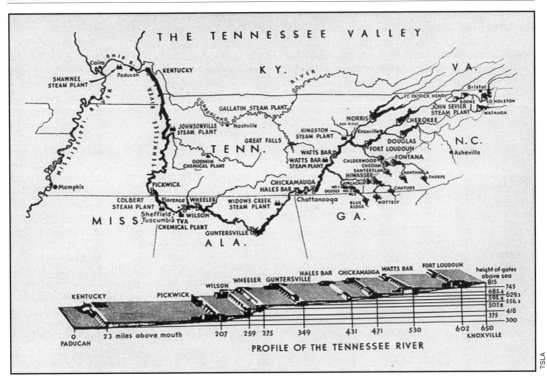

The Tennessee Valley Authority, circa 1960.

munitions during World War I and thereafter to produce fertilizer. But Republican presidential vetoes had left Norris disappointed, until the Democratic landslide of 1932. Franklin Roosevelt's vision, first expressed in a speech delivered on January 21, 1933 (before he was even inaugurated), was considerably bolder than that of Norris. Roosevelt envisioned an agency whose work would encompass all 201 counties of the Tennessee River basin reaching into 7 states—Alabama, Georgia, Kentucky, Mississippi, North Carolina, Tennessee, and Virginia. Moreover, Roosevelt's speech made it clear that he intended for such an agency to have extremely broad powers in the area of unified regional planning and economic development. TVA, in his view, was to be a bold experiment in regional development, a plan that, if successful, might be initiated elsewhere.

The TVA Act of 1933 placed the governing of the agency in the hands of a three-person board of directors, appointed by the president to nine-year renewable terms and confirmed by the Senate. As the first chairman of the board, Roosevelt chose Arthur E. Morgan, a nationally known flood control engineer and at the time president of the innovative Antioch College in Yellow Springs, Ohio. While Morgan was the utopian visionary and planner that Roosevelt appeared to want, Morgan's rigidity, paternalism,

and inability to countenance opposition would create massive internal uproar in TVA in its early years. The other two directors were Harcourt Morgan (no relation to Arthur E.) and David Lilienthal. Harcourt Morgan was an agricultural specialist who was well-known and extremely popular in the Tennessee Valley (he was a native of Canada) and president of the University of Tennessee. He spoke for farm owners and referred to land and the Tennessee River as "our common mooring." For his part, David Lilienthal was a 33-year-old attorney who came to TVA from the Wisconsin Public Utilities Commission where he had successfully battled the major regional private power companies. Lilienthal was a strong advocate of cheap electric power and strongly distrusted the kind of broad, top-down planning supported by Arthur Morgan. Conflict between the three original directors, therefore, was almost inevitable.

Arthur Morgan wanted TVA to produce cheap hydroelectric power that would be distributed by the existing private power companies, thus leaving the agency free to pursue his grander vision of broad regional planning, reforestation (to combat erosion), handicraft industries, and self-help community cooperatives (which Morgan envisioned would issue their own currency). Lilienthal was totally opposed to such naive idealism. He distrusted the private power interests (who had electrified only 3 percent of the valley's farms by 1933) and wanted TVA to distribute its electricity through municipal utility boards and public rural cooperatives (which TVA would have to create). In the many battles, Harcourt Morgan generally sided with Lilienthal, thus leaving Arthur E. Morgan increasingly isolated and frustrated. The conflict became public in 1936 when Arthur Morgan tried (unsuccessfully) to convince President Roosevelt not to re-appoint Lilienthal to a second term. Arthur Morgan then openly attacked his fellow directors for malfeasance and dishonesty, although he refused to substantiate those charges when confronted by Lilienthal and Harcourt Morgan. When Arthur Morgan instead publicly demanded a congressional investigation of the agency, Roosevelt was left with no alternative but to remove him, which he did in March 1938 for "insubordination and contumacy" (a story widely circulated in TVA was that the president chose to use the word "contumacy" because he knew most reporters would not know what the word meant and would not bother to look it up). TVA withstood the congressional investigations of May to December 1938. While Arthur Morgan may not have been a good choice to be first chairman of TVA's board of directors, his forced departure severely weakened the agency's role as a bold planner, innovator, and economic developer.

As the conflict between the directors hurt TVA from within, opposition was mounting from outside the agency as well. The most serious challenges came from the private power interests who correctly saw Lilienthal's plan of TVA power distribution through public boards and cooperatives as a death knell to its monopoly of electricity distribution. In 1934 George Ashwander *et al.*, stockholders in the Alabama Power Company, sued TVA to prevent the agency from buying facilities belonging to the power company on the grounds that TVA was unconstitutional. The first court decision went against the agency, but that decision was reversed in 1936 by the Circuit Court of Appeals and that court's ruling was upheld by the United States Supreme Court later that year (*Ashwander et al. vs. TVA*). But three months after the circuit court decision, 18 adjacent power companies sued TVA on similar grounds and won a December 1936 injunction that stopped TVA dam construction and power distribution until 1938 when the district court ruled in TVA's favor (*Tennessee Electric Power Co. vs. TVA*). The Supreme Court dismissed the suit in January 1939. Meanwhile Wendell Willkie, president of Commonwealth and Southern, a holding company which owned most of the private power companies in the Tennessee Valley, was negotiating with Lilienthal to sell the company's valley power assets to TVA. On August 15, 1939, in a public ceremony, Lilienthal handed Willkie a check for $44,728,300, TVA's share

of the $78,425,000 purchase of the properties of the Tennessee Electric Power Company.

By the end of World War II, TVA had wrought profound changes in what had been one of the nation's most economically depressed regions. Seven dams had been constructed on the main channel of the Tennessee River, nine dams had been built on the tributaries, and five dams had been acquired from the U.S. Corps of Engineers (Wilson) and the Tennessee Electric Power Company (Ocoee 1 and 2, Blue Ridge, and Great Falls). Fourteen million acre-feet of flood storage had been created, a nine-foot navigation channel existed along the entire 650 miles from Knoxville to Paducah, Kentucky (where the Tennessee flows into the Ohio River). Total electric production capacity through hydroelectric and coal-fired steam and internal combustion plants equaled 2,513,102 kilowatts (an increase of 127 percent since 1940), which by 1946 provided electricity to 668,752 households. The new city of Oak Ridge, Tennessee, part of the important Manhattan Project and which reached a high of 80,000 workers by 1945, was located in Anderson County, Tennessee, in part because of the availability of abundant electric power. Over 7,000 test demonstration farms had been set up to show valley farmers new agricultural and erosion control measures. TVA's architecture in dams, power plants, and related facilities (under the supervision of Chief Architect Roland Wank) had earned awe, respect, and prizes from other architects. By 1946 TVA had acquired approximately 1.1 million acres (less than one-third of it inundated by the lakes) and had removed an estimated 72,000 people from their land, many of whom later admitted that, while they often opposed being removed, in the long run they were economically better off. In addition, malaria had been virtually removed from the Tennessee Valley. By 1953 per capita income had risen to 61 percent of the national average. From 1933 to 1958, TVA spent approximately $2.1 billion in the Tennessee Valley, a much-needed injection of money. Although Senator Norris died in 1944 (at the age of 83), he lived long enough to see his dream become a reality.

Yet the decades between the end of World War II and TVA's fiftieth anniversary (1983) were not a golden age for the agency. Even as an almost constant stream of international visitors came to marvel at the agency's many accomplishments and to learn how similar multipurpose projects might be initiated in their own nations, TVA was beset with numerous problems that threatened one of the New Deal's brightest jewels. With the closing of the Kentucky Dam on August 30, 1944, TVA had reached its limits of hydroelectric production. Yet estimates of future electricity needs by TVA and the Atomic Energy Commission, together with TVA's need to find new projects, forced the agency into the construction of massive coal-fired steam plants, such as those at New Johnsonville, Kingston, and Gallatin, Tennessee, to generate the needed electric power. By 1954 coal-fired steam plants exceeded water power generation and by 1959 were providing approximately 76 percent of the agency's electricity output. From 1950 to 1954 Congress appropriated over $1 billion to TVA, the vast majority of it for coal-fired steam plants.

The move to coal-fired steam plants, however, revived private power company and conservative opposition, principally because steam plants theoretically would allow TVA to expand beyond the Tennessee River basin. In 1948 the Republican majorities in Congress turned back TVA's initial request for funds to build a steam plant at New Johnsonville, a decision that was reversed with President Harry Truman's 1948 election and simultaneous Democratic control of Congress. But President Dwight Eisenhower (who once referred to TVA as an example of "creeping socialism" and privately commented that "I'd like to sell the whole thing") and the 1953 Republican Congress blocked funding for a new coal-fired steam plant at Fulton, Tennessee (north of Memphis), in spite of the fact that the Atomic Energy Commission (AEC) declared that it needed the increased power.

The impasse led to the infamous Dixon-Yates incident. In 1953 a private power combination of Middle South Utilities (Dixon) and the Southern Company (Yates) proposed to the Eisenhower administration a plan whereby the combination would provide private power to the Atomic Energy Commission and certain electricity distributors (including the City of Memphis) while the government would prevent TVA from increasing its generating capacity. TVA saw this as an extremely serious threat, since it held the potential of the resurgence of private power companies to meet the increasing demand for electricity. Although the scheme ultimately died amidst charges of conflict of interest, special privilege, and political cronyism (and when the City of Memphis decided to build its own facilities), few could doubt that conservative attacks on TVA had not diminished.

By the mid-1960s TVA was the nation's largest consumer of coal, a good deal of it from strip mines in eastern Kentucky. Increased costs for coal, mounting attacks by environmentalists, and more estimates of future power needs turned the agency toward nuclear powered generation of electricity by 1966. The Browns Ferry nuclear plant was begun in 1967, Sequoyah in 1970, and Bellefonte in 1974, with more plants on the drawing boards. Since TVA had agreed with the Eisenhower administration in 1959 that all expenses for the agency's power program would be financed only through rate increases and bond issues (and not from congressional appropriations), the extremely costly nuclear program obliged the agency to go deeply into bonded indebtedness as well as institute a 25 percent rate increase in 1970. Worse, by the 1980s construction deficiencies and safety concerns had forced the closing of all the nuclear plants and a curtailment of the entire program. As expected, rate payers (who for years had enjoyed some of the lowest electric bills in the nation) were furious.

Since its founding in 1933, TVA had become accustomed to almost constant assaults from the political right. Beginning in the late 1960s, however, attacks on the agency also began coming from the left as well. TVA resisted environmentalists' charges that the coal-fired steam and nuclear plants were major polluters and/or environmental hazards. Ultimately the agency was forced to install expensive "scrubbers" on its coal plants' smokestacks. Too, although TVA had instituted plans for post-strip mine land reclamation, environmentalists claimed that water pollution was widespread and land reclamation efforts were insufficient.

Continued dam building programs on the tributaries of the Tennessee River also raised opposition. In Mills River, North Carolina, angry residents actually blocked a dam building project and forced TVA to abandon it amidst charges of "pork barrel" activities. Similarly, when the agency began work on the Tellico Dam (where the Little Tennessee River flowed into the main channel near Lenoir City, Tennessee), a loose coalition of fishing enthusiasts, local residents, Cherokee Indians (whose area burial grounds would be inundated), and environmentalists raised enough opposition to gain nationwide attention. In 1973, when University of Tennessee zoologist David Etnier discovered a three-inch perch-like fish about seven miles upriver from the dam construction (subsequently named the snail darter), environmentalists believed they had found the weapon that would stop the dam. Using the 1973 Endangered Species Act (which was passed four months *after* Etnier's discovery), environmentalists engaged TVA in a series of court battles which eventually stopped the Tellico Dam's construction. In 1979 Congress granted the dam an exemption from the Endangered Species Act and the Tellico Dam was closed on November 29, 1979, much to the disgust of TVA opponents.

In 1988 former Nissan Motors executive Marvin Runyon was appointed by President Ronald Reagan as chairman of the TVA board. In an effort to make good on his pledge of no electricity rate increases for three years, Runyon cut over 9,000 jobs from the approximately 49,000 employees on the TVA payroll. To be sure, TVA's bureaucracy was a swollen one, but the cuts produced dislocations in both Chattanooga and Knoxville.

As TVA enters its seventh decade, the New Deal agency is fighting for its existence. Chairman Craven Crowell has pledged the opening of the nuclear facilities (opposed with sit-ins by environmentalists) and keeping the agency on a sound business footing. As the New Deal is gradually dismembered in the 1990s, the Tennessee Valley Authority stands as a beacon of idealistic planning, regional economic success, and bureaucratic missteps.

W. Bruce Wheeler, University of Tennessee, Knoxville

SUGGESTED READINGS: Erwin C. Hargrove, *Prisoners of Myth: The Leadership of the Tennessee Valley Authority, 1933–1990* (1994); Erwin C. Hargrove and Paul K. Conkin, eds., *TVA: Fifty Years of Grass-Roots Bureaucracy* (1983); Michael J. McDonald and John Muldowny, *TVA and the Dispossessed: The Resettlement of Population in the Norris Dam Area* (1982); Thomas K. McGraw, *TVA and the Power Fight, 1933–1939* (1971); William Bruce Wheeler and Michael J. McDonald, *TVA and the Tellico Dam: A Bureaucratic Crisis in Post-Industrial America* (1986)

TENNESSEE VOCATIONAL SCHOOL FOR COL-ORED GIRLS opened in Nashville on October 9, 1923. Prior to its opening, the state confined African-American girls who needed correctional services in institutions with convicted adults. As a result of this practice, Frankie Pierce, an African-American activist, initiated a campaign for the establishment of a correctional school for girls.

In April 1921 the Tennessee General Assembly authorized the establishment of the Tennessee Vocational School for Colored Girls and appropriated $50,000 to purchase a site and construct a building. The state selected a 66-acre site on Heiman Street, near Tennessee Agricultural and Industrial State Normal School (now Tennessee State University). When the school opened, it served African-American girls, aged 12 through 15, from across the state, whom the courts judged to be delinquent. Frankie Pierce, the school's first superintendent (1923–1939), planned and implemented a personal development program that emphasized health, recreation, physical needs, moral training, and religion. She instilled an appreciation for the dignity of labor and encouraged the girls to become self-supporting. Nearby Hubbard Hospital at Meharry Medical College provided medical and dental care for the girls. In addition, the school employed a part-time physician to meet student health needs.

During the first year of operation, the school served 35 girls from eight Tennessee counties. These juveniles had been convicted of offenses ranging from "incorrigibility and bad conduct" to intent to murder. A fire on December 12, 1923, destroyed the contents of the school, but donations from across the state quickly replaced the loss.

As the 1928–1930 biennium ended, the school served as many as 67 girls from 16 counties. Program directors rationalized that most girls would enter domestic service after leaving the program and emphasized sewing, cooking, house cleaning, and laundering. During this same period, the school expanded its educational offerings to include grades 1–12. Of the girls who completed their sentences during this period, 34 returned to their homes, and 13 entered domestic service.

During the 1940s the school offered military training and created a cadet corps of two battalions. Increasingly, the school utilized city and county services for the girls. During the week the girls attended Haynes High School (a county school) for their high school coursework. On Sundays, the school transported them to city churches for religious services. In 1948 the school's Cosmetology Department, established in 1943, received accreditation.

By 1956–1957 the physical plant had grown from the original building to include five brick structures. That year, the State Department of Education accredited the elementary and junior high school programs of the institution, the staff of five certified instructors expanded to include a psychologist, and the curriculum added child care and commercial training (typing).

The Department of Correction desegregated all Tennessee juvenile correctional institutions during the 1966–1967 academic year and prepared to close the Tennessee Vocational School for Colored Girls, changing the name to the State Vocational School. The school initiated a pre-release cottage program, upgraded the remedial reading program, and emphasized academic subjects. During the period 1968–1970, the program added counseling and psychiatric services, and expanded recreational activities. The population increased to 103 girls, and the school encouraged parental visitation.

In 1970–1971 the school became the Tennessee Guidance and Reception Center for Children. The staff of 69 expanded to include a full-time licensed practical nurse and a full-time chaplain. The institution closed in 1979.

Evelyn P. Fancher, Nashville

SUGGESTED READING: Gary Shockley, "A History of the Incarceration of Juveniles in Tennessee, 1796–1970," *Tennessee Historical Quarterly* 43(1984): 229–249

SEE: TENNESSEE PRISON SYSTEM; TENNESSEE STATE UNIVERSITY

TENNESSEE WESLEYAN COLLEGE. The institution now known as Tennessee Wesleyan College was established in 1857, when the Holston Conference of the Methodist Episcopal Church South acquired the property of the Athens Female College, chartered in 1854 by the Order of Odd Fellows. The school continued to operate as a women's college until 1865, when it passed from the control of the Methodist Episcopal Church South to that of the Methodist Episcopal Church, a body composed of Union sympathizers. Renamed East Tennessee Wesleyan College, it initially only admitted male students, but two years later, it became coeducational.

Divisions within the church, frequent changes in leadership, and financial hardships plagued the early years. John Spence achieved some stability during his tenure as president. He strengthened the academic program and in 1867, unlike many southern colleges, the college required four years of study for the baccalaureate degree. Upon the death of former U.S. President Ulysses S. Grant, and in an attempt to appeal to potential northern supporters, the institution was renamed Grant Memorial University, an unpopular move with Confederate sympathizers.

In 1889 the Athens college merged with Chattanooga University, with the two campuses governed by a single board of trustees and chancellor, under the auspices of the Methodist Episcopal Church. Once again, the name changed to U.S. Grant University. From the beginning, consolidation brought intense rivalry and conflict. At first the school of liberal arts remained in Athens, with the schools of law, medicine, and theology in Chattanooga. When Chattanooga established a competing liberal arts curriculum in 1904, alumni and other supporters of the Athens school filed a lawsuit. The court ruled in favor of the Chattanooga campus, and the Athens branch became a preparatory school for the newly named University of Chattanooga.

The Athens and Chattanooga schools were separated in 1925, and the trustees of the Athens institution adopted the name Tennessee Wesleyan College. President James L. Robb concentrated on building a strong two-year college, which attained recognition for its academic program, particularly in the area of teacher education. The Great Depression and World War II threatened enrollment and financial stability, but returning veterans swelled the student population and necessitated expansion of faculty and facilities.

Under the leadership of Robb's successor, Dr. LeRoy Martin, Tennessee Wesleyan returned to senior college status in 1954. During the 1960s the school achieved its highest enrollment. In subsequent years, however, the school faced renewed enrollment problems because of the competition from four community colleges established within 50 miles of Athens.

Throughout its history, Tennessee Wesleyan has experienced financial and enrollment problems, but has exhibited remarkable resilience, consistently maintaining its commitment to a strong liberal arts curriculum and to the value of church-related education.
Bill Akins and Genevieve Wiggins, Tennessee Wesleyan College

SUGGESTED READING: LeRoy Albert Martin, *A History of Tennessee Wesleyan College, 1857–1957* (1957)

SEE: EDUCATION, HIGHER; HOLSTON CONFERENCE; MCMINN COUNTY; UNIVERSITY OF TENNESSEE AT CHATTANOOGA

TENNESSEE WILDLIFE RESOURCES AGENCY AND COMMISSION (TWRA) was created in 1974 through a reorganization of the Tennessee Game and Fish Commission in the latest of several attempts by the State of Tennessee to protect adequately native and game animals. Initial efforts began in 1870 with the passage of an act to protect fisheries. In the late 1880s, exploration of game and market hunting of quail were forbidden, although many counties exempted themselves from these state laws. In 1903 the General Assembly declared all game animals and fish the property of the state and named Joseph Acklen the first state game warden. Two years later, the General Assembly established the Game, Fish and Forestry Department and in 1907, set the first hunting license fees, with payment optional. In 1915 the legislature reorganized the agency and created the Department of Game and Fish.

Game and Fish was placed in the Department of Conservation when it was created in 1937, and its governing board abolished. After citizen complaints of too much interference in wildlife management, Governor Prentice Cooper reestablished the Game and Fish Commission in 1939, but the agency was still attached to the Department of Conservation. Governor Gordon Browning established an independent Tennessee Game and Fish Commission in 1949. This independent commission was a result in part of efforts by the Tennessee Federation of Sportsmen and its successor, the Tennessee Conservation League, whose members wanted to free Game and Fish from political control and the use of patronage in hiring game wardens.

In 1971 the public and media attacked the commission, charging it with fiscal extravagances and denouncing its support for the affluent hunter rather than the common hunter. In 1973 Governor Winfield Dunn appointed a special study committee to evaluate the commission's future. In April 1974, the General Assembly reorganized the Tennessee Game and Fish Commission into the Tennessee Wildlife Resources Agency, with oversight by the Tennessee Wildlife Resources Commission. In another major change, the agency was divided into a central office in Nashville and four regional offices in Jackson, Nashville, Crossville, and Talbott.

In 1997 TWRA employed more than 500 professionals in wildlife management and was directed by a 13-member commission of private citizens appointed by the Governor. License and permit fees largely fund the agency. TWRA enforces hunting, fishing, and boating laws, manages wildlife areas for game and non-game species, provides hunting and boating education, and works on wetlands protection. Its mission is the preservation, conservation, and enhancement of Tennessee's fish and wildlife for the enjoyment of all Tennesseans and visitors.

Ann Toplovich, Tennessee Historical Society
SEE: CONSERVATION; FISHING; HUNTING; TENNESSEE
CONSERVATION LEAGUE

TENNESSEE'S ARCHIVES. An archive is a repository for an organized body of records produced or received by a public, semi-public, institutional, or business entity in the transaction of its affairs and preserved by it, or its successors. The development of the archives system in Tennessee emerged from the public records system in use in British North America, specifically in the Carolina Colony established in 1663. The plantation system of land survey was particularly important, since it and other record practices traveled from North Carolina to Tennessee in the period following the American Revolution. Only vague provisions for the preservation of records were made.

The Constitutions of 1796, 1834 and 1870 recognized the Secretary of State as the chief records keeper of the state. After more than a century of neglect, the General Assembly made its first appropriation for the preservation of state records in 1907. No specific state agency was designated as the repository of state government records until 1919, when John T. Moore was appointed State Librarian and Archivist. The systematic management of state government records began in 1957, with the establishment of a Public Records Commission. It provided for the development of records retention schedules to allow the disposal of non-permanent value records and the transfer of archival materials to the State Library and Archives for permanent retention.

Records created by county and municipal government officials remained the responsibility of local government officials from the colonial period through the years of early statehood. Efforts to manage and preserve these records would not occur until the development of special agencies to provide support for municipal and county officials through the creation of the Municipal Technical Advisory Service (1949) and the County Technical Assistance Service (1973) at the University of Tennessee. In 1965 the General Assembly adopted legislation which led to the compilation and printing of the first *Tennessee County Records Manual* (1968). By means of additional legislation, counties were encouraged to establish their own public records commissions to provide for the orderly disposition of their records, and by implication, the counties were to create their own archives for the preservation of permanent value records.

In 1961 the State Library and Archives became involved in the preservation of local government records by means of a security microfilm program for bound records. This program was a response to numerous courthouse fires and other disasters, including floods, tornadoes, and earthquakes. Initially, only six counties were included, but the filming of records in all counties was completed by 1976. In conjunction with Homecoming '86 programs and activities, a new microfilm project filmed both county and municipal records for the years 1900 to 1950 for 49 counties. A later phase of the project completed 1950–1985 records for 30 counties. In 1994 the General Assembly reestablished the Local Records Microfilming Program, which provided microfilm operators to four on-site locations across the state. Projects to preserve loose records of local government are also included in the program of the State Library and Archives. As a result of an agreement with the Genealogical Society of Utah, work has begun on the processing of loose local government records for microfilming in 25 counties.

College and university archives account for another type of archival repository in Tennessee. Several public institutions of higher learning maintain an archives for the preservation of the official school records, as well as special collections of private manuscript collections. Special collections at the University of Tennessee, Knoxville, and the University of Memphis, and the Gore Research Center at Middle Tennessee State University are examples of such repositories. Private college and university archives in Tennessee include those located at Vanderbilt University, Fisk University, Rhodes College, and many others. Several colleges and universities with religious affiliations also operate a special religious archives. Lambuth College includes the archives for the Memphis Conference of the United Methodist Church, while Belmont University, Carson-Newman College, and Union University serve as archives for the Tennessee Baptist Convention. Separate religious archives are operated by the Jewish Federation of Nashville and Middle Tennessee, Diocese of Nashville, Disciples of Christ Historical Society, the Foundation for the Cumberland Presbyterian Church, the Southern Baptist Convention, and the Publishing House of the United Methodist Church.

Among the medical archives located in the state are those maintained by the Eskind Biomedical Center Library at Vanderbilt University, Saint Thomas Hospital, Meharry Medical College, East Tennessee State University, and the University of Tennessee at Memphis.

Various historical and genealogical societies have placed their records in the care of other institutions. County historical society collections are often located at the local county public library. The holdings of the East Tennessee Historical Society are housed in East Tennessee Historical Center; the Calvin McClung Historical Collection is in the Knox County Public Library; the Chattanooga Area Historical Society collection is at the Chattanooga-Hamilton County Bicentennial Library; the West Tennessee Society collections and the Mississippi Valley Collection are housed in the McWherter Library at the University of Memphis; and the Tennessee Historical Society has its collections at the State Library and Archives. The Tennessee Valley Authority maintains an archives for its records in Chattanooga.

Several private companies and corporations, including financial institutions and manufacturing firms, maintain their own archives. Examples of these include Coca-Cola, Jack Daniel Distillery, and the First American Bank.

In an effort to make historical records more accessible to the public, a directory of historical records repositories was undertaken in celebration of the state bicentennial.

John H. Thweatt, Tennessee State Library and Archives
SEE: EAST TENNESSEE HISTORICAL SOCIETY; HOMECOMING '86; MOORE, JOHN T. AND MARY D.; TENNESSEE HISTORICAL SOCIETY; TENNESSEE STATE LIBRARY AND ARCHIVES; WEST TENNESSEE HISTORICAL SOCIETY

TENNESSEE-TOMBIGBEE WATERWAY. Under construction from 1972 to 1985 by the U.S. Army Corps of Engineers, the Tennessee-Tombigbee Waterway is a 234-mile thoroughfare extending from the Tennessee River to the junction of the Black Warrior-Tombigbee River system near Demopolis, Alabama. It links commercial navigation from the nation's midsection to the Gulf of Mexico. First proposed during the colonial period, the idea received no serious attention until the advent of steamboat traffic in the early nineteenth century. In 1875 engineers surveyed a potential canal route, but issued a negative report and prohibitive cost estimates.

Enthusiasm for the project languished until the presidency of Franklin Roosevelt. Revived in 1938, the project passed in the 1946 Rivers and Harbors Act. Aided by the 1958 creation of the Tennessee Tombigbee Waterway Development Authority, an interstate compact headed by the governors of Tennessee and four other states, the project encountered further delays because of funding shortages and legal challenges. Finally, construction began in December 1972.

The Corps of Engineers divided work on the project, the largest in its history, between the Mobile and Nashville Districts. The Mobile District assumed responsibility for the 168-mile river section with four locks and dams that lay between Demopolis and Amory, Mississippi, and a 45-mile section with five locks from Amory to Bay Springs. The Nashville District had design and construction responsibility for the 40-mile divide section from Bay Springs Lock & Dam north to the Tennessee River. Although shorter in length, about half the 307 million cubic yards of earth removal occurred there. Excavation reached 175 feet in depth. Bay Springs Lock, with the highest lift

of the ten locks constructed, overcame 84 of the 341-foot difference between Pickwick Lake on the Tennessee River and Demopolis. Nashville employees also relocated two railroads, acquired 28,400 acres of land, and relocated approximately 170 people from the area.

In the early years of the project, the Nashville District, under the leadership of Euclid Moore and Richard Russell, successfully met and resolved construction challenges relating to engineering and environmental issues. Among these were groundwater removal, erosion and sedimentation, disposal of soils, and revegetation. Major excavation began in 1978, and was hampered by excessively wet weather and rising fuel prices. Construction of Bay Springs Lock commenced the following year. Work on the Divide section continued despite a series of close congressional funding votes and repeated court challenges from environmental and railroad lobbies.

Dedication of the Nashville District's Divide section took place in May 1984; the Mobile District's ceremony followed a year later. Total costs, including construction, real estate acquisition, relocations, and labor reached nearly two billion dollars.

The Tennessee-Tombigbee Waterway opened two years ahead of schedule, in the midst of an economic recession in the barge business—factors that initially resulted in a disappointingly low use of the waterway. In 1988, when drought closed the Mississippi River, however, traffic shifted to the canal. Tonnage and commercial investment along the Tennessee-Tombigbee corridor have increased steadily in the past several years.

James T. Siburt, U.S. Army Corps of Engineers
SEE: TENNESSEE RIVER SYSTEM; U.S. ARMY CORPS OF ENGINEERS

TENT CITY, FAYETTE AND HAYWOOD COUNTIES. In 1959 African Americans in Fayette and Haywood counties fought for the right to vote. The concern for voting emerged as a by-product of the absence of black jurors for the trial of Burton Dodson, an African-American farmer in his seventies, who was tried for the 1941 murder of a white man. By denying African Americans their rights to participate in the electoral process, whites eliminated them from the pool of potential jurors. To combat this injustice, African Americans in the two counties organized the Original Fayette County Civic and Welfare League, Inc., and the Haywood County Civic and Welfare League. Both leagues launched voter registration drives, and a number of blacks registered to vote during June and July. When the Democrats held their August primary, however, registered African-American voters were not allowed to cast their ballots. League members initiated the first legal action against a party primary under the Civil Rights Act of

Registering to vote in Fayette County, 1960.

SPECIAL COLLECTIONS, UNIVERSITY OF MEMPHIS. *COMMERCIAL APPEAL* PHOTOGRAPH

1957 when they filed suit against the local Democratic party.

Whites in Fayette and Haywood counties used their economic advantage to penalize African Americans, many of whom lost employment, credit, and insurance policies. Whites circulated a list of those African Americans who attempted to vote; the majority of white merchants refused to sell them goods and services, and some white physicians withheld medical care. In the winter of 1960 white property owners evicted hundreds of black tenant farmers from their lands.

African-American leaders did not surrender to the pressure tactics. With the support of black property owners, they formed makeshift communities known as "Tent City." They erected drab-green, surplus army tents, and homeless families prepared to face the cold winter winds. With no means of self-support, day-to-day existence provided a continuous strain for residents of "Tent City." Supporters from across the country helped with shipments of food and clothing. Hate groups, such as the White Citizens Council and the Ku Klux Klan, terrorized the residents by firing shots into the tents.

An exposé by Ted Poston in the New York *Post,* numerous articles in the New York *Times,* and Barry Gray's WMAC radio program brought the leagues' activities to the attention of the nation. The U.S. Justice Department filed several lawsuits against landowners, merchants, and one financial institution for violating African-American civil rights. On July 26, 1962, "landowners were enjoined from engaging in any acts . . . for the purpose of interfering with the right to vote and to vote for candidates in public office."[1]

Linda T. Wynn, Tennessee Historical Commission/Fisk University

CITATION:

(1) Memphis *Commercial Appeal,* July 27, 1962.

SUGGESTED READINGS: Richard Couto, *Lifting the Veil: A Political Struggle for Emancipation* (1993); Linda T. Wynn, "Tent Cities of Fayette and Haywood Counties, 1960–1962," in Bobby L. Lovett and Linda T. Wynn, eds., *Profiles of African Americans in Tennessee History,* (1996)

SEE: CIVIL RIGHTS MOVEMENT; FAYETTE COUNTY; HAYWOOD COUNTY; MCFERREN, JOHN AND VIOLA

TEPCO, officially the Tennessee Electric Power Company, was the largest private-sector electrical power monopoly in Tennessee's early twentieth century history. It was formed on May 27, 1922, when the Tennessee Power Company, Chattanooga Railway & Light, and the Chattanooga, and Tennessee River Power Company merged. Through outright absorption of smaller companies and stock ownership, TEPCO controlled the Toccoa Electric Power Company, Blue Ridge Corporation, Nashville Railway and Light Company, Lookout Incline Railway Company, Lookout Mountain Railroad Company, and the Tennessee Transportation Company. TEPCO was composed of the assets of 45 different Tennessee companies, some dating to the nineteenth century.

The preponderance of the hydroelectric power production units with the TEPCO system were in operation when the merger took place in 1922, and later in 1929 when Southern Cities Corporation was taken over. For example, the Chattanooga and Tennessee River Power Company had begun construction in 1905 on the dam at Hales Bar on the Tennessee River. The Eastern Tennessee Power Company had constructed Ocoee No. 1 and No. 2 and the hydroelectric site at Great Falls on the Caney River all before 1916. A number of smaller, municipal plants in Middle Tennessee, built between 1901 and 1929, were controlled by either the Southern Cities Power Company (1918) or owned by the municipalities of Cookeville and Lawrenceburg. All would be absorbed by TEPCO in 1929. TEPCO, in turn, ironically, would be absorbed by the Tennessee Valley Authority as a result of a U.S. Supreme Court decision in 1939.

Another private Tennessee power company was the East Tennessee Light and Power Company (ETL&PC), which was organized in October 1929. On June 1, 1929, ETL&PC acquired the property and assets of a number of Tennessee companies, including: Watauga Power Company, Bluff City Electric Light and Power Company, Butler Light and Power Company, and Roan's Creek Light and Power Company. ETL&PC, an interstate corporation, operated in two counties in Virginia, one county in North Carolina, and four counties in Tennessee, serving as its primary consumption centers Bristol, Virginia, and Bristol, Elizabethton, and Erwin, Tennessee. It would operate a number of facilities until 1945, when TVA would purchase its assets and add them to its public jurisdiction.

A third private sector firm, the Tennessee Eastern Electric Company (TEEC), was incorporated in June 1912. The company, soon thereafter, acquired the property and assets of the Watauga Electric Company, Greeneville Electric Company, and Jonesboro Electric Company. TEEC was the sole electrical power provider for Washington, Greene, Unicoi, Carter, and Sullivan counties in East Tennessee, including Greeneville, Johnson City, and Jonesboro as the principal cities.

But TEPCO was the largest and most important of the early Tennessee electrical power companies. The result of TEPCO's formation was essentially that everyday life for many Tennesseans began to be characterized by a full spectrum of heretofore unknown household conveniences made possible by electricity. Moreover, work altered through the introduction of water pumps, electric dairy equipment, and electric-powered cabinet making and mining equipment. Though commonplace today, the insertion of these tools and conveniences into everyday life was the result of hydroelectric development in Tennessee from 1901 to 1933.

James B. Jones, Jr., Tennessee Historical Commission

SUGGESTED READING: James B. Jones, Jr., "Pre-TVA Hydro-Electric Power Development in Tennessee, 1901–1933," *The Courier* 25(1987): 4–6

SEE: ASHWANDER ET AL. V. TENNESSEE VALLEY AUTHORITY; BURGESS FALLS STATE NATURAL AREA; HALES BAR DAM; ROCK ISLAND STATE PARK; TENNESSEE VALLEY AUTHORITY

TERA, officially the Tennessee Emergercy Relief Administration, was an important early New Deal agency in Tennessee. Shortly after the inauguration of President Franklin Roosevelt, Congress passed the Federal Emergency Relief Act on May 12, 1933, and its implementation began on May 22, with Harry Hopkins assuming the position as director of the Federal Emergency Relief Administration (FERA). The FERA program had three guiding principles: adequate relief should be given; work relief rather than dole relief should be given; and the work relief program should be diversified to allow opportunities for participants to perform activities related to their ordinary occupations. FERA had four divisions: 1) Research, Statistics, and Finance; 2) Works; 3) Rural Rehabilitation; and 4) Relations with states.

FERA distributed grants-in-aid to states according to three conditions: the state legislature had to create a state agency, which, in turn, submitted a plan that met federal approval, and the state had to provide matching funds. First, the Tennessee agency was the Tennessee State Relief Administration, and then it took the name of TERA, the Tennessee Emergency Relief Administration. TERA projects were spread across the state. At Gentry, in the Cumberland Plateau, it built a brick school. In Memphis, it distributed food, clothing, and coal to the needy; men also were hired to clean streets and dig ditches. In October 1933, Kingsport requested a $12,500 grant and loan from TERA for local relief projects.

Before TERA and other state agencies could be effectively organized and placed in operation, it became apparent to both President Roosevelt and Hopkins that the winter of 1933–1934 would be economically severe if something was not done quickly. On November 9, 1933, the Civil Works Administration (CWA) was created by executive order. It operated under Title II of the National Industrial Recovery Act (NIRA) and spent $900 million before it was discontinued in the spring of 1934. The CWA was strictly a federal agency designed to employ persons who had been receiving direct relief payments. CWA projects in Tennessee included early work on Cumberland Homesteads near Crossville.

TERA had been a partial success, "but by 1935 the economic situation had improved so little that another approach appeared necessary."[1] This became the Works Progress Administration (WPA). The WPA took over the work relief program of TERA and similar agencies in other states. The Rural Rehabilitation Division of TERA was assumed by the University of Tennessee Extension Division as of July 1, 1935. The initial efforts of the WPA were to borrow workers from TERA and gradually absorb them.

By late July, WPA had requested over five million dollars to continue rewritten TERA projects. Some delay in shifting workers from TERA to WPA required its workers to have physical exams. TERA asked for a $10,000 grant to pay for such exams. By mid-August, 8,000 physically-fit workers began working on 57 WPA projects in Tennessee.

H. Bruce Throckmorton, Tennessee Technological University
CITATION:
(1) James A. Burran, "The WPA in Nashville, 1935–1943," *Tennessee Historical Quarterly* 34(1975): 293.

SUGGESTED READING: John D. Minton, *The New Deal in Tennessee, 1933–1939* (1979)

SEE: CUMBERLAND HOMESTEADS; WORKS PROGRESS ADMINISTRATION

TERRELL, MARY ELIZA CHURCH (1863–1954), founder of the National Association of Colored Women (NACW) in 1896, was one the leading twentieth century African-American women activists. For more than 66 years, she was the ardent champion of racial and gender equality. Born into the black elite of Memphis on September 23, 1863, she was the oldest child of Robert Reed Church and Louisa Ayers. While in school in Ohio she grew aware of discrimination and resolved to excel academically to prove the abilities of African Americans and especially black women.

After graduation from Oberlin College in 1884 she took a teaching position at Wilberforce University in Ohio. A year later she was teaching at M Street High School in Washington, D.C. There she met her future husband, Robert H. Terrell. Between 1888 and 1896, she traveled throughout Europe.

In 1896 Terrell returned to the United States as an advocate of racial elevation. In the same year, she became the founder and first president of the NACW. Symbolizing unity among black women, this self-help organization offered sisterly support for its members and created programs that addressed racial problems through the elevation of black women. Terrell equated the struggle for the amelioration of discrimination with the elevation of black women.

Terrell led the NACW in establishing socially progressive institutions such as kindergartens, day nurseries, and Mother Clubs. Mother Clubs functioned as depositories and disseminators of information on rearing children and managing the home. Terrell's objective was to improve the moral standards of the poor and poorly educated, since she believed that the world judged the race through its women.

From 1896 to 1901 Terrell defined and developed her role as a "New Woman," which resulted in the development of purpose, independence, and vitality in her life. By 1901 Terrell began to move from an approach of black self-help to one of inter-

Mary Church Terrell.

racial understanding, advocating education as the way to understanding. She hoped that unbiased research and intelligent dissemination of information to both white and black peoples would promote better cooperation.

Terrell's advocacy of African-American women led to opportunities to comment on broader issues facing her race. She made many speeches on the living conditions of African Americans and highlighted their progress in spite of discrimination. In a stirring address delivered in 1904 at the International Congress of Women in Berlin, she vividly described the numerous contributions of African Americans. She delivered the speech in German (she spoke three languages fluently), receiving accolades for her depictions of African-American life and her intellectual abilities. Her speeches acted as morale boosters for African Americans, even as she exhorted them toward self-improvement.

Terrell also wrote articles and short stories on lynching, chain gangs, the peonage system, defection of mulattoes, and the disfranchisement of African Americans. In her writings, she sought to further interracial understanding by educating whites about the realities of African-American lives.

The last two decades of her life marked a transition in her position on race relations and politics.

Working on production line at Textron Aerostructures.

STATE OF TENNESSEE PHOTOGRAPHIC SERVICES

Frustrated by the economic hardships of African Americans during the Great Depression and New Deal era, dismayed by the irony that African Americans were fighting for the democracy abroad that they were denied at home, and grieved by the death of her husband, Terrell became a militant activist, working assiduously to bring a definitive end to discrimination in the United States, particularly in the nation's capital.

In her later life, Terrell led a three-year struggle to reinstate Reconstruction-era laws that prohibited racial segregation in public eating facilities in Washington, D.C. These anti-segregation laws disappeared in the 1890s, when the District code was written. On February 28, 1950, Terrell, accompanied by one white and two black collaborators, entered Thompson Restaurant; they were refused service. Terrell and her cohorts filed affidavits, and *District of Columbia v. John Thompson* became a national symbol against segregation in the United States. Her direct-action tactics of picketing, boycotting, and sit-ins proved successful and, on June 8, 1953, the court ruled that segregated eating establishments in Washington, D.C., were unconstitutional.

This ardent fighter for civil rights lived to see the U.S. Supreme Court mandate the desegregation of public schools in *Brown v. Board of Education*. Two months later, on July 24, 1954, she died.

Beverly W. Jones, North Carolina Central University

SUGGESTED READING: Beverly W. Jones, *Quest for Equality: Life and Writings of Mary Church Terrell* (1991)

SEE: CHURCH, ROBERT R., SR.; MEMPHIS; NATIONAL CIVIL RIGHTS MUSEUM

TEXTRON (CARLYLE) AEROSTRUCTURES. Names for this company have changed through the years, but the early factory site off Murfreesboro Pike in Nashville has not and the importance of this plant cannot be overstated. Nashville's Mayor Thomas Cummings (elected 1938) induced Aviation Corporation of California in 1939 to build adjacent to the Berry Field airport a factory that evolved with the needs and innovations in flight. The $9 million plant, with its projection to employ 7,000, began by manufacturing personal airplanes and military observation planes. Bought by Vultee Aircraft in 1940, the plant built P-38 Lightning fighters and became the region's first defense plant. Employing a good number of women as its aircraft workers during wartime, the Vultee Aircraft factory produced its Vultee Vengeance. This plane was used by U.S., British, and British colonial units, seeing action in Burma and India, but the dive-bomber never lived up to its expected potential.

After its wartime production, the company became the Nashville Division of Avco Manufacturing Corporation in 1949 and made parts for the Convair B-36 and Lockheed C-130. Since 1960 the Avco Corporation changed names several more times and returned to building parts for war planes. These included parts for Grumman intruder bombers, McDonnell-Douglas F-4 Phantom II fighter planes, C-141 and C-5A cargo planes, and Bell Huey (Vietnam) and Cobra (Vietnam and after) helicopter parts. At the same time, the construction of wings for Grumman and Lockheed corporate jets continued.

In the last 25 years, Avco manufactured parts of the space shuttle, wings for various U.S. and British bombers, European airbuses, as well as rocket nose parts. Its employee rolls reached the 7,000 predicted at the outbreak of World War II. Textron Inc., of Providence, Rhode Island, bought the plant in 1985 and renamed it Textron Aerostructures. The factory sold again in 1996 to the Washington, D.C.-based aerospace investment group called Carlyle, which continues to operate the facility today. As the stakes change, at least part of the pattern has remained the same. Nashville left the Depression and believed in the possibilities of growth and forward movement as an urban area and the South as a new industrial area because of the arrival of companies such as Aviation Corporation in the mid-twentieth century.

Margaret D. Binnicker, Middle Tennessee State University

SEE: INDUSTRY; NASHVILLE; WORLD WAR II

THE EMANCIPATOR, published by Elihu Embree at Jonesborough in 1820, was the first newspaper in the United States solely devoted to the abolition of slavery. Embree had previously published a weekly newspaper, *The Manumission Intelligencer,* in 1819, and it was followed by *The Emancipator* from April to October 1820. According to Embree, the purpose of *The Emancipator* was "to advocate the abolition of slavery and to be a repository of tracts on that interesting and important subject."

The Emancipator advocated gradual emancipation and colonization of slaves, reprinted the proceedings and addresses of the Manumission Society of Tennessee, and published letters, articles, and poetry related to the abolition of slavery. In his newspaper, Embree celebrated slaveowners who, like himself, had freed their slaves, and he recounted the "pitiful conditions" of many slaves to expose the institution and inhumane slaveowners.

The annual subscription rate of *The Emancipator* was one dollar per year, and it reached a circulation of over 2,000 by October 1820, with deliveries made to Boston and Philadelphia, as well as in the South. Embree mailed copies of his papers to the governors of all the southern states, but it was not well received. Many southerners erroneously thought Embree was an agent of northern abolitionist groups, sent to Tennessee to stir up trouble with his publication.

The paper ceased publication with Embree's illness in the fall of 1820; the last edition was published on October 31. *The Emancipator* was reprinted in its entirety by B.H. Murphy of Nashville in 1932.

Tara Mitchell Mielnik, Middle Tennessee State University

SEE: EMBREE, ELIHU; LUNDY, BENJAMIN; MANUMISSION SOCIETY OF TENNESSEE; PUBLISHING; SLAVERY

THE FARM is an intentional community occupying some 1,750 acres in southeastern Lewis County, near Summertown. In 1971 San Francisco resident and New Age religious leader, Stephen Gaskin, and his followers founded The Farm as a spiritual community. The group chose the Upland South for their home after several months of traveling in a caravan of brightly colored school buses in search of suitable land. Rejecting the materialism of modern society, they moved to the hilly country of southern Middle Tennessee, where they took up farming and the formidable task of establishing their utopian community.

Gaskin's teachings, an informal blend of both western and eastern religious principles, stressed non-violence and the power of good works. Enthusiastic and idealistic, his youthful supporters accepted a life of voluntary peasantry to demonstrate the concept of shared abundance as the method for providing for the needs of the world. The residents promoted vegetarianism and cooperation as the means to that end.

Honest, sincere, and industrious, the residents also tended to be moralistic. They held all possessions in common, ate no meat or dairy products, and practiced neither mechanical birth control nor abortion. They espoused natural childbirth, and The Farm's midwives, under the direction of Ina Mae Gaskin, became the vanguard, and later the center, of a national movement toward home birthing.

Despite the countrified name, few members had any actual farming experience, and the soil of the Highland Rim was not very productive. The little money remaining after the purchase of the land quickly dwindled, and the rural environment provided few opportunities for employment. When their agricultural efforts failed, the group developed a number of successful businesses, including construction, electronics, trucking, publishing, and specialty food sales.

Through hard work and near self-sufficiency, The Farm's numbers grew from 400 to 1,500 residents by 1979, but the standard of living never kept pace with the population increases. The lack of infrastructure seriously affected the well-being and success of the communal experiment, as the large numbers of newcomers overwhelmed the meager resources. The need for adequate housing, running water, sanitation facilities, transportation, and other key necessities became acute.

The recession of the early 1980s proved to be the last straw, and many residents left The Farm. In 1983 the remaining members discarded the communal system in favor of the present cooperative one, in which the land and other assets are held and maintained in common, with all residents paying a set fee for monthly dues. Under this arrangement, members retain control of their personal assets.

For the last several years, the population of The Farm has remained stable at approximately 200 people, and the businesses remain prosperous. The Farm's continued success is a clear demonstration of

the benefits of non-violence and cooperative living.
Michael Gavin, Summertown

SEE: LEWIS COUNTY; NASHOBA; RUGBY; RUSKIN COOPER-
ATIVE ASSOCIATION

THEATER has a long history in Tennessee. Early touring theater groups performed in the larger towns,
with plays such as *Child of Nature, or Virtue Rewarded*
presented in Nashville in 1807. Nashville residents
established their first theater in 1818 and during the
next two decades, performances multiplied and
became more elaborate with each passing season.
Memphis's initial theatrical performance took place
at the Blue Ruin in 1831. Nashville's Adelphi Theater
opened in 1850 as the second largest venue in the
country. A similar pattern of theater growth occurred
in antebellum Knoxville and especially in Memphis,
where troupes traveling along the Mississippi River
brought a wide variety of performers during the
1850s boom.

The Victorian age proved to be a golden era for
theater in Tennessee. Major stars such as James
O'Neill, Lillie Langtry, Julia Marlowe, Otis Skinner,
Edwin Booth, and Sarah Bernhardt performed in the
state while entrepreneurs in the four major cities, and
even smaller county seats, built theaters and "opera
houses." The Ryman Auditorium by the turn of the
century had become Nashville's premier venue;
Staub's Theater (later the Bijou) in Knoxville and the
Grand Opera House in Memphis held similar honors
in their respective cities.

Diversity marks the theater of twentieth century
urban Tennessee. In 1921 the Memphis Little Theater,
now Theater Memphis, was established. In 1931 the
Junior League of Nashville established the Nashville
Children's Theatre, later called the Nashville Academy Theatre. A huge post-World War II success, the
group opened a new 699-seat theater in 1960, the first
constructed specifically as a children's theater in the
nation. In 1949 Nashville's Circle Players were established. Led by Jackie Nicholds, the Circuit Players of
Memphis began with summer performances in 1965;
the Circuit Playhouse, Inc., of Memphis was organized in 1969 and the group opened its modern theater in 1975. In Knoxville the Bijou Theater was listed
in the National Register and restored as a modern
theater; large productions often take place nearby at
the 1920s movie palace, the Tennessee Theater. In
1971 the Clarence Brown Theater opened on the
campus of the University of Tennessee, Knoxville. It
hosts college-produced performances as well as
national traveling companies. Chattanooga's Tivoli
Theater, another National Register landmark, also
was restored for the performing arts.

The Tennessee Performing Arts Center (TPAC) in
Nashville opened in 1980. It became the state's premier theater venue and hosted the Tennessee Bicen-

tennial Arts and Entertainment Festival in 1996.
TPAC also is home to the Tennessee Repertory Theatre, which was established in 1980 and is led by Mac
Pirkle. It is the largest of the state's professional theater companies and through its Humanities Outreach
in Tennessee program, the company has brought theater to over 250,000 students.

In the latter decades of the century, important theater companies were established statewide. The Oak
Ridge Playhouse began in the 1950s. Certainly the
most famous regional company is the Cumberland
County Playhouse established by Paul Crabtree outside of Crossville in 1965. Today the playhouse's complex includes a 220-seat outdoor theater and a
490-seat Paul and Mary Crabtree Auditorium. The
Murfreesboro Little Theater once performed in a
former Boy Scout lodge building constructed by the
National Youth Administration in the late 1930s. In
1996 the company moved into the newly renovated
Center for the Arts, formerly the post office and then
city library of Murfreesboro. The Road Company was
established in Johnson City in 1975 and presented its
first performances in 1981. Important influences on
both the Murfreesboro and Johnson City companies
are the thriving drama departments of the respective
state universities located in those towns. Colleges
departments of music and drama have been invaluable in the development of theater across the state.

Locally produced theater thrives in many small
towns. Clarksville has the Roxy Theater. The Ruffin
Theater in Covington originally featured movies but
was restored in the late 1980s as a performing arts
theater. The Center for the Arts in Woodbury, established in 1991, has become regionally known for its
drama and musical productions. The Capitol Theater,
restored in 1996–1998, has recently opened as a performing arts center in Union City. Lawrenceburg is
planning a similar revival for its Art Deco-styled
Crockett Theater.

Several African-American groups have established companies over the last 30 years. The oldest
is the Carpetbag Theatre of Knoxville, established in
1969. The Blues City Cultural Center began in 1979;
it performs in Memphis as well as towns throughout the region. Stella Reed established Nashville's
Black Taffeta and Burlap in 1990 and Nashville actor
and playwright Barry Scott established the American Negro Playwright Theater in 1992.
Carroll Van West, Middle Tennessee State University

SUGGESTED READING: Clara Hieronymus, "Spotlights: 200
Years of Tennessee Theater," *Tennessee Bicentennial Arts &
Entertainment Festival Program* (1996), 20–29

SEE: BROWN, CLARENCE; INGRAM, E. BRONSON; RYMAN
AUDITORIUM; STAUB, PETER

THOMAS NELSON PUBLISHERS. In the early 1950s,
a young immigrant named Sam Moore arrived in

New York and launched his own business by selling Bibles door-to-door. His success in this endeavor provided Moore with the funds to establish the National Book Company, which merged with Royal Publishers in 1961. Moore again demonstrated his business acumen at Royal Publishing and in 1964 he purchased the Thomas Nelson American division, a British-owned company, and merged the two publishing companies.

Thomas Nelson possessed a long and distinguished name in British publishing. Thomas Nelson, the founder of the company that bears his name, migrated from Scotland to London, where he was employed by a small publisher of religious literature. Eventually, Nelson returned to Edinburgh and established his own shop. Although his early success came through the sale of second-hand books, Nelson became interested in publishing inexpensive literature for larger audiences. His first publications included excerpts from *Pilgrim's Progress, Robinson Crusoe,* and *The Vicar of Wakefield.* Nelson soon gained recognition for his publication of classic literature and eventually published over 400 volumes bearing the "Nelson Classics" name.

To meet the increasing demands, Nelson and his two sons, Thomas II and William, developed innovative publishing methods that continue to be felt in the modern publishing industry. Nelson was the first publishing company to send salesmen to individual bookshops and establish good public relations with customers. The Nelson brothers also developed innovative printing and binding processes, including the rotary press.

In 1854 Thomas Nelson II immigrated and established an office on Bleeker Street in New York, becoming the first British publisher to expand into the growing American market. With the purchase of a bindery in Camden, New Jersey, Nelson Publishers became one of the few publishers to manufacture completely in America. The company eventually expanded into the publication of Bibles, textbooks, and church literature. In the 1940s Nelson published the first editions of the American Standard Version Bible and the Revised Standard Version Bible. Since then, it has published eight other translations of the Bible.

In 1972 Sam Moore moved Thomas Nelson Publishers to Nashville, already a center for religious publishing. Since the late 1980s, the company has experienced explosive growth. It acquired Word Publishing and the C.R. Gibson gift company, which brought the publisher to a large audience. In 1997 Thomas Nelson Publishers introduced *Nelson's Electronic Bible Reference Library* on CD-ROM. The company now employs over 525 Tennesseans.

Thomas Nelson Publishers celebrates its 200th anniversary in 1998, having risen from a one-man, second-hand book seller in Edinburgh, Scotland, to become a leader in the Christian publishing industry. Today Thomas Nelson is one of the largest Bible publishers in the world, continuing a literary tradition that begins with John Bunyan and goes on to Billy Graham.

Cindy Stephens Blades, Thomas Nelson Publishers
SEE: PUBLISHING

THOMAS, ANNE TAYLOR JONES (1867–1938), Chattanooga philanthropist, was a native of Cincinnati, Ohio. Anne Jones met her future husband, Benjamin Franklin Thomas, while he was attending law school at the University of Cincinnati. The couple married in 1894 in Chattanooga. She was supportive of her husband's somewhat risky proposal to undertake the bottling of Coca-Cola. In 1904 the childless couple brought Thomas's nephew, George Thomas Hunter, into their household, where he quickly became both son and business partner.

Following the death of her husband in 1914, Anne Thomas devoted the rest of her life to charitable work and philanthropy. She was instrumental in the construction of the children's wing of Baroness Erlanger Hospital, the establishment and furnishing of a historical room in the Chattanooga Public Library, and the financing of the Pine Breeze Sanitarium. Numerous churches, schools, and charities in the Chattanooga area received contributions from Thomas. She inspired her nephew to create the Benwood Foundation in memory of her husband and herself. She died on April 5, 1938, and is buried in Spring Grove Cemetery, Cincinnati, Ohio.

Ned L. Irwin, East Tennessee State University
SEE: BENWOOD FOUNDATION; CHATTANOOGA; COCA-COLA BOTTLING COMPANY; HUNTER, GEORGE T.; THOMAS, BENJAMIN F.

THOMAS, BENJAMIN FRANKLIN (1860–1914), Chattanooga businessman and industrialist, pioneered the development of the Coca-Cola bottling industry in America. A native of Maysville, Kentucky, Thomas began his business career as a bank clerk, stone quarry operator, and manager of a hosiery mill. In 1887 he graduated from the University of Cincinnati law school and moved to Chattanooga, at the encouragement of a fellow Cincinnati graduate, E.Y. Chapin. While serving in the Spanish-American War, a popular bottled Cuban fruit drink inspired Thomas with the idea of bottling a similar carbonated beverage in America. In 1899 he and partner Joseph Brown Whitehead convinced Asa Candler, president of the Coca-Cola Company in Atlanta, to give them the exclusive rights to bottle Coca-Cola, then widely available only as a drugstore fountain drink. John T. Lupton of Chattanooga became a third partner, and the first bottling plant opened later that summer.

As the business flourished, the partners focused their attention on the creation of franchise bottling companies. In 1900 they divided the United States into franchise territories. Thomas's territory included most of the eastern United States from Chattanooga north and the Pacific coast states of California, Oregon, and Washington. In 1902 Thomas sold the Chattanooga bottling plant. His company, Coca-Cola Bottling Company (Thomas), supplied syrup to franchised bottlers across the country, in effect becoming the largest bottler of soft drinks in the world.

In 1894 Thomas married Anne Taylor Jones. Remaining childless, they invited Thomas's teenage nephew, George Thomas Hunter, to join them in Chattanooga and groomed him to take over the bottling business.

Thomas was an important economic, civic, and social influence in Chattanooga. An early promoter of real estate development on Lookout Mountain, he helped organize what became American National Bank, as well as the Chattanooga Golf and Country Club. In later life, Thomas suffered from Bright's disease. He died on June 26, 1914, in Atlantic City, New Jersey. He was buried in his hometown of Maysville.

Ned L. Irwin, East Tennessee State University

SUGGESTED READINGS: DeSales Harrison, *Footprints on the Sands of Time: A History of Two Men and the Fulfillment of a Dream* (1968); Ned L. Irwin, "Bottling Gold: Chattanooga's Coca-Cola Fortunes," *Tennessee Historical Quarterly* 51(1992): 223–37

SEE: CHATTANOOGA; COCA-COLA BOTTLING COMPANY; HUNTER, GEORGE T.; LUPTON, JOHN T.; THOMAS, ANNE T. J.; WHITEHEAD, JOSEPH B.

THOMAS, GEORGE HENRY (1816–1870), Union General, played a pivotal role in several significant Tennessee Civil War battles. Born July 31, 1816, in Southampton County, Virginia, Thomas gained local fame as a boy when he rode through the county to warn neighbors of the Nat Turner-led slave uprising of 1831. This helped him gain appointment to the U.S. Military Academy at West Point, where he graduated with distinction and became an instructor in artillery and cavalry. During the Mexican War, Thomas fought in the Second Cavalry, ironically beside several other young officers, such as John Bell Hood and Albert Sidney Johnston, who later would be his antagonists during the Civil War.

In 1861 Thomas remained loyal to his country, a stance detested by many of his Virginia friends and family members. In fact, due to Thomas's Virginia roots, federal officers were wary of giving him command. However, the methodical but resolute Thomas proved he could fight and win at the Battle of Mill Springs, Kentucky, in January 1862, where his command defeated a Confederate force from the army of Albert S. Johnston that was led by General Felix Zollifcoffer. Thomas's soldiers routed the Confederates

and Zollicoffer was killed. Mill Springs was the first significant Union victory in the western theater.

In the Kentucky campaign of 1862, Thomas again served with distinction at the Battle of Perryville on October 8. He was offered the command of his superior, General Don Carlos Buell, but Thomas demurred, accepting instead a subordinate position in the U.S. Army of the Cumberland under General William S. Rosecrans. At the end of the year, at the Battle of Stones River near Murfreesboro, Thomas's soldiers survived heavy casualties to hold the Union center—at a place known as the "Round Forest"—and to maintain control of the vital Nashville and Chattanooga Railroad line. Once again, Thomas had proven his resilence and ability in battle.

His reputation as a gifted field commander was cinched during the Battle of Chickamauga in September 1863. General Braxton Bragg's Army of Tennessee initially intended to overwhelm Rosecrans's divided army. Thomas, however, escaped from one trap at McLemore's Cove on September 9 while other Union commanders also managed to avoid confrontations. On September 18 Rosecrans concentrated his three corps along Chickamauga Creek, with Thomas's corps placed at the center. When the Confederates attacked the next day, they smashed through both the right and left flanks of the Union line by early afternoon, leaving the fate of the Army of the Cumberland in Thomas's hands. He rallied his soldiers and began to repulse repeated Confederate attacks. By 3:30 P.M., however, his command had weakened to the point that Thomas began to give ground. To his rescue came the reserve corps of General Gordon Granger. Together Granger and Thomas managed to hold their position, at least until dusk when they retreated to Chattanooga. The Battle of Chickamauga was a Union defeat, but Thomas gained the nickname "Rock of Chickamauga" for his stand, which undoubtedly saved the Army of the Cumberland from a disastrous rout.

That fall Thomas was given the command of the Army of the Cumberland, but his force was assigned a limited role in General U.S. Grant's planned assault of Confederate positions along Missionary Ridge on November 25, 1863. During the battle, however, Thomas's soldiers surged through the Confederates positioned at the base of the ridge and then, without orders, charged up the steep ridge slope, surprising the Confederates and chasing them from the field. With this rousing victory, Thomas and his men avenged their earlier defeat at Chickamauga.

After the Union's successful Atlanta campaign of 1864, Sherman in late October 1864 detached portions of Thomas's army and ordered the soldiers to return to Tennessee to defend the Union rear and the capital city of Nashville from a possible invasion from Confederate General John Bell Hood's Army of

Tennessee. A Union army under General John Scofield slowed Hood's march north at the Battles of Spring Hill and Franklin in late November, inflecting heavy Confederate casualties at the latter battle. Thomas then exasperated the Union high command by waiting for two weeks to strike the greatly weakened Army of Tennessee outside of Nashville. But when Thomas struck on on December 15–16, 1864, he left the Confederate army in shambles; the war in Tennessee was virtually over. George H. Thomas, a Virginia native, had served with distinction from the beginning to the end of that struggle, bringing victory to the Union cause.

After the Civil War, General Thomas remained in the military and was commander of the Military Division of the Pacific when he died in San Francisco on March 28, 1870.

Carroll Van West, Middle Tennessee State University

SUGGESTED READING: Francis F. McKinney, *Education in Violence: The Life of George H. Thomas* (1961)

SEE: CHICKAMAUGA AND CHATTANOOGA, BATTLES OF; FRANKLIN, BATTLE OF; NASHVILLE, BATTLE OF; SHILOH, BATTLE OF; STONES RIVER, BATTLE OF; TULLAHOMA CAMPAIGN; U.S. ARMY OF THE CUMBERLAND

THOMAS, RUFUS (1917–), legendary R&B singer, was born on March 26, 1917, in Cayce, Mississippi, just south of Memphis. He began performing in the 1930s at the Palace and Handy theaters in Memphis and as a traveling entertainer with such troupes as the Rabbit Foot Minstrels. Along with Robert Counce, Thomas formed a popular tap dance/scat singing act called "Rufus and Bones."

In the early 1950s Thomas made several recordings for Sam Phillips at Sun Records. Thomas's *Bear Cat*, reached number three on the charts, an early success for both Sun Records and Thomas. Already an established local performer, Thomas took a disk jockey job with Memphis's WDIA radio in 1954. His shows, "Sepia Swing Club," "Heebie Jeebies," and "Hoot 'n' Holler" gave initial exposure to many R&B artists.

During the 1960s Thomas played an important role in the early success of Stax Records. His duet *Cause I Love You,* with daughter Carla in 1960, was an international hit. Carla launched her solo career with *Gee Whiz* in 1961 and was billed as "The Queen of Memphis Sound."

Recording for Stax, Thomas had a top-10 hit on the R&B chart with *Walking the Dog* in 1963. Achieving this success at the age of 45, he earned the title of "The World's Oldest Living Teenager." Thomas recorded a succession of dance hits, including *Do the Funky Chicken* (1970), *Do the Push and Pull* (1970), *The Breakdown* (1971), and *Do the Funky Penguin* (1971). At the age of 80, Thomas continues to perform on Beale Street when not on tour.

Anne-Leslie Owens, Tennessee Historical Society

SEE: MEMPHIS MUSIC SCENE; PHILLIPS, SAMUEL C.; ROCK MUSIC, SOUTHERN; STAX RECORDS; WDIA

THOMPSON, FRED (1942–), U.S. Senator, Watergate committee counsel, and movie actor, was born August 19, 1942, in Sheffield, Alabama. He grew up in Lawrenceburg, Tennessee, the son of a used car dealer, and attended Lawrence County High School. He graduated from the University of Memphis in 1964 and took his law degree from Vanderbilt University in 1967. Thompson opened his law career in his hometown where he practiced until 1969 when he was named Assistant U.S. Attorney for Middle Tennessee. In 1972 he managed the Middle Tennessee portion of U.S. Senator Howard Baker, Jr.'s successful reelection campaign against Democrat Ray Blanton. The following year Baker asked Thompson to leave Tennessee for the nation's capital and serve as minority counsel on the Senate Select Committee on Presidential Campaign Activity, better known as the Watergate committee.

Thompson played an important role in the committee's affairs and it was his and his staff's work that uncovered the existence of a taping system in Nixon's White House. In a dramatic moment in the televised proceedings of the committee, Thompson asked White House aide Alexander Butterfield about the existence of a taping system and whether tapes of key conversations survived. Butterfield's affirmative answers proved to be a turning point in the course of the Watergate investigation. Thompson later described his role in the proceedings in the book *At That Point in Time* (1975).

After Watergate, Thompson took up private practice in Nashville but returned to the state political limelight in 1977 when Marie Ragghianti, the recently dismissed chair of the state Parole Board, asked Thompson to serve as her counsel in a lawsuit against the administration. Supported by Thompson and his staff's legal work, Ragghianti's testimony brought to light a scandalous cash-for-clemency system within the administration of Governor Ray Blanton. The exposé eventually helped to force Blanton from office and led to the successful prosecution of several Blanton aides.

Ragghianti later worked with author Peter Maas to write the book *Marie, a True Story.* Hollywood producers decided to make a film about Ragghianti's story, titled *Marie* (1986), and chose Sissy Spacek to play Ragghianti. They then asked Thompson to play himself in the movie. The film's success led to other significant movie offers to Thompson. He now has appeared in numerous television productions and 18 major Hollywood films, including such notable successes as *In the Line of Fire, No Way Out, Die Hard II, Cape Fear,* and *The Hunt for Red October.*

During these years Thompson's acting, despite its success, took second place to his legal and political career. He established a distinguished record as a Nashville attorney and remained politically active within the Republican party. He served as Special Counsel to the U.S. Senate Intelligence Committee and its Foreign Relation Committee. In 1994 he easily won the Republican nomination to serve the remaining two years of Vice President Albert Gore, Jr.'s seat in the U.S. Senate and decisively defeated his Democratic opponent, Congressman Jim Cooper, in the general election. Two years later Thompson won a full term in the U.S. Senate in a landslide victory over Democratic opponent Houston Gordon.

Thompson has accepted a major role in the Senate's affairs and is best known for his 1997 investigation into and public hearings about campaign funding irregularities in the 1996 presidential election. He has supported a balanced budget and actively pushed for term limits. He has served as a member of the Senate committees of Judiciary, Government Affairs, Foreign Relations, and the Special Committee on Aging. In 1997 he was appointed chair of the Government Affairs committee. He also has chaired the Subcommittees on Youth Violence and on International Economic Policy, Export and Trade Promotion. A resident of Nashville, Thompson has developed an interesting career that balances success in his chosen profession (law) with state and national success in politics and entertainment. He is the father of three grown children: Tony, Betsy (Hollins), and Daniel and has five grandchildren.

Carroll Van West, Middle Tennessee State University

SUGGESTED READING: *Tennessee Blue Book, Bicentennial Edition* (Nashville, 1996)

SEE: BAKER, HOWARD H., JR.; LAWRENCE COUNTY; TELEVISION PERFORMERS AND ACTORS; TENNESSEE IN FILM

THORNBURGH, LUCILLE (1908–), union organizer and labor newspaper editor, was born in 1908 in Strawberry Plains, Tennessee, the daughter of Mr. and Mrs. Thomas Thornburgh. After graduating from Rhea County High School in Dayton she lived in Denver, then Los Angeles, and finally Detroit, before returning to Knoxville early in the Depression.

Thornburgh was employed at the Cherokee Spinning Company, where she worked 50-hour weeks for less than $10 per week. In 1933, after President Franklin D. Roosevelt signed the National Recovery Act, which included provisions that protected the right of workers to organize, Thornburgh and seven co-workers drew up a union charter. With the help of a local union organizer, they signed up all 603 employees at Cherokee Mills. In 1934 Cherokee workers joined textile workers across the South in a general strike known as the Uprising of 1934. Knoxville workers remained out for eight weeks, but the strike collapsed following the sudden death of owner Hal Mebane, an event Thornburgh says workers interpreted in religious terms. When the workers returned, Thornburgh was blacklisted, and other mill owners refused to hire her.

Thornburgh next worked in a variety of jobs, but returned to Knoxville to take a position with the American Federation of Labor in 1943. She became the first woman to serve on the board of the Tennessee Federation of Labor and in 1947 received a one-year scholarship to study labor and economic issues at Ruskin College at Oxford University, England. When she returned, Thornburgh became associate editor of the *East Tennessee Labor News*, a newspaper she edited from 1961 to 1973. In 1995 Thornburgh was featured in the PBS film, *Uprising of '34*, which documented the general textile strike.

Connie L. Lester, Tennessee Historical Society

SEE: LABOR; PUBLISHING

THOROUGHBRED HORSE BREEDING AND RACING. As early as 1790, a number of thoroughbred stallions were brought into the Watauga and Holston settlements. Between 1790 and 1795 *The Knoxville Register* and *Star Gazette* advertised at least nine stallions as standing in what is now East Tennessee. Tradition says that the first thoroughbred stallion brought into Middle Tennessee was Grey Medley. This stallion stood the 1800 season at the Gallatin Road farm of William Donelson, a brother of Rachel Jackson, and for several years thereafter at the farm of Dr. R.D. Barry in Sumner County. Part of this farm was later Walter O. Parmer's Edenwold Stud, one of the few thoroughbred horse nurseries still operating in Tennessee in 1910.

In Andrew Jackson's day, the Tennessee Thoroughbred had no superior in the United States. General Jackson bred and owned some of the finest. Two of his best racers were Thruxton, foaled in 1800, and Pacolet, in 1808. In the spring of 1808, a proposed match at the Clover Bottom race track between Jackson's Thruxton and Joseph Irwin's Plowboy indirectly led to the duel between Jackson and Irwin's son-in-law, Charles Dickinson. The latter, an excellent shot, provoked Jackson into the duel, in which Dickinson was killed, by making scurrilous remarks about Rachel Jackson, and by complaining about how a forfeit Irwin paid was handled by Jackson.

In 1839 William G. Harding wrote that the bloodstock was "all the go" in Middle Tennessee. In the last quarter of the nineteenth century, Harding's Belle Meade Stud would become one of the great thoroughbred horse-breeding nurseries in the country. Imported Bonnie Scotland, Enquirer, and Iroquois were among the distinguished sires at Belle Meade. Most of the Kentucky Derby winners of the twentieth century can trace their lineage to Bonnie Scotland through his famous get, Bramble.

Prior to 1840, jockey clubs and race tracks were located at Beans Station, Madisonville, and Red Bridge in East Tennessee; at Clarksville, Fayetteville, Franklin, Gallatin, Hartsville, McMinnville, Mount Pleasant, Murfreesboro, Nashville, Petersburg, Pulaski, Shelbyville, and Winchester in Middle Tennessee; and at Bolivar, Dresden, Jackson, La Grange, Memphis, Paris, and Somerville in West Tennessee.

The richest stake run in the world, up to the time, was the Peyton Stake run in 1843 in a Cumberland River bottom below Nashville. Balie Peyton of Sumner County was the promoter of the event, which paid $35,000 to the winner, Glumdalditch, by Glencoe. This was considerably more that the winners of England's Epsom Derby received.

During the 1850s New Orleans's Metairie Course became the nation's premier racing center, and Kentucky bluegrass country pulled ahead of Middle Tennessee as the most important breeding center. Spring and fall races in Memphis and Nashville still were important events, however. The Civil War devastated Tennessee's stud farms and race courses. Stud books, jockey club records, blood horse association journals, and horse portraiture disappeared. Race tracks were torn up and valuable thoroughbreds were used as cavalry horses.

From the 1870s to the 1890s Belle Meade Stud and two Sumner County studs—Kennesaw owned by James Franklin and Fairview owned by Charles Reed—turned out champion thoroughbreds. Luke Blackburn, bred at Kennesaw in 1877, was one such champion. Kennesaw also produced George Kinney, only slightly inferior to "The Great Luke." Both were sons of Belle Meade great imported sire, Bonnie Scotland, as was Bramble, foaled at Belle Meade in 1875. Bred at Fairview were The Baird in 1883, Yorkville Belle in 1889, and a great broodmare, Thora, dam of Yorkville Belle. Iroquois and St. Blaise, English Derby winners of 1881 and 1883 respectively, stood at Belle Meade and Fairview during the 1890s.

A state anti-betting law, passed by the legislature in 1906, resulted in that year being the last that horse races were held in Tennessee. The incentive to breed thoroughbreds diminished, and the industry has since languished. Today Tennessee has a small nucleus of thoroughbred horse breeders. The Blood Stallion Register of 1997 lists 17 Tennessee thoroughbreds available for breeding. Favorable referendums in Shelby and Trousdale counties now allow for horse-racing and pari-mutuel betting in those locations, although no tracks have been built. It may be that Tennessee is too close to Kentucky for the industry to thrive.

Ridley Wills II, Franklin

Suggested Reading: Ridley Wills II, "The Eclipse of the Thoroughbred Horse Industry in Tennessee," *Tennessee Historical Quarterly* 46(1987): 157–171

SEE: BELLE MEADE PLANTATION; HARDING, WILLIAM G.; HORSERACING TRACKS, EARLY

THRUSTON, GATES P., COLLECTION OF VANDERBILT UNIVERSITY dates to 1907, when Gates P. Thruston (1835–1912) donated his collection of prehistoric Native American artifacts to Vanderbilt University. Containing about 1,000 objects, the collection remains a peerless assemblage of prehistoric Native American art from the Nashville area.

The majority of Thruston's collection came from a large prehistoric Native American town (A.D. 1050–1450) on the farm of Dr. Oscar Noel in Nashville. By 1890 his collection had achieved national prominence, prompting the Tennessee Historical Society to request an illustrated pamphlet. To our benefit, Thruston instead produced an illustrated book of some 380 pages. In order to place the work within easy reach of students and others, he apparently paid a large subvention to keep the price below cost.

After publication, Thruston's collection rapidly achieved international prominence. He received a bronze medal for his exhibition at the 1893 Columbian Historical Exposition in Madrid. During the 1897 Tennessee Centennial Exposition, he received a gold medal for the "finest individual exhibition in any department," and another gold medal at the later Louisiana Purchase Exposition in St. Louis.

In 1907 Thruston sought a suitable repository for his collections. He offered them to the State of Tennessee, if it would provide a suitable exhibit building. The legislature declined to provide exhibit space, prompting Thruston to donate the collection to Vanderbilt. In an ironic twist that would almost certainly have pleased Thruston, Vanderbilt and the Tennessee State Museum entered into an agreement incorporating the collection into the Museum's permanent exhibits on Tennessee's native peoples in 1986.

Kevin E. Smith, Middle Tennessee State University

Suggested Reading: Stephen D. Cox, ed., *Art and Artisans of Prehistoric Middle Tennessee: The Gates P. Thruston Collection of Vanderbilt University held in Trust by the Tennessee State Museum* (1985)

SEE: TENNESSEE STATE MUSEUM; VANDERBILT UNIVERSITY

TILLINGHAST, RICHARD (1940–), poet, was born in Memphis to Raymond Charles Tillinghast, a mechanical engineer from Massachusetts, and Martha Williford, daughter of a West Tennessee farmer and lawyer turned politician. This dual background of New England and agrarian South has given Tillinghast's poetry a strong sense of political history. He attended the University of the South, serving as an editorial assistant to Andrew Nelson Lytle at the *Sewanee Review*. He then took advanced degrees at Harvard, studying writing with Robert Lowell, the Boston poet and early disciple of the Nashville Fugitives. Lowell would become the greatest influence in his poetry, not only for his plainspoken style but also for his preoccupation with history and its subtle and often dangerous effects on the self. Tillinghast's critical memoir *Damaged Grandeur: Robert Lowell's Life and Work* (1995) is his homage. Tillinghast spent the early 1970s teaching English at the University of California at Berkeley and San Quentin Prison and since 1983 has been on the faculty of the University of Michigan's Master of Fine Arts program.

A sense of restlessness and dissatisfaction pervades much of his work, especially in his third collection, *Our Flag Was Still There* (1984). In the long poem "Sewanee in Ruins," he reacts against southern history and its "fatal romanticism / . . . / when everything burned / but the brick chimneys / and a way of talking." The myth of southern gentility provides the backdrop for the book's meditation on the Vietnam War and the nation's divided loyalties.

Like Lowell, Tillinghast sees the personal as the best access to history. His most recent book *The Stonecutter's Hand* (1995) chronicles his travels in Ireland and Eastern Europe and includes views not merely his own. In "Pasha's Daughter, 1914" a woman in Istanbul discovers that "Paradise is a bedraggled trapezoid / Of outback, its fountain a brew of leaves." When her servant enters with "six centuries / Of marches and conquests reduced to the dirt / On his cuff," she orders opium and stands at the window "to watch our empire melt in the rain." In "A Quiet Pint in Kinarva," the speaker sees Irish history contained in a "wide-eyed angel," "baptised by rain, / Outlasting Viking longboat, Norman strongbow, / Face battered by a rifle butt." Nearly all of the poems in this book are journeys of history and consciousness; travel itself, he has written, is a kind of poem.

Richard Tillinghast's poems, book reviews, and essays on a range of subjects appear regularly in the nation's leading magazines and newspapers. The recipient of numerous awards and fellowships, he is the author of two other collections of poems, *Sleep Watch* (1969) and *The Knife and Other Poems* (1980). He lives in Ann Arbor, Michigan, with his wife and four children.

Preston Merchant, New York, New York

SEE: LITERATURE; LYTLE, ANDREW NELSON; THE SEWANEE REVIEW

TIMBER INDUSTRY. Although Tennessee's earliest settlers appreciated the vast timber resources they discovered, the greatest timber extraction in the state's history occurred between 1880 and 1920. Rapid deforestation by industrial loggers during this period caused long-term environmental changes and notable revision of state and federal policies.

E. M. Copeland with sawed walnut boards for gunstocks, Alpine, 1942.

Early European settlers extolled the wonders of the rot-resistant American chestnut trees, which made up as much as 25 percent of the forest. They proceeded to build durable homes and fences from them and to clear the woods for agriculture. By the early nineteenth century, a rudimentary iron industry also found hardwood (deciduous trees) valuable to fire small blast furnaces. A typical, eight-foot square forge required a layer of charcoal four feet thick to melt 400 pounds of ore in two hours. Not surprisingly, the woods around the forges were typically cut down, and slag from such operations can still be found. Demand for wood to produce charcoal encouraged an 1809 state law that permitted ironmakers to acquire large tracts of land just for harvesting wood. In the 1830s, for example, the Tellico Plains Iron Works began harvesting trees on the Tellico River, which were used to manufacture pig iron and, eventually, cannon balls and ammunition for Confederate troops.

Large-scale timber and mining would not be profitable, however, until the railroad moved to Tennessee. Despite repeated petitions, by the 1850s the state only had 1,200 miles of track. This relatively slow entrance into the new transportation age probably protected Tennessee forests longer than the neighboring states of Kentucky and Virginia. Soldiers passing thorugh the state during the Civil War frequently commented on the verdant natural resources, particularly in the eastern part of the state; some of these men later became investors and entrepreneurs in the turn-of-the-century timber boom. As railroads began carving up the state after the war, struggling farmers picked up seasonal income by cutting and selling medium-sized species, such as locust, to the companies for railroad ties. Others sold bark from their woodlots to the nascent tanning industry.

Beginning in the 1870s, Nashville and Memphis promoters welcomed Northeast lumbermen into the state. In 1881 *Southern Lumberman*, which remains the major trade association publication for southern hardwood companies, began publication in Nashville. Nashville companies got much of their hardwood from small entrepreneurs along the Cumberland River. Enterprising men cut trees during the winter and when spring rains swelled the streams that fed the Cumberland, they floated out rafts of logs and sold them to the Nashville mills. The principal species were oak and poplar, but a few mills such as Prewitt-Spurr specialized in cedar buckets and churns. In 1910, 32 hardwood mills operated in Memphis. Furniture makers from all over the nation bought wood in Memphis, which billed itself as the Hardwood Capital of the World.

In East Tennessee, outside capitalists, such as the Scottish Carolina Timber and Land Company, from Glasgow, Scotland, also sought specialty wood, especially cherry and walnut. The company built a mill and log boom at Newport during the 1890s, but could not keep the operation solvent for long because of transportation problems. At the same time, a Michigan investor, W.E. Heyser, built a mill in Chattanooga and towed logs down the Little Tennessee to his operations. Because of the inaccessibility of the mountains, though, federal foresters Horace B. Ayres and William W. Ashe reported that the forests in the eastern part of the state remained largely intact in 1901.

The invention of steam-powered skidders and band sawmills soon improved profitability in remote locations. In Monroe County, a group of Pennsylvania businessmen operated the Tellico River Lumber Company. New York businessmen operated the Tennessee Timber Coal and Iron Company in Cumberland County. Two Cincinnati investment groups ran the Grand View Coal and Timber Company near Chattanooga and the Conasauga Lumber Company in Polk County. Wilson B. Townsend, a Pennsylvania lumberman, became interested in the Little River area after the Schlosser Leather Company financed a railroad into nearby Walland. Townsend already controlled major logging operations in Pennsylvania and coal, clay, tile, and railroad holdings in East Kentucky when he moved into Tuckaleechee Cove in 1901. He

built a railroad, mill, and company town, which residents named Townsend in his honor. As a well-financed businessman, he could afford the latest technology and so switched his operations from circular saws to band saws, which allowed cutting very thick logs with less waste. Townsend invested in steam-powered skidders that could transport oak and chestnut trees as small as ten inches as far as 5,000 feet. By 1910 his Townsend operations produced 120,000 board feet per day.

Timber barons also relied on cheap, non-union labor in Tennessee. Poor farmers moved to the temporary lumber camps and lived with their families in boxcars or "setoff" houses, eight by ten feet wide, that could be moved from site to site. In 1912 Tennessee lumber workers put in a 60-hour week for 14 cents an hour. Wages did not rise even when demand for southern hardwoods accelerated. When war broke out in Europe in 1914, the demands on southern forests, especially walnut for gun stocks, accelerated and did not abate with the return of peace.

Turn-of-the-century lumbermen took so many trees so quickly that Gifford Pinchot, head of the U.S. Forest Service, predicted that all the timber in the United States would be gone in 20 years. Such dire warnings helped lead the industry toward the National Forest; indeed, many lumbermen, including Townsend, were convinced that the Forest Service would save them money in taxes and management. The depletion of forest lands resulted in a dramatic loss of wildlife as habitat was destroyed. To protect game and improve tourism, Tennessee initiated its first game laws and, under Governor Austin Peay, established a Department of Forestry. Careless management by timber companies allowed fire to spread in the clearcut mountainsides, and erosion further damaged the land. This rapid deforestation and soil loss created high and low runoff patterns, and major flooding followed. Partially in response to swollen riverways and denuded land, the federal government in the 1930s initiated such major reforms as the Tennessee Valley Authority and the projects of the Civilian Conservation Corps as well as the designation of the Cherokee National Forest and the Great Smoky Mountains National Park.

Margaret Lynn Brown, Brevard College

SUGGESTED READING: James L. Bailey, comp., *Tennessee Timber Trees* (1962)

SEE: BLOUNT COUNTY; CHEROKEE NATIONAL FOREST; CIVILIAN CONSERVATION CORPS; CLAY COUNTY; CONSERVATION; CUMBERLAND RIVER; GREAT SMOKY MOUNTAINS NATIONAL PARK; MISSISSIPPI RIVER SYSTEM; PICKETT STATE RUSTIC PARK; RILEY, BOB; TENNESSEE RIVER SYSTEM; TENNESSEE STATE FORESTS

TIMBERLAKE, HENRY (1730–1765), colonial journalist and cartographer, was born in Virginia in 1730 and died in England on September 30, 1765. He joined Virginia military forces in 1756 and served in several campaigns during the French and Indian War. In 1761 he was assigned to troops commanded by Colonel William Byrd III and subsequently placed under the command of Colonel Adam Stephen. Stephen's mission was to retaliate against the Cherokees for their siege of Fort Loudoun and for their massacre of its garrison. In November 1761 the Cherokees concluded a truce before Stephen could launch his attack. At the peace negotiations one of the Cherokee chiefs requested that an officer journey to the Cherokee villages on the Little Tennessee River to explain the treaty and provide assurances that the colonists intended to honor it. Lieutenant Henry Timberlake volunteered to go.

After a 23-day journey down the Holston River, Timberlake arrived at the Overhill villages in early December. He was a guest of Chief Ostenaco at Tomotly, and he presented the provisions of the peace treaty to Cherokee leaders gathered in the Chota council house. He also visited Citico and Chilhowee, where he was welcomed with considerable celebration and respect. Timberlake left the Overhill country in early March 1762, reaching Williamsburg in April. In May he escorted three distinguished Cherokee leaders, including Ostenaco, to London, where they stayed until August. Timberlake remained in England until returning to Virginia in March 1763. In the summer of 1764, five Cherokees visited him, seeking an audience with the governor of Virginia and requesting passage to London. The governor denied their request, but Timberlake agreed to help them, and he and three of the Indians reached London in the fall of 1764. After the Indians departed in March 1765, Timberlake remained and died in September.

Timberlake's primary legacy is the journal he kept while living with the Cherokee. Published in 1765, the volume was probably published posthumously. His vivid descriptions and observations contained a thorough and detailed account of eighteenth century Cherokee life and became a basis for all subsequent anthropological and historical studies of eighteenth century Cherokees. Timberlake's map, entitled "A Draught of the Cherokee Country," accompanied the journal. On it he located all the Cherokee villages on the lower Little Tennessee River and provided important demographic information about village sizes, populations, and leaders. Modern studies have generally confirmed that Timberlake's map was remarkably accurate. The journal, simply entitled "Memoirs," and his map of the Overhill Cherokee country have been reprinted several times.

Gerald F. Schroedl, University of Tennessee, Knoxville
SUGGESTED READING: Samuel C. Williams, ed., *Lieutenant Henry Timberlake's Memoirs 1756–1765* (1927)
SEE: CHOTA; FORT LOUDOUN; OVERHILL CHEROKEES

TIMS FORD STATE RUSTIC PARK is a 431-acre park adjacent to a 10,700-acre lake, the Tims Ford Reservoir, in Franklin County. In 1970 the Tennessee Valley Authority finished the Tims Ford Dam to provide recreational opportunities and control repeated flooding of the Elk River. In September 1978 Tims Ford State Park was opened. It features a visitor center, 20 cabins, 50 campsites, a marina, hiking trails, a large lakeside picnic area, and various recreational facilities, including one of the largest swimming pools in the state park system.

Carroll Van West, Middle Tennessee State University
SEE: FRANKLIN COUNTY; TENNESSEE VALLEY AUTHORITY

TIPTON COUNTY. The area forming West Tennessee was part of the Chickasaw Nation until 1818, when the territory was opened for settlement under the terms of the Jackson Purchase. An 1819 act by the General Assembly divided the new territory into five districts. The first county in the Western District was Shelby, which was organized at the village of Chickasaw Bluff in 1819. Tipton County was formed from Shelby County in 1823 and named for Captain Jacob Tipton who was killed leading his men in a battle near Fort Wayne in 1791. Tipton's son, Armistead Blevins, who supervised the organization of Shelby County, was present when Tipton County was formed. Covington, situated near the center of the county, was established as the county seat in 1826. Its name honored Leonard Wales Covington, a Maryland native who was killed in the battle of Chrysler's Field in 1813.

In 1833 the *Tennessee Gazetteer* described Covington as a post town and seat of justice, 38 miles from Memphis. Covington was originally divided into 106 lots on seven streets. Most construction was of frame and log, with the exception of a brick jail. In addition to the courthouse and jail, Covington had seven stores, two taverns, a surveyor's office, three or four physicians' offices, a similar number of lawyers' offices, and 30 or 40 houses. Located on a tributary of the Hatchie River, Covington remained isolated from the steamboat trade of the nineteenth century and did not achieve commercial significance until the arrival of the Newport News and Mississippi Valley Railroad in 1873. Between 1873 and 1880, over 6,000 new residents arrived in Covington to take advantage of the commercial and industrial opportunities created by the arrival of the railroad. Economic expansion rose even faster after the takeover of the railroad by the Illinois Central in the 1890s. The town received its first telephone service and electric street lights in 1894. By 1920 Covington had a population of over 3,400 and included a weekly newspaper; three banks; an electric light plant; a water works; and a cotton mill, cottonseed oil mill, and other manufacturing enterprises. Today, downtown historic districts contain an array of architecturally significant commercial and residential buildings.

Mason, which is 13 miles south of Covington, was founded in 1858 and named for James Mason. In 1855 Mason became the first town in Tipton County to acquire rail services when the Memphis and Ohio Railroad established "Sharon Depot," later known as "Mason Depot." By 1859 the town contained four businesses, and the following year Mason hosted a campaign speech by Stephen Douglas. The town also received a visit from Jefferson Davis, President of the Confederate States, who attended services at the Trinity Episcopal Church. Mason was also the site where a regiment of West Tennessee African-American soldiers were mustered into the Union Army. By 1887 Mason was the second largest town in the county and contained 400 inhabitants.

Randolph was founded in 1823 and named for John Randolph of Virginia. Randolph undoubtedly occupied the best potential site available for waterborne commerce and provided an excellent harbor for steam and flatboats at all stages of the river. Until 1840, Randolph shipped more cotton than Memphis, as much as 35,000 to 40,000 bales annually, and became the great steamboat depot of West Tennessee. By 1834 it had its first newspaper and a population of 1,000. It had four hotels, several schools, nearly 50 businesses, and a dozen saloons.

Many factors led to the demise of Randolph. Five years after its founding, the land title was discovered to be faulty. Mrs. Ann Grambelling of New York filed suit to claim the whole town on the grounds that she had acquired a military land grant warrant that included the tract. Her case stood up in court and is of unusual interest because the warrant belonged to an African-American soldier who served in the Revolutionary War. Randolph's citizens negotiated a compromise settlement and bought their town for $8,000. More important problems that affected the town's future were Randolph's failure to secure a railroad; financial depression; an unfavorable mail route; the continuation of the county seat at Covington despite an 1852 effort to have it moved to Randolph; and the failure to secure a proposed canal connecting the Tennessee and Hatchie rivers. The final blows came in 1862 and 1865 when federal troops twice burned the town.

Today the population of Tipton County stands at approximately 40,000. The county supports a 100-bed hospital and city and county school systems. The Covington Airport has 5,000 feet of runway. Although agriculture continues to account for a significant portion of the Tipton County economy, many county residents work at one of several industrial enterprises. World Color, which prints catalogs and magazines, employs 900 workers; Charms Company has 340 employees engaged in the production of hard candy; the 250 employees of Delfield Company make food service equipment; and Mueller Fittings, LP employs 240 workers in the production of copper fittings. In addition to these large employers, several smaller manufacturers produce everything from wiring harness to business forms.

Prepared from material supplied by Angela Wallace Finley, Covington-Tipton County Tourism Bureau

SUGGESTED READING: Gaylon N. Beasley, *True Tales of Tipton* (1981)

SEE: BOYD, JOHN W.; CALHOUN, FRANCES B.; FORT WRIGHT; JACKSON PURCHASE; MISSISSIPPI RIVER SYSTEM; NAIFEH, JAMES O.; RAILROADS; THEATER

TIPTON, ISABEL HANSON (1909–1980), physicist, was born in Monroe, Georgia, June 17, 1909. She earned a Bachelor of Science degree from the University of Georgia in 1929 and graduate degrees with majors in physics and minors in chemistry from the University of Georgia (M.S., 1930) and Duke University (Ph.D., 1934). She became one of the few women in the United States qualified to teach physics. Tipton was head of the Science Department at Cox College in Georgia and taught at Ohio State University and the University of Alabama before joining the University of Tennessee Department of Physics in 1948. Tipton was widely acclaimed for her research in Raman Spectroscopy and trace metal content in human tissue, which was used to determine safe levels of radioactivity in the body. Her research garnered more than $500,000 in federal grant funding, and from it she published over 35 professional papers. She was a consultant to the Health Physics Division of the Oak Ridge National Laboratory, a position she held from 1950 until her retirement in 1972.

Tipton was a member of the Tennessee Academy of Science, serving as its secretary from 1953 to 1955 and its president in 1956–1957. She was also vice president and president (1960) of the Southeastern Section of the Society for Applied Spectroscopy. Tipton retired from UT in 1972 and moved to Long Beach, North Carolina, to devote more time to her avocation, ornithology. She died there in 1980.

Margaret Ellen Crawford, University of Tennessee, Knoxville

SEE: OAK RIDGE NATIONAL LABORATORY; TENNESSEE ACADEMY OF SCIENCE; UNIVERSITY OF TENNESSEE

TIPTON, JOHN (1730–1813), prominent backcountry era settler, political leader, and foe of the Franklin statehood movement, was born in Baltimore County, Maryland, in 1730. He served in Lord Dunmore's War, was a recruiting officer for the Continental Army during the Revolutionary War, and served as colonel of the Washington County militia. A member of the Virginia House of Burgesses in 1774, he served in the

Virginia Constitutional Convention of 1776, the North Carolina Convention to ratify the Federal Constitution in 1788, and the Tennessee Constitutional Convention of 1796. Prior to statehood, Tipton held office in the Virginia House of Delegates in 1776–1777 and 1778–1781, as well as the Franklin Conventions of 1784 and 1785, the North Carolina Senate in 1786 and 1788, and the House of the Southwest Territory in the 1790s.

After moving to present-day Tennessee in 1782, Tipton's most significant role in Tennessee history came during the State of Franklin controversy. Although at first a supporter, desirous of protecting his own land claims and those of his speculator friends, Tipton split the movement by feuding with John Sevier, the governor of the proposed State of Franklin. In 1785, when North Carolina officials demanded that frontier residents repudiate the new state, Tipton assured the governor of his loyalty. Sevier did not, demanding instead that residents express their allegiance to Franklin. Tipton and Sevier also disagreed about the proposed constitution for the new state. Finally in 1786, the two came to blows over which laws should govern the Washington County Militia, of which John Tipton was colonel.

Over the next two years, North Carolina officials largely diffused the statehood movement; yet Tipton and Sevier remained bitter enemies. In early 1788 a North Carolina sheriff, Jonathan Pugh, seized several Sevier slaves and livestock to satisfy a court judgment Tipton had instigated. Pugh took the slaves and livestock to Tipton's farm. Sevier responded with force. About 135 men accompanied Sevier to Tipton's property in present-day Washington County (the Tipton-Haynes historic site) and attempted to reclaim the slaves. In the skirmishes that ensued, Sheriff Pugh along with John Webb were killed. Two of Sevier's sons were captured but later released.

On July 29, 1788, North Carolina Governor Samuel Johnstown ordered Sevier's arrest for treason due to his wanton and unauthorized attack on several Cherokee villages. Nothing happened immediately, but on October 10, acting for a North Carolina judge, John Tipton arrested Sevier and took him to Morganton, North Carolina, for trial. That trial, however, never took place. A group of friends and Sevier's sons retrieved John Sevier from his North Carolina imprisonment and took him home. The State of Franklin movement was over, but the Tipton-Sevier feud continued into the early statehood era.

Tipton's last political office was as Tennessee State Senator from 1796 to 1799. He died at his home in 1813.

Carroll Van West, Middle Tennessee State University

SEE: FRANKLIN, STATE OF; SEVIER, JOHN; SOUTHWEST TERRITORY; TIPTON-HAYNES HISTORIC SITE

TIPTON-HAYNES HISTORIC SITE. The Tipton-Haynes Historic Site in Johnson City represents several eras of early Tennessee history. Woodland Period Indians and Cherokees first frequented the area, hunting the buffalo that traveled to its natural spring. In later years, that buffalo trail became a stage road from Jonesborough to Morganton, North Carolina. The site's cave and spring attracted James Needham and Gabriel Arthur, the first white men to explore the area, as well as the longhunter Daniel Boone. The Tipton-Haynes site was purchased to preserve the Tipton-Haynes House, a residence occupied by three prominent Tennessean statesmen: John Tipton (1730–1813); John Tipton, Jr. (1769–1831); and Landon Carter Haynes (1816–1875).

The elder John Tipton, a native of Maryland, purchased the site in 1784 and constructed a substantial log house. During the controversy over the State of Franklin, Tipton supported North Carolina and became an opponent of Franklin and its governor, John Sevier. In 1788 North Carolina authorities seized some of Sevier's slaves and took them to Tipton's house. When Sevier attempted to recover his slaves, a skirmish broke out at Tipton's house (February 27–29, 1788) between Sevier's pro-Franklin force and Tipton and the North Carolina supporters. The North Carolinians won this "Battle of the Lost State of Franklin," which marked the demise of Franklin. Tipton served in the territorial assembly and as a delegate to the first constitutional convention of the State of Tennessee, created from the territory in 1796. He also served in the first and second Tennessee General Assembly.

After the death of John Tipton, Sr., in 1813, his house and land became the property of his son, John Tipton, Jr., a resident of Sullivan County. The younger John served in the State House from 1803 to 1815 and the State Senate from 1817 to 1819.

In 1837 David Haynes purchased the Tipton property from the heirs of John Tipton, Jr. The property was then presented as a wedding gift to David's son, Landon Carter Haynes, who added a Greek Revival portico to the house and constructed a Greek Revival temple-style law office near the residence. A farmer, attorney, newspaper editor, and briefly a Methodist minister, Landon served three terms in the Tennessee General Assembly (1845–1851). During the Civil War, he served as a Confederate Senator from Tennessee, but his support of the Confederacy necessitated his removal to West Tennessee after the war. He died in Memphis on February 17, 1875.

John White of Washington County bought the Tipton-Haynes property at a chancery sale in 1871 and conveyed it to Sarah S. Simerly. After her death the property was inherited by her sons Samuel W. and Lawson G. Simerly, great-grand nephews of Landon Carter Haynes. In 1944 they conveyed a tract of 17 acres and an additional tract containing the Tipton-Simerly cemetery to the state. An additional one-half acre was purchased in 1945 to complete the acquisition of what is now known as Tipton-Haynes Historic Site. The state-owned site is maintained by the non-profit Tipton-Haynes Historical Association and was opened to the public in the early 1970s.

Kenneth Fields, Johnson City

SUGGESTED READINGS: Dennis T. Lawson, "The Tipton-Haynes Place: I, A Landmark of East Tennessee," *Tennessee Historical Quarterly* 29(1970): 105–124; John J. Baratte, "The Tipton-Haynes Place: II. The Later Years," *Tennessee Historical Quarterly* 29(1970): 125–129

SEE: BOONE, DANIEL; FRANKLIN, STATE OF; SOUTHWEST TERRITORY; TIPTON, JOHN; WASHINGTON COUNTY

TOBACCO. When the early settlers came to Tennessee and began to till the soil, the production of tobacco was one of the first crops. Since those early days, dollars received for tobacco crops have paid for farms and homes, provided money for Christmas, sent children to college, and added millions of dollars each year to the tax coffers of the state.

Tobacco is grown in 66 of the state's 95 counties. Burley tobacco is grown in all of these 66 counties, with eight counties producing dark fired tobacco. In 1996, 88 million pounds of burley and 20.7 million pounds of dark fired were produced. In addition, a million pounds of dark air cured is grown in the six counties of Robertson (630,000 pounds); Sumner (263,000 pounds); Weakley (35,500 pounds); Montgomery (34,000 pounds); Macon (22,600 pounds); and Henry (14,000 pounds).

Through the years, tobacco has ranked among the top five leading cash crops in the state and has ranked number one on several occasions. For the past 30 years, soybeans and tobacco have competed for the number one cash crop. Cotton production has made a comeback in recent years and now competes with the other two for first place. In 1996 tobacco ranked third behind cotton and soybeans, with cash receipts totaling $205.4 million.

Until 1924, burley tobacco was primarily grown only in the eastern part of the state, where smaller hillside farms made tobacco production a natural choice. Demand and the need for diversification brought tobacco production to the rolling hills of Middle Tennessee. Greene County, the location of the state extension tobacco experiment farm, leads the state in burley production, producing 8.6 million

Tobacco auction at Hartsville, 1942.

pounds in 1996. The next four top producers are Macon County with 6.1 million pounds, Claiborne County with 5 million pounds, Washington County with 4.9 million pounds, and Sumner County with 4.7 million pounds. Burley tobacco is used primarily in cigarettes for its flavor and its combustible quality. After it is harvested in the fall, burley is hung up and cured simply by the air flowing through it.

Dark fired tobacco goes into smokeless tobaccos, such as chewing tobacco and snuff. When it is harvested, it must be cured with heat inside the barn. The tobacco is hung and the floor of the barn is spread with hardwood sawdust and slabs of oak or hickory, and then the tobacco is "fired." This is a tedious process since too much heat can destroy the barn, and too little heat will cause the tobacco to mold. The bulk of the dark fired production is in Middle and Northwest Tennessee. Robertson County is the top producer with 8.7 million pounds in 1996. The other four leading counties in dark fired production were Montgomery County with 4.8 million pounds, Cheatham County with 1.8 million pounds, Dickson County with 1.7 million pounds, and Henry County with 1.3 million pounds.

Both types of tobacco require a tremendous amount of hand labor. For many years tobacco was tied in "hands" to be marketed, but for the past 20 years, farmers have been baling their tobacco. This makes it much easier to store and haul the tobacco to market. Because of the shortage of domestic labor, producers have been forced to look elsewhere for help, and migrant workers are now the norm on many tobacco farms, helping to set and harvest the tobacco crop.

In addition to providing an income for over 140,000 farmers in Tennessee, tobacco also has a great impact on the state's tax revenues. Tennessee first imposed tobacco taxes in 1925 as a "temporary" measure to help fund public schools. In the fiscal year 1995 the tobacco tax brought in a total revenue of $84.8 million, with $84 million of that used to fund education in the state.

The future of tobacco in Tennessee remains uncertain. Although farmers and researchers are looking for alternate crops, there are none presently that can approach the dollars per acre that tobacco produces. Researchers are busy studying new ways to use tobacco. They are finding that the tobacco leaf has vitamins A and E, beta carotene, proteins, and amino acids. Tobacco is also one of the easiest plants to utilize for gene manipulation. Researchers are looking at potential cancer-fighting compounds, along with possible vaccines and other substances from the tobacco plant that can be used in food and drugs.
Murray Miles, Culleoka
SUGGESTED READING: Donald L. Winters, *Tennessee Farming, Tennessee Farmers: Antebellum Agriculture in the Upper South* (1994)

SEE: AGRICULTURE; BLACK PATCH WAR; DARK TOBACCO DISTRICT PLANTERS' PROTECTIVE ASSOCIATION; GLENRAVEN PLANTATION; GREENE COUNTY; MONTGOMERY COUNTY; ROBERTSON COUNTY; WASHINGTON, JOSEPH; WESSYNGTON PLANTATION

TODD, MARY "MOLLY" HART (1904–1998). Although she rarely held elective office, Molly Todd played an important role in fashioning public policy in Nashville and Tennessee in the second half of the twentieth century. She mobilized support for reform in areas as diverse as birth control, racial integration, and metropolitan government. Her most important base of support came from the League of Women Voters. Her strategy as a reformer centered on the construction of alliances between like-minded organizations, followed by demonstrations of voting strength on behalf of targeted reforms.

Todd was born in Brooklyn, New York, in 1904 and graduated from Vassar College in 1925. Her first employment as a social worker involved birth control clinics in New Jersey and Kentucky. She moved to Nashville with her second husband, James Todd, in 1939 and took on a number of volunteer posts, including the presidency of the Tennessee Maternal Health Association and chair of the steering committee that created the Nashville Mental Health (DeDe Wallace) Center. In 1948 she helped reconstitute the Nashville League of Women Voters. As president, Todd engaged the League in vigorous campaigns to develop government support for the overcrowded county schools, library services, a family service agency, and child welfare. The League published the city's first brochure on voter education, worked to abolish the poll tax, and engaged in efforts to consolidate city and county government services.

Todd was a charter member of the Tennessee Council on Human Relations, which was organized to confront the persistence of racial segregation following the *Brown* decision. She participated in the lunch counter sit-ins, aided by her husband's quiet cooperation as an executive of Harvey's department store, a target of the protest.

Todd joined and usually held positions of leadership in an impressive number of organizations, including the PTA, the Women's Civic Forum, Church Women United of Tennessee, the Tennessee Environmental Council, the United Nations Association, and the Democratic Party. In every group she sought an agenda dedicated to social and political advancement. Todd did not see herself primarily as a feminist, but as an activist for the public good.

Defeat at the polls did not deter Todd's support of issues or candidates she considered progressive. In 1956 she became the woman's chair of Tennessee Volunteers for Stevenson-Kefauver despite the lack of enthusiasm for these candidates by the state's traditional Democratic leadership. She ran unsuccessfully for the state legislature in 1954 and again in 1960, and for Metro Council in 1965. Todd continued to advocate political goals ranging from adequate school funding to a state income tax, and from enforcement of strip mine and water control laws to repeal of the death penalty.

Anita S. Goodstein, University of the South

SEE: LEAGUE OF WOMEN VOTERS; SIT-INS, NASHVILLE; TENNESSEE ENVIRONMENTAL COUNCIL

TOQUA was an eighteenth century Overhill Cherokee village located on the Little Tennessee River in present day Monroe County. Toqua means "place of a mythic great fish." Toqua (site 40MR6) also designates a late Mississippian Dallas culture (ca. A.D. 1200–1600) village and two mounds at the same location. Henry Timberlake's 1762 map showed 32 domestic structures and a council house at the site. He also indicated that 82 warriors resided there, suggesting a total population of 200 to 300 people. American Revolutionary War forces destroyed the town in 1776 and 1780, and again in 1788 as hostilities continued after the war. Nevertheless in 1797, Duke Louis Phillipe of France observed ten houses at Toqua and wrote one of the most detailed descriptions ever made of a Cherokee council house. His brother's drawing of Toqua is the only known contemporary image of an eighteenth century Cherokee town. In 1818 only 35 Cherokees lived in the town's 13 dwellings.

In the 1970s, extensive archaeological excavations were conducted at Toqua prior to its inundation by the Tellico Dam Reservoir. The largest mound contained 16 building stages, 12 of which had multiple structures built on their summits. The second mound, built in three stages, was used primarily for mortuary purposes. Village excavations revealed a plaza, three palisades, 57 domestic structures, and numerous refuse-filled pits and burials. Excavations of the eighteenth century Cherokee occupation recorded two townhouses, ten dwellings, and a smaller number of refuse-filled pits and burials. The Toqua research contributed greatly to the description and interpretation of Mississippian period sociopolitical organization and to the understanding of Cherokee culture and culture change.

Gerald F. Schroedl, University of Tennessee, Knoxville

SUGGESTED READING: Gerald F. Schroedl, "Louis-Phillipe's Journal and Archaeological Investigations at the Overhill Cherokee Town of Toqua," *Journal of Cherokee Studies*, 3(1978): 206–220

TRAIL OF TEARS, OR *NUNNA-DA-UL-TSUN-YI* in the Cherokee language (The place were they cried), next to the practice of black slavery, is arguably the most tragic story in Tennessee history. Covering the period from May 1838 to March 1839, the Trail of Tears was the federal government's final, forceful effort to remove the Cherokees from the land on which they lived in upper Georgia and southeastern Tennessee.

After the American Revolution, white settlers had pressed westward with little regard for the Native Americans until, by 1819, the new Americans claimed over 90 percent of the land east of the Mississippi River. Whites perceived the Cherokees as the most prominent obstacle blocking their claims in parts of Tennessee, Georgia, North Carolina, and Alabama. The Cherokees had developed an agricultural economy (based in part on black slave labor) and had established a constitutional republic patterned after the United States. The capital, New Echota in northern Georgia, promised to be a center of cultural activity with increasing educational opportunities for the Cherokees.

In 1828 Andrew Jackson, whose pioneer experiences produced deep resentment against all Native Americans, was elected President of the United States. In his inaugural address, Jackson called for the relocation of all eastern Indians beyond the Mississippi River. A popular idea among white settlers, this presidential wish became federal law with the passage of the Indian Removal Act in 1830.

Compounding the problems of the Cherokees was the discovery of gold in Dahlonega, Georgia. Georgia officials immediately began devising a system of lotteries to distribute the Cherokee land and its supposed riches to white settlers. Suddenly denied the right to conduct tribal business under Georgia law, the Cherokees moved their capital to Red Clay, just across the Tennessee border. Not to be outdone, however, the Georgia governor allowed a minority group, led by Major Ridge, to gather at New Echota in December 1835 to sign a treaty, ceding all eastern Cherokee holdings to the United States for $5 million and land west of the Mississippi River. Although the lawful Red Clay representatives protested the treaty through every legal channel, the U.S. Senate ratified the Treaty of New Echota on May 23, 1836, by a single vote.

Accepting what they considered to be inevitable, Major Ridge and some other pragmatic Cherokees salvaged what they could and proceeded at their discretion to their new homeland. But the majority, led by John Ross, refused to believe the federal government would resort to force to remove them from their ancestral land.

They were wrong. After two years of pleas and threats from various United States agencies, the round-up of the Cherokees began in May 1838 with 7,000 soldiers under the command of General Winfield Scott. The Cherokees were taken—young and old, poor and rich, along with their black slaves—with whatever possessions they could quickly gather

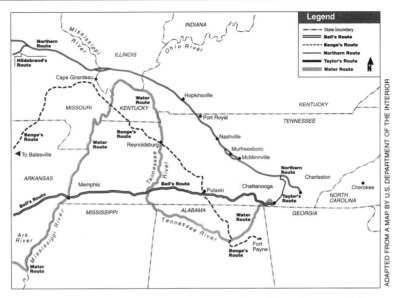

Trail of Tears passages through Tennessee. The routes terminated in Indian Territory, now Oklahoma.

ADAPTED FROM A MAP BY U.S. DEPARTMENT OF THE INTERIOR

before whites rushed in to claim their lottery winnings or to plunder what the unfortunate prisoners had been unable to take. The captives were taken to collection camps where most of them languished all summer while Indian representatives, notably John Ross, and General Scott struggled with procedures for effecting their deportation.

Originally the plan called for transporting the Cherokees by keel boats constructed for that purpose by the federal government. The proposed water route followed the Tennessee River to the Mississippi River, then up the Arkansas River to the new Cherokee territory. During the summer, three groups did leave by water from present-day Chattanooga, but they experienced great difficulty because drought had reduced the river levels. As finally organized by Ross, the mass of the Cherokees traveled by land, the first group leaving on August 28, 1838. They were followed at intervals by 12 other groups, each numbering approximately 1,000 Cherokees and blacks. The "Trail," in fact, included three routes. One crossed Tennessee to Memphis, then moved along the Arkansas River to Cherokee land. A second route went from Fort Payne, Alabama, through West Tennessee to Missouri, then down through Arkansas to Oklahoma. The third progressed through Nashville to Kentucky, Illinois, and Missouri before dropping down near the northwestern corner of Arkansas.

Escorted by soldiers on horseback, the Cherokees were not prepared for the weather or the trauma of their trek. Lacking adequate clothing and food, often moving in deplorable weather conditions, more and more fell along the way. Each campsite served as a

new burial ground, while the survivors moved on. Of the original estimated 14,000 marchers, it is believed that over 4,000 died before reaching their destination.

Long relegated to a brief reference in American history texts, the Trail of Tears has now been brought to the forefront of American awareness as Native American cultures have begun to receive the appreciation and status they deserve. In 1987 the U.S. Congress established the Trail of Tears National Historic Trail, which is administered by the National Park Service with the cooperation of a wide range of interested parties, including the Cherokee Nation. The Trial of Tears Association, a non-profit organization with headquarters in Little Rock, Arkansas, was founded in 1993 to work closely with the National Park Service in identifying and marking all of the land routes used in the forced march westward.
Ben Harris McClary, Chattanooga

SUGGESTED READINGS: John Ehle, *Trail of Tears: The Rise and Fall of the Cherokee Nation* (1988); Louis Filler and Allen Guttmann, eds., *The Removal of the Cherokee Nation* (1977)

SEE: BRADLEY COUNTY; BOUDINOT, ELIAS; BRAINERD MISSION; CHEROKEE PHOENIX; OVERHILL CHEROKEES; RIDGE, MAJOR; ROSS, JOHN; RATTLESNAKE SPRINGS; RED CLAY STATE HISTORIC PARK; TREATIES

TRAILS, HISTORIC. The trails, traces, and finally roads used by early immigrants to travel to the Cumberland settlements had two main routes. A northern route started south of Clinch Mountain (near Blaine), crossed the Clinch River (east of Oak Ridge), and continued across the Cumberland mountains to Standing Stone (Monterey). A later southern route passed by Knoxville to Kingston as settlements grew in that area, crossed the Clinch River at Southwest Point (near Kingston), and rejoined the northern route at Johnson's Stand near Standing Stone. The routes again separated near the Cumberland River, with a northern route that crossed the river at Fort Blount near the mouth of Flynn's Creek and a later southern route that crossed the Cumberland at the mouth of the Caney Fork River (near Carthage). The routes rejoined north of the Cumberland River and terminated at Nashville.

The earlier northern route from East to Middle Tennessee followed sections of an old Indian trail known as Tollunteeskee's Trail. Longhunter James Smith used this trail as early as 1766. The Cherokees claimed the territory between the Clinch River and a treaty line west of Standing Stone (Monterey) and disputed the right of whites to pass through their land without permission. James Robertson's overland trip in 1779 to establish the Cumberland settlement used the Wilderness Road through Kentucky rather than a more dangerous and direct route through the Cherokees' land.

The first formal authorization to "cut and clear" a trace for a direct route to the Cumberland settlements occurred in 1785 when the North Carolina legislature provided for a force of 300 men to protect the Cumberland settlements. These soldiers were charged with cutting and clearing a road, by the most eligible route, from the lower end of Clinch Mountain to Nashville. More direct and shorter than the Wilderness Road, it would accommodate expected increases in immigration as Revolutionary War veterans claimed their land warrants. Probably little real progress was made on this road as James Robertson continued to request protection and improvements.

In 1787 North Carolina legislators approved a second road act, which again ordered a road cut and cleared from the south end of Clinch Mountain to Nashville. Peter Avery blazed a trail to ark the route which crossed the Clinch River near present-day Oak Ridge, passed through Winter's Gap (Oliver Springs), and crossed the Emory River near present-day Wartburg. It passed through present-day Lansing to Johnson's Stand, followed a ridge to Standing Stone (Monterey), and then went on to the Cumberland settlements (Nashville). Major George Walton directed the soldiers working on this earliest road. This northern route was also known as Avery's Trace, the old North Carolina Road, and later Emery Road.

The Cherokees continued to resist white settlers crossing their land and demanded that tolls be paid. Those who refused risked losing their lives. A concern for safety caused individual travelers and families to avoid the northern route and form groups on the banks of the Clinch River to wait for an armed escort by the southern route. Both routes were still little more than traces, yet Harriette Arnow noted that a party of 100 under the protection of Kasper Mansker and other guards used the trace in 1787, a year before it officially opened.

In 1788 the North Carolina legislature passed a third act for a road to the Cumberland settlements and provided for two companies of militia of 50 men each to guard immigrants. When the road (southern route) was completed, Robertson gave notice in the *State Gazette* of North Carolina that soldiers had successfully escorted the first party of immigrants on September 25, 1788. During that year several families grouped together and made the escorted trip, including the widow of General William Davidson and Judge John McNairy and his family. Andrew Jackson also came to the Cumberland settlement during this period, having obtained an appointment as prosecuting attorney.

On July 10, 1795, the territorial legislature authorized a wagon road to be cut from Knoxville to Nashville. George Walton received the commission to determine the direct route from Southwest Point on the Clinch River, through the Cumberland Mountains to the conflux of the Caney Fork and Cumberland rivers. William Walton, William Martin, and Robert Koyle were in charge of cutting the road. This road did not meet the demands of the Cherokees for a single road from Washington District to Mero District to be authorized by the United States, so attacks on travelers and demands for tolls continued until 1799, when Tennessee legislators asked the President to designate the road and assign commissioners.

With peace obtained, the General Assembly turned Walton Road into a turnpike through legislation enacted in 1801. The requirements for a turnpike designation included measuring and erecting mileposts on the road and digging and leveling the sides of hills and mountains over which the road passed to the width of 12 feet. Bridges and causeways were to be 12 feet but on all other ground the width was to be cut to 15 feet. By 1802 Walton Road was known as a "broad and commodious" turnpike with markers set every three miles. It soon became known as the Great Stage Road and later the Cumberland Road.

Several historical markers recognize the Emery and Walton roads. At Dixon Springs, a marker commemorates these immigrant trails and the hardy travelers who used them. Just west of Cookeville, a marker identifies the Walton Road. At Blaine a marker locates the beginning of the northern route at the south end of Clinch Mountain. At Oak Ridge, on a section of the earliest (northern) route, a rock and concrete bridge was constructed in the early 1900s, and a marker for that bridge recognizes the Emery Road as one of the earliest routes used in the settlement of Middle Tennessee.

David Ray Smith, Oak Ridge

SUGGESTED READING: Harriette S. Arnow, *The Flowering of the Cumberland* (1963); A.W. Putnam, *History of Middle Tennessee* (1971); Samuel Cole Williams, *Early Travels in the Tennessee Country* (1928)

SEE: FORT BLOUNT; FORT SOUTHWEST POINT; MANSKER, KASPER; ROBERTSON, JAMES; STANDING STONE; TRAILS, NATIVE AMERICAN; WALTON ROAD; WILDERNESS ROAD

TRAILS, NATIVE AMERICAN. Animal trails crisscrossed the Tennessee region long before the arrival of humans, and the same large game animals that created the trails attracted prehistoric hunters. Early trails tended to follow lines of least resistance, avoiding heavy undergrowth, rough ground, or boggy places. In some instances, buffalo trails, such as the ones leading into the great salt lick near the future Nashville, were up to four feet wide and worn as much as two feet below ground level. However, most trails in the wooded or mountainous parts of the state were 18- to 24-inches wide and required humans to travel in single file. Although many trails had their origin as animal paths, Native Americans, rather than animals, made some high mountain trails. Above the fall lines of southern rivers, numerous trails were a preferred route for travel. Below the fall line, especially in more swampy areas and along the Mississippi, rivers were used more than trails. On the trails, travelers would cross streams at fords; if the water was too deep, they would use rafts, crude temporary bark canoes, or coracles, a round bottomed craft made of skins stretched over a sapling framework. On the larger rivers used for transportation, large dugout canoes were the preferred craft.

Early Indians seldom widened or improved trails. The large network of Indian trails, however, played a major role in allowing early European exploration of the region and access for colonial trade and settlement. These settlers, who later followed the paths with packhorses or wagons, often broadened the way. Many of the Native American trails would become the first roads of the territory and, later, routes of state highways.

Trade, war, and hunting propelled the creation of trails. By at least 2,500 years ago, trade networks brought copper from the Great Lakes region, mica from the Appalachian Mountains, shells from the Atlantic and Gulf coasts, and obsidian from the Rockies into the Tennessee region. During the Mississippian period, traders may have come from as far away as the Aztecs of Mexico. The most important exchange routes were between the sea coasts and the interior. Shells were especially prized on the interior, while deerskins were desired on the coasts, and these were traded regularly. Salt was another item of exchange, as noted by the earliest explorers.

By the late 1600s British colonists had established a major trade in deerskins with the Indians of the Tennessee region, focused most heavily out of Charles Town (later Charleston), South Carolina. The British agents traded guns and powder, woolen cloth, iron tools and kettles, dyes, beads, and rum for deerskins and other animal pelts; the Indians depended on this trade for desirable goods they did not manufacture themselves.

Archaeologist William Myer, in his "Indian Trails of the Southeast," listed dozens of documented Indian trails within Tennessee. Among the most important trails named and described by European explorers was the Great Indian War Path, used for war and trade between southern and northern tribes. It stretched from eastern Pennsylvania near Philadelphia, down the Shenandoah Valley to the upper tributaries of the Tennessee River, to the Chattanooga area and the Creek Indian country of Alabama and Georgia. At Chattanooga, the path connected to trails into Alabama, Mississippi, and Georgia. (U.S. Highway 11 follows partly along this trail.) One branch of the trail crossed through the Cumberland Gap into central Kentucky; another (the Catawba Trail) went along the French Broad River over the mountains to the middle and lower Cherokee settlements of the Carolinas. At the Little Tennessee River, another trail branched off the Great War Path at the Overhill Cherokee towns and ran over the mountains to Charleston.

In 1540 Hernando de Soto used the system of trails anchored by the Great War Path to cross the Blue Ridge Mountains from the east. His expedition picked up the trail along the French Broad, taking him to the chiefdom of Chiaha near present-day Dandridge and then south into north Georgia and the chiefdom of Coosa. In 1567–1568 the Pardo expedition followed Soto's approach, and visited towns on the French Broad, Holston, Tennessee, and Little Tennessee rivers. The Spanish built Fort San Pedro near Chiaha to command the trails and defend their colony of Greater Florida. In 1756 Fort Loudoun was built on the Little Tennessee River at the junction of the Charleston Road with the Great War Path in an effort by the British to control Cherokee movements on the paths and waterways. In 1791 the U.S. Army built Fort Southwest Point at the confluence of the Clinch and Tennessee to monitor Indian travel on the trails and rivers. Although the Great War Path system would be a major route for white and black settlement of upper East Tennessee and into Kentucky and Middle Tennessee, the Cherokees prevented settlement along the trail's lower portions until the 1830s.

Another major trail ran from the Indian towns in the present-day Nashville area to Chickasaw towns around Pontotoc, Mississippi, where it connected to other trails traversing the South. Early white explorers regarded this as a very ancient trail and called it the Old Chickasaw Trace; later settlers adopted it for their own trade use with the Chickasaws and the port of New Orleans. Eventually the trail became known as the Natchez Trace, and in 1801, with Chickasaw approval, the federal government authorized development of the trace into a national road. From the Pontotoc towns, a trail ran through Ripley, Mississippi, to the Bolivar area and on to the Chickasaw Bluffs at present-day Memphis. This trail was referred to as the West Tennessee Chickasaw Trail and appears on maps as early as 1718.

Among the important east-west trails described by Myers is the Cumberland Trace, which diverged from the Great Indian War Path near present-day Rockwood. Crossing the Cumberland Plateau on a route later followed by the Tennessee Central Railroad, the trail passed the landmark Standing Stone near Monterey and descended to the Cumberland River via one prong into the Roaring River valley and another prong down Flynn's Lick Creek. Fort Blount was built near the Flynn's Lick-Cumberland River crossing in 1784 to protect the travel of settlers from war parties on the trace.

Ann Toplovich, Tennessee Historical Society

SUGGESTED READING: William Myer, "Indian Trails of the Southeast," *42nd Report of the Bureau of American Ethnology, 1924–1925* (1928)

SEE: CUMBERLAND GAP; EXPLORATIONS, EARLY; FORT BLOUNT; FORT LOUDOUN; FORT SOUTHWEST POINT; FRENCH LICK; NATCHEZ TRACE; OVERHILL CHEROKEES; PARDO EXPEDITION; SOTO EXPEDITION; TRAILS, HISTORIC; WALTON ROAD; WARRIORS PATH STATE PARK; WILDERNESS ROAD

TRANSPORTATION, RIVER. Before the steamboat, Tennesseans navigated the Mississippi, Cumberland, and Tennessee rivers and their tributaries in canoes, keelboats, flatboats, and rafts. The original Tennessee rivermen were Cherokees, Shawnees, and other Indians, paddling their sleek wooden dugout canoes and cruder "bullboats" (made of hides and sticks) on western waters. Early European and Euro-American explorers, trappers, and traders adopted the Indian canoes and, by the middle and late 1700s, a bonafide river commerce emerged utilizing canoe, keelboat, flatboat, and raft river craft.

The keelboat was a sleek, prowed upstream craft, averaging about 60 feet in length and eight feet in width. Equipped with sails and rigging, a keelboat resembled a miniature sailing vessel or small ocean-going frigate. Keels were propelled by wind, rowing, poling, or hand-winching upstream through the herculean efforts of their crews. In 1819 it took 67 days for one crew to propel its keelboat from New Orleans to Nashville; it once took keelboat entrepreneur Andrew Jackson and his crew 16 days and a reported 20 gallons of whiskey to sail from Nashville to the mouth of the Cumberland River and back. But the heyday of the keel was short-lived as steamboats supplanted them, beginning on the Mississippi in 1811. Flatboats, however, endured well into the late nineteenth century.

Pioneer emigrants and professional boatmen alike plied Tennessee's rivers aboard flatboats. These were flat-bottomed, box-shaped craft averaging 50 feet in length and 12 feet in width. Boatmen navigated these unwieldy downstream craft as best they could with a stern oar and three additional oars, one each on the port, starboard, and bow. Their cargoes included corn, whiskey, furs, flour, hearty produce (apples, squash, etc.), and pork. Upon reaching their destination, boatmen dismantled their flat and sold it for lumber; then the crew walked home. Before 1811 Tennessee flatboatmen walked the Natchez Trace (Dr. John Bedford did so after navigating the Cumberland, Ohio, and Mississippi rivers to New Orleans in 1807). Soon, however, flatboatmen began to buy passage home on the decks of steamers.

Tennessee boatmen could more easily ply the Cumberland than the Tennessee River. The length of the Tennessee, combined with its hazardous Muscle Shoals stretch in northern Alabama, rendered it the less desirable route to the Ohio and Mississippi Valleys and the Gulf of Mexico until well into the twentieth century (and the advent of improvements by the U.S. Army Corps of Engineers and Tennessee Valley Authority).

The average antebellum Tennessee flatboatman was a white male, of English or Celtic ancestry, and 28 years of age. Exceptions included African-American (slave and free), Franco-American ("Canadian"), and Indian flatboatmen; very few women worked professionally aboard flats, though many sailed as emigrant flatboatmen. Tennessee boasted an array of experienced flatboat hands. In the nineteenth century, Edward Cason, James Stone, and Ambrose Peterman sailed flats down the Cumberland River, out of Jackson and Clay counties. A village called "Boatland" became a flatboat building center on the east Fork of the Obey River. Further west, Colonel David Crockett made an infamous flatboat trip in 1826, running aground near the Chickasaw Bluffs and nearly drowning. Boating "went so badly with me, along at the first," Crockett later wrote, "that I hadn't much mind to try it any more;" he returned home and ran for Congress.[1]

The heyday of flatboating was 1846–1847, just a few years after the infamous 1842 Memphis "Flatboat War." This "war" was actually a skirmish between flatboatmen tied up at the Memphis wharf and city officials and militiamen intent upon taxing them a "wharf fee." There was a confrontation between the militia and angry boatmen and, after an exchange of fire, one boatman lay dead. The flatboatmen eventually paid up, but the "Flatboat War" symbolized the beginning of their professional demise. Soon the combination of steam and railroad transportation ran the flats completely out of business; few returned (except on the upper, low-water portions of the Cumberland and Tennessee systems) after the Civil War. When they did return (on the lower rivers), it was in "tow" as flatboats became the wooden precursors of the modern steel river barge.

The log raft emerged to transport the timber of the Tennessee woods to lumber yards in Knoxville, Nashville, Memphis, and other commercial centers. This began in the early nineteenth century and continued until the 1920s on the Upper Cumberland and Tennessee rivers. Raftsmen built rafts in a manner similar to modern barge tows—logs were secured into "stringer" pieces, which were in turn tied together to form large rafts (on the Cumberland these "drifts" were as big as 280 feet long and 48 feet wide). Most raftsmen, like flatboatmen and keelboatmen, sailed in high water to avoid running aground. The winter schedules and freezing temperatures led to raftsmen's deaths through exposure to the elements, and raftsmen braved not only inclement weather but also snags, rocks, rapids, and cave-in banks.

While rafting endured well into the twentieth century, in most of Tennessee it also mechanized, with steamboats and, later, diesel towboats towing rafts to market. In this way, the raft became an adjunct to the steam and diesel towboat just as the flatboat had become a river "barge." Railroads and logging trucks completed the cycle of mechanization, and log and lumber rafting grew less and less important to transport on the Mississippi, Cumberland, and Tennessee rivers.

Michael Allen, University of Washington, Tacoma

CITATION:

(1) David Crockett, *A Narrative of the Life and Adventures of Colonel David Crockett of the State of Tennessee* (1834; repr., Knoxville, 1973), 195–200.

SEE: CLAY COUNTY; CUMBERLAND RIVER; FERRIES; MISSISSIPPI RIVER SYSTEM; RILEY, BOB; STEAMBOATING; TENNESSEE RIVER SYSTEM; TIMBER INDUSTRY

TRANSYLVANIA PURCHASE occurred on March 14, 1775, when Richard Henderson, a North Carolina land speculator, met with Cherokee representatives at Sycamore Shoals near the present site of Elizabethton. Henderson wanted to purchase a tract of land in what is now Kentucky and Middle Tennessee, where he planned to establish a fourteenth colony. The venture posed several problems: the Cherokees held the strongest among competing claims to the region and there was no guarantee of British recognition of the purchase, inasmuch as it represented a violation of the Proclamation of 1763. Nevertheless, Henderson had spent the previous year organizing the Transylvania Company and conducting negotiations with

the Cherokees. Four days after the conference began, the Cherokees agreed to the Sycamore Shoals Treaty, whereby they transferred to the Transylvania Company a tract of 20 million acres lying north of the Cumberland River, southeast of the Ohio River, and west of the Cumberland Mountains, with a narrow access route extending from Sycamore Shoals to Cumberland Gap. In exchange, the Cherokees received trade goods valued at approximately 10,000 British pounds, according to some scholars.

Henderson moved quickly to consolidate his claim, constructing a road to the proposed settlements and initiating a system of government under the authority of the Transylvania Company. The Virginia legislature refused to recognize the Transylvania Purchase despite Henderson's intense lobbying. In December 1776 Virginia annexed the Transylvania settlements and soon afterwards nullified the entire purchase agreement, awarding Henderson a compensatory grant of 200,000 acres.

The Virginia decision did not affect the Middle Tennessee portion of the Transylvania Purchase, and Henderson turned his attention to this region. In the winter of 1779–1780 he had a proprietary interest in establishing a settlement at Nashborough. Following his Kentucky plan, Henderson implemented a system of local government, but made no claims to the establishment of an autonomous colony. In 1783 the state of North Carolina also nullified Henderson's claim and awarded him a grant of 200,000 acres as compensation.

Michael Toomey, Knoxville College

SEE: BOONE, DANIEL; DRAGGING CANOE; LAND GRANTS; OVERHILL CHEROKEES; ROBERTSON, JAMES; SYCAMORE SHOALS STATE HISTORIC AREA; WATAUGA ASSOCIATION

TRAVELLERS REST was the Nashville home of Judge John and Mary Overton and their descendants for 150 years. In 1954 the National Society of the Colonial Dames of America in Tennessee rescued the house from threatened demoliton by the Louisville and Nashville Railroad. The railroad's Radnor Yards and mid-twentieth century suburban growth encircled the house and its remaining historic outbuildings. The Colonial Dames initiated the research of Judge Overton and his descendants and began the restoration.

In the late 1790s Overton purchased a Revolutionary War grant from the heirs of David Maxwell and proceeded to build a vernacular Federal style house. As the cellar was being dug in 1798, the workers discovered the remains of a prehistoric Native American village—arrowheads, pottery, animal bones, and human remains. As the first to examine the wealth of buried artifacts, John Overton originally named the house "Golgotha," hill of skulls. From the 1800s to 1996 several teams of professional archaeologists have researched the site and determined that a Mississippian village of 200–300 people occupied this site between A.D. 1000 and 1400. Unique artifacts from these digs have enhanced scholarship about the Mississippian peoples.

The 1799 house, and its 1808, 1828 and post-Civil War additions, plus the historic outbuildings, stand as above ground artifacts, which likewise have been vigorously "read" by historians in an attempt to portray accurately the lives of later inhabitants, both black and white. With snatches of documentation, including the 1833 death inventory of Overton, total restoration of the house to the period of the first Overtons is underway.

One of the wealthiest and most learned men of his time, Overton's large plantation thrived. Slave labor built and maintained the buildings and fields of Travellers Rest. The yard, patterns of movement within the house, remnants of tools, and the very bricks of the structures provide insight not only to the Overton slaves but their white masters as well. In its modern day role as a historic house museum, Travellers Rest and its grounds remain visual texts of the cultural, social, economic, and political history of Tennessee.

Jeri Hasselbring, Travellers Rest

SUGGESTED READING: Harry Lee Swint, "Travellers' Rest: Home of Judge John Overton," *Tennessee Historical Quarterly* 26(1967): 119–136

SEE: MISSISSIPPIAN CULTURE; OVERTON, JOHN

TREADWELL AND HARRY INSURANCE COMPANY of Memphis was the first insurance agency in the United States to be owned and managed by women. In 1910 Mary Harry Treadwell and her sister, Georgia Harry, founded the company after the death of Treadwell's husband. At the time, insurance was limited to insuring houses, businesses, and property. Most automobile owners did not have insurance on their vehicles, but Treadwell and Harry specialized in automobile insurance as a new and undeveloped area of insurance sales.

When Treadwell and Harry opened, neither woman had any business experience, but they knew many prominent Memphis families socially since their father had been a well-known steamboat captain. Riding the streetcars to the offices of various Memphis businesses, the two women wrote policies to cover a number of construction projects. When J.T. Harshan, president of the company building the second Memphis bridge, refused to consider Treadwell and Harry for insurance covering the bridge project, Georgia Harry bought a ticket on the next train to New York and returned with the contract to insure the building of the bridge. In 1917 the two women sold a policy with a $250,000 premium to the contractor engaged in the diversion of a portion of

the Holston River. They later obtained a policy for the company rebuilding railroad tracks between Paducah, Kentucky, and Memphis. As their business expanded, Treadwell and Harry purchased other Memphis agencies.

In 1926 Treadwell's sons persuaded their mother and aunt to turn the business over to them. Building on the reputation established by the two women, Treadwell and Harry became one of the largest insurance agencies in the Mid-South by the mid-1930s. Today, the grandsons and great-grandsons continue to operate the company.

Carole Stanford Bucy, Volunteer State Community College

SEE: FIRST WOMAN'S BANK; MEMPHIS

TREATIES. Relationships between Tennessee's Native Americans and the Europeans who came to settle most of the state were regulated by various treaties negotiated between 1770 and 1835. A series of ten treaties defined the areas assigned to both groups and the relationships between the parties and eventually moved Tennessee's Indian population west of the Mississippi River to present-day Oklahoma.

In 1763 the British government issued the Proclamation Line restricting settlement and fur trading without British licenses to areas east of the headwaters of the rivers flowing into the Atlantic Ocean. In 1770 British Southern Indian Superintendent John Stuart made the Treaty of Lochabar with the Cherokees that ceded land north and east of a line running along the 36 degree, 30 minute line to Long Island on the Holston River (now Kingsport) and thence northward to the Kanawa River in west Virginia. Though the line was technically the North Carolina-Virginia boundary, it actually included a small portion of what is now Johnson and Sullivan counties. In 1771, when John Donelson and Alexander Cameron surveyed the line with Cherokee assistance, the Cherokees took pity on the settlers living north of the South Fork of the Holston and agreed to the Little Carpenter modification of the Lochabar line allowing the area north of the Holston to be considered territory for legal settlement. Thus, Sullivan County was part of Virginia until 1779 and was considered a legal settlement area.

The Treaty of Sycamore Shoals was negotiated between Judge Richard Henderson of North Carolina and the Cherokees during March 1775 at Sycamore Shoals (now Elizabethton) on the Watauga River. This private treaty was illegal under both British and later American law. It was, however, one of the most influential in Tennessee history. The treaty transferred the area between the Ohio River and the headwaters of the streams flowing into the Kentucky and Cumberland rivers—central Kentucky and north central Tennessee—to the Transylvania Land Company for 10,000 British pounds of trading goods. Little Carpenter's son, Dragging Canoe, refused to recognize the sale and vowed to turn Middle Tennessee into a "dark and bloody ground," a promise he kept through his leadership of the Chickamaugas. Henderson opened the Cumberland settlements as a result of this treaty. The supplementary Watauga and Brown purchases, also made at the 1775 Sycamore Shoals negotiations, transferred ownership of lease rights to Watauga and Nolichucky to the white settlers.

Two treaties acknowledged the Cherokee defeats in 1776 and 1779 in support of the British during the American Revolution. The Treaty of Hopewell, signed on November 28, 1785, officially ended fighting between the United States and the Cherokees and ceded an area south of the Cumberland River for settlement in return for protection of the Cherokee land. Settlers moved into that land, however, and the more definitive Treaty of Holston was signed at Knoxville on July 2, 1791, by Territorial Governor William Blount. For a $1,000 annuity, later raised to $1,500 by Secretary of War Henry Knox, the Cherokees ceded all claims to the area east of the Clinch River and north of a line through Kingston to the North Carolina border.

Further cession of land by the Cherokees came at the First Treaty of Tellico signed October 2, 1798. It granted land that settlers had entered between the Clinch River and the Cumberland Plateau and between the Tennessee and Little Tennessee rivers.

Treaty negotiations often occurred at Tellico Blockhouse. The second treaty did not affect land in Tennessee, but the Third Treaty of Tellico in 1805 did. Indian Agent Return J. Meigs and Daniel Smith obtained from the Cherokees all land north of the Duck River and extended that line due east to the Tennessee River, including all of the Cumberland Plateau. A few days later, an additional payment was made to obtain the rights to operate a mail road from Tellico to the Tombigbee River through Cherokee territory as part of a Knoxville-to-New Orleans route. The same negotiations transferred a small parcel of land around the U.S. garrison at Southwest Point (now Kingston) as a desirable location for the state capital. Subsequently, the capital was moved to that site for one day, September 21, 1807, to fulfill this pledge, making Kingston one of the four official capitals of Tennessee.

The following year, 1806, the claims of the Cherokees and Creeks to the land south of the Duck River to the southern boundary of the state were purchased. Meigs and Smith paid the Creeks $14,000 for their claims, and Secretary of War Henry Dearborn negotiated the Treaty of Washington of 1806 with the Cherokees to obtain their claims for $10,000, a gristmill, a cotton gin, and a $100 annuity for Chief Black Fox.

After the War of 1812 and the subsidiary Creek War, Return J. Meigs began an attempt to persuade the Cherokees to voluntarily remove to the Arkansas area. He was quite successful, but when the Cherokees arrived in Arkansas to take possession of the land, they discovered their ownership disputed by Indians already in the area. This resulted in the 1817 Jackson and McMinn Treaty, which transferred lands along the Sequatchie River to white control along with some land in Georgia in return for secure possession of land along the Arkansas and White rivers. The U.S. government also promised to pay the expenses of Indians emigrating to the west. On October 19, 1818, Andrew Jackson and former Governor Isaac Shelby of Kentucky made the Treaty of Tuscaloosa with the Chickasaws, which has traditionally been known as the Jackson Purchase. Jackson and Shelby bribed Levi Colbert, who with his brothers had taken over political leadership of the tribe, and obtained the 10,700 square miles of territory between the Mississippi River and the western valley of the Tennessee River. This area, comprising one-fourth of Tennessee, was a Chickasaw hunting area and contained no villages. The Chickasaws traded it for $300,000 to be paid in 20 annual installments. There was an immediate rush of settlement to the area, and Jackson, John Overton, and James Winchester soon founded Memphis. Sixteen counties were established by 1824.

The next year, 1819, U.S. Secretary of War John C. Calhoun negotiated the Calhoun Treaty with the Cherokees and cleared the remaining area between the Little Tennessee and Hiwassee rivers for settlement. The only area remaining in Cherokee hands was the southeastern corner of the state in the area that now comprises Monroe, Polk, Bradley, and most of Hamilton counties.

The final treaty affecting Tennessee was the Treaty of New Echota signed on December 29, 1835, at New Echota, Georgia. It was signed by representatives of the Treaty Party among the Cherokees, who spoke for approximately 10 percent of the tribe. The leader of the signatories was Major Ridge, a Tennessean from the Sequatchie Valley area. The United States delegates included former Governor William Carroll. The treaty finalized removal plans for the Cherokees. It purchased Cherokee land in Tennessee, Georgia, and North Carolina, appropriated a portion of that money for travel expenses, used other money to purchase land for Cherokee use in what is now Oklahoma, and set aside the rest for the construction of public buildings in the new location. The treaty gave a two-year time limit for removal. John Ross of Ross's Landing near modern Chattanooga led the other 90 percent of the Cherokees to resist removal. Eventually the Trail of Tears resulted from this treaty.

Fred S. Rolater, Middle Tennessee State University

SEE: ATTAKULLAKULLA; BLOUNT, WILLIAM; CARROLL, WILLIAM; CHICKASAWS; DRAGGING CANOE; FORT

SOUTHWEST POINT; JACKSON, ANDREW; JACKSON PURCHASE; MEIGS, RETURN J.; OVERHILL CHEROKEES; OVERTON, JOHN; RIDGE, MAJOR; ROSS, JOHN; SHELBY, ISAAC; SMITH, DANIEL; SYCAMORE SHOALS STATE HISTORIC AREA; TELLICO BLOCKHOUSE; TRAIL OF TEARS; TRANSYLVANIA PURCHASE

TREVECCA NAZARENE UNIVERSITY was founded in 1901 by the Reverend J.O. McClurkan, a Cumberland Presbyterian minister, as the Pentecostal Literary and Bible Training School for Christian Workers and dedicated to training Christian workers for the United States and foreign countries. First established in Nashville in the old Hynes School Building on Jo Johnston and Fifth Avenue, the school moved to a new location on Fourth Avenue behind the Ryman Auditorium in 1905.

In 1910 the trustees enlarged the curriculum to become a four-year college and changed the name to Trevecca College, a name taken from a school in Wales founded in 1768 during the Methodist Wesleyan revival. In 1914 the school moved again to the former Percy Warner estate, Renraw, on Gallatin Road. In 1917 the Church of the Nazarene officially adopted the school. Trevecca became a junior college in 1932. In 1935 it relocated to its present site at 333 Murfreesboro Road and rechartered as Trevecca Nazarene College.

The school's program and curricular offerings expanded in 1940, with the addition of a third year of college work. In 1941 the state granted Trevecca the right to confer the A.B. degree (the first baccalaureate degrees were awarded in 1942) and approved the college's teacher education programs in 1955. The Southern Association of Colleges and Schools granted accreditation in 1969. Beginning in 1978 with the accreditation of the Physician Assistant Program, Tennessee's only P.A. program, Trevecca expanded degree programs to meet the changing needs of students: graduate programs were instituted with the master's of education in 1984, followed by the master's in religion (1987), in counseling (1991), and in organizational management (1992). A degree-completion program for the non-traditional student began in 1988. Presidents of Trevecca who served during the years of expansion and growth include A.B. Mackey (1936–1963), William M. Greathouse (1963–1968), Mark R. Moore (1968–1979), Homer J. Adams (1979–1991), and Millard Reed (1991–), under whose administration Trevecca achieved university status in 1995.

Janice M. Greathouse, Trevecca Nazarene University
SEE: EDUCATION, HIGHER; RELIGION; NASHVILLE

TRI-STATE BANK, one of the largest black-owned businesses in the state, was founded in 1946 by Dr. J.E. Walker (founder of Universal Life Insurance) and his son A. Maceo Walker. The original headquarters site at the corner of Beale Street and Fourth was also the site of Robert Church's Solvent Savings Bank and Trust, the first black-owned bank in Memphis. The building is listed on the National Register of Historic Places.

With initial assets of only $240,000, the bank has increased in size and services to the extent that current assets are closer to the $100,000,000 mark. From one small building and five employees, the bank has grown to five branches and some 70 employees. One critical contributor to the success of the institution was Jesse H. Turner, Sr. A new CPA and ex-U.S. Army officer, Turner was hired in 1949 to bring the bank's books under control. By the time he died in 1989, Turner was president of the bank and one of the first post-Reconstruction African Americans to hold local legislative office in Memphis and Shelby County. Other presidents have been both Walkers and Jesse H. Turner, Jr.

Tri-State Bank, for all its importance as a black financial institution, also played an important role in the civil rights struggles of the 1950s and 1960s. According to Jesse Turner, Jr., many local sit-ins were planned in the bank's boardroom, and bank officials often kept the vault open at night to provide bail money for protesters.

Ed Frank, Mississippi Valley Collection, University of Memphis Libraries
SEE: BEALE STREET; CIVIL RIGHTS MOVEMENT; SOLVENT SAVINGS BANK AND TRUST; UNIVERSAL LIFE INSURANCE COMPANY

TROOST, GERARD (1776–1850), geologist, was born in s'Hertogenbosch, Netherlands, on March 5, 1776. As Tennessee State Geologist (1831–1850) and the state's best known antebellum scientist, Troost promoted mining, planned transportation routes, described soils, and wrote 43 geological reports. As he traveled the state searching for geological resources, Troost also studied botany, zoology, and archaeology, publishing pioneering work in these fields.

From his arrival in Tennessee in 1827 through 1832, Troost operated the Nashville Museum of Natural History, where he displayed his personal collection of zoological specimens, aboriginal artifacts, fossils, and minerals. His principal employment from 1828 through 1850 was the professorship of science at the University of Nashville. From 1840 through 1845, he coedited *The Agriculturist,* a monthly journal of applied science. Troost was a leader in the Nashville lyceum, in the mechanics institute movement, and in anything that involved libraries. He was obsessively bookish with a private library exceeding 7,000 volumes. As his death in 1850, his natural history collection contained some 22,000 specimens, including almost 14,000 well-catalogued minerals.

Troost lived a nomadic life before settling in Tennessee. His travels began in 1794–1795, when French troops captured his home town and changed the name to Bois le Duc. Troost used both Gerard and Gerritt as his name, making it hard to distinguish his educational records. Clearly, he was an M.D., with a second diploma in pharmacy. He served as a foot-soldier, then as a surgeon in the French-dominated Dutch army, and was wounded twice.

By 1802 Troost was making pharmaceuticals at The Hague, and he was also a well-known mineral collector. From 1807 to 1810 he was based at the natural history museum in Paris, managing the royal mineral collection of Louis Bonaparte, a French-imposed king of the Netherlands. Troost traveled widely, enhancing the royal collection. In Paris he was the protégé of Abbé René Just Haüy, the father of crystallography. In 1808 he translated Alexander von Humboldt's *Ansichten der Natur* into Dutch. Eventually, Troost was skilled in Latin, Greek, Dutch, German, French, and English.

In 1810, with the collapse of the Dutch monarchy eminent, Troost left France for Philadelphia. He claimed to be on a trip to reconnoiter Java for Louis Bonaparte, but he carried letters of introduction to American scientists. In 1811 Troost married Margaret Teague of Philadelphia. In 1811 or 1812 he joined a group that planned a chemical manufacturing business at Cape Sable, Maryland. It was one of America's first chemical industries and an economic disaster; litigation surrounding the endeavor continued until the fall of 1828.

In 1812 Troost became the founding president of the Academy of Natural Sciences of Philadelphia, an office he held until 1818. Although he continued to attend Academy functions, Troost moved to Maryland by January 1814. Sometime later he returned to Philadelphia and served as one of two professors of pharmacy at the nation's first pharmacy school, the Philadelphia College of Pharmacy. In the 1820s he lectured, managed the Academy mineral collection, and mapped the geology of Philadelphia. In addition, he worked on a revision of the first geological map of North America prepared by William Maclure and wrote 15 papers for American journals.

Troost's wife died in 1819, leaving him with two small children; he married Mary O'Reilly, a widowed mother of two. By January 1826 the Troosts had settled in New Harmony, Indiana, the site of a communal experiment sponsored by the industrialist Robert Owen and William Maclure. Troost was hired at $500 per year to teach science and mathematics. Before the community declined in 1827, he lectured and wrote seven papers on regional geology.

While collecting minerals at Smithland, Kentucky, Troost met George Bowen, a friend from Philadelphia, who taught chemistry at the University of Nashville. The Troost family soon relocated to Nashville and his personal letters brim with zeal for what he called his Tennessee Citizenship. Before becoming State Geologist, Troost provided many public services. For example, he contributed the idea for a railroad tunnel at Cowan and chose the site. In 1990–1994, the tunnel served 27 to 30 trains per day, an enduring donation to all Tennesseans. His salary of $250 to $500 per year barely covered the cost of travel and research. Clearly, Troost enjoyed the labor from which so many Tennesseans have benefited and after years of wandering made the state his home.

James X. Corgan, Austin Peay State University

SUGGESTED READING: James X. Corgan, ed., *The Geological Sciences in the Antebellum South* (1982)

SEE: AGRICULTURAL JOURNALS; GEOLOGY

TROUSDALE COUNTY was the first county to be created after the Civil War and was named in honor of Governor William Trousdale. With just 114 square miles of area, it is also the smallest of Tennessee's 95 counties. The General Assembly established Trousdale County in 1870, when it carved the new jurisdiction from portions of Macon, Smith, Sumner, and Wilson counties. Despite the county's late creation, the present-day county seat of Hartsville is one of the Middle Cumberland region's oldest communities.

Settlers traveling down the Cumberland River and over the Fort Blount Trail began arriving in present-day Trousdale County in the late 1700s. Originally known as Damascus, Hartsville traces its beginnings to 1795 when several families built their homes on the east side of Little Goose Creek. Two years later, one of these families, the Donohos, built a grist mill. Another pioneer family, the Harts, built a ferry crossing on the Cumberland in 1798. By promoting settlement on the west side of Goose Creek, the Harts also helped to overshadow Damascus. With the establishment of a post office in 1807, inhabitants renamed the community Hartsville. Other antebellum communities in Trousdale County include Beech Grove, Dixon Creek, Halltown, Providence, Willard, and Willow Grove.

Early historical accounts of Trousdale County noted it for two developments: a quarry that produced high-quality grist stones for Middle Tennessee's water-powered mills and a horse racetrack at Hartsville. Horse racing there was such a popular activity that Andrew Jackson often visited the town, and the Hartsville Jockey Club hosted races in 1836 featuring 18 entries. As in much of the state, however, agriculture dominated the local economy. With four stores, by 1830 Hartsville was the central marketplace for neighboring cotton farmers. A landing south of the town was a regular stop for steamboats plying the Cumberland River. By decade's end, Hartsville was the second largest town in what was then still part of Sumner County.

Aware of the town's growing importance to the surrounding area, residents of Hartsville began to lobby for the establishment of their own county. In 1849 they convinced William B. Bate to introduce a resolution in the Tennessee House of Representatives that would amend the constitution and allow for the county's creation, but the matter died in a house committee. A cholera epidemic, which forced residents to desert Hartsville for a time, occurred that same year.

The Civil War totally disrupted the economy of Hartsville and surrounding farms. Union forces occupied Hartsville for much of the war. In late 1862 Confederate cavalry under General John Hunt Morgan captured a Federal garrison at Hartsville. Yet Morgan's raid was only a minor setback for the northern war effort, and Union troops soon recaptured the town.

Following the war, cotton ceased to be the primary agricultural product when corn, oats, wheat, and tobacco became the leading crops. With the establishment of Trousdale County and its designation of Hartsville as the county seat, the town became more prosperous. The construction of a railroad line to Hartsville in the 1890s spurred town growth in the following decades.

Throughout the twentieth century, tobacco was such a profitable agricultural product in Trousdale County that Hartsville has been the home of a thriving loose-leaf tobacco market. Besides the auction warehouses, two tobacco factories, which employed hundreds of workers, once operated in the county. Because of its identity as a leading burley producer, Hartsville once hosted the Tobacco Bowl, a high school football championship. Begun in 1954, the 1961 game drew 8,000 spectators to the community of 2,000. The tobacco factories have left Trousdale County, but in the 1990s Hartsville warehouses still market tobacco raised in neighboring counties and in southern Kentucky.

East of Hartsville, near the Smith County line, stand the mothballed structures of the Tennessee Valley Authority's Hartsville Nuclear Plant. The agency proposed the plant in 1972 and began construction five years later. It canceled the project in 1984, but not before spending two billion dollars. Today, the idle 560-foot cooling tower looms above the rural landscape, symbolizing the rancorous debate over nuclear power.

In 1990 Trousdale County had a population of nearly 6,000, over 1,000 factory workers, and just 439 farms. Notable people from the county include Montana Territory Supreme Court Chief Justice Newton W. McConnell, Edward T. Seay, a prominent Nashville attorney who briefly served as the dean of Vanderbilt University's Law School, Indiana University Head Football Coach Phil Dickens, and Casey

Wise, a member of the Milwaukee Braves baseball team that played in the 1958 World Series.

Jeffrey L. Durbin, Historic Preservation Division, Georgia Department of Natural Resources

SUGGESTED READING: Tom O. Allen, *Trousdale County Tennessee History* (1991)

SEE: CUMBERLAND RIVER; HORSERACING TRACKS, EARLY; MORGAN, JOHN HUNT; THOROUGHBRED HORSES; TOBACCO; TENNESSEE VALLEY AUTHORITY.

TROUSDALE, WILLIAM (1790–1872), Mexican War hero, Governor, and minister to Brazil, was born in Orange County, North Carolina. In 1796 he came with his parents, James and Elizabeth Dobbins Trousdale, to settle in Sumner County, Tennessee.

Trousdale first experienced military duty when he volunteered for Captain William Edwards's company of mounted riflemen during the War of 1812. Not activated until the Creek uprising in 1813, the company participated in the battles at Tallushatchee and Talladega. During the summer of 1814, Trousdale enrolled in another volunteer company that marched to the Gulf Coast in time to have an active role in General Andrew Jackson's taking of Pensacola. Continuing with Jackson to New Orleans, he went with General John Coffee on December 23 to challenge the invading British forces below the city. Trousdale engaged in a fire fight that night and on December 27 and January 1, before fighting in the decisive Battle of New Orleans on January 8, 1815.

In April 1836 Trousdale was elected major general, commanding the Fourth Division, Tennessee Militia. Two months later, preferring active duty, he raised a company of mounted volunteers for the Seminole War. When Tennessee troops met to organize, they elected Trousdale colonel, commander of the Second Regiment, First Brigade, in which capacity he led the regiment during several skirmishes with the Seminoles and in the battles of the Cove of the Withlacoochee and of Wahoo Swamp.

Ten years later the war with Mexico erupted and Trousdale accepted appointment as colonel in the regular army. He reported to New Orleans in April 1847 and took command of eight companies that he landed at Vera Cruz on June 13. Joining the march on Mexico City, Trousdale and his troops fought at Cherubusco and Molino del Rey, where he was struck in the shoulder by an escopet ball, and his horse was shot from under him. Nonetheless, five days later he led two regiments and a field battery in the successful assault on Chapultepec, the main fortress in Mexico City. His troops suffered heavy casualties, and his own right arm, hit twice, was shattered. On August 28, 1848, President James K. Polk appointed Trousdale brigadier general by brevet for "gallant and meritorious conduct in the battle of Chapultepec."

Beginning in 1820, Trousdale practiced law at Gallatin in the intervals between military adventures. In 1827 he married Many Ann Bugg; they had seven children. Trousdale unsuccessfully sought election to Congress in 1827, 1829, 1837, 1839, and 1845. He won election to the Gallatin board of aldermen 1831–1835, and to the State Senate 1835–1836. He served as a Democratic presidential elector in the 1840 campaign. His conspicuous bravery in the Mexican War returned him to the political spotlight, and the Democrats unanimously nominated him for governor in 1849. He won a closely contested race, but failed for reelection in 1851.

In 1853 President Franklin Pierce appointed Trousdale U.S. Minister to Brazil. After completing the four-year term, he returned to Gallatin and resumed the practice of law. Persistent bad health plagued him until his death in 1872. He and his family lived near the town square in a handsome Federal-style brick house known as Trousdale Place, maintained as a public shrine since 1900.

Walter T. Durham, Gallatin

SUGGESTED READING: J.A. Trousdale, "A History of the Life of General William Trousdale," *Tennessee Historical Magazine* (1916): 119–136

SEE: CREEK WAR OF 1813 AND 1814; MEXICAN WAR; POLK, JAMES K.; SUMNER COUNTY; WAR OF 1812

TUBB, ERNEST (1914–1984), pioneer of the "honky tonk" sound in country music, was born in Crisp, Texas, on February 9, 1914. After hearing a Jimmie Rodgers record, *In the Jail House Now,* Tubb determined to emulate the "Blue Yodeler" and pursue a career in country music. While hosting a radio show over KONO in San Antonio, Tubb called Rodgers's widow, Carrie, initiating a friendship that produced his first recording session in 1936, for Victor Records, Rodgers's label. During this session, at San Antonio's Texas Hotel, Tubb recorded two songs about his hero, *The Passing of Jimmie Rodgers* and *The Last Thought of Jimmie Rodgers.* Tubb became a Jimmie Rodgers imitator: he wore Rodgers's tuxedo in publicity pictures, played Rodgers's guitar during recordings, and sang a number of Rodgers's songs when he performed.

Tubb made his first Decca recordings in 1940, recording two of his own songs, *Blue-Eyed Elaine* and *I'll Get Along Somehow.* He and his wife, Elaine, moved to San Angelo and opened a bar, "The E & E Tavern," where he developed his Texas honky tonk sound. In 1941 his biggest hit, *I'm Walking the Floor Over You,* crossed over into the pop market and eventually sold a reported million copies.

On January 16, 1943, Ernest Tubb made his debut with the Grand Ole Opry at the War Memorial Auditorium. He accepted a subsequent invitation to join the Opry. During World War II, Tubb recorded hits like *Soldier's Last Letter* and *Tomorrow Never Comes.*

In 1947 Tubb opened the Ernest Tubb Record Shop on Broadway in response to demands from country fans who could not find country record stores, and he hosted a "Midnight Jamboree" on Saturday nights after the Opry from the store. The Jamboree quickly became an important part of the Nashville music scene. He also worked to change the designation of country music from "Hillbilly" to "Country and Western." In 1948 he headlined a country show at Carnegie Hall, the first country artist to do so.

After World War II, Tubb recorded with the Andrews Sisters and Red Foley, with whom he had a string of successful duets. Between 1945 and 1965 Tubb's hits included *Drivin' Nails in My Coffin* and *Waltz Around Texas.* He befriended a number of young country artists, including Hank Snow, Carl Smith, and Loretta Lynn, with whom he also recorded a number of duets. Two of his former band members, Jack Greene and Cal Smith, became country stars on their own.

Tubb hosted a syndicated television show in the 1950s and became the sixth member elected to the Country Music Hall of Fame in 1965. He performed his last show on November 13, 1982, and died September 6, 1984, in Nashville. His son Justin Tubb (1938–1998) operated the Broadway record store until his death in 1998.

Don Cusic, Belmont University

SEE: COUNTRY MUSIC HALL OF FAME; GRAND OLE OPRY; LYNN, LORETTA

TULLAHOMA CAMPAIGN. The successful Union campaign in Middle Tennessee in the summer of 1863 was a turning point in the Civil War. In just 11 days, and with very little fighting, the Army of the Cumberland maneuvered the Confederate Army of Tennessee completely out of Middle Tennessee. The campaign secured an agriculturally productive region for the Union, set the stage for the major battles around Chattanooga that fall, and led to the crucial struggle for Atlanta the following year.

The campaign was part of two years of conflict along the railroad extending from Nashville through Chattanooga to Atlanta. The first clash occurred on Stones River near Murfreesboro at the end of 1862. From a military standpoint, the battle ended in a draw, but on January 3, 1863, Confederate General Braxton Bragg retreated, moving his army south to a 20-mile long front in the Shelbyville-Tullahoma area.

The next move belonged to Union Major General William S. Rosecrans. But, despite proddings from President Abraham Lincoln, Rosecrans refused to budge from his Murfreesboro base until he was satisfied his army was ready. When Rosecrans finally moved on June 23, 1863, he followed a brilliant plan: go around Bragg's army, sever its line of supply, reinforcement, and retreat along the Nashville and

Chattanooga Railroad, and force the Confederates to turn around and fight. At the very least, the southerners would have to retreat to protect their lifeline south.

The range of hills separating the two armies figured prominently in Rosecrans's plan. Avoiding the easy advance around the hills on the western edge of the front, Rosecrans chose the difficult route directly through the hills on the east. To confuse the Confederates, he sent large parts of his army in several directions.

The Confederates held at Shelbyville and Liberty Gap near Bell Buckle, while the main Federal thrust went through Hoover's Gap on the Murfreesboro-Manchester Turnpike. By June 27, Union troops were at Manchester in the Confederate rear. Bragg had no choice but to retreat to Tullahoma. Over the next several days, Bragg's army made successive retreats to Decherd and Cowan, before the final retreat over the mountain to Chattanooga on July 3.

Incessant rain slowed the Union advance, and Rosecrans was not able to strike Bragg's army before it got away. But Rosecrans did achieve his secondary goal of forcing the Confederates out of Middle Tennessee. The battleground shifted to the Chattanooga area.

The Federals deployed about 77,000 men in the Tullahoma campaign and the Confederates 44,000. The Union losses totaled 550 captured, wounded, and killed. The Federal forces captured 1,634 Confederates, but the number of Confederate wounded and killed is not known.

Robert Brandt, Nashville

SEE: ARMY OF TENNESSEE; BRAGG, BRAXTON; CIVIL WAR; RAILROAD, NASHVILLE AND CHATTANOOGA; STONES RIVER, BATTLE OF; U.S. ARMY OF THE CUMBERLAND

TURLEY, THOMAS BATTLE (1845–1910), lawyer and U.S. Senator, was born in Memphis on April 5, 1845, to Thomas and Ora Battle Turley. His uncle was Judge William B. Turley of the Tennessee Supreme Court. After attending local schools, Turley in 1861 enlisted and served in the Maynard Rifles of Memphis, a Confederate company that joined the 154th Tennessee Regiment. Turley sustained wounds at the battles of Shiloh (1862) and Atlanta (1864) before being captured in the Battle of Nashville in 1864. He was imprisoned at Camp Chase, Ohio, from December 1864 until March 1865.

After the war, Turley enrolled at the University of Virginia, where he took a law degree in 1867. He began practicing law with L.D. McKissick, a former Confederate colonel, in Memphis. When former governor Isham G. Harris teamed with them in 1876, the firm became Harris, McKissick & Turley. After McKissick moved to California, Harris and Turley remained partners until 1886, when Turley formed a partnership with Luke Edward Wright, who later

served as governor-general of the Philippines and Secretary of War.

Although occupied with his law practice, Turley was interested in Democratic politics. In the 1896 campaign, Turley supported William Jennings Bryan, the Democratic and Populist presidential nominee and his pro-silver platform. After the death of Isham G. Harris in 1897, Turley was appointed to fill the vacant U.S. Senate seat of his former law partner. The state legislature subsequently elected him to complete the term. As a senator, Turley promoted currency expansion, sought tariff reform, and opposed imperialism. In 1900, in one of his longest speeches, Turley successfully challenged the validity of the appointment of Matthew S. Quay, a Pennsylvania Republican, to a Senate seat. Turley retired from the Senate in 1901 and resumed his Memphis law practice.

Turley married Irene Raynor in 1870. They raised five children. He died on July 1, 1910, in Memphis and was buried in Elmwood Cemetery. Turley's papers are in various collections in the Tennessee State Library and Archives in Nashville.

Leonard Schlup, Akron, Ohio

SEE: ARMY OF TENNESSEE; HARRIS, ISHAM G.; MEMPHIS; TURLEY, WILLIAM B.

TURLEY, WILLIAM B. (1800–1851) was called "the most brilliant judge we ever had" by U.S. Supreme Court Justice Horace H. Lurton of Tennessee.[1] This reputation was forged during 15 years on the Tennessee Supreme Court as part of the legendary triumvirate which included Nathan Green and William B. Reese. Samuel Cole Williams termed their "joint tenure . . . the golden era of Tennessee jurisprudence."[2]

In 1808 Turley's family moved to Davidson County from Virginia. The scholarly Turley graduated with honors from Cumberland College and opened a law office at Clarksville. Although elected to the General Assembly in 1829 as a Democrat, he accepted election as the first judge of the Circuit Court of the Eleventh Judicial Circuit of West Tennessee. He quickly earned a reputation as one of the state's best trial judges.

In 1835 the General Assembly elected Turley to the new Supreme Court created under the provisions of the Constitution of 1834. His appellate opinions were infused with his creativity and love of history, poetry, and classic literature. These decisions, along with those of his fellow judges on the court, created the foundation of Tennessee jurisprudence, and many remain controlling precedent to this day.

Although Democratic leaders urged Turley to run for the U.S. Senate in 1837, his only interest was the bench, and he continued to serve on the Supreme Court until 1850. He stunned Tennessee's legal community when he resigned in order to accept the judgeship of the newly created "Common Law and Chancery Court of Memphis."

One morning in May 1851, as Turley walked down the street in Raleigh, Tennessee, he suddenly stumbled and fell. While attempting to regain his balance by the use of his walking stick, it snapped in two under his weight, and he was impaled on a jagged half that ran through his chest near his heart. He died on May 27, 1851, after five days of torment.

Russell Fowler, Memphis

CITATIONS:

(1) John W. Green, *Lives of the Judges of the Supreme Court of Tennessee, 1796–1947* (Knoxville, 1947); 103.

(2) Samuel Cole Williams, *Beginnings of West Tennessee in the Land of the Chickasaw, 1541–1841* (Johnson City, 1930); 217.

SUGGESTED READING: Samuel C. Williams, *Phases of the History of the Supreme Court of Tennessee* (1944)

SEE: GREEN, NATHAN; TENNESSEE SUPREME COURT

TURNER, TINA (1939–), one of Tennessee's most popular performers, gained international fame and attracted record-breaking audiences with her choreographed, fast-paced dancing, her musical blend of rhythm-n-blues and pop-rock, and her electrifying stage show artistry. She has won seven Grammy Awards, numerous other music awards, sold more than 50 million recordings, and made several movies, music videos, and advertisements.

Tina Turner was born Anna Mae Bullock, November 26, 1939, in Nutbush, Tennessee, to Richard and Zelma Bullock. As a child of sharecroppers, Turner harbored a dream of leaving the poverty of rural West Tennessee.

In the late nineteenth and early twentieth centuries, Nutbush and other areas north of Memphis became a mecca for local and traveling gospel, classic blues, country blues, and jazz musicians. The performers appeared in the black churches, cafes, and juke joints that sprang up in the towns and backwoods. As a child, Turner was surrounded by music and music teachers; the Nutbush experiences served her well.

By age nine, Turner was singing in the Spring Hill Baptist Church choir. During her teen years, she sang blues with popular Nutbush native Bootsie Whitelow and his String Band. Even then, her strong voice and expressive mannerisms made her one of the most sought-after local talents.

In the 1950s, Turner developed her own distinct rhythm-n-blues style. After moving to St. Louis in 1956, she auditioned for Ike Turner's "King of Rhythm Band" and became the lead vocalist; she was 17 years old. By 1960 she had married Ike Turner, who changed her name and the name of the band to "The Ike and Tina Turner Revue" and added female back-up singers, the Ikettes. Her national popularity began in 1960 with their first Sun Records recording,

A Fool in Love. She recorded with noted British producer Phil Spector in the mid-1960s. But her best work in these years came with the Ike and Tina Turner Revue and her performing style was admired and copied by many, including Mick Jagger of the Rolling Stones. In 1972 Turner's hit *Nutbush City Limits* became a classic in Britain and Europe.

The Revue became one of the most popular crossover acts of the rhythm-n-blues during the 1960s, until its breakup in 1976, following Tina and Ike's divorce. In 1980 Tina Turner teamed with Roger Davies Management, who promoted her as a solo artist and elevated her to superstardom and the title of "Queen of Rock-n-Roll." In 1984 her song *Private Dancer* sold over ten million copies worldwide. The following February, she won the Grammy Award "Record of the Year," "Song of the Year," and "Best Female Vocal Performance" for *What's Love Got To Do With It.* Her *Better Be Good To Me* collected a Grammy as "Best Female Rock Vocal." In addition to her recording achievements, Turner, who had earlier performed in the film *Tommy*, had a starring role in *Mad Max: Beyond Thunderdome.* In 1987 Turner's "Break Every Rule" world tour closed in Osaka, Japan, after playing to four million fans during 230 appearances in 25 countries. Her South American tour played to 182,000 people in the Maracana Arena in Rio de Janeiro, the largest audience ever assembled for a single performer.

In the early 1990s, Turner performed in three world tours, "Foreign Affair," "Simply the Best," and "What's Love." A film, *What's Love Got To Do With It*, based on her book *I, Tina*, which depicted her stormy relationship with Ike Turner, received popular acclaim. Her 1996 and 1997 tour was entitled "Wildest Dreams."

Sharon Norris, Nutbush Heritage Productions Inc.

SEE: HAYWOOD COUNTY; MUSIC;

TURNEY, PETER (1827–1903), State Supreme Court Justice and Governor, was born in Jasper, Marion County, in 1827, the son of Hopkins and Teresa Francis Turney. He attended local schools in Franklin County and a private school in Nashville, and read law, first in his father's office and later under W.E. Vanable. Admitted to the bar in 1848, he practiced in Winchester in partnership first with his father, and, after 1857, with his brother. When voters defeated the secession measure in February 1861, Turney led the people of Franklin County in adopting a proposal to withdraw the county from Tennessee and attach it to Alabama. As colonel of a regiment dubbed "Turney's First Tennessee," he marched to Virginia, served under General Thomas J. "Stonewall" Jackson, and was wounded three times at Fredericksburg in 1862. Soon after his recovery, Turney commanded the eastern district of Florida, surrendering there in May 1865.

At the end of the war, Turney returned to his Winchester practice. Elected to the Tennessee Supreme Court in 1870, he held office until 1886, when he was elected Chief Justice, serving until 1893. Alarmed by the agrarian movement, Bourbon Democrats nominated Turney for governor in 1892 on the slogan "Put none but Democrats on guard." Turney defeated Republican George M. Winstead and the independent candidacy of Governor John P. Buchanan.

As governor he signed legislation that ended the convict leasing system and provided lands for new prisons. Nominated for a second term in 1894, Turney narrowly lost to his Republican opponent, H. Clay Evans. Charging fraud, Turney contested the outcome and demanded a recount. The Democratic state legislature, citing voting irregularities, declared Turney the winner by over 2,000 votes. The disputed result clouded his second term, and he never again sought public office.

In 1851 Turney married Cassandra Garner, who died in 1857, leaving three children. The following year, he married Hannah F. Graham, by whom he had nine children. He died in Winchester in 1903 and was buried in Winchester Cemetery.

Leonard Schlup, Akron, Ohio

Suggested Readings: J. Eugene Lewis, "The Tennessee Gubernatorial Campaign and Election of 1894," *Tennessee Historical Quarterly* 13(1954); 99–126, 224–243, 301–328; Samuel C. Williams, *Phases of the History of the Supreme Court of Tennessee* (1944)

See: BUCHANAN, JOHN P.; EVANS, HENRY CLAY; FRANKLIN COUNTY; TENNESSEE STATE PRISON; TENNESSEE SUPREME COURT

TUSCULUM COLLEGE is the oldest college in Tennessee, having been chartered on September 9, 1794, by the legislature of the Southwest Territory. It was founded as Greeneville College by the Reverend Hezekiah Balch and Reverend Charles Coffin, and later merged with Tusculum College, founded by the Reverend Samuel Doak and the Reverend Witherspoon Doak. After years of discussion, Tusculum became one of the earliest co-educational colleges when it admitted women in 1872.

Nine structures on the campus have been listed on the National Register of Historic Places. These include President Andrew Johnson Museum and Library, built in 1841 and the oldest academic college building in Tennessee. It is the official presidential library and contains many of the personal papers and books of President Johnson, a Tusculum trustee. McCormick Hall, named for Cyrus McCormick, who invented the reaper, was built in 1887, and Virginia Hall, one of only three buildings in the South designed by architect Louis Sullivan, was built in 1901.

Prior to leaving to become president of East Tennessee College (now University of Tennessee, Knoxville), President Charles Coffin organized the college library, which according to contemporary records contained 2,000 volumes. In spite of the Civil War and heavy usage through 1910, when this special collection was withdrawn from circulation, Tusculum College still had 1,467 of those early volumes, dating back to an incunabulum printed in 1487. Authors include John Calvin, Cotton Mather, George Fox, Pliny the Younger, and books were donated by such notables as Jonathan Edwards and Thomas Jefferson.

Under the presidency of Dr. Robert Knott, who came to the college in 1989, Tusculum reconfirmed its tradition, combining education in the liberal arts and civic responsibility as "the civic arts." This approach brings together the classical civic republicanism of Cicero, for whose villa the college is named, and the Christian heritage of early American Calvinism. Students are encouraged to develop such virtues as physical and moral courage, self-control through moderation, justice (fairness), practical wisdom, faith, and compassion, with a strong emphasis on character development and "the common good." Following the practice of the Doak founders, students enroll in one course at a time in a concentrated schedule of half-day classes for 18 days, a practice which permits extended community service projects and field trips.

The curriculum includes a number of multidisciplinary courses, while small class size encourages discussion among faculty and students. Graduating students are required to be competent in 14 areas: analytical reading, writing, mathematics, computer literacy, public speaking, critical analysis, awareness of religious heritage, arts and society, scientific inquiry, historical mindedness, environmental awareness, self-knowledge, civility, and ethics of social responsibility. The faculty is responsible for all academic activities, and all staff members teach classes.

Tusculum College serves the community with its professional studies program, which takes undergraduate and graduate programs into East Tennessee communities to help working men and women earn degrees. By taking these classes at night and at convenient locations, adult students increase their knowledge in new fields or in their chosen profession.

E. Alvin Gerhardt, Jr., Tusculum College

See: DOAK, SAMUEL; EDUCATION, HIGHER; GREENE COUNTY; JOHNSON, ANDREW; SOUTHWEST TERRITORY

TYSON, LAWRENCE (1861–1929), Tennessee's only World War I general, was born on a plantation near Greenville, North Carolina, on July 4, 1861. Tyson won a competition for appointment to West Point, and graduated from the military academy in 1883. Lieutenant Tyson served several years in Wyoming, Arizona, and Kansas and engaged in the Apache wars against Geronimo and his followers.

Tyson married Bettie McGhee of Knoxville, the daughter of railroad president Charles McClung McGhee. In 1891 McGhee secured an appointment for Tyson as professor of military science and tactics at the University of Tennessee in order to bring his daughter home. While on the faculty, Tyson took a degree in law and resigned his position in 1895 in order to practice law in Knoxville.

At the beginning of the Spanish-American War, President William McKinley appointed Tyson Colonel of the Sixth Regiment U.S. Volunteer Infantry. Tyson recruited this unit largely from Tennessee and Kentucky and served with them in Puerto Rico as commander. He was mustered out of service in 1899 with the rank of brigadier general.

In 1917 Tyson volunteered for military service again, and President Woodrow Wilson reactivated his commission, although he was 50 years old. Tyson assumed command of the 59th Brigade of the 30th National Guard Division (Old Hickory Division). Landing at Calais, the 59th were the first American troops to enter Belgium in July 1918. In September the 30th was sent to the Somme and placed in front of the Hindenburg line at its strongest point on the Cambrai-St. Quentin Canal. On September 29, the Ameri-cans in cooperation with British troops attacked the Hindenburg line. Advancing through a heavy fog behind a line of tanks, the Americans moved across the three trench lines of the Hindenburg defenses, an advance of three or four miles. They captured the entire Hindenburg system of that sector, including the tunnel of the St. Quentin canal and the German troops it housed. They defeated two German divisions and captured approximately 1,500 soldiers.

The *Nashville Banner* claimed that the 59th Brigade had been the first unit to cross the canal, therefore the first Allied unit to break the Hindenburg line. The brigade of 8,000 men lost 1,879 killed or wounded. Nine men received Medals of Honor, perhaps the largest number awarded to a single brigade. Tyson received the Distinguished Service Medal.

After the war, Tyson returned to Knoxville to his business interests and politics. He owned several textile mills and coal companies, was a director of two Knoxville banks, and in 1924 purchased the Knoxville *Sentinel*. That year, Tyson was elected U.S. Senator from Tennessee. He died on August 24, 1929, and is buried in Old Gray Cemetery in Knoxville.

W. Calvin Dickinson, Tennessee Technological University

SEE: KNOXVILLE; SPANISH-AMERICAN WAR; WORLD WAR I

U

UNICOI COUNTY, located in the mountains of upper East Tennessee, covers approximately 186 square miles, of which approximately 50 percent is owned by the U.S. government. "Unicoi" is a Cherokee word meaning white, hazy, fog-like, or fog draped. The county's principal waterway, the Nolichucky River, originates at the point where the North Toe River joins the Cane River in North Carolina. Nolichucky Gorge is now a popular center for white water rafting.

Settlers arrived in the late 1770s and quickly established farms and churches. The area that is now Unicoi County was part of Washington and Carter counties until March 23, 1875, when the Tennessee General Assembly created the new county. The county court took office in January 1876. Erwin, which was centrally located, became the county seat. The town had existed under various names including Unaka (1832), Longmire (1840), and Vanderbilt (1876). In December 1879 the name was changed to Ervin, in honor of David J.N. Ervin, who had donated 15 acres for the county seat. A mistake by postal officials, which was never corrected, recorded the name as Erwin.

Construction and maintenance of county roads and bridges proved to be a major problem for the new county. Between 1916 and 1919 macadamized roads replaced second and third class roads. Today, a modern four-lane highway links Unicoi County to Interstate 81 and to the North Carolina state line. This highway will become a part of Interstate 26 when the North Carolina link is finished in 2000.

The 1879 schools report listed one frame and 11 log school buildings in Unicoi County. Today the county has excellent schools, and school enrollment has grown from 802 in 1880 to 2,580 in 1997.

The county boasts a fully accredited Hill-Burton hospital, which opened in 1953 and was the first hospital in upper East Tennessee to install a centralized oxygen system. A library, established in 1921 and in continuous operation since, became a part of the Watauga Regional Library System in 1959. In December 1997 the library moved into facilities in the newly renovated historic Clinchfield depot.

Unicoi County experienced rapid growth once railroad construction began in 1886. Several railroads have operated trains in the county—Charleston, Cincinnati and Chicago, 1886; Ohio River and Charleston, 1893; South and Western Railway, 1902; Carolina, Clinchfield, and Ohio, 1908; and Seaboard, which became CSX, 1983. Of these lines the Clinchfield is the most important. It ran 277 miles from Elkhorn City, Kentucky, to Spartanburg, South Carolina, covering five states. Rails cross four mountain ranges and five major watersheds with 80 bridges and 55 tunnels.

Arguably, Erwin's best-known event was the hanging of an elephant in 1916. On September 12, 1916, when the circus played in Kingsport, Mary the elephant killed her trainer. Authorities decided to dispose of the elephant, but all available guns proved inadequate to the task. Authorities then requested that railroad officials hang the elephant from the large derrick used to clear train wrecks. Mary was brought to the Erwin railroad yard and hanged with a chain.

In 1897 a U.S. Fish Hatchery was established in Unicoi County and celebrated 100 years of continuous operation in 1997. The original superintendent's house has been converted to a county Heritage Museum containing memorabilia, including a fine collection of Blue Ridge pottery, enjoyed by local residents and tourists.

The Clinchfield remained the major employer until 1916 when Southern Potteries opened in Erwin. The pottery specialized in hand-painted dinnerware called Blue Ridge China. During plant construction, local people learned hand-painting, but many workers came from Ohio and West Virginia. Peak employment reached more than 1,000 during the 1940s. After World War II, imports slowly brought a curtailment in production, and the plant closed in 1957. Hand-painted dinnerware from Southern Potteries has been valuable to today's collectors.

Just as the Southern Pottery closed, Davison Chemical Company (now Nuclear Fuel Services, Inc.) located in Erwin. The plant processed uranium and thorium products and is now the major supplier of fuel for nuclear powered Navy ships. Other industries also based operation in Unicoi County, including Georgia Pacific, Hoover Precision Products, NN Ball & Roller, Morrill Motors, Specialty Tire Company, and several plastics manufacturers.

Hilda Britt Padgett and Betty Washburn Stevens, Erwin
SUGGESTED READINGS: Hilda Britt Padgett, *The Erwin Nine* (1993); Roxie A. Masters, *The Valley of the Long Hunters* (1969)
SEE: CHEROKEE NATIONAL FOREST; MURDEROUS MARY; RAILWAY, CAROLINA, CLINCHFIELD & OHIO; SOUTHERN POTTERIES, INC.

UNION COUNTY was formed in 1850 from portions of Anderson, Campbell, Claiborne, Grainger, and Knox counties. The enabling legislation was initially passed January 3, 1850; due to legal challenges and complications the county was not formally created until January 23, 1856. Shortly thereafter, Union County began functioning as a county, and county court minutes and records have since been kept.

The county name derives from two possible sources. Dr. Robert H. White, former State Historian, believed that Union County was so named because it was a union of five segments of adjoining counties. Former Union County Schools Superintendent William H. Thomas suggested in 1961, however, that the name reflected the area's support for the federal union in the political debates of the period of the county's creation.

In 1850 a small community called Liberty was near the center of the proposed new county and became the county seat. Due to the willingness of a young, brilliant lawyer named Horace Maynard to successfully defend the county in the litigation opposing the county formation, the town was renamed Maynardville. The county high school bears the name Horace Maynard High School in his honor.

Union County is bordered to the west by Anderson and Campbell counties, to the north by Claiborne County, to the east by Grainger County, and to the south by Knox County. The county is approximately 223.6 square miles in size and has three county census divisions—Luttrell, Maynardville, and Sharps Chapel—as well as three municipalities—Luttrell, Maynardville, and Plainview.

The Norris Dam project and the impoundment of Norris Reservoir had a tremendous impact on Union County. The project created jobs, trained people, and improved living conditions; at the same time, it displaced many people whose homes and property were lying below pool level or in the floodplain. Former Norris Reservoir residents still meet annually and make pilgrimages to their former homesites, cemeteries, and landmarks that can be visited when the lake level is down.

Since the construction of Norris Dam, the population and economic conditions have changed significantly. In 1930 most of the people lived and worked on farms; most were subsistence operations that barely supported the family. Over the next 20 years large numbers of people left the farms for non-farm jobs outside the county. The last 20 years have brought even greater change as the county became more closely tied to the Knoxville metropolitan area. New businesses brought new non-farm jobs into the county, and more and more people commuted to the Knoxville job market. For example, in 1990 ten new manufacturing plants located in Union County. At present about 85 percent of the work force commute to jobs outside the county. The growth of these non-farm jobs has produced a substantial population growth; the county grew from 13,694 in 1990 to 14,607 in 1994—an increase of 6.7 percent. The county is enriched by 263.6 miles of shoreline on Norris Lake and the Big Ridge State Park. Tourism and recreation continue to strengthen the economy of the county.

Yet, the county remains poorer than most in Tennessee. The county per capita income in 1989 was $8,351 compared to the Tennessee per capita income of $12,255. Although family incomes continue to rise, 18.2 percent of families remained in poverty in 1989. In 1990 the proportion of the county's adult population that attended fewer than nine years of school was 37 percent—more than twice the state average of 16 percent. The portion of the population that had a bachelor's, graduate, or professional degree was 4.5 percent. Persons 16 to 19 years of age, not enrolled in school and not high school graduates, made up 21 percent of the county population.

Union has given the U.S. Congress two members: Lafayette Ledgerwood and J. Will Taylor. Additionally, Union County is well known for its musical heritage; four of its sons are now known throughout the world—Roy Acuff, Chet Atkins, Carl Smith, and Kenny Chesney. Lois Johnson, Hilda Kitts Harrill, and Melba Kitts Greene are among the best known women entertainers.

Community organizations such as the Union County Business and Professional Association with more than 150 members, Optimist Club, Friends of Maynardville Library, Family Community Education Group, Boy and Girl Scouts, and Four-H clubs have been formed recently and are bringing about positive change in Union County.

Bonnie Heiskell Peters, Union County Historian

SUGGESTED READINGS: Winnie P. McDonald, *Our Union County Families* (1992); Bonnie H. Peters, *Union County Faces of War* (1995)

SEE: ACUFF, ROY; ATKINS, CHESTER B.; BIG RIDGE STATE PARK; BUTCHER, JACOB F.; MAYNARD, HORACE; NORRIS DAM; TENNESSEE VALLEY AUTHORITY

UNION PLANTERS BANK, the oldest existing bank in Memphis, traces its origins to the DeSoto Insurance and Trust Company, chartered in 1857. William Farrington, president of DeSoto Insurance, converted the company to banking in 1869. The company became Union and Planters Bank of Memphis, a name recalling two trusted names of the past: the Branch Union bank and the Branch Planters Bank. The bank's board of directors included some of Memphis's most talented and powerful businessmen, many of them cotton merchants. They elected Farrington as president and William Williamson, a planter and financier, as vice-president. Samuel P. Read, the only banking professional, served as cashier.

Union and Planters opened on September 1, 1869, with capital of $671,300 and a staff of four. It took over Peoples' Bank in 1869 and, in 1870, moved to a new location at 11 Madison and became the West Tennessee Depository for state funds. With 1870 dividends of 6 percent, the new bank was off to an extremely strong start. The bank survived the yellow fever epidemics of the 1870s and the bank panics of 1873 and 1893, though its board of directors changed frequently. Amid suspicions of illegal use of bank funds, the board replaced Farrington with Charles W. Goyer in 1873. Allison C. "A.C." Treadwell, a cotton agent, replaced Goyer and served until 1885. Napoleon Hill, a cotton factor and president of the Cotton Exchange, served as president from 1885 to 1897.

During the first three decades of the twentieth century, Union Planters acquired several smaller banks and became the dominant banking institution in the city. After serving the bank as cashier for 28 years, Samuel P. Read served as president from 1897 to 1915. During his tenure, Union Planters acquired the Tennessee Trust Company, raised deposits to almost $5 million, and moved into the 15-story building next door. Renamed the Union and Planters Bank and Trust Company, the bank had the second largest deposits of any bank in the city.

In 1917 Union Planters became the first Tennessee bank to join the new Federal Reserve System. By 1919, having recently acquired Mercantile National Bank, Union Planters was the largest bank in Memphis with 167 employees and deposits of $20 million. During the 1920s the bank opened a branch and purchased North Memphis Savings Bank. Frank Hayden of Guaranty Bank and Trust became president of Union Planters when it acquired Guaranty in 1924. The growing bank moved to a 12-story building at the southeast corner of Front and Madison, its headquarters since 1924.

Conditions again changed in 1928 with a run on the bank's deposits. Then in 1929 Nashville's Luke Lea and Rogers Caldwell bought controlling interest in Union Planters. The stock market crash of 1929 destroyed Caldwell's banking empire and American National Bank of Nashville acquired a large interest in the bank. Despite the depression, Union Planters remained relatively strong and contributed to the survival of Memphis Bank and Commerce. During the 1930s, Union Planters qualified for federal depositors insurance and the stockholders regained control of the bank's operations.

Union Planters benefited from post-World War II prosperity and opened 11 branches between 1940 and 1951. By the 1960s it was the largest bank in the Mid-South, ranking 44th in the nation in deposits. During the early 1970s deposits topped $1 billion. In the later 1970s and 1980s, crises produced by excessive loan write-offs resulted in a reorganization into Union Planters National Bank and Union Planters Corporation, a holding company. By 1990, under the leadership of Benjamin W. Rawlins, J. Armistead Smith, and Jackson W. Moore, Union Planters had assets of $4 billion and turned a profit of $22.7 million. Union Planters continues to be a financial leader in Memphis and the Mid-South.

Anne-Leslie Owens, Tennessee Historical Society

SUGGESTED READING: John E. Harkins, *Metropolis of the American Nile* (1991)

SEE: CALDWELL, ROGERS; HILL, NAPOLEON; LEA, LUKE; MEMPHIS

UNION UNIVERSITY, located in Jackson, is a private institution of higher learning affiliated with the Tennessee Baptist Convention and traces its lineage through two earlier institutions. Jackson Male Academy opened in 1823, and was chartered by the state in 1825. It offered a college preparatory course for the children of Jackson's more affluent citizens. In 1844 the school was reorganized and rechartered as West Tennessee College in order to gain eligibility for public land provided for in an 1806 law that settled a public lands dispute between Tennessee, North Carolina, and the federal government. In 1846 the federal government provided the state with title to certain public lands for the purpose of endowing West Tennessee College.

West Tennessee College operated until the Civil War, when both Confederate and Union troops used its facilities as a military hospital. After the war, classes reopened and continued until 1874, when the

Tennessee Baptists acquired the campus. In an effort to foster statewide unity, representatives from the General Association of Baptists in Middle Tennessee, the East Tennessee Baptist General Association, and the West Tennessee Baptist Convention met in Humboldt on March 15, 1873, and adopted a resolution favoring the establishment of a first-class college. On April 10, 1874, an Educational Convention met in Murfreesboro and appointed a committee to select a location for the proposed college. After considering several sites, the committee recommended the acceptance of the Jackson offer, which included the buildings, grounds, and endowment funds of West Tennessee College.

The new institution, named Southwestern Baptist University, opened its doors to preparatory students in September 1874, and college courses followed the next year. The General Assembly granted a charter in June 1875. On September 17, 1907, the Board of Trustees changed the institution's name to Union University, out of sentiment for an older institution of that name, which operated in Murfreesboro from 1842 to 1873. Many of the early faculty and trustees of Southwestern Baptist University were either associated with, or graduated from, this former Union University.

In the years since the school adopted its present name, the institution has maintained its strong liberal arts program and distinctive evangelical emphasis in the face of many challenges. A major fire on January 20, 1912, destroyed College Hall and Powell Chapel. In 1925 the Board of Trustees deeded all Union University property to the Tennessee Baptist Convention and secured a new charter. Hall-Moody Junior College, located in Martin, was consolidated with Union, when it closed its doors to students in 1927. In 1975 the university abandoned its College Street campus in favor of a new campus located in North Jackson along U.S. Highway 45 By-Pass.

Union alumni include the former U.S. Senator and Supreme Court Justice Howell E. Jackson; progressive era judge and founder of the juvenile justice court system in America, Benjamin Barr Lindsey; and John Dancy, senior correspondent with NBC News.

Steven L. Baker, Union University

SUGGESTED READING: Richard Hiram Ward, *A History of Union University* (1975)

SEE: EDUCATION, HIGHER; JACKSON; JACKSON, HOWELL E.

UNITED CONFEDERATE VETERANS ASSOCIATION (TENNESSEE).

In 1888 Baton Rouge druggist Leon Jastremski returned from a visit to the annual reunion of the Grand Army of the Republic (GAR) with an idea to form a similar fraternal organization for Confederate veterans. Simultaneously, a Chattanooga businessman, J.F. Shipp, sought the first national military park at Chickamauga. Together, these men invited former Confederate cavalrymen to

Tennessee officers, UCV, July 30, 1921.

TSLA. JOHN P. HICKMAN COLLECTION. PHOTOGRAPH BY THUSS

a reunion and fund raiser in New Orleans on February 13, 1888. Former horse soldiers representing local veterans' societies from Tennessee, Mississippi, and Louisiana deemed the gathering a resounding success, and laid plans to host a broader convention the following year. In June 1889, 52 delegates, representing nine separate veterans' associations, met again in New Orleans and founded the United Confederate Veterans' Association (UCV). Their constitution of 14 articles defined the organization's purpose as "strictly social, literary, historical, and benevolent." The delegates unanimously selected John B. Gordon of Georgia to serve as commander-in-chief, a position he held until his death in 1904. Other officers included Adjutant General George Moorman, Chaplain General J. William Jones, and Quartermaster General J.F. Shipp. Continuity in leadership provided the early UCV with stability and strength.

Over 150,000 Confederate veterans eventually joined the association in one of 1,850 "camps," indicating a grassroots strength to which Tennessee was no exception. Many former Confederate regiments already met informally at annual picnics across Middle and West Tennessee. By the end of the 1870s, some groups had amalgamated into larger organizations with more formal leadership structure and official programming that stressed the importance of the Confederate experience. This avid association building lent itself favorably to urban settings, and Nashville veterans formed Frank Cheatham Bivouac #1. Originally, the monthly meetings in Pythian Hall recorded an average attendance of 50 men. Many of

Nashville's most prominent ex-Confederates flocked to join the organization. By 1900 the Bivouac had swelled to 345 members and ranked first in the state among UCV camps.

In November 1885 members of Cheatham Bivouac (W.D. Gale, R.H. Dudley, Charles D. Elliott, Reverend J.H. McNeilly, William H. Jackson, and Frank Porterfield) played a conspicuous role in revamping a statewide veterans organization known as the Tennessee Confederate Memorial and Historical Association. The men expanded the original goal of funding a commemorative monument to Confederate valor and included plans to care for Confederate graves and bring living veterans into closer fraternal relations through benevolent programs for ill comrades, indigent widows, and destitute orphans. They also hoped to encourage the preparation of historical accounts of the war that would honor and vindicate Confederate actions. To meet these goals, they formed the Association of Confederate Soldiers, Tennessee, which became the first chartered organization of its kind in the South. The association met in annual state reunions that rotated among host cities in each of the three Grand Divisions. The last general UCV reunion was held in 1951.

John A. Simpson, Kelso, Washington

SEE: CONFEDERATE SOLDIERS' HOME; GRAND ARMY OF THE REPUBLIC; NASHVILLE NO. 1, UDC

UNITED METHODIST PUBLISHING HOUSE. The first Methodist publishing efforts began as the Methodist Book Concern in Philadelphia in 1789 with a loan of $600. Traveling preachers known as circuit riders delivered its publications.. The Concern later relocated to New York City and opened a second office in Cincinnati.

In 1844 sectional divisions over slavery split the Methodist Episcopal Church into the Methodist Episcopal Church, North, and the Methodist Episcopal Church, South. Southern Methodists wanted their own religious publishing house and took their battle all the way to the Supreme Court to obtain the right to publish their own religious literature. Atlanta, New Orleans, St. Louis, Louisville, and Memphis all vied to be chosen as the location of the new publishing house. Nashville was selected on May 18, 1854, at a general conference of the Methodist Episcopal Church, South held at Columbus, Georgia. The Nashville City Council was jubilant and declared that the property should never be taxed, although the denomination voluntarily chose to pay taxes on all its secular businesses. The Tennessee General Assembly granted a charter to the institution on February 26, 1856.

With money raised by subscription, Southern Methodists converted an old riverfront sugar drainery and warehouse that fronted on the Public Square.

The operation contained facilities for printing on six presses; binding; composing, drying, and pressing sheets; folding; mailing; and sales. A bookstore opened in December 1854, and book manufacturing began the following February.

The Nashville operation was the first major publishing house in the South and was well received. John Early became the first book agent and provided skilled leadership in guiding the new concern. New publications produced by the southern operation were the *Ladies Companion,* the *Sunday School Visitor,* and the *Quarterly Review.* The southern Methodist Publishing House also followed the lead of its northern competitor and published books in German and Spanish. Circuit riders continued to pack their saddlebags or new buggies with books, pamphlets, and magazines, and bookstores or depositories were established.

Both northern and southern publishing houses continued operations even after the Civil War began. When the city of Nashville surrendered to Federal troops in February 1862, the Union forces commandeered the Southern Methodist Publishing House for government printing. Part of the building was used as a stables and a harness shop for the remainder of the war. By the end of the war, the plant was in shambles. Southern Methodists retooled and began to publish again. Thirty years later, the United States Congress reimbursed the publishing house $288,000 for wartime damages.

Like other southern institutions, the church felt the financial stress of postwar Reconstruction. The Southern Book Concern could barely pay its employees and issued promissory scrip instead of money. Retired book agent John B. McFerrin was recalled when bankruptcy threatened to end church publishing. He traveled throughout the South selling Publishing House bonds to keep the Concern operating.

In 1872 fire destroyed the Southern House. The Methodists acquired additional land and with subscriptions from Nashvillians, financed a grand new building at 346 Public Square. The building rose seven stories from the riverside and four from the east side of the square.

A new concern with education in the South and with self-improvement nationally created new markets for the Southern House's publications. A summer training opportunity for Methodist adults in Chautauqua Lake, New York, inaugurated a form of adult education that came to be known as "Chautauqua." The movement used correspondence courses and circuit speakers to provide scientific, literary, and historical information as well as religious education. These educational and self-improvement movements helped foster a new era of cooperation between the Methodist Episcopal Church, North and the Methodist Episcopal Church, South and between their publishing concerns as the turn of the century approached.

In 1906 the Southern Methodist Publishing House moved all operations to new facilities at 810 Broadway. The concern built a new printing facility at 815 Demonbreun Street in Nashville in 1924. The Methodist denominations jointly produced two hymnals during the early part of the century. In 1939 the Methodist Episcopal Church, North; the Methodist Episcopal Church, South; and Methodist Protestant Church reunited, and Nashville was chosen as the site for a consolidated publishing facility—The Methodist Publishing House. In 1957 the House moved to 201 Eighth Avenue South. A merger with the United Brethren Church in 1968 created The United Methodist Church. The United Methodist Publishing House remains one of the foundation blocks of the Nashville publishing industry.

E. Michael Fleenor, Tennessee Historical Commission

SEE: PUBLISHING; RELIGION

UNITED STATES ARMY CORPS OF ENGINEERS,

first established as an arm of the Continental Army, has both military and civil missions. Since the Revolutionary War, it has provided topographic reconnaissance and mapping, fortification design and construction, and related services for American armies overseas and at home. In 1824 the work of the Corps in surveying and improving transportation logistics for frontier armies led to its congressional assignment for the improvement of navigation on American rivers and harbors.

Early engineers surveyed and mapped fortification and transportation routes for the advancing army, and these maps and routes proved useful to Tennessee pioneers. Based upon these surveys, Congress approved navigation improvements on the Mississippi, Cumberland, and Tennessee rivers before the Civil War and assigned the work to the Corps of Engineers. Using open channel clearance engineering before 1860, the Corps improved the entire course of the Mississippi River along Tennessee's western border, the Cumberland River from its mouth past Nashville into Kentucky, and the Tennessee River from the Alabama line upstream to Knoxville.

During the Civil War, Confederate army engineers fortified the rivers at Forts Henry and Donelson and established defensive positions at Tennessee's major cities. After Union forces advanced into Tennessee, their army engineers built elaborate fortifications for the defense of Nashville, Knoxville, Chattanooga, and other cities, constructed new railroads for logistics and defenses for railroad bridges, while also conducting reconnaissance and mapping for use of the armies.

During the postwar era, when Congress authorized a massive program for navigation improve-ments, the Corps again applied open-channel clearance engineering to the entire course of the Mississippi and Tennessee rivers, most of the Cumberland, and many of their tributaries. During this era, the Corps also cleared fallen trees, or "snags," and other obstructions from the Clinch, Powell, Nolichucky, French Broad, Elk, Duck, Red, Obey, Obion, and other streams to provide market access for Tennessee's agricultural, forest, and mineral resources.

Although open-channel clearance and dredging remained the Corps' method for improving Lower Mississippi River navigation, it adopted canalization for the Tennessee and Cumberland rivers near the end of the nineteenth century. To provide a minimum six-foot depth for steamboat navigation, the Corps built 15 low timbercrib dams and masonry locks on the Cumberland from its mouth to points upstream of Nashville, ending this project in 1924, when steamboat commerce died. On the Tennessee River, near the turn of the century, the Corps built two canals with locks around the major obstructions to steamboat commerce at Muscle Shoals and Colbert Shoals in Alabama, relying on open-channel clearance on river sections in Tennessee.

During the 1920s the Corps conducted comprehensive studies of the Cumberland, Tennessee, and Mississippi river basins, planning the development of nine-foot channels for towboat-barge commerce, along with flood control, hydroelectric power generation, and allied programs. The pioneering multiple-purpose project was Wilson Dam at Muscle Shoals on the Tennessee River. It was built during the 1920s as one of the nation's first projects to provide flood control and hydropower benefits in addition to navigation. The Corps was implementing its comprehensive plans for the Tennessee River, initiating construction of the Wheeler Dam in Alabama and Norris Dam in East Tennessee, when Congress created the Tennessee Valley Authority (TVA) in 1933, and assigned comprehensive development to TVA. Since the Corps had statutory responsibility for navigation, it retained this function on the Tennessee River and the lockmasters at TVA dams are employed by the Corps of Engineers.

During the 1940s the Corps managed comprehensive development in the Cumberland Valley and Ohio Valley. For flood control, recreation, and hydropower production in the Cumberland Valley, the Corps built multiple-purpose dams—Barkley, J. Percy Priest, Old Hickory, Cordell Hull, Dale Hollow, Center Hill, and others. The Southeastern Power Commission purchased electric power produced at the Corps' Cumberland valley dams and sold it at wholesale rates to TVA for distribution to local utility systems.

During World War II the Corps purchased land and constructed military installations, munitions plants, and airfields throughout Tennessee. Fort Campbell is the largest of these bases still under army management. Others, such as Sewart Air Force Base at Smyrna, were later returned to civilian management.

The Corps created special Engineer Districts during World War II and later for unique projects. Its Kingsport District managed the construction of Holston Ordnance Works for RDX projection, and its Manhattan District purchased the land and managed construction of the Oak Ridge plants and laboratories for nuclear weapons production. After the war, its Tullahoma District built facilities for aerodynamic wind-tunnel testing at the Arnold Engineering and Development Center.

The Corps essentially completed its multipurpose dam construction program during the 1970s, and the major development completed during the 1980s was the Tennessee-Tombigbee Waterway, connecting the Tennessee River, near Pickwick Dam, with the port of Mobile, Alabama. Shortening the route to the seaboard by hundreds of miles, this waterway aimed to improve Tennessee's access to international markets, but it has yet to achieve the barge tonnages predicted before its construction.

Since the creation of TVA in 1933, Tennessee has been served by two Engineer Districts, one headquartered at Nashville for the Cumberland River and the other at Memphis for the Mississippi River and its West Tennessee tributaries.

Leland R. Johnson, Clio Research Institute

SUGGESTED READINGS: Floyd M. Clay, *A Century on the Mississippi: A History of the Memphis District, U.S. Army Corps of Engineers* (1976); Leland R. Johnson, *Engineers on the Twin Rivers: A History of the Nashville District, Corps of Engineers* (1978)

SEE: ARNOLD ENGINEERING AND DEVELOPMENT CENTER; CUMBERLAND RIVER SYSTEM; FORT CAMPBELL; FORT NEGLEY; FORTRESS ROSECRANS; HOLSTON ORDNANCE WORKS; MISSISSIPPI RIVER SYSTEM; NORRIS DAM; OAK RIDGE; TENNESSEE RIVER SYSTEM; TENNESSEE-TOMBIGBEE WATERWAY; TENNESSEE VALLEY AUTHORITY; WORLD WAR II

UNITED STATES ARMY OF THE CUMBERLAND.

During the Civil War, Union forces in Tennessee were part of several different federal armies, primarily the Army of the Cumberland, the Army of the Ohio, and the Army of the Tennessee. An army from the early Department of the Missouri, under the command of General U.S. Grant, captured Forts Henry and Donelson in February 1862. By the time of the Battle of Shiloh that April, however, most of this force was known as the Army of the Tennessee, under Grant's command.

The Army of Ohio, once part of the Department of the Ohio under the command of General Don Carlos Buell, also participated at Shiloh. From this force, after the Battle of Perryville, Kentucky, in the fall of 1862, would emerge the Army of the Cumberland.

In late October, command of the army was taken away from Buell and given to General William S. Rosecrans. Upon his arrival in Nashville in November 1862, Rosecrans brought news that the Union forces gathered there would now be known as the Army of the Cumberland. The Army of the Ohio in name would resurface in 1863 as the army under the command of General Ambrose Burnside in East Tennessee. This force won the Battle of Knoxville and successfully defended the upper East Tennessee region for the remainder of the war.

From November 1862 to November 1863, the Army of the Cumberland would be the primary Union force in the state, participating in the battles of Stones River and Chattanooga in Tennessee and the Battle of Chickamauga in Georgia, and conducting the brilliant Tullahoma Campaign of 1863. After the loss at Chickamauga in September 1863, however, command of the Army of the Cumberland passed from Rosecrans to Major General George H. Thomas, whose nickname was the "Rock of Chickamauga." Thomas's army joined the Army of the Tennessee, led by William T. Sherman, during the Chattanooga battles of November 1863, a successful campaign under the overall leadership of U.S. Grant. Thomas's forces also fought in the Atlanta campaign of 1864 as part of General William T. Sherman's massive invasion force.

When Confederate General John Bell Hood launched his Tennessee invasion in the fall of 1864, Sherman detached corps from the old Army of the Cumberland, and from the Army of the Tennessee, to buttress General George H. Thomas's army in Nashville. These forces successfully defended the Union occupation of Nashville at the battles of Spring Hill, Franklin, and Nashville in late 1864. Thomas, whose reputation as a field commander is indelibly linked with the name of the Army of the Cumberland, led the final devastating Union assault at Nashville, an attack which all but destroyed the Confederate Army of Tennessee.

The Union armies in Tennessee were known for their several excellent generals, especially Grant, Sherman, Thomas, John A. McClernand, Charles F. Smith, and Philip M. Sheridan, who not only played a significant role in Tennessee but in Georgia, Mississippi, and Virginia as well as other U.S. military campaigns after the war.

Carroll Van West, Middle Tennessee State University

SEE: CHICKAMAUGA AND CHATTANOOGA, BATTLES OF; CIVIL WAR; FRANKLIN, BATTLE OF; KNOXVILLE, BATTLE OF; NASHVILLE, BATTLE OF; SHILOH, BATTLE OF; STONES RIVER, BATTLE OF; THOMAS, GEORGE H.; TULLAHOMA CAMPAIGN

UNITED STATES CHRISTIAN COMMISSION, a

project of the Young Men's Christian Association, sent almost 5,000 volunteers to the battlefields and military hospitals of the Civil War. Their purpose was to care for the spiritual and physical needs of Union soldiers, which included rescue and transportation of the wounded, nursing, and pastoral duties. Nashville became a major center for Christian Commission activities, where as many as 50 volunteers worked under the supervision of agent Edward P. Smith and his wife Hannah during the campaigns of the Army of the Cumberland. Volunteers provided first aid and loaded the injured on boxcars following the Battle of Franklin and searched for wounded men after the Battle of Nashville. At Chickamauga, one agent was captured and sent to Libby Prison in Richmond. Commission volunteers also helped with the wounded at Fort Donelson, Shiloh, Murfreesboro, Cleveland, and Chattanooga. One of these workers, Dwight L. Moody, became a prominent evangelist.

In Nashville, the volunteers served as nurses and chaplains in military hospitals, but also made two unique contributions: the Special Diet Kitchen Service and the Lending Library System. In the Kitchen Service, army cooks prepared more palatable hospital diets under the watchful supervision of Commission women. This was particularly important since Nashville had 25 military hospitals with thousands of sick and wounded men, who could not tolerate the poorly prepared fare offered by military chefs. The Library Program developed an extensive plan to bring secular and religious reading materials to Army camps in the field and to the hospitals and reading rooms of the city. These two programs, the diet service under Mrs. Annie Wittenmyer and the library system under Chaplain Joseph C. Thomas, proved so successful that they were later applied throughout all Federal army and navy commands during the Civil War.

The work of the Christian Commission has been little known or appreciated by Civil War historians who have generally ascribed almost all civilian relief work to the United States Sanitary Commission. The Sanitary Commission was a larger and more secular organization that relied on many paid agents, rather than a mostly volunteer system. Although the two agencies battled at the national level, they cooperated well in Tennessee. The Christian Commission carried out its most successful work in Middle and East Tennessee, ministering to Union troops, wounded Confederates, and civilian refugees alike.

Ralph C. Gordon, Michigan State University

Suggested Readings: William A. Armstrong, *A Friend to God's Poor: Edward Parmelee Smith* (1993); Ralph C. Gordon, "Nashville and the U.S. Christian Commission in the Civil War" *Tennessee Historical Quarterly* 50(1996): 98–111

See: CIVIL WAR; OCCUPATION, CIVIL WAR

UNITED STATES COLORED TROOPS (U.S.C.T.) in

Tennessee experienced every facet of war between

1863 and 1865. In the spring of 1863 General Lorenzo Thomas was appointed Commissioner for the Organization of Colored Troops for the Union army in Tennessee. He began actively raising black regiments in Memphis and had 3,000 troops by June. These first regiments were designated by state and race, such as the First Tennessee Volunteers infantry regiment, A.D. (African Descent). But in the spring of 1864 the Union army grouped Tennessee black troops into numbered regiments, such as the 55th U.S.C.T. By war's end, Thomas's organization had raised nearly 24,000 black troops from Tennessee and other states, filling 22 infantry regiments and eight artillery units.

Black troops contributed in a variety of ways. They met the army's occupational and logistical needs—monitoring conquered territory, watching white southerners, and assisting in the upkeep of contraband camps. Initially fearful of allowing black troops in battle, the Union army employed them as laborers, construction workers, and guards. U.S.C.T. regiments supervised black women and children crowded into disease-ridden camps outside Tennessee cities. They garrisoned forts in Tennessee, north Alabama, and north Georgia, and guarded prisoners of war. They helped recruit additional black troops. They built fortifications in Middle and West Tennessee, foraged, and performed an array of menial tasks. The U.S.C.T. guarded railroads from guerrilla raids; this duty, in fact, introduced Tennessee black troops to combat.

In December 1863, at Moscow, Tennessee, the 61st U.S.C.T. caught General Stephen D. Lee's Confederate cavalry trying to rip up the railroad near the Wolf River. A fight began, and the 61st impressively repulsed Lee's troops. Certainly the most infamous battle waged by the U.S.C.T. occurred at Fort Pillow on April 12, 1864. Confederate General Nathan Bedford Forrest invaded West Tennessee and surrounded the Mississippi River fort. Forrest's troops numbered three times the garrison of approximately 560 men. When the Confederate call for surrender was refused, Forrest's troops stormed the ramparts, entered the fort, and massacred Union troops as they tried to surrender. Blacks incurred casualties of more than 60 percent, most of whom died. The Fort Pillow massacre galvanized the U.S.C.T resolve to fight their way to freedom and stigmatized Forrest.

For the rest of 1864, the U.S.C.T., namely those regiments stationed in Memphis, fought alongside their white comrades in skirmishes against Forrest's cavalry and helped harness the general's raiders. From June to November, the U.S.C.T. participated in several engagements in Mississippi and Alabama in pursuit of Forrest. At Brice's Crossroads and Tupelo, Mississippi (June-July), Athens, Alabama (September), and Pulaski, Tennessee (September), U.S.C.T. encountered Forrest; with each engagement their combat ability improved. At Pulaski, the 14th U.S.C.T. repulsed Forrest's Confederates and gained redemption for the earlier massacre. By December 1864 the U.S.C.T. fought in heavy combat alongside white Union troops at the Battle of Nashville, where they were credited with helping to repel the Confederate charge on Overton Hill that ensured victory.

Some U.S.C.T. regiments mustered out of service as early as April 1865, while others continued in uniform until April 1866. They conducted mostly garrison and police duties in Memphis, Chattanooga, Knoxville, and Nashville, where black populations were quickly rising as a result of the exodus of former slaves into urban areas. When blacks in uniform demonstrated a pride in their service that white Tennesseans considered "uppity," violence erupted. Memphis experienced the most serious incident in early May 1866, when a two-day riot left 123 casualties, including 46 dead African Americans.

Nearly 24,000 men of color served in the Union army stationed in Tennessee and suffered almost 4,500 casualties. They persisted against ideas of inferiority professed by southerners as well as some white Union commanders. Black troops feared mistreatment, or even death, if captured and proved to themselves and their white commanders that they were fighters. Their role in Tennessee during the Civil War should be recognized as indispensable.

Kenneth Bancroft Moore, University of Alabama, Huntsville
SUGGESTED READINGS: Richard L. Fuchs, *An Unerring Fire: The Massacre at Fort Pillow* (1994); Bobby L. Lovett, "The West Tennessee Colored Troops in Civil War Combat," *West Tennessee Historical Society Papers* 34(1980): 53–70; Kenneth B. Moore, "Fort Pillow, Forrest, and the United States Colored Troops in 1864," *Tennessee Historical Quarterly* 54(1995): 112–123
SEE: CIVIL WAR; CONTRABAND CAMPS; FORREST, NATHAN B.; FORT PILLOW; MEMPHIS RACE RIOT OF 1866; NASHVILLE, BATTLE OF

UNITED STATES DAIRY EXPERIMENT STATION

was established in Marshall County in 1929. Lewisburg civic entrepreneur and cattle auctioneer Jim N. McCord, Jersey cattle farmer Jimmy Joe Murray, and Tennessee Governor Henry Horton, all from Marshall County, called upon their friend and political ally U.S. Senator Kenneth McKellar to lobby Congress for the creation of a federal dairy demonstration farm. In 1928 Congress appropriated $50,000 for the construction, equipping, and staffing of a dairy demonstration station. Horton then convinced the General Assembly to match that amount in order to acquire land for the station. Officials initially purchased the farms of R.L. Brown and R.L. Richardson, a total of 480 acres; in 1954 they purchased an additional 135 acres from Frank and Gladys Medearis.

At the time of the federal and state appropriations, Marshall Countians already had established a thriving Jersey dairy cattle business. George T. Allman introduced the animal to the county in 1871. County dairymen established the Jersey Breeder's Association, with Jimmy Joe Murray as president, in 1911. Local cattlemen later registered their pure-breds with the American Jersey Cattle Club. After the first county fair in 1919, farmers established the Marshall County Cooperative Cow-Testing Association, a voluntary association for the testing of butterfat, and reorganized the Association in 1920. During the 1920s McCord became a nationally recognized auctioneer for Jersey cattle. The Farm Bureau organized three cooperative creameries in 1924, the Marshall County Jersey Cattle Club was established in 1926, the Borden milk company opened a Lewisburg plant in 1927, and county officials and farmers organized the nation's first Jersey Production Show and the Marshall County Cooperative Creamery in 1928.

The station's first 24 Jersey cows came from Vermont, Maryland, and Louisiana. Its first superintendent was John Simms, who served until 1939. Working with the local agricultural extension agent, the federal officials assisted farmers in creating the Dairy Herd Improvement Association in 1930. Two years later, the U.S. Department of Agriculture sent 14 additional cows from its Research Herd at Beltsville, Maryland. Improvement on many farms came quickly. By 1940 the Marshall County Jersey Cattle Club published its first survey of Jersey bulls for breeding.

The station successfully promoted the breeding and production of Jersey cattle and taught local farmers how to increase the yield and the percentage of butterfat produced by their herds. Officials also experimented with alfalfa and other hays to improve pastures for the cattle. They conducted classes, traveled throughout the region to give workshops and seminars, and wrote articles about Jersey dairy production in leading agricultural magazines. Superintendent A.G. Van Horn oversaw the merger of the federal station with the University of Tennessee's Extension Service program in 1948. The following year, officials counted 12,000 Jersey cows in Marshall County alone. By the mid-1950s, also during Van Horn's superintendency, officials decided to end the importation of females to the herd as they had raised the quality of animal desired for modern dairy production. Although little known statewide, the dairy experiment station in Marshall County did, and continues to, significantly influence Tennessee's dairy industry.

Carroll Van West, Middle Tennessee State University
SEE: FARMS AND THE AGRICULTURAL EXPERIMENT STATION; HORTON, HENRY; LIVESTOCK; MARSHALL COUNTY; MCCORD, JIM N.; MCKELLAR, KENNETH

UNITED STATES PIPE AND FOUNDRY COMPANY

is one of Chattanooga's oldest manufacturing establishments and a familiar landmark on the city's skyline. The company's owners, David Giles and Caleb B. Isbester, were Pennsylvania iron men who had manufactured pipe in Nashville since 1867. Together they established the Chattanooga Pipe and Foundry Works in 1877, building a modern and efficient plant along Whiteside Street, adjacent to the city's growing rail yard.

Chattanooga Pipe and Foundry became one of the city's leading manufacturers and was recognized as one of the nation's finest iron fabricators. The company was also one of the city's top employers and engaged over 150 workers, two thirds of them black. Innovators from the outset, Giles and Isbester experimented with a number of revolutionary manufacturing techniques and even attempted to find new uses for industrial wastes—using spent tans for fuel and converting furnace ashes to fertilizer.

In 1899, following a protracted local depression, Chattanooga Pipe and Foundry consolidated with other regional fabricators to form the United States Cast Iron Pipe and Foundry Company. Later, in 1936, the company closed the old Whiteside Street plant and moved its operations to the current facility on Chestnut Street near Moccasin Bend. In 1969 the firm, now known as U.S. Pipe and Foundry Company, was purchased by the Jim Walter Corporation, a leading producer of building materials and prefab houses. U.S. Pipe and Foundry continues to be one of Chattanooga's leading manufacturers, employing over 750 workers with wages and benefits in excess of $34 million.

Timothy P. Ezzell, Knoxville
SEE: CHATTANOOGA; INDUSTRY

UNIVERSAL LIFE INSURANCE COMPANY.

Memphis-based Universal Life Insurance Company (ULICO), the second African-American company in the United States to attain million-dollar-capital status (1947), has been described as one of the "ten top Negro owned and operated business enterprises in the world" and as "the cornerstone of Negro business enterprise and financial initiative in the entire Mid-South."[1] The company was established in the Fraternal Bank building in Memphis on September 6, 1923, by Dr. J.E. Walker, former president of Mississippi Life Insurance Company. Other charter officers were J.T. Wilson, M.W. Bonner, Dr. R.S. Fields, A.W. Willis, and B.F. Booth. Only three of the men—Walker, Bonner, and Willis—remained active in the company, guiding it to its present position among African-American companies.

Universal's capital stock increased from $100,000 in 1923 to $200,000 in 1926, and the company moved to its first home-office building at 234 Hernando Street in Memphis. ULICO prospered and over the next 20 years, expanded into nine other states. During World War II, J.E. Walker served as national chairman of the War Bond Saving Club and spearheaded the purchase of $2,000,000 in war bonds. In 1952 A. Maceo Walker succeeded his father as ULICO president. In 1956 he became the only black appointed to President Dwight D. Eisenhower's Person to Person Committee.

Universal's founding goal to "build a service institution that would give jobs and financial assistance to our people" is achieved through its use of assets for civic improvements, educational scholarships, and mortgage funds. Descendants of J.E. Walker continue to operate Universal Life.[2]

Reavis L. Mitchell, Jr., Fisk University
CITATIONS:
(1) Quoted from Nat D. Williams, "On the Purchase of Excelsior" in *The Tri-State Defender* (1958).
(2) Annual Report, *Universal Life Insurance Company, 1923–1958*, pp. 9–10, 23–25.
SEE: WALKER, JOSEPH E.; WILLIS, ARCHIE W., JR.

UNIVERSITY OF MEMPHIS.

Names reflect an institution's history and the University of Memphis has undergone several name changes: West Tennessee State Normal School (1912–1925), West Tennessee State Teachers College (1925–1930), State Teachers College, Memphis (1930–1941), Memphis State College (1941–1957), Memphis State University (1957–1994), and The University of Memphis (1994–). Whatever the name, its location in Memphis favored the college. A town oriented to a rural economy and culture in 1900 became a large urban center by mid-century, and its public college expanded from a normal school to a comprehensive university.

Born during a rare moment of educational reform, the Normal's first mission was to train teachers for West Tennessee elementary and high schools. Memphis obtained the school after a vigorous competition against other regional cities. Although the state-funded institution's potential for the city was obvious, its origins were humble: three red brick buildings on an 80-acre campus just outside the city. The initial enrollment reached 300 students, many requiring a high school diploma before obtaining a teacher certificate. By 1925, however, the school accepted only high school graduates and began granting bachelor's degrees. As enrollment reached 1,000, the college set the tone for educational life throughout its area, producing excellent teachers and administrators for the rapidly expanding public school systems.

Early faculty and administrators, known as the "Schoolmen," took on the aspect of "Founding Fathers." Buildings bore their names, legends grew up about them, and former students looked back on their teaching careers with deep appreciation. The 30 or 40 faculty members were dedicated to good teaching, service, and loyalty to the school. Few placed academic specialization before guiding students, who ate with faculty at the common dining hall, saw them gathered at regular chapel programs, and participated with them in extracurricular activities. Some early traditions such as school colors, the tiger mascot, and an atmosphere of "democratic" informality have lasted.

Until just after World War II, the college paralleled its peers under the State Board of Education. Identical budgets and programs prevented rivalry between institutions. A college's destiny was related to state politics as filtered through the attitudes of governors, legislators, newspaper editors, and the governing board. Decisions made in Nashville prescribed admission policies, academic programs, and financing. Furthermore, prevailing opinion assumed that Tennessee could afford only one public university of quality.

Demographics, however significant, never determined the entire history of the college; personal leadership emerged during times of crisis to provide continuity and progress for the institution. President J.W. Brister led an old-fashioned "campaign" in the 1930s, when the Great Depression caused retrenchment and the annual budget dropped to $35,000, almost forcing the college to close. President J.B. Sanders, a nationally respected historian, overcame a second low point during World War II, when the college lost accreditation and student enrollment plunged to 200. Sanders's sterling character and the influx of veterans restored the college.

By the 1950s the college undertook a second mission by steadily expanding its offerings in liberal arts, business, and graduate work. After several futile attempts, university status was achieved in 1957. President J.M. Smith and the popular C.C. Humphreys convinced state officials and rival college supporters that metropolitan Memphis required a new mission for its college. Several factors helped bring this about: funding from other than state sources; active local support groups such as Greater Memphis State; successful NCAA basketball teams; national Greek and academic societies replacing local clubs; and the operation of a large Air Force ROTC unit.

In the 1960s and 1970s, programs, facilities, faculty, and enrollment expanded rapidly. A large-scale building program and the acquisition of additional land transformed the campus. New programs were added in graduate education, law, engineering, continuing education, and nursing. Since the 1980s, as enrollment remained stable at approximately 20,000 students, the university sought to raise standards to match its physical expansion and become a regionally recognized multipurpose university. Revised

funding formulas factored academic excellence into the university's third mission. Research grants and gifts became available; institutes and bureaus proliferated. Chairs and centers of excellence, including the Center for Earthquake Research and Information, enhanced regional research at the university.

Memphis and its university are inseparably linked, and African Americans comprise half the city's population. From eight students in 1959 to 2,000 by 1970, African-American students have helped fulfill the goal of a "democratic" opportunity for higher education. As the 1990s closed, the university had 26 percent black enrollment and was a national leader in minority-student graduation rates. Memphians have supported their university's sports programs, providing local athletic talent such as Larry Finch and Anfernee (Penny) Hardaway, the Liberty Bowl Stadium for football, and the Pyramid for basketball. Indeed, this proud tradition in intercollegiate athletics has helped bridge racial divisions. In this and many other respects, the little school of 1912 became a treasured asset.

James R. Chumney, University of Memphis
SEE: EDUCATION, HIGHER; MEMPHIS

UNIVERSITY OF NASHVILLE: See LINDSLEY, JOHN B.; LINDSLEY, PHILLIP; PEABODY EDUCATION FUND.

UNIVERSITY OF TENNESSEE was founded as Blount College, named for Territorial Governor William Blount, and chartered on September 10, 1794, by the legislature of the Southwest Territory sitting in Knoxville. Located in a single building in a frontier village of 40 houses and 200 residents, the college appears to have been an overambitious undertaking. The motivations of the founders remain unknown, but they probably followed the post-revolutionary trend of college founding in order to create an educated citizenry for the new experiment in republican government. Although seven of the first ten presidents were clergymen, the college was non-sectarian.

The college had a precarious existence. Only one student graduated, and the college depended on tuition for its financial support. In 1807 the state legislature rechartered the college as East Tennessee College and improved its financial prospects with a grant of public land. When the first president, Samuel Carrick, died in 1809, the college closed for a decade. East Tennessee College reopened in 1820, and, eight years later, moved to a new building on a hill outside town. By 1840 the institution had a new name, East Tennessee University, but its prospects continued to be uncertain. During the next 20 years, there were several presidents, and the faculty never numbered more than five. Approximately half of the 100 students

SPECIAL COLLECTIONS, UNIVERSITY OF TENNESSEE, KNOXVILLE

The University of Tennessee, circa 1900.

were enrolled in the Preparatory Department, which acted as a secondary school to prepare students for admission to the regular collegiate course.

During the Civil War the university closed; both armies successively occupied the buildings as hospitals. By the war's end, the surrounding area was bare of any vegetation. Thomas Humes, who became president of the university in 1865, had been a Union sympathizer and used his influence to secure $18,500 from the federal government as restitution for wartime damages. In 1869 the state legislature designated the university as the recipient of the funds provided by the Morrill Act of 1862. This federal act awarded states land grants or scrip for the establishment of colleges and universities that would teach agriculture, the mechanical arts, and military science. This boon to the university's fortunes made it the recipient of the annual interest on some $400,000, about $24,000.

In 1879 the state renamed the institution the University of Tennessee. In requesting the change, the trustees expressed the hope that the name change would inspire the legislature to provide regular financial support, but this generosity had to wait another 25 years. In the meantime, the institution sought to become a university in more than name by its own efforts. A somewhat hidebound and classical-

oriented faculty was reluctant to change the direction of the university, but the president who assumed charge in 1887 was not. Charles Dabney, the first president with an earned doctorate, reshaped the faculty and the institution. He successfully eliminated the preparatory department, ended the military regimen which governed student life, and began a law school and a department of education (under Philander Claxton). From 1902 until 1918, another innovation, the university's Summer School of the South, enhanced the preparation of some 32,000 regional public school teachers. In 1892 women were admitted provisionally and granted unconditional admission the following year. A zealous advocate of improved public education for both whites and blacks and the author of an influential treatise, *Universal Education in the South* (1936), Dabney proved too liberal for the trustees and left in 1904 for the presidency of the University of Cincinnati. His successor, Brown Ayres, continued to strengthen the university's academic programs and persuaded the legislature to institute a series of regular annual appropriations for the institution's operations, climaxed by the first million dollar allocation in 1917.

In the twentieth century, the University of Tennessee emerged as a modern university, with professional schools of medicine, dentistry, nursing, and pharmacy, all located in Memphis. This institution is now known as the University of Tennessee, Memphis, the Health Services Center. The Knoxville campus offers programs in agriculture, architecture and planning, arts and sciences, business, communications, education, engineering, human ecology, information sciences, law, nursing, social work, and veterinary medicine leading to undergraduate, graduate, and professional degrees. Additional campuses are at Martin and Tullahoma, where a Space Institute was established in 1964. In 1969 the University of Chattanooga, a private institution founded in 1886, was added to the newly designated university "system," with a Knoxville president and campus chancellors. From 1971 to 1979 the university maintained a campus in Nashville before it was ordered closed and merged with Tennessee State University as part of the state's desegregation program.

Despite the financial support from public coffers, appropriations never adequately funded the university. State funding currently provides about one-third of the institution's budget. An aggressive development program, instituted by president Andrew D. Holt (1959–1970), produced gifts that resulted in an endowment of more than $410 million by the end of 1996.

Apart from the admission of women at the end of the nineteenth century, the most important change in the student body came in 1952 when African Americans were admitted to graduate and law schools, under federal court order. Nine years later, the trustees voluntarily opened the doors to black undergraduates. Black enrollment currently varies from five percent on the Knoxville campus to ten percent at Memphis, and 13–14 percent at Chattanooga and Martin. In 1996 the university comprised a student body of some 42,000, more than 25,000 of them on the Knoxville campus; a faculty and staff of over 15,000, almost three-fourths concentrated on the Knoxville campus and the medical units in Memphis; and approximately 370 undergraduate and graduate degree programs.

While the university has acquired a national reputation in both men's and women's athletics—the Lady Vols basketball team having won six national championships—the institution has also produced one Nobel laureate, seven Rhodes Scholars, six Pulitzer Prize winners, two National Book Award winners, nine U.S. Senators, and one associate justice of the U.S. Supreme Court. Its 225,000 living alumni bear witness to the university's success in fulfilling its mission of preparing Tennesseans for their roles as citizens of the state and nation and helping them realize their own potential.

Milton M. Klein, University of Tennessee, Knoxville

SUGGESTED READINGS: Milton M. Klein, *Volunteer Moments: Vignettes of the History of the University of Tennessee, 1794–1994* (1996); James R. Montgomery et al., *To Foster Knowledge: A History of the University of Tennessee, 1794–1970* (1984)

SEE: BROWN, CLARENCE; BUEHLER, CALVIN A.; BUSSARD, RAY; CLAXTON, PHILANDER P.; DABNEY, CHARLES; DOUGHERTY, NATHAN W.; EDUCATION, HIGHER; FOOTBALL, COLLEGE; HERTEL, KENNETH; HOLT, ANDREW D.; KABALKA, GEORGE; MAJORS, JOHN; MAMANTOV, GLEB; MARIVUS, RICHARD; MORGAN, HARCOURT; NEYLAND, ROBERT R.; ROBINSON, THEOTIS; SMITH, HILTON A.; SUMMER SCHOOL OF THE SOUTH; SUMMITT, PAT; TENNESSEE PRESIDENT TRUST; TIPTON, ISABEL H.; UNIVERSITY OF TENNESSEE AT CHATTANOOGA; UNIVERSITY OF TENNESSEE AT MARTIN; UNIVERSITY OF TENNESSEE MEDICAL CENTER; UNIVERSITY OF TENNESSEE, MEMPHIS, THE HEALTH SERVICES CENTER; VOGEL, MATT

UNIVERSITY OF TENNESSEE AT CHATTANOOGA was founded as Chattanooga University by the Methodist Episcopal Church, North, in 1886. Strife within the church over educational policy in the South soon undermined Chattanooga University and led to its consolidation in 1889 with a rival school, Grant Memorial University in Athens, Tennessee.

In 1889 the consolidated school adopted the name U.S. Grant University. Its administrative center, undergraduate college, and preparatory department were removed to Athens, leaving the Chattanooga campus with makeshift specialty programs in business, law, medicine, and theology. Internal problems survived the reorganization. Trustees of the debt-ridden school sued its president to stop him from selling one-half of the Chattanooga campus in 1890, and the general level of teaching remained of subcollegiate grade as the number of collegiate students steadily declined to 39 out of a total enrollment of 247 in 1898.

Faculty members predicted that the school was "approaching dissolution," but the president who took office in 1898 refused to join the death watch. John H. Race, a Northern Methodist clergyman without prior experience in college administration, transformed the fractious pseudo-university into a genuine liberal arts college. Race eliminated the preparatory and specialty programs and concentrated on elevating academic standards in the undergraduate college, which reopened in Chattanooga in 1904 and six years later gained membership in the Association of Colleges and Secondary Schools of the Southern States. He raised $750,000 in capital funds, including large sums from steel baron Andrew Carnegie and the Rockefeller-funded General Education Board. He also won independence from direct control by the Northern Methodist Church. In 1909 the church transferred ownership of the school property to local trustees, who thereupon changed the name to the University of Chattanooga.

The complete severance of denominational ties came in 1935 when the university board dropped the requirement that two-thirds of its membership be Northern Methodists. Six years earlier, Alexander Guerry became the first southerner, layman, and non-Methodist to serve as university president. Under Guerry and his successors, the University of Chattanooga pursued a policy of vigorous community outreach. Town-gown relations, once chilly, grew cordial as services to the community multiplied, notably in adult education, the performing arts, and degree programs preparing students for jobs in local business. By 1945 the institution had forged an alliance with the commercial-civic elite of Chattanooga that sustained the private undergraduate college well into the 1960s.

A perplexing challenge arose in 1968 when a public institution, the University of Tennessee, announced plans to build a four-year college in Chattanooga. Faced with the choice of competing head-on with the state university or joining forces with it, trustees of the Chattanooga institution merged it with the University of Tennessee to become the University of Tennessee at Chattanooga. An unusual feature of the merger agreement was the creation of the University of Chattanooga Foundation, which retains and manages the endowment once held by the University of Chattanooga. Income from the endowment provides scholarships, distinguished professorships, and special programs not usually found on the campus of a state-supported institution. In 1996 the UC Foundation endowment stood at $65 million.

Since the merger, degree programs have expanded to include 100 at the undergraduate level and 46 at the master's level. Enrollment has climbed from 2,300 students in 1968 to 8,300 in 1996. African Americans were first admitted as undergraduates in 1965 and comprised 13 percent of the student body in 1996. Most students live within a 50-mile radius of the campus, and many are first-generation college enrollees. With a reputation for quality in undergraduate teaching and support from both private and public sources, the University of Tennessee at Chattanooga aspires to eminence as a metropolitan university dedicated to serving the Chattanooga region.
John Longwith, Chattanooga

Suggested Readings: Gilbert E. Govan and James W. Livingood, *The University of Chattanooga: Sixty Years* (1947); Linda Walker, ed., *UTC: A Pictorial Review* (1986)

SEE: CHATTANOOGA; EDUCATION, HIGHER; TENNESSEE WESLEYAN COLLEGE; UNIVERSITY OF TENNESSEE

UNIVERSITY OF TENNESSEE AT MARTIN, the only public four-year college in West Tennessee outside Memphis, traces its roots to Hall-Moody Institute, founded by local Baptists in 1900. Named for J.N. Hall and J.B. Moody, two prominent Baptist ministers, Hall-Moody offered elementary, high school, and college courses, plus training for Baptist ministerial students. By 1917–1918 the state fully accredited all courses, and the school became known as Hall-Moody Junior College.

Hall-Moody enjoyed periodic growth, but faced constant financial difficulties. In 1926–1927, after a drive to raise $75,000 failed, the college consolidated with Union University, another Baptist institution, located in Jackson, Tennessee. On June 1, 1927, Hall-Moody officially closed.

With the demise of the college, local citizens petitioned the state to establish a new junior college under the administration of the University of Tennessee. In February 1927, the state legislature passed Senate Bill 301, which provided for a junior college offering agriculture, industrial arts, and home economics. Shortly afterwards, the City of Martin and Weakley County each voted to issue $100,000 in bonds to purchase the Hall-Moody plant, secure additional land, and add new facilities.

In September 1927 the University of Tennessee Junior College (UTJC) opened with an enrollment of 120 students, a faculty and staff of 16, and a budget of $75,000. C. Porter Claxton served as executive officer until 1934. Three new classroom buildings, a gymnasium, and a steam plant were built before the Great Depression took its toll. During the depression years, enrollment declined, construction ceased, and the budget fell drastically. The low point came in 1933, when the fall enrollment dropped to 92, and intercollegiate athletics were suspended.

Fortunately for UTJC, a group of determined West Tennessee citizens petitioned the university and the legislature for an expansion of the junior college curriculum, and a new program, which included two years in liberal arts and education, was approved in 1934. Intercollegiate athletics also were reinstated. At the same time, Paul Meek became executive officer; during his tenure enrollment and facilities gradually increased.

Dark days returned with the outbreak of World War II, when enrollment again dropped to 115 students, with only 24 men. In 1942 UTJC obtained a program to train naval aviation cadets, which provided the school with sorely needed funds and held the faculty together.

After World War II, the veterans returned, and the fall quarter enrollment in 1946 surged to 649. The school quickly erected temporary buildings and added new faculty. National accolades came in 1946 when *Look Magazine* rated UTJC among the top 15 junior colleges in the nation. In 1951 the state legislators and administrators recognized area needs and elevated the junior college to four-year status, renaming it the University of Tennessee Martin Branch. The school was authorized to award degrees in agriculture and home economics. All other areas remained limited to two years until 1957, when a degree program in education was approved. Four years later majors in business administration and liberal arts were added to the curriculum.

The physical plant burgeoned to meet the needs of an enrollment which doubled during the 1950s; even greater growth occurred in the 1960s with the entry of the "Baby Boomers." By 1970 UT Martin's enrollment reached 4,622, placing the college among the fastest growing institutions in the state.

In 1967 the school's name was changed to the University of Tennessee at Martin. Paul Meek retired after 33 years of service, and Archie Dykes was appointed chancellor. In 1971 Dykes was replaced by Larry T. McGehee, who remained until 1979. Charles E. Smith assumed the helm from 1979 to 1985, followed by Chancellor Margaret N. Perry.

After a leveling of the enrollment in the 1980s, UT Martin experienced a resurgence in the 1990s and achieved a record enrollment of 5,812 students in 1995. In 1996 a four-year engineering program was implemented.

UT Martin focuses primarily on undergraduate training, currently offering degree programs in over 80 specialized fields. UTM students report a high acceptance rate into graduate and professional schools, and its alumni are located in virtually every state in the nation and many foreign countries.

Today, UT Martin's land, buildings, and equipment have an estimated value of over $143,000,000. This includes the 250-acre campus, a 680-acre

experiment farm, 44 academic and support buildings, six dormitories, and 256 apartments for married students. As UT Martin approaches its 100th
birthday, the founders undoubtedly would view
with pride the growth of the school from a fledgling one-building institution to a bustling primary
campus of the University of Tennessee system.

Robert L. Carroll, University of Tennessee at Martin

SUGGESTED READING: Neil Graves, *A Picture History of Hall-
Moody* (1975)

SEE: EDUCATION, HIGHER; UNIVERSITY OF TENNESSEE;
WEAKLEY COUNTY

UNIVERSITY OF TENNESSEE MEDICAL CENTER AT KNOXVILLE.

Fifty-four years after the city-
owned-and-operated Knoxville General Hospital
opened in 1902, it was replaced in 1956 by the University of Tennessee Memorial Research Center and
Hospital. A number of forces converged to bring
about the culmination of a nearly 12-year effort to
build a new hospital. Essential to the project's success
were the promises of radiation research after World
War II, a drive in Knoxville's medical community for
a new hospital, fresh leadership in city government
and on the Knox County Court bench, and a turnover
in the university president's office.

Opened a year after the hospital, the research
center operated as a separate entity until government
financial support for research shifted, then dried up
throughout the 1970s. Emphasis on research for the
practical purposes of diagnosis and treatment and as
a component of graduate medical education eventually brought about integration of the research center-
hospital complex.

Medical centers nationwide experienced a financial windfall with the advent of Medicare and Medicaid, which enabled the amassing of huge capital
reserves. The unfettered flow of funds from Washington freed the UT Memorial Hospital to develop costly
but effective helicopter emergency transportation,
organ transplant programs, a perinatal center, and
specialized care units. By the 1990s the now designated University of Tennessee Medical Center at
Knoxville faced serious financial cutbacks as the federal and state government altered their reimbursement policies.

The evolution of this medical center depicts the
influence of politics, social change, and financial
adjustment. At first a community hospital run
by physicians, the center has steadily moved
toward becoming a preeminent graduate medical
education facility.

Jayne Crumpler DeFiore, University of Tennessee, Knoxville

SUGGESTED READING: Jayne Crumpler DeFiore, *Miracle in the
Valley: The University of Tennessee Medical Center at Knoxville*
(1996)

SEE: UNIVERSITY OF TENNESSEE

UNIVERSITY OF TENNESSEE, MEMPHIS: THE HEALTH SCIENCE CENTER,

founded in 1911,
includes the Colleges of Allied Health Sciences, Dentistry, Graduate Health Sciences, Medicine, Nursing
and Pharmacy, the School of Biomedical Engineering,
the Bowld Hospital in Memphis; and the Graduate
School of Medicine and the Memorial Hospital in
Knoxville. UT Memphis also operates Graduate Medical Education programs in Knoxville, Chattanooga,
and Nashville; Family Medicine Centers in Knoxville,
Jackson, and Memphis; and public and continuing
education programs statewide.

The University of Tennessee, Memphis, was
formed from the merger of five medical schools:
Memphis Hospital Medical College and College of
Physicians and Surgeons in Memphis; Nashville
Medical College and the Medical Department of the
University of Tennessee at Nashville; and Lincoln
Memorial University located in Knoxville. A report
on medical education published by Abraham Flexnor
in 1910 provided the final motivation to close these
old proprietary schools and establish a new medical
school associated with the University of Tennessee.
Heeding Flexnor's advice, the Nashville campus of
the Medical Department of the University of Tennessee was relocated to Memphis and the other
schools consolidated with the new institution. The
first session was held in 1911–1912 at Lindsley Hall,
named in honor of J. Berrien Lindsley. The University
of Tennessee College of Medicine faced significant
problems in providing adequate funding, acquiring
an "A" rating from the AMA Council on Medical
Education, and gaining control of its teaching hospital from local political elites.

Now one of the nation's oldest and largest medical centers, UT Memphis includes 18 hospitals and
nearly 6,000 beds. The 2,100-member student body
receives instruction from 800 paid and 1,000 volunteer faculty in Memphis and 150 paid and 300 volunteer faculty in Knoxville. Approximately 600 students
graduate each year with baccalaureate, masters, and
doctoral degrees. UT Memphis is accredited by the
Southern Association of Colleges and Schools and
each of the appropriate professional agencies for the
various programs offered at the school. Three Centers of Excellence have received national attention for
research in microbiology and immunology, neuro-
sciences, and pediatric pharmacokinetics. UT Memphis has 35 endowed professorships, of which 19 are
Chairs of Excellence funded jointly by private gifts
and the State of Tennessee.

Connie L. Lester, Tennessee Historical Society

SUGGESTED READINGS: Marcus J. Stewart and William T.
Black, Jr., eds., *History of Medicine in Memphis* (1971); http://
chanc.utmem/admin/factsstmtutmphs

SEE: QUILLEN COLLEGE OF MEDICINE; UNIVERSITY OF
TENNESSEE; VANDERBILT UNIVERSITY MEDICAL CENTER

Early view of the University of the South showing Breslin Tower, Convocation Hall, and Walsh Hall.

UNIVERSITY OF THE SOUTH. In 1857, when it was learned that the dioceses of the Episcopal Church planned to establish an educational center, citizens of Franklin County made common cause with the Sewanee Mining Company to offer a 10,000-acre parcel, half of which was carved from the 140,000 acres given to the company by the State of Tennessee for the industrial development of the coal-bearing lands of the plateau. The Sewanee site, which met the required altitude of 1,800 feet, placed the proposed center above the malaria line and was made more attractive by the addition of a nine-mile railroad that climbed the mountain and cut across the university domain.

The plans for the center called for 30 schools or colleges offering a full range of classics and such practical subjects as agriculture and forestry. In the 1850s the wealth of southern Episcopalians and the tradition of an educated clergy made such an imaginative project seem feasible. Bishops James Hervey Otey of Tennessee and Stephen Elliott of Georgia joined with Louisiana Bishop Leonidas Polk to provide the leadership for the project. Polk and Elliott raised the largest sum ever pledged for an educational institution in America from the Louisiana diocese alone.

In 1860 the cornerstone was laid in an elaborate ceremony attended by eight bishops and several thousand people. The intervention of the Civil War disrupted plans for the university and almost destroyed the idea. By 1866 all three of the original founders were dead, the cornerstone had been blown apart, and the forest had reclaimed the clearing. When Bishop Charles T. Quintard made a quick trip through the South to raise funds to begin anew, he did not net enough to pay his expenses despite the fact that he traveled on a railroad pass.

Then Quintard's brother donated funds to allow the bishop to attend the first Lambeth Conference of Anglican bishops in England. While there, the bishop preached 250 sermons in 180 days and raised 2,500 British pounds to reopen the university. With only a week to spare before the deed to the property expired, the doors of a clapboard "chapel" opened to admit nine students and four professors. Quintard and Bishop William M. Green of Mississippi donned their ecclesiastical finery, and the tiny procession formally established the University of the South on September 18, 1868.

The poverty that characterized the South in this period produced one blessing. The institution could bring to its faculty a quality of teaching normally unavailable to a struggling college. Brigadier General Josiah Gorgas came to head the junior department and teach the sciences. Robert Dabney of Virginia taught literature. Confederate General Edmund Kirby Smith taught math. Thus was the standard of excellence set that has been the hallmark of the college. As the century closed, the University of the South, with an enrollment of over 300 students, offered coursework in the classics, theology, medicine, law, and engineering. Even the football team was impressive, remaining undefeated in 1898 and 1899.

Beginning in 1909, financial problems almost closed the school and enrollment fell to 100 students. The school continued to function through the persistence of a few teachers who worked without knowing when or if they would be paid. A military unit kept classes going during World War I. Despite these setbacks, the institution survived and continued through the years of the Great Depression. In 1938 Alexander Guerry assumed leadership of the university and returned it to full enrollment and sound fiscal condition. In the 1950s Vice Chancellor Edward McCrady oversaw a substantial building program that included new housing for faculty and students, a new library, and a science hall.

Today, enrollment at the university remains steady, the endowment has reached $200 million (among the highest per student in the nation), and the school enjoys a national academic reputation. The School of Theology, which awards several doctoral degrees annually, has moved to the Sewanee Academy campus, which was vacated in 1981 when that institution merged with nearby St. Andrew's School. Several new programs and buildings are on the drawing board, including a theatre complex to be built using funds bequeathed by dramatist Tennessee Williams in honor of his grandfather, the Reverend Walter E. Dakin, a theological student at the university in the 1890s. The Dakin Fund also sponsors programs in creative writing.

The Sewanee Review, the oldest literary-critical quarterly in America, celebrated its 100th anniversary in 1992, and the Order of Gownsmen, a student governing body unique among student organizations in this country, is now nearly 125 years old. The Sewanee Summer Music Festival is 40 years old. In the 1960s the university began admitting women students, something that previously had been permitted only in summer school. The University of the South athletes compete in NCAA Division III and are awarded scholarships on the basis of financial need, with a few honor scholarships.

The university continues its original hallmarks—ownership by the Episcopal Church, regard for the classics, a fondness for the traditions of the English universities. The military tradition is no longer a part of campus life. The campus has developed an international character as the enrollment of foreign students increases, and programs for study aboard are made available to many university students.

Arthur Ben Chitty, University of the South

SUGGESTED READING: Arthur B. Chitty, Jr., *Reconstruction at Sewanee: The Founding of the University of the South and Its First Administration, 1857–1872* (1954, rpt. 1970)

SEE: DuBOSE, WILLIAM P.; EDUCATION, HIGHER; FOOTBALL, COLLEGE; FRANKLIN COUNTY; GAILOR, THOMAS; LYTLE, ANDREW NELSON; OTEY, JAMES H.; POLK, LEONIDAS; PRUNTY, WYATT; QUINTARD, CHARLES T.; THE SEWANEE REVIEW; SMITH, EDMUND K.; TATE, JOHN O. ALLEN; ST. ANDREWS-SEWANEE; TILLINGHAST, RICHARD

V

VAN BUREN COUNTY encompasses 274 square miles straddling the Cumberland Plateau and the eastern Highland Rim. The western 30 percent of the county stands 960 feet above sea level; its limestone outcroppings have resulted in numerous caves. The best known, Big Bone Cave, was important in the early settlement period. In 1811 the discovery of bones of a giant sloth in the cave provided its name; remnants of a Pleistocene jaguar were unearthed there as well. The U.S. Department of the Interior designated the 334-acre site a Pleistocene vertebrate fossil site. It is also listed on the National Register of Historic Places because in both the War of 1812 and the Civil War saltpeter was mined there, and the well-preserved vats, tramways, and ladders remain in place today.

The other 70 percent of Van Buren County, the Plateau region, rises 800–1,000 feet higher and is generally level except where streams have cut gorges (called gulfs) through the sandstone. The Caney Fork River and its tributaries drain all of Van Buren County except for the southeast corner, drained by the headwaters of Brush Creek. The Caney Fork also creates the northern border of the county and the Rocky River serves as part of its western boundary.

Van Buren County was formed out of parts of White, Warren, and Bledsoe counties in 1840 and named for the U.S. President at the time, Martin Van Buren. Andrew K. Parker gave 50 acres of land for a county seat, and the first county court was held at the home of William Worthington on April 6, 1840. The county seat was named Spencer in honor of Thomas Sharp Spencer who had died nearby in 1794 on what became Spencer's Hill. The township was officially formed in 1850 and incorporated in 1909.

Prior to that time, the settlement had become the home of Burritt College, founded in 1848 as the first coeducational college in the South. Named for Elihu Burritt of Worcester, Massachusetts, a prominent member in the peace movement, the school was situated in Spencer to be away from the vice and corruption of city life, though many of its graduates chose moving to cities over staying in rural Tennessee. Burned during the Civil War and rebuilt, Burritt College survived until the economic failures of the Depression forced its closure in 1939.

In 1860 Van Buren County's population of 2,337 included at least 35 slaveholders who owned 239 slaves. The county supported the Confederacy with four companies, one reason Spencer was burned when Union troops took the area in 1863. Earlier, Confederate General Braxton Bragg marched the Army of Tennessee through the county on his way to Kentucky and the campaign that ended with Confederate defeat and the deaths of 12 Van Buren countians at Perryville on October 8, 1862.

An artist who captured the throes of the Civil War in his paintings, completed a half century later, was Gilbert Gaul. A native of New Jersey, Gaul inherited from an uncle a 5,000-acre farm located 12 miles south of Spencer and near Fall Creek Falls. He moved to the property in 1881 and did much of his painting there, including one piece from 1913–1914 called *Caney Fork Cabin* (now at Vanderbilt University).

What was Gaul's farm sits now within Fall Creek Falls State Park. The park, covering over 19,000 acres in Van Buren and Bledsoe counties, was proposed by James M. "Peckerwood" Taft of Van Buren County, and in 1936 construction began under the auspices of the National Park Service. The work involved the Civilian Conservation Corps, Works Progress Administration, and Resettlement Administration. In 1944 the Department of the Interior deeded the park to the state. A state natural area of 10,000 acres lies within its domain, and there are four major falls. The largest, Fall Creek Falls, drops 256 feet, a fall of 90 feet more than Niagra, that makes it the highest falls in the United States east of the Rocky Mountains. Thirty miles of trails and a public golf course ranked in the top 25 in the country exist as well as virgin forest in the Cane Creek Gulf with its gorge of 300 feet.

Van Buren County's population in 1996 was 5,046. The major road through the county, State Route 111, was paved first in 1920. Since its designation in 1973 as an "Appalachian Development Highway," it has been improved and is soon to be a major connector between Chattanooga and the Kentucky border. There are two K-12 schools in the county. The largest employer in 1997 is Camcar/Textron/Townsend Engineering Products with 430 employees.

Margaret D. Binnicker, Middle Tennessee State University
SEE: BURRITT COLLEGE; FALL CREEK FALLS STATE PARK; GAUL, GILBERT; GEOLOGY; SPENCER, THOMAS S.

VAN DORN, EARL (1820–1863), Confederate major general, was murdered May 7, 1863, in his Spring Hill headquarters by Dr. George Peters, who charged that the short, dapper general had carried on an affair with his wife while he was out of town. Van Dorn was unattended and sitting at a desk in the Matt Cheairs home, later known as Ferguson Hall, when shot once in the back of the head, apparently while writing a pass for Peters. Confederate authorities arrested Peters, but he was released and never tried for shooting Van Dorn.

Van Dorn is buried in Port Gibson, Mississippi, near the plantation where he was born, September 17, 1820. He graduated from West Point in 1842, ranking 52nd in a class of 56. His record for bravery and daring in the Mexican War and in fighting the Seminoles and Comanches led to high expectations when Van Dorn entered Confederate service as a colonel in March 1861 and then advanced to brigadier general in June and to major general in September. But Van Dorn's incompetence as an army commander turned the battles of Elkhorn Tavern (Pea Ridge), Arkansas, in March 1862, and Corinth, Mississippi, in October 1862, into important Union victories. Later, as commander of mounted infantry, Van Dorn was more effective. His destruction of the Union supply center at Holly Springs, Mississippi, along with Nathan Bedford Forrest's raid through West Tennessee in December 1862, hindered U.S. Grant's campaign against Vicksburg. Van Dorn's only notable Civil War action in Tennessee was a minor victory at the Battle of Thompson's Station on March 4 and 5, 1863.

David Logsdon, Nashville
SUGGESTED READING: Robert G. Hartje, *Van Dorn: The Life and Times of a Confederate General* (1967)
SEE: MAURY COUNTY; WILLIAMSON COUNTY

VAN VECHTEN GALLERY OF FISK UNIVERSITY. In 1888 an enterprising student at Fisk University petitioned his fellow senior classmates to join with the fledgling Fisk Alumni Association (organized in 1884) to raise funds for a new multi-purpose building for the school's campus. The unwavering dedication and persuasive eloquence of the student, William Edward Burghardt Du Bois (1868–1963), brought generous results, and an imposing brick structure in Eclectic architectural style was constructed during 1888–1889 on the western edge of the Fisk campus. The tall building with a full basement served as the gymnasium and mechanical arts building, the first such facility constructed on a black college campus.

After the university constructed a new gymnasium in 1948, the original gymnasium underwent renovation to serve as a gallery for the school's extensive collection of art. The name given the gallery honors Carl Van Vechten (1880–1964), New York music critic, novelist, and benefactor of Fisk University. It opened to the public in its new guise in November 1949.

Carl Van Vechten Gallery won international acclaim for its display of modern art. A major portion of Alfred Stieglitz's collection of modern art hangs in the gallery, because of the generosity of his widow, eminent painter Georgia O'Keeffe (1887–1986). Alfred Stieglitz (1864–1946), an accomplished photographer, magazine publisher, and influential gallery owner, supported the avant garde artists of both Europe and America and helped launch the careers of an extraordinary number of artists. In 1916 Georgia O'Keeffe had her first exhibition in his famed "291" gallery in New York. O'Keeffe married Stieglitz in 1924, and after his death in 1946 she gave Fisk University 19 of Stieglitz's photographs on chloride, as well as a major portion of his outstanding collection of modern art. Included in the collection, in addition to two oil paintings by O'Keeffe, are original works by Paul Cézanne (1839–1906), Pablo Picasso (1881–1973), Diego Rivera (1886–1957), Pierre Auguste Renoir (1841–1919), John Marin (1872–1953), Marsden Hartley (1877–1943), Charles Demuth (1883–1935), and Arthur G. Dove (1880–1948).

The Van Vechten Gallery underwent a major renovation in 1984 with funding from the U.S. Department of Commerce and other donors. Changes included the re-configuration of the interior and the addition of new systems of stringent climate control, improved lighting, and new security measures. The architectural and engineering firm of McKissack, McKissack and Thompson of Nashville designed the renovations.

The Tennessee General Assembly established an endowment fund for the gallery in 1987, making it possible for all Tennessee school children to visit the Fisk University galleries free of charge.

Reavis L. Mitchell, Jr., Fisk University
SUGGESTED READING: Reavis L. Mitchell, Jr., *Fisk University Since 1866: Thy Loyal Children Make Their Way* (1995)

Early view of Kirkland Hall at Vanderbilt University.

SEE: ART; DOUGLAS, AARON; DU BOIS, W.E.B.; FISK UNIVERSITY; MCKISSACK AND MCKISSACK ARCHITECTS

VANCE, JAMES I. (1862–1939), long-time pastor of Nashville's historic First Presbyterian Church, the largest Presbyterian Church in the South in 1914, was voted one of the nation's 25 leading pulpit ministers in 1925. A great-grandson of John Sevier, Vance was born in 1862 near Bristol. He was a graduate of King College and Union Theological Seminary. After serving three other churches, Vance began his ministry at Nashville's First Presbyterian Church in 1894. Except for a ten-year tenure as pastor of the Dutch Reformed Church in Newark, New Jersey (1900–1910), Vance spent the remainder of his career at the Nashville church.

Vance received a number of honors. He was moderator of the General Assembly of the Presbyterian Church, U.S., and head of its Foreign Mission Board. He served as chairman of the Federal Council of Churches. He was also in great demand as a guest preacher in churches throughout the country.

In his ministry, in his many books, and in his community activities, Vance displayed his insights for adapting the traditional beliefs of Christianity to the issues of the day. Vance retired in 1936 because of ill health and died three years later, mourned by the community in which he had long played such a vital role. His papers and many of his books are preserved at the Tennessee State Library and Archives.

Sarah M. Howell, Middle Tennessee State University

SEE: KING COLLEGE; RELIGION

VANDERBILT UNIVERSITY in Nashville owes its inception to the visions of a great university dreamed by the leaders of the Methodist Episcopal Church, South, in the 1850s. Efforts to realize the dream were abandoned during the Civil War and finally resurrected by the General Conference of the church in 1870. Translating the dream to reality required the efforts of two very different men: Methodist bishop Holland N. McTyeire and "Commodore" Cornelius Vanderbilt, the New York shipping and railroad entrepreneur. The creation of Vanderbilt University reflected Southern Methodism's need for better trained ministers and the South's need for quality higher education in the late nineteenth century.

In 1872 the Methodist Episcopal Church, South, granted a charter for Central University. Renamed Vanderbilt University after Cornelius Vanderbilt made an initial gift of $500,000, the school was dedicated in 1875. The school retained strong denominational ties (the first faculty and nearly all the students were Methodists), but the money, eventually totaling well over a million dollars, came from the very secular Commodore and his son W.H. Vanderbilt. Vanderbilt University vaulted to an enviable position as Southern Methodism's wealthiest university, and within the South only Johns Hopkins University had more financial resources. Vanderbilt's first chancellor, Landon C. Garland (1875–1893), in conjunction with McTyeire, president of the Board of Trust, established a biblical department that reflected the commitment of training future ministers, an academic department with an abundance of the latest scientific equipment (at the time Vanderbilt was known for the quality of its scientific apparatus), and affiliated professional schools. An immediate problem arose over the poor academic preparation of the all-male student body. Compromising with this reality, Garland allowed subcollegiate courses to be taught to prepare students for university work, but also moved to raise academic standards at the secondary level through entrance exams administered throughout the southeastern region and certification of private and public secondary schools.

Vanderbilt's second chancellor, James H. Kirkland (1893–1937), oversaw a university facing a crisis of identity, whether to chafe under denominational ties and remain a sectarian school or break free of its Methodist moorings and make a bid for national recognition. Choosing the latter, Kirkland led Vanderbilt through the bitterness of a divorce from the church in 1914. The severance of church ties ushered in a period of plentiful gifts—$1 million from Andrew Carnegie for the medical department, over $15 million from the John D. Rockefeller-funded General Education Board, and the continued generosity of the Vanderbilt family. Although women had attended classes at Vanderbilt since its founding, the university continued to be conceived as an institution for males. During the 1890s, women fought to achieve full legal equality and, during the early twentieth century led the student body in grade-point averages and university honors. During Kirkland's chancellorship, the Medical and Nursing schools led other departments of the university in achieving national reputations. After World War I, a group of Vanderbilt intellectuals, including Allen Tate, John Crowe Ransom, Donald Davidson, and Robert Penn Warren, began publishing an influential poetry journal called the *Fugitive*. After the break-up of the Fugitives, Tate, Ransom, Davidson, and Warren, joined by others at Vanderbilt, published a volume of essays extolling southern values and agrarianism entitled *I'll Take My Stand* in 1930. The Fugitives and the Agrarians gave Vanderbilt a lasting distinctiveness.

Kirkland's 44 years as chancellor established a record for leadership at a major university. He left his successor, Oliver C. Carmichael (1937–1946), a legacy of vigorous leadership difficult to follow amid the challenges of the Great Depression and World War II. When Vanderbilt's fourth chancellor, Harvie Branscomb (1946–1963), took office, he confronted problems common to southern universities of the period—inadequate facilities, provincial students, a faculty poorly paid and, outside the medical school, generally without national eminence, and low annual income. In order to benefit from the post-World War II economic boom, Branscomb and Harold S. Vanderbilt, president of the Board of Trust and major benefactor, had to steer the university in line with national norms, particularly in the area of racial integration. The dismissal of divinity student James Lawson, regional director of the Fellowship of Reconciliation and supporter of the Nashville sit-ins, caused serious divisions within the Vanderbilt community in 1960, but did not stop the slow decade-long march towards lifting of racial restrictions on admission, achieved in 1962. By the time of Branscomb's retirement in 1963, Vanderbilt drew better qualified students from around the country, had a more diverse and distinguished faculty, and had an expanded physical plant.

Alexander Heard, chancellor from 1963 to 1982, steered Vanderbilt through the difficult years of the Vietnam War, student activism, and demands for equal treatment by women and African Americans. A commitment to freedom of expression, pluralism, and increased self-government of faculty and students helped stimulate the intellectual atmosphere. In 1969 the quota that kept women to one-third of enrollment in the College of Arts and Sciences was ended. Departments began to recruit more women and minority faculty. An open forum policy brought significant and controversial speakers to campus through the annual Forum and Impact series. Major fundraising drives and campus expansions such as the absorption of George Peabody College for Teachers and the Blair School of Music demonstrated Vanderbilt's determination to achieve national stature.

Under its most recent chancellor, Joe B. Wyatt, Vanderbilt continues to define itself according to national standards, a considerable journey from its denominational and regional origins. Total enrollment in 1997 was 10,176.

Patricia Miletich, Nashville University School

Suggested Readings: Paul K. Conkin, *Gone with the Ivy: A Biography of Vanderbilt University* (1985); Edwin Mims, *History of Vanderbilt University* (1946)

SEE: AGRARIANS; DAVIDSON, DONALD; FUGITIVES; GENERAL EDUCATION BOARD; FOOTBALL, COLLEGE; GEORGE PEABODY COLLEGE; HAMILTON, JOSEPH H.; HEARD, G. ALEXANDER; LAW; LITERATURE; LAWSON, JAMES E., JR.; MCTYEIRE, HOLLAND N.; NASHVILLE; NIXON, HERMAN C.; OWSLEY, FRANK L.; RANSOM, JOHN C.; VANDERBILT UNIVERSITY MEDICAL CENTER; WALLACE, PERRY; WARREN, ROBERT PENN

VANDERBILT UNIVERSITY MEDICAL CENTER,

one of the nation's premier academic health centers, traces its lineage to the University of Nashville and to Shelby Medical College. The latter institution, open only a brief time (1858–1861), was established by the Methodist Episcopal Church, South, to provide medical education for a proposed "Central University." Shelby Medical College closed during the Civil War, and the Methodists did not renew their plans for Central University until 1872. Subsequently, the name was changed to Vanderbilt University to reflect the million-dollar gift from railroad and shipping magnate Cornelius Vanderbilt.

In 1874 the medical department of the University of Nashville was merged with that of the fledgling Vanderbilt University, providing Vanderbilt with instant recognition and securing the continuation of the medical school through the new university's ample endowment. In 1875, in the first graduating class of 71 students, ten elected to receive diplomas from the University of Nashville, 13 received Vanderbilt diplomas, and the remainder requested diplomas from both. Gradually, however, the majority of students matriculated in the name of Vanderbilt University.

In 1893 James H. Kirkland assumed the post of Chancellor of Vanderbilt University. In 1895, in response to an offer from Kirkland, the medical faculty agreed upon a new contract that would negate the joint agreement with the University of Nashville and bring the medical school under the control of the Vanderbilt University Board of Trust. A similar initiative by Kirkland in 1914 led to a court battle which granted the institution complete independence from the Methodist Church. Kirkland raised standards at Vanderbilt; in 1900, the medical course was increased from three to four years. Requirements for admission gradually rose from a high school education to a full year of college work.

These and other innovations paid off handsomely with the 1910 release of the Flexnor Report, a nationwide evaluation of medical training institutions. The report declared Vanderbilt's medical department best suited among Tennessee medical colleges to administer a course of study. The report recognized a number of deficiencies, however, including lack of laboratory space and equipment and lack of a full-time preclinical faculty. In response to these inadequacies, Kirkland negotiated a $4 million grant from the General Education Board in 1919 to reorganize the Vanderbilt University School of Medicine.

Located in downtown Nashville, the School of Medicine remained geographically isolated from the main campus. C. Canby Robinson, appointed dean of the School of Medicine in 1920, urged that the reorganized school be placed on the west campus. Robinson's innovative vision of a teaching institution and operating hospital employed the Osler-Halstead formula developed at Johns Hopkins University: a corps of full-time teachers backed by a larger, carefully selected clinical faculty. Robinson established three original departments at Vanderbilt—medicine, surgery, and obstetrics and gynecology—and three laboratories—physiological, infectious disease, and chemical. Ground was broken for the new building in October 1923, and the school opened in 1925. The faculty, house staff, volunteer faculty, and students soon established Vanderbilt's reputation for excellence in teaching, clinical research, and laboratory research. Seven of Vanderbilt's medical faculty later served as presidents of the American Medical Association.

Since World War II, Vanderbilt Medical Center has undergone numerous expansions facilitated by federal grants, an innovative faculty, and the progressive evolution of subspecialization in both clinical disciplines and basic sciences. The Learned Laboratories, which allowed additional space for graduate work, was begun in 1952 and completed in 1960. A circular hospital wing was added in 1962. The Joe and Howard Werthan Building, a new library, and laboratory space were built on 21st Avenue South. In 1977 Rudolph Light Hall was completed on the south side of Garland Avenue to provide classroom and laboratory space for medical students.

Vanderbilt Medical Center continued to expand in the 1980s. A twin-towered Vanderbilt University Hospital, with dedicated space for the Vanderbilt Children's Hospital, opened in 1980. In 1985 the Vanderbilt School of Nursing was brought under the aegis of the Medical Center. That year, the Psychiatric Hospital at Vanderbilt, a joint operation with Columbia/HCA, was completed. A new outpatient center, the Vanderbilt Clinic, opened in 1988. New medical research buildings were constructed in 1989 and 1994. In the latter year, the Vanderbilt Stallworth Rehabilitation Hospital, a joint enterprise with HealthSouth, was dedicated, and the Annette and Irwin Eskind Biomedical Library opened. In late 1997 Vanderbilt University Medical Center unveiled plans for a new Children's Hospital.

Today, Vanderbilt University Medical Center continues to enjoy regional, national, and international renown. Two faculty members, Earl Sutherland, Jr., in 1971 and Stanley Cohen in 1986, have been recognized as Nobel Laureates.

Harris D. Riley, Jr., Vanderbilt Children's Hospital

SEE: CHRISTIE, AMOS U.; CLARK, SAM L.; COHEN, STANLEY; COLUMBIA/ HCA; DANIEL, ROLLIN A., JR.; GENERAL EDUCATION BOARD; GOODPASTURE, ERNEST; MEDICINE; SUTHERLAND, EARL, JR.; VANDERBILT UNIVERSITY

VAUGHAN, JAMES D. (1864–1941), nationally significant publisher and promoter of gospel music, established the James D. Vaughan Company in Lawrenceburg, Tennessee, in 1912. Vaughan, a devout member of the Church of the Nazarene, had already published his first songbook, *Gospel Chimes*, in 1900. His Lawrenceburg-based company over its 50 years of existence would publish over 100 similar gospel songbooks, which are important because they helped to spread the popularity of gospel music, to influence later country music songwriters, and to preserve the tradition of shaped note singing. "His typical songbook," according to scholar Charles Wolfe, "contained an average of 100 songs, and a few of these were old hymns; but most of his songs were newly written gospel songs, songs produced by hundreds of amateur writers across the South."[1] The average songbook sold about 117,000 copies.

Vaughan brought a business sense to the early music industry in Tennessee. He established a singing school in Lawrenceburg, started his own record company for gospel music in 1922, and established one of Tennessee's first commercial radio stations, WOAN, in Lawrenceburg in 1924. Vaughan's records of southern music for a southern audience represent the true roots of the state's now famed recording industry.

Carroll Van West, Middle Tennessee State University

CITATION:

(1) Charles Wolfe, *Tennessee Strings: The Story of Country Music in Tennessee* (Knoxville, 1977), 52–53.

SEE: LAWRENCE COUNTY; MUSIC; SHAPE-NOTE SINGING; VERNACULAR RELIGIOUS MUSIC

VAUGHT, NATHAN (1799–1880), the "Master Builder of Maury County," is credited with the construction of many of the most imposing antebellum homes in southern Middle Tennessee. Vaught was born in Shenandoah County, Virginia, and his family moved to Rutherford County, Tennessee, in 1803 or 1805. His mother died in 1805, and his father in 1807. Vaught and his brother were placed in the care of a couple named Radford, who moved to Columbia in 1808. When Mrs. Radford died the following year, 11-year-old Vaught was bound out by the Maury County Court to cabinetmaker James Purcell to learn that trade.

In 1811 Purcell abandoned cabinetmaking and began building houses, teaching Vaught the basics of carpentry and construction. Vaught worked under Purcell as a journeymen carpenter until Purcell's death in 1821, at which time he began building houses on his own.

His excellent work soon attracted the attention of wealthy clients. Most of his earlier homes were constructed in the waning Federal style, but by the early 1830s, he was building stately homes in the Greek Revival, the new style of choice of the region's planters. His largest commissions came from the Pillow family, for whom he constructed three large Greek Revival mansions—Clifton Place (1838–1839), Rose Hill (1845), and Bethel Place (1855). He worked occasionally in other styles, an example being the eclectic Gothic rectory for the Columbia Athenaeum in 1835. In the late 1850s, Vaught acquired the necessary equipment to produce finished building materials.

Besides more than 50 homes, Vaught constructed a number of commercial buildings, storehouses, and churches. The most important of these is the State Bank of Tennessee (1839) at Columbia, a Doric temple-form building replicating the Parthenon at Athens, Greece. His public buildings included a jail (1838) and Jackson College (1859) at Columbia; he also oversaw construction of the first bridge across the Duck River there in 1822. He recorded his work in his memoirs, "Youth and Old Age," which survives today. Vaught died on April 9, 1880, and is buried at Rose Hill Cemetery at Columbia.

Richard Quin, National Park Service

SEE: ARCHITECTURE, VERNACULAR DOMESTIC; ATHENAEUM; CLIFTON PLACE; MAURY COUNTY

VELAZQUEZ, LORETA JANETA (1842–1897), Confederate soldier and spy, was born in Cuba, raised in New Orleans, and lived in Memphis at various times during the Civil War. As a young girl Velazquez developed an admiration for Joan of Arc and expressed a desire to emulate her deeds and make a name for herself as a woman of courage who would fight for a great cause.

When the Civil War broke out, Velazquez disguised herself as a man, adopted the name of Colonel Harry T. Buford, and raised a cavalry company of her own in order to be near her fiancé. In keeping with her disguise, Velazquez dressed in male clothing complete with a mustache and beard. She fought for the Confederacy in numerous battles in Tennessee and Virginia, including Bull Run and Shiloh. She also served as a special agent and a counterspy. After the war, Velazquez wrote a colorful memoir about her Civil War experiences to support herself and a young son. Some denounced the 1876 publication as a fraud. No record remains of her life after about 1880, or of the circumstances of her death in 1897.

Carole Stanford Bucy, Volunteer State Community College

SEE: SHILOH, BATTLE OF

VERNACULAR RELIGIOUS MUSIC. A wide variety of terms have been used to describe American vernacular religious music: religious ballads, hymns, spiritual songs, folk hymns, revival religious songs, gospel songs, folk tunes, and fuguing tunes. Overwhelmingly revivalistic, nineteenth century vernacular religious music began to express a distinctive American voice. For Tennessee this tradition began with the camp meeting revival songs of the early nineteenth century. Within these songs are the roots of blues, country, modern gospel, and rock-n-roll of the twentieth century.

A lack of education or musical sophistication on the part of the participants, the scarcity of songbooks, and the highly emotional nature of the meetings shaped the songs of the camp meetings that began in 1799 to 1801 in Kentucky and Tennessee. Hymnals such as those of Isaac Watts and the Wesleys, containing text only with no music, were sung to the music of secular/folk tunes which were interchangeable, and the older texts were revised by the addition of choruses. As the songs had to be sung from memory—often in call and response technique with the preacher lining out the text—they had to be simple. Techniques for easy memorization and sustained activity were refrains, formulaic tags, repetitive devices sometimes composed extemporaneously (e.g., "Where, Oh Where Are the Hebrew Children"), the verse-chorus pattern, and emotional appeal.

As religion spread over the Old Southwest the older "fasola" and the shape-note songbooks that began around 1811 provided texts for the rural areas. The original four-shape-note and later seven-shape-note books developed for unsophisticated worshippers used a system of shapes for musical notation with a leader lining out the notation for a song and the participants singing the notation through before beginning the words. Throughout the nineteenth century, shape-note singing schools were conducted all over the South, teaching a style of singing generally known as Sacred Harp singing, the name taken from the most famous tunebook—*The Sacred Harp* (1844). Several important shape-note tunebooks were published in Tennessee, including the influential *Harp of Columbia* (1845/1857) and *New Harp of Columbia* (1867). Texts were drawn from fasola book compilers or church hymnals, and melodies came from secular/folk sources or were homemade. The shape-note tradition is still very much alive in Tennessee today; a revision of *The Sacred Harp* was published in 1991.

Revivals continued to be the defining force in southern vernacular religious music throughout the nineteenth century, with the vernacular songs beginning to appear in some denominational hymnals after mid-century. The term "gospel songs" came into use in the 1870s, and some scholars credit this type of music as a unique American contribution to sacred music. These songs used the song with a refrain, verse-chorus-verse-chorus pattern, repetition of a single phrase, and a decidedly emotional appeal. The music was largely secular with many of the tunes being taken from contemporary music hall and parlor songs (i.e., *Here's To Good Old Whiskey* with *Storm the Forts of Darkness*, or *There Are No Flies on Jesus*). One of the dominant traits of continuity in American vernacular religious music is the combination of secular tunes and religious text, found from camp meeting songs to twentieth century gospel and Christian folk-rock musicals.

An older singing school tradition from the nineteenth century developed into the tradition of singing conventions in the twentieth century, including the very influential county-wide singing conventions that flourished until the late 1940s. A vital gospel music industry began in 1910 when James D. Vaughan of Lawrenceburg, Tennessee, sent a quartet to singing conventions to publicize his new songbooks. These conventions usually included singing schools capped by performances by publisher-sponsored quartets. Two Tennessee gospel music publishers—Stamps-Baxter (Dallas and Chattanooga) and Vaughan Music Company—dominated the gospel music publishing business in the first four decades of the twentieth century. Moreover, Vaughan was responsible for some of the first gospel music recordings.

After World War II, the development of technology in radio and sound recording and the attendant professionalization of gospel quartets changed religious music from a participatory music to a passive audience/professional performer music and spelled the demise of the county singing conventions. Quartets bought publishing companies that had supported the conventions and changed their emphasis. The John Daniel Quartet appeared on the Grand Ole Opry in 1942, the Homeland Quartet had a national hit with *Gospel Boogie* in 1948, and such groups as the Blackwood Brothers Quartet and the Jordanaires gained widespread popularity as performers and recording artists. Gospel music introduced solo artists, larger groups, and a variety of instruments, ultimately entering the mainstream of pop music. In the 1960s the all-night jamborees, begun in the late 1940s, became quite popular. The folk music movement of the 1960s produced contemporary Christian music artists such as Bill Gaither. Later groups such as the Imperials bridged the gap between the contemporary music world and the southern gospel world. By the 1980s gospel rock music had emerged. Rural Tennesseans still prefer the southern gospel music that combines barbershop harmonies and country music performed by a variety of groups—quartets, mixed groups of male and female performers, and solo acts—and varied instrumentation. Traditional amateur family and community gospel groups still get together for singings, perform for fees, and sell self-produced recordings.

African-American religious music has had an important place in American culture from its beginnings in nineteenth century Negro spirituals to the development of twentieth century black gospel music. Most scholars agree that the roots of Negro spirituals can be found in the white camp meeting songs, but that the performance style and the changes in songs reflect the cultural heritage of Africa and the black experience in the South. Whites placed emphasis on the words of religious songs, and blacks generally emphasized the music over the words. Black religious music has been characterized by vocal effects difficult to indicate by standard notation, elaborate vocal ornamentation, frequent melodic interjections, extreme freedom and individuality in performance, strong kinetic factors in performance (e.g., shouting and dancing), heavy improvisation, complex rhythms, and call and response/solo and chorus style. Black college singers such as the famous Fisk University Jubilee Singers firmly established the Negro spiritual during the later nineteenth century. These jubilee singers and all-black minstrel shows, along with the rise of the holiness movement at the end of the nineteenth century, constituted the roots of twentieth century black Gospel style. Black gospel music came into its own in the 1930s with such composers as Thomas A. Dorsey adding gospel lyrics to the blues and jazz traditions. Two nationally prominent black gospel composers—Lucie E. Campbell and the Reverend W. Herbert Brewster (*Surely God is Able*)—were from Memphis. Black gospel quartets began to flourish in the 1940s at the beginning of the golden age of gospel music (1945–1960), and Tennessee was prominent in the movement. Black quartets usually consisted of four to six voices, one of which was the lead singer. As black gospel flourished, quartets were all-male, all-female, or mixed. In addition the tradition included larger gospel choirs. As with white gospel music, modern technology and commercialization expanded their influence after World War II. Even as secular music influenced gospel music, gospel music influenced much of secular music—jazz, blues, and soul.

Homer D. Kemp, Tennessee Technological University
SEE: JUBILEE SINGERS OF FISK UNIVERSITY; MEMPHIS MUSIC SCENE; MUSIC; RELIGION; SHAPE-NOTE SINGING; VAUGHAN, JAMES D.

VERTREES, JOHN J. (1850–1931), Nashville attorney and vocal opponent of woman suffrage and prohibition, was born in Sumner County, Tennessee, on June 16, 1850. He attended Cumberland University and read law with W.S. Monday before being admitted to the bar. Vertrees began his law practice in Gallatin in 1870, before moving to Nashville in 1881, where he formed a law partnership with his brother, W.O. Vertrees.

Active in state Democratic party politics, Vertrees participated in several notable political controversies. During the administration of Governor William B. Bate (1883–1887), Vertrees proposed the final settlement for the state debt crisis. He served as general counsel for incumbent Governor Peter Turney when the General Assembly was called upon to settle the disputed election of 1894. The legislators declared Turney the winner over Republican H. Clay Evans by a small majority of the popular vote.

Vertrees became personal friends with future President William Howard Taft while Taft was a United States Circuit Judge holding court in Nashville. When Taft's Secretary of the Interior was investigated by a congressional committee, Taft asked Vertrees to represent the Secretary. Vertrees declined an appointment by Taft to be Governor of the Philippines and was considered by Taft for an appointment to the United States Supreme Court.

Vertrees became an active spokesman in opposition to woman suffrage. His wife, Virginia, served as the first president of the Tennessee branch of the National Association Opposed to Woman Suffrage. Vertrees believed that those who did not serve in the armed forces should not vote. In his pamphlet, *An Address to the Men of Tennessee on Female Suffrage,* Vertrees attempted to identify woman suffrage with racial equality. Vertrees died in 1931 at the age of 81 in St. Augustine, Florida. He is buried at Mr. Olivet Cemetery in Nashville.

Carole Stanford Bucy, Volunteer State Community College
SEE: BATE, WILLIAM B.; EVANS, HENRY CLAY; PROHIBITION; STATE DEBT CONTROVERSY; TURNEY, PETER; WOMAN SUFFRAGE MOVEMENT

VOGEL, MATTHEW HAYNES (1957–), Olympic medal-winning swimmer from the University of Tennessee, was born June 3, 1957, in Fort Wayne, Indiana. As a high school senior swimming for the Huntingdon YMCA in Indiana, Vogel won the 1975 YMCA National Championship in the 100-meter butterfly. Recruited by Coach Ray Bussard for the University of Tennessee swim program, Vogel had a spectacular freshman season, winning the NCAA Division I 100-meter butterfly, finishing second in the 200-meter race, and being named All-American. Vogel was the only Tennessee swimmer to make the 1976 Olympic team, and on July 21 at Montreal, Canada, he upset the world record holder and a favored teammate to win the gold medal in the 100-meter butterfly with a time of 54.35. Vogel's second medal came in the 4 x 100 freestyle relay in which the United States team took the gold with a world-record time of 3:42.22. That same year, Vogel shared honors with UT basketballer Ernie Grunfeld as Tennessee Sports Hall of Fame Athletes of the Year.

Despite a disappointing sophomore year at UT, Vogel still made the All-American team. He quit school and swimming in 1977. Returning to the University of Tennessee in early 1978, he helped the Aqua Vols capture their seventh straight SEC title and first national championship, and was again named All-American. Vogel last swam competitively in 1979. On May 9, 1996, he was inducted into the International Swimming Hall of Fame. After coaching the Atomic City Aquatic Club in Oak Ridge for more than a decade, Vogel moved in 1997 to another coaching position in California.

Margaret Ellen Crawford, University of Tennessee, Knoxville
SEE: BUSSARD, RAYMOND A.

WALDEN HOSPITAL. Prior to 1915, African Americans in Chattanooga who required hospital care were hospitalized in the basements of existing majority hospitals, such as Erlanger Hospital or Newell Clinic. In 1915 Dr. Emma Rochelle Wheeler, a physician who had practiced medicine in Chattanooga since 1905, met the need for an adequate health care facility for people of color when she opened Walden Hospital. Wheeler purchased two lots on the corner of East Eighth and Douglas streets, and using her own money, erected a three-story brick hospital. Dedicated on July 30, 1915, Walden Hospital became the first hospital in Chattanooga to be owned, operated, and staffed by African Americans and dedicated to their treatment. The hospital had a 30-bed capacity with nine private rooms containing two beds each and a 12-bed ward. The hospital consisted of three departments: surgical, maternity, and nursery. Seventeen physicians and surgeons used the hospital along with a house staff of two and three nurses. The hospital proved so successful that the construction debt was paid in less than three years.

Wheeler, one of only three women in a class of 68, graduated from Meharry Medical College in 1905. After her marriage to Dr. Joseph N. Wheeler, the two moved to Chattanooga and opened a practice on East Main Street where they treated patients there for ten years. For more than 20 years, Wheeler not only practiced medicine, but trained nurses at Walden. She founded the Nurses Services Club, a unique prepaid hospitalization plan for Club members. In addition to her medical practice and teaching duties, Wheeler also raised a family.

After almost four decades of dedicated service to the community, Walden Hospital closed its doors on June 30, 1952. Although in poor health, Wheeler continued her practice. The former Walden Hospital has been converted into apartments.

Wheeler, a pioneer black Chattanooga woman physician, died in 1957. In 1962 the Chattanooga City Commission voted to name the Housing Authority's newest residential project the Emma Wheeler Homes. In 1990 the Chattanooga African-American Museum in conjunction with the Tennessee Historical Commission placed a state historical marker at the site of Walden Hospital to honor Dr. Wheeler and the hospital.

Vivian P. Greene, Chattanooga African-American Museum
SEE: MEHARRY MEDICAL COLLEGE

WALDEN RIDGE AND SEQUATCHIE VALLEY. Sequatchie Valley is a long, arrow-straight scenic slash into eastern North America's Appalachian Plateau that divides the southern half of its Tennessee portion into unequal parts. The valley extends southwestward for about 200 miles from its northern end in Cumberland County, Tennessee, to its southern terminus in Blount County, Alabama; only the northeastern 75 miles lie in Tennessee. Sequatchie Valley is only about five miles wide, on average, and ranges from approximately 1,000 to 1,500 feet deep. The straight, linear nature of the valley is not obvious when looking up from its depths because the valley walls slope away from the bottom and are deeply incised by impressive tributary valleys, but when seen on a map or viewed from the air, it is very obvious.

Paralleling Sequatchie Valley and forming its southeast wall is Walden Ridge, the narrower of the two unequal parts into which the valley divides the Appalachian Plateau. Walden Ridge is also a relatively narrow, linear feature, but wider than the valley, averaging about eight to ten miles wide and generally rising to 2,000 feet in elevation. The ridge is almost coextensive with the Tennessee part of the valley, extending from Cumberland and Roane counties in the north to the Tennessee River gorge just north of the Tennessee-Georgia-Alabama juncture. The part of the plateau northwest of the valley is called the Cumberland Plateau, and it is wider but more dissected than Walden Ridge, especially along its western edge. North and northeast of the valley the merged, much broader plateau is called the Cumberland Plateau. In this area, the steep escarpment along the eastern edge of the Plateau is called Walden Ridge, all the way northeastward to beyond Lake City, in Anderson County.

Edward T. Luther, retired geologist, Tennessee Department of Environment and Conservation

WALKER, JOSEPH E. (1880–1958), noted physician, banker, businessman, civic and religious leader, was born in the cotton fields near Tillman, Mississippi, in 1880 and rose to become one of the most successful African Americans of his time. Walker overcame a background of poverty and worked his way through college and medical school. From 1906 to 1919 he practiced medicine in Indianola, Mississippi.

In 1912 Walker was elected president of Delta Penny Savings Bank and in 1917 president of Mississippi Life Insurance Company, which moved to Memphis in 1920. In 1923 Walker, A.W. Willis, and Dr. J.T. Wilson established Universal Life Insurance Company in Memphis. Under Walker's leadership, Universal Life grew to become one of the largest African-American-owned insurance companies. In 1946, along with his son, A. Maceo Walker, Dr. Walker founded Tri-State Bank of Memphis and was named the bank's first president.

Active in politics, Walker was a leader in the Democratic party. He was also a noted philanthropist and civic leader and helped finance the South Memphis Walker Homes Subdivision, which bears his name. He organized the Memphis Negro Chamber of Commerce in 1926 which published directories of black businesses, now a valuable resource to scholars studying early Memphis black commercial development.

In 1926 Walker was elected president of the National Negro Insurance Association. In 1939 he was elected president of the National Negro Business League. During the 1930s, *Jet* magazine listed him as one of the "10 most Influential Negroes in America."

Walker groomed his son, A. Maceo Walker (1909–1994), to succeed him in the organizations he established. Maceo Walker was elected president and chairman of Universal Life in 1952 and served in this capacity for decades. He also had a long tenure as president and chair of Tri-State Bank. When he stepped down as president of Universal Life in 1983, his daughter, Patricia Walker Shaw (1939–1985), became president of Universal Life and served in this capacity until her death in 1985. Shaw was the first woman to become president of the National Insurance Association in July 1983. Shaw's only child, Harold Shaw, Jr., currently works at Universal Life, making him the fourth generation of his family to serve this company.

Ronald A. Walter, Memphis

SEE: TRI-STATE BANK; UNIVERSAL LIFE INSURANCE COMPANY; WILLIS, ARCHIE W., JR.

WALKER, THOMAS (1715–1794), a colonial Virginian, significantly marked Tennessee through his discovery and naming of the Cumberland River in 1750 and his establishment of the North Carolina-Virginia western line in 1780. He was born in Tidewater Virginia, probably King and Queen County, on January 25, 1715. He trained as a physician and practiced that profession throughout his life, but he was also a major landowner, planter, merchant, manufacturer, land speculator, surveyor, parish leader, military man, and public official. Related by marriage to George Washington, he served as a guardian of young Thomas Jefferson. He reared a large family, and his children married into families that continued to influence America's westward development.

In 1750, as investor in and agent of the Loyal Company, a speculative land company, Walker led an exploration through Cave Gap, which he subsequently named Cumberland Gap. In his journal account of the expedition, he reported his discovering and naming of the Cumberland River and the construction of a cabin to mark the first white settlement in the area. Within three years after that journey, plans were afoot for Walker to lead an expedition to find the way to the western sea by following the Missouri River to its sources and beyond. That trip, which would have predated the Lewis and Clark Expedition by 50 years, never materialized due to the French and Indian War. During that war Walker served as commissary general for Virginia's troops and was present with Colonel George Washington, and another young soldier, Daniel Boone, when General Edward Braddock met defeat in his attempt to capture Fort Duquesne in 1755.

When peace returned, Walker became officially involved in negotiations with several Native American tribes. He represented Virginia in the Treaty of Fort Stanwix in 1768. The next year he held the same position in negotiations to adjust some errors in the Hard Labor Treaty with the Cherokee in Charleston, South Carolina. He negotiated with the Ohio Indians at Pittsburgh in 1775. Walker served in a number of political positions in Virginia throughout his life, was instrumental in founding the city of Charlottesville, Virginia, and served on the Committee of Safety, one of the early independence initiatives.

As a young man, Daniel Smith, who was to become a prominent figure in early Tennessee history, came to apprentice with Walker, initially planning to become a physician. When his interests turned toward surveying, Walker was his mentor in those activities as well. In 1780 Walker and Daniel Smith were Virginia's commissioners appointed to work with Colonel Richard Henderson of North Carolina, one of the founders of the Transylvania Company, to survey the North Carolina-Virginia line. When Henderson became disenchanted with the survey, he abandoned the effort. Part of the survey team continued to run the line, while Walker floated down the Cumberland River to French Lick, now Nashville. After the line was completed to the Tennessee River, Virginia Governor Thomas Jefferson charged Walker and Smith to proceed to the Falls of the Ohio, join General George Rogers Clark, and travel the Ohio River to its union with the Mississippi River to complete the survey, by establishing the southwest corner of the state of Virginia at the Mississippi River. An error in the survey, recognized at the time, but accepted by both North Carolina and Virginia, explains the offset in the resulting state line at its junction with the Tennessee River, still official today on maps of Tennessee and Kentucky.

After completing the survey, Walker served in political positions in the Virginia state government, before retiring from public service to live out his days at Castle Hill, his Albemarle County home. He died there on November 9, 1794.

Alexander McLeod, Nashville

SUGGESTED READINGS: Alexander C. McLeod, "A Man for All Regions: Dr. Thomas Walker of Castle Hill," *Filson Club Quarterly* 71(1997): 169–201; Harry W. Welford, "Dr. Thomas Walker: His Uncelebrated Impact on Early Tennessee," *Tennessee Historical Quarterly* 34(1975): 130–144

SEE: CUMBERLAND GAP AND CUMBERLAND GAP NATIONAL HISTORICAL PARK; CUMBERLAND RIVER; BOONE, DANIEL; SMITH, DANIEL; WILDERNESS ROAD

WALKER, WILLIAM (1824–1860) was born May 8, 1824, in Nashville and died before a firing squad in Central America. His strange, brief career earned him the sobriquet "Grey-Eyed Man of Destiny." He was controversial in the United States and feared in Central America. Trained as a physician in Pennsylvania and Paris (1843), he moved to New Orleans (1845) where he became a lawyer and idealistic newspaper editor. In 1850, after the death of his deaf-mute fiancée, Ellen Martin, Walker left for California, where he became involved in politics and emerged an advocate of Manifest Destiny.

In October 1853 Walker sailed with 45 men for Mexico. Landing in Baja California, Walker declared the Republic of Lower California independent and named himself president. In January 1854 he declared the annexation of the adjacent state of Sonora and renamed the "country" the Republic of

Sonora. Driven out of Mexico, Walker and his bedraggled forces returned to California and surrendered to U.S. troops. He stood trial for violation of U.S. neutrality laws and was acquitted. Although his expedition was a total failure, Walker was a hero to many Californians.

Walker next set his sights on Nicaragua, a fertile country with an important trans-isthmian commercial route, but in chaos due to a long series of revolutions. To circumvent U.S. neutrality laws, Walker obtained a contract from President Castellón of the Democratic party to bring as many as 300 "colonists" to Nicaragua. The colonists received the right to bear arms in the service of the Democratic government against the rival Legitimist party.

In June 1855 Walker and 57 soldiers of fortune landed at the Nicaraguan Pacific port of Realejo. With Castellón's consent Walker attacked the Legitimists in the town of Rivas, near the trans-isthmian route of the Accessory Transit Company, which Walker hoped to control. Walker's men were defeated, but armed with six-shooters and superior rifles and motivated by a boisterous spirit of derring-do, they wreaked such havoc with the defenders of Rivas that the Americans established themselves as a feared force.

On October 13, Walker took the Legitimist capital, Granada, in a surprise attack. He then negotiated the surrender of the Legitimist army, the disbanding of the Democratic army, and the formation of a coalition government with himself as Commander-in-Chief of the Nicaraguan Army. With the support of many Nicaraguans, Walker's coalition government eventually received recognition by President Franklin Pierce's administration in Washington. A bilingual newspaper, *El Nicaragüense*, was circulated in the United States, extolling Nicaragua for American colonization. Walker attracted recruits from among Americans crossing the isthmus en route to or from California.

Walker's rapid rise to power disturbed many Nicaraguans and other Central American leaders who feared he intended to "Americanize" all Central America. In March 1856 a Costa Rican army invaded Nicaragua to remove Walker. Walker's troops were defeated in fierce fighting in Rivas, but an outbreak of cholera forced the invading army to withdraw. By June, Walker's coalition government was disintegrating, and the president and various cabinet members implored Guatemala, Honduras, and El Salvador to send armies to rescue the nation. Walker retaliated by declaring the president a traitor and calling for elections with himself as a candidate.

Walker was inaugurated as President of Nicaragua on July 12, 1856, and soon launched his Americanization program. English was declared an official language; currency and fiscal policy were reorganized to encourage immigration from the United States; and *El*

Nicaragüense redoubled its recruitment efforts. Walker confiscated the estates of his Nicaraguan opponents and resold them to his American supporters. Finally, to secure support from the southern states of the United States, Walker annulled the constitutional prohibition against slavery.

Walker now faced a variety of enemies. On his inaugural day, Salvadoran troops entered Nicaragua, later joined by Guatemalan and Honduran forces. The Pierce administration refused to recognize Walker's new government. The British government encouraged Costa Rican opposition to Walker and provided arms for insurgents. Walker also made a powerful enemy in "Commodore" Cornelius Vanderbilt. Walker's lifeline to the United States was the fleet of river and lake steamers owned by the Accessory Transit Company, a lucrative Vanderbilt enterprise chartered by the Nicaraguan government. Walker unwisely agreed to transfer the charter to Vanderbilt's business rivals. In retaliation, the "Commodore" sent agents to aid the Costa Ricans when they invaded Nicaragua again in November 1856.

Walker ordered Granada razed and concentrated his forces at Rivas. The Costa Rican capture of the Transit Company steamers left Walker with little hope of reinforcement. He held out for five months against superior forces until his own army was gradually reduced by starvation, disease, and desertion. On May 1, 1857, Walker surrendered to a U.S. Naval officer who negotiated his capitulation.

Walker continued to believe himself the legitimate president of Nicaragua and mounted six return expeditions from the United States. Foiled by port authorities and bad luck, Walker was removed from Nicaragua a second time by the U.S. Navy. After an unsuccessful attempt to take the country via Honduras, he surrendered to a British navy captain, who turned him over to Honduran authorities. On September 12, 1860, Walker was executed for piracy in Trujillo, Honduras, where he is buried.

Richard C. Finch, Tennessee Technological University
SUGGESTED READING: William O. Scroggs, *Filibusters and Financiers: The Story of William Walker and His Associates* (1916)
SEE: TENNESSEANS IN CALIFORNIA GOLD RUSH

WALKER-MEADOR, JO (1928–), the first Executive Director of the Country Music Association, was born Josephine Denning in Orlinda, Tennessee. One of ten children, her early ambition was to become a girls basketball coach. She attended Lambuth College and George Peabody College and worked in a variety of jobs before being hired as the office manager and sole employee of the newly-formed Country Music Association (CMA) in 1958. In 1962 she became the Executive Director of the association and remained in that position until she retired in 1991.

Under her direction, the CMA grew from a one-person organization to an association with worldwide influence. During the 30 years of her directorship, the number of country music stations in the United States increased from 100 to 2,000, fully 25 percent of all United States stations. While at CMA, Walker-Meador initiated the Country Music Hall of Fame in 1961, Fan Fair in 1971, and the annual CMA Awards ceremonies.

In 1954 she married Charles Walker, who died in a motorcycle accident in 1967. They were the parents of one daughter, Michelle. In 1981 she married businessman Bob Meador.

Joseph L. May, Nashville
SEE: COUNTRY MUSIC ASSOCIATION; COUNTRY MUSIC HALL OF FAME

WALKING HORSE NATIONAL CELEBRATION in Shelbyville, Tennessee, is one of the largest horse shows in the world. Its physical accommodations, including 1,650 stalls for housing horses, establish it as the largest equestrian complex in America. The "Celebration," as the show is known, began in 1939, as a vision in the mind of Henry Davis of Wartrace, a longtime owner and trainer of Walking Horses. Davis witnessed a festival highlighting the crimson clover industry and wondered about the possibility of an event to celebrate the Tennessee Walking Horse.

After consulting with other owners, Davis asked for an opportunity to present his idea to the Shelbyville Lion's Club. Later the Rotary Club joined the effort, and plans went forward for the first show, scheduled for September 7, 8, and 9, 1939. After the success of the first show, it continued as an annual event and now lasts ten days, ending the Saturday night before Labor Day. Since the first show, 58 horses have been crowned "The World Grand Champion."

From the very first, the idea of a "World Series" for Walking Horses captured the imagination of owners as well as the people of Bedford County. The community organized to establish a foundation for a horse show that has become a monument to both the horses and the people who have contributed to the show's excellence.

The first show in 1939 drew 218 horses, mostly from Middle Tennessee. A decade later 610 horses entered the show. In 1996 the show attracted 2,170 entries from throughout the United States. Today's owners come from as far away as Germany and Puerto Rico. The attendance at the first show numbered perhaps 2,000; the attendance at the show in 1996 was 150,390. The seating capacity of the outdoor arena is now over 30,000 for a single performance, excluding the Calsonic Arena, which accommodates another 4,500. The prize money for the 1939 show was $2,895; by 1996 it had reached $421,850. The economic impact of the Celebration is felt throughout the year in Shelbyville, Bedford County, and the mid-state area. A recent study conservatively estimated the economic impact at $21 million.

The Celebration is the centerpiece of the Walking Horse industry. To win an award at the Celebration not only enhances the value of the horse, but brings a feeling of unrivaled accomplishment to the rider and owner of the entrant. Winners can be assured that their accomplishment will be preserved in Walking Horse history.

The Celebration sets the standard for Walking Horse shows throughout America. The size of its ring—300 feet long by 150 feet wide—has become the standard used by promoters wherever horse shows are held. Its division of entries into special classes is accepted by most other shows. Children as young as six years old to senior citizens compete in separate age divisions for coveted prizes and honors. Such an age range not only adds variety to the show, but serves as a tribute to the temperament and easy gaits of the Tennessee Walking Horse.

Duels between great horses and rivalries among great trainers have punctuated the history and contributed to the excitement of the Celebration. During the Sweepstakes Class on final night, spectators rise to their feet in tribute as beautiful and talented horses make their way around the ring. After the horses and trainers exhibit their talents, the entries line up at one end of the ring and await the declaration of "The World Grand Champion," and the victory ride around the ring.

The Celebration symbolizes many things: equine development, the establishment of a cultural tradition, and a successful economic experiment. Perhaps most of all, it symbolizes the ability of a community to focus its physical resources and imaginative leadership to establish a tradition that epitomizes the word "potential."

Bob Womack, Middle Tennessee State University
SEE: BEDFORD COUNTY; HARLINDALE FARM; MARSHALL COUNTY; THOROUGHBRED HORSE BREEDING AND RACING

WALLACE, CAMPBELL (1806–1895), East Tennessee businessman and railroad president, was a native of Sevier County and grew up in Maryville, where he attended Anderson Seminary. At age 14, he moved to Knoxville, where he was employed by a prominent merchant, Charles McClung. In 1837 Wallace entered a partnership with Matthew and Hugh L. McClung, forming Knoxville's first wholesale business, McClung, Wallace, and Company.

In 1842 Wallace bought out the McClung brothers and founded his own Gay Street wholesale business, the Campbell Wallace Company. After Wallace's company achieved success, he accepted a position on the Board of Trustees of East Tennessee College. In 1853 Wallace became the president of the

East Tennessee and Georgia Railroad. While president, he supervised the construction of the line to Bristol, which completed the railway link from Atlanta to Washington, D.C.

In July 1863 Wallace resigned as president and fled to Atlanta to avoid capture in the impending Union army occupation of Knoxville. Wallace's escape followed public criticism by the Unionist editor of the *Knoxville Whig*, William G. "Parson" Brownlow. Brownlow labelled Wallace as a militant Confederate and warned that he should either leave East Tennessee or be shot by Union supporters.

After the war, Wallace remained in Georgia. By 1866 he was superintendent of the Western and Atlantic Railroad and engaged in the rebuilding of the line that had been destroyed during General William T. Sherman's attack on Georgia. Wallace headed the Georgia Railroad Commission from 1879 to 1893. He died in May 1895.

William L. Ketchersid, Bryan College
SEE: KNOXVILLE; RAILROADS

WALLACE, PERRY E., JR. (1948–), Southeastern Conference (SEC) basketball trailblazer, was born in February 1948 in Nashville, to Perry E. and Hattie Haynes Wallace. The youngest of six children, he received his primary and middle school education at Nashville's segregated public schools. Wallace, a straight-A student and class valedictorian, graduated in June 1966 from Pearl Senior High School.

Wallace played center on Pearl's basketball team, where he was known for his slam-dunks and referred to as "king of the boards." In 1965–1966, the first year the Tennessee Secondary School Athletic Association (TSSAA) allowed African Americans to participate, Pearl romped through district, regional, and state competitions. At the end of an undefeated season, Pearl Senior High School became the first African-American team to win the TSSAA's Boys' State Basketball Tournament, posting a perfect season of 31 games and a two-year, 43-game winning streak.

Averaging 19 rebounds and 12 points per game, high school All-American Perry Wallace was recruited by more than 80 colleges and universities, but in May 1966 he signed with Vanderbilt University. Wallace became the first African-American "Commodore" to participate in varsity sports at the Nashville school and in SEC basketball.

During his freshman year, Wallace encountered segregation's "flood of hatred" during games at Mississippi State, the University of Tennessee, and Auburn University. In spite of racism, Wallace completed his freshman year averaging 17 points and 20 rebounds per game. On December 2, 1967, Wallace became the first African-American varsity student-athlete to compete in the SEC. Segregationists' ire intensified. He experienced racism at its worst, particularly at SEC schools in Alabama and Mississippi. Cheerleaders led a volley of invective racist cheers. There were threats of beatings, castration, and lynching. He endured physical abuse on the court that referees refused to acknowledge as fouls. Wallace was harangued, taunted, and threatened throughout his SEC career.

When racial malevolence confronted him, Perry Wallace mentally retreated to the north Nashville school where he last experienced the comfort and solace of community support. "On that night in Starkville, Mississippi, Perry sang the Pearl High *Alma Mater*," said his friend, high school and college classmate, the Reverend Walter R. Murray (he became Vanderbilt's first African-American administrator and board of trust member). While coaches and teammates "chose not to see the racism," Wallace said, "I . . . wanted somebody to say, you're not crazy, I heard those people . . . calling you 'nigger' and threatening to hang you, I . . . want you to know I'm with you."[1]

Struggling to stay in-bounds between whites who wanted him to fail and African Americans who expected him to be a "superstar," Wallace became the quintessential "organization man." He never retaliated against players who maliciously fouled him. Wallace realized that any perceived misconduct on his part could impede the progress of SEC desegregation. While the most noticeable person on the basketball court, he was unnoticed on the Vanderbilt campus; known by all, no one knew him. Wallace recognized that most people failed to see him as a full person; moreover, they had no concept of the problems of African Americans.

The first African American to complete four years in the SEC, Perry Wallace ended his tenure as captain of the Vanderbilt varsity team and second-team All SEC. The senior class voted Wallace Bachelor of Ugliness, an honor awarded to the most popular and most appreciated male class member. After his graduation, the universities of Alabama, Florida, Georgia, and Kentucky opened the 1970 SEC season with desegregated varsity teams.

A pioneer in the desegregation of SEC sports, Wallace earned a bachelor's degree in engineering in 1970 from Vanderbilt University. In 1975 he graduated from Columbia University's School of Law. During the administrations of Presidents Jimmy Carter and Ronald Reagan, Wallace served as an attorney in the U.S. Department of Justice. At the time of this writing, he was a professor of law at the Washington College of Law, American University in Washington, D.C.
Linda T. Wynn, Tennessee Historical Commission/Fisk University

CITATION:
(1) Perry E. Wallace, Esq., Interview by Linda T. Wynn, January 3, 1997.

SUGGESTED READING: Paul Conkin, *Gone with the Ivy: A Biography of Vanderbilt University* (1981); Roy M. Neel, *Dynamite! 75 Years of Vanderbilt Basketball* (1975)

SEE: CIVIL RIGHTS MOVEMENT; TSSAA; VANDERBILT UNIVERSITY

WALLACE UNIVERSITY SCHOOL. Nashville's Wallace University School was established in 1886 through the leadership of A.G. Adams, J.B. O'Bryan, and R.B. Throne. Desiring to establish a boys' school that emphasized character and scholarship, these men offered the position of headmaster to Clarence B. Walker, a young teacher at the University School at Charleston, South Carolina. A Hampden-Sydney graduate with a Masters degree from University of Virginia, Wallace served as headmaster until 1941, when he retired at age 82 and the school closed.

Wallace School was small and consequently had difficulty competing in athletics with prep school powerhouses, such as Battle Ground Academy; Braham and Hughes; Montgomery Bell Academy; and Morgan. Professor Wallace never encouraged athletics, fearing they might interfere with studies. Still, he remained loyal to his boys and was often seen racing up the sidelines during football games.

Each day, Wallace read to the students from a battered old Bible as part of his educational aim to produce men of honesty, integrity, refinement, and culture, who valued sound learning and scholarship. Sawney Webb, the headmaster of Webb School, believed Wallace succeeded in his goals. He praised Wallace graduates as the scholarly peers of any other school, with the additional advantage of a set of values and philosophy of life to carry them through college and the business world.
Ridley Wills II, Franklin

SEE: MONTGOMERY BELL ACADEMY; WEBB SCHOOL

WALTON, JESSE (d. 1789), pioneer soldier and settler, was born in Virginia. By the outbreak of the American Revolution, Walton was living in Surry County, North Carolina, along the Virginia border north of Winston-Salem. A patriot, Walton was active in the Surry Committee of Safety and served in the militia. His earliest service was in the procurement of arms and ammunition for the North Carolina forces. In 1776, when the Cherokees attacked Fort Watauga, Long Island, Nolichucky, and other areas in upper East Tennessee, Second-major Walton was sent with the forces under Colonel William Christian on an expedition to attack the Overhill Cherokee towns along the Little Tennessee River. Subsequently, Walton became part of the garrison forces at the newly built Fort Williams along the Nolichucky River near Jacob Brown's settlement.

In 1777 Walton purchased a farm in the region and became a friend of John Sevier, who commanded the western soldiers occupying the fort. By February 1778 Walton had been elected justice of the peace in Washington County and served on the commission charged with providing a site for the courthouse, jail, and stocks. He also was elected to the North Carolina legislature and introduced a bill in 1779 to create the town of Jonesborough, named for a North Carolina politician.

Jonesboro, as it later was spelled, was laid out by Walton and five other commissioners in one-acre lots that were sold by drawing. The original town plat showed that Walton was the largest landowner with ten lots. After founding Tennessee's first town, Walton moved to Georgia about 1781 and was killed in a battle with the Cherokees in 1789.

Fred S. Rolater, Middle Tennessee State University
SEE: JONESBOROUGH; SEVIER, JOHN;

WALTON ROAD played a major part in the settlement of the area between the Cumberland Plateau and the Cumberland River. It was not the first road through the area, but followed older paths at several points. Nevertheless, by providing an adequate and relatively secure avenue to the west, the Walton Road served as an enticement to settlers contemplating the journey.

The road was named for William Walton of Carthage, one of its surveyors and builders. In 1795 Walton, who anticipated profits from the promotion of travel along the route, secured permission from Governor William Blount for the construction of the first section of the road, which ran from the junction of the Cumberland and Caney Fork Rivers in Smith County (Carthage) to a point on the North Carolina Military Trace (Avery Trace) at Brotherton in modern Putnam County. Walton completed the project in the autumn of 1795 at about the same time he received a license to operate a ferry at the junction of the rivers.

In 1799 the General Assembly appointed Walton, William Martin, and Robert Kyle to establish a new east-west road. Completed in 1801 and officially designated as the Cumberland Turnpike, but popularly called Walton Road, it traversed over 100 miles of wilderness from Southwest Point to Carthage. The new road was 15 feet wide and free of stumps. It was to be leveled on the sides of hills and have bridges or causeways built over streams. Mile markers blazed on trees or signs appeared every three miles. Tollgates and stands (inns) were established along the route.

Spencer's Mountain at Crab Orchard in Cumberland County, named for pioneer Thomas "Bigfoot" Spencer, was the most dangerous, and the most talked about, point on the Walton Road. Although construction of I-40 destroyed the side of the mountain, Spencer's Rock still marks the path of the road up the mountain.

U.S. 70 and the railroad followed the same path as the Walton Road to descend into Roane County. The steep descent down Walden's Ridge, through Kimbrough Gap on the south side of Mount Roosevelt, received some comment from the travelers, but it evidently did not create the same intensity of fear as Spencer's Rock.

Walton Road served the traveling public into the twentieth century, providing the foundation for newer roads until the construction of Interstate 40. The Tennessee Central Railroad, built in the 1890s, followed alongside the Walton Road, particularly in Cumberland County. One way to trace the old road today is by locating the abandoned railroad bed. U.S. 70N, built in the 1920s, followed the Walton Road, and built on top of the road in several parts of western Putnam County and eastern Smith County. Putnam County contained more miles of Walton Road than Roane, Cumberland, and Smith counties that the road crossed.

W. Calvin Dickinson, Tennessee Technological University
SEE: FORT SOUTHWEST POINT; PUTNAM COUNTY; SMITH COUNTY; TRAILS, HISTORIC

WAR OF 1812. When the United States declared war on Great Britain in June 1812, Tennesseans proudly proclaimed their readiness to preserve the honor and dignity of their country. It seemed unlikely that landlocked Tennessee would be concerned about British violations of maritime rights and impressment of American seamen. The thirst for expansion, specifically for British-owned Canada in the North, and the southern desire for Spanish-held Florida, drew Tennesseans into the conflict. The acquisition of Florida would open economic possibilities through the Gulf Coast ports via the river systems of Alabama. At this time, the Creek Indians claimed Alabama, part of the Mississippi Territory.

For decades, the Creeks had become increasingly intermingled with white culture through marriage and the adoption of commercial agriculture. Just prior to the War of 1812, however, a more traditional faction known as the "Red Sticks" began promoting an anti-white campaign inspired by a visit from the great Shawnee chief, Tecumseh. Indian aggression along the frontier, encouraged by Britain and Spain, alarmed American settlers; then an attack on whites and friendly Indians at Fort Mims (near Mobile, Alabama) on August 30, 1813, stirred the outraged populace into action. The Creek War thereby became intertwined with the War of 1812.

In September 1813 Tennessee Governor Willie Blount issued a call for 3,500 volunteers. Tennesseans' enthusiastic response initiated a tradition that gave the state its nickname of the "Volunteer State." Andrew Jackson, as major general of the Tennessee militia, along with his military colleague, John Coffee, led a force into the heart of the Creek Nation with the intent of completely destroying the Creeks as a fighting force. Beginning in November 1813, a series of encounters with the Red Sticks culminated in the Battle of Horseshoe Bend on March 27, 1814. This battle left over 800 Creeks dead and ended the threat of a Creek invasion.

Throughout the Creek War, the Indians were outmanned, inadequately armed, and lacking in military discipline. In fact, Jackson's greatest threat came not from the Creeks, but from supply shortages and desertions by troops dissatisfied with their enlistment terms. Nevertheless, the victories won during the Creek War were acclaimed enthusiastically by a nation experiencing military setbacks in the North. As a reward for his efforts, Jackson was commissioned a major general in the United States Regular Army. His treaty with the defeated Creeks at Fort Jackson in August 1814 forced that tribe to forfeit nearly two-thirds of its land (about 23 million acres), which soon filled with white settlers.

Jackson next pressed on into West Florida, securing Pensacola by the end of 1814. Reports of British activities near New Orleans led Jackson's army to its final destination. This hodgepodge army, composed of backwoods militia from Tennessee and Kentucky, U.S. Army regulars, Choctaw Indians, free blacks, Creoles, and pirates, faced Britain's elite troops. Jackson's defensive strategy and the British commanders' underestimation of American fighting ability led to an English defeat at the Battle of New Orleans on January 8, 1815. Tennessee troops, under General William Carroll and the ever-present Coffee, played an active role in this American victory. Although much has been made of the fact that this battle occurred after the peace treaty was signed (December 24, 1814), it should be noted that the treaty was not ratified until February 1815. This victory catapulted Andrew Jackson to hero status throughout the country and started a political ascent that led Jackson to the presidency.

In addition to Jackson, several prominent Tennesseans played a vital role in the War of 1812. Congressman Felix Grundy was one of the principal "War Hawks," mostly Congressmen from the South and West who pressed the government for a declaration of war. James Winchester, a resident of Sumner County, was commissioned a brigadier general and led an unsuccessful invasion of Canada. Edmund Pendleton Gaines, an East Tennessean, rose to the rank of major general for his role in defeating the British at Fort Erie in 1814. Sam Houston and David Crockett, future legendary heroes, played minor roles in the war against the Creeks.

For Tennessee, the War of 1812 all but eliminated British and Spanish interference in the Southwest. It also broke the power of the southern tribes, leading to their eventual removal, and opened vast tracts of land for white settlers to exploit. Because of its political and military prominence during the war, Tennessee, for the first time, was cast into the national spotlight.

Thomas Kanon, Tennessee State Library and Archives

SUGGESTED READING: Frank Owsley, Jr., *Struggle for the Gulf Borderlands* (1981)

SEE: BLOUNT, WILLIE; CARROLL, WILLIAM; CREEK WAR OF 1813 AND 1814; CROCKETT, DAVID; GRUNDY, FELIX; HOUSTON, SAM; JACKSON, ANDREW; TROUSDALE, WILLIAM; WINCHESTER, JAMES

WAR OF THE ROSES was Tennessee's gubernatorial campaign of 1886 and pitted brothers Robert L. Taylor (Democrat) and Alfred A. Taylor (Republican). Alf had not been notably successful as a vote-getter, and his nomination was probably designed to drive Bob from the race. When Bob declined to withdraw, a Memphis *Appeal* editorial referred to the prospective race as "grotesque and unnatural." Alluding to England's War of the Roses, it asserted: "If we are to have the house of Taylor, like that of York with its white rose, and Lancaster with blood red rose; let the brothers of our house lovingly exhale the fragrance of the same flower."[1] Bob, after winning the Democratic nomination, opened the joint campaign with Alf in Madisonville on September 9. In his remarks, he turned roses into metaphors of harmony: "The red rose and the white rose bloom together and shed their odors upon the same atmosphere, and gently struggling for supremacy, glorify the twilight hours."[2] Two days later, in Cleveland, supporters began wearing red and white roses.

Myths surround the campaign. The brothers were humorous storytellers and fiddlers, but the notion that the brothers fiddled from the platform probably came from an illustration in *Frank Leslie's Illustrated Newspaper*. That the brothers played practical jokes— like speech-stealing—on one another came from Alf's imaginative account in a biography of his brother. Bob won the election with 53 percent of the vote—Alf would win the governorship in 1920—and succeeded in transforming roses into enduring symbols of good will. Over a century later, following a dispute, Democratic Vice President Albert Gore, Jr., speaking at Tennessee's Bicentennial celebration, referred to the 1886 election, presented Republican Governor Don Sundquist—his "Tennessee brother"—with a red rose, and kept a white one for himself.

Robert L. Taylor, Jr., Middle Tennessee State University

CITATIONS:

(1) Memphis *Appeal,* 19 June 1886.

(2) Nashville *American,* 10 September 1886.

SUGGESTED READING: Robert L. Taylor, Jr., "Tennessee's War of the Roses as Symbol and Myth," *Tennessee Historical Quarterly* 41(1982): 337–359

SEE: TAYLOR, ALFRED A.; TAYLOR, ROBERT L.

WARD, NANCY (1738–1822), last Beloved Woman of the Cherokees, was born in 1738 at Chota and given the name Nanye-hi which signified "One who goes about," a name taken from Nunne-hi, the legendary name of the Spirit People of Cherokee mythology. Her birth came near the outbreak of a smallpox epidemic that resulted in the deaths of approximately one-half of the Cherokees. The identity of her father is not known, but the Cherokees practiced a matrilineal tradition, and Nanye-hi's mother was Tame Doe, of the Wolf Clan, a sister of Attakullakulla, civil chief of the Cherokee nation.

In her adult years, observers described Nanye-hi as queenly and commanding in appearance and manner and as a winsome and resourceful woman. By age 17 she had two children, Five Killer and Catherine. Her husband was killed in a raid on the Creeks during the 1755 Battle of Taliwa, where she fought by her husband's side, chewing the lead bullets for his rifle to make them more deadly. When he fell in battle, she sprang up from behind a log and rallied the Cherokee warriors to fight harder. Taking up a rifle, she led a charge that unnerved the Creeks and brought victory to the Cherokees.

Because of her valor, the clans chose her as Agi-ga-u-e, "Beloved Woman" of the Cherokees. In this powerful position, her words carried much weight in the tribal government because the Cherokees believed that the Great Spirit frequently spoke through the Beloved Woman. As Beloved Woman, Nanye-hi headed the Women's Council and sat on the Council of Chiefs. She had complete power over prisoners. Sometimes known as Ghigua or "War Woman," she also prepared the warriors' Black Drink, a sacred ritual preparatory to war.

Bryant Ward, an English trader who had fought in the French and Indian War, took up residence with the Cherokees and married Nancy in the late 1750s. Ward had a wife, but since Cherokees did not consider marriage a life-long institution, the arrangement apparently presented few problems. Ward and her English husband lived in Chota for a time and became the parents of a daughter, Betsy. Eventually Bryant Ward moved back to South Carolina, where he lived the remainder of his life with his white wife and family. Nancy Ward and Betsy visited his home on many occasions, where they were welcomed and treated with respect.

Nancy Ward also became respected and well known by the settlers moving across the mountains into the Cherokee territory. James Robertson visited her home. John Sevier owed much of his military success to her: on at least two occasions, she sent Isaac Thomas to warn Sevier of impending Indian attacks. She once stopped the warriors of Toqua from burning Lydia Bean at the stake. Ward kept Bean, the wife of Tennessee's first permanent settler, at her home for a time before allowing her to return to Watauga. Ward made good use of the white woman's enforced stay and learned the art of making butter and cheese. Subsequently, Ward bought cattle and introduced dairying to the Cherokees.

Ward exerted considerable influence over the affairs of both the Cherokees and the white settlers and participated actively in treaty negotiations. In July 1781 she spoke powerfully at the negotiations held on the Long Island of the Holston River following settler attacks on Cherokee towns. Oconastota designated Kaiyah-tahee (Old Tassel) to represent the Council of Chiefs in the meeting with John Sevier and the other treaty commissioners. After Old Tassel finished his persuasive talk, Ward called for a lasting peace on behalf of both white and Indian women. This unparalleled act of permitting a woman to speak in the negotiating council took the commissioners aback. In their response, Colonel William Christian acknowledged the emotional effect her plea had on the men and praised her humanity, promising to respect the peace if the Cherokees likewise remained peaceful. Ward's speech may have influenced the negotiators in a more fundamental way because the resulting treaty was one of the few where settlers made no demand for Cherokee land. Before the meeting, the commissioners had intended to seek all land north of the Little Tennessee River. Nevertheless, the earlier destruction of Cherokee towns and the tribe's winter food supply left many Indians facing hunger. As a result of the desparate circumstances, Ward and the very old Oconastota spent the winter in the home of Joseph Martin, Indian Agent to the Cherokees and husband of Ward's daughter Betsy.

Again at the Treaty of Hopewell in 1785, Ward made a dramatic plea for continued peace. At the close of the ceremonies, she invited the commissioners to smoke her pipe of peace and friendship. Wistfully hoping to bear more children to people the Cherokee nation, Ward looked to the protection of Congress to prevent future disturbances and expressed the hope that the "chain of friendship will never more be broken."[1] Although the commissioners promised that all settlers would leave Cherokee lands within six months and even gave the Indians the right to punish recalcitrant homesteaders, whites ignored the treaty, forcing the Cherokees to make additional land cessions.

During the 1790s Ward came to be known as Granny Ward because she took in and provided for a number of children. At the same time, she observed enormous changes taking place within the Cherokee nation, as the Indians adopted the commercial agricultural lifestyle of the nearby settlers and pressed for a republican form of government. Unlike the old system of clan and tribal loyalty, the new Cherokee government provided no place for a "Beloved Woman."

The Hiwassee Purchase of 1819 forced Ward to abandon Chota. She moved south and settled on the Ocoee River near present-day Benton. There she operated an inn on the Federal Road until her death in 1822. Her grave is located on a nearby hill beside the graves of Five Killer and her brother Long Fellow (The Raven). A monument was erected on her grave in 1923 by the Nancy Ward Chapter, Daughters of the American Revolution.

David Ray Smith, Oak Ridge

CITATION:

(1) James Mooney, *Myths of the Cherokees* (1900), 490.

SUGGESTED READINGS: Pat Alderman, *Nancy Ward, Cherokee Chieftainess* (1978); Ben H. McClary, "Nancy Ward: The Last Beloved Woman of the Cherokees," *Tennessee Historical Quarterly* 21(1962): 352–364

SEE: ATTAKULLAKULLA; CHOTA; MARTIN, JOSEPH; OCONASTOTA; OVERHILL CHEROKEES; POLK COUNTY; SEVIER, JOHN; TREATIES

WARF, JOHN HOWARD (1904–1996), Tennessee Commissioner of Education (1963–1971), was born in Lewis County in 1904 and rose to political power in the rough-and-tumble world of Democratic politics in the mid-twentieth century. Warf dominated Lewis County politics in a style that earned him the label of being a "bare-knuckled political brawler."[1] He learned to be an effective political leader.

In 1963 Governor Frank G. Clement appointed Warf Commissioner of Education, a controversial move that generated considerable debate. Public school officials called the cigar-smoking Warf a political dictator, but he became the most influential Commissioner of Education in the state's history. His tenure spanned a period of phenomenal growth in higher education as the post-World War II children came of age and entered the state's colleges and universities. Under Warf's administration, new construction and expansion of faculty and programs took place throughout the higher education system. Warf was a charter member of the Tennessee Board of Regents, an agency designed to oversee all state colleges and universities outside the University of Tennessee sytem. Indelibly shaping the state's public colleges and universities, raising the standards of higher education, the Board of Regents system is now one of the ten largest in the nation. In 1992 the Tennessee General Assembly enacted a special law to retain Warf as a member of the Board of Regents, the sixth time legislators had voted to keep him on the board. Warf's lasting educational legacy is the community college system. From the initial three community colleges, the system has expanded to include 14 community colleges and numerous state technical and vocational schools.

After an unsuccessful bid for State Comptroller in 1971, Warf returned to Lewis County, where he remained active in politics until 1976. In 1994 Vanderbilt University's George Peabody School of Education presented Warf with its distinguished Peabody Award. Warf was married to Josephine Kistler Warf. He died October 27, 1996, at his home in Hohenwald.

Connie L. Lester, Tennessee Historical Society

CITATION:

(1) *The Tennessean,* 28 October 1996.

SEE: CLEMENT, FRANK G.; COMMUNITY COLLEGES; EDUCATION, HIGHER; LEWIS COUNTY

WARNER, KATHERINE BURCH (1854–1923), suffragist, was born in Chattanooga, raised in Nashville, and educated at Vassar. The well traveled Kate learned about politics through her father, John C. Burch, editor and publisher of the Nashville *American* and secretary of the U.S. Senate. She married Nashvillian Leslie Warner in 1880; the couple had three children, but all had died by 1886. Her husband's weakening health led to early retirement, and the couple devoted themselves to travel and gracious entertainment until his death in 1909.

Warner had membership in various social and civic clubs and held an office in the Tennessee Federation of Women's Clubs. After 1909, she devoted more time to the state's developing suffrage movement. Twenty years older than the other leading suffragists in Tennessee, she spoke with articulate determination at rallys, served as president of the Nashville Equal Suffrage League, and in 1918 helped amalgamate the suffrage groups in Nashville and Chattanooga that had vied with one another since 1914. Warner became that newly-united Tennessee Woman Suffrage Association's first president. She also worked to distance the image of this group from the National Woman's Party's militant one. In the summer of 1920, the nation's interest in woman suffrage focused on Tennessee as the state that would, by ratifying the Nineteenth Amendment, make it into law. Warner's ability to persuade people who favored the status quo to her point of view made her Governor A.H. Roberts's choice to lead his appointed Ratification committee. In league with the National American Woman Suffrage Association, Warner worked until the legislature ratified the amendment in August. Following this accomplishment, Warner expended her energy on behalf of the Daughters of the American Revolution until her death in 1923.

Margaret D. Binnicker, Middle Tennessee State University

SUGGESTED READINGS: Antoinette Elizabeth Taylor, *The Woman Suffrage Movement in Tennessee* (1957); Anastatia Sims, "'Powers that Pray' and 'Powers that Prey': Tennessee and the Fight for Woman Suffrage," *Tennessee Historical Quarterly* 50(1991): 203–225

SEE: DUDLEY, ANNE DALLAS; KENNY, CATHERINE T.; ROBERTS, ALBERT H.; TENNESSEE FEDERATION OF WOMEN'S CLUBS; WOMAN SUFFRAGE MOVEMENT

WARNER, PERCY (1861–1927), businessman and civic leader, followed the lead of his father, James C. Warner, who capitalized upon the New South exploitation of natural resources with his Warner Iron Corporation in the 1870s and 1880s. While working for the family company, the younger Warner developed an interest in the new areas of electric utilities and urban mass transportation. From 1903 to 1914 he presided over the Nashville Railway and Light Company, controlling all the city's streetcars. In this position, he held influence and interests in a number of Nashville businesses. Warner also involved himself in utility organizations in Memphis, Knoxville, Birmingham, Little Rock, Houston, and New Orleans and served as a director of the National Light and Power Company of New York.

Warner's marriage to Margaret Lindsley, daughter of Sarah McGavock and J. Berrien Lindsley, united new and old Nashville families. Warner inherited money and clearly enlarged those financial holdings. And though he cultivated a private collection of birds on his estate, Renraw, he also worked to save Centennial Park. Such civic-minded benevolence led to his election to the Nashville Board of Park Commissioners late in his life. Warner died suddenly and unexpectedly at age 66. As a memorial tribute, land which had been presented in the preceding year to the city to form a large public park by his daughter, Percie, and her husband Luke Lea, received the name Percy Warner Park.

Margaret D. Binnicker, Middle Tennessee State University
SUGGESTED READING: W. Clark Conn, "Waverly Place: The Study of a Nashville Streetcar Suburb Along the Franklin Pike," *Tennessee Historical Quarterly* 43(1984): 3–24
SEE: LEA, LUKE; STREET CAR ERA

WARREN BROTHERS SASH AND DOOR COMPANY. By 1853 Jesse Warren (1814–1885) and his partner Joseph Moore (1821–1871) had established a millwork machine shop on Nashville's High Street. Four years later, the nearly 50 employees of Warren & Moore were using the era's most modern steam powered equipment to produce balusters, newels, sash, doors, blinds, moldings, and dressed lumber of all kinds.

Jesse Warren, Jr. (b. 1853) and his brother Joseph M. (b. 1855) continued their father's business tradition. In 1874 they established a business at 30 South Market Street specializing in paints, oils, glass, and artist's materials, but also offering sash, doors, blinds, and other building materials. Two years later, Warren Brothers Company moved to the corner of Third Avenue and Church Street, remaining there for the next 50 years.

From 1892 to 1911 Joseph Warren also served as general manager of the Edgefield & Nashville Manufacturing Company. Sometime before 1910, Jesse, Jr.,

left the company, and according to family lore, "went west." The company continued under Joseph Warren and his descendants, Joseph Warren, Jr., (1877–1943) and Joseph Warren III (1907–1968).

In 1909, capitalizing on Warren Brothers' success in the paint business, Joseph Warren, Jr., founded the Warren Paint and Color Company. This firm attained international distinction and today continues its operations on Wedgewood Avenue, its location since the early 1920s. Around 1927 Warren Brothers moved to Broadway, before relocating to Seventh Avenue and Harrison Streets in 1936. The latter site is now a part of the Bicentennial Mall.

On May 22, 1967, Pacific Mutual Door Company purchased Warren Brothers and built it a new plant on Massman Drive, where the company began operations in 1975. Operating as an independent branch of the parent company, Warren Brothers Sash and Door company continues to distribute wholesale millwork in the Mid-South.

Michael D. Slate, Nashville
SEE: ARCHITECTURE, VERNACULAR DOMESTIC

WARREN COUNTY was established November 26, 1807, by an act of the Tennessee General Assembly, becoming the thirtieth county created in Tennessee. Settlers came to the area as early as 1800, and the new county was originally that portion of White County (created in 1806) lying south of the Caney Fork River along the Highland Rim with portions on the Cumberland Plateau on the east and in the Central Basin on the west. Warren County was organized in February 1808, and in March 1810, the County Court appointed commissioners to purchase a site for a county seat to be called McMinnville.

Warren County was named for General Joseph Warren, the first general killed in the War of Independence. McMinnville was named for Joseph McMinn, who was speaker of the Tennessee State Senate at the time the county was formed; later he served as one of the state's outstanding governors. Settlement continued at a rapid pace, and in 1810 Warren County contained 5,725 people; by 1830 it had grown to 15,351.

At the time of its creation, the county contained some 900 square miles, but this area was reduced to approximately 433 square miles from 1836 to 1844 by the creation of Cannon, Coffee, DeKalb, Van Buren, and Grundy counties. The Tennessee State Constitution of 1834 provided that, in the formation of new counties, no county boundary could be closer than 12 miles from the county seat of the former county from which the new county was to be formed. Each of the new counties established their boundaries exactly 12 miles from McMinnville, with the result, that by 1844, Warren County had acquired its distinctive round shape and its nickname of "the round county."

From its earliest days, the population was dependent upon an agricultural economy, although the terrain was not conducive to large plantations or large tillable fields. While some cotton was produced, it never dominated the county's economy. The presence of many oak, chestnut, beech, and other nut trees encouraged the raising of hogs, and settlers coupled this with the breeding of horsestock and mules. Their success in these endeavors earned Warren County the reputation as a prime source of pork and mules for the great plantations further south. A thriving orchard industry, especially apples, blossomed before the Civil War, and apple brandy became one of the major cash crops during Reconstruction. The diverse agriculture was not geared to slave labor and only 10 percent of the population was slave, while fewer than 10 percent of Warren County families owned slaves.

During the county's first 50 years, the construction of the Manchester and McMinnville Railroad, organized in 1850 and operational in 1856, represented the most important economic advancement. The establishment of the Cumberland Female College in 1850, coupled with the development of the Central Cotton factory at Faulkner's Springs, also contributed to local growth.

In 1861 Warren County initially voted against secession, but a strong anti-Lincoln sentiment quickly developed and produced a pro-secession vote in the June referendum. Warren County contributed nearly 2,000 citizens to the southern cause during the four-year conflict. A Confederate conscription center, Camp Smartt, was located south of McMinnville. As a railroad terminus to north central Tennessee, Warren County became a primary target for northern, as well as, southern armies. Repeated military activities left the area in shambles at the war's end.

After the Civil War, industrialists developed the area's mineral and timber resources. Beginning with the organization of the Caney Fork Iron and Coal Company in 1885, and continuing through the days of the Rocky River Coal and Lumber Company, a flourishing lumber business emerged, and numerous lumber manufactures, beginning with the T.F. Burrough Lumber Company, provided work and income to many area residents. Local investors in the booming George C. Brown Lumber Company accumulated substantial wealth during the early years of the twentieth century, earning for McMinnville a reputation as the "wealthiest little town in the South."

After World War I the textile and lumber industries remained the principal sources of employment. The people of Warren County soon felt the effects of economic hard times, however, and during the 1920s and 1930s many people migrated north after the failure of the Tennessee Woolen Mills, Read Hosiery Mill, Menzies Shoe Company, and Fly Overall Company.

Industry in Warren County grew after World War II. The formation of a chamber of commerce in 1950, coupled with the development of countywide electrical, telephone, and water distribution, provided incentives for the establishment or relocation of industrial plants. General Shoe Corporation built the first modern plant in Warren County in 1946, followed by Oster in 1957, Century Electric (Magnatek) in 1960, DeZurik in 1963, and Carrier Corporation in 1968. Oster's training of tool and die personnel attracted other companies, including Bridgestone, Calsonic, and Gardener Manufacturing.

A unified school system, branches of Motlow State Community College and Tennessee Technological University, and a well staffed vocational school provide the people of Warren County with a wide variety of educational opportunities. Many major Christian denominations have local congregations. An 18-hole golf course and a modern civic center have become the focus of recreational activities. A four lane connector road through McMinnville from Manchester to Cookeville displays the scenic beauty of the area's mountains and rivers. A temperate climate and adequate rainfall make the county increasingly attractive to retirees. The present population exceeds 33,000, with local banks showing assets exceeding $600 million.

Four notable Warren Countians have left their mark in American and Tennessee culture: folklorist and composer Charles F. Bryan, country music star Dottie West, journalist Carl Rowan, and writer Lucy Virginia French. The Southern School of Photography (1904–1928), established by W.S. Lively in McMinnville, was one of the first such schools in the country. Local photographers Anthia Brady Hughes and Willie Hughes left an invaluable record through their 35,000 photographs of people and everyday life in Warren County.

James Dillon, McMinnville

SEE: BRYAN, CHARLES F.; FRENCH, LUCY VIRGINIA.; LIVESTOCK; MCMINN, JOSEPH; NURSERY INDUSTRY; RAILROAD, NASHVILLE AND CHATTANOOGA; ROCK ISLAND STATE PARK; ROWAN, CARL; SAVAGE, JOHN H.

WARREN, ROBERT PENN (1905–1989), acclaimed modern American writer, was at home in all the major genres—poetry, fiction, drama, and criticism—though poetry was his dominant mode. Warren was awarded three Pulitzer Prizes, a number unmatched by any other writer, one for his novel, *All The King's Men* (1947), and two for the poetry collections, *Promises* (1958) and *Now and Then* (1978). He also received a MacArthur Prize Fellowship in 1981. The American Academy and Institute of Arts and Letters awarded him its Gold Medal for Poetry in 1985. In 1986 he was named Poet Laureate, the first in the United States to be given that title.

Warren was born in Guthrie, Kentucky, across the Tennessee state line, and educated in public schools, graduating from Clarksville high school in 1921. He entered Vanderbilt University and was adopted by the Fugitive Poets at the peak of their critical intensity. Their *The Fugitive,* a magazine of verse, ran for 19 issues through 1925. Allen Tate, Warren's roommate and life-long friend, sponsored and encouraged him in the creative climate. Warren contributed poems to *The Fugitive,* and an essay to the 1930 Agrarian symposium, *I'll Take My Stand.*

His education continued through an M.A. degree at the University of California in 1927 and B.Litt. in 1930 from New College at Oxford University, where he studied as a Rhodes Scholar. He taught at Vanderbilt from 1931 to 1934 before accepting a position at Louisiana State University. There he began a life-long collaboration with Cleanth Brooks, first on *The Southern Review,* a literary journal, then on their influential texts, *Understanding Poetry* and *Understanding Fiction.* Altogether, they shared authorship of eight texts that revolutionized the teaching of literature in the twentieth century.

During the 1940s Warren taught at the University of Minnesota. His 20-year marriage to Cinina Brescia ended with divorce in 1951. In 1952 he and writer Eleanor Phelps Clark married. With their children, Rosanna Phelps and Gabriel Penn Warren, they traveled extensively, dividing their time between Europe and New England. Warren joined Brooks at Yale in 1950 and held various appointments until his retirement in 1973.

"Prophecy," Warren's first published poem, appeared in the Camp Knox publication, *The Mess Kit,* in 1921, while he participated in a summer training program. His last collection, *New and Selected Poems, 1923–1985,* was published in 1985. Over a period of more than 60 years, during which he produced 15 volumes of collected poems in addition to verse drama and numerous individual publications, his poetic impulse was rarely absent.

The novel, *All the King's Men,* also produced as a play, an award-winning motion picture, and later as an opera, has had the greatest impact of his ten novels. Although very much of its era, the work offers powerful universal considerations of morality and modern tragedy. His last novel, *A Place to Come To,* draws most on Warren's Tennessee experiences and provides the setting of a formative period in his life.

In addition to the eight works co-authored by Cleanth Brooks, Warren wrote more than 15 analytical monographs ranging from studies of classics in the American canon to meditations on segregation and the place of poetry in the late twentieth century. Warren did much to establish that place. He died at his Vermont home on September 12, 1989.

Marice Wolfe, Vanderbilt University
SUGGESTED READINGS: Leonard Casper, *Robert Penn Warren: The Dark and Bloody Ground* (1960); Marshall Walker, *Robert Penn Warren: A Vision Earned* (1979)
SEE: AGRARIANS; BROOKS, CLEANTH; FUGITIVES; LITERATURE; TATE, JOHN O. ALLEN; VANDERBILT UNIVERSITY

WARRIORS PATH STATE PARK, located in Sullivan County, contains 970 acres on both sides of the Fort Patrick Henry Lake, a 900-acre reservoir created by the Tennessee Valley Authority when it built Fort Patrick Henry Dam from 1951–1954. Established by the early 1960s, the park has evolved into a major recreational facility for Tri-Cities residents, featuring a 18-hole golf course, 160 campground sites, swimming pool, picnic grounds, water slide, hiking trails, and a marina.

Warriors Path also includes significant historic sites. Its name reflects the fact that ancient Native American trails along the Holston River both to and from Long Island passed through the park's boundaries. It also is associated with the Wilderness Road. Fort Patrick Henry Lake is named for an earlier Revolutionary War fort, constructed in September 1776 by forces under the command of Lt. Colonel William Russell and garrisoned by troops under Captain William Witcher during the American campaign against the Cherokees. The fort was named for Patrick Henry, the famous Virginia patriot. Within the park are the archaeological ruins of Childress Town, which once stood on the banks of the South Fork of the Holston River at the Childress Ferry. On the Fall Creek Road entrance to the park is a historic gristmill, the Roller-Pettyjohn Mill, which was built in 1903. The National Register-listed mill operated until 1955.

Carroll Van West, Middle Tennessee State University
SEE: SULLIVAN COUNTY; TENNESSEE VALLEY AUTHORITY; TRAILS, NATIVE AMERICAN; WILDERNESS ROAD

WASHINGTON COUNTY was established by the North Carolina legislature in November 1777 from western territory known as the Washington District. This first county included the whole territory within the boundaries of what would become the state of Tennessee. Jonesborough, the first town in Tennessee, was selected as county seat, and in 1779, construction began on a log courthouse covered with clapboards.

Hunters came early to Washington County. Daniel Boone left tangible evidence of his hunting forays in the Boones Creek area, where settlers found a tree that bore the inscription, "D Boon cilled a bar on tree 1760." William Bean and his family became the first permanent white settlers in Tennessee in 1768–1769. Jacob Brown, who migrated from South Carolina to trade with the Cherokee Indians, later bought from the Indians thousands of acres of land on the Nolichucky River in 1775.

Following North Carolina's cession of western lands in June 1784, settlers west of the Appalachians found themselves without government. They remedied the situation by organizing the State of Franklin at Jonesborough in August 1784. John Sevier became the governor of this "Lost State," which continued until 1788. Not everyone recognized the legal authority of the new state, and a long-lived, bitter political rivalry emerged between Sevier and John Tipton, who supported the jurisdiction of North Carolina.

Early settlers quickly organized religious congregations and founded educational institutions. Tidence Lane organized Buffalo Ridge Baptist Church in 1779, the first church in Washington County. In 1780 Samuel Doak founded Martin Academy, now Washington College Academy, and established Salem Presbyterian Church in the same year. In 1789 William Nelson built on Knob Creek Road the first Methodist church, known as Nelson's Chapel, where Bishop Francis Asbury was a frequent visitor on his circuits through the region. The Quakers located their first meeting house near Telford, probably around 1800. German settlers on Knob Creek organized the first Church of the Brethren at the home of Deacon Joseph Bowman in 1799. The Immanuel Lutheran Church near Cherokee Creek and the Lamar community were established between 1800 and 1805. A revival meeting conducted by James Miller resulted in the founding of the Boones Creek Christian Church in 1825.

Washington County attracted several men associated with later state and national history. Andrew Jackson crossed the mountains and settled in Jonesborough briefly, living in the home of Christopher Taylor in 1788. While living in Jonesborough, Jackson passed the bar exam, before migrating westward to the Cumberland settlement. Quaker settlers, Thomas Embree and his son Elihu, became well known advocates of the abolition of slavery. In 1819, while living in Jonesborough, Elihu Embree published the first abolitionist journal in the United States. First called *The Manumission Intelligencer,* the name was changed to *The Emancipator* in 1820.

To improve transportation, Dr. Samuel Blair Cunningham of Jonesborough actively sought the completion of the East Tennessee and Virginia Railroad, which was accomplished in 1857–1858. Recognizing the potential for development along the railroad, Henry Johnson purchased a half acre of land along the right-of-way in 1854, where he constructed a station and a water tower. Settlement around the station led to the chartering of the town of Johnson City by the State of Tennessee in 1869.

Like other northeastern counties in Civil War Tennessee, Washington County was Unionist. A number of skirmishes were fought in the county, and Jonesborough served as headquarters for both Union and Confederate troops. Evidence of the residents' divided sentiments is readily available. The Bell-Herrin House, with its trapdoors and tunnels, is thought to have been a station along the Underground Railroad. Confederate General A.E. Jackson made his home in Jonesborough and is buried in the old cemetery. Landon Carter Haynes, a Confederate senator, lived in the former home of Colonel John Tipton. The Tipton-Haynes farm is now a state historic site near Johnson City.

After the war, both blacks and whites worked to rebuild the region. Hezekiah Hankal, a former slave, became a respected physician and teacher as well as the organizer of many Christian Churches. In the 1880s northern industrialists invested in ventures at Johnson City. General John Wilder, a former Union general in the Civil War, built a furnace to process iron ore from the Cranberry Mines in North Carolina. The ore was transported via the East Tennessee and Western North Carolina Railroad, which was completed in 1882. In the early twentieth century, capitalist George L. Carter constructed the Carolina, Clinchfield and Ohio Railway, and in 1911 he donated 120 acres in Johnson City for the location of a normal school, now East Tennessee State University. In 1974 the state established the Quillen College of Medicine at the university. In 1901 U.S. Representative Walter P. Brownlow was instrumental in securing for Johnson City one of the first National Homes for Disabled Volunteer Soldiers. Now the Veterans Administration at Mountain Home, this complex is situated on 200 acres of land and occupies 50 buildings, including a historic Carnegie Library and the Quillen VA Medical Center.

As Washington County approaches the twenty-first century, it embraces its heritage and displays a pioneering progress. In 1969 Jonesborough became the first historic district in Tennessee. In 1973 the Jonesborough Civic Trust sponsored a story-telling festival that has developed into an annual event of national importance. Politically, the county established a number of "firsts:" in 1961 May Ross McDowell was the first woman to be elected mayor of Johnson City, followed in 1976 by Grace Haws, the first woman to become mayor of Jonesborough, and in 1988 Kevin McKinney became the first African American mayor of Jonesborough.

Mildred S. Kozsuch and Ruth Broyles, Jonesborough

SEE: BEAN, JAMES B.; CENTER FOR APPALACHIAN STUDIES; CHESTER INN; DOAK, SAMUEL; DUNCAN, JOHN, SR.; EAST TENNESSEE STATE UNIVERSITY; EMBREE, ELIHU; EMBREEVILLE MINES; FRANKLIN, STATE OF; JOHNSON CITY; JONESBOROUGH; LUNDY, BENJAMIN; NATIONAL STORYTELLING FESTIVAL; QUILLEN, JAMES; QUILLEN COLLEGE OF MEDICINE; REECE, B. CARROLL; TAYLOR, ALFRED A.; TAYLOR, ROBERT L.; TIPTON, JOHN; TIPTON-HAYNES HISTORIC SITE; WALTON, JESSE; WASHINGTON MANUFACTURING COMPANY; WILLIAMS, SAMUEL C.

WASHINGTON, JOSEPH EDWIN (1851–1915), congressman, state legislator, tobacco planter, and a founder of the Tobacco Protective Association, was born November 10, 1851, at Wessyngton in Robertson County, the son of George Augustine and Jane Smith Washington. In 1873 he graduated from Georgetown College in Washington, D.C., and in 1888 earned an M.A. degree from the same school. He joined the first Vanderbilt University law class in 1874, but, although he was admitted to the bar, he never practiced law.

Politics, railroads, and tobacco defined Washington's career. He served one term in the Tennessee House (1877–1879). In 1886 he won the first of five terms in the U.S. Congress, serving from 1887 to 1897, where he sponsored legislation demanded by the state's farmers to relieve the depression in agricultural prices. Washington served as a director of both the NC&St.L Railroad and the Nashville and Decatur Railroad. In the 1870s he joined the Patrons of Husbandry and served as the secretary of the local Grange cooperative store. A nominal member of the Agricultural Wheel and the Farmers' Alliance in the 1880s, Washington questioned whether the time was "ripe" for farmers to organize. In 1904, however, he became one of the founding members (along with his brother-in-law Felix Ewing and Charles Fort) of the Planters Protective Association, an organization of dark-fired tobacco planters allied against the so-called tobacco trust.

Washington married Mary Boling Kemp of Virginia, and they were the parents of four children. He died at Wessyngton on August 28, 1915, and is buried in the family cemetery.

Connie L. Lester, Tennessee Historical Society
SUGGESTED READINGS: Tracy Campbell, *The Politics of Despair: Power & Resistance in the Tobacco Wars* (1993); Christopher Waldrep, *Night Riders: Defending Community in the Black Patch, 1890–1915* (1993)
SEE: BLACK PATCH WAR; DARK TOBACCO DISTRICT PLANTERS' PROTECTIVE ASSOCIATION; PATRONS OF HUSBANDRY; ROBERTSON COUNTY; TOBACCO; WESSYNGTON

WASHINGTON MANUFACTURING COMPANY. The origins of the Washington Manufacturing Company can be traced to 1812 when William Chester bought 260 acres near the mouth of Bumpass Cove in iron-rich Washington County and built a forge. He later sold this forge to third generation iron workers, Elijah and Elihu Embree. They operated a small charcoal furnace on the Nolichucky River which met the demands of the region's settlers. The Embrees added thousands of acres to Chester's original 260 acres and built forges, furnaces, and nail factories. By the 1820s they were widely known for their high quality cast and forged iron products. Elihu, who died in 1820, is better known for his abolitionist publications.

Elijah Embree put all his efforts into running the family iron works and created a sizable industrial empire. By the 1820s Embree's business employed several hundred men and was valued at $120,000. In 1830 Embree formed a partnership with Robert L. Blair, John Blair, William Blair, and three others which was known as the Washington Iron Manufacturing Company. After Embree's death in 1846, the company, now named Pleasant Valley Iron Works, became the largest producer of iron in East Tennessee. Over the decades, the company name and ownership changed several times. In 1917 the furnace, then owned by the Embreeville Iron Company, was wrecked and sold as scrap.

Patricia Bernard Ezzel, Tennessee Valley Authority
SUGGESTED READING: Thomas Wyman, "The British Misadventure in Embreeville," *Tennessee Historical Quarterly* 54(1995): 98–111
SEE: EMBREE, ELIHU; EMBREEVILLE MINES; WASHINGTON COUNTY

WATAUGA ASSOCIATION. By 1772 about 70 homesteads or farms had been established along the Watauga River in northeastern Tennessee (now Carter County). The area lay outside the boundaries of British colonial government and within the recognized boundaries of Cherokee territory. Disregarding the British mandate, the settlers negotiated a ten-year lease with the Indians for "all the country on the waters of the Watauga."

In 1772 the settlers established the Watauga Association to organize the region. The "constitution" of the Association incorporated the Virginia code of laws and outlined the organization of government. Five elected magistrates formed a court and conducted the business of government, including executive, legislative, and judicial matters. A clerk recorded deliberations of the court, and a sheriff executed judgments. The first five commissioners of the court are unknown, but a plausible list can be reconstructed. John Carter likely served as the first chairman. James Robertson was probably a member, and he may have suggested the name "Watauga Association." Charles Robertson and Zachariah Isbell may have been members, and the fifth member was probably either John Sevier or Jacob Brown.

The court existed for four years, regulating affairs of the Watauga community. The court probably concentrated on judicial business, since the adoption of Virginia laws alleviated the need for legislative action; the only surviving record of the Association is a lawsuit handled by the court. The court also conducted negotiations with Indians, agents of the British government, and colonial governments of North Carolina and Virginia. To provide military defense for the area, the court created and directed a militia.

For about two years general peace and order prevailed in the Watauga settlement, before lawlessness and Indian attacks disturbed the peace of the community. After 1775 the Watauga Association participated in the American Revolution. In 1777 the area became a part of North Carolina, and the Watauga Association disappeared the next year.

Since neither Virginia nor North Carolina claimed sovereignty over the area, the Watauga Association represented the first white government in Tennessee. Nevertheless, the association was not intended as a deliberate renunciation of British sovereignty, or an early attempt at independence. The lease of Indian lands specified a ten-year term, and the Watauga constitution was written in conjunction with the lease. The petition of 1776, while affirming allegiance to the rebellion against England, made no claim that the Wataugans had declared independence in 1772.

W. Calvin Dickinson, Tennessee Technological University
SUGGESTED READING: Ben Allen and Dennis T. Lawson, "The Wataugans and the 'Dangerous Example'" *Tennessee Historical Quarterly* 26(1967): 137–147
SEE: CARTER COUNTY; CARTER, JOHN; GOVERNMENT; SEVIER, JOHN; SYCAMORE SHOALS STATE HISTORIC AREA

WATKINS INSTITUTE. In 1880, 86-year-old Samuel Watkins—soldier, brick mason, brick manufacturer, and businessman—died. Reputedly the richest man in Nashville, Watkins left $100,000 and a lot at the corner of High Street (6th Avenue) and Church in trust to the State of Tennessee to establish a school where free lectures on physical and natural science would be given to promote knowledge and provide the city's poorer youth with the opportunity to acquire useful information. He stipulated that the basement and first floor of the building to be erected should be rented to provide revenue for the school. He authorized three commissioners, appointed by the governor, to equip a second-floor library and a third-floor lecture hall. The three commissioners suggested by Watkins and appointed by the governor were James Whitworth, John M. Lea, and William P. Cooper.

The commissioners soon realized that Watkins's required lectures were not reaching the intended audience. In 1889 they started the Watkins Institute Free Night School with three classes—Elementary, Primary, and Technical—which lasted for a term of four months. The overwhelming response prompted the commissioners to add additional subjects and classes to the curriculum as demand required.

Local sponsors of foreign immigrants brought them to Watkins Institute to take the elementary classes. Institute teachers soon organized separate Americanization classes to prepare immigrants for self-sufficient living and encourage them to become naturalized citizens.

In 1902 Ann E. Webber, a local business woman who was attracted by the school's ability to adapt its curriculum to student needs, transferred two store buildings to the state. She directed the income from the buildings to the support of the Night School in order to extend the term and increase the number and content of the technical courses.

From its beginning, art has played a key role at Watkins, first achieving prominence under the auspices of the Nashville Art Association. In 1910 Edwin Gardner was hired to teach in the Industrial Art Department and introduced his students to fine art, which has continued to flourish at Watkins.

The 1930s were the most successful years at Watkins. As the Great Depression took hold, people flocked to Watkins to take courses that would help them get a job, and the Institute responded with a wide variety of courses. For the next 40 years, Watkins Institute was the center for adult education in Nashville.

The high school received state accreditation in 1943. In 1976 a three-year professional course in interior design was organized, and an associate degree in Art and Interior Design was approved by the state in 1979. In 1994 Watkins merged its schools of art and interior design, forming the Watkins Institute of Art and Design, and offering programs in fine art, graphic design, photography, and an accredited interior design program. In 1995 the Watkins Film School was added to its programs.

Cornelia Walker, Nashville
SUGGESTED READING: George C. Grise, "Samuel Watkins," *Tennessee Historical Quarterly* 6(1947): 251–264
SEE: EDUCATION, HIGHER; GARDNER, EDWIN M; TENNESSEE HISTORICAL SOCIETY

WATTERSON, HENRY (1840–1921), journalist and proponent of the New South ideology, was among the last great voices in the era of personal journalism. Watterson played journalistic roles in Tennessee before moving to Kentucky where he would gain national recognition as a forceful spokesman for both the South and the Democratic Party while editing the *Louisville Courier-Journal* from 1868 to 1919.

Watterson was born February 16, 1840, in Washington, D.C., while his father Harvey Watterson, a Shelbyville lawyer and Beech Grove native, served in Congress. His mother, Talitha, was from Spring Hill. The family enjoyed close ties to President Andrew Jackson.

At age 12 Watterson edited his school newspaper. At 16 he used a press donated by his father to produce a paper he called the *New Era*. Seeking a literary career that would never materialize, he went to New York in 1856, moving to Washington in 1858, and working for several publications in both cities. He returned to Tennessee in 1861.

Politically opposed to secession, Watterson reluctantly served brief stints in the Confederate Army during the Civil War, interspersed with editing posts on four papers, including the *Nashville Banner* and *Chattanooga Rebel*. After the war, he edited the *Cincinnati Evening Post* six months.

In September 1865 Watterson returned to Nashville to marry Rebecca Ewing and become editor and part owner of the *Banner*. There he began his "New Departure" campaign urging national reconciliation, a campaign he would continue in Louisville after 1868. He retired in 1919, unable to reconcile with *Courier-Journal* owner Robert Bingham over the League of Nations. Watterson died December 22, 1921, in Florida.

Glenn Himebaugh, Middle Tennessee State University
SUGGESTED READING: Joseph Frazier Wall, *Henry Watterson: Reconstructed Rebel* (1956)
SEE: BEDFORD COUNTY; NASHVILLE BANNER; PUBLISHING

WAYNE COUNTY is located on the extreme western side of the Highland Rim, with its northwest corner extending into the Tennessee River basin. It is made up of ridges and hollows and is a plateau of about 800 feet elevation in the southwest corner of the Middle Tennessee division. Heavily wooded, the county contained deposits of iron that were still being worked into the early twentieth century.

The General Assembly created Wayne County in 1817, but the engrossing clerk failed to sign the act, and it had to be passed again when the legislature next met in 1819. The county was named to honor General "Mad" Anthony Wayne of the Revolutionary War. Created from parts of Hickman and Humphreys counties, it encompasses 338,291 acres. The first settlers in Wayne County arrived from Middle Tennessee and North and South Carolina to claim military grants, occupants' claims, and warrants.

The first county court met at the home of Benjamin Hardin on Factor's Fork where the old Natchez Trace crosses Shoal Creek. The next meeting was held at William Barnett's house on old Town Branch, where the court continued to meet until 1822. The first elected county officers were William Barnett, clerk; Benjamin Hardin, sheriff; J.M. Barnett, circuit court clerk; John McClure, registrar; John Meredith, trustee; John Hill, ranger; and William B. Payne, coroner.

In 1821 the General Assembly appointed commissioners James Hollis, John Hill, Nathan Biffle, and Charles Burns to establish a county seat. The men purchased 40 acres from William Burns for the town of Waynesboro. They sold lots and used the proceeds to build a courthouse, jail, and stocks. A century later, Waynesboro had a population of 600, several schools and churches, a bank, and a number of businesses. Today, the town's population has reached 2,400 residents. More than a dozen manufacturing plants, including Lincoln Brass Works, Inc., provide employment to several hundred workers.

Clifton was founded in 1840 and named for the high cliffs upon which it stands. Located 16 miles north of Waynesboro, Clifton was first known as Ninevah. Built on land purchased from Stephen Roach and located on the Tennessee River, the town emerged as the most important commercial location in the county. Local farmers and lumbermen shipped cotton, livestock, lumber, cross ties, and tan bark via the river from Clifton and received imported supplies which were distributed around the county by wagon. During the Civil War, on December 15, 1862, a Confederate force of 1,800 under the command of General Nathan Bedford Forrest crossed the Tennessee at Clifton to launch a 200-mile raid on Union lines and supplies in order to delay the Union campaign against Vicksburg. In 1855 the Masonic Academy was built at Clifton, and Frank Hughes College was erected there in 1906. Growth slowed dramatically from the 1920s until the 1980s. Since 1990, Clifton's growth has been revived with the establishment of a state park (Mousetail Landing State Park) to the north, the construction of a new bridge spanning the Tennessee River, the institution of a branch campus of Columbia State Community College, and the erection of a large state prison facility. Pulitzer Prize-winning novelist T.S. Stribling maintained his home in Clifton.

Collinwood traces its origins to the survey for the Tennessee Western Railroad in 1912. Investors in the Collinwood Land Company surveyed the town site on the Bud Scott farm and began selling town lots in June 1913. Collinwood was named for W.W. Collins, manager of the railroad operations in Wayne County. The town was incorporated in 1915, and the first city election brought the following men to office: Charles J. Farris, mayor; Sam V. Coltrane, city recorder; and aldermen T.A. Adkisson, J.F. Turman, Leo Forsythe, Dr. W.W. Rippy, and A.O. Lindsey. Robert L. Morrow served as marshal.

Today, the 14,000 citizens of Wayne County earn their livelihood from the lumber industry and several manufacturing concerns. Migration into the county has included retirees and families seeking a more rural setting.

Bob Rains, Waynesboro
SEE: NATCHEZ TRACE; NATCHEZ TRACE PARKWAY; STRIBLING, T.S.; TENNESSEE PRISON SYSTEM; TENNESSEE RIVER SYSTEM

WDIA. In 1948–1949 white-owned WDIA in Memphis became the nation's first all-black radio station. Its owners, Bert Ferguson and John R. Pepper, hired Nat D. Williams, the first publicly identified black disc jockey. The station aired black history segments and presented an open forum for discussion of black problems. The programming change proved successful and the station soon grew to a major 50,000-watt-station. It was the first Memphis station to gross a million dollars in a year. African Americans within its broadcast range considered WDIA as "their station."

WDIA, known as the Starmaker Station, gave exposure to many local talents. Recording greats B.B. King and Rufus Thomas worked as disc jockeys, giving exposure to such regional blues stars as Little Milton and Junior Parker and local gospel groups like the Spirit of Memphis and the Southern Wonders. Bobby Blue Bland, Johnny Ace, and Roscoe Gordon even cut some of their first records in the WDIA studio. WDIA's Teen-Town singer program recognized the talents of Carla Thomas and Isaac Hayes. Also known as the Goodwill Station, WDIA held annual Goodwill and Starlight Revues before capacity crowds, with proceeds benefiting needy African-American children.

WDIA found its niche in a segregated society. With the integration of the broadcast industry during the 1960s, the station lost its unique character. A sale to Sonderling Broadcast Corporation in 1957 and Viacom in 1986 further altered the station by implementing uniform chain-programming.

Anne-Leslie Owens, Tennessee Historical Society
SUGGESTED READING: Louis Cantor, *Wheelin' on Beale* (1992)
SEE: MEMPHIS MUSIC SCENE; MUSIC; STAX RECORDS; THOMAS, RUFUS

WEAKLEY COUNTY is located on the Plateau Slope of West Tennessee. The north, middle, and south forks of the Obion River and its tributaries drain the land westward to the Mississippi River. It is bounded on the north by the state of Kentucky, on the east by Henry County, on the south by Carroll and Gibson counties, and on the west by Obion County. Weakley County covers 576 square miles, having lost some of its land to Gibson County in 1837 and Obion County in 1870.

Weakley County was established October 23, 1823, and named for Robert Weakley II, Speaker of the Tennessee Senate. By early 1825 the organization of the county was completed, and the town of Dresden had been surveyed and platted by Mears Warner to contain a public square and 90 lots. In 1835 the General Assembly divided the county into 12 voting districts to elect justices of the peace and constables. By 1843 two new districts had been added.

The first circuit court was held in a log house on the courtyard. It was replaced in 1827 by a brick courthouse. When that structure became too small, it was replaced by a two-story brick structure in 1852. This building was destroyed by fire in 1948 and replaced in 1950 with a four-story building, including base-

ment, constructed of Alabama limestone, designed by the Nashville firm Marr and Holman.

Weakley County's first agricultural crop was corn, and by 1880 it was the state's largest corn producing county. Corn became important in the production of cattle and hogs. Pioneer farmers became engaged in cotton production as soon as the land was cleared, but county farmers steadily reduced the cotton acreage in the late nineteenth century. Since 1960 soybeans have taken the place of cotton in agricultural production and now rank as the county's leading crop. The first tobacco crop was planted in 1832. In 1980 Weakley County farmers planted 138 acres of type 22 western dark-fired tobacco. Sweet potatoes became a major crop by 1850, with 45,180 bushels produced. Almost a century later, in 1944, Weakley County ranked tenth in national production. In the early settlement of the county, farmers grew enough wheat, rye, and oats to supply their family and livestock needs. Today farmers grow more wheat in a three way rotation between wheat, soybeans, and corn. By the 1950s, modern dairying had become one of the major agricultural activities, but pressure on pasture land as it is converted to soybean production has resulted in the decline of dairying, although the county continues to be one of the top swine producers in the state.

Weakley County has five incorporated towns: Dresden, Martin, Greenfield, Sharon, and Gleason. Dresden, the county seat, was incorporated in 1827, and reported a 1994 population of 2,749. The town's first major industries were Bay Bee Shoe Company, which was established in 1948, and Dresden Manufacturing Company (1949). Dresden is the home of the 46th governor of Tennessee, the Honorable Ned R. McWherter.

Martin recorded a 1992 population of 9,246. It was incorporated in 1874, and has long sustained a reputation for its educational facilities. In addition to public schools, the town was the home to two denominational academies, McFerrin and Hall-Moody, the latter site evolving into the University of Tennessee at Martin by 1967. Fifteen industries have manufacturing plants in Martin, including MTD Products, Hubbell Lighting Company, Martin Manufacturing Company, and Martin Brothers Container and Timber Corporation.

Incorporated in 1880, Greenfield had a 1990 population of 2,105. It presently has 12 industries, the largest employers being Kellwood Company, Parker Hannifin Corporation, and Greenfield Products Company. Sharon was incorporated in 1901 and now has a population of over 1,000 residents. Nine industries operate in Sharon, the largest of which is WSW Company, a manufacturer of children's wear.

Gleason, incorporated in 1871, reported a 1990 population of 1,402. It has 10 industries, the largest employers being H.C. Spinks Clay Company and Gleason Brick Company. Known as "Tater Town" because of the large shipments of sweet potatoes that once originated there, Gleason is now recognized as the ball clay mining center of the world. Five major companies ship clay used for china, brick, and tile. In addition to the five incorporated towns, several unincorporated towns are scattered across the county, including Dukedom, Hyndsver, Mt. Pelia, Gardner, Latham, Ore Springs, Palmersville, Ralston, and Terrell.

In 1857 the Nashville and Northwestern became the first railroad to cross the county. In 1872 the NC&St.L took over the east-west line and in 1880 it merged with the L&N. Today the remnants of this line, now CSX, still serve Dresden and Gleason. Most of the tracks have been abandoned or removed. The first north-south railroad that crossed the county was the Mississippi Central in 1872. It was soon bought by the Illinois Central Railroad, which merged with G M & O in 1972, forming the Illinois Central-Gulf. Today the railroad belongs to the Norfolk-Southern Railroad Company.

Notable citizens, in addition to former governor McWherter, included Emerson Ethridge (1819–1902), U.S. Congressman and state senator and Finis J. Garrett (1875–1956), editor, educator, Congressman, and Chief Justice of U.S. Court of Customs and Patent Appeals. Another native of Weakley County is Mike Snider, a country humorist, Grand Ole Opry member, and star of the television series *Hee Haw*, who often invokes scenes and stories from Gleason in his routines.

Virginia Clark Vaughan, Weakley County historian

SEE: CORN; ETHRIDGE, EMERSON; MARR AND HOLMAN; MCWHERTER, NED RAY; MINING; SOYBEANS; TOBACCO; UNIVERSITY OF TENNESSEE AT MARTIN

WEBB SCHOOL. W.R. "Sawney" Webb, Confederate veteran and graduate of the University of North Carolina, arrived in Tennessee in 1870 to found a classical school modeled on Bingham's, his former school at Oaks, North Carolina, and similar Virginia schools. Three years later, he was joined by his brother, John M. Webb, considered to be one of the best scholars to graduate from UNC. The two brothers made an excellent team, with the strong-minded Sawney's ability to instill high moral and religious values in his students and the quieter John's skill as a classroom teacher. In 1886 the Webbs moved their school from Culleoka, Tennessee, to its present site in Bell Buckle.

The Webb School quickly achieved a notable scholastic reputation. In 1877 Vanderbilt University Chancellor Landon Garland, discussing the poor quality of students applying to Vanderbilt, singled out students from Webb School as setting the standard of scholarship to which others should aspire.

In 1946, reflecting on the early years of Vanderbilt, Professor Edwin Mims observed that the constant flow of Webb students contributed significantly to the success of the university. Likewise, Methodist Bishop Holland McTyeire praised Webb School, saying, "I know not its superior; its equal would be hard to find."

W.R. Webb, Jr., joined the Webb School faculty in 1897, after obtaining his degree from UNC and teaching English there. In 1908 "Son Will" was elevated to Co-Principal with his father and uncle. After the deaths of John Webb in 1916 and Sawney Webb in 1926, W.R. Webb, Jr., continued as Headmaster until he retired in 1952.

Webb School has experienced a number of changes in its 125-year history. Established as a school for boys, Webb began admitting female boarding students in 1973. During the tenure of Headmaster Jackson E. Heffner from 1977 to 1989, the school's physical plant was modernized, two girls' dormitories were built, and the Austin Davis-Bryant Woosley Computer/Science Building was constructed. The success of a recent capital campaign enabled the school to construct the William Bond Library and a new Student Center. Today, under the leadership of Headmaster A. Jon Frere and an outstanding faculty, the school in 1997 served 265 students in grades 7 through 12.

A. Jon Frere, Webb School

SUGGESTED READING: Laurence McMillin, *The Schoolmaster: Sawney Webb and the Bell Buckle Story* (1971)

SEE: WEBB SCHOOL OF KNOXVILLE; WEBB, WILLIAM R. "SAWNEY"

WEBB SCHOOL OF KNOXVILLE. Robert Webb, a "third generation school man," founded the Webb School of Knoxville in September 1955. From his grandfather and uncles, who established schools in Bell Buckle, Tennessee, and Claremont, California, Webb acquired a distinctive educational vision that emphasized academic excellence, a strong foundation in liberal arts, and the building of character and leadership. After a modest start as an independent secondary school for boys, Webb School of Knoxville has grown steadily and broadened its traditional commitments. In 1957 a separate girls' school was opened. Two years later the two schools moved to the current 115-acre campus. After the boys' and girls' schools merged in 1968, the new co-educational Webb School adopted an upper and middle school structure. Throughout his tenure as the school's head, Robert Webb was an influential figure in southern preparatory school circles; he is particularly remembered for his 1969 challenge to the Mid-South Association of Independent Schools to more actively promote racial integration. Since Webb's retirement in 1984, three presidents have served Webb School: Douglas

Peterson (1984–1987), William Pfeifer (1988–1995), and Arthur Scott (since 1995). Webb alumni have attended the nation's most prestigious colleges and universities and have made significant contributions in many endeavors. In 1996–1997, 730 students enrolled in grades 5–12; a new Webb Lower School will open in the fall of 1998.

Mark T. Banker, Webb School of Knoxville

SEE: WEBB SCHOOL; WEBB, WILLIAM R. "SAWNEY"

WEBB, WILLIAM R. "SAWNEY" (1842–1926), was born in a North Carolina farmhouse on November 11, 1842. His father, Alexander Webb, died when he was six years old, leaving most of his rearing to his mother. She taught Sawney the value of hard work and what it meant to be a gentleman. His older sister, "Suny," was his first teacher. His daily lessons began with a Bible reading and prayer, practices he followed as a schoolmaster.

Sawney's formal education included instruction in Latin and Greek at the Bingham School in Oaks, North Carolina. Sawney attended the University of North Carolina for several months before entering the Confederate Army as a private. During the Civil War, he survived a disabling wound in his shoulder, accepted two temporary discharges, and endured hardship, battles, and imprisonment. At war's end, Captain Sawney Webb returned home on a boxcar.

For the next five years, he juggled duties as schoolteacher, family breadwinner, and provider for the education of his younger brother, John. Sawney also earned his A.B. degree from the University of North Carolina.

The changes brought about by North Carolina's Reconstruction government convinced Sawney to seek independence and change in Tennessee. In 1870 he established a school in Culleoka. That same year, he married Emma Clary, a self-reliant and determined woman, whose encouragement and support contributed to the success of the school. In 1873 he was joined in his life's work by his brother John, an imminent scholar, who had graduated first in his class at the University of North Carolina.

When Vanderbilt University was founded in 1875, Webb School's "oldest and best boys" enrolled in the new university. At the end of the school year, Webb graduates were the only Vanderbilt students who took honors in the university's first examinations.

A decade later, in 1886, the town of Culleoka incorporated, making the sale of liquor legal within the city limits. This was too much for Sawney, an ardent prohibitionist. Sawney and his boys packed up and headed to Bell Buckle, a village 35 miles west on the Nashville & Chattanooga Railroad. On six acres of beech forest, about one-third of a mile from the depot, Sawney dug a well and built a bigger and better schoolhouse than he had in Culleoka. Leading citizens of Bell Buckle supported the move by raising $12,000 for the new school.

At Bell Buckle, Sawney, usually attired in a frock coat, continued to enhance his school's reputation for furnishing America's most outstanding universities with well-prepared students who were also gentlemen. His rules were few and simple. "Don't be a sneak. Don't do things on the sly. Don't be a me too."[1] He did not tolerate profanity, gambling, or smoking cigarettes, and was a terror to the unruly. Such boys were promptly shipped home.

By 1908 Sawney's failing health forced him to take a leave of absence from the school. In his absence, his son Will ran the school. The following spring Sawney returned with his old boyish spirit and the revival of his strength. By 1912 the state legislature chose him to fill out the unexpired U.S. Senate term of Robert L. Taylor. Once again, he turned his school over to his son Will, and headed to Washington.

After serving five weeks, Sawney returned home to worry about his boys, enjoy his family, and attend the Bell Buckle Methodist Church, where he was a devoted member. He also made speeches at various schools and accepted honorary doctorates at Erskine College and the University of North Carolina. During World War I, he served on Bedford County's draft exemption board.

In December 1926, Sawney Webb died at home at the age of 84. Memorial services were held in several locations, including Nashville. Admirers published countless eulogies to the "South's greatest teacher of boys." Old Sawney would be remembered because the school he ran in the backwoods of Tennessee was the finest preparatory school in the South and, in the opinion of Woodrow Wilson, president of Princeton University, one of the nation's finest preparatory schools. Indeed, during Webb's first 50 years, it produced more Rhodes scholars than any other secondary school in the country.

Ridley Wills II, Franklin

CITATION:

(1) Walter Stokes, Jr., " The Schoolmaker: Sawney Webb and the Bell Buckle Story, An Essay Review," *Tennessee Historical Quarterly* 30(1971): 421.

SUGGESTED READING: Laurence McMillin, *The Schoolmaker: Sawney Webb and the Bell Buckle Story* (1971)

SEE: WEBB SCHOOL

WEEMS, P.V.H. (1889–1979), internationally-known air navigator, was born March 29, 1889, at Turbine, Tennessee, the son of Joseph Burch and May Elizabeth Rye Weems. He attended Walnut Grove Country School in Montgomery County and Branham and Hughes School in Spring Hill before receiving an appointment to the U.S. Naval Academy at Annapolis in 1908. While at the academy, Weems excelled in crew, football, boxing and wrestling (he won a place on the 1920 U.S. Olympic wrestling team). He graduated in 1912 and was commissioned an ensign in the U.S. Navy. He married Margaret Thackray in New York in 1915.

In 1927 Weems served with the Aircraft Squadron Battle Fleet, began research in air navigation, and published *Line of Position Book.* From 1928 to 1930 he served as executive officer on *U.S.S. Cuyama* and wrote the textbook *Air Navigation* (1931) which received international acclaim and won a gold medal awarded by the Aero Club of France.

In addition to his military career, Weems and his wife established the Weems School of Navigation (1927). He perfected his air navigation system which included a simplified method of determining latitude and longitude by aerial observations, improvements in sextants, and adaptation of chronometers to air use. He taught air navigation to Charles Lindbergh and assisted in the aviator's global flight to determine commercial airways for Pan American Airways. In 1933 Weems went on the naval retired list and devoted his energies to perfecting his navigation system. That year he designed the first *Air Almanac.* Two years later he patented the Mark II Plotter and he published *Marine Navigation* and *Star Altitude Curves.*

Weems returned to active duty in 1942 and won a Bronze Star for his service as a convoy commander. He was promoted to captain and received the wings of Naval air navigator in 1945. He retired from active duty for the second time in 1946.

As he did earlier, Weems continued his private career in air navigation. In 1960 the American Institute of Navigation awarded Weems a gold medal in honor of 50 years of outstanding achievement in air navigation. As the space age got underway Weems taught a pilot class in space navigation at the U.S. Naval Academy (1961–1962). Weems furthered knowledge of the world through his mapping and navigation research. His papers are preserved at the Tennessee State Library and Archives.

Connie L. Lester, Tennessee Historical Society

SEE: AIRPORTS; SCIENCE AND TECHNOLOGY

WEINBERG, ALVIN (1915–), Director of Oak Ridge National Laboratory (ORNL) from 1955 to 1973, became as well-known for his ability to communicate the intricacies of science as for his research efforts. The son of Russian emigrants, Weinberg trained in mathematical biophysics at the University of Chicago. More than any other scientist of his generation, Weinberg spoke convincingly of the meaning and intent of "Big Science," a descriptive term for twentieth-century science that became commonplace among both scientists and policymakers.

Weinberg joined a team of theoretical physicists who worked together at the University of Chicago during World War II; he moved to Oak Ridge in 1945. He served as director of ORNL's Physics Division before becoming the laboratory's research director in 1948, and director of the entire laboratory in 1955.

Weinberg was one of the first to recognize the importance of exploring other research areas in addition to nuclear science and technology at the national laboratories. In the 1950s ORNL initiated the early biological studies to quantify the effects of radiation on human genetics. In the 1960s, additional programs examined the environmental impact of various energy systems, ranging from coal-fired steam plants to the desalination of sea water. During the 1970s, ORNL conducted comprehensive analyses of the potential impact of energy conservation on overall energy production and consumption.

As a scientist, Weinberg co-authored the standard text on nuclear chain reaction theory with Eugene Wigner, a Nobel laureate and one of the preeminent physicists of the twentieth century. Weinberg also proposed the development of pressurized-water reactors, which became the standard nuclear technology for naval propulsion and most commercial power generation. A vigorous proponent of nuclear energy, he first proposed the formation of the American Nuclear Society.

In 1961 Weinberg chaired President John F. Kennedy's Panel of Science Information, which produced a landmark report on the communication of science to technical and lay audiences. Entitled *Science, Government, and Information*, the report has been frequently referred to as "The Weinberg Report."

Weinberg's many publications, including the monograph *Reflections on Big Science*, vividly articulate the issues associated with nuclear energy and, more broadly, the relationship between technology and society. Speaking eloquently on behalf of the national laboratories and science, he coined phrases, such as "big science," "technological fix," "nuclear priesthood," and "Faustian bargain," now firmly embedded in the English language.

After leaving ORNL, Weinberg's influence continued as director of the Office of Energy Research and Development in President Richard Nixon's White House and as director of the Institute for Energy Analysis headquartered in Oak Ridge. His interests included efforts to increase public confidence in technology for the "second era" of nuclear energy; improvement of the prospects for nuclear diplomacy and containment in Cold War national defense; and focusing the debate over the greenhouse effect within the context of scientific knowledge and research. In retirement, he applied his communication skills to editing the papers of Eugene Wigner and the preparation of his own memoirs. More recently, he has been instrumental in the dedication of a peace bell in Oak Ridge, a gift from the Japanese government that acknowledges the powerful impact of the atom in World War II, but looks ahead to a peaceful future in which negotiations, not conflict, serve as the primary means for settling international disputes.

Daniel Schaffer, Forum for Applied Research and Public Policy, and Leland Johnson, Clio Research Institute

SUGGESTED READING: Alvin M Weinberg, *The First Nuclear Era: The Life and Times of a Technological Fixer* (1994)

SEE: OAK RIDGE NATIONAL LABORATORY; SCIENCE AND TECHNOLOGY

WELLS CREEK BASIN. This round two-mile wide (3.2 km) valley in Houston and Stewart counties is eroded in rock that once was under a meteor crater. The fertile basin has attracted people ever since Paleoindians camped there about 10,000 years ago. The soil weathered from limestone that is deeply buried outside the basin. The center rock and soil are like the ridge at Knoxville. Nearby farmland is like that near Murfreesboro and Columbia. The center rock is raised 2,500 feet (760 m). Forested hills of flinty rock ring the basin. The valley results from dissolving uplifted limestone since flint hills resist erosion. Two fault rings surround the basin: the outer one is four miles (6.4 km) from the center and touches the town of Erin.

A meteor or comet struck like an atomic explosion 95–320 million years ago. It blasted out a crater and momentarily squashed rock down and out. Seconds later, rocks rebounded up and in. The present basin has rock that jumped highest, but could not fall all the way back, because the space was filled by rock springing in from the sides. Conical fractures called "shatter cones" occur in the rock that was under the impact. The two fault rings were open cracks after the impact. They filled with rock that fell in. The crater eroded away long ago, along with at least 500 feet (152 m) of rock.

A 20 million ton meteor, or comet, striking at 25 miles (40 km) per second (90,000 mph) could blast a four mile (6.4 km) crater and make the uplift and ring faults. A stony meteor that heavy would be 900 feet (274 m) in diameter.

Richard G. Stearns, Vanderbilt University

SEE: GEOLOGY; HOUSTON COUNTY

WELLS, KITTY (1919–), pioneering female country music vocalist, was born Muriel Deason in Nashville on August 30, 1919. She learned to sing and play guitar at an early age and was performing with Johnny Wright and the Harmony Girls by 1936. In 1937 she married Wright, who gave her the stage name "Kitty Wells" after the folk song *Sweet Kitty Wells*. During the 1940s Wells focused on raising her family, occasionally performing with her husband and his partner Jack Anglin.

In 1952 she recorded *It Wasn't God Who Made Honky Tonk Angels* for Paul Cohen at Decca Records.

Ida B. Wells-Barnett.

REPRINTED FROM *HISTORIC BLACK MEMPHIANS* EXHIBIT GUIDE, UNDATED. ORIGINAL IN THE COLLECTIONS OF THE UNIVERSITY OF CHICAGO LIBRARY

This woman's answer song to Hank Thompson's *Wild Side of Life* became the first number one country hit recorded by a female vocalist. From that point through the early 1960s Wells consistently turned out hits: *Makin' Believe* (1955), *I Can't Stop Loving You* (1958), *Mommy For A Day* (1959), *Heartbreak U.S.A.* (1961), and *Password* (1964). Duets with Red Foley, such as *One by One* (1954) and *As Long As I Live* (1955), also topped the charts.

Throughout her career Wells had over 20 number one hits, earning her the undisputed title of the "Queen of Country Music." Her solo stardom paved the way for every female country performer to follow her from Loretta Lynn to Emmylou Harris. Wells entered the Country Music Hall of Fame in 1976. The Kitty Wells/Johnny Wright Museum in Madison features items from the couple's years in show business.

Anne-Leslie Owens, Tennessee Historical Society

SUGGESTED READING: Mary A. Bufwack and Robert K. Oermann, *Finding Her Voice: Women in Country Music* (1993)

SEE: COUNTRY MUSIC HALL OF FAME; MUSIC

WELLS-BARNETT, IDA B. (1862–1931), journalist, feminist, and civil rights activist, launched an anti-lynching campaign in the 1890s that made her one of the most outstanding African-American women of the nineteenth century. The eldest of eight children born to James "Jim" and Elizabeth "Lizzie" Warenton Wells, she was born a slave in Holly Springs, Mississippi, on July 16, 1862. Orphaned by the yellow fever epidemic of 1878, Wells left Shaw University (now Rust College) and, at age 16, became a teacher in rural Mississippi to support her younger brothers and sisters.

Ida B. Wells moved to Tennessee in the early 1880s and taught in Shelby County before obtaining a position in the Memphis public schools. She challenged segregated public accommodations by filing suit, in 1884, against the Chesapeake, Ohio and Southwestern Railroad after being forcibly removed from the first-class ladies coach. Although the Circuit Court ruled in her favor, awarding her five hundred dollars in damages, the Tennessee Supreme Court reversed that decision in 1887. Her eviction from the train launched Wells on a career in journalism. Writing under the pen name "Iola," she published accounts of her experience in African-American newspapers, such as the *New York Freeman* and the *Detroit Plaindealer.* Later, she presented a paper, "Women in Journalism or How I Would Edit," at the National Press Association's conference in Kentucky; became editor of the *Evening Star*; and, in 1889, bought a one-third interest in the *Memphis Free Speech and Headlight.* Two years later, she became a fulltime journalist and editor of the *Free Speech* after the school board fired her for writing an editorial critical of Memphis's inferior segregated schools.

In 1892 three African-American grocers—Thomas Moss, Calvin McDowell, and Henry Stewart—were arrested, dragged from jail, and shot to death by a mob in the infamous "lynching at the Curve." Outraged, Wells bought a pistol for protection, asserting that "one had better die fighting against injustice than to die like a dog or a rat in a trap."[1] In her editorials, the young journalist urged African Americans to leave Memphis. She exposed lynching as a strategy to eliminate prosperous, politically-active African Americans and condemned the "thread-bare lie" of rape used to justify violence against blacks. Her allegations incensed Memphians, particularly her suggestion that southern white women were sexually attracted to black men. While Wells was in Philadelphia, a committee of "leading citizens" destroyed her newspaper office and warned her not to return to the city.

Wells moved to New York, where she bought an interest in the *New York Age* and intensified her campaign against lynching through lectures, newspaper articles, and pamphlets, including *Southern Horrors: Lynch Law in All Its Phases* (1892); *A Red Record: Tabulated Statistics and Alleged Causes of Lynching in the United States, 1892, 1893, and 1894* (1895); and *Mob Rule in New Orleans* (1900). To make her anti-lynching crusade international, Wells lectured in Great Britain in 1893 and 1894, during which she wrote a column entitled "Ida B. Wells Abroad" for the Chicago *Inter-Ocean.* She also co-wrote a pamphlet to protest the exclusion of blacks from the 1893 Chicago World's Fair.

On June 27, 1895, Wells married a widower with two small sons, the prominent Chicago attorney Ferdinand L. Barnett, and they became the parents of four children. She bought an interest in the *Chicago Conservator,* which was founded and edited by her husband, and continued to write forceful articles and essays, including "Booker T. Washington and His Critics" and "How Enfranchisement Stops Lynching." Eventually, her militant views, support of black nationalist Marcus Garvey, and outspoken criticism of race leaders, such as Booker T. Washington and W.E.B. Du Bois, embroiled her in controversies. After she extolled the accomplishments of Garvey, the U.S. Secret Service branded her as a radical.

After a brief retirement from public life following the birth of her second child, Wells-Barnett continued her campaign for racial justice, the political empowerment of blacks, and the enfranchisement of women. In 1898 she met with President William McKinley to protest the lynching of a postman and to urge passage of a federal law against lynching. After an outbreak of violence against blacks in Springfield, Illinois, she signed the call for a conference, which led to the formation of the National Association for the Advancement of Colored People. She distanced herself from the NAACP, however, because of differences with Du Bois over strategy and racial politics. In 1910 Wells-Barnett founded the Negro Fellowship League to provide housing, employment, and recreational facilities for southern black migrants. Unable to garner sufficient support for the League, she donated her salary as an adult probation officer, following her appointment to the office in 1913.

An early champion of rights for women, Wells-Barnett was one of the founders of the National Association of Colored Women. In Chicago she organized what became the Ida B. Wells Club; as its president, she established a kindergarten in the black community and successfully lobbied—with the help of Jane Addams—against segregated public schools. She also founded the Alpha Suffrage Club, which sent her as a delegate to the National American Woman Suffrage Association's parade in Washington, D.C. Refusing to join black delegates at the back of the procession, she integrated the parade by marching with the Illinois delegation. Through her leadership, the Suffrage Club became actively involved in the election of Oscar DePriest, the first African-American alderman of Chicago. Her interest in politics eventually led to Wells-Barnett's unsuccessful campaign for the Illinois State Senate in 1930.

In 1918, in her unremitting crusade against racial violence, Wells-Barnett covered the race riot in East

St. Louis, Illinois, and wrote a series of articles on the riot for the *Chicago Defender*. Four years later, she returned South for the first time in 30 years to investigate the indictment for murder of 12 innocent farmers in Elaine, Arkansas. She raised money to publish and distribute 1,000 copies of *The Arkansas Race Riot* (1922), in which she recorded the results of her investigation.

Wells-Barnett continued to write throughout her final decade. In 1928 she began an autobiography, which was published posthumously, and she recorded the details of her political campaign in a 1930 diary. After a brief illness, Ida B. Wells-Barnett died on March 25, 1931, at the age of 69.

Miriam DeCosta-Willis, University of Maryland

CITATION:
(1) Alfreda M. Duster, ed. *Crusade for Justice: The Autobiography of Ida B. Wells* (Chicago, 1970), 62.

SUGGESTED READINGS: Miriam DeCosta-Willis, ed., *The Memphis Diary of Ida B. Wells* (1995); Alfreda M. Duster, ed., *Crusade for Justice: The Autobiography of Ida B. Wells* (1970); Paula Giddings, *When and Where I Enter: The Impact of Black Women on Race and Sex in America* (1984)

SEE: CIVIL RIGHTS MOVEMENT; LYNCHING; MEMPHIS FREE SPEECH; NAACP

WERTHAN, JOE (1890–1967), industrialist and philanthropist, entered the modest family business, Werthan and Company, in 1908. It dealt in scrap metal and the accumulation, reconditioning, and distribution of burlap bags to grain elevators and feed mills. In 1911 Werthan married Sadie Mai Bogatsky and their only child, Howard, was born in 1913.

Joe Werthan and his older brother, Morris, became the principals in Werthan Bag Company and, after the death of their father, engaged primarily in the production and distribution of new burlap and cotton bags. After 1918 the Werthans purchased the defunct Marathon Motor Works and converted this facility to a bag factory. In 1928 they acquired the textile bag plant, cotton mill, bleachery, and finishing plant of the Morgan & Hamilton Company.

Werthan also entered the local real estate business, acquiring residential and commercial properties. He established Warioto Farms in Williamson County for breeding, raising, and training three and five-gaited show horses. This property still remains in the family.

Werthan acquired two colonial mansions and a frame cottage on Elliston Place, which he converted to The Joe Werthan Service Center, a 250-bed facility for servicemen passing through Nashville during World War II. Funded entirely by Werthan, the facility provided beds, meals, and recreation to many of an estimated one million servicemen undergoing training in Middle Tennessee. Many friends and associates provided volunteer support.

In 1945 Werthan, his son, and two nephews established the Werthan Foundation to provide financial support to agencies in the fields of health, welfare, education, and similar endeavors. In 1951 the Werthan Foundation established the Joe and Morris Werthan Professorship in Experimental Medicine at Vanderbilt University. Werthan and his son, Howard, also co-founded the Joe and Howard Werthan Foundation, with similar purposes to the earlier organization. When Werthan, his wife, and son all died during the mid-1960s, the charter of the Joe and Howard Werthan Foundation was terminated. Vanderbilt University Medical Center became the main beneficiary of the remaining funds. A contribution of $600,000 provided for an addition to the Medical Center's facilities, which was named The Joe and Howard Werthan Building.

Albert Werthan, Nashville

SUGGESTED READING: Don Doyle, *Nashville in the New South, 1880–1930* (1985)

SEE: INDUSTRY; MARATHON MOTOR WORKS; VANDERBILT UNIVERSITY MEDICAL CENTER; WORLD WAR II

WESSYNGTON PLANTATION, located near Cedar Hill, Robertson County, specialized in dark-fired tobacco from the early nineteenth to the late twentieth century. Joseph Washington, a native of Virginia, established Wessyngton in 1796, the year of statehood, when he acquired property along Sulphur Fork Creek; his subsequent marriage to Mary Cheatham significantly expanded his property. In 1819 Joseph and Mary Washington built the manor house, a distinguished two-story, five-bay red brick example of Federal style. It is listed in the National Register of Historic Places. The cultivation and curing of dark-fired tobacco took skill, hard work, and time; hundreds of African-American slaves produced the annual crop. Washington initially relied on overland transportation to the Clarksville tobacco markets; later he turned to small steamers which traveled the local rivers.

In 1848 Wessyngton was inherited by son George A. Washington, who took advantage in the next decade of the emerging rail system, the high price commanded by African-American slaves, and the growing dark-fired tobacco market to become one of the richest men in late antebellum Tennessee. In 1860 Washington owned over 13,000 acres and his 274 slaves raised 250,000 pounds of tobacco. His real and personal estate was valued at $519,000, a property value that was 78 times the average of all property holders in Robertson County.

Like all slaveowners, the emancipation of slaves as a result of the Civil War cost Washington a large portion of his wealth, but, compared to his neighbors, Washington emerged from the 1860s as one of the region's most powerful planters. Washington maintained control over his vital African-American labor force by negotiating stringent sharecropper arrangements with his former slaves. Driving a hard bargain, Washington forced his croppers to turn over half their crop while also pledging to work for him at 65 cents a day when he needed their labor. Croppers also agreed not to work for anyone else, unless they had Washington's permission, and they agreed to tend the stables, feed the livestock, keep all fences in repair, and to donate three days of labor for every male member of the family. The market for dark-fired tobacco continued to grow in the late nineteenth century and Wessyngton continued to prosper. In 1892 the plantation passed to son Joseph E. Washington, who managed the property during the heated tobacco wars of the early twentieth century. At his death in 1915, he left the plantation to his wife Mary Bolling Kearns Washington, who owned the property until 1938.

At this time, the estate was inherited by three children of Joseph E. and Mary Washington. They managed the property until forming the Wessyngton Company in 1956 to administer the estate. It stayed in family hands through the 1970s, and was designated a Tennessee Century Farm in 1976. But when a new survey of the state's historic family farms was completed in 1986, Wessyngton had passed from the control of the Washington family. The historic estate continues to operate as a private farm.

Carroll Van West, Middle Tennessee State University
SUGGESTED READING: Carroll Van West, *Tennessee's Historic Landscapes: A Traveler's Guide* (1995)

SEE: AGRICULTURAL TENANCY; BLACK PATCH WAR; FARMS, TENNESSEE CENTURY; GLENRAVEN PLANTATION; SHARECROPPING; SLAVERY; TOBACCO; WASHINGTON, JOSEPH E.

WEST TENNESSEE HISTORICAL SOCIETY is the successor of four other historical societies. Prior to September 28, 1950, the West Tennessee Historical Society (WTHS) was an unincorporated society whose origins can be traced to the antebellum period. Organized in 1857, the Old Folks of Shelby County was the first of those organizations from which the West Tennessee Historical Society grew. The Old Folks, founded by Memphis residents to preserve the history of early Memphis, published a monthly journal titled the *Old Folks Record,* edited by James D. Davis, who also published *A History of Memphis* in 1873. The historian of the Old Folks of Shelby County was Eugene Magevney, the early Memphis educator and city alderman during the 1840s and 1850s. The society continued until the Civil War and would reorganize in 1870. In addition to preserving "authentic history" in print, the society, in 1880, acquired and provided for the preservation of Winchester Cemetery, where many of the city's early residents were buried.

Following the Civil War, the second antecedent society of the WTHS made its appearance. Founded in 1866 and incorporated in 1867, the Confederate Relief and Historical Association of Memphis chronologically overlapped the Old Folks of Shelby County. This association was not only interested in perpetuating southern history, but it also aided disabled Confederate veterans, and their widows and orphans. As its role in relief work diminished, the Association reorganized in 1869 as the Confederate Historical Association. Membership in the Association was limited to ex-Confederates "whose records as soldiers were clean, and their male descendants." Perhaps its most famous member was former Confederate General George W. Gordon, who became president of the Association in 1897. An auxiliary to the all male Association, the Ladies Confederate Historical Association, was organized on May 16, 1889. Similar to its "predecessor," the Old Folks of Shelby County, the Confederate Historical Association also perpetuated history in a more concrete sense. Following the repeal of a law which prohibited monuments to former Confederates, the Association erected a granite monument honoring Confederate dead. Once again, in 1884, reorganization occurred when the Association became Camp No. 28 of the United Confederate Veterans.

In 1900 Judge John Preston Young, who had been active in the Confederate Historical Association, was instrumental in organizing the Memphis Historical Society, which continued to focus on local history, but moved away from Civil War themes. In 1935 the Memphis Historical Society broadened its emphasis to a regional perspective when the Society became the unincorporated West Tennessee Historical Society. Fifteen years later, in January 1950, the Society voted to incorporate and received a charter from the State of Tennessee on September 7; the incorporators took over the Society three weeks later. The original incorporators were: Marshall Wingfield, Marie G. Wingfield, Lois D. Bejach, Wilena Robert Bejach, Gilmer Richardson, Enoch L. Mitchell, James A. Wax, J. Winfield Qualls, Perry M. Harbert, Roy W. Black, and John T. Gray. The first volume of the *Papers* of the Society appeared in 1947. Marshall Wingfield, one of the original incorporators, served as the president of the Society from 1938 to 1961. The Society's annual award for the best article appearing in its *Papers* is named after Dr. Wingfield.

The Society currently has over 400 individual members and 90 institutional members, and is composed of the 21 counties west of the Tennessee River. While its historical interests focus primarily on that region, it promotes and publishes histories of the state, the Mid-South, and the South.

Marius M. Carriere, Jr., Christian Brothers University
SEE: MAGEVNEY, EUGENE; UNITED CONFEDERATE VETERANS

WEST, BEN (1911–1974), mayor of Nashville (1951–1963), was born in Columbia, Tennessee, in 1911. West came to Nashville as a boy and grew up with his parents in a working-class neighborhood in the Woodbine district. He worked his way through school and attended Cumberland Law School and Vanderbilt University. In 1934 he began work as an assistant district attorney in Nashville. West ran unsuccessfully for mayor of Nashville in 1943 and won election as vice mayor in 1946 and then as State Senator in 1949.

In the Senate West introduced legislation that brought back single-member district elections, replacing the citywide election of Nashville's city council. This represented a major breakthrough for the rebirth of black voting power in city politics because it allowed minorities whose votes were concentrated in a few wards to carry elections they could not hope to win in city-wide contests. This reform was also the key to West's political future, for he would depend heavily on the reemerging black voter. With the repeal of the poll tax and other voting restrictions, and the movement of white voters to the suburbs, the political power of blacks in Nashville was increasing.

In 1951 West won election as mayor of Nashville, along with the first two African-American councilmen in 40 years. As mayor of Nashville West supported other voting reforms, particularly the campaign to reapportion rural and urban voting districts. West championed the cause of reapportionment in the landmark case, *Baker v. Carr*, by which the U.S. Supreme Court ruled in favor of the "one man, one vote" principle. This forced reapportionment of state legislatures and shifted power to woefully underrepresented cities. While mayor of Nashville, West presided over the Capitol Hill Redevelopment Project, which replaced a squalid slum and vice district surrounding the state capitol building with a green belt, parking lots, and new state office buildings. West's strong alliance with Nashville's black community also helped improve race relations and prepare the city for the challenge of the Civil Rights Movement. At one critical moment during the sit-in demonstrations of 1960 protest marchers challenged West to take a stand against segregation. He did so, and the Nashville business community quickly agreed to desegregate department store lunch counters, making Nashville the first southern city to desegregate public facilities. With his base in the old inner city, West opposed the consolidation of city and county government in 1958 and 1963. He lost reelection as mayor of the new Metropolitan government in his 1963 contest with Beverly Briley. West retired to private life and died in 1974.

Don H. Doyle, Vanderbilt University

SUGGESTED READINGS: Don H. Doyle, *Nashville Since the 1920s* (1985); Linda T. Wynn, "The Dawning of a New Day: The Nashville Sit-Ins, February 13-May 10, 1960," *Tennessee Historical Quarterly* 50(1991): 42–54

SEE: BAKER V. CARR; BRILEY, BEVERLY; CIVIL RIGHTS MOVEMENT; NASH, DIANE; NASHVILLE; SIT-INS, NASHVILLE

WESTERN STATE MENTAL HOSPITAL is the state mental hospital located near Bolivar, Tennessee. It was the last state mental hospital to be constructed and habitually the one least funded. In December 1885 the site commissioners chose the farm of Paul T. Jones as the location for the proposed facility.

The institution's patient population grew from a few hundred in the 1890s to over 2,000 in the 1960s as patients remained hospitalized for decades. Many were crowded into large dormitories and had little privacy. With a limited number of doctors and attendants and a large patient population, many were simply "warehoused."

Patients at Western received the treatments available in their period of institutionalization. These treatments ranged from hydrotherapy and insulin shock therapy to lobotomies and electric shock therapy. With the severe staff limitations, however, patients were fortunate to receive ten minutes per week with a psychiatrist.

The system for securing financing for patient care limited the operating budget. In Tennessee, there were three classes of patients: the state-pay patients, the county-pay patients, and the private-pay patients. State agencies agreed to pay for one patient out of a population of 1,000. Once this portion of the payment had been satisfied, the county was responsible for additional costs. The county payments were habitually behind, and superintendents had to engage in deficit spending to keep the hospital operating. The two most influential superintendents, Dr. Edwin Cocke and Dr. Edwin Levy, often faced political pressure from state officials, but both managed to make some improvements in the care offered at Western.

In modern times, "deinstitutionalization" produced a marked decrease in the patient population as mental health experts called for treatment of the mentally ill in local mental health clinics. Although there have been indications that this treatment has not been successful, it continues to the present time, and the indigent mentally ill continue to pose a major problem for society.

Linda T. Austin, Memphis

SEE: HARDEMAN COUNTY; MEDICINE; TENNESSEE LUNATIC ASYLUM

WHARTON, MAY CRAVATH (1873–1959), early twentieth century medical pioneer on the Cumberland Plateau, was born on a Minnesota farm. A sickly child, she was inspired and encouraged by a family friend and physician who gave her the *Home Doctor Book*. She attended Carleton College in Northfield,

Minnesota, from 1890–1893, but finished her B.A. at the University of North Dakota in 1894–1895. She studied in Europe in 1897 and taught at the University of North Dakota in 1898–1899. Finally she chose medicine as her profession, receiving her medical degree from the University of Michigan in 1905.

After graduation, she established a private practice in Atlanta, Georgia, where she met and married Edwin Wharton, a Congregational minister and missionary. In 1907 the couple moved to Cleveland, Ohio, to manage a settlement house, he as director and she as physician. In 1909 the Whartons moved to New Hampshire, where they farmed and she practiced medicine while he served small churches.

In 1917 Wharton and her husband moved to Cumberland County, Tennessee, where Edwin had been appointed as the new principal of Pleasant Hill Academy. Established by the American Missionary Association in 1884, the academy was a boarding school where disadvantaged rural youths could receive a broad education in the liberal arts and sciences as well as vocational training in agriculture and home economics. Dr. Wharton taught health and served as the academy's physician to staff and students. During the flu epidemic of 1919, however, Wharton assisted as many Plateau families as possible. She gained a reputation as a compassionate and determined doctor; she served a widely dispersed clientele, traveling on rough country roads by horseback and buggy.

Edwin Wharton died in 1920, and May Cravath Wharton decided to stay at Pleasant Hill to continue as the community doctor. Assisted by art teacher Elizabeth Fletcher and Canadian-trained Registered Nurse Alice Adshead, Wharton established a small three-room hospital almost immediately; by 1922, she had raised enough funds and had sufficient donated land to build the Uplands Sanatorium. After the construction of the Memphis-to-Bristol Highway in 1927, Wharton and her associates provided outreach programs and established small clinics in adjoining communities. A successful New England fund raising venture in 1932 allowed Wharton to build a general hospital in 1935 and the Van Dyck Annex in 1938. The hospital's name changed to Cumberland General to reflect the range of services available at the medical institution.

After World War II, Wharton was instrumental in gaining federal, state, and private funding for the modern Cumberland Medical Center. Located in Crossville, it opened with 50 beds in March 1950. Her last project at Pleasant Hill was the creation of the May Cravath Wharton Nursing Home in 1957, which later was incorporated as Uplands, Inc., a retirement village with homes and apartments. By now, Dr. Wharton's achievements had been recognized with awards from the Tennessee Medical Association and Carleton College. She received an honorary doctorate from the University of Chattanooga in 1957. Wharton died at the age of 86 on November 19, 1959.
Franklin and Betty J. Parker, Pleasant Hill

SUGGESTED READING: May Cravath Wharton, *Doctor Woman of the Cumberlands: the Autobiography of May Cravath Wharton* (1953)

SEE: CUMBERLAND COUNTY; INFLUENZA PANDEMIC; MEDICINE

WHEELER, JOSEPH (1836–1906), Confederate cavalry commander, rose from lieutenant to major general in the Army of Tennessee in less than two years. He is best known for daring raids behind Union lines in Middle Tennessee that were sensationalized at the time, but which historians have judged unproductive. Wheeler was one of the few Confederate officers to rejoin the U.S. Army after the Civil War.

Born in Augusta, Georgia, on September 10, 1836, Wheeler graduated from the U.S. Military Academy in 1859, nineteenth in a class of 22. General Braxton Bragg gave the 26-year-old Wheeler command of the Army of Tennessee's cavalry in the fall of 1862. His first flamboyant raid was a ride around the Union Army of the Cumberland on the eve of the Battle of Stones River at Murfreesboro in December 1862. In late January 1863, Wheeler struck out to recapture Fort Donelson on the Cumberland River. His leadership in that unsuccessful expedition earned him the everlasting enmity of Tennessee's most effective cavalry general, Nathan Bedford Forrest, who vowed never again to serve under Wheeler.

Wheeler commanded the cavalry during the Tullahoma Campaign in the summer of 1863, where his failure to effectively deploy his troops contributed to the Confederate loss. He served well in the Confederate victory at Chickamauga, before making his most famous raid in October—an attempt to disrupt the fragile Federal supply route into besieged Chattanooga. Wheeler's troops destroyed a large wagon train moving through the Sequatchie Valley, but followed their initial success with a wild ride across Middle Tennessee before being chased into Alabama. In the end, Wheeler had little to show for his efforts, other than an exhausted command.

Wheeler was promoted to lieutenant general and commanded the Army of Tennessee's cavalry during William T. Sherman's campaign for Atlanta in the summer of 1864. His last raid came late in the Atlanta campaign, when he led men to north Georgia to destroy the Chattanooga rail line that supplied Sherman's troops. After inflicting only minor damage, he rode off toward Knoxville, before moving into Middle Tennessee and Alabama. The raid actually benefited Sherman by removing valuable Confederate cavalry from the Atlanta area.

Wheeler was not present for the battles of Franklin and Nashville in the fall of 1864; instead, he was

TSLA

An old school bus was converted into use for Irwin's Rolling Store which operated in White County from 1945–1955.

assigned to harass Sherman on his march through Georgia and the Carolinas. Wheeler was in North Carolina when the Civil War ended in April 1865.

After the war, Wheeler lived in New Orleans for four years before moving to north Alabama, where he served eight terms in Congress (1881–1882, 1885–1900). He was commissioned major general in the U.S. Army during the Spanish-American War and served in Cuba and the Philippines. He retired from the army in 1900 and died in New York in 1906.
Robert Brandt, Nashville

SUGGESTED READING: Patricia L. Hudson, "The Old Anderson Road: Lifeline to Chattanooga," *Tennessee Historical Quarterly* 42(1983): 165–178

SEE: ARMY OF TENNESSEE; CHICKAMAUGA AND CHATTANOOGA, BATTLES OF; CIVIL WAR; FORREST, NATHAN BEDFORD; STONES RIVER, BATTLE OF; TULLAHOMA CAMPAIGN

WHITE COUNTY was established on September 11, 1806, by the Tennessee General Assembly from a part of Smith County and named for John White, one of the first settlers in the area. The Knowels, Rascos, and Swindells were among other early settlers; John H. Howell brought his family from North Carolina to a cave near Burgess Falls.

White County's first court was held at the house of Joseph Terry at Rock Island, now in Warren County. In 1809 the state legislature authorized the establishment of a county seat at Sparta. The town

was laid off by commissioners Thomas Bounds, Benjamin Weaver, Aaron England, Turner Lane, James Fulkerson, Alexander Lowry, and Nicholas Gillentine. The first courthouse was constructed of logs in 1810; in that same year, Eli Sims, a native of Ireland, came to White County. He established the county's first cotton gin, and in 1824 he and his slaves built a two-story brick house that still stands outside of Sparta and is recognized as the county's first brick dwelling.

White County furnished soldiers for the War of 1812, the Mexican War, and the Civil War. In addition to the men who served on both sides of the Civil War, aggressive partisan units on both sides settled old scores and kept the Upper Cumberland in turmoil. The most notorious of these partisans was Samuel W. "Champ" Ferguson. General Braxton Bragg also moved his army through Sparta on his way to Kentucky in 1862.

White County contained valuable natural resources in coal and timber, which were exploited fully from the 1880s to the Great Depression. Coal mines and towns were established at Eastland, Ravenscroft, Clifty, DeRossett, and Bon Air, touching the lives of thousands of residents. The first coalfield was at Bon Air, established in 1882 by Sparta resident General George Dibrell, who owned 15,000 acres in White County. But the real power behind the venture was probably the NC&St.L Railroad since its president, E.W. Cole, also served as chairman of the coal company's executive committee. The mine was an immediate success, and by 1884 the railroad extended a spur from McMinnville to Sparta. Three years later, the line was extended to Bon Air and by 1905 the branch reached the mines at Clifty and Ravenscroft.

Between 1888 and 1904 Bon Air Coal Company and the Clifty Creek Coal and Coke Company established four towns on the plateau overlooking Sparta. The Bon Air company owned at least 38,000 acres and employed 600 men from both White and Cumberland counties. Over the next two decades, the mines increased production and in 1920 White County was the sixth leading coal producer in Tennessee. In 1917 William J. Cummins and other investors acquired the properties and later established the Tennessee Products Corporation. Its headquarters was at Ravenscroft, where it operated the state's only coal shaft mine, along with a coal-distillation plant, until 1936.

Lumber was taken in vast amounts during the early twentieth century, at first in support of the continual mining expansion and then as a resource in its own right. The Sparta Spoke Factory was one of the region's largest. During World War I White County walnut was in great demand for gun stocks, which were ordered first by Allied nations and then by the federal government in 1917. To serve the increased freight traffic, the railroad built a modern depot, which is listed now in the National Register, in 1917.

Sparta grew markedly during these decades of industrial investment. Thomas L. Sperry was a leading merchant and builder. His National Register-listed home, constructed ca. 1880, overlooks the town square. A Main Street residential historic district contains popular domestic styles of the early twentieth century, including Queen Anne, bungalow, Four-Square, and Classical Revival dwellings. The construction of the Memphis-to-Bristol Highway through the town during the mid- to late 1920s also influenced the town's built environment as a new residential district developed along Gaines Street. In fact, good roads have always been important to the county's economic health. East of Sparta is the Sparta Rock House, a tollhouse that served antebellum travelers on the Knoxville-to-Nashville turnpike, first built in 1815.

White County's famous residents include bluegrass legend Lester Flatt, a member of the Country Music Hall of Fame. Its nearby recreational facilities include the Calfkiller and Caney Fork rivers, Virgin Falls State Natural Area; Burgess Falls State Natural Area, and Rock Island State Park.

Today the county population is estimated at almost 22,000 people. The Sparta *Expositor* was founded by L.D. Hill and his brother. In 1880 they sold the paper to R.P. Baker. Other owners have included James B. Snodgrass, Charles G. Sims, Floyd Bryan, Wendell Gentry, Coleman Harwell, and Bobby and Logie Anderson. Suzanne Dickerson has been the editor and publisher of the *Expositor* since 1994. The largest industry in White County is Mallory Controls, Inc., which produces appliance timers, switches, and water valves.

Carroll Van West, Middle Tennessee State University, John E. Acuff, Sparta, and Connie L. Lester, Tennessee Historical Society

SEE: ARCHITECTURE, VERNACULAR DOMESTIC; COLE, EDMUND W.; DIBRELL, GEORGE GIBBS; FLATT, LESTER, HIGHWAYS, HISTORIC; MINING; RAILROAD, NASHVILLE AND CHATTANOOGA; SPARTA ROCK HOUSE

WHITE, HUGH LAWSON (1773–1840) was a U.S. Senator whose 1836 presidential candidacy helped to establish the Whig party both in Tennessee and in the South. The son of General James White, the founder of Knoxville, White briefly served as private secretary to William Blount, Governor of the Southwest Territory, before receiving his license to practice law in 1796. The success of his law practice and the prominence of his family led to his appointment or election to several important positions, including Judge on the Tennessee Supreme Court of Law and Equity, United States District Attorney, Judge on the State Supreme Court of Errors and Appeals, State Senator representing Knox County, and president of the Bank of Tennessee in Knoxville. White's service in these offices gained for him a reputation for competence and honesty, and as a known friend of Andrew Jackson he was unanimously elected by the General Assembly to succeed Jackson in the U.S. Senate in 1825. Twice the Assembly re-elected White to the Senate, in 1829 and 1835, and both times the vote for him was again unanimous.

Upon his election to the presidency in 1828, Jackson offered White a cabinet appointment as Secretary of War. White declined, but served during Jackson's first term as one of the administration's most loyal defenders. By the beginning of Jackson's second term, however, White considered himself alienated from the administration. He openly disagreed with Old Hickory's increasing demand for conformity to the decisions of the Democratic party. Moreover, he sympathized with Whig charges that Jackson had exceeded the accepted limits of presidential power, and he apparently believed himself slighted when it became clear that the president wanted Vice President Martin Van Buren to succeed him in the White House. Despite Jackson's renewed offer to appoint him as Secretary of War, White by 1833 was acting more independently in the Senate by opposing several important administration measures. When approached by southern political leaders who had also become estranged from Jackson, White agreed to challenge Van Buren by standing for the presidency himself.

White's supporters presented him as the candidate most loyal to the original principles upon which Jackson had been elected in 1828. In particular, they charged that Jackson and Van Buren were attempting to "dictate" their will to voters by insisting that they support Van Buren simply because he had been nominated by a Democratic convention. They questioned the legitimacy of the convention since it had been packed with Van Buren delegates rather than attended by representatives of the Democratic people. The charge that Jackson was trying to force his will upon the people complemented the northern Whig party's claim that Jackson abused presidential power and acted like a monarch. In the lower South, supporters also argued that White's status as a slave owner offered better protection for slave property, although this appeal received relatively little hearing in Tennessee.

One of four candidates in the 1836 election, White carried only Tennessee and Georgia and finished third in the electoral college. By winning 49 percent of the popular vote in the southern states, however, White's candidacy divided the South's unity behind Jackson's Democratic party. Before the next presidential election, most of White's supporters joined together with northern Whigs to transform the party into a national force.

After the election, White continued to oppose "executive usurpation" and took an active role in the formation of the Whig party in Tennessee. In 1837 he testified before a House committee that Jackson had misused executive power and had exercised his influence against White in the presidential contest. When Jackson denied this charge White issued a public letter to substantiate his claims. A year later, White removed himself from consideration for the presidency and instead endorsed Jackson's nemesis, Henry Clay. When Democrats won control of Tennessee in the 1839 state elections, the General Assembly passed a series of resolutions instructing White and his Senate colleague, Ephraim H. Foster, to vote for the policies of the Van Buren administration. White and Foster both resigned rather than submit to the resolutions, but the state Whig party then named them as at-large electors for Whig presidential nominee William Henry Harrison. White accepted this nomination, but before he could campaign actively for Harrison he died of consumption at his home in Knoxville in 1840.

Jonathan M. Atkins, Berry College

SUGGESTED READINGS: Jonathan M. Atkins, "Politicians, Parties, and Slavery: The Second Party System and the Decision for Disunion in Tennessee," *Tennessee Historical Quarterly* 55(1996): 20–39; Atkins, *Parties, Politics, and the Sectional Conflict in Tennessee, 1832–1861* (1997)

SEE: BELL, JOHN; BLOUNT, WILLIAM; FOSTER, EPHRAIM; JACKSON, ANDREW; WHITE, JAMES

WHITE, JAMES (1747–1821), statesman, military figure, and philanthropist, was born in 1747 in Rowan County, North Carolina. He married Mary Lawson in 1770, and the Whites had seven children; their oldest son, Hugh Lawson White, achieved national prominence as a presidential candidate in 1836.

In 1783 North Carolina passed what came to be known as the "Land Grab Act" and opened a major portion of East Tennessee for settlement. During the next decade, White purchased over 4,000 acres in what is now Knox County. In 1786 he built a fort, and five years later, laid out a town in what eventually became Knoxville. White donated land for a town common and a Presbyterian church and cemetery. For a nominal fee, he sold land to establish Knoxville's first institution of higher learning, Blount College, which later became the University of Tennessee.

White's public service included election to the legislatures of the State of Franklin and North Carolina. He represented North Carolina at its convention to ratify the Constitution of the United States and was also a representative to the Tennessee Constitutional Convention in 1796. Elected Senator in the First General Assembly of Tennessee, he became the Speaker of that body in 1797. White resigned his seat in favor of the popular William Blount after the latter left the U.S. Senate under a cloud of scandal; he returned to the State Senate after Blount's death in 1800. His appointments include justice of the peace, Indian Commissioner of Tennessee, and member of the Board of Trustees of Blount College.

White's military career began in 1779, when he served for two years as a captain in the North Carolina militia. He was commander of the "Immortal 38" in the defense of Knoxville in 1793, against an estimated 1,000 Cherokee and Creek warriors. White served as a brigadier general with Andrew Jackson during the Creek War of 1813. The Cherokees considered White a man of honor; on at least two occasions he tactfully interceded on their behalf and prevented reprisals by hot-headed settlers.

James White died on August 14, 1821, at his farm on the outskirts of Knoxville. In 1982 University of Tennessee archaeologists excavated the farm site. White and his wife, Mary, are buried in the cemetery of the First Presbyterian Church in downtown Knoxville.

Charles Faulkner, University of Tennessee, Knoxville

SUGGESTED READING: Walter T. Durham, *Before Tennessee: The Southwest Territory, 1790–1796* (1990)

SEE: LAND GRANTS; FORT JAMES WHITE; KNOX COUNTY; KNOXVILLE; SOUTHWEST TERRITORY; UNIVERSITY OF TENNESSEE; WHITE, HUGH LAWSON

WHITE, ROBERT HIRAM (1883–1970), Tennessee's first State Historian, was born in Crockett County in 1883. He graduated from Vanderbilt University in

1910, and completed his graduate work at George Peabody College and the University of Chicago.

From 1911 until 1919 White served on the first faculty at present-day Middle Tennessee State University. There he met and married Margaret Taylor in 1917; they became the parents of two daughters, Susan (Perry) and Barbara (Humes).

After earning his Ph.D. in history from George Peabody College for Teachers, White joined the Tennessee Department of Public Health in 1930, where he served in various capacities. In January 1950 Governor Gordon Browning asked White, who was then Director of Historical Research and Writing for the Tennessee Department of Education, to compile the messages of Tennessee's governors and interpret the events surrounding them.

White had published three volumes from this enormous project when he was named by Governor Frank G. Clement to fill the new office of State Historian, created by the General Assembly in 1955. In this capacity, White continued to work on *Messages of the Governors of Tennessee* until his death; this eight-volume work became his greatest contribution to Tennessee history. In addition to his work on the *Messages*, White published *Development of the Tennessee State Education Organization, 1796–1929* and *Tennessee. Its Growth and Progress*, a textbook long used by school children. He edited *Tennessee Old and New* and wrote numerous articles for historical journals.

After a life devoted to Tennessee history, Robert H. "Bob" White died on June 7, 1970.

Walter L. Jordan, Franklin

Suggested Reading: Robert H. White, *Messages of the Governors of Tennessee*, Volumes 1–8 (1952–1972)

SEE: BROWNING, GORDON; CLEMENT, FRANK G.; TENNESSEE HISTORICAL COMMISSION; TENNESSEE HISTORICAL SOCIETY; TENNESSEE STATE LIBRARY AND ARCHIVES

WHITE, SUE SHELTON (1887–1943), suffragist, equal rights advocate, attorney, and writer, was born and reared in Henderson, Tennessee, the sixth of seven children born to James Shelton White and Mary Calista Swain White. As teachers and liberal thinkers, White's parents stressed the value of education and tutored her at home. Orphaned at age 14, White continued her education and graduated from Henderson's Georgie Robertson Christian College in 1904 and West Tennessee Business College in Dyer, Tennessee, in 1905. In 1923 she earned a law degree from Washington College of Law in Washington, D.C.

White joined the woman suffrage movement in 1912. She served as recording secretary for the Tennessee Equal Suffrage Association (1913–1918) and worked to increase support for suffrage in Tennessee. She came to believe that the policies and methods of the more radical National Woman's Party (NWP) were more effective and changed her allegiance in

1918. Moving to Washington, D.C., White became Tennessee chair of the NWP and edited the organization's newspaper, *Suffragist*. White achieved additional notoriety for participating in a suffrage demonstration in which the NWP burned President Woodrow Wilson in effigy. She was arrested and served five days in the Old Work House, a condemned jail. After her release, White joined the "Prison Special," a chartered railroad car that traveled around the country bringing the issue of woman suffrage to the people.

In June 1919 the U.S. Senate approved the Nineteenth Amendment and sent it to the states for ratification. By August of 1920, the amendment had been ratified in 35 states and needed only one additional state to become the law of the land. Eight southern states had defeated ratification, and it fell to the Tennessee General Assembly to decide the issue. White returned to the state and lobbied for ratification which was achieved on August 18.

Shortly after ratification, U.S. Senator Kenneth D. McKellar (D-TN) appointed White his clerk, later secretary (1920–1926). Continuing her interests in women's rights, White helped write the 1923 Equal Rights Amendment, sponsored by the NWP. White returned to Jackson, Tennessee, and practiced law from 1926 to 1930. She continued to be active in Democratic party politics, especially the Women's Division of the Democratic National Committee. With the election of Franklin D. Roosevelt to the presidency in 1932, White received an appointment as Executive Assistant to Mary (Molly) Harrison Rumsey in the Consumers Division of the National Recovery Administration (NRA). In 1935, after the U.S. Supreme Court ruled the NRA unconstitutional, White moved to the newly organized Social Security Administration, where she served as an attorney to help implement the Social Security Act.

After a long bout with cancer, White died on May 6, 1943, at her Alexandria, Virginia, home which she shared with Florence Armstrong, her long-term friend.

Betty Sparks Huehls, University of Memphis

Suggested Readings: Betty Sparks Huehls, "Sue Shelton White: The Making of a Radical," West Tennessee Historical Society *Papers* 48(1994): 24–34; James P. Louis, "Sue Shelton White and the Woman Suffrage Movement in Tennessee, 1913–1920," *Tennessee Historical Quarterly* 22(1963): 170–190; Marjorie Spruill Wheeler, *New Women of the New South: The Leaders of the Woman Suffrage Movement in the Southern States* (1993)

SEE: CHESTER COUNTY; MCKELLAR, KENNETH D.; WOMAN SUFFRAGE MOVEMENT

WHITEHEAD, JOSEPH BROWN (1864–1906), Chattanooga attorney and businessman, with Benjamin F. Thomas and J.T. Lupton, pioneered the Coca-Cola bottling industry. Born in Oxford, Mississippi, he received a law degree from the University of Mississippi. In the late 1880s he moved to Chattanooga, where he specialized in tax and business law. In 1896 he became involved in the New Spencer Medicine Company and served as vice president. Three years later he joined Thomas in his plan to bottle and distribute Coca-Cola. In July 1899 the two signed an agreement with Asa Candler, president of Coca-Cola Company, in Atlanta, Georgia, giving them exclusive bottling rights throughout most of the United States. In order to raise capital to open the first bottling plant, the partners added John Thomas Lupton to the partnership. The plant opened in the summer of 1899. Whitehead served as the first president of the Coca-Cola Bottling Company, chartered in November 1899.

Early in 1900 Whitehead moved to Atlanta to open the second bottling plant and continued to live there for the remainder of his life. In April 1900 the partners split the bottling territory in order to create bottling franchises. Whitehead and Lupton took the territory south of Chattanooga and the West, with the exception of the states of California, Oregon, and Washington. The two partners created such "parent" bottlers as the Dixie Coca-Cola Bottling Company in the South, Coca-Cola Bottling Company (1903) in the Southwest, and Western Coca-Cola Bottling Company in 1905 in the West. These "parent" companies granted franchises to local bottlers in what proved to be one of the most enriching and successful franchise businesses in American economic history.

Whitehead managed the bottling interests in Atlanta until his death from pneumonia in 1906 at age 42. He had married Lettie Pate (1872–1953) of Thaxton, Virginia, in 1894. They had two sons, Joe and Conkey, who both died relatively young. Lettie married Arthur Evans in 1913, and continued to be active in her first husband's affairs, especially in connection with Coca-Cola and various philanthropic works. In 1934 she became the first woman elected to the Coca-Cola Company board of directors and remained a director until her death. The Whiteheads are buried in Hollywood Cemetery, Richmond, Virginia.

Ned L. Irwin, East Tennessee State University

SUGGESTED READING: Ned L. Irwin, "Bottling Gold: Chattanooga's Coca-Cola Fortunes," *Tennessee Historical Quarterly* 51(1992): 223–237

SEE: COCA-COLA BOTTLING COMPANY; LUPTON, JOHN T.; THOMAS, BENJAMIN F.

WHITESIDE, HARRIET LENORA STRAW (1824–1903), Chattanooga business woman, was born May 3, 1824, in Wytheville, Virginia, and educated to be a teacher at the Moravian School in Winston-Salem, North Carolina. At the age of 19 she arrived in Chattanooga to teach music to one of the five children of

Colonel James A. Whiteside, a 40-year-old widower and Chattanooga's leading businessman, whom she married on February 1, 1844. A woman of strong intellectual interests, Whiteside ably supported her husband in his many ventures, in addition to bearing nine children between 1845 and 1859. When he died in 1861, Colonel Whiteside left a fortune under the control of his widow.

Whiteside acted decisively, selling what she could to pay debt against the estate with Confederate dollars. She also used Confederate money to buy tobacco that a Union friend sold in the east for greenbacks. She scarcely had time to put her husband's affairs in order before Confederate refugees began pouring into Chattanooga, followed in September 1863, by Union troops who remained in the city for the duration of the war. Whiteside, an ardent secessionist like her husband, was among those Confederate sympathizers deported to the North.

During her absence, many of her papers were lost, and when she returned to Chattanooga, she had to fight to reestablish ownership and control of her late husband's estate. Later efforts to combat a rival turnpike company on Lookout Mountain and to control access to the Point, a fracas popularly known as "The War of the Mountain Roads," earned her some public notoriety as did her divorce suit against a second husband, Varney A. Gaskill.

At the time of her death on February 1, 1903, some Chattanoogans breathed a sigh of relief because of the controversy she had engendered for the past 40 years. But one of her former attorneys, W.G.M. Thomas praised her as "an exceedingly superior woman" and "the best informed woman" of any of his clients. He also characterized her as "the best business woman I ever knew."[1]

Kay Baker Gaston, Springfield

CITATION:

(1) Kay Baker Gaston, "The Remarkable Harriet Whiteside," *Tennessee Historical Quarterly* 40(1981): 347.

SEE: CHATTANOOGA

WHITSON, BETH SLATER (1879–1930), songwriter, was born in Goodrich, Hickman County, Tennessee in 1879. Her parents were John H. Whitson and Anna Slater Whitson; her father was co-editor of the *Hickman Pioneer* newspaper. Beth Whitson began her extensive songwriting career in Hickman County. With the assistance of her younger sister Alice Whitson Norton, she composed lyrics to over 400 songs and wrote poems and short stories, many of which were published in leading magazines of the early twentieth century. Her first major hit was *Meet Me Tonight in Dreamland* in 1909, followed the next year by *Let Me Call You Sweetheart*, which is still performed today.

In 1913 Whitson and her sister Alice moved to Nashville where they continued to write and publish.

STATE OF TENNESSEE PHOTOGRAPHIC SERVICES

Lieutenant Governor John S. Wilder, 1997.

Her local biographer, Grace Baxter Thompson, remarked at the dedication of a state historical marker to Whitson's career in 1978: "She gave beauty and color and enjoyment to her community from which those qualities have been far-reaching and long-lasting."[1] Beth Slater Whitson died in 1930 and is buried in Spring Hill Cemetery in Nashville.

Carroll Van West, Middle Tennessee State University

CITATION:

(1) Marion C. Fussell, "Memorial to Beth Slater Whitson," *History of Hickman County* (1996), 322.

SEE: HICKMAN COUNTY; MUSIC

WILDER, JOHN SHELTON (1921–), Speaker of the Senate and Lieutenant Governor, was born in Fayette County, Tennessee. He attended the public schools of Fayette County, then he went to college, majoring in agriculture, at the University of Tennessee, Knoxville. His law degree is from Memphis State University (now University of Memphis) Law School.

In 1959 Wilder entered state politics and was elected to the State Senate. During the 1960–1961 boycott in Fayette County directed at local African-American tenant farmers, Wilder, unlike many of his neighbors, refused to punish black tenants by evicting them or calling in crop loans. This courageous stand temporarily impeded his political career. In 1966 he was elected to another two-year term in the Senate; he won his first four-year Senate term in 1968. He has served as a distinguished member of that body from the 85th through the 100th General Assembly and has served 13 consecutive terms as Speaker of the Senate and Lieutenant Governor of the State of Tennessee.

Wilder has been a member of many state, regional, and national commissions, associations, and committees. Some of these include the Southern Legislative Conference Executive Committee, Tennessee Industrial and Agricultural Development Commission, Tennessee Judicial Council, Tennessee Bar Association, National Conference of State Legislatures Legislative Leaders, and vice chair of the State Building Commission. In addition to his legislative work, Lieutenant Governor Wilder has an active business career as director of Health Management, Inc., director of Cumberland Savings Bank, chairman of the board of Cumberland Bank Shares, and chairman of the board of First Federal Bank FSI Holding Company, and in the management of Longtown Supply Co., a family business that was founded in 1887. He is also a Fayette County farmer and an avid aviator. Wilder married the former Marcelle Morton of Williston; they live in Fayette County and are active in the Methodist Church. The Wilders have two sons and four grandchildren.

Carroll Van West, Middle Tennessee State University
SUGGESTED READING: "John Shelton Wilder," *Tennessee Blue Book, 1995–1996: Bicentennial Edition* (1996), 9
SEE: FAYETTE COUNTY; GOVERNMENT; TENNESSEE STATE SENATE

WILDER, JOHN THOMAS (1830–1917), Union general and postwar industrialist, was born in Hunter County, New York, to Reuben and Mary Merritt Wilder. As a young man, ca. 1848, he moved to Ohio and worked as an apprentice engineer. In the late 1850s he moved to Indiana, established a foundry, and patented an improved waterwheel in 1859. When the Civil War began, Wilder joined the 17th Indiana Volunteers. He and his regiment served extensively in the western theater and gained the reputation of "Wilder's Lightning Brigade," playing a particularly significant role in the Chattanooga area campaign of 1863. In 1864 Wilder was brevetted a brigadier general.

He first was introduced to Chattanooga on August 21, 1863, when his Union forces bombarded the city. A year later Wilder resigned from the army due to illness, but he remembered the mineral-rich deposits of East Tennessee and returned to Chattanooga in 1866, ready to invest in the redevelopment of the area. The year after his return, Wilder and two associates organized the Roane Iron Works in Roane County. Later, he became involved in a number of other coal and steel companies, as well as the production of a turbine wheel that he invented. At Johnson City, Wilder built a large hotel to accommodate the businessmen he hoped would be coming to buy land from his Carnegie Land Company. Wilder also pushed for the development of the state's railroad system and developed a rail manufacturing company.

Wilder became active politically and was elected mayor of Chattanooga in 1871. He resigned the following spring, however, to focus his attention on various business interests. In 1876 Wilder made an unsuccessful bid for Congress and never sought another political office though he accepted several political appointments. In 1877 Wilder was appointed postmaster of Chattanooga and served until 1882. In 1897 President William McKinley appointed Wilder to the pension office in Knoxville, an appointment that was renewed by presidents Theodore Roosevelt and William H. Taft.

Along with other Civil War veterans, Wilder supported the development of a military park at the Chickamauga and Chattanooga battlefields and contributed to the erection of the Wilder Brigade Monument. He served first as commissioner and then as president of the Chickamauga Memorial Association in 1889.

As an industrialist, Wilder helped establish Chattanooga as an important industrial city in the redeveloping South. His civic leadership won the admiration of many, including a number of Confederate veterans, who elected him an honorary member of the Forrest camp of the United Confederate Veterans.

Wilder died on October 20, 1917, in Jacksonville, Florida, where he had gone to spend the winter. His body was returned to Chattanooga and buried in the Forest Hill cemetery.

Patrice Hobbs Glass, Chattanooga
SUGGESTED READINGS: Samuel Cole Williams, "General John T. Wilder," *Indiana Magazine of History* 31(1935): 169–203; Williams, *General John T. Wilder, Commander of the Lightning Brigade* (1936)
SEE: CHATTANOOGA; CHICKAMAUGA AND CHATTANOOGA, BATTLES OF; CUMBERLAND COUNTY; FENTRESS COUNTY; INDUSTRY; MINING; ROANE COUNTY

WILDER-DAVIDSON COAL MINING COMPLEX. Located in the rugged, isolated area at the juncture of Fentress, Overton, and Putnam counties, the five communities of Wilder, Davidson, Twinton, Crawford, and Highland Junction comprised the Wilder-Davidson Coal Mining complex which flourished from 1903 until the mid-1930s. This was the first major industrialization and the attendant culture of company towns in an area of hardy, independent people used to subsistence farming and logging. Mining in the region reached its apex during the 1920s (with 2,000 people in Wilder alone). A local labor union existed between 1919 and 1924, and labor relations were generally good, with the exception of short strikes in 1919 and 1924. During a period of great economic depression and very low labor union membership, United Mine Workers Local 4467 negotiated a one-year contract in Wilder on July 8, 1931, only to see that contract canceled on July 8, 1932. A strike initiated by the local union on July 9, 1932, spread throughout the Wilder-Davidson complex and gained national attention during a year of violence, killings, and an especially bitter winter. The strike attracted nationally prominent political and labor leaders, as well as religious and social organizations which brought aid to the workers. When, on April 30, 1933, company guards Shorty Green and Doc Thompson killed local union president Barney Graham, it effectively broke the union. Coal mining in the area never quite recovered with the exception of a short period during World War II. Horse Pound, the last active mine in the area, closed on June 1, 1951.

Homer D. Kemp, Tennessee Technological University
SUGGESTED READING: Perry C. Cotham, *Toil, Turmoil & Triumph: A Portrait of the Tennessee Labor Movement* (1996)
SEE: FENTRESS COUNTY; MINING; LABOR

WILDERNESS ROAD served as the principal route from the east coast colonies to the interior lands drained by the Ohio River. The configuration of the

Wilderness Road may be described as a broad loop, open on the north. Its eastern leg begins in Virginia near the Potomac River, stretches down the Shenandoah Valley to Staunton, and then to the Holston River, continuing to Long Island (Kingsport). The southern base of the loop extends west to Cumberland Gap and finally swings northward to the falls of the Ohio at Louisville, Kentucky. Historically, the best known segment of the road ran from the Long Island of the Holston to the Bluegrass area of north-central Kentucky by way of Cumberland Gap.

Prior to commercial and settler traffic, migrating herds of bison and Native Americans traveling between villages and hunting grounds heavily used the route. The bison sought the numerous salt licks that dotted present Kentucky and Virginia, and beat out a well-defined trace. Travelers could follow such traces on roads extending from near Roanoke, Virginia, to central Illinois. Foremost among the Indian routes in the eastern United States was the Warriors Path, which looped southward through the Gap connecting the Ohio Valley with the Shenandoah and Potomac. Branches of the road continued southeast to the Cherokee and Creek settlements. Daniel Boone traversed the road in 1769, returning in 1775 to mark it for land speculator Richard Henderson. Remnants of this early road, variously known as the lower Virginia Road, upper Virginia Road, and Kentucky State Road, are still visible.

The Wilderness Road brought travelers, skilled craftsmen, and "outside" ideas into areas across the Appalachian Mountains. Demand for improvements became a constant complaint as settlers and commercial traffic increased following the American Revolution. The route became the most direct and easiest path from the lower Ohio Valley to Philadelphia until the opening of the Erie Canal and roads across the mid-Atlantic states during the 1830s. Livestock drovers from Kentucky followed the road and its branches into the southeastern states. After 1834, a stage from Bean Station to Lexington, Kentucky, operated three times a week over the Wilderness Road, carrying freight, mail, and passengers. During the Civil War, many defensive positions imprinted the landscape, though General Ulysses Grant dismissed the road as useless for military purposes.

A semblance of order returned after the war, and modern roads began to cover the Wilderness Road by the turn of the twentieth century. Subsequently, an Object Lesson Road, then state and federal highways replaced the Wilderness Road. Efforts to locate the historic road using modern remote sensory techniques and historic accounts by travelers continue. The most ambitious attempt at Cumberland Gap National Historical Park will restore a portion of the Wilderness Road through Cumberland Gap to its 1780–1810 appearance, including vegetation along the route. The restoration project follows the construction of twin tunnels through the mountains, connecting Kentucky, Virginia, and Tennessee.

Rebecca Vial, Great Smoky Mountains National Park

SUGGESTED READINGS: Katherine R. Barnes, "James Robertson's Journey to Nashville: Tracing the Route of Fall 1779," *Tennessee Historical Quarterly* 36(1976): 145–161; Robert L. Kincaid, *The Wilderness Road* (1947, rp. 1955 and 1966); Kincaid, "The Wilderness Road in Tennessee," East Tennessee Historical Society *Publications* 20(1948): 37–48

SEE: BOONE, DANIEL; CLAIBORNE COUNTY; CUMBERLAND GAP; TRAILS, HISTORIC; TRAILS, NATIVE AMERICAN; WARRIORS PATH STATE PARK

WILDFLOWERS. Included in this category are all flowering plants (botanically, Angiosperms) that grow naturally without cultivation. Although most wildflowers are herbaceous (non-woody), flowering vines, shrubs, and trees may also be included. Most Tennessee wildflowers are native; however, many, perhaps a fourth, are alien. Many of the non-native species are of Euroasian origin and are considered weeds.

Considerable diversity occurs among the approximately 3,000 species of wildflowers found in the state. Botanists classify them into two grand groups based on their vegetative and reproductive parts: Monocots and Dicots. Monocots are generally recognized by their parallel-veined leaves and flowers with parts based on the number three. An example is an iris with these floral parts: three sepals, three petals, three stamens, and a pistil with three divisions. Besides the iris family, others of the Monocot group include the grass, orchid, lily, and other families.

Dicots have net-veined leaves and floral parts in fours or fives. Among the large, important Dicot families are the buttercup, rose, legume, heath, mint, honeysuckle, dogwood, bluebell, and the huge aster or composite family (sunflowers, coneflowers, goldenrods, and ragweeds, among others).

Tennessee wildflowers reflect the geography of the state with its variations in soil, climate, topography, and altitude. The flora of West Tennessee is much like that of the Coastal Plain region to the south. Plants of Appalachia include many with ranges that extend northward into eastern Canada. Wildflowers of Middle Tennessee are similar to those of western Kentucky and northern Alabama. Of special interest in Middle Tennessee are the cedar glades, a special ecosystem where thin soils over limestone have produced a unique assemblage of wildflowers; a dozen or so species are of global significance.

In addition to adding color and variety to the landscape from early spring to frost, wildflowers also have scientific and practical value. Botanists study plants to better understand ecological and evolutionary processes. Wildflowers of Tennessee, like plants everywhere, are a resource from which new foods, medicines, and industrial chemicals may be developed.

Conservation biologists are concerned when any plant or animal species is threatened with extinction. Many Tennessee species of wildflowers are on state or federal lists for special protection. The Tennessee coneflower, a cedar glade endemic of the aster family, was the first plant species listed as endangered by the Environmental Protection Agency. Rare species should never be picked or transplanted into wildflower gardens. Plants which have been propagated, rather than collected, can be obtained from reputable nurseries.

Besides wildflower gardening, other people learn the identification and range of wildflowers over the state. Many photograph plants, a practice which is favored over collecting. The Tennessee Native Plant Society at the University of Tennessee, Knoxville, offers opportunities for the public to learn more about Tennessee wildflowers.

Thomas E. Hemmerly, Middle Tennessee State University
SUGGESTED READINGS: Thomas E. Hemmerly, *Wildflowers of the Central South* (1990); R.W. Hutson, W.F. Hutson, and Aaron J. Sharp, *Great Smoky Mountains Wildflowers* (1995); Arlo I. Smith, *A Guide to Wildflowers of the Mid-South* (1979)
SEE: CEDAR GLADES; CEDARS OF LEBANON STATE PARK; ECOLOGICAL SYSTEMS; SHARP, AARON

WILEY MEMORIAL UNITED METHODIST CHURCH. The site of Wiley Memorial United Methodist Church, formerly Wiley Memorial Methodist Episcopal, at 500 Lookout Street has been significant throughout the history of Chattanooga. The site served as the center of community life for Ross's Landing before the name was changed to Chattanooga in 1838. During the 1863 Civil War Battle of Chattanooga, the "pepperbox" church was used as a hospital and prison by the Confederate Army and later as a military prison by the Union Army. The church received such extensive damage that it was sold to the African-American Methodist Episcopalians in 1867 for $1,000, who established the first black congregation in East Tennessee. Their first pastor was Reverend Houston.

Foundation for a brick building was laid in 1886. When arson destroyed the structure in 1887, the reconstruction became a joint effort of all the membership: women cleaned and men laid the brick. In 1901 the congregation purchased a large pipe organ, believed to be one of the first in an African-American church.

In 1978, fearing a potential roof collapse, the City Commission's Building Inspector ordered the building closed. The congregation used other buildings until 1979 when Wiley Memorial was listed on the National Register of Historic Places and city officials issued a certificate of occupancy allowing worship services to resume in the building.

Vilma Scruggs Fields, Chattanooga African-American Museum
SEE: CHATTANOOGA

WILKINSON, MICHAEL KENNERLY (1921–), a solid state physicist at Oak Ridge National Laboratory, was born at Palatka, Florida, in 1921 and attended The Citadel and Massachusetts Institute of Technology, earning his Ph.D. degree in physics in 1950. Wilkinson joined Oak Ridge National Laboratory (ORNL) as a research physicist in 1950, performing pioneering research that used neutron scattering techniques to study the physical properties of materials.

Working with the Oak Ridge Graphite Reactor, Wilkinson and his colleagues—Ernest O. Wollan, Clifford G. Shull, and Wallace C. Koehler—bombarded various types of materials with neutron beams and examined the scattered neutrons to determine atomic structures, magnetic structures, and dynamic properties of solids. His research was particularly important in providing an understanding of unusual magnetic effects that exist in various metals, alloys, and compounds. Wilkinson directed the ORNL Solid State Science Division from 1972 to 1986, developing this division into an outstanding research organization internationally recognized for its scientific capabilities. He was also involved in the development of increasingly sophisticated neutron scattering equipment and was responsible for the design and construction of several instruments in use at the ORNL High Flux Isotope Reactor.

Strongly interested in the advancement of science, Wilkinson was a member a many national scientific committees and served as a visiting and adjunct professor of physics at Georgia Institute of Technology. After his retirement from ORNL in 1991, Wilkinson became a consultant to the laboratory on research in the solid state sciences.

Leland R. Johnson, Clio Research Institute
SUGGESTED READING: Leland Johnson and Daniel Schaffer, *Oak Ridge National Laboratory: The First Fifty Years* (1994)
SEE: OAK RIDGE NATIONAL LABORATORY; SHULL, CLIFFORD G.; WOLLAN, ERNEST O.

WILLIAMS, AVON N., JR. (1921–1994), a powerful advocate for African Americans, became the leading African-American lawyer in Tennessee in the protection and advancement of the rights of blacks in education, the workplace, criminal justice, and voting. Born in 1921 in Knoxville, the fourth of five children of Avon and Carrie Belle Williams, he received his education in the Knoxville public schools and graduated with an A.B. degree from Johnson C. Smith University in 1940. He obtained his law degree from

Boston University in 1947 and a master's degree in law from the same university a year later. After practicing briefly in Knoxville, he entered a partnership with prominent black Nashville attorney, Z. Alexander Looby (1953–1969). In 1956 he married Joan Marie Bontemps, the daughter of poet and writer Arna Bontemps. They were the parents of two children, Avon N., III, and Wendy Janette.

Williams became a cooperating attorney for the NAACP Legal Defense Fund in 1949 and began a long career in civil rights activism. He served as co-counsel in the first Tennessee public school desegregation suit, filed against Anderson County in 1950 (*McSwain v. Board of Anderson County, Tennessee*). Williams assisted in obtaining admission to the University of Tennessee graduate school for four black students (*Gray v. University of Tennessee*, 1951). In 1955 he filed the Nashville school desegregation case (*Kelly v. Board of Education*), ultimately assisting in every school desegregation case statewide, except Shelby County. Williams considered *Geier v. Blanton* (1972), which brought about the merger of the mostly-white University of Tennessee at Nashville into the mostly-black Tennessee State University, his most noteworthy case. This was the first time that a court, in a higher education desegregation suit, had ordered a black college to take over a white one. It was an important symbolic victory for blacks; the former University of Tennessee, Nashville, campus was later named the Avon Williams, Jr., Campus of Tennessee State University in his honor.

Williams's practice usually involved black litigants, including cases involving black teachers deprived of their jobs, a 12-year-old boy charged with the rape of a white society woman, and numerous appeals stemming from the 1968 murder conviction of a black man tried before an all-white jury. Williams opposed the death penalty both in court and in the State Senate, and vigorously challenged the racial bias in criminal proceedings. He questioned the racial make-up of grand juries, the use of voice identification in police line-ups, and the failure to provide indigent defendants the right to free trial transcripts for use on appeal.

In 1962 Williams became active in Democratic politics, helping to create the Davidson County Independent Political Council, and later the Tennessee Voters Council, which he chaired. From 1968 to 1990 he served as a State Senator from Nashville. As Senator, he championed funding for Meharry Medical College and Tennessee State University and funding for grade school guidance counselors. He co-sponsored the law requiring public schools to teach African-American history and a law forbidding discrimination on the basis of race by utility districts in laying water lines. He was the prime mover in the passage of a state civil rights law.

In 1989 Fisk University awarded him an LL.D. degree for his achievements on behalf of African Americans. Avon Williams died on August 29, 1994, and is buried in Greenwood Cemetery in Nashville.

Lewis L. Laska, Tennessee State University

SUGGESTED READING: Don H. Doyle, *Nashville Since the 1920s* (1985)

SEE: CIVIL RIGHTS MOVEMENT; KELLY V. BOARD OF EDUCATION; LOOBY, Z. ALEXANDER; MEHARRY MEDICAL COLLEGE; NAACP; TENNESSEE STATE UNIVERSITY

WILLIAMS, CHARL ORMOND (1885–1969), educator, suffragist, and Democratic party worker, was born in Arlington, Tennessee, the third of Crittenden and Minnie Williams's six children. She graduated from Arlington's "high school on the hill" in 1903 and began teaching at Millington later that year. She served as principal of Bartlett secondary school 1904–1906, then taught at Germantown High School. Within three years, she became Germantown's principal, serving until 1912. She worked two years in the Mathematics Department at West Tennessee State Normal School (now the University of Memphis), before becoming Superintendent of Shelby County Schools, a post she held until 1922. She revolutionized the county school system, increasing its funding, adding new school buildings, and doubling school attendance. During her tenure, Shelby County's schools rose to national prominence.

Williams's rapid rise in political patronage-ridden Shelby County indicates that her family enjoyed good relations with E.H. Crump's political machine. Williams became the first Tennessee woman to serve on the Democratic National Committee. She later served as a delegate to the 1920 national convention and became the first woman in either major party to serve as national vice chairman. Williams worked closely with the Shelby County delegation in the struggle for the ratification of the Nineteenth Amendment. She remained active in Democratic politics and enjoyed a close friendship with Eleanor Roosevelt in later years.

Williams's talent and experience in partisan politics also served her well in her professional career. In 1921 the National Education Association (NEA) elected her to the presidency, making her the youngest, the first rural, and the first southern woman so elected. The success of her tenure as president immediately led to a salaried position with the NEA as National Field Secretary. She served with distinction in that office until she retired, traveling 30–50,000 miles per year, lecturing, serving on a variety of boards and committees, and writing numerous articles and two books on educational reform.

In 1935 Williams was elected president of the National Federation of Business and Professional Women's Clubs, the first educator to hold that post.

The College of William and Mary awarded Williams an honorary Phi Beta Kappa membership, and Southwestern (now Rhodes) College granted her an honorary doctorate. Following her 1950 retirement, Williams took a 10,000 mile tour of the Soviet Union, parts of the Near East, and Greece. Williams died on January 14, 1969, in Washington. Her papers are held in the Manuscript Division of the Library of Congress.

John E. Harkins, Memphis University School

SUGGESTED READING: John E. Harkins, *Metropolis of the American Nile: Memphis & Shelby County* (1982)

SEE: CRUMP, EDWARD H.; EDUCATION, ELEMENTARY AND SECONDARY; MEMPHIS; SHELBY COUNTY; WOMAN SUFFRAGE MOVEMENT

WILLIAMS, HANK (1923–1953). Few entertainers have conveyed the sincerity and realism reflected in Hank Williams's southern working class lyrics and singing style. Even fewer have enjoyed the lanky Alabaman's phenomenal degree of success. His songs permanently etched the nation's consciousness in the brief span of his career; by the age of 29, he was dead. Yet Williams's six years as a singer and songwriter broadened interest in country music and solidified the Nashville financial interests that produced it.

Born on September 17, 1923, at Mount Olive, Alabama, King Hiram "Hank" Williams seemed destined to spend his life battling poverty, ill health, and family instability. His life story achieved mythical proportions in his struggles with a domineering mother, his relationship with an elderly black street singer, and his conflicts with the ambitious wife he divorced not once, but twice.

Williams's climb to prominence made him a hardened veteran of the rough honky tonk circuit by the age of 23. He failed his first audition for the Grand Ole Opry. A proclivity for alcohol and his own undependable behavior frequently sidetracked his career. Yet his talent, particularly as a songwriter, proved difficult to ignore. Under the guidance of publishing giant Fred Rose of Nashville, Williams gradually worked his way to super-stardom. On June 11, 1949, Williams, armed with a major recording contract, several moderate hits, and a two-year round as the headliner of KWKH's "Louisiana Hayride" in Shreveport, finally performed at the famed Ryman Auditorium. He received a thunderous ovation for each of his six encores and was immediately added to the Opry roster. Over the next three years, Williams became the nation's most popular country entertainer and the leading star of the Opry.

Financial and artistic success, however, did not soothe Williams's physical and emotional anguish. An untreated congenital birth defect of the lower spine left him stooped and in constant pain. Drugs and alcohol eased his discomfort, but also accentuated his erratic personality. The Opry consequently fired him in August 1952 for chronic drunkenness, unsatisfactory performances, and conduct detrimental to the show's image. During his attempted comeback, Williams died in the backseat of a chauffeured Cadillac of an apparent heart attack on January 1, 1953. His funeral, in Montgomery, Alabama, attracted a tremendous outpouring of grief from more than 25,000 fans. In death, as in life, Williams brought attention to ordinary people, whose lives rarely resembled the affluence and homogeneity popularly associated with the postwar era.

Michael T. Bertrand, Middle Tennessee State University

SUGGESTED READINGS: Chet Flippo, *Your Cheatin' Heart: A Biography of Hank Williams* (1981); Roger M. Williams, *Sing a Sad Song: The Life of Hank Williams* (1973)

SEE: ACUFF-ROSE; ROSE, K. FRED; GRAND OLE OPRY

WILLIAMS, SAMUEL COLE (1864–1947), jurist and historian, was born in Gibson County, Tennessee, in 1864, and educated in the schools of Humboldt. Encouraged by Judge Horace Lurton—a family friend and later a U.S. Supreme Court justice—he enrolled in the Vanderbilt University law school and graduated in 1884. Soon thereafter, Williams accepted Attorney Sam Kirkpatrick's invitation to become his partner in Jonesborough. Eight years later, after his partner died, Williams moved to Johnson City, the emerging business center of the tri-states. He established an enviable reputation as a lawyer, and his clients included railroads, industrialists, and businessmen. He invested wisely in real estate, banks, and industries. Williams was appointed to a vacancy on the Tennessee State Supreme Court in 1913, and the next year was elected to a full term. He resigned to become dean of the Lamar School of Law of Emory University from 1919 to 1924.

Successful attorney, businessman, jurist, and teacher, the 60-year-old Williams returned to Johnson City, where he kept morning office hours—looking after his business interests and taking a few cases that interested him. In the afternoons and evenings, he worked at home in his comfortable library, writing the history of Tennessee from earliest times to statehood. Since 1893, he had been collecting material on the early settlers and had published ten articles in the *Tennessee Historical Magazine*, Tennessee Bar Association *Proceedings, Journal of American History,* and *Tennessee Law Review.* When he died December 14, 1947, he had written six books on early Tennessee history: *History of the Lost State of Franklin* (1924); *Beginnings of West Tennessee in the Land of the Chickasaws, 1591–1814* (1930); *General John T. Wilder, Commander of the Lightning Brigade* (1936); *Dawn of Tennessee Valley and Tennessee History* (1937); *Tennessee During the Revolutionary War* (1944); and *William Tatham, Watauga* (1947). To this list may be added some 50 articles and monographs.

In 1929 judges of the State Supreme Court, authorized by the state legislature, appointed Williams chairman of a committee to draft an official law code. *The Code of Tennessee 1932* soon became known in legal circles as *The Williams Code*.

During World War II, the "judge" helped editors of the *Tennessee Historical Quarterly* and East Tennessee Historical Society *Publications* meet their schedules. The former published nine of his articles, and the latter featured three. Elected chairman of the Tennessee Historical Commission in 1941, Williams promoted a state program placing markers at or near historical sites throughout Tennessee and encouraged the preservation of local records and private papers for students, professors, and history buffs to use in their studies of local history. One result of Williams's campaign for better county histories was the publication of *Historic Madison* (1946) by Emma Inman Williams and Robert E. Corlew's *A History of Dickson County From Earliest Times to the Present* (1956). The works of these two professional historians serve as models for amateurs and professionals.

The "judge," an enthusiastic researcher, corresponded with librarians, antiquarians, archivists, and historians who shared ideas and information with him. In 1921 and 1929 he went to England to conduct research on William Tatham. Like Henry Adams, he employed clerks to make legible copies of journals, letters, and documents. The judge wrote his books and articles in long hand, and his wife typed them. His daughter, Gertrude Williams Miller, tried to eliminate dangling participles and other errors with little success; her father had his own preferences. Although criticized for his prose and the errors in his books, Williams's contribution to the early history of Tennessee far outweighs these criticisms.

Frank B. Williams, Jr., East Tennessee State University
SUGGESTED READINGS: Pollyana Creekmore, "Bibliography of Historical Writings of Samuel Cole Williams," East Tennessee Historical Society *Publications* 20(1948): 9–15; Frank B. Williams, Jr., "Introduction to the New Edition" of Samuel Cole Williams, *Tennessee During the Revolutionary War* (1974), v–xvi

SEE: EAST TENNESSEE HISTORICAL SOCIETY; JOHNSON CITY; LAW; TENNESSEE HISTORICAL COMMISSION; TENNESSEE HISTORICAL SOCIETY; TENNESSEE SUPREME COURT

WILLIAMSON COUNTY. Centuries before whites settled in what was to become Williamson County the area was home to at least five prehistoric cultures. Over many centuries those occupants of the Harpeth Valley progressed from a nomadic existence to a settled lifestyle in fortified villages along the Big Harpeth and its tributaries. When white scouts and longhunters ventured onto the land, tribes of Cherokees, Chickasaws, Choctaws, Creeks, and Shawnees were sharing its bounty in a migratory fashion.

From the time white settlers made a frail but determined effort to wrest the area from the Indians, it was a foregone conclusion they would have the rich, well watered meadows and forests at all costs. They paid dearly for their desire to settle the region before treaties were signed, and several lost their lives to the tomahawks and arrows of those first Williamson Countians defending their hunting grounds.

By 1798 a few white settlers were permanently established in the area. Ewen Cameron built the first house in Franklin, and members of the Goff, McEwen, and Neely families made their way through the canebrake southward from Fort Nashborough. In 1799 Major Anthony Sharp sold 640 acres of his enormous military grant to Abram Maury who laid out the county seat of Franklin, named for Benjamin Franklin, on 109 acres of this property in 1800. The little village with its huddle of log cabins was half-circled by the Big Harpeth River. Franklin and Williamson County were created by the Tennessee General Assembly on October 26, 1799. Carved from neighboring Davidson, the new county was named for Dr. Hugh Williamson, a Revolutionary patriot and distinguished statesman from North Carolina.

Many of the early settlers came to take up grants awarded to them for their Revolutionary War service. Others bought land from those who chose not to settle here. Soon representatives of every honorable profession were calling the county home. Possibly its fame could be laid in part to its fine schools dotting the countryside. Franklin and Triune were noted for their male and female academies. These private schools flourished until around 1861. Attendance declined during the years of war and Reconstruction, and they were gradually replaced by the public school system.

Prior to 1861 Williamson County was the third wealthiest county in Tennessee. Its riches were derived from its productive soil, timber, and livestock. Almost wholly loyal to the South, Franklin and its surrounding communities suffered extreme hardships during Union army occupation from 1862–1865. Confederate General Nathan B. Forrest led a successful raid against a federal garrison near Brentwood, capturing 785 and valuable stores in March 1863. The Battle of Franklin was a bloody conflict fought on November 30, 1864, between the forces of Confederate General John B. Hood and those of Union General John M. Schofield. During the five hours of desperate fighting the Confederates, who made repeated attacks against strong breastworks, suffered an appalling number of casualties in both officers and men. Confederate Generals John Adams, Patrick Cleburne, States Rights Gist, Hiram Granbury, and Otho French Strahl were killed on the field. A sixth, John C. Carter, died ten days later. In some brigades all officers were killed down to the rank of captain.

Union General David S. Stanley was wounded, but no Union generals were killed.

During the war and Reconstruction, two of Williamson County's most important historical cemeteries were established. The McGavock Confederate Cemetery, near Carnton, contains the bodies of 1,481 Confederates killed at Franklin and is the largest private Confederate cemetery in America. The other notable cemetery in Williamson County is the Toussaint L'Overture County Cemetery, which is listed on the National Register of Historic Places. Although the cemetery was not incorporated until 1884, the first interments occurred much earlier, around 1869, making it the oldest African American institution in continuous use in Williamson County. The extent of destruction associated with the Battle of Franklin, the collapse of slavery, and the political upheaval associated with Reconstruction produced years of uncertainty before recovery began for the citizens of the county.

In years past Williamson County boasted some 44 communities, quite a few of which still retain their identity. However, only four—Franklin, Brentwood, Fairview, and Thompson's Station—have been incorporated as of April 1996.

Countless notable people have called Williamson County home. These include Thomas Hart Benton, Governor John Buchanan, Governor Newton Cannon, John S. Claybrooke, John H. Eaton, Bailey Hardeman, Judge Thomas Maney, John Marshall, Abram Maury, Matthew Fontaine Maury, Hardy Murfree, Randal McGavock, John McGavock, Nicholas Perkins—and many others. Daniel M. Robison (1893–1970), former State Librarian and Archivist and State Historian, was born in the village of Arrington. He initiated the useful biographical directories of state legislators in 1956.

Until recently Williamson was a rural county with very little manufacturing prior to World War II. In the 1930s the Dortch Stove Works operated in Franklin. This was followed by Magic Chef, which made electric and gas ranges on the same site. Jamison Bedding then bought the property and was in business here for many years. After CPS, APCOM, Pellican, and the Essex Group opened their plants in the 1960s, Franklin became the main manufacturing center in the county. Brentwood tends more to residential, office complexes, and service companies. General Smelting and Refining Company is at College Grove, and Four Star, which makes tobacco harvesting equipment, is at Triune.

From 1980–1990 businesses became more diversified. During that time Williamson became one of the fastest growing counties in the state, tracking 39.4 percent in major residential development, retail, office, and manufacturing. By 1996 the county reached 42 percent in those areas and in services, which include The Williamson Medical Center, doctors' office complexes, restaurants, hotels, mortgage companies, law firms, accountants, and financial institutions.

Primus, one of the largest financial companies in Middle Tennessee, is located at Cool Springs in Franklin. The largest employment site is Cool Springs Galleria, with some 3,000 employees. Population in the county has reached approximately 97,000 and continues to grow every month.

Such rapid growth and the construction of new highways, schools, and malls in rural areas, hitherto untouched by progress, have created enormous stress in many places. These developments have resulted in the loss of private homes, historic landmarks, cemeteries, springs, and open spaces. However, in the face of great odds, interested citizens are striving to preserve the best of the past as their communities move toward the future.

SUGGESTED READINGS: James A. Crutchfield, *A Heritage of Grandeur* (1981); Louise Gillespie Lynch, *Our Valiant Men: Soldiers and Patriots of the Revolutionary War Who Lived in Williamson County, Tennessee* (1977)

SEE: ARMY OF TENNESSEE; BATTLE GROUND ACADEMY; BENTON, THOMAS HART; BROWN, LIZINKA C.; BUCHANAN, JOHN P.; CANNON, NEWTON; CARNTON PLANTATION; CARTER HOUSE; CIVIL WAR; FORREST, NATHAN BEDFORD; FRANKLIN, BATTLE OF; CLEBURNE, PATRICK R.; EATON, JOHN H.; FRANKLIN MASONIC LODGE; HARLINSDALE FARM; HOOD, JOHN BELL; MAURY, MATTHEW FONTAINE; MOUND BOTTOM; NATCHEZ TRACE; NATCHEZ TRACE PARKWAY; ST. PAUL'S EPISCOPAL CHURCH; U.S. ARMY OF THE CUMBERLAND

WILLIS, ARCHIE WALTER "A.W.", JR. (1925–1988), civil rights lawyer and businessman, was born in Birmingham, Alabama, on March 16, 1925. Willis received his B.A. from Talladega College in 1950 and a law degree from the University of Wisconsin in 1953. He set a precedent (the first of many) by opening the first integrated law firm in Memphis in the mid-1950s. In 1961, when James Meredith applied for admission to the University of Mississippi, Willis was the attorney of record. He also served as a NAACP lawyer in the early 1960s during the battle to desegregate the Memphis city schools. In 1964 Willis was elected to the Tennessee General Assembly, the first African American elected to that body since the 1880s. Although he ran unsuccessfully for mayor of Memphis in 1967, Willis was instrumental in the election of Harold Ford, Sr., to the U.S. Congress in 1974.

Besides his legal work Willis was also concerned with housing issues. In 1955 he helped found the Mutual Federal Savings and Loan. Shelby County's Homebuyer's Revolving Loan Fund for low and moderate income first-time buyers was an idea he promoted. He also worked to secure funding for the Tennessee Housing Development Agency and served on the Shelby County Housing Task Force.

Willis served on numerous city, state, and national committees and commissions, including Tennessee's first Human Rights Commission in 1965 and the National Civil Rights Museum Commission which was instrumental in bringing that historic site to fruition. The Auction Avenue Bridge in Memphis was renamed the A.W. Willis Bridge in his honor. Willis died in Memphis in 1988.

Kenneth W. Goings, University of Memphis

SUGGESTED READING: David M. Tucker, *Memphis Since Crump: Bossism, Blacks, and Civic Reform, 1948–1968* (1980)

SEE: CIVIL RIGHTS MOVEMENT; FORD, HAROLD; NAACP; NATIONAL CIVIL RIGHTS MUSEUM

WILSON COUNTY was created by the third General Assembly on October 29, 1799. Its prehistoric heritage is rich. The Sellars temple mound on Spring Creek, for example, yielded an outstanding piece of pre-Columbian sculpture that has been the emblem of the Tennessee Archaeological Society. Europeans explored the land long before settlement: French trappers arrived as early as 1760, and the hunting party of Henry Scraggins passed through the area in 1765. John B. Walker led the first permanent settlers to Hickory Ridge, west of the present site of Lebanon, in 1794.

The county was named for Major David Wilson, a North Carolina hero of the American Revolution. Lebanon was named for the impressive stands of red cedar trees (actually Virginia juniper) that are characteristic of the region. In the late 1930s Tennessee and the federal government created the Cedars of Lebanon State Park in recognition of this botanical feature. Lebanon was chosen as the county seat in 1801, largely because of a large spring (still flowing) on what became the public square. The county has had five courthouses, the building of 1848–1881 having been designed by the noted architect William Strickland. Other towns and villages include Watertown, Green Hill, Mt. Juliet, Statesville, Gladesville, Baird's Mill, Norene, Cherry Valley, Shop Springs, Tucker's Cross Roads, Leeville, Martha, Bellwood, Commerce, Taylorsville, Centreville, Oakland, LaGuardo, and Maple Hill.

Although there were textile and flour mills, and even a paper mill by the 1830s, the county remained predominantly agricultural. By 1875 most Wilson County farmers owned farms smaller than 100 acres, but their county ranked first in the state in the production of wheat, sorghum, butter, and horses; second in cedar, lumber for export, grass seed, hay, barley, clover, hogs, sheep, and mules. When rail transportation came to the county in 1869, it increased the dollar value of exported forest prod-

ucts ten times. William Haskell Neal developed Neal's Paymaster corn in Wilson County, button clover was discovered here, and Major M.B. Kittrell's Tom Hal was a foundation sire of the Tennessee Walking Horse.

By 1908 industrial development reached Wilson County with the production of woolen blankets, cedar slats for pencils, denim clothing, and eventually shirts and men's socks. In 1996 Hartmann Luggage Company, TRW (Commercial Steering Division), Texas Boot, Wynn's Precision Rubber (O rings), Toshiba America, Georgia Pacific, and Bradley Candy account for the county's industrial growth. Cracker Barrel Restaurants and K.O. Lester (Pocahontas) food distributors originated in Wilson County, where they maintain their corporate headquarters. Cracker Barrel represents a unique Tennessee contribution to the national tradition of roadside architecture and roadside food service. Health care (University Medical Center) provides another major economic interest.

The county emerged as a center of education in 1842, when the Cumberland Presbyterian Church established Cumberland University. The institution in 1997 enrolled 1,100 students and included a school of nursing and a graduate school. Friendship Christian School is an expanding secondary school. In the early twentieth century, Lebanon became known as the "Little Athens of the South" because of the location of Cumberland University, Castle Heights Military Academy, and Lebanon College for Young Ladies. From 1873 to 1939 the city was particularly well known for the one-year law course offered by Cumberland University, which attracted students of law from every state and many foreign countries.

Major historical events in the county have included the start of Sam Houston's political career and his disastrous courtship, which began at a ball at a house west of Lebanon; the "stump speaking" gubernatorial debates between James C. "Lean Jimmy" Jones and James K. Polk; and a Civil War cavalry engagement between General John Hunt Morgan's Confederates and Union troops. Mussolini sent a contingent of Fascist cadets to Castle Heights in 1931. The Second Army Maneuvers director headquarters were located in Wilson County, from which 800,000 troops were supervised during the Tennessee Maneuvers (1942–1944) in preparation for service in the European Theater of World War II. Finally, the trial of Charles Sullins and Harry Kirkendoll for the shooting of Ed Collier was the first in the state to be televised (1953).

Noteworthy citizens of Wilson County who left their mark on state and nation include Governors Houston, Jones, William B. Campbell (the Mexican War hero for whom Fort Campbell was named), Robert L. Caruthers (judge, legal educator,

Congressman, Confederate governor-elect), and Frank Clement. Layula, a Lumbee, wife of Lebanon's first settler, Ned Jacobs, walked the Trail of Tears after her husband died. Alexander P. Stewart and Robert Hatton were Confederate generals. W.E.B. Du Bois, African-American leader and writer, began his teaching career in rural Wilson County. Maggie Porter Cole and Thomas Rutling were original Fisk Jubilee singers. George Wharton Winston, captain, 366th Infantry in the U.S. Army, 1918, was one of the first African-American officers in the U.S. Army. Dixon Lanier Merritt, author of "The Pelican" limerick, was a noted journalist.

Frank Burns, Garland, Texas

SUGGESTED READING: G. Frank Burns, *Wilson County* (1983)

SEE: BUCHANAN, ANDREW H.; CAMPBELL, WILLIAM B.; CEDARS OF LEBANON STATE PARK; CUMBERLAND UNIVERSITY; CUMBERLAND UNIVERSITY LAW SCHOOL; DU BOIS, W.E.B.; GREEN, NATHAN; JONES, JAMES C.; SECOND ARMY MANEUVERS; STEWART, ALEXANDER P.; STRICKLAND, WILLIAM.

WILSON SPORTING GOODS, known originally as the Ashland Manufacturing Company, was created in 1913 in Chicago as a subsidiary of Swarzchild and Sulzberger meat packing concern. The company moved into the sporting goods trade by manufacturing gut strings for tennis rackets as a means of utilizing animal by-products. The company suffered financial reversals in 1914 and, in a move calculated to capitalize upon the popularity of U.S. President Thomas Woodrow Wilson, reorganized as Wilson Sporting Goods Company under the leadership of businessman Thomas E. Wilson. The company prospered and expanded its inventory to include baseball equipment, camping gear, golf clubs, and tennis rackets.

By the end of World War I, the company had established a sales office in San Francisco and built new factories as sports became big business in the 1920s. By the early 1940s Wilson included sportswear in its product line, purchasing the O'Shea Knitting Mills in 1942. The company established subsidiary clothing mills in Tullahoma, Tennessee, and Ironton, Ohio. When those plants proved too small to handle the demand, Wilson opened a new factory in Cookeville, Tennessee, to produce professional sports team uniforms.

Located across the street from the Tennessee Central Railroad, the Cookeville plants made uniforms for professional teams in every major professional sport except boxing from 1946 to 1989. Every uniform worn by professional athletes in baseball, tennis, football, basketball, golf, and soccer came from the Cookeville plant. Each professional uniform was custom tailored to the specifications of the individual athletes, several of whom visited the facility to be fitted, including Sandy Koufax and Pete Rose. The Wilson Company hired former professional athletes as consultants to advise the company on ways to provide a better fitting uniform. The Cookeville plant also branched out into the production of college, high school, and community sports uniforms.

In 1970 PepsiCo bought Wilson and in 1989 sold the plant to AmerGroup Ltd. With the 1989 sale, the Cookeville operation declined. The 1940s building, laden with asbestos, was seen as a financial liability, and the plant moved a portion of its operations to nearby Sparta, Tennessee. Other parts of the Cookeville operation were transferred to Mexico and Indonesia. By 1989 Wilson no longer held a monopoly on the production of professional sportswear and was forced to compete with other sporting goods companies for lucrative professional contracts.

Michael E. Birdwell, Tennessee Technological University

SEE: BASEBALL, MINOR LEAGUE; INDUSTRY; PUTNAM COUNTY; WORTH, INC.

WILSON, KEMMONS AND HOLIDAY INNS. In 1951 Kemmons Wilson, his wife, and five children drove from Memphis to Washington, D.C., for a vacation. Appalled by the uncomfortable and cramped rooms with no air conditioning and the lack of restaurants and swimming pools, Wilson returned determined to build a better motel. A year later, he opened the first "Holiday Inn" in Memphis. It featured 120 air conditioned rooms and had a restaurant and swimming pool for the guests. Children under 12 years of age stayed free in their parents' room. The rooms were spacious, carpeted, offered television, a telephone, and had sturdy all-steel furniture. A distinctive bright green and orange "Great Sign" invited travelers to a night's rest; it quickly became one of the most recognized advertising signs in the twentieth century.

In 1953 Wilson formed a partnership with Memphis builder Wallace E. Johnson and invited other investors to join them to build a chain of motels. A year later, Wilson and Johnson formed Holiday Inns of America and began franchising motels. The predictable comfort of the rooms made it a first choice for travelers, and in 1967 the company began trading its stock publicly.

Wilson promoted standardization and quality control. To ensure operational uniformity he opened the Holiday Inn Innkeeping School and employed inspectors to grade each motel. Franchisees with low or failing scores had to bring their motels up to system standards or lose their business.

Wilson quickly recognized the potential for computers in the motel business. In 1965 he contracted with IBM to develop and install a "Holidex" reservation system that allowed guests or travel agents to check the availability of rooms anywhere in the system and place reservations. By 1968 there were 1,000 Holiday Inns in the United States, and the international market was growing. "The Nation's Inn Keeper" became "The World's Inn Keeper." In 1972 Holiday Inns became the first food and lodging chain to pass the billion dollar mark in revenues. In the same decade the company acquired Harrah's casino/hotel firm, making it the nation's largest gaming company. Wilson retired from the company in 1979.

Anne Leonard, Memphis Museum System

SUGGESTED READING: Eugene J. Johnson and Robert D. Russell, Jr., "Royal Oaks Motel," *Memphis: An Architectural Guide* (1990): 289–290

SEE: MEMPHIS

WINCHESTER, JAMES (1752–1826), pioneer, entrepreneur, military commander, and founder of Memphis, was born in Westminster, Maryland, and served in Maryland regiments during the American Revolution. He was wounded and captured in a raid on Staten Island in mid-1777 and imprisoned until December 22, 1780. After his release, he joined the Maryland Line and fought in General Nathaniel Greene's command until 1783, when he was discharged with the rank of captain.

Winchester came to Davidson County, North Carolina, in 1785 and settled on Bledsoe's Creek, where he built a mill, distillery, and cotton gin. When Sumner County was created by partition from Davidson in 1787, Winchester became captain of the horse, and was soon elevated to lieutenant colonel commandant of the county. In 1789 he became the first county trustee.

During the Southwest Territory era, James Winchester continued as county militia commander. Appointed to the legislative council of the territory in 1794, he was named acting commander of the Mero District Militia the following year.

When the state of Tennessee was organized in 1796, Winchester was elected Speaker of the Senate and brigadier general, commandant, of the Mero District. From 1797 to 1800, he surveyed Indian boundary lines, took the census for Mero District, and attended the meetings of the county court more often than most of his fellow magistrates. In 1800 he subdivided and platted the town of Cairo on the Cumberland and acquired an interest in a 5,000-acre tract on the Mississippi River that he and John Overton developed as the site of Memphis in 1820. Promoter of a school at Cairo, he was also a trustee of Davidson Academy, Nashville, and Sumner and Transmontania Academies, Gallatin. His various business ventures included the Sumner Cotton Factory, a riverfront warehouse, and a variety of shops, all at Cairo. He built flatboats and barges for river transportation, and in 1806 he constructed two oceango-

ing schooners near his mill on Bledsoe's Creek. After a safe passage by way of New Orleans to Philadelphia, he sold them at the latter place.

When the War of 1812 began, Winchester won appointment as brigadier general in the regular U.S. army. Assigned to the recruiting service, he yearned for a field assignment, an ambition that led to an ongoing controversy with General William Henry Harrison, and ultimately to Winchester's capture and the defeat of his army at the River Raisin on January 22, 1813. During April 1814 Winchester joined General Andrew Jackson on the Gulf Coast and took command at Mobile until the end of the war. Playing secondary roles to two military chieftains who would be future Presidents of the United States ended General Winchester's military career. He published a vindication of his acts in the northwest that charged Harrison with failing to honor his promise to rendezvous his troops with Winchester's on the fateful day of battle at the River Raisin.

After 1815 Winchester organized a steamboat company, bought and sold land, surveyed the boundary line between Tennessee and the Chickasaw Nation, and planned the city of Memphis. He died at Cragfont on July 27, 1826.

Walter T. Durham, Gallatin

SUGGESTED READINGS: Walter T. Durham, *James Winchester: Tennessee Pioneer* (1979)

SEE: CRAGFONT; JACKSON, ANDREW; MEMPHIS; MERO DISTRICT; OVERTON, JOHN; SOUTHWEST TERRITORY; SUMNER COUNTY; WAR OF 1812; WINCHESTER, MARCUS

WINCHESTER, MARCUS BRUTUS (1796–1856), land developer and first mayor of Memphis, was born on May 28, 1796, at Cragfont, the eldest son of James Winchester and Susan Black. Winchester was educated in Baltimore, but left school at age 16 to serve at his father's side in the War of 1812. He was captured with his father and others at the Battle of River Raisin and sent to prison in Quebec.

In October 1818 Winchester accompanied Andrew Jackson and Isaac Shelby to the signing of the Chickasaw Cession (Jackson Purchase) and traveled on to the Chickasaw Bluff to report on the land investment owned by his father, Jackson, and John Overton. Winchester and surveyor William Lawrence drew up a plan for a town which his father named Memphis.

Marcus Winchester made his home in Memphis, where he served as agent for the proprietors and opened the first store. He was one of the first five members of the Quarterly Court and was elected Register in 1820. When Memphis was incorporated in 1826, Winchester became the first mayor. He operated a ferry and served as postmaster until 1849 although his loyalty to the Jacksonians came under question when he supported David Crockett for Congress.

About 1823 Winchester married Amarante Loiselle (called Mary) of New Orleans, and most historians agree that she was a woman of color. They had six daughters and two sons. Possibly because of his marriage and the hardening of racial lines, Winchester's career declined. He moved with his family to his farm three miles outside Memphis and was involved in a variety of lawsuits and financial difficulties.

After his wife's death in 1840, Winchester married a 19-year-old widow, Lucy Lenore Ferguson McLean, in 1842. He served as a delegate to a railroad convention in St. Louis in 1849, and was elected to the state legislature in 1851. Winchester died on November 2, 1856.

Perre Magness, Memphis

SUGGESTED READING: Michelle Jarzombek, "Memphis-South Memphis Conflict, 1826–1850," *Tennessee Historical Quarterly* 41(1982): 23–36

SEE: JACKSON PURCHASE; MEMPHIS; WAR OF 1812; WINCHESTER, JAMES

WINEMAKING IN TENNESSEE. European settlers brought grape growing and winemaking to Tennessee in the mid-1800s. After the Civil War, the production of wine became a thriving business. J.A. Killebrew devoted an entire chapter to grape growing in his 1874 book, *Introduction to the Resources of Tennessee,* in which he also reported the 1870 Giles County wine production at 569 gallons. In 1880, according to the U.S. Department of Agriculture, there were 1,128 Tennessee acres planted in grapes, producing 64,767 gallons of wine with a value of $90,000. Tennessee's thriving turn-of-the-century wine industry ended with the addition of the Eighteenth Amendment to the U.S. Constitution in 1919.

Viticulture did not resume in earnest until the 1970s, although grapes were once again grown in Tennessee shortly after World War II. Several grape varieties were planted near Crossville in 1948 and 1953. Additional plantings occurred in 1959 and 1963. By the late 1970s grape research was being conducted at the West Tennessee Experiment Station at Jackson, the Middle Tennessee Experiment Station at Spring Hill, the Plateau Experiment Station at Crossville, and the Plant and Soil Science Field Laboratory at Knoxville. Grape production research began at the Tennessee Valley Authority Agricultural Research Farm at Muscle Shoals, Alabama, in 1974.

The first modern attempts to establish vineyards for the commercial production of grapes took place in the mid-1970s. In 1978 there were 125 acres of grapes in Tennessee. The state's first crush (or harvest) of grapes for the purpose of winemaking occurred in 1980, when the first Tennessee wineries were licensed. By 1992 there were 84 growers in the state, with over 270 acres devoted to grape production.

In 1973 the Tennessee Viticultural and Oenological Society (TVOS) was organized for the purpose of encouraging the growing of wine grapes and the development of the wine industry. TVOS was instrumental in the passage of the 1977 "Grape and Wine Law," which effectively removed wineries from the 1939 local option legislation and reduced the cost of a licensing to $50. A state tax of five cents per gallon was levied on wine produced in Tennessee from Tennessee products. No winery could sell at retail more than 5,000 gallons, or 20 percent of the wine it produced annually, whichever was greater.

In 1983 new legislation increased the amount of wine available to be sold on the premises to 15,000 gallons and stipulated that wine produced in Tennessee must be made from not less than 85 percent Tennessee-produced crops. A 1988 law reduced the amount of Tennessee products to 75 percent and permitted new wineries to use 50 percent Tennessee products for the first three years of operation. In 1985 the amount of wine that could be sold at a winery increased to 20,000 gallons annually; in 1995, the amount was raised to 40,000 gallons.

After 1985 Tennessee-produced wine was taxed at the same rate as wine produced out of state. This followed a 1984 U.S. Supreme Court ruling that struck down a Hawaiian law which imposed a 20 percent tax on wholesale liquor sales, but exempted a locally produced brandy and fruit wine. The Court ruled that this violated the Commerce Clause of the U.S. Constitution.

A Viticulture Advisory Board was created in 1985. The Board coordinates the interests of growers and advises producers. Both the TVOS and the Tennessee Farm Winegrowers Association, an organization of grape growers that was formed in 1982, are represented on the nine-member Board. Other members represent the University of Tennessee Institute of Agriculture, the Tennessee Department of Agriculture, and the Tennessee Department of Tourist Development. Two members represent the grape growers, and two members represent the grape processors. The Board is scheduled to terminate in 1999.

Today, wineries stretch across the state, from Cordova in the west to Blountville in the east. In 1996 there were 15 licensed wineries operating in Tennessee. While some are no more than expensive hobbies for their owners, others provide the primary source of income for their operators. The first licensed winery in Tennessee, Highland Manor Winery, opened near Jamestown in 1980. That winery has been in continuous operation ever since, although under different ownership.

H. Bruce Throckmorton, Tennessee Technological University

SEE: AGRICULTURE; FENTRESS COUNTY

WINFREY, OPRAH (1954–), one of the nation's most popular female entertainers, was born in Koscinsko,

Mississippi, on January 29, 1954, to Vernita Lee and Vernon Winfrey. The racially segregated town offered few opportunities for African Americans, and the Winfreys migrated north leaving young Oprah with her grandmother. At age six, Oprah joined her mother in Milwaukee, Wisconsin. Meanwhile, Vernon Winfrey was discharged from the U.S. Army and settled in Nashville, where he worked as a janitor and dishwasher until 1967, when he started a barbershop and grocery store. At age 13, Oprah, a troubled teenager, came to live with her father and his wife Velma. She graduated from East High School and entered Tennessee State University.

Active in speech and drama clubs and Miss Black America pageants, Winfrey also worked for WVOL Radio and as a reporter for Channel 5 Television. She left TSU in 1975 with one remaining requirement (a senior project), which she completed ten years later.

Winfrey worked in television markets in Baltimore, Maryland, and Boston, Massachusetts, before taking a position as the host of *A. M. Chicago*. Despite the notoriously conservative and polarized race relations in Chicago, Winfrey transformed *A.M. Chicago* into the city's most popular show. In 1986 the show was renamed *The Oprah Winfrey Show* and syndicated, soon becoming America's number-one rated talk show. In 1985 Winfrey played a leading role in the movie *The Color Purple*, and three years later launched the Harpo, Inc. production facility.

Among numerous awards and honors, Winfrey won the NAACP Image Award (1990), and the prestigious Hope Award (1990) for her generosity in time and money to feed an African village, fund scholarships, promote programs and shelters for victims of domestic violence, and her personal achievement of success in the face of adversity.

Bobby L. Lovett, Tennessee State University

SUGGESTED READINGS: Norman King, *Everybody Loves Oprah* (1987); Robert Waldron, *Oprah!* (1987)

SEE: TENNESSEE STATE UNIVERSITY

WLAC, a Nashville radio station established by the Life and Casualty Insurance Company in 1926, has shaped musical tastes in Nashville for over 70 years. Its most significant contribution to Tennessee cultural history came from the mid-1940s to the early 1970s when nighttime programming on its AM station shifted to blues and rhythm-n-blues music. Like Memphis's WDIA, WLAC in Nashville introduced whites to the sound and beat of black popular music. WLAC's powerful signal of 50,000 watts carried the programming throughout most of the eastern United States, but its greatest influence was in the South.

Gene Nobles began the tradition in the mid-1940s as he played songs requested by students attending Nashville's Fisk University and Tennessee State Agricultural & Industrial College (now Tennessee

State University). In 1947 Randy Wood of Gallatin, who wanted to add records to his local appliance store business, agreed to sponsor the program by advertising a mail-order record business. Both Nobles and Wood met with immediate success. Nobles's program had a diverse play list, including records by Eddy Arnold, Nat King Cole, and Ella Mae Morse. Wood sold these and those by other blues artists through his Randy's Record Mart, which soon became the nation's largest mail-order record business. In 1950 he established Dot Records, which recorded such artists as Pat Boone, Johnny Maddox, and Gail Storm. Randy's Record Mart remained in business until 1991.

The late night star of WLAC was John Richbourg, who hosted a two-hour show in the early morning hours. Later recognized as the "granddaddy of soul," Richbourg pushed both blues and rhythm-n-blues music and the artists who performed it, giving many their initial major radio exposure. In the 1980s Bill "Hoss" Allen maintained a part of the station's earlier tradition through his late night black gospel music program.

Carroll Van West, Middle Tennessee State University

SUGGESTED READING: Jessica Foy, "WLAC," C. R. Wilson and W. Ferris, eds., *Encyclopedia of Southern Culture* (1989), 978–79

SEE: LIFE AND CASUALTY INSURANCE COMPANY; MUSIC

WNOX: See ACUFF, ROY; CAMPBELL, ARCHIE; MUSIC

WOLLAN, ERNEST OMAR (1902–1984), pioneer physicist in neutron diffraction, was born at Glenwood, Minnesota, in 1902. Wollan attended Concordia College and the University of Chicago, where he earned his Ph.D. in 1929 under Arthur Compton in studies of x-ray scattering. Early in his career, Wollan taught physics at North Dakota State College and Washington University, and he conducted important research into cosmic rays in the United States, Europe, and South America. In 1942 he returned to Chicago as part of the Manhattan Project research team to establish radiation monitoring procedures for the safety of personnel; he invented the radiation badge that later became universally adopted. Wollan was present at the start-up of the first nuclear reactor at Stagg Field and recorded gamma-ray intensities associated with this dramatic event.

In 1944 Wollan joined the Oak Ridge National Laboratory (ORNL), where he became interested in using neutron beams from the Oak Ridge Graphite Reactor for neutron scattering research. He bombarded material with neutrons from this reactor and studied the scattered neutrons with a modified x-ray diffractometer. He and Clifford G. Shull performed pioneering research that established neutron diffraction techniques as an outstanding method for measuring nuclear properties and for determining atomic and magnetic structures of materials.

Wollan was Associate Director of the ORNL physics division from 1948 to 1964, and he retired in 1967. He served as consultant to ORNL until 1977, when he returned to Minnesota where he died in 1984.
Leland R. Johnson, Clio Research Institute
SUGGESTED READING: Leland Johnson and Daniel Schaffer, *Oak Ridge National Laboratory: The First Fifty Years* (1994)
SEE: OAK RIDGE NATIONAL LABORATORY; SHULL, CLIFFORD

WOMAN SUFFRAGE MOVEMENT. "The right of citizens of the United States to vote shall not be denied or abridged by the United States or any State on account of sex," Nineteenth Amendment, U.S. Constitution. In August 1920 the Tennessee General Assembly ratified the Nineteenth Amendment and handed the ballot to millions of American women. The amendment's jubilant supporters dubbed the state "the perfect 36" because it was the thirty-sixth state of the 48 states to approve the amendment, rounding out the three-fourths majority required to amend the Constitution. The legislature's historic vote inaugurated a new era for women and for politics and secured Tennessee's place in the annals of American women's history.

Tennessee became the final battleground in a struggle that began in Seneca Falls, New York, in 1848. The demand for the vote was the most controversial of the 12 resolutions adopted at the first women's rights convention in the United States and the only one that did not win unanimous approval. Suffrage seemed like such an outlandish idea at the time that it made feminists easy targets for ridicule. Still, women like Elizabeth Cady Stanton and Susan B. Anthony persisted and made the vote the focal point of the crusade for women's rights.

Suffragists (as the advocates of votes for women were called) faced stiff opposition, especially in the South. Long after the Civil War, many southerners continued to remember that feminism had emerged as an offshoot of abolitionism. More important, the call for women's rights challenged a precept deeply rooted in religion, law, and custom: the belief that women should be subordinate to men.

But in the South as in the North, some women resented their inferior status and joined the quest for suffrage. Elizabeth Avery Meriwether of Memphis was among the first. In the early 1870s she wrote letters to newspapers and briefly published her own journal to promote women's rights and prohibition. Meriwether attempted to cast a ballot in the 1876 presidential election, then rented a theater to explain why she believed women should have the right to vote.

After Elizabeth Meriwether left Tennessee in 1883, her sister-in-law, Lide Meriwether, took up the cause.

Lide Meriwether served as president of the state Woman's Christian Temperance Union (WCTU), and for the next 17 years she led the fight against liquor and for women's rights, both hotly contested issues. Yet the WCTU remained in the thick of the fray. Union members lobbied the state legislature, circulated petitions, and held prayer meetings at polling places where prohibition referenda were on the ballot. The temperance crusade convinced many women that they had a place in politics, and under Meriwether's leadership the WCTU endorsed woman suffrage.

Lide Meriwether founded Tennessee's first woman suffrage organization in Memphis in 1889. The second appeared in Maryville in 1893; the third, in Nashville a year later. By 1897, the year of the Centennial Celebration in Nashville, ten towns had suffrage societies. Suffragists met at the Exposition's Woman's Building in May, heard speeches by suffrage leaders from Kentucky and Alabama, and formed a state association with Lide Meriwether as president.

The state organization held its second meeting in Memphis in 1900, and Lide Meriwether announced her resignation. Meriwether had been the driving force for suffrage since the mid-1880s; her retirement was a severe blow to the struggling movement. The cause received another blow when the WCTU, under new leadership, renounced its earlier endorsement of votes for women. Prohibition gained public support, but woman suffrage remained unpopular. The temperance union sacrificed women's rights for the sake of its larger goal. After 1900 suffrage activity ceased for several years.

The movement revived in 1906, when southern suffragists met in Memphis to form a regional association. During the conference, Memphis women organized their own suffrage league, the only one in the state for the next four years. In 1910 Lizzie Crozier French who, like Lide Meriwether, had campaigned for suffrage and temperance since the 1880s, founded a suffrage society in Knoxville. The following year, women in Nashville, Chattanooga, and Morristown established local organizations. Over the next several years, suffrage clubs appeared in towns throughout the state.

In 1913 Sara Barnwell Elliott, president of the Tennessee Equal Suffrage Association, invited the National American Woman Suffrage Association (NAWSA) to hold its next convention in Tennessee. NAWSA officers accepted the invitation and asked the state organization to decide which city would host the convention. A poll of local leagues produced a tie between Chattanooga and Nashville. At an acrimonious meeting the state executive committee selected Nashville, but the dispute led to a rift in the association. The state convention in Knoxville during October 1914 split into two factions. Meeting on opposite ends of the same hall, one group elected

Lizzie Crozier French president while the other chose Eleanore McCormack of Memphis. Each claimed to be the original organization, and each side blamed the other for the rupture. French's group obtained a charter as the Tennessee Equal Suffrage Association, Incorporated (TESA, Inc.). McCormack's faction also called itself the Tennessee Equal Suffrage Association (TESA) but did not incorporate.

Both association affiliated with NAWSA, but the TESA, Inc. welcomed the national convention to Nashville in November 1914. The meeting brought some of the most famous women in the nation to Tennessee, including reformer Jane Addams, founder of Hull House in Chicago, and NAWSA president Anna Howard Shaw, a physician and ordained minister. In addition to business meetings, suffragists also hosted such social events as a barbecue at The Hermitage that featured a race between an automobile with a female driver and an airplane with a female pilot. The convention attracted favorable publicity and increased support for suffrage in Tennessee.

The two state suffrage organizations offered separate proposals to enfranchise women. TESA, Inc., lobbied for an amendment to the state constitution. In May 1915 the General Assembly adopted a joint resolution favoring the proposal, the first step in the amendment process. The resolution would have to pass again in 1917 and then be approved by a majority of voters before it could become law. Because the procedure for amending the constitution was so cumbersome, TESA joined with other groups, including the Manufacturers' Association, in calling for a convention to draft a new constitution that would, suffragists hoped, allow women to vote. The disagreement over strategy and TESA's alliance with the Manufacturers' Association, which opposed many reforms suffragists favored, widened the rift between the two state organizations.

A third statewide suffrage organization appeared in Tennessee in 1916 when Knoxville women formed a branch of the Congressional Union (later renamed the National Woman's Party). The Union represented the militant wing of the suffrage movement and never gained a large following. State chair Sue Shelton White, however, attracted national attention in 1919 when she and other radical suffragists were arrested for burning President Woodrow Wilson in effigy during a demonstration in Washington, D.C.

Opponents of suffrage—antisuffragists or antis— also organized in 1916, forming a branch of the National Association Opposed to Woman Suffrage. Virginia Vertrees of Nashville became the group's first president. When ill health forced her to resign, Josephine Anderson Pearson of Monteagle replaced her. Smaller than the suffrage organizations, the association nevertheless became a potent force because it received support from some of the most powerful political lobbies in Tennessee, including distillers, textile manufacturers, and railroad companies. Virginia Vertrees's husband John, a Nashville attorney who represented a major distillery, directed the association from behind the scenes.

Suffragists and antis faced off in 1917 when the General Assembly considered a proposal to grant women the right to vote in local elections and for president. Suffragists lobbied hard for the bill; antis worked equally diligently against it. Suffragists won a major battle but lost the war; the House passed the measure and the Senate defeated it. Suffragists then resorted to another tactic. Before the session adjourned, both TESA and TESA, Inc., renewed the call for a constitutional convention. Antis mobilized a counterattack. Convinced that a majority of men opposed votes for women, John Vertrees and others maneuvered for a referendum on woman suffrage. They hoped that a decisive defeat at the polls would put the issue to rest. The legislature refused to approve the referendum, but lawmakers scheduled an election on a constitutional convention for July. On July 28, 1917, voters overwhelmingly rejected the proposal.

A few months earlier, in April 1917, the United States had entered World War I. Suffragists threw themselves into the war effort. They sold war bonds, organized Red Cross chapters, planted "Victory Gardens," and raised money to support European orphans and provide luxuries to American soldiers overseas. The war gave suffragists the opportunity to demonstrate their patriotism and to counter the argument that women should not be allowed to vote because they could not contribute to national defense.

In 1918 TESA and TESA, Inc., reunited, and the following year they once again lobbied the General Assembly for the right to vote in municipal and presidential elections. This time they succeeded; both houses passed the bill in April. John Vertrees immediately filed a lawsuit challenging its constitutionality, but the Tennessee Supreme Court upheld the law. Tennessee suffragists had won their first major victory.

Two months after Tennessee granted women partial suffrage, Congress passed the Nineteenth Amendment. By the spring of 1920, 35 states had ratified it. If one more state approved it, women might be enfranchised in time to vote in the fall elections. When the Delaware legislature unexpectedly defeated the amendment in early June, suffragists pinned their hopes on Tennessee. They knew that they faced a difficult struggle. Although suffrage had gained popular support, strong opposition remained. Before debate on the amendment could begin, suffragists had to persuade the governor to call a special session of the legislature. Governor Albert H. Roberts had spoken against woman suffrage during his campaign two years earlier. He belonged to the antiprohibition wing of the Democratic party, and his closest advisers opposed votes for women. He feared that women would vote against him because of his opposition to women's rights and prohibition and because of persistent rumors about his relationship with his highly paid female personal secretary. Roberts faced a tough race for reelection in1920, and he knew that woman suffrage might bring about his downfall.

Suffragists and their allies mobilized. Sue Shelton White wrote the governor a letter on behalf of the National Woman's Party, and TESA sent a delegation of prominent women to meet with him. Both organizations enlisted prosuffrage politicians and officeholders, including President Woodrow Wilson. Finally, the governor capitulated. On June 25, 1920, he announced that he would convene the General Assembly in August. The governor's announcement set off one of the most heated political battles in Tennessee history. Suffragists and antisuffragists alike converged on Nashville; each side was determined to win the final battle.

Anne Dallas Dudley, Catherine Talty Kenny, and Abby Crawford Milton led the fight for the amendment. All three were leaders in TESA and in the newly formed League of Women Voters, and all were veterans of several legislative campaigns. They were skilled politicians, well versed in the realities of Tennessee politics. They received extensive support from the national suffrage organization. NAWSA President Carrie Chapman Catt coordinated the early stages of the campaign from New York. In mid-July she came to Nashville and remained until the fight was over. The National Woman's Party sent Sue Shelton White and South Carolinian Anita Pollitzer to lobby for the amendment.

The antis criticized the suffragists for inviting outsiders into Tennessee, but they called in their own reinforcements, including the wife of a former Louisiana governor and the presidents of the Southern Women's League for the Rejection of the Susan B. Anthony Amendment and the National Association Opposed to Woman Suffrage. They also received assistance from three prominent southern women— Laura Clay of Kentucky and Jean and Kate Gordon of Louisiana—who favored votes for women but opposed the federal amendment because of their commitment to states' rights. Antisuffragists established their headquarters in the Hermitage Hotel and launched a massive publicity campaign.

Both sides recruited male allies—including newspaper editors, businessmen, and politicians—and courted legislators. Suffragists repeatedly accused antis of using underhanded tactics. Early in the summer, TESA polled members of the General Assembly and identified lawmakers who promised to vote for the amendment but who might be suscep-

tible to bribes. By August, every single legislator listed as susceptible had defected to the antis.

The special session convened on August 9. The Senate was solidly prosuffrage and ratified the amendment four days later. The House delayed. Speaker of the House Seth Walker, who had originally supported the amendment, changed his mind on the eve of the session's opening, and used his power to postpone the vote. The House debated the amendment on August 17 and scheduled the vote for the following day. The galleries were packed when Walker called the session to order on August 18. In the tense atmosphere, both sides knew the vote was too close to call. A motion to table the ratification resolution ended in a tie which represented a victory for suffragists, although the real test lay ahead.

The roll call began. Two votes for were followed by four votes against. The seventh name on the list was Harry Burn, a Republican from McMinn County. Suffrage polls listed him as undecided. He had voted with the antis on the motion to table, and suffragists knew that political leaders in his home district opposed woman suffrage. They did not know, however, that in his pocket he carried a letter from his widowed mother urging him to vote for ratification. When his name was called, Harry Burn voted yes.

Suffragists also received unexpected support from Banks Turner, an antisuffrage Democrat who at the last minute bowed to pressure from party leaders, and from Seth Walker, who at the end of the roll call switched his vote from no to aye. Walker's reversal did not reflect a change of heart. It was, instead, the first step in a parliamentary maneuver that would enable the House to reconsider the ratification resolution. But when Walker changed his vote, he inadvertently gave the amendment a constitutional majority; the final tally showed that 50 of the 99 House members had voted yes. Tennessee had ratified the Nineteenth Amendment. During the next several days antisuffrage legislators attempted to rescind Tennessee's ratification, but their efforts failed. On August 26, 1920, Secretary of State Bainbridge Colby issued a proclamation declaring the Nineteenth Amendment ratified and part of the United States Constitution.

Tennessee suffragists were elated and proud of the pivotal role their state had played. "I shall never be as thrilled by the turn of any event as I was at that moment when the roll call that settled the citizenship of American women was heard," Abby Crawford Milton wrote. "Personally, I had rather have had a share in the battle for woman suffrage than any other world event."[1] The victory was especially sweet because of the deeply entrenched hostility that suffragists faced in the South; only three other southern states—Arkansas, Kentucky, and Texas—ratified the amendment in 1920. The suffrage movement in Tennessee that had begun with Elizabeth Avery Meriwether's lone crusade ended with a triumph that guaranteed millions of women the right to vote and changed the face of American politics forever.

Anastatia Sims, Georgia Southern University

CITATION:

(1) Abby Crawford Milton to Carrie Chapman Catt, 5 February 1921, box 1, folder 17, Carrie Chapman Catt Papers, Tennessee State Library and Archives, Nashville, Tennessee. SUGGESTED READINGS: Kathleen C. Berkley, "Elizabeth Avery Meriwether, 'An Advocate for her Sex': Feminism and Conservatism in the Post-Civil War South," *Tennessee Historical Quarterly* 34(1984): 390–407; Anastatia Sims, "'Powers That Pray' and 'Powers That Prey': Tennessee and the Fight for Woman Suffrage," *Tennessee Historical Quarterly* 50(1991): 203–225; A. Elizabeth Taylor, *The Woman Suffrage Movement in Tennessee* (1957); Marjorie Spruill Wheeler, ed., *VOTES FOR WOMEN! The Woman Suffrage Movement in Tennessee, the South, and the Nation* (1995); Carol Lynn Yellin, "Countdown in Tennessee, 1920," *American Heritage* 30(1978): 12–23, 27–35

WOMEN'S BASKETBALL HALL OF FAME currently is under construction in Knoxville, Tennessee and scheduled to open in March 1999. A project of the Knoxville Sports Corporation, headed by president and chief executive officer Gloria Ray, the Hall of Fame will be housed in a two-story, 30,000 square-foot building, designed by Knoxville architects Bullock, Smith and Partners. The downtown site is located near the Hyatt Regency hotel. In the *Knoxville News-Sentinel* of November 20, 1997, Bullock, Smith project designer Jeff Minton commented that the building's design is an "eclectic mix of images that incorporates some of the strengths of classical architecture, plus some imagery of more modernistic shapes and forms that give the impression of going into the future."

1220 Exhibits, Inc., of Nashville is designing the exhibits and locating artifacts for the Hall of Fame in order to cover the 100-plus years of women's basketball. Among the donors are former Amateur Athletic Union stars Patsy Neal from near Newport and Alline Banks Sprouse of Manchester. They are just two of many Tennessee women who excelled in the game at the highest levels of competition. The location of the Hall of Fame in Knoxville, in fact, reflects not only the current excellence of Pat Summitt's University of Tennessee Lady Vols, but the distinguished history of competitive basketball at the high school, amateur, and college levels in the state. Nera White of Macon County was a national star in the 1950s and the first female player inducted in the National Basketball Hall of Fame. In the last decade, both UT and Vanderbilt University have consistently ranked in the top ten of the national polls, with such state high school stars as Tiffany Woolsey and Nikki McCray at

Tennessee and Julie Powell and Paige Redmon at Vanderbilt leading the way. In the Ohio Valley Conference, teams from Middle Tennessee State University dominated the league in the 1980s just as Tennessee Technological University has dominated in the 1990s. Tennessee high school teams, such as Shelbyville Central High School, Oak Ridge High School, and Bradley County High School, have often been nationally ranked and produced many stars. Tennessee star Woolsey prepped at Shelbyville; Redmon of Vanderbilt played at Bradley County. Jennifer Azzi of Oak Ridge won a national championship at Stanford University and then gained Olympic glory as a member of the national team. Small towns and big cities across the state have contributed championship women players to schools and teams across the nation. Summitt herself played state high school basketball before starring at the University of Tennessee at Martin in the mid-1970s. "I did not think even in my wildest dreams there would ever be a place where the history of our game could be told," she told the *Knoxville News-Sentinel* on November 20, 1997. "I think this project [the Hall of Fame] will have a huge impact on the game, nationally and internationally."

Carroll Van West, Middle Tennessee State University

SEE: MACON COUNTY; SUMMITT, PAT; TSSAA

WOMEN'S CHRISTIAN TEMPERANCE UNION (WCTU), the nation's largest anti-alcohol association, held its first national convention in November 1874 in Cleveland, Ohio. Tennessean Elizabeth Fisher Johnson (1835–1883) was there. Johnson began a local union in Memphis in 1875, and Nashville women formed a similar group in 1881. On October 23, 1882, several women met in Nashville to officially establish the Tennessee WCTU, naming Johnson its first president. Johnson died only six months later, but local groups continued to organize. Although not an integrated group, Mrs. C.H. Phillips of Memphis was named president of the Tennessee Black WCTU in September 1887, as an affiliate of the white WCTU. In that year there were 130 affiliated unions—14 of them African American, 10 youth branches, and 21 juvenile societies.

Both the Democratic and Republican parties endorsed prohibition, but the measure failed to pass when brought to a vote in 1887. Discouraged by this failure, enthusiasm diminished, and membership rolls shrank. The WCTU regained some of its popularity by successfully lobbying for the 1895 Scientific Temperance Instruction Law requiring temperance education in all Tennessee public schools. WCTU members also were largely responsible for laws raising the sexual age of consent from 10 to 18, placing police matrons in city courts, establishing a state reform school for juvenile offenders, funding the Reformatory Work Home for Women, and advocating woman suffrage. The Memphis union opened an industrial school for girls in 1882, and in 1897 the Chattanooga union built the Frances Willard Home for "working girls." By 1900, despite its failure to gain statewide prohibition, the WCTU was the most powerful women's lobbying organization in Tennessee.

The murder of Tennessee politician Edward Ward Carmack helped the WCTU's efforts. Couched in language celebrating motherhood and fundamentalist Christianity, Tennessee WCTU members lamented Carmack's death, sent letters to the editors of the state's newspapers, approached their neighbors, and distributed posters. In 1909, on the day of the legislative vote, WCTU women sang hymns in the capitol's gallery when the bill was approved over Governor Malcolm R. Patterson's veto.

After 1909 the Tennessee WCTU continued its "scientific temperance instruction" and helped gain ratification of the Eighteenth Amendment to the U.S. Constitution in 1919. After the repeal of prohibition in 1933, the WCTU remained a powerful force in Tennessee, but membership never again reached the highs of the 1880s or 1910s. Its influence today is still apparent because several Tennessee counties remain "dry" or closely restrict the sale of alcohol. Throughout its history, the Tennessee WCTU provided fundamentalist Christian women the opportunity to gain significant political experience without stepping beyond the traditional female sphere.

Kriste Lindenmeyer, Tennessee Technological University
SUGGESTED READINGS: Mattie Duncan Beard, *The W.T.C.U. in the Volunteer State* (1962); Ruth Bordin, *Woman and Temperance: The Quest for Power and Liberty* (1981)
SEE: CARMACK, EDWARD WARD; TEMPERANCE; WOMAN SUFFRAGE MOVEMENT

WOMEN'S MISSIONARY UNION (WMU) was formed in 1888 as an auxiliary of the Southern Baptist Convention for the purpose of religious evangelism. Part of a trend beginning in the early nineteenth century to establish women's missionary societies within many Christian denominations, the WMU was typical of a general movement stimulated by the Second Great Awakening. Specifically, Charlotte "Lottie" Moon (1840–1912), the most famous female Southern Baptist missionary, became frustrated with the Baptist Foreign Mission Board's rule denying women the right to vote. Moon, a native of Virginia, served as a missionary in Tengchow, Shantung Province from 1873 to 1912. Resigning her position on the Foreign Mission Board in protest, Moon led the successful effort to form the WMU. Within ten years, women in Tennessee and other states supported the creation of a group to improve the quality of life and raise funds for missionary purposes.

Denied ordination as ministers, members of local WMUs felt much freer to express and practice their religious beliefs unencumbered by the presence of males, who traditionally prescribed a subordinate position for women within the Southern Baptist churches. Regular WMU bible studies served as the primary point of instruction for many women who worked as Sunday School teachers for preschoolers to adults. WMU members also have contributed significantly to the Southern Baptist Convention's mission budget. The annual pre-Christmas week of prayer and special offering for mission activities, begun in 1888, remains a signature of the WMU. Similar to other organizations formed and operated by conservative women, the WMU gave women a position of authority and influence within the male patriarchy. Today, there are 3,600 Southern Baptist missionaries in the U.S. and 3,750 in 108 foreign countries largely supported by the local WMUs like those in Tennessee.

Kriste Lindenmeyer, Tennessee Technological University
SEE: MOON, VIRGINIA BETHEL; SOUTHERN BAPTIST CONVENTION

WOODLAND PERIOD. Two of Tennessee's best known prehistoric sites, Pinson Mounds in Madison County and the Old Stone Fort in Coffee County, date to the Woodland Period (300 B.C. to A.D. 900). Anthropologist Charles Hudson concluded that the Woodland tradition represented "probably the most distinctive, the most completely indigenous culture ever to exist in eastern North America."[1]

The period was one of continuity and change for prehistoric Tennesseans. In general, Woodland peoples followed a hunting and gathering way of life similar to their ancestors of the Late Archaic era, but they also learned to exploit the region's resources in a more efficient manner. While seasonal exploitation of resources remained the norm, Woodland peoples collected and stored nuts, berries, and seeds. Remnants of hickory nuts, walnuts, butternuts, acorns, hazelnuts, beechnuts, chestnuts, grapes, persimmons, raspberries, blackberries, strawberries, blueberries, and honey locust pods have been found at Woodland period sites. They practiced a more sedentary life and built more permanent dwellings. They also demonstrated a preference for living near river flood plains. A considerably large trade network among prehistoric peoples throughout eastern North America developed. Pinson Mounds, for example, has yielded artifacts from Georgia and Louisiana.

Agricultural practices began to emerge during these centuries. The Native Americans used both native and tropical plants. Seeds were cultivated from sunflowers, sumpweeds, and chenopodiums and taken from pigweeds, knotweeds, giant ragweeds, and maygrass. Tropical flint corn was acquired about

Teacher at McReynolds School in South Pittsburg recording the weight of each student for a WPA nutrition program.

A.D. 200. Other tropical plants were the bottle gourd and squash, both from present-day Mexico, which were made into containers.

Pottery also became widespread, with local groups making their own distinctive forms and decorating them in locally distinctive ways, such as bird and serpent motifs. Luxury items included gorgets, which were flat objects of stone, copper, or wood designed to be worn on a cord and placed around the neck. They also beaded freshwater pearls into necklaces and bracelets and used them in clothing as beads. Prehistoric peoples fashioned platform pipes, a grave artifact, from stone or made them with pottery. Woodland period graves have yielded small, carefully crafted animal effigies as well.

The Woodland period tradition of elaborate burials left a lasting mark on the landscape. Native Americans built large mortuary mounds and other monumental earthworks. In some cases, bodies were buried in log tombs, which were then covered with dirt forming the mound. Some burial mounds contained only one body; others contained multiple burials. The bodies were commonly accompanied by grave goods, including pottery, jewelry, and sheets of mica. Old Stone Fort is a significant example of another type of Woodland period structure, a large

ceremonial structure whose exact purpose and use is still unclear.

Carroll Van West, Middle Tennessee State University
CITATION:
(1) Charles Hudson, *The Southeastern Indians* (Knoxville, 1976), 55. The Editor-in-Chief also relied on Hudson's general description of the period, see pp. 55–66.
SEE: ARCHAIC PERIOD; COX MOUND GORGETS; MUSSELING; OLD STONE FORT; PINSON MOUNDS; PREHISTORIC NATIVE AMERICAN ARTS; PREHISTORIC USE OF CAVES

WORKS PROGRESS ADMINISTRATION (WPA) was one of the most far-reaching and controversial programs initiated during the New Deal. Designed to put people to work, WPA received an initial Congressional appropriation of $5 billion. Between 1935 and its termination in 1943, the WPA employed approximately eight million workers and spent $11 billion.

From his headquarters in Nashville, WPA state administrator Harry S. Berry, a World War I artillery commander, launched the Tennessee program. The WPA put thousands of unskilled and semi-skilled Tennesseans to work mainly on the state's roads. Farm-to-market, rural, and city-street road projects accounted for over 60 percent of total WPA appropriations in the state. But Tennessee WPA workers also built sewer systems, bridges, waterways, dams, viaducts, and overpasses.

Eclectic in the search for worthwhile projects, WPA workers excavated ancient Cherokee earthen mounds and village sites on Hiwassee Island and unearthed a pre-Columbian Indian village near Hurricane Mills. They worked on a community house in Sparta and a home for the poor in Cookeville. Workers built several lakes, including Marrowbone in Davidson County.

Some of Tennessee's largest WPA projects reflected the arrival of the air age. WPA workers helped complete landing fields and airports at Jellico, Cookeville, Lebanon, Jackson, and Milan. They built major airports in Memphis, Chattanooga, Knoxville, Nashville, and the Tri-cities of Bristol, Johnson City, and Kingsport.

In Memphis, local political leader Edward H. Crump and U.S. Senator Kenneth D. McKellar dispensed patronage through the WPA. Besides extensive road and street work, the WPA employed thousands of men digging ditches, painting buildings, and resurfacing sidewalks in Memphis. Larger WPA projects included Crump Stadium, the city zoo, a juvenile court building, a new hospital, and several housing developments. When the flood of 1937 swept over the city's low-lying areas, the damage was lessened by the efforts of thousands of WPA workers who constructed makeshift levees and hastily-erected flood walls. WPA employees also helped care for 50,000 refugees left stranded by the flood, while Nashville WPA workers cared for the 5,000 flood victims in that city.

In Nashville WPA workers restored Civil War-era Fort Negley, completed projects at Percy and Edwin Warner Parks, helped construct a new Tennessee Highway Department building, worked at The Hermitage, and refurbished several public schools. These workers also improved city parks, built a city garage and repair building, and completed almost 25 miles of street work.

The WPA operated service and arts programs that employed a number of Tennesseans. Adult education classes, public health services, and school lunch programs hired teachers, nurses, and dietitians. In the largest cities, the WPA operated women's sewing and canning classes at domestic training centers and employed writers, actors, artists, and musicians in programs in the arts.

Young Tennesseans also benefited from New Deal initiatives. The National Youth Administration (NYA) offered vocational classes to young fulltime students and employed many others in parttime jobs. NYA youth built shops and vocational buildings in 23 counties, and gyms and recreational buildings in 13 others.

Although segregated by race in accordance with the prevailing Jim Crow standards, the NYA and other New Deal programs employed African Americans. Across the South, 750,000 unemployed African Americans worked on WPA projects, and thousands of Tennesseans were put to work this way.

The WPA ran into political trouble in 1938, when charges were made in 17 states that the agency had used funds to provide financial support for political candidates. In Tennessee, incumbent Governor Gordon Browning claimed that Crump-McKellar-backed candidates used WPA workers to bring about his defeat in the Democratic primary. Subsequent Congressional investigations revealed considerable WPA involvement in the primary as well as other irregularities. In 1939 Congress passed the Hatch Act which prohibited federal employees from participating in national elections.

Political scandals and the onset of war reduced the support and need for WPA-type employment. Ongoing WPA projects continued until the agency was terminated on June 30, 1943. During its eight years in Tennessee, the WPA employed an average of 30,000 men and women per year. Besides providing desperately needed wages, WPA construction projects built lasting monuments, such as its series of Colonial Revival-styled post offices across the state. Among its greatest contributions was a series of state guidebooks produced by the Federal Writers' Project, including *The WPA Guide to Tennessee*, an engaging chronicle of the state.

Thomas H. Coode, Volunteer State Community College
SUGGESTED READINGS: James C. Cobb and Michael V. Namorato, eds., *New Deal in the South* (1985); John D. Minton, *The New Deal in Tennessee, 1932–1938* (1979)
SEE: AIRPORTS; BROWNING, GORDON; CONSERVATION; CRUMP, EDWARD H.; MCKELLAR, KENNETH; MURALS; STADIUMS, HISTORIC

WORLD WAR I. During the interlude marked by the end of the depression of the 1890s and the entry of the United States into the First World War in 1917, Tennesseans as well as other Americans entered the twentieth century. Embracing reformism at home and imperialism abroad, Americans of this era, on the domestic front and in foreign affairs, set the nation's future course. This was Progressivism at high tide, but the philosophy that shaped it and the ideas that undergirded it spilled over at either end of its loosely established chronological boundaries. Correcting the ills of an American society struggling to make the transition from a rural past to an urban future, Tennesseans as well as other Americans concentrated on domestic issues while international relations commanded less attention. By 1917, however, ominous developments overseas could no longer be ignored.

The faraway assassination of the Austrian Archduke Franz Ferdinand in Sarajevo and the chain of

TSLA, PHOTOGRAPH BY CLAVERT

Lt. Morton B. Adams, 90th Aero Squadron, AEF, circa 1918.

events it set in motion, culminating with World War I, eventually reached into the rural communities and remote villages of the Volunteer State. Tennesseans shifted their attention from politics and prohibition to foreign affairs and distant battlegrounds. The principal European nations had been engaged in military conflict since 1914, but the United States managed to avoid direct involvement until 1917. Violations of American rights as a neutral, sympathy for Britain and France and strong cultural and historic ties with them, the diplomatic blunderings of the Germans, and economic considerations congealed. President Woodrow Wilson, a pacifist at heart, led his country into the first global war of the twentieth century.

During the Progressive era, as local and regional economies gave way to the national and international organizational structure of corporate America, a pronounced alteration in federal-state relations occurred. The creation of the National Guard, which swallowed up the old state militia units, represented a case in point. Although the militia could be called up to keep the peace at the local level or to resist a foreign invasion, it was not until after the Spanish-American War that the militia had a permanent place in the federal military. Congress, between 1900 and 1903, routinely approved appropriations for the militia, providing federal money to outfit units of citizen soldiers. With

the passage of the Dick Act on January 21, 1903, the U.S. Government officially established an organized militia that could be called into the service as a part of the regular army.

Between 1903 and 1916, other congressional legislation tied the state units even more securely to the federal government. The National Defense Act of 1916, which was intended to prepare the nation's military forces for the possibility of involvement in World War I, represented the capstone for those who had actively sought the integration of the militia into the regular army. It specified that the state units, designated as the National Guard, would pass under complete federal control in time of war or grave public emergency as determined by the commander-in-chief. Shortly after the enactment of this legislation, with revolutionary upheaval in Mexico and chaos along the border, President Woodrow Wilson ordered the National Guard into federal service. The initial call-up included almost 2,000 Tennesseans, but subsequent enlistments increased the numbers in the mobilization camp at Nashville by another thousand.

Tennessee National Guardsmen, many of whom probably still considered themselves state militiamen, made no secret of their homesickness and general dissatisfaction when they arrived in the Southwest. Both the First and the Third Regiments saw duty on the border as did three troops of cavalry and hospital and ambulance detachments. The Tennessee delegation in Congress and Governor Tom C. Rye lobbied unsuccessfully for the return of the troops by Christmas. War Department plans prevailed, the U.S. Army controlled the Tennessee National Guardsmen, and the last of them did not come home and muster out of federal service until March 24, 1917. Two weeks later, on April 6, the United States formally entered World War I. Six days thereafter, the War Department placed elements of the Tennessee National Guard on active duty; others were called up later.

When the war broke out, a relatively small number of Tennesseans already served in the peacetime armed forces, but the activation of the Guard affected hundreds of Tennesseans; still others joined of their own volition. Nevertheless, the Selective Service, commonly known as the draft, provided the greatest number of men from the Volunteer State. Both the North and the South had used the draft during the Civil War, but this marked the first time that the federal government had conscripted Tennessee civilians. The Selective Service Act of May 18, 1917, specified that military and naval forces should be recruited by lot from among adult males between the ages of 21 and 30, later expanded to 18 and 45.

Governor Rye named Major Rutledge Smith of Putnam County, who had been heading up the Tennessee Council of Defense, to direct the state's Selective Service System. Three registrations occurred on

June 5, 1917, December 14, 1917, and August 24, 1918, respectively. A total of 474,347 men reported to the Selective Service, 368,242 of whom actually completed the classification process.* The nation eventually drafted 61,069 Tennesseans, 43,730 whites and 17,339 blacks, according to figures given in Stanley J. Folmsbee, et al., *History of Tennessee* (1960). Camp Gordon, Georgia, welcomed many of these hastily created soldiers into federal service. Military and naval authorities had implemented a policy that prevented large groups of men from a single state from serving in any one division overseas. Nonetheless, the Thirtieth Division, nicknamed the Old Hickory Division in honor of Andrew Jackson, was made up of troops mostly from Tennessee, North Carolina, and South Carolina. The Thirtieth trained at Camp Sevier, South Carolina, prior to service in Europe. Elements of the Thirtieth Division played a major, perhaps even decisive role in breaking through the famous Hindenburg Line.

Most Tennesseans in the military served in the infantry, but others entered the Marine Corps, the Army Air Corps, and the Navy. Indeed, Admiral Albert Gleaves (1858–1937) of Nashville, one of the most notable sailors of this era from the land-locked Volunteer State, commanded the United States Navy Cruiser and Transport Force, which had the responsibility of convoying American and allied troops to the continent. In 1919 Gleaves was Commander-in-Chief, Asiatic Fleet. He held the Distinguished Service Medal and the French Legion of Honor. Another Tennessean, Admiral William Banks Caperton (1855–1941) of Spring Hill became commander-in-chief of the Pacific Fleet during 1916 and subsequently was involved in naval operations in the South Atlantic. World War I also featured daring young men in their flying machines, and Tennessee claimed flying aces, among them Lieutenant Edward Buford of Nashville. Two other aviators, Lieutenant Claude O. Lowe and Lieutenant McGhee Tyson, lost their lives in the line of duty. Yet another Tennessean, Colonel Luke Lea, staged one of the most colorful escapades of World War I. Colonel Lea led what American Expeditionary Commander John J. Pershing officially labeled "an amazingly indiscreet" raid into Holland in a futile attempt to capture the exiled German Kaiser Wilhelm II and bring him to justice.

The most celebrated common soldier of World War I—a Tennessean—hailed from Fentress County in the Upper Cumberlands. Of humble origin, Alvin C. York had little formal education and as a young man had indulged in the not uncommon vices of drinking, gambling, and brawling. After a religious conversion in 1915, he became a devout fundamentalist Christian who opposed war and violence. After struggling with his convictions, he was drafted and later assigned to the 82nd Division of the 328th

Infantry Regiment, where he won international acclaim for his single-handed shoot-out with a German machine gun battalion in the Argonne Forest. York supposedly killed 25 Germans, captured 132 prisoners, and silenced 35 machine guns, which earned him a promotion to sergeant and won him the Congressional Medal of Honor.

As warfare siphoned manpower out of Tennessee, it poured dollars into the Volunteer State. The U.S. Army Signal Corps Aviation Section, for example, established an aviation school near Millington in Shelby County. On November 30, 1917, the first 30 students arrived from the University of Illinois; three days later, another 75 from Princeton joined them. Most of the would-be pilots were college graduates. Student aviators trained in the JN4, known as the "Jenny," a biplane that carried two passengers. The plane featured a Curtiss OX-5 engine, a wooden propeller, and fabric covering. Park Field, the WWI training facility, contributed to the economy of Memphis and Millington, became the site of the Naval Reserve Aviation Base in 1942, and served as the forerunner for the Naval Air Technical Training Command located in Shelby County.

The World War I era also gave rise to the "war babies" in various locations around the state—industries that owed their existence to the defense effort and either ceased to exist or went into major retrenchment when the armistice came. Numerous small factories producing war materiel made their short-lived appearances. The most important facility of these years was the powder plant at Hadley's Bend—later called Old Hickory—on the Cumberland River near Nashville. It cost $80 million to construct and E.I. DuPont de Nemours Company operated it. The project brought 20,000 new workers to the Nashville area and caused a crisis in housing and transportation.

On the home front, state residents responded to the patriotic fervor of the times and organized for victory. Cooperating fully with the national government, the Tennessee State Council of Defense modeled itself after the National Council of Defense. Every county had its own council as did some six to seven thousand communities. Home Guards kept a watchful vigil over railroad trestles and bridges although saboteurs seemed to have posed no serious threat. Newspaper editors across the state rallied to promote patriotism, and nearly every county claimed "Four-Minute Men," so-called because they could deliver brief, enthusiastic orations in support of the war effort. The wonders performed by the federal food and fuel administrations and their state counterparts, which encouraged and fostered voluntary conservation of precious commodities, warded off rationing. Dr. Harcourt A. Morgan, dean of the College of Agriculture of the University of Tennessee, directed the Tennessee Food Administration. Meanwhile, public officials urged farmers to grow more crops and property owners to set aside vacant lots in urban areas for food production. Educators encouraged high school students to cultivate "Victory" gardens.

Historically, warfare has been dominated by men, but armed conflict has always impinged on women's lives as well. Some females from Tennessee entered the armed forces. Many others, black and white, worked in factories or contributed to a variety of private agencies, among them the Young Women's Christian Association, the American Red Cross, and the Tennessee Division and Davidson County Liberty Loan Organizations. The influenza epidemic of 1918–1919 inspired some of the most heroic and self-sacrificing service by women, trained and untrained, who nursed the afflicted; others drove cars and ambulances to assist physicians and public-health authorities in their efforts to combat the disease. Government officials specifically commended the emergency work of the Motor Corps Department of the Nashville Chapter of the American Red Cross. Approximately 20 million people died worldwide, including more than 500,000 Americans. The undertakers of Nashville as well as other Tennessee towns and communities found it difficult to cope with the victims. Chattanooga, for example, had experienced as many as 5,848 civilian deaths by October 19, 1918, and soldiers encamped at nearby Fort Oglethorpe, Georgia, and Chickamauga Park succumbed to influenza as well.

When hostilities ended, the home front prepared to celebrate. Women across the state, particularly in the capital, played a preeminent role in homecoming festivities. They arranged parades, block dances, patriotic tableaux, and banquets. In Middle Tennessee alone, Mrs. W.H. (Betty Lyle) Wilson, a nationally renowned cakemaker, headed a drive for the homecoming dinner that garnered ten thousand cakes. After the armistice in 1918, the 114th Field Artillery became the first of the large units to return to the state. Traveling by train from Newport News, Virginia, the troops crossed the state line on March 29, 1919. They paraded in Knoxville where more than 30,000 cheering people lined the route. Then the 114th entrained for Nashville and arrived several hours later at a siding adjacent to Centennial Park. In Nashville, when the veterans passed in review, an estimated 100,000 to 250,000 people turned out to greet them. Governor A.H. Roberts delivered a welcoming address. The troops then traveled to Chattanooga where they also received an enthusiastic welcome before being demobilized in Georgia. Other Tennessee soldiers returned to less fanfare, but citizens across the state, from Johnson City to Memphis, in many towns and cities officially greeted their returning veterans. At Jackson, a local committee of black citizens planned the largest celebration that they had ever conducted to show their appreciation for the African-American soldiers from Madison and adjoining counties.

The General Assembly voted a bonus for all who had served in the ranks, and the state legislature, city of Nashville, and Davidson County funded the War Memorial Building in the capital. One source indicates that Tennessee furnished as many as 130,915 men and women for the armed forces and experienced 3,836 deaths and 6,190 casualties. The Volunteer State also provided 3,690 officers, 110 of them female nurses. Only 288 individuals had registered as conscientious objectors; citations for bravery abounded and the state claimed six Congressional Medal of Honor recipients. Among them was Edward R. Talley of Appalachia, Virginia, who apparently had some Tennessee connections. Four of the other recipients survived the war and claimed residence: Joseph B. Adkinson of Atoka; James E. Karnes, Knoxville; Calvin J. Ward, Morristown; and Alvin C. York, Jamestown. Milo Lemert of Crossville died in service to his country, but his body was retrieved from France for final burial. Citizens of the Volunteer State had also done their share to finance the war. Every loan drive, which involved war-bond sales, including the very difficult Victory Loan of 1919, was oversubscribed in Tennessee. In the aftermath of battle, a group of representatives from division and service units of the American Expeditionary Force had met in Paris, France, from March 15 to 17, 1919, and organized the American Legion. By August 1919, Memphis Post, No. 1, set out to enlist every discharged soldier, sailor, and marine, which in Shelby County amounted to an estimated 10,000 men. Other posts soon developed around the state, and ladies auxiliaries likewise appeared.

The superpatriotism of the World War I era, fueled by such organizations as George Creel's Committee on Public Information, of which the "Four-Minute Men" were a part, encouraged a social climate that was ripe for bigotry. Intolerance, racism, and nativism ran rampant during the war years and into the next decade. Individuals of German origin suffered wartime harassment in both the state and the nation, the reborn Ku Klux Klan increased its membership in Tennessee and across the country, and race riots occurred in East St. Louis, Illinois, and Houston, Texas, during 1917, anticipating those two years later that the African-American writer James Weldon Johnson dubbed "Red Summer." During a 16-month period from April to October 1919, 20 towns and cities in both the North and South experienced disturbances that left blood in their streets. Race riots occurred in such far-flung locations as Longview, Texas, Washington, D.C., Omaha, Nebraska, and Chester, Pennsylvania. Elaine, Arkansas, and Chicago, Illinois, claimed the most violent ones of

SPECIAL COLLECTIONS, UNIVERSITY OF MEMPHIS

Crew of bomber "City of Memphis" on Guam, 1945. John J. Handwerker of Memphis, commander.

1919, but they were exceeded in intensity by the Tulsa, Oklahoma, riot of 1921—the most serious of the post-WWI years. One of the 1919 riots transpired in the East Tennessee Republican stronghold of Knoxville, Tennessee.

Margaret Ripley Wolfe, East Tennessee State University

*Numbers vary somewhat from one source to another. These statistics are from Mrs. Rutledge (Graeme McGregor) Smith, "Tennessee World War Soldiers," American Legion Auxiliary Scrap Book, 1931–1932, Tennessee State Library and Archives, Nashville, Tennessee. Mrs. Smith was the historian for the American Legion Auxiliary, Department of Tennessee, and also the wife of Major Rutledge Smith, who directed the Selective Service System in the state.

SUGGESTED READINGS: Reese Amis, *History of the 114th Field Artillery: First Tennessee Field Artillery* (1920); William James Bacon, *History of the Fifty-fifth Field Artillery Brigade* (1920); James A. Crutchfield, *Tennesseans at War: Volunteers and Patriots in Defense of Liberty* (1987); Stanley J. Folmsbee, Robert E. Corlew, and Enoch L. Mitchell, "The Volunteer State Goes to War, 1917–1918," chap. in *History of Tennessee*. Vol. 2 (1960); Rose Long (Mrs. John G.) Gilmore, *Davidson County Women in the World War, 1914–1919* (1923); Paul E. Isaac, *Prohibition and Politics: Turbulent Decades in Tennessee 1885–1920* (1965); Lester C. Lamon, *Black Tennesseans, 1900–1930* (1977); David E. Lee, *Sergeant York: An American Hero* (1985); Elmer A. Murphy and Robert S. Thomas, *The Thirtieth Division in the World War* (1936); Margaret Ripley Wolfe, "The Border Service of the Tennessee National Guard, 1916–1917," *Tennessee Historical Quarterly* 32(1973): 374–388

WORLD WAR II marks a watershed period for the United States. As one of the victors and the sole possessor of the atomic bomb, America emerged as the modern world's super power. The total war effort reshaped the state's economy drastically from a predominantly rural, agricultural economy to an increasingly urban, industrialized one. In addition to military service, the war touched thousands of Tennesseans as they migrated from the countryside and found new job opportunities in the burgeoning war industries. Tennessee played a primary role in the creation of the atomic age. Oak Ridge, which had grown out of the Manhattan Project, produced vital components of the atomic bomb dropped on Hiroshima during the final stages of the war.

More than 300,000 Tennesseans served in the armed forces; the 5,731 Tennesseans who died in the war made the ultimate sacrifice. Six Tennesseans were recipients of the Congressional Medal of Honor. Cordell Hull served as President Franklin D. Roosevelt's Secretary of State. In addition, Tennessee became the site of numerous military installations, training facilities, and prisoner of war camps during the war, and 280,000 Tennesseans worked in war manufacturing.

When World War II raged across Europe between 1939 and 1941, the United States attempted to remain neutral and at the same time become the world's arsenal of democracy. The country quickly reversed the low productivity and high unemployment of the Depression decade and converted its stagnant industries to defense production. In 1940, in further preparation for the possibility of war, the U.S. Congress enacted its first peacetime draft, the Selective Service and Training Act.

Prior to the U.S. entrance into the war, Tennessee became one of the first states to engage actively in military preparedness. After meeting Hitler during a Rotary tour of Europe in 1937, Tennessee Governor Prentice Cooper became convinced that the United States would not be able to avoid war. Governor Cooper encouraged Tennessee to prepare for the approaching war by readying the state for the infusion of war industries, military training exercises, and military bases.

Tennessee established the first state defense organization in 1940, the Advisory Committee on Preparedness. In January 1941 the state legislature created a Tennessee State Guard, the largest in the South, to provide protection for the state in the absence of the Tennessee National Guard, which had been activated as the 117th Infantry Regiment in the 30th Division. The 117th Regiment served with distinction in Europe until the end of the war.

Tennessee also designated land for potential use as military bases, an act which resulted in the establishment of Camp Campbell near Clarksville and Camp Forrest near Tullahoma. In 1941 the state bought over 3,000 acres near Smyrna, which it cleared and leased to the federal government as Sewart Air Base. During June of the same year, Major General George S. Patton conducted armored maneuvers in Middle Tennessee.

Despite Tennessee's preparations for the war, the state and the nation were equally shocked to hear the news of the Japanese attack at Pearl Harbor on December 7, 1941. The day that would "live in infamy" etched permanent imprints on American memories. Years later, Tennesseans would recall the exact moments when they first heard the news of Pearl Harbor.

Tennessee servicemen were inducted at Fort Oglethorpe, Georgia, in the early stages of the war and later at Camp Forrest. Tennessee women, who joined the Women's Army Corps, trained at Fort Oglethorpe throughout the war. Women also joined the Navy WAVES, the Coast Guard SPARS, the Women Marines, and the WASPS or Women's Airforce Service Pilots.

Hundreds of thousands of soldiers from Tennessee and across the nation trained at Camps Forrest (an induction and infantry training center), Campbell (an armor training facility), and Tyson (a barrage balloon center near Paris, Tennessee). Pilots trained at several small airports throughout the state. Major bases that trained pilots and crews were located in Smyrna and near Dyersburg. An air ferry command was located in Memphis. Millington Naval base in Shelby County was the country's largest inland naval base.

Over 20 counties in Middle Tennessee were utilized for the Tennessee Maneuvers, which were headquartered at Cumberland University in Lebanon and officially referred to as "somewhere in Tennessee." Middle Tennessee was chosen for these war games because of its proximity to the railroads and federal highways, and the similarity between its terrain and that of western Europe. Red and Blue "armies" faced each other in training exercises. More than 800,000 men and women participated in the Tennessee Maneuvers, which produced over $4 million in claims by individuals and municipalities for destruction of property by the opposing armies.

Camps Forrest, Campbell, and Tyson also served as prisoner of war camps for German, Italian, and Austrian POWs through 1946. Prisoners were also held at Tellico Plains, Crossville, Memphis, Lawrenceburg, and Nashville. At Camp Forrest, which was the headquarters for several permanent and temporary POW camps in five southeastern states, approximately 68,000 prisoners were processed. Prisoners in the camps worked in the prison hospitals and area farms, cut pulpwood, and drained malarial swamps. Several POW groups produced their own German newspapers, performed plays, wrote poetry, and often became the object of attention for curious Tennesseans.

Several hundred refugees, primarily Jews, voluntarily settled in Tennessee after their escape from Hitler's anti-Semitic laws, intimidation, and death camps. Strict immigration laws required refugees to obtain American sponsors to insure that they did not become burdens on society. Many of the Jews who settled in Tennessee found work in Jacob May's hosiery mill in Nashville.

True to the nickname of the "Volunteer State," Tennesseans supported the war not only through the armed services, but also in their homefront activities. As it became increasingly evident that the war would not end quickly, Tennesseans adjusted to the impact of total war. Encouraged by President Roosevelt's radio "fireside chats," they purchased rationed food, collected scrap metals and tires, and saved kitchen fats, which were used in the production of glycerine for bombs. Families and communities planted victory gardens and lived with shortages of gasoline, meat, shoes, cigarettes, tires, sugar, and stockings. Tennesseans invested in war bonds and practiced blackouts during air raid drills. As volunteer block captains and air raid wardens, they inspected neighborhoods for compliance. Women's clubs knitted sweaters and socks, produced soldiers' kits, and rolled bandages for the Red Cross. Communities fed, housed, and entertained soldiers. Churches, YMCAs, YWCAs, and other groups opened servicemen's lounges and canteens. Universities and colleges throughout the state experienced dramatic decreases in enrollment as college-aged men went to war, and campuses became training grounds for special units. Young and old listened to the swing sound of the big bands.

Perhaps the single most important long range impact of the war on Tennessee was its influence on the state's economy. As a result of the war, the state both accelerated and expanded its industries. Established industrial centers such as Memphis, Chattanooga, and Knoxville shifted almost entirely to war production; in addition, Kingsport mushroomed in growth as did Oak Ridge, which grew from farmlands and timbered hillsides to become Tennessee's fifth largest city by 1945.

By 1943 nearly one hundred Memphis manufacturing firms held war contracts. The two largest Memphis war production concerns were the Fisher and Ford plants, which converted from the manufacture of automobile parts to airplane parts production. Smaller, but important war manufacturers included McDonnell Aircraft, the Chickasaw Ordnance Works, and Firestone Tire and Rubber Company, which produced life rafts for the Navy. The federal government also employed several thousand civilians at Kennedy General Hospital and numerous armed services installations. Also in West Tennessee, the Milan Ordnance Center, built in 1942, employed approximately 11,000 workers in its production of shell ammunition, boosters, and fuses, as well as ammonium nitrate.

Nashville experienced a less dramatic conversion to war industry. Its only "war baby industry" was Consolidated Vultee Aircraft Corporation, which employed 3,000 workers in May 1945. Prior to the American entrance into the war, Vultee built the "Vengeance" dive bomber for Britain's Royal Air Force, and later produced the P-39 "Lightning" fighter and the O-49 observation plane for the United States. Nashville Bridge Company increased its production of mine sweepers, barges, quartering ships, cargo lighters, and submarine chasers, employing approximately 700 workers. In nearby Old Hickory, the DuPont plant produced cellophane and rayon products, including "bubblefill" for life jackets and rafts.

Chattanooga, an important manufacturing city before the war, converted to war production in its steel, ordnance, iron, textile, and chemical plants. Much of Chattanooga's industry remained relatively unchanged during the war, however, with the exception of the production of aircraft parts and ordnance supplies, the latter produced by Hercules Powder Company, which manufactured TNT.

In 1933 Knoxville became the national headquarters of the Tennessee Valley Authority, which supplied the energy for the new military industries. TVA enlarged its operations tremendously during the war; the agency constructed seven dams and a steam generating station between 1940 and 1945, increasing power generating capabilities from one to two million kilowatts. The wartime construction of the dams completed a 650-mile navigation channel connecting the Tennessee River with 6,000 miles of interior waterways. Southern Railway Systems, Fulton Sylphon, which produced temperature and pressure control instruments, and the University of Tennessee employed large numbers of workers throughout the war years. A new war-spawned industry, Rohm and Haas, produced plexiglass for airplanes. In 1939, in nearby Blount County, the Aluminum Company of America (ALCOA) expanded its plant and employed over 4,000 workers.

In upper East Tennessee, Kingsport became a major producer of explosives for the war effort. The Tennessee Eastman Company grew to be an employer of over 5,000 workers by 1949, manufacturing plastics and acetic anhydride, a raw material used for safety film. Eastman also procured a war contract from the National Defense Research Committee to produce RDX or Research Development Explosive, whose explosive capacity was 50 percent greater than TNT. Chemists at Eastman designed a method to produce large quantities of RDX, which had previously been manufactured only in small batches due to its highly explosive qualities. Further, Eastman began producing Composition B, an amalgamation of TNT and RDX for use in bombs and projectiles. Eastman produced the Composition B in the easily transportable shape of chocolate kisses. In June 1942 the federal government granted Eastman officials the authorization to construct the Holston Ordnance Works, which became the largest producer of high explosives in the world by January 1944.

Eastman's achievements in the production of explosives led to a contract to operate the Y-12 plant, one of three Oak Ridge facilities involved in the secret Manhattan Project to produce the atomic bomb. As work progressed, Oak Ridge, the "city behind the fence," experienced a peak wartime population of 75,000. The project, which employed 90,000 workers at maximum production, separated out the fissionable uranium isotope, U-235, a major component of the first atomic bomb, which was dropped on Hiroshima, Japan, on August 6, 1945.

The growth of war industry in Tennessee, concurrent with the armed service demands for all able-bodied men, created an increased labor demand along with a diminished labor supply. Consequently, the war provided a catalyst for the employment of large numbers of women. Between September 1942 and March 1944, the employment of women in several of Tennessee's chief war industries increased by nearly 21,000 or 75 percent of the expansion in these industries. Symbolized by "Rosie the Riveter," women's employment increased primarily in ordnance, textile, finished lumber, chemicals, iron, steel, aircraft, and aluminum production, as well as in communications and government agencies. Companies such as ALCOA reversed their practice of hiring women only in office positions and placed them on the assembly lines. TVA hired women as guards for its dams and downtown Knoxville buildings; females who guarded the dams were given the title, "WOOPS," or Women Officers of Public Safety. Existing seniority rights and established lines of advancement generally hampered women's advancement in production areas. Nationwide, women realized a 57 percent increase in earnings between 1939 and 1944; at $.745 per hour, their wages were still significantly lower than men's average wages of $1.159 per hour.

Federal government propaganda enticed women to work for patriotic reasons, yet the government, employers, and the public at large remained unwilling to accept the idea of working mothers, except as a last resort. In 1942 the U.S. Congress authorized limited resources for federally funded, wartime child care centers through the Lanham Act. Tennessee became a pacesetter in the South with the construction of Lanham-funded centers in Memphis, Nashville, Knoxville, and Chattanooga.

Women's wartime employment gains were usually temporary, although the war set the stage for later change. In Tennessee, women's employment increased by nearly 83,000 between 1940 and 1950; male employment during the same time increased by 110,000. Although the majority of women's war jobs in Tennessee were terminated, as the "last hired" were the "first fired," women's employment in manufacturing still was 23,000 greater in 1950 than it had been in 1940.

During the war, a number of African Americans gained notoriety for bravery in combat, while at home they experienced moderate economic advancements. Large numbers of blacks moved from rural farm areas to war production centers either in Tennessee or in northern cities. Memphis saw an increase in its non-white population from 121,550 to over 150,000 between 1940 and 1950; Nashville's non-white population increased by over 7,000 to 59,000. White housewives complained that they had lost their black maids to the war industries, which generally paid three times as much as domestic work. Despite President Roosevelt's Fair Employment Practices mandate, which required non-discriminatory hiring in the war plants, black men and women encountered discrimination. Oftentimes, blacks were employed in the least desirable positions, such as custodians, cooks, and laundresses. Tennessee's war and postwar employment figures of blacks showed strong similarities to prewar employment data, as prevailing negative and paternalistic attitudes toward non-whites remained virtually unchanged by the war.

Not only did World War II spawn industrial growth in the state, the war provided a catalyst for urbanization. Shelby County's population increased nearly 35 percent between 1940 and 1950, from approximately 350,000 to over 480,000. During the same period, Nashville's population grew by 25 percent from 257,000 to over 320,000. Between 1940 and 1950, the state experienced one of its lowest outmigration rates since 1870, while the major metropolitan areas realized a net 11 percent in-migration rate. During the 1940s, the farm population of the state decreased by over 250,000, signaling the beginning of a downward trend as the rural population dropped from 1,272,000 in 1940 to 1,016,000 in 1950. By 1960 the rural farm population had fallen below 600,000.

The war years signaled an end to the Great Depression, as bank deposits more than tripled between 1940 and 1950, from approximately $650,000 to over $2 million. Personal incomes increased from less than $1 billion in 1940 to nearly $3.3 billion in 1950. Per capita personal income nearly tripled from an annual income average of $339 in 1940 to nearly $1,000 in 1950.

In 1944 Tennessee became involved in planning for the returning veterans. Governor Cooper appointed a Committee on Postwar Rehabilitation of Veterans to organize a statewide program. The same year, the U.S. Congress passed the Servicemen's Readjustment Act of 1944, better known as the "GI Bill of Rights." This law established procedures for the reemployment of veterans as well as educational and low-interest rate benefits. As a result of the GI Bill, the postwar years witnessed a mushrooming in the size of the state's colleges and universities, and in the burgeoning suburbs.

With the conclusion of the war in September 1945, Tennesseans, along with other Americans, commemorated their war dead and looked to the future. Despite a national fear of a widespread recession, Americans reconverted from war production to peacetime production of much demanded consumer items, thus avoiding an anticipated recession. Tennessee industry as well as its cities, suburbs, and universities experienced rapid growth in the immediate postwar years. World War II, as a total war, had touched nearly all Tennesseans' lives, and the economic expansion bought about by the war would continue to have an impact on the state in the years to come.

Patricia Brake Howard, Webb School of Knoxville

SUGGESTED READINGS: Karen Anderson, *Wartime Women: Sex Roles, Family Relations, and the Status of Women During World War II* (1981); Charles W. Johnson and Charles O. Jackson, *City Behind a Fence* (1981); Patricia Brake Howard, "Tennessee In War and Peace: The Impact of World War II On State Economic Trends," *Tennessee Historical Quarterly* 51(1992): 51–65; James A. Crutchfield, *Tennesseans At War: Volunteers and Patriots in Defense of Liberty* (1987); Gene Sloan, *With Second Army Somewhere in Tennessee* (1956); Ann Toplovich, "The Tennessean's War: Life on the Home Front," *Tennessee Historical Quarterly* 51(1992): 19–50; Susan L. Gordon, "Home Front Tennessee: The World War II Experience," *Tennessee Historical Quarterly* 51(1992): 3–18; Tennessee 200, *Answering the Call: Tennesseans in the Second World War* (1996)

WORTH, INC., a family-owned baseball and softball equipment company, was founded by George Sharp Lannom, Jr., in Tullahoma in 1912 as Lannom Manufacturing Company. It began as a producer of leather horse collars and harnesses. Recognizing the decline of animal-powered farming, Lannom developed a sporting goods line in order to utilize his tannery. He started with leather footballs in 1921 and added helmets, basketballs, and then baseballs and later softballs. Naming the line "Worth," Lannom created the slogan "Another Name for Value" and masterminded the company's growth for the next 30 years. From the very beginning he had organized Lannom Manufacturing Company around the ideas of vertical integration and a 40-percent profit rule. The first insured his control over all stages of production, from raw materials to distribution; the second occasionally endangered quality levels and long-range prospects. Yet Lannom's business sense and forceful personality drove the company forward. The Tullahoma enterprise survived what turned out to be a debilitating merger in 1923 with Morrison-Ricker of Grinnell, Iowa; once Lannom gained control of the Iowa plants, he resettled in Tennessee.

In 1927 Lannom discontinued football and basketball production to concentrate on baseballs and soft-

balls. In 1933 he built a bigger factory and tannery in Tullahoma. Lannom Manufacturing employees survived the Depression, and in 1939 they produced 600 dozen baseballs daily. Lannom overcame an attempt at unionization of his employees and also foresaw the labor shortage that World War II would create. In response he opened a new factory in Puerto Rico in 1941. A second plant outside the United States began operations in Ontario in 1949.

Lannom died in 1953; two years later his son, G. Sharp Lannom III, took control of most of the Iowa-based parts of the holdings while the Tennessee-based Lannom Manufacturing Company and its Worth operations came under the leadership of Chuck Parish, Lannom's son-in-law. Over the next 20 years, Parish consolidated the holdings headquartered and directed from Tullahoma, increased his factories in Central America, and at his son's urging expanded the Worth line to include production of wood and then aluminum baseball and softball bats. Before Parish died in 1975, Worth had the majority of the U.S. aluminum-bat market and had produced the first official Little League and NCAA Collegiate aluminum bats. At the same time he maintained the cottage industry of hand-sewing baseballs his father-in-law had organized decades earlier. That tradition, much reduced, continues still.

When John Parish took over his father's position, Worth entered its most dynamic phase to date. The company's current standard, "Performance Through Technology," indicates his interest in research and development of new materials. From Worth's first polycore softball has emerged the newest Super Dot series with its lamination process that essentially makes core and cover one unit. Worth also developed Reduced Injury Factor (RIF) softballs and baseballs in the 1980s. Their batting glove has been popular with NASCAR pit crews as well, and Worth continues to experiment with the glove's material. Its aluminum alloy bats display a dual energy transfer system, what the company calls its trampoline and springboard effects. Worth's newest facility in Tullahoma opened in 1991, and it also maintains plants in other locations in North and Central America.

Margaret D. Binnicker, Middle Tennessee State University

SUGGESTED READING: Neil A. Hamilton, "Tennessee Villager in a Modern World: G.S. Lannom, Jr., Baseball and Leather Entrepreneur," East Tennessee Historical Society *Publications* 54 and 55 (1982 and 1983): 47–69

SEE: BASEBALL, MINOR LEAGUE; COFFEE COUNTY; INDUSTRY

WRIGHT, FRANCES (1795–1852) was arguably the most radical utopian thinker and activist in antebellum America. She advocated the freedom and equality of women, African-American slaves, and white working people and designed social experiments to bring the United States closer to what she considered its fundamental principles. In Tennessee, she launched a memorable attempt to find a peaceful solution to the problem of slavery through the education of slaves and the financial compensation of slave masters.

Orphaned at the age of two, Wright received a liberal education from her uncle, James Mylne, a professor of moral philosophy at the University of Glasgow, a center of the Scottish Enlightenment. Secure in the belief that all people might be educated to liberty and excited by the idea of revolutionary America and the sentiments of the Declaration of Independence, Wright first visited the United States in 1818. Her glowing account of the new nation, *Views of Society and Manners in America,* brought her to the attention of the Utilitarian philosopher, James Bentham, and the American hero, General LaFayette, and secured a place in the circles of the leading European intellectuals.

In 1823 Wright accompanied LaFayette to the United States, where she visited a number of communitarian experiments and entered an association with Robert Dale Owen and the New Harmony Community. Wright adopted the notions of cooperative labor and universal education expressed by these utopian endeavors as the means to the abolition of slavery.

In 1825, on the recommendation of Andrew Jackson, Wright purchased a tract of land outside the village of Memphis. She acquired 15 slaves and, accompanied by her devoted younger sister, Camilla, and a few like-minded friends, established the biracial community of Nashoba. Wright hoped to obtain support from white slaveowners for the community in which slaves would labor in the fields to repay their purchase price, while receiving education for liberty for themselves and their children. As a necessary compromise, Wright agreed that when slaves were freed, they would be colonized outside the United States.

The brief Nashoba experiment came to an end when Wright left the community to recover from bouts of fever and enlist support. In her absence, one of the trustees published an account of Nashoba's daily workings that offended supporters and critics. James Richardson reported the flogging of slaves, parental dissatisfaction over the loss of control over the lives of their children, sexual misconduct, and miscegenation. The experiment lost the little support it had and ended within four years, in 1829, with Wright personally escorting the remaining slaves to Haiti, where she had secured guarantees of their freedom and livelihood.

Following the collapse of Nashoba, Wright intensified her role as social critic and reformer. With Robert Dale Owen, she edited and wrote for the *Free Enquirer,* the New Harmony newspaper. She and Owen founded the Working Men's Party in New York, and Wright pioneered a day school for workers' children and a dispensary for working people. On the lecture circuit, Wright presented a vision of an egalitarian nation, made possible through a national system of education that would place all children above two years old in boarding schools free of religious instruction. She argued for the liberation of women from unjust marriages and their exclusive roles as wives and mothers, and advocated economic independence and education for women to enable them to take their places as free citizens. During a period of religious revivalism, Wright proposed a rational world, free of religious superstition and clerical power. "Fanny Wrightism" became a synonym for infidelity and radicalism, especially when, in the late 1830s, she became a partisan of the locofoco, or left wing, of the Democratic party.

Anita S. Goodstein, University of the South

SUGGESTED READINGS: John Egerton, *Visions of Utopia: Nashoba, Rugby, Ruskin, and the "New Communities" in Tennessee's Past* (1977); William H. Pease and Jane H. Pease, "A New View of Nashoba," *Tennessee Historical Quarterly* 19(1960): 99–109

SEE: NASHOBA; SLAVERY

WRIGHT, FRANCES F. (1897–), author of books for children and adolescents, was born Fannie Bell Fitzpatrick near Gallatin, Tennessee. She spent her childhood in Arizona, but when she was orphaned at 15, Fannie Bell returned to the home of her Fitzpatrick grandparents at Cages Bend near her birthplace. Neighbors fostered her literary interests through high school, observed her marriage to George Wright, and cheered the arrival of three small children.

In 1926 Wright published her first book with Cokesbury Press, and during the Great Depression, the family depended on her writing as their primary source of income. From 1930 to 1950 Wright completed regular assignments for the Baptist Sunday School Board. In 1934 she published a Lucy Ellen story in *American Girl Magazine* and continued to contribute stories about Lucy Ellen and her sister Pat through 1963. The books for adolescents grew from this material. The success of these books led her to write the Sampey Place series, five books depicting both rural life of the early twentieth century and through embedded stories, some aspects of pioneer life. She also undertook children's biographies of Andrew Jackson and Sam Houston. Wright ended her writing career at age 75, though she continued to speak to school groups.

Wright's combination of love for history and an intimate knowledge of rural Tennessee brought the past to life for generations of children. She drew upon the environment of practical farm life and the tensions provoked by life's difficulties. As social history, Wright's work reveals the conditions of both the Depression and war years without being harsh. The Downing family, whose daughters narrate these books, never suffers true disaster but a new dress is an event. The young narrators find their aspirations in daily life. When Lucy Ellen leaves college to work on the farm after her father becomes ill, it seems like the right decision for a 19-year-old girl during World War II.

Wright's work reflects the moral mid-century attitude toward literature for young people. Her protagonists may be downhearted, but they never become violent or even seriously angry. Both teenagers and children accept the concept of a rational world to which each must somehow adjust personal desires and aspirations, yet Wright never denies the strength of youth's longings.

Sara R. Lee, Brentwood

SEE: CALHOUN, FRANCES BOYD; LITERATURE

WSM, an early Nashville radio station, was the idea of Edwin Craig of the National Life and Accident Insurance Company. In the early 1920s Craig, son of National Life founding partner Cornelius Craig, watched the nationwide phenomena of radio develop into an advertising source for station owners and sponsors. Craig capitalized on this potential with the creation of a company radio station.

The fifth floor of the new National Life building on Seventh Avenue in Nashville housed an up-to-date radio station in 1925. The 1,000-watt station was equaled by only one other in the South and was stronger than 85 percent of the stations nationwide. The selected call letters stood for "We Shield Millions."

The radio station gave National Life advertising potential, community service opportunities, and support for the company's field men while promoting company identity. The first aired program included Tennessee Governor Austin Peay, Nashville Mayor Hillary Howse, National Life President Craig, and noted radio announcers from around the country.

Early programming broadcast a variety of classical and popular tunes including a quintet from Fisk University. Jack Keefe served as the radio announcer until WSM hired George Hay from the Sears station, WLS, in Chicago. Hay began broadcasting with WMC (the *Commercial Appeal* station) in Memphis prior to working for Sears.

Early radio broadcast signals were unlimited, and WSM transmitted to both coasts. Hay understood this broadcasting potential and the popularity of the barn dance programs with rural audiences. On November 28, 1925, he tested old time music with Uncle Jimmy Thompson performing an hour of fiddle music. Hay found an enthusiastic audience. On December 26, 1925, WSM formally began broadcasting old-time music every Saturday night. Dubbed the Grand Ole

Opry in 1927 by Hay, he would continue to expand the hillbilly theme.

As live audiences outgrew the original fifth floor studio of the National Life Building, the show moved to the Hillsboro Theater. Tickets for the free show became a tool for National Life agents to attract new customers. After several additional moves, the show began performing at the Ryman Auditorium, later known as the Grand Ole Opry House before moving to its present stage at Opryland in 1974.

To help fill the programming hours WSM began a subscription to the National Broadcasting Company in 1927 when the station increased its watts to 5,000. Public service remained a part of the station's mission, but promotion of National Life was prominent. The Grand Ole Opry helped to increase life insurance sales to rural customers through a new premium payment plan based on monthly rather than semi-annual payments. During World War II, the station and the company contributed to the war effort. In 1950 WSM brought the first television broadcast to Nashville. A continuing leader in country music, WSM promoted the industry by helping to develop the Country Music Association. The radio station still broadcasts the Grand Ole Opry on Friday and Saturday nights.

Lauren Batte, Nashville

SUGGESTED READINGS: J. Fred MacDonald, *Don't Touch That Dial!: Radio Programming in American Life, 1920–1960* (1991); Powell Stamper, *The National Life Story: A History of the National Life and Accident Insurance Co. of Nashville* (1968)

SEE: COUNTRY MUSIC ASSOCIATION; GRAND OLE OPRY; MUSIC; NATIONAL LIFE AND ACCIDENT INSURANCE COMPANY

WYNN, SAMMYE (1919–), educator and children's advocate, was the first black female educator to work in the Educational Opportunities Planning Center founded by the University of Tennessee, Knoxville in 1966. It trained teachers from four southern states in ways to desegregate their schools. She remained in her position when the Center became MAARDAC (Mid-Atlantic Appalachian Race Desegregation Assistance Center). At both centers, Wynn trained teachers to intereact with each other and with racially mixed students. She based her programs on the beliefs that all children need to have high expectations, and that teachers should not judge children by their racial or socio-economic backgrounds.

In 1947 Wynn earned an R.N. degree from Meharry Medical College in Nashville and established a career as a cancer researcher before coming to Knoxville in 1956 with her late husband, James W. Wynn, an educator. Frustrated by the discrimination she found in the nursing profession in Knoxville, she returned to Nashville to earn a B.S. in elementary education from Tennessee State University in 1958. In

1961 she earned an M.S. in education from the University of Tennessee, Knoxville (UTK).

Retiring from UTK in 1983, Wynn continues her teaching mission with the Career Awareness and Motivation Program (CAMP), a joint venture sponsored by the Tennessee Valley Authority and Delta Sigma Theta sorority. Through CAMP, students are exposed to successful men and women in many career fields.

Wynn also taught in the American School in Ethiopia for a year when her husband was on assignment for the U.S. Agency for International Development. She left Africa deeply affected by conditions that could not provide "even marginal help for the needs of the poor."

June Adamson, Oak Ridge

SEE: CIVIL RIGHTS MOVEMENT; MEHARRY MEDICAL COLLEGE; UNIVERSITY OF TENNESSEE

WYNNEWOOD. Overlooking the sulfur springs at Bledsoe's Lick in the Castalian Springs community, the sprawling log inn, Wynnewood, was built in 1828 for travelers passing between Knoxville and Nashville. The builders, Alfred R. Wynne, Stephen Roberts, and William Cage, located it on property owned by Wynne's wife, Almira Winchester Wynne, daughter of General and Mrs. James Winchester of Cragfont.

When the east-west traffic shifted south of the Cumberland River to Wilson County, the Wynnes purchased the interest of the others and made the inn a home for their family. Succeeding generations lived in the building until 1971, when the Tennessee Historical Commission acquired it for preservation and interpretation as a historic site.

The Wynnes operated the facility as a summer season spa, where patrons drank the water and took mineral baths under the direction and care of resident physicians. The family built additional rustic accommodations apart from the main house and added recreational facilities for bowling and tennis, but patronage remained modest.

During the latter 1800s and early 1900s, the Wynnes often leased the property to others who operated it as the Castalian Springs Hotel. With the opening of a post office in 1837, the community had changed its name from Bledsoe's Lick to Castalian Springs. The name Wynnewood was not used until the early 1940s, chosen to distinguish the property from the community and to recognize the Wynne's long tenure there.

During the Civil War, troops from both armies frequently visited the property. Some stopped to see the stump of the hollow sycamore tree in which Thomas Sharp Spencer spent the winter of 1778–1779 alone while on a long hunt from southwest Virginia. Adjoining the springs is the 16-acre site of the pre-Columbian Indian village, Chaskepi. On a hill northwest of Wynnewood was Bledsoe's Fort, built in 1784 by Isaac Bledsoe, who had discovered the springs while exploring the area in 1772.

Walter T. Durham, Gallatin

SEE: BLEDSOE, ISAAC; LOG CONSTRUCTION; SPENCER, THOMAS S.; WINCHESTER, JAMES

X

X-10, which housed the Graphite Reactor, the oldest nuclear reactor in the world, was a key component of the Oak Ridge nuclear complex. The Graphite Reactor was the world's first powerful nuclear reactor, which transformed uranium-238 into plutonium-239. The X-10 facilities also chemically separated the plutonium from the uranium. The Graphite Reactor was built in only 11 months and it produced its first self-sustaining chain reaction on November 4, 1943. Less than two months later, it yielded one-third ton of irradiated uranium a day, and in the early spring 1944 Oak Ridge scientists produced the world's first grams of plutonium. The X-10 project served as the pilot plant for larger reactors and chemical facilities built at Hanford, Washington, in 1944. Its plutonium became the nuclear explosive used in the "Fat Man" bomb dropped on Nagasaki in 1945. X-10's Graphite Reactor also produced the first electricity from nuclear energy and was the first reactor to be used for the study of the health hazards of radioactivity. Alvin Weinberg, former director of the Oak Ridge National Laboratory, observed: "the work that took place at the Graphite Reactor had ramifications for many fields of science," such as modern mammalian radiation biology, nuclear power, and neutron diffraction. Also, "it was the first place where isotopes were produced for every science you can think of."[1]

In the postwar years, the X-10 site, along with the Y-12 and K-25 complexes, evolved into Oak Ridge National Laboratory. The X-10 facility initially specialized in the design of nuclear reactors and later expanded into studies of other energy sources. The Y-12 plant became a center for precision machining, especially of nuclear weapon components. The K-25 Gaseous Diffusion Plant served as the model for additional similar plants built during the Cold War adjacent to the K-25 site and near Paducah, Kentucky, and Portsmouth, Ohio.

The Graphite Reactor at X-10 was shut down in 1963, after 20 years of use. It was listed as a National Historic Landmark in 1966, and is now open for public tours.

Leland R. Johnson, Clio Research Institute

Citation:

(1) "The Graphite Reactor," A historic site brochure prepared by Oak Ridge National Laboratory, 1992. The Editor-in-Chief also used this brochure to add material on X-10 to the earlier entry on the Oak Ridge Nuclear Complex prepared by Dr. Leland R. Johnson.

Suggested Reading: Leland R. Johnson and Daniel Schaffer, *Oak Ridge National Laboratory: The First Fifty Years* (1994)

See: OAK RIDGE; OAK RIDGE NATIONAL LABORATORY; SHULL, CLIFFORD G.; WEINBERG, ALVIN; WOLLAN, ERNEST O.

Y

YARDLEY, WILLIAM F. (1844–1924), an influential and powerful advocate for the legal rights of blacks, was the first African American to run for governor of Tennessee. Yardley was born in 1844, the child of a white mother and a black father and, therefore, legally free. He was literally left on the Knoxville doorstep of the white Yardley family, who took him in and gave him his name. Bound out to learn a trade, he attended school under the direction of an Episcopal minister. In 1869 he was teaching black children at the Ebenezer School and reading law with a white lawyer. By 1872 he had passed the bar exam and was licensed to practice. Apparently the first African-American lawyer in Knoxville, he handled mostly criminal cases for black clients. In 1870 he married Elizabeth Stone, who was part Native American, and they had four children.

Active in Republican politics, he was elected Knoxville city alderman in 1872 and served on the Knox County Court from 1876 to 1882. When the Republican party declined to nominate a candidate for governor in 1876, Yardley stepped forward as an Independent and canvassed the state with two other white candidates. He spoke boldly and eloquently against the constitutional bans on interracial marriage and interracial schooling. Although he lost the gubernatorial race, thereafter Knoxvillians referred to him as either "Squire Yardley" or "Governor Yardley."

Yardley was possibly the first African-American lawyer to take a case to the State Supreme Court (Williams, 1883). In 1885, in Eaton, he argued against requiring jail inmates to "work off" the costs of state prosecution, a practice that made poor inmates near-slaves. He lost the case, but the practice was ultimately abolished. Yardley served as co-counsel in one of Knoxville's most important criminal cases, the two murder trials (1919, 1921) of a black man who was convicted of shooting a white woman after climbing through her bedroom window. The initial incident precipitated the Knoxville race riot of 1919. Although his client, Maurice Mays, was found guilty in both trials and executed for the crime, most modern scholars conclude that Mays was wrongfully convicted.

In addition to his legal and political career, Yardley represented the Continental Insurance Company of New York and was a member of Knoxville's first fire department, serving as the second assistant fire chief, 1876–1877. In 1878 Yardley was the publisher and editor of Knoxville's first black newspaper, the Knoxville *Examiner*. In 1882 he organized and published another newspaper, the Knoxville *Bulletin*.

Wearing a Prince Albert coat and derby, Yardley remained a leading Knoxvillian for decades, hosting such dignitaries as Frederick Douglass, who called him "one of the most remarkable men that I have met."[1] William F. Yardley died on May 20, 1924.
Lewis L. Laska, Tennessee State University

CITATION:

(1) Bobby L. Lovett and Linda T. Wynn, eds., *Profiles of African Americans in Tennessee* (1996), 150.

SEE: KNOXVILLE; KNOXVILLE RIOT OF 1919; PUBLISHING; TENNESSEE SUPREME COURT

YELLOW FEVER EPIDEMICS. Epidemic diseases caused great concern for nineteenth century Tennesseans. Subject to outbreaks of cholera, smallpox, and dysentery, people lived with the stark reality of disease-induced death, especially in the growing urban areas where sanitation was often poor. For residents of West Tennessee, and particularly Memphis, yellow fever posed the greatest threat. The disease caused fevers, chills, hemorrhaging, severe pains, and sometimes a jaundicing of the skin, which gave yellow fever its name. The trademark of the disease, however, was the victim's black vomit, composed of blood and stomach acids. Although its cause was unknown until 1900, yellow fever was transmitted from person to person by the female mosquito *Aedes aegypti.* Sailors on ships from the Caribbean or West Africa, from which the disease most likely originated, docked in New Orleans, where mosquitoes spread the disease from the infected person to the local population. River traffic carried yellow fever up the Mississippi Valley as long as mosquitoes were available to transmit the disease from human to human. Reprieve came only with the first frost.

Although Memphis had been exposed to yellow fever in 1828, 1855, and 1867, nothing prepared the city for the devastation the fever brought during the 1870s. An 1873 epidemic claimed 2,000 in Memphis, at the time the most yellow fever victims in an inland city. In 1878 a mild winter, a long spring, and a torrid summer produced favorable conditions for the breeding of *Aedes aegypti,* and thus the spread of the fever. When New Orleans newspapers reported an epidemic in late July, Memphis officials established checkpoints at major points of entry into the city.

The efforts at quarantine were not extensive enough and, in any event, most likely came too late. Yellow fever cases were probably developing on the fringes of Memphis as early as late July, and by August 13 the first death was reported in the city itself. With the horrors of the 1873 epidemic fresh on their minds, roughly 25,000 residents fled the city within two weeks. The fever raged in Memphis until mid-October, infecting over 17,000 and killing 5,150. Over 90 percent of whites who remained contracted yellow fever, and roughly 70 percent of these died. Long thought to be immune to the disease, blacks contracted the fever in large numbers as well in 1878, although only 7 percent of infected blacks died. While there is still no consensus among experts explaining this racial disparity in mortality rates, it is likely that repeated exposure to yellow fever over many generations in West Africa provided many blacks with a higher resistance to the disease.

Fleeing Memphians encountered quarantines throughout the South. Some of these, like the one at Jackson, Tennessee, were successful in keeping the disease from spreading. But like the attempts at quarantine in Memphis, most of these efforts were not thorough enough. Hardest hit were the Tennessee towns along the various railroads leading out of Memphis. Germantown, Moscow, Milan, Collierville, Paris, Brownsville, Martin, and LaGrange each experienced staggering losses relative to the size of their communities. Traveling along the Memphis & Charleston Railroad, the fever even spread to a swampy slum district of Chattanooga, causing 8,000 of the city's residents to flee.

Long after cold weather brought relief from the fever, Memphis was feeling the effects of the epidemic. Yellow fever exacerbated the already dismal financial situation in the city to the point that the legislature revoked the Memphis city charter in 1879. The fever also contributed to substantial declines in the Irish and German communities as well as the general population. Despite all the horrors, however, the impact of yellow fever on Memphis was not all negative. Leaders of the black community were able to use their numerical advantage during the fever to place blacks on the police force as patrolmen for the first time in the city's history. Contrary to the prevailing trend in other southern cities where blacks disappeared from police forces soon after Reconstruction ended, blacks remained on the force in Memphis until 1895. Perhaps most importantly, after yellow fever visited the city once again in 1879, Memphis leaders embarked on ambitious sanitation reform. The fact the yellow fever did not strike the city in epidemic proportions again is less the product of sanitary reforms than of the immunity acquired by many in the Mid-South during 1878. The new sewer systems and better water supply, however, did wonders for public health as a whole, particularly in preventing outbreaks of cholera, dysentery, and other waterborn diseases.

Christopher Caplinger, Vanderbilt University

Suggested Readings: Khaled J. Bloom, *The Mississippi Valley's Great Yellow Fever Epidemic of 1878* (1993); Dennis C. Rousey, "Yellow Fever and Black Policemen in Memphis: A Post-Reconstruction Anomaly," *Journal of Southern History* 51(1985): 357–374; Lynette B. Wrenn, "The Impact of Yellow Fever on Memphis: A Reappraisal," West Tennessee Historical Society *Papers* 41(1987): 4–18

See: Cook, Annie; Disasters; Memphis

YOAKUM, HENDERSON KING (1810–1856), a Jacksonian stalwart in Middle Tennessee during the tumultuous political battles of the 1830s and 1840s, this native Tennessean later became an important personal and political confidant of Texas Governor Sam Houston and wrote the first comprehensive history of Texas in 1855. Born in Claiborne County, Tennessee, in 1810, Yoakum attended the United States Military Academy and graduated twenty-first in a class of 45 in 1832. He returned to Tennessee upon leaving West Point and married Evaline Cannon of Roane County; the Yoakums promptly moved to Murfreesboro, where Henderson undertook legal training with Judge James Mitchell.

Yoakum entered politics in 1834, publicly siding with Congressman James K. Polk in his feud with fellow Tennessee Congressman John Bell over the Speakership of the U.S. House of Representatives. Yoakum joined the Jackson-Polk Democrats, espousing the virtues of tradition and of the agrarian republic ideal. He served as mayor of Murfreesboro. In 1839 he was elected to the Tennessee State Senate, but was defeated in his reelection campaign in 1841. Two years later, Yoakum served as chair of the State Democratic Convention. Yet, increasingly dissatisfied with the Whig party's domination of regional politics, Yoakum decided to leave Tennessee after James K. Polk failed to carry the state in the 1844 presidential campaign.

He moved to Huntsville, Texas, where he opened a law office in 1845. Striking a quick, and lasting, friendship with Sam Houston, Yoakum became prominent in the Texas Democratic party and grew wealthy, owning over 10,000 acres in five east Texas counties. In 1849 he began writing his *History of Texas*, a massive two-volume study that "offered a documented and ably argued justification of the Democratic ideology of expansion and empire."[1] His history was published in 1855 and remains today an important primary source about the early history of Texas. He died in 1856 and is buried at Oakwood Cemetery in Huntsville, Texas. His friend, Sam Houston, was buried nearby in 1863.

Carroll Van West, Middle Tennessee State University
CITATION:

(1) Carroll Van West, "Democratic Ideology and the Antebellum Historian: The Case of Henderson Yoakum," *Journal of the Early Republic* 3(1983): 335.

SEE: HOUSTON, SAM; JACKSONIANS; MURFREESBORO; POLK, JAMES K.

YORK, ALVIN CULLOM (1887–1964), Congressional Medal of Honor winner and hero of World War I, was born in Pall Mall, Tennessee. The oldest of 11 children in a family of subsistence farmers, York was a semi-skilled laborer when he was drafted into the army in 1917. Having never traveled more than 50 miles from his home, York's war experience awakened him to a more complex world.

As York came of age he earned a reputation as a deadly accurate shot and a "hell raiser" who would "never amount to anything." In 1914 a close friend of York's died, and he experienced a religious conversion during a revival conducted by H.H. Russell of the Church of Christ in Christian Union. A fundamentalist sect with a following limited to Ohio, Kentucky, and Tennessee, the church espoused a strict moral code that forbade drinking, dancing, movies, swimming, swearing, and popular literature. The church also held moral convictions against violence and war. Blessed with a melodious singing voice, York became the song leader and a Sunday School teacher at the local church. The church brought York into contact with his future wife, Gracie Williams.

By most accounts, York's conversion was sincere and complete. He stopped drinking, gambling, and fighting. The American declaration of war on Germany in April 1917 tested York's new-found faith. York received his draft notice from his friend, pastor, and postmaster, Rosier Pile, on June 5, 1917. Pile

Alvin York at the tomb of Andrew Jackson, circa 1919.

TSLA. PHOTOGRAPH BY WILES

encouraged York to use the sect's proscriptions against war to obtain conscientious objector status. York wrote on his draft card: "Dont [sic] want to fight." Local and state review boards denied his case because the church was not recognized as a legitimate Christian sect.

Despite his status as a 30-year-old, would-be conscientious objector, in many ways York typified the underprivileged, undereducated conscript of World War I. York received basic training at Camp Gordon, Georgia. A member of Company G in the 328th Infantry, also known as the "All American Division," York established a reputation as an excellent marksman, who had no stomach for war. After weeks of debate and counseling, York relented to the arguments of his company commander, George Edward Buxton, and agreed that there were times when war was moral and ordained by God. He agreed to fight.

On October 8, 1918, Corporal Alvin C. York and 16 other soldiers under the command of Sergeant Bernard Early were dispatched to take control of the

Decauville railroad in the Chatel-Chehery sector of the Meuse-Argonne sector. The men misread their French language map and mistakenly wound up behind enemy lines. A brief firefight ensued, which resulted in the unexpected surrender of a superior German force. Once the Germans realized the size of the American contingent, machine gunners on the hill overlooking the scene turned their weapons on their own troops, after ordering them to lie down. The machine gun fire resulted in the deaths of nine Americans, including York's best friend in the outfit, Murray Savage. Sergeant Early suffered 17 bullet wounds and turned the command over to corporals Harry Parsons and William Cutting, who ordered York to silence the machine guns. York's efforts resulted in the capture of 132 prisoners by nine men. Although York never claimed that he acted alone, only Sergeant Early and Corporal Cutting received acknowledgment for their participation in the event; they were awarded the Distinguished Service Cross in 1927.

York's wartime exploit and humble origins captured the American imagination, not because of who he was but for what he symbolized: a humble, self-reliant, God-fearing, taciturn patriot, who slowly moved to action only when sufficiently provoked, but who refused to capitalize on his fame. Ironically, York also represented a rejection of mechanization and modernization because of his dependence on personal skill.

Yearning to return home and wed his sweetheart, York was taken aback by his New York hero's welcome. Once back in Tennessee further surprises awaited him. The Rotary Club of Nashville, in conjunction with other Tennessee clubs, planned to present the hero with a home and farm. When donations fell short of the goal, the Rotarians gave him an unfinished house and saddled him with a substantial mortgage. The organization nonetheless retained the property rights, and as late as 1922 the deed remained in the hands of the Nashville Rotary Club.

York was singled out as the greatest common soldier of World War I, but he turned his back on quick and certain fortune offered by Hollywood, Broadway, and various advertisers. He tried to resume peacetime life and the pursuit of his vision to provide practical education for children in Fentress County. During the 1920s, York went on speaking tours to promote his hopes for education and raise money for his school, the York Institute.

York also became interested in politics and used his celebrity to obtain funds to improve roads, provide employment, and promote education in his home county. In the 1932 election York changed his party affiliation and supported Herbert Hoover to protest Franklin D. Roosevelt's promise to repeal Prohibition. Once the New Deal got underway, however,

York endorsed the president's relief efforts. In 1939 he was appointed superintendent of the Cumberland Homesteads near Crossville.

With the renewed threat of war in Europe, York adopted an isolationist stance. Hollywood filmmaker, Jesse L. Lasky, had been interested in York's story since he had witnessed the soldier's welcoming parade in New York. By the late 1930s Lasky believed America had to be convinced in 1939, just as York had been convinced in 1917, that war was not only justifiable, but sometimes necessary. York's story seemed to afford a perfect example.

York announced that Lasky's planned biographical movie, *Sergeant York,* would portray his life and wartime activities, but would not be a war picture—a movie form York disliked. Nevertheless, the film that arrived in theaters in July 1941 promoted American involvement in World War II. During the shooting of the film, for which Gary Cooper as York won the Academy Award for Best Actor, even York became convinced of the world threat and supported the call for the country's first peacetime draft. Governor Prentice Cooper named York chief executive of the Fentress County Draft Board and appointed him to the Tennessee Preparedness Committee. York attempted to reenlist in the infantry, but was rejected because of age and weight. Through an affiliation with the Signal Corps, York traveled the country on bond tours, recruitment drives, and camp inspections.

York's health began to deteriorate after the war, and in 1954 he suffered a stroke that left him bedridden for the remainder of his life. The Internal Revenue Service in 1951 accused York of tax evasion on his profits from the movie. Practically destitute, York spent the next ten years wrangling with the IRS. Eventually, Speaker of the U.S. House of Representatives Sam Rayburn and Congressman Joe L. Evins established the York Relief Fund to help cancel the debt. In 1961 President John F. Kennedy, who considered the actions of the IRS a national disgrace, ordered a resolution of the matter.

York died on September 2, 1964, and was buried with full military honors in the cemetery of the Wolf River Methodist Church. The Alvin C. York State Historical Area in Pall Mall interprets the family's restored historic grist mill, the 1922 Colonial Revival-styled York home, the York grave, and other properties associated with York's life and work in Fentress County.

Michael E. Birdwell, Tennessee Technological University
SUGGESTED READING: David E. Lee, *Sergeant York: An American Hero* (1985)
SEE: FENTRESS COUNTY; WORLD WAR I; YORK INSTITUTE

YORK INSTITUTE. When Sergeant Alvin C. York returned to the United States in 1919 as the best known hero of the World War, he devoted his attention to improving education in rural Tennessee. York's tenure in the military and service overseas made him painfully aware of his own educational shortcomings and convinced him that an adequate education was the key to advancement. The initial name for the school, the York Industrial Institute (later changed to the York Agricultural and Industrial Institute), reflected York's belief that the future lay in industry. Ironically, York's Jamestown school would train students for a technological future and insure that many children would leave the region for larger urban areas.

In 1925 the Tennessee General Assembly appropriated $50,000 toward the school's construction. York, a Democrat, battled the local Republican county executives over the school's location. In 1927 local officials threatened eviction from the site, and York appealed directly to the state legislature and national media for support. As a result, the 1925 legislation was amended to give the state Department of Education oversight of York Institute.

The school opened in 1929, but even with state backing York's problems continued. Fentress County officials refused to support the school. In order to pay teachers' salaries, York twice mortgaged his home and paid the teachers directly from his own pocket. He also bought school buses with his own money because the county refused to provide them. In 1933 the Department of Education investigated charges that York was guilty of incompetence, negligence, nepotism, and bringing in outsiders. The investigation uncovered no corruption, but state officials recognized that York was ill equipped to assess the capabilities of faculty. They also discovered the enormous lengths to which York's antagonists had gone to discredit him.

The Department of Education decided that for the survival of the institution, the state would administer the school's operation. York was named president emeritus and presided over ceremonial functions. The department demanded that the school principal have a bachelor's degree, and established criteria for the selection of teachers. This action secured the future of York Institute. Today, as the only state-owned and -operated high school in Tennessee, it maintains an excellent academic and athletic record and has one of the largest high school campuses in the world, comprising over 14,000 acres. The original Institute building is listed in the National Register of Historic Places.

Michael E. Birdwell, Tennessee Technological University
SEE: FENTRESS COUNTY; YORK, ALVIN C.

YUCHI INDIANS are a North American Indian tribe belonging to the Southeastern Indian cultural group. Ethnohistorians indicate that during the historic period there were three principal bands of Yuchi: one on the Tennessee River, one in west Florida, and one on the Savannah River. The last of these relocated to the Chattahoochee River around 1715 and became part of the Creek Confederacy. The combined populations of all three groups probably never exceeded 3,000 to 5,000 persons. Unfortunately, frequent changes in location and confusion over the names applied to the tribe limits information regarding their inhabitancy of Tennessee.

The most outstanding hallmark of the Yuchis is their language, Uchean, which is distinct from all other Native American languages. While a linguistic isolate, Uchean does bear some structural resemblances to the Muskhogean and Siouan linguistic families and has occasionally been misclassified as Algonquian. Because Uchean was a difficult language to speak, most early historical sources refer to the Yuchis using a variety of non-Uchean names, including: Hogologue, Tahogale, Chiska, Westo, Rickohockan, and Tamahaita.

The Yuchis referred to themselves as Tsoyahá, meaning children of the sun. The term Yuchi probably derives from a reply yú tcí, meaning "at a distance/ sitting down," to a standard southeastern Indian salutation: "Where do you come from?"

In general, the social customs and lifeways of the Yuchi are similar to other southeastern Indians. They relied on intensive hoe agriculture of corn, beans, and squash, and hunting of white-tail deer, bear, and elk. Before 1715, the Yuchis lived in permanent towns which were considered either red (war) or white (peace). Each town typically contained a square ground, a hot house, and a ballfield, as well as one-room domestic structures. The square ground was the focus of male daily life, and it surrounded the sacred fire. The Busk, or Green Corn Ceremony, was the ceremonial focus of the year. The tribe was divided into several matrilineal clans, with important clans including the Alligator, Bear, Panther, Deer, and Wind. Marriage between a man and woman of the same clan was considered incestuous. After 1715 in Tennessee, and after the 1790s on the Chattahoochee River, social disruptions resulting from colonial pressures forced a shift in the settlement system, resulting in the Yuchis abandoning their towns and villages and living in dispersed homesteads, in a pattern similar to early American frontier settlers.

Yuchi art is classified as Eastern geometric style and is expressed in woven textiles as simple diamonds, Vs, and Ws. The diamond motif is thought to represent a rattlesnake. Certain late prehistoric gorget motifs, especially the Cox Mound style of Tennessee, some experts speculate to be expressions of the Yuchi myth of the Winds.

The earliest mention of Yuchis in Tennessee is found in the Spanish de Soto expedition narratives

(1539–1543), where they are referred to as the Chisca and located in the highlands north of the Tennessee River. The Chisca are mentioned again by the Spaniard Juan Pardo's expedition (1566–1567), where they are described as warlike mountain chiefs. In the late sixteenth and early seventeenth centuries, the Yuchis split into two groups, with one body remaining in the north and the other radiating across the southern lowlands. Interestingly, the Yuchis have an oral tradition which explains the division of the tribe, in which one group, "Trackmaster's children," remained in the original homeland, while the children of "A bear only" moved toward the southern sun.

In 1673 one band of Yuchis reportedly lived in a stockaded, or fortified town, somewhere in the headwaters of the Tennessee River, possibly on the French Broad River near the confluence with the Holston River. Two English Virginian traders, James Needham and Gabriel Arthur, visited this group, which they referred to as the Tomahittans, on an overland trading mission supported by Abraham Wood. Needham returned to Petersburg, Virginia, with some Tomahittans to formalize trade relations with Wood, while Arthur remained in the town and accompanied some warriors in a retaliatory raid against Spanish settlements in Florida around 1674.

In 1700 a Frenchman, Father Gravier, encountered a canoe of Taogrias (Yuchis) on the Mississippi River who had been trading with the Arkansea (Quapaw). In 1701 five Canadians apparently visited the Taogria Yuchi town, which was located on an island in the lower Tennessee River, near Muscle Shoals. This town had a population of about 200 men.

These Yuchis likely moved up the Tennessee River in the first decade of the eighteenth century, and by 1712 the South Carolina board of Indian trade affairs noted the presence of "Uche or Round Town people" among the Cherokees. Their town was known as Chestua and was probably located near the mouth of the Hiwassee River. The Cherokees referred to this Yuchi town as Tsistu'yi or Rabbit place. A band of Cherokees from the middle towns, led by the warriors Flint and Caesar, destroyed this settlement in the spring of 1714, possibly in retaliation for the murder of a Cherokee. The few Yuchis who survived the raid were made captives. In a hearing during May 1714, two South Carolina traders, Eleazar Wiggan and Alexander Long, were convicted of inciting the raid. After 1715 there is virtually no mention of the Yuchis in Tennessee.

Historian J.G.M. Ramsey noted the destruction of Chestua and placed the settlement at Uchee Old Fields, formerly in Rhea County. This location, near the present post office of Euchee in Meigs County, is no longer considered accurate. After 1714 some remnant Tennessee Yuchis apparently lived scattered among the Cherokees near Cleveland in Bradley County. These Yuchis continued to speak Uchean, but some also spoke Cherokee and Creek. In 1730 the population of Yuchis remaining along the Tennessee River reportedly numbered 150 men, but they had no settlement of their own.

After forcible removal of Native Americans in 1838, most Yuchis established themselves as a distinct group within the Creek Nation of Oklahoma. Anthropologists suggest, however, that a few Yuchis remained in East Tennessee as late as 1918.

C. Andrew Buchner, Memphis

SUGGESTED READINGS: Charles Hudson, *The Southeastern Indians* (1976); Günter Wagner, *Yuchi Tales* (1931)

SEE: COX MOUND GORGET; OVERHILL CHEROKEES; PARDO EXPEDITION; SOTO EXPEDITION; TRAIL OF TEARS

Z

ZIMMERMAN, HARRY (1911–1986) and MARY KRIVCHER ZIMMERMAN (1911–1986) founded in 1960 what became the nation's largest catalog showroom, Service Merchandise. Both grew up in Memphis, and, after graduating from Central High School, they married. Shortly after the birth of Raymond, their first of three children, Harry, the son of Eastern European Jewish immigrants, moved his young family to Pulaski. Middle Tennessee would be their base for over 50 years.

From his beginnings with a Ben Franklin five- and ten-cent store, Zimmerman acquired other dime stores in Tennessee rural towns and with two cousins formed a partnership, Shainberg and Zimmerman Co., that expanded eventually to ten stores. During Harry's World War II Navy tour in the South Pacific, Mary ran the business. Over the decade following his return from the service, the couple moved the family to Nashville, dissolved the partnership with his cousins, shifted into the wholesale business by selling goods directly to dime stores, began a new venture called Service Wholesale Co., and brought Raymond into the company.

Harry had also by then heard of the catalog showroom concept that originated with Sidney Lewis in Richmond, Virginia, in 1957. In this arrangement, a catalog, issued annually, advertises items that are displayed at the site of a warehouse. The customer fills in a form, and the order is processed and delivered from the warehouse by a conveyor belt to the showroom as the buyer completes the purchase. Sales clerks of traditional department stores are not needed in this setting. In 1960 the Zimmermans decided to leave the wholesale business and create their own showroom. They organized and opened the Service Merchandise Company showroom on Lower Broadway in Nashville.

The Zimmermans expanded to three stores in 1969; two years later they had five locations in Tennessee, with sales of $16.7 million. Through the 1970s the company grew rapidly, as did Best Products of Richmond and Modern Merchandising of Minneapolis. Catalog showrooms seemed to do best when sited in free-standing buildings near a shopping center in communities of at least 125,000. The "Big Three" companies chose not to compete in the same regions, and they cut expenses by printing their catalogs together. Raymond continued the Zimmerman philosophy, make a little money on a lot of sales, after his parents retired in 1981. By the time of their deaths in July (Harry) and November (Mary) 1986, Service Merchandise was a business of $2.2 billion with 300 stores across the country.

Harry Zimmerman received the B'nai B'rith National Jewelry Industry Man of the Year Award in 1974. He served on various boards due both to his business acumen and to the family belief in helping those less fortunate. At the time of his death, Zimmerman served the national Muscular Dystrophy Association as vice president. Raymond Zimmerman continues the business, adapting it recently to the changing consumer market, and the family tradition of service to others through his work with the United Way and the Tennessee Performing Arts Foundation.
Margaret D. Binnicker, Middle Tennessee State University
SEE: JEWS, URBAN TENNESSEE

ZION PRESBYTERIAN CHURCH, constructed between 1847 and 1849, is a rural church built in the Greek Revival style. The church serves the oldest active congregation in Maury County, the descendants of Scots-Irish families who moved to the area from South Carolina in 1807. They purchased 5,000 acres of General Nathaniel Greene's land grant and constructed first a log church in 1807 and later a brick church in 1813.

The present building was built of brick and locally quarried limestone. Its Greek Revival-style features include stepped gables and a recessed open vestibule. A slave gallery accommodated the African Americans in the congregation. In 1880 the church was enhanced by the addition of Tiffany stained glass.

Church relics include a small registry table, made from the original pulpit brought from South Carolina in the initial migration. Pewter mugs, china Communion plates, and Communion tokens marked "ZC" also belonged to the early settlers.

The adjoining cemetery contains more than 1,500 graves including founders of the church and veterans of the Revolutionary, Mexican, and Civil Wars. One such Confederate veteran is Sam Watkins, one of seven survivors of Company H, First Tennessee Infantry. He became famous for his recollections of the war printed in the *Columbia Herald,* and later published as *Co. 'Aytch' First Tennessee Regiment, or a Side Show of the Big Show.* Another notable feature of the cemetery is a monument dedicated to "Daddy Ben," a slave who survived hanging three times after refusing to reveal his master's hiding place to British interrogators during the Revolutionary War.

Anne-Leslie Owens, Tennessee Historical Society
SEE: MAURY COUNTY

ZOLLICOFFER, FELIX KIRK (1812–1862) was a Confederate brigadier general who attempted to pacify Unionists in East Tennessee in 1861 before meeting defeat and death at the Battle of Mill Springs in Kentucky. Born in Maury County and educated at Jackson College, he became a printer, newspaper editor, and Whig politician. During the 1830s he served as a lieutenant of Tennessee volunteers in the Second Seminole War. After service as State Adjutant General and comptroller and a State Senator in the 1840s, Zollicoffer became a power in the Whig party. In 1852 he won election to the U.S. Congress, where he served until 1859 as a states' rights champion.

In 1860 he supported Constitutional Union party candidate, John Bell, for the presidency and urged Tennesseans to remain loyal to the Union. When the state seceded, however, he fully endorsed the decision and Governor Isham Harris rewarded him with a brigadier generalship. In July 1861 Harris ordered Zollicoffer and 4,000 raw recruits to Knoxville to suppress the East Tennessee resistance to secession. Zollicoffer treated peaceful Unionists fairly, but imposed harsher measures after Union guerrillas burned railroad bridges in November.

In early autumn, Zollicoffer led most of his soldiers northward to protect the Cumberland Gap and the eastern end of the Confederate defensive line that reached from the Gap westward through Kentucky and Tennessee to the Mississippi River. By early January 1862, he and his army had crossed to the north side of the Cumberland River near Mill Springs, Kentucky. This put the Confederates in a poor position to fight an advancing Union force commanded by General George H. Thomas. On January 19, at the Battle of Mill Springs, Union soldiers routed the Confederates and killed Zollicoffer. The Confederate line in Kentucky soon collapsed and made Tennessee vulnerable to invasion. Zollicoffer was an able politician, but an ill-prepared and ill-fated commander.

Larry Whiteaker, Tennessee Technological University
SEE: CIVIL WAR; MAURY COUNTY; THOMAS, GEORGE H.

RAILROADS, 1865 AND 1997

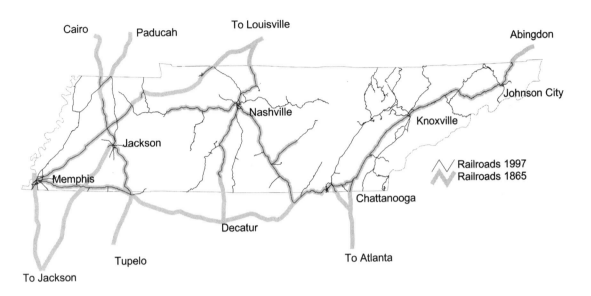

RIVERS OF TENNESSEE

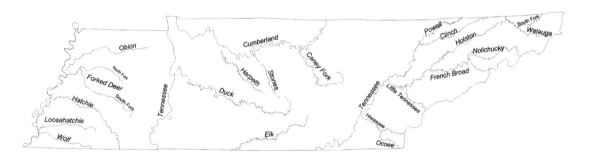

Number of Milk Cows, 1920

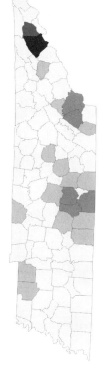

Milk cow defined as a heifer 2 years old or older

Number of Milk Cows

- 0–2,000
- 2,000–4,000
- 4,000–6,000
- 6,000–8,000
- Over 8,000

Number of Milk Cows, 1995

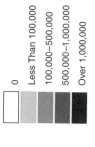

Source: U.S. Department of Commerce, Bureau of Census, 1920
Tennessee Agricultural Statistics Service, 1996

Coal Production for 1923
6,170,863 Tons

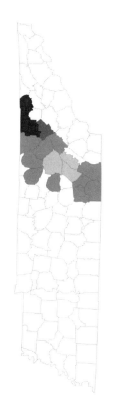

Coal Production for 1990
4,476,110 Tons

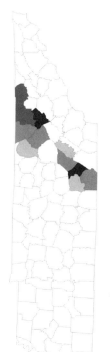

Coal Production in Tons

- 0
- Less Than 100,000
- 100,000–500,000
- 500,000–1,000,000
- Over 1,000,000

Source: Tennessee Department of Labor Annual Report

INDEX

NAACP, 680; Neyland, Robert Reese II, 688; Occupation, Civil War, 705; Ochs, Adolph Simon, 707; Overhill Cherokees, 714; Patten, Zeboim Cartter, 724; Public Works Administration (PWA), 754; Publishing, 755; Ragland, Martha Ragsdale, 764; Railroad, Memphis and Charleston, 766; Railroad, Nashville and Chattanooga, 767; Railroads, 769–770; Read House Hotel, 777; Reed, Ishmael Scott, 783; Ross, John, 811; Rowing, 812–813; Ruby Falls, 813; Sanders, Newell, 822; Sequatchie County, 834; Sequoyah, 836; Shavin House, 843; Smith, Bessie, 855; Smith, Stanton Everett, 860; Stadiums, Historic, 877; Steamboating, 883; Steele, Almira S., 884–885; Stout, Samuel Hollingsworth, 891; Street Car Era, 891; Symphony Orchestras, 902–903; Television and Movie Performers, 910; Temperance, 914; Tennessee Aquarium, 920; Tennessee River System, 944; Tennessee Wesleyan College, 963; Tennessee's Archives, 964; Thomas, Anne Taylor Jones, 972; Thomas, Benjamin Franklin, 972–973; Timber Industry, 978; Tullahoma Campaign, 995–996; United Confederate Veterans Association (Tennessee), 1003; U.S. Army Corps of Engineers, 1005; United States Colored Troops, 1008; United States Pipe and Foundry Company, 1009; University of Tennessee at Chattanooga, 1012–1013; Walden Hospital, 1025; Warner, Katherine Burch, 1034; Wheeler, Joseph, 1051; Whitehead, Joseph Brown, 1055–1056; Whiteside, Harriet Lenora, 1056; Wilder, John Thomas, 1058; Wiley Memorial United Methodist Church, 1060; Woman Suffrage Movement, 1070; Women's Christian Temperance Union, 1074; Works Progress Administration, 1076; World War I, 1079; World War II, 1082–1083; Yellow Fever Epidemics, 1090
Chattanooga African-American Museum, 398
Chattanooga Automobile Association, 250–251, 426
Chattanooga Bakery Company, **141**
Chattanooga *Blade,* **141,** 624
Chattanooga Car and Foundry Company, 293
Chattanooga Central Labor Union, 860
Chattanooga Choo-Choo Hotel, **141–142,** 398
Chattanooga College of Law, 560, 625
Chattanooga Electric Railway Company, 891
Chattanooga Fire Clay Works, 746
Chattanooga *Free Press,* **142**
Chattanooga Glass Company, **142–143**
Chattanooga Iron and Coal Corporation, 834
Chattanooga Lookouts, 398, 877

Chattanooga Medicine Company, **143,** 559, 724
Chattanooga Opera Association, 711, 903
Chattanooga Pipe and Foundry Works, 1009
Chattanooga Railway and Light Company, 390, 891, 966–967
Chattanooga Regional History Museum, 398
Chattanooga State Technical Community College, 199, 398
Chattanooga Steamboat Company, 822
Chattanooga Symphony Orchestra, 711, 903
Chattanooga Times, **143–144**
Chattanooga, 140; Chattanooga *Free Press,* 142; Cunningham Sumner A., 230; Hamilton County, 398; Jews, Urban Tennessee, 480; Lookout Mountain, 555; Miller, Randolph, 624; Ochs, Adolph Simon, 707; Patten, Zeboim Cartter, 724; Publishing, 757; Ragland, Martha Ragsdale, 764; Temperance, 913, 915
Chattin, E.W., 697
Chautauqua Movement, 114, 637, 1004
Chavis, "Chick," 478
Chayefsky, Paddy, 186
Chazen, Sol, 224
Cheairs, Matt, 1018
Cheairs, Nathaniel, 824
Cheatham, Adolphus Anthony "Doc," 478
Cheatham, Benjamin Franklin, 86, **144–145,** 335, 403, 419, 620, 672, 745, 934
Cheatham County, **145–146,** 647, 664, 724, 827, 898, 983
Cheatham Dam, 228, 351
Cheatham, Robert, 936
Cheatham, William, **146,** 1
Cheek, Leslie, 146
Cheekwood-Nashville's Home of Art and Gardens, 33, **146,** 279, 420, 577, 687
Cheeseborough, Chandra, 813
Cheesekau, 151, 844
Chemistry
Bowen, George Thomas, 80; Buehler, Calvin A., 103; Curry, Richard Owen, 230; Dabney, Charles W., Jr., 231–232; Kalbalks, George W., 497; Lind, Samuel Colville, 542; Lindsley, John Berrien, 543; Mamantov, Gleb, 568; Safford, James Merrill, 822; Science and Technology, 829; Smith, Hilton A., 858; Taylor, Ellison Hall, 906–907; Tenneessee Eastman Company/Eastman Chemical Company, 927–929
Cherokee Dam, 379, 397, 479, 720
Cherokee National Forest, **146–147**
Appalachian Trail, 22; Carter County, 130; Conservation, 202–203; Ecological Systems, 277; Johnson County, 488; Monroe County, 636; Polk County, 738; Roan Mountain State Resort Park, 798; Tennessee Scenic Rivers Program, 946; Tennessee State Forests, 949; Timber Industry, 978

Cherokee *Phoenix,* **147–148,** 755, 835
Cherokees, *also see Overhill Cherokees*
Awiakta, Marilou, 38; Basketmaking, 49; Chattanooga Medicine Company, 143; Chota, 154–155; Conservation, 203; French Lick, 343; Murfree, Mary Noailes; Nashville (Metropolitan Nashville/Davidson County), 670; Prehistoric Native American Art, 748–749; Rolley Hole Marbles, 810; Rutherford County, 818; Sequoyah, 835; Tennessee Valley Authority, 961; Trail of Tears, 984–985; Transportation, River, 988; Walker, Thomas, 1026; Ward, Nancy, 1033–1034; White, James, 1054; Wilderness Road, 1059; Williamson County, 1063; Works Progress Administration, 1076; Yuchi Indians, 1094
Chesapeake and Ohio Railroad, 773
Chesapeake, Ohio and Southwestern Railroad, 517, 525, 771, 1047
Chesney, Kenny, 1001
Chester County, 28, **148,** 152, 630, 659, 949
Chester Inn, **148–149,** 494
Chester, William, 1039
Chiaha, 720, 863, 987
Chiarugi, Vincenzo, 938
Chicago World's Columbian Exposition (1893), 352, 392, 485, 568, 921
Chickamauga and Chattanooga, Battles of, **149–150**
Army of Tennessee, 27; Bate, William B., 50; Bragg, Braxton, 86; Brown, John Calvin, 94; Chattanooga, 139–140; Cheatham, Benjamin F., 144–145; Civil War, 170; Cravens House, 216; Forrest, Nathan Bedford, 321; Franklin County, 336; Freed, Julius, 341; Hamilton County, 398; Knoxville, Battle of, 509; Longstreet, James, 554; Lookout Mountain, 555; Loudon County, 557; Patten, Zeboim Cartter, 724; Polk, Leonidas, 743; Railroad, Nashville and Chattanooga, 768; Railroads, 771; Stewart, Alexander P., 886; Tennessee River System, 944; Thomas, George Henry, 973; United States Army of the Cumberland, 1006; United States Christian Commission, 107; Wheeler, Joseph, 1051–1052; Wilder, John Thomas, 1058
Chickamauga and Chattanooga National Military Park
Hamilton County, 398; Lookout Mountain, 555; Monuments, 640; Ochs, Adolph Simon, 707; Stewart, Alexander P., 886; T.O. Fuller State Park, 904; United Confederate Veterans Association (Tennessee), 1003; Wilder, John Thomas, 1058
Chickamauga Dam, 77, 140, 309, 572, 603
Chickamaugas, **150–151**
Basketmaking, 49; Blackburn, Gideon, 69; Blount, William, 75; Chuqualataque, 158; Donelson, John, 256; Mansker, Kasper, 569; Mero District, 619; Overhill Cherokees, 714; Robertson, Charlotte

THE TENNESSEE HISTORICAL SOCIETY

The Tennessee Historical Society, publisher of *The Tennessee Encyclopedia of History & Culture*, is a private, not-for-profit membership organization established in 1849 "to collect, preserve, and perpetuate facts and events connected with the history of Tennessee." The oldest continuous cultural organization in the state, the Tennessee Historical Society welcomes everyone who wishes to be a member.

Membership benefits in the Tennessee Historical Society include:

- The award-winning *Tennessee Historical Quarterly*, presenting the best, most recent scholarship on the Volunteer State's past in an abundantly illustrated popular format—now in its fifty-eighth year.
- Significant savings on books published by the Tennessee Historical Society, such as *The Tennessee Encyclopedia*.
- Invitations to the Tennessee Historical Society fall and spring lecture series, featuring new research on our heritage.
- Inclusion in special events, tours, and workshops, recently focusing on genealogy, college sports history, and the settlement of Tennessee.

The Tennessee Historical Society owns the great artifacts and documents of Tennessee's past, including the Declaration of Rights of the State of Franklin and diner stools from the Nashville sit-ins, collections available to the public at the Tennessee State Museum and the Tennessee State Library and Archives. You help preserve this history of all Tennesseans—from East, Middle, and West Tennessee—when you join the Tennessee Historical Society. And you join the ranks of many Tennesseans whose names have been included in *The Tennessee Encyclopedia of History & Culture*—persons such as J.G.M. Ramsey, James D. Porter, Sarah Childress Polk, Frank Owsley, Stanley Horn, Mary Daniel Moore, John Lindsley, Benjamin Cheatham, Gates Thruston, and many more.

To become a member of the Tennessee Historical Society simply send your name, address, and $35 in individual dues or $45 for institutions to:

The Tennessee Historical Society
War Memorial Building
Nashville, Tennessee 37243-0084

These new member dues are good through January 31, 2000. For additional information about the Tennessee Historical Society, please write to the address above or call 615/741-8934.